3

-⟨ 88TH CONGRESS, 2D SESSION . . SENATE DOCUMENT NO. 59 ⟩-

MEMORIAL ADDRESSES IN THE

CONGRESS OF THE UNITED STATES

AND TRIBUTES IN EULOGY OF

John Fitzgerald Kennedy

LATE A PRESIDENT OF THE

UNITED STATES

Compiled Under Direction of the
Joint Committee on Printing

UNITED STATES GOVERNMENT PRINTING OFFICE
WASHINGTON : 1964

Senate Concurrent Resolution No. 69

IN THE SENATE OF THE UNITED STATES,

January 29, 1964.

Resolved by the Senate (the House of Representatives concurring), That there be printed with illustrations as a Senate document all remarks by Members of the Senate and the House of Representatives in the Halls of Congress which constitute tributes to the life, character, and public service of the late President, John F. Kennedy.

SEC. 2. There shall be printed and bound as directed by the Joint Committee on Printing, thirty-two thousand two hundred and fifty additional copies of such document, of which ten thousand three hundred copies shall be for the use of the Senate and twenty-one thousand nine hundred and fifty copies shall be for the use of the House of Representatives.

Attest:

FELTON M. JOHNSTON,
Secretary of the Senate.

Attest:

RALPH R. ROBERTS,
Clerk of the House of Representatives.

A compilation of addresses and tributes as given in the United States Senate and House of Representatives on the life, character, and public service of the late President John Fitzgerald Kennedy

Biography

JOHN FITZGERALD KENNEDY, thirty-fifth President of the United States, formerly a U.S. Representative and a U.S. Senator from the State of Massachusetts, was born in Brookline, Norfolk County, Mass., May 29, 1917; son of Joseph P. and Rose Fitzgerald Kennedy; attended the public schools of Brookline, Mass.; Choate School, Wallingford, Conn.; London School of Economics, London, England, in 1935 and 1936, and Stanford University; was graduated from Harvard University, Cambridge, Mass., in 1940; married Jacqueline Lee Bouvier, September 12, 1953; children: Caroline Bouvier, born November 27, 1957, and John Fitzgerald, Jr., born November 25, 1960; during World War II served as a lieutenant in the United States Navy from September 1941 to April 1945; PT boat commander in the South Pacific; awarded the Navy and Marine Corps Medal and the Purple Heart; author of "Why England Slept," 1940, "Profiles in Courage," 1956, and "Strategy of Peace," 1960; engaged as correspondent for a news service and covered the San Francisco Conference, the British elections in 1945, and the Potsdam meeting in 1945; elected as a Democrat to the U.S. House of Representatives from the 11th Congressional District of Massachusetts to the Eightieth, Eighty-first, and Eighty-second Congresses (January 3, 1947–January 3, 1953); elected to the United States Senate in 1952 for the term commencing January 3, 1953; re-elected in 1958 for the term ending January 3, 1965; nominated for the office of President of the United States by the Democratic Party at the convention in Los Angeles in 1960; elected President of the United States November 8, 1960, and inaugurated as the thirty-fifth President of the United States on January 20, 1961; resigned from the United States Senate December 22, 1960; died in Dallas, Tex., November 22, 1963, from the effects of an assassin's bullets while riding in a motorcade; remains returned to Washington, D.C., to lie in state for two days in the Rotunda of the Nation's Capitol; interment in Arlington National Cemetery, Fort Myer, Va.

Memorial Addresses

IN THE

Senate of the United States

IN EULOGY OF

John Fitzgerald Kennedy

In the Senate of the United States

NOVEMBER 25, 1963

The Chaplain, Rev. Frederick Brown Harris, D.D., offered the following prayer:

God of the living and of the living dead: as in this hour we bow in the shadow of a people's grief, Thou dost hear the sobbing of a stricken nation. But we come with the comfort that Thou knowest what is in the darkness, and that the darkness and the light are both alike to Thee.

For the stewardship in the brief but epochal years of the young and gallant captain who has fallen at his post, we give thanks to Thee, the Master of all good workmen. In the profile of courage, of vision, and of faith which John F. Kennedy etched upon the darkened sky of these agitated times, in his exalted place of leadership, we behold the image of our America which alone will make sure the survival of our freedom.

And now that the valorous sword has fallen from his lifeless hands, he seems to be calling to us in the unfinished tasks which remain.

> Others will sing the song
> Finish what I began
> What matters I or they
> Mine or another's day
> So the right word be said
> And life the purer made.

In the Nation's poignant loss, may there come to those whose hands are at the helm of this dear land of our faith and love the vision which fortified Thy prophet of old as he bore witness:

In the year that King Uzziah died I saw the Lord high and lifted up.

So in this year of a tragic death, may there be granted to us a vision of the preeminent spiritual verities which abide and undergird and outlast the life and death of any mortal servant of great causes who toils for a while in these fields of time in the sense of the eternal, and then falls on sleep.

We pray in the name of the risen Christ who hath brought life and immortality to light. Amen.

ADDRESS BY
Hon. Mike Mansfield
OF MONTANA

Mr. President, due to the sudden and tragic death of the President of the United States, a former colleague of ours in this body, it has been necessary to call this extraordinary meeting of the Members of the Senate before the hour formally appointed upon the adjournment of the Senate last Friday.

Mr. President, the Senate has assembled today to remark for the Record the death of John Fitzgerald Kennedy, President of the United States.

I shall be brief, for his life, too short, shut off too soon, speaks for him.

In these last hours, a profile in courage has emerged from the emulsion of his death. And the tears of those who knew him and those who did not know him will fix that profile forever in the experience of the Nation and the world.

John Fitzgerald Kennedy's courage was the human courage, the courage which all must have merely to live in this world, in the ever-present shadow of death. It was the special courage to defy the cold hand of death when it reaches out too eagerly, as twice it did—in the wounds of the war and in the grave illness of his Senate years. It was the quiet courage to accept death's finality when it would be denied no longer.

And his was an extraordinary courage. It was the courage to believe in, with all his heart, and to dedicate himself to, the attainment of the proposition that Americans—all Americans—are

1

born with an equal right to life, liberty, and the pursuit of happiness.

His was a universal courage. It was the courage of one who had bled in war to seek, unashamed, a peace of decency among all nations. It was the courage to join, before all else, the family of man and, in the joining, to affirm, before all else, the integrity of human life in the face of the powers of violence to destroy and desecrate it.

This is the profile of the man who walked among us not long ago on the floor of the Senate. This is the profile of the man who emerged to reawaken the Nation to its finest meaning. This is the man who struck new sparks of hope in a world dark with unspeakable fears.

His death, Mr. President, has fused the many faces of courage into a single profile of courage set in the enduring frame of faith and reason. This is what we have of him now. It is so little to have, and yet so much.

In a moment, I shall send to the desk a resolution of regret on the death of John Fitzgerald Kennedy. But that will not be the end. It will not be the end of our responsibility, of our debt to this decent man, this American who gave of himself until there was no more to give.

We will find, in his death, the strength to do what must be done to bridle the bigotry, the hatred, the arrogance, the iniquities, and the inequities which marched in the boots of a gathering tyranny to that moment of horror.

We will find, in his death, the strength to renew our faith in what is good in ourselves and in one another throughout this Nation.

We will find, in his death, the strength to follow the paths of reason on which he walked, until they lead us out of the morass of an all-consuming and cynical self-concern.

We will find, in his death, some of his love and reverence of life, some of his humility, some of his patience and forbearance, some of his wisdom, and some of his humor. And, so strengthened, we will join with the President in forging a new decency at home and a reasoned peace in the world.

God willing, these things we shall find, or God help us all.

Mr. President, I send to the desk a resolution which I submit on behalf of the 100 Members of the Senate.

The resolution (S. Res. 228) was read, as follows:

Resolved, That the Senate has learned with profound sorrow and deep regret of the tragic death of Hon. John Fitzgerald Kennedy, late the President of the United States, and a former Representative and former Senator from the State of Massachusetts.

Resolved, That in recognition of his illustrious statesmanship, his leadership in national and world affairs, and his distinguished public service to his State and the Nation, the Presiding Officer of the Senate appoint a committee, to consist of all the Members of the Senate, to attend the funeral of the late President at noon today.

Resolved, That the Senate hereby tenders its deep sympathy to the members of the family of the late President in their sad bereavement.

Resolved, That the Secretary communicate these resolutions to the House of Representatives, and transmit an enrolled copy thereof to the family of the late President.

ADDRESS BY

Hon. Everett McKinley Dirksen
OF ILLINOIS

Mr. President, the memory of John Fitzgerald Kennedy lingers in this forum of the people. Here we knew his vigorous tread, his flashing smile, his ready wit, his keen mind, his zest for adventure. Here with quiet grief we mourn his departure. Here we shall remember him best as a colleague whose star of public service is indelibly inscribed on the roll of the U.S. Senate.

And here the eternal question confronts and confounds us. Why must it be? Why must the life of an amiable, friendly, aggressive young man, moved only by high motives, lighted on his way by high hopes, guided by broad plans, impelled by understanding and vision, be brought to an untimely end with his labors unfinished? And why, in a free land, untouched by the heel of dictatorship and oppression, where the humblest citizen may freely utter his grievances, must that life be cut short by an evil instrument, moved by malice, frustration, and hate? This is the incredible thing which leaves us bewildered and perplexed.

One moment there is the ecstasy of living when one can hear the treble cries of scampering children over the White House lawn, the pleasure of receiving a Thanksgiving turkey which I presented to him but 3 days before the evil deed, the pleasure of conversation over many things, including his hopes for the future, the exciting fact of sunshine and green grass in late November, the endless stream of citizens coming to the President's House, the strident voice of the city rising from the hum of traffic, the animation of saluting crowds, and then the sudden strangling death rattle of dissolution. Who shall say, save that there is a divinity which shapes our ends and marks our days?

As the tumult and grief subside, as the Nation resumes and moves forward, and his own generation measures his works and achievements, what shall we say who knew him well—we in this forum, where he spent 8 years of his life—we who knew him best not as Mr. President but simply as Jack?

We saw him come to this body at age 35. We saw him grow. We saw him rise. We saw him elevated to become the Chief Magistrate of this Nation. And we saw him as the leader of both branches of this Republic assembled to deliberate over common problems.

In this moment when death has triumphed, when hearts are chastened, when the spirit reels in sheer bewilderment, what do we say now that the Book of Life has been closed?

Let me say what we have always said when he was alive, gay, happy, friendly, ambitious, and ready to listen.

He had vision that went beyond our own. His determination to effectuate a test ban treaty is a living example.

He was his own profile in courage. His unrelenting devotion to equality and civil rights attests that fact.

He was devoted to our system of constitutional government. His attitude toward the separation of church and state looms like a shining example.

He had the great virtue of spiritual grace. If at any moment he may have seemed frustrated over a proposition, it was so transitory. If he showed any sign of petulance, it was so fleeting. There were no souring acids in the spirit of John Kennedy.

If at any moment he may have seemed over-eager, it was but the reflection of a zealous crusader and missioner who knew where he was going.

If at any moment, he seemed to depart from the covenant which he and his party made with the people, it was only because he believed that

accelerated events and circumstances did not always heed the clock and the calendar.

If his course sometimes seemed at variance with his own party leaders or with the opposition, it was only because a deep conviction dictated his course.

On the tablets of memory, we who knew him well as a friend and colleague can well inscribe this sentiment:

"Senator John Fitzgerald Kennedy, who became the 35th President of the United States—young, vigorous, aggressive, and scholarly—one who estimated the need of his country and the world and sought to fulfill that need—one who was wedded to peace and vigorously sought this greatest of all goals of mankind—one who sensed how catastrophic nuclear conflict could be and sought a realistic course to avert it—one who sensed the danger that lurked in a continuing inequality in our land and sought a rational and durable solution—one to whom the phrase 'the national interest' was more than a string of words—one who could disagree without vindictiveness—one who believed that the expansion of the enjoyment of living by all people was an achievable goal—one who believed that each generation must contribute its best to the fulfillment of the American dream."

The universal expressions of anguish and agony which will well up in the hearts of people in all parts of the earth this day will linger on the evening breeze which caresses the last resting place of those who served the Republic, and here in this Chamber where he served and prepared for higher responsibility, the memory of John Fitzgerald Kennedy will long linger to nourish the faith of all who serve that same great land.

The President pro tempore. Is there objection to the present consideration of the resolution?

There being no objection, the resolution (S. Res. 228) was considered and unanimously agreed to.

The President pro tempore. The Chair appoints the entire membership of the Senate as a committee to proceed to the bier of our late President John F. Kennedy.

Mr. Mansfield. Mr. President, I ask Senators to join the leadership and proceed in a body to the bier on which our late departed colleague is now resting. I now move that this extraordinary meeting of Members of the Senate be now adjourned.

The motion was agreed to; and (at 10 o'clock and 19 minutes a.m.) the informal meeting of the Senate was adjourned.

The Senate proceeded in a body to the bier of the late President of the United States, John Fitzgerald Kennedy.

Memorial Services in the Senate
of the United States

DECEMBER 11, 1963

The Chaplain of the Senate, Rev. Frederick Brown Harris, D.D., offered the following prayer:

Our Father, God, we turn to Thee with our drained lives filled with tension for the present, anxiety for the future, with deep concern about ourselves, our Nation, and our world; and yet with a radiant hope that sends a shining ray far down the future's broadening way.

In spite of all the diversities of gifts and thought, in a common unity help us to lay aside every weight of prejudice, of pride, or of covetousness, and with glad and eager feet to march with the army that goes to free, not to bind; to develop, not to rule; to cooperate, not to dominate, until the knowledge of the Lord, who is no respecter of persons, shall cover the earth as the waters now cover the sea.

May this be a hallowed session, as this day in this Chamber, where he served the Nation, there is honored one so suddenly snatched from his great task of world leadership. We will remember him always as—

"One who never turned his back
But marched breast forward,
Never doubted clouds would break,
Never dreamed, though right were worsted,
Wrong would triumph,
Held we fall to rise,
Are baffled to fight better,
Sleep to wake."

Now at noonday, in the bustle of man's worktime, he has greeted the unseen with a cheer.

Gird us all to work in sunny hours, knowing that the night is coming when man's work is done.

In the blessed name of the world's Redeemer, who accomplished so much in so short a span, we pray. Amen.

ADDRESS BY
Hon. Mike Mansfield
OF MONTANA

Mr. President, what I had to say on the assassination of John Fitzgerald Kennedy has been said. It was said in the rotunda when his body was delivered into the trust of the Congress and the people of the Nation for a day and a night. It was said when it fell to me to give formal notification of his death to the Senate. I ask unanimous consent that both of those statements be included.

Mr. President, a flame kindled of human decency, courage and dedication does not die. The light which was John Fitzgerald Kennedy will not fail. We must not fail.

It rests with us to fashion in the glow of our grief a renewed sense of high national purpose. It rests with us to labor with humility and forbearance, with dignity and with hope to bring forth a new decency in this Nation and, in this world, a reasoned peace.

5

The ring is continuous. There is no end except that there is a beginning. There is an hour to grieve and an hour to give meaning to grief. This is the hour for those of us who live. This is the hour to end, to begin, to continue.

EULOGY BY SENATOR MANSFIELD IN THE ROTUNDA,
U.S. CAPITOL, NOVEMBER 24, 1963

There was a sound of laughter; in a moment, it was no more. And so she took a ring from her finger and placed it in his hands.

There was a wit in a man neither young nor old, but a wit full of an old man's wisdom and of a child's wisdom, and then, in a moment it was no more. And so she took a ring from her finger and placed it in his hands.

There was a man marked with the scars of his love of country, a body active with the surge of a life far, far from spent and, in a moment, it was no more. And so she took a ring from her finger and placed it in his hands.

There was a father with a little boy, a little girl and a joy of each in the other. In a moment it was no more, and so she took a ring from her finger and placed it in his hands.

There was a husband who asked much and gave much, and out of the giving and the asking wove with a woman what could not be broken in life, and in a moment it was no more. And so she took a ring from her finger and placed it in his hands, and kissed him and closed the lid of a coffin.

A piece of each of us died at that moment. Yet, in death he gave of himself to us. He gave us of a good heart from which the laughter came. He gave us of a profound wit, from which a great leadership emerged. He gave us of a kindness and a strength fused into a human courage to seek peace without fear.

He gave us of his love that we, too, in turn, might give. He gave that we might give of ourselves, that we might give to one another until there would be no room, no room at all, for the bigotry, the hatred, prejudice and the arrogance which converged in that moment of horror to strike him down.

In leaving us—these gifts, John Fitzgerald Kennedy, President of the United States, leaves with us. Will we take them, Mr. President? Will we have, now, the sense and the responsibility and the courage to take them?

I pray to God that we shall and under God we will.

STATEMENT BY SENATOR MANSFIELD
ON NOVEMBER 25, 1963
DEATH OF JOHN FITZGERALD KENNEDY,
35TH PRESIDENT OF THE UNITED STATES

Mr. President, the Senate has assembled today to remark for the Record the death of John Fitzgerald Kennedy, President of the United States.

I shall be brief, for his life, too short, shut off too soon, speaks for him.

In these last hours, a profile in courage has emerged from the emulsion of his death. And the tears of those who knew him and those who did not know him will fix that profile forever in the experience of the Nation and the world.

John Fitzgerald Kennedy's courage was the human courage, the courage which all must have merely to live in this world, in the ever-present shadow of death. It was the special courage to defy the cold hand of death when it reaches out too eagerly, as twice it did—in the wounds of the war and in the grave illness of his Senate years. It was the quiet courage to accept death's finality when it would be denied no longer.

And his was an extraordinary courage. It was the courage to believe in, with all his heart, and to dedicate himself to, the attainment of the proposition that Americans—all Americans—are born with an equal right to life, liberty, and the pursuit of happiness.

His was a universal courage. It was the courage of one who had bled in war to seek, unashamed, a peace of decency among all nations. It was the courage to join, before all else, the family of man and, in the joining, to affirm, before all else, the integrity of human life in the face of the powers of violence to destroy and desecrate it.

This is the profile of the man who walked among us not long ago on the floor of the Senate. This is the profile of the man who emerged to reawaken the Nation to its finest meaning. This is the man who struck new sparks of hope in a world dark with unspeakable fears.

His death, Mr. President, has fused the many faces of courage into a single profile of courage set in the enduring frame of faith and reason.

This is what we have of him now. It is so little to have, and yet so much.

In a moment, I shall send to the desk a resolution of regret on the death of John Fitzgerald Kennedy. But that will not be the end. It will not be the end of our responsibility, of our debt to this decent man, this American who gave of himself until there was no more to give.

We will find, in his death, the strength to do what must be done to bridle the bigotry, the hatred, the arrogance, the iniquities, and the inequities which marched in the boots of a gathering tyranny to that moment of horror.

We will find, in his death, the strength to renew our faith in what is good in ourselves and in one another throughout this Nation.

We will find, in his death, the strength to follow the paths of reason on which he walked, until they lead us out of the morass of an all-consuming and cynical self-concern.

We will find, in his death, some of his love and reverence of life, some of his humility, some of his patience and forbearance, some of his wisdom, and some of his humor. And, so strengthened, we will join with the President in forging a new decency at home and a reasoned peace in the world.

God willing, these things we shall find or God help us all.

ADDRESS BY

Hon. Everett McKinley Dirksen

OF ILLINOIS

Mr. President, the time was a few days before the vote in this body on the nuclear test ban treaty. Senator Mansfield and I made a call on the President. We were visiting quite informally in the Cabinet room. Secretary McNamara went by the window. The President asked him to join us. When the discussion was over, we stood a few paces from the others, to visit.

"Mr. President," I said, "my mind is made up. I shall support the treaty; and I expect some castigation for my vote."

He flashed a broad smile. "Everett," he said, "Have you read 'The Man and the Myth'?" "No, Mr. President, I have not." Then, with a

real chuckle, he said, "You do not know what castigation is."

I have not read the book. The John Kennedy I knew was not a myth.

Theodore Roosevelt was said to have remarked, on one occasion, that most of the world's work is done by people who do not feel well. The life of John F. Kennedy is an eloquent lesson to millions of people of things accomplished and work done by one whose life was besieged by ailments and sometimes crippling forces.

Jaundice delayed his college education. Injuries caused his rejection by the Army. Through months of strenuous exercise he qualified for the Navy. The Japanese destroyer which smashed his PT boat brought back the injury to his back. Malaria complicated his problem. The disk operation to his back in 1945 was another event in his struggle for health and vitality. His long hospitalization in 1954 and 1955 gave his family and friends real concern.

Despite these intruding forces, he was elected to Congress in 1946, 1948, and 1950, and to the Senate in 1952 and in 1958. Can anything more eloquently proclaim the determination and stamina of the man?

A presidential contest is a gruelling challenge to the mind and body of any man. Yet I know of no occasion in that contest when he relented in his vigorous pursuit of a victory. I know of no occasion when he whimpered or complained. I know of no occasion when he felt impelled to lay aside the burden of the campaign because of pain or ill health. Day after day he coursed over this land from ocean to ocean and from dominion to gulf. This is not a myth. This is not fantasy. This is the unadorned story of a man who with unquenchable zeal pursued his determination to render public service at the highest attainable level regardless of the handicaps which were his lot. This is the man who became the 35th President of the United States. This is the man who could laugh and smile through it all. This is the man who fought back the ills of the flesh, only to have his unconquerable spirit extinguished by a weapon in the hands of a fellow man with an evil brain and a black heart.

It brings back a picture of a smiling young man, at age 25, lying on a hospital cot in an Edinburgh, Scotland, hospital awaiting perhaps his 20th operation in as many months as physicians and surgeons strove to save his foot. The other had already been amputated. He had gone through illness, pain, suffering and now he was in the hands of the great Scottish physician, Dr. Joseph Lister, who had discovered a new method of treating infections. It was then, with courage high, with faith unimpaired, with the fortitude of a saint, that William Ernest Henley wrote "Invictus," a poem of force and power which has inspired millions to face the unkind blows of fate and triumph over their handicaps. In that hour when William Henley's very soul was tried in the crucible of faith this is what he wrote:

> Out of the night that covers me,
>   Black as the pit from pole to pole,
> I thank whatever gods may be
>   For my unconquerable soul.
>
> In the fell clutch of circumstance
>   I have not winced nor cried aloud.
> Under the bludgeonings of chance
>   My head is bloody, but unbowed.
>
> Beyond this place of wrath and tears
>   Looms but the horror of the shade,
> And yet the menace of the years
>   Finds and shall find me unafraid.
>
> It matters not how strait the gate,
>   How charged with punishments the scroll,
> I am the master of my fate:
>   I am the captain of my soul.

The student, the reporter, the Congressman, the Senator, the President, the PT-boat commander, John Fitzgerald Kennedy was truly the master of his fate—he was the captain of his soul.

ADDRESS BY

Hon. Leverett Saltonstall

OF MASSACHUSETTS

Mr. President, on Friday afternoon, November 22, 1963, a horrible tragedy saddened every true American citizen. We lost our President, a man whom we respected, one who was conducting the high office to which we had elected him with dignity, courage, ability, and firmness. This tragic event was doubly hard to bear because it happened in our country. Who could have believed that such an act could occur in the United States? We can only be thankful that it was apparently the action of a demented person

and not one that can be attributed to any organized group or to any failure of our way of life. This does not, of course, lessen our grief over the loss of a man in whom the country had faith and reliance, a man who was in the prime of life.

We have set aside this afternoon to pay our tribute to John F. Kennedy. When he became a Senator in 1952 I walked up the center aisle with him and introduced him to the Vice President. As his Massachusetts colleague for 8 years in this body, I came to have a relationship with him that developed into a friendship and mutual confidence in each other that lasted through the years. The late President was "Jack" to most everyone, but he was always "John" to me until he became "Mr. President." We early agreed to work together on problems that affected our Commonwealth and we often talked about these matters. I believe we did help our State by supplementing each other before committees and on the floor of the Senate. We knew we would not always agree on national questions, although we often discussed them prior to a vote. On international problems such as foreign aid, NATO, and other understandings, our feelings were generally the same.

Our Massachusetts people have a long history of courage, leadership, dedication to public service, and the ability to rise to the challenge of the times. As a student of history, John Kennedy was aware of this tradition and he became part of it. The qualities that have made Massachusetts a good place in which to do business and to bring up a family formed the historic background and tradition which so influenced John Kennedy.

He was an able man and I enjoyed the opportunity I had to watch him grow and develop during the major part of his political career. Our ages were different and so to some our relationship seemed unusual, but fundamentally we trusted and respected one another and so remained on good terms even though our partisan politics were different. Certainly he was a man of good will, a man of ideas, and yet he was a man who had his feet on the ground. He was an attractive person, never flustered, quick to understand the pros and cons of a problem, a good administrator of his office, a person who demanded and obtained good advice. No one I have ever encountered in public life could size up the public reaction to a legislative proposal more quickly or more accurately than he. One of his greatest assets was his ability to meet a person, disarm him by quick repartee, and persuade him to do what John Kennedy wanted to have done. He was always courteous and straightforward, and could be counted on to live up to his agreements.

During the long illness which he had early in his Senate service, I tried hard to see that his name was included in all that affected our Commonwealth. This I think he appreciated. It helped to strengthen the bonds between us, to make us friends and it increased our determination to work closely together to help Massachusetts. I am glad I had the opportunity to work with him as I did.

So today we like to recall our association and experiences with our late President, our respect for his intellectual and personal character, his sense of humor—and, above all, his patriotism so clearly evident in his military and governmental actions, his firmness, his decision and his understanding.

Certainly the loyalty and affection which he stimulated in his own immediate family—his father and mother, his brothers and sisters, and the vital help that he received from his good wife—helped him enormously. And they gave him this loyalty and affection because they admired and trusted him. We share their grief and sense of loss.

We who knew him will miss him. His fellow citizens will miss him and the leaders of the free world and even those behind the Iron Curtain will miss him. But his spirit and what he stood for will always remain with us.

ADDRESS BY

Hon. George A. Smathers

OF FLORIDA

Mr. President, I was too near the one we mourn to attempt to sum up his career and contributions. I will leave that to others. Poets will raise lamentations for him as Whitman did for Lincoln. Historians will fix his place in the pantheon of our Nation's heroes.

And those who speak or write the definitive accounts need never have known him personally, for great men and great tragedies touch the souls of people everywhere. The evidence was in the lines which moved endlessly past the bier in the Rotunda, reverent and inconsolable.

The tears which were shed nearly a century ago by the family and the Nation for Abraham Lincoln have long since dried. But the power of his ideals and of his tragic fate have remained to inspire the living. And some, reading his words and remembering his hopes, reach out to bigger deeds than they might otherwise accomplish.

John Fitzgerald Kennedy will likewise be a living force in generations unborn, through his idealism, his eloquence, and the terrible circumstances of his death. Because he was wise and generous in the choice of his successor, he may even prove to have been a greater immediate influence than Lincoln was on the bereaved Nation which he left behind.

There is a certain consolation in this knowledge that the causes John Kennedy believed in will be served eternally by his tragic death. More than anyone I ever knew, John F. Kennedy had a sense of history's vast sweep, and an insight into his own special role as an active figure on history's stage. And it is in history that his full measure will be known. Great men are always so far ahead of their times that seldom are they recognized for their greatness while living. Many of President Kennedy's proposals—much of his program—were received with widespread consternation. But in our lifetime we shall see many of them receive general acceptance, and many of us will wonder why we could not see their value before.

More than anyone I ever knew, John F. Kennedy desired fiercely to achieve a greatness which would be remembered beyond his own time and place. His memory will be perpetuated—but not alone in the monuments and memorials of a grateful nation. It will live in the hearts and minds of people everywhere—who saw him grasp a world which was on the brink of an atomic holocaust, and firmly and coolly hold the line, turning it back on the path of a peace with dignity.

It is one of those ironies which I think John Kennedy would have appreciated, that the killer who struck him down in the high noon of his life, also immortalized him. But it is a consolation which provides little solace to those of us who loved him, not as a public person, but as a man. I will miss the inspired leadership, the cool courage, the shining phrases, as shall we all. But the void in my heart was left by the loss of the confident, smiling, vigorous, and yet always thoughtful and tender young man with whom I shared 17 years of friendship. I regret I do not have the words for the poignancy of the loss I feel.

He was just 46. He had talents—and the energy to serve them. He had important things left to do. He had the Irish gift of laughter and of compassion. He had the loyalty and the love of a father and mother, brothers and sisters, who formed as close-knit and active family as any man could wish. He had the adoration of a radiant and gracious lady and of two beautiful, budding children—Caroline and John-John— whom he adored in return. In brief, he was alive—in a sense that few of us ever were or will be. And now he is dead. And the worst of it is that this man who was so rational, so forebearing, so forgiving should have been struck down by a mad act of hate. The finality of it is still beyond bearing.

And yet I know—we all know—that Jack Kennedy would have enjoined us to bear his death bravely and to carry on, as he said, "rejoicing in hope, patient in tribulation." Jack Kennedy loved life and lived it exuberantly. He had everything to live for. But he never shrank from what life might bring. He understood the risks and the responsibilities of living at the vortex; and he accepted them—not with bravado, not with resignation, but with calm and purposeful courage.

For he believed, without being a reckless person, that fear or self-pity make a man the prisoner of circumstance. And so, while he always knew the odds, he did not surrender to them.

It was a constant of his personality. The determined frail freshman trying for the Harvard football team, the pain-wracked swimmer in the Pacific night, the invalid who earned a Pulitzer, the courageous campaigner on a thousand hostile platforms—all of these prefigured the mettle which he showed as President.

We live in a world of danger, he told us repeatedly, "but let us not despair." And he never did. And in the moments of deepest shock and sorrow, his own family showed us how to bear the tragedy of his loss and to do what must be done.

My wife, Rosemary, and my two sons, John and Bruce—both of whom dearly loved President Kennedy—join me in extending our deepest sympathy to his parents, his brothers, and his sisters. To Jacqueline and her two precious children, whose loss is greatest of all, go our love and our prayers.

Though the empty place to which he gave such vividness, such grace, such love, can never be filled, may they—and we—find comfort in lifting high the torch which has fallen from his hand and which now and forever will light his memory. "And the glow from that fire" will indeed "truly light the world."

We shall not see his like again in our generation.

ADDRESS BY

Hon. George D. Aiken

OF VERMONT

Mr. President, in joining with my colleagues in paying respect to the late President Kennedy, I do so with full realization that eulogies in themselves may be a weak apology for some of the things we may have done or have left undone.

The only lasting mark of affection and respect we can show for John F. Kennedy will be found in the work we do during our own "little day" and the contribution which that work may make toward the betterment of mankind.

If, because of his dedication to public service and as a result of his death, we dedicate ourselves to greater service, then we will have paid him the highest possible honor.

During his first weeks in office, I was not too sure that Jack Kennedy would be a good President.

The excitement—the glamour—the abandon of many of his enthusiastic friends and supporters seemed to indicate that we might be in for a "playboy administration."

Then came the episode of the Bay of Pigs. Although he was not called upon to do so, he accepted full responsibility for the failure of that venture. From that time on it was President Kennedy. From that time on, it was apparent that the weight of his office rested more and more heavily upon his shoulders.

From that time on, he put forth an ever-increasing effort to insure national prosperity, human justice, and world peace supported by the necessary strength of our Nation.

He was called upon to meet crises both at home and in the international field. With each new challenge, he seemed to gain strength and wisdom while the burden of his office bore down with an ever-increasing weight.

It may be said that many of his objectives were not achieved during his lifetime.

Granting that this is true, it may also be said that through his thinking and through his action and his utterances an untold host of people found themselves viewing their fellowman and the world itself in a changing light.

I am content to leave to history the record of John F. Kennedy, 35th President of the United States, in the belief that history will hold his finest eulogy.

ADDRESS BY

Hon. Lister Hill

OF ALABAMA

Mr. President, as we dedicate this day to the memory of a gallant American who graced this Chamber by his presence during 8 years of his and our lives, we recall to one another the high qualities and splendid accomplishments of John Fitzgerald Kennedy, our departed friend and leader.

No quality among the many that he possessed, in my judgment, and no accomplishment among the many that he achieved, can equal his deeply devoted love of peace and his ceaseless effort to consolidate the peace of the world.

John Kennedy thoroughly comprehended the nature of the times through which we pass. He had prepared himself well for the task he entered upon less than 3 short years ago. As he grappled with all the manifold problems, threats, crises, and dangers which have confronted this Nation during his brief Presidency, he broadened and deepened his knowledge and his understanding of the awesome challenge facing mankind.

Then, just 14 months ago, he stood alone and stared more deeply than any man has ever stared into what he described as that "dark and final abyss."

It was his courage and his genius that drew us back from that abyss.

He told his countrymen:

Peace and freedom do not come cheap * * * and we are destined to live out most, if not all, of our lives in uncertainty and challenge and peril.

He told us:

Together we shall save our planet or together we shall perish in its flames.

He told us:

It is our intention to challenge the Soviet Union, not to an arms race, but to a peace race; to advance, step by step, stage by stage, until general and complete disarmament has actually been achieved.

John Kennedy conceived it to be the supreme duty of his Presidency to preserve the peace. He dedicated his full energies to binding up the old wounds of our world and to preventing infliction of new ones.

He tried by every means at his command to create an atmosphere of mutual confidence and understanding in which agreements designed to protect humanity from the holocaust could be reached and upheld.

In mounting and maintaining for our country the mightiest military force any nation has ever had, it was his solemn determination that this force shall be used only to keep the peace, to prevent war, to deter any adversary from attacking us or our allies.

Because John Kennedy seldom used the word "peace" without linking it to the word "freedom," the peace that he was seeking was not that of surrender to evil, but of the defense of freedom.

The treaty which the Senate ratified only a few weeks ago, ending nuclear experiments in the sky above us, in outer space and beneath the waters, John Kennedy intended to be only the first step toward the abolition of war as an instrument of national policy.

When the foul deed that struck him down was committed, he was already searching ahead for new ways of reducing the unbearable tensions which grip all mankind.

He saw in the exploration of outer space vast implications for the human spirit—the reactivation of the innate curiosity of the mind of man— new opportunities for the exercise of maximum ingenuity—wholly new, unexplored frontiers for American genius—an end to the suffocating atmosphere of complacency and frustration.

He knew that our age, the age of space, demands the highest order of initiative, intellectual cultivation, and attainment that has ever been required in any previous day in the history of this planet, and he urged us to follow the course of excellence in all things.

John Kennedy wanted America to lead the world toward peace, toward freedom, toward justice, toward a renaissance of civilization.

He wanted America to lead the world in unlocking the mysteries of the universe around us.

It fell to him to be our President at the moment when the revolution in military weaponry is reaching its apogee, when people everywhere have come face to face with the nightmare of the possible extinction of the human race.

Deriving from his own deep religious sentiment, carried forward by his luminous intelligence, expressed in scores of eloquent pronouncements, and sustained with ardor and bravery, the central purposes of the life of John F. Kennedy, I believe, were these:

To impel human beings everywhere to understand themselves and their fellow men, to oblige every person who loves God to give of himself rather than to demand of others, to follow the ancient Greek injunction, "know thyself," and the ancient Biblical command, "love thy neighbor," to practice rather than to preach the Gospel of the Prince of Peace, to "remark not the mote in thy brother's eye but the beam in thine own."

May God grant that we shall have the wisdom and the humility to follow in the path of peace on which he led us.

ADDRESS BY

Hon. Frank Carlson

OF KANSAS

Mr. President, as we meet to commemorate the memory of one of our famous former Members, John F. Kennedy, our thoughts bring to mind many facets of his impressive career of public service.

Those of us who had the privilege to serve with him in this body had an opportunity to ob-serve and feel his keen interest in humankind, his dedication to the preservation of this Republic, his firm and abiding faith in his God, and his determination to devote untiring effort to promote peace in the world.

Much will, and should, be said about his service to our country and the nations of the world, but I want to direct my remarks to the spiritual qualities of this great man.

For many years I have been president of the International Council for Christian Leadership, and in this position presided at three Presidential prayer breakfasts in which President Kennedy participated.

At the first prayer breakfast, March 3, 1961, following his inauguration as President, he spoke in part as follows:

I think it is most appropriate that we should be gathered together for this morning's meeting. This country was founded by men and women who were dedicated, or came to be dedicated, to two propositions: First, a strong religious conviction, and secondly, a recognition that this conviction could flourish only under a system of freedom. I think it is appropriate that we pay tribute to this great constitutional principle which is enshrined in the first amendment of the Constitution, the principle of religious independence, of religious liberty, of religious freedom. But I think it's also important that we pay tribute and acknowledge another great principle and that is the principle of religious conviction. Religious freedom has no significance unless it is accompanied by conviction, and therefore, the Puritans and the Pilgrims in my own section of New England, the Quakers of Pennsylvania, the Catholics of Maryland, the Presbyterians of North Carolina, the Methodists and Baptists who came later, all share these two great traditions which like silver threads have run through the warp and the woof of American history.

At the beginning of the second year of his administration, speaking at the annual Presidential prayer breakfast March 23, 1962, he spoke in part as follows:

I want to, as President, express my appreciation to all those whose efforts make this breakfast possible. This is only one of a worldwide effort, I believe, to build a closer and more intimate association among those of different faiths, in different countries, in different continents, who are united by a common belief in God, and therefore united in a common commitment to the moral order and as Governor Daniel said, "a relationship of the individual to the state." * * *

On our program this morning, there is a quotation from Lincoln which I think is particularly applicable today. He said, "I believe there is a God. I see the storm coming, and I believe He has a hand in it. If He has a part and a place for me, I believe that I am ready." * * * We see the storm coming; and we believe He has a hand in it.

And if He has a place and a part for us, I believe that we are ready.

This year, February 11, 1963, speaking at the 11th annual Presidential prayer breakfast, President Kennedy spoke in part as follows:

> We cannot depend solely on our material wealth, on our military might, or on our intellectual skill or physical courage to see us safely through the seas that we must sail in the months and years to come.
>
> Along with all of these we need faith. We need the faith with which our first settlers crossed the sea to carve out a state in the wilderness, a mission they said in the Pilgrims' Compact, the Mayflower Compact, undertaken for the glory of God. We need the faith with which our Founding Fathers proudly proclaimed the independence of this country to what seemed at that time an almost hopeless struggle, pledging their lives, their fortunes and their sacred honor with a firm reliance on the protection of divine providence. We need the faith which has sustained and guided this Nation for 175 long and short years. We are all builders of the future, and whether we build as public servants or private citizens, whether we build at the national or local level, whether we build in foreign or domestic affairs, we know the truth of the ancient Psalm, "Except the Lord build the house, they labor in vain that build it."

These quotations from President Kennedy reveal his sublime faith in his Creator and his dependence on his God to guide and direct him as he led this Nation through nearly three stable and prosperous years. As a legacy to him, we should rededicate ourselves to carry on in the faith that helped in dark and troublesome periods in his life of service.

As a part of these remarks, I ask unanimous consent to include an expression of sympathy adopted by the All-Student Council of Kansas University on November 23, 1963.

> The All-Student Council of the University of Kansas acknowledges with grief the tragic assassination of the President of the United States, John F. Kennedy. The very foundation of our democratic system is the peaceful settlement of disputes and change of governments. Americans and foreign students alike realize that the United States of America has lost more than a great President. The world has lost a statesman and mankind has lost a friend. The cause for which the late President died was consistent with the causes for which he fought.
>
> The country must move on, as it will of course, united behind a new President. Yet the Republic will never be the same without the leadership of this man who asked of the people the same devotion he offered them.
>
> Respectfully,
>
> JOHN E. STUCKEY, Jr.
>
> Concurred in by:
>
> REUBEN MCCORMACK,
> *Student Body President,*
> *The University of Kansas.*

ADDRESS BY
Hon. Richard B. Russell
OF GEORGIA

Mr. President, on rare occasions in history figures appear on the world stage to capture the attention and excite the imagination of all mankind.

Such a figure was John Fitzgerald Kennedy. Around him was the aura of the age of chivalry. The world saw him as the young knight with the courage of a lion and the soul of a poet who sprang almost from oblivion to world leadership and dared to challenge the dragons of war and human misery.

The tragic manner of his passing brought universal grief.

Nothing that I might say about his ability and statecraft can approach in eloquence the lofty tributes paid him by the leaders of the nations of the earth. No mortal words can reflect greater sincerity than the tears of millions of the humble who felt that they had lost a great and good friend.

It was my high privilege to have known this man personally and to have enjoyed several years of association with him. Among his other admirable attributes, he was a man of tolerance and understanding. He fought hard for those things in which he believed, but he well knew that all men would not see the same issue in the same light. He would have been the last to have expected anyone to stultify conviction merely to conform to his opinions.

This world is a much better place because he lived and passed this way. Some of his ideas and ideals will forever encourage and assist men in the quest for peace, justice, and the good life for all. May he rest in peace.

ADDRESS BY
Hon. John J. Sparkman
OF ALABAMA

Mr. President, I wish to join my colleagues in the Senate in paying tribute to the memory of our late President and former colleague in this body.

I knew Jack Kennedy when he first came to Congress. Later, of course, when he came to the Senate I came to know him even better. For a time he was a member of the Senate Small Business Committee of which I was chairman. Still later, he became a member of the Foreign Relations Committee on which I was serving. We served together on that committee and worked together until he assumed the Presidency.

I often think of Jack Kennedy as a Member of the Senate standing at his desk on the back row just under the clock. I have watched him so many times in presenting issues in which he was interested and in managing bills here on the floor of the Senate. I often watched him and was amazed at his tremendous grasp of facts in connection with any measure that he was handling. I was intrigued by his gentleness in debate, his willingness to listen with patience to the arguments that others might have and to work out differences with reference to legislation. He was an able and effective legislator— serious, conscientious, and dedicated.

So many times do I remember seeing him hobbling around the Senate on crutches or with a cane as a result of injuries received in the crash of his famed PT–109.

I have read of his experiences in the South Pacific during the war and have been impressed with the thought: Here was a man. I have read his book "Profiles in Courage" written from a hospital bed recovering from surgery that carried him to the brink of death.

It was my privilege to be closely associated with him at the time of his inauguration. I remember those friendly contacts that we had and I keep with pride on my office walls various pictures and mementos that he gave to me in connection with that inauguration.

While he was serving as President I was often in his office at the White House. I have seen the friendly manner in which he talked to adults and children with equal ease from his rocking chair.

I have seen him out on trips in Tennessee, Alabama, other places throughout the country, speaking to great crowds and then going among the people to speak to them and to talk with them.

He was a man of great intellect and sincerity of purpose. He was a man of courage as was amply demonstrated by his confrontation with Premier Khrushchev. He was truly a leader of the free world who built steadily a greater strength for our country and the free world to the end that Khrushchev openly admitted our overwhelming superiority. Through this strength he was able to push steadily for an advance toward peace. In my opinion he did more than any other person in our time toward getting the world started toward peace— a durable, universal and dependable peace. We shall remember his work, and future generations will learn of it, in the cause of world peace and will, because of it, call him blessed.

He has been taken away at the time that his free world leadership was recognized throughout the world—at a time when he was still a young man with great promise ahead. We mourn with all the world his untimely death.

Behind him he left his devoted wife and two precious children. Mrs. Sparkman and I extend to them our deepest sympathy. May God watch over and keep them.

ADDRESS BY

Hon. Clinton P. Anderson

OF NEW MEXICO

Mr. President, in May 1962, the first White House Conference on Conservation in 54 years was convened here in Washington. The President of the United States, who called that historic meeting, addressed the closing session of the Conference. With his eyes on the horizon, his thoughts on the future, John Fitzgerald Kennedy declared:

> I don't think there is anything that could occupy our attention with more distinction than trying to preserve for those who come after us this beautiful country which we have inherited.

In his first message on natural resources sent to the Congress in 1961, President Kennedy declared:

> From the beginning of civilization, every nation's basic wealth and progress has stemmed in large measure from its natural resources. This Nation has been, and is now, especially fortunate in the blessings we have inherited. Our entire society rests upon—and is dependent upon—our water, our land, our forests, and our minerals.

How we use these resources influences our health, security, economy, and well-being.

But if we fail to chart a proper course of conservation and development—if we fail to use these blessings prudently—we will be in trouble within a short time.

There are many accomplishments in many fields which can be attributed to the regrettably brief administration of John Kennedy. Foremost among these are the achievements in the wise use and protection of the Nation's endowment of natural resources. And under this heading a distinguished record was created in adding to the national parks system, new areas of recreation, historic and scenic value. President Kennedy dramatized and articulated the fact that a rapidly growing, increasingly mobile population required a vigorous program of outdoor recreation planning and development by government at all levels. I dwell on this aspect of conservation today only because it is a subject of close personal interest.

During his first 2 years of office, 13 new national parks, historic sites, memorials and monuments were authorized by Congress or created by President Kennedy by Executive order. Sometime ago I commented that the Kennedy administration was well on its way to one of the most distinguished national parks records in history.

Midway through President Kennedy's first year in office, he signed into law the act creating Cape Cod National Seashore—the first major addition to our national park system in 16 years. John Kennedy had a long and intimate tie with this stretch of sea and sand and marshland. He introduced the bill to create the park and later, as President, put his signature to the act. In another century, another distinguished son of Massachusetts, Henry Thoreau, said of the great stretch at Cape Cod:

A man may stand there and put all America behind him.

Cape Cod blazed the trail for establishment of other seashore areas. Thirty miles north of San Francisco, Point Reyes National Seashore was created, accessible to 5 million people living within 100 miles. That was in early September of 1962, and before that month was out the President's pen again had signed the act of Congress creating Padre Island National Seashore.

So from the Atlantic, to the Gulf of Mexico, and on to the Pacific shoreline, 285 miles of unspoiled seacoast have been protected for public use.

By Executive order, President Kennedy created Buck Island Reef National Memorial in the Virgin Islands, thus protecting a coral barrier reef.

And while he was stimulating the creation of recreation areas by the sea, President Kennedy also urged favorable congressional action to bring into being new parklands in interior America—in Nevada, in Missouri, in Arizona, along the Indiana lakeshore, in Utah, and on the dunes of Lake Michigan.

President Kennedy called our attention to a new natural resources problem, generally unrecognized 30 years ago. This is the necessity to encourage preservation of open space in and near our urban centers. Increasingly ours is an urban population. Even modest projections show that in merely 7 years an area roughly equal to the combined size of Maryland and Delaware will be engulfed by advancing urbanization. For the well-being of our people, the conservation of natural, green acres in and near urban centers is imperative.

President Kennedy declared in 1961 that "Land is the most precious resource of the metropolitan area." Deploring the present pattern of haphazard suburban sprawl, he won inclusion in the open-space land program in the 1961 Housing Act. Already, in 26 States, 114 grants are making communities more pleasant, better places in which to live.

The administration program for urban renewal demonstration grants induced several States to begin evaluations of their open space needs. New Jersey and Pennsylvania are studying the Philadelphia metropolitan region. Wisconsin is seeking to determine the best use of its waterfront lands with all their potential for outdoor recreation.

An early request by President Kennedy to Congress was for legislative protection of the Nation's remaining wilderness areas. Preserved, these areas will stand as living reminders of the natural wilderness from which this Nation was wrested, and as a timeless gift of immeasurable value to future Americans.

President Kennedy sought the creation of a comprehensive Federal recreation lands program and the fostering of outdoor recreation programs by State and local governments. This is underway through the new Bureau of Outdoor Recreation. And before Congress now is a Presidential request for a land and water conservation fund. This fund would provide technical and financial assistance to State and local agencies in the planning, acquisition and development of recreational sites.

When visitors go to Mount Vernon to view George Washington's home and look across the Potomac they will see much the same view that Washington saw because President Kennedy and Mrs. Kennedy took a personal interest in the preservation of the historic Potomac shoreline in neighboring Maryland.

Last May, Mr. President, I had the pleasure of accompanying a group of people very much interested in the cause of conservation to the White House. I brought my granddaughter, Mary Elizabeth Roberts, along. I mentioned to the President that she was with me because the work he was doing for her generation is going to count in the future. We stood in the sunshine with President Kennedy and discussed his interest in sound resource programs. The President said he wanted to visit some of the wilderness and other key conservation areas of the Nation. We encouraged him in his plans and in the autumn he made that tour.

Significantly, it began with the dedication of the Gifford Pinchot Institute for Conservation Studies at Milford, Pa. There President Kennedy said:

> Every great work is in the shadow of man, and I don't think many Americans can point to such a distinguished record as can Gifford Pinchot, and this institute, which is only the latest manifestation of a most impressive legacy, I think can serve as a welcome reminder of how much we still have to do in our time.

On his trip the President was primarily concerned with the need to conserve and develop our natural resources, but he saw this need in the perspective of the long-term national interest. He saw conservation as one of the basic necessities to make sure that America remained both the land of the free and the home of the brave; he saw the emerging requirement in what he called the "third wave of conservation in the United States to make science the servant of conservation as we devise new programs of land steward-

ship." But beyond this he saw very clearly that what we did in the field of conservation might not materially alter our lives in the next 3 or 4 years, but it certainly would in the decades that lie ahead.

At the White House Conference on Conservation, President Kennedy closed his remarks with a story about the distinguished French leader, Marshal Lyautey. The marshal, as President Kennedy related it, told his gardener to plant a tree. The gardener replied that it would not flower for a hundred years. "In that case," said the marshal, "plant it this afternoon."

The new parks, the new national seashores, the natural monuments preserved will stand as tribute to the encouragement by President Kennedy of wise use of God's bounty. They are an appropriate inheritance to pass on to generations yet unborn.

I have stressed natural resources because his work in that field was typical of his work in many fields. Others, I am sure, will stress those accomplishments and I would want to echo every word of those eulogies. But in my own heart and mind I cannot fail to remember first the great leadership in the effort of conservation, which centers substantially if not primarily in the West, of this son of New England whom we so reverently remember today.

ADDRESS BY

Hon. Henry M. Jackson

OF WASHINGTON

Mr. President, if a man is fortunate he may have on one or two occasions in a lifetime, the chance to work in a cause he believes in completely in company with men whom he deeply admires. I had that supreme privilege in the Government service with John F. Kennedy.

I had the good fortune to serve with him when he first came to the U.S. House of Representatives in 1947. In 1952 we were both candidates for the U.S. Senate, and were elected that year. During the presidential campaign of 1960, I was associated with him as his chairman of the Democratic National Committee. Then here in the ranks of the Senate in the last 3 years, I have been an advocate or sometimes friendly critic of his policies and programs.

Words do not come easily to express the sense of loss at the death of this happy warrior.

The whole world has recognized his special gifts dedicated to the service of his country and to a just peace. His qualities as a great public figure have been extolled by the leaders and people of every country who have paid him respect in these last weeks.

I would like today to mention a special virtue of John F. Kennedy in the office of President—he deeply understood the supreme problem of this Nation as the wise use of our great power.

For example, consider these words at the University of Washington's 100th anniversary program in November 1961:

> Diplomacy and defense are not substitutes for one another. Either alone would fail. A willingness to resist force, unaccompanied by a willingness to talk, could provoke belligerence—while a willingness to talk, unaccompanied by a willingness to resist force, could invite disaster.
>
> While we shall negotiate freely, we shall not negotiate freedom. Our answer to the classic question of Patrick Henry is still no—life is not so dear, and peace is not so precious "as to be purchased at the price of chains and slavery." And that is our answer even though, for the first time since the ancient battles between Greek city-states, war entails the threat of total annihilation, of everything we know, of society itself. For to save mankind's future freedom, we must face up to any risk that is necessary. We will always seek peace—but we will never surrender.

During the time I knew Jack Kennedy, I came to especially respect his deep interest in people. He sincerely enjoyed people. We saw this on a recent trip to the State of Washington just a few short weeks ago. He went out of his way to mingle with the crowd, to shake hands, to autograph pieces of paper. It was a special tragedy that it would be on another of these triumphal tours that he would be cut down by an assassin's bullet.

And during the days following this tragedy we have witnessed the magnificent mettle and high courage of Jacqueline Kennedy—and all the Kennedy family. We are profoundly proud of them.

Clearly, John F. Kennedy brought to the Government of the United States and to the Presidency a very special luster that we will not soon see again.

ADDRESS BY

Hon. Abraham A. Ribicoff

OF CONNECTICUT

Mr. President, many words of mourning and of eulogy have echoed eloquently across this land. The Nation's leaders and its humblest citizens have poured from their hearts the testimony of their grief, their horror at a tragedy of unimaginable proportions, and their deep sense of personal and national loss. I share that grief, that horror, and that loss.

We mourn the loss of John Fitzgerald Kennedy—a born leader, a man of brilliance, a giant among men. We have lost a great President and a rare human being. He was a man of knowledge and of vision—with a distinctive style marked by charm—and a grace tempered by wonderful wit. He brought to the Presidency a keenness of mind unmatched by all who served before him. His strength and courage were nobly translated into love of country and devotion to a world of peace and freedom. He was a young President who became for us—as for men and women and children everywhere—the symbol of a young, a free, a strong, a compassionate America.

With a sense of profound respect, we mourn our loss, and are humbly thankful for the time we knew him. For me it began in 1949. We were both young New England Congressmen. I sensed in him then the inner strength, the contained composure, indeed, the spark of greatness that so many would come to know. In days that followed we worked together, endured defeat together, rejoiced in victory together. With both the challenges of politics and the responsibilities of Government, I was proud and privileged to have had a part in helping him.

What is lost can be remembered in our minds, recalled in our words, and revered in our hearts. But what has not been lost will endure in more meaningful ways. So very much has not been lost. So very much remains.

John Kennedy rallied the forces of freedom throughout the world, and those forces and that spirit of freedom remain strong today. He led the world in a new quest for an honorable peace. He let our adversaries know that hostility meant disaster and that common understanding could lead to a decent world for all. With patience and persistence he worked to achieve the test ban treaty. The world felt and followed his leadership, and continues forward today on the course he set.

John Kennedy raised the sights of this Nation, and those sights are high today. He bid us all look with him at the unfinished business of our country, and those matters hold our attention today. He held up to us the plight of the uneducated, the unemployed, the ill and the poor. He pointed us toward the future of our cities, of our farms, of our industry, of our natural resources. The generation he inspired will never ignore these problems; we will never look away from that future.

John Kennedy set for our people a standard of excellence, a personal challenge to do our best in everything we do, and that personal challenge still lies before us today. He had the ability to lift those around him. He made us try to think more clearly, to read more widely, and weigh the facts more carefully—even to look around us at the pictures on our walls or the physical exercise we were getting—and ask ourselves if we could not do better. The generation he challenged will never cease to pursue the goals he set.

Most of all, John Kennedy caught the imagination of the young people of America, and their imagination remains fired today. He called upon those in their thirties to serve their Government, he bid those in their twenties to make the Peace Corps a reality, and he urged the teenagers to stay in school. Our Nation's youth responded to him, and the response is alive and vigorous today.

John Kennedy led us all to new frontiers and bid us cross them with him. He knew the frontiers of our continent had been replaced by frontiers of our national problems, the world and space. Those frontiers remain today, and so does his challenge to cross them.

There remains, too, the spirit of tolerance he sought by personal example to encourage throughout the land. More than any President before him, he committed the Presidency to achieving full civil rights for every American. He opposed prejudice of every kind. There was no trace of meanness in this man. There was only compassion for the frailties of others. If there is a supreme lesson we can draw from the life of John Kennedy, it is a lesson of tolerance, a lesson of conscience, courage, and compassion. And that lesson remains.

For me there remain many memories from a long association. Among the clearest is a cold and windy night 3 days before the 1960 election.

We came to Waterbury, Conn., a little before 3 o'clock in the morning on a Sunday with the man who—the following Tuesday—was to be elected President of the United States. The square in front of the hotel where we were staying was packed with people. They had been waiting for many hours to see John Kennedy.

We came out on the balcony together. The candidate spoke: the crowds responded ecstatically shouting and cheering and showing their love for this young leader. They wanted more—more—more.

But he had had a long day and he was tired. "Abe, you go out and speak," he said, and I did, but the crowd still shouted for "Jack."

So, responding as he always did, he went back to them, and spoke.

"I will close," he said, "by telling you of the letter which Lincoln wrote in a campaign very much like this, 100 years ago, when the issues were the same. He wrote to a friend: 'I know there is a God and I know He hates injustices. I see the storm coming and I know His hand is in it. But if He has a place and a part for me, I believe that I am ready.'"

"Now 100 years later," John Kennedy continued, "when the issue is still freedom or slavery, we know there is a God and we know He hates injustice. We see the storm coming and we know His hand is in it, but if He has a place and a part for me I believe we are ready."

The last "I," he changed to "we." He wanted us to be ready. He lived, worked and died to make his country ready. All that he did, all that he inspired, all that he stood for remains.

As we mourn our loss, let us dearly prize what is not lost. Now 37 years from the 21st century, we are ready for the future and all that it may bring. President Kennedy made us ready, and so by the grace of God we shall remain.

ADDRESS BY

Hon. Herman E. Talmadge

OF GEORGIA

Mr. President, the Nation and the free world still mourn the death of our late President, John Fitzgerald Kennedy. We are all filled with a deep sense of personal loss.

On this day when it becomes our sad duty to honor the memory of President Kennedy in the Halls of the U.S. Senate where he served so well and where we first came to know him, I am reminded of a splendid October morning 3 years ago in Warm Springs, Ga.

The then Senator Kennedy was vigorously campaigning for the Presidency, and I joined tens of thousands of other Georgians in welcoming this young and energetic young man to our State, and to Warm Springs, the site of the Little White House, where the great President Franklin D. Roosevelt was taken from our midst at one of the most crucial times in the history of our Republic.

John Kennedy captured the imagination of the huge throng assembled there before the white portico of Roosevelt's Georgia retreat. He won their hearts and their support of his pledge to get this country moving again.

His visit to Georgia is now legend, and I am proud to have been a part of it. And Georgians are proud that he was there.

John Kennedy knew that he was asking for the most awesome and burdensome job in the world, and he was willing and able to face this great responsibility in keeping with the best of American tradition. As he told my fellow Georgians at Warm Springs:

> I do not run for the Presidency under any expectation that life will be easy for the next President of the United States or easy for the citizens of the United States. To be a citizen of this country is to live with great responsibility and great burdens.

Life was not easy for President John F. Kennedy, and he—perhaps as much as any other of our Chief Executives—lived with great responsibilities and burdens. The President discharged his duties well, and though the dastardly assassin's bullet took him from us in the prime of life, John Kennedy has assured himself of a prominent and respected place in American history.

He died a hero's death in the service of his country, to which he had dedicated his entire life.

ADDRESS BY

Hon. Quentin N. Burdick

OF NORTH DAKOTA

Mr. President, most Americans, following the events of November 22, felt as if a member of their immediate family had died.

I felt that way. I recalled simple personal things about John F. Kennedy, as I had known him. He had paid five visits to my State of North Dakota, the final time as President of the United States less than 3 months ago.

In 1959, when I was a freshman Congressman, my teenage daughter, Jennifer, went over to Senator Kennedy's office to get his autograph.

More than a year later, Senator Kennedy, as the Democratic nominee for President, arrived at the Fargo, N. Dak., Airport. Out of a huge throng, he spotted my daughter and called, "Hi, Jenny." She was ecstatic.

This little story may seem inconsequential, but I partly judged John F. Kennedy by his kindness to my young daughter. It is only human to remember a person in this way, even when the person happens to be President of the United States.

The world has lost a tremendous human being. He was warm and friendly, firm and determined. His quick mind, his wealth of knowledge and his charming manner are no more. But we will never forget him.

John Fitzgerald Kennedy was superbly qualified for the Presidency. He had the qualities of greatness—the historical perspective, the wisdom, the sense of purpose, the ability to inspire people. And he had just begun. I am appalled by the waste. I am numbed by the magnitude of our loss.

The history books are likely to record that the paramount contribution of John F. Kennedy was to start a new trend in world relationships—

a realistic understanding by nations of the necessity for living peaceably with one another in the shadow of the nuclear bomb.

The turning point may have come in October 1962, when we learned that the Soviet Union was emplacing missiles in Cuba.

With steady nerves, but with restraint, John F. Kennedy ordered the Soviet Union to remove the missiles. The Soviet Premier backed down. The missiles were dismantled. And the whole world had heightened respect for American determination to protect freedom and halt aggression.

The tension of that crisis had a sobering effect—the stark realization that, like it or not, nations will have to coexist, or run the risk of a nuclear holocaust.

John F. Kennedy, perceiving this reaction, pressed for a further relaxation of world tension. In July, he negotiated the nuclear test ban treaty, which he termed "an important first step—a step toward peace—a step away from war." It was at this point that he was taken from us so abruptly.

The cool judgment, the respect John F. Kennedy commanded among other nations will be sorely missed, as we carry forward the unfinished work of building a more livable world.

Our responsibilities have been expressed in many ways since November 22. We have heard about the need to purge ourselves of bitterness, hatred and bigotry and about the hope that our common sorrow will unite us and uplift us.

H. A. Swenson, a member of the choir at the First Lutheran Church at Bismarck, N. Dak., was inspired to write a poem after hearing the sermon the Sunday following President Kennedy's death. It was entitled "The Lamp of Freedom":

The lamps of freedom often burn from blood by heroes
    shed.
The light of freedom is a gift from those who now are
    dead.
What does this mean to you and me who share this
    common good?
Who have not yet been called upon to give this
    precious blood.
We too must share in lesser ways to keep the fire bright.
There is so much that needs repair; there is some wrong
    to right.
With humble spirit, purpose true there is a work to do.
When we can clearly see our call and carry through.
Ours may not be dramatic spots that shake the very earth.

But in the simple, humble tasks, we need to prove our worth.

Likewise, the pupils in a small school in North Dakota caught the spirit in a resolution the day after the President's funeral. An accompanying letter read:

PEKIN PUBLIC SCHOOL,
OSAGO SCHOOL DISTRICT No. 58,
Pekin, N. Dak., November 26, 1963.

DEAR SENATOR BURDICK: I enclose a resolution from our school (grades 1 to 12).

Our school just wanted to do something. Would you take the enclosed letter and do with it what you see fit? Perhaps you would care to file it with your other papers. We seek no publicity.

Sincerely,

HENRY X. HANSEN,
Principal.

The resolution, signed by all 76 pupils and the 5 members of the faculty, follows:

IN MEMORY OF OUR BELOVED PRESIDENT
JOHN FITZGERALD KENNEDY

We, the pupils of the Pekin public school, dedicate ourselves to one special act of kindness each day for at least 1 year.

ADDRESS BY

Hon. John O. Pastore

OF RHODE ISLAND

Mr. President, unbelievable—still unbelievable—is the tragic passing of President John Fitzgerald Kennedy. In this Chamber of the U.S. Senate it seems only yesterday that Jack Kennedy moved among us—a colleague of the finest, friendliest character; an earnest youth but a statesman by every test; an ally to cherish; an opponent to command affection; a Senator who moved from our back row to the first seat of the Republic—and yet remained close, companionable to us all.

Our States were neighbors—his and mine— Massachusetts and Rhode Island—with no boundary visible to the naked eye or open heart.

Through all his years John Kennedy was a favorite of Rhode Island. He could not begin to accept the invitations we poured in upon him. When our Newport became the scene of his wedding, the romance seemed part of each Rhode

Islander's life. When he favored us with his summer presence as a man of family and as President, an enthusiastic Rhode Island had to be restrained from giving him a summer White House.

So I had the privilege here in the Senate to work often with him on measures of mutual importance.

At the close of a day of taxing debate on the Senate floor—there would come a note of thanks personally penned because he felt you had helped him. Later, the White House telephone would be personally dialed—directly and delightfully—as he seemed never to have separated himself from our midst. On occasion the President has visited this Capitol—and homesickness has led him to this very door—to peer within—smile at a speaking Senator—and whisper, "It is just as I left it."

And when we visited the White House, he would walk outside with us after the meeting, walk to the gate—and even out on the public street—to our dismay and that of the men of the Secret Service—but to the President's delight.

For John Kennedy loved people—loved to meet them face to face—hand clasping hand—winning the hearts of the world to him.

We and the world have been robbed of all this by the senseless savagery of a misfit mind.

But out of the colossal cruelty was born a closeness of our country. A life of service and a death of sacrifice united a nation, revealing the true image of America.

Even in the depths of the tragedy we saw the far-reaching vision of a leader who sought and saw his successor in a colleague who shared this Senate Chamber with him and with us.

Our country saw the John Kennedy profile of courage was a profile of good counsel, commanding the confidence of the people and the continuity of the government, implicit in his selection of Lyndon B. Johnson—guaranteed by his sharing with him all the problems and programs and potentials of administration from their first moment as a team, to their last moment in the close companionship of that day of happy beginning and finality of deepest grief.

If we speak of a people's grief in that hour, words have not yet been fashioned to tell the torment of his closest of companions—wife and mother of the little family endeared beyond cavil

to all the world—to tell of her torment or of her nobility, as womanhood has ever risen to nobility in the tragic trials of man.

I borrow the words of a religious editor of another faith to record:

In the searing and exacting duties that lie ahead, a quiet, slight young woman has given the United States an example of fortitude and strength that will not soon, if ever, be forgotten. In Jacqueline Kennedy, it has seen a pattern for its own devotion to the demands of the future.

All men bow their heads to the sacrifice and service of woman—sweet even in its sorrow—and strongest under bitterest blows.

When any of us in the Senate speak of those November hours of loss and loneliness, our words must needs be painfully personal.

What have we left of John Kennedy? Shall we count a photograph together—a flight together—an autographed volume—a family portrait—intimate letters with a signature that almost smiled as he penned it?

Yes—in our innermost hearts we shall cherish them—and as Senators and Americans we shall treasure all the imperishable words and all the unconquerable hopes of an American who shall possess the dreams and ideals of youth for all eternity.

Time shall never dim nor dull the ringing challenge of the young President at the very doors of this Capitol on the sun-splendored day of his inauguration.

Ask not what your country can do for you—ask what you can do for your country.

John Fitzgerald Kennedy asked:

What can I do for my country?

He lived for it. He died for it.

ADDRESS BY

Hon. Winston L. Prouty

OF VERMONT

Mr. President, some day in the quiet of an evening, when his toys are put aside, a young boy will ask: "What was Daddy really like?"

In that fateful moment, when time stands still and all the world descends upon her, may she who bears the burden of the answer tell no tale of office gained, of prize attained, of battle lost or won.

But speak of him who loved the Lord and saw in the least of us the traces of His majesty and in this land the glory of His handiwork.

Or if she choose another way, why then just say: "Your father, John Fitzgerald Kennedy, was a good man."

ADDRESS BY

Hon. Warren G. Magnuson

OF WASHINGTON

Mr. President, the loss to the Nation, the free world, and the free people in the captive world is great. No one in the elapsed time created, in the world, a greater respect or image for what decent people want the world to be, than John Kennedy. Can we but build on his foundation, we can look forward with some hope in this terrible tense world. His decent approach to these should be a model for the betterment of mankind. We can do what he would want by dedicating ourselves to this great cause.

His understanding of our domestic matters was based upon a simple truth. That we were a growing expanding nation and that in these changing times there would be some Americans hurt in the process. Their needs required readjustment. He believed America was strong enough morally and economically to meet the needs of the people. He knew history. He knew that any government that failed to keep up with this responsibility weakened the whole fabric of the country.

The best memorial to him would be a dedication to this basic truth.

His contribution to tolerance was enormous. During 3 years as President, he proved a Catholic can keep his religion and work a precedent, separate and independent, of each other. He was a Christian gentleman. He neither paraded nor preached his religion. He respected others' beliefs and laid no venom or intolerance to it.

He was my personal friend for many years. Even after he assumed the high office of President, he and I never lost that personal touch and on many occasions we met in that period, not on political or business purposes, but just to say "Hello" again as old friends. I will miss that.

He despised pettiness and bigotry in all human endeavor. His mind was sharp, keen, imaginative, but yet mellow as great scholars are wont to be. This may have well been his spark of greatness. Even in his relaxed moments it was there. History will make that greatness indelible in its appraisal.

To his family my deepest sympathy—but words are so futile—dedication to what he stood for will be more rewarding to me and to them.

But the ways of God work wonders. Maybe the country and the world needed a martyr to tolerance—this is a terrible price to pay. But God does reign in the heaven and thank God, the Government at Washington still lives.

Mr. President, I ask unanimous consent to insert an address by Mr. Clarence C. Dill, of Spokane, Wash., at this point.

JOHN F. KENNEDY MEMORIAL SERVICE

(Address of Clarence C. Dill, courthouse, Spokane, Wash., November 25, 1963)

Whenever an orator of ancient Athens arose to address the free assembly, he first offered a prayer to the immortal gods that no unworthy word would escape his lips. So today in the shadow of the terrible tragedy that took our President, I pray no unworthy word shall pass my lips.

We meet in this memorial service for memory and inspiration. John F. Kennedy had not passed on life's highway the stone that marks the highest point. As an English playwright said yesterday: "He was in the summer of his life." The fact is he was pressing forward with all his power, the programs he had proposed.

Although the President is dead, the program of help for the underprivileged of our own country and for the maintenance of human freedom around the world, a program to which he had dedicated his life, must be carried on. During the last 50 years our industrial, commercial, and social life has enlarged so rapidly and so enormously that new governmental remedies have been necessary for new national ills that developed from time to time.

Woodrow Wilson declared his proposed national remedies to establish the New Freedom. Twenty years later, Franklin D. Roosevelt proposed his reforms to give the American people the New Deal. Thirty years later, John F. Kennedy named his remedial programs, the New Frontier.

We are too close to the terrible tragedy that ended his career, to assess what the Nation and the world have lost, but through the gloom of grief we can discern the principal parts of the program he proposed and championed.

When Congress shall have enacted laws that will provide fully for the medical and hospital care of all the aged, and when that reform has been established to extend those same services to all our people, of whatever age, we shall have the full fruition of his dream for providing national medical and hospital service, whether it be by social security changes or some other method.

When Government and industry are able to cooperate so as to distribute the benefits of automation to aid in the employment of those affected by new machines, that will fulfill another of President Kennedy's dreams.

When all Americans, regardless of race, religion, or national origin, can be educated together, work together and have equal rights of every kind, that will be a national achievement of civil rights for which President Kennedy strove so continuously.

When all the great nations of the world destroy all their nuclear war weapons and make it an international crime for any nation to produce or possess nuclear weapons of war, so no wild man in control of any government can destroy the human race, that will be another victory for world peace which President Kennedy so much desired.

He was the symbol of youth to all the world. His Peace Corps has proved the most helpful organization for improving international relations devised by any nation during the 20th century for that purpose.

In addition to all these services to the Nation, we should recognize how well he protected his country in case of his inability to serve as President. First, he chose Lyndon B. Johnson to take his place, because he was a statesman with broad experience as a leader in the Congress, and second, he acquainted the Vice President with full knowledge of the national and international problems of the administration. As a result, despite this terrible tragedy, our land is bright today. The Nation knows and the world knows a strong man stands at the helm of the ship of state, prepared to weather any storm that may develop.

Turning now to John Fitzgerald Kennedy the man: He was born in New England, graduated from Harvard, cum laude, then studied in London and later became an itinerant observer and writer about world events. At 28 he was elected to the House of Representatives; at 38 he was elected to the Senate. He soon became one of the small number of Senators who are known outside their own States because of their independence, their ability, and their leadership. He won the Presidency at the age of 43 and was in the full flower of his leadership at the time of his death.

Television and radio had made millions of common folks feel they knew this man. It will not be easy to go on without hearing and seeing him from time to time by television in our homes. We shall miss the Boston accent of his voice that seemed a part of him. We shall miss too that eager, forward-looking attitude that he so often showed in discussing public questions. We shall miss his wit and charm in parrying political questions or his laughing at his own predicaments in his numerous press conferences. His friendly, almost neighborly style of discussing weighty subjects of legislation and international problems with seeming mastery, made his millions of listeners feel confident that he would meet all challenges with courage, intelligence, and a high sense of patriotism. He had won the respect of the leaders of the Nations of the free world. They looked to him for leadership with hope and confidence.

Although I did not know him as well personally as had I served with him in Congress, I recall an incident in the 1960 campaign when he spoke at the Lincoln Memorial at the corner of Monroe and Main at the noon hour, which like a chip of wood, shows the quality of the whole block.

At the close of his speech I tried to pilot him through the crowds to the Spokane Club. The pressure of those around us wishing to shake his hand and wish him success, was so great at times we could scarcely move at all. When I tried to apologize for not having had a police escort, he laughed and said: "Oh that's all right. I wanted this nomination and this is all a part of the fight."

During 3 years as President, he proved a Catholic can keep his religion and his work as President, separate and independent, each of the other. He was a Christian gentleman. He neither paraded nor preached his religion. On Sunday morning he took his family to the services of his church and seemed to enjoy attending services in the small, unpretentious chapels of the Virginia countryside as much as in the great cathedrals.

No eulogy should omit a tribute to the woman he chose for his wife, Jacqueline. The popularity of her beauty, her style of hair-do's and clothes with the women, were exceeded with the people only by her charming personality. The whole Nation gloried in her redecoration of the White House. She was a first lady of a different kind from all those who had preceded her, and with all this, she devoted herself to her children, Caroline and John, as her first duty.

Early in the administration, little Caroline became the beloved child of all the people. Republican leaders often said they could oppose the President and might find something to criticize about Jackie, but freely said: "There's nothing we can do about Caroline."

Little John, who came as a kind of bonus son to the winner of the presidential election, had not yet reached the age to fascinate the people, but photo flashes show boyish activities which make understandable why his doting father nicknamed him "John-John."

But it was following the crash of the assassin's bullet when he slumped upon Jacqueline's lap that brought forth her hidden strength to meet such a tragedy. She pillowed his head in her arms while his life-blood oozed away as the automobile rushed to the hospital. There, she remained at his side until life was gone. Then she rode with the casket in the ambulance to the airport. In the plane she sat beside the coffin all the way to Washington. Then she went with the body to the funeral home. She remained there until 4 o'clock in the morning when she rode with him to the White House for the last time. Not until then did she cease her vigil of Spartan-like care.

But it is that act of delicate, almost infinite tenderness at the funeral home just before the casket was to be finally sealed, of which I wish to speak especially. Alone, she went to the open casket, removed her wedding ring, placed it in his hands, and kissed his lips for the last time—a symbol of her love that would last forever. By these acts of devotion, she wrote a new and different chapter for closing the "Profile of Courage."

After this she turned over his mortal remains to the

military for funeral services and burial in that American Valhalla for heroes who have served in time of war, the Arlington National Cemetery.

In all the mythological tales of the love of gods and goddesses, in all the love stories of the kings and queens of history, in all of Shakespeare's creation of love scenes, you will not find such a beautiful, exquisitely fine demonstration of wifely love as Jacqueline Kennedy's act to symbolize her everlasting devotion.

In conclusion let me call attention to the dramatic phase of President Kennedy's taking off. It was near the close of a highly enthusiastic street parade. Just as his car approached the underpass, with his wife's words, "Dallas has been kind to you," still echoing in his ears as he smiled and waved a responding salute to the cheers of those on the sidewalks, a bullet crashed through his brain. While the automobile rolled on into the underpass, his spirit at that moment must have leaped into the skies to his heavenly home and his spirit, even now, may be exploring the space world to which he planned the astronauts should some day go.

I close in the words of James A. Garfield to a street crowd in New York City the night Abraham Lincoln was shot: "God reigns in His heaven and the Government at Washington still lives."

ADDRESS BY

Hon. Strom Thurmond

OF SOUTH CAROLINA

Mr. President, November 22, 1963, will go down in American history as a day of national tragedy. The assassination of the 35th President of the United States on that date shocked and saddened Americans of all political persuasions. That act of perfidy, evidently performed by a man whose mind was poisoned with the Communist ideology which thrives on the totalitarian idea that the end justifies the means, closed a brilliant political career of one of the most personable and popular Presidents ever to serve our Nation. There were many disagreements with President John F. Kennedy's policies and proposals; but his personal popularity, according to public opinion polls, continued at an unusually high level for a man who was continuously in the national spotlight, actively seeking approval of his proposals and actions.

I had the pleasure, Mr. President, of serving with the late President Kennedy while he was representing the State of Massachusetts in this great body. We were both members of the Government Operations and the Labor and Public Welfare Committees. I particularly remember, Mr. President, the outstanding service which the then Senator Kennedy rendered to this body when he proposed, and then served as chairman of a special committee to select five great Senators of all time from among deceased former Members of the Senate. I was impressed with the selections made by his committee and with the objective manner in which he and his committee members performed their duties in carrying out this assignment.

I have always had a high regard, Mr. President, for the late President's appreciation of history, and particularly for his Pulitzer Prize-winning book, "Profiles in Courage." This book placed before each of us serving in the Congress and in public life excellent examples of some well-known and, until then, some little-known public servants who put into practice the high ideal of willingness to stand by the courage of their convictions in seeking to fulfill the trust reposed in them by their constituents.

Our country owes a great debt of gratitude to the late President for his foresight and vision in selecting as the man to succeed him in office, in the event of such a tragedy, one of the most experienced and capable leaders I have ever known. President Kennedy made certain that his Vice President, Lyndon B. Johnson, would be more than just a ceremonial officeholder to preside over the Senate. He helped prepare his Vice President for the awesome responsibilities which descended on his shoulders on November 22, by keeping him well briefed on national policies and decisions and by utilizing his talents, not only to serve our Nation, but also to make certain that the Vice President would be able to carry on the duties of the Presidency with the least possible confusion and loss of continuity.

Mr. President, I have expressed my deep sympathy to the members of the late President's family. In closing my remarks here today, however, I wish to take this opportunity to reiterate my condolences to Mrs. Kennedy, the children, and the other members of the Kennedy family, and also the heartfelt sympathy of the people of the State which I have the honor to represent in the U.S. Senate.

ADDRESS BY

Hon. Thomas H. Kuchel

OF CALIFORNIA

Mr. President, the Senate of the United States, reflecting the poignant feelings of a bereaved Nation and of a mournful globe, pays tribute today to the life and memory of a martyred leader of America, who set his sights on the sublime cause of peace with honor for all mankind.

The late, great, and dear John Fitzgerald Kennedy, our colleague and our friend, emerged from this Chamber to become our Nation's President; and from the steps of this Capitol Building, on Friday, January 20, 1961, taking his oath of office, he cried out to his countrymen, in moving eloquence and ringing phrases, to unite and to move forward "to assure the survival and the success of liberty."

His was the same solemn charge taken before God by all his predecessors back to the beginning of the Republic.

But—

He said—

the world is very different now. For man holds in his mortal hands the power to abolish all forms of human poverty and all forms of human life. And yet the same revolutionary beliefs for which our forebears fought are still at issue around the globe—the belief that the rights of man come, not from the generosity of the state, but from the hand of God.

Thus began the Kennedy administration.

The intervening months saw the new Chief Executive set about to move toward America's goals, as he saw the light, in a whole galaxy of executive decisions and of recommendations for new laws. As in the life of any man, there were successes and failures, triumphs and tragedies, as this patriot, acting always as he believed he should, guided our country through days of peril and also through days of hope. Here, unfolding, was an exciting chapter in the life of America, where every conceivable passion, good and bad, where every conceivable feeling, constructive and destructive, made themselves heard in every area across our land.

And then, on another Friday, November 22, 1963, with an appalling suddenness, this valiant man was struck down by a mad assassin; and the people of our country—indeed, those of the whole world—stunned in disbelief and in dismay, sought to take hold of themselves, for the Government of our Nation must go on and the world must continue to turn. Our hearts poured out condolences to his widow and his children, to all his family, and to the Nation.

The late President was my friend. Courageous and intelligent, dedicated to his responsibilities and to his ideals, surely qualified for leadership, impatient at irrelevance but tolerant in disagreement with any of us, sustained by a sweet sense of humor, loved by a devoted wife and children and family, this grandson of immigrants from Ireland devoted his life to the people, and then gave that very life to the ages.

In his inaugural, the late President said:

We observe * * * not a victory of party, but a celebration of freedom.

How true. Freedom is not divisible. His earnest struggle to perpetuate our freedom, his quest for equal treatment under law for all citizens, marked no partisan boundaries. Rather did they, and do they, and shall they, stand as banners to which men of good will hopefully may always repair.

The world will not forget John Kennedy. The Senate will remember him. Perhaps, somehow, with God's good grace, this appalling tragedy may shock the American conscience into an earnest, prayerful rededication to brotherhood, where liberty and happiness may wash away all the evils which man has done to his neighbor too many times. There, I think, is the path which this lamented servant of the people would want America to tread, in memory of the zealous prayers he expressed in his all too short journey through this life.

Mr. President, I ask unanimous consent to have printed at this point in my remarks, sundry comments by the press of my State of California.

[From Sacramento (Calif.) Union, Nov. 23, 1963]

JOHN F. KENNEDY—IN MEMORIAM

A people grieve for the loss of their President, John F. Kennedy. In profound shock, the Nation offers its heartfelt sympathy to Mrs. Kennedy, the children, and all the family.

Any death of a President in office must have terrific and personal impact upon the citizens; but when it comes so abruptly in the horrible form of assassination, and to a man so young and virile as was our President, then words cannot voice our feelings nor the heart contain our emotions.

So little can be said at a time such as this. Whatever is expressed is incapable of conveying adequately confused and turbulent inner passions.

Nothing we write can alter the unalterable tragedy of the untimely death of our President. No eulogy can restore him to his family and his people from whom he was so suddenly wrenched.

Our bereavement is profound, affecting each of us individually. We offer our prayers for John F. Kennedy, late President of the United States, and pray to God in his memory and for our Nation, which now suffers the blow and the trial occasioned by his tragic loss.

Vale, Mr. President.

———

[From the Sacramento (Calif.) Union, Nov. 23, 1963]

A PROFILE IN COURAGE

Born May 29, 1917, John Fitzgerald Kennedy, 35th President of the United States, came to his untimely and tragic death November 22, 1963. Only 46 years old, he was cut off abruptly with the promise of a brilliant and dedicated life incomplete.

Only history can judge the merit of his brief span as President, but we already have lasting opinions and warm memory of John F. Kennedy, the man. His entire career was one of selfless service and devotion to the public welfare.

Son of a wealthy family, John Fitzgerald Kennedy was ever concerned with the welfare of those less fortunate. He was sensitive to the problems of the aged and sick, the needs of the unemployed, the justified aspirations of our Negro citizens, and to all whose cause deserved humanitarian championing.

Courage as well as compassion was an essential ingredient of his character. He sought no special advantage during World War II. As an officer in command of a patrol boat in the Pacific fighting, he distinguished himself.

When his ship was sunk in 1943, he saved the life of his seriously burned engineer despite his own badly wrenched back; and when the wreckage had to be abandoned, he swam to an island 3 miles away while saving another of his crew by holding the straps of a sailor's lifebelt in his teeth.

In times of peace, he showed equal fortitude and determination. It took both to challenge bigotry by running for President of the United States.

Courage was the foundation of his stand when, little more than a year ago, he defied Russia and Cuba about the Communist building in the Caribbean. He made clear our unretreating resolve to uphold our commitments to West Berlin—even as he did to other free nations on various occasions.

John Kennedy, a loyal Catholic, showed his firm moral fiber when he opposed the Roman Catholic hierarchy on the subject of Federal grants to parochial and private schools. His physical courage was of comparable fiber; he underwent a spinal operation in 1954 which nearly cost him his life, and he conducted the heavy burden of his office despite actual pain and the discomfort of a back brace.

At the age of 29, he was elected to Congress, and after twice being reelected, he won a Senate seat in 1952. In 1960, he became the youngest President in the Nation's history.

And now, at the age of 46, he is no longer with us. No man, however, left a greater heritage of pride to his family, of unstinting service to his Nation, and of consistent dedication to the ideals of peace and liberty.

No passage of time nor historical verdict is required to engrave eternally grateful memory of John F. Kennedy, respected President, upon the hearts of his fellow citizens.

———

[From the Sacramento (Calif.) Bee, Nov. 22, 1963]

THE NATION MOURNS

The entire Nation has been plunged into deep grief and shame—grief for its slain President, John F. Kennedy, and shame it could have bred an assassin capable of so cowardly an ambush.

He came to the Presidency, did Kennedy, in an hour of rising extremism and in an hour when the preachers of hate were spreading their gospels of fascism across the land and because this is a free land they were permitted to speak.

Now Kennedy is dead and a piece of America died with him. And in this hour of tragedy we think of another President who 98 years ago was felled by another assassin who had listened to the hate merchants.

Only several weeks ago another figure in American life, Adlai Stevenson, also visited Dallas and there was spat upon and hit on the head with a sign condemning Stevenson and the principles he has espoused as U.S. Ambassador to the United Nations.

These were people who had listened, too, to the preachers of hate and of fear and who wanted all of life their own way.

Another went further today. He shot and killed the President of the United States.

———

[From the Sacramento (Calif.) Bee, Nov. 26, 1963]

HERE WALKED A GIANT—IF ONLY BRIEFLY

Never has the world witnessed a more spontaneous and more overwhelming outpouring of affection than shown here in the Nation which sired him and abroad where he came to be beloved, for the late President John F. Kennedy. In his brief years he had come to touch humanity, we learn in his hour of death, as few men have touched humanity and though he died with his song only half sung his place in history is abundantly secure.

In London, citadel of political sophisticates, they cried openly in Trafalgar Square. In West Berlin, where only recently the late President ignited fire in a crowd of more than 1 million when he said: "Ich bin ein Berliner," candles dedicated to his memory lit the night like a ricocheting, vagrant meteor. In Moscow a godless state gave its permission for memorial services and a stunned Nikita Khrushchev, with all the rest of Russia, openly grieved.

Here at home through the bitterly cold night hundreds of thousands gathered in the Nation's Capital to pass by the late President's casket which rested on the same catafalque where lay another martyred President, Abraham

Lincoln, 98 years ago. There in their many ways, they paid their last respects. They felt awkward before death, as do all of us, but they wanted to say goodby, and so they came and they came and they came.

All of us are too close to this tragedy to weigh it. History will make its own assessment of Kennedy, man and President, but when it comes to writing the chronicle of his brief years and measuring him against his hour, well may it write: Here walked a giant only briefly.

Now may he rest.

———

[From the San Francisco (Calif.) Chronicle, Nov. 25, 1963]

SELF-SEARCHING BY A SAD PEOPLE

This is not America the beautiful, but America the troubled, upon which the world has looked this past weekend, and to which it has sent its leaders and heads of state for the funeral today of President Kennedy.

The great men are here to honor the late President's great qualities of mind and person, which they had learned to know, measure and respect. Yet may we not believe also that they are here to show, by the testimony of their presence, how much the example and leadership of the United States mean to them and their countries?

In the somewhat dreary discussions which we conduct in this country on our foreign relations and how much they are costing us and how little gratitude they seem to earn us and how weary we are of the burden of them, we tend to forget the force and power of the American example in the world.

President Kennedy never forgot. He never ceased striving to represent this country as strong, determined and resolute. From his inspiration let the American people take that renewed devotion of which Lincoln spoke at Gettysburg a hundred years ago when he said it was "for us the living" to carry on the work of those who have died to defend freedom.

Over this sad weekend, the people of this country, confused and bereaved by the loss of their President, have been engaged in self-searching. They have been asking themselves what forces of hatred have been let loose amongst us and how shall our freedom be preserved from the threats of these forces.

How true and apt, as if in reply to these questions, were the words of Chief Justice Earl Warren, spoken under the Capitol dome yesterday, when he said that if we are to learn from the tragedy, if we are truly to love justice and mercy, we must "abjure the hatred that consumes people, the false accusations that divide us, and the bitterness that begets violence."

THE HERITAGE LEFT BY PRESIDENT KENNEDY

The Kennedy years in the American Presidency have profoundly shaped the course of this Nation. As time passes, and as some of the still half-concealed events of the past 3 years come to light, we believe that the late President's style and judgment in dealing with international affairs will earn him an ever more secure fame.

At the same time, it seems clear that history will give him no very high score for domestic achievements—though that will not be seen as his fault altogether, rather the fault of an unresponsive and dilatory congressional system which can cheat a victorious President of his reasonable legislative hopes.

The Kennedy years began, of course, on a well-remembered, bright, cold day in January 1961, of which many people retain two outstanding memories: The sight of the greatest of American poets reading a specially written ode to the occasion, and the sound of a sharp, clear, New England-accented voice saying, "Ask not what your country can do for you; ask what you can do for your country."

This was a happy, propitious, promising moment of taking over leadership by a man of the 20th century, a man who in the vigor of youth but with the authority of the oldest of republics could challenge Khrushchev and Mao and Adenauer and De Gaulle and masses of men everywhere to make the world a fairer place for men to inhabit.

Very soon after this, the promise which had been invoked by the confident new President was blighted by the Cuban invasion fiasco. This was the one resounding error of Kennedy's foreign policy, yet out of it was eventually to spring, ironically, his most impressive success: The showdown over the Soviet arming of Cuba and the withdrawal of their missiles.

It would be foolish to say that President Kennedy alone was responsible for sparing the world from nuclear war at that moment in October 1962, but it is surely not possible to take from him the credit for having safely brought the Nation, and by extension the world, through the most perilous passage they have ever been through.

Threats and alarms of war have steadily receded since that great climactic hour. Yet it is sadly true that the country which was behind Mr. Kennedy to the man in staring down his adversary in the Cuban confrontation, failed to give him the same backing in reaching a solution of the great domestic crisis of Negro rights. For coming to terms with that revolution, we shall have to look to the new President, or his successors in office.

———

[From the San Francisco Chronicle, Nov. 25, 1963]

(By Herb Caen)

THE LONGEST WEEKEND

It is less than 72 hours since the shots rang out in Dallas, yet it seems a lifetime—a lifetime of weeping skies, wet eyes and streets, and emotions that couldn't always be kept in check. Americans are not, by nature, an emotional people; the San Franciscan prides himself on an unflagging gaiety. And yet, over the endless weekend, San Francisco looked like a city that was only slowly emerging from a terrible bombardment. Downtown, on what would normally have been a bustling Saturday, the people walked slowly, as in shock, their faces pale and drawn, their mood as somber as the dark clothes they wore under the gray skies.

I remember a famous picture, early in World War II, of a Frenchman crying uncontrollably on the Champs Elysées as the Germans marched into Paris; some people found the photo painfully moving, others criticized him for not keeping a stiff upper lip in the face of the Hun.

A grown man doesn't cry in public: It is part of the American lexicon.

But we are affected variously by various tragedies, and there were grown men crying in San Francisco—the stinging tears of sorrow and frustration. It was already the day after, but it took only a quick reminder to bring the grief back to the surface.

A man walked past the blacked-out corner window of the City of Paris, with its small white card of tribute, and tears rolled down his cheeks. At Sixth and Mission, an old woman in black passed a late newspaper headline, and suddenly sobbed. At the opera house Saturday night, Sir Malcolm Sargent and the Royal Philharmonic of London opened the concert with "The Star-Spangled Banner," and the sense of loss was felt again; all over the house, tears glistened afresh.

The longest weekend, that was to have been the big game weekend, and never have perspectives been so suddenly shattered, never have day-to-day values come in for such an excruciating reappraisal. The few people in the downtown bars sat hunched over their drinks, staring down or straight ahead. For once, in the Nation that loves humor, there was none. All at once, a city had stopped smiling.

Gray skies, and the constant gray and black of the TV screen. For the first time, in these unprecedented hours, there was total television. You were irresistibly drawn to the tiny screen, as though you expected a miracle. But there were no miracles; only the minor miracle of three networks striving valiantly, and with commendable dignity, to transmit hour after hour of unfolding tragedy, symbolized by a flag on a coffin. You were immersed in a fantasy world of honor guards standing at attention in the rain, of endless streams of black limousines, of faces that suddenly became part of your life, and to whose familiar voice and manner you clung, as though seeking reassurance.

Over the weekend that lasted a lifetime—and ended a lifetime—the faces on the screen, switching from Washington to New York to Dallas and back again, over and over, became part of your reality. Their first names joined the family: Chet, Walter, Frank, David, Frank, Martin. The harried face of the police chief in Dallas became more familiar to you than that of the man next door. You learned more about Lyndon Baines Johnson than you had ever known, or thought you would care to know. Strange and unknown orchestras and choirs came and went before your swimming eyes. History was traced and retraced—a crash course in the Presidency for millions who too often take too much for granted.

For some of us, who spend too much time at our jobs and our pleasures, and too little exploring the manifestations of greatness, the weekend provided an awakening. As always, it came too late. For those of us who seldom have the opportunity to watch TV, John F. Kennedy became more alive in death than he had been in life. For hour after hour, through the marvel of electronics, we saw the President as though for the first time. His life, compressed onto the small screen, passed before our eyes, and we marveled at his spirit, his warmth, his humor, his brilliance. He seemed vibrantly alive, and his words had a life they never seemed to possess before. We drew strength from him, and, in a way difficult to define, hope. But the lump in the throat refused to be downed.

As you watched the fine young man, the utter senselessness of the tragedy that had snuffed out his life gnawed at you. There was not even a mad nobility in the act, no glimmer or even an insane purpose. This had not been a madman in the mold of John Wilkes Booth, leaping onto the stage of a theater, crying "Sic semper tyrannis!" This was not the inevitable gloomy grandeur from which Greek tragedy is forged, nor the uncontrollable furies of Shakespeare. This had been a warped young man—"a loner," they called him—who kept saying he didn't do it. In the confusion of his own life, he symbolized nothing. Or perhaps he symbolized nothing but confusion, and that itself is a symbol of the times.

And so today, a Nation already in shock goes into official mourning, and Arlington prepares to receive another fallen soldier. He died without knowing how much he was loved—or by how many.

———

[From the Los Angeles (Calif.) Times, Nov. 23, 1963]

OUR MARTYRED YOUNG PRESIDENT

Every true American, regardless of his political philosophy, and every citizen of the world who holds mankind's good in his soul, is shocked beyond belief by the murder of John Fitzgerald Kennedy, 35th and youngest elected President.

More than just a man was slain in the streets of Dallas on Friday morning. The assassin's bullet aimed at the very heart of something we hold most dear as a free people: the majestic office of the Presidency, wherein lies our best hope of liberty here and abroad.

Mr. Kennedy, at 46, had just crossed the threshold of rich maturity as the prime defender of global integrity against communism.

He had demonstrated statesmanlike courage under devastating enemy diplomatic fire.

And he had, at home, sought a program which in principle, if not its many specifics, sought justice for our myriad population.

When the stunned shock wears off—as indeed it will, leaving only shame and sorrow—the American people must find new ways to put aside their bitter divisions, new methods to achieve noble ends.

Out of President Kennedy's martyrdom, let us all pray, will emerge new strength to drive ahead, to persevere, and to triumph over the awesome problems which confronted this young man less than 3 years ago.

We can thank our Republic's founders that the continuity of our governmental affairs continues unabated, owing to their wisdom and foresight.

This is where the assassin's bullet failed. It might wound the heart, but it could not still the inexorable beat of America's destiny.

To Mrs. Kennedy and her two fatherless children, in their terrible grief, we offer our profoundest sympathy.

To President Lyndon B. Johnson, who now assumes the monumental burden of this office, we render our hopes and prayers for strength and wisdom at a bleak and critical time.

[From the Los Angeles (Calif.) Times, Nov. 25, 1963]

EPILOG TO TRAGEDY

It did not seem possible that anything could compound the terrible ordeal of John Fitzgerald Kennedy's assassination.

But violence has begotten violence. And punishment has been visited upon the accused assassin, not by the law but by one man's twisted vengeance.

The murderer of the President deserved to die, although no penalty could be imposed that would be commensurate with his offense against the Nation and the world. Yet even the perpetrator of this most heinous crime was entitled to the due process of the law for if this right is abandoned for one, we are abandoning it for all of us.

President Kennedy died because of one man's violent hate, victim of the complete renunciation of law and order. His martyrdom will be cruelly diminished if his death does not inspire in all Americans a greater sense of common purpose and a stronger belief in the democratic process and in justice.

His murder left the Nation filled with not only grief but shame. No one man or group of men, however, can take retribution into their own hands. Nor can we permit blame for the assassination to be extended from one man to whole segments of American life.

As the ultimate manifestation of hatred and violence, the slaying of the President is a tragic warning that we cannot tolerate the bitter divisiveness that any form of extremism inflicts upon the country.

If we would honor the memory of John F. Kennedy and redeem his sacrifice, we must emerge stronger and more united.

[From the Long Beach (Calif.) Press-Telegram, Nov. 22, 1963]

JOHN F. KENNEDY

The President is dead.

We cannot write words sufficient to express the sickening shock of Americans at the manner of his death.

Only a diseased mind could conceive and execute such a deed.

The madness of one—or a few—has robbed an entire Nation of its leader.

As he fought and suffered in World War II in the service of his country, John Kennedy has died in that service.

The heavy responsibility of the biggest job in the world now falls on the shoulders of Lyndon B. Johnson.

Let us remain calm in our sadness and give the new President the support he now must have as he takes up where the efforts of a courageous and beloved predecessor left off.

[From the San Francisco (Calif.) Examiner, Nov. 23, 1963]

JOHN F. KENNEDY

The assassination of President Kennedy has overwhelmed the Nation with grief. In Dallas, Tex., that grief must be almost intolerably compounded with shame.

As now is clear the assassination was committed by a Communist fanatic unaware of the depth of evil to which such dogma could lead him. In so doing he served the Communist cause its worst setback in the 46 years since its baneful inception.

And certainly the President was the victim of insensate hatred—so depraved and vicious as to be beyond normal understanding.

He was more than a victim. He was a martyr. Not a martyr of the Democratic Party, but one who exemplified in his character, in his acts, the decency, the reason, the freedoms of his country and all its people.

The assassin is a traitor to those qualities—to Americanism as we honor it and live it. That is one of the reasons why the murder of President Kennedy is so profoundly shocking, so incomprehensibly perfidious.

It is not too much to say that John Fitzgerald Kennedy gave his life for his country, just as once before, in World War II, he was willing to give his life, and nearly did.

Mr. Kennedy was a good, courageous President. He was a good, courageous American. It is a tragedy that his career had thus to end with an assassin's bullet when he had so much more to give.

To President Lyndon Johnson we offer our fervent prayers in the momentous task that now lies ahead.

[From the Long Beach (Calif.) Independent-Press-Telegram, Nov. 24, 1963]

A MOMENT OF MADNESS

The vast majority of Americans are sane, law-abiding people who respect their President even when disagreeing with him. But the Nation has its maniacal moments. Such a moment transpired Friday as President John F. Kennedy rode through the streets of Dallas enjoying the friendly and respectful greetings of sane, law-abiding Texans. The gun of the exceptional maniac poked through a window and swerved history in its course.

A man has been arrested and charged with the murder. It is not surprising that the suspect has been associated with the fanatical activities of the extreme left, and it would not have been surprising if he had proven to be a member of the fanatical far right. Extremes of all kinds are capable of inciting weak-minded or emotionally unstable men to acts of hatred and violence.

Now that the consequences of extremism and hate have been so stunningly demonstrated, we urge those Americans who are captives of extremist groups and causes to search their minds and hearts.

It is too early and the moment too full of stress for an objective and fair judgment of the place of John F. Kennedy in history. But certainly he was one of the most intelligent, fair-minded, and friendly men ever to hold the office of President. He had a thorough knowledge and firm grasp of the facts and problems of government. He bore criticism, of which there is always more than enough for every President, with equanimity. Despite great physical discomfort, he served devotedly. He was the President, and considering all the implications of that statement, there is no need to say more.

At the time of his death, Mr. Kennedy was deeply concerned with the issue of equal rights under the Constitution for all Americans. While at this time there appears no indication that the civil rights issue was in any way related to his assassination, his dedication to this cause and the work and leadership he had given to it will surely be a factor in the ultimate achievement of the honorable goals he sought. It is an important part of his legacy to a grateful country.

Of Mrs. John Kennedy it must be said that with the death of a husband following close upon the death of a child, she has had more grief in a few short months than any woman should be required to bear. The sympathies of the Nation are with her.

Meanwhile, as the Nation recovers from its shock and goes on with the business of living, Americans can be grateful for the stability and continuity of government which their system provides. Two hours after Mr. Kennedy had slumped in his car, dead of an assassin's bullet, a new President was receiving the oath of office and pledges of bipartisan support. Government goes on; a President has died, but the Presidency and constitutional government survive.

Eyes turn now to the future. Fortunately, the new President has had extensive and practical experience in American Government. As a former Representative, Senator, and Vice President, Lyndon Johnson comes to the office with above-average credentials. He knows Washington, its officials and its processes, as well as any man and better than most.

Even so, the new President will need the aid and good will of all Americans as he adjusts himself to the responsibilities and routines of his new and awesome office. Both in memory of the fallen President and in consideration for the new one, let there be a decent period without the raucous and distracting noise of partisan politics. And in our hour of sorrow and change, let us show to the world a countenance of dignity, calm, unity, and strength—which is, despite that maniacal moment in Dallas, the true countenance of America.

[From the San Francisco (Calif.) Monitor, Nov. 29, 1963]

To a President's Son

Last Monday, young John, you saluted your father on the way to his burial.

It was your third birthday and you could not understand. But you did well to salute him. And someday you will understand why.

Someday you will understand that God gave to your father all the qualities that other men admire.

Your father had exceptional intelligence. We marveled at his grasp of facts and his clarity of expression.

He seemed to have a natural compassion for all people. It just wasn't in him to be small in dealing with others. He was the kind of man who would have had compassion even for his assassin.

Though he was rich he was one of us.

Though he had every reason to, he never took himself too seriously.

He was young, and our civilization puts great store on youth.

God had given him handsome features and an attractive personality.

He was a man of straightforward religious faith. He attended Mass as easily and unaffectedly as he did everything.

He was apparently the kind of father all fathers want to be—loving you and your sister and loved by you.

More than anyone else in our memory your father seemed to have all the qualities we expect in a hero.

And with it all he had a humility which enhanced everything else.

To all appearances God had been unbelievably generous to your father. But to whom much is given, much is asked.

A man like this doesn't just happen. He is forged out of suffering and sacrifice.

God had asked him to carry many crosses. He had suffered the loss of a brother and a sister in the prime of life. He had seen another sister burdened with a serious affliction. He had been called to endure heroic hardship in a World War. In illness he had come so close to death he was anointed. As a father he had suffered the loss of your brother Patrick.

In his chosen profession he had assumed a job at a time in history when the burdens were enough to break the back of any man.

Though he served in an arena where deeds are sometimes sordid and principles ignored, this was a man demanded by his times.

Like you will be in a few years, young John, the world today is awkward. It is an adolescent asked to grow up faster than it can. It needed a leader with intelligence far above the average; it needed a youth to keep up with the jet-speed times; and most of all it needed someone with stability to temper the wild currents that are sweeping across the world and the passions inflaming the hearts of men.

He helped us in bewildering times.

You do not understand any of this now. But may you salute your father all through your life. May you do more than that.

Please God, may you resemble him.

ADDRESS BY

Hon. Thomas J. Dodd

OF CONNECTICUT

Mr. President, John F. Kennedy, our friend, our colleague, and our President, has passed into history. His image need no longer be veiled or shrouded by the mists of partisanship or contention.

He was a man ideally equipped by nature and by training for the leadership of this Nation and of the free world in its crisis of survival.

He was born to wealth. He could have spent his days in idle pleasure and luxury or in the pursuit of some worthy but pleasant endeavor. Instead he chose the most difficult, the most demanding and the most burdensome of all careers—the path which led him to the Presidency of the United States and to that unforgettable November afternoon in Dallas.

From an early age he dedicated his life to the service of his country.

He was a complex man with enormous talents and capacities which he organized and developed through a tremendous exercise of self-discipline.

There was a marvelous balance and proportion in John Kennedy that was not a product of our age, but rather the result of a supreme lifetime effort to develop the qualities necessary to rise to the problems of our age.

He was thoughtful and reflective, yet he was a man of decision and action. He had great confidence and self-assurance, but there was nothing of conceit or arrogance in him. He was serious and solemn, yet he possessed a deep and rich vein of humor, which always flickered just beneath the surface and occasionally came into view, lighting up his face and warming all around him.

He was always in the center of action, yet he had the capacity to look at himself objectively and dispassionately as though from a distance.

He was a man of strong convictions, one who threw almost superhuman effort and commitment into the struggle to have his convictions prevail; but he was never intolerant of the views of others, never dogmatic, always modest in victory and philosophic in defeat. He demanded excellence of himself and made vast sacrifices to achieve it, yet he had a limitless compassion for the shortcomings of others.

He was a blend of the idealist and the pragmatist—idealistic in the goals he set for American society, but eminently practical in his efforts to achieve those goals.

He could meet almost any man on his own level. He was scholar and athlete, soldier and writer, hero and intellectual, statesman and politician, a family man and a solitary man. Few American hearts were so narrow or hardened that John Kennedy could not join them on some common ground.

He had a fierce love of country which manifested itself not in hollow diatribes but in a total commitment of mind, spirit and body to the high purpose of making our Nation strong and secure and of making our society conform more closely to our ancient national ideals.

It is a profound tragedy to see this beloved man, this friendly man, this husband, this father, brutally cut down in the flower of his life.

It is a deeper tragedy to see a great life, a unique life, destroyed, wantonly and senselessly, in the midst of vast achievements, and on the threshold of completion of a great design for human betterment to which he had consciously dedicated and disciplined his life.

The depth of our loss can be measured in some small way by the outpouring of emotion which plunged this Nation and most of the world into grief. What cannot be measured is the full meaning of this tragedy for our country and for the causes we uphold in the world.

For in John F. Kennedy as President there was a unique joining of the man and the office. He had the intellect to perceive coolly and clearly the problems of the Nation; the ingenuity to evolve solutions to those problems; the energy to press those solutions to a conclusion; the outward charm to win the hearts of people everywhere and the inner strength to win the respect of leaders of men.

He had 3 years of experience in the most powerful and demanding position on earth. He had mastered the job. He had the confidence of the people, the allegiance of our friends, the respect of our foes. On his shoulders rested the hope of freemen everywhere.

All this—laid in the dust by the bullets of a deranged assassin. The deeper tragedy, then, is the loss to our country and to the world. Every man, woman and child is wounded and harmed by this dreadful act.

The supreme irony of it all is that a John F. Kennedy should be slain by a Lee Harvey Oswald, for no man devoted more effort, more thought, and more care to the afflictions of the Oswalds of the world than John F. Kennedy.

Oswald was a twisted and pathetic product of the worst aspects of American life. He was the product of a broken home and a rootless life; impoverished, mentally disturbed, emotionally unstable, rejected in every phase of life, neglected by society, scorned by his fellow students and fellow workers and fellow soldiers. There were several occasions when he violently forced himself upon the attention of our various institutions.

He was not helped when he could have been helped. He was not curbed when he should have been curbed. He was allowed to sink deeper and deeper into progressive stages of rebellion and violence and finally was given free access to instruments of murder with which he killed the President of the United States.

Who has given so much attention and effort to the problems of which Oswald is representative than our fallen President? It was he who struggled ceaselessly to meet the legitimate needs of the unfortunate and the despairing—the underprivileged, the fatherless children, the juvenile delinquents, the mentally ill, the economically impoverished, the unemployed, the untrained, the unfit.

It was President Kennedy who struggled with limitless devotion and ceaseless energy to create a new American society in which there was a place for everyone, an education for everyone, a future for everyone, a job for everyone, and equal opportunity for everyone, a society in which there was adequate medical care for the sick and mental care for the afflicted.

From all sides and from all places there are reports of monuments being raised in memory of President Kennedy. It is appropriate that this should be so.

Let memorials be raised in all corners of this land which he loved so well and which loved him in return.

But I suggest that it is in pushing forward these great causes to which he devoted his life that we can best pay tribute to our fallen leader.

In the midst of the Civil War, Abraham Lincoln said something that I think expresses a thought in all of our hearts today. He was grieving over the loss of his beloved friend and ally Congressman Owen Lovejoy of Illinois. He was asked what he thought of a proposal to raise a statue in memory of his friend. Lincoln replied, "Let him have the marble monument, along with the well-assured and more enduring one in the hearts of those who loved liberty, unselfishly, for all men."

It is in the hearts of the American people and grieving millions throughout the world that the truest memorial to John F. Kennedy resides.

ADDRESS BY

Hon. Carl Hayden

OF ARIZONA

Mr. President, the many words of praise, sympathy, and rededication that are spoken today in memory of our late President can in no way lessen the tragic loss that this Nation and the world have suffered.

This is only one of the many ways in which we in the Senate can express our deep sense of loss for a man who rose from among us to become President of the United States. John F. Kennedy had the unique quality which compelled men to follow him, to listen to him, and to help him carry the awesome burden of the Presidency. He possessed the rare insight into human affairs that makes a man want to serve his fellow men in any way he can and devote his very life to that service.

We knew him in the Senate as a young man of exceptional ability and great desire, and we knew him in the Presidency as a young man of vision and determination, and we know him in death as a man who left his great dream that freedom and justice would be the destiny of all men and all nations, for the fulfillment of those who knew him and will always remember him. We will not forget, nor will we shy from the task before us. We will carry on, for such is the way of all men who love freedom.

ADDRESS BY

Hon. J. W. Fulbright

OF ARKANSAS

Mr. President, it is not easy for any of us to speak in tribute to John F. Kennedy without revealing the sharp anguish which time has not dulled. The national consciousness is heavy with fatigue from sustained and genuine grief. "Just like losing a member of the family" one heard people say and, indeed, a great loss it was to the family of man.

Even as the Kennedy family drew together for comfort and support, so each of us have felt a greater bond with one another—a bond formed of common sorrow. In that time, little more than 2 weeks ago when we could not yet comprehend the tragedy, each man somehow seemed a bit more valuable—a bit more worthy of our respect and tolerance. It was as though in his death the message of reason, tolerance, and peace, so much the essence of him, was again proclaimed. Death, the ultimate mystery, always turns men to introspection, but so much more when we grieve for one who was so much to all of us, both in person and philosophy.

John Kennedy was a political man to whom ideas were the stuff of life—to be sifted, analyzed, and refined with the scholar's precision of thought, the historian's perspective, but finally the politician's view toward accomplishment.

And he was a public man who gave himself to the public's business with zeal and enthusiasm. There was no question of his desire to assume the burdens of the Nation's highest responsibility. He sought the Presidency purposely and devoted himself eagerly to the tasks of Government.

He came to authority in a difficult and perplexing age, filled at once with the possibility of total destruction and prospects for the ultimate conquest of the age-old human enemies—poverty, disease, and hunger. He sensed these challenges and with his great faculty for communication he sought to communicate them to his Nation and to the world. The frontispiece of his book, "The Strategy of Peace," carries this quote from Lincoln:

The dogmas of the quiet past are inadequate to the stormy present. The occasion is piled high with difficulty, and we must rise with the occasion. As our case is new, so we must think anew and act anew. We must disenthrall ourselves.

It is not by chance that John Kennedy would choose these words as a preface to this collection of his thoughts on the Nation's problems—present and future. As Lincoln, he saw the newness of his time and the need for new thoughts, new questions, and new solutions.

He was an activist. The Presidency was to him a positive force in our Government and in our society and he set about to be President. Many of his chosen tasks are yet undone and many will never be fully concluded, but true to his inaugural address he began.

He set out to conclude the association of the Western democracies perceiving that strength lies in unity and seeking to achieve it through closer political, commercial, and cultural ties with our European allies. It will be left to others to conduct the trade negotiations and the political conferences aimed at this objective, but those who do will be equipped with tools he forged. Many frustrations beset him in this effort, but he persisted as we must persist to work for closer unity of the free world.

With our own Nation on the threshold of maturity he reminded us of our responsibilities to the emerging nations of the world in Africa, Asia, and especially Latin America. Many of our policies will long bear his mark. Each new Peace Corps teacher and Alliance for Progress project will be his memorial.

Above all, he forced our Nation and the world to examine the precarious position of civilization confronted with the awesome power of modern nuclear weapons and the seemingly insoluble ideological divisions which threaten to trigger them. Walter Lippmann said it well in his column of December 3:

He achieved one thing brilliantly, which is changing the course of events, and that has been to convince the Soviet Union that it must perforce and that it can comfortably and honorably live within a balance of power which is decidedly in our favor. For that John F. Kennedy will long be remembered.

The nuclear test ban treaty—the historic "first step" with the Soviet Union—was his treaty. He fostered and championed it. While treaties have not the permanence of marble, the spirit of this one is the spirit of John Kennedy and humanity is indebted to him for it.

His quest for a peaceful world won the affection of men of good will everywhere. Particularly do those who share our Western heritage grieve for him. At the conclusion of my remarks I will ask unanimous consent to have a resolution of the British House of Commons commemorating his passing printed in the Record.

He was a completely reasonable and human man whose concern for people lay at the root of his efforts to create a better life for all Americans. His legislative proposals centered on people—their economic, social, and political welfare. We should be ever grateful that from our society arise such men whose own security makes more acute their consciousness of the insecurity of others. He was endowed with this great concern and the people of America loved him for it with a love not yet come to full fruition. We do not expect young men to die and we do not expect Presidents to die at all. The editor of a weekly paper in Arkansas sensed this mood well. Tom Dearmore wrote in the Baxter Bulletin:

The shock has been so great partially because the President of the United States is a great embodiment. In his person he is a symbol of the will of the people. But there was more than that in this anguish the Nation has undergone. In his death the people have found Mr. Kennedy. Many never really knew him until they lost him.

When the history of our time is written it will be recorded that in his election and service our democracy reached a new maturity. His election—as our first President who was a Roman Catholic—evidenced a calming of the religious intolerance which has been too much a part of our history. His funeral—as though to complete the effort—brought millions through television into the church which he claimed and for which he was criticized.

And yet other prejudices plagued him. The fruition of our Nation's melancholy history of race relations fell on his shoulders. One could sense the great sorrow this caused him and one must respect the great courage he displayed in meeting this domestic crisis. His courage was manifested, in part, by his refusal to vilify the South for what is truly a national problem.

In fact, one sensed that he had a special affection for the South and its problems. Only 2 months ago he spoke in my State of the new South and concluded by saying:

This great new South contributes to a great new America, and you particularly, those of you who are young, I think, can look forward to a day when we shall have no South, no North, no East, no West, but one Nation, under God, indivisible, with liberty and justice for all. That is what we are building in this country today.

It is our tragic loss that he will not see this dream fulfilled, as fulfilled it must and will be.

He was a young man and youth responded to him. The student paper at the University of Arkansas said:

And youth identified themselves with him. They admired him, because they understood his haste and boldness. They criticized him because they felt they were his peers, entitled to judge one of their own. And all the while, they respected him, because they saw in him a leader who belonged to them, maybe even more than to the others.

Now the weight of responsibility has been lifted from him and others are left to do the tasks he so eagerly and conscientiously set out to do. It is

our gain to have known him, the country's gain to have had him lead us for awhile, and humanity's gain that such a fine and decent man should have passed through our midst.

Our prayers have been and will be with his family and his successor.

Mr. President, I ask unanimous consent that the resolution of the House of Commons, the editorial from the Arkansas Traveler, and a variety of other communications which were addressed primarily to the Senate but which came to me through the Senate Committee on Foreign Relations, from many respected leaders of the world, may be printed as follows:

HOUSE OF COMMONS, MONDAY, NOVEMBER 25, 1963—
COPY OF MANUSCRIPT AMENDMENT TO BE MOVED BY A MINISTER OF THE CROWN (PRINTED UNDER THE DIRECTION OF MR. SPEAKER)

Assassination of President Kennedy: That an humble address be presented to Her Majesty praying Her Majesty to be graciously pleased to express to the President of the United States of America the shock and deep sorrow with which this House has learned of the death of President Kennedy; and to convey their sense of the loss which this country and the Commonwealth have sustained, and their profound sympathy with Mrs. Kennedy and the family of the late President, and with the Government and people of the United States of America.

———

[From the Arkansas Traveler, Nov. 26, 1963]

A UNIVERSITY REACTS

The university campus was still Friday afternoon. People whispered as they walked into 1 o'clock classes. Some teachers lectured jerkily, briefly. Others dismissed classes filled with tension. Groups of people crowded silently around those with radios, waiting to know for certain. When the short announcement came, "John Fitzgerald Kennedy, President of the United States of America, is dead," people turned without speaking and slowly drifted away. This was the university's first reaction to the news. It was one of disbelief, then of revulsion. "No it's not true. It couldn't happen in our civilized society." Then came the realization of the baseness of such an action, the animallike violence which shepherded one human thing into taking another's life.

As the weekend went on and the primary murder suspect was caught then killed before a confession was obtained, horror and insensibility seemed to pile on one another. The sequences of events took on a thicker coat of unreality. The consequences of these events, the succession of a new President, are so widespread, so infinite they have not been grasped. The death of this dynamic brilliant man has not really been accepted, cannot be understood.

Perhaps the young will have the hardest time making any sense of this weekend. The youth never really sees death in relation to himself. How can he with a whole life of desires and plans before him? He must concentrate on fulfilling these plans; he must have done with the bothersome blocks in his way. He never dreams he might suddenly be stopped in the middle of fulfilling his goal. Yet, today the sense of death is brought home to him.

John F. Kennedy was a young man, at 46, the youngest to ever hold the office of President of this equally young Nation. He was like a character from a romantic novel. He had a brilliant mind; he had a dynamic warm personality; he had a true sincerity in his beliefs, and most symbolic of his youth, he had an indomitable will. With these qualities he attained in less than one term a greatness matched by only a handful of his predecessors. He led his people strongly and surely in an unbalanced world. He led them quickly with the haste of his youth.

And youth identified themselves with him. They admired him, because they understood his haste and boldness. They criticized him, because they felt they were his peers, entitled to judge one of their own. And all the while, they respected him, because they saw in him a leader who belonged to them, maybe even more than to the others.

———

DER PRÄSIDENT DES NATIONALRATES,
November 28, 1963.

Hon. PRESIDENT OF THE SENATE,
Washington, D.C.

DEAR MR. PRESIDENT: The National Council of the Republic of Austria has mentioned by a manifestation of mourning held on November 26, 1963, the bereavement the United States of America and their friendly nations had to suffer by the death of the honorable President, John F. Kennedy.

I have the honor to enclose the text of the speech I addressed to the National Council on this occasion. At the same time I beg you, dear Mr. President, and the Members of the Senate to present my personal condolences as well as those of the Austrian parliamentary representation on this tragical event.

With the assurance of my highest esteem I remain,
Very sincerely yours,
ALFRED MALETA,
Director, Parliament of Austria, Vienna, Austria.

———

NOVEMBER 28, 1963.

MR. CHAIRMAN: Meeting today, for the first time since the staggering events of Dallas, the Foreign Affairs Committee, before beginning its session, said a few words in homage to the memory of President Kennedy.

Its members have unanimously charged me with transmitting to you their expression of deep condolences and to inform you of the hopes which they felt with the speech of President Johnson who assumes these highest duties in the most tragic circumstances.

In reaffirming to you the personal expression of my emotion and of my sadness, please accept my warmest wishes.

MAURICE SCHUMANN,
President, Foreign Affairs Commission, National Assembly, Republic of France.

TEHERAN, *November 23, 1963.*

Hon. RICHARD B. RUSSELL,
President of the American Senate,
Washington, D.C.:

Deeply distressed by learning the tragic news of the death of the President John F. Kennedy. With profound sympathy I extend to you and to your colleagues of the Senate on my own behalf and on behalf of all my colleagues the Iranian Senators our sincerest condolences in this deeply painful circumstance through which the American Nation and the whole world suffer the loss of a highly distinguished and peace-loving personality of the modern history.

DJAAFAR CHARIF-EMAMI,
President of the Senate.

———

CANBERRA, *November 23, 1963.*

The PRESIDENT PRO TEMPORE OF THE SENATE,
Washington, D.C.:

Profoundly shocked to hear of tragic death of President Kennedy. Please accept the deepest sympathy of all Members of the Australian Senate in the great loss your country has sustained.

A. M. McMULLIN,
President of the Australian Senate.

———

OSLO, *November 23, 1963.*

The PRESIDENT OF THE SENATE OF THE UNITED STATES OF AMERICA,
The Capitol,
Washington, D.C.:

The Norwegian Storting wishes to express to the Senate of the United States its profound sympathy with the people of the United States in their grief over the death of President Kennedy.

NILS LANGHELLE,
President of the Storting.

———

BRUSSELS, BELGIUM,
November 23, 1963.

To the PRESIDENT OF THE SENATE,
Washington, D.C.:

The Dallas crime has plunged the entire people of Belgium into mourning and consternation. They are deeply touched and indignant at the tragic death of the great American President, whose eminent role in critical moments of the world's history and whose firm determination that peace in justice and honor should prevail they will never forget. Belgium recalls with gratitude the loyal friendship of the late President. It is with deep emotion that the Chamber of Representatives of Belgium conveys the feeling of the Belgian people and sends to the Representatives of the American Nation its heartfelt sympathy and sincere condolences.

A. VAN ACKER,
President of the Chamber of Deputies of Belgium.

WARSZAWA,
November 23, 1963.

Senator CARL HAYDEN,
President pro tempore of the Senate,
Capitol Hill,
Washington, D.C.:

Profoundly shaken with the horrifying news of the assassination of John F. Kennedy, President of the United States of America, distinguished statesman. I am sending you, Mr. President, on behalf of the Sejm of the Polish Peoples Republic and in my own name expressions of the most sincere sympathy. President John F. Kennedy enjoyed admiration for his efforts aiming at the consolidation of peace and promoting of international cooperation. In the person of President John F. Kennedy the American Nation has lost its eminent leader who also displayed concern in the development of the friendly American-Polish relations.

CZESLAW WYCECH,
President of the Sejm of the
Polish Peoples Republic.

———

BUENOS AIRES, ARGENTINA,
November 22, 1963.

THE PRESIDENT OF THE SENATE,
OF THE UNITED STATES OF AMERICA,
Washington, D.C.:

In the name of the Argentine Senate and in my own name I express to you the deep feeling of regret caused by the death of the illustrious President of your Nation, John F. Kennedy, whose death has so closely affected the free citizens of the world who shared the ideals of peace and brotherhood among men.

CARLOS H. PERETTE,
President of the Senate of the Argentine Nation.
CLAUDIO A. MAFFI, *Secretary.*

———

TOKYO,
November 28, 1963.

Hon. J. W. FULBRIGHT,
Senate Office Building,
Washington, D.C.:

Deep condolence for late President.

KANESHICHI MASUDA,
Japanese Diet.

———

WASHINGTON, D.C.,
November 22, 1963.

Senator J. WILLIAM FULBRIGHT,
Washington, D.C.:

I wish to express my condolences and sympathy on the tragic occasion of the death of President Kennedy.

ALI BENGELLOUN,
Ambassador of Morocco.

———

It is with profound sorrow that we have been informed of the tragic loss of President Kennedy. The entire world, in addition to the American Nation, mourns for the loss of the greatest protector of its ideals, a man who had devoted his very life to defend world peace and the prosperity and happiness of peoples.

On behalf of the Senate of the Turkish Republic and in my own behalf, I wish to extend to you, Mr. President, and to the Members of the Senate of the United States, our deep feelings of sympathy and our condolences.

ENVER AKA,
President of the Senate
of the Turkish Republic.

———

BRITISH-AMERICAN
PARLIAMENTARY GROUP,
London, November 27, 1963.

Hon. J. W. FULBRIGHT,
U.S. Senator from Arkansas, Chairman of the Committee
on Foreign Relations, the Senate Wing of the Capitol,
Washington, D.C., United States of America.

MY DEAR SENATOR FULBRIGHT: The Executive Committee of the British-American Parliamentary Group at their meeting held yesterday (November 26) in Westminster Hall, Houses of Parliament, unanimously passed the following resolution which it was directed should be sent to you, as chairman of the Foreign Relations Committee of the Senate, and to Dr. Thomas E. Morgan, Member of Congress, chairman of the Foreign Affairs Committee of the House of Representatives, namely:

"The British-American Parliamentary Group offer to their congressional colleagues their deepest sympathy on the tragic and untimely death of President Kennedy whose work for those high ideals, common to our two assemblies, they so greatly appreciated and respected. We share in the great sense of loss which has been felt throughout the world."

With kindest regard.

Yours sincerely,

Sir HOWARD D'EGVILLE,
Hon. Secretary.

———

COLOMBO,
December 4, 1963.

PRESIDENT, SENATE,
Washington, D.C.:

The Senate of Ceylon has nemine dissetiente resolved as follows begins this house desires to convey to the President and Members of the Senate of the United States of America an expression of the deep sorrow with which this house has learned of the assassination of the President of the United States, the late John Fitzgerald Kennedy, and to express their sympathy with his family and with the Government and people of the United States.

THOS. AMARASURIYA,
President.

———

ROME.

PRESIDENT OF THE SENATE OF THE UNITED STATES,
Washington, D.C.:

The death of President Kennedy is an irreparable loss not only to the United States, but to the entire community of peoples, for in him they had a most vigorous defender of the ideals of liberty and peace and of social justice in the world. His work will remain as a milestone on civilization's road and from it and our affectionate memory of him, man will in years to come obtain inspiration and instruction on the way to achieve progress and on the exaltation of the values so constantly affirmed by him. The Senate of the Republic of Italy, which remembers with emotion his recent visit to Italy, unanimously joins in the grief of the noble American Nation our friend, and shares the loss it has suffered today, which has deprived it in such a tragic manner of its first citizen.

CESARE MARZAGORA,
President of the Senate of Italy.

———

THE PRESIDENT OF THE SENATE OF THE UNITED STATES,
Washington, D.C.:

In the name of the Peruvian Senate and in my own name, I convey to you our expressions of profound sadness and sincere condolences of the irreparable loss of the illustrious President Kennedy, and at the same time, our condemnation of this atrocious crime. World democracy loses an outstanding champion, the United States an esteemed leader, and Latin America a loyal friend. We convey our deepest sympathy to you and to the Senate of the United States.

JULIO DE LA PIEDRA,
President of the Senate.

ADDRESS BY
Hon. Daniel K. Inouye
OF HAWAII

Mr. President, we meet here today as desolate men and women who have come together to eulogize a fallen leader, John Fitzgerald Kennedy.

We would extoll his many virtues in the language of the gods, had we but that gift, but as T. S. Eliot once wrote:

Words strain—crack and sometimes break under the burden—under the tension, slip, slide, perish, decay with imprecision.

We stand here bewildered in the darkness of a grotesque nightmare, the shadows illuminated only by the flickering of an eternal flame on the hills of Arlington. Yet in the infinite quality of that flame lies the legacy passed on to us by a young man who had so much more to give. Thank God that he was able to give enough.

More than anything else, John F. Kennedy taught us to be men of resolution, but also men of reason. This, he told us, is the way to world peace. He could leave no greater gift to all mankind.

John F. Kennedy rekindled within us a burning sense of our national mission, reminding us that we hold within our hands the future of the entire free world.

In his insistence that civil rights be extended to all, he mandated us to be not a nation of words—but a nation of deeds.

Here was a man, a product of our Nation's finest schools of learning; a man whose character was forged in the fire and destruction of a great World War.

When he ascended to our Nation's highest office, an entire generation was on trial. There were grave doubts in the minds of many of our people that this young man—and his generation—would be equal to the task.

We now know that the man—and his generation—met the acid test of history in a grave national crisis. But for this man, we might not exist as a nation today.

I would like to close with a few words of Vachel Lindsay:

Sleep on, O brave hearted, O wise man that kindled the flame. To live in mankind, is far more than to live in a name, to live in mankind, far, far more * * * than to live in a name.

May his soul rest in peace.

ADDRESS BY
Hon. Edmund S. Muskie
OF MAINE

Mr. President, the date of November 22 and the national tragedy caused by the wanton and senseless act of an assassin has been seared into our memories as individuals and as a nation. On that day we lost a great leader. Many of us standing in this Chamber lost a good friend.

In the days since President Kennedy's death we have emerged from the initial shock of disbelief. As a nation we have roused ourselves from the numbness of despair to a sense of resolution under a new President. In the depths of our grief we were sustained by the memory of a man of wisdom, wit, heart, and grace. We achieved new dignity as a nation through the inspiration of the President's widow, his children, and his family. We have been challenged by President Johnson to take up our tasks in the spirit of President Kennedy.

Today we pause in the course of our work to eulogize our fallen leader. For me this brings a flood of memories—of a young Senator speaking out courageously for a free Algeria—of a bright and forceful presidential candidate inspiring a crowd in a cold and snowy Maine park in the early hours of a November morning—of a new President issuing a challenge and a call to the Nation and the world on his inauguration—of a warm friend reading poetry and musing on the place of America in history as we sailed off the coast of Maine—of a thoughtful President wrestling with issues which had concerned him as a Senator and now confronted him in the new context of the Presidency—of a seasoned and vigorous world leader talking of peace and wisdom and understanding at a gathering of Maine citizens at the University of Maine less than 2 months ago—and, finally, of a man whose responsibilities encircled the globe, yet whose interests involved the needs of each State in the Union and the rights of each citizen, whatever his race, creed, or color, or economic status.

We of Maine are grateful for those golden years which John F. Kennedy gave us. They were not easy years, but they carried, with them the light of promise. President Kennedy, the man, can do no more on the unfinished tasks he set for himself and the Nation. The legacy and the promise of President Kennedy rests with us.

As Norman Cousins has written:

The ultimate tragedy of a man is represented not by death but by the things he tried to bring to life that are buried with him. The legacy of John Kennedy can be a large one—if that is the way the American people wish it to be.

We, the people, will determine whether the spirit of John F. Kennedy lives or dies; we, the people, will determine whether the eternal flame which burns on a Virginia hillside is the symbol of continuing hope or a shattered dream; we the people, must decide.

Mr. President, many tributes have been paid to President Kennedy. As an indication of the respect and affection in which he was held in Maine, I ask to have printed at this time a group of statements and editorials which have been printed in Maine, including three of my own comments to the citizens of Maine.

STATEMENT BY SENATOR EDMUND S. MUSKIE UPON THE ASSASSINATION OF PRESIDENT JOHN F. KENNEDY—FRIDAY, NOVEMBER 22, 1963

It is difficult to adjust to the shock of the news. It is impossible to comprehend the motives of one who would do this to his country. We have lost a great leader. I have lost a good friend. If I were to suggest what President Kennedy would say, if he were here, it would be: "This is a time to pray for our country." We must be restrained in our reactions; we must stand together—and, I repeat, pray for our country.

———

REPORT TO MAINE FROM SENATOR EDMUND S. MUSKIE

Hatred and virulence reached a tragic climax in Dallas, Tex., last week. As I said upon learning of the President's death: "It is difficult to adjust to the shock of the news. It is impossible to comprehend the motives of one who would do this to his country. We have lost a great leader. I have lost a good friend. If I were to suggest what President Kennedy would say, if he were here, it would be: 'This is a time to pray for our country.' We must be restrained in our reactions; we must stand together—and, I repeat, pray for our country."

As Americans, we mourn the loss of a great President, cut down in his prime. As individuals, our hearts go out to the Kennedy family. In the space of a few short months, Mrs. Kennedy lost a son and a husband. May God grant her the physical and spiritual resources she must need to persevere in the face of this tragedy. May God care for her two children.

Deep as may be our grief, we must immediately reaffirm our faith in our system of government, designed to preserve continuity even in the face of such trying circumstances. Our Republic—although its head may now be bowed in shame that this could happen here—will survive. America will continue to grow and prosper. Freedom will be maintained. However disastrous, this one insane act cannot stem the tide of freedom. I am confident that Americans of all political persuasion will unite behind President Johnson to complete the unfinished business which President Kennedy so capably and so eloquently set before us.

We, in Maine, will long remember his moving plea for peace and understanding, expressed in his address at the University of Maine on October 19.

He was a man of dignity; yet he was humble. He was a man of great intellect; yet he spoke in simple terms. He was born to great wealth; yet his great concern was for the poor, the oppressed. John F. Kennedy's place in history is secure, but all mankind is immeasurably poorer without him.

LETTER TO MAINE FROM SENATOR ED MUSKIE

DECEMBER 11, 1963.

DEAR FRIENDS: None of us will ever forget the 22d day of this past November, or the sad days of deepening, yet unbelieving awareness that followed.

The memories, though shared with hundreds of millions around the globe, will always be as personal as the tears which stung our eyes and the ache which filled our hearts.

We will remember a President who loved our country deeply, not only for what it has been and is, but also because he believed that it is America's destiny to point the way to a better world for all mankind.

We will remember a leader who dared to lead us where his understanding and his convictions told us we must go.

We will remember the voice of a man who found unforgettable words to remind us of our heritage, to express our hopes, and to summon us to the great unfinished work which is ours to do.

We will remember a warm-hearted friend whose love of home and family were symbolic of his devotion to all those who labored to serve.

We will remember him as one who loved life and lived it fully, welcoming the challenges of the Presidency and thriving on its burdens, stimulated by the wide-ranging interests of a thoroughly civilized man, appealing in the simplicity of his tastes and his clear-eyed faith in the essential goodness of his fellowman.

He believed in us and in our capacity as a people to help build a world where compassion, understanding, and reason will rule.

We will never forget him.

As we remember him, we should bear in mind these words of Norman Cousins: "The ultimate tragedy of a man is represented not by death but by the things he tried to bring to life that are buried with him. The legacy of John Kennedy can be a large one—if that is the way the American people wish it to be."

Sincerely,

EDMOND S. MUSKIE.

———

[From the Lewiston Daily Sun, Nov. 23, 1963]

PRESIDENT ASSASSINATED

An assassin's bullets have destroyed the life of the President of the United States, and changed the course of history.

The rifle shots which rang out as the official motorcade rode through the streets of Dallas, Tex., wrote a violent end to the career of President John F. Kennedy and plunged the Nation and the world into mourning.

In the few brief moments of the terrifying sound of gunfire, the President and the Governor of Texas lay wounded. America's First Lady had flung herself in front of her husband in a brave but vain attempt to shield him from the bullets which already had found their mark.

President Kennedy was in Texas as part of an effort to strengthen the Democratic Party there. He had spoken out against factionalism and strife within his party. He did not foresee that a fanatical assassin would take matters

into his own hands to strike a blow against life itself. Even the extraordinary precautions always taken to protect a President were not enough.

Violence is common to the politics of many countries. It is unusual and all the more shocking in the United States. That there were hotbeds of extremism in the West and Southwest has been a matter of common knowledge. That it would kindle the awful flames of assassination was unexpected.

The President's assassination cut short his brilliant career at its very height. He was in the preliminary stages of a campaign for another 4-year term, although he had made no official announcement of his candidacy. His visit to Texas, like the tours into other parts of the country, including the recent trip to the University of Maine, formed part of that background campaign.

Every American, regardless of party, has suffered a personal loss. America has lost an outstanding leader whose brave program for a peaceful world was the hope of all mankind.

There are no words to soothe the pain of his grief-stricken wife and family. But an America in mourning strives to share that great sorrow.

———

[From the Daily Kennebec Journal, Nov. 23, 1963]

THE PRESIDENT PASSES

Telephones jangled in every newspaper office in the land Friday—as anxious Americans sought to learn: "Is it true, what they say about the President?"

This is A.D. 1963, a supposedly civilized era.

Yet civilization's veneer is thin indeed. Friday's tragedy in Dallas brings America up short, in the realization that—for all our devotion to the rule of law, there still are mad dogs among us who obey only the law of the jungle.

It takes a brave man to be President of the United States. President Truman's temporary Washington residence, Blair House, was shot up by a handful of fanatics and Mr. Truman himself had a narrow escape. A shot fired at Franklin D. Roosevelt in 1932 killed Mayor Anton Czermak of Chicago. Theodore Roosevelt was wounded by a would-be assassin. President James Garfield was mortally wounded by gunshot. President William McKinley was killed. Abraham Lincoln lost his life to an assassin's bullet.

Yet in this day and age, many Americans had hopefully assumed that civilization had advanced to a point to which law and reason—at least in this great country—had everywhere superseded outlawry, or the taking of law into one's own hands. The assumption was premature. Anyone who reads the grim daily grist of crime news from one end of America to the other should understand how utterly uncivilized a large segment of the population still is.

The terrible news from Dallas should move every good American not only to demand a restoration of law and order everywhere in this country, but also to take direct, personal responsibility—at every opportunity—to support and assist all law enforcement agencies.

John F. Kennedy served his country courageously and to the best of his ability throughout his tragically short term of office. His sudden passing shocks and saddens all America.

And—politics or no politics—all America knows today that John F. Kennedy laid down his life for his country.

———

[From the Waterville Morning Sentinel, Nov. 23, 1963]

MAINE GRIEVES FOR A NEIGHBOR

It was 100 years ago that a gaunt President of the United States was shot in the back by an assassin.

He was President of a country torn by a civil war whose guns had only recently been stilled.

There is no evidence that President Kennedy's life was taken by a racist, but the tensions in the land today bear a frightening parallel to those which beset Abraham Lincoln.

And overlaying the civil rights issue which again divides North and South is the constant threat of nuclear war posed by the ideological differences between the Communist world and the free world.

How clear is the parallel between the times of Lincoln and the times of Kennedy will be visible only through the perspective of history to be written in another generation.

But, dim though they now may be, the outlines are there.

And only in the pages of history yet to be written can there be an evaluation of President Kennedy's place among U.S. Presidents, even as Lincoln's place was determined only by time.

Few have faced more monumental tasks than did the young man from Massachusetts. He faced them with courage and with dedication to his principles. His fateful trip to Texas was taken to support those principles.

A man of wealth, he might well have chosen the easy life of a moneyed and cultured gentleman. He did not. He chose, rather, a career of service to the country which had given him and his family that wealth.

That career has now been ended by the useless act of an assassin. The nasal New England voice through which his quick, well-trained mind was articulated will be heard no longer.

Maine has special reasons for sadness. President Kennedy vacationed on our coast and only a few short weeks ago he was made an honorary alumnus of the University of Maine.

As a man of Massachusetts he has been, throughout most of his life, our close neighbor and during his career as a Senator from Massachusetts he personally met and impressed many Maine people through his visits.

Every American today mourns the death of this President. Every heart goes out to the family which must bear the most intimate of griefs. A President has been cut down in the prime of his life, but so also has a husband, a father and a son.

———

[From the Lewiston Evening Journal, Nov. 23, 1963]

THE BLACKEST DAY

Today we, the American people, mourn the death of President John Fitzgerald Kennedy. There are no words which can be written to describe adequately the depth of emotion we are feeling over the untimely, brutal, calculated murder of our youthful President.

His near 3 years as leader of our Nation were marked by severe international crises, domestic problems that featured racial bitterness in the South and in some of our larger cities and problems involving a Congress which did not always see eye to eye with him insofar as certain important legislative matters were concerned. Despite the complex and often irritating issues which faced President Kennedy these past 3 years, he maintained a basic good humor and a sense of purpose that made his political opponents like him as a man and admire him for his persistency.

The great warmth of the late President was exemplified many times during the course of his press conferences. Many Maine citizens had a recent opportunity to witness it upon his visitation to the University of Maine where he received an honorary degree. And most remembered of all, of course, were those pictures of John Kennedy which appeared in the press and on the television screen to show him the uninhibited, loving father and family man.

Friday, November 22, 1963, will go down in American history as one of the blackest days this Nation has ever faced. It definitely represents the most tragic single event since the surprise attack upon Pearl Harbor. It was a deed most obviously undertaken by one imbued with the stark, deadly hatred which moves only within those who have taken up the cause of the lunatic left or the radical right. The assassination of President Kennedy carries within it the curse of Cain as so often witnessed to by those who are extremists. May his death bring all who have veered over into paths of intolerance and hatred back to the reality demanded of all who have faith in God; back to a realization that intolerance and hatred solve nothing, and that only love of one's fellow man possesses the virtue to bring understanding.

There are no tears shed which can relieve us of a terrible sense of loneliness and lostness. There are no emotions sufficient to disclose the measure of our sympathy for Mrs. Kennedy, 6-year-old Caroline, and 3-year-old John. Only through our prayers and our faith may we hope to walk from the valley of shadow back into the light.

Today the world shares the bereavement of John Kennedy's family and friends. May the American people of the immediate tomorrow assure the end of any similar future tragedy by dedicating themselves to the sacred task of building and preserving peace for our time at home and abroad. Then and only then may the American people proclaim that the death of this dedicated American was not in vain.

———

[From the Daily Kennebec Journal, Nov. 23, 1963]

THE GREATEST CASUALTY

Friday, November 22, 1963, was a sad and a critical day in the history of the Republic.

A century after a great President had laid down his life in the cause of racial equality another President appeared to have suffered the same fate.

It had not been determined at the time of this writing whether President Kennedy was shot by a fanatical segregationist. The point is that the war hero occupying the world's most powerful and one of its most uncomfortable positions of leadership, believed that the issues of the day called for militancy, whether it be the conflict with world communism abroad, or the struggle for civil rights at home.

A century ago the racial struggle divided the Nation and nearly brought about its extinction. President Lincoln saved the Republic, but in doing so he sacrificed his own life to the most despicable of all adversaries, an assassin.

President Kennedy realized, as many thoughtful observers have confirmed, that the Nation has been drifting perilously close to another internal explosion. He combated this drift in the two ways he knew best, as a battle-scarred soldier openly defying the forces of reaction, and as a skilled politician, carrying his case to the masses, scorning the safety of Secret Service cordons and bullet-proof bubble tops.

He paid the supreme sacrifice proving his contention that every American must take risks to protect his rights and his freedoms.

He failed to provide answers available from no other President, living or dead—why does hate displace charity in our differences between fellow Americans, and why does our generosity abroad generate universal suspicion and dislike?

As he rocked in his chair to ease the pain of his wounds, President Kennedy knew there was no soft security and no solace beyond an appeal for men of good will to search resolutely and prayerfully for a common solution to their differences.

His brutal slaying focuses attention on a vacuum in leadership that will mean many sleepless nights for Americans until it is filled by a statesman equal to its fearful demands.

———

[From the Portland Evening Express, Nov. 23, 1963]

AN INSTANT IN DALLAS

The United States is a nation in shock today.

Millions of Americans awoke this morning still at a loss to comprehend the events of yesterday; it remains all but impossible to accept the reality of that terrible moment in which was destroyed the life of the most popular President this country ever knew.

But reality it is; stark reality born in an instant of violence in the Texas city known as Dallas. John F. Kennedy, yesterday's President, is dead. Today's President is Lyndon B. Johnson, curiously enough a son of that State which will henceforth be remembered for this deed of infamy as much as for its claims to greatness.

The death of a President during his term of office brings a nation to its knees. The suddenness and malice in the violence of assassination compounds the tragedy. But it seems neither extravagant nor emotional to suggest that the death of no other President in our history, from whatever cause, could have caused so many Americans to feel so deep a sense of personal loss. No President ever has shared such an intimacy with his people as did John F. Kennedy.

The sympathy of the entire world goes out to Jacqueline Kennedy, widow, a lovely and charming lady who yesterday as the vivacious and elegant First Lady was the envy of all. That instant in Dallas has plunged her into bereavement in the most crushing event in what has been a year of great personal tragedy for her.

We pray now for Mr. Kennedy, for Jackie and Caroline and John, Junior, and all those who shared the family circle of the late President. We pray, too, for Lyndon B. Johnson, a man who through the expenditure of thousands of dollars and months of energy could not win his way into the Presidency but who, through an instant of barbarism in his home State, is thrust into that high office. The best of those among us will pray also for the man who in madness or hate has so lost his sense of balance as to commit so foul a deed.

Mr. Kennedy's innate friendliness and the very qualities which have so endeared him to Americans and the peoples of nations he has visited, have often caused concern for his safety. At home and abroad he mingled and became caught up in crowds as none of his predecessors had done. In so doing he exposed himself to innumerable dangers.

There were those, we are told, who were apprehensive about his Texas tour because it has become an area known for its reactionaries and displays of extremism. In Dallas only a few short weeks ago Adlai E. Stevenson, Ambassador to the United Nations and once a presidential aspirant himself, was insulted and molested by extremists of the street.

But it was felt that any danger that might be attached to the Presidential visit would be at the airport. But it was not so. When the evil thing was done it was not when he was caught up in the embrace of a crowd but at a moment when he was thought to be relatively safe; at a moment when all the precautions and security in the world could not alter things.

The ideals and principles which Mr. Kennedy brought to his great office will not be lost with his passing. But foremost in our tributes to him should be a firm and steadfast resolve to bring this Nation back to its proper reliance on peaceful processes, to renounce street pressures and gutter tactics which reach their most despicable example in such demonstrations as that degrading and terrifying instant in Dallas. If we do only this Mr. Kennedy will not have died in vain.

We bow today in mourning but we must not bend in despair. The grief which has seized this Nation must not be coupled with fear. The United States is not, nor has it ever been, one man. It is with considerable difficulty that we strive for objectivity at such a moment, but we must cling to the certain knowledge that our country has not been left leaderless nor given into the hands of irresponsible individuals. The changes precipitated by that cruel and senseless instant in Dallas may be less than those occasioned by an election.

The Nation, so shaken now, will go on not weakened or uncertain, but strengthened, sustained, and rededicated by the service, sacrifice, and martyrdom of John F. Kennedy.

[From the Portland (Maine) Evening Express,
Nov. 23, 1963]

A MADMAN SLAYS THE PRESIDENT, PLUNGING THE NATION
INTO GRIEF

The most incredibly tragic news that can befall a
country such as ours is the successful assassination of its
Chief Executive.

And this is the news that all Americans still numbed
by shock, are trying to grasp today.

The youthful, vigorous, personable John F. Kennedy
who rode into Texas on Thursday, fell victim yesterday
to the dread that haunts every President and his family
and his associates—the madman's bullet.

Ever since the dawn of our Nation's history it has been
fired for many reasons, or for no comprehensible reason
at all. For every attempt made on a President's life, others
are thwarted. We do not know, at this writing why the
bullet was fired at Dallas. That is far less important, right
now, than the stunning realization that the President is
dead.

So the Nation grieves, regardless of party, regardless
of religion, regardless of national origin, with Mrs. Kennedy, and his family and hers. Yet even as we mourn,
we take confidence in the strength of the American system
which has already installed his successor, Mr. Lyndon
Johnson, until yesterday the Vice President and President
of the U.S. Senate.

It is the very strength and stability of our system of
executive succession that makes assassination so futile, at
least in this day when political moderation is the rule and
not the exception in American politics. Of course, there
will be changes, but the Republic will go on.

That is for the future to bring. Today we mourn the
death of the President of all the American people, struck
down in the full flower of manhood, his potential unrealized, his ambitions for his people unfulfilled. It is a
desolate day that finds words empty to convey the full
tragedy that a single warped mind has heaped upon the
Nation, and the world.

[From the Bangor Daily News, Nov. 23–24, 1963]

THE NATION MOURNS

At one moment, a man alive, healthy and smiling; a
man waving to well-wishers as he rides with his wife in
broad daylight along the street of an American city.

The next moment, a man felled by a bullet; inert and
dying in his wife's lap as stunned witnesses gasped in
disbelief.

Thus did death come yesterday to John Fitzgerald
Kennedy at the prime of his life and of his brilliant
political career—a good man, a good American, dedicated
to serving his country in war and in peace.

There was peace in Dallas yesterday. Or there seemed
to be. Oh yes, the President was in a State where political
differences were flaring.

But when were there not political differences, when was
a President not caught up in controversy? He might be
heckled, the target of a critical wisecrack—but slain, shot
down in cold blood in his native, civilized land?

Unbelievable.

But it has to be believed. It happened. Hate brooded
in a twisted mind—brooded and planned, and then pulled
the trigger of the assassin gun.

And so today, the Nation mourns the loss of a good
man, a good American—a man who risked his life in
battle but lost it, ironically, in peace. A man slain like
another President almost 100 years ago—Abraham Lincoln—a martyr to the causes he championed.

The prayers of the Nation today are for the Kennedy
family, especially Mrs. Kennedy, who has lost an infant
son and her husband in less than 4 months' time.

[From the Portland (Maine) Sunday Telegram, Nov. 24,
1963]

PRESIDENT'S DEATH IS GRIEF MAGNIFIED

(By Len Cohen)

The death of a President is the shock and sorrow
of bereavement magnified. It is not so intense to the
average citizen as a death in his own family; but it is
a broader kind of shock for it affects the whole country,
the whole structure of society that gives people a sense
of security in their government and in their nation.

Someone who had visited the White House several
times and dined with President and Mrs. Kennedy said
Friday, "I can't believe it"—a phrase that undoubtedly
was repeated many times that day by those to whom
the late President was a warm friend as well as a
public personality.

Those who are no longer young remember, still with
vividness, the feeling of disbelief, the sense of personal loss
that flooded in on millions when Franklin D. Roosevelt
died. There was more reason for that feeling then.
Roosevelt had been President 12 years and he had become
a father image to multitudes of citizens.

I remember, too, the sense of unreality that permeated
the statehouse in Augusta only a few years ago when
Governor Clinton Clauson died suddenly after only a year
in office.

For the newsmen who were covering the statehouse
then, there was the same stark quality about the long
day when they waited for the new Governor, John H.
Reed, to arrive and take the oath—the same, in a smaller
way, that those on the scene in Dallas and Washington
must have felt on Friday.

Together with the personal shock and the unreality,
there was the whole human drama of a shift in power—
the shattering of a power structure built up by one group,
the falling of the scepter into new hands, eager to grasp
it, despite the restraint imposed by grief and respect
for the fallen Chief Executive.

And so today, my thoughts are carried back to the day
when Governor Clauson's body lay in state in the hall
of flags and citizens of Maine, great and small, filed by
to publicly express their respect and their grief.

My thoughts go back further to those 2 days of mourning that were observed by the Nation when President
Roosevelt died. All the stores in Portland were closed
those 2 days; window displays gave way to floral arrangements, from modest wreaths to great basketfuls
of flowers.

But if there was grief in the death of Roosevelt, who had worn out heart and brain in the great fights against depression and foreign enemies, there was a tragic loss in the killing of John Kennedy. For he was not the father image. He was the image of youth, of energy, of the young hero who would lead us not only against the foreign enemy but against the enemy within our own country in the form of prejudice and bigotry—in short, the enemy within ourselves.

For Maine people Kennedy held a special place. For he had come to Maine more than any President in modern times. I remember his first visit as a Senator, when he spoke to a Democratic dinner, at the end of a long evening, reading a speech perfunctorily, skipping pages to shorten it, maybe a little irked at the wearying speakers who preceded him.

I remember his coming back, to another party dinner in Augusta, as a candidate for the nomination, this time purposeful, incisive, bold, thoughtful.

He came back again, during the election campaign, radiating the confidence of the man who had won a hard fight for the nomination. He visited again in the summer of 1962, this time for a weekend of relaxation, adding little to the gradually building image of a young man of action tempered by thought. His testing in the crucibles of Oxford, Mississippi, and Cuba was still ahead. He came again, in full vigor, only last month, to receive a degree at the University of Maine.

Now he will come no more, to Maine or any other earthly place. And the people mourn him, as they mourned another President who was cut down by an assassin's bullet almost 100 years ago.

We are never prepared for death. We shall always be shocked by the brutality of assassination. And so we move forward unwillingly into the future, like children entering a dark room.

————

[From the Portland Press Herald, Nov. 25, 1963]

FREEMEN EVERYWHERE MOURNING LEADER OF UNREALIZED POTENTIAL

The Nation is still too close to the shocking tragedy enacted in Dallas on Friday to view very clearly what will happen at Washington, or in the 50 American States, or in the world at large, as the result of John F. Kennedy's murder, and the process that transfers Executive power to Lyndon B. Johnson.

Today everything but the country's heartbeat halts as we bury the martyred President. This is not a fit time to talk about politics, in the narrow meaning applied to partisan strife.

The primary task of any President is to execute the laws and take appropriate measures for national security. As the leader of a political party he is required to be a politician. As the Chief Executive of the United States, he is compelled to be a statesman. The late President John Kennedy excelled as a politician, in contrast with the personality of his predecessor. Whether he was a great statesman is too early to judge. Twenty years from now, or a half century hence, it may be possible, putting events of the 1960–63 period in correct perspective, to say that the man whose life was snuffed out 3

days ago was a great statesman as well. It may be discovered that while he made mistakes, and admitted them, he had an intuition for doing the right thing, based upon the information available at the time.

Unlike those who have no responsibility for the conduct of foreign policy in the interests of national survival, Presidents must take the long view of history, a duty rendered all the more urgent today because we must accommodate ourselves to living with other nations in the nuclear age. The Kennedy policies were built around retention and improvement of an immensely powerful military force, economic and military alliances with other free nations, programs of assistance to emerging countries unsure of their future destiny, and with a close eye to changes of a beneficial kind felt to be taking place in the world's second most powerful nation, the Soviet Union.

To carry out these policies, the late President called to his side exceptionally able men, among them Secretary of State Dean Rusk and Defense Secretary Robert McNamara. And merely to list the broad elements of the American foreign policy he pursued shows how difficult it is to evaluate their worth over a scant 3-year period. Profound changes in world history are not made that quickly, and when one adds to all of this political duties of a President, among them the necessity of dealing every day with an often rebellious Congress, there is a temptation to agree with those who insist that being the Chief Executive of the United States is simply too vast a task for a single person.

Yet there was never any indication that the late President Kennedy felt he could not cope with the burdens of the Presidency. A rich man who loved ordinary people, a fairly uncommon thing in itself, he had a great love for life, he enjoyed the accompaniments of the high office he held, he had an instinct for sensing the feelings of all sorts of minority groups, and he enjoyed playing what Frank Kent once called "The Great Game of Politics."

What kind of a record he might have made, as a politician and statesman, given 8 years in the White House, we shall never know. Yet while we mourn our own loss, his death is a great deprivation for the free world within which he moved, and which he was determined to sustain and preserve and expand against the evil forces that have assailed national sovereignty and individual freedom from time immemorial.

————

[From the Portland (Maine) Evening Express, Nov. 25, 1963]

POLICEMAN AND PRESIDENT

Two men were carried to their final resting places today, a policeman and a President.

Each man died in violence, each man died in the course of his duty. They died but a few minutes apart. But for the death of the President the policeman would not have died. But for the death of the policeman the man presumed to be the assassin of the President might not have been apprehended—and he might have not died.

Two women, in stations as vastly different as those of the men they mourned, made their final farewells to their husbands today.

They had nothing in common, these men and these women, but they had everything in common. The men, each in his own way, were keepers of the peace, protectors of the people, symbols of the law and order by which an advanced civilization lives. In those roles the two men lived and in them they died.

And the women, strangers 3 days ago but intimates in grief today, shared the duties of wife, mother, companion. One performed her duty well and the front pages of the world's newspapers noted it. The other, just as equal to her responsibilities, lived in obscurity until the 1 day of tragedy that linked them in the heart of the Nation thrust her unwillingly into the headlines.

So it has been with our Nation. To create it, to build it, to preserve it, the meek and the mighty have stood together and fallen together. And their women have mourned.

The policeman and the President stood and fell together. The widows stand apart but together. Let those women lean on the sympathy of a bereaved Nation. And may their children find proof in their time that their Nation became stronger and better because of the sacrifice of their respective fathers, a policeman and a President.

[From the Lewiston Daily Sun, Nov. 25, 1963]

NATION BOWED IN MOURNING

This day a sad nation, bowed in mourning and prayer, will bury the youngest President it ever had—a President it lost under tragic circumstances.

We will stop our normal daily activities as a solemn requiem Mass is sung for John Fitzgerald Kennedy, 35th President of the United States, in St. Matthew's Roman Catholic Cathedral at Washington, D.C. And we will grieve with his family and friends for the loss all of us feel.

That sense of loss perhaps can be expressed in how a young girl explained President Kennedy's assassination to her small playmates. "They must need 'doers' awful bad in Heaven," he said.

It is fitting, too, that President Kennedy will be buried in Arlington National Cemetery at the wish of his family and probably at the wish of many, many Americans who will visit his grave in the days, and weeks, and years to come. He was one of the Nation's war heroes and he died still in the service of his country—a vigorous fighter for freedom and the dignity of man.

Among the many world leaders, statesmen from foreign lands and officials of our own Government, joining the family of President Kennedy for the state funeral today will be representatives of countries not counted among our allies—even among our friends. These representatives, here to express the formal solicitude of their governments, should be accorded respect and courteous treatment during their stay. They came on a grave and somber mission and we should not let any incident, however trivial, mar their visit.

It already is enough to remind that President Kennedy was struck down by an assassin in a brutal barbarian assault which does not reflect the democratic and peaceful processes by which we settle our internal differences. We want the world to know our orderly and kindly ways and not picture us as an unruly ruffian. The face the United States shows to the world was of much concern to our late President.

[From the Lewiston Evening Journal, Nov. 25, 1963]

OUR FINAL PRAYER

On this national day of mourning the thoughts of the American people have been and remain directed upon the tragic, untimely death of President John Fitzgerald Kennedy. Not only is all America concentrating its attention upon the funeral and burial today of our country's youngest Chief of State, but similar consideration is being given this sad day throughout much of the world.

Chiefs of state from many nations, allied to the United States by a mutual interest in the preservation of human freedom, arrived in Washington all day yesterday. A number of important dignitaries from behind the Iron Curtain also were in attendance today at President Kennedy's funeral.

There is no question but what this young leader won the admiration and respect of Americans generally. Even though there naturally was disagreement on the part of various segments of the populace with some of his views, the vast majority of those who disagreed with John Kennedy couldn't help liking him. He was that kind of man.

The same attitude prevailed among foreign leaders who met him or who knew him indirectly through interpretation given them by their own diplomatic corps. Both allied chiefs of state and those heading up countries generally regarded as cold war foes felt respect for the American President. There is no question but what Soviet Premier Nikita S. Khrushchev, for example, admired Kennedy's firmness and determination, even though he naturally would have wished for our country to be headed by a less dedicated man.

Today we mourn our late President. In doing this we should not forget our obligation to give of our best as citizens in support of our new leader, President Lyndon B. Johnson. Such would be the wish of John Fitzgerald Kennedy, who never placed anything ahead of his duty to his country.

Our final prayer today in remembrance of our murdered President would be that all Americans might emerge from this tragedy possessed with the same desire for international peace and domestic tranquility as that which prevailed in the mind and heart of John F. Kennedy.

[From the Bangor Daily News, Nov. 25, 1963]

FROM THE FOUR CORNERS OF THE EARTH

As John Fitzgerald Kennedy is laid to his eternal rest today, sorrowing Americans can find comfort and reassurance in the great outpouring of sympathy that has come from all parts of the world.

The formal diplomatic messages were to have been expected. But there has been much, much more.

France's Charles de Gaulle will attend today's services in Washington to bid final farewell to the man who was leader of the free world as well as President of the United

States. Britain will be represented by Prince Philip and Prime Minister Sir Alec Douglas-Home. Chancellor Ludwig Erhard of West Germany will be a mourner.

Their presence is a tribute to the late President and to the Nation. But most heart-warming of all has been the spontaneous response of the world's common people.

In West Berlin, 80,000 free world men and women marched in a solemn torchlight parade, demonstrating their grief over the loss of the young and vigorous free world leader. Candles were burned in the windows of Berlin homes.

The commander of the Japanese naval craft that sunk Kennedy's PT boat in World War II—and thus very nearly taking Kennedy's life at that time—sent condolences to the Kennedy family. The camel driver friend of President Lyndon B. Johnson sent his personal message of sympathy from Pakistan. A Russian woman—a private citizen—brought an armful of roses to the U.S. Embassy in Moscow.

And it so went after the news of the late President's assassination was flashed to the far corners of the earth. The plain and good people of the world were shocked and grieved.

More than that, their words signified encouragement to the Nation that has the task of leading the struggle for freedom and justice for all men everywhere. They were speaking from their hearts. They were expressing gratitude for what this Nation has done for them. And they were rallying behind the cause which John Fitzgerald Kennedy symbolized as the President of the United States.

Today's sorrow must be borne. Life must go on. The struggle must go on. The burden is made lighter by the outpouring of sympathy that has streamed into the Nation's Capital from the plain, good people of the world. They have faith in America. This strengthens the faith of Americans in themselves.

And so now to the sad task of saying farewell to John Fitzgerald Kennedy—whose dedicated service to his country was cut short by an assassin's bullet.

[From the Lewiston Daily Sun, Nov. 26, 1963]

HEAVY BURDEN CHANGES HANDS

Many an eye shed a tear in sorrow Monday as the United States buried its 35th President and Mrs. John F. Kennedy laid to eternal rest her husband and the father of her two children.

Leaders from many parts of the world came to pay their respects and, in tribute, walked behind his casket the long half mile from the White House to the church—walked through crowds of onlookers in a display to the world of the kind of freedom that this country really possesses. Some would not have dared to appear so openly in their own lands.

Among the leaders of our Nation was one with a new job—President Lyndon B. Johnson, already burdened by the heavy responsibilities of his office. But it must have been apparent to those representatives from other countries that the United States was not without leadership; that another hand was at the helm of state even as one loosened its grip.

That this was so is due to the foresight of our Nation's founders who established the Vice Presidency—some with misgivings about its usefulness—for just such a dire contingency as did occur last Friday.

Within hours of President Kennedy's death, his office was assumed by the Vice President, and that was as it should be and as our forefathers planned it. No nation can long drift on the world's troubled waters and those waters were turbulent even then.

So on Monday the 36th President of the United States walked in the solemn funeral procession for the 35th President of the United States—probably acutely aware that he must now take up the immediate unfinished chores and plot our course for the future, aware that sorrow must be put aside for the good of a nation.

[From the Lewiston Evening Journal, Nov. 26, 1963]

A PORTRAIT OF COURAGE

There have been those who have criticized our former First Lady, Jacqueline Kennedy, as too young, too frequently pictured water skiing, and too much inclined toward high fashion. American First Ladies can expect this kind of criticism. If they happen to dress conservatively the criticism will go along another direction, including references to dowdy and uninteresting.

These past few days Jacqueline Kennedy has proved herself eminently worthy as First Lady. She has displayed the sort of courage that may be found in few people. Throughout these days from the moment she witnessed the assassination of her husband in the car with her, this tremendously brave young wife and mother has held her head high and carried through a multitude of obligations which do not confront the average woman following the death of a husband.

Nowhere along the way did Jacqueline Kennedy falter. It was she who told her two children that their father was dead. It was she who trudged the sad half mile from the White House to the cathedral where the pontifical mass was said. It was she who stood in the rotunda of the Capitol and listened to the moving words of Senator Mike Mansfield, of Montana. It was she who returned to the rotunda unannounced to be near the casket holding the body of her husband once more. It was she who stayed the night with her husband's body at Bethesda Naval Hospital in Maryland.

Today we would salute as brave an American woman as any who have been written about in history. Jacqueline Kennedy was First Lady in the noblest sense these last, sad, few days. The heart of America has gone out to her, but it was clear she had within herself those firm, sustaining foundations which ever are found in people of great character.

[From the Bangor Daily News, Nov. 26, 1963]

A TIME FOR FAITH AND ALLEGIANCE

The Nation's elected leader—John Fitzgerald Kennedy—has fallen, victim of a madman's bullet. Yesterday, he was given a hero's burial in Arlington National Cemetery. Today, America moves forward under a new President—Lyndon B. Johnson.

The Nation must move forward without faltering. And it will.

Even as the shocked American populace was mourning the death of the late President Kennedy, it was rallying behind Johnson who, as Vice President, had quickly taken up the reins of Government.

Really, the people were rallying behind more than a man. They were rallying behind the Nation and what the Nation stands for—freedom and justice.

The new Chief Executive, fortunately, is a man of proven ability—and by far better fitted through experience to step into the White House than any Vice President before him who found himself in a similar position. Johnson had a long and distinguished career in Congress. As Vice President, he has had important roles in decision and policymaking. The late President entrusted him also with important assignments in foreign lands.

Still, there is no job quite like the Presidency. The President necessarily is leader of the free world as well as of the Nation. It is a lonely job and one of awesome burdens. The President is called upon time and again in this period of world turmoil to make momentous decisions and to assume full responsibility for them.

He is going to be sorely tested in the weeks ahead. The Communist world especially is going to set out to find what manner of man he is. And, of course, there are vital issues and problems at home.

And so, in this period of transition, he is going to need the moral support of the American people. We are sure he can count upon it from the vast majority.

It is a time for faith to be reborn and allegiance to be roused and sustained. The struggle against communism must be carried on all over the world. At home, hate and violence must be purged from the Nation's life.

Today, it is essential that the Nation be united and move forward toward its worthy goals. We are confident it will.

———

[From the Daily Kennebec Journal, Nov. 26, 1963]

What Can I Do?

The words just won't come.

There's the awareness that words aren't going to do much good, anyway.

This is being written on Monday, the day of President Kennedy's funeral, when one would prefer to be writing nothing.

Augusta, like communities large and small wherever the American flag flies, is a city in mourning.

The expression, "with a heavy heart," has a literal, physical meaning, one knows now.

So much has happened—so much that is so terribly wrong—since last Friday noon in Dallas. Yet this country must learn quickly to live with its grief. John F. Kennedy certainly wouldn't have wanted us all to sit around with long faces, leaving America's work undone.

Let's think of it that way, and roll up our sleeves and get on with the job, then—the job each of us has to do: Keeping the national economy ticking, doing our part in support of the national defense, striving toward better citizenship and, in consequence, better government at every level, for our country.

When he said it, in his 1960 inaugural address, it sounded a little melodramatic—to his critics, at least. But those words of President Kennedy have taken on new meaning now:

"Ask not what your country can do for you. Ask what you can do for your country."

All right. Let's ask—every individual one of us: "What can I do for my country?" And find an answer. And work at it.

If all will do that, there will be literally no limit to the greatness America can achieve.

John F. Kennedy gave his life for this America of ours. Keeping that in mind, let anyone ask, every day from now on: "What can I do for my country?"

———

[From the Bangor Daily News, Nov. 28, 1963]

The Late President's Wish

This Thanksgiving Day will be a sorrowful one for America. The late President John F. Kennedy, who prepared a proclamation on the occasion of this traditional American observance, is dead, and the Nation is mourning its loss.

Yet, John F. Kennedy noted in his proclamation that America had much to be thankful for. And this still holds true even in a time of national tragedy. Here, using the late President's own proclamation words, are reasons why all Americans should join in thanksgiving today:

Going back to the early colonists, noted the late President, "they gave reverent thanks for their safety, for the health of their children, for the fertility of their fields, for the laws which bound them together and for the faith which united them under God * * *.

"Today, we give our thanks, most of all, for the ideals of honor and faith we inherit from our forefathers—for the decency of purpose, steadfastness of resolve and strength of will, for the courage and humility, which we must seek every day to emulate. As we express our gratitude, we must never forget that the highest appreciation is not to utter words but to live by them * * *.

"Let us gather in sanctuaries dedicated to worship and in homes blessed by family affection to express our gratitude for the glorious gifts of God; and let us earnestly and humbly pray that He will continue to guide and sustain as in the great unfinished tasks of achieving peace, justice and understanding among all men and all nations and of ending misery and suffering wherever they exist."

Let these words from the dead guide today's observances. Man is mortal, but not his principles. Let there be prayer and thanksgiving, though sorrow still hovers over the Nation.

A BRAVE AND GRACIOUS LADY

In the aftermath of John F. Kennedy's assassination, the world has been given a new and splendid insight into the character of the Nation's and President's "First Lady"— Jacqueline Bouvier Kennedy. She resolutely controlled her own profound grief and faced up to the public role which necessarily befell her. She performed the role magnificently.

The Nation first came to know Mrs. Kennedy as "Jackie"—a beautiful young woman born to wealth and elegance. She loved to ride horses, to promote the arts, to travel and to enjoy gay parties. This, in the main, was the way the Nation thought of her.

But she's "Jackie" no more. This happy phase of her life was wiped out in a terrible twinkling of time on a fateful sunlit day in Dallas. One moment a happy married woman, the first lady of a great nation; the next a young widow and a former first lady—her beloved husband of only 10 years cruelly taken from her by the assassin's gun.

Under the circumstances, she might well have crumpled, and the Nation would have understood. But duty lay before her—duty to the memory of her husband, to the Nation and to her children, Caroline and John. She did not falter. Instead, she drew upon what must have been a vast amount of spiritual strength and met the ordealing days head on.

The President had been dead less than 2 hours when she stood beside Vice President Lyndon B. Johnson as he took the oath of office which made him her husband's successor. She added several thoughtful touches to the funeral arrangements, including the inviting of John F. Kennedy's Irish kin to the rites. And there was her unannounced visitation to the President's casket as it was being viewed by the public in the Capitol rotunda. There was the silent midnight visit to her husband's grave on Monday night where the eternal flame was burning. The flame, too, was her idea.

Throughout the 4 painful days, Mrs. Kennedy was a picture of grief, but of composed grief; a grief she sought to shield from her children and from the watching world. The children were too young to comprehend, yet at times they seemed to have a sense of the tragedy and when they did she was quick to console them.

Mrs. Kennedy won the heart of a heartsick world in her last role as First Lady. If her dead husband could speak, we think he might say to her with pride, borrowing a term from his naval days: "Well done."

[From the Maine Campus, Dec. 5, 1963]

HE LIVED SO MUCH

"There was a sound of laughter; in a moment it was no more. And so, she took a ring from her finger and placed it on his hand * * * and kissed him and closed the lid to his coffin." The words of U.S. Senator Mike Mansfield will long be remembered by the millions of Americans who witnessed the tragic death of a beloved leader, a brilliant statesman, a humorous wit, a sincere man, a loving father, a giving husband who wanted that there be no room in our hearts for hatred and arrogance.

A stunned campus received the news of the assassination of President John F. Kennedy on that Friday afternoon 2 weeks ago with shock and disbelief. One young man, reluctant to turn away from a television set late that Sunday evening, said, "People find it hard to believe that he is really dead because he lived so much." It is true that he lived a lot. He lived in our hearts and it is there that we hope his spirit will continue to live.

The dazed University of Maine mourned and mourns with the rest of the world at our great loss. As so many others in the world, we feel that we have lost a true

friend. The perfect American, President John Fitzgerald Kennedy, only a little over a month ago became an alumnus of the university when he addressed the people of Maine here.

John Fitzgerald Kennedy gave of himself, "above and beyond the call of duty" to his country; he made an indelible mark of progress in the quest for world peace; he achieved the supreme position of leadership in a modern, dynamic, powerful country. We, who considered ourselves friends of the late President, will never forget his energetic youthfulness, his brilliance of perception, his unfaltering memory, his commanding personality, and his high standards for himself and his country.

We extend our deepest sympathy to Jacqueline Kennedy and to the family of our late President.

[From the Maine Campus, Dec. 5, 1963]

UNIVERSITY OF MAINE, OFFICE OF THE PRESIDENT, *Orono, Maine, November 22, 1963.*

The news of President Kennedy's assassination comes as an incomprehensible shock to the university community. Only a month ago we were honored by his presence at a special convocation on our annual Homecoming Day.

Let us learn, however, from this shattering lesson that hatred can gain control of the human mind and override justice and truth. We are prone to make heroes or villains of our public figures in such a way as to cause some citizens to lose sight of their humanity as individuals. Our civilization must take cognizance of the creation of circumstances which have led to such a terrible event as that of the death of the President of the United States and muster all the forces of reason and judgment so that such an event cannot possibly happen again.

LLOYD H. ELLIOTT,
President.

[From the Bates News, December 1963]

TRIBUTE TO PRESIDENT JOHN FITZGERALD KENNEDY

Brought to an untimely and sudden end by an assassin's bullet in Dallas, Tex., November 22—always to be remembered by this and future generations as a day of infamy and agonizing grief, but also as a day of rededication, by all Americans, to the ideals and principles which inspired and guided our late leader in his relentless struggle for unity and peace for mankind here and throughout the world. Few nations down through the centuries have had the privilege and honor of vesting their responsibilities of high government office in a man equal to his brilliance, courage, loyalty, and compassion. It is most fitting that the world measures him as a statesman of great stature. Truly, if a man is to be inspired and influenced in his pursuit of a better and constructive way of life, he has but to follow the life and deeds of President John Fitzgerald Kennedy. For they provide the undimming beacon lights for that ultimate goal. History shall surely record that society was bettered by his many endeavors in private and public life.

To be thankful for the time he spent with us, rather than to be sorrowful for his death;

To go on with the work that he began, rather than to stand mutely stricken, because he can't finish it himself;

To keep his qualities of character and personality alive within ourselves,

Rather than to let them be buried in a grave in Arlington;

Let this be our tribute to John Fitzgerald Kennedy.

ADDRESS BY

Hon. John Sherman Cooper

OF KENTUCKY

Mr. President, it is difficult to speak of John F. Kennedy. One must be careful not to give undue significance to associations and experiences in the Senate, or elsewhere, happy as they are in our memories.

The outpouring of grief and concern which attended his death does furnish insights into the regard with which he was held by the people of our country and the world.

There is shock, of course, because of the tragic circumstances of his death. We can believe also that concern is caused in part by recognition of the importance of the office of the Presidency. And we can say humbly that it reflects the importance of our country to countries and peoples throughout the world.

But at last we know that the sense of loss and concern is personal. It comes from the knowledge that President Kennedy set high goals for our country—goals, though they have not always been realized, which have given hope throughout our history to the people of the world—equality of citizenship, the provision of opportunity for all our people, and compassion for the least fortunate among us.

He had a calmness about the problems of the world. He knew they could not be settled by some swift, clear stroke; and his calmness gave assurance to our people and to other peoples of the world.

He had the courage to set in motion measures to cut through the cold war, to seek solutions of its issues, and to move toward peace.

The standards he set for our country were noble. They expressed more truly than our wealth and power the essence, the majesty, and the promise of our Republic, those goals which another martyred President said were the last best hope of man.

In time, because of his work, we shall come nearer to realization, and that, I believe, will be his best memorial.

He was an idealist and a realist, a man of reason and a man of heart, a man of courage and a man of peace.

We shall remember him as President. We shall remember always his tolerance, his essential fairness, his courtesy, his humor, the happy qualities of youth, and something about him which endeared him to us and made us love him.

I think John Mansfield's tribute is appropriate:

All generous hearts lament the leader killed,
The young Chief with the smiling, radiant face,
The winning way that turned a wondrous race,
Into sublimer pathways, leading on.
Grant to us life that though the man be gone
The promise of his spirit be fulfilled.

ADDRESS BY

Hon. Milton R. Young

OF NORTH DAKOTA

Mr. President, I join my colleagues in the Senate today in paying tribute to a most distinguished former Member of this body, the late President John F. Kennedy.

There is little I could add to the millions of words of well-deserved tribute to this great young President of the United States who literally gave his life for his country. President Kennedy was the youngest man to ever assume the Presidency of the United States. He brought to this most important office, and all of the world, great intelligence, vision, and indomitable courage. More than any other President of the United States he represented the hopes, dreams, and aspirations of the young people of this Nation.

His tremendous popularity here in the United States and all over the world is a great tribute to many causes he espoused and especially his efforts toward peace in the world. His hopes, dreams, and aspirations for a better world will live on. He left a spot in the hearts of untold millions of people that can never be filled by anyone else.

I will always cherish the memory of the warm personal friendship I enjoyed with him all during his service here in the U.S. Senate and as President of the United States. He was an exceptionally likeable person, and a friend one always felt had a real interest in him. Not the least among the fine qualities that endeared him to so many was his superb Irish wit and humor.

Mr. President, of the millions of beautiful and appropriate words written about the late President Kennedy and his wonderful wife, Jacqueline, the article written by Mr. Theodore H. White entitled "For President Kennedy: An Epilog—For One Brief Shining Moment, Camelot," seems to me to stand out above all others. It reads as follows:

FOR PRESIDENT KENNEDY: AN EPILOG—FOR ONE BRIEF SHINING MOMENT, CAMELOT

(By Theodore H. White)

HYANNIS PORT.—She remembers how hot the sun was in Dallas, and the crowds—greater and wilder than the crowds in Mexico or in Vienna. The sun was blinding streaming down; yet she could not put on sunglasses for she had to wave to the crowd.

And up ahead she remembers seeing a tunnel around a turn and thinking that there would be a moment of coolness under the tunnel. There was the sound of the motorcycles, as always in a parade, and the occasional backfire of a motorcycle. The sound of the shot came, at that moment, like the sound of a backfire and she remembers Connally saying, "No, no, no, no, no."

She remembers the roses. Three times that day in Texas they had been greeted with the bouquets of yellow roses of Texas. Only, in Dallas they had given her red roses. She remembers thinking how funny—red roses for me; and then the car was full of blood and red roses.

Much later, accompanying the body from the Dallas hospital to the airport, she was alone with Clint Hill—the first Secret Service man to come to their rescue—and with Dr. Burkley, the White House physician. Burkley gave her two roses that had slipped under the President's shirt when he fell, his head in her lap.

All through the night they tried to separate him from her, to sedate her, and take care of her—and she would not let them. She wanted to be with him. She remembered that Jack had said of his father, when his father suffered the stroke, that he could not live like that. Don't let that happen to me, he had said, when I have to go.

Now in her hand she was holding a gold St. Christopher's medal. She had given him a St. Christopher's medal when they were married; but when Patrick died this summer, they had wanted to put something in the coffin with Patrick that was from them both; and so he had put in the St. Christopher's medal.

Then he had asked her to give him a new one to mark their 10th wedding anniversary, a month after Patrick's death.

He was carrying it when he died and she had found it. But it belonged to him—so she could not put that in the coffin with him. She wanted to give him something that was hers, something that she loved. So she had slipped off her wedding ring and put it on his finger. When she came out of the room in the hospital in Dallas, she asked: "Do you think it was right? Now I have nothing left." And Kenny O'Donnell said, "You'll leave it where it is."

That was at 1:30 p.m. in Texas.

But then, at Bethesda Hospital, in Maryland, at 3 a.m. the next morning, Kenny slipped into the chamber where the body lay and brought her back the ring, which, as she talked now, she twisted.

On her little finger was the other ring: a slim, gold circlet with geen emerald chips—the one he had given her in memory of Patrick.

There was a thought, too, that was always with her. "When Jack quoted something, it was usually classical," she said, "but I'm so ashamed of myself—all I keep thinking of is this line from a musical comedy.

"At night, before we'd go to sleep, Jack liked to play some records; and the song he loved most came at the very end of this record. The lines he loved to hear were: Don't let it be forgot, that once there was a spot, for one brief shining moment that was known as Camelot."

She wanted to make sure that the point came clear and went on: "There'll be great Presidents again—and the Johnsons are wonderful, they've been wonderful to me—but there'll never be another Camelot again.

"Once, the more I read of history the more bitter I got. For a while I thought history was something that bitter old men wrote. But then I realized history made Jack what he was. You must think of him as this little boy, sick so much of the time, reading in bed, reading history, reading the Knights of the Round Table, reading Marlborough. For Jack, history was full of heroes. And if it made him this way—if it made him see the heroes—maybe other little boys will see. Men are such a combination of good and bad. Jack had this hero idea of history, the idealistic view."

But she came back to the idea that transfixed her: "Don't let it be forgot, that once there was a spot, for one brief shining moment that was known as Camelot—and it will never be that way again."

As for herself? She was horrified by the stories that she might live abroad. "I'm never going to live in Europe. I'm not going to 'travel extensively abroad.' That's a desecration. I'm going to live in the places I lived with Jack. In Georgetown, and with the Kennedys at the cape. They're my family. I'm going to bring up my children. I want John to grow up to be a good boy."

As for the President's memorial, at first she remembered that in every speech in their last days in Texas, he had spoken of how in December this Nation would loft the largest rocket booster yet into the sky, making us first in space. So she had wanted something of his there when it went up—perhaps only his initials painted on a tiny corner of the great Saturn, where no one need even notice it. But now Americans will seek the moon from "Cape Kennedy." The new name, born of her frail hope, came as a surprise.

The only thing she knew she must have for him was the eternal flame over his grave at Arlington.

"Whenever you drive across the bridge from Washington into Virginia," she said, "you see the Lee mansion on the side of the hill in the distance. When Caroline was very little, the mansion was one of the first things she learned to recognize. Now, at night you can see his flame beneath the mansion for miles away."

She said it is time people paid attention to the new President and the new First Lady. But she does not want them to forget John F. Kennedy or read of him only in dusty or bitter histories:

For one brief shining moment there was Camelot.

I join all other Americans in extending to Mrs. Kennedy and all of the family our deepest sympathy in their great sorrow.

ADDRESS BY

Hon. John L. McClellan

OF ARKANSAS

Mr. President, it is with great sadness and deep personal grief that I join in memorializing our former colleague and the 35th President of the United States, John Fitzgerald Kennedy. Our sorrow is heightened by the tragic circumstances under which he was so suddenly summoned to his eternal reward.

The horrible and cowardly act of November 22 shocked and stunned the peoples of the entire globe—both those of the free world and of the Communist sphere as well. That such an act of sudden violence and iniquitous villainy could happen in the most civilized country in the world was scarcely believable, and the United States and all humanity have suffered incalculable loss by reason of this heinous crime having been committed in our generation.

The fact that John F. Kennedy had so much to live for makes his loss even harder to bear. He looked forward to long years of rewarding and fruitful service to his country, and the American people confidently expected many more contributions to the cause of peace and freedom from this young, vigorous, and dedicated leader. To have these expectations shattered and wrenched from us so suddenly leaves us with a painful emptiness and grief.

In the past 19 days, literally millions of words of sorrow and condolence have been penned and spoken in memory of our late President, but no words are adequate to depict the depth and breadth of the tremendous void which his death has left. We, together with all civilized people everywhere, shall long mourn the loss of our great leader—a leader who championed the cause of peace, freedom, and justice for all mankind.

For 8 years, John F. Kennedy served the people of the State of Massachusetts and of the entire United States in this Chamber. During those years we all came to know him well as a hard-working and driving Senator, whose full time and attention was devoted to his duties and to the welfare of all Americans everywhere. For 3 of those years, he served with me on the Senate Select Committee on Improper Activities in the Labor or Management Field, a committee on which his brother Robert, now the Attorney General, served with marked distinction and ability as chief counsel.

Day after day that committee met for long arduous hours in meetings which necessitated equally lengthy and difficult preparation. Through it all, John F. Kennedy was dedicated and thorough—facing with courage and conviction the many challenges confronting the committee. His statesmanlike conduct, both on that committee and on the floor of the Senate, won for him the admiration of his colleagues and the good will and support of the people of the United States.

While paying tribute to our late President, we might also pause to thank him for his astuteness in selecting Lyndon B. Johnson as his running mate. He selected a man who vigorously opposed him in his efforts to obtain the nomination of his party, but in doing so, he provided the United States with a strong and capable successor.

As a longtime friend, both of the former President and of his family, I extend to Mrs. Kennedy, his children and his bereaved parents my heartfelt sympathy in this dark hour of national sorrow. Mrs. McClellan joins with me in paying homage to the greatness of our former President and in the expression of deepest sadness at his loss.

At this moment I can think of no more fitting

words of tribute than those of the American poet, Edwin Markham, who said:

He held his place—
Held the long purpose like a growing tree—
Held on through blame and faltered not at praise.
And when he fell in whirlwind, he went down
As when a lordly cedar, green with boughs,
Goes down with a great shout upon the hills,
And leaves a lonesome place against the sky.
"LINCOLN, THE MAN OF THE PEOPLE."

ADDRESS BY
Hon. James O. Eastland
OF MISSISSIPPI

Mr. President, I join my colleagues in mourning the tragic death of our late President, John F. Kennedy.

No single event in my lifetime has more profoundly shaken and stunned the people of this country and the world than has this senseless and dastardly assassination. People everywhere join with the wife and family in universally sharing the burden of grief and sorrow.

For those of us who have so long known and worked with Jack Kennedy there is a deeper and keener sense of personal loss. It seems that only yesterday he was sitting here with us. No man was ever more generally liked and respected in the Halls of Congress than was he. He was possessed with those sterling traits of character most admired by all—intelligence, courage, energy, compassion, determination, and dedication.

His life has been the realization of the American dream in its noblest and highest sense. A worthy man who openly aspired to achieve the highest office in our Republic, he accomplished the dream through that character of personal drive, initiative, and industry that has been unsurpassed in the modern history of this great Nation.

It is one of the ironies of fate that the author of "Profiles in Courage" should himself end as a shining example of one who gave the ultimate to his own country—his life.

Jack Kennedy was the rare combination of both a scholar and a man of action. The style, pristine clarity, and force of his public utterances will forever form a part of the great literature of this century. President Kennedy was one of the world's leading statesmen. He possessed a keen, analytical mind. He was honest and conscientious. This, coupled with an attractive personality, made him an outstanding man in every sense of the word.

Many of us were sometimes in disagreement with some of his programs and aims. But disagreements did not blind us to the fact that he was motivated by ideals and convictions which left no doubt in his mind that the courses of action that he pursued were for the best interest of the people. Differences of basic public issues are fundamental in the warp and woof of a democratic form of government, and without them the Republic itself cannot long survive.

Death under any circumstances is a saddening human experience. But when a young man is struck down by violence in the prime of life it becomes doubly poignant, and when that young man holds the highest office in the world's most powerful country it constitutes a national and worldwide catastrophe of the greatest magnitude. The events that have transpired since the fatal moment on Friday afternoon, November 22, have again demonstrated the awesome majesty and dignity involved in maintaining the continuity of government in these United States. The beloved wife of the deceased President played a brave and courageous role in this solemn and heart-rending drama.

If good is to come out of such great evil, it is incumbent upon all of us to rededicate ourselves to the immortal principles of liberty, justice, and freedom upon which this Republic was founded.

Again, on behalf of myself and all the people of the State of Mississippi, I extend to Mrs. Kennedy and all of the family the deepest and most sincere sympathy in this time of sorrow.

ADDRESS BY
Hon. J. Howard Edmondson
OF OKLAHOMA

Mrs. President, the date of November 22, 1963, on our calendar has been circled in black forever by the pencil of fate.

We will never forget that on that day our courageous President, John F. Kennedy, gave his life in the service of his country.

My sympathy goes out to his family, to his friends, to his fellow Americans, and to his brothers of the world.

To all, I can say I am convinced that his death was not in vain.

I doubt that any member of the Senate has seen evidence of any single act of providence that has had such a profound effect on Americans as the assassination of President Kennedy.

War in all its terrible ugliness many times has struck us with concern for our lives and property.

Depression has struck us with fear for our economic future.

Disease has struck us with apprehension for those we cherish.

John F. Kennedy's assassination has struck us with interest in an ailing American spirit.

The reflection on what happened in Dallas, Tex., has been healing.

Let us hope the cure will be permanent, for the cost of the treatment was so high that we must never pay it again.

I did not have the opportunity to serve with John F. Kennedy in the House of Representatives or in this body, as many of my colleagues did.

I did have the honor of seconding his nomination for the Presidency, and I value that act.

I marveled at his grace, his dignity, his wit.

I trusted his words.

His deeds projected the devotion of a man endowed with rare understanding—of himself, of his family, of his Nation, of his world, which is a better place because of him.

The silence his passing leaves is more deafening than all the applause his presence brought.

I saw a letter printed in one of our Oklahoma newspapers. A woman told of moving to Oklahoma from another State. Her 5-year-old son came to her and asked, "Is President Kennedy President of Oklahoma, too?"

"Oh, yes," the mother replied.

"Good," sighed the boy. "I would miss President Kennedy."

Indeed, I miss him, too.

Hon. Olin D. Johnston

OF SOUTH CAROLINA

Mr. President, it is a sad occasion for anyone when he rises to eulogize a departed friend, but when it deals with one so young and one with so much unfinished in his life such as our late President John F. Kennedy, then the occasion takes on a sadness of double proportions.

I doubt if any leader in our Nation's history had begun so much and envisioned such greatness for his Nation and was then abruptly departed from the Nation's life. In one fleeting second an irresponsible maniac murdered John F. Kennedy and robbed our Nation of its youngest President in history. However terrible as this tragedy has been for our Nation as a whole, no grief could possibly surpass that of his widow, his mother, and father, and that of his two children; for John F. Kennedy was not only a brilliant young man and an extremely efficient President, but he was also a husband, a son, and a father who exemplified the family unit.

He managed to accomplish all of his official acts and duties and still be husband, father, and son in a tender and homey sort of way. He was a great example setter and many Americans patterned some part of their life after the examples set by our late President and sometimes the members of his family.

His call for physical fitness probably affected in a real personal way more American lives than anything. His examples of showing interest in music, writing, reading, painting, and other arts kindled little fires of the finer things of life in the hearts and minds of all of his countrymen. He and his lovely wife taught many Americans the art of appreciation and in a sense created the atmosphere for a renaissance of the arts. These things represented one side of the man who the American press had nicknamed in a professional manner as "J.F.K."

Somehow, though, it seems most unfitting to apply an initial or a nickname to the late President any more as we look at him with hindsight.

It seems rather clumsy or misfitting to say in a news story now that "J.F.K." visited the Art Gallery to see Rembrandt's "Mona Lisa," or that "Mrs. J.F.K." listened last night to Pablo Casals. Certainly the millions of Americans who have visited the White House and seen the priceless treasures collected by President Kennedy and his widow realize that this was no ordinary President or an ordinary couple whom they had elected to lead this Nation and indeed the free world. He was "Mr. President" in the greatest tradition.

These fine things which the late President appreciated so much and which he wanted his compatriots to appreciate was but a reflection of one part of this unique man. He was a courageous man; he fought without fear of consequences for what he felt was right. He was wise enough to temper courage with restraint, as was exemplified in his actions and leadership during the Cuban crises. A wrong move could have set off a nuclear holocaust for the world or could have lost our Nation's position in world leadership.

In domestic affairs this courage was shown in his stand for legislative matters in which he believed, such as medical care for the aged and civil rights. Personally, I agreed with him on the medicare issue, as in many issues, and I disagreed with him on civil rights. However, never did a difference of opinion with anyone ever deter John F. Kennedy from seeking his goal or from respecting the opposing view which confronted him. He was a politician in the finest sense of the word and maintained his principles and integrity throughout all of his dealings.

It is terrible to realize that this man is no longer with us simply because some misguided individual took it upon himself to eliminate him from society.

Our official 30-day period of mourning for President Kennedy ends on December 22, but I do not believe the American people and the American Republic will ever cease to mourn his passing or fail to remember his charm, his wit, his tremendous ability to converse intelligently on practically any subject, and the great sense of responsibility which he drove home to all of us.

If we in our own lives and in our own efforts try to carry on these things, not the political or social efforts on which all of us may never completely agree, but the basic principles by which he lived, then we will do much to carry into the future these eternal flames for our Nation.

Mrs. Johnston joins me in extending to Mrs. Kennedy, the children, and others of the immediate family our heartfelt sympathy on their great loss.

ADDRESS BY

Hon. Maurine B. Neuberger

OF OREGON

Mr. President, all of us are trying to find ways to express our devotion and admiration for John Fitzgerald Kennedy. I turn to a wonderful sermon given by my own minister at the First Unitarian Church of Washington almost 20 years ago.

The late A. Powell Davies would have found John F. Kennedy an exemplary President for himself personally and for the ideals he expressed. As my tribute to our late President I would like to quote from that sermon entitled "Christmas Always Begins at Midnight":

CHRISTMAS ALWAYS BEGINS AT MIDNIGHT

(By A. Powell Davies)

LIGHT IN THE DARKEST HOUR

It is interesting to notice that in legend upon legend, and story after story, Christmas always begins, not with daybreak and the coming of the morning—but at midnight. It was at midnight that the primitive observances began—or as near it as their reckoning could bring them. It was in the darkest hour of the night—not in the glow of morning—that the shepherds of the legend heard the angels sing. And, of course, the three wise men were guided, not by the sun, but by a star.

It kindles a light, and no matter how little a light it is, the darkness cannot put it out. It says, "Be not afraid, the good and the true are stronger than anything that stands against them, and sooner or later, will prevail." If you doubt it, look backward and trace the path by which we have come; and look around you: in spite of everything, we are still on our way. The darkness is vast, truly, but across it there is a path of light—a path of moving light.

It tells a story—a thousand stories gathered up now into the Christmas story. Of an empire that was disdainful and arrogant. Of the privileged and mighty who had sold their souls for the tinsel of a moment's pomp. Of priests and temples where God was a commodity and truth a joke grown stale. They did not see that the very ground beneath their feet was slipping; so much of it was moving, and so fast. It was like the turning of the earth—unnoticed. They saw only what they looked for; things they could measure in the scales of power, and with the reckoning of gain and loss.

But there was something that humbler people could have told them; both of the old that was dying, and of the new that was newly born. For something had sung it at midnight. Something had shone in the darkest hour. A dream had been told and the hearts of men were kindling. Gentleness and brotherhood were waiting for the morning, and already in the nighttime were up on their way.

HOPE IS ETERNAL

Brotherhood—we betray it, but we cannot forsake it. Love—we disown it, but we cannot renounce it. And the dream?—even in the hour of treason, it reclaims us. For we know that sometime there shall be a world in which man's inhumanity to man is ended. A world of gladness from which all cruelty is gone, in which the joy of each is the joy of everyone, the sorrow of each the sorrow of all. There shall be such a world because there is a song that sings it at midnight, and because in the darkest hour, there comes a light to those who sit in the darkness, and new hope to those who, in the wilderness, must walk beneath the shadow of death.

ADDRESS BY
Hon. Joseph S. Clark
OF PENNSYLVANIA

Mr. President, the world has suddenly lost America's leader: a man of youth and vitality and strength; of a happy mixture of idealism and practicality; of charm, of wit, of intelligence; a friendly man committed to the causes of peace, of freedom, of equal opportunity for all.

In his inaugural address, nearly 3 years ago, President Kennedy said:

Let the word go forth from this time and place, to friend and foe alike, that the torch has been passed to a new generation of Americans—born in this century, tempered by war, disciplined by a hard and bitter peace, proud of our ancient heritage, and unwilling to witness or permit the slow undoing of those human rights to which this Nation has always been committed, and to which we are committed today at home and around the world.

No madman's bullet can be permitted to stop this memorable march of America as a part of the human race toward peace and freedom, compassion and justice under the law.

The brotherhood of man, and the fatherhood of God, call upon us to reach out loving hands across all barriers of race, religion, color, bigotry, and belligerence to all who feel as he did.

Let us in the Senate of the United States keep our hands outstretched.

ADDRESS BY
Hon. Alan Bible
OF NEVADA

Mr. President, since that fateful hour on November 22 last, certainly the United States, if not the world in general, has witnessed and participated in the greatest and deepest outpouring from human souls in modern history. The tragic and untimely death of John Fitzgerald Kennedy touched the heartstrings of Americans everywhere—men and women, young and old, rich and poor, the mighty and the humble, more than any other event which those of us here today can recollect. It is not my purpose today to attempt to add to the wonderful words, the beautiful passages, and the sincere pronouncements about this great humanitarian. However, the actual realization of what has come to pass is now fully upon this country and the world.

The expressions of grief and a great awareness that President Kennedy stood for, and fought for, the things which make our lives more worthwhile came from my State of Nevada, just as they did from elsewhere throughout this country. Illustrative of this fact is an expression in a Nevada high school newspaper which I believe speaks eloquently for the men, women, and children of my State. I wish to add to this memorial record today the sincere expression of Principal Grant M. Bowler, of the Moapa Valley High School, in Overton, Nev. I believe Mr. Bowler's words, contained in the November 27 special issue of his school's newspaper points up excellently the feeling of those at the grassroots of America, those who make up the strength and the sinew and the great body politic of the

United States. I ask that this memorial tribute be included as a part of my remarks together with a eulogy, in the same publication, written by Mr. J. G. Earl, of the Moapa Valley High School. I commend both of these expressions. The articles are as follows:

[From the Lakeside Zephyr, Moapa Valley High School, Overton, Nev., Nov. 27, 1963]

(By Mr. Grant M. Bowler, principal)

Monday, America buried the 35th President of these United States, John Fitzgerald Kennedy. His body now lies entombed in the cemetery at Arlington, Va., the final resting place of many of America's sung and unsung military heroes.

Though his earthly remains return to the soil from which it came, his thoughts, his ideals, the things he stood for, will stare all Americans in the face for generations to come.

Paraphrasing the words of the immortal Abraham Lincoln, "Though the world will little remember what is being said here, the world can never forget what he attempted to do here."

Despised by some, loved by many, and respected by all, John F. Kennedy, the youngest President of the 34 who preceded him, went to his untimely death, not knowing to what extent he had engraved his name in the annals of American history.

Never in history has one man been so dedicated to the universal freedom and individual rights of all mankind, regardless of race, economics, or religious preference.

Never in history has one man been so fearless in his belief that all men should live in freedom and enjoy the fruits of freedom.

When the bullets last Friday stopped the heartbeat of this dynamic and vigorous leader it quickened the pulse of all Americans and many millions throughout the world. It in a way made us hang our head in shame that something like this could happen here in our democratic society.

This dastardly act of assassination has brought reality into our living rooms. Through the medium of television and radio, the entire world participated with the first family in its mourning the loss of a husband, a father, and a President.

Those of our student body and faculty that saw him, in his recent trip to Las Vegas, will never forget him. On that day he delivered an address. To all that heard, it enshrined him as a truly great and humble American.

Now he is gone, he belongs to the ages, his works are now history. As we look up to observe the flag at half-mast for the next 30 days, let us rededicate our lives to the building of the America we all want and need.

As we bow our heads in respect at his passing let us pray for ourselves and our leaders, that we together, may maintain the magnificence of this great land of America, a land which all Americans feel is a land choice above all other lands.

PRESIDENT KENNEDY URGED YOUTH TO STRIVE FOR EXCELLENCE

(By J. G. Earl)

At this time of national mourning, let us look back briefly at the other U.S. Presidents who were assassinated. First, Abraham Lincoln was shot in 1865 while attending the theater. Sixteen years later, James A. Garfield was shot while entering a train station in Washington. Twenty years after that, in 1901, President William McKinley was shot in Buffalo while greeting citizens at the Pan-American Exposition. Now, 62 years later, and less than a week after his murder, the name of President John Fitzgerald Kennedy still does not seem to fit into this list of martyrs.

During my stay in Europe from 1956 until 1958, I met citizens from almost every country of the world. Starting with the unsuccessful Hungarian revolution in 1956, I saw our friends in foreign countries gradually lose respect and admiration for America. During the 34 months while John F. Kennedy was our President, we must all agree, regardless of political affiliation, that the prestige and respect of the United States in foreign countries again started on an upswing.

President and Mrs. Kennedy brought great intellect, culture, and formal education into the White House. Before attending and graduating from Harvard University, the late President attended the London School of Economics for 1 year. This formal study in economics was supplemented by experience in the U.S. Congress in later years. President Kennedy was elected to the House in 1946, directly following the Second World War. He served in the House and Senate for 14 years before his election to the world's most powerful office. He then made it clear to the American people that our economic system needed some drastic changes to keep it up to date with our modern way of life. We will undoubtedly associate the initials J.F.K. with certain economic changes of the future as our parents associated the initials F.D.R. with great changes in this field in the past.

During the past 3 years, President Kennedy was not without opponents, but no one disagrees that he was an educated, intelligent, and aggressive leader. What he recommended for America's young people was not opposed either. First, in Las Vegas recently he admonished the youth of our country to continue in school and advance educationally as far as possible, in order to be of greater benefit to our country. This does not mean just to remain in school and go through the motions of being a student, but implies a striving for excellence and scholarship. Secondly, may we long remember President Kennedy's pleas to fight communism, at home and abroad. Students, it is important that you do not become one of the growing group we call school dropouts, but equally as important that you apply all of your abilities in preparing for your future—as your future is America's future as well.

Mr. President, these expressions were sent to me in a most sincere letter by Vice Principal

Charles K. Pulsipher, of the Moapa Valley Schools; and I ask that an excerpt from his letter, again showing the depth which this great sorrow was felt, be included as a part of my remarks. The letter is as follows:

OVERTON, NEV.,
November 26, 1963.

Hon. ALAN BIBLE,
U.S. Senator of Nevada,
U.S. Senate Office Building,
Washington, D.C.

DEAR SENATOR BIBLE: Today our students of the Moapa Valley High School published a paper as a dedication to the memory of President John F. Kennedy. It occurred to me that you might be interested in knowing of the great respect our students have for this outstanding President. We mourn with you at his death and although we did not know him as you did we feel that we share your sorrow because of the closeness that television has brought him into our lives. This closeness is expressed very well by faculty and students as you can read in the special paper. Especially appropriate are the remarks by Mr. Grant Bowler, our principal, who read these same remarks to the students Tuesday in a devotional program.

Sincerely,
CHARLES K. PULSIPHER,
Vice Principal,
Moapa Valley Schools.

Mr. President, this farming community, nestled close to the country's greatest manmade lake behind Hoover Dam, is far in miles from the territory of Guam, this country's farthermost territory in the Pacific Ocean. However, the anguish was also felt in this island by other Americans. There, Gov. Manuel F. L. Guerrero, immediately after news of the President's assassination reached that island, issued a proclamation, together with a statement mourning the passing of President Kennedy. I ask that this proclamation and Governor Guerrero's statement be included as a part of these remarks. The proclamation and statement follow:

GOVERNMENT OF GUAM,
OFFICE OF THE GOVERNOR,
Agana, Guam.

PROCLAMATION NO. 63–25—THE DEATH OF PRESIDENT JOHN F. KENNEDY

Whereas the Nation and the entire free world has suffered the loss of a great and unselfish leader in the untimely death of President John F. Kennedy;

Now, therefore, I, Manuel F. L. Guerrero, Governor of Guam, by authority vested in me by the Organic Act of Guam, do hereby proclaim a period of mourning in the territory of Guam, such to last until sundown, December

22, 1963, and I ask that all flags on public and private buildings be flown at half mast during that period and I call upon all residents of the territory to pause in their daily endeavors to pay silent tribute to a great leader who died, as he lived, that our country may live up to its democratic principles of equality, opportunity and freedom; and I urge all residents to reflect upon the tremendous contributions made by President Kennedy during his short and useful life and to gain from that reflection renewed determination to work for and defend the traditions by which he lived; and I urge all residents of the territory to go to the church of their choosing and thank Almighty God for having blessed the world with such a person and pray to Almighty God for guidance for President Johnson and all other officials of our Nation during the critical days ahead.

In witness whereof, I have hereunto set my hand and caused the great seal of Guam to be affixed in the city of Agana, this 23d day of November in the year of our Lord nineteen hundred and sixty-three.

MANUEL F. L. GUERRERO,
Governor of Guam.

Countersigned:

DENVER DICKERSON,
Secretary of Guam.

———

GOVERNOR'S STATEMENT

A heartbreaking tragedy has befallen our land. We have lost a great leader.

This loss extends beyond the boundaries of our Nation and is shared by every person who loves freedom throughout the world.

The leadership of President Kennedy and his human warmth were unsurpassed.

The people of Guam have lost a true friend who, despite the pressures and burdens of his position, took a personal and active interest in the welfare of this territory at all times.

No human effort can erase this disaster; no hand can undo this wrong.

To all of us there is left only one course and that is to redouble our efforts under the leadership of our new President to further the causes of our Nation and our people in the manner typified by the life of John F. Kennedy.

Mr. President, at a Solemn Pontifical Requiem Mass at the Dulce Nombre de Maria Cathedral, in Agana, Guam, a most moving eulogy was offered by Chaplain Joseph P. Trodd, U.S. Navy. I ask that it be printed in full as a part of my remarks.

EULOGY FOR PRESIDENT JOHN F. KENNEDY, NOVEMBER 25, 1963, CATHEDRAL, AGANA, DELIVERED BY JOSEPH P. TRODD, CHAPLAIN, U.S. NAVY

In the name of the Father, and of the Son, and of the Holy Ghost. Amen.

"There was a man, one sent from God, whose name was John."

"A bad man killed my daddy."

This plaintive cry of a 3-year-old echoes hollowly through the White House halls. The world listens and grieves. The Nation is shocked and bewildered. A widow numb and unbelieving.

For John Fitzgerald Kennedy, 35th President of the United States, was murdered last Friday afternoon in Dallas, Tex. We heard this stark statement uncomprehendingly, asked why this senseless crime and then paused to assay our loss and perhaps shed a tear.

Who was John Fitzgerald Kennedy? A rich young man who might have wasted his substance? A Harvard undergraduate who might have become a playboy of our Western World? No, he became neither. He was instead a naval officer privileged to wear the Silver Star, an astute politician, a more than competent author, an able statesman, and humanitarian. His intellect was keen. His repartee incisive and at times uproarious with his crackling Irish wit.

Yet our Nation has produced many rich young men, many college graduates, many decorated officers. Why did the mantle of greatness descend upon John Fitzgerald Kennedy? Twenty years ago in the same motor torpedo boat squadrons in which he served were Larry Green, Larry Kelly, Paul Lillis, Bernie Crimmins, Al and George Vanderbilt. Surely these were men as competent and as dedicated as he. Why then did the finger of God single out John Kennedy?

We feel this.

That within him there smoldered a burning compassion for his fellow man, a fiery conviction that true peace in the world depends upon the peace of Christ in the heart. This compassion, this conviction became his mission. He toiled incessantly to teach that all men are created equal and that each, irrespective of the color of his skin is an individual with a soul precious in the eyes of God. His fidelity to his faith, his dedication to his country, his service to all marked him plainly as a doer of the word as well as a believer.

To a Winston Churchill is it given to live in greatness. To a martyr to die in greatness. A select few both live and die magnificently. Such was Abraham Lincoln. And such, we believe, was John Fitzgerald Kennedy.

For when the annals of time are weighed, history will agree, that in the manner of his dying, unwittingly he taught his greatest lesson. Here was a man, in the fullness of his strength; perhaps the most powerful single individual on earth—whose whim or nod could make a statesman or break a general who by pressing one button, could bring death and destruction to most of the civilized world.

And yet, last Friday afternoon, as he rode down a sundrenched Dallas street accepting the plaudits of thousands at the summit of his career, a finger was bent and a shot sounded.

Honor, dignity, and power faded. And in a matter of minutes a soul, naked and alone, stood before its maker.

And what of the lesson?

A poet would say "All that beauty, all that wealth ere gave, await alike the inevitable hour. The paths of glory lead but to the grave." But the Christian mindful of eternity asks "What doth it profit a man if he gain the whole world and suffer the loss of his immortal soul."

Our prayer today is this: May you, John Fitzgerald Kennedy, hear from the lips of your Saviour, "Well done thou good and faithful servant. Enter into the reward which has been prepared for you for all eternity." And then may you see a tiny figure disengage itself from the choir of angels and saints and feel its baby fingers grasp your hand and lead you to the throne of the Almighty and hear your son, Patrick Bouvier Kennedy, say, "This is my beloved father in whom I am well pleased. For here was indeed, a profile in courage."

Mr. President, in the tragic death of John Kennedy, the Senate—in fact, each and every one of us—lost one of our own. I believe each Member of the Senate has felt this grief deeply, not only because he was our colleague, but also because he went from this Chamber to the highest calling in the Government of this land. We each felt, irrespective of our political beliefs, a certain prideful warmth in his accomplishments and a certain inward grief in his defeats. Mr. President, it was my good fortune, when I first came to the Senate, to strike up a friendship with the then Senator Kennedy. Our desks were close together in the back row in this Chamber. We saw his suffering, some years ago, that kept him from this Chamber, because of recurrent complications from injuries he sustained while fighting for this country in the South Pacific waters during World War II. We marveled at the energetic campaign he waged across this land for the nomination for the Presidency, and the great vigor he displayed in winning the office of President of the United States.

It was my pleasure to have a close, personal, and warm friendship with John Kennedy, and I believe that I am better for it. The world has lost one of its greatest leaders, humanity a noble champion, and the United States of America a fearless, courageous President whose name will be enshrined forever in immortality.

The world is a better place for men everywhere because of John Fitzgerald Kennedy's great human understanding and his dauntless courage to seek for humanity more of God's great benefits.

From among the many messages of mourning that came to me from the State of Nevada, I have excerpted some representative tributes and have selected particularly fitting editorials, written in memory of the late President, which appeared in the newspapers and over television stations of my State. These editorials and statements follow:

[From the Hawthorne (Nev.) Independent-News]

A nation grieves; a world mourns.

Millions of words have been written and spoken since that dark moment on Friday morning when the President of the United States became the victim of an assassin's bullet. Yet, as so many already have said and written, words seem so empty at a time like this. And just as "empty" is used in reference to inadequate words, so does it aptly describe the physical and mental feeling of millions of peace-loving citizens in all parts of the world.

John Fitzgerald Kennedy already has been eulogized throughout the world as an exceptional man who gave his life in the service of his country, and also in the effort to lead all nations to a more peaceful existence.

Just as nations which differ with ours in philosophy gave recognition to the sincerity of the man, so have those citizens within our country who differed with President Kennedy's political philosophy and parts of his governmental program. That he was a great man in life, few will dispute; that his greatness was even more fully revealed in death, none will deny.

As Chief Executive of our great Nation President Kennedy was a symbol of leadership for freedom-loving nations in all parts of the world. That he should be taken so swiftly, so unjustly, in the prime of life, added to the sorrow of his untimely death, but even more, that he was struck down in his homeland by a cowardly sniper brought shame as well as sorrow to the Nation he loved and served.

It is not for us to attempt to recapitulate the good deeds that are to his credit. The world is well aware of that creditable record; has become more so in the past 5 years; and the story will be retold for generations to come by the historians of the world.

That we chose not to agree with many of his political beliefs and actions is a privilege that we in the United States cherish. And John F. Kennedy was a man who proved his willingness to ever protect the right of Americans to so differ.

The sympathy of a sorrowing world has been extended to his grief-stricken widow and children, his parents, and other family members. We can only repeat, in a way he would understand, the words intoned at his bier, "Eternal rest grant unto him, O Lord, and may perpetual light shine upon him."

Just as the truly united spirit of this great Nation was so evident following the tragic death of President Kennedy, it is to be hoped that the same united spirit and confidence will be displayed toward President Lyndon Johnson as he assumes the great burden of carrying on the duties of the Nation's highest office.

To use an old and general appraisal of the situation in which the new President finds himself: "The man is entitled to a chance."

This is not to imply that the traditional two-party system of checks and balances must falter during a period of crisis, but in time of crisis we are Americans first, partisans after. Thus, until the new President has been given ample opportunity to navigate his own course for our ship of state, let us be reasonable, fair, and understanding.

With the passing of time there will be occasions when the policies of President Johnson must be subjected to honest differences of opinion, not only those contentions of the opposition party, but quite likely from the ranks of his own party.

By election time next year the issues will be more clear cut—or maybe more confused—but next year will be soon enough to debate those issues in the time-honored and successfully tested American custom.

For the present, even though we have our reservations about continuance of some policies established by the martyred President, we must think in terms of what the world is thinking about U.S. leadership, and world reaction to the sudden change in our Government leadership.

This we can best do by remaining calm and confident—going forward with vigor and not in the shadow of fear—and constantly reminding ourselves of the immortal words spoken by President John Kennedy upon the occasion of his inauguration:

"Ask not what your country can do for you, but what you can do for your country."

———

[From the Paradise Press (Las Vegas) Nev.]

How futile and feeble are words when one tries to understand the monstrous events of the past several days.

Thoughts come seeping into the mind, and you try to push them away for they seem so insufficient in laboring toward comprehension of the history made in our Nation and the world.

The full force of the acts performed before the eyes of millions will not have a lasting effect perhaps for years.

But, the madness which was displayed, the motives behind a twisted mind, the cracking of guns and the barbarous, animal-like acts of so-called human beings give rise to many emotions. Sadness, disbelief, bewilderment, and anger seem to rise to the top of our experience. Of all these, anger continues to prevail.

Yes, we know that anger is the one emotion which must be drowned by common sense. But, reports coming in from all over America and the nations of the world have as an underlying current—anger.

But it was anger coupled with insanity which produced the assassination of our President, John F. Kennedy. If this be so, then let us dispel anger from our minds and thoughts. Let anger be replaced by dedication to the idea that this can never happen again. Let us also bury, once and for all, the thoughts of hate. For hate and anger are partners in crime.

Let us condemn these two criminals. Let them be judged for eternity as having no place in the American way of life.

To those who sell and spread the contraband of hate, let Americans issue a challenge to be backed with action—this Nation will no longer tolerate hate groups be they right, left, or in the middle. Hate is not choosy. It will dwell and grow like a cancer wherever it finds the right festering food.

Science and reason are conquering disease; let democracy eradicate the most devastating of all maladies—hate and anger.

It may be that the death of John F. Kennedy will be justified if it brings home to every man, woman, and child that our Nation is in grave danger if we do not grind into nothingness the elements existing in our society which caused the death of John F. Kennedy. Let us hold that his death may not have been in vain.

But, we must not let the tragic events of the last week fade away. Let not time lessen our resolve.

It is certainty that the sniveling creature who pulled the trigger and fired the fatal bullets into our President was insane. But, that should not lull us into inaction. For, there are thousands of people in this Nation who could pass a sanity test and be considered normal. Yet, they are fostering hate between people, groups, races, creeds, and religions.

Herein lies the danger for their insane acts and programs cannot be detected until they will have fired a fatal bullet in democracy and America.

Let each and every person, each and every day, each and every hour, stamp out hate and prejudice. Let us not even joke about it. Let snide remarks which give birth to the destruction of democracy be driven from our land.

We are at war. Our enemy is hate. Let us take to the battlefield now and never relinquish the day to our enemy.

——

[From the Elko (Nev.) Independent]

You look at the gray skies and you think, "even nature is in mourning in keeping with our great sorrow."

And the sun sets red and fiery angry in the west at eventide on this day of great tragedy and the thought wanders aimlessly through your numbed mind that "Even the elements are offended at the dastardly thing that earth's lowest human being has done to one of our finest citizens."

You watch a widow suffering and the tears well up in your eyes. A press camera catches a saluting 3-year-old standing erect and only half-knowing the tragedy—his own personal tragedy—of the occasion and an ever-living photograph joins hundreds of others that have been taken on this shocking weekend in America.

And again your mind wanders to thoughts that bear no logic and that have no reality in the cold, steely facts of the situation which your eyes are conveying to your mind.

Certainly the skies are gray on this day but they would have been gray and it would have stormed had not a cold, calculating assassin fired a fatal shot through the head of President John Fitzgerald Kennedy.

And the sunset would have been red and fiery on this Friday evening, November 22, 1963, whether the President had been shot or whether he had gone home to the White House that tragic November day and stepped softly into the nursery late at night to whisper a fond goodnight to little "John-John."

The awful shock of a Presidential assassination, or of sudden death close to the heart of any human being, numbs the senses and makes us prey of uncontrolled emotions. Slowly we accept the truth and resign ourselves to the world of logic from which we have been removed by shock.

When the great men have said their eulogies, when the men of God have called on their deity to take the soul from man's mortal remains, when the mourning family has returned home and has been removed from the public gaze and let to the care of loved ones, then the grim facts return, too, and slowly but surely we begin to face up to reality.

And so it is today. A great American President has been assassinated. The world has reeled in shock and sorrow. Violence has erupted in the wake of this historic tragedy to add further shock and disbelief to our numbed senses. We have been deeply emersed in sorrow and have been depressed and saddened beyond anything we have known and shared with all the peoples of earth previously.

But the ceremonies are over and the mourners have gone home. The reeling effects of time have already begun to be felt. Slowly the grinding wheels pick up speed and a busy world begins to go its way.

Few of us who die will ever cause such a long pause in the normal course of humanity's daily routine. Perhaps only one or more deaths in a century will so affect the peoples of the world.

But the passing days and months and years will close the yawning gap in human society and the world will go on, leaving only a deep scar on the history of the nations to mark the occurrence of this tragic series of events.

So it is that today we begin to look with more interest to the future than we do to the past. The work-a-day world confronts us. Our brethren are anxious to be up and doing. The demands of the present press on us and the uncertainties of the future intrigue us.

——

[From Elko (Nev.) Daily Free Press]

PRESIDENT KENNEDY IS DEAD

The world is in a state of shock because of the assassination of President John F. Kennedy of the United States.

It seems unbelievable that he is dead.

One moment he was flashing his famous smile, and in the next he was slumped limply in the arms of his wife. Within the hour he was dead, a victim of an assassin's bullets.

He was the first Catholic ever elevated to the Presidency, and his election helped to stem the march of bigotry. Many of those who opposed him because of his religion would have voted for him in the next election. His renomination for a second term to the Presidency was considered a mere formality. While polls showed that he had lost some of his popularity, they also indicated that he would be continued in office.

The greatest issue today is civil rights, an issue which will continue for many years to come. It was because of his firm stand in favor of the Negro race that he lost some of his popularity. He tempered his wishes for legislation with the hope that a bill might be passed over the objections of southern Congressmen and other opposition. The President placed the tax cut before civil rights, saying that without jobs the fight to aid Negroes would be nullified.

It was a contradictory thing that the young Democratic President, only 46 years of age, found difficulty in securing passage of legislation in a Congress which was heavily dominated by the members of his own party. The greatest stumbling block was the conservative committee chairmen, whose positions have been gained through seniority. His victory over Richard Nixon in seeking the Presidency was slim. It was difficult indeed to see where he had been given a mandate by the people. But he was a man with strong convictions on the type of legislation he desired. Much of his thinking ran into strong opposition from conservative forces throughout the Nation. This did not deter his efforts in the direction he wished to push the country.

He showed great strength of character when the chips were down in the Cuban situation and he demanded the removal of Soviet missiles from that island. But he missed a golden opportunity to unseat Fidel Castro at the Bay of Pigs. Only recently, he called upon the Cuban people to arise against Castro promising assistance from this country.

He took a step toward peace in pushing the nuclear test ban treaty. His greatest desire was to assure a lasting peace, and he went further than many Americans felt he should in seeking a better understanding with the Russians.

He was the fourth American President to be assassinated while in office. He was a perfect target for his assassin as he rode through the streets of Dallas in an open car. He had faced death before in the service of his country in World War II. He faced it many times in the past while touring the country, despite protection from those assigned to guard him. His death could mean that Presidents of the future will take greater care in shielding themselves from possible assassination. That is a horrible thought to express in America, said to be the most advanced nation in the world.

Death came to him while he was in the full strength of years. His greatest contributions to his country still lay ahead. Many of his goals had not been reached, because much of his favorite legislation was in controversy. The story is now left untold. We will never know what his future successes and failures might be. There is no doubt in our own mind that he would have been reelected in 1964. We appreciate that there were grave differences between him and many people of the country, some of it being based upon party politics alone. However, some members of his own party were opposed to liberal legislation, including the proposed tax cut. Opposition here stemmed from the fact that those of more conservative leanings wanted expenses cut before taxes were reduced.

Men and women of the world will grieve over the death of America's young President. Their sincere sympathy will go out to Mrs. Kennedy and to her two children. They have lost the guiding hand of a fine father. The Kennedy family has been famous because of its close binding ties. We can think of nothing which could bring more grief to them than the loss of this loved son.

America has lost a leader highly respected in world forums. While we will still be the seat of the greatest power of any country on earth, we are likely to suffer at least a temporary setback because his leadership will be gone.

His great consideration for the common man; his humanitarian approach to all great problems; his linking of the historical past to the present and future were among his great characteristics.

The words he spoke at his inaugural address will probably be those which will live in history longer than any of his others. He said, "Ask not what your country can do for you, but what you can do for your country."

This country has faced great losses from the death of leading men in the past. It has always risen to the occasion to meet the demands placed upon it. There will be no change today. The prayers of the Nation will be offered to Lyndon B. Johnson, now President. Those of us old enough to remember, will recall that Harry S. Truman succeeded Franklin Delano Roosevelt to the Presidency, at the time the President died in office. The new President rose to the occasion just as we are sure Lyndon Johnson will.

November 22 will go down a black day in the history of this country, but the people can be expected to meet this disaster with the same courage they have shown in the past.

[From Carson City (Nev.) Appeal]

NATION IN PRAYER

Tearful, confused, and ashamed, the people of the world's greatest nation were on their knees this morning in prayer.

The United States is mourning the death of its 35th President, John F. Kennedy.

Some unknown but God-given buffer has allowed the tragic and sorrowful news of the grotesque assassination of President Kennedy to seep into the bodies of the American people without shattering their hearts and minds.

And as the people of our Nation pray for the soul of their beloved late President and his family they also search their own soul for an answer to the insanity and sickness that allowed such a tragedy to strike.

A confused and sorrowful people trying to find an answer for an act that cannot be answered. A people seeking logic for a tragedy that has no logic.

And yet there must be some thanks given on this day of sorrow. Thanks that our Nation has not become incapacitated by a tragedy that hurts each and every one of us. We owe thanks that we have been given leaders such as the late John Kennedy and the new President of the United States, Lyndon Johnson—men who have, and will continue to keep our country great.

We must pay our respects, contemplate our sorrows and then do what the leaders of our Nation know we must do, go on.

The tragic loss we have suffered will not be forgotten. We must work harder to make ourselves and our Nation better. We must offer humility to our leaders no matter what faith, color, or political beliefs involved.

We are a humble and sorrowful society ashamed of the deeds that have marred the path of our lives and changed the course of history. But we are not (and cannot) become an angry and purposeless nation.

We must lift the cloak of darkness and sorrow that is over the hearts of all of us. The people of the United States must prove that the 35th President of this great country did not die for a people and purpose that will fail. That we will work for the goals of freedom, equality, and individualism as did the late President.

We must pray but not fear.

An assassin's bullet tore apart a piece of America's heart. A nation of concerned people will mend that heart but the ugly scar it must bear will remain.

[From Las Vegas (Nev.) Review-Journal]

PRESIDENT KENNEDY GAVE THE ULTIMATE SACRIFICE

Profound shock and deep sorrow touches all Americans today.

We have lost our President. We mourn for him as a man and as a leader. It matters not how his strides are measured in history.

It is in the greatness of this Nation that the grief which befalls us with the death of John F. Kennedy is not the grief of a few, but of all of us.

President Kennedy belonged, not to a select few, not to any political party alone, but rather to the Nation as a whole, to every American no matter what his station in life.

Tributes will be paid. They will be deserved. But the truth of what this loss means to our Nation will be found only in the hearts of the people.

Here, as in perhaps no other public figure in the Nation, indeed in the world, was a man of our times— a man who found in himself the strength to take us into the space age while at the same time coping with the great social volcano a hundred years in the making.

The mantle of the Presidency of the United States has been worn by the great, the near great, the not so great. History in time will assess him not alone as a man but more in the context of our needs, our crises, our goals, our times. And that assessment, we believe, will be that he must rank among the greats even though he was tragically prevented from carrying to fulfillment his finest work.

The ultimate sacrifice that was his to give has been given.

A great nation mourns a great leader. But our greatness does not lie in one man alone—and John F. Kennedy would be the first to remind us so.

[From Wells (Nev.) Progress]

It was a sad day for our country last Friday when President John F. Kennedy's life was taken. We wish to join with the thousands of others in expressing our sincere sympathy to members of the late President's family.

We are fortunate in having a man of the caliber of President Lyndon B. Johnson to carry on. The State of Nevada was very fortunate in having a friend in the person of President Kennedy and I am sure that things will remain the same under President Johnson's leadership.

[From the Reno (Nev.) Nevada State Journal]

A GRIEF-STRICKEN NATION MOURNS LOSS OF ITS CHIEF

The startling, unbelievable, and tragic news that President Kennedy had been assassinated in Dallas yesterday threw a pall of grief over the Nation that it has seen only rarely in its history.

War, pestilence, and other cataclysmic events have aroused the Nation in the past. But these, the people have known, they would be able to combat, to do something about.

After the assassin's bullet had founds its mark and the President's life had slipped away, it left the country with a hopeless, angry, frustrated, grief-stricken sense that there could be no action which would alleviate the pain.

The President was dead, and no power on earth, no superhuman effort could change the awful truth.

Condolences poured in upon the national seat of government from the high and the low, from both political parties, and from all faiths.

They expressed, with as much force as mere words can, their sorrow at such a monumental loss to our beloved country.

Even the arrest of a prime suspect in the assassination seemed of little consequence in the light of the gigantic horribleness of the deed itself.

The loss of the President was mirrored in the face of every pedestrian on Virginia Street in Reno. Conversation was at a minimum—for of what use is talk on such an occasion?

So it was throughout the Nation, and even throughout the world. The man who was perhaps the most powerful individual on earth was one moment waving and smiling at happy crowds and the next was dying in the arms of his wife.

As a new day dawns our Nation, stricken by grief in the loss of this vital, intelligent, and devoted patriot, and searching for some light to guide it, could well remember his stirring words at the inauguration:

"Ask not what your country can do for you, but what you can do for your country."

John Fitzgerald Kennedy gave the last full measure.

[From Yerington (Nev.) Mason Valley News]

Among the thousands of words eulogizing the late President John Fitzgerald Kennedy and the analysis of what could have motivated Lee Harvey Oswald to take the life of the Nation's Chief of State, none rang a clearer bell tone than those uttered by Chief Justice Earl Warren as he spoke in the great rotunda of the Capitol Building Sunday.

Warren laid the blame for Kennedy's assassination squarely on those in our country who foment and encourage racial prejudice, who incite to riot, who preach hatred and bigotry and infect the minds of those around them to the point where such a dastardly and despicable act would seem justifiable to such a person as Oswald.

These are the people who, in effect, killed John Kennedy; Oswald was just the instrument of that hatred and fanaticism.

If this be true—and it is without a shadow of doubt—then all of us collectively share the guilt of Kennedy's assassination. When we as a nation can shrug off the death of a Negro in the South, brutally slain, when we can ignore the riots which occurred when the law of our great land, laid down by the Supreme Court, was flouted in Alabama as a colored student sought to exercise his constitutionally guaranteed rights, when we can turn to the comic pages of the newspaper rather than become concerned when a church is bombed and youngsters killed because their skin is black, then we all share the guilt in the death of John Kennedy.

When men like Governor Wallace of Alabama can openly oppose the Constitution and a Supreme Court order and thus encourage the citizens of his State to violence and hatred, and still remain a popular political figure, it is indeed a black day for this Nation.

Wallace has declared a 30-day period of mourning in tribute to the late President. He should declare this same period as a time to resurvey the morals involved in condoning hatred which led ultimately to the death of this young leader.

Yes, we are morally responsible for the act of assassination either by condoning or ignoring the turmoil within our Nation today built on a foundation of violence.

"In the larger sense the guilt for the death of John Kennedy must rest with each of us who has permitted the spread of ignorance and fanaticism, who has joined in the flabby spirit of complacency or who has permitted the preachers of hatred to appear respectable.

"Yes, all who assume the self-righteous attitude that labels those who disagree with us as traitors and dolts prepared the way for the vile deed that snuffed out the life of our President, whom we sadly sent to his grave," aptly put by the Nevada State Journal this week.

Last Friday was indeed a black day for this Nation—a nation which attempts to hold up an image to the world of equality and freedom for all men.

It is indeed a time to contemplate President Kennedy's words at his inaugural: "Ask not what your country can do for you, but what you can do for your country."

Black is the mark on the city of Dallas, Tex., where two acts of incredible violence resulted within a 48-hour period, resulting in the loss of the Nation's President and later the murder of his accused assassin.

There seems little doubt but what Lee Harvey Oswald was indeed the man who from ambush snuffed out Kennedy's life at the peak of his career. A shocking, despicable act of violence but in the full sense no more a dastardly crime than that perpetrated against Oswald later in the basement of the Dallas police station when Jack Rubinstein committed coldblooded murder.

Equally as shocking as these two crimes was the seeming stupidity of the Dallas police force. Knowing full well that an attempt might be made on Kennedy's killer as emotions throughout the country and the world boiled, they permitted Ruby, an unauthorized person, to linger in the station for some 3 days and to be in the basement when Oswald was to be transferred from the city to the county jail.

To compound the error, they publicly announced the transfer of the prisoner, the method to be used, just when it would take place, and how.

Equally as ridiculous was the announcement that as far as Dallas was concerned the case of Kennedy's assassination was closed. A Presidential order to the FBI will continue the investigation until all available facts are known. Was Oswald a hired gun? Was his life snuffed out to keep him from talking? Was the entire episode a conspiracy? These are all questions yet to be answered.

The press played a role in Oswald's death in pressuring and prying in the line of duty for every scrap of information to feed the papers, radio, and television and, by all rights, they should have been denied the information as to when the accused assassin was to be transferred and certainly not permitted in the police station basement. Spiriting Oswald away in secret would have avoided his murder.

Despite the tragedy of last weekend, on this Thanksgiving Day, 1963, the Nation has much for which to give thanks.

As shocked as the citizenry was, and the deep, almost personal loss felt around the Nation, we can be thankful that our forefathers in their wisdom created a document known as the Constitution which provides for an orderly transition of governmental duties in times of crisis.

Had this event occurred in many nations of the world, the whole governmental procedure would have collapsed and chaos reigned. Not so in this land of ours and Lyndon Johnson, within the space of a few hours, took over the reigns of government.

We can be thankful, too, that crises seem not to destroy the American people but draw them closer together in a united front and a deeper determination to go forward and to meet problems head on. Such was the case at Kennedy's death as party politics were cast aside in the pledge of the Congress to give the new President all the cooperation and support possible.

Lyndon Johnson, while lacking perhaps the personal charm of Kennedy, certainly not an intellectual and clearly a provincial, nonetheless brings to the Office of the Presidency a tremendous background of political knowledge and achievement.

Only in the field of foreign relations will he face a fiery furnace but even here he will not be an unknown as he traveled the world extensively in his role of Vice President.

Only history will tell what kind of a President Lyndon B. Johnson will be. However, the ability he showed while leader of the Senate and the good impression he made in foreign lands will stand him in good stead.

Although he was of a different political affiliation we, nonetheless, admired this man tremendously.

We admired him not as a politician but as a loving

husband and father, a deeply religious man, an intellectual leader and a soldier who made the supreme sacrifice in service of country.

"And I heard a voice from heaven saying unto me, write, blessed are the dead which die in the Lord from henceforth: Yea, saith the Spirit, that they may rest from their labours; and their works do follow them."—Revelations 14: 13.

And finally in answer to the question posed by many: "How could this happen in a country like ours?" In what other country in the world could the assassination of a President be done with such ease? It is the American way to do things in the open, to turn the sharp eye of the public on every function, to make known all the facts whether good or bad. Heads of state in other countries would not perhaps have divulged a tour route, would have ridden in a bulletproof car, would have been spirited in and out * * * but this is not the American way.

In a country where anyone can possess a firearm * * * where the same can be purchased in any catalogue, if not in public stores, what easier place to achieve such a crime?

The American people have always been able to react to a crisis in such a manner that they bend but never break and herein lies the strength of this Nation. As shocked as all were last weekend, a return to normal was quick in coming and already this week such comments as: "There probably is an opening for chief of police in Dallas," and "Where else but Texas do they do things in such a big way?" are being heard. Such comment is not disrespectful to a departed leader but indicates the resiliency of Americans and their ability to "bounce back."

———

[From Boulder City (Nev.) News]

The Nation's leader dies at the hand of an assassin.

It is difficult to believe such could happen in a civilized country but, none of us know what goes on in the minds of people. A well-dressed, healthy, handsome man may actually be a dope addict, a maniac, a killer of men, women, children.

If there could be such a thing as an all-out drive to cure this situation in our country, it should be done now. It is a pity that a great leader be killed in the prime of his life to prove to all of us that there still lurks on our streets depraved minds, Americans who would kill.

When President Kennedy visited this area a month ago, many who watched his open car travel the route from the airport to the convention hall and back—felt he was taking a gamble against some lunatic's gun. Many of us wondered whether the security measures were detailed enough to completely shield the President.

As you watched the same sort of motorcade in Dallas, you saw the same openings for the lunatic's gun. And what didn't happen here did happen there.

A brilliant young man's life snuffed out in seconds. A nation's people brought to grief by an assassin.

Now we have President Lyndon Johnson and from all sources one learns that he should be able to steady the fears and the fallen hopes of those who felt that Mr. Kennedy alone had the answers to our Nation's immediate future.

President Johnson appears to us to be another Harry Truman. He doesn't have the educational brilliance that made Kennedy great. However, it appears he will have a way with the masses and may get much more done in Congress where for years he had the Senate in the palm of his hand.

The Ivy League influence and image around the Washington upper levels will, I believe, give way to the political machinations that one sees on the congressional levels. Possibly more laws will be passed under Johnson than under Kennedy and possibly our foreign affairs will be handled with bolder actions.

Where Kennedy's gigantic mind could fight through our international problems with brilliant words and explanations—now one may see the American stand being presented in straight-from-the-shoulder orders and demands.

Kennedy was a disciple of peace and so is Johnson, I'm sure. Johnson's western ways may prove as effective in maintaining peace as Kennedy's intellectual suavity.

Kennedy came along at the right time and proved ideal in carrying the Nation forward through difficult times. Johnson comes in and seems ideally cut out to handle the new problems before us.

Complete cooperation among all factions of our people will encourage our new President and will help him in making the transition.

Though all our hearts are weighted in grief, it is our feeling that the Nation will go on to its next steps without faltering and without serious loss or damage to our economy, our freedom, or our position as the world's leading country.

President Kennedy's short but brilliant span as our leader will be forever remembered.

He brought youth, vigor, intellect into our Government and with these he rekindled in all of us the excitement of being alive and serving the best interests of mankind.

It was a pleasure to listen to his powerful words; it was a thrill to study his face; it was heartwarming to watch him live in the world spotlight with a family that played, worked, dressed, traveled, suffered—as you and I.

The man deserved to live out his life like Truman, Eisenhower, Hoover. His presence would have added so much to mankind.

Surely, a piece of each of us died with President John F. Kennedy.

———

[From the Henderson (Nev.) Home News]

A Tragic Page in Our History

Like the rest of the Nation, Henderson was stunned by the assassination of President John F. Kennedy in Dallas, Tex., Friday.

In the Nation's highest office for less than 3 years, President Kennedy was the youngest man ever to be elected to that position and the youngest to die while President.

In slightly over a period of 12 years he rose from a post as Congressman from Massachusetts to a U.S. Senator and to Chief Executive.

Only history can evaluate his mark on its pages, but his concern for the underprivileged and for the minority groups was only matched by two other great Presidents, Abraham Lincoln and Franklin D. Roosevelt.

His career in the U.S. Navy was no less phenomenal than his rise in politics.

While blessed with wealth, his programs were constructed to aid those less fortunate and particularly those who lacked equal opportunities in this democracy.

John F. Kennedy was the fourth President to be assassinated in office—a record of which all Americans should hang their heads in shame. But in our democratic way of mingling, that dreaded possibility is always in the background.

Fortunately, in this time of need, the United States had a capable man in the office of Vice President. No man is better versed in congressional procedure. Vice Presidents of the caliber of Lyndon B. Johnson have been rare throughout our brief history.

"I will do my best with your help and God's," he said after assuming office. We can ask for no more.

___

[From KOLO–TV, Reno, Nev.]

This is a time for retrospect. This is a time for each of us to examine those things that we are made of, that drive us, that cause us to do the things we do. It is a time for each of us to make significant changes in our own lives. It cannot be wasted or washed away by time. It must come to make more meaningful the days that we are to spend here and with each other. President Kennedy passed our way. He was a man of courage; of great moral character. The past few days you were witness to an incredible scene of events and meditation. Cannot this man and these days mean more to our future thoughts and deeds than others?

It will mean more to this station—in the programs we carry, in the manner in which we address ourselves to the viewing audience.

KOLO–TV has received numerous calls and messages from persons who wished us to return to regular entertainment programing. To these persons we can only repeat some of the remarks made by Harry Reasoner of CBS news. We are not God. We are only men and only able of making men's decisions. To John Fitzgerald Kennedy we entrusted the highest offering we as citizens have. In so doing we asked him to sacrifice his life if necessary for that trust. Friday he did sacrifice his life. We, as men, can only offer respect and dedication and in so doing, make men's decisions in tribute. We are sorry it was all we had to offer.

___

[From Gardnerville (Nev.) Record-Courier]

THE GREAT UNFINISHED TASKS

(By the Reverend Robert L. Stevenson, Coventry Cross Episcopal Church, Minden, Nev.)

The tragic events of the past few days, which have seen the assassination of our Nation's 35th President, John Fitzgerald Kennedy, have cut deeply into every sensitive American heart. The traditionally festive atmosphere of a Thanksgiving Day this year will be replaced by sober soul-searching reflection and meditation.

We can truly be thankful that our Nation has shown in this hour of loss its ability to rise from adversity into united strength and solidarity.

We can be truly thankful that out of the ashes of distress has been created a new sense of purpose and rededication to American principles and ideals.

We can be truly thankful that we have faith in an Almighty God who is present in the world to give us comfort and guidance and strength.

I would humbly suggest that you and I, along with our fellow citizens across the Nation, and those whom we have chosen as our local, State and National legislators and leaders, rededicate ourselves this Thanksgiving Day to the "great unfinished tasks" ahead.

In a Thanksgiving Day proclamation for a day he was never to live to see, our late President John F. Kennedy was to write of the "great unfinished tasks of achieving peace, justice, and understanding among all men and nations."

"Today we give our thanks," he wrote, "most of all for the ideals of honor and faith we inherit from our forefathers; for the decency of purpose, steadfastness of resolve, and strength of will; for the courage and humility, which they possessed, and which we must seek every day to emulate. As we express our gratitude, we must never forget that the highest appreciation is not to utter words, but to live by them. Let us, therefore, proclaim our gratitude to Providence for manifold blessings; let us be humbly thankful for inherited ideals, and let us resolve to share those blessings and those ideals with our fellow human beings throughout the world."

Proclaiming Thursday, November 28, 1963, as a day of national thanksgiving, John F. Kennedy concluded with this prayer:

"On that day let us gather in sanctuaries dedicated to worship and in homes blessed by family affection to express our gratitude for the glorious gifts of God; and let us earnestly and humbly pray that He will continue to guide and sustain us in the great unfinished tasks of achieving peace, justice, and understanding among all men and nations, and of ending misery and suffering wherever they exist."

John F. Kennedy is dead, but his ideals and the ideals of every American President will live on for future generations to emulate, if you and I will rise to the challenge of the great unfinished tasks.

___

SERMON OF MONSIGNOR JOHN LAMBE, AT CHRISTMAS MORNING MASS, OUR LADY OF LAS VEGAS (NEV.) CATHOLIC CHURCH

The glorious days of Christmas are with us again, and the magical name brings up memories both joyful and sad—joyful, because with all Christian people—with all men of good will—we are uplifted for a time from the hard cynicism of doubt and unbelief, and we share with the simplicity of little children the glad tidings that the angels and the shepherds first proclaimed: "Christ is born in Bethlehem."

And it brings sad memories, too; for who can forget the paradise of childhood, when living with loving parents and most dear members of our immediate families, now alas no more, we shared that greatest of all family days: Christmas?

For Christmas is more than the birth of Christ; it is more than the beginning of Redemption; it is more than the beginning of Christian teaching; it is the birth of our first family—first in dignity—first in meaning—first in honor.

Because Christianity began with a family, it introduces us into that way of life for which God destines us, into that close-knit group, whose memory will never die, and where mutual love will remain forever and forever.

And so each of us, with but little difference in the total picture, celebrated our Christmas days with our own families.

In my homeland, Christmas Eve saw the setting up of the red-berried holly tree, and the lighting of the Christmas candle in every home to be a guide to the Holy Family in their search for a room in which the Divine Child might be born. And in my own house, we had the unique privilege of having a mass every Christmas morning as the very first part of our celebration. Here a congregation of 10 learned early from the Holy Family that "they who pray together, stay together." And I am sure as each one of you looks back, you will remember with sweet sadness the greatness of the love that binds you with those who are your very own.

For the family is the divine institution into which all of us are born. It is the model of perfect government. In it are contained the elements which make for godliness and Christianity. It has the ruler, the teacher, the subject. All our efforts to improve our lot in life are doomed to failure if the family is not allotted its proper place.

So it was very natural that when God devised his plan for the redemption of mankind, as part of that plan his own Divine Son would come on earth through the very human means of a family—so like our own—but of so different—the just St. Joseph, the Immaculate Mary, and the Divine Child born into that poverty so much a part of our human heritage.

St. Joseph was the ruler, Mary was the teacher, the Son of God was the subject. To Joseph the angel came in a vision to warn him to take measures for the safety of the Divine Child. And to the Blessed Mary fell the lot of guiding, if that is the proper word, the spiritual and temporal teaching of the Redeemer.

Here are the models which we must strive to copy, the ideals so unattainable, which we must strive to reach: Jesus, Mary, and Joseph.

How different it would be if fathers and mothers everywhere looked on children as gifts entrusted to them by God, whom the little Lord Jesus wants to nourish above all in the divine life. Our schools are but substitutes—the mother is the real teacher, the father is the provider and ruler. And how different the world would be if all family life was as it should be. Ah, if all the world would only come to the crib and learn.

Just 2 months ago, I said mass on the place where our Lord Jesus was laid in the manger, and there I offered mass for my little world, for all the people I ever met: priests—sisters—everybody whom I knew during my lifetime which included all of you among whom I have been working; and I trusted, as I believed, that the infinite

merits of that mass would reach out and influence the lives of all for whom it was offered. I went to the crib—because I always loved the crib—that the glory of the crib might shine on you. So come to your crib and live for a while in its reflected glory.

Come to the crib—and lest we forget—here pray often and fervently for that great President of our own faith, John Fitzgerald Kennedy, who so graced the highest office of our beloved country. Pray that his wonderful wife, Jacqueline, may continue to be a wonderful mother and that their lovely little children, Caroline and John-John, may grow up in the image of their noble parents.

Come to the crib and pray too that the successor to that high office, Lyndon Johnson, and his dear wife, Ladybird, and their two beloved daughters may continue to be living examples of sacrifice and love of humanity, that illumine the cradle of the Divine Child.

Come to the crib and learn how things should be. You have a beautiful traditional representation of it in your own parish. Visit it often. Bring your children, young, and old.

Come to the crib and rededicate your lives to the noblest ideals of fatherhood.

Come to the crib and beg the Immaculate Mary to make you a mother worthy of her.

Children, come to the crib, and learn the humility and the obedience of the Son of God who obeying the will of man lies here in a stable in Bethlehem.

Come to the crib and pray that your bishop and your priests and your sisters, who have given so much for you, may ever remain close to Jesus, Mary, and Joseph.

Come to the crib and renew your faith. Come to the crib and find hope. Come to the crib and increase your love.

Come to the crib: for here, and here alone, will you find the peace that surpasses all understanding, the peace that will be the road to everlasting happiness for you and for your loved ones.

ADDRESS BY

Hon. Ernest Gruening

OF ALASKA

Mr. President, historians of the future will have to assess in full the contribution John Fitzgerald Kennedy made to mankind. One may speculate that our late beloved President would have preferred this, for he was also a historian and history was his intimate companion. "Why England Slept," and "Profiles in Courage," will be among his monuments.

He utilized the lessons of the past, kneading them with events of the present, to create for the future. His vigilance and his actions made certain that the United States did not sleep in the face of peril. And his life both in war and in peace turned a profile in courage on the page of history.

History was his friend and we are the beneficiaries of this friendship.

For him the words engraved on the statutes at the entrance of our National Archives—"What Is Past Is Prologue" and "Study the Past"—had full meaning. An idealist, but also a realist, with a look to the future and an eye to the past, he lived in the present. Because he was a man of vision, he looked forward.

Consider his remarks in Anchorage, Alaska, September 3, 1960:

But I see Alaska, the Alaska of the future. I see an Alaska where there will be more than 1 million people. I see a giant electric grid, stretching all the way from Juneau to Anchorage and beyond. I see the greatest dam in the free world, the Rampart Dam, producing twice the electricity of the TVA, lighting the homes and mills and cities and farms of the great State of Alaska. And I see highways linking all sections of this great State. I see Alaska as the destination of countless Americans who come here not searching merely for land and gold, but coming for a new life in new cities, in new markets. I see an Alaska that is the storehouse of our Nation, a great depository for minerals and lumber and fish, rich in waterpower and rich in the things that make life abundant for those of us who live in this great Republic.

I do not say that this is the Alaska of 1961 or perhaps even of 1971. I do not say that a Democratic administration can magically bring about all of these things by itself overnight. The work must be the work of many, and the burden must be the burden of many. It will take your efforts and your help, but I think it is time we got started.

John Fitzgerald Kennedy was articulate, gallant, and courageous. He was witty, gay and high spirited. He was generous, kind and compassionate. And, when our friends across the oceans refer to him as "princely" they, too, are correct.

Moreover, he was stimulating and inspiring. Consider the immortal invocation in his inaugural address:

And so my fellow Americans, ask not what your country can do for you: Ask what you can do for your country.

My fellow citizens of the world: Ask not what America can do for you but what we can do together for the freedom of man.

This was his salutatory as President. He could have no finer valedictory.

His eloquent words he sought to match with deeds. His indefatigable quest for peace lighted the candle of the test ban treaty.

His fight for civil rights will lift our Nation to a new level of justice and racial equality.

With his lovely wife Jacqueline he made the White House the cultural citadel of America: art, music, poetry, creative expression and intellectual achievement found a new warm welcome there.

His continuing interest in the development of our resources is best noted in his own words, spoken in Anchorage, Alaska, on September 3, 1960, when he said:

The untapped energies of the American people which are more powerful than the atom itself must once again be committed to great national objectives.

Historian Arthur M. Schlesinger, Jr., writing in the December 14, 1963, issue of the Saturday Evening Post observes:

He had grown all his life, and he grew even more in the Presidency.

His was a life of incalculable and now of unfulfilled possibility.

Still, if he had not done all that he would have hoped to do, finished all that he had so well begun, he had given the Nation a new sense of itself—a new spirit, a new style, a new conception of its role and destiny. He was the most civilized President we have had since Jefferson, and his wife made the White House the most civilized house in America. Statecraft was for him not an end in itself; it was a means of moving forward a spacious and splendid America.

Statecraft is indeed the word. He was a student of and commentator on public affairs early in life, an eager volunteer in his country's war service, emerging as a battle-scarred warrior, truly a hero; thereafter a distinguished legislator in House and Senate, then President of the United States. John Fitzgerald Kennedy's public career made of politics what it should always be, a noble calling—the profession of public service.

Editorials, newspaper columns, magazine articles by the thousands in all parts of the world, and books have recorded and will continue to record John Fitzgerald Kennedy's great service to his countrymen and to the larger family of mankind. All of us in the Senate have lost a friend. I, for one, shall never forget his kindness in coming to Alaska to campaign for my election to the Senate in 1958.

America is much much richer and much much better for his having lived. It is incalculably poorer for his early and untimely departure at the height of his prowess and on the road to greater fulfillment.

Mrs. Gruening joins me in our expression of deepest sympathy for his courageous Jacqueline, for his two dear children, his brothers, sisters, and bereaved parents.

Mr. President, I ask unanimous consent to have printed editorials published in the Anchorage, Alaska, Daily Times of November 22, 1963; Anchorage, Alaska, Daily News of November 23, 1963; the Fairbanks Daily-News Miner of November 23, 1963, and November 25, 1963; Jessen's Weekly of Fairbanks, Alaska, November 27, 1963; Cook Inlet Courier of Homer, Alaska, November 22, 1963; the Juneau, Alaska, Daily Alaska Empire, November 24, 1963, and the Nome Nugget, Nome, Alaska, November 25, 1963, commenting on the service of John Fitzgerald Kennedy.

———

[From the Anchorage (Alaska) Daily Times, Nov. 22, 1963]

J.F.K. LAYS DOWN LIFE FOR HIS COUNTRY

Anchorage, along with the rest of the world, was shocked and grieved at the stunning news that an assassin's bullet had struck down President Kennedy in Texas. The 35th President of the United States died within an hour of the gunman's attack.

First word of the shooting brought a reaction of disbelief to those hearing the news—it was too stunning to be true.

The President was in Texas on a 3-day visit which had taken him to San Antonio, Houston and Fort Worth prior to the trip to Dallas, where the sniper struck.

Kennedy was the youngest man, and the first Catholic, ever elected to the Presidency. His term had been filled with controversy and therein may lie the key to the assassination. To this writing the person responsible for the President's death has not been captured. He is the fourth President to die at the hands of an assassin. The others were Lincoln, Garfield, and McKinley.

He began his political career in 1946 when he first won election to the U.S. House, representing the Boston district. He won reelection in 1948 and 1950. In 1952 he moved to the U.S. Senate when he unseated incumbent Senator Henry Cabot Lodge.

At the 1956 Democratic National Convention, Kennedy narrowly lost the vice presidential nomination to the late Senator Estes Kefauver after presidential nominee Adlai Stevenson threw open the choice to the convention.

Two years later Kennedy won reelection to the Senate by a record margin.

After sweeping the 1960 presidential primaries, Kennedy had little difficulty winning the Democratic nomination on the first ballot. That November he defeated then Vice President Richard Nixon for the Presidency.

Kennedy was not one to shirk his personal or political responsibilities. He was a naval lieutenant who played a hero's role in the south Pacific in World War II. He won the Navy and Marine Corps Medal as well as the Purple Heart.

As Chief Executive he was the first American to face possible nuclear war. He didn't hesitate to protect American interests with a show of force. Later he won an agreement from the Russians which limited nuclear tests.

The President also quickly made known his stand on civil rights. He took action in trouble spots throughout the South and he brought his forces to bear on Congress to enact a major civil rights bill to combat racial discrimination in public accommodations, schools, jobs, and voting.

Anchorage and the rest of the Nation join the Kennedy family in its time of grief for the President who died for his country.

———

[From the Anchorage (Alaska) Daily News, Nov. 23, 1963]

PRESIDENT KENNEDY'S LEGACY

The course of human events is often shaped by violence, and mankind is long inured to the experience of death and disaster. But there is something about the assassination of John F. Kennedy so irrational, so senseless, that words must fail to measure the deed, or the mind of the killer.

Whether he was a lone lunatic or the triggerman in a plot, investigation will tell. Before all the facts are disclosed, it will be unwise to jump at conclusions. Certainly no hostile government worthy of the name could have expected to profit by Mr. Kennedy's death: First, because Mr. Kennedy was a man of peace and, second, because the continuity of the American system is such that the death of a President, however calamitous, leaves the essential marrow of the Nation undisturbed.

That Mr. Kennedy should die by a fanatic's hand is peculiarly ironic, for Mr. Kennedy himself was anything but fanatical. He was a man of driving intelligence, considerable humor, and a remarkable capacity for cool detachment. He was a highly skilled politician, but he could view his role, and himself, in the broad perspectives of history—his favorite subject, and one in which he was widely read.

Like all Presidents, Mr. Kennedy aroused a measure of opposition and controversy, and like all human beings he made mistakes. But on the great questions confronting the Nation he was right. He took his stand firmly on the moral side of the civil rights issue, and he stood equally firm when the Nation was threatened by Soviet missiles in Cuba. By facing down Nikita Khrushchev at that time, he earned the lasting gratitude of America's allies and the lasting respect of its opponents.

He was cut down at the age of 46, before the full fruition of his career. The legacy he leaves to the Nation is his cool, even-tempered, rational approach to national and world affairs. There has of late come a distemper over American politics, an extremism in word and action which has assumed a disproportionate influence on the Nation's life. Mr. Kennedy was not one who subscribed to the conspiratorial view of history, to the implacable attitudes which has given rise to much of this contemporary malaise.

He was, as has often been said, a practitioner of the art of the possible. He could disagree without necessarily condemning, and oppose without questioning the opponent's motive. He was a tough man, steeled by the tests of war and of unremitting public service—public service he sought although he was born into a life where he need never have lifted a finger to exert himself. Through all of this, Mr. Kennedy remained a man without bitterness.

If his death could contribute to the amelioration of some bitterness, some of the divisive violence which has invaded American life under the pressure of momentous problems abroad and at home, it is a contribution Mr. Kennedy himself would have cherished.—R.J.C.

———

[From the Fairbanks (Alaska) Daily News-Miner, Nov. 23, 1963]

President Kennedy

Strife in the South.
A great war in progress.
An empty rocking chair.
A Vice President named Johnson suddenly becomes President.
The body of a great man lies in state as the Nation mourns his passing.
How strange it seems that these are the facts in 1963 just as they were in 1865.
Abraham Lincoln, the Republican, freed the Negro from slavery.
John Fitzgerald Kennedy, the Democrat, attempted to free the Negro from bigotry.
Both men met similar fates.
Lincoln fought the Civil War. Kennedy faced the war against communism.
Lincoln was shot in the head while sitting in a rocking chair at Ford's Theater in Washington. Kennedy too left his famous rocking chair empty in Washington when an assassin's bullets struck him in the head and neck.
Mrs. Lincoln was with the President when he was shot. Mrs. Kennedy was also with her husband when tragedy struck.
It is recorded that Mrs. Lincoln wept and fainted and cried "Oh, that dreadful house."
And perhaps now the words of President Kennedy's lovely and beloved Jacqueline will go down in history expressing the grief of all Americans when she cradled the President's head in her arms and cried "Oh, no."
Both men, mortally wounded, lived for a period of time after being shot.
A stunned Nation, caught completely unaware, could hardly believe the news, either in the case of Lincoln, or in Kennedy's death yesterday.
Even today it is difficult to comprehend this murder, for it is a double blow to the national conscience—the killing of John F. Kennedy, the man; the assassination of the President of the United States, our Commander in Chief.

Yet we will know as the days go on that no madman's bullet can stop the progress of this Nation. The rocking chair is empty as it was in 1865, but now as it did then, the country will move forward.

President Lyndon B. Johnson will take charge, and the assassin will have succeeded only in destroying a man—not the American concept of freedom and self-determination.

Our forefathers planned carefully for such tragedies as this.

No one man controls our destiny. Perhaps it is at times like this that we realize how much "In God We Trust."

America is much like a large family. We squabble frequently and fight. We have differences of opinion and we blast each other with verbal vehemence.

But in times of trouble we stand like steel. We stand united now in our anger and our grief.

Black or white, Republican or Democrat, Protestant or Catholic, all Americans are shocked.

When Lincoln died, the course of history was altered. And so is the case with Kennedy. No one can predict what changes this assassin's bullet may bring in our lives.

Kennedy and Lincoln both had small children.

Kennedy's two charming youngsters have lost a father. America has lost a leader.

Our Nation mourns with clinched fist.

But as it was in 1865, the war will be won, all citizens will enjoy their rights and another man will fill the empty rocking chair.

———

[From the Fairbanks (Alaska) Daily-News Miner, Nov. 25, 1963]

A Difficult and Somber Time

On this day we pay tribute to a man who believed in human dignity as the source of national purpose, liberty as the source of national action, the human heart as the source of national compassion, and in the human mind as the source of our invention and our ideas.

That there were and will be political disputes on the methods of fulfilling our national purpose does not take away from the shared feeling of a great destiny for this country. This national day of mourning is also, in the words of President Lyndon Johnson, a day of rededication. John F. Kennedy would have been the first to say that on such a day our ultimate responsibility is to begin looking ahead.

President Kennedy always was looking ahead. He believed we stood on a frontier of unknown opportunities and perils at a turning point in history. Never was such a statement more valid than today. He believed in Americans as all being partners in a great and historic journey. This journey continues.

Our feeling for the loss of a man is made worse by the feeling of outrage that comes with the helpless realization that a worthless character with a sick mind has murdered the President of the United States. There is other strong emotion, too, as many of us realize that perhaps never will the White House be occupied by a family of more intelligence, vitality, and elegance.

Here was a man who fought for his country, who almost died for it during the war; a man who contributed his Presidential salary to charity; who kept in trim doing pushups, playing touch football, golf, and sailing, while deploring the thought of America becoming a nation of spectators; a man of wit.

"I think the worst news for the Republicans this week was that Casey Stengel has been fired," said Kennedy during the presidential campaign. "It must show that perhaps experience does not count."

"On this matter of experience," he added, "I had announced earlier this year that if successful I would not consider campaign contributions as a substitute for experience in appointing ambassadors. Ever since I made that statement I have not received 1 single cent from my father * * *."

Yes, his sense of humor will be remembered. But more memorable will be John Kennedy's strong sense of purpose and identification with the national purpose.

"In the long history of the world, only a few generations have been granted the role of defending freedom in its hour of maximum danger. I do not shrink from this responsibility," he said. "I welcome it."

Thinking today about the man, the office, our future, and our Nation's high purpose, we can consider these words carefully as applying to each of us.

And if John F. Kennedy could speak on this day, perhaps he would repeat the words he once said:

"I hope that all of us in a difficult and somber time in our country's history may bring candles to help illuminate our country's way."

———

[From Jessen's Weekly, Fairbanks, Alaska, Nov. 27, 1963]

Life's Inexorable Course

In the span of hardly more than 72 hours, America lived through 3 days of fantastic events that made the weekend appear, in retrospect, the most nightmarish in our history. A dynamic young President was cut down by a sniper's bullet, the alleged assassin was slain in turn, and a state funeral was held to which the leaders of the free world came.

Americans wept unashamedly and their grief was shared in other lands.

Through the ears of radio and the eyes of television, the Nation observed the indescribable courage of the President's young widow, who saw her husband die and stayed beside him virtually to the end. The heart of the Nation went out to her, as she slowly climbed the Capitol steps and knelt and kissed the flag-draped casket and followed on foot the funeral cortege that took John Fitzgerald Kennedy on his last journey from the White House.

The gathering of kings and princes, presidents and premiers in Washington on Monday was a tribute not only to the fallen President, but to the unquestioned place of world leadership the United States has attained.

Stunned and shocked though the Nation is, however imponderable the fates, life follows its inexorable course. Fortunate it is that the Presidential burdens were assumed immediately by an able and tested leader. Americans may give a heartfelt response to the promise, the plea, and the prayer of Lyndon Baines Johnson:

"I shall do my best. I ask your help—and God's."

———

[From the Cook Inlet Courier, Homer, Alaska, Nov. 22, 1963]

The Shot Heard Round the World

The Nation, even the world, mourns the death of a great man, President John F. Kennedy. Whatever our views, our beliefs, the taking of a life is wrong; by whatever fashion, whatever means, for whatever reason. The broad road our Nation has been traveling at a great rate of speed under his leadership may not have been the one we thought right, nevertheless we grieve and offer a prayer for his sorrowing family. That President Kennedy was a great man, none can deny.

Now may President Lyndon B. Johnson have the courage and strength to face the challenge of the Nation and the world with directness.

In the less than 200 years of our Nation's life its history has been marred now four times by the assassination of the Chief Executive: Abraham Lincoln, James A. Garfield, William L. McKinley, and today, John Fitzgerald Kennedy.

———

[From the Daily Alaska Empire, Juneau, Alaska, Nov. 24, 1963]

Renewed Dedication

Suffering a tragedy like the assassination of President Kennedy, almost all persons want to do something to show their sorrow and respect for the one who is gone. The first thought usually is of a vocal expression of sympathy, followed by a desire to make a public gesture to show unity of feeling with the entire people, by flying the flag at half staff, or by closing the place of work, or by attending a prayer service, or otherwise by doing something different from normal which will show respect.

Beyond all the gestures and ceremonies, however—after all the expressions of respect and regret—there remains a feeling that can only be met by a measure, at least, of long-range dedication to the purposes, standards, or unfinished work of the departed one. Facing the sudden, tragic loss of President Kennedy, we find ourselves seeking the lasting ideals which he was trying to establish in concrete form for the benefit of his people and the world, both present and to come, so that we might carry these ideals on toward the goals he might have won had he not been struck down.

Seeking the meaning and momentum of his life, we find he was the first human leader entrusted with great power to risk with clear and steady judgment a confrontation of nuclear war for the protection of his Nation and the cause of freedom. We find in review that, despite disagreements at home and abroad, he stood firm against the advance of communism, yet hopeful that the good in all people would emerge, and anxious lest blind inflexibility might fail to perceive and grasp real opportunities to advance human unity and dignified peace. He held the line against communism, yet his open mind made possible the first big step—the limited nuclear test ban treaty—in guarding against nuclear contamination and destruction of mankind's home.

Mr. Kennedy saw clearly what many of us, equally sincere in opposing communism, failed to see—that ultimate victory for the dignity of man cannot be won by hasty or extreme antagonism, nor by disregard for the aspirations of confused and misguided peoples seeking in desperation a fair share of the world's goods and reasonable recognition of rights long withheld. He aided throughout the world those governments which gave consideration to the rights and needs of their people—and worked toward reform of those governments which, while opposing communism, continued to oppress their people and withhold the rights and goods to which any human being is entitled.

He stood for reasonable rights and prosperity for all the people, both at home and abroad, regardless of race or creed or condition of birth. He sought these goals, distant though they were in many situations, through the principles that have created American greatness and the greatness of human freedom everywhere, through private initiative when possible but, if not accessible by that route, through initiative of enlightened government. He stood for vigorous living, for moving boldly ahead into the adventurous future of mankind, on earth and in space.

In deep consideration for the tragedy which removed him from leadership while so many of the goals were not reached, we feel, with Alaskans and all Americans, a deep renewal and strengthening of dedication to the work he was forced to leave unfinished.

————

[From the Nome Nugget (Nome, Alaska), Nov. 25, 1963]

OF JOHN F. KENNEDY

John Fitzgerald Kennedy started his administration as the 35th President of the United States by dedicating himself to two shining goals—survival of liberty at home, and peace in a world shivering in an "uncertain balance of terror."

He invited the Communist world to join in a new beginning of "the quest for peace" before the dark powers of destruction unleashed by science engulf all humanity in planned or accidental self-destruction.

"Let us never negotiate out of fear, but let us never fear to negotiate," he said in his inaugural address that was devoted almost entirely to foreign policy and foreign affairs.

John Kennedy was born in Brookline, Mass., May 29, 1917. He received his bachelor of science degree cum laude from Harvard in 1940 and then studied at the London School of Economics. He entered politics at the age of 29, when he was elected to Congress in 1946. After winning reelection twice, he ran for the Senate in 1952 and defeated Senator Lodge. Winning reelection in 1958 by the largest plurality ever piled up for a Senate seat in Massachusetts, almost 900,000, further enhanced his political stock. He was sworn in as President of the United States on January 20, 1961.

John Kennedy and Miss Jacqueline Lee Bouvier were married in St. Mary's Catholic Church in 1953. A daughter, Caroline Bouvier, was born in 1957. Three years later there was a son, John F., Jr.

John F. Kennedy is gone—murdered by the bullet of an assassin. Our lives and the world with its seemingly never-ending series of crises, out of which arose his death, will go on, but there is now an emptiness where he once stood. All sane peoples are shocked by the manner in which this great man came to his end and all are silently speculating on their own futures.

ADDRESS BY

Hon. Wayne Morse

OF OREGON

Mr. President, the nightmarish weekend through which America recently lived will scar the memories of adult citizens for the rest of our days. We simply do not have the country we thought we had. The rest of the world knows this now, even if we may be reluctant to admit it to ourselves.

I shared the assumption of many Americans that Presidential assassination was a thing of the past. The fact that our political and moral climate still makes this heinous crime possible will give rise to much national soul searching. So, too, will the equally incredible sequel—the lynching of the accused assassin. How to eradicate political murder and lynch law from our country will occupy our thoughts for many years to come, even as we go on about the other business of Government.

For me, the greatest inspiration from the life and death of President John F. Kennedy is to be found in his own deep devotion to the principles and ideals of self-government. The tragedy of his passing does not flow from those principles and ideals, but from our failure to realize and achieve them.

I believe that like Abraham Lincoln before him, John Fitzgerald Kennedy would say that it is for the living to be dedicated to the unfinished work which both these great men so nobly advanced; and that from their deaths we should take increased devotion to the cause for which they gave the last full measure of devotion.

For as long as this Republic survives, and let us pray it will survive forever, the American people will be the beneficiaries of the statesmanship of John Fitzgerald Kennedy. He has carved in the tablets of American history inspiring challenges to all Americans who come after him to strengthen and preserve our system of representative self-government.

His insight and foresight in respect to the obligations of citizen-statesmanship which are the responsibilities of all Americans who come after him will also be a perpetual flame that will burn throughout history in the hearts of our people.

Of all the monuments that will be erected to his memory, none can ever be as symbolic of his statesmanship as his eloquent, literary writings which record for all time his political philosophy which was so in keeping with Jefferson who wrote the Declaration of Independence, and with Lincoln who penned the Emancipation Proclamation and emblazoned in American history the Gettysburg Address.

As we sat in St. Matthew's Cathedral on that sad November 25, 1963, there was placed in our hands a small memorial card containing on one side a cherished picture of the President and on the other, three short paragraphs of quotations of challenges to the American people selected from his historic inaugural address. I would let every American citizen honor the memory of John Fitzgerald Kennedy by way of rededication to the challenges of citizen-statesmanship called for in these three noble paragraphs:

Now the trumpet summons us again—not as a call to bear arms, though arms we need—not as a call to battle, though embattled we are—but a call to bear the burden of a long twilight struggle, year in and year out, "rejoicing in hope, patient in tribulation"—a struggle against the common enemies of man: tyranny, poverty, disease and war itself * * *.

In the long history of the world, only a few generations have been granted the role of defending freedom in its hour of maximum danger. I do not shrink from this responsibility—I welcome it. I do not believe that any of us would exchange places with any other people or any other generation. The energy, the faith, the devotion which we bring to this endeavor will light our country and all who serve it—and the glow from that fire can truly light the world * * *.

With a good conscience our only sure reward, with history the final judge of our deeds, let us go forth to lead the land we love, asking His blessing and His help, but knowing that here on earth God's work must truly be our own.

It is now up to the American people of his generation and future generations to keep faith with our obligations of citizen-statesmanship. We owe it to our country to ascend to the heights of President Kennedy's idealism and statesmanship and thereby prove to ourselves and the world that this great man did not live and die in vain.

ADDRESS BY

Hon. James B. Pearson

OF KANSAS

Mr. President, many Senators who have spoken today in memory of President John F. Kennedy do so as former colleagues in the Congress and as personal friends. I did not have an opportunity for such friendship. Thus my own concept and memory of the man and his work perhaps is more closely associated with that of the general public than as a Member of the Senate.

My first thought is that it is well, in a sense, that some time has passed between the date of death and this solemn occasion. The full meaning of John Kennedy's life and work was difficult to comprehend in the period of shock caused by the tragic manner of death—assassination. While all of us sought some facility to believe the unbelievable, it was difficult to put the life of the President, his impact upon our Government, and his relationship with the people, in sensible perspective.

But now we are slowly beginning to understand that it is not how long but how well one lives that counts. It is not how one dies but how one lives that has meaning.

I have often thought that the height of a man's achievement during his life ought to be measured not only by his final position of accomplishment but also by his point of beginning with due consideration for the obstacles which the uncertainties of the times place in his path. So measured, President Kennedy's life was one of great achievement.

Many others today have spoken of his courage, his intellect, his love of family and life, his appetite for work, his appreciation of good values, his sense of history, and his dedication to the

American way of life, and our system of government. These traits of character and mind he did possess.

But combined with these, I detected a capacity for sustained effort, a consistency of application of all those talents and abilities described so ably by my colleagues. Was this not his finest trait of all?

Many across the Nation have now been seeking in his deeds and words the element in his philosophy, religion, life, work, or ambition which gave him the unity of purpose and the strength required to do what he did. I would suggest that perhaps it was the admonition repeated so often by his fellow townsman, Justice Holmes, who told us all: "Have faith and seek the unknown end."

ADDRESS BY

Hon. Howard W. Cannon

OF NEVADA

Mr. President, nearly 3 weeks have passed since the death of President John Fitzgerald Kennedy, and the Nation has not yet fully recovered from the horror and indignation which grew from the most heinous crime of the century.

In almost every State in the Nation, and, indeed, in the National Capital, Americans are demonstrating their profound sense of loss through the renaming of schools, streets, airports, and other memorials.

Certainly, the fact that a brilliant young President, for altogether too brief a period, led this Nation and gave all Americans a glimpse of the promises of freedom for years ahead should not be erased from our memory. We should properly preserve his memory for as long as this Nation endures.

My thoughts today dwell on the invisible, yet powerful, memorials which could be erected to the great leader who has been taken from us. We will be a greater nation, and his legacy will be more towering than any edifice of steel and concrete if John F. Kennedy is enshrined in the national conscience as a martyr who gave his life in the enduring battle against hatred, bigotry, and intolerance.

Surely, these insidious forces guided the quick and brutal hand that struck down the 35th President of the United States.

The greatest memorial that we can give to President Kennedy is to rid ourselves, as a nation, of the fanaticism and insane rage—turned inward—which made this tragedy possible. I cannot escape the conviction that such a living memorial in the hearts of his countrymen would have been most earnestly desired by our late President.

Our Nation is made up of Americans from divergent geographical areas whose regional motives and national origins are more diverse than any other country in the world. Ours is a young nation striving, in a real sense, to find itself. Our national goals and our heritage can never be fully achieved unless we are tolerant of the views and beliefs of our neighbors. We cannot afford to set ourselves upon the Devil's work of national distrust, accusations, and suspicions of our neighbors.

These, I firmly believe, are the lessons of Dallas. We already have suffered an irreparable loss. Yet, how tragically compounded that loss would be if we lost sight of the true meaning and true cause of this tragedy.

In terms of Americanism, humanity, compassion, and decency, John F. Kennedy has left this Nation a great legacy. We are now at a turning point. Will we accept his legacy and rid ourselves of the poison which infects the national bloodstream? Will we turn from hatred and dedicate ourselves anew to the challenges—not the recrimination—that lie before us now? These are questions for each and every American to ask himself.

If these questions are answered in the affirmative; if this Nation rejects hatred and fanaticism in all forms, the greatest memorial man is capable of constructing will be erected and John Fitzgerald Kennedy will not have died in vain.

On behalf of myself and Mrs. Cannon, and of the people of the State of Nevada whom I represent, I extend our deepest sympathy to Mrs. Kennedy and her children and to the entire Kennedy family.

ADDRESS BY

Hon. Robert C. Byrd

OF WEST VIRGINIA

Mr. President, the United States of America has lost a gallant leader; West Virginia has lost a trusted friend. It is no secret that John F. Kennedy held the State of West Virginia closest to his heart, after his own native State of Massachusetts. The path that led him to the highest office in the land can be said to have begun for John F. Kennedy in the coalpits of West Virginia, into which he plunged boldly, as he plunged into all his undertakings, in order to acquaint himself at firsthand with the problems of our people.

John F. Kennedy won our hearts because of his unmistakable sincerity and his determination that the way of life which we in the Mountain State cherish must not be allowed to fall into neglect or suffer needlessly from the growing pains of a swiftly changing economy. His unshaken optimism ignited our own hopes, and his calm confidence in the ability of reasonable men to cope successfully with all human crises strengthened our own resolution embodied in our motto, "Mountaineers are always free."

John F. Kennedy reaffirmed our belief in the American way as the way in which life can be lived bravely, nobly, and in the face of a thousand dangers, heroically. He had no patience with mediocrity, no ear for the prophets of doom, no concern with the raucous outcries of the radical right or left which sought to turn aside this Nation from its destiny as the world leader of freemen, committed to the unavoidable challenge of enlarging the scope of human freedom at home and abroad.

We in West Virginia could feel at home with John F. Kennedy because we were keenly aware of his deep and essential sympathy with all men. We were drawn and held to him by the bonds that unite freemen everywhere, the bonds of the spirit. He asked for our support and help, and we gave it. He promised us that he would give himself to the task at hand with vigor, without reservation, without hesitation. No man can say that he did less.

John F. Kennedy, the man, is gone from our midst. Now he has become a legend in our land, a memory in our thoughts, a sadness in our hearts. Historians will etch his portrait with words upon the everlasting stone of time. And the calendar of life will move on.

But for us in West Virginia the shadow of John F. Kennedy will linger awhile, like the afterglow of a sunset on our mountain slopes. In West Virginia we will remember John F. Kennedy as a child might remember a special Christmas joy, as a young man might remember an ambitious dream, as an older man might remember a glorious field of battle. For he enkindled amongst us all these things: joyful hope, noble ambition, and a sense of honor. We are truly grateful.

Now the period of mourning is drawing to a close, and the happy season of Christmas will be upon us. In the broad ellipse at the foot of the Washington Monument there stands a 75-foot Christmas tree sent from the mountain forests of West Virginia. I like to think that this tree is symbolic of the place that John F. Kennedy will keep in our hearts, a place forever green and bright with the joy of the spirit.

ADDRESS BY

Hon. Frank Church

OF IDAHO

Mr. President, each of us tends to remember, in a personal fashion, the cataclysmic occasions of a lifetime. Why else is the question so commonly asked, "Where were you on Pearl Harbor Day? or V-day? or the day F.D.R. died?"

In such a fashion, each of us will remember the 22d of November 1963. Each person has indelibly imprinted in his own mind where he was, and what he was engaged in doing, when the dread news flashed that John F. Kennedy had been struck down on the streets of Dallas, by an infamous assassin.

I was at a luncheon in the State Department in honor of Senator Manglapus, of the Philippine Islands. Our host was Assistant Secretary Roger Hilsman. By strange coincidence, I was engaged in a conversation with Averell Harriman about the danger of extremism in American politics, when an attendant whispered that I had an emergency call from my office. I excused myself, placed the call back from an adjoining room, encountered difficulty with "busy signals" at the Capitol, wondered why the wires were so crowded, and then, suddenly, I was listening to the choked voice of my press secretary, Porter Ward, saying, "The President has been shot in Texas. He is believed to be either dead or dying."

The rest is a dazed memory of rushing back into the dining room to convey the sickening news. I recall how the table turned to turmoil, how the air was suddenly filled with urgent questions and protests of disbelief, how the faces in the room were pale and shaken.

Then, in the company of my colleague, John Sparkman, I remember our hurried departure and return to the Senate, where we prayed for the life of our stricken President, not knowing he was already dead.

If each of us retains a memory of that black day in terms of a personal involvement, it is not because we would blur the day with a trivial recollection, but because no one of us can fully comprehend the magnitude of our common loss.

So it is that we bear our grief, as individuals. It was often said of me that I was a "Kennedy man," a nameplate I proudly acknowledged while he lived, and one that I shall cherish now that he is dead. I took joy in his friendship, and I think I will not know his equal again. Though words are clumsy to express one's feelings, I tried to capsule my reaction to the President's martyrdom in a short tribute which I delivered at memorial services held for him at the River Road Unitarian Church in Bethesda, Md., on Sunday, November 24. I ask that these remarks appear here as follows:

It is not my purpose or place to deliver the sermon this morning. That is properly a service for your own pastor to perform. It is, rather, my purpose to say a few words in tribute to our fallen President.

I hope you will understand if I speak of him in somewhat personal terms, for this is the way I shall remember him.

He was my friend. I loved and honored him. I was proud for my country that he was our President.

John Fitzgerald Kennedy was one of those rare human beings about whom it could be truly said: "The elements so mix'd in him that Nature might stand up and say to all the world 'This was a man.'"

He was as handsome as a storied prince; his wife, Jacqueline, as fair as any princess of song or legend.

With his encouragement, she made the White House a place of impeccable beauty, where occasions of state were conducted in the style, and with a graciousness and gaiety that befits a great nation. Whenever I was present on these occasions, I never failed to marvel at the President's composure. His dignity was natural to him, and his friendliness always set his guests at ease. How unprepared they were to discover in him that endearing quality of self-effacement, which he often revealed through some lighthearted witticism, but which invariably disclosed his underlying humility. Once, in a toast to the King of Afghanistan, I recall how he explained why the Constitution limited the President to 8 years in office. The amendment had been adopted, he said, partly out of consideration for the well-being of the President, but mainly, he added with a smile, out of consideration for the well-being of the country.

Many of you will remember the celebrated comment he made to that illustrious company of Nobel Prize winners who came to dine with him at the White House. Never, he remarked, has so much talent been gathered at one time under this roof, since Thomas Jefferson used to dine here alone.

Such was the brilliance of the social life which John and Jacqueline Kennedy brought to the Presidential mansion. But more important was the kind of family life they implanted there. Somehow they managed to make that big house a home. Along with other playmates, their daughter, Caroline, and their little son, whom the President liked to call John-John, used to gather in the play yard, within easy view of their daddy's office. He was seldom too busy to be interrupted by them; he refused to permit the heavy burdens of his office to usurp his family function as a loving father. The personal attention he gave to his children, and to the needs of his grief-stricken wife, when their infant son, Patrick, died soon after birth a few months ago; the tender pictures of John-John on the south lawn awaiting his father's arrival by helicopter, or crawling through the trapdoor in his father's desk, while the President was sitting there absorbed with his evening's work; the familiar sight of Caroline clutching her father's hand as he led the family into church on a Sunday morning—all combined to present to the country the finest example of a devout and affectionate family, setting a moral standard of the highest order.

The many attributes that made John F. Kennedy such an exceptional person cannot be compressed into the short tribute I pay him this morning. Well known was his bravery in battle; his literary talents which won for him the Pulitzer Prize; the fortitude with which he bore the pain in his injured back; the ceaseless energy with which he pursued his quest for self-fulfillment through 17 years of honorable service in the House of Representatives, the Senate, and finally, the White House itself.

History will judge his greatness as a President, but already it is clear that he will be remembered for the strength of his statesmanship which saw us through the dread missile crisis in Cuba a year ago, when the world trembled on the brink of thermonuclear war. And he will be remembered too for the initiative he brought to the search for peace—for the first step along that road he made possible through the nuclear test ban treaty. Not since Lincoln has any President been so deeply committed to the cause of equal treatment for all Americans.

The tragedy of his death is heightened because it came so cruelly at the prime of his extraordinary life. It came as he was grappling with the gigantic problems of our times with the skill and courage of a young David—only to be struck down by an assassin in his own country, in a foul and cowardly murder which crosses us all with shame.

Once, when he faced a crucial primary test, in that long, arduous trek he made toward the Presidency, I asked him whether he believed in prayer. He said he did, and he seemed genuinely moved when I told him I would pray for him. Now, I think, he would want us all to pray for our new President, in faith that a national revulsion against every kind of fanaticism will wash the land clean, so that the hand of Lyndon B. Johnson may be upheld by the councils of reason and decency against the councils of ignorance, bigotry, and hate.

May God preserve this Republic and keep her sensible, strong and free.

Mr. President, it is too soon to pass judgment upon the Presidency of John F. Kennedy. But we sense that he will loom large, more so than we fully realized while he still lived. Time alone can give us a more definitive measurement.

Even now, there are those who are trying to judge his stature by examining his accomplishments in office. If this is where we should look, it still remains for future events to place his achievements as President in proper perspective. I am inclined to believe—though tomorrow could easily prove me wrong—that of the work he finished, during his brief tenure, the nuclear weapons test ban treaty will stand out above all other accomplishments. For it may well turn out to be the first benchmark on the path to peace.

During the Senate debate on ratification of the test ban treaty, I attempted to recount the earlier failures to obtain agreement, and to point up the stalwart role of our late President during the Cuban missile crisis, which, in my opinion, brought about the agreement. The words I used then somehow seem appropriate now, so I ask that the pertinent paragraphs from that address be reprinted at this point.

All of us know the sorry story of how the stalemated negotiations for a comprehensive nuclear test ban treaty ended in dismal failure; we recall how the Soviet Union, after quiet preparations, suddenly resumed testing on a most extensive scale, forcing the United States to do likewise. We remember too how the testing was accompanied by a new round of bellicose speechmaking in the Soviet Union, coupled with a hardening of Russian attitudes on every cold war front. And we shall never forget how the era culminated in a daring thrust by Khrushchev to install missile bases in Cuba, at our very doorstep. In this reckless gambit, Khrushchev in effect was asking: "If her vital interests are challenged, is the United States really willing to risk all in a nuclear war? President Kennedy's response, coming swift and sure, gave Khrushchev his answer. The world watched breathlessly as Kennedy ordered the Navy to turn back Russian ships on the high seas, even as he laid down his ultimatum that the Cuban bases must be dismantled and the Russian missiles withdrawn. Khrushchev had his answer, and he backed away under circumstances which surely inflicted the most serious reversal on the Communist cause since the end of the Second War.

I suppose Khrushchev's question had to be asked—and answered—somewhere, sometime, if a turning point in the nuclear arms race was ever to be reached. The Russians had to know whether, in a showdown situation, we actually stood ready to suffer a full-scale nuclear exchange—whether, in effect, we would sooner choose to be dead than Red. Had Kennedy allowed the Russian missile bases to remain in Cuba, then Khrushchev would have known that he could win his points, one by one, through the threat of nuclear war—that he could bluff his way to world dominion. Under such circumstances, the Russian nuclear arsenal would have had utility, after all, in advancing the objectives of Soviet foreign policy. The Russians would doubtlessly have then intensified the nuclear arms race, and we would have no test ban treaty before us today.

So the tense and terrifying days of last October may well be recorded by historians of the future as a time of destiny for the whole human race, when the fortitude of an American President won for us another chance to harness the nuclear monster, or, as Kennedy himself has put it, to stuff the genie back in the bottle, while there is still time.

Mr. President, I am not so sure, however, that we should try to measure John F. Kennedy by the work he finished, or by the degree he did, or did not, succeed in securing the enactment of his stated program. Lincoln is not remembered for the legislation he put through Congress, but for the inspiration of his leadership.

So it will be of Kennedy. What a rich literature he left us. For generations to come, when others cannot find the words that will do justice to our goals, his words will be quoted; when others falter under the burden of their duty, his example will strengthen their resolve. In less than 3 years as President, it was Kennedy, the man, who lifted the hearts of the humble, who exacted the respect of the prominent and powerful, whether friend or foe, and who fired the hopes of all who would be free.

Every land felt the force of him, and when he

fell the whole world sorrowed. The mighty came as pilgrims to march in grand procession behind his flag-draped coffin; the people, whose President he was, filed passed him in an endless stream through the Capitol rotunda, where he rested upon Lincoln's catafalque.

John Masefield, poet laureate of England, wrote:

The young chief with the smiling, radiant face, the winning way that turned a wondrous race into sublimer pathways, leading on.

And 10,000 torches were lifted in the night by the silent throng that gathered at the city hall in West Berlin, filling the great square which now bears his name.

From among the many messages of mourning that came to me from Idaho, I have excerpted some representative tributes. I have also selected certain passages from editorials, written in memory of the late President, which appeared in the newspapers of my State. I ask that they be included at this point.

[From letters and poems]

"As the greatest love can produce the greatest joy or sorrow, I realize that your privilege of serving with President Kennedy will intensify and personalize to you this thrust to the heart of every citizen. For this reason, I extend my heartfelt sympathy to you personally and pledge renewed faith in and support to the youthful aspirations for a better United States and a better world which were yours and President Kennedy's. He lived his life in honor, manhood and service. In these, he lived out several lifetimes. He can only die if we refuse the torch which he carried to light a better tomorrow." (E. LeGrande Nelson, Twin Falls, Idaho.)

"They who glimpse the effable sadness of beauty in depth—beyond sound, beyond form—knew, from the fateful words of the last inaugural, 'Let us go forth * * * knowing that here on earth, God's work must be truly our own.' That, amongst us, was another, who in the full magnificence of youth, had chosen the way that leads to Calvary." (Lillian Imler, Fruitvale, Idaho.)

"It cannot be true, were my thoughts when I heard that awful news. Then—such a waste of manhood and ability." (Mrs. John B. Harms, Wendell, Idaho.)

"Words fail to express what emotions have shaken me in the past weekend. What sorrow you have felt who have known our President Kennedy so personally. We can only hope that his death will set a new goal of citizenship for all * * * and a new meaning to the phrase, sometimes too lightly used, 'We are our brother's keeper,' for his interests were a living memorial to that creed." (Judge Frances Sleep, Sandpoint, Idaho.)

"I do not know how to write this little letter. I am so hurt over the death of a true and honest friend the world ever had, President John F. Kennedy. Every time

I watched TV it was just tears and a hurting inside me." (Herman Weisenberger, Kellogg, Idaho.)

MUFFLED DRUMS IN WASHINGTON

(By Colen H. Sweeten, Jr., Malad City, Idaho)

There's muffled drums in Washington,
    Strange stillness o'er the street;
Tear stained polished brass and robes
    Mid the silent rhythmed feet.

Horse drawn, the fallen leader lies
    'Neath the flag he held so dear.
Princes and beggars mourn their loss,
    While thousands pass his bier.

Yes, muffled drums in Washington
    Half masted flags at dawn,
Yet God is in His Heaven
    And truth still marches on.

[From the Moscow (Idaho) Idahonian]

President Kennedy will be remembered as a very human President. A very likable President. He was not given to protocol. He seldom wore a hat. When he strode to meet you he didn't wait for the formalities of an introduction, nor stand on protocol that the visitor should be introduced to the President. The writer of this comment knows, for he was privileged, just a little more than a year ago, to be surprised by this informality.

All of us have known that the responsibilities of being President have come to be of mankilling size. What most of us do not realize is that our Presidents also put their lives in the lap of the gods every day and every moment they occupy this high office.

[From the Pocatello (Idaho) Sunday Journal]

John F. Kennedy, the man, was a young, vital, courageous leader, wise beyond his years, a loving husband and father. The human tragedy of the swift and ugly assassination shames the Nation, and, in fact, the human race.

Youth and charm and grace characterized the Kennedy family in the White House. They were a part of American life, not aloof from it.

Youngest of our Presidents, John F. Kennedy fought for peace with justice, for true equality of human and civil rights. What history's verdict may be, we cannot foresee. But as a person, he embodied qualities which attracted admiration of millions, the envy and hate of few.

[From the Idaho Falls (Idaho) Post-Register]

This young, vigorous and impressively intelligent leader was silenced at the very pinnacle of his thrust for an always emerging America. He was a President who could stir his followers, excite them to dreams of New Frontier.

President Kennedy had an unusual warmth, unusual courage and patriotism. People who disagreed strenuously with him as President, admired him as a man as well as a leader.

[From the Lewiston (Idaho) Morning Tribune]

The martyred President must be judged in history, not so much by what he accomplished as by what he attempted. He had so tragically little time and so many massive barriers before him.

Perhaps no other American President prepared himself so consciously and so completely for his office. Mr. Kennedy was a master of politics, which is the necessary prerequisite for statesmanship. After his election, he laid before his country and its reluctant Congress a program for progress which is as bold as it is comprehensive.

He submitted to his countrymen imaginative new concepts in conservation and resource development, civil rights, education, public health, aid for the aging, employment, international trade and domestic economic policy, to name a few areas of his interest and competency. He demonstrated in his press conferences a continuous mastery of the varied facets of his bafflingly complex office. Many of the domestic programs he advocated doubtless will be achieved in years still to come.

In foreign policy particularly the brilliant vision of this young President surely will help guide the Nation and the free world long after his tragic death. Surely the world will listen to him anew, as it listened to Lincoln, now that he is gone:

"Let us examine our attitude toward peace itself. Too many of us think it is impossible. Too many think it unreal. But that is a dangerous, defeatist belief. It leads to the conclusion that war is inevitable, that mankind is doomed, that we are gripped by forces we cannot control.

"We need not accept that view. Our problems are man-made; therefore they can be solved by man. And man can be as big as he wants."

Or again:

"I come here today to look across this world of threats to the world of peace. In that search we cannot expect any final triumph, for new problems will always arise. We cannot expect that all nations will adopt like systems, for conformity is the jailer of freedom and the enemy of growth. Nor can we expect to reach our goal by contrivance, by fiat, or even by the wishes of all.

"But however close we sometimes seem to that dark and final abyss, let no man of peace and freedom despair. For he does not stand alone. If we all can persevere—if we can in every land and office look beyond our own shores and ambitions—then surely the age will dawn in which the strong are just and the weak secure and the peace preserved.

"Never have the nations of the world had so much to lose—or so much to gain. Together we shall save our planet, or together we shall perish in its flames. Save it we can—and save it we must—and then shall we earn the eternal thanks of mankind and, as peacemakers, the eternal blessing of God."

He left another message of special meaning this day for his grieving countrymen. He was speaking of Dag Hammarskjold and the United Nations, but he could as well have been speaking of his own beloved country and the void he now leaves in it:

"The problem is not the death of one man; the problem is the life of this organization. It will either grow to meet the challenge of our age, or it will be gone with the wind, without influence, without force, without respect. Were we to let it die, to enfeeble its vigor, to cripple its powers, we would condemn the future."

The unfinished work of John F. Kennedy awaits America. May this Nation grow to meet the challenge of our age.

————

[From the Aberdeen (Idaho) Times]

The first grief was at the loss of one so close to each of us. He represented each of us and the principles we stand for. He was a symbol to all of our way of life.

————

[From the Grangeville (Idaho) Free Press]

John Fitzgerald Kennedy was a leader among men, yet his personal appeal brought him closer to most Americans and peoples of the world than many of his predecessors in the office of Chief Executive.

The President of the United States extended to the world a warm handclasp in the name of peace. To those in need, he befriended. He was a true American, and it was his spirited approach to the problems of humanity which meant so much to the downtrodden, the poverty stricken. His image shall live for many years to come.

Americans took kindly to Mr. Kennedy and his family. The White House and its residents were next door neighbors to everyone in the United States. The affection shown to the Kennedys by the public was as real as any devotion of family life in an American home.

Mr. Kennedy met major problems while in office with a view always toward universal peace. Nothing would sway him to travel a different route. He would hold the peace to the limit.

Complicated domestic political issues did not meet with evasion when they reached Mr. Kennedy's desk. His proposals for the Nation were bold and vigorous. There was no timidity in asking for major legislation and he pressed with personal sincerity.

In this modern, space age era in which often it appears science is outdistancing the real purpose of man and swamping mankind with difficult social problems, often appearing insurmountable, it was refreshing to have in the White House a President in tune with the times.

This is not a time of hopelessness. This is a time for a reassessment of our stewardship in our democracy. And this is the time for a show of faith and thanksgiving that Mr. Kennedy left the Nation strong and dedicated to continue his deeds toward universal peace.

————

[From the Boise (Idaho) Statesman]

It is a moment in which attention is focused upon John F. Kennedy as an individual of high ideals, of dedication, and of courage.

A product of his times, John F. Kennedy was called to national leadership in a period of widely prevailing uncertainty and perhaps of epochal transition involving the clash of strongly conflicting forces. He has fulfilled his part stoutly, conscientiously, and fairly.

It has been his prime purpose to minimize the conflict and to do all within his power to make this country and the world a better place for all mankind to live.

It is perhaps that as an outstanding humanitarian his memory will be enshrined. He has been quick to respond to the appeal of human wants and needs. In his book it is the proper function of government to provide the remedy, and he has not hesitated to call upon the resources of government to that end.

In reference to the phrase that sounded like a clarion in his inaugural address, John F. Kennedy never asked what the country could give him personally; instead it has been he who has given his country and the world the last full measure of devotion.

————

[From the Rexburg (Idaho) Standard]

When a leader of great power and presence and capacity for good dies in office, the cause to which he gave leadership suffers grievous loss. President John F. Kennedy was such a man. The cause he served, and so eloquently led, was the threefold cause of human dignity and equality and freedom.

The cause he championed as acknowledged leader of the free world lives on. We who survive him can best honor his memory by doing all in our power to advance that cause, which is the very cause for which this Nation was founded.

Mr. President, sometimes, even in moments of solemn bereavement, a child will make some captivating comment. When we took our boys, Forrest and Chase, with us to the Capitol rotunda, to pay our last respects as a family to John F. Kennedy, our little boy, sensing his mother's distress, reached up for her hand and said, "Don't cry, Mommy. The guards will protect him. If these guards fall, others will come to take their place. They can never take President Kennedy away from us."

They never can take President Kennedy away from us. His memory will be guarded by every person who strives for excellence, by every mind in search of truth, by every eye that would see justice done, by every open hand outstretched for peace, and by every heart that holds freedom dear, for as long as men aspire to do God's work on earth.

ADDRESS BY

Hon. B. Everett Jordan

OF NORTH CAROLINA

Mr. President, we have not been able to bring ourselves as yet to realize fully that the late President John F. Kennedy is no longer with us.

Never before in the history of our country have our people been so shocked and saddened as we were on November 22, 1963.

We gather now to pay tribute to a human being who, in a short lifetime, came to mean so much to so many millions of peoples throughout the world.

In spite of the fact he was still a young man, John F. Kennedy had come to be a living, active, forceful symbol for freedom throughout the world.

It is impossible to express the feelings all of us have had since his tragic and unnecessary death. We are saddened beyond words.

But the greatest tribute we can pay this man today is to carry on the business of the Nation and to go ahead even while we mourn his passing.

Above all else he would want us to make the best of the situation at hand and prove beyond any doubt that our system of democracy is unshakable even at a time such as this. We have lost a great leader, a warm friend, and a courageous man, and we are deep in our sorrow, but we all know that the world is a better place in which to live as a result of his unselfish service to mankind.

ADDRESS BY

Hon. Sam J. Ervin, Jr.

OF NORTH CAROLINA

Mr. President, John Fitzgerald Kennedy was one of the bulwarks, the bright spires, the strong places.

Today we honor one of our own—one who served and served well—as a Member of this body. It was while he served here that he was chosen by the American people to take the mantle of national leadership during an awesome period of world history.

He was young, and vigorous, and wise, and dedicated to public service. Virtually all of his adult life was spent in the service of his country.

His achievements are too numerous to attempt listing; as is the case with any man so deserving of a eulogy, he does not require one.

John Fitzgerald Kennedy belonged to each of us—to every American. He was our President;

but throughout the world he belonged, in a very special way, to many others—for to them he was more than the leader of a great nation—he was a symbol of peace.

Each of us is acutely aware of the tragedy that has befallen us, and in such times we turn to our memories.

I remember him as a strong, brave young man—one who carried to his grave injuries received during World War II and endured through the years; one who offered his life for his country, first in war and again in peace. It is ironic that the first offer was refused and the second accepted; but we can be thankful for those years between the first and second offering when we had the benefit of his wisdom, his ideas, and his ideals. We grieve that his even greater potential for the years ahead has been lost to us.

I remember him for his gallant personal victory over physical disability, and I remember the standing ovation he received from his colleagues when he returned to the Senate floor on crutches in 1955. I remember his vitality, his wit, and his fine mind; and I valued his friendship.

As a public servant, I remember him as a sophisticated, polished statesman who could nevertheless communicate and identify with people of every station. He was a man of rare eloquence, strong conviction, and great courage—a diligent and dedicated colleague.

As President, I remember him not only as a political leader who met the great issues of the age, but also as one who rekindled interest in the arts, renewed concern for our national heritage, and increased respect for scholarship.

And with the confirmation of his death, I recalled the verse from Shakespeare:

Now cracks a noble heart. Good night, Sweet Prince,
And flights of Angels sing thee to thy rest.

His was indeed a noble heart, and a noble mind and a noble spirit that we shall never forget.

But perhaps our greatest legacy from President Kennedy was his dream. He said:

I believe in an America that is on the march—an America respected by all nations, friends and foes alike—an America that is moving, choosing, doing, dreaming—a strong America in a world of peace.

And this must be the dream of all of us.

Our sympathy goes out to the courageous Kennedy family; indeed, it goes out to all the Nation, for he belonged to all of us, and he was the President of all of us—and we shall miss him.

Mr. President, I ask to have inserted at this point the following articles and editorials from the North Carolina press and other news media as evidence of the esteem and affection the people of my State had for the late President.

[From the Stanly News & Press, Albemarle, N.C., Nov. 26, 1963]

A NATION IN SHOCK NEEDS PRAYER

Three shots rang out about 12:30 c.s.t., Friday, in Dallas, Tex., and the effect of them reverberated around the world within just a few minutes. A sniper, armed with a highpowered rifle, killed President John F. Kennedy and seriously wounded Governor John Connally, of Texas, who was riding in the car with the President.

The first reaction throughout this Nation was shock. It was a benumbed people who sat with their eyes fixed on television screens as the story of the dastardly crime was unfolded. The second reaction was revulsion—extreme revulsion that such a thing could have happened in this country.

John Fitzgerald Kennedy was no ordinary man. Although born to wealth, so that he could have lived in ease and luxury, he chose a path of service. Endowed with great courage, an excellent intellect, and a high sense of duty, Mr. Kennedy served his country in World War II, earning a hero's acclaim. Entering politics after the war, he distinguished himself as Congressman and Senator and served the country so well that in 1960 he was first-ballot choice of the Democrat Party for the Presidency.

History will record that he served as leader of his country and of the free world during nearly 3 years in an era when danger of a nuclear holocaust was uppermost in the minds of men around the globe. Under his leadership the Nation was spared the horror of hydrogen war, and enjoyed a high degree of prosperity and progress. Significant achievements were recorded, both at home and on the diplomatic front.

As must be said of all men in high places, not everyone was in agreement with President Kennedy. But even his severest critic could not accuse him of being insincere. His administration was dedicated to the cause of peace and sought in every way possible to further the cause of freedom.

His life of service and usefulness was cut short at 46, an age when most Presidents have not even thought of running for that high office. The youthful age at which he attained the world's most responsible office attests the ability he demonstrated and the faith which his colleagues had in his leadership.

Reaction from around the world was that of disbelief, of shock and incredulity, and this soon gave way to uncertainty about the future, for a new President was sworn in a few hours after Mr. Kennedy was pronounced dead at Parkland Hospital, Dallas.

Taking over the reins of leadership is Lyndon B. Johnson, a stalwart Texan and a man well experienced in the intricacies of the Federal Government. This Nation, if it has to experience the loss of a President, is fortunate in having as his successor a man of the ability and experience of Lyndon Johnson.

There is no way of foretelling what the future may hold

as this Nation continues to try to uphold freedom and the dignity of man around the globe.

But this we can say that Mr. Johnson is a dedicated Christian leader who has already in this dark hour, invoked the guidance of God and the support and co-operation of the people in carrying on the tremendous task of Government.

Even while our tears drop in mourning for our fallen leader, it behooves us as a people to look ahead, gather new confidence, and to rally our forces in support of our new leader. His path may not be the same as that chosen by Mr. Kennedy, but his is the responsibility for leadership. Our responsibility is that of intelligent cooperation and faithful support.

And may we pray, as did Dr. Gerner at Pfeiffer on Friday afternoon, that the enmity and hatred which prompted such a dastardly deed may give way to the spirit of Christian love and brotherhood befitting a free and democratic nation.

————

[From the Stanly News & Press, Albemarle, N.C., Nov. 29, 1963]

WHY SUCH TRAGIC HATE?

A self-styled Communist, hiding behind a sixth floor window, sighted down the barrel of a powerful rifle with a telescopic lens, and pulled the trigger three times. The President fell into the arms of his lovely young wife, mortally wounded, and the Governor of Texas was grievously hurt.

That was about 1:30 p.m. Friday, November 22, a date which will live in infamy and perhaps be known as "Black Friday."

Though the sound of the three shots was not audible over television or radio, the impact reverberated around the world in just a few hours. Friend and foe, alike, sent words of regret, of condolence.

The American people, as one individual, reeled with the incredulity of the crime and then settled themselves in front of television screens, their minds forming one big question, "Why?"

The man Dallas police say definitely killed President Kennedy, a Dallas policeman, and wounded the Texas Governor was himself shot fatally in the basement of the Dallas city hall by a nightclub operator. He died only a few feet from the spot where President Kennedy breathed his last about 48 hours earlier, in Parkland Hospital, where Albemarle's Jack Price is administrator.

There are so many loose threads of the situation, so many coincidences and unanswered questions, that one cannot help wondering if the assassin, Lee Harvey Oswald, was killed because of what he might have told police if he had lived. We may never real'y know.

On the other hand, there is a stark realization in the hearts of people everywhere of what hatred—cold and calculating enmity—can do to human personality.

Mr. Kennedy returned to Washington and to the White House, where the people of this great land paid him high tribute. Perhaps a quarter of a million men and women marched silently by his bier as it lay in state in the Capitol rotunda.

I shall never forget the sight of that spirited, prancing and impatient black horse, without a rider, following along behind the caisson bearing the President's body. In that horse it seemed I could almost see and feel the zest, the will, the spirit of the departed President, chafing at the bit and eager for action, for living.

The skies wept over Washington the day after Mr. Kennedy was killed, but the sun shone brightly as the crowds gathered to pay him tribute.

In every phase of the observance, from the time he was brought back to the White House until the casket was lowered into the hallowed earth of Arlington, in the shadows of majestic Custis-Lee Mansion, there was dignity and the aura of tribute. Symbolic of the President's influence, his widow lighted a perpetual fire at the head of his grave, which will be viewed by hundreds of thousands of Americans in the years to come.

Heads of state, kings, queens, princes, prime ministers, emperors—the most impressive array of world figures I can recall—testified to the esteem in which our President was held.

But, during it all, another figure emerged as heroic, an example for American womanhood of all the years to come. Mrs. Jacqueline Kennedy cradled the head of her dying husband en route to the hospital, rode with his body in the plane to Washington, remained near him all through the night, visited him in repose in the East Room of the White House, maintained dignity and stately composure in all her many appearances at the Capitol, the final rites, and the reception afterward at which the heads of state formally paid their respects to her.

Poise and grace were evident in her and her children, and "Jack," had he been alive to see them, would have been proud of their demeanor. "Jackie" has earned the praise of Americans everywhere in these days of mourning and loss.

It is never possible to put into words all the things one feels at a time such as this. Hearts and minds have been saddened beyond expression. Such sorrow has not gripped the Nation in many, many years, and never has a people felt so personal a loss, for John Kennedy had come into our homes and talked with us on many occasions. It was almost as if a very dear member of the family had gone beyond.

Though the loss of one so young, so brave, and so handsome must be met with deep grieving, the Nation and the world must carry on. We are fortunate to have a man of Lyndon Johnson's experience and ability to take over leadership.

But we can hope that the well-springs of hate, which beget such tragedies may be replaced by the Christian spirit of brotherly love.

————

[From the Stanly News & Press, Albemarle, N.C., Nov. 26, 1963]

JOHN FITZGERALD KENNEDY

(By George B. Weaver)

By birth a product of what has aptly been described as "the great American dream."

In early manhood, a hero through his courageous actions while in the service of his country.

By inclination, an intellectual, with rare gifts of expression and insight into human personality.

His personality, warm, friendly, almost radiant, magnetic, with a ready smile and an engaging wit.

His ambition, to serve his fellow man, to uphold freedom and justice, and to seek peace among all men everywhere.

As a father, exhibiting the love and tenderness of a fond parent, along with the faith of a devout Christian.

In middle life, elected to the highest office the citizens of the United States can offer, respected by heads of state around the world, and with a growing stature of leadership among statesmen of the world.

In death, a martyr to the causes he espoused, and perhaps as strong a testimony for right as in life. He died in the service of his fellow man and his country.

Significantly, as is so often the case, the full appreciation of what he was did not reach the minds and hearts of people in this land and elsewhere until the impact of his loss was felt.

———

[From the Benson (N.C.) Review, Nov. 28, 1963]

IN MEMORIAM

(By Dr. Gaylor L. Lehman)

Our hearts are saddened today because of the tragic death of our President, John Fitzgerald Kennedy. Last Friday afternoon we looked at each other in silent shock and stunned disbelief. Today our eyes have a glassy stare and we find the stark fact of his death still incomprehensible. As a Nation and as individuals we mourn his untimely passing and are inflamed by the insane act that caused it. In war and in peace John Kennedy offered his life to his country. Many years of leadership and greatness lay before him. His consuming desire was the triumph of freedom in our country and in the world, with its inherent right for each person to develop his talent and ability to the maximum. For this cause he lived and died.

The miracle of television made the name of John F. Kennedy a household word. His 2 years and 10 months in the office of President brought him into our homes on newscasts almost every day. It seemed as if we knew him, his wife, and his children personally. In a very real sense it makes his passing seem not only that of a President and statesman but also that of a personal friend. Whether rich or poor, unlearned or lettered, Protestant or Catholic, white or Negro, we mourn his passing. He was our President and as such he commanded our respect and our loyalty.

It is almost inconceivable that the President of the United States could be shot from ambush and murdered. In barbaric Vietnam or in the uncivilized Congo, yes; in America, no. The fact that it has happened points up the venom of hatred that exists among us—class, racial, ethnic, even religious. It speaks of the sickness of our national morality. One crazed fanatic fired the rifle. But we have all called each other too many names; we have harbored too many prejudices; we have nurtured too many suspicions. And in so doing we must bear our guilt, for it was out of this attitude that the shot

was fired. We have been unwilling to exemplify the spirit of Jesus Christ who talked about walking the second mile and turning the other cheek, and who asked that we love our neighbor as ourselves.

Today we mourn the loss of a young and great leader, brilliant in politics, yet human in qualities. It is not that we agreed with everything he said or did. It is rather that he was our President and that he belonged to each of us. Today our hearts go out and our prayers go up for Mrs. Kennedy, her children, and the family, that they may find comfort and strength amid their sorrow; for President Johnson, that he may seek and find divine wisdom and guidance to lead us in the future; and for our Nation, that individually and collectively we may find in this tragedy a new respect for those with whom we differ and a new love for God and for one another.

———

[From the Watauga Democrat]

JOHN FITZGERALD KENNEDY—1917-63

(By Rob Rivers)

The parade route was lined with friendly, cheering people as the President of the United States, the First Lady, Governor and Mrs. Connally rode along a Dallas street. Things appeared to be going well in the turbulent political tides which have ebbed and flowed in the Lone Star State. But there was the crack of a rifle, the Chief Executive slumped and the Nation was plunged into deep mourning.

Even those who liked the President least found a common ground with those who loved the Executive, in their crushed reaction to the monstrously evil thing, which could well affect the destinies of the Nation and even of the world.

Youthful, vigorous, and imaginative, Mr. Kennedy had served his country well during the agonies of the late great war and during the frenzied and dangerous age of the shaky and uneasy peace. He had served less than three-fourths of his term when an assassin's bullet struck with its crashing, searing lethality.

President Kennedy, who was no stranger to trouble and to sorrow and to family tragedy, carried into the Nation's top office a wealth of knowledge and of experience and a rare concern for the rights and welfare of the peoples of the country and of the world. Articulate, personable, and with no apparent quality of fear, he captured the imagination and esteem of his countrymen. He was thickskinned, impervious to criticism, and could make vital decisions without disturbing his sleep.

The President was not doing well with his programs in Congress. Few men of vision and change are successful right from the start when they speak freely for liberalism, and who espouse the rights of the common man, and who've believed that one race has no moral or legal right to set itself up as the master of another race whose skin comes in darker hues.

In his fight for civil rights and for the dignity of the Federal courts, President Kennedy was never swerved from his convictions, even though he was losing strength in some sections of the country. In the South, even in

North Carolina, those who've wanted to keep the status quo have railed out against the President, who would have fared badly in some of the States of the old Confederacy.

But, death in its silent, strange finality, often comes as a grim pacifier, as a sort of common denominator and those who had fought the President, tooth and nail, in and out of the Congress are now united in a common grief, the extent of which has perhaps never been equalled in the Nation's harried history.

The mysterious curtain of death has brought an amazing degree of charity and of sadness, even to his former detractors. Some of the debatable policies which he espoused with youthful vigor and without regard to personal consequences, somehow don't seem to be so tremendously wrong now that heads are bared and bowed in the stillness and hush of his tragic leavetaking. So, in the dispensation of the Father of us all, it could well be that Mr. Kennedy's death could be the means of reuniting our Nation more solidly than before in these days of our tragic sorrows, and of our common dangers.

President Kennedy was a good and a great man. He had matured in his position of power and of prestige and had met issues of monstrous magnitude with firm decisions and with courage casehardened in the caldrons of world conflict.

It is fitting that the President's body, smashed by an enemy of our country, is lying as this is written on the catafalque which first held the body of Abraham Lincoln, who himself met death as an indirect result of some of the beliefs which President Kennedy espoused a hundred years later. While the Kennedy assassination does not tie in, so far as we know, with the racial situation, most of the hatred which the late President acquired was in his efforts to implement and expand the spirit of the Emancipation Proclamation.

The sinews of a great nation are not weakened when watered by its tears, and out of a common grief should come a more purposeful perspective and a renewal of our spiritual and physical might. In our time of sorrowful reflection, we should gain strength from the unchanging purposes and high courage of our fallen President, and tranquility from Mrs. Kennedy who knelt by the catafalque which once held the body of Abraham Lincoln, kissed the flag which covered the coffin of her husband, leading her children, Caroline and John-John, one with each hand, walked resolutely from the hushed rotunda of the Capitol into the sunlight.

———

[From the Watauga Democrat, Nov. 28, 1963]

J.F.K.—HE HAD OUR ESTEEM

(By Bob Rivers)

When the white horses were drawing the caisson which held the coffin of President Kennedy through the sunshine-laced shadows of the Avenue of Presidents, our tortured mind turned back to another day long ago, when President Harding died in San Francisco's Palace Hotel. The Democrat, short handed and fairly ill equipped in those skimpy days, managed a special edition and distributed it freely, far and wide, as a public service to a mourning populace. Some years later Franklin D.

Roosevelt expired in Warm Springs, but the radio had made a special edition unneeded in a time of change. We recalled the long train trip from the west coast and the great creped engines which headed President Harding's funeral train and when the steaming, panting moguls of the shiny rails thundered through town and city and hamlet taking F.D.R. back home. There was grief, it seemed, aplenty on both of these occasions when the leaders of our country had fallen. President Harding, elected in a landslide, was popular with the masses of the people; Roosevelt was their idol, but he had little of health and vigor left.

With President Kennedy it was different from the last leavetaking of a Chief Executive. The youngest man to hold the office of crushing responsibility and of grim dangers, he perhaps hadn't yet reached the apex of his colorful career. He was not allowed to die naturally but from the tearing, rending impact of a rifle bullet. This made his going even more tragic. His youthfulness, his courageous striving for what he believed right, his tremendous mental capacity, would have seemed to portend a long tenure in the spotlight's glare.

We, who two-finger this column, liked the President from the days when he went into the political wars against what appeared overwhelming forces in his home State and won for himself a seat in the Senate. We were present when the thatch-haired Boston-trained politician was defeated for the Vice-Presidential nomination by Estes Kefauver in the convention of 1956 (which perhaps saved his political life), and took the missus on a hurried trip to Los Angeles solely to cast a delegate vote for John Kennedy for the Democratic nomination for the Presidency in 1960, thus becoming a sort of moral heretic to the vast majority of the Carolina delegation who'd gone all out for Lyndon Johnson. Fact is we got in about as bad a shape as we did in 1952 when we forsook Senator Russell and went along with Kerr Scott for Stevenson against the wishes of the kingmakers of Carolina politics. Nobody asked us to vote for Kennedy, we just liked the guy, and thought it a waste of political powder to nominate a man whose friends, at the time, couldn't have entertained a serious notion of his inhabiting the White House.

RECEPTION FROSTY

We saw Senator Kennedy at a breakfast given for the delegation. It was a kind of meet-the-candidates event, and we recall Governor Hollings, of South Carolina, being at our table when Stevenson and Symington were proposed to the delegates, and we heard Lyndon B. Johnson make a homey pitch for the support he had in his vest pocket at the time. In due time Senator Kennedy strode into the room, his bright sorrel hair standing out like a light. He walked with what someone described as that "little-lost-boy look." He spoke briefly, said he'd enjoyed being in North Carolina previously, expected to be there again if nominated "and," he said, "if I fail of nomination, I'll still come to see you, if you'll let me." He smiled the toothy good-natured Irish smile and moved away. The reception he received was not downright discourteous, or anything of that sort, but chilly like a November morning. It looked like the hundred or more people should have fetched out to the Golden State more warmth from Carolina's bright midsummer sun. But politicians being like they are, many can't abide a man running counter to their notions and few sought to shake hands with the President-in-the-making, Mrs. Rivers and we being notable exceptions, and we liked making brief talk with the man whose career we had followed with such great personal concern. Winning in a steamroller style on the first ballot, the Kennedy machine left the losers figuratively weeping in their beer.

THE OTHER RIDE—ON THE AVENUE

We'd been present on the bleak January day when the snow had been taken from Pennsylvania Avenue, so that the gay inaugural parade could proceed along the route so lately trod by the teams of pale horses. It was a glad time for all and sundry, in spite of the change in the weather, and there were tears all around in our group when a vigorous young man took the oath of office and faced up to his massive problems in an inaugural address without precedent for its eloquence and logic. "Ask not," he had shouted, and his breath was like smoke in the frigid air, "what your country can do for you, but rather what you can do for your country." Little would we have thought that his martyrdom would have been his supreme gift to the Nation.

HUMAN AND DEMOCRATIC

President Kennedy was very human and democratic. In our personal reflections we thought of having written him some time after his inaugural, offering a suggestion as to the broadening of the base of his press conferences. Back came a reply to a country editor from the Executive, with appreciation and thanks for the suggestion which he said "has a great deal of merit." And across the bottom, in the Kennedy scrawl, he penned, "would like to see you when next you are in Washington." A few weeks ago we had published a letter from President Kennedy congratulating us on the 75th anniversary of the Democrat and commending us and our family on our efforts down through the years. At home with all segments of the population, concerned over the welfare and activities of all the people, his name will be remembered for his greatness and strength.

These personal references are only intended to show the uncommon stature of the man whose tragic death we mourn. We've had a hard time keeping the tears off the typewriter these last days. Somehow they just keep coming.

[From the Charlotte (N.C.) News, Nov. 23, 1963]

JOHN FITZGERALD KENNEDY

The death of President John Fitzgerald Kennedy is a boundless tragedy. A man is dead, one of striking gifts of heart and mind and of enormous capacity for service. And with the life is lost a precious distillation of experience, judgment and wisdom that the Nation can possess only through a President acting and moving in full stride.

A disaster so profound cannot be compassed; it can only be mourned. And the loss cannot be made up. At 46, the President had decades of incalculable promise unfolding before him. Who can guess the shining acts of service the world has been deprived of by a psychotic sniper? One evil moment has ended a life of striving.

The American people wait to follow the new President with that spirit of unity and loyalty always characteristic of them in times of crisis. But only to President Johnson, thrust toward new and hard responsibilities, can the assassination seem fully credible. The gleam of John F. Kennedy's bright and buoyant spirit lingers and will not soon fade.

It is difficult even now to comprehend the swiftness of his rise in American politics and his unyielding determination to become his Nation's chief executive. Because his ambition to succeed was inseparable from his desire for the Nation to succeed, he came to personify for millions the promise and passion of a nation to remain supreme in the world.

In every Kennedy speech there always came the unquestioned accents of a patriot who loved his country.

There was a driving urgency in him, reflecting an unshakeable belief that the Nation and the world could throw off the coils of peril with unremitting faith and work. Almost from the moment of his inauguration those coils closed about the young President; in a moving speech on Berlin he admitted his astonishment at learning how terrible and awesome were the responsibilities he had sought with such unquenchable zest. Yet he was as equal to them as any man could be.

There never was any doubt, and certainly none in the Kremlin, that a threat to the freedom of America would be met with force. The President, in his finest moments, matched wits and nerves with a wily tyrant and he passed the tests with flying colors.

In the good heart and healthy mind of the President every inhabitant of the globe had a personal stake. In some measure all life was linked to his life because he possessed enough power to unhinge the world; yet neither the power nor the nightmarish problems that created it warped his spirit. On the day he lost his life the President was still carrying his gaiety and courage and, remarkably, his youth. No panic of mind or hardness of heart in the 35th President of the United States ever would have pushed mankind into the abyss. But he had found the strength and the patience to stand on the brink, and the Nation stood with him wholeheartedly. Americans had confidence in the wisdom and judgment of John Kennedy on the great issues of war or peace. He earned that confidence in trial by fire, and he deserved it.

No American can glimpse the relentless pressures and cruel choices that faced President Kennedy from his inauguration on. To reflect on them now can only deepen our grief and respect. History handed him a threatened world, a nation divided politically and a people split along racial lines. Answers of any sort were difficult; answers that would please were impossible. It was not in his power to reconcile world or national tensions; he could only try unceasingly, and he did.

But to dwell on the harshness of President Kennedy's lot would be to miss the greatness of the man. Which was that he welcomed trial, gloried in struggle and kept his faith in the face of shattering disappointments.

Those inner qualities remained untarnished to the end, and they are a large part of the legacy he leaves to a grieving nation. But not alone these. For all her internal frustrations and agony, America is a stronger nation than John Kennedy found her and the world, perhaps, is a little safer.

No President is indispensable; in the depth of its tragedy, the Nation will find new strength. But John F. Kennedy is irreplaceable, and we will tell our children that he was a rare and radiant man who loved his country fiercely and was a martyr to its service, and we will tell them the truth.

[From the Clayton (N.C.) News, Nov. 27, 1963]

(By Tom Womble)

We come in this hour to look at a man of courage—a man of dedication—a man of forthrightness. He was a man of sensitivity, a person as comfortable in the presence of political leaders as with his two children.

President Kennedy offered himself, I believe, to be used by his country and by his God.

He gave to the world a new hope for peace on the international horizon, that few others dreamed possible, along with which he gave a new sense of pride at being an American.

McGregor Barnes, historian, quoted John F. Kennedy as having said, "it will take more bravery in the sixties than ever to continue." The late President lived these words, within his life to the point that they may not be considered trivial. A back ailment proved to be only one "thorn in the flesh," of which there were many, which perplexed him throughout his 46 years. Continuous operations brought him near death's gate in 1954. This operation was for the removal of a steel plate, previously inserted, in his back. His church during these days even administered the last rites.

Years before he, as a junior-grade naval lieutenant commanding a PT-boat, had courageously saved several members of his crew, one of which had been personally towed in his teeth, having clutched in his teeth the straps of the sailor's life belt. This ordeal took approximately 5 hours.

The bravery of which he spoke can easily be identified in many areas as being desperately needed in our own land today.

John F. Kennedy's loyalty and devotion to his country is typified in his statement, "Ask not, what can my country do for me? Ask, what can I do for my country?"

This question is prominent in this tragic hour: "What can we do for our country that this great man need not have died in vain?"

First, our country must become united: pettiness cannot have a place among us in this hour.

Secondly, we must live in faith as never before. Faith that God is in control of this world and from out of these moments of upheaval and transition He shall continue to reign.

May I quote from William G. Ballentine's "God Save America" as our final thought in this eulogy to the late President of our United States.

"GOD SAVE AMERICA

"God save America! New world of glory, Newborn to freedom and knowledge and power, Lifting the towers of her lightning lit cities, Where the flood tides of humanity roar.

"God save America! Here may all races Mingle together as children of God, Founding an empire on brotherly kindness, Equal in Liberty, made of one blood!

"God save America! Bearing the olive, Hers be the blessing the peacemakers prove, Calling the nations to glad federation, Leading the world in the triumphs of love!

"God save America! 'Mid all her splendors, Save her from pride and from luxury; Throne in her heart the Un-seen and Eternal, Right to be her might and the truth made her free!"

[From the Sampson Independent, Nov. 28, 1963]

A verse for today: "Be not highminded, nor trust in uncertain riches but in the living God who giveth us richly all things to enjoy." (I Timothy 6: 17.)

PRESIDENT JOHN FITZGERALD KENNEDY

"May God rest his soul."

Americans of all faiths and all races were shocked into a prayer for the soul of their assassinated President as the news came over the airwaves on the blackest Friday in recent history.

John Fitzgerald Kennedy was 46. In the prime of life, with nearly 3 years of service as Chief Executive of the United States behind him, he was on a peacemaking mission to politically embroiled Texas, when a long-range rifle was thrust from a window and shots rang out.

The President slumped into the arms of his wife, Jacqueline Kennedy, who rode proudly beside him. He was rushed to the hospital. Specialists worked over him. Priests gave him the last rites of the Roman Catholic Church. He died within an hour of the attack.

So little did John Kennedy think that he was in any danger, that he sat beside his wife on his last ride.

Lyndon B. Johnson, who as Vice President succeeds to the Presidency, was indirectly the victim of the assassin. For it was in his State of Texas that the assassination took place which vaulted him into the White House. He was to be the host to the Kennedy's at his ranch for the weekend.

It is too early to render judgment on the 35th President. He had brought the country to its greatest peacetime strength, both in nuclear and conventional arms. He had recovered much of the loss in the space race.

On the economic front, he had seen the gross national income rise $100 billion, from $500 billion to an expected $600 billion this year. The greatest blot was the high unemployment level, that did not fall despite the Nation's great prosperity. He had achieved a certain accommodation with the Soviet Union, which somewhat firmed a shaky peace.

The Nation echoes the anguished cry of Mrs. Kennedy as the President fell into her arms, "Oh, no! Oh, no!" To her and their children, to the bereaved parents and brothers and sisters, the Nation's heart goes out. Their loss is the country's loss. May God help them, and help the country that nurtured him to his high office. And may He be with his successor, Lyndon B. Johnson, the 36th President of the United States, as he enters with heavy heart into his exalted office.

[From the Concord (N.C.) Tribune, Nov. 24, 1963]

IN MEMORIAM OF PRESIDENT JOHN F. KENNEDY—
1917–63

Words can scarcely convey the sense of horror, shock, and indignation felt when President John Fitzgerald Kennedy was assassinated Friday afternoon.

That such a thing could happen in the United States of America in this day and age is inconceivable, and even now more than a day later, remains very difficult to believe.

A bullet, fired by a cowardly murderer, cut short the life of the youngest man ever elected to the Nation's highest office. The tragic end came just at a time when it appeared that Kennedy's peaceful overtures to the Soviet Union might at long last bring relief from the pressures of the cold war.

That the late President was a controversial figure cannot be denied, but Americans, regardless of party affiliation, mourn him as a fallen hero.

Although his programs—those in effect and those on the drawing boards—drew wrath on one side and bountiful praise on the other, his acts at relieving East-West tensions should serve to place his memory deep in the hearts of all Americans.

In situations like this, we are prone to forget the things with which we disagreed and are more likely to remember only the fine qualities and deeds of the departed. Such should be the case now.

Filled with youthful energy and plans for reshaping the Nation, Kennedy took office in troubled times. And troubles he had—the Bay of Pigs disaster, Berlin, the Cuban missile crisis, civil rights struggles at home, and others.

The office matured him as only the intense pressures, obligations, and responsibilities of the world's highest office can.

Many criticized the late President for the high-powered tactics which won him the Democratic nomination in 1960, and later, the Presidency. But John Kennedy, the politician and statesman, like Jack Kennedy, the naval officer and hero, knew but one way to wage any fight— to win.

He had his successes as well as his failures and his platform raised howls of protests in many quarters, but few can doubt his personal sincerity, integrity, and courage.

An assassin's bullet killed more than a man in Dallas Friday afternoon; it killed the image of a new day in this century, for Kennedy was the symbol of youth, with its vigorous and unsullied plans for reshaping the order of things in a jumbled world.

How his death will alter the course in history is purely a matter of conjecture. However, John Kennedy was a forceful, popular man and much that only he could have accomplished has been lost to a world, now much poorer by his loss.

He took office in troubled times, but died in a period of East-West thaw, for which he was primarily responsible. As the peace-loving Americans that we are, we can only pray that the late John F. Kennedy set the stage for true world peace in the years to come.

Let us not forget the human, for in death he is not only a former President, but a loving husband and adoring father, taken from his family at the height of his success and in the prime of life.

John Fitzgerald Kennedy is dead—he is not forgotten— but now is the time to unite behind President Lyndon B. Johnson, for trying days await the new Chief Executive.

[From the Concord (N.C.) Tribune, Dec. 1, 1963]

CALLS FOR UNITY

Our new President, Lyndon B. Johnson, made a splendid appeal to the citizens of the Nation Thanksgiving night for them to "banish the rancor from our words and the malice from our hearts," so a united nation can face the days ahead.

It was a simple yet great personal appeal from the President for unity and sincerity from the people to get the job done at hand in tribute to the martyred President Kennedy.

And he made a statement that all of us must surely take to heart. He pointed out that "our homes are safe, our defenses are secure," adding "we know our system is strong."

Most of us in days past had not heard such reassuring news. Simply he was telling the people that America is strong and ready for any attack which might be mounted by an enemy.

Moved by the sudden death of his immediate predecessor, the late John F. Kennedy, he announced that Cape Canaveral henceforth will be known as Cape Kennedy, a great tribute to a young man who put America right at the top in the great outer space race.

[From the Concord (N.C.) Tribune, Dec. 3, 1963]

THE TORCH IS PASSED

It will be remembered that President Kennedy in his inaugural address, made a point of the fact that he was accepting the torch of leadership for a new generation, born in this century and veteran of its wars. The torch is still in comparatively young hands.

Lyndon B. Johnson was 55 last August 27. He was born in 1908. He, too, is a product of this century. He saw active duty as a commander in the Naval Reserve in 1941 and 1942. He is in tune with the times.

But the two men who are next in line, now "a heart beat away from the Presidency," are not of this generation. Speaker John W. McCormack, the next in line, will be 72 December 21 next. He was born in 1891. Senator Carl Hayden of Arizona, President pro tempore of the Senate and now second in line, was 86 last October 2. He was born in 1877. McCormack has been in Congress 36 years, Hayden 51. They reached their positions partly on seniority, partly on ability.

The act of succession overlooked the fact that normally the Speaker and President pro tempore of the Senate are old men who might not be able to stand the rigors of the Presidency. The old order, which made the Cabinet the immediate successors in order of Cabinet seniority beginning with the Secretary of State, had its advantages. These men share the burdens of Government with the President and they are usually young men picked for their executive ability. Now they come after the two legislative leaders.

The Congress is not likely to relinquish the succession it voted its presiding officers during the serious illness of President Eisenhower. But it should reconsider its handiwork in the light of the present outlook, should any other indisposition occur.

————

[From the Durham (N.C.) Sun, Nov. 23, 1963]

A NATION MOURNS

Dynamic, magnetic John Fitzgerald Kennedy,
Thirty-fifth President of the United States,
Young, clean, gracious, intellectual, articulate,
Is lost to the Nation and the world,
Victim of a despicable assassin's bullet.
It was a madman's act.
To his fellow-Americans ghastly and grievous.
The Republic, scarcely comprehending, weeps.
It is ironical that a courageous man
Who walked fearlessly
Among alien peoples in safety,
Walked fearlessly among his own people
And was slain.
To his family, especially his widow,
Flow sorrow, and love,
From the hearts of all the world.
None put it better than an average citizen:
"He was a great man—and a good man."

————

[From the Durham (N.C.) Sun, Nov. 23, 1963]

A BITTER, BITTER AGE

"What," many an American is asking himself and his neighbors today, "is our America coming to? How could so cruel and brutal a horror occur in the enlightened United States?"

The answer: We live in an age of passion and violence, raw passion and violence. The infection has spread to our noble democracy.

Americans will variously and instinctively, in their grief and rage and disappointment, seek to attach the stigma to someone else, thrusting away the guilt which presses in upon themselves. Many will accusingly assign the culpability for the frightful crime to this alinement or that attitude.

That will not do. Nor will it do to point the defamatory finger at any individual, even the miserable, moronic assassin.

Every human being in this country who has pondered passion and violence or who has yielded to passion and violence, thus canonizing passion and violence in our otherwise compassionate and lovely land, may feel himself contributory to November's day of infamy.

————

[From the Durham (N.C.) Sun, Nov. 25, 1963]

TAPS

John Fitzgerald Kennedy, the President,
Has been laid in his warrior's grave;
Sacred American ground in Arlington
Which he, by his life and his death,
Dedicated, consecrated and hallowed,
By his own example he illuminated
His "Profiles of Courage."
He has, in his unflinching sacrifice,
Presented a challenge to America's youth
In which he had such faith;
And to it passed a torch.

————

[From the Durham (N.C.) Sun., Nov. 25, 1963]

TWICE A HERO

Twice John Fitzgerald Kennedy went to war and twice he won his country's veneration. In the military sphere, he won his honors in the South Seas. In the civilian domain, he laid down his life.

He belongs to history and only history will comprehensively appraise his contribution to humanity. The Nation and the world today know only that a noble soul has been cut off in the very hour of his opportunity.

Worthy and understanding Americans, lamenting, place a flower on his tomb.

————

[From the Durham (N.C.) Sun, Nov. 25, 1963]

AN EQUALLY BRAVE WOMAN

No heart, American, French, Irish or otherwise oriented, which mourns the lost President, aches for him alone. Equally brave and probably more deeply loved, is the enchanting wife who survives him.

For his children, too, to whom he was so devoted and attentive and who, even at their tender ages, gave him as well as their mother their whole trust and worship, every man's heart contracts; but their lives are unformed. How tragically, cruel savages have dealt with the life of Jacqueline Kennedy.

Gracious, glowingly beautiful, marvelously composed yet joyously alive, she stood proudly yet humbly and captivatingly at his side. How sad that that sparkle should be dimmed.

————

[From the Durham (N.C.) Sun, Nov. 25, 1963]

THE WORLD BOWS ITS HEAD

Heads of state, ambassadors, ministers, emissaries variously entitled, converged on Washington today. They marched with the bereaved family behind the caisson which bore the 35th President of the United

States. In the appalling evil which has befallen our people, they stood uncovered with us.

It is evidence, undoubtedly, that a common humanity and a shared decency lie basically in the background of human aspirations and endeavors. For the moment, materialism is put aside and the hearts of a great part of the world know communion.

Men being men, it will be but an interlude; and, indeed, many in the world, and in our own Nation, continue to harden their hearts, even barely repress fires of bitterness.

Again in history, for history has many parallels of the barbarism of man, man has been shocked at the viciousness of which he is capable.

If only the remorse of this day could forever soften and temper the beings of this universe.

[From the Elizabethtown (N.C.) Bladen Journal, Nov. 28, 1963]

LET US BE THANKFUL FOR A GREAT LIFE GIVEN FOR HIS COUNTRY

America today mourns the tragic passing of President John Fitzgerald Kennedy, the 35th President of the United States at the hands of an assassin. Those who loved him and agreed with his policies, and those who opposed, all agree that the Nation has suffered a tremendous blow at a critical period in the world's history.

President Kennedy had a passion for peace and world coexistence and he used every effort at his command to bring these about. He was making great progress. Many of us realize that we probably owe our very lives during the past 3 years to the courage, strength, and intelligence of this dead chieftain.

On this day, set apart for national Thanksgiving, let us lift our hearts and voices in thanksgiving to the most high for the life of this great man and for the torch which he has lighted in a dark era in the history of the world.

Let us give thanks, too, for Vice President Lyndon B. Johnson, now the 36th President of the United States. Since he became Vice President he was very close to the late President and was well versed in the President's plans and the affairs of national interest. We can thank God that we have such a man·to follow in the footsteps of the great President.

One hundred years ago President Abraham Lincoln speaking at the battlefield at Gettysburg said, "It is for us to be here dedicated to the great task remaining before us; that from these honored dead we take increased devotion to that cause for which they gave the last full measure of devotion; that we here highly resolve that these dead shall not have died in vain; that this Nation, under God, shall have a new birth of freedom and that government of the people, by the people, and for the people shall not perish from the earth."

President Kennedy's life was dedicated sincerely as were those honored dead at Gettysburg. His vision was peace and coexistence for the world. Abraham Lincoln's words seem exceedingly fitting to be remembered at this tragic time, and in tribute to a great man of valor, of Christian faith, vision, and courage, the late President of the

United States. On this Thanksgiving Day let us one and all be grateful for his life, given for his country, and pray that his ideals for world peace may come to fruition.

[From the Forest City (N.C.) Courier, Nov. 28, 1963]

FATHER, FORGIVE THEM

The cortege moved slowly up Pennsylvania Avenue, muffled drums echoing against huge buildings and across tree-lined parks. Silent thousands watched as the flag-draped coffin passed. Millions watched over the Nation and world as the national networks carried the complete procession from the White House to the Capitol.

Only then, nearly 48 hours after the bullet crashed into the skull of John F. Kennedy, did most viewers really believe the truth of the terrible nightmare that had gripped the Nation.

The outpouring of national and world sentiment over the loss of this young, energetic, handsome leader, has been unprecedented in the history of man. It must certainly go down as one of the three most terrible losses in history, behind Jesus Christ and Abraham Lincoln.

It mattered little now that he may have been of another political party or of another faith, or of another color. It mattered not that you were for or against his program. This was our President, struck down by a hidden assailant, and this was America, the place where nothing of this nature could possibly happen.

And yet it did happen. It happened in a year when the dignity of man is supposed to have meaning. It happened at a time when America was really beginning to take full leadership in the world community.

Fear not for America is in the hands of Lyndon Johnson. He is an able statesman and experienced leader. But it is necessary that all Americans rally around the new President to assure him of the complete support of the entire country. President Johnson, for all his experience, does not have the magnetic personality or the dynamic electricity of John Kennedy. And the·peoples of the rest of the world do not know him.

However, most nations have enough faith in the American way and the constitutional government of the United States to be assured that America will not falter in this time of tragedy, regardless of who is President or which political party happens to be in power.

The death of President John F. Kennedy is a shame that all Americans will have to bear. Seeds of hate have been evident all over the Nation. Few of the perpetrators of these hate seeds would have been willing to pull the fatal trigger themselves. Nevertheless, their leadership provided the spark of hate that touched the heart of a crazed individual.

What lies ahead for America? This may well depend upon how willing Americans are to strive for continued progress at a time when unity is needed above all. For America will progress only so far as the people will let it.

Pray for our fallen leader, and pray, too, for the new President. We might also say a prayer for America in this perilous time. God grant that we have the courage and the strength to carry on, continuing to show the way to peace for the rest of the world.

[From the Forest City (N.C.) Courier, Dec. 5, 1963]

WHERE WERE YOU ON NOVEMBER 22?

What were you doing on the afternoon of November 22 when you heard the news of the assassination of President Kennedy? Chances are, the shocking impact of the news will cause you to always remember where you were, who you were with and what you were doing. There are now three incidents that are imbedded in this reporter's memory, other than personal or family. These would be, in order of occurrence, Pearl Harbor, President Roosevelt's death, and President Kennedy's assassination.

For some of our older citizens, they could add the Wall Street crash of 1929, perhaps Lindbergh's flight, the death of Woodrow Wilson, World War I, and perhaps the assassination of President McKinley in 1901.

Naturally, almost everyone has something personal that will be carried to his grave. We're speaking here of events of a national or world stature that were felt by people all over the country.

On the afternoon of November 22, I happened to be riding in my car. The radio had not been on, but for some unexplainable reason, at 1:45 p.m., I reached over and flicked it on. A reporter was excitedly giving the final details of the then unconfirmed shooting. The immediate reaction was—that crazy South America, they're always killing a president.

It took a moment for the announcement to sink in. Dallas—President shot—Governor also believed wounded. This was insane. President Kennedy was to be in Dallas today. He couldn't have been serious. Sure a lot of people are unhappy about some of the President's programs and policies, but shoot the President of the United States? Impossible. Not in 1963.

For the next 30 or 40 minutes, the networks frantically scrambled for information, for reports from Dallas, for opinions of what might result should the President die from the wounds.

Then came the pause and the announcement that spread cold chills down every spine in America: "Ladies and gentlemen, the President of the United States is dead." There was another instant of complete silence, and then the playing of the national anthem.

How do you drive with tears in your eyes? How can you explain to God the prayer in your heart one moment, and the curse that automatically followed the announcement? The answer is, you don't. You pull the car to the side of the road, and you just sit and shake your head, and ask, "why"?

There are those who are not really unhappy over the passing of John Kennedy, and even a few who admit they are glad it happened. I honestly feel sorry for these people, for they make up a part of the hate that is eating at the very heart of America.

I happen to have been a supporter of John Kennedy before his nomination. I am proud to have had the opportunity to vote for him in 1960. I was looking forward to another chance to vote for him in 1964. This black mark on America hit me hard. I make no excuses for the way I feel. There was a little bit of me that died too, on November 22 in Dallas.

[From the Greensboro Times, Nov. 28, 1963]

IN MEMORIAM, JOHN FITZGERALD KENNEDY—1917–1963

Since the beginning of man, death has been a mystery. It steals upon us like a thief in the night. It seemingly takes away the greatest possessions man has ever claimed. The graduating degrees of unbelief, shock, and distress mount into a crescendic cry of "why should such a tragedy occur?"

Many words have been written and spoken about the death of John Fitzgerald Kennedy, perhaps, than the death of any other man in history. Modern means of communications have brought this terrible breach of morality direct to the minds and hearts of individuals in all parts of the world, in an unprecedented dispatch of the events that prefaced, embraced, and culminated such a savagery by a human.

Many of these words have spoken of the causes and effects of such a crime, while many have portrayed the degree of man's failure with respect to his fellowmen. We completely concur in the stunned citizenry's condemnation of such barbarian incredulity that has blackened and saddened this Nation and world.

John F. Kennedy was the object of criticism many times in these pages, just as any public figure must expect as he leads his constituents in controversial paths. His course of action was in keeping with his personal convictions, and never would we deny the rights of an individual, especially those of such an intellect.

Perhaps we seldom consider the fact, but a President's life is a lonely and thankless task, surrounded by various actions clamoring for a different doctrine and better internal relations. John F. Kennedy was the brunt of many jokes, which he took in his stride.

While his progression from U.S. Representative to the Presidency was sparked with the most calculated details, he was not classified by most real political bigwigs as a "politician." By anyone's standards, he was a wealthy man, who never cared for expansion in this direction. By the standards of the most educated nations, John F. Kennedy was an intellect, with a never-ending desire for more knowledge and wisdom. While his was a thankless task, never did he show signs of weakness or self-confidence in his responsibilities. Here was a man of strong convictions, for following through on issues that were not always the most popular. His was a vibrant nature, adding greatly to his leadership of our Nation, and bridging breaches that separated the United States from many nations. John F. Kennedy was at the prime of his potential when his life was snuffed out, stealing from all the world a leadership that is so desperately needed at this troubled time.

It is not for us to appraise the historical significance of this life. But, if it were, we would have to say that this man will go down as one of the world's great leaders of all history. Time is the curer of historical evaluation. We believe time will prove John F. Kennedy's tenure one of complete success.

Our difference of evaluation would be this: While we have mourned with the Kennedy family and other loved ones over this assassination, we believe that this tragedy was not brought to bear on the Kennedy family so much as it was upon the American people. History has taught us to look for the good in all evil. Perhaps from this evil deed we shall salvage the good. If we do, John F. Kennedy will not have died in vain. There are many possible goods that can evolve from such a cowardly act. Not the least of these is the need for our Nation to look into the mirror at a time like this. Look long and hard. What do we see? We see wickedness and hate, love for self and pleasure, disrespect for others' rights, indifference to the problems of our fellowmen, a consuming passion for the evils that surround us.

This is the challenge that faces each of us today. If we sincerely sorrow in the midst of this tragedy, if we are sincere in our plaints, if we're really looking for the renewed destiny that lies before us, it is our conviction that John F. Kennedy would challenge each of us to clean up the wickedness that lies within our midst, dislodge the prejudice and cruelty that inhabits our hearts, and pursue with "vigor" the course which lies ahead.

It is ironic that his last message to his beloved country contained these words from Psalms, "Except the Lord build the house, they labour in vain that build it: except the Lord keep the city, the watchman waketh but in vain."

John Fitzgerald Kennedy was a man of vision and courage. His dedication remains with us to challenge our actions.

May his soul rest in peace.

――――

[From the Greensboro (N.C.) Times, Nov. 28, 1963]

THE STRENGTH OF CONVICTION

We would think the most resounding impression from the world-shattering event that occurred last week, is that given by the former First Lady and her children.

Throughout the devastating ordeal, Jacqueline Kennedy conducted herself with the same sense of courage and peace of mind that had surrounded her husband for so many years. This was the supreme test for a lady. These were the hours of greatest need by a wife and mother. The steadfast devotion for her husband was not displaced in her mourning, but was magnified, and we are certain, had her husband been present for the occasion, he would have said, "Well done, Jackie."

This is the same type of strength that her husband had displayed so many times. This was evidence of her inner strength, her complete dependence upon God, that all would be right for her husband. This was her strength of character even in her deepest grief. The rigidness with which she contained her emotions must surely have been in tribute to her late husband, and witness for her son and daughter.

We would not fail to recognize, also, the other members of the Kennedy family for their complete composure in these hours of trial. Indeed, they must have had the realization that John F. Kennedy had given his best for his country, and would live on through all eternity in his promised reward.

There are those who would point an accusing finger at this clan, saying they had failed in their outpouring of affection for their loved ones.

Conversely, we believe theirs is the strength of conviction contained in the funeral service: We would not have you ignorant concerning those who are asleep, lest you should grieve even as others who have no hope. * * * I am the resurrection and the life, he who believes in me, even if he die, shall live.

――――

[From the Greensboro (N.C.) Times, Nov. 28, 1963]

THE CAUSE AND EFFECT

The mystery of the century could be the "why" in the assassination of John F. Kennedy. Lee Harvey Oswald, while not considered a nut or maniac, was, nevertheless, deranged in his appraisal of values, for he snuffed out the life of a person who had done him no personal harm.

The cause of this senseless murder may never be known to man. That he was a loner and resented the mistreatment accorded him while serving in the Marine Corps, were apparently the key motivating forces behind his action.

With rapidly moving contemporary history, we are witnessing during our lifetime the most complex assortment of incidents than anytime in the past. Within the past decade, the transpiration of such events could exceed that of any hundred-year span during our country's entire history.

The effects of Mr. Kennedy's death could have a crushing realization of just where we as a civilized nation stand in the eyes of the world, with a reawakening of our Nation's moral responsibility.

The solidifying effect of John F. Kennedy's murder could exceed that of all expectation in causing a closer relationship between all members of the free world and possibly a goodly segment of the Communist strongholds.

Only time will tell the true scope of this deed.

――――

[From the Hamlet (N.C.) News-Messenger, Nov. 26, 1963]

ONLY HISTORY HOLDS ANSWERS TO OUR DISTURBING QUESTIONS

The President is dead.

A grieving wife mourns the death of her husband. Two small children cry in the darkness for a father they will never see again. A nation weeps in silence for its beloved leader. The world bows its head for a man, a friend.

John Fitzgerald Kennedy—the man, the husband, the father, the American, the President, the friend—is dead.

Like Americans and freemen everywhere, Hamlet residents are searching deeply into the darkened pit of reality—and even perhaps into our own disturbed consciences—for a reason on which to base this horrible crime against humanity. Many of us, even a half week after a sniper's bullet etched its infamy into the pages of history, are still hoping the dream will end. We are reluctant, perhaps afraid, to face the cold reality of this insidious deed.

Our sleepless nights are filled with questions. Why

did it happen? Who is to blame? What will happen now?

Answers to these questions lie, no doubt, somewhere in the unwritten pages of history, the same history that was jolted so violently off its course by the assassination of President Kennedy. We, as Americans, will hold the pen that writes that important chapter.

John Fitzgerald Kennedy died by an act of lunacy. He did not die in vain.

Although Friday, November 22, 1963, will always be known as one of the blackest days in American history, it will also be known as the day the spirit of democracy rose to face and defeat the challenge of death. It will be remembered as the day Americans proved to the world that even the icy finger of death cannot chill the God-loving soul of this great Nation.

With sympathy and sadness in our hearts, we must now lift the mourning veil and prepare for the future. We must rededicate our lives to the cause of peace and freedom for all men.

The President is dead, but the many perils of our time still exist. The creeping malignancy of communism spreads like wildfire through the poverty-stricken nations of Asia and Latin America. The fight for freedom and the dignity of man has never been more demanding.

In his first statement as the new President, Lyndon B. Johnson asked for our help in this fight, and for God's. God will answer. We must.

——

[From the Henderson (N.C.) Daily Dispatch, Nov. 23, 1963]

TRAGEDY FOR AMERICA

All America, regardless of partisan attitudes, was shocked and stunned by the assassination of President Kennedy in Dallas, Tex., in early afternoon, Friday. In such a time as this, we are all Americans first before being Democrats and Republicans. The killer's bullet struck down the President of the United States, not merely the leader of the majority party.

Death comes to all men. It is no respecter of persons. It is an enemy alike of the high and the low and the rich and the poor. But when the leader of the greatest nation on earth is cut down, it is a blow to all the people—in this instance to the free world and Iron Curtain countries as well.

In such an emergency, emotions rise to the surface. There is grief and a sense of loss as if a member of one's own family had been taken. First impressions are that the tragedy is hard to accept. This terrific blow emphasizes the fact that uneasy lies the head that wears a crown, whether he be King, Emperor, or President.

However much one may have differed with President Kennedy, there was universal recognition of his vigor of youth, his intellectual capacity in the grasp of problems, and his readiness to assume responsibility. He did his best to be a leader, and showed many of the qualities required of such an individual.

Mr. Kennedy's rise to power and prominence was little short of meteoric. As a politician, first in the House, then the Senate and afterward the Presidency, he stepped from star to star in achieving world stature. Always he seemed to know where he was going and to be on his way. His choice of words in getting his ideas across, his fearless pioneering, especially in the domestic political arena, his charm and personality, and his ability to mix with people, despite the pinnacle of great wealth which he inherited, were assets as he moved along the way. His knowledge of events and procedures was little short of amazing. The combination carried him to the highest office in the land, or, for that matter, in the world.

President Kennedy was the fourth American President to fall victim of an assassin. All were shot to death, Mr. Kennedy with a high powered rifle from a distance and the others with a revolver at close range. Abraham Lincoln was mortally wounded at the hands of John Wilkes Booth in a Washington theater only a few days after the end of the Civil War. James A. Garfield was shot in 1881 and William McKinley at the International Exposition in Buffalo, N.Y., in 1901. Others have died in office, but only these four were the victims of murderers.

What the assassin of a President thinks he is accomplishing is a mystery. All such hitherto have been executed for their crime, and this one almost certainly will be. About the only explanation is that these killers were fanatics. Only a few weeks ago the President of South Vietnam and his brother were assassinated. Other high officials have been in other lands. We in America had come to believe that it couldn't happen here.

What occurred in Dallas to create a day of such tragedy will be long debated. A Secret Service man and a policeman were shot to death on Friday also.

It is a tragedy unspeakable that a crime of this character should occur anywhere in this country. It is doubly so that the President was struck down in a southern city. However unjustly the accusation may be, the South will be hearing from this for months, possibly years, although the other three Presidents who were assassinated were done to death in the North. In no imaginable sense does this crime represent the sentiment of the people of the southland, who believe in justice and are law abiding. No section of the country can regret the tragedy more than this people.

Already there is widespread speculation as to the political effect of the President's death. He was advocating and pressing in Congress for a legislative program much of which was opposed by millions of people in all parts of the country. Will it suffer or will it be advanced as a result of this national tragedy? Will Khrushchev become tougher as a new hand takes the helm in this country? Will American prestige abroad suffer generally while a new Chief Executive is getting his feet on the ground? Will there be renewed defiance and new and more serious threats to American rights and to peace generally? These are questions which can be answered only in the weeks and months ahead.

President Johnson is a veteran of many years experience in the legislative halls. When in the Senate he was a master organizer. He knew how to coax his colleagues to his way of thinking. Albeit with some changes to his own liking, Johnson may be expected to follow the Kennedy line, for at least the immediate future. The extent to which he does or does not will be a factor in his efforts to appease and attract the support of the South, which was not enthusiastic about Mr. Kennedy's program, especially as to civil rights legislation.

Whether Johnson will lend his influence toward economy in Government, toward a balanced budget, and for or against fantastic spending programs will become evident as he grasps more firmly the reins of Government.

The crushing burdens of his office will bear heavily upon him. It will be remembered that he suffered a severe heart attack a dozen years ago. His 3 years as Vice President have acquainted him with the great responsibilities that now devolve upon him. But he is no novice either as a politician or as a leader. He knows his way around in affairs of Government. He realizes the necessity for assistance and for the prayers of the American people. Without these he cannot go far nor be entirely effective as Chief Executive.

For the present while, however, the country mourns at the bier of its President. The people are bowed in sorrow in the face of horrible tragedy. The crisis is upon us. Fortunately, it is not the first testing of the Nation's stamina. It has faced crises before and has found a way through. As tears are shed and as hearts are sad and crushed, it is possible to look toward the future with courage, with strength and with hope. In that spirit and in that consciousness, we can move ahead. Out of respect for a dead but respected leader, Americans can recognize their responsibilities and will meet them in the type of determination which has brought them along thus far. God being our helper and guide, we shall persevere.

———

[From the Hendersonville (N.C.) Times-News, Nov. 23, 1963]

PRESIDENT KENNEDY'S DEATH

When President John F. Kennedy was shot at 2 p.m. Friday, normally the time when the UPI teletype closes in the Times-News office, page 1 had been made up and only the women's page remained to be closed before sending them to the stereotyping department.

In the interest of time, only one-half of page 1 was made over to accommodate a story of the tragic occurrence. The President was not dead—or at least it was difficult to believe that he had gone on. The wire services had not confirmed the fact. And then came a bulletin that he had succumbed, followed by a new "lead" and a story of finality that everyone in this office hoped would not be transmitted.

The news, certainly the most important of the year and, as world events develop, perhaps the most significant of the century, again demonstrates that we are living in a hectic age in which tragedy may strike at any moment, in your lives and ours, at almost any time or place. At the height of his career, only 46 and in his first term as President, John Fitzgerald Kennedy was struck down in the twinkling of an eye within the sight of thousands. It now appears that a mistake was made in leaving down the "bubble top" of the limousine in which the President and Governor Connally of Texas and their wives were riding. There may have been other oversights, but speculation is futile now.

Although President Kennedy had many political enemies, it is difficult to comprehend how anyone not in a maniacal frame of mind could have assassinated him. We are extremely hopeful, even confident, that the assassin will be found. Meanwhile, the American people, almost to the last man, woman, and child will mourn the President's untimely death. He had led us through many crises; and while his program appeared at times to be faulty and his methods questionable in the light of established principles of American government, we believe he was a great American and that his place will not soon be as adequately filled or his influence duplicated.

It is not given to many men that they reach this exalted office or that they be cut down at the zenith of a career already distinguished. Forceful as a speaker, logical as a thinker, physically and mentally brave, unmatched as a tactician in politics and determined to do the right as he conceived it, John Fitzgerald Kennedy was a giant in world affairs and at home. Add to these and other qualities the fact that he was our President and one realizes why the Nation and the world are in mourning today.

———

[From the Hendersonville (N.C.) Western Carolina Tribune, Nov. 28, 1963]

IN MEMORY OF JOHN FITZGERALD KENNEDY WHO DIED IN SERVICE TO HIS COUNTRY

The Lord is my shepherd; I shall not want.

He maketh me to lie down in green pastures: He leadeth me beside the still waters.

He restoreth my soul: He leadeth me in the paths of righteousness for His name's sake.

Yea, though I walk through the valley of the shadow of death, I will fear no evil; for Thou art with me; Thy rod and Thy staff they comfort me.

Thou preparest a table before me in the presence of mine enemies: Thou anointest my head with oil; my cup runneth over.

Surely goodness and mercy shall follow me all the days of my life: and I will dwell in the house of the Lord forever.—PSALM 23.

"Ask not what your country can do for you, ask what you can do for your country."

He gave his all.

———

[From the Hendersonville (N.C.) Western Carolina Tribune, Dec. 5, 1963]

ONE MAN LOOKS INTO THE FUTURE

"Unforeseen events do not necessarily change or shape the course of man's affairs."—Think magazine.

To say that no one in this country even from the earliest approaches to adulthood will ever find his outlook exactly the same after 12:30 p.m., November 22 is certainly not denying the above statement, because the author meant to convey that free man, with the right of self-determination, is master of his own destiny provided he is strong.

But it is foregone to say that none of us now in adult pursuits will ever be quite the same. Everything will change, has changed in shades of degree.

Our political outlook will change. Our ability to dream with open eyes will change. Our socioeconomic concepts will change. Our religion will change. Our pursuits of daily livelihood will change.

"But we have had three such tragedies before," you say. True, and what you are today is in some degree caused by those same three murders because they, each in its time, drastically changed the destiny of a nation, even the world at large, and in so doing molded the progeny of which you are a part.

No one can say, even reliably conclude, what those fatal shots will do to us. We can only surmise:

The tax bill: It will pass the Congress even quicker than it would have done before because a nation with a sense of mass guilt and the crushing burden of "getting on with it" will write President Kennedy's favorite project into law.

Civil rights: Contrary to some opinion, the evolution begun by the 1954 Supreme Court decision was and is proceeding at a certain rate and was, in our opinion, neither slowed or facilitated, by the Kennedy administration. It was merely put into sharp focus. The Roosevelt, Truman, and Eisenhower eras contributed far more to the movement because they became the earlier, more cataclysmic phases. The increasing thunder of the Negro's self-assertion will in no wise be dampened by our recent tragedy. Some of the outer, more visible facets will change, certainly, but the wave itself will notice scarcely the tiniest backlashing ripple.

The civil rights bill: (This is the most hazardous to guess.) In our opinion it would not have passed this session had President Kennedy continued in his dynamic way. It will pass, under perhaps other, more acceptable nomenclature, during the next three convenings. Even if we're wrong, much of the essence of the bill will pass into accepted national behavior, regardless.

The lowering cloud of mass guilt which today still hangs over the Nation will be partially dispersed by manifestations, particularly in the South, of further acceptance of the Negro more than anything else as tribute to our dead President who, after all, died championing his cause.

True, it was a self-styled Marxist who pulled the fateful trigger, but the tempo of hate swirling about the head of John F. Kennedy was engendered by the passionate struggle between the races, into which both the amateur and professional Communist is eternally dedicated to step.

Cuba: Ultimate outcome unaffected. Kennedy was determined. Johnson is determined. Neither regard overt action at this stage remotely feasible.

France: President de Gaulle had a strong, personal affection for our late President, but by his actions showed that he was not in agreement with much of administration policies. The very change, coupled with De Gaulle's inscrutable, bullheaded, and intensely nationalistic concepts, will make for improved French-American relations.

Britain: The tragedy itself moved the two English-speaking peoples closer, as always during times of great national crisis on either side of the Atlantic.

The 1964 elections: President Johnson will get the nomination with merely a show of opposition, practically by acclamation. "Somehow the word 'Goldwater' just seems to go flat now," someone said last week, "like saying 'Harold Stassen,' 'John Sparkman' or 'Governor Wallace.' He's a candidate who's lost his cause."

No one on the scene now could give him a run worth the name. Time and changing tides may make it a real contest but if he chooses to run L.B.J. will succeed himself.

Robert F. Kennedy, who's made no statement other than call his new Chief Executive and pledge loyalty, is the real enigma in the wake of his brother's death. Anathema to the South, he has been too dogmatic and strongly committed to become a real political contender, even if he wants it. But it must be remembered he was the real brains and driving force behind his brother's 1960 campaign. His prowess in this respect won't be overlooked.

Hoffa and unionism: Quiet for a while, smart that they are. Knowing full well that the Kennedy brothers were closing in on the Hoffa gang they are now in a wait-and-see stage. The more respectable union leaders, Meany and Reuther, are sincerely behind the President, for the time being. Liberal-come-lately that he is, Johnson does not have the confidence of labor that his predecessor had and for this reason labor is one of the two real unknown quantities for 1964—the other being the South, a great gray area of unweighed political portent.

Congress: Literally shaken to its depths, in a wave of reaction will fall in behind the new President in unprecedented demonstration of "getting on with it," passing much legislation they would have stalled.

The new generation: President Kennedy was to the young marrieds, the svelte, smartly modern set and to the maturing teenagers as well the epitome of what they are trying to say to the world. He said it for them by his appearance, manner, mannerisms, and utterances. He was their idol whether they admitted it or not. Now that he is gone their irrepressible urge for self-assertion must find outlet in another direction, perhaps even the same direction but with more extreme and wayout manifestations. They will, on their outer fringes, get wilder, more bizarre and even weird and in the early months it will have a note of pathos in it. A ringing note they can no more subdue than they can send those fatal shots winging back into the muzzle of the $12 rifle.

Christmas, 1963: The soberest, most dedicated observance of the birth of Christ witnessed in the 20th century. If one will but turn off the kids and the TV set a moment, walk out into the chill December air during the coming weeks, carol and hymn singing may be faintly or clearly discerned from every corner of the land.

––––

[From the Hickory (N.C.) Daily Record, Nov. 23, 1963]

NONE DIED IN VAIN

Four American Presidents have died from assassins' bullets. Every one of these deaths represented a great tragedy.

Those slain prior to President Kennedy were: Abraham Lincoln, James Garfield, and William McKinley.

President Lincoln was shot in Ford's Theater, Washington, D.C., April 14 (Good Friday), 1865, by John Wilkes Booth, an actor. The President died the following day.

Sixteen years later, on July 2, 1881, President Garfield was shot by Charles J. Guiteau—an unbalanced officeseeker—as Garfield was entering old Baltimore and Potomac passenger station in Washington, D.C. President Garfield died in Elberon, N.J., September 19, 1881.

Twenty years later, September 6, 1901, President McKinley was shot by Leon Czolgosz, an anarchist terrorist, while the Chief Executive was welcoming citizens to the Pan-American Exposition, in Buffalo, N.Y. He died September 14, 1901.

The assassination of President Kennedy followed that of President McKinley by 62 years.

Lincoln was the 16th President, Garfield the 20th, McKinley the 25th, and Kennedy the 35th.

It is our studied opinion that none of them died in vain, inasmuch as the great causes for which they fought were eventually triumphant. The assassins who murdered President Kennedy have promoted, rather than impeded, the many objectives of the New Frontier toward which J.F.K. was relentlessly driving and striving.

———

[From the Hickory (N.C.) Daily Record, Nov. 26, 1963]

Life Must Go On

Not that we would change our system for the British, but their system of governmental perpetuation has points in its favor. With the passing of a monarch, there is the heartening cry: "The king is dead. Long live the king." This continuity of a regime gives a stability that has been lacking in some instances in this Nation.

The late President Kennedy's entire record emphasizes his realization of the need to face the future not the past. We are confident that it would be his wish that this Nation move toward the New Frontiers which he visualized as its destiny. Now that the obeisance due his passing has been observed, it is fitting that the Nation resume its normal activity—life must go on.

The soul searching that has occupied the Nation during these days; the frankly facing the fact that all share responsibility for the tragic murder in the fanning of hate among various groups, are bound to have a sobering effect on all and to encourage tolerance toward everything except intolerance.

We believe youths, who have probably been more deeply moved by the assassination than their elders due to their empathy with the fallen chief who was possessed of similar vigor, will be thoroughly critical of any developments in this Nation which might indicate that John Kennedy's sacrifice was in vain—that his guidelines are being ignored.

———

[From the Hickory (N.C.) Daily Record, Nov. 27, 1963]

We Should Be Thankful

On this Thanksgiving Day—Thursday—let us dwell not on what we have lost with the assassination of President John Fitzgerald Kennedy. Rather, let us be thankful for what we have gained from his life.

Even while we deplore the way he died, we can be grateful for the example he set in living. His outspoken courage was known to all, and his joy of living was a family trademark.

Everyone—those who shared his beliefs and those who scorned them—must be thankful for the strength of his convictions.

John Kennedy did not choose to die. He chose to live for his principles. He fought for these principles—and for his life—in wartime.

We have a great faith in what he termed "the calm determination of the American people," and no greater tribute can be paid to a man than to say he lived up to his faith.

In his final Thanksgiving Day proclamation, the late President said: "We must never forget that the highest appreciation is not to utter words but to live by them."

Urging expressions of gratitude to God, he begged: "Let us earnestly and humbly pray that He will continue to guide and sustain us in the great unfinished tasks of achieving peace, justice, and understanding among all men and nations and of ending misery and suffering wherever they exist."

———

[From the High Point (N.C.) Enterprise, Nov. 24, 1963]

John F. Kennedy

Even now there is still a numbness of feeling over the assassination of President John F. Kennedy. The man and his spirit are yet too much with us to accept, so suddenly and so brutally, the realization of his death. The mind records the words and the pictures that tell of what happened in Dallas Friday. The heart cries out in an anguish of disbelief.

The 35th President of the United States is dead, slain at a time when, tempered by his experience in office, he was beginning to realize the full sweep of his powers and the confidence to use those powers well for the good of the country. Certainly, his enduring mark as President was yet to come from John F. Kennedy. From the Bay of Pigs and from Vienna in 1961, he grew to face the Russians with a sure touch in Berlin and in Cuba, achieving, as a result, a new balance of respect and of confidence in our relations with the cold war adversary. In South Vietnam, the United States, under his leadership, was entering a more hopeful phase in the war against Communist subversion.

At home, the issues were economic and human, involving relationships between Government and business, and concerning the status of the Negro in the United States. In his approach to both, John F. Kennedy was hardly the man grasping for power many pictured him to be. His touch was pragmatic and, in the nature of things, political, but his principles were firm: to spur America to new heights of freedom and of achievement.

John F. Kennedy brought to the Presidency a refreshing zest for life and its pleasures. His interests were widespread; his intellect was keen. He was faithful to his church and devoted to his family. He loved to read; he enjoyed and appreciated the fine arts; he displayed a sharp wit and a love for humor. There was nothing that escaped his interest. His vigor was noticeable, with rewarding impact, on our tastes and our ambitions.

Now, John F. Kennedy is dead.

Why? The question cries for an answer. Perhaps it will never be answered. But we do well to ponder it. We should not dismiss the question by attributing the assassination to the frustrated mind of a crackpot. Let us look closely at what is happening to us. Let us examine the hate and the venom, the namecallings and the reckless accusations being hurled from both the right and the left into our body politic. Let us search the fears that may haunt our own hearts. Let us replace those fears in this moment of sadness and shame with the confidence of being Americans again.

———

[From the High Point (N.C.) Enterprise, Nov. 25, 1963]

JOHN FITZGERALD KENNEDY

John Fitzgerald Kennedy came to the Presidency of the United States as the bearer of great change. He was the symbol of something new, but he died by something as old as time—the hand of the fanatic.

He was the first man born in the 20th century to hold the office—and the second youngest in history. He was the first Catholic in the White House. He came as a naval hero of World War II who narrowly had missed death in Pacific waters, and survived a second brush with death in a grave illness 9 years ago.

To the Nation's high politics he thus brought a fresh stamp. The well-remarked "Kennedy style" was a blend of intellect, vigor, wit, charm, and a clear talent for growth.

On the always shifting, often troubled world scene, he sometimes moved with more caution than expected in young leadership. Soon after entering the White House he gamely took full blame for the Cuban Bay of Pigs fiasco as an enterprise sadly lacking in boldness.

Yet only his worst enemies withheld from him the label "courageous" when he moved resolutely against Soviet Premier Khrushchev in the great Russian missile crisis in Cuba in late 1962. And he boldly pressed for an East-West test ban treaty this year in the face of heavy charges that this imperiled our security.

In domestic affairs Kennedy won much of his program in beginning 1961, gained far less the following year, and encountered a major stalemate in 1963. The constant note against him was insufficient leadership.

But again, when 1963 brought the greatest racial crisis of this century, Kennedy—at acknowledged heavy political cost—committed himself to sweeping civil rights proposals that opened a vast new battleground.

Amid all his efforts to put the imprint of vigorous, imaginative youth upon the country's affairs in the 1960's, the late President found himself moving against a deepening background of protest, with an ugly underscoring of violence which he sought with only limited success to wipe away.

Much of this protest went to the steady encroachments of the Federal Government and its rising cost. But the bitterest reaction was white and Negro response to the enlarging racial struggle. The far right gave the mood its most perilous texture.

With the calamity in Dallas the lesson of the danger inherent in violent extremism now may be deeply implanted in America's conscience.

In this way, Kennedy in death may achieve what the living President could not do to curb the almost ungovernable rancor that increasingly discolored the politics of his brief time in power.

It was John Kennedy's good fortune to surmount many obstacles to rise to his country's highest office and bring with him the winds of a new era.

It was his final tragedy that as he labored in difficult times to use these forces for the Nation's and the world's gain, they were swiftly challenged by countering winds of bitter reaction. In Dallas, one swift gust struck him down.

The Nation thus loses a young leader whose great promise lived in the shadow of great controversy. The way he died must inescapably cost all Americans deeply in self-esteem as free men of good will.

That is the greater tragedy.

———

[From the High Point (N.C.) Enterprise]

A PRAYER

Our Father, we praise Thee for the privilege of prayer; for the assurance that Thou dost hear not only what we express with our lips, but also that Thou art attentive to the unvoiced desires of our hearts, and the longings that are known but to Thee and to us. We thank Thee that Thou hast assured us in Thy Book that if our hearts are sincere, and if we desire that Thy will be done, Thou wilt never fail to answer us according to Thy purposes.

We acknowledge Thee to be the sovereign God, and we pray that in this hour, as well as in the days ahead, that Thou wilt help us to walk by Thy guidance and to do the things that are pleasing in Thy sight. Be Thou the protector of our lives; keep us from wrongdoing; seek us when we go astray; restore our souls, and lead us in right paths for the glory of Thy name.

Let the tragic death of our late President, John Fitzgerald Kennedy, serve to remind us that Thou hast not made us to live by hatred and revenge, violence, and contemptuousness. Beget within us now a deeper love for our fellow men of all races, and a more positive concern for freedom and justice. Help us to perceive that righteousness exalteth a nation and that sin is a reproach to any person.

May our hearts be encouraged in this solemn hour that Thou art always present in the midst of the shadows of life to keep a faithful watch over Thine own, and to release Thine abounding mercy and comfort upon all troubled souls. Especially do we beseech Thee to bestow Thy ministries upon Mrs. Kennedy and the children, the other members of the Kennedy family, and all loved ones of the late President. Mercifully bring them in their deep sorrow into Thy healing and sustaining presence. Enable them to translate their bereavement whereby their faith may be strengthened and their spiritual lives enriched.

We beseech Thee to give President Lyndon B. Johnson the desire to seek Thy will and the readiness and the courage to do it. Bestow Thy guidance upon him and his advisers, and endow him with an understanding heart.

Grant that Thy benedictions may richly abide with the family of the man who was charged with the late President's death, and with the family of the late J. D. Tippit, the law enforcement officer who was killed in Dallas in the performance of his duty. We would also pray that the man who is now accused of killing Lee Oswald may seek to come to a right relationship with Thee.

Move us all to rededicate ourselves to Thee, and to the basic principles of democracy; through Jesus Christ our Lord. Amen.

Dr. Roy E. Watts,
Minister, First Presbyterian Church.

————

[From the Kinston (N.C.) Daily Free Press, Nov. 23, 1963]

PRESIDENT JOHN FITZGERALD KENNEDY

The brutal assassination of President John Fitzgerald Kennedy in Dallas, Tex., Friday has shocked and stunned the American people and the whole civilized world. It will have a profound and immeasurable impact on history.

The leader who became the 35th President of the United States at the age of 43 was a man of faith, of courage and was dedicated to keeping the peace in a world teetering dangerously close to nuclear destruction. His military service became a saga of courage as he stood by his men after a PT boat disaster in the Pacific during World War II. Although born to wealth and influence, he had a gift for understanding and loyalty to his friends that marked his entire career.

As President his New Frontier administration suffered a serious setback in the April 1961, Bay of Pigs invasion failure in Cuba. But he did not shift the responsibility to others. He bore it courageously and worked to overcome it. His confrontation with the Soviet Premier over the Cuban missile deal 13 months ago won for him the admiration of the free world, and the respect of the Soviets. Khrushchev backed down in the face of possible war with the United States. President Kennedy later went on to negotiate the test ban treaty with the Soviet Union and to pave the way for a lessening of cold war tensions.

On the domestic front civil rights struggles marked his administration. Those who did not share his views on how to handle this matter never doubted his courage or his determination to push for greater rights for all under the Constitution. His medicare, education and economic proposals for the most part are still in abeyance. But his enunciation of his views will long influence the thinking of proponents and opponents on all these issues as well. He was elected by the slenderest margin of any President in modern times; but his personal popularity remained high until his death.

Perhaps the President's most remembered phrase from his inaugural address of January 20, 1961 is "Ask not what your country can do for you, but what you can do for your country."

He loved his country and gave his life in service to it. He loved his family and he sought ever to give each member a sense of belonging and an appreciated place. He loved his church and as the first Roman Catholic ever to hold the office of President he did as much to emphasize the need for keeping church and state separate as anyone in the Nation's history.

History will assess his proper role among American and world leaders. His legacy to each American today, however, is a ringing challenge for all to do more to uphold and advance the great American ideals for which he lived—and died.

————

[From the Kinston (N.C.) Daily Free Press, Nov. 25, 1963]

THE NATION MOURNS AND SEARCHES ITS HEART

In its hour of deepest grief and anguish in this century, the Nation Monday joined the family of the late President John Fitzgerald Kennedy and the world in paying tribute to a youthful and dedicated leader who was cut down Friday by an assassin's bullet. And in that tribute there was deep soul-searching and anxiety of heart, as the people of free America pondered the shocking and bizarre events of the past 3 days.

Tragedy compounded tragedy Sunday as the suspect in the brutal slaying of the President was cut down by a nightclub operator in the sick and disturbed city of Dallas, Tex. In the church memorial services in every community in the land, in schools, colleges, and even at military installations where the grim work of keeping the peace never ends, men sought divine guidance for this hour of trial.

As the enormity of the loss crystallized in the worldwide tribute of those who trekked to Washington and Arlington Cemetery for the rites, the people sobbed in unison and asked in wounded and distraught spirit, why?

A young leader with promise, intelligence, and magnanimity of heart and spirit had been sacrificed at the altar of hate and psychopathic cunning. And before the prime suspect, who was also charged with slaying a Dallas policeman, could be tried and the full record unveiled to a bewildered world, this young man, also, was killed. The people of Dallas filled the churches Sunday in their search for guidance and direction. The Nation in essence followed suit, because all knew in their hearts that such evil is not confined to one community or to one nation in this troubled world.

Hence the message of the Scriptures comes with even more striking force to one and all. In another day and another age God's own Son was not spared. But out of that great example came the believer's greatest comfort of all. Perhaps in this period greater repentance, humility, and unity of purpose and direction may come to a divided world, torn by mistrust and violence.

Surely His promise to heal the land can and will come if mankind will put spiritual things first and seek His guidance in these days of sorrow and uncertainty.

————

[From the Leaksville (N.C.) News, Nov. 28, 1963]

LIFE OF COURAGE

Within the short span of a few tragic days, this country witnessed the assassination of its young President and the murder of the man accused of President Kennedy's slaying.

Both acts were heinous contradictions of this country's philosophy of government by law. And Lee Harvey Oswald's murder, despite the enormity of the crime he was accused of, can be condoned no more readily than John F. Kennedy's untimely death.

Whether we agree or disagree with the policies Kennedy carried out, we must agree that Kennedy was a living example of the courage of which he wrote in his book, "Profiles in Courage."

His words:

"Today the challenge of political courage looms larger than ever before. For our everyday life is becoming so saturated with the tremendous power of mass communications that any unpopular or unorthodox course arouses a storm of protests such as John Quincy Adams—under attack in 1807—could never have envisioned * * * And thus, in the days ahead, only the very courageous will be able to take the hard and unpopular decisions necessary for our survival."

President Kennedy is dead. His political career is history, and only time can tell whether the course he charted was right or wrong. There can be no doubt, however, of the courage with which he pursued that course.

President Kennedy wrote the final chapter of his book with his own blood.

It is for us now to rally behind President Lyndon Johnson and move on, despite the shame of the two deaths which this country cannot forget.

———

[From the Lenoir (N.C.) News-Topic, Nov. 23, 1963]

WORLD PAYS TRIBUTE TO ONE OF ITS GREAT

Tributes from people in all walks of life and from all parts of the world are paying tribute to the late President John F. Kennedy. His untimely death on Friday afternoon simply stunned the entire Nation and also most parts of the world when it became known that he had died of an assassin's bullet.

The people of Lenoir and elsewhere were so saddened and so stunned by the news of the tragedy that for a long time they were speechless. Many did not believe it at first until it was verified from a number of different sources.

Few people in the history of the world have done so much in the number of years which John F. Kennedy served his country. Even now it is hard to believe that one so young could reach the world's No. 1 post in government. Those who declared that he was too young and too inexperienced for the Presidency did not have to wait long until their fears were completely dispelled. He soon demonstrated that he had all of the qualities necessary to head the greatest nation on the face of the earth.

While the people of this Nation mourn his passing and extend heartfelt sympathy to his loved ones, our country must continue to move forward and to seek new frontiers of service and remain the world's leader. Since this tragedy did take place, the people of the United States realize now, even if they had not before, that in the new President, Lyndon B. Johnson, they have one of the most capable and experienced men in government. He will carry on in the true American tradition despite the great loss which he feels for his intimate friend of many years.

The Nation's newspapers today expressed the people's grief at the assassination of President Kennedy, and said the murder was "a blemish on American civilization."

Editorial comments included:

Richmond Times-Dispatch: The assassination, "coming as it does as the latest in a series of violent deaths of heads of state, is a disgrace to the United States and a blot on the good name of this country."

Indianapolis Star: "We never believed that any American could stoop to the dirty job of murder of the President. John F. Kennedy always stood for what is fine and good in the American tradition."

St. Louis Globe-Democrat: The President is "a martyr to American democracy. His murder is a blemish on American civilization."

St. Louis Post-Dispatch: The assassination is "a national tragedy of incalculable proportions. What is wrong with the United States that it can provide the environment for such an act? There is a sickness in the Nation when political differences can not be accepted and settled in the democratic way. Our democracy itself is in hazard."

Baltimore Sun: "Yesterday's first shock of horror gives way this morning to a depth of sorrow beyond expression. There is the tragedy of great tasks unfinished, of the plow stopped part way down the furrow, the house left standing in framework, the story checked mid-sentence. No one can now say what Mr. Kennedy's accomplishments would have been had he lived."

New Orleans Times-Picayune: "With the suddenness of the rifle shots, 200 million people were immersed in a great sorrow. There's no real mystery. For among human-kind there are always men of imbalance, of twisted mind, warped concepts and strange causes. Some with a deep and ugly malice toward their fellow beings. Often their hate centers upon those in high places."

New York Times: "All of us—from the country's highest leaders to the humblest citizen—all of us are still in a state of shock from this stunning blow, that even now seems unreal in its grotesque horror. John F. Kennedy died in and for the belief of those human rights to which this Nation has always been committed. No madman's bullet can stop this inexorable march of human rights; no murder, however tragic, can make it falter. In death as in life, the words and spirit of this our most newly martyred President will lead the Nation ever closer toward fulfillment of the ideals of domestic brotherhood and international peace by which his administration has been guided from the start."

———

[From the Lincoln (N.C.) Times, Nov. 25, 1963]

J.F.K., OUR 35TH PRESIDENT

Numbness of mind and body, utter disbelief, despair, silent mourning, and heartache prevail among Lincolntonians and Lincoln Countians today as they with millions everywhere in the United States and the world mourn the death of President John F. Kennedy by an assassin's bullets in Dallas, Tex., Friday.

The assassination of the President was a sickening, terrible, and despicable thing. As expressed by many, for such a dastardly act to occur in our country seemed almost unbelievable—"in other countries where there are dictators, unstable governments, yes * * * but, no, no, not ours. The United States is known the world over as the leader of Democracy. Now, how will this make us, a free country, look to the rest of the world?"

John F. Kennedy, although he met opposition to his views and programs, even within his own party in the Senate and the Congress, possessed a magnetic, vigorous personality, high intellect, charm and wit, knowledge of government that made him a popular figure in public life. He drew large and enthusiastic crowds to him wherever he went in the United States or other countries of the world. He compelled admiration from foe and friend, alike. John F. Kennedy gave dignity to the Office of the President of the United States and presented the good image. He was admired for his courage, his belief in his ideals, his dedication to the job of the Presidency.

This newspaper didn't always agree with President Kennedy's view. But, we admired him as a person of keen intelligence, charming personality and courage. He fought for what he felt was right, even when it was the unpopular view, the civil rights issue, as one example.

It could be that the tragic death of our President will bring the people of our Nation closer together, in a spirit of real, sincere unity and true American patriotism. In this hour of our Nation's great sorrow and loss, it is no time for partisan politics. There would be only one label, American. President Kennedy was just that—American, our President, a symbol of our dreams, our hopes, our freedom.

We can be calm in this time of great shock and sorrow to have faith in America, its people, and institutions. We can thank God for our blessings, His goodness bestowed upon our Nation in so many ways that the other nations do not possess, and to pray for his guidance over our new President, Lyndon B. Johnson, as he assumes the awesome responsibilities of our Nation's highest office.

[From the Lumberton (N.C.) Robesonian, Nov. 25, 1963]

LIFE TO GIVE

"Ask not what your country will do for you—ask what you can do for your country."

These words were spoken to the people of the United States in January 1961, in the inaugural address of President John F. Kennedy. They are the words most often recalled in the hours of sorrow after his tragic death in November 1963.

In the brief, intervening years, the President did what he could for his country, with all the resourcefulness at his command. What he asked of others, he demanded of himself, constantly expending his energy and vitality in the service of the Nation.

An exceptional man, John Kennedy had a capacity for greatness. It was fully realized to the extent possible within his short span of life. He was not only a dynamic political leader and statesman. He was handsome and heroic, clever, and courageous—a young man to capture the imagination of the people and inspire the youth of the land.

Reared in a superior environment, John Kennedy had the advantages of wealth and education. He lived in a way that showed he knew much is expected from those to whom much is given. He and his wife seemed born to fill the glamorous roles they played. They were as near to the hearts of the people as a storybook prince and princess of old. In the great White House of the Presidents, they kept alive the love of the arts, the humanities, and the home.

To the highest elective office on earth, President Kennedy brought youth and strength and hope and purpose, at a time when much of the world's leadership was aging. The land of opportunity had a leader with a future. The image of America was revitalized. A powerful and benevolent Nation was prepared to keep pace with a changing world in which new nations were emerging and new frontiers were opening in space.

Then suddenly, a sniper's bullet ended the career and the life of this man, whom the free world had come to know as a friend and champion, and the other world of bondage had learned to respect. The man whose bravery had brought survival in time of crisis was cut down by a shameful shot from ambush.

There was not even a semblance of misguided reason for this deed. It was a case of somebody having no better sense than to shoot the President. It was as though the progress of mankind had been halted and the machinery of civilization had been thrown out of gear, by a pebble tossed into the works.

The slender thread of one man's life has been broken, and millions have felt the impact of his fall. The world has aged more than the days on the calendar since his death, for a part of its hope and inspiration go with him as he is laid to rest. Yet the Nation he served and the people who survive can face the challenge of the future with a sustaining recollection of him, and of the courage he showed so often, in the face of obstacles and reverses and crises and evergrowing responsibilities.

Words by the tens of thousands, from people throughout the earth, have expressed the sorrow of this tragic experience, so sudden that from the President there were no last words for remembrance. But his own inaugural address, and the way he lived and died, revive the words of an American patriot at an earlier time of crisis, when this Nation was struggling to be born. His only regret was that he had but one life to give for his country.

[From the Coastland (N.C.) Times, Nov. 29, 1963]

A MIGHTY MAN AMONG MEN HAS FALLEN

When the burden of the heart is too heavy, and the mind is thick with grief, it is futile to attempt the expression of sentiment worthy of recording. In this hour we turn to the contemporary press, where we find some passages so well said that we wish to pass them on, about the loss of our great leader—our Commander in Chief.

At this time it is too difficult for us to say what should be said about so tragic and senseless a loss in leadership, decency, honesty, ability, and promise for the service of mankind. Let us read from Shakespeare in King Henry IV:

"Oh God! that one might read the book of fate,
And see the revolution of the times,
Make mountains level, and the continent,
Weary of solid firmness melt itself.
Into the sea! and, other times, to see
The beachy girdle of the ocean
Too wide for old Neptune's hips; how chances mock,
And changes fill the cup of alteration
With divers liquors! Oh, if this were seen,
The happiest youth, viewing his progress through,
What perils past, what crosses to ensue,
Would shut the book and sit him down and die."

Jonathan Daniels, editor of the News and Observer, who has moved much among the great men of the Nation, had this to say:

"DARKEST FRIDAY

"Twenty years ago the courageous young commander of a PT boat in the South Pacific narrowly escaped death in the service of his country. Then yesterday in Texas, as the youngest American President ever to die, John Fitzgerald Kennedy fell in his country's service at the hand of a more evil enemy than young Americans have ever met in war.

"Shocked Americans quickly remembered the death in the Presidency of Franklin D. Roosevelt 18 years ago. But no equal and similar tragedy has occurred in the history of America since another dark Friday nearly a century ago when Abraham Lincoln was assassinated. And not even Lincoln's death came at a time when the Nation seemed so besieged by problems and danger. Lincoln lived to see victory and peace. John Kennedy, when he died, was still leading in a far more dangerous time.

"And the death of this great, young President emphasized as nothing else could have done that the dangers around him and around us all are not merely those involving foreign menace but home malice as well.

"The death of the young and brave and beautiful is always sad. The death of the chief of the greatest nation on earth shocks men and shakes history. But John Kennedy's death carried with it not only grief but an element of terror, too. Here in a State which regards itself as especially strong in its Americanism, among thousands of good people who were cheering their pride in the Commander of their country, malice struck its shining mark. It was incredible. It happened.

"John Kennedy will be remembered long. The sacrifice of his death needs to be taken to the shaken heart of the Nation now. There can be no safety in a nation where bitterness at home impels even one assassin to his horrid crime. America's honor, greatness, and glory made the assassin's target in Dallas Friday.

"The young President is dead. The old nation is grievously wounded. Hope lies only in the unity of grief and outrage which rose in the whole continent about John Kennedy's bier. The young man died in the service of his country. His proper mourning requires the solemn understanding of the meaning in his death that the poison of hate cannot only kill a man but the dream too of an America fit to lead the world."

We also quote from the Norfolk Ledger-Dispatch, whose editor is George J. Herbert, in an editorial, entitled

PRESIDENT JOHN F. KENNEDY

"Even today, as the fuller story is being pieced together of yesterday's ghastly events in Dallas, death of President John F. Kennedy is almost too much to take in. And that, surely, has been the common reaction of heartsick Americans across this land of ours.

"The shared reaction has been one of disbelief, disbelief that it could happen, and cold anger at the dark thing that overtook this country on Friday, November 22, 1963.

"History is no stranger to assassinations. We all know, too, of the minute-by-minute vulnerability of any man in the public eye and most particularly of chiefs of state. Our minds at least are familiar with the unpleasant reality that a madman is capable of anything, and that loose among us are the few—the deranged, the misled, the fanatics—upon whom neither society's restraints nor conscience have any effect.

"But these are things we comprehend with the intellect. What happened yesterday, at the hands of an assassin deeply involved in Communist doctrine and philosophy, is new and fresh and raw and goes deeper.

"What strikes to the heart is the contrast between yesterday afternoon's black headlines, the drumfire of grim bulletins by radio and television, with their engulfing grief for a whole nation, and the bright scene of only a few hours earlier as the people of a civilized country went about their free, generally prosperous affairs in the sunshine, reading in the early newspaper editions of their young President and his smiling wife moving easily and unafraid among them.

"President Kennedy was chosen through one of our cherished democratic processes to lead all of us. No one can question that he led with all the energy and considerable talents that were his. No one can doubt that most of his countrymen admired him as a whole; felt a deep personal attachment to him and Mrs. Kennedy. Barring the unforeseen, it had been generally acknowledged that he would have been entrusted with his high office for another 4 years by those same people.

"He combined intellect with the serviceable realism of a political pragmatist. He carried great responsibilities responsibly and displayed a sense of moderation that steered the country away from many of the extremes his election seemed to threaten in 1960. He had a warmth and humor that survived all the stress and strain of his gruelling days.

"As the Cuban crisis proved, he could rise to great heights of leadership when the chips were down, with a coolness that permitted intelligent planning and with a sure insight of the kind of strength the American people had put in his hands.

"He was the President of us all. He had our allegiance and our affection.

"America mourns the loss of a President and the senseless death of a good man."

[From the Southern Pines (N.C.) Pilot, Nov. 28, 1963]

THE TRUMPET SUMMONS US AGAIN

Now, after the body of John Fitzgerald Kennedy has been laid to rest, the Nation's dark night of the soul is ending—the night of anguish that fell upon the United States with the firing of an assassin's rifle last Friday.

There is no wakening from the past week's nightmare, for it was no dream. The lifting of the darkness, indeed, makes more hideous the reality of what has happened. But light is returning and Americans must live in the world that it reveals.

"Now," the slain President has asserted in his inaugural address, "the trumpet summons us again * * * to bear the burden of a long twilight struggle, year in and year out * * * a struggle against the common enemies of man: tyranny, poverty, disease, and war itself." The words ring with added grandeur as the Nation faces a new beginning after his death.

No greater tribute can be paid Mr. Kennedy than a thoughtful, fervent, unremitting commitment to that struggle. Nor is there now, in these United States, a more potent power, to dispel the darkness and rekindle hope, than those words.

A great leader has fallen. He has been replaced, in President Lyndon Baines Johnson, by another leader wholly committed to the noble tasks so eloquently outlined by the young President on that cold January 20, 1961.

We have full confidence in Mr. Johnson's leadership. But the people of the United States should remember that the dead President said, in words that move us even more deeply now: "In your hands, my fellow citizens, more than mine, will rest the final success or failure of our course."

Mr. Kennedy is gone. But as the past week's darkness lightens, there is great comfort in this thought: the people of the United States remain—to heed, if they will, the still-echoing, strong, young voice that placed supreme importance on their own efforts in setting and holding the Nation's future course.

Mindful of this, President Johnson and the people must now, together, "go forth to lead the land we love."

THEY CAME TO HONOR HIM

The coming here of national leaders from all over the world to attend the funeral of President Kennedy is an extraordinary thing.

The young American President, who had fallen so tragically under an assassin's bullet, had been in office less than 3 years. He had accomplished a few things—and a few great things; he was cut down in the promise of so much more.

He was young, his full powers not yet come to fruition, his brilliance, his energy, his devotion even not yet fully tried. And still, from lands far and near, allied or unfriendly still, they came, the leaders, to stand beside the young leader's grave.

AN AMERICAN HEROINE

Mrs. Jacqueline Bouvier Kennedy has won the undying admiration and affection of the American people and the world.

Gallant and brave beyond belief in the ordeal of her husband's sudden assassination and the ensuing series of events and ceremonies—all occurring in the public eye—she was at once so strong and so frail, so imperturable and so touchingly and ordinarily human, that she is now, without question, the most loved woman in the land.

Not once did she falter—and it was a performance of instinct, not conscious direction. She rode with the President's body on the plane from Texas, and when the body came off the plane, she was with it, touching the casket lightly, as though reaching out for a hand, and she rode with it, in the ambulance, to the Naval Hospital.

Her Sunday night return to the Capitol rotunda, where the body lay in state, was almost anonymous among the hundreds filing by, again to reach out, touch and kiss the casket like a child seeking reassurance: a heartbreaking incident. Yet one marveled, with vast respect, at the honest, strong compulsion that sent her back there, when lesser spirits would have retired under sedation.

A British observer defined her quality throughout as "majesty." Of course, she was worthy of the term, but to us it seemed grandiose. We know only that a new American heroine is on the scene.

This is a tribute to him and to our country made doubly strong by the circumstances under which they came. For so many necessary, important persons to come to the United States at this time is another extraordinary thing. For—it must be faced—in doing so they ran a serious risk.

General De Gaulle, the new Prime Minister of Britain and Prince Philip, the Germans, the Russians, the men of the new Africa, all these and the others are controversial figures and for each one there is an "anti" group in the mixed population of the United States. In any of these groups, these lunatic fringes of the far right or the far left, there are crackpots. Every crowd, such as the multitude that lined the streets of Washington, may contain a Lee Oswald; under such circumstances, no police force, even one far less negligent than that of Dallas, can assure protection.

That these factors were well understood by the visitors goes without saying. It is a well-known fact that four American Presidents have died at the hands of assassins and others had the narrowest of escapes. This country is a violent, dangerous land, especially right now.

The leaders who came risked their lives to honor this young man. Why? To them, as he did to us, Kennedy may have stood as a symbol of the hope of peace, the hope of goodness that persists in every man's heart. In the young President's flashing energy, his strong faith in the future and the ability of youth to rebuild it in a better image, they may have recognized a touch of greatness.

These leaders from foreign lands came because they honored him and they came because of the Nation that he represented. They know its faults. They know, and judge rightly, while they scorn, its dangers, but they recognize its will for goodness, its generous heart, its steadfast belief—despite much seeming evidence to the contrary—in the worth of the human spirit.

As these great leaders stood by the grave of John F.

Kennedy to do him honor, so let us honor them; for their faith in him and in the United States which he served so well and for the generous, brave spirit that brought them here to share our grief, to stand by us in our hour of trial.

When lilacs last in the dooryard bloom'd,
And the great star early droop'd in the western sky in
    the night.
I mourn'd, and yet shall mourn with ever-returning
    spring.
O powerful western fallen star!
O great star disappear'd—O the black murk that hides
    the star!
O harsh surrounding cloud that will not free my soul.
                  —WALT WHITMAN.
(After the assassination of President Lincoln.)

———

[From the Montgomery Herald, Troy, N.C., Nov. 28, 1963]

ASSASSINATION OF PRESIDENT REMINDS CITIZENS THAT SPREADING HATRED COULD DESTROY NATION

Perhaps it has all been said already.

The President is dead and around the world millions of words have been written and spoken about the man who was the 35th President of the United States, about his contributions to mankind, and about the dastardly deed which took his life.

The shots which rang out on a crowded Dallas street last Friday were, indeed, heard around the world. The sounds of these shots, and what they mean, will reverberate for time to come.

During the long hours following President John F. Kennedy's assassination, millions of grieving Americans paused for moments of self-examination.

People thought serious thoughts. Many people wondered aloud what has happened to our civilized society. Many wondered whether they themselves have allowed seeds of hate to become sown so widely and deeply that hatred threatens to destroy this Nation's way of life.

The easiest way to write off this terrible thing, of course, is to say that the act of assassination was by the hand of a warped individual. But, we must remember that the fires of hatred, fanned by "sane" individuals, help to warp and twist other men's minds.

Friday wasn't the first time that there have been signs of hatred in Dallas. Just a few weeks ago United Nations Ambassador Adlai Stevenson was besieged by an angry mob in Dallas and spat upon. The ugly head of hatred has reared itself in other places in the land.

And, need we not kid ourselves, Dallas and other "trouble spots" are not the only spawning places for the seeds of hatred. Who among us has not been guilty, at one time or another, of uttering statements about things and people—yes, even the late President—which would tend to build hatred in our own minds as well as in the minds of others?

Freedom of speech is a precious heritage which gives all Americans the right to disagree, but we must not use this freedom to build corruptive hate which can only destroy the very things we hold so dear.

It may well be that the events of the past weekend, as tragic as they were, will result in the greatest and most lasting memorial to the late President. Not a stone and concrete memorial, but a memorial in men's minds to remind them that there is no place for hatred and malice in a civilized world.

We've a feeling that this great American would like such a memorial.

THERE'S STILL MUCH FOR WHICH TO BE THANKFUL

Still mourning the loss of a President, and still in a state of shock, Americans today pause to give thanks to the Almighty for their many blessings. It's Thanksgiving Day, 1963.

On the heels of the tragic events of the past few days many people may be inclined to feel that there is little to be thankful for this year. They are wrong.

For one thing, they can be thankful for the form of government under which we live. Not a perfect process, to be sure, it is still the best to be devised by mankind.

And, they can be thankful for their forebears who built the framework of our Government. The vivid events of the past few days demonstrate that they took their work seriously and overlooked no detail in assuring this Nation of leadership.

A President can die, but the office must continue. Last week, within minutes after President John F. Kennedy was slain there was a new President and the wheels of government continued uninterrupted.

Americans were brought close to the tragedy through the medium of television, and we believe all Americans felt a feeling of thankfulness for our Democracy.

Americans, too, on this Thanksgiving Day will want to thank God that the Nation has leadership in abundance. While we mourn the loss of President Kennedy, we are thankful that a man with the capabilities and the courage of President Johnson was standing in the wings ready to assume the awesome burden of the office.

Each citizen, of course, has many personal things for which he can give thanks. It is, indeed, a dark period in our lives, but out of the clouds of darkness there comes rays of bright hope for the future.

Let us all pause this day to give thanks for the great blessings we are privileged to enjoy.

———

[From the Washington (N.C.) Daily News, November 1963]

A NATION'S CONSCIENCE AND A BLEEDING HEART

The death of John Fitzgerald Kennedy, President of the United States, is at this very moment touching the lives of people over the world in every walk of life.

There are no mitigating circumstances surrounding his death. He was killed in cold blood, and a Nation's conscience is hurting, and it will continue to hurt for a long time. The heart of the entire world is bleeding, and with every drop of blood, there is the realization that a friend of man has given his life in the causes he deemed right and just.

It matters little the name of the assassin, or his age, color, political beliefs, or why he chose to pain the Nation's conscience or bleed the world's heart with this dastardly act.

People in America and people over the world often disagreed with Mr. Kennedy. But in America particularly we live in a land where the right to disagree is as sacred as the right to agree. Surely, John F. Kennedy would have been the last to deny that principle and the first to hold high its banner.

America has lost so very much, but this great loss is not America's alone. John F. Kennedy belonged to the world. Today wherever one lives, and regardless of what one believes, the knowledge is general that mankind has lost a great friend and a true leader.

Mr. Kennedy died fighting for the principles in which he believed. When we begin to think of how much greatness this Nation and the world have lost, the pain of shock becomes so much greater. What a brilliant young man. What a world statesman he could have been when his term of office was finished.

Men die on battlefields, and we never know what measure of greatness they might have given the world. Somewhere on the bloody beaches of Normandy or Anzio, or in the barren coldness of the 38th parallel might lie the remains of some boy, who had he lived, might have given us the cure for cancer or the key that would unlock the secret of world peace or who might have provided the leadership that would have brought political or moral or spiritual greatness to a world torn asunder. To what heights might have Mr. Kennedy gone? We'll never know, but if we could judge the future by the past, we might conclude that the opportunities ahead are limitless.

Yes, Mr. Kennedy, friend to man, champion of this time of history, and fighter to the end, lies still today. But the seeds he has grown and the paths he has explored shall one day bear a bountiful harvest of fruit.

He was our President. He died with his boots on. The mortal man is dead, but the impact lives on. And it shall live in the hearts and minds of men for a long, long time.

America mourns; the world mourns; we all have lost more than we realize.

[From the Warren Record, Warrenton, N.C., Nov. 29, 1963]

JOHN F. KENNEDY

Whether John F. Kennedy will be listed among the great Presidents of the United States history can only tell; that he was a great American there can be no doubt; but that he was beloved has been attested to by the tears of a mourning public, and the sense of depression that gripped the Nation for days following his assassination in Dallas last Friday.

Mixed with the tears and with the sense of loss has been a sense of national shame that such a thing could have happened in America.

The great and the mighty of this Nation and of the nations of the world have paid their tribute to the man, to his courage, his love of his country, his personal warmth, and his compassion for the weak. Now there remains little to say.

We think that in his death a little of us all died. We had watched him on TV, seen his pictures on magazine covers, heard his cultured voice on radio and TV until he had become almost a part of us. Even those who did not care for his views on domestic issues, admired the man as an individual, and most of us were proud that a family such as the Kennedys were in the White House.

It has been said that a man is part of all whom he has known. Certainly the memories of John F. Kennedy and his two few days in the White House will be with us the days of our life. Memory paints a picture of a young man in 1956 at the Democratic National Convention when he almost won the Democratic nomination for Vice President. We remember 4 years later his successful fight for the nomination of his party for President, how we were early won to his cause and pulled for him as the fight waged for the nomination. We remember his campaign, the TV debates, his winning the election, and his great inaugural address when he pled for the American people to "think not what your country can do for you, but what you can do for your country."

That it all had to end in such a tragic manner is truly heartbreaking.

John F. Kennedy was not only blessed with courage, stamina and an excellent mind; he was blessed with one of the truly great women of this age as his wife. People who did not like the President, learned to love his wife, for her tact, her beauty, her culture, and her courage.

Among the memories of the ceremonies connected with the death of President Kennedy, we think we shall never forget the picture of sheer courage and devotion shown by this woman. We will always remember her at the airport entering the hearse to ride to the White House with the remains of her husband. We will remember her standing before the bier of her husband in the rotunda of the Capitol, hiding her grief, as she held the hands of her little boy, 3, Monday, and girl, 6, Wednesday; and how leaving them for a moment she approached the flag-covered casket, knelt and kissed the coffin that contained the remains of her husband.

The sympathy of the Nation not only goes out to Mrs. Kennedy and her children, but to his old father and to his mother, who had already suffered the loss of one son in World War II, the loss of a daughter in an airplane crash in 1948, who have known the heartaches of a retarded child; and to his brothers and sisters making up one of America's most devoted families.

The sympathy of the Nation also goes to the new President Lyndon Johnson, who not only lost the friendship of a man whom he had learned to love but had the great problems of the world dropped into his lap with the firing of a shot. The prayers of America will be with him in his ordeal and, we believe, the support of the people.

As the last muffled drumbeat died, and the body of a beloved President was returned to the earth, the phrase that comes to us is from Horatio's farewell to Hamlet:

"Goodnight, Sweet Prince."

[From the West Jefferson (N.C.) Skyland Post, Nov. 28, 1963]

JOHN FITZGERALD KENNEDY

The tragic and untimely death of President John F. Kennedy, 46, at the hand of an assassin in Dallas, Tex., Friday brought shock and grief to this Nation and the world.

This 35th President of the United States put service above self. He was a leader who had accomplished much but who had more plans for the future. For this reason it is too soon to evaluate his real worth to this Nation and the world. History will in time record this and we believe history will prove him to be one of the greatest Presidents of all times.

He was a man known and loved, not only by Americans, but by people throughout the world. The grief over his tragic death at the hands of a sniper has been profound and been expressed by practically all countries in the world except Communist China. In West Berlin 60,000 torchbearers marched and a street was renamed "John F. Kennedy." In England, fundraising was started to erect a monument for him and a service was held in Westminster Abbey. In other countries there were more expressions of grief and sympathy.

President Kennedy championed the cause of the poor and the less fortunate, but kings, queens, presidents, and other world leaders mourned and came to Washington to his funeral to pay final tribute to this young leader cut down in the prime of life.

President Kennedy had served his country as a naval officer in war, but he was willing and ready to leave nothing undone to keep the peace of the world. But his peace was a peace of dignity and respect.

President Kennedy was a wealthy man, but he knew and understood the problems of the poor and worked for their health and welfare.

He was an educated man and realized the value of education for all Americans.

He was a fearless man of great courage and the last lines of his book "Profiles in Courage" were written with his life's blood.

He was inaugurated as President during a blizzard and brought to this Nation's Capital a real breath of fresh air. In the short period he served, less than 3 years, he has thrown out many challenges. How we accept them from his fallen hand depends upon our sense of individual responsibility.

These are indeed trying times, but they are times to rally behind the new President, Lyndon Baines Johnson, and give him the support he deserves for the heavy tasks that have been thrust upon him.

————

[From the Whiteville (N.C.) News Reporter, Nov. 25, 1963]

ASK WHAT YOU CAN DO

All the world is aware now of the atrocity committed in this country last Friday. Free people and the oppressed everywhere have lost a friend and this Nation has lost a great President and a dedicated public servant.

The courageous leader of this land's 180 million has been struck down by an assassin's unerring aim was a shot heard—and felt—around the world.

John Fitzgerald Kennedy gave his life in the line of duty and now rests with other heroes in the National Cemetery at Arlington, Va.

Some 20 years ago he was spared, prophetically, in the Pacific fighting for a cause that this Nation and its freedom-loving allies might live in peace and decency. Now he has joined many of his buddies of that frightful war.

We can ill afford the loss but the despicable deed has been done. The great promise and brilliance with which Mr. Kennedy was endowed is lost for all time. He had been honored with the highest office this Nation could give but, relatively youthful, the potential of his gift for leadership and wisdom gave great promise of strength in future years.

There were those who disagreed with some of the principles Mr. Kennedy espoused and there were those in whose hearts some phases of his domestic program created resentment, even open defiance, but true Americans bore him no hate as was exemplified last Friday. He fought for what he thought was best and proper for his fellow countrymen and not to the sacrifice of one group against another but for all people.

This outrageous act at Dallas, Tex., last Friday has brought shame to this land—haven for the depressed, home of the orphaned, friend of all who love liberty, and benefactor of mankind in many lands beyond our shores. No nation, near or remote, has been denied succor when that nation, great or weak, made its plea in good faith.

The memory of Mr. Kennedy will live for generations and many of his prophetic statements will abide forever. So it is now, in these trying hours, a time to rededicate ourselves to that soul-searching appeal he expressed in his inaugural address almost 3 years ago:

"Ask not what your country can do for you but ask what you can do for your country."

————

[From the Wilmington (N.C.) Morning Star, Nov. 23, 1963]

A NATION MOURNS ITS PRESIDENT

"He's dead."

Those words shocked a great nation and much of the remainder of the world into cold and deep silence yesterday afternoon. And it will be a long time before the numbness of the assassination of President Kennedy leaves the hearts and minds of millions of people.

The horror of the tragedy is difficult to appraise and put into words.

In one moment, a happy President was enjoying his visit to one of the Nation's fine cities. Minutes later he entered death's door. Why? Because of the warped deadly brain of a single person.

President Kennedy, like many other great men stricken down at their heights, now belongs to the ages. His supporters and his critics quietly join hands in their mutual respect as they pay homage to a man who literally gave his life for his country. This sad day transcends party lines and differences, big and small, because all Americans realize their President, dedicated to fulfilling his big and demanding role, is gone. One of the most dastardly acts of all time has taken our leader, in the prime and vigor of his life, away.

Today men of all faiths and political parties share a loss that has brought the Nation to a standstill. As these men measure their sadness, they are aware of the challenge ahead. That challenge is to act for the better welfare of the United States in the same spirit—placement of love of country and devotion to duty above all else—that motivated the life of President Kennedy.

The Nation is offered sound, moderate leadership in the new President—Lyndon Johnson. The tasks ahead for him will not be easy. He will need the people's thoughtful, unwavering support. May Americans resolve to fulfill this need as they offer their deepest sympathy to Mrs. Kennedy and the family in their darkest hour.

———

[From the Wilmington (N.C.) Morning Star, Nov. 24, 1963]

WELCOME THE NEW LEADER

As shock ebbs from the minds of Americans it is replaced with profound grief in their hearts over the assassination of President Kennedy.

Untold millions feel a personal loss as the details of one of the most dastardly deeds in history are unfolded. Regardless of whether a person liked or disliked Mr. Kennedy, if he is a true patriot his sadness is comparable to that over the loss of a member of the family if for no other reason than his reverence for the Presidency. As the deep meaning of this awesome tragedy sweeps over the Nation, good people ask themselves: What can I do, other than through my prayers, in memory of a man who gave his life for his country and in behalf of his successor, President Lyndon B. Johnson?

As that question is asked, it is likely those famous words from Mr. Kennedy's inaugural address will come to mind:

"And so, my fellow Americans, ask not what your country can do for you; ask what you can do for your country."

The first thing to do is to follow the example of true unity, regardless of partisan politics or other factors, set by the Nation's leaders in the hours following the murder of Mr. Kennedy. History has proved, time and time again, that when bitterness and selfishness are thrust aside the beauty of America's greatness in her dark hours is brilliant to behold.

Next, let there be no doubt in any mind as to the ability, desire and spirit of President Johnson to take up his tremendous responsibilities. Of all men who have stepped from the Vice Presidency to the White House, he is the best qualified from experience, knowledge and courage for the new and larger job. His many years in Government have trained him well as a skilled and respected leader. And remember, he was selected for his role by Mr. Kennedy himself.

As the Nation turns toward its new leadership, it should easily find spiritual inspiration for powerful unity and eagerness to support President Johnson in the demanding days ahead. Seldom before has the need for solidarity been greater, not only among ourselves but in demonstration to a watchful world. May it prevail every hour in behalf of the security and continued welfare of the United States as the leader of the free people of the world.

———

[From the Wilmington (N.C.) Morning Star, Nov. 26, 1963]

THE MESSAGE HE LEFT

It is over.

The massive picture, drawn for endless hours in countless scenes and words, of the martyrdom of President John F. Kennedy is no longer before the misty eyes of millions. But much of this tragic panorama is burned deep in the memory of Americans. As they look back, they feel weary in their knowledge they have suffered through a nightmare which the most fantastic fiction could not match in its incredibility.

The bizarre series of events which began with a rifle shot in Dallas last Friday is over—thank God. Its final and total evaluation is now a task for the historians.

But one thing will never be over.

It is the message in the untimely death of the 35th President of the United States.

Mr. Kennedy perhaps could deliver it better than anyone else through application of the powerful oratory he mastered so well. But his lips are cold and silent as the world mourns its loss. So others must speak. But that should not be difficult—if the speaker believes in God, the dignity of man, and the prevalence of law and order. Why? Because the message is so simple. It is:

Hate is the most powerful weapon known to man.

Modern man fears the nuclear bomb. He is just as much afraid of its vehicles of delivery. He knows planes and rockets can smash the bomb down on him and millions of his countrymen in the space of a few minutes. So as the first means of protection masses of men curb their hate as they strive for even a shred of genuine hope for eternal peace.

It was no massive nuclear bomb but a simple bullet fired from a $12.78 mail-order rifle, that ended the world of John F. Kennedy. The bullet was sent into its fatal flight by just one thing—the hate of one man for mankind.

Seldom does the Bible itself match the irony of this story in the death of Lee Harvey Oswald from a bullet in his body from another gun, only hours after the Kennedy murder.

Thus, a second merchant of hate, a man named Jack Ruby, was given the spotlight in Dallas, a city whose damnation seldom has been matched in history.

The end of Oswald was as certain as a direct hit by a nuclear bomb.

Once again, hate sent a fatal bullet into its deadly flight. It was a chain reaction.

It is readily admitted Oswald and Ruby are not average individuals. That is true—but they certainly are not the only people with hate-filled heads in this land.

Are the dastardly deeds in Dallas to be accepted as a mounting trend of uncontrolled violence? Are we to believe that the honor—and life—of the Presidency and the rights of the Constitution are worth no more than mere bullets? Is it to be that the problems of this Nation have surpassed the civilized means of solution? Is hate to rule?

Those questions are asked for the thought they may provoke.

Hate can kill nations as readily and as deadly as it kills men. Never before has it been more important for Americans to remember that—and let their highest interpretation of that thought guide them in their relations with each other and the world.

That, we believe, is the message President Kennedy left.

———

[From the Wilson (N.C.) Daily Times, November 1963]

THE NATION MOURNS FOR THE PRESIDENT

Out of the clear of everyday living came the word that the President of the United States of America, John F. Kennedy, is dead. He was killed by an assassin's bullet.

Smiling, waving and happy was the last picture he gave the people of Dallas, Tex., as he rode in the parade in his honor, in that city. This was the picture you associate with the youngest President ever to take the highest office in the land. He was young, young in spirit, often young in actions, but always vibrant, and thoughtful, and brilliant.

His young wife and their two children bring to mind the picture that is truly international, the picture of a happy family, carrying the responsibility of the biggest job on earth, with a relish and desire to carry forward for another term. For the President was in Texas on both a national and fence-mending mission.

The people of this Nation were stunned. You read over and again the words "incredible," "beyond comprehension," "unbelievable," and "tragic." While the Nation is trying to recover from the shock, the leaders of the world send words of condolence, respect and admiration for the young, but forceful leader.

It is difficult to reconcile the President's assassination with this modern age in which we live. Who his assassin is, has not been decided. It really does not matter because his deed so outweighs all other circumstances. If he was killed by a fanatic, by one either possessed of misguided national zeal or by one whose twisted mind led him to believe he was serving some cause, is of little consequence.

For we, of this age, have witnessed an event we did not think could happen. For only three Presidents before have been assassinated. The first was Abraham Lincoln, the 16th President of the United States, the President during the Civil War who was shot by John Wilkes Booth. Today he is known as the Great Emancipator. And we predict that President Kennedy will in our lifetime be called by many a second Abraham Lincoln the martyr of this age.

The other Presidents assassinated were James Abram Garfield, the 20th President who was shot in the station in Washington. He was going to Williams College, Williamston, Mass., to attend commencement exercises.

William McKinley, the 25th President was shot while attending a reception in one of the public buildings of the Pan-American Exposition in Buffalo, N.Y.

President Kennedy was a man of great ability, personality, and talent. He held the admiration of many and the respect of all. Whether you agreed with him or not, you recognized his ability and you respected his intentions. He will go down in history as a great President, and his tragic death will add luster to an already brilliant career, as a patriot, a statesman, and as the President of the United States.

From the tragedy we must come to grips with the fact that our own internal problems are more dire, more serious than those of international scope. This Nation must heal its differences. And the tragic death of the President should teach us that the strength of a Nation is built upon understanding and not bitterness, not arms but the heart. If progress is made in this direction, he will not have died in vain.

———

[From the Bertie Ledger-Advance, Windsor, N.C., November 1963]

GREAT NATIONS SURVIVE

The President is dead. His body lies buried on a hillside in Arlington Cemetery. Life and government for the people of America go on.

These are not facts that the people of Bertie County do not know. In this day of continuous on-the-spot television and radio coverage there is little that is not known throughout the land. Where these media have stopped, the daily newspapers have provided printed coverage.

What is there left for a weekly newspaper editor to say? Is there need to say anything more? In ordinary circumstances a news item so far away from the coverage area of a country weekly would go unnoticed.

But the past few days have been no ordinary days. The world has been affected in a moment of history when the President of the United States was mortally wounded.

Shocked, saddened, disgusted, sickened, grief stricken * * * these are expressions used to describe feelings yet these words seem inadequate and there are none better to describe what Americans have felt since 2 p.m., Friday.

Washington, New York, Los Angeles, Boston, Dallas have no monopoly on grief. People wept in these places. People wept too in Windsor and Colerain, in Aulander and Lewiston and in every crossroad and hamlet where this great leader was known.

These events have passed. As flags continued to fly at half mast, tears cease. A leader has fallen—a nation still stands. The future of this Nation has been affected but thank God there is a future remaining. Great leaders are mortal, great nations survive.

John Fitzgerald Kennedy was a Christian man. Perhaps in his death he accomplished something that would never have been accomplished in life. He caused millions of people to feel a need to return to God. In churches, cathedrals, and synagogues they went to pray—in tribute to his memory and in search of peace in their hearts.

It takes a tragedy to bring us to our knees for we have become a self-sufficient people who often forget The One who makes all things possible.

In sorrow we were united. Perhaps in days to come we will be united in joy. For this is America, a land where people came and still do to escape the events such as those of the past weekend. It couldn't happen here we were sure.

But it did. It happened this time in Dallas. It could happen in Windsor. It could happen anywhere in the world where regard for God's laws as well as man's laws are forgotten.

The late President was so representative of America's basic conception. He sought peace yet he was unafraid to face danger to fight for ideals. He pressed forward toward accomplishment with determination and in so doing lost personal support but gained strength for the Nation.

No more appropriate monument can be built to his memory than the eternal flame lighted at his grave by Mrs. Kennedy. We will miss him but names and personalities are soon erased.

May the eternal light at his grave be the torch to kindle a spark of love for mankind, peace, and good will that will continue this Nation on its course as:

"America, the beautiful,
The land of the free
And the home of the brave."

—LAURA HARRELL.

[From the Winston-Salem (N.C.) Journal,
Nov. 23, 1963]

JOHN F. KENNEDY

The proper epitaph for John Fitzgerald Kennedy might well be an American variant of a royal motto: He served.

He served his country as a naval officer in conditions of brutal trial and danger—a danger which called for a test of loyalty to his fellow man and all but cost him his life.

He served his State as a Senator. And though his political beginnings were unpromising, he achieved by hard work a mastery of national and world affairs that few of his contemporaries could equal.

He served the Nation again as President and Commander in Chief. In the span of less than 3 years he experienced all the grandeur and the misery of the Presidency, and he accepted both with equal serenity.

Now he has been struck down by an act of hate.

John Kennedy, as we all know, had the love of countless Americans. He knew in those exciting days of 1960 and the years that immediately followed the welcoming roar of the crowd in the streets, the frantic handclasp of the well-wishers who slipped past his bodyguards, and the "God bless you, Jack" that came from an unknown voice in the crowd.

He also knew—and let us be honest with ourselves in this moment of grief—the hatred of too many Americans. These unworthy ones held him accountable, as Americans have often held their leaders accountable in the past, for the very problems that any man in the President's office would have had to face.

Now these problems are waiting for the new President. They are familiar enough—the antagonism of the races, the malevolence of the Russians and all those they have infected with the Communist virus; the costs of national security, and all the strains in our society and the world at large brought on by the new nationalism, the Russian and Chinese revolutions, and the concurrent industrial, electronic and atomic revolutions.

There they are waiting, these problems, on the desk of President Lyndon Baines Johnson.

To meet them in a worthy way, he will need the love and the confidence of his fellow Americans.

So let there be a truce to hate.

And, conscious of our incomparable power and all that depends on it, let us unite behind our new President, raising a prayer that he will prove worthy of the trust.

[From the Winston-Salem (N.C.) Journal, Nov. 26, 1963]

A COURAGEOUS LADY

It can be truly said that nothing became Mrs. John F. Kennedy as First Lady so much as the courage and simple dignity with which she shared her grief.

Among the indelible memories of these past few days, none is etched more deeply than the sight of this slender young woman in black—bending to speak to her young children, kneeling at her husband's casket, lighting the eternal torch at his grave.

Other women have met the sudden death of their husbands as courageously. But no other woman in history, including Mrs. Franklin Delano Roosevelt, has been called on to suffer this private ordeal so publicly.

It is the price Mrs. Kennedy paid both for having been the wife of the President of the United States, whose death belonged to the people, and for living in the age of technology in which human emotions, like public events, can be viewed by millions.

Longfellow has said that "there is no grief like the grief that does not speak." And the lines of Mrs. Kennedy's silent grief were all too evident behind her mourning veil.

But throughout the long and exhausting ritual, she bore the burden of her position with a composure which we could not have asked but which has made her country proud.

There is little the Nation can say to Mrs. Kennedy as she takes off the mantle of First Lady which she wore so well—except, perhaps, to borrow the words that Abraham Lincoln once wrote to a woman who had lost her sons in battle:

"I pray that our Heavenly Father may assuage the anguish of your bereavement, and leave you only the cherished memory of the loved and lost, and the solemn pride that must be yours, to have laid so costly a sacrifice upon the altar of freedom."

[From the Twin City Sentinel, Winston-Salem, N.C., Nov. 23, 1963]

A DEATH IN THE FAMILY

A great many words have been said during the past 24 hours—some of them eloquent, but most in the simple, halting speech of people deeply grieved.

Few of us knew John F. Kennedy as a person. Many did not agree with his policies; some openly fought him. If nearly half the voters of this country had had their way 3 years ago, he would not have been President yesterday, riding in ceremonial splendor through the streets of Dallas.

But the point is, Mr. Kennedy was the President yesterday. And suddenly, stunningly, the President was dead.

Never mind now his politics, his personality, his race, or his religion. All over Winston-Salem, as in every town in every corner of the Nation, people are reacting to his death as though he had been a member of their own family.

The President of the United States is that close to the people.

In a book written for children a few years ago, Gerald W. Johnson touched on why this is so. "No country," he said, "and most certainly no democracy can last long without leadership. But in a democracy the people choose the leadership, so when all is said and done, they are responsible for it, whether it is good or bad."

We did not all help put John Kennedy into the Presidency. But all of us believe in, live by, and bear responsibility for the system that put him there. Thus believing, we hold dear both the office and the life of the man who occupies it, whatever his name may be.

So it is that the bullet which killed Mr. Kennedy yesterday has grazed the lives of us all and left its scar.

[From the Caswell Messenger, Yanceyville, N.C., Nov. 28, 1963]

CONFIDENTIALLY

(By Erwin B. Stephens)

As this is being written the muffled drumbeats in the funeral cortege of President John F. Kennedy can be heard over the airwaves, bringing a sorrowful sense of finality to one act of one of the most tragic dramas in American history.

Why did it have to happen? Over and over again the question repeats itself in the minds of millions of citizens. Why? A sense of shame and outrage swelled in the hearts of many that a shameful incident should occur in a great Christian nation. We had read about such things in other less fortunate nations; now it had happened to us.

But something of the strength and great spirit of the American people welled up to the surface as the tragic events unfolded. People of all walks of life, of all creeds and colors, came forth with a great outpouring of sympathy and expressions of tribute to one of the great men of the day.

Out of the whole tragic series of events over the week-end one can gain reassurance as to the basic strength of the people of this Nation. People who disagreed in part or in whole with the political philosophy of the President felt just as deep a sense of outrage at the dastardly crime as those who were in accord with his programs and beliefs. To everyone, this was not just a crime against the President or his party; it was a crime against all the people, for in a very real sense the Presidency is symbolic of the ideals and spirit of the American people. It holds a warm place in their hearts.

The people of America are a people of many divergent opinions, of many creeds and faiths, of divergent political philosophies. This is their strength; this is the strength of the Nation. Even the lowliest person can voice freely his disapproval of the acts of a chief executive without fear of retribution or bodily harm. Such is the freedom we possess and cherish. Such is the right that more than half the people of the world do not possess. Yet, despite such divergent opinions, in a time of national emergency or crisis, our people can unite as one, stand solid as a rock against anyone or anything that threatens our own.

Totalitarian subjects and rulers cannot understand Americans. Standing at a distance and viewing the American scene, hearing of our domestic and political squabbles, they might get the idea that the Republic is about to fall apart, that the plum is ripe for the picking. But how wrong they are. They cannot, and perhaps never will, understand how Americans can unite under stress and throw their whole resources into a common cause with zest and enthusiasm, and with a determination that cannot be deterred.

The President's death at the hands of an assassin brings into sharp focus one phase of American life which should be the concern of every rational citizen: The increase in crime and the growing trend toward violations of the laws of our land. Time and again ministers, leaders, and law enforcement officers have pointed out this trend and have sought to arouse the public to its dangers. J. Edgar Hoover, boss of the FBI, constantly sends out bulletins warning of the inherent dangers of increasing violations of the law. Our country was founded by Christian people on the foundation stone of law and order. Every violation of law, whether it be for speeding, trespassing on another's property, or for more serious offenses, chips a little more from the foundation of our Nation and contributes to the chaos which would exist if law and order breaks down. No chain is stronger than its weakest link, and any person who violates any law weakens the system which provides him, and others, with safety in his own pursuit of his goals.

In recent years we have read the statements of those who proclaimed that they would violate what they called bad laws in order to achieve what they called good ends. Such a philosophy is absurd and irresponsible and has no place in American life. It is a foreign philosophy which should never be permitted to take root in American society. Good cannot be achieved by violating the laws enacted by the representatives of the people in the interest of all the people. If we think a law is wrong or harmful, we have the right and duty to use our influence to have that law repealed by the proper authorities. That is what legislatures are for, and the process of changing, repealing, or amending laws goes on year after year in an effort to achieve greater good for more people. But when we take the law into our own hands and violate those which are distasteful to us we take the wrong stand and use our influence in the wrong way. Such a stand leads only to chaos and destruction.

[From station WBT, Charlotte, N.C., Nov. 23, 1963]

THE PRESIDENT'S DEATH

For the fourth time in the history of this country, a President of the United States has paid with his life for his fidelity to the principle that the Chief Executive of this free nation can walk among his people unafraid that even his bitterest enemy will lay a violent hand on him.

This terrible day demonstrates for all of us the failure, and the success, of our democracy. Assassination is detested by Americans of all parties and factions, and it is impossible for any of us to believe that an assassin is a man of sound mind.

Yet the President is dead—and to the extent that even one man in this Nation was so deluded as to imagine that taking the life of another would solve any problem, personal or political, our building of a civilized society has failed.

The murderer may be captured and brought to justice, but the vengeance of the law does not in the least diminish this tragedy which, by its very unexpectedness, has reduced the country to a state of shocked unbelief. His punishment cannot assuage the grief of John Kennedy's family and children or replace the shattered illusions of all of us who imagined that our society's conduct was living up to its capacity for good.

Our success lies in the fact that a blow of this kind does not upset our Government or result in wild disorder, as it would in many countries. Our new President, chastened as he must be by the stopping of that single heartbeat that separated him from the most awesome responsibility in the world, will receive the unstinted support and encouragement of the whole American people during his difficult period of adjustment.

It has been said that he who serves his country well builds his own monument. John F. Kennedy was a brilliant and personable, dedicated and courageous young man. He inspired the intense loyalty of his friends and the respect of his political opponents. He had a certain gentility that won people of all faiths, an earnestness in the service of his country that could not be denied, and a humanness that gave him that most engaging of qualities, the ability to laugh at himself.

There were many who disagreed with him violently on national or international policies, but few who were willing to credit him with any other than the highest patriotic motives. There should be none who would have denied him the right to serve as this Nation's elected leader.

The atmosphere of freedom allows the fanatic the right to life and liberty, too. But the man who turns to cowardly violence has denied our heritage, our pride as a Nation, and the God who has led us to greatness in the past.

[From station WBT, Charlotte, N.C., Dec. 4, 1963]

THE CHALLENGE OF THE FUTURE

Yesterday's headlines are growing a little more dim as we retreat into everyday reality. Let's look at them again for just a moment: "The President of the United States died of a head wound inflicted by an assassin"—"His killer was not brought to justice, but died himself by violent means"—"The new President is a man named Johnson, from a Southern State, and faces the difficult task of reconciling a nation at odds with itself."

Those identical headlines might be a week old or 98 years old. All of them apply with equal accuracy to the assassinations of Abraham Lincoln and John F. Kennedy. There is perhaps little in the string of coincidences, except for one startling reminder: that history has a way of repeating itself and of serving up a grim notice to current generations of the fact that progress has not been so great as we imagine it to be. The progress of mechanical civilization, yes—the progress of human comprehension, no.

We live in a very different world from Mr. Lincoln's so far as our external lives are concerned, but it is no different a world of the mind and heart and spirit.

The main change those 98 years have wrought is in the personal involvement of all humanity, rather than just one nation, in such a tragic event. Mr. Lincoln never left the United States, met no other heads of state or peoples of the world personally. His voice was never heard by them, his decisions as President could touch them only indirectly. Certainly, he was admired, as a character in a book might be admired, and his death was regretted, but it was a personal blow to very few outside his own Nation.

He said he lived in a nation half slave and half free, and that such a situation could not long endure. Now, we live in a world half slave and half free, and there is no reason to suppose that Mr. Lincoln's prediction for the Nation does not now apply to the world.

If the unprecedented gathering of heads of state to pray together leads us all to realize that they might as quickly gather to confer together with compassion in their hearts, rather than personal gain, then perhaps it might be said that our President's death was a sacrifice he would have been willing to make.

Even more certainly, if the people of this Nation can realize the tremendous responsibility and opportunity we have been offered, to be a leader in daring new ways rather than the hackneyed techniques of government sparring in diplomacy, the world can experience—under God—a new birth of freedom.

[From station WSOC, Charlotte, N.C., Nov. 29, 1963]

THE LESSONS WE HAVE LEARNED

From the tragic death of President Kennedy, many lessons can and must be learned by our people.

We should have learned by now that the Office of the Chief Executive is never occupied by a superman, but by a person of the same flesh and bones and feelings as ourselves. The President can be injured or destroyed, not merely by bullets, but by hatred and invective and abuse.

We have seen too how fragile one human life can be, and how it can be snuffed out in a moment of wild madness, and how the taking of that life can be a frightening loss to countless millions of men, women, and children throughout the world.

We have seen how a happy family—a courageous husband, a dauntless wife, and two marvelous young children, can be ripped apart by the blast of a single gun. And it should remind us that we all need to tie our individual families together more closely with sincere love and trust and affectionate concern. This should awaken in the hearts of all partners in marriage a resolution to cherish one another, and as parents to lavish the warmth of real devotion and understanding upon our children, and to let this same love and understanding spread to our neighbors and friends and to all mankind.

Only in this way can we make meaningful the beauty and majesty and the grand design of our democratic, constitutional system of government.

It should be obvious now that we cannot laugh or curse or blaspheme any person or any office, without demeaning ourselves and our Nation.

For this is our country, and it will stand or fall on what each of us says and does each day of his life.

As we assess the weakness and fear that we felt when our President was so abruptly taken from our midst there should be a dawning in our minds of the part that we must play if we are to make sure that such violence does not again strike our country or terror stalk our citizens in any home, any community or any State.

We have been taught a costly lesson in citizenship and the responsibilities that every person is born to inherit in our democratic government:

This Nation will be strong and healthy only so long as we individually give it strength through unselfish allegiance.

This land will be peaceful and tranquil, only so long as we insure its tranquility through law and order.

We must learn to live with one another, resisting hatred and envy, overcoming the ugly passions of arrogance and false judgment. We must not attack but support, we must not tear down but build up, preserve, and protect.

These are lessons we can learn. These are lessons we must learn if we are to keep the soul of our country clean, and make the future of our Nation secure.

[From station WSOC, Charlotte, N.C., November 1963]

UNITED WE STAND

Although we regret that it took the death of a President of the United States to do it, WSOC radio is encouraged to see the leaders of the world's democratic countries set aside disagreements and rally together in a time of crisis.

It was a moving experience to see the austere Charles de Gaulle of France, the new Chancellor Ludwig Erhardt of West Germany, Mayor Willy Brandt, the symbol of a free Berlin and many, many more of the most influential leaders of the world, all gathered together in Washington to pay their last respects to this country's late President. This indicates several things. It shows a basic unity among all of the free people of the world. It proves that for all our petty arguments and disagreements, when the chips are down, our allies can be depended on to stand behind us. And it symbolizes this country's past—and future—role as a global leader.

Our new President can now move forward in his demanding job with the full knowledge that he has the support and best wishes of the leaders of the free world.

[From station WHIT, New Bern, N.C., Nov. 29, 1963]

JOHN F. KENNEDY

Just one short week ago today John F. Kennedy was assassinated in a terrible drama that goes down as the most dastardly act of this century. The aftermath of that infamous day brought many heart-tugging episodes that will long be remembered: There was the secret service man who quickly threw himself upon then Vice President Johnson when the shooting began, at the risk of the former's own life. There was the "Profile in Courage" composure of Jackie Kennedy during the ordeal, her late and second visit to the Capitol rotunda while her husband's body lay in state. Her walk in the night following that visit, when the former First Lady's presence among thousands of Washington mourners was unknown. Also to be remembered with a tug at the heart was the irony of John-John's birthday falling on the day of his father's funeral and the military salute the little boy bravely gave at the sad occasion. The beautiful black horse in the processions to the rotunda, St. Matthews and Arlington, a high-spirited animal giving his handler a bad time every moment. The contrast in height between the tall and stately President de Gaulle and tiny Emperor Haile Selassie, standing side by side. There was also the seeming coldness of quick removal from the White House of John Kennedy's personal mementos, among them a model of his PT boat that was cut in half by the Japanese and the famous Kennedy rocking chair. And, as a climax, perhaps, there was the bugler blowing taps over President Kennedy's grave. He struck just one sour note and you knew it was because he couldn't completely control the quiver of his lips. These are the episodes long to be remembered by all who wear their heart on their sleeve.

[From station WRAL–TV, Raleigh-Durham, N.C., Nov. 22, 1963]

VIEWPOINT

Anguish alone will not suffice as the Nation's proper reaction to the news of President Kennedy's assassination. All men of sanity and humanity feel a sense of revulsion at the act of the fanatical coward who hid in the attic of a building and fired down the shots that extinguished the life of a young man who, to us, seemed to possess not merely the quality of unbounded energy, but a sort of indestructibility as well.

At this moment, of course, all Americans are united regardless of party, or philosophy, or ideals. Conservation, liberalism, right wing, left wing—all these are meaningless semantics, no longer dividers, certainly not important unless and until we respond to the question of what happened to civilization in that dark moment in Dallas.

So, in unity there is a helplessness that may assist us in groping for strength. One insane man with a high-powered rifle has exposed the incredible weakness of a nation. If we now see that weakness, if we now understand it, some consolation may be found. Men may have differed with Mr. Kennedy in his exuberant ideas about politics, government, and the quest for peace in a troubled world. But as he lies tonight in death, he has left more than a shocked and stunned nation. The manner of his death leaves America standing naked as a symbol of civilization mocked.

Every citizen will reflect upon Mr. Kennedy's life, and his death, in a personal way. Mr. Kennedy had become a part of America in a personal way. His harshest critics recognized his magnetism and persuasiveness which had drawn him into the inner circle of American life. He was not loved by everyone; still, no one doubted his courage or his stamina. He fought his political battles with every ounce of his strength. And he did it openly.

And this serves to emphasize the dastardly nature of his assassination. Jack Kennedy was killed by a coward.

As we sat alone minutes after the announcement of the President's death, a hundred images flowed through our mind. One little incident that we personally observed nearly 11 years ago came to mind as clearly as if it were yesterday. It was a cold, crisp January morning in 1953 and the quorum bells had just rung throughout the Capitol and the Senate Office Building in Washington. Members of the Senate, the old ones and the new ones, were scurrying to get to the Senate Chamber. It was oath-of-office day for 10 or 12, including a tousled-haired young man from Massachusetts who had been elected to the Senate the previous November.

Senators were boarding the subway cars which connect the Capitol with the Senate Office Building by an underground route. Visitors and employees of the Senate were being repeatedly told by operators of the subway cars to stand aside for the Senators. They had priority.

Jack Kennedy arrived to take a seat on the subway car, but the operator waved him back. "Stand aside for the Senators, son," he said. Jack Kennedy stood aside with a grin—until an observer whispered to the operator: "He's a Senator, too." The embarrassed operator got only a pat on the back and a reassurance from Senator Kennedy.

An unimportant incident? Maybe. But it is one that we will remember always. No matter how much we might have disagreed with certain of the President's views and actions, the memory of that incident provided a sense of warmth and personal affection.

Millions of words will be written and spoken about this dark hour in America's history. Many days will pass before we can stand with pride and confidence, and say to the world that we are civilized. The cause of communism has been served well by this tragedy. Freedom has suffered a telling blow.

As for our new President, Lyndon Johnson, no man has faced a sterner challenge. He needs—he must have—the prayers of a Nation of people who see the need of renewing their faith, who are willing to proclaim honestly and sincerely that "in God we trust."

[From station WTYN, Tryon, N.C., Nov. 22, 1963]

PRESIDENT JOHN F. KENNEDY

Our President, President Kennedy, the President of the United States, is dead. Shockingly and coldbloodedly shot down by an assassin's bullet.

There is not an American who does not know that this is a most terrible and tragic thing that has been done against a good man, against the great office, and against this great country, nay to every American.

The whole world will feel the impact of this foul murder, and, yet, at this time it should be a time of discipline and of careful thought to the future of our United States and to all of us and to those who remain in high offices to do their best to serve her in this hour of sorrow and of tragedy.

Let each of us, citizens of this great Nation of ours, forgetting the prejudices, the differences between us of philosophy, of faith, of petty politics, take stock of this ugly and horrible situation, joining together as free Americans to stand by those who in this time of emergency have the duty and the burden of keeping our Nation on a straight course of freedom and justice which has been handed down to us by our forefathers.

Let us not allow this dastardly and cowardly act of a madman so to unnerve us as a nation that we become bewildered and easy prey to outside interests.

Let us continue in honor, with courage, and in disciplined order, as citizens of the United States, to stand firm in the heritage of our freedoms, and in the preserving of our Constitution and way of life, with calmness, forthright commonsense, and in the unity of purpose which, as citizens of this great Nation, is our common ambition and our common goal.

Let us pray for those whose burden it is to carry on in the face of our tragic loss. May they be filled with the wisdom and the strength to bring our people and our Nation through these troubled times, and may they have the knowledge of the support and understanding and cooperation of all people everywhere.

Let us pray.

O Lord, our governor whose glory is in all the world, we commend this Nation to Thy merciful care, that being guided by Thy providence, we may dwell secure in Thy peace. Grant to the President of the United States and to all in authority, wisdom and strength to do Thy will. Fill them with the love of truth and righteousness, and make them ever mindful of their calling to serve this people in Thy fear, through Jesus Christ our Lord who liveth and reigneth with Thee and the Holy Ghost, one God, world without end. Amen.

———

[From the Nashville (N.C.) Graphic, Nov. 28, 1963]

A JOURNEY ENDS SADLY, BUT AMERICA'S ROAD LEADS ON

"And so, my fellow Americans, ask not what your country can do for you; ask what you can do for your country."

—John Fitzgerald Kennedy.

The President is dead, and a sorrowful Nation mourns his passing.

The mourning is genuine and real.

One of the most moving aspects of the tragedy which ended the life of John Fitzgerald Kennedy was that his death came as a personal loss to the lowly and the humble, no less than to the great and the near-great.

Grief and sorrow were written on faces that watched televised news reports for hours after the first announcement of his brutal assassination stunned the Nation last Friday afternoon.

In homes across the land, tears fell silently and unashamedly Monday as a flag-draped caisson, drawn by six great horses, bore John F. Kennedy to his final resting place on a sloping hillside in Arlington National Cemetery across the Potomac River from the Nation's Capital.

Part of the feeling of personal loss at the President's tragic death could be attributed to the untimeliness of his passing. John F. Kennedy died in the prime of life, at the vigorous peak of a brilliant political career.

Part of it could be attributed to the brutality and the cold viciousness of his assassination.

But there is more than this to account for the sense of personal grief that so many felt in the death of John F. Kennedy.

He held the admiration and respect of the Nation because he embodied the principles, the ideals, the hopes and the promise of America in the youth and vigor of his dynamic leadership.

Not everyone agreed with the political views of John F. Kennedy, to be sure. This newspaper has expressed opposition on several occasions to liberal legislative measures advocated by the late President.

But no one could doubt the sincerity of John F. Kennedy's convictions.

None can say that he lacked devotion to the ideals in which he believed or was unwilling to expend the full measure of his energies in the effort to achieve them.

He never asked what the country he loved so well could do for him. He asked what John Fitzgerald Kennedy could do for America.

"Now the trumpet summons us again," said Kennedy in his inaugural address, "to bear the burden of a long, twilight struggle against the common enemies of man: tyranny, poverty, disease, and war.

"Can we forge against these enemies a grand and global alliance * * * that can assure a more fruitful life for all mankind? Will you join in that historic effort?"

The President is dead. Life's brief journey ended sadly and tragically for John F. Kennedy.

Yet the Nation lives on, needing now, more than ever, the devotion and the dedicated service of free people who know in their sorrow that the road America must travel leads on toward a destiny as bright and shining as the courage and faith of their fallen leader.

———

[From the Newton (N.C.) Observer-News-Enterprise, Nov. 25, 1963]

JOHN FITZGERALD KENNEDY

"Ask not what your country can do for you—ask what you can do for your country."

These words spoken by John Fitzgerald Kennedy in his inaugural address in January 1961 gave the people of America a clear insight into the type of man that was to lead this Nation. And, until he was cut down from ambush by bullets Friday afternoon in Dallas, Tex., it can be said that President Kennedy asked not what the country could do for him but rather, he gave so much—even the supreme sacrifice—for his country.

This country has been privileged to have had a President of the caliber man such as John F. Kennedy, who in such a short period of time, gained respect of his enemies, solidified his position, both at home, and abroad, brought to America statesmanship built on a foundation of intelligence and moral integrity.

The Washington Star said of him Saturday: "He walked as a prince and talked as a scholar." These few words sum up the type man that was leading this Nation in a time of world and domestic unrest—who was giving to his country and asking not what the country could do for him.

There are so many aspects to the tragic death of the 35th President of the United States. From the beginning of his term of office until his untimely death, he was faced with one major problem after another. In this nuclear age when man attempts with all his might to live with his enemies President Kennedy reaffirmed to the whole world that this Nation was interested in the freedom of nations and the dignity of man. From the beginning he made it clear that the United States would help those freedom-loving nations of the world and that this Nation would not back down from the fist-clinching, table-top pounding of those Nations who sought to destroy freedom.

And at home, in America, decisions in domestic policy were constantly affording the President many hours of deep consternation. Though there are those who did not agree with his policies, they nevertheless would have to hold John F. Kennedy in high respect for his devotion to the causes he felt right.

Sometimes it takes a tragic incident to bring about solidarity. And we feel that through the assassination of John F. Kennedy there will come a closer, more understanding feeling about the tremendous job of the President of the United States regardless of political affiliation.

———

[From the Raleigh (N.C.) Times, Nov. 23, 1963]

IN REASON, IN COURAGE

It has come to us now to turn away from the body of a friend and begin again in reason and in courage our journey into what must be a better future for all the people of our Nation.

The grief which came to our country at President Kennedy's death will and should remain in our hearts for all the days of our lives. The shock and the terror which came to us at that first numbing news now has no place in us or in our Nation. Neither is there any place in us for the panic and the unreasoning fear which inevitably followed in the first moments after the death of the President.

There must be in our hearts now only the strength of freemen and the courage of freemen. There must be the faith of the long centuries of our reliance on the God who has walked with His people in all their hours of fear and of uncertainty. There can be in our hearts no hate for any man who walks this earth, for we have been told that we shall love our enemies.

There is danger for all of us today, danger just as sure and as deadly as the thing which struck down President Kennedy yesterday. The man who fired those shots must have done so in blind, unreasoning hatred and fear. We, as a nation, must avoid such unreasoning hatred and fear as we now assess the thing which has already happened, and as we look to the things which will come to us during the days ahead. Let there be no mistake about the fact that we will have much to do with what does come. If we act in panic and fear and hatred, we will produce the dark and evil and senseless things which men do in unreasoning moments.

We need only look back to those days almost a century ago when another President fell victim to an assassin's bullet. Abraham Lincoln had wondrous plans for the South and its people. He spoke of "malice toward none, with charity for all; with firmness in the right, as God gives us to see the right; let us strive on to finish the work we are in; to bind up the Nation's wounds; to care for him who shall have borne the battle, and for his widow, and his orphan—to do all which may achieve and cherish a just and lasting peace among ourselves and with all nations."

Lincoln did not live to nurture that charity for all, that malice for none, that firmness in the right, that binding up of a nation's wounds. Instead, the men who finally did the things looking toward reuniting the Nation did those things out of hatred and fear and malice. And because they did, we in the South are still paying terribly the bill which has come down to us every bitter day since Reconstruction.

We cannot now permit ourselves to be panicked into hasty and unreasoned actions. The events of yesterday must not be permitted to strengthen the hands of those who would take from all of us some of our freedoms simply because they are men who live by fear and not by faith in the ability of freemen to live their lives well and honestly and patriotically as completely freemen.

What happened yesterday must not be permitted to dim the shining light President Kennedy held out to all men that they should have the rights and the privileges and the opportunities their Constitution says they shall have. Make no mistake about it, there will be men who will now say piously that some of the things President Kennedy did to help men have their just and due rights under the Constitution helped stir up the unsettled conditions which brought us to yesterday. Of course, President Kennedy's efforts did help stir the anger and the conscience of this country, and for that stirring we can thank God and feel that we are the better for it.

A century ago, vengeful men and frightened men tied the hands of President Andrew Johnson as he tried to bring his South and our South back into the Nation on the terms Lincoln had in mind.

Today, a century after that tragedy of the tieing of a President's hands, we must see to it that the hands of President Lyndon Johnson are held high. We can do no less. If we do less we will regret it bitterly and our children and our grandchildren will regret it even more bitterly during all the days of their lives.

A President is dead. A new President has come in. And in this great and shaking change, there still is so little change. The old President was the servant of all the people. The new President is the servant of all the people.

President Johnson must now have the prayers and the active support of all Americans as he seeks truly to be the President of all Americans and the servant of all Americans.

———

[From the Graham Star, Robbinsville, N.C., Nov. 29, 1963]

NATIONAL TRAGEDY

Never in time of peace has this generation of Americans been so shocked as in the past week. The sorrow was nationwide and it was genuine. No need to fill this space with still another account of those events. No need to tell the miserable story again. Everyone saw it—some of it over and over again.

The late President, John F. Kennedy is gone. And it is unfair. His life was taken, but he deserved to live. The Nation's chosen leader was taken, but it deserved to be led by him. A wonderful lady's husband was taken, but she deserved to live with him. The little children's father was taken, but they deserved to have him.

Some have thoughtlessly said that the American people are responsible. This too is unfair. Was there opposition? This is the way of freedom. Were there those who disagreed with him? This is the way of free men. Was there strong feeling about the issues? This is only natural. No, if the American people are responsible, it is because we are clasping to our bosom a godless breed of men who hold to an alien philosophy which teaches them to lie, and cheat, and kill—if necessary—to overthrow us. If we are responsible at all, this is the reason.

All of the evidence we have seen points to a man who renounced his American citizenship and moved to Russia. He later returned, an avowed Marxist. If other evidence is brought forward, then it should be acknowledged, and acted upon.

In any event, faithful Americans everywhere feel—not guilty—but terribly sorry and hurt that such a thing happened.

A PART OF THE "WHY"

A 46-year-old man was murdered Friday, November 22, 1963, in Dallas, Tex. The man was John F. Kennedy, President of the United States.

The brutal killing shocked the Nation and the world, having a numbing paralyzing effect on nearly everyone.

The President was a popular man. Much of the grief occurred at the thought of the loss of this capable, young, personable leader, and Americans were filled with sorrow for his beautiful young wife and children, ages 3 and 5.

Possessed of great wealth, this man could have turned his back on mankind's problems of poverty, war, universal brotherhood, and economic growth. He could have remained aloof from all its heartaches, worries, and cares. Instead he thrust himself into the middle of them giving of his immeasurable talent and energy to work for the freedom of all men, regardless of their economic status in life, or race, for peace throughout the world.

He was truly a great man motivated by Christian ideals—a great President.

Much of the grief was felt solely at the thought of the loss of this man.

But that seemingly extra numbing chilling effect was created by the knowledge within that we all had a hand in the tragedy.

We have stood idly by while a climate of hate has been fostered and cultivated by many.

We have listened and cheered while self-seeking, ambitious demagogues ranted emotional speeches filled with phrases designed to arouse hate and set race against race. We have been amused at the sight of brutality. We have jeered and belittled efforts of people to help fellow human beings. We have allowed our news media to be used to promote such actions. We have been quick to criticize and have uttered statements not substantiated by facts against persons in authority for their crowd-pleasing effects.

Truly part of the numbing effect caused by the death of President Kennedy was each individual's conscience telling him that we have been derelict in our duty to constantly strive for the true brotherhood of men, to uphold love and denounce hate, to practice tolerance and forgo prejudice.

Americans helped nurture the seeds of hate in the brain of the maniac who killed John F. Kennedy.

As a result the Christian forces of the world lost a great leader.

It hurts and hurts deeply.

B.S.

———

[From the Rocky Mount (N.C.) Telegram, Nov. 23, 1963]

VICTIM OF AN ASSASSIN

It should go without saying that the most odious word in our language is assassin. We become acutely aware of that today as we contemplate something which could not have happened, yet it did: the assassination of the President of the United States.

Friday in Dallas, Tex., where President John F. Kennedy had gone on a mission to proclaim his ideas for the operation of the American Government, he was shot down just as a thug might have been felled in a gang dispute.

Naturally the whole Nation immediately went into mourning. Of course, you may not have agreed with many of the President's policies. In fact, there were rumblings throughout the South because of his civil rights stand. But he still was the President, the duly elected leader of us all and he had a right to complete the term in office, or as many terms in office, as the people decided he should serve.

Not since the turn of the century when President William McKinley fell a victim to an assassin's bullet had anything so awesome happened. The deed also brought back memories of Lincoln, Garfield—yet those were horrors of the past. Today, there is mute evidence, however, at the Nation's Capital because there lies the body of the youngest man ever chosen to preside over the destiny of this great Nation, the victim of an assassin's bullet.

While permitted to hold the most important elective office in the world for only such a brief span, John F. Kennedy still accomplished many things which will assure him a prominent place in history. In many long years to come, historians will recount how he faced up to the great menace of the age, Red Russia, and caused that mighty power to pack up its belongings and get out of Cuba. President Kennedy also will be remembered for his stand on civil rights, a subject which is a tender one today throughout the Southland and which will have to be weighed with passing years before its final evaluation is realized.

Today, however, all animosities should be set aside because Jack Kennedy is dead. Let all those who praised him as well as those who opposed him unite in common sorrow over the passing of our President.

At the same time, let there be a universal backing of Lyndon B. Johnson, the Vice President who has assumed the Chief Office of the land. President Johnson has a task which probably surpasses even that of Harry Truman when he became President upon the death in office of Franklin D. Roosevelt. President Johnson also merits and deserves our united support.

This country could become a shambles as frequently happens in other countries when leadership is changed through violence. Yet we hope we live in a country and in an age which will see that proper respect will be paid to our new President as he assumes the duties of the highest office in the land. And let us never forget that assassinations go hand in hand with anarchy.

———

[From the Roxboro (N.C.) Courier-Times, Nov. 25, 1963]

NEW PRESIDENT NEEDS SUPPORT IN CRISIS

What makes John Fitzgerald Kennedy's death so incomprehensible is that a little and sick mind can snuff out the life of greatness.

It happened just like that.

Little do assassins know, or care to know, that the one assassinated will likely be martyrized and that those things for which the assassinated stood so strongly will be emphasized, not for a decade, but for history.

The dastardly hand of the assassin, however, rarely strikes one who needs martyrdom. Such was the case with John F. Kennedy.

He was the personification of greatness, and he will likely take his place alongside Washington and Lincoln.

The assassin's bullet struck down not only a popular personality; it struck a blow at the integrity of the office. The office continues; the people who fill this powerful role in the free world's intricate complex change.

In a period of change in a free institution, there must be a period of unity. Nothing brings unity like such a dastardly deed.

The United States of America moves on.

The country is indeed fortunate that it moves on in the capable hands of Lyndon Johnson, a Vice President with vast knowledge of grassroots politics and a broad understanding of domestic and international issues.

We pledge to President Johnson our wholehearted support in this grave and tragic period of transition, and we are confident that he carries with him the support of every right-thinking citizen of Person County.

Now is the time for all good men to come to the aid of their country.

"And ask not what your country can do for you; ask what you can do for your country."

———

[From the Sanford (N.C.) Herald, Nov. 22, 1963]

JOHN F. KENNEDY

An assassin's bullet Friday struck down John F. Kennedy, the 35th President of the United States. Mr. Kennedy, only 46, is mourned by all of the people of the United States and no doubt most of the world. Certainly, no one anywhere feels anything but contempt for the type of man who would strike as did Mr. Kennedy's assassin.

Mr. Kennedy entered office on a surge of towering personal popularity. The new President, his strikingly attractive wife, and their children made one of the most appealing and photogenic families ever to occupy the White House. Not since the early days of Franklin D. Roosevelt's New Deal did a President and those around him become such an object of interest to an entire nation.

Undisputed personal popularity did not protect Mr. Kennedy, however, from the lash of severe criticism that accompanied some of the efforts of his administration. Nor did it rub off on Congress to the extent that the lawmakers fell over themselves to get his program passed.

In fact, his New Frontier legislative defeats in this area sometimes were impressive; his victories frequently narrow.

His great problems at the start were foreign policy and domestic economy. In 1963 both were overshadowed by the Negro question which confronted the Nation with one of its gravest domestic crises since the Civil War. However, the constant Soviet threat remained, and the President had trouble in southeast Asia and Cuba. The ill-fated Bay of Pigs invasion tarnished the bright young American President.

Today both friend and foe mourn him. His was a bright future, and he had many years ahead of him during which he could have served his country. Catching the person or persons who shot him to death cannot regain the loss this country and the world suffered Friday in his needless death.

The days ahead will be dark ones for this Nation as it mourns for John F. Kennedy.

———

[From the Sanford (N.C.) News Leader, Nov. 27, 1963]

JOHN FITZGERALD KENNEDY—35TH PRESIDENT OF THE UNITED STATES

The midday rays of a bright winter sun sparkled on a grand motorcade that rolled majestically through Dallas. A crisp breeze whipped the flags and bunting that welcomed the President of the United States to the vast Southwest. He responded enthusiastically to the warm outpouring of the love and devotion of thousands of citizens who came to cheer him along the route. Again and again he flashed his sincere smile, again and again he waved to the throngs. It was clear there was mutual respect and admiration. It was a bright day.

High above the street the warped and troubled mind of a sick man focused upon its deadly mission, a finger curled around the cold trigger and a rifle cracked sharply, then again and again. The President slumped into the arms of his wife, the Governor of Texas crumpled on the seat of the car.

The Nation was plunged into grief and a season of mourning began.

Word of the tragic event was flashed around the world by radio and television, then the free world joined us in our sorrow.

Then came the reflections. The brave and the faint, the strong and the weak, we were left helpless to express ourselves, but we tried. "He was a friend of all mankind," we said. And we said, you and I, "He was a peacemaker, a great and skillful statesman." "He was a youth of great promise, a President of great vision, a leader, a writer, a humanitarian and a servant of God." Yes, we said these things you and I, but as we watched that sad cortege travel slowly down Pennsylvania Avenue we knew we had said nothing and could say nothing that could match his sacrifice, nor could we atone for the loss.

———

[From the Shelby (N.C.) Cleveland Times, Nov. 26, 1963]

JOHN F. KENNEDY MET THE TESTS OF COURAGE

Clevelanders were not unlike free people all over the world who were stunned and saddened over the untimely death Friday of this Nation's 35th President, John Fitzgerald Kennedy.

In a weekend of mourning, the county has been at a virtual standstill out of respect to a great leader. Sanctuaries were filled to overflowing in churches on Sunday and hundreds more returned yesterday as our people instinctively turned to worship in the midst of a crisis and prayed that a change of leadership in the Executive Office in this country will reflect that of a person broadly acquainted with the affairs of this vast Nation and one who is equipped for the greatest responsibility of his life.

As a Senate majority leader and as Vice President, Lyndon Johnson's many roles in public life should find him more able to smoothly take over the reins of our Government, but he will need as never before the backing of American people and renewed strength to use his talents and his skills in the leadership he has already demonstrated as a Senator and in the Kennedy administration.

The tragedy of President Kennedy's assassination and a bereaved Nation focuses on the death of a man of quiet and true courage who charted a course through treacherous seas. Many thought he pushed too hard or drove with ruthless power, while as many others thought his views were moderate and reasonable with logic. Whatever one's views, there's no denying that he carried on his shoulders a superhuman burden that was marked with tenacity and determination. He was a fighter for justice and an apostle of peace—few can argue otherwise.

As we remain stunned and perplexed over this tragic event we think of the price we pay for the fanaticism of the misguided wretch who completed his dastardly deed. It is unbelievable that any person who has enjoyed the fruits and freedoms of America could possibly turn to such an act that for months to come will have reverberations throughout the world. To have cut a man down in his prime and at the time he held the key to so many problems is indeed the act of a madman.

While we express sincerest sympathy to the President's widow and two small children, his parents and other members of his family, we believe they are stronger today for the very reason that John F. Kennedy made them through his Pulitzer Prize-winning "Profiles in Courage," which we believe actually defines Kennedy the man.

In the book about courage and politics, politics furnished the situations and courage provided the theme. He makes clear that a man does what he must in spite of personal consequences, he tells of the satisfactions and burdens of a Senator's job, of the pressures and of the standards by which a man of principle must work and live.

We find his final paragraphs as those which exemplify the late President: "In a democracy, every citizen, regardless of his interest in politics, 'holds office'; every one of us is in a position of responsibility; and, in the final analysis, the kind of government we get depends upon how we fulfill those responsibilities. We, the people, are the boss, and we will get the kind of political leadership, be it good or bad, that we demand and deserve.

"These problems do not even concern politics alone— for the same basic choice of courage or compliance continually faces us all, whether we fear the anger of constituents, friends, a board of directors or our union, whenever we stand against the flow of opinion on strongly contested issues. For without belittling the courage with which men have died, we should not forget those acts of courage with which men have lived. The courage of life is often a less dramatic spectacle than the courage of a final moment; but it is no less a magnificent mixture of triumph and tragedy. A man does what he must—in spite of personal consequences, in spite of obstacles and dangers and pressures—and that is the basis of all human morality.

"To be courageous, these stories make clear, requires no exceptional qualifications, no magic formula, no special combination of time, place and circumstances. It is an opportunity that sooner or later is presented to us all. Politics merely furnishes one arena which imposes special tests of courage. In whatever arena of life one may meet the challenge of courage, whatever may be the sacrifices he faces if he follows his conscience—the loss of his friends, his fortune, his contentment, even the esteem of his fellow men—each man must decide for himself the course he will follow. The stories of past courage can define that ingredient—they can teach, they can offer hope, they can provide inspiration. But they cannot supply courage itself. For this each man must look into his own soul."

———

[From the Shelby (N.C.) Daily Star, Nov. 23, 1963]

THIS IS A TIME FOR AMERICANS TO RALLY TO AMERICA

Barely 2 hours after an assassin's bullet had snuffed out the life of John F. Kennedy, 35th President of the United States, Lyndon B. Johnson, the Vice President, was sworn in as President.

In this way, the chain of leadership of the United States was continued, almost uninterrupted, in a moment of confusion and crisis. It is one of the beauties of the American system of government.

The country's welfare does not depend on any one individual. It is ruled by many men, primarily the men of Congress. The President carries more influence on national and international affairs than any other person in the United States but it is the office of the Presidency which lends this prestige and influence to the individual.

The assassination of President Kennedy is a despicable thing. One bullet killed a man whom a majority of the voters who cast ballots in the last presidential election said they preferred as President. Not only did that bullet kill the most important man in the free world, it assassinated the will of a majority of the people who cared enough to vote. It is barbaric.

We seldom agreed with President Kennedy's views. But we admired him as a person of intelligence and fortitude and sincerity. He fought for what he felt was right and he fought a hard battle.

Because this is the United States of America, when we disagreed with the President, we said so. And we had no reason to fear reprisals. We live in a free society and that, too, is one of the beauties of the American system. The assassin's bullet was also a disgrace to that freedom of our society. That bullet does not fit into a way of life in which we may disagree and still live side by side and fight for the overriding common cause of building a greater nation.

Because an assassin was unable to have faith in the American system, the next few weeks and months will be a delicate time in the history of our country.

Lyndon B. Johnson will be grasping the reins of the Nation and it will take a short time for the transition to be fully accomplished. It is true that this is the moment for which his previous office has prepared him, but no man can be totally prepared for such a transition.

Therefore, it is a time for Americans to rally to America. It is a time when partisan politics should be laid aside in an effort to speed the transition. In the coming weeks, the labels Democrat and Republican should be forgotten and there should be only one label—American.

This is a time when we can all contribute to America. It is a rare opportunity to serve our country and keep her on an even keel.

What can we do in Cleveland County?

We can remain calm and have faith in this great Nation of ours. We can refuse to be panicked into selling stock in our Nation's industries. We can refuse to be carriers of rumors. We can pray to God to guide our leaders. That, too, is one of the blessings of America.

———

[From the Marshall (N.C.) News-Record, Nov. 28, 1963]

THE WORLD WEPT—WE MUST GO ON

A gala parade started in Dallas, Tex., last Friday. Thousands upon thousands waved and cheered as President John F. Kennedy, Mrs. Kennedy, Governor John Connally, Vice President Lyndon Johnson, and many other dignitaries rode by. And then it happened—an assassin fired three shots from a fifth story of a building—one shot struck and fatally wounded our President, another shot seriously wounded Governor Connally. Hysteria reigned throughout Dallas and the news swept quickly over the world. Our President is dead.

A suspect, Lee Harvey Oswald, was apprehended in a theater. He pleaded innocent but evidence mounted. He was to have been arraigned Sunday afternoon. A Dallas policeman was also slain, said to have been killed by a bullet from Oswald's gun. Oswald said "I didn't kill anyone." Evidence mounted.

Oswald, a loner, was expected to break and confess but his life, too, was ended Sunday from a shot of a pistol held by Jack Ruby, a nightspot owner with a high temper. He slipped through all security measures to fire pointblank from a few feet, struck Oswald in the stomach—he died shortly thereafter in the same hospital where President Kennedy died. Three murders in Dallas within 3 days, another charged with murder, all this in Christian America.

The skies shed tears in Washington Saturday as the world paid tribute to the late John F. Kennedy. It was a stunned world, sad, yes, tears were shed everywhere. Among the bravest were Mrs. Kennedy, and Attorney General Bobby Kennedy who remained at the side of Mrs. Kennedy. Television coverage brought all actions of excitement and sadness into millions of homes in America and abroad. Leaders of foreign countries sent messages of condolences. Over 50 countries sent representatives to the funeral of Kennedy. The world was saddened from Friday afternoon through Monday afternoon. Flags at half-mast, banks and stores closed, athletic events cancelled or postponed.

Four days seemed like 4 weeks, church services Sunday consisted of tributes. Democrats and Republicans, alike, paid tributes to a young, popular, dynamic President. A new President, Lyndon B. Johnson, succeeds the late President. Dallas feels terrible about the incident but so does the entire world. It is a sad Thanksgiving, but still much for which to be thankful—thankful we live in a country like America, despite the crackpots, assassins, and outlaws. The challenge grows, that if we are to remain a Christian nation, we must pick up the pieces, renew our allegiance to God and mankind, and march forward together to a more peaceful future.

————

[From the Mebane (N.C.) Enterprise, Nov. 28, 1963]

COUNTRY MOURNS KENNEDY

That wonderfully brilliant mind of President John F. Kennedy has been stilled for all time. The spirit which undergirded the heroic outlook of his dedicated heart will not be silenced. He challenged the Nation with his forthright statement: "Ask not what your country can do for you. Rather, ask what you can do for your country."

He met his own challenge. He paid the price.

Shame has enveloped our people that such fanatics, who have the freedoms of the Nation, should leave the power of the ballot box for that of a high-powered rifle.

Many of the American citizens disagreed with the President in every element. There are those of us who took stanch views opposed to his political philosophy. Some of us feared the rapid growth of the religious system he represented. In all of us was the recognition that he was the leader of the Nation. He was our President. He was our Commander in Chief. We join in with the millions of mourners at his passing.

President John F. Kennedy's funeral was held yesterday at St. Matthew's Catholic Cathedral in the Nation's Capital, Washington, D.C.

In the midst of the highest honors paid him he was joined with Alfred Lord Tennyson in:

"CROSSING THE BAR

"Sunset and evening star,
 And one clear call for me!
And may there be no moaning of the bar,
 When I put out to sea.

"But such a tide as moving seems asleep,
 Too full for sound and foam,
When that which drew from out the boundless deep
 Turns again home.

"Twilight and evening bell,
 And after that the dark!
And may there be no sadness of farewell
 When I embarked.

"For though out our bourn of Time and Place
 The flood may bear me far,
I hope to see my pilot face to face
 When I have crossed the bar."

————

[From the Morehead City (N.C.) Carteret County News-Times, Nov. 26, 1963]

LAMENT FOR THE LIVING

November 22, 1963.

This is written three-quarters of an hour after President Kennedy, struck by an assassin's bullets, died in a Texas hospital. This tragedy leaves us little hope for humanity.

The United States is supposed to be a civilized Nation. But the actions of one individual can drag us down to the depths, can make us feel that we have a long way to go before we are worthy of the many blessings this rich land has been heir to.

We know not why the President's murderer pulled the trigger. If it was because of Kennedy's attitude toward the Negro, it is ironic that this is the week of the 100th anniversary of the Gettysburg Address, delivered by President Lincoln, the man known the world around as the Great Emancipator of the Negro slaves in America.

The President's assassination does not solve the problems we face. His death only increases the burdens the living must now assume "that these dead shall not have died in vain."

Government of the people, by the people and for the people stands in danger of perishing from the earth, for we, by our actions are making a mockery of all those principles which we profess to hold dear.

The Nation should mourn not only for President Kennedy but for itself.

———

[From the Mount Olive (N.C.) Tribune, Nov. 26, 1963]

EDITORIALLY SPEAKING—A BLOW AT THE WHOLE NATION

Everything has been said and resaid that could describe the shock and horror of the American people, and the people of other nations, at the unbelievable act of last Friday which took the life of the President of the United States. Even so, this small voice must be added to the echo, and wring its editorial hands at such a senseless and useless tragedy.

The death of a man is always something sad, sometimes tragic, among his family and friends. But this was a blow struck at a whole nation, the savage destruction of the man a nation had chosen to its highest office to lead it through what has proved to be at once the most trying and most opportune time in its history. There can be no partisan thought of feeling at the assassination of a President of the United States. It is a shameful, massive blow to every American.

Somehow, the action of the man who 2 days later murdered the pitiful, misguided wretch who was charged with the President's death, has a little of the same repulsiveness to the average American.

In all this, one can feel sympathy, also, for the people of Dallas and of all Texas, who will suffer anguish that such a thing could happen in their midst. It will be small comfort, but it not only happened in Texas—it happened in the United States.

There is some comfort for all of us, and perhaps a warning thought, too, that this dark plot did not stem from domestic strife and differences, but was hatched in a weak, frustrated mind, contaminated and confused by alien beliefs.

Out of this dark weekend, above the tragedy, shines a monumental endorsement of the American system of government, for all the world to see. How many other nations could undergo such a crisis without public hysteria, with such calm confidence in its governmental processes, seeing its leadership change with a few minutes' notice into hands already selected by the people, without a question, without a challenge? In this example before the world may lie the most far-reaching and significant effect of these sad days.

E. B.

———

[From the Mount Olive (N.C.) Tribune]

THE MOUTHPIECE

The assassination of President John F. Kennedy last Friday, so shocking in its suddenness, so tragic in its uselessness, and so widespread in its impact, makes every newspaperman yearn for the inspiration necessary to write just exactly the right words. But, for some reason or another, words, which are our stock in trade, suddenly become empty, elusive, and hard to arrange in any order which would bring either logic or purpose in analyzing or explaining such an event.

Who, but another newspaperman, can know the frustration of failing his readers in this respect, at a time when he feels they should use him most to say for them what they would like to say? The dealers in words have filled untold columns of type, and thousands of minutes on radio and television since Friday afternoon, and in a measure, they have failed, too.

So a fresh deflating of the ego with a new realization of no greatness in one's own life, no real rising to an occasion, no worthy contribution to be remembered long after the contributor has left the scene. And there is left, after all, words that have already been written, or spoken, hundreds of times over—and yet, what newspaperman in the Nation has not faced our dilemma since Friday?

In addition to the tragedy of the President's death is the disturbing realization that our society embraces even one individual who would choose deliberate, coldblooded murder of a complete stranger, simply because he occupied the position of President. Many disagreed with him; many others did not vote for him, and many who voted for him in 1960 would not have done so in 1964. But to kill. * * *

As has so often been stated, the President was indeed intelligent. Brilliantly so. He was born with no shortage of the opportunities or means to develop his capabilities to the utmost. He took full advantage of them all.

Some have claimed for him a peculiar ability for deep understanding of Americans and their problems; yet others, while he lived, claimed he could not possibly know how the "other half" lived or felt. Only eternity will have the full answer.

Who is wise enough to know if fate dealt unkindly with a family to which it had given immense wealth, determined ambition, and talented offspring, only to stalk that same family with tragedies which money and position could not avert—even seemed to attract? Or does personal tragedy become a part of the price tag one must pay for greatness, as so often seems the case? Again, only eternity can answer.

One thing we cannot deny: with no need for the labor which produces wealth, the family's sons have chosen a field of endeavor, which, presumably, offers the heart most complete satisfaction: service to the public. Before the President's death many of their critics claimed the Kennedys served because they sought to fill a need for recognition based upon something other than the family's wealth. Nothing short of eternity knows for sure.

Mrs. Kennedy's composure during the shock of this national tragedy was remarkable. One might say that all her life's training, stemming as it did from wealth, position, and the best education, was to develop just the kind of person who would always do, say, and be the right thing. One could say, not unkindly, that for this she was born, and she was not untrue to her birth.

Of course America's heart also goes out to the Kennedy children. Nothing can replace their daddy. As one Mount Olive woman put it, "I'd rather have my daddy than all the money in the world." And so would they, and it tugs at the heart to realize the experiences ahead of them when this truism will come home to them.

Is there pity for the tragic figure of Lee Harvey Oswald,

accused of perpetrating a crime which will never be erased from the human conscience? Will anyone ever consider the sadness of an existence so hemmed in with the incomprehensible that its end would be packaged in assassination of the President of the United States?

(NOTE.—This was written before Oswald's assassination Sunday.)

Ever-widening ripples of the rifle bullet's shockwaves encompass the family and loved ones of the Dallas policeman slain shortly after the President. And the people of Dallas. Yet, no one can truthfully blame Dallas for this historic tragedy, but forever after the city of Dallas will be remembered by the world as the "Ford's Theater" of President John F. Kennedy.

Is there an avenue of escape provided by the Almighty for the Kennedy clan from the burden of hate and revenge? We truly hope so, for their sake.

Yes, President John F. Kennedy had a flare for greatness. He occupied a great position as Chief Executive of a great country, with a great birth, a great heritage, and under God, a great future. We cannot comprehend it all, nor understand it much. We say poorly what probably should not be said at all, but this one thing we do:

We sincerely pray and know you do, too, that in this period of great national tragedy and mourning the same mantle of greatness worn by John F. Kennedy will transfer with easy grace and excellent tailoring onto the shoulders of Lyndon B. Johnson, now President of the United States of America.

In this Thanksgiving week let us remember to be grateful for a country which does not fall with the fall of its great men, but one which, from its boundless resources of human spirit, can provide itself with other leaders to step into the gap of the fallen. Dear Lord, may it ever be so. Amen.

[From the Asheboro (N.C.) Courier-Tribune, Nov. 25, 1963]

PASSING OF JOHN KENNEDY—A TIME OF GRIEF, DISMAY

When the news came it lent a feeling of unreality to the moment. It was midafternoon and most people in Asheboro had only just returned to work from lunch.

Housewives were busy, their television and radio sets perhaps turned on. Possibly a frantic telephone call from a friend gave them the first report.

Others were at their desks, or machines, or working with whatever tools they earn their living.

"Shot in the head * * * probably mortally * * * now undergoing surgery."

We caught only fleeting words before the realization came that the President had been wounded by gunfire in Dallas. The tone of the newscaster was grave, face ashen and it was clear that death was thought imminent or already a fact.

Townspeople were somber, shocked as they gathered around TV sets and radios through the city. Business was at a standstill. Customers came into stores—those who hadn't heard or didn't know what else to do but finish their shopping entranced. At some counters they were given attention; mostly it was an unreal shopping day in the business district.

In business offices, workers were passing news reports among themselves. Several had small transistor radios which were turned to high volume for their coworkers' benefit.

Stories passed from hand to mouth. Rumors developed that the Vice President—though by then he was already President of the United States—had suffered a heart attack. Finally it was confirmed that the President had died from his wounds, in fact had had little chance of survival, that the Vice President had already been given the oath of office. Even then the news was difficult to grasp.

Emotion flooded the moment. First, of dismay, then of bereavement, then anger toward the killer—anger that he might have done this as an expression of ideological differences while others used the ballot box and words to express any disapproval. For a moment we felt a sense of shame for the Nation, until the saddened faces, all American, came in focus around us.

Then the emotion passed, and it was a moment to appreciate the solidity of democracy as the reins of Government passed quietly into the hands of the Vice President—and even if he too had lost his life, there would have been another, constitutionally appointed, to take his place.

Today, this week or next isn't the time to evaluate the brief performance of the late President, John Fitzgerald Kennedy.

It is a time for sympathy for the late President's young wife and family—a wife who before Friday stood beside the leader of the most powerful Nation of the world, and now as his widow, left only with memories in the absence of physical presence.

He was a dynamic man, young for the Presidency.

He was a member of an unusual family in which political instincts are keen, successfully exercised.

He had devoted his entire life to public service, first in war, then in Congress, then the Presidency.

This much we now know and can say.

But who can say in total what his mark will be on the United States, and indeed the world. It remains for the historians.

The Nation has been divided, faced with an aggressive foe pledged to destroy our freedom either by subversion or force. The divisions and the foe remain.

But the problems belong to another, now.

[From the Brevard (N.C.) Transylvania Times, Nov. 28, 1963]

A TRIBUTE TO JOHN FITZGERALD KENNEDY

It was the saddest of weekends as the world mourned the passing of the great leader of democracy, John Fitzgerald Kennedy.

Across the Nation, Americans silently wept within their hearts as the slain President of these United States lay in state in the Nation's Capitol.

Churches were filled to overflowing. People in all walks of life sought comfort that comes only from the word of the Bible and the Almighty.

The slain leader of the free Western world will live long in the hearts and the memory of those he served.

His flashing smile. His boyish-looking hair. His Harvard accent. His determination. His gestures. His vigor. His dedication to his fellow man and his country. His drive to make this great country even greater.

These things we will ever remember.

During the few, short years that he was President, he became a part of every home in America. A good friend one day; a dynamic leader in a world crisis.

Today, America has a new President. We must carry on. Lyndon Johnson has vowed to do his best with our help and with God's.

We must and we will rally to him while we mourn the passing of John Fitzgerald Kennedy.

[From the Brevard (N.C.) Transylvania Times, Dec. 12, 1963]

MULHOLLAND DELIVERS EULOGY TO LATE PRESIDENT KENNEDY

Rev. Charles Mulholland, pastor of the Sacred Heart Catholic Church of Brevard, delivered the following eulogy to the late President, John Fitzgerald Kennedy, at a special memorial service at the Brevard Elks Lodge.

The late President was a member of the Boston Elks Lodge.

The eulogy follows:

"John Fitzgerald Kennedy was in a special way one of us all. He so beckoned to the common greatness in the common man that we never realized the full size of him until he left us. Like a giant oak suddenly made leafless by a vagrant wind, we are startled by the size and strength of the rugged branches reaching to the sky and the strength and shelter that it gave us. And now this oak shall never don its green again and the emptiness, sadness, and suddenness of this realization has wrenched from us some inner vital part.

"He was born—like most of us in this century; he fought in the war that we shared in (the memory of which is now like a youthful boast); he was on the football team and unashamedly a sports fan; he was a college student; he was an Elk, he was a husband and a father and through all this there was the sickness and sadness that touches every large family (perhaps even in a larger measure—in his own). His older brother and then a sister untimely killed—a younger sister born demented. Struggles and defeats that touch us all. He was wealthy and enormously talented—characteristics which often make our identification with a person difficult or impossible. Yet, he had two great traits that are available to us all and united us to him more than we know. He loved the adventure of human life and he had the courage of his convictions.

"He did not retire to an indifferent and comfortable niche and fervently hope that life would be pleasant and gay. He ventured forth into the highways of humankind because he wanted to share and serve the life of his countrymen who traveled that highway. Like many of his fellow citizens he had a passion for politics and with a smile he gayly abandoned himself to the difficult voca-

tion of governing freemen. How easily his talents and influence could have won him the important but quiet contribution of a wartime desk job, but he was in the Pacific bearing up one of his injured sailors for 18 hours in enemy waters. He wanted to take part as much as he possibly could. 'A man does what he must,' he wrote, 'in spite of personal consequences, in spite of obstacles and dangers * * * and pressures * * * and that is the basis of all human morality.' We know that our life has involved the same choices, although less publicized and less distinguished. He further said, 'We shall bear every burden, meet any hardship, support any friend * * * oppose any foe, to assure the success of liberty.' And by his life he called us to invoke this creed in our own daily and community lives; inviting us, urging us to share in the great human adventures of our time. He did it without cant or hypocrisy, without posing or affectation, without pride or pomposity. He was just his great human self and asked that we be the same.

"He was courageous—as we should be. Not in the storybook style of blazing guns and slashing fists, but in laboring on a book while he was in a hospital bed; impatiently bearing with the price of political life; in making the difficult and unpopular decisions that often spell the doom of a political career. He stood up for us and said all the difficult words that we should say in our hearts—to troops and Governors in Mississippi; to steel presidents and labor leaders. He had that courage which saves a man from the laziness of fanaticism or demagoguery. He was a determined, but not a bitter or vindictive fighter. He was unsparing in his effort for what he thought to be right but not so that he was unsympathetic or unforgiving. He insisted that this country must be guided by the lights of learning and reason, not hate and violence. These qualities and the courage necessary for them are available to us all.

"In his last talk he said, 'This is a dangerous and uncertain world; no one expects our lives to be easy—not in this decade, not in this century.' And yet, there are times when we—you and I—look for the easy life, hope for the simple solution, the swift and easy answer to communism, poverty, and human greed.

"He deplored the confusion of rhetoric with reality; of words with deeds, and lived this dictum in his lifetime. He summoned us to be with him, to be a great people as he was a great man. To ask not what we can get, but what we can give. And his words ring in the terrible silence of his graveside; they will bring forth a golden and enduring echo if we respond to his call and his example."

[From the Davidson (N.C.) Mecklenburg Gazette, Nov. 28, 1963]

THE PRESIDENT IS DEAD * * * LONG LIVE THE PRESIDENT

It's all over now.

It's Tuesday and the world is gradually returning to normal.

We, at the Gazette, were among a handful of people in the land working yesterday.

Most of the Nation was in deep mourning * * * attending by television * * * the last rites of our late President.

But news gathering is the business of newspapers * * * and even those of us making up the staff of a small country newspaper accept our responsibility as an agency of communication, and do what we must.

Millions of words have been written and spoken about John Fitzgerald Kennedy, 35th President of the United States, since he was cut down by an assassin's bullet Friday afternoon.

Millions of tears have been shed by a grieved nation since that fateful day last week when the voice of an emotion choked radio announcer blurted out the shocking, horror-provoking news: "The President has been shot."

Thirty minutes later an unbelieving American people heard the awful tidings—"He is dead. The President is dead."

It seemed at that moment as though the world and time itself stood still, while people tried to grasp * * * struggled to understand * * * how such a terrible thing could happen in this country * * * our "sweet land of liberty."

"I can't believe it," was the cry throughout the land.

But it was true. John Kennedy lay dead in a Dallas hospital with a bullet in his head.

And it seemed strangely ironic that one born to the cradle of freedom and bred in an atmosphere of cherished liberty should be responsible for the death of this young vibrant man, who dedicated his life to the ideals of freedom and equality for all men.

The hesitant hand of fate brought a young Catholic to the highest office in the land. His margin of victory was slight, and because he was the first of his religion to serve this Nation as President, John Kennedy walked carefully, almost gingerly. He did not have time, in his brief, 3-year span of service, to become the great man many believed he could be.

So, John Kennedy, the millionaire's son, the husband of beautiful Jackie, the father of magazine illustration children, the eldest living offspring of indomitable Rose, the hero of a family of young beautiful brothers and sisters, the lucky man who had everything, lies dead and lonely in Arlington Cemetery.

And in the midst of our tragedy and grief, Lyndon Baines Johnson grasps the helm of the Ship of State.

He is another fate has singled out. A southerner who never could have attained the Presidency by a vote of the people.

Perhaps the idiotic patchwork quilt of destiny conceals a mystical tapestry too complex for mere men's eyes.

Because these two men—one a Catholic, the other a southerner—were politically handicapped. America does not trust her institutions to those who are different * * * and these men were different.

Yet John Kennedy, a Catholic, served his country well and with great honor. And now Lyndon Johnson, a southerner, begins his term as this Nation's leader. And we are reassured by history. Greatness thrust upon a man tends to transform him—to magnify his ability.

While he lived John Kennedy's voice was not always loud enough to be heard above the caterwauling of the frenzied * * * the lunatic fringes of right and left.

But now, as he lies dead, the small still voice inside each of us will not permit rest or peace.

Perhaps the voice we ignored when it was vigorous and full of life will become more insistent now that it is

stilled in death. Perhaps John Kennedy's hopes for a New Frontier in human relationship will become reality.

And perhaps this is the answer to the anguished question.

Why?

[From the Elkin (N.C.) Tribune, Nov. 25, 1963]

JOHN F. KENNEDY

John F. Kennedy, 35th President of the United States, died needlessly of an assassin's bullet molded in hate by one who knew only malevolence bred by the infection of the Communist virus.

And his death came as a stunning blow to every American who believes in the American way of life; to every foreign nation whose people cherish freedom.

In Elkin the news of the President's death came with a sense of numbing shock. Stores were quiet. People who made their way up and down the street wore solemn faces, as if they had suffered a very personal loss.

When John F. Kennedy was elected President of the United States, he did not carry Elkin as our citizens exercised their rights to vote as their conscience dictated. But when the news of his death burst like a bombshell here, all thoughts of politics were forgotten; all real or fancied dislike submerged under the very real flood of grief which swept our community.

Americans are like that. We fight and argue in political campaigns, and criticize those in power. But when the chips are down we close ranks and bring to the fore that sense of justice and fair play which underlies every heart.

The President is dead. He served his country as a dedicated public servant, forging straight ahead toward the ideals in which he believed, without fear, without faltering. That the cowardly bullet of an assassin struck him down is an act which will never be understood but must be accepted.

We have a new President now, who faces a multitude of problems. All of us should lend our loyalty and our prayers to the support of Lyndon Baines Johnson, who of all the men in the world today has the job most unenviable.

[From the Newland (N.C.) Avery Journal, Nov. 28, 1963]

MY FAVORITE MEMORIES OF J.F.K.

(By Barbara Davenport)

Disbelief is fading now, and we realize that the events of the past week are all too real. In time of tragedy and sorrow the human instinct is to turn to the past. We will all remember John F. Kennedy in some special moment:

Turning to wave from the steps beside a waiting plane.

Standing windblown before the Berlin City Hall.

Slashing the air with his hand to emphasize a point.

Walking hand in hand with a little girl named Caroline.

Announcing with pride that he was the man who accompanied Jacqueline Kennedy to Paris.

Standing in the cold one January morning and saying, "Ask not what your country can do for you, ask what you can do for your country."

My favorite memory will be a bright blue October day when he came to Chapel Hill to speak and receive an honorary degree. He was in a cap and gown as he walked across the green field at Kenan Stadium. He laughed with his audience when he announced that he came from "a small land-grant college up in Massachusetts." His robe flapped briskly behind him as he strode away from the ceremony. Every movement was alive and electric with youth. That is why his death is so hard to accept.

John Kennedy is a part of America's past now. The rocking chair has been stored away. The model of PT-109 that stood on his desk is gone. Caroline and John will not come again to entertain him with a dance in his office. The youthful dreams of the New Frontier are dead, dreams that truly lit his way to dusty death.

No one knows what history books will say about John Fitzgerald Kennedy except "he was shot down on a street in Dallas November 22, 1963," but those who lived through the past few days will carry some memory of him always. Only inasmuch as we renew ourselves in his image of tolerance and service will he live in more than history books and memory.

————

[From the North Wilkesboro (N.C.) Journal-Patriot, November 1963]

JOHN FITZGERALD KENNEDY

A dismal day in U.S. history was recorded Friday afternoon at 1:30 p.m., when John F. Kennedy, vigorous President of our country, was felled in a despicable act of murder.

It was a great personal tragedy to the Kennedy family and a tragic loss to the United States of America. There were those who opposed his views; there were few who didn't admire him for his personal charm, dedication to duty, his devotion to family, his Christian faith and gentlemanly qualities.

John F. Kennedy was an unusual man. Born into wealth, he prepared himself for public service. Blessed with a brilliant mind and vigorous optimistic view of life, he was a complete success in public affairs.

His administration was not without controversy, for it was an active one, proclaiming a bold, new era for the United States. While controversy swirled around him, his image suffered little, for he didn't resort to petty bickering. It was not his nature to do so.

Through the medium of television, the American people became closely associated with the President. They saw him in all phases of life, with his family, at affairs of state, at public functions. The people especially drew close to President Kennedy.

He was a young man, handsome, energetic, dynamic. His wife was beautiful and charming, and the Kennedy children romping through the White House captured the fancy of all.

President Kennedy was in good spirits Friday morning, telling the crowd that Mrs. Kennedy was not present because it "takes her longer to get organized," and quipping that it's supposed to "because she looks better than we do."

He was obviously pleased that Mrs. Kennedy was taking an active part in his campaign. Everywhere he went on his Texas campaign he was beaming.

But an assassin's bullet was destined to extinguish this wonderful spirit and personality.

When a reason is sought for this dastardly act, there can be none. Nothing was accomplished but utter waste and grief.

Now, in this hour of national tragedy, it behooves us to draw close to President Johnson.

He has had suddenly thrust upon him the greatest responsibility that man can bear.

It is hard for us to realize that our President could be shot down in the United States. We can only prayerfully hope that nothing like this will ever happen again.

————

[From the Raeford (N.C.) News-Journal, Nov. 28, 1963]

THE NATION IS TO BLAME

For the fourth time in history, the assassin's bullet has struck down a President of the United States.

In an unspeakable act of violence, John Fitzgerald Kennedy was slain Friday in the streets of Dallas, Tex., by a sniper who lay in wait for the Presidential caravan to pass.

The Nation mourns, and long shall mourn. For the bullet which felled our young and energetic leader also struck deep into the heart of America and the free world.

It is only of passing significance that the apparent assassin himself was slain as officers attempted to transfer him from one jail to another. The world was not deprived of an answer to the question: "Why was President Kennedy slain?"

The answer is written in the hearts of Americans everywhere.

It would be easy to write off the assassination as the criminal act of a fanatic, but in so doing, we would be closing our eyes to fact.

The Nation shares the blame.

There is in this land a growing hatred of those who would secure for all people the God-given rights of man.

President Kennedy was foremost among them. No man since Lincoln strived harder to bring to reality the brotherhood of man. And some who opposed him lashed out in venomous tongues with a resentment which was rapidly boiling into hate.

"They did not kill the President," we say of the radical right. "He was slain by a member of the lunatic left."

No. But they incited the fanatical fringe to bomb a church in Birmingham and to slay a Negro leader on its streets.

And when President Kennedy came to Texas, they did not pull the trigger. But they had murder in their hearts.

There is a lesson to be learned from this tragedy. We fervently hope that from this evil shall come good; that from this hate shall come love; that from this loss shall come gain.

That, we are sure, would be the desire of the man who said: "Ask not what your country can do for you; ask what you can do for your country."

[From the Reidsville (N.C.) Review,
Nov. 25, 1963]

There Was Another Death

The heartless murder of the President has struck dumb our Nation and much of the world. With befitting respect, we here in Reidsville add a voice to the world's common outcry of grief and indignation at this foul deed which was perhaps the inevitable climax to a summer of madness when the Nation's streets and public places became places of turmoil and danger.

But, because this is America we need have no fear that the transition of Government will not be brought about in an orderly manner. Our country will not be subjected to the chaos which would result from such a tragedy in other parts of the world.

Because this is America we were free to criticize; to oppose this, our leader, who is dead.

Because this is America we need fear no purge of those of us who may have entertained and expressed opinions different from that of the President.

Because this is America we see the mighty of the world converge on our shores in a reassuring outpouring of sympathy never before witnessed.

And because this is America we are moved today to write not a eulogy to our dead President whose untimely passing shook the world—but as he, himself, might have wished, we write instead of another death; another widow; other orphans.

In Dallas, Tex., Friday an American citizen, a police officer, gave his life in attempting to arrest the suspected slayer of this country's Chief.

Patrolman J. D. Tippitt, as much as the President, personified the American public servant. This man, just as the President, was not unaccustomed to danger. Twice before in his 11 years as a policeman he had faced death in line of duty. Normally, this man's death would go largely unnoticed outside his own city, but now the opportunity presents itself to make us mindful of the fact that his example is duplicated over and over again, throughout the Nation, year after year.

It is no sign of disrespect that today we switch from the scene of national mourning to remember this officer's careworn wife and his three children, who in the normal course of events will be quickly forgotten. "He was so good," she said. "I don't know what will happen now."

Neither do we, Mrs. Tippitt. But we do know that as long as the weaknesses of humanity spawn acts of inhumanity, men like your husband will continue to risk their lives in every community across the land, in a largely unappreciated effort to protect us, their neighbors, both the great and the small.

———

[From the Rutherfordton (N.C.) Rutherford County
News, Nov. 27, 1963]

John F. Kennedy—He Was Our President

Much has been said and written of the tragic crime against the United States—the assassination of the President.

We have little to add to what has already been said many times.

The sickening, infamous act, which has left us still stunned, should be considered as high a crime as sabotage or treason against the United States and the American system.

President John F. Kennedy was a strong Chief Executive who pushed hard for what he believed was right for the country.

Many of us did not share all of his beliefs, but that made him none the less our President.

As one Rutherfordton woman recalled her father speaking of an earlier President: "Whether he is a Republican or Democrat, whether or not I like what he is doing, he's my President."

Whether or not we agreed with the late President Kennedy, no matter what our political views, our religious faith, our race—he was our President.

All thinking people in Rutherford County and the rest of the country and the world are repulsed by the assassination and are saddened by the tragic death of the President.

We are fortunate that the American system provides for orderly "changing of the guard" in such emergencies. We are also fortunate that an experienced man is assuming the office of President.

Our new President, Lyndon B. Johnson, in his first public address after assuming this office, asked for our help and God's in this period of national crisis.

It is a time for all people to come to the aid of their country.

———

[From the Rutherfordton (N.C.) Rutherford County
News, Dec. 4, 1963]

President Kennedy

(By Dr. William T. Anthony)

Much has been said and written about the tragedy of the untimely and treacherous death of our late President. Through television and radio information and comment in fullest detail have been made available to everyone. And I realize more keenly than anyone else that I cannot presume to have anything of the smallest importance to add or to say.

Nevertheless I am obeying an impulse to think aloud in this way about a thought and reflection or two that have been and are in my mind, more perhaps for my own satisfaction than anything else.

The shock and grief at the death of Mr. Kennedy is worldwide. The crime of it and the great loss to the world pass, so it seems to me, our comprehension and realization. The shock of it is enough to move some of us even to revise and improve some of our thinking and opinions.

There are those who are now saying in all seriousness that Mr. Kennedy's death is part and result of the hate and venom and prejudice that are too common amongst us. Possibly so. I do not know. Who can tell for certain?

We have been told that all of us have a share in the guilt of it. To the extent that we do hate I suppose there is an element of truth in this. I am reminded of what Eugene Debs once said: "So long as there is a criminal class I am of it, so long as anyone is in prison

I am not free." It is enough to drive us to deep thinking and to our knees.

The office and job of the President of the United States is responsible and burdensome beyond the imagination of most of us. It is enough to inspire and fill everyone with soberness and restraint and self-command and the highest respect for the Presidency. So that it becomes impossible to think of the man in this high and lonely office without being always conscious of and assuming his integrity and sincerity and dedication to do and give his best for his country and ours.

The President is always more than the head and leader of his political party. He is the President of all of us. He needs the help and support of everyone. This is not to say that we are always to agree with him, or never to find fault with him, or even to oppose him and his measures.

But we should ever be deeply mindful of the dignity and sacredness of the presidential office. And as a supposedly religious people we should never forget to pray for our President even if we remember that we conscientiously voted against him. His task is terrifically heavy and crushing. The more we may disagree with him the greater his need of our prayers.

To pray earnestly for the President helps us to cultivate the right and just feeling about him and leads us to the deeper understanding of him that is our bounden duty to strive for.

President Johnson has asked earnestly and sincerely for the help and prayers of all of us. He has a right to this. He has great need of it. So let us pray for the President every day in our private devotions, every time that we go to church. Let us think and speak with restraint and respect about him on all occasions.

A young and good and brilliant and much-loved President and leader has been killed by an assassin's bullet. Whoever the murderer, whatever the reason and motive, how it all came about, and who of us know enough to speak responsibly and with sufficient knowledge? Mr. Kennedy is dead.

Let us all highly resolve to do away with as much as possible all wrong thinking and evil speaking. Let us pray with all our heart every day for our President that he and we together may do our best to make us a truly religious, righteous, and God-fearing people.

———

[From the Rutherfordton (N.C.) Rutherford County News, Dec. 11, 1963]

ANDERSON WRITES LETTER ON DEATH OF PRESIDENT

(EDITOR'S NOTE.—The shots that killed President John F. Kennedy have been heard around the world. Reactions to this crime, which may have changed the course of history, have come from every corner of the earth. A Rutherfordton native, Fred Anderson, who is presently studying at Oxford University, England, has written the following letter to a Chapel Hill friend expressing his feelings and those of the Englishmen around him to the Kennedy death.)

President Kennedy's death has left a dark, deep trace upon the minds and hearts of the people of England. Again and again during this tragic weekend I have wished that Americans could see firsthand how the English, and all the people of Europe, are sharing with us deeply grieved and troubled hearts over the loss we are all strained to bear. But the reaction here this weekend affirms that in spite of often ardent disapproval of American policy, in spite of complaints of American control of European affairs, in spite of manifold criticisms of our handling of our internal affairs, Europeans still feel a profound alliance with our cause and destiny and they were particularly involved with the fate of the man upon whom had been placed the responsibility of leading, not only our own country, but the entire Western world. He was our President, but we selected him to lead our country. I can see now from the somber, intense faces of Englishmen around me in Oxford, that he belonged in effect to them as well.

It is difficult to describe the feeling the small group of Americans in my college had when every act and word, every betrayed emotion, became a profound personal tribute to our countryman. In despair there was pride, and a realization of the great respect held here for the man. It was 7:30 in the evening before the news reached us, but before 11 p.m. that night the rector of our college had written a personal note of condolence to every American in the college—14 in all. Balliol College Chapel was filled at 10 p.m. the same night for prayer and tribute. Every college in Oxford has flown the British flag at half-mast since Friday. Sunday afternoon Radcliffe Square, the center of the university, was filled with people who had come to remember the late President in silence. And of course there have been long, unhappy conversations in which for once the stubborn heat of political argument has been replaced by unashamed acknowledgment of what the President meant personally to people here.

I have tried to see as best I could what it is that made the Englishman and Europeans across the channel so profoundly admire the President in particular. It seems to boil down to this, that he maintained a hopeful and even idealistic outlook for the future, an outlook and vision which he tempered with a sober and practical awareness of the means one uses in a political world to gain one's ends. This is a great tribute for any man coming from Europeans, for they among all the peoples on earth are the best-trained to know the virtue, having been betrayed by so many not possessing it during the past strife-ridden decades.

This summer Kennedy made a speech in Berlin that won him the hearts of all Germany. It was an idealistic speech, full of spirit and optimism, yet fully admitting the grave difficulties of modern Berlin in its fight to remain free. He ended every point concerning courage and freedom with the refrain, "I am a Berliner." And now we can see that everyone in Germany who heard him knew that in spirit he was. He was to Europeans a man who could translate the American ideal into terms a skeptical and wary European could appreciate and understand.

And finally we come to the essence of what was so tragic to the people here in his untimely death. The

Sunday edition of the Observer of London expresses it quite well: "When great men of state die, it is their achievements which come to mind. The tragedy of Kennedy's death is that we have also to mourn the achievements to come. There is a feeling that the future has been betrayed."

Thus there is a deep-seated sense of frustration here, much as I know there is at home.

[From the Salisbury (N.C.) Sunday Post, Nov. 24, 1963]

JOHN F. KENNEDY, A GREAT MAN

(By Homer F. Lucas)

John F. Kennedy was truly a great man.

He was just a man.

He was a man who believed all men were equal in the sight of God.

He was a man of peace.

He was a man determined, with all his soul and body, that the ravages of war would never again befall mortal man.

He was a man of love.

He was a man born to riches. He was a man who loved the ordinary man, like you and me.

He was a man of courage.

He was a man who was the butt of ridicule and nasty jokes as he displayed his courage.

He was a man of power. He was a man who never wielded, as history will evaluate, this power unjustly.

He was more than mere man to the men of the free world. He was a hope, a symbol.

He was a man who gave so much of himself to the people of the world.

He was a man of principle.

He was a kindly man.

He was a man of easy formality.

We was a man, above all, of magnificent heart.

He was a man who has passed into a new world from which no traveler, but one, has returned.

But the world which he loved and served remains.

There are times in life when time stands still.

Now is such a time.

The men of the free world, the men of love, the men of peace, and the men of courage are groping in darkness for the light.

But the light is there in the principles and beliefs of John F. Kennedy, a truly great man.

[From the Waynesville (N.C.) Mountaineer, Nov. 25, 1963]

ALL OUR ENEMIES AREN'T FOREIGNERS

It has been 3 days now since the world was shocked and sickened by the tragic murder of President Kennedy. The world is still in a daze trying to shake itself loose from what seems an unreality.

The murder appears to have been deliberate. It was apparently planned in every detail. This makes the tragedy all the more heartbreaking.

Perhaps the real motive will never be known. Maybe it will, but the damage and loss of a great man to the world will remain. Civilized men wonder in heartbreak just what could be in a man's heart to cause him to do such a barbaric deed.

This Nation was shocked beyond words and as Senator Sam Ervin, Jr., said "It just makes you sick." And as sick as the Nation still remains over the tragic news, one thing is certain, we are a united nation of solidarity, and determination in purpose and spirit.

In the days ahead, it is going to be essential to maintain this unity, as President Johnson takes over and organizes his men for the grave tasks ahead.

Very few times in the history of this Nation has there been a greater need for divine guidance than now. It has been a source of gratification to hear President Johnson and those to be closely associated with him, point to this very fact.

The tragic event of "Black Friday" will be a constant reminder for the years to come that all of our enemies do not live on foreign soil.

[From the Waynesville (N.C.) Mountaineer, Dec. 9, 1963]

TWO BLACK DAYS ON THE PAGES OF U.S. HISTORY

Thousands of citizens were unaware Saturday, December 7, that it was 22 years ago that America suffered the worst sneak attack in history as the Japanese attacked Pearl Harbor and thus plunged us into World War II.

That was a black hour in American history which will go down as comparable to another black hour, November 22, when President Kennedy was slain.

Such occasions as these come and go and we often let the years erase them from our minds. Perhaps it would be better if we would be ever aware that any tragedy can and does happen in this modern world and age.

[From the Waynesville (N.C.) Mountaineer, Dec. 9, 1963]

OFFICE OF PRESIDENT IS DUE MORE RESPECT

November 22 will long be remembered as "Black Friday" or the day of the tragic death of President Kennedy.

Historians might also record that November 22 marks another event. It could well be the beginning of an era when the American people take a different attitude toward the office of President.

In the past several score years, the average American has had a tendency to ridicule, and poke fun at the office of President as well as the man. Comedians have made the President the subject of many a joke. Records have been made which were nothing more than ridicule or belittling the man and office.

There must be a certain degree of guilt on the consciences of many an American that participated in this thing of "downgrading" the highest elective office in our land.

Peoples in other lands are taught to look with respect and with dignity to their leaders.

The tragic death of a noble man could well be the turning point of attitude of Americans on this matter.

It is way past time to correct the errors of our ways, and look up to the office of President, even if at times we disagree with policies.

———

[From radio station WBBB, Burlington-Graham, N.C., Dec. 11, 1963]

THE SENATE PUTS ASIDE ITS WORK TODAY TO EULOGIZE THE LATE PRESIDENT; AS OUR CONTRIBUTION TO THE OCCASION, WE PRESENT THE FOLLOWING "RADIOTORIAL"

The President is dead, long live the President. We hardly think there is a man living who would exchange places today with either the dead or living President. Whether we all liked all of the policies set forth by President Kennedy, none of us can deny but that he was sincere in his beliefs and his desires to help his fellow man. It must be admitted that any man who sets forth on a program to improve life for so many will face a barrier of misunderstanding, criticism, and even hate, which those who have no desire to be improved will throw up around themselves. The path of progress is a long but narrow thoroughfare which runs through a forest of doubt and fear, and those who attempt to lead the way down this narrow path are naturally the first to meet his enemy. President Kennedy met an enemy—at this point, we are prone to believe that whoever pulled the trigger that started that fatal bullet on its way, was a misguided, confused, and disarranged mental deficient. No man, or men, in this modern time could plan such a dastardly act and still be in his right senses. I also believe that, had he lived, President Kennedy would have expressed a sympathy for the man. But the President is dead, and now, long live the President. Lyndon B. Johnson has had thrust upon him the heaviest burden of any living man today. In becoming the President of the United States by inheritance, he must begin his administration below the bottom, and yet maintain it for the present, at least, at the level President Kennedy left it. In memory of President Kennedy he must justify the past and solidify the future. President Johnson, with all of his political finesse must have the full cooperation of the people and of Congress.

And Congress must also recognize the grave responsibility it faces—to pass or reject the political pets of the Kennedy administration, without offending the memory of a great President who died in the service of his country, or without endangering the political future of his successor who will die a thousand deaths in his efforts to unify a country, to say nothing of the world. How would you, as a private citizen, accept these responsibilities? And so, let us forget the past, accept the present, and look toward the future with a determination that we will all serve as good citizens, our new President, in memory of the old. The President is dead. Long live the President.

ADDRESS BY

Hon. Pat McNamara

OF MICHIGAN

Mr. President, as we rise on this melancholy occasion to eulogize our late President, John F. Kennedy, I find the terrible emotions of that dreadful day less than 3 weeks ago are renewed.

The sense of shock is still with us, and perhaps it never will be dulled much by the passage of time.

How often since has some corner of our mind sought to trick us into believing that it did not happen, that it was some bad dream from which we will awake.

But, of course, stark reality is always with us.

We have lost our President. We have lost him under circumstances of which, however ugly they may be, it truly can be said that he gave his life to his country.

We, the people, have lost a President in a most tragic manner that is an outrage against civilization.

Many of us in this Senate Chamber have an additional loss. We have lost a friend.

For many years John Kennedy was our colleague in the Senate.

Here we came to know him intimately as a warm human being, yet possessing the drive and intelligence that ultimately carried him to our highest office.

We watched this rise to the Presidency. Some of us did what we could to help it take place. Others, carrying out the vital traditions of our political system, sought to prevent it.

But when we gathered on the steps of this Capitol on January 20, 1961, to hear John Kennedy deliver his remarkable inaugural address, I am sure that all of us, all the American people, felt the spark and the promise of that eloquent message.

But that spark and that promise have been cruelly snuffed out, depriving our country, and, indeed, the world, of a leader of tremendous ability and human understanding.

I do not pretend to know how the writers of the future will treat the Kennedy administration as they compress these 3 years into the unemotional context of history.

But I do sincerely believe that our Nation—and the world—are the stronger for these 3 years. The cause of human freedom and dignity has been protected and advanced. No greater legacy can be asked of any leader.

I feel privileged to have been a participant in the Kennedy administration, and to have known and worked with John Kennedy in the Senate.

For several years we were seatmates in the rear row of this Chamber, and we served together on the Committee on Labor and Public Welfare. After he became President we cooperated on many matters of legislation and Government.

These associations are simply memories now, but they are good memories and ones that I will prize.

In paying these tributes to our departed friend and President, we also extend our heartfelt sympathies to his courageous widow, his two children, and other members of the Kennedy family.

Their personal loss is great. But if it is possible for them to find any comfort in this tragic situation, it is that their grief is shared by millions upon millions of citizens of our world.

ADDRESS BY

Hon. Vance Hartke

OF INDIANA

Mr. President, some 32 centuries ago in the Sinai Peninsula there lived and died a great and beloved leader of his people. A natural leader, he was a man who grew up in wealth, amid palace splendor. But he forsook inherited ease for a thankless, rugged life as champion of his fellow men. He became a political organizer, a lawgiver, a man with a vision of a promised land, one who walked close to God and to the common people.

At the close of his life, after many trials and tribulations suffered for the good of those he served, he stood on a mountain and looked upon the better land he had envisioned. But it was not his destiny to lead the nation further. To Moses, scripture says, the Lord spoke on Mount Nebo, saying:

I have let you see it with your own eyes, but you shall not go over there.

So it was with our great and beloved leader. The story continues:

So, Moses the servant of the Lord died there in the land of Moab.

But it also says of him:

His eye was not dim, nor his natural force abated.

And it tells the deep-felt tribute of the people whom he led:

And the people of Israel wept for Moses in the plains of Moab 30 days.

Today this Nation is in the midst of 30 days of mourning, even as were the Israelites of old. Like them, we have wept for the loss of our leader. To Americans everywhere, the shocking news was so deeply felt, that tears of grief so freely flowing, that probably nothing in history can match the surge of national, or even international, sorrow. It was as though each family had lost a member of its own, someone just beyond the intimacy of our own fireside. We are still in mourning, and it will not cease at the end of 30 days. Thousands will still journey daily, as they do today, to the white picketed enclosure on the hill in Arlington, where the eternal flame continues to burn as it keeps his memory alive.

There was tragedy in Dallas. The enormity of the crime enacted there becomes still greater tragedy in the realization that John Fitzgerald Kennedy was one, even more than the aged Moses, whose "eye was not dim, nor his natural force abated." His was the vigor of youthful prime; his was the natural force of a vital personality; his was the bright eye of unflagging interest turning to every area of human problems.

We who were his colleagues in this legislative body, we who acknowledged his leadership as President in a very special relationship, knew well his "natural force." To have lost the qualities of his leadership in these infinitely complex times, so unimaginable to the mourners for the leadership of Moses, is a compounding of our loss. For who knows, looking upon the promise of these 3 years of his Presidency, what might have been the incalculable results of another 30 years of life as a President and public leader?

There is another verse of Scripture which says:

Their young men shall see visions and their old men shall dream dreams.

Not yet old enough to dream the old man's dreams of the past, John Kennedy was still young enough to have fair visions of the future. Nor were they the apparitions of a deluded visionary. For he had looked upon the future with the eyes of both idealism and realism, focussing them together in a rare phenomenon of prophetic vision. Standing like Moses on the lonely eminence whence leadership had taken him, he looked upon that promised land of a future better America. Yet he was denied the right to enter:

I have let you see it with your eyes, but you shall not go over there.

But as with Moses, the dream, the vision, will not die. The promised land became to the Israelites a reality, and they forever remembered the leader they had mourned in the land of Moab for 30 days.

The Book of Deuteronomy closes with the death of Moses. It is followed by the Book of Joshua, which opens with these words:

After the death of Moses, the servant of the Lord, the Lord said to Joshua the son of Nun, Moses' minister: "Moses my servant is dead; now therefore arise, go over this Jordan, you and all this people, into the land which I am giving to them, to the people of Israel."

Moses had long since chosen Joshua to be his successor, and the continuation of his work was assured.

Looking out upon our own promised land, President Kennedy saw in the future a nation with greater justice for all its people, white and black alike. He looked upon a land which gave hope and promise of work for all and deprivation for none. He saw economic security where there is still too often poverty and uncertainty. His was a vision, but the vision was of a reality attainable in the future.

We now must go over this Jordan. We must leave our sorrowing on the plains of Moab and turn to Joshua, Moses' minister and the new leader of all the people, for guidance in his stead. The Israelites turned not their backs on the vision their Moses had set before them. They wept, as

we weep, but they also rallied to the challenge given them. They fulfilled the vision; they crossed "this Jordan."

Of Moses it was said:

No man knows the place of his burial to this day.

We, on the other hand, know as does all the world the burial place of John F. Kennedy. We are already spontaneously making of it a national shrine for the homage and the honor demanded by his leadership and a nation's love, mingled in these days of mourning. But to the Israelites, inspired and welded into a nation by their leader's vision, the important thing was to press on for the goals he had seen with his eyes but been denied in the flesh.

We mourn a great, young, vibrant leader:

His eye was not dim, nor his natural force abated.

The Lord let him stand on Mount Nebo and see with his eyes, but in His inscrutable way said to John F. Kennedy, "You shall not go over there."

Through Joshua, his minister, the goals of Moses lived on until the people were moved to victorious entry into the promised land. As we follow President Johnson across "this Jordan" we will be treading paths untrod before but clearly seen. When we have arrived, we will look back to the lonely tragic figure on our own Mount Nebo, to the leader who was denied his own entry to the land he sought. Then we will know that we are as fortunate as the Israelites, whose attainment of the goal owed so much to the inspiration of their dead leader as well as to the prowess of his successor.

Only a few months ago President Kennedy looked out from very near the spot where now he lies beneath the eternal flame, out upon the memorial to Lincoln, the monument to Washington, and the dome of this building where he himself once sat.

We must take new courage for the future, we must gird up our belts and follow after the vision, as his successor leads us on. President Kennedy saw the promised land; he could not enter. We must enter for him, drive out the enemies of hatred and dissidence, and build the alabaster cities of America the beautiful. In his memory, we will do so.

ADDRESS BY

Hon. Jennings Randolph

OF WEST VIRGINIA

Mr. President, in the days and nights of national mourning and personal grief since the assassination of President John Fitzgerald Kennedy, our minds and hearts have turned from the initial incredulity and shock, to sorrow, and finally to an appraisal of our national character in response to this tragic event.

Senators today have approached this time of memorial by commending the achievements of the late President who once served so well in this forum and who served also in the House of Representatives.

I recall, as do my colleagues and those in the galleries, the period of national and official mourning when the body of President John F. Kennedy lay in state in the great rotunda of the Capitol, approximately halfway between the two legislative Chambers in which he had labored. If there was one significant fact that impressed me during the period when the President was again among us in the Capitol Building, it was that more than one-third of the persons who passed reverently by his bier were boys and girls in their teens. I watched them personally as they moved slowly past, and later watched them also by television.

Citizens from every walk of life were there, expressing their sincere admiration, their genuine love, and their real affection for a fallen leader. But it was the large numbers of young mourners who left me profoundly moved. Generals and admirals, accompanied by their small children, were in the long lines trudging slowly up Capitol Hill. Citizens of high estate and low stood quietly, shoulder to shoulder, awaiting their turn to salute the slain President. And with them were the young people.

The President was a gallant man. Gallantry appeals to the youth of the United States and of the world. Youth sensed in the career of John F. Kennedy something that was good and noble.

I remember the nine young men who drove 400 miles from Huntington, W. Va., to Washington, D.C., that they might express their reverent respect—and it was that—for the Presi-dent of the United States whom they, in a degree, felt they knew and understood.

These nine youthful Americans were students at Marshall University, located at Huntington, on the western border of our State. Yet, they felt compelled to make the long trip to Washington.

I asked those young men, "Why do you come?"

They replied, "We came because we just had to come."

There were tears in their eyes as they spoke.

I remember five other young men who came from Fairmont State College, at Fairmont, W. Va. They began an automobile pilgrimage to Washington at approximately 2:30 in the afternoon and arrived at approximately 7:45 in the evening. They parked their car downtown and joined the line of grieving thousands. Eight and one-half hours later those five young men from the hills of West Virginia walked by the bier of the late President, expressing in reverent silence their appreciation for his life and their sorrow at his death.

I asked them why they came.

They replied, in essence, "He was our President, and we, as young people, felt that he was concerned with our future."

In reviewing the tragic events of last month, we have, in almost stupefaction asked ourselves, "What manner of people are we that such violence is bred in our midst?" This question, and the self-appraisals which it engenders may help to make us better men and women. But in justice to the American character, for which John F. Kennedy held such high hopes, let us also acknowledge that the same Nation which fostered his assassin, and the assassin's assassin, gave birth to John Kennedy and responded to his call for finer ways and higher deeds for humans everywhere.

Those who will write the judgment of this era will not appraise us on the basis of that insane moment in Dallas—but on the extent to which we as a nation live up to the ideals for which John Kennedy labored.

We today do not judge Athens on the basis of the bigotry and intolerance which sent Socrates to his death. Rather, we marvel at a people and culture which could produce a Socrates and his followers who nurtured his vision of the good life.

So, too, will we be judged by our commitment to the vision which our late and great President held forth for America and the world. His sacrifice will not, unfortunately, dispel all misunderstanding and rancor from our midst. For another Man, Jesus of Nazareth, died almost 2,000 years ago in order to assume the burden of man's evil, but evil is still with us.

For those of us who had the honor of knowing and working with John Kennedy, our lives have already been increased by this cherished experience. And the lives of all Americans will be enhanced if they truly understand the examples of the martyred President, and of the gallant lady who helped support him in his life and helped sustain a Nation in his death.

This example was best phrased by President Kennedy himself, shortly before his tragic earthly ending, when he defined his concept of happiness as being a life in which one utilized all his capacities in the achievement of personal excellence and public service. President Kennedy thus becomes identified with another American President, the author of the Declaration of Independence, who declared the "pursuit of happiness" to be among the unalienable rights of all.

Therefore, perhaps the most meaningful tribute to President Kennedy, and one which would create a living memorial in the hearts of all Americans, would be for all citizens to turn aside from the more shallow pursuits of pleasure, and to seek these standards of spiritual, moral, and intellectual strength which he articulated so clearly and eloquently.

And, we are moved today by an element of personal as well as official loss which millions of families sense in the passing of President Kennedy. My wife, Mary, and our two sons join me in expressing our remembrance to the relatives of the late President.

Our hearts go out to the mother and father of John F. Kennedy; to his fine sisters; to his brothers, Attorney General Robert F. Kennedy, and Senator Edward M. Kennedy, of Massachusetts. And finally, we remember his courageous wife, Jacqueline Kennedy, and her two lovely children, who have suffered a loss far beyond anything we ourselves can know. We shall be often in prayer for them.

ADDRESS BY

Hon. Albert Gore

OF TENNESSEE

Mr. President, there arose amongst us a man with grace and wit, with a style and a charm given to but few mortals. The admiration he attracted and the loyalty he won were worldwide.

Only 2 hours ago, at a luncheon at which I was the host, for visiting dignitaries from Guinea, word was given to me and to other Members of this body of the sorrow and the grief felt by the people of that faraway land. Indeed, Mr. President, from around the world we know of the heavy hearts of people who believed in President Kennedy, who trusted him, and who held him to be their champion for what is right, true, good, and brave.

Other generations of Americans have suffered the experience of the assassination of their leader. It is our burden to have seen a champion and a leader amongst all men stricken down in the splendor of his manhood, and now immortalized in the minds and in the hearts of all mankind.

Mr. President, one must wonder why—with all the agitation and the disturbances of our times, the stress and the distress, and the known dangers to leaders in such times—young men aspire to the high Office of President of the United States. I believe it is because of patriotism, pride, and the basic desire of man to win the approval of fellow men, that one is driven on. Beyond that, there are those who are intensely motivated to achieve and to do good in their time, to accomplish, and to give. Except for these motivations—such patriotism, pride, and desire—there would not have been a George Washington, a Lincoln, a Roosevelt, a Kennedy, or a President Johnson. Men thus highly and intensely motivated would, I believe, prefer to live fruitfully and dangerously, rather than obscurely in longevity.

The death of President Kennedy was a keen personal sorrow for me. We served together in the House of Representatives. We were seat mates on the Senate Foreign Relations Committee.

We served together on a special Senate committee where we joined in writing minority views. In many other ways we had official and personal associations which I treasure.

There were other moments which I shall always treasure. On one unforgettable evening, when he was then Representative Kennedy, and when the present senior Senator, the gentleman from Kentucky [Mr. Cooper], was then U.S. delegate to the United Nations, along with one other couple, the Ambassador and Mrs. Cooper, my wife and I were present at a little party at which the young Representative John F. Kennedy met a beautiful young lady, Jacqueline Bouvier, who later became his bride.

Upon that occasion, Representative Kennedy, Ambassador Cooper, and I had each recently announced our candidacies for the U.S. Senate. We compared the manner of our announcements, engaged in searching discussion of political techniques and tactics and, of course, we jested with each other as to our own foibles.

It so happened that all three of us were elected, and there was a reunion of the group on another unforgettable evening to celebrate our victories.

Ere long, the beautiful girl became Mrs. Kennedy. Then Caroline, the Presidency, and John-John. A live, vibrant, glamorous, beloved family.

Jacqueline Kennedy became an American heroine during the tragic hours following the horrible assassination. She bore up magnificently. She deported herself with the courage worthy of her gallant but fallen husband.

The works and words of John F. Kennedy have been burned into the hearts and minds of men and will last so long as America lasts.

He is a hero, now immortalized. We cherish his eloquence. His lofty ideals, the sentiments he expressed—and expressed in a manner to inspire all mankind—these are now a precious part of the heritage of our land.

To his widow, and to the little children, who may some day read the proceedings of today, I pour out all the sympathy of which my being is capable.

To his father and mother, his brothers and sisters—all of them I call my friends—I extend the deepest of sympathy. Theirs has been a great loss, but theirs has been a great privilege to have had the companionship, the love, and the inspiration of a truly good and great man.

ADDRESS BY

Hon. Philip A. Hart

OF MICHIGAN

Mr. President, today Senators will fill page after page of the Congressional Record with words, even though we are all acutely aware that words are hopelessly inadequate.

In the past few weeks millions of the world's people have worn a look of stunned despair. Certainly, nothing I could say would be a more eloquent tribute to John F. Kennedy than the grief on those faces. It is folly for me to try. And I know that many feel as helplessly inadequate for this chore as I do.

Why do we try?

Surely, the name of John F. Kennedy—like the dead at Gettysburg—has already been consecrated far beyond our poor power to add or detract.

Yet, we feel impelled to rise, one by one, and offer a few words in praise of his vision, courage and human understanding. Why do we do this? One reason, I think, is that a eulogy day gives us a chance to pour our grief into a common pool where it can be shared more readily and therefore borne more easily.

And what else? Yes, it gives us a forum to praise those attributes we most admire: vision, courage, human understanding. This may be useful. Praise provides the warmth that may nurture vision, courage and human understanding among others in our Nation, perhaps even among ourselves.

Without a doubt, these attributes deserve and need all the encouragement they can get.

But vision, courage and human understanding are easy to praise. They are abstractions. There is no lobby against them. No pickets will appear in opposition.

So perhaps for a moment we should turn our attention not to John F. Kennedy's attributes but rather to the products of those attributes. Civil rights. Tax reduction and reform. Aid to education—yes, the search for peace, the concern for our older citizens, and for an expanding economy.

President Johnson has put it simply and straightforwardly. He said that the enactment of President Kennedy's major programs would be the finest tribute we could offer to John F. Kennedy, unlike most of the stunned faces across the world, we can deliver on that one. Sometimes we feel almost sacrilegious in wishing that someone who has departed this life could tell us what he would most like to have us do in acknowledgment of his passing. I believe, without being insensitive or callous, that we can ask ourselves, "What would he like to see us doing at this moment?" I have a suspicion at this moment he would prefer to have the Senate debating the civil rights bill.

After all, can we honestly admire President Kennedy's vision without also admiring his plan for the Nation's children? Can we admire his courage without admiring his departure from the "conventional wisdom" of economics? Can we admire his human understanding without admiring his civil rights bill?

I do not say that we can admire only those men with whom we are in full agreement. But President Kennedy was not a man who ever demanded absolute conformity.

On the contrary, John F. Kennedy was a strong man—so strong that he understood fully that there are very few questions that can be given absolute answers.

His courage and vision were matched by thoughtfulness and deep insights. There was one thread of continuity in all his programs and I think it can be briefly stated like this: He sought to allow each man to fulfill completely the potential granted by his Creator.

This really was his essential goal, and the strength he showed in pursuing it was the strength of flexibility. This is what I believe history will record about him. This is what I like to believe history will record about him.

And how incredible will historians find the fact that this man's record in Congress and this man's goals in the White House were thought by some to be "soft on the Constitution."

Many have said that John Kennedy had an understanding of history. Indeed he did. He sensed, I believe, those forces which affect the destiny of nations, not merely of men.

There is one lesson of history he would hope we would understand and, understanding, react to.

There have been other great nations on the center of the world stage in the centuries which precede this, and historians indicate that not all of them had to fail. Not all of them needed to become footnotes in history, except that they dilly-dallied over making necessary reform until it was too late.

This is the kind of responsibility which happens to be ours in the Congress. It is for that reason, I suggest, that our best tribute would be to move on in the pursuit of those goals which he so dramatically portrayed for us.

Like it or not, be it fair or unfair, this Congress has acquired a reputation for inaction. Whether it is fair I do not propose to debate.

But the unhappy fact remains that we have the image of a do-nothing Congress. This is not so much because we have done nothing. It is more because we have done nothing with those pieces of legislation on which the Nation's attention has been riveted—the pieces of legislation that events and the late President dramatized before the country.

This is the situation and we cannot escape it. So essentially, my eulogy of President Kennedy consists largely of a pledge of support to President Johnson.

I join the new President in an appeal for legislation that will be a true memorial to President Kennedy—legislation of that whole litany of recommendations he gave us; legislation in civil rights, in aid to secondary and elementary schools, in youth opportunities, in tax reform—legislation that will be as bright and lasting as the flame that so many earlier mentioned, which burns now on that hillside in Arlington.

If I can be confident of anything, it is that for at least this once I can confidently speak the universal voice of the people of Michigan. Without exception, they would have me express to the Kennedy family their understanding and sympathy. For my own family, I assure each of them of a continual remembrance in our prayers.

ADDRESS BY

Hon. Paul H. Douglas

OF ILLINOIS

Mr. President, the predominant impression which I and many others formed of President Kennedy during the 15 years in Washington with him was his extraordinary composure under strain. During the strenuous and critical days of the 1960 campaign, when I was frequently with him, I never noticed the slightest sign of irritability. Similarly, in the hot legislative struggles which we have had in Congress when the President was sorely tried, he seemed to be completely free from excitement or resentment, nor did he ever blame those who differed with him or who bitterly opposed him.

Some people thought this was a proof that he did not have deep emotions and that he was not deeply concerned either with people or with issues. To my mind this was not so. It did not indicate an absence of emotions, but rather a mastery over them. The Scottish playwright, J. M. Barrie, once defined courage as "grace under pressure." If this is so—and this is certainly one attribute of courage—then John Kennedy possessed courage to a supreme degree.

This quality paid off to the greatest extent in the Cuban crisis of last year. Under that tremendous strain the President might well have been pardoned had he lost his head. He was determined to prevent any danger to the United States and to take the responsibility for an attack on the Cuban missile bases, had that been necessary, but he was also anxious to prevent a nuclear war, if this was possible. He therefore gave Khrushchev an opportunity to back down without too great a loss of face. By following this course he skirted the precipice of total war by a hair's breadth. He was able both to obtain the removal of the missiles and a reduction in Russian forces—and at the same time keep the peace. A lesser man could never have done this.

The second impression I had of the President was his extraordinary intelligence and mental ability. This was demonstrated in the way in which he handled the debate on the puzzling issue of secondary boycotts in 1959. This is the most difficult issue in the whole field of labor relations and the President came to the correct conclusions down to 100th of an inch. It was like seeing a skilled surgeon operate.

Without any reflection upon other Presidents, I believe that he ranks along with Wilson, Lincoln, and Jefferson as among the four great intellectuals in the history of our Presidency. He was widely read and a deep student of history. He was broadly versed in the poetry and litera-
ture of the Western World. He was also interested in the arts of painting, sculpture, architecture, and music. He was not ashamed to be interested in these things. He was, instead, proud to have these broad interests and to be a practitioner of some of them. He was the one public figure of our time to win a Pulitzer Prize in history. He honored those who had surpassing achievements in their fields and sought to make the American public respect them more. He raised, indeed, the whole level of our intellectual and cultural life.

His political programs were designed for the good of America and the world. It is well to create tangible monuments which will bear his name into the far future. But I think we can best create a memorial for him by our devotion to the great tasks of civil rights, the abolition of unemployment, and a more abundant life for the great mass of American citizens.

ADDRESS BY

Hon. Claiborne Pell

OF RHODE ISLAND

Mr. President, John Fitzgerald Kennedy had the sixth shortest term of any of the 34 Presidents who preceded him. He was the youngest man ever to hold that high office. Yet, history may well show that he did more than any other of our Presidents to raise the sights and elevate the spirit of our National Government and the aspirations of our people, not just in our own United States but throughout our world as well. He set a marvelous and harmonious course of domestic growth and fairness and of external peace. And, now, as we think and talk of him with grief in our hearts we find ourselves overwhelmed with sadness because his inspiring mind and presence, his vigor and sparkling life, have been taken from us so abruptly.

Our own State of Rhode Island particularly grieves because Rhode Islanders knew President Kennedy and his First Lady as friends and neighbors of long standing. He had vacationed in Newport before the war. He had received his PT boat training at Melville on our Narragansett Bay. He had visited our State in the years following the war—to speak at our Democratic dinner in 1954 and to court his future bride, whose family affiliations with Newport are deeply rooted. I remember attending his marriage in Newport in the company of my predecessor, Theodore Francis Green. And, ever since that time, President Kennedy's affection for Newport and Rhode Island grew, as did Rhode Islanders' esteem, admiration, and regard for him. He found in Newport privacy and relaxation, the two rarest luxuries that ever can be enjoyed by a President of the United States. And only a few weeks ago, he asked that arrangements be made to rent a house in Newport so that he could have a summer White House there this coming year.

John Kennedy's secure place in history has been won because he raised the sights of all Americans. The goals he set for his administration in his inaugural address just over 1,000 days before his death and only a few yards from this very Chamber were the most soaring goals that had ever been set by an American President. These were soaring goals of growth for our country, not only in physical terms, but in education and culture. These were goals, not just for our country, not just our hemisphere, but the world. Yes, even for space beyond.

It took a while for our people to fully grasp the soaring nature of these goals. Because he changed the tempo and raised the level of our aspirations, our people through our Congress hesitated at first about rising to the heights his vision made clear.

Most important, President Kennedy recognized the fact that whether we like it or not, all human beings share the same planet and the same atmosphere. As he said at the United Nations, there must eventually come some sort of international control of the nuclear weapons of death and destruction. And he eloquently laid out a path beyond this achievement to the even higher goal of the eventual and complete disarmament of the nations of our world.

For these reasons, and in this manner, he kept first things first in his mind. He always recognized that important as they are, economic growth and integration would be in vain if the human race were to suffer immolation. As a student of history, he took the long view whenever he could. What was the use of thinking only in terms of next year or the year after when we should be planning for the world of 2000?

To my mind, the greatest service President Kennedy rendered was that he raised our sights.

The tragedy of his assassination is that while his course was set, his path, his trajectory, was cut off long before all his goals could be achieved.

The best memorial we can offer President Kennedy is to keep our sights high, our heads high, to follow the course he set, but speed our tempo and to keep our eyes fixed on the vision he gave us. President Johnson has eloquently and magnificently reaffirmed these principles. As President Johnson stated, "Let us continue"—continue to bring fairness, education and a decent way of life, not just to all Americans, but to all men everywhere; continue toward a world of complete and total disarmament, a world from which the scourge of nuclear weapons is removed. Then, the year 2000 will not be our second Dark Age, but rather a golden age, a true millennium.

Finally, and speaking personally and as an old friend of President and Mrs. Kennedy, I extend all my homage to him as a grand gentleman and to her as a valiant and gallant lady. May the tone and sparkle they set so bravely continue to excite our national life for many years. And may she, their two lovely children, his parents, and his brothers and sisters all accept the utter sympathy of my wife and me and of our children.

ADDRESS BY

Hon. Clifford P. Case

OF NEW JERSEY

Mr. President, in the amount of time fairly allocable to each of us, it would be impossible adequately to express even our present impressions of the late President. In any event, it is unquestionably too early for a definitive appraisal. As has been said before, history will make that appraisal.

One thing we can be sure of is that those who loved the President—and all of us who knew him did—need have no fear that the final judgment of history will not be high indeed.

It is appropriate at this time, I think, to express merely a brief personal word. Like every other American family, our family, my wife, my children, and I, were deeply moved, were incredulous at first when we heard the news, and were shaken, as we have not often been shaken, by the news of the disaster. It was not merely because— though it was partly because—it was the death of a President of the United States. It was not just because of horror at the way in which the death occurred, or of the sadness that always exists when youth is cut off in its prime. Beyond all those considerations—and this, I know, was the experience of millions and millions of Americans—there was a very direct sense of personal involvement in the life, and then in the loss, of this man.

He had the capacity, though he was not an extrovert as many politicians are, of giving you the realization that he understood you; that he saw through what might be barriers to understanding; that he understood what you had in your mind. Very quickly there arose a feeling of mutual understanding of the sort that usually exists only between those who are most intimate and constantly in contact with one another. This was partly a matter of his keen intellect, and partly a matter of his sensitive reaction to the feelings of other human beings.

Comparable to the almost instinctive understanding that John F. Kennedy had of those with whom he came in contact was his appreciation of the problems we face in this country and that the world faces.

It is not necessary to assert—and surely he would not have been one to assert—that he had advanced us far along the road toward a final solution of these problems. Yet his understanding of them, with this fine mind of his, and his sensibilities, was, in itself, an essential step toward their resolution.

He had the understanding and the courage to state publicly the moral wrong of segregation. He did not limit his affirmation in this area merely to his duty to uphold the laws and the Constitution of this country. He recognized and stated that he was making this effort to cleanse American life of a shame and a stain and an evil thing. This required real courage, because he knew that, in the short term, he would not gain politically by that course; that in the short term he would lose. I believe he could not help make the affirmation because he saw its truth with his mind and felt it with his heart.

He had an appreciation of the great problems of the times in the field of the economy and in the field of employment, problems that no man yet knows all the answers to, arising from automation and our new technology.

While I am sure he would be the first to say he had no final answers, his awareness of these problems put him on the path of vigorous and unrelenting search for ways along which answers may lie.

In the field of foreign policy, perhaps, his awareness was most keen. He understood, surely as well as any man, and better than most, the frustrations, the dilemmas, and the paradoxes which we face, and the great dangers and difficulties faced by a world in which man can destroy himself.

While, again, he would be the last to claim he had any final answers, the very fact that we knew that he understood the problems, and saw them clearly and did not flinch from them, but had the courage to carry on and face them with gallantry and a high heart, gave this Nation, and all of us, courage to carry on.

Mr. President, Mrs. Case and I and our children and all of our family join with all those who have spoken, and for whom statements have been made, in extending to Mrs. Kennedy and the children and all the family, including our colleague in the Senate from Massachusetts, our most affectionate sympathy.

In this, Mr. President, I am joined by our former colleague, H. Alexander Smith, of New Jersey, who this morning phoned me to ask me, on his behalf and on behalf of Mrs. Smith, to express the high regard and respect which they had for John F. Kennedy, and the warm personal relations which they enjoyed, and their deep sympathy also.

ADDRESS BY

Hon. Jacob K. Javits
OF NEW YORK

Mr. President, hundreds of thousands of words have been published, and hundreds of thousands more have been spoken into the microphones of the world since John F. Kennedy was struck down in Dallas, but none of them were really adequate. Words never are in the face of sense-less tragedy.

Words cannot describe how the American people felt when they lost their President. Not until the vacuum of disbelief was filled with the horror of comprehension did any of us realize how much we identified ourselves, even apart from personal friendship, with the President— this intellectual, vigorous young man—and he would have been that if he were 80—expressing the very essence of the youthfulness of our Nation. It seems of little consequence now that there were political differences, or objections to this or that legislative product, though as far as I am concerned there was a very large measure of agreement. What matters is that feeling of loss—that personal sense of emptiness—that all Americans feel because their President was cut off in the prime of life. As a Nation, we have lost a President who understood the institution of the Presidency, gloried in its overwhelming responsibilities, and discharged his duties with dash and joy, which were an inspiration to the youth of our Nation.

But John F. Kennedy was more than that. He was a man filled with the joy of living, he was a husband, a father—and my friend.

For myself, I remember coming to Congress the same day he did. We were sworn in together on the same January day in 1947. A photograph on my office wall shows that we two, returning veterans, looked a little uncomfortable at the moment in our civilian clothes. It shows us looking at the Taft-Ellender-Wagner housing bill, and it recalls the first job we did together when we called on the National Veterans Housing Conference of 1947, which we had organized, to back this bill. It was the beginning of an association which extended throughout our careers in the House and Senate. We collaborated in many bipartisan matters, as is not unusual in the Congress. Indeed, in our service together in the Senate Committee on Labor and Public Welfare, we worked closely—as did Senator Morse and others—on the minimum wage bill, the Labor-Management Disclosure Act and other similar measures which were major aspects of Senator Kennedy's legislative career.

I am a personal witness to the fact that he was resourceful, optimistic, and creative. He became

and was my friend, and this is a deep source of gratification to me and to Mrs. Javits and our family.

Mrs. Javits, too, knew President Kennedy well and admired him greatly. She will, I know, always think of the President's graciousness and the warmth of personal friendship which he exuded.

Only a week before his tragic passing, I saw him in the Oval Room at the White House when he accepted the report of the Advisory Committee on Medical Care for the Aged, in which Senator Anderson and I joined, and issued a statement offering encouragement and help.

He was vigorous and healthy and smiling and friendly—a complete human being, concerned about other human beings who were no longer as vigorous and not quite as healthy as they used to be.

This concern for the unfortunate by a man with all the social graces and all the social status and as much power as America allows one man, was what made him so much the symbol of the youth of our country. His wife, Jacqueline, who has given Americans so much reason to be very proud of her and of all American womanhood as she reflected it, in these last mournful weeks, in the way she carried herself, has said the most beautiful tribute—that John F. Kennedy had the "hero idea of history," and that she did not want people to forget John F. Kennedy—the man—and replace him with some shadowy figure in the history books.

She need not fear that. There are already thousands upon thousands of people in the world working to keep his memory alive. I have been privileged to join with many others in this body in cosponsoring a bill to rename the National Cultural Center and make it a living, vibrant memorial to this vibrant man who loved the arts. And with Senator Humphrey, I have joined in a bill establishing a commission to insure that only the most appropriate memorials be created in his honor.

These are well-meaning, deeply sincere tokens—necessary, but still tokens. In reality it will be John F. Kennedy's youthful freshness in his aspirations for our country that will keep his memory fresh.

In a real sense we, his former colleagues in the

Congress are the only ones with the power to write words which can transform these aspirations into memorials with meaning. We can write legislative acts, like a meaningful civil rights law, which would consecrate and perpetuate John F. Kennedy's love for personal and national dignity. We can exorcise from our country—and the American people are doing that even now—those extremes of hatred and disbelief in public affairs which create a climate in which terrible acts become much more likely.

Acts such as these will be his final memorials. It is within our power to establish them. Perhaps his noblest memorial is that he would have wanted such memorials almost as no others.

So, in common with my colleagues in this solemn service—and that is what this is today—I bespeak for Mrs. Javits and my children—and I would place their names in the Record, so that as they read this Record when they grow up, I hope they will read their names in it and see that their father spoke with deep sympathy—Joy, Joshua, and Carla, to Mrs. Kennedy and the children, and to the President's father and mother and his brothers and sisters and their families our deepest sympathy on this terrible bereavement, for our Nation and for all mankind, and in the deep expectation that flowers will grow from his grave for the benefit of man.

ADDRESS BY

Hon. Frank J. Lausche
OF OHIO

Mr. President, it seems so futile to try to describe with words the profound loss the people of our country and of the world suffered in the death of President John Fitzgerald Kennedy.

Each one of us wants to pay tribute to him, but how helpless are our words compared to the great tribute that came to our departed President through the spontaneous manifestation of grief and sorrow by the people—strong and weak, rich and poor.

When the word of his death struck at home and in other nations, a pall fell over the people. They prayed, wept, meditated in silence, gathered in groups stunned and grieved. No deed in all of history brought so much grief and be-

wilderment to people everywhere as did the untimely passing of the man whom we mourn today.

His dynamism, affable attitude, and appealing and sincere smile became an integral part of the home of families everywhere, especially in our country. People felt as though they knew him intimately; that he was their personal friend.

He fought for his country in time of war and peace; did not shirk his responsibility, and was ready to stand in the front line of the fight.

In his service as a Member of Congress, he furthered the causes in which he believed, never harboring any rancor about the opposition that others might interpose against what he advocated.

In his occupancy of the office of President of the United States, he advocated action which he sincerely believed would be to the best interest of the people and the security of our Nation; the full enjoyment of constitutional rights for the citizens of our Nation was his devoted objective.

In his advocacy of favored causes, he encouraged discussion and debates, believing that out of the exchange of views there would come the adoption of programs that would richly and constructively serve the Nation.

It was not to be his lot to see the fight to the end. The grim hand of an assassin took his life on November 22. Our people are still stunned and bewildered.

He now lies in his lonely and narrow cell in Arlington Cemetery with an eternal light burning over his resting place. Mourners are wending their way to his grave, there to weep and pray. Loving, tender hands are placing tear-moistened flowers upon the ground where he sleeps.

With the dauntless courage of a leader he carried the baton on high. It has fallen from his hand, but it will be picked up by the people of our country and carried with honor and distinction to the lofty goal which he set for our country and the world.

Mrs. Lausche joins me, and I am sure the people of Ohio do likewise, in expressing condolences to Mrs. John F. Kennedy and the Kennedy family.

Beautifully appropriate to the life and death of our departed President are the words of Letitia Elizabeth Landon, English poet and novelist:

Can that man be dead
Whose spiritual influence is upon his kind?
He lives in glory; and his speaking dust
Has more of life than half its breathing moulds.

ADDRESS BY

Hon. Ralph W. Yarborough

OF TEXAS

Mr. President, our martyred leader, the beloved President John F. Kennedy, will live in our hearts forever as a gallant knight who held aloft a torch of hope for the freedom-loving peoples of the world to follow. From these legislative Halls of division and debate, he went to bold executive leadership of the Nation, then to leadership of the free world in the quest for peace, his Holy Grail. Now, after his martyrdom, he belongs to all mankind and all the ages.

President Kennedy becomes the only President in the history of the United States to achieve immortality in the quest for peace and freedom, without fighting a war. When we think of immortal leaders in this connection, the names of George Washington, Abraham Lincoln, Woodrow Wilson, and Franklin Roosevelt leap to our lips. But each fought a war to achieve greatness as a defender of peace and freedom. How much more difficult was President Kennedy's achievement—to advance the cause of peace and freedom without fighting a war.

At the end of his tragically brief lifetime, he was first in the hearts and the hopes of the world. What greater achievement can be attained by any mortal?

As Christmastime approaches, when our thoughts are always turned to family and faith, our hearts and the hearts of the world go out to the family of our fallen champion, who was so close to his faith and his family. And yet he has left to his children, to his widow, to all his family, to his countrymen, a shining heritage of vision, courage, brilliance, dedication, compassion, strength—a magnificent glow to illuminate the hopes of his family, the Nation, and all the world, for generations to come.

No country in the history of the world ever had more cause to reflect upon its course, to re-dedicate itself to humanitarian goals, to lay aside smallness, to try to see beyond the self-inflicted, constricting boundaries of time and distance, and to work for a tomorrow as bright as the eternal torch in Arlington Cemetery. President Kennedy's untimely death "tore a hole in the fabric of our society." It is the duty of all Americans of this and succeeding generations to help to repair it. Our task will be long and exacting.

In our grief we ask what course our Nation shall follow. President Kennedy, though the most intellectually brilliant man I have ever known, often turned to the Bible for higher guidance. It was a source of strength for this gallant man, as it was and is to the brave and courageous woman who was at his side in every crisis and who gave the Nation a new pride in woman's courage in the hour of the cruel taking away.

In his acceptance of the nomination to carry the banner for the Democratic Party, he quoted Isaiah:

But they that wait upon the Lord shall renew their strength; they shall mount up with wings as eagles; they shall run, and not be weary.

In his classic inaugural address, he looked again to Isaiah when he said:

Let both sides unite to heed in all corners of the earth the command of Isaiah—to "undo the heavy burdens and to let the oppressed go free."

Never have the American people been more deeply moved than by witnessing the little son of President John F. Kennedy touch his hand to his forehead in a final salute to his father. Never has the American flag had a prouder moment than when held aloft by the President's little son.

Again we may turn to Isaiah who said:

And a little child shall lead them.

Through the Bible and through the innocence of the President's little son, we find the Nation's path to true glory—we shall salute our fallen leader, we shall raise up the flag of freedom and justice, and by our actions hereafter we shall honor that for which it stands, as President Kennedy honored it both in life and in death.

In the last sentence of his last prepared speech, which was to have been delivered at Austin, Tex., on the evening of that fateful day of November 22, our fallen leader gave us our marching orders of the future in these words:

Let us stand together with renewed confidence in our course—united in our heritage of the past and our hopes for the future—and determined that this land we love shall lead all mankind into new frontiers of peace and abundance.

ADDRESS BY

Hon. William Proxmire

OF WISCONSIN

Mr. President, John F. Kennedy left this Nation a remarkable legacy. His achievements in civil rights legislation were the greatest of any American President since Lincoln. Also, he took us the initial tough and vital step toward peace in these first, infinitely dangerous years of the missile and nuclear age, in which we confront the formidable forces of international communism, including a nuclear armed Soviet Union, for the nuclear test ban treaty was a Kennedy accomplishment, both in conception and execution. As President Kennedy said early this year, the genii of the spread of nuclear weapons is almost out of the bottle, and if we do not get it back this year, 1963, we shall never get it back. The nuclear test ban treaty begins to put the cork on the bottle. Limited as it is, the nuclear test ban treaty does give us a chance to build a peaceful world of control of the immense power of destruction with which mankind has suddenly found itself. If 100 or 1,000 years from now there remains, in the nuclear age, a civilized world that can have a history, that history will recognize John F. Kennedy as being high among those who made it possible.

President Kennedy left two less noticed legacies: 23 days before he died, President Kennedy was asked to define happiness. He called it "full use of your powers along lines of excellence." And he added, "I find therefore the Presidency provides some happiness."

In a nation in which the pursuit of pleasure, fun, and easy living has become so often the accepted happiness goal of life, this reminder by the President of the solid joys of hard work, of discipline, and of determination to use every bit of talent each of us has to make us better instruments of God and country is a solid legacy that could make this a stronger and a better country.

Finally, with all the hundreds of thousands of words spoken off the cuff by President Kennedy in press conferences and in television interviews before millions of people, it is astonishing that not once did he utter a single word, so far as I can recall, which would embarrass or insult any person or in the slightest degree would demean the dignity of the office he held. This is not just a tribute to his intelligence; it is also a tribute, even more, to his sensitivity to other human beings, to his understanding, and to his sympathetic heart. This is all the more remarkable in view of the often hard-hitting and forceful encounters of the President, as in the clash with "Big Steel" and the showdown with Khrushchev and Castro over missiles in Cuba.

What a great asset this sense of the right word at the right time was in a man with the immense power of the Presidency of the United States.

Basically, the Kennedy legacy is a challenge to us to strive to live up to the ideals of equal rights for all Americans, of peace and freedom, and of dedication to personal excellence, to which he so fully dedicated his life.

ADDRESS BY

Hon. Eugene J. McCarthy

OF MINNESOTA

Mr. President, November 22, 1963, in the city of Washington was a day out of season. It was a day both of spring and of fall, both of beginnings and of endings, and of endings and of beginnings. Into the quiet of that day came the word of the death of the President.

In the days that followed immediately, grief increased in depth and in breadth, both here and throughout the Nation and the world.

President Kennedy was not merely a Washington President or a political President. He was a President in every home, every town, and every city—a President to everyone, both the very young and the very old, in the United States and in other countries of the world.

It is not for us to attempt to measure or assign the guilt for his assassination and death, for the burden of that act is too great to be borne by any one man or State or nation. Instead, that act and its consequences must be related to all our actions, and the burden of guilt must be shared by all who through the years have excited and stirred the simple and the anxious, who have raised questions and turned them about until they became suspicious, who have nurtured doubt until it bore the fruit of accusation and false charges, who have spread themselves to make a shade for fear and to save it from the light of truth until it grew to be a despairing fear of fear; by all who stood in silent acquiescence or who protested softly, too little, and too late; by all who envied him or any man or wished them ill.

We cannot rest in disillusionment or in grief. Instead, we must move on from these harsh realities, and must seek to accomplish the things for which the President stood—things made clearer by his death.   First, to accept with good heart the burden and responsibility of citizenship, and to bring to the performance of these duties, whether in the highest office of the land or in the simplest and most elementary act of citizenship, the spirit described by John Adams as one of "public happiness," which, said Adams, possessed the American colonists and won the Revolution even before it was fought, a spirit which is reflected in a delight in participation in public discussion and in public action, a joy in citizenship, in self-government, in self-control, in self-discipline, and in dedication.   Second, to seek to understand, and then to realize in some measure, his vision of the unity of Western civilization and, beyond that, a unity among all the peoples of the world.   Third, to seek to realize the potential for use in service and in perfection of all created things, an achievement to be measured, not by arithmetic or by geometry, but by the infinity of human aspirations, of human efforts, in developing and using the material resources of the earth, to the limits of science. Fourth, to seek the fullest possible development of every person—from the simple, and even from the retarded, to those with the greatest talents— making it possible for every one to achieve the goal which President Kennedy set for himself, and described in the words "the full use of one's powers according to the idea of excellence."

John Fitzgerald Kennedy demonstrated in action his realization that there must be a judgment of nations, as well as of persons.   He demonstrated his awareness of the two great facts of contemporary history—first, that the mass or the volume of current history, of the things which demand some judgment and some commitment from our Nation and from us, is greater than ever before; second, that the movement of history itself is now at a rate more rapid than ever before known.   In the face of these two ultimate facts, we are called upon to exercise, as best we can, and to the fullest possible measure to which it may be applied, the power of human reason, in attempting to give some control and some direction to life.

John F. Kennedy's entire efforts demonstrated a confidence in the future, a hope that the world of men could and would be improved, a belief in the universality of mankind and, in these far-reaching searches, a belief that there was no satisfaction except in the intensification and perfection of the life of every person.

Empty words of politicians of the past are echoed again: "The country will survive," and "the Government will stand."   These are true statements, but for some days Americans will not walk as certainly or as straight as they did in the past.   The quick step is gone.   A strong heart has stopped.   A mind that sought the truth, a will ready for commitment, and a voice to challenge and to move are ended for this age and time of ours.

This is, therefore, a time of truth for all, a time for resolution and for strong hope that what we say today may be supplemented and perfected in the future by honest historians who will trace and define the public service of John F. Kennedy.

In addition, we hope that good poets, who speak—as poets must—for each man alone, will do justice to the memory of John F. Kennedy.

ADDRESS BY

Hon. Thomas J. McIntyre

OF NEW HAMPSHIRE

Mr. President, one of New Hampshire's most respected educators, who is a historian of some note, has written me "that President Kennedy will go down in our history as one of the finest and ablest of all Chief Executives, and we who lived in his lifetime may count ourselves fortunate."

If history fastens itself upon one of the many facets that went into the greatness of John Fitzgerald Kennedy, I have no doubt that it will be his courage. As with many of the great, a thread of tragedy and suffering was woven through his life.

John Kennedy experienced much pain and loss in his brief span. And, yet, I believe he shall be remembered as a smiling, happy, self-assured man—always seeming to be in motion, a man to stir a nation from its lethargy. This was not an elder statesman drawing from the experience of a previous generation, but a young and energetic leader who had himself grown and matured with the mighty problems of the day.

The Nation and the world watched as the young leader transformed the New Frontier from idea to action. John Kennedy was called upon to handle problems as new as space and as old as equal rights. His concerns ranged from nuclear test bans to the Peace Corps; from better education for the young to better life for the old; from more help for the mentally retarded to brighter opportunities for the gifted; from firm insistence on strong defense to an uncompromising search for lasting peace.

The tributes which have been paid him in death are but a small indication of the affection and respect in which John Kennedy was held in life. The lasting tragedy is that the flame of greatness that burned in him has been extinguished from this mortal world, leaving us to wonder forever what he might have wrought.

But a flame burns still—beside the simple grave that has already become a shrine. A hundred years ago at Gettysburg, Abraham Lincoln said that "it is beyond our power to consecrate the ground in which our honored dead rest, but it is for us to take up the great unfinished tasks before us." There could be no more fitting memorial to John Kennedy.

And so, Mr. President, on behalf of the people of New Hampshire, and personally on behalf of Mrs. McIntyre and our daughter, Martha, I extend to Mrs. Kennedy, the children, and the immediate family our heartfelt sympathy.

ADDRESS BY

Hon. Margaret Chase Smith

OF MAINE

Mr. President, I cannot add anything to what has already been said this afternoon about President John F. Kennedy. I join other Senators in their tributes to him.

ADDRESS BY

Hon. Harry Flood Byrd

OF VIRGINIA

Mr. President, the death of President John F. Kennedy is a national tragedy. The Nation and the world mourn his loss.

As I reflect upon the privilege of my friendship and association with him, I find myself pondering the contradictions of life. It creates and it destroys. It affirms and it denies. It exalts and it strikes down.

It is not, of course, for us to understand the ways of Providence, and the sequence of events often is beyond human comprehension, particularly when the soul of one so prominent among us is taken.

President Kennedy was a man whose life was dedicated to the service of his country. Practically all of his adult years were spent in this endeavor—in war and in peace, in military service, in Congress, and as President.

He was engaged in the affairs of the highest office his country could bestow upon him in the prime of his life. How deeply we regret the untimely departure from among us of one so vigorous and so dedicated.

He was a man with a remarkable variety of knowledge and a well-governed mind. He was persuasive with his ideas and pursued them with tremendous native force and determination.

It has been my privilege to know his father, and to have served in the Senate with John F. Kennedy when he was a Senator. I have enjoyed his company in my home. He possessed one of the most attractive personalities I have ever known.

He was a man of devotion to his family, his religion, and his chosen work. He was a man of courage and independence. He was a man of bold talent, great enterprise, and infinite skill. He was a man gifted in the art of government.

He demonstrated deep concern for what he believed to be in the interest of the strength and welfare of his country, and proved his willingness to fight for it. His acts of office were felt around the world.

ADDRESS BY

Hon. Bourke B. Hickenlooper

OF IOWA

Mr. President, I believe the eulogies which have been given today and those which have been given continuously since the tragic events of 2 weeks ago are ample evidence of the great affection and regard which America and the world hold for President John F. Kennedy.

I do not know whether adequate words can be found to express the sense of universal shock and grief, not only in our own country, but throughout the world, that resulted from the tragedy.

I believe that most of us still feel that it is unreal. We still refuse to accept the realities of the situation. Somehow it has seemed to be a great myth.

Of course, it is not.

Those of us who knew President Kennedy, not only as President, but as a Member of Congress in this body and in the other body feel a special sense of sadness and loss. Part of that deep feeling, no doubt, comes from the fact that he was a most remarkable and almost unique young man—and I say "young man" in the sense of comparison to my own age. He possessed clarity of thought. He also had a pristine clarity of expression which enabled him to deliver those thoughts in a manner and in language that left no doubt as to his views and his purposes.

He had a driving vigor possessed by few individuals. He had a determination in political combat in advancing the goals which he thought

best for his country that probably has seldom, if ever, been equaled. These things make the tragedy so much greater. The personal acquaintance, the attractiveness of his own attitude, his cordiality, and his utter fairness in his associations with those in public life will be remembered and treasured as long as the memories of those alive will last.

I never saw him lose his temper. I never heard him make an extravagant or unwarranted expression. I have heard him many times vigorously advance his views, but always with that degree of courtesy and consideration which mark the man who has no need to be extravagant in his statements.

The tragedy is further pointed up by the circumstances under which it occurred.

While he had an outstanding record as a Member of the other body and as a Member of this body, he was going full stride into the fulfillment of the greatest political objective any man can have—that of President of the United States. He undertook the responsibilities of that office with a dedication and a seriousness which mark him as one of the great men of our time.

I believe it is only objective to say that 3 years were not sufficient for the full development of his programs or his ability. No one can say what the future will bring, but he knew the pattern which he wished to follow, and he was implementing it with a vigor and a consistency which were commendable.

In political offices there are people of divergent views. I did not belong to his party. With some of his views I could not agree. I say that in all humility and in all honesty. But I had unbounded respect for him.

The memories I have are based upon respect and admiration for a man who, in the very prime of his life and vigor, both physically and politically, had to be struck down. I still say that it is unreal, and the shock of that tragedy has not left the American people, nor will it leave the American people for an indefinite and unpredictable period in the future.

Unfortunately, I have poignant memories of the assassinations of two Presidents. I recall the shock, when I was a youngster 5 years of age, when the word came to our small schoolroom that President McKinley had been shot. I remember the sadness that universally gripped the American people at that time, a sadness not only for the individual, but also for the occurrence in our free and great American system.

I believe the frustrations which concern us now—that such a thing could happen or would happen in this country of ours—are frustrations we cannot explain, nor do we try to explain them.

President Kennedy wrote an enviable record which is indelibly inscribed in the annals of our country and of our time.

I would not pretend to say more in eulogy than the fine and articulate statements made with heartfelt motives by Senators who have previously spoken. I have a grief and a sadness that I cannot fully express. To Mrs. Kennedy, to her children, and to John F. Kennedy's family, I extend my heartfelt sympathy and condolences, and make the request that all of us be permitted to share to the utmost of our capacity in the grief which they suffer. We hope that grief can in some way be alleviated in the course of time and in the course of the great plan which we are all attempting to develop.

ADDRESS BY

Hon. John Stennis

OF MISSISSIPPI

Mr. President, among the many virtues of our late President John Kennedy, I believe the most outstanding, which will be long remembered and from which fruits will grow, was the remarkable quality he had of constant and unyielding courage.

I looked up some remarks I previously made with reference to him several years ago, in which I referred to his fine and forceful mind, which had a comprehensive grasp of all the problems of our Nation. Placing him in the White House brought that quality to finer fruit, because the opportunity was greater than I realized and greater than most people realized before he went there.

I said then, "I have great confidence in his ability, his character, and his constant and unyielding courage." That shows the trend of thought which ran through my mind at the time,

as it does now, and as it runs through the minds of many others who knew him well.

He wrote a book, quite well known. I hold a copy of that book in my hand. It is titled "Profiles in Courage."

With his very clear mind, in rare style, he brought forcefully to the attention of the reading public the lives of seven men, all of whom had served in the Congress and most of whom had served in this body. To him they personified not only personal courage, but also public political courage.

The names of those he mentioned were John Quincy Adams, Daniel Webster, Thomas Hart Benton, Edmund G. Ross, Lucius Quintus Cincinnatus Lamar, George Norris, and Robert A. Taft.

I found one sentence from his own pen in this book that was of particular interest. Referring to all these men, near the close of this remarkable volume, he said:

Some demonstrated courage through their unyielding devotion to absolute principle. Others demonstrated courage through their acceptance of compromise, through their advocacy of conciliation, through their willingness to replace conflict with cooperation. Surely their courage was of equal quality, though of different caliber.

Most of them, despite their differences, held much in common—the breathtaking talents of the orator, the brilliance of the scholar, the breadth of the man above party and section, and, above all, a deep-seated belief in themselves, their integrity and the rightness of their cause.

I have been proud of the fact that one of the men he chose from the seven around which he built the book was L. Q. C. Lamar, of Mississippi, onetime Member of the House of Representatives, a longtime Member of the U.S. Senate, a member of Grover Cleveland's Cabinet, and a longtime Justice of the U.S. Supreme Court.

Our late President developed in his book his qualities and character; and the part I have quoted was with reference to Lamar along with the others.

As he paid tribute to that statesman and that truly great Mississippian, commending him for his courage, Mississippi in turn returns the compliment to our late President, who is capable of standing alongside those he chose, or alongside those anyone else would choose, for the truly great and fine quality of courage which he demonstrated on the floor, in the White House, in the field of battle, or wherever he was.

I am glad to be one of the mediums through whom my State could pay him that compliment. At the same time, I wish to express personal grief and great regret on behalf of myself and Mrs. Stennis, as we have already done to Mrs. Kennedy and other members of the family. All members of the Mississippi congressional delegation have expressed themselves to that effect, as have others in official life in Mississippi.

I hold in my hand a copy of a telegram sent by a fine, outstanding, business executive, a fine citizen of Mississippi, which came to my attention through the Clarion-Ledger, a Jackson newspaper. I take the liberty of reading that telegram, which expresses the sentiments of many of us. It is addressed to Mrs. Kennedy and was sent following the tragic death:

Mrs. JACQUELINE KENNEDY,
White House,
Washington, D.C.:

You have the profound and sincere sympathy of all Mississippians in this time of your great personal loss shared by every loyal citizen of the United States.

We pray that God will guide you and your loved ones in His own way and by His wisdom use even this tragedy to show all of us the way to build and preserve a greater nation and a better world dedicated to His glory.

JACK R. REED,
President, Mississippi Economic Council—Mississippi's State Chamber of Commerce.

I join in those sentiments, along with all other Mississippians. The crown of glory based on courage—belongs also to the wonderful lady, his surviving wife. I think her name should be mentioned in the Record every time. She meant so much to him in life, and means so much to his family now, as well as to the Nation.

May God give eternal rest to his soul, and may that same God sustain his wife and children and enable them to see the wisdom of His ways.

ADDRESS BY

Hon. George McGovern

OF SOUTH DAKOTA

Mr. President, when Gov. John Connally was asked by NBC Commentator Martin Agronsky for his reflections on the tragic assassination of President Kennedy he replied from his hospital bed in Dallas:

Only that maybe, Martin, the President of the United States, as a result of this great tragedy, has been asked to do something in death that he couldn't do in life—and that is to so shock and so stun the Nation, the people, and the world of what's happening to us—of the cancerous growth that's been permitted to expand and enlarge itself upon the community and the society in which we live that breeds the hatred, the bigotry, the intolerance and indifference, the lawlessness that is, I think, an outward manifestation of what occurred here in Dallas.

If President Kennedy's death is not to be in vain, every American should think soberly on the meaning of the Texas Governor's words.

But while we need to remember the sad circumstances and the lessons of President Kennedy's death, we also want to remember his stirring words of hope and courage.

On a cold morning, January 20, 1961, I sat on the steps of the Capitol, 12 or 15 feet from our new President, and heard these words:

Let the words go forth from this time and place, to friend and foe alike, that the torch has been passed to a new generation of Americans.

To those peoples in the huts and villages of half the globe struggling to break the bonds of mass misery, we pledge our best efforts to help them help themselves.

I do not shrink from this responsibility—I welcome it. I do not believe that any of us would exchange places with any other people or any other generation. The energy, the faith, the devotion which we bring to this endeavor will light our country and all who serve it—and the glow from that fire can truly light the world.

And so, my fellow Americans: Ask not what your country can do for you—ask what you can do for your country.

Second only to this great inaugural, I would rate President Kennedy's magnificent speech at American University on June 10, 1963, which opened the way for the nuclear test ban treaty—that "first step toward peace."

He said in that great address:

The United States, as the world knows, will never start a war. We do not want a war. We do not now expect a war. This generation of Americans has already had enough, more than enough of war and hate and oppression. We shall be prepared for war if others wish it. We shall be alert to try to stop it. But we shall also do our part to build a world of peace where the weak are safe and the strong are just. We are not helpless before that task or hopeless of its success. Confident and unafraid, we labor on, not toward a strategy of annihilation, but toward a strategy of peace.

I will remember him for those eloquent words, his grace of manner, his quiet courage, and his consideration of others.

One personal experience particularly will stay in my mind as long as I live. On the Saturday night following my defeat in the Senate race of 1960, my wife and I were having dinner with some friends in Mitchell, S. Dak., when I was called to the phone to take a long distance call from Palm Beach. "Hello, George, this is Jack Kennedy. I am sorry about what happened to you on Tuesday," he said. "Before you make any plans, I would like to talk with you."

It humbles one to know that a great man was not so absorbed in his own moment of triumph that he forgot his friends who had stumbled.

Following that call he gave me the opportunity to serve in his administration as Director of the food-for-peace program.

In announcing the creation of the Food for Peace Office, the President said:

American agricultural abundance offers a great opportunity for the United States to promote the interests of peace in a significant way and to play an important role in helping to provide a more adequate diet for peoples all around the world. We must make the most vigorous and constructive use possible of this opportunity. We must narrow the gap between abundance here at home and near starvation abroad. Humanity and prudence, alike, counsel a major effort on our part.

In a modest, self-effacing manner, President Kennedy had said in 1957:

I will be frank with you—I'm a city boy who has never plowed a furrow. I do not pretend to be an expert on all the problems of agriculture, and I suppose some of my constituents are opposed to letting their tax dollars aid western ranchers and farmers. But I will say this: When a serious decline in farm income takes millions of dollars out of the pockets of your farmers and your towns, that is a national problem.

Actually, Mr. Kennedy had a broad concept of the role of agriculture in today's world. Speaking in Mitchell, S. Dak.—my hometown—on September 22, 1960, he said:

Fellow Americans facing a difficult future, I think the farmers can bring more credit, more lasting good will, more chance for freedom, more chance for peace, than almost any other group of Americans in the next 10 years, if we recognize that food is strength, and food is peace, and food is freedom, and food is a helping hand to people around the world whose good will and friendship we want. So you are a great source of strength to us in these great years ahead, and I come as a presidential candidate with the greatest possible hope for the future and ask you to join in a great effort on behalf of our country and the State of South Dakota. The motto of

the State of South Dakota is "Under God the People Rule." The motto of the United States could be the same. I hope in the next 10 or 20 years when historians write of our times that they will write that the cause of the people ruling under God spread in these years and became stronger, increased in strength, increased in substance.

President Kennedy's last visit to South Dakota was on August 17, 1962, when he came to our State Capital, Pierre, to inaugurate the power transmission system at the Oahe project in the great Missouri River Basin complex.

In Pierre, the President said:

I want to tell you, first of all, how much I am enjoying this opportunity to get away from Washington—to talk with local farmers and ranchers and merchants and find out what they are thinking. Those of us who serve in Washington spend too much time talking to each other, repeating the same views or listening to the same pleaders for special interests. That is why it is good to get away from Washington from time to time and to get a better and fresher perspective of what most of our citizens are thinking and doing.

In this same vein, I would hope that those who visit our country from abroad, if they want to learn the truth about America, would not confine their visits to Washington and to the great metropolitan areas of the east, but would visit this State and others like it. With all of the current crop failures behind the Iron Curtain, I think visitors from abroad should see the abundance of our fields. I think they should see our smaller towns, which show the democratic system at its best—for we started as a nation of small towns.

I think they should see this dam—the largest rolled-earth dam in the world. For this dam alone will produce enough electrical energy every year to meet all of the power needs of a city the size of Edinburgh, Scotland. This dam alone will supply enough irrigation to serve an area larger than the entire nation of Luxembourg. This dam alone will provide a magnificent reservoir lake—enriching the beauty and the recreational opportunities of this area—as long as Africa's famous Lake Victoria.

Above all, this dam provides a striking illustration of how a free society can make the most of its God-given resources. Water is our most precious asset—and its potential uses are so many and so vital that they are sometimes in conflict: Power versus irrigation, irrigation versus navigation, navigation versus industrial, industrial versus recreational. Here in the Missouri Basin, the supply of water cannot meet all of these needs all of the time. Accommodations are essential—and in 1944, under the administration of Franklin Roosevelt, a comprehensive Missouri Basin plan was authorized to fulfill all of these objectives.

This is the fifth of six great dams to control the mainstream of the Missouri River—and I can assure those of you at the upper end of the Missouri and our good friends at the lower end that it will continue to be our policy to regulate the storage and flow of water in these reservoirs in the most advantageous manner for all concerned that the most creative engineers in the world can possibly devise.

Speaking in Sioux Falls, S. Dak., at the National Plowing Contest on September 22, 1960, as a candidate for the Presidency, Mr. Kennedy drew a parallel to the election of 100 years earlier which he used on several occasions during the 1960 campaign.

He said it this way:

During the presidential election 100 years ago, Abraham Lincoln wrote a friend, "I know there is a God and that He hates injustice. I see the storm coming, but if He has a place and a part for me, I believe that I am ready." Now 100 years later, when the great issue is the maintenance of freedom all over the globe, we know there is a God and we know He hates injustice, and we see the storm coming. But if He has a place and a part for us, I believe that we are ready.

Mr. President, these and many other words of our beloved President will live in my memory for years to come.

The life and death of President Kennedy have given new meaning to the inspired New Testament words: "Whosoever shall lose his life for My sake, shall find it."

May God rest his gallant soul in peace and bring comfort to the remarkable family who loved him most of all.

And may we hear again his sadly prophetic words:

In your hands, my fellow citizens, more than mine, will rest the final success or failure of our course.

My wife, Eleanor, joins me in expressing our sympathy and our admiration to Mrs. Kennedy, the children and other members of his family.

Since the President's death, I have received numerous expressions from the people of South Dakota, on the life and death of our fallen leader. I ask unanimous consent that excerpts from the letters and messages be printed at this point. I also ask unanimous consent that several editorials selected from the South Dakota press be printed at this point.

EXCERPTS FROM LETTERS TO SENATOR GEORGE McGOVERN

From Mr. D. C. Walsh, of Miller, S. Dak.: "Certainly, President Kennedy has emblazoned for all time the answer to his own query—not what can my country do for me but what can I do for my country. What have we come to in this Nation that bigotry and personal bitterness can give rise to a disaster of this caliber? Tragic as was the event itself, it seems equally calamitous that anyone in this country would even seriously consider the perpetration of such an act. At the risk of appearing blasphemous, I wonder if at times even our Creator may view us with some feeling of disbelief."

From Mr. C. A. Sundstrom, of Alcester, S. Dak.: "I, having had no contact with this, the greatest man of our time, feel a great loss, so I can imagine how people close to him must feel."

From Mr. John Sauer, of Huron, S. Dak.: "I do not mean to prolong this letter, but I read an excerpt from a small town journalist in Minnesota that expressed my own sentiments so well that I cannot refrain from passing on to you his quotation:

" 'John Fitzgerald Kennedy was a man of grace—physical grace, mental grace, spiritual and moral grace, the grace of breeding, the grace of quality, the grace of courage, and always the grace of reason.'

"To my mind, a very fitting and true vignette of our late President's character."

From Mr. W. Neil Evans, of Watertown, S. Dak.: "I only had the privilege of meeting him once and shaking his hand, but I will always remember his firm handshake and the smile on his face as he told us we were doing a good job on the ASCS committees."

From Mr. and Mrs. Arthur Magedanz, of Revillo, S. Dak.: "We feel that the whole world is so very much better off even with this great man gone, than before, not only for what he has done, but for what he was trying to do."

From Mr. Paul H. Redfield, Madison, S. Dak.: "Beyond all doubt, John F. Kennedy was one of America's great—to America as well as to the freedom loving people of the world. Already this has been demonstrated. The ideals and principles for which he stood and fought must not be forgotten. The eternal flame must never flicker."

From Mr. Kenneth Knudsen of Irene, S. Dak.: "The leadership of President Kennedy will long be remembered by every citizen of the United States and the entire world. We trust this great injustice will be a lesson to us all, not to let hate govern our thoughts and deeds, and hereafter be constructive in our criticisms of others. If this can be accomplished, President Kennedy's fine leadership will still live with us in spirit."

From Mr. Harley Piekkola, of Newell, S. Dak.: "Somehow if you could convey the message, from this small and humble organization, that their loss is our loss, too. It is our fervent hope that the light of truth and friendship that the Kennedys lit will forever continue to grow."

From Mr. Almer Steensland, of Bersford, S. Dak.: "We certainly stand humbled before the world, not only in the assassination of the President, but in the killing of the suspect by a hoodlum before he could be brought to trial. It is simply awful."

From Mr. Sandy O. Graham, Hot Springs, S. Dak.: "The President was a good man and a good husband. May he now rest in peace."

From Mr. Maynard Engelstad, Astoria, S. Dak.: "One lesson I hope Kennedy's memory will leave us is that we must have less hate in this country and that we must grow up and live up to the principles we talk so much about."

From Eleanor McManus, Chamberlain, S. Dak.: "My sympathy goes out to his dear wife and children and I hope and pray God will take care of them. Life must go on as he always said."

From Jerry Gerdes, Rapid City, S. Dak.: "The world has suffered a grievous loss, for seldom does greatness touch a man; it brushed John Fitzgerald Kennedy, paused and laid its awesome heavy hand upon his shoulder, then, moved on, to be replaced by the hand of God, his life work not yet done—or was it? Was his courage, his leadership, his greatness, taken from us to bring to the Nation, to the world, an awareness of those things of which he spoke. We must rededicate ourselves to the principles for which he died—freedom for all men, peace for a troubled world, fulfillment of the concepts expressed in the Constitution of our Nation."

From Miss Lore Pendo, Sioux Falls, S. Dak.: "Although I am only 20 years old and not of voting age yet, I am nevertheless an American who greatly respected President Kennedy and the principles he stood for. My personal tribute to him will be my own evergrowing realization of his greatness, but more than that, I hope to someday see the fulfillment of the honor herein proposed, which John F. Kennedy so richly deserves (that the Peace Corps be renamed the Kennedy Corps for peace)."

From Prof. Allen Barnes, of Brookings, S. Dak.: "It seems that at a time of crisis such as the one which we are experiencing that most of us pledge to rededicate ourselves primarily to the service of our fellow man. * * * Many of my Spanish speaking friends have told me both verbally and in letters that the United States, through Mr. Kennedy, has a President who fully understands Latin America."

From Mr. Arvid Carlson, of Stockholm, S. Dak.: "Today I have done a lot of thinking, as no doubt we all have. However, the more I think back over the last 4 days, and yesterday particularly, the more I realize that John F. Kennedy was without question the greatest President, the greatest leader, the greatest man this country has known. His loss to our country is a promise unfulfilled, a victory not quite reached."

From Mr. John Troth, of Mitchell, S. Dak.: "If any good can arise from such an unspeakable crime, perhaps it will be the awakening of Americans to a new appreciation of their citizenship in this great Nation, and a new resolve to accept the responsibilities that accompany that citizenship. Perhaps they will now realize and truly know what John F. Kennedy meant when he said: 'We would not exchange this time or place with anyone in the world.'"

From Mr. Leo Rozum, of Sturgis, S. Dak.: "Not since our son Jim's untimely death in 1960 has anything touched me so deeply. Like millions of others we sat literally glued to the TV and radio from Friday afternoon until the close of ceremonies at Arlington National Cemetery. We shared with these millions a deep sincere grief although cognizant that God in his wisdom has assigned to each mortal an appointed hour."

(Telegrams were received from Mayor Charles E. McClean of Hot Springs, S. Dak., and Mayor John T. Barstow of Vermillion, S. Dak., asking that the sympathy and grief of these two communities be conveyed to Mrs. Kennedy and the members of the family.)

[Letter from Mrs. Olive Briles, sister of Senator McGovern]

November 27, 1963.

DEAR GEORGE: To you the loss of President Kennedy must seem even more overwhelming than it does to the rest of us because he was your personal friend as well as your President, but even to me it seems as if one of our family has died.

I keep asking myself over and over how could it happen? For the first time in our life we have had a young energetic, highly respected President and now he is snatched away.

Why? Why? Why?

The only answer that I can find is that the sins of the masses have again been borne by one. Have we become a Nation so calloused and so dominated by hate and self-interest that we are on the verge of destroying ourselves?

George Orwell in "1984" shows how a totalitarian ruler dominated a people by teaching them to hate one another. The keynote of his book is that the destruction of the humanity within a man is easy once he ceases to love. Is that what we are allowing to happen to us?

We have had repeated warnings that had we heeded might have prevented the tragedy that shocked the world and shamed America with overwhelming remorse and grief.

When little children can be murdered in Sunday School without causing a national outcry, when a brilliant Negro leader can be ruthlessly shot and little or nothing done to bring his assassin to justice, can we be shocked that that same society has produced a warped and twisted Oswald that could destroy the man who was laboring tirelessly to give him and all others a better world in which to live?

President Kennedy's death is a loss that seems greater than we can bear, but his supreme sacrifice will not have been in vain if we will now rise up and join hands—all Americans, regardless of color and creed—to resolve that "This Nation, under God, shall have a new birth of freedom"—not only freedom of worship, freedom of speech, freedom from fear, and freedom from want, but also freedom from hate.

In life President Kennedy was so dominated by love—love for God, love for family, and love for his fellowman—that he failed to comprehend the power of hate. I do not believe that the world will soon forget the man who saw the best in everyone and who envisioned the potential of brotherly love to transform the world.

Neither will the world forget the stately young widow whose trust in God and in man enabled her to transcend the natural human emotion to abhor the public that had robbed her of what she held most dear and to share with them her grief and theirs in a final tribute to her husband.

May the eternal flame that she lighted on his grave be an eternal flame in the heart of every American that will forever burn out selfishness and hatred and burn deep within every conscience the commandment of that visionary, young, and vigorous man, who decreed "Thou shalt love the Lord thy God with all thy mind, and with all thy strength: this is the first commandment. And the second is like, namely this, Thou shalt love thy neighbor as thyself. There is none other commandment greater than these."

We still have much to be thankful for in that we live in a land where there are others to take up the torch and carry on. I am sure President Johnson will do as he said—The best that I can.

With much love,

OLIVE.

———

EXCERPTS FROM SERMON DELIVERED AT THE GETTYSBURG, S. DAK., EPISCOPAL CHURCH BY REV. CHARLES GREENE, PASTOR, ON SUNDAY, NOVEMBER 24, 1963

Socrates, John the Baptist, Jesus Christ, Abraham Lincoln, Mahatma Gandhi, and John Kennedy were all men of love.

Their devotion to truth, to reality, to God, and to men carried them knowingly to the final sacrifice.

The Nation reels under the swiftness of the tragedy. The world is shocked and appalled. All mankind mourns the death of the man.

A man of courage, dedication, youth and vigor is dead, not because of hate, but because he loved his Lord and his people.

Occasionally a great man emerges to assume the reins of government, and we who so readily criticized should more properly give thanks to God for raising him up.

Today John F. Kennedy lies in state because he loved and desired to serve us. Love, not hate, has laid our President low * * * love shown in deep religious devotion, exemplary family life, sacrifice of personal fortune, and anxious concern for all men.

It is love which struck him down just as surely as it is love which brings pain to all who dare to care. And it is that very love which must continue long after his mortal remains have gone, if his life is not to have been but a vain illusion.

———

EXCERPTS FROM SERMON DELIVERED AT THE MEMORIAL SERVICE IN SISSETON, S. DAK., BY REV. EDWARD A. GILBERTSON, PASTOR OF THE GRACE LUTHERAN CHURCH, SISSETON, S. DAK.

This is not only a day of sorrow but also of repentance that we have allowed conditions to exist that would breed assassins. Everyone has the privilege of hoping that the town in which he lives may be the birthplace of a future President of the United States. We need also to remember that assassins are born and raised someplace also. This is a day for self-evaluation, not only on the national level, but also on the local level and especially the personal level.

We need well ask is Sisseton the type of town likely to be the birthplace of a future President, or rather the birthplace and the training ground of an assassin of a future President of the United States? As a nation we are nothing more than a collection of individual communities. The character of the community will be the character of the Nation.

In his inaugural address President Kennedy made this historic statement: "Ask not what can my country do for me, but rather what can I do for my country." Let us look at Sisseton in the light of President Kennedy's thought-provoking statement. What have we done for our community, particularly our children and youth, in order that we may produce good citizens, instead of a potential assassin?

———

STATEMENT BY A SECRETARY IN THE OFFICE OF SENATOR McGOVERN

The triumph of a noble spirit—this is President Kennedy's gift to America and a grieving world constituency. He was a spiritual man. He lived life well and he loved it.

He loved God and his family, the sea and books, children and animals, the theater and sports, music and good humor. Most of all, he loved us, his people, and the people of the world. He cared.

An active participant in all fields of human endeavor, he was a quiet reflector who sought solace and guidance in the written word and in contemplative ventures into history and the future that often provided the substance of decision.

His deep feeling for mankind, his intimate knowledge of human nature, his search for common ground in a world arena where only a partial prize can ever be won—he, above most of us, knew that we are merely mortal, that we are prone to error, that our spiritual incompetence can be laid to the limitations of our humanity. But he tested those limits. And he longed for peace. His search for peace and his measure of success in this ancient quest is our legacy. Man has sought peace for some 2,000 years. We thank God that he continued our pursuit. So hard did he try that his very murder is testimonial enough.

From his oval office window, his spirit looked out on a city, a nation, and a world crying for peace, longing for redemption. From another window, one looked out who deprived that world of a heart pulsing for mankind, of leadership that may never be equaled, of vision rarely known, and of a future we may never know.

But let us look to that future, leaning as did he on the past, a past which now, we can confidently know, embraces his life and his spirit.

———

[From the Daily Republic, Mitchell, S. Dak., Nov. 26, 1963]

PROFILE IN COURAGE

As John Fitzgerald Kennedy, 35th President of the United States, was laid to rest in Arlington National Cemetery yesterday, a shocked and grieving nation rededicated itself to the tasks that lie before it. That these tasks will be accomplished without further violence—generated by hate and greed and malevolence in the minds of mortal men—is the hope of all rational persons.

The martyrdom of President Kennedy, pray God, will strengthen the forces of righteousness in the everlasting battle against those of fanatic hatred. His death, we pray, will not have been in vain, but will move us to labor long and hard for those ideals which he so clearly enunciated in his brief 34 months as our Chief Executive.

For those who loved and admired the late President, the characteristics of greatness were apparent early in his administration. His greatest achievements seemed yet to come; in his brief span of national leadership he had laid the groundwork for conquering the new frontiers of democracy about which he spoke.

For the American people, Mr. Kennedy had lighted many candles to guide the way. It was not the way all were willing to follow, but it was a charted course designed to elevate this civilization to new heights. It was a grand design to attain in our time a free, disarmed world moving out of the shadows of a threatened nuclear holocaust; to attain in our time a nation in which bigotry had no place, in which there was truly a society where opportunities were equal for all without respect to race, creed or color; to attain in our time great advances in education, in economic strength, in scientific exploration, and to attain in our time a guarantee that those who labored to help us realize our aims would, in their sunset years, be spared excessive financial burdens.

History will note that President Kennedy was far more than a national leader; he was the outstanding world leader of his time. The book "Profiles in Courage," had it been written at a later time by a writer other than himself, would certainly have included him. He was true to the statement he made in his inaugural address that "we must never negotiate out of fear, but we must never fear to negotiate." He faced the crises of Cuba, the Berlin wall, South Vietnam, the autobahn blockade with courage. He stood firm in the face of threat, without panic that might have moved lesser men to calamitous action.

Surmounting each crisis, the President waited for the smoke to disperse, then moved into the clear air of negotiation, in an effort to establish, as he said also in his inaugural address, "a beachhead of cooperation in the jungles of suspicion."

An assassin's bullet has cut short this beachhead assault. It remains for President Lyndon B. Johnson and those who follow him to issue further command. It is up to them to determine whether we advance or retreat. May they be granted the wisdom and courage of John Fitzgerald Kennedy, and the great Presidents who preceded him.

———

[From the Black Hills Press, Sturgis, S. Dak., Nov. 23, 1963]

TIME FOR MOURNING

The President is dead.

A single shot has sent the world into mourning. Breathes there a man with a soul so dead anywhere in the world who does not lament the tragedy of this horrendous crime? We hope not.

The first reaction is one of shock. That such a horrible thing could happen in America seems almost beyond belief. It had happened before, but so long ago that another assassination of an American President seemed to be an impossibility. That it has happened again adds another terrible chapter to the disgraceful story of man's inhumanity to man.

Then comes the stunning realization of the dreadful loss of service to God and country which will result

from the assassin's bullet. President Kennedy was in his prime and his public career had not yet reached its zenith. He typified the youth, vigor, and imagination of his beloved country and he gave great promise of leading it to new heights of world prominence. The heart of the country was stilled with his heart. But the Nation will live and survive to realize the lofty objectives that President Kennedy espoused during his short but useful life.

The profound sympathies of the entire world go to the late President's family. Their tears, their heartbreak, their sorrow are shared by all people everywhere. President Kennedy was a family man in the truest sense, and all of America was part of his family. He was father, son, husband, brother, and our President. The loss resulting from his untimely and tragic death is virtually unfathomable.

What of the future?

Time enough for that later.

This is a time of mourning for America, and the free world.

Hurt, angered, shocked, we can only do what another assassinated President once said he did when he had nowhere else to go in times of trial—we can go to our knees and pray for the immortal soul of our lost President, for his family and for the Nation he served with dedication and devotion.

———

[From the Exponent, student publication, Northern State Teachers College, Aberdeen, S. Dak., Dec. 5, 1963]

THE NATION WEPT

As have all other Americans, the staff of the Exponent has been numbed by the shattering impact of the assassination of President John F. Kennedy. No tribute the Exponent could print in this column could match the spirit of the following poem. It was written by the Honorable Robert D. Orr, State representative of Brown County, who received his bachelor's degree from Northern and took his master's degree at the University of South Dakota. State Representative Orr wrote the poem when watching telecasts of the tragic event and agreed to the Exponent's request to publish it.

LOVE—LAUGHTER—HAPPINESS
HOPE—HATRED—BIGOTRY
TRAGIC VIOLENCE—REDEDICATION

"The Man is dead.
His immortal spirit,
Ideals,
Humanity, live on.

"In the minds, hearts,
Aspirations of fellow Americans,
Deeper meanings of a tragedy emerge.

"Disbelieving, we cried.
We prayed;
We bled.
The Nation bleeds;
It suffers, hangs its head—
Unashamed.

"It is proud, yet grieved;
Pained that law and order failed.
Monstrous violence to the restraints of freedom mitigated,
Grieved of hate, prejudice, and brutality,
Grieved for the Grievancer.

"Hurt that Man's inhumanity to man prevails;
Proud to be free, grieved to have felt guilt,
Tragically united in this hour of sorrow.

"He is martyred for a cause, for many causes,
Magnanimous:
Love for Almighty God,
His fellow Americans,
His Country,
His ideals of equality, freedom, peace;
His passion for the goodness and humanity of all men.

"Paralysis of enterprise,
The Nation wept,
Self-examined,
Reappraised.

"Friends about the world eulogized the man,
Prayed for the Nation,
Sympathized our hurt,
Were themselves hurt.

"And so we laid to rest the mortal,
While the Spirit and memory became immortal.
And the Republic rededicated itself to its task."

———

[From the Argus Leader, Sioux Falls
(S. Dak.), Dec. 5, 1963]

HERB BECHTOLD'S ROUND ROBIN

How did the average 9- or 10-year-old feel about the death of President Kennedy? We can find the answer in some of the compositions which students in Mrs. Judith Evans' fourth-grade English class at Harrisburg School wrote.

Here are some excerpts (with the original spelling):

"DEAR JOHN, JUNIOR, I heard your dad was shot last Friday when he was at a parade. But when I heard he was shot I felt like a shok hit me. My dad never even new about it until my brother told him. He was very sad. I was crying when he was buried. I hope you'll grow up to be like your daddy. But do not get shot and die like your dad. A frenid, Dennis Geraets".

"DEAR CAROLINE, when the light was shining I wondered what they were doing that for. Until they said that it was going to shine forever. Say 'Hi' to John and your mother. NADENE OPPOLD."

"DEAR JACQUELINE KENNEDY, I think I saw you going in the parade to Arlington National Cemetery and I thought it was amazing the way the soldiers folded the flag that they gave to you. I hope that you find a nice headstone for your husband's grave. PAMELA HANSON."

"DEAR CAROLINE, When you leave the White House do what mother tells you to do. I hope you grow up to be married to a nice man and some day he may be our president. You still have a long way to go so be a good citizen. DEONNE AXTELL."

"DEAR CAROLINE: You were very brave to go up and kiss his casket and so was your mother. CINDY BERNHARD."

"TO OUR FIRST LADY: I hope you get another smart husband, like your first one. PAULA ALLEN."

Patricia Dirks wrote: "When I heard that our President died. I was shockt. I prayed a couple of times that he would live. Then when I heard that Lee Oswald was found I felt good. But when I heard Kennedy died I felt shockt again. I had tears on my face."

———

[From the Pep-A-Graph, Lennox High School Paper,
Lennox, S. Dak., Nov. 28, 1963]

DON'T LET OUR PRESIDENT DIE

(By Donnis Hoogestraar)

The halls are hushed. Lockers close quietly. The former disbelief is gone from the mind and only shock and trembling permeate the atmosphere. The students of Lennox High have had the rumor reaffirmed: The President has been shot.

There is no distinction between the failing and the honor student, between the popular and the disliked, or the "rink" and refined. No, in Lennox High School each student has a tear in his eye and solemnity in his voice. All are praying, "Dear God, don't let our President die."

As classes discontinue their regular routine and radios beam for the minute-by-minute report, everyone thinks and remembers. They can see the smile and warmth of manner, hear the familiar voice, and sense the zeal of their young President. The new and extensive means of communication had made John Kennedy seem a warm and personal friend. And as the students remembered, their prayer became more fervent. "Don't let our President die."

Then came the announcement so terrible in magnitude: "President John Kennedy is dead." Tears were shed but they did not begin to express the sorrow of the school. An atmosphere prevailed that cannot be explained as students just stared, thought, and remembered.

Now Mr. Kennedy lies cold in his grave. The smile is gone; the voice silent. But he need not die. For man's body is just a flimsily built structure that houses the soul and spirit which live on after death. We prayed with great emotion, "Don't let our President die." And we can keep him alive by carrying forth the traits which made him great.

No one would daresay that he was greater than any normal man for this would mean he was supernatural. No, we thought of him as one like us: young, industrious, and most of all, common, without arrogance. So let us pick out the characteristics that made him great and make those traits live in the youth of America.

First is equality in justice. We cannot hope to solve the civil rights problem simply by making everyone treat his fellow man as an equal. This question was started centuries ago by people who lost their vision of true freedom and it will not be solved by simply enforcing a law. President Kennedy made a small dent by alining himself with the Negro. So, let us "let our President live" by defending equality.

Probably the most noticeable of his traits was his courage to stick by his convictions. Congress seldom passed his proposals to their fullest degree, but his attitude toward these beliefs did not change. He believed strongly in medicare, Federal aid to education, and civil rights— no matter what the political pressure. If we would only study the issues, decide our stand and then live by our decisions, the spirit of our President will live on.

Most of all, he was American: enthusiastic, friendly, courteous, physically, mentally, and spiritually fit. He was not infallible, but no human is. In fact, there was nothing in his spirit that we cannot have. Each one of us can take his admirable traits and let them live in America. Don't let our President die.

AMERICA'S LOSS

(By Christine Olson)

The day dawned ominous and rainy
And half of it passed away.
Crowds lined the streets;
The air was charged with excitement;
People waited to see their President.
Flags snapped in the breeze,
And down the street a band
Struck up a spirited march.
As if in respect to the guest of honor,
The clouds rolled back
And sunshine illuminated the street.
Then, there he was before us:
Our President,
Young, laughing, waving to the people.
Suddenly from nowhere a shot split the air.
Another and another,
And the scene was changed to chaos.

It is another city, another day.
Crowds line Pennsylvania Avenue
Waiting for their President.
Down the street muffled drums
Mark off a hundred paces each minute.
Then, there he is before us;
The man who was our President,
Silent forever in the embrace of death.
Seven white horses draw the caisson
On which the flag-draped casket lays.
Now it is past and gone—
And so is a great man.

Turn, my friend, turn, for this is not the end
The country marches on; the office is not void.
Pray now, my friend, for this great land,
And for the man who leads it forward.

[From the Salem (S. Dak.) Special, Nov. 28, 1963]

JOHN F. KENNEDY—35TH PRESIDENT

This community, this Nation, and this world literally stopped on Monday, November 25, 1963, to pay homage and honor to a great American, John Fitzgerald Kennedy,

35th President of the United States, who lost his life in the service of his country.

Perhaps never in all of history have so many words been spoken, so many lines written, so many prayers been said for one human being. It almost seems futile, and yet so compelling, to add any more to what we have already seen and read and heard and said.

John F. Kennedy lost his life on Friday, November 22, 1963, at the hands of an assassin's bullet. While he has now departed from the scene of this earth, his memory and his ideals and principles will live with us through our lives and with the lives of our future generations. For truly, this outstanding young man, who gave all he had for his country, will be recorded as a great American and great world leader for generations to come.

Your publisher and his family feel, as perhaps every American and world citizen does at this time, a very personal loss and very deep grief, both for the family of this outstanding man, but also for themselves and for all the people of the world.

For us, he was part of our generation. He was young, vital, religious, compassionate, understanding, firm, determined, anxious, patient, sincere, and possessed a deep feeling for the needs of all the people, not only of this country, but he sensed the need for his leadership and guidance in the world.

He was a husband and father of two lovely children. He knew the trials and tribulations of both of these responsibilities—as husband and father. He was real, earnest, honest, and dedicated. And yet, along with all these attributes were his youth and vigor.

He set an example which many of us, of his generation, admired and followed. And yet, the old and the wise, the rich and the poor, the black and the white, all revered him and gave him a special place in their walks of life and in their hearts.

We are grieved at his passing. But, as so many people have said, we are so fortunate to have lived with him and to have worked for him and to have believed in him. And as General MacArthur said, with his passing we have all lost a little of ourselves.

However, the events since that black Friday have proven to all Americans and all world citizens that ours is truly a great heritage. For even with the dreadful passing of our leader, our affairs of state remain stable, secure, and in good hands. For this is our democracy. Now President Lyndon B. Johnson is at the helm of the ship of state. As he said in his first remarks when returning to Washington, "I'll do the best I can, that's all I can do, with your help and with God's." With this sincerity and affirmation, we'll continue in our great American tradition, as a nation, strong and free.

President John F. Kennedy, in his passing, left every American a legacy which we are obligated to remember, repeat, and follow. He gave us this legacy in his inaugural address, in January 1961, when he said, "Ask not what your country can do for you, but what you can do for your country."

John F. Kennedy paid the supreme sacrifice for his country. From his example and actions, our work is put before us, to do the affairs of our lives as he did his. We certainly must always strive for that goal, just as he died for it.

[From the Lemmon (S. Dak.) Tribune, Nov. 28, 1963]

UNITED WE STAND—IN SORROW AND IN SHAME

(By F. M. Satter)

With reverberations of the assassination of President John Fitzgerald Kennedy echoing around the world, Americans—still reeling in disbelief—are attempting to regroup themselves to meet the challenges of a country which has lost its Commander in Chief.

It is indeed fitting that we should ponder this ugly act of coldblooded murder in all its perspectives. It is also proper that we should attempt to mentally probe the philosophical elements which bred, impregnated, and gave birth to the type of hatred which possessed this American-born citizen to commit such a brutal act of violence.

John F. Kennedy, as dynamic a personality to ever assume the awesome responsibilities of the Presidency, was a man who truly loved America. Even his most ardent political opponents respected the young President's dedication to the causes of freedom and his efforts to build a stronger United States. Time and time again throughout J.F.K.'s career as a naval commander and later as a statesman he openly demonstrated his willingness to give everything—even his life, if necessary—to protect America from the poisons of hatred, violence, and dictatorial factions which constantly threaten our shores.

As it came to pass it was, in fact, his life that the mysterious facets of fate decreed he lay down in the service of his country. Not in the heat of battle however, where blood is spilled and the demands of courage are momentous, but on a seemingly placid freeway in Dallas, Tex., where he was concluding a triumphant motorcade sweep through the city proper.

The bullet that winged its way to its mark and left President Kennedy bleeding and mortally wounded in the arms of his wife profoundly spelled out the uncivilized results of mankind's perpetration of extremism and racial indifference.

When will we learn that to wantonly abuse our precious freedom of speech is just as grave a crime against humanity as to deny a man the right to speak?

Let it be known, and may the hatred and bloodshed of those fateful November days in Dallas ever remind us, that the inadequacies of man's tempers are not only confined to unfounded dislike, disrespect, or harmless words. On the contrary, idle and groundless accusations against top level Government leaders, linking them to all sorts of trajtorous deeds, can only lend to sway sick minds into action.

Not long ago an eastern publication reported the whole Kennedy family should be hung. The following day the media apologized and said it meant it only in jest. But who knows what terrible repercussions those words in jest might have had on some disturbed mind.

This great country of ours, with all its freedoms and opportunities, does in fact have one poignant weakness. That being the trait of loose-lipped politicians, editors, and citizens in general to literally talk an innocent, dedicated statesman into the crosshairs of some fanatic sniper's rifle scope.

There was nothing partisan about the deadly bullet which felled J.F.K. and silenced forever the lips of a great American. Under similar foreign and domestic tensions it could have happened to any of his predecessors. The venom of hate which conquers and consumes men's minds is indeed one of the great pities of life. Ofttimes these poor misguided souls, perhaps tormented by experiences known only to themselves, are prompted to commit shocking, heinous crimes because of some careless utterance made by someone in anger.

It is therefore particularly important that we as Americans make a self-examination of our own hearts and ultimately cast out these prejudices and petty emotions.

And finally, let us pray to God that this tragic murder of our President will teach us the true meaning of human dignity. We might use the theme of President Kennedy's Dallas speech if he had lived to deliver it, when he said in part: words alone are not enough to win victories over injustice; we must say those words and then act with dispatch.

We must, as a nation, accept the moral responsibilities which our late President has placed upon our shoulders. Then, and only then, will his tragic death lose some of its sting and the indignation and shame it has brought with it.

John Fitzgerald Kennedy is dead from an assassin's bullet. Let us now then unite behind his successor, President Lyndon B. Johnson, and work unselfishly as a massive team to rebuild the decayed pillars of morality, justice, and decency which have somehow slipped away from our proud heritage.

———

[From the Arlington (S. Dak.) Sun]

TRAGEDY STRIKES THE WORLD

(By Bonnie Bennett, student at Arlington High School)

The flag is flying at half mast. Why? Because our President, John F. Kennedy, has been assassinated. Usually sitting here in my study hall desk, I can't see the flag. Now as I look at it and know the reason it is not flying at the top of the pole, I realize the tragedy of this event.

Looking first at our country, it has lost a powerful leader. He held the respect of persons all over the world. The New Frontier, "Ich bin ein Berliner," and "Ask not what your country can do for you but what you can do for your country," are but a few of the principles which have been left to our country by the former President.

As I write of Mr. Kennedy, I think of this:

"And I heard a voice from heaven saying unto me, Write, Blessed are the dead which die in the Lord from henceforth: Yea, saith the Spirit, that they may rest from the labours; and their works do follow them" (Revelations 14:13).

———

[From the Tyndall (S. Dak.) Tribune & Register]

A chapter should now be added to J.F.K.'s famous book, "Profiles in Courage," recording the story of himself—one of the most courageous of them all.

And speaking of the President's public utterances, one that he never had the opportunity to actually voice, was the one he had written for delivery in Dallas the afternoon that he was shot. In that speech, the President had written, in part:

"In a world of complex and continuing problems, in a world full of frustrations and irritations, America's leadership must be guided by the lights of learning and reason—or else those who confuse rhetoric with reality and the plausible with the possible will gain the ascendancy with their seemingly swift and simple solutions to every world problem.

"There will always be dissident voices heard in the land, expressing opposition without alternatives, finding fault but never favor, perceiving gloom on every side and seeking influence without responsibility. Their voices are inevitable."

Thus did the President bring the facts of life to a section of our Nation which had reportedly turned against him because of his determination that all Americans, no matter what color or what creed, no matter whether rich or poor, would be treated as equals under the Constitution.

——

[From the Freeman (S. Dak) Courier]

(By Glenn Gering)

The events of the past week jolted us out of our common tendency to think that things will be tomorrow as they are today. It is natural to expect to have another chance at life another day. We assume that our family, our friends, our associates will be there the same as they are today. This is a comfortable assumption. It gives us an excuse to put off doing the things we ought to do. We depend on having another chance tomorrow, so we leave a word of encouragement, unspoken; our appreciation, unexpressed; a deed of kindness, undone; an opportunity to teach, unused; a task, unfinished. We ought to be most grateful for every day we get another chance. For some the opportunity has been lost forever. Some day the opportunity will also be lost to you and me.

——

[From the Clark County (S. Dak.) Courier]

But his death has even a greater meaning to the people of the United States and the world. Perhaps never before has there been such a uniting of people as in the past few days. Protestants, Catholics, and Jews have held special services, and churches have been packed and overflowing. Republicans and Democrats have forgotten their differences during this time of crisis. People have become more aware of the loyalty they owe the Government. At a special service in Clark, people stood just a bit straighter and were giving more thought to their democracy as the national anthem was played.

Yes, John F. Kennedy leaves unfinished business, but he also leaves a heritage. He followed a path that he hoped would bring peace among nations, and his hope was for a strong democracy. These are among the unfinished duties, and it becomes the job of all of us to work for this accomplishment.

ADDRESS BY

Hon. Gale W. McGee

OF WYOMING

Mr. President, it is a sad moment indeed for us today to gather our thoughts to pay homage to a man who was once one of us and then became a leader of the Nation, and, indeed, of free men throughout the world.

John Fitzgerald Kennedy was a man of true greatness, whose passing has left us numb with disbelief and horror. In a sense we are now struggling to live with the day-to-day reality of his absence. The Nation goes on, diminished, yet unchanged. Where he was the pilot, he is now the inspiration and example; and those now entrusted with the national destiny have clear and lasting guideposts set by this great man.

We may draw strength from the fact that John Kennedy has driven these guideposts firmly and wisely, so that we have provided for us and the free world, through his foresight, new purpose and direction to our lives for years to come.

I will always count it among my real honors and privileges that I was a colleague and friend of John Kennedy. It is difficult to add to the deeply felt eulogies offered by the many friends of this remarkable man. He was a man of many talents, many interests, a man of deep feelings and strongly held convictions. He was the acme of all the values that our civilization holds dear.

Rather than try to add further words on his greatness, I suggest that his sacrifice is a call to all of us to find new courage, new hope, and new conviction to carry on the job—perpetually unfinished—of maintaining liberty throughout the world.

We may take hope from two conspicuous facts which emerge in the wake of our loss. One is in mankind around the world; the other is closer at home. The first has to do with the high esteem in which the world held him, and in which the peoples of the globe hold our Nation, the Nation he led.

Many times it has been stated that somehow the American image was a negative image, that our national faith was darkened by disparagement and criticism.

Whatever else our great President's passing in recent days has brought to light, foremost is the high esteem in which his countrymen, through his leadership, are held throughout the world.

This fact should halt those allegations made by some that our mission to try to serve mankind and freedom in the world was failing.

Quite in contrast, it not only was succeeding in the wake of a glory such as no modern nation in the world had ever enjoyed before, but that success was galvanized in the inspiration and example of the leader who has now gone from us.

In addition to that outward look, the passing of our President has required that we take a new, hard look at ourselves.

While the picture has not always been pleasant, I believe it leaves us with a positive note.

It has been easy to say that this tragedy is the work of a fanatic, a madman. Yet we must take another look at our public attitudes, at the outpourings of hate and hostility that have in themselves created a climate of intolerance and have produced aberrations which in themselves cannot absolve quickly the rest of us.

Regardless of what compelled this horrible act, we must move toward a better restraint of our emotions, and again pledge our allegiance to truth and tolerance and good government.

John Kennedy was a man whose life was symbolized by a dedication to truth and adjustment to reality. He did not expect the impossible, but neither were his goals diminished nor his principles compromised for the sake of expediency.

We can learn from these attitudes, so that sanity may prevail in a world now capable of self-destruction.

President Kennedy's "pursuit of excellence," as he often called it, has enabled us to mobilize the forces of good in our land. Above all, it is time to call a halt to the reckless downgrading of the Government of the United States and of its leaders. Without any question, the activities of some groups in our land have fostered a massive climate of disrespect for democratic government and processes. Reckless assaults on public officials, whatever the intentions may have been, bring to the surface the kind of derelicts who perpetrate the crime that has been visited upon us.

To speak of our Federal Government as though it were an enemy power; to smear the American image by casting around it a shroud of suspicion; to poison the public mind with hate and rumors; to foster panic through planting false fears only serve to create an atmosphere which breeds lunatics and inspires fanatics. The anarchy of irresponsibility can destroy a free society.

Our friend and leader, John Kennedy, now sleeps the deep sleep of history. I have no doubt that that same history will accord to him the respect and honor and eternal greatness that are his due. Even though this tragedy has brought us to the black midnight of sorrow and despair, it also augurs the approach of sunrise, of a dawn that permits us to lift our heads and renew our resolution that this great and noble man may now guide us to the new tomorrow in which he so firmly believed, and which inspired his every act. We must find, in his example, new courage to continue his work, to support his successor, to live his ideals, and to cherish his memory.

ADDRESS BY

Hon. Clair Engle

OF CALIFORNIA

Mr. President, I want to join my colleagues today on this sad occasion in memory of John F. Kennedy.

Words are inadequate tools to express the outrage and despair we all felt when President Kennedy was struck down on November 22.

We have lost one of the greatest leaders of our time. John F. Kennedy had many gifts. His presence in a room filled it with more life and gave it more wit, intellect, and charm. His presence in the political world made many things possible. It made possible a greater chance for international peace. It made possible a greater chance of eradicating poverty. It made possible a greater chance of conquering the catastrophic diseases.

When we think of the contribution to humanity that John Kennedy was destined to make in the years ahead, the tragedy of his untimely death is incalculably compounded.

My deepest sympathies go to Jack Kennedy's Jacqueline and their two children, and also to his parents, sisters, and brothers.

ADDRESS BY

Hon. E. L. Bartlett

OF ALASKA

Mr. President, although they were separated by a century in point of time, yet there were parallels, and striking ones, between John Kennedy and Abraham Lincoln. President Kennedy brought to the White House many of the qualities of leadership held by Lincoln. He had a full sense of the dignity of his office, he had the balance and perspective of history, he had a natural taste that guided his every action; and the vision that gave purpose and direction to his stewardship was tempered with shrewd realism and honest evaluation. He worked for the possible in the direction always of the ideal. "Westward look, the land lies bright."

John Kennedy was unflinching and honest, "with firmness in the right, as God gives us to see the right," said Lincoln. Kennedy was a man of courage, with courage the greater because he understood the implications of his acts and because he understood that the President must act sometimes when the full implications, the end results of his acts, cannot be foreseen. The President, after all, is human, the information supplied to him is fallible, and yet the Constitution requires that he act, that he decide, that he direct and lead the country. As he goes, so the well-being of the country follows.

This great responsibility he sought; he understood the Presidency and he sought it. John Kennedy was the first of his generation and his century to hold the office. With his inauguration the course of the United States was given over to new and vigorous hands. The wheel was seized gladly with new enthusiasm, confidence, and courage.

And, again, this great and terrible office has taken its toll.

Kennedy's Presidency was shaped by his life. Born into a family of great wealth with greater dedication to public service, he was raised to seek responsibility happily, to give to it the best that he was able. His origins and his faith gave him the character and the strength he needed.

His career was shaped by four great lessons which served him every day he was in the White House. He was in England, as a young man, to see the fateful awakening of that country from its long slumber of appeasement. The Prime Ministries of Baldwin and Chamberlain taught many people many things, but none could have learned more than did John Kennedy. The story of those years of the locust is found in that remarkable book, "While England Slept," a book as useful and instructive now as ever it was, made more significant by the fact that it was written by a college boy who was to become our President. That Munich was avoided in Cuba may have been because the President knew first-hand the awful price which Munichs command.

The courage, the daring, the loyalty, the hard perseverance in the face of adversity were fired in the South Pacific during World War II. Had John Kennedy never become President the story of his command of PT-109 would still and always be a part of the record of American heroism. He did become President, and he was served in that lonely office during the long agony of the missile crisis by his wartime experience.

After the war, as a young Senator from Massachusetts, married to a beautiful and charming girl, with the promise of everything before him, he entered a third testing. His wartime back injury flared; he was forced to spend many months on his back in a body cast. His spine was fused, a most difficult and painful operation, and he was close to death several times during his illness. This experience and the pain which was almost always with him thereafter gave him the clarity and perspective that can come from a close acquaintance with final things.

The final lessons came with the campaign for the Presidency itself. No man comes through that unchanged. In 1958 Kennedy was not well known nationally; at his death in 1963 he was grieved around the world as perhaps no man in this century has been mourned. In 1958 the people did not know him; in 1963 he was theirs. These ties with the people were made during the campaign for the Presidency. He gave to the campaign the best his intellect and body were capable of. The people responded as they always do to honesty, intelligence, and leadership. He responded to them. They gave him the personal support which sustains a man in the remoteness of decisionmaking in this nuclear age.

The character of John Kennedy, shaped by

these four trials, was ready for the Presidency. In the 2 years, 10 months he held office, in this short time, he framed the principles and the policies which will give direction to our Nation for many years to come. During the thousand days of the Kennedy administration, it was easy enough to criticize, to complain that the problems although faced were not solved, that the legislative program although proposed was not enacted, that the grand design although laid out was not yet constructed. All true. The people and the Congress were not easily convinced of the rightness of his course; the President was forced to convince and cajole, to call and to plead.

It is perhaps central to the tragedy of his early death that he was a leader not yet truly followed, a prophet not yet fully honored. The Nation and the world regret they had not listened more and followed.

And yet, it is impressive how much John Kennedy managed to achieve in this thousand days: directions were changed, corners were turned and there is now no going back: the Alianza Para el Progreso, the Declaration of Interdependence, the Kennedy round of tariff negotiations and the new trade act, efforts for tax revision and reform, a space effort second to none, and the all-out flatout determination to achieve, at last, full civil rights for all our citizens. His two greatest personal triumphs have literally changed the course of history, and for this the world will long have cause to remember John Kennedy: the Cuban missile crisis and the test ban treaty.

Ultimately what John Kennedy gave to his country is greater than diplomatic or legislative victories. The English political scientist, Walter Bagehot, once said that a nation must choose its head of state with great care for the personality and character of the leader will become the example of the country. The country in time will take on the attributes of its leader. This is Kennedy's legacy to us. By his example in these short years the strength and character of our Nation have been improved.

We are the better for having been exposed to the man. He refused to be sentimental. He maintained always the dignity of great power. He would not duck, he would not flinch. He sought responsibility joyfully. His idealism was tempered with a cool view of the possible and the perspective of history. His taste, enthusiasm, optimism, balance, courage, and vigor cannot soon be forgotten by a nation that drew so freely upon them.

Kennedy was indeed our Arthur and he made us, for a short moment, Camelot.

ADDRESS BY

Hon. Frank E. Moss

OF UTAH

Mr. President, few events in the history of our Nation have so shaken, and then so united, our people as the tragic death of John Fitzgerald Kennedy. In the black moment when he was felled by an assassin's bullet, each of us lost a little of ourselves.

I know that I also lost a great and good friend whom I intensely admired, not only for his gift of leadership, but also because he was a fine, warm human being.

I cherish now each contact I had with him, first as a colleague here in the Senate, and then as a Chief Executive who welcomed me again and again to the White House. I watched him gain in maturity and assurance, and saw in him the stuff of which the world's greatest leaders are made.

The people saw this in him too, and he became the embodiment of their ideals. Even those who did not always agree with him recognized in him an apostle for the equality and dignity of men and a leader of good will, dedicated to the cause of peace.

He seemed never to have any private, selfish motives in what he did, but to be interested only in what would advance the purposes of the Nation. There were no vindictive or mean motives behind any move he made. He was motivated by the question: "What is in the best interest of America?"

It has been said that he was the most "civilized" of our Presidents since Thomas Jefferson, and I think this is the way he will go down in history.

Now that he is gone, I find comfort in the assurance that John Kennedy enjoyed being President of these United States. I am confident that though he found the burdens of the Presidency more onerous than he had anticipated, he also found the past 3 years during which he carried these burdens the most exhilarating and challenging of his life. He was able to use his sharp and absorptive mind, his grace, his vigor, his forceful eloquence, and his wit and charm to best advantage—and he used them lavishly. On the day when he was shot, he stood at the pinnacle of life, in full realization of his great powers, and it is one of the tragedies of our times that he was not allowed to complete fully his destiny.

I find particular comfort in the warm reception which my State of Utah gave President Kennedy about 2 months before he died, and his evident relish of it. I have never seen anyone else so completely conquer a State and so thoroughly take over the minds and hearts of thousands of people in it. One could almost feel the opposition melt under the force of his personality and the brilliance of his mind. He was surrounded by eager, enthusiastic crowds, from the moment he stepped off the plane that September afternoon, until he left, the next morning. His good humor, his dignity, and his warm friendliness never left him, even though he was jostled and pushed, as he stretched his arm again and again to shake the last hand. He drew the largest crowd ever gathered at one time in Utah, and there was not a single hostile sign or outburst.

He spoke that night, in the Mormon Tabernacle, to a crowd which filled that historic structure, and flowed out into the temple grounds and the streets around, and grouped themselves before every television screen in our State. He never spoke with more persuasiveness or wisdom. I felt that he made one of his finest speeches on foreign policy, and the crowd he held spellbound appreciated the tribute he paid to them by discussing with them our Nation's most serious problems.

The rapport between President Kennedy and the people of Utah was nowhere more clearly demonstrated than in the experience of the Tabernacle choir. When the choir rose in back of the podium, to sing for their distinguished guest, no one was quite prepared for the brilliance of their performance. In their finale—"The Battle Hymn of the Republic,"—the choir seemed to sing as it had never sung before. Everyone was caught up in the glory of that singing. The President was obviously deeply touched, and rose to acclaim them. He was not satisfied with clapping his appreciation in the usual manner, but turned again and again to continue to applaud and to bow his thanks to the choir. A common response—love of great music well performed—seemed to bind the President at that moment to those who had sung so magnificently for him.

The following morning, President Kennedy was the breakfast guest of Latter-day Saints Church President and Mrs. David O. McKay, in their apartment. It was my privilege to be present. Again, I saw in full play, the force and magnetism of John Fitzgerald Kennedy. He charmed his hosts, and they charmed him. There was a meeting of minds on some questions, and an appreciation of why there were differences of opinion on others. There were sharp exchanges of wit, and a discussion filled with philosophy and fact. When President Kennedy departed, he left behind an indelible impression of brilliance, wit, sincerity, ability, independence, and strength.

John Fitzgerald Kennedy got only 45 percent of the votes in my State when he ran for the Presidency in 1960. There were many who were chilly to the intense young man from New England who dressed and talked with such understated elegance and who seemed so far removed from our open Western ways. But after his 3 years as our President, and especially after his visit to Utah 2 months ago, it was a different story. I am convinced that Utah would have voted overwhelmingly for him in 1964.

In Utah, as throughout the Nation, there was an outpouring of grief when his death was announced. After the first shock passed, stunned people in all walks of life began to try to put their grief in words. Some used the most eloquent of language, and others the most simple; but all of it came from the heart.

I wish to place at this point some examples of the editorials which were printed, the resolutions passed, the telegrams sent, and the letters written in the State of Utah on the death of President Kennedy.

John F. Kennedy lived a tough life of controversy. He stood with fortitude for the things in which he believed. He told us many times that the fight would last beyond his lifetime. How prophetic were those words. The best way we can honor him now is to get down to work and consider the cornerstone of his legislative policy—the equal rights bill and the tax bill. I think he would want us to do this beyond anything else.

But we must do more than that; we must make this country stronger and freer than it was when John Kennedy last knew it. We must expunge from our national life the bitterness and distortions which seemed to have engulfed us, and must rededicate ourselves to the values of decency and rationality for which President Kennedy stood and for which he gave his life. Only then will he not have died in vain.

The editorials, resolutions, telegrams, and letters are as follows:

[From the Salt Lake City (Utah) Deseret
News, Nov. 23, 1963]

Our Nation's Tragic Loss

The assassination of President John F. Kennedy—a senseless, stupid, revolting act—has left the Nation deeply shocked and saddened beyond the power of words to express.

It is still hard to believe that it actually happened, still harder to believe we won't wake up tomorrow and hear his familiar voice, feel his customary influence in so many ways we have come to take for granted.

It is also difficult to believe that in this era and, more particularly, in this great country there still exist a few people so deranged, who take their prejudices so seriously that they would stain their souls with the blood of murder in an insane attempt to achieve their own ends.

The death of our Chief Executive can be serious for our Nation. But now it is appropriate to remember that above and beyond all temporal leaders, we are a God-fearing people and our Nation is ruled over by one Supreme Being. As long as we adhere religiously to His commandments, all will be well with us.

Universally, our sympathy goes out to the late President's charming wife and attractive children, to his bereaved parents and friends for their great loss.

Our sympathy is also extended to the Nation and, in fact, to the entire world—for the death of the man who, by virtue of his position as leader of this country, was a prime champion of freedom. His death is everyone's loss.

In our sadness and sense of loss, however, we must take care to put aside our former differences, which now seem so petty, and unite as never before behind the men who lead this country in these troubled times.

Lyndon B. Johnson, who succeeds from the Vice Presidency to the Presidency, is particularly deserving of our support and our prayers. The Vice Presidency characteristically has not provided a completely satisfactory schooling for the Presidency. However, under President Kennedy, Vice President Johnson was given unusual opportunities to keep abreast of problems and developments both internationally and throughout the Nation. The Vice President traveled widely throughout the world and through special committee assignments was constantly kept in close touch with domestic problems and developments. This background plus his long and varied experience in government eminently qualifies him for arduous and complex responsibilities which he now faces. Morover, with his new, enormous responsibilities, Lyndon Johnson will grow in the office.

Other men in similar circumstances have stepped into the Presidency on a moment's notice, as he now does. And history bears testimony to the fact they have grown amazingly in mind and spirit in response to that challenge. Lyndon B. Johnson gives every evidence of being such a man. His capacity for leadership is well attested to by the vigor of his activities as majority leader in the U.S. Senate.

As to the assassin, he deserves only our pity and our scorn. Our pity for the irreparable damage he has done himself in his shedding of innocent blood. Our scorn because, no matter how rational he may appear to be outwardly, his is a deranged mind, and he cannot even begin to realize what he has done.

No man can know, really, the full consequences of an act such as this one. The course of history seems bound to change because of it, to be sure. But who can say how or in what direction?

The man who committed this crime against the conscience of the world put his individual will above the will of the majority that elected John F. Kennedy as President of the United States. In the process he put himself above both law and morality, which no man can do with impunity.

The deed he committed, moreover, violates some of the most sacred principles which have made America great. It violates the fundamental truth that in a democracy violence is not only repugnant but also unnecessary because our form of government provides morally acceptable, effective ways for expressing dissent—namely, through the courts, through petitioning legislatures, or at the ballot boxes.

In choosing "bullets rather than ballots," the assassin went against the very tenets of society that are designed to protect the rights not only of ordinary, law-abiding citizens but also the rights of those who, like himself, put themselves outside of civilized society and the law. It is a stirring testimony to the strength of this country that even though the assassin callously violated others' rights, he will be scrupulously protected.

John F. Kennedy will long be remembered for many things. He will be remembered for the fact that he became the first Catholic to be elected President of the United States, thus shattering—one hopes for all time—an ugly bias that had long dishonored our country.

He will be remembered as the youngest man to be elected to the Presidency.

He will be remembered for certain governmental achievements—such as winning adoption of a Trade Expansion Act that is a landmark in the long struggle to lower trade barriers between nations and bring them closer together as the brothers that they are. Also, for working out a nuclear test ban treaty which, if observed scrupulously by all, could release mankind from the fear of the nuclear shadow that has been hanging over it.

He will be remembered fighting for freedom whenever and wherever it needed a champion—whether at home on behalf of minorities being deprived of rights lawfully theirs, or abroad on behalf of peoples who have been deprived of liberty for so long they have forgotten its joys.

He was kind. He was decent. The Nation and the world owe him a lasting debt.

His life was one of unremitting service to his country—from his days as the young commander of a PT boat in the Pacific during World War II through his days as a freshman Congressman to the climax of a remarkable career that took him to the highest position and highest honor this Nation has in its power to bestow upon a man.

Part of the tragedy is that he had more to offer his country by way of future service. Even after his duties in the White House, because of his youth he would still have had years of service ahead of him as a possible adviser on national affairs and as an international ambassador of good will.

Beyond that, John F. Kennedy will be remembered with fondness not because of what he was as an elected official but because of what he was as a person. He made friends readily. Even those who disagreed with his views almost invariably liked him as a man.

Now he is gone. And now it can be said of John F. Kennedy, as it was of Abraham Lincoln when he, too, was felled by an assassin's bullet: "Now he belongs to the ages."

————

[From the Salt Lake City (Utah) Tribune, Nov. 23, 1963]

John Fitzgerald Kennedy—1917–63

America is swept today by a grief that cuts across all lines of race or faith or politics—a grief that struggles without success to express itself in words. Shock, dismay, bewilderment, anger—these and other emotions stand in the way.

John F. Kennedy was a vital, courageous young man. He was the first President of the United States to be born in the 20th century. He brought to the White House the spirit of youth. He set his sights on a better future.

And then in a matter of minutes he is dead, struck down without warning by the bullets of a dastardly assassin.

What was the reason? Who knows? Perhaps there was no reason at all. Hatred knows no rules; fanaticism creates its own warped logic.

This murder was carefully plotted. The man who pulled the trigger did not act on impulse. We hope the assassin will be dealt with as he deserves. We hope that those who abetted or inspired him do not escape. If there was a nest where the crime was hatched, then trace it down. These are people bereft of honor and principle. Vengeance? No. Stern justice? Yes. This is a land of law.

President Kennedy was murdered in Dallas. Gov. John Connally of Texas, riding in the same car, was shot down. Vice President Lyndon B. Johnson, two cars to the rear, escaped. Now he is President Johnson, heir to the many problems of John F. Kennedy.

Dallas, in recent months, has had unhappy experience with fanaticism and violence. National figures were harassed and bodily attacked by those who did not

agree with them. But these incidents were no more than ripples. The worst was still to come—the death of the Nation's President.

Yet only by chance did this horrible crime blacken the name of Dallas. It could have happened almost anywhere. President Kennedy, like every head of state, walked with Death as a constant companion. And like Lincoln, Garfield and McKinley before him, he was struck down without warning.

How will history assess the career of John F. Kennedy? History will take its time in answering. It is not for us, so close to the events, to attempt a verdict.

We can testify, however, to his courage, his ideals, his aspirations, his deep love of humanity. He fought valiantly in a great war. As President he devoted himself to the cause of peace. He sought with equal devotion to give civil rights true meaning and full scope.

It was a magnificent vision, though he was not spared to turn vision into reality.

Mr. Kennedy had been in office a few months less than 3 years. He had had one historic failure—the Bay of Pigs invasion—and one historic success—the Cuban missile confrontation with Khrushchev. But his legislative program was bogged down in a lethargic Congress. "Wait till next year" was the word on civil rights and the tax cut. And next year, the Presidency is at stake in a national election.

The political pundits were already reading the trends. Now everything is changed. There is a new President in the White House and Lyndon B. Johnson is his own man.

But matters political cannot distract us at a time of national tragedy. Loss overwhelms us. We bow our heads in brief.

John F. Kennedy was the youngest man ever elected President. His beautiful gracious wife was with him when an assassin's bullets cut him down. He leaves two young children. The White House will miss their laughter.

We should pray for the President, for his widow, for his family.

We should pray for the state of the Nation.

We should pray for President Johnson, on whose shoulders rest burdens indescribable and unimaginable.

God rest the soul of John Fitzgerald Kennedy.

————

[From the Ogden (Utah) Standard-Examiner, Nov. 23, 1963]

World Mourns John F. Kennedy

All the world joined today in mourning the brutal assassination of John Fitzgerald Kennedy, 35th President of the United States.

Millions were stunned by what Adlai Stevenson appropriately termed the "tragedy of a deed that is beyond instant comprehension."

All felt what Dwight D. Eisenhower called "a sense of shock and dismay over this despicable act."

President David O. McKay, of the Church of Jesus Christ of Latter-day Saints, spoke not only for his 2 million followers but for men and women all over the U.S.A. when he said:

"The entire Nation feels a sense of humiliation that such a tragedy could come to a President of the United States."

As the news of President Kennedy's death in a Dallas hospital flashed around the globe, the question "Why?" was repeated from thousands of lips.

The only man who could answer the question was the cowardly assassin who hid in a Dallas building until the young President, smiling and waving, came by in a parade—then pulled the trigger of his rifle.

A communism-embracing chairman of the Dallas Fair Play for Cuba Committee, Lee H. Oswald, 24, is being held as the prime suspect in the murder. But if he did kill the President, he has not yet admitted it.

To Mrs. Jacqueline Kennedy, her two children, and the late President's parents, brothers and sisters, we join in extending sympathies that their beloved "J.F.K." should be cut down in the prime of life and at the zenith of his career.

To Lyndon B. Johnson, catapulted into the White House as the 36th President of the United States, our best wishes for success in keeping the Nation—and the world—on an even keel during these perilous, bewildering times.

As he returned to Washington as President, Mr. Johnson promised "I will do my best * * * I ask for your help, and God's."

The country, in this hour of deepest grief, must provide the new Chief Executive with its help.

––––

[From the Provo (Utah) Daily Herald, Dec. 2, 1963]

MARTYR TO CAUSE OF BETTER SPIRIT

Many Americans already are saying John Fitzgerald Kennedy is our martyred President. But they differ widely on the nature of his martyrdom.

Even historians may one day define our late President as a martyr and perhaps find many reasons for doing so.

If it is to be thus, we may fairly hope they conclude that, among other things, he was martyred to the cause of a better American spirit. That spirit today is sadly flawed.

The day Kennedy was assassinated, a school teacher made the announcement to her class of 10-year-olds. The children did not exclaim in shocking disbelief. They applauded his death.

It matters not what city and region that school is in. It could have happened in a number of areas.

That it occurred at all is a measure of the strain on the American spirit in 1963.

Many people in this Nation are saying that, as a result of John Kennedy's death, we must have done with hating, with spewing out poison, with turning every controversy into mental civil war.

Whole cities are being nearly engulfed by these poisons. On some subjects and in some places, the legitimate discussion which marks a viable democracy is virtually impossible. Argument is warped out of all resemblance to reality.

All of this is utterly foreign to the true spirit of America. This democracy lives by the free choices its people make. How can they make them without discussion of alternatives? How can democracy breathe soundly if the man who raises an alternative is branded Communist or Fascist?

A nation that has no room for choices cannot have a democracy. Its essence is discussion, negotiation, compromise.

But in the lexicon of the ill in spirit, negotiation and compromise are evil words. They are seen as devices for the yielding of principle, if not the yielding to a foreign power.

In the internal conflicts which flow from this rigid outlook, political adversaries are labeled "foreign agents" or, at the very least, dupes who unwittingly serve an enemy cause.

These terrible distortions corrode American democracy at its vital core. It is a free-ranging system. It is not meant to be constricted by argument founded on the "you're either for us or against us" philosophic theme.

Patience is beginning to run thin in this country with the haters, the distorters, the cheap dispensers of "enemy" labels. None has anything to do with the real America.

If John Fitzgerald Kennedy's death can etch that truth deeply in the now greatly troubled American conscience, then perhaps we shall never have to hear again of school-children applauding the death of a President.

––––

[From the Salt Lake City (Utah) Tribune, Nov. 24, 1963]

GRIEF'S HEAVY HAND

Grief has laid its heavy hand upon Jacqueline Bouvier Kennedy. First, the death of a newborn son; now, only a few weeks later, the assassination of her husband, the President of the United States.

She is so young and beautiful, so fragile.

Mrs. Kennedy accepted tragedy with the resoluteness of a Spartan woman. Her husband, mortally wounded, slumped beside her in the car in Dallas. She rode with him to the hospital. She made the sad journey back to Washington. She bore the burden of sorrow in silence and dignity.

Our hearts go out to her, though words will not heal her woe. She is solaced by her faith in a life beyond the grave and she is not alone. There are the children. There are the memories. And time is the great healer.

––––

SALT LAKE CITY, UTAH,
December 4, 1963.

Senator FRANK E. MOSS,
Washington, D.C.:

We, the Model Congress of Highland High School, in expressing our deepest sympathy at the passing of President Kennedy, do hereby pledge our loyalty and support to those ideals for which he stood.

JACK DOBSON,
President.

––––

TRINITY PRESBYTERIAN CHURCH,
Ogden, Utah, December 2, 1963.

In behalf of the Presbytery of Utah, which represents all of the United Presbyterian Churches in the State of Utah, we extend our heartfelt condolence and sympathy to the bereaved family of the late President Kennedy.

The bullet that struck down President Kennedy has inspired already a deluge of unprecedented tributes across both the Nation and the world seldom, if ever, equaled at any other time since the assassination of Abraham Lincoln.

The tragic manner of President Kennedy's death helps to account for the unprecedented tributes in synagogue and church, but does not wholly explain it. As citizens of our beloved Nation we all share in the guilt of the President's death. We have yet to learn to disagree without being disagreeable. We have yet to learn to disagree but resolve to love. We have yet to learn that the innumerable apostles of discord ascend higher and higher on the flaming wings of so-called forums upholding either the radical far right or the radical far left. This is the price we pay, however, for our precious freedom of speech, freedom of the press, and other priceless freedoms.

So long as love and forgiveness exist among us, we may exclaim with Paul: "I am sure that neither death, nor life, nor angels, nor principalities, nor things present, nor things to come, nor powers, nor height, nor depth, nor anything else in all creation, will be able to separate us from the love of God in Christ Jesus Our Lord."

C. SUMPTER LOGAN,
Moderator,
Presbytery of Utah.

SALT LAKE CITY, UTAH,
November 25, 1963.

Hon. FRANK E. MOSS,
U.S. Senate,
Washington, D.C.

MY DEAR SENATOR MOSS: On this day of national mourning I feel the desire to take a few minutes to write to you. There are two thoughts which I wish to express. First, my deep personal grief over the death of President John F. Kennedy. Not only do I concur in the sentiments expressed in innumerable articles and eulogies across the country, but I also feel a great personal loss. Although I came to this country early in 1952 during the Truman administration, and received my naturalization papers in 1957, it was not until 1960 that I had the great privilege of voting in a presidential election. It was then, that after much searching, studying and earnest prayer, John F. Kennedy became my choice and he, in most instances, not only lived up to my expectations, but often exceeded them. The deed of that dark Friday has jolted my family and I to the depth of our souls and only the sure knowledge of a resurrection and of the working of a just God and loving Father has eased our sorrow.

Our hearts have gone out to the President's young widow, her children, and family. Today I have taken two of my six young sons, born as free Americans, to the memorial services at the tabernacle, the same building in which, as you well recall, a great man, only 8 weeks ago found friendly and kind words for a group of Americans once bitterly persecuted by their own fellow citizens because of their religion.

My second reason for writing today is to make to you a pledge. The past few days have led me to believe that America may perhaps never be quite the same. But lest I myself forget this tragic hour, let me hasten to put in writing to you, my Senator, my intentions for the future:

I, an American citizen, shall henceforth more fully endeavor to love and to pay allegiance to this my country, to honor its divinely inspired Constitution, to support its elected officials on all levels of government, to exercise my franchise in this free land, to respect the rights of all people and to extend a hand of friendship to all men, colored or white, Christian or non-Christian, to ban from my heart all impulses of hatred, to make an earnest effort to understand instead of to judge, to love instead of condemn, to live uprightly before God and men and to raise my children in this same spirit.

I realize that I could have made this pledge to myself, quietly and unobtrusively. Resolution, if shouted from the housetops are generally shallow and vain. I felt, however, that in this instance I should share this rededication with you, my duly elected Senator, whose duty it is to help bear the burden of government and whose mandate includes me as a part. Having expressed myself thusly, that burden may not feel quite as heavy to you and to me, and the hour of sacrifice of a great American takes on a new meaning.

Sincerely yours,

HORST A. RESCHKE.

A TRIBUTE TO JOHN FITZGERALD KENNEDY FROM A SCHOOLGIRL

Today we buried the man who will probably go down in history as the most famous, the most wonderful, and the most spirited President of the United States of America.

John Fitzgerald Kennedy, 35th President of the United States, fought for what he knew was right. To the Negroes, he was a symbol of equal rights. To the Nation he was a defender of the Constitution. To the world he was a symbol of peace.

The following words are taken from President Kennedy's inaugural address. He will be most famous for them because they are so spirit-lifting and so freedom-fighting: "Ask not what your country can do for you, ask what you can do for your country." These words made the whole Nation feel that the man they had voted in to office would be a good, strong, willing worker.

I was privileged to meet President John F. Kennedy, one clear September night. I had listened to his speech in the tabernacle in Salt Lake City, and afterward I went across the street to the Hotel Utah, in the Skyroom, where the Presidential reception was to be held. It was so crowded that when the President entered he was mobbed from all sides. The atmosphere of the crowd was a friendly one. President Kennedy didn't like orderly receiving lines. He enjoyed people flocking around him. People that night told me I was lucky to have met the President because many people didn't. He was smiling that night. When I shook his hand he grasped mine and held it tightly for that wonderful moment. As I dropped a curtsy and said "How do you do, Mr. President," I can remember the twinkle in his eyes. I will treasure this moment forever.

President John Fitzgerald Kennedy was a close family man. He was a wonderful father to his two children, Caroline and John, Jr. He and his little son spent many happy moments together. One of the first press conferences President Kennedy had, ended up in laughter because Caroline came out in her pajamas and her mommy's high heels.

President John Fitzgerald Kennedy will always be remembered for his courage and willing spirit in the difficult job of being the President of the United States of America.

ARDIS BEYERS.

NOVEMBER 25, 1963.

TED CANNON'S SCENE TODAY

The tragic events of last weekend had not yet transpired when Mrs. Beatrice Bennett, 750 Bryan Avenue, mailed us the following. Her note explains that she became a citizen only a year ago, and that she was moved to these lines as she sat in the Tabernacle on the occasion of President Kennedy's recent visit:

"Tonight I saw the President,
　　The Chief of all our land.
I didn't get to speak to him,
　　Or even touch his hand.
But from the crowd I saw him smile,
　　I saw him standing near,
My heart was filled with pride and joy,
　　And in my eye, a tear.

"Tonight I saw the President,
　　This man of strength and powers
I watched him as the Choir sang
　　Of this fair land of ours
America! America!
　　Oh, how my heart did ring!
On all this land so wonderful
　　What joy this man did bring!

"Tonight I saw the President
　　And all my whole life through
It's something I can dream about
　　And tell my kinsmen, too.
I love this land so beautiful,
　　It stands for all that's true.
I'm glad that for our President
　　We chose a man like you."

THE DEATH OF THE PRESIDENT OF THE UNITED STATES, 1963

The great plane came from Washington,
　　Then returned the President like a hymn
Of light to the quietness of Arlington,
　　Where dark repose must come and cherish him.

Out of the drift of air the great plane came,
　　Glinting the chief power in the whitening stream,
Bearing the letters of his country's name
　　To the city where in death he kept his dream.

The sunlight gleamed among the thronging streets
　　Where he turned and passed to find a sudden way,
The pitching storm of sorrow, the floating sheets
　　That silenced him and wrapt him from his day.

For once he heard the silver voice that came
　　Above the solemn air of his felicity
When, before the Capitol and certain fame,
　　He kept the burden of humility.

We start, and hear in the hum of coursing time
　　What time will not disclose, except bristling
And secret in a rifle's clipping mine
　　Of death, the spurt and shot, the bullet whistling.

Darkness, and all is gone, against the seat,
　　Cradled there. The wild shock, waving
Away, stills us as if yesterday were neat
　　And prim a thousand years ago, craving

To be born again and live again a better way.
　　We cannot hold it in 1 waning hour,
And it is gone, slipping from us where he lay
　　Dying, in the envy of time, the silent tower.

Then death. And now to Arlington he comes,
　　From plane and city and from the sorrow dim
And still that brought him home to muffled drums
　　And to the Nation that will cherish him.

—CLINTON F. LARSON, Provo, Utah.

ADDRESS BY

Hon. Daniel B. Brewster

OF MARYLAND

Mr. President, I rise to add my humble tribute to our late President, John Fitzgerald Kennedy. Seldom have words seemed so inadequate. A reverent silence—the kind of hush which enveloped this Hill that tragic weekend—might best express our feelings.

The life of our late President and of his family will always symbolize the great traditions of a nation proud of its heritage—unwilling to permit the slow undoing of human rights at home and abroad, but willing, in the President's own words, to "pay any price, bear any burden, meet any hardship, support any friend, oppose any foe to assure the survival and success of liberty." Our late President kept his pledge.

He bore the burdens of the Presidency with infinite good grace. He had verve, vigor, good humor, and the uncommon capacity to laugh at himself. He possessed an almost fantastic knowledge of history—and, more important, he fully understood the lessons that lie therein for all those who will but search for them. He was confident of himself, and rightly so. He was confident and morally certain that the things he believed in and the programs he espoused were right for our country and for our people.

He knew that there were no swift and simple solutions to today's complex problems, and he rightly warned us against confusing rhetoric with reality or the plausible with the possible. He was in a very real sense, the ultimate personification of the practical idealist.

He never shrank from responsibility. He welcomed it. The energy, the faith, the devotion which he brought to this endeavor did light our country. The tributes from around the world indicate this light was seen from afar.

With dedication, courage, and sacrifice, with a good conscience his only sure reward, with history his final judge, he did go forth to lead the land we love.

The now famous admonition of the inaugural address: "Ask not what your country can do for you—ask what you can do for your country," was a challenge new to many Americans, but a way of life to John Fitzgerald Kennedy.

Near the close of this address, President Kennedy spoke these prophetic words:

In your hands, my fellow citizens, more than in mine, will rest the final success or failure of our course.

In that same address, he said:

Now the trumpet summons us again.

He called on us to continue the struggle against the common enemies of mankind—tyranny, poverty, disease, and war. More than any of us, he answered that summons. With characteristic vigor, he threw himself into the fight until finally he gave his all—his life.

The sound of another trumpet echoing taps over his final resting place told us our leader had fallen. Yet the struggle to which he gave his life continues unabated. The tasks in which he asked us to join him were not finished in the first 1,000 days. They were not finished in his lifetime. They remain a challenge to every American to give more of himself to finish what we began with him.

Since the afternoon of November 25, all of us must walk in the shadow of the small, but incredibly brave 3-year-old boy who stood on the steps of St. Matthew's Cathedral and delivered that heart-wrenching last salute to one of the truly great men of our time—the 35th President of the United States—his father.

For generations, this small boy's family has served this Republic, enriched its history and all humanity. Its members have made lasting contributions to our national life.

Few families in American history have better symbolized the heritage, the traditions, the opportunities, the struggles, the courage, the achievements, and the meaning of our great country.

Our tribute, then, must be to the living as well as to the dead—particularly to Mrs. Jacqueline Kennedy, whose rare courage helped sustain us all in that terrible time.

Few of us fully realized how this extraordinary man was strengthened by the presence at his side of a truly extraordinary young woman. Many have paid tribute to her, but my good friend and former colleague in the House of Representatives, Otis Pike, of New York, said what I should have wanted to say when he recently wrote:

At a time when America should have been comforting her, she comforted America. At a time when she should have leaned on America for strength, America received strength from her. By her courage, her faith, and her fortitude she set a standard for the bereaved of all lands for all times.

By every aspect of her conduct and her bearing, a single, widowed mother poured strength into all Americans, and from the vast majority of Americans respect and love were returned.

I humbly ask Mrs. Kennedy, our colleague, Senator Ted Kennedy, the Attorney General of the United States, Bob Kennedy, our former Ambassador to the Court of St. James's, and the other members of his family, to allow us to join in their prayer:

Dear God, please take care of your servant, John Fitzgerald Kennedy.

Let us be grateful for his life. Let us recognize that the lives of all of us, of his children and of mine, have been enriched. Let us weep with his widow, salute with his son, and continue, as his family does, to serve our country through responsible leadership.

ADDRESS BY

Hon. Harrison A. Williams, Jr.

OF NEW JERSEY

Mr. President, until November 22 we thought that we would share many more days with John F. Kennedy. We thought we could continue to draw strength from his strength, wisdom from his wisdom, and inspiration from his genius. We could not know that the thousand or so days he gave to us as President were to be painfully precious because they were to be so few. He had not yet given all he had to give us, and yet he was taken from us.

Perhaps it was this that made the news so unbelievable when it came. John F. Kennedy had met many crises in his life, and always he had emerged with greater strength. He had escaped death during wartime combat. He had survived painful personal afflictions and had overcome them. He had calmed our Nation when enemies put weapons of destruction close to our shores.

Time and time again, he had helped us keep our own frailties in check, and we thought him stronger than any of us. His life, his leadership seemed to be secure to us, and yet both were taken by two bullets from an assassin's rifle.

We in this body are trying today to tell what that loss means to us. We are also trying to describe, I believe, the gifts that John Kennedy gave his fellow citizens in his lifetime.

These gifts are all that make our sadness tolerable. We must think of them.

Few of us will forget the cold Inauguration Day that began his administration. As the winds whipped about him and his audience, the new President spoke of our national mission. Man, he said, now has the power to abolish all forms of life, but this clear danger has toughened the will of those who believe that only democracy can create a world of law. The President invited every freeman to find his own way of making freedom stronger, and he spoke of sacrifice and danger. But sacrifice and danger, said our President, would make our ultimate triumph more inspiring to us and to those in nations not yet free.

John F. Kennedy accepted his own responsibility more completely than any of us. He was optimistic enough to call for a Peace Corps and an Alliance for Progress. He was determined enough to build new military strength for our Nation, and it is that strength that has led us to the beginnings of disarmament. He could not stand waste of human energies, and so he asked new programs to combat unemployment and waste of talent. He could not tolerate injustice, and so he asked for the broadest action yet taken against manmade inequalities.

Many men for many years will study the messages he sent to Congress, and we will measure our accomplishments against his requests.

Our 35th President will be remembered for what he was, as well as for what he did. We here in this Chamber have many memories of the days we spent here with him. We remember the book he wrote about six men who preceded us here.

John F. Kennedy was an authority on courage because he had his own great share of it. Each of the men he wrote about had to make decisions under great pressure, and each of them could have found reasons to take the less dangerous path. But not one of them did, and the Nation was stronger because they did not. In the White House, on many lonely occasions, John F. Kennedy made other decisions, and the world could be grateful that he was there to make them. Disciplined and compassionate, he performed the possible while he yearned for even greater accomplishment.

Mr. President, each one of us will remember John F. Kennedy in many different ways. We will remember him addressing Congress and the Nation; we will remember him at press conferences and at speaker's podiums in Washington and in city squares, in meeting rooms with chiefs of state, and on the White House property, his hand closed fast on his daughter's hand, or playing with his delighted young son.

We were interested in everything he did because we liked him as much as we respected him. And this, perhaps, is the best tribute to him.

Our loss is all the more cruel because we lived in his time. Future generations will know of our grief and they may understand it, but only we can say that we knew John Kennedy as a President and a friend. This gives us comfort as we bid him goodbye, and we need comfort now.

Mr. President, many fine editorials and articles about the late President appeared in New Jersey newspapers soon after his death. I will limit my remarks and ask that they be made a part thereof. I would like to draw attention to the comments about the courage of Mrs. Kennedy during her ordeal. To all that her husband gave her Nation, she has added one more magnificent memory.

[From the Trenton (N.J.) Times]

A GREAT LEADER IS MOURNED MANY WAYS, BY MANY PEOPLE

(By William J. O'Donnell)

President John F. Kennedy meant many things to many people.

To the little man, he was the champion of the downtrodden.

To the oppressed, he was the knight who would unshackle their bonds.

To the youth of the Nation, he was the symbol of hope and courage.

To the statesman, he was the man of peace.

To the politician, he was the tireless fighter.

To the Communist enemy, he was the roadblock to their ambitions for conquest.

To the average American, he was a loyal husband and kindly father.

Now this man of achievement belongs to the ages. This man of peace has been destroyed by violence. This man of kindness has been taken from us by hate. This man of thoughtfulness has been slain by the unthinking. This man of loyalty has been snatched away by a traitor.

To this reporter, John F. Kennedy signified all that was alive and vibrant in this challenging world. He was a man to instill confidence. He was a man to instill courage. He was a man to instill virtue and character. He was a man.

We asked others what John F. Kennedy meant to them. This is what they said:

A U.S. Congressman, Frank Thompson Jr.: "He was first a personal friend, but most important he was the symbol of the whole structure of our Government. To me he was all the American people."

A Jewish rabbi, S. Joshua Kohn: "The leader of this youthful dynamic country. One who looked forward to a better world and had the confidence to make this world a reality in the true religious spirit of all mankind."

A mayor of a city, Arthur J. Holland: "A personification of the confident and able leadership needed by our Nation and the world. A man who will always symbolize for youth a call to the pursuit of excellence. A great man who always thought of the little man."

A Federal Judge, Arthur S. Lane: "John F. Kennedy was a splendid young American, possessed of great courage, intelligence and devotion to his fellow men."

A Catholic priest, Msgr. John E. Grimes: "President Kennedy was an inspiration to me and a moving example of what is expected of a true American and a genuine Christian gentleman. He loved this country. He loved his fellow human beings. He dearly loved his family."

A housewife and mother, Mrs. John M. Smith of 54 Smithfield Avenue: "A good man is gone. He would have been a great President. His death is a great tragedy to me."

A president of a university, Robert F. Goheen: "John Kennedy was to me, above all, a man who combined clearsighted intelligence and steady commitment to the ideals of human dignity, freedom and justice. In the face of tangled and often highly recalcitrant circumstances, at home and abroad, he did much to uphold those ideals and to advance their realization in concrete terms."

A Negro leader, the Reverend S. Howard Woodson, Jr.: "To me President Kennedy was the herald of a new breed of political leadership. His forthright acts which strengthened the cause of human dignity, freedom and equality the world over translated beautiful political platitudes into realities. His death is a tragic testimony of the continuing existence of man's inhumanity to man."

A Republican lawyer, Irving H. Lewis: "Even though I am of different political faith, it is my unalterable conclusion that John F. Kennedy was a great man— unselfish in his ideal for the betterment of all mankind. His years of public service will make an indelible imprint on human affairs as long as man's accomplishments are recorded."

A Trenton barber, Peter J. Pulone, 809 Stuyvesant Avenue: "I looked upon him as my Commander in Chief. Whatever he said, I believed and followed it as an order."

A Protestant minister, the Reverend Allan R. Winn: "He bore the Nation's standard for truth and sincerity, for purposeful progress in all human relationships. As Commander in Chief of our Armed Forces, he stood ready to commit our Nation to the defense of freedom and to my personal freedom. I greatly admired his courage and bear tribute to his integrity."

A State chairman of the Democratic Party, Thorn Lord: "To me President John F. Kennedy was the symbol of kindness and tolerance. I knew him as a man who understood the essence of the Presidency. I think of him as the light of our times. I remember him as the most generous person I have ever known. I admire him as the most tremendous driving force of the 1960's."

——

[From the Asbury Park (N.J.) Evening Press]

PRESIDENT KENNEDY

A sorrowful Nation mourns the passing of its President and senses profound shame over his assassination. We had hoped that the entire Nation had grown so civilized that political opposition and even hatred would express itself only in the ballotbox. That, indeed, is the philosophy to which the great masses of people in this aggrieved Nation subscribe. Only maniacs fail to comply.

John F. Kennedy served as President for less than 3 years, and during that brief term he fulfilled his responsibilities with devotion. Even those who quarreled with his policies recognized a sincerity and fortitude that evoked admiration. His experience in the Senate had given him valuable training for the Presidency and for the aggressive leadership that he offered in his campaign for election.

Seldom has a Chief Executive been encumbered with more burdensome responsibilities. International tensions were coupled with domestic problems to challenge his wisdom and test his courage. Only history will determine the degree of success that his administration achieved. But his contemporaries can attest to the vigor and enthusiasm and conscientious effort that delineated his record.

The death of a President is always a national tragedy. In view of his comparative youth and the promise of future achievement, the passing of President Kennedy becomes an especially grievous loss. And the fact that an assassin's bullet should have claimed him carries the Nation's sorrow to the ultimate depth.

———

[From the Newark (N.J.) Star Ledger]

Of Mourning and Rededication

Today has been proclaimed a day of mourning. Americans everywhere will join in a heartfelt, sorrowful tribute to the Chief Executive so ruthlessly and viciously shot down by an assassin.

Now that the initial shock has been somewhat worn away by the inexorable process of time, the terrible enormity of the crime—with all its farflung ramifications— is only beginning to dawn on the American people.

And they are realizing, too, that the deeper the tragedy the more difficult it is to truly do it justice.

The impact of the tragedy was further brought home to millions of Americans via the television sets in their living room. They saw the flag-draped casket bearing the remains of John Fitzgerald Kennedy move slowly on a horse-drawn caisson through the streets of Washington from the White House to the Capitol rotunda.

They heard the regular beat of the hushed drums— 100 steps to the minute. And the mournful rhythm beat a tattoo the American people will not quickly forget. There have been few, if any, instances in history where so many people participated in a service marking so great a tragedy.

In many a living room yesterday it would have been hard to find a dry eye. The sight of Mrs. Kennedy, little Caroline at her side, bravely kneeling to kiss the casket of her husband will be etched for a long time on the minds of millions of Americans.

The loss Mrs. Kennedy suffered is, of course, a great one. But all of us also have suffered a great loss.

Mr. Kennedy served but a brief period in the White House. But it was an eventful period. Historians may be reluctant to pass final judgment at this early date. It was clear, however, since shortly after his inauguration that the Kennedy administration was to be earmarked by youth, vigor, intelligence, and determination to make a fresh attack on accumulated problems at home and abroad.

Seeing their young President in action, the American people had a growing confidence in his ability. Not everyone agreed with him. But no one—least of all John F. Kennedy—would have expected or wanted unanimity. The American Government provides room for disagreement and diversity. This is one measure of its strength.

But there is no room for hatred of the type displayed by the assassin who ended the President's life. When it comes to hatred, there is only room for hatred of injustice and violence.

In his few years in the White House, President Kennedy sought to end injustice and inequality in the Nation and violence from abroad. And millions of American people are undoubtedly better off today because of his efforts.

By proclamation, today is a day of mourning. It is also, by proclamation, a day of rededication. In their mourning, the American people should not overlook the obligation to rededicate their efforts to help make their country a better place for all its citizens—in a world secure in justice and freedom, removed from the threat of violence.

Perhaps such a utopia—of which man has dreamed for centuries—cannot be achieved on this earth. But this was the aim of the Founding Fathers of this Nation. And it was the aim of John F. Kennedy.

Mr. Kennedy's tragic death may have helped sharpen the full realization of fundamentals to which Americans are accustomed to give lipservice. Now is the time for all to rededicate themselves to giving much more than lipservice to the high ideals on which this Nation was founded.

———

[From the Jewish News]

Time for Rededication

The lively sense of history and national purpose which motivated our beloved President John F. Kennedy is illustrated by an anecdote of which he was fond. As he related the story, on May 19, 1780, the noontime skies over Hartford, Conn., turned from blue to gray and by midafternoon had blackened so densely that men fell on their knees and begged a final blessing before the end came. The Connecticut House of Representatives was in session. And as some men fell down in the darkened chamber and others clamored for an immediate adjournment, the speaker of the house, one Colonel Davenport, came to his feet, and he silenced the din with these words:

"The day of judgment is either approaching or it is not. If it is not, there is no cause for adjournment. If it is, I choose to be found doing my duty. I wish, therefore, that candles may be brought."

In this spirit, and with the unerring instinct of a people profoundly dedicated to democracy, let us do as President Kennedy would have wished and stand in united support of the new administration. President Lyndon Johnson bears a heavy burden, one which was assumed under horrifyingly tragic circumstances. This above all is a time for each American to respond in the courageous Kennedy tradition, to bring candles to light the darkness, to refuse to adjourn despite the staggering loss of a great leader in the parliament of mankind.

Yet, even as we recognize how we must behave at this critical juncture, in our pain and mourning we grope almost blindly for an answer to the agonizing question: Why was he taken from us? We search as well for understanding of our own tears and we find a powerful suggestion of an answer in the perceptive words of James Reston in the New York Times:

"America wept tonight, not alone for its dead young President, but for itself. The grief was general, for somehow the worst in the Nation had prevailed over the best. The indictment extended beyond the assassin, for something in the Nation itself, some strain of madness and violence, had destroyed the highest symbol of law and order."

It is not enough merely to blame the lunatic fringe elements on the far left and far right as the bearers of this "strain of madness and violence." Out of expediency of one kind or another, too many of us have come to disregard clear-cut moral issues, The frenetic climate in which the extremist of any sort thrives has tainted an inordinately large area of our national life.

This extremism and indifference we must purge if we are to be true to those magnificent things for which President Kennedy stood. In his memory, and in the name of the sacred principles which he personified, let us rededicate ourselves to American democracy.

———

[From the Jersey Journal]

JOHN F. KENNEDY

You think all the things an editorial writer is supposed to think, the awful evil of political assassination, the terrible wantonness of it, the incomprehensible fate that lets a demented marksman obliterate a President, but you keep going back to a picture of a young, vital American, President, yes, but a family man like the fellow down the block having fun with the children, weighed down with great affairs, yes, but not so much as to miss the point of a joke and have a good laugh, holder of the most august temporal title, yes, but a man you talk with as easily as you talk to the fellow beside you in the coffee bar.

You keep thinking of when first you met him, before his nomination, it was in Washington and he had just finished a landmark speech to the American Society of Newspaper Editors in which he closed forever the question of a Catholic in the White House; you intercept him as he gets out the door and tell him: "Senator, I'm from the place that is going to give you New Jersey, Hudson County." His eyes light and he says: "Fine, Neil Gallagher has been telling me about it. I'm certainly glad to meet you." His handshake is strong, friendly but he looks so boyish you wonder will the people choose him over Dick Nixon. Then he moves on through the crush. You have had the seconds he can spare.

You see him that fall in Journal Square. A crowd has waited patiently in the November cold, the largest ever packed into the square, they say. Finally he arrives, hatless as usual. You have a good view because Arthur Knaster lets you and the photographers use the windows of his law office on the second floor of the Jersey Journal

building. You are just above and behind the grandstand and you see him come up, through the crowd, onto the stand and before the microphone. You remember how that wild hair stands up on the back of his head, and think bitterly now: "This is how he must have looked to the murderer through that telescope sight" but that night who could think of him slain? The roar of that crowd as he told them how they would help him win, then a farewell smile and he is away. This was the final rally of the long outdoor campaign, the votes will be all in in little more than 48 hours, when he comes this way again he will be President of the United States.

You remember the telegram just about a year later inviting you to luncheon at the White House with the President. He is host to editors from New Jersey. The guard checking you through, the walk up the drive to the front door, noticing some peeled white paint along the driveway wall, then into the Blue Room to wait. A few minutes later the President arrives and joins his guests with their cocktails. His is tomato juice. Through luncheon he explains how "this job" keeps him too far from the people. In effect he asked, "What do you hear?" The luncheon is lively with questions and answers. Once he discusses the movie "Advise and Consent," his tone implies he would not have cast Franchot Tone as the President. You lean across to him and ask: "Mr. President, you could not get that role?" He laughs and snaps back: "I was too busy." He talks about fallout shelters and world economics and Dick Hughes' chances against Jim Mitchell. He autographs his menu because Marty Gately's hero-worshipping teenager has asked you to bring back a souvenir for her. Leaving and shaking his hand, you say: "A year ago you were fighting hard to get this job. Now that you have it, what do you think?" Suddenly he looks much older, then half whispers: "The weapons. The weapons." And you know why he seems to have an invisible weight always upon him.

And only a few months ago, at another editors' meeting in Washington, a spring evening and cocktails and a reception at the White House. He has a light word for everyone in the long line. A handshake and a word of greeting passes about Hudson and John Kenny and Bill Flanagan. The time moves on. Without suspecting, you have seen him for the last time. Six months later all that vitality and youth will be exchanged for a madman's bullet * * * and he will be a Commander in Chief slain for his country as truly as any man who ever died earning the Medal of Honor.

———

[From the Camden (N.J.) Catholic Star-Herald]

A PRESIDENT NAMED JOHN

Our age has been blessed by the presence of two Johns: Pope John XXIII and President John F. Kennedy. Both were loved and, of late, mourned bitterly in this most unhappy year of 1963. Yet the deeper sorrow was evoked by the death of our late President, not necessarily because he was greater, but because his demise was so untimely, so cruelly inflicted, so incredibly sudden.

What can we say of one whose memory has already been enshrined so fittingly by so many loving fellow

Americans and foreign leaders? How can we further exalt the life of a President whose youth belied his wisdom, whose charity tempered his courage, whose patience often camouflaged his pioneering spirit? Without doubt the highest tribute of all was given the late President by the Nation itself when, spontaneously and unanimously, it mourned his tragic passing.

To say that every American wept that day would be a gross understatement. Rather say that everywhere people of good will wept over and over again at the shocking passage of events as it was announced and explained to them. Before the sun had set on that horror-filled day of November 22, the whole world was weeping.

We have been called the ugly Americans, crass materialists bent on making money; a people allegedly oversexed, overstuffed, overstimulated. But on the day John F. Kennedy died our people displayed their innate nobility: their generosity, their tenderness, their love, their profound goodness. All commerce ceased. The TV wasteland became transformed into a panorama of a nation stricken with sorrow. Sports and social events were canceled precipitously; in the very hour of the announcement of the President's death, dazed citizens left late lunches unfinished, stopped shopping, withdrew from their labors, prayed, and wept. Unabashedly, America showed its sorrowing heart to all the world in a manner no people could ever excel. It was Good Friday again on a colossal scale.

The tribute of the people fit the man. Let us make no mistake about it; Kennedy was a great President whose greatness grew with each year. Not that we always agreed with him (in retrospect, the loss was ours), but it is the privilege of ordinary men to criticize the deeds of the greatest men. Yet who can doubt the brilliant range of his thoughts, the magnificent blueprint he presented to America to explore a new frontier? It was a masterpiece of social justice and peace for America and the world. In so many ways it heralded Pope John's two great encyclicals.

Even before the first session of Vatican II had opened, Kennedy had begun a dialog for the Catholic Church in America with all other religious groups that few of us appreciated, even today. In our brief history as a nation, no member of the Catholic hierarchy did so much to make catholicism respected in America as he did in his few short years as President. It is a special debt American Catholics must never forget.

Many of the words John F. Kennedy spoke are already immortalized. Often they were lightened by his flashing Irish wit, his frank, winsome smile. He was politician as well as statesman, knowing the practical demands of political patronage could never be divorced completely from the noblest statesmanship. He was a dreamer but not starry-eyed and impractical. He was an independent Catholic layman, who differed decisively with the Catholic bishops on the question of Federal aid to parochial education, and proved beyond the shadow of a doubt that outside the realm of faith and morals he was the keeper of his own conscience. Thereby he did more for the ultimate cause of the Catholic church than

any favorable legislation on education could ever have reaped for it.

Both Johns were too good for our times. We were unworthy of them as we were of Christ and Lincoln. For Congress repeatedly frustrated John F. Kennedy while extremists of the left and the right hated him. A similar setting could be said to have surrounded Pope John XXIII. Concerning Kennedy, clever writers lampooned him, and joked about the Kennedy clan as though it were unfitting for an entire family to be imbued with nobility. Both were sometimes despised by their own, by those who should have known better. The measure, however, of the full stature of the man was the love his family bore toward him and the love he tendered them. We recall his wife, Jacqueline, embracing him, Caroline walking hand in hand with him, and John-John crouched under his desk. We recall these scenes with pride and affection because they portrayed the great heart that accompanied the great intellect. Nor, as a parallel, can we forget Pope John's last testament wherein he spoke so tenderly of children and the love he too had for his family of brothers and sisters.

John F. Kennedy was the first Catholic President but one for whom Catholics can feel justly proud because he served all Americans with all his heart and mind as few Presidents have done. Nor can we devise any better way to conclude this tribute to him than to say it is our conviction that he fulfilled the goal he set forth in his inaugural address: "With a good conscience our only sure reward, with history the final judge of our deeds, let us go forth to lead the land we love and seek His blessing and His help and knowing that here on earth God's work must truly be our own."

———

[From the Atlantic City (N.J.) Free Press]

NATION TAKES LEAVE OF SLAIN PRESIDENT

A sorrowful Nation took leave of John Fitzgerald Kennedy as the body of the slain President was laid to rest in Arlington Cemetery and world dignitaries paid final tributes.

As citizens turn from the solemn rites to face the tasks ahead, they should rededicate themselves to the American ideals which President Kennedy symbolized. It is a time for the country to unite behind the leadership of newly sworn President Lyndon B. Johnson.

He will need the active support of all in this trying period of transition.

By striving to put an end to divisive influences, to bigotry and hatred, each of us can help assure that Mr. Kennedy shall not have died in vain.

Bruce Biossat, Newspaper Enterprise Association writer, who traveled and visited with the late President and his family on many occasions, has written for us the following editorial:

"John Fitzgerald Kennedy came to the Presidency of the United States as the bearer of great change. He was the symbol of something new, but he died by something as old as time—the hand of the fanatic.

"He was the first man born in the 20th century to hold the office—and the second youngest in history. He was the first Catholic in the White House. He came as a naval hero of World War II who narrowly had missed death in Pacific waters, and survived a second brush with death in a grave illness 9 years ago.

"To the Nation's high politics he thus brought a fresh stamp. The well-remarked 'Kennedy style' was a blend of intellect, vigor, wit, charm, and a clear talent for growth.

"On the always shifting, often troubled world scene, he sometimes moved with more caution than expected in young leadership. Soon after entering the White House, he gamely took full blame for the Cuban Bay of Pigs fiasco as an enterprise sadly lacking in boldness.

"Yet only his worst enemies withheld from him the label 'courageous' when he moved resolutely against Soviet Premier Khrushchev in the great Russian missile crisis in Cuba in late 1962. And he boldly pressed for an East-West test ban treaty this year in the face of heavy charges that this imperiled our security.

"In domestic affairs Kennedy won much of his program in beginning 1961, gained far less the following year, and encountered a major stalemate in 1963. The constant note against him was insufficient leadership.

"But again, when 1963 brought the greatest racial crisis of this century, Kennedy—at acknowledged heavy political cost—committed himself to sweeping civil rights proposals that opened a vast new battleground.

"Amid all his efforts to put the imprint of vigorous, imaginative youth upon the country's affairs in the 1960's, the late President found himself moving against a deepening background of protest, with an ugly underscoring of violence which he sought with only limited success to wipe away.

"Much of this protest went to the steady encroachments of the Federal Government and its rising cost. But the bitterest reaction was white and Negro response to the enlarging racial struggle. The far right gave the mood its most perilous texture.

"With the calamity in Dallas the lesson of the danger inherent in violent extremism now may be deeply implanted in America's conscience.

"In this way, Kennedy in death may achieve what the living President could not do to curb the almost ungovernable rancor that increasingly discolored the politics of his brief time in power.

"It was John Kennedy's good fortune to surmount many obstacles to rise to his country's highest office and bring with him the winds of a new era.

"It was his final tragedy that as he labored in difficult times to use these forces for the Nation's and the world's gain, they were swiftly challenged by countering winds of bitter reaction. In Dallas, one swift gust struck him down.

"The Nation thus loses a young leader whose great promise lived in the shadow of great controversy. The way he died must inescapably cost all Americans deeply in self-esteem as free men of good will.

"That is the greater tragedy."

29-275 O—64——12

ADDRESS BY

Hon. Stuart Symington

OF MISSOURI

Mr. President, on July 15, 1960, in Los Angeles, Calif., it was a rare privilege for me to make the following observation:

I have watched the American people, slowly at first and then with ever increasing crescendo, take to their minds and hearts the leading Democrat, the leading American of this day, John F. Kennedy of Massachusetts.

People say, "How did he do it?" Well, I will tell you how he did it.

He did it because he has just a little more courage, just a little more stamina, just a little more wisdom, and just a little more character than any of the rest of us.

Less than 2 weeks ago—just before Thanksgiving—a woman lit an eternal flame to a well-known warrior—her husband, our President—a man born early in this century, but destined, as perhaps no other, to outlive it.

Some may have envied the way he lived. Patriots will envy the way he died.

The gratitude for what he gave us, in both life and death, is what we all most intimately feel. He gave us much, and his gifts will unfold for generations to come—and be opened and cherished by our children's children.

One such gift is the reaffirmation in our time of a truth which our forefathers learned from Abraham Lincoln. It is the truth that the greatest danger to our land may not lie abroad; but here in our loss of confidence in one another, and here in our loss of respect for laws which rest on that confidence and that understanding.

The young Lincoln put it this way in an 1838 address, in Springfield, Ill.:

At what point shall we expect the approach of danger? By what means shall we fortify against it? Shall we expect some transatlantic military giant, to step the ocean, and crush us at a blow? Never.

All the armies of Europe, Asia, and Africa combined, with all the treasure of the earth (our own excepted) in their military chest, with a Bonaparte for a commander, could not by force, take a drink from the Ohio, or make a track on the Blue Ridge, in a trial of a thousand years.

At what point then is the approach of danger to be expected? The answer, if it ever reaches us, it must spring up amongst us. It cannot come from abroad.

If destruction be our lot, we must ourselves be its author and finisher. As a nation of freemen, we must live through all time, or die by suicide.

What John Kennedy by word and by example, in life and in death, has done for us, is to remind us that Mr. Lincoln was speaking in 1838 to a very large audience; because it consisted of every generation of Americans born then and to be born thereafter.

Those of us who knew him well, knew that he was a man of special grace, in action, in writing, and in thought. He had a rare humor, which often covered the depth of his fine mind. Is it coincidence, or perhaps a sense of predestination, that the last stanza of his favorite poem read:

> The woods are lovely, dark and deep,
> But I have promises to keep,
> And miles to go before I sleep,
> And miles to go before I sleep.

Now, he has traveled those miles, and he is asleep. As Cardinal Cushing said, "God rest his noble soul."

I ask unanimous consent that a poem published last Thanksgiving Day in the St. Louis Globe-Democrat be printed at this point.

THE YOUNG CHAMPION

(The following tribute to the late President John F. Kennedy was written by James W. Symington. He is a son of Senator Stuart Symington and a former Deputy Director of the food-for-peace program. Now he is practicing law in Washington.)

He came out of his corner
Like the young champion
He was.
With practiced eye and Irish smile
For a challenger
He knew,
And had beaten before.
In the Pacific
He wrestled him under a wave,
And came up spitting
Jokes. His face shimmering
With destiny.
(He wouldn't wear a hat
To shield us from his sunlight,
His blazing thought,
And the radiant challenge
Of his spirit)
They'd been locked
Like this, too,
Etherized, but straining,
Till the challenger

Was shoved away,
Goodnaturedly,
Like a dull-witted
Sparring partner
When the young champ
Suddenly remembered
An appointment.
Still, this rematch
Came too soon, granted,
The Promoter thought
It time. The Promoter
Who was Trainer besides,
And Referee
And Timekeeper
And finally, Announcer,
That this was a dream,
And the records would show
That the title really passed
A generation ago
On a beach near Rendova
Where the old challenger
Forever lost.
And failing to pin him then,
And snuff out that spark
So far from our notice,
Cannot now, or ever
Expect the mantel of years
Or any other shroud
To contain the radiance
Much less the flame.
So we file from the arena,
Comforted,
For this was truly a dream,
And his heart, his voice, his hatless glory
Are the reality,
And our white plume
Of victory.

—James W. Symington.

ADDRESS BY

Hon. Kenneth B. Keating

OF NEW YORK

Mr. President, John F. Kennedy lies in Arlington Cemetery. A stunned Nation tries to move again into the routine of living. Why? That tragic word, whispered in bewilderment and sorrow by every thinking American, is slowly fading into silence. It is a "why"? that can never be answered because the event is beyond credence, to explain it beyond the scope of a human mind.

And yet it happened. The flags at half-mast tell us that John F. Kennedy is dead.

The great of the world came to his funeral and bowed their heads in prayer. Heads of state were there—an emperor—a king—but they were not more present than his fellow countrymen who came in spirit, 190 million strong.

From the day of his election, John F. Kennedy had been an example to them—a symbol almost of their beloved country. He was young and vigorous and good to look upon, just as their country was. He was vital and smiling and assured. His love for his family, his pride in his family was like a glowing banner swirling around him through all his years in office. Americans, whatever their political differences with him, loved him for this. They admired, beyond words, that warm and close-knit family group who made the White House a home indeed.

There was laughter in the White House while the Kennedys were there. There was kindliness, there was understanding, there was love.

And there was a man.

Americans will not soon forget the dedicated service that John Fitzgerald Kennedy gave them. His eloquence, his wit, his charm will not be forgotten in this generation. They will say of him—"He loved his country, he lived for his country, he died for his country. He was our friend."

What greater tribute can a country pay, than to mourn him as a friend that is lost? And that is how John F. Kennedy is mourned today. To all of us, his death was deeply moving because his smile reached out and touched our hearts.

To those who had the opportunity to serve with him in both the House and Senate, the loss was a personal one, as well as a national one. I served with him for many years, and saw him many times, in many different circumstances. His smile and his friendship were not limited to the members of his own party, which he led with such vision and imagination, but were shared, sometimes with a wry grin, with many members of the loyal opposition.

He was born for leadership, and he achieved it. But in his leadership he never forgot that he was a father too, a husband, a soldier, a patriot— that he was, in short, an American.

President Kennedy was truly of this era. He was the first President of the United States to be born in this century. He was the youngest citizen to be elected to that exalted office. We are all proud of his tremendous achievement.

"Youth" and "Peace"—those two magnificent words were stamped indelibly on his administration. His thousand days were made splendid by his efforts for both. In the Peace Corps— which time may show to be his finest inspiration—he joined them hand in hand.

He sent them out into the world together. Was there ever before such a crusade—young America working peacefully for peace? Was there ever before such a shining example for the world to wonder at?

It must never be forgotten that when the young men and women of these United States flocked to the banner of public service and went out into the world to show by their actions "the mettle of their pastures," it was John F. Kennedy who inspired them. It was John F. Kennedy who showed them the way.

Let us therefore build for him a spiritual memorial of kindliness and understanding and peace, a testament of human rights and equality.

It is the one memorial he would have wished, who was our good neighbor in the White House.

Mr. President, I have received a number of requests, from clergymen and others, to include expressions of their tribute and grief over the death of the President. I ask unanimous consent to include, following my remarks, the text of these eloquent statements.

He Left the World Richer

(NOTE.—From the program and meditations by the Reverend Paul R. Hoover, pastor of Grace Evangelical Lutheran Church, Rochester, N.Y., in memoriam, John F. Kennedy, Nov. 24, 1963.)

We have read from the Old Testament in our worship memorial. I would now read words from the Letter of James (Phillips translation) which distill in essence the example of President John F. Kennedy:

"Are there some wise and understanding men among you? Then your lives will be an example of the humanity that is born of true wisdom. But if your heart is full of rivalry and bitter jealousy, then do not boast of your wisdom—don't deny the truth that you must recognize in your inmost heart. You may acquire a certain superficial wisdom, but it does not come from God— it comes from this world, from your lower nature, even from the devil. For wherever you find jealousy and rivalry you also find disharmony and all other kinds of evil. The wisdom that comes from God is first utterly pure, then peace-loving, gentle, approachable, full of tolerant thoughts and kindly actions, with no breath

of favoritism or hint of hypocrisy. And wise are peacemakers who go on quietly sowing for a harvest of righteousness—in other people and in themselves." (James 3,
beginning at verse 13.)

Of no man, rich or poor, high or low, ruled or ruler,
does God expect more to be said: He left the world
richer.

"Let come what will, I mean to bear it out,
And either live with glorious victory
Or die with fame, renowned in chivalry:
He is not worthy of the honeycomb
That shuns the hive because the bees have stings."

Like Biblical characters, his strength was in his purpose:
Like Abraham, he went where he was called and was
faithful in all things.

Like Moses, he led the people from doubts and fears
to confidence in the face of imponderable difficulties.

Like Joshua, he loved his country and fought and
suffered for its success.

He knew the import of Malachi's words:

"Behold, I will send you Elijah the prophet before the
coming of the great and dreadful day of the Lord: And
he shall turn the heart of the fathers to the children,
and the heart of the children to their fathers."

Like Jonathan, he met many a discouraged brother
and cheered him by giving him strength.

Like David, he had the poet's way with words and
the magic of music in them. He sang a people to
triumph of spirit and shouted on the battle of blessed
triumph.

Like Isaiah, he had the mind of a prophet who constantly pointed the world to brighter days and better
things in the future.

Like Daniel, he was true through life to the teachings
of his boyhood days.

Like John the Baptist, his desert was the loneliness of
the White House and from that desert he could cry
like John: "Prepare ye the way of the Lord, make his
paths straight."

Like Paul, he could be pricked by physical affliction.
Like Paul, from affliction he drew from the deep wells
of life to let the world know through pen and song
and service that God meets men in the voice of freedom.

Like Jesus, his Master, holding the key to power
hitherto unknown to men, he could preach the powerful
doctrine that God does not withhold from the simplest
man the importance men give only to the great.

Like Enoch, "He walked with God and he was not,
for God took him."

History will in time through the crucible of future
experience refine his image of his walk on earth. He
loved his country, his heritage, his family, his church,
his fellow men. And to the last he sought to inspire
others to share his enthusiasms and worked to the very
last moment of his busy life for the interests of the
unsaved, confused, and brutish world.

The world is richer because he lived. The world is
richer in the way he died. For even our short distance
from his fatal scene, this much is clear: he lived true to
the words of Henry Van Dyke:

"Renew the courage that prevails,
The steady faith that never fails,
And makes us stand in every fight
Firm as a fortress to defend the right."

May God add His blessing where our words fail.
Amen.

––––

OF BLESSED MEMORY

(Expression of sentiments of the Rochester, N.Y., Jewish community on the death of John F. Kennedy.)

With hearts burdened with grief, and souls seared
by tragedy, we have come to this sanctuary for prayer
and meditation.

The sun shines brightly without but our world has
grown darker and colder.

The assassin's bullet which took the life of this great
and good man sent a shudder of shock, sorrow, and outrage through our very being.

We mourn the loss of a man who rose to true greatness
through the heights of his vision, the depth of his compassion, the strength of his commitments and the nobility
of his passions.

We are all diminished in having sustained this grievous
loss.

We now ask God's light in our darkness, direction in
our gropings, guidance in our striving.

A martyred President: heroic in war, gave his life for
peace; gifted with youthful vigor and courage, dedicated his energies and abilities for the growth of understanding and amity between nations; to the manor born,
his concern was for the least among us, the disenfran-
chised, the dispossessed, the despised.

Selflessly, he gave the fullest measure of devotion to all
that is best in our national heritage.

He gave to us the gift of enlightened statesmanship,
courageous leadership, and heroic example.

It is now given to us to grant him the gift of the
immortality of inspiration by bringing into our lives, into
our communities, into this beloved land, those noble
qualities, concerns, convictions, and passions which
marked this lovely life so brief in years but so great in
influence.

––––

SERMON ON PRESIDENT KENNEDY'S DEATH

(Preached November 24, 1963, by Rev. William A. Sadler,
Jr., Ph. D., Dover Plains, N.Y.)

The darkest hour of this generation struck Friday with
cruel swiftness, casting a pall of stunned grief over the
American people, and indeed over the whole world. The
President of the United States was dead. The passing of
any man is sad. The passing of any President is an even
sadder event. Had the President been an elderly man
who died of natural causes, we would mourn deeply.
Had he been in late middle age killed in an accident like
Dag Hammarskjold, our grief would reach great proportions. He was not an old man, nor one of late middle
age. He was a young man, a remarkable man of amazing
accomplishments and with magnificent potentialities yet

to be expressed, not for his own satisfaction and gain, but for the benefit of his fellow citizens and people around the world. He was cut down in midstride. It was not an accident, but foul, calculated murder that took his life, and took from us an outstanding fellow American, a great President, a strong and courageous leader, and a magnificent representative of the highest ideals of our country and mankind. For us Christians it is an additional loss; for, his assassin struck down a brother in Christ. It is not just grief we suffer. We are struck dumb by this monstrous atrocity and our colossal loss.

The murder of the late President, John F. Kennedy, hit us like a death in the family. It was in fact just that—a death in the American family. John F. Kennedy was not merely a man—not merely a young man, a talented man, a person of wealth, a Democrat. He was the President of our country, and as such he was our representative, chosen by the people to stand for them to the world, to represent their ideals and way of life, and to stand by them as their chief leader. Because he was our President, when he was attacked, we, too, were attacked. When he died, a part of us died with him. We Americans believe that each man is created with certain inalienable rights to life, liberty, and the pursuit of happiness. The Presidential office embodies those rights and seeks to guarantee them. On Friday those rights for which our President had fought were taken from him. His earthly life was concluded, those earthly liberties canceled, that earthly pursuit ended. He did not freely give up those rights; he was savagely robbed of them. Because of the office he bore, our rights also were threatened; our ideals, our very reason for existence as Americans, were attacked. And so we suffered a double blow.

President Kennedy was not a weak man. He was not a weak President. He was a person of extraordinary moral strength, courage, wisdom, and foresight. He filled the office of the Presidency with those qualities and by so doing he helped to make our country morally stronger, more courageous, wiser, and more farsighted than before. His strength and its effects upon the American people were recognized by his adversaries; and numerous people who are marked by weakness, lack of foresight, with little concern for the extension of real justice, have vigorously opposed his principles and policies, revealing to those who observed with patience and conscience not only their lack of character but the greatness of his. President Kennedy was—is a dedicated believer, a believer in God as revealed and present in Jesus Christ. He was also a dedicated believer in the ideals of the American heritage and way of life. His Christian conscience inevitably led him to interpret American ideals in a Christian manner; and we Christians are convinced that the ideals of our Founding Fathers were meant to be interpreted that way. President Kennedy lived and gave his life for those ideals and for us, who are to continue to be led by them. What are they? Certainly they are numerous; but I want at this time to emphasize three of them.

It was reported that the Russian people, and in particular Nikita Khrushchev, were saddened and alarmed by the President's death; for, he had demonstrated forcefully that he was sincerely dedicated to peaceful existence.

The Russian people desire a peaceful world, as they have emphasized to the dismay of warmongering Chinese Communists. The Russian people recognize, and we know, that President Kennedy was a man of peace. His consistent efforts as President were directed toward the securing of peace around the world, real peace and not merely a lull in aggression and contention. His understanding of peace was informed by his Christian faith and conscience. At least each Sunday he worshipped our God who is the giver of life and who sends to His children His peace which passes understanding. This peace is no passive thing; it is, like God himself, an active mode of being. To be at peace is not to sleep; it is to exist unhindered from repressive forces that stifle and distort the soul, the life of man, and society. To be at peace is to be free to act toward the fulfillment of the destiny that God makes and gives to each of His children. Peace and freedom are inseparable. Freedom is but the expression of real peace; while peace is the condition which enables true freedom. President Kennedy believed in, proclaimed, and fostered our cherished ideal of peace and freedom.

It was not by any means easy to defend his belief, not even to some of us Americans who supposedly adhered to it. During the Bay of Pigs catastrophe he refrained from providing outright and decisive American support to the invasion forces, because such an action, he estimated, would grossly jeopardize not only the peace of Cubans, but of Americans and the world as well. In his firm stand against the Communist attempt to seize Berlin and to divide Germany permanently, as well as his resistance to the Communist endeavor to establish missile bases in Cuba, President Kennedy demonstrated his aggressive, unswerving aim to preserve the peace and freedom of the people of the Western World, when they were seriously threatened. In spite of the outcry of some nationalistic isolationists, he succeeded in his efforts to establish a peace treaty to prohibit nuclear testing in all but a few countries. He suffered the charge of hypocrisy from those who accused him of supporting warfare in other countries; yet he gave American support to actual war, such as in Vietnam, because a truce there would not effect a meaningful peace, one which respects and guarantees the freedom of individuals to pursue their separate as well as corporate destinies. President Kennedy was a crusader for peace; and, to our great loss, he became a martyr for it.

As Americans it is our role, our duty as citizens, to emulate this great leader who so nobly embodied and promoted the high ideal of peace. The forces obstructing peace and freedom in our world, and what is worse, in our land are gaining momentum to a frightening degree. These are forces which are fed by self-oriented fear and by self-regard which is disdainful of the rights of others, particularly others of a different skin color, class, or origin. They are forces which are armed with the weapons of prejudice, hatred, and the demonic desire to be superior. The war against peace is enkindled by hate; and the fires of hatred burn hot. They scorched the sense and conscience of the President's assassin, so that he committed a crime which outrages our reason and sensitivity. One month before in that same fateful city of Dallas the hateful prejudice of extremists led to the disgraceful and contemptuous treatment of another peaceful man, Adlai Stevenson, who was representing the organization designed to prosecute and to maintain world peace. This year has seen the assassinations of other peaceful men and little children and the bombing of churches. There are ugly, warring, murderous forces in our midst: prejudice, bigotry, smug self-content and disdainful superiority, hatred, and the harboring of anger that leads to the shattering of relationships and human lives. As Americans we must resist them. They do exist and can unleash havoc. It can happen here. As Christians it is our responsibility to wage war against these forces that inhabit the heart of man and do evil business in our lives. It is our responsibility, our privilege, our vocation to bless and not to curse, to settle and not to entrench our divisive differences, to be humble and not to humiliate, to be compassionate and not to condemn, to love and not to hate, to seek peace, to make it, and to keep it. The Lord who taught us to love also taught us: "Blessed are the peacemakers, for they shall be called the children of God."

A second classic ideal for which President Kennedy lived and died was justice. This, too, was an ideal interpreted and enforced by his Christian conscience. In the numerous policies which he fathered and fostered, particularly those which were vigorously discussed by politicians and often vehemently resisted, one could discern the President's deep-rooted concern for real justice. For him justice was not merely an abstract ideal; it was an obtainable goal, and he endeavored that our land and our world might attain it. It was the desire to extend effective justice to all citizens regardless of color that lay behind his strong civil rights policy. It was a dedication to justice which gave impetus and strength to his programs of medicare, education, tax reduction and reform, foreign aid, and the Alliance for Progress, as well as his vigorous support of the United Nations. In no small measure these programs aimed to enable individuals and nations to find decent and humane treatment to which they are entitled as human beings—a right which is often denied them because of lack of opportunity and funds. To assure proper medical care for the poor and aged, to provide adequate education to talented, ordinary, as well as deprived young people, to reduce inequalities in our economic system, to give aid to people and nations who are destitute of privileges we Americans take for granted, to encourage and to contribute generously to that supernational organization which was established to protect the rights of individual nations and insure fair treatment of all—these are expressions of his sense of justice which was informed by his Christian awareness of the essential command to love our neighbors as ourselves. "What does the Lord require of you," said the prophet Micah, "but to do justice, to show steadfast love, and to walk humbly with your God?" It was his responsibility and privilege, and it continues to be ours as Christians in this world, to do justice which is interpreted by love. There have been countless martyrs for justice; on Friday John F. Kennedy joined their ranks. We shall fail them and ourselves, and certainly be false to our religion and traitorous to Christ, if we do not persevere in the pursuit of genuine

justice. And do we not also believe and hope that blessed are those who hunger for justice, for they shall be satisfied?

A final characteristic of the life of President Kennedy and an ideal embedded in the true American character is courage. He demonstrated courage equal to our forefathers and pioneers in his wartime service. He manifested his deep appreciation of this virtue in his famous book "Profiles of Courage." To me, however, he exhibited the highest form of this virtue while President as he found and maintained the courage of his convictions, the courage to seek peace and to promote justice in the face of stiff resistance and stinging ridicule. Several of his programs for peace and justice suffered the most severe attacks, and he personally was abused and slandered by some of his fellow Americans. What did he personally have to gain from strong support of social security programs, from his occasional resistance to big business and other members of his own class, from his continued commitment to underprivileged nations and groups? Little personal gain, and considerable loss of political support, national affection, and mental tranquility. He stood forth with firm conviction that he was serving for the sake of right. Today we pray that he finds the blessing promised to those who are persecuted for righteousness' sake; for theirs is the kingdom of heaven.

The death of our President has caused a darkness to fall upon us; yet it is a darkness that will pass. The important question to ask now is: What kind of light will we discover and follow when the darkness lifts? We know that men are confused and led astray by lights of security, material prosperity, temporal happiness, and the sense of self-importance. These are but partial guides to behavior; regarded as most important they are lights beckoning from dead-end lanes. There are better beacons to lead us, such as the virtues of courage and the search for justice and peace. We Christians know that there is one true light, which can enlighten every man and which is the light of the world; without that light we are disastrously lost. May we Christians now more fervently than before seek that light; and grant that no clouds of this mortal life may hide from us the light of that love which is immortal and which God has manifested unto us in Jesus Christ, His Son, our Lord. Being thus illumined with the light of Christ, may our lights so shine before men that they may see our good works, our just works, our peaceful works, our courageous works and glorify our Father who is in Heaven.

Finally, this death has brought forth fears that have long lurked in our hearts. What is to become of us? What does the future hold for us? For our children? Those of us who have found the truth of God's reality and His love need not depend upon optimistic political philosophers for our ultimate reassurance. More than 500 years before the birth of Christ the Jewish people lived in exile in Babylon; it was a time for them of darkness, of uncertainty and fear. They were tremendously encouraged by God's message to them, delivered by a great prophet. It was a message that stilled their fears by deepening their faith in the reality of God's redeeming power. We who have been touched by Christ's redeeming love and reborn in His risen life will find that message more comforting and appropriate today than those to whom it was first addressed. Here is that message: "Fear not, for I have redeemed you; I have called you by name, you are mine. When you pass through the waters I will be with you; and through the rivers, they shall not overwhelm you; when you walk through fire you shall not be burned, and the flame shall not consume you. For I am the Lord your God, the Holy One of Israel, your Saviour" (Isaiah 43: 1–3).

In Memoriam: John Fitzgerald Kennedy

(By David A. MacLennan, at the Rochester Rotary Club, Nov. 26, 1963)

> "The woods are lovely, dark and deep,
> But I have promises to keep,
> And miles to go before I sleep.
> And miles to go before I sleep."

—Robert Frost in "Stopping by Woods on a Snowy Evening."

But John Fitzgerald Kennedy, 35th President of the United States, could not go the miles on this life's road he longed to travel before his sleep. Not an act of God, but an act of the demonic in a human being struck him down on what became the darkest hour of any recent year. And the lines by Robert Frost Mr. Kennedy loved became the refrain of an unfinished symphony.

Yesterday, the closing act of the drama of his death was witnessed and experienced by millions. The world saw an image of America never seen before in history, and of our celebration. If tragedy's chief purpose is to purge the soul, we ought to be cleansed of bitterness, of much that defiles and degrades men made in the image of God:

> "Solemn the drums thrill: Death august and royal
> Sings sorrow up into immortal spheres.
> There is music in the midst of desolation.
> And a glory that shines upon our tears."

Is there truly "a glory that shines upon our tears" at the death of one so gifted, so dedicated, so youthful? Nothing can diminish the enormity of the senseless, cruel crime which, as far as this dimension of life is concerned, denied him "the glory of going on, and still to be."

Yet, although he shall grow not old, as we that are left grow old, and although age shall not weary him, there is a glory, a high summons, in our late Chief's life and death.

President Kennedy, like his brave, regal wife, was marked by youthfulness not only because he was still relatively young but because he had an intellectual vigor and receptiveness to new ideas. His sense of the past was keen, he was proud of our ancient heritage and sought to conserve it; but he knew, as did a former teacher of his in college that:

> "New occasions teach new duties
> Time makes ancient good uncouth."

With patience not always found in eager youth he sought to persuade us that we must move onward "who would keep abreast of truth." President and Mrs. Kennedy came into our national life as a kind of springtime in the winter of our discontent.

> "Your old men shall dream dreams.
> Your young men shall have visions."

He not only quoted but helped fulfill.

Although he knew by cruel personal experience in the Second World War that law, whether civil or international, must have force behind it, he was a man of peace. He knew that in a nuclear-fission world, if anything goes in the way of atomic war, everything goes. One of the tragic ironies of our time is that this man who knew that successful government requires the art of compromise, this leader who won the admiration and affection of political opponents, should be the victim of hatred and violence.

Closely related to his deep concern for peace among the nations was his outstanding ability to get on with people. He was a master of the art of working with people, and many were his bipartisan conferences and programs. His infectious humor and ready wit, his charm, and unfailing courtesy toward all sorts and conditions of men endeared him to a majority of Americans, and to citizens of every nation he visited.

Our late President was an intellectual who was never pedantic, stuffy or remote from the common people. In a short time, he and Mrs. Jacqueline Kennedy did more for the arts and for artists in every field of creative culture than most Presidents could. In a world in which brains, knowledge, skill are essential to civilized living and a future worth working for, he made it not only respectable but praiseworthy to be educated and creative.

John Fitzgerald Kennedy was a fighter for justice, for freedom, for the chance of the least and lowest in our Republic to walk in dignity, enjoy equal rights and to make the most of their best. As you watched the saddened faces of Negroes both in Dallas and in Washington during the funeral march, did you think of another martyred President who also died at an assassin's hand because he believed that we were created to be free? When Abraham Lincoln's body was carried through the streets of the Capital, a Negro mother held up her child and said, "Take a long look at him, honey, he died for you."

President Kennedy was a deeply religious man. He knew that the deep sources of social justice, and personal integrity reside in God. He reverenced the reverences of others, because he reverenced the great and gracious God in whose will is our peace, and in whose service is perfect freedom.

Much more could be said. Much more has been said, and will be said. As King David said long ago of a leader who died in battle, "Know ye not that a prince and a great man was fallen this day in Israel?"

We do know. But commemoration without emulation stultifies and condemns. To praise President Kennedy's character—his faith, and high purposes, his devotion to human well-being, as he upheld our Constitution and the higher laws of God, and not to renew our own dedication, is hollow.

John Fitzgerald Kennedy sacrificed his life for his country, and for that other country which is the Kingdom of God. Must a good and great man die because most of us lack insight, moral fiber, willingness to discipline ourselves and our children in self-control? Are we so self-centered that we use persons as means to our own ends? Are we only asking but not giving a worthy answer to the question, "What can I do for my country?" Jack Kennedy already has answered the question with his life. We must respond with the service of our lives. President Johnson cannot do it all, nor can he do what we must do.

Are we men and women committed to peace, not only among nations, but among ourselves? Have we repudiated violence, so that we ourselves obey and uphold law? Will we join in redirecting the energies of our young people, whether in our privileged suburbs or in city streets into constructive channels?

When we praise President Kennedy as a champion of responsible freedom and equal justice, are we willing to follow in his train? Are we on the way with the living God who desires that we do justly, love mercy, and walk humbly before Him, or are we in the way, by our refusal to advance the best hopes of men?

Do we believe in the living God of whose grace and wisdom we have had rich experience as a nation? In one of his last addresses in Texas, our late President quoted the Bible. "Except the Lord guard the city, the watchmen guard in vain."

Do we confide ourselves to the keeping and guidance of the Lord of life and history, the righteous Father of all mankind? Do we seek to give Him our highest loyalty and obedience? Do we love America enough to practice our religion not fitfully but faithfully? With many other Protestants, Jews, Orthodox, I salute the memory of President Kennedy as a Christian man, who was scrupulously fair to all religious groups and unashamed and faithful in his own religious duty.

John Fitzgerald Kennedy could have written the lines of a poem written in the Washington he knew so well, by a noble patriot who served the Allied cause in the First World War. Relying upon Almighty God, who alone can build the house of our habitation and guard the Nation we love, let us make it our pledge in the light of the sacrifice of our late President:

"I Vow to Thee, My Country"

"I vow to thee, my country, all earthly things above
Entire and whole and perfect, the service of my love.
The love that asks no questions: the love that stands the test,
That lays upon the altar the dearest and the best:
The love that never falters, the love that pays the price,
The love that makes undaunted the final sacrifice.
And there's another country, I've heard of long ago,
Most dear to them that love her, most great to them that know,
We may not count her armies; we may not see her King;
Her fortress is a faithful heart, her pride is suffering.
And soul by soul and silently her shining bounds increase,
And her ways are ways of gentleness and all her paths are peace.
　　Amen."

　　　　　　　　　　　　　　—Sir Cecil Spring-Rice.

Address by
Hon. Jack Miller
OF IOWA

Mr. President, one could say the prayer, "Dear God, please take care of your servant, John Fitzgerald Kennedy," and the most important thoughts would have been expressed.

However, the 23d Psalm is, to me, the most consoling expression on an occasion of bereavement; and I shall read it:

Twenty-third Psalm

The Lord is my shepherd; I shall not want.
He maketh me to lie down in green pastures: he leadeth me beside the still waters.
He restoreth my soul: he leadeth me in the paths of righteousness for his name's sake.
Yea, though I walk through the valley of the shadow of death, I will fear no evil: for Thou art with me; Thy rod and Thy staff they comfort me, in the presence of mine enemies: Thou anointest my head with oil; my cup runneth over.
Surely goodness and mercy shall follow me all the days of my life: and I will dwell in the house of the Lord for ever.

Thomas Wolfe, in his immortal "You Can't Go Home Again," gives us the philosophy with which we can accept the loss of our President, and it is with these thoughts I shall close:

To lose the earth you know, for greater knowing;
To lose a life you have, for greater life;
To leave the friends you love for greater loving;
To find a land more kind than home, more large than earth—whereon the pillars of this earth are founded, toward which the conscience of the world is tending—a wind is rising, and the rivers flow.

Our late President fired the hopes and imagination of not only his fellow Americans but of the freedom loving people throughout the world. I was in Rome at the time news of his tragic death was received, and the spontaneous and genuine outpouring of grief on the part of our Italian friends was something to behold. I understand that similar reactions occurred in many of the other world capitals. It seemed as though the lights all over the earth had been dimmed.

John Fitzgerald Kennedy lived in the spirit of the poem, "A Psalm of Life" by Longfellow:

A Psalm of Life

(By Henry Wadsworth Longfellow)

Tell me not, in mournful numbers,
　Life is but an empty dream—
For the soul is dead that slumbers,
　And things are not what they seem.

Life is real! Life is earnest!
　And the grave is not its goal;
Dust thou art, to dust returnest,
　Was not spoken of the soul.

Not enjoyment, and not sorrow,
　Is our destined end or way;
But to act, that each tomorrow
　Finds us farther than today.

Art is long, and Time is fleeting,
　And our hearts, though stout and brave,
Still, like muffled drums, are beating
　Funeral marches to the grave.

In the world's broad field of battle,
　In the bivouac of Life,
Be not like dumb, driven cattle!
　Be a hero in the strife!

Trust no Future, howe'er pleasant.
　Let the dead Past bury its dead.
Act—act in the living Present.
　Heart within, and God o'erhead.

Lives of great men all remind us
　We can make our lives sublime,
And, departing, leave behind us
　Footprints on the sands of time;

Footprints, that perhaps another,
　Sailing o'er life's solemn main.
A forlorn and shipwrecked brother,
　Seeing, shall take heart again.

Let us, then, be up and doing.
　With a heart for any fate;
Still achieving, still pursuing.
　Learn to labor and to wait.

ADDRESS BY

Hon. Hubert H. Humphrey

OF MINNESOTA

Mr. President, 19 days ago, a man of reason was destroyed by an act of violence.

Today, we cannot judge John Fitzgerald Kennedy. The fact of this assassination still stuns our minds; the loss of this man still sorrows our hearts. If we seek to judge his life and work now, we must fail. Our thoughts will be like rough pebbles, unpolished by the tides of time and wisdom. Our words will be like hollow, gaudy ornaments, attached to a man's soul.

Let us leave judgment to history, and to God.

Today, we can hope only to speak of him honestly, and to remember him with respect.

If we remember his own words which expressed his own highest cause, we perhaps do best. This does not risk trying to gild what is already gold. For to me, at least, John Kennedy wrote his own epitaph: a man dedicated to "the strategy for peace."

He sounded this keynote in his first words after taking the oath of office as President of the United States. He reminded his countrymen and the world that one talon of the American eagle held the arrows of war, but the other clutched the olive branches of peace. "We shall not negotiate from fear, but we shall not fear to negotiate." These words were a fresh and memorable assertion to the world that the power of the United States was not to be feared. Peace was its purpose.

In this same inaugural address, he called us to the responsibilities of leadership for peace and justice:

> Now the trumpet summons us again—not as a call to bear arms, though arms we need—not as a call to battle, though embattled we are—but a call to bear the burden of a long twilight struggle year in and year out, "rejoicing in hope, patient in tribulation"—a struggle against the common enemies of man: tyranny, poverty, disease, and war itself.

Deeds followed these words. The Peace Corps was established. The food-for-peace program was expanded. The Arms Control and Disarmament Agency was proposed and organized. Negotiations with our adversaries were renewed. The motive, spirit, and accent of peace were carried to the far places of the earth.

John Kennedy met supreme crisis at the very brink of disaster when nuclear aggression threatened this hemisphere. The courage of peace was tested and not found wanting. Could courage and peace be combined? Could peace save its life by risking to lose it? Men must hope so, but can they believe it?

They can; and they did when they witnessed John Kennedy's devotion to peace matched by determined action.

That breathless moment a little over a year ago could have brought the exhaustion of hope, or the fears of hostility. It did neither. John Kennedy continued his initiative for peace, with the pledge that the United States would suspend atomic testing in the atmosphere.

Last June, at the American University in Washington, D.C., he reminded all peoples once more "World peace is the most important topic on earth." He continued a theme of his inaugural address:

> We shall do our part to build a world of peace where the weak are safe and the strong are just.

And he clarified our goal with eloquence:

> What kind of peace do we seek? I am talking about genuine peace—the kind of peace that makes life on earth worth living—and the kind that enables men and nations to grow and to hope and to build a better life for their children—not merely peace for Americans, but peace for all men and women—not merely peace in our time, but peace for all time.

He pressed his "strategy for peace" to the conclusion of a test ban treaty, stopping the testing of atomic weapons on the earth or above it. More than 100 nations have joined with us in this treaty.

The treaty is a frail hope as yet—frail as the dove Noah sent forth over the waters in search of land. Every day that treaty stands, however, the hope grows that the waters of war's preparation are receding. The genie of atomic power is not yet back in the bottle to use one of John Kennedy's metaphors. But despair has lost its grip upon us. A new will and resolution for peace has been born.

He again continued his "strategy for peace" last September, in addressing the United Nations. His opening words were: "We meet again in the quest for peace." He concluded:

> My fellow inhabitants of this planet, let us take our stand here in this assembly of nations. And let us see if we, in our time, can move the world toward a just and lasting peace.

In October, speaking to an audience of young people in Maine, he again recalled the American eagle and the two kinds of strength it clutches. The head of the eagle, he emphasizes, faces toward the olive branches of peace. He concluded:

> In the months and years ahead, we intend to build both kinds of strength—during time of detente as well as tension, during periods of conflict as well as cooperation—until the world we pass on to our children is truly safe for diversity and the rule of law covers all.

The theme of peace had become his hallmark. We came to expect it. His eloquence of phrase served to keep the passionate sincerity of purpose and goal from being redundant. If any scripture is ever sifted out of the torrents of the words of these years, surely his words in this high cause will survive.

He understood well the meaning of the mordant words of the Prince of Peace: "Be ye wise as serpents in order to be as harmless as doves." When John Kennedy spoke in such a vein, however, it was of a peace strong, not strident. He communicated a sense of power in the service of gentility.

In his address to the Nation on the nuclear test ban treaty, he said:

> Let us, if we can, step back from the shadows of war and seek out the way of peace. And if that journey is 1,000 miles or even more, let history record that we, in this land, at this time, took the first step.

Each of us lost a bit of ourselves at the death of the man who spoke these words, but our steps did not falter.

In remembering John Kennedy, each of us must recall his words; we must also rely on our personal individual memories of him.

I remember most clearly now my last meeting with him—on the Wednesday before the Friday of his death.

The formal meeting of congressional leaders at the White House had just ended. In that clean, precise, earnest voice, President Kennedy called out:

> Hubert, come walk with me. I want to talk with you.

He walked confidently and smoothly past the White House rose garden and toward his private office. He talked with intelligence and curiosity and concern about a problem facing the Nation and the people. His stride and his voice reflected the basic nature of the man: strength, grace, eagerness.

I was proud to walk a few steps with John Kennedy.

Today, I am aware that he never walked alone. Neither his distinctions as an individual nor his power as President set him far apart from the people of the United States. He was, perhaps, a step or two ahead of the people at times. But as an American who understood America, who brought form to its amorphous yearnings, who gave direction to its efforts, John Kennedy walked with the people.

Nineteen days ago, the worst of America struck down the best of America. For a few moments of time, violence shattered peace—fear cracked confidence—hate stood above reason.

But the worst of America did not prevail after those ugly moments. The tragedy of that day in November will not endure.

Because of the life of John Fitzgerald Kennedy, we are today a nation more fully committed to peace. Because of the death of John Fitzgerald Kennedy, we are a people more deeply determined to turn from hate and to embrace understanding and reason.

One simple line, from the book of Isaiah in the Bible, best expresses the message and mission of John Fitzgerald Kennedy:

Come now, and let us reason together.

Our fulfillment of that plea will be John Fitzgerald Kennedy's triumph.

One simple paragraph, from his book "Profiles in Courage," best describes the goodness and nobility of John Fitzgerald Kennedy:

The courage of life is often a less dramatic spectacle than the courage of a final moment; but it is no less than a magnificent mixture of triumph and tragedy. A man does what he must—in spite of personal consequences, in spite of obstacles and dangers and pressures— and that is the basis of all human morality.

Yes, Mr. President, John Fitzgerald Kennedy is gone.

He gave us strength, and the strength remains with us.

But we are a stronger nation, and a better people today because of him.

Never before has this Nation been so moved. Never before have the people so revealed themselves and their hearts.

We mourn the loss of this President. But even more, we mourn the loss of this man. The Nation's outpouring of sorrow and love for him expresses our ultimate value—the importance of the individual human being.

Our love turns toward the late President's family, to his brothers and sisters, his mother and his father, and, of course, to his dear, wonderful wife, Mrs. Kennedy. Her beautiful dignity, her constant courage and her enduring grace strengthened each of us.

At the death of John Fitzgerald Kennedy, every American felt as if he had lost a loved one.

Never before has there been such a sense of total involvement by all the people. Never before have we been so united. Never before have we been so aware of our national identity.

We are, truly, "one Nation, under God, indivisible."

With a renewed sense of unity, fortified by our common sorrow, we shall rededicate this Nation to the fulfillment of the hopes and the commitments of our beloved, martyred President, John Fitzgerald Kennedy.

ADDRESS BY

Hon. Allen J. Ellender

OF LOUISIANA

Mr. President, our illustrious colleague, our 35th President, was not a product of the log cabin. He was born rich, and in spite of that he became, among other things, a very prominent world figure, an eminent statesman, a brilliant scholar and a forceful leader.

Generally, wealth and position are the enemies of genius, and the destroyers of talent. It is difficult for the wealthy to resist the thousand allurements of pleasure. So I repeat that John F. Kennedy, in spite of having been born to wealth and high social position, became truly great—a man of the people.

Even in his youth he was a student of history. While other boys of his age were indulging in play, his fertile brain was absorbing the works of philosophers, historians, and great thinkers, both ancient and modern.

He made a fine record as a college student.

He was intensely patriotic, and when the time came to serve his country in war, in order to protect and preserve our freedom, he was not found wanting. He showed courage and bravery, unexcelled by any of those who fought by his side.

As a world leader he devoted much of his time to the pursuit of world peace. He was well on his way toward that goal when he was assassinated.

Much has been said today, as well as in the past, about his talents and accomplishments. Much will be said of him in the future. Some will be critical, but the good will so far outweigh the bad that he will go down in history as one of our great Presidents. It is tragic that an assassin's bullet deprived us of his leadership in the prime of his life. Our country and the whole world will doubtless be poorer because of his untimely death.

If to love your country more than self is goodness, John F. Kennedy was good.

If to be in advance of your time—to be an advocate in the direction of right—is greatness, John F. Kennedy was great.

If to avow your principles and discharge your duty in the midst of hostile groups is heroic, John F. Kennedy was a hero.

At the age of 46 he was felled by an assassin's bullet. He died in the land he loved and defended.

His critics cannot touch him now—hatred, bias and prejudice can reach him no more. He sleeps in Arlington, beneath the quiet of the stars.

I extend to his bereaved wife and lovely children, Caroline and John-John, my deep sympathy. They can be proud of the rich heritage of love and affection bestowed upon them when he lived, and of the mark his life will leave on the history of the world.

ADDRESS BY

Hon. Birch Bayh

OF INDIANA

Mr. President—

Let the word go forth from this time and place, to friend and foe alike, that the torch has been passed to a new generation of Americans.

The echo of this unparalleled challenge still rings vividly in our ears, yet he is gone. Tragic

as was his passing, more tragic indeed would be the hour if we who remain were content to let this sad day mark the end. If we were content to sit alone in our sorrow and sadness with personal memories which, on each reflection, renews the ache in our hearts and tears in our eyes.

I will always remember him as a world leader with profound wisdom in quest of a world at peace; as a national leader, determined that each of us and our Nation as a whole should not forget the principles of our native land, nor the price paid by others to make secure these principles.

I remember him as an example of devotion to his family and to his God.

I remember him as a great man who would always recognize a face in a distant corner of the room; as a friend who never failed to recall an easily forgotten event of some consequence in the life of a comrade.

I remember the pleasant individual conversation in a caravan and the enthusiastic outpouring of admiration from a crowd.

Some will say that John Fitzgerald Kennedy was more severely criticized by his opponents and more dearly loved by his allies than any of his predecessors.

Some will say that John Fitzgerald Kennedy was a man who lived before his time.

But I remember a man who saw America as it is today. I remember a man who saw and loved a great country unparalleled in the history of mankind. I remember a man who refused to let national pride, political expediency or vitriolic criticism blind him to the shortcomings of the land he loved.

Few of us have the inclination or courage to examine ourselves or our country; to see ourselves as we really are; to point out our shortcomings as well as our strengths; to urge that tomorrow's labors surpass today's deeds.

But I remember a man who refused to be content and complacent; a man who lived, and died, insisting that America should and could be a better place in which to live; a man who resolutely refused to follow the course of least resistance but insisted that the building of the United States of America required sacrifice from each of us—a sacrifice which he so willingly made himself.

I remember a man, a President, and a friend

who asked us for our help; help to wage the struggle against mediocrity; help to guarantee equality; help to see our land as it really is today; help to see that we build on our strengths and remove our weaknesses.

I remember a man whose challenge will continue to echo throughout this Chamber and in the ears of each of us—his colleagues—until we have carried the burden and completed the tasks which he began.

Let us remember the challenge as he said:

In the long history of the world, only a few generations have been granted the role of defending freedom in its hour of maximum danger. I do not shrink from this responsibility; I welcome it. I do not believe that any of us would exchange places with any other people or any other generation. The energy, the faith, the devotion which we bring to this endeavor will light our country and all who serve it, and the glow from that fire can truly light the world. With a good conscience our only sure reward, with history the final judge of our deeds, let us go forth to lead the land we love, asking His blessing and His help, but knowing that here on earth God's work must truly be our own.

My colleagues, in the name of God, in the name of America, in the name of John F. Kennedy, let us hold high the torch.

ADDRESS BY
Hon. Barry Goldwater
OF ARIZONA

Mr. President, there is nothing that any of us on this floor can say that would add to the eulogy paid the late President by the universal lament over his passing. So I will not attempt to explain my personal sorrow, which cannot be done.

Instead I would like to comment very briefly on one word and that word is hate. I have a feeling that I know the American people as well as any living American, and I have never detected hatred as one of their facets. Rather, I know them to be a loving people. Remembering something I wrote connected with the late President and the kind qualities of Americans, I quote it here:

President Kennedy and I are poles apart on many issues but if you assume we must also be personal enemies as well, you're entirely wrong. The fact is that while the President and I are fully aware of the gulf between us, neither has permitted these differences to develop into personal antagonisms.

Might I suggest on this day of remembrance that we remember that great quality of his which was based on love and understanding, and all of us promise in our professional, personal, and daily lives to practice more love and more understanding, not less. We must recognize, as he did, that there are two sides, sometimes more, to every question and under our concept of life everyone is allowed the possession of these opinions, so must everyone be allowed the free discussion of them.

To me the dedication of all of us to those qualities of his would be the best eulogy we could pay him.

ADDRESS BY
Hon. A. Willis Robertson
OF VIRGINIA

Mr. President, the assassination of President Kennedy was the greatest national tragedy I have experienced in more than 40 years of public service. I shared with millions of Americans a sense of shocked sadness at the untimely death of a great President.

President Kennedy had strong convictions and expressed them well. He was a brilliant son of Massachusetts and I am reminded of what another son of that great Commonwealth, John Adams, said many years ago in recommending that a young Virginian, Thomas Jefferson, draft the Declaration of Independence. Jefferson had a "felicity of expression," said his friend John Adams. The same can be said of John F. Kennedy.

I enjoyed a warm and friendly relationship with President Kennedy and wish to join with other Members of the Senate in paying tribute to a truly remarkable man whose services to his country and to the world were brought to an untimely end by the bullet of an assassin.

To his parents, who lost an outstanding son; to his wife, who lost a cherished husband, and to his children, who lost an adoring father, I extend my deepest sympathy.

Hon. Thruston B. Morton

Mr. President, along with all Americans I deplore the dastardly act of assassination that struck down President John F. Kennedy. Along with all Americans I mourn the memory of the first President of our country born in this exciting and challenging 20th century.

John F. Kennedy brought to the Presidency the vigor of youth, a broad intellectual horizon, and a dynamic talent for leadership. He had the capacity for putting to maximum use the strength and the energy, the mind and the wit, the charm and the good taste, the reverence and the dignity with which he was so generously endowed.

Let us, the living, dedicate ourselves to the proposition which he so eloquently posed on the steps of this hallowed Capitol less than 3 years ago.

Ask not what your country can do for you—ask what you can do for your country.

Hon. Herbert S. Walters

Mr. President, it is with humility and a sense of inadequacy that these words are offered, seeking not so much to give some sense to the heinous crime which has cost us the life of our Chief Executive, as to pay him earnest tribute. For we have been taught: "Be thy brother's keeper," and "Love one another as I have loved thee." And yet Cain slew Abel, and one, whose love is everlasting and all encompassing, was cruelly murdered on the cross at Calvary. From these paradoxical tenets of scripture we see that man's inhumanity to man is a perpetual mystery that will remain beyond our comprehension until God wills differently.

But, as we draw from our faith, so must we gain from our great loss in the wanton slaying of John Fitzgerald Kennedy. His was a sacrifice on the altar of humanity, for he sincerely cared for all people of all descriptions.

One who loved life as dearly as he, would not have offered his so willingly without the deepest conviction that his example would, in some way, benefit his country. In retrospect, it is clear that he was not unaware of the dangers he faced. He knew the personal risks involved as he fought fervently, ardently and so eloquently for the things in which he believed. He recognized all of this as he cast his light into dark corners where bigotry, malice and hatred needed to be ferreted out. Yet he went forward boldly and unafraid, willing to meet the challenge—his life as the pawn.

In this brief, yet interminable period, we have already learned one bitter and most important lesson: that when poisonous thoughts and hatred mate, they give birth to a despicable action. It is to our everlasting discredit that we could have spawned in our environment the twisted mentality that saw fit to cancel out the pledge of John Fitzgerald Kennedy.

One who loved his fellowman completely, his words and his ideals were a fountainhead of the rivers of truth, justice and liberty that flowed through our land. Yet, he was struck down, and as we must bear the loss, and the shame for his assassination, so must we shoulder the yoke and till the now more arid soil of our democracy, nourishing it with the little and yet so much we have left of him—this he would have wanted.

John Kennedy was his brothers' keeper in the most absolute sense. He constantly sought ways to care for the aged, the infirm, the mentally ill, the uneducated, the jobless, and the hungry. His concern for human welfare knew no geographic or racial confines and he utilized all of his youthful vigor to restore to our way of life a goodness and wholesomeness that in some way had gradually diminished through the years.

John Kennedy, leader of a great nation, executor of a priceless legacy, and skilled architect in the drafting of blueprints for a better life for all mankind, was recognized for his greatness. Yet none of this recognition will ever equal the immeasurable stature he had attained in the eyes of his wife, his daughter, and his son as their loving and devoted husband and father.

Their sacrifice is monumental, and their grief incalculable in human terms. For them, a glowing eternal memorial will replace the vital living warmth they knew. For them, the tears and homage of millions will supplant the ready wit and the easy smile. For them, consolation will be sought in prayer rather than in his arms.

The inbred strength with which they were endowed has been sorely tested during these terrible days of tragedy. America will do well to proudly follow and justly cherish their example.

We have all heard reference to John Kennedy leaving his mark as a profile in courage. Is it not appropriate and equally important for us to seek to emulate him and thereby leave for posterity our own profile in courage, giving some meaning to his sacrifice? And so we must go forward as he would have demanded of us.

We will sincerely miss him.

It is fitting at this time, I think, to include this prayer, written by Mrs. Cora Taliaferro, 200 Forsythe Street, Chattanooga, Tenn., and read to the assembled church women of St. Peter's Episcopal Church, Chattanooga, Tenn., on Monday, November 25, after President Kennedy's funeral:

Almighty God, we beseech Thee to look with mercy upon our land and its grieving people. Guide, we pray Thee, our President and all those to whom has been committed the Government of this Nation, and grant to them special gifts of understanding, of counsel and strength; that upholding what is right and following what is true, they may obey Thy holy will and fulfill Thy divine purpose. Grant, O Lord, that the sound of the shot which took the life of the President of the United States may echo in the hearts of the people of this Nation and tear away the pall of apathy and indifference to the welfare of our country; and may awaken anew a pledge of allegiance to a Republic built on law and order, of physical safety, of mental sanity, and spiritual sanctity; that we may be one people, under God, bound together with that cord of love which is a lifeline to save those weaker than ourselves; with liberty to live a life of abstinence from evil, a life of service to our fellowmen, and with justice to all men, who are our brothers. Amen.

ADDRESS BY

Hon. Len B. Jordan

OF IDAHO

Mr. President, 46 short years ago, on May 29, 1917, John Fitzgerald Kennedy was born in Brookline, Mass.

Since that day he has belonged to the Kennedy family.

On January 3, 1947, he took his oath of office as Congressman from the 11th District of Massachusetts.

Since that day he has belonged to the people of that district.

On January 3, 1953, he took his seat in the U.S. Senate as a Senator from Massachusetts.

Since that day he has belonged to all citizens of that great Commonwealth.

On January 20, 1961, he became the 35th President of the United States, the youngest man ever to be elected to that Office.

Since that day he has belonged to all the people of our great Nation.

On November 22, 1963, in the prime of his life and in a moment of personal and political happiness, he met his Maker.

Since that day he has belonged to the ages. History is the record of the ages.

Let the ages, as recorded in the pages of history, reflect the judgment of the greatness of John Fitzgerald Kennedy. I feel that he who loved history so much would have wanted it thus.

I add only this thought: Even though I disagreed with some of his policies and programs, I found his idealism inspiring, his objectives admirable. Peace and prosperity should ever be our goals.

Mrs. Jordan and the people of Idaho join with me in extending our sympathy to his father and mother, his sisters and brothers, and most of all to his courageous young widow and his little children.

ADDRESS BY

Hon. J. Glenn Beall

OF MARYLAND

Mr. President, I appreciate having the opportunity to add my voice to the voices of my distinguished colleagues paying tribute to our late President, John Fitzgerald Kennedy. The many tributes here to the late President will be sincerely spoken by saddened men who were closely associated with him.

I am one of these. It is perhaps pardonable, at this moment, to be personal. I served in the House of Representatives with John Kennedy during his entire tenure in that body. Our service in the House covered the same period. We were elected to the Senate on the same day, and were first sworn in as U.S. Senators at the same time. Six years later we both were reelected.

I knew John Fitzgerald Kennedy well. I always admired his keen intellect, his genial personality, his practical ability as a legislator, and his understanding of and unstinted fairness to those who on occasion opposed him.

President Kennedy was faithful to those things in which he believed, and he respected those who likewise were faithful to their own beliefs, even though they might disagree with him. This trait endeared him to both his supporters and his opposition.

An assassin's bullet struck down John Kennedy. The United States has lost its President and a great leader. The Nation honors him. The Nation mourns.

We extend our deep sympathy and sincere condolences, first, to the bereaved family of John Fitzgerald Kennedy, and, second, to our bereaved fellow citizens throughout the land. We all have sustained a great loss.

ADDRESS BY

Hon. A. S. Mike Monroney

OF OKLAHOMA

Mr. President, the poet Carl Sandburg said in his poem, "Washington Monument by Night":

The republic is a dream. Nothing happens unless first a dream.

The man we honor with eulogies today was by a dream possessed. John Fitzgerald Kennedy dreamed of a brighter and better world for all mankind. His life was devoted to bringing his dream to reality and to making his dream meaningful to more and more of his fellow men. Another poet, Sheamus O'Sheel, captured in musical phrases the tremendous influence of such a dream. Being, like the late President, an American of Irish descent, Mr. O'Sheel expressed it this way:

He whom a dream hath possessed knoweth no more of doubting.
For mist and the blowing of winds and the mouthing of words he scorns.
No sinuous speech and smooth he hears, but a knightly shouting,
And never comes darkness down, yet he greeteth a million morns.

John Fitzgerald Kennedy frequently described his dream. His was a dream cherished also by many millions of people throughout the world.

To different individuals his dream held different meanings. Here in our own land, and in many far away places, President Kennedy's dream was the hope for freedom. To uncounted multitudes both in the free world and behind the Iron Curtain the dream of our late President was the dream of peace and justice. But to all who shared it, his was a dream of a brighter and better world.

The dream of an American President is always important. As Editor Norman Cousins put it recently:

An American President is something special in the world precisely because American history has been something special.

John Fitzgerald Kennedy moved into the Presidency of the United States from this Senate Chamber. During his service in the Senate, he sat here in the chair next to me. Having him as a seat mate enriched my life.

His agile and perceptive mind enabled him to deal decisively with issues before the Senate. As a freshman in the Congress he did his homework, and his rate of learning was phenomenal. His quick smile, his innate modesty and friendliness enabled him to gain stature among the Members of the Senate very rapidly.

The enthusiasm which John Fitzgerald Kennedy brought to the causes closest to his heart proved contagious. In advocating and promoting legislation he seldom launched a play for short yardage. He went for the touchdown every time. With dignity and style, he transferred the spirited gamesmanship and sportsmanship of the playing field to the field of political science. Millions and millions of Americans, particularly our younger people, liked the way he played the game and liked the goals he sought. They rallied to his side and made him President of the United States.

Born to a position of wealth and blessed with uncommon talents and personal attributes, John Fitzgerald Kennedy strove as President to give his country more than he received. In view of the senseless tragedy that cut his term short, one of the most profound contributions he made was in raising the Vice Presidency to a position of unprecedented close rapport to the Presidency. This was a typical demonstration of his courage, of his willingness to face the fact that, being mortal, he should prepare for any eventuality.

In so doing, he left as a legacy to his country and the free world the essential continuity of strong leadership.

His dream is, however, the inheritance we will cherish most. It was the dream of a world free of ill will, ignorance, poverty, and disease. Such a dream can rekindle our spirits in these days of mourning and regret.

Each of us must see that the dream survives.

ADDRESS BY

Hon. Milward L. Simpson

OF WYOMING

Mr. President, America has been saddened by the tragic death of our young President. Our hearts have ached for his lovely young wife and the two precious children. Although death— the grim reaper—will claim each of us in time, it is the seeming untimeliness and awful brutality of the act which makes the President's passing so tragic and sad.

It is hard for us to realize that the vibrancy and vitality of this young man are stilled forever— but let us remember those beautiful and consoling lines from Laurence Binyon's "For the Fallen":

> They shall grow not old, as
> we that are left grow old:
> Age shall not weary them, nor the
> years condemn.
> At the going down of the sun and
> in the morning
> We will remember them.

ADDRESS BY

Hon. Edward V. Long

OF MISSOURI

Mr. President, millions of words have been written and spoken in bringing to the people of America and the world the heartbreaking story of the assassination of our late President, John Fitzgerald Kennedy.

For the first time in history citizens of the entire Nation were eyewitnesses to an unfolding national tragedy through television coverage for which even the word, "magnificent," is inadequate. Newspapers kept up with this running story in spite of tight deadlines, supplied background material, and printed some of the most touching and eloquent material we have read in our lifetime.

Yet, for this Nation which hung onto every word and picture of this tragedy, just eight words torn from the hearts of four people tell the story so graphically that none of us here will ever forget them.

They were the "Oh, no!" which was wrung from the soul of Mrs. Kennedy when she saw her husband had been shot; the "My God!" uttered by the first Secret Service man to realize what had happened; the words, "He's dead," which shattered hopes that the President might survive; and, finally, the utterance, "Dear Jack * * *", lifted from the heart of Cardinal Cushing at the funeral service at St. Matthew's.

If President Kennedy had not been a man of wide-ranging and intense but varied interests, we might well now be at the point where we would have to say, "What more can be said."

But as Chairman of the Senate's Subcommittee on National Penitentiaries, I had the opportunity to learn that this man's great compassion, which was well known, extended even to those who receive little compassion, the men and women who have been convicted of violating the Nation's laws. This facet of our late President went virtually unpublicized and little noted.

Mr. Kennedy, more than any other President, used his powers of clemency to correct inequities and to relieve hardships. During the 3 years of his administration, he reduced the sentences of more than 100 prisoners and gave full and unconditional pardons to 550 individuals who had been released from prison years ago and thereafter demonstrated good citizenship. Without exception, he approved every clemency action recommended to him by the U.S. Pardon Attorney Reed Cozart, Prison Director Jim Bennett, and the Department of Justice.

He was particularly concerned about injustices resulting from long mandatory no-parole penalties of the Narcotics Control Act. Nearly half the sentences he reduced involved drug addicts and incidental offenders who had become involved in relatively minor drug or marijuana violations and received what in some instances amounted to life sentences for their transgressions. He cut to 20 years the life sentence given a teenage epileptic addict and the 80-year sentence given to another young first offender.

He did not like to see anyone die in prison. Whenever Mr. Cozart sent him an informal note concerning a prisoner who was in terminal illness but who was not eligible for parole, President Kennedy would immediately and without redtape cut the sentence to time served so that the prisoner could return to his home and family right away.

In other instances, where the prisoner was serving a long term and had apparently rehabilitated himself although he had not yet reached the time when he would be eligible for parole, President Kennedy cut the sentence enough to advance the parole eligibility date and make possible an immediate hearing by the U.S. Board of Parole. One such individual with nine children had been in prison several years when the mother of the children abandoned them suddenly. President Kennedy promptly cut the father's sentence so that the Parole Board could take up his case and arrange his return to his children.

Because of the many cases which came to his attention, President Kennedy was vitally aware of the problems of widespread and extreme disparities in the sentences imposed for given types of offenses from one judge and one district court to another. He encouraged the judges themselves to administer justice in a more fair and equitable manner. When more than 100 Federal judges met at Highland Park, Ill., in the fall of 1961, to examine principles and procedures which would minimize sentence disparities, President Kennedy sent them a message assuring them of his complete support. He said also:

> Our citizens, high and low, rich and poor, the law abiding as well as the lawbreaker, rightfully expect the judge to exercise wisely his position and his power to preserve an orderly and just government and to use this authority as a merciful buffer for the unfortunates and the underprivileged. * * * Without the judge, our Government and our civilization would be without the vigor it must have to survive the present critical competition between systems of government, political philosophy, and social justice. Perhaps more than most elected or appointed officials he symbolizes a government that is ruled by law, a government that today seeks to associate with all nations in the creation of a world of law.

President Kennedy, in his actions and in his words, joined with another great political figure of the Twentieth Century, Winston Churchill, in the belief that one measure of a nation's virtue and strength is its treatment of the criminal. Like Churchill, he believed that "there is treasure, if you can only find it, in the heart of every man."

At this point, Mr. President, I had intended to ask permission to insert a few editorials from Missouri newspapers commenting on President Kennedy's death and what he had meant to this Nation. However, the task of selection was too great. Nearly every paper in Missouri responded in a way I have never seen equalled. Editors of large papers and small papers composed such eloquent, touching and excellent editorials that to have chosen any one, or a few, would have been an injustice to the others.

I did find a commentary, though, that for breadth and depth as well as feeling seemed to sum up the expressions of Missouri newspapermen. The writer is a nationally known Republican, Mr. Roy A. Roberts of the Kansas City Star, one of the great editors and political writers of our time.

In the Sunday, November 24, edition of the Star, he wrote a moving commentary on the death of President Kennedy, and the legend he has willed to this Nation and the world that will see his programs and philosophy live as a shrine to his memory.

Mr. President, I ask that Mr. Robert's article, entitled "Legend Will Live On," be printed at this point.

[From the Kansas City (Mo.) Star, Nov. 24, 1963]
LEGEND WILL LIVE ON—MEMORIES OF JOHN F. KENNEDY
WILL BE SPUR TOWARD HIS TWO MAJOR GOALS: WORLD
PEACE AND RIGHTS OF MANKIND—LED THE WAY—FOR-
MER PRESIDENT HAD AWESOME RESPONSIBILITIES IN THE
SPACE AGE—TIME TO CLOSE RANKS—SOBERING TRAG-
EDY MAY EASE DIFFERENCE IN AMERICAN POLITICS

(By Roy A. Roberts)

I am confident that the legend of John Fitzgerald
Kennedy, living after the man, will drive forcefully
toward his two major goals: The peace of the world
and the rights of mankind.

Even in the sorrow of the moment, it is possible to
see that in the long course of history the legend may
prove more effective than was the vibrant national and
world leadership of John Kennedy.

But what a shocking price it is to pay. What a pointless sacrifice of a human life at the hands of an assassin.

HONOR HIS MEMORY

If I know the American people—and I believe I do—
they are sentimental and they are fine. They cherish the
memory of a man and oftentimes in their midst, the
honored legend of one of their fallen fellows carries
further than did his voice, however eloquent and
powerful.

We can know, certainly, that the legend of John Kennedy will not quickly pass. In these few terrible hours it
has been inscribed on the Nation's consciousness. Both the
man and the legend have their place in history and both
will grow with the decades. Violent death, pointless
death, so often guarantees that it will be so.

And, in the case of the late President, it could be no
other way. He was first in so many things.

He was the first President elected to the space age.

He was the first Roman Catholic President.

He was, almost unique in our history, a truly urban
President.

He was the first President to carry for long—although
Dwight Eisenhower knew the burden in his later years—
the awesome responsibility of the finger on the button.
He knew that the moment of decision could come and
that civilization, in the push of the button, could be
reduced to chaos.

Throughout the story of the Republic, there has always
been the lonely man in the White House, ordained by his
people to make the decisions. The Presidency has always
been an assignment of terrible burden. But from the
other day henceforth, until man learns to control these
nuclear forces, the burden has grown and will continue
to grow. It is a time of no second-guessing and beyond
peace lies death.

Thus does the happenstance of time ennoble and enshrine the legend of the young President struck down
because of some twisted mind's decision. In sorrow, animosities are buried. From grief grows the memory that
works on for the cause.

A TIME TO RALLY

Certainly the immediate impact of the tragedy has
sobered the Nation. I hope, indeed, that it will erase
permanently some of the fierce antagonisms of the forthcoming campaign. I do know that the American people,
as they have always done in moments of emergency
past, will close ranks in this dark time. Because it has
always been thus, this Nation has reached its heights of
freedom and democracy.

But to foresee the future we must know the present.
And this, I believe, must be acknowledged as a factor
in the Nation's story yet to be told. The present Congress had made a shambles of President Kennedy's
domestic program. I have observed these matters for
half a century and I can recall no Congress that has placed
its stamp of approval on so little that a President wanted.

Frankly, you could describe the legislative situation
on Capitol Hill only as an awful mess. There are many
reasons and on a recent 10-day swing through the East,
I sought them out. I was doing so, in fact, when this
awful thing happened. I had intended to write—and in
proper time, the story can still be written—of the whys
and wherefores of the impasse between the White House
and Congress.

Yet in no way did this situation discourage John F.
Kennedy or lessen his ardor for his goals. Undaunted,
but possibly a bit frustrated, he rode off to the political
wars, confident that next year his program—built around
civil rights and a tax reduction—would win congressional
approval.

A LOOK AHEAD

It is my guess now—and it is only a guess—that this
confidence will be justified, and perhaps sooner than
expected. But not, of course, in 1963, for the days left
on the calendar simply will not permit it.

I suggest this for two reasons: The shocking end of
John Kennedy's life did not resolve the issue of civil
rights, for example. But it most certainly will remove
much of the extreme bitterness from the picture. In a
sense, the Kennedy name had become a symbol in this
fight. As symbol becomes legend, we may see a greater
sense of reason, a lessening of bitterness. And if there
is a lesson in the tragedy of Dallas, it is this: The Nation
needs more reason, less emotion in dealing with this major
problem of the rights of all citizens.

Then, another and very practical reason. Although
John Kennedy served on Capitol Hill, had many friends
there and understood the legislative process, it must be
said that he was never a member of the lodge, so to speak.
He was detached, in a sense, and certainly outside the
inner circle.

On the other hand, Lyndon B. Johnson, who now sits
in the White House, was in a similar sense the grand
master of the lodge during his later years on the Hill.
Not for decades has there been a more adept or subtle
leader of the Senate than was the Senator from Texas.
Perhaps his knowledge and understanding of the world
and of its global economy do not equal the knowledge
of his predecessor. But Lyndon Johnson knows Congress
inside and out. You see the distinct possibility of a breaking of the impasse which had become so serious that
thoughtful observers wondered whether the legislative
machinery could function in these complex times.

EXPERIENCE HIS BULWARK

L.B.J. and Mr. Sam—the late Speaker Sam Rayburn—ran a taut congressional ship for so many years. When Mr. Johnson moved from the Senate to the Vice Presidency, one fact was obvious: Those who followed him in the leadership of the lodge would not permit him to run Capitol Hill by proxy. No one realized this more than did Lyndon Johnson and he carefully refrained from interfering in congressional activities. Had he interfered, it would have been a terrific tactical error.

As President, Lyndon Johnson assumes the duty of leadership, and Congress must recognize this fact. His experience, his old associations may ease his task. In the area of domestic legislation at least, this is a significant fact of the Johnson administration.

It is hardly the time to discuss politics and it would not be in good taste. But there are a few thoughts, I believe, that may be properly expressed, toward the end of better understanding John Kennedy and his successor, and in preparation for the difficult months to come.

Certainly all preconceived notions of both parties must now go by the boards. The dope-sheets will be torn up and a new picture will develop but slowly.

KEYMAN ON TEAM

By coincidence, there was one question in my mind when I left for Washington that, once answered, sheds light on the capabilities of our new President. Did the President and his advisers, preparing for the 1964 campaign, really want L.B.J. on the ticket, or was there an intention to dump him, as some have intimated? I talked to several persons close to the top, and this, they said, was certain: John F. Kennedy did want Lyndon Johnson as his running mate. One associate of President Kennedy told me:

"Of course we want Johnson. He has been a team player. He has given the administration his complete loyalty and support. He has been self-effacing, perhaps too self-effacing, feeling that the President should always keep in the spotlight."

It was a judgment of the man Johnson and a judgment we can take at face value.

Moreover, I think it can be safely noted that the Kennedys did not anticipate defeat next year. The President and those around him recognized that a tough battle was ahead. There was the belief that John F. Kennedy had probably reached his personal low point on the political scale. It was better, the reasoning went, to reach the low point a year before the election, than either just before or just after the convention.

AT HIS BEST IN CAMPAIGN

Another point might be cleared up. Do not carry any illusions that President Kennedy had entered the political wars reluctantly or with faint heart. He may have been frustrated by the ebb and flow of world events or by the slow progress of his domestic program and the immobility of Congress. But not on politics. John F. Kennedy was a born campaigner with a deep fervor of cause and dedication.

I might recall that Franklin D. Roosevelt referred to Al Smith as the "Happy Warrior." The title stuck to the end. But Al Smith was not a happy warrior. He was a hard, snarling fighter who did not relish the political battle. John F. Kennedy, I say in the deepest of respect, was a happy warrior. And as the bullet flashed, the cheers of the crowd were ringing in his ears.

I mention these bits and pieces of politics now not because they may point to the shape of things to come, but chiefly because of the light they shed on the spirit and character of the President who gave his life and of the President who has succeeded him. There will be time enough, later, for all the politics and it will be time tinged with a deep sorrow that will linger.

I confess freely to a real liking for John Kennedy. I do not pretend to have been close to the man and I never was. But he fascinated me as few Presidents have. I did not buy everything he had to sell and certainly did not buy the philosophy of the Democratic Party on which he ran 3 years ago.

DURING TIME OF CHANGE

Looking back over those 3 years, however, I think I may say that one achievement of his too-short career was to lead his party from the outmoded ways of the New Deal into the global economy of the space age. I doubt, frankly, that most businessmen ever understood this President. I am sure I did not, for he was not an easy man to fathom.

On the surface, he was a great liberal. Yet his tax bill and his general fiscal program contained more of the moderate GOP philosophy than of the New Deal. Perhaps here we have one chief difficulty that he encountered in getting his program through Congress.

You could never size up the man on the basis of those he gathered about him. He had his circle from Harvard, liberals all. Their names made rightwingers foam at the mouth. He wanted the assistance of the liberals but he did not necessarily base policy on their advice.

Then, as Secretary of Defense, he chose Robert McNamara. It is the biggest single job in any administration (for after all, a President is, in a real sense, his own Secretary of State). McNamara is a modern industrialist, a nominal Republican and one of the strongest figures to go to Washington in decades. Excepting Robert Kennedy, McNamara probably carried more weight in the Kennedy administration than any other man.

At the economically sensitive Federal Reserve, John Kennedy strongly supported William McChesney Martin, and no one could regard Martin as anything but a sound money and fiscal man. Douglas Dillon, another nominal Republican who became Treasury Secretary, is a man who also knows money and is by no means a liberal in his economic opinions.

In matters of the deepest concern to labor John Kennedy was sympathetic. Yet he held out a restraining demand against the drive for shorter hours and too-sharp wage increases that might harm the Nation in world marketplaces.

NOT ONE-SIDED

I hesitate to label any man yet if this is a picture of the liberal, it is also the picture of a leader firmly oriented in a philosophy of real conservatism. Where John Kennedy stood in the ideological spectrum, I never could say. But this much was certain: He knew the score and he had a profound instinct for the principles and processes of government.

Then, too, the words of a man become a mark of his leadership. John Kennedy was one of our most articulate Presidents, one of the best read in history and literature. There was an element of majesty in some of his pronouncements on the world and its search for peace. I suspect that many of his speeches will live on. They were moving and if some of his words on domestic problems seemed to be aimed at the pocketbook, his words on peace spoke to the hearts of men with a real warmth. Of course, his critics said he was better at words than actions. But, I wonder, what action?

Excerpt some of the paragraphs from the speeches he made and was to have made on his final trip to Texas, and you would have a moving creed for the Nation.

History may rate the confrontation of Nikita Khrushchev in the showdown of nuclear decision as the biggest episode in the Kennedy career. But I wonder if more importance should not be given to President Kennedy's whole approach to world affairs than to one single episode, spectacular turning point that it was.

FAMILIAR WITH SITUATION

And because the new President, Lyndon Johnson, was so familiar with this whole approach, there is an element of reassurance. He sat in with John Kennedy when most of the major decisions were made. He does not face the impossible task that Harry S. Truman faced when Franklin Roosevelt died. Mr. Truman, to put it bluntly, was thrust onto the world stage unprepared, through no fault of his own, for the moments ahead.

In contrast, Lyndon Johnson knows thoroughly the Kennedy program and the men who are charged with carrying it out. To that extent, this transition in brief is easier. But it must be acknowledged that President Johnson has one liability in his new role. Our allies and our foes respect power. John F. Kennedy was elected Commander in Chief by his people. However strong his leadership may be, the new President will carry the mark of a man who succeeded to power only by the accident of another man's death. It will be thus until he is elected in his own right or until there is a new man in the White House. Especially is this a factor of importance against the background of forthcoming elections in other nations. For times of balloting are times of uncertainty and uncertainty does not create easy diplomacy.

And there is always, in national emergency or national change, an element of uncertainty for the economy. New York and Washington, I found, were thoroughly optimistic over the future. They agreed that these good times would be prolonged into the new year. So universal was the optimism that it made me feel somewhat uneasy, for trouble comes, so often, when everyone is thinking the same way. Now, we must wonder how the economy will withstand this great shock.

MORALE HAD BEEN LOW

Yet with all the optimism, there has been, in the people, a sense of frustration. National leaders I talked to in this last week said they detected a letdown feeling on the part of the public. People are weary of crisis, perhaps tired of spending money on nations that hardly can find their own place on the maps of the world. It is a case of the Nation's morale at something of a low ebb and it has been reflected, I suggest, in the savage attacks on foreign aid and spending.

In times of frustration there is a search for simple answers which so seldom are solutions. It has been reflected, I fear, in the growth of extremist groups of left and right, in the manner that the campaign, full of vituperation and name calling, had begun. It has been disturbing. We need, in a democracy, our differences of opinion but if there is a lesson of Dallas, it is this: We do not need the venom spewed by the hate groups; we need reasoned argument without vicious hatred.

And perhaps the death of John F. Kennedy may center our national thinking once more on these principles of reason and moderation in a democracy. If so, his terrible death will not have been in vain. But again, I express the common grief: What a terrible price to pay.

President Johnson deserves and will get—because it is the American way—his chance. Technically, he enters the period that politicians call the honeymoon. For him, it cannot be an extended honeymoon for the hour of national decision at the polls is not too far off.

GOOD BASIC UNDERSTANDING

I have known Lyndon Johnson much longer than I knew John Kennedy. I respect him and his ability. He, too, knows and grasps the principles of government and of democracy. He has the understanding of people that is so essential. I doubt that any new President has had so much experience in Washington and it should be of tremendous help to him in this hour of sorrow and shock.

Yet it is the stuff of a man that counts, that spells the difference between success and failure on the world stage. Certainly President Johnson starts with the good wishes and the good will of his countrymen. We can hope and pray that he will measure up to his awesome task. Yet we cannot expect this administration to be a carbon copy of the Kennedy administration. Lyndon Johnson's roots go back to the soil, not to the city. He has lived as a part of the space age; yet, he is, in contrast to John Kennedy, more in the tradition of Presidents past.

And now he must carry on where the young President left off in the moment of violence. On this middle-aged Texan falls the responsibility of world, national, and party leadership. It is a terrifying responsibility but I know that his Nation will stand united behind him in the trying months of history's ordeal.

ADDRESS BY

Hon. John J. Williams
OF DELAWARE

Mr. President, I wish to join the other Members of this body in paying tribute to our former colleague, the late President John F. Kennedy, whose life was so tragically ended by a coward's bullet last month.

We in the Senate who had known and worked with him for many years were especially stunned and shocked by that almost unbelievable act, not only because we knew the man well, but because we immediately recognized this vicious act as an attack on both our form of government and the highest office to which we can elect one of our citizens.

The fact that we may have differed with some of the policies of our late colleague does not in the least diminish our respect for his determination to pursue the goals which he sought and in which he so strongly believed.

November 22, 1963, will remain a tragic day in the history of our country—a day when the United States lost its young and vigorous leader and a day when we in the Senate lost a friend and colleague whom we had grown to know and respect so well.

ADDRESS BY

Hon. Stephen M. Young

OF OHIO

Mr. President, President John F. Kennedy, only 46 years of age, happily married, father of two children, brilliant, eager, foremost leader of the free world, died a martyr. He will no longer direct the destiny of our Nation and of freedom-loving people the world over.

John F. Kennedy was a great President of the United States. Perhaps it is too early to fix his place in history because so much of what he initiated was left for others to complete. However, two of his achievements seem likely to take root.

For the first time in this century he placed the power and prestige of the Presidency behind a downtrodden race whose second-class status demeaned the dignity of all Americans. To protect not only our freedom but the freedom of all mankind he took the world to the precipice of a war during the Cuban crisis in 1962. Khrushchev's withdrawal of his offensive missiles from Cuba was America's greatest cold war triumph.

It was also a great personal triumph for President Kennedy. A measure of his greatness lies in the fact that he followed up this triumph by deeds intended to eliminate the risk of a holocaust through madness or miscalculation—his speech at American University last June, the nuclear test ban treaty, and his other efforts toward peaceful solutions to the world's problems.

Mr. President, something else was irretrievably lost in the death of John F. Kennedy—the brilliance of his presence, the glow of his style. He brought renewed dignity to political life. His literacy, his wit, his physical grace, and his sense of history added new dimensions to the Presidency. He cherished not only learning but the learned. He brought to the Presidency a new brilliance and luster. He sparked the imagination of all Americans, reawakening in them an awareness of the great potential of our Nation.

In World War II the life of this gallant young man was saved in enemy action. In this cold war he lost his life. Why, we ask? Perhaps the answer is that hate for fellow Americans has been building up, stimulated by lunatic fringe propagandists of the radical right and radical left. There has been too much hate built up by unscrupulous demagogs—hate for President Kennedy, hate for his administration; hate for the Chief Justice of the United States; hate unbridled.

Some citizens have been tolerant of extremist elements among us, evidently, in the belief they were crackbrains, loudmouths, and habitual letter-to-editor writers who would disappear of their own accord in due time. Since the witch hunts of the early 1950's a climate was created which encouraged these lunatic extremist organizations to flourish unchallenged. Perhaps this atmosphere, which our young President sought so hard to combat, contributed to his death. If these lunatic fringe extremists of the left and right are to be restrained, they must be subject to constant exposure and relentless publicity. Unfortunately, there are too many of these patriots for profits. America is really last with them. The people of America and the entire world have poured out their grief, shock, and anger over the assassination of our President. Chief Justice of the United States, Earl Warren, expressed the feelings of many Americans in his statement on that tragic occasion. He said:

A great and good President has suffered martyrdom as a result of hatred and bitterness that has been injected into the life of our Nation by bigots, but his memory will always be an inspiration to Americans of good will everywhere.

Mr. President, it was my privilege to serve with John F. Kennedy both in the House of Representatives and in the U.S. Senate. His death meant to me not only the loss of a great President and a great leader, but the passing of a close personal friend. Let us hope that his otherwise senseless death may become meaningful in the light of history by furnishing the inspiration needed for completing his unfinished tasks. Let us complete that which he began.

ADDRESS BY

Hon. Hiram L. Fong

OF HAWAII

Mr. President, on this occasion when the Senate is honoring the memory of our late beloved President, John F. Kennedy, I, too, wish to pay tribute to my former friend and colleague. His tragic and untimely death stunned and saddened all Americans, particularly those of us who knew him both as a Member of Congress and as our Nation's Chief Executive. His sudden passing also shocked millions of persons around the globe who mourn with us. Even now it is difficult to comprehend and grasp the brutal truth that he is gone.

As others have thoroughly chronicled his remarkable life and his remarkable career, I shall not dwell upon biographical detail except to note a fact which might be overlooked, yet which endures to his eternal credit: born to material wealth, John F. Kennedy could have existed in indolent ease; but instead he chose to dedicate his life to serving his country, in war as an officer in the U.S. Navy and in peace as a U.S. Congressman, as a U.S. Senator, and finally as elected President of the United States, giving at each station the fullest measure of devotion to the people he loved and the Nation he revered. It was a mark of his ability and intellectual capacity that he grew in stature with each higher responsibility and each new post.

Then suddenly, when he was at the full height of his powers, an evil hand, from behind without warning, fired two mortal shots, depriving a wife of her husband, depriving two young children of their father, depriving our Nation of its Chief, and depriving the world of one of its great humanitarians and one of its most steadfast friends.

A man of peace was struck down by a villain of unspeakable violence.

A man of great and good will was struck down by a disciple of hatred and malevolence.

A brave and worthy personage was struck down by a craven coward.

And so the horrible news flashed forth: John F. Kennedy, age 46, mortally wounded on active duty in service of his country, felled by an assassin's bullets.

In the long span of recorded history, 46 years on life's stage are but as the twinkling of an eye. But John F. Kennedy's 46 years were crammed with action and good works which will leave their mark in the years to come.

While only time and coming events can render the final verdict on all that John F. Kennedy did, we his contemporaries know now, as we knew instantly at the time of his passing, that someone vibrant and courageous and dynamic and vigorous and imaginative and adventurous and enthusiastic and gregarious and gay and warm and witty and personable and cultured and likeable and gallant and humane and decent and idealistic and purposeful and resolute and intellectual and devout—a complete man—had passed from our midst.

Though as President he occupied our Nation's highest office and stood in the forefront of the world's leaders, John F. Kennedy remained a human being with a capacity to attend to little courtesies and endearing acts of kindness. I recall with pleasure that last October, preoccupied with the unbelievably heavy burdens of office, he took time out to send birthday felicitations to me in Hawaii. I am only one of legions of people who were touched by his thoughtfulness.

These many personal attributes he crowned with a profound sense of national destiny, giving eloquent expression to our overriding mission as a people and as a Nation: to work unceasingly for a world of peace and justice for all mankind.

Although mid-20th century America had become an affluent society, attaining the greatest good for the greatest number in history, John F. Kennedy would not let us, his countrymen, rest on our laurels, but kept prodding us and leading us toward higher goals and new frontiers of endeavor—not merely the obvious frontiers of our land, sea, and space environment, but also the frontiers of the mind and spirit.

So it was that John F. Kennedy, personifying the grandeur and beneficence of America, pressed impatiently on toward a better world where all its people would be nourished, clothed, sheltered, schooled, accepted, and accorded the liberty, equality, and dignity due them as children of the Creator.

He did not spare himself in pursuit of that goal. Last June, he journeyed nearly 10,000 miles from Washington to Hawaii and back in order to deliver a major civil rights plea in our multiracial island State. Had he given his address anywhere, it would have commanded attention. By delivering it in Hawaii, a living showcase of racial tolerance and harmony, before a conference of U.S. mayors, John F. Kennedy created a stunning impact. It was a strong message delivered personally to leaders of local communities where rests so much of the responsibility for attaining equality of opportunity for all races.

We of Hawaii were, of course, highly pleased and very proud that he had selected Honolulu as the forum for his civil rights plea.

Our only regret was that he could not have lingered in Hawaii for a visit to our neighbor islands and a rest in our mid-Pacific paradise. Despite his very tight schedule during his short stay, he found time to visit the Arizona Memorial to pay tribute to his comrades entombed in their battleship since that infamous enemy attack on December 7, 1941.

It is little wonder that, from the moment he landed until the moment he departed, the people of Hawaii received him warmly and enthusiastically without a single sour note during his visit, a tribute not only to his high office, but also to the man himself and to his outgoing and magnetic personality.

Yes, John F. Kennedy personified the spirit of America, giving it new voice, new meaning, new dimension, and new focus for Americans and for the 3 billion souls who inhabit this earth.

Although his person was struck down, his spirit—the spirit of America—endures, as it did before him and as it will long after him if we, like he, are willing to protect and preserve that spirit and pass it on to our children and to their children and to children throughout all generations, emulating in the process his courage, his fidelity, his willingness to sacrifice all, even life itself, that this spirit illuminating the world shall never be extinguished.

Now it is for us, the living, to dedicate ourselves to the unfinished business before us, as he so often exhorted.

No eulogy on John F. Kennedy would be complete without tribute to Mrs. Kennedy, whose grace, gallantry, and fortitude wrote an unforgettable and altogether fitting epilogue to his Profiles in Courage. In those dark days of supreme anguish after her husband's life was so treacherously and horribly snuffed out before her eyes, Mrs. Kennedy's serene composure, indomitable courage, and superb dignity attained awesome and heroic proportions.

She who most needed solace gave solace to others.

In this time of mourning, therefore, we honor not only a distinguished President but also his magnificent lady and from them take inspiration.

To Mrs. Jacqueline Kennedy, to Caroline, to John, Jr., to Mr. and Mrs. Joseph P. Kennedy, to our colleague Edward Kennedy, to the Attorney General Robert Kennedy, and to all the Kennedy family, Mrs. Fong and I extend our heartfelt condolences.

May you find comfort in this expression of affection, respect, and esteem for the memory of your beloved Jack.

And so, one last farewell, one final Aloha, to our fallen leader who so nobly personified the greatness and goodness of America.

ADDRESS BY

Hon. Lee Metcalf

OF MONTANA

Mr. President, it was a bitter cold day, less than 3 years ago when Senator John F. Kennedy, the President-elect rode up Pennsylvania Avenue in the inaugural parade and took the oath of office as President of the United States. It was not an auspicious start for a new administration but the ringing words of his inaugural address warmed the hearts and lifted up the spirit of the whole world:

Let the word go forth from this time and place—to friend and foe alike—that the torch has been passed to a new generation of Americans—born in this century, tempered by war, disciplined by a hard and bitter peace, proud of our ancient heritage. Let every nation know that we shall pay any price, bear any burden, meet any hardship, support any friend, oppose any foe to assure the survival and success of liberty. This much we pledge—and more.

Less than 3 years after John F. Kennedy made that pledge to our Nation, at his inaugural as our 35th President, he gave more. In the words of another President, Abraham Lincoln, President Kennedy gave "the last full measure of devotion."

I was in Washington when the President left for his last trip—to Texas. I was here when his body was returned. I joined hundreds of thousands of Americans in paying tribute to him when he lay in the rotunda of the Capitol—and when he was buried at Arlington National Cemetery. Montanans, who spent hours before their television and radio sets and read thousands of words about the untimely death of our beloved President, are as well informed as I am about the loss we have suffered. Suffice it to say that President Kennedy was a special friend of Montana.

Senator Mansfield and I were with President Kennedy on his recent trip to Montana. He was interested in the conservation, orderly development, wise management, and highest possible use of the natural resources with which we are especially blessed. He never forgot the conservation program which, as a presidential nominee, he laid down in Billings in the fall of 1960.

President Kennedy was interested in Yellowtail Dam, Yellowstone Park, Custer Battlefield National Monument. He asked about them on the airplane as we neared Billings. He talked about them, and about other key parts of Montana development, as we drove through Billings.

Because of the interest of President Kennedy, we have more parks, more recreation facilities, more forest access roads than ever before. He recommended to Congress many other proposals to develop our resources—including the greatest resource of all, our youngsters.

But when he spoke to the people of Montana he threw away his prepared speeches and spoke about what was in his heart. He talked about the test ban treaty, about peace in the world. He spoke of complicated problems which concern all citizens.

"So when you ask," he said, "why are we in Laos or Vietnam or the Congo, or why do we support the Alliance for Progress in Latin America, we do so because we believe that our freedom is tied up with theirs, and if we can develop a world in which all the countries are free, then the threat to the security of the United States is lessened.

"So we have to stay at it. We must not be fatigued."

President Kennedy was a special friend of Montanans, many of whom knew him personally. As a Senator, he had spoken in Butte and in Helena. As a presidential candidate, he had made a major speech in Billings. As President, he had visited with and spoken to many groups, including Indian leaders. His trip to Montana this fall, with speeches in Billings and Great Falls, was a return to friends. John F. Kennedy was a friend of man, a leader of men, which enriched the lives and inspired the spirit of all of us.

The epitaph of President Kennedy will be written in the accomplishments of his administration, in the courage of his leadership, in the initiative of his domestic innovations, in his boldness as an international statesman. John F. Kennedy belongs to history and the ages.

ADDRESS BY

Hon. J. Caleb Boggs

OF DELAWARE

Mr. President, I shared with my fellow Americans a very high regard for President John F. Kennedy when he was alive and along with my fellow Americans I share a deep sense of personal loss now that he has been taken from us. His death affected me, as it did millions of others, as though I had lost a member of my own family.

My association with the late President, although not a close one, dated back to the swearing in of Members of the 80th Congress in January 1947. We were both freshmen Members of the House, and I came to know him as a colleague in that great body noted for its fellowship and esprit de corps. He was always friendly. My contacts with him were always pleasant.

I was privileged to become a Member of the Senate in January 1961, when President Kennedy's administration took office. Although I am a member of the opposite party, I never failed to recognize President Kennedy's ability and dedication to the course he considered right for the country. He had my highest respect. Although he was in office only a relatively short time, his youth and vigor and personality have left a lasting imprint on our country.

His memory will always remain bright.

To Mrs. Jacqueline Kennedy and her children, and to all of the other members of the Kennedy family, I extend my profound sympathy.

ADDRESS BY

Hon. Edwin L. Mechem

OF NEW MEXICO

Mr. President, the people of New Mexico join with other Americans in paying sincere tribute to our late President, John F. Kennedy.

We were stunned beyond description by the manner in which he was taken from us. Such a deed is an attack on all of us and on our institutions and way of life.

President Kennedy was a man of conviction and principle, who fought hard for what he believed. We can take comfort in the way our fellow Americans have withstood this devastating blow. We can take confidence in the steadiness of our great Nation during this trying and dangerous period.

Even in our sorrow, shared by all Americans at the tragic death of our President, let us take renewed faith in the goodness of the overwhelming majority of humanity.

I extend my deepest sympathy to the members of the Kennedy family.

ADDRESS BY

Hon. Hugh Scott

OF PENNSYLVANIA

Mr. President, I would like to say of the late John Fitzgerald Kennedy that I knew him well, and I admired him.

He was our President, and for that reason the Nation is in deep mourning. But I knew him also as a man, and that was why I cried, as all America cried, when he was shot.

John Kennedy was young, not just in age, but in outlook. I suspect if he had lived to the fullness of man's normal span, he would still have the vigor that characterized his approach to public affairs.

This youth, optimism, and vigor permeated everything he did and, as many in this Senate remember, these qualities seemed to accompany him through the door of every room he entered.

This young man saw new frontiers and was convinced that they were just beyond the horizon. He strode forward in pursuit of them, with determination and style that carried him to the hearts of many Americans. These Americans elected him first to the House, then the Senate, finally the Presidency.

But his impact spread well beyond our own borders. We all know of the high regard heads of state all over the world had for the late President. However, I received a letter from Australia just this morning which says, in simple terms, what many persons in all stations of life thought of our late President.

My correspondent wrote:

No matter whose side you are on he was a good guy and had the guts to say and do what he thought was right.

No one knows what was in the mind of the assassin, because he also is now dead. But all evidence indicates that he was deranged.

And, as former President Eisenhower wrote in a memorial article about the late President Kennedy:

Knowing that such psychopaths are with us, we as a people do have a responsibility for avoiding fanaticism and overemotional political extremes that may tend to incite unstable individuals.

That should give us some suggestion for a fitting memorial for President Kennedy, not the only one, but one which is certainly in order in this Christmas season. Would it not be appropriate to call for a moratorium on hatred?

We are all aware of the fact that stable men are able to handle emotion, including the emotion of hatred, degrading as it is, but which can be handled and kept under control by the majority of people. But when men and women pass on expressions of hatred—of the kind that has swirled around our land, polluting our politics and our very lives—sooner or later the waves go on and reach an unstable person.

That person may be on the right or on the left. It does not matter. But those unstable men and women are capable of horrible violence because they cannot control hatred.

Each of us in our private lives can do something about it. The next time any American hears an expression of hatred or vitriol or a gangrenous kind of remark, he should not laugh nor snicker nor should he lightly dismiss evil in action. It is our duty, all of us, to condemn these things.

We as individuals and we as a nation have an obligation to condemn extremism, the kind that permits of no free discussion, that admits no diversity, that labels persons who refuse to conform to established patterns as "traitors."

This I offer as a part of my personal memorial to the fallen President. We will always cherish his memory.

ADDRESS BY

Hon. Gaylord Nelson

OF WISCONSIN

Mr. President, perhaps now that it is all over, we should remember the happy times of the past and face the sober challenges of the future.

We lived through the assassination period, numb with shock and inadequate in our grief, and then we had our spirit as a nation restored by the stately funeral and the towering courage of a great First Lady.

Perhaps now the man whose loss we feel so much would want most of all for us to look backward with a fond smile, and look forward with a brave heart.

The past is rich in memories. One memory which comes back vividly to me now is that dramatic scene at the 1956 Democratic National Convention when a wonderfully boyish John Kennedy, looking like a college freshman, climaxed an amazing drive for the vice presidential nomination by urging the cheering delegates to unite behind Estes Kefauver, who had just defeated him in a close race.

The electric personality, the tremendous ability to radiate charm to the throngs, was clearly visible on that occasion. Many of us said then that he was a man of the future.

Eventually, we in Wisconsin came to know him almost as a native son. All through the late winter and the cold, wet spring of 1960 he stumped our State in quest of the presidential nomination. The wool-shirted woodsmen in the towns of our far north got to know him over a cup of coffee, and the farmers in our rich southern counties met him over the fence.

Everywhere he went this remarkable young man and his extraordinary family won the hearts of the people of Wisconsin. That is why his death leaves such a void within us. That is why, when his young son salutes his departing funeral wagon, we salute too.

Since coming to Washington in January, I was able to visit with him at his home, and to talk with him in his office. I was struck by the same characteristics which the whole world came to appreciate: The open and friendly manner, the good humor, the spirit of confidence in the face of grave problems, and most of all, the keen mind, with its amazing breadth of interest and its storehouse of detailed knowledge.

My happiest memory of all will always be of his trip to northern Wisconsin on September 24, at the start of his nationwide conservation tour. We flew together in a helicopter over Lake Superior and the Apostle Islands, and he peered out of the window in excitement. We talked about the disappearing bald eagle and the clear blue water and the beautiful beaches, which reminded him of Cape Cod, and I was struck anew at this warm feeling for the world of nature in a sophisticated young man from Boston.

John Kennedy shared the sense of urgency many Americans have come to feel about preserving the beauty of the land in which we live. His leadership in this field will be sorely missed.

As the Nation binds up its wounds and tries to return to the tasks before it, we are all struck by the extent to which everything we do must now be recast in the light of his tragic death.

We cannot face up to any of the great issues without realizing that the vigorous young man who articulated these issues and gave them substance is gone.

He had entered all of our lives, to an astonishing degree. He had completely filled the image we have in our minds of the President of the United States, the greatest democratic office on earth. Many things will never be the same without him.

But the tasks remain.

The murder of the man who articulated the great issues of our day does not remove the issues. It simply makes them more difficult to resolve.

Some of the great burden which he carried passes on to each of us who remain behind.

The only way we can begin to replace this great loss of courage and wisdom and dedication to American democracy is to summon some of the same spirit from within ourselves.

I am confident that that spirit is there. It must be, or we would not have responded as we did to these very qualities in President Kennedy.

We loved his wit and his articulateness, we admired his courage, we marveled at his knowledge, we were moved by his deep commitment to America and to preserving the rights of men. Well then, let us live on in his tradition. Let us look within ourselves and find all we can of those same gifts we came to recognize in John Kennedy. Let each of us contribute to our country what we can of these gifts. That is the way for us to remember him. That is the way for us to face the future. That is the way he would have wished it.

ADDRESS BY

Hon. Wallace F. Bennett

OF UTAH

Mr. President, the fact of John F. Kennedy's assassination remains shrouded in an aura of unbelievability despite the complete news coverage, despite the funeral, despite the finality of his burial. We know it occurred and that life is going on in a new pattern, but we are still staggered by the awful realization that this thing happened in our midst.

Perhaps the reason for this lingering of memory stems from the nature of the man and his approach to national problems. John Kennedy concerned himself with every facet of American life. With youthful vitality he projected himself into every controversy, every decision of national import, every issue at hand. Thus, he became more widely known than most of his predecessors and his sudden removal from the scene touches all of our lives.

It is inevitable that a man of this nature would himself become a storm center of controversy, and that many would rise up to disagree with and oppose him. Such opposition has often been voiced in this Chamber by Members of the Senate including members of his party.

As a former Senator, President Kennedy understood this—indeed, he participated in the process of criticism and opposition himself when he was among us. He recognized that the right to hold honest differences of opinion was one of the privileges of freemen, and he sought to preserve that right in American life. Like any true Irishman, he is reported to have been looking toward the coming political battle in 1964 with zest and was a proven master in political strategy.

This Chamber has been the scene of the unfolding of some of his strategy, and served as an effective forum for him.

It is fitting now that this Chamber should witness a pause in the processes of controversy and strategy to see Senators unite in their determination to do honor to John Kennedy's memory. All Senators, whatever section of the country they represent or point of view they advocate, can and emphatically do subscribe to the proposition that John Kennedy was an extraordinary person whose service to his country requires extraordinary tribute.

Dwight Eisenhower once said:

To live for your country is a duty as demanding as is the readiness to die for it.

John Kennedy did live for his country, with a style and verve that enabled him to overcome serious hurdles which fate placed in his path.

He was afflicted with physical discomforts severe enough to take him to the brink of death and prevent him from performing his duties here for almost a year. Yet he fought back from that experience to wage one of the most exhausting campaigns in American history. His war record is well known, and underscores his personal sense of courage and dedication.

He suffered personal tragedy in a measure greater than most of us have known. A brother killed in war, a sister dead, a father stricken, two children lost in infancy—how many others do we know whose lives have crumbled in the face of such tragedies in the immediate family. John Kennedy remained resolute and carried on in his constitutional duty.

And so, indeed, must we. An extraordinary, impressive, exciting man has passed our way, and we are all richer for the experience of having known him. He has been brutally removed from us, and we are all poorer for the loss. Our highest tribute to him will be to carry on as he would have done were he in our place—resolutely, firmly fighting for highest principles, motivated by a dedication to the American dream of liberty for all men.

ADDRESS BY

Hon. Carl T. Curtis

OF NEBRASKA

Mr. President, millions upon millions of words have been printed and spoken concerning the tragic events of Friday, November 22, 1963. More millions of words have been printed and spoken expressing the Nation's—and the world's—sense of loss, and extending heartfelt sympathy to the family of our late President, John F. Kennedy. There is little that I can add here.

Speaking in part for my State of Nebraska, I want to say that the shock, grief and profound sorrow which engulfed our country reached the same depths in Nebraska.

It is most difficult with mere words to reflect properly the esteem and affection in which Americans hold the President of the United States. He is the supreme symbol of a governmental system, a system dear to all of us, for its institutions and principles have brought to us

the most bountiful blessings ever enjoyed by any society in all of mankind's long history. Strike down that symbol, let tragedy be visited upon the man who typifies the achievements of America, and we all are stricken.

We mourn for our late President. We mourn the loss suffered by his family and we extend to them our sympathy. We mourn the loss to our Nation and the free world of a man whose own accomplishments bespeak the greatness of our country.

We must not falter in our efforts to guard vigilantly the governmental system of which the President is the supreme symbol. Our late President would have been proud of the swift and unerring transition of leadership following his tragic death. Within a matter of minutes, the mantle of leadership passed to President Lyndon Johnson who raised anew the torch of freedom for the world to see. There was no anarchy, no political junta such as we have seen elsewhere under somewhat similar circumstances. There was no scramble for position and power.

Our forefathers had guaranteed such an orderly transition when they drafted our Constitution; and we today, in our time of sorrow, can thank our Creator for their wisdom.

ADDRESS BY

Hon. Norris Cotton

OF NEW HAMPSHIRE

Mr. President, while the Nation mourns a President, we in the Congress mourn an associate and a friend. The Nation thinks of him on the high eminence of his great office. Many of us who served with him both in the House of Representatives and the Senate cherish more the memory of those earlier years. Some of us recall his fight for health. Most of us recall his rise in this great body. I can think of no one who did not respect and admire him. A voracious reader, a master of language, a tireless worker, a fierce fighter for his convictions, he had a warmth of personality and a zest for living that endeared him to his close friends and attracted us all.

His death was untimely but therein lies one small kernel of comfort. He will never grow old. I have always remembered the words of another Massachusetts President, Calvin Coolidge, uttered just after he had lost his young son, to a friend who had suffered a similar bereavement:

By the grace of God, your son and my son will have the blessed privilege of being boys through all eternity.

The portrait of John F. Kennedy in the gallery of history will never show an old man. Unlike the rest of us, his steps will never falter, nor his eyes grow dim, nor his mind lose its keenness. He will live forever in the memory of his countrymen in the full bloom and vigor of his young manhood at the very height of his powers.

We and all who come after us will be better servants of the Republic because he lived.

ADDRESS BY

Hon. John G. Tower

OF TEXAS

Mr. President, I would like to add my voice to the many that have been raised, and will be raised, in tribute to our fallen leader, John Fitzgerald Kennedy.

Our Nation has much to learn from his brief time as our honored President. As this Senate knows, and as the people of our great and beloved land know, I was much in opposition to some of the policies of our late President. But I did not doubt the sincerity and the honesty with which he pursued what he thought was best for our country.

John Fitzgerald Kennedy was an honorable advocate and a worthy leader. He admired and respected those who did not flinch from battle, whether it be political or military. These are qualities that this Nation would do well to remember and emulate.

We shall all miss John Fitzgerald Kennedy. We shall miss his ready smile and his human warmth. We shall miss his youth and enthusiasm. We shall miss his devotion to duty.

We shall, above all, miss that leadership which said to the country that principles are worth fighting for. If we remember this, and seek to practice it, we will do honor to the memory of John Fitzgerald Kennedy.

ADDRESS BY

Hon. Gordon Allott

OF COLORADO

Mr. President, the judgment of history, more than any feeble words we may speak here, will provide the proper eulogy for the brave young man we honor today. For, in 3 short years, John F. Kennedy left his mark on time, not only by the tragic circumstances of his untimely death, but by the dedication with which he faced the task which fate had decreed should be his.

Many of us who speak here today, by right of the system that is uniquely ours, found many issues on which we felt compelled to disagree with this brilliant young leader. Yet, it is a tribute to this man, that of those of us who disagreed most with his philosophy, not one questioned his dedication or sincerity of purpose.

Mr. President, as we honor this fallen leader, struck down in the midst of his unfinished endeavors, I cannot help but be reminded of the words of Alfred Lord Tennyson, in his immortal eulogy, "In Memoriam," when he said:

God's fingers touched him and he slept.

For, truly, God's fingers touched John Fitzgerald Kennedy and he sleeps—far short of his expected lifespan. To those of us who carry on, this tragic event should create in us a rededication to the principles which have sustained men through the ages and which made this great country possible.

May God rest him and keep him, and give solace and comfort to his family.

ADDRESS BY

Hon. Karl E. Mundt

OF SOUTH DAKOTA

Mr. President, it has been said that history will be the true judge of a man's record, a man's worth, and that history will appropriately find the perspective in which a man's deeds are to be chronicled. That well may be, Mr. President, but can history even attempt to capture in the cold print of tomorrow the warmth of yesterday's fellowship and association that a man has built over the years?

Perhaps not. Perhaps that is an assignment that history cannot undertake any more than it could recall for us the vivid and excruciating pain that must have been felt by those footsore Revolutionary heroes of Valley Forge or the despair and relief that rode as dual companions in the thoughts of Abraham Lincoln in a day when brother fought brother but men were made free.

But whether history can chronicle this aspect of man's life for future generations does not lessen the impact that such a man as John Fitzgerald Kennedy has had upon us, his contemporaries, who served with him and worked with him in the common cause of good government in this Chamber and in the other body.

Each of us has his own personal recollection of John Kennedy. What we recall about this man is perhaps more important today than reciting what he accomplished and what he planned to accomplish, for these are matters of the public record—what we feel and what we think about the man are not necessarily a part of that record and I think it is most appropriate that such become chronicled for perhaps these then can make history's task not quite so impossible in relating something of the man himself.

Like many Members of the House and the Senate, I first met John Kennedy in January of 1947 when he came to the House. I served one term in the House with him and then came to the Senate.

In 1953 he came to the Senate and for 7 years was a colleague of all of us serving in this Chamber, until his election to the Presidency in 1960.

For some years he and I were on the same committee, the Select Committee to Investigate Improper Activities in Labor-Management Relations.

What is the one characteristic of this man that stands most firm in my mind?

I would term it his phenomenal capacity for growth.

Even though Jack Kennedy was a member of the other political party, and even though many of us disagreed with a number of his policies and positions, there can be no escaping the fact that he had the admiration of his colleagues, for his career represents a stirring example of the success of our American system of government.

We admired him—I admired him—for the fact that this was a man who dedicated himself to serving our country and in each of the assignments of official capacity he undertook, he grew in stature, taking unto himself the fine attributes of increasing official responsibility but yielding in return something of himself that enhanced the office he held.

I was not one of John Kennedy's closest personal friends. Some in this Chamber were, and it is they who can best speak about the very personal characteristics which gave a unique style and warmth to our 35th President.

But I was a friend in the sense that all who serve together in the Senate are friends—for that is the way—the wonderful way—of our political life. We may be opponents, but we are friends. There are no enemies here, for our political system is too sound, too strong, and so good that enmity has no room here.

The enmity that is found in our political system is that harboring in the hearts of those who do not understand the fundamental nature of our Government and therefore really are not participants. They cannot accept nor recognize that it is a broad foundation upon which our two-party system has been established and upon which it thrives.

And in this friendship of association that evolves out of service together as Members of the Senate, I have many happy recollections of Jack Kennedy and the work he carried on here.

He demonstrated early that he was a worthy proponent of the many causes he espoused and those who engaged John Kennedy in debate on matters before the Senate knew full well that they were not embarking upon some light skirmish. He was formidable and as he proceeded to the top office in our Government he grew in stature and in capacity, but even in the most trying of circumstances, he met his challenges and propounded his points without rancor.

Perhaps that is one of the heritages John Kennedy would leave to us, and to all Americans.

To try to understand a little more about the world in which we live and the people about us and to lend a little more understanding to others. He helped impress upon us all the art and the necessity of disagreeing without becoming disagreeable.

I think John Kennedy would want this as much as he would want us to continue to promote America's interests through the forums of discussion and argument, but to do it without compromise of principle or resorting to the weak reeds of vituperation which are not helpful to either cause or country.

It is indeed a tragedy that one who learned and so well practiced this capacity of being persistent without ever becoming unpleasant should be struck down by an assassin who learned only to hate our system of government and its talented and accomplished leader.

Mr. President, on this day of tribute to our late President, Mrs. Mundt joins me in extending our sympathies to the family of John Kennedy, a family which has greatly enriched the spirit of America through its contributions and sacrifices.

ADDRESS BY

Hon. Peter H. Dominick

OF COLORADO

Mr. President, I should like to add my voice to those of my distinguished colleagues in paying tribute to our late President, John F. Kennedy.

He was a man of great personal ability and energy whose approach to the overwhelming tasks of the vast executive branch of Government created in the minds of his administrators a spirit of enthusiasm, dedication, and teamwork in administering the programs and causes in which he believed and into which he put much of himself.

Both in his life as President of the United States and as the head of the Nation's first family, he added much to the average American's concept of our Chief Executive.

History will record his contribution to the great events of our time.

I join with my fellow Americans in mourning the dark deed which took the life of our Chief Executive and in expressing to his widow and family our sincerest and heartfelt sympathy.

ADDRESS BY

Hon. Roman L. Hruska

OF NEBRASKA

Mr. President, all of America found it hard—almost impossible—to believe that their energetic, youthful President, so full of zest for life and of zeal for his official duties, had been so suddenly and cruelly struck down.

Those of us who had known him in the years before he moved into the White House were even more stunned by this horrible truth.

Many honors and privileges have come to me in my lifetime. One of the most highly treasured and longest remembered will be the association I had with John F. Kennedy during his service in the U.S. Senate and during his term of office—so tragically cut short—as the 35th President of the United States.

For 6 years we served together in the Senate. Athough we were not assigned to the same committees, where there is the greatest opportunity for frequent meetings and personal consultations, we nonetheless enjoyed a cordial relationship which I shall always value.

The last time we visited was in the White House in the spring of this year. The occasion was the ceremony of his signing the congressional resolution conferring honorary U.S. citizenship on Sir Winston Churchill. The President greeted our small delegation genuinely and chatted warmly with us during the proceeding. At its conclusion, he thoughtfully offered me one of the pens which he had used. I later presented it to the Nebraska Legislature for its historical collection, together with a copy of the resolution. After the ceremonies, we stepped outside to the White House garden where the President briefly addressed the assembled group of diplomats, Members of the Congress, and other dignitaries.

During our years in the Senate, Mr. Kennedy was always friendly and cordial. We differed from time to time in issues which arose, but this did not prevent a mutual respect for each other's responsibility and duty to judge and vote on bills according to the best of our knowledge and ability. Both of us served in the Congress long enough to know that dedication to the cause of our Republic did not require that we always reach the same conclusions on national issues and legislative proposals. Unity does not require uniformity. Loyalty means more than conformity.

In fact, in such sincere differences there resides "strength, not weaknesses; wisdom, not despair."

This idea is generally recognized and accepted by Americans. That they applied it in the case of John F. Kennedy is clear, because despite the slender margin by which he prevailed in his last election, and despite the differences expressed as to various of his views and proposals, he was nevertheless accorded generous and wide acclaim at all times.

This was so wherever he journeyed, even unto his last, fateful and tragic tour.

The warm and sincere greetings expressed by the millions of people in all parts of America were, of course, due in some part to the respect of the high office he held. But, more than that, they were demonstrations of enthusiasm, admiration, and love as well as expressions of best wishes to him in his efforts. They were an outpouring from the hearts of the citizenry of their awareness of his bravery in war; his courage in peace; his constant and dedicated efforts to discharge his official duties to the best of his abilities; and his obvious concern that the interests of America be advanced.

Such a memory of our fallen leader will be precious to all of us in the years ahead. Surely in his life and works he carried on nobly and to even more superior heights the splendid traditions of the Presidency and its greatness.

So it is that the Nation mourns so deeply and grieves so sorely. Its every sympathy has been extended to the family which so bravely bore loss and so bravely carries on.

29-275 O—64——14

ADDRESS BY

Hon. Spessard L. Holland

OF FLORIDA

Mr. President, the depth of shock and sorrow which the assassination of John Fitzgerald Kennedy has brought to the Nation, and to us who served with him in this body, cannot be measured in words.

To the sadness which we feel that a life so full of brilliance, courage, strength, and promise has been ended at the height of its youth and vigor must be added the deep and lasting regret of our Nation over the tragic manner in which its end came.

I extend for myself, and for the people of Florida, my deepest sympathy to the sorrowing family of our late President.

ADDRESS BY

Hon. Russell B. Long

OF LOUISIANA

To one who at the age of 16 suffered through an assassination 28 years ago, the weight of the calamity that took place November 22 fell not totally unfamiliarly, but just as heavily.

The news of the events that happened in Dallas that fateful Friday last month swept back all the crushing memories of another day—in 1935—when Baton Rouge was the scene of murder of a top Government official. The Kennedy family would mourn the death of John F. Kennedy in 1963. How well I know that special grief. I experienced it in 1935 as a member of the Long family which mourned the passing of my father, Huey P. Long.

While it was a State—Louisiana—that suffered the loss most of all in 1935, it was a nation, perhaps a world, that bore the brunt of the loss in 1963. John F. Kennedy, who began his tenure in Congress at about the same time I started mine, had risen to become the leader of the free world, the respected pilot of the most powerful

Nation in that world. In less than 3 short years as President, John F. Kennedy had become the symbol of this Nation's greatness, its firm grasp of the present, and its continued leadership in the future. John F. Kennedy's youth, his determination, his intellect and, yes, his "vigor" had become a beacon of direction to an often haphazard world. And suddenly, John F. Kennedy was taken from us.

Most of us in our disbelief and shock could only ask why—why was he so suddenly, so prematurely, so tragically taken. My only explanation is that which I set down in a letter to Mrs. Kennedy, which I now read:

NOVEMBER 23, 1963.

Mrs. JOHN F. KENNEDY,
The White House,
Washington, D.C.

DEAR MRS. KENNEDY: Twenty-eight years ago I said my last goodbye to my father who was dying from an assassin's bullet. The intervening years have accorded me the opportunity to meditate about the sort of tragedy which took your husband on Friday.

There is no way to explain such a thing unless one has faith in God and believes in the teachings of Jesus. If it is true that there is everlasting life beyond this place of toil and tears, then we can take solace in the fact that God called a good man to a higher reward. It is hard to believe that God knows about all of these things and that He planned it to be that way; yet in time we may come to see that all of this is part of a master plan. In that case we should find comfort in the fact that He chose you and John Kennedy to play a significant role.

Mrs. Long joins me in extending our complete sympathy to you and your family.

With warmest regards, I am,
Sincerely yours,

RUSSELL B. LONG.

Mr. President, I join my colleagues in paying honor to a great leader, a good man, an outstanding American. John F. Kennedy symbolized the best there is in man, the best the human race has to offer. The legacy he leaves behind is to do what is right, to reject what is wrong, because, "here on earth God's work must truly be our own."

ADDRESS BY

Hon. Edward M. Kennedy

OF MASSACHUSETTS

Mr. President, it is indeed difficult for me adequately to express my great appreciation, and that of my family, for the heartfelt words which have been uttered this afternoon in the U.S. Senate and for the tributes which were paid so adequately and so beautifully by Members of the House of Representatives last week.

It is also difficult to express our great appreciation to the hundreds of thousands of people who have appeared at Arlington Cemetery during the past few days and weeks, and to the millions of people throughout the world who, during the past 3 weeks, have offered their consolation and their sympathy, as well as their prayers.

Many of you who spoke today were my brother's colleagues during the 8 years he was here in the Senate. You were his teachers, as well; and his career bears your imprint.

My brother loved the Senate. He respected its traditions. He read deeply of its history and the great men who made it. It was in this Chamber that he championed the causes which you have heard explained and testified to today, and about which he felt so deeply. I know that many of you stood by his side on this floor in championing these causes, and that many of you, as well, stood by his side during the hard and long campaigns, and counseled and guided him in discharging the burdens of the Presidency.

The Senate, for him, as it is for me, is the symbol of how Americans can resolve their differences through reason, instead of violence. That is why it is so important for all of us to support President Johnson in the burdens he has assumed. And if the sacrifice of life can bind the Nation together, this sacrifice will not have been made in vain.

Memorial Addresses

IN THE

House of Representatives
of the United States

IN EULOGY OF

John Fitzgerald Kennedy

In the House of Representatives
of the United States

NOVEMBER 25, 1963

The Chaplain, Rev. Bernard Braskamp, D.D., offered the following prayer:

Revelation 14: 13: *Blessed are the dead who die in the Lord from henceforth, yea saith the spirit that they may rest from their labors and their works do follow them.*

Most merciful and gracious God, we humbly acknowledge that in the life of each of us there are times of events and experiences when all our thoughts and feelings seem to impose silence.

As we assemble for prayer at this noon hour, we are not turning our eyes upon the ground whence no help can come but we are lifting them heavenward and unto Thee.

We thank Thee for the life and character and service of John F. Kennedy who walked and worked with us here in this Chamber and who now dwells with Thee in heavenly blessedness for Thou hast opened unto him the gateway to the larger life and received him into Thy nearer presence.

Thou didst not loose him when Thou gavest him to us and so we have not lost him by his return to Thee and even though his sun went down while it was yet day we believe it has risen for him in eternal glory.

On this day when his body is being carried to Arlington National Cemetery, we are not saying "Farewell" but only "Goodnight" for this is our faith that someday we shall dwell together in hallowed union and be forever with our blessed Lord in that fairer land whose language is music and where there is eternal joy.

We pray that Thou wilt give unto the members of his bereaved family and friends and to President Johnson and Speaker McCormack and to all the Members of Congress that strong faith which does not murmur or complain but which trusts and ties in courageously and confidently with the consolations of Thy grace and love and will enable them to carry on in faithfulness and fortitude.

Hear us through the merits and mediation of our blessed Lord. Amen.

Mr. Multer. Mr. Speaker, I ask unanimous consent that the eulogies to our late President delivered in the rotunda on yesterday be printed at this point.

EULOGY BY SENATOR MANSFIELD IN THE ROTUNDA, U.S. CAPITOL, NOVEMBER 24, 1963

There was a sound of laughter; in a moment, it was no more. And so she took a ring from her finger and placed it in his hands.

There was a wit in a man neither young nor old, but a wit full of an old man's wisdom and of a child's wisdom, and then, in a moment it was no more. And so she took a ring from her finger and placed it in his hands.

There was a man marked with the scars of his love of country, a body active with the surge of a life far, far from spent and, in a moment, it was no more. And so she took a ring from her finger and placed it in his hands.

There was a father with a little boy, a little girl and a joy of each in the other. In a moment it was no more, and so she took a ring from her finger and placed it in his hands.

There was a husband who asked much and gave much, and out of the giving and the asking wove with a woman what could not be broken in life, and in a moment it was no more. And so she took a ring from her finger and placed it in his hands, and kissed him and closed the lid of a coffin.

A piece of each of us died at that moment. Yet, in death he gave of himself to us. He gave us of a good heart from which the laughter came. He gave us of a profound wit, from which a great leadership emerged. He gave us of a kindness and a strength fused into a human courage to seek peace without fear.

He gave us of his love that we, too, in turn, might give. He gave that we might give of ourselves, that we might give to one another until there would be no room, no room at all, for the bigotry, the hatred, prejudice and the arrogance which converged in that moment of horror to strike him down.

In leaving us—these gifts, John Fitzgerald Kennedy, President of the United States, leaves with us. Will we take them, Mr. President? Will we have, now, the sense and the responsibility and the courage to take them?

EULOGY BY CHIEF JUSTICE WARREN IN THE ROTUNDA, U.S. CAPITOL, NOVEMBER 24, 1963

There are few events in our national life that unite Americans and so touch the heart of all of us as the passing of a President of the United States.

There is nothing that adds shock to our sadness as the assassination of our leader, chosen as he is to embody the ideals of our people, the faith we have in our institutions and our belief in the fatherhood of God and the brotherhood of man.

Such misfortunes have befallen the Nation on other occasions, but never more shockingly than 2 days ago.

We are saddened; we are stunned; we are perplexed.

John Fitzgerald Kennedy, a great and good President, the friend of all men of good will, a believer in the dignity and equality of all human beings, a fighter for justice, and apostle of peace, has been snatched from our midst by the bullet of an assassin.

What moved some misguided wretch to do this horrible deed may never be known to us, but we do know that such acts are commonly stimulated by forces of hatred and malevolence, such as today are eating their way into the bloodstream of American life.

What a price we pay for this fanaticism.

It has been said that the only thing we learn from history is that we do not learn. But surely we can learn if we have the will to do so. Surely there is a lesson to be learned from this tragic event.

If we really love this country, if we truly love justice and mercy, if we fervently want to make this Nation better for those who are to follow us, we can at least abjure the hatred that consumes people, the false accusations that divide us, and the bitterness that begets violence.

Is it too much to hope that the martyrdom of our beloved President might even soften the hearts of those who would themselves recoil from assassination, but who do not shrink from spreading the venom which kindles thoughts of it in others?

Our Nation is bereaved. The whole world is poorer because of his loss. But we can all be better Americans because John Fitzgerald Kennedy has passed our way, because he has been our chosen leader at a time in history when his character, his vision, and his quiet courage have enabled him to chart for us a safe course through the shoals of treacherous seas that encompass the world.

And now that he is relieved of the almost superhuman burdens we imposed on him, may he rest in peace.

EULOGY BY SPEAKER M'CORMACK IN THE ROTUNDA, U.S. CAPITOL, NOVEMBER 24, 1963

As we gather here today bowed in grief, the heartfelt sympathy of Members of the Congress and of our people are extended to Mrs. Jacqueline Kennedy and to Ambassador and Mrs. Joseph P. Kennedy and their loved ones. Their deep grief is also self-shared by countless millions of persons throughout the world, considered a personal tragedy, as if one had lost a loved member of his own immediate family.

Any citizen of our beloved country who looks back over its history cannot fail to see that we have been blessed with God's favor beyond most other peoples. At each great crisis in our history we have found a leader able to grasp the helm of state and guide the country through the troubles which beset it. In our earliest days, when our strength and wealth were so limited and our problems so great, Washington and Jefferson appeared to lead our people. Two generations later, when our country was torn in two by a fratricidal war, Abraham Lincoln appeared from the mass of the people as a leader able to reunite the Nation.

In more recent times, in the critical days of the depression and the great war forced upon us by Fascist aggression, Franklin Delano Roosevelt, later Harry S. Truman appeared on the scene to reorganize the country and lead its revived citizens to victory. Finally, only recently, when the cold war was building up the supreme crisis of a threatened nuclear war capable of destroying everything—and everybody—that our predecessors had so carefully built, and which a liberty-loving world wanted, once again a strong and courageous man appeared ready to lead us.

No country need despair so long as God, in His infinite goodness, continues to provide the Nation with leaders able to guide it through the successive crises which seem to be the inevitable fate of any great nation.

Surely no country ever faced more gigantic problems than ours in the last few years, and surely no country could have obtained a more able leader in a time of such crisis. President John Fitzgerald Kennedy possessed all the qualities of greatness. He had deep faith, complete confidence, human sympathy, and broad vision which recognized the true values of freedom, equality, and the brotherhood which have always been the marks of the American political dreams.

He had the bravery and a sense of personal duty which made him willing to face up to the great task of being President in these trying times. He had the warmth and the sense of humanity which made the burden of the task bearable for himself and for his associates, and which made all kinds of diverse peoples and races eager to be associated with him in his task. He had the tenacity and determination to carry each stage of his great work through to its successful conclusion.

Now that our great leader has been taken from us in a cruel death, we are bound to feel shattered and helpless in the face of our loss. This is but natural, but as the first bitter pangs of our incredulous grief begins to pass we must thank God that we were privileged, however briefly, to have had this great man for our President. For he has now taken his place among the great figures of world history.

While this is an occasion of deep sorrow it should be also one of dedication. We must have the determination to unite and carry on the spirit of John Fitzgerald Kennedy for a strengthened America and a future world of peace.

Mr. Multer. Mr. Speaker, I offer a resolution.

The Clerk read the resolution, as follows:

HOUSE RESOLUTION 571

IN THE HOUSE OF REPRESENTATIVES, U.S.,

Resolved, That the House of Representatives has learned with profound regret and sorrow of the tragic death of the late President of the United States, John Fitzgerald Kennedy, illustrious statesman and leader in the Nation and in the world.

Resolved, That as a token of honor and in recognition of his eminent and distinguished public services to the Nation and to the world the Speaker of the House shall appoint a committee of one hundred Members of the House to join a similar committee appointed on the part of the Senate to attend the funeral services of the late President.

Resolved, That the House tenders its deep sympathy to the members of the family of the late President in their sad bereavement.

Resolved, That the Sergeant at Arms of the House be authorized and directed to take such steps as may be necessary for carrying out the provisions of these resolutions and that the necessary expenses in connection therewith be paid out of the contingent fund of the House.

Resolved, That the Clerk communicate these resolutions to the Senate and transmit a copy thereof to the family of the late President.

The Speaker pro tempore. Without objection, the several resolving clauses are agreed to.

By direction of the Speaker, and by unanimous consent, the Chair appoints the following Members of the House to attend the funeral services:

Mr. McCormack, Mr. Albert, Mr. Halleck, Mr. Boggs, Mr. Arends, Mr. Vinson, Mr. Cannon, Mr. Martin of Massachusetts, Mr. Patman, Mr. Smith of Virginia, Mr. Colmer, Mr. Mahon, Mr. Cooley, Mr. Grant, Mr. Keogh, Mr. Kirwan, Mr. Poage, Mr. Sheppard, Mr. Thomas, Mr.

Brown of Ohio, Mr. Gathings, Mr. Jensen, Mr. McMillan, Mr. Mills, Mr. Kilburn, Mrs. Bolton of Ohio, Mr. Bonner, Mr. Harris, Mr. Rivers of South Carolina, Mr. Philbin, Mr. King of California, Mr. Whitten, Mr. Abernethy, Mr. Auchincloss, Mr. Dawson, Mr. Feighan, Mr. Fisher, Mr. Hoeven, Mr. Holifield, Mr. Horan, Mr. Madden, Mr. Morrison, Mr. Murray, Mr. O'Konski, Mr. Winstead, Mr. Andrews of Alabama, Mr. Rooney of New York, Mr. Beckworth, Mr. Chenoweth, Mr. Wilson of Indiana, Mr. Fogarty, Mr. Sikes, Mr. Chelf, Mr. Corbett, Mr. Byrnes of Wisconsin, Mr. Fallon, Mr. Fulton of Pennsylvania, Mr. Miller of California, Mr. Morgan, Mr. Powell, Mr. Price, Mr. Rains, Mr. Teague of Texas, Mr. Gary, Mr. Norblad, Mr. Thompson of Texas, Mr. Bennett of Michigan, Mr. Blatnik, Mr. Burleson, Mr. Donohue, Mr. Evins, Mr. Riehlman, Mr. Tollefson, Mr. Abbitt, Mr. McCulloch, Mr. Green of Pennsylvania, Mr. Aspinall, Mr. Bates, Mr. Bolling, Mr. Elliott, Mr. Ford, Mr. Willis, Mr. Saylor, Mr. Zablocki, Mr. Ayres, Mr. Curtis, Mr. Schenck, Mr. O'Hara of Illinois, Mr. Boland, Mr. Broyhill of Virginia, Mr. Frelinghuysen, Mr. O'Neill, Mr. Hosmer, Mr. Johansen, Mr. Macdonald, Mr. Thompson of New Jersey, Mr. Burke, Mr. Conte, Mr. Keith, Mr. Morse.

The Clerk will report the remainder of the resolution.

The Clerk read as follows:

Resolved, That as a further mark of respect to the memory of the late President the House do now adjourn.

The Speaker pro tempore. Without objection, the resolution is agreed to.

Pursuant to the foregoing resolution and as a further mark of respect to the deceased President, the House stands adjourned until 12 o'clock noon tomorrow.

Accordingly (at 12 o'clock and 7 minutes p.m.) the House adjourned until tomorrow, Tuesday, November 26, 1963, at 12 o'clock noon.

Memorial Services in the House of Representatives of the United States

DECEMBER 5, 1963

The Chaplain, Rev. Bernard Braskamp, D.D., offered the following prayer:

Psalm 112: 6: *The righteous shall be held in everlasting remembrance.*

O God of grace and mercy, the sudden passing of John F. Kennedy, after a brief life among us of less than half a century, and a tenure of office of only a little less than 3 years, has given clear and glorious contemporary witness and meaning to these words of sacred Scripture.

Today the Members of the House of Representatives have assembled to render tributes of praise and love to the memory of Thy servant, our President, whose mortal body has been laid to rest in Arlington National Cemetery, but whose spirit dwells in the Father's house of many mansions, leaving us to dream how wonderfully beautiful that heavenly home must be since he is there. We believe that at this very hour he is laboring and serving with all his strength and enthusiasm in the spacious and limitless fields of eternity.

As we go up and down the courts of memory and think of that brilliant and dedicated young man, whom millions in this and many other countries so dearly loved and admired, we are calling to mind especially the creative and significant part he had in history's greatest cause and challenge, the establishment of peace on earth and good will among men.

There was enshrined in his soul a deep passion for the welfare of mankind and for all the members of the human family, who are finding the struggle of life so difficult and its burdens so heavy.

By spoken and written word, by arduous toil and travel, he continually bore testimony that this was the vision which stirred his imagination and for whose fulfillment he longed and labored.

The contribution that he has made toward attaining that goal of universal peace and brotherhood will perhaps never be rightly and fully appraised by this and future generations for now we see through a glass darkly and know only in part, but someday we shall see and know the good that passed on from his life into the life of multitudes of others and how much more beautiful the world was made by his presence.

Grant unto the members of his bereaved family who were bound to him by the ties of faith and love, the consolations of Thy grace and the assurance that Thou hast crowned his life with the diadem of Thy praise and bestowed upon him Thy benediction, "Well done, Thou good and faithful servant, enter unto the joy of Thy Lord."

In the name of the Christ, our Saviour and the Prince of Peace, we pray. Amen.

ADDRESS BY

Hon. John W. McCormack

OF MASSACHUSETTS

Mr. Speaker, it can be said that the American people and the Government of the United States—both—have just passed through one of the most tragic events of our history. John Fitzgerald Kennedy, around noon on Friday, November 22, 1963, was cut down by the bullets of an assassin in one of the great cities of the country that he loved and that loved him. Here was the 35th President of the United States at a high moment of his eminence, and in the middle of the last year of what would have been his first administration, receiving the adoration and the praise of his fellow citizens. The assassin was morally blind, as blind as the bullets from his weapon, to the central fact that perhaps no leader of his people on this conflict-ridden planet since the end of World War II, and precious few before, had so completely captured the imagination of his fellow Americans, and of mankind, as this young, vigorously alive, brilliantly statesman-like champion of world peace.

The impact of a tragedy so monumental, and the high drama of the violence and the ruthlessness that surrounded it, made the whole world reel as if from a blow that had been struck at the collective brow of mankind and caught it viciously and squarely between the eyes. Not alone the unexpectedness of this calamity but the unending repercussions in the hearts of 190-odd million of his fellow Americans, and among the peoples and in the capitals of every nation in the world, produced a momentary paralysis of comprehension hitherto unknown to the psychology of mass bereavement. This President, who was the enemy of no man, suddenly called forth, by the rude ferocity of his sudden death, a flood of feeling and a depth of understanding from one end of the earth to the other, that is without parallel in the annals of time. Above all it elicited from the American people a new dimension in the quality of their character as a free nation. It called forth from them, on a superb note of dignity, a collective and a massive grandeur in their bereavement that will remain for all time one of the great phenomena of history.

It was as if the people, by the dignity of their response to the peril of the moment, strove to match in their conduct the splendid heroism exemplified in the life of their young President. This feeling of appreciation, of sympathy, of the need for abjuring panic and avoiding an almost pardonable hysteria of despair while feeling the intensest emotion of bereavement, covered the whole spectrum of American life. The political party in opposition, the leaders of practically all

the factions of American political thought—except the most rabid and the most hate-loving—responded with a degree of decency that attested to the great place John Fitzgerald Kennedy had won for himself in the minds and hearts of those who opposed him as well as those who followed faithfully what I believe was his high order of domestic and foreign statesmanship.

The American people admire courage and expect it in their leaders. This President demonstrated it—not only physically, dramatically, and actually in violent combat for his country—but intellectually and politically, in the White House, before the country, and in confrontation with the greatest nuclear power in the world, second only to our own, at the very brink of nuclear devasation.

The American people admire boldness in their leaders. This President demonstrated it again and again in his speeches, in his policies, in his negotiations with the great and the minor powers. One has but to review the list of notables who came from the far countries to attend his funeral to realize the faith he had won among the leaders of the world for the integrity of his aspirations for world peace and prosperity and the respect and prestige he had gained for his country in the great capitals of the earth. Many came personally who could have sent delegates carrying with them the highest credentials in a genuine and sincere display of condolence. All mourned the loss of a relatively young man who had proved himself a patriot passionately loving his own country, of course, but a statesman also who was concerned about the welfare and the future of all mankind.

This is no place, and the hour is too melancholy, for a review in detail. But suffice it to say that here, in the coffin now laid to rest on the soft hillside facing the Potomac, is the courage of the President who stopped the Kremlin dead in its tracks when it sought to threaten American freedom with missiles in the weak and helpless island of Cuba.

And here is the statesmanship and the courage of the President whose vision was without hate and without pique and without personal arrogance, or rancor, and who gave to mankind the greatest gift it has known since nuclear physics came into being—the gift of the nuclear test ban treaty. Much may still depend on the honor or the duplicity of the Kremlin. But through this treaty, without lessening our own strength and without committing more than we are asking the other side to commit, a step has been taken to lift the imminent threat and the unspeakable burden of war and the destruction of the earth. Is it not a tribute to statesmanship of the highest nobility and skill and the most profound integrity that the President who could compel the Soviet Union one day to withdraw its arms from Cuba, could the next day persuade it to come to terms on a matter basically affecting the status of the world's power structure?

This is the hero of the 20th century who has just been taken from us.

In every crisis that John Fitzgerald Kennedy spoke, in every crisis that John Fitzgerald Kennedy acted, he was the President extraordinary.

There rang in his words and breathed in his language the traditions of this country, and the precepts and disciplines of the Constitution which he knew as devotedly and as studiously, as a preacher of the gospel knows his Bible. When he acted in the Cuban crisis that led to the withdrawal of Soviet missiles, both his language and what his journalistic eulogists call his style had the firmness that meant business, and the reasonableness that made Soviet withdrawal possible under terms that gave the greatest possible promise of a nonviolent solution. This is what the historians of the future will put down as statesmanship. We may never know what an immense gratitude the whole of mankind owes to this brilliant young diplomat-statesman for thus, at one stroke, preserving the freedom of the West, and achieving his fixed determination to get Soviet nuclear weapons out of Cuba. All this without the firing of a shot.

Courage. There was an abundance of courage—the cool and thoughtful courage that our people admired—when in 1961 President Kennedy made plain to the Kremlin and to the whole world precisely what our position was on the matter of the East Berlin wall. The threat hung in the air that with this piece of evil demarkation standing like a prison menace between East and West Berlin, the Soviets were prepared to block access to West Berlin and the Allies in spite of long-established guarantees. At the most acute point of this menace, President Kennedy assigned Vice President Lyndon B. Johnson to the scene of the crisis. He backed him up with a formidable display of American military might in the Berlin strategic area. With the presence of the Vice President in Berlin and the evidence of military readiness, the whole of the free world on the other side of the Atlantic breathed more easily. The Kremlin was made to understand the situation in all its reality, and again President Kennedy won his point. And again the process was the process of considered statesmanship and anything but headlong, precipitate or unthought-out action.

The goal was peace—but peace with honor—and that goal, the Kennedy goal, was achieved.

President Kennedy worked with the materials at hand and with marvelous success. He had the habit of success and the design for victory from the time he came to this House as a fledgling Representative from Massachusetts in the 80th Congress in 1946, to the moment when he was felled by the assassin's bullet. He was a success at Harvard, receiving his B.S. degree cum laude. He was a notable and a dramatic success as a PT commander in World War II. His fondness and his respect for American journalism can be traced to his own tour of duty as a newspaper correspondent, and to his authorship of such works as "Why England Slept" and "Profiles in Courage," which won him the Pulitzer Prize. He was outstanding—as I personally observed—in the 80th Congress, the 81st and the 82d, and even more markedly an outstanding success as a Senator from the time of his election to the Senate from Massachusetts in 1952, to the time of his election to the Presidency in 1960.

It is no reflection on any of his predecessors to describe President Kennedy as one of the best informed, most knowledgeable, and therefore one of the most accurately articulate Presidents in the history of our country. This was a President who had taken hold of his education and whose education had taken hold of him to the immense benefit of his countrymen and to the enhancement of the prestige of the White House for all time. His state papers and his speeches, which lend themselves to quotation more easily and more effectively than the utterances of any

President since Lincoln, are examples of superior literary workmanship and a school of eloquence that can lift the heart, the dignity, the patriotism, and the distinction of a whole people. We have had strong Presidents and colorful Presidents and Presidents whom we loved as war heroes. But not until John Fitzgerald Kennedy have we had a President who belonged so wholly and so absolutely to the 20th century. He exemplified in himself, by his very breath and image, the very soul of American youth, American vitality, American courage, and American learning and tradition. Here was an American President who expressed in his every word and gesture, the inner essence of this—the freest society of all time. This was a President, who, it seemed to me, looked the way the President of a busy and an active democracy ought to look. He spoke as a President who is the head of a nation to which all mankind looks as the last great hope of earth, ought to speak.

As he will be remembered for his masterful leadership in the field of foreign affairs, our late beloved President will also be remembered for his outstanding leadership in the field of domestic affairs. His progressive recommendations to strengthen America on the domestic level, many of which have been enacted into law, and others in the legislative process of final enactment, are also a monument to his leadership.

But more than any President of our time, he fought for equal rights for all our citizens. He fought for those rights because he so deeply believed in them. There was a deep, abiding devotion to God and God's morality behind the legal social justice for which he fought. John Kennedy never thought of the brotherhood of man without relating it to the fatherhood of God, from which all virtue springs. Here was his inner strength.

There remains one note about which I can only speak falteringly, and this is the personal one. Back in Massachusetts and here in the House, both as a friend of the family and as a friend of the President, I felt a kinship born of frequent contact and intimate discussion. This is a President whom I knew as a lad in his father's house. It is God's will that I stand to speak as a mourner at his passing. For I saw

in this President a future of peace and prosperity for our country and for the whole of the free world. To see such a prospect for the human race struck down in his prime, at the very gate of massive accomplishments, brings me personally as a friend, and as a citizen, to the very edge of desolation.

What buoys us all up in this moment is the structure of our Government and the quality and the resources of our leadership. This, too, was influenced by the President who so brought the Vice President into his confidence and his activities that the transition is being effected with results that have already made the whole world feel reassured. The enemies of a free society could get no comfort out of the death of John Fitzgerald Kennedy. The strength, the vigor, the decision, and the capacity already displayed by Lyndon Johnson, have electrified our own people and the world and lifted us all out of the deep doldrums of bereavement and despair. What President Johnson is giving us is not only transition but continuity, and continuity is what mankind is looking for and what this Nation wants.

I hope I will be forgiven if I find it impossible to quit this moment of grief without a word of tribute to as remarkable an example of human courage and deportment as this Nation has probably ever witnessed. We, as a people have seen so much and been brought so close to the dreadful drama of November 22, can never forget our admiration for Jacqueline Bouvier Kennedy, the widow of the President. I know of no way to lessen her agony. She is the living proof that as John Fitzgerald Kennedy was a success in war and in peace, in politics and in statesmanship, so he was a success as a husband and a father. The modern communication media helped the whole world to see a quality in human character that must restore respect for human nature in the most pessimistic among us. This young woman proved herself a patrician capable of a display of grace under pressure beyond anything our world has seen in its time.

And I might say, looking through the pages of history, I cannot find therein any lady who underwent the terrible experience that Mrs. Kennedy endured—riding with her loved husband—

chatting—joy—happiness—love—then the sudden bullet. And then embracing her husband in her bosom in his dying moments.

It was because of all this that I say the American people and their Government have just passed through one of the most tragic, and in the majestic bearing of Mrs. Kennedy, one of the finest hours in our history.

ADDRESS BY

Hon. Carl Albert

OF OKLAHOMA

Mr. Speaker, on Friday, November 22, for the fourth time in the history of this Republic, our Chief Executive had been struck down by an assassin's bullet. On that day of darkest tragedy the most beloved man of this generation bowed his head for the last time and said "goodby."

On Monday, as the autumn evening descended over the slopes of Arlington, taps sounded the final solemnity to the President's funeral pageant attended by a sea of mourners—plain and royal, ordinary and exalted, a grieved family and thousands of heart-heavy citizens.

Mr. Speaker, the death of the President and these tributes have moved me to an emotion I cannot express. For the first time in my life have I felt such grief. For the first time have I begun to comprehend the shock and sorrow of the generation that lived through the martyrdom of Abraham Lincoln.

Our hearts and prayers go out to the wonderful family of our late beloved President, to Mrs. Kennedy whose courage and devotion have inspired the world, to the children, to the father, mother, brothers and sisters, and other relatives of our departed leader. May the love of God, which passeth all understanding, sustain them in their sorrow.

The life and deeds of John Fitzgerald Kennedy will forever illuminate the pages of American history. This son of the 20th century, who was destined to live less than two thirds of the allotted span, was also destined to compress into his short

years one of the most remarkable records in all the annals of time.

The rhythm of his life astounded us. He moved with the pace of one who had so much to do, so little time in which to do it. Never stopping even to catch his second wind, he hastened to meet responsibility after responsibility. Already having taken time out to fight a war and to recover from the wounds of battle, he came to the House of Representatives in 1947, the youngest Member of this body. In 1953 he was the youngest Member of the U.S. Senate. In 1960 he was the youngest man ever elected President of the United States, and less than 2 weeks ago, he became the youngest President ever to die in or out of office.

When he came to serve in the House of Representatives he was—as has been said many times in thousands of words—a hard working, dedicated, brilliant, and articulate young man. But these were not the qualities that set him apart—not his youth, his elegance of form and manner, not his matchless zest for life, his vast intelligence nor even the simple goodness of a Christian gentleman. No, Mr. Speaker, it was not any one of these qualities, impressive though they all were, which set John Kennedy apart. It was rather that they should all come to dwell in one man.

John Kennedy was a man of tough mind and tender heart, of great passion and iron self-discipline. A man for work and a man for play. A man for joy and a man for suffering. A man for the heads of state and a man for little children. A man for the old and ill, a man for the youthful and strong.

Such was the man mourned the length and breadth of land and sea—behind whose funeral caisson united representatives of most of the world to walk together in grandly silent tribute.

John Kennedy stirred peoples long quiescent and despairing to rise and demand a place in the community of free men.

In his own country he called his people to join with him in preparing for a new era in time.

For John Kennedy felt in his deepest soul that we were entering a new epoch in the history of man.

He believed literally that the world stood at the bar of the universe—that we had collided head on with immeasurable distance and yet-to-be-fathomed mysteries of a new frontier.

He believed that this event demanded a fuller implementation of our traditional concepts and goals and a fuller development of the potentialities and opportunities of all men.

In his inaugural address in 1961 he bid us join him in a "celebration of freedom." For John Kennedy, the "celebration of freedom," its fulfillment and its extension, was the be-all, end-all of his life. To him freedom could not be circumscribed or limited. It belonged to the humblest man in the most distant corner of the globe.

John Kennedy was not a man who limited freedom by fences and boundaries, justice by color or name, peace by politics or geography.

He has written his personal translation of democratic government into the hundreds of programs he devised and pressed—national and international, economic and social, scientific and military, educational and cultural.

One year ago in his State of the Union message he reported that we had made "steady progress in building a world of order in Berlin, in Laos, in the Congo, in Cuba" and that "at home, too" we had made "good progress in handling our economic problems and heading off a recession." "But," he continued, "we cannot be satisfied to rest here. This is the side of the hill, not the top."

During his brief sojourn in the White House, President Kennedy stamped an indelible imprint on every phase of American public life. As one who knew the horrors of war, he waged an unrelenting battle for world peace on every front. The Alliance for Progress, the Peace Corps, the test ban treaty—all testify to his grasp of world problems in this generation and loom as monuments to the far-seeing constructive quality of his statesmanship.

His leadership in the cause of world peace was recognized worldwide. At his death, the shock of a world crying for peace was expressed by 83-year-old Irish playwright, Sean O'Casey, who wrote a friend in New York City:

What a terrible thing has happened to us all. To you there, to us here, to all everywhere.

Peace, who was becoming bright eyed, now sits in the shadow of death; her handsome companion has been killed as he walked by her very side. Her gallant boy is dead.

A devotee of the principle of religious freedom and of the separation of church and state, John Kennedy did more than any man in our time to erase the blot of religious bigotry from our land.

A firm believer in the ideals expressed in the Declaration of Independence, he has done more than any American since Abraham Lincoln to give them substance. Calling upon the moral resources of this country, he made it the mission of this generation to remove the last vestiges of slavery.

John Fitzgerald Kennedy gave America and the world a rallying point to rededicate themselves to liberty when dedication seems to have faltered—to be courageous in the pursuit of justice when courage seemed to have waned—to be hopeful of peace when peace had become fragmented. In his youth and strength, his love and courage, he gave all that mortal man can give—all in the cause of freedom and justice.

The challenge of the death of President Kennedy was expressed in his own state-of-the-Union message when he said:

Now the time has come * * * to translate the renewal of our national strength into the achievement of our national purpose.

On November 22, John F. Kennedy passed the torch to us. President Johnson has dedicated his administration to the unfinished task. In the fulfillment of our responsibilities in this day and this generation, this House, under God, can do no less.

ADDRESS BY

Hon. Charles A. Halleck

OF INDIANA

Mr. Speaker, I think my reaction to the first report I received that the late President John F. Kennedy had been shot was shared by virtually every American citizen: a total disbelief that the news was true.

Even as we stand here today in tribute to the 35th President of these United States, there is to me a strange quality of unreality about the events which have transpired since that awful day in our national history, Friday, November 22, 1963.

But the assassination of President Kennedy was real—tragically real—and we as a nation are stunned by the sad truth—that this was no nightmare to be forgotten with the dawn.

We, as a great people, are bereaved, and the people of the world share our loss.

I recall a conversation I had with a newspaper friend a few days after the death of our late President.

In attempting to assess the deep shock and sorrow of every man, woman, and child capable of understanding what had happened, he said something like this:

I think every President carries in his being a little piece of every one of us. And when a terrible thing like this happens to him a part of us is somehow lost, too.

This seems to me an expressive way of describing how Americans feel about the death of John F. Kennedy.

Certainly, in a relatively short time, President Kennedy had identified himself with Americans in all walks of life, and they with him.

There was no question of his great love for America, her heritage and her traditions.

And there was never any question about his unwavering faith in America's future.

As a nation we are immeasurably poorer at his loss.

The John F. Kennedy I knew, first as a Member of this House of Representatives, later as a Member of the other body, and finally as our President, had all the attributes we generally associate with success in the field of public service.

His war record established his courage and his devotion to his country and his fellow men.

His record in the Congress of the United States established his high intelligence, his energy and his sense of purpose.

Beyond that, I found him to be a young man of much personal charm and graciousness, whose ascendancy to the highest office in our land did not, so far as I ever knew, affect his genius for being most thoughtful of others, be they of high or low stature.

The achievement of becoming the youngest President in the history of our Republic is perhaps the greatest testimonial to John F. Kennedy's determination to serve his country to the ultimate of his capacities—capacities which were considerable.

He and I differed on matters of political philosophy. We did not agree on what might be the best means to serve the best ends.

But as combatants in this great arena, neither of us, to my knowledge, ever ascribed to the other a dishonesty of conviction or of purpose.

It is not for any of us to question the wisdom of a Higher Power who has taken from our company a devout servant.

But we all sorrow that he is gone, with heartfelt compassion for the fine family he leaves to mourn.

Who can say that his work was unfinished?

Perhaps the ideals of peace, freedom and good will among men for which he labored will be pursued henceforth with even greater diligence by all men everywhere, to the end that John F. Kennedy, like the innumerable other Americans who have served valiantly, shall not have died without cause.

This is the way of history.

ADDRESS BY

Hon. Hale Boggs

OF LOUISIANA

Mr. Speaker, as we gather here in this, the highest theater in the world, to commune together in grief and in remembrance, so many scenes come back to my mind from the years in which I knew, loved, and trusted this magnificent leader of mankind.

Nineteen hundred and forty-seven—the first glimpse of a tall, gangling, boyish, smiling broth of a boy, sent by his neighbors to the Nation's Capital to speak and work in their behalf.

He was a young man, his body wracked with pain from a war wound that never went away, who on sight was a warm, relaxed, buoyant new friend—a friend who trusted and was trusted in return.

I came in time to know his father and his grandfather. I treasure the picture that hangs in my office of the President's grandfather, well known to our colleagues here from the great State of Massachusetts. I remember the occasion in 1947 when he asked me to go to Boston to talk to the Clover Club. I spent a great deal of time preparing a serious speech, but when I arrived there I realized I should not be serious. And I have had hanging in my office ever since a picture of the President taken in that year of 1947, a gangling boy standing next to his Irish grandfather, "Honey Fitz," and inscribed thereon in the handwriting of the President:

To my dear friend, Hale Boggs, in memory of the night we were both in Clover.

I remember so many other things. I came to know his father and his mother. I remember her coming to my city of New Orleans in 1960 when the President was seeking the Presidency. She met there with a group of ladies from my hometown and my home State of Louisiana—friends of mine and friends of my wife. Her charm, her courage, and her knowledge of our country which she and her husband had translated and transmitted to her great son, charmed and captivated all the ladies of my town, despite the fact that they had been reared in what we value and prize as our southern tradition, and she, of course, had been reared in the New England-Irish tradition.

So many things have happened. A lovely wife that all of us loved and who has been described as one who brought majesty to our country during the last few years. There is one who said she came to Washington as a beautiful girl, but leaves official life as a beautiful spirit.

I remember one day after one of our White House breakfasts the President brought in Caroline and, in the tradition of little girls, she had been taught to curtsy. She curtsied to Mr. McCormack, she curtsied to Mr. Albert, and to Senator Mansfield, and to Senator Humphrey, and to Senator Smathers. I think even to me. But she did not curtsy to the then Vice President, now President, Johnson. He said:

Why, Caroline, didn't you curtsy to me?

And in little-girl fashion, she said:

I forgot.

The real reason was that she considered the Vice President a member of the family. She, too, had this magnificent quality of grace that the President gave to all with whom he was associated.

There are so many memories, memories of the man that come fleeting back to me. Many of you served here with him, and knew him when he served in the other body, and watched him as President. We remember his fight to go to the U.S. Senate against odds which were considered difficult at that time, but which he overcame through hard work and quiet confidence in his own ability.

We remember the wide range of efforts, covering the whole panorama of American life, which he undertook as a Senator. I served with him as a member of the Joint Economic Committee, and there I became aware of his fabulous knowledge of the economy of this country and of the world.

Will you forget that day in Chicago in 1956 when he barely missed the call to national leadership, a defeat which he accepted with the grace, with the composure which characterized his life. Or can any of you ever forget the excitement of Los Angeles, when this man was nominated to the Presidency, and with determination he called out to all of us to get moving forward?

Or can any of you forget some of his TV performances? I remember Mr. Sam Rayburn's muttering to some of us, and I quote almost his exact words:

My God, the things that boy knows.

Imbedded in our memories like an etching, I am sure, in that day in January 1961, when a young President, his hair waving in the blizzard wind, called the Nation to action as he himself entered his last battle. And only last October a year ago when the world trembled on the verge of the ultimate holocaust, our valiant leader, alone in the world's most awful loneliness, became a giant as he turned the corner of peace with a courage and a patience and a calmness and a determination unequaled in our time.

So many, many things to remember this man for. Unruffled and unhurried, he always had time to hear another's problems. Witty and urbane, he was also warm, thoughtful, and eternally considerate to his fellow man. Burdened by problems heavier than any one man should ever be called on to carry, his faith in his country and in its future never faltered. A giant himself, he made all men taller. He gave us back a sense of purpose.

A few weeks ago, I think at his very last press conference, he was asked to appraise his job, and this is what he said:

Well, I find the work rewarding. Whether I am going to stay and what my intentions are and all of the rest, it seems to me, is still a good many months away. But as far as the job of President goes, it is rewarding, and I have given before this group the definition of happiness of the Greeks, and I will define it again. It is full use of your powers along lines of excellence. I find, therefore, the Presidency provides some happiness.

That was his quote.

Yes, there was excellence, Mr. Speaker, but there was also humanity and love. And how the Nation responded in life and in death.

Will any of you forget the Sunday just a little more than a week ago when we gathered in the rotunda of this great, historic building and listened to the words of Senator Mansfield, the Chief Justice, and our distinguished Speaker, and watched that bereaved, majestic lady and those lovely children pay their own tributes?

And can you forget the people who came from everywhere and how they stood through the cold of the night and how they were still there when they took him away the next morning? I found it hard to believe that they would stay there through the sunset and would still be there after the rising of the sun.

Oh, yes, Mr. Speaker, so many memories, so many personal memories. I remember so many things that he did for all of you. Some of you would come to me from time to time, and I was honored when you did, and you would ask me some simple thing, and there was never a time that this man did not understand, whether it meant autographing a picture, signing a book, writing a letter, sending a greeting, or shaking hands with a constituent, whatever it may have been, he was never too busy to respond to the demands of our people.

Again I remember that Cuban crisis. I see sitting here that great statesman from the State of Georgia, and I remember coming from one of those meetings with Admiral Vinson, and his remarks about the steely calmness of this man who was directing the destiny of all of mankind. I

think that when history is written that act will figure as one of the decisive acts in all the history of mankind because that could very well have been the decision that prevented a holocaust which could have destroyed all of mankind.

To add just a personal note. Just a few weeks ago my mother was visiting in Washington. My mother, my wife and her mother went to the White House about the time of our Tuesday breakfast. I asked the President if he would greet them—I thought for just a moment. But in typical fashion, he personally called them into his office.

It was a beautiful fall day and we looked out on the famous rose garden and on the fall flowers that were blooming there. The President turned to my wife and said:

Lindy, how long do the chrysanthemums bloom in the fall in Washington?

Then he looked across and pointed to the magnolias and he told us about Andrew Jackson planting them. Yes, his interests even encompassed the trees and the plants in that garden.

Then he took us into the Cabinet Room and he explained to those ladies so dear to me, about the table that had been designed by Jesse Jones so that all who were seated at it could sit as close as possible to the President to hear what was going on. I became concerned about the amount of time he was taking—but he summoned Mrs. Evelyn Lincoln, and God bless her, and asked for a photographer. So I have that prized possession for my mother and my wife's mother and my wife and myself.

Then finally our last breakfast was on November 20. We talked about many things, including the feuding among Texas Democrats. He said that would create interest and would bring a lot of people out. That remark so truly reflected the temperament of the man. He always looked at the optimistic side of every problem. It was so typical of him. Then he said—I think I shall always remember this because it was the last thing he ever said to me:

Things always look so much better away from Washington.

As I recalled that meeting and the people who sat there, I thought of the thousands and thousands of people all over the world who loved this man. But I thought, none loved him more than the members of his own staff whom he took to these meetings year in and year out—Larry O'Brien, Kenny O'Donnell, Ted Sorenson and Pierre Salinger—and that list is anything but inclusive or exclusive.

How do you define such a man, Mr. Speaker? No one can, really. Because he means something different to every person. I think what he best symbolized was an understanding of people and of his country and of the world in which we live. He knew, as he said so many times, that we had to move ahead. He knew that as a static society we would perish. He grew as a Congressman. He grew as a Senator. He grew as a President.

He had the capacity for growth, just as he knew that our country had the capacity for growth.

He faced awful problems—a growing population, overflowing cities, automation, unemployment, racial tensions at home, the threat of nuclear war, civil strife, and revolutions abroad. He described it all in his last news conference as "an untidy world."

Yes, Mr. Speaker, he is gone, but his spirit, his courage, his inspiration will live with every American as long as there is an America and as long as there is an American.

Another great American, also felled by an assassin's bullet, told us in his time what those who come along must do, and I quote:

> It is for us the living rather to be dedicated here to the unfinished work which they who fought here have thus far so nobly advanced. It is rather for us to be here dedicated to the great task remaining before us—that from these honored dead we take increased devotion to that cause for which they gave the last full measure of devotion—that we here highly resolve that these dead shall not have died in vain, that this Nation under God shall have a new birth of freedom, and that government of the people, by the people, for the people, shall not perish from the earth.

Mr. Speaker, now, when our grief is unsolaced and our loss seems unbearable, let us really move ahead, remembering what he taught us by his example: To die for one's country is the supreme sacrifice, but let us now here assembled remember that if we live in our country, well and wisely and actively, we die for it, too.

John Fitzgerald Kennedy did both.

Mr. Speaker, I include an address made on Monday, December 2, before the National Women's Democratic Club, here in Washington by Mrs. Hale Boggs, former president of the club, and Mrs. Boggs was selected to deliver this eulogy for the club.

It follows in full:

EULOGY REMARKS ON THE LATE PRESIDENT, JOHN FITZGERALD KENNEDY, BEFORE THE WOMEN'S NATIONAL DEMOCRATIC CLUB, DECEMBER 2, 1963

(By Mrs. Hale Boggs)

A week ago today (it seems an eternity), on a sunny slope in Arlington Cemetery, where L'Enfant once looked across the Potomac to envision the Federal City, where Robert E. Lee paced making his agonizing decision, at a spot he had called the prettiest place on this earth, John Fitzgerald Kennedy, naval hero, Congressman and Senator from Massachusetts, 35th President of the United States, before the greatest assemblage of world dignitaries ever gathered to honor an American statesman, was laid to rest among our honored dead. Then Cardinal Cushing, his life-long spiritual adviser, committed "our dear Jack" to the company of the angels; American boys from the various branches of our military forces lovingly and expertly folded the flag that had draped their precious burden; his valiant widow lighted a torch and with the assistance of his two brothers, in whom he placed so much affection and confidence, ignited an everlasting flame.

President Kennedy would have approved every word and every motion because they were most appropriate in the affectionate mourning of the man and in the honor due the leader of the free world. For he was always personal in his interest and always pertinent to the occasion, whether he greeted a group of youngsters as "fellow members of the CYO" or admitted that he was "the man who had accompanied Jacqueline Kennedy to Paris," or whether he inquired about the hospitalized child of a White House staff worker, or declared, while looking calmly down the nuclear gun barrel during the Cuban crisis, that the United States wished for peace, but was prepared for war.

It was this very pertinence that identified him with his times. He tapped the great resources of learning available in a free society, and used to intelligent advantage the computers and the opinion polls, the helicopters and jet planes of a modern technological nation. President Kennedy had a style that was perfect for our times—an understated elegance, a sparkling wit, an enduring charm, an amazingly absorptive mind and a retentive memory on a wide variety of subjects, and most of all, a joyful love of life and a real love for the most challenging job in the world.

He understood the world in which we live: the constant threat of nuclear carnage; the ideological struggles all over the globe; the bursting desire of peoples everywhere to be free; and he also understood perfectly America's role in this world. He knew that our military and economic strength must be maintained but that it must be matched by moral restraint and high national purpose. He knew that we must at last reassure the rights of every American; else we could not have self-respect, nor could we expect the emulation of our system by other nations. He knew that we must move America forward, and his identity with the young will assure our destiny in the future. His influence on the young caused a general reawakening of an interest in politics; and more importantly, he opened up to them new and effective channels of service through the Peace Corps, through an accelerated summer Government employment program, through the various areas of relieving the human needs of the old, the infirm, the school dropouts, the mentally ill, the mentally retarded, and through encouraging participation in music, the sciences, and the arts.

Among the hundreds of messages that have poured into my husband's office perhaps the most enchanting was from a young Algerian professor who felt that John Kennedy was "a modern American chevalier with a beautiful lady for an ornament." And true knight he was—dedicated to God, devoted to the service of his country, faithful son, courtly husband, affectionate father, loyal and generous friend, who was willing to give his life that right might prevail.

In weak imitation of his splendid style, I feel that no tribute from this club to President Kennedy's memory would be appropriate without expressing the personal appreciation of its members to Mrs. Kennedy, one of our two honorary presidents. Her stoic composure and unfailing grace gave to American women everywhere a renewal of the strength and the pride they sorely needed in an hour of sorrow and dismay. And she assuaged the grief of a nation by following the suggestions of Isaiah, one of President Kennedy's favorite Biblical references, who said:

"Give unto them beauty for ashes, the oil of joy for mourning, the garment of praise for the spirit of heaviness."

We now place with Caroline our collective hand in hers to comfort her, and with little John we salute our departed leader, and bid adieu to our beloved friend.

Mr. Speaker, President Kennedy appealed to all men, all races, and all nations, but he particularly appealed to young people. It is my pleasure to include a very moving tribute paid to him by a 16-year-old resident of the beautiful city of Lafayette, La. This young man is Joseph E. Le Blanc, Jr., and his tribute follows in full:

JOHN F. KENNEDY

On November 22, 1963, John Fitzgerald Kennedy was assassinated. To many, we lost merely a political leader; but to many more, we lost John Kennedy, the man. Though opposed by some in action, he was loved by all in virtue, and seldom before has any one man come so close to fulfilling the ideal of Americanism. He did more than what his superficial duties exacted of him, and actually reached into and captured the hearts of the American people. In bygone eras, when men such as Al Capone and Babyface Nelson were idolized, corruption and vice held the minds of young Americans in an iron paw; but with the coming of John Kennedy to the Presi-

dency, a new image has assumed the pinnacle of American achievement, one of morality and of courage, of sincerity, and of dedication.

He was a true martyr for his cause, in every sense of the word, and had he been blessed with time, he undoubtedly would have proved successful in accomplishing his aim, the strengthening of an America bound by equally free men. John Kennedy revived the flame of equality enkindled by our forefathers of long ago, and caused this irrepressible fire to glow brighter than ever. We, as true, noble American citizens, must carry unfalteringly this torch of freedom handed us by John Kennedy, and if we should choose to extinguish this flare of fraternity among all men, then we shall be failing not only Mr. Kennedy, who worked so hard for us, but also ourselves, who are left to utilize the fruits of his labor.

Did this fine man, in the prime of his life, die in vain? Did he give his life for American ideals only to have them cast aside by uninterested, inactive American citizens? Let us prove both to ourselves and to the future generations in whom President Kennedy expressed such complete confidence that this leader of our Nation, this champion of the American way of life, did not die in vain. Let future generations be able to look back on the late President Kennedy and say—here was a man.

JOE LE BLANC, Jr.

Mr. Speaker, I now include text of the eulogy by Richard Cardinal Cushing; an article by Theodore H. White; and an article by James Reston in the New York Times for November 23, 1963.

[From the New York (N.Y.) Times, Nov. 25, 1963]

THE TRANSCRIPT OF CUSHING'S EULOGY

(NOTE.—Following is the text of Richard Cardinal Cushing's eulogy of President Kennedy on a nationally televised mass from Boston as recorded by the New York Times through the facilities of WOR radio.)

In the name of the Father and of the Son and of the Holy Ghost. Amen.

My dearly beloved, friends in Christ, and guests:

A shocked and stricken world stands helpless before the fact of death, that death brought to us through a tragically successful assault upon the life of the President of the United States.

Our earliest disbelief has slowly given way to unprecedented sorrow as millions all over the earth join us in lamenting a silence that can never again be broken and the absence of a smile that can never again be seen.

For those of us who knew the President as friend as well as statesman, words mock our attempts to express the anguish of our hearts.

It was my privilege to have been associated with John F. Kennedy from the earliest days of his public life, and even prior to that time, my privilege to have watched him mature with ever-expanding responsibility, to have known some of the warmth of his hearty friendship, to see tested under pain and loss the steely strength of his character.

I have been with him in joy and in sorrow, in decision and in crisis, among friends and with strangers and I know of no one who has combined in more noble perfection the qualities of greatness that marked his cool, calculating intelligence and his big, brave bountiful heart.

TRIBUTE AS WORLD LEADER

Now all of a sudden, he has been taken from us and I dare say we shall never see his like again.

Many there are who will appropriately pay tribute to the President as a world figure, a tribute due him for his skill in political life and his devotion to public service.

Many others will measure the wide interests of his mind, the swiftness of his resolution, the power of his persuasion, the efficiency of his action, and the courage of his conviction.

For me, however, it is more fitting and proper to recall him during these days of mourning as husband and father, surrounded by his young and beloved family.

Although the demands of his exalted position carried him often on long journeys and filled even his days at home with endless labors, how often he would make time to share with his little son and sweet daughter whatever time would be his own.

What a precious treasure it is now and will be forever in the memories of two fatherless children. Who among us can forget those childish ways which from time to time enhance the elegance of the Executive Mansion with the touching scenes of a happy family life?

Charming Caroline stealing the publicity, jovial John-John on all fours ascending the stairs of an airplane to greet his daddy and a loving mother, like all mothers, joyfully watching the two children of her flesh and blood, mindful always of three others in the nurseries of the Kingdom of Heaven.

At the side of the President in understanding devotion and affection behold his gracious and beautiful Jacqueline. True always to the obligations of her role as mother, she has given new dimensions to the trying demands of being America's First Lady.

The pride in her husband which he so eminently justified, was plainly reciprocated in his pride of her. The bonds of love that made them one in marriage became like hoops of steel binding them together.

From wherever men may look out from eternity to see the workings of our world, Jack Kennedy must beam with new pride in that valiant woman who shared his life, especially to the moment of its early and bitter end.

It will never be forgotten by her for her clothes are now stained with the blood of her assassinated husband.

These days of sorrow must be difficult for her—more difficult than for any others. A Divine Providence has blessed her as few such women in history by allowing her hero husband to have the dying comfort of her arms.

When men speak of this sad hour in times to come, they will ever recall how well her frail beauty matched in courage the stalwart warrior who was her husband. We who had so many reasons for holding her person in a most profound respect must now find an even wider claim for the nobility of her spirit.

One cannot think, my dearly beloved, especially one such as myself, of the late President without thinking also of the legacy of public service which was bequeathed to him by his name and his family.

FAMILY DEDICATION

For several generations in a variety of tasks, this republic on one level or another has been enriched by the blood that was so wantonly shed on Friday last. Jack Kennedy fulfilled in the highest office available to him the long dedication of his family.

It is a consolation for us all to know that his tragic death does not spell the end of this public service but commits to new responsibilities the energies and the abilities of one of the truly great families of America.

What comfort can I extend to their heavy hearts today—mother, father, sisters, brothers—what beyond the knowledge that they have given history a youthful Lincoln, who in his time and in his sacrifice, had made more sturdy the hopes of this Nation and its people.

The late President was even in death a young man— and he was proud of his youth. We can never forget the words with which he began his short term as President of the United States:

"Let the word go forth," he said, "from this time and place, to friend and foe alike, that the torch has been passed to a new generation of Americans—born in this century, tempered by war, disciplined by a hard and bitter peace, proud of our ancient heritage."

No words could describe better the man himself who spoke, one whose youth supplied an almost boundless energy, despite illness and physical handicap, whose record in war touched heroic proportions, whose service in Congress was positive and progressive.

It was against this personal background that he continued by saying:

"Let every nation know * * * that we shall pay any price, bear any burden, meet any hardship, support any friend, oppose any foe to assure the survival and success of liberty. This much we pledge and more."

All that the young President promised in these words, he delivered before his assassination. He has written in unforgettable language his own epitaph.

A FULLY HUMAN LIFE

Two days ago, he was the leader of the free world, full of youth, vigor, and promise, his was a role of action, full of conflict, excitement, pressure, and change; his was a fully human life, one in which he lived, felt dawn, saw sunset glow, loved, and was loved.

Now in the inscrutable ways of God, he has been summoned to an eternal life beyond all striving, where everywhere is peace.

All of us who knew personally and loved Jack Kennedy—his youth, his drive, his ideals, his heart, generosity, and his hopes—mourn now more for ourselves and each other than for him.

We will miss him; he only waits for us in another place. He speaks to us today from there in the words of Paul to Timothy:

"As for me, my blood has already flown in sacrifice. I have fought the good fight; I redeemed the pledge; I look forward to the prize that awaits me, the prize I have earned. The Lord whose award never goes amiss will grant it to me—to me, yes, and to all those who have learned to welcome His coming."

John F. Kennedy, 35th President of the United States of America, has fought the good fight for the God-given rights of his fellow man and for a world where peace and freedom shall prevail.

He has finished the race at home and in foreign lands alerting all men to the dangers and the hopes of the future, pledging aid in every form to those who attempted to misinterpret his words, to misunderstand his country, to become discouraged and to abandon themselves to false prophets.

He has fulfilled unto death a privilege he made on the day of his inauguration—a privilege in the form of a pledge—"I shall not shrink from my responsibilities."

Far more would he have accomplished for America and the world if it were not for his assassination here in the land that he loved and for which he dedicated and gave his life.

May his noble soul rest in peace. May his memory be perpetuated in our hearts as a symbol of love for God, country, and all mankind, the foundation upon which a new world must be built if our civilization is to survive.

Eternal peace grant unto him, O Lord, and let perpetual light shine upon him.

In the name of the Father and the Son and the Holy Ghost. Amen.

———

[From the Washington (D.C.) Daily News, Dec. 4, 1963]

FOR ONE SHINING MOMENT THERE WAS CAMELOT

(By Theodore H. White)

(NOTE.—The following is from the current issue of Life magazine where it appears under the title, "For President Kennedy, an Epilogue.")

HYANNIS PORT.—She remembers how hot the sun was in Dallas, and the crowds—greater and wilder than the crowds in Mexico or in Vienna. The sun was blinding, streaming down; yet she could not put on sunglasses for she had to wave to the crowd.

And up ahead she remembers seeing a tunnel around a turn and thinking that there would be a moment of coolness under the tunnel. There was the sound of the motorcycles, as always in a parade, and the occasional backfire of a motorcycle. The sound of the shot came, at that moment, like the sound of a backfire and she remembers Connally saying, "No, no, no, no, no."

She remembers the roses. Three times that day in Texas they had been greeted with the bouquets of yellow roses of Texas. Only, in Dallas they had given her red roses. She remembers thinking, how funny—red roses for me; and then the car was full of blood and red roses.

Much later, accompanying the body from the Dallas hospital to the airport, she was alone with Clint Hill—the first Secret Service man to come to their rescue—and with Dr. Burkley, the White House physician. Burkley gave her two roses that had slipped under the President's shirt when he fell, his head in her lap.

All thru the night they tried to separate him from her, to sedate her, and take care of her—and she would not let them. She wanted to be with him. She remem-

bered that Jack had said of his father, when his father suffered the stroke, that he could not live like that. Don't let that happen to me, he had said, when I have to go.

AN ANNIVERSARY REMEMBRANCE

Now, in her hand she was holding a gold St. Christopher's Medal.

She had given him a St. Christopher's Medal when they were married; but when Patrick died this summer, they had wanted to put something in the coffin with Patrick that was from them both; and so he had put in the St. Christopher's Medal.

Then he had asked her to give him a new one to mark their 10th wedding anniversary, a month after Patrick's death.

He was carrying it when he died and she had found it. But it belonged to him—so she could not put that in the coffin with him. She wanted to give him something that was hers, something that she loved. So she had slipped off her wedding ring and put it on his finger. When she came out of the room in the hospital in Dallas, she asked: "Do you think it was right? Now I have nothing left." And Kenny O'Donnell said, "You leave it where it is."

That was at 1:30 p.m. in Texas.

But then, at Bethesda Hospital, in Maryland, at 3 a.m. the next morning, Kenny slipped into the chamber where the body lay and brought her back the ring, which, as she talked now, she twisted.

On her little finger was the other ring: A slim, gold circlet with green emerald clips—the one he had given her in memory of Patrick.

There was a thought, too, that was always with her.

"When Jack quoted something, it was usually classical," she said, "but I'm so ashamed of myself—all I keep thinking of is this line from a musical comedy."

"At night, before we'd go to sleep, Jack liked to play some records; and the song he loved most came at the very end of this record. The lines he loved to hear were: 'Don't let it be forgot, that once there was a spot, for one brief shining moment that was known as Camelot.'"

She wanted to make sure that the point came clear and went on: "There'll be great Presidents again—and the Johnsons are wonderful, they've been wonderful to me—but there'll never be another Camelot again.

"Once, the more I read of history the more bitter I got. For a while I thought history was something that bitter old men wrote. But then I realized history made Jack what he was. You must think of him as this little boy, sick so much of the time, reading in bed, reading history, reading the knights of the round table, reading Marlborough. For Jack, history was full of heroes. And if it made him this way—if it made him see the heroes—maybe other little boys will see. Men are such a combination of good and bad. Jack had this hero idea of history, the idealistic view."

But she came back to the idea that transfixed her:

"Don't let it be forgot, that once there was a spot, for one brief shining moment that was known as Camelot—and it will never be that way again."

LEST THEY FORGET

As for herself? She was horrified by the stories that she might live abroad. "I'm never going to live in Europe. I'm not going to 'travel extensively abroad.' That's a desecration. I'm going to live in the places I lived with Jack. In Georgetown, and with the Kennedys at the Cape. They're my family. I'm going to bring up my children. I want John to grow up to be a good boy."

As for the President's memorial, at first she remembered that, in every speech in their last days in Texas, he had spoken of how in December this Nation would lift the largest rocket booster yet into the sky, making us first in space. So she had wanted something of his there when it went up—perhaps only his initials painted on a tiny corner of the great Saturn, where no one need even notice it. But now Americans will seek the moon from Cape Kennedy. The new name, born of her frail hope, came as a surprise.

The only thing she knew she must have for him was the eternal flame over his grave at Arlington.

"Whenever you drive across the bridge from Washington into Virginia," she said, "you see the Lee Mansion on the side of the hill in the distance. When Caroline was very little, the mansion was one of the first things she learned to recognize. Now at night you can see his flame beneath the mansion for miles away."

She said it is time the people paid attention to the new President and the new First Lady. But she does not want them to forget John F. Kennedy or read of him only in dusty or bitter histories:

For one brief shining moment there was Camelot.

[From the New York (N.Y.) Times, Nov. 23, 1963]

WHY AMERICA WEEPS—KENNEDY VICTIM OF VIOLENT STREAK HE SOUGHT TO CURB IN THE NATION

(By James Reston)

WASHINGTON, November 22.—America wept tonight, not alone for its dead young President, but for itself. The grief was general, for somehow the worst in the Nation had prevailed over the best. The indictment extended beyond the assassin, for something in the Nation itself, some strain of madness and violence, had destroyed the highest symbol of law and order.

Speaker John McCormack, now 71 and, by the peculiarities of our politics, next in line for the Presidency, expressed this sense of national dismay and self-criticism: "My God! My God! What are we coming to?"

The irony of the President's death is that his short administration was devoted almost entirely to various attempts to curb this very streak of violence in the American character.

When the historians get around to assessing his 3 years in office, it is very likely that they will be impressed with just this: his efforts to restrain those who wanted to be more violent in the cold war overseas and those who wanted to be more violent in the racial war at home.

He was in Texas today trying to pacify the violent politics of that State. He was in Florida last week trying to pacify the businessmen and appealing to them to believe that he was not antibusiness. And from the beginning to the end of his administration, he was trying to damp down the violence of the extremists on the right.

It was his fate, however, to reach the White House in a period of violent change, when all nations and institutions found themselves uprooted from the past. His central theme was the necessity of adjusting to change and this brought him into conflict with those who opposed change.

Thus, while his personal instinct was to avoid violent conflict, to compromise and mediate and pacify, his programs for taxation, for racial equality, for medical care, for Cuba, all raised sharp divisions with the country. And even where his policies of adjustment had their greatest success—in relations with the Soviet Union—he was bitterly condemned.

The President somehow always seemed to be suspended between two worlds—between his ideal conception of what a President should be, what the office called for, and a kind of despairing realization of the practical limits upon his power.

He came into office convinced of the truth of Theodore Roosevelt's view of the President's duties—"the President is bound to be as big a man as he can."

And his inaugural—"now the trumpet summons us again"—stirred an echo of Wilson in 1913 when the latter said: "We have made up our minds to square every process of our national life with the standards we so proudly set up at the beginning and have always carried at our hearts."

This is what the President set out to do. And from his reading, from his intellectual approach to the office, it seemed, if not easy, at least possible.

But the young man who came to office with an assurance vicariously imparted from reading Richard Neustadt's "Presidential Power" soon discovered the two truths which all dwellers on that lonely eminence have quickly learned.

The first was that the powers of the President are not only limited but hard to bring to bear. The second was that the decisions—as he himself so often said—"are not easy."

QUOTED MORLEY

Since he was never one to hide his feelings, he often betrayed the mood brought on by contemplating the magnitude of the job and its disappointments. He grew fond of quoting Lord Morley's dictum—"Politics is one long second-best, where the choice often lies between two blunders."

Did he have a premonition of tragedy—that he who had set out to temper the contrary violences of our national life would be their victim?

Last June, when the civil rights were at their height and passions were flaring, he spoke to a group of representatives of national organizations. He tolled off the problems that beset him on every side and then to the astonishment of everyone there, suddenly concluded his talk by pulling from his pocket a scrap of paper and reading the famous speech of Blanche of Spain in Shakespeare's "King John":

"The sun's o'ercast with blood: Fair day, adieu.
Which is the side that I must go withal?
I am with both; each army hath a hand,
And in their rage, I having hold of both,
They whirl asunder, and dismember me."

There is, however, consolation in the fact that while he was not given time to finish anything or even to realize his own potentialities, he has not left the Nation in a state of crisis or danger, either in its domestic or foreign affairs.

WORLD MORE TOLERABLE

A reasonable balance of power has been established on all continents. The state of truce in Korea, the Formosa Strait, Vietnam, and Berlin is, if anything, more tolerable than when he came to office.

Europe and Latin America were increasingly dubious of his leadership at the end, but their capacity to indulge in independent courses of action outside the alliance was largely due to the fact that he had managed to reach a somewhat better adjustment of relations with the Soviet Union.

Thus, President Johnson is not confronted immediately by having to take any urgent new decisions. The passage of power from one man to another is more difficult in other countries, and Britain, Germany, Italy, India and several other allies are so preoccupied by that task at the moment that drastic new policy inititatives overseas are scarcely possible in the foreseeable future.

At home, his tasks lie in the Congress, where he is widely regarded as the most skillful man of his generation. This city is in a state of shock tonight and everywhere, including Capitol Hill, men are of a mind to compose their differences and do what they can to help the new President.

Accordingly, the assumption that there will be no major agreements on taxes or civil rights this year will probably have to be revived. It is, of course, too early to tell. But it is typical and perhaps significant that the new President's first act was to greet the congressional leaders of both parties when he arrived in Washington and to meet with them at once in the White House.

Today's events were so tragic and so brutal that even this city, which lives on the brutal diet of politics, could not bear to think much about the political consequences of the assassination.

Yet it is clear that the entire outlook has changed for both parties, and the unexpected death of President Kennedy has forced Washington to meditate a little more on the wild element of chance in our national life.

This was quietly in the back of many minds tonight, mainly because President Johnson has sustained a severe heart attack, and the constitutional line of succession places directly back of him, first Speaker McCormack, and then the President pro tempore of the Senate, 86-year-old Senator Carl Hayden, of Arizona.

Again this note of self-criticism and conscience has touched the Capital. Despite the severe illness of President Eisenhower just a few years ago, nothing was done by the Congress to deal with the problem of Presidential disability.

For an all too brief hour today, it was not clear again what would have happened if the young President, instead of being mortally wounded, had lingered for a long time between life and death, strong enough to survive but too weak to govern.

These, however, were fleeting thoughts, important but irritating for the moment. The center of the mind was on the dead President, on his wife, who has now lost both a son and a husband within a few months, and on his family which, despite all its triumphs, has sustained so many personal tragedies since the last war.

He was, even to his political enemies, a wonderfully attractive human being, and it is significant that, unlike many Presidents in the past, the people who liked and respected him best, were those who knew him the best.

He was a rationalist and an intellectual, who proved in the 1960 campaign and in last year's crisis over Cuba that he was at his best when the going was tough. No doubt he would have been reelected, as most one-term Presidents are, and the subtle dualism of his character would have had a longer chance to realize his dream.

But he is gone now at 46, younger than when most Presidents have started on the great adventure. In his book, "Profiles in Courage," all his heroes faced the hard choice either of giving in to public opinion or of defying it and becoming martyrs.

He had hoped to avoid this bitter dilemma, but he ended as a martyr anyway, and the Nation is sad tonight, both about him and about itself.

There is one final tragedy about today: Kennedy had a sense of history, but he also had an administrative technique that made the gathering of history extremely difficult. He hated organized meetings of the Cabinet or the National Security Council, and therefore he chose to decide policy after private meetings, usually with a single person.

The result of this is that the true history of his administration really cannot be written now that he is gone.

He had a joke about this. When he was asked what he was going to do when he retired, he always replied that he had a problem. It was, he said, that he would have to race two other members of his staff, McGeorge Bundy and Arthur Schlesinger, Jr., to the press.

Unfortunately, however, he was the only man in the White House who really knew what went on there during his administration, and now he is gone.

ADDRESS BY

Hon. Leslie C. Arends

OF ILLINOIS

Mr. Speaker, there are no words by which we can fully express the shock and deep sense of loss felt throughout the world with the assassination of John F. Kennedy—the beloved President of all of us. Even at this hour, as he rests in peace in the national burial ground of our country's fallen warriors for the cause of freedom, we can hardly believe that such a monstrous act would be committed. We keep asking ourselves: Why? Why? For what purpose?

In a brief moment there was taken from us not only the head of a great nation, not only a world leader. There was taken from us a young man whose life was filled with meaning and purpose. There was taken from us a man, endowed by the Maker of all men everywhere, with the rare qualities of intellect and personality that encourage and inspire men everywhere.

He has not lived and died in vain. His words and deeds live after him to encourage and inspire us in our unfinished task.

The untimely death of our President has brought us to an immediate realization of his greatness. It has also brought us to a fuller realization of the greatness of our system of government and our people. In a quiet, somber, orderly manner we have proceeded with the affairs of state under a new President. And this is how our late President would have it.

I extend my personal sympathy to Mrs. Kennedy, the children, and the family.

ADDRESS BY

Hon. Carl Vinson

OF GEORGIA

Mr. Speaker, a little over 3 years ago a young man with spring in his step, determination in his eyes, firmness in his voice, an overwhelming sense of humanity in his heart, and a burning desire to lead the United States of America to even greater heights, spoke at Warm Springs, Ga.

John Fitzgerald Kennedy was seeking the office of the Presidency of the United States. On that day, which I remember so well, he said:

I do not run for the Presidency under any expectation that life will be easy for the next President of the United States or easy for the citizens of the United States.

To be a citizen of this country is to live with great responsibility and great burdens. The United States must be true to itself, it must meet its own responsibility. It must build great strength in this country because it alone defends freedom all around the globe.

The American people listened to this youthful-looking man who possessed the vigor that so characterizes our Nation; they expressed their trust and confidence in John Fitzgerald Kennedy, and they elected him the 35th President of the United States.

In his first appearance before the Congress we can all recall his fateful and prophetic words:

Before my term is ended, we shall have to test anew whether a nation organized and governed such as ours can endure. The outcome is by no means certain. The answers are by no means clear. All of us together—this administration, this Congress, this Nation—must forge those answers.

Eight months later he stood before the United Nations General Assembly to eulogize the late Dag Hammarskjold. He said:

His tragedy is deep in our hearts, but the task for which he died is at the top of our agenda. A noble servant of peace is gone, but the quest for peace lies before us.

These words spoken by President Kennedy are words that describe the greatest goal John Fitzgerald Kennedy sought for this Nation.

Just two months ago he said:

Let us complete what we have started, for as the Scriptures tell us, "no man who puts his hand to the plow and looks back is fit for the kingdom of God."

There is no person in America who denies the sincerity of purpose of John F. Kennedy. No person doubts his dedication to the cause of freedom; his love for his fellowman; his goals for the betterment of America; his understanding of the problems of his fellow citizens; and his objective of a better life for freemen everywhere.

In addressing the Congress in May of 1961, President Kennedy, recognizing the challenge of the future as no man before him, said:

The great battleground for the defense and expansion of freedom today is the whole southern half of the globe—Asia, Latin America, Africa, and the Middle East—the lands of the rising peoples. Their revolution, the greatest in human history, is one of peace and hope, for freedom and equality, for order and independence. They seek an end to injustice, tyranny, and exploitation. More than end, they seek a beginning—a jungle road to bring a doctor when a child is ill—a schoolhouse to unlock the mysteries of knowledge—seed and fertilizer, jobs and food, a chance to live and be more than just alive.

This was the vision of John F. Kennedy for the future of the world. This epitomizes his incomparable sense of humaneness for his fellowman.

John Fitzgerald Kennedy became President of the United States in a time of peril, and soon he faced the challenge of Cuba, the problem of South Vietnam, the tinderbox of India, the wall of Berlin, the ambitions of the Soviet Union, and the poverty of parts of the free world that might have opened their arms to communism in a move of desperation.

He knew that this Nation was the leader of the free world, and was the single focal point for the universal goal of world peace and freedom.

He knew that this goal could not be achieved by a nation that rested on its laurels; he knew that the burden of responsibility placed upon our shoulders by the events of this century required, in fact, demanded, an ever forward moving America.

He knew that our economy had to expand, and he also knew that traditional barriers among nations had to be eliminated.

He was an American, through and through, who responded to the challenge of our time as no man before him.

All of us who knew John F. Kennedy watched him grow in stature, and in leadership, as he assumed the reins of Government and led the Nation in its goal of peace, prosperity, and progress.

The Nation can be grateful that he was permitted to be one of us so that he could leave his imprint—an imprint so indelible and so impressive, that his name now joins that small select group of very great Americans to whom this Nation owes an everlasting debt.

John F. Kennedy is no longer with us; he was cut down by an assassin's bullet; his wisdom; his humanity; his ambition for America; his thoughtfulness; his quiet humor; his dignity; his vigor; his foresight; his leadership are gone. But no one can deny that the good he has done for the Nation, and the world, will live on forever.

No one could look upon the hundreds of thousands of faces that waited to view his bier in the rotunda of the Capitol and question the love and affection which the American people held for him.

He was a man who could stand with kings, but talk and walk with the people of this Nation from every street of life.

The strong and the mighty; the weak, and the unimportant understood him, loved him, respected him, and mourn his death.

Probably no man in the history of the world has ever achieved such universal greatness in such a short period of time.

John F. Kennedy leaves behind a courageous, but sorrowing wife and family. But in her sorrow, Mrs. Kennedy displayed a courage that has inspired every citizen of this Nation. Her grief was shared by millions of people throughout the world. But the manner in which she met the shock of her husband's assassination and the mournful days that followed will be remembered, admired, and respected in the years ahead.

Mrs. Kennedy has become a symbol of courage to which every American can point with pride while sharing, with deep conviction, her sorrow.

John F. Kennedy also leaves behind goals yet unattained, but he has set the course for the Nation for generations yet unborn.

The American people are headed on that course and though there are shoals in the channels of progress in the years ahead, there is no question that we will one day enter the harbor of universal peace and world understanding. When that happens, the master of our destiny in that respect here on this earth will have been John Fitzgerald Kennedy.

ADDRESS BY

Hon. Clarence Cannon

OF MISSOURI

Mr. Speaker, in all our history nothing has so shocked the Nation and the world as the tragic death of our beloved leader.

When the annals of these critical days are written, he will rank as one of the greatest in that long line of distinguished men who have occupied the office of the Presidency down to this or any future time.

But had John F. Kennedy never been President, he still would have been one of the outstanding men of his time.

Every war has produced heroes, and the legendary stories of heroic accomplishments have come down to us from every battlefield. Lieutenant Kennedy's remarkable salvage of every man of his command when survival seemed hopeless, after PT boat No. 109 had been lost by enemy action, is one of the all but incredible achievements of the war. And he carried to the end the disabilities incurred in that historic disaster.

He was a most uncommon man—a man of engaging presence and magnetic personality. It was said of him that he walked like a prince and talked like a scholar. He was indeed a scholarly man. In addition to other notable academic honors, both during and after his undergraduate days, he wrote a book at that early age, "Why England Slept," of such unusual merit that it was in demand throughout Europe and America. His "Profiles in Courage" was awarded the Pulitzer Prize. And, of course, his "Strategy of Peace" is found in every library in America and Western Europe.

Among the leaders of the world, among all the executives of state, kings, presidents, and premiers, who today direct the affairs of nations, he was outstanding, not only in position and prestige and power, but in the realization of great ideals and aspirations in national and international precepts and policies.

The devotion and majestic dignity of Mrs. Kennedy at the most tragic crisis of her life, in the greatest bereavement that could befall her, add luster and laurel to the family and the Nation on this terrible occasion. To her and the children we extend our deepest sympathy. Our hearts go out to them.

But the man who struck him down did even a greater disservice to our form of government. The strength of democracy depends on the acquiescence of those who in a campaign have differed from the verdict of the voting majority. President Kennedy, above all others was a notable example in that respect. When at the Chicago Convention in 1956 he lost by the narrowest possible margin—it could not have been closer—the nomination for the Vice Presidency of the United States, he accepted it smilingly, without evidence of regret or disappointment, and cooperated in that campaign as heartily as if he had himself been on the ticket.

This untoward act of force and violence has served to disturb the long-established custom by which, after every election, however bitterly contested, we conform and concur, regardless of any previous convictions we may have had or statements we may have made, in the decision of the majority. This is the soul and essence of democracy and democratic government.

It is a relief to know that this unspeakable crime was the individual act of one twisted and disordered mind and that no party or faction or group or organization prompted or promoted it. It was insanity. It was not American.

The Nation still lives. And he still lives—in the hearts and memory of the people—in the enhanced stability of the Government to which in his brief administration he gave such added impetus, and for which he died.

It is for us who are left behind to close ranks, to present a united front and "to continue," as he admonished, in the development and achievement of loyal and patriotic citizenship.

He died as he would have preferred to die—in the press of strenuous events—in the harness and with his face to the front—on the crest of recovery from threatened recession—and in the hour of his greatest fame and acclaim.

ADDRESS BY

Hon. Torbert H. Macdonald

OF MASSACHUSETTS

Mr. Speaker, I rise to join with my colleagues of the House in paying our small tribute to President John F. Kennedy. I know that other speakers will extoll President Kennedy's great leadership, his eminence in our chosen field and his well deserved stature as a world figure, indeed his position as the world's most powerful man. Since I know that his place in history has been so solidly carved out that he will join that historical group of legendary leaders of our country, I will not dwell on that aspect of his life. I do know that my generation has lost its leader and his like will not be seen again in our day.

I would, therefore, like to pay tribute not to President Kennedy, but to Jack Kennedy, the man. I have known Jack Kennedy intimately for over 28 years. As my college roommate, war companion, as an usher at his wedding, as a godfather to my oldest son, as one who sat with him in Los Angeles at the news of his selection as our party's leader, and as one who walked that terrible distance from the White House to St. Matthew's Church, and as a total and complete friend, I think that I am somewhat qualified to discuss the sort of a man that our President was. I have seen him grow and mature physically, mentally, and morally. I have been blessed by a sharing of his joyous moments, his sorrows, his triumphs, his hard times and through a melding of all these, I have come to know and understand the best person I have ever known. Many people now just remember Jack Kennedy at the pinnacle, but I can remember the hard, difficult, arduous and sometimes tragic road that took him to that pinnacle. I have shared with him the grievous loss of members of his beloved family, Joseph Patrick Kennedy, Jr., his equally beloved sister, Kathleen, the loss of his youngest son and have seen out of these experiences the forging of a man of indomitable strength, will-power, and serenity.

I suppose I am now engaged in a matter of which Jack Kennedy would not approve, namely, publicly displaying emotion and an expression of love, which is so closely felt and held in my heart. His was a nature that was so hardily forged that he would not, and perhaps could not, reveal to the world the depth, warmth and serenity of his emotions. For Jack Kennedy was, among other things, a Spartan, even though he was Irish to the core. The pain of body which he knew and endured so well was never reflected in any of his words. But I believe that his insight into the needs and hurtful emotional pains of other people had been woven into his fiber from the cruel experiences he suffered, both during World War II and at the time of his excruciatingly painful back trouble and operation. The concealing of his emotions was not a purposeful thing, but an ultimate expression of his belief in the rationality of life. He understood better than most of us that with good, some bad always follows, and that pleasure often is the companion of pain. I know it was the pleasure of many of you to have served either with or under Jack Kennedy and I know that pleasure is one of the chief reasons for the terrible pain that many of us feel on this melancholy day.

I am very proud that Jack is the godfather of my oldest boy, one of the newest generation, for I feel confident that Jack's life, his dedication to the principles in which he so firmly believed, by which he lived and, perhaps, for which he died, will be a challenging inspiration for those of the generation to follow us. A devoted husband, father, son and brother, his love was returned doubly by those he loved and I am sure it must be of some solace to all his family to know that we and the Nation mourn him so deeply and so personally. Their loss is our loss, our loss is the country's loss. Life will, of course, go on, but life will never be the same for me or for many millions of our people. It always seemed to me that being President was just one of the things that Jack Kennedy could have done. The qualities that distinguished this man from all others, the grace, the brilliance, the fortitude, the understanding and compassion which he brought to this high office, would have made him a brilliant man in any field he chose. But his qualities will not be forgotten, nor will they, in my judgment, ever be duplicated again.

In the same way that the eternal light shines from the ground near his grave, in the same way will life and the love which he kindled in our hearts and minds glow on forever. As is said in our shared religion, may he rest in peace, may perpetual light shine upon him, and may God have mercy on his soul.

ADDRESS BY

Hon. F. Bradford Morse

OF MASSACHUSETTS

Mr. Speaker, it is not given to every generation to have a political leader of the quality of John F. Kennedy. For those of us who knew his firm handshake, his ready smile, his keen wit and his youthful wisdom as he campaigned across the Commonwealth of Massachusetts the loss is particularly acute. He was a loyal friend, an honest and honorable opponent and a dedicated public servant.

John F. Kennedy had an ability to stand outside himself and survey the sweep of American history. He knew how to build upon the greatness of the past and how to profit from the errors of those who came before. He was able to operate within the realities of today without losing sight of the vision of tomorrow. But perhaps most important of all he truly understood the 20th century. He spoke of a new generation of Americans "born in this century, tempered by war, disciplined by a hard and bitter peace, proud of our ancient heritage, and unwilling to witness or permit the slow undoing of those human rights to which this Nation has always been committed, and to which we are committed today." This new generation was not to be defined in terms of age but in terms of an understanding of the inexorable development of human events.

Western civilization has faced its most severe challenges in this century. The best of its virtues is reflected in the drive for independence by the emerging nations of the world; the worst of its vices in World War II. President Kennedy understood the modern world. Although he recognized the challenge to freedom posed by the Soviet bloc, he also knew that there must be room for diversity in a world so vulnerable to annihilation. He knew that we can defend freedom without sacrificing internal liberty or world peace, and that we must serve the cause of democracy at home before we can represent it abroad.

We who stand in the House today to pay tribute to our fallen President cannot help but reflect on the mortality of man, the continuity of nations, and the responsibility of public service. We cannot put aside our grief and return to our usual tasks—our tasks are his and they are those of the Nation. We cannot achieve the goals of equality, justice, and peace solely by the way we live as private individuals—we are charged with the attainment of the supreme goals of a great nation.

There are no words to express our grief—each of us has sustained a loss which cannot be expressed here, or in any other place, except in our own hearts. We can best honor John F. Kennedy by dedicating ourselves to the pursuit of excellence: to the nobility of ideal, majesty of purpose, and to the highest standard of integrity in public service.

We are bereaved, but not bereft. For it is in our power to help achieve the high ideals of this Republic—by the way we conduct ourselves in this Chamber.

To Mrs. Kennedy and his children we extend our deepest sympathy, our admiration for their courage and strength in the face of tragedy and our pledge to work in peace for the attainment of the high aims of the American experiment in which John F. Kennedy believed, and for which he gave his life.

ADDRESS BY

Hon. Edward P. Boland

OF MASSACHUSETTS

Mr. Speaker, I am pleased that our friend and colleague, the gentleman from Massachusetts, Congressman Macdonald, was recognized to lead off the tributes of the Massachusetts delegation to our late, beloved President John Fitzgerald Kennedy.

No one in this House knew President Kennedy better than the gentleman from Massachusetts, Congressman Macdonald. No one could have offered a more personal and moving testimonial.

Mr. Speaker, John Fitzgerald Kennedy was my friend as well as my leader. I traveled with him to many places in this country and to some nations across the Atlantic Ocean. I was privileged to share with him private moments of relaxation and reflection, as well as public occasions of controversy and triumph.

He was a friend to the people of my district long before he became President. They knew him as their Senator and advocate who had shaken their hands, attended their functions, worshiped with them and always listened sympathetically to their problems.

Our personal loss is great, but it is insignificant compared to what the Nation and the world lost when this dynamic life was cut short, so soon, by so brutal an act.

John F. Kennedy did not shrink from the burdens of the Presidency. He welcomed them as an opportunity to make America mean more to its people and to the world. The programs he advocated for education, medical care, civil rights, and economic strength will be an inspiration until the day they become law and a source of strength to the country from then on. The Peace Corps, the Alliance for Progress, the nuclear test ban—all of which he originated and fought for—have alined our Nation with the hopes and aspirations of people throughout the globe.

Mr. Speaker, America lived under the leadership of John F. Kennedy for only 2 years, 10 months, and 2 days. It was not a long period, as time is measured, but it will shine out in the history of our Republic as long as men have the capacity to admire courage, to desire progress, and to perceive greatness.

Mr. Speaker, I cherished John F. Kennedy in intimate affection. I honored him as a political associate and ally. I took pride in him as a glorious contribution of my great Commonwealth, Massachusetts, to the Nation. I deeply mourn the loss of my friend. I bewail the loss of his magnificent abilities to the public life of America. But my heart, heavy as it is, rejoices in the fact that Massachusetts has been privileged to contribute such a hero to the United States. His patriotism embraced every inch of American soil and every single American citizen. His loyalty was not limited to the land and people of Massachusetts, nor to those who shared the Irish origins in which he took a just and honorable pride. He loved his country with a deep and abiding passion and constantly his great talents, his keen intellect, his persuasive voice, and his physical strength were all used to the fullest to make our Nation and the world a better place in which to live.

Mr. Speaker, I join in paying tribute to Jacqueline Kennedy. At no time within the memory of man has such a burden of grief blanketed a wife and mother. And never has anyone stood so erect, so majestic in such anguished hours. She has set an example and inspiration that can never be surpassed.

Mr. Speaker, the entire Kennedy family has given this Nation an example of devotion, dedication, and decency. Our Nation is the richer for it.

Finally, Mr. Speaker, I express to this House the gratitude of the Commonwealth of Massachusetts for the moving and magnificent expressions that have echoed this Chamber today—and the days of the past 2 weeks. The people of Massachusetts are grateful for the honors and tributes that the world, this Nation, and this city have heaped upon its most famous and most beloved son.

Mr. Speaker, I ask permission to include at this point one of John Fitzgerald Kennedy's greatest state papers—his inaugural address. I further ask that a communication of John Kenneth Galbraith be included. It is one of the finest pieces on President Kennedy and penned by one who knew him intimately and under varying circumstances.

The Inaugural Address

Vice President Johnson, Mr. Chief Justice, President Eisenhower, Vice President Nixon, President Truman, reverend clergy, fellow citizens:

We observe today not a victory of a party but a celebration of freedom—symbolizing an end as well as a beginning—signifying renewal as well as change. For I have sworn before you and Almighty God the same solemn oath our forebears prescribed nearly a century and three quarters ago.

The world is very different now. For man holds in his mortal hands the power to abolish all forms of human poverty and all forms of human life. And yet the same revolutionary beliefs for which our forebears fought are still at issue around the globe—the belief that the rights of man come not from the generosity of the state but from the hand of God.

We dare not forget today that we are the heirs of that first Revolution. Let the word go forth from this time and place, to friend and foe alike, that the torch has been passed to a new generation of Americans—born in this century, tempered by war, disciplined by a hard and bitter peace, proud of our ancient heritage—and unwilling to witness or permit the slow undoing of those human rights to which this Nation has always been committed, and to which we are committed today at home and around the world.

Let every nation know, whether it wishes us well or ill, that we shall pay any price, bear any burden, meet any hardship, support any friend, oppose any foe to assure the survival and success of liberty.

This much we pledge—and more.

To those old allies whose cultural and spiritual origins we share, we pledge the loyalty of faithful friends. United, there is little we cannot do in a host of cooperative ventures. Divided, there is little we can do—for we dare not meet a powerful challenge at odds and split asunder.

To those new states whom we welcome to the ranks of the free, we pledge our word that one form of colonial control shall not have passed away merely to be replaced by a far more iron tyranny. We shall not always expect to find them supporting our view. But we shall always hope to find them strongly supporting their own freedom—and to remember that, in the past, those who foolishly sought power by riding the back of the tiger ended up inside.

To those people in the huts and villages of half the globe struggling to break the bonds of mass misery, we pledge our best efforts to help them help themselves, for whatever period is required, not because the Communists may be doing it, not because we seek their votes, but because it is right. If a free society cannot help the many who are poor, it cannot save the few who are rich.

To our sister Republics south of our border, we offer a special pledge—to convert our good words into good deeds, in a new alliance for progress, to assist freemen and free governments in casting off the chains of poverty. But this peaceful revolution of hope cannot become the prey of hostile powers. Let all our neighbors know that we shall join with them to oppose aggression or subversion anywhere in the Americas. And let every other power know that this hemisphere intends to remain the master of its own house.

To that world assembly of sovereign states, the United Nations, our last best hope in an age where the instruments of war have far outpaced the instruments of peace, we renew our pledge of support, to prevent it from becoming merely a forum for invective; to strengthen its shield of the new and the weak, and to enlarge the area in which its writ may run.

Finally, to those nations who would make themselves our adversary, we offer not a pledge but a request; that both sides begin anew the quest for peace, before the dark powers of destruction unleashed by science engulf all humanity in planned or accidental self-destruction.

We dare not tempt them with weakness. For only when our arms are sufficient beyond doubt can we be certain beyond doubt that they will never be employed.

But neither can two great and powerful groups of nations take comfort from our present course, both sides overburdened by the cost of modern weapons, both rightly alarmed by the steady spread of the deadly atom, yet both racing to alter that uncertain balance of terror that stays the hand of mankind's final war.

So let us begin anew, remembering on both sides that civility is not a sign of weakness, and sincerity is always subject to proof. Let us never negotiate out of fear. But let us never fear to negotiate.

Let both sides explore what problems unite us instead of belaboring those problems which divide us. Let both sides, for the first time, formulate serious and precise proposals for the inspection and control of arms, and bring the absolute power to destroy other nations under the absolute control of all nations.

Let both sides seek to invoke the wonders of science instead of its terrors. Together let us explore the stars, conquer the deserts, eradicate disease, tap the ocean depths, and encourage the arts and commerce.

Let both sides unite to heed in all corners of the earth the command of Isaiah—to "undo the heavy burdens (and) let the oppressed go free."

And if a beachhead of cooperation may push back the jungle of suspicion, let both sides join in a new endeavor: creating not a new balance of power, but a new world of law, where the strong are just and the weak secure and the peace preserved.

All this will not be finished in the first 100 days. Nor will be it be finished in the first 1,000 days, nor in the life of this administration, nor even perhaps in our lifetime on this planet. But let us begin.

In your hands, my fellow citizens, more than mine, will rest the final success or failure of our course. Since this country was founded, each generation of Americans has been summoned to give testimony to its national loyalty. The graves of young Americans who answered the call to service surround the globe.

Now the trumpet summons us again—not as a call to bear arms, though arms we need—not as a call to battle, though embattled we are—but a call to bear the burden of a long twilight struggle, year in and year out, "rejoicing in hope, patient in tribulation"—a struggle against the common enemies of man: tyranny, poverty, disease, and war itself.

Can we forge against these enemies a grand and global alliance, north and south, east and west, that can assure a more fruitful life for all mankind? Will you join in that historic effort?

In the long history of the world, only a few generations have been granted the role of defending freedom in its hour of maximum danger. I do not shrink from this responsibility—I welcome it. I do not believe that any of us would exchange places with any other people or any other generation. The energy, the faith, the devotion which we bring to this endeavor will light our country and all who serve it—and the glow from that fire can truly light the world.

And so, my fellow Americans: Ask not what your country can do for you—ask what you can do for your country.

My fellow citizens of the world: Ask not what America will do for you, but what together we can do for the freedom of man.

Finally, whether you are citizens of America or citizens of the world, ask of us here the same high standards of strength and sacrifice which we ask of you. With a good conscience our only sure reward, with history the final judge of our deeds, let us go forth to lead the land we love, asking His blessing and His help, but knowing that here on earth God's work must truly be our own.

———

[From the Washington (D.C.) Post, Nov. 25, 1963]

A COMMUNICATION

(By John Kenneth Galbraith, professor of economics at Harvard University and former Ambassador to India)

In these last few hours hundreds, thousands of men have tried to write about John F. Kennedy. This is not wholly a ritual of the modern newspaper, one of the final rites of the great. Millions of people on this dark and sombre weekend want to read of, and then to reflect, on this man who was so profoundly a part of their lives. This wish the papers are seeking to serve.

My justification for this brief word is not that of a

friend but of a writer who knew the President a trifle better than most of those who must tell of him in these days.

No one knew the President well. In a sense no one could for it is part of the character of a leader that he cannot be known. The rest of us can indulge our moments when we open the shutters to our soul. We are granted also our moments of despair—the despair, indeed, that we felt on Friday when that incredible flash came in from Dallas. But a Kennedy or a Roosevelt can never turn the palms of his hands outward to the world and say: "Oh God. What do we do now?" That armor which insures confidence in power and certainty in command may never be removed even for a moment. No one ever knew John F. Kennedy as other men are known.

But he carried his armor lightly and with grace and, one sometimes thought, with the knowledge that having it without escape, at least it need not be a barrier before his friends and associates. He surprised even friends with the easy candor with which he spoke of touchy problems, half-formed plans, or personal political dangers. Without malice or pettiness he contemplated the strengths and weaknesses of high officials and influential politicians. He was constantly and richly amused by the vanities of men in high places. He freely discussed ideas the mention of which would make most men shudder. Last summer during the visit of President Sarvepalli Radhakrishnan of India, in a social moment before a formal dinner, mention was made of some woman politician. He turned and asked me why there had been so few women politicians of importance—whether women were poorly adapted to the political art. Here surely was a politically ticklish subject; women are half the voting population and might not react well to wonder at their political shortcomings. I struggled to come up with examples—the first Elizabeth, Mrs. F.D.R., one or two others. The President admitted the exceptions but good humoredly returned to the rule. He knew he could discuss an interesting point without anyone proceeding to argue that he was against the 19th amendment.

"The political campaign won't tire me," he said in the spring of 1960, "for I have an advantage. I can be myself." He had learned one of the hardest lessons of life which is that we all have far more liberty than we use. And he knew beyond this, that others because they admired it would respect the informality with which he passed through life. No President ever said so much to so many friends and acquaintances and so rarely had to disavow or explain.

John F. Kennedy was much interested in writing. This, I think, provides one small clue to understanding. Good writing requires a sense of economy and of style and the absence of vanity which allows a man to divorce his writing at least a little from himself. A writer can be interesting when he is speaking to others; he is rarely if ever interesting, when he is speaking to himself except to himself.

Mr. Kennedy hated verbosity. Though he rejoiced in politics he hated the wordiness of the political craft. He never, at least in his adult life, opened his mouth without having something to say. Never even in conversation did he speak for the pleasure of hearing his own words and

phrases. Many of us have a diminished interest in the words of others. Mr. Kennedy was the rare case of the man who applied the rules with equal rigor against himself.

The Kennedy style, though it involved detachment from self, involved no self-deprecation. In the early years when he was enlisting followers, he did not offer a program for universal salvation. He was suspicious of all resonant formulas from whatever source—he rightly regarded some of the liturgy of American liberalism as corrupt. It is trundled out at election time as once were the candidate's trains, urged in a torrent of words and then put away for 4 years. His case again had the merit of candor. He said, essentially, I am a man worth following, you can count on me to be honestly better at the art of government than any other possible contender, and, an important detail, I know how to get elected.

That he was qualified in the art of government there will never be any question. His style called for unremitting good taste and good manners. It called also for a profound commitment to information and reason. He did not think that man had been civilized as an afterthought; he believed it was for a purpose. Perhaps there are natural men, those who have the original gift of art and insight. Mr. Kennedy without being so rude as to say so would believe such pretension to be an excuse for laziness. His reliance was on what men had learned and had come to know. What Mr. Kennedy had come to know about the art and substance of American Government was prodigious. I first knew Jack Kennedy 25 years ago when I was a comparatively young tutor and he was an undergraduate in Winthrop House at Harvard. He was gay, charming, irreverent, good-looking and far from diligent. What no one knew at the time was that he had the priceless notion that education never stops. Some of us who later worked with him on economic issues—farm policy, interest rates, Federal Reserve policy, the control of inflation, other arcane or technical matters—used to say that we had observed three stages in his career in the House and more particularly in the Senate: The first was when he called up to ask how we thought he should vote; the second was when he telephoned to ask 15 or 20 quick questions as to what lay behind the particular action or measure; the third was when he did not call at all or inquired as to why, as he had gleaned from an article or a letter to the Times, we seemed to be acting on some misinformation. My colleague, Prof. Carl Kaysen, who has worked in the White House these last years, has said that when asked who is the most knowledgeable of the President's advisers he always felt obliged to remind his questioner that none was half so well-informed as the President himself.

Mr. Kennedy knew that knowledge was power; no one, of course, will ever imagine that this was his sole reliance. Knowledge without character is worthless—or worse.

Departments and individuals, in approaching the President, invariably emphasize the matters which impress them most. Mr. Kennedy knew how to make the appropriate discounts without anyone quite realizing they were being made. He had a natural sense for all of the variables in a problem; he would not be carried away by anyone.

Like all men of deep intelligence, he respected the intelligence of others. That was why he did not talk down to the American people; it was why he was contemptuous of the arm-waving circus posturing of the American politician which so many American newspapermen so much admire right up to the moment of final defeat.

The President faced a speaker with his wide gray-blue eyes and total concentration. So also a paper or an article. And, so far as one could tell, once it was his it was his forever. This, of course, was not all.

Knowledge is power. But knowledge without character and wisdom is nothing, or worse. These the President also had, and also the highly practical capacity to see when part of an argument, being advanced by a department, bureau, or zealot, was being presented as the whole. But I come back to the group of issues, the breadth of information and the power of concentration. Perhaps these come naturally. I suspect, in fact, that few men in history have ever combined natural ability with such powers of mental self-discipline.

ADDRESS BY

Hon. Silvio O. Conte

OF MASSACHUSETTS

Mr. Speaker, as we meet here today to pay tribute to the memory of John Fitzgerald Kennedy, we pay tribute to a continuing force among us. For the finest thing that we can say about the late President is that, in a very genuine sense, he is with us here today on the floor of the House where his admirable career had its beginning and where he gave his state of the Union addresses.

These addresses, Mr. Speaker, were model surveys of plans, programs, and policies of a vigorous young man who lived actively the life of the mind and one who attempted to fuse the ideal with the real into programs that were part and parcel of the great American tradition. Few people agreed with all of his ideas, but many people were to agree with most of them.

It will be the place of history to record how successful his brief tenure as Chief Executive of our land was and how meaningful many of his programs will become with the passage of time.

We can already say with certainty, for example, that the dream of the Peace Corps has become a reality. We do not know, on the other hand, whether the Alliance for Progress will develop into the kind of a program and demonstrate the great potential that it has. And on and on—these and other judgments will be made by the ultimately objective hand of history.

We can remember him now as one who believed in the career of politics and equated the word "politics" with good government.

This was true of the young John Kennedy at Choate and later at Harvard, and during his graduate work at the London School of Economics. Soon after his commendable career in the U.S. Navy, he was to go into the rough and tumble politics of the Boston area, an area that has been called an advanced school of political science.

The young man obviously was a man of destiny, and his election to this body from the 11th Congressional District in Massachusetts was the beginning of one of the distinguished careers in the history of American public life.

Few of us would have thought that such an amazing career would have been possible, but John Kennedy demonstrated that it was. And we can remember him with a great deal of pride for innumerable things and incidents.

It seems incredible to me that just a short while ago I had a wide-ranging discussion with him during the ground-breaking ceremonies for the Robert Frost Library at Amherst College in Massachusetts. He had come there to pay tribute to the poet whom he loved, and after the ceremony, we talked about legislation and he expressed intimate detail of issues which confronted the Nation, issues which were, in a real sense, his own plans for the extension of American social progress and progress around the world—the free world in which he had become the indisputed leader.

All of us have our own private prayer for the late President and for the surviving members of his family.

As a recent issue of Commonweal magazine so profoundly stated:

The loss of a President is more than the loss of its most important officeholder and the symbol of its law and order, as stunning as that is in itself. It is also the loss of a man—in this case—with a peculiarly apt set of talents and convictions for our time.

The editorial goes on to state, quite basically, that he was a man of our time, who understood the problems of our time. While we may have had different interpretations of how certain policies could have been executed, he stood squarely in line with those whose view of the world was broad, and not narrow.

It was one of peace, and not hate. It was also one of hope, and in summing up, I would like to quote from a statement made by Mark Van Doren, in Cornwall, Conn., just over the borders of the Berkshires where John Kennedy loved to visit.

Mark Van Doren, the distinguished poet and writer, said, at the conclusion of his public statement:

> The oneness of the world is what we are now feeling; and fearing, if we doubt that it can soon enough be good, at least within the limits of mankind's capacity.
>
> But there are fears and fears, noble and ignoble; and the noblest fear is that which each of us can have lest he himself fall short of being as sensible, as reasonable, as steadfast, and as loving as he can. It is not for others to be these things to the limit of possibility. It is for ourselves, each one of us, whoever, whatever, and wherever he may be.
>
> Goodness—

Van Doren said, and we all must agree—

> begins at home. If it is not there, it may be nowhere. The clearest sign that it is there, the unmistakable sign, is our fear that we ourselves have not been all that we could be. This is a noble fear, another name for which, when hope and faith come with it, is humility. Hope and faith, and not despair, upon which fear can feed until it fills the world. Hope and faith, the final cure of fear; along with knowledge—all of which we can possess—and charity: the rarest, the most difficult, and still therefore the greatest of these.

My deepest sympathies go out to the wife and family of the late John Fitzgerald Kennedy.

ADDRESS BY

Hon. Joseph W. Martin, Jr.

OF MASSACHUSETTS

Mr. Speaker, several days have elapsed since the tragic assassination of our late President, John Fitzgerald Kennedy, yet it still seems impossible to believe that death has taken from us one of the great leaders of our time.

Jack Kennedy was a young and vital man. I have known two generations of his family be-

fore him and watched him grow to manhood in my home State of Massachusetts.

His maternal grandfather, John F. Fitzgerald, was once mayor of Boston, and I knew him well. His father, Joseph P. Kennedy, is known to all of us for his contributions to the public service. When I served as Speaker of the House in 1953, I had the honor to appoint him to the Hoover Commission. The Fitzgerald and Kennedy families have lived and loved politics for many generations.

Our late President was introduced to public service in the House of Representatives at the statehouse in Boston. When he returned from naval service after World War II, he visited our House Chamber with his Grandfather Fitzgerald. And State Senator Leslie B. Cutler from my district escorted him to the rostrum for an introduction. There began a remarkable career— Congressman, U.S. Senator, President.

In 1946, as Speaker, I was privileged to administer the oath of office to two youthful Congressmen, President Kennedy and Richard Nixon.

Although the late President and I were faithful to different political parties, we shared a common love of Massachusetts and our country. We worked together for many programs we believed to be for the common good.

The world and all of us will miss his dynamic leadership, his ability to keep his eye on great goals, his genius at keeping the peace in troubled times, his dedication to equal rights for all Americans.

Massachusetts had a special love for this man. His support transcended party lines. His remarkable wife and his fine children deserve our heartfelt grief.

But the best expression of our sorrow is renewed dedication to the goals of his eventful life. The eternal flame that now glows on the hillside in Arlington must not only be a glimmer of physical warmth, but a beacon of hope to a world locked in the throes of change.

His name will be remembered by future generations because it has been affixed now to our launching site in Florida. It must be remembered also for the great contributions that the late President and his wife have made to cultural activities and the fine arts. I had the privilege of joining this week in filing legislation to name our National Cultural Center in his honor.

This Kennedy Center will be an appropriate memorial. Future generations that visit Washington will not only remember the vigor with which this young man pursued political goals, but they will remember now that Robert Frost read poetry at his inauguration, that artists and writers were his close friends and frequent visitors at the White House, that the White House itself was transformed into a place of beauty and artistic achievement during his residency there.

He was ever a strong champion for the improvement of arts, science, and our cultural life.

Mr. Speaker, I wish to record my sorrow at his passing and my deep sympathy for his family in their bereavement.

ADDRESS BY

Hon. James A. Burke

OF MASSACHUSETTS

Mr. Speaker, on Friday, November 22, 1963, the assassination of President John Fitzgerald Kennedy brought shock and grief to both great and humble people throughout the world.

The Commonwealth of Massachusetts, of which I am honored to be a native, and Representative from, lost a son in whom its pride had constantly increased. From that day in 1943, during the Second World War when a young Navy lieutenant commanding a PT boat performed a heroic rescue, until that unhappy day when his life was extinguished, the Nation was nobly served by John Fitzgerald Kennedy. In 1946, at the age of 29, he was elected a Representative from Massachusetts to the U.S. Congress. After serving three successful terms in the House of Representatives, he was elected, in 1952, to the U.S. Senate. In the short span of 8 years he was elevated to the country's highest position, and became the 35th President of the United States.

The entire Nation lost a leader, who was in the midst of his task of exploring new frontiers and fulfilling his pledges to carry America forward. Under the leadership of President Kennedy, new force was given to the search for ways to expand an economy which had already outdistanced any other system in providing high living standards for its peoples. New recognition was brought to certain national problems which had received relatively little attention, such as the problem of mental retardation. Most important, new progress was made in conquering the greatest single domestic problem of the United States, the problem of insuring equal opportunity for all. Such problems as these, many of which had long been the subject of despair, received vigorous thrusts forward toward solution under the administration of President Kennedy. Now there is a void in the hearts of people throughout the land because this beloved man, who had accomplished so much, and who held the promise of accomplishing still more, is gone. As much as any one man could be, he was the indispensable man of our times.

The sadness and mourning at the death of President Kennedy is not confined to the United States, as the free world has lost a chief proponent of its goal of liberty for all. Under his leadership the determination to defend freedom from every threat, the determination to maintain the strength necessary to defend freedom was proved at many outposts around the world and decisively in Cuba. Freedom was also given an unforgettable push forward by President Kennedy when he implemented such programs as the Alliance for Progress, designed to correct some of the basic conditions which have been inimical to freedom. Now, there is aching in the hearts of freedom-loving people throughout the world because this distinguished leader is gone.

President Kennedy's energy, dedication, and sacrifice for his country will long be remembered as a glowing tribute to what one man so young, so vital and so rich in spirit could accomplish in the short time that he was allowed to be our Chief Executive.

We, who knew him closely, will always remember him for his championship of equal rights, wisdom, warm humor, high judgment and deep love for his country and people.

ADDRESS BY

Hon. Philip J. Philbin

OF MASSACHUSETTS

Mr. Speaker, the tragic death of President John F. Kennedy has brought unspeakable shock and deepest grief to people all over the world and it is with heavy heart that I join my colleagues in the House today in this solemn ceremony to mark the life, works, service and principles of a very great American whom I was privileged to call my friend for many years, going back to his service in the House after World War II, his distinguished service as U.S. Senator from Massachusetts and later as President and world leader.

The focal point of the sad events of the weekend before last was centered here in this majestic Capitol where the President's body lay in state. The unprecedented funeral ceremonies were thronged by the largest crowds in the history of our Capital City and in the rotunda on Sunday night, I saw vividly the great and silent grief of thousands upon thousands who came to pass by his bier.

That night to make the short trip from the rotunda to my hotel, it was necessary for me to travel in the opposite direction almost to the District of Columbia Stadium, almost 25 or 30 blocks from the Capitol, before I could find a detour that would bring me to my destination.

Along the streets the people were massed four and five deep in a long winding trail of 3 or more miles in a long wait that would take them the whole night through in bitter cold before they could pass in review in a matter of a few seconds in a last personal tribute to their fallen leader.

Washington has never seen anything like this, nor will it see anything like it again. The magic of television could not capture this great silent mass of solemn people, thousands upon thousands in number, waiting the night for this last mark of respect and devotion to a great American. This had to be seen and, of all the stirring and moving events of those sad days, I have impressed upon my memory the vast sorrowful multitude waiting silently in the night to pay their last respects to our beloved President.

I was among those Members of the House designated by the gentleman from Massachusetts, Speaker John W. McCormack, to represent this body at the solemn funeral services at St. Matthew's Cathedral, which was thronged with the heads of state and distinguished leaders from the great powers of the world, high Federal and State officials and close friends of the President. As elsewhere in the Nation, a cloud of sorrow hung over the many mourners, great and little, and it was clear that all Americans had been stunned, shocked, and moved by deepest sorrow into a personal, collective grief.

Thus, a great Nation mourned its stricken leader and a sorrowing people openly expressed its profound bereavement as the Nation and the world paid an unforgettable tribute to a great leader who had left an indelible impress upon history.

The inspiration of President Kennedy's courageous, stirring leadership will live through the years to strengthen and sustain our great Nation and time will enrich the greatness of this outstanding American, who shall always be remembered for his vision, his courage and his dedication to freedom, peace, and the cause of humanity.

It seems but yesterday that he was sitting here with us, an esteemed colleague and dear comrade. We saw him—vital and dynamic, touched by the spark of destiny, moving inexorably to greatness, to the other body and to the White House.

Just a few days ago, we saw and talked with him as he conducted the great office of President, honored leader of our great Nation, recognized everywhere as the most articulate spokesman and courageous leader of the free world.

How impressive was his magnetic personality, how appealing his alert mind; how appreciated the lightning of his ready wit; how admired his lofty ideals, his intrepid courage, the sweep of his altruism and concern for all those unable to speak for themselves; how inspiring his battle for social justice, for equality of right and opportunity, for the cause of the poor and the oppressed, his determined struggle for peace and order and a world organized on the rule of law, his firm resolve to preserve the integrity and security of our Nation and the free world, to uphold the basic moral and ethical principles of the American way of life and Western civilization in the God-fearing values and traditions of our forebears and our Constitution.

Now he is gone, though we who loved him and the whole world that hailed him hardly can believe or accept it. He is gone—gone to that land "from whose bourn no traveler returns" to the heavenly reward of eternal life with his Creator.

No longer will the smiling, handsome face of this revered Galahad of the 20th century appear before us in real life. No longer will his confident voice and stirring, noble words move and inspire us in the struggle for human betterment and peace. No longer will his message of hope, faith, and aspirations for suffering humanity be publicly expressed to bring solace and renewed devotion to the cause of freedom and justice for all.

But his spirit lives on in human hearts, in our hearts. It will never die. More vibrant in death than in life, it will be the rallying call for the forces of enlightenment and progress, the light of reason and advancement, delivering men and women from the shackles of ignorance, fear, and doubt, and guiding humankind to new pathways of understanding, cooperation and brotherhood under the fatherhood of God.

The name and contributions of John Fitzgerald Kennedy will go down the long, unbroken channels of history like a great, gleaming beacon light casting its warming light of toleration and justice over the Nation and the world and showing us, and unnumbered generations yet to come, the way to plenty, prosperity, amity and peace.

Out of the pathos and sorrow of this sad hour, out of the inutterable personal grief we who were his friends so poignantly feel, out of the disbelief of the world that this great shining standard bearer of lofty human causes has gone from us, let us all lift up our hearts in faith and submission to the will of our Divine Master.

Let us pray for our great, good and dear friend and his bereaved wife and family. To them, suffering as they are under the heavy burden of personal sorrow and irreparable loss, let our deepest and most heartfelt sympathy go out to all members of this afflicted family—his devoted wife who has borne her grief with dignity and majesty; the young daughter and son, yet unaware of the true measure of their loss; his great, distinguished father and devoted, loving mother sorrowing for the son who brought the immortality of history

to their name; his esteemed, distinguished brothers, his able partners in his memorable tasks; his gracious, beloved sisters who were also proud, valuable members of his team, and all members of his family whose loss is so shocking and so profound.

Let us join as a proud, united and dedicated band of believers and achievers in carrying forward the torch of inspiration which has fallen to us from his failing hand.

Let us go forward for his great cause—for justice, for freedom and peace for our own Nation and the world. Thus we can best honor the blessed memory of the great John F. Kennedy.

In the touching words of the contemporary Massachusetts poet, Mr. Anthony Cama:

How splendid glows his torch; how haloed is his cross.
He is not gone. He is with us to stay.
He is the dream of battles faith has won.

His indomitable spirit, lofty ideals and great achievements will aways be with us, our country and the world.

Mr. Speaker, my heart is sorrowful with deepest grief for the loss of a dear friend and honored leader.

May the good Lord, whose understanding and love consoles and strengthens us, bring him rest, peace and happiness in his eternal home.

ADDRESS BY

Hon. Thomas P. O'Neill, Jr.

OF MASSACHUSETTS

Mr. Speaker, it is with diffidence that I rise at this time. Words are certainly meaningless tools of expression when one tries to fumble for the proper phrase to convey deep sentiment. What can one do at a time like this except to pray for the assistance of the Lord for the soul of John F. Kennedy and pray for the strengthening of our country, and offer prayers that will bring solace to the members of the bereaved Kennedy family.

Like all of you, I mourn the passing of a dear friend, a friend whom I have known since the first day he entered into the public life of this Nation.

It is less than 2 weeks ago that this great Nation of ours was rent by remorse and silence. In the deltas and the cane breaks, in the prairies of the West. In the tenements of the East, the Nation was shocked and silenced.

To be with silence is to be with God—for in the hearts and minds and on the lips of men there were fervent prayers for the soul of our departed President.

Yet during these trying hours, I cannot help but think of the words of the poet, Robert Frost, a great favorite of our President John F. Kennedy. Robert Frost on his 80th birthday made this statement:

Despite our fears and worries, and they are very real to all of us, life continues—it goes on.

And as we watched on television and as we watched in person, one could not help but think that the transition of Government is really cruel to a certain degree—but life continues and the Government continues. But that is the way John Kennedy would have wanted it. That is one of the reasons why this Nation of ours is as great as it is and it is because of this stability of Government in this time of remorse that we have been able to continue on.

When I think of John Kennedy, I knew him so well—the philosophy and creed by which he lived: "Thou shalt love thy neighbor," "I am my brother's keeper." He truly lived by the Golden Rule—"Do unto others as you would have them do unto you." "No one saves us but ourselves; no one can and no one may. We ourselves must walk the path; teachers merely show the way." He has been a great teacher to the Nation, to the world.

I am reminded of the prayer of St. Francis of Assisi, which truly Jack Kennedy lived by.

Lord, make me an instrument of Thy peace. Where there is hatred let me show love. Where there is injury, pardon. Where there is doubt, faith. Where there is despair, hope. Where there is darkness, light. Where there is sadness, joy.

O Divine Master, grant that I may not seek to be consoled as to console, to be understood as to understand, to be loved as to love, for it is in giving that we receive, it is in pardoning that we are pardoned, and it is in dying that we are born to Eternal Life.

I cannot refrain from expressing that the President was blessed with a wonderful wife, Jacqueline, and a marvelous family. May God's blessings be upon them.

ADDRESS BY

Hon. William H. Bates

OF MASSACHUSETTS

Mr. Speaker, it was the greatest drama of the century, perhaps of many centuries—a tragedy—that unfolded before him; but no one, not quite three, could understand. He was only a little tot standing at hand salute and he was too young to know.

An emperor, a chancellor, presidents, queens, prince of state and church, a mourning world was the cast. No one, not Aeschylus, nor Sophocles, nor Euripides, nor Shakespeare, nor Dumas, nor Beaumarchais had ever attempted to rival this. This list of characters was too rare to be assembled together in such quick fashion—and as mere bystanders—in any work of fiction. Only in reality, where they could be recognized as living figures of history, could their presence be believed—at least by us. But this little fellow—he was too young to know.

Never so widely throughout the world was the word so quickly spread, nor the sorrow so profoundly felt. Pictures have now come back to us from distant lands, where, although this man never learned their tongue, he somehow captured their heart. Someday this little fellow will glean from this a real sense of pride—but today, he is just too young to know.

Only those of us who have long witnessed the uncertainties and tragedies of life could accept the reality of this procession which had shaken the world. You and I accepted it, not as a fact that could be readily understood, but rather as a matter of blind faith that we neither questioned nor clearly perceived. The deed had been done, but why? He is too young to know.

This is not the first time, nor shall it be the last, when the Commander in Chief will fall when his life is far from spent. Philip of Macedon, Julius Caesar, Abraham Lincoln, James Garfield, William McKinley, as heads of government, had fallen before. The price of leadership is great and uncertain. The price of freedom is never paid. Another downpayment on liberty has been made. Someday, this little boy will understand as we understand. But, Mr. Speaker, do we really understand? Do we really understand?

Our former President was a master of verse and an advocate of the arts. His expressions were graphic and destined to be found among the treasures of world literature. Robert Frost was one of his great favorites. Both the man and his poems were a highlight of President Kennedy's inauguration in 1961.

Perhaps Frost would be more widely acclaimed; perhaps his words would have lasting fame if he had lived and his pen would write and capture the pathos of this dreadful experience. However, he could not have more keenly felt the loss, nor fashioned a more heartfelt phrase than came from the lips and pens of the average American. Among those who turned to verse to pay a tribute deeply felt and richly deserved was Anthony Cama, of Lynn, Mass., in his poem entitled "A Martyr for Humanity" which in part, follows:

As truly as this Nation is his birth,
  As truly as this Nation is his bed;
The stars are weeping on the anguished earth—
  "Our President is dead."

Drop gently, tears and sorrow, great our loss,
  Let every heartache clasp its hands and pray.
How splendid glows his torch; how haloed is his cross.
  He is not gone. He is with us to stay.

He is the dream of battles faith has won,
  A father's love, a husband's treasured part,
America is proud of such a humble son,
  His noble service; his devoted heart.

As truly as this Nation loved his mirth,
  As truly as he lived and died and bled,
The world is weeping; mourns the sobbing earth—
  "Our President is dead."

A light has gone out, but a greater light has lit the world.

ADDRESS BY

Hon. Harold D. Donohue

OF MASSACHUSETTS

Mr. Speaker, 13 fateful days ago, about this hour, a torrential wave of anguish suddenly swelled up in the street of an American metropolis. With the lightning speed of electronic sound its floodwaters of strickening grief rolled out and into every hamlet of the Nation; overflowing our shores it spread its shocking, sickening sorrow among the peoples and the princes, and even the dictators, of every country in the world.

John Fitzgerald Kennedy, the 35th President of the United States, was untimely dead.

The composite boundlessness of this unique man's coordinated capacity of intellect, courage, vision, personality, faith, humaneness, culture and character discourages and dismisses any unending inventory of his separate virtues and talents.

He could astound the most learned with the eagle swiftness of his perception and the scholarly details of his knowledge.

He could warmly share a homely anecdote with the untutored.

For the honor of mankind he dared the arrogance of tyranny to thunder open the earth for the perishment of all upon it, while he patiently pointed toward the path of understanding to prevent it.

He could forgo the tempting machinations of expedient accomplishment to self-effacingly strengthen the foundations of the free government he was dedicated to preserve.

He could uplift the wholesome laughter of assembly on a celebrating day. He could bow down his worshiping head in lonely, suppliant prayer on a night of fearful danger and decision.

He could fling forth the challenge of cooperating effort to rid the world of "tyranny, poverty, disease, and war itself," while he cursed in condemnation the dark powers that harass and hinder this blessed happening.

He understood the need to encourage the culturing influence of the poet while he rigidly repelled the debasing barbarity of the tyrant.

His wit was tempered, his humor was warm, and his infectious smile of tolerance reflected the clean breath of the freedom he so valiantly protected for the sake of all on earth.

The sudden passing of this great spirit erupted the spontaneous recognition of personal nobility his presence had delayed. He walked with even step among the humble and moved with towering stature above the mighty.

He was a leader of men and a servant of God and this poor world will not soon see his like again.

The extent of the universal tragedy that has

befallen us cannot yet be fully realized but, as emphasized in the December 7, last, issue of the America magazine, it is perhaps best prophesied in this briefly pertinent passage from the third act of Shakespeare's "Hamlet":

The cease of majesty Dies not alone, but like a gulf doth draw What's near it with it. It is a massy wheel Fixed on the summit of the highest mount, To whose huge spokes ten thousand lesser things Are amortized and adjoined; which, when it falls, Each small annexment, petty consequence, Attends the boisterous ruin.

This attendant ruin need not and must not be. Let the word go out, from this Chamber and through these walls that echoed to his tread, that we shall not stop, we shall not be weary, we shall not rest, we shall not relax, until the fullest measure of each of his aims "to assure the survival and success of liberty" here and everywhere has been indelibly inscrolled upon the brightest pages of all our legislative history.

Looking toward the eternal flame that marks his tomb let us solemnly pledge ourselves to the unswerving and unshrinking welcome of this united responsibility because by our common action we can insure that the glow from that flame will everlastingly "light the world" to new horizons of tolerance and decency, of progress and peace.

Only in this manner can we prove to all who come after that this generation was worthy of the life of President John F. Kennedy and guiltless of the shame of barbarous death. And now, in custom, what feeble words can we or have we to say to, or of, the partner of his glory.

"She walked in beauty" beside her fallen warrior and the splendor of her stride portrayed for all the world to see the majestic grandeur of "woman," God's fairest creature.

The inspiring observance of a troubled daughter's comforting little hand, and the solemn salute of a small but stalwart son, in accord with noble heritage, vaulted the watching world to heights of compassion hitherto and hereafter unparalleled.

Mr. Speaker, I entered this Congress on the same day as John F. Kennedy and was privileged to work closely with him throughout these near 17 years past. I, with others of like privilege, have suffered a deep personal loss beyond belabored expression.

I join with all my colleagues here in extending heartfelt sympathy to our late and beloved President's widow, Mrs. Jacqueline B. Kennedy, his daughter, Caroline, his son, John, Jr., his parents, his brothers and sisters. We prayerfully ask Divine Providence to grant them the extraordinary grace of faithful understanding and resignation to the holy will that designed the destiny of this sacrifice of husband, father, son and brother.

From boyish wartime decorated skipper of a small boat to the seasoned peacetime commander in chief of the Ship of State, within 20 short years, he has now been hastily summoned as aide to the Almighty, to be, no doubt, from the parapets of heaven, the continuing guardian of the land he served under the Lord he loved.

May the great soul and spirit of John Fitzgerald Kennedy rest in peace until we meet again in the House of Resurrection presided over by the Eternal Father of us all.

ADDRESS BY

Hon. Hastings Keith

OF MASSACHUSETTS

Mr. Speaker, I sincerely wish to join in heartfelt tribute to a great American, John Fitzgerald Kennedy. The Nation, indeed the whole world, was stunned by the cruel and senseless crime of November 22. Those of us from Massachusetts and particularly in my district at Cape Cod, which the late President in many ways considered his home, have felt the added personal grief that comes from the loss of a good friend and neighbor.

The loss, of course, extends far beyond the bounds of our personal sorrow. America and the free world has lost an able leader. His unique personal prestige outside of America will be missed, as will his intellectual, keenly professional approach to the awesome responsibilities of the high office he held. John Kennedy conveyed a sense of excitement that quickened the tempo of political life everywhere.

It will be a long while before we fully recover from the tragedy that has befallen us. We pray to God, however, that in the end we will be stronger fortified with the strength we found in an hour of crisis and in the rich legacy of courage and dedication left us by a martyred President.

We must take this occasion to rededicate ourselves to the high principles of human dignity, of liberty and to the continuing cause of peace and good will that were guiding beacons in the purposeful life of John Kennedy—that will be the finest tribute we could pay his memory.

ADDRESS BY

Hon. Emanuel Celler

OF NEW YORK

Mr. Speaker, it is sad indeed to express our sentiments on this day of mourning for our late, lamented President, John F. Kennedy. Words cannot describe our personal grief and the sorrow of the Nation, if not of the world at his passing.

Here was a young man of greatest promise struck down at the height of his career. He was a man who could walk with kings, but not lose the common touch. His credo was for the forgotten man. Indeed, his philosophy was well summed up in a paragraph taken from his immemorial inaugural address:

Now the trumpet summons us again—not as a call to bear arms, though arms we need—not as a call to battle, though embattled we are—but a call to bear the burden of a long twilight struggle year in and year out, "rejoicing in hope, patient in tribulation"—a struggle against the common enemies of man: tyranny, poverty, disease, and war itself.

He was a man that wanted peace—not peace at any price, but peace with honor. He proposed that both sides, meaning the Soviet side and our own, should unite and explore problems that confront both, instead of belaboring those problems and thus divide and widen the breach between us.

He realized that he could not make effective in the short space of his tenure of office the gigantic plan he had for us and for the world, and he said:

All this will not be finished in the first 100 days. Nor will it be finished in the first 1,000 days, nor in the life of this administration, nor even perhaps in our lifetime on this planet. But let us begin.

He was meek, but only in the sense that "the meek shall inherit the earth."

If stark tragedy had not directed the fatal bullet that felled him, there is no telling to what further pinnacles of achievement he would still have risen.

He had an uncanny sense of history that unerringly guided him in his daily tasks.

He was kind and benign. He had a grace of manner. Indeed, he could charm a bird out of a tree.

Latterly, I had occasion frequently to be with him at the White House in conference with Members of the House. The purpose of these meetings was to solidify support for the civil rights bill. Our late President, anxious that all Americans should have the same rights, sought to convert some Members. He never threatened, raised his voice or hectored. He sought in quiet, firm tones, to win over. He accepted refusal to join with him in stoic manner. His modesty, demeanor, infinite patience, keen persuasion did, however, cause numerous Members to come over to his side.

He was possessed of a self-deprecatory sense of humor. We recall that when he went to Europe with his dear wife Jacqueline and both were acclaimed, he said he was the man that accompanied Jacqueline Kennedy to Europe.

At Denver, Colo., he was guest of honor at a $100 plate fundraising dinner for the Democratic campaign chest. He said he was touched with the reception given him and added that those present were more "touched" than he. His delicate trend of humor always stood him in good stead.

He knew the frustrations of the office of the President, but also knew its victories and the victories compensated for the many disappointments. He often quoted Lord Morley, who, in effect said, "politics is one long second best, where the choice often lies between two blunders."

John F. Kennedy has not died in vain. His words will ever be emblazoned upon the tablets of history. The record of his deeds will glow with time. We are the better for his passing through our midst.

We extend to his dear wife and children and the members of his family our heartfelt sympathy.

ADDRESS BY
Hon. Wilbur D. Mills
OF ARKANSAS

Mr. Speaker, the moving tributes which have been paid during the past 2 weeks and during this meeting today to the late John Fitzgerald Kennedy who was taken from us under such tragic circumstances reflect the deep feeling of all our people over this said event.

When a Nation loses a courageous leader, there is always a deep sense of shock and loss, and a keen feeling of sadness. When the event occurs under sudden, unexpected, and tragic circumstances, the shock, the loss, and the sadness are all the greater.

John Fitzgerald Kennedy proved his courage in war, in peace, through periods of serious sickness, and under the harsh, unyielding, and continuous pressures of the most important and difficult job in the world today.

I will not undertake to try to find the words today to frame all the thoughts which come to my mind. Others have eloquently spoken of his attributes of statesmanship, his moral firmness under the most trying of pressures in foreign affairs, and of the qualities of his leadership during the past 3 years.

I simply want to say, Mr. Speaker, that I was privileged to meet often with our late President over matters falling within the sphere of the committee of which I have the honor to be the chairman. Because of the nature of the problems which came to our Committee on Ways and Means, I counseled with John Fitzgerald Kennedy over many aspects of these particular legislative issues. During these many meetings, in the discussions he always kept foremost the public interest to be served by the legislation under consideration. In addition he always evidenced a very keen insight into the details of the legislation and how the public interest could best be served, not only by the broad objectives but also by the details.

I have a deep sense of personal loss. I join in the expressions of sadness which have been here given, and I again extend my deepest feeling of sympathy to Mrs. Kennedy and her children. They can take solace from the knowledge that John Fitzgerald Kennedy as the 35th President of the United States left a heritage of courage and leadership which will properly be accorded a high place by those who in the future record the accomplishments of our great Nation.

ADDRESS BY
Hon. Oren Harris
OF ARKANSAS

Mr. Speaker, on the sloping hillside in Arlington Cemetery, just a short pace down and in front of historical Lee Mansion, now lies in eternal peace our late, beloved President, John Fitzgerald Kennedy. There glows the eternal flame as symbolic of the light of lasting peace on this earth to which he had so dedicated his life.

As we reflect this terrible, awful tragedy which profoundly shocked the Nation and the world and stunned and numbed the conscience of the American people, our hearts go out for Mrs. Kennedy, Caroline, and John, Jr., as well as the entire family. They have our sympathy in the deep sorrow they bear. Our prayers are for them that they will be sustained as they and the Nation mourn the loss of this loved one, our leader, our President.

Mr. Speaker, in the aftermath of a national tragedy, realization is followed by concern. It is to the everlasting credit of our country and our leaders that concern rarely gives way to consternation and panic. It is a fitting tribute to our late President that the citizens of the United States in their sorrow and indignation set about the solemn task of paying their last respects with dignity and effected the transition of Government leadership with firm dedication to established principles.

Never in recent years have we been bound so closely together as a nation as we were during the awful weekend beginning on November 22.

On the day following the death of John F. Kennedy, I addressed a letter to my constituents that expressed some of what we all felt—the tragedy, the loss—the anger. But on that morning another feeling was born—the feeling of determination that is now so evident.

On this day of reflection and tribute I would like to include my thoughts on that Saturday morning as the Nation picked itself up and continued.

Saturday, November 23, 1963.

It is dark and dreary in Washington today. The weather reflects the gloom that has settled over the Nation's Capital. The whole world mourns the sudden death of President Kennedy at the hands of an assassin in Dallas. The despicable and incredible act has shocked the Nation beyond description.

Throughout the Capital astonishment was followed by a dull sort of paralysis. Radios and television sets suddenly appeared and each one attracted a small somber group. Routine work was forgotten. Special editions of Washington papers were delivered and disappeared in minutes from the newsstands. Throughout the day nothing penetrated the deep melancholy that gripped the Capital. Churches remained open all night. In the Catholic churches every available candle was lit. Aimless groups and individuals gathered near the White House, stayed a while and wandered away. Today many offices normally busy are closed and many normally closed are working, as everyone seeks his own way of meeting the emotional impact of yesterday's tragedy.

Last night the body of the late President rested in the naval hospital at Bethesda and today lies in repose in the East Room of the White House where the family, the Cabinet and the Congress will pay their respects. This afternoon I will join the others passing through the East Room in tribute and admiration for the man and the office held. I have been asked by Speaker McCormack to be one of those representing the House of Representatives attending the funeral and paying final respects to the President.

The body will lie in state in the Capitol Sunday and Monday morning until 10 when it will be removed to St. Matthew's Cathedral for the solemn pontifical Requiem Mass at noon.

I knew President Kennedy from our service in the House of Representatives for 6 years. I knew him as a Senator. I have known him as a President. Through the long association I admired him as a Member of Congress in the House and Senate, as President of the United States, and as a friend.

"If ever there was a time to pray, it is now, for our President, and for our country."

This prayer echoes throughout the country in expression of the deep sorrow of our people and sympathy for Mrs. Kennedy and the family. It expresses an even deeper faith of our people in our sustaining belief in God and the future of our country.

It is in the midst of these dark moments in the life of our country that Vice President Lyndon Johnson has taken office as the 36th President of the United States. Our prayers are with President Johnson as he is so suddenly and unexpectedly catapulted into the vast responsibilities of a great, strong, progressive, dynamic, and powerful country.

Regardless of the political differences that exist in the country he deserves the wholehearted and unanimous support of the people of America in his effort to guide the ship of state through the turbulent waters to a more calm and peaceful sea.

When this tragedy flashed throughout the country it was immediately assumed that it was the handiwork of someone associated with the segment of our people who had sharp political differences. The assumption proved to be erroneous. Apparently the dastardly act was committed by one who had attempted to defect and spent 3 years in Russia and who was an admitted leader in the pro-Castro, Communist-supported regime in Cuba.

This tragedy should be a reminder to all of us that even though we have our political differences, which become sharp and deeply imbedded in the minds of our people, our enemy—the real threat to our future is in the Communist philosophy of those committed to our destruction.

There have been dark moments in the life of our Nation before. Our people as a nation have met and overcome crisis after crisis. I have no doubt that we will emerge from this one as a stronger nation with even greater determination for the future well-being and security of our people—and a better understanding among the nations and peoples of the world.

ADDRESS BY

Hon. Abraham J. Multer

OF NEW YORK

Mr. Speaker, by direction of the Speaker, at the suggestion of our leadership, on November 25, 1963, it was my high but most painful, most sorrowful, privilege to present to this House the official resolutions on the death of our late and beloved President, John Fitzgerald Kennedy.

With a heart still overflowing with grief, I again join our colleagues in this further tribute to a great and a good man.

I first met John F. Kennedy immediately after I became a Member of the 80th Congress.

I was quickly drawn to him as a man. The world will long remember him for his great intellect, his keen wit, his fine manner, his good deeds, his many kindnesses.

I will best remember him for his love—a love born of deep respect for his family, his fellow man, for all humanity, love of, not for, authority, and of the dignity, the rights, and the privileges of others.

I am a better man because of the opportunity to have known him and to have worked beside him and for him.

My coreligionists have for centuries uttered a special prayer for those who have fallen in battle, from which I recite:

And the work of righteousness shall be peace and the effect of righteousness, quietness, and confidence forever.

We close the Kaddish, our prayer for the dead, thusly:

May the Father of Peace send peace to all who mourn, and comfort all the bereaved among us.

Impressed, as all of us were, by the magnificent stallion which followed the President's caisson in the funeral procession, my good friend, Rabbi Louis I. Newman, has written a poem, eloquently expressing a feeling for the symbolism of that riderless horse. Permit me, Mr. Speaker, to repeat it here:

THE RIDERLESS HORSE

(By Louis I. Newman, Nov. 25, 1963)

A horse dark of hue wears a blanket of black;
Its saddle is empty; its guiding reins slack;
Its footsteps move sidewise; the touch at its head
Is strange to a creature so lovingly bred.

A sword in a scabbard is strapped to its side,
A sign its commander has made his last ride;
His stirrups and boots are turned backward, to tell
A soldier has fallen. Brave martyr, sleep well!

A horse walks alone, 'mid the music of grief,
Bewailing the loss of a gallant young chief,
Shot down in the battle, his arrows unsped,
His mission unfinished, his message unsaid.

Oh, mourn for the leader so heartlessly slain,
Whose voice could command, yet so wisely restrain!
Oh, mourn for the steed, of its master bereft,
That looks for its friend to the right and the left.

Our Nation is trembling, a riderless steed,
That yearns for a hand that can halt and can lead.
Oh, symbol of majesty, honor, and pride,
How long shall we weep, now our chieftain has died?

Alas for the warrior who lies in his tomb,
Alas for the horse in its vestment of gloom!
But hail to the horseman who mounts to his place,
The saddle refilled for the challenging race!

And when this great charger is freed from its bonds,
Behold how it leaps and with ardor responds!
Oh, thus may our country, still bowed under pain,
Courageously take up its burden again.

Let us say together: May the memory of John Fitzgerald Kennedy be for a blessing forever.

ADDRESS BY

Hon. Robert N. Giaimo

OF CONNECTICUT

Mr. Speaker, the hearts and minds of men have suffered a grievous blow. From among us has gone a truly great man. The ability to be great is given to few men, but it was given in abundance to John Fitzgerald Kennedy, and through him, to his country.

In the days of numbing shock and sorrow which followed his death, I am sure that each of us searched his mind for adequate words, for personal consolation, for courage. He was our leader, all could say. He was our friend, many could say. He is gone—no one can bring himself to say.

It is inconceivable, unforgivable, that it happened. And it hurts almost too much for words.

For days, people throughout the world stood with the faraway looks and tears in their eyes which spoke silently but eloquently of their deep sorrow, their anger and their ineffable anguish. People would stop me on the street and say "I'm so sorry. I remember when I saw him." It was never necessary to ask them whom they meant.

In our agonizing attempts to regain perspective, we took our memories of this man and mourned him with deep personal grief. There were many memories for many people. There are the memories of the man who sold him apples on the road to New Haven—the first time, in 1960, because a brilliant young candidate for the Presidency needed a quick snack; the second time, in 1962, because a brilliant young President remembered that the man was waiting for him. That man will always remember John Fitzgerald Kennedy. And so will the men whose hands he shook; the women whose smiles he returned; the children whose heads he patted. I will remember how good it was to be his friend and his follower. My daughter will remember that he often stopped to ask how she was. All of us have our intensely personal memories of this brief glimpse of greatness—the cherished mementos to last a lifetime.

From the flood of memories and tears, it is the little things about the man that we remember first and most poignantly—the smile, the witty remark, the unfailing thoughtfulness, the power to inspire the minds, hearts and love of people.

Now we also remember the towering principles for which he stood. We remember his unswerving dedication to efforts to assure the rights of all men to live in dignity and freedom. We remember that he had the courage to be strong; the conviction of purpose to reason. We remember that he gave to this country an image of poise, graciousness, maturity, and culture. We remember that he had absolutely no doubt that the future can and will belong to those who plan and plan well, to those who dedicate the present to the welfare of posterity.

There is so little that can be said that has not been said. The country has lost a matchless leader; the cause of freedom, its most ardent advocate; the future of man, its most determined champion. It is incomprehensible that this man, with his flawless sense of history, his unique ability to comprehend and command, should not be permitted to continue the work he so brilliantly began.

Because there seems to be no sane reason for this tragedy, we are determined that there will be living results. We are not a nation that accepts such a needless loss. We cannot just accept the fact that he is gone. We must not.

If we must search for blame—and it is inherent in us that we must—let us all share it. Let each of us who has ever known a complacent moment bear the blame. Let each of us who ignored the fury of hate and extremism bear the blame. And let each of us who thought more of self than the rights and future of others bear the blame.

There was dignity, warmth, purpose, and principle in the man we mourn. We as a nation must adopt these qualities as our own or else we will bear the opprobrium that history could say he was too good for us. If we do not perpetuate the principles for which he lived and died, if we do not strive to meet the goals he set for us, we do ourselves and this magnificent man's memory a disgraceful disservice.

If his brave and gracious widow can derive any consolation, it must lie in the fact that millions mourn with her and promise that the memory of John Kennedy will live in the hearts, minds, and actions of man everywhere.

What of his monuments? Thucydides said:

To famous men all the earth is a sepulcher. Their virtues shall be testified not only by the inscription on stone at home but in all lands wheresoever in the unwritten record of the mind, which far beyond any monument will remain with all men everlastingly.

This is, in truth and in perpetuity, John Fitzgerald Kennedy's monument.

To the country he led and loved, let us swear to continue his principles and to meet his goals.

ADDRESS BY

Hon. William L. St. Onge

OF CONNECTICUT

Mr. Speaker, I join with my colleagues in this sad tribute to our late beloved President John Fitzgerald Kennedy, whose passing was so tragic and untimely. His death is a terrible blow to the American people and to freedom-loving people everywhere. Although nearly 2 weeks have gone by since he was brutally torn from our midst, I still cannot bring myself to the realization that our country and the world have suffered this most horrible loss.

I believe that the needless and incredible death of President Kennedy may well prove to be the most shameful and dastardly act in our Nation's history during the 20th century, just as the assassination of Abraham Lincoln was the most shameful and dastardly act of the 19th century. The death of President Kennedy will leave a great void and a gaping wound in the hearts of men of good will all over the world.

In assessing the enormity of this crime of the century, the noted columnist Walter Lippmann wrote as follows:

The only solace for the Nation's shame and grief can come from a purge of the hatred and venom which lie so close to the surface of our national life. We have allowed the community of the American people to be rent with enmity. Only if and as we can find our way back into the American community can we find our way back to confidence in the American destiny.

We have lost much more than the life of one individual and the services of a most able leader. We have sustained great loss of faith, reason, and inner peace. We have lost much of heart, courage, and noble values which we inherited from our forebears. It will take many years to recoup these losses.

In his short life of only 46 years, our martyred President has shown us the true meaning of courage and patriotism. He has given us a new sense of purpose and a new inspiration. He has given us new ideals and new goals. We must strive to attain these goals, to fulfill these ideals, and to continue to seek inspiration from the examples he set for all mankind—even though he is no longer with us in body, but only in spirit. The strength of his indomitable spirit will surely strengthen us all in the years ahead.

In the speech he never delivered in Dallas, President Kennedy had in the text of his address which was issued later the following observation:

In a world of complex and continuing problems, in a world full of frustrations and irritations, America's leadership must be guided by the lights of learning and reason—or else those who confuse rhetoric with reality and the plausible with the possible will gain the popular ascendancy with their seemingly swift and simple solutions to every problem.

These words are both a legacy and a warning we must never forget. It is a legacy that we must hold high the lights of learning and reason, which have made our Nation great. It is a warning that we must stamp out the hatred and the bigotry of the left and the right, the evil forces which seek to rend our Nation asunder and to bring it down in ashes. John F. Kennedy clearly foresaw this danger and he warned his countrymen. Those who hated Kennedy cut him down before he was able to warn the Nation of their evil schemes.

In this hour of national bereavement, let us rededicate ourselves to the ideals for which John F. Kennedy labored so hard—the building of a world of peace and freedom, a world of brotherhood and genuine understanding, a world of morality and loving kindness for all mankind. I pray that God, in his infinite wisdom, will guide us to this kind of a world.

To the courageous widow of our martyred President, Mrs. Jacqueline Kennedy, to her young children deprived so untimely of their loving father, and to the members of the Kennedy family, we express our deepest sympathy. We pray that God will give them the strength to bear this great bereavement, which all of us

share with them. May they be consoled by the fact that his memory will always live in the hearts of the American people and his name will always occupy a glorious place of honor in the history of our Nation.

And now let us resume the task of building our Nation. For as President Kennedy said in his famous inaugural address nearly 3 years ago:

With a good conscience our only sure reward, with history the final judge of our deeds, let us go forth to lead the land we love.

This is what John F. Kennedy wants us to do.

ADDRESS BY

Hon. Emilio Q. Daddario

OF CONNECTICUT

Mr. Speaker, we meet today, in the House of Representatives, where John Fitzgerald Kennedy once served, to pay tribute to the memory of our martyred 35th President. In the tragic days that followed his violent death at the hands of an assassin, our press, our clergy, and the people have eulogized him many times over. It remains for us, his partners in Government, to contemplate the lessons which his life and works have bequeathed to the Nation.

To those of us from New England, who knew him well as a neighbor, his ties were especially close. He had attended Choate School in Connecticut, and he visited us often in public life. He had attracted the fervent admiration of our people even before running for the Presidency and winning the campaign as our Chief Executive.

His early career had given him an apprenticeship for affairs of state. With education at Harvard, Stanford, and London, he had acquired scholarship. As the Ambassador's son in London, he had observed the movement of great tides of history. He made a perceptive study of the reactions of people in a democracy to the threat of fascism, a study which he documented in an analysis of why England slept as war approached. He served his Nation in the South Pacific and the mark of his character was, perhaps, best exemplified in the dramatic adventure that befell him there.

He had come to the helm of state in 1960, tested in the crucible of war and warmed by the comradeship of conflict. He had been born while the United States was engaged in one world war and he, like the generation of young Americans who gave him their loyal support, had known well the gathering storms of the Second World War and the persistent, bleeding struggle of the subsequent years. He was of that generation. He became its leader. With their help he assumed with confidence and coolness the mantle of leadership for the world's most powerful nation.

He had concern and compassion for all Americans. He devised and fought for a program which would build a better country, a stronger United States. He made progress, but his most difficult task was to get America to look to its hopes, rather than its fears. The doubts, uncertainty, and inertia that marked the Nation whose direction he had assumed were reflected in the razor-thin margin of his victory and that, in turn, was reflected in the obstacles and barriers that were waiting along his path.

He ignited the spirit of the younger men of his own generation who saw the possibilities as he outlined them. He drew to him a staff of exceptional merit, whose loyalties could be dedicated to the common peace. In his messages of cogent and comprehensive reasoning, it was the work of many men who contributed to the sense of urgency and motion, but this staffwork was the lengthened shadow of one man.

These messages, which came to the 87th Congress at a furious pace, set forth the problems and the solutions that he recommended. Out of them were hammered programs to strengthen our social security and minimum wage laws, to rebuild areas particularly hard hit by chronic unemployment, to encourage world trade and world peace, to support education, to control water pollution.

In each of these successes, and in others that he himself would not attain, our democratic system reflected both its strengths and its weaknesses. For our Constitution does not permit the Executive to dominate the process of Government. Instead it requires that each proposal undergo the thoughtful and considered scrutiny of the Congress, and be subject to the best suggestions that may be made. This process may be twisted and tortured into delay, and there were those who fought each and every proposal, some on principle, some for politics.

It was here, too, that the conflict between the new generation and the old was most apparent. The Congress is the product of tradition, and great reliance is placed on seniority. Age often confers wisdom and experience, and such seniority has merit. Yet younger members chafe at the deliberate pace which seniors prefer, especially in the full sense of the importance of the goals toward which we must move.

On several occasions recently, I have seen references to programs in which President Kennedy was reported to have told associates that it would be well to get at it, since this or that specific program might well be the only memorial they would leave. This, too, I think, reflects the spirit and vigor of the generation tempered in war, for those who knew command and responsibility at a young age understood that time is one resource which may not be hoarded or reserved. Once foreseen or anticipated, an objective deserves attack and conquest. When John Hersey wrote his memorable account of John Kennedy's survival in World War II, he began his report with the words:

Our men in the South Pacific fight nature, when they are pitted against her, with a greater fierceness than they could ever expend on a human enemy.

It was the dedication of our late President, with his apparently inexhaustible energy, to the fight for a better country, that we must celebrate today. We must pledge ourselves to an unrelenting attack upon the forces of war, disease, ignorance and the imperfect.

John Fitzgerald Kennedy was the architect of a better and greater United States. He envisioned the world as it must be, as it ought to be, within the limitations of the best information we have available to us today. These are the precepts of imagination and possibility which must be taught to our young and which, through President Kennedy's particular attention to the youth of our Nation, are bound to have an ever-widening impact. For years and decades to come, men will be reaching into the store of his plans and programs for inspiration.

We must do all we can to record and pass on the lessons which his work embodied. I was disturbed to read in a recent article by James Reston that much may be lost to history because of the informal way in which the late President conducted affairs of the greatest moment requiring rapid reflexes and response. I would hope that some of the personal recollections of our leaders may enter the Record today. The memories of our distinguished Speaker, who observed the late President's public career throughout his lifetime, or of the esteemed gentlemen from Georgia, who walked with the President in the rose garden, deserve to be recorded. President Johnson should be encouraged to find the resources in the Executive Office, perhaps through the use of Dr. Schlesinger, or Mr. Holborn, to assemble a broader record, through interviews and the collection of documents, to cast a greater light upon such a man.

In my capacity as a member of the House Committee on Science and Astronautics, I was particularly impressed with the late President's understanding of the possibilities of science and the importance of the space program. He had delegated direction of the latter program to his most important aid, the Vice President, but he did not lose sight of the goals for which we worked. In one of his last public appearances, he discussed this question at the dedication of the Aerospace Medical Health Center at Brooks Air Force Base in Texas.

He told, to illustrate his point, an Irish story of Frank O'Connor, who had learned as a boy to face the challenge of a wall that seemed too high, too doubtful, by scaling his cap over the wall so that he had no choice but to follow it. And so, President Kennedy said, we have tossed our cap over the wall of space, and we have no choice but to follow it.

The work which President Kennedy charted will be carried out in years to come. The John F. Kennedy Space Flight Center will be the scene of many successful efforts. Let me say that I am not thoroughly convinced that he would have wanted the cape on which this flight center is located to be named after him as well. His sense of history would have respected the traditional name which has earned such wide recognition across the world through our space successes.

It would be more fitting if we named only the Center and then looked out and determined that the point on which our first astronaut lands on the moon would assume the name of Kennedy. And yet that too can be done.

I have mentioned the President's awareness of the uses of science. He had gathered the resources of the executive research establishment to help identify the problems we face and to decide upon solutions. He was not one who thought we could undiscover the atom; he worked unceasingly to find out how we could make use of these resources to improve our way of life. He had warned and emphasized that recent scientific advances have not only made international cooperation desirable, but they have made it essential.

President Kennedy's term of office was tragically short. One landmark may stand high to historians who review this work in later time. For John F. Kennedy worked vigorously for peace, and for a better understanding among peoples of the world. He was resolute in defense of American principles, but he coaxed and led on the way to peace. Just a few short months ago, at his urging, the Senate approved our part in a ban on nuclear tests—tests which had threatened to poison the atmosphere and despoil the world in which our children are to live. This was a step intended to free mankind from the dangers and fears of radioactive fallout.

His service in the White House changed him, as it must all men who assume those formidable responsibilities. He acquired a new and greater sense of the power of the office. Yet he never lost the grace and wit that had characterized his life. He faced the calumny and hatred heaped upon him by a tiny minority with steadiness and integrity. I recall with a sense of repugnance, the hysterical campaign of mail and telegrams that reached us in the Congress at the close of a long session 2 years ago crying that Congress should remain in session to prevent his seizure of tyrannical power. I have only pity for these little minds. Perhaps the martyrdom of our President will serve to wipe out that shame by forcing these people and all our people to a better understanding of what the United States must mean. President Johnson, in his appeal to the Congress, has set these medicines to work, and we all hope for a more reasoned approach to the political efforts of our leaders seeking to bring about a better nation.

I have heard many people wonder why John Fitzgerald Kennedy, who was born to wealth and a comfortable life, would have sought the position of President, why he entered politics and engaged in the tiresome, rugged engagements that mark the political scene. Perhaps he said it best himself in the speech at Boston on November 7, 1960, when he asserted that—

I run for the Presidency of the United States because it is the center of action, and in a free society the chief responsibility of the President is to set before the American people the unfinished public business of the country.

And he had no illusions, for he warned that on the shoulders of the President elected in 1960 would rest burdens heavier than had rested on the shoulders of any President since the time of Lincoln. These explanations should be received with particular understanding among us here, who have also moved toward the center of action in behalf of our people and our country.

John Fitzgerald Kennedy, whose memory we honor today, assumed the responsibilities of power with a full understanding of their nature. He was a member of a generation that has earned recognition in its own right, regardless of race, religion or color, among Americans. He was sometimes described as a Brahmin of Boston, out of respect to his attainments and to the Yankee traditions among which he flourished, but it was his achievement as one of the new breed, born of a tradition of immigrants who have made their mark in this land of opportunity that stands foremost as a mark to those who follow.

He was of a new generation, toughened by war, but compassionate for the people; decisive in action, but flexible in studying the courses which were open to him. His cultural attainments and his interests in the arts were, with those of his gallant lady, to set standards which this Nation must strive to emulate. Above all, he was a man, enthusiastic about the delights of physical sports, aware of the sensibilities of others.

He has left a legacy of personal devotion to the greatest good of our country and of our people. Given the continued progress of our youth in the lessons he has taught, his kind will pass this way again, and in that we may take the greatest comfort.

ADDRESS BY

Hon. John S. Monagan

OF CONNECTICUT

Mr. Speaker, a furtive assassin has brutally murdered John F. Kennedy and we meet today to honor our late President.

Our friend, our leader, the gay warrior and dauntless standard bearer is:

> dead ere his prime
> young Lycidus, and hath not left his peer.

Others may celebrate his political victories, his legislative achievements or his diplomatic triumphs. I shall mention none of these. Instead, I shall testify to the style and quality of the man.

He was indeed "a parfit, gentil Knight," a Lancelot in the modern world of politics. In the midst of partisan strife or internecine feuding he maintained serenely his concept of the ideal executive. Recognizing the need to give hard knocks and to press an adversary without flinching, he nevertheless retained a grace, a cleanliness and a style that we shall not soon see again.

He brought gusto and zest to the job of being President. With his lovely wife he swept out the corners and opened the windows and spread a new light around the Presidency. He lent to it a unique bravura and surrounded it with a romantic quality that was pervasive—yet, almost intangible.

> We people on the pavement looked at him
> For he was a gentleman from sole to crown,
> Clean favored, and imperially slim.
> And he was always quietly arrayed
> And he was always human when he talked;
> But still he fluttered pulses when he said,
> "Good morning," and he glittered when he walked.

In the spell which he wove was something of the poetry, the imagination and the creativeness which came to him through his Celtic forebears.

His loss is a tragic one, indeed, both for us his friends and for our country. Yet may we not find solace in knowing that he will to us and to history always be young and bright and fair?

He gave to the Nation the incomparable gifts of freshness, of vigor, of idealism and of faith. How much better to remember always the youthful profusion of this endowment which he lavished upon us.

Never will he "swell the rout of lads that wore their honors out, runners whom renown outran and the name died before the man."

Like the John Keats of Shelley's "Adonais":

> He has outsoared the shadow of our night
> Envy and calumny and hate and pain,
> And that unrest which men miscall delight,
> Can touch him not and torture not again;
> From the contagion of the world's slow stain
> He is secure, and now can never mourn
> A heart grown cold, a head grown gray in vain.

STATEMENT BY REPRESENTATIVE MONAGAN ON NOVEMBER 26, 1963

Mr. Speaker, I share in the national and world-wide grief at the death of President Kennedy, but I also feel a very personal sense of loss at his passing. Having served in the two Congresses during his Presidency, having campaigned with him, having seen his popularity, his vigor and his selfless interest in the welfare of the people, I have felt a close identification with him. It has been a sad experience for me to have shared in the mournful ceremonies here in Washington.

In a larger sense, however, President Kennedy's tragic death is a loss to our whole country. With constant cheerfulness, unfailing courage and faith in America, he pressed for measures which would benefit the average citizen of this country and bring peace to the world.

We shall retain our pride in his achievements and our conviction that he has laid firm foundations upon which future generations may build.

In his great inaugural address, which we heard with pride less than 3 years ago, President Kennedy said that all work on national problems would not be finished in the first 100 days of his administration—nor in the life of that administration—but he urged the Nation to begin that work upon the complex problems which he described.

It will be to his eternal credit that in the brief space of time allotted to him he made a noble beginning.

In the words of Whittier:

> And now he rests; his greatness and his sweetness
> No more shall seem at strife
> And death has molded into calm completeness
> The statue of his life.

Mr. Speaker, on the day of the funeral of our late President, John F. Kennedy, officers and members of the U.S. 8th Army in Seoul, Korea, attended a mass for President Kennedy. The eulogy was delivered by the Right Reverend Monsignor (Col.) J. S. Chmielewski, Catholic chaplain of the 8th Army.

Colonel Chmielewski is well known in the Nation's Capital having served 4 years as chaplain of the Military District of Washington before leaving for Korea in August of this year.

With permission to extend my remarks, I include at this point the magnificent tribute paid to our late President by Monsignor Chmielewski in his eulogy.

EULOGY FOR JOHN F. KENNEDY

(By Chaplain (Col.) J. S. Chmielewski, Seoul, Korea)

Your Excellency, right reverend monsignors, reverend fathers, General Howze, distinguished guests, fellow Americans and friends: The world was stunned last Friday by the tragic death of John F. Kennedy, 35th President of the United States. To those of us serving in the Armed Forces, his death meant the loss of the Commander in Chief. This frontline duty soldier went to give an account of his stewardship to his supreme commander. I feel sure that Almighty God, in reviewing the records of this great and heroic soldier-statesman, perceived in him many noble and sterling qualities. If we were to enumerate some of them, in my humble opinion, we would first mention courage. The late President was imbued with and understood well the virtue of courage which he aptly described in his book, "Profiles in Courage." But more than writing about courage, he better exemplified it in his life. He faced one crisis after another in the span of less than 3 years as President of the United States, and invariably forced his opponents to relinquish ground whether it was in Cuba, Berlin, Asia, or within his own country. Such courage could come only from a sincere dedication to high ideals and a deep religious conviction. As someone said, "Courage is fear that has said its prayers."

John F. Kennedy was also a just man; he strove to render to each and everyone what by right was his due. He recognized that the rights man enjoyed were God-given and must not be violated. Thus the mainspring for all his actions, for all his virtues—particularly patriotism and justice—was a deep and reverent religious faith. He knew that such a faith spurred on our forefathers who launched the United States on the road to greatness. He was not ashamed of his faith, he went to church regularly and fulfilled his religious obligations. This was his source of strength.

The late President Kennedy was also a man of great hope for the future of the world. He reminded me by his youthful appearance of a young boy aboard a ship that was caught in a vehement storm. The waves were rolling high and threatened to engulf the reeling vessel in the mighty depths. The young lad showed no signs of alarm, with calm defiance he watched the uproar of the elements. And, asked if he did not fear the storm, he answered with assurance. "No, my father is at the rudder." What sublime confidence, what candid trust of the young man in his father. He fears nothing in his presence; he believes in his father's readiness and ability to help. This is the type of unlimited confidence the late President had in Almighty God, his Father and our Father.

If John F. Kennedy were to speak out to us at this moment from the great beyond after having conferred with the Supreme Commander, I wonder what he would have to say. Surely he would remind us that we must be loyal to the cause for which he so valiantly fought. He lost his life that man would be free and at peace with his fellowman and God. He died that man could freely serve his God and one day be united with Him for all eternity. If we were to say that he lost his life for his country, the late President would correct us and say, "I did not lose it, I gave it." For did he not say in his inaugural address, "Ask not what your country can do for you but what you can do for your country." He gave us the great example of patriotism, he gave his all for the country he loved so much.

The people of the Republic of Korea have expressed a sense of deep sorrow in the death of the President of the United States. They saw in him a great world leader. Toward him they felt a sense of deep gratitude, since he wholeheartedly continued to reinforce the defenses of the Republic of South Korea against the intrusions of communism. It was he who provided the aid program to assist Korea to regain economic stability. As the first citizen of our country, President Kennedy has given of himself, he generously supported the many welfare activities of the religious bodies working in Korea, for example, the Church World Services and the Catholic Relief Services. He made possible the shipment of needed supplies into Korea through the hand-clasp program. He has encouraged Americans to give to the world's needy, and especially to the Korean people, through CARE. His example made it possible for others to lift their vision and support agencies that are helping the weak, the homeless, the widow and the orphan, as all of us know.

In closing, I would like to paraphrase the words of another great President, Abraham Lincoln. May we from the honored dead gather increased devotion to the cause for which he gave the last full measure of devotion. May we all join in prayer to our merciful and omnipotent Father to reward John F. Kennedy for his unselfish devotion to duty, his dedicated patriotism, and let us ask our merciful Father to sustain those who are left to mourn his life.

ADDRESS BY

Hon. Abner W. Sibal

OF CONNECTICUT

Mr. Speaker, President Kennedy was one of the most remarkable men ever to serve in public

life in this country. The world will never be the same because he lived.

President Kennedy was a rare combination of physical vitality, limitless personal courage, a creative intellect, a restless, probing imagination, and ardent patriotism. He was an activist who sought to use the Government as a refined instrument for the people's good.

He was impatient at the thought of unused talent and national capacity and insistently and constantly pressed his fellow citizens to make the most of their vast personal and national resources.

He could not bear to see suffering go unattended nor injustice go unavenged. He dared to experiment.

He filled the Nation's Capital and the chambers of government with youth and laughter as well as with a sense of high purpose. He graced the arts with his educated patronage and stimulated the Nation's sense of beauty.

To the world, he gave an image of America's youth and energy.

As he lies now in the silence which comes to us all, I think there is truth to the old Greek saying, "Those whom the Gods love, die young."

ADDRESS BY

Hon. Bernard F. Grabowski

OF CONNECTICUT

Mr. Speaker, the mortal man, John Fitzgerald Kennedy, has left us.

Our Nation and the world are in mourning. All mankind is poorer because of his death.

This man who was our President lives on, not only in the immortality God offers us, but in all those whom he touched.

The values for which John Fitzgerald Kennedy spoke and fought are still with us. They live in both his words and remembered deeds. They live in all American hearts and minds and in the hearts and minds of all the people of the world.

In grief we are united with all humanity, we join to mourn the tragic loss of a dedicated, noble man.

By his notable achievements during an unexpectedly brief term of office, John Fitzgerald

Kennedy left a profound mark on the course of human affairs. His efforts were directed toward the noblest of man's dreams; justice, freedom, equality, and the brotherhood of man.

John Fitzgerald Kennedy came to office to face domestic problems, world political upheavals, the great ideological struggle and the problem of human destiny. He faced them boldly.

John Fitzgerald Kennedy said that he wanted to be known not only as the President who prevented war—but who won the peace. He had expressed a bold thought and held a bold hope. He faced a situation, that in this nuclear age, had made the choice quite clear. It was, simply, to strive and work in every possible way for world peace and not to continue toward the stockpiling of nuclear weapons and world frustrations and hatreds.

John Fitzgerald Kennedy knew that we could not have an overnight cessation of antagonisms and hostilities. But he knew, that for the sake of future generations, we would have to make a start, a beginning.

He followed his dream, and because he did, we have begun what may be a long journey, a hazardous journey. But, we have started, and because of this the world may be a better place for future generations.

John Fitzgerald Kennedy was a man of his age, an eloquent spokesman for our era, who was concerned with history and our posterity.

There are many programs he requested which we must now act upon and, as President Johnson has said, now is the time for action. The torch has been passed to us and we will try to carry it as bravely as our lamented President did.

If we have learned a lesson from this tragic event every American must now join together. We must, all who love this country, all who seek justice and implore mercy, unite to erase the hatred that clouds men's minds. We must cease making accusations, false and malicious, which lead men to violence. If this can be achieved our beloved President will not have died in vain.

If not, if we continue to be divided by hate groups, if we cannot disagree yet live harmoniously, then we have learned nothing from our crushing loss.

Let us move forward to achieve the Nation and world John Fitzgerald Kennedy envisioned and is now unable to share with us.

Let us never forget our heroic President standing bareheaded and unafraid, requesting, at his inauguration:

That we ask not what our country could do for us—but what we could do for our country.

Let us face the future as he did, unafraid and with faith in ourselves and in our Nation.

ADDRESS BY

Hon. George H. Mahon

OF TEXAS

Mr. Speaker, there are several of us in the House at this time who accompanied the late President John F. Kennedy on the last trip of his life and were with him when the tragic shots rang out that took his life.

On this trip President Kennedy was relaxed and cordial, he was elegant and charming in his manner. He was a picture of confidence and poise. He was good humored, humble, and patient. He was magnificent in his public utterances. The throngs who saw him were pleased and inspired by his presence. In his every action he reflected credit upon the great office which he held.

Mr. Speaker, I shall not undertake to speak at length—I had great admiration and respect for the President and I simply want humbly to join with others here in paying tribute to the memory of one I was privileged to call my friend, the late President of the United States.

ADDRESS BY

Hon. John F. Baldwin

OF CALIFORNIA

Mr. Speaker, on behalf of the citizens of my district, and of my own family, I would like to express my deepest sorrow at the tragic event which brought to such a sudden and untimely end the life of President John F. Kennedy. The citizens of our Nation had elected him to serve as our leader, our President. He was a loyal, dedicated American. The assassination of the President was a blow not only to his family but to our entire Nation. His loss is a grievous one. It is a shocking thing that the person responsible for this terrible act was unwilling to allow our Nation to function as a democracy. The citizens of my district and my family join with me in extending our deepest sympathy to Mrs. Kennedy and her two children at this tragic time. May our Creator give them strength to meet the future as He gave them strength during the 3 days preceding the funeral of the President. Their courage and moral strength during those 3 days was an inspiration for our whole Nation.

ADDRESS BY

Hon. Herbert C. Bonner

OF NORTH CAROLINA

Mr. Speaker, "We shall pay any price, bear any burden, meet any hardship, support any friend, oppose any foe to assure the survival and the success of liberty."

These are immortal words of our late, beloved President John F. Kennedy, who fell to the senseless marksmanship of a psychopath on that ugly, infamous day of November 22, 1963.

These words and many more splendid words were uttered during his inaugural address on January 21, 1961, when he was sworn in as the youngest President of this great country.

Many of us here served with Jack Kennedy when he was a Member of this House. Many of us, older than he, remember him as an eager, restless, young man who was going places. I am sure that none knew at that time of the heights he would achieve. But with an indomitable will, a sense of destiny, and a never failing good humor he went on to the Senate—and from that vigorous battleground to the campaign that led him to the highest office in the land.

Mr. Speaker, the genius of our political system has somehow made all our Presidents great.

Relatively mediocre men have—with history thrust into their hands—met the challenge. In every case our Nation has moved forward in greater or less degree. But John F. Kennedy knew where he was going from the beginning.

Over the span of my years on Capitol Hill—which exceeds by a little bit that of our great new President—I have often recognized the ingredients of greatness. Some are born with them. Some acquire them.

The tousled haired young man from Massachusetts who attended his duties in the House from November 1946 to November 1952, when he went to the Senate, was a man of patriotism—in action.

Yes, there are many of us who knew him; many of us who somehow felt his dynamic influence. But, many of us did not appreciate, in the fullest sense, those qualities until he burst upon the world stage as President of the United States—and became, through his own personal powers, a new and vital force for the advancement of this Nation—and the world.

This Nation—and the world—mourns the wasteful death of John F. Kennedy, who dwelt with us so brilliantly for much too short a time. The lost years of his normal promise are things we will long ponder.

What would they have meant had he been given a full chance to show his mettle?

His record, the words, the philosophies, which he left behind set examples and goals by which to live and to aspire.

On this sad requiem day, as in all the long days since the 22d of November, let us thank God that John Fitzgerald Kennedy came this way.

And let us thank God, too, that the American ideal contains the firm, strong thread to keep our system going forward under a vigorous, able person like Lyndon Johnson, on whom the mantle falls. President Johnson has received the torch to carry the flame of liberty.

Mr. Speaker, I join with all the other Members of this body in expressing my deepest sympathy and admiration to that great and noble young woman, Jacqueline Kennedy, who was the source of so much inspiration to her husband—as she has been to all of us since his untimely death.

ADDRESS BY

Hon. Michael A. Feighan

OF OHIO

Mr. Speaker, the untimely death of President John F. Kennedy has inscribed a sad and tragic chapter in the history of our great Nation.

Our beloved President was a source of strength, inspiration, and hope for our people and for countless millions of others in many distant lands. The full measure of our loss is indescribable, for his lifework embodied the spirit of heroism, dedication, brilliant and confident leadership, and unselfish devotion to the highest American ideals. It is little wonder that the shocking news of his death struck our people a blow that can be compared only with the shock of Pearl Harbor.

The stature of John F. Kennedy loomed large on the world stage. During the course of a short 2 years and 10 months as our President, the quality of his leadership made of him a giant among giants. In all the things that he did, his abiding confidence in the noble cause he led was matched by an uncommon inner confidence in his abilities to meet and resolve the many challenges confronting our Nation and the free world community. And these attributes of true greatness shone through the daily test and trial of his leadership like a bright silver lining in an overcast sky. The course of his journey through life was charted by the steady and certain guidance of Divine Providence on which he depended and which he constantly sought.

John F. Kennedy was an unyielding champion of peace with freedom and justice for all men and all nations.

John F. Kennedy was a tireless fighter for human rights, equal dignity, and equal opportunity for all the people of our Nation.

John F. Kennedy was an implacable foe of poverty, disease, illiteracy, injustice, and all forms of tyranny.

John F. Kennedy was blessed by his Maker with many rare talents and he happily turned those talents to a life of labor for the benefit of his fellow men.

These immortal lines of personal dedication, spoken by our late President in closing his inaugural address, resound today as a clear trumpet's call to this generation of Americans:

With a good conscience our only sure reward, with history the final judge of our deeds, let us go forth to lead the land we love, asking His blessings and His help, but knowing that here on earth God's work must truly be our own.

Our country has lost one of its most noble souls and gifted citizens. Our memory of him as the architect of a heroic age in an era of uncertainty and fear will never die. May his noble soul find peace and comfort in eternal rest.

I join the people of our saddened land in expressing condolences to Mrs. Kennedy and her dear children and to all the members of the Kennedy family in this hour of national mourning.

ADDRESS BY

Hon. Frank Chelf

OF KENTUCKY

Mr. Speaker, in the gracious words of our late and beloved friend and President, John F. Kennedy, "thank you, thank you so very much" for your recognition of me so that I might say a few words of eulogy with respect to our fallen and martyred leader.

Among the many very real and beautiful talents that President Kennedy possessed, such as honor, integrity, courage, intelligence, wit, humor, dedication, loyalty, ability, youth and many, many others, he had a genuine love and respect for his fellow man. In my opinion he had more consideration for others than any man I have ever known in any office high or low. If you will please pardon the personal reference let me give you an example. The President and I were personal friends. Our friendship dates back to when we served together as young Members in this House. I was elected in 1944 and he came to Washington in 1946. Whenever I had a birthday he would send me a letter of congratulations. Each time he did so his staff would write the salutation "Dear Congressman Chelf" and invariably the President in his own handwriting would cross out the "Dear Congressman" and write in "Dear Frank." He was not only considerate but a kind and generous person as well.

For instance, when my dear brother, Henry Lee Chelf, passed away, a personal letter of condolence came to me from the President. Truly it was one of the sweetest, most considerate acts of kindness ever done me. His greatness was his deep humility.

Mr. Speaker, I could speak for hours on this great and good man, but I know that President Kennedy is now sitting in a special room, looking out at all of us from a special window, from a special rocking chair fashioned of love, immortality, and eternity—yes, he sits in God's own presence and in God's own mansion. Why? Because President John Fitzgerald Kennedy "let his light so shine that men might see his good works and glorify our Father, which art in heaven."

Our beloved President lived an exemplary life, one of moderation, courage, of kindness, of gentleness, one that was free of hate, malice, and bigotry. He read and loved the Bible and I am sure that he has said to Almighty God many times these words from the book of books:

Let the words of my mouth and the meditations of my heart be acceptable in Thy sight O Lord my strength and my redeemer.

It is no wonder that all the world was stunned by his sudden tragic death.

We are all better men, better women, better legislators and we are a better country because John Fitzgerald Kennedy passed our way and served approximately "a thousand days" as our President. And thank Thee, dear God, for his selection of Lyndon B. Johnson as his running mate. Bless him and guide him now and always.

To all members of his family, and most especially his stoic, gallant, magnificent widow and his lovely, wonderful, well-mannered children, Caroline and John, Jr., I extend my deepest sympathy. "May their leaf never wither and whatsoever they do—may it prosper."

ADDRESS BY

Hon. William H. Natcher

OF KENTUCKY

Mr. Speaker, the heart of our Nation is heavy today. A great American is dead and a grateful nation bows is solemn tribute. The death of our President, John F. Kennedy, is too tragic for words.

Into a world darkened by ideological struggle and actual conflict, his clarity of vision, intellectual honesty and indomitable courage brought a clear shaft of light and hope. In these times when many of the problems confronting this country and the world seem almost incapable of solution, we can ill afford to lose a man with the experience, ability, integrity and statesmanship of our late President. He had no peer in his knowledge of public affairs. His honesty and fairness were proverbial. It was these qualities which led to his rise to power and to a position which commanded the confidence of millions of Americans.

The passing of this great American is a great loss to this Nation and to the free world. To his grieving family we can offer only the comfort that John F. Kennedy won an assured place in history and a permanent resting place in the hearts of all good men.

ADDRESS BY

Hon. John J. Rooney

OF NEW YORK

Mr. Speaker, it is with a deep feeling of sadness at the untimely loss of our beloved President, John Fitzgerald Kennedy, that I this afternoon join my colleagues in these eulogies. Really, I cannot find the words to adequately express the reaction I had when I first heard the tragic news on that fateful afternoon of November 22, 1963. The feeling of utter helplessness I had then, overcomes me again today in trying to find words to properly express the sadness I have suffered in the passing of John Fitzgerald Kennedy.

The moving tributes from my distinguished colleagues certainly indicate the high esteem, admiration and respect that was felt for President Kennedy and there is little that one can say which would not be repetitious. The most fitting tribute we as a nation could give to our late President would be for each and every citizen to strive to bring to an end the hatred which incites destruction and death, for President Kennedy's dream was to have a peaceful world in which his children and ours could live. In the words of

Abraham Lincoln, whose life was a great inspiration to President Kennedy:

Let him have the marble monument along with the well-assured and more enduring one in the hearts of those who loved liberty, unselfishly, for all men.

I am indeed proud to be able to say that John Fitzgerald Kennedy was one of the finest friends I have had in my lifetime. I first came to know him when he became a Member of this body in January 1947. I worked closely with him on a number of matters, including his legislation to separate airmail pay from subsidy moneys for the airlines. He helped me in connection with the erection of the beautiful statue in honor of Comdr. John Barry, the father of the American Navy, unveiled in September 1956 at Crescent Quay, Wexford, Ireland. It was this statue on which President Kennedy placed a wreath last June. At his invitation, I had the privilege to meet with him for a few days at his father's home in Palm Beach at Christmastime in 1960 following his election to the Presidency of the United States. I also had the great privilege of being one of the Members of this House invited to attend his wedding at Newport, R.I., in 1953.

During those hectic days following November 22 when our country was grasping for something of which it could be proud, we found that something in the strength, endurance and devotion of Mrs. John F. Kennedy. My heartfelt sympathy and prayers are with her, Caroline and John John, and the entire Kennedy family in their great loss.

ADDRESS BY

Hon. Joe L. Evins

OF TENNESSEE

Mr. Speaker, the flag of our country and the hearts of our people continue to fly at half-mast because of the death of John F. Kennedy, the late President of the United States.

I join with my colleagues in mourning his passing and in paying a brief but sincere tribute to his memory and to his life of dedicated service to our country.

I was shocked and saddened, as all the world was shocked and saddened, to learn of his un-

timely passing—to know of this most terrible tragedy which took the life of the young, brilliant 35th President of the United States.

In his passing the cause of freedom has suffered an irreparable loss.

A truly great hero and champion has fallen in our midst.

Reflecting in the afterglow following this tragic event, it is well that we consider the moral implications of conditions in the world which produced such a national tragedy.

The country may well fasten the blame on a single individual and attribute to him a diseased and depraved mind. History may possibly label this era as an era of hate and suspicion and an age which produced an unhealthy climate filled with the venom of hate in which the assassination of the President was but a single expression.

Perhaps the death of John F. Kennedy will signal the beginning of the end of the hate period in America and in the hearts of men everywhere. If such a condition would occur, then the President's life would have been given for a most noble purpose unparalleled and unequaled in time.

In the year that John F. Kennedy first ran for Congress from Massachusetts, I also ran for Congress—from Tennessee—and after the election in 1946 we came together as classmates in 1947 to the 80th Congress. It was my privilege to work with "Jack" Kennedy and to come to know him as a warm and personable friend.

In our freshman class he was elected president of the Young Democrats of the 80th Congress and was early marked as a man of destiny.

My esteem and respect for him continued to grow and increase over the years. Our friendship continued through his terms of service in the House and in the Senate and during his years in the White House.

Born of wealth he might have chosen a life of relative ease—a life with few problems and many comforts. Instead he chose a career of public service—predicated upon the choice of the electorate—and a life filled with service to the cause of democracy and our country.

He brought to this life of service a great intellect, dedication, and immense courage.

He was taken from us in the prime of life while at the height of service but his 46 years were filled with accomplishments and with rich contributions to his country—the America which he loved with intense devotion.

America and the free world have lost a great leader, and I have lost a personal friend.

I am proud to have known John F. Kennedy.

I am proud to have walked in the Halls of Congress and to have served with him.

John F. Kennedy the man is dead—but, John F. Kennedy the patriot will live forever.

The principles for which he lived and died will continue to shine forth as a perpetual monument to this great and good man. His place in history as a dynamic, forceful, and foresighted President is assured. His brilliance and eloquence will serve as a continual reminder to Americans of the ideals and goals to which our country can aspire. I believe these goals are best summed up in the words of the late President himself when he said in his inaugural address:

And so, my fellow Americans, ask not what your country can do for you—ask what you can do for your country.

As the Nation observes the official period of mourning for our late President, I extend my deepest sympathy to Mrs. Kennedy and the other members of his family in their bereavement.

ADDRESS BY

Hon. Seymour Halpern

OF NEW YORK

Mr. Speaker, on Friday, November 22, a devastating blow was struck at every one of us.

On that day, and for days thereafter, there were stunned, unbelieving looks on the faces of the people: crowds in the street, mourners in the President's funeral procession; wherever you looked you saw shock and incredulity.

The bullet of the assassin had come like a wind of hurricane force out of clear skies, to strike down our wise and beloved leader, and to endanger our Ship of State in the difficult navigation of the waters of national and international affairs.

We are all shaken, not only by the sudden tragic loss of a courageous and vital President, but by the realization of how powerless our pre-

cautions of police and other guards have proved against the spite and ingenuity of a viciously twisted mind. This silly little man, cocksure in his own warped and opinionated ideas, has taken the life of one of the leading human beings of the world, and deprived the people and nations of the world of a great man's inspiring strength and energy and guiding wisdom in the good fight for peace, justice, and human dignity.

Tragically, the rule of law in our country has been grossly violated, first by the brutal assassination itself, second by the shooting down in cold blood of the policeman trying to apprehend the suspected assassin, and third by the murder of the handcuffed suspect himself.

But in noble contrast to this breakdown of order and justice, in these sudden and violent events, we see the entire Nation, and the vast majority of the nations of the world, joining in a dignified, orderly, and impressive series of actions. In the honors paid to the slain President, in solemn processions and in lying in state, in the religious rites of his church, in the presence of high officials and heads of state of many countries at his funeral, we see recognition both of the intrinsic value of the man and of the dignity of his office. No assassin's bullet could reach or damage either that value or that dignity.

In Mrs. Kennedy's behavior we see the utmost love for her husband combined with a noble concern for the welfare of our country, and a touching courtesy toward all who came to mourn her husband's death. Our hearts and prayers were with her during those long hours of terrible anguish, and our love and sympathy will always be with her and her children in all the days ahead. Our grief and our profound sympathy go out to all the bereaved members of the Kennedy family, who set an unforgettable example for us all of the strength, warmth, and beauty of a close and loving American family.

In these sad and turbulent events we see, too, our ship of state surviving the sudden shock, and once more breasting the waves, as a new captain, experienced and conscientious, takes the wheel. In this reaction to the tragic event, we find a great consolation. Our party differences, our conflicts of opinion about various governmental measures taken or under consideration, give way for the time to our basic loyalty to the American democratic system of government. The transition from one administration to another has been marked, not by any conflict or irregularity, but by an ease and good will springing from our universal devotion to constitutional principles and the democratic process. Leaders of both parties have affirmed their unhesitating loyalty to our new President, the line of succession is known and accepted, and the necessary steps have been taken to prepare for any such transition in the future.

The people of America today send up fervent prayers to God that our new captain be given the strength and wisdom he will need to carry on the great task that has so suddenly become his responsibility. In our prayers, we recall with mournful gratitude the great sacrifice made by our late captain, President John F. Kennedy, in his constant and strenuous efforts to keep our ship of state on a smooth and steadfast course.

John F. Kennedy was a Democrat, and a great one. I am a Republican, but proud to recognize, in this standard bearer of the rival party, a sincere and stalwart American. I can say in all honesty that he lived up to the great American tradition of bipartisanship, whenever matters of great importance to our Nation were involved, and put the interests of America above any personal, regional, or partisan considerations. His love and his shining courage were at the service of his country, as much when he served in the Presidency as when he served in the Navy.

John F. Kennedy was a practical idealist, a great statesman, and a brilliant world leader. This is not at all to say that he was not a politician, or that he was not a man devoted to his political party. He had a conviction of the rightness of a certain body of principles that he associated with that party, had developed personal and professional associations, and knew how to work in and with that party toward the attainment of national goals. He was a politician in the best sense of the word, and proud of it. He respected the two-party system, as I know every Member of this body does, and realized that as long as we have two thriving, competing, potent parties, this Nation and its liberties will be safe. His words and his actions made plain that he realized that politics is the science of government, and that good politics means good government. Partisan politics, for him, did not transcend, but served, the ideals of

freedom, justice, brotherhood, and the dignity of man.

From the very first moments of his Presidency, John F. Kennedy made of his youth a banner and a rallying cry. He took pride in being the first President born in this century, and issued a ringing call to the young people of America to join him in a vigorous, active response to the new challenges of today's world. Characteristic of this attitude of infectious courage were the words from his inaugural address that immediately preceded his well-known and often repeated peroration:

Ask not what your country can do for you—ask what you can do for your country.

We must not forget that preceding this call to duty, and underlying it, was John F. Kennedy's bold and clear-eyed vision of the dangers and difficulties that face America in the world of today.

In the long history of the world—

He said—

only a few generations have been granted the role of defending freedom in its hour of maximum danger. I do not shrink from this responsibility—I welcome it. I do not believe that any of us would exchange places with any other people or any other generation. The energy, the faith, the devotion which we bring to this endeavor will light our country and all who serve it—and the glow from that fire can truly light the world.

President Kennedy brought to his office courage, vigor, high ideals, intelligence, and the charm and elasticity of youth. He brought into his administration young men with new ideas, and explosive energy. A spirit of hope and energy and activity emanated from the man, pervading not only his immediate surroundings, but the whole Nation. Young people were inspired by his example and exhortations to undertake their own tasks, to form their own decisions, to assume their rightful share of responsibility for America and for the world. And everywhere in the world was felt the impact of John F. Kennedy's character and personality. Men and women, great and small, recognized his qualities of essential goodness and trustworthiness, felt an affection for him and an identification with him, and responded to the appeal of his nature.

As we participate, in the time ahead, with our

new President, Lyndon B. Johnson, in the Government of our great country, we know that the waters will not always be tranquil. We shall continue to face difficulties and dangers abroad, and varied troubles at home. Of course we shall not always be in agreement on what measures are best for surmounting these difficulties and dangers, and for dealing with our domestic troubles. But as President Johnson takes command, in these difficult times, we pledge to him our respect for his person and for the dignity of his office, and our loyalty to him as the visible symbol of the majesty of our Nation. The prayers of all Americans go up to God that he may be granted strength and wisdom as he leads us in the days ahead.

ADDRESS BY

Hon. Chet Holifield

OF CALIFORNIA

Mr. Speaker, for the fourth time in our 188 years of national existence, a President of the United States has been slain by an assassin's bullet. Four Presidents, each of whom were elected by a majority of our citizens to lead us in times of peace or war, have been struck down by four murderers. Four individuals at four different times took upon themselves the awesome responsibility of making the personal decision to destroy the highest official in our structure of Government.

We have elected men to the high offices of President and Vice President 47 times. Lyndon Baines Johnson is our 36th President. He is the fourth Vice President to succeed to the Presidency because the President was assassinated. Abraham Lincoln, James A. Garfield, William McKinley, and now John Fitzgerald Kennedy comprise the list of assassinated Presidents of the United States.

There have been several attempts on the lives of other Presidents, attempts which fortunately were not successful.

My remarks today will not be directed toward praise alone of John F. Kennedy. Any praise which I might give would be inadequate to express my appreciation for his contribution in

ideas, in high ideals, and quality of dedication to country.

Neither could I express my grief, the grief of my family, and the grief of my constituents at this tragic loss. This grief is augmented by the tears of millions throughout our country and the world.

It is beyond my poor talents to express the sympathy which all of us extend to his courageous wife in this time of deep sorrow. To the President's family we extend also our heartfelt sympathy.

Today I wish to go beyond the words of praise and sympathy which expresses the deep emotions we all possess.

I wish to direct my words toward analysis of the basic foundations and superstructure of a society which can at one and the same time produce a beloved citizen such as our former President and at the same time produce an individual who, given the opportunities and freedoms of our society, will nevertheless spurn those opportunities and freedoms, and destroy with an assassin's bullet our President.

I adopt this procedure because no tears or words of praise which I might give will wash away our grief nor will my poor words ennoble his character or memory. Perhaps it is better that we turn away from our sorrow and face the problems and opportunities which we have, and try to correct society's defects for the benefit of the people our President served and loved.

How do we explain, in this country with its great belief in government by majority election of public servants, the assassination of our President, this throwback to the age of violence when national leaders were assassinated almost as an ordinary procedure?

We can only explain these sporadic acts of violence as the result of the fact that men have not reached the goal of self-control as individuals or as nations. Murder, hate, violence, and evil still lurk in the background of the mind. Its repression from overt act or expression depends on the degree of stability and nobility of the human mind.

In our society, we have moved too slowly in the field of understanding the social sciences. We have moved too slowly in the treatment of mental diseases and mental retardation.

We have moved too slowly in eradicating from

our country the slums and cesspools of ignorance, poverty, and disease which breed twisted minds that are unable and unwilling to face the pressures of our time. As long as we refuse to face the problem areas in our society with realism and with the determination to improve those defective areas, just that long will we be faced with the results of our indifference.

Total protection, from deliberately planned assassination of high public officials, probably can never be obtained in any kind of society. Such protection in a free society is much more difficult for many reasons. Most of our public officials are men of substantial personal courage. They resent and refuse to live behind bulletproof shields. They accept the risk of death in an environment of freedom rather than accept the restrictions for security which could be imposed on their daily lives for greater personal protection.

With this realization in mind, however, we should take all reasonable precautions which are endurable to protect the lives of our President and other high officials from danger. I am sure the President's security people will strengthen, wherever possible, their protective care of the President and his personal and official family.

There is an obligation of society—of each citizen—which can and should be discharged. The collective obligation of society can be strengthened by eradicating ignorance of the mind by education. It can eliminate the slum environment which breeds poverty and sickness of body and mind. The cost of correction of these areas of neglect and limitation of opportunity can never, never equal the cost of crime, sickness and unemployment, the cost of which we now must pay. The tempo of society's collective action must be increased.

The basic responsibility for improvement of our social environment rests upon the individual citizen.

In the final summation of the value of a society, we must always turn to its component units, that is, the individual citizen must be informed. The citizen must participate in government.

The citizen must assume the responsibilities of expending time and dollars in collective and personal efforts to improve the society in which we must live. The responsibilities of the citizen in a free society are many. They are many because our society becomes daily more complex. Time and space do not permit the enumeration or evaluation of a good citizen's responsibilities.

At this time I comment on a grave and growing factor in American political life.

A representative constitutional type of government such as ours, is, in my opinion, the most rewarding type of government yet devised. It offers more individual opportunity. It offers a better and wider base of economic rewards. More important, it provides greater individual freedoms and liberties.

If these statements are true, and I believe their verity cannot be challenged, then we must as citizens understand the political philosophy which supports our basic structure of government.

Basically our structure of Federal Government is divided into three parts, executive, legislative, and judicial. The executive and legislative parts are directly under the control of the citizens. The citizens elect their policymaking officials. Every 2, 4, and 6 years, the voting citizens select and elect their President, Senators, and Representatives. The judicial part of our Government, under our Constitution, has its personnel selected by the President and approved by the Senate. Therefore, its basic existence stems from the citizens' choice of a President and their Senators.

The citizens' choice of Federal representatives, President and Vice President is in turn based on the principle of majority choice. It is equally important that the minority accept the majority's choices. I cannot emphasize too strongly the importance of this basic principle of our form of government. Unless we accept it and live by it, our form of government cannot long endure. It has provided the basic procedure of transition from President to President, from U.S. Senator to succeeding Senator, from U.S. Representative to succeeding U.S. Representative. These transitions have occurred without strife, violence, or armed conflict between groups of citizens. Even when elections have been very close, as in the 1960 presidential election when less than one-tenth of 1 percent of the votes gave John F. Kennedy the majority over Richard M. Nixon, the principle held steadfast. The people accepted the principle of majority selection and election.

Transition from Republican Party control passed quietly to the control of the Democratic party. The quiet acceptance of the minority—by such a narrow margin—was a proof of the maturity of the citizen electorate and a testimonial to our constitutional strength.

From the executive and legislative sections of the Federal Government let us turn to the judicial section, the Supreme Court and its subordinate Federal courts. Here again we find the principle of majority decision at the highest level of our judicial system, the Supreme Court of the United States.

The actions of the executive and legislative branches of government must be in harmony with the Constitution of the United States. The citizen has the ultimate right of appeal against those actions to the Supreme Court if a constitutional controversy is actually involved.

The Supreme Court cannot legislate. It can and must interpret the existing law in relation to our basic constitution. While the interpretation frequently gives final meaning to legislated enactments, it need not be the final determination of legislative purpose and intent. The Congress can always enact new laws for the purpose of changing the Supreme Court's decisions. As long as the new law is in harmony with the Constitution, it can and does clarify, modify or nullify existing law. When the Supreme Court is again confronted with a similar or different problem, it must take into consideration the new action of the Congress.

I have made this very brief exposition of some of the basic principles of our structure of constitutional Federal Government for an important purpose. I have sought to lay a foundation of understanding and appreciation for the structure of government per se. I believe that our national destiny depends on the preservation of our basic structure of constitutional government, such as I have described.

Unless the structure is preserved—unless its procedures are safeguarded—unless its laws and decisions are respected, our Government will be destroyed.

There is abroad in our land forces which seek to destroy the confidence of our citizens in the integrity and efficacy of our traditional structure of government—in the efficacy and values of its procedures and in the integrity of its elected and appointed officials.

At this point, I want to clearly state that there is a distinct difference between the criticism of a law enacted by the Congress and a criticism of Congress as an institution of constitutional government.

There is a clear difference between the criticism of a Supreme Court decision or a difference in belief as to the validity of a Supreme Court interpretation of a law, and the vicious, intemperate criticism of the Supreme Court as a constitutional body.

There is a sharp difference between the criticism of any official act of an elected or appointed official of government and a vicious, intemperate and usually unfounded attack on the character and integrity of a particular official in government.

I will go even further and say that I would not curtail the right of any person or communication media from criticizing any elected or appointed official of government for any personal offense against the laws or moral standards of our society. It is necessary that the right of criticism be zealously guarded for the protection of our basic institutions and liberties. But those who use the freedom of press and word also bear a responsibility for the preservation of truth and justice. A public official can be destroyed by the spreading of innuendoes, snide stories, and unfounded rumors. Those who use these dangerous methods strike a blow at the integrity and the character of men who represent, in the public mind at least, the personification of government.

If these indefensible tactics persist, it will become more and more difficult to obtain the services of responsible men for public service in Government.

Neither do I believe that criticism should be prohibited against any public servant for an official vote, act, or decision. But, I say let that criticism be based on the merits which are involved in the case and not based on a vicious attack against the motives, integrity, or patriotism of the person who made such vote, act, or decision.

There are too many people today who seek simple answers to complicated national and international problems. They seek and accept the simple answer—the vicious statement—the character-assassinating explanation.

These people seek their kind for comfort and mutual encouragement. They organize in action groups of the Communist and extreme left. They organize in the hate groups of the extreme right.

Whether left or right, they are impatient with constitutional procedures and functions of orderly government. They seek not only to discredit a President, a Senator, or a Representative by character assassination and personal defamation—they seek to destroy confidence in the structure of government. They offer vague and untried substitutes for orderly and proven methods of evolutionary change.

These extremists of the left and right go much further than logical argument and explanation of position. They forsake the calm appeal to reason and the sane methods of persuasion. They adopt the tactics of the fanatic. They adopt the tactics of the Communist cell or the Nazi storm troopers. They disrupt civic meetings and organizations with violence of word and deed. These extremists operate their printing presses and mimeograph machines night and day, spewing out their vicious poison into the homes of our citizens.

These are the hate groups, frequently hiding behind innocent front names of various kinds. They purloin decent words such as "Christian," "peace," "American," "constitution," "freedom," and "liberty" and embody them in their titles of organization, for the purpose of recruiting the simple or unwary.

Their doctrine is the doctrine of hate—hate of the President, hate of the Congress, hate of the Supreme Court, hate of the United Nations, hate of the Jews, hate of the Catholics, hate of all religion, hate of liberals, hate of conservatives, hate, hate, hate.

This river of hate—this ocean of venom—is threatening the basic structures of our Nation. The strong mind, the well balanced and informed mind, can evaluate its evil and reject it.

The indifferent mind can close its ears and turn carelessly away.

The simple mind or the unbalanced mind too often accepts it and becomes victim to its poison.

These are the minds that twist and writhe under the stimulus of hate until only destructive action can give them relief from their emotional torment.

In this Nation as in every nation under the sun, we have our share of weak minds, simple minds, unbalanced and twisted minds. These people are sick people in mind if not in body. The solution for their care or cure is neither simple nor

cheap. They will be with us in the future as in the past.

These twisted minds cannot control the stimulus of hate. They cannot cope with the vicious lies and denunciations against public officials, public policies, and public institutions. Lee Harvey Oswald's mind was twisted by hate. He hated our institutions. The fact that he subscribed to the doctrine of the extreme left is no more pertinent than had he subscribed to the doctrine of the extreme right. The pertinent point is that his mind was twisted with hate. His act of violence against the President was embedded in his hate for our institutions and our public officials.

Lee Harvey Oswald was the end result of subversive beliefs and the doctrines of hate. His deed of violence was the evil fruit from the tree of hate.

Let all of those who spread the doctrine of hate take note. The seeds they plant today will inevitably produce the evil fruit of hate and violence tomorrow, or some future tomorrow.

President Lyndon Johnson, in his first address to the joint session of Congress on Wednesday, November 27, 1963, said:

The time has come for Americans of all races and creeds and political beliefs to understand and respect one another. So let us put an end to the teaching and preaching of hate and evil and violence. Let us turn away from the fanatics of the far left and the far right, from the apostles of bitterness and bigotry, from those defiant of law, and those who pour venom into our national bloodstream.

Along with every other loyal citizen, I know we can say, "Amen." I know that we too can "highly resolve that John Fitzgerald Kennedy did not live—or die—in vain."

ADDRESS BY

Hon. Ogden R. Reid

OF NEW YORK

Mr. Speaker, today we are met in simple tribute to John F. Kennedy. All America sits here too—expressing, I believe, a sense of personal loss.

Throughout the world these past days, people from all walks of life have mourned too.

Here in the House we join in extending our deepest condolences to Mrs. Jacqueline Kennedy and the family. From her grace, courage, and fortitude we take fresh inspiration.

Mr. Speaker, as a young President, John F. Kennedy truly articulated the dreams of America and inspired young men and women to new dimensions of service in the cause of peace. His hopeful and courageous approach to the future will long live in the hearts of the people.

Who can forget his call to a new generation of Americans—"ask not what your country can do for you—ask what you can do for your country."

Who can forget his injunction "to invoke the wonders of science instead of its terrors" in exploring the stars, conquering the deserts, eradicating disease, tapping the ocean depths and encouraging the arts and commerce.

Who can forget his recognition of the great truth that our "revolutionary beliefs"—including the rights of man—"come not from the generosity of the State but from the hand of God."

Now that he has passed—but with us still—let us remember his imperatives:

First. That "our strength as well as our convictions have imposed upon this Nation the role of leader in freedom's cause."

Second. That "continued Federal legislative inaction—on civil rights—will continue, if not increase, racial strife—causing the leadership of both sides to pass from the hands of reasonable and responsible men to the purveyors of hate and violence."

Third. That in building the peace—"together we shall save our planet or together we shall perish in its flames" and that "it is our intention to challenge the Soviet Union, not to an arms race, but to a peace race; to advance step by step, stage by stage, until general and complete disarmament has actually been achieved."

Finally, do not his words before the Massachusetts Legislature bear relevance to each of us here in the Congress:

Of those of whom much is given, much is required. And when at some future date the high court of history sits in judgment on each one of us—recording whether in our brief span of service we fulfilled our responsibilities to the State—our success or failure, in whatever office we may hold, will be measured by the answers to four questions: were we truly men of courage—were we truly men of judgment—were we truly men of integrity—were we truly men of dedication.

And now, Mr. Speaker, in this hour of stark tragedy for our country, may we stand as one man back of our President and our Government. May Almighty God guide and sustain President Lyndon Johnson.

ADDRESS BY

Hon. Paul C. Jones

OF MISSOURI

Mr. Speaker, as we are gathered here today to pay tribute to the memory of a young courageous hero, my prayer to God is that he has not died in vain. I have neither the words nor the eloquence of speech to express the feelings that I have experienced since hearing the first report, that came over the radio to which I was listening at the time, that our President had been shot. "Who" and "why?" were the first questions to enter my mind. Incredulous, I reasoned, that here in the United States, an assassin's bullet would be the means of extinguishing the life of the President of the United States. But as the minutes and hours passed, with the news bulletins of the rapidly developing events of the day, I began reminding myself of the increasing evidences of hatred, bigotry, distrust, and lack of respect for constituted authority which apparently has been growing in this country for sometime. It was then that I began to reluctantly admit to myself that such a tragedy was possible. Was this God's way of shocking this Nation into a realization of the responsibilities of each of us as individual members of what had been presumed to be an enlightened and intelligent society? Was it His way of reminding us that we as a Nation had so far departed from the ways of decency, that we were approaching a moral degeneration that would eventually and inevitably result in the decline and fall of the United States of America, the last hope for millions of people who were being forced to live not only in a world of turmoil, but under conditions that prevented them from enjoying the peace, the freedom and the many advantages of life that were synonymous with the United States? In the almost 2 weeks that have passed since that tragic day, including the traditional Thanksgiving season, we have come to realize that despite the great loss which this world has suffered, we still have many things about which we can be thankful. The uninterrupted transition which has occurred in the President's office has demonstrated to the world that our system of Government is sound and stable, and to me at least it has demonstrated that the Founding Fathers who originally established this Government and drafted the original Constitution, were acting under the guiding eye of a benevolent Creator. Our prayers, during the past few days have been for our new Commander in Chief, that God may continue to give him the wisdom, the understanding, the courage and the strength, to lead this Nation in the direction that He would have us go; that we may continue to be an inspiration to other nations, less fortunate, to convince them, through our actions and our deeds, and not through force or compulsion, that our way is one that they may safely follow. And, yes, Mr. Speaker, our prayers are for the widow and the children of our late departed friend and leader. Mrs. Jacqueline Kennedy has demonstrated to the world that she is a tower of strength, a most remarkable woman by any standard. Nothing that we can say or do here today can assuage her grief, and none of us can fully understand the agony and torture that she has borne during these trying days, or even the days ahead, but I know it is the hope and prayer of all of us that during the days and years to come she will have every reason to believe, and that her children as they grow into maturity will realize that the sacrifice which this husband and father made, has left its imprint upon all posterity, and that President John Fitzgerald Kennedy did not die in vain. May his soul rest in peace, and may God's richest blessing be upon his family and all those he loved.

Mr. Speaker, I am including herewith an editorial, written by Jack Stapleton, Jr., publisher of the Daily Dunklin Democrat, of Kennett, Mo., which appeared in that publication on Monday, November 25, 1963.

John Fitzgerald Kennedy

John Fitzgerald Kennedy was laid to rest today.

And his life has become a part of the heritage of America, to be told and retold down through the ages of this Nation and of the world.

A sobbing Nation today paid its last formal tribute to John F. Kennedy, but in the days and years ahead, there will be many more tributes paid to the 35th President of the United States of America.

Although the events of the last few days hang like a nightmare over the minds of Americans, there is enough reality in the events since Friday to make us realize there has indeed been a tragic death in the American community, that a void has been left in the Nation's leadership, that a man with a great vision for world peace and brotherhood has lost his life in the cause of freedom and human dignity.

Even if we cannot understand the reasons for them, Americans everywhere have begun to realize the significance of the death of John Fitzgerald Kennedy. There is a new President in the land, and by virtue of his experience, his devotion and his dedication to public life, Americans somehow feel that Lyndon B. Johnson will be a great President in his own right.

One of the reasons for this sense of security in the new President is the record of the one he succeeds. From the office of the Presidency, John F. Kennedy had assumed the leadership of not only these 50 States but of the entire free world. This mantle of leadership came not only because he was the Chief Executive of the United States of America, but because he displayed those qualities of determination, intelligence, fortitude and bravery for which mankind grasps and so often fails to achieve.

As elaborate and grandiose as all of the formal eulogies were, they were echoed time and time again by every American who has often wept silent or open tears since the assassination last Friday. For it was with the average citizen that one could find the perfect tribute, the heartfelt sorrow of his death. As one Washington woman said as she stood across from the White House last Friday night, sobbing quietly, "He belonged to all of us, he belonged to all of us." A man standing beside her turned and replied, "Yes, we know that now."

In a real sense, the death of John F. Kennedy is a martyrdom which gives promise of returning America to an emotional stability which has been too long lacking in this nation of ours. For in America, where civilization has reached a zenith in so many areas of life, we have too often forgotten that the cause of freedom demands the best in us, and the best from us, if we are to measure up to our responsibilities as citizens.

Like a cancer has grown the hate, the grumbling, awful hate which blackens men's hearts with violence, both in word and deed. The strident cry of the alarmist, the racist, the hatemonger, the extremes of both sides have too often turned American against American. A breeding of suspicion has been cast over the land until it has festered for so long that hate and discontent have become a part and parcel of the American community as much as affluence and progress.

The admonition, "Thou shalt love thy neighbor as thyself" has been a mockery in American life for too long; the struggle for mankind's freedom around the globe has come second, nay third or fourth, in too many lives, in too many minds, in too many hearts.

When this hate is exposed, as it was Friday in all of its stark terror, America can too often see itself mirrored in the actions of a madman. And the awful consequences of this hatred, this contempt for others, this lack of Godliness in our lives is then held up for America to see.

By the grace of God, may we see before it is too late and all of mankind stands before judgment.

It is too early to judge critically the administration of the 35th President. Proper reflection, intelligent analysis, free of emotion, will be required to make a proper appraisal. But to every American, the dedication of John F. Kennedy to the cause of human freedom around the world is inescapable. During his relatively short tenure, he led this Nation through some of its most trying times. His record of leadership in this single, most-important phase of his office has seldom, if ever, been surpassed. The direct confrontation, for the first time in the world's nuclear age, between the free world and the Communist world is of such major importance that it may well mark the most significant date of the 1960's. That direct confrontation with a nuclear power that seeks our destruction was of such awesome proportions that many Americans still cannot grasp its full meaning. It was the 35th President of the United States who, as only he could do, ordered and directed that confrontation. And in all of the events of reality of last April, the awful truth of mankind's destiny stood fully in focus. For this moment, John F. Kennedy may well have been divinely created by his God.

Blessed be the poor in spirit—blessed be those who weep this day for John F. Kennedy.

Blessed are they that mourn—may they understand the cause for which he died and embrace it forever in their hearts.

Blessed are the meek—may the qualities of our fallen President be a part of our minds, our bodies and our souls, now and always.

Blessed are they which hunger and thirst after righteousness—may they lead us through a period of hate to the land of peace and forgiveness.

Blessed are the merciful—may the quality forever be America's.

Blessed are the pure in heart—for they shall be divinely ordained to carry the banner of peace and love.

Blessed are the peacemakers—and may we as mankind emulate them from this day on.

Blessed are they which are persecuted for righteousness sake—for theirs is the Kingdom of Heaven.

God bless John Fitzgerald Kennedy.

God bless America.

ADDRESS BY

Hon. Clement J. Zablocki

OF WISCONSIN

Mr. Speaker, the assassination of President Kennedy is a tragedy for our Nation and for the cause of human freedom throughout the world. As no one else in our time he was able to awaken in the hearts of our people an awareness of the tasks we must perform before America's ideals can become a reality for all men.

He called our attention to the unfinished business of our society; he spoke of the long twilight struggle for the freedom of man; he asked that we consider what we can do—and should do—for our country. During the brief time he spent in the White House, he devoted himself with rare courage and energy to the attainment of the promise of America—both for our people and for those of other lands.

I knew President Kennedy as a leader and a friend. We met in 1948 when I entered Congress. Later it was my privilege to assist him in the Wisconsin primary and in the presidential campaign, on his road to the White House. We met frequently in the past 3 years, most recently upon my return in mid-October from the fact-finding trip to southeast Asia. At that meeting, as before, I was impressed with the youthful vigor, clear thinking, and historical perspective of President Kennedy. As Cardinal Cushing said in eulogy of him: "We shall not see his like again."

In President Kennedy's death, we have lost a friend, a good man and a great leader. Let us pray that with his passing we shall not also lose the will which he awakened within us, the will to follow the course which he had set for us. For if that should occur, then President Kennedy's death will go down as one of the most tragic events in our Nation's history.

I am confident, however, that our people will rally from this stunning blow to once again move forward under the able leadership of President Lyndon Johnson. In our journey we have as our beacon the symbolic eternal light that flickers by the grave in Arlington Cemetery where lie the mortal remains of John Fitzgerald Kennedy.

As we mourn his loss, let us rededicate ourselves to the ideals and principles for which he fought. May God have mercy upon his soul and the United States of America which he served so well.

To Mrs. Jacqueline Kennedy, the children and the Kennedy family go our sincere prayers that the good Lord may assist them in their great trial and sorrow.

Mr. Speaker, exercising the general permission to revise remarks and to include editorials eulogizing our beloved, late President John Fitzgerald Kennedy, I join with my colleague, the distinguished gentleman from the Fifth District of Wisconsin, Congressman Reuss, in placing the editorials that appeared in the Milwaukee Journal and Milwaukee Sentinel at this point.

[From the Milwaukee Journal, Nov. 23, 1963]

JOHN FITZGERALD KENNEDY

A stunned people and a shocked world stand transfixed in the presence of a most monstrous and senseless crime—assassination of the leader of earth's greatest nation. There have been Presidents shot before by cowards and idiots, but the killing of John Kennedy appalls and numbs the mind as that of Abraham Lincoln did.

Politics and policies have no relevance at this moment. Here was a brilliant young man of great ability, great determination, great ideals for the future of America and the free world. His elevation to the Presidency had captured every imagination, and was a hope and a promise to millions on all the continents.

The mind almost repels belief that suddenly he is gone. Though he will be ably succeeded and the world will go on, the murder of the President in his young prime, still in the midst of his first term and of a dangerous era, so much to do and so little time, is stark catastrophe.

Words fail. There is no room even for rage at the murderer. For this moment, the heart can do no more than share in spirit the terrible grief of the young widow and two little children, and pray God's strength for President Lyndon Johnson.

[From the Milwaukee Journal, Nov. 24, 1963]

JOHN FITZGERALD KENNEDY

The tragedy of the assassination of John Fitzgerald Kennedy will be with us and the world for a long time. This young, vibrant, eloquent man was leader not only of the United States but of the free world. The measure of the loss is still smothered by the impact of shock and the horror of the crime that took him.

President Kennedy was the vanguard of youth that was ready to take over the leadership of nations from the tired and aging men whose roots go well back into the beginning of the century. In a real sense his was the voice of the future and of a new and better world. That voice, always articulate, often moving, was listened to by men everywhere.

For the United States the tragedy is personal and bitter. Not all men liked the policies of the President. But few did not admire him as a human being. He and his family had brought a warmth and a vibrancy to the White House which had lacked them for too long.

But there are many who also admired him for his policies and his ideas and ideals. They looked to him as a hope in an uneasy world. There were many who loved him. The heart of every American will go out to his family, which loved him most.

There is so little that can be said when a great man has gone. The void always seems so tremendous, the future so dark, the fears so sharp. The country will go on, of course, for it is a great country of great strengths. The sun that goes down will give rise to new suns.

History has yet to deal with John Fitzgerald Kennedy. One can guess that it will deal well. He was a new type of political leader emerging from the old—freer of emotion than most, a pragmatist. He saw the world clearly, and while he aimed high he had the realism to accept the limitations of men and events.

The problems that men created, Mr. Kennedy said, can be solved by men. His no longer is the responsibility. It passes to other shoulders, and it is heavy. As the Nation mourns it will do well to take to heart the words that President Kennedy spoke in New York City only a few days ago:

"My fellow Americans, let us be guided by our interests, not our indignation. Let us heed the words of Paul the Apostle to the Galatians:

" 'Let us not be weary in well doing,' he wrote, 'for in due season we shall reap, if we faint not.'

"And let the word go forth—to all who are concerned about the future of the human family—that we will not be weary in well doing and we will faint not; and we shall, in due season, reap a harvest of peace and security for all members of the family of man."

[From the Milwaukee Journal, Nov. 28, 1963]

OUR UNFINISHED TASKS

Eighteen days before he was assassinated, John F. Kennedy issued the Presidential proclamation of Thanksgiving Day for 1963. The document bears the marks of his gift for the felicitous strong phrase. It may now be reread as a sort of testament, telling what he would have us do.

After recounting how the tradition grew along with the Nation's population, plenty, and power, Mr. Kennedy wrote:

"Today we give our thanks most of all for the ideals of honor and faith we inherit from our forefathers—for the decency of purpose, steadfastness of resolve and strength of will, for the courage and humility, which they possessed and which we must seek every day to emulate.

"As we express our gratitude we must never forget that the highest appreciation is not to utter words but to live by them."

And after the formal "Now, therefore," setting Thanksgiving on this fourth Thursday of November pursuant to law, the late President added a sort of postscript:

"On that day let us gather in sanctuaries dedicated to worship and in homes blessed by family affection to express our gratitude for the glorious gifts of God; and let us earnestly and humbly pray that He will continue to guide and sustain us in the great unfinished tasks of achieving peace, justice and understanding among all men and nations, and of ending misery and suffering wherever they exist."

[From the Milwaukee Sentinel, Nov. 23, 1963]

TRAGIC LOSS

There are no words to express the Nation's shock.

One can only feel, each in his own heart and mind, the reaction to the assassination of President Kennedy.

Therefore, we do not attempt to set down here any words to describe the sorrow that besets America, and indeed the world. This we leave to each person, to mourn individually in his own way.

Not this! President Kennedy assassinated! Even as we write this, we find it impossible to believe.

But it is true.

The country will be a long time recovering from the numbness that gripped every citizen as the tragic news. in agonizing bits, came out of Dallas, Tex.

So vigorously did President Kennedy apply himself to the job of being President of the United States that it will take time to realize that he has been removed from the stage and out of the role into which he had poured his life.

He was very real in Wisconsin. We learned firsthand of his consuming drive to serve his country in its highest office.

Having gone into every nook and byway of this State in search of the votes that were to put him well on the way to the Democratic nomination, Mr. Kennedy was personally known by and held a special relationship with many Wisconsin residents. Wisconsin mourns the tragedy acutely.

Mr. Kennedy's death is a tragedy in countless ways, but perhaps most of all because he has been cut down in his prime.

Even Mr. Kennedy's most severe critics would have to concede that the man had grown greatly in the nearly 3 years he was given to hold office, until at his assassination he was becoming as much the statesman as he was the politician.

Now, as we write this only a few hours after the event, is not the time to be making any judgments about the record of President Kennedy. History will do that.

This is so because as the initial shock of the tragedy wears off, some idea begins to form of the magnitude of the influence Mr. Kennedy's assassination will have on the lives of us all.

Time enough for that. For now, for us all, there is nothing to do but mourn—and pray.

———

[From the Milwaukee Sentinel, Nov. 25, 1963]

OUR NATION

To U.S. President assassins, past, present, and God forbid, future:

How can your crazed mind be made to understand that you can kill a man but you can't kill the President of the United States?

Four times now you have mortally wounded the Nation's Chief Executive. Yet the office of President of the United States has remained filled and the Nation has gone on.

You have, to be sure, rocked the ship of state. Each time, the ship shudders. But each time she has stabilized herself and has sailed on. So it will be this time. So it would be again, if your madness should erupt yet once more.

Thirty-five Presidents, four assassinated. That is a rate of one in nine. It is appalling enough of itself, but

all the more so in the light of what we so proudly hail as the American way of life.

We like to think that our system of government and society is the most enlightened the world has seen. An assassination shakes our faith in that system. Is the price of individual freedom the freedom for an individual to put a shot through the head of state?

Brutal as it sounds, perhaps that is the price. To prevent you, the assassin, from firing the fatal shot would require a police state condition that would be absolutely intolerable and would completely negate our precious democracy.

Still, neither can a society that believes itself to be civilized tolerate your madness. What can be done to stop you? It is humanly impossible to identify you in advance. Or is it?

For you—the potential assassin—are one of us, or will be in the generations to come.

That is why you—each of us, really—must be led to understand that the American system of government is not like any other sort of government—not a kingdom, not a dictatorship, not a state ruled by a power elite.

The United States, rather, is a democracy, a republican form of government, based on the consent of the governed; a government of laws, not men. None of this source of power can be destroyed, the way a man, however high or however low, can be destroyed.

On this funeral day, when the Nation's grief is deepest with the burial of John Fitzgerald Kennedy, it is for us, the living, to search our own hearts, and in the process thereby to strengthen our faith, in ourselves, in our trust in God.

In this way lies the only hope of preventing you, the assassin, from infecting the American society with the cancer of hate.

ADDRESS BY

Hon. Carl D. Perkins

OF KENTUCKY

Mr. Speaker, no public figure has ever captured the hearts, the confidence, and the support of the people it is my privilege to represent in the Congress like John F. Kennedy. We in eastern Kentucky felt very close to him—close enough that some of the pain, anguish, and complete sense of loss being felt in the hearts of the late President's family now grips our own hearts.

When I was first elected to Congress and assumed duties on January 3, 1949, one of the first individuals that I met was the Honorable John F. Kennedy, Congressman from the State of Massachusetts. Like myself, he was assigned to the Committee on Education and Labor on which he had served in the preceding Congress. During the 81st Congress we had many controversial subjects before the committee. Of the present committee membership only the chairman and I, out of 31 Members on both sides of the aisle, were members of the committee at that time. Some of the most controversial pieces of legislation in the House of Representatives were considered by our committee in those years, particularly the minimum wage legislation, Federal aid to education, Federal Employment Practices Act, and amendments to the so-called Taft-Hartley Act that had been enacted in the previous Congress. During the years 1949–50 our committee was presided over by the gentleman from Michigan, John Lesinski. Many night sessions were held because the hearings were conducted by the full committee; in other words, the chairman did not assign any of this controversial legislation to subcommittees but decided the full committee should hear all the witnesses on minimum wage legislation and changes suggested in the Taft-Hartley Act. I shall always treasure the warm working relationship I have had with that fine statesman since those days of the 81st Congress in 1949.

His 46 years of vibrant activity is an enduring message conveying again to all who will listen that even a tragically short life can be rich and full.

The late President, John Fitzgerald Kennedy, will go down in the annals of history as truly a man of the people—a man who not only espoused freedom for all men but also was greatly concerned about the lack of economic opportunities and substandard living conditions in many areas of our country. He turned the eyes of the Nation to the Appalachian region where automation and economic changes in the coal and other industries has extracted its toll of human discomfort—high unemployment—low family incomes. The people of the Appalachian area have felt that John F. Kennedy was truly their President.

Mr. Speaker, evidencing the regard that eastern Kentuckians had for our late President are many expressions of the people as carried in the newspapers serving the eastern Kentucky area which I would like to have inserted following my remarks.

In conclusion, Mr. Speaker, I extend my deepest sympathy to Mrs. Kennedy and the family.

[From the Louisville Courier-Journal, Nov. 23, 1963]

JOHN F. KENNEDY—1917–63

President Kennedy is dead, in the 46th year of his life and the third of his presidency. A stunned and grieving Nation cannot, at once, assess the reasons why.

John Kennedy came upon the national scene in a time of change. The face of our world was altering all around us, the temper of our Nation was changing in ways not always understandable. The greatest gift he brought us was the gallantry with which he met that spirit of change, the earnestness with which he sought the ways of peace abroad and at home.

The makeshifts and compromises of the postwar era were falling apart when he became President. He had to chart new lines, to watch for new currents, to make us aware of aspirations still unmet and wrongs neglected too long.

At home and abroad the obstacles to progress were dismaying in their magnitude. But to a man of intelligence and humanity the sicknesses which beset our body politic, the rancors that divide Americans into glaring, hostile camps were evils to be overcome at all costs, even, as it turned out, at the cost of life itself.

The years and the energies of John Kennedy's presidency were dedicated to an effort to bind up the wounds of his world and his time, to heal the divisions that separate man from man. He sought an easing of tensions within the world community, the creation of an atmosphere in which East and West could grope their way toward understanding and an avoidance of nuclear holocaust. He sought within his Nation a middle ground on which labor and management could meet for the economic welfare of both. And he sought to touch within the hearts of men a charity and a decency that would permit man to live with his fellow man.

He was a strong man, impetuous and given to the occasional outbursts of temper that mark strong men. His feeling for the right phrase, his articulateness and the saving note of wry gaiety which saved his occasional rhetoric from any pomposity have been matched in our time only by Franklin Roosevelt.

Underlying this surface grace and humanity of utterance was an intellectual courage, a moral toughness that made him respected in his own country and by the world at large. His words were heeded even by those who disagreed with them. His willingness to take desperate risks for peace impressed men who had earlier questioned the force of our will for peace. The epitaph history will write must take account of these facts and the progress he had made, as it will note the sacrifice demanded of him in the end.

Stunned by his death, the Nation must now face the awesome questions that such a calamity poses. Shall we continue to try to heal the wounds of the world? Are we capable of the tolerance and patience and intellect that the search for peace demands? Can we honor the concepts of dignity and decency and brotherhood on which our Nation was founded? Or shall we be sacrificed, as our President has been sacrificed, on the altar of man's refusal to live with man?

Of the new President, taking office under circumstances so tragic, one may say the Nation is fortunate that his experience is wide, his goals are those for which President Kennedy fought and that he has the courage to walk the high and lonely path his predecessor has marked out. May God be with him.

––––

[From the Louisa (Ky.) Big Sandy News, Nov. 28, 1963]

A BELOVED PRESIDENT LAID TO REST; HIS SUCCESSOR TO CARRY ON BY THE HELP OF GOD

Residents of Louisa and Lawrence County joined a shocked nation and world in mourning the death of John Fitzgerald Kennedy, 35th and youngest President of the United States, who was felled by an assassin's bullet Friday, November 22, while on a speaking tour of Texas and died, a short time after the ambush shooting, in Parkland Hospital, Dallas.

The news of the tragedy here and elsewhere was met with disbelief at first, but when it became a reality the stunned citizens joined a stunned nation and his family in mourning his untimely death which deprives the Nation of one of its greatest leaders.

Texas Gov. John B. Connally, who was also shot as he sat side by side with the late President in the open car, is reported to be recovering from his wounds.

These heads of governments were reportedly slain and wounded by Lee Harvey Oswald, a former marine whose records show he was twice court-martialed while in the service and received an undesirable discharge so he could accept citizenship in the Soviet Union. Oswald died 48 hours later from bullet wounds inflicted by Jack Ruby, an operator of two striptease joints in Dallas. He is now in custody, charged with murder.

The 24-year-old Oswald, a native of New Orleans, La., a self-styled Russian and a member of the Fair Play for Cuba Committee, married a Russian girl. He was the father of two small children.

Many beautiful and touching tributes from across the Nation and around the world were paid the late President. Many have praised Mrs. Kennedy and other members of the Kennedy family for the courage they displayed in their trying hours. Perhaps one of the most touching scenes was when John, Jr., 3-year-old, saluted a farewell to his daddy, thus becoming the brave soldier his father would have wanted him to be.

As a means of expressing their loyalty, devotion, and grief, some churches have conducted memorial services, church bells have tolled and on Monday, the day declared by the new President Lyndon B. Johnson, as a day of mourning, was observed here by closing business places, city, county offices and city and county schools. Heads of city and county governments, Lawrence County Bar Association, ministerial association, parent-teacher organization, superintendent of schools, both political parties, Democrat and Republican, were invited by the News to express their sympathies and views and all have responded. Their expressions are incorporated in this story.

EULOGIES

LAWRENCE COUNTY BAR ASSOCIATION

Being aware that no statement, by it, could hope to add any vital significance to the private and public condolences offered to the bereaved family of our assassinated President, and that words cannot adequately express our feelings of the loss of this great intellect from the leadership of our Nation and the world. Nevertheless, we believe such a baseless atrocity against law and order should be an occasion for every citizen to cry out in shame for the sins of omission which would generate such wanton destruction.

It is inconceivable that any citizen should be so ignorant of our system of "government under law," or believe that an objective for good or evil, could be achieved by taking the life of our President or any other public officer, or that such hatred could be generated against the one holding an office as to create a desire in any mind, no matter how depraved, to remove him by an assassin's bullet.

In mourning the loss of our leader, we should each be rededicated to the faith of our Founding Fathers that this Nation, under God, shall grow under law into a country of freedom and justice for all.

C. F. SEE, Jr.,
Secretary,
Lawrence County Bar Association.

LAWRENCE COUNTY DEMOCRATIC CHAIRMAN

Like millions of other Americans, I cannot express in words the shock of the late President's death and the way it was brought about.

I believe history will record the name of John F. Kennedy alongside those of Thomas Jefferson, Abraham Lincoln, and Franklin D. Roosevelt, for his dedicated service to his country, and his efforts toward world peace and equal rights for all men.

Mr. Kennedy and his young family were the image of America itself. This young couple, highly trained, very capable and willing, were eager to meet each responsibility of their high calling. John F. Kennedy will be missed throughout the world.

JOHN B. PATTON,
Chairman, Lawrence County Democrat Party.

LOUISA MINISTERIAL ASSOCIATION

The Word of God says, "Thou shalt not kill." The murder of the late President John F. Kennedy was a violation of God's Word. The breaking of God's law is sin and sin always results in hurt, damage, misery, sorrow, and loss. The murder of our Chief Executive served to amplify and magnify the results of sin until our Nation and the entire world have seen these results. We have viewed them with horror and disbelief. They have brought an ache to our hearts, a lump to our throats, and tears to our eyes. We have genuinely mourned the loss of our President.

May the awfulness of this act of murder be etched into our minds and hearts. It has cost us the life of a talented, brilliant, and energetic young leader. May President Kennedy's tragic death shock us into the realization that our Nation cannot afford the wages of sin.

His death is symbolic of a moral decay which is eating away at the very moral fiber of our Nation. Our sin is sapping our true strength. His death is symbolic of our losses.

Let us turn to God through Jesus Christ. It is only here that we find the spiritual powers for living above sin. May we come to fear sin with all of our hearts and to dread its wages. May we come to love God and realize that He is able to save us from sin. Let us as individuals submit ourselves to the will of God through Jesus Christ. Only then will we be able to bring our beloved Nation under the will of God that we might truly serve Him. May God have mercy upon us as a nation for our sinfulness.

W. L. STRATTON,
President, Louisa Ministerial Association.

LAWRENCE COUNTY JUDGE

Lawrence County Judge J. J. Jordan said, "This is the most deplorable thing that has ever happened to this Nation and the world. It is unbelievable that this could occur in a free country. I know the rich and poor, State and county, will miss John F. Kennedy as he has done so much in 1962–63 for the depressed area of eastern Kentucky by appropriating money for building roads and bridges in Lawrence County which would have been impossible for the county to have financed. Myself and the fiscal court deeply feel this loss."

LAWRENCE COUNTY REPUBLICAN CHAIRMAN

Roy Potter, chairman of the Lawrence County Republican Executive Committee said, "I am deeply disturbed by this unforgettable tragedy. It is almost unbelievable that this terrible thing could happen in our freedom-loving country.

"My heartfelt sympathy goes to the entire Kennedy family in their bereavement."

CITY OF LOUISA

We extend our deepest sympathy on behalf of all the citizens of Louisa, Ky., to President Kennedy's family and the Nation, and to pray for the guidance and direction of our new President Lyndon B. Johnson, and that we may have peace and good will among all nations.

CLAUDE T. WILSON,
Mayor, City of Louisa.

LOUISA PTA

Mrs. Andrew York, president, said: "Members of the Louisa Elementary Parent-Teachers' Association join the Nation in expressing sympathy to all the members of the Kennedy family, in the passing of our late President, Mr. John F. Kennedy, and pledge their full support and prayers to their new President, Mr. Lyndon B. Johnson. Let us remember that the American way of life is the only one capable of insuring peace and security. The battle for human rights is being borne by our children and youth."

She continued: "There has never been a time in the history of the parent-teachers' association when it was so important that every member give urgent attention to the vital issues of human relation programs, as in the coming year."

"A good man never dies—
In worthy deed and prayer,
And helpful hands and honest eyes,
If smiles and tears be there;
Who lives for you and me—
Lives for the world he tries
To help—he lives eternally,
A good man never dies."
—JAMES WHITCOMB RILEY.

LAWRENCE COUNTY SCHOOLS

The assassination of President John Fitzgerald Kennedy left the free world stunned beyond words. The greatest leader of the free world, of this generation, is lost to civilization because his assassin was not taught the principles of democracy by his parents, his church, his school, or the other organizations with which he came in contact during his short life.

We, as American citizens, should render the man who replaces him as President of these United States the benefit of our prayers and our undivided support until that office is reaffirmed as the symbol of the security of the free world.

W. A. CHEEK,
Superintendent, Lawrence County Schools.

President Kennedy's death could not have come at a more crucial time in our Nation, but, in the words of the late James A. Garfield (an assassinated President in 1881), "Fellow citizens, God reigns and the Government in Washington still lives."

Following the ceremonies at St. Matthew's Cathedral, Monday, by Richard Cardinal Cushing, Archbishop of Boston, an old friend of the Kennedy family, the late President now rests in beautiful Arlington Cemetery near the resting place of another great President, Abraham Lincoln, who succumbed to a bullet fired by another assassin, John Wilkes Booth, on April 14, 1865.

The funeral ceremonies were attended by representatives of governments around the Nation and from most of the countries of the world. Over his resting place will burn an eternal flame, lit by his widow, assisted by two of his brothers, Robert and Ted.

[From the Hazard (Ky.) Herald, Nov. 28, 1963]

A TIME TO EVERY PURPOSE—A TIME TO MOURN, A TIME TO GIVE THANKS

"To every thing there is a season, and a time to every purpose under the heaven * * * a time to be born, a time to die * * * a time to kill, and a time to heal * * * a time to weep, and a time to laugh * * * a time to love, and a time to hate * * * a time of war, and a time of peace"—Ecclesiastes 3.

The season is Thanksgiving, a time of joyful praise to the Lord for His bountiful goodness, but now a time of mourning for the dead man who loved these words from the Holy Bible.

President John Fitzgerald Kennedy had "his purpose * * * his time to live, and his time to die." We who mourn cannot understand why this man's talents were taken from this earth, and in such tragic manner, shot down from ambush by a little man dissatisfied with his own world and others. A horrendous deed that leaves not only this Nation but the world in a state of shock and disbelief that such a thing can take place in America, the land of the free, man's last, best hope on earth.

Violence of this nature is a thing abhorred by true Americans. Therefore the second violent act just 48 hours later, which claimed the life of the accused killer was almost as repugnant to us as the President's assassination. It was simply more violence, an act which sealed the man's lips forever before justice could be meted through our courts. It profited nothing. Violence never does.

As we ponder over John Kennedy's being plucked from our midst in the very flower of his life, our "whys" are too many to be answered, as they always are. The inexplicable divine plan is never revealed except in God's own time. Therefore, it behooves each of us to respect this man's memory for his contributions to humanity, and for the example he set as a man of faith and character.

So let us mourn, and rightly so, but let us also learn from his greatness of spirit. Let us acquire some of his tolerance and understanding for our fellow men, regardless of their race, creed, or color. This was the great task to which he bent his vitalities. It's what John Kennedy would have wanted for tribute.

The torch has been passed to other hands. Another leader, President Lyndon B. Johnson, quickly assumed the reins of government. His experience points to his ability to carry on with full measure of success. We trust every American will do his small part to assist, in the city, on the farm, or the small town such as ours.

So on this Thanksgiving Day, we can find much for which to be thankful. Not the least of our blessings is the American system of government, which never faltered while paying the highest tribute to our leader.

We join the world in paying tribute to John Fitzgerald Kennedy, who gave his life to his country. On Thanksgiving Day, let us rejoice in his good works, his portion on this earth, and pray God's blessing on the man who is now President.

It is the season for giving thanks.

———

[From the Hazard (Ky.) Herald, Nov. 28, 1963]

DEATH OF A PRESIDENT

A shot rang out through the crowd that day.
It took the life of our President away,
An assassin's mind was poisoned it seems
Against our country's future, hopes and dreams.
The world was shocked, grief-stricken and stunned,
And with all our prayers, nothing could be done.
This too was a shot heard 'round the world—
For in no time the news was hurled
Across the sea to many a land
Where people who heard couldn't understand
Why in America, the land of the free,
Such a thing that happened, they couldn't see.
Our loss is great, but we still must go
On and on and let our faith grow
For in America, the land of the brave
Our red, white and blue is still free to wave.
And our Government by the people has not perished
And thanks be to God, we've still this to be cherished.
                              —IDA LEE HANSEL.

Composed November 23, 1963.

[From the Hazard (Ky.) Herald, Nov. 28, 1963]

COMPARISON OF TWO PRESIDENTS

NOVEMBER 25, 1963.

Through the assassination and death of our 35th President, I have heard and read various comparisons between President Kennedy and our 16th President, Abraham Lincoln. From two books I have both well worn with age, called "Heart Throbs" and written around the turn of the century, I find the following on the death and assassination of Lincoln:

GARFIELD ON THE DEATH OF LINCOLN

"There are times in the history of men and nations when they stand so near the veil that separates mortals and immortals, time from eternity, and men from their God that they can almost hear the breathings and feel the pulsations of the heart of the Infinite. Through such a time has this Nation passed. When 250,000 brave spirits passed from the field of honor through that thin veil to the presence of God, and when at last its parting folds admitted the martyred President to the company of the dead heroes of the Republic, the Nation stood so near the veil that the whispers of God were heard by the children of men. Awe stricken by His voice, the American people knelt in tearful reverence and made a solemn covenant with God and each other that this Nation should be saved from its enemies; that all its glories should be restored. It remains for us, consecrated by that great event, and under that covenant with God, to keep the faith, to go forward in the great work until it shall be completed. Following the lead of that great man, and obeying the high behests of God, let us remember:

"He has sounded forth His trumpet that shall never call retreat;
"He is sifting out the hearts of men before His judgment seat;
"Be swift, my soul, to answer Him; be jubilant, my feet,
"For God is marching on."

And his closing statement in his New York speech was: "God reigns, and the Government at Washington still lives.

                              —"JAMES A. GARFIELD."

The above seemed so true today on the assassination and death of our late President, I am moved to submit same to your paper to be published if you see fit.

                              Mrs. IDA LEE HANSEL,
                              Hazard, Ky.

———

[From the Maysville (Ky.) Daily Independent, Nov. 23, 1963]

THE UNFORGETTABLE MAN

John Fitzgerald Kennedy is now immortal.

As an assassin's bullet sped the President of the United States to stand in judgment before Almighty God, tears mingled with our prayers for the loss of this earthly leader. On this dread day of November 22, 1963, time stopped before he could fulfill the hope of greatness every American knew he had. Countless millions prayed for his soul:

"Eternal rest grant unto him, O Lord, and let perpetual light shine upon him."

John Kennedy is the only President who ever shook our hand or allowed us to break bread with him. We, who are nobody, had been asked for our advice and left his presence humbled as if we too were another Atlas weighted down by the burden of a world too heavy to support.

Yes, John Kennedy was the Mr. President by whose side we walked into the state dining room to eat food that might have been ambrosia. He was Mr. President who went up in the elevator with us to show, on an impulse of course, the bedroom of another great hero, Abraham Lincoln. With love, John Kennedy touched this sacred memento or some other symbol dear to him and to Jacqueline. Thinking back now to that day, there seems now a prescience of tragedy we shall never forget.

We need more than tired, defaced words in this time of sorrow to try to capture the essence which was John Kennedy.

None of us shall be able to do it. For who can say with sureness what was the spirit of a man who knows now that there is no greater love than to lay down his life for another?

John Kennedy was like that. Despite all the frailties of man, and he had his share of them, he already had proved in his short 46 years his invincibility to death. Already familiar with personal pain and the heartbreak of the loss of a son, and, yes, familiar too with the bitter taste of failure of some of his dreams, Jack Kennedy had experienced a long preparation for yesterday's tragedy. Now in his final trial he has proved his indestructibility.

If in dying, the magnificence of his vission can yet be executed by the peoples of these United States, he shall not have died in vain. If his death brings us the wisdom of which we have such a terrible need, he shall yet live.

We loved him. So did you.

———

[From the Morehead (Ky.) News, Nov. 28, 1963]

THE PUBLISHER'S PEN: APPROPRIATELY WE DEVOTE THIS COLUMN TO JOHN KENNEDY

Morehead, and this area, like the rest of the United States and most of the civilized world, was at a standstill in shock and near unbelief from Friday afternoon through the weekend as an assassin's bullet removed a great and courageous leader from this earth.

John Fitzgerald Kennedy was, in our book, the greatest President of all, even though many of his programs are unfinished. Perhaps our evaluation, and grief, is deeper because he was the only President that we knew personally.

While he was a candidate for the Presidency—the Democratic nominee—it was our privilege to spend 4 days with his public relations corps, many of whom are now on the White House staff.

Later, we attended a dinner for about 20 newsmen in the White House. The place cards had each individual's name engraved in gold (protocol for state dinners) and we were only one seat removed from the President. Our friend, and colleague, J. T. Norris Sr., publisher of the Ashland Daily Independent, sat next to President Kennedy.

We recall our one question during that 2-hour forum. It was: "Mr. President, we recently heard a speaker who was a member of, and official representative of the Strategic Air Command, say that our greatest danger was Russia destroying our nuclear bases before we could get our planes off the ground, and he further indicated that we were not keeping enough of these planes, fully loaded with nuclear bombs in the air 24 hours a day. Could or would you, comment on this?"

The President answered: "First, let me say that Mr. Khrushchev and I are agreed that in the event of nuclear war that society and humanity as we know it will be destroyed. Specifically, answering your question—I will say that we do have sufficient planes in the air for the SAC to retaliate and destroy Russia, or any aggressor. We would destroy each other."

A week later we read in the newspapers that SAC had more than doubled, perhaps trebled, the number of planes in the air at all times. Of course, this had already been ordered by the President before our question.

Last year we traveled with the White House press on a mission much like the one at Dallas where a little punk fired that fatal and historic shot from a mail-order rifle. We were included in one press pool that rode in the same plane that took Mr. Kennedy to Texas and returned with his body.

We could write columns about the security measures taken by the Secret Service that we saw firsthand to protect the President. It was evident that the greatest concern was vulnerability of Mr. Kennedy when riding in an open car. We heard it mentioned several times that the mountains of western Pennsylvania through which the President was traveling at the time were one of the real danger spots, that a sniper could be hidden on a mountain side, or toss explosives from a steep cliff.

Concern of the Secret Service reached a climax at Washington, Pa., where about 30,000 had gathered. The platform was unusually high. The Washington Hotel, just across the street, was cleared of all but the first floor and we heard members of the Secret Service say after the speech finished, "We're glad that one is over."

The White House press corps, including Presidential Press Secretary Pierre Salinger, went out of their way to entertain and advise us, probably because we were a country editor among big-name writers.

We have preserved the White House and White House press memos for our grandchildren. Where else, in all the world, could a rural, grassroots editor of a weekly newspaper be accorded such red carpet treatment, including a personal Christmas card last year from John Fitzgerald and Jacqueline Kennedy.

MOURNERS

A report is on the desk that church attendance in Morehead, and perhaps all this area, may have reached an alltime high Sunday as people gathered in houses of the Lord to mourn the passing of President Kennedy and pray for our new leader, Lyndon Baines Johnson.

MEDITATION

Also at hand, and to the credit of a great nation, is that business in the Nation's bars and liquor stores fell off 50 percent or more, over the weekend. Most people prayed and meditated instead of trying to drown their deep sorrow.

MUST HAVE HURT

Casting back, we recall that Glenn W. Lane, Democratic county chairman, was the first outspoken and effective ally of Mr. Kennedy in Rowan County. Mr. Lane sold himself at the 1956 National Convention in Chicago when Mr. Kennedy barely lost the nomination for Vice President.

FOND MEMORY

The January 1961 inauguration of President Kennedy witnessed a blizzard at the Nation's Capital. Somehow, two choice inaugural platform tickets were obtained for Mr. and Mrs. Lester Hogge, deans of the considerable delegation from Rowan County and eastern Kentucky. After the inauguration Mr. Hogge said: "That was the greatest speech (Kennedy's) ever delivered. * * * He will go down in history as one of the great Presidents of all time."

UNTIMELY?

Many think the assassination almost ruined the founders' day program marking the 40th anniversary of Morehead State College. President Adron Doran announced the death of the President shortly after the program started at the fieldhouse. Almost in unison, the 3,500 present gasped and said "Oh, no." But at every founders' day in the years to come, people will recall the simultaneous events in 1963.

APPROPRIATE

Gov. Bert Combs had handed news media the text of his founders' day speech containing high praise for MSC, its president, regents, and progress. He discarded the speech, said a few words, and then appropriately asked the college chaplain, Dr. Gabriel Banks, to lead the assemblage in the Lord's Prayer.

POSITION OF POWER

One of the closest friends and allies of President Lyndon Baines Johnson is Kentucky's former Governor and former U.S. Senator Earle C. Clements. It is certain that Clements, presently legislative chairman of the Maritime Union, will have a powerful voice at Washington and will confer often with the President on domestic policies as he has through the years. It is probable that Kennedy's death will result in realinements of the Ned Breathitt administration and Democratic policy in Kentucky.

PROCLAMATIONS

It is rare that we observe proclamations requesting all business places to close. We had two within 3 days. County Judge W. C. Flannery and Mayor Eldon T. Evans issued a proclamation for business to halt from 2 until 4 o'clock Friday in observance of MSC Founders Day. Mayor Evans signed a proclamation Sunday requesting the same thing from noon until 2 o'clock Monday during the funeral and burial of President Kennedy.

UNUSUAL

Our youngest granddaughter is 3 years old. During her brief life the United States has had three presidents— Dwight D. Eisenhower, John Fitzgerald Kennedy and now Lyndon Baines Johnson. In the event President Johnson does not succeed himself she will have seen four different presidents when still 4 years of age.

COMMUNICATIONS

The assassination of President Kennedy will also go down in history as the finest coverage by newspapers, television, and radio of any event. Many Americans did not learn of the assassination of Abraham Lincoln for 2 or 3 days. The reports then were so confused that waves of rumors and misinformation spread that the Government in Washington had been overthrown.

IN CONCLUSION

History may record that President Kennedy, a Roman Catholic, did more than any other man to effect an understanding between all religions and all churches in the world.

———

[From the Prestonsburg (Ky.), Floyd County Times, Nov. 28, 1963]

THIS TRAGEDY POSES MANY QUESTIONS

What shall we say now, almost a week after the tragic event occurred?

Mere words, with all their shades and tones, have been employed by others, and they are inadequate. Our addendum to the great day of grief would be equally inadequate. Those intangibles of the human spirit cry out for expression but so often are inexpressible.

Then let us turn to facts, which in themselves are sad enough.

The President of the United States has been stricken down by cowardly attack engendered of hatred. The Governor of the State of Texas lives but not because the gunman who sought the deaths of the two men willed it so. Less than 48 hours later, the man accused of the President's assassination has himself been gunned down at a time when he was as defenseless as was his victim.

Is there something basically wrong with a country which has lost four of its 35 Presidents to guns in the hands of murderers and where attempts have been made on the lives of at least two other Presidents, one former President and one candidate for the Presidency. This question is asked in the purview of history which shows that in all the centuries-long annals of England not a King or Prime Minister has ever been subjected even to attack.

It is true that the mentally deranged have figured in some Presidential assassinations, but England has its deranged, too.

Is "gun law" still a basic idea of American justice? Can it be that, for all our progress and industrial genius, there remains in the deep recesses of darkened minds the idea that the gun is needed as the arbiter of differences, political or personal? Or that, as in the slaying of the accused killer of President Kennedy, gun-justice satisfies the needs of society? Are the orderly processes of government fit only for the scrap heap if they do not suit our individual tastes?

These senseless murders pose many questions which will intrigue sociologists, psychologists, and students of government as well as the ordinary citizen. They may never be fully answered, and we do not attempt all the answers, much less to pontificate.

What causes one man to take the life of another? Except for those who engage in mortal combat as members of a country's armed forces, either sudden anger or dark, brooding hate must be considered the motivation for such violation of the person of another and of the laws of the land. Then whence came the hatred which cost John F. Kennedy his life?

Remember that rightwingers hate as violently as the left. Remember the tensions of the times—the passions arising because of divergent ideologies, the class hatreds as well as the racial, the swirling and apparently endless conflict involving so many and composed of so many evil ingredients.

Veritable "hate campaigns" are waged. Presidents are the special targets of secret and public abuse. Unstable minds and characters are inflamed to action.

And political campaigns have deteriorated into their own particular brand of "hate campaign." In Kentucky, for instance, the intelligence of the voter is flouted, the real issues of political campaigns have been tossed aside, and character assassination has become a familiar and disgusting tactic. Many astute political observers have become convinced that the collective mind of the electorate has become so conditioned that a calm appeal to reason is helpless in the face of a demagogic appeal to the emotions.

Politicians, the old pros of politics, can remain more or less detached and if affected emotionally only in superficial degree by such donnybrooks. But to many of unstable character and emotions the "hate campaign" remains after the real campaign has ended.

Then again one wonders how truly Christian is so-called Christian America. One wonders if all of us, including the millions of citizens who are shocked by wanton murder or other violence, do not share some of the guilt. How far does our Christianity extend? The passive absence of hatred leaves a void unless there is the active presence of love.

Dallas, Tex., has its problems. It cannot shed the blood-red stigma of murder with which it has been stained. But "it can happen here," or in any other part of this country.

For there is no protection for President or the lowliest against the heart which fills itself, or has been loaded with, the venom of hate. We cannot preach hatred in one breath and turn it off as we would a faucet. The true Christian principle which recognizes every human being as equal in the sight of God, regardless of his color, his politics, his intellect, his ideals or even his acts, is the only hope that the genus homo will ever escape the rule of fang and claw.

[From the West Liberty (Ky.) Licking Valley Courier, Nov. 27, 1963]

Is It Fate? Is It the Turning Point in World History? Will America Measure Up?

In 3½ days of a fateful weekend Americans experienced nearly the full gamut of human emotions—from stunning shock to despicable shame, with noble grandeur in between.

It was Friday afternoon when the first flash came, "President Kennedy Has Been Shot."

From this first shock that stunned our complacent belief that "it can't happen in America," through Sunday when his handcuffed assassin was so despicably murdered in the Dallas police court station with cameras picturing it all to the world, through the solemn funeral mass and burial in Arlington as crowned monarchs and potentates from most of the nations of the globe bowed with Americans in respect—most Americans were glued to their television.

And, seeing it all, nearly the full gamut of human emotions, they experienced the deep pathos of tragedy, marveled at the magic majesty of Jacqueline Kennedy, shed a tear as she and Caroline kissed the flag on the bier, and another when John, Jr., 3, saluted as they bore his father's coffin to the caisson, felt the grandeur that is America as the funeral procession moved across the Potomac to Arlington, Lincoln's tomb in the distance.

Never in history have so many millions been drawn directly, through modern communication media, into the vortex of such saddening and sobering dimensions.

It has left a soberer citizenry—and provoked a lot of needed soul searching.

Our failure to fight back at hatemongering that has sickened our society; our complacency, and our attachment to the fast buck and equating comfort with freedom—these have bred a false way of American life.

But, as the wounded Governor Connally said—John Kennedy in death may accomplish what he could not in life. He had revived again the ideals of the human race, freedom for all men.

Belatedly, Americans are just now realizing he was a Spartan warrior placing the full power of the strongest government on earth on the side of the common man. One of the ironic facts of our time is that the rest of the world knew, especially since the Cuban missile crisis, Kennedy to be a strong, resolute and wise leader.

Americans in large part had been blinded by hatemongering, so slyly spread that it perplexed our citizenry, fanned little prejudices into hatreds. This was gnawing at our Nation's vitals, consuming our Union which alone is a democracy's strength.

Other nations divined Kennedy's greatness; so did Americans of good will, except those perplexed and blinded by hate and intolerance.

Else why did the heads of most nations of the globe make pilgrimages to Washington to honor the fallen leader? And why did more than 250,000 from over the Nation file past his bier under the Capitol dome, the line growing longer through a wintry night? And why the hundreds of thousands who lined the streets to watch his coffin pass? And why the half million who visited his grave in 1 day? And why does this steady stream continue past his resting place in Arlington?

It may have been fate. It may have been the will of the gods that kept Lt. John Kennedy alive during the 5-day ordeal in the South Pacific when a Jap destroyer shot his PT boat in two and he saved his crewmen in heroic manner. A divine will that kept him alive for a nobler mission.

For in a postwar troubled era he brought stability between nations threatening a holocaust of nuclear war, and he raised again the hopes of the human race for freedom for all men.

But some in their greed for power dissented. Knowing that emption, not reason, rules the race, they spread hate, the hate that is easily distilled against one who sought civil liberties for citizens whose skin was unlike theirs, and whose religion was different. This hate was consuming our democracy.

Did it take assassination to awaken a people to the sickness that is consuming our Union?

No other event, not even Pearl Harbor, has so absorbed the emotions of America.

Is it fate? Is it that America is to have another chance if—if her citizenry can be awakened by a shock back to their senses of common decency and the ideals of human freedom that spawned our democracy?

The world is waiting, and watching, and weighing. This may be the pivot time in world history. Will Americans measure up to their destiny?

Call it good luck—or the favor of the gods, as you will. America was blessed with a calm and wise second in command.

Vice President Lyndon B. Johnson upon becoming President has steadied a wavering world in a midnight of tragedy and doubt—and has asked "the help, the strength, the prayers" of his people as well as God's guidance.

And to dispel the sickness of a people that kill their Lincolns and their Kennedys, he has asked the people of America to "banish the rancor from our words and the malice from our hearts," and thus rid the Nation of "the burden of hate and prejudice we have borne too long."

The shock of John F. Kennedy's assassination may mark the turning point in world history, if—if Americans measure up.

————

[From the Licking Valley (Ky.) Courier, Nov. 27, 1963]

To Honor Him Whom Hatred Felled

Much has been said in the wake of President Kennedy's shocking death about banishing hatred and rancor from this land. No one to our knowledge has expressed it more eloquently than the president of Indiana University, Elvis J. Stahr.

"I would suggest," he told an overflow audience at memorial services in the Indiana University auditorium Monday, "that we shall best honor the memory of (John F. Kennedy) from this day forth if we strive, as he did, each as best he can, to eliminate bigotry and hatred and prejudice and intolerance from our minds and hearts, to

uphold freedom and free institutions in our own land and for people everywhere."

Such words, unfortunately, cannot be expected to penetrate minds encased in utter fanaticism. But they should give pause to those whom Chief Justice Earl Warren had in mind, standing beside Mr. Kennedy's flag-draped casket in the rotunda of the Nation's Capitol, he said: "Is it too much to hope that the martyrdom of our beloved President might even soften the hearts of those who would themselves recoil from assassination, but who do not shrink from spreading the venom which kindles thoughts of it in others?"

————

[From the Sandy Hook (Ky.) Elliott County News, Nov. 26, 1963]

Memorial Service for President Attended by Many in Sandy Hook

The Sandy Hook Methodist Church was the scene for an impressive and beautiful memorial service for President Kennedy held at 10 a.m. Monday, November 25.

Rev. James Medley spoke the memorial tribute and ended with the prayer from the ritual for the President of these United States, after which the congregation stood and joined in the singing of the national anthem with the church organ.

Reverend Medley's text and excerpts from his tribute follow:

"Blessed is the nation whose God is the Lord." Psalms 33: 12.

"Blessed are they that mourn; for they shall be comforted." Matthew 5: 4.

There is much in the ethic of Jesus that is paradoxical. Few reasoning people see in mourning the source of blessedness. This morning, I want to help in reaching an understanding of this paradox as we study it in the context of the Sermon on the Mount and apply it in the context of the sudden and tragic passing of John Fitzgerald Kennedy, 35th President of these United States of America.

Having presented the foundation stone of Christian experience in the statement, "Blessed are the poor in Spirit, for theirs is the kingdom of God," Jesus grants insight for growth in that kingdom.

The tragedy of sin can only be viewed properly in retrospect. Those who are blinded by sin unforgiven cannot see it in true perspective.

Blessed happiness can be the part of all who admit sinfulness and place personal faith in the Christ.

Blessed are they that mourn as we do for John Fitzgerald Kennedy.

Our mourning brings us to the point where we know that as a nation we cannot express ourselves except in prayer. Some prayers will be orderly. Some prayers will be marked by the hysteria of grief. We shall be comforted in the fact that God hears both. The Holy One of Israel is aware of our dilemma and cares for us. This care is a reality for each personal faith in Christ. We pray that it might become the corporate experience of our Nation.

John Fitzgerald Kennedy committed himself to the

role of making peace. He seemed to have incorporated in his personal being the salient features of men with profiles of courage. Underprivileged men the world around are indebted to him for his efforts to bring freedom from want and peace of mind that comes to those who need never look with envy upon a favored America.

His stability of character has added much to the possibility of establishing peace among races and religions in our Nation.

His personal bearing of integrity has added much to the area of peace now enjoyed between labor and management.

His passing makes us the recipients of a fresh determination to make this world the peaceful kingdom of our Lord and our Christ.

I think it entirely proper and practical for us to reaffirm our faith in the historical gospel of the Sermon on the Mount and to pray earnestly for the 36th President of these United States of America, Lyndon Baines Johnson.

———

[From the Maysville (Ky.) Daily Independence, Nov. 23, 1963]

All Mourn—Dastardly Act, Says Stunned Community

The work-a-day world of Maysville died yesterday with the assassination of President Kennedy. Business was at a standstill as townspeople lived through the half-hour agony that preceded the moment he was shot and the awful numbness that followed the word he had died.

What had seemed important a moment before, no longer had any significance. The streets of the city became almost deserted as people went home to pray and to follow on television every terrible related fact.

Mayor T. T. McDonald at once directed the flag on Market Street and at city hall to be flown at half mast. County Judge John P. Loyd did likewise.

Soon after the confirmation of the President's death, the bells at St. Patrick Church began to toll. At 6 p.m. the Episcopal of the Nativity tolled its dirge of sorrow. Civic leaders were as one in their expressions of sorrow.

The Right Revered Monsignor Leo B. Casey termed the assassination a senseless, despicable act and a tragic one. He said the world had lost a great leader and an apostle of peace.

No sooner had word of the tragedy spread like wildfire through the countryside, than the children at St. Patrick school went to St. Patrick Church. There led by Father Casey and the Reverend Robert Wendeln the children recited the Rosary and prayers for the dead.

At St. Rose of Lima Church in Mayslick, where 40 hours devotions are being held, the church was filled with a multitude of prayerful citizens offering petitions to God for the repose of the President's soul. The bell there also tolled.

The Reverend Robert Peck, of the Church of the Nativity, said a mass of requiem would be said Sunday and that public prayers would be offered Sunday afternoon.

The Reverend T. Howard Kinston, of the First Baptist Church, in expressing his shock and sympathy, said he felt it must be the act of some insane person and not representative of the citizens of the country.

The Reverend James Rucker, of the First Presbyterian Church, expressed sympathy for Mrs. Kennedy and the President's family as he said that he felt "a personal responsibility that we can let matters get to such a stage."

Superintendent of City Schools Earle Jones said, "It made me sick down deep in my heart that in a civilized country such a terrible thing could happen" and that he hoped it would be the last.

Circuit Judge John A. Bresta, who was in Augusta when apprised of the tragedy, termed it "a barbaric thing" and that it gave him a sense of "numbness and disbelief." He quoted the president of the U.N. "that all of us should pause and look to our country and at the democratic process." He added his prayers for the family and the success of President Johnson.

Mayor McDonald and Judge Boyd said they would proclaim public days of mourning to conform with what will be done at the national level.

Doctors, lawyers, merchants, and chiefs—the common man so to speak that each represents—went about in a daze after the tragedy. For a little while, it was as if hope had died in a senseless world. Poignant were the words of sympathy uttered for Jacqueline Kennedy. To everyone it seemed that a beloved friend was gone.

The public meeting of sanitation district No. 1 for interested citizens was also canceled. "No one felt like talking," Chris Kilgus, chairman of the board of commissioners, said.

———

[From the Pike County (Ky.) Times, Nov. 28, 1963]

Gloom Pervades Land When Kennedy Killed—President's Death Stops Area Meeting—Colonel Cochran Reviews Flood Control Problems; Stream Snagging Viewed

The incredulity, shock, and deep sorrow with which word of the assassination of President Kennedy was received here last Friday afternoon was typical of the emotions experienced in every nook and corner of America and in almost every country of the world.

An almost palpable gloom settled over the land. Beginning with the first announcement that the President and Governor Connally of Texas had been shot in Dallas, Tex., millions sat as if transfixed before television sets. Wherever others went or gathered here, there was one topic of conversation.

Official Frankfort reacted as did the ordinary citizen. The State flag atop the Capitol was lowered to half-mast. Governor Combs, at Morehead at the time for a Founder's Day address at Morehead State College, discarded his prepared speech to speak movingly of the martyred President and the gravity of the hour for the Nation.

At Pikeville, where many Floyd Countians were attending a hearing conducted by the U.S. Corps of Engineers on flood control on the Big Sandy and its tributaries, word of the tragedy abruptly ended the meeting before testimony was introduced.

On Sunday churches over the land joined in expressions of grief and in prayers for the Kennedy family, the new President, Lyndon B. Johnson, and for the Nation. In Prestonsburg a lone blast of the fire department siren was the signal at 11:15 a.m. to worshippers at the various churches to unite in 2 minutes of silent prayer.

Then, Sunday afternoon, came the second shockwave when television viewers saw murder committed before their very eyes as Lee Harvey Oswald, prime suspect in the President's assassination was gunned down in the Dallas police station by a nightclub operator.

Monday, the day of national mourning proclaimed by President Johnson, saw businesses closed here, streets as deserted as they will be Christmas morning. Doors of local churches, however, remained open as an invitation to any who wished to enter for prayer or meditation.

So, in brief, have the days passed. And still the tragedy, the strange chain of violence which in one Texas city saw a President slain, a Governor wounded and finally, a prisoner shot down, continues its hold on the minds of millions.

————

[From the Paintsville (Ky.) Herald, Nov. 27, 1963]

A NATION IS WARNED BY THE UNSPOKEN WORDS OF AN ASSASSINATED PRESIDENT

The triple tragedy in Dallas and the slaying of our President have shocked the world and brought grief and sorrow to the people of the United States. Death is natural even for one so young, but these three deeds of smoldering resentment and madness, are ominous and threatening, and strongly suggestive that all is not well with us. Our citizens turn guiltily to look within their own hearts for the causes.

Only last week one of the Nation's leading newspapers carried separate articles on the rapid increase of crime in the State of Texas and the lack of efficiency on the part of law enforcement officials in Dallas. One writer pointed to the loose Texas State law on acquiring firearms. But Texas with its high crime rate is not alone among the States. J. Edgar Hoover of the FBI has repeatedly warned of the Nation's increasing lawlessness and juvenile delinquency, attended by the unconcern, lack of cooperation with police officials and the general apathy of the people.

We believe the bullets in the gun of the accused Lee Oswald were molded by our society and that his sick mind and soul were creations of this society. The 24-year-old Oswald who enlisted in the U.S. Marine Corps at the age of 17 appeared frank and open in his deep resentment and his contempt for the system that made him as he was.

This youthful, accused assassin of President Kennedy and alleged slayer of a Dallas law official was not unlike the Billie Sol Estes and hundreds of others in top circles of business and government from the grassroots to Washington who operate under the cloak of hypocrisy and deceit until the sands run out in their sordid hourglass. The frank disdain, the youthfulness of Oswald, his apparent lack of remorse cause us with a sense of guilt to turn and look within ourselves for the answer to the Oswalds in our midst.

We must weed out in our small hamlets, our rural areas, and our crowded cities over this Nation, the seeds of violence, the greed and hatred of the innocent. Even in our small communities there are vile and despicable deeds by elected officials and civic leaders, carefully carried out under the protection of the law or the secretive darkness. And here in these small communities are the same hate and resentment that pulled the trigger of the assassin's gun in Dallas last Friday. The same hatred took the life of a policeman to leave a widow and three young children; it took the life of an accused assassin without benefit of trial. The same hatred is in our midst.

The late President Kennedy in his speech prepared for Dallas citizens, stopped by death before its delivery, concluded with spiritual truths handed down through the centuries. Taken from Psalms, these words carry a warning and a prophetic message to the American people: "Except the Lord keep the city, the watchman waketh but in vain." The President was warning as did that inspired writer more than 2,000 years ago, that if we keep the faith, if we let the Lord keep our beloved country, our defenses will not be in vain.

President Kennedy is gone but this was his parting message. May it be inscribed in the hearts and souls of every citizen of this blessed land.

The crime of Lee Oswald is shared with every individual who makes up our society. If the death of President Kennedy serves to awaken us to a nationwide soul searching, and a revival of righteousness, then he will not have died in vain.

————

[From the Journal Enquirer, Grayson, Ky., Nov. 28, 1963]

HISTORY PAUSES TO MOURN—CARTER COUNTIANS PAUSE WITH NATION TO PAY TRIBUTE TO SLAIN PRESIDENT KENNEDY

When a television program is interrupted, and the word "bulletin" is flashed on the screen, a certain amount of anxiety exists.

Probably the anxiety will never be as high again, however, as it was last Friday afternoon when newsmen confirmed that President John F. Kennedy, 35th President of the United States, had been assassinated as he was riding in a motorcade through the outskirts of Dallas, Tex.

As was the case throughout the nation—and, indeed, the world—the news was received with shock and disbelief.

In Grayson the word came about 1:45 p.m., shortly following the lunch hour. Little was accomplished for the remainder of that day.

At Prichard High School in Grayson—and other schools in the county—the news stunned students and faculty alike. Some students broke into tears. Radios were pressed into service to obtain details.

Carter County schools were dismissed on Monday, day of the former President's funeral.

Along the business districts of Grayson and Olive Hill, people gathered to tell those who had not heard. "Isn't it terrible" was the expression used over and over. After first reports were ended and it was announced the President was dead, a wave of stunning shock prevailed. Throughout Carter County communities, area residents gathered in stores and various neighborhood places to join their thoughts concerning the President's assassination.

Regular church services throughout Carter County on Sunday included prayers for the Kennedy family and for the new President, Lyndon B. Johnson.

Special memorial services were held Monday in Carter County.

In Grayson, the Bagby Memorial Methodist Church was jammed with businessmen and residents who gathered to pay tribute in a special community service.

Most business houses were closed from 9:30 until noon.

Participating in Monday's service were host minister K. R. Dillon; Jay D. Cooper, minister of the First Church of Christ; William Scott, minister of the Church of the Nazarene; Melvin Hester, minister of the Bayless Memorial Presbyterian Church; and J. C. Stephens, minister of the First Baptist Church.

Dillon, in bringing the memorial devotion, urged Americans to take another look at their lives. He asked that citizens draw strength from the tragedy by stamping out hatred in individual lives. He also called on the nation to pray for President Johnson as he assumes the responsibility of leading the free world.

———

[From the Bath County (Ky.) News Outlook, Nov. 28, 1963]

A SHAME TO SHARE

Twenty years ago, the late Ernie Pyle so poignantly described his feelings upon seeing his American foot-soldier buddies brought down out of the Italian hills, their lifeless bodies draped across the backs of burros.

Wrote the immortal war correspondent:

"It makes you feel ashamed to be alive."

That is the same feeling that struck us Friday upon hearing the news of the Nation's great tragedy, the cold-blooded murder of our President, John F. Kennedy. It made us feel ashamed to be Americans.

In a crisis like this, we are not Republicans, Democrats, segregationists, conservatives, liberals—we are all Americans. We share equally in the grief and shame of this despicable act. Even though we live in a country where we have learned to expect the most unusual, nothing in our lifetime has touched us so deeply or shocked us so greatly.

Friday, November 22, 1963, will go down in history as the day of infamy in our generation, even overshadowing the nightmare havoc of Pearl Harbor 23 years ago. It is a day that marks a terrible blot on our country's rich and prideful history. It is a day we will have to live with, as badly as we would like to erase it from the calendar. It is a day to make all Americans realize their need for strong patriotism, a strong desire for unity and an even stronger faith in God.

The reaction of the people of Hometown, Owingsville, Ky., U.S.A., must have been almost universal. The flag at the post office was quietly lowered to half-staff, business came to a near standstill, sober-faced people gathered in small clusters, listening to the latest news and talking in whispered tones. There were tears, heads shaken in bewilderment and disbelief. The shroud of sadness loomed like a blanket of fog over a country not easily moved by emotion.

That a twist of fate should permit the demented mind of one bad apple to snuff out the young life of a great American statesman in his prime is a great mystery to most of us. It takes faith in the divine providence to accept this as having some meaningful purpose known only to our Maker.

But by our apathy toward extremists, hate-peddlers and Communists we have contributed toward this end and must share the blame and shame of this day of infamy. Let us hope President Kennedy's death will not have been in vain. If it makes us more vigilant, more cognizant of the dangers that beset our national security and freedoms, more tolerant of each other in our political convictions, more affirmed in our Christian way of life and more dedicated to making this world a place of peace and understanding, then his passage will have a meaning.

We believe it has a meaning for all of us to see and follow.

———

[From the Bath County (Ky.) News Outlook, Nov. 28, 1963]

LETTER OF SYMPATHY TO PRESIDENT'S WIDOW

The sentiments of Owingsville were expressed by Owingsville Mayor Robert W. Gilmore in the following letter to Mrs. Jacqueline Kennedy:

NOVEMBER 25, 1963.

Mrs. JACQUELINE KENNEDY,
White House,
Washington, D.C.:

We the citizens of Owingsville, Ky., join with the rest of the world in our expression of sympathy. Your personal loss in a husband and father, we know seems unbearable. The citizens of this Nation shall always remember him as a great leader.

Words such as these will come to you from kings and queens, leaders of great nations eloquently expressed by great statesmen. Perhaps this message will be from the smallest city of the group but even though small, there will be none more sincere and genuine than this message from the heart of our people. We think of ourselves as "The little town with a big heart." And at an hour such as this we extend it all to you.

ROBERT W. GILMORE,
Mayor.

———

[From the Ashland (Ky.) Daily Independent, Nov. 23, 1963]

DEEP SORROW AND A SENSE OF GUILT

The nation is joined as one today in sorrow. Prayers arise from the hearts of Americans of every race, creed and type of political belief. They implore merciful comfort for the wife and family of the murdered John F. Kennedy. They ask that strength and inspiration be given President Johnson as he assumes his new responsibilities. They seek the aid and blessing of Almighty God for our Nation, as a great leader is lost.

In all of these we join. Many times during the past 24 hours the words of Walt Whitman, wrung from him in anguish on the death of Lincoln, have been recited, beginning "O Captain, my Captain our fearful trip is done."

· With all of this there arises in our hearts a vague sense of individual guilt. How could we, a free, self-governing people, have permitted conditions to exist which made possible such diabolicly-planning assassination of our President? Three times before presidents have been brutally murdered. On several other occasions attempts upon the life of a Chief Executive have narrowly failed.

In our anxiety to permit freedom of thought and opinion to every man, have we not permitted small but powerful groups to exist in our midst, which recognize no law nor orderly processes of change provided by our system? The relatively few thousands of these agents of destruction live among us and labor with the deadly intent of destroying the liberties of 190 million people.

We need more realistic recognition of this menace. What happened in Dallas on Friday could happen again. Not only our Chief Executive could be destroyed, but our vital defenses could be made useless with relative ease by these agents and saboteurs of our enemies. If we would protect our liberties we must tighten our security methods within our country. We have been warned of this by J. Edgar Hoover and others many times. If any good can arise from the tragic murder of our President, perhaps it will be a sadly needed strengthening of our internal security safeguards.

ADDRESS BY

Hon. Ross Bass

OF TENNESSEE

Mr. Speaker, while campaigning for John F. Kennedy for President in 1960, I described him in this manner:

A man with the intellectual level of Thomas Jefferson, the courage of Andrew Jackson, the dedication to purpose of Woodrow Wilson, the vision and leadership of Franklin Roosevelt, and the fortitude and decisiveness of Harry Truman.

Now I know I was right. He can now be described as a composite of greatness.

I liked him as a man. Loved him as an American. Enjoyed him as a friend. Admired him as a leader. Supported him as a President.

An assassin's bullet has taken Jack Kennedy but his influence will live for generations.

I will miss him greatly.

May his family be consoled in the memory of his great works.

ADDRESS BY

Hon. Dante B. Fascell

OF FLORIDA

Mr. Speaker, "The world is very different now." President John Fitzgerald Kennedy spoke thus in realistic and prophetic appraisal on January 20, 1961.

Our great American, President John Fitzgerald Kennedy, is now gone, and, Mr. Speaker, the entire world is indeed very different as a result of the events of Friday, November 22, 1963.

In that short space of time John Fitzgerald Kennedy set for himself and all Americans great goals for a better America and a better world. He was a man of indomitable courage and keen and far-sighted historical vision. He set for himself, for all Americans, and for all peoples challenges sufficient to call forth the best in every man, woman, and child—a clean-cut and hard blast of the horn for unity, peace, and action.

Sparks of action—electricity of purpose—these are the benchmarks of a man who dedicated his life to work for his beloved country.

All this—

He said—

will not be finished in the first 100 days. Nor will it be finished in the first 1,000 days, nor in the life of this administration, nor even perhaps in our lifetime on this planet. But let us begin.

And, Mr. Speaker, begin he did. The leader chose the road, charted its course and asked his people to join him and join him they did, not only Americans, Mr. Speaker, but people in all parts of the world joined. They sparkled with new enthusiasm, they looked upward with new hope and spirit. For they saw in this young, fearless, idealistic yet realistic leader, the crusader, the new frontier, the new hope for all mankind.

I am proud that history will record that this great American did so many great things, accomplished so much for so many people in so short a period of time.

But, Mr. Speaker, all this is cut short. What years of dangerous wartime service could not do, an assassin's bullet did in a split second.

My wife, children, and I who knew him personally, grieve with millions of Americans and for some of these I am honored to speak in these hallowed halls today. But with a great outpouring the likes of which the world has never seen, Americans and others have spoken eloquently for themselves.

HIS CHAIR IS STILL

(By Donna Davis, Miami)

The rocking chair sits empty now,
 No stalwart frame to hold;
No vigorous movement to allow
 A point, a plan unfold.
A strong young warrior poised there
 In earnest motion without cease,
Fighting for freedom everywhere
 Dreaming of a world at peace;
The rocker there was not to rest
 Nor rest on laurels won
But rather ready for the test—
 Chart the course of state to run.
I do not think his chair is still
 But speaks of courage so sublime
His acts live on and history will
 Tell nobly of this man—this time.

———

JOHN F. KENNEDY

(By Judy D. Cooper, Miami)

You were the greatest of them all Mr. Kennedy
You were the greatest of them all I know.
You helped us out so very much and there was such
 a short time to go
You helped to bring us from the bottom to the middle,
 and then almost to the top
You did or tried to do the things you said you would
And just by that I know you could
Because you tried the way you should.

———

ALL THE WORLD KNOWS WHY

(By John L. Perry, Miami)

She didn't cry
She didn't sigh
She only lost her smile
But all the world
Was praying
She'd regain it in a while
For she'd lost one
The world would mourn
For wanting all men free
I'm writing this for Jackie
So all the world knows why
When Jackie smiles
Her face just tells
Her heart another lie.

HE FOLLOWED TO INFINITY

(By Jean Quinn, Miami)

He stood so tall, with sadness all around,
The beat of the drums, the only sound,
This sailor with face so sad and strong,
Took his place where he belonged
His name to me, is unknown,
I only remember, the pride that was shown,
As he followed the caisson, his step never lagged
For he proudly carried his President's flag.

———

LONG MAY HE LIVE

(By Madelynne Cooper, Miami)

Our leader has fallen, and long may he live,
He'd not question why, but for us to forgive,
This world will be a better place, for it has been honored
 by his touch,
Oh dear Mr. President, we all loved you so much!
God bless America, long may our flag wave,
For here in this country is a marked grave,
Of a man who asked little and gave so much,
The world will be better, having been graced by his
 touch.

———

LOVE OR HATE

(By Albert L. Citero, Miami)

The falling tears of a mourning world,
Were caused by hate, its wrath unfurled,
First, the President, then the law,
Next the assassin, hate killed them all.
If love had only replaced the hate;
Oh God, please teach us before it's too late.

———

A PRAYER FOR A PRESIDENT

(By Mrs. George A. Pikari, Miami)

He was a man we all did love,
He sought his guidance from above,
In his views he shone a light.
Some say that he was wrong
But he did what he thought was right.

A great man, a family man,
And both in such a way,
That he will be remembered,
Forever and a day.

Bow your head and say your prayer,
For your President JFK,
For by his death his goal was reached,
He showed us all our need for Peace!

DOLOR

(By J. Carlton Barnette, Miami)

Daybreak again!
Another day to live through,
Passing the hours somehow,
Until the inscrutable shades of night
Bring blessed sleep.

Life holds no peace for me,
My eyes no gladness see,
Where once was happiness, my heart
Is saddened now and filled with nought
But deepest grief,
Our President, John Fitzgerald Kennedy,
Is dead,
Struck down by a cowardly assassin's
        bullet.

May he rest in peace.

————

(From the Miami Herald, Nov. 23, 1963)

OUR SORROW IS THE WORLD'S: JOHN FITZGERALD KENNEDY

Wherever the somber sound of voice or the grave face of type reached yesterday, people recoiled in horror and in shock.

President John Fitzgerald Kennedy was dead of an assassin's cowardly bullets. In the freest land in the world death had come by sneak attack to the people's Chief Magistrate.

No one can say at this writing what was the motive of the killer. It is hard not to take account, however, of the climate of hate in which men struggle to govern.

We differed with Mr. Kennedy on many occasions. Where these differences were noted, the President offered game and gay rebuttal.

A gentleman always, and ever a scholar, he lent dignity (spiced with a certain boyish humility) to the greatest office in the gift of the people. One might quarrel with his policies but never with his encyclopedic knowledge of government.

The Nation's sorrow is the world's, also.

Under this President the United States had been moving in the direction of peace with freedom.

Like his predecessors, he was conscious of America's role of leadership thrust upon it by the fortunes of war (which he shed blood to help win) and the circumstances of unrivaled prosperity.

What more can one say as a young man is struck down in his prime in an act of such suddenness that the country is left reeling?

May God be with the 35th President of the United States.

And may He be with his successor, upon whom the nearly intolerable burden falls, Lyndon B. Johnson.

————

[From the News Leader, Homestead, Fla., Nov. 24, 1963]

WHEN THE WORD CAME

A President is shot and the world seems to slow down to await word of the human body's battle for survival.

The word comes. The President is dead.

The world seems to stop momentarily.

Even after the waiting and the announcement of the worst there still is a state of disbelief—or of not wanting to believe.

Then slowly but surely the realization sets in, damply in many instances.

Heads are bowed in prayer and flags are lowered in mourning.

The talk, as it has been from the first announcement, is subdued, but gradually the voices return to normal.

You think about it. Your heart goes out to the family. You wonder about the Government.

But there's work to do, and you know that the man in his midforties who almost made the supreme sacrifice for his country in World War II but survived that to become one of our most knowledgeable and energetic Commander in Chief would want, even in death, the business of the country and the millions of people who make it up to continue.

After the shock you realize there's the future to look to. The President had often reminded us of that.

So for a moment you look ahead. One of the first things you see is Thanksgiving Day.

And you wonder perhaps how his family will find much to be thankful for in this Thanksgiving Week.

But even they must find some thankfulness in the prayers and sympathies the people of the world over are offering. And they must be thankful that one of their own has been able to achieve so much and do so many things in such a few years.

And the country?

Whether you agreed with the President or not on many things there is the knowledge that he was a man who acted on facts as he knew and understood them, and he made every effort to get all the facts all the time.

Perhaps one of the things we can be most thankful for is the fact that he chose his biggest competitor for nomination to the office to be his Vice President. That person of course now is our President.

This Thanksgiving Week will be a week of mourning for John Fitzgerald Kennedy.

But it will also be a week of giving thanks for our system of government that insures an orderly continuation of the business of this Nation.

————

[From the News Leader, Homestead, Fla., Nov. 28, 1963]

INDIGNATION WILL FADE, BUT WE CAN MAKE A VOW

What is it that causes a mind to slip over the brink to the point that the body which houses it will viciously attack and kill a little girl, or from a hiding place shoot to death a president of his country?

If we knew the answer to such questions perhaps tragic events of recent days could have been avoided.

But we don't know, and the shock and indignation of the two recent crimes that have touched us closer and deeper than usual gradually will fade for most of us as we go about the business that must go on if life is to be worthwhile.

But as the shock and indignation are dulled, it is appropriate that we vow to ourselves to practice more the spirit of brotherhood—to love when hate momentarily seems in order; to forgive when we are tempted to take vengeance; to give when we are tempted to take; to be courageous in moving ahead when a step backward seems easier.

———

[From the Jewish Floridian, Nov. 29, 1963]

PRESIDENT KENNEDY'S TRAGIC PASSING

We mourn the tragic passing of John Fitzgerald Kennedy. The Nation has lost an outstanding leader: a young and vigorous man; an intellectual, who brought a breath of fresh air to the erstwhile distant formalities of the White House; an author, whose knowledge of history helped set the course for our future as a people; a President, whose years belied his capability, and whose easy manner disguised his courage.

Our 35th President of the United States is gone. The Nation laid him to rest in Arlington on Monday. It is difficult to believe that he has passed. And yet, the presence of President Lyndon Baines Johnson in the White House today tells us it is a fact—that the unbelievably tragic circumstances of last weekend were no fantastic piece of fiction, or even a page torn from the distant American history book of yesterday or tomorrow.

Saddened as we are by his death, we give thanks that the Nation is now in the hands of President Kennedy's capable successor. A man with a devoted record of service to his country, running over the course of many decades, Mr. Johnson comes to the President's office well steeped both in the demands and the intricacies of the position he has taken over.

The Nation, grieved, is now a nation solidly behind President Johnson, sorrowful in the memories of its youthful leader assassinated so brutally and so purposelessly, but assured that the United States of America can successfully withstand tragedies even as profound as this.

———

[From the Miami Times, Nov. 30, 1963]

THE NATION MOURNS

The assassination of our dear beloved President, John Fitzgerald Kennedy, on November 22 in Dallas, Tex., coming so unexpectedly, struck the Nation—nay the whole world, a stunning blow.

The dastardly deed was committed by Lee Harvey Oswald at 12:30 last Friday.

As ye editor entered the Times' office shortly after 1 o'clock he observed quietness. Everybody's eyes were centered on the television. What's wrong? he inquired. Came the sad reply: "President Kennedy has been shot. He is dead."

It was undoubtedly one of the sad moments of ye editor's life. He glanced at the figures on the press. Checked, they showed but 6,400 copies of the Times printed. A change of makeup was ordered for the first page, and not long after newsboys who were waiting were on the streets announcing the sad intelligence— President Kennedy is dead.

The man who committed this hideous crime was arrested, but he too fell a victim of an assassin's bullet. He was shot Sunday by Jack Ruby, a barroom owner,

as Ruby got through a crowd of newsmen on the basement of the Dallas police station.

This was unfortunate. Far better would it have been if Ruby had allowed the culprit to be brought to justice.

The FBI and other authorities are investigating. It is hoped that they may be able to find sufficient evidence to unravel what was really behind the assassination of President Kennedy and perhaps, Oswald.

The body of the President was taken to Washington, where funeral services were held on Monday and the mortal remains placed in Arlington National Cemetery.

Special services were held in churches throughout the Nation. In Washington the services were at St. Matthew's Cathedral. While the body was at the White House and Capitol thousands upon thousands went and paid their respects to the President.

Millions saw the funeral cortege on television and heard the high terms in which bishops and others spoke of President Kennedy.

During the funeral service ye editor was practically glued to his chair looking at television, as he is certain many others were.

Heads of Government from most countries attended this funeral and later were received and thanked by Mrs. Kennedy.

During the ordeal Mrs. Kennedy has proved herself to be an extraordinary person. Her calmness under such trial could be an example worthy of emulation.

May God continue to bless her and her children.

There has been so much said over television and radio, so much written and printed in our daily newspapers that this humble scribe finds little left to say. However he will say that little.

President Kennedy was a champion for the underprivileged. His fight for human and civil rights has been emblazoned upon the hearts of millions, never to be forgotten.

President Kennedy was a man among great men; a President among great Presidents; and a Christian among Christians.

May he rest in peace and light perpetual shine upon him.

———

[From the Voice, weekly publication of the Diocese of Miami covering the 16 counties of south Florida, Nov. 29, 1963]

BISHOP CARROLL MOURNS KENNEDY

(The following statement was issued by Bishop Coleman F. Carroll from Vatican City, where he is attending the second session of the Second Ecumenical Council.)

VATICAN CITY.—I am deeply shocked by the news of the tragic death of President John F. Kennedy, as indeed are all Americans and citizens of other nations.

We grieve for our country which has lost a courageous, able and tireless leader, and for the world which has looked to him for leadership and courage in the never ending struggle for peace and freedom. Our hearts go out to his bereaved wife and to his family. We beg God to console and strengthen them in their severe trial.

We Catholics in south Florida who considered him a neighbor and fellow parishioner have added reason to feel keenly his untimely death.

I am sure it is the prayer of all Americans that God may grant John Fitzgerald Kennedy a full measure of peace and a fitting reward for a life characterized by total dedication to duty and fidelity to his God and country.

With this unexpected crisis in government the burden of leadership has been placed on the shoulders of Lyndon Johnson. He will stand in need in these critical days not only of the vast and varied experience of his public life but of divine guidance and assistance.

We pledge President Johnson the full support of our prayers that God may give him the wisdom and courage for the attainment of peace and the recognition of the rights of all men.

COLEMAN F. CARROLL,
Bishop of Miami.

———

[From the Miami News, Nov. 30, 1963]

FLORIDA PAPERS SAID:

A cross-section of editorial comment on President Kennedy's assassination from daily newspapers in Florida:

Gainesville Sun: "Mr. Kennedy's greatness was hewn from the same rock as that of the Great Emancipator, Abraham Lincoln. * * * When struck down in Dallas, Practical Politician Kennedy was rebuilding fences which Idealist Kennedy had knocked down."

Clearwater Sun: "It is incomprehensible that this could happen in America, the land of the free and the home of the brave, the stronghold of democracy, a nation to which the entire free world has looked, and received leadership in time of deepest tragedy."

Ocala Star-Banner: "We have taken issue with President Kennedy on a great many of his programs. But in our country, political differences are not necessarily personal differences. * * * Even when we disagreed with him we couldn't help sympathizing with him because of his impossible position."

St. Augustine Record: "The shots that were fired at President Kennedy should be a warning that our country has enemies from within—Communists, pro-Castro supporters and the like who seek to destroy or enslave our Nation."

Lakeland Ledger: "The terrible thing that happened * * * surely has moved the American people to more serious reflection as to the basic importance of showing proper respect for the high office of the Presidency."

Orlando Sentinel: "The bullet which struck the young President was felt by each of us, and a part of us was lost when he died."

Palm Beach Post-Times: "A sense of outrage pervades this community where John F. Kennedy was a friend and neighbor in addition to being President of the United States. His murder seems a personal thing."

St. Petersburg Times: "* * * Since 2:39 p.m., Friday, November 22, our destiny as a nation, and much of the destiny of the free world has been in the hands of President Lyndon B. Johnson. Fortunately * * * the Presidency has fallen into capable hands."

Sarasota Herald-Tribune: "A piece of each of us died at that moment. Yet in death he gave of himself to us."

Pompano Sun-Sentinel: "Perhaps the fact that so many of us have had the chance to see violence in action will serve to cool the blood and ease tensions which have strained our Nation. Let us pray that this may be."

Tampa Tribune: "How could it happen? It could happen because in a free society it is not possible to search out and quarantine every festering mind which may develop a murderous resentment against the President or the national policy he represents."

Daytona Beach Morning Journal: "The good people of the Nation must begin anew on our task—the task of driving out the hatred and fear and scorn that can become trigger happy."

Jacksonville Times-Union: "Bullets prove only who lives, not who is right, and this attack does great disservice to the cause of those honest men and women who have sought to change the policies of this Government by lawful means."

Fort Lauderdale News: "That President Kennedy had his quota of political opponents goes without saying. * * * But how anybody could let their personal or political beliefs drive them to the point of coldbloodedly murdering the President of our Nation is neither understandable, rational, nor excusable in any sense of the words."

Key West Citizen: "The greatest memorial that the world could erect to our late President would be one of a lasting peace and understanding among the peoples and nations of the earth."

Hollywood Sun Tattler: "There is no easy way to forget. * * * The Nation can but seek to evidence the same type of courage which characterized the President it mourns."

———

[From the Hialeah-Miami Spring (Fla.) Home News, Nov. 27–29, 1963]

BLACK FRIDAY: A DAY OF NATIONAL SHAME

Not since the night that John Wilkes Booth pulled the trigger in Ford's Theatre, has the world's mightiest nation been as close to prostration as it appeared to be last Friday afternoon.

His visit to the Miami area only 4 days earlier still fresh in the minds of Dade Countians, President John F. Kennedy lay dead in Texas.

Countless citizens of our generation remembered the stun and shock of December 7, 1941, but the numbness that set in following last Friday's announcement of President Kennedy's assassination sent all reeling.

Senseless, needless, and utter waste of valued human life were just a few of the first reactions that came to a dazed public.

Then, as the first shock wave wore off and a partial emotional balance was restored, memories poured forth.

The man chosen by the electorate to be the symbol of democracy and of a free society became victim of an assassin's bullet in his own country where, by all sane and logical reckoning, he should have enjoyed the fullest measure of safety.

That the assassin met a similar fate offers no consolation to a mourning Nation. An "eye for an eye" cannot return the President to his Nation, nor can it bring back a devoted father and loving husband.

But the black deed is done, and the world repaid it Monday with probably the highest tribute ever tendered any leader in any time.

Now, in deepest mourning and emotionally drained, we must set aside our humiliation, bury our remorse and resume President Kennedy's dedicated purpose of showing the way to the free world.

We must also rally around the new President, Lyndon B. Johnson, to give him the support he so urgently needs in this hour of great crisis.

——

THE WORLD FAMILY CAME TO MOURN

From the far corners of the globe they came.

From 53 countries they traveled to the United States on their melancholy mission.

Kings, presidents, prime ministers, foreign ministers, defense ministers—they came here not for political advantage or financial gain—but to pay final homage to the American President.

They came to our Nation's Capital for the solemn services at which the assassinated President was to be laid to rest—the shocked-haired young American whose soaring ideals had won their admiration and whose firm courage had exacted their deep respect.

Such a coming together of the world's mighty leaders had never happened before. Such a concourse of the world's top governing men in one place—at one time— for one purpose—had never been witnessed in all history. And it might never be again.

The leaders, who came from all the continents, were joined by a bond, a bond of sorrow over the loss of the beloved U.S. President, the man who had dedicated himself to preserving human freedom and world peace.

The powerful leaders came from lands where various shades of political philosophy prevailed. Yet they walked in the funeral cortege from the White House to the cathedral, as simple human beings, in sympathy and grief for a suddenly bereaved family and a suddenly bereaved nation.

Like many another, we yearn to believe that from the grotesque and awful tragedy the Kennedy family and our Nation suffered last week—a tragedy of such magnitude that the mind is stunned and the emotions numbed—some droplets of good will come.

Like millions of others, we yearn to believe that the untimely death of this remarkable person and magnetic leader has not been in vain.

We long to believe this, to ease the pain and sense of futility that clutches us at the thought of the mindless atrocity that has been perpetrated.

We want to believe this because John Fitzgerald Kennedy, as we conceived him, would be happy to have it so.

Thus we harbor the hope that in the unplanned meeting of the world's heads of state at the bier of our assassinated President, the start of a rapport was lighted.

If each leader of state saw in the other, a simple human being groping toward a better life for his people, perhaps he can now regard him more kindly. If each leader of state saw in the other not the sinister, formless "enemy" but a vulnerable man as himself—perhaps his fears of him will diminish. If each leader of state saw the lines of

worry and weariness lining the face of the other—perhaps his resentments will give way to sympathy. The common knowledge that the others are all human clay, all subject to the Great Leveler, can conceivably be the basis for the easing of hostilities and an eventual building of peace for mankind.

We would like to believe that such a spark was lighted at the somber and highly moving ceremonies at which John F. Kennedy was laid to rest.

We would like to see it as a translation into human terms of the eternal torch that burns at his Arlington grave.

——

[From broadcasts over WTVJ–TV, Miami, Nov. 25, 1963]

FOUR DAYS OF TRAGEDY: A SUMMATION

With this program, we are nearing the end of nearly 4 continuous days of reporting by television what most certainly is one of the most dramatic and important events in history—the assassination of our 35th President.

Never before has such a tragic moment of existence been shared by so many. The momentous series of events etched forever in the minds of millions of Americans are never to be forgotten, and the events should not be forgotten.

First, on Friday, we listened anxiously for reports from Parkland Memorial Hospital where the President struggled vainly for life. Then came news of his death and the dramatic flight to Washington on Air Force 1 with the newly sworn President, Lyndon Johnson, on board with Jacqueline Kennedy and the late President's body.

Television transmitted the arrival at Andrews Air Force Base. Then the dignitaries of the world poured in— General de Gaulle, Lord Home, and others. We saw their arrivals. Then yesterday, at the lunch hour, came the incident which more than any other pointed up the ability of television to transmit to millions the scene of action. In this case, the basement of the Dallas City jail and the unexpected killing of Lee Harvey Oswald. A burlesque club owner, of all people, putting a climax to the story—a story which all along had really been unbelievable.

At about the same hour, TV cameras in Washington showed us the cortege moving from the White House to the Capitol. We watched as Mrs. Kennedy stood in the White House portico holding the hands of Caroline and John, Jr. Then the casket was carried up the Capitol steps. In the Rotunda, another moment which brought tears to the millions watching—Mrs. Kennedy moved forward to kiss the flag of her beloved country— the Nation for which her husband gave his life, truly in the line of duty.

Through the day and night we saw thousands of citizens file past the bier—paying last respects. Those of us watching at home did the same.

Then came the final coverage still fresh in our minds— the funeral mass; young John, Jr., outside the church saluting his father's casket; the long trip to Arlington; the Lincoln Memorial, hovering in the background, giving a sense of history to the proceedings; the playing of the dirge; the flyover of Air Force jets; the final volley of shots; playing of taps, and the folding of the American flag. It was over.

At the State Department we saw the new President of the United States, Lyndon Johnson, as he began his new duties by greeting the largest number of royalty, heads of state, and government leaders ever assembled in this country.

At the moment this Nation and its people continue their headlong rush into history.

I would just like to leave this thought: That because of television and what we have been able to see first-hand since Friday, all of us will be prepared to move ahead with a new sense of purpose. We have a better understanding of our role as individuals and as citizens of this great country.

PRESIDENT KENNEDY: HIS ACCOMPLISHMENTS LIVE

"It is for us the living, rather, to be dedicated here to the unfinished work which they who fought here have thus far so nobly advanced."

And so, almost 100 years ago to the day, Abraham Lincoln, himself to be assassinated, turned from the tragedy of death to the future and the molding of a great nation.

It does seem appropriate to pause, however quickly, to reflect on what our young President began and what we must continue and complete.

As President Kennedy so poetically expressed his first day in office, that this is a new generation of Americans born in this century, so we must recall not only his classic words but his deeds.

His steadfast efforts toward world peace and human rights; a Peace Corps, that now sustains thousands of idealistic but realistic Americans in a hundred lands— taking with them the zeal and sincerity of purpose that accomplishes more than all the words in the language or all the promises in the mind.

The Alliance for Progress, a firm, steady hand of help extended to the nations of Latin America, to assist them in their efforts to become strong and independent partners in freedom.

The first President to make a governmental study of juvenile delinquency to try to assess the reasons and causes for it.

The first to address an administration's attention to the cause of women in America—their progress, their opportunity.

The President who finally brought to fruition the dream of men since the atom was turned into a weapon— the nuclear test ban. The abrupt halting of a headlong weapons rush that seemed inevitably turned to war. But perhaps what John Kennedy brought to the highest office in the Nation was a new sense of youth and vitality. For the first time in most Americans' recollection, the young, prosperous, and most free nation in the world was in the hands of an equally young, dynamic, and thoughtful man.

Not perfect, to be sure, our young President, but from his most eloquent moving inaugural address to his last in Dallas, he was always the figure of what made America great—the zest of life, the course of purpose and, maybe the most important, the use of new ideas.

John Kennedy brought to the Government of America a quality not usual in its workings but sorely lacking. He turned the minds of men to more than just politics and vote getting.

From the universities and corporations of America there was the move to put the best man in the right place in government, regardless of political payment or due.

And before we close this partial list of his accomplishments, a word concerning our First Lady and mother—his wife, Jacqueline.

Surely one of his greatest accomplishments shall be numbered that she was his wife. For millions of Americans who themselves have fallen into grief, her courage and pure spirit will never be forgotten. Truly tonight, and always in memory, she leads her Nation in spirit and soul.

But what to do of this fallen hero—our dead President?

To mourn him too much is to detract from the work he began. He surely would be the first to call short this sorrow. We then must anticipate his spirit of purpose and devote ourselves to keeping alive that new sense of being which he lived and died.

Mr. Speaker, John Fitzgerald Kennedy dedicated his life to us. He did all for his country, but that is not all. Mrs. Kennedy and her children dedicated their life to him and through him to all Americans. We must forever be inspired by her courage, determination, and dedication to the ideals and responsibilities of J.F.K., the man, the husband, the father and the President of the United States. No woman more completely joined with her husband and stands now at his side in history.

Mr. Speaker, it is for us not to forget. The eyes of courage are upon us. All mankind and history wait and listen.

Mr. Speaker, he began—it is for us to carry on. There is work yet to be done.

Fortunately, immortal words of John Fitzgerald Kennedy will forever stir Americans to action. Who will ever forget?

And so, my fellow Americans, ask not what your country can do for you; ask what you can do for your country.

Will we pick up and carry forward the baton of these moving words of John Fitzgerald Kennedy on Friday, January 20, 1961:

We dare not forget today that we are the heirs of that first Revolution. Let the word go forth from this time and place, to friend and foe alike, that the torch has been passed to a new generation of Americans—born in this century, tempered by war, disciplined by a hard and bitter peace, proud of our ancient heritage—and unwilling to witness or permit the slow undoing of those human rights to which this Nation has always been committed, and to which we are committed today at home and around the world.

Let every nation know, whether it wishes us well or ill, that we shall pay any price, bear any burden, meet any hardship, support any friend, oppose any foe, in order to assure the survival and the success of liberty.

This much we pledge—and more.

With God's help let us resolve here today that we will.

ADDRESS BY

Hon. Kenneth J. Gray

OF ILLINOIS

Mr. Speaker, greater love hath no man than this, that he is willing to lay down his life for his friends.

With these words in mind, I rise today with a deep and sorrowful heart to join my colleagues in tribute to the greatest leader I have ever known, John Fitzgerald Kennedy. Like a giant oak tree that has stood as a landmark giving refuge from the heat of the day and providing a special character of a total environment, a great man served his nation. Just as the complete worth of a magnificent tree is seldom fully appreciated until the ravages of time take their toll so it is with this great man, John F. Kennedy.

Now that my dear friend and leader is dead, his role in leading this Nation and truly improving all of our lives is more crystal clear today than ever before. His was a life filled with deep devotion to mankind, blessed with imagination and depth of insight which was complete with a courage that never faltered.

John Fitzgerald Kennedy was a true leader of a great people. He believed a responsibility was a sacred privilege and that life had true purpose and personal significance only when devoted to the welfare of all men.

Mr. Speaker, for him there was no room for the defeatist, no room for the weary, the despondent, the retreater or the sinner. John Fitzgerald Kennedy faced life possessing firmness without harshness.

He faced life with vision, without daydreaming; confidence without brashness; courage stripped of vanity.

Now that the great oak tree has fallen, let us recognize as never before the debt every person in this Nation owes to this great man.

We of southern Illinois can look throughout the hillsides and see progress in agriculture; we can see the mark of this man for all time to come. Possibly we can honor him best by resolving to fight hard to be worthy of the mantle of leadership he has now passed on to us.

I would like to dedicate the following short poem to his memory:

> John Fitzgerald Kennedy,
> His life is a beautiful memory,
> His absence a silent grief,
> He sleeps in God's beautiful garden,
> In sunshine of perfect peace.

To his courageous wife and loving family I want to extend my heartfelt sympathy and that of my constituents and my family and to thank them for sending this great man our way.

ADDRESS BY

Hon. Ken Hechler

OF WEST VIRGINIA

Mr. Speaker, it was a glorious spring in 1960 in West Virginia. The laurel-decked hillsides sparkled. When the early morning fog had lifted from the mountaintop airports, planeloads of news commentators, political experts, and curious visitors debarked and headed for the hills and hollows. This was political primary time in West Virginia, the primary which started John F. Kennedy on the road to the White House.

West Virginia, the 35th State in the Union, made John F. Kennedy the 35th President of the United States. It was on this battleground on the 10th day of May 1960, that the future President scored a smashing victory which buried the so-called religious issue.

The strong affection between West Virginia and President Kennedy was not due to the primary alone, even though the intensive week in April and May 1960 enabled both the candidate and the people to get to know each other intimately. In West Virginia, President Kennedy recognized a State which received its birth of freedom in the turbulence of the Civil War, and where the spirit of freedom and self-help burned bright in the breasts of its mountaineers. He saw that God blessed our State with rugged mountains, and he put black diamonds in them all. In West Virginia, President Kennedy saw an unfulfilled potential. He worked tirelessly as President of the United States to help all of God's children realize their potential, in West Virginia, in West Berlin, and all over the world.

Whether he was dealing with one person, with a group, with a community, with a State, or with any nation or the people of the world, the mainspring of President Kennedy's philosophy was how to help them realize their most noble capabilities.

Here was a man who knew more about our Nation's past than any occupant of the White House, yet keyed his every action to what it would mean for the future. That is why the closest thing to his heart was the youth of the world. He was a builder for humanity's future. His interest in and concern for young people extended across the board. Since he was perhaps the most completely educated man of this generation, he had a deep and personal understanding of the importance of education. He looked on education as an essential of national strength in the future, and as a source of personal fulfillment for the human beings of the Nation. He worked to perfect vocational education, job training, youth employment, and measures to reduce juvenile delinquency. He worked for young people to live in a better world in the future.

Cynics have termed people like this "do-gooders." The implication is usually left that such dreamers will sap the initiative of free men by spoon feeding them. One only had to watch the interaction of young people with President Kennedy to realize that this could never happen with him. He invited, challenged, and demanded of the young people of America and the world more than any other leader of modern times, and they responded and will continue to respond.

Have you seen the hordes of young people who stood in line, hour upon hour in the cold, to pay their last respects to the President? Have you seen the radiant enthusiasm on the faces of the young people with whom he has talked?

I remember Ravenswood, W. Va., on a Sunday in the spring of 1960, when a woman's club reception was augmented by an eager group of high school students. I remember every Monday morning during the summers of 1961, 1962, and 1963, standing with a group of West Virginia high school students at Andrews Air Force Base, and to watch their inspired looks as the President waved at them or sometimes would stop to speak with them, as he returned from a weekend at his beloved Hyannis Port.

President Kennedy awakened in young Americans an interest in and awareness of their Government, the necessity to participate, and the nature and value of our Nation's ideals. Like Theodore Roosevelt, he quickened the appreciation and understanding which young people hold for the Nation's noblest virtues. His presence kindled a flame of eagerness to learn, as he did, and for young people to dedicate their lives to purposeful activity, as he did.

It was with a group of my students from Princeton University that I first met this man some 15 years ago. He was serving his first term in the House of Representatives, after a surprising primary victory over eight opponents in the Boston area. His office was delightfully disorganized. By studiously refusing to enter except through the door to his private office, his staff could rarely discover whether or not he was in. Just as his secretary was announcing that Congressman Kennedy was not in, he appeared at his office door bearing a tray from which he was just finishing lunch. "I can save lots of time this way," he announced. On numerous occasions, I have watched him since, "saving time," almost as though he realized he must work fast to fulfill God's purpose on earth.

The interview almost fell flat on its face, because this man had a wonderfully mischievous sense of humor. Our class was studying "Legislatures," and before we could get the first question out, the Congressman asked: "What kind of a group is this?" I answered rather quickly: "This is a group in 'Legislatures'." He shook his head sadly and responded: "Now, that is very unusual. In all my years in school, I never heard of a group in legislatures." He engaged in very light banter and needling for a few minutes, apparently to establish whether the professor was a stuffed shirt, and then suddenly turned the conversation in a way which made the students feel they had the most important teacher in the business. Those who were fortunate enough to know this man best can appreciate both of these wonderfully human qualities—his quick and delicious sense of humor, always tempered by a sensitive consideration for the feelings of others.

As I looked at this very thin, sophomoric-looking legislator, his face slightly yellowed by the atabrine he took for wartime malaria, I wondered just what motivated him to get into politics when his father's millions could have launched him on any of a dozen other careers. I paused at the doorway to ask, as my students were leaving. He glanced out of the window in a preoccupied, imperturbable way, and answered casually: "Oh, I guess it's a sort of an obligation."

With John F. Kennedy, life was a dedicated obligation, and he always talked about it with deliberate understatement.

One of our West Virginia tributes to President Kennedy was penned by the editor of the Charleston (W. Va.) Gazette, who has summed up the late President's life in terms of the single word "sacrifice." Under unanimous consent, I include the article by Harry Hoffmann, editor of the Charleston Gazette:

Lessons for Public in Kennedy's Life
(By Harry Hoffmann)

John F. Kennedy in his brief, brilliant, and tragic career in public life, constructed a legacy that provides for this generation and for posterity lessons to be learned by people in all walks of life and in all nations.

In the millions of words that have been written around the world since that black Friday in Dallas, Tex., this seemingly has been all but overlooked except in what the individual may deduce on his own in reading of the purpose and achievements of the young man from Boston.

Did not the course which John Kennedy set for himself teach us all something about our responsibilities to our Government, to our fellow citizens, to the world?

Here was a man born to wealth. He could have led a carefree life, irresponsive to the needs of other people and safe from the calumny and abuse that, in the American tradition, seems to be a burden of those who offer themselves in public service.

He could have gravitated from seashore to mountain resort, from one continent to the next, from one social funfest to the other—all without worrying about where the next dollar was coming from to buy whatever he may have desired.

He could, in what too often has become the tradition of those born to wealth accumulated by a father

or a grandfather, have led a wasteful life of fun and frivolity.

Instead, he chose to make something of his life—not for himself but for others. So it was that, when an old back injury made him ineligible for enlistment in the armed services in World War II, he committed himself to demanding exercises to strengthen his back so that he would be acceptable.

And, after the experience that brought him so close to death in the South Pacific, he resisted what might be the normal temptation to adopt the easy life provided by inherited wealth and chose to offer himself in the public service—first in the House of Representatives, then in the Senate, and finally in the excruciating burdens of the Presidency.

He well know the price of his decision for, in the preface of his book, "Profiles in Courage," he included this quotation from Edmund Burke:

"He well knows what snares are spread about his path from personal animosity * * * and possibly from popular delusion * * *. He is traduced and abused for his supposed motives. He will remember that obloquy is a necessary ingredient in the composition of true glory * * * that calumny and abuse are essential parts of triumph."

John Kennedy, putting aside the safe and happy life that wealth could provide, was willing to risk the hazards of public life and high office. In so doing, he and his family experienced the slander and the abuse he had anticipated—and in the final analysis, by choosing a purposeful life instead of a wasteful one, he sacrificed his life to the cause.

This was the key to his life and to his success—sacrifice. He not only accepted it; he welcomed it, even when the position to which he was born gave him every reason to avoid it.

For this, much of the credit must go to his parents and to the upbringing they provided. They had the means of avoiding sacrifice and giving their children whatever they wanted.

Instead, they taught them that there was a purpose in life, and they had to compete with each other and with the world, that they had to fight for a position of their own and for what was right, that they had to know living was something more than a selfish pleasure.

In this sense, Joseph and Rose Kennedy, the parents of the martyred President, are the real heroes in the saga and the tragedy of John Kennedy—and thus a lesson is provided for parents everywhere: don't safeguard your children from sacrifice, but attune them for sacrifice.

John Kennedy, the man and the President, had other qualities to provide lessons for this generation and those of the future. He had physical courage, as demonstrated by his wartime service, and moral courage, as exemplified by his decision in the Cuban crisis and his stand on civil rights.

In the first instance he was willing to avoid an excuse, and instead went out of his way to jeopardize his life to serve his country; in the second, after the success of his decision on Cuba, he was so determined not to damage the future world prospect by any humiliation of Khrushchev that he completely failed to bring home to the American people the magnitude of the victory which he had won. He was also ready to give up votes to further the cause of racial equality.

What is the first lesson to be learned by the people of West Virginia—the people of the State he made such an effort to help—from the life John Kennedy chose for himself?

The answer might be in the single word, "sacrifice," or in a willingness to avoid an easier life and stand for public service. But the question may well be answered through another question:

How long has it been since you have taken the trouble even to vote in an election? Or, better still, when have you made the effort to learn the respective qualifications of the candidates before voting?

For those who have wondered why this man of moral strength and judgment and courage should be taken from us at a time when his qualities could best serve the world, the answer may be in the lessons he leaves for us by his decisions and service in life.

A quotation from his "Profiles in Courage" of 1955 seems proper to point up the lessons of his life and his chosen course of living it:

"The courage of life is often a less dramatic spectacle than the courage of a final moment; but it is no less than a magnificent mixture of triumph and tragedy. A man does what he must—in spite of personal consequences, in spite of obstacles and dangers and pressures—and that is the basis of all human morality."

This is the true purpose of politics. Can there be any better lesson than that to gain from the life of John F. Kennedy? And what will be our fate if we fail to take heed?

Mr. Speaker, I also include a column by Bill Wild in the Huntington (W. Va.) Herald-Dispatch for December 2, 1963:

REFLECTIONS ON A MOMENT IN HISTORY

(By Bill Wild)

A week ago John Fitzgerald Kennedy, an exciting, challenging President, went to his grave, a martyred hero's plot, in Arlington National Cemetery. The deed which put him there and the national reaction stripped the English vocabulary bare of words and terms which would be properly expressive. Larger than life as President, his shadow looms larger still. Historians are already looking forward to the coming battle between "facts" and the inevitable "myths."

Huntington is among the relatively few (many, but still relatively few) places in the Nation which got a closeup of J.F.K. in the heat of close-up battle action before he moved behind the barriers which inevitably come to surround persons of enormous prominence. We would like to recall a moment or two of that time almost 3 years and 7 months ago at the start of the West Virginia primary battle which was to "make" Kennedy.

Huntington was a Nixon town. It had earlier eagerly received the GOP hopeful. Now moving in this April 1960 was the still-new Kennedy State organization, more effective than it knew, full of self-doubts, attractive to amateurs and idealists, despised by many "regulars." Now the candidate comes into view in this account:

"A trifle ill at ease at the gates of the H. K. Porter Co. steel plant as he greeted workers, Senator Kennedy leaped to the top of his car just a block away to bring cheers and laughter to a throng of Marshall students."

A crew of still-doubtful out-of-town newsmen accompanied him, gathered "background" from local yokels and found confirmation for their dispatches to the Nation that the campaign in West Virginia was going to be a close thing for this youthful, and Catholic, upstart.

A press conference at the Hotel Prichard preceded a reception for the candidate. Whatever might have been newsworthy comment was lost in the din. Out-of-town reporters asked about West Virginia. West Virginia reporters asked about Quemoy and Matsu. One hard-of-hearing reporter took copious notes on things no one else could hear. A worried young county organization functionary named David Fox, Jr., asked that the conference conclude so the reception could go on, thereby grievously insulting a New York Times man who considered it his privilege, as senior among those present, to declare the little gathering at an end. Subsequent events developed this impression printed a few days later:

"Senator Kennedy brings to campaigning a different kind of tirelessness * * * than does Minnesota's Senator Humphrey * * * Senator Humphrey, an energetic political hummingbird always nervously on the move, is up against a different kind of bird. Kennedy is a robin, head cocked to one side, eyes carefully appraising the ground ahead, then, jump-jump-jump moving in quickly to strike hard."

During the reception a lifelong Republican was instrumental in seeing to it that the late Col. George S. Wallace, watching from the sidelines with his chin resting on the great cane he carried, was properly and formally introduced to the young candidate.

A brief speech established the picture which was to become familiar later from the television debates.

"The man should be watched in action as he ponders questions shot at him, lets his head drop * * * as his eyes seem to be trying to pick the words out of the air, and then, generally looking his questioner full-on, answers rapidly and almost never with hesitation. His hands * * * are used sparingly to emphasize only the most important points or strongest of feelings. Generally, the right hand does the gesturing and either impales the air or chops it to bits. The left hides a good deal in a great flannel pocket, emerging * * * only in moments of gravest crisis, usually something Republican."

Even then there were indications that this man could put together a powerful party organization beyond the scope of a more articulate liberal such as Senator Humphrey. There was this evaluation:

"Kennedy has the more formidable philosophy in that it is more realistic; it is flexible enough to fit well into several regional Democratic patterns. It carries the assurance that compromise, while perhaps distasteful, is still not impossible."

A powerful image of idealism was emerging even then. The candidate was described as "someone who could be voted least likely ever to be found in a smoke-filled room, who makes the words 'let the people pick the candidates' sound like a crusade."

The reception was over and one of those curious opportunities for a reporter arose which occurs maybe once a decade. Everyone streamed from the Prichard ballroom doors except the young candidate, a reporter and two eager Democratic admirers, Mr. and Mrs. Robert K. Emerson. There was perhaps 5 minutes of three-cornered conversation during which the reporter fervently hoped that, against all odds, he could corner the candidate alone. The Emersons, after all, two votes, won out. The interlude was brief for, in a short time, the organization streamed back again seeking its hero and the future President was swept away, to history.

Mr. Speaker, I include a column written by H. R. Pinckard in the November 24, 1963, issue of the Huntington (W. Va.) Herald-Advertiser:

(By H. R. Pinckard)

I will always remember John Kennedy as I saw him last April at a White House reception for the American Society of Newspaper Editors.

It wasn't a formal reception. Mrs. Kennedy was not in Washington and the President had not been scheduled for a "set" appearance. The guests trooped through the White House on a tour most of us had made several times on previous trips to Washington—the women pausing to examine paintings, furniture and china, as women will, and their escorts nervously trying to urge them on, as men will.

Most of the throng eventually congregated in a large and almost barren room at the rear of the White House. This room was on the first floor and just outside the windows could be seen tools and wheelbarrows that gardeners had abandoned at the 5 o'clock quitting time.

On a long table at one end of the room was the usual assortment of hors d'oeuvres—cheese and crackers, shrimp on toothpicks, olives and pickles. There were two kinds of punch, white and purple. The waiters pointed to them, saying "This one is, this one isn't."

The chattering in the big, barren room finally reached the point where it exceeded the sound barrier and I decided I had had enough of it. My luck was good, for as I approached the big entrance hall near the main door of the White House, I saw Mr. Kennedy just entering.

The Marine Corps orchestra was playing in the main hall and the President paused to listen and to smile cordially at some young girls who were gathered around the musicians.

In that incredibly quick way that throngs collect around a celebrity, the President was almost instantly surrounded, but I managed to work my way to his side. "I'm from West Virginia," I said. "I remember shaking your hand as you stood on the corner of Tenth Street and Fourth Avenue in Huntington. You were with Brother Bob and you were running hard to win the West Virginia primary."

Mr. Kennedy smiled and shook hands warmly. "I'll always remember West Virginia with the kindest recollections," he said. "That was where I started * * *. How are things out there?"

Well, what do you tell a President at a time like that? I said things were fine with us in Huntington, though perhaps not so good in the coal fields and in some other areas of distress.

In a moment he was literally swept away as the guests from other parts of the White House discovered their host and descended upon him.

I watched him as this flood of humanity rolled in from all sides, breaking only slightly to avoid doing the President physical damage.

He seemed so young, so boyish, so modestly surprised at this acclaim—which must, of course, have been an almost daily occurrence. Yet he had a kind of inner serenity and outward poise that couldn't be shaken. He was always the master of the situation, never its victim. He invariably—perhaps instinctively—said the right thing, made the right gesture, seemed always to be glad to shake a hand, return a smile, answer a question, respond to a conversational sally.

I have seen many people struggle with admiring crowds—Presidents, generals, movie stars, champions of this and that. But none had this man's aplomb, his keen attentiveness to the individuals that make up a clamorous crowd, his way of showing that this was a sustaining and appreciated part of his life and his mammoth job—not a boring interlude to be endured and made the best of.

Many thought, some said, that it was hard to believe that this handsome young man had taken the measure of Nikita Khrushchev in the Cuban crisis—just 6 months before.

It was a natural observation. But the longer you watched those blue eyes and that firm jaw (now busy in amiable chatter) the more you realized that even in friendliness they did not yield all of the inner man. Those eyes could turn cold and that chin could be stubborn and resolute.

Perhaps this was the afterthought. But I am sure that many in that gathering gained the same impression. And even as I did, they must have had the sick-stomach feeling when they learned, on Friday that he was dead.

Mr. Speaker, I include an editorial from the Huntington (W. Va.) Advertiser for November 23, 1963:

NATION MOURNS PRESIDENT'S DEATH

The news of the shooting of President Kennedy in Dallas, Tex., struck every community of the Nation with stunning force yesterday and echoed throughout the world with a shocking sense of personal grief and anxiety over his condition.

The scenes of people crowding about wire service machines in the newsroom of the Huntington Publishing Co. and about radios and television sets in homes and stores here were reenacted in thousands of towns and cities.

There was deep shock beneath the tension of veteran newsmen accustomed to handling stories of tragedy and disaster that tear the heart. Dispatches from Dallas said sobs were heard in the corps of correspondents assigned to the presidential party.

During the long moments of suspense while crowds waited for news from the hospital, there were words of hope and then cause for deepening anxiety as two priests arrived, presumably to administer last rites of the Catholic church.

At last the word came that the President was dead.

In fleeting thoughts during their tension people had already been considering the possible consequences upon the lives not only of officials but of millions of people in this country and around the earth.

In this hour of shock and grief even those with the most complete information will be unable to say what course events will take in the delicate balance of international affairs.

No doubt President Johnson will continue the general line of domestic and foreign policy laid down during the years of President Kennedy.

But for the present thoughts will dwell upon the personal aspect of the tragedy of the attractive and highly popular young President's being shot down beside his wife in a moment of triumph and acclaim.

The "Oh, no!" that she cried in anguish and the picture of her cradling him in her arms will remain for life with all those who read the accounts.

People of West Virginia felt a particularly heavy sense of loss because they had seen so much of the young candidate during his primary and presidential campaign in 1960.

He appeared at Huntington several times, talked with many people personally and addressed gatherings attended by those of both parties.

One reason he won the primary campaign was that he was able to communicate to the people his sincere sympathy for those suffering through the years of chronic heavy unemployment.

His impressive victory in the primary effectively cleared the way for his nomination, and he never lost an opportunity to express his gratitude to the people for their support.

Even before his inauguration he began to fulfill the promise he had made of economic assistance by appointing a task force headed by Senator Paul H. Douglas, of Illinois, with Senators Robert C. Byrd and Jennings Randolph, of this State, as consultants to formulate a program of aid.

The group presented its recommendations on January 1, and as one result of the study, the bill for creating the Area Redevelopment Administration was the first offered when the Senate convened.

Under this agency and other programs initiated during the Kennedy administration millions of dollars have come to the State not just in emergency relief but for permanent improvements establishing a sounder base for the economy.

The humane action to aid the people of West Virginia was typical of the various phases of domestic policy designed to stimulate economic growth and create new jobs.

Among the most important measures now pending before Congress are those for reducing taxes, extending civil rights to all classes, providing medical care of the aged, and granting much-needed aid to public schools and institutions of higher learning.

President Kennedy's eloquent and forceful appeals for such measures will assure him a notable place in American history not only as a humanitarian but as a man of clear vision who recognized the vital needs of people in an increasingly complex social and economic order.

In the field of international relations, also, the young President charted a course that will give him towering stature among those who throughout history have stood resolutely for freedom against the encroachments of tyranny.

His ultimatum forcing Premier Khrushchev to remove his ballistic missiles from Cuba will be remembered as an achievement cracking the monolithic unity of the Soviet Union and widening the ideological breach in the Communist empire.

The tense days during the eye-to-eye confrontation while the fate of the human race trembled in the balance will live among the most critical in modern times.

The calm courage of the young President, along with the solid support of the people of the United States and the free world, helped open the way for the later nuclear test ban treaty and for perhaps further accommodations between East and West.

On the basis of these achievements, President Kennedy's place in history will be that of a strong man of far vision whose assassination at the early age of 46 was a heavy loss to the people of the world as well as those of the United States.

The shocking tragedy underscores the view expressed on this page today by Walter Lippmann that representative democracy is failing to solve the complex problems of nations in this perplexing age.

There has been entirely too much fanaticism in the political arena. Extremists of both right and left have gained a hearing far beyond the justification of their mental processes.

No doubt President Kennedy is a victim of the crackbrained hatred generated in the boiling cauldron of radicalism or mental confusion, just as the assassinated Presidents before him have been.

There is no way to eliminate such dangerous people, but those of sounder minds and more temperate judgment can avoid inciting them to violence by keeping their own good sense in control of their emotions.

There is particular need in this hour of national sorrow and world crisis for people to lay aside the animosities that have divided the Nation as well as both parties and to concentrate on the public welfare.

Differences on means of meeting problems will always exist but there should be no thought of reaching a solution through violence. This should be constantly on the minds of political candidates and orators during the heat of the national campaign just getting underway.

Meanwhile the Nation is fortunate that President Johnson has had wide experience in the problems of government during his years as majority leader of the Senate and as Vice President.

He will be able to take over with a sure hand and continue the business with only the interruption that the national tragedy imposes.

No doubt he will benefit from the popular unity that a crisis always brings to an intelligent free people and perhaps will be able to bridge the coming days of transition more easily because all good citizens will move closer together from the sobering shock that violence has caused them.

Mr. Speaker, I have referred to the fact that President Kennedy always turned his eyes toward the future. Nothing better illustrates this than his great vision and imaginative grasp of this Nation's space program. He was determined that America to remain preeminent among nations must master space and sail on this new ocean. He refused to be deterred by his short-sighted critics who failed to recognize the bold progress which the challenge of outer space could provide. History will record the courage and the foresight which President Kennedy showed in mobilizing the Nation's resources to make America first in space.

It would take pages to set forth the many different interests and activities of President Kennedy, and the fields in which he lent leadership. His interests and knowledge were as wide as Jefferson's. He brought a realization to our minds that we as individuals should work together regardless of race, color or religious faith. To the many people who criticized him for "going too far" in the field of human rights, he calmly replied that his stand would probably lose votes, but he clearly indicated that this was a matter of moral principle.

This great man with a compassionate heart worked tirelessly to ease the burdens of the aged through a program of medical care, and to launch a new program to combat mental retardation. It was in West Virginia that stark poverty moved him very deeply. "Imagine," he said to one of his assistants one night, "just imagine kids who never drank milk." Two weeks to the day before his tragic death, he made some informal remarks before the Protestant Council of the City of New York, as the council conferred on President Kennedy its first annual "Family of Man" citation for his support of human rights. President Kennedy chose as his text this theme: "Our Obligation to the Family of Man." He referred to a newspaper article which he had read on poverty in the Appalachians, and mentioned "schools which were without windows, sometimes with occasional teachers, counties without resources to distribute the surplus food we make available."

It was this compassionate heart of the great President which was illustrated in his very first official act after taking the oath of office: the Presidential order that additional emergency food relief be sent to West Virginia and other areas of need. In quick succession, a whole series of additional measures were taken to help West Virginia and other areas with high rates of unemployment. He launched the area redevelopment program. Under this program, Huntington, W. Va., my hometown, became the first place for the administration to undertake a retraining program for the unemployed. West Virginia now has about 40 such retraining projects underway or completed. New employment was created through industrial and commercial loans, and public facilities loans. When ARA took hold perhaps too slowly, President Kennedy a little over a year ago launched the highly successful accelerated public works program, which has enabled communities across the Nation to build new streets, water and sewer systems, public libraries and other buildings, hospitals and health facilities. To West Virginia, this program has provided a tremendous shot in the arm, as about $40 million has been awarded in matching funds for some 275 projects which have provided work for the unemployed and have made these communities better places to live, as well as more attractive for new industry.

During the 1960 campaign, John F. Kennedy many times referred to the fact that the State of West Virginia had contributed more volunteers in proportion to population during the Korean war than any other State, and that West Virginia also suffered more casualties than any other State in the Union in proportion to its population. Senator Kennedy then referred to the fact that per capita West Virginia stood near the bottom of the list in the per capita amount of prime military contracts awarded.

I recall one occasion when Senator Kennedy was due to address a breakfast in Huntington, attended by his brother Robert. Although Robert arrived on time, Senator Kennedy's plane was late. In the period of time while the audience was waiting, one of his Huntington campaign supporters picked up an issue of U.S. News & World Report and started to read off the small amounts of defense contracts awarded to West Virginia in comparison with other States. When he came to the State of Massachusetts, this Huntington supporter read off a rather substantial figure, and paused with slight embarrassment, only to have Robert Kennedy interrupt with this comment:

That proves that Massachusetts has had excellent representation in the Senate.

After John F. Kennedy was elected President, the entire picture was changed. West Virginia now stands 26th in the Nation instead of close to the bottom in per capita prime military contracts. And great plants like the Food Machinery Corp. in South Charleston, manufacturing armored personnel carriers and other vehicles for the Army, are providing employment for thousands of West Virginians.

Mr. Speaker, many volumes will be written about the wonderful woman who served as First Lady of the Land, and by her qualities Jacqueline Kennedy has earned the title of "First Lady of the World." I recall the first time that I met Mrs. Kennedy at the Democratic National Convention in Chicago in 1956, at the time when her husband, as a U.S. Senator, came within an eyelash of being nominated as the candidate for Vice President of the United States. At the time, what deeply impressed me was the detached serenity and deep principle of this woman of talent and intelligence, whose conversation was so refreshingly different in an atmosphere of highly competitive presidential politics. Her comments were never cynical, but she seemed to be able to put everything into grand perspective, and to glorify what to surface observers looked like a mad scramble for delegates. Then I remember January 2, 1960. The cameras and the floodlights were set up in the caucus room of the Senate Office Building. A still-shy and slightly diffident looking young U.S. Senator walked into the room, and his hands shook as he read a prepared statement to announce what was no secret: that John F. Kennedy was throwing his hat into the presidential ring. I looked around the room to see who had come to witness the launching of Senator Kennedy's campaign for the presidential nomination. Only one other Member of the House of Representatives was there, Representative Edward Boland, of Massachusetts, who asked me: "Does this mean that you are publicly supporting Senator Kennedy?" At that stage I was just an observer and a fence-sitter, and I told Eddie: "No, I am just here to watch a great campaigner in action, but I can tell you this: he has lots of

friends and supporters in West Virginia." Then I glanced around and saw a beautiful lady dressed in a red coat, calmly sitting by herself in the front row. Nobody was with Jacqueline Kennedy, nobody from the press came up to interview her, few people seemed to recognize the woman who a year later would become the First Lady. I sat down quietly beside her and introduced myself again. Once more, she conveyed that wonderful spirit of quiet confidence which gives strength to men to work for their goals and ideals. I came away with the impression that, in any campaign, she would not provide the ordinary type of handshaking and small talk but would really contribute something new. I started to imagine the role she might play in West Virginia, or perhaps in the White House itself. I did not dream that she would go down in history as the First Lady with the deepest understanding of the history of the White House, and the First Lady who with her illustrious husband brought a new culture and stimulus to the arts, music, and literature.

Mr. Speaker, at this point I include a column from the Huntington, W. Va., Herald-Advertiser of December 1, 1963, written by Bill Belanger:

"Real courage instead of being a man with a gun in your hand is when you know you're licked before you begin, but you begin anyway and see it through no matter what. You rarely win. But sometimes you do."

I was reading this paragraph in Harper Lee's "To Kill a Mockingbird" and trying to forget about what had happened. I was trying to realize that television commentators had not slipped when they were saying "President Johnson" instead of President Kennedy. And then it came through in the crazy mixed up way that everything comes to my mixed up brain; Harper Lee's paragraph about real courage was the kind that the late President Kennedy had.

I'd admired him, not so much for his bravery in a PT boat fighting in the war, but for standing against the crowd who ridiculed him for trying to help them. I admired him because he took a dirty word—in our land—like "culture," and another dirty word "intellectual" and made them not merely fashionable but sought after in the true meaning.

For years we Americans have written ourselves off as a crass class of people, historically too young to have intellectual roots, or a culture of our own. Anyone who dared to like art and good music had better be prepared to defend himself, to show he wasn't a sissy. Some Presidents have paid lipservice to cultural affairs by donning boiled shirts for one opera a season or an art exhibit. But the impression they wanted to give was they were too much "he" men to really like such stuff.

But Mr. Kennedy made no pretenses. He liked art and music and I suppose what really endeared him to me was that he even went with his wife to the ballet. No red-blooded American can get away with that? I guess it took a Kennedy to do it.

He apparently agreed with Bacon's ideal of the "whole man"; he advocated physical fitness programs so that we could be even more mentally alert to use our opportunities for education.

The making of the "whole man" which has long been carried out by the Great Books of the Western World reading program is now filtering down for younger readers. A set called "Gateway to the Great Books" has been published by Encyclopaedia Britannica, edited by Robert M. Hutchins and Mortimer J. Adler, father of the Great Books idea.

In 10 volumes it has the great writings selected by the GBWW editors. It serves as bridge to the Great Books, being a complement to them, having some of the same writers but not their same writings. There are contributors like Ernest Hemingway, Joseph Conrad, Thomas Mann, George Bernard Shaw, Ibsen, and Eve Curie. There is a graded reading plan too. And the editors assure the reading can be enjoyed by most 16- and 14-year-olds.

But that is not the real value of the set.

It is worth every penny of the $69.50 just for the introductory essay on reading written by Robert Hutchins. From it you will learn—and don't think you can't learn—the difference between knowledge as facts and knowledge as inquiry. He makes the point beautifully that the greatest enjoyment, greatest fun in life is learning. He implies the means of getting an education in the true sense is more enjoyable than the end.

Hutchins shows literally how Xenophon and Prescott are better than any western and no more difficult to read. The curse of education today, he shows, is the need for group study with its consequent demand for adjustment. The fast learner is bored waiting for the slow to catch up so they both can go on. The slow learner is bored by frustration.

Plans like "machine education" which are really not machines but a plan to permit individual progress through self-teaching are only partly the answer.

A practical education is not one that aims to transmit information but one that leads to understanding, he concludes. And while we agree with him we must admit the idea has been expressed before—in the Bible: "The man that findeth wisdom is the man that findeth understanding."

Mr. Speaker, in reviewing the thoughts which flash across my mind in an unorganized fashion, I cherish many memories of John F. Kennedy in West Virginia. There was the April day when his plane landed in Parkersburg, W. Va., and the able director of his West Virginia campaign, Robert P. McDonough of Parkersburg, squeezed me into the front seat of his station wagon next to Senator Kennedy as he rode to an early-morning reception at the Elks Club. It takes a lot of effort for a man under such heavy pressure to be

graceful so early in the morning, but I was amazed at his knowledge of West Virginia, his quick absorption of facts, and once again the breadth of his interests. I paid a man a few dollars to drive my convertible from Parkersburg to Charleston so I could fly with the candidate's plane and pick up their motorcade from Charleston to Huntington. The first thing which struck me when we got on the plane was the difference between this candidate and other presidential candidates with whom I had traveled in the past. The first thing he did was to pick up a map of West Virginia, and to start asking questions and making casual comments which revealed his deep understanding, not only of the politics, but the economics, culture and history of the State.

"Tell me about Mingo and the Indians," he said as he put his finger on Williamson, and then he proceeded to tell us all more than the combined knowledge of the staff and correspondents on the plane. His alert finger ran across to Logan County—a machine-controlled county where John F. Kennedy engineered one of the great surprises of the primary by pulling a 3 to 2 victory out of the primary fire. He mused, half to himself, "The Iroquois Confederacy produced great characters like Cornplanter and Sequoia and, last but not least, Logan." Then without any apparent reason, he glanced out of the plane and quoted this sentence: "Who is there to mourn for Logan? Not one." I still do not know who or what he was quoting, but months later, while glancing through Morison and Commager's "Growth of the American Republic," I found both of these references which his insatiable mind had retained.

Debarking at the Kanawha Airport, the motorcade took a swift ride to Morris Harvey College where the young candidate addressed a student assembly. He asked for questions. A student with a strident voice, reading from a slip of paper, asked him rather provocatively whether his Catholic religion would interfere with his oath of office, and asked why he had declined to attend a Philadelphia fundraising dinner in 1950 for the Chapel of the Four Chaplains. The question did not sound like the type of question a student would formulate himself, nor was it posed with the courtesy which has come to be associated with most West Virginians. Many students were visibly embarrassed. I wondered, as I watched Senator Kennedy closely, just how he would handle such a question. He smiled ever so slightly and met the question head-on. He answered it so directly, so clearly, so completely and so forcefully that the audience gave him a prolonged ovation which I am certain surprised even the candidate.

After a stiff luncheon for contributors in Charleston, the motorcade started driving along Route 60 to Huntington. I wanted very much to have Senator Kennedy visit Marshall College, but there were no definite plans, and everyone realized that the backward rule prohibiting candidates from visiting the campus would make it impossible for him to set foot within the gates of Marshall. On the spur of the moment, I telephoned a Marshall student, Bobby Nelson, and asked him if he would see if he could round up a few students to wait just outside the Marshall campus gates along about midafternoon. Nelson said he would try. Along the way between Charleston and Huntington, the candidate blithely yielded to local entreaties that he stop by a few farms and get photographed with some local politicos. The motorcade became completely disorganized. "First time in history anybody has been lost on Route 60 between Charleston and Huntington," grumbled a United Press reporter.

Hundreds of students swarmed along Third Avenue in Huntington waiting for almost 2 hours for the satisfaction of seeing the young candidate. It was a completely unplanned, spontaneous tribute arranged without official announcement and spread by word of mouth. After a brief stop at the H. K. Porter Steel Co., Senator Kennedy saw the great wave of students at the Marshall gates and started walking toward them. They poured across Third Avenue, blocking traffic and swarmed around him. He cheerfully leaped up on the hood of an automobile to make this prophetic statement to 500 cheering students, "Ken Hechler tells me that Marshall will soon be a university." After a few preliminary remarks, which rang out loud and clear despite the lack of a microphone, he asked for questions. Here he was at his best, stimulating and stirring, never preaching or talking down, but leaving each one of his listeners with part of himself—and above all, the inspiration to go out and learn more.

Perhaps in this review of what John F. Kennedy stood for, and his relation with West Virginia, I place too much stress on the great primary campaign of 1960. But I agree with the assessment by Arthur Edson of the Associated Press, one of those who covered the West Virginia primary, who wrote after the Democratic Convention:

If our political disputes are ever remembered as our battlefields are now, West Virginia will become a national shrine. For it was in West Virginia's beautiful mountains, in its thriving cities, in its impoverished coalfields that the decisive battle was fought that gave Senator John F. Kennedy the Democratic presidential nomination.

West Virginia will always be grateful to John F. Kennedy not only for the concrete accomplishments which he wrought in providing jobs for West Virginians, but more particularly in what President Kennedy stood for. Many, many times I stood on the edge of a spellbound crowd, watching this vigorous and high-principled man, who so often would end his talk with one of his favorite quotations from Robert Frost:

> The woods are lovely, dark and deep
> But I have promises to keep
> And miles to go before I sleep—
> And miles to go before I sleep.

ADDRESS BY

Hon. William S. Moorhead

OF PENNSYLVANIA

Mr. Speaker—

I weep for Adonais—he is dead.
Oh, weep for Adonais. Though our tears
Thaw not the frost which binds so dear a head.

The great Republic weeps and grieves for the loss of an inspiring and courageous leader. Courage in battle is a rare and important quality. That he had, but even more significant, he was a profile in political courage.

Back in 1932, Walter Lippmann described such courage in political leaders when he said:

It is not necessary to talk softly to the people and to pamper them as if they were invalids. One has only to look back and see how the real leaders of men have talked to their people in a time of crisis to see how false it is to offer men mere optimism and reassurance.

By entitling his administration the "New Frontier," he offered us not "mere optimism and reassurance," but a challenge to look squarely at the problems which menace us, and then, with intellectual integrity and political courage, seek a solution to them.

He insisted upon excellence in every aspect of his administration, upon trained competence and upon idealism tempered by the need for effectiveness.

Never before have the American people seen such youthful flair as that which President and Mrs. Kennedy brought to the White House. Unique among occupants of the White House the Kennedys had the courage to try and to succeed in inspiring the American people to seek new heights of intellectual and cultural understanding.

Cuba tested his political courage first in failure and then in success. After the Bay of Pigs he had the courage to assume full responsibility rather than to search for a scapegoat to absolve himself. In the October 1962 Cuba crisis he had the courage necessary to force Nikita Khrushchev to pull his nuclear missiles out of Cuba before the eyes of the world, but he was also so politically courageous that he did not push the Soviet leader into a corner. In the triumph of Cuba the same restraint that earlier had marked his acceptance of bitter defeat led directly to the successful negotiation of the nuclear test ban treaty. He honored his inaugural commitment: "Let us never negotiate out of fear but let us never fear to negotiate."

On the domestic scene, his political courage was equally magnificent. The summer of 1963 was a period of racial discontent. Though he was aware that his support of a strong civil rights program could tear apart his party and cost him his reelection, he moved courageously toward a program which he believed to be right.

A young man born in this century and tempered by war, he brought to the White House a wisdom far beyond his years. In 1960 his political wisdom, his political courage, his sense of history and his deep understanding of our constitutional form of government led him to request—nay, even demand—that his strongest opponent for the presidential nomination should receive the nomination for Vice President of the United States.

Today, in Lyndon Baines Johnson all Americans benefit from that political wisdom, from that political courage.

Despite his wisdom and despite—or possibly because of—his courage, he was destroyed by a movement of hatred.

Hatred, bigotry, intolerance, and fanaticism in any form were an anathema to this man of reason as they are to all who cherish constitutional freedom.

From him who did not shrink from his responsibility of defending freedom in its hour of maximum peril, let us take new energy, new devotion, new consecration to replace violence, hatred, and extremism with rational discussion, moderation, and understanding of all the traditions for which John Fitzgerald Kennedy and this Nation stand.

America has lost a hero but, unto eternity, America will always remember the light which his life and his Presidency gave to us—

Say: "With me died Adonais; till the future dares forget the past, his fate and fame shall be an echo and a light unto eternity."

ADDRESS BY
Hon. J. Edward Roush
OF INDIANA

Mr. Speaker, as I rise to speak on this most solemn occasion, I am aware that I speak not only my own sentiments but that I give expression to the feelings and sentiments of the people I represent for at this moment, and on this occasion, we feel with one heart and we express that feeling with one voice. What we say is accompanied with a prayer and cry unto God. The Psalmist said:

Hear my cry O God; attend unto my prayer
From the end of the earth will I cry unto Thee
When my heart is overwhelmed; lead me
To the rock that is higher than I.

At this moment, etched in my memory—as they will be forever—are feelings, sights and sounds which have attended these dark and tragic days. There was that shock of the terrible news, "The President is dead"; there was that moment when I walked into the East Room of the White House where President Kennedy rested in death as did President Lincoln 99 years ago; there were those acts, sights and sounds which said so much and can never be forgotten; there was that expression of love as a young widow pressed her wedding ring unto the cold, cold hand of her beloved; there was the night long shuffling of feet, hundreds of feet, thousands of feet, which was the whisper of the American people saying farewell to their President as they filed by the black velvet draped catafalque in the rotunda of the Capitol; there was the riderless horse following the slow-moving caisson bearing the body of his fallen captain; there were the tears rolling down the cheeks of men, women and children; there was the little girl who, while thousands watched, walked slowly and alone onto Pennsylvania Avenue and spread her flowers in the path of the funeral cortege of her President "cuz I love him"; there was the sound of the muffled drums as they beat out the cadence to which the great of the world marched up that hill and into Arlington Cemetery, John F. Kennedy's final resting place; there was the sound of taps which echoed throughout the world as we bade farewell for the last time to our fallen leader.

In the tears rolling down the cheek of the little colored boy, in the prancing, impatient, proud and riderless horse, and in the salute of the great men of the world we saw in death what John F. Kennedy symbolized in life.

John F. Kennedy brought to America a new compassion for the lot of our fellow man, a new respect for the rights of all men and a new hope for the brotherhood and dignity of man. He aroused in us a sense of urgency. He expressed and exemplified an idealism which was American through and through. His vitality and enthusiasm were inspirations which have made their mark on us all, for friend and foe alike have hastened to associate themselves with this new generation to which the torch has been passed. To those who love freedom in this world his message came through loud and clear that "we shall pay any price, bear any burden, meet any hardship, support any friend, oppose any foe, in order to assure the survival and the success of liberty."

Now he has been taken from us but his idealism, his work and his dream for America and, yes, for the world, is left for us to continue. This he would want us to do. This we pledge to do for he was our friend and gave so much. "Greater love hath no man than this, that a man lay down his life for his friends."

All, all the people of the world were his friends.

ADDRESS BY

Hon. Arnold Olsen

OF MONTANA

Mr. Speaker, it is with deep sorrow that I join my colleagues and pay high tribute to my beloved friend and leader, John Fitzgerald Kennedy.

I learned to know him first, as did most Americans, in 1956, at the Chicago convention of our Democratic Party. I was attracted by his radiant personality— emitting both youth and wisdom— and I sought him out. Thereafter, Mr. Kennedy came to Montana. We became more closely and personally acquainted. Finally, while I was making my first run for Congress, I personally led the campaign to win Montana's 1960 State Democratic Convention endorsement and Montana's Democratic delegation to the National Convention for Mr. Kennedy for President. I mourn his loss as a close and dear friend—but I think all men of good will mourn, whether they personally knew him or not. Taken in a temporary triumph of madness and violence, all men of good will are hurt and offended and mourn the more.

Mr. Kennedy loved his fellow man. Therefore, he dreamed great and practical dreams. Because he loved, he knew the needs of people, and because he knew, he championed their cause—the needs of the poor, the sick, the aged, the young he cared for; and he encouraged the rich and able too. Because he lived, more people have a better standard of living, the country is stronger and healthier and happier. More people have homes. The health of many is better cared for. More people eat better, and are better clothed and sheltered and schooled. He did work for every facet of our lives. He made our defenses of our country stronger and still had time to work for peace in the world.

His words of 1 week before his assassination I will remember well: "Marshal Lyautey, the great French marshal, went out to his gardener and asked him to plant a tree. The gardener said, 'Why plant it? It won't flower for a hundred years.' 'In that case,' the marshal said, 'plant it this afternoon.'" Mr. Kennedy said "That is what we have to do."

So in Montana, as everywhere, he inspired all of us to do the practical things of today and at the same time do what must be done for 100 years from now. Yes, and he said, "For a thousand years from now." His last visit to Montana, he advised us again of our need for natural resources development—of the land, the crops, the forest, and the great rivers. He thought we should clean the water, and keep it clean; and clean the air and keep it clean. Daring dreams, but oh so practical. We miss him, and we thank God's grace that he passed our way, in our time. He inspires all of us to continue devoted service to all of mankind.

Mrs. Olsen, my children, my mother, all my loved ones join the prayers of everyone for John Fitzgerald Kennedy, for his devoted widow Jacqueline and for his children and his loved ones.

ADDRESS BY

Hon. Wm. J. Randall

OF MISSOURI

Mr. Speaker, our hearts are heavy with grief and mourning for our President fallen by an assassin's bullet. From the hour the news flashed, the shock almost defied expression. The dominant reaction, repeated over and over again, was one of disbelief. Our inner mind kept telling us the news just couldn't be true but then, when we saw the flag-draped coffin of our former President, we knew it was not a nightmare or a bad dream, as we had preferred to think, but that our loss was real.

Not only is it a real loss but a great loss. For some, it was a personal loss, but for all of us collectively, it was a great national loss. The entire free world suffered in the brief span of a few seconds. What a senseless waste of experience and talent was tossed away so suddenly. A truly great national asset was forever lost in those few short seconds.

Our great leader is gone but everyone of us will have the pleasant privilege to look back on a man whom we knew had a great heart and a great mind. He was a man of warmth, poise, high motives, and great courage. As proof of his courage and vibrant spirit, he ruled against riding in the bubble-top limousine or armored car. This vibrant personality loved people from all walks of life and wanted to be near and close to them. It is for this very reason the American people will never forget the image of John Fitzgerald Kennedy.

I think one of the greatest tributes made to the late President came from German Chancellor Erhard who said, "Whenever we picture him in the mind's eye, we feel a breath of wind over our heads and against our cheeks."

No leader of modern times ever received the spontaneous outpouring of respect and affection shown our fallen President. Over 250,000 people stood in line, throughout the night, to pass through the rotunda in respect to their national hero. The following day 1 million people lined the streets of Washington with bowed heads as the caisson passed through the city streets from the Capitol to the cathedral and then to Arlington Cemetery.

As we look back upon the life of our great leader, we realize that he was an idealist to the extent that he sought a nation and a world of justice, dignity, and peace. We are also mindful he was a realist knowing these goals could not be realized in his administration or perhaps in our lifetimes. But somehow, someway, he thought we should start toward this better world.

John Kennedy was struck down in the summertime of his life. In an instant one killer deprived us of a great statesman and then another robbed us of the proper course of justice of which this country has been so proud.

But John Kennedy would not have us look back but instead look ahead, because he looked ahead. All of his speeches were filled with hope for America's future. One of the most significant things we should observe in eulogy of John Fitzgerald Kennedy is to take a look not only at his friends but at the enemies he made. He was a man who liked to be liked, but he was willing to court dislike and disfavor; to be a resolute leader of what he thought was right. The enemies he made were bigots of race, class, and religion. Those who hated him tell us much of what kind of man was John F. Kennedy.

Perhaps never has a nation lived a chapter of its history as that of the 72 hours from noon Friday, November 22, until just after noon Monday, November 25. Historians in the future will appraise this period but, for the time being, all of us were taught by these 72 hours that we all had a more remarkable President than we ever realized or understood. We learned, too, how much the rest of the world respected him, which was proved by the extraordinary appearance of 220 foreign leaders at his funeral.

Finally, as we look back, we have the lesson of the courage and dignity of Jacqueline Kennedy in her ordeal. Not to be omitted is the gallant example of the tiny children and in particular the small boy when, on the steps of St. Matthews Cathedral, he stood erect and gave a salute to his father, that stirred millions.

Those of us who had the personal privilege to talk with him on occasions will cherish these pleasant memories the rest of our lives. Those who knew him will silently repeat the words of Richard Cardinal Cushing uttered at the Cathedral when he said "May the angels, dear Jack, lead you to Paradise." Millions of words have been said and written, but all of us will repeat, again and again, along with Cardinal Cushing, as he turned away from the grave at Arlington, the simple words "He was a wonderful man."

To Mrs. Kennedy and her dear little ones, we individually, along with the Nation, extend our heartfelt condolences. Our deepest sympathy goes out to them. May God sustain them in their hour of sorrow.

ADDRESS BY

Hon. William F. Ryan

OF NEW YORK

Mr. Speaker—

The testimonies were vast that when the news came that he had been killed, that he was dead, that he had gone from them and would never speak again—there was shock, they were stunned, there was nothing to say, they could sit silent and weep.

The tears came—and nothing to say.

When they said "It is terrible" or "God help us" or "It is too bad" or "Good God, how sad" it was not as though they were talking to others but rather as though they were moaning to themselves and knowing very well no words were any use.

Thousands and thousands would remember as long as they lived the exact place where they had been standing or seated or lying down when the news came to them, recalling precisely in details and particulars where they were and what they were doing when the dread news arrived.

Those are the words of Carl Sandburg, describing what occurred throughout the land in the aftermath of the Black Friday, April 14, 1865, when Abraham Lincoln was shot. He might as well have been speaking of that other Black Friday, November 22, 1963, when John F. Kennedy was taken from us.

On November 22, 1963, America was shocked, stunned, silent, and in tears. An American President had been murdered, a sacrilege against the people. A buoyant, vibrant, and creative spirit, the President of all Americans, had been struck down, his work unfinished.

Abraham Lincoln and John Fitzgerald Kennedy embodied the best hope of mankind that reason, tolerance and human decency would prevail. When unreason, intolerance, and violence took their lives, doubt was cast upon that hope, and Americans grieved for themselves and all mankind.

The grief at the death of President Kennedy will be with us, as Adlai Stevenson said, until the day of ours. But mourning is not enough. We must move forward with strong and active faith in advancing the goals he set at home and abroad.

Mr. Speaker, the Presidency of John F. Kennedy ended, almost before it began, in grievous tragedy. What heights of accomplishment he might have reached in the future years will now be forever unknown to us. He is now like those whom Laurence Binyon laments in his poem, "For the Fallen":

They shall grow not old, as we that are left grow old:
Age shall not weary them, nor the years condemn.
At the going down of the sun and in the morning
We will remember them.

The full measure of the greatness of John F. Kennedy lies today in the hands of the people of our Nation. He is to be measured by the rightness and magnitude of the goals that he set for his administration and for the American people beyond the span of any one man's executive leadership. But he is to be measured in the final analysis not only by these goals, but by how nearly the United States in response to his challenge approaches to the accomplishment of these goals.

In his eloquent inaugural address, now grown

familiar to our ears and deeply treasured in our hearts, John F. Kennedy told us:

All this will not be finished in the first one hundred days. Nor will it be finished in the first one thousand days, nor in the life of this administration, nor even perhaps in our lifetime on this planet. But let us begin.

This call to action was followed by a statement to which the recent tragedy has given pathos and added urgency:

In your hands, my fellow citizens, more than mine, will rest the final success or failure of our course.

John F. Kennedy summoned us to meet the challenges of our time. He knew that the sixties demanded new ideas, new approaches, and new leadership. He did not shrink from this responsibility—he welcomed it.

John F. Kennedy never underestimated the ideological challenge we face in the world, but he knew also that it could not be met with inflexible dogma. In his American University speech on June 10, 1963, he called for purposeful perseverance toward peace. This policy led to the nuclear test ban treaty, which may well be remembered as the monument to his administration.

President Kennedy's administration was marked by the civil rights revolution. He recognized that 100 years after Abraham Lincoln, emancipation was not a fact, and he urged Congress to act. And act we must, not only in tribute to John F. Kennedy, but to keep faith with the American people and the ideals of our first revolution.

Let us honor the immortal spirit of John F. Kennedy by continuing along the road he charted. Let us be strengthened in our aspirations for human dignity and freedom by his dedication to the goal of full equality for all of us and his firm resolve to put us on the path to peace.

When he took office on that beautiful and exhilarating day in January 1961, President Kennedy said:

Let the word go forth from this time and place, to friend and foe alike, that the torch has been passed to a new generation of Americans.

Let the word go forth today that the torch is still burning. We of the Kennedy generation have accepted it and will carry it forward toward that New Frontier of equal rights, peace, and social justice for which he lived and died.

Hon. Robert L. Leggett

Mr. Speaker, it is paradoxical perhaps that the cataclysmic termination of the life of the 35th President of the United States, John F. Kennedy, has presumptively been caused in the Dallas heartland of much of the extremely conservative right by a young man apparently dedicated to the radical left. Many have been quick to indict and convict those of the right and left in a supposed natural effort to attach some blame for this most spectacular example of man's inhumanity to man.

There has been admittedly over the past series of months of this session a crescendo of indictments of American foreign and domestic policy by many persons who can charitably be labeled as intolerants. The loyalty to the Constitution of many public elected officials including myself has been doubted. The President himself has been accused of vacillation to the Soviets and being too soft on our Latin Communists to the south. It was ironic therefore that the President's presumed assassin should apparently be motivated by the fact that the President was not sympathetic to these alien interests.

I would caution the country, even with the preliminary showing that has been made, to be cautious in indictment and only include therein the offenders where probable cause indicates their culpability. Perhaps this issue has been laid to rest. Surely patriotic Americans will have died in vain if we forsake our democratic institutions including presumption of innocence and the requirement that guilt be proven to a moral certainty and beyond a reasonable doubt in a stampeding effort to vindicate a wrong. To say the least, it seems unrealistic to presume a teetering dictator to the south planned this assassination of the fine late President who has only been accused of being too reasonable.

Neither should this crime against the people of America affect the rights of a free people to express themselves. Rightly, our Supreme Court has determined that the rights under the Bill of Rights and particularly free speech, should not be abridged unless a clear and present danger is presented to life, limb or national security.

There are those who might suggest that this tragedy is in some way related to extremism and, for this reason, both the right and left should be cautioned. This tragedy, I believe, is related only to insanity which could find solace perhaps among either faction of our national parties.

Let us not martyr John Kennedy for any one of his particular causes. Our late President need not be martyred because he gave so much during his lifetime and tenure of leadership. The causes which he espoused stand alone without the ghostly support of our late President, and certainly if these causes do not so stand, John Kennedy would be the first to modify his position.

I think that for many of us, the last few days have produced an end-of-the-world atmosphere as great as mortal man will ever realize. The President's wife and family have the solace of knowing that all segments of the Nation join them in grief and sorrow.

The President, a friend of people in life, perhaps will only truly be appreciated in death. His cause in life was the cause of people—fundamental rights of people which some have unfortunately interpreted as opposing the rights of property. The President acknowledged last week that there was in fact a deadlock in our system on the civil rights issue that had sterilized the Congress. He stated that however dark it looks now, "Westward look, the land is bright" and he hoped that America truly would be brighter by next summer. It is hoped by many that this mortal man should not have died in vain, that in some way this sacrifice of the very best that this country can produce might somehow anneal some of the wounds which have arisen in the moral fabric of the United States of America.

We are fortunate indeed to have had a President in truth and fact as Vice President who has stepped forward according to law to fill the legal void created. With cooperative help of all Americans he will be successful.

The void in our hearts, however, perhaps will never be replaced. John F. Kennedy stood for more than a program for people; he stood as a living symbolic image of a day-to-day considerate, compassionate response to the requirements of a country both domestically and internationally.

Time, of course, stands still for no man and no one understood this better than the late President. Even now, we must continue to chart the course of a free America.

ADDRESS BY

Hon. Edward J. Patten

OF NEW JERSEY

Mr. Speaker, it is now 2 weeks since we were shocked by the horrible assassination of John F. Kennedy. He would be happy to know that in these 2 weeks his death brought out the "goodness" in America. In a sense, because of newspapers, television, and radio, every American attended his funeral services. He would have seen the entire Nation turn to prayer—millions of our men wept openly and were not ashamed. The American people filled every church and synagogue over and over again.

The whole world was shown that the American people have great respect for the office of the President, our Congress, and our Supreme Court. Our democratic processes were tested—this great Government continued on in orderly fashion, supported by a united people. There was no doubt we showed the high morals we possess—time and time again we went over every word he uttered that inspired us. The people in my district of New Jersey loved John F. Kennedy. As their Representative I pledge to work here in Congress that we should leave a fitting memorial for our late President.

He wanted peace and freedom for all the people of the world and to that end he established the Peace Corps, the Alliance for Progress, and urged foreign aid. He supported the United Nations and asked support for our space programs. He knew we needed these programs in order to live in peace and freedom. He promised we would try to wipe out unemployment; care for the aged; raise the standard of living for all Americans and to this end he asked for the $11 billion tax cut so the economy of this country could function freely and create employment.

He urged this Nation, as no other man in our time since Abraham Lincoln, to solve our racial problem and he sought the passage of civil rights legislation so all Americans could be first-class citizens. We here in Congress should provide a real memorial to John Fitzgerald Kennedy by carrying out his program.

ADDRESS BY

Hon. Claude Pepper

OF FLORIDA

Mr. Speaker, it was the evening of Monday, November 18, 1963, when the President, John F. Kennedy, returned to the White House from a day in Florida inspired by the warmth of hands and hearts he had received from the people of Tampa and Miami. I was the last to shake his hand as he left the helicopter and thanked me for a page advertisement which Mrs. Pepper and I had inserted in the paper that day to welcome him to Miami. He strolled rapidly toward the south entrance pausing only warmly to return the greetings of his faithful dogs and entered. The master of the house was home again and happy.

And then came Friday—a day which, too, will live in infamy—and he was struck down on the streets of a great city in his own land. The bullet pierced the brain from which had come the wit and wisdom which had challenged the admiration of the world and had become a lasting part of the literature and the lore of the race. Without a sound he fell into the arms of that fairest of ladies, Grecian goddess, with Spartan spirit, who in tragic minutes was changed from laughing and loving wife to mourning widow.

A short time before he had stood majestic in his figure, like noble Lancelot, tall and strong and unafraid, symbol and champion of the eternal Camelot, chiefest knight of all the round table of the world, dedicated to the service of God and good. And then suddenly, too young to die, he was dead. The voice which had charmed millions was now forever silent and the hand which had turned miracles was forever stilled. He survived war to be killed in peace by an enemy of his country.

We who contemplate those who thought or wrought this heinous deed asked the question, as does humanity, as history forever shall, as Pilate asked of those who clamored for the death of Jesus, "what have you to say against this man?" And rolling over the hills and valleys and oceans of time, ever following the sun, as long as men shall tell tales of foul deeds and epic eras comes the answer: he revered God and he worshiped Him; he believed in the Bible and he lived by it; he loved the Constitution and he upheld it; and in his heart he had compassion for his fellow man.

For these things did he who fired the fatal shot, each who wished him dead; and each who rejoiced in his death, kill him.

We of all faiths can forgive if we cannot forget. And we, too, can pray and pray do we now with all our hearts that somehow God's mysterious chemistry has made it possible for the tears which have fallen from the eyes of the millions who have mourned his passing to wash away the stains of hate from the hearts embittered toward him.

And may the memory of that undaunted but anguished widow and of his half-orphaned children—little John gallantly saluting his dead father on his third birthday, and brave, beautiful little Caroline comforting her grieving mother at the funeral service—may these moving memories somehow soften the hearts of those who turned only harsh hands and raucous words against him; and may his sacrifice purify and cleanse and make more contrite the heart of this great Nation.

And, may this land he loved be better because he lived in it and led it and died for it.

Now, Mr. Speaker, we take our leave of our brave leader and noble friend in the words of the sorrowing Horatio to the fallen Hamlet:

Good night, sweet prince, and flights of angels sing thee to thy rest.

ADDRESS BY

Hon. Neil Staebler

OF MICHIGAN

Mr. Speaker, President Kennedy lifted the horizons of his countrymen and of people all over the world. He demonstrated that economic growth could be quickened. He brought a renewed sense of public responsibility and public trust. He brought warmth, sympathy, and a sense of urgency into the improvement of human relations. He brought balance and strength to the problem of world understanding. In all of these areas and many others, he stirred the conscience, raised the expectations, and evoked the energy to strive toward excellence—national excellence, personal excellence.

He was particularly the spokesman of the younger generations throughout the world. To them, the world's flaws have not been glossed over and shortcomings remain glaring anomalies. To them, his call to get on with the task of meeting the problems and improving the circumstances of our time will be heeded for generations to come.

I am told that when the news that there would be a flame lit on his grave reached people in a number of foreign lands, the streets immediately filled with people who had lighted torches. For millions of people, perhaps hundreds of millions, John Kennedy lighted a torch. The penumbra of those flames will spread through time.

ADDRESS BY

Hon. Charles McC. Mathias, Jr.

OF MARYLAND

Mr. Speaker, the murder of John Fitzgerald Kennedy was more than the trespass of one man against another. It was more than a crime against a wife and children. It was more even than a blow against all humanity.

It was an act which struck at the Constitution of the United States itself—that Constitution which established our great Republic and provided the manner in which we choose our Chief Magistrates, and the manner in which from time to time we may replace them.

It was an act medieval in its horror. The assassination of a head of state is outlawed and outlived as a means of terminating temporal power.

When I first heard the news of President Kennedy's assassination, I was attending the President's Appalachian Regional Conference in Hagerstown. The speaker on that occasion was to have been Under Secretary of Commerce Frank-

lin D. Roosevelt, Jr. As soon as I had been advised that President Kennedy had been wounded I told Secretary Roosevelt the sad news. We made an announcement to the group gathered there for lunch and we both immediately felt that we should get to a place where we could follow events and be of service in any way possible.

It was all too soon that the announcement was made—the President had died. This unbelievable fact, even more unbelievable because of the vitality and youth of the President, was hard for the country to absorb as a reality. On the following day, Mrs. Mathias and I joined our colleagues at the White House to pay our respects. We were met at the door by one of President Kennedy's naval aides and with slow ceremony escorted through the state rooms of the White House into the East Room where the coffin lay in state.

In the very presence of death it was impossible not to accept the reality of death. What had been so unbelievable to the news became, unfortunately and sadly, fully believable.

By the ceremonies which began at this point, our Republic was not only expressing its sorrow at the passing of a great citizen, but it was expressing its profound shock and its indignation that this crime could have taken place— a crime which violates the organic and fundamental moral law of God and man.

The next act in the sad drama occurred on the following day when the President's body was moved from the White House to the Capitol. On Sunday the entire Congress gathered solemnly in the rotunda under the great dome. There, in muted light, surrounded by the pictures of the great events which represent more than three centuries of American history, we waited together for the unfolding of yet another chapter in the history of America. You will all remember that as we waited we could hear through the stone walls of the Capitol the drums and music of the funeral cortege approaching Capitol Hill. When the great bronze doors opened, the casket was brought in to rest upon the Lincoln catafalque. No human heart within that great hall could be untouched and unmoved when Mrs. Kennedy, following the coffin of her husband and clasping the hands of her children, came forward to bid farewell with dignity, with grace, and with beauty.

On the following day the Congress again gathered in the rotunda accompanied by members of the Cabinet, former Presidents, and many of those who had taken great parts in the life of this Nation. We gathered in complete quiet. The eloquent men, the great orators of the Congress, all stood silent with heads bowed and centered in attention and emotion on the casket carrying the body of the 35th President of the United States. As the pallbearers bore the casket from the rotunda every soul in that assemblage was wrenched by the human suffering of Mrs. Kennedy and of her children—that suffering which she subdued because the wife of a President is not even allowed the privilege of an expression of her grief, but must uphold the traditions of the office to which her husband had been called.

In the afternoon, Congress went to Arlington National Cemetery to bid farewell to John F. Kennedy. I was struck by the fact that the Members of Congress gathered on the grass under an ancient oak tree, gnarled, almost leafless—standing on the hill below the home of George Washington Parke Custis in that sunny afternoon as if they were gathering in a country churchyard. There was a simplicity about the fact that these Senators and Representatives—Members of the greatest legislative body in the world—stood there, bareheaded for the most part, waiting for the body of the Chief Magistrate of this Republic to be borne to its final resting place.

It was a simplicity reminiscent of the early federal period of our Nation when the patriots—Washington, Jefferson, Adams, Madison, and all the rest lived their lives in simple grandeur.

From the hillside we saw the funeral cortege coming across Memorial Bridge. And what a procession—representing the peoples of the world—President de Gaulle, Prince Philip, Prime Minister Home, King Baudouin, Emperor Haile Selassie, all these—come to salute a great man and a great nation. The day seemed in tune with the event. As we stood by the grave at Arlington the sun moved over our heads and touched the top of the trees. The shadow lengthened and it was, indeed, a time for farewell.

How rightly typical of a Republic—what a scene to emphasize the dignity of man—there, not separated by position, rank or favor, the leaders of the nations gathered as one family to pay a last tribute. It was a moving testimonial to the office of the Presidency, to its 35th occupant and to the Nation over which he presided.

I believe that the greatest monument that any President can ever have reared to his memory is that the Constitution passes intact from his hands to his successor's, and, I believe, the greatest act of memoriam any citizen can render is to resolve anew that the life and work and greatness of the Republic shall continue.

This is the monument that every American can help to build. This is the monument that will endure and will commemorate the life of dedication which is required of and freely given by a President of the United States.

In this city we have reared great marble temples to our national leaders of the past. One of the greatest is to Abraham Lincoln, a memorial which inspires me anew every day I pass it.

Yet Abraham Lincoln is known to millions throughout the world who have never and will never see the Lincoln Memorial. It is the principles of freedom and democracy, that he proclaimed and supported, and the Constitution and the Republic that he supported which make his name a household word in all nations of the world.

But all Americans since Lincoln's day have helped to build this monument. By our respect for freedom and self-government we have helped to rear this monument.

Just so, I propose that all Americans take part in erecting a similar monument to John Fitzgerald Kennedy. By the care with which we continue the institutions he held dear, we shall preserve his memory in a medium more lasting than stone.

The struggle for the maintenance of freedom was a historic task of John F. Kennedy. Freedom may well be lost, if Americans ever slack in this constant and unremitting contest. To recognize the gifts that freedom confers, and to observe the discipline that freedom imposes is the duty of every American, but it is also a contribution to the memory of John Fitzgerald Kennedy.

ADDRESS BY

Hon. John A. Blatnik

OF MINNESOTA

Mr. Speaker, it is truly difficult for me to express my feelings about the tragic assassination of John Fitzgerald Kennedy. When it was finally announced that the President had died, I was filled with heartbreak and grief. The days which have since passed have done little to dull the pain of that tragic hour.

In life President Kennedy gave of himself to his utmost, with great courage, devotion, total dedication born of deep conviction. With greatest determination he worked to give full freedom to all the people of our country and to build up our domestic strength to support the tremendous requirements necessary to sustain us in world leadership. He dedicated himself to seeking peace, freedom, and the blessings of a good life for our own people and the people of the world.

John F. Kennedy and I came to Congress together 17 years ago; I came to know him well and his gracious wife Jackie, whose courage and fortitude during these dark hours was perhaps the greatest tribute to his memory. The mark this man made upon our world is exhibited no more poignantly than in the expression of personal grief felt by so many in so many lands.

A most striking element of the death of our President was the discovery that on God's earth there were events which transcended the struggle which preoccupy us in our daily lives. Certainly it gave us pause to ask, "Can we look into our own hearts and say that we are doing all that we can for our beloved country?"

As we make the pilgrimage to the grave where is lit the eternal flame, there burns within us the memory of a great man. But beyond a memory there will be hope—hope for a world which will carry on in his spirit his basic humanity, his kinship with the peoples of the world—hope and confidence in the enduring greatness of America.

Truly, it can be said that greater love than this no man hath, that a man lay down his life for his friends and for his country.

Mr. Speaker, I wish to include with my remarks a most moving editorial by Miss Veda Pokikvar, editor of the Tribune-Press in my hometown of Chisholm, Minn.

HE, TOO, BELONGS TO THE AGES

The voice of our captain has been stilled.

Our Nation grieves in shocked disbelief at the swift and tragic death of President John Fitzgerald Kennedy.

The world mourns with the crying skies, and the sad dirge of the winter wind.

On the streets of the world, men, women, and children of every color and creed stand together weeping unashamedly, yet in remorse that, in a civilized generation of humanity, such infamous action as the assassin's bullet could even come to pass.

Each crucial period in the history of mankind has given rise to men of kaleidoscopic leadership, and a vision that magnetizes and rebuilds the finest in human ingenuity. The various eras have had their outstanding leaders and great Presidents, but, without a doubt, historians will write of perhaps the greatest, John Kennedy. The world's problems were his problems and, in the loneliness of his trusted office, he approached each challenge with a courage and forthrightness that is not given to many men to enjoy or endure.

Millions of people believe in peace. But few pursued it with such vigor and keen analysis as did the President. He worked for this cause with a firmness that commanded the respect of friend and foe. The entire world was his threshold, and his deep belief in freedom convinced him that only by working together, as people of good will, oblivious to color of skin, greed, and hatred could we achieve the ultimate in man's dream.

In his three dynamic and historic years of the Presidency, the Chief Executive exemplified the beacon in the lighthouse, sharing his brilliant knowledge, his radiating kindness, and his humble goodness with the peoples of the world. His love for the United States was a masterpiece of patriotism. His piece of tapestry was the globe of nations and illimitable space. He wove the threads into a chapter of profound human leadership that has no peer. All those who love freedom, must be free; the starving must be fed; the uneducated, educated; the misguided, directed; those blind to justice made to see the righteousness of justice for all; and those steeped in hatreds and prejudices, mellowed in the understanding for the dignity of man.

The Divine Master must know that the piece of tapestry on earth has not been completed, and yet, in this unfinished work remains a challenge of unequaled significance. Our Nation—yes, the world—has lost a leader, a molder of good crucibles, a husband and father who exemplified the highest ideals of family life, and an American patriot who will stand with the musketed soldiers at Valley Forge; with the men of the Blue and Gray in the war of emancipation just a hundred years ago; with the hopeful khaki-clad armies of World War I; and the patriotic dreamed-filled youth of World War II. We stand today, with heads bowed, knowing that we must complete the task. This world cannot long exist, half slave and half free; two-thirds starving and one-third fed; two-thirds uneducated and one-third educated. Man was meant to be free, to live as a brother, and to share in the riches of the good earth. This, President Kennedy believed, and this, we must all believe.

Our fears must be assuaged by the inner candle glow of knowledge that death is not the end—it is only a long sleep. The sun has set for America's most indefatigable President. He now belongs to the ages, and has left for all mankind a blueprint for peace.

We have work to do. We must not—we cannot—fail.

Mr. Speaker, I also include an editorial by my very good friend, Marty McGowan, editor of the Appleton Press, Appleton, Minn.

PRAYER FOR THE NATION AND ITS FALLEN LEADER

All Americans today feel saddened and ashamed. They are saddened because they have lost their President. They are ashamed that one among them would be so savage as to kill the President. They are further ashamed because the suspected assassin was murdered before he could be given a trial.

There is grief for the family of the President, the young widow bereft of her husband so early in life, and the two children who have lost their father.

The Nation is also the loser. Its great leader has been taken from the scene at such a young age, even before he completed his first term, and before his full potential could be realized. The question of what would happen to this young man after he had completed what were expected to be 8 years in the White House at an early age was answered by a sniper's bullet Friday.

The feeling of shame comes that there are still those in this Nation who would stoop to violence on their President. This is a nation having the highest standard of living with the most culture. Such things are not supposed to happen here; they are only for unstable South and Central American nations or those of Asia.

It may never be known the real reasons for the assassination but the crime must be attributed to a deranged mentality, as is usually the case with such killings. In a polyglot nation of 130 million there are bound to be a few crackpots.

The Press was not among the most ardent admirers of President Kennedy either before or after his election because of what this paper considered his failure to understand the great problems of the vast agricultural Midwest. This inability would be understandable in a man with no financial worries raised in an eastern manufacturing State.

Yet the Press did have the utmost admiration for the work of President Kennedy in other fields. He excelled in foreign relations where an innovation was the Peace Corps, which put the work of peace on a personal basis. That it was succeeding is manifestly evident. He also kept the cold war cool when the peace of the world was threatened with missiles in Cuba.

President Kennedy also excelled in civil rights. His efforts were long overdue but these same efforts were pushed with the vigor that characterized all his work and with a disregard for the political consequences.

For his work in these two fields alone will President Kennedy be most remembered. These efforts will also put him in the category of great Presidents.

Born to wealth, President Kennedy could have loafed through life and made no contributions for the betterment of his fellow man. Had he done so, he might be alive today.

But instead he offered himself and his labors to a lifetime of service. Nearly killed once in the wartime defense of his country, he was saved then only to be cut down later after greater service in the highest office the Nation can bestow on one of its citizens. He died Friday on another field of battle.

There will be little joy in the United States on this Thanksgiving Day. Yet there are still some small consolations to be found for which to be thankful.

This Nation has the system of government that can survive such a wrenching to its roots. It has another man well trained to step in and fill the breach. He has taken over and the Nation moves on.

The Nation can give thanks for this today as it also utters another prayer in memory of its fallen leader.

ADDRESS BY

Hon. Roman C. Pucinski

OF ILLINOIS

Mr. Speaker, it is with a deeply wounded heart that I rise today to join my colleagues in paying tribute to our late and beloved President, John Fitzgerald Kennedy.

I speak here today in behalf of all the people of the 11th Congressional District on Chicago's northwest side, who join me in acknowledging the great loss our Nation has suffered in the death of President Kennedy.

John Fitzgerald Kennedy had the unique capacity to understand the problems of all people; and for this reason he was respected by all people regardless of their political views, their religious beliefs, or their racial background.

His untimely death has been mourned by all, and so today I extend condolences to his survivors not only for Mrs. Pucinski and myself, but in behalf of every single person residing in my congressional district.

The Washington Post, shortly after the tragic death of President Kennedy, in an article entitled "A Promise of Power Wisely Used," stated that:

President Kennedy gave our Nation an exhilarating vision of political dignity.

There will be many epitaphs written in his behalf and I think this epitaph certainly belongs in the forefront.

The Post stated:

However he had to zig and zag, the goal he sought was peace, and his methods were those of reason. Those who admired him never doubted his earnestness, though they were sometimes impatient with his caution.

He now belongs to history, and his confidence that time would soon bear him out, bringing the country to where the land was bright, remains imponderable. So does his buoyant faith in reason.

For the most savage irony is that this apostle of enlightenment, this advocate of rational discourse, was cut down by the very fanaticism that as President he sought to contain.

He paid with his life in a cause that remains in doubt. The last page of his biography must be written with what Vergil called the tears of things.

Mr. Speaker, perhaps another meaningful epitaph that belongs to John F. Kennedy is that he dared to dream.

He dared to dream of a world aglow with peace; he dared to dream of a world prospering from the blessings of freedom; he dared to dream of an America, strong, prosperous, free, educated, caring for its aged, opening new opportunities for its youth.

He sought an America where every citizen could develop his own full talents without discrimination because of his race, his age, the color of his skin, or because of his religious beliefs.

Yes, Mr. Speaker, President Kennedy left us a legacy—a legacy based on intellectual courage and honesty; a legacy which summons all Americans to his courage in carrying out his magnificent dream for a greater America.

President Kennedy wrote his own "Profile in Courage."

Even though there were those, yes, here in this very Congress, and in his own political party, who admonished him that he was moving too swiftly; that he was working with strokes too broad for the canvas to carry; that he was too impatient with the normal pace of our democratic process; that he should curtail his awe-inspiring program for America.

President Kennedy insisted on moving forward because he had promised America a New Frontier. He himself said his program would not be completed in "the first 100 days or even the first 1,000 days," but he asked us to begin.

He urged and got from Congress, at least from the House so far, a historic tax revision program which gives new meaning to capitalism and the free institutions it represents.

He fought without compromise for civil rights legislation and admittedly risked his own political future in an almost spiritual belief that democ-

racy cannot survive if all of our citizens are not free to seek equal opportunities.

Above all, Mr. Speaker, he had the courage to propose a concept for understanding in world relations, even with our most bitter enemies, in those areas where America's own security was not diminished.

President Kennedy has already built his own monument when he successfully worked through Congress the controversial nuclear test ban treaty; the Peace Corps, and the Disarmament Agency, which for the first time gives our Nation a systematic approach in the search for peace.

But man perhaps is incapable of envisioning the full glory that awaited America had President Kennedy been able to carry out his entire inspiring program. Imagine what great opportunities await our Nation with enactment of his program of medical care for our aged; the youth opportunities bill; amendments to the Manpower Retraining Act; the mass transit program; improved conditions in our educational institutes both at the secondary and higher education level; the President's program for aid to the mentally ill; his efforts to improve labor-management relations; his magnificent desire to help mankind explore the mysteries of the moon and the rest of the universe.

Yes, Mr. Speaker, President John Fitzgerald Kennedy has already built his monument to a greater glory for our Republic.

Civilization will never be able to fully understand the monstrous attack upon this President by a hate-filled individual who took his life. The Chicago Sun-Times, in an editorial written moments after the President's death, analyzed this particular aspect of this tragedy in words much more eloquent than I could hope to compose. It is for this reason, Mr. Speaker, that I request the Sun-Times editorial titled "America Weeps" and written by that newspaper's chief editorial writer, Robert E. Kennedy, be included at the conclusion of my own remarks.

The most unfinished business that faces our Nation today in the wake of this great tragedy is to make sure that hate never again becomes so much a part of our national fabric as to lead to another Lee Oswald.

Mr. Speaker, in paying tribute to John Fitzgerald Kennedy we cannot help but to also pay tribute to his gallant and heroic wife, Mrs. Jacqueline Kennedy. In the depth of her tragedy, Mrs. Kennedy, through her stature and her majestic behavior, has given all of us as Americans the strength we needed in our moment of greatest despair.

The spirit of President Kennedy lives on both in his wife and wonderful children. It also lives on in a grateful nation. We as a nation are so much the richer today that both President Kennedy and Mrs. Kennedy have touched all of our lives albeit much too briefly.

May our late President rest in peace and may his wife and his children be to all of us a constant reminder of his noble character.

Our Nation can offer a profound prayer of thanksgiving to the Almighty that in the wake of this great tragedy with the death of President Kennedy, we have been blessed with a worthy successor in President Lyndon Baines Johnson.

[From the Chicago (Ill.) Sun-Times, Nov. 23, 1963]

AMERICA WEEPS

(By Robert E. Kennedy)

President Kennedy lies dead, a martyr in the cause of democratic government.

His countrymen weep in sorrow and in anger.

The immensity of the crime can hardly be grasped in these hours of confusion that inevitably have followed the assassination of the Chief of the most powerful nation in the world.

The Nation is left temporarily without a leader. Vice President Johnson will assume the heavy burden of the Presidency and the policies of the Nation will undergo no imminent change. But inevitably the assassination will change the course of history, not only in the Nation but in the world.

And it should change the temper of our times. At the moment the motive that lurked in the twisted mind of the killer is not, of course, known.

But the deed in Dallas was different only in degree of importance from such acts of violence as the bombing of houses of worship, racial murders and only last month, in the same city, the degrading assault on U.N. Ambassador Adlai Stevenson.

All of these acts of violence are the work of persons who, fundamentally, do not believe in a democratic government operating under a rule of law.

The preachers and whisperers of hate and disunity, who undermine confidence in our Government and our public officials by irresponsible attacks on their sanity and loyalty, plant the motives in the heads of those who pull the triggers and toss the bombs.

Those who impugn the motives of our national leaders, who defy the courts and distort the operations of the United Nations would not themselves do violence. But they engender the kind of hate that must have been in the eyes that lined up Mr. Kennedy's head in the crosshairs of a rifle sight yesterday.

The awful loss that hate visited upon the Nation and the world should inspire all Americans to join together in this hour of shock and mourning in a reexamination of the national conscience.

The right of dissent, the exercise of free speech, the criticism of the President and other public officials high and low, must not corrode into sullen rebellion that breeds violence. All Americans, those who agree with their Government's policies and those who disagree, must stand together on this fundamental and demonstrate this unity by action as well as words. The purveyors of hate must acknowledge the danger they create.

When we speak of the purveyors of hate we obviously are not speaking of the President's regular political opposition, those persons in his own party and in the Republican Party who had disagreed with many of his views and policies and who also grieve for Mr. Kennedy. We are speaking of the extremists from both parties who go beyond the pale in their opposition and criticism.

The Nation owes a great debt to Mr. Kennedy, who gave his life in the service of his country as surely as a soldier on the frontline. And to Mrs. Kennedy and the President's family the American people offer their hearts. The personal tragedy of an assassination seldom has been as heartbreakingly evident as in the scene that followed the shooting; Mrs. Kennedy holding the President's head in her lap and weeping "Oh, no."

No, it should never have happened in America. That it did must weigh heavily on America's conscience. And if it brings a reawakening and a real change in the temper of our times Mr. Kennedy will not have died in vain. This is a prayer in which all Americans can join.

[From the Washington (D.C.) Post, Nov. 24, 1963]

A PROMISE OF POWER WISELY USED: JOHN F. KENNEDY GAVE US AN EXHILARATING VISION OF POLITICAL DIGNITY

(By Karl E. Meyer)

He came in with a snowstorm and the symbolism was flawlessly right on Inauguration Day, January 20, 1961. There was no premonition of tragedy, but rather a sense of rebirth in a Capital mantled in beauty as the oldest President yielded office to the youngest man ever elected Chief Executive of the United States.

It was much more than a change of administration. It was also a change of generations, a change of outlook— and, most immediately apparent, a change of style. When John Fitzgerald Kennedy became 35th President of the United States, he appeared to fulfill Robert Frost's augury that an age of poetry and power was commencing in Washington.

But the poetry is now hushed, and the promise of power wisely used is now an unfinished chapter of a history entitled, "Let Us Begin." We are left with memories of a singular and gifted man, memories that sustain us, following a tragedy as unspeakable as it was incomprehensible. None of us suspected that in retrospect the inaugural show would seem a shroud.

Every President is a bundle of men—the chief of state, who admonishes us to be better than we are; the taskmaster of a bureaucracy; the champion of a party and, not least, in this case the father of a family whose every trivial habit was watched and copied by the Nation. More than most, President Kennedy made of these fragments of official functions a harmonious whole.

This swiftly became apparent during the first hundred days. If he did not give us a New Deal, he did provide an exhilarating vision of the dignity of political life. In every aspect of government—small and large—he insisted on trained competence, on grace and integrity, on idealism tempered with a shrewd awareness of the possible. If the substance of his program did not differ dramatically from his predecessor's, it surely contrasted in style.

A STANDARD OF ARTICULATENESS

The most obvious element of that style was articulateness. The clipped cadences of the inaugural address set the standard for his other great utterances as President. They also reflected the man, a man who could be ambiguous but who was seldom diffuse or banal.

"He brought an unsparing instinct for reality to bear on the platitudes and pieties of society," Mr. Kennedy once said of Robert Frost. The words applied to the President at his best.

Yet more fundamental than eloquence were Mr. Kennedy's sense of history, his courage, his temperance, his belief in reason—and all of these were laced with a potent dram of wit. The President did not excel at slapstick or sarcasm; his weapon was irony, which he used like a rapier, and sometimes so deftly that the victim only slowly became aware that his head had been figuratively separated from his neck.

His favorite foil was the press, but, unlike some other great men, his sense of humor extended even to himself. He was never more memorably engaging than at the White House correspondents' banquet in May 1962, at which he mockingly protested the rise in ticket prices for the dinner—this, after the press had parodied his own attack on big steel.

Only the other day, though it feels like a chasm of time, Mr. Kennedy deflated Barry Goldwater by remarking that the Arizona Senator had spent a busy week in, among other things, selling the TVA and interfering in the Greek election. With his death, President Kennedy has left Washington not only a sadder but also a colder place.

The courage in office was untheatrical and was the more impressive for its understated quality. Though President Kennedy had his share of Irish temper, his nature was not choleric and his anger seldom soured into rancor. But when he felt personally betrayed, or when he believed that a deep principle was involved, he could display a spinal fortitude that belied his need for a rocking chair.

As a Presidential candidate, he made what was probably his greatest speech before an audience of Protestant clergymen. The subject was religious bigotry; his delivery blended passion and precision; the place, ironically, was Texas.

As President, his courage was twice tested by Cuba—first in failure, then in success. Perhaps the most morally impressive moment was his acceptance of full responsibility for the debacle at the Bay of Pigs—and his refusal to redeem a fiasco at the risk of American blood and a world war. And though the defeat cut cruelly and deeply

into his self-esteem, he disdained making a ritual scapegoat of any adviser.

In what was at once his greatest and most perilous moment as Chief Executive, Mr. Kennedy forced Nikita Khrushchev to pull nuclear missile bases out of Cuba before the eyes of the world—but he did not push the Soviet leader into a corner. He honored his inaugural commitment: "Let us never negotiate out of fear. But let us never fear to negotiate." In triumph, he showed the same restraint that earlier had marked his acceptance of bitter defeat.

Domestically, the strength of his backbone was demonstrated during a summer of racial discontent. Though the President was aware that his support of a strong civil rights program could rend his party and cost him popularity, he accepted both risks with calm—with an almost awesome equanimity.

This detachment frequently drained the drama from his gestures and gave a misleading coldness to his Presidency. Yet that was an indispensable element of the Kennedy style—an abhorrence of posturing. As President, he placed more confidence in the verdict of history than in the clamor of the crowd. And the sense of history was perhaps the secret of his serenity.

President Kennedy was a prodigious reader who was steeped in the records of the past and absorbed by the literature of the present. His chief military aide, Brig. Gen. Chester V. (Ted) Clifton, was astonished to discover that Mr. Kennedy even glanced critically over the monthly list of books recommended to service officers and that he read, in galley proof, books like Barbara Tuchman's "Guns of August."

From his reading, the President acquired a sense of detachment about himself and about the limits of his power. To his liberal friends, this trait was at once exasperating and winning; to them, he sometimes appeared more a Hamlet than a Hotspur. Like Lincoln, he seemed to feel that he was as much controlled by events as controlling events. In death, his view has acquired a poignant authority.

His favorite biography was Lord David Cecil's "Melbourne," a book about the urbane Whig who was Queen Victoria's first Prime Minister. In both the flattering and unflattering sense, the choice disclosed something of Mr. Kennedy's definition of himself. For the Whig aristocracy, like the President's own family, blended moderate liberalism, an attitude of noblesse oblige, a conventional if broad-ranging interest in the arts and a coolness about excessive commitments.

Above all, the leaders like Melbourne who dominated British politics in the early 19th century were temperate men. They wanted to civilize power as much as to use it. They regarded noisy public dispute as a mark of political failure, not as a device for compelling consent.

SYMPATHETIC POLITICIAN

In his relations with fellow politicians, as well as with the press, Mr. Kennedy showed a reluctance for turbulent combat. A gifted craftsman in politics himself, he understood the political problems of others.

When a President of Argentina campaigned for office on a platform calling for a cancellation of contracts with foreign oil producers, Mr. Kennedy's restrained reaction testified to his fraternal feeling for another elective official's need to keep a promise.

The same tolerance marked his relations with a Congress nominally dominated by his own party. He could be tough in private, but his voice was soft in public. Through all the vicissitudes of political life, he retained an abiding faith in the power of reason to affect the destiny of men. It was President Kennedy who saw to it that a "hot line" was installed in the White House to give reason a chance before mankind plunged over a brink.

His belief in human intelligence gave a glow to his style. More, perhaps, than any other President since Thomas Jefferson, Mr. Kennedy cherished not only learning but the learned. His ideal of Government seemed to be part academy, part precinct club. His mind was open to fresh ideas, and his official residence was open to anybody—from Nobel laureates to lowly subordinates—who could impart a ferment.

THE CHILLING HEIGHTS

It may be that when he took the oath of office, John F. Kennedy was still the carefree playboy of hostile propaganda, though the evidence is to the contrary. Lincoln was also a more ambitious politician than a prophet of freedom when circumstances contrived to make him President on the eve of civil war.

But the heights chill as well as elevate, and before long Mr. Kennedy comprehended the responsibility in his hands. In two speeches—at the United Nations in 1961 and at American University only a few months ago—the President disclosed his troubled reflections about a world that modern weapons could turn into a flaming pyre.

In private discussions, the President tirelessly iterated his feeling that mankind walks a narrow ledge. However he had to zig and zag, the goal he sought was peace, and his methods were those of reason. Those who admired him never doubted his earnestness, though they were sometimes impatient with his caution.

He now belongs to history, and his confidence that time would soon bear him out, bringing the country to where the land was bright, remains an imponderable. So does his buoyant faith in reason.

For the most savage irony is that this apostle of the enlightenment, this advocate of rational discourse, was cut down by the very fanaticism that as President he sought to contain.

He paid with his life in a cause that remains in doubt. The last page of his biography must be written with what Vergil called the tears of things.

THE INAUGURAL ADDRESS

Vice President Johnson, Mr. Chief Justice, President Eisenhower, Vice President Nixon, President Truman, reverend clergy, fellow citizens:

We observe today not a victory of a party but a celebration of freedom—symbolizing an end as well as a beginning—signifying renewal as well as change. For I have sworn before you and Almighty God the same solemn oath our forebears prescribed nearly a century and three-quarters ago.

The world is very different now. For man holds in his mortal hands the power to abolish all forms of human poverty and all forms of human life. And yet the same revolutionary beliefs for which our forebears fought are still at issue around the globe—the belief that the rights of man come not from the generosity of the state but from the hand of God.

We dare not forget today that we are the heirs of that first revolution. Let the word go forth from this time and place, to friend and foe alike, that the torch has been passed to a new generation of Americans—born in this century, tempered by war, disciplined by a hard and bitter peace, proud of our ancient heritage—and unwilling to witness or permit the slow undoing of those human rights to which this Nation has always been committed, and to which we are committed today at home and around the world.

Let every nation know, whether it wishes us well or ill, that we shall pay any price, bear any burden, meet any hardship, support any friend, oppose any foe to assure the survival and success of liberty.

This much we pledge—and more.

To those old allies whose cultural and spiritual origins we share, we pledge the loyalty of faithful friends. United, there is little we cannot do in a host of cooperative ventures. Divided, there is little we can do—for we dare not meet a powerful challenge at odds and split asunder.

To those new States whom we welcome to the ranks of the free, we pledge our word that one form of colonial control shall not have passed away merely to be replaced by a far more iron tyranny. We shall not always expect to find them supporting our view. But we shall always hope to find them strongly supporting their own freedom—and to remember that, in the past, those who foolishly sought power by riding the back of the tiger ended up inside.

To those people in the huts and villages of half the globe struggling to break the bonds of mass misery, we pledge our best efforts to help them help themselves, for whatever period is required—not because the Communists may be doing it, not because we seek their votes, but because it is right. If a free society cannot help the many who are poor, it cannot save the few who are rich.

To our sister republics south of our border, we offer a special pledge—to convert our good words into good deeds—in a new alliance for progress—to assist free men and free governments in casting off the chains of poverty. But this peaceful revolution of hope cannot become the prey of hostile powers. Let all our neighbors know that we shall join with them to oppose aggression or subversion anywhere in the Americas. And let every other power know that this hemisphere intends to remain the master of its own house.

To that world assembly of sovereign states, the United Nations, our last best hope in an age where the instruments of war have far outpaced the instruments of peace, we renew our pledge of support—to prevent it from becoming merely a forum for invective—to strengthen its shield of the new and the weak—and to enlarge the area in which its writ may run.

Finally, to those nations who would make themselves

our adversary, we offer not a pledge but a request: that both sides begin anew the quest for peace, before the dark powers of destruction unleashed by science engulf all humanity in planned or accidental self-destruction.

We dare not tempt them with weakness. For only when our arms are sufficient beyond doubt can we be certain beyond doubt that they will never be employed.

But neither can two great and powerful groups of nations take comfort from our present course—both sides overburdened by the cost of modern weapons, both rightly alarmed by the steady spread of the deadly atom, yet both racing to alter that uncertain balance of terror that stays the hand of mankind's final war.

So let us begin anew—remembering on both sides that civility is not a sign of weakness, and sincerity is always subject to proof. Let us never negotiate out of fear. But let us never fear to negotiate.

Let both sides explore what problems unite us instead of belaboring those problems which divide us. Let both sides, for the first time, formulate serious and precise proposals for the inspection and control of arms—and bring the absolute power to destroy other nations under the absolute control of all nations.

Let both sides seek to invoke the wonders of science instead of its terrors. Together let us explore the stars, conquer the deserts, eradicate disease, tap the ocean depths and encourage the arts and commerce.

Let both sides unite to heed in all corners of the earth the command of Isaiah—to "undo the heavy burdens (and) let the oppressed go free."

And if a beachhead of cooperation may push back the jungle of suspicion, let both sides join in a new endeavor: creating not a new balance of power, but a new world of law, where the strong are just and the weak secure and the peace preserved.

All this will not be finished in the first 100 days. Nor will it be finished in the first 1,000 days, nor in the life of this administration, nor even perhaps in our lifetime on this planet. But let us begin.

In your hands, my fellow citizens, more than mine, will rest the final success or failure of our course. Since this country was founded, each generation of Americans has been summoned to give testimony to its national loyalty. The graves of young Americans who answered the call to service surround the globe.

Now the trumpet summons us again—not as a call to bear arms, though arms we need—not as a call to battle, though embattled we are—but a call to bear the burden of a long twilight struggle, year in and year out, "rejoicing in hope, patient in tribulation"—a struggle against the common enemies of man: tyranny, poverty, disease and war itself.

Can we forge against these enemies a grand and global alliance, North and South, East and West, that can assure a more fruitful life for all mankind? Will you join in that historic effort?

In the long history of the world, only a few generations have been granted the role of defending freedom in its hour of maximum danger. I do not shrink from this responsibility—I welcome it. I do not believe that any of us would exchange places with any other people or any other generation. The energy, the faith, the devotion which we bring to this endeavor will light our

country and all who serve it—and the glow from that fire can truly light the world.

And so, my fellow Americans: Ask not what your country can do for you—ask what you can do for your country.

My fellow citizens of the world: Ask not what America will do for you, but what together we can do for the freedom of man.

Finally, whether you are citizens of America or citizens of the world, ask of us here the same high standards of strength and sacrifice which we ask of you. With a good conscience our only sure reward, with history the final judge of our deeds, let us go forth to lead the land we love, asking His blessing and His help, but knowing that here on earth God's work must truly be our own.

ADDRESS BY

Hon. Everett G. Burkhalter

OF CALIFORNIA

Mr. Speaker, Arlington National Cemetery was chosen as the last resting place for the mortal remains of our respected and revered President John Fitzgerald Kennedy. The ever-present symbol of the always burning eternal flame, which was so eloquently chosen by his thoughtful and devoted wife, Jacqueline, shall serve in the ages ahead to remind all mankind and especially those in our democratic Nation of the ideals and ideas of true freedom and peace that the President espoused while he served as the elected Chief Official of this great free Republic.

His stay was so short but his works, deeds, and thoughts will endure forever where free men and women gather to work toward a world free of prejudices and hate and fear and where the word "peace" can have a daily meaning of strength and not be circumspect in its allegiances.

A path once trod is much easier to follow. President Kennedy in envisioning the new horizons to be explored in this 20th century world, whether they be on this planet or on the surface of others, in his ringing cry for the conquering of these new frontiers had the courage and wisdom to blaze the trail so those of us who followed could find it easier to attain these self-same pinnacles of human understanding and love for all mankind, whether or not we shared their particular native tongues or native customs.

President Kennedy has given us all a responsibility and another stone of American heritage to place in the building of a greater understanding in the edifice of our still unfinished shrine and fortress of a meaningful democracy. Each of us in his own way can mix the mortar that will hold this heritage in place for time immemorial, but all ingredients of hate, intolerance and bigotry must be banished from this true mortar of liberty and equality to assure a firm, sound and binding medium for future generations of free Americans to build on with confidence.

Words are so meaningless unless backed by actions and deeds. I feel that Mrs. John Fitzgerald Kennedy will find more solace and understanding, in the days ahead if she can see deeds and actions that are put into motion to finalize the dreams that our beloved President had hoped to achieve in his elected term of service to the people, country and ideals of this our land which he loved so well. May Caroline and John-John in their majority, know that the Nation as well as the world in which they exist is better because of the courage and convictions that their daddy had when they were his adorable, lovable playmates in the Oval Room of the House that is home for all of our American dreams and achievements.

In this tragic moment of sorrow and grief Mrs. Burkhalter and I extend our prayers and heartfelt sympathy to Mrs. John Fitzgerald Kennedy and children and to Ambassador and Mrs. Joseph P. Kennedy and to Attorney General Robert Kennedy, Senator Edward Kennedy, Eunice Shriver, Jean Smith, Patricia Lawford and their families on the death of the President John Fitzgerald Kennedy, one so dear and close to each and every one of them.

Our democracy is a living thing, one of its greatest leaders, President John Fitzgerald Kennedy, has died in its service. May his supreme sacrifice be the birth of a new and better understanding amongst all of us. Time will prove it was not in vain.

ADDRESS BY

Hon. James C. Wright, Jr.

OF TEXAS

Mr. Speaker, when the petals of a rose are crushed, a fragrance lingers in the atmosphere. The life of John Fitzgerald Kennedy inspired and beautified our world. It was the finest and most perfectly formed rose in our garden. Now, so unspeakably crushed in the full flower of its beauty, its fragrance is all about us.

How unreal it seems. How beyond our capacity to fathom. How incongruous and paradoxical that in the cosmic fitness of things so premature and untimely an end to so great a life would come at such a time and in such a seemingly senseless way.

Ushered in on the falling flakes of a snowstorm on that bracing January day in 1961, 3 short years of his invigorating leadership of our Nation have come to a halt.

Yet as deathless as immortality are some of the things he said. His blithe and refreshing spirit will be with us for generations to renew our faith when we are tired, to rekindle our hopes when we would despair.

One hundred years from now, the children of this land will still recite and apply to their lives the timeless words of that inauguration address:

My fellow Americans: Ask not what your country can do for you—ask what you can do for your country.

So long as the fires of freedom burn on earth, free men still will find their inspiration renewed in the memory of his challenge:

My fellow citizens of the world: Ask not what America will do for you, but what together we can do for the freedom of man.

So long as men hope and dream of peace, they may find direction anew in the words spoken in his fine hour in October of last year:

Our goal is not the victory of might, but the vindication of right—not peace at the expense of freedom, but both peace and freedom, here in the hemisphere, and, we hope, around the world. God willing, that goal will be achieved.

So long as there are men and women of compassion, they will find confirmation of their faith in his message to Congress in 1962 wherein he said:

For we are not developing the Nation's wealth for its own sake. Wealth is the means—and people are the ends. All our material riches will avail us little if we do not use them to expand the opportunities of our people.

And never will the Nation be able to forget his timely reminder:

If a free society cannot help the many who are poor, it cannot save the few who are rich.

John F. Kennedy was a far greater man than

many ever fully realized. Not only was he our youngest President, but surely one of the most intellectually gifted.

Some of us had the rich privilege to know him as an extraordinarily fine human being. He was approachable and warm. You could talk to him and he would listen. He was a man of sparkling humor, capable of friendship and deeply loyal. He loved his country and believed earnestly in its future.

On Friday morning, November 22, which today seems an eternity ago, none could feel but that the Nation and this man who so perfectly symbolized it were in their finest hour.

On that morning, I had the privilege of walking with him through a glamorous hotel lobby and across the street to a waiting crowd, tumultuous with the joy of seeing their President. In that inimitable way in which he gave himself, we walked past the speaker's stand and directly to the people. It was his joy to go among them, to shake their hands, to feel the press of their hopes and aspirations.

There were accompanying him that morning a little group who never will forget the warmth of his personality and the depth of his humanity. Raymond E. Buck, president of the Fort Worth Chamber of Commerce, State Senator Don Kennard, Mrs. David O. Belew, Jr., the State executive committeewoman, Texas Gov. John B. Connally, and President Kennedy's devoted friend and capable fellow laborer, our then Vice President Lyndon B. Johnson.

The President was relaxed, in the high spirits of his characteristic good humor, vibrant and outgoing at his very best, a President sharing himself with his people.

As he talked, another crowd awaited at a breakfast. But he would not bring himself to leave, so hungry were the people assembled in a drizzling rain to hear him and to clasp to themselves forever the imprint of his personality.

Almost whimsically, I thought of the words of that last stanza of his favorite poem:

> The woods are lovely, dark and deep
> But I have promises to keep,
> And miles to go before I sleep,
> And miles to go before I sleep.

Everywhere he went the throng crowded about. The people sensed that this was, in solemn truth more profound than the mere utterance of words, their President.

Never has there been a man more loyal to the hopes and dreams of his people. Never has there been one more able to articulate the finer essence of their spirit. Time will not tarnish nor age decay the ever-fresh example of this man, plucked off in the full flower of his youth.

America will never be so young again, but when we are old we still can remember the words that he spoke and the deeds that he did.

So helpless do we feel to comfort or give solace to those who loved him most—his incredibly brave young widow and their children. She has represented us nobly in this moment of our tragic trial when all the world looked on and saw her unflinching courage in the face of adversity so stark as to beggar description.

But John F. Kennedy would not have us to look back. His faith was in the future. His hope was in tomorrow. And all of our tomorrows will have more than a little bit of him.

We cannot linger in the paths of our reflections, and he would not have us do so. There is work to be done, and a torch to be lifted from his hands and carried on into all the tomorrows that stretch beyond the horizon. Tempted though we are to linger longer in the moment, we hear again his words as he quoted Robert Frost:

> The woods are lovely, dark and deep
> But I have promises to keep,
> And miles to go before I sleep,
> And miles to go before I sleep.

Can we from this unutterable tragedy find light for the way? Can there emerge from this circumstance which defies mortal understanding a beacon to lead us? Perhaps from this traumatic shock the Nation may learn a new tolerance. Lest his life shall have been in vain, may we find in this a new sense of unity and a new dedication to the national purpose.

May the bitter, howling winds of divisiveness and the occasional gusts of hate be stilled among us. May we in this hour and tomorrow and tomorrow be able to repeat again the prayer murmured by Aristophanes among the ruins of the

Greek temples devastated by the Peloponnesian wars:

> From the murmur and subtlety of suspicion
> With which we vex one another
> Give us rest;
> Make a new beginning
> And mingle again the kindred of the nations
> In the alchemy of love;
> And with some finer essence of forebearance
> Temper our minds.

The Scriptures tell us "Greater love hath no man than this, that he lay down his life for his friends."

John Fitzgerald Kennedy, the 35th President of the United States, who gave strength to his people and drew strength from them, who exposed himself to the Nation at such unrestrained sacrifice of his own comfort and repose, has laid down his life for the Nation he loved.

May we seek to be worthy of so grand a sacrifice.

ADDRESS BY

Hon. Thomas E. Morgan

OF PENNSYLVANIA

Mr. Speaker, we will long remember the terrible sense of shock and sorrow as well as that of deep personal loss which we felt on learning of the tragic assassination of President John Fitzgerald Kennedy. The sense of sudden shock will fade in time, but that of personal bereavement will stay with us.

The spontaneous expressions of tribute and condolences of countless Americans as well as people in other lands have been a vivid demonstration of the measure of esteem and affection that President Kennedy inspired. Our hearts, and those of people of good will everywhere, go out to our widowed First Lady, her little children, and the others of the Kennedy family, in their grief. We share their deep sense of loss.

History will assess the impact of President Kennedy as going far beyond the comparatively 3 short years he served as Chief Executive. His leadership was composed of a great and rare blend of courageous dedication to high principles, depth of understanding, wisdom, and kindness of heart. To know him was to admire, respect, and like him.

The world is truly enriched by the example given us by our late President. He was a most remarkable man in many ways. His tremendous energy, his quickness of mind and his determination enabled him to overcome at various times opposition, illness, and adversity. He demonstrated an abiding interest in his fellow men. His endeavors in their behalf never faltered.

President Kennedy's firmness with the Soviet during the Cuban crisis may well have been the turning point in the long and difficult struggle to preserve the peace. All his foreign policy reflected his determination to achieve his best in efforts to build world conditions in which our democracy could survive as a nation of free and independent people. His domestic policies were reflected in his proposals for legislation designed to improve the business climate and create improved and increased opportunity for employment. He was also a stanch advocate of physical fitness, stressing health-building exercise for the young, and urging adequate care for the aged.

Yes, while the world is poorer for his loss, it is still enriched by the impress of his character and personality upon our civilization. The mantle of destiny had been placed on his shoulders and he wore it with a gracious dignity and wisdom. I am proud to have been his friend, to have served with him in the Congress and under him as our President. John Fitzgerald Kennedy, already enshrined in the hearts of his fellow men, will be recorded by history as brightening the pages of our time.

ADDRESS BY

Hon. John L. McMillan

OF SOUTH CAROLINA

Mr. Speaker, we were all shocked and distressed to learn of the tragic passing of our beloved President, the late John Fitzgerald Kennedy. It is rather difficult to realize at this late date that such a tragedy could happen in the United States. We are supposed to be one of the leading civilized countries in the world and it is generally understood among all people that we can and should be able to disagree on about every problem confronting our country and our personal affairs without being disagreeable.

I had the distinct honor of serving as chairman of the House District Committee during the time our late President, John Fitzgerald Kennedy, was serving as a member of the District Committee. Congressman Kennedy as I addressed him at that time was one of our most active Members and was very cooperative with me as chairman of the Committee at all times.

I was able to work with President Kennedy after he was elected to serve as our President and on several occasions he personally called and asked me to come to the White House and discuss problems confronting the District of Columbia and other problems confronting the country with him when no one was in the room with me except the President. I never repeated to anyone any of the conversations that we had since he had requested a private conversation with me.

I had explicit confidence in our late President and think that he will go down in history as one of the most brilliant men who ever served as President of the United States.

We did not always agree on certain proposals pending before the Congress and I did not always agree with some of his policies and I am certain he did not always agree with my policies and votes; however, this did not lessen my great respect for John Fitzgerald Kennedy as a man and as our President.

President Kennedy was a gentleman under all circumstances and no one could ever point their finger at any discrepancy of any type that he participated in during his long public service.

We all fully realize that President Kennedy could not handle all the problems confronting this country and our foreign relations with other countries without some assistance. I am certain that if it had been humanly possible for him to handle all the affairs on the homefront and the problems overseas we would have a better country to live in at the present time.

The world was shocked over the tragedy and as long as we have mentally deranged people and people who are not stable roaming the streets and byways of this country it will be dangerous for a President or in fact any person to travel without some protection. I have wondered on numerous occasions in previous years why the President of the United States was allowed to ride up and down Pennsylvania Avenue with the top down on his automobile when any "crackpot" could have shot him from the roof of any building on Pennsylvania Avenue.

I always disapproved of any President traveling over the United States in individual States for the purpose of campaigning or making public appearances as a man in this position already has more responsibility and work at the White House than he can possibly bear or transact.

My deepest sympathy goes out to Mrs. Kennedy and their two children, also to the President's distinguished father and mother, and his brothers and sisters.

ADDRESS BY

Hon. Robert N. C. Nix

OF PENNSYLVANIA

Mr. Speaker, my remarks are limited by the magnitude of my sorrow. This leader whom the world has lost came to us out of the mystic womb of time, fashioned out of superb intellect, sparkling wit, and an incomparable grace. A person of heroic stature chosen by destiny for high service to humanity. Only in the crucial moments of mankind's life is it given the rest of us to walk, talk, and be inspired by a leader who is endowed with qualities that transcend those bestowed upon the rest of us. Only, it seems, in periods of a hundred years is the mold out of which mankind is fashioned, modified by God and a greater portion of the infinite injected into the soul of a finite being, so it was with John Fitzgerald Kennedy.

Such leaders in sparing numbers have appeared on the world scene in times of our most crucial struggles. We of the 20th century have shared for a brief moment an image of greatness such as we will never see again—for now he is committed to the immortality of the ages.

Today, we see the worldwide consensus of his greatness. Today, we note that no barrier of race, creed, or nationality intrudes upon the common suffering at this time of our fellowship in anguish. And, Mr. Speaker, although the progress of man as recorded in history is known to me; although I am aware of man's inhumanity to man; despite my knowledge of man's predilection to look within himself for greatness, to close the doors of his mind and heart even when that which is his salvation is freely offered, I yet ask myself over and over again—why? Why? I can not find the answers. I do not know that I shall ever find them, but I do know that I must say to my colleagues and to men everywhere as has been said before: That the purveyors of hate and intolerance, the peddlers of bigotry, as well as those who wrap themselves in the mantle of indifference, are coconspirators in a deed so foul that it revolts the conscience of mankind. They have permitted, both actively and passively, men of incomparable evil to inject venom into the bloodstream and the nerve centers of some of our fellow countrymen. They have prostituted the faith they claim to possess and they have made a mockery of the American dream.

Mr. Speaker, it would be unseemly for me to proceed further, and it would be unthinkably cynical for me to live without hope for the future of our country. Let me, therefore, say in closing:

The wicked are the chaff which the wind driveth away. Therefore, the wicked shall not stand in the judgment, nor sinners in the congregation of the righteous; for the Lord regardeth the way of the righteous, but the way of the wicked shall perish.

ADDRESS BY

Hon. James H. Morrison

OF LOUISIANA

Mr. Speaker, more than any other President in history, John Fitzgerald Kennedy was an integral part of this body. He loved Washington. He loved the men and women who labor in these halls, and his love of his fellow man and his country seemed unending.

And yet, Mr. Speaker, I think it highly probable that we—even we who knew him best—underrated his greatness. We were so close to him that we could not accurately estimate his great stature.

We were prone to think of John Fitzgerald Kennedy as a dear friend and colleague who had been elected to the Presidency of the United States and was therefore the leader of 200 million Americans. We could not entirely grasp the fact that his leadership, and his responsibility, extended to the whole of humankind, to the free world and even to the world that is not free.

When we first learned the dreadful news of his assassination, we felt, primarily, a personal loss. Then we began to comprehend the national loss. But it took a little longer to grasp the fact that ordinary men and women in every walk of life, in every corner of the free world, were mourning him as fully and as personally as we were.

A Japanese farmer walks 18 miles, with his family and through the night, just to stand silently in prayer before the American Embassy in Tokyo. Bus drivers in Warsaw, when they hear the news, halt their vehicles and burst into tears. A hundred thousand students in West Berlin carry memorial torches through the night. Men and women in London on the streets break into uncontrollable sobs. In every capital of the world, grieving citizens line up before American embassies and consulates to sign a book so that the bereaved citizens of this country will know they share with us their great sorrow.

Never before in the history of man has the death of a leader caused a deeper or a more universal grief.

John Kennedy once said that a nation reveals itself by the men it honors. He was speaking of another when he said it, but the phrase applies with such poignant truth to himself. Without completely realizing it, Americans were enlarged and glorified because they had seen fit to honor John Fitzgerald Kennedy and to choose him as our leader.

We have often been blest with idealists and greatness in the White House, but John Fitzgerald Kennedy was the most articulate and the most dynamic magnificent idealist we have ever had as our President. He gave our national ideals vibrancy and vigor and he gave them meaning with his masterful leadership.

He believed passionately in peace and he believed passionately in freedom. And the glory of the man is that he saw no conflict between the two.

He believed in the potential of the individual.

He believed in the reality of hope.

He believed in thought. He believed in reason. Just because reason so often fails, he would not permit himself to entertain the belief that it never works.

He believed in laughter and he believed in life.

He believed in an obligation to generations yet unborn, to provide them with a good earth and a decent world.

Above all, he believed in God.

And, Mr. Speaker, he believed in all this so strongly and so completely that the rest of the civilized world—its leaders and its ordinary citizens—came to realize that the people of the United States shared these beliefs with their President. We, the American people, were indeed revealed by the man that we honored.

At the moment we feel that our tragedy is total. But, great as our sorrow is, it need not be total if we pledge ourselves to work for the accomplishment of what John Kennedy tried to do.

The ultimate tragedy of a great man is not represented by death. It is represented by the things he sought to bring to life. It is up to us, Mr. Speaker, and to the American people to complete the vast programs for the benefit of this great Nation and all mankind which John F. Kennedy had started. It is up to us, and to the American people, to give life to the ideals and to the purposes of the great man whose memory we cherish so dearly.

We mourn the death, with all our heart, of a great friend, a great President, a great world citizen. We extend, with all our heart, the hand of condolence to his bereaved widow and his children. May his spirit and his greatness live on forever.

ADDRESS BY

Hon. Charles E. Bennett

OF FLORIDA

Mr. Speaker, the Nation has experienced a great tragedy in the horrible murder of its beloved leader, President John F. Kennedy. Like most of my colleagues here in the House, I knew

him as a personal friend. This is true, in a very real sense, for all Americans, because he was truly interested in the welfare of us all.

Many suggestions have been appropriately made for memorials to his memory. Regardless of what may be done on those proposals, each of us can create for President Kennedy a memorial in our own hearts by channeling our thoughts to love and understanding among mankind, in our time and wherever we may be. By so living we may lessen the tensions and provide the solutions of many of our problems.

ADDRESS BY

Hon. William G. Bray

OF INDIANA

Mr. Speaker, I join my colleagues in paying tribute to a former Member of this body.

No American is unmindful of the tragic loss which President Kennedy's death has brought to this Nation.

Yet those of us in this body also remember him as a former colleague.

When I first came here as a Member of the 82d Congress, John Kennedy was in his third term. As it turned out it was his last term in the House, for he thereafter successfully sought election to the Senate.

Those who knew him in those years know that he grew greatly in maturity and ability as he continued to move into greater responsibilities. Even in those years he was liked and respected.

When he entered the White House a decade later, although he was the youngest man to be elected to the Presidency, he possessed a maturity and an experience well beyond his years.

No one can adequately measure just what his contributions to America might have been had he lived a full span of years.

Instead this young and promising leader was cut down by a mad assassin, who had fed himself on the hatred and destructiveness of communism.

Lee Oswald's act is the complete antithesis of our free traditions, which are honored and preserved in this body, and which were exemplified by our late President.

In a free society we cannot always be safeguarded from a madman.

This was recognized and accepted by John F. Kennedy. This risk, as he knew, is part of the price of freedom.

We can greatly honor John F. Kennedy by continuing his fight against the forces of darkness, typified by his Marxist assassin, which still threaten the world with tyranny and slavery.

ADDRESS BY

Hon. T. Ashton Thompson

OF LOUISIANA

Mr. Speaker, I know that I represent the feeling of all of those from my district and of Louisiana in expressing my heartfelt regrets at the loss of the late John Fitzgerald Kennedy. The freshness of his approach to the manifold problems of this country and his constant vigilance in keeping the security of our people will be an inspiration forever to those who love America.

The greatness of our system of government and the fortitude of our people will insure the perpetuity of things for which President Kennedy devoted his tireless and enlightened efforts.

The memory of his dedication to duty and his love of country will certainly influence future generations to strive to follow in his footsteps of progress.

In speaking for the people whom it is my privilege to represent, I wish to extend my sincere sympathy to President Kennedy's bereaved family on the occasion of their irreparable loss which was so keenly shared by people throughout the world.

ADDRESS BY

Hon. Richard H. Fulton

OF TENNESSEE

Mr. Speaker, it is hard to add much to the moving words of tribute that have been paid here this afternoon; however, I am grateful for the honor of joining my colleagues in expressing my sense of loss and shock at the tragic passing of President John F. Kennedy.

He brought to Washington and the Nation a new appreciation for excellence—excellence in statesmanship, excellence in intellect, excellence in devoted service to his country and to free men everywhere. It was this pursuit of excellence that brought to Washington a brilliant and dedicated new generation of public servants—men who continue to serve. I extend my sympathy to his family and all those near and dear to him.

In closing I would just like to add that I will cherish throughout my lifetime the privilege of having had the honor to serve in this distinguished House of Representatives during a portion of President John F. Kennedy's administration.

ADDRESS BY

Hon. Graham Purcell

OF TEXAS

Mr. Speaker, so much has been written and spoken about our late and beloved President Kennedy, and his short life was so full of accomplishments and great moments, that I feel incapable at a time like this to try to express my admiration for him, my deep sense of loss at his death, my sincere sympathy for his family, and my hope that the memory of him will live in people of good will everywhere throughout the ages.

It still seems almost impossible that he is gone from us. This young and vigorous man had risen to the pinnacle of his chosen career of public service. He gained the highest office in the land and the most important office in the world today in a shorter time than did any before him. He served in that post with honor and dignity. Born in a time of crisis, he served his Nation with a dedication few men possess.

His military career exemplified his courage and his love for his fellow man, as did his whole life. He almost gave his life in the Pacific to save his comrades. He was a hero who could have satisfied himself with having served his Nation with distinction. But this was not enough for John Fitzgerald Kennedy.

Born to privilege, he was trained for service, service to his Nation and to all mankind. He served with a vigor seldom equalled. Throughout his career in the House of Representatives, the U.S. Senate, and his 3 years as President of the United States, he gave his Nation all his energy and mental ability. No task was too difficult, no burden too great.

During their 3 years in the White House, President and Mrs. Kennedy enriched the cultural life of our Nation beyond measure. This was only a small part of their total effort, but their impact in this field will never be forgotten.

Even in death our beloved President continues to serve. That tragic event on the 22d day of November, just 13 days ago, has bound this Nation together in a unity we were not able to accomplish before. We hope and pray that it is a permanent unity, that we will not forget so soon as we are apt to do.

God grant that a new and permanent spirit may be born in us, that our President shall not have died in vain, "that there shall be a new birth of freedom in our Nation, so that government of the people, by the people, for the people, shall not perish from the earth."

Our President was but a mortal man. But he was an extraordinary mortal. He had faults as all men do. But he had a love for people, a desire to serve, a dedication to ideals, and a brilliance to comprehend that was unique, and vital, and needed.

To those of us who had the pleasure of knowing him personally, his death is a more personal loss, perhaps. We knew him as a warm and understanding person. We will miss him.

For all Americans, and for freemen everywhere, we have not only lost a dedicated leader, we have lost a true friend. May he rest in peace.

ADDRESS BY

Hon. Dan Rostenkowski

OF ILLINOIS

Mr. Speaker, "For dust thou art, and into dust shalt thou return." This is a simple truth we all must face one day, and although we recognize it, we shut it from our minds until it touches someone near. It is then we experience the grief accompanying it. However, when these expected moments arrive the sorrow and grief we experience is relieved through tears that we shed. It is one of the mysteries of the mind that grants this relief. But as mysterious as the mind can be, in that it motivates our very actions, there are moments when all of its mysteries cannot produce the answer to an accepted fact—when it fails in its task to accept the reality that is placed before us.

The loss of someone near and dear is always a painful experience, but when the loss is unexpected and sudden, no mortal can understand it and they want so much not to accept it. It is a shock that dulls our senses. It leaves us in a state of limbo.

Thus it was on November 22, 1963. A shock wave rumbled that reached to the far corners of the world. It was a deep shock, so deep that a state of paralysis seemed to engulf everyone that it touched. It will go down in history as the day the world stood still. President John Fitzgerald Kennedy, Chief Executive of the United States, had been assassinated.

When the news of his tragic death was announced, the world was stunned. Many wanted to cry, but the shock was so great that the tears would not form. We were numb.

What is the significance of the reaction that took place? Considering that in the history of mankind many tragedies have occurred where lives were lost through sickness, plague, war, and human error, one might feel that we have conditioned ourselves to this eventuality. Yet the modern world had never experienced the loss of a leader who was recognized as the "protector of peace." A man who was dedicated not only to serving his country, but to serving all mankind. One who chose to lead this life, for he had ideas and far-reaching vision to bring about a peaceful existence amongst humanity. His love for his fellowman has been recorded in his service record during World War II. Even then he was ready to sacrifice his life for his country. But it was not to be. Rather, he was to be spared to carry on in a more important role with far more reaching effects.

President Kennedy was groomed for his office. He had the experience of serving in both bodies of Congress and he made certain he was fully aware of our country's needs and position in the world.

In accepting the Presidency of the United States, he was more determined in his desire to improve conditions both here and abroad. For through a program of action, which he had carefully planned, the dream of peace and prosperity could one day be a reality. He became the hope of the oppressed, the poor, and the helpless. But more so, he became the hope of the future for all humanity.

Why then should this great man be taken from us in the prime of life? Many answers have been given to this question, but I wonder if there is not a real significant meaning to the one answer that could be the right one. The answer that this tragedy was put before us as a message from our Maker to return to His acknowledgment.

In recent years the world has grown to live in fear, greed, and hate. It has strayed from the everlasting teachings of faith, hope, and charity and our purpose in life on earth was being lost. We had to be awakened from this hypnotic state and returned to the path of righteousness.

It could very well be that the death of President Kennedy, before the eyes of thousands of our citizens, before the eyes of the world, was the message we were to receive. For as I have said, November 22, 1963, was the day the world stood still. But it only stood still with respect to the material things in life. It moved toward the spiritual things we were forgetting.

Never in the modern history of the world have so many stopped to take time to enter their houses of worship and silently pray for the repose of one human soul. Although their actions were in behalf of this man, I am sure a soul searching took place.

If this be the answer to the question, "Why was this great leader taken from us?", then I hope that this message will resolve ourselves to return to normalcy.

Although we have lost a great leader, his spirit will never die. His life is the everlasting light at his gravesite. Let us look to it as a symbol of guidance toward achieving the goals designed by the man for which it burns.

John Fitzgerald Kennedy will be missed but he will never be forgotten. He was a martyr for a cause—a cause for peace and love amongst mankind.

Let us carry on in his felt absence.

ADDRESS BY

Hon. Walt Horan

OF WASHINGTON

Mr. Speaker, as a Republican I am particularly pleased to have the opportunity to pay my own personal respects to our late President John Fitzgerald Kennedy.

The reaction to his senseless assassination was one of national shock and yet one of national unity. There was a closing of the ranks following this great tragedy. I believe, as his spirit now looks down upon us mortals who remain here, that he approves.

John F. Kennedy loved this Nation passionately and held high hopes for its immediate future and ultimate destiny.

There are, of course, those of us who may differ with the ways and means of determination to keep this Nation great—a fitting place for the land of the free to be and for the home of the brave to be located.

ADDRESS BY

Hon. James C. Corman

OF CALIFORNIA

Mr. Speaker, on behalf of everyone in my district, I join with my colleagues in eulogizing our late President, John F. Kennedy.

The Presidency of John F. Kennedy lasted only slightly more than 1,000 days, but it was a time of greatness for our United States. Now it is ended by an assassin's bullet, but the national purpose which he gave the Nation will live on.

In his campaign, President Kennedy pledged to face squarely the challenges of the 1960's. His domestic program and foreign policy show how successfully he kept his word. Never before in our history has a President accomplished so much for the Nation in so short a time.

Immediately on taking office, President Kennedy moved boldly to invigorate our sluggish economy through the new area redevelopment program, needed public works projects, and legislation for tax reduction and reform. As a result of these actions, the gross national product has been increased $100 billion in less than 3 years. For the past 34 months, there has been a steady upward trend in the economy.

President Kennedy believed the evils of segregation and discrimination have no place in our national life. He eradicated them from public housing through an Executive order, removed barriers to employment opportunities in government and private industry by enforcing a policy against prejudice with every means at his disposal, and proposed to Congress the most sweeping bill on civil rights in the Nation's history. President Kennedy gave top priority to this legislation because he believed the immoral practices of segregation and discrimination were preventing us from fulfilling the ideals of the Constitution and hampering us in our role as leader of the free world.

President Kennedy's foreign policy brought us a step nearer to lasting peace. In 1961, our conventional military forces were in a sad state of disrepute. This weak link in our armor was a threat to our security because it gave us no choice between nuclear holocaust and surrender. President Kennedy initiated the special forces program and today the soldiers of this unit are expertly assisting the South Vietnamese in their struggle against Communist insurgents. He also increased our nuclear arsenal to the point where we now have absolute superiority over any potential enemy. President Kennedy demonstrated that he would use our military might to combat threatened aggression in the Berlin crisis of 1961 and the Cuban missile crisis of 1962. This policy of seeking peace through strength was proved correct with the signing of the limited test ban treaty. It showed that the Soviets recognized overt aggression would avail them nothing and they should seek a detente. The Treaty of Moscow was the first positive step toward a lasting peace in more than 10 years.

President Kennedy's contribution to the Nation should not be measured solely in terms of policies adopted or programs proposed. He brought an energy and drive to government which had been missing for many years. He gave Government service a dignity and respect long absent. He provided inspiration for those at every level of service.

John F. Kennedy was a brilliant and articulate President. His inaugural address, his speech at the U.N. on disarmament, his address at American University, and his remarks to the Nation this past June on civil rights will surely be ranked among the great orations of our time. President Kennedy had the power to uplift men's spirits and touch their most noble instincts. It was he who conceived the idea for the Peace Corps as a group of dedicated people working for human betterment around the world. This organization, which has been so successful, will be a lasting memorial to his Presidency and the ideals for which he fought.

But, Mr. Speaker, it is not enough that we honor the accomplishments of President Kennedy. We have an obligation to him and to the entire Nation to learn an invaluable lesson from the tragic and frightening experiences of recent days.

The principles on which our open society is based, respect for law and order, rationality and freedom of ideas, have suffered an agonizing blow. The fabric of our society has been brutally torn by this monstrous assassination. We ask ourselves in shocked disbelief, How could such a thing happen in our country?

To answer this question we must look within ourselves, individually and collectively and identify those who are responsible for the low level to which our national life has sunk. Those extremists who have preached hatred, fear, and distrust must accept a large portion of the blame. By questioning the loyalty and dedication of our national leaders, they poisoned the minds of decent people across the country and so set the stage for the savage events which took place in Dallas. These extremists are guilty of subverting the most sacred principles of the Constitution. Surely now, all must realize that we must repudiate extremists of both the left and the right and unite behind men of reason and good will who can lead the country forward along the path set forth by President Kennedy.

The responsibility for this terrible deed extends beyond the disseminators of evil and divisive propaganda. A measure of guilt must be borne by everyone who sat by and allowed a scurrilous remark against the President or the Chief Justice of the United States to go unchallenged, by each citizen who smugly neglected his duties to his fellow man and to his community, and by all those who failed to speak up and support the laws of the United States and the orders of the Federal courts when they were defied by local officials.

No one can completely escape blame for what has occurred. Thus it is incumbent on each of us to pledge to eliminate from our national life those forces which have led us to this dark time in our history. On his last trip to Texas, President Kennedy warned against those who spread passion and violence. He pleaded for reason and understanding.

In his inaugural address President Kennedy said, "Ask not what your country can do for you—ask what you can do for your country." We have his answer. He died in the service of his country like the heroes of Gettysburg, the Aisne-Marne campaign, Iwo Jima, and the battle for Seoul. Let us make sure he has not died in vain.

ADDRESS BY

Hon. Harris B. McDowell, Jr.

OF DELAWARE

Mr. Speaker, as the sun began to descend from its meridian on November 22, 1963, John Fitzgerald Kennedy's moments on this planet were quickly fleeting. His labors were nearing an end. His vision was about to be closed.

Suddenly, as from the ground yawning at his feet, Death, the phantom, with all the accouterments of his terror, leaped upon John Fitzgerald Kennedy, the youthful, vibrant, and dynamic 35th President of the United States.

At the turn of the road in Dallas, Tex., a transient glimpse of the violent agitation of sudden death was revealed to thousands of American lookers-on—a scene flashing in and out of their unbelieving eyes for the briefest instant, telling its own dreadful tale and sweeping it forever into the minds and hearts of a shuddering and mournful humanity.

His back at that moment was turned to us; not by sight could he any longer communicate

with the waiting peril. But from the ominous crack of an assassin's fusillade, too truly had his ear been instructed that all was done as regarded any effort of his. Already in resignation, John Fitzgerald Kennedy had rested from his struggle. And perhaps in his heart he was whispering, "Father, which are in Heaven, do Thou finish above what I on earth have attempted."

The specter of death mixed itself already in John Fitzgerald Kennedy's early manhood with the heavenly sweetness of life. Yet, upon our beloved President, as upon other mortals scattered in the vast field of eternity, fell too powerfully and too early the vision of life.

A certain rabbin upon the text, "Your young men shall see visions, and your old men shall dream dreams," inferred that young men are admitted nearer to God than old men, because vision is a clearer revelation than a dream. President Kennedy was a visionary—a man young in years but perhaps old in hours because he lost no time. In the conduct and manage of his actions, he did not embrace more than he could hold. Nor did he stir more than he could quiet, nor did he fly to the end without consideration of the means and the degrees.

John Fitzgerald Kennedy possessed a rare and deep insight into the history of man and the world, without which there is no recognition of the understanding of the rapture of life. No marble, no gilded monuments of kings and princes shall outlive nor war's quick fire shall burn the living record of the memory of John Fitzgerald Kennedy.

When old age shall this generation waste,
Thou shalt remain, in midst of other woe
Than ours, a friend to man.

ADDRESS BY

Hon. Charles S. Joelson

OF NEW JERSEY

Mr. Speaker, words are insufficient instruments to capture and convey the essence of a human being—especially when the human being is a man of the nature of John F. Kennedy.

We mourn the passing of a man of spirit, gallantry, wisdom, and verve. He made this Nation's Capital and many capitals throughout the world brighter and more stimulating in the time of his brief young life.

I am eager to eulogize John F. Kennedy in works rather than words. I am yearning to speak eloquently with the single syllable "aye" for equal opportunity, for expanded democracy, for new frontiers of economic security, for a peaceful world.

As our late President so often told us, the path is long and arduous. It is not for the bigoted, nor the cynical, nor the easily discouraged. But I am grateful to know that there are many of us who are willing to follow it. That is our best memorial to our vigorous young leader. If we do not tire, if we accomplish, we will be insuring the place of John F. Kennedy in the history of the country he served so well.

ADDRESS BY

Hon. W. R. Hull, Jr.

OF MISSOURI

Mr. Speaker, we have assembled here today to pay honor to a man, the late President John Fitzgerald Kennedy, who exemplified the most noble qualities of American statesmanship and American citizenship.

John F. Kennedy was born to wealth and comfort, yet he dedicated his life to the poor and the uncomfortable of this Nation and the world. During the last World War he suffered enduring wounds in defense of the humanitarian principles which have sustained this Nation since its inception. In 1963, he gave his life for these same best standards of our American ideals.

All of us in this Chamber knew John Kennedy. Each of us has shared the shock and the sorrow produced by his death at the hands of an unprincipled coward. Every American, regardless of political persuasion, must surely feel a sense of personal loss, as we do here, at the passing of so vibrant, so courageous, and so duteous a leader as John F. Kennedy.

Like each of you, I have lived through some of the grandest and the saddest scenes of time.

We each of us have shared human triumph and human despair. We have seen human strength contend against human weakness, and we have learned to appraise the different qualities of the human heart, the different things that are great and grand in this world.

I have traveled to and fro across my beloved Missouri countryside, marveling at the diversity of its topography and the immutable strength of its people. And I have always thought that was wonderful.

I have been at my home in rural Missouri and looked at the red maples in their torrid autumn dress, and listened to the birds and enjoyed the quiet and tranquillity, and I thought that was wonderful.

I have traveled this country over and much of this world over, from Atlantic to Pacific, with all the myriad scenes of grandeur. And I thought these were wonderful.

I have listened to oratory and music so magnificent that it appeared to me that "the human spirit seemed to be separated entirely from the gross things of this earth and it seemed to my spirit there was nothing but love and laughter and beauty and spirituality and holy things in this life," and I thought that was wonderful.

But the greatest and most wonderful thing I have ever seen in this life is a man who possesses a good and God-fearing character with a warm sympathy for the unprivileged, with an understanding of human rights, with an undivided love for his country, with intelligence and culture and wit, and with the courage to fight for his convictions even when in a position of ultimate responsibility and ultimate vulnerability.

On behalf of the citizens of northwest Missouri, on behalf of my family and myself, I extend heartfelt condolences to President Kennedy's courageous wife, his lovely children and his devoted family.

A great poet once wrote about such a man as John F. Kennedy:

> Were a star quenched on high,
>   For ages would its light,
> Still traveling downward from the sky
>   Shine on our mortal sight.
>
> So when a great man dies,
>   For years beyond our ken,
> The light he leaves behind him lies
>   Upon the paths of men.

ADDRESS BY

Hon. Don Fuqua

OF FLORIDA

Mr. Speaker, I stood there on the hillside.

To my right and to my left I could see an almost endless sea of crosses.

Below was a small plot of ground, flowers covering an enclosure bordered by a white picket fence. A flame burned brightly at the head of the grave, at the foot a sad but proud guard of honor.

I had come to Arlington National Cemetery to join with the thousands of others who have formed an almost continuous line to pay their respects to John Fitzgerald Kennedy, the 35th President of the United States, in his final resting place.

I watched for a long while from the hillside, as a steady stream of Americans trudged up the embankment. It was quiet, it was reverent, it was sad—but in a sense, it was proud.

Proud of the man whose memory this silent march commemorated.

Gazing into the distance, I saw the Lincoln Memorial. I saw the Washington Memorial. I saw our Nation's Capitol. This Capitol represented to me the dynamic spirit of these United States, that men can live in peace and freedom, that they can live with a stable government of democracy tragically proven again in these past few days. The memorial to Washington reached skyward, symbolizing the unceasing spirit of freedom of the man who helped found this Nation on a dream. The Lincoln Memorial honors the man who preserved this Nation, who gave it a new birth of freedom, and who died as did John Fitzgerald Kennedy, serving the land he loved so well.

And just below me burned the flame.

I was deeply moved, as have been all Americans at the events of these past few days. The youngest man in the history of our land to be burdened with the duties and responsibilities of the most powerful and important position man can bestow, had been struck down by a cowardly and dastardly deed.

I thought back over the years to a young man who had served his Nation so valiantly in time of war. Naval Lt. John F. Kennedy was willing to lay down his life for his beloved country in time of war. He was a hero in the American mold, and his story, and that of the men of *PT-109* have become a part of the American tradition.

Looking at our Capitol through the slowly gathering haze, I could see in my mind's eye, a young man serving his Nation in the Congress of the United States, first in the House of Representatives and then in the Senate.

He was then called by America to lead this great Nation in the most trying and difficult times that man has ever known.

He called to us in his inaugural address for new resolve, for new dedication. He said:

Together let us explore the stars, conquer the deserts, eradicate disease, tap the ocean depths and encourage the arts and commerce.

He called for "a new world of law, where the strong are just and the weak secure and the peace preserved."

Destiny was not to allow him to serve out even his first term. I do not know why it had to happen, but I do know that we are all poorer because he has died, but knowing just as well that we are all richer because he lived.

I thought of his brave widow, who, for each of us bid him farewell and silently closed the coffin. Truly then did he, too, belong to the ages.

The band of gold which she placed on his still finger seems to me to be symbolic somehow for each of us. The circle has ever been a symbol of eternity, never ending, never ceasing, our faith in the eternal. And because of our faith in God, we know that this has been His will.

We grieve for his bereaved and gallant widow, his children, his family. Theirs is a sorrow that we all share. Their grief is our grief and we bear it with them.

Looking again from that hillside at the Lincoln Memorial, I thought of another American President who had given his life for his country. And the endless procession of white crosses I saw in the gathering dusk below, each also represented a life given for each of us in the defense of freedom, for the American way of life, for the eternal hope of tomorrow when all men will live in peace and brotherhood, blessed by our Heavenly Father.

John Fitzgerald Kennedy is gone from us. But his spirit should never be allowed to die. His words will cry out through the ages:

Ask not what your country can do for you—ask what you can do for your country.

Our beloved President now lies in honored glory with the remains of thousands of American heroes, some known only to God, those who gave their lives for you and for me.

He died a hero, serving his Nation and its people.

As I descended the hillside to return to Washington, the silent line of mourners continued to press on toward the grave, silently to honor his memory and his sacrifice. A saddened and quiet multitude descended the hill, joining in a silent march from the grave.

Looking back at the flickering eternal flame, I felt that from this life, and death, America should gain a new measure of devotion and resolve. This flame, burning ever brightly, represents the true spirit of America, ever new, ever rekindled as the torch is passed to new generations, in the spirit that all men can someday live in a world of peace and prosperity.

Let us now pray for the man who has assumed the awesome responsibilities that only the President of these United States can bear.

Let us learn from this tragedy. Let us move bravely, as he would have done, to the future.

The spirit of John F. Kennedy can never die as long as America lives. For truly, it was and is the spirit of tomorrow.

Mr. Speaker, Dr. Gordon W. Blackwell, the president of the Florida State University, Tallahassee, Fla., is one of America's most outstanding educators. At a memorial convocation in memory of our late President, John F. Kennedy, Dr. Blackwell made the following remarks, which I feel is a moving tribute to his life and work:

REMARKS AT MEMORIAL CONVOCATION FOR JOHN FITZGERALD KENNEDY

(By President Gordon W. Blackwell, Florida State University, November 25, 1963)

The shocking, unbelievable events of the past 3 days must have special meaning for each of us. Each has his own interpretation; each, his own emotional reactions; each, his own thoughts on the import of all this.

For those of you who are away from the comforting mooring of home and family, it has doubtless been a particularly trying time.

Many well chosen words have been written and spoken in these days. Impressive and richly deserved tributes to our late respected leader have been made by many who are eminently capable of so serious a responsibility.

Now, as these tragic events reach their denouement, one wonders what more of significance can be said. Perhaps we can look beyond the confusion of the moment, the personally felt shock, the deep feeling of sympathy for the bereaved, the clear impression of Mrs. Kennedy's devotion and courage. And as we look beyond these fleeting, transitory emotions, perhaps we can see something which will give comfort and hope.

Certainly the opportunity to participate intimately in these tension-filled events through the miracle of instantaneous communication has left each of us emotionally drained. But perhaps also the experience has left us stronger, better persons.

We have had the intimate experience of corporate sharing of deep grief, not only with Americans but with all men who believe in human goodness and the dignity of man. The familiar words of John Donne have never been more poignant: "and, therefore, never send to know for whom the bell tolls; it tolls for thee." Perhaps through this tolling we shall come to be less self-centered as individuals.

Especially have the young among us, I believe, experienced a renewed dedication to the principles upon which this country must stand if it is to remain the world's chief bulwark of freedom for the mind and the spirit. For John Fitzgerald Kennedy, as few other Presidents in American history, was identified with the vigor, the imagination, the excitement of the young at heart and the young in action. His familiar face was that of a young man. His courageous wife, the epitome of youthful beauty and creativity, typifies the cultured, well-educated woman. With their two lovely children, the image of the first family has been that of the ideal young American couple.

So Mr. Kennedy and his wife have had a profound meaning for young America. As the news of his death spread around this campus on Friday afternoon, students began to gather at the religious houses, and a few hours later crowded into the First Presbyterian Church for a memorial service. It was clear that these young people had been profoundly affected by the news of the President's death.

There can be no question but that the late President caught up the enthusiasm of the young with his warm personality, the brightness of his mind, and his love for sports and the out of doors. He carried them forward with the vigor of his thinking which matched his vibrant personality. He said to them, as to all of us: "Ask not what your country can do for you; ask what you can do for your country." This question which he posed was no idle rhetoric, for he provided not only the inspiration but also some of the avenues by which many young Americans could find their own answers to the question. I think particularly of the Peace Corps, an instrumentality through which Mr. Kennedy brought into reality the proposition, advanced by William James three generations earlier, that for young people there should be a moral equivalent for war. Through the Peace Corps, self-sacrificing young Americans have moved into the far corners of the earth to represent their country on the front lines of ignorance and sickness and poverty.

But in an even larger measure President Kennedy helped to identify public service in government as a proper career ambition for youth, a career, like the other professions, deserving its fair share of the best talent and the best brains coming from our colleges and universities.

And so we mourn today America's youthful President, one of the youngest ever to hold the office, the one leader of modern times more than any other with whom young people could identify most closely, the one whose own life charted courses for them of both inspiration and action.

As an institution of learning, too, we respect and honor the qualities of his intellect, a mind that was well trained, quick to perceive, able to penetrate the complex problems that were his daily routine. He stood for the right of all to educational opportunity which would enable them to develop to the fullest their God-given talents. His leadership made brighter the prospects for strengthening higher education as a vital national resource.

Scholar, author, Pulitzer Prize winner—John Fitzgerald Kennedy, in the short number of years in which he lived such a full life, helped to create a new respect for intelligence, for the disciplined mind. For this all colleges and universities are grateful.

As students and teachers we mourn this man who was both an interpreter of the American way of life and a warrior for American ideals. Against the background of war we saw his profile of heroism; against the background of international crises, we have seen him move with courage no less inspiring. Time and time again he desperately sought to bring to America and to the world an understanding of the larger meaning of the ideals for which he first risked his life in the service of his country.

And I believe it took no less courage for him to make decisions on the domestic issues which confronted him than it did to swim through the hostile waters to save the men in his command. Walter Lippmann observed some months ago that seldom in American history has a leader been so quick to perceive the true nature of major social changes. He faced issues squarely; he laid his political future on the line without hesitation as he attempted to lead the Nation through a most difficult stage in its domestic development. He took what he believed to be a sound middle course, one that was both legally and morally based, and, as a consequence, he was fiercely attacked from both the far left and the far right. At the end, it was only a question from which side the bullet had come.

As we ponder the kind of climate which is conducive to assassination and counter-murder, we see anew the danger of extremists who preach fear, hatred, and bigotry without regard for law and order. The divisiveness which threatens our country can be laid directly to such extremists. Perhaps we have now been shocked into seeing these groups for what they really are.

The late President's violent death appears in one light as yet another incident where people who differ resort to violence rather than reason. Especially in a university do we have a responsibility to stand for the resolution of differences around the conference table, not on the streets, through negotiation, not the bomb or the sniper's bullet. But the opportunity of the conference table must be provided, and representatives of groups in conflict, no matter what the issue, must be willing to sit down to reason together. This is the civilized way, the intelligent way. This is the only way by which violence can be avoided.

In this memorial convocation, then, we pay homage to the memory of the youthful and martyred President who gave so much; who in his shortened life symbolized the values that we are charged with teaching and learning; who in his death has challenged the Nation to reexamine its ideals and how they shall be achieved.

The slaying of the President was an aggression against all freemen. In mourning this senseless and tragic death, let us reaffirm more boldly our belief in a purposeful life, in liberty and justice for all, and in the dignity and brotherhood of man. As students and as teachers of new generations, let us move with firm resolve to replace fanaticism with tolerance and prejudice with understanding, so that each of us may retrieve from these tragic days something of personal significance and lasting value that this community, this State, this Nation—yes; even this world will become truly a better place in which to live.

ADDRESS BY

Hon. John Lesinski

OF MICHIGAN

Mr. Speaker, I shall never forget that tragic and dark day of November 22 when, with you in the House restaurant here in the Capitol, I heard the dreadful news about the assassination of our 35th President, John Fitzgerald Kennedy. It was, and still is, extremely difficult to believe that such a terrible thing can happen in the United States today. But happen it did and a great leader was taken from us.

John Fitzgerald Kennedy was born to wealth and could have chosen a career in any field, but he chose the most difficult one of all, that of public service. And he served boldly and courageously, both in war and in peace. He was a strong and fearless leader, both in war and in peace.

The entire world recognized his outstanding character and qualities and our loss was also their loss, mourned even by our enemies.

To his bereaved widow and family I extend my heartfelt condolences.

Hon. William E. Minshall

Mr. Speaker, human grief cannot be assuaged by human words. It is beyond anyone's power to dispel the shock and anguish suffered by the Nation, the intimate friends, the family, in the death of our late President.

We in the House of Representatives who were loyal opposition to some of his policies mourn in the loss of John F. Kennedy the departure of a brave and dauntless, and beloved, adversary.

His ideas delighted many, affronted others, astonished some, disappointed a few, challenged everybody. He crystallized important issues, cleared the field for honorable dispute; he gave the Congress and the American people a chance to make their own clear-cut decisions. He breathed new life into both great political parties. He drew the battlelines distinctly between Democratic and Republican philosophies and defended his own with vigor, imagination, skill, and courage.

The young and energetic man in the White House carried his convictions into the home of every citizen, stirring an interest, an excitement, an anticipation unparalleled in this generation. By throwing down the gauntlet to keen minds of every shade of opinion, he drew forth the finest efforts of men of all political faiths. He aroused millions of Americans, who had grown indifferent, to a new awareness of the Federal Government's impact upon their individual lives.

John Fitzgerald Kennedy enjoyed the clash of political controversy; he thrived on the sharp abrasive of partisan conflict. He knew, with his lively valuation of American history, that out of controversy and conflict have emerged the United States most noble achievements and most splendid triumphs.

In sincere tribute to his memory, let us keep aflame the torch of controversy among good and honest citizens. Let us honor him, as he did honor to other great Presidents of the past, by striving with intelligence and integrity, with unwavering devotion and calm patriotism, with the courage of our convictions, to maintain and preserve this most perfect of unions.

Hon. Don H. Clausen

Mr. Speaker, we all seek the exact phrases to express our great sorrow at the shameful loss of a President of the United States. While thinking about this, I received yesterday a letter from one of my constituents, Joyce Torrence Conley, of Crescent City, Calif. Mrs. Conley said that "out of their fullness of heart, people do many different things. The fullness in mine spills over into poetry." Indeed it does, Mr. Speaker, and in this time of sadness I take leave to use the words of Mrs. Conley to express my sentiments to this House:

THE PEOPLE SPEAK

We, the Nation, mourn.
We mourn a gallant leader who is gone,
Shot down so brutally while in his prime.
We weep for him.
But even more we weep for loved ones left behind
And for ourselves, the Nation—
For the world.
The loss indeed is great.
We cannot estimate
Its implications;
Still we must accept and carry on.
We bow our heads in grief and pain.
We must, regrettably, bow, too, in shame,
For guilt is on us everyone—
Guilt that a Nation blessed so bountifully
Could foster such an act as has been done,
Guilt that, lethargic, we
Have shirked responsibility.
Our President is dead; we grieve.
And in our hearts we vow that he will be
Forever living in our memory—
That his example we will not forget—
That we, in facing duty, will learn devotion yet.
We make a pledge that his shed blood
Will somehow be a bridge to brotherhood.

———

To Mrs. Jacqueline Kennedy

What is there of comfort
In words at times like these?
Alas! None that we know.

And yet we speak.
We, the people, speak that you may know
The deed that grieves you so
Grieves too the world.
Our hearts are rent
For you—your children—
For the life that's spent.
Nought that we can offer you can e'er replace
The missing voice—the missing face.
Nothing can we do save walk in pride.
That this brave man gone from your side
Did walk in honor,
Did discharge his duty's harsh demand
With dignity and courage.
Let us pray his sacrifice this day
Will be an inspiration to us all
That we too may rise in honor
At each sound of duty's call.
First lady—Our Lady—
From this day forward you will ever be
First lady in our hearts.
Beyond all others you
Are all the name's significance imparts,
And we pay tribute to true majesty.
We know the burden of the public view,
And we—who loved him too—
Express our gratitude that you
Have shared with us in grief.
Your courage and your grace—
The sorrow in your face—
These rend our souls apart;
Alas, nought we can say
Can ease the awful sadness in your heart.
All we can do is vow your loss will not be vain
By striving, as did he,
To bring the world to brotherhood again.
Our Lady, forgive us in that we
Have made of you an ideal.
'Tis not an easy thing to be!
Pedestals are cold and barren homes
For those in occupancy.

———

TO MRS. KENNEDY AND MRS. TIPPITS

I offer you, the lonely ones, my sympathy.
Your loved one was as dear to you as mine are dear to
    me.
Yet what is there that I can do or say
To help you in your anguish on this day?
I know that you do not expect me to pretend
The deed he did was less than shameful—wrong.
But wrongfulness still does not alter love that's strong;
So now you weep and bear the burden of his sin.

And I—I too must cry.
As parents weep when brothers war,
As Adam grieved for Abel—and for Cain,
So too must I.
Three sons—two honored—one dishonored—I have lost,
And still another yet may die.
God help us all.
God help us all.

        —JOYCE TORRENCE CONLEY.

ADDRESS BY
Hon. J. Irving Whalley
OF PENNSYLVANIA

Mr. Speaker, no words can express how shocked we were to learn of the unexpected death of our President, John Fitzgerald Kennedy. The tragic event of November 22 caused sorrow throughout the world and each family in the United States felt they had lost a loved one, for the President belonged to us all.

President Kennedy was a man of intelligence and courage. He was a man of vision and unlimited energy. His great energy, intellect, and human qualities combined to mark him with the genius of leadership.

I wish to extend to Mrs. Kennedy and to all the family the sincere sympathy of Mrs. Whalley and myself.

ADDRESS BY
Hon. James Harvey
OF MICHIGAN

Mr. Speaker, I speak not only for myself but for all the citizens of Michigan's Eighth District as, in some small way, we, too, pay tribute to our late President, John F. Kennedy, in this special session of the United States House of Representatives today.

The tragic death of our President sent our Nation and, for that matter, the entire world into a state of shock. The news of his passing was incredible, unbelievable. But as we must, our Nation has slowly but surely recoiled from the tragedy. All our people have demonstrated true Americanism in closing ranks behind President Lyndon B. Johnson in a critical period.

Literally thousands of words have been spoken and many more will be written in eulogy of our late President, and many more thousands will be heard and read in the days ahead, for all Americans will not soon forget the terrible tragedy of the assassination.

Because I am honored to represent Michigan's Eighth District, I believe it is most fitting that the sincere, heartfelt words of another citizen from there also be included in this tribute. I am taking the liberty of inserting a letter I received from a dear friend, Rev. Wilfred G. Sawyier, pastor of the First Presbyterian Church, Ionia, Mich. His letter, dated November 23, 1963, the day after the death of the President, read as follows:

> DEAR JIM: I thought you might be interested in the enclosed poem, written through unashamed tears last night. Our memorial services here express the shock and grief we all feel at this hour. We don't have to be of the same party to recognize greatness.
>
> Cordially,
>
> BILL.

Mr. Speaker, Reverend Sawyier's letter and poem are among many, many letters received from residents of the Eighth District. His poem, I believe, represents the feelings of all people throughout our Nation and the world:

ON THE DEATH OF OUR PRESIDENT

A man touched by greatness and thrust into
The middle of the splendor and agony of the world
Is dead.
Even saying it and repeating it hardly makes
It true. For didn't he just a yesterday
Walk the hallowed halls of our nations shrines,
Talk to great and small at the world's crossroads,
And kneel in humility before His God?

He really never ate the bread of hunger * * *
But compassion for the hungry moved him to action
He could never be in the tormented skin of his darker
 brother
But he suffered and perhaps died—with his tears for them.
Thank God he never knew in this beloved land
The heavy hand of tyranny
But he agonized—and perhaps died—for the freedom of
 others and other lands.

He was no angelic being—just one of us.
The flaws were there for those, so willed, to pick at, and
 he did not need to fear the said unhappy circum-
 stance, that "all men speak well" of him.
He had the shadow of death brush over him;
Once on the heroes sea and nameless other times.
He knew sorrow, as only the bereaved can know it.

Yet, through it all, he was a great man in a high place
 with a noble purpose.
He had said that "the cost of freedom is high."
And, for him it cost dear, for the free hand that struck
 him down with demented anger, feared freedom.
Whether freedom for some within our land, or freedom
 for others in foreign shackles,
It matters not—
Their hope of freedom cost him his life.

The years, we pray, will treat him kindly;
But it really matters little!
For the Christian God he worshipped will treat him
 kindly;

Even as His love gave and sustained, it will continue his
 life.
And God will give strength to those who, bewildered,
 are left behind to grieve;
And the one who takes the helm of State!

God grant that each may deeply ask, not
"What can my country do for me?"
But, like him, "What can I do for my country?"
This will make more bearable the fact—
That though still a nightmare—
A man, touched by greatness and thrust into
The middle of the splendor and agony of the world,
Is dead!

—W. G. SAWYIER.

IONIA, MICH., *November 22, 1963.*

ADDRESS BY

Hon. Richard H. Poff

OF VIRGINIA

Mr. Speaker, these were the thoughts that came to me as Mrs. Poff and I stood before the catafalque in the great rotunda of the Capitol, the dimensions of which have ever struck awe in the hearts of Americans: The greatness of man is measured by many yardsticks. One is his fear of God; President Kennedy measured the full height. Another is his love of country; President Kennedy measured the full depth. Another is his devotion to his wife and children; President Kennedy measured the full scope. Another is the strength of his convictions; President Kennedy measured the full length. Another is the respect he holds for the convictions of those who disagree with him; President Kennedy measured the full breadth. In all these dimensions, President Kennedy measured up to greatness.

Not the least important of these yardsticks is the latter. The man who, while holding strong convictions of his own, can honor other men whose convictions are different is the man every man should strive to be.

The thoughts which came to me as we watched Mrs. Kennedy leave the graveside in Arlington National Cemetery I translated into a telegram addressed to her:

> All Americans are proud that, even in her most terri-ble travail, America's First Lady conducted herself as always as a great lady. Mrs. Poff and I beseech God's guidance and comfort on you and your children.

The thoughts which came to me as President Lyndon B. Johnson addressed a joint session of Congress were these:

America is one Nation under God—one people with one President. As patriotism is due America, loyalty is due America's President. In every way consistent with individual conscience, every citizen, both in and out of Government, must rally to President Johnson's leadership and must never be found guilty of opposition for opposition's sake. And yet, loyalty does not demand servility. Indeed, President Johnson would be the first to despise a sycophant. As one who recognizes that most questions have two sides, he welcomes opposition of the constructive variety. And as a former Member of both Houses of the Congress, he knows better than most that the compromises hammered out on the anvil of debate in the legislative halls by 535 men and women, all with different viewpoints and each representing a constituency different from all the rest, best promotes the long-range welfare of the Nation as a whole.

ADDRESS BY
Hon. Charles S. Gubser
OF CALIFORNIA

Mr. Speaker, the millions of words which have been written about our recent national tragedy have never come close to describing the vivid individual feelings of every American. Each of us will wear the indelible imprint of our personal feelings within our own conscience—and it will never be erased.

The magnificent funeral, which for the first time brought Americans to the ceremonial maturity which distinguishes Europeans, was indeed a fitting tribute to President Kennedy as a man and to the Presidency. But in many ways the events of the days which followed the funeral and the manner in which the affairs of State have continued constitute an even greater tribute.

At the time of tragedy the business of Government could not stop and give way to national grief. As we paid last respects and left the East Room of the White House on that rainy Saturday of November 23 and walked past the playground of the Kennedy children, it was possible to see the heads of President Johnson's Cabinet at work over the elliptical table of the Cabinet Room. Somehow this starkly necessary job was not offensive to the somber ritual underway at the opposite end of the White House. To the contrary it seemed quite in keeping with the vitality and enthusiasm with which President Kennedy approached everything he did. It was the way he would have wanted it.

The transition from leadership by President Kennedy to that of Lyndon Johnson has been unbelievably smooth. Today we are a united people and in being such we continue to pay the highest possible tribute to our late President.

There will still be opposition to parts of his program. But opposition will not desecrate his memory. Mr. Kennedy thrived upon opposition and he loved it. The position he fought so hard to achieve would have held less meaning for him had it not been won for a hard price after a struggle against strong opposition. Regardless of how strongly he may have felt over parts of his program, I am sure he would not wish it to be legislated without honest and vigorous debate.

Today we are a more prideful people. Mrs. Kennedy's magnificent demeanor throughout her ordeal has served to buttress the pride of every woman and man's pride in woman. In recent weeks it seems that every American has taken stock of moral values and principles of Americanism. Latent patriotism has swelled into demonstrative pride in country. And the mere expression of that pride has stimulated Americans to greater things.

The country did not stop—it kept moving and is still moving.

And by keeping it moving we are truly paying the highest compliment and respect to President Kennedy. It is the way he would have wanted it.

ADDRESS BY
Hon. John R. Pillion
OF NEW YORK

Mr. Speaker, it is entirely appropriate for the Members of this House of Representatives to assemble here, today, to express the grief of the people of this Nation.

It is the Members of this House who are so intimately associated with the emotions and the sensibilities of our people.

President Kennedy, himself, served with honor and distinction in this House. He earned the admiration and the profound respect of those who served with him in both the House and the Senate of this Congress.

We rise here, today, from all parts of this land representing a people united in common sorrow.

President Kennedy was truly great. He had a grandeur of spirit, a nobility of mind, a generosity of heart, and the courage of action. He sought to sublimate and to activate this Nation toward higher concepts. President Kennedy was, at all times, motivated by an urge to improve the lot of mankind.

President Kennedy's messages to this Congress had a common thread. They formed a pattern that sought a political, social, and economic betterment for all peoples of all nations.

As the first President of the Roman Catholic faith, he gave assurance that a Catholic citizen could serve this Nation in that high office with complete fidelity and devotion.

President Kennedy was a symbol of hope to the less fortunate peoples of the world. He fervently and sincerely sought a just peace between divided peoples, conflicting national interests, and antagonistic social systems.

President Kennedy bequeathed to this Nation a new destiny for greatness, new paths toward world peace.

Spiritually, President Kennedy lives on. He will continue to walk with this Nation toward the achievement of our peoples' aspirations for freedom, peace, justice, and equality.

ADDRESS BY
Hon. Charles M. Teague
OF CALIFORNIA

Mr. Speaker, on behalf of the people of the 13th District of California, I join my colleagues in expressing our sorrow at the tragic assassination of President John Fitzgerald Kennedy.

We all extend deep sympathy to members of his family.

ADDRESS BY
Hon. Joseph M. McDade
OF PENNSYLVANIA

Mr. Speaker, I join with all Americans, and with men of good will everywhere, in expressing the shock and grief felt by the tragic assassination of President John Fitzgerald Kennedy.

We saw in the morning the joyousness and youthfulness of this young man, our President, as he went to visit and to speak among his people in Texas. We saw in the night the melancholy procession of a coffin slowly carried to the White House, when he returned dead to all his people in the Capital of the Nation.

Two children lost a father in a way they cannot comprehend. A wife lost a husband in a depth of horror that is beyond comprehension. We lost a President, but in a way that we can indeed comprehend. His death has turned our eyes back upon ourselves, and I believe that all Americans have renewed most profoundly their dedication to the principles which have made this country the most noble experiment in the history of mankind.

If it is true that adversity builds character, as I believe it does, then this tragedy can become a living challenge to every one of us, to build the greatness of America in the future in our lives, as others have built the greatness of America in the past in their deaths.

We have seen his widow, steeped in grief, giving the entire world a new meaning to courage and dignity. These things we shall not forget.

The editorial writers of the 10th Congressional District of Pennsylvania have expressed their horror in far more literate language than I could hope to emulate. I, therefore, include the editorials to which I have referred.

[From the Scranton Tribune]

OUR PRESIDENT IS DEAD

The President of the United States is dead.

He was assassinated by a fanatic.

The entire Nation and the free peoples of the world are in mourning.

The brutal, callous manner in which the life of President John Fitzgerald Kennedy was snuffed out defies belief.

Shock mingled with outrage swept the Nation and spilled into the far corners of the planet. The acknowledged leader of the free world, gunned down in a great city of the greatest Nation of that free world. What a horrendous crime was perpetrated, what a dastardly blow to befall this Nation.

The vision of a vigorous man of 46, his body slumped in the arms of his wife and life draining away with each heartbeat, was almost too much to bear. Women, and strong men too, wept. It was as if his death had personally touched the lives of every American.

It was a sad hour for all of us, regardless of party affiliation, regardless of one's political beliefs, or creed or color.

President Kennedy was the very epitome of the ideal American—a man with strength of character, firm resolve, and a dedication of purpose that was not lost on world leaders.

President Kennedy, in the very prime of life, the Executive head of a Government which has prided itself the world over as an orderly, representative Government of the people, by the people, for the people—the very words of another President shot to death by another fanatic—has, too, been assassinated.

We join all our fellow citizens in remorse, in regret, and in deep mourning for this terrible tragedy.

———

[From the Tunkhannock Republican and New Age, Nov. 28, 1963.]

THANKSGIVING AMID GRIEF

"The Lord hath given, the Lord hath taken away: blessed be the name of the Lord."

These words, uttered by the sorely pressed Job, should be in the hearts and minds of all grieving Americans on this Thanksgiving Day. They express an abiding faith in God which we most urgently need in the face of the unspeakable tragedy of last Friday.

Mortal man should not attempt to question the methods of God. We should not ask of God why John Fitzgerald Kennedy, a young, vigorous man of immense courage, intelligence and dedication, should be so abruptly halted in the midst of his labors. We should not ask why his wife and children will be deprived of the husband and father they loved so deeply. We should not ask why God has allowed the striking down of this selfless man who was born to serve—who could have lived out his years in idleness and pleasure had he not been devoted to the cause of his fellow man.

Grieve him we shall, and the shocked disbelief on the faces of young and old, regardless of party affiliation, as the Nation waited in hushed silence for word from Parkland Hospital in Dallas; the unashamed sobbing which was heard as the death of John F. Kennedy was revealed, indicate that the Nation's grief will be long with it.

But even as we join in mourning this latest martyr to man's refusal to lift himself from the realm of the animals, we must face this Thanksgiving Day with hearts full of gratitude for his bounty to use.

It is easy to give thanks when all is going well. It is much more difficult to turn to the Lord in thanksgiving when grief and suffering are predominant.

But Job—who suffered far more than most men—could do it. So must we.

Aside from our material blessings, we must give thanks for hope and faith—that God has not turned away from us, that His will shall be done, and that this Nation, under God, shall continue—despite its terrible loss—to provide leadership for the free world and hold out hope for the downtrodden.

So even as we commit to God the soul of John F. Kennedy, we must, again, echo Job's words, "The Lord hath given, the Lord hath taken away: blessed be the name of the Lord."

———

[From the Towanda Daily Review, Nov. 23, 1963]

DEATH SAD BLOW TO WHOLE WORLD

Unbelievable as it seems, President John F. Kennedy is dead.

News that an assassin's bullet had cut him down while he was visiting Dallas, Tex., Friday afternoon came like a thunderbolt out of the blue. It is hard to conceive of a tragedy which could have caused greater genuine grief throughout the world. First reaction was a stunned silence. Then many swallowed a "lump in the throat" and others gave way to tears.

Sadness was not confined to members of his own political party by any means. We frequently differ on political issues but that is what gives this Nation its strength; debate brings out the best for the good of all. No one knew this better than President John F. Kennedy and he always helped to give important questions a thorough airing. Above all, he was an American.

Our deepest sympathy goes out to the President's widow and his little children. Their grief is almost unbearable. When Mrs. Kennedy entered the hospital with her husband her clothes were bloodstained from the President's wounds. What a horrible experience for any woman, let alone the wife of the Chief Executive of the world's greatest nation. And our hearts go out, too, to little Caroline who is old enough to realize that her daddy has gone, never to return. The only solace of the family can be the knowledge that President Kennedy, youngest man ever elected to the Presidency, will go down in history as a great man.

The President had a great and abiding faith in the future of America and was determined to do his best to promote its best interests not only at home but everywhere around the globe. His stanch patriotism could never be questioned by even the most partisan politicians. He was forthright in giving his views and expected others to be the same. His word was as good as his bond and he had worldwide respect even in nations which opposed American ideologies. Complications throughout the world as the result of his untimely death may be far-reaching.

On the home front Lyndon B. Johnson, who succeeded to the Presidency yesterday, will face many serious problems which President Kennedy had tackled vigorously but which still are unsolved. One of these deals with civil rights and it is to be hoped that Mr. Johnson will be able to find a solution. If he can, nothing would be a more fitting memorial to the late President. He firmly believed in the brotherhood of man and that all men have inherent rights to a dignified, free existence.

As John F. Kennedy becomes a name in the history books, his existence on this mortal sphere at an end, his memory will linger on for years to come. Most of those now alive will never forget his tousled head, the famous Kennedy smile, the pointing finger as he spoke, and the accent that could not be mistaken anywhere.

Friday, November 22, 1963, will indeed go down as one of the blackest days in the annals of the United States, if not the entire world.

———

[From the Troy Gazette, Nov. 28, 1963]

ASTOUNDED, STUNNED

The booming noises persisted, and the instreaming sunlight of that Sunday morning made slumber no longer a joy.

Arising and dressing, the booming noises continued in no particular pattern, excepting to indicate some sort of a contest. Curious, a walk along the row of slumber-laden beach cottages to the Waikiki Beach, was taken. It's the Navy on practice maneuvers and a gun battle. But so close to shore? Then, as a youngster pointing toward Pearl Harbor, to his mother, saying: "There's another one," you got the idea quickly. Pearl Harbor was aflame, asmoke, exploding.

Turning on heel, steps were retraced more rapidly. Now, a radio announcement would pierce the otherwise still morning. All firemen report to stations immediately. All police * * *.

At home again, a quick switch of the radio dial— then, "This is no false alarm, this is the McCoy * * * Pearl Harbor is being bombed. Repeat." Webley Edwards, of Honolulu radio station, was declaring over the radio.

The phone rang. The duty officer tersely stated: "Report for duty immediately." "Yes, sir."

That was Pearl Harbor, December 7, 1941.

Last Friday, November 22, 1963, some 22 years later, another stunning event occurred. The President had been shot.

Only, it was different now. Twenty-two years ago the shock was allayed by duties that occupied the mind and body. I was in military action.

Last Friday was different. You waited, after the first shocking, brief announcement was made. You waited, thoughts racing, for word that the President was not seriously wounded. Then, it came. "He is dead."

But, you still did not believe it. You wanted to know how it had occurred, where and when. And, who did it?

Subsequently, you caught bits of information, pieced them together as you listened to radio and television announcements. And then, you were stunned, numbed. And, you wondered: The President of the United States assassinated? And by an American? It was not possible. Then, you wondered, just how permanent, how sure are we.

The death of President Kennedy occurred in Dallas, Tex., at 1 p.m. It was 2 p.m. in Harrisburg when Governor Scranton interrupted the speaker to say: "The President has been shot three times, according to radio. Nothing further has arrived."

The Governor was at a luncheon held in the Penn-Harris Hotel, attended by over 90 editors and publishers of Pennsylvania newspapers. The occasion was an information meeting on the newly formed "100,000 Pennsylvanians for the Promotion of Economic Growth."

The program was underway. Luncheon tableware had been removed and the speakers had commenced their deliveries.

A telephone buzzed twice before the receiver was lifted. Soon one of the Governor's aids at the luncheon went to the phone. Finished, he approached the speaker's table at which sat some dozen dignitaries, including the Governor and his wife. The man from the Governor's office leaned over, head between the Governor and his wife. He whispered.

Mrs. Scranton raised her hand toward her face which showed "horror reaction." The Governor's face became graver.

The speaker continued. Only a handful in the large room knew what had happened. The phone rang again. This time, only one ring. Again, a trip to the Governor's side. He nodded, then arose and interrupted the speaker, to make the first announcement.

His second announcement, about a half hour later, came while he was delivering the main address on "100,000 Pennsylvanians." His aid stood beside him, awaiting a break in the Governor's speaking. It came, and he turned to his aid, listening, nodded, then finished the thought he had been developing. It completed, he stopped, and said:

"The President is dead. In view of the circumstances, I think we should terminate our session. Let us stand in silent prayer."

Each publisher and editor in that large room heard words of the speakers, but his mind was racing over events connected with the wounding of the President, and the consequences. The words of the speakers were like background radio sounds; they were there, but you did not hear exactly what was being said.

Those publishers and editors who could not leave for their own communities immediately, sought radio, or television outlets, to learn more details. Those who came by autos equipped with radio sets must have turned on these sets and listened as they drove homeward.

Those who traveled far, had a longer session of it, for there was practically nothing on the air except news about the assassination. And, you went to bed, late that night, absolutely dead-tired, shocked, and stunned as probably did millions of Americans and other people of the world who had heard the day's tragic news—CDA.

———

[From the Canton Independent, Nov. 28, 1963]

GRIEF-STRICKEN AMERICA, FREE WORLD LOSE LEADER

A panorama of history swept around the world on Friday as the President of the United States was assassinated while visiting in Dallas, Tex. John Fitzgerald

Kennedy, our 35th President, was dead at 46 years of age, on his 1,000th day as President of this great Nation.

In less than 1 hour after his airplane landed at Dallas Love Field, the President and Texas' Gov. John Connally were shot and by 1 p.m. c.s.t., Friday, November 22, the President was dead. The Governor is recovering at Parkland Hospital, Dallas, following surgery.

Mrs. Kennedy accompanied her husband on the Texas tour, following a time of mourning from the loss of their infant son Patrick Bouvier. Her gracious manner was applauded by the Texans. In 1 short hour tragedy hit her home and the Nation.

The grief of Americans joined by the citizens of the world seems to have united peoples of races, creeds and nationalities.

President Kennedy was a symbol of the younger generation. He was courage, champion of human rights, a man of peace and dedication, a leader of the New Frontier and Peace Corps.

Mrs. Kennedy, a shy, cultured woman, added much glamour to the White House and became a symbol of fashion as well as outstanding example as a wife and mother. Her interests in fine arts opened a new era in America's life and she endeavored to preserve early American heritage as well as restoration of the White House.

From the time of the fatal shooting of the President, she rested his wounded head in her lap, spent every hour with his body and marched behind his casket to the cathedral on Monday.

The circle of death continued as a Dallas patrolman gave his life in attempting to pick up a suspect, Lee H. Oswald, 24. Then on Sunday as Oswald was being moved from the city jail to the county jail, Jack Ruby took Oswald's life.

Sorrow of this week will be remembered for centuries to come. The heads of government from around the world sent delegates to share with Mrs. Kennedy, Caroline and John, as well as other members of the family, the loss of this great American, John F. Kennedy.

[From the Forest City News, Nov. 28, 1963]

IN MEMORIAM

As the news of the death of our President, by assassin's bullet, reached Forest City last Friday afternoon, it was received with a feeling of complete and utter disbelief by our citizenry. Up and down Main Street small groups of people gathered still unable to realize the full import of the tragedy. Unashamedly, tears of shock and grief, dotted the faces of a number of passersby. A lone flag, flying at half mast, at the corner of Main and Dundaff Streets lent a somber emphasis to the great tragedy which had befallen our country.

The shock was deepened by many thoughts. First, the youthful exuberance which had been introduced into our American way of life. Here, for the first time in many years, the White House in Washington had heard the scamper of little feet in the person of 3-year-old John and 6-year-old Caroline. In addition the flashing beauty of our First Lady, endowed our Government with a new life and feeling. Here was a closely knit family group,

which in one fleeting second was torn apart and exposed to an agony not often experienced by anyone.

Secondly, our shock was compounded by thoughts that this heinous deed could happen at this time; the 20th century, 1963. Surely, things like this couldn't happen in our United States. Yes, it could happen to Abe Lincoln in 1865, to Garfield in 1881, and to McKinley in 1901, and it could happen in Vietnam, to the Diems, but it could never happen here. Well, it did happen here, and this is the 20th century. A crime such as this has no time, or no place. It can happen and it has.

A leader, a statesman, and a family man has been removed from our land. Mr. Kennedy always called himself a child of the times. Tempered by the depression and matured by war as we all of this century have been. We will never forget this horrifying deed and we can but hope that a higher purpose will be served through his sacrifice.

In the democratic tradition, a new man has stepped forward to assume the awesome duties of the Presidency. Lyndon B. Johnson, a man of vast experience in Government, has been thrust into a responsibility, which is completely incomprehensible to us, on a moment's notice. To fulfill these duties he will need the prayers and support of every man, woman, and child in this country. The days ahead may be difficult, but we can endure.

We can but join with the peoples of the world in our sincere and heartfelt grief and sympathy to the family and close associates of John Fitzgerald Kennedy, that he may rest in peace after his difficult trial in life. He will be remembered always, by we who have lived in this era. Let this coming Thanksgiving Day bring a new meaning to our lives and a fresh understanding of the problems facing us and we can truly say that his death, "shall not have been in vain."

[From the Carbondale News, Nov. 28, 1963]

THE PRESIDENT IS DEAD—PRESIDENCY REMAINS

John Fitzgerald Kennedy, 46, succumbed to an occupational hazard at 2 p.m., Friday, November 22, eastern standard time.

The lunacy of assassination proved to be a communicable disease and 48 hours later the primary suspect in the killing of the President himself was cut down by a one-man lynching party.

Three Presidents before Mr. Kennedy died of wounds inflicted by assassins, all succumbing to gunshot wounds.

Abraham Lincoln was shot in Washington by John Wilkes Booth April 14, 1865, and died April 15.

James A. Garfield was shot in Washington July 2, 1881, by Charles J. Guiteau and died September 19.

William McKinley was shot by Leon Czolgosz in Buffalo, N.Y., September 6, 1901, and died September 14.

An attempt on the life of Franklin Delano Roosevelt resulted in the death of Chicago's Mayor Anton Cermack.

An attempt on the life of Harry S. Truman failed.

Every President lives from day to day in the shadow of death at the hand of a fellowman.

Yet the striking down of Mr. Kennedy sent a numbing shock across the entire Nation.

It seemed inconceivable that such a vigorous young man

should have ceased so abruptly to live, to have had his life's blood spattered upon his lovely young wife, to have taken such abrupt leave of two attractive young children, themselves personalities at an early age.

Our Thanksgiving editorial already had been written, set in type, and the page made ready for the press. In essence we said that the Nation had much to be thankful for, this Thanksgiving.

First reaction in the News office and shop was that events had made the Thanksgiving editorial inappropriate. But sober second thought said no, that despite the Nation's terrible loss we still should be thankful.

Thankful that our system of government provides an orderly succession of Chief Executives in event of death of the President in office.

Thankful that the new President is a man of strong character, broad experience in government, and thorough training for his succession.

We mourn our loss.

And we give thanks.

[From the Sayre Evening Times, Nov. 23, 1963]

AMERICANS STAND UNITED IN MOURNING FOR KENNEDY

Americans stand united today as seldom in the Nation's history, in mourning the death of assassinated John Fitzgerald Kennedy, and in horrified revulsion at the manner of his passing.

In life, President Kennedy was a highly controversial figure, capable of arousing both wild enthusiasm and sharp opposition. But in death, felled by an assassin's bullet, he was recognized only as the martyred President of all Americans, and the feeling of grief and loss was universal.

Americans of every walk in life from the mightiest to the lowliest, of every shade of opinion—political, religious, economic—of every race and of every national background, became as one in the feeling of shock and sadness.

It is impossible at this early moment to say with certainty what was the full impact upon the country of President Kennedy during his few short years in office. Only the passage of time will permit a historical objective assessment of his administration.

But it can be said with confidence that much of what he did will live on to affect the welfare of the Nation—and of the world—far into the future. The Alliance for Progress of which he was the chief architect will continue the effort of bringing all of the American nations closer together in cooperative effort. And it may be considered a certainty that the Peace Corps of which he was the father will remain an active effort over the coming years to show the true American image to the people of other lands.

President Kennedy will be remembered as a vigorous President, one not only willing but eager to fight for his beliefs and his ideals. He will be remembered as a man of deep and loyal devotion to the country he loved, and tireless in his efforts to advance its welfare and the welfare of its people.

What he might have accomplished had he lived to complete his term and perhaps serve an additional 4

years in the Presidency can now never be known. But every American is fully cognizant of the fact that his work was cut short by an assassin in complete negation of every tenet of the democracy on which this country is founded, and his death comes as a matter of personal loss to every last citizen of this land.

President Kennedy will be enshrined in memory as a martyred President, one who died in the service of his country just as truly as any man who has fallen in battle.

[From the Scranton Times]

NATION MOURNS

In every home across the length and breadth of America there is today deep sorrow—a grief almost to the point of numbness. And around the world, wherever men cherish freedom and respect its champions, there is also sincere mourning and a sense of deep loss.

For the United States and the world have lost one of their great leaders. President John F. Kennedy fell victim to an assassin's bullet yesterday in Texas. The news of this tragedy and the realization of the heinous crime behind it shocked the Nation. Throughout the country, as newspapers and television and radio stations carried the fateful news to the people, strong men unashamedly wept and found a lump in their throats as they tried to talk. For John F. Kennedy was not just a lofty figure, aloof in his high station; he had won his way into the hearts of his countrymen of all classes, of all races, of all political parties in our great Nation.

Their sympathy went out immediately to his bereaved wife, the mother of his two children, and to the other members of the Kennedy family. Theirs is the deep personal loss; the President's death by cruel assassination in the prime of his manhood is the loss of all our people.

Americans have long revered their Presidents who made their way from humble origins—Lincoln and his log cabin birthplace, as an example—to the highest public office in the land.

But John F. Kennedy brought a new image to families of great wealth. He recognized the responsibilities which great wealth imposes. His father, who created the family fortune, had instilled that sense of responsibility in all his sons. John F. Kennedy saw his opportunity to fulfill it in the dedication of his life to public service through good government. His preparation for the Presidency included terms as a Congressman and a U.S. Senator.

In the cold war he assumed great burdens as he moved into the White House. He was the recognized spokesman of the free world, the symbol and the voice of human liberty. He was a seeker of peace but practical enough to know that the best defense is in armed strength. He kept America strong and sought to do the same for our allies. His negotiation of the test ban treaty with Soviet Russia was a mighty contribution to the cause of world peace.

It is a reflection of President Kennedy's high character, his great talents in government and his devotion to America's highest ideals that the religious issue which was so heated in the 1960 campaign no longer exists. He was the first Catholic to be elected to the Presidency, yet only a few short days ago in New York City he was honored by an award from one of the country's lead-ing Protestant organizations.

With his background of wealth, John F. Kennedy was moved by concern for the common man. His legislative program was an expression of this concern. Medical care for the aged, public works projects to give jobs to the unemployed, measures to aid the physically handicapped and the mentally retarded were close to his heart, as he had shown.

That President Kennedy should die at the hands of an assassin is an ironical twist of fate considering the risks he endured as commander of a Navy PT boat in the Pacific area during World War II. He emerged from that conflict, with an injury that remained for life, as one of its outstanding heroes.

John F. Kennedy is dead and today Lyndon B. Johnson is President of the United States by succession. The prayers of every American will be for him as he takes over the crushing burdens of his high office; but he will find encouragement to meet his heavy task in the fruits of his long association with the man whom he succeeds and in the knowledge that the American people will pledge him their allegiance in every action for the wel-fare of the Nation.

Fortunately for the people of the United States, Lyndon Johnson is a man well versed in the art of government. His service as Vice President for the past 3 years, coupled with a vast knowledge of legislative and administra-tive affairs gained as majority leader of the Senate, makes him exceptionally well qualified to take over as the Nation's leader in this hour of emergency.

———

[From the Wayne Independent, Nov. 25, 1963]

PRESIDENT KENNEDY'S MESSAGE

The assassination of President Kennedy casts a somber shadow over the coming Thanksgiving holiday. As this community and the Nation mourn the death of its leader, heavy hearts may find it difficult to feel the true spirit of Thanksgiving.

Yet, in his Thanksgiving proclamation issued more than a week before his untimely death, the President asked the Nation to offer thanks to God, not only for material blessings, but for those of the mind and soul.

Concerning the former, he pointed out, "Today we are a nation of nearly 200 million souls, stretching from coast to coast, on into the Pacific and north toward the Arctic, a nation enjoying the fruits of an ever-expanding agri-culture and industry and achieving standards of living unknown in previous history. We give our humble thanks for this."

But the President asked, too, that Americans "be humbly grateful for inherited ideals." He continued, "Let us resolve to share those blessings and those ideals with our fellow beings throughout the world."

He went on to trace the establishment of Thanksgiving as a national holiday and pointed out that the country has made great strides in both its population and power. "Yet, as our power has grown," he added, "so has our peril." He asked that prayers be offered for guidance "to sustain us in the great unfinished tasks of achieving peace, justice, and understanding among all men and na-tions and of ending misery and suffering wherever they exist."

This vital man has made an indelible impression upon the mind and heart of the Nation, in his short period in office—short in relation to other Presidents, only five of the other 33 men who were President having served for briefer periods. He seemed closer to the people of this area because thousands saw him personally at Milford less than 2 months before his untimely death.

The plea of this young President now dead, for prayers of guidance and thanksgiving rings out louder than before.

ADDRESS BY

Hon. Robert A. Everett

OF TENNESSEE

Mr. Speaker, words are not at my command to express the feelings of the people of our con-gressional district in the tragic death of President John Fitzgerald Kennedy.

His death is certainly a great loss to our dis-trict, our State, our Nation and the world.

To best describe the feelings of our section, I quote from a letter that I received from a senior at the Martin branch of the University of Tennes-see, which is located in our congressional district:

What does one say to a friend and neighbor about the tragedy that has beset our Nation, and the world? When I first heard that Mr. Kennedy had been shot, I asked God to take away my breath and give it to him. It is not my place to question our Maker, but I just cannot understand why He would allow such an act.

I did not agree with all of Mr. Kennedy's policies, but I highly respected his firm stand on his beliefs and con-victions, for a man's worth is not measured by his size, color, or shape, but by his deeds and actions.

I guess that's why I'm writing this way to you. For your actions and deeds are of the highest caliber.

Our Nation has lost a great man. I feel that there is something I must do, but at the same time, there is a feeling of complete helplessness. I wish that my thoughts and feelings could be put into adequate words, of which there are none, to express the profoundness of this occa-sion. His death shall not have been in vain. It will serve as a reminder of the high ideals which were ham-mered and forged by our forefathers into the form of the greatest country and people the world has ever known. May God bless his soul, and, in the same instance, give us of earthly life new courage and assured guidance to continue to strive, to sweat, and, if necessary, to fight, for those beliefs we hold most dear.

May his epitaph read, "Ask not what your country can do for you, but ask what you can do for your country."

On November 23, I received a telegram from Mr. Shannon D. Faulkner, superintendent of the

Tipton County schools, which also expressed our sentiments:

The great tragedy which has befallen us by the death of our· President gives cause for a period of mourning in the schools of Tipton County, Tenn. I hereby declare an interruption in the activities of Tipton County schools until Tuesday morning, November 26, and suggest that each student, parent, and teacher reflect on the implication of this grave hour in the history of our country. Although burdened by grief, we have the greatest confidence in President Lyndon B. Johnson and his ability to carry our country forward in the historic tradition of our Founding Fathers. May God help us all in this endeavor.

To Mrs. Kennedy and the family I want to express my deepest sympathy.

ADDRESS BY

Hon. Victor A. Knox

OF MICHIGAN

Mr. Speaker, the shock and grief that swept our Nation at the untimely death of John Fitzgerald Kennedy are still very much with us. The numbness has not completely worn off. The feeling still remains that the events subsequent to midday on November 22 are all part of some hideous nightmare. Through our modern communications media, nearly all our citizens were made witness to this strange and tragic drama. Throughout those terrible 4 days one could not help feeling, and desperately hoping, that when the weekend was over all would return to normal, and we would find that these things never really occurred. And yet they had.

It is too soon to adequately and completely analyze President Kennedy's stewardship. Only the passage of time will give us the perspective so vitally necessary for that task. Some impressions of Mr. Kennedy, as President, as politician, and as a man, remain with me. With each succeeding year, John Kennedy grew and matured despite the awful pressures and burdens of the Presidency. He brought devotion to duty, persistence, and imagination to the post that demands them most heavily. And whether one agreed with Mr. Kennedy or not, one respected him, for he was the President.

Even as one battled him, one found himself, grudgingly perhaps, admiring him. His sense of timing, his choice of phrases, and his intuition were unmatched.

But it is John F. Kennedy as a man that will be most sorely missed and it is in this sense that his death was most tragic. He was cut down in the prime of life, with many years of useful service to the Nation still ahead of him. His youth and vitality, his marvelous sense of humor, his warmth, intelligence, and casual dignity were reflected in being in his presence. His great courage was wonderfully reflected in that shown by his wife Jacqueline and the children in their days of trial and grief. The Presidency will carry on, and will be well filled by other men. There will be other great politicians and statesmen. But there will not be another John Kennedy.

His life taught much, but his death, tragic though it is, can teach more. It has pointed out, as perhaps no other event could, both the weaknesses and strength of our form of government. It was the very freedom he loved in this Nation that allowed him to be cut down. Yet it is the strength arising from that freedom that allows us to carry on. One is hard put to think of anywhere else on earth that the events of the recent past would not lead to civil strife or near panic which would rip other nations asunder. Perhaps we must pay this tragic price for our freedom. Yet John Fitzgerald Kennedy did not shirk from it, nor did any of his predecessors. Out of this tragedy we can draw hope, and from that moment of weakness, our Nation has drawn strength for the tasks which lie ahead. For John Fitzgerald Kennedy, it is our fervent prayer that he may rest in peace.

Mr. Speaker, the people of our Nation have reacted in their own way at the tragic event of November 22. One of my constituents from Roger City, Mich., sent a poem to the editor of the Presque Isle County Advance which expresses the feeling of so many in the loss of President Kennedy. I insert the poem written by Betty Wojtaszek:

POEM BY BETTY WOJTASZEK

On that dreadful day in Dallas,
  In the fall of sixty-three,
Thousands gathered on the street,
  To cheer John Kennedy.

The motorcade moved slowly,
  On this last and fatal ride,

So all could see the President,
   And Jackie by his side.

Three shots rang out, so suddenly,
   A cause for great alarm,
"Oh, no," cried our First Lady,
   Her wounded husband in her arms.

The crowd was stunned and praying
   John Kennedy would live.
A man who helped our Nation,
   With all he had to give.

They waited sick with sorrow,
   That the news, they would not dread,
But their hopes died with these fatal words
   "Our President is dead."

Tears fell, by the millions,
   For this great and noble man,
The leader of our country,
   And for who our country stands.

He's gone, but not forgotten,
   And these words are all well meant,
We hope he'll hear them from above,
   God bless you, President.

ADDRESS BY

Hon. Robert L. F. Sikes

OF FLORIDA

Mr. Speaker, the death of President John F. Kennedy was one of the great tragedies of modern times. I would not have thought it could happen here. The President's leadership in the fields of foreign affairs and national defense had contributed significantly to improved prospects for peace in the world and encouraged greater prosperity at home. There was a brighter hue in the world around us; strong promise of a better tomorrow. Then he was struck down.

The impact of this young man's leadership upon the world is best illustrated by the fact that 220 heads of state and high ranking officials came to Washington for his funeral. Very probably we in America failed to fully grasp the dynamic energy, the great enterprise, the powerful leadership given our Nation by President Kennedy.

In company with most of my colleagues, I differed with him on occasions. That is one of the treasured rights of a democracy. We can respect our leaders, we can admire them personally, we may even support them with enthusiasm, but we reserve the privilege to assert our own beliefs and those of our people at home when we feel it is right and proper to do so.

It is a tribute to John F. Kennedy that our country has reacted with courage and vigor to press forward following his death. The chaotic events which began with his assassination would have created panic in many parts of the world. For a few hours the people of this country were stunned. They could not grasp the significance of what had happened. But the firmness with which President Johnson took the helm of government and the smoothness of transition to the new administration were reflected in a tremendous outpouring of determination to go forward in the Kennedy tradition. This is in part a barometer of the Nation's resiliency to adversity, but it is also a tribute to the man who had led us upward and onward for 3 years. And, I am sure the world took note of this reflection of confidence by our own people in our own country.

Out of that stunning rush of events, some things stand out—none with more dramatic clarity than the courage and devotion of Jackie Kennedy. If she had critics, they were silenced during those long grief-stricken hours from the time the assassin's bullet found its mark until the President's body was laid to rest, in Arlington. She is a great lady, and the Nation's pride in her is as great as the vast outpouring of sympathy it offered her.

John F. Kennedy was struck down needlessly, senselessly. His work is done, but his spirit and his leadership are our heritage. The life of our country goes on. Its work must go on. We shall have to stand and work more closely together as Americans to make up for the great loss the Nation has suffered.

ADDRESS BY

Hon. Sherman P. Lloyd

OF UTAH

Mr. Speaker, in September 1963, just a little more than two months before his death, John F. Kennedy came to my district, the Second District of Utah, and received a tumultuous welcome. He spoke to an overflow crowd of cheering citizens in the Mormon Tabernacle in Salt Lake City and was a breakfast guest of President and Mrs. David O. McKay of the Church of Jesus Christ of Latter-day Saints—Mormon. His visit was bathed in friendship and good will. On behalf of my district where he will be remembered so well, I join in these eulogies.

His handsome grace and expression, his concern for human beings, his talented mind, his patriotic devotion to America, his responsible projection of the United States in the leadership of the free world, the testimony which he gave to the principle of free men governing themselves, brought to this Nation a respect from legions of righteous men throughout the world. As a result, the ice of the cold war had shown signs of thaw, and a season of spring was developing in which men of diverse opinions were gaining confidence in finding peaceful solutions.

While knowing that fanatics walk the earth and may appear at any time at any place, he vigorously and joyfully battled for public office and public expression. He fanned into flames much dormant interest in democratic government and spurred participation in political action.

At his assassination his wife set a standard of bravery under the blows of indescribable shock, torment, and grief of lost love.

With my son, I viewed the miles long, wide line of mourners, waiting patiently through a cold night for the privilege of paying tribute at his bier and I sensed that John F. Kennedy had become nobly enshrined in the history of our Republic.

ADDRESS BY

Hon. James C. Healey

OF NEW YORK

Mr. Speaker, we have said goodby to a brilliant young President. We mourn him here in the Congress as we try to resume our legislative work, but our hearts are heavy with sorrow.

We mourn John Fitzgerald Kennedy as a friend and as a former Member of this body. We mourn for his young widow and children, for his parents and other members of this close and affectionate family. And we mourn for our Nation that has lost a dedicated and courageous Chief Executive, and for the world that has lost a great humanitarian and leader for peace on earth.

Unafraid of responsibility and unremitting in the performance of his awesome tasks, he brought to the office of the Presidency, youth, vigor, and a forward look. He was a man of persuasive ability, he had political dignity, eloquence of speech, wit, and charm. He saw troubles ahead, but was calm and determined, and he had great faith in America. He had said just before his election as President: "We will need in the sixties a President who is willing and able to summon his national constituency to its finest hour, to alert the people of our dangers and our opportunities, to demand of them the sacrifices that will be needed." In John F. Kennedy we had such a President. His record of performance in the short time he was in the White House had brought our country a long way, but it was only the beginning for him; he was taken from us harshly and suddenly at the pinnacle of his leadership. His untimely death made me think immediately of the words of Poet Robert Frost, whom the President admired so much, and I believe this was one of his favorites of Mr. Frost's poems:

> The woods are lovely, dark and deep,
> And I have promises to keep,
> And miles to go before I sleep.

Surely our young President, who had just begun to blaze the trail of the New Frontier, must have felt that he had miles to go before he slept.

John F. Kennedy was a warm and friendly person. He was a devoted husband and father, and a religious man. He forgave quickly and he bore no grudge or envy. It was my privilege to consider him a friend and to know him personally. He had asked me to the White House on several occasions in the past few years, sometimes on legislative matters and sometimes for social functions when my wife accompanied me. We had visited him in his home in Palm Beach. Last February when I was ill and hospitalized, his personal notes of good wishes and his beautiful bouquet of flowers brought me happiness. This was a man with tremendous responsibilities, daily burdened with work, problems, and decisions, who somehow found time to personally and warmly touch on the lives of so many. His telephone call to former Vice President John Nance Garner to wish him happiness on his birthday—only a matter of hours before the black hour of his death—was an example of the type of thoughtful, personal deed he so often performed.

A short time after my release from the hospital, he wrote to express thanks for my support of one of his proposals:

Although you were far from well, you were present in the House on Wednesday to vote in support of the administration's position. * * * This is to express my personal appreciation and my admiration for your strong sense of loyalty and responsibility.

This from a man who had no equal when it came to loyalty and responsibility.

Our beloved late President was a champion for world peace; probably his greatest goal was harmony and understanding among the nations of the world, and among our own American people. He had said:

However undramatic the pursuit of peace, that pursuit must go on. Peace and freedom do not come cheap. * * * Let us not be petty when our cause is so great * * * let us not quarrel among ourselves when our Nation's future is at stake * * * let us stand together with renewed confidence in our cause * * * and determined that this land we love shall lead all mankind into new frontiers of peace and abundance.

Though he was criticized by some, he was instrumental in bringing about the nuclear test ban treaty and he was hopeful it would prove a lasting and major deterrent to a destructive nuclear war. He had great hopes for the advancement of our space program and the peaceful use of atomic energy. In his inaugural address, he said:

Let both sides seek to invoke the wonders of science, instead of its terrors. Together let us explore the stars, conquer the deserts, tap the ocean depths, and encourage the arts and commerce.

He was determined to keep his promise to the people of West Berlin. He stood firm against Soviet Russia on the Cuban crisis. He saw his Peace Corps program acclaimed a successful contribution to humanity throughout the world. He sought approval of a civil rights program "to achieve equality we have talked about for a hundred years," and he asked Congress for education bills "that would bring the light of learning to every home and hamlet." He said:

America's leadership must be guided by the lights of learning and reason. Liberty without learning is in peril, and learning without liberty is in vain.

He wanted a tax bill that would keep our national economy from faltering; and he had asked Congress for a foreign aid bill that "would make it clear that we do not intend to forfeit our responsibilities to this hemisphere or the world." He had repeatedly urged approval of medical care under social security for our aged citizens.

My respect and admiration for President John F. Kennedy was deep. His wonderful memory will live in my heart. I will remember him as "a profile in courage."

My family and I extend heartfelt sympathy to Mrs. Kennedy, to young Caroline and little John, and to other bereaved relatives. They have our prayers for the strength and comfort that only the Almighty can give.

ADDRESS BY

Hon. Eugene J. Keogh

OF NEW YORK

Mr. Speaker, the bereavement of the entire free world has been so intense that most of us still have difficulty in finding words adequately to express our sense of grief and loss occasioned by the tragic assassination of our late, beloved President John F. Kennedy.

Seventeen years ago, almost to the day, when John F. Kennedy arrived in Washington for the first time, as a Representative-elect from Massachusetts, those of us who were serving in this body at that time were immediately attracted to him by the many facets of his outstanding character. Since then he has become known to the world; and the traits that first endeared him to his colleagues in this House brought him the highest honor the citizens of this country can bestow—the Presidency of the United States.

To say that John F. Kennedy was a good man seems insufficient, but when we recall that millions of people—upon recovering slightly from the horrendous shock of the news of the President's untimely death—blurted those words through their tears, we have some appreciation of the meaning of that phrase. That spontaneous tribute summed up in two words, which can rarely be so universally applied to a man, all those attributes of character that adorned John F. Kennedy and that he bore with such grace.

He was naturally good. As Aristotle observed many centuries ago, the goodness that comes by nature is bestowed by a divine agency on certain people who truly deserve to be called fortunate.

We shall never again see John F. Kennedy, but the good that he has done in his lifetime will live on and touch the lives of generations yet to come.

The genius of President Kennedy was his ability to accomplish great things for his country and his people in the face of long odds. One attribute of his character which enabled him to turn back the slings and arrows aimed at defeating his objectives was a wit that he had inherited from a long line of Celtic forebears. It was the manifestation of his wit on many occasions that so endeared him to million of Americans.

The world today is the poorer for his passing, but it is immeasurably richer for his having been with us during these past years.

There is no need for me to enumerate the fine accomplishments of John F. Kennedy. Others have done that today and much of it is known without the retelling. I only want to stand here in reverence to the memory of a good man and express my own sense of bereavement.

To the wonderful family of President Kennedy, I extend my most heartfelt condolences. Their sorrow is shared by all of us. Perhaps never has any family in our history shared in the prayerful remembrances of so many million Americans. Their grief can be less unbearable in the knowledge that it is also the grief of all Americans.

ADDRESS BY

Hon. William J. Green, Jr.

OF PENNSYLVANIA

Mr. Speaker, rarely in the history of America has one man blazed his path of glory across the horizons of this Nation in so short a time and with such momentous impact as did John Fitzgerald Kennedy. He was fashioned of the heroic stuff of which great Americans are made. Yet we who knew him best can testify before all the world that here was a man of gracious charm, broad intellect, and rare wisdom, a man with all the courage, faith, and compassion which real manhood forever requires.

And as if aware of the tragic limitations which destiny was to impose upon him, he swept with power and purpose out of the mists of relative political obscurity to burst upon the consciousness of the American people as few men before

him have ever done, symbolizing in his vigor, his leadership, and his vision a new generation of Americans.

In many ways, John Fitzgerald Kennedy was the living embodiment of the American dream. Born to wealth and prominence, he, nevertheless, became the champion of the poor and downtrodden. Of Irish immigrant ancestry, he fused within his own personality those characteristics for which Americans have become world famous, while giving voice and form to the yearnings of all his countrymen regardless of their backgrounds. As a young man in England, he witnessed firsthand the ravages upon the human spirit of tyranny and oppression, even as the first rumblings of war swept through Europe. Later, he went on to experience for himself the awful agonies of combat and its aftermath while fighting in the South Pacific.

In all of his formative years, it is difficult to find a time when John Kennedy was not testing himself, when he was not sharpening and perfecting his moral and intellectual capacities for that fateful moment when he would keep his long-appointed rendezvous with destiny as President of the United States. His entire life became a hymn of preparation for the brief but critical months of service he would undergo as leader of the country he loved so dearly and for which he finally gave every last ounce of devotion that there was in him to give.

Though he wrote three books, he considered himself no author. Though he was a decorated war hero, he was no militarist. Though he served with honor as a distinguished political figure, he was no politician. But, first and foremost, he was a great patriot. Above personal ambition, above party affiliation, above petty conceits, John F. Kennedy will forever be a challenge and an inspiration to all those patriots, present and future, who would take their place among history's honor roll of the brave and the good.

Though many men are called to serve their God and their country, a very few men in any generation are chosen to walk the solitary path to glory which he walked. His entire life was a noble overture to his sudden and tragic death.

No man so captured the imagination of his age as did John F. Kennedy. No man so mirrored the ideals and aspirations of the American people as did he. When John Kennedy died, people the world over felt hope within them die.

When John Kennedy was struck down, men everywhere saw reason and sanity and understanding being struck down with the same brutal senselessness and violence.

But the ideals which were so much the immortal part of John F. Kennedy shall endure beyond the grave. The assassin's gun and the assassin's bullet has not been made which can destroy freedom's dream—a dream that is indelibly impressed upon the minds and hearts of men. The dream of freedom shall endure so long as man himself endures.

On January 20, 1961—nearly 3 years ago—John F. Kennedy said:

Let the word go forth from this time and place, to friend and foe alike, that the torch has been passed to a new generation of Americans. * * * Let every nation know, whether it wishes us well or ill, that we shall pay any price, bear any burden, meet any hardship, support any friend, oppose any foe to assure the survival of liberty.

John Fitzgerald Kennedy has borne his burden. Now let us take up ours. With God as our shield, with freedom as our cause, let us labor to create a new and even greater America so that historians, in the years to come, will not find us unworthy of the sacrifice made by one of the noblest men of this or any other age.

ADDRESS BY

Hon. William S. Broomfield

OF MICHIGAN

Mr. Speaker, to eulogize our former President, John F. Kennedy, is a task which simple words cannot master. The man, himself, was his own eulogy.

All of us look at the world and beyond in new dimensions and perspectives because of John F. Kennedy. His breadth of vision, his depth of intellect and the height of his spirit will be remembered as long as there are men on this earth.

More than any other man, President Kennedy understood that civilization no longer has a choice between peace and war. There is only the choice between peace and annihilation.

President Kennedy was a hero in war. He knew the meaning of battlefield courage. But more important, and infinitely more difficult, he was a hero in peace in a continuing battle in which there are few if any discernible victories and many defeats.

Most important, President Kennedy saw. He had the vision and the imagination to see the future of our Nation in its broadest perspective. His vision was not a daydream like fantasy of little substance, but a solid, tangible pattern of peace, justice, opportunity, and freedom which showed the way to progress for millions in our Nation and the world.

He saw that, just as it is impossible for a man to exist in a vacuum, so is it impossible for a nation to exist alone in the world, divorced from friends, encircled by enemies, even if that nation is the richest and the freest the world has ever known.

John F. Kennedy died a hero in a battle which will continue for decades and possibly centuries. The battle is for freedom, for dignity, for the right of each of us to realize his full potential.

His horizon stretched far beyond the shores of our Nation and, indeed, beyond the reaches of this small planet on which we live.

Now it is up to us not to lose sight of the goals John F. Kennedy has set for us. He was truly a pathfinder on the dangerous road to peace.

ADDRESS BY

Hon. John M. Slack, Jr.

OF WEST VIRGINIA

Mr. Speaker, many have been the tributes paid to the late President John Fitzgerald Kennedy, and no words of mine could hope to match the hundreds of scholarly expressions which have come from all over the world to add luster to his memory.

Yet, I must add these few words because the people of my State and my congressional district were privileged to know him under exacting conditions, and he walked among them on many occasions with smiling countenance and purposeful stride, en route to the White House.

In the fateful West Virginia primary campaign of 1960, they voted their confidence in him and provided the catalyst that changed a hazardous prospect into an ultimate victory. He came to them as a man with a purpose, seeking support and understanding for his objectives. He left with them an impression which will survive as long as there remains alive even one among the thousands who shook his hand.

They were impressed by his clear understanding of the vast national problems which confront us, by his compassion for those who have not shared in our material progress, and most of all they admired his courage, both physical and spiritual, present in quantity and combination not often granted to any leader in our Nation's history.

Throughout a strenuous campaign in which his entire future hung in the balance, it was remarked that he never spoke an unkind word. But he spoke often in praise of others, and whoever gained his support was proud of it, and carried those words of praise with him as a buffer against adversity.

Now his days have been numbered and he has passed on to a greater journey. Like Halley's Comet which crosses the heavens only once each 75 years, we may not expect to soon see his equal in human resources enter on this stage again.

But each of us knows from the career of this man that, as long as the citizenry of this Republic continues to bring forth such men, then like the fire which drives the comet on its trajectory through the universe, our national spirit is unquenchable, and we shall remain invincible.

ADDRESS BY

Hon. Fred B. Rooney

OF PENNSYLVANIA

Mr. Speaker, although I am a relatively new Member of this legislative body, it was my great honor to have known and been associated with our late, beloved President, John F. Kennedy, for many years before my election to the Congress.

I first met him in 1956. I came to know him better in the years intervening.

In 1958, the President—then serving as a Senator from Massachusetts—came to Easton in Northampton County in my district to make a public appearance.

Then, as always, he impressed the people of my area in Pennsylvania as a man of enormous compassion and magnificent insight into the great difficulties confronting mankind in modern society.

In July of this past year, following the death of my great and esteemed predecessor, Congressman Francis E. Walter, I was selected to be the Democratic nominee to fill the vacancy in the Congress.

Throughout the campaign in July, I made it perfectly clear that I was strongly and unswervingly allied with the President's policies, in general, and with his desires for a strong civil rights measure and a tax cut to stimulate our economy, in particular.

I ran, during that campaign as a liberal Democrat—against the advice, I might add, of several persons within my district. I do not regret having done so—and I believe that the actions of my constituents in electing me to this seat by a 7,000-vote margin would indicate that they agreed with me in that respect.

I am convinced, today, as I was in 1960 at the Democratic National Convention, that my party nominated the two men best qualified—by experience, by temperament and by native intelligence—to serve all the people of this Nation as their highest officials. There should be no doubt in anyone's mind, now—if there ever was before—that Lyndon Baines Johnson and John Fitzgerald Kennedy were allied philosophically in the single struggle to make the American dream a reality.

But President Kennedy did not live. He was cut down by some quality of madness, some maniac's reasoning that none of us here in this room will ever fully understand.

Now the assassin is dead, killed by a man who must have lacked the same ability to reason and the same lack of faith in a free society.

Three men lie dead, restored to the earth of their origins, stilled in the ashes of eternity—one of them among the most humane and compassionate and intelligent men ever to walk the path of righteousness in this country, the second a man of delusion and disenchantment, bitterness, and blind bigotry, the third a brave police officer who was murdered in the line of duty.

We have put John Fitzgerald Kennedy's body to rest now in Arlington Cemetery. But his soul will not rest, his spirit walks the Halls of this Congress today and we must not let his memory rest and die away within us, within our minds and hearts. It is—and it must be—a bright flame burning at the center of our collective conscience, as Congressmen and as his countrymen.

To understand the meaning of John F. Kennedy's life we must understand, also, the lives and thoughts of those men who first set down the principles of this great Nation.

Washington, Jefferson, Paine, Patrick Henry, Adams—these were men who recognized the grandeur of America and the greatness of its challenge. They knew—as did Lincoln, as did the two Roosevelts and Woodrow Wilson—that the very nature of this Nation would be such that its business would never be truly finished, that each challenge, once met, would give way only to another challenge—and that it was America's eagerness to be challenged which set it apart, totally and triumphantly, from every other nation ever created on the face of the earth.

No man in our time so thoroughly understood the underlying meanings of this free society.

No man in our time was ever more willing to meet the challenges it conveyed upon him, and upon us, as our birthright.

No one gave more freely of himself, in life. No one has left us a greater legacy, in death.

Less than 2 weeks have gone by since John F. Kennedy's earthly body was placed in a grave at Arlington. Less than 2 weeks have gone by since we watched, with the final flagging energy of a nation sapped of tears and mourning, as a great lady of youth and beauty stood beside that grave and said a last goodby.

Less than 2 weeks.

And yet the voices are already rising across the land, saying that it was a terrible, tragic thing—but, after all, none of us were really to blame.

Is that true? Is that really true?

Can we say, in good conscience, that there is no blame upon this Nation, that those who spoke with hate and malice and bigotry before can be absolved of guilt in this senseless, futile killing?

I pray that none of us here in this room believes that the death of John Fitzgerald Kennedy was an accident of fate.

That it was the work of insanity, we do not and will not deny.

But even the most insane deed is committed in the right climate of opinion. And the climate of opinion in a country is created by many forces, not just a few.

There will be many memorials to John F. Kennedy. Some of them will be just, lasting, and fitting tributes to a man who cared more deeply about this country than anything in his own life.

One of those memorials has already been proposed to this Congress and I am in full agreement with those who wish to see the National Cultural Center become the John Fitzgerald Kennedy Memorial Center. No President in America's history believed more firmly that the strength of our country was founded upon its intellectual and esthetic development.

Less than 2 months before his death, President Kennedy flew to Milford, Pa., in Pike County, in my district. He went there at the beginning of a great nationwide tour in the interests of conservation. He went there to dedicate a research center commemorating the life and work of a great Pennsylvania Republican Governor, Gifford Pinchot, who was our State's first genuine conservationist.

But he went, also, to remind us that the majesty and grandeur of our natural surroundings must be preserved, that we must do all within our power to prevent the ravages of floodwaters such as those that laid waste to Pike and Monroe and Northampton Counties in Pennsylvania during Hurricane Diane in August of 1955.

He believed, with all his heart, in the continuing greatness of America, in its people and in the dream which made it possible.

He loved people, too—and it was a basic part of his personality to want to be with them wherever they were, in crowds, on the streets, or at the seashore. I remember that beautiful September 24 of this year when John F. Kennedy finished his formal talk at Milford and stepped down to shake hands with the hundreds of men and women who had come to hear him.

There were many young people there that day—just as there were here after his death. They came, I think, out of love for him, out of respect for him and the office he held—and out of understanding. For he was the first man in many years who could tell the youth of this country that America was still a young nation and make them believe.

It was the core of his being which spoke to all America when he talked of moving forward to meet the great, unfinished business of our country.

That is why he was so concerned with the development of Tocks Island Dam and national recreation area on the Delaware River in my district in Pennsylvania.

And that is why I am humbly hopeful that his

family and the Members of the Congress may look with favor upon a proposal to give his name to this magnificent reservoir and recreation area. It will be the largest of its kind in eastern America. It will serve between 20 and 30 million people—approximately 11 to 15 percent of our total national population.

I can think of no more dignified or fitting means of keeping his memory alive in the minds of such a large segment of the American people.

Surely, it is obvious that John Fitzgerald Kennedy took with him in death the prayers and blessings of the vast majority of citizens in this country. He was loved in life by countless millions, not only here, but in other nations beyond our borders.

He is loved, in death, as few men have ever been.

He will be remembered, for his cause was the fulfillment of America.

ADDRESS BY

Hon. Robert McClory

OF ILLINOIS

Mr. Speaker, in participating today in the eulogies to the late John Fitzgerald Kennedy, I want first to point out that these remarks are in behalf of all who make their homes in the 12th Congressional District of Illinois. The grief which accompanied the President's passing came to each household, each family, and indeed, each individual. These expressions today on the floor of the House of Representatives follow the many personal letters, newspaper editorials, and radio and television programs, all dedicated to the memory of President Kennedy and to his life and work.

An obvious explanation of the general outpouring of sorrow and sympathy is that the President was the leader of our Nation. The thought that anyone would presume to assassinate the head of our Nation is deplored and rejected by all. Our initial unbelief was soon followed by deep individual and personal grief. I doubt that the emotional impact which we experienced during the dark days following the President's assassination will ever leave us.

President and Mrs. Kennedy and their children have endeared themselves to the Nation as a whole. On my several personal contacts with the late President, I found him to be a most friendly and warm individual, a person who expressed concern and interest in others. In addition, he was one who attracted the most friendly attitudes on the part of others. He was well liked—and assumed that others liked him—as they did.

These personal attributes of the President make his death the more tragic and more heartrending. That anyone would harbor feelings of hostility to the extent of wishing to inflict on him physical harm or violence was surely beyond his belief. The entire world has been stunned and shocked by the brutal slaying of our President.

The sorrow of this hour is assuaged by the knowledge that in the Spirit, life is eternal, and that however it may appear to mortal eyes, in the eyes of the Divine Power which governs us all— man is forever alive. As a spiritual man of God, John Fitzgerald Kennedy lives.

ADDRESS BY

Hon. Leonard Farbstein

OF NEW YORK

Mr. Speaker, at this moment in history when the world reels in shock at the insensate, cruel, and brutal murder of our beloved President, it becomes a bounden duty to assess our role in this day and in this crisis.

As a nation and a people, joined by the peoples of the world, we pay fitting tribute to this man who gave unstintingly of his time, his mind, his energy and, indeed, his very life, to insure peace in this world and a better life for its people. This is as it should be.

But this is also a moment of truth and we cannot escape it. We must with all sincerity examine our hearts and our consciences. It is inescapable that we all share to some degree a collective responsibility for the continued reservoirs of hate and ignorance that can bring forth such a crime.

John Fitzgerald Kennedy was a man. He was a man who dared to meet the challenges of our times. His name and his deeds will live as a magnificent monument to the determination of this Nation and our people to realize the immortal promise of the American dream—a free people and a free nation—devoted to the pursuits of peace and the betterment of mankind.

Now he has given his life to these ideals.

The American people will even now look to those within whose power it resides to erect a lasting memorial to this American whose memory will remain a beacon light along the paths of democracy.

Mr. Speaker and Members of this House, I propose that we join, not as Democrats—not as Republicans—but as citizens of this great Republic, in enacting into law that program which will live as the greatest memorial to the ideals and hopes of John Fitzgerald Kennedy.

In closing, I would like to recall the words of the Prophet Isaiah:

And thine ear shall hear a word behind thee saying, this is the way, walk ye in it.

ADDRESS BY

Hon. Donald G. Brotzman
OF COLORADO

Mr. Speaker, on behalf of the people of the Second District of Colorado, which I represent, I join my colleagues on both sides of the aisle in expressing our sorrow over the tragic assassination of the late President John F. Kennedy and extend our sympathy to the members of his family.

ADDRESS BY

Hon. Byron G. Rogers
OF COLORADO

Mr. Speaker, never in the history of our Nation has a death affected the lives of so many people as the untimely, senseless murder of President John Fitzgerald Kennedy. He was indeed a man of courage, brilliant intellect, and a dynamic leader. His death brought shock and sorrow to all of us and plunged the entire Nation into deep mourning.

He had youth, charm, a zest for life, and leadership the White House has seldom known. He had courage in war and in peace and he had

the wits to confound those at home or abroad who would despoil his beloved country.

Like Jefferson, he kept faith with the common man's ability to exercise his own freedom. His was an abiding conviction that all citizens have a right to equality.

During his short time as our leader, he achieved greatness. To each problem that was presented, he sought a solution. Each solution helped America retain her position in world affairs.

For the first time in the history of the world, the citizens of the bereaved Nation have been able to see the deep lines of grief etched upon the faces of the peoples of this and other nations and to hear, firsthand, their expressions of regard and concern.

It is highly significant that in this great tragedy even those who have disagreed with the President and his philosophy of government are as sincere in their grief as those who marched side by side with him as he stood at the helm of the great Nation.

The people of the United States and the world will forever mourn his untimely death. They will pay proper recognition to the contributions he has made to help mankind and maintain a free America.

I extend my sympathy to the family.

May his soul rest in peace.

ADDRESS BY

Hon. Katharine St. George
OF NEW YORK

Mr. Speaker, after the tragic assassination of President John Fitzgerald Kennedy, I wrote a letter to my constituents. This letter expresses my feelings then and expresses them now and I ask unanimous consent to place this letter at this point.

This is not the usual newsletter. It is just a word to let you know of my participation with you in the shock and grief at the dastardly assassination of our President.

Never has there been such an outpouring of sympathy, sorrow, and indignation in the Nation's Capital. At the White House everything was quiet and impressive. In the East Room that most of us have usually associated with gay occasions the great catafalque draped with the flag was in the middle of the room with the huge candles at the four corners and the guard of honor immobile, like statues, with their eyes fixed on the ground. Many of us knelt for a brief moment at the foot of the catafalque and prayed not only for our President, who had been taken in such a tragic manner, but for his bereft family. Mrs. Kennedy has been magnificent throughout and the heart of the Nation goes out to her. Owing to television and radio, we were all very close at the time and no one will ever forget Mrs. Kennedy's face as she stood near President Johnson on the plane as he took the oath of office or when she left the plane at Andrews Air Force Base and got into the ambulance that took the late President's body to Bethesda Naval Hospital. There is a saying in the hunt country that Mrs. Kennedy loves so well that: A thoroughbred never lets you down— she surely has proved herself true blue during these tragic days.

And now the 35th President of the United States is left to the ages, and in the words of the poet:

"The tumult and the shouting dies;
The captains and the host depart;
Still stands thine ancient sacrifice,
An humble and a contrite heart."

Yes, certainly John Fitzgerald Kennedy gave the last full measure of devotion to our country and this will be remembered after much else will be forgotten.

ADDRESS BY
Hon. Edward R. Finnegan
OF ILLINOIS

Mr. Speaker, little can be added to that which has been so eloquently spoken here today. What is so deeply felt by millions of Americans and many millions more the world over requires but few words.

John Fitzgerald Kennedy is dead.

"He cometh up, and is cut down, like a flower"—and the people lament.

We ask ourselves, what purpose, what reason serves this twist of fate? Why was one, whose superior capacity for leadership of and good will toward the brotherhood of man, taken so violently from us in the summer of his life by a loathsome assassin?

The guilt for this atrocity is borne in part by all of us, and well it should be. For we are not as far advanced from the uncivilized periods of this world as we should like to think. We must give pause in our thoughts on this date and earnestly hope and pray that from this great tragedy a lesson has been learned. A lesson that shall not be forgotten.

But no matter what new resolves for improvement emerge from this tragic experience, we have lost that which cannot be recovered. We have lost a great and good man, and one feels as did Horatio upon the death of Hamlet:

Now cracks a noble heart.
Good night, sweet Prince; and flights of angels sing thee
to thy rest.

ADDRESS BY
Hon. Donald Rumsfeld
OF ILLINOIS

Mr. Speaker, the people of the 13th Congressional District of Illinois share the profound shock and grief that our Nation and, indeed, the world has experienced as a result of the still unbelievable and terribly tragic assassination of President John F. Kennedy. He commanded the respect and admiration of all who met him as a man of conviction who respected the convictions of others; a formidable politician and born competitor who did much to raise the level of respect for politics and politicians; a man of dedication, who faced his many difficult tasks with enthusiasm and a zest for living; a man devoted to his country.

As the Nation goes forward in these still troubled times, all of the fine qualities which he exemplified will help us fulfill the hopes and aspirations which all of us hold for our country and its people.

ADDRESS BY
Hon. Ronald Brooks Cameron
OF CALIFORNIA

Mr. Speaker, my mail of November 26 brought the following letter, which I believe to be as eloquent a tribute to President Kennedy as has been written:

RONALD BROOKS CAMERON,
House Office Building,
Washington, D.C.

DEAR SIR: My family and I have been deeply disturbed by the death of President Kennedy.

It is difficult to put into words, but perhaps it is like

our reaction to a breeze that moves through the forest; it rustles the leaves and stirs the surface of a pond; we feel its presence and grow accustomed to it. Then it stops, and we are impressed by the stillness. The presence of Mr. Kennedy was like a clean, fresh breeze that moved the leaves of our society and stirred the surface of its culture. That presence is gone, and I can only wonder at the stillness and express to you my support of his principles, and to encourage you in continuing your efforts to implement them.

Sincerely,

Mr. TERRY L. WORTHYLAKE.

WEST COUINA, CALIF.

ADDRESS BY
Hon. Robert T. Stafford
OF VERMONT

Mr. Speaker, I rise here today in behalf of the people of Vermont to pay tribute to our 35th President of the United States, John Fitzgerald Kennedy.

No new words can be added to the thousands which have been expressed so eloquently by so many since that tragic event of November 22.

There does seem to be one more fitting tribute which should be made, however. As you know, President Kennedy and Vermont's beloved Poet Laureate, Robert Frost, shared life's greatest hopes.

Frost spoke of some of these at President Kennedy's inauguration here nearly 3 years ago. The President honored Frost publicly at later events. Both have now gone on.

In tribute to John Fitzgerald Kennedy, I should like to read the following verse written by his friend from Vermont, Robert Frost.

ESCAPIST—NEVER

He is no fugitive—escaped, escaping.
No one has seen him stumble looking back.
His fear is not behind him but beside him
On either hand to make his course perhaps
A crooked straightness yet no less a straightness.
He runs face forward. He is a pursuer.
He seeks a seeker who in his turn seeks
Another still, lost far into the distance.
Any who seek him seek in him the seeker.
His life is a pursuit of a pursuit forever.
It is the future that creates his present.
All is an interminable chain of longing.

ADDRESS BY
Hon. Thomas M. Pelly
OF WASHINGTON

Mr. Speaker, a Member of Congress did not have to be of the same political persuasion of a New Frontiersman to admire the warm personality and fine qualities of leadership of John F. Kennedy, 35th President of the United States.

Future historians will assure Mr. Kennedy the place in history which he so richly deserves. But I venture to say that far beyond the memories of any of us who live today his name will be venerated as a great humanitarian and upholder of human rights.

For myself, I would express admiration on one count which I feel deserves special mention. Respect of a people for the highest public office—the Presidency—is evidenced by the universal grief of our people and the orderly transfer of authority from the slain President to his successor. This, I believe, is a vital prerequisite to preservation of freedom and democracy. So in paying my tribute to the life and accomplishments of John F. Kennedy, let me point up especially this particular aspect of his service. Our late President lent dignity to his high office and this in itself was an important contribution to our Republic. He brought the people, through his televised and personal appearances, close to the White House and gave them an understanding of national problems. His words reached the people and respect for the office of President has been sustained on a very high level.

Mr. Speaker, because of this, I was restrained when I disagreed with Mr. Kennedy. I freely debated issues where there were differences with his administration but I honored him and his views as did other members of my party. We differed in approach but never with objectives. He was for peace. We are for peace. He was for human dignity. We are for human dignity. He was for a better life for our citizens and mankind. We are for a better life for our citizens and mankind. He was for a strong America. We are for a strong America.

Only did we quarrel at times over the best means to achieve these common objectives.

Now with Lincoln and other noble leaders of the past, he belongs to the ages. The American people of all creeds, races, and political views have been drawn together by our sorrow. We remain drawn together seeking the same objectives to which Mr. Kennedy was dedicated. We are left by the tragic assassination a united people under God and in this time of grief each of us must rededicate ourselves to our beloved country. That is what John F. Kennedy would wish. That is the way it will be.

ADDRESS BY

Hon. James D. Weaver

OF PENNSYLVANIA

Mr. Speaker, the 35th President of the United States, John Fitzgerald Kennedy, will be remembered in history as a victim of the "cold war"— a victim of an assassin schooled in communism.

Through his youthfulness, vigor, leadership, his gracious wife, Jacqueline, and their two lovely children, the Presidency was given a new concept.

These assets along with a keen mind, an eloquent speaking technique, a pleasing appearance, and his theme of moving the United States forward, projected President Kennedy into the hearts of his countrymen. He became one of this Nation's most popular Presidents.

The shock of his death still remains in the minds of many. All of us who felt the effect of this horrendous act will never erase it from our memories.

Not everyone agreed with his policies; but the President in carrying out his responsibilities did so as a great American who had the best interests of the Nation at heart.

His quality of leadership that I admired most could be best illustrated in his firm handling of the Cuban crisis in which his bold moves saw the Soviet Union retreat from American strength and power.

Mrs. Weaver and I will never forget the sadness that filled our hearts as we expressed our personal sympathy and that of the people of the Erie, Crawford, and Mercer Counties at the White House, Capitol rotunda, and Arlington Cemetery. Mrs. Jacqueline Kennedy and her children,

Caroline and John, truly deserve the respect of this Nation for the dignity they displayed during this moment of personal grief, shared by the entire world. Mrs. Kennedy was truly a "profile in courage."

His death was a profound loss to the Pennsylvania 24th Congressional District. My sentiment and that of our people is reflected in the editorials appearing in the press in the Mercer-Crawford-Erie district.

Following are some of the writings:

[From the Erie Times, Nov. 23, 1963]

ODDS AND ENDS

(By Ed Mathews)

We didn't always agree with him.

We were like a great deal of other people.

We felt that he was politically activated on many of the things he did.

On the other hand we admired him.

We thought he was a great President.

We doubt if there will be another President like him.

We felt as though he was someone we knew on a personal level. We didn't but he had the overwhelming power to make you think you did.

We remember the last time we saw him. He spoke to the American Society of Newspaper Editors at their annual convention in Washington and when he finished he spoke to each and every member.

He was a politician, a good one.

He was a man who couldn't possibly have been beaten in 1964.

He was a symbol of what was the new fighting look in a young vigorous country.

He was a war hero who was lucky to survive.

He died as a man in the service of his country.

He died at the hands of the type of man he abhorred— the mixed-up type who thought other countries much better than his own.

He died on a political trip—which he enjoyed—to help Texas, the home of his successor.

When he died a little of each and every one of us died with him.

We were with a group of newspapermen attending a meeting to improve the economy of the State of Pennsylvania when the news first was announced. Gov. William Scranton was on the speaking platform and we happened to be sitting with his press secretary, Jack Comny. A hurry-up call took him away from the table. Then he approached the Governor with the news. We watched the expression on the Governor's face and then we told Mary Scranton that it was easy to see a great tragedy had taken place. The time was 1:40 p.m.

We thought it was some member of the family by the look on Mr. Scranton's face. Then the Governor interrupted the speaker to say:

"Gentlemen, I have some news for you. It isn't good.

"The President of the United States has been shot three times in the head."

Almost to a man there was a reaction: "Oh, my God!"

Arnie Goldberg of Uniontown summed it up when he said, "I feel sick to my stomach and we can't do a damn thing about it."

We realized how helpless a President is—even with the elaborate precautions of the Secret Service when a maniac with a gun is set on killing him. And you realize how united a country is behind a President in time of trial.

It wasn't too much longer the final word came. Then it was like a morgue. Newsmen used to big stories quietly moved away not knowing which way to turn.

It was a time when you wanted to be with one closest to your heart.

In short it was awful.

November 22 continued and it was nearly 6 p.m.—a mere 5 hours after the assassination and a President and his wife were getting off a plane at Andrews Air Force Base. It was not the one who left shortly before. It was Lyndon B. Johnson and Mrs. Johnson.

The body of the former President and his grieving wife had preceded him to a waiting ambulance from Bethesda Naval Hospital.

The country had gone through a horrible day in its history—but it already had a new President. It would continue to go on.

Somehow, as you watched, you knew it—but somehow, too, you found it hard to believe because of the man in the casket—J.F.K.

The world was a poverty-stricken place.

————

[From the Farrell (Pa.) Press, Nov. 29, 1963]

IN MEMORIAM

It was slightly past 2, Friday afternoon, November 22, when word rang around the world that our beloved President John F. Kennedy was assassinated. People just couldn't believe it. Thousands of men and women burst into tears, grieving at the thought of losing a President who has done so much and still had much to be done, but now will not have the opportunity to fulfill this mission.

Radio and television kept a constant continuity on his untimely passing and the public was well informed on all details. Churches and synagogues were jammed and the Nation went to prayer services.

The largest attended funeral in world's history was held Monday afternoon in Washington. President Kennedy now rests in Arlington National Cemetery with thousands of other veterans who gave their lives for their country. Millions attended the funeral by television and radio and were saddened by this terrible murder in these United States.

The Farrell Press joins millions of Americans in extending our sincerest sympathies to his courageous widow Jacqueline and the Kennedy family. With Mr. Kennedy's successor, President Lyndon B. Johnson, at the helm, we know America will continue to go forward and meet every crisis well, in the true American tradition.

[From the Meadville (Pa.) Tribune, Nov. 26, 1963]

A NATION GRIEVES

It was almost as though Americans, stunned by the swift turn of events of the past few days, could not fully comprehend that an assassin's bullet had taken the life of their President. But the burial of his body yesterday shocked all of us into the realization that President John Fitzgerald Kennedy no longer is our leader.

In death, President Kennedy unified the Nation as it never has been united except in times of national emergency. This dynamic, boisterous, exuberant country was brought to a virtual standstill by deep, heartfelt grief that manifested itself yesterday.

Bereavement knew no party lines. People of high and low estate were emotionally upset. Protestants, Catholics, and Jews offered prayers, each in his own way, and Americans of no religion at all paused to contemplate their loss. All of this Nation, regardless of national origin or color, shared together feelings of personal grief as though each of us had lost a member of his family.

Indeed, the death of President Kennedy might be compared to the loss of the head of a household. For was he not the head of the American household? Did not each of us look to him for guidance and leadership, even though we may not have been in accord with his decisions? Did we not depend on him for our national security and our well-being both as a nation and as individuals? Our aspirations for peace, freedom and prosperity—and, indeed, the hopes of many throughout the world—were personified in him.

The name of President John Fitzgerald Kennedy will be entered indelibly in the history of this Nation. But time and events do not stand still, and the mantle of authority has passed to President Lyndon Baines Johnson. While we may grieve over the death of his predecessor, our loyalty and our confidence now are transferred to the new President. If the unity achieved by sorrow could be committed to the support of President Johnson and the course he takes to advance our national welfare, the memory of the late President Kennedy would be well served.

————

[From the Sharon (Pa.) Herald, Nov. 23, 1963]

JOHN FITZGERALD KENNEDY

A nation, indeed a world, united in sorrow, mourns today the death of John Fitzgerald Kennedy, 35th President of the United States, martyred by an assassin's bullet.

For millions upon millions, his loss is a keenly personal one, the shock of which only now is being felt.

For this is the kind of man John Fitzgerald Kennedy was: As with all who are firm of conviction and strong in leadership, he could and did engender hate; what other force could have moved the demented mind of his assassin to commit his monstrous crime?

Yet, because of these same qualities, he could and did excite in millions throughout the world who felt their lives touched by him deep and abiding affection, profound respect and heartfelt admiration. It is these who now kneel beside the late President's wife and his family as they turn to the God of all for His comforting hand and His guidance in their hour of sorrow.

The Nation in anguish today asks itself: How could this be? How could this act of madness happen among us who live in a society in which stability in government, orderliness and tolerance are the touchstones of a way of life envied the world over? Are we a damned people?

The answer surely must be that we are not, for then how could the Republic survive? We are, rather, a people who harbor in their midst some so poisoned in both mind and heart they are incapable of understanding either the meaning of liberty or of discharging the responsibilities of freedom. The Republic, by the very nature of its foundation in freedom, is ill-equipped to guard against these.

History in its own good time will assess John Fitzgerald Kennedy as President. The first child of this century to achieve the Presidency, he brought with him to this noblest and yet most awesome of offices his youth, his keenness of mind, his soundness of heart and the firm determination to usher the country into a new era.

However one views his policies and programs, few will deny he was equal to the tasks of the Presidency. From the outset of his administration he was beset by the staggering problems of our times. Abroad, the threat of nuclear destruction hanging over all mankind, the Communist colossus, the deteriorating Western alliance, Cuba; at home, the lagging economy and persistent unemployment and that gravest of all domestic problems, the relations between the white and Negro races which another martyred President nearly a century before also was unable to solve—all these and scores of others tested him and he did not turn aside.

History, we believe, will look with favor upon John Fitzgerald Kennedy during the 2½ years he occupied the White House. If his life was cut short before he was able to achieve the goals he set for himself and his country, it was long enough for him to set the Nation on a course from which, for better or for worse, it will be unable to turn. Indeed, the assassin's bullet which ended his life fixed the Kennedy era into history. It will last long after him.

Now, the monumental task of leading the Nation, particularly through this troubled hour, falls upon the shoulders of President Lyndon B. Johnson, so recently the Vice President. He has accepted the responsibility, gravely, humbly asking for the help and the support of his fellow countrymen—and for God's.

Americans all, though burdened with the grief for their dead President, will respond unstintingly to the appeal of their new President. For at this hour there can be no Republicans, no Democrats, there can be no whites or Negroes, no northerners or southerners—there can only be Americans. Only in this way will the Republic be preserved.

———

[From the Corry (Pa.) Journal, Nov. 23, 1963]

He Cared for the People

A writer of words is a poor craftsman to tell of greatness.

The indelible pen with which history writes will leave for posterity the unchangeable record of President John Fitzgerald Kennedy. Then will a determination on the balance scales be made.

Historians will record that President Kennedy led our Nation when we reached for the moon.

But we believe that he will be judged on the blueprint he fashioned for the people; for the Negro and the colored races when the world was watching; for the aged and the sick when no one but our own too-quiet conscience was watching; for the jobless when crushed and defeated spirits were watching; for the untrained, unlearned youth when posterity was watching.

For these he will be remembered long after other accomplishments of his short Presidency are forgotten.

And history will recall that he cared for the people.

———

[From the Titusville (Pa.) Herald, Nov. 23, 1963]

A Tragic Loss

The assassination of President John Fitzgerald Kennedy comes as a profound shock to all citizens of the United States and the free world. Although there were many who differed with him on matters of high policy, all true Americans admired his stamina, his articulateness, his longtime devotion to public service, his political adroitness, and his warmth of personality. The Nation has suffered a serious loss with the violent death of President Kennedy, the youngest man ever to be elected to its highest office. The Nation now mourns his tragic passing and extends its prayers and deepest sympathy to his fine family.

———

[From the Albion (Pa.) News, Nov. 27, 1963]

A Weekend of Tragedy

The 35th President of the United States was mortally wounded by an assassin in Dallas, Tex., Friday. He died at about 1 p.m. within 30 minutes of the shooting.

At 3:30 p.m., after a 2-minute ceremony, Vice President Lyndon B. Johnson was sworn in as the 36th President, while standing in a plane at Dallas. His first Executive order was: "Now, let's get airborne"—to Washington to assume the reins of Government.

The suspected assassin, 24-year-old Lee Oswald, was captured within an hour after the shooting. Forty-eight hours later he was fatally shot by Jack Ruby, a Dallas nightclub owner, while he was being moved from the Dallas city to county jail.

The late President's body was flown to Washington with his wife and President and Mrs. Johnson early Friday afternoon. He lay "in repose" in the White House Saturday, and Sunday was taken to the Capitol Rotunda. An estimated 250,000 grieving persons passed through Sunday, Sunday night, and until 9 a.m. Monday.

He was buried in Arlington National Cemetery after services in St. Matthew's Cathedral. Heads of state and representatives of 55 nations were among those present. It was a weekend of world mourning.

[From the Erie (Pa.) Lake Shore Visitor, Nov. 29, 1963]

FALLEN HERO

Millions of words have been written and spoken in the past 6 days about the life and character of the late President John F. Kennedy. His courage, vigor, intellectual prowess, dedication and skill as the leader of the free world have all received full and richly deserved praise.

One of the most remarkable aspects of his career was the unaffected way he fulfilled his duties as a Catholic and a family man. Unashamedly and with neither ostentation nor attempts at secrecy, the personal side of his life was lived without any posing or posturing.

The whole Kennedy family has given the world an example of closeknit family life that the world badly needs. They have proven beyond any possible quibble that Catholicism is in no way incompatible with political life.

In the stunned and confused atmosphere which followed last Friday's dark deed it has been impossible to look with complete objectivity on the life of the statesman, but it does seem clear that his example should and probably will have an influence long after things return to normal.

Normal, wholesome family life has been at a discount in recent decades and it is a part of his greatness that President Kennedy with all his other great qualities was still the well-rounded, normal family man who has been too rare. He wore his private responsibilities almost gaily, but he always wore them.

We have always as a Nation cherished our heroes, and John F. Kennedy will be long remembered as an authentic one. In a century which has often not been very selective in the popular heroes or heroines it idolized for a brief moment, the late President stands head and shoulders above the crowd on whom the spotlight has fallen.

The responsibilities of the Presidency are, to repeat the shopworn phrase, truly awesome. It is a part of the measure of his greatness that Mr. Kennedy shirked none of them, public or private.

R.I.P.

[From the Erie (Pa.) Times, Nov. 25, 1963]

PRESIDENT KENNEDY

The unreal dream has become substance.

John Fitzgerald Kennedy, 35th President of the United States, was buried today in Arlington National Cemetery alongside other heroes who have given their lives for their country.

Lost to us is his compassion for the afflicted, his warmth for the young, needy and aged, his courage and leadership in times of international stress.

He left a legacy of courage and dignity. His own life was a story of pain surmounted, of heroism in the face of danger and of personal sorrow in the death of his infant son.

The tragic chain of senseless violence took three lives and accomplished only a national tragedy.

The assassin of the President died in the same violent manner, never actually comprehending the magnitude of his evil deed.

President Kennedy's widow has been a shining example of courage and fortitude in her personal grief.

It is as though she were taking our hand to comfort and solace us through the period of our national trial.

We must turn now and take up the tools of our daily lives to carry on as President Kennedy would have wished.

We are the greater people and Nation for having known him, even for so short a time.

[From the Greenville (Pa.) Record-Argus, Nov. 25, 1963]

WE MUST LOOK FORWARD

The British have a way of saying it that we Americans might revise a bit and adopt for our own use in this dark day. The President is dead. Long live the President.

The implication, of course, is acceptance of the fact that our President, John F. Kennedy, is dead but our new President, Lyndon B. Johnson, lives and we wish him well.

These are times that try men to their utmost. Times when it seems almost as if the world had stopped. But it hasn't stopped. All men, the world over, can only sorrow at the loss of John Kennedy to an assassin's bullet. His death will have far-reaching effects on the many complex problems the United States faces.

However, we must remember, and there's no doubt that Lyndon Johnson remembers, the world will go on. Vietnam won't disappear during our grief. The Berlin problem will be there tomorrow just as it was Friday morning. Castro and his Communist friends in Cuba won't go away. These and the many other perplexing problems the United States and President Kennedy faced together are still there.

They are no longer President Kennedy's problems. They fell on the broad, Texan shoulders of Lyndon Johnson at 2 p.m. Friday. They rest there now.

There have been many eulogies since the death of President Kennedy. But all men in every station have felt the same inadequacy of expression.

His former political foes, men with whom he had fought battle after battle right up to the very moment of his passing, wept. They recognized John F. Kennedy for what he was—a great man—despite their political differences. They felt the same pangs of sorrow as were felt by every man, woman and child in the Nation.

Those who lived through that black Friday will never forget it. The emotional shock was almost more than many could bear. Men's minds and hearts were shaken by extreme sorrow and at the same time anger and shame that this horrible thing should happen in the United States.

Today they laid John F. Kennedy to rest. He was a man of courage and expected every other American to be the same. He had seen death close by before and came back to win the highest office in the land. His success didn't dim his courage nor did it alter his faith in mankind. His patriotism was unchallenged. To him, the love of his country was part of life. He believed all Americans had felt the same.

Because he was the man he was, President Kennedy would wish nothing more than for Americans to unite in their common sorrow, shake off the cloud of grief and move forward. He was not a man to look back. The future was what counted. His philosophy, though difficult at times to accept in this regards, is sound. It is the philosophy all Americans must adopt.

President Johnson has assumed the role of the highest office in our Nation. He has full knowledge of the turmoil that exists in the world. He also knows he faces a monumental task. Let all men make him aware he has our prayerful support.

America cannot afford to dwell in the past. The present won't wait for us. The future presses in too quickly. There are jobs to be done and men must be at them. The finest memorial we Americans could raise in memory of John Kennedy is a monument of a strong, united nation, its loins girded with the courage with which it was built, striving with even more vigor to preserve democracy.

His dream was of a free world. It is now our responsibility to see that dream come true. Lyndon Johnson, with the help of God and man, will lead us toward the realization of that dream.

The President is dead. Long live the President.

———

[From the Edinboro (Pa.) Independent, Nov. 28, 1963]

PRESIDENT SLAIN—SHALL HE HAVE DIED IN VAIN

In Dallas, Tex., on the afternoon of November 22, 1963, a young man died in a hospital emergency room from wounds caused by an assassin's bullet.

What had been the body of an energetic young American man, now lay stilled in death.

Thus died John Fitzgerald Kennedy, the 35th President of the United States of America.

We are benumbed and grief stricken.

His kind of faith in our future and his unshakable belief in peace should confidently move us forward into a better society.

His civil rights program will require all our skills, tolerance, and understanding, in order that it may become fact, and not fancy.

Most definitely we want to retain the atmosphere of "a new era" in the White House which he and his family brought about. We should seek to prevent a loss of impetus and tempo on his outstanding programs, i.e., the Peace Corps, tax reform, stable prices, Manpower Development and Training Act, urban renewal, 10-year city program, etc.

We feel strongly that Americans of all parties should cooperate, wholeheartedly, on these programs in order to better our own survival as a nation, and to prove our good faith and intentions to the international community.

As President-elect, in 1960, he said, "In the * * * challenging, revolutionary, 1960's—the American Presidency will demand more than ringing manifestos issued from the rear of battle * * *. In the coming years we will need a real fighting mood in the White House * * * a man who will not retreat."

On January 30, 1961, in his state of the Union address, he said to a joint session of Congress, "It was here * * * that I gained both knowledge and inspiration from your wise and generous leaders. * * * Let every man and woman of our National Government say with pride and honor: I served the U.S. Government in that hour of our Nation's need.

"We greet healthy controversy as a hallmark of healthy change."

John F. Kennedy was a knowledgeable young man with almost unlimited energy. He possessed an unflinching determination to "get America moving again." He discerned the future of our country and our world with objectivity and logical analysis.

He perceived the mistakes and blunders of some of our country's past leaders, and took concrete steps to rectify them, and to make them right.

His stanch courage in the face of adversity and extremely trying conditions, was demonstrated during his first 90 days as our President, and has continued apace.

He was a dutiful son; a loving father, and a thoughtful and considerate husband.

Yet, he paid in full the penalty of leadership, in the form of criticism, detraction, the shafts of the envious few, and death by the stealthy, squeezing trigger finger of a hidden killer.

His vibrant words of courage, "To state the facts frankly, is not to despair the future nor indict the past," bespeak him well.

As fellow Americans, we are obligated to work unceasingly, with the greatest devotion and self-sacrifice, toward the realization and fruition of his aims, programs, plans, and ideals. Now, more than ever before in our history as a nation, we must present a united front to the entire world community, as he would have desired it.

Our job is: "To state the facts frankly" dedicating ourselves to the principles that the things he stood for are made a part of our American heritage.

If we fail—our young immortal pioneer will have died in vain.

In his own words, "We pray that we may be worthy of the unlimited opportunities that the Infinite has given us."

We also pray: That his inspiring image will remain undimmed for all eternity.

———

[From the Erie Morning News, Nov. 26, 1963]

THE FINAL PRAYERS SAID, TAPS HAVE BEEN SOUNDED

Our tears have fallen without shame.

Our last goodby has been said.

President John Fitzgerald Kennedy has been committed to the care of God and history.

It is painfully difficult to make any attempt to put the tragic events of the past few days in focus, or to begin to grasp the depth to which each of us has been affected.

This we know now. There is no American whose life was not altered during the 2 years and 10 months that President Kennedy was our leader.

The course of human events which seemed so inalterably directed toward holocaust and doom despite our resistance, suddenly was diverted to a new mainstream.

It is still too early to tell whether the river of life moves toward a real world of peace, or just a new plateau in the cold war.

Too much still depends upon our antagonists.

It would be completely impossible for any succeeding leader to negate the work of peace that has President Kennedy's indelible touch on its face.

Mere records will show that the late President was less than successful in his attempts to carry out many domestic changes, and that some of his strongest political opponents were of his own party.

But even political failures in our land are not without their advantages to the Nation as a whole, for by the very working of our system the open debates and discussions help many to a clearer vision of the needs of the people.

Where his domestic plans went astray in the simmering national forge, his successes as the leader of the free world were from the beginning bathed in a brilliance that unfortunately peoples of many foreign lands saw and recognized long before his own Americans did.

This we can only regret as all too many Americans must do now when it is too late.

For our last goodby has been said.

———

As We See It

(By Frances Moore, editor and assistant publisher, Allied Newspapers, Grove City, Pa., November 25, 1963)

By the time this is in print the body of President John Fitzgerald Kennedy will have been laid to rest on a hillside overlooking the scenes which were a part of his daily life. Even now almost 3 days after that dastardly deed that so suddenly brought to an end, the young, enthusiastic, and courageous life of our President—it doesn't seem quite possible that it all happened.

We take so much pride in our civilization, and in our democracy. We take for granted the fact that we can agree or differ as the case may be, with our leaders, yes, even with the President—yet live at peace with one another, on friendly terms. Then some anarchist fires a volley of shots, and our President dies. This can't happen in these United States, we tell ourselves. But it did.

The man who was accused of the unspeakable deed later died in the same manner, but not before he killed a police officer, who also was a husband and father of young children. One of the many thoughtful and considerate acts performed by Jacqueline Kennedy, in her time of deepest sorrow, was that of sending a message of sympathy to the bereaved wife of the slain policeman. Her consideration for others has shown itself in deed and word almost from the very moment when death took the First Lady's husband from her. Those who have always admired her, admire her more; and those who have ofttimes been critical, have learned to admire her deeply during these days. And she has been, in truth, the First Lady.

Regardless of political differences, the populace, as one, felt the horror and shock when the news of the shooting first came over radio and television shortly after 1:30 Friday afternoon. They didn't matter then, those differences—a gun-carrying maniac had fired a shot that took the life of a man riding smilingly along a Dallas, Tex., street; riding in an open car because he loved to ride that way; riding without protection of bulletproof glass; riding so that he could put out his hand and touch a close bystander; riding so, because this was the United States of America and so he was safe from sniper's bullets—and this man was our President.

We ask why? And this we will never know, perhaps, since the man accused of firing the fatal shot also has been silenced by death, death at the hands of another murderer. This Nation has felt shock before at the loss of Presidents by assassins, and maybe those who lived then felt shock and sorrow as deeply as we who live today feel at the death of President Kennedy. It would seem that they must have, but as we feel now, it seems impossible that our country has ever before been subjected to shock so deep and so full of horror.

The people were shocked when on April 12, 1945, news was received of the death of President Franklin D. Roosevelt, and the Nation mourned. But he died a natural death, even though suddenly, so the shock was not coupled with the horror of deliberate killing. An attempt had been made to take the life of this President, too, but the sniper was not so accurate—and another man died, instead.

The first President to die by an assassin's bullet was Abraham Lincoln, 16th President, shot April 14, 1865, and died the following morning. James A. Garfield, the 20th President, was shot on the second day of July 1881, and lived until the 19th of September. William McKinley, the 25th President, was assassinated since the turn of the century. His death took place September 14, 1901.

If anything can be realized by thinking back over this history it is that, in spite of shock and loss of good men, our Nation does go on and does continue to grow. One of the first speakers we heard after the first hours of awful news on Friday, said with great earnestness, that what we must know is that, although we have lost our President, we still have our country.

Now, if ever, we can see the value of our system of succession. We have a President. We have at the helm one who has had many years of experience in Government and who is fully aware of current affairs. And certainly no President has ever taken office who had the prayers of so many people as does Lyndon B. Johnson. A young man—in his early twenties, well known and very close to this scribe—said on Saturday, "All we need to do is pray." If young men know that, our country is in safe hands.

ADDRESS BY

Hon. George M. Wallhauser

OF NEW JERSEY

Mr. Speaker, I rise to pay my respects to our late President, John Fitzgerald Kennedy, and to extend my deep sympathy to his fine family.

Much will be written and said about the life and career of President Kennedy, but in substance the record will show:

John Fitzgerald Kennedy was a great and dedicated American and person. He was a dedicated son, husband and father. He was a dedicated legislator and Chief Executive. His deeds in life were good ones. His aspirations for his Nation and its people were good ones. Love and respect for his fellow man were paramount.

This will be the record. It is the kind of record that all of us would like to achieve and leave as a legacy to our families, our friends, and our Nation.

ADDRESS BY

Hon. Charlotte T. Reid

OF ILLINOIS

Mr. Speaker, at this time I want to add my remarks to those of my colleagues. This is a tragic time in our history; and my deep and profound sympathy goes to all members of the late President's family.

ADDRESS BY

Hon. Clarence E. Kilburn

OF NEW YORK

Mr. Speaker, it is incredible and terrible that in this great free land of ours a murder of our President could take place.

As we all know, President Kennedy was our President. He was the President of all the people. He was trying to do his best for his country. He was young, extremely intelligent and worked all the time for all of us.

It is heartbreaking for us all that a crazy wretch could, in a matter of minutes, so affect our lives, our country and the world.

My heartfelt sympathy, along with that of everyone else, goes to his courageous wife and family.

ADDRESS BY

Hon. James F. Battin

OF MONTANA

Mr. Speaker, tragedy begets tragedy. Calm begets calm. The President has gone to his great reward but the shock still hangs over the Nation. We mourn him as a leader of our country and as a person. He was the leader of the greatest country of the world today.

To meet such an untimely death at the hands of an assassin is beyond comprehension. We all take pride in the courage and composure of Mrs. Kennedy. She of course suffered the greatest loss.

The Nation and its people must go on and, without doubt, will. This is the fiber of the Nation and the strength of its people. This is what makes our country great.

Words are not adequate to express my personal feelings. Though I disagreed with him on political matters, he was my President, he was the President of all Americans.

My heart and that of my family, as well as that of all Montanans goes out to his loved ones. He did indeed pay the supreme sacrifice for his country.

ADDRESS BY

Hon. Craig Hosmer

OF CALIFORNIA

Mr. Speaker, today we meet to eulogize our late President, John Fitzgerald Kennedy, who was foully murdered in Dallas, Tex., on November 22. It seems like such a short time ago that he was alive and planning for his future and our future. Now he is part of history and lies in Arlington National Cemetery.

An assassin's bullet struck him down. It would be impossible to evaluate the greatness of the man at this time in history. He occupied the White House for but 3 short years. He did not have the time to see most of his plans brought to fruition. We can only guess what the outcome of his projects and grand designs might have been.

The suddenness of his death at the hands of a madman tinged by Communist philosophies at first brought great shock and then great grief to the whole Nation. It is unbelievable that such a monstrous atrocity could happen in a civilized country. The late President symbolized the hope in mankind for true peace and true freedom. His death is a loss not only to America but to the world. Every American, regardless of political viewpoints, has suffered a personal loss. President Kennedy requested and encouraged vigorous debate on the programs and projects he proposed. I was one of those who vigorously opposed his views relating to the nuclear test ban treaty. Because he invited such opposition and debate, and because others and myself accepted such invitation, the molding of our opposite viewpoints which eventually occurred resolved the issue in a much more satisfactory manner than otherwise it could have been. The debate was keen. It was on the issue. It was wholly without rancor or personal animosity on either side. The national interest was served, the issue was distilled to its essence, and safeguards were defined—all in accord with the highest tradition of open, democratic debate and discussion that characterizes American public life.

John Kennedy was not the father image. He was a man who belonged to us and our age. Now a foul deed has placed him in history.

During this period of mourning for our murdered President the Nation's thoughts turn to ways in which we as a people and as a society can better serve. President Johnson eloquently expressed this in his address to us by saying: "Let us here highly resolve that John Fitzgerald Kennedy did not live—or die—in vain." It is our duty and responsibility to see that the institutions which make up our great and mighty Nation are protected and perpetuated. It is our duty to see that the Kennedy children who have lost their father do not lose their birthright as well. Indeed, that our own children do not lose their heritage of freedom.

The Nation is fortunate that at this time of crises a man well-trained and skilled in the art of Government stood ready to assume the massive burdens of the Presidency. The firm strength and dignity with which Lyndon B. Johnson grasped the reigns of Government was reassuring both at home and abroad.

When we received the news of our President's death it seemed that nothing more could touch us or shock us for a long time, for it was a numbing blow. Then in just a day and a half his assassin was mortally wounded in view of the whole Nation. This Marxist fanatic was denied due process of law and the country was denied the right of knowing the truth. It was a second deep wound in our way of life. Now there are many things which we will never know with assurance from the assassin's lips.

President Johnson has appointed a very representative seven-man Commission to investigate the terrible tragedy which took John Kennedy's life. Like the rest of the Nation we are waiting to hear their report and learn all the facts in the case which can be uncovered.

But now we must take up our responsibility as citizens and legislators and see that the foundations of our country are strong. We must make sure that hate and subversion are not eroding our institutions.

John Fitzgerald Kennedy who was cut down so early in life will surely go down in history as one of our most tragic Presidents. In closing, I would like to use the words of the man whom we are eulogizing because I am sure he would want us to remember our responsibilities and would again urge us on by saying: "Peace and freedom do not come cheap, and we are destined to live out most if not all of our lives in uncertainty and challenge and peril."

ADDRESS BY
Hon. Paul B. Dague
OF PENNSYLVANIA

Mr. Speaker, the shock felt by the Members of this House was well-nigh universal and I have yet to find anyone so politically partisan as to confess to a lack of acute distress when he heard that our 35th President had been struck down in cold blood by the hand of a psychopathic killer. And we certainly do this great, decent American's memory a definite disservice when we try to link his death to the honest legislative opinions of sincere citizens, be they of the left or of the right.

The word of President Kennedy's tragic death came to me as I was entering my hometown post office. There I met one of the clerks coming out who told me he was going to lower the flag because our Chief Executive had just been shot to death. And all I could do was to remove my hat and stand there in bewildered numbness as our flag came down in tribute to the passing of the one man who symbolized all that we as a free people hold dear.

A scant hour later I gave this statement to the press and radio:

> The death of our President has brought the Nation to the verge of its greatest grief in my lifetime. Some fanatic has struck down a great statesman, a great leader, but equally as frightening has been the blow we have seen struck at all of our sacred symbols.
>
> I have been immeasurably shocked by the President's assassination and I know that I speak for the half million residents of this congressional district when I extend to Mrs. Kennedy and her children our heartfelt sympathy and condolences. May a merciful and all-compassionate Creator have them in His tenderest care.

The next few days, along with all of the free world, I stumbled through a series of tributes to this fallen leader, culminating in the moving ceremonies as his body was laid to rest in Arlington. Thereafter I addressed a personal letter to Mrs. Kennedy on behalf of Mrs. Dague and myself and since then I have continued to remember them in my prayers.

What more can I say? There is nothing that we can add in tribute to this decent American who has been so wantonly cut down at the peak of his service. But throughout it all John Fitzgerald Kennedy has symbolized for us everything that this Republic of Sovereign States stands for and his murder remains an attack on our priceless heritage, on all that we are committed to. Perhaps the periodical, National Review, has summed up for us better than most the real threat with which we are still faced.

> The assassination of President Kennedy was the act presumably of a madman, heir to the madman who killed Lincoln and McKinley and, for that matter, Christ, reminding us that the beasts are always with us, and that they continue to play decisive roles in history and in human affairs.

John F. Kennedy rests in hallowed peace, his memory enshrined in the hearts of his countrymen. The Nation lives. Let us get on with the job of keeping our heritage secure.

ADDRESS BY
Hon. Elford A. Cederberg
OF MICHIGAN

Mr. Speaker, it is with deep sorrow that I join my colleagues in paying our deep respect for our late President, John F. Kennedy.

This country became great by the hammering out on the anvil of public debate the great issues of our time. President Kennedy was an honest and eloquent spokesman for his viewpoint. The Nation has lost a great leader.

I express to Mrs. Kennedy and the family, on behalf of all citizens of the 10th Congressional District of Michigan, our very deepest sympathy.

ADDRESS BY
Hon. George A. Goodling
OF PENNSYLVANIA

Years ago, as a teacher in high school, it became my sad duty to attend the funeral of a student. She was a senior who appeared to have a great potential and was admired and respected by all who knew her.

An elderly minister used a very fitting but little known passage of scripture for the basis of his remarks:

> Her sun went down while it was yet day.

Friday, November 22, 1963, will always be remembered as a day of infamy not only in the United States but in the entire world. It was a day of sincere grief and righteous anger. It is incredible that such a heinous and dastardly act should have been committed in an enlightened nation.

Many did not agree with the political philosophy of the President. None could question his sincerity or devotion to duty. He gave unselfish service. All have a responsibility in seeing to it that his sacrifice may not have been in vain.

The sun of John Fitzgerald Kennedy did go down while it was yet day.

A poem by a constituent, Mrs. Sarah Ann Knaub, York, Pa., written during the funeral procession of our late President, appears appropriate:

AND THEY TOOK THE YANKEE HOME

When emissaries of this mighty land,
Among the many hued peoples of the world have
    traveled,
They frequently have had to face the stinging
Placards of a venomous crowd, saying "Yankee, Go
    Home."
There are slinking forces alive in the world
Waiting, lurking, jabbing, stabbing, trying to
Divide our Nation from the world—indeed divide the
    Nation from within.
On that Friday of infamy a sign was
Seen among the crowd saying, "Yankee, Go Home."
A bullet sent on its way by one whose hatred may have
    been fed by those who would
Annihilate the Yankee, made it necessary
To take the Yankee home.
His widow uttered a cry—heard round the world—
And she took the Yankee home.
But the end is not yet.
Consider how they took the Yankee home.
To the sound of muffled drums,
On caisson slowly drawn—that all
The world might see and pay respect
To our dead leader.
And the world did see—the leaders of the world did
    come.
They came and marched to muffled drums as
They took the Yankee home.
From France, from England, Germany, Japan,
Belgium, Ethiopia, from all the cultures of the world.
Who dedicated his living as we dedicate his dying to the
    cause of world peace.
The leaders of the peoples of the world marched—
    together:
And will long remember
When God took the Yankee home.

—MRS. SARAH ANN KNAUB.

ADDRESS BY
Hon. Albert W. Johnson
OF PENNSYLVANIA

Mr. Speaker, as each day goes by the enormity
of the tragedy that befell this Nation in the tragic
death of President John F. Kennedy becomes
more and more apparent.

You find it in the expressions of his fellow
man. It has a lingering and powerful influence
in our schools, churches, national assemblies, in
our newspapers; yes, in every walk of life.

As each day goes by we all endeavor to extend
in some way our sympathy to his bereaved family
to try to make their burden lighter and lessen
their great sorrow.

It is fitting that today this House of Representatives of the Congress of the United States pauses
in its deliberations to memorialize our dear departed President.

I have picked out several editorials in newspapers which reflect the sentiment in the 23d
District of Pennsylvania, which follow:

[From the Kane Republican, Kane and Mount Jewett,
Pa., Nov. 29, 1963]

TO HONOR HIS MEMORY

When a leader of great power and presence and
capacity for good dies in office, the cause to which he
gave leadership suffers grievous loss. President John F.
Kennedy was such a man. The cause he served, and so
eloquently led, was the threefold cause of human dignity and equality and freedom.

Though President Kennedy is dead, struck down most
foully by an assassin's hand, the cause he championed as
acknowledged leader of the free world lives on. We
who survive him can best honor his memory by doing all
in our power to advance that cause, which is the very
cause for which this Nation was founded.

Guidance for the difficult time ahead may be taken
from the immortal words spoken by Abraham Lincoln on
that solemn occasion at Gettysburg almost exactly a century
ago. For President Kennedy died in defense of freedom
as truly as did those who fell on that historic field of
battle. In these days of profound national sorrow it is
appropriate to reflect on Lincoln's exhortation to his
fellow Americans "that from these honored dead we
take increased devotion to that cause for which they gave
the last full measure of devotion—that we here highly
resolve that these dead shall not have died in vain."

To resolve thus and to act thus—that is the task to
which we must now turn our minds. This is so even
though grief and a deep sense of loss will far outlast the
initial period of outraged shock at the murderous act in
Dallas. We cannot permit ourselves the luxury of
heedless sorrow. The forces that work against the
realization of man's highest dreams remain strong and
malignant. Those forces must now be countered with
new dedication, so that President Kennedy's martyrdom
in the fullness of life shall indeed not have been in vain.

The heaviest burden falls upon Lyndon B. Johnson,
who became President the moment John F. Kennedy
succumbed to the assassin's bullets. But all citizens must
in some measure share that burden. In his first public
utterance as Chief Executive, President Johnson said
this to the American people: "I will do my best. That
is all I can do. I ask your help—and God's." It is a
commitment, and a challenge, worthy of the best that
is in all of us.

———

[From the Derrick, Oil City-Franklin-Clarion, Pa., Nov.
25, 1963]

TIME OF DEDICATION

John Fitzgerald Kennedy, the United States youngest
President, will be laid to rest today as the Nation mourns
his tragic death.

The shock of President Kennedy's assassination will be with us for a long time; in a sense the rest of our lives.

That moment when the news was received will remain engraved in our memories as in the case of Pearl Harbor. No one could remain aloof from the emotional impact of this senseless deed. To their credit, children seemed to respond most appropriately—with prompt, wholesome tears.

The thoughts of Americans, in their sorrow, turn particularly to two individuals. First, to Jacqueline Kennedy. The horror of her experience wrings the heart. This courageous lady, who brought charm and gaiety to the national scene, was plunged in the wink of an eye into the terrible crisis for which nothing can prepare the strongest man.

She bore herself nobly. Beyond question, the time will come when Mrs. Kennedy will draw deep solace from the fact that she was there, comforting her husband in his last moments. The sympathy that has gone out to her and her children from all the world, is beyond measure.

The mind's eye turns, too, to the new President, Lyndon Johnson, in taking up his burden. To his own prayer, we add ours: God grant him wisdom and strength to know and to do the things that must be done.

This should, of course, be a time of reunion, a time of general dedication, when Americans of all persuasions draw closer in their mutual need.

If the death of President Kennedy engenders bitterness among the people he served, we shall betray his sacrifice. If it brings new resolve to meet the challenge together, John F. Kennedy may rest content.

————

[From the Warren County (Pa.) Observer, Nov. 25, 1963]

OBSERVATIONS: COMMON LOSS

(By Bob Walsh)

For the past 3 days we have lived as a nation in concert. We have set aside our differences and even those whose philosophies of government, economics, and perhaps we should include religion, were not parallel to those of our late President, have added their voices to the torrential expressions of praise and respect which have occupied much of the television time.

Some will label this hypocrisy, and there is little doubt that there is a measure of it to be found wherever humans are involved. But we prefer to believe that it represents a large degree of respect. Respect for an opponent in some cases, but also a previously unexpressed esteem by many who believed that here was a leader of whom we could be justly proud.

These days have proved that we may not be in complete agreement on all issues, but we are in agreement that there must be action. We honor this young man for his courage to act and the intellect and integrity which supported it. Though each of us might have a different way of attaining the desired ends, most of us would support such a leader once our Nation were committed.

UN-AMERICAN?

We have written that this tragic act was un-American. This is not altogether true. It is true in the sense that the American way is not one of violence and that we do not believe in resolving our differences through riot and military actions. It is true that whatever an assassination may represent, its purposes never are attained through such an action.

It is American in that it is limited to the death of one official, and not the overturn of a government. It is American in that it tends to bring us together in a more closely knit relationship as a nation.

It is American because such an act would be much more difficult to manage in nations which are less free and where the carrying of weapons or the permit to use them is very limited. It is American because an assassination in most nations would necessarily be accomplished by the military, thus representing not a personal whim, but a desire on the part of a political group.

In fact, the very characteristics which ease the way of the assassin in the United States make the violence represented extremely un-American.

WHY?

The question constantly asked is why this costly loss of life is allowed to occur if our God is just. If this question is being put to the predominantly Christian share of our population the answer is an easy one. History, and specifically the Bible, plainly reveal that the leading figures in man's background often are lost at a relatively young age.

But many of those who have contributed the most, accomplished much of it, and sometimes almost all of it, through their deaths, which at the time caused others to ask, "Why? Why?"

We have lost a very strong crutch. It has been taken away from us suddenly, not allowing us time to dwell on how we will manage. We now must walk without that crutch, both as a nation of people who should be better informed today about what is going on in government than they were 3 days ago, and as leaders who must forget much of their petty politicking and resolve the problems before us with wise, positive action.

The death of President John F. Kennedy reaches many of us because of our vicarious tendencies. He represented a promising young gentleman, well informed, courageous, and personable. He had an obviously good family relationship, much as the average American family either has or would like to have. He was many of us personified if we could shape our lives without the effort he represented. Or even with such effort. All of us are not so blessed.

And perhaps it is this personal aspect that has brought a share of the grief into each of our lives and has made it seem almost a part of our homes. At least this is the way it has been with millions of Americans whose sense of a great loss this past weekend has been deeply felt.

Why? We shall learn the answer to that even as we help shape it through our own actions in the days to come.

[From the Warren (Pa.) Times-Mirror, Nov. 25, 1963]

JOHN FITZGERALD KENNEDY

As the shadows of evening fall across this day of mourning, we shall all settle down to hope for a brighter tomorrow.

We no longer hope that we will awake to find that it has all been a bad dream; a joke in bad taste. But we do hope that, from this tragic event, the assassination of the President of the United States, we shall achieve a new dedication of purpose.

John Fitzgerald Kennedy was the youngest man ever elected to the Presidency. He was a man of controversy. He aroused violent likes and dislikes. He was a man with a purpose and a program—a program which some disagreed with.

Yet in that instant when a bullet slammed into his brain, he became simply a man; and in that same moment, we all became just one thing—Americans; not Republicans or Democrats; Americans, not Catholics, Protestants, Jews, black, white or yellow or red, but simply, Americans.

We were so stunned, so unbelieving, so stricken with grief that this young, vital man had been mercilessly cut down in the very prime of life, that we had little emotional room to work up a deep hatred for the arrogant, twisted, vicious dog who destroyed him.

We learned the deep truth of John Donne's lines: "Send not to see for whom the bell tolls. It tolls for thee." Indeed, all of America was diminished by the death and by the manner of the death of this man who was our 35th President and the 4th to fall to the bullet of an assassin.

Texans, particularly residents of Dallas, are stricken not only with grief, but with shame and guilt; shame that in their city, the fabulous "Big D" of song and story, a man like the assassin could live unnoticed among them, to spring into sudden, infamous notoriety by pulling the trigger on a rifle.

We all share that guilt and shame, because there must be something very wrong with a Nation which can allow such an individual to grow to manhood without the attention of the police or the mental hospitals.

There is something wrong with an America which can take back to its soil a man like the killer; a man who had renounced his American citizenship, married a Russian woman and who, when he had been refused Russian citizenship, came crawling on his knees to the American Embassy to ask permission to go "home" and to even borrow the money to do so from embassy officials.

What went on in the mind of this killer as he was growing up? Why didn't someone notice him—someone understand that in the darkness of his mind he was hatching a deadly hatred which would find such terrible expression?

Yet we are a tolerant people, even as John Fitzgerald Kennedy was a tolerant, open-hearted man. Just as his own openness led him to ride through Dallas with the bullet-proof plastic bubble of his car stowed away, so did the tolerance of our society permit a mad dog Marxist to grow up among us.

There are ironies in this murder which strike deep. The right wing had accused Mr. Kennedy of being too friendly with the Communists, yet it was an avowed lover of communism that killed him. Mere logic would have made it seem more likely that his death, if it was to come like this, would have come at the hands of some diehard segregationist, or some hate-filled right winger like the one who only a few weeks before, had assaulted and insulted Adlai Stevenson in that same city.

The world is sadly out of joint when, in the midst of great prosperity, great culture, great promise, we can suddenly be thrust back into the Middle Ages; back to the time when drug-crazed youths, obeying the commands of the Old Man of the Mountain, first brought the word assassin into the lexicons.

It is a thing almost as incomprehensible as the deed itself.

As for the man whose life was taken, what can one say? We have disagreed with some of his policies, as we have disagreed with many men in power. But like any American, we mourn his death and the manner of his passing. Perhaps the best that anyone can say is to quote the words of a little Yankee lawyer as he closed in death the eyes of another President who had fallen to a mad dog's bullet:

"Now he belongs to the ages."

ADDRESS BY

Hon. James C. Auchincloss

OF NEW JERSEY

Mr. Speaker, it is difficult to express adequately one's feelings when a tragedy is so immense and so intense that it affects intimately our whole Nation and in a real way the entire world. The human mind is incapable of expressing itself under such circumstances and words in any language are entirely inadequate. In a situation of such poignant magnitude one instinctively turns to Almighty God and calls on Him for faith and comfort, guidance and courage. Such an attitude is evident everywhere today on all sides and if any possible good could come as a result of this tragic assassination, it is this renewal of our faith in the God we trust.

The late President Kennedy was a remarkable man, gifted in many ways and respected by everyone. It was not always that I agreed with his philosophy of government and perhaps his methods, but his patriotism and sincerity were never questioned and there was never doubt about his loyalty to the ideals which have made our Nation great. He was a real leader of men and although he was persistent in advancing his own ideas, he saw the point of view of those in opposition to him. I can recall few men of my time who have made a greater impression on more people than did President Kennedy. His thinking was challenging and stimulated the imagination of all our citizens. Indeed I am convinced that his mind was so active he was an enigma to those who would overthrow our form of government and baffled them. Above all he was a Christian gentleman.

People everywhere, shocked by the unexpected crisis which confronts the world by his death, have expressed real, sincere and deep sympathy. Men and women have forgotten their political differences, and overcome by loyalty to America and with confidence that his work was not in vain, are united and determined to carry on in the best tradition of our beloved country. As an example of the universal feeling I append to these remarks a telegram I received from the First Aid and Rescue Squad, Matawan, N.J., which reads as follows:

May we ask you, * * * to convey, when you think the time and place to be proper and fitting, our feeling of sympathy to Mrs. Kennedy and her family.

As further evidence of the universal feeling which is held throughout the country, I add a poem written by a good friend of mine, Paul T. Flood, of Winter Park, Fla., who is a stanch Republican, but above all a loyal American:

JOHN FITZGERALD KENNEDY—NOVEMBER 22, 1963

Would I had words to write a threnody
To honor John Fitzgerald Kennedy.
History must fully judge his acts—
I am too close—must deal with facts
Distorted by hearsay and sniping,
By petty malcontented griping.
Should he have died a World War hero
When his survival chance seemed zero?
What star of fate, what gesture callous
Beguiled him on to die in Dallas
Of bullet fire from ambushed gun?
Must we suppose his work is done?
No! No! We all helped trip that hammer!
Our national voice must lose its stammer,
Must rise in swelling, vibrant tone
Until his dream comes to its own!
Dear Jack, enjoy your rocking chair
In peace, in clear celestial air,
With certain knowledge that your drive,

Your grasp of history stays alive;
You gave us in your youth and prime
What we must carry on through time.

ADDRESS BY

Hon. Omar Burleson

OF TEXAS

Mr. Speaker, since today is especially set aside for tributes to the late President, John F. Kennedy, it seems appropriate to insert a proclamation issued by the Honorable R. R. Kelley, mayor of the city of Stamford, Tex., located in my congressional district.

It is with appreciation and justifiable pride that I make this request. The proclamation of Mayor Kelley followed a memorial service held at the First Baptist Church in Stamford on Monday following the death of our late President. It was issued on behalf of the sorrowing citizens of that city, and it pleases me to present it here, that others may know of this action:

PROCLAMATION OF THE CITIZENS OF THE CITY OF STAMFORD, TEX.

With our hearts today we proclaim our sorrow as citizens of Stamford for the death of our President, John F. Kennedy, joining in the bereavement of this our land of free men, the United States of America, and may we with bowed heads today renew our allegiance to our Nation before God, for the solemn event of November 22, 1963, at Dallas, Tex., has happened and cannot be denied and must be remembered as the day on which for a tragic moment the imperfections of man tarnished by hatred, malice, and distrust merged to take the life of our President. This moment of personal tragedy for the family of John F. Kennedy is magnified by the tragedy and bereavement felt by each true American that this sorrowful event could happen in our land and it is clear that not one of us can deny our duty to America, faithful to our heritage, that we must move forward along the road of reason toward faith in our God with charity and good will toward all men and against all bigotry and all evils that afflict our town, our Nation, and our world.

Therefore, this day is proclaimed as a day of mourning in the city of Stamford, Tex., for our President, John F. Kennedy, that we may in his memory give our best for America in the days ahead in support of our Nation under the leadership of President Lyndon B. Johnson with God's blessing.

Given under my hand and seal of office this 25th day of November A.D. 1963.

R. R. KELLEY,
Mayor, The City of Stamford, Tex.

ADDRESS BY
Hon. Steven B. Derounian
OF NEW YORK

Mr. Speaker, for the fourth time in the history of our Nation a President has been assassinated, and now this generation shares the shock and the grief experienced by other Americans before us in the wake of such a terrible tragedy. We are understanding of the great sorrow that now consumes the parents of John F. Kennedy, his wife and children, brothers and sisters, and all who held him dear, and our hearts go out to them.

We are ashamed, too, that a fellow American could have so defiled our Nation by committing this barbarous act. He had learned, as a Marxist, that assassination was a recommended method of Communist action.

But through this whole nightmare our Government and its people have performed in the highest tradition and we have, spontaneously, shown the whole world the strength of our Constitution and demonstrated the unmatched qualities of a true Republic. Never for a moment did the structure of our Government tremble. We have moved from one President to another with absolute confidence. We have a great deal to be proud of.

Our way of government and our way of life met the greatest possible test magnificently. We are able, therefore, even now, to look ahead to the future with pride and hope. And this, I am sure, is exactly what President John F. Kennedy would have wanted.

ADDRESS BY
Hon. Herman T. Schneebeli
OF PENNSYLVANIA

Mr. Speaker, as we reflect on the fine qualities of John F. Kennedy, we are impressed by the breadth of his character—compassionate, dynamic, religious, genteel, witty, warm and

vibrant, intellectual, resourceful. We could continue at length.

This was a great man, struck down in the prime of life as he was just hitting his stride. The blow was sudden and vicious, shocking and unbelievable. Assuredly, the Kennedy family is now aware of the great love which the American people, and the entire world, held for our late President.

As a nation, we are fortunate in having Lyndon B. Johnson, an able and experienced statesman and legislator, as our new President, and to him we pledge our support and understanding.

ADDRESS BY
Hon. Frank J. Becker
OF NEW YORK

Mr. Speaker, now that almost 2 weeks have passed since the tragic assassination of our late President John F. Kennedy and the murder of his assassin, I, like millions of Americans, have been offering my prayers for the repose of the soul of John F. Kennedy, and for Almighty God to bring strength and comfort to his widow, children, and family.

Words of sympathy carry very little meaning, but one message I bring to all people, speaking for myself. In politics and in my position as a Member of the House, I have had many differences of opinion with our late President, but never have I allowed these differences to reflect disrespect upon the Presidency or the individual holding that office. Why this fine young man should have had his life snuffed out in such a horrible manner, we will never really know. The answer will remain with our Maker.

ADDRESS BY
Hon. Frank J. Horton
OF NEW YORK

Mr. Speaker, a vigorous young man who began his successful career in public office in the House of Representatives has been taken from us. The tragic assassination of President Kennedy was an act of such violence to our way of life that no American will ever forget it.

The murder of President Kennedy was a dastardly blow at a brave man and an attack on the American system of government. The presidential office is the greatest elective office of our democracy—it is sacred to our citizens. Even a verbal threat directed at the President is a threat to that which we hold near and dear.

Perhaps there is no more fitting time than now to emphasize to our fellow citizens the distinctions in political life to which President Johnson referred last week in his address before the joint session. He said:

Our American unity does not depend on unanimity.

The qualities which unite us as Americans are at the very foundation of American government. They are our constitutional principles.

Public figures and their attitudes for one another have little connection with whatever partisan differences may separate them on the issues which they are elected to decide. This characteristic of judging policies apart from personalities brings to our democracy one of its finest and most distinguishing features. Freemen resolve their differences in the arena of fact where they meet in an atmosphere of mutual personal respect.

John Kennedy believed in the American dream as much as any man ever has. He fought valiantly for its realization.

Then a demented mind that had expressed preference for a totalitarianism system which threatens freedom the world over shot down that valiant fighter. Time can never diminish the cry of "Why?" that all of us uttered on that dreadful day.

In expressing this tribute to the memory of our late President, Mr. Speaker, I would like to include with my remarks the text of the weekly column I released this week to the news media in my congressional district:

THE LATE JOHN F. KENNEDY

Our Nation's heart is heavy. A man who brought enthusiasm and verve to the country's highest elective office has gone to his last reward. The assassination of President John F. Kennedy was a senseless and heinous act. His assassin did violence not only to a man but to a noble democratic institution.

I was in Rochester when the news of the President's death came. My initial reaction was doubtless the same that many had: this was some cruel joke, it just could not have happened. Then, disbelief turned to horrible shock and grief.

After sending a message of sympathy to Mrs. Kennedy and other members of the Kennedy family, I felt it essential to wire President Johnson pledging my full support to him as he was summoned to defend the Constitution in this time of national crisis. Then I immediately returned to Washington.

The Saturday following the President's death was a sorrowful occasion. The leaden skies over the Nation's Capital and the steady rain spoke their own mournful message.

Many of my colleagues gathered in the Capitol in small groups on Saturday morning. Some there had witnessed the tragedy of the day before. They found words escaped them when they tried to talk about what had happened. Nobody pressed for information. We knew from the news media the tragic sequence of events.

That afternoon, I joined hundreds of other Congressmen and Senators in a solemn journey to the White House. We went to pay our final respects to a man who had served his country faithfully.

I could not help but be struck by the contrast of this visit to the White House and the last time I had been there a few months ago. On that occasion, President Kennedy had held an evening reception for the new Members of Congress.

I recalled going in the same entrance and being greeted by the President. He and I had engaged in a few minutes of conversation. We had discussed the needs and interests of our Nation and its people. It had been an occasion to remember. Men from opposing political parties gathered as friends.

Now, the door of the White House was draped in black. There was no lively conversation. There was no conversation. We walked into the East Room, near the room where the President and I had talked on that earlier occasion. Each of us paused at the casket and then moved on. There was little said on the trip back to Capitol Hill.

Sunday and Monday were days of grief for the country, too. The sadness brought by President Kennedy's death was evident on every face.

I was in the Capitol rotunda when the honor guard bore the casket from the Lincoln catafalque to the caisson, and the cortege began the last trip from Capitol Hill. Somehow, you felt the sorrow of the President's death and the need for the country to dedicate itself to carrying on the business of freedom.

Now, that the remains of President Kennedy have been laid to rest in Arlington National Cemetery and a new administration takes the reins of Government, I feel each of us must personally accept the obligation of working for the goals that are our heritage. The bitter divisions which too frequently have occupied people in the recent past should be forgotten. Strong partisan feeling should spring from love of country, not from hate directed at opponents.

America is fortunate to have a system permitting the kind of continuity of government we are seeing today. Our memorial to John F. Kennedy should and can be, therefore, assuring the imperishability of the U.S. Government.

ADDRESS BY
Hon. Harold M. Ryan
OF MICHIGAN

Mr. Speaker, it is difficult to reconcile ourselves to the fact that our beloved President, John Fitzgerald Kennedy, will no longer be with us.

Never before have the hearts of so many millions of Americans been so touched and saddened as by the death of a beloved leader.

Our President is dead. The leadership of the Nation continues under the hand of a new Chief Executive, backed by a grieving great Nation, united in sorrow, but welded into a strength to carry forth the best of American ideals.

The sudden, tragic, and violent death of President John Fitzgerald Kennedy has stunned the people of America and those of the entire free world. The news of the terrible tragedy reaching into homes, business places, meetings, conferences, and street corners was met with a general feeling of astonishment, horror, and disbelief. As the initial shock wore off, it was replaced by a general feeling of suppressed anger, frustration and deep personal loss—a feeling that when he died, a part of us died with him. Not only had the Captain of the Ship fallen, but a beloved and respected leader had become an honored martyr.

Here in our own United States the impossible turned into reality. President Kennedy had become a victim on the altar of freedom and justice through assassination. He was a victim of the times in which we live, and all society must bear a portion of the blame.

Surviving the battles and holocaust of war, having fought and conquered physical disabilities and seemingly insurmountable social and political obstacles, he was struck down by an assassin's bullets after serving nobly for 2 years, 10 months and 2 days in the highest post our country had to offer.

President John F. Kennedy's martyrdom will forever remain a tribute to the high ideals he set as his objective. During his short lifetime, his dedication to these high objectives has insured him an everlasting place in history.

From this time forward he will live in the hearts of his fellow Americans.

We shall miss him for many reasons; foremost because of his love for his God, his country and the millions of Americans who considered him their leader and their friend.

We willingly share with his family and especially his young and bereaved wife and lovely children, the terrible sorrow that has befallen them.

As our President, he belonged to us—to all of the people of this Nation. No person could ever fill the void created by the foul deed of a perverted, twisted mind whose well-aimed shot brought to an end the close family and patriotic ties that surrounded him.

John F. Kennedy, the first President of the Catholic faith, demonstrated that he was indeed a good Christian, and also that his kind of Christianity was a strength to his serving the whole people of the whole Nation under the Constitution and under God.

I close with a poem which is truly symbolic of his belief in God and which perhaps best expresses his concept of life and death.

A VOICE FROM HEAVEN

I am home in heaven, dear ones;
Oh, so happy and so bright!
There is perfect joy and beauty
In this everlasting light.

All the pain and grief is over,
Every restless tossing passed;
I am now at peace forever,
Safely home in heaven at last.

Did you wonder I so calmly
Trod the valley of the shade?
Oh! but Jesus' love illumined
Every dark and fearful glade.

And He came himself to meet me
In that way so hard to tread;
And with Jesus' arm to lean on,
Could I have one doubt or dread?

Then you must not grieve so sorely,
For I love you dearly still;
Try to look beyond earth's shadows,
Pray to trust our Father's will.

There is work still waiting for you,
So you must not idly stand;
Do it now, while life remaineth—
You shall rest in Jesus' land.

When that work is all completed,
He will gently call you home;
Oh, the rapture of that meeting,
Oh, the joy to see you come!

ADDRESS BY

Hon. J. Vaughan Gary

OF VIRGINIA

Mr. Speaker, I join my colleagues today in paying a tribute of respect to our departed President, John Fitzgerald Kennedy, who was so ruthlessly felled by the bullet of a foul assassin on November 22. In our expressions here on the floor of the House we are also voicing the sentiment of millions of Americans throughout the United States and countless millions of people throughout the world. The full effect of his untimely death will not be known for many years to come, if ever. History will record his determination, vigor, and courage, and his accomplishments will give him a prominent place in the hall of fame, notwithstanding the fact that he had such a limited time within which to implement his far-reaching programs.

His untimely death came as a severe shock and a personal loss to all of us who had the privilege of working with him. Many of us have fond recollections of him as he served with us in this House. His attractive appearance, genial personality and personal charm ingratiated him with all who came in contact with him. His dedication to public service was an inspiration to all who worked with him.

Our hearts go out to his charming wife who labored so effectively with him during his life and displayed such magnificent grace and courage at the time of his death. Her demeanor set new standards of womanly devotion and dignity which touched the hearts of millions.

We also grieve for his two attractive children who have been deprived of the wise and sympathetic guidance of a kind and loving father.

The outpouring of high foreign dignitaries at President Kennedy's funeral was evidence of the admiration and respect he enjoyed throughout the world. This popularity, due in part to his magnetism and charm, also resulted from his firm action in the Cuban situation when firmness was required, and his sincere interest in the cause of world peace as evidenced by his sanction of the test ban treaty and other international negotiations for the promotion of a better understanding among nations.

We are most fortunate in having such an able and strong leader as President Lyndon B. Johnson to succeed him. But we should never forget that it was President Kennedy who recognized the importance of a capable and able Vice President fully informed and trained for the role and the responsibilities of the Chief Executive.

The news of President Kennedy's assassination reached me in my office here in Washington as I was preparing the radio talk I make to my constituents each Saturday night. My thoughts of that grim moment remain as my tribute to the man we eulogize today and I would like to record them here as they were carried November 23, 1963, by radio station WRVA in Richmond, Va.:

> In this time of anguish and mourning in our country, I speak to you with a heavy heart. I know that you share the sadness that has enveloped all our fellow citizens and, in a sense, the entire world because of the assassination and the death on yesterday of our President, John Fitzgerald Kennedy. The stunned lack of realization of yesterday has turned today to a great and vacant sense of sorrow. I know you will understand my loss for words to adequately express my own grief.
>
> The dastardly deed that took place in Dallas will be deplored by every American. President Kennedy's tragic and untimely death will be a great loss to this Nation and will be seriously felt throughout the world. It is a deep wound that we must bind with a pledge to continue his work for peace, justice, and freedom if meaning is to be given to the high purpose he pursued.
>
> President Kennedy was a great and good man and an exceptional leader who provided this country with wise direction in a period of great international stress. He served his country in war and peace and it was a dedicated service. He was my friend and I cherished his friendship. It was my high privilege to work with him when he was in the House of Representatives. It is still difficult to believe that he has been struck down at an age when he had so much left to give to his country.
>
> The work of the Congress will continue with what I feel will be a new sense of dedication. For now we must rally behind President Johnson, who asked yesterday, on his arrival in Washington, for our help and that of God. I ask you to join with me in pledging that help at a time when it is sorely needed.

ADDRESS BY

Hon. Porter Hardy, Jr.

OF VIRGINIA

Mr. Speaker, I am one of those who shared the privilege in January 1947 of being a freshman Congressman with John F. Kennedy. During that first term, our offices were not far apart on the third floor of the Old House Office Building. I enjoyed the friendly association we had during those years when he was in the House, and although our contacts were infrequent after he moved over to the other side of the Capitol, I took great pride in welcoming him to Virginia's largest city, Norfolk, in my district during his successful campaign for the Presidency. I look back upon that particular visit with a great deal of pride and satisfaction as well as to the privilege of serving in the Congress during the peak of his public career when he was our President.

Joining my colleagues in paying tribute to this truly great American, who was our friend, I would like to quote editorials from the two newspapers in my district. The Norfolk Virginian-Pilot carried an eloquent memorial to John F. Kennedy and his contributions to the world in its editorial "To Light the Lamps of Our Time":

In scarlet and blue and green and purple, three by three the sovereigns rode, with plumed helmets, gold braid, crimson sashes and jeweled orders flashing in the sun. After them came five heirs apparent, 40 more imperial or royal highnesses, seven queens and a scattering of special ambassadors from uncrowned countries. Together they represented 70 nations in the greatest assemblage of royalty and rank ever gathered in one place, and of its kind, the last—Barbara Tuchman, "The Guns of August."

The Kings who followed a black riderless horse on May 20, 1910, when Britain buried King Edward VII and those who followed another black riderless horse when President John Fitzgerald Kennedy was buried yesterday alike mourned men who were central to their time.

After the death of Edward VII there were but a few years left to the age of comfort and established order to which historians have given his name, and much of the royalty represented in his funeral procession was snuffed out in the upheaval.

In 1914, when the guns of August began to roar, Viscount Grey stood by his study window and said to a visitor, "The lamps are going out all over Europe, we shall not see them lit again in our lifetime." When the lamps went out, the hopes of men for a world at peace dimmed and flickered, not to be revived until a war had been fought to make the world safe for democracy, and another and greater had to be fought over the embers of the first, and a police action fought in Korea, and a host of lesser wars.

The great came from all over the world yesterday to pay their respects to the man who had begun to light the lamps in our time.

A dozen members of reigning royal families, 18 presidents, 35 foreign and defense ministers, representing 53 nations, they came to mourn the man who embodied the hope of a peaceful tomorrow for the whole world.

Far more than Americans realize, the 46-year-old President with the boyish good looks, the father of two young children, the man with the quick mind and ready wisecrack, represented freedom and generosity and man's good will to man for the entire free world and for those who aspired to freedom in the lands of the unfree.

To the Berliners who lit candles in thousands of windows in honor of the man who had only recently told them, Ich bin ein Berliner; to the Africans and the British and the Irish; to the millions who felt his loss as a personal stab and sought to express their sympathy in some way, he was the good man who tried to bridle the forces of unlimited destruction and find a path to the sunny uplands.

It was to the generation who talk of World War II as their war, and to those younger yet who hope to be spared their war, that Mr. Kennedy particularly seemed to speak. It is their idealism and intelligence that he mustered, and they grieve for his brave young widow with special understanding.

In the few months between the Cuban confrontation and the assassination of the President so senselessly last Friday, there seemed to be the beginnings of the chance of reaching some understanding, the chance of lighting lamps for tomorrow. That hope must not be buried with the President.

Let us look to the first few lamps that John Kennedy lit throughout the world.

The Norfolk Ledger-Star has beautifully expressed our pride in our great President and departed friend in a tribute entitled "Shoulder High We Bring You Home":

"Today, the road all runners come,
Shoulder high we bring you home,
And set you at your threshold down,
Townsman of a stiller town."
—A. E. HOUSMAN,
To an Athlete Dying Young.

Thousands of mourning Americans today, as yesterday, passed by the bier in the rotunda of the Capitol where lay in state the body of John F. Kennedy, touched by destiny for the ultimate reach of fame and of tragedy.

The two are almost one in the light shed by the brief candle of his life. It was tragedy that first started him to ultimate fame, for John Fitzgerald Kennedy walked in the shadow of his brother, Joseph P. Kennedy, Jr., as long as his elder brother lived. It was Joe Kennedy on whom their father counted to make the Kennedy name even more famous. It was only when Joe was killed in World War II that Jack Kennedy fell heir, some say unwillingly, to the role of public service his father planned for the eldest son.

So the gangling Kennedy cadet, so full of charm, so full of life, who in the beginning may far rather have chosen his own way, was thrust by tragedy onto the path that led to fame and prestige and power, with all the cares and troubles of an office whose demands are really known only to those who hold it, onto the path that led to his own ultimate tragedy.

During the years between the decision to seek public office since Joe could not, the young man prepared himself for the demands and opportunities of political life. He was well equipped. He had an inquiring mind. He was an intellectual. He was widely read. He surrounded himself with other intellectuals on whose knowledge and mentality he honed fine his own.

His wit, his intellect, his charm, added to a prodigious political organization, led him to the highest and most responsible position in the free world. Except for the first Cuban crisis, the disaster at the Bay of Pigs, when it appeared to many that American policy was paralyzed, he led his administration with ability and with courage through the minor crises and the major crises. America stood tall, every man and woman in it, in the Cuban showdown in October 1962. There has been criticism, since, that later on the country did not require of the Russians what at first we seemed to require; but in the moment of the missile challenge and in moments since at the Berlin wall and checkpoints, America has stood grim and fast.

From that steadfastness has developed what Khrushchev has chosen to call the "spirit of Moscow." It represented a softening, as history since the end of World War II is assessed, of historic Russian obstinacy. The President moved slowly into this new area, and he moved cautiously. He was not going to be taken in by any suggestion that a mere thaw meant all sweetness and light forever.

For linked with the Kennedy intellect, whose tools were logic and reason, was also a deep-seated pragmatism. Almost, one might say, a touch of fatalism. A man reached high, but settled for what was within his grasp; in a complex world no one person is in control of events always.

History will assess the less than 3 years of this 46-year-old man's Presidency chiefly in terms of foreign policy. There were no great turns, as history records them, in his domestic successes. Most of his ideas had not come into law.

But there was a domestic success about his shooting-star career that blazed so brightly and was extinguished near its zenith that will mark for a long time the place he held.

He brought spirit and zest and learning and intellectual pursuit to the White House where it has too rarely been seen. He created a leadership for art and drama, and his brave and lovely wife for taste and discrimination, and he brought to the highest office of the land a youthfulness that, whatever one thought of his policies, swelled the hearts of nearly all with pride and affection. He was easy to oppose as a politician; as a person he was easier to love.

His personality and presence shone with a bright and golden light. He was gay. He had the gift of laughter. He was active. "Vigor" was a favorite word, and he used it in an intellectual as well as physical context.

Not everyone was a devotee of the mystique that already had begun to surround him in his lifetime. But the seeds of legend were there and they will sprout and grow and flower now. Today the Nation thinks of the ultimate reach of fame and of tragedy that overtook John F. Kennedy. But townsman of a stiller town though he may be in the ultimate democracy of death, the shining legend will remember him in other words of Housman's:

"The time you won your town the race,
 We chaired you through the marketplace;
 Man and boy stood cheering by,
 And home we brought you shoulder-high."

ADDRESS BY

Hon. Dominick V. Daniels

OF NEW JERSEY

Mr. Speaker, a great redwood has fallen in the forest. A massive tree has been felled by an unfeeling hand and has left us numb with remorse. The sound of the fall was echoed round the world. It was the sound of the fall of our late President—John Fitzgerald Kennedy.

Our sorrow is a deep well and leaves us with an infinity of emptiness. The loss of our leader makes us feel like fatherless children, something strangely unexplainable. We are mystified.

Yet with all the tragedy that has unfolded, we are grateful for our small blessings. We were blessed first when John Fitzgerald Kennedy was born in Brookline, Mass., May 29, 1917. We were blessed again when he became our 35th President and served us faithfully for almost 3 years.

He exemplified courage as a way of life during his full-worked days on earth and exhibited that same courage until his final hour.

He believed in humanity for all men and proclaimed from his Presidential chair their unequivocal right to it.

He strengthened our faith, not only of goodness in man, but in high office. He maintained his own simplicity though there was no demand for it.

He took upon himself enormous tasks and responsibilities, and by his acts as a man wrote a new meaning for the word "duty."

He fought first with his body and later with his mind for the preservation of American ideals, and survived 4 arduous years of military combat.

He gave us peace on our land by his deeds and in the midst of its greatest enjoyment was shot down by an act known and expected only in wartime.

Why was this despicable deed perpetrated and carried to fruition? Why is the history of man besmirched with the untimely death of good men? Why must the good perish and the evil survive?

For some, conformity or violence is a single creed. For some, violence is their only byword. For some, death is their only answer in seeking solution.

But let us firmly restate and give full warning, as times demand strong action, that this Nation has no room for violent dissenters but a peaceful settlement of all differences in a manner dictated by law.

All humanity is rightly convulsed by this vicious deed which has severed the cord of life between a great man and his people—between a great man and his family.

But something strangely mystical has happened to us through all of this. It is as if the final shattering of our late President's life on that fateful black Friday caused his spirit to seep out and pervade a whole nation of people, and even the world.

He shall and will be missed, without doubt. But a small part of our fair President still lives in the heart of each of us today.

He was a great man, as well as a great leader. Our servant, as well as our master.

ADDRESS BY

Hon. Page Belcher

OF OKLAHOMA

Mr. Speaker, last week a great nation's spirits bent low and the world's head bowed in humble sympathy as the news of President John Kennedy's untimely death filled the corridors of this era.

With stunned faces and puzzled eyes, Americans everywhere quickly turned back the pages of time to reminisce and talk in low tones of this young man's life—his quick rise to fame—his ascension to the highest office and honor this Nation has to bestow. Hearts echoed a lonely cry as the realization dawned that no longer could we hear J.F.K. speak with "vigah"; no longer would we hear the spontaneity of his wit; no longer could we feel the impact of his tireless nature. President Kennedy had passed from our sights.

And then, just as our hearts strained to an almost unbearable point, we took courage—from Mr. Kennedy's own example—and "looked forward," realizing that the future of a "nation under God" falters not, however great the blow, but ever unfolds in progressive steps.

I knew John Kennedy personally. I served with him in the House of Representatives before he went to the U.S. Senate. Our philosophy of government was radically different, but I knew him to be a hard working, energetic young man and his dedication to public service gave to this country a Navy lieutenant, a Congressman, a Senator, and a President. But more than these offices this dedication poured forth upon American thought a youthful love of life and all the good it has to offer. Indeed, he had opened the door of public thought and strode in, with an easy and winning smile and lively eyes, an elegant quote and a political quip, warming the hearts of thousands not only in the United States, but around the world.

ADDRESS BY

Hon. Winfield K. Denton

OF INDIANA

Mr. Speaker, would it not be wonderful if we could only waken and find that what we experienced on that bleak Friday afternoon was but a terrible dream; that it was a forewarning, perhaps to make us better appreciate the greatness that was among us. But alas, this cannot be. What is done must be accepted. Bitterly, and with deep regret, but nonetheless accepted.

In the words of Omar Khayyam "The moving finger writes, and having writ moves on."

How can one express the sorrow felt at the passing of such a great man as John Fitzgerald Kennedy, 35th President of the United States?

Were he only an intellectual one could compose suitable poetry or prose that might, perhaps, do justice.

Were he only a courageous citizen, veteran of a great war, and hero, one might inscribe his name among other heroes and that might suffice.

Were he only a fine example of a dedicated patriot one could, perhaps, erect a statue or monument that would suffice.

Were he only a loving father and husband one

could commiserate with the bereaved family, share in their sorrow, miss the departed, and perhaps that might suffice.

But President John F. Kennedy was all these, and more.

All these attributes were combined with many others to make him a shrewd and capable leader of men.

We must all remember the vigorous, well planned campaign that led him through the nomination and election to the office of the Presidency.

We must marvel at the way he surrounded himself with capable and efficient aides and advisors and pushed this country forward. How he strived for improved conditions both at home and abroad and how he worked for world peace.

We must remember that in almost all things he attempted he was a great success.

What made this man the great and able leader that he was?

I would like to remember his great friendliness, his capacity for work and for play. And I cannot forget the world of experience he gained while serving as a Member of the House, and of the Senate. Experience and knowledge that he put to good use in the office of the Presidency; remembering the trials and tribulations of Members of both Houses, and trying to make their jobs perhaps a little easier.

The dastardly deed that took from us our beloved President, John Fitzgerald Kennedy, will not soon be forgotten. It was an almost unbelievable shock to the entire country, yea to the whole world.

The tribute paid to President Kennedy by the leaders of the world was indeed heartwarming. It showed not only the respect with which they held for this man but also the respect they hold for this Nation, which President Kennedy worked so hard to strengthen.

Although John Fitzgerald Kennedy is gone, his influence and spirit live on. And I am sure that we shall all hold dear the memory of our departed colleague and try to live up to the standards of devotion to our country which he set.

Many times he said he would willingly give up his life for his country.

Let us now vow that although he was called upon to make this supreme sacrifice he did not die in vain. Let us always remember those words from his inaugural address and to heed them in our daily deliberations on the problems of this country. "Ask not what your country can do for you. Ask what you can do for your country."

ADDRESS BY

Hon. John J. Rhodes

OF ARIZONA

Mr. Speaker, with the passing of President John F. Kennedy this Nation loses not only its first citizen, but one of its most able sons. The intellect given by the Almighty to President Kennedy impressed itself upon the records of this House, the other body, and on the Presidency. Seldom in the history of the world has one so young been placed by his fellow men in positions of such high influence. Seldom has one so placed made such a profound impact upon his country, his fellow citizens, and the world.

The Creator also endowed President Kennedy with all of the charm usually attributed to the Irish. His personality endeared him to his countrymen and to his friends.

His passing is not only a great loss to the United States of America and to Americans, but to the entire world. Most especially, it is a blow of the first magnitude to his wife, to his young family, to his mother and father, and to his sisters and brothers. To all of them, and to all of the Americans who felt that in a great sense this man was theirs, Mrs. Rhodes and I extend our deepest sympathy.

ADDRESS BY

Hon. Joel T. Broyhill

OF VIRGINIA

Mr. Speaker, the assassination of John Fitzgerald Kennedy will forever rank among the most infamous crimes ever perpetrated against humanity. Regardless of political persuasion or personal philosophy, we all recognize that this deed took from us a great intellect who, without doubt, would have written boldly across the pages of history. And history will be the final judge of the magnitude of these times and the impact this man had upon them.

I am personally convinced the tragic loss of President Kennedy will be profound and that the shape of things to come will bear the indelible imprint of his personality.

I join with the people of Virginia and of the Nation in mourning his death and our hearts go out to his widow and children.

ADDRESS BY
Hon. Walter Norblad
OF OREGON

Mr. Speaker, I wish to join with my colleagues in paying tribute to the late President John F. Kennedy.

In 1947, Mr. Kennedy and I were freshmen Congressmen. Although we were on opposite sides politically this never affected my personal friendship with him, nor my high respect for him as a Member of Congress and later as our President.

Our Nation, and indeed the entire world, have lost a great man who labored so much for the betterment of all mankind.

Mrs. Norblad and I extend to Mrs. Kennedy our deep heartfelt sympathy in her courageous bereavement.

ADDRESS BY
Hon. Ben Reifel
OF SOUTH DAKOTA

Mr. Speaker, on Friday, November 22, South Dakota joined the world in mourning the tragic loss of President Kennedy.

The citizens of South Dakota felt they knew this man, even though few of them had met him. On some issues their views differed from his, but throughout his nearly 3 years in the White House they respected John F. Kennedy as their President. He was the leader of the Nation and the free world. Like all Americans, South Dakotans felt they knew him as a person and now they feel a deep personal loss.

John Kennedy visited South Dakota on three separate occasions—once as a U.S. Senator, once as a candidate for the Presidency, and once as the President of the United States.

On June 19, 1960, Senator Kennedy addressed a State convention of the American Legion at the Sioux Falls Coliseum.

Three months later, Candidate Kennedy addressed an estimated audience of 75,000 persons at the national plowing contest near Brandon. Rain poured down the day before Senator Kennedy's appearance and the field had become a sea of mud. As he began to speak, the rain resumed. Anticipating the address the following day by Vice President Richard Nixon, Senator Kennedy reminded his audience with characteristic wit that the rain falls on Democrats and Republicans alike.

President Kennedy's last visit to South Dakota was on August 17, 1962, when he dedicated power facilities at Oahe Dam near Pierre. It was a bright and radiant day, typical of the Dakota prairie country, as the President delivered his "power on the line" talk.

Senator Kennedy was adopted by the Sioux Nation on his first visit to the State. He received a colorful headdress and the name "Chief Eagle."

Indeed, South Dakotans felt they knew this man. They respected and honored him as the elected President of the United States.

Born to wealth, John Kennedy strived to serve those not so generously endowed. With sensitive consciousness, he vigorously sought to advance those ideas which he so fluently expounded and in which he believed.

The tragic death of the President has given pause for Americans to think twice about the future. As so ably put in one South Dakota newspaper, the episode in Dallas "does not cast a shadow on the whole of America." The shadow lies on the fringe—on the edge of extreme of both the left and the right. It is here that the violence and hate and bigotry lie.

If, by his passing, we are reminded of our duty to the truths of our heritage, our devotion to God and country, our obligation to a free society in order to keep it free, our rededication to "the great task remaining before us," then John F. Kennedy did not die in vain.

May God bless his memory.

Hon. William T. Cahill

OF NEW JERSEY

Mr. Speaker, the assassination of John Fitzgerald Kennedy, the 35th President of the United States, in Dallas, Tex., on November 22, 1963, shocked the entire world. The death of any President is a crushing blow to any nation but the demise of President Kennedy at age 46, at the very height of his physical and intellectual capabilities had the impact of a hydrogen bomb on all of the people of the United States. I suppose every Member of this House will forever remember exactly where he was and what he was doing on November 22, when the awful news of the fatal shot was broadcast in sad and ofttimes tearful words throughout the Nation. All Americans were stunned. Our minds were seared as if by a hot iron by the news. None of us will ever forget that moment. Most of us likewise will never forget the man. For John F. Kennedy was indeed a man to remember. For those of us in the Congress who came to know him, it was a tremendous personal loss. President Kennedy was many things to many people. He was at one and the same time a devoted husband, an obedient son, a loving father, a courageous President and an inspiring world leader. Few men in the history of the country and indeed the world accomplished what he did in 46 short years. A war hero, a Pulitzer Prize winner, an author and intellectual, a Member of the House of Representatives for 6 years and of the U.S. Senate for 8 years, he was elected by his fellow citizens at the age of 43 to lead the greatest Nation in the world at the most dangerous and difficult period in the world's history. In spite of every accomplishment, however, President Kennedy still possessed the virtue of humanity and the love of fellowmen that made him accessible and loved by all the peoples throughout the world. Possessing all material things, he spent most of his life fighting for those who had little of the world's possessions. He was truly a champion of the underdog, the needy and the oppressed. He truly "walked with kings yet had the common touch." President Kennedy had already earned his place in American history. His martyr's death, however, will forever enshrine him in the hearts of all present and future Americans. Many of us must ask: "Why was this young, able, personable and dynamic leader taken from us in our day of greatest need?" Only God of course knows the answer to that question. Most Americans, however, will find some comfort and solace in the thoughtful words of Bishop Fulton Sheen who wrote concerning President Kennedy's death, "Nothing is as democratic as death for all of a sudden there is no distinction between Jew or Greek, male or female, Socialist or totalitarian, Republican or Democrat. All suddenly realize the wickedness of the world in which we live. Not until we see what is done to the humanity loving do we grasp the frenzied hate which will not be stilled by the tears of a little John or the whimpering sadness of a Caroline. Everyone now says: 'The world has lost a great leader.' True, but in the greater tomorrow we may speak of 'Our second emancipator.' It takes a sacrificial death to break down the walls of division. When some men refuse to acknowledge others as their equals under God words will not unite them. It takes blood. It took a Lincoln's blood to unite a nation; it has taken a Kennedy's blood to prepare for the equality of men in that same nation. This is the mystery of his death, the price men destined for greatness have to pay to prove that love is stronger than hate."

The death of President Kennedy must serve as a warning to all peoples everywhere. Life indeed is short and eternity is forever. Hopefully, President Kennedy's sacrificial death will be the inspiration needed to encourage all of us to live together in brotherly love and to devote ourselves to more useful and unselfish lives so that we in our own way may carry on the work commenced by President Kennedy. I join all Americans in expressing sincere sympathy to Mrs. Kennedy and the entire Kennedy family.

Hon. W. Pat Jennings

OF VIRGINIA

Mr. Speaker, the late President John F. Kennedy was a friend of the people in the Ninth

District of Virginia, which I have the privilege of representing.

We, the people of the Ninth, gave a majority of our votes to the Democratic nominees of John F. Kennedy and Lyndon B. Johnson in the election of 1960.

We in the Ninth shared the deep shock and sorrow that came to the Nation and the world with the assassination of President Kennedy. It is impossible to find adequate words to convey our grief—to adequately summarize our respect for the Office of the Presidency and the man who occupied it so ably for almost 3 years.

Perhaps the most fitting tribute I can make to the late President is to record his concern for the problems that face the people of districts like mine and to express our gratitude for this concern.

That John F. Kennedy, son of a wealthy family, an Irish Catholic, and New England Yankee, would understand the needs of southwest Virginia's coal miners, family farmers, and small businessmen was in itself remarkable. But he did more: First, he conveyed his sense of caring to these people; he won, as I said, a majority of their votes for his Presidential candidacy. Second, he translated his care into economic action programs that have benefited and will continue to benefit my people and their counterparts across the country for generations to come. Thirdly, and most important, he included us not only in his practical programs to improve our economic lot, but also in his dream of moving America forward educationally, spiritually, and culturally.

Last month, in tribute to his friend, Poet Robert Frost, our late President said:

I look forward to an America which will not be afraid of grace and beauty * * * which will steadily enlarge cultural opportunities for all of our citizens * * *. which commands respect not only for its strength but for its civilization as well. And, I look forward to a world which will be safe not only for democracy and diversity but also for personal distinction.

The President was speaking to an audience at Amherst College in Massachusetts, but we in Virginia's Ninth District knew he was speaking to us as well.

While still a Senator, John F. Kennedy went to my district and addressed a dinner meeting there. In his comments he said that it is "better to light a candle than to curse the darkness."

The Bristol Herald-Courier, in editorializing on the President's death, mentions this dinner and the President's comments. I herewith include this editorial in these brief remarks:

[From the Bristol (Va.) Herald-Courier, Nov. 24, 1963]

JOHN F. KENNEDY: TOUCHED BY FATE

"I do not pretend to say that the future will always be easy," President Kennedy said in an address here in 1958 while still a Senator. "There will be crises, there will be problems."

But, he continued, "we can go forward to a new and better America, never satisfied with things as they are, daring always to try the new, daring nobly and doing greatly."

In the face of a "somber and uncertain future," he implored, "we ask you to bring candles to illuminate our way."

That future was not easy; it was filled with crises and with problems; it was more somber and uncertain than any believed possible on that blustery Friday evening in March little more than 5 years ago.

There have been candles along the way, sometimes burning brightly, sometimes flickering in those ebbtides which grace, at intervals, the lives of all men.

But now the candles are multiplied a thousandfold. Unbelievably, shockingly, tragically, malevolently, the future of which Mr. Kennedy spoke has ended for him. He is dead, and there remains only the heartbreak of mourning and the beginning of an assessment which will not end in our lifetime.

John Fitzgerald Kennedy was touched by fate and possessed of those qualities which, in fine blend, lift men up and make them great.

He could inspire a nation and a world with his words. He could restate the cause of freedom, the purpose of these United States of America. And he could draw visions of the best that men can become if they but bend themselves to the task. "Let us begin," he said.

John Kennedy did not succeed in his every effort. No one can, for there are some problems which men cannot solve, and only the courageous choose to try. He chose to try, and in the trying to brave the slings and arrows— and finally the bullets—which came his way.

But while he did not succeed, at least he began. And though he cannot finish, at least he has made men more mindful of their own agonies and of the agonies of their fellows at home and abroad. And men so mindful are men more willing to wrestle with those seemingly insoluble problems which grind conscience and spirit.

He was a leader without contemporary peer, a man loved and hated with equal passion, a man who challenged men to meet him at the water's edge and fight against the tides which wash humanity with tyranny and grief.

Some fought with him. Others fought against him. But all now mourn, forgetful of political passions, unified as Americans are always unified in time of tragedy.

This is such a time.

We in the mountains of southwest Virginia are not given to excesses of emotion. But, in the tragic loss of our President our sorrow has no bounds.

As President Kennedy's casket was lifted from the caisson and carried to its final resting place in Arlington National Cemetery, an Air Force bagpipe band played the doleful hymn, "The Mist Covered the Mountain." In southwest Virginia, where we loved Jack Kennedy, and where we needed his understanding, his faith, and his courage, mist does indeed cover our mountains as we grieve our loss.

ADDRESS BY

Hon. John D. Dingell

OF MICHIGAN

Mr. Speaker, I join hundreds of millions of people around the world in sorrow at the brutal and untimely death of our beloved President, John Fitzgerald Kennedy.

History will recall as a part of his epitaph that he was among the greatest of our Presidents. His good works for equality of all men, his drive for adequate social legislation, and a decent standard of living for all Americans, and his efforts to secure a meaningful and lasting world peace with freedom for all, speak louder than any words that can be said by his friends and admirers.

The shot that snuffed out his life robbed the United States of an effective and well-beloved leader, who had successfully recast, for the better, the image of the United States around the world, and denied Americans, and the world, the leadership of a man who had only begun to make his contribution to mankind.

God be merciful to John Fitzgerald Kennedy. He was a great President, and a good man. Americans everywhere pray for the repose of his soul and for strength and peace for his grieving wife and family.

ADDRESS BY

Hon. Lucien N. Nedzi

OF MICHIGAN

Mr. Speaker, our Nation grieves. We grieve for our beloved and martyred President, John F. Kennedy. There was stunned disbelief at the terrible deed, then anguished hope that he

would somehow survive, then a feeling of deep emptiness and sorrow. We who served under him, we who loved him, we who shared him with free men and women everywhere, can hardly yet believe that he is dead.

We are yet numb at this, one of the greatest tragedies in the history of mankind. And, in the solemn words of Adlai Stevenson, we "will bear the grief of his death to the end of our days."

By a twist of fate, I was in Texas with the Presidential party the day before the terrible tragedy. There was President Kennedy and his beautiful and courageous wife, in top form. Oh, the brilliance of the man. Oh, the wit. Oh, the style. Fortunate the Nation which had such a leader. So much of our optimism for the future, I thought, was wrapped up in this man who was so young, so much a man of action, with so much greatness yet before him. Then, in a split second, all of it was snuffed out. Up to that split second, any one of dozens of conceivable circumstances of fate could have intervened to make that fatal second impossible—but, to our grief, none did. Thus it was that, still stunned, still hoping it was all a bad dream, we came to the gravesite on the cold slopes of Arlington. Here, where he had just 2 weeks before honored our war dead, we gathered to pay our last respects—the humblest of men and the greatest of men, heads of state and anonymous citizens, merged in silent and grieving tribute.

An old proverb says: "A tree is best measured when it's down." The enormity of this disaster, the dimensions of its consequences, is hour by hour growing on us. The greatness of John F. Kennedy, mankind's love for him, the miracle of his great personal qualities, our compassion for his dear wife and children, has no bounds. The work of our Nation will go on because it must go on. But the world will never be quite the same for any of us.

ADDRESS BY

Hon. Melvin R. Laird

OF WISCONSIN

Mr. Speaker, President Kennedy is dead. The untold grief that has gripped the Nation and the world is beyond measure. Our Chief Executive, the leader of 190 million people, has been taken from us. The head of the leadernation of the free world has been struck down by an assassin's bullets.

Even yet, the magnitude of the deed—in fact, the reality of the deed—is incomprehensible. Since its perpetration, the whole world, it seems, has acquired an aura of unreality. Words are inappropriate, expressions inadequate. Words cannot possibly be fashioned to convey the deep sense of grief and loss that has come to every American, to every human being.

Our President is dead, and the hand that allegedly took him, itself now lifeless, quit this world without a hint of the reason for this unreasoning act.

Mr. Speaker, in the person of John F. Kennedy was embodied the office of the President of the United States. As an American citizen, I am outraged at this unspeakable blow to the very heart of our Republic. As an elected public servant, every fiber of my being cries out against this unbearably heinous crime. As a Republican, I join with my colleagues from across the aisle in mourning the untimely loss of their party leader who was the President and leader of us all.

To his wife and children, to his mother and father, to his brothers and sisters, to his many close, personal friends, who must all carry on as the country and the world must, I offer my deepest and most heartfelt sympathies.

To Almighty God, whose inscrutable will is often obscured to those of us who remain behind, I offer my prayers for our late President, and for his bereaved family and country.

And to our new President and to all who must pick up the reins and carry on with a continuity that must be a wonder to all the peoples of the world, my support in this trying but sure and steady period of transition is pledged.

ADDRESS BY

Hon. Thomas N. Downing

OF VIRGINIA

Mr. Speaker, the death of President John F. Kennedy is an awful truth that our Nation has found almost impossible to bear. Our Nation's

heart has bled. Yet, we are a courageous people in a Nation that has long survived under a constitutional form of government, and we will survive the loss.

Our people loved and respected John F. Kennedy. They were proud of the vigor and the vitality, the youthful enthusiasm, that he stamped on our national image. He was intelligent and he was earnest and he cared about the people. The people responded to him as the epitome of the new pioneer who would lead them to the New Frontier.

John F. Kennedy was born with hereditary riches, yet he dedicated himself to elevating the impoverished; he was blessed with hereditary intelligence, yet he believed that knowledge should be available to all mankind; he was nurtured to an early understanding of political ideologies, yet he knew that America should be an example for men—a government of the people, by the people, and for the people.

The continuing heart and the continuing hopes of our Nation—what has been called the genius of America—will attach themselves most naturally to men with a sense of history and an ability to place personal power and prestige below the Nation's aspirations. John F. Kennedy understood the genius of America. He put his Nation above his party; he revered freedom above personal security, and he tolerated no threat to peace.

Even a world as complex as our world must be still only a world of men. John F. Kennedy lived as a President, but he died as a man. There is a oneness that we all can feel in death—perhaps as there can never be in life. Our Nation felt it, each one of us felt it. One hundred and ninety million Americans knew the sorrow of our loss as if we were one when the man, John F. Kennedy, died. He was our President, and we sorrowed, but he was a man and our sorrow was even greater.

A poet has written that old men go to death, but death comes to the young. No man can truly choose his life or his death. He can only do his best. John F. Kennedy lived proudly and courageously; he died proudly and courageously. Death made his life brief, but he was beloved by his people and he has found an early immortality.

Men who live near the sea know that smooth seas never make skillful mariners. John F. Kennedy lived by and loved the sea, as a man who would rather be a skillful mariner than dwell on calm seas. Sailors say that God is closest to a man at sea. The awesome power, the strength of the sea, the beauty of the sea help mold the character of men who, like John F. Kennedy, had learned to live bravely and die, even on adverse seas.

John F. Kennedy is no longer our President, but he is still our beloved friend. His death makes time seem shorter and days seem longer for all of us. We will miss him, but his demise—so unbearable a few days ago—may be eased if we recall, with Joseph Hall, that Adam, the first sinful man, did not die first; Cain, the first evil man, did not die first. Abel, a righteous man, was the first to die. God must love the ones he takes first.

ADDRESS BY

Hon. Jackson E. Betts

OF OHIO

Mr. Speaker, many words have been written and spoken about the tragedy of President Kennedy's death and I want mine to be among them. No one can experience a sad event such as this and feel that he has adequately expressed himself. Plainly and simply I join those who mourn the untimely passing of a young and eloquent leader. But the greatest tribute is not so much in our words as in the silent respect the entire Nation exhibited during the ordeal of the days immediately following the assassination. I saw it in the faces of the grief stricken who waited in front of the Capitol and the throngs that lined the route of the flag-draped casket as it was taken to Arlington Cemetery. It was also manifest in the leaders of foreign nations who humbly followed the cortege on its last journey. I mention this because it expresses much more effectively than I can the unity of the American people and the respect of the rest of the world in paying tribute not only to the fallen President but also to the great Nation of which he was the head.

ADDRESS BY

Hon. Alexander Pirnie

OF NEW YORK

Mr. Speaker, since the tragedy of November 22 the world has poured out its heart in grief. Much has been spoken and written about the admirable qualities of John Fitzgerald Kennedy as a man and as our President. Only history will confirm his greatness and mark that fateful day as one of the darkest in the life of our Nation. As our country's leader he symbolized our hopes and purposes as well as those of the free world. The heavy responsibilities of his great office have been borne by all his predecessors but John Kennedy brought to the Presidency at a critical hour an unprecedented youthfulness and vigor which cloaked him with a special appeal. Under his leadership, the Nation and the free world had so much to anticipate. In so many fields America stood on the brink of new achievement. Thrilling breakthroughs were occurring in space technology and visible signs of a thaw on the cold war seemed apparent. Hope and thanksgiving were in our hearts. Then the blow was struck. Those hopes were crushed by the cowardly bullet fired by a wretched assassin whose mind was warped by the very communistic doctrines which divide the world and which we have sworn to oppose.

He left many enduring contributions but the Peace Corps best symbolizes his noble concept of public service as man's highest privilege and greatest responsibility. It will remain a living memorial to its founder.

Foremost, we admired his courage. As PT boat commander and as Commander in Chief, he ignored personal danger in his commitment to duty. He died in the service of his country and deserves the praise due a hero and the honor owed a martyr.

Saddened as we are by his death, we are proud of the reaction of our Nation. His grieving family, our new President, all of Government and, indeed, all our people have responded with a display of courage, unity, and dedication which gives heart to all the world. America will march on. Our national fabric is strong and our concept of free society deeply rooted.

Mr. Speaker, many will endeavor to express their great sorrow at the tragic passing of our beloved President, but few will find words adequate to do so. The impact of such an event is so deep and so special as almost to defy expression.

An assassin's bullet has robbed our Nation and the free world of a young and vigorous leader. Without warning, and while the cheers of thousands were ringing in his ears, his brilliant career came to an end. A cowardly, criminal act has done that which enemy action so nearly accomplished in the dark waters of the South Pacific.

In the intervening years, John F. Kennedy lived an exciting, useful, and memorable life. The youngest man ever to be elected President, he demonstrated a poise and resourcefulness which belied his years. He worked hard at his task. He was articulate and forceful. He made friends at home and abroad. He was dedicated to his public service, and to it, he made the supreme gift of self. This, a grateful, yet sorrowing Nation, will remember.

In our grief we should particularly remember the sorrow within the family circle. Our hearts go out to his wife and children who have been robbed of a young husband and father. Little Caroline and John-John have crept into the hearts of millions. They and their brave mother will be remembered in our prayers.

We trust this sad hour will cause us to be even more dedicated to the welfare of our country and the preservation of all that is best in our national life.

ADDRESS BY

Hon. Samuel S. Stratton

OF NEW YORK

Mr. Speaker, words are most difficult to find today to express the sorrow and loss that all of us here feel at the tragic death of our friend and beloved President, John F. Kennedy. Yet inadequate as any words may be, I rise to join in paying my own tribute to one of the greatest men who has ever occupied the American Presidency.

Mr. Speaker, John F. Kennedy was a unique person and brought a unique spirit to the Presidency. Others have mentioned this quality—it was a lift, a special quality of grace, a kind of personal style that we have never quite seen before and perhaps shall never see again.

This indeed, as Theodore H. White wrote in this week's issue of Life, was "for one brief fleeting moment, Camelot." All of us in this House have felt that unusual quality. No President ever did more to create a warm and understanding relationship with Members of the Congress. Without in any way detracting from the awe and respect in which we always hold his great Office, he and Mrs. Kennedy made us come to regard the White House not as a national shrine nor some top cold war command post, but as a gracious home where friends could meet and come to know each other better. He was not only our leader, he was also our dear friend.

Mr. Speaker, the tremendous outpouring of grief from Americans all over our country and from people in every walk of life all over the world, have shown how well John Fitzgerald Kennedy, even in a comparatively brief period of service in his great Office, had established the same warm and intimate relationship with millions of persons who were never privileged to know him as well as we have been.

Mr. Speaker, of course John Fitzgerald Kennedy will go down in history as one of our greatest Presidents. His life was an embodiment of the courage which he so much admired—not only physical courage, but moral courage too. His cool and calm courage during the Cuban crisis last October marked one of the real turning points in our Nation's history and perhaps in the whole cold war. It was the same cool and calm courage he displayed in the Solomon Islands back in 1943; it was the same courage he displayed in riding through the streets of Dallas on November 22 without the slightest regard for his own personal safety.

Because he was cut down so early in his life and so early in his Presidential career, John F. Kennedy did not complete the work he had set out on January 21, 1961, to do. But John Kennedy knew this was to be true. The tasks he set for himself and for our Nation were tasks that would not soon be fully achieved. "We shall not complete this job," he told us, "in the first 100 days or in the first 1,000 days. We may not see it completed," he said, "perhaps even in our lifetime or in the life of our generation. "But," he said, "let us begin."

Mr. Speaker, John F. Kennedy was given only about that first 1,000 days to get his program and his country started toward the bright goals and objectives he so clearly saw ahead.

Under John Kennedy, Mr. Speaker, we did begin, as he asked us to do. And now that John Kennedy has been taken so suddenly from us it is up to us who are left behind to carry on that great work which he so nobly began. Perhaps we too may not be able fully to complete that work either, but we must certainly do our best to push it forward as he would wish us to do.

When John Kennedy died his ideals and his objectives ceased, Mr. Speaker, to be purely personal or even partisan aims. They became a part of the goals of our whole American democracy and our great tradition. And it is up to all of us, regardless of geographic location or party, to join in working to build that world of freedom, of peace, of equality, of growth, and of continuing improvement.

This is surely no easy task, Mr. Speaker, but we who loved President Kennedy, we who were privileged to know him and to work with him, we who gather here today to pay him our humble tributes—surely we can do no less. And as we here in this House and those millions of others in every part of the world, join together to bring into being the kind of America and the kind of world to which he was so deeply committed, we shall be giving him the greatest possible tribute and shall be truly remembering his memory in the days to come.

Mr. Speaker, in pausing to remember President Kennedy, there come flooding back to my mind those lines of the poet, Lawrence Binyon, written in memory of all young men who have given their lives in the service of their country:

> He shall grow not old
> As we that are left grow old;
> Age shall not wither him
> Nor the years condemn.
> At the going down of the sun
> And in the morning
> We will remember him.

ADDRESS BY

Hon. Martha W. Griffiths

OF MICHIGAN

Mr. Speaker, the people of the 17th District of Michigan, as I am sure the people in the rest of America were numb with shock and grief when they learned that their President, John F. Kennedy, had been assassinated.

No words of remorse are sufficient. No words of sympathy and love to his widow, his children and his family are adequate. I agree with President Johnson that the proper way to show our respect for our late brilliant President, who sought in his time the brotherhood of man and peace in the world, can best be done by passing his programs immediately.

ADDRESS BY

Hon. Leonor Kretzer Sullivan

OF MISSOURI

Mr. Speaker, the shock and the sorrow which we have felt in these last 13 days will remain in our memories as long as we live. We shall never cease regretting that John Fitzgerald Kennedy was not spared long enough to complete his work on the many imaginative ideas which characterized his administration. We shall never know, of course, to what heights of greatness he would have ascended if he had been able to serve two full terms in office.

But while our hearts are heavy as we contemplate the might-have-beens in the promising future of so able a man as President of the United States, we have now had nearly 2 weeks in which to put into some perspective the greatness which he had already achieved.

The eulogies which have appeared in news media of every shade of political opinion have attested to the courage, the integrity, the imagination, the decency of this man who for nearly 3 years stood as the exemplar of leadership in the free world. Many things about President

Kennedy's administration have been singled out in these past 13 days for particular attention and comment: The energy with which he pursued the cause of freedom and of understanding on the international level; the intelligence and ability of the men and women he selected for high office in his administration; the greatness with which he spoke and wrote of the meaning of American democracy; his cool and intelligent handling of critical and explosive threats to our security and to peace—the list of his achievements in office is long and impressive.

Even those who strongly opposed him politically have freely acknowledged the great gift for leadership which he brought to the Presidency. Americans without exception will remember not only the events of the past 13 days but also their deep personal involvement in those events. As the years go by, the drama surrounding the death and the burial of John Fitzgerald Kennedy will remain vividly alive to all who witnessed any part of that drama—whether in Washington as participants in one of the most moving episodes in American history, or whether as viewers of history-in-the-making on a television screen.

The sorrow with which we bade farewell to our fallen Commander-in-Chief in the battle for freedom is tempered by what I can only describe as a sense of joy and exultation that we have been privileged in our lifetime to have had a man of such unique talents serving as the leader of our country during a period of great danger and of great challenge.

Few men since Jefferson were able to breathe such life into the principles of American democracy—to make them meaningful to our citizens. His eloquence ranked him among the most effective spokesmen we have ever had for American idealism. The sincerity of his convictions has touched the hearts of all mankind. Negroes who write to me call him the Second Emancipator; Jews, Catholics, Protestants unite in praising his spiritual qualities—his humanity, and his respect for the dignity of the individual.

History will ultimately assess John Fitzgerald Kennedy in ways none of us can now foretell. His political innovations—such as the Peace Corps, his ability to communicate to the American people and to the peoples of other nations his commitment to decency and to human rights and to peace, the vast store of knowledge which

he brought to his tasks in the most burdensome and demanding job in the world—these things, among many others, will keep President Kennedy's memory bright as a shining example of excellence among America's great public men.

One of the finest things President Kennedy did for his country and for his people, for all Americans, was to reestablish the concept of politics as an exciting force, a stimulating outlet for brilliance and imagination, a form of activity which can bring not only challenge but pleasure to those who, like John F. Kennedy, find a nobility in public service for public good.

Prior to his administration, we were often told, we who serve in elective office, that politics had no appeal to youth. Youth, we were told, looked upon political activity as self-serving and somehow not quite respectable.

But from the moment John F. Kennedy came upon the national scene as a candidate for President of the United States, this concept began to change. It was not merely because he was unusually young for the role he sought to play. Rather, it was the fact that John F. Kennedy reached out to youth and enlisted them as participants in politics as the most exciting aspect of American life, whether or not they were old enough to be voters. He made the history books come alive. He took patriotism off of a marble pedestal and put it into our daily lives, by translating into action and example the truths of our heritage which sometimes .become lost in platitudes.

Mr. Speaker, when we met in bitter cold on the steps of the Capitol of the United States on that January day nearly 3 years ago to install a new President, we knew from his inspiring inaugural address that we were participating in what would be a great new chapter of American history. And when we met in the rotunda of the Capitol a week ago Sunday to say farewell to the mortal remains of John F. Kennedy, we knew we had been privileged, as few Congresses were privileged, to have worked with greatness in the office of President of the United States. A chapter had ended, but the lessons learned and the achievements recorded in that chapter of American history represented by the administration of John F. Kennedy will forever fortify the people of this country in facing the perils, the challenges, and the opportunities of new eras under new leaders, but under the same basic principles which have always guided the United States of America.

Miss him? Yes, Mr. Speaker, those of us privileged to know John Fitzgerald Kennedy and to work with him in great causes will forever miss his bright smile and great gifts for leadership. Our country will miss him. The world will miss him. But there will always be joy in our hearts when we remember not how he died but how he lived, and what he accomplished, and how he loved the job in which he served with such magnificent skill.

ADDRESS BY

Hon. Willard S. Curtin

OF PENNSYLVANIA

Mr. Speaker, today we all join in remembrance of the memory of the late President John F. Kennedy, who was struck down by an assassin's bullet on November 22.

He was the fourth President of these United States whose term of office was cut short by such a despicable act.

The late President Kennedy served his country with ability and distinction both in the military service during World War II and later in the Halls of Congress and then in the Office of President.

This tragic assassination left this country in a state of shock, sorrow, and dismay which will be with us for a long time.

The sympathy of the world has gone out to the late President's family.

ADDRESS BY

Hon. Melvin Price

OF ILLINOIS

Mr. Speaker, the term our late President Kennedy was allowed to serve was short—2 years, 10 months, 2 days. I am sure it is the sense of this House that he crowded into this brief span so much activity, such urgency of purpose, such vitality of spirit, that he left a permanent imprint on our Nation.

Many of us in this House today served with John Kennedy when he was one of us, a Repre-sentative from Massachusetts. Many knew him when he moved to other fields of public activity. We have all known him in the Presidency to which he brought both zest and wisdom, both courage to act and patient resolution in seeking to persuade others to act.

It has been said by some, because he did not wear his emotions on his sleeve, that he failed to convey in his programs a sense of moral commitment that could warm other men's souls. The criticism, if that is what it is, has always seemed to me a dubious one. Here was a President who could talk about poverty in America and a stronger minimum wage law to a labor convention, where it would be expected, and then hit the same theme of poverty in America to an entirely different audience, such as the group of scholars and writers and intellectuals recently gathered at Amherst College for the ground-breaking ceremonies for a new library honoring the memory of the poet Robert Frost.

There was no political need, assuredly, for John Kennedy to curry favor with his academic audience by discussing the obligation of our best educated and most-favored citizens to play their part in meeting the problem of poverty. But that is precisely what he did. He was deeply disturbed by the discovery, in cold statistics, that we have vast quantities of "inherited poverty" as well as "inherited wealth" in this country, and he urged the young men of Amherst College in their future lives to help do something about it. To me, that spells a moral commitment to the achievement of a moral end.

The people, in any case, very often have a sure instinct for the style and the flavor of their leadership. Their estimate of John Fitzgerald Kennedy's leadership was measured in the outpouring of personal grief when he was senselessly and most savagely struck down. Men wept tears not only for his youth, for his lovely young wife and his children, for his family, but for the harsh fact that he was not allowed to finish his work. Men and women the world over wept in personal grief because they recognized in him a man of peace, a man worthy of trust even in other nations.

There were two incidents that, for many, spelled out John Kennedy's courage and integrity, and both of them are connected with the sorry situation in Cuba.

With one, we are still entirely familiar—how

he forced the removal of Soviet missiles and rocket launchers from Cuban bases with the utmost frankness to the American people and with the utmost candor to the Soviet Union, while pushing the deployment of our military strength to the exact point where it would produce the necessary results without leaving the potential enemy no way to pull back from the danger.

The other incident was, in its time, a disaster— the Bay of Pigs episode, which left us all ashamed and unhappy and with a feeling that our affairs were in disarray. I was never prouder of John Fitzgerald Kennedy than when he stood before his first press conference after that sad event and bluntly acknowledged that whatever blame attached to any officials should be laid at his door. He was our Chief Executive, he had allowed the plans to proceed, he had made other decisions— the responsibility was his, as always it must be a President's ultimate responsibility for the decisions to go or to stop, and he took it, publicly and without hesitancy.

We shall be legislating in this Congress for years to come, I believe, in the area of proposals first urged on us by President Kennedy or perhaps renewed after a long lapse.

Some of them are most certain to be acted on by us in the upcoming 2d session of the 88th Congress, including proposals of great sweep and significance in such fields as human rights and the education of our young people. Our actions, I have no doubt, will constitute in their way a kind of legislative memorial, and in the broadest possible sense they will be actions in the public interest, and for the general welfare.

As for the rest, John Fitzgerald Kennedy brought a style to the Presidency that emphasized those things that are finest in our traditions, those things that ennoble, the things that are good and wise. His term was short, he was most brutally cut down, and nevertheless he has most powerfully influenced the ongoing of our people.

ADDRESS BY
Hon. John L. Pilcher
OF GEORGIA

Mr. Speaker, it is my sad purpose today to speak of the loss of our late President, John Fitzgerald Kennedy.

When historians of the future look back on this era, they will see throughout our land the indelible footprints of a relatively small band of giants who towered over their fellow men in ability, in leadership, in devotion to duty. Because of these men, our Nation has continued to grow and prosper. Yes, Mr. Speaker, giants have left their unmistakable marks on this, our present age, and among their number was the late John Fitzgerald Kennedy, our 35th President of the United States of America.

The shocking news of his death reached me at my home in Meigs, Ga., within just a few minutes after he expired at the hospital to which he had been rushed immediately after the assassin's bullet felled him. My home county paper, the Thomasville Times-Enterprise, called me for a statement shortly thereafter, and I would like to quote my immediate reaction to his death as carried therein on November 22, 1963:

U.S. Representative J. L. Pilcher, of Meigs, today said the shooting of President John F. Kennedy and Gov. John Connally in Dallas today "was the most dastardly crime anyone could commit."

Congressman Pilcher, who was contacted at his home in Meigs, declared: "This was the most awful crime I can think of—a tragic blow to our country.

"John Kennedy has been the most dedicated public official I have ever known. He loved his country with a passion. With his experience in both the House and Senate, he knew more about the Federal Government than any man who has been President in decades.

"Whether you agree or disagree with his philosophy, whether you are a Republican or Democrat, you know this crime constitutes irreparable damage to our country at a crucial time like this.

"The President's philosophies of government are the same as those of Vice President Lyndon B. Johnson—and I am sure those same philosophies will continue.

"Lyndon Johnson is the protege of, and was carefully tutored by, the late Speaker Sam Rayburn, Mr. Democrat.

"All of us should pray for our new President, for the family of John F. Kennedy, and for divine guidance for our country."

Our late President was a charming man. He was a sensible man and he was a dedicated man. Soon after his nomination, it was my pleasure to meet with him as I am sure did many of my Democratic colleagues.

I will never forget his response when I said I was a Democrat and planned to remain a Democrat and would support his candidacy. I assured him that while I intended to support him for the Presidency that as between all individuals there would be times when I would scrap him when I thought he was wrong, but that I would scrap for him just as hard when I felt he was right.

As with all big men, his attitude was that he did not expect anyone to agree with him all of the time and would have very little respect for any man who would compromise his convictions. He was a gentleman beyond question, and this mark of a great man is further amplified by his attitude that men could disagree without being disagreeable.

After 2 years, 10 months and 2 days of service to his Nation and to the world, as President of the United States, this fine young man came home for the last time on November 22, 1963.

The light created by this dynamic man toward which every eye in the free world had become focused and dependent for comfort and courageous leadership had gone out. It was broken by an assassin's bullet. Yes, broken by the hand of a person who was so out of tune with a free society in the most enlightened and moralistic nation of people who ever graced the face of the earth that he brought unto himself the will to substitute a bullet for a ballot. Men of good will, men who truly appreciate freedom, men who love the concepts of democracy do not react as savages.

We do not know what causes some people to act one way and yet others to act another way. But, I am sure that being the great and compassionate man he was, if John F. Kennedy could be returned and speak to the Nation here at this moment, he undoubtedly would, in the manner of all compassionate and understanding men, dismiss the tragedy by saying to those who would seem to forget or disregard the Biblical teachings that man should respect and honor the lives of others, that "hate is for those who are too weak to love."

All of the world will greatly miss this distinguished man. I join my colleagues in extending heartfelt condolence to President Kennedy's devoted wife, his children, and other members of the family. Their grief is shared by all of us who had the good fortune to know him.

ADDRESS BY

Hon. Frank M. Karsten

OF MISSOURI

Mr. Speaker, it was my privilege to know and work closely with our beloved late President,

John F. Kennedy, for many years. His untimely passing is a great personal loss to me, for I have lost a wonderful friend.

I recall our first meeting more than a decade and a half ago, at the beginning of the 80th Congress, when John Kennedy and I began our service as new Members of the House. We introduced ourselves to each other and as new Congressmen with very similar political philosophies we immediately became close personal friends.

Because of a back injury, he was accustomed to sitting on the first aisle and I spent many hours in the seat alongside of him. He served as a member of the Committee on Education and Labor, which was one of the most active committees of the 80th Congress, and I remember our long discussions and his outstanding work on complex labor legislation.

Later, the people of Massachusetts sent him to the other body and through the years we always kept in close touch with each other. After he became President, on occasions at the White House he would call me aside to talk for a moment or two of the days when we served together in the House.

John Kennedy was endowed with a gentle personality that attracted people to him. He had a wonderful sense of humor and a ready wit. The good natured twinkle in his eyes radiated friendship and understanding. Those who were his opposition, no less than those who were his intimate associates, always recognized in him a rare crusader for the human race. His ideals were inspired by his love of his fellow man and his absence is keenly felt by mankind all over the world.

About 3 years ago, he spoke in my home city in St. Louis and, as I reflect upon the things he said that day, I think of the ancient lines:

Men judge by the complexion of the sky
The state and inclination of the day.

He drew a parallel between 1860 and 1960 and this is what he said:

One hundred years ago Lincoln wrote a friend, "I know there is a God and He hates injustice. I see a storm coming, but if He has a place and a part for me, I am ready."

In 1960, we know there is a God, and we know He hates injustice, and we see the storm coming. But if He has a place and a part for us, I believe we are ready.

In our sadness we are heartened only in the knowledge that the courage of great men outlives them, to become the heritage of our people. President Kennedy's courage still lives and upholds the high ideals and noble purposes for which he lived and died.

ADDRESS BY
Hon. Harold C. Ostertag
OF NEW YORK

Mr. Speaker, I desire to join you and the Members of this House of Representatives in tribute to a great man and great American. The assassination of President John F. Kennedy has been one of the most shocking and tragic experiences in our lifetime and in the history of our Nation. The sadness of the occasion will be with us for a long time to come. We all hope and pray that this catastrophe will never again be repeated and that our Nation will be able to dissolve the feelings and attitudes which could have nurtured such a tragic event.

To all of us, the assassination of our President was utterly unbelievable. We are a people who pride ourselves on selecting our political leaders through free elections by the people. Political assassination is completely alien to the traditions of freedom and liberty which we have developed over a period of 200 years. Only a madman could commit such a heinous crime in this day and age.

President Kennedy's death was a stunning and terrible blow to our country and to the world, to persons of all creeds and political beliefs, to those in all walks of life. He held the most powerful and responsible position in the world today, and yet all this might and power could not protect him from the vengeance of a single sniper.

The President was an alert, vigorous, intelligent, searching leader. He dedicated himself to moving the country ahead with programs he felt were in the national interest. Though there are those who did not always agree with his proposals or policies, none of us failed to respect and admire him and his efforts for our country.

In addition to his predominant public role, the President was also a beloved husband, father, son, and brother. All Americans extended their deepest sympathy to the members of his family, and hopefully the burden of their sorrows was lightened in some small measure by the knowl-

edge that millions of mourners shared their grief. Certainly, the members of the First Family revealed a strength and devotion during this period which was an inspiration for all of us.

We can take solace during this time at the inherent strength of our form of government which provided for the immediate accession of the Vice President to the Presidency. Continuity of Government was maintained, even in this tragic time, and confusion and doubt were held to a minimum.

Our country lost an alert and energetic President at the apex of his service to the Nation. He made the supreme sacrifice in serving us all. Now we have taken a new President and he has moved swiftly and confidently to pick up the fallen reins of Government.

Mr. Speaker, as Representative of the 37th New York District, may I take this means to extend the heartfelt sympathy of the people of our area to the late President's family.

We will mourn the passing of President Kennedy for a long time to come; at the same time we extend our hands in cooperation and support to our new President to advance the best interests of our beloved country.

ADDRESS BY
Hon. Harold T. Johnson
OF CALIFORNIA

Mr. Speaker, I was deeply shocked and grieved about the great tragedy which has struck this Nation and the free world, the taking of the life of President John F. Kennedy. There is no doubt in my mind but what President Kennedy will go down in history as one of the greatest Presidents this Nation has ever known.

During his short time in office, he accomplished much for the benefit of all freedom-loving people. He was truly a world leader who was making great progress in furthering the true cause of peace through understanding among the people of the world; through personal leadership and imaginative programs which gave the people of this Nation an opportunity to express in person the true spirit of the United States of America.

Here at home he was a national leader with a

tremendous knowledge about the diverse problems of a vital, complex nation.

I, of course, representing an area in which natural resources play such a vital role in the welfare of our State and people, worked closely with the President in this field. He was a true leader in the wise utilization and management of our natural resources.

Mr. Speaker, President John F. Kennedy has set an example of sincere, unselfish service to his country and his fellow man for all of us, whether we be in private or public life, to follow.

The Nation and the world will sadly miss this great man, and I extend my deepest sympathy to Mrs. Kennedy, her children, and all members of the Kennedy family.

ADDRESS BY

Hon. J. Arthur Younger

OF CALIFORNIA

Mr. Speaker, it is not given us, and fortunately so, to comprehend or foretell tragic events which occur daily, and all the more so such a catastrophic atrocity as took the life of our late President, John Fitzgerald Kennedy. Only the sustaining assurance in the existence of a Supreme Ruler of the universe supplies the spiritual consolation for such an unlooked for tragedy. Our deepest sympathy and prayers go to the bereaved family. It is well to remember in connection with this unbelievable occurrence God's word to Noah as recorded in Genesis 9: 6:

Whoever sheds the blood of man by man shall his blood be shed for God made man in His own image.

ADDRESS BY

Hon. Ben F. Jensen

OF IOWA

Mr. Speaker, the brutal, tragic assassination of John F. Kennedy, our late President, was a grievous shock to all good Americans, and to millions of his admirers across the seven seas.

My heartfelt sympathy and that of my wife and family is extended to Mrs. Kennedy, her children, and to the entire Kennedy family.

John F. Kennedy was a most sincere, deeply religious gentleman.

May the same God who called their loved one to his heavenly home, give the family strength to bear the great loss they have sustained.

God rest his soul.

ADDRESS BY

Hon. Carl Elliott

OF ALABAMA

Mr. Speaker, John Fitzgerald Kennedy was mortal, and now he is no more. But the ideals and the ideas for which he labored and died are immortal. He stood for the dignity of man, for the freedom of the human spirit, for decency, for universal understanding.

These ideals, which are as old as civilization and as immediate as today, cannot be extinguished by a sniper's bullet even as they could not be stamped out by the hate-filled acts of other evil and irrational men who have befouled the pages of history.

For all his brilliance, for all his wisdom, John Kennedy could not have understood the twisted mind which caused him to be struck down in the summer of his life. There was less hate about John Kennedy than any other person I have ever known.

There was no room in his heart for hatred. He met hate with compassion; he turned aside virulence with sparkling wit; he loved the challenge of political debate, but his mind recoiled at the thought of vituperation.

One of the remarkable things about John Kennedy, I think, was his capacity to understand the other fellow's point of view. He was too big a man to let personal difference of opinion control his emotions. In my own meetings and conversations with him, I could detect no trace of vindictiveness against any individual, against any group or against any region. He freely recognized the right and, yes, the responsibility of his contemporaries to disagree and disagree strongly with some of his policies and programs.

John Kennedy has now gone from among us. But he left a call to duty for all Americans, a call summed up best, perhaps, in these lines from his inaugural address:

With a good conscience our only sure reward, with history the final judge of our deeds, let us go forth to lead the land we love, asking His blessing and His help, but knowing that here on earth God's work must truly be our own.

All too soon, his work on this earth done, John Fitzgerald Kennedy awaits the verdict of history. He will be judged by the inflexible guidelines that he himself had set down:

Of those to whom much is given, much is required. And when at some future date the high court of history sits in judgment of each one of us—recording whether in our brief span of service we fulfilled our responsibilities to the State—our success or failure, in whatever office we may hold, will be measured by the answers to four questions: were we truly men of courage—were we truly men of judgment—were we truly men of integrity— were we truly men of dedication?

ADDRESS BY

Hon. Watkins M. Abbitt

OF VIRGINIA

Mr. Speaker, the entire Nation was shocked upon the assassination of our President in Dallas on Friday, November 22. The entire free world was saddened beyond expression.

When I first heard the news I was unable to comprehend or realize what had happened. It was unbelievable to me that such could happen in America.

Our Nation has suffered a great loss. The free world will miss him tremendously.

John Fitzgerald Kennedy was a brave soldier who defended his country in time of war fearlessly, wholeheartedly and voluntarily. To say he was a brave soldier is putting it mildly. He was a great statesman and whether one shared his philosophy, political or personal, he was recognized as a great scholar, a strong leader, and a dynamic President, who worked hard for what he believed to be right and best for the Nation.

We all mourn his loss and extend to his loved ones our heartfelt sympathy in their sorrow.

ADDRESS BY

Hon. Ralph J. Scott

OF NORTH CAROLINA

Mr. Speaker, I rise to express my personal shock and sadness occasioned by the loss of our great President, John F. Kennedy, and also to convey similar expressions from the people of my district.

As the depth of our feelings increases, the adequacy of words as a method of expression decreases. Today we find them so grossly inadequate as to seem superfluous and of little use except as a device for observing the requirements of formality.

The tide of feeling which arose with the news of President Kennedy's assassination has been too deep and full for "sound or foam."

John F. Kennedy was inaugurated as President of the United States during a disturbed and tumultuous period in a world divided on many issues, small and great. He knew that the responsibilities of the Presidency would perhaps be heavier than in any period of our history. In his inaugural address he said that he would not shrink from but would welcome these awesome responsibilities, and by his every word and act thereafter proved that he did indeed welcome them.

Whether one agreed with him on specific issues or not, none has ever doubted or questioned his vigorous and unswerving loyalty to the very highest ideals and aspirations of all Americans, as well as all of the freedom-loving peoples of the world. It will take a long time for us to fully understand and evaluate the extent of the loss we have sustained.

The first news of the President's tragic death left us shocked, dazed, in stunned disbelief, and found us unable or unwilling to accept as fact an event which has no parallel in human history. Alternately, we have felt indignation and sorrow, resentment and sadness, anger and bereavement, and at all times the deepest sympathy for the widow, the children and all members of the Kennedy family.

The poise and fortitude exhibited by Mrs. Jacqueline Kennedy throughout the ordeal so suddenly and tragically thrust upon her has become a subject of nation and even worldwide admiration and wonder. Surely, she has been possessed of and sustained by a strength not her own. Any who may have doubted now know that she not only held the title "first lady" but that she deserved it well indeed.

John Fitzgerald Kennedy was our President, honored and respected by all: He was also husband, father, son, and brother. May the days ahead bring to his valiant widow and to every member of his family a full measure of comfort and surcease from the sorrow occasioned by their sad loss.

ADDRESS BY

Hon. John C. Watts

OF KENTUCKY

Mr. Speaker, the life of John Fitzgerald Kennedy has been taken from us. The ideals to which he devoted himself shall live on. They shall not perish from this earth so long as man endures.

John Fitzgerald Kennedy was a patriot in the greatest American tradition. He gave unsparingly of himself to those ideals which he truly believed would strengthen America. He gave totally of himself in direct combat against this Nation's mortal enemy during World War II when evil then, too, tried to triumph. He gave totally of himself in this very House of Representatives where we stand today; and in the Senate, when utilizing the democratic processes our forefathers bequeathed us, he fought for those measures he believed would enhance this great Republic of ours. He gave totally of himself in the Presidency where he exerted all effort humanly possible to guide this United States and the world back from the brink of total nuclear destruction, but without placing in jeopardy the rights and freedom of man.

The well-aimed bullet of a mad-driven assassin struck down our President in the prime of life. This act of evil has provoked all men to search their souls and rededicate their lives to fulfilling those ideals on which our forefathers founded this Nation, and to which John Fitzgerald Kennedy has now given his life.

The dignity, love, and courage which Mrs.

Jacqueline Kennedy has displayed in this hour of trial, has given added meaning and depth to her husband's whole life. By her every action, she has obliterated the evil of that moment in Dallas. She has symbolized, for all the world to behold, the triumph of good over evil.

May the evil, violence, and hatred which erupted in Dallas be interred with the assassin.

May the eternal flame illuminate and guide us along that path to freedom and dignity ennobling the lives of all men, first chartered by our forefathers and so joyously traveled by President Kennedy.

May abiding power for good always be at the helm of our Nation.

In rededicating ourselves to America and all for which it stands, do we honor our slain President and commit him to immortality.

ADDRESS BY

Hon. William M. Tuck

OF VIRGINIA

Mr. Speaker, when the dreadful news of the assassination of our late President, John Fitzgerald Kennedy, was broadcast over the Nation, I was on my way back by automobile to my home in southern Virginia. The tidings came like a clap of thunder out of a clear sky. I was stunned and shocked beyond all description, and upon arriving at my home I found the same consternation and disbelief on the faces of my family, my friends, and neighbors.

Foremost on my mind as I listened to the details on what the assassin's bullet had done was thought of the effect it would have upon the Nation, as well as upon the late President's wife, children, and the members of his family. To be deprived in such a way of a loved one in the prime and glory of manhood, at a time when he was in the midst of official duties, waving in acknowledgment of the cheers of the throng, is a toll we do not like to associate with American politics and our generous and cherished way of life.

I have only the highest praise for the widow. Her display of courage and fortitude at this time of sadness will certainly go down in our annals as an example for bereft women over the world for many years to come.

This assassination took away from us one of

the most personable Presidents in the period of my memory. Mr. Kennedy came into office at a crucial period in world history. Not always did his expression of policy fall upon friendly ears, but he listened to his opponents courteously and patiently. He was a man of courage, and his most disarming weapon was a smile that radiated good will and friendliness.

As I think of this tragedy, I join millions of others in a feeling of abhorrence that it should have brought death to such a young man occupying such an exalted position. But his end did not come before he had made his mark in life, before he had advanced to the ranks of those public servants who will be long remembered.

His tragic passing at such a youthful age reminds us all of the certainty of death and the magnitude of eternity. As the noted poet, Henry Wadsworth Longfellow, so deftly phrased it:

> Life is real! Life is earnest!
>   And the grave is not its goal;
> Dust thou art, to dust returnest,
>   Was not spoken of the soul.
>
> Art is long, and Time is fleeting,
>   And our hearts, though stout and brave,
> Still, like muffled drums, are beating
>   Funeral marches to the grave.
>
> Lives of great men all remind us
>   We can make our lives sublime,
> And, departing, leave behind us
>   Footprints on the sands of time.

ADDRESS BY

Hon. James Roosevelt

OF CALIFORNIA

Mr. Speaker, "nothing is true except as a man or men adhere to it—to live for it, to spend themselves on it, to die for it."

Four days before his death, John F. Kennedy thus quoted his favorite poet and fellow New Englander, Robert Frost, and pointed out that "we need this spirit even more than money or institutions or agreements."

This was the spirit in which John Kennedy lived—as a young naval officer selflessly risking his life for those under his command, as a Member of both bodies of the Congress, and as our President.

Within the all too brief time given to him to bear the massive responsibilities with which this age of chronic crisis has invested the Presidency, John Kennedy accomplished much.

But an attempt to summarize in terms of treaties signed, or laws enacted, misses the essential greatness of this man.

Some 30 years ago, one of his predecessors in the Presidency issued a call for "prophets of a new order of competence and courage."

John Kennedy was such a man; devoted to excellence, supremely courageous.

He sensed that the problems confronting the Nation demanded greatness of the American people.

It was a special grace in President Kennedy that he was able to capture the best in our Nation's heritage within the measured stanzas of his restrained eloquence. He laid before his people dreams and hopes to which all could aspire. He inspired the Nation. "Let us begin," he said, and thousands of America's young people took up the fight against ignorance, disease and poverty in the villages of Africa, the jungles of southeast Asia—wherever people needed help. He brought to the task of leading us a sense of fierce immediacy, a demand that each of us give of our best, to help hew out new frontiers of freedom.

He touched the hearts and minds of all Americans, everywhere. Because of this each of us—not just here in the Nation's Capital, but on the streets, the farms, in the shops and factories—everywhere in this broad land he loved so well, every American feels a personal grief, a sharp sense of loss because of his untimely death.

The peoples of the world mourn him, too. Instinctively, they seemed to have perceived that here was a good and wise man dedicated to peace and the furtherance of global human understanding.

Lastly, may I add a personal word. I had known the late President as a personal family friend when he was a very young boy and man. I had the opportunity to watch his development, to see him grow as one would watch a young tree grow into sturdiness and majestic strength. It is not often that one has the privilege of seeing close, at firsthand, a human being emerge and attain the stature of true greatness. Mrs. Roosevelt and I have a very deep and intense feeling, therefore, when we realize that we have said goodby to him forever.

Hon. Thomas J. O'Brien

Mr. Speaker, grateful for all time should the United States be for the service and sacrifice of John Fitzgerald Kennedy, the President of courage and wisdom, whose vision and foresight in domestic and foreign affairs elevated his country in the eyes of the world.

A public servant, faithful to all mankind, his term of service as the President of the United States was brief but crowded with achievements that history and humanity will recognize in proper stature.

Before his terms in Congress and the U.S. Senate, he distinguished himself in the military service of his country.

He was a man of great valor. He was a man of prudence. He was a man, above all, who feared God, and only God.

For the loss of President Kennedy the United States is poorer today; yet with his interment in Arlington National Cemetery all of him could not be interred. As though it were willed to every citizen of our great country, his courage, his valor, his farsighted wisdom remain and are remanded to us.

Let every citizen of this great country recognize and hold dear in his heart, these gifts; for they shall become the American's heritage.

To his undaunted widow, Mrs. Jacqueline Kennedy, in her fortitude, there is a greatness that awes all. May she in her deep grief find comfort and consolation in the love and affection of her children and be blessed by a merciful God.

Hon. Robert E. Jones

Mr. Speaker, in recent days we have paused, each of us, to reflect on the significance of the terrible calamity which befell this country with the murder of John Fitzgerald Kennedy.

When an assassin's bullet cut down the President, shock waves engulfed all of us and extended far beyond to people in every area of the globe.

I felt the loss of this vibrant and handsome man in many ways and even now it is difficult for me to sort out my personal reactions to that dastardly crime of November 22.

But one result of the tragic event is as clear to me now as when news of the assassination was first broadcast.

We have not only lost a great and energetic leader, we have lost a man of peace.

John Fitzgerald Kennedy dedicated himself, through words and actions, to the achievement of an honorable world peace—peace through strength, not peace through weakness. He was consumed by a desire to lead us from darkness toward the dawn of a new era of world understanding, based upon freedom, decency, and humanitarian principles.

Our young President faced an awesome task and no one realized this more than he. Peace was his dream, yet he was not a dreamer. No one knew better than John Fitzgerald Kennedy what this Nation faced in the painful progress toward peace. No one was more aware of the whirlpools and craters that we must conquer, the cliffs we must scale, the jungles we must traverse, as we moved toward the dawn of peace.

In his relentless drive for world amity and fellowship, John Fitzgerald Kennedy was a realistic man and a patient man.

He first told us of his dream and then he took us by the hand and at the time of his death he was guiding us, inch by inch, toward a new and glorious day in world history. His touch upon us was both gentle and strong.

He tolerated neither laggards nor impetuous front-runners.

He vigorously opposed the apostles of gloom and doom and sharply rejected the philosophy of those who sought peace at any price.

Now, this man of peace is gone.

This fact, to me, represents the greatest wound we and the people of the world have suffered in the death of John Fitzgerald Kennedy.

But in our grief and sense of great loss, I ask that we not forget that he has placed us—all of us—on the right track. He has headed us in the direction of peace.

So let us now proceed on the true course set by John Fitzgerald Kennedy. I have the feeling that his footsteps will always be there to guide us.

Hon. Otto E. Passman

Mr. Speaker, as I join today with my colleagues in paying tribute to the life and memory of our late President, I am moved to the thought that "the measure of a life is in the quality, and not in the length of it." And, although John F. Kennedy's life on earth was tragically ended in the prime of his manhood, his life was indeed of the very finest quality.

It was my privilege to know "Jack" Kennedy personally over a period of 17 years. We were administered the oath of office in the House of Representatives at the same time in 1947. Through the period that elapsed since then, we developed and maintained a cordial personal relationship while frequently and vigorously differing on numerous political, legislative, and other governmental issues and policies. I shall always cherish my association with this dedicated man and, so long as I live, shall remember, with appreciation, his warm personality, his enthusiasm, his brilliance, and his sincerity.

John Fitzgerald Kennedy possessed the basic attributes which are necessary for leadership; and frequently—both as a Member of Congress and as President—those sterling qualities shone forth brightly, cloaking him in the aura of greatness.

Along with each of my colleagues and Americans everywhere, I deeply mourn the death of the President, and am appalled at the despicable act which took his life. And also, along with my colleagues and others who had known John Kennedy well through the years, there is a profound personal sadness and grief in my heart. But I believe, Mr. Speaker, that we shall find from the terrible tragedy of President Kennedy's dastardly assassination a lesson for all men—a lesson which will find us all dedicated to a more vigorous and courageous striving to live up to the fundamental principles of Americanism, and to build a civilization of law and order and respect for human dignity and life.

And, even though words are inadequate on such an occasion as this, I wish to join now in expressing to Mrs. Kennedy, our late President's devoted and courageous wife, and to each one of the members of his family my heartfelt sympathy and sincere condolences. May God's grace sustain and strengthen them.

And may they, as well as all Americans, find comfort in their faith of the certainty of eternal life. For, as Victor Hugo expressed this great truth:

The tomb is not a blind alley; it is a thoroughfare. It closes on the twilight, opens on the dawn.

President Kennedy's dauntless spirit lives on, and it will continue to live so long as the spirit of freedom remains alive in the hearts and minds of mankind.

Hon. Joe D. Waggonner, Jr.

Mr. Speaker, though the Nation and, indeed, the world is still filled with poignant grief over the passing of our distinguished President, the memory of his warm personality, his engaging smile, and his intense dedication still buoy the people.

Time will not erase the impression he left upon this Nation for he will be judged for the deeds he did and the dreams he dreamed.

I did not share the years of acquaintance with him as many of you here in the Congress have, but in the brief hour our paths crossed I learned quickly the reason for the devotion he inspired in those around him. I understood the magnetism of his personality. I felt the wave of enthusiasm that radiated from him.

That the world rushed to his side in the final agonizing hours of his life must give his family comfort against distress and consolation that, in his time, brief as it was, he became one of the most honored of men.

I join my colleagues on both sides of the aisle to mourn his passing.

Hon. James A. Byrne

Mr. Speaker, we are assembled to pay honor to a man who restored self-confidence to a free world, who defended freedom with all of his strength, and whose energy was spent making the United States a strong and dynamic country for us all—no matter of what race, color or creed.

It is impossible to describe in sufficient terms my deep feelings of sadness in the loss of our great President, truly a great American, John Fitzgerald Kennedy.

This brilliant young man in the short time he served as President fulfilled the promise he made in his inaugural address January 20, 1961, that he would not shirk from his responsibilities in "the role of defending freedom in its hour of maximum danger."

From that day on John Fitzgerald Kennedy set out to establish a real peace the world over, a true peace built on a foundation of true brotherhood wherein each man is his brother's keeper.

The energy, the faith and devotion that John Fitzgerald Kennedy put forth in this endeavor has reflected upon our Nation as a beacon light of freedom to influence the whole world in its fight for liberty. This has been evidenced in the reverence shown by the people of the world who have given expression to their grief in many ways—in the dedication to his memory of edifices, public works, parks, and thoroughfares.

Generations still unborn will reap benefits from programs he instituted here at home and abroad.

His tragic death has, indeed, left this world poorer in the loss of his genius and leadership.

In behalf of my entire congressional district, I extend my heartfelt expressions of sympathy to the most courageous woman of this age, Jacqueline Kennedy, and her lovely children in the loss of a devoted husband and father.

May eternal rest be granted upon him, O Lord, and let perpetual light, shine upon him; may his soul rest in saintly peace, a peace well earned—for which he fought so valiantly to achieve for all men and all nations.

ADDRESS BY

Hon. George H. Fallon

OF MARYLAND

Mr. Speaker, all of us are sad over the assassination of President Kennedy. Although his articulate voice has been stilled forever, it shall never be forgotten. The individual, the Nation and the world mourn the loss of this truly remarkable man.

John Fitzgerald Kennedy was a great President. He achieved a new level in quality in the White House that may never be matched. His courage, intelligence, and dynamic leadership were the qualities that endeared him to the people and won him world respect.

On November 14, 1963, I had the distinct and memorable pleasure of accompanying the President to the formal opening of the Maryland Northeastern Expressway and the Delaware Turnpike. We rode in his helicopter, leaving the White House at 3 o'clock p.m., and arrived at the ceremonies in the late afternoon. It was cold and chilly, but despite the weather, he was greeted by a large and enthusiastic crowd. The people loved him. His passing was a great personal loss to me.

We shall miss his articulate voice, his remarkable candor, the warmth of his personality, his wit, and the many wonderful and colorful characteristics that were the makeup of this energetic and likable man.

We shall miss his interviews with the press. I particularly liked them. We shall miss seeing the kind father with Caroline and little John-John. We shall miss the graciousness and elegance that he and Mrs. Kennedy brought into the White House.

We shall miss President John Fitzgerald Kennedy. But, as he would expect us to do, we shall carry on.

ADDRESS BY

Hon. John F. Shelley

OF CALIFORNIA

Mr. Speaker, with braveness, honor, and disbelief, we have laid to rest John Fitzgerald Kennedy.

Days ago I stood with the countless numbers of Americans who gathered at his final resting place. I stood with those Americans and shared their sorrow and their hope. I knew that he was gone physically—but I knew and know, as they do, that those things for which he lived are not dead with him.

John Fitzgerald Kennedy was a 20th century renaissance man. To catalog his interests is to catalog the range of human thought itself. To enumerate his virtues is to spell out the goodness in man. To speak of warmth, of strength, of compassion, of charity, of loyalty to friends, family, and country, is to speak of John Fitzgerald Kennedy.

His was an exemplary life. He was a consummate statesman and a devoted family man.

His life and works are a source from which we can each of us replenish our own strength for the tasks that confront us.

ADDRESS BY

Hon. Ray J. Madden

OF INDIANA

Mr. Speaker, today our Members are paying tribute to the memory of our martyred President. No man in history has risen to such phenomenal success in governmental leadership or world respect and renown as our departed President John F. Kennedy.

No man in modern times has demonstrated such remarkable talent to lead the people of our Nation, and indirectly, the nations of the world, on a program of international understanding for future world peace as the man whom we memorialize today.

President Kennedy's contribution to his country was not confined solely to serving in our Congress or as President. His heroic deeds as a member of the Armed Forces in World War II will forever stand alongside the records of our most outstanding military heroes of the past. As a lieutenant in our Navy, his deeds of valor in the South Pacific have already been recorded in the annals of newspapers, magazines, books, and a cinema called "PT 109." He received Navy and Marine Corps decorations for his heroism and was the recipient of the Purple Heart.

In January 1947, John F. Kennedy was sworn in as a freshman Congressman. He was assigned to the Committee on Education and Labor in the 80th Congress. I was a member of that committee and served with this youthful member during his first session in this legislative body.

He as a freshman soon demonstrated his natural ability as a legislator. He worked hard and diligently on the busy legislative schedule and devoted long hours to his district, State, and Nation.

Time and space do not permit a review of his record as Congressman, Senator, and President.

It is sufficient to say that no man in our Nation's history has made even a close approach to duplicating his extraordinary ascendancy in political and official life.

At the age of 30, he was sworn in as a "rooky" Congressman from Massachusetts and on January 20, 1961, 14 years later, he took the oath as President of the United States.

The multimillion words spoken and written about the abilities of this remarkable genius in government have sufficiently recorded his accomplishments and achievements for all posterity to revere and admire.

Although he was assassinated in the prime of his life, by a mentally twisted fanatic, his influence on our Nation's future economy and well-being has been implanted in the minds of millions and will live on and bear fruit for generations yet unborn.

His success in educating millions throughout the globe on building a solid foundation for world peace has not been in vain.

History reveals that our greatest Presidents and statesmen—George Washington, Abraham Lincoln, Benjamin Franklin, and others—were slandered and maligned during their lifetimes.

In 1722, Benjamin Franklin wrote a letter to his old friend, Joseph Galloway, with whom he had shared a shattering political defeat a few years previously. The letter read:

We must not in the course of public life expect immediate grateful acknowledgment of our services. But let us persevere through abuse and even injury. The internal satisfaction of a clear conscience is always present, and time will do us justice in the minds of the people, even of those who at the present are the most prejudiced against us.

Monuments will decay, buildings will disappear, portraits fade, and words written or spoken are soon forgotten. But the deeds, accomplishments, and programs of our young martyred President John F. Kennedy will live long in the future, and his memory will continue in the minds and hearts of millions of his fellow countrymen.

May the immortal soul of our great leader

whom we memorialize today enjoy forever the rewards of blissful rest and peace.

ADDRESS BY

Hon. William A. Barrett

OF PENNSYLVANIA

Mr. Speaker, at God's command and by His hand, our dearly beloved President, John Fitzgerald Kennedy, was led from this mortal earth into the Kingdom of Heaven. We often question the wisdom of the Almighty because we do not understand. We are shocked and cannot comprehend why a man of such talent was called from a troubled world to a place beyond the horizons where there is no pain, no sorrow or strife.

We say it cannot be. But it is. He has gone away for a while. He had laid down his burdens of office for a well-deserved rest. His service is now to his God and Creator.

Our Nation mourns this tragic loss, but it is strengthened by the friendship extended by other Nations and other peoples.

My family and I are deeply grieved. We have prayed for Mr. Kennedy and his courageous widow. Our sympathies are with her and the children in this hour of sorrow and we hope they are comforted by the strength of our grief.

God giveth John Fitzgerald Kennedy and God taketh John Fitzgerald Kennedy. "Thy will be done on earth as it is in heaven."

ADDRESS BY

Hon. Charles A. Vanik

OF OHIO

Mr. Speaker, for the Members of the House today is a day of recollection on the life and works of our late President, John F. Kennedy. A great memory now begins on the countless deeds of his life which have left their imprint on this generation and upon history.

During his time in the Presidency, President Kennedy radiated justice, strength, trust, and wisdom in the struggle for the best kind of an America and for peace throughout the world.

The people of Cleveland had a special affection for our late President. He was a frequent visitor; he was seen by hundreds of thousands. In Cleveland, President Kennedy was welcomed by the largest and most enthusiastic crowds in America. The devotion of our people to the President was complete and unrestrained.

President Kennedy first came to Cleveland in February 1957 to address the annual meeting of the National Conference of Christians and Jews. At this very time, world attention was focused on the Suez Canal crisis and the violence between Arab and Jew in the Middle East. He stoutly opposed the use of sanctions.

A year later, in 1958, the late President made a brief visit to Cleveland to discuss his new book, "Profiles in Courage." Immediately after the luncheon meeting, he rushed to Washington to vote for the postal pay raise bill. As he left the luncheon he said:

"I have a strong suspicion that if I am absent on this important vote, the postmen of Massachusetts may not always ring twice."

In September of 1958, the President addressed the annual steer roast of the Democratic Party in Cleveland. At that very time, when the islands of Quemoy and Matsu were under fire and hotheads suggested a war with Red China, the President said the islands were not vital to Formosa and not worth fighting for. History has clearly approved the wisdom of this position.

In 1959, the President made two April visits to Cleveland. During the course of his earlier visit and in reply to a newsman's inquiry about the prospects of his candidacy in 1960, he stated:

January is the time for a serious candidate for the Presidency to declare himself.

Later that month, he returned for another visit to an author's luncheon in Cleveland where he stated:

I am not certain that all my fellow politicians would share my enthusiasm for these literary gatherings. But let us not forget how much the world of literature has always meant to the statesmen of America.

September 1959, the President again addressed the Democratic gathering in Cleveland and before enthusiastic unprecedented crowds, he delivered a fighting speech of a candidate, poised for the Presidency, prepared and ready. Our enthusiasm for his candidacy needed no formal announcement.

In 1960, in the midst of the presidential campaign, the President returned to Cleveland as the Democratic nominee. Over a quarter-million people lined the streets along a 12-mile route to the park at which he spoke where another 100,000 persons were assembled. To a cheering crowd of supporters, he stated:

If you think America is a great country that can be a greater country, a powerful Nation that can be more powerful, if freedom can be held higher, then I want your help.

On October 19, 1962, the President made his last and only appearance as President in Cleveland. When he spoke on the Cleveland Public Square, he said in a typical bit of humor:

Fellow Democrats—and Republicans who are passing through the square.

Later in his speech he spoke in support of the medicare bill, but he had more serious concerns on his mind. The next day he cut short his campaign plans and returned to Washington for the most vital decisions of his life—the Cuban crisis was at hand. In hours, he rallied the American people to the danger of a nuclear war. He defied Russia on the Cuban missile crisis and won a bloodless victory. This was America's finest hour—we did not negotiate out of fear.

It is impossible to assess at this time the many vital contributions which President Kennedy gave to this country and to the world. He shook off the notion that America was either too tired or too obese to move forward. The spirit of the New Frontier administration stimulated a better moral and physical fitness on the part of the Nation and all of the people. The search for betterment and perfection was becoming contagious. People thought more of the plight of the unemployed at home and the hungry and unhoused abroad. Eager young people joined the Peace Corps to spread good will and progress in far-off places. Service to the Government again became a proud endeavor. Distressed areas received new hope on the preservation of their communities. The march on urban slums and juvenile delinquency became a crusade against crime and the misery of slums. America was indeed moving forward—and liking it. The captain at the helm of the ship of state was using every bit of sail to keep the country on a forward course.

Undoubtedly, the nuclear test ban treaty, ratified September 24, 1963, constituted the greatest achievement of all because it developed areas of agreement out of a wilderness of irreconcilable conflict. It demonstrated the President's capacity to negotiate a hard bargain. It was a giant step toward peace and world understanding. Our President was now strong in changing the course of history. Among the aging leaders of state, he had come forward at an hour of need to wisely move the entire world toward more reasonable things.

As one citizen and on behalf of the people whom I represent, I must express profound sorrow at the events which cut short a life so necessary and so meaningful. But I must also express gratitude for having seen and known the dynamic spirit of President Kennedy. That spirit will live in each of us for the rest of our lives, and each of us in our turn will pass it on to those who succeed. Such spirit needs no eternal light—it is eternal.

ADDRESS BY

Hon. Don Edwards

OF CALIFORNIA

Mr. Speaker, the world has lost a great man. One is tempted to go on, to try to enumerate his accomplishments, his qualities, and all of the things we loved and respected in him. But our best writers, our most fertile minds, have been humbled in their attempts to put our loss into words. Just as the name Abraham Lincoln is now a synonym for goodness and greatness, the name John Fitzgerald Kennedy will one day occupy that same place in our vocabulary, and we will not have to try to tell of him, as we are trying to do today.

When he was serving his country as a young lieutenant in the South Seas he was a member of a fraternity of people, most of whom are unknown to each other, but who have left a special kind of kinship to our late President. I am talking about the thousands of American service men and women who served on ships sailing between the tropical islands with strange names like Eniwetok, Tinian, and Babelthaup and who lived for months and years on coral islands that could have been more accurately named Tedium and Apathy.

Mr. Speaker, I would like to speak for them and for my constituents. I will not name those who have written to me of their grief. There are too many. The words they have used are the familiar words we have heard from the great and the humble—courageous, wise, strong, gentle, concerned, beloved. He was all of these but there was something else—something that keenly affected those who knew him and which reached out to everyone who watched him campaign or conduct a press interview. It was an intensity, a joyfulness about life itself, that made the world seem a better place to live in. He served us all with a grace and good humor and gave his life trying to make it a better world.

ADDRESS BY

Hon. Joseph E. Karth

OF MINNESOTA

Mr. Speaker, the death of John Fitzgerald Kennedy and the events since the tragedy of November 22, 1963, have caused much reflection upon the qualities of this fine man who as President of the United States for only 2 years and 10 months nevertheless has already made a most significant mark in world history.

His cool courage and his analytical appraisal of complex facts and forces during the Cuban crisis last year effectively convinced the Soviet Government of our Nation's determination to save freedom for the world even in face of the gravest threats of nuclear war.

President Kennedy's forthright action on the crisis in Cuba won for our Nation gratitude, admiration, and respect. The wanton assassination of this great leader rightly caused, first, revulsion and, then, despair in people in other lands who came to look upon John Fitzgerald Kennedy as the epitome of American strength and determination.

Americans have a right to be proud of John Fitzgerald Kennedy who embodies the virtues of which they are proudest. He had the vision, intellect, energy, ideals, ambition, wisdom, compassion, wit, courage, love of justice and mercy, the toughness, the sense of proportion, and the many other characteristics which we so admire in our leaders.

He practiced in his chosen craft of politician and statesman with pride and consummate skill to the benefit of his countrymen and to those economically and legally disadvantaged persons who sought—and found in John Fitzgerald Kennedy—a stout champion for their cause. It is they who are the poorer for the martyrdom of our late President. The plain people in other lands have instinctively sensed their loss and have poured out their sorrow and their sympathy in ways which best express the intense emotion of their personal bereavement.

The remains of John Fitzgerald Kennedy rest fittingly in hallowed ground with those other heroes who dedicated their lives to the service of our Nation, but his spirit shall long serve as inspiration.

A special tribute is due to Jacqueline Bouvier Kennedy who quickly overcame the trauma of watching her beloved husband die in her arms and led the country through the pomp and ceremony of the President's funeral.

The majesty of her presence turned a Nation transfixed by the awful horror at Dallas to what in effect became a reconsecration of our democratic institutions. We are very much in debt to Jacqueline Kennedy for her magnificent participation in a most tragic situation.

History alone will make the final judgment, but I am confident the greatness of President Kennedy and his short administration will be a brilliant chapter in the American chronicles of which he was so appreciative a student.

ADDRESS BY

Hon. Lindley Beckworth

OF TEXAS

Mr. Speaker, there are no words that can adequately express the great sorrow which is in our hearts occasioned by the assassination of our beloved late President Kennedy.

I heard President Kennedy at each of his speakings in Texas. It was my privilege to be on his plane during his last flight—the one between Fort Worth and Dallas. He was very cheerful, confident, and pleasant. He seemed pleased by the kind of receptions he and Mrs. Kennedy had been accorded.

I would say in essence that his response was that of a person who was very optimistic for the future of Texas, the future of our Nation and the future of the free world.

I know we all are grief stricken to the greatest degree. May God help us to bear the great burdens which have come to each of us as a result of the assassination of the late great President Kennedy.

In this connection it is my hope and my prayer that our present great President and native Texan, President Lyndon B. Johnson, will have the aid and help of the people of this Nation and the people of the free world in such a manner that success likewise will crown his efforts as our Chief Executive. I have great confidence in President Johnson; he can and will do an excellent job as our President.

Colonel Carl Estes is the able publisher of the Longview News-Journal. I desire to include his splendid editorial that appeared in the Sunday, November 24, issue of his Longview News-Journal.

The Russell Laschingers and Ray Greens are publishers of my home county seat newspaper, the Gilmer Mirror. I desire to include their splendid editorial that appeared in their paper on November 28 and also a reprint of a Dallas Times Herald editorial that appeared in the Gilmer Mirror.

[From the Longview (Tex.) News-Journal, Nov. 24, 1963]

OUR PRESIDENT

(By Carl L. Estes)

Our President is dead, and as a people we are bowed in grief and respect. But we are thankful that in the unity of this common grief we can say to our new President and to each other: Long live our President.

Our city, State, and Nation, indeed the whole free world, was shocked and saddened by the death Friday of President John F. Kennedy. The circumstances were such as to numb the senses of all decent-minded men and women. A slinking coward, tentatively identified as a leftwinger and admirer of Soviet communism and Red Dictator Fidel Castro, of Cuba, coldbloodedly assassinated the man who in person and position had stood in the breach as chief leader of the forces of freedom against the Communist conspiracy to subjugate the world.

We people of Texas are the more deeply saddened because this tragedy occurred while our distinguished President was visiting in our State. Texans often have been divided in their views of some of his policies and programs, but there has been no division in our respect for him as our President and as a dedicated American.

In war, Mr. Kennedy and the writer fought in the Pacific in common cause and each carried home the scars of battle earned in defense of the high principles of democratic freedom, which includes the right to disagree. In peace, we have disagreed on many things, all in the interest of individual freedom and national safety; but we have stood together and the President has had our admiration and respect in the great essentials of love of country, our homes, our churches, and our God.

We spoke out in admiration and praise and urged all Texans to give the fullest support when President Kennedy stood up to Communist Khrushchev in the Berlin and Cuban crises. We now call attention to the fact that President Kennedy is due the honor of a national hero, for he has died on the firing line of the cold war in his country's service.

While all of us here in Texas may feel that sudden death is too good for the cowardly murderer who pulled the trigger from ambush, we expect to see that he is accorded the consideration which leftwing revolutionaries are unwilling to give others—courthouse justice before a jury of citizens, not a firing squad at dawn on orders of a dictator. We feel quite sure that President Kennedy would have had it so.

John Fitzgerald Kennedy was a patriot. He fought for his country and proved himself a determined and resourceful man of war. In peace, he sought opportunity and faithfully served his country, holding nothing in selfish reserve.

He was a devoted family man. Under the heavy duties and great stress of his office, he often was shown as watching his children at play and giving them his personal attention and interest. He always insisted that Mrs. Kennedy accompany him on his journeys, near and far, and he rested and vacationed with his family when opportunity presented.

Mr. Kennedy was an active and dedicated churchman. He was loyal to his church in attendance and worship even under the intense pressure and demands of his high office. He stood foursquare for Christian unity.

It is both in admiration of his many fine qualities and respect to him as our President and to his good family that our business and editorial offices will be closed during the funeral services between 11 a.m. and 12 noon Monday (Longview time). Wouldn't it be a fine show of public respect if all businesses would close for this solemn period?

While we all are deeply grieved, history waits for no man and vigilance calls us to duty. The example we need is before us in the courageous action of Mrs. Kennedy who, though numbed in grief at her great loss, stood in bloodstained clothing beside Vice President and Mrs. Lyndon B. Johnson as he was administered the oath as President.

President Johnson literally is a man on the spot in the hall of history. Seldom does a national or world leader have duty so suddenly thrust upon him. Never has a new President faced more trying and difficult problems, with our Nation infiltrated and the whole world on the brink of flame from the Communist world conspiracy.

As President, Mr. Johnson brings to the office an unmistakable spirit of courage. He has demonstrated it not alone on the political front in public life but also face to face with the enemy on the war front. He saw service in the Pacific in World War II and, before being officially recalled to Washington, won the Silver Star for gallantry in action.

As the wheels of our American Government and leadership begin to roll under the direction of our new President, it behooves all of us as patriotic citizens to unite behind Mr. Johnson and give him the support and understanding he must have in order to lead our Nation firmly and effectively. This will be a natural thing for the writer to do, because ours were the first newspapers in east Texas and among the few in Texas which supported Johnson when he made his original campaign for the U.S. Senate.

We here again pledge to President Johnson our help and understanding in all ways in which we may be able to serve the cause of freedom and national safety and peace in the world. Long live our President.

––––

[From the Gilmer (Tex.) Mirror, Nov. 28, 1963]

WE LIVE SO HE SHALL NOT HAVE DIED IN VAIN

We looked into the jaws of death this past weekend. The black, sickening news of the murder of John Kennedy was akin that of a member of our own family. He was that familiar, and for most of us, that well admired.

Why? The exact workings of a psychotic's maddened mind can never be known, and stupidity which followed tragedy in Dallas made this certain as the assassin was also murdered.

But our system exposes our political leaders to these type goons, with only minimum amount of protection. We would not have a free society were it otherwise.

Every leader of any national cause in America is exposed to the crackpot, the extremist, the "nut" as most of us would say. But we cannot shrink from these minute few, and still have our open, free, responsible society.

We can—those who mourn and grieve—gain assurance that the President who died so suddenly, at the height of gaiety, the family who lost so hideously, and the Nation who suffered so grievously, faced all these dangers with high courage.

Surely he knew there were those who would try this. Certainly he knew the emotions were high around him, and the threats and risks uncertain, but lurking. But he took them in his stride. We must do likewise in our own lives to be true to his faith and his inspiration, and now his memory.

There are those who would pull the trigger today which not only would snuff out a national leader, but a whole nation. And John Kennedy knew it better than any of us.

There were those who said "He's a one-termer."

In one sense they are now right. But his words, actions, deeds, and efforts, in a wide range of endeavors in our diverse Nation, will now live far longer than a one-term President. As it was said of Lincoln, after his murder, "he now belongs to the ages."

It seemed a few months ago that things were piling up, and some unseen fate seemed to know something. For John F. Kennedy was rushing from here, to there, to elsewhere, with a hundred things going at once, trying to finish them before something happened. He was, as it turned out, in a race with a tragic destiny.

Those unfinished things we know will be done, and in his name. He set this Nation on the right road for this decade, perhaps longer. We have only to reread his thoughts, his words, his urgings, to stay on the right path.

As for the whys, ifs, recriminations, and reasons of the horrible Dallas murder, that cannot be undone, even if the failures of responsible people are found. It is a terrible setback, of course, to have found a man almost perfectly suited to the national leadership, then let a deranged marksman sit unmolested in a window. It cannot be undone, however. The world is full of ifs.

We must live with memories, with inspiration, with the example of courage, and with one of the most clearheaded moral guides we have found in national leaders today. These are the trail marks blazed by John Kennedy, who did more in less than 3 years as President than any other man in our history.

To those who still bear hatred, rancor, venom, spite, and bitterness toward him, we say—and he would, too— "This is a free America," or "Ameriker" as was his style. And this is our strength and our weakness, this democracy of ours.

Its weakness is the weakness of all democracies, which cannot protect themselves (or their leaders) as a dictatorship can. And for the short haul, the dictatorship can act more efficiently.

Democracy's strength lies in the historical fact that history has marched on sturdy legs of people who govern themselves. No matter the mistakes, the horrible mistakes, they are in the van of the future. And the dictatorships—even though they may protect their leaders— end in calamity, sorrow, or despair.

John Kennedy shall not have died in vain, if we as Americans follow the marks of the 20th-century world leadership he blazed in so few months as our President.

––––

[From the Gilmer Mirror, Nov. 28, 1963]

DEATH'S SAD INTIMACY

In death, Dallas has found a new love and respect for John F. Kennedy. And feeling the sad intimacy of his death that we do, we of Dallas also have a sudden, close, and indissoluble tie with his memory. John F. Kennedy and Dallas will forever be together on the pages of history.

It will be generations before the memory of him is relegated to the past. There was a magnetic quality, often noted, which drew attention to John F. Kennedy. It was a quality of destiny which bespoke exciting and important things in his personality, which hinted always of the future.

It was this quality of destiny which marked his career from its beginning. He became a national figure almost from the moment he strode onto the Washington scene as a freshman Congressman in 1947. His storybook heroism during the war, his precocious political ingenuity evidenced while still a collegian, his American good looks combined with this essence of excitement to mark every move of the man—in private as well as public.

By 1956 his importance was such that even in comparative youth his name on the Democratic party ticket as Vice President was considered only logical. And it took no bold prophet to predict his nomination for the Chief Executive's chair, even in 1956, for the race of 1960.

That campaign carried America's imagination back to the breathless early days of Franklin D. Roosevelt in searching for a suitable comparison. Not since Roosevelt, and seldom before, has a President's individuality been so identified with his administration.

John F. Kennedy was a controversial, at times impolitic, figure in the political ring. He made many enemies, it is true, but it was almost exclusively as the Chief Executive that he made them, not as Kennedy the person. This was the paradoxical factor of his career—that he was hated impersonally and loved fervently in a personal way.

But he was straightforward, which helps explain this paradox. He never soft-pedaled or side-stepped. No one can charge the memory of John F. Kennedy with the grayness of hypocrisy.

And he was bold. His noblest hours were those when he stood firm and strong in the face of our Nation's foes and said to them, "No more."

John F. Kennedy was distinctive in looks, manner, and speech.

This contributed to the enraging of his enemies and the endearment of his friends. His hatless, athletic way of moving about the Nation kept America alive to his youth. A mimicking artist became rich and famous just by imitating his famous accents. "Cuber" and "vigah" will remain for decades as crisp trademarks of his speech.

He was granted that journalistic accolade which only the familiarly great receive, identification by initials only. JFK is one with FDR. His bushy profile was accomplished easily by a few artist pen strokes.

In short, his was a figure history became instantly conscious of—and time will not soon diminish.

ADDRESS BY

Hon. Howard W. Robison

OF NEW YORK

Mr. Speaker, the tragic event on Friday, November 22, and the deeply moving scenes that followed it have left their mark upon us all. It has been an unforgettable experience—one evoking the memory of another American President of courage and devotion to the duties of that office who, with his self-appointed tasks likewise unfinished, was also taken away from us nearly a century ago.

Within the fortnight, Columnist James Reston, writing in the New York Times, had commented on the late President's failure to move key portions of his legislative program through this Congress, and had speculated that this might be so because "he—President Kennedy—has touched the intellect of the country but not its heart."

Perhaps if one were to confine himself to political programs and policies, this was true. However, the spontaneous and obviously sincere outpouring of national grief that marked the shocking and senseless killing of John F. Kennedy, the President, has seemed to demonstrate beyond all doubt that the people of the United States have now taken John F. Kennedy, the man, to their hearts.

One could and did differ with President Kennedy—as I and many another here have on occasion—but one could not do so without an appreciation of his tolerance of honest differences over means, his patience in the midst of adversity, the breadth of his intellect and the keenness of his wit, and, of course, the encompassing warmth and vitality of his personality.

It has been reported that Mr. Kennedy, who greatly admired the work of the poet, Robert Frost, had as his favorite that one of Frost's verses that concludes with these lines:

> The woods are lovely, dark, and deep
> But I have promises to keep,
> And miles to go before I sleep,
> And miles to go before I sleep.

Some observers have thought to explain this Presidential choice as indicative of the possibility that Mr. Kennedy had some premonition about the brevity of the opportunity for leadership that was to be his. If this was so—and who is to say that it was not?—it may help to explain why Mr. Kennedy, an architect of change with eye fixed on distant goals, seemed so often to exhibit an inner need to hurry.

Out of that same sense of urgency may well have also come his approach to the Presidency which, in his own words, he regarded as "the wellspring of action in the American constitutional system."

To such a man, the reluctance of this and the previous Congress to adopt his programs and policies with a greater alacrity than they displayed must have been more frustrating than he permitted himself to reveal. In part, of course, his forebearance from congressional criticism had to stem from the political realities of his situation. I should like to think, however, that it stemmed from his understanding that the Congress was—by its own lights—also only playing its part in that same American constitutional system.

In his splendid inaugural address, he acknowledged that the goals he had set himself and the Nation might not be achieved, "in the life of (his) administration, nor even perhaps in our lifetime on this planet." But, he urged, "let us begin."

One does not have to completely agree with the desirability of those goals, nor with the means John F. Kennedy sought to apply to attain them, to share in the tragic realization that he was destined to make only that "beginning." Perhaps this fact, as much as anything else, has contributed to the feeling of emptiness to which so many of us have confessed during those first few days.

However, the stream of life flows endlessly on, and we are—unwittingly and sometimes unwillingly—an integral part of it. Although none can help but wonder at the ways of Divine Providence, nor still the cry of "Why?" we can take comfort from the fact that our God is the same God, yesterday, today, and forever, and from the inalienable fact that our Republic still stands.

Our prayers in the first days of our loss were for our fallen President, for his children and for the other members of his family, and particularly for that unforgettable gallant lady who was his wife, and whose great dignity and courage as his widow had been of such inspiration to us all.

As our prayers now turn—as turn they must—to our new President and to those who will counsel and guide him, let us also pray for our Nation—that, out of these sad hours, it may have found new resolution and its people a renewed sense of common purpose.

Mrs. Robison joins me in expressing our deepest sympathy, in this, their continuing time of sorrow, to Mrs. Jacqueline Kennedy and her children, and to the other members of the immediate family of the late John F. Kennedy.

ADDRESS BY

Hon. John E. Fogarty

OF RHODE ISLAND

Mr. Speaker, in these sad and sorrowful days following the death of John Fitzgerald Kennedy,

much has been said and written of him as a scholar, statesman, gifted intellect, professional politician in the truest sense, and world leader.

As one who had the opportunity to work closely with him for 6 years in the House of Representatives and in more recent years during his service as a United States Senator and finally as our Chief Executive, I not only enjoyed a close working relationship with him but I also came to know him as a good personal friend. In assessing the all too short period spanned by this experience, I can echo the sentiments of those who laud John F. Kennedy for his statesmanship, courage and world leadership in the great East-West confrontation just a few months ago. I can echo the sentiments of those who say that this young man brought to the White House a spirit of dedication and zest for public service unparalleled in modern times. And I can subscribe to the affirmations of those who point to his leadership on the domestic scene that will inspire this Nation for generations to come.

Though it may be true that John Fitzgerald Kennedy may achieve a status of greatness in the eyes of history for his resolute stand against encroachment of the Western Hemisphere by those who would break the peace or for his courageous leadership in quest of the unfinished business of our martyred Chief Executive a century ago, I am deeply impressed and thankful for his contributions to the public good in another sphere of activity.

I refer, of course, to the vision and resolute actions which Mr. Kennedy brought to bear on problems of vital importance to all of us—our children, and ultimately to the Nation and the entire world—health and medical research. His efforts to improve the health of our people and people everywhere took many forms. Though he spoke out more frequently and more forcefully on the subject of better health than any of the 34 Presidents of the United States who preceded him, he did not fight this battle with words alone. It was just 29 days after his inauguration as President that he took the first step to bring into being—via legislation—the National Institute of Child Health and Human Development to provide a focal point for research on a wide array of health problems that had long been neglected.

This year—in fact, just a few weeks prior to his untimely death—three legislative proposals of greatest health significance to this Nation were enacted into law. I am convinced that none of these beneficial programs would have been enacted without the President's leadership and support. The first of these, the so called Health Professions Education Assistance Act—which I had championed unsuccessfully for many years—will stand as one of the living monuments to Mr. Kennedy's deep interest in the health of our people. The other two bills—among the last to be signed by President Kennedy—provide the framework for all-out campaigns against two of our most perplexing health problems: mental illness and mental retardation. Today, over 5 million Americans are afflicted by mental retardation and almost 1 of every 2 hospital beds is taken by a person suffering from mental illness. Thus, these programs in which John F. Kennedy believed so deeply but never saw developed stand to improve the lives of millions of Americans who will know this man only through their history books.

One other point should be made in a brief assessment of Mr. Kennedy's love and concern for his fellow man. It may be considered by some to be relatively easy to do the things and say the things that will result in new programs for improvement of the public health. Mr. Kennedy—in word and deed—went far beyond this commitment. As a son, as a father, as a brother, he knew well the heartbreak of one who is helpless in the face of medical mystery. And so, he not only gave his leadership, vision, and official support to the furtherance of medical research; he gave lavishly of his own time and resources to help support the attack on disease, disability, and untimely death.

Thus, John F. Kennedy as a friend and public servant emerges as one who devoted his entire life to that of giving. When there was war, he gave bravery; when there was peace, he gave service; when there was uncertainty, he gave inspiration; when there was vacillation, he gave vigor; and when there was hate, he gave his life.

All of us—as individuals and as a nation—are better off because John Fitzgerald Kennedy walked here.

ADDRESS BY

Hon. George E. Shipley

OF ILLINOIS

Mr. Speaker, in his infinite wisdom, Almighty God has seen fit to take from us a great man who loved, and was beloved by, all humanity.

No man could possibly fill the tremendous void left by the passing of that noble soul. No words can ease the aching hearts of untold millions of every race, creed, and color. The world knows it has lost a heroic champion of justice and freedom.

Tragic fate has thrust upon us grave responsibilities. We must carry on. Our departed leader never looked backward. He looked forward and moved forward. That is what he would want us to do. That is what America will do.

So much blood has already been shed for the ideals which we cherish and for which John Fitzgerald Kennedy lived and died.

Here in America, President Kennedy labored long and hard to achieve a social order worthy of our great heritage; in his time tremendous progress was made for the really democratic way of life. Let us rededicate ourselves today, the forward looking people of America, that there will be no relaxation in our efforts to improve the lot of the common people.

That is what John Fitzgerald Kennedy was striving to do and this was as Americans must strive to do also. John Kennedy never ceased his struggle to preserve and maintain our American way of life. He devoted himself to long hours of hard work, true uncomplaining self-denial and sacrifice, to rise to a position of influence, prominence and esteem. Indeed, he was a man of action, a doer, a man of intensity, striving relentlessly to accomplish worthwhile things for the people of America and the world.

The news of the sudden death of our President came as a hammer blow; it had a paralytic effect upon me and my family. I feel sure that most people throughout the Americas and the world felt the same way I did when they first learned the tragic news. A pall of gloom settled over our hearts and the world. His sudden death in the prime of life, when he had just reached a plateau in his life which gave promise of a long and distinguished career, not only saddened America, but the world.

During World War II, John Fitzgerald Kennedy fought with many honors to preserve American liberty. Returning home, he recognized the need of fighting to assure an American future of freedom and vitality, firmly anchored on the steadfast rock of our Constitution. With the vigor of his youth, the brilliance of his insight into historic truths, he was well armed for the living Constitution.

I never knew John Kennedy to qualify or apologize for his faith in the continued ability of Americans to determine freely their own and their Nation's destiny. I never knew John Fitzgerald Kennedy to bow to political expediency. He put the best interest of the country above all else. John Kennedy died in the triumph of knowing that the people of America had given him an overwhelming mandate to carry the battle of freedom to the world. He died in the knowledge that his was a righteous and live cause.

It is rare that one so young in years should be so wise in action. John Kennedy knew where he was going, and knew how to get there. The intensity of his drive and the sincerity of his belief led him many places where others would fear to tread.

He was primarily devoted to his country in time of war, and completely dedicated to it in time of peace.

This young man was truly a prince among men. On one occasion King David said to his servants, upon the happening of the death of Abner, "Know ye not that there has fallen a prince and a great man this day in Israel." And so we ourselves now note that upon the death of John Fitzgerald Kennedy there fell a prince and a great man of our country, one who was high in intellectual attainments and totally dedicated to the service of his country in time of peace.

We have heard many tributes to this young man; however, there is one he truly deserves. It is a tribute expressing how great an American John F. Kennedy was. John Kennedy was genuine; he was genuine in all his thinking and all his doings, he was a man of genuine convictions, with courage to express and stand by those convictions.

The lines of a great American poet come to mind that are inscribed upon a memorial for Abraham Lincoln and they apply also to John Kennedy. They are: "Here is a man posed against the world, a man to match the mountains and the sea."

In future years there will be great memorials erected for this prince among men; however, he leaves a living memorial. In his brief 46 years, this remarkable young man wrote a noble record of courage and faith in the United States which will inspire men to carry his battle flag, so long as American liberty is cherished.

On one occasion I approached him on a matter which concerned Illinois residents. He knew immediately of the situation and grasped an extremely complex problem in a very few minutes and assisted me in taking necessary steps to solve the problem.

Although he will not be with us in person, the imprint of his association with us as a man of great character, courage, and friendly spirit will remain. I shall always cherish having known him. I extend my deepest sympathy to his wife and children. May the good Lord give them supporting strength in their hour of great loss.

Our religious faith and our basic beliefs teach us that life, the true life of the soul is not terminated by death. John Kennedy has layed aside his physical form. He has gone from us in life's prime, but his spirit is with God who gave it.

ADDRESS BY

Hon. Charles H. Wilson

OF CALIFORNIA

Mr. Speaker, on the afternoon of Friday, November 22, in the city of Dallas, Tex., the President of the United States was murdered in cold blood.

It is difficult, if not impossible, for me to find fresh thoughts to express at this time. Hundreds of thousands of words are being written in tribute to John F. Kennedy, and messages of sympathy have poured into Washington from all parts of the world. An unprecedented gathering of royalty and foreign heads of state participated in the funeral ceremony, and thousands are continuing to pay their last respects to our fallen Commander in Chief at Arlington National Cemetery.

Almost everything that can be said about John Kennedy has already been set down. Our Nation weeps, and in the months and years to come the tributes will continue for it is true to say that never in our time has our country been so shocked and inwardly tormented.

John Kennedy was a complex man. There were many facets to his character and personality. Combined within his person was the hardheaded political realist; the shy and boyish introvert; the crowd-pleasing and crowd-loving extrovert; the orderly, disciplined mind of the scholar; and the introspective loneliness of the creative artist. Always in evidence, moreover, was the rich vein of his humor. More than any other President in this century, John Kennedy loved a joke and he could laugh at himself as readily as he could laugh at others.

In my opinion, this often hard to fathom but very human man will be long remembered for the style and polish he brought to the Presidency. Not since Franklin Roosevelt and Winston Churchill has a major world leader been so accomplished in the use of the English language. The major Kennedy speeches were classical in their simplicity, and in his speeches, messages, interviews, and other papers the President left the world a large volume of eloquent words and phrases defining and illuminating the political, economic, and social issues of our age.

The artistic talents of President and Mrs. Kennedy were also well demonstrated. In the less than 3 years of his administration, President Kennedy and his remarkable wife transformed the White House. Once again the presidential mansion became the center of our social and cultural life, and due to their good judgment and taste the venerable old building was refurnished and redecorated until it became a living symbol of American history. From the wallpaper to the furniture, room by room, the White House now portrays the story of America and all her Presidents. This legacy to the Nation will be ever appreciated.

Historians in the years to come will speak of John Kennedy's great promise, and they will speculate on what might have been. It is my belief that if the Kennedy administration had been allowed to complete its course its record would stand with any in our history. John Kennedy had the touch of greatness, and the accomplishments of the past 3 years bear witness to this fact.

John Kennedy will receive much attention in the years ahead. He was the youngest man ever elected to the Presidency, and the first member of his religious faith to be so elected. Barriers of any kind were just one more challenge for him, and we have seen nothing like his dynamism and exuberance for more than 50 years.

The President was nominated for his high office by the Democratic National Convention in my home city of Los Angeles. I participated in that convention, and shared in the color and excitement of the labor election victory. Therefore, in a very personal way I felt that John Kennedy was my President.

This young warrior represented all that was best in our society, and his tragic death has touched us all. I find that the most fitting words were expressed by a junior member of the administration in a recent television interview. Speaking for all members of our generation, he said:

Yes, we will continue. We will go on. But we will never be young any more.

ADDRESS BY
Hon. Elmer J. Holland
OF PENNSYLVANIA

Mr. Speaker, I, too, want to join with my colleagues in this formal expression of the Nation's grief over the loss of our late President.

And—in these days of sorrow—I cannot help but also express my utmost respect and heartfelt pride for his widow, Mrs. Jacqueline Kennedy. Her bravery—her courage—her dignity—and her willingness to share her husband with the people of the Nation, as well as the world, are far beyond the realm of duty.

By her conduct throughout those trying days and her considerate understanding of our loss, she has established for us an outstanding example of selfless devotion to one's nation and one's principles. I hope her sacrifice will not be in vain.

May I say—that in my 30 years in public life— never have I seen our Nation, indeed the world, so bereaved.

Our late President was a citizen of the world, and he was the hope of this troubled world.

His youth, his fresh approach to "old, tired problems," his realization that we could—and would—find a common ground on which peaceful international relationships can be established; his belief in the equality of all men and his desire to see all enjoy equal opportunities; his appreciation of the need of more and more education, for us here in America as well as for those in our newer undeveloped nations throughout the world; his joy of living and his wish for all others to share that joy; his concern for the aged, the infirm, the halt and the lame—these, Mr. Speaker, as well as his zest to meet every challenge, these have been denied all peoples of the world—because of a dastardly act of one person. One individual—whose instincts to hate had been so well nurtured and so well cultivated by the "lunatic fringe" that all reasoning ceased to exist.

That lunatic fringe, those steadily increasing groups of fanatics, have indeed acquired another "distinguished" devotee in the person of the assassin.

Those people who fear what is ahead and who want to ignore the future; those people who not only wish to keep the status quo but hope to regress to the good, old days when the health of the mule in the mines was of more concern than the health of our aged and our children; those people who are so intent on fighting "isms"—but are so anxious to return to the days of cheap labor, ill-fed and ill-housed families, undereducated children and desperate parents; those people who are not intelligent enough to realize and recognize they are advocating the best breeding grounds in the world for the birth of alien "isms"; those people—throughout the Nation, wherever they may be—can carry with them the responsibility for this act, committed by a receptive student of hate, and they can share their shame at their clandestine gatherings.

For those of us who believed in John Fitzgerald Kennedy—this is our opportunity to erect a living memorial to him.

Let us rededicate ourselves to carry this Nation forward to those broad horizons which John Kennedy had set as his goals.

Let us fan the flame and rekindle the fire of the true American spirit to help those who need aid and to help those others so they may eventually be able to help themselves.

Let us carry on John Kennedy's quest for peace on this earth and his desire for international cooperation in the exploration of space.

Let us assure the younger generation that educational opportunities will be available to adequately prepare them to become the leaders of this Nation when it is their turn to accept those responsibilities.

Let us—without further delay—provide first-class citizenship for all of our people and insure them opportunities for equal education and employment.

I firmly believe that John Fitzgerald Kennedy would prefer such a memorial as this, for, as a young and energetic man, he liked action and results.

This, Mr. Speaker, is our opportunity to show our people and the people of the world that our youngest President did not give his life in vain.

ADDRESS BY

Hon. Daniel J. Flood

OF PENNSYLVANIA

Mr. Speaker, John Fitzgerald Kennedy is dead and we are the bereaved.

The words I have spoken are words I never conceived of saying, words I never dreamed of hearing. Yet, they are true. And it is with profound sorrow and a deep sense of loss that I join my colleagues in the House, and citizens of this Nation and the world in mourning him.

We have had 2 weeks to absorb fully the nightmarish events of November 22. But our imaginations almost reject the knowledge of that day and what ensued. A whole Nation sat hypnotized by television and radio for 4 days, watching, but not believing, not wanting to believe. A pervading atmosphere of unreality surrounds this international tragedy, this national ordeal.

And it is a personal grief we feel for John Fitzgerald Kennedy, an intimate sense of loss. The qualities he brought to the Nation and to his office were unique and valuable. We have not only lost a President who demonstrated his sagacity and greatness, but a man whose personal being came to mean more to a country than the affection its leader can normally hope to expect.

In a short 3 years, his own youth and vitality

permeated an entire Nation, stimulated the interest of young people in government affairs and indeed in generally seeking to achieve, precipitated the growth of enthusiasm for energetic pursuits of the body and the mind. The Peace Corps symbolized the Kennedy years and the Kennedy influence. The response of the Nation can only be characterized as overwhelming and it reflects the appeal of Kennedy the man to the public imagination.

There were many qualities which endeared him to his country and the world. The sheer personality and character of John Kennedy left indelible impressions on the United States. One sensed that, in his pursuits, he recognized that he was in the eyes of the Nation and had the responsibility to set an example to our youth.

He had a wit at once pungent, subtle, and kind—a wit revealing his capacity for self-evaluation and perception. Wit arises in one's ability to rise above a subjective, personal level and observe oneself on the stage of life. It reveals an interested, reasoned detachment and steadiness of judgment. That John Kennedy possessed these characteristics, he demonstrated time and again.

He had a mind—fertile and active, disciplined and practiced. There has been, perhaps, no other President who combined in such a happy mixture both intellectuality and pragmatism. He surrounded himself with men, not only accomplished, but brilliant and talented. When he spoke to the American people his appeal was not on an emotional plane, but it was nonetheless as effective as an impassioned plea for support. He accustomed the American people to hearing of the complicated issues involved in our national survival. His technique was a challenge to us— a challenge not to shirk thought and consideration, a challenge to react on a rational, reasoned basis, not on a lesser emotional plateau.

He had a keen sense of history, the possession of which will reveal itself in the years and generations ahead, even though he was fated to serve so briefly. His decisions were made with a comprehension of the broad sweep of history, with a world view so rare to those who occupy positions of power and authority.

Youth was the keynote of these 3 years. Not callowness and inexperience that are usually associated with this universally envied commodity, but appreciation and a sense of responsibility toward it. The world that John Kennedy hoped to build by his actions was a world that our young people would want to live in and build further in turn. He hoped to release energies in the country's youth that would dare them to seek responsibility. He thought ahead to the generations of the future as well as concerning himself with the problems of the present. Such enacted and proposed programs as the Peace Corps, its domestic counterpart, the National Service Corps, the drive for youth employment, the emphasis on improving our education, and, of course, the conviction that all our citizens must be on an equal footing with equal treatment and opportunities before we can truly succeed in our works—these all were consistent with the philosophy and beliefs of John Fitzgerald Kennedy.

He was our President for a brief—all too brief—time. But he will be remembered and loved. He will be remembered for his charm and grace and wit and intelligence. But most of all he will be remembered in the time to come for his idea—his plan for the future of the country he loved so well, his belief that all our children should be given the opportunity equally to choose their future course and to share in all that our country can offer.

A man's brilliance and service and dedication are, indeed, sufficient for history to deal kindly with him. And for these alone would he be remembered. But a man who, in addition, is a builder of the future, is truly blessed. John Fitzgerald Kennedy was such a man and in his death we have suffered a bitter blow. We shall miss him.

ADDRESS BY

Hon. Fernand J. St Germain

OF RHODE ISLAND

Mr. Speaker, one of history's greatest men has been taken from us. Seldom have the words "We share your grief," been so sincere from so many.

I am sure that all the people of Rhode Island join Mrs. St Germain and me in expressing deepest sympathy to Mrs. Kennedy and the late President's family. However, at this time of great loss, may I also express my sympathy to all the people of Rhode Island, of the United States and to all the freedom-loving people of the world.

History has shown us that in time of great need, God has provided men to fill the need. Such a man was John Fitzgerald Kennedy.

The President was close to all of us; not only to those of us who were honored to have known him personally, but to all who admired him, loved him, and had faith in him.

We must take heart. Pray for the soul of the late President; pray for the health and well-being of our new President, Lyndon Baines Johnson; pray that God bless him and guide him upon his succession to this great office of trust and responsibility.

We shall deeply miss John F. Kennedy who was certainly a profile in courage.

One of President Kennedy's most outstanding characteristics was his love for the American people. He shared their hopes, sorrows, dreams, and aspirations. They, in turn, loved and revered him to a degree seldom seen in the annals of our Nation's history. A fitting example of this great feeling is expressed in a letter which I have received from one of my constituents. It should be pointed out that this lady did not have the benefit of a formal education and most of her years have been spent in a textile plant to supplement her husband's income in order to feed, clothe, and educate their children. Her letter follows:

DEAR FRED AND RACHEL: Our sorrow is beyond expression as we share with Mrs. Kennedy the loss of her dear husband and our beloved President. Our only consolation is that he walked hand in hand with God, and took upon his broad shoulders the suffering and poverty that mankind was enduring. His life was sacrificed to eliminate this condition and find a solution to overcome the sufferings of this human race. His death was not in vain, because others will continue the programs that he had to leave behind. I never dreamt that I would be enclosing this note within this envelope. We still cannot face reality and realize that he is gone from us. His smiling face we cannot forget. God must have a special seat for him in Heaven among the great saints and prophets. He lived as God's chosen apostle and shall never be forgotten by those who loved him so dearly.

I know how great your sorrow must be. We will all share it together and God will give us all the courage we need to face such a great loss.

Sincerely yours,

———— ————

This simple but beautiful tribute gives eloquent voice to what is in all our hearts and minds at this sad time. We pray that Almighty God will give him peace and that perpetual light will shine upon him for all eternity.

Hon. Michael J. Kirwan

Mr. Speaker, we gather here to pay tribute to a great leader—John Fitzgerald Kennedy—the 35th President of the United States.

Words are inadequate to express my true feelings for this great leader—I feel I have lost a member of my family. I was privileged to be in this great legislative body in 1947 when John F. Kennedy arrived as a freshman Congressman from Boston. I watched him work and grow in the 6 years he served in the House of Representatives. I saw him fight and conquer insurmountable odds to be elected to the Senate of the United States, and there he continued to work and grow. I watched him again overcome obstacles and barriers unparalleled in history to be elected President in 1960. I watched him as he assumed that great burden, and he continued to work and grow, and I prayed that he would be granted divine light and guidance to continue his noble effort to accomplish the goals he envisioned for this great country of ours. In 3 short years he set new goals for all mankind, new vision for the free world, and new hope for peace on earth. Now he is gone—yet, his hopes, dedication, and goals for all the world are an inspiration to go forward to achieve these goals he so clearly desired.

It was a privilege to know this great man, and I extend to his widow, children, and family my deepest sympathy.

Hon. Compton I. White, Jr.

Mr. Speaker—

The great man, with his free force direct out of God's own hand, is the lightning. * * * The rest of men waited for him like fuel, and then they, too, would flame.

The spirit of those words, written by Thomas Carlyle, could very well have described our Nation's departed President, John Fitzgerald Kennedy.

His life personified the aspirations, the honor, the courage of all mankind and prompted lesser men to greater deeds. His leadership, faith, and confidence in our country, and our people, and our heritage never once faltered even in the light of other significant tragedies which are so much a part of our world today. His grasp of the problems of the 20th century were met without hesitation or excuse, and he well understood the destiny that our forefathers set forth for our Nation.

My first visit with the late President, then a Senator from Massachusetts, was in the early months of 1960 during one of his four trips to the State of Idaho. It was an interesting, educational visit, and we compared Idaho's local problems in perspective with those of the Nation and the world. His knowledge, frankness, candor, and willingness to speak freely were encouraging, and his words of advice were gratifying and appreciated.

He told one crowd of Idaho citizens that "we need people who can look ahead, men who believe in the future, men who are willing to try something new." John F. Kennedy exemplified this. He said that "Lewis and Clark did not travel this area on a mission they thought would be easy," and it can be said that John F. Kennedy knew the difficulties of his mission, too:

Today the frontier they explored has been pushed aside. We stand on the edge of a new frontier—and we need more men to cross the mountains.

* * * * *

With your help, with many hands, we can make for all the Nation a living reality of this State's inspiring motto: "Esto Perpetua"—may this State endure forever.

That State and this Nation and the world will endure. They will endure because of persons with the wisdom and foresight of our departed friend and leader. Even though his horse is now without rider, the memory of John Fitzgerald Kennedy will linger on forever. We are wiser because of him. We are more tolerant. His words and deeds will be repeated for generations to come and his actions will indeed be recorded in the archives of great men.

All Idaho shares the sorrow of this tragedy. One astute observer, William Johnston, editor of the Lewiston, Idaho, Tribune, had this to say:

[From the Lewiston (Idaho) Morning Tribune, Nov. 23, 1963]

WHAT COULD HE DO FOR HIS COUNTRY?

"And so, my fellow Americans: Ask not what your country will do for you—ask what you can do for your country."

—*John F. Kennedy.*

Slowly, among the shocked and sorrowing people of the world, the incredible news congealed into aching understanding that a great American President is dead.

One moment he was with us—a warm, kindly, human leader who mingled smilingly with crowds, shared his wit and wisdom without malice or meanness, and symbolized for all mankind a courageous, proud, friendly America. The next moment he was gone.

The terrible deed was the consequence of horrible hallucinations in one twisted mind. Yet, the shameful act was born in a climate of falsehood and hatred. The fierce, reckless accusations and the angry defiance of law and elected authority among other citizens feed the delusions of assassins and terrorists. Every hysterical hate cult in this land of free discussion and majority decision share the shame.

It was a question, in those long moments of suspense, whether the assassin was an ugly, ultimate caricature of the Kennedy-haters of the left or the right. Was the fatal bullet fired by an assassin whose soul had been poisoned by the President's crusade for civil rights and economic opportunity for all Americans? Or was this the foul crime of a brain warped by the ugly dreams of totalitarian communism? Americans should have learned something in the suspense. The answer could have come from either side. The left and the right become indistinguishable at the stage where hate supplants reason and terror supplants law.

The martyred President must be judged in history, not so much by what he accomplished as by what he attempted. He had so tragically little time and so many massive barriers before him.

Perhaps no other American President prepared himself so consciously and so completely for his office. Mr. Kennedy was a master of politics, which is the necessary prerequisite for statesmanship. After his election, he laid before his country and its reluctant Congress a program for progress which is as bold as it is comprehensive.

He submitted to his countrymen imaginative new concepts in conservation and resource development, civil rights, education, public health, aid for the aging, employment, international trade, and domestic economic policy, to name a few areas of his interest and competency. He demonstrated in his press conference a continuous mastery of the varied facets of his bafflingly complex office. Many of the domestic programs he advocated doubtless will be achieved in years still to come.

In foreign policy particularly the brilliant vision of this young President surely will help guide the Nation and the free world long after his tragic death. Surely the world will listen to him anew, as it listened to Lincoln, now that he is gone:

"Let us examine our attitude toward peace itself. Too many of us think it is impossible. Too many think it unreal. But that is a dangerous, defeatist belief. It leads to the conclusion that war is inevitable, that mankind is doomed, that we are gripped by forces we cannot control.

"We need not accept that view. Our problems are manmade; therefore they can be solved by man. And man can be as big as he wants."

Or again:

"I come here today to look across this world of threats

to the world of peace. In that search we cannot expect any final triumph for new problems will always arise. We cannot expect that all nations will adopt like systems for conformity is the jailor of freedom and the enemy of growth. Nor can we expect to reach our goal by contrivance, by fiat, or even by the wishes of all.

"But however close we sometimes seem to that dark and final abyss, let no man of peace and freedom despair. For he does not stand alone. If we all can persevere—if we can in every land and office look beyond our own shores and ambitions—then surely the age will dawn in which the strong are just and the weak secure and the peace preserved.

"Never have the nations of the world had so much to lose—or so much to gain. Together we shall save our planet, or together we shall perish in its flames. Save it we can—and save it we must—and then shall we earn the eternal thanks of mankind and, as peacemakers, the eternal blessing of God."

He left another message of special meaning this day for his grieving countrymen. He was speaking of Dag Hammarskjold and the United Nations, but he could as well have been speaking of his own beloved country and the voice he now leaves in it:

"The problem is not the death of one man; the problem is the life of this organization. It will either grow to meet the challenge of our age, or it will be gone with the wind, without influence, without force, without respect. Were we to let it die, to enfeeble its vigor, to cripple its powers, we would condemn the future."

The unfinished work of John F. Kennedy awaits America. May this Nation grow to meet the challenge of our age.

So appropriate are the words of Mr. Johnston as are the words of Mr. Kennedy in his book, "Profiles in Courage":

> The courage of life is often a less dramatic spectacle than the courage of a final moment; but it is no less than a magnificent mixture of triumph and tragedy. A man does what he must—in spite of personal consequences, in spite of obstacles and dangers and pressures—and that is the basis of all human morality.

John Fitzgerald Kennedy now belongs to the history of our Nation. May the eternal light now burning over his grave at Arlington National Cemetery continue to remind us throughout the ages of his hopes and dreams of peace and good will for all mankind and our continuing efforts to make them come true.

ADDRESS BY
Hon. Joseph P. Addabbo
OF NEW YORK

Mr. Speaker, unbelievable and shocking was the murder of President John F. Kennedy. A catastrophic moment and an entire nation and world suffered a loss and experienced great sorrow and mourning. History and the future can only prove the real greatness of John Fitzgerald Kennedy—President, father, husband, son, brother, war hero.

Yes, the evil event of November 22 still remains unbelievable as a bad dream, but it is no dream, it is the raw, ugly reality that there was such a man as the murderer of our President. This unbelievable murderer who could harbor such thoughts and hatred changed the entire course of human events.

John F. Kennedy's life was dedicated to the people of this Nation as a war hero, legislator, and President. He could have led a peaceful life in luxury without harassment, without ridicule, but he chose the life of dedicated service to his country and fellow man. He sought programs and legislation he believed necessary to help all mankind, the Nation, and bring about world peace.

Though his programs were not in accord with everyone's beliefs or desires, I believe all respected him and in his death felt a part of each of us went with him.

I thank God and the people of my district for having given me the opportunity to have known John F. Kennedy personally—his friendliness, his understanding.

As we reflect on these past dark and sorrowful days, we remember a strong gleaming light as the warmth and strength of sunlight standing beside the sorrowful dark cloud—it is a lady of great majesty and strength—the grieving widow—Mrs. Jacqueline Kennedy. I believe great strength was given to all by this great First Lady and our prayers should include continued comfort for her and their two wonderful children.

Through the life and death of our President John F. Kennedy and the great majesty of his and our First Lady, Mrs. Jacqueline Kennedy, I believe we can and should rededicate ourselves to the building and working for the basic principles on which this Nation was founded, the brotherhood of man, and love of country.

Words cannot really express what Mrs. Addabbo and I know nearly all feel in the loss of our President John F. Kennedy or lessen the grief of this loss. We extend to Mrs. Jacqueline Kennedy, Caroline and John, Jr., his parents, our

Attorney General, Robert F. Kennedy, our colleague, Senator Edward Kennedy, our heartfelt sorrow and pray for the repose of his soul and comfort upon them that mourn.

I believe what we all feel was aptly put by a constituent of mine, a child, Maria Papa, of Ozone Park, N.Y.:

A GREAT LOSS

We lost a man, a man so great,
A man that no one could ever hate,
And, yet our disbelief is strong,
Though we did not know him long,
They mourned his death far and wide
For a good and grateful man had died.
And now we must quietly pray
To help our Nation on its way.

ADDRESS BY

Hon. Herman Toll

OF PENNSYLVANIA

Mr. Speaker, as Mrs. Toll and I traveled down on the train from Philadelphia to Washington that bleak, drizzly Saturday morning, November 23, to pay our last respects to our fallen leader, our recollections went back to other meetings with John Fitzgerald Kennedy:

To our first introduction in 1956 to the then Senator Kennedy in Chicago at the Democratic National Convention, when I substituted for Councilman Finley in voting for the Democratic candidate for Vice President.

To a meeting in 1958 in the office of Congressman Keogh, of New York, where I was invited by Congressman William J. Green, Jr., and he asked me some questions about Philadelphia.

To Los Angeles, July of 1960, after the Democratic Convention, when campaign pictures were taken with him and the then Senator Johnson after their nomination as our party's leaders. Later the campaign pictures with him at the White House.

To later that fall when it was my privilege to appear with him on the platform at Cheltenham Avenue and Washington Lane in Philadelphia, where he spoke to more than 25,000 people, and I rode with him through my district.

To the gay, memorable receptions which we attended at the White House. His friendly and informal manner, which Mrs. Kennedy shared. The annual prayer breakfast where he spoke.

The annual St. Patrick's Day Party and the annual gym party for Members of the House. He showed up at many places where I did not expect him to be, and always greeted all Members from both political parties.

To meetings in the East Room of the White House where he personally briefed hundreds of Members of the House on important legislative matters, such as the tax cut bill. Always his explanations were clear and precise.

To a meeting during the 87th Congress when I, as one of the sponsors of the arms control and disarmament bill, was called to the White House along with various other Members to attend a meeting with the Chief Executive. At that time he helped us to prepare some of the language of the bill, including the title.

To a meeting just a few weeks ago, on the second story porch of the White House, the famous Truman porch, to discuss with him and 14 other Members of the House the civil rights situation.

To two other meetings with the late President and some of my committee colleagues in the White House Cabinet Room to discuss the provisions of the new civil rights bill. He helped us to get the bill out of the full committee and to keep the equal employment opportunity provisions in it. That was a major accomplishment because the opposition was very strong.

And then to my last meeting with the President on October 30 when the Philadelphia congressional delegation was invited to ride with him on the Presidential plane en route to Philadelphia where he was the speaker at the Democratic dinner held at Convention Hall. He came to our seats in the plane to chat with each of us.

As we neared Washington, the words of the Senate Chaplain the day before came to mind:

Our Father, Thou knowest that this sudden, almost unbelievable news, has stunned our minds and hearts as we gaze at a vacant place against the sky, as the President of the Republic like a giant cedar green with boughs goes down, with a great shout upon the hills, and leaves a lonesome place against the sky.

Since first elected to public office in 1950, I have served in two legislative bodies with four executives. His executive manner was like no other—warm, friendly, knowledgeable. I truly believe he was an idealistic man and his philosophy of "do what you can for your country" certainly supports this belief.

Young in years but mature in judgment, fair to all people, dedicated to his country and its citizens, he labored hard and well for the security of our Nation and for peace in the world.

As the members of the Philadelphia congressional delegation walked up the White House steps to pay our last respect to John Fitzgerald Kennedy, the rain continued to come down. Even the heavens wept.

Mr. Speaker, it is fitting, I believe, to include a resolution adopted December 2, 1963, in the Senate of Pennsylvania. The resolution, which memorializes the Congress of the United States to declare November 22 as President Kennedy Memorial Day, is as follows:

RESOLUTION

The 22d day of November will go down in history as the anniversary of the day that the people of the world were thrown into deep sorrow upon hearing of the assassination of President John F. Kennedy.

It was a day of sadness for all and will linger in the minds of mankind for many years to come.

It would be most fitting for the Congress of the United States to set aside November 22 of each year as a day when the people of our Nation can rededicate themselves to the ideals which were set forth by our 35th President; therefore be it

Resolved, That the Senate of the Commonwealth of Pennsylvania memorialize the Congress of the United States to declare November 22 as President Kennedy Memorial Day; and be it further

Resolved, That a copy of this resolution be forwarded to the Speaker of the House of Representatives and President pro tempore of the Senate in Washington, D.C., as well as each Member of the Congress from the Commonwealth of Pennsylvania.

I certify that the foregoing is a true and correct copy of Senate Resolution Serial No. 9, introduced by Senators William J. Lane and James S. Berger on behalf of the entire membership of the Senate and adopted by the Senate of Pennsylvania the 2d day of December 1963.

MARK GRUELL, Jr.,
Secretary, Senate of Pennsylvania.

ADDRESS BY

Hon. Joseph M. Montoya

OF NEW MEXICO

Mr. Speaker, today I am reminded of words uttered about the United States more than a century ago by John Bright. He said:

Every 4 years there springs from the vote created by the whole people a President over that great Nation. I think

the whole world offers no finer spectacle than this; it offers no higher dignity.

Our admirer from Great Britain said it well, Mr. Speaker. My words could convey no greater dignity nor offer any comparable tribute to that already bestowed on John Fitzgerald Kennedy by his countrymen, for he has held the Office of President of the United States.

I would, therefore, address myself to the dignity and immeasurable tribute which our late President Kennedy has paid to the American people. With the approving roars of a demonstrative city still echoing in his ears, he sacrificed his life. He gave it for those many who stood cheering that they might have courage; he gave it for this Congress that we might show wisdom; he gave it for mankind that we might have peace; and, he gave it for his assassin that he might have justice.

What manner of man was John F. Kennedy that he offered his precious blood for ordinary commonsense—so much in exchange for so very little? He, himself, answered that question in a simple few words when he wrote:

A man does what he must—in spite of obstacles and dangers and pressures—and that is the basis of all human morality.

He penned those words in praise of others, but they truly describe him.

He traveled the road of progress, a tempestuous journey breached by many blind intersections, but without fail he took direction from a map not plotted for mere expedience but for truth and right.

None but a man inextricably bound to his fellow man could have so lived and died for mankind. The Presidency was a welcome burden to John F. Kennedy because he felt as one with each man and with all men. Unemployment, bankruptcy, thirst, hunger, fear, despair; it made no difference. "There but for you, go I," was his battle cry, and throughout this land we are better for his charge.

Now, John Kennedy is gone and we are led by a new commander of ability and virtue, who has been sharpened by trial and tempered by experience.

He urges that we continue our journey of progress. This Republic wants to move; she pulls to run a mile ahead. For the path is warm and the lead is strong. There is a sense of strength and a rebirth of purpose, for John Fitzgerald Kennedy strode down that way and it is not yet cold or devoid of hope.

ADDRESS BY
Hon. Richard H. Ichord
OF MISSOURI

Mr. Speaker, the American people have lost a great and courageous leader. John Fitzgerald Kennedy was a very strong President who sought to incorporate his high ideals and standards into American society and to diffuse his high veneration for Christian principles and tradition into all our institutions.

John Fitzgerald Kennedy was a politician, a man well versed and experienced in the science of government, and even though his tenure of office was shortened by a meaningless, unintelligible act of a reactionary extremist, the comparatively short time he held the Presidency will record him in history as a true statesman. His influence in only 2 years, 10 months, and 2 days in the highest office in our land is probably unexcelled by any other Chief Executive. We mourn a great man who had limitless potential, and the true impact of the tragedy will not be fully felt for years to come.

These and many other words eloquently eulogizing our late President have been spoken and written since his remains were interred in Arlington National Cemetery. A master journalist in my district, publisher of the Rolla Daily News, Mr. Edward T. Sowers, perhaps, has best evaluated the situation and the event, and I borrow his words, appropriately entitled "Hail to the Chief—And Farewell," which so adequately express my own personal sorrow and regret for the needless loss of a great man:

One of President Kennedy's last official acts was, as Commander in Chief, to send Operation Big Lift on its way to demonstrate to the world our great strength and determination to preserve peace. This picture of Jack Kennedy as he reviewed the bombers and tankers before takeoff is the way I wish to remember him—a rugged, hatless, bronzed warrior for freedom.

As we sadly bow our heads in shame and say hail and farewell to the Chief, let us remember to eliminate our weakness within while we build our physical strength without—strength and the courage to use it—as President Kennedy helped build it, and left it, for our use.

As this is written, the funeral cortege with many world heads of state has just passed the Lincoln Memorial where the inscription says, "Now He Belongs to the Ages."

Moments later, the 20th century symbol of the doctrines we live by, fight for and die to preserve is buried in Arlington Cemetery. If we merit it, by our actions in the future, we shall build a memorial perhaps in stone, but, more importantly, in the hearts and minds of free men and women everywhere—and shall keep the eternal flame of freedom—the torch which President Kennedy's brave widow lighted—burning forever over his grave, and eventually, throughout the world.

ADDRESS BY
Hon. Thomas L. Ashley
OF OHIO

Mr. Speaker, the agony begins to abate, but a heartsick nation will know deep sadness for many years to come.

The world mourns John Fitzgerald Kennedy because it has lost a gallant and gifted leader. Our bereavement is this and more. We grieve a President whose spirit and style reflected so splendidly the best that America stands for and the destiny we seek to fulfill in these difficult years of the 20th century. We grieve for his courage and dedication, his vitality, his sanity and wit, his confidence in his country and himself.

Perhaps the most immediate measure of this remarkable man is the extent to which each of us, each American, feels not only a sense of personal loss but an obligation to give more fully of ourselves, as he did, for the common cause of mankind.

Mr. Speaker, John Fitzgerald Kennedy was a man of rare vision and ability, a strong President in a period of great challenge. History will accord him a proud place. May it also relate that those who mourned him kept faith, and that through their efforts, as well as his, the hopes and ideals of civilization were advanced.

ADDRESS BY
Hon. Frank M. Clark
OF PENNSYLVANIA

Mr. Speaker, future historians will give to John F. Kennedy, our beloved President, his merited recognition as a great leader in a period when there was need for great leadership. His ability, his courage, his vision, his indomitable drive, his tolerance, and his great warmth are known to the present generation. But John F. Kennedy was more than a great leader of men. He was a faithful husband, a doting father, and a friend always patient and understanding with those upon whom he so lavishly bestowed his friendship. Despite the heavy burdens of his office and the demands upon his time, he was always available to those who sought his help as I and so many of you well know. In his tragic and untimely death, the Nation and the free world have lost a great and able leader and those of us who knew him well have lost a valued and true friend.

ADDRESS BY

Hon. Tom Steed

OF OKLAHOMA

Mr. Speaker, a stirring tribute to the late President John F. Kennedy was delivered at memorial services at Oklahoma Baptist University, Shawnee, Okla., by the president of the institution, Dr. James Ralph Scales.

More than 900 students, faculty members and townspeople gathered for the service at the Raley Chapel at Shawnee. Here is the complete text of that tribute:

A "PROFILE IN COURAGE": SPECIAL TRIBUTE GIVEN TO PRESIDENT KENNEDY

(EDITOR'S NOTE.—"Profile in Courage," a stirring tribute to the late President John F. Kennedy, was delivered Sunday in a special memorial service at Oklahoma Baptist University by Dr. James Ralph Scales, president of the university. More than 900 students, faculty and townspeople gathered for the impressive service in the beautiful Raley Chapel. Here is the complete text of that tribute.)

The youngest of our Presidents to be elected, the youngest to die, John Fitzgerald Kennedy cannot be measured in the days of his years. He was a man of quality, a man of character, a man of intellect.

To the end of his life, he remained faithful to his great loyalties; his country, his family, his religion, his school. In the conduct of his affairs, he brought honor and glory to all of these. But he was not the prisoner of these allegiances; his was not a parochial outlook. His spacious vision extended beyond the boundaries of his own land and encompassed the family of mankind.

He had a grand sense of history, and an endless fascination and respect for the institutions of our democracy; the courts of law, the Congress in which he served 14 years, the Presidency he sought and helped to fashion.

His was a reverent, almost mystical feeling for that office. He enjoyed power, and did not hesitate to use it. History will judge whether he used it wisely. When the balance is struck, I am persuaded that the judgment will be favorable.

The Presidency belongs to all of us. Every incumbent is cherished as the symbol of a great nation. As I read American history, every President has been enabled by his work, even the poorest of the succession. The responsibilities of this awesome office are a refiner's fire that burns away the dross of pettiness and malice.

Because the hopes and fears of mankind settle upon his shoulders, the President is every citizen's kinsman. When a President dies, as General MacArthur noted in his tender message to Mrs. Kennedy, something within us dies. The most obscure of us, of whatever section, of whatever race, or whatever party, has a personal relationship to the President.

This then is my personal testament. President Kennedy, though he once shook my hand, did not know me; but I knew him.

I first met him in a book he wrote, "Why England Slept." It was his senior thesis at Harvard, an important book that traced the consequences of appeasement in the years before 1939. This young man, only an indifferent student his first 2 years, was gripped by the excitement of scholarship and its relevance to world events. His experience should be an inspiration to other young men to use their God-given gifts, to realize that even in their extreme youth, they can perform worthy public service, just as Mr. Kennedy performed a public service in arousing his fellow man in an hour of grave menace to civilization.

I next knew the future President in World War II as I sat in the coding room of my ship, breaking low-priority dispatches about some minor action in the Solomons, an action that was to become famous as the heroic exploit of *PT–109.* I did not even recall the commander's name, but I had seen nests of these little boats in tropic harbors as their tired, disheveled crews rested for the next mission. There is a comradeship of men at arms that transcends all barriers. We proudly identify ourselves with the occasional hero of our branch of service, and sublimate our own dull tasks in the achievements of a Sergeant York, an Audie Murphy, a Jack Kennedy.

I remembered the impact of young Senator Kennedy's next book, "Profiles in Courage." Its theme is his life's theme. Writing that book was itself a study in courage, for it was done in racking pain. But pain and sorrow were no strangers to the Kennedy family. For all their wealth and power, they have known the tragedy of violent death, the tragedy of losing children, the tragedy of an afflicted child.

I was a member of the convention in 1956 when Mr.

Kennedy sustained his only political defeat. But I remember the roaring excitement of that afternoon, and the gallantry of Senator Kennedy as he moved to make unanimous the nomination of his successful foe, the late Estes Kefauver.

And who among us does not recall the campaign of 1960? We shall not review it here, for our purpose today is to unite and not to divide our people. On both sides it was a titanic exertion, with punishing schedules, television debates, exhiliration and despair. Indefatigable energy and courage aplenty were present in the four patriotic Americans, who led the two national tickets; and not a little courage was quietly shown by millions of voters who felt the tug of ancient loyalties, even as they weighed the pounding issues of war and peace. Once the choice was made, we closed ranks in the great tradition of a free society, and acclaimed a new President—just as we prayerfully close ranks today.

Those who "lost their vote," no less than his friends, expressed gratification that the ghost· of second-class citizenship for human beings of any faith was at last removed.

And so my private memories have long since merged with yours. Except for two treasured souvenirs, a Christmas card from the Kennedys, with a picture of little Caroline; and a beautiful letter from the President saluting me on my inauguration and the completion of this chapel. (Both of us were inaugurated in blizzards in the year 1961, but there the parallel ends. Mine was inside, his was outdoors. Mine is a much humbler, and safer, presidency.)

President Kennedy's legacy is the sanity he exemplified in public life in a time of violence. He will not have died in vain if, in the soul-searching that is now going on, the American people return to reason and decency; if we recover our natural optimism; if we reject extremism in every form; if we ignore the intimidating and strident voices of those who would poison the wellsprings of public discourse; if we scorn the slander, name calling, spitting, and howling; if the national soul is cleansed and the national purpose is renewed.

Once our hearts resonated to the noble words of Jefferson, bugling forth the right of men to life, liberty, and the pursuit of happiness. It can be so again. We shall differ, but the debate must be conducted in decency and in reason.

In his last, undelivered address at Dallas, the President said "Reason and learning must be the guides to American policy." As he embodied reason, he also exemplified learning. He cared for the quality of American education. He was an activist, brought up in the tough school of Boston politics, yet he retained the nobility of the scholar. A finely tempered integrity prevented his dramatizing some of the public issues that swirled about him. Robert Frost once advised him to "show a little less Harvard and a little more Irish." But the spirit of learning prevailed in the Kennedy style. An urbane, 20th century man thus joined the list of the presidential intellectuals, Jefferson and Wilson. And the forceful stylists, Lincoln and the two Roosevelts.

There are only a few great state papers which are remembered by every patriot. Among these treasures we think of the Declaration of Independence, the Constitution (especially the Bill of Rights), Washington's and Eisenhower's Farewell Addresses, Wilson's and Roosevelt's war messages, Monroe's State of the Union speech enunciating the famous doctrine of hemispheric solidarity; Jackson's proclamation denying the South Carolina ordinance of nullification; Theodore Roosevelt's "standing at Armageddon and battling for the Lord" as he launched the Bull Moose Party; Lincoln's Farewell to Springfield, the immortal Gettysburg Address, and the letter to Mrs. Bixby, who had lost four sons in battle; Woodrow Wilson's Fourteen Points; F.D.R.'s Four Freedoms and his annual message in the blackest days of World War II when, in ringing accents, he rallied the Nation with the words:

"The state of this Nation is good;
"The heart of this Nation is sound;
"The hope of the Nation is strong;
"The faith of this Nation is eternal."

And we remember the classic inaugurals: Jefferson's first ("This country, with its institutions, belongs to the people who inhabit it"); his second ("With malice toward none, with charity for all"); Wilson's first ("This is not a day of triumph, it is a day of dedication"); Roosevelt's of 1933 ("The only thing we have to fear is fear itself"); and of 1937 ("I see one-third of a Nation ill fed, ill clothed, ill housed").

President Kennedy ranks in eloquence with the best of these. Who among us did not respond to the calm but resolute message in October 1962 when he threw down the gauntlet in the Cuban crisis? Who was not convinced of our national failures when he gave moral leadership to the battle for human rights in a moving and compassionate address of last June?

And who did not thrill to the trumpet summons of his great inaugural, "My fellow Americans: ask not what your country can do for you—ask what you can do for your country"?

Tirelessly, patiently, despite many discouragements, misunderstandings, and cruel challenges, he proceeded to advance the cause of peace, making good on his inaugural appeal, "Let us never negotiate out of fear. But never let us fear to negotiate."

In a time of national soul searching and apprehension, we take renewed spirit from the pledge he made then, and devoted superhuman energy to fulfill:

"Let the word go forth from this time and place, to friend and foe alike, that the torch has been passed to a new generation of Americans—born in this century, tempered by war, disciplined by a hard and bitter peace, proud of our ancient heritage.

"Let every nation know, whether it wishes us well or ill, that we shall pay any price, bear any burden, meet any hardship, support any friend, oppose any foe to assure the survival and the success of liberty."

The word has gone out, and freedom stands.

Every nation does know, and in tribute to the strength of this country and the faithful servant who preserved it these 3 bitter years, there will assemble in Washington tomorrow the most notable group of rulers in recent world history.

The youngest to serve—the youngest to die. In our hearts he will be forever young.

"He shall grow not old, as we that are left grow old;
Age shall not wear him, nor the years condemn.
At the going down of the sun and in the morning,
We will remember him."
    (Adapted from Laurence Binyon's "For the Fallen.")

ADDRESS BY

Hon. Thaddeus J. Dulski

OF NEW YORK

Mr. Speaker, on November 22, 1963, an assassin's bullet was fired that echoed around the world.

Almost immediately, unbelievable accounts of President Kennedy's assassination flooded the airwaves. I would need a novelist's skill and a poet's words to adequately describe my emotions. I felt as if the entire world was standing absolutely still for a moment. And then came the word we all feared but did not want to hear—that he had left us. Our country lost a great leader, and I lost a good friend.

Despite his short term in the Presidency, he has left an indelible mark on the history in our time. He set out to make the United States of America an even better place in which to live, and to promote peace and good will among the family of nations so they, too, might have a fuller, richer life. His programs, his plans, his endeavors—all were designed to achieve this. He championed the causes of peace and the rights of man with undaunted courage. Is it any wonder then that the whole world has put on its mourning dress and shares the sorrow of every grieving American?

I first met the late President when he was a Senator. I was most impressed with his innate friendliness, his vivacious personality, and his illimitable storehouse of wisdom. Our paths crossed much more closely when he was a candidate for the Presidency in 1960 and campaigned in our city of Buffalo. After his election as President, I visited with him on several occasions, and in the fall of last year he honored us again by coming to Buffalo for our annual Pulaski Day observance. He witnessed one of the greatest crowds that had ever turned out to welcome an official.

I want to quote the last words of our late beloved President's inaugural address:

With a good conscience our only sure reward, with history the final judge of our deeds, let us go forth to lead the land we love, asking His blessing and His help, but knowing that here on earth God's work must truly be our own.

And to the very last, this is what he did.

Mr. Speaker, to his brave widow and his family, we offer our deepest sympathy.

ADDRESS BY

Hon. James W. Trimble

OF ARKANSAS

Mr. Speaker, it is with sadness that I join with my colleagues today in tribute to our late, great President, John Fitzgerald Kennedy, our former colleague in the House of Representatives. His tragic death has shocked all of us, the Nation, and the world.

While he served less than 3 years the impact of his service will be felt throughout the centuries.

He was a friend to all of us, and I join with others in deep sympathy to the family, especially to his widow and children. They have every reason to be very proud of him, as we all are.

ADDRESS BY

Hon. Leo W. O'Brien

OF NEW YORK

I am humbly grateful for the opportunity to add a tiny tile of tribute to the national mosaic of sorrow, which has been formed by the tears of millions of my countrymen.

In the final analysis, the greatest scholar and most gifted orator among us cannot approach what the great mass of Americans, speaking simply and from the depths of their hearts, have already said.

Haltingly and movingly they have said what John F. Kennedy would have appreciated most—"He was our friend, as well as our President."

My heart has been touched by the letters which

have come to me in recent days, letters containing urgent pleas for direction of the senders' sorrow. Some have proposed monuments; many have simply stated that they want to take up arms against the dark demons of hatred who achieved an unholy sacrifice of something precious to us all.

One hesitates to rummage in the debris of senselessness for words of consolation to a bereaved family or a bereaved Nation. And yet, in the grand design which men cannot comprehend, is it not possible that our fallen leader, in his martyrdom, won a mighty battle against the forces of darkness and malice and intolerance?

I do not believe John F. Kennedy ever hated anyone. If he hated anything it was hatred itself.

During recent months, many of us, hypnotized into immobility, watched a blight creep over our land. False prophets arose among us and preached the devil's doctrine in the name of patriotism. Wrapping the flag about their shoulders, they set themselves up as infallible, daring to judge the patriotism of their fellow men. Restlessly, they cast about for a man on horseback.

They railed at the President, the Supreme Court, the Congress. Those who differed with them were traitors and there were hints of violence, rather than debate; lynching rather than law.

Is it any wonder, Mr. Speaker, that this slimy river of hate reached into the tortured minds and produced the most shameful crime of our generation?

We have always had extremists in our midst, some moving in the dark shadows of communism and some posing as the final arbiters of right and wrong.

So long as they remained only ugly sores on the body politic, they constituted no cancerous threat to our society and way of life.

Their menace became real and frightening when some of our good people began to echo their slogans. Some were willing to accept the enticing labels on the package, such as anticommunistic, economy, and antisocialism, ignoring the deadly poison within the package.

Then came the awful day in Dallas.

The shot which struck down our vibrant young President and plunged our Nation and much of the world in grief also shattered into a million pieces the growing lure of the extremists for the "good people."

The tragedy of Dallas showed us the terrible end to which hatred could and did lead us.

Mr. Speaker, our President died and no words uttered today can bring back our friend. But, from the terror of it all, we have forged a new resolve, a resolve to bury once and for all the temptation of believing, ever, that the end justifies the means and that patriotism belongs to a self-anointed few.

President Kennedy died that we might learn these truths. We pray to God that we will not soon forget what we have learned.

ADDRESS BY

Hon. John Jarman

OF OKLAHOMA

Mr. Speaker, John Fitzgerald Kennedy was a Member of this body when I first came to the House of Representatives in January of 1951. I watched with great admiration the events and activities that took him to the U.S. Senate and then on to the White House as our President in the span of but a few years.

I pay tribute today to my former colleague and friend, not only as a great national leader, but as a dynamic and courageous leader of the free world. He led us well in our survival struggle with the Communists. He earned the respect of men of all nations and awakened their faith in his purposes. He laid a firm foundation on which to build a better and more secure world. I am sure at this time he would not want us to reflect on what might have been, but instead to meet the challenges to come with firm convictions and renewed dedication.

People around the globe are saddened by the tragic and untimely death of this able and dedicated man. His strong faith in his country and his quest for peace will be a lasting inspiration for men of good will everywhere. The United States of America has lost a great President and the whole world has lost a warm and devoted friend.

Hon. Lester R. Johnson

Mr. Speaker, Friday, November 22, 1963, will be recorded as one of the blackest days in our Nation's history. For within a few horrifying and unbelievable moments on that black Friday, an assassin's bullet had robbed the United States of our beloved President, the world of a distinguished leader, and the Kennedy family of a loved one.

As a Member of the House of Representatives, I was privileged to serve with President Kennedy during his days in the U.S. Congress. As a fellow Democrat, I was glad to work with him for the successful outcome of the 1960 election. Since that time, I have been honored to have him as my Chief Executive.

The entire Nation shares a deep sense of loss which is both public and personal. Our public grief is for the loss of a President who, in less than 3 years' time, had made giant strides toward translating his ideas and ideals into reality for the good of the United States and the free world. Our personal grief is for the loss of a dynamic, brilliant and vital young man, whose murder has deprived his young family of a husband and father and has left all of us poorer indeed.

Mr. Speaker, President Kennedy's tireless efforts for peace and a better life for the citizens of the United States and the world brought successes which will stand as living monuments to the greatness of the man. Even in death, he left us with an indelible message against hate, bigotry and violence.

As our new President, Lyndon B. Johnson, pointed out so effectively in his first message to Congress, it is for those of us who remain to continue the good work which President Kennedy began. The concluding sentence of Psalm 15 states prophetically:

Teach us to number our days, that we may apply our hearts to wisdom.

In these dark and disturbing times, I feel we must all keep in mind that it is better to light one small candle in the world than to curse the darkness. The eternal flame which burns at President Kennedy's grave in Arlington National Cemetery will serve as a constant reminder that he lived by such a noble philosophy.

Hon. Edward A. Garmatz

Mr. Speaker, so much has been said and written about John Kennedy in the past 2 weeks, it doesn't seem possible that anything has been left unsaid. However, I would like to add my few words of tribute to his memory.

We came to the House together in the 80th Congress and at that time I was impressed with what I considered his youthful enthusiasm, his elan. I was confident that the duties and responsibilities of the office would soon take their toll of these admirable characteristics. How wrong I was you well know.

His service in the House and Senate provided a good background for the office of the President. It gave him an excellent opportunity to be in close touch with the people and to recognize their needs, their hopes for a better standard of living, greater security. Possibly this accounts for the fact that despite his having been brought up by an ultraconservative father, he became one of the most liberal Presidents we have had. His program, his admiration, was devoted to improving the health, the welfare, the conditions of all of our citizens.

There has been some criticism about the delay in fulfilling all of his campaign pledges. But how many past Presidents succeeded in accomplishing so much in such a short period of time? He has to his credit an increase in social security benefits for the elderly and disabled; an increase in the minimum wage; the Peace Corps; increased unemployment benefits; a manpower retraining program; aid for construction of medical schools; and financial assistance for medical students. In addition, considerable progress has been made on civil rights and tax reform and reduction. Could anyone reasonably expect more?

We shall never know how much more might

have been accomplished by the end of his first term. However, we do know very well what he hoped to see accomplished. Since President Johnson has stated he will pursue the same program, and has the same aims and hopes for our people, the Congress can build on the excellent foundation which has been laid by John Kennedy, for the good of all of our citizens, our country, and the entire world, and as a fitting tribute to his memory.

ADDRESS BY

Hon. Charles A. Buckley

OF NEW YORK

Mr. Speaker, on Friday, November 22 last, on a sunlit day in the city of Dallas, Tex., the 35th President of the United States, John Fitzgerald Kennedy, was assassinated. A great American was struck down in his prime. There was taken from this Nation and from the world a young, vigorous leader. This act which brought about the death of President Kennedy was an act of unparalleled viciousness that will rank as one of the most monstrous deeds in all recorded history.

The emotional shock and the sense of loss we have suffered and still suffer as a result of President Kennedy's passing will be with us for a long period of time. The death of any individual is always a sad occasion but the death of a man such as President Kennedy, who meant so much to his country and to the world, is tragic. It is doubly tragic when we look around us in this day and age and see the need for the leadership that President Kennedy represented.

I can recall John Fitzgerald Kennedy as a youthful Member of this House. I followed his career as he moved to the Senate and then to the highest office this country can give to any individual. I can recall John Fitzgerald Kennedy as he was in Congress with all that youthful zeal and drive that was still burning within him on the day he died.

I can see him during the presidential campaign of 1960. I was privileged to be one of his earliest supporters and I can see him now addressing a Democratic rally at the corner of Fordham Road and the Grand Concourse in my home borough of the Bronx, N.Y. I recall the crisp, sharp delivery, the intelligence behind his remarks and the enthusiasm with which the crowds greeted him in every available spot to see and hear this man whom they sensed to be a true leader. He was not only respected but loved by all who knew him. There was within him that intangible something that is reserved only for the great and by which men in high office are able to communicate with the people they represent.

John Fitzgerald Kennedy had a sense of history. He knew full well that the program he advocated would not come into being overnight. He knew it would not be finished within his lifetime or possibly within the lifetime of those who would follow him. He knew, however, there must be a beginning, a beginning to a program that would really provide a better world for all of us who live in it today and all who will follow us in the years to come. If we can follow this path he has laid out, if we can really by our deeds implement his ideas, I believe that will be the greatest tribute we can pay President Kennedy.

If we can see to it that in the days to come every effort will be made within this country and throughout the world to reach a peaceful solution to the problem of mankind; if we can eliminate the dark seeds of discord and hatred which have been sown by those who know nothing but fear and who would attempt to tear us apart; if we can continue to move forward on a path that will provide better living, better housing, and a greater spirit of unity for all of us, then truly John Fitzgerald Kennedy will not have died in vain. For we all must realize that which John Fitzgerald Kennedy sought is what all of us in our inner selves seek. His goal was really the goal of all of us—a better world for all.

Mere words such as these are inadequate to express my feelings today. It was my privilege to know President Kennedy and his family. To them on behalf of Mrs. Buckley and myself I extend our deepest condolences.

I am proud to have lived in a time when I could have known such a man as John Fitzgerald Kennedy. I am certain that in the years to come when the history of these days is written those who write it and who look back upon this era will fully recognize the greatness of this man. President John Fitzgerald Kennedy may have died in Dallas on November 22 last but that for which he stood will be as alive in the ages to come as it was when he himself was expressing these ideas to all of us.

ADDRESS BY

Hon. Bob Casey

OF TEXAS

Mr. Speaker, as we assemble here today to pay tribute to our fallen leader, President John F. Kennedy, my heart is filled with sadness and sympathy. Sadness and sympathy for his grieving but courageous wife, who gave a nation strength when strength was needed—for a son and daughter, who, like our people, will find the terrible cost of an assassin's bullet to be a lifetime of grief.

To this great family, we can only say that the prayers of our people are with you, and this tragic loss you have borne is shared by each and all of us.

Like most of our people, I was swept with shocked waves of disbelief, horror, and shame at the swift unfolding of the tragedy that struck our land. Our people cried open and unashamed, as news of the President's death came. My grief was not only for the loss of the man, although that in itself was great enough, but also because something evil had been loosed in our land, and the shame of it was overwhelming.

My sorrow was heightened by the fact that only a few short hours before I had welcomed President and Mrs. Kennedy to Houston. I shall remember forever the way the people of my hometown took this warm, vibrant man and his wife to their hearts in a wonderful reception.

In the sorrowful days that followed President Kennedy's death, my memory kept returning to highspots of his brief 3 years in office. The things I remembered, surely, were not his greatest achievements, but were ones that had left a lasting impression with me that I shall cherish all of my days.

I remembered the bitter cold January inaugural, as I sat with my colleagues at the Capitol,

and being struck with the tremendous vitality of this man delivering a call to all America that will ring down the halls of recorded time.

I recalled the feeling of pride as I watched this man stride into the House Chamber, vigorous and confident, a picture of strength in a time of uncertainty, to deliver his first state of the Union message.

Again, I pictured the days after his inaugural and felt anew the electric excitement that swept through Washington, the sense of urgency, the feeling of getting the country moving again.

My thoughts went back to another Houston visit, and the feeling of pride I had in seeing President Kennedy walk into a meeting of Protestant ministers, who had honest and sincere questions concerning his responsibility to his faith and to his country. The deftness and dispatch with which he handled the interview, his candid answers, his frank demeanor, nonplussed even his greatest critics and it was in fact the turning point of his campaign.

I doubt if anyone, even those blinded by animosity, would question this man's courage. But I recall vividly the deep emotions he stirred within me as I watched him apprise the Nation of the threat we faced, and the action he was to take, during the Cuban missile crisis. And I remembered again the courage it took for this man to shoulder full responsibility for this problem of Communist Cuba, partly inherited, and admitting in effect that he was not infallible and had listened to poor advice.

John F. Kennedy had, I feel, the attributes of greatness and had time been more generous, would have realized it to its fullest within his lifetime.

Surely it is no secret that during his 3 years in office the ardor of some of us here for his administration cooled somewhat. But it was influenced not by the man himself so much as by the decisions of those who surrounded him.

My admiration never ceased for the strength, the courage, the intellectual honesty and warm good humor that set President Kennedy apart. Here was a leader that even in disagreement I viewed with an honest sense of pride and great respect.

As my colleagues know, we of Texas were not

the earliest of President Kennedy's supporters, for in the preconvention days we pressed for our own great native son, Lyndon B. Johnson, for this high office. But even at the hour of that defeat, I felt renewed faith in my own judgment as President Kennedy picked this great American to be his Vice President. Even now, in this tragic hour of grief, our people give thanks for the courage and foresight of our fallen leader in selecting a man so eminently qualified to lead our country in the dark days ahead.

Mr. Speaker, it is with endless sorrow that we see the closing of such a brief chapter in our Nation's history, one that had opened with such high hope and brilliant promise.

We cannot break faith with this man who asked so much of us—and gave more. As we stand here in sorrow, let us rededicate ourselves to the principles on which our Nation was founded and must survive—of justice, and liberty, and freedom, of one Nation indivisible under God. Certainly our pledge to eradicate fear and extremism that divides us would be a living memorial to President John F. Kennedy, and the promise for a better world of brotherhood would burn as bright as the eternal flame that lights the final resting place of this great man.

Surely no words could better express our responsibility in the task ahead than those uttered by President Kennedy on that bitter cold inaugural day of January 20, 1961:

In the long history of the world, only a few generations have been granted the role of defending freedom in its hour of maximum danger. I do not shrink from this responsibility—I welcome it. I do not believe that any of us would exchange places with any other people or any other generation. The energy, the faith, the devotion which we bring to this endeavor will light our country and all who serve it—and the glow from that fire can truly light the world.

And so, my fellow Americans, ask not what your country can do for you; ask what you can do for your country.

My fellow citizens of the world, ask not what America will do for you, but what together we can do for the freedom of man.

Finally, whether you are citizens of America or citizens of the world, ask of us the same high standards of strength and sacrifice which we ask of you. With good conscience our only sure reward, with history the final judge of our deeds, let us go forth to lead the land we love, asking His blessing and His help, but knowing that here on earth God's work must truly be our own.

Mr. Speaker, we here can resolve no less than this.

ADDRESS BY

Hon. Carlton R. Sickles

OF MARYLAND

Mr. Speaker, the man had noble thoughts. The man spoke with eloquent words. The man did courageous deeds.

He envisioned a world where men could live in peace and prosperity; a world where the fear of a nuclear holocaust would be removed; a world where poverty, disease, prejudice, and ignorance would be conquered.

He spoke of need to use wisely the knowledge we have for "man holds in his mortal hands the power to abolish all forms of poverty and all forms of human life"; of the need to control nuclear weapons "before the dark powers of destruction unleashed by science engulf all humanity in planned or accidental self-destruction"; of the need for Americans to "bear the burden of a long twilight struggle—a struggle against the common enemies of man: tyranny, poverty, disease, and war itself."

He acted to ban the testing of nuclear weapons in the face of false accusations of treachery and weakness; to extend basic human rights to all Americans arousing the bias and bigotry of those who seek someone to hate and a scapegoat for their own prejudice and ignorance; to balance the human budget by providing the opportunity for more jobs, better health care, and educational opportunity for all with ability despite bitter criticism from the shortsighted.

John Fitzgerald Kennedy was a great man who harbored no little thoughts.

John Fitzgerald Kennedy was a great President whose words and deeds will leave an indelible mark on the scroll of our history.

John Fitzgerald Kennedy was a great American who gave his last mortal breath to preserve the life of his country.

ADDRESS BY

Hon. Thomas G. Morris

OF NEW MEXICO

Mr. Speaker, the sad and tragic events of the last few days have seemed like a continuous nightmare to all Christian men and women. All freedom-loving people in every land have lost a great and wise champion—a champion who placed service to this land of ours we call America above his own personal health and liberty. Hundreds of thousands of words will be written and spoken about President Kennedy's character and deeds but none will adequately express the profound respect and admiration he enjoyed among those of us who were privileged to know him personally.

One of the most outstanding characteristics of the late President that will always remain in my memory was his eminent courage to act in the face of danger with wisdom, straightforwardness and logic. Until the very instant a murderer snuffed out his life, this courage shone forth like a knight in armor—bright as a star on a dark night—for all the world to see.

President Kennedy had the physical courage not only to survive the sinking of his ship during World War II, but also to lead his men to safety. This was a man who had the courage to seek the nomination and to be elected to the highest office in any democratic country despite the handicap of his religion. This man we mourn today had the courage to risk his life every time he made a public appearance.

But our late President displayed the greatest courage known to mankind when he looked down the nuclear gun barrel at the Soviet Union and said, "remove your offensive weapons from Cuba or face the terrible consequences which will follow." Very well did he know what the consequences might be but equally well did he understand the meaning of political slavery, lack of intellectual freedom and the dismantling of this Nation's sovereignty. Those of us who have witnessed a nuclear explosion realize what great courage this action required and we hope and pray that no other American will ever be called upon to display this type of courage.

To Mrs. Kennedy, the Kennedy children, and to all of President Kennedy's family, Mrs. Morris and our children wish to extend our deepest sympathy. Let us hope and pray that this tragic experience will awaken our countrymen to a true understanding of tolerance toward our fellow man so that America will regain her composure and find even greater wisdom and strength.

ADDRESS BY

Hon. James J. Delaney
OF NEW YORK

Mr. Speaker, the entire civilized world has expressed its heartfelt grief at the loss of our beloved President, John Fitzgerald Kennedy. However, I do not think that a more eloquent tribute has been paid his memory than that which I witnessed in the streets of New York City on that terrible November day.

There I saw thousands of New Yorkers, in the streets and on the subway, shocked by the loss which each of them felt so personally. At first they refused to believe and then, believing, they fell silent. People hurrying along the city's sidewalks suddenly walked softly. Jostling subway crowds suddenly became orderly and quiet. Many bowed their heads in silent prayer. Some wept openly and in the eyes of all there were tears.

I cannot hope to match this great tribute paid John F. Kennedy by his people. Neither can I hope to equal the many fine words of eulogy poured forth in his honor, but I would like to express my strong sense of personal loss.

He was my friend long before he was my President and I grieve deeply at his passing.

John F. Kennedy possessed not only dignity and intellect, but great personal warmth, understanding, and wit. I had never seen nor do I expect to see again the combination of zeal, vision, and dedication that he possessed.

John Kennedy captured America's imagination with his dream of the New Frontier and America followed him forward toward that dream. Under his leadership the sprawling giant of American industry surged ahead to greater peacetime heights than it had ever known. The young responded to his call and set out to bring the fruits of democracy to underdeveloped countries around the globe. He stiffened the spine of this mighty Nation and showed the world that America was willing to risk all-out war to fight the encroachment of communism and that this free land was equally willing to lead the world to peace through nuclear disarmament.

John F. Kennedy believed in the dignity of man as the source of national purpose, the liberty of man as the source of national action, the human heart as the source of national compassion, and the mind of the freeman as the best source of invention and intellectual progress.

He translated these beliefs into a strong anti-Communist foreign policy, an effective Defense Establishment, and a domestic program designed to give equality to all Americans, reduce unemployment, educate tomorrow's citizens, combat mental illness, and give old age the dignity it should possess.

To John Kennedy, liberalism was not a party creed or political platform, but an attitude of mind and heart, a faith in man's ability through the experiences of his reason and judgment to increase for himself and for all mankind the amount of freedom and justice and brotherhood which all men deserve.

When we look on the life of John F. Kennedy we see the prophecy—the destiny—in much that he said and did. He told us that this decade would be a hazardous experience, that we would live on the edge of danger. For him the most terrible danger has been realized.

He is gone now. The warmth and the vibrancy are no more and all mankind has lost a brother. However, his dreams live on and the plans he set forth for moving this country forward are still very much alive. The Government stands firm and, thanks to our democratic system, a strong and honorable man has stepped forward to lead.

John Kennedy was particularly fond of a statement made by Abraham Lincoln shortly before the Civil War. Lincoln said:

I know that there is a God and that he hates injustice. I see the storm coming. But if he has a place and a part for me, I am ready.

John Fitzgerald Kennedy was ready to meet the storm of this decade and, indeed, God had a very important place for him.

We sorrow deeply at his passing, but we thank Almighty God that he was here.

ADDRESS BY

Hon. Walter S. Baring

OF NEVADA

Mr. Speaker, for all decent Americans of all political views, the death of President Kennedy was a tragedy which we will remember all our living days. No matter how much conservatives disagreed with the policies of his administration, which was our right as citizens, we respected the constitutional office of the President, admired the individual who had served his country bravely in wartime, and wished nothing but personal happiness for Mr. Kennedy, his wife, and children.

The tragic way in which the President was removed from his high office was in a manner which no good man or woman in America would ever want or even think could ever happen. Not only was this a dastardly blow at a brave young man, but also a tremendous jolt to our American system. The assassin who fired at President Kennedy fired at our system of government, at our Republic, which is nearest and dearest to the hearts of all Americans.

Moreover, our hearts go out to Mrs. Kennedy and the young children in their deep sorrow and loss.

Mr. Speaker, I remember Jack Kennedy when he was a Member of our body back in 1949 and 1950. We were personal friends. His smile and personality set him off as a leader among men. About a year and a half before he filed for President, he called me over to his Senate office for lunch and on that occasion stated, "Walter, I am going to run for President. What can you deliver me from Nevada in the way of convention votes"?

While I had read newspaper and magazine articles that his name had been mentioned as a Presidential candidate, I do not believe I had given it complete consideration, but when he so positively put it to me, I liked it, and I told him, "Jack, I will deliver you at least half of the delegation votes from Nevada." This, Mr. Chairman, I was able to do at the Los Angeles Convention, and in the election that followed I want to point out that Nevada was one of the Western

States which carried President Kennedy to victory.

Personally, being a Jeffersonian States Rights Democrat, I differed with President Kennedy on numerous occasions relative to legislation, but we always maintained our personal friendship. His tragic death has so stunned the world that only history will fully reflect the impact of this dark event, and people will always wonder why his life had to be thusly taken.

Mr. Speaker, since President Kennedy's death, I have not been able to think of anything other than the words spoken by a bystander who saw the assassination. I have heard many fine words of oratory today, and I have read many masterpieces of eulogy in the newspapers, but I cannot forget the statement of the bystander who said, "He was looking so happy," as the parade went by, "and then came that awful look." It is a sad time in our history and words are not adequate to express any part of what took place.

ADDRESS BY

Hon. Victor Wickersham

OF OKLAHOMA

Mr. Speaker, may I quote from the words of our late President:

I call upon all of you to join us in a journey to the new frontier. The voyage is a long and hazardous one, but we are all partners in a great and historic journey.

These were the words of John Fitzgerald Kennedy, who served his country well.

He was a young President, full of vigor, and his journey to the new frontier had indeed been hazardous. He narrowly missed death in the defense of his country in World War II, again in a serious illness 9 years ago. His dangerous voyage continued through his years as President by his being committed to sweeping civil rights proposals at acknowledged political cost. His historic journey ended November 22 with many accomplishments behind him.

I want above all else to be a President known—at the end of 4 years—as one who not only prevented war but won the peace—as one of whom history might say: He not only laid the foundations of peace in his time, but for generations to come as well.

These were the words of John Fitzgerald Kennedy, who served his country well.

He will be remembered for his untiring efforts in working toward world peace. This was his most pressing goal. His actions to thwart the spread of communism in the Vietnam area, his firmness at the Berlin wall and his quick, but firm action to stop the flow of atomic missiles toward Cuba were recognized by all inhabitants of the free world as real acts of courage. His work in this regard, as leader of the free world, earned him the gratitude and praise of people the world over. Millions of persons in other countries mourned his passing as if they too had lost a leader, and indeed they had. History will tell us that John F. Kennedy laid the foundations of peace in his time and for generations to come as well.

Let the word go forth from this time and place, to friend and foe alike, that the torch has been passed to a new generation of Americans—born in this century, tempered by war, disciplined by a hard and bitter peace, proud of our ancient heritage—and unwilling to witness or permit the slow undoing of human rights to which this Nation has always been committed.

These were the words of John Fitzgerald Kennedy, who served his country well.

The torch has been passed. The eternal flame stands lighted across the Potomac in Arlington National Cemetery for all to see. John F. Kennedy's death must mean something to us all, or he will have died in vain. The people of the United States now have the torch, it is up to us to make good use of it.

I extend my deepest sympathy to all the members of the late President's family.

ADDRESS BY

Hon. Robert W. Hemphill

OF SOUTH CAROLINA

Mr. Speaker, a great man has passed to the great beyond and we who are his friends and admirers find an emptiness in our hearts that can never be filled.

We come today to salute the magnificent effort, the sterling image, that his life, before he was President, and while he was President, presented and which lingers today as a bright star over a horizon filled with the darkness of gloom and distress over the loss of this man; an irreplaceable loss to his wonderful family, his legion of friends and admirers, his Nation, and his time.

I find it most difficult to find even one adjective of praise that has not already been applied. In each instance I find most properly, that in describing this man, what he did, what he proposed, the heritage he gave, and the hope he left, only superlatives are used. I have no new word of praise, but I feel no plagiarism in echoing the wonderful tributes which he, and his purposeful life, so richly deserve.

Now I reflect on some of the instances I was privileged to be a part of. When he came to Charlotte, N.C., in 1960, in the midst of the campaign, I was privileged to be present, and on the platform. I saw John Kennedy as the candidate, and having had limited experience in politics, recognized readily the strain, the tired eyes, the baggy trousers, and the tense determination to win. Despite the strain upon him, he was able to smile, he was able to inspire, he impressed that he could lead, and he was most happy that day at the reception in the coliseum at Charlotte.

Later he did honor to my State by visiting Columbia, S.C., and in front of the State Capitol made a magnificent impression before a crowd that waited more than an hour just to see and hear him. The newspapers played down that visit, but if honesty has its place in their records, now, they must admit that he was everything a candidate for President should be on the platform in Columbia that day.

We had known Jack Kennedy in South Carolina before. I am proud to refresh the memory of those assembled here today that he had been given an honorary degree by the University of South Carolina, which is my own alma mater. We had recognized his ability as a historian, as a leader, and his contribution to the constructive analysis of what a statesman should be, and what history should present.

On another occasion, I was at the White House to discuss a matter with him. I apologized for taking the time. I remember his telling me that he always had time for his friends, and he did.

The world is a better place because of his life, not only today, but for the future generations. In death, as in life, he has impressed all of us, and like others who gather in this Chamber today to do him honor, well knowing we can probably never do him justice, I am grateful to a benevolent Master that this man lived and served in my time.

To Mrs. Kennedy and the entire family, Mrs. Hemphill and I express our deepest and continuing sympathy. May they find comfort in reflection of a life truly lived for the betterment of mankind, the promotion of peace, and the improvement of civilization all over the world.

ADDRESS BY

Hon. A. Fernós-Isern

OF PUERTO RICO

Mr. Speaker, it was the 80th Congress, the first in which I had the honor to serve, and it was the first Congress in which John Fitzgerald Kennedy served, and it was then when I had the opportunity to know that most promising young man from Massachusetts.

In the course of the years, he successively became U.S. Senator and President of the United States. In all those years there were a number of occasions when I discussed with him matters concerning Puerto Rico. Always I found him interested, understanding, sympathetic.

Twice did he visit Puerto Rico; first, as a Senator and then as President. Twice again I had the honor to greet him in the name of the people of Puerto Rico whom I represent.

He was the President of the United States, and as such he always had the respect of the people of Puerto Rico. But the people of Puerto Rico saw much more in him; they saw a great leader in the battle for freedom for all men and peace for all nations, and they saw a friend, a warm friend, their friend, always willing to help. When the cruel, sorrowful news reached the island, the people went in shock, speech was lost, eyes filled with tears; it seemed as though all life had ceased. The official mourning proclamations were duly issued, the flags were lowered to half-mast, but, even before that, schools and stores had closed, public amusements stopped, radio and television programs canceled, except those giving the sad news. The churches filled to capacity, and this continued for days.

I visited Puerto Rico the day following the funeral services, and the ambient was of profound sorrow and grief and despair, of actual paralysis. There was a general sense of helplessness. There was only one topic of conversation—the great loss, the unbelievable tragedy. President Kennedy had given Puerto Rico full attention and recognition. Now Puerto Rico was expressing, in a heartfelt way, its full recognition of the stature of the beloved President.

In these brief words, for they should be brief, let me express, in the name of the people of Puerto Rico, that to them someone very dear has ceased to be. That they accept the awesome reality because they must, but reality seems to them a nightmare from which they wish to awake, and they dream they will awaken from it.

ADDRESS BY

Hon. Neal Smith

OF IOWA

Mr. Speaker, in view of our position in world affairs, the loss of our President is a mournful occasion for the entire free world. When President Eisenhower had a heart attack, the Nation prayed that he be saved and he was; but, President Kennedy's death was so quick and so violent as to add shock to dismay.

At first it seemed that the only thing we had left to be thankful for was that an able and experienced Vice President would firmly grasp the reins of Government; that the same society that produced a Lee Oswald and a Jack Ruby also could produce a John Kennedy and a Lyndon Johnson.

Although President Kennedy had already reached the most powerful office on earth, he was assumed to have more years of service ahead of him than behind him. The sudden calling of such a vigorous and youthful President and the common assumption that he would render great service to the Nation for many years after completing two terms as President, dramatically reminded everyone how transitory life is for all of

us and how we are all subject to immediate call.

But even in passing, the President did something no living man has done. His violent death caused almost the entire world to pause collectively long enough to observe where we have been going. Never have so many world leaders assembled at one funeral; never has one man gained such stature and prestige after only 3 years as the leader of a country; and never have so many citizens of all countries of the world mourned and paid tribute to the leading apostle of peace so sincerely that a greater feeling of brotherhood became evident everywhere.

During all of the several occasions when I had the pleasure of talking with or working with John F. Kennedy when he was a Senator and as President, it was most evident that no man was ever more able or willing to serve his nation. It was evident that he lived to serve his fellow man. His deep sense of responsibility and understanding and his intense desire to serve were responsible for the great and good ultimate impact he has left upon the world. We share the deep and profound sorrow of his devoted wife and family and I wish to join my colleagues in extending a deeply felt expression of sympathy to them.

ADDRESS BY

Hon. Jacob H. Gilbert

OF NEW YORK

Mr. Speaker, we meet in one of the most tragic hours of our Nation's history and in one of the most sorrowful moments in the history of the House of Representatives. We meet to pay honor to the memory of President John Fitzgerald Kennedy, a truly great President who gave his life for his country.

The shock of his assassination was felt not only throughout our Nation, but in every part of the globe. The headlines screaming "President Is Shot Dead" will be forever emblazoned upon our memories. We were a nation stunned, and our first reaction was one of disbelief—we could not believe that such a horrible tragedy could befall our brave, young leader and ourselves.

We are benumbed by grief and millions of people of good will the world over are joining us in our mourning. Many people in the 22d District of New York whom I have the honor to represent have written me expressing their profound sorrow and love for President Kennedy, and I speak for them as well as for myself in offering this eulogy.

President Kennedy in his inaugural address pictured for us the New Frontier and filled us with hope for a better world and with a zest to achieve the goals he set; his enthusiasm, his courage, his strength of character, his love for humanity, his vibrancy, his love of life, all combined to make him the strong and trusted leader whom millions came to admire and love. He thought of all those who needed help—the oppressed, the poverty stricken, the jobless, the youth of our Nation, the sick and elderly, and suggested practicable programs for their benefit. He believed in the dignity and equality of all human beings.

He sought the Presidency, not because he loved power, but because he felt that he could use that power effectively to secure peace and the survival of human beings in the world; peace was always of a foremost concern to him.

John Fitzgerald Kennedy was a highly talented author and historian. He was a brilliant legislator in the House and Senate before becoming our President. He was in the White House not quite 3 years, but in this short span of time he proved himself to be a man of wisdom, great knowledge, and a fearless Chief Executive; he was a reasonable man and sought the solution of local and world problems through reasonable and responsible discussion and action. He earned the trust of other nations, as was evidenced by the large number of heads of state and dignitaries from 92 countries who came to Washington for his funeral and who walked behind his body for the half mile from the White House to St. Matthew's Cathedral. They came to pay honor to a world leader they had come to respect, for they knew he had earnestly sought for peace among all nations.

He was willing to die for his country—he saw heroic service in World War II and at that time his life was miraculously spared. It is cruel beyond words that while on a friendly mission of good will, in peacetime, he was shot down by a murderer filled with unfounded hatred and fanaticism; these evils he had, as President, sought to curb and contain.

John Fitzgerald Kennedy excelled in all the roles his life demanded of him—as the youngest man ever to serve our Nation as its President and ruthlessly struck down before he could accomplish all he set out to do for us, he has nevertheless set the finest examples of good citizenship, tolerance, and responsibility toward our fellow men. We knew him to be a devoted husband and a loving and understanding father.

The dastardly act of the assassin was meant to kill our President; it was also meant to shatter our ideals, our faith in our Nation's institutions and our ability to achieve the true brotherhood of men for which we aim. It has also shocked us into the realization that there is indeed a sickness in this country which must be cured, and this is the job of each and every American. Blinding hate, bigotry, discrimination, malevolence, are undermining our Nation, and if our Nation is to survive, these forces which would destroy us must be overcome and conquered. These forces brought about the death of our beloved President Kennedy; if we earnestly work to rid ourselves and our Nation of such evils and strive toward the kind of nation our martyred President prayed and worked for, then he will not have died in vain.

Many memorials have been suggested to honor President Kennedy. No more precious or beautiful monument could be created for him than the fulfillment of his dreams, his plans, his programs, for the benefit of this country, which he so dearly loved. Passage of the civil rights bill, now, would please him more than any monument of stone. He was a man of purpose and action; he would prefer that we act speedily on those matters which were his chief concern rather than be idle in grief for him.

Our hearts go out to the young widow and the children of our slain President. Mrs. Gilbert, our three children, and I extend to them our deepest sympathy, as well as to all members of the former President's family.

And now, even as we say a sad farewell to our beloved John Fitzgerald Kennedy, it is important that we stand united behind our 36th President of these United States, Lyndon Baines Johnson, who has asked our help in the difficult days ahead. We pray that under his able leadership our Nation will achieve that greatness envisioned for us when he made the plea that all

Americans "understand and respect one another." And when we do this, we carry out one of President Kennedy's dearest wishes.

ADDRESS BY

Hon. Jeffery Cohelan

OF CALIFORNIA

Mr. Speaker, there are truly no words to describe the loss we have suffered. The death of John Fitzgerald Kennedy is a tragic setback not only to the country he loved and served so well, but to the cause of freedom and justice throughout the world.

Sophocles once said, "One must wait until the evening to see how splendid the day has been." John Kennedy had made a beginning but he had only begun. He had laid the foundation of a program to make the American ideal a reality, here and wherever freemen are prepared to grasp the torch of liberty, of progress, of equality and self-determination.

His life was cruelly snuffed out before the task could be its own monument to his statesmanship, his courage and his determination. But in this all-too-brief period the Government and the American people had already begun to feel the impact of the man.

American foreign policy had become more aware, more alert and more adaptable. No practical step toward peace was left untaken or unexplored, while a vigilance was maintained and the security of the Nation advanced.

At home a sluggish economy was confronted and challenged. The dread disease of discrimination was attacked, and grudging progress toward final victory was begun.

John Kennedy was a man of courage and compassion, of keen intelligence and decisive action. He understood the world in which he lived, the Nation which he loved, and he gave the full measure of his life in their service—for their security and freedom. He was an American, but he was also a citizen of the world.

No more fitting epitaph could be made for this good man and great President than the one he delivered at his own inauguration—an epitaph which will excite the hearts and minds of Americans for all time to come:

> In the long history of the world, only a few generations have been granted the role of defending freedom in its hour of maximum danger. I do not shrink from this responsibility—I welcome it. I do not believe that any of us would exchange places with any other people or any other generation. The energy, the faith, the devotion which we bring to this endeavor will light our country and all who serve it—and the glow from that fire can truly light the world.

Mr. Speaker, the personal loss which Mrs. Kennedy and the family has suffered is deep and crushing. But the loss is overpoweringly ours as well, for John Kennedy was not only President of the United States, he was part of us all.

So let us dedicate ourselves anew to that for which he lived, and for which he gave his life—peace, understanding, justice, freedom in a free and open society with a will to tolerate diversity and to withstand tension. Let us dedicate ourselves to this "profile in courage" so that his death will not have been in vain.

ADDRESS BY

Hon. Walter Rogers

OF TEXAS

Mr. Speaker, a man destined for history's immortal stamp was John Fitzgerald Kennedy, a President to be well remembered as long as our Nation lives for the courage, the intelligence, the dignity, grace, and good humor with which he carried the staggering burdens of his office.

How very much our country has lost with his passing.

How much we who knew him will miss him.

How well we all will remember him.

But John Fitzgerald Kennedy's memory will be served poorly if we Americans do not now pledge to strive together, in cooperation and optimism, to find solutions to the wide range of problems confronting our Nation and the world. In his own search for these solutions, President Kennedy personified the American ideal of tolerance and moderation, and it is in this spirit that we must carry on. We may propose and dispose and differ, but can we all resolve to do so in the American way?

Let us not forget that the target of the assassination was not only John Fitzgerald Kennedy, the President, the man, but also was all for which John Fitzgerald Kennedy stood for and which this country must continue to stand; the bullets were aimed also at the institutions of freedom, of democratic government, of justice under law. Let we who hold the responsibility for guiding the Nation's destiny rededicate ourselves to the pursuit of constructive courses to resolve our differences of view, and to do our best to impress upon our fellow citizens the need for respectful understanding of these differences.

Our Constitution was the product of moderation; in its formulation it represented the coming together of ideas as to an establishment of government under which freemen could live out their lives in peace and justice. On the one bleak occasion in American history when the coming-together processes of moderation failed us, and differences remained unreconciled, a bitter and bloody civil war resulted. In the century since, our institutions of government were strengthened along with other phases of our national life, and it seemed to most citizens—until November 22, 1963—that We the People of the United States had formed a more perfect Union, had established justice, had insured domestic tranquility, had provided for the common defense, had promoted the general welfare, had secured the blessings of liberty to ourselves and our posterity.

Our best memorial to John Fitzgerald Kennedy would be to give our very best efforts toward the fulfillment of these goals expressed in the preamble of the Constitution.

ADDRESS BY

Hon. Basil L. Whitener

OF NORTH CAROLINA

Mr. Speaker, it is with a sense of profound sadness that I join my colleagues today in paying my deep personal respects to the memory of our late President, John Fitzgerald Kennedy.

The people of the United States and the free world have lost a great leader in the tragic passing of President Kennedy. Although he had been President of the United States for less than 3 years at the time of his death, his services in behalf of the people of his country and in the cause of freedom throughout the world stand as a lasting monument to his memory.

John Fitzgerald Kennedy was young in years yet he possessed a maturity of person and a philosophy of government and life that was far beyond a man of his age. He believed strongly in the dignity of man and in the economic and social progress of all mankind.

Our late President was proud of the fact that his Nation was a young country and a world leader. He took pride in our advanced society and in our democratic institutions of Government. Although John Fitzgerald Kennedy was a profound student of history, his face was pointed to the future. He realized that in the future lay the bright hope of his country and the progress of all mankind.

He approached the tasks of his high office with vigor and enthusiasm and with a high sense of dedication to the great mission his country had in the free world. He realized the dangers which threatened our society; yet he was open to conciliation and compromise so long as our vital interests were not threatened. He advanced the cause of peace in the world by constantly seeking new avenues of mutual understanding among nations while at the same time taking strong action where armed aggression threatened the cause of freedom.

John Fitzgerald Kennedy possessed in his soul the humanity of Abraham Lincoln, the intellectual greatness of Woodrow Wilson, and the understanding of human nature so well exemplified by our beloved late President, Franklin D. Roosevelt.

The American people have lost a great leader, and the world has lost a champion of freedom. The ideals of peace, freedom, social and economic progress for all men for which John Fitzgerald Kennedy labored will not be soon forgotten by his grateful countrymen and people throughout the world who looked to him for leadership.

He was a bright light of hope in a world beset with much gloom and despair. He gave to the Presidency of the United States a new meaning. His high office was brought closer to the people, and they responded with love and a sense of deep personal friendship.

John Fitzgerald Kennedy is dead. His soul has gone on to immortality, and his memory has been enshrined forever in the hearts of freedom-loving people.

> Master, I've done Thy bidding,
> And the light is low in the West,
> And the long, long shift is over;
> Master, I've earned it—Rest.

ADDRESS BY

Hon. W. R. Poage

OF TEXAS

Mr. Speaker, not too many years ago a bushy-headed young man ofttimes occupied a seat on the front row to the Speaker's right. He was a Representative from the State of Massachusetts. He was friendly and intelligent, but few of us who served with him could foresee the height to which he would rise. He moved across the rotunda and took a seat in the U.S. Senate, where it was not long until the whole Nation was recognizing him as an outstanding leader.

In 1956, along with other delegates from Texas at the Democratic National Convention in Chicago, I voted for him for Vice President. He was not the nominee, but from that day forward, he was very definitely in the public mind whenever men considered the 1960 presidential race.

In 1960 I felt that Texas offered the Nation its greatest leader. I did all I could to secure the nomination for the man who now occupies the Presidency. I failed, but I knew that we had been defeated by a worthy foeman. We left Los Angeles, knowing that the Democratic Party had an outstanding ticket and those of us who were not successful at the convention realized as never before that the party's candidate was a man of untiring energy, of towering intellect, of integrity, of commonsense, and possessed of the common touch. I was happy to give that candidate my wholehearted support.

In January 1961 John F. Kennedy became the 35th President of the United States. In less than 3 years he made an imprint on our history far surpassing that of many who served the Nation much longer. He became the very tangible symbol of world leadership. But his achievements were not his alone. Fortunately, the Nation and the world recognized that he had the love and the help of a great lady, and the people shared their love and admiration of our President with his wife and his family.

Two weeks ago yesterday President and Mrs. Kennedy flew from Washington to Texas. It was Mrs. Kennedy's first official visit to the State. More than 9 million people joined in extending a sincere welcome to their President and their First Lady. On the next day a warped mind of a Communist renegade planned the assassination of our beloved leader.

Wherever there are people of good will around the world there was grief and despair, and wherever there were Texans, there was deep hurt and humiliation that such a cowardly and cruel thing could have occurred in our State.

Of course, we recognize that great as the loss has been to the Nation and to the world that the keenest and most personal loss was that sustained by his wife, but never in history has there been a more magnificent example of dignity and courage than that of Mrs. Jacqueline Kennedy. To her we all extend our most sincere sympathy, and for her we pray.

The memory of John F. Kennedy will long remain bright throughout our land. We, his friends of many years, can today but add our testimony to his great qualities of leadership character.

ADDRESS BY

Hon. Henry B. Gonzalez

OF TEXAS

Mr. Speaker, John F. Kennedy, 35th President of the United States, is dead, a hero and a martyr. Only history can tell the measure of this man, but I believe that he will be judged among the greatest men of our time. Years must pass before the length of his shadow can be known, but I believe it will be a long one. And though he is gone from among us, as long as there is a flaming torch in Arlington his spirit will survive; as long as the hills stand over the valleys, his voice will echo its eloquent and urgent call to duty and service.

The voice and spirit of John F. Kennedy proclaimed for us new goals and new ideals, and it is for us who remain to heed his call and keep our eyes on the horizons he pointed to, and beyond which he has gone. It is for us to see the visions his eyes once saw, and to strive to complete the work he began.

For my part, I can only mourn his loss and vow to live by the light his life has given us.

Such men as John F. Kennedy are all too rare, and it is not easy for our limited visions to compass the measure of him. But before we can see his visions and dream his dreams we must make an effort to know what he stood for and who he was. It is not in my power to plumb the depths of our late President, nor to comprehend what he meant to the world. I can only estimate his measure as a man.

We measure a man in any number of ways, none of which can bespeak true accuracy. But of all the estimates of a man's worth and stature, surely courage is one of the best indicators we have.

There are many kinds of courage, and it can honestly be said that John F. Kennedy was lacking in none of them. For he knew a great deal about courage, having lived through infinite dangers; and he studied courage, having known and studied courageous men.

No man living today can say that he lacked courage in the face of pain and danger to himself. Only courage of an extraordinary kind enabled him to survive and save his fellow seamen from death at the terrible hand of war and in the depths of the lonely sea. And this same courage enabled him to smile in the face of the pain he so often knew as a result of those nights and days of war.

Courage of another kind was required of this young man as a Congressman and Senator. But he knew political courage as few men did; his study of it became one of the great books of our time. Only a man of great courage such as he was could understand it as he did.

History will record John F. Kennedy as a courageous man because of the unflinching calm with which he carried this Nation through the first nuclear confrontation in history. As the world edged toward holocaust during those terrible October days, he did calmly and quickly what had to be done, and won a victory whose dimensions we do not yet realize.

It must take an extraordinary kind of courage to hold the highest office in the land—most powerful in the world—yet John F. Kennedy enjoyed his burden. Not many Presidents in our history reflected the joy and exuberance he did while wrestling with the great problems of our time, and all time—peace, poverty, and all the others.

The courage to survive untold pain and peril, to face unafraid perhaps the most dangerous crisis of all time, to laugh in the face of misfortune, to stand for morality when expediency might have done, and to smile and actually enjoy the crushing burden of the Presidency. This was the courage with which John F. Kennedy lived and by which he must be measured.

Men are measured by standards other than courage, and these are legion. Deeds, words, intellect, capacity, energy, and leadership are all among the things that go into the shadow and substance of a great man.

The deeds of John F. Kennedy were cut short in his most promising time, but the things he did in his lifetime gave him greatness and they foreshadow what might have been. Which of his accomplishments are most meaningful, only time can tell. Perhaps it is enough to say that this, one of our youngest Presidents, proved himself equal to men far older and more experienced than he and proved himself as wise as any. No recitation of what he did in his lifetime is as meaningful as the simple fact that his accomplishments were enough for all mankind to recognize him as a leader of great wisdom and great vision, of wit and resourcefulness, of energy and nerve. Let his tribute be the respect showed him by the world and its leaders, and their weeping when he died.

Great words were also a mark and measure of the man. Few who heard it will ever forget the inaugural address of John F. Kennedy. Thousands of young people responded to his call to duty and service, heeding to the immortal call: "Ask not what your country can do for you—ask what you can do for your country." Nor will we ever forget those strong and measured cadences that he urged us forward with throughout his term of office. Even in his last speeches, he called us forward and exhorted us to shoulder the burdens of peace and world leadership.

He was also a man of great intellect and had a deep capacity to understand, as few men do, our world and our times. His glittering intellect and capacity have already become legend, and I will not dwell on it here.

Beyond all this, John F. Kennedy was beloved for his unceasing interest in human beings, young and old, and strived constantly for means to better utilize the human resources of this country. He was a patron of many causes, but above all he was a patron of learning, of scholarship, for he knew that knowledge is the key to man's hopes for survival and advancement. He also knew that a full man must know and respect the past, must master history or be forced to repeat it.

Beyond all else that he was, our late President was a loving husband and father; all America, even the world, shared the love and joy he had in his family. He loved his family enough to warm us all, and we were the better for it.

He was a man of strong courage, of action, of great word, and greater deed.

By any measure, John F. Kennedy was a great man. History will judge him well, and his shadow across the breadth of time will be long.

We must go forward, even with the loss of our beloved President. As we go, we will be guided by the light of his greatness and inspired by the echo of his words.

ADDRESS BY

Hon. D. R. (Billy) Matthews

OF FLORIDA

Mr. Speaker, so much has been so eloquently said and written that it seems impossible to add further to the national and international expressions of sadness because of the passing of our late President. I should like, however, to express my personal grief and to wish for his brave widow, and the other beloved members of his family, the blessings of divine providence to be with them and to sustain them because of their indescribable loss. I should also like to insert a letter that I wrote to my constituents entitled "John F. Kennedy—In Memoriam":

JOHN F. KENNEDY—IN MEMORIAM

NOVEMBER 26, 1963.

DEAR CONSTITUENT: With millions of other Americans, my first reaction to the assassination of President Kennedy was one of shocked disbelief. There followed a feeling of indescribable sadness. This vibrant young man, gracious

and understanding, invariably cast his shadow on all who knew him. His life—a profile in courage—was so dedicated to the service of his country that he had no time to hate. He accepted the noble challenge so eloquently expressed in his inaugural address when he said, "Ask not what your country can do for you; ask what you can do for your country."

One of the last visits your Congressman had with President Kennedy concerned a project in our district. It was then after working hours, about 5:30 p.m., but this leader had time to talk of local affairs because no matter how demanding the task of foreign policy, he wanted to help the American people achieve a more abundant life.

With my wife, Sara, I attended the sad rites at the White House Saturday afternoon, the mournful ceremony in the rotunda of the Capitol on Sunday afternoon, and the melancholy interment in Arlington National Cemetery on Monday afternoon. My most vivid impressions of these heart-rending hours were the unbelievable composure of Mrs. Kennedy, Caroline, and little John; the grief of a million people who were a part of these somber historic events; the tributes from the representatives of 92 other Nations; and the emphasis on the spiritual need of this Nation, so prayerfully expressed by so many.

The Nation mourns the passing of President Kennedy. We cry out, as did Walt Whitman after the assassination of President Lincoln, "I, with mournful tread, walk the deck my captain lies, fallen cold and dead."

The only consolation in this sad hour is the feeling that the ship of state has a skillful pilot in the person of President Lyndon B. Johnson. This dedicated and able American has visited in our district many times. We know him and respected him. The transition of government is now completed. This continuity guaranteed by our Constitution must inspire us all to be worthy of our citizenship.

Let us resolve with the help of Almighty God to give more to our country than we take from it—so that we may deserve the final and full sacrifice made by John F. Kennedy.

Sincerely, your Congressman,

D. R. (BILLY) MATTHEWS.

ADDRESS BY

Hon. Robert B. Duncan

OF OREGON

Mr. Speaker, the ways and means of the Almighty are not for us to question. It is a sad fact that it is most difficult to believe when that belief is most needed. Now is when America and every American needs that belief and faith the most.

It is rather for us to be grateful for the few short years John F. Kennedy was permitted to be among us. It may well be said of him what can be said of few—"He left the world a little better than he found it."

What better epitaph can be written? What better memory can be left?

Our heartfelt sympathy goes out to his remarkable and devoted wife, his lovely children, his mother and father and all members of the family.

ADDRESS BY

Hon. Thomas G. Abernethy

OF MISSISSIPPI

Mr. Speaker, the assassination of John Fitzgerald Kennedy was a black day in the history of our country. The dastardly act removed from our midst a young man of unusual brilliance, one who had attained the highest office in our land at the youngest age of any of his predecessors.

The life of our late President was marked with achievement and success, from his days as a student to his last days as the leader of the American people. In the interim he had distinguished himself as a soldier, author, Representative in the U.S. House of Representatives and later as U.S. Senator. Seldom will his record be equaled, if ever again, in the history of our country.

Mr. Speaker, I often found myself in disagreement with President Kennedy. I opposed much of his policies and programs. But I am happy to say, Mr. Speaker, that while I frequently disagreed on policy, our disagreement was never personal.

I knew him personally as a Member of this House. He had a remarkable memory for people, particularly his associates in the Congress whom he always warmly addressed by their given names.

While John Fitzgerald Kennedy had achieved great heights in politics, his greatest achievement was as a father and head of a family. He was very devoted to his wife and children. Busy and burdened as he was, he never let the day pass that he did not devote at least a part thereof to the interest of his family and particularly his two small children, Caroline and John.

We regret his passing. We condemn the act which took him away. Indeed such is not the way to protest in a civilized society. It was terrible. It left this entire Nation and the world saddened and terribly shocked.

ADDRESS BY

Hon. Gerald R. Ford

OF MICHIGAN

Mr. Speaker, the ignominy at Dallas was a tragedy for the United States and the world. Little can be added to the millions of words that have been spoken and written in expressions of shock, and of sympathy, and of support—of shock that such a crime could take place in our country, of sympathy to the family, and to all of us for whom John F. Kennedy was "Mr. President," and of support to Lyndon Johnson upon whom the responsibilities of the Presidency have fallen.

I first met Jack Kennedy in January 1949 when I came to Congress and was assigned an office across the corridor from his on the third floor of the Old House Office Building. Frequently during the ensuing 4 years we walked and talked together as we went to and from the House Chamber. Although on many fundamental issues we held different viewpoints, I always respected his ability and valued his friendship.

From 1953 to 1960 while Mr. Kennedy served in the Senate I saw him less frequently but whenever we met he was most cordial and congenial. Following his election to the Presidency in 1960 I had several close and intimate contacts with him. In the summer of 1961 during the consideration of the controversial foreign aid authorization bill, Mr. Kennedy asked me to come to his office in the White House for a conference on the legislation. This half-hour session with the President on an important legislative problem will remain one of the highlights of my experiences in the Nation's Capital. For 30 minutes just the two of us talked about his proposal to finance the development loan part of the mutual security program by the "back-door-spending" method. He was friendly and extremely well informed on the technical details of our differences. Although we did not see eye to eye on the controversy, I well remember his fairness and kind consideration of my views. The memory of that discussion in the President's White House office was vivid as we stood before the bier in the East Room on that solemn Saturday afternoon.

In full realization that I vigorously disagreed with President Kennedy on many basic issues of public policy, I did appreciate his friendship and I do commend to all people as a fitting tribute to his memory these words from his eloquent inaugural address:

And so, my fellow Americans, ask not what your country can do for you: Ask what you can do for your country. My fellow citizens of the world: Ask not what America will do for you, but what together we can do for the freedom of man.

As we now proceed to carry on the Nation's business, we do so with a renewed sense of our responsibilities as American citizens. This sentiment was so well expressed in a recent letter on the President's death from a friend in a small Michigan town that I conclude with his statement:

At this sad time of history, it is our aim to be the best kind of citizens—faithful to God, loving our fellow men, serving our country and defending it to the last by every effort, no matter how small, including the education of our two children in the right way.

ADDRESS BY

Hon. Glenn Cunningham

OF NEBRASKA

Mr. Speaker, mere words cannot convey the shock which we all felt when we learned that a madman had shot the President. Inside all of us, all across the Nation, is the memory of this moment when the stunning news was first given us. It was unbelievable then. It still is.

We have taken the President's wife and children to our hearts since that moment. Her strength has given us all the realization that life goes on. And we recall the anguished words of the Senate chaplain, who prayed in those terrible moments when word of the shooting was received but before we knew the bullets had been mortal, "God lives. And the Government at Washington still stands."

As we thus look to the future, we find there have already been appropriate actions taken by men and governments to honor the memory of the late President. More will be considered, some in these Halls of Congress in which he served.

Yet I think that he would have been pleased if Congress would take action on several things connected with his tragic death.

For example, had he been seriously injured and disabled but not killed, who would have acted as President while he was still alive but unable to carry out his duties? The speed with which President Johnson was sworn in—a very necessary speed—shows how important it is that someone have the power of the Presidency at all times. Crucial decisions can be made and certain other constitutional duties performed only by the President; yet we have no provisions for Presidential decisions when the President is disabled.

It would be well also to have a thorough investigation of the Oswald type, the leftists and pro-Castro element he represented in our country, to determine just what type of threat they pose. It is essential that all possible information be available so the American people can understand the nature of this radical element in our midst.

There is also much concern over the fact that it is not a Federal crime to assault or kill the President or Vice President, yet it is a Federal crime to kill an FBI agent or Federal marshal, U.S. judge or U.S. attorney, Secret Service agent, or certain employees of the Interior and Agriculture Departments. Many feel that the same provision should be extended to an assault on or assassination of a President or Vice President.

The sentiments in Walt Whitman's "O Captain! My Captain!" in my opinion, express the feelings of this Nation which has lost its leader:

O Captain! My Captain!

O Captain! My Captain! our fearful trip is done,
The ship has weather'd every rack, the prize we sought
  is won,
The port is near, the bells I hear, the people all exulting,
While follow eyes the steady keel, the vessel grim and
  daring;
But O heart! heart! heart!
O the bleeding drops of red,
Where on the deck my Captain lies,
Fallen cold and dead.

O Captain! my Captain! rise up and hear the bells;
Rise up—for you the flag is flung—for you the bugle
  trills,

For you bouquets and ribbon'd wreaths—for you the
　　shores a-crowding,
For you they call, the swaying mass, their eager faces
　　turning;
Here Captain! dear father!
The arm beneath your head!
It is some dream that on the deck,
You've fallen cold and dead.

My Captain does not answer, his lips are pale and still,
My father does not feel my arm, he has no pulse nor will,
The ship is anchor'd safe and sound, its voyage closed
　　and done,
From fearful trip the victor ship comes in with object
　　won:
Exult O shores, and ring O bells!
But I with mournful tread,
Walk the deck my Captain lies,
Fallen cold and dead.

　　　　　　　　　　　　—WALT WHITMAN.

ADDRESS BY

Hon. John Dowdy

OF TEXAS

Mr. Speaker, these are sad days in our beloved
country. In a troubled world, torn by strife and
turmoil, with street demonstrations, riots, sedi-
tion, atheism, murder and assassination, we were
shocked a few days ago by a Marxist rifle shot—
a shot truly heard around the world—which took
the life of the President of the United States.
The tragedy is such that, even yet, it is hard to
believe it really happened.

President Kennedy, in the prime of his life,
full of the vigor of which he was so proud, acknowledging the plaudits of crowding throngs,
most of whom had never before seen a President
in person, was struck down, never knowing what
had hit him—dying in the arms of his adoring
wife, who, dismayed and distressed, was awed
with unreality and unbelief, even as she held close
his body, as its spirit returned from whence it
had come.

Assassination is all too common in these modern times—in this age which we so proudly call
enlightened and civilized. Being prone to dis-
parage such events in other parts of the world,
holding to the vain thought that "it cannot happen here," we are abruptly pulled up with horrible proof—it has happened here. Every effort
is made to protect the life and limb of the Presi-

dent—yet history has repeated—it is again revealed there is no assurance—no insurance—
against the assault of the assassin.

Our country was founded on the principle that
our differences be settled by ballots, rather than
by bullets and bayonets. The Communist does
not hold to that principle. Mr. Kennedy is the
victim of the vicious cold war, which has claimed
its sacrifices, just as surely as any war we have
ever fought.

As our Nation mourns the untimely death of
our President, my heart goes out to his little children, and to Mrs. Kennedy. Her grief can only
be known to one who has himself suddenly been
confronted with the loss of life's companion.

ADDRESS BY

Hon. Catherine May

OF WASHINGTON

Mr. Speaker, on behalf of myself, my family,
and the people whom I represent in my part of
the State of Washington, I wish to join my colleagues today in this tribute marking the tragic
and untimely death of President John F. Kennedy. On this occasion I would first of all convey our heartfelt sorrow and deep sympathy to
the late President's wife and children, and with
this sympathy a tribute, beautifully expressed in
these words that appeared in an editorial in one
of my newspapers:

> Perhaps the bravest lesson of all comes from Jacqueline
> Kennedy, whose courage in her ordeal has been beautiful
> to watch. She has set a noble example for those who
> pick up the burden from her fallen husband.

There are many facets to the grief that all of us
have felt since the terrible day that President Kennedy was assassinated because of senseless action
by unreasoning passion. Certainly our grief is
based on the untimeliness of this loss—a brave
and vigorous young leader struck down while he
still had a long and important way to go to fulfill
his destiny in American history. But it seems to
me that herein lies an important cause for hope,
too. Hope that this tragic event will, in the final
analysis, inspire all the people of our Nation to
unite so that we can provide the most fitting memorial of all to John F. Kennedy. That me-

morial—a national determination to join the battle against man's inhumanity to man.

May the black day of November 22, 1963, stand as eternal reminder to every American that all wars are inward. That we must fight until we have vanquished within ourselves the intolerances, the prejudices, the hates—all those things that cause us to commit crimes against our fellow man.

Within the reach of each of us is this opportunity to give John Fitzgerald Kennedy this chance to reach his hoped for destiny in history.

ADDRESS BY

Hon. Odin Langen

OF MINNESOTA

Mr. Speaker, I rise today to join my colleagues in punctuating a chapter in the history in this House and Nation. A chapter that relates the birth, life, and death of a President. John F. Kennedy was that President.

While his Presidential life was short in historic latitude, it has no parallel in historical design. Our memory is not strained to recall the birth of his Presidency by election and inauguration, and many still thrill to the enthusiastic response of the Nation as he accepted the mantle.

There followed in equal magnitude a Presidential service in a character that was commensurate with the vigor, color, and dispatch that was so evident at its birth. A restless Nation and world taxed every resource of decision, action, and future vision.

There was the brightness of sunshine and darkness of storm that strains the vitality and tenacity of a leading Nation in a troubled, confused, and struggling world. To chart its course in these unmapped waters at times defied man's understanding with demands of judgment and comprehension that only providence could properly provide. Yet, under the sharpest fire and stubborn resistance the Presidency must of necessity respond with faith and convincing confidence to a demanding people.

To be so taxed in the youth of a Presidency should by all known standards bear rewards of future sufficiency with time for the glory of recollection. But the historic chapter of John F. Kennedy's Presidency, while so well written, has no such consistency, for it was rather to be hastily and brutally ended. The sinful weakness of men even in the atmosphere of divine freedom was to prematurely claim him, his strength, and his faith at the crest of achievement, as if to avenge and yet give credence to the weak and the unfaithful.

While it is not for us to judge or evaluate this destiny in terms of righteousness, it is for us to recognize and take heed that we may be guided by its worldly example. The blemish of the act on humanity, the Nation, and the world will not easily erase, but will fade with a rebuilt character in mankind and its behavior. Such character must be founded on Christian morals and faith emphasizing man's freedom to be thusly guided, rather than directed by his weakness to govern.

May the memory and review of this chapter serve all people to live with respect, faith, and regard for each other in free societies and nations.

Where our attempts to punish and reward may be replaced by forgiveness and the tranquillity of a faith in God; for only then will peace and justice prevail throughout the world. To seek this objective will bring peace to John F. Kennedy's memory.

ADDRESS BY

Hon. Albert H. Quie

OF MINNESOTA

Mr. Speaker, it has been a time of shock, unbelief, realization of loss, and finally the grim and impressive ceremonies by which we paid our last respects to the President of the United States.

The death of President John F. Kennedy affected all of us deeply, regardless of political affiliation, for an attack on the President is an attack on our Nation.

The President was killed by a man who did not

understand that political issues are not resolved by violence, but are hammered out on the anvil of debate, tempered by understanding and packaged in compromise.

During the entire brief administration of President Kennedy, human rights as they affect the individual overshadowed all other legislative discussion. It seems fitting that the Congress should now recognize that hate, based on matters of race, color, or creed, is not a fit companion of the 20th century, and that we should act quickly in the area of civil rights.

There were qualities in President John F. Kennedy that all of us admired. First, he was a man who was willing, ready, and able to fight for the things in which he believed. Many of us, even some in his own party, often disagreed with him. But Americans love a man who will fight hard for what he believes. President Kennedy showed his respect for men who would stand up for their convictions. He even wrote a book, describing and praising outstanding acts of individualism.

President Kennedy, then, stood for what he believed. It is a lesson for us all.

In his speeches, President Kennedy often spoke of the individual.

In his most famous remark, he told the individual American to "ask not what your country can do for you, but what you can do for your country."

This, certainly, is a sentiment to be honored.

On many occasions, President Kennedy showed the Nation and the world that he believed in God.

We can do him honor by remembering that in the tragic hours following his death we turned as a nation to our churches and our God—the only place where we could find understanding and solace.

There is no question but that God and religion and the dignity of man is the very basis of our right to govern ourselves. Let us, as time softens this blow, never confuse separation of church and state with separation of God from this Nation.

We should remember in honor to President Kennedy and to all Americans who died that we might live in freedom under God, that we must ultimately turn for guidance and aid to the Highest Authority of all.

ADDRESS BY

Hon. Glenard P. Lipscomb

OF CALIFORNIA

Mr. Speaker, our Nation and the world were thrown into despair and sadness November 22, 1963, when an assassin's bullet ruthlessly claimed the life of the 35th President of the United States, John F. Kennedy.

His tragic death has brought about a personal sense of loss to countless millions of people.

Mr. Kennedy had many attributes—an intellect of high order, dedication, a strong desire for public service, and many more. All of these qualities stood him in good stead in his rise to the Presidency. Those who have differed with him on issues and policies nevertheless found him to have an engaging, likable personality. He worked with dedication for those things in which he believed.

I first met Mr. Kennedy, then Senator Kennedy, in the 84th Congress when we both served on a conference committee discussing a measure which eventually became Public Law 84–863. This law embodied one of the major recommendations of the Hoover Commission, to modernize Government budgeting and accounting procedures. Mr. Kennedy exhibited a deep interest in legislation of this type.

Above all else, when his life was taken Mr. Kennedy was President of the United States. He was serving each and every one of us. We pay respect here this afternoon to both the man and the high office he held.

And as we move forward President Kennedy's memory will live in the hearts and minds of all of us.

ADDRESS BY

Hon. William E. Miller

OF NEW YORK

Mr. Speaker, we who knew him will never forget the warm and youthful vitality of John F. Kennedy, characteristics which earned him the devotion of vast multitudes of his countrymen.

The words spoken here today, like the many tangible memorials which have been, and later will be, dedicated to his name, can never adequately memorialize the profound dismay of the civilized world over President Kennedy's death at the hands of an assassin.

In his brief tenure of the Presidency, John F. Kennedy was confronted by great, surging tides of social change and by national peril of unprecedented gravity, both offering challenges to tax even the most seasoned leaders.

It is for us to join together now and seek the sound and lasting solutions to the problems our late President articulated so well.

ADDRESS BY

Hon. William L. Springer

OF ILLINOIS

Mr. Speaker, I have been in the House of Representatives for 13 years. Many of you here today have been in this House much longer.

All of us realize that many come and go. There are always a few of whom we become especially fond and miss their going.

I can remember when I first came to the House, John Kennedy had been here 4 years. I can still remember the first day I ever saw him. In the House the two parties were split over an agriculture bill. When the time came for a vote the Republicans stood in a body. At first, as I looked around, there were no Democrats standing. When I looked back again there was just one on his feet. That was John Kennedy. He showed me that day that he was his own man. He was independent enough that when he believed he was right he crossed party lines—even if he were the only member of the party who would. I can still remember a colleague going over to him and joking with him about being the only Democrat to vote with the Republicans. John Kennedy smiled and stood his ground.

In the Senate he often reflected more of this intellectual temperament. It was against his grain to have to be for something just because other people were for it when he thought it was wrong.

When he went to the White House he grew in stature spiritually and intellectually. He was almost a different man this last year than he was on January 20, 1961. He loved to surround himself with people of his same temperament. He had little use for second-raters. He could tolerate mistakes, but they had to be based on some conviction.

In the last year you could see the mellowing process at work and the maturity that came from solving difficult problems. I think it was in this period that he came to be loved and tremendously admired by not only his colleagues in the House and Senate but by people generally.

John Kennedy was a friendly man and by that I do not mean being friendly with the thought that he could influence you. He was friendly because he was that kind of a person.

John Kennedy was a gentle and kind person and I can point to many personal experiences that prove this to me. Although our political philosophies were poles apart I respected him and I am sure he did me. These are the relations which people in the Congress never forget about other Members with whom they have rubbed elbows over a period of many years.

I personally will miss John Kennedy, not only because he was a great man, but also because he was one of the least affected persons that I have ever known. I am not surprised at the popular image which he created throughout the country as a statesman, as a father, and as a husband.

We will miss John Kennedy here in the House of Representatives because for a long time he was a part of this body and when one of us dies a part of this body goes with him.

I am grateful for having known John Kennedy and I am thankful for the contribution that he has made to this House and to the people of this country. Men with his stature and personal charm are just that rare.

ADDRESS BY

Hon. George Meader

OF MICHIGAN

Mr. Speaker, on the bright, crisp afternoon of November 25, I stood below Lee-Custis Mansion on the hill in Arlington Cemetery and looked toward the Lincoln Memorial across the bridge waiting for the cortege to appear. I thought—this cannot be real; it must be a horrible dream; in this land of the free, the true and the brave—alert to defend itself—this brutish episode is impossible.

What venom, zeal, efficiency, and planning struck down with a little bullet not only an intelligent, able, personable young American but, at the same time, degraded the highest office in the world—the Presidency of the United States.

A devoted Marxist—refused Soviet citizenship because his fanaticism would be more useful in America than in Russia, where there are already sufficient Communists—pulled the trigger on a $12.78 mail-ordered rifle with telescopic sight—three times and cut down this young man and this Nation—and seriously wounded the Chief Executive of a proud and independent State.

Why?

What now?

A President assassinated.

All Americans have had the same sensation of sickness at this senseless sharpshooting.

Why? Who?

It is not that this is the first President to be assassinated. It is the fourth. Lincoln was the first.

But was this the individual act of a Marxist madman?

Possibly we will never know the complete accurate truth—even though State and Federal law enforcement agencies, and a Presidential Commission, to be headed by Supreme Court Chief Justice Warren, are investigating.

The character of the affair—so incongruous—so insensate—so incomprehensible, evil and malevolent—has rocked and shocked the American ethic and the American mind.

SHAKESPEARE'S "KING RICHARD THE SECOND," ACT III, SCENE II

KING RICHARD. Of comfort no man speak:
Let's talk of graves, of worms, and epitaphs;
Make dust our paper, and with rainy eyes
Write sorrow on the bosom of the earth;
Let's choose executors and talk of wills:
And yet not so—for what can we bequeath
Save our deposed bodies to the ground?
Our lands, our lives, and all are Bolingbroke's,
And nothing can we call our own but death,
And that small model of the barren earth
Which serves as paste and cover to our bones.

For God's sake, let us sit upon the ground
And tell sad stories of the death of kings:
How some have been depos'd, some slain in war,
Some haunted by the ghosts they have depos'd,
Some poison'd by their wives, some sleeping kill'd;
All murder'd: for within the hollow crown
That rounds the mortal temples of a king
Keeps Death his court, and there the antick sits,
Scoffing his state and grinning at his pomp;
Allowing him a breath, a little scene,
To monarchize, be fear'd, and kill with looks,
Infusing him with self and vain conceit
As if this flesh which walls about our life
Were brass impregnable; and humour'd thus
Comes at the last, and with a little pin
Bores through his castle wall, and farewell king!
Cover your heads, and mock not flesh and blood
With solemn reverence: throw away respect,
Tradition, form, and ceremonious duty,
For you have but mistook me all this while:
I live with bread like you, feel want,
Taste grief, need friends: subjected thus,
How can you say to me I am a king?

ADDRESS BY

Hon. Wayne N. Aspinall

OF COLORADO

Mr. Speaker, sorrowfully and prayerfully, I join with my colleagues of the House today in paying a tribute to the life and services of our martyred President, patriot, coworker, and friend, the late John Fitzgerald Kennedy. Sorrowfully, because I weep with the rest of the world for what has befallen us. Sorrowfully, because of my personal sympathy for the widowed mother and sweet children and the other members of the families who lost their loved one at the hands of a thoughtless and hate-filled monster of the human race. Prayerfully, because the United States of America, which I personally have served and loved for so many years, has shown a side to her body politic which I did not think could be a part of us. Prayerfully, because I earnestly beseech the Almighty that the personal and collective hate which led to the foul deed may be removed from the life of a people whose high resolutions call for liberty, freedom, and justice to all. I weep not for my generation today for it, too, is approaching the brink of the grave and what ideals it has had for a better world are about to go with it into the halls of eternity, but I do weep for the younger generations who follow who have found in our lately fallen President not only those ideals for a better world but a dedication of purpose to activate them in the interest of all members of the human race. Our late President was challenging that divine spark which is most noticeable in the young before it becomes tarnished and dimmed by the earthly cares which beset mankind. That these ideals and encouragement have received the setback that they have is the real tragedy of this hour.

Mr. Speaker, on an occasion such as this, words are so inadequate for the average person to express what is truly and really in his heart. It is not the lips that give the tributes. It is the heart that prompts those who would try to write on the pages of history how they feel about the loss we have suffered. So, like many of my fellow citizens, I stand almost mute before my colleagues in the sadness and despair that has been visited upon us. The pages of eternal history will be filled with the recitation of our late President's deeds and his utterances—his innumerable deeds of unselfish service to his fellow man and his statement of principles so high and noble. There is no need to record them in this ceremony in which we are presently engaged. Others far more qualified than we shall set them down for those who follow after. As for me, I shall be content to say to you that during my remaining waking hours I shall always hear the clarion call of service voiced so eloquently by our fallen leader when in resonant tones he spoke to America:

And so, my fellow Americans, ask not what your country can do for you, ask what you can do for your country.

He offered his life many times for his country and he finally gave it. No man can do more. The debt we owe to him and his can never be fully repaid. But in trying to make our country a better Nation for all, we can at least make certain that he and the other martyrs before him have not lived in vain.

Part of his strength came from the understanding, talented, charming and heroic woman with whom he shared his successes, heartaches and service. Seldom has the world experienced such a heroic and tragic personality. To me, she is the epitome of gracious and true womanhood. To her and their children and the families of each

who have been caught in this incredible event of history, Mrs. Aspinall and I send our most sincere and deepest sympathy.

ADDRESS BY

Hon. Charles R. Jonas

OF NORTH CAROLINA

Mr. Speaker, on behalf of all the people of North Carolina's Eighth Congressional District, and on behalf of my family and myself, I join my colleagues today in paying tribute to the memory of our late President John Fitzgerald Kennedy.

It is always an occasion for mourning when untimely death removes a colleague or high Government official from a position of responsibility given to him by his fellow citizens. This occasion is all the more sorrowful not only because of the brutal and senseless way in which President Kennedy was murdered but because he was still a young man, energetic and vital, who had every right to anticipate many years of future service to his country.

This fact compounds the tragedy and deepens the sense of grief which has touched the country and the world since the terrible events that transpired on last November 22. President Kennedy was the first man born in this century to have been chosen for the highest office in the land and he was permitted to serve less than 3 full years in the high office to which he was called by his countrymen.

During the relatively brief period that John F. Kennedy was permitted to serve as our 35th President, he had succeeded in making a tremendous impact on the minds of the people of our own country as well as of the world. He had great personal charm which, coupled with a friendly manner, and with a quiet dignity and reserve, endeared him to all with whom he came in contact. He had a quick wit that included an ability to poke gentle fun at himself. Added to these qualities was the strength of an active and inquisitive mind. These personal characteristics were easily conveyed to all the people through the modern media of communications. He also made excellent use of the more traditional written word and in this set a standard which will be difficult to match. Throughout President Kennedy's tenure of office he faced problems of transcendent importance to the country and the world. The supreme tragedy of the event we mourn today, aside from the personal loss suffered by his immediate family, was that he was not permitted to live long enough to view in retrospect the completion of the tasks he had begun.

This is a time to remind ourselves and all our people, as well as the people of the world, that although differences of political philosophy divide us we are one in our devotion and dedication to our country; and we are one in our determination to preserve the security of our country and the freedoms we enjoy as American citizens, whatever honest differences we may have about how to insure these goals.

It is a shame that it takes a tragedy of this magnitude to bring home to all of us that we can have but one President at a time and that whoever he may be at the moment all loyal Americans unite with him in his efforts to promote the interests and security of our country and a just and lasting peace throughout the world.

Mrs. Jonas joins me in extending deep and heartfelt sympathy to Mrs. Kennedy and her children and in a prayer that God will comfort them in the days and years that lie ahead.

ADDRESS BY

Hon. Otis G. Pike

OF NEW YORK

Mr. Speaker, I pray that never again within my lifetime shall this beloved land be forced to undergo such a convulsion as shook it on Friday, November 22, with the monstrous act which resulted in the death of President John F. Kennedy.

President Kennedy had appealed to the higher motivations in all of us. He sought to move us to actions based on the essential brotherhood of mankind. He asked us to think not of ourselves but of the oppressed, the hungry, the diseased, the poor, and the elderly. To those of us who heard what he said, his life was a sermon, and because all of us are human beings, we all too

frequently applauded the words which he gave us without acting upon them.

His death brought to the people of America and to the people of the world first, disbelief, next, shock, then dismay, and now, hopefully, a rededication to those goals and to those high ideals which he so eloquently set forth.

Into my office has poured mail from my district and from friends all over the country and all over the globe. It is perhaps as fitting a testimonial to the universal appeal of President Kennedy that I received this letter from a Protestant minister, the Reverend Herbert Perry, doing missionary work in southern Rhodesia, Africa:

DEAR OTIS: News of President Kennedy's death reached here less than an hour after it happened (about 10 o'clock last evening, our time). We were of course deeply shocked and moved, while we stayed up listening to the Voice of America through the night.

This morning finds us bleary eyed and shaken, but stanchly proud of our country—and of Kennedy himself, who seemed such a good symbol of all that America really means and stands for.

I think I shall always remember him with respect and gratitude, and with the feeling that we have been deprived of a leader as near to being essential to our future well-being as a nation as any man can be. It can't be denied that there's a note of angry resentment and perplexity in our prayers, but neither can it be denied that there's also a note of gratitude for having been given such a man at such a time. Our prayers also go out to the Nation, the Democratic Party, as well as to his family and many friends. But as he knew so well, prayers by themselves are far from adequate to the tasks and challenges facing our Nation and the world today. With something of his energy, zeal, and dedicated action in all of us, our civilization will perhaps become more worthy of such men as he.

Fond regards,

HERB.

NOVEMBER 23, 1963.

This eloquent tribute speaks my own thoughts better than I can say them.

ADDRESS BY

Hon. Horace R. Kornegay

OF NORTH CAROLINA

Mr. Speaker, as we gather here today on this most solemn occasion to pay tribute to our late President, John Fitzgerald Kennedy, and to express our grief and shock over his untimely and tragic death, we are keenly aware that the one to whom these tributes are paid does not belong to the Congress, the Federal Government, or indeed the Nation—he belongs to the ages. The scope and magnitude of the effect of President Kennedy's death on the civilized world is one of the imponderables. The canvas containing the imprint of his life and personality is so broad that it cannot be nationally contained.

As for my own tribute here today, let me say that there are times in the lives of men when through the medium of poetry we can best express the thoughts that lie within our innermost selves. The poem by Walt Whitman, "O Captain! My Captain!" holds for me the deep emotional impact experienced in learning the terrible news of John Fitzgerald Kennedy's death:

O Captain! My Captain! Our fearful trip is done.
The ship has weather'd every rack, the prize we sought
    is won.
The port is near, the bells I hear, the people all exulting,
While follow eyes the steady keel, the vessels grim and
    daring;
But O my heart! heart! heart!
O the bleeding drops of red,
Where on the deck my Captain lies
Fallen cold and dead.

I am reminded of the concluding words in the message which President Kennedy had designed for that fateful day in Dallas and which he was never to deliver, and how fitting these words were to the personality of the man, who ever looked to Providence for guidance for his personal life and for that of his beloved country:

Except the Lord build the house, they labor in vain
that build it: except the Lord keep the city, the watchman
waketh but in vain.

Along with my colleagues, I had the sorrowful privilege of attending the final sad rites for John Fitzgerald Kennedy, and I observed with a feeling of comforting satisfaction what a noble and magnificent site Mrs. Kennedy and the family had chosen for his last resting place. No more appropriate site in the vicinity of Washington could have been found. As one stands on the gently sloping hillside in the Arlington National Cemetery, the earthly resting place of many of the Nation's heroes, and gazes over the beautiful waters of the Potomac to the Nation's Capitol, the memorials to Lincoln and Jefferson and Washington, the splendid grandeur of the scene grips the

throat and heart, and the lines of William Wordsworth come so quickly and so aptly to mind:

Earth has not anything to show more fair:
Dull would he be of soul who could pass by
A sight so touching in its majesty:
This city now doth like a garment wear
The beauty of the morning; silent, bare,
Ships, towers, domes, theaters, and temples lie
Open unto the fields, and to the sky;
All bright and glittering in the smokeless air.
Never did sun more beautifully steep
In his first splendor, valley, rock, or hill;
Ne'er saw I, never felt, a calm so deep!
The river glideth at its own sweet will:
Dear God! the very houses seem asleep;
And all that mighty heart is lying still!

Our hearts, and the collective heart of the Nation and the civilized world, go out to Mrs. Kennedy and her children and to all the Kennedy family, for John Fitzgerald Kennedy was a man of many parts, and one of his most important and endearing parts was his devotion and his close ties to his family. Mrs. Kennedy has borne her most grievous bereavement with a courage and a nobility worthy of the magnitude of her loss. President Kennedy now lies in a family plot, with his two small children by his side. His widow and his surviving little girl and boy, who are cradled in tenderness in the world's sorrow, may now visit the place where not only a President lies, but where a President lies with his family.

As we recall the charm and the vitality and the intellect and the accomplishments of this man, let us momentarily close the chapter of his interment with Stevenson's moving "Requiem":

Under the wide and starry sky
Dig the grave and let me lie,
Glad did I live and gladly die,
And I laid me down with a will.

This be the verse you grave for me:
Here he lies where he longed to be;
Home is the sailor, home from sea,
And the hunter home from the hill.

ADDRESS BY

Hon. James A. Haley

OF FLORIDA

Mr. Speaker, it is appropriate that we, as the representatives of the people, are gathered here today to pay tribute to the young man who was the 35th President of the United States, for the people of the Nation—without regard to race, creed, or political faith—mourn the cruel death of John Fitzgerald Kennedy.

No mere words of mine can add to the flood of tributes which have poured from full hearts the world over—the hearts of great leaders of great nations but also the hearts of the men and women in the street—since President Kennedy was laid low by bullets senselessly fired by an assassin with a fevered mind.

As in the case with all of us in this House of Representatives in which Jack Kennedy first served as an elected official of this country, I am grieved by his death, angered by its manner, and share in the national shame that a thing such as this could happen in our country.

I am particularly grieved for John Kennedy the man, the husband, and the father. None of us, I am sure, can ever forget the courage and dignity with which his widow, Mrs. Jacqueline Kennedy, bore her grief and shock from the time of her husband's death until he was laid to rest in Arlington National Cemetery on a day of majestic sadness. She had more to bear than most of us; she bore her burden better than most of us. I am certain also that none of us will forget the bewildered sorrow of the President's children, who had so obviously adored their daddy— and had been adored by him. My heart goes out to them—as must, I am sure, the hearts of all of us here today, and of all Americans.

I would hope that for their sakes, and for the sake of our President who has been struck down in the summer of his life and in the service of his country, that we in the Congress, and all of the citizenry we represent, will not let this tragedy deter us from our purpose of keeping this great and free Nation, and of maintaining its leadership in its quest for the freedom and dignity of all mankind, and peace and good will on this earth.

I believe that our slain President would want us to do this for the country he served. I do not believe that those of us spared to continue serving it could build a better memorial to John F. Kennedy than to achieve through our actions a better country and a better world.

ADDRESS BY

Hon. David N. Henderson

OF NORTH CAROLINA

Mr. Speaker, President John Fitzgerald Kennedy is dead and even as we say it with our mouths and hear it with our ears, we cannot truly accept it in our hearts.

Of his death, many words have been spoken and written.

Of his life, each of us holds his own special memories.

Our Republic will be the richer for his service to it and the poorer for his untimely passing.

We grieve with his widow and family but admire their spirit and unflinching courage of which our departed leader displayed his own full measure.

This is a time for looking backward without stopping and moving forward without stumbling. The torch of liberty flickered briefly, but was quickly revived by those who indomitably refuse to let the death of this great man halt the march he led.

There are those who would cast blame upon many people and many concepts for the tragedy which has befallen us. There are those who deplore the weakness of the moral fiber of this proud Nation because this act has occurred.

Let it be remembered that John Fitzgerald Kennedy met his death not at the hands of a rebellious army or mob; not by the action of a massive throng or even a small group; but because of the twisted mind of one unfortunate creature; unable, even, to decide where to place his national allegiance.

All elements of America's citizenry mourned our President's death and the mighty of the world marched behind his widow to his funeral.

He left our Nation as strong as he found it; united, steadfast, free, determined to fulfill its destiny and a little further along the road to lasting peace.

ADDRESS BY

Hon. Lionel Van Deerlin

OF CALIFORNIA

Mr. Speaker, I can understand the feeling expressed today by more senior Members—men who served alongside our late President here in Congress, and who therefore feel the loss of a close personal friend. For newer Members such as myself, knowing the man only as President, prevented this same easy personal friendship. The Presidency is indeed a lonely pinnacle.

And yet what an influence the Kennedy leadership has exerted on all of us. It has elevated the whole tone of government.

There was, first of all, the man's mental brilliance. His range of knowledge and clarity of thought shone through every meeting with press or public, and in every official utterance. I have twice watched Mr. Kennedy address great crowds without manuscript, yet with an orderly arrangement of ideas and perfect syntax.

Clarity of thought, in some men, offers no assurance of good works. It was the Nation's good fortune that, in John Kennedy, a brilliant mind was matched by a devotion to public service. Materially blessed by the accident of birth, this man could have chosen the easy life; instead, the story of his career reveals a long series of deliberate choices—choices resolved consistently in favor of exacting study, of hard work, of physical danger, of political risks. He despised the lazy, the mediocre, the satisfied.

Finally—and perhaps most of all—the name Kennedy will remain a synonym for courage. There was the raw personal courage of a PT commander whose craft was smashed in enemy action. There was the courage required in meeting, head on, the threat of a hostile arms buildup in Cuba. And there were more subtle, in some ways more difficult demands for courage—the courage to face squarely some ancient prejudices built on religion and race. In refusing to flinch

before bigotry, John Kennedy may have left his most lasting mark.

Mr. Speaker, let us hope that the eternal beacon of Arlington will continue to send its glow across the river—that in its light, those of us who were elected under the Kennedy banner, and all who serve in Congress, may be better, more high-minded and more courageous men.

ADDRESS BY

Hon. Clark MacGregor

OF MINNESOTA

Mr. Speaker, those of us who stood in Arlington National Cemetery on the afternoon of November 25 were deeply moved by two emotions as we watched a family, a nation, and the world's leaders pay their final tribute to President John F. Kennedy.

We felt first a great sorrow that the life of such a lively and youthful national leader should end so cruelly and suddenly. Mr. Kennedy had qualities of greatness. He stimulated the enthusiasms and the imaginations of many of our people as few other American Presidents have ever done. Our hearts go out to Mrs. Kennedy and to their children. They will continue to symbolize the youthful spirit of our lost President.

Our second emotion was one of national pride. Two such incredible and fantastic acts of savagery as America had witnessed might well have sparked a serious outbreak of general violence among a less stable people. While deploring what did happen, we should take some satisfaction in seeing that as a nation our commonsense prevailed and our governmental continuity was carried forward.

It was surely that national strength of continuity together with the spirit of John F. Kennedy which brought such a great representation of the world's leadership to Arlington National Cemetery that day.

We have lost a President, but we have gained a fresh new understanding of our national purpose. On behalf of the residents of Minnesota's Third Congressional District, and of the members of my family, I extend deepest sympathy to the surviving members of the family of John F. Kennedy.

ADDRESS BY

Hon. Eugene Siler

OF KENTUCKY

Mr. Speaker, since our President was cut down 13 days ago in the cruelty of an attack that shocked the world, this Nation has drunk deeply of its cup of bitter grief and poignant sorrow. Our remorse has been quite moving and very real.

Of course, many of us disagreed with President Kennedy on various subjects. And even now in the sound stability of our individual minds we feel that whatever was unwise or unconstitutional before this dark specter of death cast its shadow over the Capitol is still unwise and unconstitutional. Yet all of us greatly respected the President and unanimously we honor him today with our eulogies. None of us would ever have wished the slightest physical detriment to come upon the leader of our Nation or any of his outstanding family. And we pour out our heartfelt sympathy to Mrs. Kennedy and all members of the Kennedy family over their loss and the bitterness of this experience.

One reason I would honor President Kennedy today and forever is because he followed his country's flag in time of war. In the holocaust of a deadly war, some of the scions of very wealthy families do not offer to sacrifice themselves and their careers. But John Kennedy did so and no doubt even went beyond the call of that which was strictly his duty. He was true to the highest traditions of all the patriotic men and women who ever helped America survive in time of armed conflict.

President Kennedy was also a good exemplification of the American family man. He cherished his children and seized every opportunity to enjoy something of a happy homelife with his wife and little ones. And thus he projected himself as a good image of the well-being and success of the family leader here in our country. He will long be remembered for this idealistic conception he presented before the face of the Nation.

And now John Kennedy has gone through the valley of the shadow of this life and has ascended the sloping hillside up to that topmost height where life lets go and life at last is born. There he should find all the dreams that he ever lost on toilsome earth. And those, we feel, will be good dreams out there in the continuity of eternity.

ADDRESS BY

Hon. Ralph R. Harding

OF IDAHO

Mr. Speaker, in all probability John Fitzgerald Kennedy will be one of the most widely quoted of our past Presidents in the speeches that will be delivered in America in the next 100 years. This is because a man with his rare combination of talents only comes along once every 100 years.

I first met Senator John F. Kennedy at Boise, Idaho, in 1958. I had the opportunity to renew our acquaintance in September of 1960 at Pocatello, Idaho, when he was seeking the Presidency and I was a candidate for Congress from the Second District of Idaho. I had the pleasure to visit with Senator Kennedy on political issues and the progress of our campaigns.

I was so impressed that the night before election after I had invested several thousand dollars and many months of hard work in my own campaign for Congress, I told my wife that, "If only one of us can win tomorrow, I hope that it will be John F. Kennedy because the country needs his leadership." I was fully convinced that this great American had been blessed with those "once in a hundred years" qualities of leadership.

He had a great sense of humor. I now can remember both privately and publicly many of the remarks of our late President that enlightened the burdens that his listeners were carrying. Never anything vulgar or smutty, but always light and refreshing.

He was a powerful reader. His rapid reading rate of over 2,000 words per minute and 99 percent comprehension filled a mind that was constantly questing for knowledge. It enabled him to keep up with the experts on the many complex problems of national defense, international relations and domestic prosperity.

He loved people. President Kennedy was the gregarious, outgoing type. He could not get off an airplane or go through a crowd without responding to the friendly persuasion that led him to shake hands, no, speak to and show an instant interest in a person who was a complete stranger. It was this love of people, an outward friendliness, that enabled him to win in a West Virginia primary that had many of his stanchest supporters convinced that he would never win.

He had enthusiasm for work. President Kennedy was a young man, eager, anticipating, vibrant, and enthusiastic. He was alive. To a nation that was used to Presidents in their sixties, this young President in his midforties provided a picture of activity, bounce, and movement. He stimulated others around him to respond to the challenges of the offices that they held.

He exuded confidence. While the President was youthful and energetic there was something about his personality that gave everyone an assurance that he could handle the job. All was well as long as he was at the helm. Even though he was lighthearted and gay, on occasions when toughness, determination, and resolution were needed, he showed that he had these characteristics in ample quantities. Whether he had to face Khrushchev over missiles in Cuba, the big steel companies over increased steel prices, and a hike in inflation, the labor leaders who were insisting on a cut in the 40-hour workweek, Jack Kennedy was able to meet their challenges with an air of confidence that enabled him to emerge the winner.

He was truly a man that comes along only every 100 years. I look back now on the many little experiences I have had at the White House, the stag parties in the House gymnasium, his addresses to the Congress, and two chance encounters at the funeral of our late Speaker Sam Rayburn in Texas and recently on the back lawn of the White House when the President broke away from his intended course to walk out of his way, shake hands, and visit briefly with me.

I am exceedingly grateful for this friendship that I have enjoyed with one of God's choicest sons and of America's greatest leaders. I am grateful also that I have been one of his stanch-

est supporters in the Congress, not only because I was supporting a program that was preserving the peace and moving the Nation progressively toward increased prosperity, but also because it was the program of a great President.

We are all going to miss our late President John F. Kennedy, but the greatest way that we can assure our appreciation for the life of this great man is by rededicating ourselves to the ideals in which he believed—a strong America with equal rights and opportunity for all Americans regardless of race, creed, or color. By following his exhortation, "Ask not what your country can do for you, ask what you can do for your country," with meaningful action we too make John F. Kennedy's ideals our ideals.

Mr. Speaker, the following are some of the many outstanding tributes that were paid to our late great President in the newspapers of Idaho:

[From the Blackfoot (Idaho) News, Nov. 26, 1963]

He Got the Country Moving

The bewildering shock felt by citizens in all walks of life following the assassination of President John F. Kennedy has been shared by the writers and news commentators of the Nation. Even those who knew him well have appeared muted and dumb.

Perhaps the terrible exhibition that proved an anarchist with a twisted and perverted mind can strike through the most careful protection given the Captain of the Nation has been a greater shock than can immediately be understood or borne.

A man whom most of the people of the Nation had come to look on as the guardian of our rights and our peace and as a great and good man has been stricken dead.

It is frightening to think that any one of our citizenry, given the proper twisted mentality, has such power to strike a blow at the entire Nation by striking down its chosen representative.

As we have taken counsel of our fears we have become introspective. What is it in our national character that permits the growth side by side of the highest idealism ever to find fruit in a national culture, and beside it the radicalism and hatred that more often than in any other land kills our greatest chosen leaders?

God save America, and save us from our hatreds. As we ponder the meaning of the death of John F. Kennedy we have all wondered what is in our own hearts that makes possible the horrible and frightful in our national life.

Many men of abilities with words will try to tell what the life and example of John F. Kennedy meant to the United States and to the world. Each of us would like to speak an expression of gratitude. Poorly expressed though it may be I should like to add a word of appreciation for what I think he has done for our country.

Prior to the year 1960 he was to me simply a young eastern politician with an enthusiastic local following. As a member of the opposite political party, there was considerable indifference toward his effort to achieve the nomination of his party for the highest office of the land.

It is well to remember the context of the times. To me it seems the most important task was the preservation of peace in the world. At the helm was President Eisenhower, perhaps not a great President, but a good man who appeared to be approaching greatness by his determination to let his heart rule in assuming the road to international conciliation.

Alarm grew as it became apparent that elements in this country were as willing to prevent the approach to conciliation as were some of our opponents. Then came the culmination of reaction with the sickening U–2 affair; its clumsy handling by the men around President Eisenhower and the apparent blasting of further efforts toward conciliation.

The voice of the then Senator Kennedy gave evidence that hope might yet remain. Here was a man to be watched.

During the infighting prior to the Democratic National Convention, the man Kennedy appeared blurred by his political organization that was awesome in its efficiency. But with the nomination secured, John F. Kennedy emerged to speak hope, courage, and good cheer with his promise to get the country moving again.

There was one small incident in the campaign that brought home to me the fact that Kennedy was the man the Nation needed.

In the course of the fall of 1960, the Reverend Martin Luther King, the great civil rights crusader, was taken into custody in a city of Georgia. Circumstances surrounding the case indicated that his life might be endangered, as the life of any outspoken Negro is in danger in some sections of the United States.

Senator John F. Kennedy called Mrs. King offering her assurance that he would do all in his power to insure the safety of her husband; then called the Governor of Georgia to point out to him that the Nation's eyes were upon the State.

Some chose to call that an act of political expediency.

As one who is proud that the blood of abolitionist forebears runs in his veins and who has revered Abraham Lincoln as the statesman of modern history who cared most for the common man, I thrilled to a man with political courage who reacted from the heart in a case where more votes were likely to be lost rather than gained.

(Do you remember his message to the Nation the night of the riot on the campus of the University of Mississippi? And the reaction later reported by its central figure, James Meredith, the object of unlimited hatred and scorn, who for the first time in his life felt the majesty of the power of the United States on the side of a Negro, and who thrilled to the words "Mr. Meredith" from the lips of the President.)

I consider it fortunate that on two occasions it was possible to meet in rather small groups with John F. Kennedy. The first was at the press conference in Pocatello held in connection with one of the first political speeches of his campaign of 1960. The other was in company with a small group of Idaho newspaper publishers invited to dinner with him at the White House.

At the first I was impressed with his youthfulness; his idealism; his utter honesty. ("What is Burns Creek? I've never heard of it.")

At the latter I was impressed by his growth in 2 years; by the easy manner in which he carried the burdens of his office; by his grasp of the situation; by his utter frankness in answering any question; by the fact that he did not hesitate or say that anything was off the record. (The plea for discretion came later from Pierre Salinger.)

Such affairs are valuable perhaps in the process of confirming or reversing opinions formerly held. From both I emerged confident that the man who had been the center of all eyes was worthy: in the first case of a chance to assume the burden of the Presidency; in the second that he was doing a good job.

In the 2 years and 10 months that John F. Kennedy was President of the United States I felt that the peace of the world was secure in his hands because I felt sure he thought the thoughts of the average man and woman much better than they could think or express them.

As a Protestant, proud of much of the heritage of the Reformation, I am grateful to him for a demonstration of the unity of our common Christian heritage.

As a citizen of the United States I proudly claim that he fulfilled his promise to get the country moving again. He has pointed the direction of humanity, of brotherhood, of decency. The country has started moving along those lines.

It will move faster because of his martyrdom. I believe this devoutly and can see no other explanation of the meaning of his death.

————

[From the Idaho Falls Post Register]

THE UNSPEAKABLE LOSS

The President dead. No one could believe it at first. But as the wire services haltingly unraveled the shocking assassination of President Kennedy Friday, incredulity slowly turned to revulsion.

Who would do such a thing? Why?

In the fevered brain of an assassin, reason has long since been assassinated itself—killed by the worst malignancy of the human race, extremism. In this emotional myopia, weird causes are justified, might makes right, the end justifies the means, and hatred is purified. And tragically, in this mental blur, the assassin often conceives himself a patriot of some kind.

Extremism is the total antithesis to this Nation's grand covenant, a nation under law. Within the scope of the law, you may criticize the President or castigate his programs, and maneuver for his and their defeat. But, all within the pale of the law.

In Dallas, Tex., Friday, November 22, 1963, an ugly symbol of extremism in effect proclaimed: I am the only right; there is no law but mine and the gun.

It may turn out to be a most isolated symbol—but just as ugly.

This incredibly inhumane thing which happened in Dallas Friday can never be explained. No explanation suffices. This young, vigorous, and impressively intelligent leader was silenced at the very pinnacle of his thrust for an always emerging America. He was a President who could stir his followers, excite them to dreams of new frontiers.

President Kennedy had an unusual warmth, unusual courage, and patriotism. People who disagreed strenuously with him as President, admired him as a man as well as a leader.

Only two impulses survive in the forlornly bleak aftermath—one of inexpressible sympathy for the Kennedy family, especially Mrs. Kennedy, and a prayer for our new President.

A strange, stifling hush settles over the land as the Republic makes its transition sadly but firmly to a new leadership. New frontiers, challenged so aggressively by President Kennedy, await a new matching in America.

Certainly Friday, November 22, was a black day in the history of this Nation and the world.

———

[From the Rigby Star]

HERE AND THERE

(By Hope)

America hung its head in grief and shame Friday after an assassin's bullet in Dallas, Tex., took the life of President John F. Kennedy.

"Brutal, despicable, unbelievable, incredible," were the general reactions of the mass of American people as they rallied from the first shock of the news. Whatever their politics, their religion, their station in life, they were shocked and saddened, for this was not only the death of the President of the United States, but of a husband, father, son, and brother, an American who had served his country from the war in the South Pacific until the moment of his death. And his death came through an assassin's bullet, a fanatic, who had forsworn allegiance to this Nation.

There are very few who are not genuinely grieved that this young, intelligent, and energetic President was felled while on a mission of good will and friendliness. Unlike the three other Presidents of the United States who were assassinated, President Kennedy is said to have died immediately—the others lingered on for a time.

If, out of the tragic death of President Kennedy, the people may learn that hate is a cancer upon the heart of the human family; that unless we as a people and a nation become more appreciative, more loyal, more dedicated to upholding the ideals of this country, we are going to fail. Moral degeneration can and will set in.

Fifty-three nations, including kings and queens, came to pay homage to our martyred President. A day of national mourning was set aside that we Americans could revalue our aims and purposes in life. Now we are in a 30-day period of mourning for President Kennedy and the world in retrospect will see the picture of Mrs. Jacqueline Kennedy, her magnificent courage and dignity during the days just past.

I asked a Rigby high school senior his reactions: "I just couldn't believe that it could happen in America, we were stunned." It has happened here. Let's take stock of ourselves.

[From the Rexburg (Idaho) Standard, Nov. 26, 1963]

TO HONOR HIS MEMORY

When a leader of great power and presence and capacity for good dies in office, the cause to which he gave leadership suffers grievous loss. President John F. Kennedy was such a man. The cause he served, and so eloquently led, was the threefold cause of human dignity and equality and freedom.

Though President Kennedy is dead, struck down most foully by an assassin's hand, the cause he championed as acknowledged leader of the free world lives on. We who survive him can best honor his memory by doing all in our power to advance the cause, which is the very cause for which this Nation was founded.

Guidance for the difficult time ahead may be taken from the immortal words spoken by Abraham Lincoln on that solemn occasion at Gettysburg almost exactly a century ago. For President Kennedy died in defense of freedom as truly as did those who fell on that historic field of battle. In those days of profound national sorrow it is appropriate to reflect on Lincoln's exhortation to his fellow Americans "that from these honored dead we take increased devotion to that cause for which they gave the last full measure of devotion—that we here highly resolve that these dead shall not have died in vain."

To resolve thus and to act thus—that is the task to which we must now turn our minds. This is so even though grief and a deep sense of loss will far outlast the initial period of outraged shock at the murderous act in Dallas. We cannot permit ourselves the luxury of heedless sorrow. The forces that work against the realization of man's highest dreams remain strong and malignant. Those forces must now be countered with new dedication, so that President Kennedy's martyrdom in the fullness of life shall indeed not have been in vain.

The heaviest burden falls upon Lyndon B. Johnson, who became President the moment John F. Kennedy succumbed to the assassin's bullets. But all citizens must in some measure share that burden. In his first public utterance as Chief Executive, President Johnson said this to the American people: "I will do my best. That is all I can do. I ask your help—and God's." It is a commitment, and a challenge worthy of the best that is in all of us.

———

[From the Arco (Idaho) Advertiser, Nov. 28, 1963]

APOLOGY TO A PRESIDENT

The cruel and senseless murder of President Kennedy shocked the world, and well it should have. To those of us in Butte County the news was heard in shocked disbelief, and then accepted in numbing grief.

Our President is dead, and forever it must be.

With acceptance of death came compassion for his widow and the two children who will grow up with only vague memories of the great man who was their father. And we selfishly wonder what the sudden changes in the Nation's leadership will mean to us.

Our President is dead, but his high ideals, his compassion for mankind the world over live on. Many of us were critical of the office and for this there is no shame. Sometimes in pettiness we heaped bitter scorn upon the man, and we would have those words unspoken.

It is a judgment against us that this man had to die to bring out much of the decency in mankind. It may be hoped that this tragedy may enlarge the desire in all people to unite in a world free from hatred and bigotry and greed. That we may now realize and put aside the petty differences and unite to carry on John Fitzgerald Kennedy's hopes of a world of freedom, equality, and love.

We have the power. May God grant us the will.

[From the Owyhee Chronicle]

MANKIND WALKS A NARROW LEDGE

The tragedy which deprived America of its President should awaken all to the shocking price of fanaticism and hate-filled thinking and arouse in each of us a reevaluation.

The late President Kennedy often reiterated "mankind walks a narrow ledge." Never before have Americans walked a narrower ledge than we walk today. Never before have we faced a more compelling need to erase this mesmerism of hate which turns race against race, brother against brother, culminating in this tragic event.

The savage irony is that President Kennedy, who had buoyant faith in reason and was an advocate of rational discourse, was cut down by the very fanaticism that as President he sought to contain.

But his death will not be in vain if it becomes the turning point toward a rational approach to the solution of today's crucial issues—if it has shocked us back from the brink of the ledge.

[From the Idaho Statesman]

OUR LEADER HAS FALLEN

Profound shock and deep and bitter sorrow occasioned by the enormously tragic death of President John F. Kennedy must inevitably be shared by every rightminded individual.

In the gloom that is spread over the Nation and the world, philosophical and political difference in which he was inevitably involved pale now into insignificance as all of us are united in a common grief.

It is a moment in which attention is focused upon John F. Kennedy as an individual of high ideals, of dedication and of courage.

A product of his times, John F. Kennedy was called to national leadership in a period of widely prevailing uncertainty and perhaps of epochal transition involving the clash of strongly conflicting forces. He has fulfilled his part stoutly, conscientiously and fairly.

It has been his prime purpose to minimize the conflict and to do all within his power to make this country and the world a better place for all mankind to live.

It is perhaps that as an outstanding humanitarian his memory will be enshrined. He has been quick to respond to the appeal of human wants and needs. In his book it is the proper function of Government to provide the remedy, and he has not hesitated to call upon the resources of Government to that end.

In reference to the phrase that sounded like a clarion in his inaugural address, John F. Kennedy never asked what the country could give him personally; instead it has been he who has given his country and the world the last full measure of devotion.

So our leader has fallen, victim of one who could not have been other than a demented and tortured assassin. So in the tradition of nations we now must rally around a new leader and press forward toward the achievement of our national destiny.

[From the Idaho Sunday Journal, Nov. 24, 1963]

ASSASSIN'S BULLET TAKES A COURAGEOUS LEADER

The hopes and fears of 180 million Americans center upon the Presidency of the United States with a white heat. Controversy and conflict is a part of the intense pressures upon the solitary man who bears the burden of that exalted office. Love, and hate, too focus there. We know now, with stunned bewilderment, that one warped mind can rob our Nation and the world of its elected leader in an instant. We are reminded "In the midst of life, we are in death."

John F. Kennedy, the man, was a young, vital, courageous leader, wise beyond his years, a loving husband and father. The human tragedy of the swift and ugly assassination shames the Nation, and, in fact, the human race.

Youth and charm and grace characterized the Kennedy family in the White House. They were a part of American life, not aloof from it.

Youngest of our Presidents, John F. Kennedy fought for peace with justice, for true equality of human and civil rights. What history's verdict may be, we cannot foresee. But as a person, he embodied qualities which attracted admiration of millions, the envy and hate of few.

His lovely and gracious wife, his charming children, are bereft, and the heartfelt sympathy of all reaches futilely out to them.

Profound changes no one can foresee were set in motion by the deadly aim of the assassin.

But the headlong pace of history waits not. Lyndon B. Johnson is now our President. Even in the hour of his grief, the weight of office begins its unremitting pressures.

We can be thankful for the enduring structure of our Government that does not falter or fail under the stress of change and grief.

We can be thankful that President Johnson is as well prepared as any man can be to assume the mantle of leadership. He has courage and strength, experience and faith.

We can pray for the unhappy family President Kennedy was forced to leave. We can pray for God's help which President Johnson besought in taking the oath of office. In doing so, we pray for the world and for ourselves.

Mr. Speaker, I am proud to join my colleagues and the above representatives of the Idaho press in paying tribute to our late and great President John F. Kennedy.

On behalf of all of the people of Idaho, I want

to express our sympathy to his beloved and courageous wife and companion. Her courage and
bravery have been eloquently described in the
following editorial:

[From the Gooding (Idaho) Leader, Nov. 28, 1963]

OUR NATION GOES ON—A WOMAN'S COURAGE

(By Herb Love)

Among the tragic events of the past few days one fact
has become more and more apparent—the courage of
Jacqueline Kennedy. Perhaps one in a million could see
her husband shot at her side, hold his bleeding body in
her arms, accompany him to the hospital and then home
to Washington and attend all the last services of that
husband without evidence of tears or hysteria.

Those who viewed the scenes as eyewitnesses or by
television have marveled at her incredible composure and
at her iron control of her emotions and actions.

Her bloodstained dress that she wore through those first
long hours might well be preserved as a symbol of the
bravery of an American woman.

She has been an exceptional First Lady, serving the
United States well in securing the friendship of other nations. Her education and training and personality helped
her husband, the President, in many ways.

Her courage will long be remembered. She has gained
the love and respect of all Americans.

To this lovely lady, Jacqueline, their two children, Caroline and John, Jr., his wonderful parents and outstanding and talented brothers and
sisters, I offer the sympathy, condolence, love, and
prayers of the people of Idaho.

ADDRESS BY

Hon. Ed Edmondson

OF OKLAHOMA

Mr. Speaker, we meet today to honor one of the
noblest Americans of our Nation's history, John
Fitzgerald Kennedy.

As 35th President of the United States, John F.
Kennedy had to contend with some of the most
terrible challenges and dangers our Republic has
known. The nature and gravity of those Presidential burdens are known in part to all of us,
but I doubt if any man who has not held our Nation's most exalted office can fully appreciate
them.

For me, the greatest quality of our country's
35th President was his courage.

In a time which sorely tried the soul and spirit
of every thoughtful man, John Fitzgerald Ken-

nedy faced danger and conflict with high courage
and true gallantry.

The quality of bravery which he exemplified
as a Navy lieutenant in World War II served
the Nation well in the years of John F. Kennedy's
service as President.

During this brief but memorable period our
Nation and the world stood at the precipice of
thermonuclear war, and saw many parts of the
world torn and divided by strife and revolution.

The calm, determined courage with which
President Kennedy faced and dealt with these
crises will be an enduring inspiration to every
American, just as I am sure his brave example
inspired our late President's gallant widow in the
trying days which have followed the tragedy of
November 22.

To the family of our late President, and especially to his fine children and their brave mother,
I join my colleagues today in this expression of
deepest sympathy.

In closing, Mr. Speaker, I would like to quote
several lines from the poem by David Randolph
Milsten, written in tribute to John Fitzgerald
Kennedy:

> The world will know and long remember
> That peace was his constant goal,
> Surely for such an illustrious son
> There is an immortal role.

> If prayer can be the passport
> To the presence of Almighty's grace
> The whole universe has joined to
> See him safely to his place.

> Dear God, his soul is yours forever
> He has come to you without despair
> And we pray that what he sought
> Will be waiting for him there.

ADDRESS BY

Hon. John Young

OF TEXAS

Mr. Speaker, in this hour of great national sorrow, I take this opportunity and time to join my
colleagues in paying tribute to our late, beloved,
and respected President, John F. Kennedy—the
latest martyr in the cause of freedom. Our sorrow is, of course, exceeded by the pride and respect that we hold for this great American. Few

men in history, at his age, have left such an impress on the times nor such a mark of leadership and courage as a matter of course in his everyday existence. In his everyday life, John Kennedy displayed such a purity of purpose that his very nature seemed to exclude any consideration of fear or uncertainty. The fortitude that brought him through the greatest war of all time characterized his conduct of the greatest office of all time—the Presidency of the United States.

In this day of labels, many were applied to the President, but no label, save that of "American," was properly applicable. Liberal, conservative, or moderate—whatever the issue—if the matter was of consequence to the Nation, one could always be sure that President Kennedy would do whatever to him appeared to be in the best interest of the country.

We sorrow in his passing, Mr. Speaker, but his legacy of courage and love of country will always be with us.

ADDRESS BY

Hon. G. Elliott Hagan

OF GEORGIA

Mr. Speaker, I still find it hard to realize that John Fitzgerald Kennedy is dead. November 22 and the days since—just as the life and activities of John F. Kennedy—will long live in the minds of citizens in the First District of Georgia as well as other parts of the Nation and the world.

Some of the most eloquent tributes to our late President have come from the pens of citizens in the district which I am privileged to represent in the Congress of the United States.

I include a few of the many editorials which have been published in connection with this tragic event in our Nation's history:

[From the Savannah Morning News, Savannah, Ga., Nov. 23, 1963]

JOHN F. KENNEDY

To a country which he served both in bloody war and in uneasy peace, as a young Navy lieutenant, as a Member of Congress, and then as President, John Fitzgerald Kennedy gave the full measure of his devotion.

When he was slain yesterday by an assassin's bullet, the 35th President of the United States was 46 years old.

He had not completed his first term in office, and he had much more to give to his country and to his fellow Americans. His loss is a national tragedy which words are too flimsy to describe.

Our Nation is outraged by the evil which was committed on Friday, November 22, and which will live forever in our memories. We are shocked, grief stricken. We bow our heads in mourning and in prayer for our slain leader's family, and we ask ourselves, "How could this happen here?"

But it has happened, and the grieving Nation must also pray for the man who has succeeded to the Presidency with all its awesome responsibilities and travail.

The grave tasks to which John F. Kennedy dedicated himself now rest in the hands of Lyndon Baines Johnson, who will need the strength and support of a united nation to help him carry on.

That John F. Kennedy should have died in such a manner, that a President of this country should be the victim of such a crime, is the greatest tragedy of all. But Mr. Kennedy was a man of courage who had risked his life more than once in the performance of his duties, and we recall the moving words he spoke in his inaugural address: "Ask not what your country can do for you, ask what you can do for your country."

No man could do more than to lay down God's greatest gift, life, in his nation's service. So it was with John Fitzgerald Kennedy, 35th President of the United States.

———

[From the Savannah Evening Press, Nov. 23, 1963]

JOHN FITZGERALD KENNEDY

John Fitzgerald Kennedy, 35th President of the United States, the youngest man ever elected to the Nation's highest responsibility, is dead from an assassin's bullet.

Many Americans still find it difficult to accept the awesome truth of what has happened. Yesterday morning he was the vital leader around whom the course of national and world events revolved. Today he is dead and Lyndon Baines Johnson is President.

The enormity of events that have taken place in the last few hours is so vast that words are incapable of encompassing its significance. The full implications cannot even be guessed at this time.

Perhaps President Johnson's simple eloquence, stemming from his personal grief and profound understanding of the responsibility that had suddenly and unexpectedly been placed upon his shoulders, is all that can be said at this time: "I will do my best. That is all I can do. I ask your help—and God's."

John Fitzgerald Kennedy's personal popularity was something the poll takers and analysts had tried in vain to chart. That his presence struck a responsive chord in millions of Americans is undeniable. He was an embodiment of mid-20th century generations now in charge of the destiny of this Nation, and as such he was a symbol of hope for new conditions which are still evolving and which are yet to be fully comprehended.

Whatever reservations and doubts there may have been about President Kennedy's specific proposals for meeting the challenges of our times, there was an implicit appreciation of his willingness to live in the present and look toward the future. He saw the second half of our century as offering a "New Frontier" for American aspirations, and political sloganism aside, it was a phrase that captured the imagination of a nation born in a pioneering spirit of freedom and individual opportunity.

Every American today is searching himself for the full implications of the tragedy played out on the crowded streets of Dallas, Tex., early in the afternoon of November 22, 1963. There will never be a way to understand the motives of the man who pulled the trigger, the confused thoughts which led him to take the life of a young and vibrant leader of the people of the United States, a man whose career has already affected the course of world history and which contained resources for future effectiveness in man's quest for peace and security that will now never be known.

A burning new page of American history was written in the confusion and numbing shock of yesterday's swift events, and now all a saddened America can do is to turn toward the future.

Parties and politics, policies and programs have been set aside to pledge President Lyndon Johnson the support and assistance he will need in bridging the abyss which opened up so suddenly before him. America has always responded to such challenges with a strength and unity of purpose that has continually confounded those who fail to understand our way of life. The American people will do so again. The world will once again be witness to the elements of greatness that have made America what it is.

"Ask not what your country can do for you, ask what you can do for your country."

So said John F. Kennedy on the day he took office as President of the United States. His words have a significance on this day after his tragic death which every fellow American will heed.

———

[From the Bulloch Herald and Bulloch Times, Statesboro, Ga., Nov. 28, 1963]

THE GREATNESS OF JOHN F. KENNEDY EMERGES IN DEATH BEFORE THE EYES OF MILLIONS OF AMERICANS

Because a madman chose Friday, November 22, to kill John Fitzgerald Kennedy, the President of the United States, the man who in life created currents of controversy wherever he moved, now in death emerges as a man who has attained a cohesive influence over the American people. The Nation with its attention focused on TV screens saw this emergence as thousands and thousands of people let their prejudices and animosities go with the wind as they grieved, not just for the President of the United States, but for a man, for a woman, for a family.

We may know, as we do, that among so many people as there were on the streets in the city of Dallas that day, there will always be one who will erupt in violence; that is why, even in an orderly and peaceful society, we must make provisions to protect the President from men of twisted minds and convictions. Nonetheless, it is an event we guard against in disbelief that it will happen; indeed, it was this disbelief, shared by the President himself, that helped let it happen.

All the more, then, when it does happen, we stand in sudden shock not only before the death of a man but before the blow that assassination itself strikes at the very roots of our ways. That it should happen in our country above all others, seems to leave us naked before ourselves as well as our enemies.

Thus it is that now the people mourn for a man and for the Nation.

It is agreed that Mr. Kennedy was a man of force and direction. There was greatness in him that many refused to concede because their prejudices and strong feelings colored their appraisal of him. To call upon a tired cliche, "You may not have agreed with him but you had to respect him," was a widespread acceptance of him and his ideals.

John F. Kennedy was convinced that his political course was the right and best one for his country. Right or wrong, he was a man who put his convictions into action. And it now would seem that the future might prove him more right than wrong.

It is our sincere conviction that John F. Kennedy was a great man, and we share with the millions of Americans who were drawn together by the shock of his death, their grief, and sense of loss.

And we draw comfort with a bereaved people from what came afterward.

Surely and swiftly the institutions of an ordered society moved to fulfill their functions. At once the American people had a new President, and without a tremor all the vast machinery of Government moved under a new hand. Through all the change it was done with hardly a conscious thought of what a miracle it was.

Lyndon Johnson became President and brings to the office a love of country, a deep sense of responsibility, and an instinct for the reconciliation of views that sometimes divide us. He brings to the office long political experience gained in the House of Representatives and in the Senate and as Vice President. He was prepared for just this tradition.

And shining through it all was a lady who but a few hours before had cradled her husband's head in her hands. Instinctively she came to stand in public beside the new President of the United States while he took the oath of office. Her courage in so doing did honor to herself, her husband, and her country.

Such then are the ways our Nation moves forward after tragedy. Men pass and are mourned, but they leave behind them that which abides. This is the way, we think, that John F. Kennedy would have had it be.

The President is dead. Long live the President.

———

[From the True Citizen, Waynesboro, Ga., Nov. 27, 1963]

A TIME FOR GRIEF, A TIME FOR PRIDE

(By Wilkes Williams)

A thousand men die in a mining accident and some people in the world take note. One man dies and the entire world is shocked, bewildered, bereaved and saddened. Never in history has one single event so moved the human race as this assassination of an American President.

This is the result of what one young man has done with his life. This man, John Fitzgerald Kennedy, as leader of the greatest nation on earth, held out to the people of the world the hand of friendship. He represented a beacon of light in a dark sea, the messenger of freedom, the hope that sustains life.

He traveled the world over to show oppressed people everywhere the warmth and sincerity of the nation that produced him. He looked into friendly and unfriendly faces of many nationalities thousands of miles from home and told them of the peace-loving, law-abiding people he represented.

He told of his nation's heritage, the individuality of his people, their love of God, country and freedom, and of their generosity. He spoke with a sense of pride and never a note of shame.

He told of the unique system by which they govern themselves. And in all these things he told the truth.

If, then, he did tell the truth, that his people are God-fearing, peace-loving people, why is this great American dead—assassinated in the heart of his own country?

Now, and in the months ahead, literally thousands of reasons, factors, and theories will be forthcoming. Political factions, religious differences, racial strife, all will find their way into the stream of reasons and analysis behind this dastardly act. But let it be said now that this was not an act of an American city, a section of our country, or the American people. It was the crime of one man. A man who could have been in any city, any State, or any country.

Certainly the Communist nations of the world will capitalize on this tragic event. They will emphasize the brutality of the act. They will hold every American up as the assassin, evil, cruel, and selfish.

This propaganda will no doubt cause many people of the world to wonder what type nation this can be for such a thing to happen. In fact, Americans themselves will search their souls for the answer.

Let the people of the world, including Americans, take note—

It is a nation where 3 years ago almost 50 percent of the people did not support this man for President, yet, they have followed him and now unanimously they sincerely mourn him.

It is a nation where 180 million people are free enough to be told of the terrible act and secure enough not to panic.

It is a nation where the people in this time of crisis have not had to wonder who would take control of their Government. They knew who it would be.

It is a nation where no thought had to be given to wholesale slaughter of Government officials in a grab for power when its President was murdered.

It is a nation where the assassinated President's family is loved and respected by the mass of the people and will always hold a place in their hearts.

It is a nation where one of the first acts of the new President was to seek the advice of two past Presidents, one from his party, one from the opposition party.

It is a nation that vengefully wanted to punish the guilty party, yet clung to a principle beyond the shadow of a doubt and overwhelmingly condemned the man who took it upon himself to execute the obviously guilty assassin.

It is a nation where the closeness of the people and their leaders, combined with certain freedoms they both consider essential, might have made possible this dreadful deed.

It is a nation, complex and simple, that in such trying times, when its newspapers are filled with stories concerning heads of states, on the same page can still tell of a little boy walking down the corridors of the White House saying, "Now I don't have anyone to play with."

It is a nation capable of criticizing its President, booing him in public, voting him out of office. Yet, when a foreign nation threatens its shores with missile bases, it becomes a united nation standing solidly with its President even in the face of a nuclear war.

These things we feel John Fitzgerald Kennedy believed, and if he could speak today, he would remind us of them.

It was a great nation into which this man was born 46 years ago.

It is a great nation that mourns him now, and it will be a great nation that perpetuates his memory and preserves his ideas in the future.

It is a natural thing that we are overcome with compassion, sorrow, and sympathy, and feel the heavy burden of this great loss.

But, as Americans, we should not confuse these emotions with feelings of shame either for our country or its institutions.

We can mourn the man, condemn the deed, and still be proud Americans.

———

[From the Pembroke Journal, Pembroke, Ga., Nov. 28, 1963]

John Fitzgerald Kennedy Pays the Price

The assassination of President Kennedy on the streets of Dallas, Tex., on Friday afternoon, when he was riding in a motorcade with his wife, Governor and Mrs. Connally of the State of Texas, who was also shot by the assassin, is one of the darkest blots in the American history, and especially bad for the great State of Texas. The President of the United States died within an hour after being shot, and the Governor of Texas is in a serious condition in a Dallas hospital.

John Fitzgerald Kennedy, a young President, who believed in what he believed and was willing to fight for it, and of course some of the things he fought for were not popular the world over, and there were many in the South that would not have voted for him again, still they respected the man, and condemn the man, or men back of his assassination.

President Kennedy was important to the entire free world, and he meant a great deal more to all of us, than many of us knew, or would admit. His death is a loss to many countries, and when the news flashed around the world of his assassination, although it was midnight in France and many other countries, the rulers and leaders of these countries sent wires of their sorrow and grief, which proved the respect that the entire free world had for this great leader.

His passing places our country in a precarious position, we have many things facing us in the immediate future, that it is going to take an iron hand, and a dedicated man to the principles he believed in.

The Journal joins all the other newspapers of America in paying tribute to this great leader, who was cut down by an assassin's bullet, in the prime of life, and at a time when he was so badly needed by all the free world.

[From the Darien News, Darien, Ga., Nov. 28, 1963]

ECHOES OF A DALLAS GUNSHOT

The crack of a rifle in a Dallas street last Friday has brought echoes from all over the world. These echoes, like those of the Navy sonar, have given indications of the nature of the objects from which they came.

The message of shock and concern from Moscow indicates that even in the midst of avowed atheism there remains a semblance of basic human decency and an appreciation of greatness among those of opposing political persuasions. When the news came to the Kremlin, regular television broadcasts were interrupted, the announcement was made, and an interlude of somber organ music was played.

From certain southern Governors who had taken public stands against the philosophy and policy of the Kennedy administration in regard to civil rights there also came expressions of shock and sympathy, indicating their respect for human life and their appreciation of outstanding political leadership in those who do not agree with themselves.

The only death which has ever had a greater impact upon the human race was that of Jesus of Nazareth. Cries of dismay and anguish from around the globe indicated that the human race is at last beginning to realize its essential kinship, and that men—wherever they are found, and to whatever racial, political, or national group they belong—are, if they are men at all, an integral part of a worldwide humanity. This, in itself, is an indication that the dream of John F. Kennedy is in the dawn of its realization.

The story would not be complete, however, without mention of the ominous echoes which bounced off the rottenness of the world, and which were even more nauseating than the sound of the shot itself. These sickening echoes took the form of such phrases as, "Old man Kennedy is dead," "Have you heard the good news?" or "I'm not shedding any tears." These were reflections not upon the man of whom they were spoken, but of the venom of the hearts out of which they were spoken. They were manifestations of what newsman Chet Huntley described as "the ominous popularization of hatred" which has characterized American politics during recent years. This crowd has abandoned the Bible principle of love and brotherhood, and has preached that in some cases love is a vice and hate a virtue. Such a man was Kennedy's assassin. Such a man is Jack Ruby. And such are the men who applaud acts of violence, wherever they occur.

Let Americans thank God this Thanksgiving season that those among us who believe hate is the solution to our problems are in the minority. If it were not so,

God would surely have long since said to us, as he did to ancient Jerusalem. "O Jerusalem, Jerusalem, thou that killest the prophets, and stonest them which are sent unto thee, how often would I have gathered thy children together, even as a hen gathereth her chicks under her wings, and ye would not! Behold your house is left unto you desolate."

Most of the world feels today that our house is indeed left unto us desolate. But already the Nation, and the free world, are rallying around President Johnson. Our desolation shall be healed. An eagle has fallen, and the worms come out to gloat—but there will be other eagles. The army of darkness has won a battle, but the forces of light will win the war.

Truth is stronger than a lie. Love is stronger than hate.

[From the Bryan Countian, Pembroke, Ga., Nov. 27, 1963]

JOHN FITZGERALD KENNEDY

A man is dead. A man—created in the image of God—lies in his final resting place; the victim of an unimaginable crime against God and mankind.

John Fitzgerald Kennedy died at the hands of an assassin; his death an unthinkable, unbelievable tragedy; a tragedy which shocked the Nation and the world into a state of numbness.

President Kennedy was much more than a man; he was a leader of men and nations; the living image of democracy for countless millions throughout the world; but, above all, he was a true humanitarian.

Words, perhaps, are futile in the face of this tragic event. We can only pray that God will give us the wisdom and ability to examine ourselves so that we may discover the terrible fault in our society capable of producing such a despicable deranged soul as the creature who murdered our beloved President.

John Kennedy will never be forgotten; the whole world mourns the loss of this great man, and our hearts go out to his family in their hour of sorrow.

[From the Springfield (Ga.) Herald, Nov. 29, 1963]

THE WAY IT LOOKS TO ME

(By Ruth Lee)

Yes, I have wept with you, the Nation and the world, during these past few days. I wept unashamedly—our Nation has suffered a great loss, and if we had failed to feel it personally, certainly there would have been a great deal wrong with us as a nation.

On an occasion such as we have experienced we must rise above personalities, and personal differences; and yes, even sectional differences. We must show that we are one nation, under God; and I believe that we have.

No matter how much you or I, or anyone else, may have differed with John Fitzgerald Kennedy, he was our President, duly elected under our laws.

There have been many that have implied many things during this time concerning his death. In my own heart I can only feel that it was the work of one wretched and tormented soul, who felt that he must have personal vengeance, for something for which he must take the full responsibility himself.

The one implication that must be seen is that this is the high price of liberty that our country has once again paid. A liberty that goes to all persons, whether they be deserving of it or not. The liberty that was enjoyed by the apparent assassin though he had renounced his country, though he had failed to serve with honor in his country's service, and though he was outspoken against the policies of our country and saw fit to take up the cause of one of our most violent enemies, Cuba.

Yes, that is the price of liberty; a price that I am sure President Kennedy all too well realized he might be called to pay.

While we differed with Mr. Kennedy; if we made the effort to study the man we must have realized that he was not an ordinary man. He had a vision, and was willing to make every effort to see it a reality; and we must respect him for that. We, in our short-sightedness, many times failed to realize that in all that he did he had to have the backing of the Congress or the courts. The next months and years will prove, I fear, on some grounds, that all of his actions were not just personal action because he personally felt they must be done, but that they were supported by many of our other national leaders.

Be all this as it may—the point at the present is that we lost our leader, and no nation can do this, especially under such terrible circumstances, without losing some part of themselves.

I make no attempt to write a eulogy, or defend the man—history will evaluate him, and persons more capable of fitting eulogy have voiced that the world over. But I feel impelled to say that we as a Christian people could have faced the situation in no other way but that of mourning the dead, and of sympathy for those loved ones he left behind.

I am told that there are those who found no sorrow in the tragedy. I can only feel sorrow for them—anyone that is incapable of some sort of sorrow or grief on such an occasion is more to be pitied than even those who personally suffered the loss. Are they so radical in their thinking that they could not rise above their personal hatred for a man and realize that a nation, and yes, even the world, had lost a leader? If we are to call ourselves a Christian nation and a Christian people we must practice a Christian love and compassion.

Some have said that they did not feel that all of the ceremonies and, as they put it, "the goings on" were necessary. This was our President that we buried, not an ordinary man. This was part of our national custom; we would have done less than we ought, if we had failed to carry it out. I am sure the Kennedys had no need for the ceremony that went with it—surely their grief would have been easier to bear in their own privacy. Mrs. Kennedy was known for her shying away from public view. I feel that their sharing their final moments as they did was a sacrifice on their part, but they must have realized that he was a man that belonged to the Nation and to the world. And the world did come to pay its final respects.

Surely, Mrs. Kennedy has made for herself a new place in history with her remarkable and unbelievable composure during these trying hours. Many have tried to imitate her in the past in dress, etc.; they would do well to take a lesson from her grace, dignity, and sense of duty in trying times.

Once again, the Nation has proved its greatness—tragedy has served to bring about a national unity that is not often known. We have seen our national leaders lay aside their differences and pledge their effort to see that our national image is carried forth in the high honor and impact that it, by all rights, must deserve. This in itself is perhaps the greatest eulogy of all to be given to the late President.

Our Nation has probably never gone through such a shocking experience, and as the full realization of its reality settles on us all—may we all pray to God that we, as a Nation, will be spared such tragedy in the future.

[From This Week in Savannah, Savannah, Ga., Nov. 29, 1963]

VOICE IN THE WILDERNESS: A TRIBUTE TO J.F.K.

(By O. J. Murry)

A star fell from out of the heavens this day.

The world—and God—are the sadder for it. For somewhere the celestial machinery that guides the paths of stars had gone awry. A malfunction of hatred and violence, of malice, prejudice, and evil turned out this light at the height of its glory.

Yes, a light has gone out—a light of hope—and of courage—and of faith to free men everywhere. And, yes—to men who are not free.

There have been other stars at other times—guiding wise men to a Saviour, the adventurous and faithful to new lands—stars for spiritual and for mortal guidance.

God, in His infinite wisdom, has provided many stars. When one falters and fades away in a brilliant burst of glory, there is another to take its place. Such is the tradition and heritage of America.

Perhaps the paths of the stars that guide the destinies of men will someday cross again. Then all men will be led to a heavenly reunion where their souls can join with the heavenly chorus in praise of Him who is Creator of us all.

So we say—look up. Look up, ye who are heavy laden; ye who are sad of heart and of mind and spirit. There is a new star in the Heavens this day, a star that may well be the living spirit of John Fitzgerald Kennedy, 35th President of these United States.

[From the Claxton (Ga.) Enterprise, Nov. 28, 1963]

JOHN F. KENNEDY

We are yet too close to John Kennedy to truly measure him and his impact on history. Only time will assess this value.

We found ourselves poles apart in our philosophy of government, and far apart many times in its application to the people of our country.

Yet we deeply mourn his passing, and feel a great personal loss, for we never doubted his courage, or his conviction, or his deep love for this, our country.

As truly as if he were felled on the battlefield, or in

the explosion of a naval vessel, he gave his life in the service of his country and in the defense of an ideal that he held dear.

For this we respect him and admire him, and to the measure in which a great country like this is made up of its members, we have lost a part of our country.

Out of the hatred and bitterness that brought his death—let us rise up as men dedicated to liberty, to make of this Nation an even greater bulwark of freedom for all men.

Like the mythical phoenix, may the dove of peace rise from the ashes of our grief as a nation, and bring to men everywhere the blessings of the one who said, "My peace bring I unto you."

———

[From the Metter (Ga.) Advertiser, Nov. 28, 1963]

IN MEMORY OF OUR PRESIDENT, JOHN F. KENNEDY

He disappeared in the dead of winter;
The brooks were frozen, the airports almost deserted,
And snow disfigured the public statues;
The memory sank in the mouth of the dying day.
O all the instruments agree
The day of his death was a dark cold day.
Far from his illness
The wolves ran on through the evergreen forest,
The peasant river was untempted by the fashionable quays;
By mourning tongues
The death of the poet was kept from his poems.
But for him it was his last afternoon as himself,
An afternoon of nurses and rumors;
The providences of his body revolted,
The squares of his mind were empty,
Silence invaded the suburbs,
The current of his feeling failed; he became his admirers.
Now he is scattered among a hundred cities
And wholly given over to unfamiliar affections;
To find his happiness in another kind of wood
And be punished under a foreign code of conscience
The words of a dead man
Are modified in the guts of the living.
But in the importance and noise of tomorrow
When the brokers are roaring like beasts on the floor of the Bourse,
And the poor have the sufferings to which they are fairly accustomed,
And each the cell of himself is almost convinced of his freedom;
A few thousand will think of this day
As one thinks of a day when one did something slightly unusual.
O all the instruments agree
The day of his death was a cold dark day.

———

[From the Millen (Ga.) News, Nov. 28, 1963]

JOHN FITZGERALD KENNEDY, MAY 29, 1917– NOVEMBER 22, 1963

Multiplied millions of words have been spoken and written within the past few days in bringing the sad news of the assassination of our late President, John F.

Kennedy; and in praise of his leadership as the Nation's 35th President. Tributes have been made by men in high places throughout the world. We cannot add to the sentiments that have already been expressed.

We were shocked as millions of others were on Friday when the news of the tragedy became known to one and all. There was a tug at your heart because of the tragic loss to the Nation and the world of this great leader.

We were privileged to occupy the same platform with him once, and again to breakfast with him, still while he was Senator, and from this association we learned that he was a family man, a man with a vision and a man willing to give his all for his country; he loved people, despite the fact that he was independently wealthy; and he wanted to see above all else a world at peace. He worked hard at the job. We found it easy to disagree with some of his programs and some of his proposed legislation. But we never hated and we were not disagreeable because we disagreed. The man was honorable, conscientious and above all a worldwide statesman. Our Nation and the world shall miss his leadership.

No better tribute can be given than that which comes from the pen of the newly named poet laureate of Georgia, and we quote:

"TRIBUTE TO THE LATE PRESIDENT

"In Arlington where other martyrs sleep
He rests in peace. Oh, say not he is dead!
The nations gather there to pray and weep,
Recalling burning words that he has said.
His image, and the cause for which he stood,
Is etched in gold upon each stricken soul,
His vision of a worldwide brotherhood
And principles that make all mankind whole.
The chief is dead? No, he shall never die!
His voice will thunder down chaotic years
Echoing like a warrier's battle cry,
Shattering the dark labyrinth of man's fears.
Oh valiant one, so much you had to give,
Yourself—that other men might better live!
    "—*Agnes Cochran Bramblett.*
"FORSYTH, GA., *November 25, 1963.*"

———

[From the Swainsboro (Ga.) Forest-Blade, Nov. 27, 1963]

TRAGEDY WITHIN A TRAGEDY

The death of John F. Kennedy is all the more tragic because the lesson it offers will most assuredly be missed by the majority of American citizens.

His assassination was more than the result of a gun fired by a misguided, warped young Marxist. It is, at least in part, the product of a society that feeds upon hatred and utter disregard for the rights of others and for the God-inspired principles upon which this Nation was founded.

There is within modern-day America a growing urge to destroy or hurt those who disagree with us, whether it be politically, socially, or religiously.

As an example, take the use of economic boycotts by groups of people against businesses and institutions whose owners either refuse to endorse the principles or give in to the demands of the group.

Is this not economic assassination, robbing the business owner of his rights to life, liberty, and the pursuit of happiness?

And we do not speak only of the much-publicized Negro boycotts, for even here in Swainsboro at least one group of white people has threatened use of such a boycott if a store owner did not refrain from saying that Georgia's gaming laws should apply to them as well as to all other citizens.

The Forest-Blade can speak first hand, also, for we have been threatened with violence on more than one occasion in recent years because we publicized the illegal activities of certain individuals.

Indeed, one or two governmental officials have even insinuated they will withhold payments of just debts to the Forest-Blade if we continue to publicize grand jury presentments beyond the mere legal requirements.

Pastors seeking to elevate the moral tone of the community have also been threatened or been publicly ridiculed for their efforts.

The tragedy of the President's death is not that America has lost its leader or that a family will weep; rather, the real tragedy is because we will not see in it a warning of a deadly danger.

We are rapidly becoming not a Nation of laws, but of men.

———

[From the Sylvania (Ga.) Telephone, Nov. 29, 1963]

May God Save America From Hate

One person, probably conceived and born in hate, certainly reared and trained in it, with malice and aforethought, designed and planned in a warped and wicked mind to kill the President of the United States. The success of his atrocious plan shocked the entire world more, in our opinion, than any other like event in the world's history.

Whatever one's political evaluation of President Kennedy may have been, it must be acknowledged that he was the world's most powerful voice for the freedom and peace of all people. His energy, sincerity, ability, and dynamic personality will be missed in the councils of the nations.

Words completely fail us in trying to express our contempt for the person, or persons, who conspired to kill our beloved and respected leader. We shudder to think of the future consequences of such hate. We are alarmed that organizations, built upon hate, rooted in the extremes of every issue, can thrive in America. One person can kill the leader, but organized hate can make demons of thousands and bring destruction to entire nations.

Even more contemptuous than the lone assassin are those groups who as apostles of hate incite the passions of the gullible for their own financial or political profit. Every American has felt the creeping venom of it in his everyday business and social intercourse as the passions of men are freely and publicly exposed in verbal explosions.

Someway and somehow, with God's help, those grouped apostles of hate, who set race against race, creed against creed, and class against class, must be halted.

America has always been able to rise to the demands of the crisis of the moment. We have every confidence that the political leadership will quickly close the ranks and the United States with President Lyndon B. Johnson at the head will assume its position among the nations of the world as the true leader in the mission for peace and freedom.

We average Americans must be ever aware that love only has the force to bring peace and understanding among our people and the people of the world, and only God has the infinite wisdom to guide us to the solution of our differences. Any other direction can but lead to our dissolution and decay as a Nation.

May God save us from hate.

———

[From the Screven County News, Sylvania, Ga., Nov. 28, 1963]

The President Is Dead

An eternal light burns on the grave of President John F. Kennedy in Arlington National Cemetery, while millions share grief of sorrowing loved ones.

MANSFIELD GIVES CAPITOL TRIBUTE

Following is the text of a tribute to the late President Kennedy delivered by Senator Mike Mansfield, Democrat, of Montana, Sunday:

"There was a sound of laughter; in a moment, it was no more. And, so, she took a ring from her finger and placed it in his hands.

"There was a wit in a man neither young nor old; but a wit full of an old man's wisdom and of a child's wisdom, and then, in a moment, it was no more. And, so, she took a ring from her finger and placed it in his hands.

"There was a man marked with the scars of his love of country, a body active with the surge of a life far, far from spent and, in a moment, it was no more. And, so, she took a ring from her finger and placed it in his hands.

"There was a father with a little boy, a little girl, and a joy of each in the other. In a moment it was no more, and, so, she took a ring from her finger and placed it in his hands.

"There was a husband who asked much and gave much, and, out of the giving and the asking, wove with a woman what could not be broken in life, and, in a moment it was no more. And, so, she took a ring from her finger and placed it in his hands, and kissed him and closed the lid of a coffin.

"A piece of each of us died at that moment. Yet, in death he gave of himself to us. He gave us of a good heart from which the laughter came. He gave us of a profound wit, from which a great leadership emerged. He gave us of a kindness and a strength fused into a human courage to seek peace without fear.

"He gave us of his love that we, too, in turn, might give. He gave that we might give of ourselves, that we might give to one another until there would be no room, no room at all, for the bigotry, the hatred, prejudice, and the arrogance which converged in that moment of horror to strike him down.

"In leaving us—these gifts, John Fitzgerald Kennedy, President of the United States, leaves with us. Will we take them, Mr. President? Will we have now the sense and the responsibility and the courage to take them?

"I pray to God that we shall and under God we will."

———

[From the Montgomery Monitor, Mount Vernon, Ga., Nov. 28, 1963]

THE WASTE OF HATE

Hate, the horrible force of ignorance in action, has blindly struck down a young President, husband and father—John F. Kennedy. The initial disbelief, shock, and concern which we have felt in this tragic loss is centered in the question, Why did this happen?

More than any American leader in recent history, Mr. Kennedy stirred in the people of the United States a new sense of vision, energy, and leadership. His administration brought a return of American prestige as leader of the free world and a reawakening of the promise of American life to millions of people in this country.

His youth, his family, and his imaginative and able appointees were subjected to a closer and a more adoring scrutiny than the American public has given any chief of state in recent years. And yet there were those who, guided by hate, set themselves in opposition to everything that this man, whom we mourn, stood for. What is the nature of this terrible force—hate?

Hate, among the strongest of man's negative emotions, begins in ignorance and fear, is nourished on intolerance and bigotry, and reaps a wasteful harvest of death and destruction.

Hate breeds intolerance and leads to a lack of concern for the things which concern others. People who recognize their own faults are usually tolerant of those same faults in others, but the hater generally finds something in others on which to pin his own sense of guilt and shame.

Hate leads to aggression, in which the control of thinking over behavior is so reduced that force is the only way of dealing with a tension that one cannot control.

Hate often springs from unconscious motives. Since it is often unconscious, hate is hard to deal with. One cannot catch himself at it. For that reason, many people refuse that there is any such thing in their own personality. The more self-deception involved in hate, the more likely it is to be harmful. In the mind of the hater his position always seems to be obviously true. The hater refuses to examine the evidence of both sides of an issue, especially the other side. In effect, he cuts off all new learning.

Hate breeds cowardice. Truth and the courage to speak it have been all too rare in history. We should strive to develop a picture of ourselves as those who would rather know the truth than be comfortable.

Hate deadens the power of creative thinking. Regular trips into the world of ideas can be an exciting activity rather than a dreary chore. Mr. Kennedy's mental alertness, imagination, and interest in foreseeing causes and consequences of events, coupled with his vigor, were in the highest tradition of the educated man and the mature personality.

Hate leads to a feeling of separation. Separation from our fellow man, estrangement from God, even the loss of self-respect are the products of hate. The deepest need of man is the need to overcome his separateness, to leave the prison of his aloneness. The full answer to the problem of existence lies in true and mature love.

What is mature love? It is union under the condition of preserving one's integrity, one's individuality. Love is an active power in man, a power which breaks through the walls which separate man from his fellow men, which unites him with others. Love makes him overcome the sense of isolation and separateness, yet it permits him to be himself.

John Fitzgerald Kennedy manifested those qualities of character and competence that are the measure of mature love and of greatness. He was too big to stoop to return the hate hurled at him by rabid fanatics. His confidence in faith and reason transcended the carping pettiness of partisan critics. His dedication to this country was but suggested in his heroic actions as commander of the ill-fated PT 109 in World War II. Later, a lesser man might easily have given up his career in public life, when recurring back injuries laid him low.

The pattern of the late President's domestic programs and the foreign policies he pursued were not the vain motions of an unthinking, unfeeling demagog. Indeed, each of these programs bear the unmistakable stamp of Kennedy's convictions of their desirability and reasonableness in overcoming the common enemies of man—tyranny, poverty, disease, and war itself—which he enumerated in his inaugural address of January 20, 1961. He did not shrink from responsibility—he welcomed it. And at the time, he asked the citizens of the world not what America can do for them, but what together we can do for the freedom of man. That question remains before us.

This time of mourning symbolizes not the victory of hate over a good man, but rather a reconsecration of a nation to those ideals of truth, faith, hope, and justice which President Kennedy and a host of other Americans have given their lives to defend and perpetuate.

ADDRESS BY

Hon. Roy A. Taylor

OF NORTH CAROLINA

Mr. Speaker, it was a tragic hour in American history when John F. Kennedy, young, vigorous President of our country, was murdered by an assassin.

Possessed of great wealth, this man could have turned his back on the problems of mankind. He could have remained aloof from all of the world's heartaches, worries, and cares. Instead, he thrust himself into the middle of them, giving of his immeasurable talent and energy to work for the freedom of all men and for peace throughout the world.

There were those who opposed his views, but there were few who did not admire him for his intellectual gifts, his courage, his fine qualities of character, and his dedication to human dignity, world freedom and the brotherhood of man.

I was impressed by the expressions of respect and worldwide grief coming from all parts of the world and by the attendance of some 220 world leaders at the Arlington funeral. These leaders showed great respect for this country and seemed to agree that the soil of America had never received a more courageous, more dedicated and finer American citizen.

John Fitzgerald Kennedy knew how to build on the experience of the past, how to face the realities of today, and how to dream and plan for a better tomorrow. Like a man of destiny, he did not shrink from the burdens of leadership. He welcomed them. He gave so much because he loved his country and his fellow man.

I salute his gallant and dynamic spirit and pay tribute to his wise leadership during a period of crisis in our national life. Though in office less than 3 years, he will be remembered as one of our greatest Presidents and greatest world leaders.

As expressed by President Johnson in his speech before Congress, let us hope that "the tragedy and torment of these terrible days will bind us together in new fellowship."

ADDRESS BY

Hon. John C. Kluczynski

OF ILLINOIS

Mr. Speaker, the sadness of a mourning Nation over the tragic death of John Fitzgerald Kennedy continues to be felt in strong testimony to the love and admiration of our country for this great leader.

The tragedy of his death is heightened because it came so cruelly at the prime of his extraordinary life. It came as he was grappling with the gigantic problems of our times with skill and courage, moved only by high motives, guided by broad plans, and impelled by understanding and vision.

But as the tumult and grief subside, as the Nation resumes and moves forward, and as his own generation measures his works and achievements, what shall we say who knew him? History will judge his greatness as a President, but already it is clear that he will be remembered for the strength of his statesmanship, for the initiative he brought to the search for peace, for the selfless energy with which he pursued 17 years of honorable service in the House of Representatives, the Senate, and finally in the White House itself.

He was his own profile in courage. Well known was his bravery in battle during the war and the fortitude with which he bore the pain in his injured back during the grave illness of his Senate years.

This was a courage that went beyond physical courage. It was the special courage to believe in, with all his heart, and to dedicate himself to the attainment of the greatest of goals of mankind.

This courage was the courage of a man who emerged to reawaken the Nation to its finest meaning. It was the courage of one who struck new sparks of hope in a world dark with unspeakable fears. His was the courage to affirm the integrity of human life and equality and to seek a rational and durable solution.

With his death our constant prayer should be that his sincere efforts for the peace and happiness of our Nation and the world may not have been in vain.

We must find, in his death, the strength to follow the paths of reason on which he walked, and the strength to forge a new decency at home and a reasoned peace in the world.

ADDRESS BY

Hon. John O. Marsh, Jr.

OF VIRGINIA

Mr. Speaker, the death of President Kennedy was truly a national tragedy and certainly every American felt a measure of the deep grief and sense of loss experienced by his family.

In the shock of such an event as this was dramatized the dual life of the individual who occupies the highest position the people of this Nation can bestow. Not only did we see John F. Kennedy as the President of the United States, but also John F. Kennedy as a son, father, and husband.

Not only did this Nation mourn the passing of the Chief Executive, but the hearts of his people were touched by a special sadness in the knowledge of the particular loss suffered by those who knew him best and loved him most. The gripping scenes of his children shortly after his death transmitted a sense of anguish that shall not be soon forgotten.

That John F. Kennedy loved his country and was prepared to give it his best each day, there could be no doubt. He committed his abilities and his energies to the fullest in war and in peace. He knew the awesome responsibilities he had assumed in the Presidency of the Nation fated to hold the leadership of the free world in a nuclear age. His chief hope, undoubtedly, was that he could contribute significantly to the establishment of a stable peace in the world, but he recognized the unhappy essentiality of keeping the Nation well girded against nuclear attack through the maintenance of a deterrent power balanced as between nuclear and nonnuclear capacities.

It was particularly fitting, therefore, that the guard of honor in his funeral procession and at his burial should include members of the Army Special Forces. A green Special Forces beret left at the grave testified eloquently in its silence to Mr. Kennedy's active personal interest in the development of means within our Armed Forces to cope with unconventional warfare techniques wherever ·they might be employed against the free world, and, if required in the defense of freemen, to employ surpassing ingenuity in multidimensional warfare against a devious, crafty, and resourceful enemy.

As the Nation mourns a slain leader, it gains reassurance, by strange and perhaps meaningful coincidence, from the words of another leader, also fated to be slain, uttered 100 years, almost to the day, before the tragic event in Dallas:

Government of the people, by the people, for the people, shall not perish from the earth.

ADDRESS BY

Hon. Stanley R. Tupper

OF MAINE

Mr. Speaker, there are in this world people who by nature and temperament are activists— the "doers" in our society—impatient with the status quo and always seeking to enrich the lives of all of us.

Our late President, John F. Kennedy, was such a man.

The great men in our history have not been negative people who fear change and lack trust in government and its institutions. They have been men who trusted the will of the people and recognized that our Federal Government represents the people. Those having the greatest impact upon our Nation over the years since the American Revolution have been men who did not shrink from war or threat of war when the situation demanded it, but who unceasingly sought peace—men who knew that a government such as ours demanded that all people be given equal rights, and realized that we could not long deny dignity to one class, or finally it would be lost to all men.

History will assess the contribution of John F. Kennedy, but in my opinion the standards he set were the standards of greatness.

It was in May of 1961 that I first had an opportunity to talk at some length with the late President and to "size him up" as we say in New England. After this meeting I wrote a newsletter to my constituents in which I said:

When the President entered the room he seemed somewhat tense but quickly broke into a wide smile as he greeted a few Members he knew well. He looks to be in the very best of health—tanned by the Florida sun—and by any standards younger looking in person than on television.

As he made his way around the room, many of the characteristics of the man were obvious. He is still basically a rather shy and reserved person. This is something he does not feign, nor can he completely overcome it. Frankly, I find this an appealing side of the man. There are too many gladhanders and backslappers in politics today. The Presidency demands dignity. In this respect I found President Kennedy not unlike former President Eisenhower.

At that time, he went out of his way to make sure he did not neglect anyone. It would have been easy, and perhaps natural, for him to give the bulk of his time to those with whom he had served in the House, but he did not. A cynic would say this was just good politics, that he has a program to sell. But I believe the President is too good a politician to think he could influence many congressional votes with this device.

Being only a few years younger than the President, I marvel that he has such a quick grasp of so many entirely unrelated subjects. His reputation as a gifted student of government and history is well founded. Watching him and hearing him talk, I thought what an awesome responsibility to be assumed by such a young man. For despite all his advisers, he is the final voice in making decisions affecting every American and many people in other countries. There will doubtless be many times that I will disagree with his conclusions on particular issues; but, after meeting him, I will not question his sincerity.

In my last newsletter a few days after the President's assassination, I recalled the many courtesies he had extended to me at White House functions and wrote of my last conversation with him during a flight to Maine where he was to receive an honorary degree at our State university only a few weeks ago. In my last newsletter I wrote:

President Kennedy was a warmhearted human being.

At times I have been mildly criticized by some of my constituents for not being partisan enough. I have always felt that I could personally contribute more to my district and State by seeking bipartisan cooperation wherever possible, particularly in view of the fact that Maine has only two Members of the U.S. House of Representatives. On the occasions when I have disagreed with the administration of our late President, I always tried to do so in a constructive affirmative way. I am thankful that I never made hateful and disparaging remarks about the late President as so many did. Vitriol and meanness have no place in our political life.

John F. Kennedy set our ship of state on the right course. Now that his hand has left the tiller, it is for another to safely bring us through troubled seas.

ADDRESS BY

Hon. John V. Lindsay

OF NEW YORK

Mr. Speaker, I wish to join in eulogies for the late President being stated on the floor of the House of Representatives today. I have spoken before on the subject in this Chamber, and what

I said then, out of deep sadness, need not be repeated, except that it is right and proper for the House to pay this additional tribute to the memory of our late President, a young man who stood for much, who died too early, and who leaves a bereaved family and country. The very genuine expressions of deep sorrow expressed by people all over the world, and by their leaders, were very remarkable testimonials to the life of John F. Kennedy and the worth of America under his leadership.

In this period of mourning all of us continue to pray for the comfort, and are thankful for the courage, of the young President's young widow, and we stand behind the new President in the critical period of transition.

Mr. Speaker, we read every day of new proposals for memorials to the late President. They vary in nature, but most of them take shape in tangible forms, in concrete or steel. Some are good proposals, some are less good. It seems to me that the greatest memorial that can be created to the memory of the late President would be the bettering and strengthening of institutions and processes by which this Nation may conduct itself under the rule of law, by which justice may be done, by which tyranny is shut out, and bigotry and hatred erased. If we wish to build a great memorial to John F. Kennedy, let us do these things in his name.

ADDRESS BY

Hon. Ray Roberts

OF TEXAS

Mr. Speaker, I rise today to extend my deepest sympathy to Mrs. Jacqueline Kennedy, her two small children and other members of the Kennedy family.

I rise also to say how deeply I personally feel the loss of John Fitzgerald Kennedy. It is a tragedy not only that he was struck down by an assassin while serving as President of the United States of America. Not only that he was a magnificent leader, respected and loved both in the United States and abroad. Not only that he was a man who was contributing so much to our world. But also that he had so much ahead in life, yet was killed before reaching the peak of his capacities, his talents, his intellect, his energies. This is a part of the tragedy also.

We can only guess what we have really lost with the death of this man. And we can only say that we know our loss is great.

ADDRESS BY

Hon. James C. Cleveland

OF NEW HAMPSHIRE

Mr. Speaker, the assassination of President John F. Kennedy was a great national tragedy. However, in times of crisis the unity of the American people is a solid, significant, and reassuring fact of life. As a government of law, not men, we carry on despite a deep sense of grief and loss. We can all take pride in the dignity of Jacqueline Kennedy who helped to restore our faith in America after it was so suddenly shattered by a savage, senseless act of assassination. It is a time of soul searching. All Americans can only pray that, as a result, the safety of our Nation and the freedom of the world will be enhanced.

Perhaps the best way to truly eulogize President Kennedy would be for us, each in our own way, to the best of our abilities, and according to our individual principles and beliefs, to rededicate ourselves to the cause of government to which he dedicated his life and for which he gave his life.

ADDRESS BY

Hon. Clarence D. Long

OF MARYLAND

Mr. Speaker, President Kennedy, who risked his life in World War II to defend America, finally gave it 20 years later to make a better America. President Kennedy's death follows the pattern of the other actual and attempted assassinations in our history. When intense hatreds burn in the minds of millions of people—somewhere, somehow, a mentally diseased person resorts to this kind of terror. The individuals and groups who have fed the fires of these hatreds bear on their consciences the death of a brilliant and kind President.

Of President Kennedy's manifold accomplishments, the Nation will particularly remember his contributions to our national security; and his calm leadership during the Cuban crisis; his championship of excellence in national life—especially in the arts and sciences; and, though born to wealth, his concern for the poor, the sick, the blind, the unemployed, and the mentally retarded.

President Kennedy believed that America must go forward if it is to survive and he gave his talents to the growth of our nation. In 3 short years he was not able to complete his great work, but what he began, let us carry on.

ADDRESS BY

Hon. Homer E. Abele

OF OHIO

When the news of the death of our President reached me at McMurdo Sound in the Antarctic, I was shocked and saddened that such an evil deed could be committed. In attending a Memorial Service for the President at Christchurch Cathedral, New Zealand, many persons expressed to me their profound sorrow for the President's family and their good will for the people of the United States. When Admiral Reedy spoke in the church service in honor of our President, servicemen, public officials, and people in general manifested in a variety of ways their loyalty and great sense of grief at the death of the President.

The tragic and untimely death of our late President John F. Kennedy deprived the Nation of the services of a great and good man. His sense of responsibility, his keen intellect, his respect for the dignity of all mankind, and his willingness to labor for the ideas of ideals for which he lived and gave his life will live in the minds of men of good will throughout the world.

His work as a devoted servant of the people was a magnificent illustration of his philosophy that our people must be more concerned about how to serve the Nation. Because of his loyal service to his country in both peace and war, it could have been said of him in the tragic hour of his death, "well done thou good and faithful servant."

ADDRESS BY

Hon. William M. McCulloch

OF OHIO

Mr. Speaker, the President, our former colleague, was felled by an assassin's bullet. It was a tragic death, especially for one so young, who had so much to do and, for the doing, he had so little time.

The good John Fitzgerald Kennedy has done will live long after him, and millions of people scattered throughout the world will have been helped, yes, will have been uplifted by his coming their way.

Throughout the world, there is mourning and deep sorrow. John Fitzgerald Kennedy has gone to the world of eternal peace, the peace he so earnestly sought in our time, for all people everywhere.

ADDRESS BY

Hon. Frances P. Bolton

OF OHIO

Mr. Speaker, so much has been said in these past days about our late President, John Fitzgerald Kennedy, that one hesitates to add even a word. Yet I would do so.

Many years ago Mrs. Joseph P. Kennedy and her children came to my Florida home for swims and the like, so I knew them casually when they were young. Just before "Jack" entered the House a mutual friend brought him to see me, and among other things we discussed his election. Young, eager, full of energy, it was good to know that one of his intelligence was taking his citizenship seriously.

After he came he was ill—very ill—and one wondered if he could pull through. But he did— and went on to the Senate and then to the high-

est office in the land. With him went his energy, his eagerness, the urge within him to change some of the things he thoroughly disapproved, and plant the seed for those in which he deeply believed.

Then suddenly all that energy, all that vivid life ended. One wonders why. Must we not believe that even the tragic cutting off of such a life in the fullness of its youth and service may direct the people of this country to a more serious willingness to get at the heart of the problems that confront us? Was that perhaps why he was born and why he so tragically died?

Surely, the most difficult matter that we as Americans must solve is how to change the individual men and women that peace may be so deeply rooted in their hearts that America will pull herself back onto the road that leads to her original goals: trust in God, respect for the individual and the law, and united among her people; that she by her very life, may bring peace to a confused and tragic world.

ADDRESS BY

Hon. Frank T. Bow

OF OHIO

Mr. Speaker, I wish to associate myself with those who mourn the death of our late President.

It is always difficult to accept the passing of a friend. It is particularly difficult when he is young, energetic, and in the prime of life, with everything to live and fight for. It was a devastating blow to lose the President of the United States at the hands of an assassin.

I recall with pleasure the cordial relationship we enjoyed over the past 14 years, a relationship that persisted despite a growing difference in our political viewpoints. I recall particularly an occasion several years ago when I had the opportunity to help him in a time of political difficulty, and I shall always prize the autographed copy of "Profiles of Courage" which he sent me in appreciation.

Much has been said about the tragedy of a career cut short, and no one can deny that it is tragic even though he had already accomplished more than most men could hope in a full lifetime. To me the greater tragedy, therefore, is the personal tragedy that has been visited upon this family, for the assassin could do nothing more cruel than deny our friend the right to guide his children and see them grow to womanhood and manhood, surely the most precious gift any man can enjoy. My heart goes out to the children, to Mrs. Kennedy, and the other members of this family who have suffered so grievous a loss.

ADDRESS BY

Hon. Paul F. Schenck

OF OHIO

Mr. Speaker, Friday, November 22, 1963, started out the same as most every other day in the offices of the Members of Congress during the session—stacks of mail had been received, each Member and his staff were busy preparing answers to the letters, ordering Government documents requested by constituents, calling Federal agencies and committees for information on the status of legislation and programs already in operation so as to advise a constituent properly with regard to some personal problem. Some staff members were studying committee hearings and reports to develop important information helpful to their Representative or Senator in his consideration of legislative measures. The Member himself was attending a meeting of his committee, discussing proposed bills with his colleagues, meeting with constituents individually or in groups interested in a particular legislative proposal, working on amendments he felt would improve a measure under consideration, or he might be working out the language of a new bill he wanted to introduce. Throughout the Halls of Congress every Member was engaged in some official duty connected with his responsibility as a legislator. In other words, it was a typical workday at the U.S. Capitol.

Suddenly, in the midst of all the routine phone calls that come in constantly during the usual working day comes one into my office from the daughter of one of my secretaries who was home from school that day on account of illness and who was listening to the radio when the startling news of the shooting of President Kennedy was broadcast. All work stopped while the whole office staff and I sat in stunned silence. Someone had the presence of mind to get out the small transistor radio from the cupboard where it is kept for use by the staff members who want to hear special messages delivered before joint meetings of the House and Senate.

Little did we think it would ever be used to tell us such shocking and unbelievable news that our President had been assassinated. The shock was felt almost simultaneously throughout the world due to our wonderful communications system today and I am sure that every listener had the same reaction as we did in our offices and homes here in the Nation's Capital. No one could understand or immediately accept as a fact that in this country of ours such a tragic event could possibly occur.

Gradually, as the details of the tragedy were recounted over and over and the first plans were announced, Americans everywhere united in the usual traditional manner when disaster strikes and each in his own way prayed and renewed his dedication to his Government.

It is at a time like this that we most appreciate the foresight of the founders of this country who worked out the provisions of the Constitution. Too often we are only concerned with the precious privileges, freedoms, and opportunities it provides. Now we are grateful for its provision for continuity of Government when the Nation's leader is gone. Had the event that took place on November 22 occurred in many other countries, complete chaos and revolutions would inevitably result. Under our Constitution, however, it took only a matter of minutes to put the reins of Government in the hands of the Vice President to whom the oath of office was administered on the plane that was bringing the deceased Chief Executive back to Washington. In his saddened and stunned state of mind, he accepted the responsibilities of the office of the Presidency.

It became my sad privilege to visit the White House on Saturday afternoon, November 23, to express my sympathy in person to Attorney General Robert Kennedy and his two sisters before going to the East Room where the body of the late President John Fitzgerald Kennedy lay in repose in the flag-draped casket. I stood for a moment in silent prayer for him, his family, and our Nation. All around the fence surrounding the White House thousands of people from all walks of life stood in silent tribute.

It was a solemn and moving sight. Thousands of others joined them as the funeral cortege with the flag-draped casket containing the body of the President on the horse-drawn caisson and the honor guard moved along the route to the Capitol where the body lay in state. The same hundreds of thousands of mourners lined the streets of Washington, standing with bared and solemnly bowed heads in prayer, as the body of the President was borne to St. Matthews Cathedral for the service and thence to its final resting place in Arlington National Cemetery.

The heads of foreign states and members of the diplomatic corps of nearly all the nations of the world, the Governors of all our States, clergymen of all faiths, the highest officials of the United States, including the legislative, executive, and judicial branches, gathered together in the great cathedral to join with close personal friends and the family of the late President to pay honor and tribute to the memory of the life and service of this great man. As one of those designated by you, Mr. Speaker, to be an official representative of the House of Representatives, it was my sad privilege to join in the imposing religious service. Included in the 1,200 people, who occupied every possible seat in the cathedral, were high dignitaries from all over the world. They represented the largest group of important personages ever to be gathered together in any one nation. This not only shows the high respect in which our late President was held by the leaders of other countries who came to pay tribute to him, but it is indicative of the prestige our Nation enjoys among the people of the world who appreciate and understand our form of government and our ideals.

Ever since the day of the burial thousands have continued to visit the grave of the late President to silently pay their personal respects to his memory and to pray for the continuance of the great traditions of our history.

Though President Kennedy met an untimely death at the hands of a crazed maniac, the leadership and responsibility for the affairs of the Nation passed from the hands of one man into the hands of another with scarcely a ripple in the administrative functions of government. By divine grace and the wisdom of our Founding Fathers 174 years ago, the Constitution of the United States continues to serve and protect us all. We should be ever mindful of and grateful for the life and service of each of our past 35 Presidents. We should renew our pledge to so live and act that our Nation will continue to be the greatest in the world and that the rights and privileges of each and every citizen will always be recognized, observed, and protected.

As we reflect upon the tragic event that rocked our Nation and the world, let us, Mr. Speaker, also avow our devotion to a system of government that allows free and open disagreement with our leaders on the national scene. We, as true Americans, at the same time, unite in our love and respect for John Fitzgerald Kennedy, the man, who died in the service of his country.

ADDRESS BY

Hon. Delbert L. Latta

OF OHIO

Mr. Speaker, when I first heard the news that President Kennedy had been assassinated, I could not believe it. I could not believe it because I did not want to believe it. When this ghastly news was finally confirmed, I wondered aloud why anyone privileged to live under our form of government would want to take the life of our President.

Why such a cruel, inhuman, barbaric, and senseless act would be committed in the United States was beyond my comprehension. The answer partially came when the suspected assassin was apprehended. This awful crime had been done by one adhering to a philosophy of government foreign to ours. To learn this cannot give solace or comfort to the President's widow, his children, or to a grieving Nation but I am certain that John F. Kennedy would like to know that he was not betrayed by one believing in the same principles and form of government for which he fought, worked, and died.

In the words of one of my constituents, President and Mrs. Kennedy brought a "special some-thing" to the White House. This "special some-thing" shall be missed and not soon replaced. It was separate and apart from the many Gov-ernment programs espoused by the President. In short, it was something human and involved personalities. You do not replace these things.

On behalf of all the people I am privileged to represent, Mrs. Latta, and myself, I again extend our deepest sympathy to Mrs. Kennedy, the Ken-nedy children—little Caroline and "John" John as he was affectionately referred to by the Presi-dent—and to the other members of the Kennedy family.

ADDRESS BY

Hon. Robert Taft, Jr.

OF OHIO

Mr. Speaker, the shocking death of John F. Kennedy, deeply reflected as it was in the uni-versal outpouring of mourning throughout the world, affected everyone, whether a citizen hav-ing no personal contact, one who knew him only as an acquaintance, or those who knew him well. Even those who differed with him on pub-lic issues admired him as a vital and committed American who accepted the philosophy that the duties of those in high office transcend partisan limitations.

Our Nation and the world have been enriched because of his demonstration of deep dedication to public service. He has left an example to all of us, but more particularly to those who were privileged to serve in the Government now and in the future.

High tribute should also be paid to Mrs. John F. Kennedy for her steadfastness, resolution, and devotion during the trying hours of her bereave-ment and the unifying influence that she portrayed.

On behalf of those I represent in Ohio, and individually, I express the deep sense of shock and sorrow experienced because of the death of John F. Kennedy. We all share in the tragic loss of the Kennedy family and those close to them, and we extend our deep sympathy to them.

ADDRESS BY

Hon. Clifford G. McIntire

OF MAINE

Mr. Speaker, this is a day for paying tribute to the memory of the late President John Fitzgerald Kennedy.

I want to join with my colleagues in paying respect to our former President and in further respect make reference to two memorial ad-dresses delivered for President Kennedy.

One such address was presented by Dr. Fred-erick W. Whittaker, president of the Bangor Theological Seminary, Bangor, Maine, and the other by Rev. Peter M. Kemper, pastor of the First Baptist Church of Pittsfield, Maine.

I introduce these addresses for I sincerely feel they appropriately pay eminent tribute to our late President.

SUNDAY MORNING SERMON, NOVEMBER 24, 1963,
FIRST BAPTIST CHURCH OF PITTSFIELD

(By Rev. Peter M. Kemper, pastor)

"Blessed is the nation whose God is the Lord." (Psalm 33: 12.)

How much does it mean to us who take our blessings for granted? How much does it really mean to us when we stand with hand over heart and "pledge allegiance to the United States of America?" Does it send chills up and down our spine, or do we say it quite indifferently? "One nation, under God, with liberty and justice for all"?

How does it affect you when we stand and sing the hymns that we have sung this morning?

"O beautiful for pilgrim feet,
    Whose stern, impassioned stress
A thoroughfare for freedom beat
    Across the wilderness!

America! America!
    God mend thine every flaw,
Confirm thy soul in self-control,
    Thy liberty in law!"

Stunned, shock, disbelief, sorrow, anger—these emo-tions engulfed America and the world like a great tidal wave. With shattering impact the news of the assassina-tion of John Fitzgerald Kennedy, President of the United States of America, rocked the capitals of the world—an act which outrages decent men everywhere. Our differ-ences in a time like these are dissolved in shock and in sorrow. We no longer think of the petty things that sometimes divide us and keep us apart. The little things that seemed so big have faded into insignificance.

Emotions grip the world; many have called it the

most tragic circumstance since the assassination of Abraham Lincoln.

Hate and jealousy brooded in a twisted mind—brooded and planned, and then overcame as a finger squeezed the trigger of the assassin's $12.78 rifle, obtained from a Chicago mail-order house, advertised in a national magazine.

The irony of President Kennedy's death is that this short administration was devoted almost entirely to various attempts to curb this very streak of violence in the American character. The Nation today mourns the death of a citizen who risked his life in battle but lost it, ironically, in peace—a martyr, like Abraham Lincoln, to the causes he championed.

Words are certainly inadequate to express our shock and sorrow. This morning we cannot but help think of some of those who are so personally involved. Uppermost in our thinking would be Mrs. Jacqueline Kennedy who lost both a son and a husband within a few months. She was faced with the grim task of telling her children—Caroline and John, Jr., what had happened to their daddy last Friday in Texas.

Overshadowed, and almost forgotten, is the family of the Dallas Police Department detective sergeant, J. D. Tippit, age 39, shot to death by Lee Harvey Oswald, 24, being held by the Dallas police as the assassin of John Fitzgerald Kennedy, age 46—the youngest President of these United States of America, and the youngest President to die in office. Officer Tippit leaves three children and a wife—children whose ages are 14, 10, and 5 * * * Mrs. Tippit in her own hour of grief, sent her condolence to Mrs. Kennedy and said, "Express my sympathy to Mrs. Kennedy. I know how she feels."

We would also remember Gov. John B. Connally of Texas, his wife and those who stand by the vigil of his bedside. He is expected to make a complete recovery from his physical wounds sustained at the same time of President Kennedy's assassination.

But I hope that we as Americans, as Christians, as Baptists, as residents of Maine, of Pittsfield—do not forget Lyndon Baines Johnson. He took the oath of office a short time after the assassination and thus became the 36th President—the oath administered for the first time by a woman, Judge Sarah T. Hughes. In the first Presidential statement at the airport, President Johnson said, "I will do my best."

In tragic times such as these, it calls upon our own faith, our own belief, and our own trust in God. How often we have repeated, as we have read from the coins of our Nation, "In God we trust." We have witnessed the smooth transition of Government. It has been marvelous. It makes us even more proud to be Americans. When the first announcement shocked the world, just a few moments after that tragic event, people all over the world followed—on radio and television. We were there. The Nation, the world, has shared personally in this sorrow.

President Lyndon Baines Johnson has proclaimed tomorrow a national day of mourning for the late President, John F. Kennedy. He has requested that the respective places of divine worship be open and has encouraged and challenged the American people to bow in submission to the will of Almighty God and pay their homage.

This church will be open all day tomorrow. We invite you to come, to stay as long as you might desire, to bow in silent prayer and meditation. Pray for those whose names we have mentioned this morning, so very personally and intimately involved in this experience. But then may we take the suggestion of President Johnson and pray God's continued blessing upon America and upon us as individuals; to rededicate ourselves, first as Christians and then as American citizens, to these truths we hold so dear and so faithful.

There are many personal things that touch our minds and hearts in times such as these.

I don't believe we will realize the impact of what has transpired, and what is transpiring, but we can thank God that through the clouds that overshadow, the veil of tears that sometimes blurs our vision, we can yet see the faithful, eternal hand of God leading us.

Friday and Saturday, and even this morning, I found myself, like many Americans, glued to the TV set and a slave thereunto. As President Johnson took his oath of office and took upon his shoulders great responsibilities of our Nation, I could not help but think of a personal experience. I hope you will forgive me for mentioning it this morning. On Tuesday, the 22d of May 1962, a very historical day in my life, the Chaplain of the Senate, Dr. Frederick Brown Harris, introduced me to the then Vice President of the United States, President of the Senate, Lyndon B. Johnson, a tall man from Texas with a warm smile and a firm handclasp. We sat in the corridor outside the door leading onto the Senate floor and talked about many things. One of the remarks which he made—and I can never express the feeling that came over me when he said it—"Another man called Peter will lead us in prayer today." I would never be able to describe, either, the feeling that was mine as I walked onto the Senate floor, and I realized the tremendous obligation and responsibility that was mine, not only for that moment but each day and each moment of my life. "Another man called Peter will lead us in prayer."

History will endeavor to calculate, to summarize, to evaluate all that has transpired. But history will never be able to tell the impact this has made on the hearts and lives of the American people—an impact that will cause us to renew our dedication and consecration to God Almighty and to this wonderful land of ours, this great America.

God help us that we will not take our blessings for granted. God help us, also, to say "God bless America."

John F. Kennedy was a family man. We have been impressed, regardless of difference in religious affiliation, by the fact that he did not neglect church attendance and personal religious discipline.

Are we going to be good citizens of our country because we are good citizens of the Kingdom of God? Christian principles were behind the movement for freedom of our forefathers. As those pioneers moved across the country the church took the lead. Life and its institutions must be understood in the light of God's will and God's law. These experiences bring us closer to Him who is the resurrection, our hope, our light, in whom is our faith.

"Righteousness exalts a nation; but sin is a reproach to any people" (Proverbs 13: 34).

"Blessed is the nation whose God is the Lord" (Psalm 33: 12).

———

A TIME FOR PRAYER

(Memorial address honoring President John Fitzgerald Kennedy by Dr. Frederick W. Whittaker, president of Bangor Theological Seminary, Bangor, Maine, delivered in the Beach Chapel, Nov. 26, 1963)

This is a time for prayer—prayer of thanksgiving for the life and work of President John Fitzgerald Kennedy; prayer of intercession for his eternal well-being and for the sustaining of his loved ones; prayer of penitence for the guilt which all Americans share in the assassination of our President; and prayer of petition for divine guidance of the Nation and its new Chief Executive. Prayer is our only sanctuary after a weekend of violence, shock, disbelief, grief, and sorrow which no one of us will ever forget. On the eve of this Nation's traditional day of gratitude it will not be easy for us whose lives have suddenly been saturated with sadness to review our faith and to sing praises to our God. But we shall turn from the darkness to the light because we know that under divine providence gloom cannot for long overshadow hope.

John Fitzgerald Kennedy, in the moment of his cruel and untimely death, may have set in motion moral and spiritual forces which will guide the peoples of the world to a new era of mutual understanding and peace. His assassination by one of his own countrymen may have so dismayed the citizens of our beloved land that we shall seek and find new ways of living together in brotherhood from shore to shore. Chief Justice Earl Warren has called President Kennedy a great and good man. His greatness was shown in a life-long series of "profiles of courage," in his dealings with other nations through a rare combination of strength and compassion, and in his fearless support of the rights of minority groups within the United States. His goodness was readily recognized through his love for his family, his concern for the senior citizens of our country, and his willingness to mingle with the people as friend to friend even at the risk of his life. Very few men in so short a period of time have captured the minds and hearts of such a worldwide multitude. Testimony to this fact was given by the representatives of 53 foreign states and the millions of Americans who have wept for him and brought him tribute. Our first prayer, then, should be of thanksgiving for the life and work of our departed leader.

As Christians we believe that death does not end our individual existence but that by faith we inherit the everlasting life promised by God through Jesus Christ. Thus with confidence we may utter our prayer of intercessions for President Kennedy and for the sustaining of his loved ones. There is no doubt he was a man of religious conviction and one who was strengthened in his private and public acts by the teachings of his church. Our petitions for his eternal well-being will be echoed around the earth

and with the assured hope that they will be answered. When news of the President's death was finally accepted as true by a stunned and disbelieving world, the early reactions of many took the form of anguished sympathy for the widow and for the fatherless children. That Mrs. Kennedy has been aware of this universal concern has been abundantly clear to all who have seen the majestic beauty and dignity of her composure in time of deepest grief. The spiritual stature of the first lady has been a source of inspiration and courage to innumerable men and women of lesser faith. God has indeed spoken through her abiding love for her husband and the obvious survival of that love beyond the grave. Yet we shall want to pray for Mrs. Kennedy, for her young ones, and for the members of the President's family in their present bereavement; and ask that the Holy Comforter may be with them steadfastly in the long days and years which are to come.

There is another prayer we must utter before the Creator and Judge. It is one of penitence and supplication, of begging forgiveness of the guilt which all Americans share in the assassination of our President. One man in a city far away fired the fatal shot. But my conscience has been burning within me ever since that fateful Friday. Do I not speak for you, too, and for countlesss others when I say that we and our fellow countrymen are implicated in this murderous crime because we have left undone those things which we ought to have done and we have done those things which we ought not to have done? Have we not been responsible for the development in our land of a climate of hatred, intolerance, lust, suspicion, dishonesty, intemperance, violence, and a host of other evils which served as a breeding place for the angry or misguided killing of our Chief Executive? Have we not condoned the glorification of sex, of lawlessness, and of greed for material possessions in our literature, our legitimate stage productions, our moving pictures, and our television fare? Have we not waited almost a hundred years since the assassination of another great American President before beginning to redeem his death by granting at last a measure of real freedom and equality to our Negro citizens? Have we not established an unnecessary and an unhealthy enmity among political parties in our Nation by seeking first to be partisan Republicans or Democrats rather than first to be loyal Americans, and by irrationally hurling at one another the epithets Communist and Fascist, leftwing and rightwing, liberal and conservative? Have we not in our religious communities sought to dwell in splendid isolation as Protestants, Roman Catholics, and Jews instead of acknowledging our common heritage and joining hands to take our best spiritual insights into the world for the uplifting of our bewildered society? And do not our affirmative answers to these questions have relevance to the terrible tragedy which engulfs us? We are, indeed, standing in the need of a prayer of penitence.

As those who seek forgiveness from above we shall be most worthy of God's blessing if we now and for the future rededicate ourselves as a nation in a commonwealth of nations to those ideals and high purposes for which our fallen President gave his life and met his death. To this end our final prayer must be a petition for divine guidance of the people of the United States and of our new leader.

President Lyndon B. Johnson has been unexpectedly charged with a responsibility of great magnitude, but there is welcome evidence that he is prepared for the task. One of his most challenging legacies is the problem of racial justice and peace. That he intends to follow in the footsteps of his predecessor on this issue was made manifest by the then Vice President at Gettysburg on last Memorial Day where he declared at the close of an address marking the centennial of Lincoln's Emancipation Proclamation: "Until justice is blind to color, until education is unaware of race, until opportunity is unconcerned with the color of men's skins, emancipation will be a proclamation but not a fact. To the extent that the proclamation of emancipation is not fulfilled in fact, to that extent we shall have fallen short of assuring freedom to the free."

Our new President will surely need the help of the Almighty in the solution of this and a host of other vexing problems. He will also need the assistance of a people under God united in labor for holy and righteous causes. And so this day, in honor and memory of "a great and good man" we offer our prayers of thanksgiving, of intercession, of penitence, and of petition for divine guidance. Yet may we know that after our prayers are answered and the divine guidance has been given we cannot escape the awesome fact set forth by President John Fitzgerald Kennedy in his inaugural address: "Here on earth God's work must truly be our own."

ADDRESS BY

Hon. Milton W. Glenn

OF NEW JERSEY

Mr. Speaker, it seems to me that on this day set aside for tributes to our late President, John Fitzgerald Kennedy, it would be appropriate to hear from those in my constituency, the Second District of New Jersey, through editorials and otherwise, as to the great loss which our Nation has suffered. It is, therefore, with considerable respect that I submit the following editorial which appeared in the Atlantic City Reporter and which has been so well written by its publisher and editor, Charles E. Seel. It certainly indicates how many of my constituents feel about the awesome tragedy which occurred on November 22.

THE DAY THE WORLD STOOD STILL
(By Charles E. Seel)

It has been a week since—and still the Nation mourns. We look back in retrospect at this intolerable tragedy. "Friday, 2 p.m., November 22, 1963."

The shocking report that spread like the proverbial wildfire—"The President has been shot."

All matters else paled to insignificance.

Imaginations stubbornly balked at the fantastic incredible news.

"Such a thing couldn't possibly be true—not our President," was the expression of skepticism on the faces of everyone who heard and rejected it as a false rumor.

All was a vague jumble of chaotic impressions.

Then came the heartbreaking report that reverberated around the world: "The President is dead."

It was at this moment that it seemed as though the world had stopped rotating on its axis.

"The world stood still."

The rush and bustle of daily doings—the banterings and chuckles a short time before, echoed off into a morbid silence.

A listlessness mixed with pain, sorrow and pity permeated the atmosphere.

All public places seemed to empty as if by robot command—some gathering on street corners to speak in low tones—other hurried to the sanctity of their homes—all stunned by the sudden calamity that beset our country, which we considered so powerful and guarded.

NO SADDER WORDS OF TONGUE OR PEN

The inexhaustible marathon of wordage on radio, TV, newspapers with their vivid and chronological presentation of facts and events, as all verbally marched down the road to the assassination, the capture and arrest of the charged assassin, the assassination of the assassin, and, after this, more of the infinite, endless melange of on-the-spot news coverage and now there is but little else to say. They all sit back in a comatose state of fatigue from their gloomy reveries—tired, haggard, and to say any more would suffer them to phraseological quagmire.

Newsmen, commentators, their quavering voices throbbing with sad emotion as they went about their duties—men to whom events of the most sensational nature is just part of a day's work, were seen, as they propounded their stories, to flick a "dewdrop" from a corner of their eye.

It all started last Friday, November 22, 1963, at 2 p.m.

A day of infamy that will live in the minds of our people from here to eternity.

There is a saying: "Be it grief or sorrow—the passing of time will make it less." But not this tragic deplorable day of infamy—this day is one that time shall never suppress.

The Nation wept: It wept not in the sense that a President had been assassinated. To some it was like having a family loss—an endeared and beloved child or relative. To others it was a calamitous vanishing of something unexplainable—an image—or better, a symbol—a symbol of peace—of citizens' rights—a symbol of our country's power and security. Now gone.

And gone, too, is the alleged assassin.

However, to us, this is not where the story ends.

In dallying in maudlin regret and looking back at the ironic turn of events we become aghast at our country's manifestation of helplessness?

A crime, so serious, diabolical, and damnable—the ease with which it was perpetrated by an insignificant communistic "germ" with a $12 rifle? Inconceivable absurdity? But it happened.

All the facts of why such a thing could happen are still hopelessly fogged.

The death of the assassin closes the door to many questions.

This is indeed most regrettable, for even though we all hoped with incarnate hate, that the alleged assassin would die—and a most sufferable death, we believe that his murderer's quixotic impulse thwarted efforts of our FBI to learn more from Lee Harvey Oswald.

That perhaps this crime was not merely the vengeance of a bestial fanatic—but a well-planned plot of intrigue—that Oswald was only the maddened scapegoat?

Thus it all leaves us with a bewilderment of feelings.

Is it a complacency on our part that makes us such easy prey to our enemies?

This may be an indelicate thought, and perhaps we will be criticized for so saying, but we are beginning to think that the great "freedoms" we so enthusiastically herald are a bit too free.

Much too free to the likes of the anti-American "Oswald," who openly declared his love for. communism and Cuba.

Much too free to a rupture-headed rabble rouser name of Lincoln Rockwell who leads a pistol-packing race-hating group with headquarters a few miles from our National Capitol—and a group who call themselves "Nazi-Americans."

"Nazi-Americans" mind you. How our law enforcement agencies and our Government can shut their eyes, and stomachs, to the linking of such a blood-stained name as Nazi to that of America is a glaring example of how indifferent we are and to whom we grant our much-touted freedoms. Our freedoms have reached the stage where they are being vulgarized by too perpetual a-parroting. Especially so to our self-avowed enemies.

Our despair is in seeing groups of impudent, insolent, and insidious Red fanatics, parading our city streets, and waving anti-American slogans and challenging the frustrated police to arrest them, with claims that our Constitution gives them the right of freedom of speech.

Their Communist leaders must chuckle as they rule with an iron hand of oppression, and observe the weakness we display to their puppets.

Puppets did we say?

Every Red—every anti-American in this country today is a potential assassin and murderer—and yet, we grant them the freedoms of our Constitution which only rightfully belong to the citizens of our country.

We will perhaps, in history and on the record, refer to our beloved President's death as an assassination.

This we reject with indignation.

We call his death murder—and in the worst degree. Out-and-out well-planned murder—premeditated—prearranged with professional integrity—and not the impetuous action of an enraged vengeful crank. We firmly believe that "Oswald" was merely a means to an end. There are hundreds like him.

With the swearing-in of the new President, Lyndon Johnson, we believe the time has come, to make the needed modifications to our many "freedoms."

We must tighten up on our loose freedoms to conform with these critical times.

We are no longer fighting Indians—and the crack in our Liberty Bell grows wider each day with laughter, as our enemies keep abusing and using our laws to further endanger our country as they destroy us from within.

When so dastardly a crime of lawlessness and violence can be so easily accomplished, on our own city streets, by such a wretched, vile, contemptible "nothing," then, unless we have all become callously deaf, we certainly can hear the "bells-of-alarm" ringing.

We no longer live in a world of melody and softness.

This is an era of madness and folly, and we are faced with enemies on all sides who are aggressive, nefarious, and pathological liars; who subtly speak of negotiations and bargaining on the one hand, but deal in monotonous negations and contradictions in order to nullify and destroy.

Our patriotism and reverence for our constitutional freedoms is pleasurable and wholesome, but in this day and age it has become ponderous and unwieldy.

The paltriness of our penalties against the crimes of our enemies is humiliating. Death to a dedicated fanatic is anticipated, and for him an easy way out compared to the enormity of his crime.

We've got to get tough. "Rough-on-rats."

We must stand up on our good ol' American legs and yell t'hell with Commies—all Commies who menace the life and peace of our Nation.

Let us for a change hand out a few "bloody noses," instead of sitting by and licking our wounds, hoping that the day will arrive when our enemies will become more docile, tactful, and conciliatory. This day will never be, unless we harden our convictions into resolves.

We must begin by expelling any and all anti-Americans from our country. We must dig them out of their ratholes by the scruff of their filthy necks—and if necessary order that our police officers and security men, beat-the-living-hell-outa'-them, if they act aggressive and sullen and scream for a copy of our Constitution and their rights.

Then deport them to their enslaved countries where they belong.

We say, "enough of this cacophonous, grudging, miserable squabbling. Stop all this abuse and slander—the South against the North—the left wingers and right wingers with their arrogant and overbearing claptrap. Such clamorous and wild shenanigans are playing us right into the hands of our enemies.

If we wish to survive as the greatest, freest, and most democratic nation in the world, and retain leadership over free people, we must hold all else in abeyance for the moment, and join hands with one paramount purpose in mind—to make it clear, to everyone everywhere that we are a united people, ready, willing, and able to demonstrate our strength and determination to deal, and harshly, in order to maintain world leadership and respect. Let us no longer be played the patsy—let's get tough.

We feel, and most strongly, that if we do, our great and beloved President John F. Kennedy will not have died in vain.

ADDRESS BY

Hon. Garner E. Shriver

OF KANSAS

Mr. Speaker, in his address to the joint session of the Congress a week ago, President Johnson declared:

Today in this moment of new resolve, I would say to my fellow Americans, let us continue.

Following the terrible tragedy which deeply shocked and saddened all Americans, we have witnessed the continuation of Government and national leadership under President Johnson which is essential to the survival of the Republic and the way of life which we cherish.

However, as the Nation recovers its composure and resumes the business which must be done, we will continue to carry in our hearts the memories and appreciation of John F. Kennedy. President Kennedy was the leader of the greatest country of the world today. It is difficult to understand how assassination could occur in a civilized and free land such as ours.

Although I was not in agreement with him at all times on his policies and political positions, he was my President, he was the President of all Americans. He was sincere and dedicated to his convictions and ideas; and he respected those who held opposing views.

Mr. Speaker, I join with the citizens of my district in mourning the death of President Kennedy. Mrs. Shriver and I have conveyed our heartfelt sympathy to Mrs. Kennedy, her children and the Kennedy family. We pray that God will bless them and our Nation.

It seems appropriate to repeat some of the words spoken in prayer by the Chaplain of the U.S. Senate shortly following the assassination of President Kennedy:

Hold us, we pray, and the people of America, calm and steady and full of faith for the Republic in this tragic hour of our history.

God save the state and empower her for whatever awaits for the great world role she has been called to fill in this time of destiny.

ADDRESS BY

Hon. Bob Dole

OF KANSAS

Mr. Speaker, our late President John F. Kennedy was a politician in the finest sense. Politics was a profession of endless fascination and highest importance to him. He laid careful plans for winning—and serving in—the Presidency, a position so trying that scholars have said, "No man is good enough to be President, but someone has to be."

To this profession and position of power, unmatched in the world, John Kennedy brought not only the standard requirements in good measure, but some rare additional qualities.

As stated in the Washington Evening Star:

He brought gaiety, glamour, and grace to the American political scene in a measure never known before. That lightsome tread, that debonair touch * * * that beguiling grin, that shattering understatement. He walked like a prince and he talked like a scholar. His humor brightened the life of the Republic. When finally elected, he saw no reason to hide his wit. It glinted at every press conference. His public statements were always temperate, always measured. He derided his enemies—he teased his friends. He could be grave, but not for long. When the ugliness of yesterday has been forgotten, we shall remember him smiling.

The mood following his assassination was universal. My hometown paper the Russell Daily News editorialized, "whether one was a member of Kennedy's party or shared his views was no longer important. Even his opposition respected him and the place he had earned in the world's affairs."

The Attica Independent muses:

It is indeed a sad trait of man that only after death is a person recognized for what he truly was in life * * * his most ardent foe and his most outspoken ally, together, tell the world that he was truly a great man.

Comments the Hutchinson News:

John Kennedy had a way of making America feel its greatness.

From the Norton Daily Telegram:

Nearly all Americans have come to have a lot of affection for the most youthful of American Presidents, the man with the boyish grin who aged so fast in our service. President Kennedy had the power of leadership.

The Pratt Daily Tribune says:

Though many differed with him on the handling of some of these problems, no one could deny him the respect due him for his vigor and doggedness in facing these momentous obligations.

Kennedy was schooled in the art of government and politics. He understood an honest difference of opinion as part of the American way of life.

Over and over the comments refer to his courage. From the Advance Register, of Wichita:

No one can deny he faced the task of serving his Nation courageously, unhesitatingly, unstintingly.

The Northwestern Kansas Register makes reference to his book, "Profiles in Courage," saying:

Surely he fitted as well as any of the list of Presidents who had never failed—come what might—to take a conscientious stand.

The Glasco Sun surmises:

Why was President Kennedy killed? The reason probably lies in the fact that he was one of the most courageous Presidents of our time. He fought vigorously for what he believed was right, regardless of the opposition.

The Ellsworth Reporter says:

He will be remembered as one of the most outstanding men in our history. The Nation mourns the passing of a courageous leader.

The Hugoton Hermes:

He will not be known as our best President, * * * nor our worst. He will, I think be one of our strongest in terms of world reputation.

Outstanding are the comments about his personality. The Larned Tiller and Toiler:

John F. Kennedy brought to the office a youthful vitality, he was debonair, often radiant, but dignity and good taste were also faces of his character. He and his wife, Jacqueline, gave to the White House an intellectual and cultural atmosphere that was perhaps without precedent. He was himself a writer of distinction, and he shared with Mrs. Kennedy an appreciation of the other creative arts which she cultivated and encouraged as First Lady.

The Prairie Drummer:

John Kennedy was a President very close to the people of the United States. His wartime heroics, youthful personality—all led to immense respect from millions.

The Spearville News:

John Fitzgerald Kennedy was a man of courage, personality, power, and vast capabilities. He was young and filled with hope for peace. He loved life, he loved his country and her people and the people loved him.

The Kinsley Mercury:

As President of this country he was naturally considered a great man. And yet—what made him great came from within himself.

The Great Bend Daily Tribune:

He was not without opponents, not without critics, but beneath it all was a respect for the man because, while they opposed him and were critical, his opponents knew he was sincerely trying to do what he thought best.

The Lyons Daily News:

With the tragic event comes the stark realization that when a man is elected President of the United States he becomes an exposed human being with prestige of such eminence that it is beyond comprehension.

The Smith County Pioneer:

As this shocked Nation started to recover there came the realization—and admission—even by political enemies, that here was a great statesman and probably the most cultured man who ever held the office of President.

The Western Kansas World:

Truly we can say President Kennedy gave everything a single individual could give for his country and for the freedom and peace of the world.

The Downs News:

We gather here to reaffirm our faith in the democratic processes as they oppose the tyranny that suggests, "I can kill the man with whom I disagree."

These are but a few of the highlights of the flood of editorial comments in western Kansas papers, each recognizing in some form the late President's strength in and love of politics. It is important to the individual and the country, that politics be studied with the same sense of dedication successful men bring to the profession of farming, teaching, law, or medicine or any other.

We live in a country—in a world—of enormous complexity. The strength of a democracy is in its enlightened electorate and the complexity of modern life makes this ideal very difficult to achieve. During such a time, the professional politician, whether you agree or disagree with what he always says or does, is important. President Kennedy was such a person. His knowledge, his brilliant mind, his continuous study of politics, were of great importance and while many have these qualities, few have all the ingredients necessary.

His feeling of identification with people, his great interest and fondness for great crowds of humanity, his tolerance of the differences of human beings, was the wonder of John Kennedy.

The three previous Presidents assassinated shared many of the same qualities, and strangely each was slain during a period in his administration when there was peace, prosperity, and happiness. Furthermore, on the day the crime was committed, each was unusually happy, pleased with the progress, and held in great favor by the crowds who came to see them. Finally, each was slain by a person with little or no reason for the act or hope of gain once it was accomplished.

What is done is tragically history and as the Nation mourns and all hearts go out to Mrs. Kennedy, the children, and all members of the Kennedy family, little can be said but let us recall the statement of Daniel Webster, carved in granite above the center door of the House of Representatives Press Gallery. It is a challenge to all now as it must have been to then Congressman John F. Kennedy when he first reflected upon it:

Let us develop the resources of our land, call forth its powers, build up its institutions, promote all its great interests and see whether we also in our day and generation, may not perform something worthy to be remembered.

Presidents that could be classified as an intellectual. This characteristic is evident in his literary manuscripts, his prepared speeches, as well as his extemporaneous remarks. Few other persons have I heard employ such a broad vocabulary as did the late President and have the faculty of selecting exactly the right word to accentuate the point he wished to make.

These things being said, I think it would be inappropriate not to mention my philosophical differences with the former President. As I have recited in earlier commentary, my differences with him were in principle, not in prejudice.

There is no question that his administration for only 3 brief years will leave a very critical imprint on American society. The cowardly assassination deprived his party, his country, and the world of a final judgment on what he might have contributed to mankind had his life not been taken. He shall be missed as our selected leader, as a friend and as a political adversary, but most important, it should be recorded that his disappearance from world politics will create a void that is discernible to all mankind for the present and for a time in the future.

ADDRESS BY

Hon. William H. Avery

OF KANSAS

Mr. Speaker, it is premature to attempt to evaluate the place that the late John Fitzgerald Kennedy, President of the United States, will hold in the history of this Nation or world as events are recorded by future writers. It is not too early to make several observations.

First, he was a man dedicated to public service. This was manifested through his military service in time of war and more recently in his rapid ascendancy in public office.

Further, probably few other national leaders have been as colorful as he in their own inimitable ways. No doubt this was due in part to his youth, but more particularly to his natural vivaciousness and a tremendous capacity for work. This particular capacity was not limited to John Kennedy but seems to be a common tendency through the entire Kennedy family.

History will probably record him as one of the

ADDRESS BY

Hon. Robert F. Ellsworth

OF KANSAS

Mr. Speaker, certainly John Kennedy was an extraordinary man. His assassination was a body blow to our ideals of free government. It was a sharp and painful human loss, too, especially to those of us who had met and known and worked with him, if only for 3 short years, here in Washington.

The thing about President Kennedy's assassination that hurt many of us more than anything else was the cutting off of his immense aliveness. As a man, as a politician, as President, he was alive and sensitive to his world as few of us are. And people everywhere seemed to be able to understand this, even though they had never seen him in person.

His vitality came through to large numbers of people in an immediate way. For example, he came to my hometown, Lawrence, Kans., in the late 1950's to speak to a student convocation at the University of Kansas. Even though he was then a young and junior Senator, our student body and faculty, as well as the citizens of the town, responded unforgettably to the excitement of John Kennedy's aliveness.

Then too, his aliveness and warmth called up an exuberant response from those who met him individually. Certainly this was true of Mrs. Ellsworth and me when we met and visited briefly with him at White House social occasions. His warm and friendly liveliness came through to me again one afternoon at the White House when he and I interrupted a legislative working session to visit about mutual friends in Springfield, Mass., where I had once practiced law.

But above all, John Kennedy was alive to the tides of changing ideas, to the shifts of political and social facts, to the sweep and rush of world history. People everywhere in the world, who are themselves sensitive and alive in any degree to what is going on in the world, know the world is changing. They knew that John Kennedy knew it, too; and they sensed he was doing his best to deal with the world. Here was a young man, born in this century, steeped all his young life in the study of history, fully alive and sensitive as well to the world of ideas as to the world of brutal power.

Not that all of us always agreed with every direction of his lively responses to the world; far from it. But he did respond. He couldn't help responding, so alive was he. And all people everywhere—even his opponents—granted that, and felt at his death a rude and human shock.

As the news of John Kennedy's assassination came to me over my car radio less than 2 weeks ago, I felt that shock.

As Mrs. Ellsworth and I walked solemnly past his casket and catafalque in the White House East Room, with the giant chandeliers and the fireplace draped in black crepe, where before we had danced to gayest music, we felt that shock.

And as at last the representatives of the American people, the Members of the Congress, and our families, joined his sad widow on the hillside under the giant oaks at Arlington that bright, cold November Monday afternoon, we shared that shock again, this time with all the great from all the world. Just as taps echoed finally

from higher up the hill, the afternoon sun slipped down behind the crest and a very real chill indeed settled over Washington, and over our beloved Nation.

Yet so powerful and so beautiful was John Kennedy's aliveness that I cannot think he would have wanted us here now to bear the pall of that chill for long. After all, he died as he would have wanted—in the heat of the battle for a lively appreciation of the world by all of us. There he was in Dallas, moving freely and openly among the people, surrounded round about by his friends supporting him and his enemies attacking him.

Let us commit ourselves today to being as alive and responsive as we can be, and with that let us be warm and human and loving and understanding. Let us not suppose we have to agree with each other all the time, nor even with all of our late President's ideas—he never asked that, even in life.

But, because of him and of his hero's death, we will forever after give more respect, and more honor and glory than ever before, to those men and women who are alive as he was to ideas, to facts, to history, and to men and women as individuals and as part of the sweep of our human history.

ADDRESS BY

Hon. Joe Skubitz

OF KANSAS

Mr. Speaker, there are times when it is difficult to translate into words the thoughts which we carry in our hearts and minds. For me, this is one of those occasions.

November 22, 1963, and the event which transpired on that tragic day has left its mark upon our Nation's history—a mark which time may dim but can never erase. But I cannot in my own heart feel that all America should be adjudged guilty for the act of one warped mind, and I do not think that John F. Kennedy would want it so.

I did not know John F. Kennedy intimately. But anyone who was privileged to see him and hear him will never forget his wit, his smile and his personality. He served his country as best he knew how. No man can do more. His dreams, his aspirations and his goals for a better America in a world living in peace were shared by all of us. But so long as man has a free mind, honest differences will develop as to the methods, procedures and programs which should be followed in achieving these national objectives.

John Fitzgerald Kennedy is gone. But as surely as the night follows the day the spirit of John F. Kennedy will live on. His work is finished. The heavy burden now falls upon the shoulders of his wife, Mrs. Jacqueline B. Kennedy. To those of us who attended the services in the rotunda of the Capitol, the courage, the fortitude and the majesty of Jacqueline Bouvier Kennedy, wife and mother, will long be remembered. Men and women cried unashamedly as they watched her kneel and press her lips to the flag which draped the casket of her beloved husband.

My deepest sympathy is extended to Mrs. Kennedy, to Caroline and to John. I pray God has given them the courage, the will and the understanding to carry on, as I am sure that John F. Kennedy, husband and father, would have so wished.

ADDRESS BY

Hon. Edward J. Derwinski

OF ILLINOIS

Mr. Speaker, as we pay tribute to our assassinated President, John F. Kennedy, we realize the inadequacy of words and recognize the justifiable duplication that is produced. In the 2 weeks since the tragic assassination of the President, the Nation has expressed shock, sorrow, and respect for the late President.

Mrs. Derwinski and I extend to Mrs. Jacqueline Kennedy, her children, and the Kennedy family our deep personal sympathy. Despite the natural preoccupation with governmental complications caused by the assassination, we recognize the great personal loss that Mrs. Kennedy and her children suffer, and certainly the citizens of the country manifested understanding and sorrow in the personal, as well as in the official nature of the tragedy.

The nationwide feelings of shock and sorrow can be very vividly recognized as we read the editorial comment from publications across the country. I include at this point editorial comment, eulogizing President Kennedy, that appeared in numerous independent community publications in the Fourth Congressional District of Illinois:

[From the Blue Island Sun-Standard, Nov. 28, 1963]

NOVEMBER 22, 1963, WILL NOT BE FORGOTTEN

There is not one of us who will ever forget where we were or our surroundings—November 22, 1963—when the awful impact of the assassination of John F. Kennedy, President of the United States, finally became a part of our consciousness.

Who can forget the intoning of the radio announcer who said, last Friday, "two priests who have just left the hospital said that the President is dead"? Those few words changed the irrevocable, shocking possibility into a hard, unyielding actuality.

There has been no President since Lincoln who perhaps was so openly villified and ardently disliked by certain elements—his very youth and vigor, the multiplicity of activity of the Kennedy family—all seemed to add certain resentments to his career.

On the other hand, it took his brutal, untimely death to bring forth the new general appreciation of what this comparatively young man did for the world which last October wavered on the brink of atomic war. He stood steadfast in his talks to Khrushchev in a manner which demonstrated the same inherent courage he personally displayed years before, in World War II.

The signing of the test ban treaty was another great accomplishment and victory of statesmanship he displayed during the past 3 years of worldwide crisis.

His extensive travels, particularly his trip to West Berlin and other troubled spots on the globe—all accomplished with safety and acclaim—made doubly horrible the fact that he should be cowardly murdered in an American city.

Sorrow is intermingled with indignation in knowing that such violence should exist against a head of state—our head of state. We are sure that everyone feels personally affronted, as well as aggrieved.

John Dryden, famous English poet, wrote a poem—strangely enough, for Saint Cecilia's Day—November 22. The title was "A Song for Saint Cecilia's Day, November 22, 1687."

> "As from the power of sacred lays
> The spheres began to move
> And sung the great Creator's praise
> To all the blest above:
> So when the last and dreadful hour
> This crumbling pageant shall devour
> The trumpet shall be heard on high
> The dead shall live, the living die
> And music will contain the sky."

It was a coincidence to read over those lines on November 22, 1963, exactly 276 years later, even though the context is not particularly applicable to the assassination of a President of the United States, still those sonorous last phrases of Dryden's poem might well be repeated as a form of requiem.

[From the Harvey Tribune, Nov. 24, 1963]

JOHN FITZGERALD KENNEDY

A saddened America mourns the tragic death of President John Fitzgerald Kennedy and joins in worldwide prayers for the late Chief Executive and his family. A shocked America strives in vain to comprehend the base wickedness leading to so inexplicable a horror as his assassination.

If any seed of comfort can be derived from this great sorrow, it must be the common bond which so emphatically overrides political partisanship and all other considerations at times of great adversity. On our late President's death, we stand united, as we had stood united under his dynamic leadership in time of peril.

As Chief Executive of the United States, John Fitzgerald Kennedy was the President of all Americans. As an individual, he was a man whose magnetic personality and courage won respect in addition to that accruing from the dignity of his office.

A measure of his character is the fact that he had given much of his short life to public service when the responsibilities were grave.

It is in this light that we add our humble words to the countless others coming from those in all stations of life who have lost their President.

And it is with an abiding faith in the fabric of American leadership and American principles that we confidently expect our new President, Lyndon B. Johnson, to receive unreserved cooperation at every hand as he performs his duties in these trying times.

[From the Lemonter, Nov. 28, 1963]

A GREAT AMERICAN DIES

It will be a week Friday since John Fitzgerald Kennedy, the 35th President of the United States, was slain by an assassin at Dallas, Tex.

News of this horrifying event stunned the civilized world. Horror, bewilderment, shock, and grief gripped all as word of the tragedy spread. It was as if some strange vacuum had been loosed, draining emotions and leaving people empty and dazed.

John F. Kennedy was a man who had captured the affections of the public. One might disagree with his political views and policies but at the same time like and admire the man. He was colorful, engaging and dynamic. He was an intelligent, shrewd leader—an intellectual with the common touch. One couldn't help but like President Kennedy. Millions who had never seen him in person considered him as a personal friend.

That he had endeared himself to all people was demonstrated by the spontaneous tears, evoked in all nations when news of his death was flashed over the air.

The late President was confronted with great and grave problems almost from the time he took office 34 months ago. He faced them with courage and fortitude.

The duties and responsibilities of the Presidency are terrific, physically as well as mentally. President Kennedy was further handicapped by a spinal injury incurred in college days, aggravated by his war service and further worsened by the grind of official rounds and the public demands upon his strength. As a result the late President suffered considerable pain but he kept it hidden and never hid behind it.

President Kennedy was a great American, a man devoted to the cause of peace, who endeavored to serve all according to his lights and aims. In time his place in history will be evaluated but there can be no dispute that he was a great leader, a man who loved people and in turn was loved by them.

Speaking for the people of the area we wish to extend the deepest and sincere sympathy to the family of our late President.

May his soul rest in peace and light perpetual shine upon him.

[From the Markham Bulletin, Nov. 28, 1963]

AN EDITORIAL

Some of the initial shock of Friday's heinous assassination has by now worn off. Realization that things are as they really are is being established. The true impact of the tragedy—of course—remains unknown. History must now finally assess the greatness of our former President. Certainly the bereavement of this country has been felt by all. The tributes have been made, but words cannot suffice to fully convey the sense of loss felt by citizens of this country.

All will recognize that President Kennedy's brief tenure encompassed all the truly profound issues of our time— and that upon him was thrust the responsibility of establishing policy that would influence all generations unborn, as well as all living beings on earth. Weighty responsibilities indeed—and perhaps unfair responsibility for any mortal.

Our former President met these duties with great personal courage; as a patriotic American, with utmost belief that his decisions were considerate of the best interests of the free world, and predicated upon the laws of our land. Surely it would be unfair to have expected his executive decisions to have been popularly supported by everyone. Maybe others could have executed his position better. This is doubtful, and the awesome burden of proof will now fall to those who will succeed him. Our prayers must be extended to these Americans.

Our former President combined his vast array of talents with personal warmth and compassion. A rare and wonderful combination—totally diverse from the dark forces that triggered Friday's atrocity. These forces are the manifestations of our imperfections: capacity for hate, greed, perversion. In all of us there are degrees of wrong: imperfections which make possible in our society the ultimate sin of murder. In some portion we can all share the blame of Friday's disaster.

On this Thanksgiving eve it would seem appropriate to be grateful that we were given such a leader as John F. Kennedy; that other brave and intelligent men will follow and guide this great country; that within the vast,

vast majority of mankind there dwell forces for good far exceeding the resident evil; that as long as there is life there will always be this great exertion for right over might.

We might also pray that Friday's tragic sacrifice will not have been made in vain. That somehow from the depths of the grief and sickness that surrounds this loss there will emerge meaningful recognition of man's capacity for and need to love.

———

[From the Park Forest Reporter, Nov. 27, 1963]

And Now, Eternal Peace

Five days have passed since the world was stunned by the shocking international tragedy when an assassin's bullet on Friday took the life of our beloved President, John Fitzgerald Kennedy.

The esteem in which he was held by fellow Americans and nationals of many foreign lands was demonstrated by the tremendous outpourings of sympathy and concern which emanated not only from the capitals of the world, but also from villages and the hinterlands all over the globe.

Across the length and breadth of our Nation, millions of grief-stricken men, women, and children mourned the passing of President Kennedy as though he were a member of the family. His 34-month tenure as our Chief Executive endeared him to all peace-loving people—those who agreed with his political philosophies as well as those whose party affiliations or foreign philosophy brought them into conflict with his views.

What manner of a man was Mr. Kennedy that he, at a youthful age of 46, should earn such worldwide acclaim and immortality?

It is left for history to record the scope of his deeds, but the personal excitement he created and the strength of character he displayed will long be remembered by those who were touched by his magnetism.

Culturally an intellectual, President Kennedy, born into a millionaire family, possessed the simple graces which made him sincerely devoted to a cause which championed for a better America and a better world. His humility, his faith, his compassion for the underprivileged both here and abroad, his zeal toward a fulfillment of complete citizen rights for all Americans, regardless of their origins and the color of their skins did not make him most popular in some sections of the Nation, but he steadfastly refused to give ground until his cause triumphed.

His humor, wit, and charm added a new dimension to our Nation's top office.

His role as a husband and a father would qualify him for an all-American role, regardless of the competition. With wife Jacqueline, they made a couple without counterpart among the heads of all the world's nations.

Millions of words have been written and spoken since that dreaded black Friday of last week, eulogizing the world's most popular citizen in the postwar years. To repeat them now would be unnecessary.

In life he worked so earnestly for a lasting peace on earth. Deservedly he has earned eternal peace. There is no higher reward.

[From the Riverdale Advertiser, Nov. 25, 1963]

In Peace and Honor Rest You

The death of John Fitzgerald Kennedy can in no way destroy the sincerity of his thought for his country and for his fellowmen. Certainly it may be said of him that he did what he felt was right for him to do for the welfare of all of us and he did by his deeds and words, the very best he could do. No man could have done more than that.

———

[From the Sauk Village Review, Nov. 28, 1963]

Editorial

(By Lee Staley)

Wiser, more learned and profound men than I have already written about President Kennedy's assassination. But I felt a personal and moral obligation to our readers to express my thoughts.

I do not believe that the full impact or significance of what occurred last Friday in Dallas, Tex., was immediately felt by the stunned citizens of the free world.

A great and noble man had fought in two wars—in World War II as a naval officer fighting for the ideals of liberty for the country he loved—in the cold war as President of the United States fighting for the freedom and human dignity of mankind. He lost his life on the battlefield of humanity.

Now we must put forth our combined efforts to help maintain the peace and ideals of this courageous leader.

We must help our new President Lyndon Baines Johnson pick up the reins of our fallen President.

May God help him guide the reins to a peaceful world.

———

[From the Suburbanite-Economist, Nov. 27, 1963]

He Shall Live On

President John Fitzgerald Kennedy has joined the Nation's heroes in Arlington Cemetery while his country and the world continue in the throes of the most poignant grief ever known on a global scale.

Not even his most fervent admirers realized that he was the idol of peoples of all levels everywhere. Cables report natives in Europe, Asia, Africa, and South America wept unashamedly on the streets, in houses of worship, or wherever they gathered.

To foreigners, he was the undisputed champion of all that is just, fair, and right, and they looked to him to lead the world back to peace.

To Americans he was regarded similarly, but, in addition, as the young leader who would correct the wrongs from which the Nation has suffered since its founding.

Now an eternal light burns on the cemetery slope at his grave. It can be seen from the Nation's Capital City, and it is to be hoped it will serve future governments as a reminder that the people want done the things this great man stood for and fought for.

His name has taken its place in history with those of George Washington and Abraham Lincoln. It will never be forgotten.

[From the Worth-Palos Reporter, Nov. 28, 1963]

IT'S UP TO US, NOW

Throughout these last tragic days, we have asked ourselves desperately "Why?"

Through all the horror, all the grief, each one asked each other, "Why?" Shock and disbelief echoed with each asking.

Now, because the evident assassin is dead, it may never be known what sickness twisted him so. It is for us, then, to turn from questioning to resolution. To give meaning to this martyrdom by the way we live and act.

This is not the first time one man has been a sacrifice for all men. Will we go through eternity letting our best and bravest die for us? Or can we learn, slowly and through terrible pain, some lesson from each one?

No man now living is untouched by John Kennedy's lifeless hand. Unless that touch reaches to our hearts and makes each one of us in some way better, we will be writing our own answer to that desperate "Why?" We will be answering, "For no reason."

FOR GALLANTRY

A recurring theme expressed by every one of the newsmen who brought us the terrible details of tragedy has been admiration for Jacqueline Kennedy.

She has acted throughout as though each citizen of the country was a member of John Kennedy's family, and has let us mourn with her in dignity. Each of us has traveled with her through that bright Friday morning. We have followed her into shock as she cradled her dying husband in her arms.

Our hearts have ached for the wife who walked, dazed but resolute, beside her husband's coffin. And we have wept for the mother whose little daughter turned to her in bewilderment to learn what to do next as she knelt in the great rotunda.

Mr. Speaker, these editorials express fully the feeling that was obvious during the tragic weekend of the President's death. The President, with his energy and ability to communicate with the public, reflected an image of the Presidency of which the public was justifiably proud.

The overwhelming shock that all Americans felt was reflected in the statement, "I didn't think anything like this could happen here." The totally unexpected tragedy caused all Americans to reappraise the national scene, and reevaluate their understanding of our national heritage. In that reevaluation, they recognize the deep roots and true greatness of the Nation that has exhibited itself in the days of national sorrow that marked President Kennedy's death.

The fact that the assassin was motivated by Marxist philosophy was duly recognized by the public, and in the moment of national tragedy we note the reaffirmation of faith in the American way of life and the determination to maintain a world of freedom and peace to achieve the goal of ultimate victory of justice over the tyranny of communism.

It is truly fitting and timely in the memory of the late President Kennedy that we rededicate ourselves to the necessary triumph of free-world philosophy over the diabolical Communist ideology.

I know I speak the sentiments of all the people of the Fourth Congressional District of Illinois and express their profound sorrow in the tragic loss of President Kennedy.

To Mrs. Kennedy and the late President's family, I convey on behalf of the citizens I represent their deep personal sympathy and understanding, and with all Americans, we renew our determination to build America on the solid foundations of the past and demonstrate the stability of the Nation in surviving this tragic assassination.

ADDRESS BY

Hon. J. Edgar Chenoweth

OF COLORADO

Mr. Speaker, I wish to join my colleagues in paying tribute to the memory of our late President John F. Kennedy. I was deeply shocked and saddened when I learned of the tragic event which took his life. His assassination was a grievous blow to our Nation and brought overwhelming sorrow to all of our people. It is still hard to believe that such a tragedy could occur in this country.

It is difficult to understand why the President should be cut down, without warning, at the peak of his career. The people of this country hold their President in great affection and respect. This is true regardless of political affiliation and they were completely unprepared for the shocking news which reached them on November 22. The Nation united in sincere grief for its stricken President.

I liked President Kennedy and always enjoyed a visit with him. He always had the same friendly greeting and was a most congenial person. It is not difficult to understand why he had so many friends, not alone in our own country, but throughout the world. He had a charm and grace which attracted people of all types to him.

President Kennedy was a most welcome visitor to Colorado. He visited our State several times, and on each occasion received a most cordial reception. He had many friends in Colorado, and in my congressional district, who deeply mourn his untimely death.

I recall that in August of last year President Kennedy came to Pueblo in my district to help us celebrate the authorization of the Fryingpan-Arkansas Transmountain water diversion project. He signed the bill at the White House on August 16, 1962, and came to Pueblo the next day. I am proud to have in my office one of the pens he used to sign this bill. The people of my district greatly appreciated the support President Kennedy gave this project, and he was accorded a most enthusiastic welcome. It is now proposed that the Pueblo Dam, an important feature of the project, be named in his honor.

The last trip of the President to Colorado was in June of this year, when he went to Colorado Springs to address the graduating class of the Air Force Academy. Over 30,000 persons gathered in Falcon Stadium to greet him, and thousands lined the streets to extend their welcome on his way from the stadium.

Mr. Speaker, I had the great honor of serving in the House with Mr. Kennedy. I recall how diligently he worked for the district in Massachusetts which he represented. I remember on one occasion the hard fight he made on the floor for funds for a flood control project in his district.

I was not close to President Kennedy politically, since we belonged to opposite political parties. However, I had great admiration and personal affection for him. His tragic death was an irreparable loss to our Nation.

Mrs. Chenoweth joins me in extending our deep personal sympathy to Mrs. Kennedy and the children, and the other members of the family.

ADDRESS BY

Hon. John Bell Williams

OF MISSISSIPPI

Mr. Speaker, in the prime of his life and at the point where he could render his greatest service to his country, John Fitzgerald Kennedy was taken from our midst.

All America was saddened over the senseless assassination of our President by a Communist sympathizer. The motivation for such a barbaric act can be understood only by the twisted mind of an anarchist.

We mourn his death and we deeply sympathize with his wife, his children, and his family.

One of the finest tributes I have seen paid to John F. Kennedy was by the Vicksburg, Miss., Evening Post. In an editorial on November 23, 1963, the Evening Post commented on his death and I truly believe that the sentiments expressed in that editorial to be representative of the feeling of the people of Mississippi.

Mr. Speaker, I include the editorial as a part of my remarks:

JOHN FITZGERALD KENNEDY

Only yesterday, in the full flush of manhood, John F. Kennedy was President of the United States, the acknowledged leader of the free world. Today, he lies cold in death, the victim of an assassin's bullet. Yesterday, in many of his proposals and programs, he faced a vigorous opposition. Today, in death, he finds 180 million people completely united in their horror at his tragic death. Yesterday he was the loving father and husband. Today the family circle is broken, never again to be regained.

The manner in which President Kennedy met his death will always remain in our annals as a crime of dastardly proportions. Not only was he wantonly murdered—that fatal shot was directed at the people of the United States, who had entrusted him with their leadership. It was a blow against American principles and freedom. It was the work of a warped and twisted mind. It was the act of one completely out of tune with every vestige of decency. November 22, 1963, will go down in our history as another day of infamy.

John Fitzgerald Kennedy was in his 47th year, and in the 3d year of the Presidency. He had brought a new concept to the Presidency, new ideas, new programs, both in domestic and international affairs. He was a controversial President in that many of his policies met with strong and vigorous opposition, but he was a man of courage, a man of sincerity, a man dedicated in his beliefs. Classed as a liberal, he was faced with mounting conservative opposition, and criticism of his administration was loud. But he met the criticism with courage and with a faith in his own ideas and ideals. The courage he had displayed as a naval officer in World War II never failed him when he assumed the tremendous burdens of the Presidency. He was called upon to stand up to the Reds' on more than one occasion. This he did unflinchingly and with firmness. He was the first President to have the full responsibility of warding off, or plunging the world into, a nuclear war. No one man in history had a greater burden to bear than that. John F. Kennedy met that responsibility, and the dreaded nuclear war did not materialize.

The cowardly attack upon this great leader has left a nation stunned and dazed, that such a thing could happen in a free country. The cry of the Nation now is that the guilty be apprehended, and that the world will know that under our American system, political or other differences will never be settled by violence, but only through the free and open discussion of opposite views can there be a resolution of differences in the true American tradition.

As John F. Kennedy comes back to the White House today in death, a saddened and deeply affected nation mourns his passing—it mourns the fact that his service to his Nation has been so tragically terminated—it mourns with his devoted wife and his children orphaned at such an early age—it mourns with his parents and the other members of his family—it mourns for America in one of her saddest hours.

John Kennedy, in his inaugural address, pleaded with his countrymen to give to their country. Yesterday he gave his all. His life was offered as a sacrifice on the altar of devotion to his country. Upon his tombstone should be inscribed "Killed in action," for in a very true sense he died the death of a hero.

His soul, troubled and weighed down by the awesome responsibilities of the Presidency, is now at rest. May a merciful God grant him an eternity of the peace for which he had given such dedicated service.

ADDRESS BY

Hon. William M. Colmer

OF MISSISSIPPI

Mr. Speaker, the bullet from the assassin's gun that felled President John F. Kennedy on that beautiful fall morning in Dallas, Tex., only a few days ago, was a national tragedy. Death as a result of natural causes is always a sad event, but when a young man, and particularly a young man who is President of the United States, is struck down at the hands of an assassin, it is most reprehensible.

On the morning of November 22, President John F. Kennedy rode down the street of Dallas,

Tex., a happy man with the vigor of youth, with virtually the world at his feet. He was the leader of the greatest and most powerful nation in the world; he was possessed of wealth, power and happiness; he enjoyed the love and adoration of his parents, brothers and sisters as well as his charming wife and infant children. He had everything to live for. His popularity was worldwide; even those who did not share his philosophical views respected this young President of ours.

Mr. Speaker, it is difficult sometimes to understand the scheme of life and death. It is certainly most difficult to understand the motivation of this warped-minded individual who fired the fatal shot. And yet, we know that throughout the recorded history of mankind every generation of men has been plagued with such types of depraved human beings. Unfortunately, President Kennedy's tragic death is not without precedent in the comparatively short life of this Republic; as witness the unfortunate and tragic deaths of Presidents Lincoln, Garfield, and McKinley. In each instance, these four Presidents died at the hands of assassins of dubious objectives conceived by unbalanced minds. Possibly the greatest parallel in this most recent national tragedy is that of President McKinley who died at the hands of an admitted anarchist. The obvious murderer of President Kennedy was an admitted Communist.

Mr. Speaker, as one who honestly and sincerely but regretfully differed with our lamented President, as thank God it is our right to do under the American political system, I also was one of those who had a genuine affection for the President and, like all other Americans of good will, Mrs. Colmer and I join in extending our sincere sympathy to his family.

ADDRESS BY

Hon. Charles B. Hoeven

OF IOWA

Mr. Speaker, the entire Nation was shocked beyond expression at the sudden and tragic death of President John F. Kennedy. It is almost inconceivable that such an assassination of an

American President could occur in this enlightened age of American history.

I first became acquainted with President Kennedy when he joined us in the House of Representatives in 1946 and thereafter followed his career in the Senate and in the White House with keen interest. Truly he served with great honor and dignity.

John F. Kennedy's warm personality, genuine sense of humor, and outstanding intellect won for him the admiration of a world of friends. The whole world will continue to mourn the untimely passing of this great American and fine Christian gentleman.

ADDRESS BY

Hon. William K. Van Pelt

OF WISCONSIN

Mr. Speaker, in this historic Chamber, where John Fitzgerald Kennedy served as a young Congressman and prepared himself for the destiny that led him not only to the highest office in the land but also to an untimely and tragic death, I wish to join my colleagues in paying tribute to his memory; also to extend my sincere condolences to his brave widow and his family.

No American could fail to respect him for his energy, his great ability, and his deep devotion to what he deemed to be his patriotic duty. I admired him for his unselfish dedication to public service and for his bravery as a young Navy lieutenant risking his life in the defense of this Nation.

And now he is gone, "Leaving his death as an example of noble courage, and a memorial of virtue, not only unto young men, but unto all his Nation."

ADDRESS BY

Hon. Harlan Hagen

OF CALIFORNIA

Mr. Speaker, my wife and I join the millions of decent people worldwide in sorrow over the death of John F. Kennedy.

Truly the world has lost a great statesman, who—in his rather brief career as our President—accomplished much good according to Christian principles and the other ideals to which we adhere as Americans.

I was privileged to know the late President through conversation in my district and at the White House and learned the same respect for him that was learned by his more intimate acquaintances. My feeling is that here was a man of great humility, compassion for humanity, and tolerance and understanding of the strengths, weaknesses, and needs of people in every walk of life.

He could, without question, express the ideals of our democratic Republic better than any President since the time of our Founding Fathers and his spoken and written observations on the affairs of the Nation and the world will be textbook material for scholars forever.

Our sorrow for John F. Kennedy is matched by an admiration for his widow. Inevitably the wife of a great public man stands somewhat in his shadow during his lifetime. In the grim days following the death of her husband, however, Jacqueline Kennedy demonstrated qualities of courage, devotion, and dignity which will live in the memory of all of us. I am certain that her reactions under stress inspired millions of Americans to lead better lives in the service of our society.

ADDRESS BY

Hon. O. C. Fisher

OF TEXAS

Mr. Speaker, I fully share the feeling that has been expressed here today concerning the tragic death of President Kennedy. His loss is mourned by the entire Nation, and indeed by the entire world where freedom, liberty and justice are respected. His life was dedicated to those principles.

It was my good fortune to have been rather closely associated with John Kennedy when he first came to Congress in 1947. He was a hard fighter for what he believed in. Everything he did was honorable and fair. There was nothing petty or small about that great American. The result was that he commanded respect and admiration in everything he did. Whether one agreed with him or not, he was respected as a worthy adversary and an able and energetic advocate.

As President he gained the confidence of freedom-loving people all over the world. He held high the banner of hope for freedom and tranquillity in this troubled world. It is indeed a terrible thing to contemplate his loss at the very peak of his career. I join with my colleagues in an expression of condolence to the surviving widow and children.

ADDRESS BY

Hon. Rogers C. B. Morton

OF MARYLAND

Mr. Speaker, at this late hour on a day set aside to eulogize our late President, it is difficult to add to what has been said without repeating the thoughts and phrases of others.

The story of John Kennedy, the man—his capacity for leadership—the dynamics of his personality—his devotion to duty—all have been articulated and documented by speakers and authors of great renown. In fact, it is probable that more words than ever before concerning one man have been written in the press of the world and spoken to the world through the media of television and radio about his life—his death—and the reaction of people everywhere to the horror of his sinister assassination.

Among the civilized people, grief is universal.

Should we in this hour of shock and moment of despair linger in a vague, subconscious hope that something can be undone that is done, time will not wait for us. We cannot recast the challenge of today. The press of new people being born every hour, demanding as they grow new opportunity to become a part of a higher order of civilization—the demands of nations for a larger share of the world's bounty, for independence but with protection; for aid but without obligation—the ever-present conflict between man's concept of freedom and his reaction to law and discipline—the awareness of these forces were a part of the total understanding within John Kennedy. His willingness to enter the arena to fight for his solutions, to accept the scars of battle as part of the job and to give of himself to motivate others is what I hope history will hold high in its reflection of the man.

America's strength and, most important, her future contribution to the development of man's lot on earth is the product of the forces which unite us as a people and a nation. These forces are strengthened, not weakened, by the partisanism of our politics. The differences of opinions and philosophies which conform us into a society of individuals rather than a herd are the dynamics of our ability to govern ourselves. We have the capacity to unite—unite in purpose—unite in fellowship, and yes, unite in grief and tribute because by open debate and by resolution of our differences through the honored processes of our system we have achieved this right to unite. The unity here today in grief and tribute is without bond, or control, or influence by any imposition, foreign or domestic. It is the product of free men working, thinking, and differing, but within the design of our Constitution.

Mr. Speaker, in final tribute to our late President we must recognize this crime of his death for what it is. Does it represent the imperfection of our system? Was it motivated by some wild extreme of our normal differences? On this, sir, may I quote in part the words of the Senator from Kentucky [Mr. Morton], when he said on November 25 in the Senate:

It was not a flaw in the American system or the American character that struck down John Kennedy. It was not the sin of a city or of its citizens. It was not a tragedy that struck from some dark stain of violence on the American system or in the American soul. And we do not serve the best interests of our Nation, of truth, or of the memory of a murdered President by letting wrongly placed recriminations overcome the good sense of this great Nation and its people.

To prejudge the crime is in itself a departure from the principles of our law. The mechanism has been set up to provide history with the truth. Let it function in due course.

Coupled with patience, there must be resolution on our part to accept the problems of the day, to keep moving toward the American horizon—

a better day for men everywhere. Let us be able to say today and tomorrow, "this man did not die in vain."

ADDRESS BY

Hon. B. F. Sisk

OF CALIFORNIA

Mr. Speaker, the people of the United States were stunned by the tragedy of November 22, 1963. Their shock and disbelief gave way only slowly to an outpouring of grief of a magnitude and universally shared depth and quality we shall not again witness in this generation. Perhaps the grief of many is deeper through their realization of the qualities of a man only upon his passing.

My personal sorrow is the greater because of my opportunity to know this fine man and to appreciate the courage and determination with which he served us. During the climax of his all too brief years he brought to the Presidency a direction, a purpose, and a leadership we desperately needed in these perilous times. History will recognize his qualities and pay tribute to John Fitzgerald Kennedy as one of our greatest Presidents, a leader sent to us in time of crisis. Sadly, he cannot now share in seeing his work carried forward to fulfillment, but we can see that it is carried forward. We can here determine that our country shall realize those ideals for which he fought and for which he gave his life. We can here determine that his wisdom, tolerance, and dedication to the highest ideals of our country shall not be in vain. We can see that the bitter, vacant place in the hearts of the people of America shall be slowly filled to overwhelming with a renewed faith, and confidence in America and a determination to carry our country to the destiny in which John Fitzgerald Kennedy had abiding faith.

Our grief is too heavy upon us to understand the inscrutable will which has taken him from us. My faith tells me that will intends we shall be brought closer to the realization of those profound and everlasting truths for which our Savior

also died. Out of sorrow, may we draw closer together, find love and confidence in each other to replace bitterness and hate. This shall be our witness to those who loved him, whose sorrow we deeply share, that John Fitzgerald Kennedy lives in the good works we shall carry forward.

ADDRESS BY

Hon. Don L. Short

OF NORTH DAKOTA

Mr. Speaker, I join with all Members of the House of Representatives today in expressing sorrow at the tragic assassination of our President. I say our President because John F. Kennedy was my President, regardless of the fact that I am a member of the opposite political party. This is a facet of our Government that is often overlooked by people not familiar with our American form of government. In the tradition of our freedom we compete strenuously through our political parties to elect those who will be the leaders of our Government. Once elected, however, these duly elected officials are the representatives of all the people not just of those who voted for them. Thus, John Kennedy was my President even though I was not one of those who supported him in his efforts to become President of the United States. I admired his courage and ability and even though I often disagreed with his proposals, he had my deep respect.

I feel a loss, as I am sure all true Americans feel a deep loss that this vigorous, articulate, aggressive young man was taken from us. When we ask why such a tragic event can happen, it is perhaps appropriate to reflect that a higher power makes these decisions and it is not for us to reason why. We can ask what influence prompts a demented human being to perform such a dastardly act. Is the assassin also one of God's children?

I am not endowed with an ability with words to add to what has already appropriately been said here today. My heart goes out particularly to Mrs. Jacqueline Kennedy and the two lovely children who have lost a husband and a father. A new President has taken over the responsibilities of guiding our Government and this great country will go on. The father and husband cannot be replaced.

On behalf of the people of North Dakota, whom I have the honor to represent, and my wife and I, I want to express deepest sympathy to the members of the entire Kennedy family in this hour of their great loss. John Kennedy is gone from among them, but the pride in this distinguished member of their family will live on.

ADDRESS BY

Hon. John W. Byrnes

OF WISCONSIN

Mr. Speaker, I join my colleagues in paying tribute to the memory of John Fitzgerald Kennedy.

The assassination of President Kennedy, a courageous and dedicated leader, will ever remain one of the great tragic episodes in American history.

As a Nation, we have had taken from us the youth and grace and charm he brought to the Nation's highest office. An indomitable spirit and the sheer joy of living shone through his every word and act. His warmth and gentle sense of humor will be sorely missed in a land where these qualities are often underestimated.

Those of us who so often found ourselves engaged in battle with President Kennedy have been deprived of a worthy opponent who never failed to command our deepest respect. He loved the hard and bitter give-and-take of political life, and he transmitted this zest to friend and foe alike. He recognized, more than others, the need of his office and the country it served for debate and criticism and he never allowed disagreement over policy or issues to turn into petty personal animosity.

The tragedy of John Kennedy, and our tragedy, is that this man of so many virtues and such outstanding ability should be struck down so early in a career which held the promise of greatness.

We mourn his passing. Our hearts go out to his brave widow and children and to his family in their hour of sorrow and bereavement.

ADDRESS BY

Hon. Edward J. Gurney

OF FLORIDA

Mr. Speaker, the finest tribute to the late President Kennedy which I have run across were two editorials appearing in newspapers in my district, the Orlando Sentinel and the Titusville Star-Advocate.

These express far better than I can, what the people of my district feel about the tragic assassination of President John F. Kennedy. I feel it fitting therefore to insert these editorials:

[From the Titusville (Fla.) Star-Advocate, Nov. 25, 1963]

WITH A FULL HEART

The name of John Fitzgerald Kennedy, 35th President of the United States of America, has indeed been inscribed in the "scroll of the immortals."

As he is laid to rest today in Arlington National Cemetery, with full military honors, countless millions of people, from all walks of life the world over, feel a sense of grief and personal loss in the tragic death of this ambassador of world peace and understanding among nations.

That the life of our young Chief Executive should be snuffed out by an assassin sniper's bullet in Dallas, Tex., last Friday—here in the freest land on earth—the most highly civilized country in the world—in the culmination of a campaign of hate, the very hate which John F. Kennedy abhorred and worked so tirelessly to eradicate—surely has an unknown significance in this dark hour of grief.

Mr. Kennedy was a deeply religious and dedicated man, with tremendous enthusiasm and a dynamic personality, and in his short 34 months as President, exerted his untiring efforts for peace and understanding and abhorred the hate prevailing among peoples of different races and faiths, not only here in America, but throughout the world. He had, thusly, become an international symbol of good will.

We differed with the late President on many issues, but this in no wise lessened our respect for him and the high office which he held with dignity. He was truly a gentleman and a scholar as well as an able leader.

The record of John Fitzgerald Kennedy stands upon its merits—he served his country well in the time of World War II as commander of PT-109; he served for 14 years in the Congress of his country; and upon becoming our

35th President, gave his life for his country in the cause of peace and understanding in the year of our Lord 1963.

His life was truly patterned on the "last mile principle." May he not have died in vain.

———

[From the Orlando (Fla.) Sentinel, Nov. 23, 1963]

PRESIDENT JOHN F. KENNEDY

Every American in every walk of life feels a deep sense of loss today.

The death of the President touches each one of us, regardless of race, creed, religion, or political party.

We did not always agree with the President, but we never doubted his honesty, his sincerity and his devotion to his country—all the way from PT–109 to the White House.

He almost died during World War II for the country he loved.

And yesterday he did.

The way Mr. Kennedy died profoundly shocked all Americans. Men wept unashamedly at this wanton murder of a young President, a loving father and a devoted husband.

Mrs. Kennedy's lost cry of despair echoed in every heart throughout the land.

Justice must be swift for the assassins of President John Fitzgerald Kennedy.

The presence in this country of men with minds like that is a more dangerous threat to the preservation of freedom than is the Soviet Union with all of its atom bombs and missiles.

Young Mr. Kennedy tried mightily in the biggest job in the world.

He wanted to be President and he worked hard at it. That the measures he thought would benefit the human race were not more widely accepted by Congress was not his fault, for he labored at being President, and at bringing his job closer to the people, as hard as anyone before him has done.

He liked people. All of his person-to-person visits, his handshaking with huge crowds, his motorcades and many trips were not entirely political.

He believed if he took the issues and his warm personality to the citizens that they would understand and join him.

And they did. Few people who ever met the President failed to like him. Even at a distance his magnetic personality captured friends for him to the confusion and irritation of Mr. Kennedy's political opponents.

The Nation now has a new President, Mr. Lyndon B. Johnson, and the Nation wishes him well.

Mr. Johnson was not always a John F. Kennedy supporter, but he too was captured by the deep genuine warmth of J.F.K. and became, in the campaign days of 1960 and since, one of his most devoted admirers.

No man, it is said, is indispensable. The Nation will go on, and go forward as it has for 200 years.

But for many of those years ahead the people will remember the young President cut down in the prime of life by a madman's bullet. And none of us will ever understand the burst of hatred in which it was fired.

ADDRESS BY

Hon. Paul G. Rogers
OF FLORIDA

Mr. Speaker, the entire Nation and the world mourns the passing of our late President, John Fitzgerald Kennedy, as do the people of Florida and our own Sixth Congressional District, where we considered the President and his family as neighbors and friends.

The winter White House at Palm Beach was familiar to all and Palm Beach had witnessed not only the comings and goings of the President but his growth and development from childhood, as a teenager, college student, war hero, Congressman, Senator, and President up until the weekend prior to his tragic death. For this reason we will remember John F. Kennedy the man as well as the President.

Few men in our history have brought such a feeling of warmth and friendship as did John F. Kennedy. Representing the young, vigorous man overcoming wartime danger and personal illness by determination and strong will to reach the highest office of this Nation, he was an example to the world of what we hoped was the best in all Americans. He was able to face life and his personal and official responsibilities with strength and at the same time show tenderness and love for all, especially young people.

Many will remember most clearly the last few public appearances and photographs of him with his family as a mirror of the man. By his Veterans Day visit to Arlington he paid honor to our war dead and at the same time demonstrated a father's pride in the child who will have to defend our freedoms in the future, as did the father and honored war dead in the past. That the young son learned well from this experience was demonstrated to all by his salute to his father just 2 short weeks later.

A few days later, new photographs showing father and daughter and son again delighted us. The Presidency has been said to be the loneliest job in the world, and yet we could see the satisfaction given to him by his children at these moments.

On the very day of his death he showed his great devotion to his wife by his comments to the crowds outside the hotel and at the breakfast meeting, and as they drove together through the streets of Dallas.

The people of Palm Beach and all Florida will remember, as will those of Washington, Hyannis, and Middleburg, a young father and his family attending church together on a Sunday morning, looking very much like any other American family with the deep religious heritage of our Nation's forefathers.

We will remember the smile, the quick wit, the firm handshake, the steady gaze from bright, alert eyes and the personal interest taken by this man in our problems.

A group of schoolchildren will remember the time taken by their President for participation in a "People-to-People" film, after he had learned of it during a weekend visit to Palm Beach. The request had been, as so many must be, routinely regretted by a staff member.

On this personal level, and through the success of the Peace Corps, John F. Kennedy will be remembered for his abiding faith in the young people of this Nation and the world. They returned this respect by the open outpouring of emotion at his passing. Perhaps the most memorable fact about the million people lining the streets of Washington on the route to Arlington was the number of young people who had come from near and far to pay their respects to the man who had given them example and a high standard by which to live.

Millions of words have been said, when we know in our hearts words cannot express our feelings. To that which has been said we can only pray, "May he rest in peace," and to his family, "God be with you." This has already manifested itself in the courage and strength which we have all witnessed and which will be an inspiration for years to come.

ADDRESS BY

Hon. Donald M. Fraser

OF MINNESOTA

Mr. Speaker, the pulsing beat of muffled drums has passed—bittersweet notes of "Taps" have faded on the wind—the clattering caisson has borne its lifeless burden to its last resting place on a quiet slope looking across the Potomac.

Our late, our honored President, John Fitzgerald Kennedy, rests in peace there now—where his mortal shell will stay until new bugles call every man to that final judgment day.

Now our television sets stand mute as we seek to blot out the horrors of these last days, when one foul deed piled on another, stunning the Nation and the world. The drama of the assassination of the leader of the free world still holds a nightmare grip. Did it really happen here?

We still half expect to see that shock of hair, that gleaming smile, to hear that cultured voice plead with us to help get the Nation moving again. How can it be that this our leader is gone—with his grand plans unfinished, his dreams on drawing boards, his legislative program snarled in congressional morass?

How unfathomable are the ways of the Lord, who has chosen to take from us His gifted son, John Fitzgerald Kennedy, at the crest of his career? But who are we to question the hand of God? Indeed, had not this man drunk fully a cup of life that overflowed with draughts enough for many men?

Uncommon was his rearing; in a home of wealth and luxury he was taught discipline, manly piety, a competitive spirit, a love for learning and a fierce pride in his Irish forebears. His schooling was the finest money can buy. Gifted with a fertile mind and pen, he was achieving success in literature when the heroic death of his eldest brother handed him the mantle of a family tradition of political success.

In the swift years that followed he became a wartime hero in his own right, a canny political campaigner, a Member of the U.S. Senate, a Pulitzer Prize-winning author, the head of a most charming family, and, shattering the political prejudices of a bygone day, the first President of the United States to be a member of the Catholic faith.

Then, as the leader of the mightiest temporal power on earth, he moved the Nation forward, striving for new frontiers of justice, charity and love for all mankind. Even as he held the world's greatest nuclear striking power in his hand, he captured the imagination of the Nation and the respect of friend and foe around the planet.

In less than 3 years as President he stamped his forceful personality on the tablets of history. He launched the Alliance for Progress to help our Latin American neighbors help themselves. He stayed the military arm from committing the might of the United States to intervention in Cuba during the bloody Bay of Pigs debacle. Then, buckling on the Nation's breastplate and nuclear armor, he confronted the Russian terror, slavemaster of half the world, and forced withdrawal of its rocket threat from the Western Hemisphere.

Picking up where another assassinated President left off one century before, he proclaimed a new emancipation seeking equal justice under law for our Negro brothers. He forged an international bond of friendship and mutual assistance in the Peace Corps, where dedicated Americans of all ages ask only what they can do for their country—and their fellow man.

As if all these things were not enough, John Fitzgerald Kennedy demonstrated, for all the world to see, a model family life. His wife, Jacqueline, fulfilled her goal of providing a happy home life for her husband and family. She and her husband brought charm, warmth, music, culture and gaiety to the first home of the land. He was a devoted husband and a loving father, and he practiced his religion without fear or public show.

Are not these deeds more than enough for any single life—however short? We submit they are. Despite our tears for the bereft little family—its head, husband and father gone—we can resume our daily tasks firm in the knowledge that this young man for the ages has built an image of vigor, courage, intellect and compassion, which men always and everywhere may admire and seek to emulate.

Let us accept as our own the standard he laid down for his brief but meteoric career as President of the United States:

With a good conscience our only sure reward, with history the final judge of our deeds, let us go forth to lead the land we love, asking His blessing and His help, but knowing that here on earth God's work must truly be our own.

Truly, we have been blessed because of the days John Fitzgerald Kennedy served his Nation and the world. Let us claim his fallen torch and keep the flame alive.

Mr. Speaker, these words came from the pen of Bernard Casserly, editor of the Catholic Bulletin for the St. Paul archdiocese. I could not add to their eloquence.

Mr. Speaker, we have lost a great leader. John F. Kennedy loved his country; and his countrymen loved him. He was a man of compassion and of determination. He brought to us his conviction that our Nation could fulfill its destiny as the leader of free men.

He was of a new generation, which has seen the tragedy of two world wars and the futility of efforts to prevent those wars. His understanding of history led him to search boldly for new paths to peace with honor. He knew that the people of this Nation want peace, and he worked with imagination and determination to secure it.

He understood the dynamics of our Nation's economy and he acted to keep it serving the welfare of the people. The jobless, the sick, the elderly—all those for whom our Nation has not yet fulfilled its promise—these are the people whom he sought to aid.

He spoke with conviction about the need to banish hate and bigotry and acted to translate the American ideal of equality into a living reality.

Above all else, he brought a new spirit to our Nation. He enlarged our horizons, and taught us that we can, when we will, find within this Nation a greater fulfillment of our own lives.

Let us then rededicate ourselves to the goals for which he worked—peace with honor, the elimination of hate and bigotry, and an abundant life for all. His sacrifice shall not have been in vain.

ADDRESS BY

Hon. Joe Pool

OF TEXAS

Mr. Speaker, the effort to find language for our mute agony has brought many Americans nearer to the lucid prose which was one of the distinguishing marks of the late President himself. I will not try to find words of my own. Instead, I would like to claim as mine, too, the words of a new citizen of the United States, Mrs. Lottie Adams, of Electra, Tex., who wrote me this letter to tell me what she felt. I think it is a lovely expression of the thoughts of many of us, and I want to share them with you.

DEAR MR. POOL: Just 2 weeks ago I received your congratulations as a new citizen of this beautiful free land, but only today I sealed my oath, sharing the pain of the millions of freedom-loving people all over the world, over the tragic death of our beloved President Kennedy.

The tremendous loss I feel is not only for our President, but also for the husband and father of such a wonderful family, as Jacqueline and her two children. I also am a widow with two children: a boy, 3 and a girl, 6. I lost my husband in a car accident in July 1961; he also died practically in my arms. So you see why I identify my sorrow with that of Mrs. Kennedy. I live through all the anguish all over again.

I sent my warmest wishes of sympathy to the Kennedy family. At the same time I wish to congratulate our new President, President Johnson. We all know what a hard job fell on his shoulders but we all have confidence in him for as long as we the citizens of this glorious country have a right to vote, there shall be a striving for a free world, for we all, millions of us owe it to the memory of a courageous brave American, our beloved President Kennedy who died for this goal.

May God lead us and guide us always.

Sincerely,

MRS. LOTTIE ADAMS
(A new citizen of the U.S.A.).

ADDRESS BY

Hon. James G. Fulton

OF PENNSYLVANIA

Mr. Speaker, John Fitzgerald Kennedy was a fine President with his principles and far vision. We in Congress greatly admired his high integrity, his strong convictions and his dedication to the overwhelming responsibilities of the Presidency.

Under President Kennedy's leadership, many advances were made for America. He achieved a higher standard of living for Americans, progress in international understanding, and safety and security for our good country and the people. President Kennedy worked hard to maintain historic landmarks for which he will long be remembered. His family life, his devotion to Mrs. Kennedy and his children, Caroline and John, are hearthstones and symbols of which all the people of our country can be proud. His wonderful

receptions at home and abroad, and even on the day of the terrible event is indeed a credit to the Kennedy family, the U.S. Government and the American people.

The respect of world leaders, which he had quickly won, was great evidence of his power, intellect and ability to negotiate and reach reasonable compromises between nations, peoples and all mankind. President Kennedy had strong devotions to all Americans, loyalty to our allies and successful administrative ability. One of the chief characteristics of President and Mrs. Kennedy is that they never forgot their old friends.

It has been a real privilege to have served in Congress with President Kennedy, to have been part of the administration of the Federal Government under his leadership, and I will always remember his kindness, his personal interest and friendship with humility and pride.

My best wishes in this sad hour go out to all the Kennedys who have given one of the fine members of their family in the cause of American freedom and security.

Long may President Kennedy's high name, high principles and warm friendly personality be remembered by this generation and generations to come.

ADDRESS BY

Hon. John J. Flynt, Jr.

OF GEORGIA

Mr. Speaker, today we pay tribute to John Fitzgerald Kennedy, late President of the United States.

Shortly after noon on Friday, November 22, 1963, the world was stunned when word was received that the President had been shot. Half an hour later the announcement of his death brought a combined feeling of shock, disbelief, and grief. It seemed as if a giant pall had fallen over our land.

Looks of horror and utter disbelief took the place of normal expressions and smiles. Tears came to the eyes of old and young.

Each of us remembers the exact time and place he first heard the news. Some were driving in automobiles and slowly pulled over to the roadside and stopped. Many were at dining tables for the noon meal. Others were at work in accustomed places. Nearly all experienced the same shocked and stunned reaction.

Suspense gave way to sorrow and grief. The realization that the President was dead brought a numbness that defies description.

Gradually the shock was replaced by the realization that there must be a manifestation of composure and control lest our national grief turn to national panic.

My own thoughts recalled the words of James Abram Garfield who, in announcing the death of President Lincoln, said, "God lives, and the Government in Washington still stands."

There must be and there would be orderly transition and the reaffirmation of the strength and stability of our Government.

Our Nation has suffered a grievous loss of its Chief Executive, cut down in the very bloom of his life by an assassin's bullets. I have suffered the loss of a personal friend. I remember many exchanges of evidence of friendship between us. I vividly recall exchanges of pleasantries in which his tremendous good humor and wit were scintillating. I also recall very serious discussions during which we either agreed or strove earnestly to resolve any differences.

He gave to America and to Americans a new kind of leadership. It was the dynamic and courageous leadership of a dedicated young man, mature beyond his years. He gave of himself and he gave to his country. He brought into the Office of the Presidency a brilliant intellect, a boundless enthusiasm, and a tremendous capacity for growth.

Endowed with a keen mind, sharpened by a fine education, matured by wartime service in our Nation's Armed Forces, seasoned by the experience of 6 years in the House of Representatives and 8 years in the U.S. Senate, at 43, he became the 35th President of the United States.

On a cold January day in 1961, he took the oath of office and delivered an inaugural address which became indelibly impressed on the minds and hearts of men. In it he said, "Now the trumpet summons us again."

On the tragic moment of that Friday afternoon in November 1963, the trumpet once more summoned John Fitzgerald Kennedy. This time to eternal rest.

It cannot be that he died in vain. Out of the period of mourning—personal and worldwide—which follows his death there must surely come a solemn rededication to those principles which underlie our system of government. With this rededication may there come a growth from strength to greater strength.

ADDRESS BY

Hon. Clark W. Thompson

OF TEXAS

Mr. Speaker, I have read and heard some of the very finest tributes ever paid to mortal man inspired by the assassination of John F. Kennedy.

Suddenly we have come to realize that in addition to the man we knew first as a colleague in the House, then as a Senator, and finally as our President, was one of the truly great men of all time. No one in history has made such an impact on the world and the loss which we have sustained at home and abroad can only be compensated for if we carry on as best we can the efforts in behalf of humanity on which he so ably launched us.

With all of the greatness which we are realizing and recognizing more and more with each passing day, my mind keeps returning to some of the intensely personal little things which he did for people. The warmth of his personality was evident whenever one was fortunate enough to be near him. It was the sort of warmth that can only come from the heart. It had to be genuine or it could not have impressed us as it did.

I keep recalling our last conversation shortly before his Texas trip. A comparatively minor decision with reference to the rice industry had been referred to him for final action. Somehow he knew that it was of tremendous interest to me and my people in Texas. He took the trouble to phone me personally to tell me that our request had been granted. He had done the same thing some 2 years earlier when a similar decision was in the making and he called me at my home in Texas, to personally give me the news. Just a few weeks ago, in the early morning hours, his naval aide called me at home and said the President wanted me to know that within an hour or two he would announce the appointment of Lt. Gen. Wallace M. Greene as new Commandant of the Marine Corps. He thought it might be nice for me, an old marine, to have the word a little ahead of the public announcement. Somehow he knew that Wally Greene and I had served together years ago and that I held him in very high regard.

To some, these little personal touches may seem unimportant. To me, they tell a story of a basic attribute of one of the greatest men we will ever know.

Now just one parting thought. A military commander when he takes over a new assignment is taught to immediately choose and thoroughly train his second in command. This understudy must be prepared to step immediately into the commanding officer's shoes in the event of an emergency. One of the greatest services that the President ever did for his country was to thoroughly inform his Vice President of all of the responsibilities that might conceivably fall on his shoulders. Certainly President Kennedy never dreamed of the tragedy that lay ahead of him but the fact that he took no chances and that he used his Vice President and informed him just as a military commander would have informed his next-in-line enabled our new President to move forward without the loss of a single stride.

The spirit of this great man will live in our hearts always and our lives will be enriched because we knew him.

ADDRESS BY

Hon. Joe M. Kilgore

OF TEXAS

Mr. Speaker, history will write the verdict on the presidential administration of John Fitzgerald Kennedy—on the actions he took, the policies he followed, the programs he proposed. But we have no need to wait for the verdict of the historians to know that the late President was a man deeply beloved by his fellow Americans,

and by those men all over the world who cherish freedom.

His personal popularity as a living man was repeatedly evidenced. His hold on the heartstrings of Americans in every walk of life has been demonstrated during the days since his tragic death. Millions of people have expressed their deep sorrow and their compassion by attending memorial services that have been held not only in the great centers of population but in the small towns and villages of America and in country church houses.

Yes, and from all over the world, heads of state came to express officially their great personal respect as their people poured out their own feelings in ceremonies and services in the four corners of the world.

This is as it should be. The late President was a man who liked to be among people and who drew strength from them. No one can doubt that who ever saw him going out to the people of the country either as a candidate or as President.

Thus, Mr. Speaker, Americans now are mourning not only for a President but for a man as well—a human being of courage, a man who possessed the charm and outgoingness that drew people to him, including those people who differed with his political philosophy.

This outpouring of grief speaks more than words of the warmth, the courage, the faith and of the concern for his fellow man possessed by John Fitzgerald Kennedy.

Removed now from the concerns and troubles of this world, may his soul rest in peace. And may this Nation wrest from the tragic sacrifice of this young man's life a new resolve to hold firm to the course laid down by the Founding Fathers.

ADDRESS BY

Hon. Thor C. Tollefson

OF WASHINGTON

Mr. Speaker, all America mourns the loss of its President, a good man and a strong leader, John F. Kennedy. The profound sympathy of the

Nation goes out to his courageous widow and children. The President's life was snuffed out by an assassin's bullet in the prime of his life. God alone really knows why such a tragedy should happen in a nation like ours. We do know, however, that the Nation must go forward—there is work to be done—our Republic must survive. Let all of us seek the guidance of the Almighty in the critical days and years ahead.

A timely editorial appearing in a recent issue of the Bremerton Sun, a newspaper published in my congressional district, calls our attention to the fact that we have a task at hand. I include it with my remarks.

THE TASK AT HAND

The long, agonizing weekend is over.

The people of America, stunned and silenced by the slaying of our President, resumed today the business of the living.

A new President tackles in earnest the official business of state and picks up the pace of America, slowed by the tragic events of the last few days.

The funeral procession has completed its awful task and the church bells are stilled again.

It is time now to look ahead with the memory of the destruction of hate still fresh in our minds.

Some good has surely come from all this.

Americans, drawn together in their common sorrow, may stay together in their common prayer that what has happened may shock all Americans into the realization that our way of life is too precious to sacrifice on the altar of bigotry and hate.

The shocking example of revenge exacted by a Dallas innkeeper in what he incorrectly presumed to be an act of glory should startle all of us into a rededication of our determination to have justice by law and not by emotion.

The agonizing ordeal suffered so bravely by the widow of the President is an inspiration for all Americans.

The sight of the new President, his head bowed in grief and his shoulders carrying the burden of his new responsibilities, should recharge us all with loyalty and unity.

The recollection of the Kennedy children, still too young to fully comprehend the meaning of what they saw, reacting with typical childlike indifference, exemplifies for all of us the cherished unit of American life that is the hope of the future.

Above all, the horrifying events of the last few days will, we hope, shock Americans out of their smug complacency and bring home with brutal impact the sure knowledge that to ignore our greatness is to lose it; to foster hate and greed and bigotry is to give life to the forces of destruction; to sneer at our principles of justice under the law for all Americans is to play into the hands of our enemies.

It is time for each of us to get to work at the job of keeping this Republic safe.

ADDRESS BY

Hon. F. Edward Hébert

OF LOUISIANA

Mr. Speaker, the greatest and most sincere tribute that I can pay to the memory of the late President Kennedy is to stand here today with a heavy heart of sorrow and a silent prayer for the salvation of his immortal soul.

Like those martyred Presidents who have gone before him, he now belongs to the ages, and no words of mortal man can bring him back.

What more can I say than has been said here today by those who knew him, admired him, respected him, and loved him.

How hollow and meaningless would feeble words falling from my lips be compared to those strong words spoken here today.

How can I adequately say something that will ease the pain of the wife he loved and who loved him?

What can I say that will make those bereaved children understand the magnitude of the tragedy that cloaks their little bodies?

No, nothing can be done to return life to his lifeless body, but those who now live can use the life which remains in them to pray to God for his eternal rest and to God for the comfort of the family, so dear to him, which he left behind.

This we can do and must do in this our moment of national grief.

ADDRESS BY

Hon. Ralph F. Beermann

OF NEBRASKA

Mr. Speaker, it was with a profound sense of shock that my fellow Nebraskans and I heard of the tragic assassination of President Kennedy. An atmosphere of utter disbelief fell over us all. It just did not seem possible that this young and dynamic individual had been taken from our midst. His personal magnetism had caused millions to identify themselves with his every deed and made his passing a personal as well as a national tragedy. Although historians will have to evaluate John Fitzgerald Kennedy's contributions to mankind, his contemporaries will not soon forget his driving force.

I wish to extend to Mrs. Jacqueline Bouvier Kennedy and her children our deepest sympathy. Further, I wish to say to them that we Nebraskans share their sorrow.

ADDRESS BY

Hon. Robert P. Griffin

OF MICHIGAN

Mr. Speaker, I know I speak for all the people of Michigan's Ninth Congressional District as I add my voice to the tribute being paid here today to a beloved President.

John F. Kennedy was as warm and friendly as he was courageous. All who knew him, whether they agreed or disagreed with his programs, were bound to admire and respect him.

Mr. Speaker, at a time like this, it is natural for each of us to look back upon his personal relationships with John Kennedy. As a House Member of the opposite political party, I had the privilege to become closely associated with John Kennedy when he served in 1959 as chairman of the 14-man Senate-House conference on labor reform legislation. It will be recalled that the legislation before that conference was controversial, to say the very least.

Serving as chairman of that particular conference was not an easy task, and the meetings went on and on over a 12-day period. He did an excellent job in presiding over the conference and working to bring divergent points of view toward a consensus. During that period, a friendship developed between John Kennedy and me—a friendship which followed him into the White House and continued until his life was so abruptly ended by the dastardly act of an assassin.

Mr. Speaker, those of us in the Congress have lost a good friend. The Nation has lost a vigorous leader.

To Mrs. Kennedy and to the family of our late President, I extend the deepest sympathy of everyone in the district I am honored to represent.

ADDRESS BY

Hon. John J. McFall

OF CALIFORNIA

Mr. Speaker, God gave us John F. Kennedy to be our President for 2 years, 10 months, and 2 days.

Now on a hill overlooking the Lincoln Memorial an eternal flame flickers over his grave in Arlington Cemetery.

In the darkness, from the Memorial dedicated to the ideals of freedom and justice for which Lincoln also gave his life nearly a century ago, is visible the tiny beacon of John Kennedy's grave.

It will be an eternal reminder to free people all over the world that the struggle to make those ideals a reality is a continuing one.

In the brief span of his Presidency, he revitalized our country, charted new and far-reaching goals and gave us peace based upon dignity and strength.

During these hours of self-examination and rededication to the ideals that John Kennedy espoused, our consolation must come in the form of thanks for having him with us as long as we did. We can find comfort in the knowledge that although he was on earth only a brief period, he led a complete life.

His own words in his book about his brother Joe are an appropriate epitaph for the President himself:

> It is the realization that the future held the promise of great accomplishments for Joe that has made his death so particularly hard for those who knew him. His worldly success was so assured and inevitable that his death seems to have cut into the natural order of things. But at the same time, there is a completeness to Joe's life, and that is the completeness of perfection. His life as he lived * * * could hardly have been improved upon.

As a sorrowful Congress turns its attention again to the ordinary business of government—and it must—we are solaced by the legacy of thoughts and actions he left us as an articulate Chief of State.

We can best serve his memory by striving to accomplish his objectives for the peace of the world and the future of mankind.

ADDRESS BY

Hon. William C. Cramer

OF FLORIDA

Mr. Speaker, on November 22, 1963, two shots heard around the world snuffed out the life of a young and vigorous President.

Although I disagreed with many of his policies, it is with sincere candor that I can say my respect for the man himself never diminished; for Mr. Kennedy was a skillful practitioner of the noble political profession and a standout American whose love for the give-and-take of politics made him a challenging competitor in the great two-party system that is ours.

During the days following the President's assassination, the Communist press was reported as saying that the people who opposed Mr. Kennedy's policies "are now hypocritically praising him." How strange it is to us that the Communists do not understand that Democrats and Republicans are Americans first. And how strange it must seem to the Communists that it was Mr. Kennedy who, as a leader of men, exemplified this ideal—this give-and-take of ideas that were distilled into programs contributing to America's ever-increasing greatness.

It will be history that decides Mr. Kennedy's record as President. But there is not one of us here today that cannot truthfully say here and now that John Fitzgerald Kennedy, while serving as our First American, was an American first, that he served with great distinction, with love of country, and without fear in the best traditions of the practice of the art of statecraft.

I know of no higher tribute.

ADDRESS BY

Hon. Arch A. Moore, Jr.

OF WEST VIRGINIA

Mr. Speaker, as our Nation continues its mourning for our late President, I would like to express the particular grief which the people of West Virginia feel for our fallen leader. It was in West Virginia that John F. Kennedy sur-

mounted some of his greatest obstacles to the Presidency of the United States. No one can ever forget the memory of this courageous young man who captured the hearts of so many West Virginians in his brilliant quest for the presidential nomination and then the Presidency itself. In turn, we can always take great pride in the undoubted affection he had for us.

Now he is gone—taken from us by one of the most villainous acts in American history—but his memory will be with us forever. Here was a man who carried on the noble traditions of his predecessors in office—a man who was suddenly taken from us in the prime of life. No matter what our political persuasion may be, all Americans feel a deep personal loss in President Kennedy's untimely death. Amazing in all of this was the strength our country received from the truly majestic bearing of Mrs. John F. Kennedy. Surely history will record that in one of our Nation's most tragic hours, she made it one of our finest hours.

Finally, we can all take strength in the knowledge that our Republic remains strong, our Government remains stable and our people remain confident in the face of a great national tragedy.

ADDRESS BY

Hon. August E. Johansen

OF MICHIGAN

Mr. Speaker, it was only a week before the tragic event that I wrote in a newsletter, referring specifically to Members of Congress: "We are all mortal—physically and politically."

No one could have then imagined that a scant 7 days later this common mortality of all men would be so terribly dramatized in the person of the President of the United States, under circumstances thus tragic, senseless, and wicked.

"We shall pay any price," President Kennedy had said in his inaugural address. The words he then spoke for the Nation speak now for him. He himself has paid the supreme price—the price which is always a hazard of the Presidency—the price paid thrice before by Presidents of the United States.

I was privileged to sit as a member of the official

delegation named to represent the House of Representatives at the funeral of President John F. Kennedy.

It was an awesome gathering. Three Presidents of the United States were there. Assembled were the great of the earth as man reckons greatness—potentates and presidents and princes and ministers of state.

Death was there—and grief.

And the most awesome presence of all—faith.

Faith in the institutions of our Government which survive unscathed the blow of violence—and faith, as well, in the immortality which conquers even death.

Symbol and substance of constitutional continuity is President Lyndon B. Johnson.

In his stewardship as Chief Executive he is charged—by the oath he took so unexpectedly—"to preserve, protect, and defend the Constitution of the United States."

To the best of his ability. So help him God.

He assumes that awesome responsibility and task with the sincere good will and earnest prayers of his countrymen.

ADDRESS BY

Hon. John M. Murphy

OF NEW YORK

Mr. Speaker, John Fitzgerald Kennedy on November 22 possessed everything a man could gain from this mortal life. He held the highest position afforded any man. He had a beautiful wife, two small children, wealth, power, brilliance, personality, and charm. In his body was a zest for living, a reason for existence, and work to be done. The cheering crowds which he so dearly loved, the smiles on the people's faces on which so much admiration was written were the last crowds and smiles he would see.

In the darkness of ignorance, prejudice, one man sat among the books of learning, of democracy, squinting in the radiance of the sun. He aimed a cheap rifle with a cheap bullet in its chamber. He touched his finger on the trigger and in one second in endless time, snuffed out the light of brilliance. President John F. Kennedy was dead. John Kennedy lost all that the world could offer—but we too have lost.

John Kennedy left much behind. In his short time of leadership in the New Frontier, he forged through the virgin woods of hate, ignorance, strife, and poverty. He felled trees, cleared the land, plowed and planted seeds—seeds of progress, of brotherhood, of peace. The task now rests upon all Americans to continue to nourish these seeds and reap from the foresight brilliance, and greatness of President Kennedy. Let us nourish seeds of newness and of courage.

The pioneer of the New Frontier was the light of the bonded, the liberator of the chained and imprisoned, the hope of the diseased world, the inspiration of the free world, the friend of the friendless, the hope of the hopeless, and the courage of the weakened.

From the many letters I have received from our fellow Americans, I want to quote from just a few. A grammar school girl:

> I could only cry.

A high school senior:

> The world will long remember President Kennedy, our Nation will always revere him. It is a shame that it required his death for many people to wake up and realize his great achievements, something you and I knew from the beginning of his years in the White House. His desire for peace, yet without surrender; his desire for a better educated people; his work for civil rights; the prosperity of the economy, point toward one thing, as did his death, and that is his love of the United States and the betterment of it. I myself hold the opinion that no President since Abraham Lincoln worked as fervently for the Nation than did John Fitzgerald Kennedy.

A new college graduate:

> I doubt that any man has had a more powerful impact on the emotions of so many. In life he was respected as well as questioned. In death, he has been elevated to an almost "God-like" quality. His demise has rekindled in the hearts of all Americans our real purpose—peace through justice.

And a combat Army colonel:

> We in the Army have lost a great Commander in Chief—one who answered every challenge of the past 3 years in a true professional manner. History will prove John Fitzgerald Kennedy as worthy of a position aside Washington and Lincoln.

And now the eternal flame burns brightly at Arlington National Cemetery where our beloved President rests. His memory shall burn brightly in each of us. His ideals have been etched in the hearts and minds of all people. Let us now proceed through the darkness using the torch of John F. Kennedy to light our torches. Let us not be content until all Americans hold the light of hope in their hands for the world to see—until the world is freed from the chains of human bondage. In his Inaugural Address, President Kennedy said, "Let us begin"—we have begun and the road of our journey is infinite—let us continue—continue on the path he chose. Let us have the courage for correction, the desire for decision, and in his memory, move on to new frontiers.

ADDRESS BY

Hon. John Kyl

OF IOWA

Mr. Speaker, last week my home community, like almost every single community across the Nation, held memorial services for President John F. Kennedy. The several churches participating presented a service which provided a deep and meaningful experience. My own brief, inadequate address delivered during that service follows:

Abraham Lincoln said it—in the month of November, exactly 100 years ago—the words are as fresh, as true on this day, as they were a century ago. "It is for us the living to be dedicated here to the unfinished work. * * * It is for us to be dedicated to the great task remaining before us."

Sadness has walked the land. Our shock has been so great we are almost ashamed to seek solace, consideration, or comfort. We want to share the grief of the entire Nation.

In these past days, Americans have shared a variety of emotions. First, every American shares a common, personal loss engendered by the death of the man who was our President—our leader. As President, because of the nature of this Nation and the nature of the man, John Kennedy held a close personal relationship with the citizens. This is always true, not because all individual Americans view a particular President in the same light—but because we all view the holder of that high office

with respect, with honor, and with love. These feelings are far deeper than the adulation we pay to celebrities in other fields of endeavor because the President is ours—and we are his. He represents the people, deriving his powers from the consent of the governed. Of greater significance is the realization that for peoples of all the earth—the President's image is our image. We are identified in his identity. People of foreign nations see America—see us—in our President. Small wonder that Americans follow with interest what the President eats for breakfast—what the First Lady wears on a particular day. From the moment a newly elected President and his family step inside the White Georgian Mansion on 16th Street and Pennsylvania Avenue in your Nation's Capital, their personal, private life is lost. They live in public. They belong to the public. Every sniffle—every sneeze or headache becomes public business. The President becomes a personality without individuality. He becomes an almost indefinable something. His name could be anything, for he is Uncle Sam, who in reality is everybody.

According to recent reports Dwight Eisenhower noted the fact in this manner. Just after his inauguration, his secretary reported that Gen. Omar Bradley was on the phone. The President picked up the phone and said, "Hello Omar." And then, General Bradley, classmate at West Point, comrade in arms, beloved friend, answered, "Mr. President, this is Omar Bradley." Then, said Mr. Eisenhower, I realized the lonesomeness of the job. I was no longer Dwight D. Eisenhower, I was "Mr. President."

Harry Truman sometimes referred to the White House as the most lavish prison in the world, thus describing his separation from his former life.

Is it any wonder then, this sense of personal tragedy which has enveloped us all as our young President, John Kennedy, has been taken from us? Is it any wonder that we so deeply appreciate the personal courage and majesty of our First Lady, Mrs. Kennedy, who has borne tragedy with such dignity through the trying hours—who twice, in only a few months, has walked with death?

Too, our pride has been hurt. We say, "This sort of thing can't happen here." We must suppress those other emotions of hate, anger—the urge for revenge which surrounds the nature of our President's death. For if America is to be adversely judged by a lawlessness which prompted or permitted assassination of the President, the desire for, or the accomplishment of revenge compounds the essence of lawlessness.

The other emotional aspect of the moment is our apprehension, our fear, our wondering about the present and future welfare of our Nation. You need harbor no fear.

The greatness of the U.S. Government, the wisdom of those unbelievably understanding men who laid our foundations, have again been demonstrated. A free nation remains free because all men have an opportunity for greatness, for leadership and for service. This Nation, therefore, always has a reserve of leadership—trained, experienced, capable and devoted. President Lyndon Johnson knows America. He knows government. He has had opportunity to face both foreign and domestic problems, and to participate in decision-making. His perception is great.

Perhaps some of you would have preferred a different leader. Be not dismayed. I have a favorite musical composition which I like so much that I have several recorded versions. I listen to one and I say, "This is perfect." Then I listen to another with a different conductor and find things I like better—some things I like less well. Our American symphony will have a different conductor, and the performance will be harmonious.

On Wednesday, President Johnson will ask the Congress for cooperation and for understanding. This he will receive. It will be demonstrated for all the world that this Government is in business with strength, with leadership to do what is right for our people and for all the world's people.

We cannot compare the assassination of our President with those acts of violence which occur so often in other lands where governments are overthrown. Our Government cannot be overthrown by a single act or a series of violent acts. It will not be lost until the people sleep. Asleep we are not.

May I also note the renewed evidence that ours is a spiritual nation—a nation which automatically turns to God in time of need. Would that we could remember this need is constant and eternal—that in the words of the hymn, "I need Thee every hour." How weak is the flesh, how undying the spirit.

It is ironic that our tragedy has occurred in the week of a national holiday—a family holiday with religious overtones—the season of Thanksgiving. Perhaps it is fortunate that we will soon be entering the holy season when all our feelings will be submerged in that all-pervasive, indescribable spirit of Christmas—the season of peace on earth, good will to all men. For that is the season when our feet return to the ground so our thoughts might be more lofty.

Our President, John F. Kennedy, is gone. When he departed, he took something of us with him, and he left something of himself with each of us. Therefore, on this day, "Go not to ask for whom the bell tolls. It tolls for thee."

I join all American citizens in praying that Almighty God will attend the needs of this great Nation of free men and that we may be ever worthy of His grace.

ADDRESS BY

Hon. Harold D. Cooley

OF NORTH CAROLINA

Mr. Speaker, strange and mysterious are the vicissitudes of human life. Frail and precarious are our best holds upon human happiness. A few short days ago a young man lived and labored and loved. By his life he beautified the altars of freedom. Wherever he went, throughout the troubled world in which we live, he made a broad thoroughfare for friendship. Today he sleeps in the solemn silence of the grave. Yes, his soul sleeps in peace. Until the end of time men and women will cherish the memory of this illustrious man. We cannot beautify his character, nor can we dignify his life. We can only commune with his spirit. We shall always remember his genius, his labor, his wonderful achievements, and the beauty and simplicity of his life. His life was a blessing to the world in which he lived.

Having known our late beloved President for many years, and having enjoyed his friendship during the time he was our colleague here in Congress, I knew his true worth and I cherished his friendship. His record, though brief yet dynamic, was written on the hearts of men and women throughout the world. By the nobility of his soul and by the exalted purposes of his life he shall be remembered through countless ages. His contributions to the cause of peace were great and grand and all of those who love freedom owe him a debt of gratitude. He was a child of the universe and he believed that the world with all of its sham, drudgery and broken dreams was still a beautiful world. He never suffered fears born of fatigue and loneliness, but he always nurtured strength of spirit to shield him in misfortune, and with courage, vision and fortitude he stood forthright before the world as a champion of the cause of peace. By his life he made the world a better place in which to live and when his soul moved across the crystal sea into the great beyond the whole world grieved. Truly he was one of God's noblemen.

When I think of our fears and our tears, I am reminded of something I heard on the floor of this House many years ago:

They say that life is a highway; the milestones are its years, and here and there is a tollgate where we pay our way with tears. It's a high road and a rough road and it leads near and far. But it leads at last to the golden town where the golden houses are.

When I think of the great sorrow we all have suffered, and of the life and the death of our beloved statesman, the first citizen of the world, John Fitzgerald Kennedy, my favorite song comes back to me:

Oh, heart of mine, we should not worry so;
What we missed of calm we could not have, you know,
What we met of a stormy pain and sorrow's driving rain,
We can better meet again if it blow.

For we know not every morrow can be sad.
So forgetting all the sorrow we have had,
Let us fold away our fears and put by our foolish tears,
And through all the coming years just be glad.

Just be glad that we have known and loved and here labored with Jack Kennedy whose soul has entered upon a new career in the regions of immortality. The tomb cannot enclose the fine virtues nor retain the influences of our departed friend. The unseen spirit will escape from the portals of the tomb to bless and enrich the lives of those who knew him and felt the tolerance and the kindness of his heart. His character was a tower of strength and his heart was the core of his greatness.

To his lovely and lonely wife, may I express my sincere and heartfelt sympathy. I hope that the love and sympathy of his friends will soften the sorrow she is now suffering. May the Lord of Mercy bless and sustain her as she goes forth to face the world alone.

ADDRESS BY

Hon. Kenneth A. Roberts

OF ALABAMA

Mr. Speaker, on the night of January 19, 1961, Washington was visited by one of its heaviest snowstorms. Literally hundreds of cars were abandoned along the roads, streets, and boulevards in and around the Capital City.

No one would have dared to predict that the next day would see bright sunshine and clear skies. Clear and bright came Inaugural Day. It seemed to symbolize the beginning of a new era in American Government.

The new 43-year-old President, John F. Kennedy, did not disappoint the millions who witnessed the swearing in of a young vibrant new Chief Executive.

His inaugural address was brief but full of challenge for the people of our times. He recognized the period of crisis which all mankind was facing. He recognized the problems of poverty at home and mass misery abroad. He painted in clear strokes the danger of total destruction.

He asked that both sides "begin anew the quest for peace, before the dark powers of destruction unleashed by science engulf all humanity in planned or accidental self-destruction."

It was a speech that contained assurance for our friends and recognized the dangers from our enemies. He did not threaten our enemies nor did he give them any reason to believe that America was afraid.

He welcomed the opportunity to serve his countrymen and the world.

Especially did he, in a few words, call upon all Americans for their aid and support. These words will be repeated as long as America holds aloft the beacon light of freedom for all the world to see.

Looking back to this day and the events which are now a part of history, I think all of us know what President Kennedy meant when he said:

And so, my fellow Americans, ask not what your country can do for you; ask what you can do for your country.

It was my privilege to be associated with this leader of men in an effort to do something about the twin problems of mental retardation and mental health. His great interest in this subject led to the enactment of a bill which will, I hope, become a landmark of legislative action in a totally new effort which will return millions of Americans to their homes as a result of new techniques, new drugs and adequate personnel in the long-neglected field of mental health.

This legislation will bring hope to the hopeless and will enable millions of America's neglected children to have care and treatment for the first time in the history of this Nation.

It would be difficult to select or choose the monument by which President Kennedy will be remembered but I believe that he would have chosen this effort as one of his contributions nearest his heart.

I am grateful to have had a small part in this effort.

The entire Nation shares in the bereavement of the entire Kennedy family and, particularly, his beloved wife, who, through a most trying time conducted herself in a manner reflecting one intimately associated with greatness.

Hon. John H. Dent

Mr. Speaker, at a time when one wishes to convey a most sincere expression of loss one becomes painfully aware of the inadequacy of words with which to give voice to true feelings.

With millions of others around the world I grieve over the loss of our late President. Yet, this grief is tempered by the fact that our system is so organized as to prevent any gap in leadership. Therefore, my grief is occasioned even more by the loss of a great man, a kind man, a gracious man, a loving husband and father. For if our system provides for continuity of leadership, it cannot provide us with the characteristics and qualities which were uniquely those of John Fitzgerald Kennedy.

I grieve because a dastardly act has deprived us, and untold future generations, of the many contributions which John Kennedy was destined to make for the benefit of all mankind. Most assuredly would those contributions have been made. For we know now how completely this sensitive man had committed himself to the ideal of the brotherhood of man.

My heart is heavy with the realization that this courageous man should be the victim of so brutal and so cowardly an act. Those fanatical forces against which our late President stood so resolutely cannot claim other than a hollow and shameful and silent victory. Indeed, his death cannot and must not fail to have us band together to insure that his efforts shall not have been in vain. We must, by our reactions to the great loss we have suffered, give testimony to the fact that we are a people governed by the rule of law. While we permit and encourage diversity of opinion we can no longer by our inaction permit and encourage the growth of minds twisted by hate and bigotry and exploited by fanatical haters. Our task is clear. Let us be as resolute as was John Kennedy and let us heed the admonition of President Johnson to honor the late President's memory by acting now to remove from our national life all traces of hate and evil and violence.

Finally, as we meet at this time of grief, let us make known that we shall not forget John Fitzgerald Kennedy. Let us make known that while future historians will judge him with a detached objectivity, we, here in this Chamber, judging on the basis of personal knowledge of our former colleague can and do attest to his greatness.

Hon. John B. Anderson

Mr. Speaker, it is certainly with the utmost humility that I approach the task of offering a eulogy of our late President, John F. Kennedy. Literally millions of words have been written and spoken in both poetry and prose since the tragedy of his assassination. It is truly at a time like this that we remember the words of another President spoken almost a century ago:

> The world will little note, nor long remember what we say here, but it can never forget what they did here.

And a little later in that same immortal address Lincoln said:

> It is for us the living, rather, to be dedicated here to the unfinished work which they who fought here have thus far so nobly advanced.

Now that some of the shock and horror has begun to subside we must nevertheless seek to take up the task of making America a better place in which to live and the world a more peaceful planet on which men may dwell without the constant dread of atomic annihilation.

John F. Kennedy was taken from the American people and his high office by the bullets of an assassin, a self-confessed Marxist and Communist who was consumed with passion and hatred for a fellow human being. This is truly the tragedy of our age—that in a world which has enjoyed such unparalleled scientific and technological progress in recent decades—the ungovernable rages of men are still capable of causing acts of barbarism and violence of the most primitive nature. Can there be any doubt in anyone's mind that there are truly monumental tasks yet undone.

John F. Kennedy brought intelligence, vigor, and great personal charm to the office of the Presidency. He was extremely talented in the art and science of Government, and even those of us who differed with him on specific political issues sensed that he respected and admired an honorable opponent. Even as he believed that diversity of thought and opinion must be allowed to flourish in the world outside the United States, even so I know he believed in our two-party system and in the role of a loyal opposition.

Mr. Speaker, I truly believe that our American heritage will be richer because John F. Kennedy lived. It is not merely respect for the high office which he held, but also respect for the man that prompts me to express my personal grief at his premature passing. My wife joins me in expressing to Mrs. Kennedy, the two Kennedy children, and other members of the Kennedy family both our heartfelt sympathy and the assurance of our prayers for the future.

ADDRESS BY

Hon. James G. O'Hara

OF MICHIGAN

Mr. Speaker, millions of eloquent words have been written and spoken about our late and beloved President, his death and his impact upon America, its citizens and freedom-loving men everywhere. It is difficult to say anything which has not been said before—and said much better. Words come hard at a time like this and they never seem quite adequate to the task.

I knew John Fitzgerald Kennedy, although we were not close personal friends. Our acquaintanceship was not of long enough duration to establish such bonds. But I knew him well enough to like him as a person, trust him as a leader, and admire him as a President.

The sudden and violent death of President Kennedy has taken from the American people a great leader, from the free world one of its leading statesmen, and from his wife and children a devoted husband and father.

His death struck deep into American life. It was a stunning blow to the heart and mind of a great nation. The tremendous outpouring of grief is evidence enough of this. Here was a man who, with his wonderful family, had captured the heart of America. Here too was a man—a young man—who had kindled the hopes and aspirations of free men and women, and those who long to be free, in all parts of the world.

Who can forget the stirring pledge of his inaugural address on that cold day in January less than 3 years ago:

Let the word go forth from this time and place, to friend and foe alike, that the torch has been passed to a new generation of Americans—born in this century, tempered by war, disciplined by a hard and bitter peace, proud of our ancient heritage—and unwilling to witness or permit the slow undoing of those human rights to which this Nation has always been committed, and to which we are committed today at home and around the world.

The world was to learn that here was a man who meant what he said.

As much as any President in our history, I believe John Kennedy symbolized the basic idealism, the faith, the vision, and the yearning for peace with justice of the American people. The undertakings of his administration—innovations like the Peace Corps, the Alliance for Progress, the nuclear test ban treaty—these are among the deeds for which President Kennedy will be judged by history. But, as important as deeds in these difficult times are commitments—expressed not only in action but also in words.

It was through words—eloquent, but meaningful, from the mind and from the heart—that our late President spoke for us to friend and foe. And the world understood. For John F. Kennedy spoke the universal language—the language of freedom and justice.

Few of us will forget his triumphant tour of Western Europe and his "I am a Berliner" address. This, to our friends abroad, was the voice of America speaking—speaking out forcefully for a world of peace, a world of law.

To millions of them and other millions here at home, John Fitzgerald Kennedy personified the United States of America. His youth, his ideals, his creative efforts reflected the qualities of the Nation for which he spoke. It is for this reason that his death had such a tremendous impact in every corner of the globe. All over the world the man on the street had confidence in President Kennedy and expected that this vigorous young leader of a vigorous young nation could help "build a world of peace where the weak are safe and the strong are just."

We know not today how John Fitzgerald Kennedy will be judged by history, although we believe the judgment will be generous. We can, however, read the message written on the faces of freedom-loving men throughout the world since the tragic events of November 22. We see there an almost universal devotion to an outstanding leader taken from us before he could fully realize the greatness that was in him.

ADDRESS BY

Hon. James T. Broyhill

OF NORTH CAROLINA

Mr. Speaker, the tragic circumstances of the death of President John F. Kennedy has plunged the Nation and much of the world into confusion and grief. Perhaps no event in this century has so struck the conscience of men of good will as this senseless and barbaric act that struck down the President of the United States.

All of us here share a feeling of shock and dismay that this could happen in a nation which has been founded upon respect for dissent, freedom of speech, freedom of political opinion, and freedom of philosophical choice in our elected leadership. The act of brutal violence outrages every American.

I have not always agreed with the legislative recommendations of President Kennedy. Yet, he was a vigorous and articulate exponent of his political philosophy. He symbolized a thoughtful America searching for new pathways into this Nation's future.

Beyond the shock of national mourning, our sorrow extends to the personal tragedy and loss sustained by Mrs. Kennedy, the President's children, and the family left behind. Even now, we cannot properly assess the nobility and strength of spirit which has borne Mrs. Kennedy through this terrible ordeal.

The revulsion to the despicable act the world has witnessed is a demonstration by the American people of their instinctive devotion to government

by law and the totality of their allegiance to the processes of democracy.

A deeply saddened Nation now moves on as a new President takes the helm. All Americans speak and pray as one that President Johnson's burdens will not be beset by new and unforeseen problems, and that the transition to his administration can be accomplished smoothly.

ADDRESS BY

Hon. Burt L. Talcott

OF CALIFORNIA

Mr. Speaker, the record will show that I was often in disagreement with the legislative program of President Kennedy. But, on November 22, 1963, the assassin killed my President.

I hate the assassin for his deed. If hating under these circumstances is wrong, I trust I shall be forgiven when the truth is made known to me.

Tears at death are the price we pay for many wonderful, happy experiences shared during life. If there had been no happy moments shared during life, there would be no sadness at death. The universality and enormity of the demonstrations of our Nation's sadness is a solemn measure of the respect and admiration which he properly enjoyed.

Mrs. Talcott and I convey our heartfelt and genuine condolences to Mrs. Kennedy, who was simply magnificent throughout her inordinately tragic and difficult ordeal. President John F. Kennedy passed on to his children a rich heritage of courage, dedication and patriotism. Few children will inherit greater treasures.

ADDRESS BY

Hon. Laurence J. Burton

OF UTAH

Mr. Speaker, since the untimely death of John Kennedy, many speeches have been made and many beautiful phrases have been uttered to memorialize and honor our slain President.

This is a time when the outstanding personal qualities of our late President should be recognized and his accomplishments praised.

This is a time when his widow, children, and family should be comforted.

This is a time when many pertinent and searching questions should be asked of every American, and a time when valid answers must be given.

Of all the tributes I have read, none has asked more pointed questions nor supplied wiser answers than those contained in a letter to the editor of the Ogden Standard-Examiner on November 25, 1963.

Mr. Speaker, I ask unanimous consent to include that letter by Mr. and Mrs. Donald D. Stout, of Layton, Utah.

DEEDS OF KINDLINESS

EDITOR, STANDARD-EXAMINER:

The assassination of President Kennedy came as a deep stab to us who have not been political supporters of him; at a moment like this, politics and differences are swept aside. We feel the pain that comes when lifeblood rushes out of one so young, so full of vitality and leadership, a youthful husband and a father.

We think of him as he came here a few short weeks ago when we and the hosts beside us waved joyously, and the stalwart young President of the United States of America arose in his car, waving back and smiling broadly. In that moment we knew without doubt that we could love the person even though we didn't agree with all his politics.

We feel shame at his assassination. The evil deed is done. We cannot restore the life to the murdered President. Yes, the criminal will be caught and punished; that is the least that society can do.

Yet we can do more than merely mete out justice to the murderer. We can do something to prevent the hate, the malice, the greed for blood that lies behind assassinations. Let us start anew with self-government in our homes; let us make clear to our children that there is a difference between liking a man and embracing his politics, or his religion, or his philosophy, or creed. We can approve of the man even though we do not endorse, necessarily, all that he does.

When our children quarrel or fight, let us seize this as an opportunity to increase their understanding of each other; to help them communicate more peaceably with each other. Let us, ourselves, refrain from evil speaking of others. When we must disagree with others' policies or viewpoints, let us make it clear that we do not hate nor dislike others personally.

Let us teach respect and reverence for the office of President of the United States, regardless of politics.

Let us plant and nourish daily small deeds of kindliness as a memorial to the man who had his own life cut short in this service—John Fitzgerald Kennedy, President of the United States of America.

Mr. and Mrs. DONALD D. STOUT.
Route 2, Box 177, Layton.

ADDRESS BY
Hon. Ancher Nelsen
OF MINNESOTA

Mr. Speaker, it was a dark day in the history of a great Nation when we faced the incredible fact that our President had been assassinated, a dark blot on this Nation that such a thing could happen in our midst. We mourn this tragedy as a great personal loss to all of us, as a grievous loss to his family, and as a tremendous loss to the Nation.

John F. Kennedy served his Nation to the best of his great ability, and died in its service. I join sorrowfully in paying him tribute.

ADDRESS BY
Hon. Robert W. Kastenmeier
OF WISCONSIN

Mr. Speaker—

Never send to know for whom the bell tolls: It tolls for thee. Any man's death diminishes me because I am involved in Mankinde.

So wrote John Donne in the beginning of the 18th century, and today we may well echo those words about John F. Kennedy for the bell tolls for all of us. Indeed all America and much of the world mourns the loss of President Kennedy for he was a man of considerable courage and fine intellectual attainment who expressed the dreams of America and inspired young men and women to new dimensions of service in the cause of peace—and security from war. He knew that the people of this Nation want peace above all else, and he worked with imagination and determination to secure it. Thus spoke he,

It is our intention to challenge the Soviet Union, not to an arms race, but to a peace race; to advance step by step, stage by stage, until general and complete disarmament has actually been achieved.

Though born to wealth and personally removed from deprivation or want, he understood and was genuinely concerned with the welfare of the common man. Better still, he understood the dynamics of our economy and felt it must serve the welfare of the people—the jobless, the sick, the elderly.

Above all, he spoke with conviction and fervor about the need to banish racial hate and bigotry and challenged the Congress to translate the American ideal of equality into a living reality. In these prophetic words he asserted that:

Continued Federal legislative inaction will continue, if not increase racial strife, causing the leadership of both sides to pass from the hands of reasonable and responsible men to the purveyors of hate and violence.

If by his tragic and shocking death, he has made us more aware of our shortcomings; if by his untimely passing we are made to realize the imperative urgency of fulfilling his mandate, then he will not have died in vain.

I can think of no more fitting tribute or monument to the memory of our late President Kennedy than to translate into law those national goals and purposes which he spoke and expressed so well, and I fervently hope that we will emerge from this tragic experience with renewed hope and high resolve for a stronger, more democratic and better America.

ADDRESS BY

Hon. George M. Rhodes

OF PENNSYLVANIA

Mr. Speaker, in the tragic death of President John Fitzgerald Kennedy, the world has lost the greatest leader of these troubled and dangerous times in which we live.

He had the spark, the fire, and the drive that together with his brilliance, patience, knowledge, understanding, character, ability, kindness and courage gave him many qualifications that few men in all history have possessed.

The sorrowing millions at home and abroad are shocked and saddened, for in President John F. Kennedy lived their fondest hopes for human progress, social justice, world understanding, and peace.

We have lost a great national leader and all of us have lost a good friend.

In his brief 3 years as Chief Executive, President Kennedy's accomplishments were enough to earn him the title of one of our country's great Presidents. His wisdom, energy, spirit and dedication have placed him in the company of revered Presidents such as Thomas Jefferson, Abraham Lincoln, Theodore Roosevelt, Woodrow Wilson, and Franklin Roosevelt.

His major accomplishment was bringing the goal of world peace closer to reality. It is a mark of his greatness that he put at least a small crack in the Iron Curtain. On foreign policy he showed both restraint and firmness that brought respect and admiration at home and abroad.

President Kennedy's greatness was affirmed when, against powerful opposition, he successfully negotiated a limited nuclear test ban treaty with the Soviet Union.

By this act, the President affirmed to the world that a strong America does not view the quest for peace as a weakness. He showed the world that America's national security did not require excessive numbers of nuclear weapons or the pollution of the atmosphere with its hazards to the health of our children.

One of the President's greatest achievements, as Prof. Henry Steele Commager, prominent American historian at Amherst College, told the country in summing up Mr. Kennedy's accomplishments, is that President Kennedy made the sense of public service and public enterprise a goal to America's young people. Not since the early days of President Franklin Roosevelt's New Deal have young Americans felt that service to the public should be the cherished goal of those who want to aid the cause of freedom and progress.

Without doubt the President's many words of wisdom, expressed with deep conviction and great courage, will echo throughout the land. Knowing President Kennedy as I did, I could not help but feel that no other President in our entire history possessed so many of the good and high qualities required for leadership. He was extremely well informed on every important issue. His contribution to our Nation and to the world has been tremendous. His greatness will grow with passing time. It was my privilege to know him as a giant among men and as a personal friend.

It is over a week now since the President was slain, but it is still difficult to believe that John F. Kennedy is no more. The last time I was with the President was at the White House 3 weeks before his death.

I had an invitation from him to participate in the signing ceremonies of a bill which he sponsored, and in which he was very much interested. As an assistant Democratic House whip, as a member of the Health Subcommittee, and as a Senate-House conferee, I played an active part in getting this legislation through Congress. It was a bill to authorize construction of community health centers and facilities for the treatment and care of the mentally retarded and mentally ill. In Washington at the annual banquet of the national leaders in this field, this legislation was hailed as the greatest achievement of the 88th Congress. President Johnson also mentioned it on Wednesday in his address to the Congress and the Nation.

I recall a lovely evening last summer when I spent more than 3 hours on the famous east portico of the White House with the President and several other House Members who were invited for an informal discussion. Before we left the President escorted us through the family living quarters.

I have known three Presidents, but none was I closer to than President Kennedy. We first met when we took the oath of office in the 81st Congress nearly 15 years ago. Later that year we visited the Pocono Mountains in Pennsylvania where we shared the speakers' platform at Unity House, the summer camp of the Ladies' Garment Workers' Union.

Last year the concern and the support of the President was of much help to me in my reelection campaign, after the merging of Berks, Schuylkill and Northumberland Counties into one oversized congressional district.

As an active member of the Kennedy team in the House, I had frequent contacts with the President and his staff members.

Last year I was invited to the White House lawn to make a trip with the President by helicopter to Harrisburg, where he was scheduled to speak at the annual State Democratic dinner. That day there was an important bill on the House floor. The session lasted into the evening. Because of the importance of this bill, in which the President was deeply interested, and because of my duties as a House whip, it was not possible for me to travel with the President as I would have liked to do.

Together with my wife, I visited the White House with other Members of Congress to pay respect to the departed President. As my wife and I left the bier, we were met by the President's brother, Attorney General Robert Kennedy, who greeted us softly. It was most difficult to speak on this sad occasion.

On Sunday evening, we returned to Washington to be on hand for the funeral ceremonies the following day. On arriving in Washington at midnight we were amazed at the great throng of people waiting in long lines to enter the Capitol where the President's body was lying in state.

After some difficulty in getting through the crowds we went to the rotunda of the Capitol where people were silently passing the bier with saddened faces and tearful eyes.

The next morning, Mrs. Rhodes and I were back in the rotunda of the Capitol as preparations were being made to take the President's body on the final trip to the White House, then to St. Matthew's Cathedral for the pontifical low mass, and then to Arlington Cemetery for the final resting place.

Before the body was taken from the Capitol, and as we stood nearby, the President's widow and his two brothers, Attorney General Robert Kennedy and Senator Ted Kennedy, knelt before the bier just before the honor guard began to remove the casket.

With other House Members and their wives, we journeyed to Arlington Cemetery in special buses and then to the site near the place of burial. It is difficult to describe the apparent feeling of sadness of those along the route of the funeral parade, past the Lincoln Memorial and over Memorial Bridge and to Arlington Cemetery where the hillsides were packed with sorrowing crowds. There near the famous Lee Mansion and the Tomb of the Unknown Soldier were the important heads of states from many nations. They had come to pay their final respects and tribute to a man who was loved by so many, not only in his own country but by the mighty and the lowly from all corners of the earth.

Two days later President Johnson told the Nation in his address before a joint session of Congress that he would carry on the program to which President Kennedy was dedicated. It was quite evident to me as I listened to President Johnson's remarks that the death of President John F. Kennedy will have a powerful impact on

Congress, for the legislation for which he fought.

Mr. Speaker, with permission of the House, I include a number of splendid editorials pertaining to the death of President Kennedy and the ideals, principles, and objectives for which he gave his life:

[From the Harrisburg (Pa.) Patriot]

THE PRESIDENT—LET US PRAY FOR OURSELVES, TOO

When the first news came, it hit all of us. Hard. Some of us wept. Most of us felt like crying. It is always this way when the lightning hits our Presidents. It hits us, too, in a special way. Our Presidents are so much a part of our lives. Above all Americans, our Presidents embody so much that all of us hold close and dear. Wherever our Presidents stand, we stand, too. Whatever the burden they carry, we carry it, too. And the power and the glory.

Some of us found this out for the first time, perhaps, when the thunderbolt struck down John F. Kennedy in Dallas. Others of us of another generation, remembering an April day in 1945 when the thunderbolt struck down Franklin D. Roosevelt, recognized it once again.

Some of us wept. Most of us felt like crying. For President Kennedy. For his wife. For his little children. And for ourselves and our country.

When the lightning strikes, suddenly and unexpectedly, it hits all of us.

The storm had swirled around John F. Kennedy in dissent and even anger. A very few among us excoriated his name. Especially in the Deep South where civil rights was becoming a flaming issue, too often consuming reason and simple human decency in its fire.

In our Deep North, too, where a few among us have spewed out deprecations and accusations right up to the ugly charge of treason. They have done all of this in the name of patriotism and Americanism, as if John F. Kennedy did not really know or care or try to lead us in the cold war against communism.

And so very many among us stayed silent while the lunatic fringe lashed out in passion and hatred.

It is little wonder that so many of us wept and so many of us felt like crying. For President Kennedy and his family. And for ourselves and our country.

We have prided ourselves so long and so much because, as a free people, we settle our arguments and conduct the institutions of our freedom in reason and in law. And we are reassuring ourselves that President Kennedy was struck down as Lincoln was before him, and Garfield, and McKinley, by a crazed man.

Those of us who believed in John F. Kennedy are heartsick. Those of us who were only waiting for next year to try and vote him out of the White House are heartsick, too. He was every American's President. He was, in his very special office, every American. The bullets fired by the fanatic hit us all.

Today many of us are praying for John F. Kennedy, the 35th President of the United States, and for Lyndon B. Johnson, the 36th President, who has picked up the terrible burden—and the power and the glory, too.

Let us also pray for ourselves.

Let us resolve to shed our silence when the extremists and the fanatics cut loose with their wild and reckless oratory, their completely baseless charges, their rumors and their ugly innuendo.

Let us speak out for reason, and right, and simple human decency, and let us regard our fellow Americans and the man who leads our Nation in trust and compassion and respect—whatever the differences we may have among ourselves and whatever issues divide us.

The finest monument any of us can erect to the memory of President Kennedy will be to do all we can to extinguish the passions and the hatreds which smoulder in this wonderful country he served so very well and loved so very much.

———

[From the Washington (D.C.) Evening Star, Nov. 26, 1963]

INTELLIGENCE WAS HIS HALLMARK—KENNEDY'S MIND WAS CONSTANTLY ON FIRE; MEMORY AND READING WERE PRODIGIOUS

(By Eric Sevareid)

What was John F. Kennedy? How will he stand in history? As this is written, hours after his death, it is hard even to assemble thoughts, easy to misjudge such a complicated human being.

The first thing about him was his driving intelligence. His mind was always on fire; his reading was prodigious; his memory almost total recall of facts and quotations. A friend of mine once crossed the Atlantic on a liner with the Kennedy family, years ago. She remembered the day 12-year-old Jack was ill in his stateroom; there lay the thin, freckled little boy—12 years old, and reading Churchill's early, other books scattered about his bed. His was a directed intelligence; he did not waste his energies; he always seemed to know where he was going and he put first things first.

John Kennedy's intellectuality was perhaps the hallmark of his nature, even more than his youth; the thing that made him different from so many Presidents. But few thought of him as an intellectual in the sense of one seeking truth for its own sake; he sought it, in order to act upon it. He was that rare and precious combination, the man of contemplation as well as the man of action. He had a sharp sense of history from his immense reading, and was acutely conscious of what his own place in history might be. In a sense, he lived for that; much of his personal correspondence as President suggested his awareness that those letters would be part of the American archives and story for all time.

He brought a new style into Government; he surrounded himself with intellectuals, as did Franklin Roosevelt in his first years; but in his personal style he was more like President Theodore Roosevelt. Like the first Roosevelt, President Kennedy believed in action; he had no patience with those who were tired or skeptical or cynical; no patience with those who could not keep up mentally or physically.

He became, with his young and beautiful wife, the symbol of America as he and most of us like to think of

America: itself young, itself always hopeful, believing, and believing that Government could change the face of our land and our lives and that America could do more than any country in the world to change the face and the nature of the world itself.

He showed no signs, even after 3 years in office, of growing tired, either in body or spirit * * * but the built-in obstacles to practical achievement were—and remain—prodigious and complex. He began some new practical courses of Government action—as with the Peace Corps and the Alliance for Progress; these, perhaps, were more imaginative than his domestic conceptions; in any case, it is in the domestic field that his difficulties were the greatest and progress the slowest.

Early on, he showed that his way would be to try to conciliate and persuade the Congress, and to compromise with it where he had to, rather than to try bulldozer tactics. Of his bold actions, his nuclear confrontation with the Soviet Union over Cuba was the boldest, one of the boldest and most successful acts of statesmanship the history books will ever tell the future about.

But at bottom, Mr. Kennedy was a cautious, prudent man. He liked to have all his ducks in a row before he fired. However vibrant in his political behavior, he was, in his deepest emotional nature, a conservative human being. Rarely did the people become aware of his deep feelings about anything. When he spoke to the country by radio or television his head usually ruled his heart. Only in very special circumstances, as on the day of brutal events in Mississippi, did passion rise in his voice as he spoke. This is why some professional observers said that President Kennedy had opened his mind to us, but not his heart * * * that therefore, politically, he had not captured the heart of the people.

If that was so, it is so no longer; the heart of the people is with the young President in death; with all of his family.

The tears of the country are with them; its hopes are with the new President.

———

[From Pottsville Republican]

John F. Kennedy

John Fitzgerald Kennedy came to the Presidency of the United States as the bearer of great change. He was the symbol of something new, but he died by something as old as time—the hand of the fanatic.

He was the first man born in the 20th century to hold the office—and the second youngest in history. He was the first Catholic in the White House. He came as a naval hero of World War II who narrowly had missed death in Pacific waters, and survived a second brush with death in a grave illness 9 years ago.

To the Nation's high politics he thus brought a fresh stamp. The well-remarked "Kennedy style" was a blend of intellect, vigor, wit, charm, and a clear talent for growth.

On the always shifting, often troubled world scene, he sometimes moved with more caution than expected in young leadership. Soon after entering the White House, he gamely took full blame for the Cuban Bay of Pigs fiasco as an enterprise sadly lacking in boldness.

Yet only his worst enemies withheld from him the label "courageous" when he moved resolutely against Soviet Premier Khrushchev in the great Russian missile crisis in Cuba in late 1962. And he boldly pressed for an East-West test ban treaty this year in the face of heavy charges that this imperiled our security.

In domestic affairs Kennedy won much of his program in beginning 1961, gained far less the following year, and encountered a major stalemate in 1963. The constant note against him was insufficient leadership.

But again, when 1963 brought the greatest crisis of this century, Kennedy—at acknowledged heavy political cost—committed himself to sweeping civil rights proposals that opened a vast new battleground.

Amid all his efforts to put the imprint of vigorous, imaginative youth upon the country's affairs in the 1960's, the late President found himself moving against a deepening background of protest, with an ugly underscoring of violence which he sought with only limited success to wipe away.

Much of this protest went to the steady encroachments of the Federal Government and its rising cost. But the bitterest reaction was white and Negro response to the enlarging racial struggle. The far right gave the mood its most perilous texture.

That is the greater tragedy.

With the calamity in Dallas the lesson of the danger inherent in violent extremism now may be deeply implanted in America's conscience.

In this way, Kennedy in death may achieve what the living President could not do to curb the almost ungovernable rancor that increasingly discolored the politics of his brief time in power.

It was John Kennedy's good fortune to surmount many obstacles to rise to his country's highest office and bring with him the winds of a new era.

It was his final tragedy that as he labored in difficult times to use these forces for the Nation's and the world's gain, they were swiftly challenged by countering winds of bitter reaction. In Dallas, one swift gust struck him down.

The Nation thus loses a young leader whose great promise lived in the shadow of great controversy. The way he died must inescapably cost all Americans deeply in self-esteem as freemen of good will.

———

[From The Reading (Pa.) New Era, AFL-CIO Paper]

Why?

(By Bob Gerhart)

As memories of emotion-packed scenes starting in Dallas and ending in Arlington continue to flash through my mind, I constantly ask myself the simple question, "Why?" And then when the finality of this tragic slaying of our beloved President, John F. Kennedy, sinks in and another man moves into the White House, the anger and bitterness that mingled with grief and sorrow give way to a feeling that we must get on with the job.

Maybe it is the electronic journalism called television that is responsible for our feelings. Cameras were there when a bleeding young man was cradled in the arms of a loving wife and mother while an open car sped 100 miles an hour to a hospital. In our very living room all of us watched the sombre events unfold—a returning of the body to Washington that same day; the dramatic escort of President Kennedy's body from the White House to the Capitol rotunda; the all-night vigil which saw the face of America move silently past the bier in the heart of our democracy; the moving events in St. Matthew's Cathedral where Cardinal Cushing commended President Kennedy's soul unto God; the melancholy beat of muffled drums as the horse-drawn caisson left the Cathedral with the mortal remains of the leader of the free world; and finally, interment of President Kennedy's body in Arlington Cemetery, shrine of the Nation's honored dead.

And then, almost stealthily it was all over and the inexorable movement of time was inaugurating a new period, a new administration in American life, leaving the period from last Friday to Monday evening with a nightmarish quality—also as if you had to shake yourself occasionally to eradicate the disbelief. It couldn't happen, it wouldn't happen, but it did.

There now can be no doubt as to the love our people held for President Kennedy. Despite all the antagonism created in the press and by the hate cult that was being encouraged of high places reminiscent of the Roosevelt-haters of two decades ago, despite the bitterness which responsible individuals held against him over the civil rights controversy, despite the assaults on the entire Kennedy family by the hate elements of the extremist right wing including at least one presidential aspirant—despite all of these things, President Kennedy was loved by the people.

The outpouring of emotions over the weekend in front of the cameras which recorded the tragic event was a far more potent testimonial to this man's closeness to the common people than all the Gallup polls and political prognostications which, by and large, were controlled and manipulated by the very people who wanted to defeat him by what apparently has become standard format in American political life—namely, character assassination. The very least that should evolve from this bodily assassination of the President of the United States is a reappraisal of what has been happening to the democracy which we say we cherish.

Can there be any doubt that the hatreds inflamed on our political scene by reckless assaults on public figures for partisan political advantage was not to a great measure responsible for the climate in which a man by the name of Oswald found justification for his horrible crime? Just review the guilt by association devices and the dirty tactics employed in the recent election right here in Reading and Berks County and you have a pretty good idea of what we mean. Discussing the issues is no longer the American way. All you do today is call the other guy a crook and then lumps everyone on his side together and you have a formula for winning elections. And is it merely a coincidence that this is the method employed by one of our major parties consistently to achieve power and control at local, State, and National levels?

Even Vice President Nixon, in his brief eulogy for President Kennedy, lamented the atmosphere in which the assassination took place and called on the American people to "reduce hatred that has driven men to this terrible deed." It is no secret that Dallas is the hotbed of the radical right in the South. Not only is it a center of unlimited wealth but it is the cradle of numerous extremist movements which embark upon forays into the far reaches of America, preaching hatred and spewing vituperation in its wake.

Hate movements take many forms. Its ugly head may appear in the religious arena where innocent clergymen may be duped into serving as its tool under the guise of advancing Christianity. What a mockery. It may appear in a Hitlerian mask seeking to divide Protestant, Catholic, and Jew. It may appear cloaked in the American flag preaching a doctrine of hatred for foreign lands and advocating a cruel isolationism by withdrawing from the United Nations. It may appear in the form of the billboard which I saw recently on the outskirts of Harrisburg boldly exhorting passersby to "Impeach Earl Warren," Chief Justice of the U.S. Supreme Court.

Adlai Stevenson, U.N. Ambassador to the United Nations, revealed in an interview with Martin Agronsky, NBC newscaster, that after the threat to his own life in Dallas, recently, he thought about the cloud of hate that hovered over the Texas city and then called the White House urging them to cancel out the President's trip. Stevenson said he was reacting to instinct. However, the President decided to go there anyhow to see whether he couldn't provide the moderating influence to bring warring parties to their sense. Maybe he has now done so in martyrdom.

Yet, even though our Nation shudders at the thought of what has happened in this great land of the free— "it can't happen here, only in South America, Europe, and Asia, we said"—can you imagine that there are people like the man in a local industry who called the assassination "my best Christmas present"? Hatreds may have temporarily been submerged in the sea of grief that engulfed the Nation. But make no mistake. The attitudes are still present because they are in the hearts of some people.

And what meaning does the President's slaying have to us here in Reading and Berks County? Has it mellowed the hearts of those who espoused President Kennedy's legislative cause yet permitted petty rivalries and bitterness to split and divide us? Will there now be a reappraisal, a new approach? Will we be able to rise above the bickering and envy to mold a sensible spirit of cooperation for the future? President Kennedy's unexpected death is forcing the Nation to take a new look and make a new beginning under the leadership of President Lyndon B. Johnson. Can we do less here at home?

———

[From Time magazine]

How Sorrowful Bad

In halting English, a Moslem telegraph operator in the Middle East tapped out on the telex: "Is it correct Kennedy killed pls?" When New York replied, "Yes, an hour ago," the Moslem signed off, "How sorrowful bad."

As the shadow of the news spread across the world, was received everywhere with stunned disbelief. The mpress of Iran broke into tears, as did the President f Tanganyika, and countless anonymous men and omen. Along Rome's Via Veneto grief sounded peratic. "E morto." People called to one another, nd at a cocktail party the guests put down their glasses nd began to recite the Lord's Prayer.

Wherever monarchs still ruled—in the United Kingom, in Jordan—formal court mourning was proclaimed. Hardly a nation in the world failed to order the rites of olling bells and lowered flags. Theaters and sports renas closed down on individual impulse. With the ews of Kennedy's death, a Viennese ice show halted in nidperformance; in Belgium, a 6-day bicycle race was nterrupted; in distant Nepal, the ceremonial opening of leprosarium was postponed.

Everywhere, bars, cafés and restaurants emptied long efore closing time. Strangers spoke to each other in hort, simple phrases—"Poor Jackie," or "How awful," or It can't be true." The phones of Americans abroad ever ceased ringing, as foreign friends and acquaintnces—or even total strangers—called to offer sympathy. The streets in front of U.S. embassies were jammed with nourners who stood in line for hours to write their ames in books of condolence. Some brought flowers, ut many searched out an American diplomat merely to hake his hand.

MONSTROUS ACT

One by one the statesmen joined the chorus of comniseration. As Big Ben tolled every minute for 1 hour a gesture normally reserved for deaths in the royal amily, Prime Minister Sir Alec Douglas-Home said: There are times when the mind and the heart stand till." From Sir Winston Churchill came a statement: The monstrous act has taken from us a great statesman nd a wise and valiant man." The words still seemed o carry the old, sibilant indignation of the ancient lion. iberia's President William Tubman cabled: "The urn f grief has been opened and is being filled with tears of riends the world over." Israel's David Ben-Gurion only sked: "Why, why?"

Almost by reflex, people rushed to disclaim even renote complicity in the murder. "Thank God it wasn't a Negro," said a Negro in Toronto. Many others insisted n reading into the event their own political passions. Statesmen in Africa, Asia and elsewhere insisted that the leed must have been done by a racist, and that Kennedy was a martyr like Lincoln or Gandhi. And Nehru could not resist remarking that the murder gave evidence of "dark corners in the United States, and this great tragedy s a slap for the concept of democracy."

GOLDEN BOY

The mourning voices first of all were for the President of the United States, regardless of his name or dentity. For in a sense far beyond daily foreign policy squabbles, he is to much of the world the protector of he weak, the benefactor of the poor.

Because of the changes in the cold war climate that occurred during his administration, millions, even on the enemy side, mourned John Kennedy as a man of peace. But above all they mourned him for his person. Perhaps even more than his own countrymen, other peoples saw in him the embodiment of American virtues—youth, strength, informality, good looks, the idealistic belief that all problems can eventually be solved. A Southern Rhodesian paper called him "the golden boy," and Common Market President Walter Hallstein said that Kennedy "personified the most beautiful qualities of his people."

Possibly more than any other President in U.S. history, he had set out to charm the world, and he had succeeded in convincing many a nation that it was his special favorite.

Alive, John Kennedy had been particularly idolized by the citizens of West Germany, who received him last June as they had no other foreign leader. When the President told a crowd of 150,000 West Berliners, "Ich bin ein Berliner," the German people were his. Dead, John Kennedy was instantly enshrined by Germans as a hero. On the night of his assassination, 25,000 West Berlin students assembled and marched on city hall, where Mayor Willy Brandt, exhausted from a trip to Africa, told them: "I know how many are weeping tonight. We Berliners are poorer tonight. We all have lost one of the best."

West Germany's Chancellor Ludwig Erhard was on his special train returning from a Paris meeting with Charles de Gaulle. A scotch and soda at his elbow, he was briefing himself for a trip to Washington to see Kennedy, scheduled for this week. When Erhard's press chief came suddenly into the car and blurted out the news that Kennedy was dead, Erhard sat in stunned silence. Finally he murmured, "Unfassbar, kaum fassbar [Inconceivable, hardly conceivable]."

UNDER FIRE

In Paris, the news reached President de Gaulle in his private apartments at the Elysée Palace. He turned on his TV set. When Kennedy's death was confirmed, De Gaulle—himself twice the target of assassination attempts—called in his staff. His face drawn and pale, he dictated his statement of condolence: "President Kennedy has died like a soldier, under fire." Russia's Red Army Choir, performing at Paris' Palais des Sports, interrupted its program for the announcement of the death and then, after a moment of silence, sang a Schubert lied in Kennedy's memory.

In Geneva, Swiss citizens jammed traffic by abandoning their cars in the middle of the streets to snatch up newspapers. An old woman, tears staining her cheeks, cried, "What an age we are living in."

In Spain, no foreigner has ever won the public's heart as had Kennedy. Said a Madrid editor, "Nothing has jolted me so much since the start of our own civil war." Americans were sought out for a pat on the shoulder, a comforting phrase such as "Hombre, lo siento mucho [Man, I feel deeply]."

Italy was locked in a political crisis when the news came. Premier Aldo Moro promptly adjourned his attempts to form a Cabinet with leftwing Socialist Leader Pietro Nenni. Emerging from the meeting, 72-year-old

Nenni, with tears in his eyes, said: "These are little affairs of ours, in the face of this tragedy for the whole world." At the Vatican, Pope Paul went to his private chapel to pray for the wounded President and, after the news of his death, said mass.

To Ireland, John Kennedy was the apotheosis of the country's hopes and history—the great-grandson of a poor emigrant who had stormed the ramparts of the New World and won its highest honor. He was looked upon, said the Irish Times, "as a younger brother and with great affection."

REICHSTAG FIRE

On the other side of the Iron Curtain, Chairman Nikita Khrushchev and two aides drove to the U.S. Embassy in Moscow. Dressed in black and looking noticeably depressed, Khrushchev spoke for 19 minutes with U.S. Ambassador Foy Kohler, reminiscing about the slain President. Khrushchev's wife Nina cabled Jacqueline Kennedy. The genuine dismay in Russia was soon modified by politics, when it turned out that the prime suspect was a self-declared Marxist who had lived in Russia. Said one Soviet journalist suspiciously: "Is this affair being whipped up in the press? Is the situation grim?" Said another Russian taking up what sounded like an emerging propaganda line: "Remember that they found a Communist who started the Reichstag fire."

In the Middle East, one Iraqi was amazed: "We are used to this kind of thing in Arab countries. But in America?" In the Congo, East Katanga's President Edouard Bulundwe and his entire cabinet, together with their seldom seen wives, trooped into the home of the U.S. consul. "This is how we behave in Africa when a great chief dies," explained Bulundwe as they sat stiffly in the drawing room. "President Kennedy will be mourned in even the smallest village of our country as a man who cared for and worked for the blacks."

It was the same in Asia. In Thailand, authorities sent sound trucks into the villages to spread the mournful news that Prathanathibodi [President] Kennedy was dead. In Saigon, people were more shocked by Kennedy's death than they had been by that of President Diem; and Buddhists held special memorial services and prayers. In Japan, technicians were up before dawn to receive the historic first transpacific TV broadcast from the United States, which was to have included a personal message from the President. Instead, the voice of a Japanese newsman in Manhattan reported the news of Kennedy's death.

In all of Asia, Red China was almost alone in its determined lack of sympathy. Peiping radio carried the Kennedy story without comment. The Hong Kong Communist New Evening Post sneered that Kennedy had "used a two-faced policy to promote an imperialist war course."

VANISHING BAITERS

Even Cuba proved less surly than Red China. Fidel Castro deplored the murder, said he had no reason to wish for Kennedy's death, but conceded that "perhaps" Cuba might have had motives "to feel like it" and vaguely suggested that "reactionaries" were really to blame. Elsewhere in Latin America, all the Yankee baiting seemed

to disappear for the moment. A sense of pessimism about the future gripped Brazil, and the downtown streets of Rio de Janeiro were filled with people whose tight faces, glazed eyes and unaccustomed silence revealed their feelings. In the favelas (shantytowns) on Rio's outskirts, samba bands called off their rehearsals for the carnival, and President João Goulart said about Kennedy: "I kneel before his memory."

The most eloquent Latin American voices were those heard in the street. A janitor in Quito, who had been listening to the news on radio, refused to read his newspaper because "it's too painful to go over such a sad story again." Despite later revelations about the crime, most Latin Americans persisted in believing that Kennedy had been slain because of his support for Negro rights. In Buenos Aires, women cried, "Qué barbiridad," and old men made sad, futile gestures with their hands. Said one grieving Colombian: "It seems as though all the Presidents in all the Latin American countries have died."

To the north, throughout Canada, theaters and arenas closed their doors, and large cities became hushed with a curious quiet. Prime Minister Lester Pearson was just about to open a session of Parliament when he was handed a note. He threw it on the top of his desk, slumped back in his seat and seemed at a loss for words. His voice broke as he said: "The world can ill afford at this time in our history to lose a man of his courage."

History's more precise appraisals would come later, as would the resumption of all the world's usual enmities. But for a brief time at least, the U.N. General Assembly, standing in silence, was in a mood to agree with U.S. Ambassador Adlai Stevenson, who said: "All of us who knew him will bear the grief of his death to the day of ours."

[From the New Era]

THE AMERICANS

(By Jere L. Gabrielle)

It's 2:30 in the morning of Monday, November 25. You're tired. You're emotionally drained by the events of the past 2 days. Your eyes are smarting under the strain of watching, watching, watching. Your ears somehow absorb the repetition of the macabre events that have transpired. You know you should hit the sack but you sit there transfixed, tired eyes glued to the television screen.

Actually you don't really know why you sit there trying to stay awake at 2:30 in the morning. You tell yourself it must have become a habit that started on Friday afternoon. Just one of those crazy ideas that you might miss something if you stopped staring.

Then through the haze of your clouded thoughts you suddenly realize what really holds you there. It isn't curiosity. It isn't a stubborn desire to sweat this out to the bitter end. It is people. You, sitting there in the comfort of your living room, are enjoying the privilege of a front-row-center look at America.

The voice of the commentator interrupts your reverie to tell you that people are silently passing before your eyes at the rate of about 5,000 an hour and that the prospects of the thousands who wait, in a line that extends for some

miles, of ever getting a chance to see what they came to
e are pretty slim.

Then the impact of this procession of human beings—
mericans—really hits you like a ton of bricks. These
lks, moving past the flag-draped casket are not curiosity
ekers. That kind would not wait out in the chill air
f night for hours and hours just to say that they passed
rough the rotunda of the Capitol Building at 2:30 a.m.,
look at a flag-draped coffin.

These folks are here because they want to be here.
here is a compulsion, an inexplicable motivation that
as moved them to this short minute in history.

Perhaps a desire for personal affiliation with the event
the answer to some. To others, perhaps it is the desire
r conclusive evidence that this monstrous thing has
eally happened. Some may feel that they must see, or
uch, physically the only remaining material evidence of
hat is a closed chapter in their lives.

But as you watch the faces you know that without
xception there is a spiritual link between each man,
oman, and child in that endless shuffling procession and
e man whose remains lie beneath that American flag.
es, a spiritual link. A spark, however great or small, of
nderstanding and love, of feeling that here was your
rother, someone who thought as you do, someone who
as tied in, however remotely, with your own personal
spirations, someone who had somehow shared with you
sorrow, exultation, ambition, and most of the other
motions evidenced in the complexity of your life.

Those who passed and prayed knew that this man had
rayed. Those who wept knew that this man must have
ept on occasion. Those carrying infants asleep on their
oulders knew that this man had carried his own children
ften on his shoulder.

The very young knew that this man was in tune with
hem. The very old, the lame, the blind knew that this
an had held out his hand to them. Catholics felt a
pecial spiritual brotherhood for him because he was a
atholic but those of other creeds thought of him as their
wn special brother also.

The face of bigotry was absent from this scene. There
as no segregation in this face of America. The black
nan and the white man shuffled slowly side by side and
gether they stopped for their personal look or prayer.
he man they came to see was really the image of those
ho looked at him. It was like a look into a spiritual
nirror.

Yes, I was looking at the face of America and it made
ne proud. All the quips and jokes and the ugly stories
nd the hatred faded into nothing. In their place there
ose only the countenance of the thousands upon thou-
ands whom I must believe are, in essence, imbued with
he same dignity and purpose as the man to whom they
ere paying homage. And I know, because of this, that
ny country will endure forever.

Our President, who battled to outlaw the use of nuclear
eapons costing millions of dollars and capable of destroy-
ng millions of humans in one fell swoop, was murdered
y a guy with scrambled eggs in his head, with a $12.75
nail-order rifle and a couple of 20-cent shells. But that
nan was not in the procession that I saw on Monday at
:30 a.m. His face, thank God, is not the face of
America.

ADDRESS BY

Hon. Hugh L. Carey

OF NEW YORK

Mr. Speaker—

There is an appointed time for everything, and a time
for every affair under the heavens.

A time to be born, and a time to die; a time to uproot
the plant.

A time to kill, and a time to heal; a time to tear down
and a time to build.

A time to weep, and a time to laugh; a time to mourn,
and a time to dance.

A time to scatter stones, and a time to gather them; a
time to embrace, and a time to be far from embraces.

A time to seek, and a time to lose; a time to keep, and
a time to cast away.

A time to rend, and a time to sew; a time to be silent,
and a time to speak.

A time to love, and a time to hate: a time of war, and
a time of peace.—Ecclesiastes 3: 1–8.

His time was at hand. On a summer night in
Los Angeles, his party called him to be its candidate for the Presidency of the United States. I
watched him as he stepped from the darkness of
the night into the brilliancy of the convention
doorway. He left uncertainty behind; his was a
sure and swift movement into the center of his
people and on up to their leadership.

It was his right and time to lead and he had
seized it. It had not been conferred upon him;
he had won it over all. He had gone into the
winter of New England, the rains of Wisconsin,
and the hills of West Virginia and carried the
day. Cynics said he could not be nominated.
Skeptics said he could not win. His faith was
against him. His youth would defeat him. He
knew America better than they. Because of his
faith in God and in his fellow man, he rejected
the cynic and dismissed the skeptic. Because he
was young and had the vision of tomorrow, he
knew he would prevail.

He went forth from that convention with the
message that it was better to light a candle than
curse the darkness and his flame fired the Nation.
Now it will never be extinguished.

He vowed that he would get this Nation moving. In 1,000 days he kept that vow.

He banished uncertainty and wore the mantle
of world leadership with determination. There
was a way to peace along a path of strength and
he found that way. With more power in those

young and sensitive hands than any man had ever held before, he fashioned a bond of nations against the spread of ultimate destruction.

He assessed the Nation's needs and neglected none. The health of our children and our elderly were his concern. He knew that only an educated people could truly enjoy the dignity and rights of free men and he planned for that. He seized the equalitarian doctrine that was rooted in our heritage, reaffirmed it and did not flinch. He ran the risk for what was right. We will have a new birth of freedom because he lived as he believed that all men are equal before God.

He had a sense of history and he knew it was his time to lead us, that his time was at hand.

I saw him last in the Lincoln bedroom. He had called us around him, 12 of the people's Representatives, to discuss the Nation, district by district.

We met on the Truman balcony and we spoke to him of the national needs. He seized and sized each case, every detail, weighed and recommended, evaded nothing. No man who ever lived in the White House was close to the people of the United States, knew them better, loved them more, or served them with greater devotion. We went from the balcony to the Lincoln room and he spoke with reverence of the martyr President. He pointed to the portrait of Jackson whom Lincoln admired as he admired Lincoln.

A strong President himself, he revered a strong and martyred President.

I left him at the Lincoln room and I was sure as always that our Nation had chosen wisely and well. We had made him our President, he had chosen the hour. We had called him to lead, he had called us to sacrifice. We had sought strength, he cast out weakness. We looked for peace, he chained the monster of war. We searched for a way through dark and dangerous hours, he gave us light and sureness.

We made him our President, he made our President immortal.

With the warmth of the flame of the new fire at his resting place let us cherish the hours he was among us.

Through that flame let malice be seared away and hatred purged from the land.

John Fitzgerald Kennedy, hero, martyr, President of the United States must be more than re-

membered. His words must be followed and his works begun well finished.

To his widow, Mrs. Jacqueline Kennedy, and the family of our late President, our gratitude and feeling is unbounded.

We know now that at his side was a gracious lady who helped him to help us. In our most tragic hour we, too, borrowed on her courage. What would we have been without him? What would we have done without his great and grand lady?

STATEMENT BY HON. HUGH L. CAREY ON NOVEMBER 27, 1963

Mr. Speaker, I believe there is no need to recount for the people of my State and my community, any part of the tribute, the funeral and requiem or the burial at Arlington. In the East Room of the White House, in the great hall of the people at the Capitol rotunda, and finally at Arlington Cemetery, I was there humbly in person and all the world was there more vitally in spirit.

This message is simply to pledge the continuum of that spirit.

Thank you, thank you very much, Mr. President.

This is the day we press on. Twenty-four hours after the mortal part of President John Fitzgerald Kennedy was placed before the altar of God for his requiem, we resumed the business of the Congress in which he served so long and well.

Because he led us for a thousand days our aims are high, our goals clear. We have no time for the indulgence of self pity that he was with us so short a time or so swiftly departed. Rather let us reflect on our fortune that he was here in our dark and dangerous hours. In his name, let us be impatient with futility of the present and move to the high promise of the future. If his sacrifice is to have full meaning, our pace must be urgent, our steps determined.

We mourn and our memories of the moments we spent with him are precious to us no matter how brief. Because they are precious, I will share mine on another day and set them forth so they will not be lost to our children and my countrymen. But at this time as we approach the day set for Thanksgiving let us have one recollection.

As he walked among the people he loved with outstretched hand and his smile of friendship, he was not silent. While he had a special word of wit, of intimacy for some, these words he had to all:

"Thank you, thank you very much." "Thank you" was his constant expression to the children, the men and women, the crowds, the country, because his heart was full of gratitude for their high honor, for their support, but most of all for the opportunity to serve mankind which he had firmly sought and fully won.

Now as we press on in that same service, if we pause, let it be only for gratitude, for thanksgiving. Let us now respond.

Thank you, Mr. President.

For the faith in God and fellow man your life personified, we are grateful.

For the unity and strength you left us as a country, we are grateful.

For teaching us that there must be an end to venom as a means of vengeance and hurt for the sake of hate, we are thankful.

For the lesson that we measure mortality in the mystery of eternity not in days but in deeds, we are thankful.

For your interest in our children, your concern for their education, your determination that the handicapped among them who "had felt the hand of fate would never be victims of neglect," we are grateful.

For the path to peace you found amid the thicket of tension and threat of war, we are most grateful.

For your words and works, your "Profile in Courage," which you brought to life in your own sacrifice, we are most grateful.

For your judgment, that favorite word of yours which guided us toward well-being for all men, toward order and understanding in the whole world, we are most grateful.

For your heroism in war and peace which won you your rightful resting place among our brave departed you will be well remembered.

But above all, Mr. President, we give you thanks for the self you left to lead us in the person of your wife and family.

For Mrs. John F. Kennedy who raised us from despair and summoned up in all of us the spirit we needed and did not have, for her example, her calm, her love, and, hopefully, her forgiveness.

On Thanksgiving Day to you, Mr. President, Mrs. John F. Kennedy, and all your family, thank you, thank you very much. Thank you.

ADDRESS BY

Hon. Phil M. Landrum

OF GEORGIA

Mr. Speaker, the tragic death of John Fitzgerald Kennedy has deprived the world of its youngest, yet its most effective leader in the quest for peace. His intellectual attainments, his wide knowledge and articulate speech, his courage and his compassion commanded respect and admiration throughout the world from friends and foe alike. Within the short space of 3 years as President of the United States he became the world's most respected and effective spokesman. His life was a symbol of freedom throughout the world.

And while he had become a world figure let us not overlook the fact that here at home his public and private life set the very highest standard of conduct for public officials. As Columnist Richard Wilson said of him last August:

The world is much concerned, as it ought to be, with standards of human conduct. Moral, ethical, and spiritual questions are sharply presented in many different ways. They arise in the private and public lives of officials here and abroad, in the revolution of religious theology and dogma, in the morality of nuclear policy, in the relationships between the races, and, most of all, in the ordinary complexities of modern life.

In this vortex of changing standards and values, when the individual finds himself troubled so much of the time, the conduct of the President of the United States provides a temporal precept and example.

President Kennedy, in his public and family life, has set the very highest standard of American conduct. One need not agree with all, or any, of his policies to recognize that in his behavior, attitude, and demeanor he provides the needed example that the troubled or misguided may turn to with respect and admiration.

Despite the reality of the sad days following his assassination I find it difficult to believe that he is dead. Even so it is more difficult to understand that the catastrophe did occur in our land and in our time. As millions in stunned disbelief upon hearing of his death exclaimed, "Why?"—so must we today and every day continue to ask, "Why?"

When we answer this question we will have fulfilled our obligation as public officials and provided in some measure that the life and deeds of John Fitzgerald Kennedy shall not have been lost.

Hon. Frank Thompson, Jr.

OF NEW JERSEY

Mr. Speaker, at this moment I could wish for nothing more than to be a poet or writer, for only as one of them could I find the words to express my grief over the loss of our beloved President, John F. Kennedy. In expressing my grief I would be expressing, also, the feelings of my family, my constituents, and my friends and acquaintances in an appropriate manner.

But I am not a poet, Mr. Speaker, and platitudes would never do for me at this moment. I will limit myself therefore to a few simple words. I knew John F. Kennedy well and I loved and admired him. I worked harder for his election in 1960 than I have ever worked for anyone, or than I ever shall again. My constituents approved of President Kennedy long before he was elected to that great office and they showed it by giving him a great majority of their votes, their unstinting support and above all, their loyalty and deep affection. They will miss him terribly, as will the Nation and, indeed, the world.

I am consoled by the fact that it was my privilege to know, to work for, and to support John F. Kennedy. He was deserving of far greater things than I could ever have given him and I regret only that I shall no longer have the opportunity to serve him, for to do so was to serve the Nation and the people of the world. I shall be mindful always of the things he stood for and I shall do everything possible to see that those things come to pass. By doing so perhaps I can show his brave widow and children the depth of my affec-

tion for John F. Kennedy and the things for which he stood. I could never express these feelings with words but I might be able to with deeds which last longer than mere words. My wife, my family, and all of our friends join me in this expression of loss and of our heartfelt sympathy to President Kennedy's family.

Hon. Benjamin S. Rosenthal

OF NEW YORK

Mr. Speaker, it was John Fitzgerald Kennedy who said at a news conference on March 2, 1962:

There is always inequity in life. Some men are killed in war, and some are wounded, and some may never leave the country. * * * It's very hard in military or personal life to assume complete equality. Life is unfair.

No more telling meaning could have been given to these words than the death of John Fitzgerald Kennedy.

President Kennedy gave his life in the service of his country. In that service he had won the love, affection, respect, and esteem of his fellow Americans and fellow citizens of the world. We mourn his loss, and grieve for his family and for ourselves.

John F. Kennedy assumed the Presidency with our hopes and his determination. He was proud and warmhearted, literate and articulate, dynamic and vital. He acknowledged that no experience can possibly prepare you adequately for the Presidency, and yet we know now that no man in our times could have had a greater preparation for the Presidency. The beauty and eloquence of his inaugural address assured all the world that the United States had chosen a President who would wear the traditional robes with grace and distinction. The inaugural address was but a first step in a long succession of profound and inspiring pronouncements—pronouncements that have already led to deeds in commemoration of his ideas and ideals.

It was this man among men who taught us that national security and freedom, and efforts for the preservation of the peace of mankind are all singular objectives of our people. It was his determination, and his alone, that permitted the execution of the nuclear test ban treaty, a first step in the breaking of the nuclear deadlock that threatened to engulf mankind. Surely, his dreams for world peace and understanding were never more eloquently expressed than at American University earlier this year when he said:

And if we cannot end now our differences, at least we can help make the world safe for diversity. For, in the final analysis, our most basic common link is that we all inhabit this small planet. We all breathe the same air. We all cherish our children's future. And we all are mortal.

John F. Kennedy's mission, and in fact his performance, was to advance the cause of all humanity. He was mindful of man's inhumanity to man, and determined to correct the world's inequities.

It was he alone among the free world's leaders who, more than any other, understood the revolution and rebellion of the underprivileged.

It was he who gave meaning and direction, and offered hope and help to those who sought to play their proper role in our society.

It was he who was both resolute and determined in dealing with threats from our antagonists, and at the same time and with the same degree of determination to lead the fight to "get the nuclear genie back into the bottle."

It was he who gave the American minorities the new hope for dignity, respect, and confidence that was too long overdue.

Indeed, he offered special inspiration to those of his generation. He was made for these times, and these times were made for him. He loved this land and its people, and they in turn offered to him their blessings in exercising the leadership that they willingly bestowed upon him.

The incredible tragedy of his death, and abruptness with which his life was terminated, leave a deep emptiness in the fabric of our life. Time may heal the pain we suffer, but it shall never replace for us Americans the loss of our good friend, and our devoted and distinguished leader.

America has lost a noble son, but we shall remain loyal to his ideals, his hopes, his dreams, and his memory.

ADDRESS BY

Hon. Edith Green

OF OREGON

Mr. Speaker, I have listened to the eloquent remarks made so far today in tribute to our late President. If I may paraphrase President Johnson's remarks last week in this very Chamber: I wish with all my heart we were not here this day doing what we are doing.

A witless act by an ignorant assassin struck down John Fitzgerald Kennedy—the fourth President of the United States to be slain. Ironically, he was a victim of a fanaticism his cool, sensitively honed intelligence abhorred and rejected.

Certainly, at this moment Shakespeare might well have written for Americans the words he placed in the mouth of King John:

> Of comfort no man speak
> Let's talk of graves, of worms, of epitaphs.
> Make dust our paper and with rainy eyes
> Write sorrow on the bosom of the earth.

Some of us grieve, because we knew John F. Kennedy as an able political leader and a kindly father and a civilized man. He gave us a glimpse of promise and fulfillment in our national life; gave us surcease from what Matthew Arnold once called "this strange disease of modern life, with its sick hurry, its divided aims, its palsied hearts."

Others among us grieve because, although they owed him no political allegiance, he was the President of us all. We all should grieve because most terribly the office of the Presidency, itself, has been damaged.

Private emotion, however, cannot redeem dastardly acts. There was grief and sorrow aplenty when a town mutinied in Mississippi because a Negro American wished to attend a State university that barred Negroes. Two men were slain in the civil strife. There was surely grief and sorrow when Medgar Evers was slain by a racist, thereby stopping his own fight to translate into performance the promises of our Declaration of Independence and the Constitution. There was abundant grief and sorrow when Negro children were murdered in a church bombing one Sunday morning in Birmingham. What means our private grief and sorrow when it does not prevent the recurrence of the preventable?

There is entirely too much private sorrow that is uncoupled to individual, tangible, contributions to public decency and responsibility.

There is a contribution each can make in this difficult hour by realizing that however profound our sorrow, it is to no avail unless coupled with a public act that condemns and rebukes extremes in word and deed.

And so the President of all the American people is gone—struck down in the summer of his life. A man who lived by the dictate that courage is grace under pressure.

All over the Nation, Americans mourned. It was as if collectively the Nation mourned in company with Jacqueline Kennedy. At a moment when this Nation desperately needed a proud and beautiful act, the Nation found it in the deportment of Mrs. Kennedy as she walked behind the flag-draped caisson bearing her husband's body. Certainly, she showed her profile in courage.

Portland and Oregon mourned no less than other communities and States in the Nation. Moving sermons and addresses were given. Memorial services were held. Constituents and friends sent letters.

Typical were these:

This terrible loss comes to me as though it were one of my immediate family.

Please convey my feeling of loss; I would gladly have given my life for his.

The Reverend Robert H. Bonthius, pastor of Westminster Presbyterian Church, Portland, spoke feelingly in his sermon of tribute:

It is fitting that we remember John Fitzgerald Kennedy this morning, giving thanks to God for those gifts which he used in the service of this country and the world, and asking God that whatsoever was honorable and excellent in his leadership may be bestowed upon his successor. We remember his courage in war and in peace, the range of his mind and his capacity for amassing information and organizing it for policy decisions, his willingness to assume public and personal responsibility for serious mistakes, his boldness in times of international crisis, his concern for the weak and underprivileged and those deprived of civil rights. We recall his coolness in controversy, his broad human sympathy,

his ability and willingness to draw upon the talents of both political parties for important missions across the world. We remember that he gave no special favors to one religion or one church at the expense of another. Perhaps more than all else, we recall his sense of destiny, his deep persuasion of the mission which this country has before it, his eloquent voicing of that mission to all nations, inviting in particular the Soviet Union to consider new proposals for arms control, disarmament, and peace. He could not rest or let the country rest when there was so much yet to do and be as Americans in a new and promising though threatening age.

Four lines of Robert Frost, a friend of the President's and a favorite poet, were written by Mr. Frost for himself. They might be applied also to John Kennedy:

> "And were an epitaph to be my story
> I'd have a short one ready for my own.
> I would have written of me on my stone:
> I had a lover's quarrel with the world."

Rabbi Emanuel Rose of Congregation Beth Israel in Portland said at a memorial service for the late President on November 25, 1963:

The uniqueness of John F. Kennedy is not to be found in the frailties common to all mankind, but in the particular strengths of the man. John F. Kennedy was a strong man. He was strong in his ideals. He was strong in his commitments. He was strong in his philosophy. He was strong in his determination to make real his philosophy. It was—in my opinion—his most obvious characteristic "his youth" which was his particular uniqueness in this office.

It is in the nature of man that with the passing of years he becomes more complacent, for he has learned, perhaps due to disappointment, the emotional necessity of accepting more of what is. But with youth there is a greater zealousness. The visions of youth evoke more intensive action. It is the youthful vision which stimulates faster progress. It is the youthful vision which is less able to accept the status quo. It is the youthful vision which is less influenced by that rationalization which results from lengthier years.

Although historians will long argue the point—was it the mere accident of time and circumstances, or was it John F. Kennedy, the man, who in his young years under his Presidency was able to secure a nuclear test ban treaty—yes, deliberations lasted for many prior years, but could they not just as well have continued through more years without arriving at a successful conclusion? Is it accident of time alone that the strongest civil rights bill of any administration has been presented to Congress? Is it accident of time alone that the mental health bill was presented to Congress—which will have profound impact upon our Nation? Is it accident alone that a Peace Corps came into being under his administration? Here was a man of deep commitment. He was, in the words of the Chief Justice, Earl Warren, "a fighter for justice," "an apostle for peace." His zealousness for his vision of America, his energetic dedication to his dreams for his Nation are the seal of his uniqueness as the 35th

President of the United States. To be sure, his appeal to America toward the fulfillment of the American dream was not new, but it was fresh and vigorous. He was free of the shallow triteness of superficial nationalism, but suffused with a profound understanding of national integrity and individual dignity. He was emotionally distant and apart from the flag wavers, but intellectually akin to the deeper meaning of the Stars and Stripes. His vocabulary was void of ballyhoo cheapness, but his speeches were weighted with literary acumen.

The Portland Oregonian on November 26 was moved to comment editorially:

The maniacal events of the past weekend, which brought into counteraction the enduring strengths of the American people—faith in God, unswerving loyalty to our ways of life and government, the disciplined courage of a widowed First Lady, the compassion of a multitude—have left us all drained of emotion.

Drained, but not empty. From the ashes of our sorrow and anger rises a new sense of dedication. The lawlessness of the jungle will not prevail. Although there are savages among us, new ways will be found to restrain them. Our national purpose will not be blunted by the irrationalities of the few. There will be no gain to our enemies here or elsewhere in the world from the assassination of President Kennedy and the stupidity of the Dallas police in allowing the murder of his assassin. This Nation draws together in shock and adversity. The democratic ideal is as tough as it is rational. It will grow stronger until all the world learns that mankind cannot live without it.

Its sister paper, the Journal, editorialized on November 23:

Tragically Mr. Kennedy did not have time to prove what his place in history might become. But he will be remembered as a courageous leader, one who proved his bravery in the face of death as a naval lieutenant in World War II and who in the White House faced crisis after crisis with the same kind of bravery.

It has been easy to find fault with some of Mr. Kennedy's decisions and policies. Now it is just as easy to forget the fault-finding. The President is a martyr to the causes in which he believed. Nothing that happens from now on can take this role from him.

On November 23, 1963, the Portland Reporter gave this accounting:

We do not know John F. Kennedy's last words, but we know what he intended to say. In an advance copy of the speech he was to make in Dallas, were the words:

"There will always be dissident voices heard in the land, expressing opposition without alternatives, finding fault, but never favor, perceiving gloom on every side and seeking influence without responsibility."

Kennedy was to say that these voices were preaching doctrines wholly unrelated to reality and that they "apparently assume that words will suffice without weapons, that vituperation is as good as victory and that peace is a sign of weakness."

Men of good will seek to resolve differences by discussion and persuasion. Tragically there still are those of unbalanced minds with power to change the future of the world.

Let us now accept the reality of the deed and dedicate ourselves anew to creating a better world.

John Fitzgerald Kennedy, our 35th President. A Japanese destroyer tried to kill him by ramming the PT boat he commanded. It failed. But one of his fellow Americans succeeded.

ADDRESS BY

Hon. Joseph G. Minish

OF NEW JERSEY

Mr. Speaker, the late President Kennedy left millions of Americans grieving at his passing as though they were his immediate survivors, as though he had been a member of their own families, a brother, son, husband, even a father. This genuine grief and sense of loss are felt for many reasons. In the first place, he had often been in the homes of many Americans by way of their television screens, as a Senator, as a presidential candidate, and as President of the United States. He seemed to belong in those homes just as he seemed to belong in what became for a time his own home, the White House.

His personal characteristics were such as to endear him to millions here and abroad. He was handsome, his smile was radiant, his mind quick, his speech clear, his voice strong, his humor apparent, his courage unquestionable and his dedication to his country and its people obvious. Some of his charm and grace was derived from the fact that he liked his awesome job so very much. He was a born leader. He knew it, and so did his country and the world. In losing him we have come to realize more accurately and much more fully how much he meant to all of us. The trust, the admiration that people in all lands held him in was revealed by the unprecedented outpouring of grief in the whole family of man.

Mr. George Gallup, whose public opinion polls have charted the President's ups and downs in the affections of Americans since his candidacies in the presidential primaries of 1960, said the other day that:

> During the nearly 3 years of his term in office, one group stood solidly behind the President—the majority of the American public.

Strangely enough, so it would seem, the high point of approval of John Fitzgerald Kennedy came in the aftermath of the ill-fated Cuban invasion attempt in the Bay of Pigs. Yet on examination this is not strange at all, but is rather an example of the American tradition of loyalty and stanchness in a crisis. The American people rallied around their new leader when they knew that the breaks had gone against him.

Since there will be many who will praise him for his triumphs, and only silence now from those who criticized him, it may be well to say a few words about the unhappy episode. Of course, he assumed all responsibility for any errors of judgment which had been made. Constitutionally the responsibility was his, and he accepted it and bore the critical onslaught with characteristic grace and good will.

It has been noted that only in this one instance did the President rely wholly on the judgment and advice of the experts. Of all who opposed the Bay of Pigs invasion he had felt the gravest skepticism; yet he accepted his responsibility when it turned out that the people who knew the most were shown to know the least, and no mistake of a similar nature or a comparable magnitude was subsequently made. He learned things quickly, well, and for good. The second Cuban crisis revealed him in his full stature. As Joseph C. Harsch, the noted columnist, has observed:

> That moment of the Cuban crisis grows larger in perspective as it recedes into the past. It stands out on the record of the past as the watershed between the period when the possibility of nuclear war ever was present in our lives and the period when the danger seems itself to be a major deterrent.
>
> Mr. Kennedy gave the West, indeed all the world, the priceless gain of release from fear of inevitable nuclear war. He gave us all a chance to look and think and plan ahead in an atmosphere of confidence and relief.

Just as he struggled so unceasingly to achieve a world of law and order, so at home he fought to insure that every American should enjoy the equal rights and equal opportunity guaranteed by our Constitution. A truly civilized man, he recognized the human dignity and worth of every individual and he sought to elevate our national standards to the lofty goals he envisioned. A devoted and solicitous son, husband, and father, he knew the importance of the family and wanted every family to enjoy a decent standard of living and the better things of life. He was the champion of the working people and sought the abolition of exploitation and misery.

President Kennedy summarized his goals in his brilliant inaugural address:

> Now the trumpet summons us again—not as a call to bear arms, though arms we need—not as a call to battle, though embattled we are—but a call to bear the burden of a long twilight struggle, year in and year out, rejoicing in hope, patient in tribulation—a struggle against the common enemies of man: tyranny, poverty, disease, and war itself.

We grieve that he has been taken from us so prematurely before he could achieve all he hoped to achieve in the cause of peace and freedom and equality. He has left us a noble legacy, and our finest tribute to this great man would be to dedicate ourselves as he did to the building of a world of peace and brotherhood.

One of the most moving tributes to the President came in a very short interview over Washington's Station WTOP. Daniel P. Moynihan, Assistant Secretary of Labor, was interviewed by WTOP Reporter Harold Walker. This is the way it went:

> Mr. WALKER. Is there any meaning you can find in what has happened?
>
> Mr. MOYNIHAN. I suppose the point that cuts deepest is the thought that there may not be. * * * You know the French author, Camus, when he came out at the end of his life, he said the world was absurd. A Christian couldn't think that, but the utter senselessness, the meaninglessness. * * * We all of us know down here that politics is a tough game. And I don't think there's any point in being Irish if you don't know that the world is going to break your heart eventually. I guess we thought we had a little more time. * * * So did he.
>
> Mr. WALKER. Is the New Frontier leaderless?
>
> Mr. MOYNIHAN. No, sir. We have a leader. He is the President. If we learned anything from John Kennedy, we learned to serve the President. I think that the single, one thing that some of us are holding to, to keep our minds together, is that we will do exactly as the President wishes us to do in exactly what capacity he indicates.
>
> Mr. WALKER. Will the New Frontier still be able to realize its dream?
>
> Mr. MOYNIHAN. Oh, we're no good at answering questions like that. You speak of dreams. You recall the passage from "The Tempest":
>
> "We are such stuff as dreams are made of."
>
> Well, you know that passage begins, "Our revels now are ended."

ADDRESS BY

Hon. Al Ullman

OF OREGON

Mr. Speaker, John F. Kennedy was uniquely a man of his time who spoke not just the words of this day and age but somehow breathed the spirit of this complex 20th century world. When he died a little bit of all of us died, not just in our own country but around the world.

When I returned from the White House on that sad Saturday afternoon following the tragic events in Dallas I sat down and wrote a letter to the people of my State. This is what I said to them:

DEAR FRIENDS: As I stood with bowed head before that lonely flag-draped coffin in the east room of the White House, my heart cried out "Why, oh God, Why?"

This was a good man, a man of faith, a man of courage. He was not a man of violence, nor of guile, nor of conceit, but a man of restraint and dignity, a tolerant man, one who loved life, who loved people, who wanted to help them, not hurt them. He was my friend. He was America's friend. His whole life is a testimonial to his love of country—a life almost in its entirety dedicated to public service both in war and peace.

In every way he was a man of good will, a moderate and a Christian. His personal philosophy was to win—but fairly and according to the rules—to persuade with argument and facts, to appeal to the heart as well as the mind, to give unstintingly of himself—to ask no more than he himself was willing to give.

He was of this time and this age. No one in public life so well typified the mood and spirit of our day. He spoke for millions of people, articulately, compassionately, naturally. His voice was theirs. He was one of them.

Who then could commit this monstrous act? How could it happen, here, in the mid-20th century, in the greatest free nation on earth, the cradle of democracy, the haven for the world's oppressed and downtrodden, the world's hope for freedom and justice for all men?

Is the fault only with the assassin who pulled the trigger or does the guilt go deeper? Is it not in fact with every man and every organization that has sowed the seeds of hate throughout our land? Is it not with every tongue that has spread the venom of distrust, and disrespect for our laws and institutions? Is it not with every radical and extremist, whether of the left or of the right, who spreads doubt and suspicion in our midst? Is it not with every deceiver who has fanned the flame of intolerance and preached the gospel of hate, and every idle tongue that has thoughtlessly wagged to defame the face of our leaders and our institutions? Do not they all share the guilt in this terrible crime?

The man who pulled the trigger was preceded in the act a thousand times by all those who preach violence, hatred, and intolerance—by the extremists, the fanatical fringe, the character assassins, and the hate peddlers of our day. The President has died. The people of this Nation must now cleanse themselves from the disease of hate or he will have died in vain.

Let us not forget too quickly. We have a tested and able leader to assume the great responsibilities of the Presidency, but because of that let us not too soon turn our thoughts away from what happened and why. It is for us as individuals and as a nation to examine our own conscience and to dedicate ourselves anew to those great principles of truth, tolerance, understanding, justice, and love that were taught us by the Prince of Peace, and that have guided our Nation these many years.

President Kennedy typified those principles as much as any other American of our time. We would do well to build a monument to this good and great man—each one of us—in our own hearts—a monument of dedication to those great principles he so well exemplified. John F. Kennedy gave his life for his country. We owe him much, but especially we owe him this.

Mr. Speaker, America has suffered a great and irreparable loss. In our hour of grief we are infinitely proud of Jacqueline Kennedy who has shown us nobility of character in these hours of grief that will remain for all time a living inspiration to men and women everywhere. May God be good to Mrs. Kennedy and the children and all members of the family and may all of us help to pay the debt we owe by becoming more faithful servants of the land we love.

ADDRESS BY

Hon. Homer Thornberry

OF TEXAS

Mr. Speaker, I join the leadership and my colleagues of the House in paying tribute to the memory of that great and noble American, President John Fitzgerald Kennedy.

Much is being said on this floor today about our martyred President. No words of mine can accurately or adequately describe my thoughts about him.

Like many of you I knew him first when he was a Member of this House, then as a U.S. Senator, and then as our President. I admired him greatly and liked him very much.

It was my privilege to accompany him across Texas in the 1960 presidential campaign. I was honored when I could present him to the welcoming throng of Americans who met him at the Austin, Tex., Municipal Airport just after he had made the courageous and magnificent appearance before the Houston Ministerial Conference. I was never prouder of an American than I was of Senator Kennedy that evening.

I shall always remember with pride the great honor he afforded me when he appointed me as U.S. district judge for the western district of Texas.

I am glad that I had the opportunity as a Representative in the Congress of the United States to support him as the leader of this Nation and of the free world. Not only was I shocked but saddened beyond words when I first realized in Dallas that our President was dead.

Little did my colleagues from Texas and I realize that when we accompanied him to our State on November 21 and 22 that we would be close to the tragedy of his death. There is no way to tell of the shock and grief we experienced.

President John F. Kennedy is now immortal. History will record his greatness. All I can say here is that I am thankful I knew him and that I could serve in a small way to make his tremendous task easier. My family and I are grieved for his incomparable widow and children and his remarkable family.

ADDRESS BY

Hon. Charles A. Mosher

OF OHIO

Mr. Speaker, one of my earliest memories is of my father's enthusiasm for the late Teddy Roosevelt. I remember his reading to me the reports that Roosevelt sent back from his African trips, as published in a magazine which was a prime influence in our home at that time, but is no longer published, the old Outlook. And my own first boyhood involvement in politics was in active support of Roosevelt's Bull Moose campaign.

I mention that, Mr. Speaker, because it has seemed to me that President John F. Kennedy had something of the same "flair" that characterized Teddy Roosevelt, an abundant vitality of body and spirit, combined with both idealism

and pragmatism and intellectual capacity of a high order, which I found very attractive and even exciting.

Both men were quick and vocal in their recognition of social and economic problems which they felt threatened our Nation, and both vigorously espoused what they considered to be the effective and necessary reforms to solve such problems. Both also roused up strong opposition.

I will not attempt to press too far any recital of the similarities between these two great national leaders, Teddy Roosevelt and Jack Kennedy. They were different in many ways. But, Mr. Speaker, I do say that in my own impressions they had much of the same impact. They were similar in their ability to express ideas and ideals excitingly, and to capture the imagination and the support, especially of people who are young, imaginative, idealistic, full of energy and ambition, interested in creating a better world.

Yes; President Kennedy attracted me greatly as a person, even though I was not of his political party and even though I sometimes found myself thoroughly disagreeing with him. I believe he would be the first to appreciate that honest criticism has its rightful place in any sincere eulogy, and therefore I submit it shows no lack of respect for me now to say that I found exciting and admirable Mr. Kennedy's skill and eloquence in the use of words and ideas, but at the same time I was frequently distressed and disappointed by the actual solutions he offered for this Nation's problems.

His solutions too often seemed to lack originality and inventiveness. His proposal of the Peace Corps, I am quick to admit, is an exception to that rule. But too often I felt discouraged and frustrated when, after he would lift the Nation to heights with his calls for action, the specific programs he proposed would be largely mere repetition of the old New Deal remedies, emphasizing increased Federal expenditures and increased concentration of authority and responsibility in the Federal Government.

Perhaps the very fact that John Kennedy so relished the world of ideas and ideals and so enjoyed intellectual discourse, made him suspect in the eyes of some people. It is said that Americans are suspicious of intellectuals, and that the Congress mirrors such popular suspicion. That alone might be an important reason why the

Kennedy legislative program had met with such public apathy and had made so little progress in the Congress, at the time of his tragic death. But my own personal appraisal is this, he was eminently successful in his statement of the problems and in his eloquent insistence that the problems must be met, and then he was too lacking in originality in the action he took to follow up on those words. He will be remembered much more as an idea man than as an action man.

Nevertheless, Mr. Speaker, all of us here must admit that something wonderful was lost to each of us, was lost to all of America and to the world, when that dastardly assassin's bullet snuffed out with such shocking abruptness the vitality and the ability to excite and inspire which so characterized President Kennedy's leadership. And I for one will be quick to forget the ways in which I disagreed with him, but I will remember forever with gratitude and inspiration the young President's extraordinary "flair." As one of the newspaper editorials said on the day following President Kennedy's death, "He walked like a prince and talked like a scholar." It is those qualities in him—and many more—that will forever linger in my own memory.

I am humbly grateful that it was my privilege to come to Washington and serve here, even in a very small way, while John F. Kennedy was our President. It has been an unforgettable experience for all of us.

Jack Kennedy was much, much too young to die. His less than 3 years as President did not give him an opportunity to show the full range of his talents or of his capacity to be effective, even though he matured very rapidly in that impossibly difficult office. The assassin did not give him a chance to become one of the great Presidents, but even we whose admiration for him was tempered with occasional criticism, must admit that he might well have become one of the great Presidents, if he had been given the time.

Mr. Kennedy's own acute sense of history, and the delightful way he had of being able to laugh at himself, would mean, I suspect, that he himself would agree he had not yet achieved true greatness. He was an exceptionally ambitious young man, in the best sense of that word "ambitious," and he certainly understood his potential niche among the greats of history. It is a mockery, a terribly unfair thing that he was not allowed sufficient time.

But in death, he is not the greatest loser. We and all the world are the real victims of that assassin's bullet. The nature of the world in which we live and the course of history itself, are suddenly changed by the death of President Kennedy. It is a very real personal tragedy for each and every one of us.

Having lost our young President, Mr. Speaker, we have lost one of the most eloquent, articulate exponents of political ideas and ideals that this century is likely to know. In his brief time as President, Mr. Kennedy's impact upon all of us has been deep and indelible. I know that I speak the feelings of my own 13th Congressional District in Ohio when I say that all of us are deeply grieved by his death. In each of us there is profound sympathy for Mrs. Kennedy and for the children and brothers and sisters of the late President. The close ties by which that extraordinary family are united and by which they work together are an inspiration to all of us, and will undoubtedly continue to be.

We grieve for our lost President, Mr. Speaker, but in closing these brief remarks, let me say that the people in my district also join me in looking to our new President with loyalty and with hope, and with prayers that he may be given the strength and the wisdom which now more than ever we Americans so desperately need.

ADDRESS BY

Hon. H. R. Gross

OF IOWA

Mr. Speaker, with all citizens of this country I was shocked and grieved by the wanton slaying of President Kennedy.

I first met our late President when he was a Member of the House of Representatives and, while I did not agree with his position on many issues then, nor later as President, I recognized him as an able Christian gentleman, loyal to his country and dedicated to his purposes.

It seems inconceivable that he should be struck down so tragically and violently in the prime of life.

I extend sympathy to his widow and especially to the children who have been made fatherless.

ADDRESS BY

Hon. John W. Wydler

OF NEW YORK

Mr. Speaker, John Fitzgerald Kennedy is now a part of history. The God that made him has taken him, and God's will be done.

No words can portray the shocking events of the last few days nor set forth the grief of our Nation. Each family in America feels a loss of a loved one, for the President belonged to us all. Let us measure our sorrow, however, by the agony of his brave wife and family who have lost a beloved husband, father, brother, and child. Our prayers should be for them.

President Kennedy was a man of intelligence and charm, a brave man and a dedicated one. His wit, his confidence, and his ability will be missed. We mourn him.

The Presidency, however, never dies. Our strength lies in the fact that we are a nation of laws, not men. The new President has assumed his full responsibilities. Our country is scarred but intact. Our hopes are high. Our faith is secure.

As we pray and mourn together, it is time for us to assume our full responsibility. Let our Nation draw closer together, more united, more dedicated.

The measure of a man is the effect he has on the lives of others. In life and death President Kennedy served us all. He told us we can do better, and I believe that history will show this Nation rose from its sorrow to stand taller than it ever did before.

ADDRESS BY

Hon. Bruce Alger

OF TEXAS

Mr. Speaker, we of Dallas want to join in remembrance of our late President, John F. Kennedy. We decry the violence and deplore the action of a twisted mind so filled with a foreign ideology and hate for all that is good in America that he could find release only in the murder of the President.

The most fitting memorial to John F. Kennedy is a rededication on the part of all Americans to the preservation of this Nation and its fundamental ideals, a pledge to hold freedom dear, and to subject all the issues which confront us to careful study and decision on merit determined only on what is good for America and all its people.

ADDRESS BY

Hon. Harold R. Collier

OF ILLINOIS

Mr. Speaker, little did any of us dream when we concluded legislative business for the week on Thursday, November 21, that we would find ourselves engaged in the sad but fitting and proper respect we have here today. As we pause to pay solemn tribute to our late President, John F. Kennedy, we cannot help but feel the great impact that the tragic event of his assassination left upon millions of people around the face of the world.

When death takes one whose role in the destiny of our Nation and the world was so important, it is indeed a time of deep sorrow; but when that death comes in the sudden and shocking manner that it did to our late President, it is one of the historical tragedies of all time.

The assassin's bullet which struck down the 35th President of the United States snuffed out the life of a brilliant young man who was in the prime years of his life. Beyond the limited tenure of his office as Chief Executive, there is no doubt that he was destined to play a leading role in the affairs of this Nation and the world for many years to come. Now we shall never know how great an effect that role might have been in the future. But we do know that in the comparatively short years of his public service he left an indelible mark upon the records.

Like many Members of both legislative bodies, I had philosophical differences from time to time with programs recommended and supported by the Kennedy administration. Honest differences of opinion in dealing with the many complex problems of our time are certainly understandable. The late President frequently expressed his disagreement with programs and policies of President Eisenhower's administration when he served in the legislative branch of government. And this is as it should be in a nation that is established on a system of checks and balances and upon the fundamental representative form of government.

We who deeply respected the late President Kennedy's pursuit of his own deep convictions in providing legislative and administrative solutions to the many problems facing the Nation know that he respected the right of others to pursue their convictions in those things that they sincerely felt were in the best interests of the country. And while often our approach to handling the problems may have been different, we shared the recognition of these existing problems.

The late President Kennedy was dedicated to the policies and programs which he supported. He did so even in the face of opposition, in some cases within his own political party, and naturally to that of his political opponents as is so normal in a political system with two major political parties embracing somewhat divergent political philosophies.

John F. Kennedy fought for his country in time of war and in peacetime stood stanch in his belief in his dedication to strengthening the United States of America in its international conflict with the Communist world.

To his courageous widow, lovely children and beloved family, I extend my condolence and prayers. They have indeed been burdened with a loss and heartache which will remain with them forever.

ADDRESS BY

Hon. Henry S. Reuss

OF WISCONSIN

Mr. Speaker, the bitter events that began with the assassination of our beloved President, John F. Kennedy, on November 22, have very force-

fully reminded us how fragile are the things we prize most in this world. The tragedy reminds us how the inscrutable forces of evil impinge upon our best efforts to order our society rationally.

In the old story, the flame had flickered symbolically in the cathedral's niche for centuries. It could have been snuffed out at any time. But it burned on and on until one day an evil man entered the sanctuary and blew it out.

The President of an open democracy believed that he could communicate with his people best by going freely among them. Then an evil man shot him as he rode through the city of Dallas.

Like the flame of truth and justice, life—even of the most exalted—is fragile in a world where there is violence and hatred.

And now the President's body has been buried in the goodly company of heroes at Arlington.

Now we can only pay tribute to John F. Kennedy and to his memory.

We loved this man: his truth telling whether it was accepting full responsibility for the Bay of Pigs, or his never-delivered speech in Dallas calling for an end to the fanaticism and hatred that were rending the Nation; his taste for literature and history, music and the arts; his gaiety and high spirits; his tolerance and freedom from rancor and grudge bearing.

I shall particularly remember two tributes that came on the day he was buried—the ambassador of a new-founded African nation who said to me "My people mourn him, too"—and a cable from my friend, Walther Casper, head of the West German Peace Corps which John F. Kennedy had done so much to stimulate:

In this hour of grief to you, the United States, and all mankind, we shall try to fulfill President Kennedy's heritage by continuing our German Peace Corps work.

He was a President in the great mold of Washington and Jefferson and Lincoln and F.D.R. Yet the time allotted him did not permit all the accomplishments that his greatness promised. But as a realist as well as an idealist he always knew that his work would not be finished.

In his inaugural address he sensed the limitations of his office.

All this will not be finished in the first hundred days. Nor will it be finished in the first thousand days, nor in the life of this administration, nor even perhaps in our lifetime on this planet. But let us begin.

The beginnings are surely with us. The Soviet power turned back at Cuba yet with the restraint that avoided a nuclear showdown; the challenge of equal opportunity for all Americans boldly accepted; the foundations for full employment and the general welfare at home, for trade and aid abroad, well laid. These are no inconsiderable foundations.

So let us turn aside from the bloody Gehenna of Dallas and ask ourselves to capture the truthfulness and taste, the high hopes and the high courage of John F. Kennedy, and to apply them to our problems of economics and ethics, race relations and peace on earth, in the trying days that lie ahead.

Like no other event in our times, the death of President Kennedy has inspired an outpouring of grief. Some expressions of a people greatly moved have been drawn together in the following article from the December 2, 1963, issue of the Milwaukee Journal:

THE GRIEVING PEOPLE SPEAK

Hundreds of letters have been written to the Journal about the death of President Kennedy, many by persons who have never been moved to write letters for publication before. Because it is impossible to publish all of them in their entirety, the following excerpts have been chosen to indicate the range of feeling among Wisconsin citizens on the tragic event and its aftermath.

From a northside Milwaukee man:

"I am not a reporter, but I experienced a sensation which made me feel how close we people of this country really are when a tragedy befalls us.

"I walked into a store and heard a colored man explain to his 3-year-old son, 'We have lost the greatest friend we ever had.' I heard a lady tell a salesman, 'I am sorry. I don't want to look any more. I just don't feel I could concentrate on anything today.' This woman had tears running down her cheeks."

From a Milwaukee housewife:

"I shall deeply miss and mourn President Kennedy as though I would my own husband or child. I never met him, only heard and saw him on TV and in the papers, but he was to me, as countless others, a beloved and respected person. Let us hope and pray his death will not be for nothing. Somewhere in all this is a lesson; let us look for this hidden message."

From a South Milwaukee mother:

"Since Friday, almost every person I've talked with has expressed a furious hatred for the murderer of President Kennedy. Interviews with people of Dallas show an open feeling of hate.

"But how many of these people have gone to church and sat quietly in prayer? Have they asked themselves why and how such a bizarre chain of events could happen in our Christian America? Have they let their young children hear them utter these disgusting expressions of hate?

"Christ rode in a similar triumphant procession before His tragic crucifixion. But did God put hate into the hearts of the true mourners? I believe Christ's prayer was, 'Father, forgive them, for they know not what they do.' Certainly He did not teach the hate that seems to be in the hearts and minds of so many people in our country."

NOW IS THE TIME WE SHOULD NOT PANIC

From a 13-year-old Menomonee Falls girl:

"Yes, there has been a great loss, not only to Jacqueline and family, but to many nations. I think now is the time that we should not panic, but think of the future and look forward in hope that many more leaders will come as strongly minded as John F. Kennedy."

From a Waupaca housewife:

"I strongly feel, as most of the Nation must feel, that President Kennedy fought the evil in our world with one of our most powerful weapons * * * love. The good that has been done by this love can never be wiped away by a mere bullet. It's almost as though the bullet, in shattering the man, spread his goodness, justice, patience, and love throughout the world. Who could do more?"

From a Milwaukee man:

" 'Blessed are they who mourn, for they shall be comforted.' This truth was etched indelibly into the minds of a stunned and sorrowful people by the eloquent nobility and dignity of a young wife and mother, in very fact comforting all of us in the awesome silence of her own deep and tragic grief. She sustained us in our loneliness.

"May we now, in grateful acknowledgment of her unparalleled example, offer this woman our own fraternal comfort in return."

OUR GAIN MUST SURPASS OUR LOSS

From a Milwaukee housewife:

"From this terrible, black weekend of numbness and utter dismay has come to the citizens of our young Nation a deep and renewed patriotic sense of unity and rededication. It is almost unbelievable that a few short days of abandonment of daily pursuits and frantic living could give way so readily to complete reflection as to why we are here and our real purpose for living.

"Our gain must surpass our loss, as great and tremendous as it is. Our concentration must be on the ideals for which our dear President died, and not on the conditions or reasons for which he died."

From a Marquette University student:

"We begin to realize we must live in this world and start to believe in something. We must stand for something. No longer can we go on letting events pass by without realizing their significance. What kind of power is invested in mankind? Will we use our power as Lee H. Oswald did, or will we channel it in a direction that will preserve the human race, that will make one human proud to be part of the other?"

From a 17-year-old Milwaukee girl:

"There is a freedom song that has become popular in recent years called 'We Shall Overcome.' I sincerely hope that the new President Johnson, and more important, all American people will make this simple song their theme. Then the eyes of the world will look with favor upon us, because we will have achieved what our beloved President strived for: Peace based on the brotherhood of man."

From a Racine housewife:

"President Kennedy loved all people, even our foe. He loved all and wanted to give all he could. Now, Mrs. Marina Oswald is left with a name and two children. Was she left to provide a future for these children? What is going to happen to the Oswald family? Let it not be written that she was condemned for her name."

SPIRIT CAN BE BORNE TO ALL NATIONS

From a Waukesha man:

"Now the body lies in a hero's grave. The soul has been lofted to companionship with other departed great. But the spirit is not interred. It is free, as vital and eager as during life.

"The spirit lives on. It will not die as long as men can find shelter for a bit of it in each of their hearts. It can be borne to all nations, to all corners of the earth and beyond. It need never cease the quest for enduring peace which began as it pulsed in the mighty, compassionate heart now stilled."

From a University of Wisconsin student at Madison:

"So often it is only after death that we recognize a man's real qualities, and now we look at John Fitzgerald Kennedy and Abraham Lincoln and think:

"Both were killed by the assassin's bullet * * * both were followed to the Presidency by a Vice President named Johnson * * * both were killed during periods of tension—the Civil War then, the cold war now * * * both were instrumental in the rights of the Negro * * * both had a highly developed sense of humor * * * both were men of a deep faith in God * * * both left us addresses we will long remember * * * and most important, both believed in the basic human dignity that united all men."

From a West Allis man:

"Violent means to end political or social problems of any kind always bring tragedy, and whether the life or lives thus forfeited are those of a state dignitary or the average man, the end results are always the same.

"Perhaps the martyrdom of Mr. Kennedy will do something to halt or brake the headlong rush of otherwise intelligent nations into a holocaust of nuclear destruction. May he not have died in vain."

BEAVER DAM WOMAN, MAN FROM WEST BEND

From a Beaver Dam woman:

"Surrender your heart to those qualities which claim it today—
Sorrow, in the loss of a monarch in human inspiration and dignity;
Sorrow, for the ruthless severance of a holy union, which, among men,
Is the cup of strength from a benevolent God;
Regret, for action too long withheld; regret, for truth too long denied;
Shame, for the yoke of responsibility that rests now, too late,
Heavy, heavy, on each of us, for each of us—one to the other."

From a West Bend man:

"As he died in search of this thing people call peace, a question is asked: Is there peace? Yes, and if all free men will unite, there will be peace. This is not an easy thing to ask of some people.

"It may mean that bigots will have to surrender their cause—perhaps they can find some other pastime. It will mean that racists will have to, if this is at all possible, realize that they live in a country that they did not inherit. When they got here, the trail was blazed by the blood of people of God's creation, be they red, black, white, or yellow."

From a Waukesha man:

"Their silent faces told that they had lost a son.
The world wept for one so young, so near with his devotion.
They asked, 'Why?' when caught in death's emotion,
And the spirit of dedication and love and will they knew
Answered: 'Ask not what the world can do for you.'"

ADDRESS BY

Hon. Barratt O'Hara

OF ILLINOIS

Mr. Speaker, an angel of peace and human understanding has passed our way and we have touched his garment.

On November 22, 1963, his mission on earth tragically ended, the soul of John Fitzgerald Kennedy was freed from finite limitations to continue in immortality the work of peace on earth, good will among men, that was the purpose of his creation.

Peace on earth, good will among men, it is the goal of our prayers that will be reached.

And the soul of John Fitzgerald Kennedy, gone only from the vision of the eye, will continue to lead us on, us who in his days on earth touched his garment.

John Fitzgerald Kennedy brought to the office of President of the United States a spirit of dedication to the service of his country which shall live in the hearts of all Americans forever. He dedicated himself to the task of making life better for all of us. He would improve the lot of mankind not only materially by wiping out poverty, ignorance, and disease; his sights were set upon the day when a lasting peace would free the minds and hearts of men to build "progress, human rights, and world law."

In his address before the American University, June 10, 1963, President Kennedy defined the peace he envisioned:

What kind of peace do I mean and what kind of peace do we seek: Not a Pax Americana enforced on the world by American weapons of war. Not the peace of the grave or the security of the slave. I am talking about genuine peace—the kind of peace that makes life on earth worth living—and the kind that enables men and nations to grow and to hope and build a better life for their children—not merely peace for Americans, but peace for all men and women—not merely peace in our time but peace for all time.

A student of history, he made history. He was a trail blazer. In promoting legislation to aid the unemployed, to make opportunities for our youth, to assist depressed areas, he was building upon established foundations. In establishing the "hot line" between Washington and Moscow, in supporting a Peace and Disarmament Agency, and in the negotiation of a nuclear test ban, and in building the Peace Corps, he carried the United States and the world across the threshold of a new era in human understanding.

Again we turn to his own words:

According to the ancient Chinese proverb, a journey of 1,000 miles must begin with a single step. My fellow Americans let us take that first step. Let us, if we can, step back from the shadows of war and seek out the way of peace. And if that journey is 1,000 miles or even more, let history record that we, in this land, at this time, took the first step.

The brief administration of John Fitzgerald Kennedy, while serious in purpose, was colorful and exciting. His keen, ready wit, his brilliant intellect, made every speech a classic and his press conferences a delight.

The irony of it all lies in the fact that despite his effort to build peace and good will, to promote human rights, it was hate that killed him; the blind bitter hatred of which Birmingham was the symbol; the hatred which manifested itself in the extremist both of the right and of the left. In his last speech at Fort Worth he said:

This is a dangerous and uncertain world—no one expects our lives to be easy—not in this decade, not in this century.

John Fitzgerald Kennedy died to make a better world of peace on earth, good will among all men. If we can dedicate ourselves to the achievement of his goals, he shall not have died in vain.

Mr. Speaker, our hearts go out to all the members of the family of President Kennedy. No family in our national history ever was more closely knit together. Family affection is a precious thing. Love for and loyalty to family is akin to love for and loyalty to country. It is in the noblest of American traditions.

The story of those dreadful, sorrowful days will be told and retold throughout the centuries and the names of John and Jacqueline Kennedy forever will be linked together in one of the world's imperishable love stories.

Mr. Speaker, the distinguished majority whip, the gentleman from Louisiana [Mr. Boggs] in his eloquent and moving remarks, made mention of the maternal grandfather of our martyred President.

When I came to the Congress in 1949 John Kennedy was commencing his second term in the House. At the time I was taping a half hour radio program for Chicago, and my young colleague from Massachusetts always responded with instant willingness and a smile to my request for participation. On occasions this was at considerable inconvenience to him, and to no personal advantage since mine was a local radio program that did not reach his constituency.

My fondness for him was deepened by the reports that came to me of his kind, gentle, considerate treatment of the men and women working in his office. One day I said to him: "Jack, you get your sweetness from your grandfather." I was referring to his mother's father, mayor of Boston at the time of the Spanish-American War. He was a man "all heart" and deeply beloved by the low and the high. He had been one of the idols of my boyhood.

Two weeks before his death, on the afternoon of Friday, November 8, I saw President Kennedy for the last time. It was at the White House, and although for the President it was a very busy day, he had, in the sweetness I shall always associate with his memory, set aside a quarter of an hour to meet and chat with Archie House, the newly elected commander in chief of the United Spanish War Veterans, who in 1898, just turning 16, had gone with me, 2 or 3 months his junior, to the siege of Santiago in Cuba. To me it was an occasion freighted with tender sentiment to introduce my buddy of so long ago to the President of the United States. I had never seen the President looking better. He seemed filled with the vibrancy and cheer of life. When we were leaving, and the President was shaking hands with Archie, he mentioned his long friendship with me, and added: "Barratt knew my grandfather." Those were the last words of President Kennedy that I was to hear. "Barratt knew my grandfather." And now they are among the treasures of my memory, associated with my words to him at the commencement of our friendship: "Jack, you get your sweetness from your grandfather."

President Kennedy's naming of his yacht, the "Honey Fitz," and his insistence on the full spelling out of his middle name—Fitzgerald—indexed his pride in and his affection for his grandfather.

An angel of peace and human understanding has passed our way and we have touched his garment. I know of no other way of expressing what is in my mind and heart.

ADDRESS BY
Hon. Peter W. Rodino, Jr.
OF NEW JERSEY

Mr. Speaker, "to every thing there is a season, and a time to every purpose under heaven."

The world—the humanity—and the country he loved and served so well shall never forget him or his name—his aims and aspirations, his noble endeavors and his dedicated efforts for the sake of mankind. He will be a memory forever in the hearts and minds of free men and in the hearts of his countrymen.

His was a true greatness—a greatness born of constant courage and deathless dedication in a crusade for great ideas and greater ideals. For his was a soul fired with a deep sense of mission in the endless and enduring struggle of his fellow man—to achieve brotherhood through understanding and understanding through brotherhood. Though recognizing the need for strong action in the name of freedom, he was unfailing in his pursuit of peace.

Believing that God's work on earth is "truly our own" he sought to bring from out of the darkness, light; from despair, hope; and out of hatred, love. And so he uttered wise words, did great deeds, and suffered noble sorrows for the cause of his country and the world.

He asked of his country only one thing—that he might be able to give: to give of himself—and this he did in the fullest sense for in its cause he truly laid down his life.

Though he has fallen, this knight in shining armor, his torch shall burn brightly and forever, and its eternal light will glow from generation to generation—as a beacon lighting the way for men of good will.

ADDRESS BY
Hon. Mark Andrews
OF NORTH DAKOTA

Mr. Speaker, the assassination of John F. Kennedy on Friday, November 22, 1963, has brought a time of great sadness to all Americans. It is a most shocking thing to have a man dedicated to public service shot down in the prime of life.

Our thoughts and prayers are with the Kennedy family. The personal sorrow is shared by all of us as Americans.

This is a moment for reflection on the strength that is America. The continuity that our Constitution provides made the transition of Government possible. The most fitting memorial we can provide for President Kennedy is to work together to strengthen this country we all love so well.

Hon. Florence P. Dwyer

Mr. Speaker, only now are we beginning to understand what happened on that cataclysmic Friday, the 22d of November, when violent death removed the 35th President of the United States from his commanding position in America and the free world. For only now are we beginning to emerge from the numbness and the listlessness which cloaked so many of our people following the shock of sudden and tragic death.

So, only now can we begin to appreciate and define, with some measure of objectivity, the extent of the loss which has befallen the Nation as a result of the assassination of John F. Kennedy.

And only now, as events of the past 2 weeks slip into focus, can we begin to assess the consequences of the murder of a man and a President who attracted affection and widespread admiration and also inspired in others some deep misgivings, but toward whom no one could remain indifferent.

It is fitting, therefore, that we undertake this task of appreciation and assessment here in the Chamber from which the youthful Congressman began his historic climb to the height of mature statesmanship. At the same time, we owe it to this man with a sense of history and a respect for words to see him whole and deal justly with the facts. His life, I think, suggests that he would as quickly spurn the sticky, the sentimental, the emotional desire to canonize him, as he would resent slander and regret the failure to understand what he was trying to do.

What is it then, Mr. Speaker, that our country has lost and what manner of man is he whom we mourn in the death of President Kennedy? Others among us knew him personally far better than I. Yet, since he was preeminently a public person—one who sought, enjoyed and understood the public nature of the office he held and who never seemed to seek refuge from the public spotlight in a false claim to privacy—the public record of what he did and said—as well as what he did not say or do—may provide us with everything we need to know, as opposed to everything we might like to know. On the public record,

therefore, it is clear that the United States has lost a remarkable President and a gifted human being. Whether or not all agreed with each of his specific objectives or with the means he chose to achieve them, there is no doubt that he operated in the best postwar and postdepression American tradition of seeking peace and justice through national strength and the sharing of our national abundance, and of promoting equality and opportunity here at home through the judicious balancing of private and public activity.

In broad outline, these are national aims which are and have been generally accepted by the great majority of our people, and so President Kennedy's uniqueness lay not so much in making these purposes his own as in the style and spirit with which he articulated them and the way in which he pursued them.

There was a sureness of touch about the way the President managed the country's foreign affairs, a coolness and confident poise under pressure, an impressive grasp of detail wedded to a deep understanding of the historic moment and of the limitations and opportunities which influenced the directions we can take.

He saw in the cool light of reason, without sentiment, both the problems and the promise of our land and our people. He understood what we could be and do if ever we could assure equality, remove discrimination, improve education, provide enough jobs, protect the unfortunate, conserve our natural resources, make our cities truly habitable, and lift our aims to match our potential. We may have differed at times with his strategy, his tactics, or his timing, but his ideals had an undeniable splendor.

He was no visionary. His dreams—if, indeed, they could be called dreams—were made of solid stuff, the product of an active intellect, tempered by an acute awareness of what at any one time was practicable. He was said to have lacked passion and fire and warmth and deep feeling. Possibly so—but he was strong in the more reliable area of the intellect.

For President Kennedy was a man of ideas—not so much the creator or the innovator as the appreciator, the collector, the user of ideas. He admired excellence and honored the excellent, and ceaselessly searched for both in everything he did. He respected and understood the political process in all its frustration and ambiguous complexity as the interplay of power and personality, the essential means of translating ideas into action.

Conversely, he distrusted the emotional, feared the irrational, and was unimpressed by the cliches and platitudes of the doctrinaire left and right.

There was a special flavor and spirit about this man—restless, alert and aware, fresh and full of vigor, a word with which he shall forever be identified. There was grace too, and good taste. In partnership with his lovely wife, he inspired new zest and hope in the cultural and intellectual life of America whose leaders and practitioners sensed his interest and understanding and joy in what they were doing. A lot of good things happened in America during the Kennedy years, Mr. Speaker, not alone because he distinctly encouraged them but because he helped create an atmosphere in which the arts and science and the imagination could flourish.

John F. Kennedy possessed another great gift, Mr. Speaker, the gift of honesty in seeing himself and others as they really were, the rare ability to diminish himself momentarily from the hubbub and confusion of the Presidency and look at himself and his associates in the cold gray light of objectivity. He seemed never to be self-satisfied or complacent and despite the partisan nature of much of his job he could recognize the sincerity and perhaps the rightness of many who disagreed with his programs and policies.

In the perspective of his death, the capacity of this young President to grow and mature has come strongly to the fore. We have been abruptly and permanently denied the opportunity ever to know fully just what kind of President he might have become. But we have seen the tremendous changes that transformed Kennedy the campaigner into Kennedy the President. There was his greater awareness of the difficulties of his office, his increasing recognition of the need to consider many and varied points of view, his developed understanding of the limits as well as the powers of his position. The tedious process of reaching rational decisions about public policies and of obtaining consent to controversial proposals was rapidly maturing this gifted young man and now we can only speculate about what he might ultimately have meant to the Nation and the world.

In all that he was and was becoming, President Kennedy reflected the still youthful quality of our

country. He, like all of us, was tested by the unending problem brought by our technological superiority and confounded by the shrinking world we live in. That his urgent search for the proper balance between national security and international responsibility, between public needs and private rights, was proceeding in the right direction has been certified by the unprecedented expressions of grief and loss and tribute which have poured forth from every corner of the earth. People everywhere seemed instinctively to regard him with hope and trust.

This is what we have lost, Mr. Speaker, and the loss has been a grievous one.

But in our losing we have also gained.

We have marveled at the gallantry of his young widow who, in the moment of her greatest grief, has carried herself with simple dignity and quiet courage and true majesty.

We have been enabled to look into our own hearts and minds in this time of national tragedy and challenged to remove the vestiges of bitterness and hate and suspicion.

We have been freed from the frequent distortion of the immediate and permitted to view our recent past more broadly and more accurately.

We have rediscovered the fundamental unity of our people as they shared experience of national shock and mourning.

And we have demonstrated anew to ourselves and to the world the soundness and stability of our political institutions which allowed us to make the difficult transition of leadership with certainty and sureness.

In mourning the loss of John F. Kennedy, Mr. Speaker, we are conscious chiefly of what he was and what he might have been, but we also have ourselves to think of. To be true to ourselves and to our responsibilities we must get about our work—the work to which he devoted the last full measure of himself.

ADDRESS BY

Hon. Wright Patman

OF TEXAS

Mr. Speaker, only history many years hence can possibly give to the story of mankind the full and accurate evaluation of John Fitzgerald Kennedy's contribution to the freedom and the peace of the human race. Here under the pressure and the immediacy of the vast problems that confront us I believe the tendency is to undervalue the full dimension of what the late President Kennedy has wrought for the good of the free world.

And this undervaluation is taking place in spite of the enormous mountain of feeling and sentiment, bereavement and indignation, that is stirring in the souls of men everywhere on this earth. For President Kennedy has effected a series of breakthroughs on the brutality of national and international history in our time that marks him, in my humble judgment, one of the great statesmen of American history.

The meaning of his service as President of the United States is not to be found wholly in a kind of tabulation table of his accomplishments in terms of so many laws passed, and so many goals actually attained in all their completeness. The meaning of his service rather, as I see it, is in the enormous strides into the future that seemed impossible until he came along and that plowed new ground for a relatively peaceful world of peace and prosperity.

Nor was his service lacking in formidableness in the area of actual legislation on the statue books, and actual negotiations for peace on the international stage where the lives of tens and hundreds of millions of people were involved. Even in the cold terms of bookkeeping and statistics the hard facts show that in 1961 in the first year of the Kennedy administration Congress passed no less than 154 major laws, laws that in their totality had a profound effect on the American economy and the American way of life along progressive lines. In the second year of the Kennedy administration Congress passed 148 major laws—that was a year ago in 1962. And in the first 6 months of 1963 this Congress passed some 29 major laws.

This record, looked at through any manner of microscope, critically or with applause, may be said objectively to constitute on the whole an accomplishment of the first magnitude. The Kennedy administration was a working administration. It was a working administration that sought, as the President's personality revealed, to achieve its ends by calmness, by reason, by persuasion, and by good humor. Occasionally under the pressure of immense human and material forces strong tactics were employed to forward what seemed to the administration a vital and significant goal.

But the meaning in all its aspects of the personality of a man like John Fitzgerald Kennedy was such as to win him approbation, even affection, and support in many quarters both at home and abroad.

At home even in the area of business where some hostility was said to exist and an area with which I have some familiarity, the Kennedy personality acted—as I look back—like the balm of Gilead. This does not mean that there was a state always of untarnished harmony but it does mean that the President felt it his duty to uphold the dignity of the White House. And this he did splendidly and magnificently and with great aplomb. And then in the sphere of practicality the President did for business, in my judgment through the regular executive channels, as much as he did for any other segment of American life and the American economy. And his whole heart and his whole soul was devoted to the American people. He himself, shortly before he was felled by the assassin's bullets, delineated his service to business and contiguous areas. He said:

> We have liberalized depreciation guidelines to grant more individual flexibility, reduced our farm surpluses, reduced transportation taxes, established a private corporation to manage our satellite communication system, increased the role of American business in the development of less developed countries, and proposed to the Congress a sharp reduction in corporate as well as personal income taxes, and a major de-regulation of transportation.

When I say the "balm of Gilead" I can imagine no more soothing lotion than these practical measures for the alleviation of the problems of our business community. They were definite. They were concise. They had the quality of touching problems at specific points and correcting situations that called for more enlightened legislative and executive treatment. Except for pending legislation—not abandoned legislation— pending legislation, this proved an immensely effective program and history will so honor it.

Yet this is—all of it—hardly more than a fragment of the work that President Kennedy actually put in for the good of our country, the good of the free world, the good of mankind now and for posterity. Will mankind ever forget, both this generation and generations to come, the skillful and adroit, the human and the wise, handling of the Cuban situation by President Kennedy? Of course the Kremlin backed down and was stopped and of course Khrushchev retreated.

But the sensitive and careful handling of this incredible potential world bomb is a tribute to statesmanship that comes close to the highest order of human genius. That fateful October in 1962 put all the qualities of the President to the supreme test. The President ordered a blockade that meant halting the Soviet Navy at sea and that could bring mankind to the day of doom. We had nuclear missiles at our very doorstep and these had to be removed.

The finesse of the Kennedy management of the problem was such as to permit the pride of the Soviets to effect their evacuation of missiles from Cuba without too much injury to their self-esteem. The main object was freedom for mankind and an end to the threat of nuclear enemy proximity to American shores. But the almost equal companion goal of the Kennedy strategy was to make it possible for the aggressive forces in the Soviet Union to be so handled from Washington as to provide them with a path out of the dilemma short of war.

And of course history knows with what success this was accomplished.

There was another confrontation of almost equal peril in 1961 when President Kennedy made sure that the Soviets would not again cut off Allied access to Berlin in the light of the threat presented by the East Berlin wall. The President, as has so often been noted, shipped highly mobile troops into the disputed area and assigned his eminently competent Vice President—Lyndon Johnson—to the Berlin crisis to reassure the German people and the free world of the sincerity and the firmness of our intent.

And of course history knows with what success the President's ends were accomplished.

It is in the very fact of this background of crucial confrontations, bringing the two greatest powers on earth to the very verge of war, that President Kennedy and his administration put over the now historic nuclear test ban treaty. This may go down as the prime achievement of his life. Should the Soviet Union fail to live up to its commitments on a matter of such immense moral and human significance, for itself as well as the whole world, it will forever expose itself to the suspicion, the contempt and the distrust of the human race, of all political

faiths and all forms of government. It seems incredible to me that this treaty will not hold.

What the President has left behind for this generation apart from his achievements in domestic legislation and foreign diplomacy is the example of a great and a good man. He delighted in the Presidency and in his family. He exuded faith in the good things of life and he was a man of religion. The whole world came to his funeral, so to speak, and the honor that was conferred upon him in death reflected prestige upon the whole of his record as a President and his qualities as a man. We will never forget the poise and the dignity of the widow through this unspeakable calamity. Mr. Speaker, as we see the mantle fall upon the shoulders of the gifted and competent President Lyndon B. Johnson, who is raising our hopes and lifting our hearts, we can reflect upon the inherently tough structure of our Government, but nothing—just nothing—can expunge the feeling of irretrievable loss in the death of John Fitzgerald Kennedy.

ADDRESS BY

Hon. R. Walter Riehlman

OF NEW YORK

Mr. Speaker, the tragic death of President Kennedy was a shocking event to the whole Nation and to those of us who served with him in Congress.

John F. Kennedy was elected to his first post of national responsibility the same year I was. We both arrived in Congress in 1947.

I worked with him and I respected him. He labored diligently for the people of his congressional district and, I am sure, served them well.

His great drive and interest elevated him to the Senate and then the Presidency, the highest position Americans can bestow on their political leaders.

He was devoted to the philosophy and the causes he believed in and he gave unsparingly of himself to attain his goals.

It is a sad day indeed when a comparatively young man is struck down in the prime of life by an unbalanced, self-appointed executioner.

And, especially sorrowful is the loss to his devoted wife and his little children.

President Kennedy's death is a loss to the Nation and the entire world.

I extend to his family my heartfelt sympathy in these days of their bereavement.

ADDRESS BY

Hon. Paul Findley

OF ILLINOIS

Mr. Speaker, the tragic death of President Kennedy had unusual meaning for the district I represent. My district, the 20th Illinois, is the heart of the land of Lincoln. It includes Springfield, Abraham Lincoln's home. It includes the countryside Lincoln traveled as a youth and as a country lawyer. It includes a city, Quincy, where one of the famous Lincoln-Douglas debates occurred. Virtually all this area was in the district which Lincoln once represented in the House of Representatives.

And so, the people of this area know better than most the sorrow that comes when a President of the United States is slain.

Ninety-eight years ago Springfield knew the sorrow of bringing home for final rest the remains of President Lincoln. And today Springfield mourns anew. President Lincoln—like President Kennedy—was killed in the prime of his life and in the prime of his service to his country by an assassin's bullet.

Springfield had sent young Lincoln to Congress and had seen his rise to national fame in the debates over slavery. On February 11, 1861, the citizens of Springfield received Lincoln's affectionate farewell, as the President-elect entered the train that was to take him to the White House. Four years later he returned to Springfield in a coffin.

The Illinois State Journal of Springfield reported the news of Lincoln's rise to fame—and the news of his tragic death. Lincoln wrote:

The Journal paper was my friend, and of course its editors the same.

The same newspaper reported the news of Kennedy's rise to fame—and the news of his tragic death. The present-day publisher of the Journal, Jack Heintz, spoke for all in the Land of Lincoln when he cried out with these words:

What kind of a man is this? At 1 p.m. I look out my window at a street Christmas decoration which is now black. A man has died at the hands of a madman. The skies are darkened by a drizzling rain which echoes my despair. What manner of man is this who would differ so violently with a father, a husband, a country's leader who would do but what he felt in his heart was best for his fellow American, fellow man? May God have some mercy on his soul to the end of his violent, misshapen, and maniacal days.

Yes, Lincoln's Springfield, and all in the district I represent, mourn anew.

The Journal's companion newspaper, the Illinois State Register, the same day carried this front-page black-bordered editorial:

NATION IN STATE OF SHOCK AT PRESIDENT'S TRAGIC DEATH

Our beloved President is dead, victim of a bullet fired by a cowardly assassin. John Fitzgerald Kennedy, 35th President of the United States, who had survived the ordeals of war as a gallant hero, went to his death as he led this Nation in a quest for peace.

The people of the United States, numb with shock at the tragic manner in which our President died, mourn as one. Our hearts go out in sadness and deep sympathy for the President's family in their bereavement. The death of President Kennedy is a loss to all humanity, a loss made even more tragic by the manner in which he died.

This dastardly crime shook to the core even the most calloused, and the entire Nation poured out its grief unashamedly at the news of the President's death, and mingled with the tears were emotion-filled outpourings of anger at the psychopathic killer who had pulled the trigger to fire the bullet that snuffed out the life of the President.

John Fitzgerald Kennedy, the fourth President of the United States to die at the hands of an assassin, had experienced in his 46 years the role of successful lawyer, author and recipient of a Pulitzer Prize, of Senator of the United States and of President of the United States. He had experienced personal suffering and hardship in the military service of his country; he provided leadership with the quality of greatness during this cold war period of international political strife with the Communists; and, he was a husband and father, a role dear to his heart. He was a man of integrity, a man of honesty, a man of deep conviction and sincerity.

In a moment of tragedy, his life ended. But the principles in which he believed, and for which he fought, will live on in the hearts of all who live on to fight the battle President Kennedy considered his greatest goal, the quest for peace.

In this hour of bereavement, we join with all Americans in their sorrow and in their prayers for our fallen leader, President John Fitzgerald Kennedy.

ADDRESS BY

Hon. Charles E. Chamberlain

OF MICHIGAN

Mr. Speaker, we have had 13 days in which to try to comprehend and accept the reality of the incredible tragedy of the assassination of President Kennedy. Yet, it still remains beyond our grasp. And no doubt it will remain so until the history of our country is forgotten.

My own feelings and thoughts are echoed in the sorrow and sense of loss shared by my fellow citizens of the Sixth Congressional District of Michigan as expressed in two editorials last Wednesday, November 27.

Today I would but add to those sentiments, the thoughts of David Lawrence, appearing in the December 3 issue of U.S. News & World Report, as they strike me as being both fitting and proper and worthy of recording on this memorial occasion.

THE INCREDIBLE TRAGEDY

(By David Lawrence)

The American people and the peoples of the world mourn the death of President John F. Kennedy.

For the assassin's bullet ended the life of a young man whose sincerity of purpose, dedication to duty, and devotion to what he believed was right characterized his service to the United States. Even as he had responded to the cheers of the crowds and had ridden happily in an open automobile through the streets of Dallas, Tex., he reflected the confidence of a man with faith in his fellow citizens.

What shall we say of the insane impulse which caused a despicable individual to destroy the President of this great country? Americans, regardless of party or faction, believe in morality and in respect for human life.

Three times before in American history a President has been killed while in office—Abraham Lincoln, James A. Garfield, and William McKinley. In each instance, individuals of an erratic or unbalanced mentality were responsible. This strange hand of fate has taken from the White House four men of dedicated character. It is difficult to understand these tragic events in our history. For as a President is removed from this mortal life in a few minutes, there emerges a feeling that life and sudden death, even in high office, are beyond the comprehension of our finite minds.

We do know that every year the number of crimes committed by deranged individuals is increasing. Can we not devise some means of detecting in advance the symptoms of such behavior in our society?

The Secret Service has grappled with this problem for decades. Observation of the houses and buildings along a parade route, inspection in advance, and a multitude of bodyguards close at hand have evidently provided no sure preventive.

It was during a theater performance in Washington, on the night of April 14, 1865, that Abraham Lincoln, sitting in the presidential box, was shot by an erratic individual, who was subsequently killed for his crime by soldiers in pursuit of him.

James A. Garfield was shot by a disappointed office-seeker as he was entering the railroad station in Washington on July 2, 1881. His assailant was hanged.

William McKinley was shot by a man who came up to shake hands with him after a presidential speech at the Pan-American Exposition in Buffalo on September 6, 1901. The revolver was concealed beneath a big handkerchief and thus escaped notice. The assassin, an anarchist, was electrocuted.

These happenings cast a cloud of gloom over the whole of our country. But somehow we do not seem to be able to forestall such incidents.

One wonders whether Presidents will venture hereafter to make public appearances except in halls and auditoriums under tight security guard. But our Presidents have been brave men who seem to feel that they must go before the people and take the risks that come with the duties of high office.

John F. Kennedy had that spirit of bravery and felt that he must see the people frequently, without regard to danger. On these pages in 1959 there was printed a detailed story of Lieutenant Kennedy's heroic exploits as commander of a PT boat in the Pacific during World War II. He was never governed by fear. His personal courage has been demonstrated on more than one occasion.

Mr. Kennedy came into office at a crucial time in world history when emotions ran high and differences of opinion on domestic and foreign questions were deepseated. But no President has tackled as many problems and such a variety of delicate and difficult issues as those into which John F. Kennedy delved so deeply during his 34 months in office.

President Kennedy listened patiently to his advisers and showed a remarkable familiarity with detail. Perhaps his outstanding characteristic was his readiness to listen to the arguments of those who disagreed with him. If a resolution of differences were possible so as to lessen friction and bring about an agreement, he conscientiously sought such a solution. He had shown the same attitude when he was in the Senate and in the House.

Mr. Kennedy manifested, in other words, a spirit of mediation and a desire to attain out of every controversy the maximum good for the public. For he adopted again and again the maximum that "half a loaf is better than none."

In world affairs, Mr. Kennedy exhibited a rare quality of patience and restraint. Whatever setbacks his administration may have encountered around the world, the fact remains that he tried his utmost to preserve peace for his country while maintaining the military strength so necessary to deter an enemy.

It is hard to believe that our President is dead at 46. It is hard to believe that this man who sought so earnestly to serve his country should be cut down in the prime of life.

This is an incredible tragedy.

ADDRESS BY

Hon. Richard S. Schweiker

OF PENNSYLVANIA

Mr. Speaker, as I looked up at the Capitol dome from the rotunda awaiting the arrival of Mrs. John F. Kennedy to come for her husband's body, I could not help but think of the thousands of people who passed under this great dome to pay their respects in that brief space of time from Sunday afternoon until Monday morning while the President lay in state.

In a sense, it was ironic that so short a time had been available for these many people to view the President's body, because it was symbolic of the fact that there was so little time available on earth for John F. Kennedy to accomplish his work. He served only 2 years and 10 months as President of the United States and lived only 46 years. There was so much to do for John F. Kennedy and so little time in which to do it.

And then, later that same day, as my wife and I awaited the arrival of the funeral cortege at Arlington Cemetery, I could not help but think once again of the sad tragedy of it all.

Immediately after the President's body was carried past us at Arlington Cemetery, a large group of nearly all the leaders of the free world walked within a few steps of where we were standing, to pay their last respects to the President.

One could not help but be impressed with this great assemblage of free world leaders who thought so much of our late President to pay their personal tribute in this dramatic and unique way. Never in modern time had so many leaders of the free world been assembled in such a short time. No doubt this in itself was probably the greatest tribute that President Kennedy could receive from his contemporaries.

This assemblage demonstrated the great respect and admiration which they held for the youngest President of the United States ever to be elected to this important office.

Another remembrance of this tragedy hit deeply within me as I glanced up from his grave to see that striking giant, Air Force 1, pay its last respects by flying low over his grave and dip its wing as a final tribute to its great chief.

All of these sad experiences made me wonder how such a horrible tragedy could have befallen our country during these enlightened times. It gave me pause to reflect on this dastardly act.

Our system of government is based on a differing of opinions. Such a divergence is healthy and necessary in our Republic, but fanatical extremism which engenders bitterness and hatred in depraved minds cannot only take the life of a President but the life of our country as well.

While I have not always agreed with President Kennedy, I admired his articulation of ideas, his devotion to duty, his strong leadership, and his exercise of responsibility.

My wife and I join with millions of Americans in mourning the death of our President and extend to his family our deepest sympathy in their tragic loss—a loss that will be felt throughout the world.

ADDRESS BY

Hon. Edna F. Kelly

OF NEW YORK

Mr. Speaker, in every hamlet, town, and city across the land, for the past 14 days, the people of our Nation have paid their respects and their tribute to our late President, John F. Kennedy. In the lonely reaches of their hearts, in the privacy of their homes, and in public gatherings, they have mourned the passing of a leader who, in a brief span of less than 3 years, had left his indelible imprint upon the course of our national history.

We are met today to record those sentiments— our personal feelings and those of our constituents—in the permanent congressional proceedings. I speak, therefore, not only for myself but also for the people of the 12th Congressional District of New York, whom I represent here. And in so doing, I want to voice the sorrow and anguish which fill our hearts. The death of

President Kennedy was a tragedy for each of us and for our Nation. In a larger sense, it was also a tragedy for the cause of human freedom throughout the world.

President Kennedy belonged not only to us and to the present, but also to the world and to the future. In his person, he combined some of the best characteristics of the many nationality strains which comprise our great Nation. He was conscious of the spiritual, cultural, economic, and political values of countries whose birth predates that of our own Nation.

He was even more deeply steeped in that rare blending of different cultural heritages achieved in the United States which we know as the American tradition. In addressing himself to the problems of our day, in shaping the policies and the goals of the Government which he headed, he drew on both. He embraced the highest ideals of Western, Judeo-Christian civilization. And he was loyal to the institutions and the traditions which our unique experiment in human freedom and democracy produced upon the American soil. Thus, while serving his country, he served mankind.

President John F. Kennedy worked for, and died for, the implementation of the principles of human dignity, justice, and freedom. He fought against the denial of the basic human rights to people everywhere. It is now up to us to continue the task for which he gave his life. It is up to us to rededicate ourselves today to the attainment of these principles so that he will not have died in vain.

My prayers at this time are for Mrs. John F. Kennedy. I pray that God will send to her His choicest blessings to help her carry this cross—the death of her beloved husband, John F. Kennedy.

ADDRESS BY

Hon. W. J. Bryan Dorn

OF SOUTH CAROLINA

Mr. Speaker, the first time I met John F. Kennedy was rather significantly in the White House. We were invited by President Truman to the White House in the fall of 1946 as young Dem-

ocratic nominees to the Congress. Mr. Truman wished to give us a bit of encouragement and a round of picture taking before the November elections. This was my very first contact with any of the future young Members of the 80th Congress.

On that September day, I remember well meeting John Kennedy for the first time. I was impressed then with his friendly manner and warm disarming smile. He was a bit shy and slightly gaunt from wartime service in the Pacific and from a tough, rough and tumble Boston campaign. Kennedy at that time moved cautiously and somewhat awkwardly in high political circles. At that time he was and looked like a kid.

Mr. Speaker, the last time I saw John Kennedy was late last August, again in the White House, as President of the United States. My mother had never met any President, and Mr. Kennedy very graciously granted us an appointment. The President came out alone and met us in the Cabinet room. My mother, Mrs. Dorn, and one of my sons, Jennings, were with me. The President remonstrated with me for not bringing all of my five children and twice asked about my younger boy, Johnson, age 3, whom some of the neighbors called John John because of a resemblance to the President's son. My mother who had seven boys in World War II offered the President her sons again, if needed, in Berlin, Cuba, or throughout the world. The President's smile vanished, and he expressed the hope they would never be needed. The President asked us to come into his office and told about the desk, a gift from Queen Victoria, and other items in the office. Then we talked about John C. Calhoun, Clemson College, and football.

The President went into Mrs. Lincoln's office and asked for five fountain pens with his autograph which he personally gave to our son, Jennings, for each of my children. It was awfully quiet in the White House that day and strangely lonely. The President followed us rather wistfully and seemed not to want us to leave. He asked about the South and about the coming campaign. I observed he was no longer the kid I had met that day in September 1946. He was a grown man at last in the flower and bloom of manhood. He was heavier, filled out, and more handsome with a becoming grayishness around the temples. He was confident, sure of himself, and looked like a President of the United States.

Between that first meeting in 1946 and the one last August, I talked with Jack Kennedy many times. I saw him upon social occasions. I saw him on the floor of the House, and I noticed for the first time the jabbing forefinger so characteristic of his speaking style.

I remember a long talk alone with him during the Korean war in the Imperial Hotel in Tokyo, Japan. He had just flown in from a conference with Nehru in India. Kennedy that day expressed grave concern about the Far East and the advances of communism. He was fearful the United States was creating a dollar image rather than an image of freedom, good will, and individual liberty.

I remember appearing with Representative Kennedy as a rather nervous witness before the vitriolic Tom Connally who was serving as chairman of a Joint Senate Committee of the Foreign Relations and Armed Services Committees on the question of troops to Europe. I remember his pushing through a crowded White House reception last winter to assure Mrs. Dorn and me the stories in the New York Times and Wall Street Journal were untrue about my being placed on his purge list. He assured me I was on no purge list of his—that we might differ on certain issues but we would always be friends.

John Kennedy is gone. He was stricken down by a misguided, deranged, Marxist assassin— one who in his warped mind was a follower of Fidel Castro and his ingenious schemes to subvert the Western World.

Washington will never be the same to me. President Kennedy represented an era—the era of television in politics for the first time, the era of downtown parades in open convertibles, the era of political glamour.

John Fitzgerald Kennedy was an intellectual. He was brilliant. He was well-groomed, well-mannered, and cultured. He was gracious and hospitable. He loved the typical American. He was a man of humility and charm.

Mr. Speaker, John F. Kennedy was my President and my Commander in Chief. He was a man of unquestionable integrity, and patriotism. He loved the United States and all of its people. I will miss him so long as I live.

Mrs. Dorn joins me in my most heartfelt sympathy to Mrs. Kennedy, his lovely children, and to his mother, father, brothers, and sisters.

Hon. Frank C. Osmers, Jr.

Mr. Speaker, what is there to say? All of us who served here with John Fitzgerald Kennedy have suffered a great personal loss.

While we all must die, what a tragedy it is that this wonderful man should be taken from us in the prime of life and under such dreadful circumstances.

It matters not what our political beliefs may be in a time like this. Those of us who knew him have lost a good and noble friend and the Nation has lost an outstanding leader.

It is my sincere conviction that he would want us to move forward toward solving the Nation's problems without breaking step.

Once again, in this hour of our mourning, we can thank the founders of our Nation for their wisdom in providing for the orderly transfer of Executive power in our Constitution. We can also be thankful that our new President, Lyndon B. Johnson, is a man of known ability and vast experience.

Hon. Samuel N. Friedel

Mr. Speaker, there are no words which can adequately express our profound grief at the sudden and tragic death of our beloved President, John Fitzgerald Kennedy. Persons much more eloquent than I have tried to express their sentiments and those of our Nation in these dark hours, but what can we say that will do justice to the man?

Although born to great wealth, raised amid gracious and cultural surroundings, and educated at America's oldest and most renowned institutions, he sought not a life of ease and leisure, but a life completely dedicated to the service of his country and his fellow man. It is not only we in America who mourn his loss. The whole world is enveloped in grief because this great champion of the people has been snatched from our midst, and to our everlasting shame, by an assassin's bullet.

Public service was John Fitzgerald Kennedy's calling. To us here in the House of Representatives, where he served for 6 years, he was a source of inspiration. When he was later elected to the Senate from his native State of Massachusetts, we recognized full well that here was a man of destiny, which subsequent events proved.

John Fitzgerald Kennedy was a man of this century. In his brief term as President of the United States he made an indelible mark on the history of our time. We will remember him as a distinguished champion for peace in the world. The tragedy of his loss is increased because he was taken from us at the very time when he was contributing the most any man could to the cause of world peace. He understood the need of our time to transform ideals into reality and he magnificently began the long and difficult task of accomplishing this objective.

He reminded all Americans of the great principles that liberty could not be cheaply preserved. That vigilance and the willingness to make personal sacrifice are the eternal price to be paid for freedom. He set an example for courage and sacrifice. He showed us that Americans must always be willing to shed their own blood to preserve those things which we hold sacred: Freedom, liberty, and independence.

Because the life of President John Kennedy has been so senselessly and tragically cut short, our Nation has been cruelly deprived of part of its greatness and the life of every American is now poorer. With his death, a very precious part of each of us has died.

President Kennedy's inspiration, his tremendous courage, his integrity and the warmth of his feeling for his fellow man will be a beacon to those of us who share his convictions. And his hopes for the future of our Nation. For I believe he has left us with an inspiration that will serve throughout our own lifetime, and our children's and for generations to come. He inspired us to achieve greatness as a nation and good will and understanding as a people. He lit the lamp of peace and he showed us that the most noble and courageous thing a mighty nation can do is to attempt to find peace, with honor, for all men.

Mr. Kennedy's own life was the greatest example of unselfish and devoted service to his country. He was truly a man of greatness. He understood both the terrible perils and the magnificent promises of our times and he inspired greatness in all Americans. He often reminded us that actions, and not mere words, will be history's measure of this generation of Americans. He urged Americans to give, rather than take from their country. In the cause of his country he gave all that any man can give to his Nation—his life.

For his efforts on behalf of our own citizens and for the benefit of suffering humanity throughout the world, John Fitzgerald Kennedy has earned a lasting place among the truly great men of history. Even though an eternal flame was kindled at his last earthly resting place, another flame will forever burn brightly in our Nation's memory to illumine the future course of our leaders to help achieve a world freed from tyranny, aggression, senseless prejudice and bias. We can truly say that the world is a better place for all of us because of John Fitzgerald Kennedy.

Perhaps President Kennedy's best epitaph can be drawn from his own statement that:

> Whether you are citizens of America or of the world, ask of us the same high standards of strength and sacrifice that we shall ask of you. With a good conscience our only sure reward, with history the final judge of our deeds, let us go forth to lead the land we love, asking His blessing and His help, but knowing that here on earth God's work must be truly our own.

President Kennedy gave more to our Nation than he asked of us. He gave his life, and his sacrifice is our mandate to carry on his work.

ADDRESS BY

Hon. Roland V. Libonati

OF ILLINOIS

Mr. Speaker, it was a happy couple that received the applause and warm greetings of the friendly Texans all out on the streets to welcome them to their city. It was a gala day—the weather was reflected in the silver lined clouds with quivering streaks of golden sunshine. The parade of autos moved on flanked by the cheering citizens.

Upon approaching the dispersing point, suddenly a sharp crackling of spewed lead was heard, thrice echoing its message of fatality. A lady moaning lament of wounded love was seen caressing her mate's blood-smeared face—head bleeding, resting in her lap—then a racing motor moving the car in speed toward medical aid, and so he died. Thus the fates wafted the purple crepe of mourning over the peoples of the world. Many prayed to their God for deliverance; others, in tearful reverence, wept openly for his greatness; and still others cursed the fates, stunned at the great loss; and those who loved him most, felt a part of self had died with him.

The leaders of nations, friend or foe, paid him high public homage. The common people of all nations were bereft for the loss of a friend who loved the little people—the poor, the sick, and the enslaved who looked to him for hope and help.

And, so proud Texas tilts its flag in grief that this foul bloody deed has stained its sacred soil— and the Nation's soul cringes, seered by the flame of hate, also bears its brunt of responsibility. The shock was great, the pangs of regret deep, but the Government still lives, and tradition dictates it must go on. The sad experience spurs each American to aspire to greater gains in our President's dedication to lead the freedom-loving nations to peace, and to support the spirited patriots of these captive nations enslaved who seek liberty—that they may not lose hope, we must move forward to the goal that our martyred President sought for all men—that peace and liberty would prevail among the nations of the world.

Mr. Speaker, only history can measure the true loss suffered by the freemen of the world in futura before the death of President John F. Kennedy. He kneeled in humility before the altar of freedom, and pledged with action to rid mankind of the inhuman standard of inequality. He revered and respected God's law, that the inherent quality of man in character were of necessity an adjunct to his likeness in being.

President Kennedy was the intellectual aristocratic type of scholar whose vast knowledge of government equipped him with an infallible insight into its operational problems. He had a meticulous knowledge of national and foreign affairs. His speeches were carefully prepared and presented with a strength of feeling that reflected his deep sincerity and power of logic. His public utterances in support of legislative proposals in defense, civil rights, medicare for the aged, tax cuts, welfare legislation for the poor, and also, labor, unemployment, public works for depressed areas, and education showed him to be knowledgeable in the Nation's needs to go forward and also proved him to be a master of invective and sarcasm. He fortified his speeches with facts and figures to carry his point to the people. His grasp of public questions was swift, comprehensive, and positive. As an orator, President Kennedy's fame is established—few Presidents of our country matched his attractive and magnetic influence over an audience. His strong features—boyish and handsome—with tousled brown hair—heaped—his blue eyes fired with the sparks of sincerity—words flowing as easy and smooth as Bostonian colloquialisms interspersed would permit, transfixed his listeners. His diction—a message for the common man was simple, clear, and forceful—to the educated he was classical in expression.

He was decisive in his ability to meet any emergency that would arise—as in the Cuban crisis. He was always prepared—his intellect never failed him, even at the news conferences. His answers were clear and to the point. His high sense of humor was most perceptible in turning aside a question or questioner. His most noteworthy speeches represent the superlative oratorical effort in forensics, and will be placed among the historical documents of our Nation.

The loss of our young President, vigorous in mind and body, in the prime of life, a national figure of the highest type, respected, admired and trusted by the leaders of the free world in these critical times of trouble in world affairs emphasized to the Nation and the Congress, the need to solidify our forces in a unified front, and to go forward in the accomplishment of his aims for which he so valiantly fought and died.

The courage and loyalty displayed by Mrs. Jacqueline Kennedy throughout the perilous and sanguine experience, and the subsequent ordeal at the funeral ceremonies, gained the admiration, sympathy, and love of every American, and the people of the world; the true mother with her darlings at her side, statuesque in bearing, facing her grief with regal acceptance of tragedy, like the Madonna at the Crucifixion, stood in silent adoration of her love with a dignity that captured the hearts and emotions of millions throughout the world. No one can deny that as the late lamented President passed through the Portals of Oblivion, a deep sense of pride for her permeated his very soul. May God in His omnipotent wisdom bless the future of our Nation, and grant everlasting peace to our martyred President for which he so valiantly struggled to achieve for mankind and nations.

I dedicate to his memory the following stanzas:

HE PASSED THIS WAY TOO SOON

Every hurt—a tear, a moan, a sigh
E'en though of noble mien
Like the stranger, leaves the scene
Every man is born to die.

Every joy, a smile, a twinkling eye
Greatness seems to be God's loan
One was called before his turn
Every man is born to die.

Every courage, holds freedom high
Mortals ever for him pray
Nations mourn this tragic day
Every man is born to die.

ADDRESS BY

Hon. Wayne L. Hays

OF OHIO

Mr. Speaker, a bright flame marks the final resting place in Arlington National Cemetery of one of freedom's most ardent and eloquent advocates. The voice once so familiar in these halls is now hushed in tragic death. While its sound no longer greets our ears, its bold and fervid enunciations will never be forgotten.

That heroic devotion to truth and justice, to equality and fraternity, we so often admired, and which is exemplified by countless acts and incidents extending through years of an active existence, is a most worthy example for all good men.

The principles which he professed and the work which he performed, professions and practice being in perfect harmony, will in all future time and in all nations render the name of John Fitzgerald Kennedy a synonym for human liberty.

His oratorical powers, general information, and keenness of wit gained for him a worldwide affection. As an advocate he was quick and powerful. Laying hold of the strong points in a cause, he presented them in a succinct and comprehensive manner. He was always an ardent friend of public improvement and universal education, a bitter opponent to human slavery and oppression.

The grand blows which he struck in his great battle for liberty and justice will long survive him and leave their impress upon all lands, strengthening the purpose of the toiling and struggling millions on earth. His successful life-battle should teach us the value and self-sustaining power of a career consecrated to the best interests of his country and his fellowmen.

In this impressive hour, while reviewing his heroic and unselfish acts, let us renew our vows of fidelity to the great principles which he so long, so ably, and so faithfully maintained. Let us here, and now, pledge our lives anew to the cause of human liberty and human progress, resolving that no obstacle nor selfish interest shall cause us to falter, so that when we too pass away the benedictions of mankind shall bless us, as they now bless him for whom we mourn, and it shall be said of us as it is now said of him: "He hath not lived in vain."

The image of John Fitzgerald Kennedy needs no monument. The imprint of his mind is upon the history of his country, and is more ineffaceable there than all the dedication we authorize in his memory. It is the Lincolns and the Kennedys, the humanitarians and reformers who die with their boots on. As policies are bigger than men may it be the legacy to our great Nation that much of what our late President initiated will go forward.

ADDRESS BY

Hon. Bill Stinson

OF WASHINGTON

Mr. Speaker, John F. Kennedy was born when the world was in a time of heavy crisis. Later in life, in another crisis, he answered the call of his Nation to defend the principles and ideals upon which our Nation is founded. He served with honor.

His country again called upon him to serve

when he was elected to represent the people of Massachusetts to the U.S. House of Representatives and later in the U.S. Senate.

The people of our Nation then deemed it right to honor him with the highest office and greatest responsibility of the land. To this challenge he gave his life.

It has been written:

No man is competent to judge in matters of a kingdom until first he has been tried; there are many things to be learned in the depths which we may never know in the heights.

During this time of tragedy we must measure these depths that we, in turn, may travel those heights. From this deep trial, perhaps we, too, shall be declared competent to judge a nation.

No greater love hath a man than to lay down his life for his brother. By this death we are challenged to live—to work for right and justice—to guard our heritage, and to provide continued leadership to a dark and searching world.

ADDRESS BY

Hon. Harley O. Staggers

OF WEST VIRGINIA

Mr. Speaker, a bright and shining figure in the image of Plato's philosopher-rulers has been struck down. It is the essence of the image that the guardian of the state possess vast disinterestedness, perceptive understanding, swift insight—that "divine madness" which reaches valid conclusions before the premises are fully stated. Power in President Kennedy's hands was only a means to an end—and that end was the enrichment of human life. Born to privilege, inured to prestige, he was trained for service—to the Nation—to all people. He carried with him the sure knowledge that the blood in his veins was derived from the same almighty parent, and was no better than that of the humblest citizen. His intelligence recognized that simple fact, and he built his life to conform with it.

The President led us to an open window through which he pointed to the dawn of a new day, a day from which the clear light of reason and selflessness had burnt away the clouds of misery and injustice and oppression which have lain heavily over the human race through the centuries. That day could be approached only through a "long twilight" of toil and sacrifice and devotion. To reach it, new and untried paths would have to be hewn through seemingly insuperable difficulties. The bright spark of his unique personality had lit up the prospect, and we were almost persuaded that the end was worth the effort. And then he was cut down.

In our hour of anguish, two thoughts bring some little comfort. The first is that only a half-crazed individual could have perpetrated the foul deed. The act was the venom of a mind so egocentric that it could view the normal operation of economic and social laws as expressing a personal vindictiveness toward itself. Such a mind strikes out blindly, irrationally, with a demoniac futility. Its victim is simply the most conspicuous object in sight.

And yet there is a terrifying and half-expressed, half-suppressed, dread that we are all somehow involved in the act. We instinctively turn a searching eye on our inner souls, and ask the troubling question: Have I, myself, by word or deed, whether intentionally or unintentionally, contributed to the confusion and suspicion in this Nation, confusion and suspicion which seems to prefer contention to orderly progress?

Whence arises the second source of comfort in our distress. In the shock which removed this deed from the realm of the unbelievable to the fact of reality, there is opportunity to pause and think. This Republic was established by men who eblieved in the platonic tradition. The true questions which divide us today concern the public policies and procedures which are appropriate to the needs of the time. Prejudice and bias and selfishness will not discover the answers, nor will they put them into execution. We have a new opportunity to examine them all in the cold light of reason, and with an acute awareness of the practical potentialities which this age of enlightenment and of technical competence offers us to make what changes we will. Unanimity of agreement to rational examination is not a function of a free society. But, once decisions have been arrived at by rational processes, unanimity of action is. The thing that must become unbelievable today is that while we loll in the luxury of plenty and power, we should permit "the bounty of heaven to be split" by fratricidal emotionalism.

On last Saturday, the heavens wept unrestrainedly as if in attempt to wash away all traces of bitterness and ugliness in our relations with one another. In the late evening, a cooling wind swept back the clouds, and along with them, we hope, the clouds of passion in men's souls which obstruct their view of a beneficent infinity. Bright stars appeared, and a crescent moon hung in the western firmament. On Sunday morning a new day—a holy day—dawned in glory and brilliance. May it be a symbol.

On a gentle hillside, and in full view of the seats of the mighty on this continent, there flickers a glowing flame. It, too, is a symbol, a symbol of the indomitable spirit of our departed President and leader. May the thoughts and efforts of all of us be dedicated to the determination that the bright spark which our fallen President kindled shall never go out, but that it shall grow stronger and clearer until it leads us through the long twilight to a more perfect day.

It has always been an inspiring thought that out of evil may come good. The Judeo-Christian tradition assures us that sacrifice is never in vain, and that the ways of providence, however inscrutable, are righteous altogether. The last speech prepared by John Kennedy on that fatal November day contained the words:

Except the Lord keep the city, the watchman waketh but in vain.

If good comes out of his sacrifice, he would bow in humble submission. We trust in God.

ADDRESS BY
Hon. George F. Senner, Jr.
OF ARIZONA

Mr. Speaker, there is so deep a sense of loss, so great a sense of grief that I cannot yet find the words that will give a full measure of meaning to the tragedy we have suffered.

To what my colleagues are saying here today, and to what the world has already said I can now only add—Farewell, my beloved President, I will miss you.

ADDRESS BY
Hon. Robert T. Ashmore
OF SOUTH CAROLINA

Mr. Speaker, John Fitzgerald Kennedy has joined the ranks of those patriots whose lives have been spent that others might live to enjoy the fruits of their battles. It is a most tragic and unfortunate fact that death is often the sacrifice of those who would promote a better life. All Americans must admire and respect him for his untiring energy, great ability and sincere devotion to what he believed to be his patriotic duty. He unselfishly dedicated himself to public service.

While he served as Chief Executive of our Nation he manifested strong convictions and sincere leadership, not only for America but the entire free world. His assassination is one of the greatest tragedies of this century. Both friend and foe were stunned with the unbelievable announcement that our President had been shot. Grief, sorrow, and sympathy immediately descended upon the civilized world.

We will long remember President Kennedy's contagious smile, sparkling humor, bright eyes, spontaneous gestures and aggressive leadership. This intellectually powerful young man showed tremendous courage both in war and in peace. His action in the face of the enemy on the field of battle stamped him as a wartime hero. But I am convinced that his highest ambition was to go down in history as the President who did most to bring lasting peace to all mankind.

ADDRESS BY
Hon. Spark M. Matsunaga
OF HAWAII

Mr. Speaker, the horror of the incredible tragedy which recently enveloped the Nation—and the world—still hangs over our head as an inenarrable pall. The senseless assassination of our beloved President John Fitzgerald Kennedy ended the career of a young, vigorous American in the prime of his life. The youngest man ever to be elected President of the United States, he had dedicated his life to serving his fellow beings unswervingly, unselfishly, unstintingly, with the highest code of morals and ethics as his guide.

As President, he reiterated again and again to the heads of other nations and to the peoples of the world the sincerity of our country in its desire to be their friend, to help them in their troubles, and to give them the assurance of assistance in friendship, whenever they felt the need.

From the days of his wartime service as a young naval officer on a PT boat, he had offered his complete time, service, and devotion to his country and his fellow men. He added in large measure to the dream of mankind—the attainment of the brotherhood of men in a world of peace.

He was mankind's man, a champion of the poor and lowly and of the rich and exalted, and though he walked with kings he never lost the common touch.

John F. Kennedy was the finest product of American democracy. He was a President in the truest of American traditions. Possessed of great intelligence and rare courage, he gave eloquent voice and meaningful action to the conscience of America and to the dream of mankind. His deeds and spoken words will forever serve as an inspiration to men of good will everywhere in striving to reach greater heights.

To honor his memory let us heed his many words of wisdom, among them these:

> With a good conscience our only reward, with history the final judge of our deeds, let us go forth to lead the land we love, asking His blessing and His help, but knowing that here on earth God's work must truly be our own.

President Kennedy will go down in history as one of our greatest Presidents of all times. Just as Abraham Lincoln, almost a century ago, laid down his life to make men free, so did John Fitzgerald Kennedy give up his life to free his fellow men from the chains and shackles of prejudice.

We have lost a great President; indeed the entire world has lost one of the greatest leaders it has ever known. He gave voice to the conscience of America and to the dream of mankind; he gave action to the conscience of America and

to the dream of mankind. His unwavering courage and enlightened leadership will forever inspire men of good will everywhere to greater heights.

To Mrs. Kennedy and her children and to the entire Kennedy family, I wish to convey the deepest sympathy and condolences of the people of the State of Hawaii and mine.

In Jacqueline Kennedy, American womanhood, long epitomized by the pioneer's wife, has blossomed into full bloom for the entire world to behold in admiration. Burdened by the grief known only to a bereaved wife, she drowned the woes of life in her own tears to others never shown. As the First Lady of our land, she walked in composed dignity as if guided by that same hand which inspired the rare courage and genius of her late husband.

ADDRESS BY

Hon. Edward R. Roybal

OF CALIFORNIA

Mr. Speaker, I would like to join with millions of my fellow Americans and countless millions of people throughout the world in paying final loving tribute to the memory of our martyred 35th President, John Fitzgerald Kennedy.

It is still almost impossible to believe that John Kennedy, that young, dynamic, vibrant, and courageously statesmanlike champion of peace, is no longer with us—but has fallen before the merciless bullet of an assassin—now, to rest forever among the country's greatest heroes in the hallowed ground of Arlington National Cemetery.

The stirring words he spoke, the high causes he represented, and the bold actions he took during the short years he was permitted to spend among us, will live on to renew our own faith, and the faith of future generations of Americans, that the democratic heritage we treasure can be as meaningful and effective in the space age as it was in the early years of the Republic.

President Kennedy himself had said it:

> The energy, the faith, the devotion which we bring to this endeavor will light our country and all who serve it—and the glow from that fire can truly light the world.

And John Kennedy spoke to all men in tragically prophetic words when he expressed the secret of America's great past, as well as the key to its bright future:

> We shall pay any price, bear any burden, meet any hardship, support any friend, oppose any foe, to assure the survival, and the success of liberty.

Now John Kennedy, himself, has paid that ultimate price, he has sacrificed his life to assure the survival of the ideals of freedom and liberty that give meaning to America.

On November 22, he passed the torch on to us, the living, to continue the struggle in which he gave the last full measure of his devotion.

We remember the words of his magnificent inaugural address when he said:

> In your hands, my fellow citizens, more than mine, will rest the final success or failure of our course.

In future years, President Kennedy will be remembered for the vitality and brilliant promise he brought to the task of governing a democracy.

He will be remembered for the great search for peace he carried on in an age and in a world threatened with nuclear destruction.

Who can forget his words to the Congress in reporting on negotiations that ultimately led to the signing of the nuclear test ban treaty?

> A journey of 1,000 miles must begin with a single step. My fellow Americans, let us take that first step. Let us, if we can, step back from the shadows of war and seek out the way of peace. And if that journey is 1,000 miles or even more, let history record that we, in this land, at this time, took the first step.

In international affairs, John Kennedy represented a force for reason, for strength, and for compassion. He sought to make the world safe for diversity, in a world that put a premium on conformity.

He will be remembered for new and imaginative efforts to achieve the goals of peace and prosperity around the globe. The Peace Corps, the Alliance for Progress, and the food for peace program, all bear the mark of his untiring work.

Domestically, President Kennedy visualized his Nation as a young country trying to realize its full potential and secure for all its citizens the blessings of the great promise of America.

With a tremendous drive and determination he promoted the cause of equal rights and equal opportunities for all Americans. He strove to revitalize our national economic growth rate to provide the training and the jobs necessary for full employment in an age of rapid technological change and onrushing automation.

He greatly expanded our military capability while launching the country into the space age with characteristic vigor and with a characteristic goal of world leadership.

Realizing that the ultimate success of the American democratic experiment depended on the quality of its citizens, President Kennedy advocated major new programs designed to assure that American education from the first grades on through advanced graduate work would be second to none.

And he and his lovely wife Jacqueline have served as a constant encouragement to the arts as an essential civilizing influence in our national life.

Just a few months ago he expressed what was his own democratic philosophy of the arts:

> Art establishes the basic human truths which must serve as the touchstones of our judgment. The artist becomes the last champion of the individual mind and sensibility against an intrusive society and an officious state. I see little of more importance to the future of our country and our civilization than full recognition of the place of the artist. If art is to nourish the roots of our culture, society must set the artist free to follow his vision wherever it takes him.

One of President Kennedy's favorite passages from Scripture was quoted at his funeral service:

> There is an appointed time for everything, and a time for every affair under the heavens; a time to be born and a time to die; a time to plant and a time to uproot the plant; a time to kill and a time to heal; a time to tear down and a time to build.

The greatest memorial which we can create for President Kennedy is to see that this is a time to heal—and a time to build.

President Kennedy's eloquent inaugural address of January 20, 1961, will always remind me of the true greatness of this courageous American.

These words will be etched in the proud annals of our history as a beacon light to which we can return in times of trial and difficulty for light and direction:

> We observe today not a victory of party but a celebration of freedom—symbolizing an end as well as a beginning—signifying renewal as well as change. For I have sworn before you and Almighty God the same

solemn oath our forebears prescribed nearly a century and three-quarters ago.

The world is very different now. For man holds in his mortal hands the power to abolish all forms of human poverty and all forms of human life. And yet the same revolutionary beliefs for which our forebears fought are still at issue around the globe—the belief that the rights of man come not from the generosity of the state but from the hand of God.

We dare not forget today that we are the heirs of that first revolution. Let the word go forth from this time and place, to friend and foe alike, that the torch has been passed to a new generation of Americans—born in this century, tempered by war, disciplined by a hard and bitter peace, proud of our ancient heritage—and unwilling to witness or permit the slow undoing of those human rights to which this Nation has always been committed, and to which we are committed today at home and around the world.

Let every nation know, whether it wishes us well or ill, that we shall pay in price, bear any burden, meet any hardship, support any friend, oppose any foe to assure the survival and the success of liberty.

This much we pledge—and more.

To those old allies whose cultural and spiritual origins we share, we pledge the loyalty of faithful friends. United, there is little we cannot do in a host of cooperative ventures. Divided, there is little we can do—for we dare not meet a powerful challenge at odds and split asunder.

To those new states whom we welcome to the ranks of the free, we pledge our word that one form of colonial control shall not have passed away merely to be replaced by a far more iron tyranny. We shall not always expect to find them supporting our view. But we shall always hope to find them strongly supporting their own freedom—and to remember that, in the past, those who foolishly sought power by riding the back of the tiger ended up inside.

To those peoples in the huts and villages of half the globe struggling to break the bonds of mass misery, we pledge our best efforts to help them help themselves, for whatever period is required—not because the Communists may be doing it, not because we seek their votes, but because it is right. If a free society cannot help the many who are poor, it cannot save the few who are rich.

To our sister republics south of our border, we offer a special pledge—to convert our good words into good deeds—in a new alliance for progress—to assist free men and free governments in casting off the chains of poverty. But this peaceful revolution of hope cannot become the prey of hostile powers. Let all our neighbors know that we shall join with them to oppose aggression or subversion anywhere in the Americas. And let every other power know that this hemisphere intends to remain the master of its own house.

To the world assembly of sovereign states, the United Nations, our last best hope in an age where the instruments of war have far outpaced the instruments of peace, we renew our pledge of support—to prevent it from becoming merely a forum for invective—to strengthen its shield of the new and the weak—and to enlarge the area in which its writ may run.

Finally, to those nations who would make themselves our adversary, we offer not a pledge but a request: that both sides begin anew the quest for peace, before the dark powers of destruction unleashed by science engulf all humanity in planned or accidental self-destruction.

We dare not tempt them with weakness. For only when our arms are sufficient beyond doubt can we be certain beyond doubt that they will never be employed. But neither can two great and powerful groups of nations take comfort from our present course—both sides overburdened by the cost of modern weapons, both rightly alarmed by the steady spread of the deadly atom, yet both racing to alter that uncertain balance of terror that stays the hand of mankind's final war.

So let us begin anew—remembering on both sides that civility is not a sign of weakness, and sincerity is always subject to proof. Let us never negotiate out of fear. But let us never fear to negotiate.

Let both sides explore what problems unite us instead of belaboring those problems which divide us.

Let both sides, for the first time, formulate serious and precise proposals for the inspection and control of arms—and bring the absolute power to destroy other nations under the absolute control of all nations.

Let both sides seek to invoke the wonders of science instead of its terrors. Together let us explore the stars, conquer the deserts, eradicate disease, tap the ocean depths, and encourage the arts and commerce.

Let both sides unite to heed in all corners of the earth the command of Isaiah—to "undo the heavy burdens (and) let the oppressed go free."

And if a beachhead of cooperation may push back the jungle of suspicion, let both sides join in creating a new endeavor, not a new balance of power, but a new world of law, where the strong are just and the weak secure and the peace preserved.

All this will not be finished in the first 100 days. Nor will it be finished in the first 1,000 days, nor in the life of this administration, nor even perhaps in our lifetime on this planet. But let us begin.

In your hands, my fellow citizens, more than mine, will rest the final success or failure of our course. Since this country was founded, each generation of Americans has been summoned to give testimony to its national loyalty. The graves of young Americans who answered the call to service surround the globe.

Now the trumpet summons us again—not as a call to bear arms, though arms we need—not as a call to battle, though embattled we are—but a call to bear the burden of a long twilight struggle, year in and year out, "rejoicing in hope, patient in tribulation"—a struggle against the common enemies of man: tyranny, poverty, disease, and war itself.

Can we forge against these enemies a grand and global alliance, North and South, East and West, that can assure a more fruitful life for all mankind? Will you join in that historic effort?

In the long history of the world, only a few generations have been granted the role of defending freedom in its hour of maximum danger. I do not shrink from this responsibility—I welcome it. I do not believe that any of us would exchange places with any other people or any other generation. The energy, the faith, the devotion which we bring to this endeavor will light our country and all who serve it—and the glow from that fire can truly light the world.

And so, my fellow Americans: ask not what your country can do for you—ask what you can do for your country.

My fellow citizens of the world: ask not what America will do for you, but what together we can do for the freedom of man.

Finally, whether you are citizens of America or citizens of the world, ask of us here the same high standards of strength and sacrifice which we ask of you. With a good conscience our only sure reward, with history the final judge of our deeds, let us go forth to lead the land we love, asking His blessing and His help, but knowing that here on earth God's work must truly be our own.

In this spirit, therefore, let us face the future with confidence, and resolve with President Lyndon Johnson that "John Fitzgerald Kennedy did not live—or die—in vain."

ADDRESS BY

Hon. Charles E. Goodell

OF NEW YORK

Mr. Speaker, all Americans were stunned and agonized by the sudden, senseless, violent death of our President. We grieve and are sick at heart that such an abominable thing could occur to him and to us. We salute his bravery, his brilliance and his patriotism. We marvel, humbly, at the majestic fortitude of his wife and family.

Under the darkened sky of these black-bordered days since the President fell, I have talked with many of John Kennedy's former colleagues and friends in the House of Representatives and the Senate of the United States. Many of them differed with Mr. Kennedy on matters of public policy; all of them respected his qualities of mind and wit and heart. The differences of conviction amongst us never engendered the bitterness and gall of hatred and bigotry. His colleagues miss him and mourn his tragic death more than words can express.

As I reminisce upon the almost 3 years that I served in the U.S. Congress while John Kennedy was President, I think less about our differences than about our agreements. Yes, we differed, and I will continue to differ on issues affecting the health and life of our country. But our ultimate objectives were always the same. On many occasions we in the Congress of both parties were able to substitute legislation for the President's proposals that accommodated our differences in the best interests of the people. I think, for instance, of the Manpower Retraining Act, of the higher education bill, of vocational education, of defense expenditures, of equal pay for women, of a tax cut and, this year, the need for civil rights legislation. Yet, on those many issues where differences of philosophy extended beyond the reach of accommodation, we shall miss John F. Kennedy as a worthy and articulate adversary. God grant that he may rest in peace and be cherished forever in the hearts of his countrymen.

We turn to thee, O God, who are from everlasting to everlasting, grateful that a riderless steed, upon which millions have gazed with appalled eyes, is not a symbol of a leaderless nation, and that history assures us that in every crisis, Thou dost raise up men to carry on Thy mission for the redemption of humanity.

Thus the Chaplain of the U.S. Senate opened the proceedings the morning after President Kennedy's funeral. We can all be thankful that Lyndon Johnson has the competence and the seasoned background to provide a reasonably smooth transition in this time of national crisis. From the moment of tragedy, all Americans were aware that a strong and steady hand was at the helm. President Johnson's moving and forceful address to the joint session of Congress symbolized our unity to the entire world. He well understood when he spoke that differences of conscience and conviction will persist among our people as long as we are "the land of the free and the home of the brave." As President Johnson so concisely put it:

Our American unity does not depend on unanimity.

One of John Kennedy's favorite words, and one of mine too, in describing democracy is the word "diversity." As we strive to dispel hatreds and bitterness from our ranks, let us never strive for conformity. Vigorous dissent and public debate are the very touchstones of our American experience and American success. We have bigots and hate mongers in our midst. We always have. Hate is a horrible emotion, severing all meaningful ties to God and to man. It must be controlled, moderated, understood, and intelligently attacked. Let us keep this in perspective, however. If the survival of our country depended upon the complete eradication of hate and bigotry in every individual, we would never have survived into the 19th century. With all of John Kennedy's strivings for change in the things he disliked about our system, he never doubted the essential strength and rightness of America. The haters are not, and never have been, in the mainstream of American life. I sincerely believe that the general temper of our society today is typified by growing understanding and compassion for others. Our achievements are less than perfect, our efforts often less than effective, yet it is hard to think of a time when there has been so much concern by so many for the dignity of all men. In the dread aftermath of a black chapter in our history, let us not lose sight of the qualities that marked the reaction of the overwhelming majority of Americans to the President's death. That reaction was not one of violence and hate, but an outpouring of deep, earnest and personal grief. This does reflect the true temper of the American people.

ADDRESS BY

Hon. Alec G. Olson

OF MINNESOTA

Mr. Speaker, John F. Kennedy as a young man turned away from other careers and chose one of public service. In this career he attained excellence. His hope was peace and toward this end he selflessly devoted his fine intellect, his vast energies—in a word, his life. An assassin's bullet snuffed out this young life and shocked and saddened the world. That this sorrow was universally shared without regard to political philosophy, national origin, or creed is the best measure of the reality he was able to give his hope for peace in the few years permitted him.

The tragic events of November 22 will be written indelibly into our history books. Beyond this, I hope, will be preserved the memory of his

example as a son, as a husband, as a father, and as a public servant.

It was my privilege to know him and my honor to serve under him.

ADDRESS BY

Hon. William B. Widnall

OF NEW JERSEY

Mr. Speaker, since the unbelievable and incredible tragedy on November 22, 1963, took place, the Nation and the world have been stunned and cannot seem to realize that our young and vigorous leader has been taken. As one, the people of our country have united in their grief. It was a tragedy that touched all our homes and caused a soul-searching reappraisal of our lives.

President John F. Kennedy symbolized the vitality and youthful vigor of what has been called the American experiment. He saw a country 188 years young, and sought to move it forward to a greater maturity, both at home and abroad. It was his sense of history and his belief in the destiny of this country, that provided him with his guidelines for action, and stimulated his eloquent appeals for peace and progress.

By now, many words have been spoken of our late President's abilities, virtues, and accomplishments. Little more can be added to the eulogies and the beautiful tributes that have already been expressed. If there is little left unsaid, there is still much to be done.

We can all take comfort, in our hour of grief, that the constitutional framework remains, and that it has functioned so well in the face of adversity. In the years ahead as America moves forward, as it must and will, each of us has a part that can be played in helping to fulfill the great promise of our Nation.

In the future, the means with which we choose to pursue our common goals will not always correspond with those proposed by our late President. Yet there can be no greater living memorial to John F. Kennedy than an America tolerant of differences, strong in its ability to wage meaningful debate on the nature of society without resort to violence or demagoguery, and confident that the democratic process he used and helped us to perfect will carry this Nation to its true destiny.

ADDRESS BY

Hon. Richard T. Hanna

OF CALIFORNIA

Mr. Speaker, he lies now unmoved by tears, yet still we weep. Tears of sadness to give relief for deep felt grief too strong to be contained. Tears of bitterness surging with the sense of loss. Loss of that spirit, that leadership, that promise of a young and gifted President. Tears of sympathy streaming the cheek at thought and sight of friend without this friend, family without this son or brother, wife without this husband, child without this father. So we weep for this man who lies beyond the reach of grief.

He lies now and knows no more of pomp and pageantry, yet still we parade. Moving compulsively in long lines, we mark the loneliness of our loss. Marching in the ways devised by man to render homage. Marching in massive tribute to testify, we adjudge this life to have been both good and great. He sees no flag and yet they are unfurled. Do honor to his loyalty to this our land. For he paid the highest price that from a patriot devotion to duty can extract. His fellow citizens, therefore, call for pageant recognition. He misses the cadence of the count and still we move in mournful, measured steps. We come finally to that last resting place where other gallant men occupy the hallowed ground, Arlington National Cemetery. So we parade for him who lies but does not see the banner blow or hear the bugle's final blast.

He lies now and hears no praise, yet still we raise our voice to laud him. Praise to assure his friends and family that the good he did will not be interred with his remains but will live on to do him, them and his country great and lasting credit. Praise to assure the widow and the orphan that we support and share a pride that will last longer than the sorrow of his tragic passing. Praise to assure ourselves and all the world this life now gone was lived rich in service; fruitful both of promise and performance. So we praise this man who lies beyond the sound or pleasure of our voice.

He lies now untouched by prayer, yet still we pray. Prayers of strength for those touched personally by this passing. Seeking support for that majestic lady who now must stand alone and those little children who yet must learn the measure of their loss. Prayers of anguish wrung from the universal guilt that none escapes. Painfully knowing in this tortured hour that we are members of the family of man and that we are, indeed, our brother's keeper. Prayers of mercy, supplications for the forgiveness, the understanding, and the peace we did not offer when they were ours to give and which now only a gracious Father can extend. So we pray for this man whose judgment is of his own making and whose mercy lies above our small powers.

It is then for us the living, rather than for him who lies in death, that tears are shed, pageants pass, praises are pronounced and prayers are patterned. We hope that our tears assuage some human grief, our pageantry deepens with dignity the impact of this life upon the living, our praises warm those left cold by this cruel loss, our prayers win us some mercy from Him who is most merciful. No weeping we do, no pomp we show, no praise we sing, no prayer we lift can affect the judgment to which our President, John Fitzgerald Kennedy, now has passed. It is for us the living to learn from our tears, to be motivated by our marching to do more, to realize the hope that sings through our praises and to find in our prayers that the strength of our tomorrows lies within us. With God's help that strength can be summoned and with His help it will be summoned. Then perhaps we can truly reach this man in that place where now he lies.

ADDRESS BY

Hon. Henry C. Schadeberg

OF WISCONSIN

Mr. Speaker, I wish to add my voice to those of my colleagues in expressing my personal shock and sorrow over the assassination of President

John F. Kennedy. When I heard the report on the radio I was aware that it was my President who had been the victim of this diabolical deed. The right hand of Christian fellowship and love of my family is added to mine as it is extended to Mrs. Kennedy and the bereaved family.

The office of the President of the United States stands as a symbol of law and order before the world. It is the image of a country committed under faith in God to the preservation and extension of the dignity of the individual. The death of our President, tragic as it is for the family and for our Nation, will not be in vain if we are determined to bring to reality the ideals of which he so forcibly spoke. Let us labor to keep America strong in the cause of right as we see it. This is the only fitting memorial for one who has served our country in its highest office and died while in the service of his country.

ADDRESS BY

Hon. William T. Murphy

OF ILLINOIS

Mr. Speaker, while attending the burial services of John Fitzgerald Kennedy in Arlington Cemetery, I noted the stately figure of Gen. Charles de Gaulle, the President of the Republic of France, standing at the bier. His appearance called my attention to the fact that two of the foremost leaders of the free world were present—one alive and one dead. On further reflection I realized that in a short period of 6 months the free world had lost four out of five of their outstanding leaders, namely, Dr. Konrad Adenauer, former Chancellor of the Republic of West Germany, retired on October 15, 1963; the Honorable Harold Macmillan, former Prime Minister of Great Britain, resigned on October 18, 1963; the Honorable Amintore Fanfani, former Premier of the Republic of Italy, resigned on May 16, 1963. And now the Honorable John Fitzgerald Kennedy, the late President of the United States of America. My thoughts turned back pages of history to the year 44 B.C. when Julius Caesar, ruler of the Roman world, and the foremost leader of the

world at that time fell victim at the hands of an assassin. History tells us of the momentous impact on the entire world through that great loss.

How will the world of today accept the death of John Fitzgerald Kennedy who was the foremost spokesman of the free world? His untimely death has created a vacuum in world affairs, making it necessary for every nation to reevaluate its foreign policy. The peoples of the world received the tragic news with heartfelt sorrow. They knew of his vital contributions to the security of the free world. In the field of general welfare, the people of the world knew of his great interest in assisting other countries to become independent and self-supporting and to achieve economic and social progress through free institutions.

With the death of John Fitzgerald Kennedy, the world has lost a mighty champion of peace and good will.

My family and I join the people of the world in extending our heartfelt condolences to Mrs. Kennedy and to members of the late President's immediate family in their hour of bereavement.

ADDRESS BY

Hon. Earl Wilson

OF INDIANA

Mr. Speaker, the bullet from the assassin's gun that felled President John F. Kennedy on that beautiful fall morning in Dallas, Tex., only a few days ago, was a national tragedy. Death as a result of natural causes is always a sad event, but when a young man, and particularly a young man who is President of the United States, is struck down at the hands of an assassin, it is most reprehensible.

On the morning of November 22, President John F. Kennedy rode down the street of Dallas, Tex., a happy man with the vigor of youth, with virtually the world at his feet. He was the leader of the greatest and most powerful nation in the world, he was possessed of wealth, power, and happiness; he enjoyed the love and adoration of his parents, brothers, and sisters as well as his charming wife and infant children. He had everything to live for. His popularity was worldwide; even those who did not share his philosophical views respected this young President of ours.

Mr. Speaker, it is difficult sometimes to understand the scheme of life and death. It is certainly most difficult to understand the motivation of this warped-minded individual who fired the fatal shot. And yet, we know that throughout the recorded history of mankind every generation of men has been plagued with such types of depraved human beings. Unfortunately, President Kennedy's tragic death is not without precedent in the comparatively short life of this Republic; as witness the unfortunate and tragic deaths of Presidents Lincoln, Garfield, and McKinley. In each instance, these four Presidents died at the hands of assassins of dubious objectives conceived by unbalanced minds. Possibly the greatest parallel in this most recent national tragedy is that of President McKinley who died at the hands of an admitted anarchist. The obvious murderer of President Kennedy was an admitted Communist.

Mr. Speaker, as one who honestly and sincerely differed with our lamented President, as thank God it is our right to do under the American political system, I also was one of those who had a genuine affection for the President and, like all other Americans of good will, Mrs. Wilson and I join in extending our sincere sympathy to his family.

ADDRESS BY

Hon. Robert T. McLoskey

OF ILLINOIS

Mr. Speaker, the entire Nation, yes, even the world was shocked at the untimely passing of John Fitzgerald Kennedy, the 35th President of the United States.

The ensuing grief and bewilderment which an assassin's bullet brought transcends party lines, and persons from all walks of life, both Republican and Democrat, have asked the question which confounds us all—why must it be? Only the passing of time and history itself will record what his place may be.

It is only honest to say that many Americans did not concur with his interests. I would be less than candid if I did not point out that my concept of the role of Government differed with his, and though on occasion I took exception with his philosophy of government, never at any time did I question his sincerity or motives in desiring to reach his objectives.

While I differed with him I respected his viewpoint as I am sure he was always able to see the other person's view. There were no sour grapes in the spirit of John Kennedy.

No one can deny that he was active and aggressive in the pursuit of endeavoring to bring his programs to fruition. Most certainly he was a thoughtful and engaging young man.

A man of great determination, gay, friendly, and happy—ambitious beyond end but apparently always willing to listen to reason.

I am sure that he was the leader of a generation who felt he must contribute something to the fulfillment of an American dream. This he attempted to do.

Surely he will be missed, and I am sure, while we mourn his passing, we shall always remember the fullness of his patriotism and the untiring dedication he gave to his country's interest.

ADDRESS BY

Hon. Ed Foreman

OF TEXAS

Mr. Speaker, I rise today to express the heartbreak, grief, and sorrow shared by west Texans and folks around the world over the tragic incident that took the life of our President on November 22.

Although I did not always agree with his philosophy or his legislative recommendations, President Kennedy was a vigorous and articulate exponent of his political philosophy. He was truly an outstanding young American and the world mourns his untimely death.

Our thoughts and prayers are with Mrs. Kennedy and her little children during these trying times. May God bless, love, and comfort them.

Hon. E. Y. Berry

OF SOUTH DAKOTA

Mr. Speaker, both on my own behalf and in behalf of the people of western South Dakota I join my colleagues in expressing our grief and sorrow at the unconscionable assassination of John F. Kennedy, the 35th President of the United States.

While I liked and admired the man and his exceptional ability, I disliked and disapproved of many of his policies and programs. At the same time, however, I, as did many of my colleagues, recognized the personal ability and personal influence of this brilliant young man struck down in the prime of life.

I extend our sympathy to his widow and our deep feeling of compassion to his children who have thus had their father snatched from them.

Hon. Albert Thomas

OF TEXAS

Mr. Speaker, as we sit in this Chamber, each with a heavy heart, it is most difficult for me to realize that John F. Kennedy is dead.

Less than an hour before he was assassinated, he joined 8 or 10 of his friends on his airplane as it was preparing to set down in Dallas. He was cheerful and deeply appreciative of the warm and tremendously large reception he had received in San Antonio, Houston, and Fort Worth. He was anxiously awaiting the same warm reception by thousands of people in Dallas.

His death instantaneously brought to the surface the deep fundamental respect, admiration and devotion which the people of the United States and nearly every foreign country felt for him. That devotion, respect and appreciation of the man and his great work will make his memory stand out in American and world history. I shall not mention here his renowned

works—volumes can and will be written on that subject.

I had the high honor and privilege of introducing him in Houston to a crowd of some 3,500 diners and one of the largest radio and television audiences on record in Houston, some 14 hours before his death. At that time I said, "This great leader will go down in history as one of the greatest men the United States has produced."

The human response to his tragic death from all over our Nation and the world clearly indicates that history will record John F. Kennedy, alongside George Washington, Abraham Lincoln, and Franklin D. Roosevelt, as one of our greatest Americans and one of our greatest Presidents.

My family joins me in extending to one of the bravest women I have ever known, his wife, Mrs. John F. Kennedy, and to little Caroline and little brother, John, our sympathy and understanding in their great loss.

Hon. Julia Butler Hansen

OF WASHINGTON

Mr. Speaker, thousands of brilliant words have been spoken and written in tribute to President Kennedy—for his magnificent leadership, brilliance, and humanity. I, too, want to join the distinguished leaders of this House of Representatives in paying a deep and sincere tribute to President Kennedy and to his courageous widow.

From my own heart, and from the hearts of the sorrowing people of my district, comes the deepest sympathy and our love to Mrs. Kennedy.

One single, simple sentence speaks eloquently for so many of us—the moving words of Theodore White in this week's Life magazine: "for one brief, shining moment there was a Camelot." These words will forever bring me the memory of faces, young and old, as they passed through our Capitol where the body of our President lay on that ice-cold November night—faces sorrowing, yet in their way reflecting some essence of the great spirit John Fitzgerald Kennedy left mankind. The spirit which was a shining symbol of faith and hope in a brighter, better world. Those faces said that they, too, saw Camelot.

ADDRESS BY

Hon. Alton Lennon

OF NORTH CAROLINA

Mr. Speaker, the incredible and shocking news of the tragic death of President Kennedy stunned the civilized world.

The portrayal by modern news media of the sequence of events that followed even beyond the 21-gun salute and taps, sounding over the hills of Arlington National Cemetery, plumbed the depths of human emotions of mankind everywhere—perhaps to the greatest degree in history.

Countless eloquent words have been written and spoken in tribute to the life and work of our late President. He served his country well; he sought peace with justice for all nations. This brilliant, dedicated, and courageous young leader built his own monument—a monument to inspire his present and future countrymen.

The people of North Carolina have in many ways expressed their sorrow over this national tragedy. I extend my personal sympathy to all loved ones of the President.

ADDRESS BY

Hon. John C. Kunkel

OF PENNSYLVANIA

Mr. Speaker, President Kennedy's assassination is a tragedy touching the heart and mind of every American. The wanton destruction of this gay, ardent, vivid young man at the zenith of his powers first stunned us, and then left us with a deadening feeling which continues to persist. I believe this same effect has been felt by people throughout the world who had been inspired by his ideals so eloquently expressed.

I mourn the loss of this fine young man who was so boldly steering our ship of state through the turbulent waters of domestic troubles and international strife.

I had the privilege of knowing him since he first came to Congress. I watched his brilliant career, admiring his courage and ability.

My deepest sympathy goes out to his wife and his two lovely young children at this time of their great sorrow, and to the other members of his family.

My heartfelt prayers go out to Almighty God for President Johnson, our new Commander in Chief, as he takes over the gigantic problems now facing the Nation. Fortunately, President Kennedy had seen to it, with foresight, diligence, and care, that President Johnson made the contacts and undertook the responsibilities which equipped him to step into the breach fully armed for the tasks ahead. This is one more thing for which we can thank our late President, John Fitzgerald Kennedy.

ADDRESS BY

Hon. Olin E. Teague

OF TEXAS

Mr. Speaker, as deeply as most of us loved and respected John Fitzgerald Kennedy, it would be that people who knew him so well may have underrated his stature. The intense grief that his mindless assassination has created throughout the free world has borne home to most of us the devotion and affection with which this young President was held by people in all walks of life in every land where freedom is cherished.

Perhaps this was best summed up in a personal letter written by the great Irish playwright, Sean O'Casey. Mr. O'Casey, writing to an American friend, said:

> What a terrible thing has happened to us all. To you, there; to us, here; to all, everywhere. Peace, who was becoming bright-eyed, now sits in the shadow of death: her handsome champion has been killed as he walked by her very side. Her gallant boy is dead.

It was a curious thing about the character and personality of John Fitzgerald Kennedy that everyone, even those who lived in far-distant lands, thought of him as a warm personal friend whom they had known all their lives. There was no great difference between the public image of President Kennedy and the private image. The public personality was merely a clear projection of the vibrant spirit that animated the man in his personal relationships.

As we mourn his assassination, Mr. Speaker,

each of us in this body cherishes personal memories. For instance, it was my privilege to fly with him in the Executive Compartment of the airplane that carried him from Fort Worth to his rendezvous with destiny in Dallas. With the easy familiarity which his manner induced, we spoke about the importance to the Nation of our space program. As always, he was magnificently informed about the subject and fortified his contagious enthusiasm with extensive factual data. It was an inspiring conference and one that I shall always remember with pride modified by sorrow.

We came to Congress together, Mr. Speaker, in 1946 and, despite the fact that we sprang from different sectors of the country, and from different backgrounds, and despite the fact that we had basically different opinions on some issues, we were good friends, always. We served 6 years together on the District Committee, and I clearly recall the idealism with which he approached the task of trying to solve the problems that chronically beset the Nation's Capital. Many Members of the Congress consider service on the District Committee an onerous and thankless task. Typically, John F. Kennedy considered it an important challenge in the field of human relations.

On several occasions we put on the uniform of the Washington Senators together to play in the annual charity baseball game against our friends on the other side of the aisle. He played in these games, I believe, with a little more seriousness than did most of us. John F. Kennedy never saw any sense in engaging in any contest, athletic, mental or political, unless one played to win. And, until the cowardly murderer struck him down, he was a consistent winner in everything he attempted.

More than any President in our history, he was one of us. He was part and parcel of the Congress, and the Congress was a permanent element in his bloodstream. This was so apparent when—after his election to the Presidency—he would call us to the White House for conferences. He always understood what was possible of accomplishment in our deliberations, and what was not. He respected our judgment; he understood our problems; he treated us as friends and colleagues.

With his death, every one of us, Mr. Speaker, died a little.

We have lost a great leader.

We have lost a great friend.

And the entire free world has lost a living symbol of courage and decency. Indeed, as Mr. O'Casey said, the handsome champion of peace was killed as he walked by her very side. Her gallant boy is dead.

ADDRESS BY

Hon. Robert H. Michel

OF ILLINOIS

Mr. Speaker, I should like to add my tribute this afternoon to the many eloquent ones which have been said in memory of our late President, John F. Kennedy.

The stunning news came to me as I had started my drive back to Illinois on that fateful Friday, November 22. I was between Hagerstown and Hancock, Md., when the confirmed report came over the radio that the last rites had been administered and that the President had died. I pulled off the side of road to control my shock and emotion and sought out the first telephone that I might phone my wife. Neither of us could talk very intelligently but we did decide that I should turn back and return to Washington.

I shall never forget that drive back to Washington along Route 240 which I had driven so many times. Cars were pulling off to the side of the road in numbers and those still on the road were just poking along. It was quite obvious that drivers were listening intently to their radios for every fragment of news. As I turned onto Embassy Row, down Massachusetts Avenue, I never before have noticed so many flags representing foreign countries and all were drawn to half mast. I guess there never has been so tragic an event that has touched so many capitals around the world and certainly attests to the stature this relatively young man achieved in so short a time.

His being taken from our midst in such an awful manner reminds us how the course of history seems to be charted more by accident than by design, and of the Biblical Scripture which tells us that these events can happen "within the twinkling of any eye." Rhetoric and prose are so inadequate at a time like this but I do want to simply add the profound sympathy and condolences of our family to those untold numbers which have gone out and continue to be said for Mrs. Kennedy, the children, and the entire Kennedy family.

ADDRESS BY

Hon. L. H. Fountain

OF NORTH CAROLINA

Mr. Speaker, I know I cannot add anything of significance to the very eloquent and moving words which have already come from the saddened hearts of so many Members of this House over the untimely, the unnecessary, the tragic and shocking death of our late President of the United States, John Fitzgerald Kennedy.

However, I would betray every impulse of my nature if I did not express my own deep sorrow and pay my poor flower of tribute to the many bouquets of friendship and affection which have been offered here in his memory.

Like many others, I was honored with the privilege of seeing and being with him on a number of occasions, both public and private. He was always gay and cheerful. As someone has already said, "you could see a laugh coming in his eyes before you could hear it from his lips." He was always hungry for information and one of the best listeners I have ever known. In fact, he was a questioner. He posed the questions and complimented you by listening to your answers. The fact that he was so well informed can probably be attributed to his inquiring nature.

The world is a poorer place with the passing of this gallant leader, whose true greatness will never fully be known. We are saddened all the more because our beloved President has been taken from us at a time when his star was strongly in the ascendancy and his efforts for world peace and a better society were only beginning to bear fruit. Even so, his contributions are impressive and John F. Kennedy is destined to become a legend in our time.

In so many ways, the President was a study in contrasts. He was a humble man and a person of aristocratic bearing. He was a very warm human being and yet reserved. He was gentle and he was forceful. He was practical and he was idealistic. And he expressed himself with both eloquence and simplicity.

All of us were touched in one way or another by the courage and the example of this young President, who was wise beyond his years. Those of us who had the privilege of meeting with him occasionally will remember him as a soft-spoken man of great charm and good humor who would rather hear an opponent's views than criticize his thinking. One could and did differ with President Kennedy, but one could not do so without appreciating his openminded receptiveness to differing points of view which characterizes the scholar.

John F. Kennedy, the President, had political opponents, but I cannot believe that John F. Kennedy, the man, had any enemies. Even the man who assassinated him must have had a twisted, distorted, and confused mind. He was mentally and spiritually sick. Those who fought the President and his programs in the political arena would, I believe, be the first to acknowledge his sense of fairplay and his dedication to the democratic ideals and institutions of the country he loved so well. More than any of us realize, during the days and months and years that lie ahead, all of us will miss John F. Kennedy more and more.

The dignity and courage of our late President are traits shared equally by his noble, gallant, and beautiful widow. Mrs. Kennedy's inspiring example during these trying days will remain in our memories forever. May she find some solace in the knowledge that each of us shares her bereavement and joins in her prayers.

ADDRESS BY

Hon. Cornelius E. Gallagher

OF NEW JERSEY

Mr. Speaker, the United States, indeed the whole world, has passed, in recent days, through a long, dark, and dismal corridor. Having emerged once again into the light, we are left still in our grief and surrounded by the shrouds of mourning, grim reminder of the tragedy that haunts us—with the heritage of John Fitzgerald Kennedy.

As we might expect, this is no ordinary heritage of material value, for this was no ordinary man. The heritage of John F. Kennedy is a challenge to all Americans, to men everywhere, to continue, even though he no longer leads us, the efforts to attain the goals he had set not only for himself, but for every citizen of the United States.

Few men in history are touched with greatness which, we all know, to be a combination of many talents of wisdom and courage, and of knowledge, of purpose and dedication, and of understanding and compassion. All these and more our late President possessed in abundance.

Perhaps history shall remember him best for having sought, above all else, the betterment of mankind. In perilous times and possessing power over the most awesome weapons ever created, he sought peace for the world.

In a land of plenty, he sought an equal share of our goods for all men—to aid the aged, to care for the ill, to educate the illiterate, to assist the underprivileged, to guarantee the constitutional rights of every citizen.

He promised to get America moving again. Maybe we just seemed to have stopped but many people here and abroad thought we did. Both friend and foe wondered whether our forward motion had ceased. Many questioned the future of our Nation and the system which made it great. They wondered whether the great changes taking place throughout the world foredoomed a free, competitive society. They wondered whether communism was not truly the wave of the future. They wondered if we were not too well off to protect ourselves, too liberal to fight, too tired to care. They pondered and then equated the Rise and Fall of Rome with the history of the United States. They felt that America would lose its freedom by default.

The inauguration of John F. Kennedy as President changed all this. Not only was America moving, but the spirit of our motion thrust ahead. We had a new President, a new leader who instilled vitality, confidence and faith in our Nation and our system. He demonstrated with great clarity that the United States of America as a Nation was still in its early ascendancy.

He looked upon communism, not as an ogre too fearsome to behold but as something that contained within itself the seeds of its own destruction and that what was needed most was time and patience and strength. For he believed that the answer to communism rested not with the Communists but within ourselves provided we had faith in ourselves.

John F. Kennedy's time ran out all too soon, but the legacy he left America was faith, confidence, and a renewed belief in ourselves. The legacy he left the world was a future for freedom.

ADDRESS BY

Hon. John E. Moss

OF CALIFORNIA

Mr. Speaker, we who are the Members of this distinctive parliamentary body today have had a great privilege in knowing and working with John Fitzgerald Kennedy. Our close association with our late beloved President assigns to us at this moment the role of evaluating the man. The wanton taking of his life by an assassin has assigned to history, to the generations of the future, the role of evaluating John Kennedy the President.

As a contemporary of the late President, I enjoyed an all too brief association with him. I found it an inspiring experience. No leader of our time was so completely a part of the 20th century. No leader of our time so fully understood the significance of the American role in the second half of the 20th century. No leader of our time was so obviously the master of the complexities of this most difficult and too frequently frustrating era. President Kennedy had an unusual zest for the challenge, however awesome that might be, in the high position he occupied for less than 3 years. This fact was so clearly stated in his own words in his inspiring inaugural address on January 20, 1961, when he said:

In the long history of the world only a few generations have been granted the role of defending freedom in its hour of maximum danger. I do not shrink from this responsibility—I welcome it.

This was truer at the moment of death than at the time of inauguration. The outpouring of sympathy, the obvious grief evident throughout the civilized world, attested to the success of his efforts to minimize those things which divide the peoples of our time and build upon the opportunities which tend to unite mankind.

President Kennedy was a man of unusual intellectual capacity and yet he was a most comfortable person to be around because he understood not only the problems of his generation but the generation itself. Perhaps no President in his public utterances so phrased his statements as to make them fully quotable as did President Kennedy, yet few have shown the humor which characterized the dialogue of his administration. In fact, within a few hours preceding the senseless act of assassination, the President demonstrated the keenness of that wit, the delightful turn of a phrase, whether designed to have you laugh with him or at him. There was nothing pompous about John Kennedy, yet in the fullest sense he was the President and carried that role with every dignity befitting the office. He worked hard; he never ducked a fight and he enjoyed both to the fullest.

All America, yes, and I guess the greater part of the world has taken pride from the young President with his beautiful wife and very attractive family. All have enjoyed the delightful antics of Caroline and the President's beloved John-John. All have been proud of the regal dignity of Jacqueline Kennedy, and while the Kennedys became a political issue, all have enjoyed the vigor of the President's brothers and sisters. Nevertheless, none would deny the dedication of this family to the welfare of all our citizens. This was a vital family unique in the American political experience and we are all the poorer because of the tragedy of Dallas.

At the very moment when the world was beginning to sense the magnitude of his achievements, the success of his international policies and the almost spectacular emergence of a healthier domestic economy, we were robbed of the leadership of this vital young intellect. But even in that moment of darkest despair, the unusual insight of the President was again demonstrated when we witnessed a new President taking over the onerous burdens so unexpectedly thrust upon him, because the choice made by John F. Kennedy in Los Angeles in 1960 was a wise choice. He had wanted Lyndon Johnson as his running mate—a selection made with utmost care, a deliberate assessment of the needs of the Nation. The President's wisdom in that choice each day becomes more apparent.

President Kennedy, the first man of my generation to achieve the Presidency, afforded all who lived through his brief tenure in office an experience of enrichment. Let us hope, Mr. Speaker, that we will most thoughtfully review his many public statements, his carefully conceived programs recommended to this Congress, and after a more deliberate evaluation of them, make a renewed dedication to make them work as he knew they would for the benefit of all mankind.

Mr. Speaker, a tribute to President Kennedy would not be complete without mention of the great courage of his widow. Her conduct from the moment tragedy struck should make every American more proud. Perhaps no woman in history was ever called upon to play a more difficult role under more brutal or tragic circumstances. No one could have done it better. The British press stated that Jacqueline Kennedy gave the American people something they lacked. That something in their words was "majesty," but however we characterize it, Mr. Speaker, we must recognize that the grief felt by each of us was only a small part of that felt by her. How many of us with our small part of the burden could have conducted ourselves with the grace, the courage, and the majesty of Jacqueline Kennedy?

I am pleased to announce to the Congress that the Sacramento City Board of Education on November 27, 1963, acted to honor our late President in a most fitting manner. All of us who were privileged to work with the late President knew of his vital concern to provide education for all the people of the United States. Therefore, it is most fitting that a new senior high school in Sacramento is to be named the John F. Kennedy Senior High School.

Mr. Speaker, I conclude my remarks with the resolution adopted by the Sacramento City Board of Education:

RESOLUTION BY SACRAMENTO BOARD OF EDUCATION

Whereas John Fitzgerald Kennedy was a great statesman who served as America's eloquent spokesman throughout the world in our country's search for peace and security for all mankind; and

Whereas John Fitzgerald Kennedy was a true champion of education and the equality of educational opportunity for all, regardless of color, creed, social or economic status; and

Whereas John Fitzgerald Kennedy was most articulate in his support of good citizenship, physical and mental fitness, vocational competence, and of improved living standards for all citizens; and

Whereas John Fitzgerald Kennedy had become known and respected as a true champion of freedom, justice and understanding in America and among all nations; and

Whereas John Fitzgerald Kennedy, with all his great responsibilities as the head of our Nation, still gave continued evidence of love of children and family and a deep concern for the values of home, community, church, and schools; and

Whereas John Fitzgerald Kennedy endeared himself through his sincerity, his high principles and his ennobling example to young and old alike: Be it therefore

Resolved, That the Board of Education of the Sacramento City Unified School District, on behalf of all pupils and the entire district staff does herewith express sincere and heartfelt sympathy to Mrs. Jacqueline Kennedy, daughter Caroline, son John F. Kennedy, Jr., and all members of the Kennedy family; and be it further

Resolved, In order to perpetuate in this Sacramento community the memory of a great and renowned man, a new senior high school, now in progress of planning and soon to be built shall be known as the John F. Kennedy Senior High School; and be it further

Resolved, That the Board of Education of the Sacramento City Unified School District of Sacramento, Calif., in special meeting assembled, does approve this resolution in sincere tribute to John Fitzgerald Kennedy, 35th President of the United States of America, whose tragic death brought deep sorrow to all loyal Americans and to the entire world; and be it further

Resolved, To adjourn this meeting of the board of education in honor and sincere tribute to John Fitzgerald Kennedy, our late esteemed President.

We hereunto set our hand and seal on this 27th day of November 1963.

THE BOARD OF EDUCATION OF THE SACRAMENTO CITY UNIFIED SCHOOL DISTRICT.

By Jewel W. Blucher, president; Genevieve N. Didion, vice president; Marie E. Babich, M.D.; John Quincy Brown, Jr.; Alba Kuchman; Gladys R. Paulson; Milton L. Schwartz; and F. Melvyn Lawson, superintendent and secretary.

Memorial Tributes

IN THE

Senate of the United States

IN EULOGY OF

John Fitzgerald Kennedy

Memorial Tributes in the Senate
of the United States

TRIBUTE BY

Hon. Carl Hayden

OF ARIZONA

The President pro tempore laid before the Senate a joint resolution of the Legislature of the State of Arizona, which was ordered to lie on the table, as follows:

HOUSE JOINT RESOLUTION 1

A joint resolution on the death of John Fitzgerald Kennedy, 35th President of the United States

Whereas on the 22d day of November, in the year 1963, John Fitzgerald Kennedy, the 35th President of the United States, was stricken down by an assassin's bullet and

Whereas the 26th Legislature of the State of Arizona, now convened in its second regular session, desires to record for posterity by this resolution both respect and tribute to the memory of our departed President: Now, therefore, be it

Resolved by the Legislature of the State of Arizona:

John Fitzgerald Kennedy typified the exemplary American by devotion to his country, by devotion to his family, by participation in the affairs of government, and by concern for the welfare of people both in America and throughout the world.

He gave much in the defense of his native land against the foul designs of the enemy, and he joined with his fellow Americans in preparing again for conflict if it came, but he also joined with his fellow Americans in seeking the peace so that men, women, and children, wherever their abode, could accomplish the fulfillment of their lives without want or fear.

Many have and will pay tribute to our fallen President for his devotion to the public welfare and many have and will pay tribute to his devotion to public service because he was not lacking in the sincerity of his resolutions and the courage of his efforts to secure their fulfillment.

His fellow Americans recall in retrospect his devotion to his lovely and accomplished wife who shared with him and with pride observed the honors which a grateful people conferred upon him, and they will recall how Caroline and John not only kindled the warmth of his fatherly love but they also recall the affection for them imprinted in the hearts of people everywhere.

But now, alas, the hopes, aspirations, and ambitions of a valiant President have been thwarted. Just a few weeks ago he commanded the respect and leadership of a free world, full of youth and promise. His was a role of action filled with conflict and anxiety. Never did people anywhere, free or slave, doubt his dedication to the dignity of man and the value of their freedom, and it was the nobility of this dedication that could have inspired him to proclaim to the world upon his inauguration: "Let every nation know * * * that we shall pay any price, bear any burden, meet any hardship, support any friend, oppose any foe, to assure the survival and success of liberty."

John Fitzgerald Kennedy was dedicated to God, to his country, and to his fellow man. He fought valiantly in war and in peace to preserve that dedication. He accepted the truism that all men are created equal and fought until the end to convince people everywhere that discrimination between persons because of race or creed is violative of every historic document inscribed and proclaimed by the patriots who founded this Nation.

The legislature of the State of Arizona, in further tribute to our fallen President, requests and directs the secretary of state of the State of Arizona to transmit copies of this resolution, under his hand and the great seal of the State of Arizona, to the President of the United States, to the President of the Senate of the United States, to the Speaker of the House of Representatives of the United States, and to Mrs. Jacqueline Kennedy, the widow of the late President.

Passed the house January 13, 1964, by the following vote: 79 ayes, 0 nays, 1 not voting.

Passed the senate January 14, 1964, by unanimous vote.

Approved by the Governor, January 15, 1964.

Filed in the office of the secretary of state, January 15, 1964.

TRIBUTES BY

Hon. Mike Mansfield

OF MONTANA

Mr. President, during the past few days a great number of telegrams and letters have reached me. They are expressions of regret on the tragic death of President Kennedy. Some came to me in my capacity as majority leader. Others in my capacity as a Senator from Montana and still others as a friend to turn to in order to give voice to a profound grief.

The telegrams came from Canada and from many countries in Latin America. They came from France, Denmark, Germany. They came from "just simple Montana people," from Indian tribes and from an association of sergeants at the San Antonio Air Base and from student associations in my State. They have one characteristic in common—an outpouring of a deep grief at the terrible loss. It is a grief which cannot be comforted by words. It can only be made to recede by a rededication to the purposes for which President Kennedy strove—a more decent nation in a more decent world.

Mr. President, I ask unanimous consent that a selection of telegrams and letters be included as follows:

HELENA, MONT.,
November 22, 1963.

Senator MIKE MANSFIELD,
Senate Office Building,
Washington, D.C.:

Although we are just simple Montana people we wish to extend our deepest sympathy to Mrs. John F. Kennedy and family, the greatest President since Franklin Delano Roosevelt. May God be good to us as we will need all of His grace in the months to come.

Mr. EDWARD J. WORDAL.

————

BILLINGS, MONT.

Senator MIKE MANSFIELD,
Senate Office Building,
Washington, D.C.:

I am extremely proud of your actions in this time of tragedy.

Express our support for you and President Johnson in the future.

BILL SPEARE.

BOZEMAN, MONT.,
November 22, 1963.

Senator MIKE MANSFIELD,
Senate Office Building,
Washington, D.C.:

Mannix Electric, Inc., and each employee requests you to extend every condolence to the Kennedy family. Also, we want you to know we have the utmost confidence that you will see, after proper and full investigation is conducted, that the responsible people will be made sorry they executed this plot.

CON MANNIX,
President.

OTTO ZEIER,
DAVID R. BRUCK,
DAVID ANDERSON,
FRANK A. HAYS,
FLORENCE A. WILLIAMSON,
CARL NUBER,
Employees.

————

GREAT FALLS, MONT.,
November 22, 1963.

Hon. MIKE MANSFIELD,
U.S. Senator, State of Montana,
Senate Office Building,
Washington, D.C.

DEAR MIKE: The assassination of our President John F. Kennedy has shocked the citizens of our city. We feel a very personal loss since he visited here with you in September. Knowing that you already are carrying a heavy load, we want you to know that we join the mourning Nation and extend sincere sympathy to Mrs. Kennedy and the children.

MARIAN S. ERDMANN,
Mayor, City of Great Falls, Mont.

————

GREAT FALLS, MONT.,
November 22, 1963.

MIKE MANSFIELD,
Senate Majority Leader,
Washington, D.C.:

The deepest sympathy and the prayers of the sisters of the College of Great Falls are with you and Congress. May the memory of the great man gone to God be a beacon of inspiration in your effort to preserve and extend the blessings of justice and liberty for all.

SISTER RITA,
Sacred Heart President,
College of Great Falls.

————

MONTREAL, QUE.,
November 22, 1963.

SPEAKER OF THE SENATE,
Washington, D.C.:

The council, mayor, and all the citizens of the city of Westmount share your loss of a tremendous leader.

C. H. DRURY,
Mayor, City of Westmount.

GREAT FALLS, MONT.,
November 22, 1963.

Senator MIKE MANSFIELD,
Senate Office Building,
Washington, D.C:

The student body of the College of Great Falls shares your grief at the passing of our President. Please convey our sincere sympathy to the President's family and friends. May God bless and guide you in the difficult days ahead.

Sincerely,

ARLEN D. STUBES,
Body President,
College of Great Falls.

———

WESTFIELD, N.J.,
November 22, 1963.

MICHAEL MANSFIELD,
Senate Office Building,
Washington, D.C:

Huguette in France but know she joins Anthony, Peter, myself in wanting to tell you and Maureen how deeply grieved we are at this monstrous act and we pray the President, with God's help, will continue to work with your help like his predecessor for the peace on earth and good will of mankind.

RUPERT.

———

OAKLAND, CALIF.,
November 23, 1963.

Hon. MIKE MANSFIELD,
The Senate, Washington, D.C.:

My prayers for your strength at this time of deep sorrow and new responsibility are with you and Maurine. May God be with you.

MAXINE B. SCOTT,
Hotel Caremont.

———

NOVEMBER 22, 1963.

SENADO ESTADOS UNIDOS,
Capitolio, Washington, D.C.:

Konrome Transcribir ustedes siguiente resolucion aprobada unanimidad Senado Nacional Bolivia bipuntos articulo primero rendir su homenaje postumo al gran Presidente John F. Kennedy lider de la hermandad en el mundo muerto alevosamente por mano criminal por defender los derechos de igualdad libertad y mejores condiciones de vida del ser humano. Articulo segundo izar el pabellon nacional en el parlamento durante tres dias como dolorosa expresion del sentimiento del pueblo Boliviano. Articulo tercero hacer llegar al senado Norteamericano el texto de esta resolucion camaral.

Atentamente,

FEDERICO FORTUN SANJINES,
Presidente Senado Nacional.

———

MONTEVIDEO, URUGUAY,
November 22, 1963.

Etat al Senado de los Estados Unidos de America, Washington, D.C:

El Senado de la Republica Oriental Del Uruguay presenta a esa alta corporacion sus mas sentidas condolencias por la muerte del ilustre Presidente John F. Kennedy, que priva a esa eignisima nacion y al mundo, de una de las mas altas expresiones de la democracia y del derecho. Y de un celoso cultor de las supremas idealidades del hombre y de los pueblos.

MARTIN R. ECHEGOYEN,
Presidente Senado.

JOSE PASTOR SALVANACH,
Secretario.

———

BUTTE, MONT.,
November 23, 1963.

Hon. MIKE MANSFIELD,
Senate Majority Leader,
Washington, D.C.:

Express our deepest sympathy to Mrs. Kennedy—Kennedy family and members of the administration.

Dr. and Mrs. HARRY G. FARRELL.

———

BUTTE, MONT.,
November 23, 1963.

Senator MIKE MANSFIELD,
Washington, D.C.:

Please convey our sincere sympathy to the Kennedy family on their tragic loss and the Nation's loss.

Sincerely,

FRANCIS X. DOLAN,
DENNIS F. DOLAN.

———

CORAL CABLES, FLA.,
November 23, 1963.

MIKE MANSFIELD,
Senator from Montana,
U.S. Senate, Capitol Building,
Washington, D.C.:

On behalf of the Cuban Medical Association in Exile I express to you our deepest condolence for the death of President Kennedy, victim of a treacherous crime.

Dr. ENRIQUE HUERTAS,
President, Cuban Medical Association in Exile.

———

SAN ANTONIO, TEX.,
November 23, 1963.

Hon. MIKE MANSFIELD,
U.S. Senator, Washington, D.C.

DEAR SENATOR MANSFIELD: We, the airmen of the U.S. Air Force, join with you and the Nation in mourning the loss of our Commander in Chief, John F. Kennedy, President of the United States. That this Nation, under God, should suffer indignity and shame of this nature when we strive so hard with all our sources to create peace and nonaggression in all the world. It is incomprehensible.

May our combined prayers provide solace for the bereaved families of our great leader.

BENNY W. McGEHEE,
President of the Air Force Sergeant's Association.

GREAT FALLS, MONT.,
November 22, 1963.

Hon. MIKE MANSFIELD,
Senate Office Building,
Washington, D.C.:

Please convey Cascade County's deepest sympathy to the Kennedy family for you and for our new President Johnson go our prayers for strength and wisdom in the days ahead.

DEMOCRATIC CENTRAL
COMMITTEE, CASCADE COUNTY,
JOHN McLAUGHLIN.
Mrs. P. J. GILFEATHER.

———

KOEBENHAVN,
November 23, 1963.

The CONGRESS OF THE UNITED STATES,
Capitol, Washington, D.C.:

The Parliamente of Denmark wishes to express its heartfelt condolences on the tragic death of President John F. Kennedy.

GUSTAV PEDERSEN,
President of the Folketing.

———

NOVEMBER 23, 1963.

CAPITOL,
Washington, D.C.

Our whole sympathy belongs to the greatest President of the United States, John F. Kennedy. May God bless him always.

FAMILY PATAN,
FAMILY KNOBLOCK,
Western Germany.

———

TOKYO, *November 23, 1963.*

Senator MIKE J. MANSFIELD,
U.S. Senate, Washington, D.C.:

Wish to present my profound condolence to the President Kennedy's death.

YANG IL-DONG.

———

MEXICO CITY, MEX.,
November 24, 1963.

Senator MIKE MANSFIELD,
Senado de Los Estados Unidos,
Washington, D.C.:

A la profunda consternacion causada por el innoble crimen cometido en la persona senor Presidente Kennedy seguira luto mumdial para quienes admiramos portentosa magnitud del estadista que habiendo sido el mas insigne abanderado de las causas nobles y justas coma séra por siempre para digma del bien y la paz universales. punto sirvase aceptar mis.

As sentidas condolencias por la perdida irreparable ha sufrido pueblo y gobierno Norte Americanos.

Punto respetuosamente,
DIPUTADO LIC ROMULO SANCHEZ MIRELES,
Presidente Gran Comision.
H. CAMARA, *Diputados.*

PARIS,
November 22, 1963.

Senator MIKE MANSFIELD,
U.S. Senate, Washington, D.C.:

Our deepest sorrow and condolences.

ROBERT and SUZANNE LOUPPE.

———

GUANAJUATO, MEX.

Senator MIKE MANSFIELD,
Senador de Los Estados Unidos,
Washington, D.C.:

Unome profunda pena pueblo Norteamerica y sentimiente munidal por muerte excelentisimo Senor Presidente del nacion punto atentamente gobernador constitucional del estado.

LIC JUAN JOSE TORRES LANDA.

———

GUADALAJARA, MEX.

Senator MIKE MANSFIELD,
Edificio Del Capitaolio,
Washington, D.C.:

Unome duelo General Perdida Gran Ciudadano America Presidente Kennedy abrazolo sentidamente.

Senador GUILLERMO RAMIREZ VALADEZ.

———

LONG BEACH, CALIF.,
November 24, 1963.

Senator MIKE MANSFIELD,
Former MSU History and Political Science President,
Senate Democratic Leader, Washington, D.C.:

What happened in Dallas, Tex., yesterday is not only a national tragedy; it is a national disgrace. We hang our heads not only in mourning but in shame. So another fragment of the American dream is ripped away before our eyes by ignorance, hate, and murder. Is mankind forever to be ignorant, hateful, and capable of such heinous acts. Oh, Lord, are we Americans to destroy our magnificent testimonial of what free and democratic people can do?

JIM BEAKEY,
MSU Graduate Teacher.

———

GUANAJUATO, MEX.

Senator MIKE MANSFIELD,
Senado de Los Estados Unidos,
Washington, D.C.:

Reuegole aceptar mis sentimientos por muerte excelentisimo Senor Presidente Estados Unidos punto atentamente Secretario Privado C. Gobernador Guanajuato.

MARCOS AGUAYO DURAN.

———

HAVRE, MONT.,
November 23, 1963.

Senator MIKE MANSFIELD,
Old Senate Office Building,
Washington, D.C.:

Extend our deepest sympathy for the Kennedy family. The loss of our great President is felt by the tribe for his untiring efforts for the Indian people.

EDWARD EAGLEMAN,
Secretary, Business Committee.

Mexico City, Mex.,
November 23, 1963.

Senador Mike Mansfield,
U.S. Senate, Washington, D.C.:

Con profunda consternacion he recibido la noticia del asesinato del Senor Presidente Kennedy su gran amigo-punto acompanolo en su pena y por su conducto expreso mi stentida condolencia a todos su colegas del senado puto un abrazo fraternal.

Senador Manuel Moreno Sanchez.

November 25, 1963.

Sympathy as we have all lost a great leader and friend. If and when you see Lyndon please also convey to him our sympathy and warm wishes for the great task that lies ahead of him.

Affectionately,

Jane and Charlie.

Mexico, *November 23, 1963.*

Mr. Mike Mansfield,
Senate Office Building, Washington, D.C.:

Juego a usted aceptar mis mas sentidas condolencias por la muerte de su gran Presidente y muy querido amigo mio John F. Kennedy punto lo saludo afectuous amente punto Secretario Agricultura.

Julian Rodriguez Adame.

November 22, 1963.

Dear Mike: Our hearts are heavy with grief and our minds refuse to believe that our President has been killed.

A first reaction is one of desire for vengeance—an agonized cry against persons or factions which could have been responsible.

Mr. Kennedy has been a good President, and one can only hope that our Nation will give sober thought to our future.

We send our message to you, expressing our sorrow, since you knew him as a friend and since you may let the family know how we Montanans feel.

One can hope that through or because of this tragedy, our people will draw closer to the American hearth in unity of action and peace.

Sincerely,

——— ———.

Leon, Gto.,
22 de Noviembre de 1963.

Senador Mike Mansfield,
U.S. Senate,
Office of the Majority Leader,
Washington, D.C.

Querido y fino amigo: No habiendo podido comunicarme en estos momentos telefonicamente con usted, séáme permitido—usar este medio para presentar por su conducto al Senado de su País mi más profunda condolencia por la pérdida irreparable que acaban de sufrir no solo los Estados Unidos y México, sino el mundo entero, del más preclaro paladin de la libertad y de la democracia, Señor Presidente John F. Kennedy.

Guardo en mi corazón y mi memoria las deferencias y atenciones que para mi tuvo el Señor Presidente tano en Washington como en México, y siempre pediré al Todo Poderoso por su alma.

Reciban sus compañeros de Gámara y usted, repito, mis mas respetuosas y cariñosas condolencias.

——— ———.

Memorial Resolution

We, the Missoula County, Mont., Democratic Central Committee, gathered in special memorial meeting on this day, November 23, 1963, at 10 a.m., do hereby express our shock over the assassination of President Kennedy. We are stunned and bewildered by this harvest of hate and political immaturity.

For comfort we turn to his courage in seeking peace and justice for a troubled world. We ask, in his words, what we can do for our country. Our answer is a call upon men of good will everywhere to put down their hates, to seek a resolution of differences in a fashion consistent with the dignity of man.

For hope we turn to his successor and pray that God will give him wisdom and courage as he assumes his new burden of Government.

We do, hereby, pledge to President Lyndon B. Johnson our full and energetic support in the days ahead.

We offer our deepest sympathies to Mrs. Kennedy, her children, and the Kennedy families. We offer our assurance that in President Kennedy's memory we will continue to find inspiration.

Thomas F. Murray,
Chairman, Missoula County Democratic Central Committee.

Attest:

Adeline Barton,
Secretary.

Missoula County,
Democratic Central Committee,
Missoula, Mont., November 23, 1963.

Senator Mike Mansfield,
U.S. Senate, Washington, D.C.

Dear Senator Mansfield: I am enclosing a copy of the memorial resolution adopted this morning by the Missoula County Democratic Central Committee.

The original has been forwarded to Mrs. Kennedy.

Sincerely,

Thomas F. Murray,
Chairman.

Rabat,
November 23, 1963.

Senator Mansfield,
U.S. Senate, Washington, D.C.:

Presentons condoleances les plus emues suite deces du President Kennedy heros de is paix heros de la liberte et grand ami du peuple Marocain.

Le Comite Provisoire de la Chambre
des Conseillers,
Du Maroc.

RIO DE JANEIRO,
November 25, 1963.

Senator MANSFIELD,
U.S. Senate,
Washington, D.C.:

Still under the impact of Friday's tragic event. We wish to convey, dear friend, our deepest sympathy.

ELIZINHA and WALTHER MOREIRA SALLES.

CUTBACK, MONT.
November 25, 1963.

Hon. MIKE MANSFIELD,
Senate Majority Leader,
Washington, D.C.:

To see and hear you give the eulogy in the Capitol for our great and beloved friend most touching in my sorrow. We have lost him but have President Johnson and you. In this hour of darkness and challenge God bless both of you.

WALTER WETZEL,
Chairman, Blackfoot Tribe.

MISSOULA, MONT.,
November 25, 1963.

Senator MIKE MANSFIELD,
U.S. Senate,
Office of the Majority Leader,
Washington, D.C.:

The Associated Students of Montana State University do hereby express our regret over one of the gravest tragedies that has befallen our Nation in the lifetime of many students at Montana State University, the death of John F. Kennedy. We only hope that former President John F. Kennedy, who served during his time of Presidency as an inspiration for the youth of America, because he himself was a young man and because of his ability to work unceasingly for the United States of America, will continue to serve in history as a man with ideas that will inspire students toward building lives of promise.

RICK JONES,
President, Associated Students of Montana State University.

POPLAR, MONT.,
November 26, 1963.

Senator MIKE MANSFIELD,
Washington, D.C.:

A humble tribute to President Kennedy, the greatest white father of the vanishing race, shall always be remembered for his New Frontier pace, he has joined the great chiefs at their happy hunting ground, leaving us a cultural transition that may never be found, his love and understanding devotion to all mankind shall never be forgotten throughout the ages of time, divine hopes in a redeemer of his integrity, will enlighten the spirit of preservation in perpetuity. The American Indians shall forever cherish his virtue, especially those of the Assinniboine and Sioux.

AUSTIN BUCKLES.

WOLFPOINT, MONT.

Senator MIKE MANSFIELD,
Senate Office Building, Washington, D.C.:

We have no words to tell of our grief for the passing of our martial President but only to know that in spite of his physical absence from us the ideals and examples he set shall not die and cannot be taken from us. Please convey this message to the Kennedy family. Letter follows.

CHIEF FIRST TO FLY,
JOSEPH WEFIT,
Representing Indian People of the Fort Peck Reservation, Wolfpoint, Mont.

WASHINGTON, D.C.,
November 21, 1963.

DEAR MIKE: I write at once to share our grief on this tragic day. God rest the soul of John Kennedy and comfort his widow and the family. This loss is profoundly distressing to us all; and I pray that we may learn yet again to value properly what he dedicated himself to do and consider how best to carry out the unfinished task. May God bless our country and guide its people and their representatives and comfort us in our sorrow.

Devotedly your friend,

ANDREW.

MONTREAL, QUEBEC,
November 23, 1963.

SPEAKER,
U.S. Senate,
Washington, D.C.:

The IUE Canadian General Electric Conference Board, meeting in Montreal, learned with indescribable shock and mortification of the untimely and unwarranted passing of the President of the United States. We share the mourning of his passing with all people the world over who have come to admire his unmatched capabilities and capacity to promote peace and the well-being and equality of mankind everywhere. As we pray for the happy repose of his soul, our prayers and deep condolences go out to his widow and the President's entire family in this hour of monumental grief. You may be sure that all Canadians feel the same sense of immense loss for this great man and good neighbor to the south of us.

HAROLD DAVEY,
Chairman.
ROBERT ORR,
Secretary.

MEXICO CITY, MEXICO.

Senator MIKE MANSFIELD,
Senate of the United States,
Washington, D.C.:

I beg you to accept my most sincere condolence on the death of President Kennedy, great guardian of the world's peace, and defender of the human rights in the United States.

Sincerely,

MANUEL J. SIERRA.

Mr. President, the death of President Kennedy was a profound shock not only to this Nation but to people everywhere. Many in other lands shared the grief which we experienced. Some expressed this shock and grief with great sensitivity and very deep feelings.

In this connection, I invite the attention of Senators to an article by Mr. Eric Nicol on President Kennedy's death which was referred to me by Mr. James J. Flaherty of the Great Falls Chamber of Commerce. Mr. Nicol's tribute to Mr. Kennedy appeared as a column in the Vancouver Province which is published in Vancouver, British Columbia. It is a moving and eloquent comment which reveals not only the high esteem and affection in which the late President was held by our northern neighbors but also the sense of bitter loss, so similar to our own, which his death occasioned among Canadians.

I ask unanimous consent that the editorial referred to be printed as follows:

A Tribute

"Never send to know for whom the bell tolls."

Our grief, this numbing November weekend, was sharpened I think by our sensing that violence has won out over reason.

The assassin's bullet sought the brain, the seat of man's only hope against the tyranny of superstition, hate, and the prodding demons of war. From President Kennedy's superb mind the missile sped on to lodge in the hearts of all of us.

The head that was doing its level best to lead us out of the primitivism of emotional response—in my judgment, was his characteristic preface to a statement—lost out to a bolt-action rifle as crude in its lethal purpose as a stone age club.

Because most of us identified ourselves gratefully with the young President's intellectual strength, his determination to make reason the master of the tumultuous forces threatening to sunder the world, the ripping away of that support by a sole agent of the powers of darkness has made the loss more than a matter of simple sorrow for the passing of a great nation's leader.

By extension we recognize the sniper's rifle as the symbol of nuclear war, triggered by some madman at the least expected moment.

In last Friday's triumph of extremism, of passion, of the irrational and irrevocable act, we see that America is not Harvard. It is also Dallas, Tex. It is the country where the gun is still more widely admired, as the instrument of policy, than is power of intellect.

The author of the New Frontier was felled in the heartland of the old frontier. The violence and stupidity of the TV western has won out over the lonely struggle of a brilliant man to stimulate his fellow countrymen to abandon the path of valiant ignorance.

President Kennedy is the lucky one. He died young, without suffering, at the height of his powers. He will never know the bitterness of the downgrade of glory. Whom the Gods love die young.

What we mourn today, consciously or otherwise, is our surviving him to live in a world which, when it dies, will very likely be destroyed from ambush.

In the textbook warehouse of all our accumulated knowledge and wisdom there squats this ape creature, chewing on fried chicken and waiting for the moment to squint down the 'scope.

We cannot give up our effort to flush him out. But we have felt the scalp crawl on the back of our neck even as we witness, today, the grieving of an entire globe. In death, the face in the flag-draped coffin looks strangely like our own.

"Therefore never send to know for whom the bell tolls; it tolls for thee."

Mr. President, I ask unanimous consent to insert an outstanding sermon by Rabbi Henry Segal, of Temple B'nai Israel. This sermon was delivered before a gathering of more than a thousand persons who assembled spontaneously before noon on the national day of mourning proclaimed by President Johnson. The physical miles separating the B'nai Israel Synagogue in which these people had gathered for a memorial service, and St. Matthew's Church in which world figures had gathered for the funeral services for John Fitzgerald Kennedy, were dissolved by the grief that bound both congregations in spiritual unity.

Memorial Tribute Honoring the Memory of John Fitzgerald Kennedy, 35th President of the United States of America, Delivered on Monday, November 25, 1963, at 11 a.m. at B'nai Israel Synagogue, 16th and Crittenden Streets NW., Washington, D.C., by Rabbi Henry Segal

On January 20, 1961, the great American poet, Robert Frost, declaimed the poetic augury which he had penned, that with the inauguration of John Fitzgerald Kennedy as the 35th President of the United States, an age of poetry and power was commencing in Washington.

On this 25th day of November 1963, 2 years, 10 months and 5 days after that cold, snow-mantled and sun-drenched day of promise, when, alas, the heavy pall of gloom, in the wake of sudden dark and bloody tragedy, has hushed the poetry and cut off the power of this great young profile in courage, we recall a verse from another beautiful poem from the pen of Robert Frost, "Stopping by Woods on a Snowy Evening," in which we discern a parable, poignantly depicting the shockingly incredible character of this unspeakable tragedy.

> "The woods are lovely, dark and deep,
>   But I have promises to keep;
>   And miles to go before I sleep,
>   And miles to go before I sleep."

On Friday, November 22, 3 short days ago, this young and fearless champion of freedom started out in the company of his young, beautiful, and lovely helpmate, full of life and vigor, cheered by the friendly welcome of thousands who came to watch him gallantly continuing his eloquent intellectual combat with the forces of hate and bigotry. He was deeply aware of the "promises he had to keep," confident in the hope that he still had "miles to go before he slept, miles to go before he slept." Our Nation and the whole world shared his hope and confidence, and looked forward to the many more miles he had to go, the many more years of brilliantly competent and dedicated service that he had in him yet to give to an eager, free world sorely in need of a true champion such as he was. The future looked bright and promising, and the victories he had won for freedom and peace thus far seemed to augur greater and more decisive victories he would yet help the free world win in the months and the years ahead. And all of a sudden, out of nowhere, it seemed, death-dealing shots rang out and found their deadly mark in the stately, regal frame of this brave and intrepid warrior, cutting his life off at its prime, and leaving his loving wife widowed, his darling children orphaned, and a nation and a whole world bereft of their most formidable and distinguished defender against the sinister forces of darkness.

With heads bowed in sorrow, hearts heavy with grief, and eyes blurred by tears of weeping, we, together with millions all over the world, have these past 3 nightmarish days watched the lifeless, mortal remains of this classically immortal leader being brought back to this beautiful and historic Capital of our Nation, the scene of his beautiful and happy family life, and the arena of his brillant and triumphal career as a leader of men, to be borne on his final journey to his eternal resting place in the hallowed ground directly across from the memorial honoring another great martyred champion of human freedom, Abraham Lincoln.

At the close of his inspiring biography of Abraham Lincoln, Carl Sandburg, the sage American poet, very significantly entitles the chapter in which he tells of the tributes voiced about the great emancipator after his death by the hand of a deranged assassin, "A Tree Is Best Measured When It Is Down." Perhaps unbeknown to himself, Carl Sandburg was thus paraphrasing a Hebrew proverb: Bi'nefol eytz rom ve'nisso yeyro'eh el nochon komoso, u'vemoss odom godol neyda el nochon geduloso ve'tzidkoso—"Just as when a tall, sturdy and stately tree is felled, one can best measure its true height, so, too, when a great man dies, it can best become known how truly great and righteous he was." This has been sublimely true of the 16th President of the United States, Abraham Lincoln, the true stature of whose greatness has grown immeasurably with the passing of the years; and this is also unquestionably true, and will become ever more manifestly true of the martyred 35th President of the United States, John Fitzgerald Kennedy. Our rabbis of old were wise with the sense of history when they said: Gedolim tzaddikim be'missosom yosseyr mi'be'chayeyhem—"The great, righteous spirits among men are greater after death than during their lifetime." Not only is this true because the legend of a famous man's life grows, but

because only in the passing of time can his true greatness be revealed.

The loss which has now been inflicted upon us and upon the whole world is an immeasurable and irreparable one. But time will prove more and more how very severe a loss this is, for it will tell how great was the influence of John Fitzgerald Kennedy upon his time, how deep and abiding was his mark upon history, and how truly creative were his achievements. Whatever we have loved, honored and benefited by in this great and good man, is ours for as long as life shall last for our Nation. What he was and did has become part of us, "interfused with our lives, blended with our hearts, minds and memory, joined to our souls," and merged with the rich legacy of our priceless American heritage. There is in us—there must be—the resolve that the good we knew and revered in him shall live in ourselves, and be passed on to the generations yet to be, immortal with God and with men.

When Abraham Lincoln died a martyr in the cause of human freedom, over doorways, in store windows, on arches spanning streets, were signs on which ran the legend, in the words of the Book of Genesis about the first Abraham, the Patriarch of Israel, "And The Lord Blessed Abraham In All Things"—V'adonoy beyrach es avrohom ba'kol.

That was positively and profoundly true of John Fitzgerald Kennedy. God blessed him, indeed, in all things. God blessed him with attractive good looks, and he cultivated in himself a good conscience. God blessed him with a brilliant mind, and he nourished in himself a great heart. God endowed him with the blessing of eloquence of speech, and he employed it to express the sincerity and truthfulness of his spirit. God blessed him with the gift of prophetic vision, and he used it to show a whole world the way to righteousness. God blessed him with an unmatched personal charm, and he carried himself with impeccable dignity and self-respect. God blessed him with a wonderful family, and he reciprocated with unswerving loyalty, love, and respect. God blessed him with the vigor and dynamism of youth, and he never failed to defer with deep reverence to those older than he. God blessed him with the gifts of greatness, and he bestowed their fruits on others with goodness. God brought him into riches, and he chose to be generous in sharing them with others less fortunate. God blessed him with wisdom, and he broadened it with a holy curiosity that thirsted for more and more knowledge and understanding. God blessed him in the fullest measure, but he chose to be himself a blessing unto multitudes not so richly blessed. He made us see the truth that God dwells not in temples made of stone and mortar, but in the great hearts and noble spirits of richly gifted men.

He gave us and all of humanity at fearful cost to himself a vision, a hope, a promise of a beautiful and good world of tomorrow, a tomorrow that he, alas, cannot now return to share. He infused in us the aspiration to make man's brightest dreams come true, dreams that for him must now, alas, remain unfulfilled. He "paid for our dreams with his blood, the blood of youth, pulse, and passion. This was the cost to him, the cost unspeakable." God grant that we be worthy.

To him, as to us, "life on earth was fair and right." He loved the busy world and the works of its people. He loved his home, his family, his intimates, and his friends. He loved life, but more than life itself, he loved "the vitrue that mankind must live by," the truth that he saw being trampled, the freedoms that he witnessed being stifled, the visions that he beheld being blurred, profaned, and forgotten. "He loved honor and duty, and he gave to honor and duty his 'last full measure of devotion.'" With undaunted courage he fought for what he believed, and died giving battle to hypocrisy.

He strove for truth, and when he found it, spoke it without fear. "When he saw evil, he cried out against it. He felt in his own heart the pain of injustice done to others, and he condemned oppression and fought for liberty."

He had "the power and the outreach of mind," with which he strove to light "the dark places of fear and ignorance," giving new understanding to multitudes, and leading us all to a "rediscovery of our unused resources."

He remembered with gratitude the "benefits which came to us from bygone ages, and he strove to make us worthy of our inheritance," by teaching us how "to sow much that shall be worth harvesting in the future."

He was part of all that looked and moved forward, and he inspired us to grope toward new frontiers, and to toil for better days to come.

He had a friendly face, showing a warm heart. He could make high professions real by joining them to high attainments. He could voice beautiful and eloquent words, revealing noble thoughts. He "weighed his words carefully, and his words carried weight with men everywhere." He was truly a great voice, not a mere echo.

He understood that man cannot have "peace without pain, security without sacrifice," and that we must assume the responsibilities of peace, so that we may be spared the frightful cost of war.

Above all, he strove to show all "other nations of the world an America to imitate," the image of a nation that truly prizes freedom and denies it to no one, the likeness of a people that loves fair play and deals honestly with all, and that keeps undimmed man's faith in God and in man.

He chose rather to "fail in a noble cause that must in the end succeed, than to succeed in an unworthy cause that must ultimately fail." Without fear he answered the call of duty, and joined battle with wrong, that right might triumph.

May the supreme sacrifice he made in this battle inspire us to melt away all bitterness and hate, to turn all harshness into gentle compassion and mercy, to displace all enmity with friendly understanding. If so much that was so precious in this great and good man can so soon be lost, may we forever cherish what remains with us as the priceless legacy of his life, and, by its inspiration learn to cultivate, nurture and help to increase the things precious in the lives of all the children of man.

As John Fitzgerald Kennedy goes to meet his Maker, the Lord will surely welcome him into the illustrious company of the great and noble spirits of all time, with the verdict about his life and work, "well done."

May the "poetry and the power" of his life not have been hushed and cut off forever, but may it live in us, as his spirit shall keep marching on. May we help fulfill the promises he strove so hard to keep before he went to sleep for we have many "miles to go" before we shall merit to receive from God and from history, likewise, the verdict about our performance of the great tasks remaining before us, "well done."

TRIBUTES BY
Hon. Wayne Morse
OF OREGON

Mr. President, I have received a letter and a series of telegrams from individuals and chambers of commerce in my State expressing profound sorrow of the shocking, tragic assassination of our late great President, John F. Kennedy. I ask unanimous consent that the telegrams may be printed as follows:

SALEM, OREG.,
November 25, 1963.

Hon. WAYNE MORSE,
U.S. Senator,
Washington, D.C.:

The composition of this telegram has taken considerable hours after which we come to our first conclusion: That the citizens of the United States of America and peoples of the world have lost a dedicated and beloved man. Our heartfelt sympathy to the members of the Kennedy family.

STANLEY GROVE,
Manager, Salem Area Chamber of Commerce.

———

FLORENCE, OREG.,
November 25, 1963.

Senator WAYNE MORSE,
Senate Office Building,
Washington, D.C.:

We know that both yourself and Gov. Mark Hatfield consider that you represent all of us in Oregon in your expressions of sympathy to the Kennedy family and to our Government caused by the loss of this great and good young man. We must reaffirm that ours is a Government of law and that acts of assassination or subversion must be prosecuted to the fullest extent of the law.

HOWARD CAMPBELL,
President, Florence Chamber of Commerce.

———

EUGENE, OREG.,
November 23, 1963.

Senator WAYNE MORSE,
Washington, D.C.:

DEAR MR. SENATOR: As one of your supporters from Eugene, Oreg., we regret the horrible loss of a fine man. Please convey our condolences to the First Lady of the land, and stand by us. We need good men.

A REPUBLICAN.

PORTLAND, OREG.,
November 23, 1963.

Hon. WAYNE MORSE,
Washington, D.C.

DEAR SENATOR MORSE: Mrs. Hannah and I want to express sorrow and concern at the tragedy which struck our Nation today in the assassination of our President. His death is a personal loss for all of us and the hate which motivated this crime is a poisonous sore in our society. More than ever we are grateful for your strength and statesmanship and pray for your good health that the President and our country may continue to have the benefit of your wisdom and courage. May God bless you and our other leaders in this time of trouble.

Sincerely,

JAMES B. HANNAH.

NOVEMBER 23, 1963.

Hon. WAYNE MORSE,
Senate Foreign Relations,
Washington, D.C.:

Profoundly consternated please receive retransmit our condolences your coleaders Government in this grave hour which afflicts world.

LUIS GONZALEZ FAMILY.
Senator ALFONSO LARA.
Senator EUGENIO GOMEZ.

LIMA, PERU,
November 23, 1963.

Senator WAYNE MORSE,
Washington, D.C:

Es esta hora de dolor para el mundo democratico presentole profundo pesar.

[Translation]

In this hour of grief for the democratic world, I express to you my profound sorrow.

CELSO PASTOR.

YAKIMA, WASH.,
November 25, 1963.

Senator WAYNE MORSE,
Washington, D.C.:

The climate of the country is such that it needs the comfort of inspiration. Give us the opportunity for which we long to ease the passion in our hearts. Can you not make concrete use of our nobler concepts of democracy by setting up a monument to the man worthy of his breadth and scope to which the peoples and the nations of the world can subscribe.

J. E. KOSTINER.

GRANTS PASS, OREG.,
November 22, 1963.

Senator WAYNE MORSE,
Washington, D.C.:

The assassination of our President is the most tragic thing that has ever happened to our country. Mr. Morse, may I suggest that you do everything in your power to have the portrait of President Kennedy depicted upon the silver dollars which will soon be minted.

C. G. MURRAY, Jr.

Mr. President, I also ask that a letter from the mayor of the city of Glendale, Oreg., may be printed at this point.

CITY OF GLENDALE, OREG.,
November 23, 1963.

Hon. WAYNE MORSE,
U.S. Senator,
Washington, D.C.

DEAR SENATOR MORSE: As our Oregon representative, in our U.S. Senate, we as a city, would ask that you relay our condolences and sympathy, to Mrs. Kennedy, during this tragic ordeal.

We realize, that through better chosen words, you will be better able to do this. Also to express the monumental loss, to our Nation, the world, our State and not least of all to our city. What a tragedy that such a brilliant, humanitarian leader's and statesman's life should be lost, while serving his country so well.

You may rest assured that this community's prayers will be with Mrs. Kennedy, yourself and the remainder of our leaders, during this great time of trial and stress, within this great Nation of ours.

Thank you, in advance, for doing this most difficult job, during a most difficult time.

Sincerely yours,

RALPH E. PLACE,
Mayor.

In part the letter says:

DEAR SENATOR MORSE: As our Oregon representative in our U.S. Senate, we as a city, would ask that you relay our condolences and sympathy, to Mrs. Kennedy, during this tragic ordeal.

We realize, that through better chosen words, you will be better able to do this. Also to express the monumental loss, to our Nation, the world, our State and least of all to our city. What a tragedy that such a brilliant, humanitarian leader and statesman's life should be lost, while serving his country so well.

I do not know how anyone could use more beautiful, more eloquent language than the mayor used in this letter. I would not attempt to improve upon it. Therefore, when I received the letter, I forwarded it immediately to Mrs. Kennedy.

Mr. President, the best poetic tribute to President Kennedy which I have yet seen has been written by Mr. Howard C. Zimmerman, of Eugene, Oreg.

I HEARD THE DRUMS

I heard the drums in Washington—
    Muffled, marching, slow;
I saw the kings and princes come,
    Bereaved that he should go.
I paused beside the catafalque
    To touch the mournful bier;
I thrilled at honor humbly paid
    For service rendered dear.

I wept within the Capitol
  Among the pressing throng;
I lifted grief as sacrifice
  In the chalice of a song.
I followed caisson step to step
  Along the avenue;
I dignified with silent tears
  The only chief I knew.

I listened to the bugler's taps,
  The cannoneer's salute;
I patterned sunbeams on the lips
  And tombstones standing mute.
I bowed my hatless head in shame
  To know the need for praise,
A growing spirit crushed to dust
  In the summer of his days.

I watched the kings and princes leave,
  The presidents depart
I stood alone beside a flame
  To reconstruct my heart.
I searched for deathless, faithful truth
  Across bleak Arlington.
I touched the shadow of his hope;
  I rose and journeyed on.
    —Howard C. Zimmerman.

Mr. President, I wish to call attention to a beautiful eulogy given by Elder Bryant A. Alder at the memorial services honoring President Kennedy, held in Portland West Stake, Church of Jesus Christ of Latter-day Saints, on Monday, November 25, 1963.

I have found it to be a very moving eulogy and I ask unanimous consent that it be printed.

Memorial Services for President John F. Kennedy Held in Portland West Stake, Church of Jesus Christ of Latter-day Saints, November 25, 1963

For the past 72 hours, through the medium of radio, television, and the printed word, we have been witness to a historic incident—one in which America needs to bow its head in sorrow and shame. The assassination of President John Fitzgerald Kennedy brings to all Americans the full measure of grief which each of us experiences in the loss of a loved one. And at the same time causes us to bow our heads in shame that this could happen, as it has done to three other Presidents, in this cultured and democratic land.

This day has been declared by our new President as a day of mourning for our late President. There has already been much mourning—there will undoubtedly be much more in the days to come. No more than has already been said could possibly be said here of value, of the merits of the man who has been lost, or the principles that have been jeopardized by this unspeakable act in Dallas, Tex.

Anything which I might say regarding his accomplishments would be secondhand and merely repetitious—but this is an hour of great tragedy, grief, and personal loss to every citizen of this great country. And so it is only

proper that we gather here, at the recommendation of the president of this great church, to pay our honor and respects to the memory of the young, fallen President. Whatever political beliefs we may individually possess, or whatever our differences of opinion might have been on various subjects—on this particular occasion we are all united.

In the few short years he walked on this earth, President Kennedy realized an almost incredible number of accomplishments, and will be remembered unpredictably far into the future for his dedication to the call which was made of him to direct the affairs of this Nation.

Probably a summary of his attitude could be expressed in one statement made in his inaugural address: "Ask not what your country can do for you—but what you can do for your country." And certainly no man could give more for his country than his life.

But our thoughts today should be more with those who mourn him in the close relationship of life—his family and loved ones. In the minds of many people when they see a talented and gifted young person such as this taken prematurely in life, the question naturally arises: "Why did God snatch him away from this earth?"—and the answer might come that when you go forth into your flower garden to pick a bouquet, you never select the withered and drooping flowers, but always look for the brightest and gayest buds and fresh blossoms. Maybe God does that at times, too. If heaven is just an extension at a higher level of what we see here on earth, then heaven is not solely an old people's home. It must also contain babies, and toddlers, and teenagers, and young people—not just the aged.

Certainly, as taught by all the prophets of ancient and modern times, Mrs. Kennedy and her children can expect to be reunited with their husband and father at some later date. Life here on earth would hold very little promise if this were not so. Surely, if one can judge by their outward demonstration of devotion to beliefs, they believe in God and the resurrection which Jesus underwent here on earth.

Of course, that doesn't stop their tears or their mourning. Neither did it prevent Jesus from weeping at the tomb of his friend Lazarus. For farewells are fraught with sadness, even while we realize we are under the everlasting will of God.

As Latter-day Saints we believe in a literal resurrection. We do not entertain the idea, as many in the world do, that the resurrection will be a spiritual one only. The promise of the Lord is that we shall receive our bodies again. We look upon death merely as a temporary separation of the spirit and the body. We do not look upon death as the end of our individual existence. On the contrary, knowing Christ to be our prototype, we have the assurance that death is only temporary, and that there will come a time after death when we shall again receive these same bodies which we possess here upon the earth, and that the union of spirit and body shall never be dissolved. The bodies we shall receive will be immortal, and the spirit and body united will constitute a living soul—and this should offer to Mrs. Kennedy and all those who mourn great solace and comfort.

This is the time when every man, woman, and child under the protection and blessing of free government should bow his head in prayer of rededication to all that we hold so dear. It is so easy to take for granted all the good our country gives us. It is so easy to become involved in unimportant details of minor individual interests that we forget, or fail to appreciate, the tremendous magnitude of the rights and privileges granted us by our Constitution. The greatness of the United States as an outstanding, dynamic, and progressive nation, lies in the sound principles of the American Constitution. Some people may still argue that our Constitution is not a perfect one. This statement does not contain a great .amount of evil, due to the fact that if this be true, there are methods of changing it as has been done in the past. Our greatest concern should be that these changes—if changes become necessary—are made for the benefit and interest of all people.

At this particular time, probably every American is asking what influence will this incident have upon the future of this country—and if I were to editorialize certainly the only answer that can be given is that his death is a tragedy of unknown proportion—it may shape the course of our lives in ways we do not now understand. However, the days and weeks which follow will require that all men, whether in high positions of Government leadership, or just we as ordinary citizens, demonstrate our faith in the strength of the United States system of government.

"This is our country." Almost 190 million American people should thrill with the significance of these four humble words. "This is my country." America is a land of promise. It is a land choice above all other lands upon the face of the earth—and we as Latter-day Saints have far greater understanding and appreciation of this statement than does any other group. The men and women who have taken an active part in the building of these United States have made contributions to our lives far greater than our abilities to ever comprehend and appreciate.

Yes, we have lost a President this day—but we have not lost a country, or a nation, or the principles thereof. Tragically, Mr. Kennedy did not have time to prove what his place in history might become. But he will be recommended as a courageous leader, one who proved his bravery in the face of death as a naval lieutenant in World War II, and who in the White House has faced crises after crises with the same kind of bravery. His insistence in recent months to want to get close to the people and shake their hands was a source of great concern to the members of the security guard, and probably his own reluctance to use special protective measures in the motorcade was a contributing factor in his death.

The President is a martyr to the causes in which he believed. Nothing that happens from now on can take this role away from him. He accomplished a great many things in a few years he walked in this life. These things will remain as a tribute to him.

In II Timothy is recorded a statement which probably best expresses the sentiments that John F. Kennedy would have felt prior to his leaving us. "The time of my departure is at hand. I have fought a good fight, I have finished my course, I have kept the faith; Henceforth

there is laid up for me a crown of righteousness, which the Lord, the righteous judge, shall give me at that day; and not to me only, but unto all them also that love His appearing."

I think Edgar A. Guest best explains what we must do when sorrow comes:

"WHEN SORROW COMES

"When sorrow comes, as come it must,
In God a man must place his trust.
There is no power in mortal speech
The anguish of his soul to reach.
No voice, however sweet and low,
Can comfort him or ease the blow.

"He cannot from his fellow men
Take strength that will sustain him then.
With all that kindly hands will do,
And all that love may offer, too.
He must believe throughout the test
That God has willed it for the best.

"We who would be his friends are dumb;
Words from our lips but feebly come.
We feel, as we extend our hands
That one power only understands
And truly knows the reason why
Such a man as this must die.

"We realize how helpless then
Are all the gifts of mortal men.
No words which we have power to say
Can take the sting of grief away.
That power which marks the sparrow's fall
Must comfort and sustain us all.

"When sorrow comes as come it must,
In God a man must place his trust.
With all the wealth which he may own,
He cannot meet the test alone.
And only he may stand serene
Who has a faith on which to lean."

I think our united prayer this day should be to rededicate ourselves to a determination to help keep this Nation forever free, a place where men and women can build homes and rear families with faith and confidence. I would hope that we could rededicate ourselves to the determination to help keep this a land where children of all ages, sects, and creed, regardless of wealth, position, or family—may have the privileges of a free education.

I think that we should rededicate ourselves to living at peace with our families, our neighbors, and our associates, for no nation can be a happy, free nation, if its people war among themselves in their domestic or neighborhood relationships.

And for those who are responsible for the tragedy which permits us to assemble this day, I think we should recall the words of the Lord given to our modern prophet: "My disciples, in days of old, sought occasion against one another and forgave not one another in their hearts; and for this evil they were afflicted and sorely chastened. Wherefore, I say unto you, that ye ought to forgive one another; for he that forgiveth not his brother his trespasses standeth condemned before the Lord; for there remaineth in him the greater sin. I, the Lord, will forgive whom I will forgive, but of you it is required to forgive all men. And ye ought to say in your hearts— Let God judge between me and thee, and reward thee according to thy deeds." (Doctrine and Covenants 64: 8-11).

The grief of the Kennedy family is shared by countless millions throughout the world. He has now taken his place among the great figures of the world. We can truthfully say that we are better off because he has passed our way. In the name of Jesus Christ, Amen.

Mr. President, I ask unanimous consent to insert a moving and beautiful eulogy of President Kennedy delivered by Prof. Joseph F. Smith on November 25, 1963, at a memorial service at the Mormon Tabernacle in Honolulu, Hawaii.

A DIGEST OF REMARKS MADE BY JOSEPH F. SMITH AT A MEMORIAL SERVICE FOR PRESIDENT JOHN F. KENNEDY, BEFORE A CONGREGATION OF MORE THAN 2,000 AT THE LATTER-DAY SAINTS TABERNACLE, HONOLULU, HAWAII, NOVEMBER 25, 1963

Fewer than 80 hours ago, John Fitzgerald Kennedy was alive and was the President of the United States. At this hour, his body, torn by an assassin's bullets, lies in Arlington, the national cemetery dedicated as the burial ground for American heroes who have given their lives in their country's service.

At this moment here in Honolulu, geographically remote from Dallas, and even further removed from Washington, you and I are met in memorial service. I would ask, "To what purpose?"

A memorial service affords opportunity to pay tribute to the deceased, but if this service does no more than that, if a man elected to the Presidency of the United States be robbed of his life by a heinous deed, and you and I in memorial service do no more than pay him memorial tribute—even with sincere mourning—our tribute will be no more than gesture.

The Nation, during the past 3 days, has lain under a pall of gloom and of grief: gloom, that in this country dedicated to freedom, assassinations can be; grief for a President of the United States cut down in his prime, and for a family bereft.

In contemplation of the events of the past few days, can anyone of us here wholly absolve himself from responsibility? Let us grant for the moment, that the assassination was the sole deed of a young man confused to the point of madness, will this wholly absolve you and me from responsibility? Are not the violence and the vandalism, the robbery and the rape, the industrial hatreds in Honolulu, this town of yours and mine, a part of a national sickness of which the murder of John Fitzgerald is another part?

This hour is fittingly a time of tribute and a time of mourning, but it must be more than that. It must be an hour of sober reckoning and of solemn resolution. Tragically, it cannot be an hour of restitution. The sin is a national sin; a nation is affected. May I note here, in passing, that I do not specifically condemn Lee Harvey Oswald for the crime. Whatever his action, he has been deprived of his right for trial by law. The man who shot him is equally guilty with him who fired the fatal bullets at the President. Twice in the space of 3 days, the international spotlight has illumined the abrogation of law in a country supposedly committed to government by law. Have you and I no responsibility in the matter? Indeed, this is a time of reckoning for you and me.

Last Friday on the floor of the Senate, the first words to be spoken in announcing the death of the President came from Senator Wayne Morse, of Oregon. He said, "If there was ever an hour that every American should pray, this is the hour." And I would repeat that if there was ever an hour that every Latter-day Saint should pray, this is the hour, because we have a particular responsibility, a very especial responsibility, for the preservation of law and order in this country. We know—thanks to divine revelation—that this is a land choice above all other lands. It is a land designed for the rebuilding of Zion. This is our responsibility.

The Savior, when asked what was the greatest commandment, replied, "Thou shalt love the Lord with all thy heart, might, mind and strength. This is the first and great commandment and the second is like unto it: Thou shalt love thy neighbor as thyself."

Brethren and sisters, are we adequately abiding the second of these commandments? Until we do, we are not keeping faith with our responsibility. Until every one of us within the area of his particular influence is so abiding, he cannot abide the first. This we must set about more diligently to do.

It is fitting that in this time of resolution we paraphrase another great and martyred President: That you and I, that we here highly resolve that the 35th President of the United States shall not have died in vain; that we here dedicate ourselves to the preservation of the land through righteousness. The Hawaiian words come to mind: Ua mau ke ea o ka aina i ka pono—the life of the land is preserved in righteousness.

Righteousness is never passive. Lassitude, lethargy, indifference, neglect, unconcern—these are insidiously potent allies of unrighteousness. What boots our present grief if it moves us not to more dedicated effort to bring greater order to our immediate house?

If the land shall be preserved in righteousness, it will require your loyalty and mine, your love and mine, your unremitting labor and mine.

That we make irrevocable resolution toward this end is my prayer in the name of Jesus Christ. Amen.

Mr. President, I ask that a poem written on the occasion of the death of President Kennedy be printed. It is titled: "The Kennedy Star," and was written by Rex Trowbridge of Sisters, Oreg.

THE KENNEDY STAR

There's a new star in heaven tonight,
An orb in outer space—silvery bright:
Symboled for all the world to see,
A martyr's mark, the light of liberty.

There's a new star in heaven tonight,
Triumph of right o'er the devil's might;
The roll of muffled drums, flags unfurled;
"Ring Freedom's Bell!" heartbeat of the world.

Bells for our martyr—ring,
Marking mankind's travail:
"Oh death, where is thy sting?"
God's mercy will prevail.

"Flame of freedom," in heaven tonight,
Beacon of hope, and celestial light:
Let your heart be thrilled anew—
"The Kennedy Star" is shining for you.

Mr. President, Mr. William E. Bradley, chairman of the Democratic Central Committee of Multnomah County, Oreg., has brought to my attention a resolution adopted unanimously by the committee on December 5.

Because of the very fine sentiments expressed in the resolution concerning our late beloved President, John F. Kennedy, and the resolution's endorsement of the forward-looking legislative program President Kennedy sought on behalf of the people of the United States, I ask unanimous consent that Mr. Bradley's letter of December 6, containing the central committee's resolution, be set forth at this point.

DEMOCRATIC CENTRAL COMMITTEE,
Portland, Oreg., December 6, 1963.
Hon. WAYNE MORSE,
Senate Office Building,
Washington, D.C.
DEAR WAYNE: The following resolution was unanimously adopted by the Democratic Central Committee of Multnomah County at its meeting last night. I thought that you might be interested in it.

Whereas the late great President Kennedy had dedicated his life to the establishment of conditions of peace and dignity for human existence everywhere, and

Whereas President Kennedy, preoccupied with international relations, had only partially accomplished his aims to secure these objectives on the home front, and

Whereas President Johnson has emphasized his purpose to carry forward the same tradition of our late President: Now, therefore, be it

Resolved by the Multnomah County Democratic Central Committee, That the Congress of the United States be urged to enact into law as a memorial to our late great President, those programs—such as civil rights, aid to education, tax reduction, medical care for the aged—for which he fought so valiantly; and be it further

Resolved, That like-minded Americans everywhere be urged to write their Senators and Representatives in the Congress of the United States, to erect this memorial to a great American.
Sincerely,

WILLIAM E. BRADLEY,
Chairman.

TRIBUTES BY

Hon. Clinton P. Anderson

OF NEW MEXICO

Mr. President, Emma Lee McLeod, a teacher in the schools at Los Alamos, N. Mex., during the days when the country was filled with grief because of the assassination of President John Fitzgerald Kennedy, wrote a tribute. Friends of hers have suggested that it ought to be put in our permanent record and I, therefore, ask unanimous consent that the tribute be printed as follows:

THIS DAY
(By Emma Lee McLeod)

Death drove in through doors
That had been opened by the hearts
Of men. These doors were hinged with
The faith that gives another breath
To the dying—that gives another
Note to the symphony—that gives
Another prayer to the mourning.
These were the eternal doors whose hinges
Open only inward.
And today they have opened again.
The promised glories were waiting,
The angels and saints—those
Who had been the earth's big and little
And those who had been divided by class
And race and religion—those
Who had known poverty and hatred and
Persecution—those who had been
Members of a minority were here together.
The victories of the heavens
Enveloped the newcomer.
Here was peace—peace—
Eternal peace—at last,
But yet too soon
For those who still breathe
Fear and hatred.
Could their hearts be less bitter today?
Could their minds be less warped?
For if such is so,
The race was finished well.
The price of victory was paid
The reward of eternal life has been given
And a new star [1] has risen in the heavens
To proclaim this day.

Mr. President, in houses of worship through the land Americans have attended services in memory of our late President, John Fitzgerald Kennedy. Last Monday, the Jal (N. Mex.) Gen-

---

[1] Discovery of a new star was announced at Palomar Observatory on Nov. 25, 1963. Although the star will be assigned its technical number, it will be named "The John F. Kennedy Star."

eral Ministers' Association conducted a united memorial service at the First Methodist Church in Jal. At that service a poem written by Jenie Burke on the day after the assassination of President Kennedy was read. The poem is entitled "Requiem," and is a moving statement of the deep sense of loss felt by all Americans.

REQUIEM

How can I write
When the depth of my sorrow
Is torn with surges
Of frustration and anger—
When the tear almost shed
Loses itself in the void
The very chasm of my grief—
How can I write
What justice can be wrought
On the evil one
Who did this thing—
No power of civil society
May redress the wrong
No counter violence assuage our hurt—
The voices of powerful men
Sound small and weak
Each in a measure echoing
The thought all would speak—
To honor him is brief and pitiful
Unless we meet the challenge of the war he fought
Against man's abuse of man of the hope he brought
To the tired, the sick, the oppressed of the peace he sought
For an anguished world power possessed—
How then can I write
Except that we bury him
In simple dignity befitting his estate
Among the unknown heroes
And their silent comrades of our wars
Yet in this hallowed place
Will echo through the corridors of time
The war he fought
The hope he brought
The peace he sought.

—JENIE BURKE.

TRIBUTE BY

Hon. Robert C. Byrd

OF WEST VIRGINIA

Mr. President, I wish to have printed an item which appeared recently in the St. Albans (W. Va.) Advertiser.

A DEATH IN THE AFTERNOON

(By Deane Morrison)

In Dallas, Tex., President John F. Kennedy is shot to death on the afternoon of Friday, November 22, 1963.

That death in the afternoon was the most tragic episode involving a President of the United States since Abraham

Lincoln was mortally wounded in Ford's Theater in Washington, D.C., 100 years ago.

Millions of people the world over were shocked and saddened by the vicious, brutal, coldblooded murder of our President.

It is indeed a terrible tragedy that there should be in this Nation an individual so unbalanced, so twisted and torn in this heart, so demented in his mind and emotions, that he would take a powerful rifle and with it commit such a wicked and evil crime.

John F. Kennedy and his wife came to St. Albans on the evening of April 30, 1960.

At that time, of course, Mr. Kennedy was a candidate for the nomination, on the Democratic ticket, of President of the United States.

Mr. and Mrs. Kennedy appeared at the St. Albans Junior High School Auditorium and there both of them spoke briefly.

On that evening Mr. Kennedy had a severe infection of the throat, and for that reason he did not speak as long as he had intended.

Nevertheless he did speak for a few moments, and many local people heard him, and heard Mrs. Kennedy, and shook hands with them and talked to them briefly.

This is a great Nation, a great country and President John F. Kennedy became a part of its history.

His death is a great tragedy.

President John F. Kennedy was the most powerful individual in the modern world.

Both those who agreed with him and supported him, and those who disagreed with him and fought him, were all saddened and outraged and shocked by his death.

Written in St. Albans by Deane Morrison on November 23, 1963.

TRIBUTE BY

Hon. Thomas J. McIntyre

OF NEW HAMPSHIRE

Mr. President, each of us has his own thoughts and feelings of loss this day. But I believe a brief editorial in a newspaper in my State of New Hampshire has set down in words the thoughts and feelings of a great number of Americans. I ask unanimous consent to have printed an editorial from the Portsmouth, N.H., Herald, of November 23, 1963, entitled "A Tragic, Needless Death."

A TRAGIC, NEEDLESS DEATH

There are no words that give adequate expression to the feeling of shock and sorrow brought by President Kennedy's death. The suddenness of the event, in all its infamy, seems too much to grasp. The sense of loss is too great.

But it isn't only a reaction of remorse and bewilderment that occurs. There is also one of anger and indignation. For the American people have been confronted with the terrible truth that a President of the United States can't do his duty as he sees it and remain safe in his own land.

Complaint is not made here, either, of any lack of precautions to protect the President. He was as well guarded as practical circumstances would allow. But at a time when so many fanatical-minded citizens put reason aside to embrace the extremes of discord, depravity becomes a greater menace than the best security can overcome.

It is in such a rabid atmosphere that lunatics take license to practice violence. They are encouraged by the sound and fury of organized malcontents who somehow are credited with respectability, yet who have no real purpose but destruction.

It makes no difference whether the extremism runs to left or right. When the Nation's laws and institutions are scorned, when the elected leadership is treated to open and vicious abuse, when the rights of fellow citizens are ruthlessly trampled upon, the particular direction of political leaning is a matter of small consequence.

What counts is the fact that such extremism exists at all, and that the fact of its existence leads to a crime so foul as to take the life of a President.

While it cannot be said that President Kennedy's death was a direct result of conspiratorial evil, neither can the idea be disallowed that the present state of political emotions was at least partially responsible. That is, to the extent of further perverting an already demented mind.

It is too late now, however, to think of what might have been. President Kennedy is dead, a victim of the hate he devoted his life to counteracting. What matters in the aftermath is that his death was not in vain—and to this end there is fervent hope that the fomenters of malevolence and disunity will have cause for earnest soul searching.

Meanwhile, the prayers and sympathies of all good Americans will abide with the Kennedy family. They have so much to mourn, but in the years ahead comfort will come from the knowledge they shared the life of one of the Nation's greatest men.

For the new President, Lyndon B. Johnson, there can only be the solemn hope that he will enjoy the good health to bear the heavy burden that fate has handed him. It's a blessing to the country that one so skilled in the demands of leadership occupies the place of succession.

The task ahead will not be an easy one, but President Johnson—thanks to Kennedy's wisdom—is properly prepared for it.

TRIBUTES BY

Hon. A. Willis Robertson

OF VIRGINIA

Mr. President, it was my privilege last Sunday to hear an inspiring sermon by Dr. R. B. Culbreth, pastor of Metropolitan Baptist Church, in

which, after deploring the passing of a great President, he appealed to the people of our Nation to rededicate themselves to the service of our Lord and Master. I ask that the full text of that sermon may be printed as follows:

THE DEATH OF OUR PRESIDENT

(Sermon preached by Dr. R. B. Culbreth, pastor, Metropolitan Baptist Church, Sixth and A Streets NE., Washington, D.C., Nov. 24, 1963)

Scripture: Isaiah 6: 1–13.

Not since Jesus Christ died on the cross in Jerusalem has a death affected the lives of so many people as the untimely, senseless murder of President John F. Kennedy. Regardless of our political belief, he was our President, and a little bit of each of us died with him. He was indeed a man of courage, brilliant intellect, and a dynamic leader. He had won the respect of most of the nations, even our enemies, and had become a symbol of freedom to millions from many nations. His death brought shock and sorrow to all of us, and plunged the entire Nation—and much of the world—into deep mourning. "Greater love hath no man than this, that a man lay down his life for his friends" (John 15: 13).

This message is not an effort to condemn the man who pulled the trigger that felled our President, even though much could be said about our laxity regarding the sinister forces of evil that are evidently growing within our land. It was from this same pulpit that the Honorable Strom Thurmond, of South Carolina, warned about the growing menace of communism. We can be grateful that the warped mind that planned this murder was bred on the evil powers of communism rather than the foul racial prejudice, or the equally foul religious prejudice. Atheism produces communism. Prejudice breeds hatred; hatred can result in murder.

Does the Bible have anything to say to us in this tragedy? Can God speak to our hearts in the midst of our sorrow? Yes, praise His name, He can. Day is usually preferable to night, but night has some advantages over the day. In this night of gloom and of national tragedy God's love can shine brightest.

We have a parallel in the Bible to our day. Around the middle of the eighth century B.C. the good King Uzziah died. Perhaps the young man, Isaiah, had gone to the Capitol to view the body, then to the funeral of the only King he had ever known. Feeling the great need of prayer he then went into the temple to pray. It was here that he had an experience with God and his life was changed. Let us take a closer look at Isaiah's experience and pray that we may have a similar one. May we center our thought around four words: Revelation, prostration, purification, and dedication.

I. REVELATION

"In the year that King Uzziah died I saw the Lord." O God, may it be that in the year that President Kennedy died, people will see the Lord. In this dark, tragic hour you would think that people would flock to the church seeking God as did Isaiah. When he came seeking, he saw the Lord.

What kind of a God did Isaiah see? First of all, he saw a God that was still on the throne—"high and lifted up." The King had been toppled from the throne, but God was still reigning. We need to see this matchless truth today. Our brilliant young President has been dethroned by the assassin's bullet, but the God of this universe is still on His throne. He can never be dropped by the enemy's shots.

When Jesus was facing the crucifixion He told His disciples that He would soon leave them, but that the Comforter, the Holy Spirit, would come, and the world could not seize Him (John 14: 17). The world could and did seize Jesus, death did seize Mr. Kennedy, but death cannot touch our God. He is still on His throne.

Isaiah also saw a God that was majestic and described him in these words: "His train filled the temple. Above Him stood the seraphim: each one had six wings; with two he covered his face, and with two he covered his feet, and with two he did fly."

"Seraphim" are burning messengers of God. The wings are symbolic. The two that covered his face mean "reverence"—necessary in any true worship. America needs to rediscover this sense of reverence for God. So many things have crept into our national life and worship that many think of God as one of us, rather than the Almighty, omnipotent creator of this universe.

The two wings that covered his feet suggest humility. This is a lesson sorely needed by all Americans. We have a very exalted opinion of ourselves. We have read of other nations deposing their leaders, and with smugness have said that we are a too sophisticated and civilized people for that to happen to us. But it did happen and we are humbled by it personally and by its possible effect upon our image abroad. Humility before God is not a sign of weakness, but strength, and we need to get back to it.

The two wings that enabled the seraphim to fly suggest unhindered action and service. Too many of us run hot and cold in our devotion and service to God.

Not only did Isaiah see a God who was still on His throne and a God who was majestic, but also a God who was thrice holy. Holy means separate or apart, different. God is different from men. His ways are not our ways and His thoughts are not our thoughts.

If America can get a vision of God through our President's death, then he will not have died in vain. If his passing will shake us from our spiritual lethargy and make us realize our spiritual poverty, then his death will produce good.

II. PROSTRATION

When Isaiah had the vision of God he realized a deep sense of sin both personal and social. This is the natural followup of a vision of God. Our own weakness and unworthiness parades before our eyes as we compare our relationship to God.

One is not often conscious of dress until he is in the presence of others who are dressed better, and the same is true of speech. It is equally true that we are not conscious of our sins, shortcomings, and spiritual needs until we get into the presence of God.

Thoroughly smitten with his own lack, Isaiah cried out,

"Woe is me, for I am undone, because I am a man of unclean lips, and I dwell in the midst of a people of unclean lips: for mine eyes have seen the King, the Lord of hosts." He could never get away from the sense of sin. His lip-service and that of his people paraded before his eyes and he fell prostrate before God.

America needs a vision of God and a sense of sin. We have become a great and powerful people, chosen, I believe, of God to be a blessing to all nations. But our greed and lust, and trust in military might alone could be our undoing. Our record of murder, divorce and crime precede our witness for Christ abroad and cause our missionaries' lips to give hollow sounds when they tell others about how God can change human lives for good. America needs to fall on her knees before God crying with Isaiah, "Woe is me."

III. PURIFICATION

It is one thing to have a vision of God and realize a sense of sin, but the real test comes in what you do about it. Many people admit they are sinners and need God, but few are doing anything about it. Repentance is a broken and contrite heart and very few people like to have their hearts broken and pride dethroned.

If sin is to be dealt with, it must be done drastically, "so as with fire." Fire consumes and purifies. It must be dealt with "from above." One of the Seraphim took from the altar a live coal and laid it upon the mouth of Isaiah. This drastic action was symbolic of purification. "Thine iniquity is taken away, and thy sin is purged." America's hope of survival lies in this direction. Our sins are grievous in God's sight. We must let Him deal with us, as did Isaiah, with coals taken from the "heavenly altar." Let us pray that through the death of our President, God shall lead us to confession of sin and purification.

IV. DEDICATION

When a person sees God, realizes sin, and receives forgiveness the next step is dedication. Isaiah heard God calling for volunteers for His service—"Whom shall I send, and who will go for us?" Quickly he found a voice for the deep emotions within him and responded, "Here am I; send me." God said, "Go and tell this people." This same God, speaking in the same voice, under a similar circumstance is calling each of us to speak for Him. Will we hear? Will we obey? Will we do it? If so, then our Nation, so dearly loved by us all, and for which John F. Kennedy gave his life, shall accomplish His purpose for us as a nation. These things can only come as people surrender to God. It was belief in God that led us to greatness and it is a return to the Bible and personal belief in, and acceptance of the Christ of the Bible, that will preserve our greatness and make us as a nation a fit servant of God.

Mr. President, I ask unanimous consent to have printed a telegram from Mr. James F. Tindall, president, Virginia Press Association, expressing sympathy over the tragic death of President Kennedy.

MARION, VA.,
November 22, 1963.

Senator WILLIS ROBERTSON,
Senate Office Building,
Washington, D.C.:

On behalf of the newspapermen of the Commonwealth of Virginia, may I express profound regret and deep sympathy for our Nation and its leaders on the tragic death of our President. May God grant us strength to seek unity and humility in our efforts to help mankind.

JAMES F. TINDALL,
President, Virginia Press Association.

TRIBUTES BY

Hon. Ralph W. Yarborough

OF TEXAS

Mr. President, on the last journey into Texas by the late President of the United States, the beloved John Fitzgerald Kennedy, a series of five major addresses were planned by President Kennedy. Two brief, unscheduled addresses were also delivered.

The first address was delivered at dedication ceremonies for the Aerospace Medical Health Center at San Antonio, Tex., on Thursday afternoon, November 21. The second address was made in Houston later Thursday, in the early evening before the League of United Latin American Citizens at the Rice Hotel. It was brief and had not been on the original schedule. The third address was also in Houston at a testimonial banquet for Representative Albert Thomas at the Coliseum Thursday night, November 21. The great appreciation banquet was in honor of Representative Albert Thomas for his 27 years of effective service in the U.S. Congress.

On Friday morning, November 22, the President made another short, unscheduled address to a large crowd in an open square in front of the Texas Hotel at Fort Worth, followed by his main address at a breakfast in Fort Worth sponsored by the Fort Worth Chamber of Commerce. All of these five speeches were attended by thousands.

The speech that President Kennedy had prepared for delivery for Friday noon, November 22, at the vast Trade Mart in Dallas was undelivered, as the assassin's bullets snuffed out the President's life while the President's automobile in which he was traveling with Mrs. Kennedy was about 4 minutes away in time from the Trade Mart. The Dallas meeting was sponsored by three nonpartisan groups.

The only political meeting as such that President Kennedy was to address in Texas was a banquet sponsored by the Texas State Democratic Executive Committee, to have been held Friday night, November 22, in my home city of Austin, the State capital. A great welcome awaited President Kennedy in Austin, a welcome denied the people of Texas as well as President and Mrs. Kennedy, by the heartless acts of a murderous assassin.

Mr. President, it was my honor and privilege to travel to Texas with the President and Mrs. Kennedy on the Presidential jet on November 21 and 22 and to travel in all the motorcades. The Vice President—now President—and Mrs. Lyndon B. Johnson traveled on another jet, but took part in all of the meetings and motorcades.

At San Antonio, President and Mrs. Kennedy went by motorcade from the International Airport to the School of Aerospace Medicine, through the heart of San Antonio, and then on to Kelly Field by motorcade, a total distance of about 22 miles.

President Kennedy was seen by more people than ever seen in any other parade for a person in San Antonio. At Houston, the motorcade went from the International Airport to the Rice Hotel. Thursday night on arrival at Carswell Air Force Base, President and Mrs. Kennedy again led an open motorcade the 15 miles to downtown Fort Worth. Though this was about 11 o'clock at night, many thousands of people met the President's plane at Carswell, many thousands more lined the roads and streets the 15 miles to Fort Worth. Thousands more stood outside the Texas Hotel at Fort Worth or jammed the corridors and main lobby to see the President.

On Friday morning, the 22d, many additional thousands came out to line the streets and roads to cheer the President and Mrs. Kennedy on their 15-mile motorcade route back to Carswell Air Force Base. At Dallas at noon, hundreds of thousands of friendly people massed in dense throngs on every street to show their love and affection for the President and Mrs. Kennedy.

The President had passed through all the downtown tall building area and passed the last high-rise building on the parade route, only to be cut down from behind by rifle fire by an assassin lurking in a dark corner of the sixth floor of the last high-rise building.

Mr. President, in the six motorcade rides in four Texas cities on November 21 and 22, President Kennedy had been seen by more than 10 percent of the entire population of the State. It was a warm, friendly enthusiastic greeting. I rode in each of those motorcades. I saw the people exulting, cheering, waving, calling to the beloved and esteemed President. More people in Texas had seen President Kennedy in these 2 days than had ever seen any one man on a similar visit to Texas before. President and Mrs. Kennedy had traveled more than 65 miles in open motorcade in Texas.

Mr. President, because of the governmental messages they carry, and the historic interest in these last speeches by President Kennedy, I ask unanimous consent that the series of seven speeches by President Kennedy including both Fort Worth speeches and the speeches prepared but undelivered at Dallas and Austin be inserted at this point.

REMARKS OF THE PRESIDENT AT DEDICATION CEREMONIES, AEROSPACE MEDICAL HEALTH CENTER, BROOKS AIR FORCE BASE, TEX., NOVEMBER 21, 1963 (AS ACTUALLY DELIVERED)

Mr. Secretary, Governor, Mr. Vice President, Senator, Members of the Congress, members of the military, ladies and gentlemen, for more than 3 years I have spoken about the New Frontier. This is not a partisan term, and it is not the exclusive property of Republicans or Democrats. It refers, instead, to this Nation's place in history, to the fact that we do stand on the edge of a great new era, with both crisis and opportunity, an era to be characterized by achievement and by challenge. It is an era which calls for action and for the best efforts of all those who would test the unknown, and the uncertain in phases of human endeavor. It is the time for pathfinders and pioneers.

I have come to Texas today to salute an outstanding group of pioneers, the men who man the Brooks Air Force Base School of Aerospace Medicine and the Aerospace Medical Center. It is fitting that San Antonio should be the site of this center and this school as we gather to dedicate this complex of buildings. For this city has long been the home of the pioneers in the air. It was here that Sidney Brooks, whose memory we honor today, was born and raised. It was here that Charles Lindbergh and Claire Chennault, and a host of others, who, in World War I and World War II and Korea, and

even today, have helped demonstrate American mastery of the skies, trained at Kelly Field and Randolph Field, which form a major part of aviation history. And in the New Frontier of outer space, while headlines may be made by others in other places, history is being made every day by the men and women of the Aerospace Medical Center, without whom there could be no history.

Many Americans make the mistake of assuming that space research has no values here on earth. Nothing could be further from the truth. Just as the wartime development of radar gave us the transistor, and all that it made possible, so research in space medicine holds the promise of substantial benefit for those of us who are ~~earthbound, for our effort in space is not as some have~~ suggested, a competitor for the natural resources that we need to develop the earth. It is a working partner and a coproducer of these resources. And nothing makes this clearer than the fact that medicine in space is going to make our lives healthier and happier here on earth.

I give you three examples: First, medical space research may open up new understanding of man's relation to his environment. Examples of the astronaut's physical, and mental, and emotional reactions teach us more about the differences between normal and abnormal—about the causes and effects of disorientation—in metabolism which could result in extending the lifespan. When you study effects on our astronauts of exhaust gases which can contaminate their environment, you seek ways to alter these gases so as to reduce their toxicity, you are working on problems similar to those we face in our great urban centers which themselves are being corrupted by gases and which must be clear. And second, medical space research may revolutionize the technology and the techniques of modern medicine. Whatever new devices are created, for example, to monitor our astronauts, to measure their heart activity, their breathing, their brain waves, their eye motion, at great distances, and under difficult conditions, will also represent a major advance in general medical instrumentation. Heart patients may even be able to wear a light monitor which will sound a warning if their activity exceeds certain limits. An instrument recently developed to record automatically the impact of acceleration upon an astronaut's eyes will also be of help to small children who are suffering miserably from eye defects, but are unable to describe their impairment. And also by the use of instruments similar to those used in Project Mercury, this Nation's private as well as public nursing services are being improved, enabling one nurse now to give more critically ill patients greater attention than they ever could in the past.

And third, medical space research may lead to new safeguards against hazards common to many environments. Specifically, our astronauts will need fundamentally new devices to protect them from the ill effects of radiation which can have a profound influence upon medicine and man's relations to our present environment.

Here at this Center we have the laboratories, the talent, the resources to give new impetus to vital research in the life centers. I am not suggesting that the entire space program is justified alone by what is done in medicine. The space program stands on its own as a contribution to national strength. And last Saturday at

Cape Canaveral I saw our new Saturn C–1 rocket booster, which, with its payload, when it rises in December of this year, will be, for the first time, the largest booster in the world, carrying into space the largest payload that any country in the world has ever sent into space. That is what I consider.

I think the United States should be a leader. A country as rich and powerful as this which bears so many burdens and responsibilities, which has so many opportunities, should be second to none. And in December, while I do not regard our mastery of space as anywhere near complete, while I recognize that there are still areas where we are behind, at least in one area, the size of the booster, this year I hope the United States will be ahead. And I am for it. We have a long way to go. Many weeks and months and years of long, tedious work lies ahead. There will be setbacks and frustrations, disappointments. There will be, as there always are, pressures in this country to do less in this area as in so many others, and temptations to do something else that is perhaps easier. But this research here must go on. This space effort must go on. The conquest of space must and will go ahead. That much we know. That much we can say with confidence and conviction.

Frank O'Connor, the Irish writer, tells in one of his books how, as a boy, he and his friends would make their way across the countryside and when they came to an orchard wall that seemed too high and too doubtful to try and too difficult to permit their voyage to continue, they took off their hats and tossed them over the wall—and then they had no choice but to follow them. This Nation has tossed its cap over the wall of space, and we have no choice but to follow it. Whatever the difficulties, they will be overcome; whatever the hazards, they must be guarded against. With the vital help of this Aerospace Medical Center, with the help of all those who labor in the space endeavor, with the help and support of all Americans, we will climb this wall with safety and speed, and we shall then explore the wonders on the other side. Thank you.

———

REMARKS OF THE PRESIDENT AT DEDICATION CEREMONIES, AEROSPACE MEDICAL HEALTH CENTER, BROOKS AIR FORCE BASE, TEX., NOVEMBER 21, 1963 (AS PREPARED FOR DELIVERY)

For more than 3 years, I have spoken to the American people in terms of the New Frontier. That is not a partisan term. It is not the exclusive property of either Democrats or Republicans. It refers instead to this Nation's position in history today—to the fact that we stand on the edge of a great new era, filled with both crises and opportunities, an era to be characterized by both grim challenges and historic achievements. It is an age which calls for doing and daring, and for the best efforts of all who are willing to explore the unknown and test the uncertain, in every phase of human endeavor. It is a time for pathfinders and pioneers.

I have come to Texas today to salute an outstanding group of pioneers—the men who man the Brooks Air Force Base School of Aerospace Medicine and the Aero-

space Medical Center. The trails which they blaze and the paths which they open hold the key to man's success in the environment above—the key to further progress in aerial flight and to further exploration of space.

It is fitting that San Antonio should be the site of this Center and school, at which we gather today to dedicate this complex of buildings. For this city has long been the home of the pioneers of aeronautics. It was here that Aviator Sidney Brooks, in whose memory this base was named, was born and raised. It was here that Charles Lindbergh and Claire Chennault and so many other heroes of pioneer aviation received their early training.

The tales and memories of Kelly Field and Randolph Field form a major part of aviation history. And in the new frontier of outer space—while more headlines may be made by other men in other areas—history is being made every day by the unsung heroes of this Aerospace Medical Center, without whom there could be no headlines.

But too many Americans make the mistake of assuming that space research has no values here on earth. Nothing could be further from the truth. Just as the wartime development of radar gave us the transistor and all the products it made possible, so research in space medicine holds the promise of substantial benefits for those of us who are earth-bound. For our effort in space is not, as some have suggested, a competitor for the national resources needed to improve our living standards. It is instead a working partner and coproducer of those resources. And nothing illustrates this point better than the fact that almost every field of medicine may profit in some way from aerospace medical research. Permit me to cite three examples, familiar to all of you but not fully realized by all Americans.

First, medical space research may open new avenues of understanding of man's relation to his environment. Examinations of the astronauts' physical, mental and emotional reactions can teach us more about the differences between normal and abnormal—about the causes and effects of disorientation—about changes in metabolism which could result in extending the life span. When you study the effects of our astronauts of toxic gases which can contaminate their environment, and seek ways to alter these gases to reduce their toxicity, you are working on problems similar to those we face in the pollution of the air in our urban centers. Already air pollution is contaminating 7,300 communities in the Nation, in which lives 60 percent of our population—and aeromedical research into atmospheric conditions offers some hope of assistance in our efforts to control this menace.

Second, medical space research may revolutionize the technology and techniques of modern medicine. Whatever new devices are created, for example, to monitor our astronauts—to measure their heart activity, their breathing, their brain waves and their eye motion, at great distances and under different or difficult circumstances—will also represent a major advance in general medical instrumentation. Physical examinations under conditions of stress and activity will then be possible, permitting an earlier detection of danger signals. Heart patients may even be able to wear a light monitor that will sound a warning if their activity exceeds certain limits. An instrument recently developed to record automatically the impact of acceleration upon an astronaut's eyes will also be of help to small children who are suffering miserably from eye defects but are unable to describe their impairment. Also, by the use of instruments similar to those used in Project Mercury, this Nation's private as well as public nursing services are being improved, enabling one nurse now to give more and better attention to critically ill patients than several nurses could formerly do in the absence of these instruments.

Third, medical space research may lead to new safeguards against hazards common to many environments. Specifically our astronauts will need fundamentally new devices to protect them from the ill effects of radiation. Those devices will be equally available here on earth—not, we hope, for purposes of civil defense but for safeguarding the increasing use of nuclear energy for peaceful purposes. Also, new sterilization techniques—developed to prevent the contamination of other planets by men traveling from our infected and infested earth—may be used here on earth to protect our food from botulisms.

These are but a few examples of the benefits we can hope to obtain through this one vital part of space research. Albert Einstein once said that the life sciences must keep pace with the physical sciences, or else all mankind is in jeopardy. And here at this Center we have the laboratories, the talent, and the resources to give impetus to vital research in the life sciences. For the formidable engineering and medical task of launching and sustaining a man in space provides a useful and commanding focus for the development and coordination of the most advanced concepts of both engineering and medical research; and I believe that the new information and techniques to be produced will provide enormous benefits for us all.

I do not say that we know with any precision how and where space medicine will contribute to medicine here at home. It is the nature of scientific research and exploration that we cannot know—any more than we could have known that research related to radar would eventually lead to the transistor. But what we do know is that fundamental research has always led to new and vital applications—that our whole modern technological society was formed from such unpredictable applications—and that we have every reason to believe that space research, including medical research, will continue that unbroken pattern.

Nor am I suggesting that the entire space program is justified as a means of advancing medical research. The space program stands on its own as a part of our national strength. But I am confident—and the history of scientific endeavor justifies this confidence—that as a valuable byproduct this effort in space medicine will benefit in scores of ways our everyday lives here on earth.

Space medicine is still an infant science—but no other frontier of medicine is more exciting. In determining the need and role of various human parts, their creation and their possible substitution, you shall be probing the origins of life itself. And thus both the ancient past and the distant future—both the beginning and the end of this world and others—may be viewed under the microscopic eye of this and similar schools.

Let us not be carried away with the grandeur of our vision. Many weeks and months and years of long, hard tedious work lie ahead. There will be setbacks and frustrations and disappointments. There will be pressures for our country to do less and temptations to do something else. But this research must and will go on. The conquest of space must and will go ahead. That much we know. That much we can say with confidence and conviction.

Frank O'Connor, the Irish writer, tells in one of his books how, as a boy, he and his friends would make their way across the countryside, and when they came to an orchard wall that seemed too high to climb, too doubtful to try, too difficult to permit their journey to continue, they took off their caps and tossed them over the wall—and then they had no choice but to follow them.

My friends, this Nation has tossed its cap over the wall of space—and we have no choice but to follow it. Whatever the difficulties, they must be overcome. Whatever the hazards, they must be guarded against. With the vital help of this Aeropsace Medical Center, with the help of all who labor in this space endeavor, with the help and support of all Americans, we will climb this wall with both safety and speed—and we shall then explore all the wonders and treasures that lie on the other side.

REMARKS OF THE PRESIDENT BEFORE THE LEAGUE OF UNITED LATIN AMERICAN CITIZENS, THE RICE HOTEL, HOUSTON, TEX., NOVEMBER 21, 1963

Mr. Chairman, Mr. Vice President, Mrs. Johnson, ladies and gentlemen, my wife and I are very proud to come to this meeting. This organization has done a good deal for this State and for our country, and I am particularly glad that it emphasizes not only the opportunity for all Americans, a chance to develop their talents, education for boys and girls, so that they can pursue those talents to the very end of their ability, but also because you remind Americans of the very important links that we have with our sister republics in this hemisphere.

One of the things which I have taken the greatest interest in has been attempting to pursue an example which was long neglected, and that was the one set by President Franklin Roosevelt to emphasize that the United States is not only good neighbors, which we were in the 1930's, but also friends and associates in a great effort to build in this hemisphere an alliance for progress, an effort to prove that this hemisphere, from top to bottom, and all of the countries, whether they be Latin or North American, there is a common commitment to freedom, to equality of opportunity, a chance for all to prove that prosperity can be the handmaiden of freedom, and to show to the world a very bright star here in this country and, indeed, in the entire hemisphere. So I am glad to be here today.

In order that my words will be even clearer, I am going to ask my wife to say a few words to you also.

REMARKS OF THE PRESIDENT AT TESTIMONIAL DINNER FOR
CONGRESSMAN ALBERT THOMAS, THE COLISEUM, HOUS-
TON, TEX., NOVEMBER 21, 1963

Congressman and Mrs. Thomas, Mr. Vice President, Governor Connally, Senator Yarborough, Congressman Casey and the congressional delegation of Texas, ladies and gentlemen, when I came to the House of Representatives in 1947 as a fairly young Congressman from Massachusetts, I heard the old saying that you spend the first 6 months in the House of Representatives wondering how you got there, and the next 6 months wondering how everybody else got there.

I spent the first 6 months as expected, but I must say that I never wondered how Congressman Thomas got there. It has always been clear to me. When I read the report that Congressman Thomas was thinking of resigning, I called him up on the phone and asked him to stay as long as I stayed. I didn't know how long that would be, but I wanted him to stay because I thought that he not only represented this district with distinction, but also he served the United States.

The Presidency has been called a good many names, and Presidents have been also, but no President can do anything without the help of friends, and I must say in the 3 years that I have been in this office, the 3 years really since I was here in Houston that night in this hall, I don't know anyone who has been a greater help in trying to get the job done, not just for Houston and not just for Texas, but for the entire United States than Albert Thomas, and I am glad to be with his friends here tonight. He may not be so well known outside of this district in Texas and Washington, but I can tell you that when he rises to speak in the House of Representatives they listen, so do some Senators, and so do we down at the other end of Pennsylvania Avenue.

He has one of the longest records of seniority in the House and also one of the shortest biographies. He has been consistently loyal to his party, but he has always stayed above partisan rancor. His record serves his constituents, but it serves the United States. He has helped steer this country to its present eminence in space. Next month when the United States of America fires the largest booster in the history of the world into space for the first time giving us the lead, fires the largest payroll—payload—into space giving us the lead. It will be the largest payroll, too. And who should know that better than Houston. We put a little of it right in here.

But in any case, the United States next month will have a leadership in space which it wouldn't have without Albert Thomas. And so will this city. He has been a stickler for efficiency in Government, but he has also been for progress and growth.

He is 65 years of age this month, but has a young man's interest in the future and a young man's hope for his country, for he has lived with change and he has sought to channel its force instead of combating it. He understands, as any Texan does, the meaning and importance of growth, for he has served one of the fastest growing countries and States and cities in the Nation. And those who oppose progress should look at Houston and look at Texas.

When he went to the U.S. Congress in 1936, some 27 years ago this month, this city had less than 200,000 people. But Albert Thomas had a vision of a modern Houston which now has a million people, and is growing stronger every day. He was not satisfied, nor the people of this city, with a channel which carried less than 30 million tons a year. He foresaw that this city, despite the fact that it is located 50 miles from the sea—and I come from a city that is on the sea—yet this city today ships second to the city of New York around the world. And that is in part because of Albert Thomas. And he and you were not content with an airport serving a handful of passengers and an industry of less than 300 planes carrying passengers of less than a half billion revenue miles. He foresaw that that industry would provide 6 times as many planes, employ 19 times as many people, and serve more than 33 billion passenger miles a year. Here in Houston the number of passengers who go through your great International Airport have quadrupled in the last 15 years. This city has looked forward with hope and commitment, and those who say "No" in Houston or in Texas or in the United States are on the wrong side in 1963.

Finally when Congressman Thomas went to the House of Representatives in 1936 he did not confine his sight to a Texas of less than 6 million people, a Texas doing less than $500 million of manufacturing, a Texas in which 37 percent of its population lived on the farm. By 1963, that population had dropped to 7 percent, the population of this State exceeds 10 million, the value of your manufacturing has climbed to $6 billion, and Texas today is 1 of the 10 most highly industrialized States in the Union.

Many of the products and employers of this State and city were wholly unknown when Albert Thomas went to the House—electronic machinery, sophisticated instruments, and preparations for the exploration of space. But those are the industries which helped this State reach its highest peak of prosperity in 1962, except for 1 year—1963. In Texas and the Nation, change has been the law of life. Growth has meant new opportunities for this State. Progress has meant new achievements. And men such as Albert Thomas, who recognize the value of growth and progress, have enabled this city and this State to rise with the tides of change instead of being swept aside and left behind.

There were in 1936, as there are today, those who are opposed to growth and change, who prefer to defy them, who look back instead of forward. But Albert Thomas and those who work with him did not heed that view in the midthirties, and this city, this State, and this country are glad that they did not. And we dare not look back now, if 27 years from now, in the year 1990 a new generation of Americans is to say that we, too, looked forward.

In 1990, for example, this Nation will need three times as much electric power as it has today, four times as much water, and that is why we are developing the Canadian River and the San Angelo, and the Columbus Bend, and other Texas river projects, and seeking at Freeport to find an economical way to get fresh water from salt, and building antipollution plants throughout this State and Nation, in a new and expanded program. In 1990 the need for national and State parks and recreation areas will triple, reaching a total very nearly the size of Indiana. That is why we are creating Padre Island Seashore, and adding refuge.

In 1990 your sons, daughters, grandsons, and grandchildren will be applying to the colleges of this State in a number three times what they do today. Our airports will serve five times as many passenger miles. We will need housing for a hundred million more people, and many times more doctors and engineers, and technicians, than we are presently producing. That is why we are trying to do more in these areas, as in the thirties, Albert Thomas and Franklin Roosevelt and others did those things which make it possible for not only Texas but the entire United States to prosper and grow, as we do in the 1960's.

In 1990 the age of space will be entering its second phase, and our hopes in it to preserve the peace, to make sure that in this great new sea, as on earth, the United States is second to none. And that is why I salute Albert Thomas and those Texans who you sent to Washington in his time and since then, who recognize the needs and the trends today in the 1960's so that when some meet here in 1990 they will look back on what we did and say that we made the right and wise decisions. "Your old men shall dream dreams, your young men shall see visions," the Bible tells us; and "where there is no vision, the people perish."

Albert Thomas is old enough to dream dreams, and young enough to see visions. He sees an America of the future, in the lifetime of us; all with 300 million people living in this country with a $2 trillion economy which will happen in this century. Even more important, he sees an America, as do we all, strong in science and in space, in health and in learning, in the respect of its neighbors and all nations, an America that is both powerful and peaceful, with a people that are both prosperous and just. With that vision, we shall not perish, and we cannot fail.

Behind the Speaker's desk in the House of Representatives there are words from a great speech by a great citizen of my State, Senator Daniel Webster. It says, "Let us develop the resources of our land, call forth its industry, develop its resources, and see whether we also in our time and generation may not perform something worthy to be remembered."

Albert Thomas didn't need to read those words. He has performed something worthy to be remembered.

Thank you.

———

REMARKS OF THE PRESIDENT BEFORE A CITIZENS' RALLY IN FRONT OF THE TEXAS HOTEL, FORT WORTH, TEX., NOVEMBER 22, 1963

Mr. Vice President, Jim Wright, Governor, Senator Yarborough, Mr. Buck, ladies and gentlemen, there are no faint hearts in Fort Worth, and I appreciate your being here this morning. Mrs. Kennedy is organizing herself. It takes longer, but, of course, she looks better than we do when she does it. But we appreciate your welcome.

This city has been a great Western city, the defense of the West, cattle, oil and all the rest. It has believed in strength in this city and strength in this State, and strength in this country.

What we are trying to do in this country and what we are trying to do around the world I believe is quite simple, and that is to build a military structure which will defend the vital interests of the United States; and in that great cause, Fort Worth, as it did in World War II, as it did in developing the best bomber system in the world, the B-58; and as it will now do in developing the best fighter system in the world, the TFX, Fort Worth will play its proper part. And that is why we have placed so much emphasis in the last 3 years in building a defense system second to none, until now the United States is stronger than it has ever been in its history. And secondly, we believe that the new environment, space, the new sea, is also an area where the United States should be second to none.

And this State of Texas and the United States is now engaged in the most concentrated effort in history to provide leadership in this area as it must here on earth. And this is our second great effort. And in December— next month—the United States will fire the largest booster in the history of the world, putting us ahead of the Soviet Union in that area for the first time in our history.

And thirdly, for the United States to fulfill its obligations around the world requires that the United States move forward economically, that the people of this country participate in rising prosperity. And it is a fact that in 1962, and the first 6 months of 1963, the economy of the United States grew not only faster than nearly every Western country, which had not been true in the fifties, but also grew faster than the Soviet Union itself. That is the kind of strength the United States needs, economically, in space, militarily.

And in the final analysis, that strength depends upon the willingness of the citizens of the United States to assume burdens of citizenship.

I know one place where they are, here in this rain, in Fort Worth, in Texas, in the United States. We are going forward.

Thank you.

———

REMARKS OF THE PRESIDENT BEFORE THE FORT WORTH CHAMBER OF COMMERCE, TEXAS HOTEL, FORT WORTH, TEX. (AS ACTUALLY DELIVERED), NOVEMBER 22, 1963.

I know now why everyone in Texas, Fort Worth, is so thin, having gotten up and down about nine times. This is what you do every morning.

Mr. Buck, Mr. Vice President, Governor Connally, Senator Yarborough, Jim Wright, members of the congressional delegation, Mr. Speaker, Mr. Attorney General, ladies and gentlemen, 2 years ago, I introduced myself in Paris saying that I was the man who had accompanied Mrs. Kennedy to Paris. I am getting somewhat that same sensation as I travel around Texas. Nobody wonders what Lyndon and I wear.

I am glad to be here in Jim Wright's city. About 35 years ago, a Congressman from California who had just been elected received a letter from an irate constituent which said: "During the campaign you promised to have the Sierra Madre Mountains reforested. You have been in office 1 month and you haven't done so." Well, no one in Forth Worth has been that unreasonable, but in some ways he has had the Sierra Madre Mountains reforested and here in Forth Worth he has contributed to its growth.

He speaks for Fort Worth and he speaks for the country, and I don't know any city that is better represented in the Congress of the United States than Fort Worth.

And if there are any Democrats here this morning, I am sure you wouldn't hold that against him.

Three years ago last September I came here, with the Vice President, and spoke at Burke Burnett Park, and I called in that speech for a national security policy and a national security system which was second to none, a position which said not first but, if, when and how, but first. That city responded to that call as it has through its history. And we have been putting that pledge into practice ever since.

I want to say a word about that pledge here in Fort Worth, which understands national defense, and its importance to the security of the United States. During the days of the Indian War, this city was a fort. During the days of World War I, even before the United States got into the war, Royal Canadian Air Force pilots were training here. During the days of World War II, the great Liberator bombers, and which my brother flew with his co-pilot from this city, were produced here.

The first nonstop flight around the world took off and returned here, in a plane built in factories here. The first truly intercontinental bomber, the B–36, was produced here. The B–58, which is the finest weapons system in the world today, which has demonstrated most recently in flying from Tokyo to London, with an average speed of nearly 1,000 miles per hour, is a Fort Worth product.

The Iroquois helicopter from Forth Worth is a mainstay in our fight against the guerrillas in South Vietnam. The transportation of crews between our missile sites is done in planes produced here in Fort Worth. So wherever the confrontation may occur, and in the last 3 years it has occurred on at least three occasions, Laos, Berlin, and Cuba, and it will again—wherever it occurs, the products of Fort Worth and the men of Fort Worth provide us with a sense of security.

And in the not too distant future a new Fort Worth product, and I am glad that there was a table separating Mr. Hicks and myself—a new Fort Worth product, the TFX. Tactical fighter experimental—nobody knows what those words mean, but that is what they mean, tactical fighter experimental—will serve the forces of freedom and will be the No. 1 airplane in the world today.

There has been a good deal of discussion of the long and hard fought competition to win the TFX contract, but very little discussion about what this plane will do. It will be the first operational aircraft ever produced that can literally spread its wings through the air. It will thus give us a single plane capable of carrying out missions of speed as well as distance, able to fly very far in one form or very fast in another. It can take off from rugged, short airstrips, enormously increasing the Air Force's ability to participate in limited wars. The same basic plane will serve the Navy's carriers, saving the taxpayers at least $1 billion in costs if they built separate planes for the Navy and the Air Force.

The Government of Australia, by purchasing $125 million of TFX planes before they are even off the drawing boards, has already testified to the merit of this plane, and at the same time it is confident in the ability of Fort Worth to meet its schedule. In all these ways, the success of our national defense depends upon this city in the Western United States, 10,000 miles from Vietnam, 5,000 or 6,000 miles from Berlin, thousands of miles from trouble spots in Latin America and Africa or the Middle East. And yet Fort Worth and what it does and what it produces participates in all these historic events. Texas, as a whole, and Fort Worth bear particular responsibility for this national defense effort, for military procurement in this State totals nearly $1¼ million, fifth highest among all the States of the Union. There are more military personnel on active duty in this State than in any in the Nation, save one—and it is not Massachusetts—any in the Nation save one, with a combined military-civilian defense payroll of well over a billion dollars. I don't recite these for my partisan purpose. They are the result of American determination to be second to none, and as a result of the effort which this country has made in the last 3 years we are second to none.

In the past 3 years we have increased the defense budget of the United States by over 20 percent; increased the program of acquisition for Polaris submarines from 24 to 41; increased our Minuteman missile purchase program by more than 75 percent; doubled the number of strategic bombers and missiles on alert; doubled the number of nuclear weapons available in the strategic alert forces; increased the tactical nuclear forces deployed in Western Europe by over 60 percent; added 5 combat-ready divisions to the Army of the United States, and 5 tactical fighter wings to the Air Force of the United States; increased our strategic airlift capability by 75 percent; and increased our special counterinsurgency forces which are engaged now in South Vietnam by 600 percent. I hope those who want a stronger America and place it on some signs will also place those figures next to it.

This is not an easy effort. This requires sacrifice by the people of the United States. But this is a very dangerous and uncertain world. As I said earlier, on three occasions in the last 3 years the United States has had a direct confrontation. No one can say when it will come again. No one expects that our life will be easy, certainly not in this decade and perhaps not in this century. But we should realize what a burden and responsibility the people of the United States have borne for so many years. Here a country which lived in isolation, divided and protected by the Atlantic and the Pacific, uninterested in the struggles of the world around it, here in the short space of 18 years after the Second World War, we put ourselves, by our own will and by necessity, into defense of alliances with countries all around the globe. Without the United States, South

Vietnam would collapse overnight. Without the United States, the SEATO alliance would collapse overnight. Without the United States, the CENTO alliance would collapse overnight. Without the United States, there would be no NATO. And gradually Europe would drift into neutralism and indifference. Without the efforts of the United States in the Alliance for Progress, the Communist advance onto the mainland of South America would long ago have taken place.

So this country, which desires only to be free, which desires to be secure, which desired to live at peace for 18 years under three different administrations has borne more than its share of the burden, has stood watch for more than its number of years. I don't think we are fatigued or tired. We would like to live as we once lived. But history will not permit it. The Communist balance of power is still strong. The balance of power is still on the side of freedom. We are still the keystone in the arch of freedom, and I think we will continue to do as we have done in our past, our duty, and the people of Texas will be in the lead.

So I am glad to come to this State which has played such a significant role in so many efforts in this century, and to say that here in Fort Worth you people will be playing a major role in the maintenance of the security of the United States for the next 10 years. I am confident, as I look to the future, that our chances for security, our chances for peace, are better than they have been in the past. And the reason is because we are stronger. And with that strength is a determination to not only maintain the peace, but also the vital interests of the United States. To that great cause, Texas and the United States are committed.

Thank you.

————

REMARKS BY THE PRESIDENT AS PREPARED FOR DELIVERY TO THE DALLAS CITIZENS COUNCIL, THE DALLAS ASSEMBLY, AND THE GRADUATE RESEARCH CENTER OF THE SOUTHWEST, AT THE TRADE MART, DALLAS, TEX., NOVEMBER 22, 1963

I am honored to have this invitation to address the annual meeting of the Dallas Citizens Council, joined by the members of the Dallas Assembly—and pleased to have this opportunity to salute the Graduate Research Center of the Southwest.

It is fitting that these two symbols of Dallas progress are united in the sponsorship of this meeting. For they represent the best qualities, I am told, of leadership and learning in this city—and leadership and learning are indispensable to each other. The advancement of learning depends on community leadership for financial and political support—and the products of that learning, in turn, are essential to the leadership's hopes for continued progress and prosperity. It is not a coincidence that those communities possessing the best in research and graduate facilities—from MIT to Cal Tech—tend to attract the new and growing industries. I congratulate those of you here in Dallas who have recognized these basic facts through the creation of the unique and forward-looking Graduate Research Center.

This link between leadership and learning is not only essential at the community level. It is even more in-dispensable in world affairs. Ignorance and misinformation can handicap the progress of a city or a company—but they can, if allowed to prevail in foreign policy, handicap this country's security. In a world of complex and continuing problems, in a world full of frustrations and irritations, America's leadership must be guided by the lights of learning and reason—or else those who confuse rhetoric with reality and the plausible with the possible will gain the popular ascendancy with their seemingly swift and simple solutions to every world problem.

There will always be dissident voices heard in the land, expressing opposition without alternatives, finding fault but never favor, perceiving gloom on every side and seeking influence without responsibility. Those voices are inevitable.

But today other voices are heard in the land—voices preaching doctrines wholly unrelated to reality, wholly unsuited to the sixties, doctrines which apparently assume that words will suffice without weapons, that vituperation is as good as victory and that peace is a sign of weakness. At a time when the national debt is steadily being reduced in terms of its burden on our economy, they see that debt as the greatest single threat to our security. At a time when we are steadily reducing the number of Federal employees serving every thousand citizens, they fear those supposed hordes of civil servants far more than the actual hordes of opposing armies.

We cannot expect that everyone, to use the phrase of a decade ago, will "talk sense to the American people." But we can hope that fewer people will listen to nonsense. And the notion that this Nation is headed for defeat through deficit, or that strength is but a matter of slogans, is nothing but just plain nonsense.

I want to discuss with you today the status of our strength and our security because this question clearly calls for the most responsible qualities of leadership and the most enlightened products of scholarship. For this Nation's strength and security are not easily or cheaply obtained—nor are they quickly and simply explained. There are many kinds of strength and no one kind will suffice. Overwhelming nuclear strength cannot stop a guerrilla war. Formal pacts of alliance cannot stop internal subversion. Displays of material wealth cannot stop the disillusionment of diplomats subjected to discrimination.

Above all, words alone are not enough. The United States is a peaceful nation. And where our strength and determination are clear, our words need merely to convey conviction, not belligerence. If we are strong, our strength will speak for itself. If we are weak, words will be of no help.

I realize that this Nation often tends to identify turning points in world affairs with the major addresses which preceded them. But it was not the Monroe Doctrine that kept all Europe away from this hemisphere—it was the strength of the British fleet and the width of the Atlantic Ocean. It was not General Marshall's speech at Harvard which kept communism out of Western Europe—it was the strength and stability made possible by our military and economic assistance.

In this administration also it has been necessary at times to issue specific warnings—warnings that we could not stand by and watch the Communists conquer Laos by force, or intervene in the Congo, or swallow West Berlin or maintain offensive missiles on Cuba. But while our goals were at least temporarily obtained in these and other instances, our successful defense of freedom was due—not to the words we used—but to the strength we stood ready to use on behalf of the principles we stand ready to defend.

This strength is composed of many different elements, ranging from the most massive deterrents to the most subtle influences. And all types of strength are needed—no one kind could do the job alone. Let us take a moment, therefore, to review this Nation's progress in each major area of strength.

I

First, as Secretary McNamara made clear in his address last Monday, the strategic nuclear power of the United States has been so greatly modernized and expanded in the last 1,000 days, by the rapid production and deployment of the most modern missile systems, that any and all potential aggressors are clearly confronted now with the impossibility of strategic victory—and the certainty of total destruction—if by reckless attack they should ever force upon us the necessity of a strategic reply.

In less than 3 years, we have increased by 50 percent the number of Polaris submarines scheduled to be in force by the next fiscal year—increased by more than 70 percent our total Polaris purchase program—increased by more than 75 percent our Minuteman purchase program—increased by 50 percent the portion of our strategic bombers on 15-minute alert—and increased by 100 percent the total number of nuclear weapons available in our strategic alert forces. Our security is further enhanced by the steps we have taken regarding these weapons to improve the speed and certainty of their response, their readiness at all times to respond, their ability to survive an attack and their ability to be carefully controlled and directed through secure command operations.

II

But the lessons of the last decade have taught us that freedom cannot be defended by strategic nuclear power alone. We have, therefore, in the last 3 years accelerated the development and deployment of tactical nuclear weapons—and increased by 60 percent the tactical nuclear forces deployed in Western Europe.

Nor can Europe or any other continent rely on nuclear forces alone, whether they are strategic or tactical. We have radically improved the readiness of our conventional forces—increased by 45 percent the number of combat ready Army divisions—increased by 100 percent the procurement of modern Army weapons and equipment—increased by 100 percent our ship construction, conversion and modernization program—increased by 100 percent our procurement of tactical aircraft—increased by 30 percent the number of tactical air squadrons—and increased the strength of the Marines. As last month's Operation Big Lift—which originated here in Texas—showed so clearly, this Nation is prepared as never before to move

substantial numbers of men in surprisingly little time to advanced positions anywhere in the world. We have increased by 175 percent the procurement of airlift aircraft—and we have already achieved a 75 percent increase in our existing strategic airlift capability. Finally, moving beyond the traditional roles of our military forces, we have achieved an increase of nearly 600 percent in our special forces—those forces that are prepared to work with our allies and friends against the guerrillas, saboteurs, insurgents and assassins who threaten freedom in a less direct but equally dangerous manner.

III

But American military might should not and need not stand alone against the ambitions of international communism. Our security and strength, in the last analysis, directly depend on the security and strength of others—and that is why our military and economic assistance plays such a key role in enabling those who live on the periphery of the Communist world to maintain their independence of choice. Our assistance to these nations can be painful, risky, and costly—as is true in southeast Asia today. But we dare not weary of the task. For our assistance makes possible the stationing of 3.5 million Allied troops along the Communist frontier at one-tenth the cost of maintaining a comparable number of American soldiers. A successful Communist breakthrough in these areas, necessitating direct U.S. intervention, would cost us several times as much as our entire foreign aid program—and might cost us heavily in American lives as well.

About 70 percent of our military assistance goes to nine key countries located on or near the borders of the Communist bloc—nine countries confronted directly or indirectly with the threat of Communist aggression—Vietnam, Free China, Korea, India, Pakistan, Thailand, Greece, Turkey, and Iran. No one of these countries possesses on its own the resources to maintain the forces which our own Chiefs of Staff think needed in the common interest. Reducing our efforts to train, equip, and assist their armies can only encourage Communist penetration and require in time the increased oversea deployment of American combat forces. And reducing the economic help needed to bolster these nations that undertake to help defend freedom can have the same disastrous result. In short, the $50 billion we spend each year on our own defense could well be ineffective without the $4 billion required for military and economic assistance.

Our foreign aid program is not growing in size—it is, on the contrary, smaller now than in previous years. It has had its weaknesses—but we have undertaken to correct them—and the proper way of treating weaknesses is to replace them with strength, not to increase those weaknesses by emasculating essential programs. Dollar for dollar, in or out of government, there is no better form of investment in our national security than our much-abused foreign aid program. We cannot afford to lose it. We can afford to maintain it. We can surely afford, for example, to do as much for our 19 needy neighbors of Latin America as the Communist bloc is sending to the island of Cuba alone.

IV

I have spoken of strength largely in terms of the deterrence and resistance of aggression and attack. But, in today's world, freedom can be lost without a shot being fired, by ballots as well as bullets. The success of our leadership is dependent upon respect for our mission in the world as well as our missiles—on a clearer recognition of the virtues of freedom as well as the evils of tyranny.

That is why our Information Agency has doubled the shortwave broadcasting power of the Voice of America and increased the number of broadcasting hours by 30 percent—increased Spanish language broadcasting to Cuba and Latin America from 1 to 9 hours a day—increased seven-fold to more than 3.5 million copies the number of American books being translated and published for Latin American readers—and taken a host of other steps to carry our message of truth and freedom to all the far corners of the earth.

And that is also why we have regained the initiative in the exploration of outer space—making an annual effort greater than the combined total of all space activities undertaken during the fifties—launching more than 130 vehicles into earth orbit—putting into actual operation valuable weather and communications satellites—and making it clear to all that the United States of America has no intention of finishing second in space.

This effort is expensive—but it pays its own way, for freedom and for America. For there is no longer any fear in the free world that a Communist lead in space will become a permanent assertion of supremacy and the basis of military superiority. There is no longer any doubt about the strength and skill of American science, American industry, American education and the American free enterprise system. In short, our national space effort represents a great gain in, and a great resource of, our national strength—and both Texas and Texans are contributing greatly to this strength.

Finally, it should be clear by now that a nation can be no stronger abroad than she is at home. Only an America which practices what it preaches about equal rights and social justice will be respected by those whose choice affects our future. Only an America which has fully educated its citizens is fully capable of tackling the complex problems and perceiving the hidden dangers of the world in which we live. And only an America which is growing and prospering economically can sustain the worldwide defenses of freedom, while demonstrating to all concerned the opportunities of our system and society.

It is clear, therefore, that we are strengthening our security as well as our economy by our recent record increases in national income and output—by surging ahead of most of Western Europe in the rate of business expansion and the margin of corporate profits—by maintaining a more stable level of prices than almost any of our oversea competitors—and by cutting personal and corporate income taxes by some $11 billion, as I have proposed, to assure this Nation of the longest and strongest expansion in our peacetime economic history.

This Nation's total output—which 3 years ago was at the $500 billion mark—will soon pass $600 billion, for a record rise of over $100 billion in 3 years. For the first time in history we have 70 million men and women at work. For the first time in history average factory earnings have exceeded $100 a week. For the first time in history corporation profits after taxes—which have risen 43 percent in less than 3 years—have reached an annual level of $27.4 billion.

My friends and fellow citizens: I cite these facts and figures to make it clear that America today is stronger than ever before. Our adversaries have not abandoned their ambitions—our dangers have not diminished—our vigilance cannot be relaxed. But now we have the military, the scientific, and the economic strength to do whatever must be done for the preservation and promotion of freedom.

That strength will never be used in pursuit of aggressive ambitions—it will always be used in pursuit of peace. It will never be used to promote provocations—it will always be used to promote the peaceful settlement of disputes.

We in this country, in this generation, are—by destiny rather than choice—the watchmen on the walls of world freedom. We ask, therefore, that we may be worthy of our power and responsibility—that we may exercise our strength with wisdom and restraint—and that we may achieve in our time and for all time the ancient vision of "peace on earth, good will toward men." That must always be our goal—and the righteousness of our cause must always underlie our strength. For as was written long ago: "except the Lord keep the city, the watchman waketh but in vain."

REMARKS OF THE PRESIDENT AS PREPARED FOR DELIVERY TO THE TEXAS DEMOCRATIC STATE COMMITTEE, THE MUNICIPAL AUDITORIUM, AUSTIN, TEX., NOVEMBER 22, 1963

One hundred and eighteen years ago last March, President John Tyler signed the joint resolution of Congress providing statehood for Texas. And 118 years ago next month, President James Polk declared that Texas was a part of the Union. Both Tyler and Polk were Democratic Presidents. And from that day to this, Texas and the Democratic Party have been linked in an indestructible alliance—an alliance for the promotion of prosperity, growth, and greatness for Texas and for America.

Next year that alliance will sweep this State and Nation.

The historic bonds which link Texas and the Democratic Party are no temporary union of convenience. They are deeply embedded in the history and purpose of this State and party. For the Democratic Party is not a collection of diverse interests brought together only to win elections. We are united instead by a common history and heritage—by a respect for the deeds of the past and a recognition of the needs of the future. Never satisfied with today, we have always staked our fortunes on tomorrow. That is the kind of State which Texas has always been—that is the kind of vision and vitality which Texans have always possessed—and that is the reason why Texas will always be basically Democratic.

For 118 years, Texas and the Democratic Party have contributed to each other's success. This State's rise to prosperity and wealth came primarily from the policies and programs of Woodrow Wilson, Franklin Roosevelt, and Harry Truman. These policies were shaped and enacted with the help of such men as the late Sam Rayburn and a host of other key Congressmen—by the former Texas Congressman and Senator who serves now as my strong right arm, Vice President Lyndon B. Johnson—by your present U.S. Senator, Ralph Yarborough—and by an overwhelming proportion of Democratic leadership at the State and county level, led by your distinguished Governor, John Connally.

It was the policies and programs of the Democratic Party which helped bring income to your farmers, industries to your cities, employment to your workers, and the promotion and preservation of your natural resources. No one who remembers the days of 5-cent cotton and 30-cent oil will forget the ties between the success of this State and the success of our party.

Three years ago this fall I toured this State with Lyndon Johnson, Sam Rayburn, and Ralph Yarborough as your party's candidate for President. We pledged to increase America's strength against its enemies, its prestige among its friends, and the opportunities it offered to its citizens. Those pledges have been fulfilled. The words spoken in Texas have been transformed into action in Washington, and we have America moving again.

Here in Austin, I pledged in 1960 to restore world confidence in the vitality and energy of American society. That pledge has been fulfilled. We have won the respect of allies and adversaries alike through our determined stand on behalf of freedom around the world, from West Berlin to southeast Asia—through our resistance to Communist intervention in the Congo and Communist missiles in Cuba—and through our initiative in obtaining the nuclear test ban treaty which can stop the pollution of our atmosphere and start us on the path to peace. In San Jose and Mexico City, in Bonn and West Berlin, in Rome and County Cork, I saw and heard and felt a new appreciation for an America on the move— an America which has shown that it cares about the needy of its own and other lands, an America which has shown that freedom is the way to the future, an America which is known to be first in the effort for peace as well as preparedness.

In Amarillo, I pledged in 1960 that the businessmen of this State and Nation—particularly the small businessman who is the backbone of our economy—would move ahead as our economy moved ahead. That pledge has been fulfilled. Business profits—having risen 43 percent in 2½ years—now stand at a record high; and businessmen all over America are grateful for liberalized depreciation for the investment tax credit, and for our programs to increase their markets at home as well as abroad. We have proposed a massive tax reduction, with particular benefits for small business. We have stepped up the activities of the Small Business Administration, making available in the last 3 years almost $50 million to more than 1,000 Texas firms, and doubling their opportunity to share in Federal procurement contracts. Our party believes that what's good for the American people is good for American business—and the last 3 years have proven the validity of that proposition.

In Grand Prairie, I pledged in 1960 that this country would no longer tolerate the lowest rate of economic growth of any major industrialized nation in the world. That pledge has been and is being fulfilled. In less than 3 years our national output will shortly have risen by a record $100 billion—industrial production is up 22 percent—personal income is up 16 percent. And the Wall Street Journal pointed out a short time ago that the United States now leads most of Western Europe in the rate of business expansion and the margin of corporate profits. Here in Texas—where 3 years ago, at the very time I was speaking, real per capita personal income was actually declining as the industrial recession spread to this State—more than 200,000 new jobs have been created—unemployment has declined—and personal income rose last year to an alltime high. This growth must go on. Those not sharing in this prosperity must be helped. And that is why we have an accelerated public works program, an area redevelopment program, and a manpower training program—to keep this and other States moving ahead. And that is why we need a tax cut of $11 billion, as an assurance of future growth and insurance against an early recession. No period of economic recovery in the peacetime history of this Nation has been characterized by both the length and strength of our present expansion—and we intend to keep it going.

In Dallas, I pledged in 1960 to step up the development of both our natural and our human resources. That pledge has been fulfilled. The policy of "no new starts" has been reversed. The Canadian River project will provide water for 11 Texas cities. The San Angelo project will irrigate some 10,000 acres. We have launched 10 new watershed projects in Texas, completed 7 others and laid plans for 6 more. A new national park, a new wildlife preserve, and other navigation, reclamation and natural resource projects are all underway in this State. At the same time we have sought to develop the human resources of Texas and all the Nation—granting loans to 17,500 Texas college students—making more than $17 million available to 249 school districts—and expanding or providing rural library service to 600,000 Texas readers. And if this Congress passes, as now seems likely, pending bills to build college classrooms, increase student loans, build medical schools, provide more community libraries, and assist in the creation of graduate centers, then this Congress will have done more for the cause of education than has been done by any Congress in modern history. Civilization, it was once said, is a race between education and catastrophe—and we intend to win that race for education.

In Wichita Falls, I pledged in 1960 to increase farm income and reduce the burden of farm surpluses. That pledge has been fulfilled. Net farm income today is almost a billion dollars higher than in 1960. In Texas, net income per farm consistently averaged below the $4,000 mark under the Benson regime—it is now well above it. And we have raised this income while reducing grain surpluses by 1 billion bushels. We have, at the same time, tackled the problem of the entire rural economy—extending more than twice as much credit to Texas farmers under the Farmers Home Administration—and making more than $100 million in REA loans. We have not solved all the problems of American agriculture—but we have offered hope and a helping hand in place of Mr. Benson's indifference.

In San Antonio, I pledged in 1960 that a new administration would strive to secure for every American his full constitutional rights. That pledge has been and is being fulfilled. We have not yet secured the objectives desired or the legislation required. But we have, in the last 3 years, by working through voluntary leadership as well as legal action, opened more new doors to members of minority groups—doors to transportation, voting, education employment, and place of public accommodation—than had been opened in any 3-year or 30-year period in this century. There is no noncontroversial way to fulfill our constitutional pledge to establish justice and promote domestic tranquillity—but we intend to fulfill those obligations because they are right.

In Houston, I pledged in 1960 that we would set before the American people the unfinished business of our society. That pledge has been fulfilled. We have undertaken the first full-scale revision of our tax laws in 10 years. We have launched a bold new attack on mental illness, emphasizing treatment in the patient's own home community instead of some vast custodial institution. We have initiated à full-scale attack on mental retardation, emphasizing prevention instead of abandonment. We have revised our public welfare programs, emphasizing family rehabilitation instead of humiliation. And we have proposed a comprehensive realinement of our national transportation policy, emphasizing equal competition instead of regulation. Our agenda is still long—but this country is moving again.

In El Paso, I pledged in 1960 that we would give the highest and earliest priority to the reestablishment of good relations with the people of Latin America. We are working to fulfill that pledge. An area long neglected has not solved all its problems. The Communist foothold which had already been established has not yet been eliminated. But the trend of Communist expansion has been reversed. The name of Fidel Castro is no longer feared or cheered by substantial numbers in every country—and contrary to the prevailing predictions of 3 years ago, not another inch of Latin American territory has fallen prey to Communist control. Meanwhile, the work of reform and reconciliation goes on. I can testify from my trips to Mexico, Colombia, Venezuela, and Costa Rica that American officials are no longer booed and spat upon south of the border. Historic fences and friendships are being maintained. Latin America, once the forgotten stepchild of our aid programs, now receives more economic assistance per capita than any other area of the world. In short, the United States is once more identified with the needs and aspirations of the people to the south—and we intend to meet those needs and aspirations.

In Texarkana, I pledged in 1960 that our country would no longer engage in a lagging space effort. That pledge has been fulfilled. We are not yet first in every field of space endeavor—but we have regained worldwide respect for our scientists, our industry, our education, and our free initiative.

In the last 3 years, we have increased our annual space effort to a greater level than the combined total of all space activities undertaken in the 1950's. We have launched into earth orbit more than four times as many space vehicles as had been launched in the previous 3 years. We have focused our wide-ranging efforts around a landing on the moon in this decade. We have put valuable weather and communications satellites into actual operation. We will fire this December the most powerful rocket ever developed anywhere in the world. And we have made it clear to all that the United States of America has no intention of finishing second in outer space. Texas will play a major role in this effort. The Manned Spacecraft Center in Houston will be the cornerstone of our lunar landing project, with a billion dollars already allocated to that Center this year. Even though space is an infant industry, more than 3,000 people are already employed in space activities here in Texas—more than $100 million of space contracts are now being worked on in this State—and more than 50 space related firms have announced the opening of Texas offices. This is still a daring and dangerous frontier; and there are those who would prefer to turn back or to take a more timid stance. But Texans have stood their ground on embattled frontiers before—and I know you will help us see this battle through.

In Fort Worth, I pledged in 1960 to build a national defense which was second to none—a position, I said, which is not "first, but," not "first, if," not "first, when" but first—period. That pledge has been fulfilled. In the past 3 years we have increased our defense budget by over 20 percent; increased the program for acquisition of Polaris submarines from 24 to 41; increased our Minuteman missile purchase program by more than 75 percent; doubled the number of strategic bombers and missiles on alert; doubled the number of nuclear weapons available in the strategic alert forces; increased the tactical nuclear forces deployed in Western Europe by 60 percent; added 5 combat ready divisions and 5 tactical fighter wings to our Armed Forces; increased our strategic airlift capabilities by 75 percent; and increased our special counterinsurgency forces by 600 percent. We can truly say today, with pride in our voices and peace in our hearts, that the defensive forces of the United States are, without a doubt, the most powerful and resourceful forces anywhere in the world.

Finally, I said in Lubbock in 1960, as I said in every other speech in this State, that if Lyndon Johnson and I were elected, we would get this country moving again. That pledge has been fulfilled. In nearly every field of national activity, this country is moving again—and Texas is moving with it. From public works to public health, wherever Government programs operate, the past 3 years have seen a new burst of action and progress—in Texas and all over America. We have stepped up the fight against crime and slums and poverty in our cities, against the pollution of our streams, against unemployment in our industry, and against waste in the Federal Government. We have built hospitals and clinics and nursing homes. We have launched a broad new attack on mental illness and mental retardation. We have initiated the training of more physicians and dentists. We have provided four times as much housing for our elderly citizens—and we have increased benefits for those on social security.

Almòst everywhere we look, the story is the same. In Latin America, in Africa, in Asia—in the councils of the world and in the jungles of far-off nations—there is now renewed confidence in our country and our convictions.

For this country is moving and it must not stop. It cannot stop. For this is a time for courage and a time of challenge. Neither conformity nor complacency will do. Neither the fanatics nor the fainthearted are needed. And our duty as a party is not to our party alone, but to the Nation, and, indeed, to all minkind. Our duty is not merely the preservation of political power but the preservation of peace and freedom.

So let us not be petty when our cause is so great. Let us not quarrel amongst ourselves when our Nation's future is at stake. Let us stand together with renewed confidence in our cause—united in our heritage of the past and our hopes for the future—and determined that this land we love shall lead all mankind into new frontiers of peace and abundance.

Mr. President, I have received in my office a copy of the official messages of tribute from France to the late, beloved President John Fitzgerald Kennedy. In addition, there are comments from French newspapers and other expressions of public opinion. These touching tributes from our great sister republic in Europe, and from the first nation to come to the aid of the embattled colonies in our War of Independence, move the American people with all our old sentiments of love for our ally, France.

General de Gaulle, by coming to the funeral of our late President, and leading the march of foreign dignitaries behind the casket of our late President, won new esteem and affection from the American people.

I ask unanimous consent that the following publication from Ambassade de France, entitled "France's Tribute to the Late President Kennedy," be printed.

FRANCE'S TRIBUTE TO THE LATE PRESIDENT KENNEDY— GENERAL DE GAULLE'S STATEMENT—OFFICIAL MESSAGES—GENERAL DE GAULLE ATTENDS THE FUNERAL— FRENCH PUBLIC OPINION

General de Gaulle's statement on the death of President Kennedy:

"President Kennedy died like a soldier, under fire, in the line of duty, and in the service of his country.

"In the name of the French people, ever the friend of the American people, I salute his great example and his great memory."

OFFICIAL MESSAGES

Message to Mrs. Jacqueline Kennedy from General and Madame de Gaulle: "The great sorrow that has just befallen you distresses my wife and myself to the bottom of our hearts. Rest assured that we are with you in our thoughts and in our prayers. President Kennedy shall never be forgotten."

Message to President Lyndon Johnson from General de Gaulle, President of the Republic:

"The death of President Kennedy is a source of deep sorrow to the French people, who held in the highest esteem this great head of State, illustrious servant of freedom and of the destiny of mankind.

"In the face of a misfortune which so profoundly affects your country and which concerns all the peoples of the world, and at a time when fate bestows upon you the more than ever loyal and confident friendship of France for the United States of America."

Message to President Lyndon Johnson from M. Georges Pompidou, Premier:

"Deeply moved by the tragic loss experienced by the United States on the death of President Kennedy, whose courage and great gifts as a statesman were admired by all, the French people wish to convey to you the grief felt by all my fellow countrymen.

"Rest assured that at a time when under such cruel circumstances you take up your high office, my colleagues of the French Government and myself join with you in a feeling of most grieving and most loyal friendship."

Message to Secretary of State Dean Rusk from M. Maurice Couve de Murville, Minister of Foreign Affairs:

"Profoundly shocked by the news of the act which has just cost the life of the President of the United States, may I assure you that I deeply share in your mourning and in that of the Government and the American people. Mindful of the welcome that President Kennedy extended to me only a few weeks ago, I can appreciate the extent of your sorrow.

"All my countrymen join with me and share in the feelings of friendship toward your country which have existed for two centuries."

Message to Secretary of Defense Robert McNamara from M. Pierre Messmer, Minister of the Armed Forces: "Upon hearing of the tragic death of President Kennedy, I ask you to accept the condolences of the French Armed Forces and also my own personal, sincerest and grieving condolences."

Message to Gen. Maxwell Taylor, Chairman of the Joint Chiefs of Staff, from Gen. Charles Ailleret, Chief of Staff of the French Armed Forces:

"May I express to you, and request that you convey this message to the Joint Chiefs of Staff, the shock and indignation of the French armed forces on hearing the news of the outrage against President Kennedy.

"May I also express to you my deepest personal sorrow at the death of the President of the United States who welcomed me such a short time ago with so much friendliness and warmth."

Statement by M. Roger Seydoux, permanent representative of France to the United Nations, before a plenary session of the United Nations General Assembly, held on November 27, 1963, to pay homage to the memory of the late President Kennedy, "All my compatriots, for whom the visit in Paris of Mr. and Mrs. John Kennedy remains a bright memory, turn toward the people of the United States, our everlasting friend. We wish them to know that their trial is our trial, their sadness our sadness, their mourning our mourning. Ours also is, despite the heavy loss they must bear, their steadfast faith in the future as is steadfast our confidence in their great destiny."

Statement by the French Premier, M. Georges Pompidou (the statement by the French Premier was broadcast over French television and transmitted to the United States by satellite via the Pleumeur-Bodou relay station):

"The stupefaction engendered by a despicable assassination, the indignation at seeing President Kennedy struck down by the side of his young wife in the fulfillment of his duties as a humane and liberal head of state, is accompanied by a great sadness also felt in our hearts: sadness because, once again, blind violence has triumphed; sadness because a great and friendly people is plunged into mourning; sadness because the free world has lost one of its surest guides.

"In these tragic hours, all France is at the side of the United States in anger, in grief, and, despite everything, in confidence also for the future."

Statement by French Foreign Minister, M. Maurice Couve de Murville (the statement was carried over the three major American television networks. It was transmitted by the communications satellite Relay:

"It was with the most grievous impression of shock that we all, in Paris and in France, heard the appalling news of President Kennedy's cold-blooded murder. Many elements combined in our thoughts: the terribly premature disappearance of a statesman of the first magnitude, the death of a man who was the incarnation of youth and vitality, the awful tragedy that hit a glamorous and lovable family, the general feeling of a blow inflicted to a great country for which France has, from the beginning, felt the closest friendship, further reinforced by comradeship in three wars.

"For me, who had the privilege of long talks with President Kennedy, the memory will not pass of his friendliness, his eagerness, his wisdom and his courage.

"Believe me when I say that we, the French people, today all grieve and pray together with the American people."

Statement broadcast over American television by M. Hervé Alphand, French Ambassador to the United States:

"The tragic death of President Kennedy has deeply moved the French people, forever the friend of the American people. Your sorrow is our sorrow and this sorrow we share with Mrs. Kennedy and her family, tonight we pray with them.

"The President had always displayed toward my country a great fondness, particularly on the occasion of his visit to Paris in 1961.

"For me it was also a personal friend who always showed me a profound affection and understanding.

"As General de Gaulle said today, he died as a soldier. We shall never forget his example or his memory, the memory of a great man."

GENERAL DE GAULLE ATTENDS PRESIDENT KENNEDY'S FUNERAL

The Presidency of the Republic issued a communique on November 23 announcing that General de Gaulle, President of the Republic, would attend the funeral of President Kennedy. He would be accompanied by M.

Maurice Couve de Murville, Minister of Foreign Affairs; Gen. Charles Ailleret, Chief of Staff of the French Armed Forces; and M. Etienne Burin des Roziers, General Secretary of the Presidency of the Republic.

FRENCH PUBLIC OPINION

France mourns President Kennedy

On the personal orders of General de Gaulle, all flags on public buildings were flown at half staff from 9 a.m. on November 23.

In paying this respect to the memory of President Kennedy, General de Gaulle departed from French tradition, which requires flags to be flown at half staff only during the funeral of a head of state of an allied or friendly power.

On November 23, the Paris Municipal Council sent a telegram to Mrs. Kennedy in which it told her that the city of Paris was in mourning. In addition, a member of the council proposed that the name of John F. Kennedy, defender of the fundamental freedoms of man and who fell for these freedoms, be given to a street in Paris. The council unanimously adopted this proposal on November 28.

In addition to messages of condolence addressed by official French circles to Mr. Charles Bohlen, many people from all walks of life, veterans' associations, French-American associations, and others sent messages of sympathy to the U.S. Embassy in Paris.

Among many expressions of sympathy, mention should be made of a group of between 2,000 and 3,000 students of all nationalities who went to sign the register of condolence in the U.S. Embassy in Paris.

A service in the memory of President Kennedy was held on November 25 in the cathedral of Notre Dame de Paris. It was attended by the U.S. Ambassador and Mrs. Bohlen and by Madam Charles de Gaulle. M. Georges Pompidou, French Premier, the President of the Senate and Madam Gaston Monnerville, members of the Government and members of the diplomatic corps in the French capital were also present in the great cathedral which was unable to hold the crowds of Parisians who wished to attend the service and who overflowed into the square in front of the cathedral, where members of the Garde Républicaine, swords unsheathed, formed an honor guard.

The French press

The entire French press without exception reflected the feeling of affliction among the French people at the death of President Kennedy. Raymond Aron in Le Figaro of November 23 wrote: "The assassination of J. F. Kennedy affects all mankind. * * * He wanted to be one of those statesmen whom history remembers because they accomplish their task. * * * He will leave a memory which will not be unworthy of the grandeur which he dreamed of achieving."

In an editorial of November 23, Combat wrote: "The crime committed yesterday is the worst one can imagine, since the man it struck down was a symbol in the eyes of hundreds of millions of our contemporaries."

Also on November 23, France-Soir wrote: "Like lightning, anguish and grief have hit the world. The hearts of men and women sank, at the same moment, in every country and on all continents. * * * All peoples weep also and above all for this man who, in the words of Pope Paul VI, 'defended the liberty of peoples and the peace of the world.' "

La Nation of November 25 published the following editorial comments: "He was one of the great men in this world. * * * A man with a personal fortune for whom it was possible therefore to have narrow views and yet he was more aware than millions of others of man's fate, a man above all who had the courage to direct his actions in tune with his heart."

Paul Bastid, in l'Aurore of November 25, wrote: "There was in the personality of John Fitzgerald Kennedy a kind of lucid fire in the service of liberty and peace which commanded admiration and sympathy. He devoted himself entirely, with the energy of his temperament and of his age, to causes that are dear to us."

Le Monde, in an editorial in its November 26 issue, said: "He leaves an inspiration, a style, a line from which America will not easily stray." In the same issue, the French poet and Nobel Prize winner Saint John Perse wrote: "Kennedy * * * was an athlete running in a race against fate. He fought fairly and squarely always and his encounter with death came with his face uncovered."

The next day Le Monde published an editorial containing the following comment: "The gesture by the President of the Republic who, right at the outset, decided to be present at the funeral of a man whom many considered his rival, has come opportunely to show that, in difficult time, he intends to behave as a loyal friend of the United States. He had already proved this during the Cuban crisis."

Eulogy pronounced by M. Jacques Chaban-Delmas, President of the French National Assembly

At the opening of the November 26 sitting, in the presence of Mr. Charles Bohlen, U.S. Ambassador to France, M. Jacques Chaban-Delmas, President of the French National Assembly, pronounced the following eulogy of the late President Kennedy:

"John F. Kennedy was not only the world's most powerful head of state. He was also an exceptional man.

"The murder of this hero, who fell in the flower of his youth, who knew what power and glory was, this murder in which the fate of the ancients finds expression has already taken on an historic amplitude and its echo will never die away. No, we shall not forget John F. Kennedy.

"Yesterday, in Washington, France expressed her grief through the presence of the most famous of her citizens, he who, without a doubt, already belongs to history and continues to forge the future.

"Today, the National Assembly shares as one in the mourning of the United States and of its Congress. It participates with emotion in the sorrow of the Kennedy family. Deeply shocked, it pays its respects before the anguish of this charming, worthy and courageous young woman who brought a little of the gentleness of France into the harsh existence of America's first citizen.

"Tomorrow it will be up to each and every one to pursue his task in defending and expounding the great principles shared by our two countries, principles in whose respect President Kennedy lived and also died."

M. Maurice Couve de Murville, Minister of Foreign Affairs, associated the Government with the words of the National Assembly: "The homage paid by the National Assembly marks the share taken by the French people in the mourning of the American people and shows the esteem and affection for the President who died in the line of duty."

More than 400 Deputies stood and observed 1 minute's silence. Meetings were suspended for 1 hour as a sign of mourning.

Mr. President, the U.S. News & World Report of December 2, 1963, published an article, "The Incredible Tragedy," by David Lawrence, worthy of preservation in the permanent archives of this Nation. This is a fine tribute to the memory of our gallant fallen leader, the late President John Fitzgerald Kennedy. I ask that it be printed as follows:

THE INCREDIBLE TRAGEDY

(By David Lawrence)

The American people and the peoples of the whole world mourn the death of President John F. Kennedy.

For the assassin's bullet ended the life of a young man whose sincerity of purpose, dedication to duty, and devotion to what he believed was right characterized his service to the United States. Even as he had responded to the cheers of the crowds and had ridden happily in an open automobile through the streets of Dallas, Tex., he reflected the confidence of a man with faith in his fellow citizens.

What shall we say of the insane impulse which caused a despicable individual to destroy the President of this great country? Americans, regardless of party or faction, believe in morality and in respect for human life.

Three times before in American history a President has been killed while in office—Abraham Lincoln, James A. Garfield, and William McKinley. In each instance, individuals of an erratic or unbalanced mentality were responsible. This strange hand of fate has taken from the White House four men of dedicated character. It is difficult to understand these tragic events in our history. For as a President is removed from this mortal life in a few minutes, there emerges a feeling that life and sudden death, even in high office, are beyond the comprehension of our finite minds.

We do know that every year the number of crimes committed by deranged individuals is increasing. Can we not devise some means of detecting in advance the symptoms of such behavior in our society?

The Secret Service has grappled with this problem for decades. Observation of the houses and buildings along a parade route, inspection in advance, and a multitude of bodyguards close at hand have evidently provided no sure preventive.

It was during a theater performance in Washington, on the night of April 14, 1865, that Abraham Lincoln, sitting in the Presidential box, was shot by an erratic individual, who was subsequently killed for his crime by soldiers in pursuit of him.

James A. Garfield was shot by a disappointed office-seeker as he was entering the railroad station in Washington on July 2, 1881. His assailant was hanged.

William McKinley was shot by a man who came up to shake hands with him after a Presidential speech at the Pan-American Exposition in Buffalo on September 6, 1901. The revolver was concealed beneath a big handkerchief and thus escaped notice. The assassin, an anarchist, was electrocuted.

These happenings cast a cloud of gloom over the whole of our country. But somehow we do not seem to be able to forestall such incidents.

One wonders whether Presidents will venture hereafter to make public appearances except in halls and auditoriums under tight security guard. But our Presidents have been brave men who seem to feel that they must go before the people and take the risks that come with the duties of high office.

John F. Kennedy had that spirit of bravery and felt that he must see the people frequently, without regard to danger. On these pages in 1959 there was printed a detailed story of Lieutenant Kennedy's heroic exploits as commander of a PT boat in the Pacific during World War II. He was never governed by fear. His personal courage has been demonstrated on more than one occasion.

Mr. Kennedy came into office at a crucial time in world history when emotions ran high and differences of opinion on domestic and foreign questions were deepseated. But no President has tackled as many problems and such a variety of delicate and difficult issues as those into which John F. Kennedy delved so deeply during his 34 months in office.

President Kennedy listened patiently to his advisers and showed a remarkable familiarity with detail. Perhaps his outstanding characteristic was his readiness to listen to the arguments of those who disagreed with him. If a resolution of differences was possible so as to lessen friction and bring about an agreement, he conscientiously sought such a solution. He had shown the same attitude when he was in the Senate and in the House.

Mr. Kennedy manifested, in other words, a spirit of mediation and a desire to attain out of every controversy the maximum good for the public. For he adopted again and again the maxim that "half a loaf is better than none."

In world affairs, Mr. Kennedy exhibited a rare quality of patience and restraint. Whatever setbacks his administration may have encountered around the world, the fact remains that he tried his utmost to preserve peace for his country while maintaining the military strength so necessary to deter an enemy.

It is hard to believe that our President is dead at 46. It is hard to believe that this man who sought so earnestly to serve his country should be cut down in the prime of life.

This is an incredible tragedy.

Mr. President, Dr. Jenny Lind Porter, who has been selected as poet laureate of Texas for 1964, author of several volumes of poetry and of many separate poems printed in magazines and journals all over the world, now associate professor of English at Southwest Texas State College, has written a beautiful tribute to our martyred President, the late John F. Kennedy.

Dr. Porter has compared the spirit and dreams and hopes for a land and a people held by the Poet Robert Frost and John F. Kennedy. Her comparison, under the title, "The Poet and the President," was printed, with photographs, as the lead story on the front page of the feature section of the Austin American-Statesman on Sunday, December 15, 1963.

J. Frank Dobie, writer, philosopher, folklorist, author of many books, pamphlets, articles, sage of the southwest, historian of the cowboy and his environment, now a consultant to the Library of Congress in the field of American culture, an admirer of the late John F. Kennedy, has written feelingly of the effect of the sudden loss of Kennedy—"a citizen of the world." Mr. Dobie's tribute was printed under the title "Summing Up" in the book section of the Austin American-Statesman for Sunday, December 29, 1963.

Mr. President, I request unanimous consent that Dr. Jenny Lind Porter's article "The Poet and the President" and J. Frank Dobie's article "Summing Up" both be printed in full at this point.

[From the Austin (Tex.) American-Statesman, Dec. 15, 1963]

THE POET AND THE PRESIDENT

(By Jenny Lind Porter)

(NOTE.—Dr. Jenny Lind Porter, Poet Laureate of Texas for 1964, is assistant professor of English at Southwest Texas State College. Her biography appears this winter in the new issue of the Dictionary of International Biography, just published in London. She appears regularly on KLRN–TV with a program called "The Poet Laureate and the Poets.")

This could be called a tribute to John Fitzgerald Kennedy through the lines of the poet who read at his inauguration—Robert Frost. Who of us would have thought that day, watching the octogenarian poet and the boyish, handsome, 43-year-old President, that each was soon to complete his "gift outright" to the Nation? And they were magnificent gifts. In this month, December, when we talk of the gifts of the Magi laid at the feet of the Christ child, we can remember that we may follow Kennedy and Frost on a trail of the modern Magi, through a land that realizes westward because we have laid our dreams at the master's feet and are fully aware that a princely star looks down on Cape Kennedy and that frankincense and myrrh have come in great mailbags to a Dallas police station for the widow of Officer Tippit. Our country, such as she is, such as she will become, is perhaps more prayerful this week than it has ever been, more soul searching, and more humble.

Frost and Kennedy had much in common. Each was a visionary, a dreamer. Naturally, for the poet; not so naturally, with a President. Out of our 36, those Presidents possessed of great dreams and similarly endowed with courage and social conscience and eloquence number only 4 or 5: one thinks of a Jefferson, a Lincoln, an F.D.R., a Kennedy.

> "We are the music makers
> And we are the dreamers of dreams,
> Wandering by lone sea breakers
> And sitting by desolate streams.
> One man, with a dream, at pleasure,
> Shall go forth and conquer a crown;
> And three with a new song's measure
> Can trample an empire down."

John Fitzgerald Kennedy, a millionaire's son, might have chosen the easy route of champagne and yachts and silk suits. Instead that redheaded Irishman chose to fight for his country in war and in peace. Frost has a poem about how a great man surveys life as if it were a road that forks; in his spiritual calm, this man faces the struggles which the little-traveled road presents, and he sets forth upon it rather than upon the broad highway. So Kennedy set forth to war, to foreign countries, and even to Dallas, for one must commit himself, and he must not live in fear. Had he taken the other road, he might not lie with a flame over his grave at Arlington Cemetery—but recollect that the flame is over his grave, and over our lives, and over our Nation—indeed, over the earth, because of a safe road not taken. Total commitment to an ideal is a beautiful, awesome thing.

> "Two roads diverged in a yellow wood,
> And sorry I could not travel both
> And be one traveler, long I stood
> And looked down one as far as I could
> To where it bent in the undergrowth;
>
> "Then took the other, as just as fair,
> And having perhaps the better claim
> Because it was grassy and wanted wear;
> Though as for that the passing there
> Had worn them really about the same,
>
> "And both that morning equally lay
> In leaves no step had trodden black.
> O, I kept the first for another day,
> Yet knowing how way leads on to way,
> I doubted if I should ever come back.
>
> "I shall be telling this with a sigh
> Somewhere ages and ages hence:
> Two roads diverged in a wood and I—
> I took the one less traveled by,
> And that has made all the difference."

John Fitzgerald Kennedy was a great humanitarian. He loved people, and he was shining with that love when translated to another sphere. This is true of Frost, too: "Earth's the place for love. I don't know where it's likely to go better." Of his students, he said, "I'm very thick with 'em." You and I recall President Kennedy's concern that artificial barriers erected by race and creed should be obliterated for national harmony. Thomas Browne used to say that he was in England everywhere.

President Kennedy won hearts when he sympathized with the people of Berlin, saying in fellow feeling, "Ich bin ein Berliner." One thinks of Frost's kindred understanding in "Mending Wall."

Something there is that doesn't love a wall. Frost tells us that he and his Yankee neighbor would go along the stone wall which divided their properties (and which nature kept tumbling down) and repair the gaps—senselessly, it seemed to him, for after all—

> "He is all pine and I am apple orchard.
> My apple trees will never get across
> And eat the cones under his pines, I tell him.
> He only says, 'Good fences make good neighbors.'
> Spring is the mischief in me, and I wonder
> If I could put a notion in his head:
> Why do they make good neighbors? Isn't it
> Where there are cows? But here there are no cows.
> Before I built a wall I'd ask to know
> What I was walling in or walling out
> And to whom I was like to give offense.
> Something there is that doesn't love a wall,
> That wants it down."

To Frost it was as if the Yankee farmer were out of place in his stonelaying as a Druid priest in New England. When Kennedy looked at the wall, he saw its dark blot on progress and civilization. The same compassion he applied to the race question in America.

We had in Kennedy a man who loved his work. Frost said that he wanted to "lodge a few poems where they'll be hard to get rid of, like pebbles." They both were men of ideas, philosophical, thoughtful men, who wanted to communicate. "Triumph in poetry," Frost warned, "comes in facing up to darkness. You had better decide what is worth failing with as well as what is worth succeeding in." Both Frost and Kennedy wanted knowledge put to work. "Piling up knowledge," according to Frost, "is as bad as piling up money indefinitely. You have to begin sometime to kick around what you know." "And don't dry up," he admonished an audience of teachers. "A prune can never become a jucy plum by any amount of soaking. Better not to dry up in the first place." Everyone knows the story of how Frost employed seamstresses to convert the varicolored silk and satin hoods from his 33 honorary doctorates into a pair of stunning patch-work quilts. Kennedy was a Harvard graduate, with many honorary degrees, but he kept going—reading, traveling, talking with people. I find his spirit in Robert Frost's "Two Tramps in Mud Time," where the poet reminds us that we must come to work with a spirit of love as well as with a thought of our daily bread. Kennedy didn't need the salary he made at the White House to feed Jacqueline and Caroline and John-John; Frost didn't need to earn his living chopping wood, as the lumberjacks did who wanted to do his work for pay and take the ax from him. Love and spiritual hunger have their claims.

> "Only where love and need are one
> And the work is play for moral stakes.
> Is the deed ever really done
> For heaven and the future's sake."

When Frost was young, he knew great suffering. He was born March 26, 1874, in San Francisco, but his father was from Massachusetts—another Kennedy tie—and after the father died in 1885, Mrs. Frost and the two children came back to New England to live with Grandfather Frost. In 1895, Frost and Elinor White were married (she died in 1938), and Grandfather Frost bought a farm in Derry and told the young man he must not sell it for 10 years. "Nobody can make a living from writing poetry," said Grandfather to Robert. "I'll give you a year to try." "Give me 20," was the quick reply. In 1912 Frost sold the farm and went to England on a shoestring, taking his family along—and with the publication of "A Boy's Will" and "North of Boston," at last, at age 39, his career was launched. So both Frost and Kennedy—the latter with his earnest pursuit of career, his family sorrows, and his back ailment—grew through sorrows perhaps unknown to the public which sees only their fame and not their heartaches. Each man came into his real soul stride in his thirties. Each lost several children. Each had family griefs and times when it looked as if the shadows would engulf him.

> "I have been one acquainted with the night.
> I have walked out in rain—and back in rain.
> I have outwalked the furtherest city light.
> I have looked down the saddest city lane."

Spiritual to the core, each survived hatred and jealousy; for these come to one who is a distinct individual.

> "Some say the world will end in fire,
> Some say in ice.
> For what I've tasted of desire
> I hold with those who favor fire.
> But if it had to perish twice,
> I think I know enough of hate
> To say that destruction ice
> Is also great
> And would suffice."

But the eternal flame conquers the ice of hatred. Kennedy was not afraid that harmony wouldn't prevail. He faced our friends and foes with that firmness and sweet, shining look born of a man who gets down on his knees. With the same optimism, Frost answered reporters who feared atomic destruction. "If we all went up in an atomic explosion," he said, "when we came out the other side and brushed ourselves off, somebody would say, 'Wasn't that something?'" "You can't exterminate us," he continued, "we're like lice or bedbugs." The President was just as hopeful, just as witty.

Each man was a friend of wind and sea and trees and stars. "This must be the most beautiful place in the world," President Kennedy told a friend of the vista in Arlington Cemetery where he was later buried. The river and the trees spoke to him, even as the tree in Frost's poem:

> "Tree at my window, window tree,
> My sash is lowered when night comes on;
> But let there never be curtain drawn
> Between you and me.

> "Vague dream head lifted out of the ground,
> And thing next most diffuse to cloud,
> Not all your light tongues talking aloud
> Could be profound.

> "But tree, I have seen you taken and tossed,
> And if you have seen me when I slept,
> You have seen me when I was taken and swept
> And all but lost.

> "That day she put our heads together,
> Fate had her imagination about her,
> Your head so much concerned with outer,
> Mine, with inner, weather."

John Fitzgerald Kennedy was a hero, fittingly given a hero's last tribute. Frost wrote a poem called, "A Soldier," which describes the hero as a fallen lance that lies pointed as it plowed the dust, and ends:

> "But this we know, the obstacle that checked
> And tripped the body, shot the spirit on
> Further than target ever showed or shone."

Somehow, as I wrote this, I felt the presence of Robert Frost, and I knew that the poet would want me to close this tribute to President Kennedy with the reminder that he has given us the torch for a new generation and that we can look at his example and shut our eyes and think of the lady in the harbor, with the inscription beside her torch—"Give me your tired, your poor, your huddled masses yearning to be free * * * I lift my lamp beside the golden door * * *" and admit that the responsible Americans have—

> "* * * Promises to keep
> And miles to go before (they) sleep."

[From the Austin (Tex.) American-Statesman, Dec. 29, 1963]

SUMMING UP

(By J. Frank Dobie)

The last long night of a long year has almost passed. As I look back, I seem to myself increasingly unimportant. I went to California and worked for a month with nothing else on my mind but a book that I have at last finished—to be published away along in 1964. During the year I have seen cherished friends, gone hunting, read some fine things, read things that incensed me, watched the pageant of life pass by.

Nothing experienced went into so deeply or will remain so deeply impressed on my mind and in my nature as the sudden vanishing of our President, John Fitzgerald Kennedy, at Dallas, Tex., a little past high noon on November 22, 1963. During the weeks that have passed since he was killed, contemplation of his noble nature has made me feel "a richer woe." I never met him or saw his face except through the mediums of television and photography, but to me, as to millions of others, he personified hope, growth, humanity, superb intelligence, wonderful understanding of nations and peoples.

Like Benjamin Franklin and Thomas Jefferson, he was a citizen of the world. It is true that he came out of

Massachusetts, but who thinks of him as belonging to Massachusetts? While the Republic was still young, Alexander Hamilton said that for President a man was needed who could "think continentally." Times have so changed and spaces have so shrunken that now the President must think globally. John F. Kennedy's thinking compassed the world and looked far into space.

He never spoke to Buncombe County. When he spoke to the United States of America, he spoke also to nations of the world, as in his inaugural address: "My fellow Americans: ask not what your country can do for you; ask what you can do for your country. My fellow citizens of the world: ask not what America will do for you, but what together we can do for the freedom of man."

For him freedom was—is—a state of life far beyond the bare differences between being and not being a slave—the difference that Lincoln's Proclamation of Emancipation achieved 100 years ago. In June 1963, President Kennedy said: "If an American, because his skin is dark, cannot eat in a restaurant open to the public; if he cannot send his children to the best public school available; if he cannot vote for the public officials who represent him; if, in short, he cannot enjoy the full and free life which all of us want, then who among us would be content to have the color of his skin changed and stand in his place? Who among us would then be content with the counsels of patience and delay?"

Compassion was a word familiar to John Kennedy. I dreamed a dream in which a lad from the sticks, unfamiliar with travel, was inducted into the army and given a ticket that would carry him from a place in southern Texas a thousand miles north. He appeared to be about 18 years old. In the strange ways of dreams, his color was indeterminate; now white, now brown, now black. He was shy, bashful, ignorant of travel procedure. He sat alone in the train all day. Night came. He had not a bite to eat. He was hungry. A man walked down the aisle by the lad and stopped. The man smiled, not at all patronizingly, and spoke. The lad stood up. The man was plainly President Kennedy. "You look lost and hungry," he said. "I am going to the diner to eat. Come with me."

His words were not in an accent the lad was used to, but they expressed a concern for fellow human beings that he understood and that went into him. All this was just a dream. Presidents do not walk alone down the aisles of railroad cars. They are transported in special airplanes. The act and the words in the dream would, nevertheless, have been in character for John F. Kennedy.

Compassion was not—is not—enough. Kennedy laid strong emphasis on knowledge and thought; on cultivated intellect. The good hearted who are ignorant can no more govern than a ditchdigger can pilot a jet-propelled airplane. Some Frenchman spoke of the "intellectual and spiritual aura" that Kennedy moved in. He did not make the White House a "prison" occupied by a man holding "the loneliest job in the world." He was at home there. He and Jacqueline Kennedy made it so bright that its brightness lighted the land. They brought a new style to Washington, even if obstructing chairmen of legislative committees—brought to power by

an outmoded seniority system—never felt it. They seem barricaded against the brightness of intelligent vitality.

Under President Lyndon Johnson they have continued to block government. The blocking powers have been set against the Kennedy-Johnson policy of treating openly nations that discard "venomous hatreds." No country is the czar of the whole world. In the words of Kennedy, "If we cannot end now our differences, at least we can help make the world safe for diversity." The New Frontier has proved itself something beyond a political tag. It has changed many minds holding the stubborn opinion that any approach on America's part with communist powers is no better than carrying the Munich umbrella of appeasement.

John F. Kennedy, in my judgment, revealed himself in no higher form than in choosing—always with excellence in mind—individuals to go with him. Two chosen ones stand out; the woman of marked dignity, brightness and judgment who became his wife and the man of extraordinary competence, fidelity, and understanding who became his Vice President and then our President.

President Lyndon Johnson will not fail in bringing freedom of life to more individuals and in forwarding peace to our own and other nations of the world. In the words of a prayer I heard my father decades ago say over and over, "Bless those in authority over us."

Mr. President, Dr. Gaston Foote, one of the most learned and devout men in Texas, a great leader at the First Methodist Church of Fort Worth, preached a moving memorial service to the memory of our late martyred President, John F. Kennedy, on Sunday, November 24, at Fort Worth, Tex. I ask that Dr. Foote's memorial tribute to the late beloved John F. Kennedy be printed as follows:

OUR PRESIDENT—A MEMORIAL SERVICE,
NOVEMBER 24, 1963

(By Gaston Foote)

PRAYER

Eternal Spirit of God, source of all light and life, the sudden cataclysmic events of the world have driven us to our knees. We humbly kneel at Thy feet today because, if we were not willing to come, we were forced to come. Our desolation and bewilderment has commanded us to seek Thy presence for Thou alone art the source of our strength. The frailties of man are apparent all about us. We are but passing shadows in the mighty parade of human history. Only Thou art from everlasting to everlasting.

We offer our prayer, O God, for our sin-sick world. Millions of Thy children of every race, color, and creed have been stunned by the events of the moment. Perplexed by problems without solution, buffeted by sorrow, baffled by bullets of hate, we feel a dreadful sense of loneliness when men of great promise and power are taken from our midst. Bless the sorrowing peoples of the earth whose hope of freedom from the tyranny of oppression and poverty was centered in the devotion and the courage of the late President of the United States, John F. Kennedy.

We offer our prayer, O God, for our own beloved country. We are a people of many nations. The cultural heritages of the entire world flow within the bloodstream of our beloved America. From Boston to San Diego, from Seattle to Miami, we are a varied people. But we are a united people in that we rejoice in our liberties and glory in our sacred traditions. May we never cease to thank Thee for the noble heritage of our forefathers, bequeathed to us as free citizens of a free country. We bless Thy Holy Name for such men as Washington and Jefferson and Lincoln who conceived a country that was, itself, conceived in liberty and dedicated to the proposition that all men are created equal. We bless Thy Holy Name for John F. Kennedy, who so nobly and fearlessly epitomized this spirit of democracy with liberty and justice for all. We thank Thee for his strong heart, his indomitable courage, his untiring zeal, his unalterable belief in the American dream.

We raise our prayers to Thee, O God, for his beloved family. Bless his stricken father on his bed of affliction. Deal Thou graciously with his devoted mother. Hold within the hollow of Thy loving hand the gracious First Lady whose grief is beyond our power of comprehension. Fill with Thy love the great vacancy in the hearts of his beloved Caroline and John, Junior. May the united prayers of the Nation sustain them in this, their darkest hour.

We raise our prayers to Thee, O God, in behalf of John Connally, Governor of our great State. Bless the doctors and the nurses who assist the Great Physician in bringing him back to health and usefulness. Put Thine arm of love around the shoulders of his devoted wife, his sons, his daughter in this hour of trial.

We raise our prayers to Thee, O God, in behalf of our new President, Lyndon B. Johnson. Keep him in the strength of Thine undergirding love and sustain him in his momentous decisions by Thine infinite wisdom. May all of the finest resources of all of the people in America be put at his disposal that he may rise to greatness in this great hour. May he truly be our President, under the leadership of God.

We commit our lives, our fortunes and our future into Thy hands as we pray in the name of our crucified and risen Lord. Amen.

EULOGY

Four times in the history of the United States a President has died of an assassin's bullet. Abraham Lincoln was killed by John Wilkes Booth in 1865 while attending a play in the Ford Theater in Washington. James A. Garfield was shot by Charles J. Guiteau in 1881 while waiting to catch a train in the railroad station in the same city. William McKinley was killed while attending a reception in Buffalo, N.Y., by Leon Czolgosz. And now our own beloved President John F. Kennedy has been killed by an assassin's bullet.

As one of millions upon millions of persons who mourn his passing, I should like to lift up some of the many admirable characteristics of his short, eventful life.

He was a family man. He came from a closely knit family of nine children. When the Kennedys all gathered at the family retreat at Hyannis Port, it must have been quite a hilarious occasion. And no man seemed to be more devoted to his own little family than our President. Despite the press of duties of the state which would have destroyed the ordinary man, John F. Kennedy took time to be with his children. Caroline, as familiar to most of us as are the children of our neighborhood, seemed to be "daddy's girl." John-John was the apple of his eye. It was not unusual for Washingtonians to see the Kennedys strolling across the White House lawn holding the hands of their two children.

In many ways the President showed his devotion for his brilliant and beautiful wife, Jackie. She in turn must have been extremely proud of her illustrious husband. One can well imagine what a different United States we would have if all our families were as devoted to each other as were the members of our first family.

Our President was a religious man. He never insisted that his faith be practiced by those of other faiths but he insisted on practicing his faith. Seldom did a week pass without some news photographer snapping a picture of the President, either alone or with his family, entering a church door for divine services. He did not take time out for worship to be seen of men but rather to get himself a clearer vision of God.

Moreover he was a devoted student of the Holy Scripture. His speeches were filled with quotations from the Prophets, the Psalms, the Gospels and the writings of Paul. Like his predecessor, Abraham Lincoln, he made wide use of the eternal truths recorded in Biblical literature.

What a reproach our President's record at church is to some of us. We frequently say we are too busy to attend church. But with the intolerable burden of the responsibilities of state upon his shoulders he found time for God.

Our President was a man of sympathetic, human understanding. Born to wealth, he never lost the common touch. His sincere sympathy seemed always to be with the poor. He said, "If a free society cannot help the many who are poor it cannot help the few who are rich." His major social legislation was in behalf of the poor, the sick, the unemployed, the exploited.

One reason for his sympathetic understanding was the many sorrows in his own life. His older brother, whom he idolized, was killed in World War II. A sister was killed in a tragic plane crash. His father almost died of a stroke 2 years ago. Barely 3 months ago he buried part of his own heart in a little grave in Boston when his second son died before he was 2 days old. As if this were not enough, he suffered throughout his entire adult life from an injured back. When he spoke feelingly of the needs of his fellow Americans, there was a ring of utter sincerity in his voice.

John F. Kennedy was a man of great wisdom. His mind seem to be on fire. It sparkled with a scintillating brilliancy. He was a prodigious reader and had the uncanny ability to read with great speed and clear understanding. He could dip down in any period of American history and feel completely at home. His choice of words was superb, his profundity of thought was startling. Yet he was not bookish. He did not seek truth for truth's sake; rather for the sake of action in today's world. He knew whereof he spoke and sought to lead the Nation into greater fields of endeavor.

Our President was a man of great courage. He wrote a significant book, entitled "Profiles of Courage" which, in retrospect, epitomizes his own life. Upon enlistment in the Navy he was given a desk job in Washington. Quickly tiring of his routine labors he finally became captain of a PT boat in the Pacific. The boat was cut in two by the enemy and he and his crew floundered for hours in the water. He swam for miles to an island dragging an injured member of the crew behind him holding in his teeth a strap of his comrade's lifesaver.

In his inaugural address he numerated the hardships through which Americans must pass to effect world security. Then he said, "I do not shrink from this responsibility, I welcome it." Hardly had he taken his seat in the White House when the Cuban crisis broke in all its fury. At the time when we needed a strong hand at the helm of the Ship of State John Kennedy was equal to the occasion. We were perhaps never closer to world holocaust than when the voice from Washington said to Mr. Khrushchev, "We demand that the offensive weapons now in Cuba be removed." The quarantine of the island and the turning back of the ships from Russia laden with war supplies is familiar to us all. Only a man with great courage could do that.

He showed no less courage amid problems of a domestic nature. When the hands of history pointed to the University of Mississippi crisis as one that demanded immediate settlement the words from Washington were loud and clear. Said the President, "We have every right to disagree with the law of our land; we have no right to defy it. Defiance of any law upon which we disagree would lead to defiance of all law." Once again a courageous voice had given stability in a critical hour.

Our President was a committed man. He spoke to the youth of America about the American dream as being something yet to be realized. He challenged us all to make democracy real not to 85 percent of the American people but to all of them. He challenged each of us to make our individual contribution to human welfare by the words: "Ask not what your country can do for you but what you can do for your country." In the establishment of the Peace Corps he challenged youth to change its image of the "Ugly American" to one of service above self. He was committed to the great American dream.

He was committed to world peace. His efforts were conciliatory, calculated to calm. He said "Let us never negotiate out of fear but let us never fear to negotiate." Stanch supporter of the United Nations, he felt that peaceful negotiation was infinitely better than provocative irritation. He gave the supreme measure of his devotion to his country under the leadership of his God.

And now the assassin's bullet has found its mark. Hate pulled the trigger that killed him. And we who have let emotion rather than reason lead us, we who were quick to be critical and reluctant to help, we who were blinded by our prejudices have allowed hate groups to grow up in our midst until the very atmosphere has been conducive to producing the tragedy that has befallen.

I call you to an altar of penance in this our darkest hour. Let hate give way to love and vindictiveness give way to valor. Rise up, O men of God, with love in your heart for all of your fellow Americans everywhere and with knees bowed in penance and your hand in the hand of God, act and live as men worthy of our great tradition.

There is no benediction to this service. After you have knelt at the altar, let only the benediction of God go with you into the dawn of a better tomorrow.

Mr. President, Dr. John Barclay, minister of the Central Christian Church of Austin, Tex., a devout and scholarly man, delivered an invocation at the inauguration of President John F. Kennedy in January 1961.

After the cruel assassination of President Kennedy occurred November 22, this distinguished clergyman delivered a moving sermon on November 24, 1963. I agree with Dr. Barclay's estimate that "We would not see President Kennedy's like again in this century." It is a thoughtful message, voiced in sorrow, but filled with love and understanding. I ask unanimous consent that the inauguration invocation and the sermon of November 24, entitled, "A Vital, Living Memory," be extended in my remarks.

INVOCATION AT PRESIDENT KENNEDY'S INAUGURATION, JANUARY 1961

(By Rev. Dr. John Barclay, pastor of the Central Christian Church, Austin, Tex.)

Eternal God, our Father, we pause again to acknowledge that in Thy presence we are living and moving and in Thee alone we have our being.

We are thankful for the great and good men raised up by Thee to lead us in the past. Bless these leaders of recent decades, still with us, who have led us through these tumultuous times, to live out their years with the consciousness of the admiration and appreciation of a grateful people.

We thank Thee for our country, for the manner in which Thou didst lead our fathers to establish this Nation in which all men have equal rights to life, liberty, and the pursuit of happiness. Help us to so unite duties and rights that there may develop in all our people a new maturity that will continually produce life more abundant, liberty more responsible, and spiritual satisfactions more abiding.

Our Father, we pray for the Congress and the courts and all public servants, that there may come from their deep dedication and high patriotism a new inspiration for all Americans.

We thank Thee, our Father, for the two men whom we have elected to lead us, who today assume the almost unbearable responsibilities of their exalted offices. We thank Thee for their high intelligence and their characters made great by hard work and devoted services to their country in war and in peace.

Bless them with vigorous health, great strength, and courageous boldness to lead our Nation out into a new era and into a new frontier. Help them to lead us to return to the virtues of our fathers: industry, honesty, and frugality.

Under their leadership may we recapture the faith of our fathers and their spiritual optimism that problems are soluble, that what ought to be can be, that neighborly potential is inherent in mankind.

FAMILY SUPPORT SOUGHT

Our Father, we pray Thou will bless Lyndon B. Johnson and add Thy strength to his strength as he continues to lead men of divergent views to reconcile their differences in the interest of the common good of our Nation and of all mankind. Add Thy wisdom, grace, and power to his great abilities, and may his willingness to serve bring strength and help to the President.

May the beauty, understanding, and spiritual support of his family continue to bless his life all his years.

We pray, Our Father, for John F. Kennedy as he assumes the heavy burden of great leadership in these ominous times. Bless his family that in all the turmoil of his public life they may be for him an oasis of quiet peace and rest.

When he faces great and solemn hours of decision, decisions upon which may hang the fate of all mankind, when he must ascend the lonely pinnacle, help him then to know that he is not alone; that Thou art with him to guide him in making decisions of wisdom and righteousness for his Nation and the whole world.

May the magnitude of his leadership inspire tens of millions of Americans into a dedicated involvement in their country's progress. And may peace crown his years. In the Master's name, we pray. Amen.

——

A VITAL, LIVING MEMORY

(By John Barclay)

Friends, we come this morning to worship God and to remember in sorrow and grief our slain President. I am sure we all deplore the increase in violence in these postwar years. Much of it is motivated by economic greed as in bank robberies, and in various types of stickup jobs. Political hatred as a motivation for violence has been greatly increased in this generation. This type of hatred has now climaxed in the assassination of President Kennedy. This happens because the Nation is being brainwashed by certain newspapers and by radio and TV commentators and as these editorials and other approaches are poured into people's minds day after day, there builds up a sense of hatred that may turn into violence. This situation marks out clearly the task of the pulpit and the church generally for years to come. It is simply this, we must reach, and preach, and practice this great principle that the law of love must become our way of life. We must continually preach against the sin of hate.

The New Testament is very clear on this. It says, "he that hateth his brother is a murderer." This we must remember. We can become mad, I mean literally unbalanced, through hatred. If we hate Lyndon Johnson; if we hate Ralph Yarborough; if we hate John Tower; if we hate John Connally, we are doubly sinners. It is a sin to hate any person, for every person in the world is the child of God. It is a sin to hate anybody, because it may lead to murder. It is a particular sin to hate people whom we have elected to lead us in public office, for this is a sin against democracy, and both are sins against God. If we have not learned yet how to be good citizens in a democracy where we speak with our votes, and change governments with our votes, then we are still children, in government. This has led to the assassination of other Presidents—three others, and two other attempts. This country went for nearly 75 years without an attempt to assassinate a President; then at the close of the Civil War, it began. Since Alfred the Great was crowned King of England in 871—and he was the first person ever to speak of England as one country, as a single land—and from then until now, nearly 1100 years, there has been no assassination of a British sovereign.

Friends, we must learn the deeper meaning of democracy that politics is the way of life in America. It is the art of the possible. The people elect their Governors, their Presidents, their Congressmen, their Senators, their city councilmen. We elect those that lead us. The very fact that we elect them puts us under a peculiar obligation to respect their leadership and most of all to respect and admire the offices which they fill. We must respect the office of authority in government and the way of dissent must be by nonviolence and voting.

There seems to me there is a double tragedy in the death of John F. Kennedy. First, his youth, his ability, his almost perfect preparation for the Presidency, the great fulfillment of his task now goes unfinished. This is the first tragedy.

The second tragedy is his depth of greatness in a new worldwide setting of opportunity; this was lost to our world. I sat and listened to him on that blustery, cold day as he gave his inaugural address, and there he pictured his vision of our country in a new frame of reference, in the world setting of tomorrow. I sat there and thought of two great men who were sitting on the platform. These men I had admired; men that I had often saluted in my heart because they were courageous men. I am speaking, of course, of General Eisenhower and ex-President Truman. These men had to make terrible decisions and they made them. They were great leaders and great Americans. But Mr. Kennedy was the first man to be President who was born in this century and as he finished this address, it seemed to me that his mind and his plans and his vision, were in the history of the future. Here was the stream of time into which his leadership and genius would be poured. This man in his 3 short years in the Presidency gave an image of America to the world that I believe will be an image in fulfillment for the rest of this century.

First, he wanted to talk about peace, like his predecessors, from the standpoint of strength. This we have. But it was a peace of reason that he wanted, and he was reasonable, in seeking it. His representatives at the peace conference have published now the "American Blueprint for the Peace Race," which is one of the most intelligent and forward-looking and hopeful documents that has ever come from the State Department. I hope you will read it word for word. It is a 35-page booklet. This is the dream of the future for mankind—to get out from under this nuclear cloud of fear and dread. That was first: that in our generation we begin to secure the peace for mankind. And his second great ideal was prosperity; to get the economy going; to lift up every year more hundreds of thousands of people who will live on a comfort level of life where they enjoy the good things that are created in our land. And the third was like unto it; namely, national sharing. He said to the Congress just the other day that "I cannot do my duty as President of this land if you are going to cut foreign aid, and cut and cut and cut." This was part of his program. This is a part of his ideal of life that he knew first in his family—simply, that if you have wealth, you must match it with responsibility. This is not just for persons; this is for nations. No rich nation in a poor world can ever be secure and safe, and this was a great, new ideal begun in the days of Mr. Truman and continued in the days of his successor and continued also by Mr. Kennedy. But this was his ideal to see not only our land lifted up, but also the whole world to a new level of prosperity, and mutual helpfulness.

And then he had a fourth very great ideal upon which he staked his very life, his political life; namely, that every citizen's rights should be respected by the people and protected by the Government. Friends, this image of his country was personified in his own life. The flowers in the baptistry this morning are red roses because we want to symbolize his courage and his love and his sacrifice. His was a pure life, with a certain mature innocence. He knew that if somebody wanted to kill him, he could. There is no way to completely protect a President. But he never could make up his mind that anybody wanted to kill him. So he traveled more freely probably at times than he should have. His was a simple but strong and sincere faith in God; his religion was expressed by his churchmanship. The record shows that in nearly 3 years in the Presidency he never missed a Sunday going to church. Wherever he was in the world, he arranged to be close enough to a church to attend it, when Sunday came.

However difficult was his life, and however heavy the burdens of responsibility of his office, he felt that there was a duty that he had to his God, to his family, and to himself that he needed to worship; that he needed to go to church and experience again, as all Catholics do at the mass, the crucifixion of our Lord. In this he gave an example to all of us, to all of his citizens. He was just not satisfied to give his money to his church; he gave it his personal attention and his time. You have probably heard on the television what people have thought all over the country. I have this quotation from an Austin high school boy—which moved me deeply. He said, "Somehow I felt so safe while he was alive." He probably had never thought this before he died. He just went along taking things for granted and then when this tragedy struck—quickly—here in our own Texas, it stunned him, and then as he thought back, he felt that this man could lead us in ways of peace and mutual helpfulness.

And questions are being asked—not just by high school students and children, or college students, but by all of us. They are asking the question: Is there really anything to the doctrine of divine providence? Does God care? Does He care whether this man was protected; whether this other man with evil thoughts should kill him like that [snaps fingers]—and probably a second after the bullet hit, he was never aware of anything. Does God care about these things? And, of course, we answer: God does care. God cares about us all, whether it is the President of the United States or a nameless and an unknown peasant, that falls; God cares. Jesus went into this with such infinite detail, that He said: "The very hairs of your head are numbered. Not a sparrow falls without the Father's concern." This is the very basis of our religion. Then why does it happen? This is the price of freedom. When God divided His sovereignty with mankind and gave us freedom, then we help make the decisions about life and what happens in life.

What is left of John F. Kennedy? Tomorrow in a great formal ceremony before members of almost all the nations of the world they will inter his body among the immortal dead of this Nation there in Arlington. I know many of you have gone over there into the cemetery and paused on the front porch of Robert E. Lee's home. There many of the great and immortal dead of our country lie buried. And there they will inter his mortal remains, and that is what goes. But what stays—what remains? What is left? And this is the important thing. This is the thing that every preacher tries to say to people who are sorrowing at a funeral—this is difficult at times, because the spiritual atmosphere is not thrown around funerals as much as we would like, but what we are saying is that his vital, living memory continues to live. The glory of his life, his high purposes, his courage, his sacrifice, his high sense of duty, his great vision live on in all the people that loved him and followed him.

Thirty years ago I heard a story of a man who had come back from China. He had gone way out in the western province of China, Sikiang, and he said he saw there on the semidesert a little hut and way in the distance there was something shining on the top of the roof. When he got there he saw "Standard Oil" on the piece of tin that was on the roof, that was what was shining. But this herdsman asked him in; they had language difficulty but one thing he understood—there on the wall of this hut way out in western China was a picture of Abraham Lincoln, who had been slain 70 years before by an assassin.

This man and his family who were destined to live in poverty and squalor all their lives had some touch of dignity put into their souls by the fact that they could admire and get some inspiration from this man that came up from poverty, came up from the people, and yet became one of the great and dynamic men of history. The deathless quality of love and honorable character, and service to others live on. Indeed these are released by death. This we have always known about Jesus. As long as He was Jesus of Nazareth, He could be in only one place at a time; He could talk only to one group; He could heal only one person at a time; He had the limitations of the flesh, the limitations of time and space; but as soon as He rose from the dead, and became an immortal soul, He was freed from these limitations and Jesus could dwell in a hundred million minds at the same moment and He could bring healing and health and inspiration to millions around the world at the same time. And this is what is released in death—the limitations of the flesh. And we take this as the perfect case in the world. But there is no reason why we should limit this truth and not take this same ideal and apply it, take this same truth and apply it to the good and the great of all generations. Because out of this outpouring of life into the stream of humanity there goes this spiritual food, this mental lift, this guidance of the spirit for people not only who knew him, of people who were present, not only his contemporaries but if he is great enough, if he lifts his soul high enough in life, he lives on forever in other lives made better by his presence.

This morning as we close this memorial to our fallen President, I want to carry on a tradition that has been in this church since its beginning, 116½ years ago, we have never closed a worship hour in this church without opening the doors of the church to any who would come in and join us, either by letter or statement or the simple confession of Christ's saviourhood. Come and walk with us in this high tradition of our Saviour.

TRIBUTES BY

Hon. Eugene J. McCarthy

OF MINNESOTA

Mr. President, much has been said and written in memory of and in tribute to our late President, John F. Kennedy, in the sad and overcast days since his death. One of the most moving tributes I have read was delivered by Daniel F. Foley, national commander of the American Legion, at a joint Legion and Auxiliary memorial service held in Minneapolis on November 23. Commander Foley pointed out that "President Kennedy gave his life for his country as surely as if he had died in combat," and pledged the American Legion to a continuing and active role in the struggle for justice and freedom as the best memorial to our late President. I ask that Commander Foley's remarks be printed as follows:

REMARKS BY DANIEL F. FOLEY, AMERICAN LEGION NATIONAL COMMANDER, AT A JOINT LEGION AND AUXILIARY FALL CONFERENCE MEMORIAL SERVICE IN BEHALF OF PRESIDENT JOHN F. KENNEDY DELIVERED AT THE PICK-NICOLLET HOTEL, MINNEAPOLIS, MINN., NOVEMBER 23, 1963.

National President Mrs. Johnson, my fellow Americans, for some time, I have looked forward to this conference, for the wanderer yearns for home. To be home with members of my own department, where the Legion spirit is deep and where the Legion heart beats strongly.

But today we are sad. The heart of America is sad. The soul of freedom aches. Our President has died—a martyr for the cause of justice and of freedom, not just here in the United States, but throughout the world.

It is the character of the true American to love justice and to jealously regard the highest rights of man as a creature of God.

The sincere, determined efforts of President Kennedy to promote justice among men everywhere will speak well for him before the tribunal of divine justice.

It is the inborn desire of all men to be free, and throughout all of our history brave men and women of great courage have and do defend the cause of freedom. Defenders of the cause of freedom daily lay their lives on the line that freedom may endure.

President Kennedy gave his life for his country as surely as if he had died in combat, and all men of good will are crushed by this tragic event.

But again the great character of the American people, their deep love of God and loyalty to country will spring forth in all its fullness, for all the world to see, in this time of crisis.

Let no one think for a fleeting moment that this Nation will be divided in this hour of challenge.

Whatever differences of a political nature or disagreement on issues that may exist are quickly set aside as all Americans rush to accept the challenge these tragic circumstances have thrust upon our Nation.

One of the hallmarks of a free society under constitutional government is its continuity. What dictatorship can face the people of the world and say it speaks from the freely expressed will of the people?

But here in this Nation, which has now seen eight Presidents die in office, some at the hands of the assassin, such as Abraham Lincoln, James Garfield, William McKinley and now John Kennedy, the Government of the United States continues on—confident and courageous are its people—dedicated and sincere its leaders.

It is this desire to perpetuate freedom that has inspired the American Legion in its many years of fruitful service. We pledge ourselves to foster and perpetuate a 100-percent Americanism, maintain law and order, to promote peace and good will on earth, to safeguard and transmit to posterity the principles of justice, freedom and democracy. Devotion to these principles characterizes the service which John Kennedy has left to all the ages, for his life work was filled with courage, compassion for others, a deep sense of justice and a love of freedom, as God willed it when He created man.

Into the stream of challenge, created at this hour, the American Legion, a powerful force for good, may well face its most crucial hour—its most difficult test.

We believe it to be the responsibility of every American to be an active participant in the affairs of the present, in a responsible manner. Every man who would enjoy the rights and privileges of citizenship in a free society must discharge the accompanying duties and responsibilities of citizenship. It is the total business of our life's work to be always consistent with the ideals of freedom, which encompasses a love of God—love of country—regard for the rights of others, and a renewed realization of our great responsibility to preserve for our children and our children's children down through the ages an America forever strong and forever free.

The Legion has the great challenge now, if it is to contribute significantly in these moving times, to hold its head high in service to the high cause of freedom, set an example for others to follow in all our actions, in all our utterances and so conduct ourselves in all of our posts across the length and breadth of the land, that our people will always see our work at its best and our ideals at their loftiest.

By so doing, we show reverence to the memory of our dearly loved President, who has fallen, and give hope and encouragement to our new President, who now assumes the awesome responsibility of leadership.

In this hour, so sad to us all, in this hour which challenges us so, we say for all men to hear:

Though the forces of evil, lawlessness, and hatred may beat with all their fury upon the breasts of liberty—

This Nation will endure strong in justice.

This Nation will prosper rich in compassion.

This Nation will stand down through the corridors of time secure in freedom.

Mr. President, a recent issue of the Nation contained a memorable poem by Wendell Berry on the death of President Kennedy. I ask that the text of this poem, entitled "November 26, 1963," be printed as I believe it is worthy of preservation along with the many other fine tributes to our late President.

November 26, 1963

(By Wendell Berry)

We know the winter earth upon the body of the young
    President, and the early dark falling;
We know the veins grown quiet in his temples and wrists,
    and his hands and eyes grown quiet;
We know his name written in the black capitals of his
    death, and the mourners standing in the rain, and
    the leaves falling;
We know his death's horses and drums; the roses, bells,
    candles, crosses; the faces hidden in veils;
We know the children who begin the youth of loss greater
    than they can dream now;
We know the nightlong coming of faces into the candle-
    light before his coffin, and their passing;
We know the mouth of the grave waiting, the bugle and
    rifles, the mourners turning away;
We know the young dead body carried in the earth into
    the first deep night of its absence;
We know our streets and days slowly opening into the
    time he is not alive, filling with our footsteps and
    voices;
We know ourselves, the bearers of the light of the earth
    he is given to, and of the light of all his lost days;
We know the long approach of summers toward the healed
    ground where he will be waiting, no longer the
    keeper of what he was.

TRIBUTES BY

Hon. Sam J. Ervin, Jr.

OF NORTH CAROLINA

Mr. President, the Reverend Mr. R. F. Smith, Jr., pastor of the First Baptist Church of North Wilkesboro, N.C., made a touching statement concerning the untimely death of President John F. Kennedy at a service conducted at his church on November 24, 1963. Some of those who were privileged to hear this statement have called it to my attention and have suggested to me that it is worthy of reproduction in order to assure its wide dissemination. I share their view, and for this reason ask unanimous consent that Mr. Smith's statement be printed at this point.

On the Death of John F. Kennedy, President

(The following words were spoken during the 11 o'clock worship service, November 24, 1963, and again at the Union Memorial Service at the First Methodist Church, 12 noon, November 25, 1963, by our pastor. They are presented here upon request of many members.)

The 35th President of the United States is dead.

The horrible tragedy which stunned our Nation into shocked disbelief, paralyzed the free world and numbed the imprisoned souls behind the Iron Curtain, finds in no language adjectives capable of describing the wrongness of it all.

The bullet that cut its way into the head of our President has cut way into our hearts with jagged edges that have torn our tissues and brought sadness to our souls and tears to our eyes.

We are part of a nation and a system that declares all men are free—free to speak, free to believe, and free to criticize those in power.

From the halls of Montezuma to the shores of Tripoli; from Bunker Hill to Kings Mountain; from Bull Run to Gettysburg; from the trenches of France to the foxholes of Belgium; from Pearl Harbor to Iwo Jima; from Seoul to Heartbreak Ridge; our grandfathers, our father, our brothers, and our sons, have fought, shed crimson blood, and died that this Nation and its system of freedom might not pass from the land.

In such a system we campaign, we debate, we criticize, and we vote. And whether we win or lose in a political campaign is beside the point to thinking men and women, because the President, regardless of his political affiliation, becomes our President.

He is a man—a man with human frailty and weakness—but he is more than a man.

He is a symbol—of a nation; a symbol of freedom; a symbol of freemen; a symbol of a free and powerful country.

And when the blast of the assassin's rifle bored its way into the head of John F. Kennedy to seal his lips forever—it was my President who died; it was my

President who was cut down; and with that blast every American died a little—and every hope for freedom was dimmed a little—and every battle our fathers fought in was tainted a little.

Is it, then, a time for hate—a time to organize vigilantes and go witch hunting? No, this would be to tear down what our fathers have fought for and our President believed in.

But it is a time to rethink our role as parents and leaders in this world.

The bullet fired from the assassin's gun was molded in a furnace of a growing boy who perhaps read the wrong books or gave the wrong interpretation to what he read.

The bullet was fired, not with his finger, but from his mind—from his heart. And the task of every parent—every leader—is to fill hearts with love and understanding—fill their minds so full that there will be no sweltering furnace hot enough to melt the bulwarks and ramparts of reason and justice and hearts so cold as to mold bullets.

And if we do this, he, and the thousands before him, will not have died in vain. I do not understand how such a thing could happen in America—in Christian America—in the Bible Belt of the South—I don't know. I am numbed. I find myself staring with glazed eyes of disbelief into outer space.

My heart goes out to a lonely and widowed wife—to his two children the same age as mine—to a 3-year-old boy who will never know what it is to have a daddy to show him how to hold a baseball bat and to throw a body block and to toss a basketball.

But I have found comfort in the immortal words of James Russell Lowell:

> "Truth forever on the scaffold,
>   Wrong forever on the throne;
> Yet that scaffold sways the future
>   And the dim, dark unknown
> Standeth God within the shadows
>   Keeping watch above his own."

Mr. President, on November 22, 1963, the Senate of the Dialectic and Philanthropic Literary Societies of the University of North Carolina adopted a resolution expressing the deepest sympathy to the family of the late President John F. Kennedy and declaring support for his successor, President Lyndon B. Johnson. I ask that this resolution be printed at this point.

A RESOLUTION OF THE UNIVERSITY OF NORTH CAROLINA CONCERNING THE DEATH OF JOHN FITZGERALD KENNEDY

Whereas President John F. Kennedy has served this Nation with courage and dignity for 3 years in times of great foreign and domestic turmoil; and

Whereas the President exhibited great devotion and meticulous attention to his duties even up to his final hour, often in the face of acid criticism; and

Whereas he never faltered in his faith and belief in the dignity of all humanity and he proved his conviction by living a life of unceasing struggle against complacency and half-truths; and

Whereas he met an untimely death at the hands of a despicable and misguided assailant: Now, therefore, be it

Resolved by the Senate of the Dialectic and Philanthropic Literary Societies meeting in joint session, That we are deeply shocked and dismayed by the untimely passing of a great American and a noble human being. We express our deepest sympathy to the family of John F. Kennedy for their great loss and do hereby declare our united support and encouragement to President Lyndon B. Johnson.

Respectfully submitted.

LESLIE W. BAILEY, Jr.

Passed by acclamation, November 22, 1963.

HUBERT W. HAWKINS, Jr.,
President.

TRIBUTE BY

Hon. J. Caleb Boggs

OF DELAWARE

Mr. President, a high school senior from my State, Miss Geraldine Marie Quigley, of Wilmington, has written a poem in honor of the late President Kennedy. It is very well done. It reflects not only her sentiment but, I am sure, those of millions of her fellow Americans. I ask to have this poem, "Tribute to a Fallen President," printed as follows:

TRIBUTE TO A FALLEN PRESIDENT

> No ears can hear, nor tongues can speak
>   That which has taken place;
> But only weeping silently
>   We turn a tear-stained face.
>
> Our hearts are heavy, our minds are sad;
>   Our Nation stilled and crying
> Turned its face to God, to pray
>   For a hero who lay dying.
>
> The country loved, and then it lost
>   A gentle, noble soul;
> And a pang of sorrow swept the land
>   As mournful church bells toll.
>
> We lost the life, the man is gone,
>   But his gallant spirit stays
> To lead his people safely
>   Through dangerous, hate-filled days.
>
> A hero both in war and peace
>   He died a hero's death,
> And for his beloved country
>   He gasped his dying breath.
>
> Oh, merciful God, we pray You
>   Hear our prayers so fervent,
> And into your gentle hands receive
>   The soul of this Thy servant.

No more to meet with chiefs of state,
　Nor leaders of foreign sod,
For on this fateful day, in death,
　Our President met with God.

Requiescat in pace.

　　　　　　　　　　—GERALDINE MARIE QUIGLEY.
WILMINGTON, DEL.

TRIBUTES BY

Hon. Vance Hartke

OF INDIANA

Mr. President, the death of John F. Kennedy has evoked among our people a great emotional stirring. Some reflect this in a tear, others with words of great eloquence. Throughout the land, uncommon tributes are being paid an uncommon man.

Hundreds of my constituents in Indiana have been moved within the past week to express, through my office, their shock and their deep condolences. I would like at this point to cite three such instances.

The first is an editorial read on radio station WXLW, Indianapolis, on the day of the President's assassination; the second, a moving message by Rabbi Frederick A. Doppelt, of the Congregation Achduth Vesholom, Fort Wayne, delivered on the day of the President's funeral; and third, two resolutions presented by the Young Democrats of Indiana, John D. Bottorff, president.

I ask unanimous consent, Mr. President, that these three statements be printed as follows:

EDITORIAL—ROBERT D. ENOCH, NOVEMBER 22, 1963

This is a dark day for the United States—and for each one who calls himself an American. The President is dead, the victim of an assassin's bullet. Each of us mourn his death, and grieve for those closest to him.

Our heads are bowed in shame, in the knowledge that such a deed can happen here.

The cloak of civilization is yet too thin a garment. The pride we have taken in our expanding worlds of intelligence has lost touch with the humbleness, the love, and the moral consciousness of the true servants of God.

It is a time for prayer. It is a time of soul searching. It is a time for rededication to the faith of our fathers that founded this Nation.

We weep for John Fitzgerald Kennedy, and pray for him and his family.

We pray for our Nation.

TEMPLE SERVICE OF NATIONAL MOURNING FOR JOHN FITZGERALD KENNEDY, MONDAY, NOVEMBER 25, 1963, 11 A.M.

A solemn and saddened congregation filled the sanctuary of the temple to capacity for a brief service of mourning preceding the funeral services for John F. Kennedy in Washington, D.C. Rabbi Frederic A. Doppelt delivered the following message:

"THE MEASURE OF KENNEDY'S LIFE

"What is the measure of a man's life? How shall we measure especially the life of John F. Kennedy? By time or eternity? By the number of years he spent on this earth which were altogether too few and fleeting, or by how he used his brief and precious time to bring eternity down to earth?

"Let us measure it by his consummate devotion to the highest office in these United States which he ennobled with ability and integrity, and graced with dignity and humility—for that was the true measure of Kennedy's life.

"Let us measure it by his unyielding determination to honor our historic commitment as a nation under God that liberty and justice are the birthright of every man of every color and every creed in this land—for that was the true measure of Kennedy's life.

"Let us measure it by the courageous dedication of his position and power to the biblical vision of a world where nation shall not lift up sword against nation, and of a time when the Fatherhood of God will reign over the brotherhood of man—for that was the true measure of Kennedy's life.

"By mere length of time, his span on earth was only a mere handbreadth in the vastness and expanse of the universe. But when measured by the greatness of his soul and excellence of his deeds, the life of John F. Kennedy was a holy moment in the conscience of humanity which will abide as a living force unto all eternity.

"May his soul be bound up in the bond of life eternal."

———

RESOLUTION OF THE YOUNG DEMOCRATS OF INDIANA, ADOPTED NOVEMBER 24, 1963

Whereas John Fitzgerald Kennedy, 35th President of the United States of America, at all times stood as an inspiration to all Young Democrats, for his love for his country and its people; in the best of times made his fortunes our fortunes, in the worst of times exhibited valor surpassed by none, attempted by few, and recognized by all.

Now, therefore, the Young Democrats of Indiana resolve that as he loved his country and its people, we weep for him; as he was fortunate, we rejoice at it; as he was valiant, we honor him; offering tears for his love, joy for his fortune, and honor for his valor.

Resolved this 24th day of November 1963.

　　　　　　　　　　JOHN D. BOTTORFF,
　　　　　　　　　　　　　　President.

———

RESOLUTION OF THE YOUNG DEMOCRATS OF INDIANA, ADOPTED NOVEMBER 24, 1963

Whereas Lyndon Baines Johnson, 36th President of the United States of America, has asked that the people of the Nation lend him their support in these perilous times, has asked that we pray for divine help and guidance;

Now, therefore, the Young Democrats of Indiana, recognizing that Young Democrats have a particular duty and desire to answer our President's call, resolve that we lend to Lyndon Johnson our uniform and unrelenting support; we offer our prayers for him and the Nation.

Resolved this 24th day of November 1963.

JOHN D. BOTTORFF,
President.

Mr. President, I have recently received a copy of an address delivered at a community memorial service held in Howard Hall, Frankfort, Ind., on November 25. The citizens of Frankfort, like those in so many communities all over the Nation, gathered on that morning in tribute to the late President Kennedy in order to express in united fashion the grief and mourning which has touched us all.

The address was given by the Reverend Charles W. Ridlen, pastor of Frankfort's East Side Christian Church. It is a thoughtful tribute, full of dignity and beauty appropriate to the occasion, reflecting a spirit worthy of our consideration.

PRESIDENT KENNEDY

We come today to honor the memory of our late President, John F. Kennedy. We, the people of the Frankfort community, hereby express our deep regret and sorrow at this hideous crime against freedom and humanity. We convey to the Kennedy family our heartfelt sorrow and sympathy.

We have all been shocked and angered by the horror of our President's death, as he was so cruelly cut down by the cowardly assassin's bullets.

President John F. Kennedy has now answered his own fateful challenge as he said, "Ask not what your country can do for you, but ask what can you do for your country?" In that final and full measure of devotion, he has answered with his all. No man can do more. He has died as he had lived, giving himself completely in devotion to the task he saw before him. In this he has displayed a soul and character of great strength and drive templed in a fragile house of clay. He overcame injury and illness that would have left lesser men whining for pity, but he asked no quarter in the great struggle of life.

He seemed always possessed by the urgency of his mission, as perhaps he sensed his rendezvous with death as in the words of the poet—Alan Seeger:

"I have a rendezvous with Death
At some disputed barricade,
And I to my pledged word am true,
I shall not fail that rendezvous."

He had met head on with courage those forces which he had seen, but this he did not see. He had fought with vigor and stamina to survive against the forces of the sea and jungle, but this he could not fight.

He had guided with skill and determination those events over which he had control, but this course could not be altered.

President Kennedy died as a soldier at his post of duty; his was not a martyr's death but that of a soldier of valor on the battlefield of life. As he fulfilled his duty, he calmly accepted the accompanying risks and dangers. He understood the hazard, yet felt the call of duty even stronger. May our Nation now follow his example in this brave act. May we answer the call of duty for freedom's sake and face the hazards of courageous action.

May I point out to you this morning, by way of contrast, the qualities that make our Nation great. Firstly, in our President we see a man who believed in God. He trusted in Him, he worshipped Him, and sought His divine aid and counsel in life. He lived in obedience to the disciplines of his faith in Almighty God and died in the good graces of his church. His accused assailant believed there was no God. He was a dedicated and avowed Marxist. He trusted only in the theories of men. He worshiped power and power-maddened men. He sought comfort in revolution and death. He lived in disobedience to the laws of Almighty God and died by the gun, as he had lived.

Secondly, our President believed in the worth of a man. He believed that man was created in the image and glory of God. He was sensitive to the needs of men and sought to provide for those needs. He had purpose in his heart to help men in need wherever they were and pursued this to the last moments of his days. He tried to ease the hunger and ignorance of the world. He endeavored to bring about an order in the world wherein men would live without war. In sharp contrast, his accused assassin saw no value in a man. He saw man as a creature for production, as a purely materialistic being without a soul. He was sensitive only to his own needs and desires. He took and did not give. He tried to ease no suffering but has caused great grief and sorrow. This cowardly assassin sought to build the new order on the ashes of dead men and a ruined world.

Thirdly, the contrast is most vivid in the way of action of these men. Our President moved and worked under the law, the law of the land that has stood the test of time. Though he was often peeved and chafed by the slowness of the powers of law, he understood that right could only come by being true to the law of our great Republic. He thus restrained the impatience of youth and waited to accomplish a greater good. The stark terror of the assassin's deed is seen, as he makes himself a law unto himself and snuffs out life without the least regret. This coward was afraid to await the verdict of men and time and so committed such an immense crime against humanity and liberty.

Thus may we learn the bitter lesson of today as to what makes our Nation great: Our faith and trust in Almighty God; the value and worth of a man; a government regulated by law.

Was President Kennedy great? This question we leave to time and history for only they can answer. No man has been called great in his own day, for the test of time must be applied to his ideas and works. Was he great or not, we cannot say today. But this we can say, he was well known to us all. President John F. Kennedy has been in my home many times. I have listened to him with a concerned interest as he spoke his plans and desires for our country. I have had opportunity to argue the point, to disagree with the logic and to oppose the judgments of his position. I feel I have had a part in hammering out the hard problems of state, as the President visited in my home. The electronic marvels of our day have made this possible and have made the President more personal. He was my President; he was my Commander in Chief, as I served in my country's Army. As the President, I loved and respected him as I am sure all of Frankfort did.

We falter for words in this attempt to express our feelings to the family of our fallen hero, President John F. Kennedy. We can only give to you the warm love and comfort of our hearts and pray God's blessing of strength and assurance for you.

May each of us carry with us now the memory of our beloved President, John F. Kennedy, as we think of the words of that great hymn, "America the Beautiful."

"O beautiful for heroes proved in liberating strife,
  Who more than self their country loved
    And mercy more than life.
  America! America! May God thy gold refine,
  Till all success be nobleness and every gain divine.

"O beautiful for patriot dream that seems beyond the
    years
  Thine alabaster cities gleam, undimmed by human tears.
  America! America! God shed His grace on thee,
  And crown thy good with brotherhood from sea to
    shining sea."

We now deeply and solemnly honor the memory of President John F. Kennedy. He gave all that he could give.

Mr. President, many eulogies to President Kennedy have been penned and not a few have been preserved. I ask unanimous consent to have one more printed.

This tribute in verse is perhaps unique, for it is not only a better literary effort than some of those by nonprofessional writers, but it is the outpouring of a working man and union officer. He is Bruce Kingery, who has been for the past 14 years shop chairman of United Auto Workers Local 292, the Delco Radio local, in Kokomo, Ind. Mr. Kingery is also education chairman for this 5,000-member organization and Democratic committeeman from the city of Kokomo's 24th precinct. I am happy, Mr. President, to be able to draw attention to this expression of sorrow for our late President, which is at the same time to considerable extent a credo for a better day in America.

EULOGY

(By Bruce Kingery)

A part of you and me is dead
With his passing, for we knew him
And he knew us, we felt ourselves
So much a part of him, that life
Was more meaningful and God was good
Unto our land, and the destiny
Of this land of ours most truly seemed,
For the brief space of life that he
Was at its helm, the fulfillment years
Of mankind's dreams and hopes and prayers
To walk at last among the gods.

He was of giants,
Who walked among
The mighty ones of our space and time
And knew no peer in all the world
In the common aspirations of all mankind:
An end to wars, the finale to
All the plagues that cast their blight
Upon all the races of all humanity—
These were the goals he was dedicated to.

An end to poverty, he had to have
Compassion born of more-than-man:
The understanding, pity and sympathy for
The downtrodden masses of all this earth,
In order to know and to understand
The depth of deathless struggle against
The apocalyptic forces that rule and sway
So great a portion of the human tide
Of the planet, that Saros should
Forevermore be its lot and name.

He had to know of masses, steeped
In wretched poverty—and he knew it well,
Enough to forego a definite life of ease
In order to place his name among
Those awesome products of mortal womb,
Who, inspired by heaven, step out to meet
The challenge of the world—and embattle it.

An end to pestilence and disease
Were oaths he took, we swore with him,
To realize within each our own allotted span
And time of life, to put an end
To the crippling diseases and infirmities
That have plagued the hapless of this earth
From dawn's first day, throughout the time
Of all its existence, unto this age,
And, with him before us, showing the way,
We embarked upon the long and arduous road
Toward that goal of all our goals.

The end of ignorance, bigotry, hate;
What gigantic strides along the way
Our President took to totally eliminate
These basic causes for man's wars on man!
What genius was his! He lit the torch
And led a people and a land
Away from the pitted depths of gloom

And darkness of poverty, disease, and war,
And all the ills that plague mankind,
That mire him in the muck and mud
Of despair, when his very soul would reach
Out for the turrets of grace that rightfully
Are man's own natural heritage.

He led this people, and all the host
Of mankind unto the new, bright dawn
Of morning sunlight—for the dark is not
A match for sunlight, nor ever was.

He walked with heroes.
As one of them—
For he gave of his very life, itself,
In watery battleground in time of war,
Laying his life upon the line
Wherein all heroes have laid their lives
Since mankind first died for noble cause.
Who, living through history's gravest and greatest war,
To achieve his country's most cherished prize,
Fell—sudden prey to senseless hate
And died the martyr's death in peace—
Time, struck down by blind, unreasoning wrath
And venom-inoculated bigotry.

What debt we owe his small ones and
His widow, that all our lives might be
Spent in solemn remembrance of
Such singular act of senseless depravity,
Nor can, nor should we e'er forget
That the end result of all that hate,
Bigotry, ignorance, and rank prejudice
Implies—has left a lonely vigil in all the nights
For all her life to his grieving widow and
Fatherless loneliness for small children, who,
In their innocent childhood, cannot comprehend
That mortal frailty has bereft them of
A living father's deathless love.

Time—and the act itself have pressed
Upon our minds, our hearts, our very souls,
Such haunting innocence of each small child
And ineffable courage of woman and widow that
The indelible stamp of eternity
Shall remember such courage and innocence
For all time that was and is to be:
The epitome of sacrifice and nobility.

Such is the nature of man that he
Must kill the thing he cherishes most;
He destroys the good and retains the base
Things, for, were Time itself, compressed into
Minuteness—a few short hours ago
Man left his cold, dark caves behind
And when the pressures and duress of life
Leave him bewildered, still seeks sanctity
Among the caves—and cares not for the distant stars.

Yet the deed is done, nor can we part
With the memory of even a minute of it
Any less than we can seek to relegate

All to forgetfulness and undo that
Which is done, by willing that it were not so.

At times, throughout the infinite space
And moments of mankind's passing dream
Which mortals call: Life (and perhaps it is)
There comes a flaming, starlike meteor
That passes across the limited horizons of
Man's limited vision, as this man did.
(And so few like him, far too few,
To change the preordained destiny
Of man into something of higher, nobler mien)
And, like such meteor, through blackened skies
Causes man to look upward from whence he came,
Surely—And in looking upward, take hope anew
To higher endeavors than he deemed self capable of.

Such a man was this, the ages own
Him now forever but there was a time
When Camelot's dreams held but for a spell
The bright promise of better things to be,
For him: because he dared to dream the dreams;
For us: because we chose to share.

The meteor dies, for its short space
And span of existence across the skies
Is far too brief—but its inanimate
Self cannot be truly compared unto
The life and time allotted to
Heroes, such as this man, President
John Fitzgerald Kennedy was, for he,
Though dead, not truly died,
He, though gone, is inspiration unto
Those generations that, following his lighted way,
Shall see and know what lies beyond
The farthest acme of mankind's dearest hopes;
Shall see and know what kind of life
That God ordained for those who walk
The new frontiers of planet, time and space,
With human hands and hearts and minds
Dedicated to human progress for all mankind
To God's greater glory, that the spirits
Of unselfish souls like his might not
Have truly lived and died in vain.

Mr. President, we all know that the tragic death of President Kennedy has stirred the entire Nation as nothing in recent history. The grief we have felt has been unlimited by class, color, creed, or age.

Among the outpourings and tributes which have come to me is one signed "Anonymous" which contained a poem composed by Peggy Anna Moore, 12 years of age, a resident of Georgetown, Ind. Because it illustrates the feelings of the young, paralleling those of their elders, I ask that this poem may be printed. Peggy Anna Moore has titled it simply, "He Died."

He Died

(By Peggy Anna Moore, age 12)

A soul was taken from us the other day,
To a much better place so far away.
He died to keep our Nation free,
He died for you, he died for me.
He helped to make our Nation grow,
Although he was killed in doing so.
He died so that our honored flag
May lead the nations and not lag.
He died so that the younger generation
May one day help to rule the Nation.
He died to give the "States" a key,
To keep us in true unity.
So let him not have died in vain,
Let not us use a crutch or cane,
To lean upon to avoid responsibility.
We dedicate this to John Fitzgerald Kennedy.

Mr. President, it has been my good fortune to make the acquaintance of Arthur Franklin Mapes, a fellow Hoosier from Kendallville, and I value his friendship highly. He is well known throughout Indiana for his poetry and is the author of our official State poem.

On the assassination of President Kennedy, Mr. Mapes was inspired to write a poem entitled "He Moved the World" which I believe to be one of the most touching tributes to our fallen leader which I have seen.

He Moved the World

A constant flame, a gleam of light,
A flame eternal, burns tonight;
A flame that flickers, yet reveals
The glory of his great ideals.

His heart gave love, his words gave hope,
He furnished light for those who grope
In darkness yet, that they might find
A lasting peace for all mankind.

He moved the world with strength of truth.
He loved the aged and the youth.
He showed concern for those in need
Regardless of their race or creed.

With courage and sincerity
He struggled for equality,
From those who would his dreams reject
Came admiration and respect.

He smiled through sorrow, laughed at gloom,
He visioned yet a world in bloom,
When dreams of lust and hate were ended,
When man could live as God intended.

If every man would hoe his row
The weeds of hate could never grow;
The world would be a garden grand,
And peace would bloom in every land.

—Arthur Franklin Mapes.

Mr. President, the assassination of President Kennedy deeply moved the people of this country and expressions of sympathy continue to be voiced throughout the land. Many of my fellow Hoosiers have sent their condolences through my office.

Few of the tributes which have reached my desk are as poignant and meaningful as that embodied in a newspaper column written by Mrs. Mary D'Andrea, society editor of the Logansport (Ind.) Pharos-Tribune.

News and Views

(By Mary D'Andrea)

Words are inadequate in a time of great sorrow.

The loss of this Nation's President was one of inexpressible grief and frustration for the millions who considered him not a Republican or a Democrat, not a Catholic or a Protestant, but a leader of all men.

"Logan-land" residents expressed themselves in silent and solemn tribute, in special services in all churches, in a memorial service at Berry Bowl, in the display of the American flag at half mast or with black crepe, and in written words, lines of poetry.

Some of the poetic tributes to the late President, John F. Kennedy, are recorded here. Three of the local authors prefer to remain anonymous.

Black Friday

From Washington to Dallas and back
This day for our Nation was very black
It was Nov. 22nd, the year 1963,
It will never be forgotten, but go down in history.

It started with a big parade
With our President in a motorcade
In the State of Texas, on a Dallas street
Never thinking his fate he'd meet,
When all of a sudden, above the cheers
A shot rang out that brought us tears,

And now he's gone, and left us sad
This youngest leader we ever had
But our Nation lives on and is stronger today,
Because we had him—J.F.K.

—Sara Rivers.

To Kill This Nation

How do you kill this Nation?
Murder its leader?
Oppress its people?
Purge its name?
Destroy its flag?

How do you kill this Nation?
Benedict Arnold tried betrayal.
John Booth tried murder.
Adolf Hitler tried war.
Nikita Khrushchev tried intimidation.

How do you kill this Nation
If it is loved?
If it is free?
If it is Christian?
If it is America?

How do you kill this Nation?
Only when you destroy peace.
Only when you destroy the last American.
Only when you destroy the world.
Only when you destroy God.

————

A Shot Was Fired

A shot was fired
An irrational act of man
Upon mankind
And though it was but one
It pierced the hearts of millions
Slaying a part of each.

A shot was fired
Producing not the death desired
But giving life anew
Through grief
To build men's lives
With courage and with love.

A shot was fired
In death to martyr
But in life
To give
A hundredfold
That which it was meant to destroy.

————

If Daddy Had Been There

The day was gloomy in spite of the sun,
People crowded around everywhere
But John-John missed only one
His Daddy was not there.

"Why do all these people come?"
Was John-John's puzzled look.
It wasn't a day for fun; besides,
He'd rather look at a picture book.

Daddy always read to him
Before he went to bed
But last night all seemed grim
So he left the words unsaid.

John-John couldn't understand
When Mommy wouldn't play his favorite game
Because Daddy wasn't home yet, and
Things just weren't quite the same.

"Daddy gone away?" he asked.
Recalling 'copter trips of the past
He always liked to watch for him
And be there when the "chopper" got in.

John-John knew something was wrong
When he didn't see Daddy in that throng
Even as Mommy held his hand tight
John-John knew something wasn't right.

The church was filled with people
But only sad tolling came from the steeple
And after Mass, the horses pranced in pairs,
Everything would have been just fine, if Daddy had
been there.

The tiny tears came slow, then fast,
And Mommy soothed him as in the past
Why he was crying he did not know
And when Daddy comes he would tell him so.

The tears went away like Mommy said they would,
He stood very tall and as straight as he could,
He remembered the times on Daddy's knee
And he knew today was far from carefree.

The little hand went up to a youthful brow
And unshed tears were forgotten now.
His salute was solemn and given with care,
He knew Daddy would be proud, had he only been there.

————

From Twelve Mile we received a portion of a letter from a former resident of that town, Mrs. Myrna Kay Hoch, who wrote to her parents, Mr. and Mrs. Castle G. Farley, relating her reactions and impressions in passing the bier of the late President Kennedy. Her letter in part:

"I guess you are all interested in hearing about the trip to Washington. I'll try to explain the best I can. We got in line about 9 p.m. Sunday (November 24) walking 3 miles to find the end of it. People were standing from six to nine deep, all huddling together to keep warm. Among those waiting were babies a few months old and oldtimers supporting themselves with canes; even two or three were in wheelchairs.

"The majority of those waiting were middle class (in a manner of speaking); a few were wearing diamonds and mink and some were very obviously poor.

"One man had his family of 13 children there. The little boys were dressed in suits, topcoats and snap-brim hats; the girls in frilly Sunday dresses and hats. They all waited throughout the night, the tiniest sleeping in their parents' arms.

"There were people speaking languages I've never heard spoken before. The waiting itself was an education. People talked and laughed during the early part of the night while we were still out of sight of the Capitol, but as we got closer and closer they became quiet and orderly almost to the point of being unbelievable.

"A few times a group of 20 persons or so would try to break into the line and then these people who were so quiet and orderly became almost maniacs, pushing, shoving and cursing. It frightened me—I just knew some one would be hurt but fortunately no one was.

"When we finally got on the steps of the Capitol and were filing in, both men and women were crying and no one was ashamed. I've never before had the feeling that I had as I walked by the casket. A hundred things flashed through my mind, among them how I jokingly referred to him as if he were a personal friend, about Jackie, Caroline and even Macarone.

"The flowers were beautiful although most of them were in the corridors off of the rotunda. I could write six more pages and still the description of feelings wouldn't be complete. It was one experience I'm sure I shall never forget."

Mrs. Hoch is the wife of Capt. Virgil I. Hoch, stationed at Dover Air Force Base in Delaware, where the couple resides with their three sons. Captain Hoch's parents are Mr. and Mrs. Marshall Hoch, rural route 6, Logansport.

TRIBUTE BY

Hon. Herman E. Talmadge

OF GEORGIA

Mr. President, on November 24, on the eve of the late President John F. Kennedy's funeral, Dr. James P. Wesberry, pastor of Morningside Baptist Church in Atlanta, delivered a heart-warming television message dedicated to the memory of our slain President. Dr. Wesberry's message is as follows:

MESSAGE DELIVERED BY DR. JAMES P. WESBERRY, PASTOR, MORNINGSIDE BAPTIST CHURCH, ATLANTA, IN MEMORIAL SERVICE ON EVE OF PRESIDENT JOHN F. KENNEDY'S FUNERAL, SUNDAY NIGHT, NOVEMBER 24, 1963

The heart of our great Nation has been broken by a deep sorrow. The body of our great President, John F. Kennedy, lies in state under the dome of our Nation's Capitol. Multiplied thousands of people have already passed in review and will, and tomorrow, the day of President Kennedy's funeral, has been declared a day of national mourning.

How quickly and shockingly momentous world events take place. Little did any of us think that we would come to this Thanksgiving Sunday bowed in grief over the untimely and tragic death of our brilliant and gifted leader. Full of life and completely dedicated to the service of the Nation and to the freedom and peace of the entire world, the President of the United States was cruelly and brutally shot and killed by an assassin in Dallas, Tex., last Friday, and now the assassin is dead.

It is as unbelievable as it is shocking—and yet we know it is true. How hard it is for us to believe that such a thing could happen in so-called Christian America. We find it so difficult to believe that we are living in a land where such a thing as burning churches, bombing a synagogue or church, and murdering a President could happen. To think that he who gave his life so freely and who carried within his office the greatest power on earth could have his life snuffed out in such an atrocious way.

This sadly reminds us that the awful sins that helped to crucify the Lord of glory on Calvary over 1900 years ago still lurk in the human heart, and there are yet evil forces that would tear down and destroy everything for which Christ stands and upon which America was built.

President Kennedy commanded the respect, love and admiration of the world. His was a great faith—a true profile of courage. His sacrificial death has a sobering effect upon our Nation and our world. America can never be the same after such a tragic, staggering blow. Whatever comfort there may be in it, God is great enough to make the wrath of man to praise him—out of evil good can come. As great as President Kennedy was in life, he is many times greater in death. This is a better world today because of his life and death and America has been brought closer to God.

Senator Wayne Morse was right when he said just before the Senate was recessed Friday: "If ever there was an hour when Americans should pray, this is the hour." This sort of thing humbles us all and causes us to hear again God say, "If my people, which are called by my name, shall humble themselves, and pray, and seek my face, and turn from their wicked ways; then will I hear from heaven, and will forgive their sin, and will heal their land." Only time will reveal Mr. Kennedy's contribution to the unity of our world, of the nations, of religious denominations, to brotherhood, justice and peace.

The universe is full of vicarious suffering. One thing lays down its life for another. This is true in the vegetable world as well as the animal world. Everything is bought with a price. Men lay down their lives sometimes in single heroic acts of martyrdom, sometimes by years of patient, self-denying service—the physician, the school teacher, the engineer, the statesman. Only God knows the price many pay to serve—mothers and fathers, husbands and wives.

Oh, what a price they pay as they suffer and sacrifice for the well-being of their children. This is the nature of atonement, and in every corner of the world it is spelled out like a dim and broken inscription on the fragments of human life. Everywhere this vicarious principle is at work. "Except a corn of wheat fall into the ground and die, it abideth alone; but if it die, it bringeth forth much fruit."

We find this at the very summit of all being. "Without the shedding of blood there is no remission of sins." We do not expect our great Creator to ignore this vicarious principle with which He has filled the world. He, too, suffers and sacrifices for his children. The throne of God is one of self-sacrificing love. "The Lamb is in the midst of the throne" is a "Lamb slain from the foundation of the world." There is the blood of the Cross. There is a voice saying, "Father, forgive them."

Father Damien, at the age of 18, joined the Society of the Sacred Heart. When he finished training he asked to go as a missionary to the Hawaiian Islands. Deeply moved by the sad condition of the lepers on the Island of Molokai he went to live among the minister to them. "No matter," he said to those who opposed his going, "it is the call of God and of human need, and I am going." He lived with those unhappy people the rest of his life, contracted the dread disease and died from it, disfigured almost beyond recognition, after 26 years of devoted service. Like his Master, whose spirit he had caught, he gave himself for lepers through long years of faithful and loving ministry. So it has been with many others, such as, David Livingstone, giving his life to

Africa; Wilfred Grenfell, of Labrador; Lincoln, Garfield, McKinley, and now John F. Kennedy.

Nothing short of this experience of earnest service and unflinching sacrifice for the triumph of God's will can interpret to us today the meaning of the sacrifice of Christ on His cross.

Every man or woman who has ever tried to do these things in any measure knows only too well that there can be no salvation either from sin or from the misery sin entails on guilty and innocent alike save by the vicarious sacrifice of some brave, generous servant of righteousness and benefactor of his fellows. This great doctrine of vicarious suffering is self-evident to every man who ever fought entrenched and powerful evil or sought to rescue the wicked from wickedness. To those who know nothing of giving themselves for others this doctrine, like all deeper spiritual truths, remains an unintelligible and impenetrable mystery.

The first man I talked to after the tragic news that our President had been shot said, "I feel guilty myself, as if I had a part in it." Don't we all? For we are all responsible citizens or should be.

This is not the only crisis our Nation ever faced. There have been many others. It was a sad day in America over a hundred years ago when a troubled minister wrote to the Secretary of the Treasury of the United States and suggested that the recognition of our undying faith should be printed in some form on the coins of our Nation. "This," he wrote, "would relieve us from the ignominy of heathenism. This would place us openly under the Divine protection we have personally claimed. From my heart I have felt our national shame in disowning God as not the least of our present national disasters."

Upon receipt of this eloquent plea the Treasurer wrote the Director of the Mint in Philadelphia saying, "No nation can be strong except in the strength of God, or safe except in his defense. The trust of our people should be declared in our national coins."

The Director of the Mint ordered that a motto be prepared expressing in fewest words this national recognition. Several mottoes were tried, but in 1864 there first appeared on a U.S. coin, a 2-cent piece, the words, "In God We Trust." These immortal words symbolize the faith and righteousness that exalts a nation, and have a ring of timelessness as though they had been given to our Founding Fathers upon tablets of stone.

Blind indeed are they who would pull this standard down. It must be maintained at all costs. The ancient landmarks for which we are most grateful, and for which our Nation stands and which have made America great, must never be removed: The Bible, church, home, Christian schools, the Lord's day, Sabbath, prayer.

No people every suffered greater hardships than our pilgrim fathers. Of 102 immigrants who landed on that bleak, rocky, storm-tossed shore of Cape Cod in the winter of 1620, almost half of them died during the first year. They built seven times more graves than they did homes. Only God knows what they suffered during that cold, hard winter. There was sickness, hunger, depression, death, bitterness, sorrow, loneliness, and separation from native land. But of all that history records regarding them, there is nothing written more indelibly than their faith in Almighty God.

For many this may seem like a midnight hour, but let us, like the Psalmist say, "At midnight I will rise to give thanks unto thee because of Thy righteous judgments." And remember, as long as our trust is really in God, all things work together for good—and as He has blessed our Nation in times past, so will He go with us as we face the future, for it is He who says, "Be strong and of good courage, fear not, nor be afraid of them: for the Lord thy God, he it is that doth go with thee; He will not fail thee, nor forsake thee." Deuteronomy 31: 8.

TRIBUTE BY
Hon. Frank Carlson
OF KANSAS

Mr. President, many excellent articles were written following the assassination of our late President, John F. Kennedy.

Mr. Robert M. Schrag, assistant editor of the Mennonite Weekly Review, wrote a splendid article entitled "A Moment in History" which I wish to call to the attention of the Senate and ask that it be printed as follows:

A MOMENT IN HISTORY

The doleful drums rolled on Pennsylvania Avenue. When a President had ridden in triumph, a military caisson bore him slowly along in death. John F. Kennedy was gone, and a world mourned.

The awesome drama was played from beginning to end on one long November weekend. On Friday noon the President was in Dallas, vibrantly alive. A few hours later he was back in Washington, dead. Time, space and history itself were foreshortened in a technological age.

"A bad man shot my daddy," said John F. Kennedy, Jr., 3 years old the day of his father's funeral. "His world was strangely different, in little ways a child notices but does not understand," wrote the UPI. General MacArthur summed up everyone's personal sorrow: "When he died something died within me."

America's self-confidence was shaken. In a country of law and reason and light, the dark and brutal spirit of the jungle possessed the heart of an assassin with a mail-order rifle. A nation accustomed to smugly lecture its Latin neighbors about their violent politics drew itself up short for a searching look at its own soul. What were we coming to? The deep melancholia of an entire people called forth Shakespeare's lines:

"For God's sake, let us sit upon the ground,
And tell sad stories of the death of kings."

John Kennedy was not a king, but no Caesar ever had more power to decide the fate of nations—the might of the nuclear thunderbolt. During his brief 3 years in office, the force of the atom had once again been contained, however precariously, and the world was grateful.

His successful efforts for a nuclear test ban treaty raised the hopes of fearful humanity.

The U.S. Chief Executive was more than a national symbol, for he identified himself with the larger cause of mankind. "I am a Berliner," he declared last June to the throngs in beleaguered West Berlin. A marked contrast to the aged leaders of Europe, the young President and First Lady inspired the world with a spirit of youthful optimism.

Among the ironies of this moment in history was the obvious parallel to President Lincoln, assassinated on Good Friday, 1865, after preserving the Union in the Civil War. Though separated by a century of change, Lincoln and Kennedy faced many of the same basic domestic problems. Kennedy, a strong civil rights advocate, was martyred in the centennial year of Lincoln's Emancipation Proclamation. The London Times described the late President as one "who felt that he was challenged to carry forward the implications of Lincoln's work and who in this last year, has been seen wrestling with the critical issues of race and national unity."

With the numbing shock came also a sense of national rededication to making real the ideals of American civilization, and of Christianity itself. John Kennedy's goal of national brotherhood—transcending even racial barriers—was elusive during his lifetime. Now, at his death, it seemed strangely closer to realization.

In the three grief-filled days from her husband's death to his burial, Jacqueline Kennedy was a model of courage. The darkly veiled young widow bravely led a unique gathering of the world's dignitaries from the White House to St. Matthew's Cathedral for the funeral. Following the requiem mass, quotations were read from the Kennedy inaugural address ("Ask not what your country can do for you—ask what you can do for your country") and from Ecclesiastes ("A time to be born and a time to die").

It was the making of a legend. The statue of the Great Emancipator looked down upon the somber yet majestic funeral procession as it wound past the Lincoln Memorial toward a hero's grave across the Potomac. And the drums rolled.

TRIBUTES BY

Hon. Everett McKinley Dirksen

OF ILLINOIS

Mr. President, Mr. Talmage S. Wilcher, chairman of the Americanism Committee of the Virginia State Elks Association, delivered a tribute to the late President John Fitzgerald Kennedy in connection with the Know Your America Week. The ceremonies were held at the Arlington-Fairfax Lodge of the Benevolent and Protective Order of Elks on November 30 and I ask unanimous consent that Mr. Wilcher's tribute be made a part of my remarks.

SPEECH OF TALMAGE S. WILCHER, GENERAL CHAIRMAN FOR NORTHERN VIRGINIA, KNOW YOUR AMERICA WEEK COMMITTEE, AND VIRGINIA STATE CHAIRMAN, ELKS ASSOCIATION OF VIRGINIA (AMERICANISM COMMITTEE), DELIVERED AT A SPECIAL MEMORIAL SERVICE FOR BROTHER JOHN F. KENNEDY, AT THE END OF KNOW YOUR AMERICA WEEK PROGRAM AT NEW ELKS HOME, ARLINGTON-FAIRFAX LODGE, NOVEMBER 30, 1963

Chairman Herman C. Anderson, distinguished guests, Monsignor Heller, Reverend Smith, Rabbi Golinken, it is with a sad heart that I attempt to address you all on this most solemn occasion, the martyrdom of our great leader and President. First I must say that I am a Republican. But John F. Kennedy was my President too. Now I have another President; he is a Democrat, but he is my President also.

We in America stand as a unit, that is why America is great; as Americans, we stand as a whole, regardless of creed, color, religion, or political preference. Our State Elks association, our great lodge, the All American Conference To Combat Communism, the National Council of Citizenship, are fighting a battle for all of us, to save our country from the specter of communism, hate, greed, selfishness, ignorance, and fanaticism. We are fighting to save our children from hate, ignorance, and the little-thinking people who would destroy us. If we give them the chance, there is no future for any one of us.

The Elks is not a one-man organization, it is not an exclusive club for the benefit of a few, it is not an organization to satisfy the egomaniacal expression of ignorant, selfish men. It is not an organization that caters to a few to the detriment of the whole. We have a mission. That mission is positive Americanism. The inculcation and exemplification of American manhood, with brotherly love, of justice, charity, and fidelity.

Without a mission, little men fail. While on the other hand men with a vision can and will prevail over ignorance. Let's get it straight: we, the people of the United States, can truthfully say: I am proud to take those ringing words for my own, proud to be a part of a great hope, a great confidence that man is and of right, ought to be free.

I am an American, free to work, free to build, free to speak, free to worship. I have faith in America because I know that America is right, because I believe in freedom, because I accept and enjoy the tremendous responsibility and great blessings of America for myself, my family, and my nine precious grandchildren, and their offspring to come. I am proud of America. Millions have lived for it. Millions have sacrificed for it. Millions have died for it, including our beloved brother, John F. Kennedy, President of the United States. In the light of those very sacrifices, I am proud to say that for me and my family we are dedicated Americans. In conclusion let me say and repeat the great poet who is unnamed:

"God give us men. A time like this demands strong minds, ready hands, men whom the lust of office cannot buy, men who have honor and men who will not lie. Tall men, sun-crowned men who live above the public fog in private duty and in public thinking, for while the rabble with their thumbworn creeds, their large possessions and little deeds. Lo freedom weeps, while wrong rules the lands and waiting justice sleeps. God give us men. Men of dependable character, men of sterling worth, then all the wrong of men shall be redressed and right over might shall rule the earth. God give us men."

In these final hours, of a great planned celebration, when all the world seemed to turn upside down, in minds of men, in the hearts of the young, in the schools, in the churches, in the business places, the frustrations, the tears, the sorrow, let us not forget there is a lonely, widowed mother, with her two young and beautiful children. Because a maniac, with hate in his heart, killed a man, her husband, a President, a father.

Mr. President, Mr. William J. Simonini, who is retired from the U.S. Air Force, has written a beautiful tribute to the late President, John Fitzgerald Kennedy, which is at once a tribute also to our Republic. It does merit inclusion in the tributes of this body, and I ask unanimous consent to have it made a part of my remarks.

OUR GOD, OUR HOME, OUR GOVERNMENT—A TRIBUTE TO OUR LATE PRESIDENT, OUR NEW PRESIDENT, OUR EX-PRESIDENTS, OUR LATE PRESIDENT'S WIFE AND FAMILY, OUR CABINET, AND MEMBERS OF CONGRESS

(By William J. Simonini)

A few days ago, November 25, 1963, I stood on a hill overlooking Washington, D.C.'s, Arlington Cemetery. From horizon to horizon, my eyes saw row upon row of small white crosses marking the graves of soldiers who fought so bravely for their country. But today another soldier was being buried among the other small white crosses. His name was John Fitzgerald Kennedy, 35th President of the United States. As I observed the last rites of our beloved Commander in Chief, and as the sounds of "Taps" echoed into the distant hills bordering the Potomac, my heart saddened, I turned my head toward the Capitol. As I looked on the towering marble building, a mist gathered in my eyes, as, standing there, I thought of its tremendous significance, its powers there assembled, and the responsibilities there centered—its President, its Congress, its courts, its gathered treasure, its Army, its Navy, its Air Force, and its more than 180 million citizens. All this I could see clearly before me, because of an assassin's bullet. This picture would have been unclear a day before. I saw before me our new President, our ex-Presidents, dignitaries from all over the world paying tribute to our late President. As the last note of "Taps" faded across the still green Virginia country-side, this last sound, above all, convinced those who refused to believe that our young Commander in Chief, including myself, was gone forever.

It seemed to me the best and mightiest sight that the sun could find, on this sad day, in its wheeling course was the majestic home of our Republic—the Capitol. Our Nation was hit hard by the loss of its titular head, but it has taught the world its best lessons of liberty—and I felt that if wisdom, justice and honor abided therein, then the world would stand indebted to this temple (the Capitol)

on which my eyes, filled with tears, rested, and in which the ark of my covenant was lodged for its final uplifting and regeneration.

And as I gazed, the memory of the great Capitol, and a great ex-President laid to rest, slowly faded from my mind. Forgotten during this crisis its treasure and its splendor, I slowly walked down the still green hill and I said silently to myself: "Surely here—here in the homes of the people of this great land is lodged the ark of covenant of my country. Here is its majesty and its strength. Here the beginning of its power and the end of its responsibility."

In sacrifice and denial let us keep them free (our homes) from debt and obligation. Let us make them homes of refinement in which we shall teach our daughters that modesty, and patience, and gentleness are the charms of woman. Let us make our homes temples of liberty, and teach our sons that an honest conscience is every man's first political law. That his sovereignty rests beneath his hat, and that no splendor can rob him and no force justify the surrender of the simplest right of a free and independent citizen.

And above all, let us honor God in our homes—anchor the family close to His love. (Remember President Kennedy and his wonderful family were always close to their creator.) Build His altars above our fireplaces, uphold them in the set and simple faith of our fathers and crown them with the Bible—that Book of Books in which all the ways of life are made straight, and the mystery of death is made plain. The home is the source of our national life, this and nothing else will the Capitol be. This, not Secret Service agents, will prevent future assassinations. Our homes need a good housecleaning. Let's make each home in America a temple of democracy. Let's read and follow the Good Book—if we do our country will always be strong.

In closing, our late President gave his life fighting hate, poverty, and ignorance. Our new President is now engaged in continuing this fight. But he needs our help, if we help him God will help all of us automatically. So, let's start by improving our standards in our home. And our Congress, which has worked so hard, and which we have given very little credit for. They have pulled us out of two serious crises—they are valiants for the 180 million people, they are the best the country can offer. This pertains to the Cabinet and Supreme Court members as well. But we at home must sustain this drive. We must vote and encourage others to vote, we must help our growing towns and cities by volunteering our time and services without pay. We must keep our churches strong, and, above all, we must strive for the highest family standard, and our weapon is the Bible. If we follow God's teachings we will eliminate hate, greed, and jealousy which, in turn, will make us become humble. Lincoln remarked, "No man can become great without first becoming humble." And to be humble you can't hate. And remember, I say again, "What the home is, this and nothing else will the Capitol be. What the citizen wills, this and nothing else will the President be."

WILLIAM J. SIMONINI,
U.S. Air Force (Retired).

TRIBUTES BY

Hon. Abraham A. Ribicoff

OF CONNECTICUT

Mr. President, the State of Connecticut knew President John Fitzgerald Kennedy well. I ask unanimous consent to include various editorials from Connecticut newspapers which pay tribute to our late President. These editorials truly reflect the love and respect all the people of Connecticut had for President Kennedy.

[From the Hartford (Conn.) Times, Nov. 23, 1963]

JOHN F. KENNEDY

The young President of the United States, John Fitzgerald Kennedy, was murdered from ambush by a hate-tortured misanthrope.

The backwash of this crime is sobering the American people who, in recent years, have been more and more expressing their anxieties and fears about public policy in reckless, even sick, political behavior.

The prime suspect appears to be a confused and paranoiac promoter of Fair Play for Cuba. This organization has been known to attract persons of far-left affiliations and was, at one time, partially financed from Cuba proper. The suspected assassin was reportedly active in the Cuban sympathy movement after having been denied Russian citizenship.

But this aberration had been preceded by others, suggesting a dangerous and pathetic instability of mind and emotion. That a President of the United States should die at such hands deepens our humiliation and heightens our grief.

Between the extremists of the right and of the left in this country the late President tried nobly to illuminate and to explain the realities of modern problems; to hold the majority on a course of reason; to isolate and to shame those who would employ spittle, and sickening slogans, and riotous conduct as political weapons.

Mr. Kennedy's inaugural proclamation that we must never negotiate from fear but also never fear to negotiate was turned against him by jingoes who still believe that they can blow down the Communist monolith with hot air.

His steely and deadly earnest response to the Soviet missile buildup in Cuba and his contempt for the perfidious Castro enraged the self-exiled minority in American society who cling to the deception that Castro's revolution was genuine, wholesome, and necessary.

The President's eloquent appeal for practical brotherhood as a first fundamental in civil rights and equal justice before the law won him the contempt of Dixie.

The humiliation at the Bay of Pigs. The detestable wall across Europe. The throbbing carbuncle of Cuba. The indissoluble power of the ruling class and moneyed interests of Latin America. The worsening domestic economic future charted for the United States. These challenges were faced by the late Mr. Kennedy with patience, with reason, with firmness and with programs.

But he was finding himself more and more whipsawed between extremes. He was hobbled by equivocation and indecision in Congress and within large areas of public opinion. And he was being abandoned by faithless colleagues who started drifting from the President's side to save their own hides.

It is only now, when this young man is lifeless and mourned, that some shocked Americans will cool down and listen to what he had to say.

Now the vicious gossip about the Kennedy dynasty will not evoke such cruel laughter.

Now the hope and the commonsense, the humor and the idealism, the courage and the insights of what Senator Russell called this brilliant and dedicated young statesman will get the hearing, posthumously, that they have always deserved.

Mr. Kennedy's first 3 years in the White House were interpreted as disappointing by some of his friends. He was damned for moving too slowly in civil rights. Then when he moved, after the violence at Oxford and Birmingham, he was cursed for precipitating tensions with no plans for allaying them.

The President was on the right side in the great debate over the moral challenge inherent in the race crisis—and no man of conscience, of ethical awareness, of scientific reasoning or religious conviction could deny it.

But the rightness of his cause became lost in the fierce and cynical maneuvers of special and regional interests; in the muck of political contention; in the howling tribalism of party factions—stirred to a kind of semantic madness by the narcotic of unreasoning dissent.

Well, John F. Kennedy did not live beyond the age of 46. He was not allowed the grace of even one full term in the office he had won, and which he had enriched and enlivened with great intellectual and cultural attentiveness.

Although personally popular for his masculine charm and the exciting glow cast by his beautiful wife and their utterly normal family, John Kennedy was denied the full attention and the respect that his ideas, his modern idealism, and his vastly researched plans warranted. Too many people were searching for too easy answers—and they still are.

Perhaps as we review the tragically shortened career of this young man, we can think more objectively about the real content and portent of the issues upon which he discoursed so solemnly and, at times, so futilely. That would seem to be the least measure of gratitude and devotion that we can pay to John Fitzgerald Kennedy, the 35th President of the United States, whose life was yielded to a fanatic's gun in Dallas, Tex., November 22, 1963.

ROBERT W. LUCAS.

———

[From the Hartford (Conn.) Courant, Nov. 23, 1963]

DEATH OF A PRESIDENT

Not since the assassination of Abraham Lincoln has the lightning of fate struck down a President with such swift unexpectedness as yesterday in the streets of Dallas. This senseless murder leaves one awed and numb. Here is a change in the leadership of the country that no one expected and that no one can have wanted—surely not even that twisted, malignant spirit in human form that caused it.

What does this portend? What effect will this tragedy have on that surging tide of racial change whose sweep will still, inevitably, make real for America's Negroes as well as whites that historic affirmation that all men are created equal? What effect will this blow have on legislation? What on the Presidential election that is less than a year away? Still more, what new directions will it give to that titanic struggle that dominates the last half of our century—the cold war?

The answers to these questions, and many more like them, are unknown. At the moment one comes back only to the blow itself. There looms the human drama. At one moment President Kennedy was enjoying the accustomed, carefree routine of being a visitor among some part of the American people. And those people, no matter what their party, always find their hearts quickening at the sight of the President. In the next instant the hand of death struck, from nowhere. Half an hour later the youngest man ever to be elected President of the United States lay dead. Almost surely he had ahead of him 5 more years in office, and that full place in history, reserved for those who are two-time Presidents. We remember the confident young man of the inaugural, on that frosty day less than 3 years ago delivering to a listening, watching Nation, what may well be that one of his speeches to live in history. There followed the familiar course of partisan political battles—a tripartite battle it was, what with the backward tug of the southern wing of Mr. Kennedy's own party.

Now all that has fallen away, and there is only awe and stillness.

There remains the bereaved family—two young, fatherless children. Even both of the President's parents remain to mourn. And there was the President's wife, one moment gay with life, the next sheltering the bleeding head of her husband in her arms.

For a moment the turbulent stream of history is stilled. This event calls to mind our earlier President Johnson, Andrew, who likewise came in office by the accident of a madman's bullet. We think of the new President, Lyndon Johnson, suddenly confronted with uncounted responsibilities. He is an older man than his predecessor, and he has known illness. But then President Eisenhower, too, has had a heart attack, and he lives.

Such an event as this highlights the almost casual way we choose our Vice Presidents. Yet this country has lived through such swift, sharp turns in its course before in the century and three-quarters of the Constitution. Today the future is a question mark. All we can do is say, after the fashion of the peoples of old when death brought them the uncertainty of a new ruler: Long live the king.

There are two schools of thought as to what shapes history. One holds that men make events, the other the reverse. This last view was written by Tolstoi in his "War and Peace." The tide in human affairs is what shapes the future, he argues, and it inevitably calls up leaders who ride its crest. Probably the truth lies halfway between this view and the other, that great men bend our course to their will. We can be sure that the next half decade, at least, will be different from what it would have been if yesterday's blow had not struck. Yet there are clearly also great historical forces at work, in this country and in the world. They are forces that will not be denied, no matter who is in office.

This is a time for all of us to open our hearts and our minds, to be generous to the new President, as he faces the darkness ahead. We are a people who do not seem to feel ourselves called to greatness. We are given to seizing the main chance, to letting George do it, to not wanting to be involved. Perhaps now we shall be shocked into a more sober awareness of our duties as citizens. Faced with this tragedy, let us for the moment at least push hate and fear aside. Let us mourn him who has left us. Let us uphold him who succeeds him. Indeed, let us make a quiet resolve to do our part to see that, in those familiar words whose centenary we have just observed, this Nation shall have a new birth of freedom. And, we might add, of courage, and devotion, and strength.

———

[From the New Haven (Conn.) Register, Nov. 25, 1963]

A NATION MOURNS ITS SLAIN PRESIDENT

John Fitzgerald Kennedy, 35th President of the United States, is dead, killed by an assassin's bullet in Texas. The entire free world, of which he was the leader, mourns a man whose sincerity, convictions, integrity, and courage were never challenged.

The assassin struck at more than the President. He aimed his fatal bullets at every American. President Kennedy was shot because he represented you and me. He was our President. Because he was, he died. He was not slain because he was John Fitzgerald Kennedy, the individual. He was murdered because he was our President, our personal representative in national and world affairs. It is because of this that the tragedy strikes into every home and heart in the United States and outside the Nation where freedom burns.

It is ironic that Mr. Kennedy should survive enemy attacks as commander of PT–109 in World War II only to be slain by a madman in his own land.

Mr. Kennedy died as he lived—dramatically. Fate, so kind to him for 46 years, suddenly turned cruel. He did not seek to be dramatic, the role was destined for him. He filled the role nobly with distinction to himself, his family, his Nation, and his God.

Mr. Kennedy's brief but active career was one of public service. Had he so elected he could have followed a life of complete leisure. But he loved his Nation and his fellow man. He served them in the House of Representatives, the Senate, and the Presidency, the greatest honor any nation can confer upon one of its citizens.

In a world that is mad, it must be expected that some of its madness will rub off upon others. It was such an individual whose bullet snuffed out the life of a truly great man and added his name to those of Abraham Lincoln, James A. Garfield, and William McKinley as assassinated Presidents.

When a man of the stature and character of President Kennedy suddenly leaves this world he loved, there is little that can be said. Mr. Kennedy wrote his own epitaph in life.

When another chapter is written in "Profiles in Courage," it will be about John Fitzgerald Kennedy, public servant, statesman, war hero, and father.

[From the New Haven (Conn.) Journal-Courier, Nov. 25, 1963]

A MARTYRED PRESIDENT

A Nation placidly going about its noontide affairs until the dark hour of last Friday's assassination of President John F. Kennedy, attends upon his funeral today following a weekend of shocked bereavement.

A week in which Americans normally would be approaching the mixed solemnity and festivities of Thanksgiving Day has been blighted by a murder, a monstrous crime which touches upon the lives, the homes, the families of all. The prayers for the dead and for a beloved President are on millions of lips and welling from millions of hearts this morning.

John Fitzgerald Kennedy in the 46 years of his American boyhood, youth, and manhood was one of those marked by destiny for a role in history, not alone of his own United States but in the annals of the free world and of free men. His fellow Americans, the great and the humble everywhere, find it incredible that the assassin bullet from a sniper's gun would close so abruptly, so dreadfully, the final chapter of this too brief biography— would make of him the fourth of our martyred Presidents.

In an eventful and dramatic life of public prominence and service John Fitzgerald Kennedy has been no stranger to the plaudits of the crowds, the accolades accorded our national heroes, the distinctions designating the famous. In death, he has received the most honest, the most sincere, and the most heartfelt of tributes, an outpouring of a Nation's love and affection, esteem, and recognition. The eulogies of personal friends and admirers, of political supporters and political adversaries, have been one in their mutual expression.

Today the martyred President lies in a flag-draped casket in the Nation's Capitol. The burdens and responsibilities of his office have been thrust upon a new and sorrowing President. Governor Dempsey has proclaimed this a day of mourning in Connecticut.

The sympathies of our people, individually, and collectively, for the family of the slain president, Mrs. Kennedy, his young daughter and son, his parents, and all who survive him, are echoed in this proclamation. Let this day be observed in our State as the Governor requests us.

[From the Bridgeport (Conn.) Post, Nov. 23, 1963]

THE NATION'S TRAGEDY

Tragedy stalked nakedly in Texas yesterday when an assassin's bullet took the life of President Kennedy, as he pressed his previously triumphant speaking tour in the Lone Star State.

But this grim tragedy concerned not only its noted victim, and the Governor of Texas who was wounded by the same rifle burst, but extended to ever-widening circles throughout this country and the free world—yes, even to Communist nations.

The tragic event also placed an overwhelming burden upon Lyndon B. Johnson, who yesterday took the oath as President, as domestic and world problems have moved toward crossroads in which vital policies must be developed and decisive actions taken.

The current issues are too well known to be enumerated here, but some of them are taxes, medicare, Cuba, Vietnam, Cambodia, Berlin, and myriad others. The new President, even though he may have been in close confidence with the martyred President, and is familiar with pending situations, must shoulder the task ahead and maintain the fine balance that has kept us, thus far, out of direct conflict on the international front and out of recessionary trends at home.

Thus the sudden and ghastly death of President Kennedy cast a pall over the world. In world chancelleries lights burned fitfully. In the churches, prayers were offered for the assassinated Chief Executive, and in the hearts of his countrymen, regardless of politics, there was sorrow.

This sorrow was not only for the untimely passing of a young and vigorous President. It contained also a somber feeling of worry over what portends despite the normal American optimism that everything will work out satisfactorily.

In his inaugural address President Kennedy enunciated a major precept of patriotism.

"Ask not what your country can do for you, ask what you can do for your country."

A few days ago former President Eisenhower added this sentence to that precept:

"To live for your country is a duty as demanding as is the readiness to die for it."

On both counts, President Kennedy has set the example. None can gainsay that he lived and performed his duties faithfully as he saw them, and at the end, he gave his life.

[From the Bridgeport (Conn.) Telegram, Nov. 23, 1963]

MARTYRED PRESIDENT

A tragedy beyond words struck our Nation yesterday when President John F. Kennedy was assassinated. Beyond words, indeed, for there are no words to describe the unconscionable deed, or the overwhelming grief of millions of Americans.

The facts are so stark, and so wretched, they strike all of us in a shocking manner, deeper and more poignant than any other type of sorrow. The President of the United States, young, vigorous, intelligent, personable— assassinated by the hand of a wanton, pitiless, secret foe.

This awful death, which links the President to the ranks of our martyred dead, is a profound personal and woeful loss to all of us.

Yesterday, millions of Americans differed, which is their political right, in the nature of our democratic government. And moments after President Kennedy had concluded a powerful political address and began a motorcade procession in Dallas, he slumped, virtually in the arms of his young wife, a maniac's victim.

A hush spread from Dallas over the Nation as the tragic message reached city and hamlet and tears welled spontaneously. There were then no differences of political opinion, no Democrats, no Republicans. All Americans were awed by that mysterious sense of loss that comes with death, but more especially such a cruel death.

To Mrs. Kennedy, on her first trip with the President after her own personal suffering, and to their lovely, now fatherless children—our hearts go out—we can say no more.

[From the Bridgeport (Conn.) Sunday Herald,
Nov. 24, 1963]

A Great Man Dies and Yet Lives on

"For all flesh is as grass, and all the glory of man as
the flower of grass. The grass withereth and the flower
thereof falleth away."

Thus does the scripture on which John Kennedy's
church and faith were founded counsel us regarding the
fleetingly transient character of human life, and warn us
that even in the fullest flower of mind and body—even
in the prime of life—the grass and the flower may die
with cruel abruptness.

But the same scripture and the same church that warn
of fear and pestilence, agony and death, teach also that
life is eternal. The seed lives on; the seed of John Kennedy's greatness was his immortal soul.

And the flower lives on in our mind's eye. The flower
that is noble and beautiful may perish as does the flesh,
but its image lives on from generation unto generation, as
long as men have memories of the great and the good.

The flower lives on as the remembrance of a President
with courage to face a revolution whose proportions were
as cataclysmic in their way as the other great revolutionary
chapters in American history were in theirs.

Nor was it just courage, but a determination to vouch-
safe equality and opportunity to the Negro as no President
other than Lincoln had done before.

The flower of a great life lives on, too, in other images
of courage which men will identify with John Kennedy
as long as history is read—the courage to stand up firmly
to an aggressive totalitarian power when doing so could
have meant imminent nuclear annihilation.

And the courage, too, to stand up to corporate in-
transigence when its demands for greater profits could
have had catastrophic effects on the economy.

His courage we shall remember, and his nobility of
character, and the strength of his patience with men and
circumstances that often made the Presidency a painful
ordeal.

And the flower of a great life lives on in the image of a
man of great compassion. Never has any administration,
indeed, any head of any government anywhere, exerted
so much leadership in behalf of the physically and mentally
and culturally disadvantaged.

More than any President, John Kennedy viewed as one
of the key roles of Government that of an agent of a
humanitarian society lending its encouragement and support to those unable to fend for themselves.

Those who were dearest to President Kennedy have
from childhood been steeped in an unshakable faith that
the souls of the good live on eternally. And Americans
of every faith who know of John Kennedy's works know
that the flower of this noble spirit cannot really die, for its
roots are grounded in enduring greatness.

[From the Waterbury (Conn.) Republican,
Nov. 23, 1963]

John F. Kennedy

"Eternal rest grant unto him * * * and let perpetual
light shine upon him."

The shock and horror at the death by assassination of
John Fitzgerald Kennedy, 35th President of the United
States of America, confounds this Nation and the world
of nations.

His death has struck profound tragedy in the soul of
America. Stunned as must be every feeling human,
sympathy flows to the members of the Kennedy family
in their most excruciating hour.

Yesterday's cruel history has enervated Americans and
made awful pause in the lives of citizens bereaved of their
President. The Nation mourns and wonders, and mixed
with sorrow is the pulse of outrage at so despicable an act,
a deed all the more chilling because of the pathos of its
context. No one can visualize Mrs. Kennedy cradling
her husband's head and not feel emotion physically.

As of this writing the man who committed the murder
of John F. Kennedy is not positively identified, but he will
be the object of this Nation's wrath as he has been the
agent of its terrible loss.

Lyndon Baines Johnson, because of the murder in his
native Texas, which could have claimed his life too, has
been sworn in as the new President of the United States
in solemnity and grief, and to him devolve the awesome
duties of Chief Executive in an hour of personal and national distress.

What can and will be said and written about John F.
Kennedy the man and John F. Kennedy the President
will be here left to less trying hours. His death has jolted
the fabric of all contemporary affairs and few things in our
national and international life will be unaffected.

At this hour, while our country absorbs the shock and
the body of President Kennedy lies in state, grief holds
dominion. The President held a special place in the
hearts of the people of Waterbury, a place now darkened
by his death. He promised, at his second electrifying appearance on the green just over a year ago, that he would
come back to Waterbury at 3 o'clock in the morning—to
speak to the people of a city he had identified with his
presidential victory and whose enthusiasm had evidently
touched him. The crowd roared and there was no doubt
in any observer's mind that Waterbury would have been
there again in November 1964, if it had to brave a
firestorm.

Perhaps, a year from now, there will be somebody on
the green in symbolic waiting.

John F. Kennedy is dead. Let us mourn.

[From the Waterbury (Conn.) American, Nov. 23, 1963]

John F. Kennedy

Why?

Persistently, hour after hour, this question pushes itself
to the forefront.

Why?

The shocking news of the assassination of the 35th
President of the United States, John Fitzgerald Kennedy,
is almost unbelievable. The rational mind tries futilely
to tell itself that this has not really happened—not in the
year 1963 in a nation which considers itself civilized
and a leader in the fight for human freedom.

Yet the facts are there—cold and harsh and inescapable.

John Fitzgerald Kennedy, aged 46, a citizen, a veteran,
and a statesman is dead.

The youngest man ever to be elected to the Presidency of the United States, the first President to profess the Roman Catholic faith, a man of courage, conviction, and ideals; a man with a warm smile, a strong handclasp, and an overwhelming personality has suddenly been taken from us by the act of a maniac—and the whole world shudders.

Why?

We wish we knew.

But, failing to understand, we must necessarily turn to what lies ahead. Presently we are confronted with tragedy and sorrow and grief—and they will be with us for many months to come.

Even as we individually experience a sense of physical illness—an experience multiplied millions of times over in homes all across the Nation—we must be aware that John F. Kennedy was such a man as to point a friendly finger toward his countrymen and say, in effect:

"Keep punching."

The causes for which he fought and pleaded are still with us. They will not disappear because he has passed, nor will they be relegated to oblivion because his hand has lost its strength.

Ideas and ideals live on long after the men who conceive and support them leave these mortal shores. Even out of the present tragedy there is hope extant—and John F. Kennedy was nothing if not a man of hope for the future, for the improvement of the lot of his fellows, for peace and brotherhood among men.

We must mourn his passing—but we must not let our sorrow obscure the fact that he was a man of faith, a man who did not believe that he had all the answers, but only that he had an opportunity to lead in what he conceived to be the right direction; to set a course which others could follow, leading toward a better and brighter world.

We are stricken—but we would be letting him down if we failed to pursue the objectives which he so fervently and conscientiously sought.

We grieve for his family and his close friends—yet all the while knowing that they must hold close to their hearts a special share of the gratitude of a nation for his stalwart and courageous leadership in times that tried men's souls.

────

[From the Ansonia (Conn.) Evening Sentinel, Nov. 23, 1963]

JOHN FITZGERALD KENNEDY

When the fact of the President's death had penetrated the shock most of us experienced yesterday, there followed a sickening feeling as we contemplated the human depravity that could coldly undertake so cowardly a deed.

The dreadful news that an assassin's bullet had slain John Fitzgerald Kennedy, 35th President of the United States, in his 46th year, stunned his fellow citizens and the civilized world almost to disbelief. The lethal attack from a cowardly ambush struck down a leader whose approach to the difficulties that beset our times often invited controversy, yet his high courage, sharp intelligence, dedicated devotion to the good of his country as he saw it and decent family life earned almost universal respect from his fellow Americans.

The President's triumphal cavalcade had moved through Dallas streets lined with tens of thousands cheering him and his good and loyal wife. Moments later he was dying in her arms. The sympathy of Americans goes out to Mrs. Kennedy in her sudden sorrow that is almost beyond comprehension.

Those who saw what was happening in that Dallas street could hardly believe their eyes. None was more stunned than Vice President Lyndon B. Johnson, the native Texan, who had sought the Presidency in vain in 1960 and was now to have it thrust upon him through a national tragedy. As he undertook the onerous obligations of the Presidency, the Nation's new Chief Executive spoke with sadness and humility. The country, he said, had suffered a sad loss and he a personal one. The world shares the loss, he said, with Mrs. Kennedy.

"I will do my best—that is all I can do. I ask your help and God's," the new President said.

The youth, vigor, and buoyancy of President Kennedy had commanded wide admiration. His self-possession in the face of crisis had rallied the Nation in the eyeball confrontation over the Cuban missiles. He had given far more than lipservice to the principle that American liberties are the right of all Americans regardless of race.

President Kennedy was the first of Roman Catholic faith to be elected to the Presidency. Only 2 weeks ago he had been recognized by a representative body of the Protestant churches of the country with an award that testified to their sincere respect for him.

The news of his assassination was received around the world with deep sense of shock. No one ever knows the full extent to which a bullet directed by malice may alter history.

As the world mourns John F. Kennedy's tragic death, and recommends him to God in its prayers, men of good will everywhere will also pray earnestly that his successor, President Johnson, may find strength, courage and divine help to guide our ship of destiny on tomorrow's troubled seas.

────

[From the Bristol (Conn.) Press, Nov. 23, 1963]

THE NATION MOURNS

John Fitzgerald Kennedy, 46, the 35th President of the United States, is dead.

A saddened nation is still in a state of shock at the tragedy in Dallas which shook the entire civilized world. The bullet of a psychopathic sniper sped from an upper floor of a warehouse overlooking the presidential motorcade, and in a fraction of time dealt the lethal blow which snuffed out the life of the Chief Executive of the greatest free nation on the face of the earth.

Two hours earlier at his home in Uvalde, Tex., former Vice President John Nance Garner, giving a press interview on the occasion of his 95th birthday, had said that he believed that John Kennedy would prove to be one of the greatest Presidents this Nation ever had.

Truly, in the midst of life we all face death.

Disbelief, shock, grief and anger that such a terrible thing could happen in this land of ours were the sensations which swept the Nation in that order.

Although the predominant feelings of the people are of grief at the loss of a popular President and sympathy for the bereaved family, it would most certainly be the fervent wish of the late President that the Nation's business is paramount and must be carried on regardless.

President Lyndon B. Johnson is deserving of the consideration and support of the entire Nation as he undertakes the tremendous burden which we place on our highest government official.

Yet time is not so fleeting that we cannot take a moment to cherish the memory of a vigorous leader, a great humanitarian, a Christian gentleman who loved his fellow man and was dedicated to promoting the best interests of the Nation which he served so well for far too short a time.

For John Fitzgerald Kennedy was all of these.

A courageous young chief of state has died in the service of his country.

May he rest in peace.

————

[From the Danbury (Conn.) News-Times, Nov. 23, 1963]

THE WORLD MOURNS

Many an American awakened this morning with a vague hope that this had all been a bad dream, that the tragic events of Friday, November 22, 1963, had not really taken place.

But the disbelief so evident yesterday with the first reports that President John F. Kennedy had been shot in Dallas had long given way to worldwide sorrow and to horror at a monstrous deed.

Sorrow with and sympathy for Mrs. Jacqueline Kennedy and her two young children, now fatherless for their third and sixth birthdays next week. And for the grieving parents and other members of the closely knit Kennedy family. Indeed, sorrow for the Nation itself.

And horror at the infamous act which snuffed out the life of a young, vigorous and popular President in the prime of his life.

This was the fourth assassination of an American President in a little more than 98 years. As a world tragedy it ranks with the national tragedy of the first assassination, that of Abraham Lincoln.

It is ironic that John Fitzgerald Kennedy, who had worked so hard, and with such perseverance, to avert world violence, which could culminate only in nuclear war, was himself the victim of violence.

Yet, as we look back over events of the past few years, this in a way is not surprising. In far too many instances, in this country and in this hemisphere, extremists of the right and of the left have found persuasion unavailing and have turned to violent means.

The attack on Ambassador Stevenson, also in Dallas, was one recent instance. Bombings and shootings elsewhere—most noteworthy the murder of four Sunday school tots in a Negro church in Birmingham—were another.

The national horror at the assassination of President Kennedy should have the salutary effect of turning all from the path of violence and toward the path of peace which he unfailingly pursued.

Genuine sorrow surged through the nation yesterday and continued to swell today. Here, as elsewhere, people felt as if they had lost a member of their own family. Events were canceled, bells tolled and prayers offered.

President Kennedy will be remembered for many things—for his heroism as a PT boat commander in World War II, for his intellectual and literary qualities, for his service in the Senate, for his political "savvy" and tireless campaigning.

He will be best remembered, of course, for his nearly 3 years as President, his championing of liberty, his advocacy of human rights, his constant striving for world peace and national prosperity.

John Fitzgerald Kennedy, 35th President of the United States, died Friday in the line of duty. The world mourns a great leader, the country a truly great American and New England one who was outstanding among its many famous sons.

————

[From the Greenwich (Conn.) Times, Nov. 25, 1963]

A NATION MOURNS

The United States has passed through the saddest, most grief-stricken weekend in its entire history. The 35th President of the United States, John Fitzgerald Kennedy, was buried this afternoon in Arlington National Cemetery.

John F. Kennedy died on Friday afternoon in Dallas, Tex., a half hour after a sniper's bullet hit him as he rode alongside his wife in a happy motorcade. As the news quickly spread throughout the Nation, Americans were stunned. Heads shook in disbelief. It was difficult to understand. How could such a thing happen in the United States?

A deep, dark sorrow and despair descended on the land. The loss of the President is a personal thing to each and every American. The relationship of a President and his countrymen cuts across all lines of parties and creeds. The assassin's bullet brought a personal, heartfelt grief.

Words cannot describe the national horror. John F. Kennedy, who was dedicated to and worked so hard for peace, for the avoidance of world violence, for tolerance, became the victim of hate and violence.

John Fitzgerald Kennedy typified the emergence of the world into a new era, the space age. Young, fiery, courageous, determined, and able, he was a man who persevered in standing for what he thought was right. His youthful exuberance coupled with high intelligence and with deep devotion to his country, caught the fancy and imagination of America and the world.

We will never know the dimensions of greatness that John F. Kennedy might have reached in the coming years. The effects of his loss on the Nation and the world in the immediate future cannot be assessed at this time.

His comparatively brief career was one of public service—in the House of Representatives, the U.S. Senate, and the Presidency. He easily could have chosen a life of leisure instead. But as his career and stature grew, his dedication centered on human rights and the equality of men. ————

[From the Manchester (Conn.) Evening Herald, Nov. 23, 1963]

JOHN F. KENNEDY

The youth of him and the gallantry of him are tied in together.

They made a beautiful human combination to be ruined by one mad bullet plowing its way through his bone and flesh.

He was young, and he was gallant, and he was full of a dry sophisticated humor.

Perhaps the humor helped make him seem the most intelligent President of our times.

He could usually see himself, and one who sees himself can see others well, including his opponents.

There was a time when some of us were a little frightened of his youth. We thought that, when he actually got into the cold war battle he had talked about so much, he was at first nervous and uncertain. But when we saw him settle down, and blood himself, until he got to be able to fight with magnanimity and tolerance toward his enemy as well as considerable mastery.

But even when that judgment he was always talking about may have been a little uncertain, he never lacked for courage. He had the best kind—the courage to be gentle, the courage to go calmly against an hysterical general trend of surface nonsense, the courage to take the full and single responsibility for a mistake which may have been created by many.

He had the courage always to be himself.

He had the supreme courage to make himself the leader in the direct and necessary assault on one of the great barriers unworthily surviving in this democracy of ours.

When he had dared to fight that battle, and had won, the main domestic effort of his administration pressed on toward a second great battle of the same nature.

These domestic battles, the other great battle being fought in the whole world, were such as to breed extremist emotions in the minds of men, or to enlist the partisanship of sick men in search of extremist emotions.

Yesterday some of this irrational ugliness took the shape and concentrated power of a bullet.

When a culprit is found guilty, there will also be some guilt for the climate which produced and inspired him.

Let us try to cleanse ourselves, not merely by condemnation and punishment, but by trying to make some of our own living a tribute to the memory of this clean, gallant, literate, humor-gifted, excellence-dedicated young leader.

All the qualities in John F. Kennedy seemed to add up to one final denominator.

He was a civilized man, who fought against barbarism at home and abroad.

This was in his character as well as in his action. His hope for and belief in the possibility of a world in which men treated each other as civilized human beings was the dominant theme of his living.

The degree to which our living still falls short of that civilized state became the mark of his dying.

The horror of the sacrifice to which he headed, combined with the nobility with which he followed his path of duty and principle toward whatever the danger might be, made the imperfect torch of civilization flame higher as he passed it on.

———

[From the Meriden (Conn.) Journal, Nov. 23, 1963]

THE ASSASSINATION OF A PRESIDENT

John F. Kennedy, President of the United States, has been cut off in his prime by the bullet of a vile assassin.

The whole Nation sorrows today for the loss of this vital young leader who, like other martyred Presidents, has given his life for his country.

The office of President is one of great risk. The man who fills it is always in danger. Security precautions, as it has been demonstrated again and again, are never an absolute safeguard. A high-powered rifle, with telescopic sights, in the hands of a sharpshooter with the will and the desire to kill, can penetrate the screen of safeguards set up by the Secret Service.

When Franklin D. Roosevelt, Mrs. Roosevelt and Senator Maloney, with Gov. Wilbur Cross drove into Crown Street Square in an open car, all of the surrounding buildings were searched for their protection. Again when President Harry S. Truman spoke from a platform in front of the Record-Journal building, the President's guards surveyed every spot from which a rifle might have been trained upon him. Yet those who occupied the platform remarked that it would have been easy for an assassin, mingling with the crowd, to have plunged a knife into his back or to have shot him at close range. A President takes such risks everywhere he goes. He lives in constant danger, and knows it. If he thought of his own safety at all times, he would be a craven unfitted to be the Chief Executive of a great nation. President Kennedy, a World War II hero, was a brave man—as brave as any President we have ever known.

All Americans, regardless of their political affiliations, have a deep sense of personal loss in this tragedy. They mourn for a great man who stood by his beliefs and proclaimed them to the world. They mourn that he can never achieve the goals for which he had fought. They sympathize with his bereaved wife, his fatherless children, his parents, his brothers and sisters, the whole closely united Kennedy family.

Now comes the turning of the page, the beginning of a new chapter. Lyndon B. Johnson has been sworn in as the President of the United States. It is a matter of record that the new President aspired to the office which he now occupies when he contested with John F. Kennedy for the Democratic Presidential nomination. It is a matter of record that, despite the keen competition between these able men, prior to and at the convention, it was Kennedy who chose Johnson as his running mate. Whatever their differences had been, the pair achieved close harmony in their relationship as President and Vice President.

The Nation should close ranks behind President Johnson at this critical moment of history. He is a man of proven ability and long experience in government. We feel sure that he will acquit himself well in the position which has been thrust upon him.

———

[From the Meriden (Conn.) Morning Record, Nov. 23, 1963]

THE NATION MOURNS

We in the United States of America are completely stunned. So catastrophic is the assassination of the President that we are unable as yet to assess the measure of our loss. The suddenness of it all is appalling.

Nearly a century ago Lincoln was assassinated as he sat

in the theater. The next morning he was dead. Some years later President Garfield was shot soon after taking office. He lingered for some months but died as a result of the attack. Just after the turn of the century, President McKinley fell at the hands of an assassin. Again there was a gap between the crime itself and resultant death—time in which to condition a country's reflexes to the tragedy. This unhappy Friday noon the end came almost at once with dreadful finality.

How tragic is such a death. How wasteful of the youth, vigor, talent, experience, and capability for growth in leadership of this man who has served us diligently and faithfully for nearly 3 years in the highest office of the land.

Few of us either in his own party or of the opposition have agreed with John Kennedy on every one of his policies and activities as Chief Executive. Americans are independent thinkers. There seldom is unanimity and there hasn't been during this administration. But, as our President, Mr. Kennedy has had our full allegiance. He won our admiration as a hard worker, quick thinker, and courageous official. We quickened with pride in him for the speediness of his rise as a world figure. We have loved his image as an adored and adoring parent, as a husband justifiably proud of his lovely and talented wife, as a man of personal charm and brilliant intellect.

The loss cannot be measured. Our hearts ache for Mrs. Kennedy who has graced the White House these past 2 years and 10 months. We grieve for the two young Kennedys who had to share their daddy with the public and who will have only childish memories of his glowing figure to carry with them through the years. Our sympathy goes to President Kennedy's parents and to his devoted brothers and sisters. Everybody shares in their bereavement. And we are sorry for our United States that is meeting a national tragedy of great proportions, as we pay our last respects to a man whose life has been snuffed out by a dastardly deed.

———

[From the Middletown (Conn.) Press, Nov. 23, 1963]

JOHN KENNEDY

John Fitzgerald Kennedy, the 35th President of the United States, is dead of an assassin's bullet. He died with the quest of reason in his mind, with the vision of peace in his eyes, and with the hope of a more perfect union for all Americans in his heart.

All this he sought for us with gallantry and grace, with charm and wit, with energy and purpose, and with the unwavering knowledge that this Republic, as he once said, is "unwilling to witness or permit the slow undoing of those human rights to which this Nation has always been committed, and to which we are committed today at home and around the world." May it be so, as we try to orient ourselves in this overpowering hour, that this should be his remembrance.

Our citizens are still stunned beyond all belief; as Adlai Stevenson said, an event such as this is beyond instant comprehension. Here in our land of great civilization the fires of hate have burned so intensely that our President is dead. Willy Brandt in Berlin said it first: A light has gone out.

This is the sad truth. There will be many men in the future of our country who can fulfill the constitutional role of the Presidency with reason, intelligence, and good heart, certainly there have been such in the past. But few men could articulate and personify all that is the best about this country, and refresh for all disbelievers, the truth that this is a youthful, vigorous country whose destiny lies not in the past but in the great years to come.

That is why, perhaps, his death means so much to us all. His work was unfinished. His hopes had been defined, but only a few had been culminated. Even those who disagreed with his methods, often agreed with his aims.

At his inaugural he touched upon the dilemma of the man of the 20th century in a world beset by the cold war. "Let us never negotiate out of fear," he said. "But let us never fear to negotiate." To a world struggling in misery, he described the pragmatic reasons for our help: "If a free society cannot help the many who are poor, it cannot save the few who are rich."

In office, he tried to give national reality to the challenge as he saw it: "Since this country was founded, each generation of Americans has been summoned to give testimony to its national loyalty. The graves of young Americans who answered the call to service surround the globe." In peace he tried to approach this higher testimony.

Now that globe has one more grave.

When the tragedy slammed into the consciousness of America yesterday, the reaction of most people was that the deed must have been done by a John Bircher or a zealot in the cause of segregation. It now appears that this was not the case, and that there is a strong possibility that the lunacy of the left, and not the right, was responsible. In one sense it makes little difference, because assassinations are always the child of extremism. There is no radical cause for which an American President should die, because it is our national judgment that he should live to fight the fight for which he was elected.

Walt Whitman, writing in 1865 upon the death of Lincoln, said it rightly in: "O Captain! My Captain!"

"My Captain does not answer, his lips are pale and still,
My father does not feel my arm, he has no pulse nor will,
The ship is anchored safe and sound, its voyage closed
    and done,
From fearful trip the victor ship comes in with object
    won;
Exult O shores, and ring O Bells!
But I with mournful tread,
Walk the deck my Captain lies,
Fallen cold and dead."

As if to insure that our ship of state does not falter, Democrats and Republicans, Protestants and Catholics and Jews, southerners and northerners, easterners and westerners, white and Negro, all were united yesterday in grief and silent pledge to the Republic, while around the world, queens and pontiffs expressed their bereavement. In Berlin, in that separated enclave of freedom, the candles are to be lit at night in memory, and even also in Moscow, the captain of the guard who stands over Lenin's tomb, expressed sorrow at the death of the man who had tried, with principle, to bring peace to all men.

President Kennedy yesterday was in Texas, a land that shelters many who felt little comity with his views. He believed he should go there and he had prepared a short speech that will rank with his best. But instead of giving it, he was shot down, falling unconscious into the arms of his wife. For her presence, we should not grieve, she would have wanted it no other way, her heart would only have been heavier if she had not been there. Nor should we think thoughts of vengeance, nor have misguided regrets as to why it happened. Lincoln died because of his compassion; it would have advanced no cause to have President Kennedy martyred in the service of civil rights or constitutionalism or even anticommunism.

Now, as well, we have to countenance the ugly fact that the individual accused of the murder of the President was a self-avowed Marxist, an ex-patriot resident of the Soviet Union, and the local chairman of the Fair Play for Cuba Committee, an organization which was purportedly originated in the country by a gift of $5,000 from Raul Castro, the brother of Fidel Castro. Nations have gone to war for as much; the comparison of the assassination of Archduke Francis Ferdinand in Sarajevo, the flashpoint of World War I, is not inexact. But we think we know what the President would have wished, and it is not the easiest way to purge our sorrow.

It is a time, we say, to recall what is probably the best known passage of any inaugural address, given as Lincoln reached the pinnacle of his eloquence at his second inaugural: "With malice toward none, with charity for all, with firmness in the right as God gives us to see the right, let us strive to finish the work we are in, to bind up the Nation's wounds * * * to do all which may achieve and cherish a just and lasting peace among ourselves and with all nations."

For now we have a new President, even if our struggle be constant. May God protect him.

———

[From the Naugatuck (Conn.) Daily News, Nov. 23, 1963]

DAY OF INFAMY

Yesterday will forever be remembered as a day of infamy. It was a moment of reckoning for the assassins because they will be punished for the murderous attack on President Kennedy. The tears of the Nation fall heavily today and each will imbed in the soul of the Nation. President Kennedy was the image of our country. Whatever he said, whatever he did, so said and did the Nation. Yesterday time stood still. A nation was shocked mute for a period of horror, and when it realized the impact of what had happened, it wept. The blatant response of a people to what is a calamitous incidence rose above the awful din of an energetic world, and a black page in history was recorded. We cannot know the ordeal of a President but there must have been many hours of fretful sleep; many hours of fears and apprehension. But like every other President before him, Mr. Kennedy waded through the mire of criticism, censure, and festoons of Executive duties. His reward was death at the hands of assassins. We do not pretend to understand the motive nor the reason therefor, but we do

know that we have lost a leader of the highest caliber. No matter what our political affiliation may be, whatever we have felt in our hearts toward him when he acted according to his judgment, such acts perhaps contrary to our beliefs, we have now just cause to lament our loss. There is no eulogy more fitting than to say of him: that he mastered our ship of state to the best of his ability, and if he erred, it was because we, the followers, strayed perhaps too far from the path which he took, believing always that the path would lead to more fertile pastures. Though he walked alone at times, he walked in the light of perseverance. Though he may have faltered at times, he was but human. Though he be dead, he lives, for the beacon of his character, his strength, and his wisdom, shines forever to light our paths as we go on without him. Truly this Nation is impoverished by his untimely death. But we, who believe that God so made man that he would require servitude, and in that servitude all must resolve in the ultimate good to be weighed in the great balance, are solaced nevertheless by the knowledge that President Kennedy was needed elsewhere to fulfill a destiny that was marked for a brief period here on earth. He is gone, but his works live on.

———

[From the New Britain (Conn.) Herald, Nov. 23, 1963]

A MARTYR TO DEMOCRACY

Grief hangs heavy over America today.

We mourn the death of a great man, a respected man, a prince among men.

Just as another great President fell before the assassin's sinful shot some 98 years ago, John Fitzgerald Kennedy died yesterday.

He was slain while in the full flower of his life, in a moment of joyfulness, at a time when his leadership had won him the love and friendship of uncounted millions around the globe.

It was an inconceivable deed. It was a gross, shocking, horrible moment that spun this Nation cyclonically into disbelieving horror. It was an act of hate, all the more violent because ours is a land of reason, of love and understanding. Yet, because we have believed so strongly in democracy, because we have recognized the right of men not to agree, we have allowed the haters to exist in our land.

Our dead President Kennedy is a martyr to democracy.

John Fitzgerald Kennedy believed in peace and freedom. He dedicated his stewardship to those ends, bearing on his own shoulders the massive weight of attempting to achieve justice for mankind even while under the shadow of the possibility of a nuclear holocaust. Yet he bore the burden with dedication, with a savor for the job, with a growing command of the complexities of the world.

Mr. Kennedy was for the little man. He fought hardest for those programs and policies which would have taken the burdens of life, insofar as was possible, off the shoulders of the oppressed and the poor. This sense of Christian charity permeated his very being.

At this moment, we are all Americans first. Not Democrats or Republicans or northerners or liberals or conservatives. We are simply Americans, the children of God, mourning a lost leader. It is as though we have lost a member of our own family: a father, a brother, a son.

Thank God for the wisdom of our Republic that our leadership, even under such terrible crisis, can pass smoothly and without panic, to qualified men. We pray for Lyndon Baines Johnson, our new President.

And we pray, too, that the ideals for which John F. Kennedy gave his life did not die with the firing of that bullet.

[From the New London (Conn.) Day, Nov. 23, 1963]

JOHN F. KENNEDY

The grief, the sense of outrage, at the assassination of President John F. Kennedy, are universal in this country today.

The tragic circumstances were appalling. They stunned millions, first hearing the news and unable to believe it. It seemed incredible, devastating—that a young man in the prime of life, who had been vigorously touring numerous parts of the country and recently Texas, could now lie dead, the victim of a sniper. The apparent ease with which it was done, the fact that Mrs. Kennedy was in the car, the wounding of the Texas Governor—all these make the shock more staggering.

Almost without a single exception Americans react with unbelieving wonder and helpless anger to such a thing as this—a rarity in their more or less orderly lives. In this Nation's long history there have been other attacks upon Presidents, but none with the immediate deadly effectiveness of this one. In other shootings the people have had a little time to absorb the shock, before the death of the Chief Executive.

Political divisions and partisan ideas are forgotten by the people at a time like this, as they try inadequately to express their deep sympathy for the family, their grief over this incomprehensible tragedy. They will, also, loyally pledge their cooperation in this Nation's time of crisis—the transition from the administration of John Kennedy to Lyndon Johnson, which under the best of circumstances will present problems. They will grieve also, it seems likely, over the needless sacrifice of a young man, representing a dedicated and highly intelligent effort to lead his country to peace and prosperity.

The needless angle is, as a former Chief of the Secret Service recently said, that any determined crank, with real ability as a marksman, could assassinate any President we have had in modern times. This follows because of the way in which the Chief Executive appears, relatively unprotected, in the midst of large crowds. The tragic circumstances suggest an earnest appraisal of this situation.

There is incalculable loss to the world, not just to the narrow confines of this Nation. Freedom-loving people everywhere had reason for faith and hope in a brightening ideal of real, democratic government under the inspiration of a hardworking American leader. The intelligence, the qualities of leadership, the inspiration offered by this dynamic young Executive had a profound bearing upon their lives.

However, much the American citizen feels the loss, his thoughts must turn to the personal tragedy inflicted on Jacqueline Kennedy and the two young Kennedy children. Mr. Kennedy was a devoted husband and father, a model of parenthood in the way he found time, despite the demands of a busy life, to meet the needs of his family.

Indeed, Mrs. Kennedy herself set an example of courage and reliance in a higher authority during the terrible experience in Dallas and the subsequent return with the President's remains to the White House. Perhaps there is a lesson here for all Americans.

In truth, life goes on, the man's ideas and ideals live beyond the shadow of death. Mr. Kennedy, born to wealth and with no need for further material advantages, concentrated on service to his Nation. The memory of him can only serve to strengthen America's resolve to face its problems with courage.

[From the Norwalk (Conn.) Hour, Nov. 23, 1963]

PRESIDENT KENNEDY

A shocked and sorrowful Nation today mourns the tragic death of John F. Kennedy, 35th President of the United States, who was fatally shot by a cowardly, hidden assassin Friday afternoon in Dallas, Tex.

President Kennedy joins the other martyred Chief Executives who fell from assassins' bullets—Lincoln, Garfield, and McKinley.

In Norwalk, like elsewhere all over the world, news of President Kennedy's death cast a pall of sorrow and brought tears to the eyes of hundreds.

President Kennedy, 46, was the youngest man ever elected to the Presidency, and was the first Roman Catholic ever to hold that Office.

Few will ever forget him at his inauguration when he dedicated himself to two shining goals—survival of liberty at home and peace in a world shivering in an "uncertain balance of terror."

Many important events occurred during his administration: His pledge to fight if necessary to maintain Americans' rights of access to Red-surrounded Berlin; manned flights into outer space; and abortive invasion of Cuba by U.S.-aided refugees; increase in the minimum wage from $1 an hour to $1.25; Social Security benefits increased; organization of the Peace Corps; moratorium with Russia on nuclear bomb testing; his showdown with Khrushchev to force Russia to remove nuclear weapons from Cuba.

In the present session of Congress, many of President Kennedy's proposals—income tax reduction, foreign aid, etc., met with a rough reception.

These and the other proposals of his program—what will happen to them now? And how will this affect the delicate balance of the chiefs of state in the cold war—De Gaulle, Erhardt, Home and Khrushchev—in their almost endless negotiations?

But these are, as of the moment, minor considerations compared to the fact that the democratic world not the United States alone, has lost a leader who proved himself fearless in the Russian crisis, a man of intense feeling for the underdog, and a man with the intelligence, imagination and force to fight his way toward all his objectives.

Political friends and foes alike agree on President Kennedy's patriotism and sincerity. His shocking death will never be forgotten. His love of country should be a shining example to all of the youth of our Nation.

[From the Norwich (Conn.) Bulletin, Nov. 23, 1963]

A NATION'S SORROW

A sniper's bullet, fired from ambush, plunged the Nation and the world into sorrow as it cut down John Fitzgerald Kennedy, President of the United States, while he rode with his wife and Gov. John B. Connally of Texas in a motorcade at Dallas, Tex., early Friday afternoon. Mortally wounded in the head Mr. Kennedy was taken to a Dallas hospital where he died some 20 minutes later. Governor Connally was gravely wounded in the chest by the assassin.

The Nation in its deep mourning at the tragic death of its young President stands appalled and stunned to think that such a thing could happen in a Nation as civilized as ours. Despotic rulers have fallen at the hands of the assassin since the world began, but no one could conceive that it could happen here. There must have been deep hatred in the heart of the man who so ruthlessly fired the shot that took the life of the President. It is unthinkable that anyone, unless mentally ill, could commit such a despicable act.

The assassination of President Kennedy was one of the most tragic in the history of the Nation, largely because of the suddenness that death came. Other Presidents have died at the hand of an assassin but they did not die until sometime after they had been shot, and the people were prepared for the news of their death. Yesterday, it was only a space of minutes after the news spread that the President had been shot that word of his death was flashed across the Nation and to the world.

A young man in the prime of manhood John F. Kennedy had achieved the ultimate in the field of politics— the head of the greatest Nation on earth. He had achieved this highest office in the Nation by surmounting obstacles that had defeated many who aspired to the office before him. He was born of a wealthy background; he was considered of the intelligentsia because of his Harvard background; he was the son of a man of great political influence and he was a Catholic. It was his simplicity, his youthfulness and his charming personality that carried him to the heights.

President Kennedy, although severely criticized both by members of his own party and by the Republicans, was dedicated to the interests of the Nation. In fact, his dedication extended beyond the boundaries of America. He thought in terms of world harmony; he strove to help the faltering economy of lesser nations, he was dedicated to the advancement of world peace. But there were times when he could be firm in world crisis, not to say tough. When elected there were cries that he was too young for the duties of President, but he proved his critics wrong. He performed with the efficiency of an older man; he was a student of national and international politics.

John F. Kennedy has gone and the Nation mourns; the world mourns and there is sadness everywhere. Even in Soviet Russia there is respect for the memory of Mr. Kennedy; President de Gaulle of France with whom he differed is saddened; in other nations, in Latin America where Mr. Kennedy visited there are expressions of grief and sympathy. Seldom has a President of the United States met and made friends with the leaders of other nations as the late President. To say that he was not loved by all the international leaders may be putting it mildly but there is certainty that he was respected.

Here in America he was beloved by many and respected by all. Everyone is shocked at the sudden termination of his life and the sympathy of the Nation goes to his wife and children and to his parents. We add our small tribute to a man who has given his all to our Nation and our sympathy to those who were near and dear to him.

––––

[From the Stamford (Conn.) Advocate, Nov. 23, 1963]

JOHN F. KENNEDY

John F. Kennedy, President of the United States, died yesterday by an assassin's bullet. At the age of 46, he was a man of vigor, good health, and joy of life. His death brought disbelief, shock, dismay, and national sorrow.

He was born to great wealth. With his joyous disposition, he could have spent his life in self-pleasure without criticism. Instead, after an outstanding war record, he entered the field of politics, in which for generations his family had been prominent. He achieved immediate success. He became the youngest man ever to be elected to the highest office in our Nation.

Along with his political New Frontier, he brought to Washington a new, youthful spirit which the whole Nation, regardless of political persuasion, took to its heart. His devotion to his wife, his affection for his children gave the Nation assurance that all the old values were not dead. His sorrow over the death of an infant son became a national sorrow.

He was the first Catholic elected to the Presidency. For all time, he put an end to the false fear that a Catholic in the White House would be controlled by a Pope from Rome in secular affairs.

John F. Kennedy came to high office in trying times. The free world was tiring of the effort demanded of it to fight the cold war. This caused a weakening of needed ties. New states emerged, with loud voices, little power, and no economic viability. Their people needed help if they were to rise from poverty which was destructive to human dignity. Twenty million Negro Americans determined that now was the time to join their white fellow citizens as full partners.

These waves for change placed complex burdens on the youthful shoulders of the President. He shouldered them with courage and deep, human sympathy.

Gen. Douglas MacArthur said that on learning of the former President's death, a small part of him died with him. All Americans, in sympathy with the closely knit Kennedy family, feel with the General the loss of the personification of youthful vitality that John F. Kennedy had made part of the national way of life.

––––

[From the Torrington (Conn.) Register, Nov. 23, 1963]

A NATION MOURNS

John F. Kennedy's career as President of the United States ended yesterday, when a senseless murderer assassinated him in Dallas, Tex.

The slaying of our Chief Executive struck the Nation with horror, leaving all of us shocked and saddened.

President Kennedy fulfilled the duties of President with dignity and distinction. His youth and vigor indicated he could continue to serve his Nation in distinguished manner for years to come.

It seems unbelievable that, in a free society such as ours, the career of the head of our Nation could be ended in such a manner. We all regret the occurrence, and angrily hope that the person responsible will be brought to justice quickly and properly.

We join people everywhere in mourning the death of John F. Kennedy. Our sincerest sympathy goes to his wife, his children and other members of his family.

And, as we mourn this death, we also express sincere hopes for success to Lyndon B. Johnson, who succeeded to the Presidency because of the despicable act in Dallas.

President Johnson's task is a difficult one. May he have the ability and strength to cope with it, and may all Americans give him the support he needs to guide the United States to new and greater heights.

————

[From the Willimantic (Conn.) Daily Chronicle, Nov. 23, 1963]

LEGACY OF A PRESIDENT

"Are you sure? I'm shaking. Is it possible?"

That is the way one woman responded to the news of President Kennedy's death. The President who had mingled with crowds in Berlin, Cologne, Paris, Dublin, London, and San Jose with fearless abandon, was killed by an assassin's bullet in Dallas, Tex.

Adlai Stevenson, U.S. Ambassador to the United Nations, can count himself lucky. When he was in Dallas recently he only got hit on the head with a poster carried by an angry picket. But who envisioned a sniper's bullet for the President?

John F. Kennedy was the youngest man ever elected President of the United States. He brought to this Nation a symbol of a new generation. He came to office at a time when the new age of technology and space was breaking over the civilized world. His phrase "The New Frontier" stirred the imagination of his people.

President Kennedy was a war hero in the greatest tradition. It was not that he won great battles, but that he risked his life for a member of his crew in the South Pacific. That regard for the individual is a hallmark of American tradition and President Kennedy not only preached it, he knew whereof he spoke.

It is ironic that Abraham Lincoln who freed the slaves was shot and so was President Kennedy who almost went down in history as the President who gave the Negroes equal opportunity.

President Kennedy will not leave behind him any great program which he pushed through Congress. He was cut down before his potential could be realized. He will be remembered in history for his dramatic Cuban stand that forced the Russians to take their missiles home. The Peace Corps was a startling innovation and a tremendous success. The Alliance for Progress is on a rocky road but the new emphasis on Latin America was a change in foreign policy.

There were contrasting symbols associated with President Kennedy. His famous word "vigah" became common wherever Americans gathered. His liking for a rocking chair started a new trend in home furnishings. President Kennedy touched a nerve deep within his people.

John Fitzgerald Kennedy brought to the Presidency a sense of history, a love for the arts and sciences and a respect for intelligence. It seems to us that a whole generation has been inspired by these Kennedy ideals. Perhaps there is no bill in Congress, no monument to point to, but Kennedy's intangible ideals impressed the young and old alike. "Ask not what your country can do for you, but what you can do for your country." These few words from President Kennedy's inaugural address gave the Nation renewed inspiration.

There is a new respect for intellectual achievement in the Nation, a reverence for art and a new optimism about the future. The cold war will be long and burdensome, but President Kennedy seemed to give the Nation confidence we can win it.

Our Nation will go on. But the Nation will not soon forget the spirit of the New Frontier. May its momentum carry us forward in the generation ahead.

We join with the world in offering our sympathy to the President's wife and her two small children. The world will miss him—how much, only the future will tell. ————

[From the Winsted (Conn.) Evening Citizen, Nov. 23, 1963]

TO HONOR HIS MEMORY

When a leader of great power and presence and capacity for good dies in office, the cause to which he gave leadership suffers grievous loss. President John F. Kennedy was such a man. The cause he served, and so eloquently led, was the threefold cause of human dignity and equality and freedom.

Though President Kennedy is dead, struck down most foully by an assassin's hand, the cause he championed as acknowledged leader of the free world lives on. We who survive him can best honor his memory by doing all in our power to advance that cause, which is the very cause for which this Nation was founded.

Guidance for the difficult time ahead may be taken from the immortal words spoken by Abraham Lincoln on that solemn occasion at Gettysburg almost exactly a century ago. For President Kennedy died in defense of freedom as truly as did those who fell on that historic field of battle. In these days of profound national sorrow it is appropriate to reflect on Lincoln's exhortation to his fellow Americans "that from these honored dead we take increased devotion to that cause for which they gave the last full measure of devotion—that we here highly resolve that these dead shall not have died in vain."

To resolve thus and to act thus—that is the task to which we must now turn our minds. This is so even though grief and a deep sense of loss will far outlast the initial period of outraged shock at the murderous act in Dallas. We cannot permit ourselves the luxury of heedless sorrow. The forces that work against the realization of man's highest dreams remain strong and malignant. Those forces must now be countered with new dedication, so that President Kennedy's martyrdom in the fullness of life shall indeed not have been in vain.

The heaviest burden falls upon Lyndon B. Johnson, who became President the moment John F. Kennedy succumbed to the assassin's bullets. But all citizens must in some measure share that burden. In his first public utterance as Chief Executive, President Johnson said this to the American people: "I will do my best. That is all I can do. I ask your help—and God's." It is a commitment, and a challenge, worthy of the best that is in all of us.

Mr. President, I have been deeply moved by the messages I have received on the death of our late President. So many of them express our feelings poignantly and eloquently. I include a poem of beautiful simplicity which came to me from Bloomfield, Conn.

ONE MAN ONE G-D

One man is dead.
I did not know him; I never saw him.
His death has hurt me.

One shot has killed him.
I did not see it or even hear it.
His death has frightened me.

One man has killed him.
I do not hate him.
His deed has stunned me.

One woman has no husband.
I do not know her.
Her tragedy is mine.

One girl and boy have lost a father.
I need no pity.
My pity is with them.

One country has lost a President.
I love this country—it is mine.
Its loss is my loss.

One tear turned into many.
I cried for him.
His death perplexed me.

One man will be remembered.
I see the flag at half-mast.
His memory lives.

One belief is not ruined.
I know our faith will save us.
His G-d is my G-d.

—*Judith Anne Wright.*
Bloomfield, Conn.

Mr. President, on Monday night, November 25, the day of the funeral services for our martyred President, John F. Kennedy, I attended a Jewish community memorial service for President Kennedy, conducted under the auspices of the Greater Washington Rabbinate and the Jewish Community Council of Greater Washington. Among the 4,000 persons in the overflow crowd was the President of Israel, Shneor Zalman Shazar. Rabbis Norman Gerstenfeld, Martin S.

Halpern, Eugene J. Lipman, Stanley Rabinowitz, and Lewis A. Weintraub led the assembly in reading the order of the service; tributes were presented by Mr. Justice Arthur J. Goldberg, of the U.S. Supreme Court, and by the Honorable Myer Feldman, deputy special counsel to the President. Cantor Raphael Edgar chanted the memorial prayer.

The contents of this memorial were so meaningful and so moving, that I ask unanimous consent to use the order of the service and the texts of the tributes.

A JEWISH COMMUNITY TRIBUTE FOR OUR MARTYRED PRESIDENT, JOHN F. KENNEDY

(Under the auspices of the Greater Washington Rabbinate and the Jewish Community Council of Greater Washington, November 25, 1963, 8:30 p.m., at the temple of the Washington Hebrew Congregation, Massachusetts Avenue and Macomb Street NW., Washington, D.C.)

RESPONSIVELY

Lord, what is man, that Thou hast regard for him?
Or the son of man, that Thou takest account of him?
Man is like a breath,
His days are as a fleeting shadow.
In the morning he flourishes and grows up like grass,
In the evening he is cut down and withers.
So teach us to number our days,
That we may get us a heart of wisdom.
Mark the man of integrity, and behold the upright,
For there is a future for the man of peace.

PSALM 23—A PSALM OF DAVID

The Lord is my Shepherd; I shall not want.
He maketh me to lie down in green pastures;
He leadeth me beside the still waters.
He restoreth my soul;
He guideth me in straight paths for His name's sake.
Yea, though I walk through the valley of the shadow of death,
I will fear no evil, for Thou art with me;
Thy rod and Thy staff, they comfort me.
Thou preparest a table before me in the presence of mine enemies;
Thou has anointed my head with oil; my cup runneth over.
Surely goodness and mercy shall follow me all the days of my life;
And I shall dwell in the house of the Lord forever.

AMERICA—FOUNDED ON BIBLICAL PRECEPTS

We hold these truths to be self-evident, that all men are created equal, that they are endowed by their Creator with certain inalienable rights, that among these are life, liberty, and the pursuit of happiness.

Have we not all one Father?
Hath not one God created us?
Why do we deal treacherously, a man against his brother?

We, the people of the United States, in order to form a more perfect union, establish justice, insure domestic tranquillity, provide for the common defense, promote the general welfare, and secure the blessings of liberty to ourselves and our posterity, do ordain and establish a constitution for the United States of America.

Justice, justice shalt thou pursue,
That thou mayest live in the land which God giveth thee.

Congress shall make no law respecting an establishment of religion, or prohibiting the free exercise thereof; or abridging the freedom of speech, or of the press; or the right of the people peaceably to assemble, and to petition the Government for a redress of grievances.

Proclaim liberty throughout the land,
Unto all the inhabitants thereof.

Of all the dispositions and habits, which lead to political prosperity, religion, and morality are indispensable supports. Where is the security for property, for reputation, for life, if the sense of religious obligation desert the oaths which are the instruments of investigation in courts of justice? And let us with caution indulge the supposition that morality can be maintained without religion.

It hath been told thee, O man, what is good,
And what the Lord doth require of thee:
Only to do justly and to love mercy,
And to walk humbly with thy God.

For happily the Government of the United States which gives to bigotry no sanction, to persecution no assistance, requires only that they who live under its protection should demean themselves as good citizens in giving it on all occasions their effectual support.

Righteousness maketh a nation great,
But sin is a reproach to any people.

We here highly resolve that these dead shall not have died in vain—that this Nation, under God, shall have a new birth of freedom—and that government of the people, by the people, and for the people, shall not perish from the earth.

Behold, how good and pleasant it is
For brethren to dwell together in unity.

With firmness in the right as God gives us to see the right, let us strive on to finish the work we are in, to do all which may achieve and cherish a just and lasting peace among ourselves and with all nations.

Let justice well up as the waters,
And righteousness as a mighty stream.

In the future days which we seek to make secure, we look forward to a world founded upon four essential human freedoms: freedom of speech and expression—everywhere in the world; freedom of every person to worship God in his own way—everywhere in the world; freedom from want which will secure to every nation a healthy peacetime life for its inhabitants—everywhere in the world; freedom from fear, which means a worldwide reduction of armaments to such a point and in such a thorough fashion that no nation will be in a position to commit an act of physical aggression against any neighbor—everywhere in the world.

And they shall beat their swords into plough-shares,
And their spears into pruning-hooks,
Nation shall not lift up sword against nation,
Neither shall they learn war any more.
But they shall sit every man under his vine
And under his fig tree;
And none shall make them afraid.

WORLD PEACE

It shall come to pass at the end of days
That the mountain of the Lord's house shall be established
As the top of the mountains;
It shall be exalted above the hills;
All the nations shall flow unto it.
And many peoples shall go and say,
"Come, let us go up to the mountain of the Lord."
God will teach us His ways,
And we will walk in His paths;
God shall judge between the nations;
He shall decide for many peoples.
And they shall beat their swords into plowshares,
And their spears into pruning forks.
Nation shall not lift up sword against nation;
Neither shall they learn war any more.
The Lord will break the bow and the sword
And the battle out of the land;
He will make the people to lie down in safety.
Violence shall no more be heard in your land.
Neither desolation nor destruction within your borders.
All your children shall be taught of the Lord.
And great shall be the peace of your children.
They shall not hurt nor destroy in all God's holy mountain,
For the earth shall be full of the knowledge of the Lord,
As the waters cover the sea.
The work of the righteous shall be peace,
And the result of righteousness, quietness and confidence forever.
Then shall they sit every man under his vine
And under his fig tree,
And none shall make them afraid,
For the Lord Himself hath spoken it.

FOR A REDEDICATION OF AMERICA TO HER TRADITIONAL IDEALS

Let America be America again.
Let it be the dream it used to be.
Let it be the pioneer on the plain
Seeking a home where he himself is free.
Let America be the dream the dreamers dreamed—
Let it be that great strong land of love,
Where never kings connive nor tyrants scheme
That any man be crushed by one above.
O, let my land be a land where Liberty
Is crowned with no false patriotic wreath,
But opportunity is real, and life is free,
Equality is in the air we breathe.

O, let America be America again—
The land that never has been yet—
And yet must be—the land where every man is free,
The land that's mine—the poor man's, Indian's, Negro's—
    we
Who made America,
Whose sweat and blood, whose faith and pain,
Whose hand at the foundry, whose plow in the rain.
Must bring back our mighty dream again.
And yet this oath I swear—
America will be!
Out of the rack and ruin of our gangster death,
The rape and rot of graft, and stealth, and lies,
We, the people, must redeem America.
We, the people, must redeem
The land, the mines, the plants, the rivers,
The mountains and the endless plain—
All, all the stretch of these great green states—
And make America America again!

                                    —*Langston Hughes.*

TRIBUTE BY HON. MYER FELDMAN, DEPUTY SPECIAL
COUNSEL TO THE PRESIDENT

I do not intend to eulogize him; others far more articulate than I have done it during the past 2 days and will do it in the future.

Nor do I intend to ask the question which must trouble all of us at times like this: "Why?" The rabbis in their wisdom should answer that for us.

Nor do I intend to answer the question of his place in history. Historians have already begun to make these judgments, and I leave to their mercies this task.

But there is a custom common among learned Jews that I should like to pursue. After one whose life has touched them has passed away they gather together and exchange recollections of that person. John F. Kennedy touched the lives of all of us, and I should like to share with you some of my memories.

I saw truckloads of flowers delivered to the White House yesterday, and I saw beautiful floral pieces decorating the hillside at Arlington Cemetery when he was laid to rest. But I thought of his joy as he looked out the french doors of his office and delighted in the beauty of the flower garden, the pride that he took in its reconstruction, and his pleasure in the beauties of nature. I saw John-John walk down the aisle of St. Matthew's Cathedral. But I remembered a morning only 2 or 3 weeks ago when John-John appeared at a business breakfast in the White House and sat in the chair that was reserved for the Secretary of State. The President, who had just decided upon the transfer of thousands of men thousands of miles, was unable to move John-John out of that chair.

I saw the silent crowds along the route we drove in a motorcade to the cemetery. But I thought of a hundred other motorcades, and of the impossibility of restraining John F. Kennedy from leaving his seat and walking along so that he could meet the people along the way. I thought of how, when arriving at an airport, he insisted upon walking to the barriers to shake hands, in spite of the pleas of Secret Service men. He felt that those who took

the trouble to come to the airport were entitled to more than a fleeting glimpse of their President.

I saw the Negro pallbearers carrying the casket. But I remembered that day a little less than 3 years ago when he asked why there were no Negroes in the Coast Guard unit in the inaugural parade. This was quickly corrected.

I saw the preoccupations all around me, both in the funeral procession and in the airplane flying over the Pacific, where I learned the news. But I thought of the many preoccupations engendered by times of crisis. In the midst of one of the most severe, he was told of a letter from the widow of a postal employee who had died of cancer, leaving several small children. He learned that the husband had been so active in helping others he had been unable to accumulate any resources. President Kennedy dictated a response which assured her that a cold Government had a warm heart.

I saw the forlorn dogs on the White House lawn. And I thought of the kind manner in which he would call to them and bring them inside so that he could feed them a delicacy and send them on their way.

I thought of his flashes of wit and how these lightened the burden of everyone around him.

These were all random thoughts. They came to mind in connection with almost every incident during the past 2 days. They represented a man so full of compassion and understanding, so creative in mind, so courageous in spirit, that no one his life has touched, be it ever so lightly, will ever be the same. We are all the better for his having been with us.

Now it is up to us to pick up the torch which he lighted and follow along the way which he charted.

TRIBUTE BY MR. JUSTICE ARTHUR J. GOLDBERG,
U.S. SUPREME COURT

In the Book of Ecclesiastes, chapter 9: 12, it is said, "For man also knoweth not his time, as the fishes that are taken in an evil net, and as the birds that are caught in the snare, so are the sons of men snared in an evil time, when it falleth suddenly upon them." Friday was an evil time. Sunday was an evil time. Today our country has engaged in a day of national mourning; it has also endured a day of national shame.

It is a cardinal principle of our democracy derived from Biblical teachings that it is an inalienable right of man, as a child of God, to have human dignity. The assassination of our great President on Friday was a supreme violation of human dignity; the killing of the man charged with the assassination Sunday was a violation of human dignity too, for on Friday life was taken, the great commandment "Thou shalt not kill" was violated; and on Sunday a life was taken too without due process of law. Human dignity on both occasions was violated.

Today's day of mourning was different from that day of mourning when we buried our great President Franklin Roosevelt, because while our grief today was equally great, it was compounded by humiliation—humiliation lacking when Franklin Roosevelt was buried. If, in a new country in a remote corner of the world, the head of state was assassinated and if the man charged with the killing was himself assassinated a few days later while in the custody of the police, we would say to ourselves, in all self-righteousness, that the country was not fit to govern; that it was uncivilized. What are we to say to ourselves as a nation?

John F. Kennedy, 2 weeks before his inauguration, stood in the assembly of his native State of Massachusetts, and gave a speech in which he quoted Pericles' statement to the Athenians, "We do not imitate, but are a model to others." John F. Kennedy proudly said of our country, "We are a model to others, we do not imitate." An assassination is not an act of a people, another killing is not an act of a people, but in a very significant sense, we are all responsible for these terrible happenings—all of mankind is responsible. The dominant characteristic of our modern times is the cheapness of human life. The dominant characteristic of the present age is the lack of respect for the human being—our forgetfulness of the human dignity with which God endowed every human being. More people have been killed, more exterminations have taken place, more massive barbarism has occurred in the world since the beginning of World War II than has ever been recorded in the history of civilization.

There is another saying from Ecclesiastes, "Sorrow is better than laughter, for by the sadness of the countenance the heart is made better." Let us use the occasion of the sad, sad passing of our great President to make the heart better, to make the heart more responsive to what is needed in the world. And what is needed in the world more than any other thing is love and not hatred, because in a real sense, hatred is what caused the terrible events of the last few days.

Our late President, John F. Kennedy, was a man of love; he was not a man of hatred. He devoted himself in the international affairs to the elimination of hatred between nations, to the cause of world peace and world justice. He devoted himself, in domestic affairs, to the elimination of hatred between the people of this country, to the cause of equality and brotherhood. The President is a victim of the unfinished tasks of his own administration. Would that he had lived out his full days and his full time, so that he could have witnessed a more peaceful world and, in the words of our Constitution, a more perfect union. But he was snared in an evil time, and he knew not his time as indeed we know not our time.

We owe it to the memory of our martyred President to rid our Nation of the evil forces of hate and bigotry and violence. In the book of President Kennedy's speeches, which he called "To Turn the Tide" he wrote, "Neither wind nor tide is always with us. Our course on a dark and stormy sea cannot always be clear, but we have set sail, and the horizon, however cloudy, is also full of hope." Today, our course is on a dark and stormy sea, and the horizon is cloudy. We must make it full of hope, full of hope for a better world, full of hope, for freedom, for justice, for order, for peace. These are the ends of organized society, these are the ends for which President Kennedy gave his life, these are the ends to which we must all rededicate ourselves anew.

Memorial Prayer—"El Molei Rahamim"
[Translation]

O merciful God who dwellest on high and art full of compassion, grant perfect rest beneath the shelter of Thy divine presence among the holy and pure who shine as the brightness of the firmament, to John Fitzgerald Kennedy, President of the United States, who gave his life for his country and for humanity. May his soul be bound up in the bonds of eternal life. Grant that his memory ever inspire us to noble and consecrated living. Amen.

———

America, the Beautiful

O beautiful for spacious skies,
  For amber waves of grain,
For purple mountain majesties
  Above the fruited plain!
America! America!
  God shed His grace on thee,
And crown thy good with brotherhood
  From sea to shining sea!

O beautiful for pilgrim feet,
  Whose stern, impassioned stress,
A thoroughfare for freedom beat
  Across the wilderness!
America! America!
  God mend thine every flaw,
Confirm thy soul in self-control,
  Thy liberty in law!

O beautiful for patriot dream
  That sees beyond the years,
Thine alabaster cities gleam,
  Undimmed by human tears!
America! America!
  God shed His grace on thee,
And crown thy good with brotherhood
  From sea to shining sea!

TRIBUTE BY

Hon. Daniel K. Inouye
OF HAWAII

Mr. President, I received yesterday a copy of a sermon given November 24 at the Star of the Sea Church in Honolulu by Father John H. McDonald. It is never too late for us to read such a message and I earnestly commend this sermon to all my colleagues.

Behind the Mask of America in Mourning Hides the Cancer of Hate

Death is abroad in our land today, and sorrow in the whole world. This is a strange thing, that good men everywhere and those, by all accounts, not so good are shocked numb by the death of one man.

We modern sophisticates are used to violent death. News media list dozens: death on the highway because of drunkenness and irresponsibility, death in places of business, death from jealousy, death from lust, death from greed. How many times in a few years have we learned of the violent death of some other head of state, a husband and father, earnest and devoted for all we know. And not this reaction.

The universal outrage at the senseless, cruel thing that happened Friday cries out for explanation. Not for 100 years has the world felt anything so deeply. Why?

Because for the first time in several lifetimes we are face to face with the full malice of hate, face to face with a crime entirely worthy of Satan himself, who is the personification of hate.

Had our President died violently as the result of the plotting of the leaders of an unfriendly power, were he assassinated through the machinations of the evil forces at work in our own land, we could accept the fact more readily and with less outrage. But this is not the fact.

What really happened during one dreadful half-second on Friday? All of these things happened: A young man in the full prime of a vigorous life was murdered. A wife and two small children lost forever the husband and father they loved and needed. The greatest military force in the world lost its Commander in Chief. One hundred and eighty million Americans lost their Nation's President in the most perilous times that Nation has ever known. The hundreds of millions of men and women of the free world lost the leader to whom they could look with faith and trust for the courage and wisdom and strength to continue the struggle to make all mankind free. And a thousand million enslaved humans behind the Iron Curtain of despotism were deprived of the most significant force for good their desperate struggle for liberty has yet known.

His greatness is almost beside the point. It is a fact that he was all of these things; and it is a fact that on Friday, he was destroyed, in a split second, by the twitch of a finger guided by the hate-filled little mind of a miserable creature mankind had never heard of and will, please God, soon forget.

This is the "why" of the world's grief and outrage. All of these really dreadful things are the result of one sin of hate. There is great malice in every sin; but the sin of hatred can be infinite in its malice and scope, for any of us. There is no limit to it. We can hate one man, or a hundred, or a hundred million, or the whole universe including God himself.

God intends some great, universal good to result from this tragedy. And this must be part of what He intends: that you and I and the world realize that one sin of hate can affect the lives of every man, woman, and child in the world.

What about your hates and mine? (For we have all hated.) Deep in our hearts we know that we must share responsibility for the death of our President. Have we turned our thoughts or raised our voices against a fellow man—we have hated. Have we (in our homes, our places of worship or business, our communities) been guilty of

bigotry and intolerance? These are other names of hatred. And hate engenders hate. Singly our little hates have small effect: taken together they have provided the climate in which thrives the big hate, on the right, on the left, in the center, that can explode into Friday's cruel and tragic death.

If our Nation is so sick that it is not sickened by the wanton murders of our President and his murderer, God help us. We must banish hatred and try to love as Christ loved. We must fight for justice and freedom and peace as John Kennedy fought for them. We must rise up in holy anger at the cynical hatred that exists in high places—even now. We must atone for past hatred.

There is a personal good that has come for me from Friday's outrage, and I feel compelled to pass it on to you. History records that some 2,000 years ago a woman stood on a knoll outside the walls of Jerusalem and watched her son pour out his life in a violent death because his vision was, as John Kennedy's was, greater than the vision of smaller men. Although I have tried hundreds of times to fathom what she felt and what she said, I have been unequal to the task until last Saturday morning. And then I read that as Jacqueline Kennedy bent over the stricken body of her husband she whispered, "Oh—no." This must be what Mary felt and said at the foot of the cross.

TRIBUTE BY

Hon. George A. Smathers

OF FLORIDA

Mr. President, approximately a year ago it was my distinct privilege to have been able to arrange a luncheon with the late President of the United States, John Fitzgerald Kennedy, and Martin Andersen, editor and publisher of the Orlando Sentinel.

Martin Andersen is a prominent civic leader in middle Florida, as well as a courageous, forthright and highly respected editor and publisher. Though we have differed on occasions, he is my friend of many years standing.

Upon the death of our late and great President, Martin Andersen wrote a remarkable editorial entitled "A Luncheon With a Courageous Man" in which he captured with the precision of words the true essence of John Fitzgerald Kennedy as he really was.

I ask to have this editorial inserted, because of its unique insight into the characteristics of our late President that have won the hearts of the American people and the countless millions throughout the world.

A Luncheon With a Courageous Man

(By Martin Andersen)

No matter whether you agreed with him on all his policies or not, you had to admire John F. Kennedy.

He had a certain tough courage which is difficult to define, because it was a sort of courage which carried him forward in behalf of his beliefs in the face of great criticism from a large segment of the public and a large segment of the country.

He was a controversial figure, as he had to be, because he was bold enough to step up and stand out for his new and revolutionary concept of government and rights for all the people—with no thought to creed or color.

And yet, when the cowardly assassin's bullet cut him down from ambush yesterday, the Nation was shocked in its grief. Strong men and strong women wept after exposing themselves to hour after hour of the TV exposure of the tragic story. Others, too stunned to cry, thought of this young man's widow, his children, his mother, father, brothers, sisters and thought mostly of his great and sincere ordeal for his country.

President Kennedy was not a strong man physically. He was at death's door during World War II, after a Jap destroyer had cut his PT boat in half and left him for dead in an ocean of sharks. Ever since that time his back gave him trouble. There were times when he could hardly walk, so great was the pain in his repaired and wounded spine. But he did walk and he did travel and he did work and he did speak and argue and fight for his program and he courageously kept his suffering mostly his own secret.

We sat to the immediate right of the President one day at a luncheon in the White House some 2 years ago, with a group of six or seven other Florida publishers.

We occupied that seat of honor because our name came up first alphabetically. Greater publishers with larger newspapers, more circulation and more money were scattered around the table farther away. But President Kennedy followed the protocol of the alphabet and there we were not only in the White House for the first time in our life but we were having lunch with a President for the first time in our life and we were also closer to him than anybody else—except the man on his left.

The group of us arrived ahead of the President and were in a sitting room when he arrived. Senator Smathers introduced all of us to the President and as he gave us a firm, warm handclasp he called our names as they were announced by Senator Smathers. A waiter brought around cocktails. Martinis and scotch and bourbon and sherry. Most of us had a cocktail of strong liquor but the President took a small glass of sherry wine.

He never finished his drink, even though several minutes of conversation passed and some of the crowd took a second cocktail.

This was a busy man. There was trouble in Vietnam. There was trouble in Berlin. There was trouble in Africa and the Cuban thing and the Bay of Pigs fiasco had just passed. The President had plenty on his mind. But he appeared calm and collected and talked first to one and then to another of us, just about like a district governor of a Rotary Club would do. There was, of course, a certain austerity about the scene. There is no denying that we all held him and the high office he represented in awe. And we all addressed him, with care, as "Mr. President."

When I speak of the President's certain tough courage, I refer to his stand on Cuba.

We began asking him questions about his next move on that island, shortly after we were seated at the round table.

I am not going to quote the President because Senator Smathers announced before the luncheon that this was just an informal social gathering and not a press conference in any sense of the word.

But the President gave us to understand that he did not give air protection or an air offensive to the invading Cuban fighters at the Bay of Pigs for the simple reason that he did not dare risk a counter military move in Berlin or elsewhere or in "ten other spots" which Russia was able to initiate and which possibly would wind up in the last world war to be fought by modern man.

The popular thing before him of course was a marine landing on the island of Cuba and the elimination of Castro.

He admitted that this could be done—at that time— in 10 days of fighting.

He seemed to think that Castro, if given plenty of rope, would hang himself. And we would have been saved all the lives of several thousand Marines in Cuba plus the lives of perhaps several hundred thousand of Americans in "local wars" or incidents in a dozen different spots all over the universe.

At the time I disagreed with his plan, but later on, as I began to mull his program over in my mind, I realized the chance he would have been taking to invade Cuba. Not a personal risk, but a risk of many thousands of others. And we understood, as we thought over the situation months later, that the President was willing and able to let the Castro crisis ride for awhile and perhaps erase this problem in some other manner.

Right or wrong, such a move demanded a strange sort of courage. The country, and Florida in particular, was crying for action and hollering about the Reds being just 90 miles away. But the President was able to ride with the punches as he understood there is more to the problem of running our country and keeping the peace than teaching this bearded upstart a lesson. He had more information than I had and more information than any of us around that table had. He also had a program and his program was aimed at peace and survival and the prevention of unnecessary killing of American boys in a dozen little wars all around the world.

We looked down at the President's shoes as we sat there and listened to him banter questions put to him by the publishers.

The shoes looked old to us. They were brown and had not been shined, it appeared, for several days. They must have been comfortable shoes and we surmised that he must have argued with his butler or valet about wearing them day after day as any ordinary American will wear his favorite shoes and, being the busiest man in the country, he just didn't have the time nor the inclination to get them shined.

I think he had on a brown suit. Neat enough but it did not appear any more expensive than our own. He wore a shirt with a slight pinstripe and a blue necktie.

He appeared to be not in too good health. And shortly after our visit, he did go to bed with a cold or some other slight illness.

He was a bundle of nerves and as he talked, he played with a piece of toast with his right hand, breaking it in small bits there on the table. He drank milk and after his lunch he pulled out a small cigar, little longer and a little fatter than a cigarette. He did not offer anybody a cigar, but a little later, the waiter passed cigars and cigarettes.

After the luncheon he guided us into the elevator and we got off on a higher floor and there was his beautiful wife.

"Why didn't you come down and have lunch with us?" he asked her.

"I would have, if I had known about it," she replied.

Then the two of them paraded us through the various rooms of the White House, Jackie explained each room and each piece of furniture and each picture.

There was no hurry.

The President and his wife appeared to have all the time in the world. Just like your next-door neighbor. We wound up on a portico looking out over what I would call the spacious backyard of the White House. Workmen were putting up collapsible seats for some affair scheduled for the next day.

There seemed to be no end to the job of being President—either for John Fitzgerald Kennedy or his wife.

He belonged to the people.

One may disagree with some of his policies, but he had the size and the touch of greatness. He cared naught for money and on most occasions carried none with him. Lyndon Johnson used to chide him during the campaign that he, Lyndon, always had to pay for the drugstore lunch they would eat on the fly.

He belonged to the people and the people loved him as an individual, because he was a warm, charming human being with a beautiful wife and two wonderful children. And because he was fundamentally a great American who believed in rights for all of the people.

TRIBUTE BY

Hon. Daniel B. Brewster

OF MARYLAND

Mr. President, 24 days have now passed since the death of President John Fitzgerald Kennedy.

Both the House and the Senate have devoted a day to eulogies for our fallen leader. Thousands and thousands of words have poured forth from citizens and dignitaries at home and abroad in praise and condolence.

My attention has recently been called to a eulogy delivered by the Very Reverend William-M.J. Driscoll, S.J., president and rector of Georgetown Preparatory School on the occasion of the school's Requiem Mass, Monday, November 25, 1963. This brief tribute has impressed me as among the most distinguished I have read. It is for this reason that I ask unanimous consent that it be printed as follows:

EULOGY FOR PRESIDENT JOHN F. KENNEDY

(Delivered by Very Rev. William-M.J. Driscoll, S.J.)

"Now the trumpet summons us again * * * not to bear arms, but to bear the burden of a long struggle, year in and year out, rejoicing in hope, patient in tribulation—a struggle against the common enemies of man: Tyranny, poverty, disease, and war itself * * *—asking His [God's] blessing and His help, but knowing that here on earth God's work must truly be our own."

Thus John Fitzgerald Kennedy sounded the trumpet call as free world leader against these common enemies when he became the 35th President of these United States on January 20, 1961, and he added: "Can we forge against these enemies of man, tyranny, poverty, disease, and war, can we forge a grand and global alliance, north and south, east and west, that can assure a more fruitful life for all mankind? Will you join in that historic effort?"

A young, dynamic leader of men—extremely intelligent, competent, hard working; eloquent, courageous, temperate; witty, yet serene; with a balanced sense of history which indicated that he knew he both controlled events and also was controlled by them; devoted to the place and use of reason and its power in sifting the destiny of nations and of men; humane, kind, charitable, understanding; a respecter of all persons and their inalienable, God-given human rights; a great lover of human life, of human freedom, of human unity, of human betterment, of international and domestic peace, and most assuredly, a great lover of God.

Not to merely pledge good words, but to do good deeds; not to rest safely neutral, but to oppose any foe for the survival of liberty; not to belabor what divided, but to explore what united; not to ignore the heavy burdens of the poor, the starving, the miserable, the suppressed—either at home or abroad, but to "undo these heavy burdens, and let the oppressed go free"; not to create a new world power, but a new world of law, "where the strong are just, and the weak secure, and the peace preserved"; and to do all of these things for one reason only: because it was right. And why was it right? Because it was God's work; for as he said so well "here on earth God's work must truly be our own." These were the principles and purposes of our great leader.

The world has always needed big men, men big enough to lead the rest, to inspire the rest of us to follow them into reflected greatness. Without such giants, we are truly "sheep without a shepherd"; our end is chaos and calamity; our path remains unlighted by the stars. But with such leaders, we are lifted up, we find direction, inspiration; we are blasted off the launching pad and propelled almost past the moon; our heartbeat quickened and our realization charged, we almost come to know by convinced personal experience in our contact with our leader that "God created us men just a little less than the angels; and crowned us with honor and glory." And we are inspired then to work to bring about a new creation in ourselves and in the world, helping to prepare for the coming of the world's Lord at time's end. For our vision is from convinced leaders who surpass themselves in performing and inspiring in us petty men noble deeds for our fellow men.

A truly great, active, zealous leader who strives to make his vision of a better world come true, lives in the grateful hearts and in the continued striving of his people and of the world for the ages. When such a leader is taken away, we all feel poor, deprived, less than before; for we have lost something of ourselves.

We have personally, each one of us, lost his greatness, reflected in us. When such a leader dies, we are diminished; but when he is swept away by such a tragedy as we have experienced, as unspeakable as it is incomprehensible, we are crushed; we are lost; we, too, almost die.

Some men are so captivated with God's gift of life to them, that diamond sparkle of immortality, and are so saturated with its purposefulness and how they can best use it for good, that they exert all of their human powers, responding completely to every moment, as though they disdained to make a response which was less complete, less worthy of this divine gift. Such a man we have known; he has been our leader. What an accusation he is, vibrant with the joy of life, uncompromising in his purposefulness, to us who live halfheartedly. Be our mediocrity in the development of our minds and talents in the pursuit of new knowledge as students, or in hesitation in following to the hilt what we come to know is our true vocation in life, or in the determined growth in our Christ-like appreciation and sacrifices of our fellow men, their needs and their rights and their woes, his life of purpose and complete response accuses us personally. "You have not joined this historic alliance," he says to each of us.

Our leader whom we have lost was one of highest and most completely dedicated purpose; he was such a leader because of such high purposes: "Here on earth God's work must truly be our own." Although John Kennedy walked like a prince, talked like a scholar, and was born seemingly destined to be President * * * if this had not been God's plan for him in life, he would have been a leader anywhere because he was a completely dedicated and purposeful man: "Here on earth God's work must truly be our own."

And so he challenges us, his people, to take up the same purpose and complete dedication, to live in the height of our powers. "Will you join in that historic effort?" When he passes from us, that is loss indeed. If we have really heard him and caught his message, our purposeful and dedicated lives will be his abiding monument.

Grateful indeed are we to God who sends us betimes men both wise and good, such as our President, to lead us. Yet—they all pass. The life they briefly possess disappears from our ways, and they are seen no more. And then we come to know that truly only life remains, the life of One who exulted to walk our soddy earth and enlighten all men with His touch and word. His was the life whose vital spark was and is so contagious that we can, even as President Kennedy, still be quickened by its current. Though we lose men of greatness and their inspiring lives, One remains who is Life Itself. "I am the Life." And He also is our Leader: "I am the Way." And He came to lead us to the fullness of life, that "more fruitful life for all mankind": "I came that all men may have life and have it more abundantly."

The death of a great leader is a clarion call to Christian men everywhere who wish to give themselves for a great cause. To rise to such heroic tasks tomorrow, each one of us must respond today in the school that makes leaders, that ultimately made Mr. Kennedy, the school of Christ the Leader, where our President caught, and where we can catch a vision that will make us surpass ourselves.

Surpass ourselves * * * surpass ourselves! Listen: can you not hear an echo, muted by soft falling inaugural snow which now seems to cover yesterday almost like a shroud: "Now the trumpet summons us again. So let us begin anew. It may not be finished in our lifetime on this planet. But let us begin. Can we forge against these enemies of men, tyranny, poverty, disease, and war, can we forge a grand and global alliance that can assure a more fruitful life for all mankind? Will you join in that historic effort, knowing that here on earth God's work must truly be our own."

Listen! Listen! For there is another echo. From another, an earlier inaugural address delivered 2,000 years ago in the sunny spring on distant Palestine's rolling hills. The words are faint, but they are clear. Listen to what they say in answer:

"Blessed are the poor in spirit; blessed are those who mourn; blessed are the patient; blessed are those who hunger and thirst for holiness; blessed are the merciful; blessed are the peacemakers; blessed are those who suffer persecution in the name of right; the kingdom of heaven is theirs.

"Blessed are you, John Kennedy, when men revile you, and persecute you; be glad and lighthearted, for a rich reward awaits you in heaven."

TRIBUTES BY

Hon. J. Glenn Beall

OF MARYLAND

Mr. President, I ask unanimous consent to have printed a poem written by one of my constituents, Mr. Joseph F. Spalla, of Baltimore. The poem, written in the style of Walt Whitman's "Oh Captain, My Captain," is a tribute to the late President Kennedy.

Our Captain Lives

(On the style of Walt Whitman's "Oh Captain, My Captain")

Say thou the captain doth not speak?
E'er in mortal silence held?
Pray not that this be so,
Tis told he waits on sunlit heights,
Cross 'Tomac's green banked rill,
Yes! There! There! There he stands,
Mid Arl'n'ton's valored band.
Oh say! Say not! Say not to us!
Our beloved captain's dead.
Say thou the flashing smile, unruly lock,
Shall ne'er more be seen?
That "vigahed" voice forever dimmed
Neath mournful tread of saddened feet?
Oh say! Say not! Say not to us!
Our beloved captain's dead.
For short tenure he strode,
The forecastle's embattled tenement,
There commanding with brave stand,
The destined course of this God favored land.
A Madonna knelt, no sign revealing.
The tragic aura of her woe,
'n pressed a circlet made o'gold
In our captain's stilled hand.
A covenant death could not void
Twas in that moment made.
Lo! She leaves! She leaves him not!
Daily to his side she goes,
To abide n'whisper tender words
That only he should know.
O shriven day! O grieved loss!
Engraved upon our hearts will stay.
Stay thy hand! Thou forlorn fate!
Turn back the pierced shards in flight,
Return to us our captain brave
To lead our way these peril'd days.
O tiara'd mother of our shores,
Thou harbored dame of liberty
Lift up thy beaconed torch e'er higher,
To guide our captain on his way.
Console us in our grief O mother,
Assuage our murderous pain this day.
"Hush! Hush! My people! Hear me!
My son, your brother, passed by this way,
And stopped to bid the time of day.
I told him to be faithful, I told him to be free,
For nowhere in this wide wide world
Will be found one such as he."
"Yes," she seems to whisper
With vibrant voice aglow,
"He lives! He lives! He lives in immortality!"

Mr. President, since the tragic assassination of our late President, Americans young and old have tried to express their grief in various ways.

One such expression in the form of a poem has been composed by Miss Diane Love, the 16-year-old daughter of Dr. and Mrs. E. Justin Love, of Montgomery County, Md. Miss Love's poem, entitled "And in a Moment It Was No More," was published recently by her school newspaper, the Immaculata News.

I ask unanimous consent that this poem from the paper of the Immaculata High School, Washington, D.C., be printed as follows:

And in a Moment It Was No More

(By Diane Love)

It came as lightning,
    Swift and bold,
And held for men
    A grief untold.
Bow your heads
    And to God do pray
For our President
    Has passed this way.
A bullet of hate
    In a gun of fear
Took from us
    A man, so dear.
Bow your heads
    And to God do pray
For our President
    Has passed this way.
He's gone from us
    But leaves behind
The thoughts and ideals
    Of his great mind.
So, in tribute to him
    Let us do what we can
To strengthen peace
    And the brotherhood of man.
Bow your heads
    And to God do pray
For our President
    Has passed away.

TRIBUTE BY

Hon. Kenneth B. Keating

OF NEW YORK

Mr. President, a constituent of mine, Miss Kay Magenheimer, was moved to express the feelings of grief and awe that moved our Nation when we lost our President. Her poem, "Ask Not," was printed in the Rosarian of the Queen of the Rosary Academy, in Amityville, N.Y. Mr. President, I ask unanimous consent that this poem, "Ask Not," be printed as follows:

Ask Not [1]

(In Memory of John Fitzgerald Kennedy)

"No man while I live
And behold light on earth
Shall lay violent hands on thee" [2]
My country, my liberty.

Grieving unspeakably
For all creation;
For his country's sake, for dying liberty
And our children's unseen fate,

This man—this beacon for humanity—
With heart cast of oak and daring
Made his great resolve
And nailed his colors to the mast.

Above the thunder of the wild sea
Breaking against his bleak New England coast
His voice rose to shake the mighty halls of earth
To rouse men from their sleep.

So little time for Hera's charge;
So short, so short a time for glory
As if some great maternal Thetis
Had foretold this immortal story:

Our mighty Achilles lies dead
In the arms of his gallant Love;
Slain by some malignant spirit
Before the victory's claimed.

Rise up! Rise up, America!
Before it is too late.
His young, strong hand no longer
Shields us from an evil fate.

The only hand that can save us
Is the One he held—as his son held his.
America! America! Awake!
Before it is too late.

—Kay Magenheimer.

(Note.—Achilles is the greatest hero of the Greeks who was killed in battle, just before the fall of Troy. His mother was Thetis. Hera, in Greek mythology, is the goddess-patroness of marriage.)

Written on the date of burial: Nov. 25, 1963.

TRIBUTES BY

Hon. Jacob K. Javits

OF NEW YORK

Mr. President, I have been sent, by the well-known author and poet, James T. Farrell, a beautiful poem about the late President Kennedy.

[1] From Mr. Kennedy's inaugural address: "Ask not what your country can do for you. Ask what you can do for your country."

[2] From the Iliad of Homer.

John Fitzgerald Kennedy

He rode, smiling, in sun and triumph.

Six seconds
Of naked tragedy
And of the ultimate, terrible beauty of death—

He was no more,
We wept in the solitudes of our silence,
With the solidarity of grief.

—James T. Farrell.

Mr. President, I ask unanimous consent to have printed at this point a eulogy of the late President Kennedy which I have received from Manhattan Chapter No. 23 of the National Association of Retired Civil Employees.

John Fitzgerald Kennedy, 35th President of the United States

(Eulogy of our late President John F. Kennedy delivered by John H. Sheehan, member of the executive committee, Manhattan Chapter No. 23, New York, N.Y., National Association of Retired Civil Employees, at the regular chapter meeting, Wednesday, Dec. 18, 1963)

On November 22 while visiting Texas to aid in solving the political differences in the Democratic Party of that State, President John F. Kennedy was shot down by an assassin's bullet thus ending the short term of 3 years as our national leader. What benefit could result to the assassin or those similarly motivated by hatred and ill will because of the administration's bill in Congress now being considered.

All of us know the statements made by the Governors of Alabama and Mississippi through the press and on television in opposition to the decision of the Supreme Court in the integration of the schools. Their defiant activities were completely hostile to the administration's effort to enforce the Court's decree thus stimulating discord among the people of the South.

His death made an indelible impression on Americans and to the world beyond. The fact he governed—made our country's decisions and the courage indicates the confidence which he possessed abundantly. At the time of the Bay of Pigs fiasco in Cuba for which his opponents severely criticized him although not to blame, he assumed the responsibility without passing the onus to others in the CIA. Although serving less than 3 years he demonstrated his ability to exercise the full authority of his high office so capably that the world is in a large measure indebted for the brief leadership of John F. Kennedy.

The high spirited ideals which were so well exemplified by him during his career will be missed at home and abroad. The frequent appearances on television during the meetings with the press and the flash of the Kennedy grin in making responses so readily will be of immeasurable loss to millions of his admirers who were fascinated by his wit and thoroughness of his prompt replies. The New Frontier is now behind us but we shall remember the statement at his inauguration: "Ask not what your country can do for you, ask what you can do for your country." When he was inaugurated he predicted that his dream of a new America would not be achieved in the first 100 days— nor in the life of this administration, nor even perhaps in our lifetime on this planet and how prophetic this became in so short a space of time. But he said let us begin— which he did so nobly until his death.

John Kennedy was possessed of the attributes that manifest his qualifications of greatness to an extraordinary degree. Let us recall the showdown with Khrushchev in Cuba in 1962 when we were on the edge of conflict that might have resulted in nuclear war, the confrontations over Berlin, the sending of troops to Vietnam, the release of Professor Barghoorn by the Soviets, to suitably estimate the courage of our leader. At home he had to face the adversaries over civil rights which threatened him with political suicide and yet he never flinched in the performance of his duties. A man's greatness may not be easy to measure at close range. It is not measured by how much other men may agree with him—nor how little. It is measured by how strongly he stands for his convictions and how effectively he pursues the goals he sees above and ahead.

A leader may command the art of persuasion to a large extent but eventually discussion must close with the decision to be made solely by him. After due deliberation he must stand by it and cause it to be carried through despite the protests of those who cannot be persuaded. He must draw apart from others in reflecting on the import of his views and seek the loneliness which the person of supreme power has to undergo in directing the ship of state through troubled waters. This is the faith one must have in a good cause from which follows the power of making his decision.

On June 9, 1961, the President said in an address that of these to whom much is given—much is required. And when at some future date the high court of history sits in judgment on each of us—recording whether in our brief span of service we fulfilled our responsibilities to the state—our success or failure, in whatever office we may hold, will be measured by the answers to four questions: (1) Were we truly men of courage; (2) Were we truly men of judgment; (3) Were we truly men of integrity; (4) Were we truly men of dedication.

In his last speech at Fort Worth on November 22 before going to Dallas, he stated that we in this country, in this generation, are—by density, rather than by choice— the watchmen on the walls of world freedom. We ask, therefore, that we may be worthy of our power and responsibility—that we may exercise our strength with wisdom and restraint—that we may achieve for our time and for all time the ancient vision of peace on earth, good will toward men. That must always be our goal— and the righteousness of our cause must always underlie our strength.

The tragic death has brought home to most Americans that they had in John F. Kennedy a more remarkable President than they had understood. Too few of the American people realized the importance of the measures he advocated to solve the problems at home and abroad to advance the cause of peace for all mankind. The revelation of how much the rest of the world respected him; the extraordinary spectacle of 220 foreign leaders at Arlington Cemetery expressed more worldwide grief and concern than anyone knew existed. Another important memory is the courage and dignity of Jacqueline Kennedy throughout her ordeal. Well done thou good and faithful servant that you may now enjoy the rest and blessing for a job well done.

TRIBUTE BY

Hon. Norris Cotton

OF NEW HAMPSHIRE

Mr. President, on November 24, 1963, at the Cathedral of the Pines, at Rindge, N.H., there occurred a most solemn and impressive tribute to the memory of President John F. Kennedy. The memorial remarks were delivered by the Reverend Robert W. Little, copastor of the United Church of Christ, Keene, N.H., and are especially moving. I ask unanimous consent that the Reverend Mr. Little's remarks be printed.

A Memorial for John Fitzgerald Kennedy

(By Rev. Robert W. Little)

We have gathered here without regard to our racial, creedal, or political background to pay the tribute of our commonly held love and respect for the life of John Fitzgerald Kennedy, 35th President of the United States of America.

We gather with heavy hearts, filled with sorrow, and with minds that are shocked by the senseless tragedy which has visited us in the death of our President.

It would be presumptuous of me to assume the task of attempting to speak an adequate tribute on your behalf in this memorial service. I shall not attempt to do so. Your very presence here speaks more eloquently than any spoken word can do of the tribute you yourselves would pay if you were standing in my place.

Yet the very fact that we are here together speaks its own words of truth. Let me try to express, on your behalf, these words.

One word of truth your presence speaks is this: You care very much, or you would not be here in this bitter cold. You are here today to express the same feeling those who stood all night long outside of the White House on Friday night were expressing; the same feeling those who have been going in and out of churches across the land for prayer have been expressing; the same feeling those who placed lighted candles in their windows in Berlin were feeling. You feel the need to do something which says you care about what has happened to our President and to his family and his associates. It is the expression of love, of respect, of grief.

A second word of truth your presence speaks is part and parcel of the first. It is this: You care about what has happened to our President, for John F. Kennedy belonged to you. He belonged to all of the American people. He served and himself respected us all, whatever our faith or color or political persuasion.

Indeed, as the expressions which have flowed into Washington from all parts of the earth since the moment of his death testify, John F. Kennedy was also a world citizen, held high in the esteem of men of many nationalities. The whole world shares our grief and joins us in the tribute of love and respect.

It is right that a memorial service in his honor should be held in this place, dedicated to the worshipful use of all people, without restriction as to their race, or creed, or national origin. It is a proper reflection of the meaning of the life of President Kennedy that this service is being led by Christian and Jew, white man and Negro, Protestant and Roman Catholic.

So do we embody, in our physical presence. the word of truth you feel in your hearts that John F. Kennedy was our President, belonging equally to all. We are grateful to Dr. and Mrs. Douglas Sloane for this opportunity to express our common tribute as symbol of the truth which is felt this day the world around.

Our presence here together this day speaks a third word of truth. It is this word: John Fitzgerald Kennedy died on our behalf and in our place.

It is yet too soon to know for certain what misguided jungle of evil thoughts directed the mind of the man whose finger pulled the trigger of the weapon which ended so abruptly the President's life.

But I dare to speak for you the truth that his hatred did not center upon John F. Kennedy, the man. It was focused, rather, upon John F. Kennedy, the President, the living symbol of American hopes and aspirations. The hatred, then, is directed toward all of us together. The President is truly martyr, receiving into his own body on our behalf whatever revenge for real or fancied wrong the assassin sought from the American people.

Our grief is real, for we know that this martyrdom has been suffered in our own place. A man of great courage stood before the world and proclaimed the strength and fiber of the American dream of peace and freedom for every man. He stood there for you and for me. He died in our place.

We have no other choice than to match his courage by our own, bringing to the cause of freedom, as he challenged us in his inaugural address, an energy, faith, and devotion which will light the Nation and set up a glow that can truly light the world.

The fact that we are free to gather here today speaks one further word of truth—hatred is a bitter passion which cannot win the victory its victim seeks to achieve.

Whatever we may eventually learn of the cause behind this senseless act, the destruction of the physical being of our President will not destroy the ideals which he and the American people hold in common.

There will be no anarchy, no abandonment of free government, no outcry from the citizens to compromise the American dream.

Even in the midst of shock and grief, we pledge our devotion and support to our new President, Lyndon B. Johnson. The Government goes forward. Our people, as your presence here testifies, become all the more determined to carry forward to fulfillment our common hopes and aspirations of justice for all peoples.

Hatred cannot win the victory it sought. Let us heed well this truth which here our very presence speaks. Let none among us fall victim to hatred's bitter course, seeking to revenge our grief upon whatever cause, or whichever group, has already seemed unworthy in our sight. For then shall America lose the very victory for peace, and freedom, and justice which John F. Kennedy so vigorously sought, to which he devoted the splendid intellect of his mind, and for which he died.

May the soul of John Fitzgerald Kennedy rest in peace.

May his family be supported by the comfort of Almighty God.

May our prayers for him, for them, and for our country be acceptable unto God.

May God give strength and wisdom to Lyndon B. Johnson, and to all leaders of our Government.

May each one of us so devote himself to the cause of liberty, justice and peace that the life we honor today shall not have been given in vain.

TRIBUTE BY

Hon. Edmund S. Muskie

OF MAINE

Mr. President, the shock of our late President's tragic death still pervades every phase of American life. Each of us has tried to express his grief in his own way. Some have the eloquence, the gift of expression, which the rest of us wish we possessed. Miss Kathleen Watson, of Bath, is one of those who has used her talent to express in poetry, something of the feeling which all Americans experienced when President Kennedy was struck down. I ask that Miss Watson's poem, "Who Was This Man?" be printed.

Who Was This Man?

Why has a nation bowed its head?
    Why is a world in sorrow?
Why does a woman walk alone
    Today and each tomorrow?

Why did a morning filled with joy,
    With laughter and with cheers,
Turn from a day to darkest night,
    To emptiness and tears?

Who was this man from whom we weep,
    Whose spirit will not die,
Whose tragic loss has made men pause
    To pray and ask God "Why?"

Who was this man beside whose grave
    A flame shall always burn,
Which thousands pass in silent grief
    And know not where to turn?

Who was this man who walked with us
    And taught us to be brave,
Who asked of us great sacrifice,
    And what he asked—he gave?

Who, if we could but speak to him,
    To ask him on this day,
"What can we do to honor you?"
    Would smile and then would say:

"Weep not for me, America;
    My task is not yet done,
But light the torch and follow me,
    And victory will be won.

"First rid your hearts of bigotry
    And fears that still remain,
For if you will but keep my dream,
    My death was not in vain.

"No monument of marble stone,
    No statue ever could
Bestow more honor on my name
    Than peace and brotherhood."

Who was this man who gave us hope
    Of peace and then was gone?
Who was this man so wise, so good?
    —A servant God called "John."

                —Kathleen D. Watson.

TRIBUTES BY

Hon. Paul H. Douglas

OF ILLINOIS

Mr. President, on Christmas Day last the Mount Sterling (Ill.) Democrat-Message published a moving comment on the character and work of the late President John F. Kennedy. This essay, written by Editor Sid Landfield, points out with deep understanding why the Nation's loss is so great. I think it should be widely read now and in the future, for it is an impressive demonstration of the deep and lasting affection held for John F. Kennedy throughout the land.

A LITTLE BOY NAMED JOHN-JOHN

"Tell me a story, Daddy," might be the most appropriate theme for Christmas, for after all, here is a holiday intended mainly for children. And what a nice Christmas present to be told a wonderful story by your father.

There are tens of thousands of little boys in our Nation who will not be able to say "Tell me a story, Daddy,"—these youngsters are without fathers and among them is a little fellow of 3 whose dad loved to call him John-John.

This little boy, blessed in many ways, lost his great and his wonderful father on November 22, 1963.

If we were in the company of young John-John we would volunteer to tell this boy a story: a magnificent story and most of all a true story. We'd begin this way:

John-John, once upon a time there was a little boy who wanted to grow up to become President of the United States. Now there's nothing too unusual about that ambition, because thousands of young Americans cherish that hope. But our little boy realized his ambition and though he was to serve his country but a very short time, the impression he would leave would be indelible through the generations and all around the world. Now what do you suppose this little boy who grew up to become President possessed that made him so unusual and so vital?

Well, he had imagination. And he had humor. And he had understanding.

Each of these qualities is a wonderful possession, but to have all three, and the ability to use them together, would make a man as wise and as great as Abraham Lincoln. Our hero had the ability to use these three qualities as a unit.

As with Mr. Lincoln, people scoffed at this man. Some even hated him. When in tragedy he died, a few even applauded and cheered.

In life, they sneered at him, derided his family, castigated his most solemn principles. It was not disagreement, it was awful hate.

But like we said, this man had humor.

In life, they predicted he would wreck things, tear down institutions, weaken our structure.

But like we said, this man had imagination.

In life, they deplored his insistence on equality for all men. They used vile language and they used violence many ways.

But like we said, this man had understanding.

John-John, if this man could have lived but another 5 years, in order to serve out his full term as President and a second full term, then all the people of this Nation—and all the people of this great big world would have gained in stature and in compassion, for he was a once-in-a-hundred-years kind of a leader.

As you grow older, John-John, the idea one day might come to your mind that you would like to grow up to become President of the United States. This is a noble aspiration for any youngster to have. If this idea should come to your mind, who would your hero be? Who would you like to fashion yourself after?

Well, young man, the reason we brought the subject up, and the reason we tell you these things, is because we should like to suggest that you fashion yourself after this great President we are telling you about—that you allow that man to become your ever-present hero and inspiration.

At this time, people will little note that the President we refer to takes his place alongside Mr. Lincoln as the 1–2 of all Presidents. At this time, not enough people fully realize that here was a man who desired equality—and justice—for all men more than he wanted life even. You see, this man had money—great wealth; he had charm and exciting personal appeal; he had youth and he had health. This man could have lived the easy life. He could have been famous, and liked and loved by millions in many fields.

But this man had understanding. People were his job. Nothing else.

Dear little boy, this is an absolutely true story we tell you this Christmas. Will you remember all the time? Will you tell it and retell it to others as you grow up? Will you live it?

Now ask us some questions, John-John. Ask us anything.

Who was the man, you ask? What was his name?

Well his name was John, like yours. And Kennedy like yours. But then—that's a perfectly common name, isn't it? There are all kinds of people named John Kennedy.

Why did this man die, you ask?

Well, John-John: your religion teaches you beautifully why 2,000 years ago another man died. As you grow older and are better able to understand such things, you will be able the better to relate these two happenings.

Who killed him, you ask?

Well, the record says a man killed him—with a rifle. But really, it was like the story of the death 2,000 years ago: the people killed him.

Do you know the man real well, you ask?

No. You never got to know the man real well because you were so young. But—the man knew you real well. He knew all about you, John-John—all about you.

Did he love you, you ask.

Yes, he did, young man. Like a father. Like a President. As much as he loved life. No more questions now, John-John * * * it's Christmas time: time for happy thoughts and gayety because you're only 3 years old.

So * * * goodnight, John-John—and happy dreams.

Yes, we'll tell you some more stories about the great man and wonderful President at another time. Lots of people will tell you stories about him as the years go by. Your mother has much in store for you—she'll tell you the most happy things about this man, as you grow older * * * and as you get imagination, and humor, and understanding.

Merry Christmas to John-John in the year of his Lord 1963.

Mr. President, one of the best editorials I have seen concerning the death of the late President John F. Kennedy was printed in the Tazewell County (Ill.) Reporter for Thursday, November 28, 1963. I ask that this editorial be printed so that others may read it as well.

WHY? WHY?

Why? Why?

This mournful dirge will ring down the long corridors of eternity and still go begging for an exact answer.

Why? Why?

In that split second before the light was forever extinguished, this inscrutable question may have entered that magnificent tomb which was the brain of John Fitzgerald Kennedy.

Why by the stealth borne of cowardice did the assassin squeeze the trigger which launched the fatal bullet on its dreadful path? Why when confronted with insurmount-

able evidence of his guilt did he choose to deprive the country of the important but twisted logic behind the deed?

Little does it matter now that he paid the extreme penalty at the hands of another assassin. The question of his guilt and the certainty of his ultimate punishment by the society he betrayed were already sealed.

But lost forever is the imparting from his own lips the vital information of what factors are at work in our society which drive men to such lengths. For, though we seemingly stand on the heights and gaze down into the chasm of his iniquity, perhaps we too have the blood of the President upon our hands.

Though we kept the prayerful watch and draped the colors at half-mast, what will the morrow bring? Will we look the black man in the face and recoil? Will we say to the Jew, "You killed Christ"? Will we tell our neighbors around the world, "Get along as best you can, for the burden is too heavy for us"?

Will our legislators continue to belabor those hallowed halls with minuscule and divisive interpretations of how best to chart the course of a great nation on a perilous voyage? Or, will statesmen rise and grasp the torch so recently fallen on the blood-stained street at Dallas?

A just God grant they may. Then, truly, meaning will be given the fervent hope of John Fitzgerald Kennedy: "Let the word go forth from this time and place, to friend and foe alike, that the torch has been passed to a new generation of Americans."

And, what of the man himself? Is it finished with the placing of his mortal remains beneath the sod on a wind-swept slope in Arlington National Cemetery? There he will keep the vigil with thousands of others who died in the service of our country.

Those who note the flight and fall of the lofty eagle will, in mind's eye, visit this spot again and again. And, with the passage of time, the breadth and height and scope of the martyred man will emerge to be savored and reflected upon by those unashamedly in love with America.

For, despite the circumstances of wealth and position, he was a man who held out the hand of greatness to a nation too hesitant to grasp it and, at times, reluctant to make the sacrifices attendant upon it. By catchword and cleverly implanted doubt, we were often cautioned to suspect his motives.

It is ironic that perhaps the most moving summation of his life and creed are from another country. The Vancouver, B.C., Province said:

"He chose the glory road, the road chosen by those who have the look of eagles, the high and dangerous road that winds beside chasms and precipices that daunt lesser men."

Not in our time have we seen such an outpouring of grief at the passing of one man. The death of Franklin D. Roosevelt, who led us in the dark days of the depression and the difficult times of war, is the closest analogy. Though shocking and sad, his passing was from natural causes due to infirmities generally known.

But, here we have a man senselessly cut down in the vigor of manhood with great triumphs ahead; a man who leaves behind a grieving young widow and two children with the pap of infancy scarcely gone from their lips. He brought all the forces of a giant intellect to bear upon the awesome task he undertook with complete dedication to the ideal that he was President of all the people.

And how stands the Nation? We can all thank on bended knee the foresight of the founders of our great Republic who provided for the orderly transition of Executive authority. The mantle of leadership flows naturally from shoulder to shoulder, decade upon decade, without strife or civil insurrection and the Nation endures.

Just as the memory of those great forefathers endure and the intent of their handiwork becomes clearer with the ages, so will this Nation endure the winds of change and momentary calamities which buffet her. While we have seen, and will see, differing interpretations on the founding precepts handed us, we need have no fear so long as the core of their meaning is preserved.

With the course of our national purpose pointed aright and the minds of our leaders attuned to the hopes and aspirations of our people, we may take renewed dedication in those immortal words: "Government of the people, by the people, for the people shall not perish from the earth."

In epilogue, we have one more sacred obligation before us this day. We must not slight nor tarnish the glory of that other martyr who died with the President that fateful November day.

J. D. Tippit, who died by the same hand which slew the President, has earned a niche in the memory of his countrymen. He was killed while carrying out the highest tradition of our Nation's law enforcement agencies. He was the instrument serving as intermediary between the actual and the philosophical in a concept that this is a Nation of men and laws.

As thousands of military graves throughout the world testify, there can be no nobler death than that imposed by faithful performance of oaths taken. Officer Tippit epitomizes to the highest his fallen Commander's admonition:

"Ask not what your country can do for you. Ask what you can do for your country."

So mote it be.

TRIBUTE BY

Hon. John Sherman Cooper

OF KENTUCKY

Mr. President, I ask unanimous consent to have printed a newsletter written by my wife, Mrs. John Sherman Cooper, on the late President John F. Kennedy, which was published in many Kentucky newspapers.

LETTER FROM MRS. JOHN SHERMAN COOPER

November 25, 1963.

I have just come from the President's funeral. The house seems very still after the cathedral crowded with the mighty of the nations, followed by the long, slow procession past the Lincoln Memorial over the bridge to Arlington Cemetery. The afternoon was so bright and fair that the thousands of baskets of flowers, which had been sent regardless of the family's wishes, belied the autumn leaves and gave the impression of springtime. John and I mourned not only for our President but also for our friend. He was your friend too. Because it is so easy to forget, I am going to mention some of the things he did for Kentucky.

On January 21, 1961, Senator Cooper, Republican, of Kentucky, said on the Senate floor:

"I am glad that President Kennedy in his first Executive order acted to improve the amounts, variety, and nutritional quality of food distributed to needy families. For 3 years, I have urged this action by the Department of Agriculture. * * * I think it humane and appropriate that the first act of the new President was to help the neediest people of the Nation."

Also, in the beginning of 1961 he requested TVA to locate a steam plant in Knox and Bell Counties, on the Cumberland River, to stimulate the economy of southeastern Kentucky. TVA, however, had made a prior decision to locate the plant in Tennessee, but the President wanted it for Kentucky. This year, after the floods in eastern Kentucky, John and I went to visit the disaster area. After having seen the terrible devastation, John went to the President, who, at his request, gave increases in funds for flood protection for eastern Kentucky. As you know, one of President Kennedy's last official acts was on November 13, when he said:

"I have today met with Gov. Bert Combs, of Kentucky, and members of the Kentucky congressional delegation to discuss a crash program designed to bring special attention to the especially hard-hit area of eastern Kentucky—the most severely distressed area in the Nation."

There have been many times in the last 3 years that I have asked the President or Mrs. Kennedy to give our State special consideration. I am sure that the thousands who heard the Lexington Youth Symphony or saw the Berea dancers perform on the White House lawn will never forget the honor it gave our State—an honor which every other State in the Union is trying to attain and which was made possible because I asked Mrs. Kennedy to bring it to her husband's attention. It would be impossible to mention the endless special White House tours and other marks of friendship and consideration. In fact, I have never had "No" for an answer in courtesies for Kentuckians. Although we belong to different political parties, John Kennedy was not partisan in friendship. Even when he came to Kentucky during a recent senatorial campaign he had good things to say about my husband, both at the airport and at the dinner in Louisville, which is most unusual in the heat of a campaign. I wish all of you had known him. This poem by Molly Kazan was printed in the New York Herald Tribune; it gives you another glimpse of him.

"I think that what he gave us most was pride.
It felt good to have a President like that:
Bright, brave and funny and good looking.
I saw him once drive down East Seventy-second Street
In an open car, in the autumn sun
(As he drove yesterday in Dallas).

His thatch of brown hair looked as though it had grown
    extra thick
The way our wood animals in Connecticut
Grow extra fur for winter.
And he looked as though it was fun to be alive,
To be a politician,
To be President,
To be a Kennedy,
To be a man.
He revived our pride,
It felt good to have a President
Who read his mail,
Who read the papers,
Who read books and played touch football.
It was a pleasure and a cause for pride
To watch him take the quizzing of the press
With cameras grinding—
To take it in his stride,
With zest.
We were privileged to see him on the worst day (till
    yesterday),
The Bay of Pigs day,
And we marveled at his coolth and style
And were amazed at an air (that plainly was habitual)
    of modesty
And even diffidence.
It felt good to have a President
Who said, It was my fault.
And went on from there.
What was spoken
Was spoken well.
What was unspoken
Needed to be unspoken.
It was none of our business if his back hurt.
He revived our pride.
He gave grist to our pride.
He was respectful of intellect;
He was respectful of excellence;
He was respectful of accomplishment and skill;
He was respectful of the clear and subtle use of our
    language.
And all these things he cultivated in himself.
He was respectful of our heritage.
He is now part of it."

TRIBUTE BY

Hon. Stephen M. Young

OF OHIO

Mr. President, I have been asked by the District of Columbia chapter of the Federal Bar Association to include a resolution that was passed on December 4, 1963, by the board of directors of that chapter memorializing the late President Kennedy.

It is most fitting that a bar association of Government attorneys pass such a resolution because among his many other great qualities the late President Kennedy stood for thorough and ethical legal procedures within the forces of the Government, and he stood for the rule of law rather than the rule of individuals. His assassination was an unspeakable crime against the Nation. His passing is justly mourned by the legal profession.

JOHN FITZGERALD KENNEDY: "A WRIT FOR FREEDOM"

Resolved, The District of Columbia chapter of the Federal Bar Association on behalf of its members join the Nation and the world in expressing sympathy in the tragic loss of the President of the United States, John Fitzgerald Kennedy.

Being a man of great intellect, he has raised the sights of our people in innumerable ways. In his inaugural address he renewed our pledge to enlarge the area in which the writ of the United Nations must run for the freedom of man and, through his distinctive vision, gave strong recognition that man is about to embark into a new world of law where the strong are just, the weak secure and the peace preserved.

Our Nation and the universe will move on, being a better place because of John Fitzgerald Kennedy. The legal profession is now more cognizant of its heritage and will earnestly seek to accomplish his most noble desire—a world of peace and freedom under law. To this end, we shall urge that the International Court of Justice be given greater jurisdiction over the disputes among nations and among men as well as greater power to enforce more meaningfully its writs and judgments.

Subscribed this 4th day of December 1963, at Washington, D.C.

CYRIL F. BRICKFIELD,
President.

TRIBUTES BY

Hon. John J. Sparkman

OF ALABAMA

Mr. President, there have been innumerable eulogies of our late, beloved President, but I was particularly impressed with one I read a few days ago, published in a weekly paper in Alabama, written by a young girl, a high school student, by the name of Cam McCurry.

The subject of her little article is "Reflections of a Tragedy." She lives in Oneonta, Ala., and I presume this article was published in the

Oneonta newspaper. I ask that it may be included at this point.

REFLECTIONS OF A TRAGEDY

(By Cam McCurry)

From the events of this past week, we, the citizens of the United States of America, should have gained a lesson. Such a tragic event has brought to us a numbness, a disbelief, but from this we have gained a feeling of unity. A great man has died. He was killed by an assassin's bullet. Such a senseless, dastardly deed. He died as he lived, courageously.

How can decent men believe such a thing has happened in these United States? And we ask ourselves the unending question, Why? Why did this sickening thing happen?

I believe it happened because we, the people of the United States, let our minds and hearts stray—stray from the lesson of love Christ taught to the ways of hate, the ways of sick, stupid men. How can we, people who call ourselves Christians, intelligent people, sit in judgment on this one man, the man who pulled the trigger of a gun that cut down a great man, John F. Kennedy, when we helped to load the gun and we planted the idea in his mind? Yes, we did. We let ourselves hate so that we might as well have handed Lee H. Oswald the loaded gun.

The man, the good, kind man, is dead. But he died a hero, a martyr for the cause of freedom and of justice, freedom for his country, and justice for his fellow man. May God grant that his spirit live within us and from his courage may we gain the courage to do away with the strife and hate between man and unite America once more in freedom and in courage.

Mr. President, I have before me another eulogy, from Radio Station WAMI of Opp, Ala. Mr. Jim Williams, the manager of WAMI, on the occasion of the assassination of President Kennedy, gave an editorial over that radio station.

Every community throughout the United States is in deep mourning today—mourning for our leader and President, John Fitzgerald Kennedy, cut down by an assassin's bullet early Friday afternoon in Dallas, Tex. President Kennedy made an indelible mark and profound image on this Nation and the world during his comparatively short 46 years. He did this by seeking out his country's needs, our world problems, and according to his sincere convictions, implementing the measures that would make this a better country for all mankind, a safer world for our children, grandchildren, and future generations. President Kennedy, having a deep compassion for all of the world population, and at the same time respecting the differences of opinion that are rampant in the 20th century, may, indeed must, have found his job frustrating many times. It has been said that the post of our Presidency is a lonely spot for any man. Every action taken by President Kennedy, it seems, was a step he thought would bring a better understanding among the peoples of the universe, and an effort to get all men to meet on a common ground, a mutual ground where they could live in dignity with themselves and in peace with their fellow man. On the world scene, he commanded respect for our Nation, yet he conveyed to people everywhere his eagerness to search for a world where all men could live in self respect and in peace. President Kennedy was many things to many different individuals. History is a factual report of the past, and it seems that tomorrow's history will read something like this. John Fitzgerald Kennedy, U.S. President, from January 20, 1961, until November 22, 1963, convinced reasonable men throughout the world that America wanted peace on earth and good will toward man. During the coming weeks, probably, his 3-year-old son will ask for daddy or perhaps seek to locate daddy's new office. Unlike "John-John," as he was called by his father and our President, we realize that the answer won't come and that his office will not be found, but many Americans, in childlike bewilderment, will join "John-John" in asking: "Why?"

I have also received a tribute to the memory of President John F. Kennedy, delivered by Paul-Henri Spaak, Minister of Foreign Affairs of Belgium, before the U.N. General Assembly on November 26, 1963.

A TRIBUTE TO THE MEMORY OF PRESIDENT JOHN F. KENNEDY, BY PAUL-HENRI SPAAK, MINISTER OF FOREIGN AFFAIRS OF BELGIUM, BEFORE THE U.N. GENERAL ASSEMBLY, ON NOVEMBER 26, 1963

Mr. President, the assassination of the President of the United States has shocked the women and the men of my country more than it was possible to imagine. They wept, for the human tragedy. They worried about the possible political consequences.

When death strikes one of the great of this world who has arrived at the end of his career, whose work is done, one accepts the inevitable. One bows before this foreseen fatality. But when death blindly strikes the man who is in full possession of his faculties, whose personality is growing, from whom one still expects so many things, then stupefaction and revolt fill the heart and the mind.

John F. Kennedy has already given us a great deal but we were confident that we could expect much more still.

Amidst the elder statesmen, he represented a new generation. He symbolized youth in the ascent, youth that affirms itself.

As I have seen him and as I think I understood him, he was a rare combination of courage and imagination, of daring and composure. He had the will that would not give in on essentials, and the desire not to let any occasion escape to better international relations.

Like so many great Americans, he believed in democracy, he cherished freedom and wanted peace.

He did not shrink from any responsibilities. He accepted them, on the contrary, with a kind of contagious and touching enthusiasm.

In the few conversations I had the rare privilege to have with him, I felt my affection, my esteem and my admiration for him constantly grow.

I like to remember that the first time I met him he let me talk, the second time he questioned me, the third time he gave me his advice, the fourth time he took the decision.

Thus, gradually, his personality developed. The qualities of the heroic officer of the great war, of the young Senator, of the President of the United States grew into one. The statesman was born.

Since his life was too short for his work to be complete, he will remain essentially the man who fostered the legislation on civil rights and the equality of races, the man who without bravado but with a rare composure, faced a great danger that menaced his country, and still more, the man who signed the Treaty of Moscow which brought to the world a glimmer of hope.

He was cordial and simple and had an extraordinary presence. I still cannot accept the idea that he is no more. Immobility, nothingness, are so contrary to the vitality and the ardor which he represented. How can we accept the idea of the death of John Kennedy, when he was so extraordinarily alive and when he could have remained with us for a very long time?

To his family, to his friends, to his advisers, to his compatriots, we express not only our profound condolences. There is much more. Their sorrow is our sorrow. Their loss is also our loss and the man whose memory we honor today was not only the President of the United States of America; he was a citizen of the world who belongs to us like he belonged to them.

John F. Kennedy, 35th President of America, we will cherish your memory a very long time. We will be inspired by your example. In the great struggle that we will carry on for the ideal which was common to us, you will remain our companion until the day of victory.

TRIBUTE BY

Hon. Edward M. Kennedy

OF MASSACHUSETTS

Mr. President, the members of the Federal House of Deputies of Brazil passed a resolution in connection with the assassination of President Kennedy which they asked me to bring to the attention of the Congress.

I ask unanimous consent that the English translation forwarded to me by the deputies be printed and appropriately referred.

[Unofficial translation]

Senator EDWARD KENNEDY,
Senate of the United States of America,
Washington, D.C.:

The undersigned, Members of the Federal House of Deputies of Brasil, address to the United States Congress,

through your good offices, the expression of their earnest wishes for the thorough identification of the true motives and authors of the brutal act which took the life of the democratic leader John F. Kennedy, outraged the free conscience of the peoples of the world as it did that of the generous American people and gravely jeopardized hopes for peace and peaceful coexistence among all races, classes, religious faith, and political ideologies throughout the world.

NAMES OF SIGNERS

João Doria, Breno da Silveira, Rolando Corbisier, Getúlio Moura, Bento Gonçalves, Antonio Bresolin, Ary Alcântara, Ruben Alves, Clay Araújo, Campos Vergal, Geremias Fontes, Manoel Almeida, Francisco Macedo, Geraldo de Pina, Theódulo de Albuquerque, Chagas Rodrigues, Ivan Luz, Sergio Magalhães, Doutel de Andrade, Clemens Sampaio, Mario Maia, Fernando Gama, Epitácio Cafeteira, Rogê Ferreira, Helio Ramos, Valério Magalhães, Benedito Vaz, Josaphat Azevedo, Plínio Sampaio, Clovis Pestana, Ortiz Borges, Francisco Julião, Janduhy Carneiro, José Esteves, Paulo Coelho, Hélcio Maghenzani, Benjamin Farah, Paulo Mansur, Lírio Bertoli, José Maria Ribeiro, Miguel Buffara, Antônio Anibelli, João Herculano, Antonio Feliciano, Guilhermino de Oliveira, Abrahão Sabbah, Almino Afonso, Carlos Murilo, Palhano Saboia, Audizio Pinheiro, Floriceno Paixão, Castro Costa, Pereira Lúcio, Antonio de Barros, João Veiga, Padre Nobre, Nogueira de Rezende, Silvio Braga, Pedro Marão, Marcelo Sanford, Machado Rollemberg, Olavo Costa, Zacarias Seleme, Leão Sampaio, Padre Vidigal, Renato Azeredo, Medeiros Neto, Nelson Carneiro, Mario Lima, Orlando Bertoli, José Carlos, Adrião Bernardes, Geraldo Freire, Geraldo Mesquita, Wanderley Dantas, Daso Coimbra, Max da Costa Santos, Floriano Rubim, Leopoldo Peres, Henrique Lima, Manso Cabral, Tuťy Nassif, Gil Veloso, Clodomir Millet, Arruda Câmara, Tabosa de Almeida, Celestino Filho, José Freire, João Alves, Lamartine Távora, Artur Lima, Viera de Melo, Djalma Passos, Josaphat Borges, Braga Ramos, José Carlos Teixeira, Costa Lima, Zaire Nunes, Estelio Maroja, Ramon de Oliveira, Batista Ramos, Emmanoel Waissmann, Cesar Prieto, Lister Caldas, Rui Lino, Paulo de Tarso, Jales Machado, Ari Pitombo, Arnaldo Garcez, Levy Tavares, Segismundo Andrade, Nicolau Tuma, Américo Silva, Heitor Cavalcanti, Benedito Cerqueira, Temperani Pereira, Osmar Grafulha, Wilson Roriz, Cândido Sampaio, Moisês Pimentel, Garcia Filho, José Sarney, Sussumu Hirata, Mario Covas, Raphael Rezende, Paulo Freire, Magalhães Melo, Regis Pacheco, Dinar Mendes, Emílio Gomes, Alceu Carvalho, Derville Alegretti, Armando Carvalho, Alberto Aboud, Wilson Chedid, Oscar Cardoso, Mello Mourão, Tourinho Dantas, Elias Carmo, Celso Passos, Cardoso de Menezes, Aderbal Jurema, Aloísio Nonô, Lourival Batista, Anísio Rocha, Miguel Marcondes, Fernando Santana, Jaeder Albergaria, Horácio Betônico, Wilson Falcão, Celso Amaral, Edgard Pereira, Unirio Machado, Afonso Celso, Heraclio do Rêgo, Manoel Novaes, Necy Novais, Luna Freire, Wilson Martins, Pedro Braga, Aécio Costa, Moreira da Rocha, Océlio de Medeiros, Oziris Pontes, Neiva Moreira, Guerreiro Ramos, Renato Medeiros, Armando Leite, Haroldo Durate, Raimundo de Andrade, Ivan Saldanha, Milvernes Lima, Oséas Cardoso, Simão da Cunha, Marcial Terra, Perachi Barcelos, Marco Antonio, Roberto Saturnino, Raymundo Brito, Waldemar Guimarães, Burnett Paiva Muniz, Ferro Costa, Cid Carvalho, Esmerino Arruda, Pereira Nunes, Mendes de Moraes, Milton Brandão, Bivar Olinto, José Menck, Paulo Maranini, João Ribeiro, Maia Neto, Gadhil Barreto, Athié Coury, Lino Morganti, Amintas de Barros, Ozana M. Coelho, Chagas Freitas, Gabriel Hermes, Amaral Furlan, Osmar Dutra, Eurico Ribeiro.

TRIBUTES BY

Hon. Claiborne Pell

OF RHODE ISLAND

Mr. President, in the past few weeks, I have received many communications from my fellow Rhode Islanders consisting of expressions of grief as a result of our recent national tragedy. The extremely sad circumstances which surrounded the loss of our great President, John Fitzgerald Kennedy, have led many Rhode Islanders to express their thoughts in many different ways. Some desire construction of a suitable memorial, such as the National Cultural Center. Others wish the minting of a coin or the naming of a square in order to commemorate our late President. However, the majority of the citizens who have written to me from my State have expressed their grief in a more personal manner. Along this line, I have received two rather exceptional communications which are symbolic of the thoughts of all Rhode Islanders during this period of national mourning. Therefore, I ask unanimous consent at this time, Mr. President, that two poetical eulogies, which have been written by the Reverend Jessie Koewing Brown and Patrolman Robert E. Taylor, both of the city of Providence, be printed.

A NATION MOURNS

A Nation sadly mourns; we bow our heads in grief,
As in death's cruel cold embrace, lies our beloved Chief.
So truly dedicated he, so dauntless, young, and brave,
Must he forever silent be, in a martyr's lonely grave?

Ah no, his spirit calls us, we see him through our tears,
He bids us carry on his work, he gently stills our fears;
He says "take up the burden where I had to lay it down,
And together we will fight and win, and gain a victors'
    crown.

"We must ne'er negotiate through fear, nor fear to
    negotiate,
Our forefathers' dream of liberty we must perpetuate,
It is a lonely battle, this fighting for world peace,
But trust in God, keep praying, and may your faith
    increase."

And so the spirit of John Kennedy will lead us in the way
To worldwide peace and understanding, and bring a
    brighter day;
But the challenge is a great one, we must abolish fears
    and hates,
And give our all as he did, to these United States.
With grateful hearts o'erflowing we thank Thee Lord for
    him
Whose faith, intelligence, and love, endeared him to all
    men:
God rest his stalwart soul in peace, and to his loved ones,
    God be good,
And in his memory may hands 'round the world, be
    joined in brotherhood.
                —Jessie Koewing Brown.
November 24, 1963.

A TRIBUTE TO JOHN FITZGERALD KENNEDY

Dear God, send forth the inspiration I need
To write poetic words the whole world can read.
Just simple words from my deep, saddened heart
About John F. Kennedy, whom from life did part.

A man so much loved by one and all.
A symbol of peace that stands so tall.
Has now passed on from the living race
To join great men at a far distant place.

Arriving in Dallas with a large motorcade,
'Twas a heart broken city in which history was made.
From a building up high the fatal shot came
The assassin we know, without trial, without name.

On his death bed, for life they did fight
Two priests near by gave the last rites.
His final breath gone Jackie reached for his hand,
Placed on his finger her gold wedding band.

A mental picture now comes to mind
Of a Texas boy holding a sign.
It said, "Yankee Go Home," painted in red
A few moments later, John Kennedy lay dead.

He did return home, in Air Force One
A casket of bronze, beneath the bright sun
His wife as always there by his side,
What a stout hearted woman he chose for a bride.

I'll say in closing of he who is gone
In our hearts, our minds, he will always live on.
Now dear God, our prayers shall be
For strength and guidance to his bereaved.
           —Patrolman Robert E. Taylor,
    Providence Police Department, Providence, R.I.

Mr. President, among the tributes to our late President John F. Kennedy, one which has touched me deeply is a poem by Miss Mary McGann, of Newport, R.I., presently a student of Newton College, Massachusetts. The poem was published in the December 27, 1963, edition of the Providence Visitor, from my State of Rhode Island.

In meaningful fashion the poem links words by Robert Frost with President Kennedy's achievements, and it appeals to me particularly as representing the regard and affection which he inspired among our country's youth. The youthful spirit, in its quest for learning and self-expression, has a great significance in our times and in our Nation; and with these thoughts in mind, I ask that this poem be printed.

A SACRED MEETING

Robert Frost, arise—awake,
And meet your favorite son,
Greet the man whose battle won
You were there to commemorate.
Greet him, Poet Laureate—verse maker old and wise—

"The land was ours before we were the land's"
Or so you said, he asked us to give to that land
Of ourselves—all we had;
And he gave more
And you heralded in verse the New Frontier, the one
  he gave.

"But I have promises to keep, and miles to go before
  I sleep"
Promises to us his people; and he never slept—
Till now, he sleeps in eternity.
From Berlin where a wall would keep back freedom—

"Something there is, that doesn't love a wall."
He looked ahead, that the world would be free—
That all men as brothers would never fight—

"The deed of gift was many deeds of war."
Now, Robert Frost—knower and writer of life,
He's there with you; for he gave of himself outright—
"For this is love and nothing else is love."
                                        —Mary McGann.

TRIBUTES BY

Hon. J. W. Fulbright

OF ARKANSAS

Mr. President, on November 25 the European Parliament, the parliamentary arm of the six countries joined together in the European communities, paid tribute to the memory of the late President Kennedy.

The speeches of the President of the Parliament and some of his distinguished colleagues have been reprinted in a special brochure, copies of which have been sent to the Senate. A copy has been sent to each Senator's office. In order that the eloquent statements of these high European officials may have a wider audience, I ask that they be included as follows:

TRIBUTE TO JOHN F. KENNEDY, PRESIDENT OF THE UNITED
STATES OF AMERICA

ADDRESS DELIVERED BY MR. GAETANO MARTINO, PRESIDENT
OF THE EUROPEAN PARLIAMENT

Ladies and gentlemen, John Kennedy, the young and well-loved President of the United States of America, died tragically at the hand of an assassin in his own country while carrying out the duties of his high office. He was one of the most enlightened, noble and generous figures that have guided American policy since the Declaration of Independence, one of the most brilliant and courageous men, richly endowed with creative spirit and irresistible energy that have been called upon to play a predominant part in world politics—one of the loftiest and most inspiring spirits that have been born to uplift the condition of mankind.

Today, all that he stood for dominates our world. Time will neither diminish nor efface his achievement.

During the 3 years he was President, his name was linked to events of fundamental importance. He had already secured a permanent place in history as President of the New Frontier—of a political concept and form of government aimed at promoting the consolidation and defense of freedom and democracy on American soil, through the enrichment and development of the principles and ideals that nourish and foster them and, through a relentless struggle against the factors that threaten their life and progress. These are poverty, ignorance, disease, discrimination, and social injustice. The New Frontier has meant a return and an appeal to that spirit of loyalty, courage, solidarity, and manly enterprise which distinguishes the expansive aspect of the American Nation and provided it with the moral basis that insured its progress in freedom, equality, and order.

The driving force given by President Kennedy to American domestic policy exemplified the loftiest Christian and liberal virtues. This policy knew no hesitation, respite or compromise with internal opposition. Kennedy was convinced that a man should always carry out his duty and that in this lay the basis of all human morality. Not only with the civil rights bill, but also with his antiracial discrimination, educational, economic, and social policies, he sought to give a new and richer content to liberal and democratic institutions.

The spirit of the New Frontier inspired not only domestic policy but also, I feel, above all, American foreign policy in the past 3 years. This is why the tragic end of John Kennedy's life has left its mark on the minds not only of the American people, but also of all citizens of the free world, indeed all civilized mankind.

President Kennedy will be remembered as the fearless champion of the freedom of the peoples of the West and the initiator of the great aim of conciliation and relieving tension. He proved this at a time in international relations fraught with difficulties and grave uncertainty—the Cuba crisis—when he gave a measure of his firmness in defending the principles and the very foundations of the free world. Until then, he had not been spared the accusation that he could not accurately assess the forces that threatened the free world and that he was not as firm as his predecessors toward the unscrupulous and deceitful policy of the adversary. But when 13 months ago the defenses of the free Western World were exposed to a dire threat, he did not hesitate to adopt, on his own personal responsibility, the measures necessary to overcome it. His action showed that there are limits to democratic tolerance which cannot be ignored without involving the risk of setting off a world conflict.

I do not know whether the policy adopted by Kennedy at the time of the Cuban crisis was the origin of his tragic death. It was certainly the policy that ushered in a new phase in international relations which, while it has strengthened the moral forces of the West, has also permitted mankind—through the agreement, even if only partial, on nuclear tests—to discern a new light that raises the general hope of a brighter, less uncertain future.

There is an aspect of Kennedy's policy which I should like particularly to mention. We who live and work in a part of Europe that has already achieved a certain degree of unity, which we are endeavoring with all our might, and despite all obstacles, to consolidate and extend, also remember President Kennedy as the determined advocate of full European unity, and this not as an end in itself but as an instrument for consolidating the solidarity of the Atlantic peoples and as a decisive step toward complete union of the free world, inspired by that peace in which people live side by side in mutual respect and work together with mutual consideration.

In his historic speech at Philadelphia on July 4, 1962, Kennedy called for closer links between America and Europe as a first step toward achieving the grand design of the association of the Atlantic peoples. In noble and impressive terms, he appealed to the Europeans to carry out a creative and resolute action—the construction of their new House—while at the same time he exhorted the Americans to think no longer in continental terms but in intercontinental terms. He firmly maintained that only if we united could we play our part in building a world based on law and on freedom of choice, banishing war and coercion.

The unification of Europe is in the interest not only of America but of the entire free world, indeed of all men anxious to reach at last a safe haven of peace. Such a united Europe, linked to America by indestructible bonds, would serve as an inexhaustible fund of energy and progress.

The basic concepts and themes of the Philadelphia speech have been embodied and amplified in the no less memorable speech of June 25, 1963, in the Paulskriche at Frankfurt. In that speech Kennedy reaffirmed the historical necessity—as well as the profound common interest of the free peoples—in creating a Europe permanently united and integrated in an Atlantic association of independent States which would also share responsibilities and decisions, all equally united in the task of defense and the arts of peace. This was no pipe dream: the association could have been achieved, he maintained, by taking concrete steps to solve the problems that face us all, whether military, economic or political. The association is not so much an attitude as a process—a continuous process which becomes accentuated over the years as we dedicate ourselves increasingly to our common tasks.

In reaffirming the absolute need for solidarity between the United States and Europe, Kennedy did not neglect to express the hope in continued talks with the Soviet world with a view to relieving tension. But he expressly asked those who look upon themselves as our opponents to understand that in our relations with them we are not bartering the interests of one nation for those of another, as the cause of freedom is common to us all. He did not underestimate but frankly recognized that the obstacles to hope are grave and threatening. And yet the goal of world peace, he concluded, should now and always inform our decisions and inspire our intentions. * * * We were therefore all idealists, all dreamers. He felt that it should not be said of this Atlantic generation that it had left ideals and dreams to the past, and firmness of purpose and decision to our opponents.

Ladies and gentlemen, during my recent official visit to the United States, as President of this Parliament, I myself had direct and conclusive evidence of President Kennedy's will to help build a united Europe, to struggle alongside us against the failures and myths of a barren and divided past, to seek with us the most appropriate means for overcoming our dissensions which he hoped would be temporary and incidental. He wanted to be informed of all serious and pressing problems that faced the European Community and wished to reaffirm explicitly, during our talks, his full support for the work of the European Parliament.

With the death of Kennedy the cause of European unity has lost a great friend and ally. In paying reverent tribute to his memory, while the American people renders its last homage to its President, I believe that it is our duty to resolve jealously to cherish the message he has left us and to continue on the path that he helped to open up and which he frequently described as the only one offered by history which alone can preserve, for us and for our children, the freedom and dignity of man—that is the basis of all that makes life worth living.

———

ADDRESS DELIVERED BY MR. L. DE BLOCK, SECRETARY OF STATE FOR FOREIGN AFFAIRS OF THE KINGDOM OF THE NETHERLANDS, PRESIDENT IN OFFICE OF THE COUNCILS OF MINISTERS OF THE EUROPEAN COMMUNITIES

Mr. President, ladies and gentlemen, President Kennedy's tragic death has moved us deeply and fills us with great sorrow. The Councils of the European Communities join in the sympathetic words which you, Mr. President, have just expressed in memory of the man who was so cruelly killed.

The emotion his death has caused all over the world

shows the extent of the loss we have suffered. We all share in the deep grief which has overtaken the American Nation.

John Kennedy's enthusiasm and drive were for millions of his contemporaries the symbol of youth. This youthfulness, combined with outstanding qualities of courage and intelligence, expressed itself above all in his broadness of outlook. He was also a symbol of justice and peace which, as the President of the most powerful Western democracy, he strove to promote with a deep sense of reality and responsibility which is the characteristic of great statesmen.

Above all, however, he was the statesman who, inspired by ideals of freedom and human dignity, gave the world new hope for a lasting peace among men. For us, Europeans, he was also the man who realized how necessary it is for Europe to unite. He supported our nations in their endeavor to achieve the economic and political unification of Europe. At the same time, he was convinced that the New World and the Old World should combine their efforts to defend their common ideals of freedom and peace, and strive together for greater prosperity in the world.

The 3 years during which President Kennedy bore his heavy responsibility have left his own mark on the international policy to which he gave a new inspiration.

His tragic demise has not allowed him to develop all his talents and to fulfill the great task he had set himself.

John Fitzgerald Kennedy is no longer with us, but his life and work will remain for us, Europeans, and for every nation sharing his ideal, a living source of inspiration. May he rest in peace.

———

Address Delivered by Mr. W. Hallstein, President of the Commission of the European Economic Community

Mr. President, ladies and gentlemen, the man in honour of whose memory this House is assembled here today was more than the President of a great and powerful Nation. He was a man whose resolution, whose deeds, whose counsel were directed to us all—to the entire free world and not least to Europe.

Although only 3 years have elapsed since he first took office, his Presidency appears to us in retrospect to have spanned an entire epoch. Seldom can the American people have pinned such high hopes on a new President. Seldom can a new head of state have been as fervently acclaimed as was John Fitzgerald Kennedy, a radiant, dynamic personality imbued with inexhaustible optimism, a man on the threshold of his prime who had promised to lead his people to the New Frontier. New Frontier—the term has an intimate ring in American ears, stirring up memories that have long since passed into history. The New Frontier is no rigid boundary-line immutably staked out; rather does it conjure up a vision of illimitable horizons, an escape from an order of things that has grown old and sluggish, that is slowly grinding to a standstill; a challenge to turn our eyes to the future, to brave the

unknown, to prepare ourselves for hardship, trials and also adventure.

But Kennedy courted adventure not merely from a desire to change the established order or from a love of danger. The dazzling vistas revealed to him as he mounted the pinnacle of power held the key to what he called "the great human adventure" where "freedom is more than the rejection of tyranny, prosperity is more than an escape from want." Kennedy was one of the great American reformers who pinned their faith on the power of thought, the triumph of reason, the goodness in man. His resolution, like his every endeavour, sprang from the conviction that, as the American philosopher Emerson once put it, "there is an infinite worthiness in man." Kennedy was no fanatical reformer abandoning himself to a planner's irresponsible dreams. He had that rare, inestimable gift, a creative political imagination, the power to discern possibilities, to recognize what was feasible, what was essential.

Only a man who is conscious of his responsibilities is in a position to gage what can and what cannot be done. If we compare the pictures of President Kennedy taken immediately after his election, showing a man vibrant with joyous, almost carefree energy, with those of later years, we see at once that his features bear the imprint of the burden of office—stupendous if only on account of the multiplicity and complexity of the tasks—of the fearful knowledge that on his shoulders lay the responsibility for the fate not only of his own country but of the free, indeed of the entire world. He could not, as he once remarked, afford the luxury of free advice, the luxury of indecision. His responsibility was one of decision.

He never shirked that responsibility, particularly where it involved courage, contention or trials of strength. He followed the dictates of his conscience, even at the risk of alienating voters and endangering his personal prestige.

The conviction that "there is an infinite worthiness in man" enabled him to embark on his great reforms for the unification of the American peoples—a mission animated by the very spirit of the American Constitution with its insistence on equality, on the indivisibility of the freedom of the individual. Kennedy sought to establish a new social order in which man would be master of his fate. He strove for a world at peace, for "a world where peace is not a mere interlude between wars but an incentive to the creative energies of humanity." Thus he formulated a "strategy of peace" and did not hesitate to tread the brink in pursuing a policy of easing tensions, a policy of equalization where a false step, an ill-timed concession, might have precipitated a plunge into the abyss.

It is to President Kennedy that we Europeans are indebted for the idea of the Atlantic partnership—a link, on an equal footing, between the new continent and the old, a community designed not as an end in itself but as a model of a peaceful order, itself an essential factor for the peace of the world.

Nobody has expressed this concept more lucidly than Kennedy himself in the now classic utterances of his speech in Philadelphia on July 4, 1962, commemorating the American Day of Independence.

This amounted to a rejection of domination—a rejection

of domination where it could well have been imposed, an offer of a partnership that went beyond the mere sharing of power, a project of full give and take between equals. It is only now that we perceive the full implication of his offer, an appeal to us, which we cannot afford to ignore, to create the conditions necessary for the Atlantic partnership, and therefore for a peaceful order, right here on the old continent, thus justifying the faith placed in us by the New World, the world of the departed President.

In rendering homage to the late President Kennedy and offering our deepest sympathy to the family and Nation that mourn him, we take to our hearts the challenge thrown out by him about 6 months ago when, as spokesman of the free world, he once again conjured up for us a vision of a world where peace and universal freedom reigned:

"So we are all idealists. We are all visionaries. Let it not be said of this Atlantic generation that we left ideals and visions to the past, nor purpose and determination to our adversaries. We have come too far, we have sacrificed too much, to disdain the future now. We have sacrificed too much."

The late President himself fell a sacrifice to his office. Let us answer his call. Let us hold on to what has been achieved. Let us help to crown his great achievement.

___

ADDRESS DELIVERED BY MR. E. MEDI, VICE PRESIDENT OF THE COMMISSION OF THE EUROPEAN ATOMIC ENERGY COMMUNITY

Mr. President, ladies and gentlemen, the death of President Kennedy has filled the world with sorrow. He fell on the threshold of the new vistas that are opening up for mankind, in the fulfillment of a lofty mission of peace, justice, and understanding among the nations.

Our European Community—closely linked to the noble American Nation, which made and is making such a great and fundamental contribution to civilization and progress—shares the general grief.

President Kennedy has clearly shown the world the enhanced value of scientific research and peaceful development when combined with the highest human virtues. In following his lead, Europe is in unison with the other nations.

Hate propaganda generates death but love of our fellow men, as preached by those who have become its martyrs, will open up the paths of life. President Kennedy ranks with the noblest and worthiest figures in history. He gave us a shining example of faith in God and man by pointing to the arduous road of courage and sacrifice.

To our generation, to you the youth of future generations, President Kennedy's message is: to preserve life we must be prepared to sacrifice it.

___

ADDRESS DELIVERED BY MR. D. DEL BO, PRESIDENT OF THE HIGH AUTHORITY OF THE EUROPEAN COAL AND STEEL COMMUNITY

Mr. President, ladies and gentlemen, the high authority wishes to express its sorrow at the death of the American President.

It is not for us in this hall to ask why he was killed and whether it was the result of the destructive urge of a revolutionary ideology or the uncontrolled and criminal initiative of a lunatic. Abraham Lincoln also remains unforgettable although he too was assassinated by a histrion who, by some grotesque irony, described himself as a gentleman of the south.

We are only interested in the heritage which Kennedy leaves to Europe.

The President of the United States of America successfully concluded a cycle which began in the now remote past with the Declaration of Rights of Virginia when the United States was born in the struggle against the relics of European despotism.

Since those days relations between the United States of America and Europe, albeit always peaceful, have almost constantly been strained. If the United States of America made her contribution of blood in the first and in the second World Wars, she did this for the fortress America, which had here in our countries its own outposts to safeguard and defend. With John Kennedy, however, a purely instrumental consideration of Europe on the part of the United States came to an end.

Those among us who rightly ask that relations based on equality should be established between Europe and the United States of America, have been able to observe, particularly over the last few years, the extent to which the American John Kennedy was also a European, advancing with us at the same quick pace and with the same determination.

The high authority would like to express its distress, and also its solicitude for Kennedy's young children for whom he will always remain the best of guides, for his wife, who gave such a spontaneous example of the way in which a brave heart faces grief, and for the people of the United States of America to whom we feel as close in their hour of misfortune as at the time of their victories.

Mr. President, there have been countless numbers of words written about the assassination of President Kennedy. We all, I think, felt upon the President's death a sense of great personal loss and grief and attempted to express it in our own way. One of the most poignant messages which has come to my attention was written by Mr. Harold C. Miller, who many of the Members of Congress will remember as the long-time administrative assistant to our late colleague, Senator Harley M. Kilgore, of West Virginia.

Harold Miller, a veteran himself of the war in the Pacific, as was President Kennedy, attempted to set forth his feelings in a statement written on the day following the assassination. His statement was printed in the Washington papers, but in order that the message it expresses may receive wider distribution, I ask that it be included.

It Rained in Washington Today

(By Harold C. Miller)

It always seems to rain after a terrible tragedy. It comes not with fury, but steadily, softly it tries to wash away the horror the mind cannot fully comprehend.

The blood streaked veteran of every battle knows it well. The weeping widow, once so vivacious, stands with blood streaked clothing.

Why? Why? Why?

The cry goes out through the land. The horror of it is so great the mind is stunned. There is no comprehension, no understanding of the terrible carnage.

It has happened. It is over. The steady fall of raindrops tries to wash away a memory too horrible to relate. It is over. Pay heed to your folly. This is the message of a gentle God trying to sooth His troubled children.

Life must go on.

Each citizen must try to find his own soul in this carnage.

John Fitzgerald Kennedy has died in the quest for human dignity and peace. This man has given the full measure of his life. Can we, the living, say the same?

The rain falls steadily.

November 23, 1963.

Mr. President, Mr. Sam Faubus, one of my esteemed constituents and a good friend, recently wrote one of the most succinct and eloquent tributes to President Kennedy that I have seen. This tribute to our late President appeared in the Madison County Record, which is published in Huntsville, Ark. The Madison County Record is owned by the Governor of Arkansas, who is the son of Mr. Sam Faubus.

Sam Faubus was introduced to President Kennedy when the President dedicated the Greers Ferry Dam in Arkansas this fall. I ask unanimous consent that the letter by Mr. Faubus be printed as follows:

Combs, Ark.

Dear Editor: I am stunned and bewildered. I don't seem to be able to realize that the bright-eyed, dark sandy-haired young man that greeted me with a smile and a warm handshake and told me he had received a nice letter from my daughter, Bonnie, in California, only a few days ago, now lies murdered by the hand of an assassin.

When history has rendered its verdict it will place the name of John Fitzgerald Kennedy as one among the greatest Presidents this country has had since the time of Abraham Lincoln. He has done more for peace and freedom in the 3 short years he has been President than any man in our Nation's history.

Children will read about John Fitzgerald Kennedy in their history books for generations to come, and men believing in liberty, justice, and freedom, will revere his name throughout the entire world.

Sam Faubus.

TRIBUTE BY

Hon. Pat McNamara

OF MICHIGAN

Mr. President, there have been many fine tributes paid to our late President, John F. Kennedy. One of these, which I found particularly appropriate, was written by John Herling, Washington correspondent and editor of John Herling's Labor Letter. I ask unanimous consent that the text of Mr. Herling's tribute be printed as follows:

The Most Tragic News of Our Lifetime

We have all lost our President, and many of us a personal friend. Jack Kennedy lived life with zest and intelligence. He gave to all of us a renewed sense of the challenge, the laughter, and the danger of life. He brought into public career the importance of private dedication. His gaiety was always tinged with the imminence of uncertainty. He was serious without pompous solemnity. He was natural in demeanor but his demeanor was one of easy dignity. He was often fierce in private anger and scorching in his estimate of those whom he thought proved unworthy of trust or who tried to nail him or his friends to a double cross.

He was a wealthy young man; in his own lifetime he witnessed the transition of his family from middle income to great fortune. But an overriding fact about John Kennedy is that the aura of suffering hovered over him constantly. In his youth he was not too robust, and was rather introspective. During the war his great deed of daring for which he is remembered was a rescue operation of his comrades. He came out of the war with a smashed back which nearly cost him his life on the operating table 10 years later. Its dull ache plagued him all his remaining days. But it was not only personal suffering that he endured, he had a sense of folk suffering. He never forgot, and indeed many refused to let him forget, that he came out of a minority group. His father once said, "When will people stop calling us Irish-American and just call us American?"

The paternal anger was understandable. He was fighting for his children's rights. But the son turned his origin into a status symbol. His psychological insight made him understand the frustration and the yearning and the aspiration of all men of all groups who were hit by prejudice and who day after day were shot down by the glaring eye of the bigot. He understood full well that deprived men and women do not, indeed, cannot act always from the highest motives. But as a practical politician, he sought to convert dross into a new creative element.

His relations with the trade union movement were easy and spontaneous, and were based on a fundamental respect for the people in it, and for the historical and humanitarian posture of the American trade union development. He frequently felt that organized labor did not take sufficient advantage of its strength and position, while he never hesitated to indicate where he thought that important opportunities were lost either through carelessness, or lack of sensitivity. Just as he himself had a great sense of history, so he constantly sensed the significant place in history of the American labor movement.

He was a great reader. He was avaricious for learning. He admired men of ideas who acted to make them real. He was constantly exploring the geography of his own mind, and of the minds of others. When people like myself wrote a column, or a letter, we flattered ourselves that we were being read by the usual people, plus one. He sometimes would talk to newspapermen about something they wrote, and would give them as much time as he might an ambassador, or indeed, a head of state. Like a good newspaperman, which he once was, he sought to comfort the afflicted, and he never hesitated to afflict the comfortable, if he thought they deserved it.

We all died a little—Oh, more than a little—when John Fitzgerald Kennedy was killed in Dallas. He had added to our self-respect, he had made us stretch our mind and our spirit even as he stretched his. We were fortunate as a people to have lived with Jack Kennedy and that Jack Kennedy grew into our lives. He might have perished in the Pacific war, he might have died on the operating table, but instead he lived on to be President— and he died when and as he did. We who used to ask him questions now will have to ask them of his successor. But for a long time, there will be an ache in the asking, and in that room, we shall hear the echo of that brilliant, gallant, and thoughtful man who today looks toward us from Arlington, and we to him.

J.F.K.'S LEGACY TO LABOR

Just a year ago in the same East Room of the White House where John Kennedy lay dead, the young President strode in with a confident, half-smiling, half-appraising look on his face to talk to 600 invited labor leaders. He looked out at them and then grinned widely. The faces before him were familiar. He knew personally more trade union men of national and local importance than any President before him. While President Franklin Roosevelt surely understood the nature and purpose of the labor movement, he was never really acquainted with many local leaders outside his own State. But J.F.K. knew them.

They warmed to him and he to them.

On that November day in 1962, the purpose of the meeting was to talk about civil rights and about organized labor's responsibility in the field. Mr. Kennedy said:

"I want to express my warm welcome to you in this historic room, and to express my great appreciation to you for your effort in joining together to commit ourselves once again to the goal of equal opportunities for all.

"This," he said, "is a cause you understand very well. The labor movement, after all, was originated by those who were being denied their equal opportunity. Whether it was because they were working 12 hours a day, 6 or 7 days a week, whether it was because they were immigrants, whether it was because of one reason or another, the labor movement began as a union of those who were the least privileged in our society.

"So it seems to me very natural that those who took into their ranks and, indeed, built their ranks upon immigrants, upon women who were exploited, upon men who worked too long, upon young people who were put to work under adverse conditions, old people who were dismissed when they were too old to sustain the burdens of long employment—that the labor movement could be, as it has been for the last 30 years, the natural center and core of the effort to provide better opportunity for all of our fellow citizens. Whatever their racial descent, whatever their religion, whatever their color, whatever region of the country they come from, this is a cause to which labor has been associated for many years."

He turned to Lyndon Johnson, and said: "I want to commend the Vice President for his long efforts with all of the people of our country in making this cause more successful; the labor movement itself, and the Secretary of Labor Willard Wirtz. This is something you know all about. This is something you are doing. This is something we can all do better on."

Then with great emphasis he said: "The work of the labor movement isn't done. When the work of the labor movement is done, then all of you might just as well go home and stay in bed. The work of the labor movement goes on. It is wholly unfinished.

"There are too many areas of our country where there isn't equal opportunity, where people aren't adequately paid, where they work too long, where their rights are not guaranteed, and as long as that is true, there is need for the American labor movement.

"So I ask you to join in an old cause and a new one— and that is to make sure that in the ranks of labor, labor itself practices what it preaches. This is true of labor; it must be true of all of us."

TRIBUTE BY

Hon. E. L. Bartlett

OF ALASKA

Mr. President, I was moved in reading the letter written on the morning of the day when tragedy befell us, and the world, in the death of President Kennedy by a young man from Alaska who is studying in Germany.

Richard Gillam, honor student and Stanford University junior, is one of 60 Stanford students studying abroad for 6 months. The letter written in Stuttgart, Germany, was directed to his father, Byron Gillam, in Anchorage. Its text is worthy of a wide audience and I ask unanimous consent that the letter be printed following my remarks:

I am writing this letter on the morning of President Kennedy's death. I am writing because I wish to express my feelings to someone a bit closer to the situation han I. I am writing because I think a breathless moment in our history has been reached. I am writing because today—and perhaps only last night for a few terrible moments, or seconds—the world must suddenly view itself as it is. And I am writing because a great and good man has been destroyed.

He was a man who more than anyone of our century embodied the hopes and aspirations of mankind—he was the only figure in modern world history that would have spontaneously inflamed over 60,000 West Berliners—in a city directed microscopically by the hate of the world—to express their grief in a milling, unbelieving demonstration on the very spot where this man, only a few months before had said, "I am a Berliner."

And, my father, Berlin is the world today—2 million flickering candles in an otherwise dark city have marked the ascension of this world's—and I mean Berlin's—Christ on earth.

It is trite, and so very true to say that he was an idea, a very needed idea in a world which it appears must ever again be snatched from the jaws of a ravaging entity that feeds on darkness and spews billowing mush-oom-shaped clouds of destruction.

It is unconceivable that this event should have occurred, but it has—and the eternal inevitable and unanswerable question is why, why, why—?

And it matters not from which fountain of evil the assassin stemmed—as Mr. Cronkite (news analyst Walter Cronkite) so eloquently expressed—they have all participated and have all pulled the trigger.

In the early 1930's, the madman of all history came to power because he burned the Reichstag and blamed the Communists; the magnitude of evil then unleashed may never be comprehended but let us now at least realize that we are all morally accountable for yesterday's monstrosity because if we don't realize this fact we are only compounding the now manifest unrights in the history of man.

America will survive the crisis because it is a strong country. But we can survive either under the reactionary and stunting philosophy of isolationist self-centeredness and pragmatic, hatemongering opportunism or under a philosophy which I can only describe as one of hope, love, and intense world concern.

The man to carry on this philosophy I cannot name, but I hope to God, America, that you wake up, because you can either destroy or recreate yourself within the span of these coming precarious months.

The people of Europe realize this and are waiting. Last night the air was pervasive with confusion and fear. Crowds milling around the few still open newsstands could not and did not want to believe what they heard. People parked about American Embassies throughout this continent prayed that the reality which they already knew was true was not true.

It seemed that a vital, elemental stay of reality had suddenly been smashed away, and a humanity in free fall clutched at all straws offering promise of support—yet last night there were no straws.

Viewed soberly in the light of a new morning, we begin to pull ourselves together. We begin to hope again. We find new references, a severely tried political system shows signs of pulling itself together also, and the world waits.

We may well be at a great crossroads in the path of human existence—we face the complexity of infinity in choosing our course—may we have the courage and wisdom, to find the right. And may we never forget the "why" of this great and terrible lesson we have been given.

TRIBUTES BY
Hon. Frank E. Moss
OF UTAH

Mr. President, as a fitting part of the 14th biennial National Convention of the Young Democratic Clubs of America held last week in Las Vegas, Nev., a memorial tribute was paid to the late President of the United States, John F. Kennedy. More than 1,500 young men and women of our Nation gathered there to hear a stirring memorial address by the senior Senator from Nevada, Hon. Alan Bible. Because I feel that Senator Bible has so completely spoken the sentiments of us all in this eulogy, I ask that it be printed in full following my remarks.

MEMORIAL TRIBUTE ADDRESS TO PRESIDENT JOHN F. KEN-NEDY BY U.S. SENATOR ALAN BIBLE, DEMOCRAT, OF NEVADA, AT 14TH BIENNIAL NATIONAL CONVENTION, YOUNG DEMOCRATIC CLUBS OF AMERICA, JANUARY 31, 1964, FLAMINGO HOTEL, LAS VEGAS, NEV.

President Allan Howe, distinguished guests, and fellow Democrats all, mine today is a solemn task. Were that I stood here not in memoriam but only with a rallying call.

But, I ask, would John F. Kennedy—would the legacy that the 35th President of the United States left to Americans, and particularly young Americans such as yourselves, want us to tarry long in the sorrow of his passing?

John F. Kennedy's incisive answer, crackling with an Irish glint in his eyes, would be: "There is work to be done, mountains to be climbed, bridges to be built, races to be won."

But, I believe he would not deny us the privilege, as we linger today for a few minutes, to pay him honor and dedicate ourselves to those principles and ideals for which he fought and died.

Since that fateful hour on November 22 last, certainly the United States has been joined by most of the world in witnessing and participating in the greatest and deepest outpouring from human souls in modern history. His tragic and untimely death touched the heartstrings of Americans everywhere—men and women, young and old, rich and poor, the mighty and the humble.

In paying a memorial tribute for this entire convention today here in my home State, I do so with the deepest sense of humility which has come my way during my lifetime. It is not my purpose to attempt to add to the wonderful words, the beautiful phrases, and the sincere pronouncements about this great humanitarian.

Each of us, who knew John Kennedy as a personal friend, as a dynamic leader of our party, or as the President of the United States, know full well we have been touched by a great man and a great moment in world history. Only on rare occasions do figures appear on the stage of our world who capture the attention and excite the imagination of all mankind. To each of us, John Kennedy probably represented something innately good in different ways. For many of us, around him was the aura of the age of chivalry. Some saw him as a courageous, young knight who dared to challenge war and human misery everywhere.

To others, John Kennedy was a magnetic leader who possessed the ability and the dauntless courage to forge ahead in spite of obstacles. Controversy did not sway his direction. He brought to the Government of the United States and our world a very special luster that we will not soon see again.

With the passage of 70 days since his tragic death, this country and the world has moved along. Others must take up the challenges and the tasks as has been the sinew and strength of our way of life.

It is not for us to attempt to recapitulate his great deeds. His leadership throughout the free world was probably unequaled by any American President.

Certainly, John Kennedy probably did more than any man in our time toward getting this world started toward peace—a durable, universal and dependable peace.

One of his hallmarks was his youth. In it most Americans, if not the leaders of the world, saw in him an ability to attempt to do those things which all men have a great desire to do—to build a more decent, understanding civilization for mankind everywhere. No man in modern history has created a greater respect or image for what decent people want the world to be.

Only months ago, John F. Kennedy spoke a few short blocks from where we sit today. His message was one of hope and one of challenge for us here in a growing Western United States, for our country generally and for the world. May I recall for those members of the National Young Democratic Committee the words of President Kennedy to you in the new flower garden at the White House on April 26, 1963. And I quote:

"I think that the purpose of any political party is to serve a great cause and I think the cause in the 1960's is to see if domestically we can develop and manage our economic society so that we do not move from recession to recession with continuing and ever-increasing unemployment, with millions of young people coming into the labor market, with millions of others trying to go to our colleges, with millions still unemployed. With a history of recessions in 1958 and 1960, all these make important the development of an effective national economy which offers an opportunity for all of our citizens on a basis of equality, and makes that one of our most difficult and pressing challenges in the 1960's.

"Now all this can be done and must be done under our system by a party which has responsibility. We have the responsibility now in the Executive, in the House and the Senate and I am asking your help not only in mobilizing the people of this country to comprehend what our program means, but also to make it possible for those Democrats who believe in progress—and most of them do or they wouldn't be Democrats—that you will do your part to assist them in 1964 to get our citizens registered, to get them out to vote, to make them understand that this is an important election and it does go to their welfare."

Now as this great convention helps to gird our party for our important November elections this year, I know that the image of John Kennedy and his dynamic example of what youth can bring to this world will be the greatest memorial possible.

Can we but build on his foundations and permit such to be a model for the betterment of mankind. We can do what he would want us to do by dedicating ourselves to this great cause.

It was my good fortune when I first went from the State of Nevada to the U.S. Senate 10 years ago, to strike up a friendship with the then Senator Kennedy. Our desks in the Senate Chamber were adjoining. I saw his suffering that kept him from his Senate duties because of recurrent complications from injuries he sustained while fighting for his country in South Pacific waters during World War II.

We marveled at the energetic campaign he waged across this land for the nomination for the Presidency, his great vigor displayed in winning that office and his tremendous inward and personal growth in rising to the many responsibilities that great office demands. The world is a much better place for all mankind because he passed our way. Many of his ideas and ideals will forever encourage and assist men in the quest for peace, justice, and the good way of life.

The world lost one of its greatest leaders, humanity a noble champion and our country a fearless, courageous President whose name will be enshrined forever in immortality.

Taps that sounded over his grave that sunny November day at Arlington National Cemetery spelled eternal rest for John Kennedy, the man. But for John Kennedy, the martyr, they sounded the reveille of action to search out more of God's great benefits.

John F. Kennedy was not a man of inaction. The torch which he threw down on that tragic November 22 has been grasped strongly and firmly by the man he chose as his successor, Lyndon B. Johnson—a torch still held high for all the world to see. Certainly the greatness for which John Kennedy gave so much is pointed up by the mastery with which his successor has gone so far to prove that America can forge, not one, but more than one man of greatness in a single era.

And let me close this memorial tribute with several paragraphs from a moving eulogy delivered by Chaplain Joseph P. Trodd, U.S. Navy, at a solemn pontifical requiem mass at the Dulce Nombre de Maria Cathedral at a far Pacific Ocean base in Agana, Guam, on November 25:

"Within him there smoldered a burning compassion for his fellow man, a fiery conviction that true peace in the world depends upon the peace of Christ in the heart.

This compassion, this conviction, became his mission. He toiled incessantly to teach that all men are created equal and that each, irrespective of the color of his skin, is an individual with a soul precious in the eyes of God. His fidelity to his faith, his dedication to his country, his service to all marked him plainly as a doer of the word as well as a believer.

"To a Winston Churchill is it given to live in greatness. To a martyr to die in greatness. A select few both live and die magnificently. Such was Abraham Lincoln. And such, we believe, was John Fitzgerald Kennedy.

"For when the annals of time are weighed, history will agree, that in the manner of his dying, unwittingly he taught his greatest lesson. Here was a man, in the fullness of his strength; perhaps the most powerful single individual on earth—whose whim or nod could make a statesman or break a general, who, by pressing one button, could bring death and destruction to most of the civilized world.

"And yet, last Friday afternoon, as he rode down a sun-drenched Dallas street accepting the plaudits of thousands at the summit of his career, a finger was bent and a shot sounded.

"Honor, dignity, and power faded. And in a matter of minutes a soul, naked and alone, stood before its Maker.

"And what of the lesson?

"A poet would say 'All that beauty, all that wealth ere gave, await alike the inevitable hour. The paths of glory lead but to the grave.' But the Christian mindful of eternity asks 'What doth it profit a man if he gain the whole world and suffer the loss of his immortal soul.'

"Our prayer today is this: May you, John Fitzgerald Kennedy, hear from the lips of your Savior, 'Well done thou good and faithful servant. Enter into the reward which has been prepared for you for all eternity.' And then may you see a tiny figure disengage itself from the choir of angels and saints and feel its baby fingers grasp your hand and lead you to the throne of the Almighty and hear your son, Patrick Bouvier Kennedy, say:

" 'This is my beloved father in whom I am well pleased. For here was, indeed, a profile in courage.' "

Mr. President, I have read no more moving tribute to our late great martyred President and his valiant First Lady than the one given at the Utah State University on January 7 of this year by President Hugh B. Brown of the Church of Jesus Christ of Latter-day Saints. President Brown represented the Mormon Church at the Kennedy funeral. He felt deeply the grief and shame which engulfed the country, and counseled against extremists who impugn the motives of dedicated leaders.

He urged, also, that we seek a historian's perspective in the conflict with communism, and keep "cool heads, strong hearts, dauntless courage, and mutual confidence if we are to bridge the dark days."

The speech is an eloquent appeal for loyalty to our institutions and our country. I ask unanimous consent that it be included as follows:

MEMORIAL SERVICES FOR PRESIDENT JOHN F. KENNEDY, JANUARY 7, 1964, UTAH STATE UNIVERSITY

(By President Hugh B. Brown)

President Chase, members of the faculty, distinguished guests, and fellow students, because it was my privilege to attend the funeral service of President John F. Kennedy, you have honored me by asking that I participate in this memorial service.

With thousands of others, I was deeply moved by the dignity and solemnity of the funeral and memorial services, where kings, presidents, prime ministers, and heads of state from most of the nations of the world had assembled to mourn with the American people and to pay honor to a truly great world leader.

First may I pause to pay tribute to one who is living. I have never seen a finer demonstration of courage, fortitude, and faith than I saw in the rotunda of the Capitol Building in Washington, D.C., when a tragic heroine, clasping the hand of her little daughter, walked calmly into the enclosure, knelt for a moment by her husband's casket, kissed the flag, and with admirable poise and head erect, left the building.

From the moment following that awful rifle shot when she cradled his head in her blood-stained lap, through the vigil at the hospital where he died, sitting by his body during the plane flight to Washington, supervising the preparations for the funeral, the march to St. Matthew's Cathedral and then to the rites in Arlington National Cemetery—through it all she displayed courage, dignity, and self-discipline, which had been so characteristic of her husband and which are now revealed as innate and mature virtues of that valiant first lady, Jacqueline Kennedy.

While the last year has in many respects been a happy and prosperous one, we were stunned and grieved by the shocking tragedy which occurred in Dallas on November 22, when the most promising young man of this generation was cruelly shot down by an assassin.

Our whole Nation was engulfed by a wave of horror, grief, and shame, but as President Eisenhower said: "Our country quickly absorbed the shock and closed ranks behind the new President. Thanks to the foresight of the Founding Fathers who provided in our Constitution for an orderly succession to the office of President, there was no faltering of our Government or hiatus in our Executive leadership. Once again our democratic system demonstrated to the world that although any political leader may pass suddenly from the scene, the institution of the Presidency itself continues firm and secure." This fact proves that the American political system is tough and resilient.

It is well that we remember when we speak of the Government that it is, after all, what Theodore Roosevelt declared it to be: "The Government is us. We are the Government, you and I."

Let us think for a moment of the real meaning of our Constitution, of our Declaration of Independence and the things for which they stand, and of our glorious flag which is an emblem. Just what these things stand for is well stated by a modern author as follows:

"The flag for which the heroes fought, for which they died, is the symbol of all we are, of all we hope to be.

"It is the emblem of equal rights.

"It means that this continent has been dedicated to freedom.

"It means universal education; light for every mind, knowledge for every child.

"It means that the schoolhouse is the fortress of liberty.

"It means that governments derive their just powers from the consent of the governed, that each man is accountable to and for the government. This responsibility goes hand in hand with liberty.

"It means that it is the duty of every citizen to bear his part of the public burden, to take part in the affairs of his town, his county, his State.

"It means that the ballot box is the ark of the covenant; that the source of authority must not be poisoned.

"It means that every citizen of the Republic, native or naturalized, must be protected; at home, in every State; abroad, in every land, on every sea.

"It means that all distinctions, based on birth or blood, have perished from our laws; that our Government shall stand between labor and capital, between the weak and the strong, between the individual and the corporation, between want and wealth, and give and guarantee simple justice to each and all.

"It means that there shall be a legal remedy for every wrong.

"It means national hospitality; that we must welcome to our shores the exiles of the world, and that we may not drive them back. Some of them may be deformed by labor, dwarfed by hunger, broken in spirit, victims of tyranny and caste—in whose sad faces may be read the touching record of a weary life—and yet their children, born of liberty and love, will be symmetrical and fair, intelligent and free."—From "The New Colossus," by Emma Lazarus.

How often we have read on the Statue of Liberty these poignant words:

"Give me your tired, your poor, your huddled masses yearning to breathe free, the wretched refuse of your teeming shore. Send these, the homeless, tempest-tost; I lift my lamp beside the golden door."

Herbert Hoover gave us this summation:

"America means far more than a continent bounded by two oceans. It is more than pride of military power, glory in war, or in victory.

"It means more than vast expanse of farms, of great factories or mines, magnificent cities, or millions of automobiles and radios.

"It is more even than the traditions of the great tide westward from Europe, which pioneered the conquest of a continent.

"It is more than our literature, our music, our poetry. Other nations have these things also.

"Perhaps the intangible we cannot describe is the personal experience, the living of each of us, rather than in phrase, however inspiring.

"The meaning of our America flows from one pure spring. The soul of our America is its freedom of mind and spirit in man. Here alone are the windows through which pours the sunlight of the human spirit.

"Here alone is human dignity, not a dream, but an accomplishment."

To this continent for nearly three centuries, three centuries and a half, men of all races have migrated and no one has been forced to come. Curiously most who did come escaped from some dissatisfaction, disappointment, or disillusionment, from poverty, hunger, fear, inequality, oppression, bigotry. These came to America, millions from every land, and here they found what they sought most; freedom to live their own lives as they chose.

There are other governments in the world, totalitarian in their nature, which have sworn to bury us, who feel they can overtake us, outdo us, supersede and subjugate us. It is of the utmost importance that the youth of our land become aware of the dangers that threaten us, aware also of the strength of our position and the source of that strength, be alerted to the responsibilities that rest upon them to preserve our land and our form of Government for future generations.

Herbert Hoover emphasizes the need for us to instruct our youth in the faith of our fathers when he said: "A nation is strong or weak. It thrives or perishes upon what it believes to be true. If our youth is rightly instructed in the faith of our fathers, in the traditions of our country, in the dignity of each individual man, then our power will be stronger than any weapon of destruction that man can devise."

Freedom is a live and growing plant which must be nurtured, cultivated, pruned, and kept fruitful. Freedom, like life, is a process, a growth where the new is perpetually crowding out the old. There is a constant wearing away and renewing. The beautiful blossom of today is by tomorrow wilted and dry and must fall by the next tomorrow and be forgotten, while the new bud comes and is heralded for its brief day. So the freedom of today, if not kept up to date by adjustments to suit new seasons and new occasions, may dry and become musty, and actually become serfdom.

Freedom without discipline is a delusion and spills over into license, where law is not respected and where decorum is not known. When, however, in the name of discipline, men are robbed of their right to think or speak or act; when the will of the few is imposed on the many; when the dignity of the individual is denied and responsibility to God rejected; then communism will flourish and the people become slaves.

If you are to enjoy those inalienable rights with which you are endowed by the Creator, you will not fawn before flattery, cringe before denunciation; nor will you yield to your own lawless impulses.

Sometimes the immigrants or refugees from other lands see this America of ours against a background which is alien to us and some of their definitions of our country and our liberties cause us to realize that we may be too close to the forest to see the trees. Hear this from a German refugee: "Americanism is not a birthplace nor a birthright; it is a vision in the brain, a cry in the heart, a flame in the soul. He who lives it may have it, and he who lives it not may never have it, though he may have the names of all the patriots on his family tree."

And then listen to a Frenchman, still loyal to his beloved France: "With no disloyalty to my beloved France, I embrace America. I salute its courage and audacity, its kindness and good will, its turbulent energy and unquenchable zest. I love America because I find here both the freedom that ennobles life and the discipline without which freedom becomes anarchy."

You are all familiar with the words of Walt Whitman, with his characteristically rugged prose-poetry. He said:

"Sail, sail thy best, oh ship of Democracy
Of value is thy freight—
'Tis not the present only, the past is also stored in thee:
Thou holdest not the venture of thyself alone—
Not of the Western continent alone:
Earth's resume entire floats on thy keel, O ship—
Is steadied by thy spars;
With thee, time voyages in trust.
The antecedent nations sink or swim with thee,
With all their struggles, martyrs, heroes, epics, wars.
Thou bearest the other continents; theirs,
Theirs as much as thine is the destination port triumphant,
Steer then with good strong hand and wary eye,
O helmsman—thou carriest great companions.
Venerable, priestly Asia sails this day with thee, America,
And Royal feudal Europe sails with thee—
How can I pierce the impenetrable blank of the future;
I feel thy ominous greatness, evil as well as good.
I watch thee advancing, absorbing the present, transcending the past.
I see thy light lighting and thy shadow shadowing as if the entire globe
But I do not undertake to define thee—hardly to comprehend thee."

Those of us who went through two World Wars and thought we had fought a war to end wars and to make the world safe for democracy, those of us who saw the subjugation of nations and the pitiless occupation of free lands by tyrants, realize that we must never seek peace by submitting to slavery.

After two World Wars and our experience in Korea, and now in the midst of a continuing cold war, we are coming to realize that our best defense lies in the moral strength of our people. In a recent issue of Sunshine magazine appeared the following:

"Despite the most costly rearmament program in the history of the world, the rising tide of crisis and confusion continues to threaten to engulf America and the cause of freedom.

"Yet, from their discouragement and disillusionment, the American people are beginning to remember something they have too long forgotten—that only from their moral strength can they generate the power to preserve their precious way of life, and to keep alive the flames of freedom which, in the chaos of the world around us, symbolized the one hope for liberty-loving peoples everywhere.

"In recent years, we have heard more of our leaders— military, political, and religious—call for the reawakening of the true American spirit in our people."

America is great in proportion that she makes sure that she will have great men in the next generation.

Let us beware of extremists in this land of ours, groups who attack the integrity and impugn the motives of some of our greatest patriots. Let us not be deceived into accepting their un-American and undemocratic philosophies even though they carry some anti-Communist banners. President Eisenhower wrote:

"Democracy is nothing but the opportunity for self-discipline. We owe it to ourselves to be deeply interested in political issues, to be thoughtful about the policies of our country—but we are simply endangering our democratic system when we go to extremes, deal in vilification, make threats against our own officials, and incite violence and lawlessness. The individual who unthinkingly goes to such extremes in weakening the whole structure of self-government."

We hope the young people of this institution, this State, and of our country will be loyal to our institutions, loyal to our leaders, and dedicated to the principles set forth in our Constitution. All of us are opposed to communism, but we do not fight communism best by weakening and dividing our own forces or destroying the faith of others in the integrity of our leaders.

Let us seek rather the historian's perspective and see this conflict with communism, not as a holy war, but as a difficult and perilous struggle with an implacable foe. We live in a diverse world in which there is a diversity of economic systems, political creeds, and philosophic faiths. We know, in part at least, what a nuclear war would mean. To avoid it is the common interest of all mankind and this interest must transcend all conflicts of ideology and national ambition. We need cool heads, strong hearts, dauntless courage, and mutual confidence if we are to bridge the dark abyss.

Let us conclude with a paragraph from a speech which President Kennedy prepared for delivery on that fatal day in November—a speech he was not permitted to deliver, but he left us this sublime paragraph:

"We in this country, in this generation, are—by destiny rather than by choice—the watchmen on the walls of world freedom. We ask therefore that we may be worthy of our power and responsibility—that we may exercise our strength with wisdom and restraint—and that we may achieve in our time and for all time the ancient vision of 'peace on earth, good will toward men.' That must always be our goal—and the righteousness of our cause must always underlie our strength. Or, as was written long ago: 'Except the Lord keep the city, the watchman waketh but in vain.' "

Thus President John F. Kennedy speaks to us from among the thousands of other living whom we call dead. They gave their lives for freedom. They now pass to us the torch as he did. We must hold it high and not break faith with him or them. Their task—our task—will not be finished until universal and permanent peace is established on the earth. Thank you.

Mr. President, Louis W. Larsen, one of the great poets of my State of Utah, lived up to his reputation as a "living poet" when he wrote the stirring lines he entitled "Eternal Flame," in memory of a man who was truly loved throughout the world, President John F. Kennedy.

I am sure that the many thousands of people who have waited in line at the Arlington Cemetery on a cold day to pay their respects to our fallen Chief will agree that President Kennedy's "journey" was one indeed "forever charted for the brave."

I ask unanimous consent that Mr. Larsen's "Eternal Flame," as it appeared in the Salt Lake Tribune on December 1, be included as a living tribute to a man who is very much alive in the hearts of all Americans.

[From the Salt Lake (Utah) Tribune, Dec. 1, 1963]

ETERNAL FLAME

(By Louis W. Larsen)

The flame eternal marks a path
    Where footprints came a little way,
To end as though some voice of wrath
    Had summoned men to bend and pray.

The journey to the distant land,
    Forever charted for the brave,
Is signaled by a gentle hand
    That lit the flame beside a grave.

TRIBUTE BY

Hon. Warren G. Magnuson

OF WASHINGTON

Mr. President, all Members of Congress and every American will long remember those fateful days last November. Many of us were asking, "Why?" Many of us were asking, "What is this that has pierced me?" And many of us experienced a feeling of inadequacy in our attempts to properly express our feelings at that time.

We have all been privileged to hear, and to read, numerous tributes to our late President. To me, none is more eloquent than a poem written by one of my constituents, Mrs. Edna Leal Williams, the night of November 25th.

Mrs. Williams, highly talented housewife, is the wife of one of the Northwest's most experienced labor leaders. It is my understanding from the information that came to me that she was so upset by the tragedy that beset us all that she could not sleep and that she composed

this remarkable tribute during the period of 1 night. Of course, I am going to see that a suitable copy of this tribute is personally delivered to Mrs. Kennedy.

Entitled "Dies Irae, Dies Illa," "Day of Wrath, That Dreadful Day," it is my humble privilege to ask unanimous consent that Mrs. Williams' poetic tribute be included so that it may be preserved for all time, and so that others may also have an opportunity to read it.

DIES IRAE, DIES ILLA

What is this that has pierced me?
Oh, no, please God, no.
Our gay and gentle knight is hurt.
His love holds on, the grasp grows weak,
He is gone.
With leaden heart we watch as home he soars.
We weep, we weep.
His love goes with him
That he be not alone.
The box is sealed, the flag unfurled.
Our knight pauses yet a while
That all may say farewell.
His love comes in. Oh, tear, oh, tears.
The lament wails round the world.
The great file by.
And now we hear the roll of the caisson.
His love is there that he go not alone.
The black steed prances.
Why this containment? Where is my master?
We must away, there is much to do.
The caisson rolls and his love follows.
The bells toll, weary,
The muffled beat of drums is heard.
The step heavy.
Trees weep, leaves softly drift to earth.
Our knight again pauses in his farewell.
Oh, love.
All night they come, and on into the morn
His flock, with mournful eye.
There is not time enow
That all who love come by.
Time grows more dear
And his love comes near.
The caisson rolls, midst resplendent accompaniment.
He pauses to make ready for his Master.
His great and good friend with sacred vessel greets him
His love is there with him, to enter.
The organ sounds, sweet voice the Ave Maria intones.
His great and good friend chants the Requiem.
Dear Lord, sweet Lord, I am not worthy.
And his love receives her Lord.
Sweet knight, we cannot tarry.
Time is dear, time is dear.
And so, with heavy heart all proceed
Accompanied by muted drum and dirge.
And yet his love is strong.
Now, all is done. No more is left.
Save that our knight again pause briefly.
Then, to rest.

The bagpipes wail, the cannon roars,
The rifles crack out in triad.
And, o'er the sky, our knight's winged friends come by
For one last sweet salute.
His eagle dips low.
The taps sound out.
Oh, dear heart.
The flag is folded, and with each fold the end draws nigh.
His love clasps it to her heart.
Farewell, farewell.
But lo, wait, not all is lost.
A torch appears with flame eternal.
Quickly, his great and good friend consecrates the fire.
Our knight be not forgotten.
His flame burns on and on
In heart, in spirit, in love.

EPILOG

Awake, awake, oh Nation ours
Lest all be lost!
The foe we seek is not without
But gnaws instead within.
Arise ye legions who love
And sound the cry that fells the enemy.
We love, we love, we love.

TRIBUTES BY

Hon. Leverett Saltonstall

OF MASSACHUSETTS

Mr. President, at the suggestion of students and teachers at Swampscott High School, I ask unanimous consent to include a splendid tribute in memoriam to our late President, John F. Kennedy, written by Lola Kramarsky, president of the National Hadassah.

In Memoriam—John Fitzgerald Kennedy, 1917–63

(By Lola Kramarsky)

Every church and every synagogue in this country was filled with mourners and worshippers on November 23, and for days thereafter. Yet America is said to be a secular country. America is said to be a Protestant country. Its President was a devout Catholic. America is called a factionalized country. Yet every American from north to south, east to west, from mansion to hut, from the mightiest to the humblest, was united in bereavement and tragedy, in bewilderment and sorrow, at the death of John Fitzgerald Kennedy, the man, and the President of the United States of America. He who strove to unify the country in greatness of purpose, in firmness of discipline, in nobility of resolution, as befits a nation of freemen, united them in mourning at his death; and in sorrow at the brutality and anarchy of his assassination and the hatred and lawlessness it spells.

President Kennedy was the symbol of courage and reason in a world riddled with fear and unreason. He was the epitome of brilliance, style, elegance, in a world grown drab and mediocre. He was the personification of youth and vigor in a world grown aged and weary. He added compassion to statesmanship and magnanimity to prudence. He wore leadership with grace, and authority with charm. Our allies saw in him an American-made symbol of hope for the future. Our adversaries saw in him America's strength, its pride, calmness, confidence, courage, and resolution.

He represented the highest aspirations of this land of freedom and greatness and voiced them in eloquent and inspiring phrases. And he understood how wide is the gap between man's aspirations and human performance.

A sorrowing nation has now only one thing to do. We must stand united behind the new President, each one of us, Christian and Jew, Negro and white. We must prove to ourselves, to our friends, and our foes that when John Fitzgerald Kennedy spoke of our hope for a world of liberty and equality, decency and justice, discipline and law, his was the authentic voice of the American people.

Mr. President, I include a poem entitled "Our President, John Fitzgerald Kennedy" which was published in the February issue of the Union Postal Clerk, a national magazine of the United Federation of Postal Clerks, as the official tribute of that organization.

Our President, John Fitzgerald Kennedy
1917–63

(By William F. McDonough)

Then on his grave she tenderly kindled the eternal flame,
As if to purge the malice at Dallas of its enduring shame.

On a lovely Arlington hillside the President rests in sleep,
While the world and a mournful Nation fervently pray and weep.

Grieving the folly of hatred imbued in the assassin's crime,
And the tragic cost of martyrdom, the price of a hero's shrine.

Nearby the historic Potomac flows, wending its way to the sea,
Cradle of this Nation's sorrows and guardian of their majesty.
A stillness envelops the gravesite, as sentries guard their Chief,
And the river seems to be whispering a requiem in sheer disbelief.

Adown from the sloping hillside another haunting memorial stands,
The towering Lincoln temple, the most hallowed in all the land.
Two kindred souls in life and death, who heeded their country's call,
Apostles of the ideal of freedom with liberty and justice for all.

Short years ago, how short they seem, he gave us his
American dream,
An eloquent credo of new frontiers, provocative in scope
and theme.
A dream that embraced the rights of man, humane, noble,
and just,
With a promise to meet every challenge worthy of man-
kind's trust.

"Let us create a world of law," he said, in his famed
inaugural plea,
Pledging to bear any burden or risk in the survival of
liberty.
A new leader had grasped the helm, a new banner had
been unfurled,
With an inspired hope and purpose, "that would truly
light the world."

In the crucible of civil rights and summitry he rebuked
the unjust,
Knowing that peace and equality for all was his most
sacred trust.
As long as freedom is denied and the people's rights are
enslaved,
Let no timid, tortuous epitaph impoverish the President's
grave.

Alas, his dream is suspended, but a gathering momentum
makes clear,
He inspired a mighty impetus toward his goal of the New
Frontiers.
And these nobly conceived horizons shall manifestly
become secure,
Impelled by a nation's conscience that can no longer
injustice endure.

And unlike the one brief shining moment in the legend
of Camelot,
His name will be cherished forever, and his needs never
forgot.
When the verdict of history is rendered and the final
chapter is told,
Let it extol his love for the people which he prized above
riches and gold.

EPILOG

And on his grave she prayerfully kindled the eternal
flame,
As if to purge the malice at Dallas of its enduring shame.
Shine on O' blessed beacon; shine on through peace and
strife,
Symbol of a gallant torchbearer; emblem of an heroic life.
—William F. McDonough.

TRIBUTES BY

Hon. Quentin N. Burdick

OF NORTH DAKOTA

Mr. President, I was moved by an item that
appeared in the November 29, 1963, edition of the
Mandan, N. Dak., Pioneer:

PRESIDENT'S DEATH DEEPLY FELT BY SCHOOLCHILDREN

How did the death of the President affect the children
of the country? Ask their teachers. They know. They
observed the youngsters' reactions, for it happened during schooltime.

Children are too young to understand much about
political philosophies but this they knew and expressed
in their simple ways. That their President worked hard
for peace. That their President tried hard to help the
Negroes. That hate makes men do terrible things.

One little boy, an 8-year-old in Miss Martha Huber's
third-grade room at Mandan's Roosevelt School, expressed his feelings in a poem which he wrote and then
shyly showed to his teacher saying: "It isn't very good
but would you read it?"

It was good—for an 8 year old. And it spoke eloquently of the feelings of all children. Here it is:

"A GREAT MAN—JOHN F. KENNEDY"

"On a good, good day,
Something happened in a strange, strange way.
It happened in a car,
From a window not far.
And when it happened,
It made us get saddened.
He was good and great
But was killed by hate."

The poem was written by Mark Seerup, son of Mr.
and Mrs. Virgil Seerup, 1009 Northwest Second Street.

Mr. President, Larston Farrar, a Washington
writer, described the tragic circumstances of November 22 in a dramatic and colorful way. I
ask that the tribute written by Mr. Farrar be included as follows:

THE SLEEPING PRINCE—A TRIBUTE

(By Larston D. Farrar)

There lies today, in deep repose beside a flaming torch,
a prince among the people of the earth.

There is restlessness in the land. Grief is evident
everywhere.

Many minds think sad thoughts—of sympathy and
condolence. Others think terrible thoughts of revenge.

All men wonder.

Hearts are heavy with the burden, and with questions.
How can a prince fall so quickly? Why couldn't he
grapple wtih his adversary? What cruel fate kept him
from a chance to strike back?

He had been a fighter all the years we knew him.

At first, he was fighting on the football field. He
tested his flesh and his drive against those who stood
in his way, or strove to stop him. He could not be
stopped.

Then he fought a war of ideas—with himself and
with others. Some were good ideas; others could not
stand the heat of argument. In the crucible and fire of
time and debate, many ideas were winnowed out, like
dross falling from pounded metal. Some proved not to
be of steel. Yet, others lived, and stood out—gleaming
and sharp.

Then he fought a war of weapons. He learned about boats and bayonets and bullets. Hot metal and cold steel. He never flinched.

But he was not impregnable. Or impervious to pain. He fought a war against injury and illness. It never ended.

Later, he entered into the perennial war of words. He won it against some of the sharpest adversaries, on battlefields from East to West. The steel became stronger and more tempered. He learned how to sharpen and harden words, so that they could both pierce and glitter. The prince had many swords.

Then, the greatest test of all, he led us in our war of nerves. He chose to be out front—on the firing line, all the time—against enemies foreign and domestic. Or did we shove him there? No matter. This was the true test. In it, he excelled as he had never excelled before. He did not falter. He had been the prince of a family, the brightest of the clan, the best of the litter. Now, he became a true prince of the people.

He met every challenge that mattered. The others he scorned.

This prince was many men. He was a tender and devoted father. A handsome and loving husband. A slave to duty and responsibility. A Spartan in spirit, inside. He was beautiful in body and lithe of limb. He moved with purpose and sureness. He spoke with confidence and strength and sincerity. He smiled a smile with a hint of sadness. People believed him, and believed in him, because he believed both in his words and in himself. And in them. He was a prince who knew what to say, and how to say it, and said it.

This prince of many moods was blessed to find a princess strong and courageous. Another Spartan. She was beautiful and proud and desirable. And yet she was humble and thoughtful and kind. She loved children. She was devoted to him, and she believed in him. Their faith moved mountains.

The end came like lightning out of the blue. There were no clouds. No thunder. And yet, blood was flowing, and he was falling into her tender arms. The incredible became credible. The unbelievable became reality. She was holding him, while he fought for his life. But even a prince must perish. We live our lives like a tale that is told.

He is stretched out. There is no pulse. Anguish fills her heart, but she is strong. She takes off the sacred wedding band, puts it in his lifeless hand and kisses it tenderly.

The prince is asleep. It is time for him to rest. There is no more hope—on earth—for him. There is only hope for the country, for the people, for life, and liberty, and the pursuit of happiness. The dream is ended. This is the awakening. But the prince sleeps on.

What frantic and feverish brain could plan such a monstrous and savage act? The policemen ran here and there. Minds began to work. Distances were measured. People contributed bits of information. The pieces began to fall into place. The man who would deliver such a blow could not do it out of one morning's plans. He had to have a background of nursing grievances and thwarted vengeance.

It came from hate.

He hated himself because he did not understand and he hated others because they would not or could not stop to help him understand. He was lost before he was born. He was the victor and the victim. The prince had been struck down. But this tortured mind could not feel triumph. The dark and devious plan had worked. Yet, the victor could not beat his breast and scream his defiance.

The prince was cut down without a chance to strike back. He had no premonition, no inkling, no chance. He never even saw his challenger.

This was the swift and terrible hand of fate at work. The time, the place, the killer, the opportunity, the trip, the unused hardtop, the slowness of the car, the deadly accuracy of the rifle, the speed of the bullet, the brightness of the sunshine, the clearness of the target, the bitter determination behind the finger that pulled the trigger, the sharp eyes, the half-used mind that could not see things in focus, the shift of the prince's head at the right moment.

All meant that the hand of fate was at work.

No one could bring it back and replay the scene. No one could talk to the killer and help him to see straight. No one could stop that deadly trickle of blood. No one could retrace a step.

The moving finger had written.

The great void was not a void. The prince had not been hurt. He had gone to sleep, after living his life. The restless heart is at rest. The backache is gone. The rocker is stilled in its swing.

The victory is his.

He had done what he had lived to do. He worked to become the prince of the people. In the manner of his death, he won every heart. This was the last full measure of devotion. Greater love hath no man—no prince— than this, that he lay down his life for his friends, his countrymen.

A prince should not be craven before the people. He could not be a prince, hidden under a bubbletop. If the prince were to live in fear, how could he be a brave leader, a prince? He had to move in the open and face the people.

They wanted to see him.

He wanted to see them.

He had to die, as he did die, a hero's death.

There was no other way.

That is why the prince now can rest so beautifully in repose. He can sleep in peace. He proved that a man can live like a prince, marry a true princess, and then die like a prince, and all the time be a man.

This was no spectacular, staged in Hollywood. The script had not been polished and repolished. The prince was no makebelieve actor, repeating rehearsals until he was perfect. He was schooled and trained to lead—by fate, through men. He wore the mantle of his offices proudly from the first.

He never flinched. He could not flinch, even when he fell in the lap of his beautiful princess. He had to live as he did live. And he had to die as he did die.

And all of his life led to his death.

The prince is asleep. He has served every moment of

his time. He now can rest in peace. The wars are all over for him. No more bruising battles. No more icy waters. No more intellectual joustings. No more cares. No more tears.

The prince is asleep.

Hon. Harrison A. Williams, Jr.

OF NEW JERSEY

Mr. President, during the unhappy days after November 22 many fine tributes were paid to President Kennedy. One of the most eloquent I have seen is the moving address which Rabbi Gershon B. Chertoff, of Temple Bnai Israel in Elizabeth, N.J., delivered to the students and faculty of Union Junior College on the day before Thanksgiving.

It was hard for all of us to think of giving thanks so soon after the tragedy which shattered the Nation. But Rabbi Chertoff's inspiring address has demonstrated that this Thanksgiving was a time to be grateful for the heritage of reason and knowledge which President Kennedy left us, and to which we must now dedicate ourselves. I ask unanimous consent that Rabbi Chertoff's Thanksgiving tribute to our late President be included.

ADDRESS BY RABBI CHERTOFF

It goes against the grain to celebrate our country and sing its praises so soon after our martyred President has fallen cold and dead. How shall we offer thanks when on the silent ground lies the silent slain? We weep for the voice of hope that was stilled, we grieve for the promise not completely fulfilled, we mourn for the burgeoning greatness that had not yet reached its climax.

In the President's death there is not only tragedy, but also transfiguration. America was always promises, and continues to be. And now that he belongs to the ages, the President's words, along with those of the two Roosevelts, Lincoln, Jefferson, and Washington, have become testament rather than tool, and are part of the American scriptures that have always inspired America to break a lance with the future and laugh at fears for the morrow.

For us of the academic and scholarly community there is particular consolation. In his last prepared address for Dallas, which was undelivered but published, the President spoke directly to us. In it he emphasized the indispensable link between leadership and learning.

"Ignorance and misinformation can handicap the progress of a city or a company," he wrote, "but they can,

if allowed to prevail in foreign policy, handicap this country's security. In a world of complex and continuing problems, in a world full of frustrations and irritations, America's leadership must be guided by the lights of learning and reason—or else those who confuse rhetoric with reality and the plausible with the possible will gain the popular ascendancy with their seemingly swift and simple solutions to every world problem."

The pursuit of learning and the exercise of reason—these are the tasks of the academic community and are inseparable from the civilized life.

You are being trained in the life of reason, so that you might be civilized. You are being taught to think. Thinking is a sophisticated activity. The authentic thinker recognizes the complexity of problems and does not seek simple (simplistic) answers. He has a feel for subtleties and is willing to live with partial solutions. He respects differences of opinion and has the wit and wisdom to agree to disagree. We never achieve this goal in its entirety, but if we make the attempt, we cannot wholly fail.

The barbarian on the other hand does not even make the attempt. The connoisseurs of violence, from Faubus to Wallace to Barnett, together with their followers and predecessors who created the atmosphere for Oswald's act, are the true primitives. They devaluate everything about life except the instruments for defacing it. They confuse their own rhetoric with reality. They think with their fists and persuade with a gun, they spew words of hate and defy the law, in a vain attempt to force simple and swift solutions where there are none. They are extremists because they cannot live with the frustrations and irritations of continuing problems. Their cult of force, if successful, would bring about the dethronement of reason, the closing off of discussion, the denial of the rights of opposition, and an end to democracy.

The late President Kennedy's appeal to reason and learning, his very martyrdom, calls us back to the faith of our Founding Fathers and might very well serve as the text for Thanksgiving. His challenge recalls the "decent respect to the opinions of mankind" that animated the authors of the Declaration of Independence. They rested their case before mankind on a common belief in self-evident truths, in reason, and in the moral ideas of Western civilization shared by educated men everywhere.

It is for us the living to dedicate ourselves to the unfinished work to which they were committed and which our martyred President so nobly advanced.

On his last sad journey, from which he did not return, the President stopped at Tampa, Fla., where he addressed the business community He deplored the attitudes of those businessmen who were interested only in their business and not in the business of government. To them "the balance sheet and profit rate of their own corporations" were "of more importance than the worldwide balance of power or the nationwide rate of unemployment." And he quoted to them the passage from Dickens' Christmas Carol in which Ebenezer Scrooge is terrified by the ghost of his former partner, Jacob Marley. And Scrooge, appalled by Marley's story of ceaseless wandering, cries out, "But you were always a good man of business, Jacob." And the ghost of Marley, his legs bound by a chain of ledger books and cash boxes, replied: "Business? Mankind was my business. The common welfare was my business. Charity, mercy, forbearance, and benevolence were my business. The dealings of my trade were but a drop of water in the comprehensive ocean of my business."

Charity, mercy, forbearance, and benevolence, together with a passion for justice and an acceptance of the yoke of the law, these are the ingredients out of which democracy is made. They will not be achieved unless we eradicate from our minds and hearts the egotism that restricts our concerns to our own private affairs alone and hardens our hearts to the common weal.

Democracy is a sophisticated doctrine, beyond the reach of the barbarian, the connoisseur of violence. It demands the educated heart as well as the educated mind. It is no wonder that we falter and fail. But if in the words of the Preamble to the Constitution we are to promote the general welfare and secure the blessings of liberty to ourselves and our posterity, then in the words of President Kennedy, "whether we work in the White House or the statehouse, or in a house of industry, or commerce, mankind is our business and if we work in harmony, if we understand the problems of each other and the responsibilities that each of us bears, then surely the business of mankind will prosper, and your children and mine will move ahead in a secure world, and one in which there is opportunity for them all."

The ancient commentators in their quest for universal meaning in Scripture interpreted synonyms which the careless eye sees as nothing but trifling, as being rife with subtleties. In the Bible when a man has passed away, Holy Writ usually describes him as having died. But when King David died he is described as having "slept with his fathers."

The distinction according to the commentators is momentous. The expression of "sleeping" was used in the case of David because he left a son like himself, who walked in the ways of his father and continued his noble deeds. Therefore David did not truly die, but lived on in the reflected life of his son. But when a man's ideals and his style of life are not carried on by worthy successors, then he dies with the death of his ideals.

Democracy is forever precarious and unstable, and in no manner does it promise a tame idyll or a static utopia. The violence that destroyed the President and tore the fabric of our society is the price we pay in failure for the vision of the ideal society. We now know bafflement, tragedy, sacrifice, and defeat. But we may well know fulfillment if the President will not have died, but will have slept with his fathers.

Our efforts will consecrate his unhappy end if we dedicate ourselves to the unfinished task begun by our Founding Fathers, that the President set before himself. Let us here firmly resolve that from this honored dead we take increased devotion to that cause for which he gave the last full measure of devotion. Then he shall not have died in vain, and this Nation under God shall have a new birth of freedom, and violence shall be no more.

TRIBUTE BY

Hon. J. Howard Edmondson

OF OKLAHOMA

Mr. President, many poems and other tributes have been written about the late President Kennedy since his assassination on November 22, 1963.

One which I felt was very moving was written by David Randolph Milsten of Tulsa, Okla., and printed in the Tulsa World.

Mr. President, I ask unanimous consent that Mr. Milsten's poem, "John Fitzgerald Kennedy," be printed as follows:

JOHN FITZGERALD KENNEDY
(By David Randolph Milsten)

It is hard to conceive the enormity
  Of the events which have taken place,
The full impact of our Nation's loss
  Was reflected in every face.

The assassin's deed was swiftly done,
  Dastardly malicious, brutal and quick
It left us stunned in icy shock
  And turned our stomachs sick.

Man could not tell to others
  The supplications to be said
Yet, propelled by broken hearts
  They whispered, "Our President is dead."

Through the miracle of television
  In the homes of our treasured land
They came to know the beloved Chief
  And extended him their hand.

He championed the cause of civil rights
  And vigor sparked his eyes
Now closed to the mortal world
  As in death's repose he lies.

Prime Ministers, Kings and Princes
  Joined with thousands to appear
And bestow the honors due him
  As they mournfully passed his bier.

The world will know and long remember
  That peace was his constant goal,
Surely for such an illustrious son
  There is an immortal role.

If prayer can be the passport
  To the presence of Almighty's grace
The whole universe has joined to
  See him safely to his place.

Dear God, his soul is yours forever
  He has come to you without despair
And we pray that what he sought
  Will be waiting for him there.

TRIBUTES BY

Hon. George McGovern

OF SOUTH DAKOTA

Mr. President, since the death of President Kennedy, many eloquent words have been written and spoken by our finest citizens.

No writer has come closer to expressing my own feelings about the President, his life, and his death than Mr. William Attwood, who writes in memory of the President in the December 31 issue of Look magazine.

Bill Attwood, who served as Ambassador to Guinea during the first 2 years of the Kennedy administration, now represents the United States on a special assignment to the United Nations. I ask that Mr. Attwood's article be printed as follows:

IN MEMORY OF JOHN F. KENNEDY

(By William Attwood)

I never knew Jack Kennedy very well. I was not what they called a New Frontier insider or even an old friend. Over the past 4 years, I don't think I talked with him more than 20 times. So do not read on if you are expecting one of those intimate portraits.

I knew him as a boss—and he was a darn good one. You knew where he stood and what he wanted. You could always get to him when you had to, and when you did, you knew that he was interested in what you were doing and in what you had to say. I've just been looking at a note he sent me a few weeks before he was killed. He simply wanted to let me know he'd read an article I'd done for Look, and had liked it. And at the end he wrote, "Many thanks."

Many thanks. Well, I think perhaps it's my turn now to thank Jack Kennedy. Not for any personal favors—I don't mean that. He did make me Ambassador to Guinea, and I spent a couple of hard and satisfying years there, but I'm not thanking him for that. What I'm grateful for is something not as tangible: It's for having made me and my generation—some of us, anyway—feel alive, exhilarated and prouder to be Americans than we've ever been before.

This is no small thing. It takes a lot to give you this kind of feeling when you're past 40 and have, as they say, been around.

The funny thing is that Jack Kennedy seldom acted as if he were trying to inspire or stir up the people who worked for him. Maybe that's why he succeeded. Maybe we reacted to him and to his style of doing things because he was always cool, always restrained, always himself, and never, in the slang of our generation, corny.

I remember flying into El Paso on his plane during the 1960 campaign. It was night and we were late, and a crowd of 7,000 people had been waiting at the airport for hours. They wanted to yell and cheer, and they wanted him to wave his arms and smile and say something about the Texas sky and stars. But he just strode out of the plane and jabbed his forefinger at them and talked about getting America moving again. And then he turned and climbed into a car and drove away.

A few days later, when I saw him on the plane, I told him the crowd had felt let down and suggested that the next time he should at least wave his arms the way other politicians did and give people a chance to get the cheers out of their throats. Kennedy shook his head and borrowed my notebook and pencil (he was saving his voice for the day's speeches) and wrote, "I always swore one thing I'd never do is—" And he drew a picture of a man with his arms in the air.

Jack Kennedy could never pretend to be somebody he wasn't. He couldn't even put on funny hats or Indian feathers like other candidates. He had his own personal, down-beat style, and all who met him got used to it, and the country got used to it, too.

It was a style that had class—in the very best sense of that word. In Boston, where he started the long political journey that ended in Dallas, they loved him for it. Outside an Irish tavern on East Broadway in Boston, after President Kennedy died, a court clerk named Patrick Hines was trying to talk away his tears:

"Oh, I remember when he used to come marching down this street in a parade, and boy, he had that walk, and no hat, and— 'My name is Jack Kennedy, I'm a candidate for Congress,' and girls used to flock around him—young, young, personality second to none—God, we'll miss him."

Outside of Boston, I don't suppose many Americans had yet learned to love him the way they loved F.D.R. or Ike (I'm sure he was embarrassed by the affection of those who did)—but even his political opponents liked and respected him, and that's what he really wanted.

Jack Kennedy was cool, but not cold. He sought the Presidency, he used to say, "because I want to get things done," and he was anything but cool and detached about these things, these measures that he believed would make America stronger and the world safer.

Civil rights was one of the things he cared about, and I'd like to be able to thank him now for these words he spoke last June:

"If an American, because his skin is dark, cannot eat lunch in a restaurant open to the public; if he cannot send his children to the best public school available; if he cannot vote for the public officials who represent him; if, in short, he cannot enjoy the full and free life which all of us want, then who among us would be content to have the color of his skin changed and stand in his place? Who among us would then be content with the counsels of patience and delay?"

The day before, he had been speaking of the search for peace in a world divided between rival political systems:

"Let us not be blind to our differences, but let us also direct our attention to our common interests and the means by which those differences can be resolved. And if we cannot end now our differences, at least we can help make the world safe for diversity. For, in the final analysis, our most basic common link is that we all inhabit this small planet. We all breathe the same air. We all cherish our children's future. And we are all mortal."

This was the speech, they say, that induced Khrushchev to sign the test ban treaty. So here's something else to thank Jack Kennedy for.

He was tough, too, and God knows we needed a tough President as we entered the sixties. I first glimpsed his toughness a few weeks before he was nominated. We were having dinner in Washington. I had been doing some work for Adlai Stevenson, and Kennedy wanted to know why Stevenson was holding back, instead of supporting him for the nomination. I told him that some of Stevenson's friends thought the convention might deadlock, and they wanted him to be available, just in case. Also, people were talking about a Stevenson-and-Kennedy ticket.

Kennedy dismissed this possibility. He had the first-ballot votes all but sewed up, and if by some chance he couldn't make it, he would never settle for anything else. He was running for the Presidency, period.

I started to say something about how some people thought he wouldn't refuse the second spot if it came to that, but he cut me off in midsentence. His eyes were cold and his voice—as flat as a slap—ended the conversation, "Yes, well, you can tell them they're wrong."

I have a feeling that the Soviet Ambassador saw that look and heard that voice during the Cuban crisis last year, just before the Russian ships turned around in mid-Atlantic.

The whole world can be thankful for that.

Jack Kennedy understood this revolutionary era we live in. We knew he did on that cold, sparkling afternoon in January when he stood on the steps of the Capitol and flung out the words that still stir me as much as any words I have heard.

"Let the word go forth from this time and place, to friend and foe alike, that the torch has been passed to a new generation of Americans, born in this century, tempered by war, disciplined by a hard and bitter peace, proud of our ancient heritage, and unwilling to witness or permit the slow undoing of those human rights to which this Nation has always been committed, and to which we are committed today at home and around the world."

Around the world. He was respected around the world because he was trusted—and because of him, those of us privileged to represent our country in the world were trusted, too. It was a wonderful time to be an American abroad. How often I can remember being able to say, with pride, in Africa, "I know this is what President Kennedy believes—this is what we Americans stand for." I remember the foreign minister who told me: "Let me know what we can do to help your President. We need him as much as you." And I remember, at the United Nations in New York, the day he died, all the African hands gripping mine, the eyes full of tears.

He talked the language of the young leaders of this turbulent new world because, in his midforties, he was one of them. I saw some of these leaders at the White House and talked to them later. They thought of him

as a friend. He knew their problems and made them understand ours. It was because of President Kennedy, because they had talked to him and knew what he was trying to do, that the leaders of black Africa have been so understanding of the torment and the violence of our own struggle for freedom and equality here at home.

Out in the world, Jack Kennedy's memory will also live on, for years to come, wherever the Peace Corps is, for that was his idea and, I suspect, one of the most enduring legacies of his administration. For the Peace Corps volunteers, I'm sure, as for most of us who were serving overseas when he was President, it was good to know he was back there in the White House, cheering us on, in his own way, by making the decision and fighting for the legislation that would help us in our work.

Like Harry Truman, he could make up his mind, and he didn't pass the buck. He made you want to try harder because you knew he was trying all the time. Those of us who worked for him usually felt we were hitting on all cylinders, and glad to be. He often spoke of the ancient Greeks' definition of happiness—"the exercise of vital powers along lines of excellence in a life affording them scope"—and some of us were able, under his leadership, to appreciate that definition for the first time. And I'm grateful for that.

Jack Kennedy was so much a part of everything we did in Washington that the day after his death, waiting at the State Department before going over to the White House, I still found it hard to believe, impossible, really, that the President would not be there to greet us in his office. He had been dead, after all, less than 24 hours. It wasn't until I walked into the darkened East Room and saw the flag-draped casket that I fully realized that we had lost him—and what an unexpectedly personal loss it was for someone like me, who had known him so fleetingly.

The Kennedy administration was an exciting time to be alive, and a good time to be busy. I think the Johnson administration will be, too, for the new President has the experience and the drive, and the Nation now has the momentum. But my thoughts are still turned to the years just past, rather than to the years just ahead. All I know, as I end this memoir, is that I shall always be proud to have been involved with the history of this time—the New Frontier period, as the historians will surely call it—and that my children—the two old enough to have worn Kennedy campaign buttons and the one soon to be born—will also remember and be proud of what their father was doing in the early 1960's.

So I have that to thank Jack Kennedy for, too.

And now, with Christmas almost upon us, I find myself thinking of last Christmas and the present I brought back to my 11-year-old daughter from the White House. It was a note from the President in answer to a letter she had written him. She had it framed, and it has been on her bedside table ever since. The note is signed, "Your friend, John F. Kennedy."

She never met the President, but she always thought of him as her friend, and she was crying that terrible weekend because her friend was dead.

This Christmas, I think a lot of Americans, like my daughter, feel they have lost a friend. They have.

Mr. President, as we all know, the shock of the death of the late President Kennedy affected Americans of all ages. One of the finest tributes I have seen was the reaction of a young 12-year-old schoolgirl, Emily Ann Barnes, of 184 Asbury Avenue, Carle Place, Long Island, N.Y. This child captures the significance of the President's death in words of wisdom far beyond her years—words which were written solely as an outlet for her emotions, meant only for her own solace. Her father, Sullivan Barnes, brought them to my attention, and I ask that her short reflection be inserted here.

November 22, 1963.

It started out as a regular Friday morning. I started to school early to see Mr. Jacquenot, but missed him. Nothing special happened in the morning nor in the afternoon until in last period, math, we were taking a quiz on fractions, when about 2:10 p.m., a boy yelled into our classroom. He said: "Hey, Miss Ludlow, Kennedy was shot." Everybody laughed. We all thought he was kidding. Miss Ludlow went out for about 5 minutes which is unusual during a test. She came back, real flushed and red. She said: "There is a rumor that the President and the Vice President have been shot." Now no one laughed. About 2:20, Mr. Coop announced over the intercom what had happened: "Vice President Johnson has been shot in the arm and President Kennedy in the head. It is not determined what their condition is." Everyone groaned. In the head. We waited tensely for about 3 or 4 minutes. Finally the intercom blasted out the fatal words: "President Kennedy is dead." At this time, many students' and teachers' eyes filled with tears. Mr. Coop started to say something else and then stopped. Finally the secretary came on sharply: "Would the janitors please lower the flags to half mast." It was true. They were not rumors but hard, true facts. We never finished that test. The halls were frightfully quiet. No one said a word, just looked at each other in quiet mourning. Many students sobbed outwardly but we were all saying inwardly, "Why, Why?" He was so nice. Always considerate, no matter what the situation called for. Patience, help, love, all these and many more were in the President. He always had a smile on his young face. The bushy hair, deep circles, broad shoulders, and Bostonian accent so many times imitated are no longer with us. Why? A rifle answers a part of this question. A rifle found in a building from where the bullets came. Fingerprints and more and more evidence, but still no answer. The man accused was killed before trial by still another human whose ideals were different from ours. This man is now accused of slaying the man who slayed our dear President. Can this horrible thing go on? Yes, it can, unless tomorrow we turn to God.

Mr. President, some of the most thoughtful statements made on the death of President Kennedy were offered by three bishops of the Methodist Church.

The December 19, 1963, newsletter of the Mitchell, S. Dak., Rotary Club carries a statement by Bishop Edwin R. Garrison, of the Dakota area of the Methodist Church. The January 1964 issue of the Methodist magazine, Together, includes a tribute to the late President Kennedy by Bishop John Wesley Lord of the Washington area. The December 1963 issue of the New England Methodist publication, Zion's Herald, carries the address by Bishop James K. Matthews of the Boston area which he delivered at the Washington Cathedral on November 24.

Mr. President, I am proud of the leaders of my church as represented by the moving statements of these three great bishops. I ask that the three statements be included here.

[From the Rotary Whistle, Mitchell (S. Dak), Dec. 19, 1963]

Our first word must concern our bereavement in the death of President Kennedy. Every person of religious faith will pray for the Kennedy family. We will likewise pray for President Johnson. May God have mercy on this land of ours, forgive each one of us for our trespasses and set our feet upon the path of righteousness, justice, and mercy.

These tragic days are a byproduct of a serious flaw in our American behavior. We call ourselves a civilized people. Our material standard of living is the highest in the world. In comparison with other nations we lack nothing which our money can buy. We are a nation of churchgoers in a sense no other nation can claim. Why, then, do our leaders fall before gunfire as in no other country where the political and economic stability approaches our own? The truth is that we are a people of irresponsible thought and unbridled language. We think in irrational extremes. Whoever disagrees with a fellow-citizen stands the risk of being tagged as subversive. All too often we accept the idea that the end justifies the means even if it means disregarding somebody's constitutional rights. In political campaigns we make charges and counter charges. One man is said to be "soft on communism." Someone else is called a Fascist. Campaigners imply that if the opposition wins the election, the country will be lost—so go the diatribes.

Most of this loose talk is sheer rhetoric—intended to jolt voters out of their lethargy. It is proven on the day after election when the loser shakes hands with the winner and pledges his support. But the damage has been done. In every community there are emotionally disturbed persons who may be triggered to violence by irresponsible language.

This goes on all the time in our public life situations which should call for sensible discussions—race and international relations, management and labor controversies. Public speaking platforms and mail boxes are deluged with appallingly bitter language.

Now add to this our peculiar insistence upon the right of every citizen to carry a gun, combined with a love of shooting scenes in movies and TV, and you have the making of explosive disaster.

For some time there has been the most irresponsible kind of talk in our country. Sometimes from Governors of States, now and then also from so-called ministers of the gospel there has been a continual stream of words which beget violence. Some people sit by their radios and television sets and mutter approval and seethe in malice. Then some psychotic soul takes it seriously enough to pick up a gun and put words into action. It is time we Americans grew up. When they are crossed little children blaze out in violent words and action. But when we grow up, we are to put away childish things.

It is time to practice our Christianity and to remember that in His Sermon on the Mount, Jesus declared that a person sins in thought and word as well as in deed: "You have heard that it was said to the men of old, you shall not kill, and whosoever kills shall be liable to judgment, but I say to you that every one who is angry with his brother shall be liable to judgment; and whoever insults his brother shall be liable to the council, and whosoever says, 'You fool' shall be liable to hell fire."

Message of Bishop Edwin R. Garrison.

A Tribute to John F. Kennedy

(By John Wesley Lord, bishop, Washington, D.C., area, the Methodist Church)

By invitation of his brother, the Attorney General, I attended the funeral service of the late President John Fitzgerald Kennedy at St. Matthew's Cathedral in Washington, D.C. The universal sadness that had cast its pall over the entire world seemed focused there as members of his family, heads of state, Government officials, and friends bowed in unutterable grief. President Kennedy had lived to serve this age; now he was being given to the ages.

Methodists around the world mourn the death of a great and good President. Though it came suddenly and tragically by the hand of an assassin, his death places upon all of us the burden of achieving the suffrage of the free human spirit to which President Kennedy was committed. He will be remembered as a man of deep religious faith, articulate intelligence, and redoubtable courage. A kindly, peace-loving man, he nevertheless dared to risk a nuclear war when his conscience clearly dictated this to be the only way of meeting a threat to our national security.

With his well-trained, disciplined mind and an inner security born of deep spiritual resources, President Kennedy never lost faith in the ultimate integrity of humanity. He believed that, in a world filled with malice, there could be a meeting of minds among people of differing ideologies; that there was no gulf that could not be spanned, given time, patience, and intelligence; that men not under the stress of fear still can control events; and that right will triumph.

On June 10, 1963, the President delivered a historic commencement address at Methodist-related American University in Washington. He spoke on strategy of peace, directing his message to those who say it is useless to speak of peace or world law or world disarmament until the leaders of the Soviet Union adopt a more enlightened attitude. It was his conviction that we could show the way for the Soviet Union to adopt that attitude.

The President urged also that we rethink our attitudes toward peace itself. To believe that peace is impossible or unreal is dangerous and defeatist. This leads to the conclusion that we are gripped by forces we cannot control. But we need not accept that view. Man's reason and spirit often have solved the seemingly insolvable, and they can do it again.

These are the thoughts and this is the faith of a man who had not lost his belief in the essential goodness and reasonableness of humanity. He was a lover of peace, which he defined as a process, a way of solving problems, requiring only that men live together in mutual respect. Against a heritage of hate, the late President bequeathed his country and the world a new heritage of mutual toleration, in which may be found peace with justice.

The President concluded his American University address with a verse from the 16th chapter of the Book of Proverbs: "When a man's ways please the Lord, he maketh even his enemies to be at peace with him." On occasion he would call to the White House the religious leaders of the Capital area. Implied and often expressed in these briefings was the truism that the real problems the Nation faced were not so much political or military as they were spiritual. It was the task of religion, he indicated, to create the climate in which real solutions could be found.

It will be the verdict of history, I expect, that President Kennedy was a champion of the unprotected. No occupant of the White House felt more deeply the burden of the dispossessed. He knew that indifference to suffering is the explosive factor in history; and against tremendous odds and apathy, he championed the cause of civil rights for all men everywhere.

In the slow task of building a world community, he was ever on guard that our country's rightful concern to preserve national security and national values did not betray our international responsibilities. He sensed so clearly the terrible travesty of our times: that there may be more substance in our animosities than in our love, and that we have learned to hate better than we have learned to love. As he said in a late 1961 speech, "Let our patriotism be reflected in the creation of confidence rather than in crusades of suspicion."

Some 200 years ago, John Wesley wrote: "He who governed the world before I was born shall take care of it, likewise, when I am dead * * *. My part is to improve the present moment." Man of peace, guardian of the unprotected, lover of mankind, John Fitzgerald Kennedy will be remembered as a man who indeed did improve the present moment.

The Gift of a Man—A Protestant Interpretation of the Life and Death of John F. Kennedy

(By Bishop James K. Mathews)

(NOTE.—An address presented at the interdenominational service at the Washington Cathedral on November 24 in memory of the late John Fitzgerald Kennedy, President of the United States.)

Today, Americans can have but one thought; for we have been present at a new crucifixion. A people who could endure the villainous murder of Medgar Evers without undue remorse, who could observe the slaughter of the innocents by a bomb in a Birmingham church and not really cry out for justice, have called for a yet more costly sacrifice—that of the President of their country. Truly, then, Americans are weeping not only for him but for themselves.

We react, indeed, in anger and sorrow; but do we react sufficiently in repentance? To fail to miss the message of God in this tragic hour would be to allow yet another martyr to have died in vain.

For martyr he was, as surely as those who have died for their vision in earlier ages: a martyr at the hands of extremists of every kind, as well as at the hands of the comfortable captives of the status quo which most of us have become; a martyr to those who enjoy prejudices a century out of date, and those who refuse to live in the day which God has given to us.

To take seriously the death of a martyr is to take the meaning of that death upon ourselves. For in his mortal wound is our own hurt and the hurt of all mankind.

We are a proud, and even arrogant, people who have told ourselves that this sort of thing could not happen here. In more primitive periods of our history, yes. Among more primitive peoples even today. But not here. What could not happen has happened and it has happened to us all.

More than this, all of us have had a part in the slaying of our President. It was good people who crucified our Lord, and not merely those who acted as His executioners. By our silence, by our inaction, by our willingness that heavy burdens be borne by one man alone, by our readiness to allow evil to be called good and good evil, by our continued toleration of ancient injustices, by our failure to address ourselves to this day—by these means we all have had a part in the assassination.

In particular measure, we of the church must bear a heavy share of responsibility. For we are those who speak for God. We are His people and the sheep of His pasture. We are the Body of Christ, which bears His wounds. We are sentinels of civilization, but we have failed to sound the alarm. We have been conformed to the social order we were supposed to have informed. Alas, the garments of the slayer are at our feet. Therefore, "the time has come for judgment to begin with the household of God."

Our Lord says: "Every one to whom much is given, of him will much be required." This word of God is a summons to accountability, just as the events of these days are a summons to accountability. For all too long now we have not been called to account: either to one another; or to the world; or to God. We have been ready to receive abundantly of God's grace, but it is when the demands of that grace are upon us that we fail to measure up.

We call this Thanksgiving Sunday, when we are supposed to acknowledge the mercy of God. It is not really a question of whether or not it is proper for us to celebrate Thanksgiving at such a tragic hour as this. The fact is that we as a people have allowed Thanksgiving,

as a significant day, to be lost long ago. It has been reduced to feasting and football. It has become "a pleasant interlude between leaf-raking and snow-shoveling." This holiday, far from being a holy day, has become a hollow day. Having eaten our fill, and that in the midst of a hungry world, we are left with an empty feeling.

Fundamentally, we have been seized by a forgetfulness of nationwide proportions. Abraham Lincoln told a war-torn Nation in his Thanksgiving Proclamation in November 1863: "We have forgotten the gracious Hand which has preserved us in peace and multiplied and enriched and strengthened us, and have vainly imagined in the deceitfulness of our hearts that all these blessings were produced by some superior wisdom and virtue of our own. Intoxicated with unbroken success, we have become too self-sufficient to feel the necessity of redeeming and preserving Grace, too proud to pray to the God that made us."

If this was true then, how much more is it true today, exactly 100 years later? So it was that in President Kennedy's Thanksgiving Proclamation of November 1963, he said: "* * * as we express our gratitude, we must never forget that the highest appreciation is not to utter words but to live by them. Let us therefore proclaim our gratitude to Providence for manifold blessings—let us be humbly thankful for inherited ideals—and let us resolve to share those blessings and those ideals with our fellow human beings throughout the world."

Yes, we have been seized by forgetfulness. No wonder we debate about our national purpose. No wonder we worry about what other nations shall think of us as a people. Is it not here that we have lost our way? We have forgotten who we are. We have forgotten whose we are. We have forgotten whence we have come. Therefore we do not know where we are going.

"Much has been given to us," yet we have been a thoughtless and thankless people. I do not mean merely that we have been given abundant harvests and a proud heritage. These, we have come to take for granted. Rather, we have been given a man. And this man has been, in an astonishing way, a symbol of the changing world in which we live, a constant flowing river of change which has not left any part of earth untouched.

For John Fitzgerald Kennedy represented and embodied a brandnew world. Indeed, he grasped for it by means of the image of the New Frontier, not merely as a political implement, but as a present reality. So radically has the whole climate of mankind changed that one could almost say that a person living at the beginning of this century would have been more at home in Julius Caesar's time than in our own. This cultural revolution in which we find ourselves was that for which our late President stood.

Again, he made valiant efforts to give a new sense of mission to us as a Nation. This does not mean that he solved all our problems for us but that he was, by virtue of office and by deliberate intent, in the very middle of the dramatic struggles that characterize our age. This sense of mission, involving the welfare of all civilization, has scarcely ever been as well articulated as it was in his inaugural address. Nor has a more imaginative token of it been created than the Peace Corps. So it was that one Peace Corps volunteer said last Friday, "I myself am a part of the legacy he left to the world." Young Americans, in particular, seemed to catch what this man symbolized.

Moreover, he invited and encouraged a new human dignity—a freedom for man now. If this was to have meaning, through Americans, throughout the world, it had to have substance now within our own borders. Therefore, the Negro citizens, patient for a hundred years, were encouraged by President Kennedy to become a new people. That is to say, they have decided to be the free people our Constitution and the Gospel of Jesus Christ say they are. When men determine to be free, there is an unanswerable quality about their determination.

From the Hebrew-Christian perspective, all of this is the work of God. For God is a God who acts in history; indeed, who makes history and gives meaning to human events. The President saw precisely this when he declared, "Here on earth God's work must truly be our own."

We have assuredly been given much in our day, but some factors in our national life have said "No" to it all. They have said "No" to a brandnew world; "No" to national involvement in the whole process of civilization; "No" to the fulfillment now of human dignity. For all this, the high price of martyrdom has been paid. A martyr is, literally, a witness, and this is the witness we have been given.

Great gifts demand great responsibility. For "every one to whom much is given, of him will much be required." What, in the light of this sacrifice, does the Lord require of us? All human kind will be watching what we do in response, for when a people takes its own history seriously, every man's history is involved.

First of all, we who have been forgetful are called to recollection and return. We have come to take God for granted, have tried to encase Him in the past and to capture Him in our creeds. Meanwhile, He is at work, as always, in the present orders of society.

Let us recall that we are a people by heritage dedicated to law and order and to equality under law. This was by specific intent. For 343 years ago this very week, the Pilgrims landed on Cape Cod. Their navigation had been faulty, and they had missed the territory for which they had been granted authority. Some of the colonists considered that they were, therefore, under no law. Then, by deliberate act, they made themselves equal under law, by creating the Mayflower Compact. In this they promised to "covenant and combine ourselves together into a civil body politic, for our better ordering and preservation and furtherance of the ends aforesaid; and by virtue hereof to enact, constitute and frame such just and equal laws, ordinances, acts, constitutions, and offices, from time to time, as shall be thought most meet and convenient for the general good of the colony, unto which we promise all due submission and obedience."

They were, therefore, a covenanted community: in acknowledging God, they acknowledged one another. By self-conscious promises, each held himself before God as responsible to his neighbor in a common endeavor. We are summoned by the martyrdom of our President to renew such a covenant of equity, under law, which is basic to any true community.

Secondly, in the light of this sacrifice, we are called to receive the very realities which it symbolizes. Therefore, we must embrace this new world of radical change and possibility. For it is offered to us as the gift of God.

Moreover, if this is to be a meaningful sacrifice, we are called as a people deliberately to involve ourselves in the whole enterprise of humanity. For, in a degree unparalleled in earlier centuries, we owe ourselves to the world. Merely to preserve ourselves as a nation is to lose our identity. But to give our lives in the service of total civilization is to find ourselves. For it is only in our mission together that we are a nation.

Again, in view of this martyrdom, we are called to a deepened fulfillment of the dignity of every person. There can no longer be any second-class people of any kind, anywhere. Only through acknowledging this dignity for all—without any exception—can any one of us possess dignity himself. So it is that integrity may return to us and we can be the nation we have pretended to be.

What I have said is that we have been present at a new crucifixion and that we all have, in fact, contributed to it. Our crucified Lord enables us to understand the cruciform nature of all human existence, and He endows even the most senseless event with cosmic meaning. But the Christian is not allowed to speak of crucifixion without speaking also of resurrection. This can only be realized by our embodying, as living sacrifices, that which was embodied by the one who was slain. That is to say, we are to confront life and the world with a new openness, a new awareness of our true identity and responsibility as a nation, and a new readiness to acknowledge the validity of every human being.

Finally, let us receive the torch that has been "passed" to a new generation of Americans. "For this generation," as John Fitzgerald Kennedy himself so clearly expressed it, "would not exchange places with any other people or any other generation. The energy, the faith, the devotion which we bring to this endeavor will light our country and all who serve it—and the glow from that fire can truly light the world." That never-dying torch has now been lighted by a martyr for his people. For this man not only uttered words but lived by them. "Every one to whom much is given, of him will much be required." Amen.

Mr. President, on Sunday, December 1, members of the Sioux Falls Elks Lodge gathered in memory of deceased members of the lodge.

At this memorial service, Circuit Court Judge Francis Dunn offered a fitting eulogy to the late President Kennedy. Judge Dunn is one of the Nation's finest citizens and public servants. He possesses a brilliant mind, a keenly developed sense of justice, and warm heart. He was a strong supporter and friend of John Kennedy and I am sure that our beloved fallen President would have deeply appreciated what Judge Dunn said about him. The eulogy by Judge Dunn follows:

On Friday, November 22, 1963, John Fitzgerald Kennedy, 35th President of the United States, and a brother in the Benevolent Protective Order of Elks, fell before an assassin's bullets. In just a few moments this most vigorous young man, acknowledged leader of the Western World, was reduced to a lifeless bundle.

Since that fateful hour, hundreds of people have spoken millions of words in eulogy of this great man—I intend to add only a few. Each person who has spoken has touched on one common theme—the feeling of personal tragedy that this assassination has brought to them. I can understand this feeling. I touched this man's hand but once, yet his death brought deep and personal grief to me as though I had lost someone near and dear to me. And the reason is that I had, indeed, lost someone near and dear to me. I had lost the idol of youth, the image of greatness that had been placed before me since childhood by my parents, by my teachers and by my spiritual advisors.

For here was the perfect image of young American manhood; tall of stature and handsome, with a warm winning smile and a glowing personality that would melt an iceberg.

Here was a man of great intellect; blessed with a keen mind—he had cultivated that mind with formal education and voluminous reading until he was a veritable walking book of knowledge.

Here was a man of courage who in time of hot war when his PT boat was shot from under him, and with a painful injury to his back, swam for miles towing an injured shipmate to safety; and who in time of peace and cold war, has stood up to the tyrants of the world until they gave ground before him.

Here was a man born to enormous wealth, yet with the greatest compassion for the lame, the ill, the aged, and the unfortunate.

Here was the most powerful man in the Western World, yet he unashamedly and regularly fell on his knees and asked God for guidance and strength.

Here was a true family man who has publicly stated that his greatest duty on earth was being a parent, and who found some time from each of his crowded days to spend with his beloved Caroline and John-John.

And finally, here was a patriot of the highest order, who fought valiantly in time of war, fought brilliantly for peace in our times, and died serving the great America that he loved.

I do not suppose that John F. Kennedy ever had much time to attend Elks meetings in Boston or in Washington, yet I submit that he lived and died according to the finest principles of this great order. Today we mourn the passing of a brother.

Mr. President, one of the finest tributes to the late President Kennedy I have seen was written by Mr. Arthur Schlesinger, Jr., for the December 14 issue of the Saturday Evening Post.

Mr. Schlesinger, a special assistant to the President, is one of the Nation's most brilliant historians. He writes with a unique insight and sensitivity. I ask unanimous consent that his article be printed at this point.

[From the Saturday Evening Post, Dec. 14, 1963]

(By Arthur M. Schlesinger, Jr.)

A EULOGY: JOHN FITZGERALD KENNEDY

The thing about him was the extraordinary sense he gave of being alive: This makes his death so grotesque and unbelievable. No one had such vitality of personality—a vitality so superbly disciplined that it sometimes left the impression of cool detachment, but imbuing everything he thought or did with intense concentration and power. He was life affirming, life enhancing. When he entered the room, the temperature changed; and he quickened the sensibilities of everyone around him. His curiosity was unlimited. The restless thrust of his mind never abated. He noticed everything, responded to everything, forgot nothing. He lived his life so intensely that in retrospect it almost seems he must have known it would be short, and that he had no time to waste. Or perhaps it was that, having lived closely to death ever since he swam those lonely, terrible hours along Ferguson Passage in 1943, ever since he nearly died after the operation on his back in 1955, he was determined to savor everything of life.

He was a man profoundly in earnest. Yet there was never a moment when his manner was not informal, reverent, rueful and witty. He took life seriously, but never himself. He cared deeply, but his passion was understatement. No heart ever appeared on his sleeve, though only the unaware could have concluded that this meant there was no heart at all. He mistrusted rhetoric, and he detested histrionics. But the casualness, the dry humor, the sardonic throwaway lines, the cool precision in press conference, the sense of slight distance from emotion, the invariable courtesy and the inextinguishable gaiety—none of this could conceal the profound concern and commitment underneath.

His whole life gave him that concern. He came from a religion and race which had known discrimination and persecution. He came from a family which in its energy, its warmth, its subtle and disparate solidarity had nourished his capacity for competition, for tenacity and for affection. Education developed his intelligence and awakened his historical imagination. This was most important; for he saw the movement of events as a historian sees them, not as a morality play, but as a complex and obscure interaction of men and values and institutions, in which each man's light is often dim but each must do the best he can. As a senior at Harvard he wrote an honors essay to explain why Great Britain was so poorly prepared for the Second World War. The book was published the next year, and he wrote in the introduction: "In studying the reasons why England slept, let us try to profit by them and save ourselves her anguish." He had the insight and the sense of language which could have made him a distinguished historian, but his was the nerve of action.

The hard experience of war deepened and toughened him. He was, of course, an authentic hero, a man of valor and hope. As a young skipper on a PT boat, he displayed his capacity for command, which always meant, for him, not the compulsion to bark orders, but the capacity to enlist confidence and assume responsibility. After the war, he was broken in health but lively in spirit. Though his father had been one of the most successful businessmen of his time, something had saved the older Kennedy from the ethos of the business community; he inspired his children with the belief that serving the Nation was more important than making money; and it was the natural thing for young Lieutenant Kennedy, pale and shaken from the war, to run for Congress from 11th District of Massachusetts. I had been a classmate of his older brother at Harvard and had been aware of John Kennedy, who was a sophomore when I was a senior; but I first knew him when he became the Congressman from the district in which I lived. One remembers the quick intelligence, the easy charm, the laconic wit. One did not then see the passion and power which lay underneath.

I have always felt that in these years John Kennedy perhaps thought he was going to die because of the unresolved trouble with his back, and that he was therefore determined to have the best possible time in the days left to him. This was his season of careless gaiety, of Palm Beach and Newport, of dances and parties, and he married the most beautiful girl of them all. But the trouble with his back remained; and in 1955 he underwent a long and complicated operation—a double fusion of spinal disks with ensuing complications. He received last rites and nearly died. But he fought through, as he had fought through the waters of Ferguson Passage, When he recovered, he knew that he would live. My guess is that at this point he decided to become President of the United States.

HE WANTED TO USE POWER

There used to be a fashion of criticizing John Kennedy for being ambitious, as if anyone ever became President of the United States who had not schemed and labored to that end. Of course he wanted to be President. But he wanted to be President not because he wanted power for its own sake: He wanted to be President because he wanted to use power to advance the purposes of the Nation. He was a supreme politician. He loved the flicker of tension and persuasion, the cut and thrust of political infighting, the puzzles of political strategy. He also came to love campaigning. He always seemed a little surprised by the ardor of the crowds which flocked to see him; but he gathered strength from them as they gathered strength from him.

But, overriding everything else, he had a vision of America, of what this country might do and might be, and he had a vision of the world. He saw this Nation as a noble nation, rising above mean and ugly motives, subordinating private selfishness to public purpose, raising the standards of existence and opportunity for all its citizens. He was always receptive to new experience, and

new experience steadily deepened his sense of what America must do to fulfill the vision. Thus the primary campaign in West Virginia in the spring of 1960 gave his understanding of poverty and his determination to eliminate it new concreteness and urgency. He never could understand the complacent rich who, so long as they had everything they needed for themselves, were content to starve schools, medical services, and social services for their less fortunate fellow citizens. In one of the last talks I had with him, he was musing about the legislative program for next January and said, "The time has come to organize a national assault on the causes of poverty, a comprehensive program, across the board."

So, too, the agony of the Negroes transformed another abstraction into cruel reality, and so he committed himself to the battle for civil rights. He did this not for political reasons, because he always believed it would lose him many more votes than it would gain him. He did this because it was necessary to keep the faith of American democracy and preserve the fabric of American life. He did this because he felt with cold passion that it was the right thing to do.

These things deeply preoccupied him, but what preoccupied him most, I believe, was the peace of the world and the future of mankind. His historian's perspective made him see the conflict with communism not as a holy war but as a difficult and perilous struggle for adjustment and accommodation. The world, he deeply believed, was in its nature and its historical movement a diverse world— a world which had room for a great diversity of economic systems, of political creeds, of philosophic faiths. He respected the distinctive values and traditions, the distinctive identities, of other nations and other societies. He felt that as the possessing classes in the American community had an obligation to the weak and defenseless, so the possessing nations had an obligation to the nations struggling to emerge from the oblivion of stagnation and want. And he saw this not just as a moral obligation but as a social necessity. "Those who make peaceful revolution impossible," he once said, "make violent revolution inevitable."

Above all, life must survive on this planet. He knew what nuclear war would mean, and he believed that the avoidance of such a war was the common interest of mankind—a common interest which must transcend all conflicts of ideology and national ambition. This common interest was the bridge across the dark abyss. His deepest purpose was to strengthen that bridge against the storms of suspicion and fear, and to persuade his adversaries that, if each nation and people respected the integrity of the rest and accepted the reality of the world of diversity, if nations abandoned a messianic effort to remake the world in their own image, peace would be possible, and humanity would endure.

These hopes, I believe, guided him in his terrible task. In the midst of his crushing burdens, he moved always with grace, composure and cheer. His office reflected his own serenity in a world of chaos. He was a man born to the exercise of power, but also a man born to the responsibility of power. He immersed himself in the issues, understood what mattered and what did not, mastered the necessary information and dominated the process of government. I have so often seen experts come before him, men who had worked on problems for months or years, and I have seen him penetrate at once to the heart of the issue, and then place it in a wider context, raising questions of significance which the experts had not thought about. His presence pervaded Washington, and he infused the laborious and opaque machinery of government with a sense of his own standards, his own imagination and his own high purpose. With all this, his kindness, his consideration, his gaiety and his strength were absolute.

He had grown all his life, and he grew even more in the Presidency. The ordeal of the first Cuba made possible the triumph of the second Cuba. He broke new paths in a dozen sectors of national policy—in civil rights, in economic policy, in the reorientation of military strategy, in the reconstruction of foreign aid, in the exploration of space, in the encouragement of the arts. But the bright promise of his administration, as of his life, was cut short in Dallas. When Abraham Lincoln died, when Franklin Roosevelt died, these were profound national tragedies; but death came for Lincoln and Roosevelt in the last act, at the end of their careers, when the victory for which they had fought so hard was at last within the Nation's grasp. John Kennedy's death has greater pathos, because he had barely begun—because he had so much to do, so much to give to his family, his Nation, his world. His was a life of incalculable and now of unfulfilled possibility.

Still, if he had not done all that he would have hoped to do, finished all that he had so well begun, he had given the Nation a new sense of itself—a new spirit, a new style, a new conception of its role and destiny. He saw America, not as an old nation, self-righteous, conservative, satisfied in its grossness and materialism, but as a young nation, questing, self-critical, dissatisfied, caring for greatness as well as for bigness, caring for the qualities of mind, sensibility and spirit which sustain culture, produce art and elevate society. He was the most civilized President we have had since Jefferson, and his wife made the White House the most civilized house in America. Statecraft was for him not an end in itself; it was a means of moving forward toward a spacious and splendid America.

And so a crazed political fanatic shot him down. With this act of violence, and with the violence that followed, the idea of America as a civilized nation—the idea which John F. Kennedy so supremely embodied—suffered a grievous blow. The best way to serve his memory is to redeem and revindicate the values of decency, of rationality, of civility, of honor—those values for which he stood through his life and to which in the end he gave his life.

Mr. President, Molly Kazan, wife of the distinguished theatrical producer, Elia Kazan, died on December 14 of a cerebral hemorrhage. Before her death, she wrote a beautiful poem setting forth her feelings about the life and death of the late President Kennedy. I ask unanimous consent that her poem entitled "Thanksgiving 1963" be printed at this point.

(The following poem, entitled "Thanksgiving 1963," was written by Molly Kazan after the death of President Kennedy. It was read originally as part of a church service.)

I think that what he gave us most was pride.
It felt good to have a President like that:
Bright, brave, and funny and goodlooking.
I saw him once drive down East 72d Street in an open
    car, in the autumn sun (as he drove yesterday in
    Dallas).
His thatch of brown hair looked as though it has grown
    extra thick, the way our wood animals in Con-
    necticut grow extra fur for winter.
And he looked as though it was fun to be alive, to be a
    politician, to be President, to be a Kennedy, to be
    a man.

He revived our pride.
It felt good to have a President who read his mail, who
    read the papers, who read books and played touch
    football.
It was a pleasure and a cause for pride to watch him
    take the quizzing of the press with cameras grind-
    ing—take it in his stride, with zest.
He'd parry, thrust, answer or duck, and fire a verbal shot
    on target, hitting with the same answer, the segre-
    gationists in a Louisiana hamlet, and a govern-
    ment in southeast Asia.
He made you feel that he knew what was going on in
    both places.
He would come out of the quiz with an "A" in econom-
    ics, military science, constitutional law, farm prob-
    lems, and the moonshot program and still take
    time to appreciate Miss May Craig.

We were privileged to see him on the worst day (till
    yesterday), the Bay of Pigs day, and we marveled
    at his coolth and style and were amazed at an air
    (that plainly was habitual) of modesty and even
    diffidence.
It felt good to have a President who said, "It was my
    fault."
And went on from there.

It felt good to have a President who looked well in
    Vienna, Paris, Rome, Berlin and at the podium
    of the United Nations;
And who would go to Dublin, put a wreath where it
    did the most good and leave unspoken the satis-
    faction of an Irishman en route to 10 Downing
    Street as head of the U.S. Government.

What was spoken was spoken well.
What was unspoken needed to be unspoken.
It was none of our business if his back hurt.

He revived our pride.
He gave grist to our pride.
He was respectful of intellect;
He was respectful of excellence;
He was respectful of accomplishment and skill;
He was respectful of the clear and subtle uses of our
    language;
He was respectful of courage.
And all these things he cultivated in himself.

He was respectful of our heritage.

He is now part of it.

He affirmed our future.

Our future is more hopeful because of his work but our
future is not safe nor sure.

He kept telling us that.

This is a very dangerous and uncertain world.

I quote. He said that yesterday.

He respected facts.

And we must now live with the fact of his murder.

Our children cried when the news came. They phoned
and we phoned.

And we cried and we were not ashamed of crying but we
were ashamed of what had happened.

The youngest could not remember any other President,
not clearly.

She felt as if the world had stopped.

We said, "It is a shame, a very deep shame."

But this country will go on more proudly,

And with a clearer sense of who we are and what we
have it in us to become,

Because we had a President like that.

He revived our pride.

We are lucky that we had him for 3 years.

TRIBUTES BY

Hon. Philip A. Hart

OF MICHIGAN

Mr. President, sometimes the most eloquent
tributes are those voiced by children. They are,
indeed, the most lasting on many occasions.

I received from Jo Ann Johnson, of the fifth
grade of the Central Grade School, Negaunee,
Mich., a longhand letter which reads as follows:

> FIFTH GRADE ROOM 202,
> CENTRAL GRADE SCHOOL,
> *Negaunee, Mich., January 29, 1964.*

Hon. PHILIP HART,
*Senator from Michigan,
Senate Office Building,
Washington, D.C.*

DEAR SENATOR HART: Miss Carter's fifth grade is
sending you a biography of President Kennedy. Every
one in Miss Carter's room put this book together. We
hope you will enjoy reading it.

> Sincerely yours,
>
> JO ANN JOHNSON.

The enclosure of which she speaks, the biography of President Kennedy, prepared by that
fifth grade, I ask to have inserted at this point.

JOHN F. KENNEDY, OUR 35TH PRESIDENT

(By Grade 5, Room 202, Central Grade School,
Negaunee, Mich.)

The boys and girls of many schools have been learning
sayings of great leaders. Here is one that children
later on will be learning:

"Ask not what your country will do for you. Ask
what you can do for your country."

This story is about the great leader who said that.

John Fitzgerald Kennedy was born in Brookline, Mass.,
on May 29, 1917, to Joseph and Rose Kennedy. After
he was finished high school, he went to Harvard University. He was among the people with the best marks.
Because he had good marks, he graduated cum laude in
1940.

Mr. Kennedy joined the U.S. Navy when he was 24
years old. In World War II he was on a boat called the
PT–109. At one time a Japanese boat came and cut his
PT–109 into two pieces. Lieutenant Kennedy saved a
man's life by putting a strap btween his teeth to pull
the man. He swam 5 miles to an island. By doing these
things even though he was injured, he earned the Purple
Heart and other medals.

Mr. Kennedy married Jacqueline Bouvier in 1953. They
had two children, Caroline and John. They also had a
baby named Patrick, but that baby died soon after his
birth. The Kennedy's named their plane the Caroline,
after their daughter.

John F. Kennedy was elected to Congress. From 1947
to 1953 he was in the House of Representatives, and
from 1953 to 1961 he was in the Senate. These are the
two parts of the Congress of the United States.

Mr. Kennedy wrote some books, one of them when
he was sick. After his injuries while in the U.S. Navy,
he had to spend some time in the hospital. He wrote
a book called "Profiles in Courage." Before that he had
written "Why England Slept." He also wrote papers on
"Strategy of Peace." He got a prize for writing "Profiles
in Courage."

In 1960, Mr. Kennedy was elected President of the
United States. He was inaugurated in January of 1961.
As the 35th President of our country, he did many good
things for America and the world. He worked with other
nations because he wanted to keep the United States
from having war.

Our President wanted to settle the Berlin question with
Russia so the wall could be torn down. Also, President
Kennedy insisted that missiles be removed from Cuba.
He did this because they might damage North and South
America. He also started the Alliance for Progress with
countries in the Western Hemisphere. The nations wanted
to work together to improve conditions.

President Kennedy started the Peace Corps, which helps
countries to start a new and better life. This organization sends people to other countries to help them in
getting schools, clothes, food, and many other things.

The President signed a test ban treaty, outlawing nuclear
testing in the air, with Great Britain, Russia, and others.
He did this because he wanted our country to make
friends. Do you know another reason? The nuclear
tests leave poison in the air and people breathe it in.

People were getting lazy. President Kennedy said that Marines used to walk 50 miles. He said that we need to be physically fit. Many people went on a 50-mile hike.

The President suggested some plans. His education bill is a plan to help the schools. Congress passed parts of the plan to help colleges, science study, and defense areas where more children came to the schools. He wanted money for all of the public schools.

President Kennedy worked hard for the civil rights bill. In this he could be compared with Lincoln. He believed that everyone should have equal rights, no matter what his color or race. He thought that Negro children should be able to go to the same school as white children. President Kennedy was trying to carry on the work Lincoln had begun over 100 years ago.

John F. Kennedy spent long hours working for our country and traveling to many places. He wanted to make friends with our own people and those of other countries. He didn't want war.

On a tour of Texas, President Kennedy, along with Vice President Lyndon B. Johnson, Governor Connally, and their wives, visited in Houston, Fort Worth, and then in Dallas. After getting off the plane in Dallas at Love Field, Mrs. Kennedy received a bouquet of red roses. President Kennedy shook hands with many people. Some had signs saying, "Welcome, Mr. President." Everywhere he went he was welcomed by huge crowds.

Everybody was excited when the President was riding down the street in the motorcade. People were shouting and cheering the President. All of a sudden a gun was fired from the sixth story of a huge building. Two more shots rang out. President Kennedy and Governor Connally had been hit.

Then the cars sped on faster until they reached the hospital. Doctors and nurses were able to help Governor Connally, but at 1 p.m. the world heard the sad news. President Kennedy was dead. Everywhere people were shocked.

A plane carried the President's body to Washington, D.C. Mrs. Kennedy, Mr. Johnson, and Mrs. Johnson were also on the plane. Before the plane left, Mr. Johnson took the oath of office and became President of the United States.

At the White House, U.S. leaders came to honor President Kennedy. Drums were beating and people were mourning for their beloved President. His coffin was put on a caisson pulled by silver-gray horses. The cortege was going down Pennsylvania Avenue. At the U.S. Capitol Building, the coffin was placed on the stand on which Lincoln's coffin was put when he died. Thousands of people paid their last respects to the President in the Capitol rotunda.

President Johnson ordered that Monday was to be a day of mourning. People came to Washington, D.C., from all over the world to honor the 35th President. There were presidents, princes, kings, queens, and ministers.

The President's funeral was at St. Matthews Cathedral on Monday, November 25. Some of the people, including leaders of many nations, walked behind the caisson to the church, just as people did at the time that Lincoln died.

Afterward, in the procession, they took John F. Kennedy's body on the caisson to the Arlington National Cemetery. There was a 21-gun salute because he was a hero in the Navy. Fifty jets flew over the cemetery to represent the 50 States.

Mrs. Kennedy lit a flame that will burn forever by the grave of the President to show that John F. Kennedy's spirit is everlasting.

John Fitzgerald Kennedy was a noble gentleman and a great leader. He loved our country. He was very courageous, worked hard for America, and died for our country.

President Kennedy believed in freedom and lived in a way that showed he believed in equal rights for all. He made friends with everyone of all colors. He thought that the skin may be different but the hearts are the same. He showed that he liked people by always wanting to be around them. He liked to talk to people and shake hands with everyone he met. He enjoyed living, and he couldn't keep still. He liked to have fun and play with his children because he loved them. The President, like many other people, enjoyed sports. One of the sports he liked was touch football, which he played with his family.

It was in his first speech as President that he said: "Ask not what your country will do for you, ask what you can do for your country." And he did just that.

We are thankful for our 35th President of the United States.

Our fifth-grade class studied Walt Whitman's poem "I hear America Singing." Then we wrote a poem of our own about hearing America singing today, today's song of work and play. We include it in our story because it shows the sounds of America that President Kennedy heard:

"I hear America singing the songs of work and play:
Men sing while working for their country.
Carpenters sing while building a house.
Cars sing a song as they go—Honk! Honk!
Scientists sing as they work.
Men sing while drilling and digging for ore.
Firemen sing while putting out a fire.
Men sing while blasting rocks for a new highway.
A woman sings as a man plays the piano.
A man sings while fixing his car.
Children sing while working puppets.
Witches sing on Halloween night.
Little girls sing while playing jump rope.
Roller skates sing while children play.
In school I hear happy children singing.
The songs of work and play are glorious, beautiful, and
    gay."

Mr. President, Jo Ann hopes that I enjoyed reading the biography. I did. I feel confident that Senators who now will have an opportunity to read it will share the same pride and reaction that I felt on reading it. I take great pride in the mature performance of these children in Negaunee.

Mr. President, I have been requested to insert the resolutions of the National Council of the Federal Bar Association, the Capitol Hill Chapter of the Federal Bar Association, and the United Nations League of Lawyers, memorializing the late President John Fitzgerald Kennedy. These resolutions are not only appropriately worded, but they bear a significant message from the legal profession in respect of a great President who believed in the rule of law rather than the rule of men.

RESOLUTION OF THE NATIONAL COUNCIL OF THE FEDERAL BAR ASSOCIATION ADOPTED UNANIMOUSLY, NOVEMBER 27, 1963

John Fitzgerald Kennedy was a great American President, dedicated to principles of the rule of law, of freedom, and the equality of men; and consecrated to their fulfillment. He was a strong and qualified leader and an inspiring head of the Executive Department. Let it be recorded here that we so regarded him, and that we share the depth of the sense of loss and sorrow of all Americans because of his tragic and untimely passing.

Let it further be recorded here that he has by his devotion, courage, and determination set for us, as lawyers and as servants or former servants of the general government, an example which will continue to urge us toward these goals through all the time which can be foreseen.

PRAYER

Our help is in the name of the Lord, who made heaven and earth.

Give unto the Lord, O ye kindreds of people; give unto the Lord glory and strength.

Honor and majesty are before Him; strength and beauty are in His sanctuary.

Let us pray.

Blessed and glorious Lord God Almighty, by whose power, wisdom, and love all things are sanctified, enlightened, and made perfect, be merciful unto us. We beseech Thee to cause Thy face to shine upon us.

O Thou who are the Creator and lover of all men, by whom all souls do live, we give thanks to Thee for having permitted John Fitzgerald Kennedy to dwell and work among us, recalling all in him that made others love him. We thank Thee for the goodness and truth that have passed from his life into the lives of others and made the world richer for his presence. We bless and praise Thee for the example he has given us of personal integrity and courage and of hope and love and devotion to duty for this our country, and of love and concern for Thy people everywhere, not only for their physical well-being but also their intellectual and spiritual well-being, and for his constant desire for and effort to bring Thy peace to this world.

Grant we beseech Three to his widow and children and to the other members of his family the comfort of Thy presence and the ministry of Thy Holy Spirit, renewing within them the gifts of patience and enduring love. Grant that Thy strength and consolation may be given them and endue them with holy thoughts and a loving hope.

We thank Thee that deep in the human heart is an unquenchable trust that life does not end with death, that the Father, who made us, will care for us beyond the bounds of vision, even as He has cared for us in this earthly world.

O Lord our God, in whom light for the darkness resideth for the Godly, we pray Thee in this troublesome time to grant that the spirit of wisdom may save our President, Lyndon Baines Johnson, from all false choices, and that in Thy light he may find light for his guidance, and in Thy straight path he may not stumble.

We beseech Thee O God to forgive those national sins which do so easily beset us, our wanton waste of the wealth of soil and sea, our desecration of natural beauty, our heedlessness of those who come after us if only we be served; our love of money, our contempt for small things and our worship of big things, our neglect of backward peoples and minority groups, our cults of hate for those whose views differ from ours and our pride of life. We humbly beseech Thee that we may prove ourselves a people mindful of Thy favor and glad to do Thy will. Endue with the spirit of wisdom all those to whom in Thy name we entrust the authority of government that there may be justice and peace at home, and that through obedience to Thy law we may show forth Thy praise among the nations of the earth; and, Beloved Father, grant each of us guidance to recognize and strength to bear our individual responsibilities.

Now unto the King Eternal, immortal, invisible, the only wise God, be honor and glory forever and ever. Amen.

UNITED NATIONS LEAGUE OF LAWYERS

Whereas the sudden and untimely death of President John Fitzgerald Kennedy occurred on November 22, 1963, at Dallas, Tex.; and

Whereas President Kennedy had long actively supported the purposes and objectives of the United Nations to the furtherance of which the United Nations League of Lawyers is also dedicated; and

Whereas President Kennedy has performed outstanding service in furthering the humanitarian purposes of the United Nations not only in the United States of America but throughout the world by supporting national and international programs to eliminate disease, to eliminate unjust discrimination between peoples based on race, color, creed or national origin, to provide education and to house and promote the welfare of the young and the aged; and

Whereas President Kennedy was for many years a strong leader in activities designed to promote world peace and has brought about adoption of measures such as the nuclear test ban treaty, the Alliance for Progress and has taken steps in support of the splendid work and the continuance of the United Nations; and

Whereas the death of President Kennedy has caused great sorrow and a feeling of loss to people throughout the world who had been encouraged by his devotion, courage and determination in support of the objectives above set forth and of the rule of law in the world:

Resolved, That we, members of the United Nations League of Lawyers, hereby express our feeling of concern over the crime against the United States and against free peoples throughout the world that was committed in the assassination of President Kennedy, and our feeling of sympathy to his family and to the people of the United States of America, and at the same time hereby memorialize and commend to high esteem the memory of the late President John Fitzgerald Kennedy.

———

RESOLUTION OF THE CAPITOL HILL CHAPTER OF THE FEDERAL BAR ASSOCIATION MEMORIALIZING THE LATE PRESIDENT JOHN FITZGERALD KENNEDY

Whereas the late President of the United States John Fitzgerald Kennedy was a great President and leader who was dedicated to the principle of the rule of law; and

Whereas he sponsored, supported, and was dedicated to measures to improve the welfare and equality of mankind and to insure peace in the world; and

Whereas this chapter of the Federal Bar Association feels that all functions of the chapter of a social or quasi-social nature should be canceled during the official 30-day period of mourning for the late President of the United States; and

Whereas this chapter has scheduled a December monthly luncheon meeting and has made preparations together with the Empire State chapter for a large reception in the New York Yacht Club, New York City, on the evening of December 18, 1962, in honor of the Federal judiciary; and

Whereas as lawyers, the members of this chapter wish to express our sympathy in the great and tragic loss of the late John Fitzgerald Kennedy: Now, therefore, be it

Resolved, That this chapter hereby memorializes and commends to high esteem the memory of the late John Fitzgerald Kennedy as a truly great President of the United States.

It is directed that the aforementioned events of the chapter be canceled and that a copy of this resolution be forwarded to the widow of the late President as a token of sympathy and of great respect.

TRIBUTES BY

Hon. Karl E. Mundt

OF SOUTH DAKOTA

Mr. President, recently I have received a copy of a most moving tribute to our late President John F. Kennedy. Delivered by Pastor H. Clarence Johnson to the Kiwanis Club of Ortonville, Minn., on November 26, it was also delivered as a Thanksgiving Day message in Tabor and Grace Lutheran Churches in Strandburg and La Bolt, S. Dak., on November 28.

This is a most eloquent memorial tribute to President John F. Kennedy.

No one speaks in these days or even thinks—in these days of mourning, these days of grief, and even in these days of a shared sense of guilt for the taking of a life. The life of a person whose only object in life was to live for the welfare of his country and for the benefit of humanity.

One cannot help but have all of his thoughts, and all of his speaking, colored by the somberness and the sobriety of these days through which we have passed. I suppose that if it were not for the fact that during these days that I was in the process of preparing a talk for the Kiwanians at Ortonville, which I had opportunity to deliver on Tuesday, I do not know whether this particular message would be my Thanksgiving message to you or not.

But, I've searched my heart and soul these days asking the question—when one thinks of the very sordid nature of the crime that has been committed in a civilized nation one cannot help ask—for what shall we be thankful and render thanks to God? And then, one cannot help but allow the thoughts to begin to gather, and then the answer begins to come. And in the middle of this answer that comes to us is the image of a man. The image of a man whose life will likely mark the pages of history, comparable perhaps, to men like George Washington and Abraham Lincoln.

And, I would give thanks today for some of the ideals, as well as the accomplishments, of President John Kennedy. I would give thanks, first of all, for the faith of this man: A faith which he didn't carry about offensively—ever. A faith which he didn't hold up as something to be cherished over and above the faith of other men. But a faith to which he constantly bore witness, unashamed. But with it all, a faith that lacked bigotry.

Here was a man that, it seems to me, was born for the hour. Not for the time in history when division was the order of the day. Not for the time in the development of our country when, almost of necessity, there had to be the springing up and the growth of diverse groups of religious, almost religious factions, as it were. Religious elements of every kind spring forth in a new and fertile ground of liberty that we have known in these United States. It could hardly be otherwise for when those who left their home countries to seek a land where they might have their liberty, and worship God according to the dictates of their consciences, it could hardly be otherwise. The very rigor of these people meant that they would give birth to independence. And I suppose it's true, I'm sure it's true, that in no nation have there been as many expressions of various kinds of a faith of people as we have found under the name of Christendom in this country. This is not the day in which we live.

And here, it seems to me, a man of firm faith and loyalty to his own particular church, nevertheless, personifies the ecumenical age in which we live. This is the day when men do not look for their religious convictions to divide. But the age in which, into which you and I have been ushered, together with this great leader who met his untimely death, is a day when we look for our religious convictions to unite; to bring together, and to make whole.

Along with this I think, then, of President Kennedy's, shall we say, fraternalism, with the proper connotations to that word. A man who indeed wanted to be brother not only to his countrymen, but to all the peoples of the whole wide world. He was thinking first and foremost of the general well-being of all people. Treating mankind, applying in his relationship the Golden Rule toward all of us.

In the next place, I thank God for the fidelity of this man: For his faithfulness to what was reiterated again by President Johnson yesterday—the American dream. (Incidentally, I want to say here that anything I say that sounds like President Johnson's message yesterday is purely coincidental because these notes were written before I listened to him yesterday. And, as a matter of fact, in its essence delivered at the Kiwanis Club Tuesday.) I said, I thank God for the faithfulness, the fidelity of our martyred President to the American dream. This man had caught the vision of what was in the heart and in the mind, which it couldn't realize fully how it would develop, and how it would unfold, and how it would grow, and finally blossom into its fullness, when they framed the Constitution of these United States. When they put in words something like this—that this Nation was to stand for the inalienable rights to life, liberty, and pursuit of happiness of all mankind.

Here was a man who saw within such a dream, who found in it, a challenge to which to dedicate his life. Just written lines can often very conveniently be tucked away in the closed chapters of history and not come into vital meaning in the expression of the life of a society. That which could happen to the Constitution of the United States, that it could become and be thought of only as written sacred words—just as we have sometimes been guilty of in the church, of thinking of our Bible only as sacred written words—and almost untouchable as far as full application in the lives of men.

I see in his fidelity, also, his vision of putting into living practice the meaning of those words that were once written in the Constitution. We have to grant that there is, that there is a time when we can only progress by stages. Maybe it's always true, and it was certainly true at the time of the writing of the Constitution of our country.

I just discovered this past week, in paging through some history pages, that a surprising thing happened at the time when the Constitution was framed. In setting up the form of government, in setting up a representative type of government, in the South where the slaves were found, only two-thirds of those slaves were counted in the census. In other words, as I understand it, what was actually done—if their particular community would have a hundred slaves only 66 of them would have to be counted in the census. And so, in a sense, one-third of them were completely and entirely forgotten. It was necessary that the North had to settle for this kind of a halfway satisfying proposition in order to get the new Nation underway. And with this, there was also an agreement passed that

there would be no law that would be passed the first 20 years prohibiting the importing of more slaves.

Just as President Kennedy expressed himself in his beautiful inaugural address—that he gave at the time of his inauguration when he challenged America to at least begin toward the goal that he envisioned—so we must recognize that our forefathers realized then that theirs was only a beginning; and that there is an ideal in the American system that we're always reaching, we're always progressing, we're always growing toward that goal of which we dream and for which we pray.

We can also say such things as this about our martyred President—we can thank God for his fortitude. For few men, it seems to me, have had the energy, and the ambition, and determination, that he displayed. But there is another phase to this gratitude that ought to be ours today. And that is that John Kennedy does not stand alone today expressing himself, in a way, and now giving us memories, in a way, for which we shall be very grateful.

There is a counterpart to this, and this is—I thank God today for the American people. I thank God for the oneness of the American people in a crisis. All of the free world, as well as all of humanity, could not but recognize the unity that actually exists among this generation today and with this unity a beauty and a dignity, I do not know how else to describe my impression. We can get good impressions today of what goes on—through the medium of television and radio. In this scene that so many of us witnessed in the grief, and the sorrow, and the mourning, of a nation, in which we all participated; the attendance, as if we were there in person, almost, at the burial service. This is something for which we thank God today.

In epitomizing this, for some strange reason, there was in the White House a young wife of a President who, by the way, as far as I know was unknown a few years ago. But now she has risen to a place where she shall never be forgotten. She shall be recognized for meeting a situation with beauty of character, and poise, and dignity, and honor, and, if you please, nobility. It did not spring from a particular line of kings such as was thought necessary at one stage in history in the world, if there was to be that kind of womanhood demonstrated. But, here is one who had come, we hardly know from where, who now stood to mourn and to play her role; for it's necessary at times, even in sorrow and grief, to be strong enough to play the role that has fallen upon our shoulders. I think we shall have to agree and thank God that there is this kind of character present in our society today. When it is possible for such character to be generated and borne through the years in which we have lived, then I see there is great hope—despite the shame that we feel today—there is great hope for America.

One could also see the things that are to be regretted and grieved, such things as are still present in our society—such things as the hostility bred in an Oswald. Or, what to me is equally serious, the anarchy and lawlessness in a Rubenstein. But perhaps these—these dark spots only tend to set in bold relief the reality of the glorious age in which God has called us to live.

There is then, a third place. Besides thanking God for the ideals of our former President, and the character of today's generation of people in this country, I would like to observe, also, that I thank God for a new partnership that I see in church and state. Now, please note, I did not say union of church and state—for that American ideal, the American dream, will best be fulfilled if church and state stand separate. But, the fact that we believe that we have been called to be separate identities does not mean that we cannot stand strong and God-like in the partnership that we must seek to establish as a nation. Together, the church and state. The one representing temporal society, and then the other representing the eternal kingdom of God. Neither is to rule or subdue the other, or to be either embarrassed or reluctant to walk together down the unfolding pages of American life— as we saw in our hour of grief, effective, beautiful. May we seek, friends, to see in this tragic hour some of the hopeful things that God would have us see.

I want to close by saying two things. That is, first of all, one of the problems that I had as I was thinking about preparing this talk, I couldn't remember who I voted for in the last election. And, I can't. I know I voted for Roosevelt, once or twice, I know I voted for Eisenhower. But for some strange reason, I cannot recall when I went into that wonderful place of privacy that we have in the American life—the voting booth—I can't remember what I finally decided, as to what side to place the X. I guess I shall never know. And I say that for this reason, that I hope that there has been no gleaning on the part of anybody there's politics in my thinking today. And I have tried to leave this particular—in fact, we have a glorious way of balancing the conservative and the liberal that we certainly want to cherish, and want to keep. And I wouldn't want to predict—I made a little prediction in my own mind that, sometime when I'm not in the pulpit I'm going to pass it on to some of you—of what I think is going to happen in the next few months, or few years.

Of course, politics is only an instrument to the shared life in the American way. And so, we may debate, and we may argue, and we may tussle, with the problem of what is the greatest way, the rights of future pages of American history. But, it is wonderful to know that we stand united as a people.

God will bless such a people and use such a generation. Amen.

TRIBUTES BY

Hon. Hubert H. Humphrey

OF MINNESOTA

Mr. President, "Let the Alliance for Progress be President Kennedy's living memorial," said President Johnson in his first official public statement. These words were spoken to all the peoples of the western hemisphere. To the United States they say, "let us continue," and to those south of the Rio Grande they say "let us continue."

Did these words fall on unhearing ears? The record we in this hemisphere write next week, next year, and from then on will tell whether we heard, and heeded, but the grief of our partners in the Alliance over the loss of our President gives proof of their commitment to this task, and to this hope.

Reports of their grief are flowing to Washington from the capitals and villages of the Latin American countries.

As President Johnson's words of reaffirmation reached the Latin cities, expressions of confidence and gratitude accompanied the expressions of grief. I offer a sampling, so that we may know the quantity and quality thereof, and pay heed to the strength of this partnership.

ARGENTINA

The shocking, tragic death of President John F. Kennedy plunged the Argentine people into a trauma of unprecedented proportions and evoked an outpouring of deeply touching expressions of condolences.

For the first time since his inauguration— October 12—President Illia gathered his entire Cabinet together to issue a decree invoking an 8-day period of national mourning and to declare the day of the funeral an official holiday. Personal visits and telephone calls expressing sympathy for the Kennedy family and the American people deluged the Embassy and the homes of its officers. Books, opened for signature at the Embassy Chancery and the residence drew long lines of people, many standing for hours, to record their grief. Some 5,000 letters, cards, and telegrams have been received from all over Argentina. Over a hundred floral offerings, ranging from elaborate wreaths to simple bouquets placed by children, flooded the chancery. Some 40,000 portrait photographs of President Kennedy were handed out by USIS in response to requests. A solemn Requiem Mass at the Buenos Aires Cathedral was attended by President Illia, top officials, diplomats, and a crushing capacity crowd on the day of the funeral. Other churches, of all denominations, held memorial services at one time or another during the week. Practically all top officials of the present government and the last government, as well as political leaders of all persuasions—Peronist, Christian Democrats, Socialists, and so forth—personally paid their respects to the Ambassador. The Ministry of Education named the National Normal School for Modern Languages after President Kennedy in a formal ceremony on November 28, and all Argentine national schools held special classes on November 29 on the contributions of President Kennedy to the cause of world peace. The foregoing serve merely as indications of the sincere and deeply emotional reaction of Argentina to this tragic event. The national mourning brought official and political activity nearly to a standstill, with attention universally focused on the assassination, the funeral, the attendant developments in the United States, and a widely voiced marveling at the manner in which the people and Government of the United States took the tragedy in stride, named the new President and carried on.

President Johnson's address to Congress received top billing in all papers. The influential La Prensa calls the President's speech "a piece of singular worth that can be considered his first victory." Asserts this means "leadership of the great Republic has changed neither course nor level," and hails the speech as a "political message of singular beauty" and as coining phrases that will last as models of expression and norms.

La Nacion, November 28, observes Johnson "not a President by mere chance" and "entering presidential stage with dignity of a master in his legitimate domain."

Said La Razon:

The President is dead, but another man identified with his ideals and principles is already at the helm, and within the Democratic Party and the administration the spirit of teamwork continues * * * based on the presence of men of thought and action, advisors noted for their scholarly qualities and intellectual devotion, who from now on will apply themselves to the programs and plans which they conceived in simple and friendly comradeship with the young statesman whom humanity has lost * * *. It is certain that in the United States everything will go on as if John F. Kennedy was still at his White House desk.

RIO DE JANEIRO, BRAZIL

News of the death of President Kennedy was received with shock and sorrow throughout Brazil, and with considerable speculation as to what the death meant in terms of Brazilians and their interests. President Goulart decreed 3 days of national mourning, personally called on Ambassador Gordon on Friday evening, and offered a Requiem Mass at Planalto Palace in Brasilia on November 25. Governor Lacerda called on the Ambassador immediately upon hearing the news and decreed 5 days of mourning in the State of Guanabara. Tribute is still being paid to the late President in municipal chambers, State legislatures, and the National Congress, which on November 27 initiated a motion to recommend President Kennedy for the Nobel Peace Prize for 1963.

Public reaction was, to all appearances, overwhelming. Crowds flock to the Embassy and the Consulates for news. Four of Rio's morning dailies issued special editions on Friday evening, and up to 80 percent of the regular editions of all Rio papers through November 26 was devoted to news from Dallas and Washington. Rio's radio and television stations were, and still are, on strike. News to the city's radio audience was supplied in special and lengthy broadcasts by Government-owned Radio Nacional, and from stations in Niteroi, São Paulo and Belo Horizonte, which on Friday and Saturday devoted almost all of their air time to coverage of the events. Outpouring of sentiment from all over Brazil was expressed as for over 2 days radio announcers read message after message from civic, social, sports, commercial, industrial, and professional associations, private citizens and public officials. Special memorial services were held and reverential minutes of silence were observed throughout the nation. In various cities housewives lit candles in their windows on the night of President Kennedy's funeral.

SÃO PAULO, BRAZIL

Paulistas forgot politics when the news came of President Kennedy's death. Few cities in the United States could have been more deeply upset. Public figures flocked to the Consulate General, often in tears, till late at night. Crowds gathered where news was available downtown. Another in the succession of petty political crises seemed to die in the bud. Brazilians called at the homes of American friends. Americans were stopped on the streets for condolences. The press ran what is said to have been the biggest extra edition in years. A Gazeta changed its customary red headlines to black.

All commentators agreed that John F. Kennedy had appealed to Brazil as had no other American President except F.D.R.

On Monday, the Legislative Assembly held a special commemorative session. Its President then flew to the United States with condolences, as did Auro Moura Andrade, President of the Federal Senate. The capital city and many smaller towns announced the intention of naming streets, squares, and schools after President Kennedy.

SALVADOR, BRAZIL

The shock of the news of President Kennedy's assassination is still reverberating throughout the district. The Governor of Sergipe sent a telegram stating that 5 days' official mourning were declared in that state. Three days' mourning were declared by Governor Lomanto for Bahia. The expressions of grief cut across all party and ideological lines. Local commentators and orators have likened the President to Pope John XXIII, Lincoln, and Roosevelt, as a figure who had shaped the destiny of the world.

President Johnson's prompt assurances that the Alliance for Progress will be carried on with vigor have been very welcome.

COLOMBIA

Colombian reaction to President Kennedy's death was shock, grief, and initial disbelief. Mourning was widespread, and deep seated, with perhaps more surprising manifestations of grief and desire to honor the dead President from the common people, than even from the country's leaders.

A 3-day mourning period was immediately declared by President Valencia, and a requiem mass was celebrated on Monday with the attendance of Valencia, the diplomatic corps, the Cabinet, and other high Government and military officers.

On November 22, President Valencia sent a message to President Johnson stating that—

As the days pass, the figure of President Kennedy will grow in the consciences of men as the most determined paladin of liberty, of human rights, of understanding, and harmony among men and peoples, and of world peace.

A flood of telegrams, letters, and phone calls from Colombian groups and individuals reflected this sentiment.

Perhaps the most touching manifestation of solidarity was the decision of the citizens of Ciudad Techo to change the name of their housing project to Ciudad Kennedy. The project was inaugurated by President Kennedy in December 1961. The Colombian national housing authority, which has the primary responsibility for the Alliance-sponsored project, seconded the name-changing proposal.

The chancellery announced that a book for those wishing to sign would be placed at the Embassy. In 3 days more than 1,800 people used this way of expressing sympathy. The signers represented all strata of Colombian society from day laborers and soldiers to bankers and political leaders.

The former President of Colombia, Alberto Lleras Camargo, a man who knew John F. Kennedy and who knows Latin America, put it this way:

Never has a President of the United States devoted so much and such affectionate interest to Latin American affairs, particularly to the affairs of the less fortunate * * * he was the principal author of the alliance, its defender and supporter. His enemies sought to hurt him through the alliance, knowing him to be more vulnerable there than in any other part of his program. For Latin America, Kennedy's passing is a blackening, a tunnel, a gust of cloud and smoke. Until it dissipates, until someone takes up the fallen banner, there will be uncertainty and danger in that part of the world.

COSTA RICA

Immediately upon hearing of the death of President Kennedy on November 22, President Orlich, accompanied by several of his closest advisers, called on the Ambassador to present condolences. Within hours, the Council of Government, "profoundly and grievously moved by the tragic death of the President of the United States, Mr. John F. Kennedy, and feeling the sentiments of sorrow of the Costa Rican Nation," decreed 5 days of national mourning. Within hours, too, the Legislative Assembly had paid final tribute to the President and dispatched a delegation to call on the Ambassador to express its sympathy. Thousands of messages poured in via telephone, telegraph and mail as well as through cards left at the Embassy and chancery. Masses and Protestant services were held during the official period of mourning which ended November 27 with a state funeral service attended by the President, Cabinet, Justices of the Supreme Court, legislators, the diplomatic corps and guests at the Metropolitan Cathedral. Statues of the former President have been proposed in San Jose and in several towns.

Deputy Alberto Canas expressed the deep feeling of the Costa Rican people when he said of President Kennedy that—

When this man spoke, he was saying in a loud voice and beautiful prose, that which we, simple citizens in a small country, were thinking and yearning for. And that sensation, we are sure, has been common to all the simple citizens of the land.

DOMINICAN REPUBLIC

El Caribe reported the tragedy in an extra edition Friday evening. The following day the paper carried a front-page editorial stating that—

Kennedy had undertaken the mission of defending freedom, social justice, and peace in the Western World as an example of American democracy.

The editorial added that—

His death means the offering of one more martyr in the defense of these principles, which are the principles of a free people.

Listin Diario ran a moving biographical editorial entitled "John F. Kennedy, a Profile of Courage." The editorial suggested that "his legacy of justice, courage, and liberty may be converted into a spiritual inheritance, not only for the United States but for all the countries of the world."

ECUADOR

Ecuadorans of all classes, professions, and regions were stunned and universally grieved by the death of President Kennedy. As one Ecuadoran put it, never in the history of the Nation has the death of a world figure so moved and distressed the people. Many donned mourning immediately, and men as well as women were seen weeping in the streets. Flags appeared at half-mast in all parts of Quito, and the grief of the people seemed almost a tangible thing throughout the long, gray, November afternoon.

Reports of the assassination first reached Quito by radio at approximately 2 p.m. on Friday, November 22, and within a half hour a stream of visitors, faces drawn with grief and bewilderment, began to pour through the Embassy gates. Throughout the afternoon and into the evening they came, including the four junta members, Ministers of State, the diplomatic corps, former Presidents and Foreign Ministers, delegations of students, military, businessmen, clergy, and others, most of whom were received personally by the Ambassador. Equally impressive were the numbers of workers, shopkeepers, taxi drivers, men from every walk of life, many in tears, who came or telephoned, each with his own tribute to the man, each expressing an obviously profound sense of personal loss. An estimated 200 to 300 people visited the Embassy during that Friday afternoon, some only to drop cards, some to say a few words of sympathy to the Embassy officers in the lobby to meet them. These visits, both at the Embassy residence and the Chancery, have continued unabated.

The normal rhythm of life in the capital city slowed and seemed almost to halt as the horror of the events in Dallas became known. The strike at Central University, which, in any event, had failed, with only a small minority of the students participating, lost its steam entirely; public absorption in the President's death was total. All other activities and problems seemed tasteless and insignificant.

No single event in memory has received greater news coverage in Ecuador than the assassination of President Kennedy. Immediately following the President's death, all radio stations interrupted their normal programing and carried nothing but news bulletins, memorial programs, and appropriate music. Most stations devoted themselves entirely to relay of the VOA Latin American Spanish transmission. On the afternoon of November 22, for example, 25 of the 26 Guayaquil radio stations were noted to be relaying VOA. During the following 2 days 65 stations throughout Ecuador relayed VOA sporadically, breaking into programing with VOA bulletins. President Kennedy's funeral services—attended by Ecuador's Foreign Minister—were carried in their entirety by a known 91 stations, the largest network in Ecuadoran history. A 2½-hour TV memorial to President Kennedy was shown in Guayaquil and Quito on Saturday evening, November 23, and film coverage of President Johnson's inauguration, as well as President Kennedy's last major address—to the Inter-American Press Association in Miami—were shown on TV in these two cities on November 26. Several newspapers published extra editions on November 22, and all papers devoted almost the entire front page and several interior pages to President Kennedy on November 22 and the 3 days following. To date, in Quito alone, 217 paid announcements expressing condolences have been published in the press by various public and private organizations.

Religious ceremonies honoring President Kennedy began on Saturday, November 23 and have included, thus far, an English language mass at the Quito Anglican Church and innumerable Catholic masses which will continue throughout the officially proclaimed 8 days of national mourning. The focus of religious activity, however, and perhaps the climax of Ecuadoran emotion over the loss of the former President was a pontifical requiem high mass offered by the Embassy and other U.S. missions and said by the Papal Nuncio at the National Cathedral on the morning of November 26. Attended by the junta, Ecuadoran dignitaries, and the diplomatic corps, this mass was a profound tribute to the dead President as an estimated 4,000 to 5,000 Ecuadorans, most of whom had to stand throughout, filled every corner of the cathedral and overflowed into the plaza outside where they listened to the mass and the Nuncio's moving eulogy over loudspeakers. Many were weeping.

The personality of President Kennedy, his programs, ideals, and family life seem to have struck a chord deep within even the simplest, least sophisticated Ecuadoran. The genuine and unreserved grief throughout all strata of Ecuadoran society, down to the last "common man," resulting from his death have revealed the fund of good will, perhaps previously unguessed; for the deceased President and his programs. Although criticism of various U.S. programs in Latin America had been expressed in Ecuador, as elsewhere, and sometimes these voices of criticisms are the only voices heard, there now is little doubt that there exists a wealth of faith in the Alliance for Progress and good will for the United States, which were manifested so vividly only in the spontaneous emotional aftermath of a President's tragic assassination. President Kennedy's death, which was felt as a personal blow to almost every Ecuadoran, has demonstrated the hope of the common man in Ecuador in the one great idea given them by a lost idol, the Alliance for Progress proposed to them by the North American President, John Fitzgerald Kennedy.

EL SALVADOR

Local political developments were completely overshadowed by the tragic news of President Kennedy's death. Many expressions of condolence were tinged with concern over the future of U.S. relations with Latin America, particularly because of the late President's personal identification with the Alliance for Progress, but President Johnson's assurances regarding the continuity of U.S. policy have gone a long way to assuage these fears.

With the arrival of the first reports of the President's death came several personal inquiries from President Rivera to the Chargé, urgently requesting whatever information was available.

On the morning of November 23, President Rivera visited the Embassy with the President of the National Assembly, the President of the Supreme Court, the Foreign Minister and other high dignitaries. He delivered a eulogy to the assembled Embassy staff and the other officials, in which he officially declared a 3-day mourning period.

A memorial mass was conducted at the cathedral on November 25. It was attended by the diplomatic corps, government officials, Americans and Salvadorans of all social classes spontaneously demonstrating their grief.

Thousands of letters and telegrams were received at the Embassy expressing the great sorrow of people from all walks of life.

Salvadorans gathered in groups throughout the center of town and in the markets, overcome with the loss of their friend.

Press reaction to President Kennedy's death was continuous and complete for at least 4 full days. Editorial and news comment on radio and TV, as well as press, was exclusively and deeply sympathetic.

FRENCH WEST INDIES

Martinique and Guadeloupe mourned John Kennedy as one of their own, and the colored people of the islands seem to have placed his memory beside that of Abraham Lincoln in the pantheon of the benefactors of the Negro race. The imagination of humbler folk has established a causal connection between the fact of his assassination and the fact that in life he took up the cause of Negroes. They have concluded that in some sense he was martyred for them.

A solemn high Requiem Mass was sung for the repose of his soul on Monday evening, November 25, in the cathedral of Fort-de-France. The church was packed 20 minutes before services began, and 200 to 300 people crowded outside; this in a town of 80,000. The fervor and intentness of the worshippers, mostly Negroes, was almost palpable.

Groups of 20 to 30 people have been continually in attendance at the USIS window display of photographs of the funeral of the President and of major events in his life. When some move on, others take their place. A good half of them are young people under 20. All week, people have filed in to sign the book of condolences, most of them writing a word of tribute to President Kennedy and of sympathy to his widow and family. Thursday, when schools were closed here, high school students queued up to sign. Repeatedly they would ask for a photograph of the late President.

The wave of shock and sympathy that followed the news of the assassination embraced people of all categories and every social condition, colored and white. Hundreds called personally to present condolences, hundreds of others sent telegrams, cards or letters of sympathy. The principal of a boys' orphanage drove some distance to sign the book of condolences and to say that her young wards had put the institution's flag at half mast immediately upon learning of the President's death, and the president of the local taxi drivers' union, in mourning black, called personally to express the sorrow of his members. Heads of every imaginable kind of association called or wrote on behalf of the membership, people composed poems to his memory, and a town council passed a formal motion of homage saying that President Kennedy "joins the lineage of the great benefactors of humanity."

The French civil and military officials were animated by a chivalrous desire to pay fitting respect to the memory of a man they greatly liked and respected. The prefect and all his ranking associates came in full dress uniform to the mass sung in the President's honor, as did the commanding general and some 20 of his senior officers. The general, at his own initiative

and not at our request, had an honor guard and the military band in front of the cathedrals, and the two national anthems were played before the official procession entered the nave of the church.

GUATEMALA

The shocking news of the assassination of President Kennedy, and the President's funeral, monopolized Guatemala's attention this week. The Embassy and other U.S. Government agencies received hundreds of telegrams, letters, telephone calls, and personal visits of condolence from representatives of all sectors of Guatemalan life; and many labor, student, commercial, and other organizations issued formal proclamations of sorrow and indignation over the terrible crime.

The Government of Guatemala, in a proclamation which eulogized the late President and took special note of his efforts to promote the development of Latin America and of his consideration for Guatemala, declared 3 days of national mourning.

Diario de Centro America, the Government newspaper, declared that—

Central America keeps for Kennedy its highest affection and will not forget that he was the first President of the United States who honored the Isthmus. For Latin Americans he, who was the youngest U.S. President and the first Catholic in the White House, will always be remembered as the creator of the 10-point plan that, in the historic meeting of Punta del Este, was transformed into the monumental Inter-American Program of the Alliance for Progress—the first collective strike against the viciousness of economic underdevelopment.

HONDURAS

The assassination of President Kennedy November 22 caused shock and profound grief throughout Honduras and completely overshadowed internal concerns throughout most of the week. The Government decreed 3 days of official mourning and late in the day Chief of Government Col. Oswaldo Lopez made a statement over a nationwide radio hookup, warmly praising President Kennedy as a true friend of Latin America and lamenting his shocking and untimely death.

The report of the assassination was immediately followed by visits to the Embassy, and also the AID and USIS offices, from individuals and representatives of organizations offering their condolences. The Embassy has also received several hundred telegrams and letters of condolence and a number of floral wreaths.

MEXICO

The death of President Kennedy caused an unprecedented manifestation of shock and grief in all sectors of Mexican life. Immediately upon the receipt of the first bulletin on the assassination, arrangements were made for Mexican television stations to hook up directly with U.S. networks via microwave. The Mexican television audience was given approximately 14 hours daily of direct broadcasts from the United States in this unprecedented public service coverage and at considerable cost and loss of revenue to the Mexican stations.

More than 4,000 Mexicans from all walks of life came in a steady stream to sign the condolence books in the Embassy lobby, while many dignitaries personally presented their condolences to the Ambassador. The Embassy switchboard was jammed on the day of the assassination and calls offering condolences continued to be received throughout the weekend. Large numbers of Mexican families followed the funeral mass on television in their homes, many of them kneeling in prayer before their sets. Most churches in Mexico offered special masses and services in memory of the President, and the mass at the Basilica of Guadalupe, where President and Mrs. Kennedy worshiped during their visit here, was attended by an overflow crowd including a large part of the diplomatic corps. Another mass was held at the National Cathedral and special services were scheduled at Protestant churches and synagogues throughout the city.

The press was completely dominated by the tragic news and subsequent events, and was filled with eulogies of the late President. Almost every editorial declared that the world has lost a great statesman and they spoke of President Kennedy as a true friend of Mexico.

There are now numerous reports of movements underway to name a street in Mexico City, a park, and a school after President Kennedy, and a report has also been heard of erecting a statue of him in Mexico City.

Excelsior:

We are sure that under the Presidency of the ex-Senator from Texas the relations between the White House and Mexico will continue friendly. Clear indication of this is his declaration of friendship made to the Government and people of Mexico.

In another editorial:

Notwithstanding that John F. Kennedy left behind a formidable luminous star in the White House, President Johnson will not be a poorly defined and opaque figure. He is a capable citizen and worthy of his post. A man of political vocation and great skill.

La Prensa: Banner headline: "Forward the Alliance, Says Johnson." The paper editorially cited Johnson as a true friend of Mexico and said:

The only thing desired is that he maintain the ideals of Kennedy.

Novedades:

The neighboring country continues its forward march, still carrying the spiritual havoc of its tragedy, but with a singleness of purpose and a resolve to rise above adversity. This is an example of a moral consistency and an institutional strength which highlights the excellent features of a solid and harmonious democracy.

NICARAGUA

The practically unanimous demonstration of mourning for the late President John F. Kennedy, which has been exhibited by all sectors of Nicaraguan life, is overwhelmingly impressive. It is hard to imagine how Nicaraguans could or would have shown deeper and more genuine sadness if the assassinated Chief of State had been a well-loved President of Nicaragua itself.

President Schick issued a proclamation expressing profound regret and decreed 8 days of official mourning in Nicaragua. He also canceled all public observances of his birthday the following day, November 23.

In a great variety of official and unofficial circles the reaction was likewise prompt and spontaneous. The Nicaraguan Military Academy canceled the gala dance with which it was going to cap the climax of its anniversary celebrations on November 22. The professional baseball league, with the season in full swing, canceled all games for the day in Nicaragua's No. 1 sport. The Club Terraza, one of Managua's principal social clubs, postponed until December the annual debutante ball for which Managua's Garden Club had spent hundreds of dollars and scores of hours in preparation.

The Ambassador and other Embassy personnel began to receive telephone calls and personal visits in ever-increasing numbers as soon as the tragic news came over all Managua's radio stations, which canceled programs to play funeral music between news bulletins the rest of the day. In the late afternoon the Ambassador and Mrs. Brown, accompanied by personnel of the Embassy and other U.S. Government missions here, received a constant flood of visitors expressing condolences at the Embassy residence.

Meanwhile, Nicaraguan press and radio organs have been outdoing each other, not only in news coverage of the startling events but also their own expressions of regret and mourning. Editorials in all the daily newspapers and broadcasts by prominent local radio commentators have produced several notable examples of unusual eloquence

The tragic death of President Kennedy was clearly felt throughout Nicaragua. The Ambassador has attended Requiem Masses at Leon and Granada. Eyewitnesses have told us of the sincere consternation felt by peasants in rural areas when news of the tragedy reached them. The Embassy has been swamped with telegrams of regret and condolences from all over the country, coming from local officials, schoolteachers, and ordinary citizens.

In all the tremendous display of Nicaraguan emotion, no event was more touching than the visit to the Embassy chancery on the afternoon of November 25 of some 200 children from the Larreynaga public school, who had marched 6 kilometers from their school in an outlying district of Managua, carrying American and Nicaraguan flags linked with black ribbon, and led by the school principal and four teachers. Under the principal's direction, the school children marched to the Embassy flagpole, each boy and girl carrying a flower or two, which had been picked from woods and fields and were half wilted from the long hot march in the children's hands. At the base of the flagpole with its half-masted flag, they deposited their flowers in the form of letters until they had spelled the Spanish word "dolor"—"grief."

Standing then by his pupils' flowers, the principal made a heart-warming speech of tribute to President Kennedy on behalf of his school, its teachers and pupils and pupils' parents, from a very humble section of the city. After the reporting officer attempted a grateful reply and the students closed their ceremony singing the Nic-

araguan national anthem, they reassembled for the 6-kilometer march back home. Behind them by the flagpole they left their wilted wild flowers and an overwhelmed little group of Americans.

PANAMA

The Government of Panama and its people joined the rest of the world in displaying deep sorrow and shock at the death of President John F. Kennedy.

The National Assembly on November 23 approved a resolution "sharing the deep sorrow of the United States to which Panama is linked by special bonds." Assemblymen then paused for a moment of silence and adjourned the session for the remainder of the day as a tribute to the fallen President. In public statements, letters, telegrams, and press releases, civic and professional organizations, political parties of every coloration, labor unions, schools, businessmen's groups, government agencies, the supreme court, political and society leaders, and the man in the street have voiced their shock and dismay at what they consider a tragedy for the United States and all the world. School children, government officials, and citizens from every walk of life have called at the Embassy for expressions of sympathy and to sign the condolence book. A special Requiem Mass November 25 at Panama City's Metropolitan Cathedral was thronged by Panamanians and Americans.

PERU

All local events were subordinated to the tragic death of President Kennedy during the past week. The reaction of the Peruvian Government was immediate. President Fernando Belaunde Terry was conducting a Cabinet meeting when he was informed and immediately drove to the Embassy accompanied by his entire Cabinet to express his shock and dismay to Ambassador Jones. Belaunde declared November 25 a day of official national mourning. His visit to the Chancery was followed by a stream of visitors from both high and low who wanted to show their deep sense of regret and solidarity with the United States. The three American churches in Lima held memorial services on Sunday, and on Monday a High Requiem Mass in honor of President Kennedy was said in the church of Santa Maria Reyna attended by the President, the Prime Minister, the Presidents of both Houses of Congress, the President of the Supreme Court, Cabinet Ministers, members of the Diplomatic Corps, and private citizens from all walks of life. The Congress also passed a resolution calling for the award of the Nobel Peace Prize to President Kennedy. The love and respect held by the people of Peru for the late President were also evident in the outpouring of messages and spontaneous demonstrations of grief and loss from all sides.

The people of Arequipa took the sudden death of President John F. Kennedy as a personal loss. From all walks of life—authorities, professional men, businessmen, teachers, students, trade unionists, laborers, and the poor—came to the consulate and to the consul's residence, to express their grief and sympathy, often in tears. Telegrams, letters, cards and telephone calls flooded the consulate to manifest condolence. Many Arequipenos canceled social engagements and flew the Peruvian flag at half-mast with a black ribbon above it to demonstrate their deep sorrow. The Cathedral of Arequipa, which held its first Requiem Mass for a foreign President on November 25, was packed with mourners. Religious services were also held throughout the city in honor of President Kennedy. The mayor proposed that a street of Arequipa be named after the late President.

URUGUAY

Uruguayans in general respected President Kennedy highly and a large majority gave him their sympathy and even affection. His death, therefore, struck this small country perhaps as deeply as the death of one of its own leaders. The National Council of Government met in special session Friday evening, November 22, as did the Senate and the Chamber of Deputies. Speakers of all political persuasions eulogized the President, and the Parliament, at the request of the NCG, unanimously voted the day of the President's funeral a day of national mourning. Perhaps more significant and more meaningful was the reaction of the people of Uruguay, from the humblest to the wealthiest. Many expressed their sorrow and condolence for the American people in a flood of messages and calls on the Embassy, including a silent march of some 3,000 people from the center of Montevideo to the Embassy residence on November 22, a distance of about 2 miles.

VENEZUELA

The image of President Kennedy was far greater in Venezuela than the Embassy realized. The outpouring of condolences from all sectors of Venezuelan life, from President Betancourt to humble campesinos, took the form of telegrams, letters, telephone calls, and personal visits. Hundreds paid their respects to the Ambassador at the residence and at the chancery, where guest books were signed. Despite the fact Venezuela was in the final stage of a heated, emotional political campaign, the country seemed numb with the news. Political parades and speeches were stilled for 3 days of Venezuelan mourning, even though last weekend was expected to see the climax of political activity. Venezuelans were choked with emotion. News coverage here of the President's assassination and the funeral was probably the most complete of any major event in history. All radio stations played funeral music during the 3-day Venezuelan mourning period, and 52 of them were hooked up to the USIS radio studio for direct relay of the Voice of America broadcast of the funeral. Newspapers and magazines devoted page after page to news and features on President Kennedy and President Johnson. All television stations carried hours of programing on President Kennedy, including newsreel coverage out of Dallas.

On November 26 Venezuelan authorities announced that the newly built AID-financed housing project being dedicated that day near the Caracas area is being named "Barrio John Fitzgerald Kennedy" to commemorate the late President's leadership in the Alliance for Progress.

All these words are not in vain, or mere bombast, as our partners realize as well as we what is ahead. In the words of one envoy who heard President Johnson's pronouncement—reported by R. H. Boyce, Scripps-Howard staff writer:

> Johnson is wise to continue the Alliance program. He couldn't quickly change it if he wanted to. The Alliance is a program already underway. Its ideals are perfect. Its success depends on how well those ideals are practiced—on both sides of the Rio Grande.

Mr. President, during the past several weeks I have received many letters from the young people of my State expressing their own distress at the tragic death of our late President.

To these young people, as to their parents, John Kennedy stood for a future of peace, of service, of commitment to ideals. To these young people, he stood for what was best and fine and decent in our political life. His death moved them deeply and it is important to acknowledge their efforts to express their grief.

The high school paper in Albert Lea, Minn., dedicated an entire issue to the late President. It showed great maturity and understanding on the part of the students.

Mr. President, as recognition to all the young Americans who mourn President Kennedy, I ask that the editorial by Joan Graham of Albert Lea be printed as follows:

Irony Should Sober Citizens

(By Joan Graham)

The body of a great man lay in state in a giant rotunda in Washington, D.C., and a quarter of a million people waited outside in the cold for a chance to file past his coffin.

The body of another man lay in a Fort Worth funeral home, but nobody came—not even his immediate family.

A funeral was held in St. Matthew's Cathedral in Washington, D.C. It was attended by hundreds of dignitaries from all parts of the world, and carried on coast-to-coast television. Millions mourned.

That same afternoon another funeral took place somewhere in Texas. Another man was buried, but there were no dignitaries. There were no mourners.

A little girl knelt with her mother and kissed the coffin of her daddy. A little boy saluted it.

Two other children, undoubtedly unaware of the fact that their father was dead, paid no such respects. Nobody paid respects.

The man to whom the homage was paid loved and was loved by all. People of all races and walks of life were saddened by his tragic death because they felt that they had lost a leader who had discarded personal prejudices and respected them because they were human beings like himself. He represented love and all that is good and just—and the people wept.

The other man—the one in Texas—was loved by no one. He represented hate, prejudice, arrogance, violence, disrespect, and all that is evil.

What a dignified and wonderful world it would be if everyone would adopt the standard which they so admired in John Fitzgerald Kennedy, and denounce those which they despised in his assassin.

Mr. President, many of the young people who have written to me of their feelings on the death of the President have enclosed poems which they have composed. One of the young teenagers who has sent a poem is Linda Jean Miller, a student at Northeast Junior High School in Minneapolis.

Mr. President, as another indication of the impact of the President's death on our young people, I ask that Miss Miller's poem be printed as follows:

Portrait of a Great President

The world now mourns a precious man,
Who under his world freedom plan
Brought greater union to us all,
That peace on Earth might be our call.

A man of love and faith was he,
Who led, that man might peaceful be.
His courage and his wisdom great
Saved every land from tragic fate.

Tasks of challenge he did take,
For this a greater world would make.
His smile, his face, his friendly wave
Man ne'er forgets. His life he gave.

His voice, his words, his love of life,
Rang out in speech through lasting strife.
"Ask not what your country can do for you,
But what, for your country, you can do."

Let shine the flame of freedom's light,
That all the lands may shine as bright.
E'en though in silence he does lie,
He in our hearts shall never die.

His strength had come from Heav'n above,
With gifts of power, peace, and love.
His great ideals are set for all,
That a world of liberty may never fall.

He was humble, which made him truly great,
He was kind, which changed most people's hate.
He loved mankind, and they in return
Loved him, who let peace's light yet burn.

For no man did as much as he,
To make our world more great and free.
A dedicated man of priceless worth,
Our President Kennedy has left this earth.
　　　　　　　　　　　　—*Linda Jean Miller.*

Mr. President, many eulogies and statements have been made, here and all over the world, wherever men have attempted to communicate their sorrow to others. The words have reflected the deep shock and grief which the world suffered due to the death of our beloved President, John F. Kennedy.

Last Tuesday the entire day was set aside to eulogize the President; but still there are thoughts unsaid, sorrow unassuaged.

The Cooperative League of the United States released a statement which is noteworthy for its positive tone and its resolution in the face of calamity. It is a pledge, on the part of 15 million Americans that they will persevere, that they will dedicate themselves anew to the ideals which President Kennedy so ably characterized in his words and demonstrated in his actions. This is the spirit which now must fill all American hearts. Though the man is gone, the tasks he set for himself and for the country yet lie before us. He would have us continue.

Mr. President, I ask that the statement of the Cooperative League of the U.S.A. be made a part of these tributes.

VOORHIS ASSERTS COOPERATIVE'S SUPPORT OF NEW UNITY IN NATION

(On behalf of the Cooperative League of the U.S.A., the member organizations of which encompass some 15 million U.S. families, Jerry Voorhis, executive director of the league, issued the following statement Monday, November 25.)

In the name of the Cooperative League of the United States and on behalf of its several million thoughtful and devoted members, this statement is made and this pledge affirmed:

First. We share with every true citizen of our country an overwhelming sense of grief and shame. Our President has been struck down. In the very midst of his work for peace, for equality, for freedom, and for a better life for man, the gun of a miserable assassin has murdered him.

John F. Kennedy died a martyr to the cause of the welfare of his fellow human beings.

Not since the murder of another great President, Abraham Lincoln, at a time and under circumstances all too similar to those of this hour, has our Nation appeared in such a tragic light before the world.

What, then, shall we do?

We shall herewith resolve with all our souls that, in Lincoln's own words, "these dead shall not have died in vain."

We shall begin by seeing clearly that both President Lincoln and President Kennedy were killed in the midst of their work for human reconciliation and for the equal dignity of all human beings. And we shall solemnly dedicate ourselves to working with quadrupled effort to put these principles into practice in the everyday activities of life. As it happens, they lie at the very core of the objectives to serve which the Cooperative League of the U.S.A. exists. Had we worked with greater effect toward reaching them, the President might not have had to die.

Second. We shall dedicate ourselves to helping to bring about the "real change in the temper of our times" for which the Chicago Sun-Times, in an editorial of sheer greatness, called with these words:

"Those who impugn the motives of our national leaders, who defy the courts, distort the operations of the United Nations, or advocate a change in our form of government, might not themselves do violence. But they engender the kind of hate that must have been in the eyes that lined up Mr. Kennedy's head in the crosshairs of a rifle sight.

"The right of dissent, the exercise of free speech, must not corrode into sullen rebellion that breeds violence. All Americans, those who agree with their Government's policies and those who disagree, must stand together on this fundamental and demonstrate this unity by action as well as words."

Third, we reaffirm our own stand on this fundamental of unity within diversity. The longstanding policy of open membership of the Cooperative League does not mean that the organization countenances persons whose beliefs commit them to actions which would destroy the very cooperatives in which they have been accepted in membership.

This stand is spelled out in the membership policy of the Cooperative League of the U.S.A. as follows:

"Membership in cooperatives is open to all people of good will regardless of race, creed, or economic status. But cooperatives are not called upon to admit to membership * * * persons who hold beliefs which render it impossible for them to desire the success of cooperatives as a basic solution to human problems.

"Therefore, it is the policy of the Cooperative League of the United States that no person who holds to a belief in totalitarian government, whether Communist or Fascist, is eligible for or properly admissible to membership in an American cooperative society."

In times like these there can be no room within our cooperative organizations for those who, whatever their professions to the contrary, are necessarily committed to objectives as foreign to those of true cooperatives as night is to day.

Fourth, we shall find in our new President, Lyndon B. Johnson, a man as worthy by experience, by nature, and by character to assume the awesome burdens of the Presidency in these tragic hours as providence and the good judgment of men could have provided us. To him we pledge, as to every President, but especially to him in present circumstances our support, our labors, and our unswerving loyalty.

And fifth, we shall go forward in a spirit which was—perhaps prophetically—outlined in an editorial in the official magazine of the Cooperative League, Co-op Report, only 3 short weeks before the tragedy of November 22. The editorial reads in part as follows:

"All of us must fulfill one primary duty, of understanding why those with whom we disagree think as they do.

"If we—all of us on both sides of every issue—do this, honestly and fairly, we shall learn to respect once more the rights and opinions of others, and to treat and regard them as good citizens—however sharply and deeply we may disagree with them.

"Our Nation never needed a basic unity of purpose and unity of spirit as it needs them now. Those who destroy that unity by hate, bitterness, false accusation and name-calling, should consider whether in their drive to have their own way completely, they are not in the process going to make it impossible for our American rights and freedoms to continue to exist at all.

"It's a hard and often not very satisfying role—but what our country needs now is a larger and larger number of reasonable middle-of-the-roaders who will work as hard as the extremists do, who will hold those extremists in check and blunt their unreasoning bitterness—and save our Nation from the tragedies of civil strife which now threatens to engulf us."

If the struggle of the forces of freedom and peace against

tyranny and violence is to be won for freedom in the world today, it will be won by the methods of John F. Kennedy and those who carry forward the principles and ideals for which he stood. We pledge ourselves to carry forward that struggle by those methods.

Mr. President, not only was it remarkable that there was such a universal outpouring of deep sorrow at the assassination of our late President John F. Kennedy, but the quality of the tributes were so high. We have all read many which have enriched us. Recently, I was moved again by a eulogy delivered by Bishop Kellogg in the Cathedral Church of St. Mark, in Minneapolis, Minn.

[From the Minnesota Missionary, December 1963]

A Eulogy—John F. Kennedy

(By Bishop Kellogg)

A few days ago, the postman brought to my door, as I imagine to the doors of many of you, a magazine with a nationwide circulation. The date on the cover was December 3, 1963—magazines always seem to bear an advance date—but that was not what was important; the important thing was the cover picture: It was a picture of a handsome little boy, who today has his third birthday, and his equally handsome father.

On the day that this magazine with this picture came to my door, it was just another magazine with a joyous and meaningful picture. However, now it will become, I am sure, one of the most cherished and treasured pictures in history. It is an unforgettable picture. The little boy's name was "John-John," and the equally handsome father's name was John Fitzgerald Kennedy, 35th President of the United States.

Then, came Friday, November 22, and a shot rang out like a clap of thunder. It left that little boy without a father, and it left the father without the breath of life. Above all, it left a Nation without its elected leader, and shocked, and stunned beyond belief.

When the shock had passed a little, one's mind roved back to 98 plus years in time to April 14, 1865, also a Friday, when a shot was fired in Ford's Theater in Washington, which also deprived a little boy of his father, and a Nation of a great leader, and left it in mourning, and in shock.

As one looked upon the picture of Lee Harvey Oswald on the front pages of the newspapers, he could not help but think of that other Presidential assassin, John Wilkes Booth. They had much in common. They both were disturbed men, in whose hearts, hate—the result of wounded pride and imagined wrong—lingered until it flowered in tragedy. Both men were contemptuous of constituted authority.

Lincoln was 56 when an assassin's bullet felled him. John Fitzgerald Kennedy was a decade younger, 46, when a dreadful and violent act resulted in his death. Though their Presidencies were a century apart, these two men had much in common, besides the fact that their lives were taken by assassin's bullets. They both believed in, and fought hard to the best of their ability, and the fullness of their strength, for the dignity of human kind, and for the equality of all men under God, regardless of color, creed or race. Both the 16th and the 35th Presidents believed with all their hearts, and fought with all their might, and with all their wisdom for equal justice and equal opportunity, for all men.

Last Friday, as I listened to the radio and television announcements, and subsequently, read the newspaper reports of what happened on that grim day of infamy, I was reminded of "Jim" Bishop's book "The Day Lincoln Was Shot." Before our very eyes, the events of that fateful day passed in review in all their stark reality, and in trigger-quick succession.

The morning of April 14, 1865, dawned soft and sunny on the Nation's Capitol. The lilacs were in eager bloom. The willows clothed their graceful boughs with a new green—spring had come. The war was over. There was no longer any doubt of that. Early on that very morning, final word had come, and everyone rejoiced. Even the countless multitude who were mourning their beloved dead felt the common thrill of a new joyousness. James Russell Lowell wrote to his good friend, Charles Norton: "The news, my dear Charles, is from Heaven." Lincoln was the happiest of all. There was a new spring in his step; the bowed shoulders were uplifted.

Last Friday in Dallas, likewise, was a sunny and soft day, Jacqueline and John Kennedy were together. Their cup of happiness was full to the brim. It was a joyful day, and the sun in the sky was reflected in their faces, just as it must have been reflected in their hearts, too. Then, the shot rang out. There was a careening and mad dash to Parkland Hospital. It was too late.

John Fitzgerald Kennedy served his country both in peace and war. In war, he was wounded, and this wound left him with an almost intolerably painful back. While recuperating after one of the operations, which was performed to remove the injury, and to restore full usefulness, Mr. Kennedy wrote a book entitled "Profiles in Courage." Although I am sure he himself never so thought, the title of this book more nearly provided a title for his own life, than any other which could be suggested.

During the 2 years, 10 months, and 2 days of his Presidency, John Fitzgerald Kennedy was confronted with many occasions which required consummate courage, as well as consummate leadership and tact. Among these, of course, there were those last days of October and the first days of November, 1962, when he and his colleagues stood eyeball to eyeball with the Russians over the removal of the missiles from Cuba. In an autumn of anxiety, he exhibited that there was, within him, an invincible summer.

Whatever may be said or written to commemorate John Fitzgerald Kennedy, it will be inadequate. Whatever building or monument may be constructed in his name will fail to measure the fullness of his stature. The most fitting memorial—the one enshrined in the hearts and minds of his family, his numberless friends, and the people of this Nation—will be the continuation of the great projects to which he dedicated himself so completely and so wholeheartedly.

Let all of us strive to keep alive and bright the memory of this courageous and dynamic man who, in a short time, fulfilled a long time and became a great leader among men.

It is far too early to measure his achievements, or the impact of his Presidency, either upon this Nation or upon the world. It also is too early to measure what his loss will mean, both to the progress and stability of the Nation, and to the progress and stability of the world. Nevertheless, regardless of the political philosophy to which each one of us may subscribe, if we are honest, we know that he was a courageous man—a towering pine among the trees of mankind—a fitting mast for the ship of state. By martyrizing him, the assassin insured his historic immortality.

Today, at his funeral in Washington, the great and powerful of the earth have gathered to salute and to pay tribute to his memory. Not since that day, more than 60 years ago—May 20, 1910—when 9 rulers of Europe, several heirs apparent, and 40 imperial and royal highnesses, representing 70 nations, assembled in London for the funeral of King Edward VII—has so much rank been gathered together, as has gathered today in Washington, representing 91 nations, to salute and pay tribute to John Fitzgerald Kennedy. But this gathering of rank is more than a salute and tribute to John Fitzgerald Kennedy—it is a salute and tribute to the United States of America, the land of the free, and we hope that it also always will be the land of the brave.

Our prayers and profoundest sympathy go out to the bereaved family—to Caroline, and little John-John; but most of all to the beautiful and dry-eyed widow, who, last Friday, just before the casket was closed, leaned over and kissed her husband, took off her wedding ring, and pressed it into his hand; a symbol of a love and loyalty that not even an assassin's bullet could destroy. It also would seem appropriate and fitting that, in our prayers, we ask Almighty God to forgive not only the assassin, and the assassin's assassin, but all of us, for whatever responsibility we as a people may have had in this tragedy, praying that He will bless, keep and preserve our country, bringing to people of all religions, concord, peace, and unity of spirit.

On the night of April 14, 1865, as the President and Mrs. Lincoln sat in Ford's Theater, where they had gone to see Laura Keene in "Our American Cousin," many plans went through Lincoln's mind. Among them was to go as soon as circumstances would permit to Palestine. A yearning had come over him to tread those holy fields over whose acres walked those blessed feet nailed for our advantage on the bitter cross.

He looked at Mrs. Lincoln, and said that there was no place he wished to see as much as Jerusalem. The word was but half finished on his lips. She heard him whisper "Jeru." Then, a bullet as cruel and senseless as that one fired last Friday, sped all too straight to its mark. Abraham Lincoln started for Jerusalem, but it was: "Jerusalem, the golden—the home of God's elect."

And, I believe, that John Fitzgerald Kennedy now is embarked on the same glorious journey to the same glorious place.

Mr. President, Dr. Jerome B. Wiesner, the special assistant to the President for science and technology, has written a deeply moving eulogy of the late President Kennedy which appeared in Science magazine, on November 29, 1963.

His remembrance of President Kennedy perceptively captures the true spirit of a man whose vision and outlook made it easy for him to understand the social significance of modern science and technology.

In this age of technological revolution we are fortunate to have such wise and dedicated men as Dr. Wiesner serving as science adviser to the President.

I share with him this sense of great loss he felt for a leader who, though he had no background or training in scientific matters, nevertheless, had a quick, almost instinctive understanding of problems once he was given the facts.

I ask unanimous consent that the article by Dr. Wiesner be printed at this point.

[From Science magazine, Nov. 29, 1963]

JOHN F. KENNEDY: A REMEMBRANCE

"His respect for science as an instrument of good was one of the Chief Executive's distinctive qualities"—Jerome B. Wiesner.

(The following was written especially for Science by the late President's special assistant for science and technology.)

Never have I been given a more difficult task. To put into words the true spirit and charm and intelligence of John F. Kennedy would be impossible even for a writer far more gifted than I. It would take the telling of many tales, a description of his handling of problems large and small, a detailed history of his 3 brief years as a world leader, to show his true greatness.

I have just returned from Arlington National Cemetery where thousands of people from all over the world paid their last respects to the man who had given them so much hope. It was a beautiful, cold, sunshiny day, the kind he loved. One could almost call it a New England day. The day was like the President, radiant and crisp. He added something indescribable to every occasion; his smile brightened it, his humor livened it. He had a quick and often sardonic humor and a quick mind. To these he added an optimism about the future and a determination to bring out the maximum capabilities of our people, and, indeed, of all mankind. He was an intelligent, educated man. He was a kindly man. I never knew him to do a mean thing to any person. He was never too busy for a word of greeting. He had a strong temper but one that subsided quickly. Challenged, he responded firmly. Big problems were never allowed to submerge the small, today's problems to obscure tomorrow's. At the height of the great crises of his tenure—the Bay of Pigs disaster, the resumption of nuclear testing by the Soviet Union, Mississippi, Birmingham, the confrontation with the Soviet Union over the missile installations in Cuba—he still talked about the future. He retained his monumental interest in the details of the ongoing business of government. He read an amazing amount, and seemingly remembered it all. He often asked about obscure stories concerning science buried in the New York Times or the London Observer or any one of the dozens of papers and periodicals he somehow found time to read.

VISION AND OUTLOOK

I met Jack Kennedy while he was a Senator from my home State of Massachusetts. He needed advice on technical matters, particularly military technology and nuclear test ban, issues then occupying much of my time. I agreed to help largely because friends asked me to and because he was my Senator. I heard from him only infrequently at first and saw him even less. But even those brief contacts caused me to admire him, so that I readily agreed to join up and provide what little help I could when he became the Democratic candidate for the Presidency. Many things impressed me then and drew me to him. There was, of course, his charm but there was much more. I was most impressed by his quick, almost instinctive understanding of problems once he was given the facts. His background ill prepared him for an interest in scientific matters, yet his interest was lively. He was, in fact, then a member of the Harvard University visiting committee. Obviously unprepared to understand the theory of scientific subjects, he tried to get a physical feel of the matter. For example, he was forever trying to get someone to explain electromagnetic propagation comprehensibly. He didn't call it that. He wanted to know how radio worked. But when one tried to answer, one learned that the question was not about electron tubes or transistors or coils—these were manmade things which he could believe—but why and how did nature really allow energy to be sent through space.

Someone called him a truly modern man, this first American President to be born in the 20th century. And he was that. He had confidence in and used the modern tools. In a real sense technological marvels gave him his chance to be President. Without the airplane and television, he would not have been able to wage his successful campaign in 1960. And he never forgot this. His vision and outlook made it easy for him to understand other products of technology. President Kennedy, better than any political figure I have known, understood the social sigificance of modern science and technology.

As I try to remember the things that impressed me most about the President, four qualities stand out: his intelligence, his hopefulness, his sense of history, his striving for excellence. All of us who worked with him were proud of him. His very appearance, his composure, his sensitivity for every situation led us to an ever-growing admiration. He was the President from the very beginning, and as he was tested in his terrible job, he grew.

His vision and perfectionism may best be seen in his speeches. He had a vision of what he thought the world could be, and he projected this in his poetic prose. His inaugural address set the plan for his administration, and he strove consistently to reach the goals he set then. He said, "To those peoples in the huts and villages of half the globe struggling to break the bonds of mass misery, we pledge our best efforts to help them help themselves, for whatever period is required—not because the Communists may be doing it, not because we seek their votes, but because it is right. If a free society cannot help the many who are poor, it cannot save the few who are rich."

And about the arms race, "Finally, to those nations who would make themselves our adversary, we offer not a pledge but a request: that both sides begin anew the quest for peace, before the dark powers of destruction unleashed by science engulf all humanity in planned or accidental self-destruction. * * * Let both sides explore what problems unite us instead of belaboring those problems which divide us. Let both sides, for the first time, formulate serious and precise proposals for the inspection and control of arms—and bring the absolute power to destroy other nations under the absolute control of all nations."

Much of President Kennedy's hopefulness was derived from his conviction that science provided our Nation with vast powers for good. In the inaugural speech, he summed this up with, "Let both sides seek to invoke the wonders of science instead of its terrors. Together let us explore the stars, conquer the deserts, eradicate disease, tap the ocean depths and encourage the arts and commerce." He was ever pressing to put technology to work. In foreign affairs, for helping other nations, for insuring our security, in seeking solutions to our domestic problems, he looked to science for the clues.

NATIONAL ACADEMY SPEECHES

Twice he responded to invitations to speak before the National Academy of Sciences, and, as far as I know, set a precedent for presidential attendance at academy functions.

On April 25, 1961, the President, in dedicating the new wing of the academy, disregarded his prepared text and in an eloquent extemporaneous talk revealed his sensitive understanding of the necessary cooperation between the Government and the scientific community. In calling upon the academy and the scientific community, the President remarked:

"This country must move forward, and most of the areas where we must move forward involve most sophisticated problems which your experience and training can help us to solve. One of the problems, it seems to me, of a free society is the fact that all of the questions which we must decide now are extremely sophisticated questions. It is difficult enough for those who hold office, either in the administration or in the Congress, to attempt to make a determination between alternate courses of action—fiscal policy, monetary policy, agricultural policy, international policy, disarmament, arms control, all the rest, all of these involve questions to confound the experts. For those of us who are not expert and yet must be called upon to make decisions which involve the security of our country, which involve the expenditures of hundreds of millions of billions of dollars, we must turn, in the last resort, to objective, disinterested scientists who bring a strong sense of public responsibility and public obligation. So this academy is most important."

Again, on October 22, 1963, a month to the day before the tragic events in Texas, the President appeared before the academy on the occasion of its anniversary convocation and he emphasized the importance of basic scientific investigations, the contributions that science can make to international objectives, and the interdisciplinary and intercultural aspects of science in playing its role in modern society. He also dwelt on a theme that he many times expressed, the need for applying the results of scientific and technological advances to the conservation and development of natural resources. During his relatively brief stay in office he gave physical meaning to these objectives.

On the subject of basic scientific research, the President said in his last academy speech:

"But if basic research is to be properly regarded, it must be better understood. I ask you to reflect on this problem and on the means by which, in the years to come, our society can assure continuing backing to fundamental research in the life sciences, the physical sciences, the social sciences, on natural resources, on agriculture, on protection against pollution and erosion. Together, the scientific community, the government, industry, and education must work out the way to nourish American science in all its power and vitality."

President Kennedy regarded international scientific cooperative activities and scientific exchanges as one of the strongest bridges to other nations, and at the academy celebration he expanded on this view. "I would suggest that science is already moving to enlarge its influence in three general ways: in the interdisciplinary area, in the international area, and in the intercultural area. For science is the most powerful means we have for the unification of knowledge, and a main obligation of its future must be to deal with problems which cut across boundaries, whether boundaries between the sciences, boundaries between nations, or boundaries between man's scientific and his humane concerns."

He closed his talk with an anecdote that revealed the strength of his conviction about the importance of basic research to the country's future when he remarked, "the great French Marshal Lyautey once said to his gardener: 'Plant a tree tomorrow.' And the gardener said, 'It won't bear fruit for a hundred years.' 'In that case,' said Lyautey to the gardener, 'plant it this afternoon.'" "That is how I feel about your work," said the President.

BASIC RESEARCH AND MANPOWER

Under the President's leadership there has been a substantial strengthening of the basic research grants of the National Science Foundation in recognition not only of the need for the results of such research, but also of the essential role of basic research in the training of new scientists. In a news conference on January 15, 1962, the President expressed his concern about the future adequacy of our scientific and technical manpower in referring to a study of Soviet technical manpower that had just been published by the National Science Foundation. He said, "This has been a matter of some concern to me for some time because one of the most critical problems facing this Nation is the inadequacy of the supply of scientific and technical manpower, to

satisfy the expanding requirements of this country's research and development efforts in the near future." He called upon the President's Science Advisory Committee, in cooperation with the Federal Council for Science and Technology, to report as quickly as possible on the specific measures that could be taken to develop the necessary, well qualified scientists and engineers, and he reinforced his personal concern with the words, "To all those who may be within the sound of my voice or who may follow your stories in the papers, I want to emphasize the great new and exciting field of the sciences." Following a submission of the Science Advisory Committee report of December 1962 on needs for graduate training in engineering, mathematics, and physical sciences, the President's 1964 budget for the National Science Foundation reflected his acceptance of the PSAC judgment of the importance of increased support for graduate education. This is also reflected in his proposed legislation to increase the number of fellowships under the National Defense Education Act, and in his extemporaneous remarks at the National Academy celebration he expressed his deep disappointment in the failure of the Congress to support this program.

SPACE PROGRAM

During his administration he made persistent efforts to strengthen the U.S. space program. He saw in it the opportunity to serve many national needs. He was firmly convinced that Soviet space supremacy had greatly weakened the United States in its foreign affairs. He saw military hazards in a lagging space capability. He saw the exploration of space as one of the great human adventures of this century, and he appreciated the important scientific possibilities of space exploration. He dedicated this Nation to a massive space program with a firm target of a manned lunar landing in this decade. This is a costly program and his decision to undertake it was not made lightly. He talked to hundreds of people in the process of making his decision and he weighed the costs with real concern. In the end he became convinced that the United States could not remain second in this important field. Despite continual review, he remained convinced of the correctness of this course.

Yet with the closing of the gap between United States and U.S.S.R. outer space capabilities, he followed through his inaugural theme with the proposal to the U.S.S.R. for a joint moon venture.

He also followed through on his inaugural hopes of conquering the deserts, and the national efforts at desalinization were greatly reinforced, along with a stepped-up program of underlying basic and applied research to overcome the barriers to economic desalinization.

NATURAL RESOURCES

In the field of natural resources, the President early in his administration took steps to accelerate the pace of the national program in oceanography, and at the same time provided leadership and backing both for congressional support and for a coordinated, balanced, and imaginative interagency approach to oceanographic research. An old sailor, he had a special interest in this research. He got a particular pleasure when the Presidential yacht *Williams-*

burg was converted into an oceanographic research vessel. For a film on oceanographic research just completed, the President provided the opening and closing lines. Recently, after I had recovered from the consequences of a sailing accident, inaccurately reported, he offered to give me lessons in sailing and press relations. He called upon both the National Academy of Sciences and the Federal Council for Science and Technology to study and make recommendations for strengthening the Federal efforts across the broad horizons of natural resources in the land, sea, and air so that they can better serve the needs of the American people.

Early in his administration, too, the President lent substance to his desire to encourage commerce through science and technology by initiating a national program to strengthen civilian technology, including the appointment of an Assistant Secretary of Commerce for Science and Technology. In remarks prepared for delivery in Dallas, never given, the President pointed out that communities possessing the best in research and graduate facilities tend to attract the new and growing industries. He congratulated those who recognized the relationship between leadership and learning and the need for community support for the advancement of learning underlying the creation of the forward-looking Graduate Research Center of the Southwest.

President Kennedy's interest in international aspects of science was again highlighted in his September 20, 1963, address to the United Nations, where he urged a world center for health communications to warn of epidemics and the adverse effects of certain drugs; regional research centers to advance common medical knowledge and train new scientists and doctors for new nations; and a cooperative system of satellites to provide communication and weather information on a worldwide basis. As a result of his initiative, work has already begun in the world meteorological organization to develop the outlines of a world weather system and to strengthen basic research in atmospheric sciences on an international basis.

In connection with technical assistance to newly developing countries, the President was instrumental in bringing about closer attention to the need for research underlying the planning and execution of the AID program. This was reflected in the formulation of his Alliance for Progress program with its emphasis on science education, and in the establishment of the Office of Human Resources and Social Development in the Agency for International Development.

There are numerous other examples of President Kennedy's interest in promoting the development and application of science on an international basis, ranging from his initiative in establishing the United States-Japan Science Committee and his encouragement of the scientists' Pugwash movement, to his request for specific studies from his Science Advisory Committee, including a study of the problem of hoof and mouth disease in Argentina, the problem of water logging in Pakistan, and most recently his initiation of a study of the boll weevil problem in cotton production, a matter of international as well as national concern.

ARMS CONTROL

I have already referred to the President's strong conviction about the need for bringing about adequately safeguarded international arms control, a matter that occupied a very substantial part of his time from the very first days of his administration. The whole world can be thankful for two major accomplishments that flowed from his efforts, two monuments to his labors on the road to peace—the Arms Control and Disarmament Agency and the Nuclear Test Ban Treaty—which can inspire us to persist in the efforts to avoid the nuclear holocaust that so haunted him. One of his first acts was to propose to Congress the creation of the Arms Control and Disarmament Agency, the world's first governmental activity dedicated solely to the study of disarmament problems. As a result, the U.S. Government now has a small cadre of professionals in this extremely complicated and important field.

The signing of the nuclear test ban treaty gave the President enormous satisfaction. For him it proved that meaningful disarmament steps were possible, and it justified the hundreds of hours of debate and study, the deep disappointments along the way. His striving for this treaty, begun in the first days of his administration, weathered many bitter disappointments and was the subject of much unjust criticism. He could hardly have been blamed had he abandoned hope after the Russians resumed nuclear testing in the summer of 1961. Characteristically, though, he continued his attempts to work out an acceptable agreement. The question of the need for further nuclear tests in order to enhance our national security involved highly technical issues and extremely controversial ones as well. So did the capabilities of nuclear test detection systems. The President made himself an expert on these subjects. He listened to many briefings and more debates. He talked to experts with every possible view and finally formed his own conclusions.

In the process he also achieved an understanding of the role of scientific advice in policy matters. In his last National Academy address he said, "As the country had reason to note in recent weeks during the debate on the test ban treaty, scientists do not always unite themselves on their recommendations to makers of policy. This is only partly because of scientific disagreements. It is even more because the big issues so often go beyond the possibilities of exact scientific determination.

"I know few significant questions of public policy which can safely be confided to computers. In the end, the hard decisions inescapably involve imponderables of intuition, prudence, and judgment."

The President called the nuclear test ban treaty a small first step. Since its signing the nations of the world have also responded to his call for a pledge to prohibit the placing of nuclear weapons in orbit. He hoped that these agreements would be followed by many more.

President Kennedy not only understood the need to invest resources for extending our understanding of science and its applications but also saw the need for institutional change to guide and assist the mounting governmental involvement in science and technology to serve national objectives. He shared the view that the Federal scientific enterprise would be best served by strengthening the individual agencies whose missions required the exploitation of science, rather than by the creation of an all-encompassing department of science. Toward this end he sought the inclusion of a technically educated individual at the policy level in each department which is heavily dependent upon science for the accomplishment of its mission. The evolution of the Office of Science and Technology also reflects this policy of building strength in the individual agencies. On March 29, 1962, after much discussion, he sent a message to the Congress providing for reorganization in the field of science and technology. He pointed out that the evergrowing significance and complexity of Federal programs had earlier necessitated several steps for improving the organizational arrangements of the executive branch. The President believed that the creation of the Office of Science and Technology would facilitate communication between the executive branch and the Congress. The wisdom of the President in making this proposal is being increasingly realized through the activities of its director, in its close collaboration with the Bureau of the Budget, its presentations to congressional committees, and through its leadership in initiating long-range planning of research and development within the Federal agencies. To assist this work, the National Science Foundation has created an Office of Resources Planning, and closer ties with the National Academy of Sciences have been established through its newly created Committee on Science and Public Affairs.

These are only the highlights of President Kennedy's broad interest in science and technology and the tangible forms they have taken. Although much progress has been made, much more needs to be done. But because of his interest and support we have a stronger base upon which to extend the already impressive contributions of American science and technology.

Mr. President, many Americans have expressed their grief at the tragic assassination of President Kennedy. The distinguished commentator Richard Rovere has written one of the most moving of these valedictories. In a few short paragraphs Rovere gives us a touching picture of the late President's human qualities—the depth of his knowledge and interest in the world around him, his sharp wit, and the winning directness of his manner. I ask that this tribute by Richard H. Rovere from the New York Review of Books for December 26, 1963, be printed.

[From the New York Review of Books, Dec. 26, 1964]

A TRIBUTE TO PRESIDENT KENNEDY

(By Richard H. Rovere)

I was not one of the Washington journalists who knew him well and saw him often. Before his nomination, I knew him scarcely at all. The first time I sat down alone with him was only a few days before his election. He had had a wild day campaigning in and around Phila-

delphia. He had shaken so many hands that his own right one looked like raw beef. One woman, running alongside his car, had held on to avoid losing her balance and perhaps being run over. There was a chance that he had dislocated a shoulder. It hurt badly. Around midnight, I joined him at supper in his cabin on the *Caroline*. After getting me settled, he said, "What do you know about Taper?" I couldn't imagine what he meant. I had to ask him. "Taper," he said, "you know, the one who writes that column in the Spectator." I was at the time a correspondent for the London Spectator, and Taper was a pseudonym used by Bernard Levin, a political writer for that magazine, who has since become theater critic for the London Daily Mail. I told him what I knew, which wasn't very much; Kennedy said he admired Levin and would enjoy meeting him.

I had three talks with him in the White House. There were several more "Taper" incidents. "I ran into Kahn the other day," he said once. I wracked my brain. Herman Kahn, the thermonuclear-war man? The Aga Khan? But wasn't he dead? Aly Khan? Otto Kahn? Dead, too, wasn't he? Could it be a friend of mine, another Herman Kahn, a historian in the National Archives? Mohammed Khan of Pakistan? Who the hell was Kahn? He could see me struggling "Jack Kahn, you must know him, on the New Yorker? He was in here doing a Talk of the Town story. He was talking to my secretary about my going to theaters in New York. I've been wondering about the piece. Do you know when it's going to come out?" I knew nothing about it.

Another time, he seemed mildly and inexplicitly upset about a New Yorker piece that had appeared—a profile of Pablo Casals by a man whose name really was Taper, Bernard Taper. "It was interesting," he said, "but I figured it must have been written a long time ago. It wasn't up to date." Thinking fast, I assumed he meant that it had not said enough about the Casals concert in the White House. I asked him if that was it. "No, no," he said, and he went on to explain that in three or four places it had described arrangements in Casals' life that had changed in recent months. He seemed to feel that the New Yorker was somehow losing its grip if it couldn't be au courant in such matters. "Who is this Taper?" he said. I told him a bit, mentioning that this Taper and Pierre Salinger were friends, having worked together as reporters in San Francisco. He went on with something like, "What did you make of that last Norman Mailer piece?"

Once, when I felt that I had really taken up more than enough of his time, I tried to prepare the way for my leaving with what would have been a lame and elaborate opening. What I meant to say was something like this—that I would really worry about the country if I thought that its President was putting in a lot of time talking with someone like me about Norman Mailer, Bernard Taper, and so forth. I forget how it went, but I got out just a few words, like "Mr. President, I'm taking up too much of your time. I think that if—."

"You think," he said, "that I wouldn't be much of a President if I spent much of my time this way."

Mr. President, probably nowhere in the world was the death of President Kennedy felt more profoundly than in Latin America. His passing was mourned by old and young, by rich and poor, by high government officials in the capitals and lowly peasants in the country. President Kennedy symbolized a new era in relations between the United States and Latin America, a new understanding of the problems of a continent in the throes of a social and economic revolution.

In Chile an important national federation of workers published a special edition of their newspaper dedicated to President Kennedy, proclaiming in bold headlines: "Though His Body Is Dead His Spirit Lingers On."

Another group that has felt deeply the impact of President Kennedy and his death is the rising generation of students, artists, writers, and intellectuals in Latin America. In Latin America as in the United States, President and Mrs. Kennedy had and still have a special appeal to younger people and people in the artistic, literary, and intellectual worlds. President Kennedy realized that the success of his grand strategy for cooperation with Latin America, the Alliance for Progress, depended on more than economic development. He realized that for the Alliance to succeed it must have a political content, an ideological substance. It must come to symbolize the hopes and aspirations of both the elites and the masses of Latin American people. President Kennedy himself was the symbol of the hope and imagination which is needed. As the symbol of hope and imagination, he is today a mythological hero among the people of Latin America. And this includes among the impatient, idealistic youth who have been and are even today strongly critical of certain aspects of North American life.

And it is significant that 2 days before his death, President Kennedy met at the White House with a group of young Latin American writers, artists, and intellectuals who had been brought together by the Inter-American Committee for a symposium on problems of the hemisphere. He engaged in a wide-ranging discussion with them on problems of the Alliance for Progress. Following this meeting he arranged for them to continue the discussion with the Attorney General. Later that day it was my privilege to spend about an hour and a half here in the Senate with this group of brilliant, impatient, critical, and idealistic young people.

Some of them would no doubt be considered radical. They are impatient with the older ruling groups of Latin America. They are intent upon seeing radical changes in their own societies. They ask uncomfortable questions and they demand penetrating answers. It was part of President Kennedy's accomplishment to recognize that their questions cannot go unanswered, that indeed they themselves will play a major role in shaping the institutions of their societies in the decades ahead.

One of the group that met with President Kennedy has written one of the most moving tributes to the late President that has appeared. Writing in the current issue of Americas, Dr. Rafael Squirru, a dynamic young Argentine artist and writer who is now providing bold new leadership in the Department of Cultural Affairs at OAS, describes the "deeper reality" that President Kennedy represented for his generation of Latin American people. Part of President Kennedy's appeal in Latin America, Dr. Squirru notes, lay in the mythical quality that surrounded his person. Even before his death Mr. Kennedy had left the aura of a mythical figure—a man who would bring peace to the world, who would launch a program of help to foreign countries that would give them opportunity to achieve their destiny in dignity and freedom. As the author of this article perceptively remarks, President Kennedy is revered not only for what he accomplished in physical and material terms through the Alliance for Progress, but more so for what he inspired in terms of hope and imagination for the peoples of Latin America. Men like President Kennedy, the author tells us, are often revered like gods. This is because it is the one way that men have of expressing "the gratitude that men feel for those who have lightened their burden, all too oppressive, all too insipid, all too dull without that ray of light that myth kindles."

For those who would like to appreciate the reaction of the leaders of Latin America to President Kennedy's death I commend this article entitled "A Deeper Reality" by Dr. Rafael Squirru to their attention.

A DEEPER REALITY

(By Rafael Squirru)

Among the books published during 1963 that created a stir in the United States is one entitled "J.F.K.: The Man and the Myth," by an author whose name I do not recall. The most important thing about this book,

I believe, is the title—"The Man and the Myth"—and I suppose that what the author implies is that one thing is the myth created by Mr. Kennedy and another quite different thing is the man himself. It is precisely the impossibility of divorcing these two factors that makes me wary of the criticism implied by the author. The whole key to the understanding of a personality such as that of the late President of the United States is precisely that of grasping the total identity between man and myth. And this requires realizing the significance of myth in general and what it implies. There is a superficial notion that myth is something equivalent to nonreality, to make-believe, to nontruth; a notion springing from despising the value of the imagination as opposed to that of reason and analytical knowledge. The whole point of mythology is that not only is it not removed from reality but that on the contrary it is a way of penetrating a deeper reality than that of the factual world.

If it be true, as I believe it is, that Mr. Kennedy created a myth regarding himself as a public figure, the lesson to be derived from the achievement is not one of disparagement regarding Mr. Kennedy's conduct but on the contrary one of deep admiration for a man able to transcend inert reality and enter the living reality of the imagination and poetry.

I find it extremely significant that Mr. Kennedy was used quite often by pop artists in many of their works as the kind of image that coincided with the sensibility which this school displays. The central point about pop art in the United States, the main preoccupation of this group of creators, is that of the all too thin frontier that separates art from reality, understood as everyday reality. The pop artist is obsessed with the presence of art in everyday life and of life in everyday art. He will take a comic strip and almost without changing it he will endow it with a subtle quality that transforms a craftsman's drawing into one of valid esthetic quality worthy of the name of art. Art is and will always be inseparable from personality; that is, the personality of the artist, which can manifest itself in such a way as to become, though present, hidden in the work of art. This hiding of the personality is an important characteristic in the classical world: the artist, apparently purporting to portray nature, conceals himself through the use of forms familiar to the eye, which has led many to believe that art was but a reproduction of something that was already there. I say it is symptomatic of the personality of Mr. Kennedy that his image should have been validly appropriated and used by the pop artists as one where factual reality and the world of dream actually met.

Although I met President Kennedy only twice, I was very much impressed by the mythical quality that surrounded his person like an aura not easily grasped by the physiological eye. Mr. Kennedy moved in a world of dream because he himself was partly dream. He played the part of Mr. Kennedy so well that, in fact, to a great extent he actually became Mr. Kennedy, and when I say this I mean the Mr. Kennedy of his own dream; this man who would bring peace to the world, who would launch a program of help to foreign countries that would give them the opportunity to achieve their destiny in dignity and freedom. Perhaps it is true, as many critics say, that none of these high goals was actually accomplished, but it would be more true to say that a much higher accomplishment was reached: these goals fired the imagination of those to whom he promised this kind of redemption.

That Mr. Kennedy is idolized by millions in different parts of the world today is a fact that ought to make us stop and think. After all—and at the risk of being considered a cynic or a skeptic—the truth is that what can be done for man to better his lot is always rather little. What really counts is not so much, therefore, what can be achieved in a material sense as what can be reached in terms of hope and imagination. The human being is frail and needs this daily bread even more than that of flour and crumb. We must be thankful for those who have had the power to create myth. Mankind has often revered them like gods themselves and this is no idle caprice of the human soul. It is one way of expressing the gratitude that men feel for those who have lightened their burdens, all too oppressive, all too insipid, all too dull without that ray of light that myth kindles.

Whoever wishes to analyze Mr. Kennedy through the microscope will fail to see him because he can be seen only through the telescope. It is in the world of the stars that such men exist, and it is up and not down that we must look to find them.

Mr. President, I would also like to call to the attention of my colleagues another excellent article appearing in the same edition of Americas, devoted to President Kennedy. In this article, Americas, which is rapidly becoming an important medium of communication between younger writers in North and South America, brings together the reaction of six men who were familiar with President Kennedy's work in the Latin American area, and gives their comments about "What was Kennedy's greatest accomplishment?" The reaction of these six people, chiefly North Americans and many who worked with President Kennedy in the Alliance for Progress program is very similar to that of the younger Latin Americans whose views I referred to earlier. They comment on the "atmosphere he created, on the idealism he imparted to all, the climate of opinion he left behind him wherever he went."

As his colleague and friend Arthur Schlesinger, Jr., says, President Kennedy gave the United States a new conception of itself—or rather he was able to "revive for our age the oldest conception of this Nation, as a young, resolute and progressive democracy dedicated to certain self-evident truths—that all men are created equal, that they are endowed by their Creator with un-alienable rights, and that among those rights are life, liberty, and the pursuit of happiness."

Mr. President, I ask that this article be inserted at this point.

WHAT WAS KENNEDY'S GREATEST ACCOMPLISHMENT?—SIX REPLIES TO A QUESTION FROM AMERICAS ASKED ON NOVEMBER 27, 1963

Richard L. Coe, drama editor, the Washington Post: "Invisible, evanescent is the world's most potent force. Though the Americas were thousands of miles from conflict, all were aware of World War II's events, all can sense cold war attitudes. This force is called atmosphere, felt, unseen.

"It was this invisible, unweighable substance John F. Kennedy created and which historians will never fully grasp. It followed an atmosphere of which his predecessor, Dwight D. Eisenhower, can take pride, a climate of peace but nonetheless curiously self-satisfied, a fullness of age.

"Though it was dramatically vivid seconds after one knew he had gone, President Kennedy's peace was of a different kind—dynamic, questing. It was a peace of youthful idealism, the avowal that if right were done, right would result. This implies values in excellence.

"This value of excellence, whether in balancing international claims, winning elections, honoring artists or collecting stimulating companions quickened the world of John F. Kennedy.

"It was a sense of quality, a shirt stud or a witticism, a strong stand or gracious tribute, which gave his brief era that sense of distinction historians are likely not to see when they assay the accomplishments of President Kennedy. New climates will intervene. His was morning sunshine."

Richard N. Goodwin, Secretary General, International Peace Corps Secretariat: "His greatest accomplishment was that he gave us the strength to believe we were better than we had thought."

Teodoro Moscoso, U.S. Coordinator, Alliance for Progress: "We are still too much in the grip of the tragedy that befell us on November 22 to judge what were the most significant of John F. Kennedy's accomplishments. The clouded eye of the present cannot separate them, nor decide among them. That they were substantial—and will be enduring—few even now can doubt.

"To his times, he gave style, skill, and deep intelligence. He sensed drift—and gave a firm direction—in an era of subtle and complex change. He fought for civil rights, for education and against human misery and backwardness. He helped abate the threat of nuclear war.

"But for me, his understanding of the problems of our times was most convincingly demonstrated in his efforts to strengthen and give a new resilience to the ties among the nations of the New World—ties that had been allowed to slacken and chafe thin in the years since World War II. Through the Alliance for Progress, he gave new dimensions to the inter-American system. His legacy, in this hemisphere, is a continent committed to change and to the goals of prosperity and social justice in freedom."

Norman Podhoretz, editor, Commentary: "In my opinion, President Kennedy's most important accomplishment was his success in negotiating an atomic test ban. I believe that this treaty will come to be seen as the first significant step in the direction of arms control, and perhaps also the first notable move in the direction of a workable Soviet-American rapprochement."

Arthur Schlesinger, Jr., Special Assistant to the President: "Perhaps John Fitzgerald Kennedy's basic accomplishment as President was to give the United States a new conception of itself—or rather to revive for our age the oldest conception of this Nation, as a young, resolute, and progressive democracy dedicated to certain self-evident truths—that all men are created equal, that they are endowed by their Creator with unalienable rights, and that among those rights are life, liberty, and the pursuit of happiness.

"In President Kennedy's view this was what the United States was all about—this was the American commitment and not just to the American people but to all mankind. Thus he led the great campaign within the United States to assure equal rights to all American citizens, regardless of race or color. And, as he called for progress and justice at home, so he saw the United States as the bearer to the world of a revolutionary faith in freedom and diversity and as the shield and partner of all free nations in the tasks of liberty, abundance, and peace. It was this vision which strengthened his determination to help all nations defend their independence against aggression and which animated the great creative programs of his administration—the Alliance for Progress, the Peace Corps, the test ban treaty, and the disarmament effort, and the new emphasis on cultural and intellectual exchange."

Arturo Morales Carrión, Deputy Assistant Secretary for Inter-American Affairs: "It is too early to tell, in view of his many initiatives. His masterful handling of the Cuban missile crisis will mark him, in my opinion, as a great statesman. His concern for economic development and social justice will show him to be a true humanitarian. He will also be remembered for having 'rediscovered' Latin America as a partner of the Western World and for having felt so deeply and supported so strongly the aspirations and hopes of the peoples of our hemisphere."

Memorial Tributes

IN THE

House of Representatives
of the United States

IN EULOGY OF

John Fitzgerald Kennedy

Memorial Tributes
In the House of Representatives
of the United States

TRIBUTES BY

Hon. John W. McCormack

OF MASSACHUSETTS

Mr. Speaker, under leave to extend my remarks, I include the following address by Bishop James K. Mathews, Methodist Bishop of New England, at the interdenominational service at the Washington Cathedral, Washington, D.C., Sunday, November 24, at 4 p.m., in memory of the late John Fitzgerald Kennedy, President of the United States:

THE GIFT OF A MAN: A PROTESTANT INTERPRETATION OF THE LIFE AND DEATH OF JOHN F. KENNEDY

(By Bishop James K. Mathews)

Today, Americans can have but one thought; for we have been present at a new crucifixion. A people who could endure the villainous murder of Medgar Evers without undue remorse; who could observe the slaughter of the innocents by a bomb in a Birmingham church and not really cry out for justice, have called for a yet more costly sacrifice—that of the President of their country. Truly, then, Americans are weeping not only for him but for themselves.

We react, indeed, in anger and sorrow; but do we react sufficiently in repentance? To fail to miss the message of God in this tragic hour would be to allow yet another martyr to have died in vain.

For martyr he was, as surely as those who have died for their vision in earlier ages: a martyr at the hands of extremists of every kind, as well as at the hands of the comfortable captives of the status quo which most of us have become; a martyr to those who enjoy prejudices a century out of date, and those who refuse to live in the day which God has given to us.

To take seriously the death of a martyr is to take the meaning of that death upon ourselves. For in his mortal wound is our own hurt and the hurt of all mankind.

We are a proud, and even arrogant, people who have told ourselves that this sort of thing could not happen here. In more primitive periods of our history, yes. Among more primitive peoples even today. But not here. What could not happen has happened and it has happened to us all.

More than this, all of us have had a part in the slaying of our President. It was good people who crucified our Lord, and not merely those who acted as His executioners. By our silence, by our inaction, by our willingness that heavy burdens be borne by one man alone, by our readiness to allow evil to be called good and good evil; by our continued toleration of ancient injustices, by our failure to address ourselves to this day—by these means we all have had a part in the assassination.

In particular measure, we of the church must bear a heavy share of responsibility. For we are those who speak for God. We are His people and the sheep of His pasture. We are the Body of Christ, which bears His wounds. We are the sentinels of civilization, but we have failed to sound the alarm. We have been conformed to the social order we were supposed to have informed. Alas, the garments of the slayer are at our feet. Therefore, "the time has come for judgment to begin with the household of God."

Our Lord says: "Every one to whom much is given, of him will much be required." This word of God is a summons to accountability, just as the events of these days are a summons to accountability. For all too long now we have not been called to account: either to one another; or to the world; or to God. We have been ready to receive abundantly of God's grace, but it is when the demands of that grace are upon us that we fail to measure up.

We call this Thanksgiving Sunday, when we are supposed to acknowledge the mercy of God. It is not really a question of whether or not it is proper for us to celebrate Thanksgiving at such a tragic hour as this. The fact is that we as a people have allowed Thanksgiving, as a significant day, to be lost long ago. It has been reduced to feasting and football. It has become "a pleasant interlude between leaf raking and snow shoveling." This holiday, far from being a holy day, has become a hollow day. Having eaten our fill, and that in the midst of a hungry world, we are left with an empty feeling.

Fundamentally, we have been seized by a forgetfulness of nationwide proportions. Abraham Lincoln told a war-torn Nation in his Thanksgiving proclamation in November 1863: "We have forgotten the gracious Hand which has preserved us in peace and multiplied and enriched and strengthened us, and have vainly imagined in the deceitfulness of our hearts that all these blessings were produced by some superior wisdom and virtue of our own. Intoxicated with unbroken success, we have become too self-sufficient to feel the necessity of redeeming and preserving grace, too proud to pray to the God that made us."

If this was true then, how much more is it true today, exactly 100 years later. So it was that in President Kennedy's Thanksgiving proclamation of November 1963, he said: "As we express our gratitude, we must never forget that the highest appreciation is not to utter words but to live by them. Let us therefore 'proclaim our gratitude to providence for manifold blessings—let us be humbly thankful for inherited ideals—and let us resolve to share those blessings and those ideals with our fellow human beings throughout the world.' "

Yes, we have been seized by forgetfulness. No wonder we debate about our national purpose. No wonder we worry about what other nations shall think of us as a people. Is it not here that we have lost our way? We have forgotten who we are. We have forgotten whose we are. We have forgotten whence we have come. Therefore, we do not know where we are going.

"Much has been given to us," yet we have been a thoughtless and thankless people. I do not mean merely that we have been given abundant harvests and a proud heritage. These, we have come to take for granted. Rather, we have been given a man. And this man has been, in an astonishing way, a symbol of the changing world in which we live, a constant flowing river of change which has not left any part of earth untouched.

For, John Fitzgerald Kennedy represented and embodied a brandnew world. Indeed, he grasped for it by means of the image of the New Frontier, not merely as a political implement, but as a present reality. So radically has the whole climate of mankind changed that one could almost say that a person living at the beginning of this century would have been more at home in Julius Caesar's time than in our own. This cultural revolution in which we find ourselves was that for which our late President stood.

Again, he made valiant efforts to give a new sense of mission to us as a nation. This does not mean that he solved all our problems for us but that he was, by virtue of office and by deliberate intent, in the very middle of the dramatic struggles that characterize our age. This sense of mission, involving the welfare of all civilization, has scarcely ever been as well articulated as it was in his inaugural address. Nor has a more imaginative token of it been created than the Peace Corps. So it was that one Peace Corps volunteer said last Friday, "I myself am a part of the legacy he left to the world." Young

Americans, in particular, seemed to catch what this man symbolized.

Moreover, he invited and encouraged a new human dignity—a freedom for man now. If this was to have meaning, through Americans, throughout the world, it had to have substance now within our own borders. Therefore, the Negro citizens, patient for a hundred years, were encouraged by President Kennedy to become a new people. That is to say, they have decided to be the free people our Constitution and the Gospel of Jesus Christ say they are. When men determine to be free, there is an unanswerable quality about their determination.

From the Hebrew-Christian perspective, all of this is the work of God. For God is a God who acts in history; indeed, who makes history and gives meaning to human events. The President saw precisely this when he declared, "Here on earth God's work must truly be our own."

We have assuredly been given much in our day, but some factors in our national life have said "No" to it all. They have said "No" to a brandnew world; "No" to national involvement in the whole process of civilization; "No" to the fulfillment now of human dignity. For all this, the high price martydom has been paid. A martyr is, literally, a witness, and this is the witness we have been given.

Great gifts demand great responsibility. "For every one to whom much is given, of him will much be required." What, in the light of this sacrifice, does the Lord require of us? All humankind will be watching what we do in response, for when a people takes its own history seriously, every man's history is involved.

First of all, we, who have been forgetful are called to recollection and return. We have come to take God for granted, have tried to encase Him in the past and to capture Him in our creeds. Meanwhile, He is at work, as always, in the present orders of society.

Let us recall that we are a people by heritage dedicated to law and order and to equality under law. This was by specific intent. For 343 years ago this very week the Pilgrims landed on Cape Cod. Their navigation had been faulty, and they had missed the territory for which they had been granted authority. Some of the colonists considered that they were, therefore, under no law. Then, by deliberate act, they made themselves equal under law, by creating the Mayflower Compact. In this they promised to "covenant and combine ourselves together into a civil body politic, for our better ordering and preservation and furtherance of the ends aforesaid; and by virtue hereof to enact, constitute, and frame such just and equal laws, ordinances, acts, constitutions, and offices, from time to time, as shall be thought most meet and convenient for the general good of the colony, unto which we promise all due submission and obedience."

They were, therefore, a covenanted community: in acknowledging God, they acknowledged one another. By self-conscious promises, each held himself before God as responsible to his neighbor in a common endeavor. We are summoned by the martyrdom of our President to renew such a covenant of equity, under law, which is basic to any true community.

Secondly, in the light of this sacrifice, we are called to

receive the very realities which it symbolizes. Therefore, we must embrace this new world of radical change and possibility. For it is offered to us as the gift of God.

Moreover, if this is to be a meaningful sacrifice, we are called as a people deliberately to involve ourselves in the whole enterprise of humanity. For, in a degree unparalleled in earlier centuries, we owe ourselves to the world. Merely to preserve ourselves as a nation is to lose our identity. But to give our lives in the service of total civilization is to find ourselves. For it is only in our mission together that we are a nation.

Again, in view of this martyrdom, we are called to a deepened fulfillment of the dignity of every person. There can no longer be any second-class people of any kind, anywhere. Only through acknowledging this dignity for all—without any exception—can any one of us possess dignity himself. So it is that integrity may return to us and we can be the nation we have pretended to be.

What I have said is that we have been present at a new crucifixion and that we all have, in fact, contributed to it. Our crucified Lord enables us to understand the cruciform nature of all human existence, and He endows even the most senseless event with cosmic meaning. But the Christian is not allowed to speak of crucifixion without speaking also of resurrection. This can only be realized by our embodying, as living sacrifices, that which was embodied by the one who was slain. That is to say, we are to confront life and the world with a new openness, a new awareness of our true identity and responsibility as a nation, and a new readiness to acknowledge the validity of every human being.

Finally, let us receive the torch that has been passed to a new generation of Americans. For this generation, as John Fitzgerald Kennedy himself so clearly expressed it, "would not exchange places with any other people or any other generation. The energy, the faith, the devotion which we bring to this endeavor will light our country and all who serve it—and the glow that fire can truly light the world." That never-dying torch has now been lighted by a martyr for his people. For this man not only uttered words but lived by them. "Every one to whom much is given, of him will much be required." Amen.

Mr. Speaker, I include a beautiful and expressing poem, a tribute to and in commemoration of our late beloved President John Fitzgerald Kennedy, which came from the mind of and written by George N. Welch, president of the Charitable Irish Society of Boston, Mass.:

A Tribute to John Fitzgerald Kennedy, 35th President of the United States

It was a lovely day in Texas,
In Dallas, a cultural town,
The multitudes were gathered
To see the President and Jacqueline
And receive them with welcome profound.
The welcome was tumultuous
And all was going well
When suddenly shots rang out
And on the gathering cast a spell.

For the President was shot and dying
And the Governor wounded too
By the hand of a fanatic
With a distorted sense of view.
Now he has gone from us
And our lives are filled with pain
For nowhere in this vale of tears
Shall we see his like again.
Superbly endowed by heritage
Education and training
For the greatest office of all
Made it almost imperative
That John F. Kennedy answer the call.
The call that came from the people
Throughout the length and breadth of the land
That J.F.K. should be our President
And on that office place his brand.
As our President he has striven
With all his might and main
To bring peace and order
Throughout the world,
And for this he was cruelly slain.
So we pay him this tribute
Futile though it may seem
As we long for the glint of humor
That in those Irish eyes did gleam.
Taken off in the bloom of his manhood
With his herculean tasks undone,
The awesome responsibility ended
His race of life prematurely run.
But wherever real men gather
Throughout the entire world,
They will talk of his courage and wisdom
And manners beyond compare,
These things he had in abundance
They were part of his daily fare.
We shall miss his encyclopedic memory
And his analytical, panoramic mind.
As well as his humble approach to problems
When answers were hard to find.
The mighty and the humble
Have paid tribute at his bier,
Heads of state from far off places
Have come to shed a tear.
We have lost a great President,
And in the annals of time
His stature will increase and grow,
Until the world regards him
One of our greatest men
In this planet here below.
This valiant warrior for peace
And the brotherhood of man,
Has joined the ranks of the martyred
During his short earthly span.
May the symbolic flame
Which burns o'er his grave
Be as eternal
As his unquenchable spirit.
May the Great God above
Receive his valiant soul,
And give him the peace and serenity
Which was his earthly goal.

Mr. Speaker, Miss Miriam Gilbert, 11-year-old daughter of my dear friend and colleague, Representative Jacob H. Gilbert, of New York, has written a beautiful poem in memory of our martyred President, John Fitzgerald Kennedy. The children of our Nation have also been greatly saddened by the tragedy of his death, and I feel certain that Miriam has expressed the grief and thoughts of her contemporaries in the lines she has composed. I am pleased to include her poem.

A EULOGY FOR PRESIDENT KENNEDY

(By Miriam Gilbert)

The world died with him
On that cruel November day.
His memory in our hearts
Will forever stay.
He was the Naval hero of PT 109
For that he won a medal for his gesture so fine.
But then he was stricken with malaria and an injured back
Even then courage he did not lack.
He became a Member of Congress, then President of the Nation
But he never had this expectation.
The world died with him
On that cruel November day.
His memory in our hearts
Will forever stay.
He was a man of dignity, good will and determination.
He fought against all kinds of discrimination.
He fought for civil rights, his most important bill
It would please him most now if that wish we would fulfill.
The world died with him
On that cruel November day.
His memory in our hearts
Will forever stay.
He negotiated with the Communists, and soon they did find
He was a man with a very skillful mind.
He prevented us from a war against our greatest foe.
If he hadn't done that we'd have suffered a terrible blow.
The world died with him
On that cruel November day.
His memory in our hearts
Will forever stay.
In public, Jackie held back her tears of grief
While inside her there were cries of disbelief.
Why did this have to happen to me?
John-John standing there bewildered as can be—
Caroline might have known what it was about,
But even in her mind there was probably some doubt.
The world died with him
On that cruel November day.
His memory in our hearts
Will forever stay.

Be brave Jackie, John-John, and Caroline
Live your lives with zest.
For he has gone to God's Heaven
Where he will find eternal rest.

TRIBUTE BY

Hon. Carl Albert

OF OKLAHOMA

Mr. Speaker, a column entitled "The Grief of Maria" from the Buenos Aires Herald, an English language newspaper of Buenos Aires, Argentina, has been sent to me by the Honorable George O. Huey, our American consul in that city. In the words of Mr. Huey, the article demonstrates that "perhaps we have not been as unsuccessful as it sometimes seems in reaching the minds and hearts of the little people whose responses are seldom recorded." The reams of copy which poured from the typewriters of many eminent journalists recorded every conceivable reaction, both their own and that of persons of varying degrees of distinction, but mostly of those highly articulate. Maria was scarcely literate, but through the plainness of her language shone the greatest sentiment and most sincere tribute which could be paid to our deceased President, and that transcending the boundaries of country, culture, and station.

The article is as follows:

THE GRIEF OF MARIA

On the day of President Kennedy's funeral Maria Baez went out and spent the last 280 pesos in her purse on flowers.

These she arranged on the dresser of her tiny room before a photograph of the dead President cut from a magazine.

"I cannot think what else I can do, señora," she said. "He was such a good man."

Thus Maria Baez, 42-year-old cook in service, paid her rich tribute to a man familiar to her only in photographs.

The middle-aged husband and wife who employ Maria told me that on the day that President Kennedy died she appeared tearfully in the sitting room doorway and said: "Madame, sir: I would like to express to you my deepest condolences over the death of your President Kennedy. I have just heard the terrible news from the porter."

Grief was written on her face; sorrow had bowed her head.

Her employers were touched by the obvious depths of

feeling over a tragedy so remote from her own narrow world.

The señor was moved to rise from his chair and take the woman's hand. "Your sentiments are those of kindness, Maria," he said softly. "But you know, President Kennedy was not our President. We are not Americans."

"I know, señor," said Maria, "but is this not a tragedy for all the English-speaking people? I have seen you, sir, made silent by grief. For you it is also a sad personal moment."

Thus expressed herself a woman to whom the world has not shown much kindness since, at the age of 9, it sent her out to earn a living.

Maria Baez cannot read nor write. What she knows of the world is gleaned from her small bedside radio and the pictorial press, and the conversation of the tradesmen and servants who people her small world.

Maria knows nothing of politics or of the intricate affairs of men. She knows only that there are evil men and good ones—and that the man they called President Kennedy was a good one.

Yet Maria also prayed for the man who struck the President down. She prayed with the words of one without religious instruction or congregational ties. Her prayers were of those whose faith is inborn and not directed.

Her employers marvel that a woman who has known so much of what is known as cruel in this world exudes no ill and only good. Her thoughts are for others. She weeps for them though she knows that none will weep for her.

And so Maria Baez mourned for a man, who was a son and a father, a great man whose greatness she did not understand; but a man who in his greatness was a good man.

So Maria, who has never seen the mountains or the sea, shed her tears for that good man beyond the mountains and the sea.

TRIBUTES BY

Hon. Hale Boggs

OF LOUISIANA

Mr. Speaker, in connection with the assassination of the President of the United States, I include newspaper and other articles which were published subsequent thereto:

[From the Washington Daily News, Nov. 27, 1963]

THIS WAS MR. KENNEDY'S THANKSGIVING MESSAGE

President Johnson yesterday urged that the late President Kennedy's November 5 Thanksgiving Day proclamation be read in houses of worship as a memorial tomorrow. He also asked the press to "make it available to all the American people." It follows:

"Over three centuries ago, our forefathers in Virginia and in Massachusetts far from home on a lonely wilderness, set aside a time of thanksgiving. On the appointed day, they gave reverent thanks for their safety, for the health of their children, for the fertility of their fields, for the love which bound them together and for the faith which united them with their God.

"So too when the colonies achieved their independence, our first President in the first year of his administration proclaimed November 26, 1789, as 'a day of public thanksgiving and prayer to be observed by acknowledging with grateful hearts the many signal favors of almighty God' and called upon the people of the new republic to 'beseech Him to pardon our national and other transgressions * * * to promote the knowledge and practice of true religion and virtue * * * and generally to grant unto all mankind such a degree of temporal prosperity as He alone knows to be best.'

"And so too, in the midst of America's tragic Civil War, President Lincoln proclaimed the last Thursday of November 1863 as the day to renew our gratitude for America's fruitful fields, for our national strength and vigor, and for all our singular deliverances and blessings.

"Much time has passed since the first colonists came to rocky shores and dark forests of an unknown continent, much time since President Washington led a young people into the experience of nationhood, much time since President Lincoln saw the American Nation through the ordeal of fraternal war—and in these years our population, our plenty, and our power have all grown apace. Today we are a nation of nearly 200 million souls stretching from coast to coast, on into the Pacific and north toward the Arctic, a nation enjoying the fruits of an ever-expanding agriculture and industry and achieving standards of living unknown in previous history. We give our humble thanks for this.

"Yet as our power has grown, so has our peril. Today we give our thanks, most of all, for the ideals of honor and faith we inherit from our forefathers—for the decency of purpose, steadfastness of resolve and strength of will, for the courage and the humility, which they possessed and which we must seek every day to emulate. As we express our gratitude, we must never forget that the highest appreciation is not to utter words but to live by them.

"Let us therefore proclaim our gratitude to providence for manifold blessings—let us be humbly thankful for inherited ideals—and let us resolve to share those blessings and those ideals with our fellow human beings throughout the world.

"Now, therefore, I, John F. Kennedy, President of the United States of America, in consonance with the joint resolution of the Congress approved December 26, 1941, designating the fourth Thursday in November in each year as Thanksgiving Day, do hereby proclaim Thursday, November 28, 1963, as a day of national thanksgiving.

"On that day let us gather in sanctuaries dedicated to worship and in homes blessed by family affection to express our gratitude for the glorious gifts of God; and let us earnestly and humbly pray that He will continue to guide and sustain us in the great unfinished tasks of achieving peace, justice, and understanding among all men and nations, and of ending misery and suffering, wherever they exist."

[From the Denver (Colo.) Register, Dec. 8, 1963]

DALLAS PRIEST RELIVES PRESIDENT'S FINAL HOURS—
FATHER HUBER POINTS TO OUTBURST OF LOVE IN CITY
WHERE J.F.K. DIED

(By Very Rev. Oscar L. Huber, C.M.)

The great day set for the visit of the President of the United States, John Fitzgerald Kennedy, had arrived. Dallas had worked feverishly to make this the most enthusiastic welcome ever to be given a President of the United States. On TV at 11:35 a.m., I saw his arrival at Love Field and heard the enthusiastic welcome given him. Then I walked down to Lemmon and Regan Streets, about three blocks from Holy Trinity Church, to await the motorcade that would bring the President along the planned route that would end at the Dallas Trade Mart, where a sumptuous luncheon and a splendidly arranged program were to highlight his visit.

There both sides of the streets were lined with people eagerly awaiting the President—there also were the children of Holy Trinity school, their teachers, the Daughters of Charity, and lay teachers. Soon the car carrying the members of the Presidential party passed by. The President and Mrs. Kennedy were waving and smiling to everyone and these gestures of good will were enthusiastically returned by the happy onlookers along the way. It was a thrilling moment for me as I had never before seen a President of the United States.

I returned to the rectory—ate a brief lunch—had just finished when Father [James N.] Thompson, C.M., one of my assistants, who had finished his lunch previously and was watching the motorcade on TV—came to the refectory and announced that the President had been shot. We went to the recreation room where we heard, over TV, the President had been taken to Parkland Hospital—this hospital is within the confines of Holy Trinity parish. Within a short time we were on our way to the hospital. Shortly after we left the rectory, a telephone call came from someone at Parkland saying Mrs. Kennedy was requesting a priest to administer to the spiritual needs of the President. Within 10 or 15 minutes we were at the hospital. Father Thompson parked the car while I was escorted by a policeman to an emergency room where I found the fatally wounded President lying on a portable table. He was covered with a sheet that I removed from over his forehead before administering the last rites of the church.

Because of the President's condition, I administered conditionally the Sacraments of Penance and Extreme Unction, followed by the Apostolic Blessing. After this I recited for the President, from the ritual prayers for the dying and for the repose of his soul, to which was added: "Eternal rest grant unto him, O Lord, and let perpetual light shine upon him. May he rest in peace. Amen."

During these ceremonies, Mrs. Kennedy was standing beside the President. She and others in the emergency room answered the prayers with which they were familiar. Mrs. Kennedy bent and seemed to kiss the President and then, I believe, placed on his finger her wedding ring. This, I have been told, signifies: "Together in life, together in death." Soon after this, followed by Mrs. Kennedy, and others who were present, I walked from the emergency room to the adjoining corridor. Sorrow and consternation bowed the heads of everyone present. The silence that pervaded the corridor was mute evidence that another President of the United States died at the hand of an assassin. Yes, it was evident—the President was dead.

During this most trying ordeal, the perfect composure maintained by Mrs. Kennedy was beyond comprehension. I will never forget the blank stare in her eyes and the signs of agony on her face. I extended my heartfelt sympathy and that of my parishioners to her. In a low tone of voice she thanked me graciously and asked me to pray for the President. I assured her I would do so. Shortly after this Father Thompson and I returned to Holy Trinity rectory.

At 5:30 the same afternoon of his death, I offered a Requiem Mass for the repose of the President's soul. Sunday morning at 9:30 a Requiem High Mass was offered for the President. On Monday, the National Day of Mourning, a Requiem High Mass was offered at 8:45 with Holy Trinity schoolchildren in attendance. In the evening at 5:30, a Solemn Requiem Mass was offered in the presence of an overflowing crowd.

I believe that in every place of worship in Dallas, Catholic, Protestant, and Jewish, services, attended by unprecedented crowds, were held for the President on the National Day of Mourning. To me this was a marvelous expression of love, devotion, and deep-seated respect for the President of the United States. The fantastic interest of the people shown by the meticulous preparations made for the visit of the President, merits for them a lasting place in the hall of loyalty. A striking demonstration of sorrow can be seen by the great number of wreaths that decorate the spot where the President was assassinated.

The people of Dallas, along with the whole world, deeply mourn the loss of our President of the United States, John Fitzgerald Kennedy. May God grant him eternal rest. Likewise, may God lead the new President of the United States, Lyndon Baines Johnson, safely along the arduous paths that lie ahead of him.

———

[From the New Orleans States-Item, Nov. 23, 1963]

OVERWHELMING TRAGEDY: ASSASSIN'S BULLET CLAIMS
PRESIDENT

What can be said that would pass as adequate comment on the tragedy of President Kennedy's assassination?

So overwhelming is the impact of his slaying at Dallas that full realization of what the assassin's bullet wrought cannot be expected to be grasped immediately.

But shock, rejection of the deed, grief, and a sense of shame that this sort of thing happens in the United States today are reactions shared by everyone—and properly so.

The people of this Nation recoil from acts of violence. Their disapproval of such methods as a means to eliminate an official from office is paramount to any feeling they may have about the official's policies.

We grieve that John F. Kennedy has joined the ranks of the martyred Presidents, Abraham Lincoln, James A. Garfield, and William McKinley.

In so doing, he gave his life for what he believed.

And such strength of conviction must be respected, even by those whose beliefs may differ in great degree and whose convictions are also unwavering.

Mr. Kennedy injected into the Presidency a winning type of personal diplomacy that comprised a new formula for solidifying Western relations on the grassroots level.

The young and dynamic head of an attractive young family, the Chief Executive brought to the White House a vitality and an atmosphere of family life that hadn't been known there since the dawning years of the 20th century.

And he died as surely in the service of his country as had he fallen in military service. All but those whose gnawing rancor has overpowered Judeo-Christian ethic will say as much.

Out of this senseless bloodshed comes a burning truth which Americans cannot escape: Hate breeds more hate and, unstemmed, it and blood spill over into the streets.

For President Lyndon B. Johnson, the position suddenly thrust upon him is necessarily even more complex than it was for his predecessor. May the prayers of a nation, brought together by bonds of sympathy, rest with him as they rest with the family of the late President.

The scar of yesterday's tragedy can never be erased but Americans of good will can see to it that American principle is again enshrined.

———

[From the New Orleans (La.) Times-Picayune,
Nov. 25, 1963]

A PRESIDENT DEAD—ALL MUST SUFFER

A few rifle shots rang out near a Dallas underpass around midday Friday. But the sound moved 'round the world with the impact of a nuclear bomb.

The President of the United States had been assassinated. John Fitzgerald Kennedy was dead.

With the suddenness of the rifle shots, 200 million people were immersed in a great sorrow. At home and almost equally abroad, people were engulfed in perplexity. Who would want upon him the blood of John Kennedy, kindly man, humanitarian; the blood of a President and statesman, the most influential spokesman for the Western World? A crime so useless, so futile, so destructive to the peace of mind of countless millions—how could a thing like that happen in a country like the United States?

But after all, there's no real mystery. For among humankind there are always men of imbalance, of twisted mind, warped concepts and strange causes, some with a deep and ugly malice toward their fellow beings. Often their hate centers upon those in high places. This time the target was President Kennedy, just as thrice before Presidents of the United States had died upon the evil impulses of such assassins.

People everywhere shiver and grieve at the President's death. It is a very personal loss for most, as well as the loss of a leader. While the Nation mourns, the greatest grief, as always, overwhelms the President's family, whose members all of us wish we could console.

Vice President Lyndon B. Johnson was sworn in as President a couple of hours after the tragedy Friday. How the change will affect the affairs of state or U.S. policies abroad, one can only surmise. History tells us that the jitters will wear off soon and orderly processes will resume.

Meantime, the horror of Friday, November 22, 1963, holds the Nation in a vise that will not loosen immediately—not in these troubled days when we suffer for the crime that has been perpetrated among us.

———

[From the New Orleans (La.) Times-Picayune,
Nov. 25, 1963]

A DAY OF MOURNING

A national day of mourning proclaimed by President Lyndon B. Johnson, coincident with formal funeral services in Washington for John Fitzgerald Kennedy, will find citizens of the United States somewhat recovered and ready to pay their respects today in a thousand ways to the memory of a dynamic Chief Executive brought to untimely end.

In his successor, they have a man qualified by long years of active dealing with the affairs of the country in legislative halls at Washington; the personal choice of the late President for second position in the executive branch; a Vice President who, thanks to the enlightened policy instituted by Mr. Eisenhower, and its adoption by Mr. Kennedy, became so conversant with affairs of state and world conditions that he can take the reins with far greater assurance than ordinarily would be the case.

But as if to pile outrage on outrage and shock on shock, an assassin came forward on the Sabbath to murder the alleged assassin of Mr. Kennedy, depriving the law of its proper course. The same police department that so promptly corralled the prime suspect and with other enforcement agencies built a circumstantial case that at least saved the Nation from a period of uncertainties, wild accusations and unfounded suspicions: The same police failed somehow to shield it and its prisoner from a second unforgivable crime.

The accused individual never admitted guilt. If this was brutality against brutality, coldbloodedness against coldbloodedness, stupidity against stupidity, with no more chance given one victim than another, it nevertheless grievously affronted justice; and it may very well have circumvented it, in that otherwise the full truth of the primary crime might more readily be established.

Needless to say, pursuit of all facts and possibilities remains imperative in this connection, as it does with regard to the second slaying. Judgments, meanwhile, must remain in suspense.

New Orleans is as unhappy to be associated in nativity with the late suspect as Dallas is to have been the scene of tragedy; as our new President must be, that it occurred in his own State. But there is, of course, nothing but unhappiness connected with the entire, ghastly event. The wound that was fatal to John Fitzgerald Kennedy was a wounding of the sensibility of all Americans, wedded to the principle of a Chief Executive serving and representing all the people, and thus identified with his safety and security. The wound fatal to his alleged killer scars another foundation of our common faith. There was far too much to mourn as it was.

[From the New Orleans (La.) Times-Picayune,
Nov. 26, 1963]

KENNEDY'S SPEECHES PUT HIM AMONG HANDFUL OF PRESIDENTS

During the dramatic unfolding of the great tragedy in which the American people have shared, one of the commentators observed that John F. Kennedy was the most articulate President since Abraham Lincoln.

He overlooked, to be true, Woodrow Wilson, a profound scholar, and Franklin D. Roosevelt, a fluent phrasemaker, but he was on solid ground.

For John F. Kennedy indeed brought intellectual brilliance, wide knowledge, and sound scholarship to the White House, as was often noted.

Carl Sandburg, the poet and biographer of Lincoln, expressed it beautifully and ably in a foreword to a collection of President Kennedy's speeches, published in 1962 under the title, "To Turn the Tide." Said Sandburg:

"Not often has a President of our country had, besides content and substance to his speeches, the further merit of style as such. We recur to Jefferson, Lincoln, Wilson, the two Roosevelts, and we are near the end of the list. In the opinion of many, Kennedy belongs among those always having good solid content, often color and cadence in style, and there are moments in the cause of human freedom when his words move with a measured passion."

A few quotations from John F. Kennedy's early speeches in office may remind us that his words did indeed "move with a measured passion."

Eleven days before assuming, as he called it, "that high and lonely office," President-elect Kennedy addressed the Legislature of his native Massachusetts and pledged to characterize his administration with "courage, judgment, integrity, dedication."

The courage of which he spoke was "to stand up to one's enemies, and * * * to stand up, when necessary, to one's associates, the courage to resist public pressure as well as private greed." His idea of judgment concerned, "the future as well as the past * * * our own mistakes as well as the mistakes of others, with enough wisdom to know what we did not know, and enough candor to admit it." His concept of integrity envisaged "men who never ran out on either the principles in which we believed or the people, who believed in us, men whom neither financial gain nor political ambition could ever divert from the fulfillment of our sacred trust." Dedication consisted of "an honor mortgaged to no single individual or group, and compromised by no private obligation or aim, but devoted solely to serving the public good and the national interest."

In President Kennedy's inaugural address, undoubtedly one of the great inaugural speeches, he reaffirmed the faith of the Founding Fathers "that the rights of man come not from the generosity of the state but from the hand of God."

And then President Kennedy directed his words across the Iron Curtain and there could be no doubt in friendly chancelleries as well as in the Kremlin as to what they meant:

"Let every nation know, whether it wishes us well or ill, that we shall pay any price, bear any burden, meet any hardship, support any friend, oppose any foe to assure the survival and the success of liberty."

He called for an end to the deadly atomic race "to alter that uncertain balance of terror that stays the hand of mankind's final war." He called for "a beachhead of cooperation" to "push back the jungle of suspicion." He urged: "Let us never negotiate out of fear, but let us never fear to negotiate." And the keynote of his speech is as valid today as it was yesterday and will be for endless tomorrows:

"And so, my fellow Americans, ask not what your country can do for you; ask what you can do for your country."

In the light of events, this is a call for all factions in American life to rally behind the successor of John F. Kennedy—President Lyndon B. Johnson.

[From the New Orleans (La.) Times-Picayune, Nov. 25, 1963]

PRESIDENT'S SLAYING THROWS PALL OVER 61ST TULANE-LSU GAME

The senseless, brutal killing of President Kennedy cast a pall over the 61st football game between Tulane and LSU.

As far as I'm concerned, the game should have been postponed until next Saturday. Apparently close to 10,000 ticket holders felt the same way, for although 64,000 seats were sold for the game, the attendance was estimated at 55,000 over the loudspeaker. I'd like to bet it didn't exceed 50,000. Threatening weather may have kept some at home, but the likelihood is that they didn't have any stomach for football in such a moment of national tragedy.

And for those who were there—or so it seemed to me, because that's how I felt—it was just another football game, not the Tulane-LSU game.

One may rationalize until he's blue in the face that the late John F. Kennedy, himself, a lover of sports, would have wanted the game to go on. Most of the other, but not all, self-respecting universities in the country didn't feel that way and why Tulane and LSU chose not to line up with the vast majority of these schools is anybody's guess.

I said it was just another game. As a Tulane fan, who hasn't seen his team beat LSU since 1948, it really didn't make much difference how it came out. As Tulane lost again, 20 to 0, I found little or no cause to grieve in the face of national grief. What is a lost game when we've lost a President? Had Tulane pulled the virtually impossible, an upset, I doubt if the long denied victory would have brought any feeling of exaltation to me. Does one, can one, feel personal joy while experiencing the impact of an unbelievable national catastrophe?

Normally, I would have devoted this space to the Tulane-LSU game. I will stop here after saying that LSU was a bigger and better and faster team than Tulane and demonstrated it ably and that Tulane, although outmatched, was not outclassed nor outfought.

News of President Kennedy's death came over my car radio Friday as I was driving up to Baton Rouge for a meeting. As the airport slipped by, the first flash came and then, mile by mile, the dreadful story unfolded. Everyone to whom I spoke at Baton Rouge or when I got home had the same reaction. This was a monstrous thing, cruel to a nation, and to a family. And anyone with an honest heart, whether he be pro-Kennedy or anti-Kennedy, liberal or conservative, Democrat or Republican, must have done some soul searching since the fatal shots were fired.

There are those who hated John F. Kennedy with a blind hatred, because they opposed his policies. Can't one have an honest opposition without hatred and venom?

There are those who encouraged disrespect for the law because they didn't like the law any more than they liked Kennedy.

On the other hand, there are those who idolized Kennedy and were perhaps as blind in their idolatry as the Kennedy haters were blind in their hatred.

But the true stature of the man who was the youngest elected President of the United States is shown by the worldwide shock and dismay over the news of his assassination and by the glowing tributes of world leaders, most of whom had flown into Washington for today's funeral.

The consequences of an irresponsible, cruel act—the aim of a gun, the pressure of a trigger finger—were far reaching, for not only a nation, but the free world mourns. And more intimately, three families have been shattered by the gunfire by Lee Harvey Oswald.

First it was the Kennedy family—suddenly bereft of a son, a husband, and a father.

Then, when Oswald was trying to get away, he killed Policeman Tippitt, bringing shattering grief to the officer's family.

And when Jack Ruby killed Oswald in a bizarre development in this tragic story, he brought extra grief to the already grief stricken mother, wife, and children of the President's assassin.

From Oswald's initial shot stemmed a chain of grief which circled the world, starting from the Kennedy family and ending with his own.

———

[From the Washington (D.C.) Post, Nov. 26, 1963]

TODAY AND TOMORROW: MURDER MOST FOUL

(By Walter Lippmann)

The first need of the country is to take to heart the nature of this unspeakable crime. There is no public crisis at home or abroad which demands such instant attention that it cannot wait until we have collected ourselves and can proceed deliberately. But there is a searing internal crisis within the American spirit which we have first to realize and then resolve.

The American future depends upon it, and our capacity to govern ourselves. What we have to realize is that, though speech and gossip and rumor are free, the safety of the Republic is at stake when extremists go unrestrained. Extremists may profess any ideology. But what they all have in common is that they treat opponents as enemies, as outside the laws and the community of their fellow men.

What happened in Dallas could, to be sure, have happened in another city. But it must be said that the murder of the President was not the first act of political violence in that city but one in a series. The man who is now the President of the United States was manhandled by his fellow Texans. The man who represents the United States at the United Nations was spat upon.

In this atmosphere of political violence lived the President's murderer, himself addicted to the fascination of violence in his futile and lonely and brooding existence. The salient fact about him was his alienation from humanity, from country, family, and friends. Nothing within him, it would seem, bound him to the President or to the Governor as human beings. No human feeling stayed his hand.

In his alienation Oswald turned to the left. But that was incidental. Those who assaulted Lyndon Johnson and Adlai Stevenson had turned to the right. The common characteristic of all of them was their alienation, the loss of their ties, the rupture of the community.

An extremist is an outsider. For him the Government in Washington is a hated foreign power and the President in Washington is an invading conqueror. There is no limit, therefore, to his hatred which feeds upon the venom of malice, slander, and hallucination. In Dallas today there is much searching of conscience, and well there should be. For Dallas has long been conspicuous for its tolerance of extremists, and for the inability of its decent citizens, undoubtedly the great majority, to restrain the extremists and restore a condition of honest and temperate and reasonable discussion.

It was comforting, therefore, to read on Sunday that the mayor of Dallas, Earle Cabell, had said that "each of us, in prayerful reflection, must search his heart and determine if through intemperate word or deed we might have contributed in some fashion to the movement of this mind across the brink of insanity."

We must all follow the mayor of Dallas in that prayerful reflection. For it is only too easy to forget that in a free country there must be not only liberty and equality but also fraternity.

The only solace for the Nation's shame and grief can come from a purge, or at least the reduction of, the hatred and venom which lie so close to the surface of our national life. We have allowed the community of the American people to be rent with enmity. Only if and as we can find our way back into the American community will we find our way back to confidence in the American destiny.

We must stop the flow of the poison that when men differ, say about taxes or civil rights or Russia, they cannot be reconciled by persuasion and debate, and that those who take the other view are implacable enemies. In the light of this monstrous crime, we can see that in a free country, which we are and intend to be, unrestrained speech and thought are inherently subversive. Democracy can be made to work only when the bonds of the community are inviolate, and stronger than all the parties and factions and interests and sects.

I wish I felt certain that the self-realization into which grief has shocked us will endure when we go back about our business. The divisive forces of hatred and ungovernability are strong among us, and the habit of intemperate speech and thought has become deeply ingrained. It is deepened by the strains of war and the frustrations of this revolutionary age, by the exploitation of violence and cruelty in the mass media, by the profusion of weapons and by the presence of so many who know how to use them.

But I do have much hope in the healing arts of Lyndon Johnson. We can turn to him with confidence. For his great gift is in finding the consensus without which the American system of government, with its States and regions, its checks and balances, is unworkable.

To find the consensus among our divided and angry people is his historic opportunity. To restore the internal peace of the United States is his unique mission. That done, all else will be manageable.

———

[From the Washington Post, Nov. 26, 1963]

KENNEDY SLUMPED OVER AND SAID NOTHING: CONNALLY DESCRIBES ASSASSINATION: "FROM GREAT JOY TO GREAT TRAGEDY"

DALLAS, November 27.—Texas Gov. John Connally, wounded during the assassination of President Kennedy, said today that after being shot the President "slumped over and said nothing."

"As I turned to the left, I was hit. I knew I was hit badly. I said, 'My God, they are going to kill us all.'

"Then there was a third shot and the President was hit again. Mrs. Kennedy said 'Oh, my God. They killed my husband. Jack, Jack.'

"In the space of a few seconds, great joy and anticipation was turned to great tragedy."

Connally, in an interview from his hospital bed—the first since he was shot while riding with Mr. Kennedy last Friday—said he has had many thoughts since the tragedy and one of the most important was why Mr. Kennedy's life was taken and his was spared.

Connally recalled:

"It was a great morning. The crowds were great in Fort Worth. There were huge throngs in Dallas.

"Dallas was real warm, real understanding, and real appreciative.

"The ovation for Kennedy was tremendous.

"The President and his wife both remarked about how warm it was.

"Not 30 seconds before the President was shot, Nellie (Mrs. Connally) had said to the President that no one could say that Dallas did not love and appreciate him.

"Kennedy answered her, 'You sure can't.' "

Then Connally described the actual shooting.

Connally said he did not think the assassin was after him only.

"The man did what he intended to do—he shot both of us," the Governor added.

Connally said that perhaps the President, through his death, was asked to do something that is hard to do in life, and that is:

"To shock and stun a nation and its people and the world to what is happening to us through this cancerous growth of extremism."

"This is the only answer I can give you on why he is gone and I am not," he added.

He said the world should avoid the type of extremism that breeds hatred.

"The genesis of our self-destruction—if we are going to be destroyed—comes from this extremism," he added.

Connally wept and dried his eyes with a towel during a pause in the interview, the first portion of which lasted 5 minutes.

NOT TOLD OF DEATH

The Governor said he was not told that the President was dead until Saturday, the day after the assassination.

"But it was no news, I was almost sure he would be after those two shots."

"My first conscious thoughts were, 'My God, what a horrible tragedy in a space of a few minutes.' It makes you ponder and wonder if you are making the contribution you should make to society because you never know when a thing like this can happen."

Connally said a monument should be built to President Kennedy, "but I hope that the people build not in the sense of absolving themselves. The monument should be through patience, tolerance, knowledge, human understanding, and dignity."

The Governor said he had been very close to the new President, Lyndon Johnson, serving with him in the Navy during World War II.

"I thought how ironic it was that the man who defeated him (for the Democratic nomination) named me Secretary of the Navy and on the day of the tragedy Johnson became President of the United States."

Asked to give his opinion of President Johnson, Connally said he was a person "of many complexities."

He said that President Johnson had a great understanding of human nature, was a man of his convictions and was forever working for perfection.

"No man ever assumed office better equipped to carry out the duties of the Office of President."

Connally said Mr. Johnson was born of hard times and his days of school were arduous.

"But he walked with many people of many nationalities and he understands the heartbeat of this Nation as no other man in this position has," Connally said.

NEWSMEN SEARCHED

Connally's interview late this afternoon in Parkland Hospital was conducted by Martin Agronsky of the National Broadcasting Co., picked by Connally as a good reporter. Other reporters watched the interview on a closed television circuit as a part of the interview plan.

Prior to the actual news conference two still photographers and one silent movie cameraman were allowed in Connally's room. Newsmen were checked thoroughly and searched before being allowed near the door.

"We were asked not to reveal the location of the bed in the room or the other security measures that had been taken," a photographer said.

———

[From the Wall Street Journal, Nov. 26, 1963]

NO TIME FOR COLLECTIVE GUILT

In the shock of these past few days it is understandable that Americans should find their grief mingled with some shame that these events should happen in their country.

We all stand a little less tall than we did last Friday morning.

Yet, for our own part, we find past understanding the remarks of some otherwise thoughtful men who, in their moment of shock, would indict a whole Nation with a collective guilt. It seems to us that they themselves have yielded to the hysteria they would charge to others, and in so doing show that their own country is past their understanding.

Any one who has been reading the newspapers, listening to the radio or watching television has heard these men; they include public commentators, Members of our Congress and men of God. And the substance of what they charge is that the whole of the American people—and by inclusion, the ways of the American society—are wrapped in a collective guilt for the murder of a President and the murder of a murderer.

A Senator said that the responsibility lay on "the people of Dallas" because this is where the events took place. A spokesman for one group of our people said the Nation was "reaping the whirlwind of hatred." One of our highest judges said the President's murder was stimulated by the "hatred and malevolence" that are "eating their way into the bloodstream of American life." A newspaper of great renown passed judgment that "none of us can escape a share of the fault for the spiral of violence." And these were but a few among many.

Such statements can only come from men who have not been broad in the land, neither paused to reflect how the events came about nor observed in what manner the whole American people have responded to tragedy.

A President lies dead because he moved freely among the people. He did so because he was beloved by many people, respected by all, and because everywhere people turned out in great numbers to pay him honor. In a society of tyranny the heads of state move in constant fear of murder, cordoned behind an army of policemen. It is the fundamental orderliness of the American society that leads Presidents to move exposed to all the people, making possible the act of a madman.

In the tragedy there is blame, surely, for negligence. In retrospect, perhaps, it was negligent of a President himself not to be aware that there are ever madmen in the world; yet it is a negligence born of courage and confidence. It was negligent of the police authorities, perhaps, not to search and cover every corner, every window, which might shield a madman; yet it was a negligence born of years of proven trust in the crowds of Americans through which Presidents have safely moved.

It was most certainly a terrible negligence on the part of the local police authorities which permitted one man to take vengeance into his own hands. It was an outrageous breach of responsibility for them to have moved a man accused of so heinous a crime in so careless a fashion. It was outrageous precisely because all the American people were themselves so outraged by the crime of assassination that anyone who knew these people ought to have known that one among them might be deranged enough to do exactly what was done.

Yet the opportunity for negligence came because here the accused was being treated as any other accused, his detention in the hands of local police, the procedures those followed for the ordinary of murders. In another land he would have been efficiently buried by a secret police in a Lubyianka prison, never again to be seen or heard of until his execution.

One might say, we suppose, that some of this negligence could be laid to all of us. It is, after all, the eager interest of the people in the persons of their leaders that brings them into open caravans, and it is the desire of the people to follow the normal ways even in murders of state that left the accused to bungling local police.

In sum, there is in all of this—let there be no mistake—much to grieve, to regret, to blame. We can't escape remorse that there are madmen in our midst, that a President is dead, that we have been denied the right to show in open court the virtue of a free society. Now we pay the price of all sorts of negligence.

But this is something different from the charge in the indictment. It is more than nonsense to say that the good people of Dallas, crowding the streets to honor a President, share a murderous guilt; or that the tragic acts of madmen cast a shadow on the whole of America. Such an indictment is vicious.

Of reasons for shame we have enough this day without adding to them a shameful injustice to a mourning people.

[From the Clarion Herald, New Orleans, La., Nov. 28, 1963]

THE LAST FULL MEASURE

"Every day is a good day to be born and every day is a good day to die."

With serene faith, Pope John XXIII accepted the illness that on June 3 of this year terminated his brief but brilliant term as Supreme Pontiff.

His words are a consolation as all mourn the tragic death of another world leader on November 22—John F. Kennedy, President of the United States.

It is a consolation sadly needed, for humanly speaking, the passing of President Kennedy seems far more untimely.

The Holy Father died at 82. In his short reign he achieved a greatness that few men in history have reached in decades. In his "Pacem in Terris," completed not long before his death, he left a heritage of hope for world brotherhood and peace. In his convoking of the Second Vatican Council he challenged not only the church but the world to a renewal of faith, to a refashioning of spiritual forces to meet the needs of a world in turmoil, to a uniting of all men in the brotherhood of Christ and the fatherhood of God.

President Kennedy died of an assassin's bullet at 46. He achieved greatness in the service of his country as a naval officer in World War II, followed by distinguished performance as U.S. Representative and Senator, and by truly notable service as President and world leader. Yet his work had only begun. As experience ripened into greater wisdom his native gifts of intelligence, courage, and leadership, how much more could he have wrought for America and for the world.

Upon the strong shoulders of Pope Paul VI fell the mantle of Pope John. Ably has he carried on the mission of the church and especially the concern to complete the ecumenical council.

To Vice President Lyndon B. Johnson are committed the responsibilities of Mr. Kennedy. With his training and experience there is no doubt that President Johnson will prove an able leader. But Kennedy's genius will be sorely missed, particularly in the struggle to make completely effective the American democratic ideal of full equality for all.

This struggle began a century ago with the efforts of another President, Abraham Lincoln, who also was prevented from completing his mission by an assassin's bullet. Just 100 years ago this month Lincoln made his immortal address at Gettysburg, concluding with this charge to the Nation:

"It is for us the living rather to be dedicated here to the unfinished work which they who fought here have thus far so nobly advanced. It is rather for us to be here dedicated to the great task remaining before us— that from these honored dead we take increased devotion to that cause for which they gave the last full measure of devotion—that we here highly resolve that these dead shall not have died in vain, that this Nation under God shall have a new birth of freedom, and that government of the people, by the people, for the people, shall not perish from the earth."

The "last full measure of devotion" given to America by these two great Presidents today is a charge upon the conscience of all Americans that they shall not have died in vain.

——

[From the Washington (D.C.) Evening Star,
Nov. 29, 1963]

TEXT OF MESSAGE—END HATRED, JOHNSON ASKS

(NOTE—Following is the text of President Johnson's personal Thanksgiving Day message to the American people, delivered over nationwide television and radio networks.)

My fellow Americans, on yesterday, I went before the Congress to speak for the first time as President of the United States.

Tonight, on this Thanksgiving, I come before you to ask your help, to ask your strength, to ask your prayers that God may guard this Republic and guide my every labor.

All of us have lived through 7 days that none of us will ever forget. We are not given the divine wisdom to answer why this has been, but we are given the human duty of determining what is to be, what is to be for America, for the world, for the cause we lead, for all the hopes that live in our hearts.

A great leader is dead; a great Nation must move on. Yesterday is not ours to recover, but tomorrow is ours to win or to lose. I am resolved that we shall win the tomorrows before us. So I ask you to join me in that resolve, determined that from this midnight of tragedy, we shall move toward a new American greatness.

More than any generation before us, we have cause to be thankful on this Thanksgiving Day. Our harvests are bountiful, our factories flourish, our homes are safe, our defenses are secure.

We live in peace. The good will of the world pours out for us, but more than these blessings, we know tonight that our system is strong, strong and secure. A deed that was meant to tear us apart has bound us together. Our system has passed. You have passed a great test. You have shown what John F. Kennedy called upon us to show in his proclamation of this Thanksgiving: That decency of purpose, that steadfastness of resolve, and that strength of will which we inherit from our forefathers.

What better conveys what is best for America than this. On Saturday when these great burdens had been mine only hours, the first two citizens to call upon and to offer their whole support were Dwight D. Eisenhower and Harry S. Truman.

Since last Friday, Americans have turned to the good, to the decent values of our life. These have served us. Yes; these have saved us. The service of our public institution and our public men is the salvation of us all from the Supreme Court to the States. And how much better it would be, how much more sane it would be, and how much more decent and American it would be if all Americans could spend their fortunes and could give their time and spend their energies helping our system and its servants to solve your problems instead of pouring out the venom and the hate that stalemate us in progress.

I have served in Washington 32 years—32 years yesterday. I have seen five Presidents fill this awesome office. I have known them well and I have counted them all as friends: President Herbert Hoover, President Franklin Roosevelt, President Harry Truman, President Dwight Eisenhower, and President John Kennedy.

In each administration, the greatest burden that the President had to bear has been the burden of his own countrymen's unthinking and unreasoning hate and division. So in these days, the fate of this office is the fate of us all. I would ask all Americans on this day of prayer and reverence to think on these things. Let all who speak and all who teach and all who preach and all who publish and all who broadcast and all who read or listen—let them reflect upon their responsibilities to bind our wounds, to heal our sores, to make our society well and whole for the tasks ahead of us. It is this work that I most want us to do, to banish rancor from our words and malice from our hearts, to close down the poison spring of hatred and intolerance and fanaticism; to protect our unity North and South, East and West; to hasten the day when bias of race, religion and region is no more; and to make the day when our great energies and decencies and spirit will be free of the burdens that we have borne too long.

Our view is outward. Our thrust is forward, but we remember in our hearts this brave young man who lives in honored eternal rest across the Potomac. We remember him; we remember his wonderful and courageous widow that we all love. We remember Caroline and John and all the great family who gave the Nation this son and brother.

And to honor his memory and the future of the works he started, I have today determined that Station No. 1 of the Atlantic Missile Range and a NASA Launch Operation Center in Florida shall hereafter be known as the John F. Kennedy Space Center.

I have also acted today with the understanding and the support of my friend, the Governor of Florida, Farris Bryant, to change the name of Cape Canaveral. It shall be known hereafter as Cape Kennedy.

On this Thanksgiving Day, as we gather in the warmth of our families, in the mutual love and respect that we have for one another, and as we bow our heads in submission to Divine Providence, let us also thank God for the years that He gave us inspiration through His servant, John F. Kennedy.

Let us today renew our dedication to the ideals that are American. Let us pray for His divine wisdom in banishing from our land any injustice or intolerance or oppression to any of our fellow Americans whatever their opinion, whatever the color of their skins—for God made all of us, not some of us, in His image. All of us, not just some of us, are His children.

And, finally, to you as your President, I ask that you remember your country and remember me each day in your prayers, and I pledge to you the best within me to work for a new American greatness, a new day when peace is more secure, when justice is more universal, when freedom is more strong in every home of all mankind.

———

[From the New Orleans (La.) Times-Picayune, Nov. 30, 1963]

BISHOP SCORES HATE CLIMATE—CALLS ON AMERICANS TO RECOGNIZE GUILT

The Episcopal bishop of Louisiana called upon Americans to recognize their guilt Friday night at a service of prayer and meditation occasioned by the assassination of President Kennedy.

The Right Reverend Girault M. Jones told worshipers at the Church House on St. Charles Avenue, "We have so completely forsaken the Biblical precepts of charity and of brotherhood that what was once a close-knit society is coming apart at the seams."

"We know that hatred leads to violence, and yet we have been willing to risk such consequences. We have identified political policies with one man, we have personalized worldwide social unrest by this man's image, we have shared in gossip, in offcolor jokes, and in deliberate misrepresentation * * * all in such a way as to plant the seeds of personal hatred, and to nurse them into flower," Bishop Jones said.

"America has created a climate of suspicion and of hatred in which no man is permitted to be himself," he told worshippers at the service, held by the Greater New Orleans Federation of Churches and the New Orleans Ministerial Union.

Stating the "American way of life" cannot "stand the test of world scrutiny," Bishop Jones continued, "and now we must admit what can happen in the Congo, or in the Dominican Republic, or in Vietnam * * * can also happen here."

"This is a tragic day. We grieve the loss of a President, and we would honor his memory. We grieve for his family, and we would offer sympathy. We grieve for

this Nation, and indeed for the world, and would pray that out of this shocking experience, God will recall us to Himself," the bishop concluded.

Other clergymen who participated in the service were the Reverend Dr. G. Avery Lee, pastor of St. Charles Avenue Baptist Church; the Reverend Dr. Alex W. Hunter, minister of the First Presbyterian Church; the Reverend Herbert L. Polinard, minister of the St. Charles Avenue Christian Church, and the Reverend George Wilson, executive secretary of the Greater New Orleans Federation of Churches.

The Reverend W. K. Sisk, Jr., minister of the Elysian Fields Baptist Church, presided.

———

[From the Washington (D.C.) Post, Dec. 1, 1963]

ASSASSINATION PLUS SOCIETY ALSO SUFFERED TWO GREAT WOUNDS

[By Roscoe Drummond]

Everyone who has spoken and written about the misshapen events that have engulfed us—assassination and then murder on top of assassination—have avowed and prayed and predicted that, as a people and as a nation, we would emerge from the shock and shame of these events a better people and a better nation.

I believe this will prove to be true. But neither words of wrath nor words of expiation nor words pious and wishful thinking will make it so. Words will do little and words without deeds will do nothing.

Jesus taught that man must be judged by his fruits, not by his protestations. And Paul, in his letter to the Philippians, after commending us to think on whatsoever things are pure and honest and just and of good report, instantly added the higher command:

"These things, which ye have both learned and received, and heard, and seen in Me, do, and the God of peace shall be with you." (Philippians 4: 9)

If we are to learn some good from these horrible events, we must fix clearly in mind the exact wounds that have been inflicted upon our society and upon our Nation.

The murder of the President is grievous enough. But great wounds were inflicted upon our whole democracy.

1. The assassin's bullet struck from the hands of the 68,836,385 citizens who went to the polls in 1960 their precious right to have a President of their own choosing and an administration by the consent of the administered.

2. The murderer's bullet struck from the hands of the accused assassin, the most precious guarantee of a free society, an open trial in open courts by a jury of his peers.

These are two grievous wounds to the fiber and fabric of what most Americans cherish as the pillars of our social compact: a knife wound at our process of democracy, a knife wound at the process of justice.

After Jack Ruby shot Lee Harvey Oswald as he was surrounded by Dallas police in the basement of the city jail, you no doubt listened to the many interviews in the street which television recorded. Not a few of them expressed their praise and pleasure at the murder of the accused assassin. In almost the same words, each said, "I believe in an eye for an eye, a tooth for a tooth; I'm glad he got it."

Are they, when they think it over? Our criminal law is based, in part, on the Old Testament moral law of an eye for an eye, the doctrine that punishment must fit the crime. But who shall determine the guilty? An enemy, an avenger, a crackpot—or a court of law? Ruby acted to sentence Oswald before he was tried—and the American social compact was torn asunder as it has been torn too often in recent years.

I believe that the point of beginning is to be a little less sure that we alone are right and that those who disagree are automatically wrong. I share the view that the words and actions of the extremist right and the extremist left have sown seeds of hatred and violence in the land. But even here I would draw with great care the lessons from the acts of hideousness we have recently experienced.

There is no evidence that the assassination was the act of a racist. There is no evidence that the assassin was influenced to commit his act by the seeds of hatred which extreme racists have sown and which have come to fruition in the murder of Medgar Evers and the Negro schoolchildren in Birmingham.

We don't know what went on in Oswald's twisted mind and, because Ruby took the law in his hands, we never will know.

But we do know that the words of President Johnson need to be taken to heart by all of us: "Let us put an end to the teaching and preaching of hate and evil and violence. Let us turn away from the fanatics of the far left and the far right, from the apostles of bitterness and bigotry, from those defiant of law and those who pour venom into our Nation's bloodstream."

Why shouldn't we?

————

[From the Baltimore (Md.) Sun, Nov. 23, 1963]

The President

John Fitzgerald Kennedy is dead, and the Nation mourns him. Yesterday's first shock of horror gives way this morning to a depth of sorrow beyond expression. We can at this moment only look back briefly, and try to look forward briefly, and look into our own hearts as individuals and as a people.

President Kennedy loved the life that has been taken from him. That is what we think of first, remembering him. The pictures that come back are the lively ones: the candidate fighting with a kind of cheerful ferocity for the great office in the performance of whose duties he died; the President laughing, sailing, throwing himself into a speech, joking with his children, reveling in a world full of things to see and hear and think about and above all, do. Life and color and, to use his favorite word, vigor, went with him everywhere. He was greatly endowed by fortune and, unlike many men so endowed, knew it. Complaint and repining were no part of him. Lethargy was no part of him. This quality of vividness, which captivated first the country and then much of the world, makes it seem all the more incredible that he should have been struck down, at the peak of his abilities, gone at an age when most men of his stature are still but on their way toward high achievement.

His death is a tragedy with many facets. The country's first thoughts go to his family, his gentle wife and his young children, only just old enough to understand that their father and companion is gone; his close-knit band of brothers and sisters, his parents, who now lose a third child dead too young. That for all of us is the personal aspect: in loss, all mankind is kin.

There is the tragedy too of great tasks unfinished, of the plow stopped part way down the furrow, the house left standing in framework, the story checked mid-sentence. No one now can say what Mr. Kennedy's accomplishments would have been had he lived. We do know that he was a strong man in a crisis, and the graver the crisis the stronger the man. Berlin in 1961 and Cuba last year are the memorable examples, written forever in our history: at those breathless moments President Kennedy held the Nation's fate in his hands, and the hands were firm. We do know that in shocking national failure, as with the Bay of Pigs, Mr. Kennedy could take upon himself the full burden of responsibility. We do know that he left his country stronger in the world than he had found it, and more confident of its destiny. We do know that when internal discord arose to threaten our tranquillity, because of wrongs left too long unrighted, he faced the issue gravely, squarely, and honestly, leading the country in another crisis, a crisis this time of the national conscience. Thus the record so far. What the rest might have been we shall never know.

Regret for a life's work cruelly cut off, and horror at the way Mr. Kennedy died, and grief over personal loss, are not enough. We must resolve as a nation that the story in which Mr. Kennedy was for all too short a time the chief actor shall continue, and grow brighter and more honorable, until the blots of bitterness and hatred no longer stain its pages.

The Government of the United States continues; that Government of which a President is at once master and servant. Any one man's passing is, in the long life of this democracy, but a missed heartbeat. Mr. Kennedy, who had looked death in the face oftener than most, who was a scholar of the Constitution and a pragmatic politician, knew that as well as anyone. To every President the existence of the Vice Presidency is a constant reminder of the continuity of the Republic, though men are mortal. It must have crossed Mr. Kennedy's mind, from that moment more than 3 years ago when he asked Lyndon Johnson to run for office with him, that his old Senate colleague, his political rival and friend, might through an accident of history be his successor.

Upon President Johnson now falls this weight of office. Only one other man in the United States knows how heavy the mantle is when it falls suddenly upon the shoulders. Harry Truman, in 1945, spoke for Lyndon Johnson today when he asked his hearers, if they ever prayed, to pray for him now.

————

[From the Christian Science Monitor, Nov. 27, 1963]

Kennedy's Great Work—Its Impact Abroad

(By Joseph C. Harsch)

London.—John F. Kennedy did not have time to achieve everything he hoped to achieve. The biggest single waste in terms of statecraft is that he will not have the chance to use in what might have been his second term the influence and prestige which he had gained during his first.

The immediate damage is minor, since, in effect, a recess had been called in diplomatic affairs. The week of the assassination opened with a restatement of the world balance of power by Secretary of Defense Robert S. McNamara which had the effect of closing the season. The Soviets would hardly be expected to negotiate in the wake of an announcement of decisive Western superiority in both conventional and nuclear weapons.

Even without the McNamara speech the chances of useful or constructive diplomacy during the balance of this year and 1964 were uncertain. Great nations do not often negotiate over major issues when elections are in the offing. Had Mr. Kennedy been spared, he might have been able to do little more until after the November elections next year than others apparently can do now. It appeared probable to be a period of waiting.

But had he won his reelection substantially, he would have possessed such influence and prestige as few statesmen in history ever have achieved. It would have been an advantage to himself and his country of significant value—a credit to be spent for the greater security of his country, of his allies, and of the world.

An English workman who knew me to be an American stopped me on the street and offered me his sympathy on my loss and told me that when he heard the news he wept. I asked him why, and he said, "He was one of us. He was a good man. And I felt safe while he was there."

Many "felt safe while he was there."

That feeling of safety was not an old condition; it was a very recent condition. It can be dated from the Cuban crisis of October a year ago. Until Cuba, the duel between Soviet Premier Nikita S. Khrushchev and Mr. Kennedy was unresolved and relentless. At some point there had to be the decisive confrontation, the final test of strength.

That moment of the Cuban crisis grows larger in perspective as it recedes into the past. It stands out on the record of the past as the watershed between the period when the possibility of nuclear war ever was present in our lives and the period when the danger seems itself to be a major deterrent.

Mr. Kennedy gave the West, indeed all the world, the priceless gain of release from fear of inevitable nuclear war. He gave us all a chance to look and think and plan ahead in an atmosphere of confidence and relief.

Perhaps not everyone realized the achievement until the man who had gained it was gone. Surely the workman on the street did not realize until the blinding moment of tragedy that he indeed had felt more safe and secure over a whole year for the first time since the last great war ended. When the climactic moment came, he understood it and could articulate it.

In one sense that achievement remains for the greater safety of all. The clock can scarcely be turned back entirely to the dark and dangerous times before the Cuban confrontation. The essential facts of these new times remain unaltered and undamaged. It is reasonable to assume that diplomacy can resume its work once the various political uncertainties of the next year are resolved.

But there already will have been two Presidents in the White House in Washington during a span of 2 years and 10 months and there is now a possibility of three in 3 years. The chance of much achievement until this time of change is over is not large.

The evil work in Dallas has taken from us all the opportunity Mr. Kennedy had earned for himself and the human race to use a longer period. None other can use it for him as he could have used it. It takes the better part of 4 years to make a President.

Mr. Kennedy had only just emerged in his full stature as the leading statesman of the world when hatred struck him down. This is the heaviest loss to the world.

———

[From the Washington (D.C.) Post, Nov. 25, 1963]

Go, Stranger

(By Joseph Alsop)

Of all the men in public life in his time, John Fitzgerald Kennedy was the most ideally formed to lead the United States of America.

Such, at any rate, is this reporter's judgment, perhaps biased, but at any rate based on long experience and close observation, and no longer possible to suspect as self-serving. To be sure, judging Kennedy was never easy, for he was no common man, to be judged by common standards.

Courage, intelligence, and practicality; a passion for excellence and a longing to excel; above all, a deep love of this country, a burning pride in its past, and unremitting confidence in the American future—these were the qualities which acted, so to say, as the mainsprings of Kennedy the President.

Kennedy the man, Kennedy the private face, was half the enemy and half the reinforcement of Kennedy the President. He had an enviable grace of manner and person. He enjoyed pleasure. After Theodore Roosevelt, he was the first American President to care for learning for its own sake. After Abraham Lincoln, he was the first American President with a rich vein of personal humor—which is a very different thing from the capacity to make jokes.

This strange, dry, detached, self-mocking humor no doubt aided him to assess men and events; but in his public role, it was a handicap. Certainly it was not the same sort of handicap as Lincoln's humor, which actually prevented great numbers of otherwise intelligent persons from taking Lincoln seriously.

President Kennedy's humor instead inhibited him from showing the depth of his feelings. Any public exhibition of emotion gave him gooseflesh. So foolish people said he was a cold, unfeeling man, although few men in our time have had stronger feelings about those things that mattered to him.

After his country, what mattered most to him was to live intensely, with purpose and effect. He was in some sense the ultimate personification of the observation of Justice Holmes: "Man is born to act; to act is to affirm the worth of an end; and to affirm the worth of an end is to create an ideal."

The ideal that Mr. Kennedy affirmed in action was singularly simple; for no man was ever more contemptuous of the theological complexities of ideology. (It was hard to know, indeed, whether he held a more sovereign contempt for the doctrinaire mushiness of the extreme American left or for the doctrinaire hate-preaching of the extreme American right. He was slow to anger, but these made his gorge rise.)

His ideal could be completely summed up in only a score or so of words—a nation conceived in liberty and dedicated to the proposition that all men are created equal; the proud stronghold of a new birth of freedom; and the standing promise to all men that Government of the people, by the people and for the people shall not perish from the earth. The noble, ancient phrases, the pieced-together tags from the finest of all American utterances, are as well worn by now as antique coins, whose legend is illegible. But, he could read the legend still. He still took this definition of our Nation's purpose with perfect literalness and this was the ideal that his actions sought to affirm.

Whereas, Franklin Delano Roosevelt took office when the Nation was clamoring for leadership and crying out to be shown a new course, John Fitzgerald Kennedy took office in a time of violent—yet hardly comprehensible, change.

Too many, then as now, confronted the vast revolutionary processes of our time either with fatty complacency or with shrill, embittered indignation. His task was therefore a hard task, and he was untimely cut off before his task could be half done.

Yet if we look at our country and the world in which we live—if we honestly compare the prospects now opening before us with the prospects as they seemed when Mr. Kennedy's Presidency began—we can see that there has been a new birth of hope.

It is perhaps pardonable, at this moment, to be personal. Speaking for myself, I have not dared to hope as I do now since those first months of the Korean war, when such overly high hopes were born from a strong sense that America was grandly accomplishing a high, historic service. That service had its heavy price.

I still remember watching the wolfhound regiment through a long, hard fight, and how the bodies of the fallen were carried in when the fight was won, and how I suddenly could think only of Simonides' epitaph that was inscribed, for all to read, on the tomb of the dead Spartans at Thermopylae:

"Go stranger, and in Lacedaemon tell
 That here obedient to the laws we fell."

But the President who is lost to us, like those men who were lost so many years ago, was no drilled, unthinking Spartiate. He was the worthy citizen of a nation great and free—a nation, as he liked to think, that is great because it is free and this was the thought that always inspired his too brief leadership of this Republic.

[From the Shreveport-Bossier City (La.) Journal, Nov. 25, 1963]

MICKLE ATTACKS HATEMONGERS

"The stage had been set for someone to murder President John F. Kennedy somewhere. It could have happened to Shreveport."

So spoke Dr. Joe J. Mickle, president of Centenary College, this morning, in addressing a memorial service at the college for the assassinated Chief Executive.

"I make these statements," said the educator, "because John F. Kennedy was much hated—hated both by the Communists and the professional haters of Communists.

"Judging by certain editorials, letters to the editor, an avalanche of filthy printed material, certain radio and television programs and political speeches by any number of candidates for offices in our States, John F. Kennedy was the personification of almost all evil.

"Thus it is that our thinking has been warped by an almost endless stream of words of suspicion and hatred. Hatred and violence have ridden unchecked across our land. Eventually this constant stream of destructive criticism, suspicion, hatred, and violence begins to take its toll; and faith in our Government, our churches, our schools, and our international organizations so vital to world peace and security is undermined. Thus, a climate has been created in which almost any person of warped mind or emotionally disturbed may feel that he is rendering a great service by sending a bullet crashing through the brain of a Government official.

"We can honor a great American, John F. Kennedy, only if we individually and as a nation bow our heads in introspection, humility, and repentence before Almighty God," Mickle said.

Elsewhere in Shreveport and Bossier City, residents joined with the fellow Americans in the national day of mourning for the late President.

From 11 a.m. to 1 p.m., the business life of the community came to a virtual standstill. The Shreveport Civic Center, Bossier City Hall, and many stores and business establishments were closed during the period out of respect to the slain Chief Executive.

Banks, Federal and State offices were closed for the day. So were Caddo Parish public and parochial schools. Bossier Parish schools will be closed throughout the week because of a previously announced teachers' meeting and the Thanksgiving holiday.

———

[From the Christian Science Monitor, Nov. 27, 1963]

A SCENE UNDUPLICATED

(By Richard L. Strout)

WASHINGTON.—Pictures and sounds and music told the story better than words.

The Nation, emotionally depleted, went back to everyday life—to routine jobs, to holiday shopping, and to television commercials, but with a new President and ache when it thought of a former one and with a sense of guilt that it could not quite define but could not eliminate.

Above all, the Nation had watched a brave woman, Mrs. Jacqueline Kennedy, representing it among visiting kings, presidents, and dignitaries—a woman who had seen her young husband slain at her side only 3 days before but who somehow managed from an inner spring of strength and self-control to put her sense of duty above her personal grief and to redeem in personal dignity some part of the shame and ignominy the Nation felt.

VERY DETERMINED CROWD

The story of the day can never quite be duplicated in this restless Capital. Scene after scene unfolded, then blurred into one another, and finally ended with the evening starlings, flying in as usual from across the Potomac against a fiery sunset.

Sometime during the day the White House announced that President Johnson, as one of his first acts in office, had sent to Nikita S. Khrushchev, Soviet Premier, a message pledging to continue the efforts for peace of his predecessor, John F. Kennedy.

The Johnson message replied to one of condolence and sympathy from Moscow.

Long before this announcement of state, however, the patient crowds had collected and waited and shuffled in the freezing weather all night long for a chance to file past the bier of President Kennedy. It was placed on the Lincoln catafalque in the great echoing rotunda of the hushed Capitol.

Officials were awed at the queue which, by midnight, extended back 30 blocks. At 2 a.m., and 3, at 4, and again at 5, the police warned the shuffling throng that there was little chance of getting in before the great bronze doors shut at 9 a.m. But still they came and came.

At the end, with the grotesqueness that mingles with tragedy, the line was hurried past the casket in a kind of lope.

All during Sunday dignitaries from four quarters of the globe had been gathering in Washington; so many, so varied, and so subdued that often they went to their embassies virtually unrecognized: 22 presidents or prime ministers, 3 reigning kings, and the princes and princesses of 9 countries.

SOVIET EMISSARY

There was stately President de Gaulle of France, rotund Chancellor Ludwig Erhard of West Germany, and wily Anastas Mikoyan, Soviet First Deputy Premier, who came on a special flight from Moscow as Premier Khrushchev's personal emissary.

From Britain there was Prince Philip, Prime Minister Alec Douglas-Home, and opposition leader Harold Wilson. There was beautiful Queen Frederika of Greece, picturesque Emperor Haile Selassie, and Premier Hayato Ikeda from Japan.

Then somewhat before noon, down historic Pennsylvania Avenue came the roll of drums, and the crowds, lined 10 to 20 deep, craned to see the military procession and cortege, moving from the Capitol to the White House, from whence it would go on to St. Matthew's Roman Catholic Cathedral.

The grief was genuine but it was different from that which greeted the bier of Franklin D. Roosevelt on his final ride.

DIFFERING EMOTIONS

For Roosevelt, the crowd made no effort to hide its sobs, as though for a father or protector. For President Kennedy, it was poignant rather than overwhelming. The feeling toward this gay, graceful young man evidently did not go so deep as to the wartime President; it was the tragedy of a broken home and lost opportunity rather than the vivid personal identification to the President of 12 years. Above all, it was a crowd eager to see Mrs. Kennedy.

Soldiers, sailors, airmen, marines, and special service detachments moved precisely, with black-draped drums. The journey was in two parts. The procession came to the White House that seemed to be keeping a kind of silent vigil of its own. And there Mrs. Kennedy and her family and the visiting dignitaries left cars and walked behind the procession to the cathedral.

Crowds were so dense along the streets that those in the rear could not see. Many heard only the clatter of the horses, the cadenced scuff of soldiers' feet, and the Air Force band playing "America, the Beautiful."

At many times at the cathedral and later Mrs. Kennedy stood with her two brothers-in-law, Robert Kennedy and Edward Kennedy.

Caroline and John Jr., wearing blue coats, arrived in a car and joined their mother. Her thoughts were toward her children; she comforted John who cried at one point.

A BOY'S SALUTE

At another time she bent over as the band played, and he stepped forward, holding a pretended salute.

She seemed composed as she emerged after the sonorous Latin service and waited while the coffin was placed back on the caisson for its final ride to Arlington. She held the hands of her two children, Caroline sobbing. Bells pealed softly.

Two former Presidents and old opponents, Dwight D. Eisenhower and Harry S. Truman, chatted on the cathedral steps. They were asked by Senator Kennedy to speak to Mrs. Kennedy and came forward briefly to say a few quiet words of comfort. Then they entered the same car for the ride to the cemetery.

CENTER OF SCENE

It was around Mrs. Kennedy that the scene turned. It was she that the hushed and almost awe-struck crowd followed with its eyes.

In the solemn serenity of Arlington cemetery the simple headstones of soldiers from all America's battles lie in ordered sequence.

The sky was so clear that vapor trails of airplanes were like sweeping chalkmarks on a blue board.

So on a brilliant November afternoon, in which shadows gradually lengthened, John F. Kennedy, of Massachusetts, came to rest at last, some of his work done, most undone, in a career cut short in senseless tragedy.

Shortly before midnight, Mrs. Kennedy slipped out of the White House and rode to Arlington National

Cemetery to place flowers on her husband's grave. A perpetual flame on the grave was burning through its first night.

The only meaning to all the shock and horror at the end came from the posture of his wife, Jacqueline, a woman long considered beautiful, but who came through the ordeal with ennobling dignity.

A PROCLAMATION

(Mayor Victor H. Schiro issued the following proclamation today designating Monday, November 25, 1963, as a day of sorrow in New Orleans in memory of the late President John F. Kennedy.)

Whereas the sudden and untimely death of John Fitzgerald Kennedy, the 35th President of the United States of America, has cast the dark pall of sorrow and regret over the city of New Orleans; and

Whereas the assassination of our Chief Executive ranks with the vilest crimes of this generation and as such brings down the resentment of law-abiding people everywhere; and

Whereas citizens of this community abhor and do condemn this truly un-American act which snuffed out the very life of the man chosen by this great Nation to be its duly elected President and Commander in Chief; and

Whereas law-abiding citizens are outraged at this dastardly crime which removes from his place of high esteem the leader of this Nation, a man who had not yet attained his true and ultimate mark in life:

Now, therefore, I, Victor H. Schiro, by the powers vested in me as mayor of the city of New Orleans, do hereby proclaim the day of President Kennedy's funeral service, Monday, November 25, 1963, to be a day of sorrow, and urge all citizens to publicly and privately mourn the passing of our Chief Executive.

On this sad occasion, and in tribute to our late President, I have ordered that city hall and all municipal offices be closed and I request that all American flags, displayed on public and private buildings, homes, institutions, etc., be flown at half-mast during the period of local and national mourning.

I urge all municipal employees, as well as all citizens, to observe Monday, November 25, as a day of prayer and reverence so that God, in His infinite wisdom and goodness, might: bring peace and eternal rest to the soul of President Kennedy; that the President's wife, Mrs. Kennedy, and his family might be sustained in this hour of bereavement; that our new President, Lyndon B. Johnson, might be given strength and guidance in this hour of crisis; that our Nation might be greater united to meet the challenges that face us today and in the days to come.

In addition, I recommend that all places of amusement and business be closed on Monday, November 25. Where it is not possible to close certain business establishments because of undue hardship on employers or employees, I request that at 11 a.m., c.s.t., on the above date that a 5-minute period of silent prayer be observed.

VICTOR H. SCHIRO,
Mayor.

[From the New Orleans (La.) Times-Picayune, Nov. 25, 1963]

BOGGS DESCRIBES SHOCK, SADNESS IN WASHINGTON—SAYS FREEMEN EVERYWHERE LOST FRIEND

(By U.S. Representative Hale Boggs, House majority whip)

WASHINGTON, D.C.—This is a day I never thought I would see. I shall always remember each sad detail.

I had had a busy week. On Sunday, Speaker (John W.) McCormack's brother had died in Boston, and Congressman (Carl) Albert spent the week as Speaker pro tempore, and I was acting majority leader. This meant constant attention to floor details.

Today, however, the House was not in session, and I thought I would take care of several of my many requests from constituents.

I got the news (of the President's death) in a Government agency office downtown. Immediately, the Capitol switchboard was swamped, and the streets of Washington almost instantly were jammed with people.

I hurried to Speaker McCormack's office. He had just returned today from his brother's funeral in Boston. Already, the Secret Service had quietly moved in to protect his person. (He is now next in line of succession to President Johnson.)

FLOOD OF RUMORS

Already, he was complaining about the Secret Service agents. I told him that they would be with him from now on whether he liked it or not.

We were flooded with rumors. One was that the Vice President, now President Johnson, had suffered a severe heart attack. This visibly shook the Speaker and caused grave alarm among all of us. Fortunately, this dreadful rumor was unfounded.

Soon the word came that President Kennedy's body would arrive at Andrews Air Force Base in nearby Maryland at 6:05 p.m. Congressman Carl Vinson, of Georgia, the dean of the House; Speaker McCormack and I went out to the base together. Other cars brought the other congressional leaders.

Soon, out of a clear and crisp autumn night, came the beautiful Air Force red-white-and-blue jet No. 1. Awaiting it were the dignitaries of the world who represent their Governments in Washington; Representative Charlie Halleck and Senator Everett Dirksen, the Republican leaders of the House and the Senate, were standing right next to me.

WEEP FOR WIFE

As the brown casket carrying the body of our young President was moved from the plane, the great and the near great wept openly for the brave Mrs. Kennedy, who followed behind the casket, and for the man who had given his life for America.

The President's body was then taken to the Bethesda (Md.) Naval Hospital.

The congressional leaders then went to the White House for a meeting with a grave and saddened Texan who now becomes the loneliest man on earth. Present from the

Senate were Senator (Mike) Mansfield, the majority leader; Senator Dirksen, the minority leader; Senator (Hubert) Humphrey, the majority whip; Senator (Thomas) Kuchel, the minority whip; and Senator (George) Smathers, the Senate deputy whip.

And from the House, there were Speaker McCormack, Majority Leader Carl Albert, Minority Leader Halleck, and myself.

ALL PLEDGE HELP

The new President asked for our help. He asked for a united country. He said he had been in touch with former Presidents Eisenhower and Truman and they had said they would come to Washington.

We pledged our help, and each of us, on leaving President Johnson, said, "God bless you, Mr. President."

As I left, the White House was dark except for a light in the nursery. The rocking chair in the President's office was now empty, and a lump came into my throat. I remembered on Wednesday, just the day before yesterday, at our usual weekly breakfast, the vibrant health of our President. I remembered his interest, as always, in every detail of the legislative program; his quiet comment on his warm reception the day before in Florida, and his concern for the Speaker and the loss of his brother.

As I drove away, I said to myself, I have lost a friend. The Nation has lost a peerless leader. And freemen everywhere have lost him too.

Mr. Speaker, I include herewith a splendid article written by Mr. Tom Fox of the Clarion Herald in New Orleans. It gives further insight into the warm and friendly nature of our late great President. The article follows in full:

FRAYED-COLLAR FRIENDSHIP—KENNEDY WARMTH OUTSTANDING MEMORY

(By Tom Fox)

Because great men are always judged on a yardstick of great deeds, America and the free world will remember John Fitzgerald Kennedy for the big things he accomplished in life.

Yet I will remember the slain 35th President of the United States not for his varied achievements but for a little incident that took place 3 years ago.

As news of his assassination spread across the world that black Friday in November, my thoughts raced back to Evansville, Ind., where, on a rainy October afternoon, I spent an hour with Kennedy. He was Senator Kennedy then and he was campaigning for the White House.

I was a sportswriter and fun and games were my beat. Vice President Richard Nixon had come to town and my editor barked out an assignment: "Go out and talk to Nixon about sports."

Nixon was a sports buff. He forgot about the big issues for a few minutes and talked about Ted Williams and Stan Musial and Sammy Baugh. It was a good interview, easy and relaxed. My editor was impressed.

Five days later Jack Kennedy came campaigning in Evansville.

"We've got to give the Democrats equal space," the editor said. "See if Kennedy likes sports, too."

It was not an easy assignment.

"That [sports] is not the contest this year," Kennedy said. He told me the voters should hear his views on foreign policy, the Cuban situation, unemployment, civil rights.

"Why sports?" he wanted to know.

I asked Kennedy if he could beat Ike playing golf. He seemed irked by the question.

"That's not the contest this year," he said and turned to field a question from a battery of political reporters. I was a one-man sports minority. I needed a fresh approach.

I stood back and sized up the handsome young Senator. He was wearing a brown herringbone tweed suit, a white oxford cloth shirt with blue stripes, and a blue knit tie. I looked at the shirt a second time. I had discovered a weak spot in the Kennedy armor.

The collar was badly frayed at the neckline. Jack Kennedy, seeking the highest office in the free world, was campaigning in a shirt with a frayed collar.

I edged closer to Kennedy.

"If you'll give me your collar size and sleeve length I'll buy you a new shirt," I said.

Kennedy seemed puzzled at my offer.

"Why," he asked, wrinkling his forehead, "would I be in need of a new shirt?"

"Because," I said, whispering into his ear, "the one you have on is badly frayed at the collar."

He drew back. He felt the neckline. He felt it again.

"Do I have that one on?" he asked. I nodded.

He tried to push the frayed edge inside the neckline. I told him my offer still stood. "Oh, no, no," he said, "I have other shirts on the plane."

Kennedy turned to the other reporters, but he took a double take and smiled at me. "Thanks, anyway," he said. The infectious Kennedy grin, the billboard smile that was to win the love and admiration of millions of men of good will the world over, got bigger and bigger. Jack Kennedy was laughing heartily, laughing at himself.

"You're very observant," he said. "Tell your editor I said you should be covering politics."

Perhaps the incongruity of the frayed collar struck Jack Kennedy's Irish sense of humor, for thereafter he talked on endlessly about sports.

He was explaining how his wife Jacqueline, broke an ankle in a game of touch football at Hyannisport * * * and then a minister began the invocation to open the Evansville political rally on the courthouse square.

"Just a moment," Kennedy said, bringing a finger to his lips and bowing his head in meditation.

When the prayer was over, Kennedy continued the story. "Jackie," he said, smiling, "I just got racked."

The last time I saw Jack Kennedy alive he was in the private compartment of his plane, taking off the shirt with the frayed collar. He seemed tired and drawn.

"The competition in athletics is very similar to the competition in politics," he said as I was leaving. "But you pay more in politics—physically."

People will remember John Fitzgerald Kennedy for many things. The sports buff will tell you he made touch football as popular as Coca-Cola. Wall Street may recall the gusto with which he backed down the steel interests. Diplomats will remember his courage in forcing Red missiles out of Cuba. History, perhaps, will acknowledge him as another Lincoln, a young Roosevelt, a latter day Jefferson. His church will regard him as a noble son.

But I will always remember John Fitzgerald Kennedy on that rainy October afternoon he came to Indiana campaigning for the Presidency in a frayed shirt collar.

In the wake of his tragic death, it's the only memory of the man that I can recall and somehow manage to smile.

TRIBUTE BY

Hon. Joseph W. Martin, Jr.

OF MASSACHUSETTS

Mr. Speaker, many fine tributes to our late and beloved President, John F. Kennedy, have appeared in the press of our Nation and have been heard from the pulpits of our churches. One of the most moving delivered in my district has been called to my attention by Alderman-elect Edward C. Uehlein of Newton and was written by the Reverend William Foley, rector of the Church of the Good Shepherd of the Waban section of Newton, Mass.

The sermon exhorts the American people, in memory of the late President, to rise to our highest ideals. I offer the final portion of this inspiring address.

The final veil of the Israelites was the veil of complacency. After Moses destroyed the calf, the people grew penitent. And God made a covenant with Moses and the people that He would be their God and they His people. The people rejoiced greatly. But, as the days became months and the months years, prophets rose up amongst the people because the law that Moses had given them had remained graven on stone and never entered their hearts. They had become a complacent people of outward observance, instead of inward truth, of law without love, of tight lips and loose morals, a people that knew all the words of God but never let them enter their lives.

We too have tended to become a complacent people. We have grown sleek and fat, happy in our material splendor and complacent about our spiritual nature. This is the kind of decay that has preceded the fall of the greatest civilizations known to man. They didn't have to be bombed out of existence, they just got so rotten that they fell of their own weight.

When the people of a nation are no longer roused by the revelations of a Valachi, the appalling rate of promiscuity, the suppression of minority groups, when people no longer speak out and take action against the decay of spiritual values, then they are dead already, and the righteous God shall bury them—perhaps even using a Russia, or a Red China, as His instrument. For the righteous God shall make no complacent compromise with evil.

If our 46-year-old President is not to have died in vain, we must rouse ourselves and turn our blinded eyes to the One who can heal us, who can lift us up and take the veil from our eyes so we can see again. His name is Jesus Christ. He has been taking the veils from people's eyes for centuries, showing them the fresh vision of a new and greater life. For in him all veils have been removed, and we can see God face to face—if only we are dissatisfied enough with the veils of a narrow life to come to Him and believe.

TRIBUTES BY

Hon. Edward P. Boland

OF MASSACHUSETTS

Mr. Speaker, I offer the following editorial from the Saturday Review. Its brilliance and depth need no comment of mine.

THE LEGACY OF JOHN F. KENNEDY

An American President is something special in the world precisely because American history has been something special. A nation founded on a decent respect for the opinions of mankind is bound to attract reciprocal sentiments. And when an American President gives life to the central purpose built into the design of that Nation, the purpose being to advance the human cause on earth, it is natural that profound feelings of human oneness should be released.

The Japanese farmer and his family who walked 18 miles through the night in order to stand silently in front of the American Embassy in Tokyo; the Warsaw busdriver who, upon being informed by a boarding passenger of the terrible news, halted his vehicle and wept openly; the elderly woman in Dublin who cried because her own body could not have intercepted the bullet; the students who carried memorial torches in Berlin; and the people everywhere who could only sit quietly with their sorrow— all this is more than a world expression of sympathy. It is a reminder of what this country is all about. It makes real the connections, seen and unseen, between the United States and the human community—connections that were basic in the thinking of the men who fashioned this Nation.

John Fitzgerald Kennedy didn't superimpose himself upon American history; he fitted into it just as it fitted into him. He didn't have to wander through government archives looking for records of ideas and acts that had gone into the making of the American purpose. This knowledge was part of him and he put it to work.

Related to this knowledge was the awareness that his office was a repository of the hopes of many millions of people everywhere and not of Americans alone. He believed deeply and often said that the national interest and the human interest went together.

At his command was immediate obliterative power, more power by far than had ever been collected in one place at one time. In the American arsenal were thousands of explosives, some of which contained more force than all of the bombs and shells in all the previous wars in history put together. In toto, this destructive force represented the equivalent of 30,000 pounds of TNT for every human being on earth.

He regarded this power not as a source of true security, for, as he said, a nation's security could shrink even as its atomic might would expand. The power—not in our hands alone but in the hands of other nations—had to be brought under world control. It could not be unilaterally discarded—this would not create safety or sanity; it would have to be eliminated as part of a genuine world security system under law.

In this sense, John F. Kennedy as President was confronted with issues involving human destiny. Woodrow Wilson used to say that his constituents included the next generation. The question before John Kennedy was whether there would be a next generation at all—here or elsewhere. This for him was not a melodramatic pact; he was not the melodramatic type. But it was a fact nevertheless and it never left him. He knew that his job was connected to the whole of the human future. No greater burden had to be sustained by any man in the history of the race.

He was caught between two worlds. One was a New World trying to be born, a world in which human political evolution might arrive at a point where the world could at least be made safe for its own diversity. The other world was the old and volatile one in which nations acted and reacted according to their sovereign dictates, a world in which superior violence was often the only arbiter. Before the New World could be brought to full growth, the Old World had to be subdued or transformed. But in that old world were thrusts and churnings, themselves the culmination of a long historical development.

John Kennedy came into office at a time when most of the world's peoples were shopping for a revolution. He knew he had to identify the United States with the desire for freedom of a billion people; he had to make this identification convincing to those who were then or had been under the domination or control of the nations with whom the United States had been closely linked for almost two centuries. He did everything he could to accelerate the historical process of national freedom.

But he knew, too, that the issue went beyond independent statehood; it had to do with a conception of man himself. Did man own himself? Was government instituted to protect and cherish the concept of individual sovereignty, which is to say, a free man? Or was man a unit in a vast organism to which he was subordinate and secondary? In either case, man had to be fed,

housed, educated, developed. These needs were insistent. Which ideology had most to say to him?

John Kennedy did not minimize the extent of the ideological challenge. But he knew he could not meet it with obsolete information and concepts. He knew that the Communist world was itself in a condition of upheaval. He knew how important it was for the United States to make a correct assessment of these changes, for the wrong decisions could help create a conjunction of the two Communist forces. In this event, the center of gravity would be in Peiping, with its fanatical hatred of the West in general and the United States in particular, and with a readiness to pursue policies that added greatly to the likelihood of nuclear war.

John Kennedy's policy, therefore, was to close off every possible opening through which the Soviet Union might advance its national or ideological interests to the detriment of other nations, and to keep open every channel through which sensible arrangements by the two countries might be made in their joint interest and in the human interest. One example of this policy was Cuba. Another was the nuclear test ban. Both seemed to point in starkly opposing directions, yet both were part of the same basic purpose; that is, a determination to resist encroachments and a determination to explore every opportunity to build a durable peace.

This policy was never better articulated by the President than in his June 10, 1963, American University commencement talk. It tried to cut through the insanity of mounting nuclear stockpiles and mounting antagonisms. It tried to apply a human perspective to grave international problems. It tried to speak directly to the Russian people, not lecturing or scolding but giving full weight to their ordeals and difficulties and recognizing that common hopes can dissolve even the oldest enmities. The full text of this talk was published in the Soviet press.

The June 10 talk led in a straight line to what was perhaps the President's greatest triumph in the area of foreign policy. This was the successful fight, in his words, to get the nuclear genie back into the bottle. He had to obtain Soviet adherence to a nuclear test ban treaty and then he had to obtain Senate ratification, and he did both. He regarded this treaty not just as an end in itself but as a possible wedge into far more difficult and consequential problems between the two countries.

Questions of human destiny, world political upheaval, and ideological struggle were not the only burdens carried by the young President. Inside the United States, another historic process was approaching its culmination. The American Negro was emancipated from slavery but not from humiliation. He received his liberation but not his rights. He was not so much freed as cast adrift. He was accorded no place of essential opportunity or dignity. And the same ground-swell that a hundred years earlier has culminated in what another martyred President had called a fiery ordeal was beginning to make its tremors felt.

People today forget that Lincoln was condemned by many of his contemporaries because he didn't move faster, because he seemed to temporize, because he spent so much energy on persuasion. But Lincoln knew his main job was to hold the country together, appealing to reasoning people on both sides and trying to effect a profound transition without insanity or national tragedy.

The same men who have no hesitation today in acclaiming Lincoln for his leadership on the issue of human rights have no difficulty in denouncing John Kennedy for acting as Lincoln acted. John Kennedy tried to find the answer, not to force a solution. His job, no less than Lincoln's, was to keep even the bitter and basic issues from producing a national convulsion. He knew that fundamental questions of human rights could not and should not be deferred any longer. And he accepted the need to find every opening, develop every resource, command every initiative in that direction. But always in front of him, to paraphrase Madison, were the purifying but enfeebling limitations to the Presidential office in bringing about fundamental change.

John Kennedy did not find an answer to the dilemma, any more than any of his predecessors did. He could state the moral issue; he could use the full powers of the Executive office and even of the National Guard to attempt to carry out the laws; but always he had to contend with the raw fact that the ultimate power was in the hands of the people themselves. The legislative process was only one reflection of this fact. The whole mechanism, often mysterious and always intricate, by which an idea gains acceptance and becomes living history, was another.

If the people looked to the President, the President looked no less to the people. He knew that on most big issues he would be helpless without them. Not that he expected public opinion to define every great question, carry it forward, move it triumphantly through the Congress, and deliver it to him for final signature. He saw his role and the role of public opinion as a process of creative interaction. He accepted the job of stating the case and giving it the proper degree of urgency. But the public also had the job to respond—one way or the other.

James Bryce, in his study of American institutions a half century ago, called attention to the relative ease with which the democratic process could be overloaded with pressure groups—to the point where the process would have difficulty in functioning. By the time John F. Kennedy came to the White House, the Presidency had become less a powerful pivotal station for affecting history than an arena for the most complicated balancing act in modern times. One set of pressures had to be weighed constantly against another. Movement in one direction was immediately met by resistance from another. Even the smallest legislative journey was a vast exercise of multiple force, pulling or pushing.

The original design for the Presidency had called for a proper number of checkpoints on the Executive power, but it never anticipated that ultimately the checks and pressures would multiply to the point where the President would spend most of his life running a gantlet.

To sustain this kind of battering, a man must have love for his job or a superhuman disposition. John Kennedy had both. It is doubtful that any President ever paid more attention to his homework or tried harder to comprehend the full dimensions and all the implications of any decision he had to make. His press con-

ferences were remarkable demonstrations of a man in full command of his office, prepared to answer questions covering literally hundreds of topics. Generally, he would begin by making sure he had understood the question thoroughly. He would state the arguments against his position, frequently better than they had been stated by an opponent. Then he would proceed to meet these arguments one by one, not by characterizing them but by providing relevant fact. He rarely left a sentence or an idea uncompleted. And always there was the effort to state a problem in reasonable terms in a way that might appeal to reasonable men.

The key to John Kennedy was that he was in the American rationalist tradition. Not every problem had an answer but every problem had its origins and component parts, each of which called for weighing and grading, and all of which were related to one another in a way that increased the probability of a workable answer.

The American Founding Fathers believed that a government, like man himself, was highly delicate and had to be carefully nurtured. The result was an ingenious system under which the individual had greater protection against excesses or encroachments by officialdom than existed almost anywhere else on the face of the earth.

But the design was not without its inevitable flaws. The rationalist Founding Fathers did everything they could to protect the individual against government, but they had no way of protecting government against the irrational individual.

One man with a gun could create chaos, could shatter the brain of the man whose decisions were critical to the life of that community, and could lay a burden of grief on the hearts of millions.

Confronted with this fact, some people now wonder whether the rational design ought not somehow be changed. Some may even say that the design is no longer workable. John Kennedy would be the first to remind them that not even the most totalitarian society can protect itself altogether against a man with a gun. Indeed, with his sense of history, he would be certain to point out that totalitarianism almost automatically fosters such violence, for that is often the only way to change it.

Is there then nothing we can do to halt and expunge the obscene and spreading violence? Is there no way to keep the face of the Nation from being pockmarked and blistered by men putting their tempers to triggers? Is the shape of America to be determined by a barroom brawl?

There is something we can do.

We can reexamine the indifference to violence in everyday life.

We can ask ourselves why we tolerate and encourage the glorification of violence in the things that amuse us and entertain us.

We can ponder our fascination with brutality as exhibited hour after hour on television or on the covers of a thousand books and magazines.

We can ask why our favorite gifts to children are toy murder weapons.

We can ask whether we are creating an atmosphere congenial to the spiraling of violence until finally it reaches a point where living history is mauled and even our casualness toward it is pierced.

We can resensitize ourselves to the reality of human pain and the fragility of human life.

There is something else we can do at a time of emptiness and national deprivation.

We can be bigger than we are. We can rise above the saturating trivia, redefine our purposes, and bring to bear on problems that combination of reason, sensitivity, and vision that gives a civilization its forward movement. Our ideals are all right, W. Macneil Dixon once said, but they are unreal until they become articulate.

We can give not just added protection but added dignity to public office and reduce the sense of loneliness of public servants who are regarded as easy game for the predatory attacks of extremists.

The best defense against mushrooming madness is to carry on, to strengthen the belief in a rational society and in the natural sanity and goodness of man, to take all reasonable precautions but not to allow the precautions to distort or disfigure our lives. "The fact that reason too often fails," Alfred North Whitehead said, "does not give fair ground for the hysterical conclusion that it never works."

The sense of tragedy over the assassination of the President will not soon be dispelled, but in due time we may find warrant for some consolation in the fact of orderly succession, a miracle in itself, built into the structure of Government. Even more basic is the fact that there is nothing to stop the American people from giving life to the ideas and purposes of the man whose memory they now cherish. The loss of John F. Kennedy becomes a total one only if our understanding of what he tried to do is emptied from our minds.

One of the unique characteristics of a free society is that it can assign immortality to a concept, an ideal, a set of working principles. If the impact of John Kennedy is confined to the circumstances of his death, then the tragedy is indeed a total one. But if there is accord with his purposes, then this may be a solvent for our grief.

John Kennedy believed in peace. He believed in freedom. He saw no conflict between the two. He believed in the creative potential of the individual man. He believed in the reality of hope. He relished laughter and the vigorous life of the mind. He loved life, and by life he did not mean segregated life; he meant all life. He believed in thought. He believed in reasonable exchange. He recognized obligations to people not yet born—to help provide them with a good earth and a decent world.

The ultimate tragedy of a man is represented not by death but by the things he tried to bring to life that are buried with him. The legacy of John Kennedy can be a large one—if that is the way the American people wish it to be.—NORMAN COUSINS.

Mr. Speaker, I know that all of our congressional offices have been deluged by mail from our constituents expressing their very deep feelings over the death of our late beloved President. All of these people have been bound together to share the overwhelming grief that our Nation and the world has experienced. Many of these expressions of sorrow have been shown in poetry. I include two poems that came across my desk this morning.

Rev. Thomas F. Curran, pastor of St. Patrick's Church and chaplain of Elder Council Knights of Columbus in Chicopee Falls, Mass., composed and delivered at the Elder Council memorial service to John Fitzgerald Kennedy on Sunday November 24, 1963, the following poem:

IN MEMORIAM

A new frontier for him is crossed,
    Pray God he's gained a goal
He richly earned while we have lost
    A leader with a soul
Whose intellect and noble will
    Sought only love and peace
The heart of every man to fill
    That wars and hate might cease.

A leader he was naught to gain
    For self, who needed naught,
Happy and in an instant slain
    By one with hatred fraught.
A nation grieves, a nation reels,
    A nation kneels to pray
For one whose honest, strong appeals
    Were for a better day.

So valued and so highly priced
    A life, with much to give,
Is taken much like that of Christ
    Who died that men might live.
Freed from the prison with white walls
    That claims a man's whole being
Where the whole welfare stands or falls
    Of men who are unseeing.

Pray God that as his body's free
    From care and long endeavor
So may his noble soul now be
    To live with Thee forever.
The flag he loved flies at half-mast
    Alight from lamps above,
Pray God with him all hatred dies
    And men may learn to love.

Mr. Speaker, the following poem comes from Joseph A. Novak, formerly of Chicopee, Mass., and now of Santurce, P.R.:

IN DALLAS

A shot rang out in Dallas
    That traveled 'round the globe
And struck a billion hearts and more
    From Cape Cod to Nairobi.

For a great man fell in Dallas
   A man whose life was good,
A noble soul whose words and deeds
   On earth spelled brotherhood.

Then a cry went up in Dallas
   And in each city and nation
Condemning this wanton and senseless act
   And recording earth's indignation.

But prejudice in Dallas,
   Hatred and greed in all men,
Were the real cause of a martyrdom
   Which may well occur again.

For the guilt of a man in Dallas
   Was the guilt of men everywhere,
And so it will be forevermore
   Until man can love and share.

Only then may one say in Dallas
   Only then can mankind acclaim
That John Fitzgerald Kennedy
   Did not die in vain.

Mr. Speaker, millions of messages of sympathy poured into Washington following the untimely death of our late beloved President John Fitzgerald Kennedy.

Today, I received probably one of the most touching and genuinely sincere messages that I have read so far. It came in the form of an anonymous letter from one of my constituents in Three Rivers, Mass., who signed it as "A Member of Christian Church." Enclosed was a $20 bill as an offering in memory of the late President Kennedy, and an expression of sorrow that the writer could not afford the expense of attending the late President's funeral in Washington, D.C. I will personally see to it that this money offering from a sincere, humble, and grief-stricken citizen will be used for the purpose in which the anonymous sender intended.

Mr. Speaker, under permission granted, I include the following anonymous message of sympathy:

DEAR SIR: In memory of our late President, of grieve and sorrow that extends over all the world and the whole remaining family we all have our sympathy to share in all sudden tragic unexpected emergencies of our great and beloved late President, of whom will never be forgotten. I extend my small donation as a gift as all that I could afford at this time. I am sorry that I could not afford the money to travel to Washington, D.C., funeral.

A MEMBER OF CHRISTIAN CHURCH.

Mr. Speaker, poems are being penned continuously in memory of the late beloved Chief Executive, President John Fitzgerald Kennedy. A poem that I think profoundly expresses the sentiments we all share concerning the late President Kennedy was written by Brian F. King, a creator of verse and distinguished columnist for the Springfield (Mass.) Sunday Republican, and appeared in that newspaper last Sunday, December 1, under the title "In Memoriam":

IN MEMORIAM

In Arlington a skylark wings
Its lonely way across the sky, .
And wind-swept grasses sigh and grieve
O'er graves where gallant heroes lie;
They whisper of the shameful deed
That called a valiant heart to rest,
And bend to kiss the hallowed soil
A mourning nation's tears has blessed.

In Arlington there is no hate,
Its aisles are steeped in peace and pray'r;
In comradeship its heroes sleep,
For all is ever tranquil there.
God grant its sacred vales will bring
To him who lies there, shrined, alone,
Surcease from ev'ry mortal care,
While we atone—while we atone.

In Arlington a songbird trills,
Its small voice pure and crystal clear;
It sings his hymn of love and faith,
Of bright tomorrows, free from fear;
It sings of his love for God and man,
And falters as, with troubled grief,
Its sweet crescendo sings the dirge
Of a sad farewell for a martyred Chief.
         —BRIAN F. KING.

Mr. Speaker, our late beloved President, John Fitzgerald Kennedy, has been eulogized throughout the country in newspaper editorials and in church requiem services. One of the most thoughtful sermons, which aptly pays tribute to President Kennedy's work of upholding man's personal dignity through civil rights legislation, was delivered by Rev. Donald L. Garfield, rector of St. Peter's Episcopal Church, Springfield, Mass., while conducting a Requiem Mass for the late President on Sunday, November 24:

REQUIEM FOR THE PRESIDENT

"The righteous shall be had in everlasting remembrance: they will not be afraid of any evil tidings."

Across this land today, indeed throughout the civilized world, men of good will are commending John Fitzgerald Kennedy, his wife and family, his successor in office, and our country, to a care beyond human reach. However we worship God, however we voted for President in 1960 or will vote in 1964, we stand united in giving thanks for the integrity and courage of the man who in 3 years made so telling an impact on all who love freedom and uphold man's personal dignity. As you and I offer Christ's sacrifice—full, perfect, and sufficient for the sins of the whole world—we offer it for the repose of a great soul, a sheep of Christ's own fold, a lamb of his own flock, a sinner of his own redeeming. "Receive him," we pray, "into the arms of Thy mercy, into the blessed rest of ever-lasting peace, and into the glorious company of the saints in light." There, he will not be afraid of any evil tidings—nor need we fear. For the righteous shall be had in everlasting remembrance, and the good work begun in him and in all who have laid down their lives in the serv-ice of our country, will be made perfect through Jesus Christ our Lord.

The work which was John Kennedy's greatest—the work which no Christian can quarrel with—was the work of upholding man's personal dignity. Call it what you will: civil rights, racial equality; but put it in practice as God gives you to see the right. The principle of equal opportunity to serve and be served comes from the Saviour who shed His blood and thereby made all men to be of one blood—to be brothers and sisters because we are sons and daughters of one Father—our Father and His. If John Kennedy's life work, and his death, will call us to seek out one another, to know one another and therefore serve and live in peace with one another, then he will not have died in vain.

One hundred years ago, dedicating a cemetery for the men who died at Gettysburg, President Lincoln said: "The world will little note, nor long remember, what we say here, but it can never forget what they did here. It is for us, the living, rather to be dedicated here to the unfinished work which they have, thus far, so nobly advanced. It is rather for us to be here dedicated to the great task remaining before us—that from these honored dead we take increased devotion to that cause for which they here gave the last full measure of devotion—that we here highly resolve that these dead shall not have died in vain; that this Nation under God shall have a new birth of freedom; and that government of the people, by the people, for the people, shall not perish from the earth."

These are familiar words—familiar ideals. Fellow citizens, fellow Christians, what have you and I done to translate ideals into everyday acceptance? Can we point accusing fingers at others who obviously, shockingly, be-tray the ideals of our country without looking at ourselves, our own hidden motives, our acceptance of things as they are, our reluctance to stand solidly and openly for human dignity, and to see justice done to all men? Great em-pires have crumbled because little men betrayed them with little sins—a letting go of truth so gradual as to go unnoticed. Great ideals can become empty flag waving unless you and I apply them where it is not easy, where it may make us lose face and favor with those we thought were friends.

Your children, our country, face a future which is in your hands and mine, and what we do day by day will shape it. What we do this afternoon when representa-tives of religious groups of Springfield look at their role in inter-racial understanding will help to shape our fu-ture, and I ask your prayers for that conference. What you do when you go back to your neighborhoods, to your school or shop or office, and what you and I do when we come together in St. Peter's Church to worship our one God and Father, will have still more to do with the fu-ture—good or evil—of this city, our country, God's world. "No man is an island," we go forward together, or we fall back into the anarchy which martyred our President.

To God's mercy we commend him in this mass and in the prayers we shall offer after mass at the catafalque that symbolizes the presence of his body and joins us with those who can be physically present with it tomorrow. Incense burning itself out before God rises as a symbol of sacrifice. Water sprinkled on the bier is a sign of spiritual cleansing. We offer incense and holy water, praying that Christ's sacrifice may purge his soul, so that it may be presented pure and without spot before God.

To God's mercy, also, we commend his family and our country, knowing that if we live uprightly we need not be afraid of any tidings, however evil. It is for us to be here dedicated to the great task remaining before us: a task which a century has not completed and only another century of increased devotion may accomplish—that this Nation under God may have a new birth of freedom.

> "Judge eternal, throned in splendor,
> Lord of lords and King of Kings,
> With thy living fire of judgment
> Purge this land of bitter things;
> Solace all its wide dominion
> With the healing of Thy wings."

Mr. Speaker, 2 years ago, France, the oldest ally of the American Republic, gave our late be-loved President, John Fitzgerald Kennedy, and the First Lady, Mrs. Jacqueline Bouvier Kennedy, one of the most tumultuous, most affectionate, and warmest receptions ever seen or recorded in ancient Paris. The United States and France to-gether have shared a special affinity for each other ever since the French gave moral support and financial assistance to the American colonists in their revolution for freedom and independence. The French people and government held Presi-dent Kennedy in special and unique esteem. The French Ambassador to the United States, His Excellency M. Herve Alphand, has prepared a brochure of France's tribute to the late President Kennedy, including the statements of Gen. Charles de Gaulle, President of the Republic of France, official messages, and French public opinion:

General de Gaulle's statement on the death of President Kennedy:

"President Kennedy died like a soldier, under fire, in the line of duty and in the service of his country.

"In the name of the French people, ever the friend of the American people, I salute his great example and his great memory."

Message to Mrs. Jacqueline Kennedy from General and Madam de Gaulle:

"The great sorrow that has just befallen you distresses my wife and myself to the bottom of our hearts. Rest assured that we are with you in our thoughts and in our prayers. President Kennedy shall never be forgotten."

Message to President Lyndon Johnson from General de Gaulle, President of the Republic:

"The death of President Kennedy is a source of deep sorrow to the French people, who held in the highest esteem this great head of state, illustrious servant of freedom and of the destiny of mankind.

"In the face of a misfortune which so profoundly affects your country and which concerns all the peoples of the world, and at a time when fate bestows upon you the highest responsibilities, rest assured, Mr. President, of the more than ever loyal and confident friendship of France for the United States of America."

Message to President Lyndon Johnson from Mr. Georges Pompidou, Premier:

"Deeply moved by the tragic loss experienced by the United States on the death of President Kennedy, whose courage and great gifts as a statesman were admired by all, the French people wish to convey to you the grief felt by all my fellow countrymen.

"Rest assured that at a time when under such cruel circumstances you take up your high office, my colleagues of the French Government and myself join with you in a feeling of most grieving and most loyal friendship."

Message to Secretary of State Dean Rusk from M. Maurice Couve de Murville, Minister of Foreign Affairs:

"Profoundly shocked by the news of the act which has just cost the life of the President of the United States, may I assure you that I deeply share in your mourning and in that of the Government and the American people. Mindful of the welcome that President Kennedy extended to me only a few weeks ago, I can appreciate the extent of your sorrow.

"All my countrymen join with me and share in the feelings of friendship toward your country which have existed for two centuries."

Message to Secretary of Defense Robert McNamara from M. Pierre Messmer, Minister of the Armed Forces:

"Upon hearing of the tragic death of President Kennedy, I ask you to accept the condolences of the French Armed Forces and also my own personal, sincerest and grieving condolences."

Message to Gen. Maxwell Taylor, Chairman of the Joint Chiefs of Staff, from Gen. Charles Ailleret, Chief of Staff of the French Armed Forces:

"May I express to you, and request that you convey this message to the Joint Chiefs of Staff, the shock and the indignation of the French Armed Forces on hearing the news of the outrage against President Kennedy.

"May I also express to you my deepest personal sorrow at the death of the President of the United States who welcomed me such a short time ago with so much friendliness and warmth."

Statement by M. Roger Seydoux, Permanent Representative of France to the United Nations.

Before a plenary session of the United Nations General Assembly, held on November 27, 1963, to pay homage to the memory of the late President Kennedy, Mr. Roger Seydoux, Permanent Representative of France to the United Nations, made the following statement:

"All my compatriots, for whom the visit in Paris of Mr. and Mrs. John Kennedy remains a bright memory, turn toward the people of the United States, our everlasting friend. We wish them to know that their trial is our trial, their sadness our sadness, their mourning our mourning. Ours also is, despite the heavy loss they must bear, their steadfast faith in the future as is steadfast our confidence in their great destiny."

Statement by the French Premier, M. Georges Pompidou:

The following statement by the French Premier was broadcast over French television and transmitted to the United States by satellite via the Pleumeur-Bodou relay station:

"The stupefaction engendered by a despicable assassination, the indignation at seeing President Kennedy struck down by the side of his young wife in the fulfillment of his duties as a humane and liberal head of state, is accompanied by a great sadness also felt in our hearts: sadness because, once again, blind violence has triumphed; sadness because a great and friendly people is plunged into mourning; sadness because the free world has lost one of its surest guides.

"In these tragic hours, all France is at the side of the United States in anger, in grief, and, despite everything, in confidence also for the future."

Statement by French Foreign Minister, M. Maurice Couve de Murville:

M. Couve de Murville made the following statement over the three major American television networks. It was transmitted by the communication satellite relay:

"It was with the most grievous impression of shock that we all in Paris and in France, heard the appalling news of President Kennedy's cold-blooded murder. Many elements combined in our thoughts: the terribly premature disappearance of a statesman of the first magnitude, the death of a man who was the incarnation of youth and vitality, the awful tragedy that hit a glamorous and lovable family, the general feeling of a blow inflicted to a great country for which France has, from the beginning, felt the closest friendship, further reinforced by comradeship in three wars.

"For me, who had the privilege of long talks with President Kennedy, the memory will not pass of his friendliness, his eagerness, his wisdom, and his courage.

"Believe me when I say that we, the French people, today, all grieve and pray together with the American people."

Statement broadcast over American television by M. Hervé Alphand, French Ambassador to the United States:

"The tragic death of President Kennedy has deeply moved the French people, forever the friend of the American people. Your sorrow is our sorrow and this sorrow we share with Mrs. Kennedy and her family, tonight we pray with them.

"The President had always displayed toward my country a great fondness, particularly on the occasion of his visit to Paris in 1961.

"For me he was also a personal friend who always showed me a profound affection and understanding.

"As General de Gaulle said today, he died as a soldier. We shall never forget his example or his memory, the memory of a great man."

General de Gaulle attends President Kennedy's funeral

The Presidency of the Republic issued a communique on November 23 announcing that General de Gaulle, President of the Republic, would attend the funeral of President Kennedy. He would be accompanied by M. Maurice Couve de Murville, Minister of Foreign Affairs; Gen. Charles Ailleret, Chief of Staff of the French Armed Forces; and M. Etienne Burin des Roziers, General Secretary of the Presidency of the Republic.

FRENCH PUBLIC OPINION

France mourns President Kennedy

On the personal orders of General de Gaulle, all flags on public buildings were flown at half staff from 9 a.m. on November 23.

In paying this respect to the memory of President Kennedy, General de Gaulle departed from French tradition, which requires flags to be flown at half staff only during the funeral of a head of state of an allied or friendly power.

On November 23, the Paris Municipal Council sent a telegram to Mrs. Kennedy in which it told her that the city of Paris was in mourning. In addition, a member of the Council proposed that the name of John F. Kennedy, defender of the fundamental freedoms of man and who fell for these freedoms, be given to a street in Paris. The Council unanimously adopted this proposal on November 28.

In addition to messages of condolence addressed by official French circles to Mr. Charles Bohlen, many people from all walks of life, veterans' associations, French-American associations and others sent messages of sympathy to the U.S. Embassy in Paris.

Among many expressions of sympathy, mention should be made of a group of between 2,000 and 3,000 students of all nationalities who went to sign the register of condolence in the U.S. Embassy in Paris.

A service in the memory of President Kennedy was held on November 25 in the cathedral of Notre-Dame de Paris. It was attended by the U.S. Ambassador and Mrs. Bohlen and by Madame Charles de Gaulle. Mr. Georges Pompidou, French Premier, the President of the Senate and Madame Gaston Monnerville, members of the Government and members of the diplomatic corps in the French capital were also present in the great cathedral which was unable to hold the crowds of Parisians who wished to attend the service and who overflowed into the square in front of the cathedral, where members of the Garde Républicaine, swords unsheathed, formed an honor guard.

The French Press

The entire French press without exception reflected the feeling of affliction among the French people at the death of President Kennedy. Raymond Aron in Le Figaro of November 23 wrote: "The assassination of J. F. Kennedy affects all mankind. * * * He wanted to be one of those statesmen whom history remembers because they accomplish their task. * * * He will leave a memory which will not be unworthy of a grandeur which he dreamed of achieving."

In an editorial of November 23, Combat wrote: "The crime committed yesterday is the worst one can imagine, since the man it struck down was a symbol in the eyes of hundreds of millions of our contemporaries."

Also on November 23, France-Soir wrote: "Like lightning, anguish and grief have hit the world. The hearts of men and women sank, at the same moment, in every country and on all continents. All peoples weep also and above all for this man who, in the words of Pope Paul VI, 'defended the liberty of peoples and the peace of the world.'"

La Nation of November 25 published the following editorial comments: "He was one of the great men of this world. A man with a personal fortune for whom it was possible therefore to have narrow views and yet he was more aware than millions of others of man's fate, a man above all who had the courage to direct his actions in tune with his heart."

Paul Bastid, in l'Aurore of November 25 wrote: "There was in the personality of John Fitzgerald Kennedy a kind of lucid fire in the service of liberty and peace which commanded admiration and sympathy. He devoted himself entirely, with the energy of his temperament and of his age, to causes that are dear to us."

Le Monde, in an editorial in its November 26 issue said: "He leaves an inspiration, a style, a line from which America will not easily stray." In the same issue, the French poet and Nobel Prize winner St. John Perse wrote: "Kennedy * * * was an athlete running in a race against fate. He fought fairly and squarely always and his encounter with death came with his face uncovered."

The next day Le Monde published an editorial containing the following comment: "The gesture by the President of the Republic who, right at the outset, decided to be present at the funeral of a man whom many considered his rival, has come opportunely to show that, in difficult times, he intends to behave as a loyal friend of the United States. He had already proved this during the Cuban crisis."

EULOGY PRONOUNCED BY M. JACQUES CHABAN-DELMAS, PRESIDENT OF THE FRENCH NATIONAL ASSEMBLY

At the opening of the November 26 sitting, in the presence of Mr. Charles Bohlen, U.S. Ambassador to France, M. Jacques Chaban-Delmas, President of the French National Assembly, pronounced the following eulogy of the late President Kennedy:

"John F. Kennedy was not only the world's most powerful head of state. He was also an exceptional man.

"The murder of this hero, who fell in the flower of his youth, who knew what power and glory was, this murder in which the fate of the ancients finds expression has already taken on a historic amplitude and its echo will never die away. No, we shall not forget John F. Kennedy.

"Yesterday, in Washington, France expressed her grief through the presence of the most famous of her citizens, he who, without a doubt, already belongs to history and continues to forge the future.

"Today the National Assembly shares as one in the mourning of the United States and of its Congress. It participates with emotion in the sorrow of the Kennedy family. Deeply shocked, it pays its respects before the anguish of this charming, worthy and courageous young woman who brought a little of the gentleness of France into the harsh existence of America's first citizen.

"Tomorrow it will be up to each and every one to pursue his task in defending and expounding the great principles shared by our two countries, principles in whose respect President Kennedy lived and also died."

M. Maurice Couve de Murville, Minister of Foreign Affairs, associated the Government with the words of the National Assembly:

"The homage paid by the National Assembly marks the share taken by the French people in the mourning of the American people and shows the esteem and affection for the President who died in the line of duty."

More than 400 deputies stood and observed 1 minute's silence. Meetings were suspended for 1 hour as a sign of mourning.

Mr. Speaker, one of the most profound appreciations of our late beloved President, John Fitzgerald Kennedy, that I have read appears in the December issue of the American Ecclesiastical Review, a monthly magazine for the Roman Catholic clergy, and published here in Washington at the Catholic University of America. The tribute was written by the Reverend David G. Granfield, a member of the Order of Saint Benedict, who lives at St. Anselm's Benedictine Abbey in Washington, and who comes from my home city of Springfield, Mass. Under permission previously granted, I include Father Granfield's tribute to President Kennedy:

JOHN FITZGERALD KENNEDY—1917–63

A servant of the people, strong in mind and spirit; a brave and resourceful Navy lieutenant in a fighting war, a heroic Commander in Chief in the cold one; born to riches, educated for success, graceful in speech, pointed in wit, noble in his patriotism, familiar with suffering, yet youthful in his vigor and indefatigable in his work; courage he valued highly, justice he loved deeply; powerful among the mighty, he was humble with the poor; catholic in his talents and in his visions, he was, above all,

Catholic in his religion, not confusing what is Caesar's with what is God's; a seasoned judge of good men, a patient but unrelenting opponent of evil ones; a gentleman by breeding, a diplomat by nature, he was a gifted statesman, and finally, by the will of the people of the United States, a beloved President; a golden legend in his lifetime, John Kennedy won the undying love of his fellow citizens by his sacrificial death; leaving behind two young children and a lovely First Lady, he died a martyr to the cause of equality and peace. May his blood heal the wounds of hate and violence that have rent the fabric of the state; last of all, may John Fitzgerald Kennedy who hungered and thirsted after justice now have his fill for all eternity; great peacemaker that he was may he rest in joy and peace among the children of God.

Mr. Speaker, in his annual Christmas message to his flock in the Roman Catholic archdiocese of Boston, Richard Cardinal Cushing, a close personal friend of our late beloved President, John Fitzgerald Kennedy, again paid tribute to President Kennedy for his unstinting labors on behalf of "peace on earth." Under unanimous consent, I include Cardinal Cushing's message, taken from the Boston Herald of December 20:

CARDINAL PRAISES KENNEDY'S NOBILITY

Richard Cardinal Cushing, in his annual Christmas message, entitled "The President of Peace," said last night that "We can begin to see an international orchard of good fruit growing out of the tragic martyrdom of our much loved and sorely missed young President, John F. Kennedy."

TURNED THE HEARTS OF MEN

The cardinal's message:

" 'The people that walked in darkness, have seen a great light. To them that dwelt in the region of the shadow of death, light is risen.'

"The test ban treaty, the prevailing price of wheat, a heartening pause in the mad, incessant rush to arm, the talk of butter instead of guns emanating from Moscow, slashed budgets in the Pentagon—all this accumulation of positive thought and action regarding disarmament has surely turned the hearts of men, in this Christmastide, toward genuine sentiments of peace on earth, good will among men.

"Gradually, in our cautious optimism about world peace, we can begin to see an international orchard of good fruit growing out of the tragic martyrdom of our much-loved and sorely missed young President, John F. Kennedy.

"If his administration accomplished nothing else—and certainly there have been many other fine achievements—his legacy to us of a more stable peace alone would enable his memory to be resplendently enshrined in the minds and hearts of all men."

PERSONAL CHARM

"John Kennedy's irresistible personal charm, his penetrating intellect and nerves of steel in varied dialog with Khrushchev and the other key leaders of the world, have yielded worldwide easement where there was paramount tension, universal hope where there was widespread fear.

" 'We arm to parley', J.F.K. used to say, citing the words of Churchill. And parley he did, strong in the strength of America's embattled traditions and vast resources. Yet he always 'parleyed' with greater emphasis on the will to win, not by guns and bombs, but in the arts of peace and the works of peace.

"We can certainly advance the educated guess that so very much of the domestic and moral instability which plagues our families, our religious practice, our school decorum, has been due to the terror and fear implanted in the human spirit by the constant threat of holocaustal atomic war."

WALKING IN DARKNESS

"J.F.K. knew, in the words of Isaiah, that all too many members of the human family walked in darkness and in 'the shadow of death' because of dread of the H-bomb.

"Beset by sore domestic problems though he was: civil rights, the unfinished business of Abraham Lincoln; aid to education in which the common interest alined him against many of his coreligionists; the liberals versus the conservatives, with life-long friends arrayed on both sides; always he knew that world peace in a climate of dignity and justice was the mightiest challenge of his high calling.

"National unity in wartime is easy; national unity in time of peace is difficult, yet much more productive of the positive things to which all Americans stand dedicated; a full dinner pot, educational opportunity for all, a big brother generosity to those peoples and nations in need of our overflowing abundance."

AMERICA'S ROLE

"Our late President knew with profound conviction that America could not adequately fulfill its democratic destiny in a climate of war. Peace, peace with justice and dignity, this is and has ever been the prerequisite of America's role in a free and prosperous community of nations.

"The current lessening of world tensions gives the fact of history to J.F.K.'s oratorical pleas to make a beginning, take one step forward, even in the face of 100 years of uncertainty.

"In this happy, annual commemoration of the birthday of the Prince of Peace, let us also commemorate a noble American and constant follower of the Christmas star, under which he, like the shepherds and the wise men, harkened to the message of 'peace on earth to men of good will.' "

Mr. Speaker, one of the finest poems about our late beloved and lamented President John Fitzgerald Kennedy, that I have read, was written by Mrs. Molly Kazan and was printed by the New York Herald Tribune the day of the Kennedy funeral and reprinted on Thanksgiving Day.

THANKSGIVING 1963

(By Molly Kazan)

I think that what he gave us most was pride.
It felt good to have a President like that:
bright, brave and funny and goodlooking.

I saw him once drive down East Seventy-second Street
in an open car, in the autumn sun
(as he drove yesterday in Dallas.)
His thatch of brown hair looked as though it had grown
    extra thick
the way our wood animals in Connecticut
grow extra fur for winter.
And he looked as though it was fun to be alive.
to be a politician,
to be a President,
to be a Kennedy,
to be a man.

He revived our pride.
It felt good to have a President
who read his mail,
who read the papers,
who read books and played touch football.
It was a pleasure and a cause for pride
to watch him take the quizzing of the press
with cameras grinding—
take it in his stride,
with zest.
He'd parry, thrust, answer or duck,
and fire a verbal shot on target,
hitting with the same answer, the segregationists in a
    Louisiana hamlet and a government in southeast
    Asia.
He made you feel that he knew what was going on in
    both places.
He would come out of the quiz with an "A"
in Economics, Military Science, Constitutional Law,
    Farm Problems and the moonshot program
and still take time to appreciate Miss May Craig.

We were privileged to see him on the worst day
(till yesterday),
the Bay of Pigs day,
and we marveled at his coolth and style
and were amazed at an air (that plainly was habitual)
of modesty
and even diffidence.
It felt good to have a President
who said, It was my fault.
And went on from there.

It felt good to have a President
who looked well in Vienna, Paris, Rome, Berlin
and at the podium of the United Nations
—and who would go to Dublin,
put a wreath where it did the most good
and leave unspoken
the satisfaction of an Irishman
enroute to 10 Downing Street
as head of the U.S. Government.

What was spoken
was spoken well.
What was unspoken
needed to be unspoken.
It was none of our business if his back hurt.

He revived our pride.
He gave grist to our pride.
He was respectful of intellect;
he was respectful of excellence;
he was respectful of accomplishment and skill;
he was respectful of the clear and subtle uses of our
        language;
he was respectful of courage.
And all these things he cultivated in himself.

He was respectful of our heritage.
He is now part of it.

He affirmed our future.
Our future is more hopeful
because of his work
but our future is not safe nor sure.
He kept telling us that.
This is a very dangerous and uncertain world.
I quote.   He said that yesterday.

He respected facts,
And we must now live with the fact of his murder.

Our children cried when the news came.   They phoned
        and we phoned
and we cried and we were not ashamed of crying but we
        were ashamed of what had happened.
The youngest could not remember any other President,
        not clearly.
She felt as if the world had stopped.

We said, it is a shame, a very deep shame.
But this country will go on
more proudly
and with a clearer sense of who we are
and what we have it in us to become
because we had a President like that.
He revived our pride.
We are lucky that we had him for 3 years.

TRIBUTE BY

Hon. Harold D. Donohue

OF MASSACHUSETTS

Mr. Speaker, I would like to include a very
timely article stressing the great contribution of
our late President, John F. Kennedy, to the revival of culture in this country and the world,
that appeared in the November 26 issue of the
Worcester, Mass., Evening Gazette, authored by
Mr. Ivan Sandrof, the distinguished literary editor of the combined Telegram-Gazette newspapers. The article follows:

WORLD OF CULTURE HAS LOST AN ENTHUSIASTIC
SUPPORTER

(By Ivan Sandrof)

The death of John F. Kennedy struck down not only a
President of the United States and a statesman, but a
scholar. Bookmen, savants, poets, prosemen, actors,
musicians—the entire world of culture, have reason to
mourn, for not since the days of Jefferson have the arts
had a more warm and enthusiastic supporter.

The active support of our culture was more than shared
by Mrs. Kennedy. This year, for example, the White
House appointed a special consultant on the arts, August
Heckscher. The President was in favor of the National
Cultural Center to be built in Washington.

The cultural events at the White House are too familiar
to repeat. But the image made its point; culture had assumed a new, national dignity and importance. It was
said well by Heckscher, who observed that the President
cared about the life of the mind; he cared for excellence in
all fields. And so he was led to care for the arts, which
he felt to be bound up with the well-being and the vitality
of the Nation.

A WRITER HIMSELF

"He reminded our writers and poets, our musicians and
painters and actors and playwrights that what they aspire
to and achieve is of central importance to us all."

Perhaps it all stemmed from a deep-rooted drive, the
creative urge of the writer. Kennedy's book, "Profiles in
Courage," won the Pulitzer prize for biography in 1957.
His friends said this honor meant more to him than any
other.

There is reason to believe that he once considered a
career as a writer. Looking back, there are clues. At
his inauguration, the late Robert Frost, poet, was in the
spotlight. Only last October 26 President Kennedy was
in Amherst to honor the opening of the Robert Frost
Memorial Library.

ONETIME REVIEWER

Edward A. Laycock, veteran book editor of the Boston
Globe and one of the best known critics in New England,
recalls a shy young man who once asked if he could review
books, and did for a time. His name was John F.
Kennedy.

And so the clues appear and reappear that he loved the
written word. Rocking away in his favorite chair, he
read widely and well—perhaps the happiest moments of
his Presidency.

While he was Senator, after 1953, Kennedy delivered
a memorable speech calling for an end of war between
writers and politicians. Among his telling points: "We
award medals and memorials to distinguished civil servants, to famous military men, to outstanding scientists,
and, of course, to retiring politicians—but nothing to distinguished authors. I have serious doubts that a national
poet laureate could ever get Senate confirmation," he said.
"We subsidize beetgrowers, silver miners, fertilizer spread-
ers, and even honeybees—but not authors."

PEACE BY RECOGNITION

Senator Kennedy affirmed that "Peace between these
longtime enemies will be achieved not by an accentuation

of our differences but by a recognition of our similarities, of all we have in common, of all we share and should share."

He disclosed that the Nation's first great politicians included most of the Nation's first great writers and scholars. "The founders of the American Constitution were also the founders of American scholarship. The works of Jefferson, Madison, Hamilton, Franklin, Paine, John Adams, and Samuel Adams * * * influenced the literature of the world as well as its geography. Books were their tools, not their enemies."

He decried the fact that there were not more men of political courage, willing to go out on a limb for what they believe, and the rise of awareness in a modern politician "that what he says but never writes can almost always be denied; but that what he writes and never remembers may someday come back to haunt him."

A POINT MADE

To prove his point, he told the story of a famous Senator of half a century ago who had become so accustomed to political caution and guarded opinions that when he went to see the Siamese twins he warily asked the guard at the exhibit, "Brothers, I presume?"

And again, he invoked a similarly inclined and similarly cautious Senator of a generation ago, William B. Allison, of Iowa, about whom it was said "that if a piano were constructed reaching from the Senate Chamber to Des Moines, Allison could run all the way on the keys without ever striking a note."

The President-to-be stressed again how inextricably entwined are the professions and the fates of our politicians and writers, and pleaded for "the synthesis of our efforts and talents [that] may provide a greater service to the cause of freedom—a bulwark to meet the challenge of the future."

Those watching television Sunday saw a man in a drenching rain pushing a dolly from the White House with two rocking chairs, topsy-turvy, the rockers upside down. Here was the full malignant finality: He would rock and read no more.

And the final bitter irony. The assassin did his dirty work in a warehouse of books and sat on a carton of books as he rested his rifle on the window sill and brought to an end the head of the Nation.

TRIBUTES BY

Hon. Hastings Keith

OF MASSACHUSETTS

Mr. Speaker, while I realize that the constituencies of all of my colleagues deeply felt the loss of the President, his tragic death had a tremendous personal impact in my district, for—as I have noted—he was a part of it.

With this in mind, I think it would be most appropriate to include a sampling of the many editorials and articles which appeared in the newspapers throughout southeastern Massachusetts and Cape Cod.

The first is from the Standard-Times, of New Bedford, and was published on November 23, the day after the fatal shooting:

JOHN F. KENNEDY

The American people are in shocked disbelief that President Kennedy is dead. He was the symbol of America's vitality, a man who drove himself day and night to lead the free world through some of its most trying hours.

That was wiped out in a terror-filled moment in Dallas. A sniper's bullet proved once more that the President of the United States is not invincible even though he is the repository of more power than any other person in the world.

The assassin, somehow, thought his miniscule of discontent was greater than the hopes and aspirations of millions of Americans who praised, admired, worked for and, yes, loved the President.

Tragedy had dogged Mr. Kennedy much of his life. An elder brother, Joe, was killed over France while on a special air mission during World War II. A sister, Kathleen, died in an airplane crash. It was only 3 months ago that the President's own son died, shortly after birth.

As a Harvard student, Mr. Kennedy injured his back playing football. He was badly wounded by enemy action in the South Pacific in 1943, for which he was awarded the Purple Heart. While on a Pacific island he contracted malaria, from which he suffered periodic attacks for several years.

None of these deterred John F. Kennedy.

He wrote "Profiles in Courage" in longhand in a hospital bed while recuperating from a spinal operation. His wartime injury did not prevent him from campaigning for a House seat and was not going to diminish his contributions as a U.S. Senator from Massachusetts. Nor did a painful back discourage him from maintaining a rigorous schedule in the 1960 presidential campaign.

While in Canada, Mr. Kennedy injured his back once more. His pace never slackened. He was a living "profile in courage."

At this moment, Mr. Kennedy's widow and family are in their loneliest hours. Messages of condolence, letters of sympathy from round the world, and the tears of those close to the late President cannot fill the void in their lives.

Massachusetts mourns its brave native son. The Nation joins in the mourning for John Fitzgerald Kennedy.

Next, Mr. Speaker, a particularly well-written tribute from the Wareham Courier of Wareham, Mass.:

HIS LEGACY IS GREATNESS

Never before has one human being been mourned by so many throughout the world.

Never has there been such a spontaneous and universal expression of genuine grief. It became increasingly obvious that the assassin's bullet unleashed an emotional floodgate, the likes of which had never been known on this earth. It also became evident that John Fitzgerald Kennedy had achieved a stature, in a lifetime shorter than most, unparalleled in history.

Even those who, prior to the deed which plunged the world into darkness temporarily, were at the opposite political pole, or who would have denied a personal liking, suddenly discovered they harbored a steadily growing, sincere affection for this young man who wore the cloak of maximum responsibility and world leadership so grace· fully. They, too, fought to hold back tears of sorrow.

John Fitzgerald Kennedy epitomized the American dream—that the Presidency is within the reach of anyone, regardless of race, creed, or color.

This young man, who was overtaken by destiny too soon, grasped the reins of Government of the greatest country in the world at a time when the greatest threat to survival faced that country. He held with a firm hand, and kept us on the road, avoiding the abyss of an-nihilation which faced us at every turn.

For his Americanism, for his leadership, for his timeless example of what a God-fearing man should be, we offer the words spoken regularly at the end of each of his press conferences, and which we now utter with a much deeper meaning, "Thank you, Mr. President."

For its special Thanksgiving edition, the Old Colony Memorial of Plymouth, Mass., noted that while life goes on "remorselessly," and that a tragedy of timeless implications had befallen the Nation, we owe a debt of gratitude to this coun-try's founders for a Constitution that insured the continuity of Government:

THANKSGIVING DAY, 1963

The murder of the President and all its attendant cir-cumstances have added up to the most harrowing public event that most of us shall ever know.

This was a tragedy of antique power, with timeless im-plications. Who now can doubt the workings of Providence?

Life goes on remorselessly. The darkest pall must dis-perse, the sun shine again. Yet Thanksgiving, 1963, can-not be like most, coming so closely as it does on the heels of this dreadful happening.

A great leap into the dark has been taken. Gone is a brave and clear-minded man, who strove with all his might to help and keep us. The bitterness of his taking lingers in the mouth and will not wash away.

Therefore, this year we must look outside our own circle for other things besides family togetherness, abun-dance of food, and traditional comforts to be thankful for.

Our gratitude must go to the Founding Fathers who, with great foresight, in making the Constitution insured the continuity of our Government, and with it our national life. The banner fell. But swiftly it was raised again.

We have cause for thanks, too, in the fact that our new President is a man of great experience, strong and wise enough to take over the great burdens of Chief Magistrate.

Then there is one more, final reason for thanksgiving. This is the certain knowledge, demonstrated on massive scale, that in crisis the people of America feel and react as one, and so doing draw the whole world in their train.

During the first hours after the President's death a great emptiness came on the land. But soon into the air stole intimations of a slow, sad music, the music of the people, murmuring as one. And presently the mighty and the weak, the few and the many, closed ranks, like the closing of a giant fist.

With this, quite spontaneously, affirmed by the very heart and instinct of all Americans, the President's death became felt as a kind of sacrifice, and the legacy of his hopes took on an even greater urgency than when he had lived.

For reasons inscrutable John Fitzgerald Kennedy has been reduced to dust and a cruel blow visited upon his beloved wife and children, his family and all who loved or liked him. Yet this same blow shocked all Americans into a unique awareness of their nationhood, warned them in terrible depth of responsibilities too often neglected.

This last circumstance has nothing, of course, to do with gratitude. Rather it calls, on this 1963 Thanksgiving Day, for meditation on the final meaning of this life, and a tally not of benefits, but of things worth living—and dying—for.

The famed Vineyard Gazette on Martha's Vineyard hailed the late President for his candor and for representing, as he did, "the utter routing of bigotry."

A MEMORIAL IN THE HEARTS OF MEN

He will be forever young. His youth will live in the pages of history, and this is not a small or unimportant thing. Amid frustration and erosion of the spirit, gravity and crisis, the abundance of John Fitzgerald Kennedy's fresh spirit and optimism will supply the strength of his unforgettable example.

All else aside, he represented too the utter routing of bigotry. In candor of language and behavior, in the context of his personal and official life, it was inconceivable that he would abate in the least from his own faith, or that he would seek to impose it upon others. Catholics, Protestants, and Jews were free to support his policies, and they did; they were as free to oppose his policies, and they did.

The best memorial that can be erected to him is a larger sense of humanity in the hearts of men and women. The things that bind together are more important than the things that rend apart. What diminishes humanity for one, diminishes it for all.

The lesson has been taught for some 2,000 years, but it has not yet been completely learned. May not this tragedy, the dimensions of which are so hard to conceive, bring home again and in the new light of our times, the force of the spirit and ethic which alone can justify and fulfill our common heritage.

The base newspaper at Otis Air Force Base, where *Air Force 1* made many landings, carried the following tribute from the wing commander, Col. Rudolph B. Walters:

It it difficult during this time of national sorrow to find words capable of expressing the depth of the grief felt by all persons at Otis AFB.

Each person here felt particularly close to President Kennedy, partially due, perhaps, to his frequent visits here. This tragedy has struck us a deep personal blow.

As for myself, I feel that—in addition to losing my Commander in Chief—I have lost a personal beloved friend.

COL. RUDOLPH B. WALTERS.

My predecessor in Congress, former Congressman Donald W. Nicholson, now in retirement at his home in Wareham, Mass., served in the House with the late President and counted him a personal friend. The Wareham Courier printed the following tribute from Congressman Nicholson:

It was with overwhelming shock and sadness that I heard of the untimely death of President Kennedy. I considered him a personal friend and I used to call him "Johnny." Besides his outstanding ability as a legislator he was very much a friend and thoughtful of all, as everyone can testify.

Speaking for an area of Cape Cod that John Kennedy knew well, the Provincetown Advocate and New Beacon of Provincetown expressed the shock and remorse felt throughout the land:

[From the New Beacon, Nov. 27, 1963]

HAIL AND FAREWELL

Ask not what your country can do for you, but ask what you can do for your country.—John F. Kennedy.

"He did a great job as President." These were the words of Town Manager Walter E. Lawrence as he reflected upon the sudden and tragic death last Friday of President John F. Kennedy. "His loss is a tragedy for the country and the world," Mr. Lawrence continued. "He was a good, clean, honest, intelligent, young man, whose conduct of affairs met with the approval of his countrymen. Again, his death was indeed a tragic loss."

We echo these words. That such a man, who, in the prime of his life was leading his country ever forward, meeting the problems of the century, both foreign and domestic squarely, and solving them, had evoked nothing but praise from his fellow countrymen of both high and low station.

The late President was a friend of the people. He liked to shake their hand. When there was a problem he told them about it straight from the shoulder, and just what he intended to do about it. He was idolized and mobbed by the younger citizens wherever he went.

Also, the diplomats of the world came to know him as a tactful and resolute negotiator, who wouldn't back down, and always stood up for what he thought was right.

His life as a family man, a loved and loving father to his two children is well known. Much time was spent with Caroline and John, Jr., as much as the affairs of state would allow. Their loss is indeed great.

But to Mrs. Kennedy, the solid Jacqueline, who stayed with her husband from the time of the fatal shot until the final taps at Arlington National Cemetery, go our heartfelt sympathies. This strong wife was forced to control her feelings and emotions, so that her husband's funeral would be a period of national solemnity, rather than hysteria. To this end she was admirable.

The cape, the State, the country, and the world has lost one of its most dynamic citizens of the 20th century. To him indeed should go the Nobel Peace Prize. As we go forward into the sixties and seventies, let us walk upon that road which he set out to travel, that road that may be paved with ruts and curves, but at its end we will find his goal, and surely our goal—peace and freedom for the whole world. This is his legacy to us. Let us use it well.

———

[From the Provincetown Advocate, Nov. 28, 1963]

CAPE END STUNNED BY TRAGIC EVENTS—SCHOOLS, BUSINESSES IN MOURNING

Even now Provincetown is quiet, drained of emotion, and still unbelieving.

The news of the assassination of President Kennedy on Friday afternoon came over television and radio minutes after it happened in Dallas, Tex., and it came to an incredulous cape end town far out in a November Atlantic.

First to feel the onslaught of the ghastly tragedy was the town telephone switchboard. Chief Operator Frances Raymond said that suddenly every line flared red, and she had to call for additional help until the force was doubled and every board position filled.

Gradually the streets of the town emptied, and cape enders sat at their radios and TV sets getting more news as soon as it was broadcast. There they stayed for most of the weekend through the tragic drama unfolding in Dallas and Washington.

As soon as reason began to return, many Provincetown people turned to their churches with questioning hearts, and they began to plan for their own mourning. Some places closed immediately and remained so through Monday, though most of the shops and offices closed for the day of the funeral. All schools, too, closed on Monday.

In all churches there were memorial services. At the Universalist Church here in Provincetown in place of the scheduled Thanksgiving message the service was devoted to John F. Kennedy as it was at the Truro Congregational Church. The Church of St. Mary of the Harbor held a memorial service Friday night and a requiem communion service on Monday noon. The Provincetown Methodist Church held a memorial service on Monday during the time of the services in Washington.

Over in Wellfleet the Methodist Church was opened on Friday night for prayers, and on Monday held a communion and prayer service at 3 p.m. The Christian Union Church in North Truro held a memorial service at 12 o'clock noon on Monday.

At the church of St. Peter the Apostle in Provincetown on Sunday night there were evening devotions and recitation of the rosary offered for President Kennedy and a requiem funeral high mass was held Monday night. In Wellfleet there was a funeral mass on Monday night at Our Lady of Lourdes Church and in Truro at the Sacred Heart Church, and at the Church of Our Lady of Perpetual Help in North Truro there were funeral masses at 8 a.m. on Monday morning. The First Church of Christ Scientist held memorial services at Orleans on Monday afternoon.

Two other fine Cape Cod newspapers published editorials that should be included in this small collection. The first, from the Cape Codder, published at Orleans, comments on the violence of the act, and the cruel irony that a man who stood for tolerance and good will was struck down by a moment of hate:

WHAT OF HATE, FRIENDS, WHAT OF HATE?

Why is the sense of loss so great? Why does it curl the heart with a pain that will not be quenched? We think it must be because the loss is, one and at the same time, personal and for the world of man. We grieve for our finite selves and for the infinite world. This is almost unbearable grief because we measure the loss not for ourselves alone but for man everywhere. Something in all mankind was killed by that hateful lead pellet and we all know it.

As and if we know this, there lies the hope. Perhaps—just perhaps—the incredible futility and waste of this mad act may serve to bring home the good this man worked for, a good whose essential was the eradication of violence among men and the hate that spawns violence. His death out of hate and through violence may demonstrate as nothing else could the necessity of bringing about the aims he stood for.

Let there be no mistake about this fact: The hate that killed him is the responsibility of all of us. It will not be fobbed off on the head of the madman who pulled the trigger. It is the same hate and violence that denies the brotherhood of man, that would pit brother against brother in bloodlust rather than tolerate the negotiation of honest differences of opinion between rational men. It is the mark of Cain that we all bear.

What he stood for was a great tolerance, a sense of feeling that encompassed the plight of our Negro citizens in their eminently just search for equality as well as the desperate struggle of all men for peace that would spare nuclear destruction. The great irony is that because of these things he was the object of hate when to all men of good will—and they are multitudinous, in the North and in the South, in the East and in the West—he should have been universally loved.

Now, in death, he is loved. Is it too late?
Hear the tolling bells?
Hear the muffled drums?
They toll, they beat for all of us.

The Dennis-Yarmouth Register made noteworthy comments on the late President's youth and the inspiration his youthful service has been to the young people of the country:

FIRE FROM A DARK FRIDAY

By the time this is printed, volumes will have been written and spoken about the events of the past week.

The Nation, under the practiced hand of President Johnson, will have ceased its trembling. The people, having purged their guilt through the mechanisms of mourning, will be composed.

In all probability there is nothing left to be said that could add to the eulogies or to the marvelous articulateness of President Kennedy himself, as passages of his speeches are played back over the radio and television and in our minds.

Nevertheless, one thought arises insistently from the fact of our President's youth. His death would have been more bearable if it had not been for that.

For we are left forever to speculate what might have been, what contribution might have come from a President of the United States, only just come to the peak of extraordinary personal ability.

This thought of youth colors another fact. The excitement aroused by this unusual President infected most deeply young people, people who will increase in places of power and influence for decades to come. His death, still so preposterous, must sooner or later come into perspective. It is the young people who must draw from it a meaning.

It was this generation which could light a fire, he said. The rifle shot extinguished one blazing figure. But could we hope it also kindled the fire of which John F. Kennedy spoke, kindled it among those best able to make it bright? Isn't that the only possible meaning?

As the Nation rearranges itself without President Kennedy, to face a world suddenly drab and tense, we should be looking beyond the shame and degradation of last week. We should look for the flame, and this time unfailingly nourish it.

The Nantucket Inquirer and Mirror tells of the impact of the President's death on that island, where he was considered a neighbor. The newspaper has characterized John Kennedy's greatness as resting in large part upon "his stature as a political idealist whose aspirations were the goals that the community at large wants ultimately to attain. The quarrels he had with his political adversaries usually concerned the timing and mechanical methods proposed to accomplish his ultimate objectives and not the ends themselves." I think all of us can agree with that statement:

THE KENNEDY TRAGEDY

Severe shock and profound grief struck the Nation on Friday, following the assassination of President Kennedy. Good citizens here and everywhere extend deep and affectionate sympathy to Mrs. Kennedy and her children, to the President's parents, to his grandmother, and to his brothers and sisters.

The shooting of the President was the first of two acts of violence last week that contorted the posture of the United States as the world's outstanding society successfully based upon the rule of law. In the first one, a shot from the assassin's rifle overthrew the administration. In the second, the President's alleged assassin was himself summarily executed by one who chose to arrogate to himself the functions of the judicial process.

Had President Kennedy put less faith in the American people, it seems likely that the tragedy of his death would have been avoided. But he was apparently misled by the warmth of his Texas reception and he neglected to take advantage of measures and equipment available for his personal protection. In an unfortunate, though understandable. effort to return the friendship and good will being expressed by the people of Texas, he seems to have cast caution aside and his assassin took advantage of the opportunity thus offered.

In the light of what has happened, there should be imposed upon our Presidents a firm duty and obligation to observe security regulations prescribed for their protection by the officers placed in charge of their personal safety.

The violent, extra-legal execution of President Kennedy's alleged assassin could easily have been prevented if the local police had used ordinary care. There can be no excuse for moving the accused only at a time calculated to satisfy and accommodate representatives of the press, radio, and television. There was no reason for making a public spectacle of the accused by dragging him through a corridor filled with a milling throng of excited people.

The halls could and should have been cleared because the accused was entitled to protection. On the record he deserved no sympathy, but the State of Texas and the city and county of Dallas had a duty and an obligation to see that he was treated in accordance with the law.

The impact of President Kennedy's death has been very great here on Nantucket as it has been throughout the Commonwealth, the Nation, and the world. He was a distinguished neighbor who brought fame and prominence to the Nantucket Sound area. But more importantly, he was an admirable and attractive man because he was young, poised, cultured, handsome, articulate, magnetic and dynamic. Possessed of all these qualities, he was a statesman who appealed to many world leaders as the one among them who might best be able to guide the world to peaceful solutions of its problems.

In his time, President Kennedy was certainly a great man, but his administration was a short one and much of his program remained unfinished when he died. Whether he has attained historical greatness only time will tell.

President Kennedy's present greatness rests in large part upon his stature as a political idealist whose aspirations were the goals that the community at large wants ultimately to attain. The quarrels he had with his political adversaries usually concerned the timing and the mechanical methods proposed to accomplish his ultimate objectives and not the ends themselves.

The simplicity of the short ceremony in and by which the administration passed to the hands of President Johnson was impressive. But much more so were the solemnity and ceremonial majesty of the return of President Kennedy's body to Washington and to the White House, its removal to the Capitol and its lying in state there in the great rotunda, the filing past by a vast throng of loving, reverent citizens to pay their humble respects, the funeral services and finally the burial itself, each of these episodes was planned and executed with dignity, discrimination and grace and together they satisfied the people of the United States that their late President was being accorded the reverence and respect that they knew the man and office ought to have.

Throughout her tragic ordeal Mrs. Kennedy maintained magnificent composure. A most attractive young woman of unusual beauty and dignity, she, with her charming children, Caroline and John Jr., commanded tremendous admiration and sympathy from everyone.

The personal courage she so naturally and unwittingly displayed was at least equal in excellence and quality to the political courage extolled so ably in her husband's fine work "Profiles in Courage," so she has amply earned the love and affection of the American people.

As its tribute to the late President, the Barnstable Patriot, which is published in Hyannis, printed a poem by Albert Epstein:

RIGHT MAKES MIGHT

(By Albert Epstein)

(Reprinted from the February 8 issue of the Barnstable Patriot as a tribute to the late John Fitzgerald Kennedy).

I did not know where fate had cast me;
A Voice called, a Voice—There was nobody—
"Lincoln, enshrined in his memorial,
Will comfort and sustain you;"
I journeyed to his shrine.
Lincoln looked down upon me,
His eyes—the mystery of compassion,
His sad face brightened, illuminated by his gentle smile;
Serene, weighing carefully each word,
Kindness, wisdom, and understanding, faith,
Glorified his thoughts;
"Fear not.
Tyrants cannot destroy us,
Our Constitution or our Bill of Rights,
Degrade free men,
Transform them into slaves;
Our sacred boys have not died in vain.
With abiding faith in our heritage,
With humble pride in our achievements,
With eternal vigilance,
With the guidance of Almighty God,
Freedom, the Dignity of Man, will be preserved.
Convey your message to our countrymen,
Reveal it to the world,
For all men cherish Freedom.
Fear not—
Evil shall not emerge triumphant,
God wills the Brotherhood of Man."

Representative of the reaction in the South Shore area of my district, I wish to include in these proceedings a poem from the South Shore Mirror and an editorial from the Hull-Nantasket Times, as well as excerpts from a column, "How

It Looks From Here," written by John Bond, editor of the Rockland Standard:

[From the Hull-Nantasket Times, Nov. 28, 1963]

WHAT WE CAN DO

"Ask not what your country can do for you, but what you can do for your country, and, people of the world, ask not what can America do for us, but what can we do for all mankind."

The above inspired words, of course, are from the inaugural address of our late beloved President John Fitzgerald Kennedy.

And after the shocking tragedy and almost unbelievable events of black Friday, November 22, in which the young Chief Executive was cut down in the vicious and cowardly act of a fanatical psychopath, shock waves of horror spread throughout the world, and millions who loved honor, decency, and John F. Kennedy bowed their heads in grief and murmured prayers in their native tongues.

"What can we do, what can we do," echoed from memory of the President's inaugural words and blended in cadence with the measured tread of the marine guards removing the President's body from the plane to the ambulance, pathetically followed by his bereaved widow, and again in the beat of the military drums as the cortege proceeded to the Capitol from the White House on Sunday, and to the last resting place for national heroes, the Arlington National Cemetery on Monday.

As President Kennedy's body was lowered into his grave, amidst worldwide sorrow, the answer to what we can do again came from his gallant soul and high spirit as left in his words from the inauguration: "In your hands, my fellow citizens, rather than mine will remain the future success or failure of our final course," and also from his speech prepared for delivery, but never delivered on Black Friday at Dallas:

"We in this country, in this generation are—by destiny rather than choice—the watchmen on the walls of world freedom. We ask therefore, that we may achieve in our time and for all time the ancient vision of 'Peace on Earth, Good Will Toward Men.' That must always be our goal—and the righteousness of our cause must always underlie our strength. For, as written long ago: 'Except the Lord keep the city, the watchman waketh but in vain.' "

Hatred, bigotry, racial and ethnic prejudice and warped personal rancor, greed, and spite must be made the objective of permanent correction, and its poisonous effect eliminated from all relations between men and nations.

Furthermore, experts in the fields of science, psychiatry, religion, and social welfare must merge their forces more effectively and constantly in a determined drive to reduce and eventually remove completely the basic causes which have given rise to the increasing wave of irresponsibility, immorality, and the wave of crime and violence which have erupted throughout our land.

Then truly we shall be keeping faith with the basic principles upon which our Nation was founded, and upholding the request of our martyred President by not only asking, but proving, what we can do for all mankind.

[From the South Shore Mirror, Nov. 28, 1963]

THANKSGIVING

Thank you, Mr. President.
Thank you for broadminded courage.
For believing that Baptists would vote for Catholics,
For upholding constitutional religious freedom,
For friendships with Billy Graham and Cardinal Cushing,
Thank you for broadminded courage.
Thank you, Mr. President.
Thank you for physical courage.
For PT 109 determination,
For motorcades and quiet demonstration,
For braving chance assassination,
Thank you for physical courage.
Thank you, Mr. President.
Thank you for civil rights courage.
For sacrificing votes for rights of others,
For sharing a most certain Evers bullet,
For losing political life before the physical,
Thank you for civil rights courage.
Thank you, Mr. President.
Thank you for peace-minded courage.
For calm determination banning Cuban missiles,
For clean test ban air, the gift of treaty,
And "fear-not" drive to try negotiation,
Thank you for peace-minded courage.
Thank you, Mr. President.
Thank you for New Frontier courage.
For dollar concern to win foreign aid for others.
For Peace Corps youth now spread the world around,
For being a Berliner, a UN'er, a frontiersman,
Thank you for New Frontier courage.
Thank you, Mr. President.
                                    —REV. CHARLES W. LUDEKING,
                                                      Baptist Church.
NORTH SCITUATE, MASS.

———

[From the Rockland Standard, Nov. 28, 1963]

HOW IT LOOKS FROM HERE

Whatever you were doing between 1:30 and 2 o'clock on the afternoon of November 22, 1963, you will remember it the rest of your life. You will remember it because it was about midway of those hours that you heard the awful news that President John F. Kennedy had been shot in Dallas, Tex.

For me November 22 started like any other Friday afternoon. Shortly before 1:30 I got into my car at Scituate Harbor to drive to Marshfield for the weekly meeting of the board of selectmen at 2 p.m. As usual the car radio was on and Bruce Bradley had just commented that Saturday would mark the 60th anniversary of Enrico Caruso's debut at the Metropolitan Opera House in New York City. With his usual whimsey Bruce took note of the occasion by playing a swinging number that could have been "Jumpin' at the Woodside."

Before the tune was over there was a break for a news bulletin. A tense voice announced that UPI in Dallas had flashed: "President Kennedy has been shot by a sniper—possibly fatally." A few fragmentary details followed. Then a CBS network alert confirmed what seemed too terrible to be true. The President had, indeed, been struck down by an assassin's bullet. How seriously he was hurt was not at once apparent. The grave voices of the reporters in Dallas were ominous.

Mr. Bond then described in detail the reaction he met from various townspeople—a shocked disbelief—and concluded on this fine note of tribute:

I realized as I talked to people, all of them sober faced and sad, that this young man whose loss had stunned the world, was more than a political leader of the highest magnitude. Despite deep and bitter differences that whirled about him in his office as President and leader of the free world, he had in less than 3 years at the vortex of world events won the respect and affection of many of those who politically disagreed with him. He was indeed a good man.

A few sentences from the Brockton Enterprise characterize very well the sense of personal pride that those of us from Massachusetts felt in the achievements of a beloved native son:

President Kennedy was from our State and whether or not you differed from him politically, there was that feeling of pride that a man from Massachusetts was in the White House. The President had visited Brockton before attaining the Presidency and many in our city were privileged to regard him as a friend. While campaigning for his seat in the Senate, President Kennedy made it a point to bring out that former Mayor Charles M. Hickey was a second cousin.

Men, women and citizens of all walks of life have had something to say about President Kennedy's death. We can add nothing to their eloquence. Sympathy for the Kennedy family transcends politics, transcends everything. This is a dark hour. Our hearts are heavy.

Mr. Speaker, our hearts are indeed heavy. I know that there are perhaps hundred of other articles and editorials that could be properly made a part of this tribute. I have not attempted to pick out the best, by any means, but only a few articles that I felt would be representative of the reaction in an area that was well known to the late President—an area that was proud he considered it his home and made it the site of the vacation White House on many occasions.

Volumes have been written about this sad event and the loss to the Nation. Yet, all of us recognize that at such times words are inadequate substitutes for the deep feelings we have experienced.

Perhaps the best tribute we can pay the late President would be to, each of us, join with the Hyannis Board of Selectmen in the resolution they have offered:

We hereby highly resolve that John F. Kennedy shall not have died in vain; that each one of us, under God, shall do everything possible to eliminate any ideas of hatred, intolerance, or revenge in our hearts to the end that government of the people, by the people and for the people shall not perish from the earth.

Mr. Speaker, from the Cape Cod Standard-Times, a fine editorial they published upon receipt of the tragic news:

DEATH OF A PRESIDENT

A Nation is still aghast by the virtually incredible assassination of its President.

John Fitzgerald Kennedy, a Cape Cod colonist by affection, was shot down yesterday in Texas, shot down in the prime of his being in a horrifying burst of gunfire that stunned the entire world.

The President was waving from a limousine when the treacherous attack deprived the world of an acknowledged leader.

It couldn't happen—but it did.

And that it did left the country utterly shocked in disbelief. The country hoped against hope, when the President was taken into a hospital that he would emerge alive, that he could continue his vigorous tenure in the White House.

It was not to be; a remarkable career had been ended by an assassin's bullet.

For it was a remarkable career that had been shared in happy days from youth to this summer with his Cape Cod neighbors. It had seen him rise through the U.S. House of Representatives and the Senate to the Presidency of the world's greatest power. All had thrilled, on a bitterly cold day in January 1961, to one of the most inspiring inaugural addresses ever delivered. All had trembled, with him, only a year ago, on the precipice of nuclear war involving Cuba.

And now he is gone to his Maker, deprived, in a tick of history, of his tremendous joy of life, of his supreme confidence that this could be made into a better world.

It happened and mankind mourns him and presses its sorrowing condolences on a bereft family.

TRIBUTE BY

Hon. F. Bradford Morse

OF MASSACHUSETTS

Mr. Speaker, many of my distinguished colleagues have during the last several weeks eulogized our late President, John F. Kennedy.

Under leave to extend my remarks at this time I take pride in bringing to the attention of my colleagues an editorial entitled "A Final Tribute" written by Mr. Andrew A. Minahan, editor of the Merrimack Valley Advertiser, Tewksbury, Mass.

Mr. Minahan, a distinguished newspaperman in Massachusetts, reflects upon the events of the tragic weekend of November 22, 1963, in a sympathetic tribute to our late President.

His article, which appeared in the December 5 edition of the Advertiser, follows:

A FINAL TRIBUTE

(By Andrew A. Minahan)

Over a week of national solemnity and contrite sorrow by a stunned Nation has passed since the shocking assassination of our late bereaved and martyred President, John F. Kennedy. Millions in the Nation and throughout the world witnessed on television and were deeply moved by the Christian fortitude, the indomitable Spartan courage, the enduring and magnificent bearing of the President's beautiful young widow, Jacqueline, during the trying days and nights she had to inwardly suffer every second she was observed on television. Her stamina, her mien, were never equaled or excelled by any celebrity in the public eye.

Her display of unquestioned love and devotion to her husband, to the kissing of his casket; the scene of Caroline wiping the tears from her eyes after the services at the cathedral; the military salute of 3-year-old son to the casket as it was being carried out by the bearers, a last salute to his beloved Dad, were heart-rending memories that will live long in the minds · of those who witnessed these dramatic events.

The public will miss the image the late President created on his television appearances, especially his news conferences at the White House—a man with a vibrant, sparkling personality. * * * with a distinctive appealing voice * * * somewhat musical at times, a voice that many TV comedians tried to mock * * * that effused an understanding, sympathetic heart * * * a voice when tuned to a pitch in great heights of oratory in times of crises * * * captivated the Nation more than any other President with the exception of Franklin D. Roosevelt.

He was idolized by the vast score of newspapermen who were assigned to Washington, even many who did not agree with his political philosophies. His ever infectious, gracious smile; his keen intellectuality that members of the press say was never equaled in their memory; his quick perception that could quickly analyze tricky, confusing, embarrassing questions by some critical members of the Fourth Estate which usually brought forth a humorous evasive answer in reply, were among incomparable, unequaled features of his press relations that delighted the members of the newspaper fraternity.

The members of the press place President John F. Kennedy on the highest pedestal as the most considerate, the smartest, and the most beloved man with whom they had ever had relations in Washington.

Having personally known this great man, and members of his family, having the honor and privilege of being part of his campaign press committee in 1960; having been offered a position in his administration in Washington after his election, I, too with the other newspapermen who knew, idolized, and respected him, join with them in unison when they pray:

"Requiescat in pace." "May he rest in peace."

TRIBUTE BY

Hon. Philip J. Philbin

OF MASSACHUSETTS

Mr. Speaker, under unanimous consent to revise and extend my remarks, I include herein a most appealing, inspiring eulogy, in poetic form, of our late, much lamented, dear and great friend, President John F. Kennedy. This very moving poem is entitled "Farewell."

This beautiful, metered eulogy was written by Dr. Charles H. Bradford, one of the greatest surgeons and medical leaders in the Nation, and will have extraordinary appeal to people everywhere who admired and loved our great President.

Dr. Bradford is an outstanding doctor and one of the greatest medical and humane leaders in the country.

Of a famous Massachusetts family, tracing back to the first Governor of our Commonwealth, he is of the Harvard College class of 1926, a great football player and hammer thrower, member of Phi Beta Kappa, magna cum laude graduate, also equally distinguished in the Harvard Medical School.

He is now a very famous orthopedic doctor in Boston. He is a twin brother of Mr. Edward Bradford, another fine Harvard athlete in football and track, and the brother of the Honorable Robert Bradford, the very able, distinguished former Governor of Massachusetts.

All the Bradford boys have had great collegiate and service records in time of war. Dr. Bradford was a paramedic and made many parachute jumps behind the enemy lines during World War II.

His father, Dr. Edward Bradford, founded an institution which has done immeasurable good for crippled children, the renowned Massachusetts Hospital School for Crippled Children at Canton, Mass., where the famed Mr. N. V. Swede Nelson has been trustee for the past 22 years.

Dr. Bradford has given most unselfishly the best part of his life to the care and treatment of handicapped children and other afflicted people.

He was a close friend of my late, much-admired friend and great football player-coach, Mr. Charles F. Crowley, of Harvard, Notre Dame, and Columbia.

To my mind, Dr. Bradford is one of the greatest Americans of our time, and it is with genuine feelings of pride, as well as deep appreciation, that I include his beautiful, touching poem on President Kennedy.

PRESIDENT JOHN F. KENNEDY

(By Charles H. Bradford, M.D.)

1. SOLEMN MEMORY

Sadly, the Nation's flag, at half mast flies,
Telling of grief, greater than we can say;
For, deep within, a painful sorrow lies,
Too heavy and sincere to pass away.
A strong, wise, friendly, brave, and hopeful man,
Bearing the burdens of the Chief of State,
Has come now to the end of his life's span,
Cut off, in his best years, by tragic fate.
In solemn gratitude, we strive to tell
The thanks that, from our hearts, he has deserved,
Who, leading us through stormy trials, fell
With full devotion to the cause he served.
In years to come, when grief has stood aside,
Our people still, will guard his name with pride.

2. WAR SERVICE

When war first called, he sacrificed at once
His place of rank, and influence, and wealth;
Accepting arduous duty that confronts
More toilsome tasks, straining his strength and health.
His patriotic spirit never sought
A service that from peril might be free;
But in the front line combat zone, he fought,
Meeting the foe in battle, on the sea.
And when, from desp'rate risks, his craft was downed,
He organized the rescue of his crew;
And by indomitable courage, found
Means of escape, to join the fight anew.
In hardship, valor, and true sacrifice,
He paid more than his share of victory's price.

3. STUDIES, THOUGHTS, VISION

His active mind, in scholarship, pursued
The complex lessons history had taught;
And from a wealth of studies, he reviewed
Life's deeper meaning, and more basic thought.
Out of this background, his broad vision grew,
Sensing the principles that guide a state;
And from his own experience, he drew
Ideas that would a New Frontier create.
In a more personal historic mood,
The profiles of his countrymen, he scanned,
Marking the urgent crisis where each stood,
And the firm courage, great events demand.
By such wide knowledge trained, he dared to meet
Tasks where the greatest leaders must compete.

4. WORLD LEADERSHIP

When finally, he reached the topmost place,
Over the ramparts of the world, he watched,
Meeting conflicting powers, face to face.
With calm, bold moves, that every challenge matched.

By his undaunted leadership, he showed
That freedom's cause was resolute and strong,
And that no hostile threat would be allowed
To shake the truths, supporting it so long.
His quiet fortitude has left behind
An aim; a goal, that stands before us still;
By building common sympathies, to find
That the world's peace lies in the world's good will.
Though with still-grieving thoughts, his loss we feel;
Still-waiting time will cherish his ideal.

5. FAREWELL

So bid him now farewell; but not goodbye.
The purposes he built must never die.
Great men, great hearts, great thought continue on
Long after we who thrilled to them are gone.
Into our heritage, he now has passed,
Joining the men whose work will always last.

TRIBUTE BY

Hon. Joseph P. Addabbo

OF NEW YORK

Mr. Speaker, since the tragic day of November 22, 1963, when our beloved President, John F. Kennedy, was struck down by an assassin's bullet, there have been many eloquent editorials and tributes to him. We give pause to reflect upon how this horrible act could have occurred in this day and age.

Under leave to extend my remarks, I include an editorial from the November 23, 1963, issue of the Long Island Press which, I believe, should be read by every American:

WE ALL HELPED PULL THE TRIGGER

In the past hundred years, 19 men have held the proud office of President of the United States. Of the 19, 4 were assassinated—Lincoln, Garfield, McKinley, and now John F. Kennedy. Two more narrowly escaped being murdered: Franklin D. Roosevelt and Harry Truman. Still another, Theodore Roosevelt, by then an ex-President, was wounded, though not fatally.

Seven presidents out of 19, slightly more than 1 in every 3, have been the targets of assassins. This is a ghastly record hardly to be equaled in the unruly Balkans or among the wildest desert dynasties, or in the jungles of Africa. Yet it is the record of the United States of America, leader of the West, the world's bulwark, the hope of mankind and the shining pinnacle of civilization.

We are rich—richer than half the world dreams of ever being.

We are generous—pouring out money all across the earth.

We are educated—with so many Ph. D.'s that if laid end to end they would reach to the moon.

But we are not disciplined, we are not thorough-going, we are not tough enough with ourselves or with our children.

We go for the big and the easy. We let our children slither and slide through schools where everything is made as soft as possible. We create a national atmosphere in which the queer become queerer and are encouraged to deviate in the name of tolerance.

We make discipline impossible of enforcement; we applaud interpretations of the law so broad that minor offenders are left free to grow into major criminals.

Yesterday all this caught up with us. Our President, in the full vigor of life, was shot down. We cannot excuse ourselves by saying that the assassin must have been mad. True as this may be, it is we who have encouraged the madness.

We have been a nation which has tolerated the wildest vilification of our public men. We have become used to the preaching of hatred. Let it go on, we have said; our people are too intelligent to be taken in.

Yet in the grim aftermath of Mr. Kennedy's assassination we must acknowledge that we have let social evils flourish not because we are too tolerant but because we were too lazy to fight them; too busy making the comfortable dollar.

Yesterday's martyr was a man trying to lead us out of our moral morass. He was young, intelligent, vigorous, and indefatigable. Before his fellow citizens he held aloft the torch of a real Americanism * * * an Americanism based on spiritual courage, on moral fiber, and on plain hard work.

In his dedication to mankind he dared to defy powerful elements within his own political party. He was a standard bearer for human freedom in every quarter of this world, and above all a stalwart champion of his Nation, the man who faced down Russia time and again. And he spoke always to the best that is in us, striving to rekindle the spirit that carried the United States to greatness.

Perhaps the tragedy of his death will reawaken us. Perhaps the horror of yesterday will shock us out of our lethargy.

Possibly we shall even see a reaction from hatreds; and if this occurs, let us prayerfully hope that President Johnson will be able to seize upon it and channel it into constructive social action.

To Mr. Kennedy's stricken family, we can only offer our hope that the consolations of their religion will carry them through the terrible days ahead. Their loss is beyond estimating. Not only did a President die yesterday; a son died and a brother; a grinning young war hero died, a youthful Senator died; a young lover, a husband, a father who had just built a new house, a father who took the kids to church on Sunday.

So brave a life, so debonair, so full of accomplishment and so big with promise of still greater things. Wiped out * * * murdered * * * a victim of the system we have helped create.

TRIBUTE BY
Hon. William H. Ayres
OF OHIO

Mr. Speaker, under leave to extend my remarks, I include the following article from the NPC Record:

A LOOK BACK: PRESIDENT KENNEDY AND THE PRESS CLUB

(NOTE.—The tragic news from Dallas, November 22, caused particular sorrow at the National Press Club, many of whose members had reported the activities of President John F. Kennedy and some of whom were with the presidential party that fateful day. The following was written by NPC Historian John Cosgrove (Broadcasting Publications) who recalls the club's association with the late President on a happier occasion almost 2 years ago.)

As I walked through the East Room of the White House that Saturday evening to pay my last respects to the assassinated President, thoughts of another memorable Saturday night passed through my mind.

It was the night of January 28, 1961, just 1 week after his spectacular inauguration as the Nation's 35th President, that John F. Kennedy paid personal tribute to the National Press Club. He stopped by to wish me well on my inauguration as the club's 53d president, and to pick up his membership card. Earlier that evening, News Secretary Pierre Salinger brought over the President's $90 check, the initiation fee for a nonactive member.

Mr. Kennedy's surprise visit electrified the East Lounge. We were having dinner when he arrived. It came about like this:

Pierre Salinger told me in response to earlier discussions about 4:30 that afternoon that the President would stop by but to keep the secret to ourselves. I was bursting, but later told my wife, who then understood my long absence from the receiving line while secret service agents, Pierre and I made a hurry-up inspection tour of the club.

We had a prearranged signal—a long ring on the East Lounge phone when the President left the White House. That meant that Pierre and I would have time to leave the East Lounge and arrive at the F Street entrance to greet Mr. Kennedy.

Unfortunately, the Presidential limousine made better time than anticipated, and when we reached the street lobby, the President was there, alone, pacing in front of the elevators. Smilingly, he inquired, "Where have you been?"

En route to the East Lounge via the 13th floor corridor, he graciously stopped for a handshake or to exchange pleasantries with well-wishers.

As I presented him with nonactive card No. 2973, the President praised the club for sticking to its principles and rules, for having "the decency to charge me initiation fee and dues." Many other memberships have come his way since the November elections, he noted, often with no mention whatever of any costs.

Mr. Kennedy said that he was happy to become a member, that he had originally started in journalism, but gave it up for politics because he felt accomplishments could be more readily realized in politics. Also, he hoped that in the final analysis that he would have lent some dignity to both professions.

The President's appearance in the East Lounge was brief, but he did manage to greet head table guests which included Speaker Sam Rayburn and Chief Justice Earl Warren. He had to leave before the swearing-in ceremonies, and in departing looked at me directly and said: "I'm sorry that I can't stay longer, be sure to keep your hand on the Bible." There had been considerable discussion as to whether he had his hand on the Bible when the Chief Justice swore him in just 8 days previously.

The event marked the first participation of a U.S. President in a club inaugural, and added another link to the unbroken chain of Presidents who have belonged to the National Press Club. The line extends back through Woodrow Wilson. William Howard Taft became a member after he left the Presidency.

Membership possibilities were originally discussed with Pierre Salinger the day after John F. Kennedy, Jr., was born, and Pierre told me he felt that the President-elect would be happy to be proposed for nonactive membership.

I had the forms prepared, and Mr. Kennedy was proposed by Sol Taishoff, Broadcasting Publications; seconded by Ted Koop, CBS News; sponsored by Bill Lawrence, ABC News, then with the New York Times.

The Board of Governors approved the election on January 23, and the bulletin board informed the membership with this announcement:

"John F. Kennedy, a former newspaperman, now in politics, approved for nonactive membership."

A few days after the NPC inauguration I received a letter from the President which said in part:

"I was delighted to be able to stop briefly to accept my membership and to see my colleagues of the press under less menacing circumstances than usual. For better or worse we are likely to have a close association for some time to come, and I am most happy to be a member of the Press Club."

The feeling was mutual, Mr. President.

TRIBUTE BY

Hon. William A. Barrett

OF PENNSYLVANIA

Mr. Speaker, under leave to extend my remarks, I would like to include the text of the sermon by Father George E. O'Donnell of the faculty of St. Charles Borromeo Seminary, Over-

brook, at the memorial mass for President John F. Kennedy at the Cathedral of SS. Peter and Paul, Philadelphia, on November 25, 1963:

HIS MEMORY REMAINS

The memory of him shall not depart away, and his name shall be in request from generation to generation.—Ecclesiasticus XXXIX 13.

In the days when it was customary to put glowing tributes of praise on tombstones, a wise man (Oliver Goldsmith) suggested that everyone should write his own epitaph, that he should express it in the most commendatory terms, and then spend the rest of his life living up to it. Few men have lived worthy of their hopes and promises.

Our Blessed Saviour, of course. He said: He came into the world to do the will of him who sent him. In the crisis of the Garden that will prevailed and on the Cross He could say, "It is consummated." In terms of meaning for the world Our Lord expressed the will of the Father, which was His own, when He said, "I am come that they (my flock, men) may have life, and have it more abundantly." And the epitaph above the empty tomb will always read, "I am the resurrection and the life."

What an example of reliability Our Saviour gave the world. All the promises that were made about Him in the Old Testament—His birth, His life, even the manner of His death—He fulfilled to the letter. Then His own fulfilled promises: His cures, "I will come and cure him"; His raising of the daughter of Jairus and His friend Lazarus from the dead; His going up to Jerusalem when He knew it meant His crucifixion: His promise to give His flesh and blood, His giving them at the Last Supper and on the Cross; and greatest of all promise and fulfillment, His resurrection from the tomb on the First Easter.

When we speak of other men in the same breath with Christ, we dare not forget that He is immeasurably above us; but on the other hand neither should we forget that He said, "I have given you an example."

THE SUPREME QUESTION

The Supreme question which all humans must meet and answer is this: "What shall we do with our lives?" The answer of Christianity is ever the same: "You shall give them away." In normal times this means devotion beyond duty to the welfare of others. In heroic times it means the acceptance of death that others may live. It is the highest degree of charity. "Greater love than this no man hath that a man lay down his life for his friends."

By this standard we may measure the life and death of our beloved President, John F. Kennedy. In devotion to God, to country, to the welfare of all men he meets the test of Christian heroism. For the quality of his reliability in his promises let all Americans recall the famous words of his inauguration, "Ask not what your country can do for you; ask what you can do for your country," and then supply as his epitaph, "I have given you an example."

Our hearts go out in sadness and sympathy to the bereaved relatives and friends of President Kennedy. At the tomb of Lazarus our Lord wept, not for Lazarus— whom He was about to bring back to life—but for Martha and Mary and because Lazarus was His friend. Again at Naim He had compassion on the mother of the dead youth. So our prayers go to Heaven today for strength to his loved ones to bear the burden of grief.

At the time the shots were fired, Mrs. Kennedy is reported to have turned to the President and cried out, "Oh, no." A stunned world, "I can't believe it. I can't believe that he is dead." If by "dead" is meant the final disintegration of the body and the annihilation of his soul, if by "dead" is meant the end of all he was and stood for in his life, then we shall say, "We can't believe that he is dead." By the faith we shared with him we are confident he will rise again to the embrace of his Saviour, and by our devotion to his ideals he will live in us for the life of our Nation.

"The memory of him shall not depart away, and his name shall be in request from generation to generation."

TRIBUTE BY

Hon. Robert R. Barry

OF NEW YORK

Mr. Speaker, many of my distinguished colleagues have today eulogized our late President, John Fitzgerald Kennedy. Their words will ring throughout this great land.

One of the finest, most sympathetic tributes to our late President has been written by Alberto Gavasci, a distinguished Boy Scout leader and a columnist for the Home News & Times of Yonkers, N.Y.

I take great pride in quoting Mr. Gavasci's heartwarming tribute:

(By Alberto Gavasci)

John F. Kennedy, Scout: Our President was a Tenderfoot Scout. As a boy he lived close to Yonkers, just across the Bronx River Parkway in Bronxville. He was a member of troop 2. His former scoutmaster, Donald MacKinlay, once said, "He was a regular Scout."

On Friday night, November 22, a group of institutional representatives of the Yonkers district Boy Scouts of America, met to renew our beliefs in scouting. At the close of the meeting I asked permission to say a few words. I asked the assembled group to rededicate themselves to the high moral and spiritual beliefs of the Scout movement, and to the human dignity and understanding of mankind that President Kennedy had stood for. We all rose for a moment of silence in respect for Scout President John F. Kennedy.

This summer I visited Ephesus in Turkey, Asia Minor, the city where John the Apostle built his first church.

I viewed the ruins of this once great city, cradle of Christianity, and with deep insight I understood the mission of John the Apostle. These words in poetic illustration of John Ephesus I dedicate to our late John F. Kennedy:

"Trace the steps of John Apostle, religion bent
Through Ephesus, Antioch, empire cities great—
His thundering words proclaim to those reverent
Along streets, alleys, gardens from morn 'til late.

"The Spirit of Christ touches the mighty and the low
Sowing words of love, good to merchant and foe.

"The glittering sunlit marble columns sprinkle light
On opposite black-green hills of sage and olive trees
With deep noon shadows cast on the temple site,
Goddess Diana stands alone in lattice frieze.

"Apostle John lifts his voice to speak and teach
'Christ and God is One,' he dares to preach.

"He builds his first church and six more will stand—
For citizens follow his footsteps crying, 'John is here
To save souls with love,' our time is sand,
Scattering in the wind, and falling everywhere.

"John the Apostle walks and prays rebirth
Opening mortals' eyes to God's alert.

"Ephesus port of call for Nomad and Roman
Falls to destruction, waste, and the ocean leaves.
But, John's church remains as an holy omen,
That man will love, live forever in God's eaves.

"Ephesus in stone, tradition and church of Christ
Is alive in the hands of John, Apostle of God's Might."
ALBERTO P. GAVASCI,
Yonkers Scouter.

TRIBUTES BY

Hon. Ross Bass

OF TENNESSEE

Mr. Speaker, as we all know only too well, the tragic and untimely death of our late and beloved President, John F. Kennedy, has brought sorrow and grief into the hearts of all Americans, and indeed, into the hearts of all peoples throughout the world. Capt. Lewis E. Moore, Jr., chairman of the history department of the Columbia Military Academy, an institution in my congressional district in Tennessee, delivered a speech to the student body at special memorial services held for our late President which is an outstanding expression of the sentiments which we all share at this time. Therefore, under leave to extend my remarks, I would like to submit the following.

Speech Delivered by Capt. Lewis E. Moore, Jr., Chairman of the History Department of Columbia Military Academy to the Faculty and Student Body of CMA at Special Memorial Services, Monday, November, 25, 1963, at the School, 11 a.m.

At 10:15 p.m. on the evening of April 14, 1865, President Abraham Lincoln sat in the Presidential box at Ford's Theater in Washington intently watching a performance of "Our American Cousin." Suddenly and without prior warning John Wilkes Booth, an American actor of note, burst into the Presidential box and at point blank range fired a pistol shot into the head of the Great Emancipator. Mortally wounded Lincoln died 9 hours and 15 minutes later—a victim of the irrationality of a man whose only defense was his desire to be remembered by history. In a split second of time this deranged egotist had erased the life of the one man who could have begun the work of reconciliation in the South which fruits might have been a truly united nation with equal rights and opportunities for all citizens rather than today's hatred and fear that characterizes our relations with the descendants of the slaves of 1860.

On a railroad platform at the Washington railroad station on July 2, 1881, President James Garfield was shot by a mentally unstable and disappointed office seeker, Charles J. Guiteau. The life of a duly elected President of the United States was snuffed out by one whose only service to humanity was his selfish feeling that he above all men deserved a position in the Government of the very country whose President he cowardly killed. Present on that railroad platform on that ominous day stood Robert Lincoln, Secretary of War, the only surviving son of Abraham Lincoln.

On September 6, 1901, while attending a reception at the Pan-American Exposition in Buffalo, N.Y., President William McKinley was shot by Leon Czolgosz, an anarchist, one whose political beliefs led him to hate all governments, even that Government under whose protection he had been free to commit such a dastardly act.

On November 22, 1963, while enthusiastically waving and smiling to thousands of Dallas Texans who thronged his parade route, President John Fitzgerald Kennedy fell victim to an assassin's bullets fired cowardly from a window some 75 yards away, from a rifle with the aid of a telescopic sight. Within the hour a man, whose entire adult life had been dedicated to public service, was dead—killed apparently by an openly avowed pro-Castro Communist sympathizer, Lee Harvey Oswald, who used the freedom of an open society to commit a crime whose implications will remain of unknown proportions for years to come. Oswald, himself, fell before an assassin's bullet nearly 48 hours later. America will not know for weeks, and perhaps never fully know, the real reason for or all those involved in the plot to assassinate our President.

Who was this President whose death has caused so much worldwide mourning? Descended from Irish immigrants to the United States whose father, controversial Joseph Kennedy, amassed one of our Nation's largest fortunes, the deceased President was born on May 29, 1917. He graduated cum laude from Harvard in 1940 and then studied at the London School of Economics.

While abroad he wrote an analysis of England's attitude before the start of the Second World War entitled "Why England Slept." He was 23 years old. In 1957 his writing talent received further recognition when his book, "Profiles in Courage," was awarded the Pulitzer Prize for biography. During the Second World War Mr. Kennedy received the Navy and Marine Corps Medal and Purple Heart in connection with the now historic PT-109 incident in the South Pacific.

At the age of 29, Mr. Kennedy was elected as a U.S. Representative from Massachusetts, an office he held for three terms. In 1952 he was elected U.S. Senator from Massachusetts, a position he held until his election to the Presidency in 1960. At 43, John F. Kennedy became the youngest man ever elected President of the United States. He became—last Friday—the youngest President ever to die in that office.

As is the case with all Presidents, in varying degrees, Mr. Kennedy had many domestic and foreign problems facing him when he took office in January of 1961. Among those things for which our revered former Chief of State will long be favorably remembered are these:

He forcefully called the hand of the Russians when in October 1962 he instituted a naval blockade of Cuba, warning Russia that aggressive troops and weapons must be withdrawn from that island 90 miles off our shore.

Mr. Kennedy will long be remembered for the creation of an international Peace Corps in which the youth of America can give of its talents and energies to help the under-developed and backward areas of the world to advance toward a higher standard of living.

He was instrumental in negotiating a nuclear test ban treaty with Soviet Russia which gives to the world hope that nations with nuclear potential will not continue to spew the atmosphere with the dreadful possibilities of radioactive death.

Mr. Kennedy had an unswerving loyalty to the American policy of containment of communism reflected in his determination to keep South Vietnam and West Berlin from falling into Russian Communist hands.

He was consecrated to the ideals of equality of opportunity for all citizens as embodied in the Declaration of Independence which so magnificently laid the philosophical groundwork for the "American dream" in that eventful year of 1776.

In 1962 and 1963 Mr. Kennedy twice stood true to his constitutional duty and in the face of unpopular reaction in the South took the necessary action to insure that the "laws be faithfully executed".

Mr. Kennedy's realization of his position as representative of the public interest was no more evident than in his condemnation of the proposed steel price increase in 1962. His action in the face of influential big business opposition brought condemnation ringing down on his head from the Nation's leading industrial figures.

Mr. Kennedy's victory as the first Roman Catholic to win the Presidency was a monumental victory for tolerance over prejudice—a milestone on the path toward the realization of the "American dream".

Can any such impressive list of accomplishments be drawn up for his suspected assassin? There can be none. This man who at one time tried to obtain Russian citizenship can make claim to only one major distinction—he killed a president * * * or did he? Yes, you heard correctly. Did he? Strong indications are that Oswald pulled the trigger on the murder weapon but who or how many placed his finger there and helped exert the pressure which sent the fatal bullet on its despicable mission?

It would not be completely false to say that everyone, some of you included, whoever hated a fellow American, or who ever wisecracked that "someone will get that Negro lover" or who ever preached disregard for the laws of the land, or who ever called for the hanging of Chief Justice Earl Warren, or who ever indifferently said "Everybody in politics is crooked" helped Oswald pull the trigger. Yes, you, whoever and wherever you are, helped create the climate of opinion which encouraged a murderous personality to summon up the necessary disregard for civilized society to point a rifle at the exposed head of the President of the United States and in a moment snuff out the life of the man that Americans had elected to the highest office in their power to give. The assassin took the processes of government into his own hands and defied our democratic system of election. He destroyed the votes of millions of Americans. A minority of one has taken our most precious possession—the vote—away from us and yet some people, some of you, laughed, and in so doing gave your approval to an act which signifies the awesome possibilities of an armed dictatorial state where no man has a voice in how he is governed but rather he must bow before the threat of force. We say it can't happen here—but also we said that the events of last Friday could not happen in America.

It is a credit to this student body that most of you felt a genuine remorse and sense of loss when news of the President's assassination reached you. Let us hope that your feelings of sadness came from a true sense of pride in our political system—our world's last best hope. Let us hope that you realized that after the votes are counted * * * be you Democrat or Republican—the victor becomes the president of us all and can expect—not our blind allegiance, but rather either our enlightened support or at least forbearance realizing that if we do not favor the incumbent president we will have an opportunity to select a different one through the peaceful method of free election. Let us hope that you realize that violence begets violence in which no one or no thing is safe. Let us hope that you are dedicated to the continuance of this, the greatest governmental system yet devised by man—a system which emphasizes the idea of peaceful evolution by means of the ballot box as opposed to the system of revolution by force. To those of you who shed a tear for the intellectual, witty, vibrant, and warm-hearted young man who so ably served for so short a time as our Chief Executive, we commend you; to those who would find pleasure in the events of the past days, we can only hope that it is youthful immaturity which motivates your actions. If it is not, then we pray that our system will be able to survive in the face of such complete unawareness of the danger of such attitudes.

The United States of America will survive this crisis as it has survived others. We will miss the young President who brought the warmth of a loving husband and father to the historic halls of the White House, but, as provided for in our constitutional system, we immediately, upon the passing of Mr. Kennedy, elevated one to replace him. No man, however great, is inexpendable. Our system is sufficient to the task at hand. President Lyndon B. Johnson, a man of unique qualifications, having served as Representative, Senator, Senate majority leader, and Vice President, will, our prayer is, have the strength and endurance to handle this, the most exhaustive position in the world.

On January 20, 1961, the city of Washington was buzzing with the excitement of the inauguration. Today there is only sadness there as hundreds of thousands file by the unopened casket which rests on the same catafalque which bore the weight of the assassinated Lincoln 98 years ago.

Today over the land much will be said to pay respects to a brave leader prematurely fallen. Perhaps here today we would better pay an enduring tribute to his memory if we recall the challenge he hurled at Americans on that January day almost 3 years ago:

"Ask not what your country can do for you, but ask rather what you can do for your country."

God give us strength to examine our own attitudes and determine that we will do positive things for our country:

We will try to make ourselves better-educated and informed citizens.

We will take part in the political activities of our State and Nation.

We will try to wipe out hate and prejudice in all areas of our lives.

We will stand for equal justice for all.

We will rededicate ourselves to constitutional government which emphasizes peaceful evolution by the ballot rather than violent revolution by force.

We will take renewed pride in being Americans.

If we do these things faithfully, then the 35th President of the United States will not have died in vain. If we fail to do these things, the weeds will grow tall over the grave in Arlington, and John Fitzgerald Kennedy's memory will fade, fade, fade away.

Mr. Speaker, of the many tributes which have been paid to our late beloved President, John Fitzgerald Kennedy, I think the sermon delivered by Dr. Wallace E. Fisher, senior pastor of the Lutheran Church of the Holy Trinity, Lancaster, Pa., is one of the most outstanding and expressive which I have had the privilege to read. I would like, therefore, to share this sermon with my colleagues, and Dr. Fisher's remarks follow herewith:

JOHN F. KENNEDY, 1917-63

John Fitzgerald Kennedy, 35th President of the United States, projected an image of the splendid American. It is fitting and proper in this Christian service that we take cognizance of his person and his leadership.

In a society of fragmented persons, the fullness of President Kennedy's person was striking: intellectual curiosity, moral sensitivity, social consciousness, political sagacity. Unlike many activist leaders, Mr. Kennedy was an intellectual; indeed, on occasion he could be philosophical like Jefferson and Lincoln and Wilson before him. But in an age when some intellectuals are content to toy with ideas, to fondle them as ends in themselves, John Kennedy was remarkably decisive; he coveted results. Rarely precipitous, often cautious, he cleanly made significant decisions. This rare combination of intellectualism and activism—a vigorous commitment to the "strenuous life"—was reminiscent of another dynamic leader, Theodore Roosevelt.

Deep, quite emotion gave added dimension to his thoughts, public addresses, deeds. Unostentatiously he worshiped the Christian God, honoring Christ's church as a vehicle of God's grace. Few Presidents have been as disciplined in corporate worship as Mr. Kennedy. Further, this emotionally healthy man was devoted to his wife and children. He enjoyed to the hilt and accepted responsibly his parental relationships with Caroline and John. His generous, delightful, public recognition of his accomplished wife was positively refreshing. Not least among the Kennedy contributions was the image of an exciting marriage, responsible parenthood, and stable family life. The Kennedys were indeed America's First Family. May the Holy Spirit support and sustain that grief-stricken home, cruelly broken by an assassin's bullet.

Now, an observation on Mr. Kennedy's leadership. No one, of course, can appraise it fairly at this juncture. His administration, launched on an evenly divided vote of the electorate and less than 3 years old in the moment of his tragic death, had only begun to reveal its structure. A later generation of historians will evaluate that structure. But one suspects that the style of his administration will affect future administrations, and the evidences of his personal leadership are plainly discernible.

When the Bay of Pigs enterprise turned into a debacle, President Kennedy accepted full responsibility. That is leadership. As Birmingham seethed and exploded regularly, as the Old South threatened political anarchy, as the Washington freedom march took shape, President Kennedy called for the most comprehensive civil rights legislation in American history. He did so in the full knowledge that this would disrupt his party in the South and offend the complacent and bigoted in every corner of America. That is leadership. On the international front, he resisted the hot-heads and ignored the political illusionists. He examined the Cuban situation methodically, spoke cautiously for weeks, studied the frightening alternatives, and then knowledgeably took the first step toward possible nuclear war if Soviet Russia continued to use Cuba as a missile base. That daring, realistic confrontation showed a quality of leadership reminiscent of Mr. Lincoln's costly decision to preserve the Union by force. Honest men differ with John F. Kennedy's decisions; some charge him with moments of indecision. But no responsible person will deny that Mr. Kennedy was a leader. The 35th President of the United States has won a firm place in that select band which historians call strong Presidents. May his successor be equally strong.

We remember John Fitzgerald Kennedy gladly and gratefully as one who exercised responsibly the leadership inherent in the Presidential office, and exercising that leadership, paid with his life. We remember gratefully his gracious wife who enriched the Presidential office in a score of ways, but never so significantly as in the hour of her husband's tragic death. We remember prayerfully Caroline and John, Junior, whose enthusiastic escapades pointed to a happy family in the White House. We remember gratefully Mr. and Mrs. Joseph P. Kennedy who reared their children to avoid casual living and to serve their country in war and peace. Finally, we remember the late President's Roman Catholic Church which taught him the ways of God, sustained him during hard days, and now offers the comfort of the resurrected Christ to his bereaved family.

John Fitzgerald Kennedy—complex person, devoted husband, exuberant father, dedicated citizen, bold leader—projected an image of the splendid American. May the impact of his person inspire America's youthful and adult citizenry to project that image, too. Forgetting, therefore, the things which ought to be forgotten (for the political arena is a bruising place) and remembering the many things that ought to be remembered ("ask not what your Nation can do for you; ask what you can do for your Nation"), let us campaign actively for human rights and freedom and honorable coexistence. These were his aims; they cost him his life. They should cost us something.

But this tragic event—the assassination of a president in a civilized, free society—calls serious citizens not only to remember their fallen leader but to face up to inescapable historical realities.

First, this Nation has forgotten in its sudden affluence and growing cynicism that the Office of the President of the United States has built-in risks for any incumbent. Four Presidents have been assassinated; three have died in office. One President's wife, Rachel Jackson, died, exhausted by the viciousness of the election campaign. Every incumbent has been harassed, vilified, hindered, hurt. The hour should be at hand when our citizenry view their presidential candidates and elected executives more maturely—giving them sympathetic respect, assessing their awesome responsibilities, cooperating intelligently and generously, and learning to pray daily for them. Critical judgments must be made; free society cannot long exist without them. But such judgments must be made responsibly, respectfully, fairly honestly, openly.

Second, no responsible American will view the tragic events at Dallas simply as bizarre happenings. Ignorance, prejudice, envy, and willful self-interest have fanned too many fires of hatred in too many places to let Americans rest complacently. These widespread emotional fires not only produce multiple character assassinations by innuendo and slander; they also incite fanatics and warped minds to infamous deeds: a wall of shame in Berlin, an alien society in Cuba, a murdered Negro leader and the broken bodies of little children in a bombed church in Birmingham, the assassination of an American President on the open streets of an American city, the senseless killing of a Dallas policeman, the vengeful murder of the assassin. Guilt is corporate. Soul-searching and repentance and mended ways must become our national mood. Lee Oswald's death will not assuage Jacqueline Kennedy's grief nor restore the father of Caroline and John, Jr. But the Kennedy family will find meaning and purpose in the President's death if this Nation rises with new resolve to work creatively for human rights and freedom and honorable coexistence. And that national mood originates and emanates from the complex of American communities like Lancaster or it does not emerge at all. Mr. Lincoln speaks to us, a generation mired in arrogance, pride, prejudice, affluence, multiple fears, and ad-interim ethics: "With malice toward none, with charity toward all; with firmness in the right as God gives us to see the right, let us bind up this Nation's wounds."

Finally, this tragic event reminds Christians that while some humans beings can and do emerge as decisive leaders only Christ has the power to save; that human leaders pass away and only God remains as the ground of all existence; that justice and brotherhood are illusions outside God's Kingdom. If, therefore, our citizenry chooses this sad, bleak moment to repent of those things which they have done and ought not to have done, and to repent of those things left undone which ought to have been done; and if our citizenry looks more eagerly to God in the conviction that apart from Him they build to no avail, then Mr. Kennedy who lived creatively shall not have died in vain.

Now we, in the company of our fellow Christians in St. Matthew's Catholic Church in Washington, commit John Fitzgerald Kennedy to Almighty God from whose creative hand he came, and to Christ whose resurrection is every man's best and only hope, and to the Holy Ghost who calls and fashions responsive persons for eternal life with Him who made and redeemed them. Amen.

TRIBUTE BY

Hon. Page Belcher

OF OKLAHOMA

Mr. Speaker, under leave granted, I wish to insert the following Memorial to J.F.K., written by Miss Carolyn Woods, a senior at Enid High School, Enid, Okla.

MEMORIAL TO J.F.K.

He was a man.
And yet he was more than a man.
He was a symbol of peace and security to a troubled
    world
A symbol borne forth in all nations
Loved by every nationality
Praised by all religious
Yet, he was more.

He was a statue
A statue of love and light
In a world of hate and anger
A statue placed in every country
Raised by friendly hands
For all to view
Yet, he was more.

He was a child
A child of wisdom and knowledge
In the great classroom of experience
A child yearning and hoping
For the answer of right and justice
And yet, he was more.

He was a teacher.
A teacher of deeds and good works
A teacher in the world of the teachless
Striving for the enlightenment of the masses
Through the spreading of righteousness
Yet, he was more.

He was a husband and father
The provider of bread and protector of life
To a small, loving, close family of four
Yet, his love extended to another already
Bedded in the arms of the earth
Yet, he was more.

He was a writer
A writer of tragedy and fame
Collector of two Pulitzer prizes for his written words
About the teachings of experience
Learned by him first hand
Yet, he was more.

He was a statesman
Winner of political fame
Representative of the masses he loved and worked for
A servant of the people
Wrapped up in their desires and ideas
And yet, he was more.

He was an Irishman
Entwined in tradition of family lineage
Favorite son of Ireland's thousands
For whom only months before they had cheered and
Now were to weep and pray
Yet, he was more.

He was a son
Stepping to the place of an older brother
The pride of an aged stricken father
The favorite of two brothers and four sisters
The hero of numerous nephews, nieces, and cousins
And yet, he was more.

He was a President
Opposed on policies by some
Leader of a New Frontier on an old continent
Founder of international movements
Respected by young and old, rich and poor
Yet, he was more.

He was a guest
In a city of American people
A guest who was waved at and
Later victim of an Italian rifle's bullet.
Principal figure of a hospital race.
Then he was dead.

Today he is again a symbol
A symbol of dedication to a cause men have died for.
Slumbering in death along with other national heroes
Has not quenched his teachings
He is a dedication of the world to peace and hope.

The life breath is gone from his lungs
The heart of this leader beats no more
Yet his silenced hope for peace in a troubled world lives on
It is to this goal that John Fitzgerald Kennedy would
    have us dedicate our lives.

He was a symbol, a monument, a teacher
Child of wisdom, father of love
A statesman and writer dedicated to right and justice
A son, a guest, a dedication
Yet, he was more,
He was an American.

                —CAROLYN WOODS.

TRIBUTE BY

Hon. Charles E. Bennett

OF FLORIDA

Mr. Speaker, I wish to congratulate Caleb King, Jr., editor of the Florida Times Union, on the excellent editorial published in the November 25 edition of that paper. It was truthfully there said that "A man of courage and ability has fallen in the service of his country." Having served with Mr. King in World War II, I know that when he paid this tribute to our fallen leader, President Kennedy, he is conscious, as am I, that the President died as a soldier for his country, as truly as any recipient of the Congressional Medal of Honor. Soldierlike, Mr. King observes that "life must go on" and we must all "stand strongly behind" our new leader. The late President Kennedy would have been the first to say that. The editorial reads as follows:

WE MUST STAND TOGETHER IN THIS HOUR OF SORROW

A grim and sorrowing Nation will honor the late President, John Fitzgerald Kennedy, in solemn rites in Washington at noon today. The grief, which every American shares with the widow and family of the late Chief Executive, is in no way assuaged by the knowledge that justice is moving swiftly to exact retribution for the dastardly crime.

All Americans may, however, take justifiable pride in the way in which our Nation has drawn together in this hour of mourning and in the spirit of bipartisan cooperation which the Congress has pledged to President Lyndon Johnson upon his succession to the office lately held by a young and vigorous leader.

Many Americans are inclined to view the theory of bipartisan support with skepticism. The theory was

devised by President Franklin D. Roosevelt to meet the emergencies and needs of World War II, but it has not always been successfully applied since his time.

But, bipartisanism is an honorable policy for all to follow in times of national crisis and tragedy, such as this Nation is now experiencing. In such times there can be no thought but that which is the best for the Nation as a whole.

In these modern times it is hard to decide where domestic and foreign policies end or begin. It used to be said that domestic policies ended at the water's edge, but now those things which affect us internally often affect us externally as a nation. The President's murderer has, therefore, changed all our history in the single, treacherous pull of a trigger.

No one can say with certainty what the changes will be nor how they will affect all of us or all free men in the world.

The new President has in brief and solemn words sought the bipartisan support of Congress, the help of the people, and the aid of Almighty God. The trials which now face him are many and great and upon their successful resolution much depends.

In the final analysis life must go on. A man of courage and ability has fallen in the service of his country. None can explain or understand why he should have been called upon to make this supreme sacrifice, to all it appears a useless and senseless waste of a life dedicated to service.

We may all give meaning to the life of the late President, so tragically shortened, by pledging ourselves anew to stand strongly behind President Lyndon Johnson and to offer prayers for the comfort of the living and a safe voyage through these perilous times for our Nation.

TRIBUTE BY

Hon. Frances P. Bolton

OF OHIO

Mr. Speaker, Mary Mills is a nurse serving overseas with AID as a public health nursing advisor and instructor. She has been in the service of her country many (18) years, has spent some time in Liberia, Beirut, and Cambodia. She is now in Hue, Vietnam.

In writing me recently she enclosed a copy of her account of the memorial services for the late President, John Fitzgerald Kennedy. It seems to me this respect paid by our American citizens abroad to our assassinated President must have had great meaning, not only to the Americans over there but also to the citizens of that war-torn country. I would like to share with you the account by Mary Mills:

MEMORIAL SERVICES FOR THE LATE PRESIDENT JOHN FITZGERALD KENNEDY, MONDAY, NOVEMBER 25, 1963, HUE, VIETNAM

Yes, there was something we could do in Hue, Vietnam: Representatives from the Consulate and our military headquarters came by the house on Sunday evening to tell me that there would be a memorial service for our late President on Monday morning at 11 (11 at night there). By morning I knew what to do. I had the driver cut some sprigs of boxwood from the garden, and armed with the big brass punchbowl, I was off for our military headquarters. The officer on duty was not certain if flowers would be used since it was to be a military ceremony but that he would find out and let me know. Leaving his office I ran into the commanding officer who not only welcomed the idea but insisted that I remain and have breakfast with him which I politely refused because I did not have the time. He did insist that I at least have a cup of tea with him. From there I went to the market to buy flowers. En route to the school I passed by my French teacher's to give them the information about the ceremony. Back at school I suggested that a student representation of one student from each of the four classes prepare themselves to accompany me to the ceremony at 10:45. The instructors and the administrative assistant along with my immediate staff were invited to accompany us. It was suggested that we all go in uniform.

I stopped and gathered some fern and a beautiful little running flower with delicate white blossoms from the Sister's residence which is near our school. My driver helped me with the floral arrangement. In the main entrance of the military headquarters through which the guests passed, on a table beneath a large draped picture of the President, I did the most beautiful (I think) arrangement I have ever done. Never have I given the care and attention to such an arrangement. The table was covered with a white tablecloth and on either side of the huge copper punchbowl were tall candelabra. To the right of the picture was the American flag. The part of the cloth which hung over the table was garlanded in black. The flowers consisted of lilies, a delicate white flower, a few pale pink roses, and the boxwood and fern. Those were the only flowers used since the service was strictly military and held out of doors. Even the rains were kind to us; it was a heavenly morning.

At 10:45 two cars took us in a group, to the military headquarters. Surprisingly, there was a special seat for me with my name pinned on it, but most important of all there was the place of honor reserved for my staff and students. It so happened that with us appearing in uniform and our group representing the only Vietnamese appearing in a small group, quite an impression was made on both the Vietnamese and some of the others.

It was a touching and most impressive ceremony; in 20 minutes it was all over. The chaplain had performed what must have been for him, as was true for others throughout the world, a painful but honored duty. The Vietnamese Band (military) played the Funeral Dirge,

Taps, and our National Anthem. During our minutes of silent prayers following the chaplain's eulogy and prayer, certainly there must have been unisonous in silence that united us in his honor and memory; that we would reaffirm our faith and rededicate our efforts and our lives to help carry out the mission begun by him and yet common to us all, the continuing search for the fulfillment of a just and lasting peace, that we would come to recognize the true worth of all mankind irrespective of the differences that may separate us, and that human dignity and freedom would become our symbol and a reality not only for our own country but for mankind. If we can so bind up our wounds and suffering for this great loss through such a dedication, then his short life and tragic loss would not have been in vain. Some people finish their work on this earth in a much shorter period of time than is necessary for some of us who spend most of our lives trying to destroy others while at the same time not realizing that the tragic loss is that of our own lives. And so, while there is still time, let us put forth an all-out effort to become men of good will.

MARY MILLS.

HUE, VIETNAM.

TRIBUTE BY

Hon. John Brademas

OF INDIANA

Mr. Speaker, I would like to include in my remarks the text of a sermon preached by the distinguished religious leader, the Reverend Dr. W. A. Visser 'T Hooft, General Secretary of the World Council of Churches, at a memorial sermon for President John F. Kennedy at St. Pierre Cathedral in Geneva, Switzerland. The sermon follows:

"AN IMMENSE COMPLAINT FILLS THE EARTH"—THEIR DEEDS FOLLOW THEM

(By W. A. Visser 'T Hooft)

(W. A. Visser 'T Hooft is General Secretary of the World Council of Churches. This sermon was preached at a memorial service for John F. Kennedy at St. Pierre Cathedral in Geneva, Switzerland)

With my voice I make supplication to the Lord. I call out my complaint before Him. I tell my trouble before Him.

—PSALM 142: 1–2.

This is exactly what we have come here for this morning. Since last Friday an immense complaint fills the earth. Have we not all been deeply impressed and moved by the unanimity of that complaint? We have discovered that even in our divided world it is still possible to have the experience of being of one mind, of seeing the Iron Curtain and the gulf between the continents and the tension between the races vanish for a time as we become simply one great human family.

What lies behind that unanimity? Simply that we have lost a man whom we needed so very, very much. Had we not all been grateful that this young President of the United States had had the courage and the imagination not merely to speak of peace but to act in such a way that the international climate began to become less intolerable? Had we not followed with passionate interest his struggle to give to the Negroes of America the human rights they had desired for such a long time?

His disappearance is not only a loss for our American brethren but for us all. The future, already so uncertain, becomes even more threatening when such a man is taken away from us. The world is now even more out of joint than it was already. Everyone feels it—men of all races, nations, and confessions, some by political insight, some merely instinctively. That is why we are in the midst of an experience that is so exceptional—the whole of humanity mourning together.

But that is not all. We are not only weeping about the death of a statesman on whom we counted and from whom we expected so much. Such a complaint could be egoistic, and expression of self-pity.

THE HUMAN DRAMA

We think also and especially of the human drama and all that it means for his family and all those who have loved him. Here was a man who had really succeeded in the truest sense of that word and whose success could only call forth our admiration. For it is a noble ambition to want to bear the greatest and heaviest responsibility that exists in one's own country. He had undertaken his overwhelming tasks with tremendous energy. He hoped to realize great things for his country and for the world. But before he could make his full contribution the thread of his life was cut, and cut in the most irrational manner. His wife, who had also shown remarkable courage, and his young children remain behind.

James Reston has written that America weeps because the very man who had tried to make violence cease became the victim of violence. Had such a man not deserved a better fate? Must history in its worst aspects repeat itself ad infinitum? Must lives such as those of Abraham Lincoln and Mahatma Gandhi and John Kennedy always end in this way? If that is possible, then everything is possible. How can we suppress in our hearts the feelings of revolt that life appears so meaningless, that we can count on nothing, that history seems to be nothing else than a tale told by an idiot.

The men of Holy Scripture know these sentiments. Our psalmist says that his life has become a prison and that there is no longer any refuge. But he does not let himself be enclosed within his distress. He does not merely share it with his fellow men; he pours out his complaint before God and tells Him his trouble.

That is what we must do today. We must have the courage to address our complaint and even our sense of revolt to the only good address. For God knows how to listen. We could even say: "Ecouter est Son metier" (listening is His job). He will not say to us that we have

no right to complain. He will let us pour out everything that we have on our hearts.

But then He will give us His answer. That answer will not be an explanation. We will never know why his family, his country and humanity had to lose the man who seemed more indispensable than anyone else. But God will say to us that it is precisely because we live in a world where such things happen that He has sent His Son and that that Son died on a cross. The obscurity is not abolished, but in that obscurity there is a light for those who have eyes to see the light of Christmas that shines in the darkness.

THAT DIVINE ANSWER

If we accept that divine answer, we will no longer have that terrible sentiment of complete solitude before a blind fate. The great secret of the men of the Psalms is that as they tell their trouble to God they discover that God not only listens but identifies himself with men and enters himself into their sufferings, that the infinite compassion of God has found its full expression in the coming of the Son who is willing to suffer and die for us.

Let us therefore not be ashamed to complain, but let us pour out our complaint before God. Then there will come a moment in the conversation when God will ask us a question: I have listened to your complaint, but is there in your heart not also a place for gratitude? Could you not also think of that great thing, the example given by a man who accepts willingly some of the greatest responsibilities a man can carry and who then devotes himself completely to the task of giving peace and justice and freedom a real chance in the world? For such a man can still exert a profound influence after his death. The very depth and unanimity of the world's distress is already a powerful demonstration of that influence.

Let us then promise to make sure that President Kennedy's vision continues to lead us. The shock the world has received must become a salutary shock that leads us to the decision to work more faithfully, more wholeheartedly for the great objectives John Kennedy had made his own. We must do whatever we can to insure that the great word of Scripture may be confirmed:

"And I heard a voice from heaven saying, 'Write this: Blessed are the dead who die in the Lord henceforth.' 'Blessed indeed,' says the Spirit, 'that they may rest from their labors, for their deeds follow them.'"

—Revelation 14: 13.

TRIBUTE BY

Hon. Jack Brooks

OF TEXAS

Mr. Speaker, a great many moving tributes have been paid our beloved late President; I believe the record would be incomplete, however, if the tribute paid by State Senator Dorsey B. Hardeman at the Park Heights Baptist Church on November 25, 1963, were not included.

Senator Hardeman has served long and ably in the Texas Senate and has distinguished himself to all Texans by his devotion to duty and steadfastness of purpose.

I offer for the consideration of our colleagues the remarks of Senator Hardeman:

In this trying hour, we are assembled to pay our tribute of respect to the memory of John Fitzgerald Kennedy—American.

Words at my command are wholly inadequate. The lurid scenes of last Friday in Dallas need not be repeated. The tragedy, and its accompanying grief, have reached the flaming ramparts of the world.

Of President Kennedy's death it may be appropriately said that he has passed—

> "Out of the strain of the doing
> Into the peace of the done,
> Out of the thirst of pursuing
> Into the rapture of won."

Fulsome flattery would be distasteful to him, yet some broken sentences of veneration and love may be indulged to the sorrow which oppresses us.

Our late President struck down in the maturity of his powers and his fame, with marked accomplishments and unmeasured opportunities for additional achievements apparently awaiting him, with great designs uncompleted, surrounded by the proud and affectionate solicitude of a great constituency, succumbed to the assassin's lethal messenger, which beckoned him to depart. His sun went down at noon, but it sank amid the prophetic splendors of an eternal dawn.

President Kennedy expressed the creed of patriots in the immortal words, "Ask not what your country can do for you, but what you can do for your country."

No mortal has more to give for his country, and for the cause of freedom, than life itself. That, he gave. President Kennedy belonged to a breed of strong and resolute men to whom history has only been willing to entrust the care of freedom, and to which he was so valiantly dedicated.

I cannot attempt to grasp and sum up the aggregate of the service of his public life at such a moment as this; it is needless. His life requires no moralization. It conveys its own lesson. That we shall all cherish his memory there can be no doubt. May his death be the prelude of an America united, and let us treasure, even more, the compact which his faith made with the God of his fathers and with his allegiance to right and peace as he understood it.

As the gigantic figure that envelops men within the folds of his dark mantle, and even with the robe drawn about him, President Kennedy seems so unshrouded that—

> "Nothing can cover his high fame but heaven;
> No pyramids set off his memories
> But the eternal substance of his greatness;
> To which I leave him."

But midst the sadness of this dark and tragic event, with the sounds and emblems of mourning encircling the earth, there is assurance. We can feel secure, and confident for the future, as the leadership of our country passes into the capable and experienced hands of President Lyndon B. Johnson.

This occasion is our opportunity to offer our firm support and friendship to and for our President, as he moves to the monumental task awaiting him. He has my profound sympathy and he will continue to have my earnest support in all his efforts for the welfare and glory of our beloved country.

His legislative, diplomatic, political, and native abilities have provided him with the experience and valuable knowledge peculiar to the office of President, gained from his close association with Presidents Roosevelt, Truman, Eisenhower, and as the right arm of President Kennedy available in no other man on the American scene, to lead America in the enjoyment of her free institutions and to the full fruition of our ideals.

President Johnson, as he has solemnly requested, needs the help of God and the support and prayers of all Americans in the discharge of the tremendous burdens now devolving upon him. He asks no more; he deserves no less.

As this contribution to the service of respect for the slain John F. Kennedy, a victim of hate, is concluded, there comes to mind the words of the Master, himself a victim of hate, who declared, "They hated me without a cause" (John 15: 25).

Let us, therefore, in this hour of travail, find fresh bonds of brotherhood and of union in the treasured memory of our fallen leader and attempt to assuage the bitterness which too often marks unavoidable differences of opinion; let us resolve to banish from our midst the cruel hatred that is visited upon mankind through prejudice and bigotry.

Under the dynamic leadership of our President, Lyndon B. Johnson—American, Texan—let us go forward in unity for the greatness of America and the glory of God.

TRIBUTES BY

Hon. Joel T. Broyhill

OF VIRGINIA

Mr. Speaker, memorial services for the late President, John F. Kennedy, were held at the Lutheran Church of the Redeemer, McLean, Va., on November 25, 1963, at 11 a.m. Whether partisan or nonpartisan, sympathetic or blasé, we can all benefit from the remarks of Pastor H. Alvin Kuhn as they were delivered at that service. The complete text of his message is printed verbatim:

So many words have been spoken on radio and television and so many written in the newspapers about the tragic events of the past few days and the persons immediately involved in them, that I do not need to add to that number. It is not necessary, nor proper, that a eulogy be read, for our purpose is not to glory in the life of a man, regardless of the office he holds, but to renew our trust and faith in Jesus Christ in whom all men stand revealed as sinners, dependent upon the grace of God, and in whom all men may find hope and comfort in time of sorrow.

As the Christian Church, our primary task is to declare God's saving act in Jesus Christ to the living, that in Him we and they may find the strength and the courage we need in times of personal or national crisis.

The life of John F. Kennedy now belongs to God and to history. His work on earth is done. But his family, his friends, the citizens of the country and world he led, live on. It is to them and to us we proclaim again the victorious words of our Lord, "I am the resurrection and the life. He that believes in Me, though he die, yet shall he live."

It is to them and to us that we repeat the assuring words of the Apostle Paul, "For I am sure that neither death nor life, nor anything else in all creation will be able to separate us from the love of God in Christ Jesus our Lord."

The wife and children of John F. Kennedy, the wife and children of Police Officer Tippit, the wife and children of Lee Harvey Oswald, their fathers and mothers, brothers and sisters, close friends, and acquaintances— and we, too—have been caught up in a wave of events that could overwhelm any person whose life is not anchored in the life of Him who died and rose again, Jesus Christ, our Lord. It is for them in particular that we pray, even as we pray for ourselves, our new President, and our country.

As the earthly body of one we here honor is placed among the thousands who have given their lives for their country, it is fitting that we pause to show our respect for the man, and the office he held. But the mark of our Christian faith lies not in our losing ourselves in helpless grief, but, rather, in our rededicating ourselves to the tasks God gives us among the living. In life we stand in the midst of death; but our faith is sure, our hope is firm, our will is resolute, for we live and move and have our being in God.

Amen.

Mr. Speaker, I have received a letter and enclosure from Janet Hess, age 15, of 406 Meadow Lane, Falls Church, Va. The style of the letter and the literary skill demonstrated by this young lady in composing the enclosures is of such significant magnitude that I would like to share this refreshing young talent with my colleagues in the House of Representatives. Janet was obviously and sincerely moved by the tragic death of our late President. So touching was her tribute, I commend it to you without further comment:

In Appreciation

A wave stopped short,
    A red rose bent,
A gifted man,
    A life half spent.

A shock of hair,
    An infectious grin,
A battle hard fought
    But no time to win.

A saddened woman,
    A darkened face,
A determined courage,
    A religious grace.

A brave little girl,
    A confused little man,
A salute to his father,
    Who guided our land.

A flag flying low,
    A head held high,
Showing John F. Kennedy
    Never can die.

———

[From the Falls Church High School Jaguar
Journal, Dec. 19, 1963]

An eerie gray haze filtered through the expansive windows in the upper Cherry Street lobby. This was a Friday afternoon, by tradition the time for students to prepare for the fun of the upcoming 2 days. This was the weekend of the frolicking junior-student powderpuff game. This was the weekend the Falls Church auditorium was to echo with laughter from the first play of the year.

But these things were not to be. The halls were crowded but silent as students left the building, stunned beyond comprehension. This was not the day for laughing. This was the day for mourning.

This was the day John Fitzgerald Kennedy died.

On the never-ending calendar of time, a span of 46 years would seem insignificant and, in most instances, is so. But John Kennedy was not an insignificant man. In his short life on this earth, he became the youngest man ever elected President—and the youngest ever to die President. Ironically, it was exactly 13 months before his death that he went before the American people and the people of the world to describe, in a crisp but reassuring voice, the crisis in Cuba which at any moment could have exploded into nuclear holocaust.

Most of us changed our connotation of him after that memorable October day. Before, he was a dynamic politician with an attractive family. Afterwards, he was a man of maturity and wisdom. We realized the burdens he bore, not only as a leader of the world but as the bulwark insuring the future of our generation and country.

The assassination of President Kennedy is deplorable enough, but coupled with that of his accused assassin, it would seem to make a mockery of everything he stood for. It's our responsibility to show the lack of validity in such a position. President Kennedy said, "Let us begin."

Lyndon Johnson said, "Let us continue." We say, "Let us know what the youth of America can do, and we shall do it."

This is the least we can do for our country and for its late President.

TRIBUTES BY

Hon. Hugh L. Carey

OF NEW YORK

Mr. Speaker, under leave to extend my remarks, I include the following:

A MEMORIAL TRIBUTE TO MR. KENNEDY

(Delivered at Borough Hall, Brooklyn, December 6, 1963)

"When a high heart we magnify
And a sure vision celebrate
And worship greatness passing by
Ourselves are great."

These lines were penned by John Drinkwater in tribute to Abraham Lincoln. They are words eminently befitting John Fitzgerald Kennedy, our President, so young, so full of hope, so quickly fallen, now resting among the Nation's heroes in our Nation's noble field of honor.

John Kennedy had a high heart, he was a fine human being, and for that alone we will surely miss him. What gaiety, what honest love of give-and-take he brought into American politics. Ruling has always been a sober business and it takes a big man to hold power and yet enjoy it. It takes a great-hearted man to be solemn when life and death hang in the balance, to be decisive when destiny knocks, to be clear when the issues are confused, to read much and yet not be bookish, to be an intellectual without losing the common touch, to laugh without being shallow, to enjoy the full life given our generation of Americans and yet never to forget that "from those who have been given much, much will be required" in the long, last judgment of history. We have lost a man with a high heart.

We would be remiss to forget in our praise the high heart of the lady of the White House and her children. Never could we be prouder of our First Family than in the hour of their deepest grief. Other nations have their symbols of royalty, people of majesty, sense of honor, devotion to duty. In a mother and daughter kneeling quietly at a bier, in a tiny son saluting the last mortal remains of his father, we have known that this land, to which the commonest of men have come for shelter and opportunity, can and has produced an aristocracy, a royalty second to none.

The poet speaks of Lincoln's sure vision. We are here today to salute the idealism, the sure vision of our fallen leader. John Kennedy had a vision of a new and greater America and a new and better world for all mankind. He was possessed of a dream that our children would live in a land without racial injustice or second-class citizenship, a dream of freedom, stoutly defended but generously offered to the submerged poor of the earth in every continent, every clime. He took to heart the angels' song of "peace on earth, good will toward men." He made us all feel we were a Nation of forerunners, bound for a finer tomorrow. He followed a star to which he never played false. He knew that without vision the people always perish.

So we have seen greatness passing by, passing all too suddenly from our mortal sight, and having seen such greatness we resolve ourselves to be a bit greater in the days ahead. The business of being free men in a free land is yet unfinished. The high heart that was his must be ours now, driving from our own hearts all rancor, all hatred, all fear of change, all extremism, all selfish gain at the expense of the common good. And the sure vision must be ours, also, for we can all too easily forget the dark lessons of these last 2 weeks and fall back into the old ways of mediocrity and public apathy.

God grant that John F. Kennedy shall not have died in vain, nor lived among us in vain. We are a great people if we have the courage to be great. Ours is the most exciting age in the history of man, and those who stride ahead without fear toward its frontiers, wherever those frontiers may be, are those who will win and claim the splendor and glory of this age.

I know others have spoken of their nation's "finest hour" as being in the black days of war. My fellow citizens, I think two weekends ago was our finest hour, as Americans in this century. We were a humbled people, a shocked people, a united people, a people who turned quietly back to the God our fathers had known. We saw greatness passing by, laid to rest by the muffled drums of time, and we resolved ourselves once more to be great.

HARRY H. KRUENER.

Mr. Speaker, it is my privilege to include a sermon by Rev. Raymond Shelvin, assistant pastor at St. Francis Xavier R.C. Church, Brooklyn, N.Y., delivered on the occasion of a solemn month's mind Mass for President John F. Kennedy on December 21, 1963.

This memorial Mass was attended by thousands of residents of the Brooklyn area and was arranged by the Democratic organizations of the third and eighth assembly districts.

Fittingly, it was attended by public figures and citizens of all political beliefs.

I believe that Father Shelvin's moving and meaningful words are an impressive tribute to our departed friend and late President:

If there is anything that arouses the sympathy of people it is when a great and good person suffers an injustice. Some of the most lovable personalities of history have been men and women who have suffered much. The human heart has an instinct for justice and the human mind finds its greatest joy in honor.

Thus on November 22 when the news of President Kennedy's assassination was broadcast throughout our Nation, every American rebelled with righteous indignation at the thought of this injustice. Here was a man who typified all the traditional ideals of every American. Whether we subscribed to his political thinking or not, everyone felt that this is the way every American should be: Genuinely loyal to his country, sincerely conscientious in his duties to his family, and firmly devout in the practice of his religion.

Who has not marveled at his spirit of dedication to the American cause. On how many different occasions did he challenge his countrymen to come forth and give honest, efficient service to their country. "Ask not what your country can do for you * * *." Speaking to a group of teenagers who had assembled at a CYO convention in New York, he said: "I hope that all of you will serve * * * serve not only your families, your church but also your country. Our country has been very generous to us and we must be generous in return to it."

And then as a father, it was obvious that he delighted to be with his family. In these days when men seem to be indifferent about family unity, his devotion to his family and to his home was exemplary. In spite of a heavy workload of huge responsibilities, his family was very important to him and in return he was very important to his family. By giving attention to them, he received attention from them. By giving affection to them, he received affection from them.

And all this flowed from his sense of duty to his God. A person conscientious in his duties to his God can't help but be a good citizen and a good father. Here was a man who had the burdens of a great nation on his mind and yet regardless of where he was or what he was doing, he would always fulfill his Catholic obligation of going to mass on Sundays. He recognized himself as a creature of God and thus he had the obligation of giving service to God.

We have lost a great man. America has suffered a great tragedy. But instead of this being a great loss to us, it might turn about to be a considerable profit. Tragedy is often the mother of character—it is often the seeds of great virtue. So perhaps as America looks at this man and looks at his personal qualities, America might acquire more loyal Americans; American homes might profit by having more conscientious parents; and, finally, America might become stronger by having greater respect and devotion to God.

TRIBUTE BY

Hon. Emanuel Celler

OF NEW YORK

Mr. Speaker, Fur Center Synagogue, the spiritual pivot of more than 10,000 persons com-

prising the industry's population, preponderantly of Jewish faith, has expressed the poignant sorrow of its congregants, trustees, the industry at large, in the following memoriam. This memoriam appeared in Fur Age Weekly, following memorial services at Fur Center Synagogue in New York, which were marked by an overflowing attendance:

IN MEMORIAM: JOHN FITZGERALD KENNEDY

A part of the heart of every person in the Nation, and of many in enlightened areas of the world, has been interred with the mortal but heavenly blessed remains of our late President.

Prematurely and savagely plucked from our midst; ruthlessly deterred in his world-enriching mission in life; leaving his loved ones crushed by sorrow universally shared; the rich heritage he left behind is gradually discernible through the Nation's tear-glistening eyes.

Although our late lamented President has been taken to the bosom of his Maker, our hearts brighten with high hopes and renewed faith in his ideals.

The seeds of racial tolerance, global friendship in the cause of freedom in all lands, sown by him in the fertile soil of brotherly love, should by our tender and dutiful nurturing yield a bountiful harvest of world peace and new dimensions to human dignity.

This much we owe to our departed leader, a great man and renowned statesman; above all a good man, indeed a good man.

The trustees, officers and congregants of Fur Center Synagogue, unanimously resolve to perpetuate the memory of our Nation's late President by erecting in the new synagogue building, a suitable plaque, and other form of memorial, as a symbol for posterity, that his memory is enshrined in Fur Center Synagogue, as it is in the hearts of all men of dedicated purpose—Jew and non-Jew alike. November 22, 1963.

Alex A. Bernstein, Chairman, Building Committee; Nathan Farber, Chairman, Fund Raising Committee; Albert J. Feldman, Cochairman, Fund Raising Committee; Harry Metzger, President; Charles Baum, Executive Vice President; Murray Greenberg, Secretary; Rabbi Samuel Blech; Abe Fried, Treasurer; Herman Gitters, Vice President.

TRIBUTE BY

Hon. Charles E. Chamberlain

OF MICHIGAN

Mr. Speaker, we have just lived through a tragic period in the life of the Nation. It has been one of those intense moments in our history when we as individuals in a vast pluralistic society have come to fully realize ourselves as citizens of a single community bearing common experiences. This commonality of sentiment and understanding is echoed in the many statements, often even of similar phrasing, spoken by national and world leaders and private citizens as well. This reiteration discloses the very great and common personal feelings these words convey however often they are repeated. In order that the record may reflect the deep sentiments of some of Michigan's citizens as this tragedy becomes history I would like to include editorials contained in the Lansing State Journal for Saturday, November 23, 1963, and the Flint Journal for Saturday, November 23, 1963. The editorials follow:

[From the State Journal, Nov. 23, 1963]

JOHN F. KENNEDY

The Nation today mourns the sudden and violent death of its young President.

The earthly life of John Fitzgerald Kennedy was cut short Friday by an assassin's bullet as the presidential motorcade passed through cheering throngs in Dallas, Tex.

The American people received with a sense of profound shock the news of the assassination of the President and the wounding of Gov. John B. Connally, of Texas, who also was struck by the bullets fired from ambush.

A man of strong convictions and a courageous fighter for what he believed to be right, Kennedy, like many of the Nation's Presidents, was a controversial figure.

But there was never any doubt as to his devotion to America and the ideals it seeks to uphold throughout the world.

Some Americans, perhaps, had come to believe that this country was immune to the degree of turbulence that has led to the brutal slayings of leaders of other nations.

The tragic fact is that Kennedy is the fourth of this Nation's Presidents to die at the hands of cowardly assassins and that attempts have been made on the lives of two other Presidents.

No words can adequately express our shock and sorrow at the death of the vigorous and earnest young American who served his country and the cause of freedom in war a heroic PT boat commander, and in peace a Member of the House of Representatives, the U.S. Senate and, finally, as Chief Executive.

We join with all Americans in expressing our deepest sympathy to the President's bereaved young wife and to all the members of his family.

We hope and pray that this tragedy may have a sobering effect upon the fanatical extremists who believe their causes can be advanced by bloodshed and violence.

Americans now join in prayer that President Lyndon B. Johnson will have the benefit of divine guidance as he assumes and seeks to discharge the awesome responsibilities of the Presidency and the leadership of the free world.

———

[From the Flint Journal, Nov. 23, 1963]

JOHN F. KENNEDY ANSWERS TRUMPET OF
HIGHER SUMMONS

"We shall bear any burden, meet any hardship, pay any price * * * to assure the survival and the success of liberty."

So spoke John F. Kennedy upon being sworn in as President of the United States.

Friday he paid the supreme price.

He gave his life in his country's service.

The President's death at the hands of an assassin left the Nation shocked and grief stricken almost beyond comprehension.

It is difficult to grasp the magnitude of the tragedy that struck the hearts of all Americans; to fathom the severity of the loss our country and the entire free world has suffered.

It is beyond estimating.

It could not have happened. But it did.

Without warning, with frightening suddenness, the vibrant, exuberant spirit of the youngest, most-influential leader and champion of freedom in the world today was stilled, his life snuffed out.

Gone, now, is the enthusiasm and zest with which John F. Kennedy met every problem and challenge.

Gone is the personal magnetism which he possessed in rare quantity and with which he cemented close friendships, even among political foes.

Gone is the indomitable courage, displayed in both military and civilian service, that helped to strengthen the moral fiber of those who looked to him for leadership in time of crisis.

Gone is the fresh and spontaneous interest which he inherently displayed in the troubles, the hardships, the disappointments and the hopes of little men and humble people of every race and every walk of life.

There were those who disagreed with some of his policies and actions. But few could deny that this young man, who preferred public service to a beckoning life of idleness and ease, possessed vision to understand clearly the crises of our times and the resoluteness to boldly meet each crisis as he was convinced it should be met for the good of the country he loved.

His underlying policy was clear. It was forged from a deep conviction that only in a world in which there is room for equality and freedom can we hope to preserve for ourselves and others the only way of life which Americans believe to be worth living. Even those who sometimes questioned his methods had a profound respect for his devotion to the ideals for which he worked and fought.

In accepting without reservation the most burdensome responsibility of our time, this dedicated young statesman faced every challenge unflinchingly, almost with relish. He seemed to thrive on pressure. He possessed a unique

arm. Even under fire he combined a rare affability
d informality with a winning smile, succeeding in
ansforming austerity into personal warmth.

Rarely has this country been led by a President with
ore political astuteness, with such superbly persuasive
ility.

Still he put his personal convictions ahead of political
in when he went before the people with his civil rights
ll. Even realizing the possible ramifications at the polls,
 placed his personal influence and the weight of his
fice squarely behind an all-out demand for an end to
cial discrimination in every segment of community life.

"Let it be clear, in our hearts and minds, that it is not
erely because of the cold war, and not merely because
 the economic waste of discrimination, that we are
mmitted to achieving true equality of opportunity.
he basic reason is because it is right."

John F. Kennedy's courage and inner strength were
ver displayed more dramatically than in that hour.
ot even in his alerting his fellow Americans to the
ssibility of all-out war during the Cuban missile crisis.

An appraisal of this youthful President, struck down
en before attaining the peak of his dedicated career, is
possible at this time. This must be left to the pages
 history.

But of one thing grieving Americans can be certain.
hn F. Kennedy devoted his heart, body, and mind to
lfilling the solemn oath he swore before them and
lmighty God.

At that time, as our newly sworn-in President at age
, he said "* * * the trumpet summons us * * * to
struggle against the common enemies of man: tyranny,
verty, disease, and war itself."

In harking to that summons, he followed his own
ea to his fellow Americans. He asked himself what
 could do for his country, and he set about doing what
 believed would best serve to fulfill its commitments.
Friday, John F. Kennedy answered a higher summons.

In our hour of sadness, and beyond, our constant prayer
ould be that his sincere efforts for the future peace and
ppiness of our Nation, and of the other nations of
e world, may not have been in vain.

TRIBUTE BY

Hon. Frank M. Clark

OF PENNSYLVANIA

Mr. Speaker, I would like to include in my
marks an editorial from the News Tribune in
eaver Falls, Pa., in my congressional district
y Mr. James March, editor.

Mr. Speaker, our hearts will be heavy for a
ng, long time in the loss of our beloved Presi-
ent and friend. This editorial by Mr. March
xpresses the thoughts and feelings of all of us.

JOHN F. KENNEDY

We are all, like swimmers in the sea,
Poised on the top of a huge wave of fate,
Which hangs uncertain to which side to fall;
And whether it will heave us up to land,
Or whether it will roll us out to sea.
                              —MATTHEW ARNOLD.

The high and the low, Americans all, with any sense
of responsibility at all are saddened by the heinous
murder of the President of the United States.

No matter what one's political faith may be, the
death of a President is a loss to the Nation and to the
world and a personal tragedy to many.

John F. Kennedy along with his ability as an outstanding leader was endowed with great personal charm. On
two occasions he visited Beaver County briefly. Everyone who heard him speak here will never forget his
personal magnetism.

His New England "Ameriker" and "Cuber" and his
stabbing finger to emphasize a point were another kind
of charm.

Part of the personal popularity of the President and
Mrs. Kennedy was that they brought gayety and life to
the White House. They were young, they were rearing
children, they liked the theater, the arts, sports, were
devoted to their parents—qualities with which millions
of Americans could identify.

The Kennedy clan with all its wealth, prestige, and
power knows only too well the anguish of grief in the
loss of loved ones as do most families.

It is particularly hard to reconcile the death of a
family man in the prime of life and the only salvation
for those personally affected is to learn to accept and
not to question.

Those who believe the words of Jesus who said that
not one sparrow falls to the ground without the Father's
notice, do not question the wisdom of God, no matter
what the burden, or anguish they may have to bear.

The length of one's life is not the greatest factor.
The use made of the time allotted man on earth is of
utmost importance. The President did not squander his
time or talents and will serve as an inspiration for generations to come.

We join the closely knit Kennedy family in their
sorrow.

TRIBUTES BY

Hon. Jeffery Cohelan

OF CALIFORNIA

Mr. Speaker, I take this time today to share
with you a letter I received from a very dear
friend. It was my great privilege some years
ago to study in Great Britain where I worked
with the distinguished Prof. S. G. Raybould of

the University of Leeds. He writes from Leeds, England:

THE UNIVERSITY, LEEDS,
November 25, 1963.

DEAR JEFF: I feel I must write at this time to at least some of my American friends to send our profound sympathy to you in your terrible loss. Throughout this country there is a deep feeling of personal grief and bereavement, and sense of tragedy, such as we felt when Hugh Gaitskill died—perhaps even deeper; and an awareness, of course, of the greater loss to the whole world. But beyond all that, I'm sure there is great sympathy for the people of America, as well as for the President's family and household, such as can rarely, if ever, have been felt by the people of one country for those of another.

I wish there was more I could say. But I suppose it's a measure of the tragedy that there isn't.

Yours most sincerely,

SID.

Mr. Speaker, the student body of Willard Junior High School in Berkeley, Calif., can be proud of the editorial staff of the school newspaper. The editors of Scoop published a memorial edition on Tuesday, November 26, following the memorial holiday weekend. These wonderful youngsters gathered over the weekend and channeled their feelings of distress and sorrow into this special mimeographed edition.

IN MEMORIAM—JOHN FITZGERALD KENNEDY

(By Martha Simpson)

John Fitzgerald Kennedy died Friday, November 22, leaving behind him records of great accomplishment during his office as 35th President of the United States. The death of this great President went not unmourned, for he was dear to the heart of not only his family, but to all people of the United States, which he, prudently and confidently had guided through unending local and national crises since his inauguration on January 20, 1960.

Special announcements being broadcast from Dallas reached Berkeley a little after 11, Friday, the 22d of November. First, word came that the President had been shot, then that these sad tidings meant that the President, John Fitzgerald Kennedy, was dead.

The reactions of Willard students here were those of anger, shock, and sorrow. Some students left Willard to attend special Mass held in his honor that afternoon. Others remained at Willard that day and tried to participate as usual in classes. The teachers, also feeling tense and grieved, tried to maintain classes. Mr. Shearer sent around bulletins urging the students to continue classes as normally as possible and consoling them in their sorrow.

We, the people of the United States, mourn the death of our late President, but now we must prepare for the future, under the guidance of Lyndon Baines Johnson, former Vice President. Even in our deepest sorrow we must pledge our support to Lyndon Johnson, our new President, and have confidence that he will guide ᵤ with prudence through the next difficult years.

————

(By Sheila Reinke)

On May 29, 1917, John F. Kennedy was born, and o November 22, 1963, he died, a great man and a grea leader. He was born in Brookline, Mass., of a wealth Catholic family.

Kennedy entered politics in 1946 and was elected t the House of Representatives. In 1952, after a lon period in the House, he became Senator fron Massachusetts.

In 1953 he married Jacqueline Bouvier. They late had two children, Caroline, now 6, and John Fitzgeral who is just 3.

In October 1962, he put up a blockade against Cuba and stopped all trade of the United States with tha country, in order to rid Cuba of Russian missiles. Ken nedy got Peace Corps aid for underdeveloped countrie passed a bill for $600 million aid program to Lati America, and created the Alliance for Progress. He late got Russia to sign a limited nuclear test ban treaty.

In the 3 years he was President many great things wer done.

A little less than a century ago Abraham Lincoln wa shot down. There is a parallel between Lincoln an Kennedy. Both Presidents worked for equal rights fc all races, colors, and creeds.

————

(By Dan Roberts)

At around 12:30 in the afternoon of Sunday, Novem ber 24, 1963, a Dallas nightclub owner shot and kille Lee H. Oswald, the alleged assassin of our late Presiden John F. Kennedy. This happened while the Dallas polic were trying to move Oswald from the Dallas city jail t the larger county jail.

This crime shows us that not only are there people wh will kill the President of the United States, but that ther are certain citizens who do not have enough confidenc in the government of their own country to let that gov ernment use its legal machinery to convict the Presi dent's slayer.

As a lot of our readers know, an interdenominationa service was given in the park in front of the Berkele City Hall on Sunday, November 24. After the servic several people were interviewed on their opinions of th murder of Oswald. The general theory was that eve though it was fairly definite that he was the assassin c our late President, Oswald should have been able to enjo the right of every American citizen to be judged by group of his own equals.

The crime that was carried out in the basement c the Dallas City Hall was almost as terrible as the one tha snatched up the young life of the late John F. Kennedy Killing the leader of this great Nation was a crime almos unparalleled in history. On the other hand, the murde of Lee H. Oswald was tragic in its own special way.

Jack Ruby, the murderer of the alleged assassin, no only took away an American's right to a free trial, bu also killed the one possible source of light on the basic motives and organization of the assassination.

America, land of the free, and home of the brave, and a haven of justice, should raise its mighty voice not only in grief over the death of its youngest President, but in anger over the flouting of the laws set up by our forefathers.

———

(By Matthew Barr)

The President is dead. We have lost one of the foremost leaders the White House has ever held. The assassination of John Fitzgerald Kennedy has left a wake in the minds and acts of the American people.

Few other Presidents did as much for civil rights as he did. He was one of the Presidents who did not shrink under the great burdens of the Presidency. The test ban treaty, the lessening of the cold war tensions, foreign aid, taxes, all these subjects had been dealt with fairly and justly by Kennedy during the 2 years and 10 months he held office. Everything was going well: the future seemed bright when Kennedy was shot down last Friday.

The irrational violence that we have experienced in the slayings of President Kennedy and Oswald prove this: the whole Nation needs a reeducation. This sounds wholly silly at first, reeducating the Nation of 185 million people—but when you think it over, about the reactions of the people on civil rights, you may think it a good idea to teach people that all human beings are entitled to equal respect.

Sensible people who respect democracy must stand up for our equal rights now, or we may find ourselves washed away in a flood of chaos.

TRIBUTES BY

Hon. Emilio Q. Daddario

OF CONNECTICUT

Mr. Speaker, one of the finest poets in the United States is a former professor of mine at Wesleyan University and a man who has attained national recognition in the arts, in the academic world, and as an elected official. He is the former Governor and Lieutenant Governor of Connecticut, Wilbert Snow.

Following the death of our late President, John F. Kennedy, Governor Snow wrote a brief poem in his memory. It was published on the cover of the January 1964 issue of the Wesleyan Alumnus magazine, and drew my attention immediately. It is one of the best statements I have seen to express the image of a young man struck down in the midst of his promise.

I had an opportunity to discuss this poem with

Governor Snow recently and I asked him in particular about the use of two words. One was "Eshcol" in the line—"Loving the wine of Freedom's Eshcol brook." His idea was that the wine of freedom should be made from the biggest and best grapes. He got the impression from the Book of Numbers in the Bible, chapter 13, verses 23–24:

> And they came unto the brook of Eshcol, and cut down from thence a branch with one cluster of grapes, and they bare it between two upon a staff. * * * The place was called the brook Eshcol, because of the cluster of grapes which the children of Israel cut down from thence.

The other word was "ichor" in line 6 of the poem which reads: "As the ichor of our old New England schools." Governor Snow explained that the ichor fluid took the place of blood in the bodies of the gods in Greek mythology. His purpose in this use, therefore, was to cite the individual freedom which the President loved and which has been nourished in him by the old schools, Choate, Princeton, and Harvard, that he attended.

I have found this poem most inspirational and I believe all Members should read it and reflect upon it:

J.F.K.

(By Wilbert Snow)

Greek runner on whom people loved to look,
    World Consul with a youthful mind and heart,
Lover of wine from Freedom's Eshcol brook,
    A Renaissance man whom the world of art
Enriched and widened and endowed with balance,
    As the ichor of our old New England schools
Gave Emersonian luster to his talents,
    And honed his humerous Irish foil for fools.
New man of this new day, he shamed us all
    By keeping faith with the American dream;
He trusted it and labored to install
    An order that would bring the sorry scheme
Of old world hatreds to an end. Stars, mourn
    That such a radiant soul from earth was torn.

Mr. Speaker, I have had the opportunity to read a most penetrating and sympathetic remembrance of our late President John Fitzgerald Kennedy, with special reference to his interest in and respect for science. This monograph appeared in the magazine Science, which is the publication of the American Association for the Advancement of Science, and I have asked unanimous consent so that all our Members may read it.

JOHN F. KENNEDY: A REMEMBRANCE

(By Jerome B. Wiesner)

(His respect for science as an instrument of good was one of the Chief Executive's distinctive qualities.)

Never have I been given a more difficult task. To put into words the true spirit and charm and intelligence of John F. Kennedy would be impossible even for a writer far more gifted than I. It would take the telling of many tales, a description of his handling of problems large and small, a detailed history of his 3 brief years as a world leader, to show his true greatness.

I have just returned from Arlington National Cemetery where thousands of people from all over the world paid their last respects to the man who had given them so much hope. It was a beautiful, cold sunshiny day, the kind he loved. One could almost call it a New England day. The day was like the President, radiant and crisp. He added something indescribable to every occasion; his smile brightened it, his humor livened it. He had a quick and often sardonic humor and a quick mind. To these he added an optimism about the future and a determination to bring out the maximum capabilities of our people, and, indeed, of all mankind. He was an intelligent, educated man. He was a kindly man. I never knew him to do a mean thing to any person. He was never too busy for a word of greeting. He had a strong temper but one that subsided quickly. Challenged, he responded firmly. Big problems were never allowed to submerge the small, today's problems to obscure tomorrow's. At the height of the great crises of his tenure—the Bay of Pigs disaster, the resumption of nuclear testing by the Soviet Union, Mississippi, Birmingham, the confrontation with the Soviet Union over the missile installations in Cuba—he still talked about the future. He retained his monumental interest in the details of the ongoing business of Government. He read an amazing amount, and seemingly remembered it all. He often asked about obscure stories concerning science buried in the New York Times or the London Observer or any one of the dozens of papers and periodicals he somehow found time to read.

VISION AND OUTLOOK

I met Jack Kennedy while he was a Senator from my home State of Massachusetts. He needed advice on technical matters, particularly military technology and nuclear test ban, issues then occupying much of my time. I agreed to help largely because friends asked me to and because he was my Senator. I heard from him only infrequently at first and saw him even less. But even those brief contacts caused me to admire him, so that I readily agreed to join up and provide what little help I could when he became the Democratic candidate for the Presidency. Many things impressed me then and drew me to him. There was, of course, his charm but there was much more. I was most impressed by his quick, almost instinctive understanding of problems once he was given the facts. His background ill prepared him for an interest in scientific matters, yet his interest was lively. He was, in fact, then a member of the Harvard University Visiting Committee. Obviously un-

prepared to understand the theory of scientific subjects, he tried to get a physical feel of the matter. For example, he was forever trying to get someone to explain electromagnetic propagation comprehensibly. He didn't call it that. He wanted to know how radio worked. But when one tried to answer, one learned that the question was not about electron tubes or transistors or coils—these were manmade things which he could believe—but why and how did nature really allow energy to be sent through space.

Someone called him a truly modern man, this first American President to be born in the 20th century. And he was that. He had confidence in and used the modern tools. In a real sense technological marvels gave him his chance to be President. Without the airplane and television, he would not have been able to wage his successful campaign in 1960. And he never forgot this. His vision and outlook made it easy for him to understand other products of technology. President Kennedy, better than any political figure I have known, understood the social significance of modern science and technology.

As I try to remember the things that impressed me most about the President, four qualities stand out: his intelligence, his hopefulness, his sense of history, his striving for excellence. All of us who worked with him were proud of him. His very appearance, his composure, his sensitivity for every situation led us to an ever-growing admiration. He was the President from the very beginning, and as he was tested in his terrible job, he grew.

His vision and perfectionism may best be seen in his speeches. He had a vision of what he thought the world could be, and he projected this in his poetic prose. His inaugural address set the plan for his administration, and he strove consistently to reach the goals he set then. He said, "To those peoples in the huts and villages of half the globe struggling to break the bonds of mass misery, we pledge our best efforts to help them help themselves, for whatever peiod is required—not because the Communists may be doing it, not because we seek their votes, but because it is right. If a free society cannot help the many who are poor, it cannot save the few who are rich."

And about the arms race, "Finally, to those nations who would make themselves our adversary, we offer not a pledge but a request: that both sides begin anew the quest for peace, before the dark powers of destruction unleashed by science engulf all humanity in planned or accidental self-destruction. * * * Let both sides explore what problems unite us instead of belaboring those problems which divide us. Let both sides, for the first time, formulate serious and precise proposals for the inspection and control of arms—and bring the absolute power to destroy other nations under the absolute control of all nations."

Much of President Kennedy's hopefulness was derived from his conviction that science provided our Nation with vast powers for good. In the inaugural speech, he summed this up with, "Let both sides seek to invoke the wonders of science instead of its terrors. Together let us explore the stars, conquer the deserts, eradicate disease, tap the ocean depths and encourage the arts and commerce." He was ever pressing to put technology to work.

In foreign affairs, for helping other nations, for insuring our security, in seeking solutions to our domestic problems, he looked to science for the clues.

NATIONAL ACADEMY SPEECHES

Twice he responded to invitations to speak before the National Academy of Sciences, and, as far as I know, set a precedent for Presidential attendance at Academy functions.

On April 25, 1961, the President, in dedicating the new wing of the Academy, disregarded his prepared text and in an eloquent extemporaneous talk revealed his sensitive understanding of the necessary cooperation between the Government and the scientific community. In calling upon the Academy and the scientific community, the President remarked:

"This country must move forward, and most of the areas where we must move forward involve most sophisticated problems which your experience and training can help us to solve. One of the problems, it seems to me, of a free society is the fact that all of the questions which we must decide now are extremely sophisticated questions. It is difficult enough for those who hold office, either in the administration or in the Congress, to attempt to make a determination between alternate courses of action—fiscal policy, monetary policy, agricultural policy, international policy, disarmament, arms control, all the rest, all of these involve questions to confound the experts. For those of us who are not expert and yet must be called upon to make decisions which involve the security of our country, which involve the expenditures of hundreds of millions or billions of dollars, we must turn, in the last resort, to objective, disinterested scientists who bring a strong sense of public responsibility and public obligation. So this Academy is most important."

Again, on October 22, 1963, a month to the day before the tragic events in Texas, the President appeared before the Academy on the occasion of its anniversary convocation and he emphasized the importance of basic scientific investigations, the contributions that science can make to international objectives, and the interdisciplinary and intercultural aspects of science in playing its role in modern society. He also dwelt on a theme that he many times expressed, the need for applying the results of scientific and technological advances to the conservation and development of natural resources. During his relatively brief stay in office he gave physical meaning to these objectives.

On the subject of basic scientific research, the President said in his last Academy speech:

"But if basic research is to be properly regarded, it must be better understood. I ask you to reflect on this problem and on the means by which, in the years to come, our society can assure continuing backing to fundamental research in the life sciences, the physical sciences, the social sciences, on natural resources, on agriculture, on protection against pollution and erosion. Together, the scientific community, the Government, industry, and education must work out the way to nourish American science in all its power and vitality."

President Kennedy regarded international scientific cooperative activities and scientific exchanges as one of the strongest bridges to other nations, and at the Academy celebration he expanded on this view. "I would suggest that science is already moving to enlarge its influence in three general ways: In the interdisciplinary area, in the international area, and in the intercultural area. For science is the most powerful means we have for the unification of knowledge, and a main obligation of its future must be to deal with problems which cut across boundaries, whether boundaries between the sciences, boundaries between nations, or boundaries between man's scientific and his humane concerns."

He closed his talk with an anecdote that revealed the strength of his conviction about the importance of basic research to the country's future when he remarked, "The great French Marshal Lyautey once said to his gardener: 'Plant a tree tomorrow.' And the gardener said, 'It won't bear fruit for 100 years.' 'In that case,' said Lyautey to the gardener, 'plant it this afternoon.' That is how I feel about your work," said the President.

BASIC RESEARCH AND MANPOWER

Under the President's leadership there has been a substantial strengthening of the basic research grants of the National Science Foundation in recognition not only of the need for the results of such research, but also of the essential role of basic research in the training of new scientists. In a news conference on January 15, 1962, the President expressed his concern about the future adequacy of our scientific and technical manpower in referring to a study of Soviet technical manpower that had just been published by the National Science Foundation. He said, "This has been a matter of some concern to me for some time because one of the most critical problems facing this Nation is the inadequacy of the supply of scientific and technical manpower to satisfy the expanding requirements of this country's research and development efforts in the near future." He called upon the President's Science Advisory Committee, in cooperation with the Federal Council for Science and Technology, to report as quickly as possible on the specific measures that could be taken to develop the necessary, well-qualified scientists and engineers, and he reinforced his personal concern with the words, "To all those who may be within the sound of my voice or who may follow your stories in the papers, I want to emphasize the great new and exciting field of the sciences." Following submission of the Science Advisory Committee report of December 1962 on needs for graduate training in engineering, mathematics, and physical sciences, the President's 1964 budget for the National Science Foundation reflected his acceptance of the PSAC judgment of the importance of increased support for graduate education. This is also reflected in his proposed legislation to increase the number of fellowships under the National Defense Education Act, and in his extemporaneous remarks at the National Academy celebration he expressed his deep disappointment in the failure of the Congress to support this program.

SPACE PROGRAM

During his administration he made persistent efforts to strengthen the U.S. space program. He saw in it the opportunity to serve many national needs. He was firmly convinced that Soviet space supremacy had greatly weakened the United States in its foreign affairs. He saw military hazards in a lagging space capability. He saw the exploration of space as one of the great human adventures of this century, and he appreciated the important scientific possibilities of space exploration. He dedicated this Nation to a massive space program with a firm target of a manned lunar landing in this decade. This is a costly program and his decision to undertake it was not made lightly. He talked to hundreds of people in the process of making his decision and he weighed the costs with real concern. In the end he became convinced that the United States could not remain second in this important field. Despite continual review, he remained convinced of the correctness of this course.

Yet with the closing of the gap between United States and U.S.S.R. outer space capabilities, he followed through his inaugural theme with the proposal to the U.S.S.R. for a joint moon venture.

He also followed through on his inaugural hopes of conquering the deserts, and the national efforts at desalinization were greatly reinforced, along with a stepped-up program of underlying basic and applied research to overcome the barriers to economic desalinization.

NATURAL RESOURCES

In the field of natural resources, the President early in his administration took steps to accelerate the pace of the national program in oceanography, and at the same time provided leadership and backing both for congressional support and for a coordinated, balanced, and imaginative interagency approach to oceanographic research. An old sailor, he had a special interest in this research. He got a particular pleasure when the Presidential yacht *Williamsburg* was converted into an oceanographic research vessel. For a film on oceanographic research just completed, the President provided the opening and closing lines. Recently, after I had recovered from the consequences of a sailing accident, inaccurately reported, he offered to give me lessons in sailing and press relations. He called upon both the National Academy of Sciences and the Federal Council for Science and Technology to study and make recommendations for strengthening the Federal efforts across the broad horizons of natural resources in the land, sea, and air so that they can better serve the needs of the American people.

Early in his administration, too, the President lent substance to his desire to encourage commerce through science and technology by initiating a national program to strengthen civilian technology, including the appointment of an Assistant Secretary of Commerce for Science and Technology. In remarks prepared for delivery in Dallas, never given, the President pointed out that communities possessing the best in research and graduate facilities tend to attract the new and growing industries. He congratulated those who recognized the relationship between leadership and learning and the need for community support for the advancement of learning underlying the creation of the forward-looking Graduate Research Center of the Southwest.

President Kennedy's interest in international aspects of science was again highlighted in his September 20,

1963, address to the United Nations, where he urged a world center for health communications to warn of epidemics and the adverse effects of certain drugs; regional research centers to advance common medical knowledge and train new scientists and doctors for new nations; and a cooperative system of satellites to provide communication and weather information on a worldwide basis. As a result of his initiative, work has already begun in the World Meteorological Organization to develop the outlines of a world weather system and to strengthen basic research in atmospheric sciences on an international basis.

In connection with technical assistance to newly developing countries, the President was instrumental in bringing about closer attention to the need for research underlying the planning and execution of the AID program. This was reflected in the formulation of his Alliance for Progress program with its emphasis on science education, and in the establishment of the Office of Human Resources and Social Development in the Agency for International Development.

There are numerous other examples of President Kennedy's interest in promoting the development and application of science on an international basis, ranging from his initiative in establishing the United States-Japan Science Committee and his encouragement of the scientists' Pugwash movement, to his request for specific studies from his Science Advisory Committee, including a study of the problem of hoof and mouth disease in Argentina, the problem of water-logging in Pakistan, and most recently his initiation of a study of the boll weevil problem in cotton production, a matter of international as well as national concern.

ARMS CONTROL

I have already referred to the President's strong conviction about the need for bringing about adequately safeguarded international arms control, a matter that occupied a very substantial part of his time from the very first days of his administration. The whole world can be thankful for two major accomplishments that flowed from his efforts, two monuments to his labors on the road to peace—the Arms Control and Disarmament Agency and the nuclear test ban treaty—which can inspire us to persist in the efforts to avoid the nuclear holocaust that so haunted him. One of his first acts was to propose to Congress the creation of the Arms Control and Disarmament Agency, the world's first governmental activity dedicated solely to the study of disarmament problems. As a result, the U.S. Government now has a small cadre of professionals in this extremely complicated and important field.

The signing of the nuclear test ban treaty gave the President enormous satisfaction. For him it proved that meaningful disarmament steps were possible, and it justified the hundreds of hours of debate and study, the deep disappointments along the way. His striving for this treaty, begun in the first days of his administration, weathered many bitter disappointments and was the subject of much unjust criticism. He could hardly have been blamed had he abandoned hope after the Russians resumed nuclear testing in the summer of 1961. Characteristically, though, he continued his attempts to work out an acceptable agreement. The question of the need for further nuclear tests in order to enhance our national security involved highly technical issues and extremely controversial ones as well. So did the capabilities of nuclear test detection systems. The President made himself an expert on these subjects. He listened to many briefings and more debates. He talked to experts with every possible view and finally formed his own conclusions.

In the process he also achieved an understanding of the role of scientific advice in policy matters. In his last National Academy address he said, "As the country had reason to note in recent weeks during the debate on the test ban treaty, scientists do not always unite themselves on their recommendations to makers of policy. This is only partly because of scientific disagreements. It is even more so because the big issues so often go beyond the possibilities of exact scientific determination.

"I know few significant questions of public policy which can safely be confided to computers. In the end, the hard decisions inescapably involve imponderables of intuition, prudence, and judgment."

The President called the nuclear test ban treaty a small first step. Since its signing, the nations of the world have also responded to his call for a pledge to prohibit the placing of nuclear weapons in orbit. He hoped that these agreements would be followed by many more.

President Kennedy not only understood the need to invest resources for extending our understanding of science and its applications but also saw the need for institutional change to guide and assist the mounting governmental involvement in science and technology to serve national objectives. He shared the view that the Federal scientific enterprise would be best served by strengthening the individual agencies whose missions required the exploitation of science, rather than by the creation of an all-encompassing department of science. Toward this end he sought the inclusion of a technically educated individual at the policy level in each department which is heavily dependent upon science for the accomplishment of its mission. The evolution of the Office of Science and Technology also reflects this policy of building strength in the individual agencies. On March 29, 1962, after much discussion, he sent a message to the Congress providing for reorganization in the field of science and technology. He pointed out that the ever-growing significance and complexity of Federal programs had earlier necessitated several steps for improving the organizational arrangements of the executive branch. The President believed that the creation of the Office of Science and Technology would facilitate communication between the executive branch and the Congress. The wisdom of the President in making this proposal is being increasingly realized through the activities of its director, in its close collaboration with the Bureau of the Budget, its presentations to congressional committees, and through its leadership in initiating long-range planning of research and development within the Federal agencies. To assist this work, the National Science Foundation has created an Office of Resources Planning, and closer ties with the National Academy of Sciences have been established through its newly created Committee on Science and Public Affairs.

These are only the highlights of President Kennedy's broad interest in science and technology and the tangible forms they have taken. Although much progress has been made, much more needs to be done. But because of his interest and support we have a stronger base upon which to extend the already impressive contributions of American science and technology.

TRIBUTE BY
Hon. Dominick V. Daniels
OF NEW JERSEY

Mr. Speaker, never could it be more truly said than of our late President: He has captured the imagination of our youth. And so it is as testimonials of love, of reverence and respect for John Fitzgerald Kennedy pour into our office from our younger generation. Two of these testimonials represent some of the finest sentiments from youth ever expressed.

The first inclusion comprises the opening remarks of a Boy Scout troop, which identifies itself with the late President, as he himself was a Boy Scout once. These remarks were followed by 1 minute of silence at an opening ceremony of a meeting of Cub Pack 43, sponsored by the Kiwanis Club of Hoboken, N.J.

The second inclusion is a poem written by a West New York, N.J., eighth-grader, Frank Leanza.

John F. Kennedy was the first Boy Scout ever to become President of the United States of America. Like you, John F. Kennedy was a boy, loved fun, games, and activity. Like you, he raised his hand in the Scout oath and law, not so important that he became President of our Nation, as that, when he became a man he never stopped living by that code. Each point of the law was exemplified in his life, each phrase of the oath he followed in his daily life, he was an example to each of us, not so important what we become, but how we live whatever we become, tomorrow and next day and next week, and beyond. May each of us live the oath and law as to fulfill and bring to the world that for which President Kennedy gave his life, ours is the responsibility to build on the heritage which is ours.

JOHN FITZGERALD KENNEDY

(By Frank Leanza)

That October we were on the brink,
Would the Ship of Liberty sink?

In Cuba were the missiles and IL–38's,
In the hands of J.F.K. lay our fates.

Like a block of granite he stood his ground,
Then Russian ships turned 'round.

There followed a relieving sigh,
For the moment danger had passed by.

He risked his popularity,
So in the South all could be free.

In Birmingham and in Albany,
He did his best so all would be free.

He said: "All equal, all the same,"
The segregationists he put to shame.

James Meredith was a boy who wanted an education,
Getting it was filled with many a trial and tribulation.

So on the campus of Ole Miss a battle was fought,
For in America, liberty is always sought.

Now he is dead,
So let it be said:

He was great, he was grand,
He was the best in the land.

His spirit and ideals shall live on and be infinite,
He asked not what he could do for his country,
He did it.

TRIBUTE BY

Hon. John H. Dent

OF PENNSYLVANIA

Mr. Speaker, under leave to extend my remarks, I would like to present Senate Resolution 9, introduced in the Senate of Pennsylvania, on December 2, 1963, by the Honorable William J. Lane and James S. Berger, in memory of our beloved President, as follows:

RESOLUTION

DECEMBER 2, 1963.

The 22d day of November will go down in history as the anniversary of the day that the people of the world were thrown into deep sorrow upon hearing of the assassination of President John F. Kennedy.

It was a day of sadness for all and will linger in the minds of mankind for many years to come.

It would be most fitting for the Congress of the United States to set aside November 22 of each year as a day when the people of our Nation can rededicate themselves to the ideals which were set forth by our 35th President; therefore be it

Resolved, That the Senate of the Commonwealth of Pennsylvania memorialize the Congress of the United States to declare November 22 as President Kennedy Memorial Day; and be it further

Resolved, That a copy of this resolution be forwarded to the Speaker of the House of Representatives and President pro tempore of the Senate in Washington, D.C., as well as each Member of the Congress from the Commonwealth of Pennsylvania.

I certify that the foregoing is a true and correct copy of Senate Resolution Serial No. 9, introduced by Senators William J. Lane and James S. Berger on behalf of the entire membership of the senate and adopted by the Senate of Pennsylvania the 2d day of December, 1963.
MARK GRUELL, Jr.,
Secretary, Senate of Pennsylvania.

TRIBUTE BY

Hon. Samuel L. Devine

OF OHIO

Mr. Speaker, among the eulogies for our late President John F. Kennedy, one of the most objective was given by Bob Sherman, news editor of radio station WMNI in Columbus, Ohio, on November 23, 1963. The eulogy follows:

THE ASSASSINATION OF PRESIDENT KENNEDY: A EULOGY

Good evening, this is Bob Sherman, WMNI news "Current Events and Comments." Tonight, John Fitzgerald Kennedy, 35th President of the United States, 1917–63, in memoriam.

When Franklin Delano Roosevelt addressed the Congress of the United States on December 8, 1941, he assessed the events of the day before as ones which would cause December 7 to live in infamy.

I can think of no more adequate language to denote the day before this Saturday, November 22, 1963.

I am still in a state of stunned amazement, the people I see around me now, as I am certain the people around you, reflect the same ashen somberness which has suddenly cast a pall over the faces of all Americans and our friends around the world.

At 1:30 in the afternoon, on a sun-bathed, crowd-lined street in Dallas, Tex., a portion of the world's light went out; John Fitzgerald Kennedy is dead. The heinous crime which took the life of America's 35th President is an event which no Americans, save a fringe of lunatics and insane fanatics, can either justify or find satisfying.

I am profoundly sorry. I speak for all of the people associated with WMNI in extending our heartfelt condolences to the family of the President at this time of grievous personal loss.

I first met John Kennedy, the handsome junior Senator from Massachusetts, in Boston, at a reception for news reporters in 1957. A handshake, an almost automatic, yet deeply warm smile, this was my first observation, and a final impression. I saw him again in a television studio in Parkersburg, W. Va., in 1960. For 2 weeks, a bevy of reporters and I followed this amazing, hardworking strenuous man over the mountain State, traveling in a very old bus, over equally archaic and never-comfortable roads. Being one of the junior members of a large reportorial crew of men like Edward P. Morgan of A.B.C., W. H. Lawrence of the New York Times, and Clark

Mollenoff of the Des Moines Register, it did not frequently fall my fortune to ask a question. But when I did acquire the hard-campaigning candidate's attention, he was always fair to me as if I represented the big networks, not just a smalltown radio-TV news department.

Even if he is not in Washington, regularly covering the White House beat, I think a reporter somehow feels closer to the public officials, particularly the President. I think he feels closer than the average private citizen. Can you imagine how many times, I, for instance, have said "President Kennedy" in the last 3 years? I can't estimate the number. I do know that it has been sufficient to create an almost pavlovian habit that will be arduous to alter.

A vicious sniper's bullet yesterday in Dallas created the necessity to break that habit.

As I mentioned, I believe reporters, because of the nature of their tasks, or perhaps due to the requirements of their profession, feel a closer affinity toward a President than the ordinary citizen. For this reason, and principally because it has been our custom, and I am speaking of the journalists of America, as a body, this evening, I would like to present, if I may humbly solicit your indulgence, this reporter's analysis of the past, tragic, grief-filled hours.

John Kennedy's political program was controversial. I am afraid that to some unsophisticated ears that analysis might seem almost unkind now in lieu of his untimely death. However, I don't think so. It is unfortunate that the word "controversial" has become something to be feared in America. John Kennedy took a stand, he promoted and advanced a political creed and philosophy. This is honorable, judging not the feasibility or the advisability of his political principles or his economic policy. Americans must respect him for—indeed—it requires courage to be controversial.

John Kennedy's contribution to mankind may not and probably will not be his legislature program, his "Peace Corps," his appointees or even his books and essays, but in my opinion, the three short years he was at the center of the world stage, he made his finest donation to humanity, by standing resolutely for his ideals, and firmly by his principles. He was a man of action, and therefore, he generated a reaction. I know he caused people to think. He caused the American political pulse to quicken a bit or so and pumped fresh blood into the mainstream of honest American political liberalism. As a result, John Kennedy helped to create a new conservative political force. His contribution is this: he made people choose up sides. He, because of his stand, caused others to take a stand. The immortal Dante wrote centuries ago, "the hottest places in hell are reserved for those who in a time of moral crisis, refuse to take a stand." John Kennedy was not one who failed to meet the basic quality of that kind of statesmanship.

To debate here the individual assets and liabilities of John Kennedy's program would be a premature act on the part of this commentator. However, to assume that with his death too succumbed the head for future argumentative deliberation over his programing would also be equally fallacious and wholly improper.

Omar Khayyam penned the words, "and the moving finger writes and having writ moves on," and so it does.

The clock of history continuing to advance. Not one second which has slipped by can be reattained, not even that split second during which the fatal shot was fired into the brain of the late President can be brought back from the clutches of immortality. To hope, as I heard a Detroit priest express it, last night, "that from this personal tragedy, we might construct some good."

What beneficences can result from the death of a man, I cannot say, but, his survivors can hope, and well they should do so.

I hope Americans will not choose to feel disgraced by this event; collectively, or even individually, society is not responsible for this crime. While it is true that a climate of political disagreement exists in America, it is intemperate to regard the actions of one man, a killer, as indicative of the moral character of either the genuine left or the sincere right on the national political spectrum. When society hangs its head in shame and offers a hasty self-indictment because of a single maniac's dastardly deed, that society is only pitying itself. America has no cause for shame. If we hang our heads, it should be for the purposes of prayer in behalf of John Kennedy's soul.

Perhaps the single thing that will be wrought from the tragedy is understanding of our real cause. The preservation of liberty at home and expansion of freedom to the oppressed millions abroad. Also, the vital need to better know our enemy. Let the American people take honor to themselves for the fact that only in this Nation could so horrible an event as the killing of the chief of state occur without subsequent chaos and complete confusion in the normal processes of democratic institutions. This is not to say that the President's death is not cause for concern and remorse, but it is to reassert that the American system can survive such a serious wound and continue to function.

Realizing and knowing now that the assassin represents a philosophy so alien to our way of life that we are repulsed by its prospects * * * perhaps this brazen and brutal killing will cause our people to open their eyes and their minds to the type of degenerate filth that causes the Marxist tributaries to pollute the rivers of freedom, decency and dignity. Today, we are saddened, but aroused people; if history follows its heretofore inevitable course, then tomorrow the majority of our people, I am sorry to report, will return to their dank stations of apathy and the dark cellars of complacency.

The evidence which points accusingly at the agent to be a devotee of an alien conspiracy demonstrates again that the Marxist movement has not yet appeased its insatiable appetite for human blood. This, the American people must not forget. Let us, however, hope that this event as unnecessary and despicable as it was, can cause a new union for the promotion of what our forefathers called the common good, a refurbished offensive against the dangers of apathy.

John Kennedy said, "We cannot solve all of our problems today, but let us begin." We might well launch the crusade by making a more strenuous effort to open, to expand the channels of meaningful communications between divergent political factions. We might hoe out the weeds which Aristotle described as "despair and irresolution," and instead, replant the seeds of cooperation in the interest of heaping a bountiful harvest of honest disagreement, but, within an atmosphere conducive to victory over the enemy. That enemy, whose deranged devotee has slain our President, either by design or by coincidence, is totalitarianism. An Asian monarch once assembled his wisest advisers to uncover the simple, irrefutable truth. After much study, they presented the monarch with a stone tablet upon which were inscribed these words: "And this too shall pass away."

This is true of individuals, it is now accurate of John F. Kennedy, it will, one day, be true of you and me. It need not, however, be true of freedom.

The task is clear, the objective is elusive, the road is long and hard, but, without putting aside differing ideas of how to achieve our goal, but, through wider respect for each other and deeper dedication to our goal, "let us begin."

Our task is to roll back the tide of tyranny, our objective is to shore up the bulwarks of freedom, and to choose prudently our path on the pitfall-pocked road of experience. The President's death must not give rise to an intemperate demand for alteration of our Constitutional Republic, but, it should serve warning for all to see that the fanatical Marxist movement will resort to murder in the streets in an effort to establish their will by attempting to demoralize our American character. Our righteous indignation is warranted at this tragic time, yet it must not drain dry the cup of understanding.

At the same time, it is also fitting and proper to recall that the challenge issued on January 20, 1961, now contains additional poignancy and new pertinence, "ask not what your country can do for you, but what you can do for your country." This clarion call for citizenship, issued by a now deceased statesman, nearly 3 years ago, can be, should be our guidelines for future national endeavors. I join all Americans in praying for the fulfillment of this dream, and begging God's guidance so that we might start, "let us begin."

TRIBUTES BY

Hon. John D. Dingell

OF MICHIGAN

Mr. Speaker, pursuant to permission granted, I am offering the memorial address for the late President John F. Kennedy delivered by Rabbi Moses Lehrman at Congregation B'Nai Moshe November 25.

MEMORIAL ADDRESS FOR THE LATE PRESIDENT JOHN F. KENNEDY, DELIVERED BY RABBI MOSES LEHRMAN, MONDAY, NOVEMBER 25, 1963, AT A SPECIAL MEMORIAL SERVICE AT CONGREGATION B'NAI MOSHE, OAK PARK, MICH.

We have had an extended Yom Kippur and Tisha B'av combined during the last 3 days. Three days of bewildering shock and stunning meaningless confusion held us in its grip. Perhaps history in the future will manage to extract some reasonable meaning out of this catastrophe—a meaning crystallized in our collective resolves to cast aside all pettiness, selfishness, and vanities, and work as one to bring our world nearer, nearer, however slow, to the doorsteps of the fulfillment of a vision nurtured by our martyred President—the freedom and security of man.

In the meantime the smog of horror still chokes our hearts and stifles our thoughts. The words of David in his eulogy for the slain King Saul and Jonathan rise out of the pages of the Bible, reverberate across the centuries and ring in our ears "How are the mighty fallen in the midst of the battle," and David continues his lament for his beloved friend Jonathan "I am grief stricken over you, my brother, you have been very dear to me." These moving and sorrowful words might as well be on our lips today.

I know that I am reflecting the crushing experience of all our people in America as well as those beyond our shores who struggle for the dignity of man, as I, feebly, attempt to portray my own bewilderment. When the final news of the death of our President reached my ears, I screamed out—"It can't be true. Unbelievable. Unbelievable." Upon the realization that it was no nightmare, but stark reality, I broke down and sobbed hysterically. When I recovered somewhat, I stood in the family room, staring helplessly into a vast emptiness. "Why" I asked myself, "do I feel so totally crushed? Is it because we have lost our head of state in so tragic a fashion?" That is so, indeed. That is sad enough—the interruption of the career of a man who stood at the helm of our Government during the most critical days of a free world. But there is a great deal more than that. I was proud to be identified with a way of life which John F. Kennedy so thoroughly and magnificently represented. I was proud each time he appeared before the world on the screen. The miracle of TV made him a frequent visitor in our home. Here was the President in our very living room, so close to us, not a distant symbol locked up in an ivory tower, but a glowing personality, a cheerful countenance, cultured, witty, dynamic, speaking to us and with us. He had grown on us. We grew accustomed to his face, his smile, his sincerity, and idealism. He had become so much a part of our household.

His keen intellect was an inspiration and a stimulation to me. As he spoke to us, I would see before me more than a statesman, a political head of state. I visualized him as a great poet, a gifted linguist, a master of composition, capable of expressing profound thoughts in most eloquent style. At times, I imagined him as a philosopher who so ably captured the very secrets of the art of deep living and presented it so vividly and so simply.

I pictured him, at other times, as a religious teacher whose identity with our sacred literature was so marked in his appeals for rededication to the cause of man's highest aspirations. Isaiah and Hosea and Micah found lodging in the depth of his soul and in the breadth of his vision. With Isaiah he looked for the day when the sword will be turned into a pruning hook and man will not learn the art of war anymore. With Micah he translated the goals of man's striving on earth into doing justly, loving mercy, and walking humbly with God.

Thus I sensed a kinship with John F. Kennedy which becomes more real in a commonness of ideals and values than in a mere biological relationship. I considered him one of us striving for the fulfillment of the same goals, dreaming the same dreams of peace and brotherhood and working toward their attainment.

I saw in him the warm being whose acclaim did not go to his head. We all recall the intimate scenes describing his visit to distant relatives in a small town in Ireland. We watched him participate in a humble family reunion, cutting the cake and handing out slices to the humbler members of his family. He was not ashamed of his poor relatives, going out of his way to bring prestige to distant cousins at the hands of the most important man of our day. How happy he must have made his less glamorous relatives feel. What greatness. Indeed, with the prophet he taught the world a lesson in "walking humbly with God."

Several weeks ago, I had received an invitation to a dinner in New York, sponsored by friends of the Weizmann Institute at which President Kennedy was to be the guest of honor. In his impossible schedule of activities he had found time even for the Weizmann Institute of Israel. Thus, my kinship for the late John F. Kennedy, and thus I underwent the crushing experience at his tragic and untimely passing. Already historians are anticipating the place that John F. Kennedy will hold in the history books of the future. The rare combination of the courage of a Lincoln, the intellectual drive of a Wilson and the statesmanship of an F.D.R. guarantee his place among the immortals of all times. The late President will, for generations to come, maintain a place of honor reserved for brilliant and prophetic leadership in the annals of history.

What prompted John F. Kennedy to leave a life of comfort and security to take up the perilous road of leadership? It is always a source of stimulation to ponder upon the qualities of greatness and to behold the motivations which lead a man to give of himself unto a cause. Above everything else, there is an inner voice which summons the man to rise to the hour of destiny and to follow the call wherever it may take him. He must keep faith with himself and his God at whatever the cost may be to his personal comfort.

The voice is heard "Set my people free" and it grips him and masters him and never leaves him until his mission is done. That is the basic feature of great leadership. He cannot rid himself of that compulsion. He is captive in the hands of God. Such was the call that came to John F. Kennedy. He obeyed the voice and chose the perilous course. There was no alternative for him. He was aware of the responsibilities and uncertainties which lurked on all fronts and in his own words "I do not shrink from this responsibility. I welcome it." The security, the peace and future of his country were at stake.

It was not an extemporaneous impulse that hurled him into the thick of battle. It was a commitment begun in the earliest days of his life. All of us recall his self sacrificial heroism as an officer in the Navy on the PT boat which he commanded and which was blown up in battle. His life then hung in the balance as he feverishly labored to save his crew. This heroism on a global scale was manifest in him a year ago in October. Who can forget his courage as he faced the Nation with the gravest decision made in the history of all mankind—a decision to preserve the dignity of America and at the same time to risk atomic warfare. Who of us did not tremble with the President as he solemnly said "I am not unmindful of the risks involved." Think of the gruesome days which followed—the terrifying possibility of global war and its aftermath. This responsibility John F. Kennedy bore with the courage, and glory of a David, a Lincoln and a Roosevelt.

It was not given to him to complete his mission, but the success of his enlightened and heroic thrusts into a no man's land of apathy toward the emancipation of man is historically assured. His name will live forever in the annals of man's highest levels of attainment. It is up to us to make this attainment more real.

When President Kennedy's coffin was taken from the White House yesterday, the announcer very movingly said "President Kennedy has left the White House for the last time." These words pierced me to the very core as it did every American who listened—"for the last time." Yet something was left unsaid—"His spirit has not left it." It will hover over the White House, the Capitol, Washington, Detroit and the whole free world.

It has also been said that a piece within each of us died with the President. Permit me to add to this truth. A portion of John Fitzgerald Kennedy remains within each of us. Let us never forget that. Let us never forget that.

Mr. Speaker, pursuant to permission granted, I would like to include in my remarks one of the most touching memorial tributes which I have seen to our beloved late President, John F. Kennedy, by Rabbi Richard C. Hertz, of Temple Beth El in Detroit on Friday evening, November 29, 1963, entitled "Why We Mourn":

WHY WE MOURN—A MEMORIAL TRIBUTE TO PRESIDENT JOHN F. KENNEDY

(By Rabbi Richard C. Hertz)

One week ago we came here dazed and stunned by the tragic news of President Kennedy's assassination. In the few hours that had elapsed since 2 o'clock on that fateful Friday afternoon, we groped for words to express our shock, our horror, our disbelief that such a monstrous, depraved deed could be perpetrated against our President. We turned to God for comfort because there seemed nowhere else to go. Then we turned to television too. And for 3 solid days all America sat glued to the screen, unwilling to leave for fear of missing one detail of the grim, unfolding tragedy. Television made the sorrow a deeply personal experience for all America. By the time Monday night came around, we were emotionally drained. We had so completely identified ourselves with the personal tragedy of John F. Kennedy, with Jacqueline Kennedy, with Caroline and John, with Robert and Edward and the entire Kennedy family, that we felt as if one of our own family had been shot. John F. Kennedy had become a part of us, and something of us was buried Monday in Arlington.

Our Nation has been in mourning all week.

WE MOURN FOR JOHN FITZGERALD KENNEDY

He was so young, so vigorous, so energetic, so witty, so full of high hopes for a better world, so eager to give his country so much of himself.

When he took the oath of office on Inauguration Day, it was as if a young Greek god had snatched up the torch of leadership and Apollo-like, he went forth up Pennsylvania Avenue into a brave new world. His meteoric career inspired youth to public service in the Peace Corps. The young people of America are especially in mourning for one of their own, for he gave them an excitement of expectation.

He was a martyr to the cause of civil rights and human rights. The Negro saw in him a champion of emancipation 100 years after it had been proclaimed. People of all creeds and races rallied to his standard. They eagerly identified with him in the battle for justice and equality on behalf of the underprivileged, the disinherited, and disadvantaged, the oppressed and the exploited.

He brought a sense of history to everything he did. His intellect, his Harvard training, his gift for communicating, marked him a man of his generation, an eloquent spokesman for that strange new world which the Second World War had ushered in. More than any President since Woodrow Wilson, he believed in the power of ideas. His quick intelligence gave him an extraordinary grasp of the vast scope of the presidential office. His deep intellect molded a philosophy of government that rare oratorical powers of eloquence enabled him to articulate with grace and with distinction. He was deeply concerned over the preservation of peace, the necessity for nuclear disarmament, the insistence on peaceful negotiation of differences with allies no less than with adversaries.

He was himself a profile of courage. Whether in overcoming personal and physical pain or in persevering in political life, his singlemindedness of purpose, his sense of personal duty to face high responsibility enabled him to say on that cold January day of his inauguration:

"In the long history of the world, only a few generations have been granted the role of defending freedom in its hour of maximum danger. I do not shrink from this responsibility—I welcome it. I do not believe that any of us would exchange places with any other people or any other generation. The energy, the faith, the devotion which we bring to this endeavor will light our country and all who serve it—and the glow from that fire can truly light the world.

"And so, my fellow Americans, ask not what your country can do for you, ask what you can do for your country.

"My fellow citizens of the world, ask not what America will do for you, but what together we can do for the freedom of man." John F. Kennedy wrote his answer with his own blood on the streets of Dallas, Tex.

WE MOURN FOR JACQUELINE KENNEDY

This beautiful, gracious, regal-like woman who brought so much of her own esthetic character into the White House gave a majestic object lesson to all America in courage, self-control and dedication. She too had a sense of history and understood that though other women have lost their husbands in the prime of life, her husband belonged not only to herself but to the people of the world. Her justifiable pride in his achievements and her immeasurable loss were seen in every closeup of her controlled face. She too was a living profile in courage.

WE MOURN FOR LITTLE CAROLINE AND JOHN-JOHN

When Jacqueline Kennedy took Caroline and John, Jr. by the hand and led them up the steps of the Capitol rotunda to pay their last respects to the flag-draped coffin, those children walked right into the hearts of all America. Nothing could surpass the poignancy of little John asking for another small flag for his daddy—or the look of confidence and security Caroline found in the eyes of her mother as she grasped Caroline's hand tightly and looked down at her as if to say, "Watch me and do likewise."

WE MOURN FOR AMERICA'S DISRESPECT OF LAW AND ORDER

The assassination of the President by a sniper from a tall building was horrible enough, but to have the suspect apprehended and then shot down while under police protection, the way other prisoners have been lynched in the South—that was the supreme blot on our country that compounded national tragedy into monstrous outrage.

What a price America must pay for fanaticism and lawlessness. Violence begets violence—and where does it all end?

America prides herself on the democratic concept of "equal justice under law." Even in this case, the world saw unmasked on TV—live—an example of how Western vigilante justice operates. Lee Oswald had not confessed; he had not been brought to trial; he had not been defended; he had not been sentenced. At the very moment that cooler, grief-stricken minds were calling for traditional American protection of our laws with full opportunity for his defense before a properly constituted court, millions saw on TV a monstrous Texas western carried out live on the screen, as Lee Oswald was shot in an outrageous breach of police responsibility—with the crowd outside shouting its murderous approval of this disgusting, appalling killing.

WE MOURN FOR OUR NATION

This dastardly deed was perpetrated in our country, the so-called land of freedom and equality before the law.

A horrible scar was inflicted upon our country that made this civilized country look uncivilized. We lost face with ourselves and with our world. We saw an image in the world's mirror and we did not like what we saw. We mourn for our own shame as well as for our sorrow. This happened not in South Vietnam nor in some Latin American cesspool of revolution, but in the proud State of Texas.

We kept asking ourselves: How can this happen in America? What is happening to our country? Where is the respect for law and order? Has hate and prejudice so warped the minds of America that reason is gone, justice is gone, decency is gone, freedom is gone, public safety is gone? Is ours to be an age of fanaticism and bigotry? What kind of sickness of soul has come over America? Where will strife and bitterness lead us? What will unreasoned violence do to the democratic fabric of our life? What will be the new America if lawlessness and racism persist in this country, if unstable and warped minds can take the law into their own bloody hands? Where is the dream of America?

WE MOURN FOR OURSELVES

A part of us went into the grave with John F. Kennedy. We ourselves are guilty of his murder. All of us in America had a part in the slaying of our President. We are guilty by our silence over the forces of primitive hatred that have eaten their way, cancerlike, into the bloodstream of American life. We are guilty by our inaction, by our willingness that heavy burdens be borne by one man alone; by our readiness to allow evil to be called good and good evil; by our continued toleration of ancient injustices. We are guilty because we think we are good people, but good people willing to do nothing to undo evil. Now we have to learn all over again that bystanders are not innocent, for now the consequences have caught up with all of us.

If there is any hope at all, any lesson to be learned from the shock of this tragedy, it is perhaps the realization of how a free and civilized nation must live up to the responsibilities of personal citizenship.

The shock that stunned America may in the long run be the means of awakening people of this country to their full moral responsibilities. The memory of our martyred President will not wither but will grow in meaning and intensity. The assassination of President Kennedy, like Lincoln's, will not be forgotten. But maybe people will now realize more soberly that hatred spawns bigotry, that freedom will not be denied human beings any longer simply because their skin is black. John F. Kennedy in life may mean even more in death if his martyrdom arouses people to a greater unity, a greater sense of dedication to our public responsibilities as citizens. President Kennedy died for his country. We are asked only to live for our country—to put aside our passions and our prejudices, and recognize the human right of all people, all classes, all religions, and treat our neighbors as Americans all.

When I first heard the grim news of the assassination my mind went back exactly 100 years ago, almost to the day, November 19, 1863, when Abraham Lincoln boarded a special train out of Washington to journey to Gettysburg, there to dedicate a new cemetery where so many fallen heroes of the Blue and the Gray lay recently buried. Edward Everett had been chosen the orator for the day, and for 2 solid hours he held forth in masterful eloquence. Then the President was called on for a few appropriate remarks. Mr. Lincoln rose to his full height, took out of his stovepipe hat a few scraps of paper, and looked out upon the crowd with those sad eyes of tragedy, with words that seem so appropriate at this hour:

"The world will little note nor long remember what we say here, but it can never forget what they did here. It is for us, the living, rather, to be dedicated here to the unfinished work which they who fought here had thus far so nobly advanced. It is rather for us to be here dedicated to the great task remaining before us—that from these honored dead we take increased devotion to that cause for which they gave the last full measure of devotion, that we here highly resolve that these dead shall not have died in vain."

A few months later, the War Between the States was officially over, but reprisals, hate, and revenge were not quelled. One evening when a weary Mr. Lincoln went out to Ford's Theater for a rare moment of recreation, he was shot by a wild assassin, John Wilkes Booth. All during the night he battled for life; but as morning came he closed his eyes. Mr. Lincoln was dead. Standing over him, to the end, was Secretary Stanton. As Mr. Lincoln breathed his last, Secretary Stanton exclaimed, "Now he belongs to the ages."

This we say of John F. Kennedy: "Now he belongs to the ages."

As our prayers go out to our new President, Lyndon B. Johnson, for wisdom and divine guidance, so we take renewed hope from President Johnson's moving words to the Congress on Wednesday and to the Nation yesterday, Thanksgiving Day. We have a new captain to guide our ship of state—able, dedicated, experienced, decisive in action and humble in his responsibilities.

With Longfellow, we pray:

"Thou, too, sail on, O Ship of State,
Sail on, O Union, strong and great!
Humanity with all its fears,
With all the hopes of future years,
Is hanging breathless on thy fate!
Our hearts, our hopes, are all with thee,
Our hearts, our hopes, our prayers, our tears,
Our faith triumphant o'er our fears,
Are all with thee—are all with thee!"

John Fitzgerald Kennedy is gone—but he is not truly gone. His spirit goes marching on in the hearts of a grateful nation,

"The tumult and the shouting dies;
The captains and the kings depart—
Still stands Thine ancient sacrifice,
An humble and a contrite heart.
Lord God of Hosts, be with us yet,
Lest we forget, lest we forget!"

Mr. Speaker, under unanimous consent, I am offering a memorial tribute to our late President read to the Wayne County (Mich.) Board of Supervisors on November 26, 1963, by one of its members, Dr. Broadus N. Butler. Dr. Butler, a distinguished citizen of Detroit, is assistant to the dean of the Wayne State University College of Liberal Arts:

IN MEMORIAM: JOHN FITZGERALD KENNEDY, PRESIDENT
OF THE UNITED STATES

(By Supervisor Broadus N. Butler)

At the height of the first ray of hope for a new national climate of brotherhood, democracy, and opportunity in this tragedy ridden 20th century comes the assassination of the one President of the United States who has symbolized not only for America, but for the world, the ideal of executive leadership toward the full recognition of human dignity.

This has been a century in which the respect of person and human dignity has been trampled unto death and degradation in some dramatic way in each generation. This century has seen three major international wars take millions of lives, untold numbers of smaller wars add up to more millions. It has seen genocide in the extermination of 3 million Jews in Germany, the rise of communism and massacres in Asia, the assassination of Mohandas Gandhi in India, apartheid and the killing of thousands of black Africans, particularly in Angola and South Africa. It has suffered killings, riots, and more than 50 bombings of churches and schools—killings of men, women, and children—in the United States. The past decade of this century has seen this violence go unmitigated and unpunished in our own Nation. It has watched the overthrow, by violence of government after government throughout the world.

John Fitzgerald Kennedy tried in less than 3 years to write a chapter of human dignity and equality of opportunity for all into our national life. He tried to see and move optimistically toward a new climate of brotherhood and hope at least in our own land, if not throughout the world.

We must now face finally and ultimately the stark fact that it is no joke that fanatical forces of the right and the left have tried and are still trying to write an obituary for this great, overgrown and, they think, dying Nation. One hundred years ago, Abraham Lincoln told this to the 19th century Americans in the Emancipation Proclamation and in the Gettysburg Address. He tried to set this Nation in the direction of freedom and respect for person, and they killed Mr. Lincoln.

In this centennial year of the Emancipation Proclamation and the Gettysburg Address—98 years after the assassination of Abraham Lincoln—the ablest and most dedicated spokesman for those ideals in the 20th century was suddenly shot from the same kind of darkened crevices of hate.

They killed President Kennedy. The same hands; the same forces. The same harbingers of hate, greed, tyranny, avarice and arrogance demonstrated again and beyond a doubt that they will still stop at nothing to prove that the American creed of democracy and brotherhood is not viable—that America will die before she will be free. And, like Mr. Kennedy, she will die unless we acknowledge this shocking reality. We must finally know that the extreme right would rather see the Nation dead than see one Negro free; the extreme left would rather kill the Nation than see one American free. That was the essence of the meaning of the assassination of

Mr. Lincoln. That was the essence of the failure to implement the original Declaration of Independence. That is now the essence of the meaning of the death of President Kennedy.

The President is not dead; the Presidency lives. But the only President since Abraham Lincoln who devoted so much of his executive resources and moral suasion to give real meaning to civil rights, equal opportunity, and human freedom is dead. No, we say in disbelief. It cannot be. But, it is.

In our time, there is one and only one significant difference between America and Germany, Italy, Japan, and the other countries that died of their own involvement in violence. America and America's creed of freedom revived and saved them. America retrieved them with men, the ideology of freedom, and with all the moral power and economic resources that it takes to recover a dead society from itself and infuse it with a new vision of life and hope—a new freedom from its own ashes. Now, it is America. Can America save America? Will God? Will Americans? This time it is we, ourselves. What will we do now?

Goodby, dear Mr. President. May your soul and your memory—your ultimate sacrifice—save a people and a nation so great as ours that cannot otherwise save itself from its own domestic violence. Will those who could not learn from the deaths of Christ, of Lincoln, of Gandhi now see that the shot of hate that pierced John F. Kennedy, was aimed to kill Thee.

Americans, be of good judgment and firm dedication to complete his unfinished task. In the transition from John Fitzgerald Kennedy to Lyndon Baines Johnson there is one great comfort for our saddened Nation. The Presidency moves from strength, courage and moral integrity to continued strength, courage and moral integrity in the quest for democracy, for domestic brotherhood, and for international peace.

Our hearts go out to the President's family and especially to Mrs. Jacqueline Kennedy who has suffered the double personal tragedy of the loss of a son and a husband in so short compass.

May the wisdom of our departed President rest upon and give strength to our new President, Lyndon B. Johnson. May his soul and purpose pervade the whole American citizenry across the land to remove the hate and bigotry which besets us. May the people of America now see the light and learn the truth that his martyrdom beams forth so clearly to us. Cannot we hark the painful miracles of this year? Cannot we heed the words of our great and departed exemplar who implored us to "Ask not what your country can do for you. Ask what you can do for your country."

Jesus Christ said, in effect, "If you will love God, you must love one another." Every recent martyr has echoed, "If you will love one another, you must love me." Let every American learn to love—to respect the person and dignity of—one another.

(Read to the Wayne County Board of Supervisors, Tuesday, November 26, 1963.)

Mr. Speaker, pursuant to permission granted, I would like to include in my remarks a memorial tribute to our beloved late President at Adas

Shalom Synagogue in Detroit, Mich., by its distinguished rabbi, Jacob E. Segal, an eminent churchman and community leader.

I believe that the sincere and touching tribute to our beloved late President by this outstanding American merits recognition.

IN MEMORIAM—JOHN FITZGERALD KENNEDY, 35TH PRESIDENT OF THE UNITED STATES

(A memorial tribute by Rabbi Jacob E. Segal, delivered at Adas Shalom Synagogue, November 25, 1963)

At 12 noon today, in our Nation's Capital, the final act of a tragic drama will begin to play itself out before the eyes of the world. A solemn cortege will wind its way from the White House to the National Cemetery at Arlington. There John Fitzgerald Kennedy, 35th President of the United States, cut off by a madman's bullet, will be laid to rest.

We have gathered here now in a private prelude to that final act on the national stage. We have gathered here as a Jewish congregation, to give voice to our common grief—to the broken hearts, the sundered love and the shattered spirits which we share with all Americans and with men and women of good will everywhere, at the sudden incredible passing of our valiant young President.

The devastating bulletins which on Friday afternoon began to inundate and darken our homes and offices— the cataclysmic bulletin that made last Friday the blackest Erev Shabbos in America's history—these bulletins, in spite of a grief-drenched weekend, still ring in our ears like a grotesque fantasy, a savage nightmare from which at any moment we hope to awaken.

Why is this news still so new, so incredible? Is it simply because the leader of a Nation has suddenly died?

No, that cannot be all. This news is still so incredible because it was the single most unlikely, most inconceivable tragedy that could have struck the world.

As a British televised tribute touchingly put it last night, if any elder statesman, American or foreign, had died, it would have been a shock and a major tragedy— yet somehow capable of absorption and belief.

But, that this young man, so vital and vibrant, so handsome and brilliant, so athletic and dashing, so literate and eloquent, so active, so full of grace and wit and charm, so mature yet so youthful, so wise and courageous, yet so boyish and dynamic;

That this young man, whose essential nature was reflected in the word "vigah";

That this young President—who in less than 3 years rose to be the acknowledged leader of the free world and the protagonist of an America respected even by the enemy;

That this young and vigorous husband, this loving son, this doting father of two beautiful little children;

That he should have been snatched away by a madman's bullet, was the most unlikely, unacceptable news that is still at this moment impossible to accept or believe.

Yet, though our conscious mind refuses to believe it, something else in us tells us it is true, after all.

In a kind of half-dream world we have been drawn together here on less than 1 day's notice to pay our respects, as Americans and as Jews, to the memory of the leader who, we cannot believe, has fallen.

The fact that so many have gathered here to honor his memory, is a measure of how honorable his memory is—of how great an honor the remembrance of his life may yet shed upon this Nation and the world.

But the fact that we have come to the synagogue is a measure of something else. It is a measure of our desperate need to find comfort in the House of God. In an hour of infamy and sorrow, we Americans of all faiths, and even those of no particular faith—have nowhere else to turn—except to God.

We somehow cannot get Lincoln out of our mind, when we think of the young President who was martyred on the streets of Dallas.

We cannot forget the sublime irony that the Gettysburg Address was delivered by Lincoln 100 years ago last Tuesday, and that 100 years have gone by since Lincoln signed the Emancipation Proclamation.

I am not invoking the magic of numbers. Yet in some meaningful way history has come full circle again:

If Lincoln was a martyr to the cause of human liberty, if his signing of the Emancipation Proclamation made him the target of an assassin a year and a half later—

Then it may be equally true, alas, that John Kennedy's courage in proclaiming a second emancipation for the Negroes and the underprivileged of our time;

His vigorous stand for the cause of civil rights;

His willingness to lead the battle for all human rights;

Engendered the kind of violent opposition and insane bitter hatred which created the immoral climate in which an assassin could dream of performing his demoniac act of murder.

We cannot help thinking of Lincoln as the backdrop for Kennedy, when we read again the poignant lines which Edwin Markham wrote at the death of Lincoln:

"And when he fell in whirlwind he went down
As when a lordly cedar, green with boughs
Goes down with a great shout upon the hills
And leaves a lonesome place against the sky!"

How prophetic and biblical those words sound. How reminiscent of the Psalmist who, when he sought comfort from God, cried out:

"I will lift up mine eyes unto the hills,
From whence shall my help come?"

Our help, our comfort will come, if we lift up our eyes unto the hills;

If we honestly gaze at the lonesome place which has been left by our martyred young President "against the sky";

If we study and cherish the story of his young meteoric and brilliant life against the sky of eternal moral values;

If we cherish his valiant deeds against the horizon of those moral ideals and commitments—to truth and justice, to peace and human freedom—which were the guiding stars, the moral heavens by which John Fitzgerald Kennedy charted his course.

His ideals and commitments were many, and the galaxy of his stars was bright. But the two that shone brightest and most steady were his two north stars: world peace, and equal human rights for all the citizens of this land.

His place against the sky may seem lonesome now that this lordly cedar has fallen. But in that lonesome patch of sky we can still see—

If we only have the will and the courage to look we can still see those two stars, and many others beside them beckoning to us with their unfailing light, as they beckoned to him before he was cut down.

I could not help thinking of this last night when in my mood of sorrow I turned to a treasury of American poetry and read again Walt Whitman's stirring ode on the death of Lincoln, his tragic yet triumphant "O Captain, My Captain."

"O Captain! my Captain! our fearful trip is done,
The ship has weather'd every rack, the prize we sought
    is won,
The port is near, the bells I hear, the people all exulting,
While follow eyes the steady keel, the vessel grim and
    daring;
But O heart! heart! heart!
O the bleeding drops of red,
Where on the deck my Captain lies,
Fallen cold and dead.

"My Captain does not answer, his lips are pale and still,
My father does not feel my arm, he has no pulse nor
    will.
The ship is anchor'd safe and sound, its voyage closed
    and done,
From fearful trip the victor ship comes in with object
    won;
Exult O shores, and ring O bells!
But I with mournful tread,
Walk the deck my Captain lies,
Fallen cold and dead."

The poem rings true emotionally. Yet some of its lines are not yet fulfilled:

"Our fearful trip is not yet done,
Our ship has not yet weathered every rack,
The prize we have sought is not yet won!
Though our captain lies fallen, cold and dead,
That prize—
Of a universal peace, and secure and equal human rights
Remains yet to be won!"

We may yet win that prize—if we gird ourselves with his vision and his courage, with his love of all people as creatures equally made in the image of God.

As Lincoln and Kennedy kept mingling in my mind last night, I recalled those other even greater lines written by Walt Whitman, when he beheld the coffin of Lincoln winding its way across the fields and meadows of this land, back to its burial place:

"When lilacs last in the dooryard bloomed,
And the great star early drooped in the western sky in
    the night,
I mourned, and yet shall mourn with ever-returning
    spring.
Sure to me you bring,
Lilac blooming perennial and drooping star in the west,
And thought of him I love.

"Over the breast of the spring, the land, amid cities,
Amid lanes and through old woods * * *
Carrying a corpse to where it shall rest in the grave,
Night and day journeys a coffin.
Coffin that passes through lanes and streets,
Through day and night with the great cloud darkening
    the land,
With the pomp of the inlooped flags with the cities
    draped in black * * *
With processions long and winding and the flambeaus
    of the night,
With the countless torches lit, with the silent sea of faces
    and the unbared heads * * *
With the tolling, tolling bells' perpetual clang,
Here, coffin that slowly passes,
I give you this sprig of lilac."

I could not help thinking of these lines, because all through this dismal week, and through the coming months and years, so many bereaved individuals, so many bruised and loving hearts of men, women and children in this land will feel like saying to John Fitzgerald Kennedy: "I give you this sprig of lilac."

We have all been impressed by the royal pageantry of dukes and emperors, of queens and generals, who in solemn pomp have descended upon Washington this weekend.

But far more impressive was the sight of those hundreds of thousands of humble, ordinary people who filed past the flag-draped catafalque in the rotunda of the Capitol— all day yesterday and all through the night, even to this moment—including some young students I know personally, who have made the tearful journey from the University of Michigan to Washington—to wrest a tender glimpse of the coffin, to give the fallen leader their own little "sprig of lilac."

I could not help thinking of comfort when I read John F. Kennedy's Thanksgiving proclamation, which appeared in the Detroit News on Thursday, November 21— the day before he left us.

"Over three centuries ago, our forefathers in Virginia and in Massachusetts, far from home in a lonely wilderness, set aside a time for thanksgiving. On the appointed day, they gave reverent thanks for their safety, for the health of their children, for the fertility of their fields, for the laws which bound them together and for the faith which united them under God.

"Today we give thanks, most of all, for the ideals of honor and faith we inherit from our forefathers—for the decency of purpose, for the courage and the humility, which they possessed and which we must seek every day to emulate.

"As we express our gratitude, we must never forget that the highest appreciation is not to utter words but to live by them.

"Now, therefore, I, John Fitzgerald Kennedy, President of the United States, do hereby proclaim Thursday, November 28, 1963, as a day of national thanksgiving.

"On that day let us gather in sanctuaries dedicated to worship and in homes blessed by family affection to express our gratitude for the glorious gifts of God; and let us earnestly and humbly pray that He will continue to guide and sustain us in the great unfinished tasks of achieving peace, justice and understanding among all men and all nations and of ending misery and suffering wherever they exist."

The President asked us to gather in our sanctuaries to thank God. We have gathered instead to intone a prelude to his funeral.

Yet if we truly want to honor his memory, we dare not entirely ignore his summons. Alongside our grief, we must force our trembling lips to utter a prayer of thanksgiving, that this man has lived among us.

The best way to frame our thanks is to dedicate our lives to that vision of glory which he invoked so nobly in his inaugural address. On that frigid day in January 1961, John Kennedy stood in the whirling snow in the shadow of the Capitol dome—in whose rotunda he has lain in state all day yesterday and all through the night—and chanted forth his dream and his faith, for all the world to hear:

"In the long history of the world, only a few generations have been granted the role of defending freedom in its hour of maximum danger. I do not shrink from this responsibility. I welcome it. I do not believe that any of us would exchange places with any other people or any other generation. The energy, the faith, the devotion which we bring to this endeavor, will light our country and all who serve it, and the glow of that fire, can truly light the world.

"And so, my fellow Americans, ask not what your country can do for you—ask what you can do for your country.

"With a good conscience our only sure reward, with history the final judge of our deeds, let us go forth to lead the land we love, asking His blessing and His help, but knowing that here on earth, God's work must truly be our own."

With this summons ringing in our hearts, let us rise in prayer for our martyred President, and ask God for the courage and the will to make His work truly our own.

TRIBUTES BY

Hon. Thaddeus J. Dulski

OF NEW YORK

Mr. Speaker, daily editorials have appeared in our newspapers throughout the country, reflecting the deep sense of loss our Nation has suffered in the tragic and untimely death of President John F. Kennedy.

Under leave to extend my remarks, I wish to include two excellent editorials which were carried in Buffalo's newspapers last week. These follow.

[From the Buffalo (N.Y.) Evening News, Nov. 23, 1963]

A MARTYRED PRESIDENT

The sense of incredulous shock and total tragedy that swept over a stunned nation with yesterday's terrible news from Dallas has been so universally experienced and so widely articulated that further words today could add no more than a trite echo.

The assassination of President Kennedy was a dastardly deed so senseless, so utterly devoid of any rational service to any conceivable cause, that it had to be an act of lunacy. But what precisely motivated the assassin, what sinister influences or psychopathic hates had worked him up to plot and do this thing—these are questions that still cry for answers on the day of grief and anger that follows the first day of shock.

Probably no other tragedy in our time has triggered such a profound sense of public disbelief. Death, to this young President so full of life and future, came so swiftly, so suddenly, so incongruously. In speeches that morning, he had sparkled with wit and zest. Texas had given him its warmest, most festive welcome. Just at the mortal moment, the wife of its Governor was happily chiding him, "You can't say Dallas is not friendly to you today." Then the shot, the slump, and his life, his Presidency, were over.

This assassination will inevitably be compared with the others—of McKinley here in Buffalo in 1901, of Garfield in the first months of his term in 1881, of Lincoln nearly a century ago, an act that brought another Johnson so unexpectedly to the Presidency. But of the four, we venture to predict that history will regard the striking down of John F. Kennedy as the most tragic in its timing. For Garfield's Presidency had hardly begun, and both McKinley and Lincoln had finished full terms and had the sense of fulfillment that decisive reelection gave them.

Of Lincoln, indeed, Walt Whitman could write, before his Captain "lay fallen cold and dead," that his "ship has weather'd every rack, the prize we sought is won; the port is near, the bells I hear, the people all exulting."

But for President Kennedy, the journey was only well begun. Some reefs were safely past, but the heaviest weather lay ahead. The prize of reelection, of a second term mandate, was only dimly perceived on the far horizon. And the safe port, the bells, the people all exulting—whether any of this could have been written of President Kennedy, history now can only speculate.

While today's journalism must defer to tomorrow's history for definitive judgments about the Kennedy Presidency, however, some things in appreciation can be said with assurance even now.

High among them is an enumeration of the great qualities of mind and spirit this young man brought to the Presidency—courage, both physical and moral; a high sense of purpose and patriotism; intelligence, cool and analytical; judgment, daring on occasion but usually balanced; an immense self-confidence tempered by a penetrating wit and disciplined by the wisdom to face and profit by his own mistakes; and with all this, a charm of manner that put on his administration a unique stamp of dash and verve.

By all the tangible yardsticks available, moreover, the state of our Union has fared well under this foreshortened Presidency. Our national economy has functioned at a steadily advancing pace; our national strength is high, militarily beyond compare with that of any combination of would-be foes. Where foreign threats were clear, we have resolutely faced them down. If the world has not been made measurably safer for free peoples, it is certainly not measurably less so. At home, while his leadership had yet to spark enough response from Congress to bring much of his domestic program to fruition, he will doubtless be best regarded by history for this year's moral leadership and appeal to national conscience in the field of civil rights.

What distinguished the Kennedy Presidency more than anything else, however, was its style. Here was a White House filled to overflowing with youth and vigor, charm and sophistication, a Presidency of culture and taste and deep regard for human achievement in all the enduring areas of art, literature, science, and intellect.

It is in this area, of course, where the Kennedy Presidency was a team effort, its magic touch deftly supplied by the beautiful and gracious First Lady. And it is to her and her children, that the Nation's heart pours out its deepest sympathy in this day of their tragic bereavement.

[From the Buffalo (N.Y.) Courier-Express, Nov. 26, 1963]

JOHN F. KENNEDY—MARTYR TO HATRED

Our President has been laid to rest. The brief but intense period of national grief is ended. Life in these United States will go on.

No one who sat before the television screen and watched the incredible unfolding of this horrible weekend could escape a sense of shock that these things could happen in this Nation. And no one can escape a share of the blame. For this Nation, a symbol of all that is great and good in Western civilization, a golden land of opportunity, must expel the hatred which caused this despicable act.

This propensity for hatred is prevalent not just in Dallas, not just in Texas, but everywhere. In Buffalo, in New York, in every corner of the Nation. It was not enough to oppose. We had to hate. Nationalistic hates. Racial hates. Hatred of unions by management and of management by labor. Hatred of the Birchites and hatred by the Birchites. Hatred of the Kennedys; hatred of Goldwater; hatred of Communists; hatred of Catholics, of Protestants, or Jews, or atheists. Hatred of modern art or modern music. Hatred of anything that did not conform to our basic beliefs.

Each of us can say: "No, not I." But each of us who told or laughed at a hate-inspired joke or story, each of us who spread or listened without complaint to a hate-inspired rumor or report helped to prolong and promulgate the wave of hatred which culminated so tragically on the streets of Dallas.

May God grant that life will not go on as before, that each of us will be able to view the death of John Fitzgerald Kennedy as a symbol of the futility and corrosiveness of hatred, that we can oppose without rancor, dispute without venom, that we conduct our lives in public and in private in accord with the phrase so often spoken in connection with our new President, Lyndon B. Johnson: "Come let us reason together."

Let us resolve in this hour of national mourning to pluck the hatred from our hearts and in so doing give new meaning to the resolution uttered 100 years ago by another martyred President that "these dead shall not have died in vain."

Mr. Speaker, one of my personal friends, Hon. Frank E. Wendling, supervisor of the 11th ward, Buffalo, N.Y., recently introduced a resolution at a meeting of the board of supervisors in the city of Buffalo.

The resolution encompasses the many thoughts that have been expressed since the tragic death of our beloved President, John F. Kennedy.

Recent tragic circumstances compel us at this time to reappraise and reevaluate our Nation, its foundations, and institutions, and its people.

Magna Carta began "by the grace of God" and "in the presence of God."

The Declaration of Independence reaffirmed that all men are endowed by their creator with certain unalienable rights and that governments are instituted among men to secure these rights.

These documents and their concepts became the very bedrock of our Nation.

The United States came into being to secure the blessing of liberty for ourselves and our posterity, and in article 2 vested executive power in the President of the United States of America.

At a high time in our history, John Fitzgerald Kennedy was chosen as our Chief, and vested with the awesome powers and responsibilities of that high office.

The scope of that leadership extended beyond our geographic boundaries, and our President is the leader of freemen everywhere and the hearts and minds gain strength and courage from the torch of liberty held in his hand.

In a world torn by strife, bitterness and insecurity John Fitzgerald Kennedy looking toward new horizons accepted the challenge of the sixties and became our 35th President.

Sworn to uphold our Constitution and our laws, this young man of strength and courage and vision came forward, accepted the burdens and moved ahead into dangerous and uncharted waters.

Peace with dignity, rights of fellow man, love for neighbor, respect for others all gathered with an abiding belief in a Supreme Being with recognition of His supremacy became the credo to lead our Nation and the world from darkness to light.

Symbolically his public life in this capacity lasted for 3 years.

However, the forces of hate and bigotry, and bias, and prejudice had too long gone unattended in the hearts of many men.

With valiant effort, he strove to rekindle in his people humility before God, understanding among men.

He showed us the way, but his candle alone was not enough and we must rededicate ourselves and our Nation to the cause and the flame which flickers must be joined by all of us so that his supreme sacrifice will have not been wasted on an unappreciative mankind.

He could give no more than his life; he gave no less.

He told us among many other things that we shouldn't ask our Government what it could do for us, but rather should ask what you can do for it.

We must profit from the presence of this man in our midst, and his life, his energies, his ideas, ideals and spirit must go forth in all of us everywhere.

Let us think of Friday, November 22, 1963, not as a day of despair and hate or we forget him and his message too quickly, and his supreme sacrifice will have been wasted among us.

Wherefore, it beehoves us to set aside a day annually for each man to meditate in his own way, to examine our individual consciences, to remove blackness, bitterness and hate from our hearts and instill therein a dedication of love and understanding for our fellow man so that all peoples everywhere can truly learn by our example and we can secure for our posterity a world for all mankind that will meet not only the challenge of the sixties but thereafter; now, therefore, be it

Resolved, That this, the Erie County Board of Supervisors memorialize the Congress of the United States of America to set aside as a national holiday the 22d day of November as one of memory and remembrance and re-evaluation and dedicated to the spirit of love and freedom throughout this great Nation and among our peoples.

FRANK E. WENDLING,
Supervisor, 11th Ward.

Mr. Speaker, a resident in my district, Mr. Joseph C. Carson, of Buffalo, N.Y., writes poetry as a hobby. He is also a great humanitarian, and is active in civic and charitable affairs.

Mr. Carson has sent me two of the poems he has composed, one following the inauguration of President Kennedy in 1961, and the other following the tragic assassination of our beloved President:

JUST FRIENDLY KIND: AS YOU LEAD THE WAY

Best wishes, Mr. President
    As you lead us on our way
And may God's guiding grace be yours
    In all you do and say.

May Congress and the Senate
    Each lend a helping hand
To make your burdens lighter
    In a way you'll understand.

We find at each election
    Those that win and lose
The meaning of democracy
    Is to have the right to choose.

And what we all should realize
    As we play the game
That when the contest's over
    We're Americans just the same.

So let us pledge to do our best
    And mean it when we say
Hand in hand—throughout the land
    We're with you all the way.

May you find the road to the future
    Paved with blessings from above
That will guide your way to a brighter day
    In this wonderful land we love.
                            —JOSEPH C. CARSON.

MARCH 1961.

———

DEDICATED TO OUR LATE PRESIDENT, JOHN FITZGERALD
KENNEDY: HE PASSED OUR WAY

Well done Thy noble servant
    Your task on earth is o'er
Though you left us for the great beyond
    You will live forever more.

Your words and deeds are a volume
    With pages edged with gold
That through the years the world will find
    A treasure to behold.

We will miss you gallant leader
    More than words can ever say
We are asking God to help us
    And lead us on our way.

We are asking God to grant the peace
    You strived so hard to gain
And to make it everlasting
    So you labored not in vain.

You left us fondest memories
    Few others ever will
That will echo through the ages
    Although your voice is still.

God called you to that distant shore
    Your helping hand is gone
But the guiding light you left the world
    Shines on and on and on.
                        —JOSEPH C. CARSON, 1963.

Mr. Speaker, a dear friend of mine, Buffalo and Washington attorney, Vincent M. Gaughan, was the principal speaker at the interfaith memorial service for our late President, John Fitzgerald Kennedy, held at the Trinity Episcopal Church in Hamburg, N.Y., on Sunday, December 22, 1963. The service was held in conjunction with the candlelight service, marking the end of the national mourning period at the Lincoln Memorial in Washington, D.C., and addressed by President Lyndon B. Johnson on that same day.

Mr. Gaughan was a friend of our late President for the past 15 years and served as his advance man in the presidential campaign of 1960, and in the congressional campaign of 1962.

One of Mr. Gaughan's last assignments for President Kennedy was to serve as the special representative of the President at the independence ceremony held in Dahomey, Africa, last August.

On the President's last trip, Mr. Gaughan had preceded him to Texas, where he had worked on the arrangements in Austin. The President was scheduled to arrive in Austin on the night of November 22.

The deep sorrow which Mr. Gaughan felt at President Kennedy's death was expressed in these poignant words, which I think will be an inspiration to all of us.

Under leave to extend my remarks, I include Mr. Gaughan's eulogy which follows:

EULOGY OF PRESIDENT JOHN FITZGERALD KENNEDY

(By Vincent M. Gaughan)

We meet today in this holy place to honor our fallen captain. Our minds are troubled and our hearts are heavy because our captain was not only our leader who buoyed our courage in the heat of battle, he was also our loved and cherished friend, who walked and dwelt amongst us, giving freely of all he possessed.

He gave us counsel and understanding. He gave us a new dignity, a higher hope, a greater vision. And finally, with his last breath, he gave us the most priceless gift of all—his life.

Today, the shadow of the man falls long and dark across this Nation.

Be not sad, dear friends. It is altogether fitting that we meet this day to take down the black shrouds of mourning and death, to be replaced with the joyful boughs of evergreen, symbol of everlasting life.

The cool, crisp voice, the graceful laugh, the mortal man are gone. Yet he lives—he lives.

He lives forever in the hearts of all who love their God and serve their fellow man.

He will live in generations yet unborn, to whom he will be a towering inspiration, beckoning them through endless time to seek a fuller life and a better world.

Charles Dickens once wrote:

"When Death strikes down the innocent and young, for every fragile form from which he lets the struggling spirit free, a hundred virtues rise in shapes of mercy, charity, and love to walk the world and bless it."

This is a season of holiness. This is the season of Christmas joy that down through the ages has held out to mankind the promise of a new birth, through which the whole world is born again. Let us now, each in his own humble way, in the spirit of the Prince of Peace, firmly resolve to make the assassin's bullet that brought death and final ending to our martyred President bring new life and a new beginning to this Nation.

Let us resolve to replace unreasoning hate and distrust in our national life with love and understanding.

Let us resolve that no act or word of ours will ever encourage the bigot to transgress the rights and privileges of another human being, be he pauper or prince, black or white, Jew or gentile.

Let us resolve to continue the assault on poverty and quest for peace for which he so nobly lived and nobly died.

Let us resolve to continue the ecumenical spirit which brings me, a Catholic, to an Episcopalian pulpit.

No library, no eternal flame, no renaming of a space agency, no road name, or school name will be so appropriate a monument as this. No monument built of stone and mortar will last as long or mean as much as this monument of the heart and mind.

A commander has fallen. A new one steps in to fill the breach. The battle goes on.

But before we turn away from the flag-draped caisson, the empty saddle, the turned boots—before we turn our thoughts to the tasks at hand—let us consign his spirit to He who loves him best, with the prayerful plea:

"Dear God, please take care of your servant, John Fitzgerald Kennedy."

TRIBUTE BY

Hon. Carl Elliott

OF ALABAMA

Mr. Speaker, the mayor and City Council of Vestavia Hills, Ala., has adopted a resolution of condolence on the untimely death of former President John Fitzgerald Kennedy.

The resolution is as follows:

RESOLUTION OF CONDOLENCE

Whereas an assassin did take the life of John Fitzgerald Kennedy, President of the United States of America on November 22, 1963, at Dallas, Tex.; and

Whereas the citizens of Vestavia Hills, Ala., join with their fellow Americans in mourning the assassination of our President, and deploring the godless philosophy which caused his murder; and

Whereas the citizens of our community desire to express their most sincere condolences, prayers for surcease from sorrow and wishes for the future welfare and happiness of the bereaved widow and children of the President: Now, therefore, be it

Resolved by the City Council of the City of Vestavia Hills, Ala., in regular session assembled, That we join in silent prayer to God for our departed President and, that we do, by this resolution, express our personal sorrow and deep sense of loss of the bereaved family of John Fitzgerald Kennedy; and be it further

Resolved, That a copy of this resolution be spread upon the official minutes of the City Council of the City of

Vestavia Hills, Ala., and the original be sent to the widow, Mrs. Jacqueline Kennedy.

Unanimously adopted in regular session this 2d day of December 1963.

ROBERT M. GUILLAT, *Mayor.*

Attest:

HENRY G. GALLIMORE,
City Clerk.

TRIBUTE BY

Hon. Joe L. Evins

OF TENNESSEE

Mr. Speaker, the shocking and tragic news of the untimely death of President Kennedy has shaken the feelings and emotions of the world. In my own State of Tennessee, on Sunday, November 24, prior to the funeral of the President, a memorial service was held in Nashville, the capital city of Tennessee, which I was privileged to attend along with the Governor of Tennessee, The Honorable Frank G. Clement, members of his cabinet, members of the Supreme Court of Tennessee, and representatives of all religious faiths and leading public officials of Tennessee who were in attendance and participated.

The vast War Memorial Building of Tennessee was packed to capacity, including the galleries with standing room only. Governor Clement made the observation that it was the largest crowd he had ever witnessed in this vast auditorium.

On this occasion, Mr. Speaker, The Honorable Weldon B. White, distinguished justice of the Supreme Court of Tennessee, gave the principal memorial address and eulogy on the life and public service of the late President John Fitzgerald Kennedy. Judge White's address is a beautiful memorial to our late President, which I feel many will want to read.

The memorial address to the late President Kennedy follows:

MEMORIAL TO JOHN FITZGERALD KENNEDY—1917–1963

Governor Clement, Lieutenant Governor Bomar, former Governors Cooper, McCord, and Buford Ellington, Congressmen Richard Fulton and Joe Evins, distinguished members of the Cabinet, member of the general assembly of the State of Tennessee, fellow members of the judiciary, State and Federal, Mayor Briley, members of the Metropolitan Council of Nashville and Davidson County, the clergy of all faiths and all creeds who are with us on this platform here today, members of the press, radio, and television, and members of this audience, numbering more than 3,000, and fellow Tennesseans:

It is an honor to have been selected by the committee on arrangements to deliver this memorial address. I speak the sincere and deep sentiment of all loyal patriotic Tennesseans in saying that the flag of our country and the heart of our people fly at half mast because—

The President of the United States is dead.

These sad and meaningful words were broadcast and rebroadcast by all news media to a sorrowful nation and a shocked world, the real victims of an assassin's bullet, on November 22, 1963.

Born to wealth and educated by the masters, he possessed a love of country, a dedication to public service, and a responsive feeling for the welfare of the average American citizen far beyond that of most men.

Answering his own conscience, and his Nation's call to duty in World War II, he gave his best efforts and almost his life in valiant service of this country that he loved so dearly.

Returning to his home in Boston at the close of the war, and despite his injuries and consequent suffering, he became active and fruitful in the political affairs of his State and our Nation, meeting with such success that he finally attained the Presidency, the pinnacle of success. He was the youngest man ever elected President of our country.

At his inauguration in January 1961, he outlined a program of ideals and goals which he hoped to gain during his administration. He then pursued them vigorously and wholeheartedly with his every resource of spirit, mind, and body. He was a strong and resolute man.

Rebuff at home and abroad failed to daunt his courage or swerve him from these ideals or his chosen path and determined goal. He felt that this country, nearing 200 million, had sufficient natural resources and technological capability to provide an excellent standard of living for all of us, and, at the same time, maintain our place in the sun.

He foresaw the need of other nations to know of and be acquainted with our institutions, our people, our purposes, and our democratic way of life. The Congress of the United States joined with him in creating the Peace Corps to travel abroad and to lay before the people of foreign lands our ideals and our way of life. The success of the program is known to all.

He foresaw, too, that the cause of human progress would be advanced by acquiring knowledge of outer space and all the mysteries that lie there. Great strides are being made toward this end of our program.

In confrontations with powerful leaders of other strong nations he stood erect and unbending in the belief shared by all Americans that the world can live in peace through the Rule of Law rather than suffer by the Rule of Force. But, he convinced those same leaders that if Force be necessary we Americans stood with him.

This type of leadership, decisive action and resolution demonstrated to the enemies and friends of our country that we want and desire peace—not peace at any price—but peace on terms honorable and just to all.

The 35th President of the United States, the Honorable John Fitzgerald Kennedy, is now dead but he and his ideals remain a part of the heritage of this great Nation. He was stricken down in the discharge of the duties of his office. Mrs. Kennedy, another great soldier, was at his side and gave him comfort and strength in his last moments. Her stanch devotion then and in the hours after his death gives to her a unique place in our history.

We salute you, too, Mrs. Kennedy. You discharged your every duty to the President of the United States, your husband, and to the office you have graced for the past 3 years despite many hardships and personal losses.

Robert Frost, the poet and the personal friend of President Kennedy, said:

"Despite our fears and worries—and they are very real to all of us—life continues * * * it goes on. In these three words I can sum up everything I have learned in my 80 years about life" said Mr. Frost, "it goes on."

We recognize, as Mr. Frost did, that life does go on.

The drafters of our Constitution knew that the life of a nation does not stop at the passing of a man, even a great man. It has to go on, and for this purpose provision was made for succession to the presidency. Within the space of 2 hours after the death of Mr. Kennedy, the Vice President, Mr. Lyndon B. Johnson, with his hand upon the Bible, and with Mrs. Johnson on one side and Mrs. Kennedy on the other, subscribed to the oath of office as President of the United States. And, within the space of another 2 hours, he stood in the Capital City and gave to the American people this humble statement:

"I will do my best. This is all I can do. I ask for your help, and God's."

What more can we Americans ask of any man than that he seek our help and invoke the blessings of God upon assuming the obligations, duties, and responsibilities of this, the highest office occupied by man. We of all faiths, creeds, and color are united in our grief at the passing of our President.

We must be equally united in our support of our new President who will need our help and that of Almighty God in maintaining and pushing forward this growing and maturing American society in its quest for educational, cultural, and economic advancement and political stability.

We should bear in mind that our institutions do not rest on thin air. They rest on sacrifice, character, ideals and faith. Being an American is more than just being a citizen of a country. It is being a member of a strong, progressive, vibrant living society in which every man has respect for the other and the Government has respect for the integrity of all.

At the time when we grieve over the death of our President, it is fitting that we pray to God that He grant to us as individuals the wisdom to "know ourselves" and from that knowledge to rid ourselves of all bitterness, hate and resentment that may be in our hearts, lest their acid eat into our physical being and corrode our spirits; and that He help us not to be frightened by the problems of the day, but rather to be a part of the answer and not a part of the problem.

I think it most appropriate to quote the last paragraphs of the speech prepared for delivery by President Kennedy to the Dallas Citizens Council, the Dallas Assembly and the Graduate Research Center. He was to have said:

"Our adversaries have not abandoned their ambitions—our dangers have not diminished—our vigilance cannot be relaxed. But now we have the military, the scientific and the economic strength to do whatever must be done for the preservation and promotion of freedom.

"That strength will never be used in pursuit of aggressive ambitions—it will always be used in pursuit of peace. It will never be used to promote provocations—it will always be used to promote the peaceful settlement of disputes."

Mr. Kennedy continued:

"We in this country, in this generation, are—by destiny rather than choice—the watchmen on the walls of world freedom. We ask, therefore, that we may be worthy of our power and responsibility—that we may exercise our strength with wisdom and restraint—and that we may achieve in our time and for all time the ancient vision of 'peace on earth, good will toward men.'"

So ends the last speech prepared by our President.

In Switzerland, I am told, there is a church among the Alps far up on the mountainside and in it there are no lights or lamps. When the time comes for evening service one can see the villagers coming from their homes, each one bearing his own light. At first there is only a glimmer in the darkness, but when they have all arrived for the service the little church is aglow with the combined light of many lamps and candles.

Many of us have only a small light. John F. Kennedy had a large light. A gun in the hand of a man with a diseased and depraved mind has snuffed out the bright light of this forceful, courageous, and dedicated man.

In our grief over this great tragedy we must remember that America like the little church in Switzerland has no light at all, save as we bring our individual lights together for its improvement and the betterment of man.

To the family of Mr. Kennedy we, Tennesseans, extend our sympathetic understanding.

To our new President, Mr. Johnson, we, Tennesseans, pledge our loyalty and support in the troubled and difficult days ahead.

WELDON B. WHITE,
Associate Justice, Supreme Court of Tennessee.

(The above address was delivered in the War Memorial Auditorium on Sunday afternoon, November 24, 1963.)

TRIBUTES BY

Hon. Leonard Farbstein

OF NEW YORK

Mr. Speaker, under leave to extend my remarks, I would like to include an editorial written by my good friend, Abraham Schlacht, editor and publisher of the East Side News. Mr. Schlacht did not affix his name to this particular editorial because he wanted it to be the general expression of the newspaper.

This is a typical characteristic of Abraham Schlacht, a man who has worked tirelessly and unceasingly in behalf of the people of the East Side of New York, most of the time without making known his efforts. However, fame has a way of singling out for recognition even the most unassuming of individuals. In the case of this outstanding journalist, his address on the occasion of the presentation of an award to him by the East Side Post Jewish War Veterans, later incorporated as an editorial entitled "Freedom Versus Apathy," was considered for an award by the Freedoms Foundation at Valley Forge.

His editorial in memory of our late President speaks for the people of that area of New York which is known worldwide as New York's East Side—the melting pot of the Nation. I commend it to my colleagues:

IN MEMORIAM, JOHN FITZGERALD KENNEDY—1917–63

A week ago today our great President fell at the hands of an assassin, and the Nation has not yet recovered from its tragedy.

Our hearts still overflow with grief at the loss of our Commander in Chief—John Fitzgerald Kennedy, a sacrifice to the cause of freedom.

Our hearts go out, too, to Mrs. Jacqueline Kennedy and her two children, Caroline and John, Jr., who have suffered their greatest blow.

Mrs. Kennedy will ever be remembered for the manner in which she bore her hour of sorrow.

From the beginning to end of this tragic event, she reflected a stoic air and dignity that can never be erased from our memory.

Since the days of the Great Emancipator no other President's death has struck the Nation with such shock and horror as did the senseless assassination of our President.

No other President has left the world with such hollowness and meaninglessness as did the death of the late President.

And no other in the annals of this generation has held the world spellbound, and no other has championed and symbolized the hopes of our youth and that of the world as did our stricken commander.

To all of us, his passing is our personal tragedy.

In eternal glory lie the mortal remains of our immortal President in Arlington National Cemetery.

They rest on an open hillside among tall, bare elms, and a slight distance away stands a solitary cedar.

As one looks about from the grave of the President,

one can see several hundred feet away thousands of our honored dead, and the floodlighted columns of the Custis-Lee Mansion. One cannot help but sense a quiet, awesome feeling of deepest solemnity pervading the cemetery grounds.

At the head of his grave burns an eternal flame, and around it is a multi-array of flowers.

Let us trust that the light of this flame will cast its peaceful rays in the hearts of all men everywhere.

And without a doubt millions of people of all races and creeds from every clime will make their pilgrimages to honor his memory.

The American people cannot forget those moving words which he delivered in his inaugural address:

"Together let us explore the stars, conquer the deserts, eradicate disease, tap the ocean depths and encourage the arts and commerce."

Which other leader in American life has expressed so aptly in so few words?

Which other in this generation, we ask, has expressed in such simple and stirring language the things that lie closest to the average human heart.

The image of the late President can never be forgotten from our memory.

Who among us can ever fail to recall his winsome smile, his humor, often displayed at public places and press conferences; his repartee and brilliance in debate, and his knowledge and mastery of problems of state?

Moreover, who can ever forget his innate sense of refinement, and, in particular, his unwavering steadfastness in the face of national peril?

He will live on not for decades, but for centuries, so long as human beings love peace, righteousness, and mercy.

May his soul repose in peace. May his memory ever abide in our thoughts. May his principles, for which he so ardently toiled, for ourselves and for humanity, become a reality. May his memorial, reflected in his utterances and deeds, be a glowing light ever to behold and an inspiration to this and to all future generations.

For the people's safety and domestic tranquillity, let us dedicate ourselves anew to make these United States a haven of peace and good will, where hate and bitterness shall be forever obliterated, and where all are Americans, first and always.

Mr. Speaker, under leave to extend my remarks, I am pleased to include the eulogy in memory of our late President, John F. Kennedy, delivered by Rabbi Harry J. Kaufman, spiritual leader of the Beth Sholom Congregation of Washington, D.C., on November 25, 1963:

With bowed heads and broken hearts we join America in the recitation "Boruch Dayon Hoemes" on the passing of a great and good leader, President John Fitzgerald Kennedy.

A sad and senseless national tragedy has come to pass, nurtured by a climate of derision, indifference, and hate that has become part of our contemporary scene.

This supreme loss echoes in our souls the incisive lament of the teachers of Israel—

"Oy Ledor Sheovad Manhigo"
"Oy L'sfisono Sheovad Karbonitoh"

—*Talmud* (*Baba Bathro*) 91: *B.*

"Woe to the world that has lost its leader and woe unto the ship that has lost its pilot."

President Kennedy was not only the leader of our generation but was the confident pilot who guided the distressed ship of a faltering humanity.

Our loss is incalculable even as this tragedy is unfathomable. Most trying times have come upon us.

God is the source of life and the author of history. His will prevails. He sets the times and raises up the men to live in these times. We cannot question His action, what remains for us is to reexamine our conduct.

In the book of Genesis we read, "And Jacob was left alone." A dreary night envelops him as he is overcome by a dismal loneliness; but the struggle for survival must go on.

Faith becomes his most potent defense against the onslaught of a mysterious adversary. He is stunned, he understands not why nor wherefore this comes to be, but he continues indomitably, battling for God, for himself, and for humanity. Though gravely hurt he carries on and vanquishes his adversary, as a new dawn emerges.

The time is today, the struggle is in the present. The anguish is ours as the mystery of these sorrowing happenings eludes us, but we too must carry on until the light of a new dawn will reveal itself to us.

Great men become the fabric of a nation. Its martyrs set the tone of its ideals and dreams.

Through the life of John Kennedy we were given a glimpse of a world that could come to be; a world of dynamic vigor, adventure, discovery, hope, and worthiness, of children laughing and men working together in a harmony of decency, purpose, and fulfillment. A world that can cast aside cruelty, ugliness, and hatred as the inevitable pattern of man's life on earth.

A beautiful dream has been broken. The inspiring vision has been shattered and we have become poorer by his death, even as we were made richer by his life.

We have been taught that the righteous are not memorialized by words but by works, not by august monuments but by monumental actions. not by lamenting dirges but by lofty deeds.

The greatest of our goals and the noblest of our purposes have been sown in tears and born in agony. As the prophet, Jeremiah, cries out "Refrain thy voice from weeping and thine eyes from tears—for there is yet great reward in thine actions." Tears cannot bring John Kennedy back but he can continue to live with us and through us by our consecrated devotion and attainment of the great causes he served.

May the Comforter of all sustain and protect this great land and our new President and may He bestow His loving grace upon the valiant and courageous First Lady and her dear children and the family of our great President.

May He, who is the source of all strength and wisdom, embolden our resolve to make real in our lifetime, the yearnings, the hopes, and dedicated goals of our Lincolns and our Kennedys that from this anguish "This Nation, under God shall have a new birth of freedom."

> "Were a star quenched on high
> For ages would its light
> Still traveling downward from the sky
> Shine on our mortal sight
> So, when a great man dies
> For years beyond our ken
> The light he leaves behind lies
> Upon the path of men."
>
> —*Longfellow.*

TRIBUTES BY

Hon. Dante B. Fascell

OF FLORIDA

Mr. Speaker, all the people of the Fourth Congressional District of Florida express their intense regret for the tragic death of the late President Kennedy; and they extend their heartfelt sympathies to Mrs. Kennedy, the children, and the family. The following editorials speak eloquently and are representative of the intense feelings, and the thoughts and prayers of the people I am honored to represent in the Congress of the United States:

[From the Miami News, Nov. 23, 1963]

WE MOURN FOR OURSELVES AND FOR THE WORLD

The President of the United States and the leader of the free world is dead.

The prayers of millions follow President John Fitzgerald Kennedy in death, and beseech guidance for his successor, President Lyndon Baines Johnson.

We mourn for President Kennedy's family, a notably close family even in a Nation where close families are the norm.

We mourn for our country, which must undergo a difficult change of leadership in critical times.

And mostly, we mourn for ourselves, who have been denied the fullest potential of a brilliant young President.

We have been denied by what Winston Churchill has rightly called a monstrous act, whose full impact is only beginning to seep into the hearts and minds of the Nation.

In late years it has been axiomatic that the man who occupies the highest position in the United States occupies the most powerful position in the world.

America has been fortunate that the men who have held this lofty office have treated it as a sacred trust. Certainly it was treated so by John Fitzgerald Kennedy.

Only rarely in the course of our history have we been blessed with a President whose qualities of leadership combined to inscribe his greatness forever on our national shrines. Jefferson was one of these, and Lincoln was another. And more and more you are going to hear Mr. Kennedy's name mentioned as one of the great ones.

He had youth, charm, and a zest for life and leadership that the White House has seldom known.

Surely no President faced larger problems than John Fitzgerald Kennedy, and none met his problems with greater optimism.

It was a measure of his leadership that he never hesitated to attack a problem merely because that problem seemed insoluble, and Heaven knows many of them must have seemed just that. They would have crushed a lesser man into inactivity.

He had courage in war and in peace, and he had the wits to confound those at home or abroad who would despoil his beloved country. He had brilliance when only brilliance would suffice.

Like Jefferson, he kept faith with the common man, believing in the common man's ability to manage his own freedom.

Like Lincoln, he had an abiding conviction that all citizens have a right to equality. Despite his certain knowledge that this conviction was unpopular in much of the Nation, he supported it to the fullest. This was a demanding test of his integrity, and he passed it in his own way as nobly as Lincoln passed his.

America is a great Nation, and it is one of the blessings of our democracy that our Government endures even such catastrophes as this. These are times when we rally together behind our new leader.

The President is dead, God save the President.

[From the Key West Citizen, Nov. 24, 1963]

As the World Mourns

As the world stands bowed in grief today over the untimely death of one of the alltime great leaders of the world, our President, John Fitzgerald Kennedy, the real stature of this protagonist of peace is beginning to emerge as other world leaders pour out their hearts in sympathy.

Sympathy, first of all to the bereaved family; then to the Nation he has led so well for 2 years and 10 months, and, lastly, to the whole population of the world, a world which has lost a mighty champion of peace and good will among all peoples.

For the first time in the history of the world, the citizens of the bereaved Nation have been able to see the deep lines of grief etched upon the faces of the peoples of this and other nations and to hear, first hand, their expressions of regard and concern.

It is highly significant that in this great tragedy even those who have disagreed with the President and his philosophy of government are as sincere in their grief as those who marched side by side with him as he stood firm at the helm of this great Nation.

John Fitzgerald Kennedy, with firm determination and courage seldom found in mortal man, confronted the might of Soviet Russia and won his way, thus earning great respect for himself and for our Nation throughout the world.

He fought valiantly for the betterment of the people of his own nation and for the bringing about of equal opportunities for all.

As in the case of all great national tragedies, the world faces a time of readjustment and, we pray, self-examination.

As we mourn the passing of one great American, we turn our thoughts and prayers to the one upon whose broad shoulders the mantle of peacemaker has fallen.

Our Nation shall long remember John Fitzgerald Kennedy for the deeds he did and the light he shed upon a dark and troubled world.

People are wont to erect great memorials to leaders who have passed on to the Great Beyond. The greatest memorial that the world could erect to our late President would be one of a lasting peace and understanding among the peoples and nations of the earth.

Even as we are bowed in sorrow let us each dedicate ourselves to the unfinished task of the 35th President of the United States.

[From the Miami Beach Daily Sun, Nov. 24, 1963]

Our President: His Bequest to Us

You cannot stop an idea with a bullet.

In the numbness of President Kennedy's assassination, this is perhaps our only solace.

Our President died for freedom Friday. He was killed by hate; whatever particular label it may bear is only incidental.

What killed him was the fury of the small minds which cannot tolerate anything different from themselves, any outlook different from their own, any aspirations with frontiers beyond their own crimped view.

John Fitzgerald Kennedy gave voice as have few political leaders in this century to the cravings of all Americans for a job, for an education, for the right to move freely about one's own country as a full-fledged citizen of this Nation.

Mr. Kennedy was a fighter, a trait which served him well in election but which ennobled him in times of national need such as the Cuban crisis. He articulated for us all the resolution necessary to back down a murderer named Khrushchev in Cuba.

Memorials may well be raised to our late President. They really are but a postscript for even in death he left us with a living one: He cared enough for his fellow man to insist on a better way for him and his posterity.

[From the Diario Las Americas, Miami Springs, Fla., Nov. 24, 1963]

John F. Kennedy

When the world learned the tragic news of the assassination of the President of the United States, John F. Kennedy, a profound spiritual commotion invaded all the civilized peoples of the globe, who recognized in him one of the most outstanding figures of contemporary mankind. John F. Kennedy was, more than a President of the United States of America, an extraordinary man, a statesman of lofty intellect, a great master of the oratory, a renowned warrior of liberty, a noble defender of human equality and dignity.

When his life was a promise for his country and for the world, an irresponsible assassin fired the weapon that cut short the thread of President Kennedy's existence, plunging the United States and all those who on the face of the earth have their heart in the right place, into deep and confusing consternation. In a matter of a few minutes a Communist assassin caused the physical disappearance of a man of eminent qualities, of superior intelligence and of upmost human sensibility, whose ideas and intentions will vibrate forever in his exceptional speeches, which were a model of pronouncements for their impeccable style and for their unmistakable ideological depth. The Communists have assassinated an illustrious defender of democracy and of the just social replevins, but that does not mean that they have been able to kill the ideal and work of John F. Kennedy, which from now on will have more meaning in the remembrance and admiration of all the peoples on earth.

The man who triumphantly defied death as hero and patriot in the Second World War, lost his life when, in the fields of peace, he struggled for the prevalence of the principles that ordered his actions in the feat of the Pacific Ocean that was and will always be a source of pride for the United States. The enemy's bullets respected the life of a then very young John F. Kennedy, perhaps to permit humanity to see at the White House in Washington a ruler of the elevated hierarchy of the one who, with his death, has just darkened with mourning the flags of all the civilized nations of the world.

In the life and death of John F. Kennedy there are lessons to be learned. In his life won the will to excel, the talent, the goodness of sentiment, the impassioned love for the fatherland and for the cause of liberty, his devotion in study, his political vocation in the function of democracy. His accomplishments will be source of inspiration for those wanting to climb to the heights of the supreme values of patriotism and of the spirit. In his death is, once more, the hard lesson of what the Communists are capable to do. The coldness of crime, the calculation for the execution of a savage act that stands for anticivilization. And in the face of those proofs of Communist monstrosity, the United States and the free world should react in a determined action of combativeness and defense.

Diario Las Americas joins with profound respect to the immense grief of the people of the United States in these sad moments of their history, and expresses its sentiments of deep sorrow for the death of this illustrious head of state who will figure in universal history as one of the most enlightened personalities of the 20th century.

May in the peace of God rest the soul of John F. Kennedy, so that he may enjoy in eternity the quiet and light that corresponds to those who, like him, were an example of spiritual excellence.

TRIBUTES BY

Hon. John E. Fogarty
OF RHODE ISLAND

Mr. Speaker, our late President, John Fitzgerald Kennedy, was a good friend of Providence College in my State of Rhode Island, which is so ably administered by its president, the Very Reverend Vincent C. Dore, O.P., and in all of the words of eulogy that have been expressed following the untimely death of the President, I am particularly proud of the high tribute that has been accorded him by the college. On Monday, November 25, Providence College honored the memory of our late President by a solemn mass of requiem which was attended by the entire student body, faculty, college personnel and many friends and relatives of the college. On that occasion the Very Reverend Vincent C. Dore, O.P., celebrated the mass and delivered the eulogy for President Kennedy which I believe ranks as one of the finest tributes of the many that have been made. Under leave to extend my remarks I would like to include a copy of the student newspaper of Providence College, the Cowl, which contains the eulogy:

[From the Providence (R.I.) Cowl]

PRESIDENT KENNEDY ASSASSINATED, BURIED IN ARLINGTON YESTERDAY—NATION AND WORLD SADDENED—PROVIDENCE COLLEGE MOURNS LOSS

Following a pontifical requiem mass offered by His Eminence Richard Cardinal Cushing, archbishop of Boston, in St. Matthew's Cathedral in Washington, D.C., the casket containing the body of John Fitzgerald Kennedy was laid to rest in Arlington National Cemetery yesterday afternoon.

The President was assassinated last Friday afternoon in Dallas, Tex., during a motorcade through the downtown area of that city. He succumbed to his wounds within an hour of being shot.

The alleged assassin, Lee Harvey Oswald, was murdered on Sunday by a Dallas nightclub owner, Jack Rubenstein, while the Dallas police were transferring him to another jail.

While the casket lay on a catafalque in the East Room of the White House during Saturday, two priests knelt beside it in silent prayer. Earlier in the day, mass had been offered in the East Room for the family and close friends of the President.

From Sunday afternoon at 2 p.m. until yesterday morning at 10 a.m., over 100,000 people filed through the rotunda of the Capitol to view the casket placed on the Lincoln catafalque.

At times, the line of people waiting to enter the Capitol and view the solemn scene extended over a 30-block-long area. Those waiting in the chill Washington air on Sunday evening were numbered at approximately 300,000.

At Providence College, the students began their weekend-long observance of the President's assassination with an all-night vigil in the Chapel of Aquinas Hall on Friday.

Starting at 10 p.m. on that evening, members of the Providence College student community said the rosary continuously through the night until 7 a.m. on Saturday morning when mass was then offered for the repose of President Kennedy's soul. Masses were also offered at 8 and 10 a.m.

Yesterday morning at 9:30 a.m., a solemn high requiem mass was offered for the late Chief Executive in Alumni Hall. The celebrant of the mass was Very Rev. Vincent C. Dore, O.P., president of the college. Following the Gospel, Father Dore delivered a eulogy for the assassinated President.

––––

[From the Providence (R.I.) Cowl]

PRESIDENT OF PROVIDENCE COLLEGE EULOGIZES PRESIDENT

(The following is the eulogy for President Kennedy which was delivered by the Very Reverend Vincent C. Dore, O.P., president of the college, at yesterday's requiem mass in Alumni Hall.)

On this sad day in our Nation's history, you are assembled to assist me in offering the holy sacrifice of the mass, in solemn requiem, for the repose of the soul of John Fitzgerald Kennedy, 35th President of the United States.

Providence College mourns with deepest sorrow the death by an assassin's bullets of our Commander in Chief, the President of the United States, on Friday, November 22.

Our martyred President was a courageous leader of our people who ennobled our Nation as a virtuous individual; as a devout man who loved his family; and as a scholar, author, and world statesman of high ideals, lofty aspirations, and noble deeds.

He ennobled our Nation and the world by his constant adherence to the principles of liberty, justice, and equality and their application to all men and nations.

May the blood of his martyrdom on the altar of patriotism be the seed from which will spring a greater universal understanding, a higher moral social order, and wider horizons and brighter frontiers of peace and justice and freedom throughout the world.

John Fitzgerald Kennedy was indeed one of God's great noblemen. May his memory ever be held in benediction and may his immortal soul rest in peace.

As we bow our heads in sorrow, let us lift up our hearts to the glory of the resurrection and ask almighty God to sustain and comfort in their great loss—his young widowed wife, his little children, his parents, and their entire family. Let us also include in our prayers the family of the valiant Dallas police officer who lost his life in dedication to his line of duty on that tragic day.

With our fellow Americans and with all men and nations of good will throughout the world we unite through prayerful petition and supplication to almighty God that He may bless our new President, Lyndon B. Johnson, and grant him health and strength and wisdom to bear the heavy burdens placed upon him and to carry forward under God and with God's help and grace, the destiny of our beloved America.

––––

[From the Providence (R.I.) Cowl]

MEMO FROM THE EDITOR

America's light of liberty to the world shone, and it was extinguished. The symbol of freedom to the Nation and the peoples of the world was, and then it was no more. John Fitzgerald Kennedy, our President, had been taken from us.

Unbelieving, we sat before our radios and televisions and hoped against hope that what we had heard was no more than a terrible dream. Could this man, so universally respected and loved, have been so suddenly and cruelly removed from our midst?

Words failed us as we sat stunned and incredulous. This, we said, could not have happened here, today.

Difficult indeed is it for me, as it is for so many, to find words to express so great a loss. The loss is not so great, so shocking, so unbelievable, because a man died. Neither is it such because a President died. Rather, it is because this man, this President, died.

The spirit of our late President is such that it will not soon fade. For, President Kennedy was, in death as in life, so much a part of our generation, so much a part of us.

FRANK DEVLIN.

Mr. Speaker, under leave to extend my remarks, I would like to include an address delivered by President Francis H. Horn of the University of Rhode Island at memorial services for our late President, John Fitzgerald Kennedy, on November 25, 1963, at Edwards Hall.

MEMORIAL SERVICE FOR PRESIDENT KENNEDY, NOVEMBER 25, 1963

The Nation's new President, Lyndon B. Johnson, has proclaimed today, the day of the funeral service of our late President, John F. Kennedy, a "national day of mourning throughout the United States." He has urged that people assemble "in their respective places of divine worship, there to bow down in submission to the will of Almighty God, and to pay their homage of love and reverence to the memory of a great and good man." The Governor of our State, John H. Chafee, similarly has requested that memorial services be held this morning in all the schools of Rhode Island.

We have gathered here together not only in response to these requests, but also because we as a university community, so terribly grieved by the tragic death of President Kennedy, feel the need deep within us for a university ceremony of tribute to the gallant leader who has been snatched so suddenly from us. Each of us in the last few days, regardless of political affiliation or ideological convictions, has responded with tears, if not openly, at least inwardly, to the sad events of last Friday. Many have already participated in memorial services in our respective churches. But it is especially appropriate that we as a university, an institution which for over eight centuries has been dedicated to the search for truth and the meaning of life, engaged in the preparation of leaders for society, and consecrated to the advancement of the welfare of all mankind, should pause to mourn one who has demonstrated so effectively in his own life the ideals for which universities exist.

It is particularly fitting that our university should mourn today for President Kennedy. He had special ties to Rhode Island through Mrs. Kennedy's family, through his close personal friendship with the members of the Rhode Island congressional delegation, and through his frequent visits to our State. We had hoped to see him here often next summer. This hope, along with so many so much more significant for the world and its future, ended in Parkland Hospital in Dallas at 2 p.m. last Friday.

The initial shock, the disbelief, indeed, the horror, of the assassination are now pretty largely over. We have lived for 3 days with the headlines, the radio announcers, and the TV screens. Through the magic of the TV cameras, we have witnessed the historic events which will end with the interment this afternoon in Arlington National Cemetery. We have been moved by both the monumental worldwide outpouring of grief for President Kennedy and by the truly magnificent courage of Mrs. Kennedy, to whom our admiration and our affection go out with our prayers for her and her two children. We have read and listened to the tributes, to the recital of things achieved and goals unaccomplished, to the preliminary and tentative evaluation of Mr. Kennedy's place in history. There is no doubt both as to his stature as one of the great leaders of our time and as to the warm human qualities of the man. It has been rightly noted that John F. Kennedy has with his own death written the final chapter to his "Profiles in Courage."

It is not my intent at this memorial service, therefore, to attempt to add to the tributes. I think it not inappropriate, however, if I take this occasion to make several observations, of special significance to a university audience.

First, it seems to me that John F. Kennedy should remain a continuing inspiration to the youth of the world, especially to college students. No one of our day exemplified so thoroughly the ideal of the well-rounded individual, or as the ancient Greeks put it, the possessor—and user—of "a sound mind in a sound body." Yesterday's Journal, in Frank Lanning's superb tribute, referred to him as the "personification of youth, by word and act an ardent advocate of athletics and, by example, an apostle of sportsmanship." Yet he graduated from Harvard "cum laude" and published a best selling book the year

of his graduation and subsequently another which won him the Pulitzer Prize. Elected to Congress, at 30, to the Senate at 35, he narrowly missed nomination for the Vice-Presidency at 39, and was elected President at 43. One must go back into history to discover one so young whose impact on his time was so great. In a world in which youth questions its role, shuns personal ambition, and is skeptical as to what any single individual can accomplish, the life and example of John F. Kennedy should stand as a beacon to all our young people calling them to lives of greater and nobler achievement.

Second, no modern President, not even Franklin Delano Roosevelt, demonstrated so thoroughly as did President Kennedy a commitment to the life of the mind, the promotion of which is the basic reason for the existence of universities. The most perceptive of newspaper columnists, James Reston, in his first statement after the President's death, wrote that he was "a rationalist and an intellectual." The speech he was on his way to deliver in Dallas when he was struck down, stated that learning and reason must guide American policy. The goal of any university is to promote learning and to develop the rational power of its students, with the ultimate objective of bringing greater wisdom into the affairs of men and of nations. John F. Kennedy, a man of action who brought the world to the brink of nuclear war and who used the full power of his high office to uphold the constitutional rights of the Negro, was one who based his actions upon knowledge and upon reason and believed others should do the same. His example is one for us to hold high to the generations of students passing through our institutions of higher education in the decades ahead.

Third, and finally, we must keep the memory of President Kennedy ever bright for his commitment to peace. Though he risked war, his ultimate goal was a world truly at peace, one in which the fatherhood of God and the brotherhood of man had become realities. In his own words, he called upon all to join him in the endeavor to establish "a new world of law, where the strong are just and the weak secure and the peace preserved forever." He has set us on the high though torturous road toward that goal; he has charted the course not only for future statesmen and Presidents, but for all of us ordinary citizens everywhere. The sacrifice of his life will not have been in vain if his goals and his ideals remain ever before us.

Today, we must not only mourn President Kennedy—though this we do with sad hearts. We must also, as President Johnson said in his proclamation, make this a day of "rededication." President Kennedy, he said, would not have us shrink from carrying on his work beyond this hour of national tragedy." If John Kennedy could speak to us today from beyond the veil, would he not have us ask ourselves, as he asked the Nation in his inaugural address: "Ask not what America can do for you and for me, but what we together as Americans can do to bring peace to the world and freedom for all mankind."

John F. Kennedy must remain in the hearts and minds of us all; but more, each of us must pledge to work vigorously for those major goals of a better world which he held most dear. Our hopes and prayers must therefore go out, as Mr. Kennedy would have them go out, to his friend and successor, our new President, Lyndon B. Johnson, to whom now falls the task of leading us toward those goals. This too is a part of our meditations in today's service.

The President asked that we gather in our places of worship for these services. The University of Rhode Island has no chapel, but it does have chaplains. Consequently, to lead us in prayer on this solemn occasion we have the university's four chaplains or their representatives.

We shall now proceed to our service of prayer and meditation.

(Our service of mourning for John F. Kennedy and of rededication to the ideals for which he lived and died will conclude with the benediction.)

TRIBUTES BY

Hon. Donald M. Fraser

OF MINNESOTA

Mr. Speaker, among the many tributes and memorials to our late President, John F. Kennedy, the following meditation by Pastor Alton Motter of Minneapolis deserves to be read and remembered by all Americans. Pastor Motter has recently been chosen as the new executive secretary of the Minnesota Council of Churches. His intense commitment to the welfare of man is reflected in his searching question, "Have we the will, the sufficient sense of responsible citizenship to take up where he left off?" I especially commend this message to my colleagues and hope our actions will indicate we have responded affirmatively:

A CHALLENGE TO THE SOUL OF AMERICA

The President is dead. How that news has tested the faith and courage of every American in these days. As we gathered in our sanctuary to find strength and comfort, every word of song and scripture spoke to our souls in an extraordinary way, making the reality of Christ and of faith stand out bold and fresh.

(In the special service of commemoration and dedication held on America's National Day of Mourning on Monday, an overflow congregation heard a memorable meditation delivered by Pastor Alton Motter.)

There is a time in the life of a nation when the grief which encompasses it is too great to be expressed in words. We are in the midst of such a time now.

Most of us believed that the assassination of a President belonged to the struggling stages of our past, that it was something for history books—Lincoln in 1865, Garfield in 1881, McKinley in 1901. But 3 days ago it happened, and, within minutes, the young and vital life of President John F. Kennedy came to an end.

But in a very real sense, the assassin's bullet killed not only our President; it killed a part of each of us. It was an attack, as was the murder of the murderer since then, upon our democratic procedures, upon our respect and reverence of human life, upon our hopes and dreams.

As we think of the awfulness of the deed which caused his death, we can think only of the words of our Lord from the cross: "Father, forgive them, for they know not what they do." For it seems clear that only a warped life could commit such a crime; that only a hate-filled personality could bring such sadness to a nation and to the world. What a price to pay * * * for the poison of hatred.

There is, in this great national tragedy, deep and challenging implications for all Americans, but especially for all Christians in America. For it is the Christian's business to overcome hatred, to conquer fear, to provide the inner disciplines which can bring the kind of social and spiritual security which makes murder unnecessary. My friends, how our world cries out for the qualities of Christian love—the kind of compassionate love which can bring justice and freedom and peace to every person, to every race and to every nation of the earth.

This day, then, should be not only a day of mourning for the untimely death of our departed President—for his widow and his children, for his family and his colleagues—this it should be and is. But it must be more: It should be also a day of rededication to the quality of love revealed in Jesus Christ, our Lord, and the ways that love can survive and conquer the evils of our time. "America, America. God mend thine every flaw, Confirm thy soul in self-control, Thy liberty in law."

President Kennedy worked faithfully and diligently to remedy some of the evils of our time: to bring equality of opportunity to all races; to reconcile the differences between nations; to bring hope to the economically dispossessed; and to encourage man's search and struggle for the more abundant life. Have we the will, the sufficient sense of responsible citizenship to take up where he left off? To support such efforts of our new President as he makes his way into the future?

This, then, is truly the hour to recall the words of our martyred President: "Ask not what America can do for you; ask, rather, what you can do for America."

Mr. Speaker, December 22 marked the end of the 30-day period of national mourning for our late, beloved President. While we in America mourn the loss of a great citizen and leader, the world joins with us in tribute to a man whose stature knew no national bounds, whose concern was always for the dignity of man wherever he may be.

A recent article by H. O. Sonnesyn, editor of the North Minneapolis Post, contains two letters written by Danish and German students expressing their country's grief and shock over the assassination. Both are remarkable letters, reveal-ing the deep friendship these nations felt for President Kennedy. I commend them to the attention of my colleagues.

PEN PALS SHARE IN SORROW—YOUTHFUL DANE, GERMAN, WRITE OF J.F.K.'S DEATH

Judy Gallagher, daughter of Mr. and Mrs. Francis Gallagher, 5400 42d Avenue North, Robbinsdale, has two pen pals, one in Germany and the other in Denmark. It was interesting to read the letters written by them to her after the death of the late President John F. Kennedy. The Denmark pen pal wrote his letter on the very same day he heard about the death of the U.S. President.

The Denmark pen pal said:

"I just only will tell you that I have heard about the murder of the President of the United States. I was the first in my family, I think one of the first in Denmark who knew about President Kennedy's death. I was lying ill in bed at this time. I tried to find some music and heard an American station. The time was 7:52 p.m. and then the speaker said, 'Here we are with a special news.' Then it comes. 'The President of the United States of America was shot today.' My heart got up in my neck. I jumped quick out of my bed and ran to my mom and pop in the living room and cried that the President was dead. At first they would not believe me, but at 8 o'clock the news from the Danish radio comes and then they must believe me.

"I know that I can say for all the Danish people that we are very, very sorry. It is going to our hearts that a so beautiful, clever and busy man, who has done so much good should be dead right now. Mom was very near to cry, and there was being a remarkable silence in the room. The speaker who said it had trouble to say he was dead. The time is now 9:30 p.m. at the November 22, 1963. I think that all TV stations have broken their programs. We have seen pictures from the murder over the German TV. We are thinking of his wife and his children.

"I think that you and me are feeling the same. We must think a little of what happened."

Her German pen pal wrote the day after the assassina-tion. He started his letter by addressing:

"Family Gallagher:

"It is afternoon stillness in a German province. The second night comes over Europe and the second night over America. It is 17.00 h local time, that is 12.00 h eastern standard time. Three snow-white candles are standing in my room. When it is 19.00 o'clock then I put these in the windows of this room, and I set these on fire.

"On this night at 07.00 I have heard a transmission from my hometown. The spokesman was the mayor, Willy Brandt. He gave orders that all Berliners put at 19.00 burned candles in the windows. And I am also a Berliner.

"With greatest dismay the free world, and especially the Berlin inhabitants, have received the message of the death of the President of the United States of America.

"John Fitzgerald Kennedy. In the Federal Republic and in West Berlin is ordered state mourning. All flags are on half mast.

"A great man went out of our middle. A friend of the German people. A fellow citizen of the Berliner. We can be very proud of him. To 03.00 local time in the morning I hear the informations of the Voice of America and American Forces network Europe.

"John F. Kennedy is dead. But in our hearts he lives on."

The German pen pal also wrote this line in German. We have spelled some of the words in the American way so they would be easier to decipher.

Judy's two pen pals are only 17 years old. We think it was indeed remarkable that youths of this age in foreign lands pay such beautiful tributes to the late President John F. Kennedy. The speed with which they conveyed their regrets after they had heard about the death of our President is also remarkable. We are wondering how many of us would have shown the same spirit these two teenagers did had the table been reversed. We think it is a rather remarkable display of international friendship.

TRIBUTES BY

Hon. James G. Fulton

OF PENNSYLVANIA

Mr. Speaker, I would like to include in my remarks the moving poem composed and read by Irvin R. Lindemuth, pastor of the Birming-ham Congregational Church, 25 Carrick Avenue, Pittsburgh, Pa., on Sunday, November 24, 1963:

IN MOURNING AND IN MEMORY OF JOHN F. KENNEDY, PRESIDENT OF THE UNITED STATES—HE WAS ONE MAN

(By Irvin R. Lindemuth, Pastor, Birmingham Congrega-tional Church)

He was one man. Mortal man was he,
With love of life, love of home, love of family,
Love of country, all life means
To all who love it. Many dreams
Were dreamed when he was but a boy.
Perhaps some day, in some strange way, his Nation would
    employ
The very gifts he had to give, the very life he had to live.

War came then, cruel curse of men;
Man became a beast again.
No one wins, when man kills man.
Because man sins, some higher plan
Is needed so that all men gain,
And man can be a man again.
He must have prayed to be unafraid.

Trained and talented, wise
Beyond his years, youth could not disguise
The hopes and dreams of men like him.
Even the Presidency could not dim
The boyish smile, the ruffled hair,
The outstretched hand, the inward prayer.
He was a man of God's own plan.

Religious? Yes, he knew
Religion's teachings, like me, like you.
Many opposed his different faith,
But there is little difference in God's grace.
Men are what they are born in race and creed.
A nation saw the higher need,
Heard him, stirred him.

Let this be said: he, too, was man.
But man is part of God's own plan.
The world today is so ashamed.
Let one more mortal man be named
Among the dead who died that others
Might look on all men as their brothers.
He was one man. Mortal man was he.
But God gives immortality.

Mr. Speaker, under leave to extend my remarks, I include the following television and radio editorial:

THE PRESIDENT'S DEATH

KDKA brings you an expression from Harold C. Lund, vice president of Westinghouse Broadcasting Co., Fred E. Walker, general manager of KDKA–Radio.

President Kennedy is dead. It is a shock to people in Pittsburgh and everywhere throughout our Nation and the world.

Another President, Lincoln, nearly a century ago, died the same way, at the hands of an assassin, fighting for the same cause, the principle on which this Nation was founded, that all men are created equal and entitled to live that way.

We think it appropriate at this time to remember the words of President Lincoln, at Gettysburg—100 years ago. He said and we quote: "We here highly resolve that these dead shall not have died in vain, that this Nation, under God, shall have a new birth of freedom and that government of the people, by the people, for the people, shall not perish from the earth."

President Kennedy was in Texas fighting for that same cause. We fervently hope and pray that his death will hasten the day when all men indeed can live as equals. Then, he shall not have died in vain.

Mr. Speaker, I include the excellent editorial of my longtime friend, John J. Edwards, owner of the West Side News, 229 Wyoming Avenue, Post Office Box 1042, Kingston, Pa., concerning our beloved late President John F. Kennedy. The editorial follows:

One of the most distressing aspects of the untimely death of President John F. Kennedy is the fact that no man on earth had more good to live for than he. His life was dedicated to that which is good and his every effort in public life seemed to be aimed at improvement in the welfare of his fellow human beings. In addition, his personal life promised to go on being an exceptionally happy one.

President Kennedy's personal characteristics were contagious. His vigor, his enthusiasm, his optimism, and his good humor all seemed to have their influence upon his fellow citizens, and certainly they were responsible for his having become so endeared to his fellow citizens.

Always with President Kennedy it was to smile and to keep busy, busy, busy. He had so much to do and so little time that he couldn't even be bothered with a hat and topcoat. He wanted his fellow Americans to be busy also and to be physically fit through exercise. He was the President who had a poet, the late Robert Frost, as a speaker at his inauguration and he and Mrs. Kennedy were active sponsors of music and the arts.

So, his personality and his leadership have left what we hope will prove to be indelible marks on the face of the Nation, and we hope that the high principles for which he stood so firmly will be maintained in our Government and national life.

TRIBUTES BY

Hon. Cornelius E. Gallagher

OF NEW JERSEY

Mr. Speaker, so much has been spoken, so much has been written of the tragedy of November 22—the assassination of a young and beloved President. Most of what was said and written was eloquent and this was to be expected, for John F. Kennedy was a man who by his very nature evoked eloquence.

Much of what men expressed in this period of national grief should be preserved. I would like to include a copy of an editorial written by a friend of his, Mr. Eugene Farrell, that appeared in the Jersey Journal, published in Jersey City, N.J., on November 23, 1963. These are warm and personal words, a remembrance of a great leader not alone for his greatness, but for his own warmth and friendliness, a friendliness that the people of one city like so many cities the world over will cherish for years to come.

JOHN F. KENNEDY

You think all the things an editorial writer is supposed to think, the awful evil of political assassination, the terrible wantonness of it, the incomprehensible fate that lets a demented marksman obliterate a President, but you keep going back to a picture of a young, vital American—President, yes, but a family man like the fellow down the block having fun with the children, weighed down with great affairs, yes, but not so much as to miss the point of a joke and have a good laugh, holder of the most august temporal title, yes, but a man you talk with as easily as you talk to the fellow beside you in the coffee bar.

You keep thinking of when first you met him, before his nomination. It was in Washington and he had just finished a landmark speech to the American Society of Newspaper Editors in which he closed forever the question of a Catholic in the White House; you intercept him as he gets out the door and tell him: "Senator, I'm from the place that is going to give you New Jersey, Hudson County," his eyes light and he says: "Fine, Neil Gallagher has been telling me about it * * * I'm certainly glad to meet you." His handshake is strong, friendly, but he looks so boyish you wonder will the people choose him over Dick Nixon. Then he moves on through the crush. You have had the seconds he can spare.

You see him that fall in Journal Square, a crowd has waited patiently in the November cold, the largest ever packed into the square, they say, finally he arrives, hatless as usual, you have a good view because Arthur Knaster lets you and the photographers use the windows of his law office on the second floor of the Jersey Journal Building. You are just above and behind the grandstand and you see him come up, through the crowd, onto the stand and before the microphone. You remember how that wild hair stands up on the back of his head and think bitterly now: "This is how he must have looked to the murderer through the telescope sight" but that night who could think of him slain? The roar of that crowd as he told them how they would help him win. Then a farewell smile and he is away. This was the final rally of the long outdoor campaign * * * the votes will be all in in little more than 48 hours. When he comes this way again he will be President of the United States.

You remember the telegram just about a year later inviting you to luncheon at the White House with the President. He is host to editors from New Jersey. The guard checking you through, the walk up the drive to the front door, noticing some peeled white paint along the driveway wall. Then into the Blue Room to wait. A few minutes later the President arrives and joins his guests with their cocktails. His is tomato juice. Through luncheon he explains how "this job" keeps him too far from the people. In effect he asks "What do you hear?" The luncheon is lively with questions and answers * * * once he discusses the movie "Advice and Consent," his tone implies he would not have cast Franchot Tone as the President * * * you lean across to him and ask: "Mr. President, you could not get that role?" He laughs and snaps back: "I was too busy." He talks about fallout shelters and world economics and Dick Hughes' chances against Jim Mitchell. He autographs his menu because Marty Gately's hero-worshiping teenager has asked you to bring back a souvenir for her * * * leaving and shaking his hand, you say: "A year ago you were fighting hard to get this job. Now that you have it, what do you think?" * * * suddenly he looks much older, then half whispers: "The weapons. The weapons." * * * and you know why he seems to have an invisible weight always upon him.

And only a few months ago, at another editor's meeting in Washington, a spring evening and cocktails and a reception at the White House * * * he has a light word for everyone in the long line * * * a handshake and a word of greeting passes about Hudson and John Kenny and Bill Flanagan * * * the line moves on * * * without suspecting, you have seen him for the last time * * *

6 months later all that vitality and youth will be exchanged for a madman's bullet * * * and he will be a Commander in Chief slain for his country as truly as any man who ever died earning the Medal of Honor.

Mr. Speaker, eloquent words beyond counting have expressed the sorrow and the deep sense of loss our Nation suffered in the tragic death of President John F. Kennedy. I am inspired by a splendid editorial which appeared on November 25, 1963, in the Jersey Journal, published in Jersey City, N.J. It suggests that perhaps the finest tribute to a great President would be to follow in our daily living the examples he set in his short lifetime and to help put in motion the programs for the betterment of mankind which he proposed. The editorial follows:

A Day To Pray

This day of national mourning is a day to pray.

In churches everywhere there are special services this day in memory of our slain President. It is a way to perpetuate his memory in each one's own heart.

In the last 72 hours a shocked, a grief-stricken people have put forward many ideas to honor his memory. One can be sure that schools, streets, parks, and buildings will be named or renamed for him. He has earned much more than this kind of superficial tribute from all of us, however earnestly we mean it.

The day he took office, he told us: "Ask not what your country can do for you, but what you can do for your country."

There would be our finest tribute to him: To do for our country our very best. To pursue high ideals with vigor and sincerity. To be stanch in times of crisis as he was only 13 months ago when he defused Cuba. To be physically fit, as he wanted us to, perhaps even to be able to walk a bit instead of driving every time there is an errand to the corner. To be intellectually honest with ourselves; doing more than mouthing phrases about equality, actually not running away when interracial preachings must be put into practice. To be the kind of good family man he was—son, husband, father. To enjoy life wholesomely as he did, the arts, culture, hobbies, exercise, sport, afloat and ashore, indoors and out.

It is a day to pray and to hope that something of the good qualities of the man we mourn somehow miraculously will cloak all of us.

TRIBUTE BY

Hon. Edward A. Garmatz

OF MARYLAND

Mr. Speaker, many tributes have been paid to the late President Kennedy and all of them very fitting and certainly well deserved. To these I would like to add one written by Joseph L. Manning, secretary-manager of the Independent Retail Grocers & Meat Dealers Association of Baltimore, and published in their magazine, the Maryland Grocers' Skirmisher.

He Was Like David Facing Goliath

In a way he was like David and the world of unrest was like Goliath. He had no fears—because he knew his cause was a righteous one. He faced the colossal problems that confronted him unafraid. His weapon of right like David's was small in comparison to a vast world of bitterness, hatred and greed. Yet in the short time allotted him, he set down for all of us a pattern of courage and determination to make this a better world to live in. Long after he is gone we will remember that his martyrdom at the hands of an assassin was a flaming, unforgettable page in history. That this assassin, born of despair, fear and hate was but a symbol of the people who did not understand John F. Kennedy's place in history.

It was obvious from the start that this great man who faced death in combat sensed that he was a man of destiny, and that time was running out. Like Lincoln his path of "glory" was blocked by overwhelming burdens and heartaches, yet he always gave the impression that these obstacles were part of the play and that he as the principal actor must always convey to the audience a feeling that the show would go on to a happy ending. His courage and confidence were tremendous in the things he believed were right. He never flinched in facing the trials and tribulations that were his as President of the United States.

There were problems he could have bypassed had he belonged to the lesser greats in our history, but he faced them all head-on because, he believed that his generation was a generation of destiny and that the task though great was a duty that he was sworn to and would carry out. Your secretary was honored and privileged to be in his company on several occasions when he was the U.S. Senator from Massachusetts, and twice after he became President. On every occasion he displayed a warm and friendly spirit and always seemed interested in the other fellow's problems.

I recall so vividly when, as a member of a reception committee, along with Mayor Thomas D'Alesandro, we met the Senator and Mrs. Kennedy at the Friendship Airport and escorted them to the Emerson Hotel where he spoke in behalf of Adlai Stevenson, who was then the Democratic candidate for the Presidency. We drove them to the hotel and it was one of the most pleasant rides I have ever experienced. Both of them acted as if they had known us for years and their manner had all of us at perfect ease.

Another time after he became President, attending the Press Club banquet in Washington, D.C., I had the pleasure of talking to him before the banquet. It was a great thrill that he remembered me and when he asked me about the Friendly Sons of St. Patrick in Baltimore and whether or not I was still rendering Irish songs I, of course, was very happy and overwhelmed and it was a night I shall long remember and cherish.

No man was ever more human and warm than he. And only God knows why he was taken so suddenly from our midst. While we are all aware that his name and memory will be carved eternally in the pages of history, his wife, Jacqueline's name will also be etched beside his. Her courage under fire when her husband was slain at her side, and her fortitude in the ceremonies that followed profoundly touched the hearts of her countrymen. May her shadow never lessen.

As I watched his casket being lowered into the grave on television, his undying words echoed loud and clear: "Ask not what your country can do for you, ask what you can do for your country." Greater love hath no man than to lay down his life for his people.

Most sincerely,

Joseph L. Manning.

TRIBUTE BY

Hon. Robert N. Giaimo

OF CONNECTICUT

Mr. Speaker, under unanimous consent, I would like to include in my remarks a memorial address to our late President by the distinguished mayor of the city of New Haven, the Honorable Richard C. Lee.

This very hall has rung with stirring eulogies to our lamented leader, and I feel that Mayor Lee's is as touching and inspiring as any we have yet heard. From President Kennedy's numerous speeches he has selected a few tremendously pertinent quotations, which suggest to us, as well as quotations can, the essence of the man. I wish to congratulate Mayor Lee on this moving address.

Remarks of Richard C. Lee, Mayor, City of New Haven, at the Memorial Service for President John F. Kennedy, Woolsey Hall, Sunday, November 24, 1963

We gather this afternoon in one of the most solemn moments of American history, for not only has America lost its President, but the free world has lost a great leader, and we—the people of this Nation—have lost a symbol of all that is decent and warm, courageous and dedicated.

None of us in this hour of world tragedy is equipped with the simple eloquence which can express our pain, our anguish, and our sorrow. We can find comfort only in realizing how much he brought to this Nation, and with what courage and dedication he served the cause of freedom and democracy.

John Fitzgerald Kennedy; J.F.K.; Jack; the President of the United States; politician, humanitarian, soldier, father, husband, statesman; but, as well, an articulate and eloquent champion of the rights of free people everywhere.

His words have ringed the world.

Hear him now—January 20, 1961: "In the long history of the world, only a few generations have been granted the role of defending freedom in its hour of maximum danger. I do not shrink from this responsibility; I welcome it. I do not believe that any of us would exchange places with any other people of any other generation. The energy, the faith, the devotion which we bring to this endeavor will light our country and all who serve it, and the glow from that fire can truly light the world."

In 1956, in "Profiles in Courage" "without belittling the courage with which men have died, we should not forget those acts of courage with which men * * * have lived. The courage of life is often a less dramatic spectacle than the courage of a final moment; but it is no less a magnificent mixture of triumph and tragedy. A man does what he must—in spite of personal consequence, in spite of obstacles and dangers and pressures—and that is the basis of all human morality."

And then, again, written as if to offer us now on this day of national tragedy, in this hour of our grief, these words:

"To be courageous * * * requires no exceptional qualifications, no magic formula, no special combination of time, place, and circumstance. It is an opportunity that sooner or later is presented to us all. Politics merely furnishes one arena which imposes special tests of courage. In whatever arena of life one may meet the challenge of courage, whatever may be the sacrifices he faces if he follows his conscience—the loss of his friends, his fortune, his contentment, even the esteem of his fellow men—each man must decide for himself the course he will follow. The stories of past courage can define that ingredient—they can teach, they can offer hope, they can provide inspiration. But they cannot supply courage itself. For this, each man must look into his own soul."

On January 9, 1961, as President-elect of the United States of America, he appeared before the State legislature of his home State of Massachusetts. In discussing the challenge before public servants, he summarized his own credo in these few lines as he approached the office which would lead, ultimately, to his death:

"Courage, judgment, integrity, dedication * * * these are the qualities which, with God's help, this son of Massachusetts hopes will characterize our government's conduct in the 4 stormy years that lie ahead. Humbly I ask His help in this undertaking; but aware that on earth His will is worked by men, I ask for your help and your prayers as I embark on this new and solemn journey."

But perhaps more symbolic even of what he believed, of how he spoke, are these words of January 20, 1961:

"And if a beachhead of cooperation may push back the jungle of suspicion, let both sides join in creating a new endeavor, not a new balance of power, but a new world of law, where the strong are just and the weak secure and the peace preserved.

"All this will not be finished in the first 100 days. Nor will it be finished in the first 1,000 days, nor in the life of this administration, nor even perhaps in our lifetime on this planet. But let us begin."

In the words of the Secretary of War in the administration of Abraham Lincoln, "Now he belongs to the ages."

And we who remain behind, seeking solace, and comfort, and inspiration, hear, again, what he offered to us just 3 short years ago as advice and counsel:

"In your hands, my fellow citizens, more than mine, will rest the final success or failure of our course. Since this country was founded, each generation of Americans has been summoned to give testimony to its national loyalty. The graves of young Americans who answered the call to service surround the globe.

"Now the trumpet summons us again—not as a call to bear arms, though arms we need; not as a call to battle, though embattled we are; but a call to bear the burden of a long twilight struggle, year in and year out, 'rejoicing in hope, patient in tribulation,' a struggle against the common enemies of man: tyranny, poverty, disease and war itself."

Everyone has his cherished memory of the President. Some of these memories are widely shared with millions of Americans. Others are not so widely known. I give you, from among my memories, one of his favorite bits of history, as he recounted it in one of his early addresses in Connecticut some years ago.

Then a Member of the U.S. Senate, he was talking of public service and dedication, of the necessity for choosing as elected leaders people who would lead, people who believed in the cause of justice and freedom, people indefatigable in their pursuit of that which was right and good and necessary for America. His words were these:

"Long years ago—indeed, in another century—this was stated well by one of the Founding Fathers of the then tiny democratic nation of Colonial States. The century was the 18th; the year was 1780; the time of the day was noon, when, suddenly, over the city of Hartford, Conn.— then a little town—the sky began to blacken, and by 3 in the afternoon, it was as dark as night.

"Many people of devout and passionate religious beliefs thought then that the day of judgment had arrived, and prepared themselves to meet their Maker. On this day, the Connecticut House of Delegates was in session, and some of the more religious of their members thought, in deference to this day of judgment, that the House should adjourn. But the Speaker of the House, Colonel Davenport, rose to his feet, and addressed the members as follows:

" 'Gentlemen, the day of judgment is either here, or it is not. If it is not, there is no cause for alarm. If the day of judgment is here, I prefer to be found at my duty. Mr. Clerk, bring candles and let us proceed.' "

Ladies and gentlemen, on Friday, November 22, the day of judgment arrived for the President of the United States. He was found at his duty. May he rest in peace.

TRIBUTES BY

Hon. Edith Green

OF OREGON

Mr. Speaker, as the tributes to John F. Kennedy continue to pour across my desk, it is apparent that his memory, above all else, is associated with the fight against the forces of hatred and bigotry. Over and over again runs the theme of bitter sorrow combined with newly formed or renewed determination to join that battle he so gallantly led. The tribute sent me on behalf of 250 members of the Oregon chapter of the National Association of Claimants' Counsel of America eloquently summarizes the substance of hundreds of grieving messages.

A TRIBUTE TO THE SPIRIT AND MEMORY OF JOHN FITZGERALD KENNEDY

The assassination of John F. Kennedy on Friday, November 22, stunned and shocked men of good will everywhere. The memory of his brutal, high-noon, murder while riding in a motorcade on the streets of Dallas, Tex., will remain with each of us until the end of our days. We will long remember where we were and what we were doing when we learned of the shooting.

The initial impact of the news was often disbelief that such a thing could come to pass. As disbelief was dispelled by stark reality—then a hope and a prayer that the wounds were not serious or fatal—a hope that soon was ended by the announcement that "The President Is Dead."

John F. Kennedy—the 35th President of the United States—the youngest man ever elected to that high office—the leader of all our people—a man young in vitality, wit, charm, and zest—a man devoted to freedom and to the dignity of all men everywhere of every race, color, or creed—was dead. The litany of what he stood for and fought for could go on. But it would be a litany for the dead as John F. Kennedy had just been spun off from the midst of the living by two blasts from a rifle. A rifle that had been shot from the six-story ambush of a city warehouse on a sunny November day in Dallas, Tex.

The forces of evil (whatever they might later prove to be) had triumphed over the forces of good.

The pallor of profound grief spread over the world to the very edges of Red China. Yet, within 48 hours, this profound grief was to be shattered by the bizarre and by the ugly as the alleged assassin was himself gunned down and murdered in the basement of the Dallas city jail. And all within sight of millions of TV watchers as they sat in their living rooms on that Sunday morning. Violence and hatred on top of violence and hatred.

A little more than a week ago, John F. Kennedy was laid to rest in Arlington National Cemetery. You and I have now had time to recollect on that awesome and awful long weekend in November. You and I, as lawyers and citizens, have seen not only brutal murders, but we have witnessed the hateful shattering of two great principles—the integrity of the Presidency of the United States and the integrity of due process of law. These two institutions—orderly democratic government and due process of law—are the foundations of our noble profession.

We, of all men, should be in the forefront to protect and promote these fundamentals of the good life. This we can do as lawyers and as men of good will. It is not a program for the other fellow. It is a program for you

and for me. That is for whom this bell tolls. It is a personal dedication. A dedication that we will not remain silent or inactive when we hear words or see deeds or acts of hatred and bigotry. Let us resolve that the dignity of man is not only an ideal. It is our way of life.

In the year 1963, the flowers of evil have bloomed. They have bloomed for the ambushed Medgar Evers in Mississippi. They have bloomed for the four little bombed Sunday School children in Birmingham. They have bloomed for those generous and noble law school students who, last summer, were harassed in the South while trying to gain the Negroes' constitutional rights to vote. And now les fleurs de mal have bloomed for John F. Kennedy.

In the year 1964, may the flowers of evil wither on the vine.

To John Fitzgerald Kennedy, let us reverently say: Requiescat in pace.

To ourselves, let us resolutely say: May we not rest in peace until we have fulfilled our resolution to run the good race against hatred, prejudice, and bigotry in all their evil forms and shapes.

JIM KENNEDY,
President, Oregon Chapter of NACCA.

Mr. Speaker, the shot heard round the world in 1963 carried sorrow to every corner of the earth. To those Americans in foreign lands November 22 brought to their lives a special agony. Far from home and friends, standing on alien ground, it must indeed have seemed for a moment as though they, too, had been dealt a fatal blow. But then the ragged edges of grief were made endurable by the spontaneous, embracing, warm and healing sympathy of newly found friends. Under unanimous consent, Mr. Speaker, I would like to include the memorial tribute of one such American to his late President, John F. Kennedy. It was presented at a Thanksgiving Day service in Indonesia by Monroe Sweetland, of Portland, Oreg., now professor at the Universitas Padjadjaran.

JOHN FITZGERALD KENNEDY—IN MEMORIAM

Among the favorite quotations of John F. Kennedy, 35th President of the United States, are the lines from his New England friend Robert Frost.

"The woods are lovely, dark and deep.
But I have promises to keep—
And miles to go before I sleep."

In his few crowded years our late President keenly relished life itself and lived it fully—the woods of life were, for him, "lovely, dark, and deep." How resolutely he fulfilled his promise. He went many, many miles indeed before the end—and now he sleeps.

There is no need to dwell today on the utter tragedy, the circumstances of his death, nor even the poignancy of this heartbreaking event. Every person feels these facts acutely as a wounded nation, and the whole world pours out its emotion in sympathy to the shattered family—to Mrs. Kennedy and the children, to his father and mother, his grandmother, his brothers and sisters.

We Americans react alike on few occasions, but this is one of those few. Emotions of shock, grief, humiliation, disbelief, anger, outrage, and helplessness are commingled in all of us. Differences of party and principle are merged. We react as Americans—but we in Bandung react as a very special group of Americans in a foreign land, doubly sensitive to the implications of this week, terrible for our Nation and, for its relationships with other peoples.

There is one acknowledgment to be made this day—on this Thanksgiving Day—which I know is in the hearts of all Americans here. This is to voice our deep gratitude to the people of Indonesia for the outpouring of regret and sympathy given to each of us. To an amazing extent the warmth and vitality of the Kennedy personality had radiated deep into the ranks of the people around us. We Americans can never forget the visits to our homes which began as the tragic word from Texas was broadcast, the throng which overflowed the memorial Mass, and even the passers-by on the street or on the campus who grasped our hand to say a few words of respect and regret. These are a measure of American prestige and influence, to be sure, but even more, they measure the extent to which John F. Kennedy was able to project his sincerity, warmth, and genuine interest in people. Seldom has the leader of a nation had this special endowment in so generous a portion. In a few short years the image of leadership of the free world has been given warmth and character, symbolized by this young man in a world where every other major state is led by men a generation his senior.

The warmhearted genius of this great American was not a mere happy accident. Born into a family of wealth and position, he might have chosen a life of affluent indolence. But some inner purpose motivated him from early years toward public life and service. He studied at Harvard and at London School of Economics. He learned much of statecraft from his father's years as U.S. Ambassador at the Court of St. James. He learned of practical politics from his mother's remarkable family, observing what was good and what was to be avoided in State and local government in turbulent Boston.

He won a seat in Congress as a very young man, proceeding to the U.S. Senate where he quickly became one of its most effective Members. In 1956 he very nearly won the Democratic nomination for Vice President, and in 1960 he won each of the seven hard-fought primary elections which he entered. This led to his nomination, and in November 1960, he broke traditions all along the line to win election as our 35th President.

As President of the most powerful Nation on our earth and the acknowledged leader of the free world it would be easy for the people of the free world to regard him as an institution. But somehow he was able to come through in the public mind as a man—a man capable of love, mistakes, humor, pain, anger, joy, and sorrow. He had known, in common with many of his generation the world around, the horror, degradation, and futility and personal agony of war. His own heroism, his demonstrated physical and moral courage, were fused in the terrors of battle and death.

In his adult years John F. Kennedy had the security and happiness of marriage to a truly exceptional woman. Together they knew the joys and sorrows of parenthood. Jacqueline Bouvier Kennedy has given a new dimension to the role of First Lady. Her beauty, her youth, her grace, talent, and culture add brilliant luster to the legend of the White House family at home and abroad. For John F. Kennedy, the man, those who knew him personally will be forever thankful that his years were shared in love and companionship with this woman. Her courage and dignity today would be a source of great pride to her husband. Indeed, an epilog to John F. Kennedy's best-selling book "Profiles of Courage," in which he reviewed the lives of brave American men, might well be inscribed now to his magnificent young widow.

Only history will be our judge, as John F. Kennedy said on January 20, 1961, as he took his oath of office. But already it is apparent that in less than 3 years the leadership of this young man has indeed established new frontiers—has lifted up the horizons of his own people and of all men, everywhere. Two profound achievements have already been established in history as the torch is passed to his trusted successor, President Lyndon B. Johnson:

First, the trend toward mutual atomic annihilation has been halted by a treaty between the two powers possessing massive atomic capacity.

Second, the full strength and moral leadership of the Presidency has been thrown into the ending of legalized segregation and discrimination under the flag of freedom. Racialism has been the most insulting and offensive defect in our national image, the most vulnerable weakness in our leadership of freemen. In Indonesia and among the large majority of mankind the suspicion of racial arrogance attached to us Americans as to our European cousins, with echoes from the oppressive days of colonialism and imperialism sounding down the years. Now an American President has renewed the appeal of American democracy at home and leadership abroad as he has thrown the moral strength of his leadership into the balance on behalf of freedom. On this basic point I will read you the concluding lines of his stirring and practical message to Congress on June 19, outlining his civil rights proposals:

"I ask every Member of Congress to set aside sectional and political ties, and to look at this issue from the viewpoint of the Nation. I ask you to look into your hearts—not in search of charity, for the Negro neither wants nor needs condescension—but for the one plain, proud, and priceless quality that unites us all as Americans: a sense of justice. In this year of the Emancipation centennial, justice requires us to insure the blessings of liberty to all Americans and their posterity, not merely for reasons of economic efficiency, world diplomacy and domestic tranquillity, but, above all, because it is right."

As Americans on this Thanksgiving Day we may be

thankful, too, for many other legacies from the brief years of our young President. Already written into the patriotic adages of America was his ringing challenge in the inaugural address: "Ask not what can your country do for you, but what can you do for your country." And out of that concept came the American Peace Corps with a capability for good which has even now only begun to be developed.

On the occasion, only 3 weeks ago, of the 1963 award by the Protestant Council to President Kennedy as having made this year's most profound contribution to the family of man, the President discussed our obligations as Americans around the world. Every single one of us Americans in Indonesia and in southeast Asia is involved in the implications of his address on that occasion. In conclusion I will excerpt some of the stirring words from that address, in the President's own effective and personal style, for their pertinence to our work here, and the future of our Nation in the world.

"The family of man is not limited to a single race or religion, neither can it be limited to a single city or country. The family of man is more than 3 billion strong. It lives in more than 100 nations. Most of its members are not white. Most of them are not Christian. Most of them know nothing about free enterprise or due process or the Australian ballot. If we are to promote the family of man, let us examine the magnitude of our task." (He then reviewed the major factors of the task as he sees them.)

Then he concludes:

"Some say they are tiring of this task, are tired of world problems, are tired of hearing that those who receive our aid disagree with our diplomacy. But what kind of a spirit is that? Are we tired of living in a free world? Do we expect to make it over in our own image? Are we going to quit now because there are problems not yet solved?

"Surely the Americans of the 1960's can do half as well as the Americans of the 1950's. Surely we are not going to throw away our hopes and means for peaceful progress in an outburst of petty irritation and frustration.

"My fellow Americans: Let us be guided by our interests, not our indignation. Let us heed the words of Paul the Apostle to the Galatians: 'Let us not be weary in well-doing', he wrote, 'for in due season we shall reap, if we faint not.' Let the word go forth—to all who are concerned about the future of the human family—that we will not be weary in well-doing and we will faint not; and we shall, in due season, reap a harvest of peace and security for all members of the family of man."

We Americans indeed live a good life, perhaps the freest and healthiest and best on the globe. For this, on our Thanksgiving Day, we are grateful. But we are thankful, too, that men like John Fitzgerald Kennedy can rise up amongst us, help us to be true to the best in our rich traditions.

Surrounded by the good life, we Americans find the woods around us, in the words of Robert Frost, "are lovely, dark, and deep." But as a nation and a people we, too, "have promises to keep—and miles to go before we sleep."

TRIBUTE BY

Hon. William J. Green, Jr.

OF PENNSYLVANIA

Mr. Speaker, the tragic death of our late President, John F. Kennedy, has left upon this Nation a shock that will prevail for generations to come.

It was particularly felt by our youth of standing age. In their display of love and reverence for our youthful President who represented the ideals they cherished and hope for in mature life. In the shadows of his glowing consideration for our national youth, as indeed for children of other lands, many have become creative in their individual rights, as did Catherine Kennedy Haugh, of Philadelphia, who contributed her beautiful poem, "Even Heaven Cried," to the memory of a noble and dedicated man.

EVEN HEAVEN CRIED

She looked upon a lady
   Standing tall in pride
But standing all alone
   And even Heaven cried.

She looked upon a little girl
   Who had stood at his side
Who'd lost the one to teach her
   And even Heaven cried.

She looked upon a little son
   So proud and starry eyed
Who didn't know how much he'd lost
   And even Heaven cried.

She looked upon a nation
   Whose tears could not be dried
Such waste, such shame, such pain, such grief
   And even Heaven cried.
           —CATHERINE KENNEDY HAUGH.

PHILADELPHIA, PA., *November 23, 1963.*

Mr. Speaker, as national consternation and grief emanating from the sudden and tragic death of the beloved John F. Kennedy subsides into a period of meditation and composure, we review with wonder and amazement the tremendous impact this courageous and dedicated President had on people of all ages and in all walks of life.

It was a dedicated personal feeling, sufficiently close that his departure was akin to the loss of an immediate member of one's own family.

Such expression was deeply and personally felt by all those fortunate enough to be present when a young priest, Father O'Malley, delivered the following eulogy to the late President during a late November retreat at Woodstock College, Md.

JOHN F. KENNEDY

There was a man sent by God, whose name was John. * * * He was not the light, but—in his way—he gave testimony to the light.

Perhaps the spirit of this weekend is captured best by A. E. Housman's poem to an athlete, dying young:

> "The time you won your town the race.
> We chaired you through the market-place;
> Man and boy stood cheering by,
> And home we brought you, shoulder-high.
>
> Today, the road all runners come.
> Shoulder-high we bring you home,
> And set you at your threshold down,
> Townsman of a stiller town."

I don't know whether you cried on Friday. I'm not ashamed to say I did. I don't know why. I didn't really want to. I didn't really know him. And yet, somehow, he was mine.

I suppose this possessive feeling is the result of a kind of cruelty of the press, that opens up a prominent man's life and lets us enter, and know him, and love him. It was strange to me—and almost irritating—that when I heard the news I realized that, at the very moment of his death, I had been looking at pictures of the President, beaming at his little boy. And I had thought to myself, "Yes. That's it. That's what a man looks like."

At first, the news had to be untrue. It was like watching a great athlete stop in the middle of a race, and turn and walk away. It was too big to take in, all at once. And I began to realize a little of what Peter must have felt that night in the garden, when he saw the first torches coming through the trees—This isn't happening. There were all those palms and all those voices crying Hosannah. He's too young. He's too good. We love him.

And then, when the news became undeniable, the question became—Why? Why a good God could allow such a monstrous thing to happen.

TRIBUTES BY

Hon. James A. Haley

OF FLORIDA

Mr. Speaker, with permission to extend my remarks, I would like to include a prayer which was a part of a special requiem mass said for the late President Kennedy at the Church of the Epiphany, Venice, Fla., on November 24, 1963.

JOHN F. KENNEDY, PRESIDENT OF THE UNITED STATES

As a fruit of exceptional beauty and promise is plucked from the tree before it has reached the peak of its destined maturity so has our President been shorn of life as he ascended steadily and surely the ladder of greatness.

This man—in the very prime of life—with vast intellectual powers, remarkable gifts of personality and a comprehension of history and the Presidency that few possess has been snatched from us. It leaves us stunned and shocked beyond the power to express.

A thousand and one lessons will come home to us in the days to come. The eternal question of "it might have been * * *" will restlessly turn up in our thinking. If I may interject one small thought among the many that will cross your mind; How much more important it is to express our loyalty, our fidelity, our allegiance, our devotion, our affection, our cooperation, our love for our leaders while they are with us. When the all-knowing hand of God takes a soul unto himself with numbing suddenness we poor humans grope to express our grief and our sense of loss and we hasten to display our fealty and dedication. The feelings of love, devotion, respect, honor and loyalty that have hidden deep within us bubble forth in a great physical outpouring. Yet think how we could have eased that awesome burden of responsibility on his shoulders had we but expressed these feelings in proper time.

May the noble example of this dedicated man inspire in this Nation a renewal of those eternal Christian truths and those American qualities that he knew so well and which he exemplified with such distinction.

May Almighty God grant him eternal happiness in Heaven.

Mr. Speaker, with permission to extend my remarks, I would like to include a eulogy which was a part of a special requiem Mass which was said for our late President, John Fitzgerald Kennedy, at St. Raphael's Church, Englewood, Fla., on November 25, 1963.

A whole nation and all the world mourns today the untimely death of John F. Kennedy, late President of the United States. He loved his country, he loved its people, he loved humanity. John F. Kennedy is dead, but the spirit of John F. Kennedy will go on forever. He fought for his country in war. He fought for justice and the rights of all people, including his own. He waged a battle for peace and went down fighting with flags flying and bands beating.

Greater love than this hath no man than that a man lay down his life for his friends. The world and the Nation are thankful to God this day in the midst of its tears and desolation. Thankful to God are we for the noble, courageous, and generous soul, who gave everything—even his life—that men and women everywhere be happier, more abundant and live in harmony with their fellow men. His great belief in the brotherhood of man and the fatherhood of God is his rich heritage to all men of good will. All right thinking people must surely realize the deep, abiding conviction that possesses the soul of this great leader.

Today our hearts reach out and only ask him, as he meets his Maker face to face to pray for a grief stricken Nation that God may guide its destinies in the hands of another great American, Lyndon B. Johnson. May we pray fervently that God who in His inscrutable ways has seen fit to take our President in his best years, comfort and console his wife, the parents, the loved ones of this just man. May God help us remove from our midst hatred and bitterness against which John F. Kennedy fought so hard. To him it was a greater challenge, a more glorious battle than the PT boat 109 battle of World War II. There he had to fight for justice, for liberty and for peace. He fought for them nobly, against all opposition, as President of the United States. His was a dedicated life, a life spent for others. He knew what suffering was, and did his best for the sick. The underprivileged of the world were near to his heart. He had one hate—injustice. He had one love—peace.

Were he to speak this morning, he would probably say to us, "Grieve not, let not your hearts be troubled, justice will prevail, peace can be achieved. Preach it from the pulpits, say it in the streets, shout it in your hearts and homes—justice will conquer injustice, love will destroy hate, tolerance will win over intolerance, that the peace of Christ may reign forever in nations as well as in men."

May the soul of John F. Kennedy find that peace in death that he so ardently fought for in life. May his soul rest in the eternal splendor of God. He has fought the good fight, he has finished his course, he has kept the faith. Well done thou good and faithful servant, because you have been faithful over a few things, I will place thee over many. Enter John Fitzgerald Kennedy, President of the United States, into the joys of the Lord.

TRIBUTE BY

Hon. Wayne L. Hays

OF OHIO

Mr. Speaker, under the leave to extend my remarks, I include the following poem written in memory of the late President John F. Kennedy by Miss Marty Hale, the "Old Spinner," of Steubenville, Ohio:

IN MEMORY OF JOHN F. KENNEDY: HE PASSED OUR WAY

He passed our way and left for us a smile,
    A handshake that was friendly and sincere.
There seemed no barriers nor wall between,
    He had a voice that seemed to draw us near;

Not a sophisticate with put-on airs,
    A manner that was warm and down to earth,
These were the sort of things we loved him for,
    The thing for which the whole world knew his worth;

Our leader and our friend he went his way.
    And left us saddened as we saw him go;
A wave of hand, a smile and he was gone,
    His country stunned beneath the crushing blow.

With heart and soul he sought to do God's will;
    And as we watched his cortege pass today,
With silent prayer for those he left behind,
    We thanked the good Lord that he passed our way.

He passed our way and left his legacy,
    A touch of God we had not known before;
The years will find the world remembering
    His own to love his name forevermore.

He left for us the will to carry on,
    And right the wrongs for which our country cries.
His dauntless spirit will keep urging us,
    Like the eternal flame that never dies.

His loved America will dry her tears.
    Another hand will carry on, his way;
And as we strive our hearts repeat these words,
    The world is better that he passed our way.
                                    MARTY HALE.

TRIBUTE BY

Hon. James C. Healey

OF NEW YORK

Mr. Speaker, with permission, I would like to include in my remarks a very splendid eulogy to our beloved late President, John F. Kennedy, which was delivered by Attorney Louis L. Schwartz at the memorial services at the Jewish Center of Highbridge, 1178 Nelson Avenue, Bronx, New York, N.Y., on Monday, November 25, 1963. Mr. Schwartz, a long-time friend of mine, is the very able president of the Jewish Center of Highbridge, in my congressional district. Rabbi Nathan Taragin, also a very dear friend, is spiritual leader of the center and, in addition, is chaplain of the Lebanon and Morrisania City Hospitals. I am pleased to include the eulogy which follows:

MEMORIAL SERVICES IN TRIBUTE TO JOHN FITZGERALD KENNEDY, MONDAY, NOVEMBER 25, 1963

(By Louis L. Schwartz, Esq.)

One hundred years ago, our Nation was torn asunder by ideological differences which were then being tested on the field of battle; hundreds of thousands were engaged to determine whether this Nation under God will survive.

It finally culminated in eventual success after a titanic struggle for the rebirth of a new Nation, dedicated to the proposition, among other things, that all men are created equal.

But as the Nation celebrated its rebirth of freedom and began its task of rebinding its wounds, an assassin's bullet cut down its leader, raising passions to new heights and making the task more difficult.

But the dead past buried its dead; the Nation's wounds were healed, and progress and prosperity rose our Nation to the greatest in world leadership.

As our Nation was torn asunder by two different ideologies over a century ago, so we find the entire world at this time, gripped in violent passions of two schools of political and economic beliefs.

Into this world was thrust John Fitzgerald Kennedy, 35th President of the United States; young (he was but 43 years of age when inaugurated), full of vigor, highly educated and from a family of great wealth, he soon met the challenge; he overcame the handicap that sometimes come to persons of extreme wealth and immediately sought to improve the lot of oppressed and economically deprived people all over the world. He inaugurated a worldwide system of self-help by sending thousands of our young people all over the four corners of the world as a Peace Corps army to train natives of economically backward countries to develop themselves and raise their standards of living, production, education, and sanitation.

On the domestic front, we will remember him well for his struggle to bring adequate medical care to all our elderly citizens in a broad program of social medical insurance.

We will always remember him for being one of the greatest champions of civil liberties, equality of opportunity in jobs, homes, education, and public places, for peoples of all faiths, national origin or color.

Himself the first President of the United States of a minority religious belief, he was soon put to the test of meeting issues in which his own religious followers differed from the construction of our constitutional separation of church and state, and he showed his greatness by adhering to the accepted principles of law enunciated by the Supreme Court of the United States as being the last word on the subject.

In the great crisis of the internal affairs of the Vietnam Government, he was foremost in demanding that as a condition for further financial support from our Government, religious liberty be restored to the peoples of that unfortunate country.

For many months, he watched, in silence, the reports of the vast fleet of Russian ships entering Cuba, just 40 miles south of the Florida peninsula, for the so-called purpose of bringing in supplies to build a new seaport in Cuba. When the final acts of installations were completed and discovered to be the construction of missile bases to launch atomic weapons at the United States and the Panama Canal, he stood up to Khrushchev with the solemn warning that either these bases be dismantled and removed, or else face the fierce consequences of meeting the might of American power.

That he was solely devoted to bring peace to this troubled world is strongly borne out by the record; he knew war—its bitterness and consequences—for he, himself, was in the midst of it (almost at the cost of his own life).

At his inaugural he said:

"Let the word go forth from this time and place to friend and foe alike, that the torch has been passed to a new generation of Americans—born in this century, tempered by war, disciplined by a hard and bitter peace, proud of our ancient heritage—and unwilling to witness or permit the slow undoing of those human rights to which this Nation has always been committed, and to which we are committed today at home and around the world."

He had put full meaning into these words by looking for every avenue open, and to explore every opportunity in the cause of peace. In his crusade for peace he entered into negotiations that led to the eventual agreement banning nuclear explosions in the atmosphere, and the construction of a direct line of communications between the White House and the Kremlin to prevent an accidental war.

The test ban treaty was Mr. Kennedy's monumental achievement on the long road ahead of us toward peace and disarmament.

While it is a beacon in a stormy sea, his untimely passing ended his efforts to further calm the angry waters of discontent still manifest in the world today. The light of reason all over the world was extinguished by the sudden snap of a trigger, but search for everlasting peace must never end.

He was cut down in the prime of his life and far from giving us the greatest in him; he had known personal losses and tragedy—the loss of his brother in the service of our country, the serious illness of his father, and the recent loss of a newly born son—yet with all his personal sorrows, he kept those to himself and never let them interfere with the affairs of state; truly the mark of a great man, one of strength and character; he maintained his winning smile and his affability all during his personal trials and tribulations.

Now, we have met in the hour of our great loss and affliction, first to pay homage of love to the memory of our great leader and secondly to seek peace within our own souls; to see if we can find the solutions to the problems which bore so heavily on the shoulders of John F. Kennedy.

His words, uttered at his inaugural, still resound in the minds and memory of all who witnessed the event on television:

"In the long history of the world only a few generations have been granted the role of defending freedom in its hour of maximum danger. I do not shrink from this responsibility; I welcome it. I do not believe that any of us would exchange places with any other people or any other generation. The energy, the faith, the devotion which we bring to the endeavor will light our country and all who serve it, and the glow from that fire can truly light the world. * * * Ask not what your country can do for you, ask what you can do for your country."

We, therefore, the Jewish Center of Highbridge, in mourning the tragic loss of John Fitzgerald Kennedy, 35th President of the United States of America, assembled in public worship, now pledge ourselves, in his honor and blessed memory, to carry his ideals on a new sense of purpose to the American people; to remove the shackles of hatred and violence that has poisoned the minds and hearts of some of our people; that the birth of freedom, gained 100 years ago on the field of battle shall inure to all our peoples, of all faiths, national origin, cultures, and color, and that all men shall walk with their heads erect in the image of God.

TRIBUTE BY

Hon. Robert W. Hemphill

OF SOUTH CAROLINA

Mr. Speaker, under leave to extend my remarks, I include an article written by Mr. Jim Oliphant, and published in the Spartanburg Journal:

IN SPRING THE NEW, TENDER MOUND WILL HAVE A COAT OF IRISH GREEN

(NOTE.—Herald State Editor Jim Oliphant traveled to Washington to report on President Kennedy's funeral. Here, in brief requiem, is his tribute to a man named Kennedy.)

(By Jim Oliphant)

ARLINGTON CEMETERY.—I would like to come again to this sloping hillside and gaze once more across the river to where he used to live, where there was a happy game on a wide, wide lawn and where there were smiles instead of tears.

I would choose springtime, not fall, to climb this hill and see where a man named Kennedy found a resting place.

Perhaps then the grief would not be so tight and the tender mound of earth that covers the man named Kennedy will carry a coat of Irish green.

I would choose a quiet Sabbath afternoon to wind through these drives past the olive-drab bell tower when the barren old oak just below this hallowed ground would once again show its color.

It would be good to come here when the sound of hoofbeats does not bring tears and a black riderless horse does not deepen the lump that is 2 days old in the throat.

I would like to mingle among the warriors resting here without being stifled with sorrow at the sound of a far-off bugle. Only a quiet visit would I want, just a

little while and then go back down the hill and watch the river flow its endless route.

It would be good to walk along Washington streets—down Pennsylvania Avenue—and see people smile, not weep, and perhaps that time will come although it now seems so far away.

Give me a day when a little girl named Caroline and her brother John, a little older perhaps, can smile again as they walk in other places with a beautifully brave mother named Jacqueline.

Let me come back some day to listen again to the bird song in the trees when the boom of cannon doesn't slice the heart to shreds.

But don't let me forget a chill November afternoon when the six gray horses pulled the ancient caisson and its flag-covered casket to the foot of the hill and a widowed mother found relief in tears.

I would want to forget the reasons that brought him here, remembering rather the wonderful and vast throng that sorrowed as one and remained faithful to the end to the man they called their own.

TRIBUTE BY

Hon. A. Sydney Herlong, Jr.

OF FLORIDA

Mr. Speaker, under leave to extend my remarks, I would like to include a letter written to the entire student body of Mainland Junior High School of Daytona Beach, Fla., by my friend John F. May, the principal.

Mr. May periodically communicates with the students with such letters. His latest letter went to the students on Monday, November 25, and I commend it to the Congress as a well-written and thoughtful commentary:

NOVEMBER 25, 1963.

DEAR STUDENTS OF MAINLAND JUNIOR HIGH SCHOOL: I am writing this letter to each of you, hoping that you will read it and keep it for many years to always remind you of what a privilege it is to be an American and the responsibilities that go with it.

You have lived the past 3 days in what will probably go down in history as the most disgraceful days of our great country.

We were thinking toward Thursday and another Thanksgiving Day, which started in 1621 by the Pilgrim Gov. William Bradford, when news came that our President had been shot. This should cause us to be ever more thankful that we live in a nation where great men give their lives for their country.

I would like to point out to you that since our first President, George Washington, was elected on April 30,

1789, we have had four of our Presidents assassinated, and all four of the assassins had many things in common. Most of all they carried hate and bigotry in their hearts.

The first President assassinated was Abraham Lincoln by John Wilkes Booth in Washington, D.C. John Wilkes Booth shot and killed President Lincoln because of his stand against the South during the Civil War.

The second President assassinated was James Abram Garfield by Charles Julius Giuteau in Washington, D.C., by a disappointed officeseeker who had wanted to be appointed U.S. Consul to Paris.

The third President assassinated was William McKinley in Buffalo, N.Y., by Leon Czolgosz, a factory worker who was an anarchist. An anarchist is a person who wants to overthrow an established government and live without laws.

The fourth and last President assassinated was John Fitzgerald Kennedy in Dallas, Tex. The alleged assassin was Lee Harvey Oswald, a professed Communist who also held a grudge against our form of government and had been given an undesirable discharge from the Marine Corps.

In a study of all four assassins we find that there was hate and bigotry in their lives and they had a resentment toward our democratic form of government.

John Wilkes Booth resented President Lincoln because he tried to preserve the Union and had to take a stand against the South. He was an actor in bad health and without a regular job. This hate for the President and our Government led him to murder.

Charles Julius Guiteau shot President Garfield because he did not get the position he wanted so his hate drove him to commit murder.

Leon Czolgosz shot President McKinley because he did not respect our form of government and by shooting our President he felt he could overcome much of the hate in his heart.

Through Lee Oswald I hope you students will learn a lesson that will remain with you throughout life. The teachers and I are continuously trying to get you to be better citizens and to prepare yourself for life. Lee Oswald is an example of a student that had a distaste for school. He quit school at an early age and then blamed our country for his not being able to make a living. He, himself, was not accepted in our society because he would not let people help him.

We try so hard to teach you to be good students, to accept your neighbors, to live with each other and to accept your position in life. There is too much hate in our everyday life where there should be more love for our fellow man.

I hope and pray that each of you will not let President Kennedy's life be lost in vain. I sincerely believe that had Lee Oswald had the proper training in school and church that we would not be grieving the loss of our President.

Always remember the words of President John F. Kennedy in his inaugural address when he said, "Don't ask what your country can do for you, but what you can do for your country."

A fellow American,

JOHN T. MAY.

TRIBUTE BY

Hon. Elmer J. Holland

OF PENNSYLVANIA

Mr. Speaker, I would like to include in my remarks two eulogies for our late President, John F. Kennedy, that were delivered and printed in the 20th Congressional District of Pennsylvania shortly after the tragic passing of our President.

The November 28 issue of the Greek Catholic Union Messenger, published in Homestead, Pa., was dedicated to President John F. Kennedy.

The editor, Michael Roman, was the author of the eulogy which I believe expresses fully the innermost feelings of the Greek Catholic community and their intent to carry forward the ideals of our late President.

At the memorial services held at St. John's Byzantine Catholic Cathedral in Munhall, Pa., on November 25, the Very Reverend Monsignor Basil N. Smochko, S.T.D., delivered a noteworthy review of John Kennedy's life and his contribution—during his short stay in this world—to all of mankind regardless of color, of creed, of nationality. His words show the great respect and great love the people of the Byzantine Catholic community have for John Kennedy—and for the Office of the Presidency by their prayers for the new President which are offered in sincerity and high esteem.

MAY ALMIGHTY GOD GRANT PRESIDENT JOHN F. KENNEDY ETERNAL REST AND BLISSFUL REPOSE

(Text of eulogy delivered on November 25, 1963, by Very Rev. Monsignor Basil N. Smochko, S.T.D., vicar general of Pittsburgh diocese.)

My dear friends in Christ, at this hour of national grief over the tragic death of our beloved President, John Fitzgerald Kennedy, it is befitting to draw inspiration from the words of our blessed Saviour, when He said, "Blessed are the peacemakers, for theirs is the kingdom of Heaven."

John F. Kennedy, the first Catholic President of the United States of America, will go down in history as the peacemaker of humanity. In the acceptance and fulfillment of his office as President, he molded his noble ideals of faith and devotion to the responsibility in the realization of openness of heart to all men and faced the ills of the world with courage and conviction.

We have gathered together today in this cathedral church to pay homage to and to offer our prayers for one who was a great American and world leader, the 35th

President of the United States, John F. Kennedy. And President in a certain sense embodies these very United States of America and all its citizens within himself and any harmful blow to that President cannot help but affect each and every American as well; and because of the position of this country as the leader of the free nations throughout the world, such a tragic blow cannot help but have its effect on the entire world as well. This is precisely what we have experienced during the past 4 days. President Kennedy's untimely and meaningless assassination has left the United States and the rest of the world in a state of shock and confusion. So many Americans have commented: "I just can't believe it." How can America—so great, rich, wonderful, the envy of civilization—still have within itself a streak of instability and violence capable of so brutal an action? Our hearts today bleed with sorrow and compassion for Mrs. Kennedy, her children and the entire Kennedy family.

Though not all of us may have agreed with all of his political proposals or ventures, nevertheless, we respected and admired our late President for many reasons, among them his keen intelligence, his remarkable eloquence, and his wit. But of all of President Kennedy's many qualities, there were three in particular which enabled him to win the hearts of people the world over. The first of these was his basic openness toward people, which indicated not merely a political politeness but rather a true sincerity. This openness toward others was not limited to national and world leaders nor to socialites, but was unselfishly given to the common man, woman, and child as well. He was a personable President and he will long be remembered for this trait.

Secondly, President Kennedy's life can indeed be called a profile in courage. His heroic experiences as a naval officer, the calmness he displayed through dangerous operations in hospitals, and the manner in which he faced the important issues of his various political offices, all indicated a courage second to none. In the end, he sacrificed himself for the freedom upon which this country was founded. He was as much a martyr to his country as any soldier on the field of battle.

And finally, President Kennedy was a man dedicated to the service of God, his country, and his family. His dedication was clearly exemplified in all of his efforts as Representative, Senator, and President. His untiring zeal for justice, freedom, and peace were completely in accord with what our late and beloved Holy Father, Pope John XXIII, presented in his two social encyclical letters, entitled "Mother and Teacher" (Mater et Magistra) and "Peace on Earth" (Pacem in Terris). The year 1963 will be remembered in history for the loss of two great men, who, although they have left this world physically, their deeds shine as guiding stars for present and future generations—our Holy Father of blessed memory, Pope John XXIII, the Pope of goodness, and John F. Kennedy, the President of peace, who have given to the young and old a refreshing purposeness of life and have brought joy and dedication to the lives of men in this atomic and space age.

The similarity of the ideals of these two great men in history is evident from a comment of President Kennedy on Pope John's encyclical "Pacem in Terris," of which he said, "This document clearly shows that on the basis of one great faith and its traditions there can be developed a council on public affairs that is of value to all men and women of good will. As a Catholic, I am proud of it, and as an American, I have learned from it."

This example of dedication the tomb cannot hide, this spirit of sacrifice the tomb cannot hold and this spirit of courageous responsibility, which our late President instilled in our age, the death of the body cannot suffocate. May we all join with our gloriously reigning holy father, Pope Paul VI, who said, "We pray God that the sacrifice of John F. Kennedy may assist the cause promoted and defended by him for the liberty of all peoples and peace in the world."

When a loved one dies, we can turn in only one direction to receive the consolation which we seek. That direction is heavenward, in the Person of our Heavenly Father. Only faith and trust in our Personal, Loving, and Merciful Father can soothe our sorrow and give us the stability to go on. In the words of our Divine Saviour: "I am the resurrection and the life; he who believes in me, even if he die, shall live; and whoever lives and believes in me, shall never die." (John 11: 25–26.) And the book of the Apocalypse tells us that in Heaven, "God will wipe away every tear from their eyes. And death shall be no more; neither shall there be mourning, nor crying, nor pain anymore, for the former things have passed away." (Apocalypse 21: 4.) May Almighty God grant to President Kennedy eternal rest and peace.

But, my dear friends in Christ, our present sorrow cannot allow us to stop; we must push on. Our faith and trust that Almighty God continue to bless and guide this Nation must be combined with our best efforts as responsible citizens. As Pope Paul VI remarked just 2 days ago: "We deplore with all our heart this event. We express the hope that the death of this great statesman does not bring harm to the American people but reinforces its moral and civil sense and strengthens its sentiments of nobility and concord." America needs strong leadership backed by a strong people. Indeed, we must place the welfare of our Nation above our position and personal considerations so that we may give our loyal support to our new President, Lyndon B. Johnson, as he undertakes the tremendous burdens of the White House. May God always bless him and guide him.

In conclusion in behalf of our beloved Bishop Nicholas, the priests, religious, seminarians, and faithful of our Eparchy of Pittsburgh, we express to Mrs. John Kennedy and the bereaved family of the President, our heartfelt sympathy and assure them of our prayers for the repose of his soul. May Almighty God accept the soul of this great peacemaker into His Heavenly Kingdom and eternal joy.

IN REMEMBRANCE OF THE MARTYRED PRESIDENT OF THE UNITED STATES

Like all loyal Americans, we of the Greek Catholic Union were deeply saddened by the assassination of our beloved President, the Honorable John Fitzgerald Kennedy of happy memory.

We were saddened, stunned, and perplexed because our young and vibrant leader was stricken down in his prime, slain by a cowardly assassin who without warning swooped down upon his prey.

Yes, a courageous hero who miraculously escaped death in World War II, met an untimely demise while receiving the plaudits of his fellow countrymen.

It was hard to believe, to comprehend, but it did happen and he has gone to his eternal reward.

But his death will not be in vain if we shall take lessons from his exemplary life as a courageous leader, a loyal American, a loyal member of his church, a devoted husband, father, and son.

It will not be in vain if we, too, learn to bear our burdens and tragedies in such majestic fashion as did his faithful wife in these recent trying days.

Likewise, his death will not be in vain if we follow in the footsteps of the leaders of our Nation and of the world who—despite their religious and political beliefs—came to pay final and deserving tribute to a martyred President.

On this Thanksgiving Day we should also express our gratitude to God for allowing us the privilege, even though it was brief, of having John Fitzgerald Kennedy as our President. We should also dedicate ourselves to labor unceasingly—as he did—for a stronger and better America and for a peaceful world.

It is our fervent belief that we can show no better final tribute than this.

May Almighty God comfort the bereaved and may He grant eternal rest and blissful repose to our departed President.

TRIBUTE BY

Hon. Walt Horan

OF WASHINGTON

Mr. Speaker, under leave granted to extend my remarks, I am pleased to include a sermon delivered last Sunday at Chevy Chase Presbyterian Church by the assistant minister, the Reverend Robert Clyde Curry.

This sermon was but one of thousands delivered on a Sunday but 2 days removed from the tragic event of last Friday. This sermon, like the others, undoubtedly replaced one already prepared. Many of them, I have read, were excellent and reflected something of the greatness of this Nation, its tremendous and ultimate unity.

Washington, D.C., is a church-going city, and last Sunday Washington's churches were crowded. Chevy Chase Presbyterian was one of these. We listened intently as Reverend Curry

spoke from his heart and with fiercely honest conviction.

At the earnest suggestion of others who heard this fine sermon, I am pleased to include it in my remarks.

THE PEOPLE OF THE MAN—IN MEMORIAM, JOHN FITZGERALD KENNEDY (MAY 29, 1917–NOVEMBER 22, 1963)

John Fitzgerald Kennedy has died. He has been taken from our lives and from our history. The last rites of his communion have been administered. We declare with them the words of assurance from "The Book of Common Worship" of our communion:

"Unto the mercy of Almighty God, we commend the soul of our brother departed, in the sure and certain hope of the resurrection to eternal life; through Jesus Christ our Lord. Amen."

The shock and shame of our President's death stuns and angers. We are stunned to think that one so great and so young could be destroyed so easily. Anger boils with intensity and self-righteousness as we strike out at the deed, the individual, at the place, the time. Weak we become as we weep openly or within for the life of another human being untimely dead; for his wife, his daughter and son, his close-knit family, his future. We are made fearful and anxious because leadership has been lost, the course of history profoundly altered. And what of our history? What of the "land of the free and the home of the brave?" A leader has been lost. Another shall arise. A President has been killed. What he believed in is enmeshed in policies and programs yet to be realized. But what of the land? He is dead, but we, the people, live on. He is gone, but the land remains. His life has been sacrificed—but our life continues. What of our land and her people?

In this memorial to John Fitzgerald Kennedy let us look at the "people of the man." Let us honor and memorialize him by looking at our people, our Nation whom he served, whom he loved, as whose leader he died. In his death, perhaps, we, the people, shall learn.

WHEN SHALL WE LEARN THAT TOMORROW IS ALWAYS TOO LATE?

The psalmist writes concerning the length of life, "three score years and ten and if by reason of strength they be fourscore." No matter what the length of life cries the psalmist, "Teach us, O Lord, to number our days, that we may apply our hearts unto wisdom." "* * * that we may apply our hearts unto wisdom." Does it always demand a tragic crisis for us to see, to know, to do the good? Is it only when a church school is bombed and children are killed or when a President is shot or personal tragedy strikes that we will apply our hearts unto wisdom? That suddenly the superficialities of our lives are stripped from us and we see what is true, what is of import, what is of value. Numbering our days does not mean sitting and crossing off blocks on the calendar. It means knowing, knowing that tomorrow is forever, today is now. It means knowing that life never, never stands still nor waits. It means beginning to live is not going to take place at the next party, the next stage in life, or after the next hurdle is passed, or beyond the present crisis. Life is going on now. Numbering doesn't mean listing, it means knowing the limitations. We work within our own lifespan only, no one else's. The numbering is important if only to make this clear again.

But the numbering is necessary if we are ever to apply our hearts unto wisdom. If we realize the ultimate limits then, perhaps, we can attempt to approach the immediate problems with wisdom, with insight, with courage. This is the psalmist's plea—"teach us to number our days, that we might apply our hearts unto wisdom." That we might live wisely.

Tomorrow is not only forever, it is always too late. Tomorrow is too late for one segment of our society to be accepted as men. Tomorrow is too late to remove the stigma of hate, of cruelty, of persecution from any man. Tomorrow is too far away and too slow in coming for dreamers of great dreams. Today may already be too late.

Tomorrow is too late to talk peace—for tomorrow may never come. There may be no tomorrows if today there is no peace.

Tomorrow is too late to apply our hearts unto wisdom for the wisest possible decision of our lives are needed this day.

We need to number our days.

A local newspaper had no obituary prepared on President Kennedy. On the other living Presidents such was on file. Not for Mr. Kennedy. He was too young to die. How wrong they were, and yet, how right. For he lives as a man for whom no obituary would be necessary. The man who numbers his days and applies his heart to wisdom lives not for the final number, not for infinity, but for the expression of wisdom in his life now.

When will our people learn, when will we learn that tomorrow is always too late?

WHEN WILL WE LEARN THAT SACRIFICE IS DEMANDED OF US ALL?

The words when first spoken rang with authenticity. They have since been mocked and questioned. It has been noted how little they have been realized in practical politics. Yet their truth has never been lessened.

"Ask not what your country can do for you; ask only what you can do for your country."

The direction is right. The way is hard. These words were not and are not intended for the relief roles of the Nation or for the aged or for the minorities, all of whose needs are so very real. They were and are directed to every citizen who permits his Nation's destiny to be decided without either personal effort or personal concern.

Little there is that we can do as part of the mass of men. Little there is that we can affect from positions relatively unimportant and obviously removed from the power structures of our community and Nation. Little there is that the complexity of our life permits the individual, the one, to do.

And these are very real barriers. Each of us must face them. Yet just as surely the sacrifice that is demanded most is the agonizing reappraisal of our national and our personal goals. We must submit ourselves, our practical beliefs, our way of life to honest confrontation with the life that ought to be and the God who rules us all. This is never easily done nor lightly undertaken.

This Thanksgiving season must find us on our knees. Not to thank God for things. Not to thank God that we are not like other men—Communists, poor, uneducated, unsophisticated, unclean, hungry, naked. But to thank God that we are exactly as other men. To thank God that with all men we stand before Him and Him alone, as our God. To thank God that with all men we stand before Him in need and in hope, in confusion and in certainty; in desperate sorrow and anguish, but at least—at least before Him in love.

Sacrifice is sacrifice only when it costs. Of personal anxiety there is much. Confusion and questions abound. Only as we reach out to our brother with our abilities, our concern, our interest, our time, energy, and money will the action be sacrificial. It is not enough to put our gift on the long pole of the United Fund and reach out, giving, but clean; helping, but untouched. We must physically take ourselves there and bring their needs here. These two dare no longer be mutually exclusive. The sacrifice now will be real. And this is not sacrifice in a morbid, depressing sense at all. This is sacrifice that converts the life, that turns the life around, that lifts the life up. That which was or those who were hated and despised, that which was or those who were avoided and disdained, are enveloped in our love and our concern.

This agonizing reappraisal and sacrifice each of us must do. Do it for our personal goals as well as those of our Nation. Such an act cannot help but touch and affect every institution—our families, or communities, our churches, our Nation, our world. We need to recall that the prayer—"let this cup pass from my lips" was uttered in the same breath with "not my will but thine be done." And that both were raised to God in the dark night of a garden filled with death and despair, yet from which the hope of the world was to come.

"Ask not what your country can do for you. Ask only what you can do for your country."

"Ask not what you can get. Ask only what you can give."

These words ring with truth and judge us rightly in this season. When will we learn that sacrifice is demanded of us, each one of us now?

WHEN WILL WE LEARN THAT GOOD IS GOOD, BAD IS BAD, AND PEOPLE ARE BOTH?

We are a black and white culture. This has no reference to race. It means only that we tend as a people to view others, but not ourselves, as either good or bad. We identify our enemy by his badness. The popularity of westerns on television has pointedly illustrated this characteristic. Here identification of good and bad is easily and simply accomplished.

As much as we would have life be one great cineramic continuous "Winning of the West"—it is simply not this way. There is good. There is right. There are standards. Our sense of the right as a Nation has been outraged by the murder of our President. Our people and the peoples of the world unite in identifying this act as despicable, as horrible, as heinous. We know good and we know bad. And we know people, or at least we know one person, ourselves.

And we know that we are good. We know that we are not murderers. We know that we are not evil.

We know that we are not murderers, except that we do hate and our Lord has called such hate "murder of the heart." We are not evil. We are not bad. Except with the Apostle Paul we must cry out "The good that I would, I do not, but the evil which I would not, that I do."

When are we to learn that good is good? That there is right? And that bad is bad? That there are wrongs, and no matter how one rationalizes or excuses them from their lives, they remain wrong? And that we, the people, are both? When will we learn to distinguish between the sin and the sinner? When will we learn that the greatest tragedy that can befall a man is not death, but to be isolated from his fellows by hate? When will we learn that hate breeds hate even when of self, and leads only to destruction? When will we learn that people beginning with ourselves are both good and bad?

The death of our President must be attributed to a warped mind. Only such a one could have done such a thing. That the accused man is of the political far left may save the face of many. But political far left or political far right, both have evidenced a contempt and a hate that leaves one anxious of his Nation, fearful of his people. If we are involved in either of these extremes the hate that finds expression through them must be revealed. What causes these pockets of hate to be so difficult to confront is the political and religious cloak behind which they hide. That cloak has been ripped from the face of our land since early Friday afternoon. We Christians, citizens of this land, must lead the way. We must stop the mouth of the slanderer. We must halt the malicious and destructive hatred of men wherever we find it beginning with ourselves. This may mean that soon, perhaps today, you and I are going to confront a friend or a neighbor or perhaps a stranger with—"You are wrong. You have misjudged. You are involved in a deep hate." And more honestly we are going to be confronted by a friend, perhaps a neighbor, or only the voice of a stranger over the television saying—"We are wrong. We have misjudged. We are involved in a deep hate."

Some mornings we stride into this sanctuary ready to lift our voices in robust praise to Almighty God. The stronger and more vigorous the hymn the more it encourages the expression. To offer a prayer of confession fits neither the mood nor the theology. Another morning we confront the whole service with only the need to be cleansed, to be forgiven, to be loved once more. Both are needed, for we are children, children of the light and children of the dark.

WHEN WILL WE LEARN THAT CHRIST'S GOSPEL OF GOD'S LOVE IS FOR THE WHOLE WORLD?

The women was an adulteress. "Go and sin no more."
The man was a tax collecter. "Come and follow me."
The rich man was confused. "Sell, give and come."
The holy man was unctuous. "Pray simply—Our Father—."

The brother was a prodigal. "Kill the fatted calf and come let us be merry."

The disciples were afraid. "Peace I leave with you. My peace I give unto you."

Who were those people to whom the good news was brought? Who were these people that responded? Who went and sinned no more? Who forsook all and followed after? Who sold and gave? Who learned to pray humbly? Who lost their fears and found only courage? They were people. People in and of the world who needed to know and to feel the love of someone for them.

It is incomprehensible that God should love all. We cannot understand what this love is or means. What we can understand is that God loves us, loves me. And as significantly, loves you. It is this love that is for the whole world.

Love has an odd characteristic. It shrivels, dies into hate if it finds no expression, no sharing. The love of our God can never be dogmatized. Can never be ritualized. Can never be held in a stone building or a rigid denominational pattern. The love of God denies dogma, for someone not worthy of love is always loved. The love of God forsakes ritual for its forms are as varied as we are. The love of God escapes the tabernacle, even when built to his glory, for in its shadows outside its walls hover the "beloved of the Lord." And his love has no name except our own.

What dare we feel for Mrs. Kennedy and her children? Her life and her tragedy? Deep grief. And we weep with her. Her loss is ours and the world's. But more, we know God's love for her shall not fail. His love for us shall not fail. "Faith, hope, love abide, these three, but the greatest of this is love."

Paul writes to the Christians at Rome:

"Everyone who calls upon the name of the Lord will be saved. But how are men to call upon Him in whom they have not believed? And how are they to believe in Him of whom they have never heard? And how are they to hear unless there is a proclaimer. And how can men proclaim unless they are sent."

How can the love of God for the world be made known unless there are those who believe? How can the love of God for the world be told except those who believe be sent. How is the love of God to be taken to the world unless and except we take it? Will we learn, we who are Christ's followers, that the love of God is for the whole world, but it must be taken to that world? The message needs messengers. The gospel needs tellers. The love needs vehicles. When we learn, then we shall indeed be Christ's men—God's ambassadors.

When will we learn that Christ's Gospel, the good news of God's love, is for the whole world?

The President is dead. His soul we commend to the care and love of Almighty God.

To whom shall we commend the soul of this our Nation? In whom shall we find her life? It is in us, the people of this man and the people of God, that the answer must be found.

In a speech never given, the President quoted the second verse of the 127th Psalm.

"Unless the Lord watches over the city, the watchman stays awake in vain."

To it we must add the prior verse—"Unless the Lord builds a house, those who build it labor in vain."

Unless the Lord builds the Nation, those who build it labor in vain. The people of this man, the President of the United States—John Fitzgerald Kennedy, dare not labor in vain.

TRIBUTE BY

Hon. Craig Hosmer

OF CALIFORNIA

Mr. Speaker, in its December bulletin the Long Beach Bar Association paid its respects to the memory of the late President John F. Kennedy in the following touching words written by Attorney Blaine Nels Simons:

IN MEMORIAM TO JOHN FITZGERALD KENNEDY

Goodbye—
To father, husband, son,
Too soon, too soon your race is run
Time's sands run out, the battle done.
Goodbye—
And in those few and fleeting years
We hope you felt, throughout the din of cheers,
The deep affection proved now by our tears.
Goodbye—
Sleep on in peace beneath Virginia's sod,
And pity us who on life's highway still must trod,
Not knowing, as do you the loving arms of God.
Goodbye.

—B. N. SIMONS.

TRIBUTE BY

Hon. George Huddleston, Jr.

OF ALABAMA

Mr. Speaker, the tragic assassination of President John F. Kennedy has brought unparalleled grief and sorrow to our Nation and, indeed, the world. Gone from our midst is an outstanding citizen and a leader who was the personification of the youth, vigor, and vitality of the country which selected him as its President.

My hometown in Birmingham, Ala., joins the Nation and world in an expression of sorrow to the family of the late President Kennedy and a voice of hope and unity for tomorrow to President Lyndon Johnson.

Through a letter dated November 26, 1963, Mayor Albert Boutwell sent to the members of the Alabama delegation, first, statement of the mayor of the city of Birmingham, November 22, 1963; second, city of Birmingham proclamation dated November 23, 1963; third, statement of the mayor to the council, November 26, 1963; and fourth, resolution adopted by the Birmingham City Council on November 26, 1963.

I respectfully insert the above-named documents on behalf of the city of Birmingham.

STATEMENT OF THE MAYOR OF THE CITY OF BIRMINGHAM, NOVEMBER 22, 1963

I sincerely believe that almost every man, woman, and child in Birmingham, regardless of how deep their personal political feelings may run, are shocked and saddened as I am by this terrible tragedy.

I speak for the city government of Birmingham, for myself, as mayor, and for President M. E. Wiggins and his fellow council members, in expressing to the President's personal and official families the depth of the sorrow and sense of tragedy that we share with them and with the people of the United States. In the name of the city government and the people it represents, I have sent a telegram of condolence to the President's wife and children, to express to them our sympathy in this time of their personal loss and personal grief.

Whatever forces may lie behind this terrible event, whatever persons may have inspired the striking down of a President of the United States, we can have no other feeling than one of sorrow and deep regret.

For the President's wife and children and the members of their families our hearts go out. We pray to Almighty God that He will, in His infinite compassion, comfort and strengthen them. And for the Nation we pray that divine providence will watch over and guide us in the troubled hours that will be the inevitable consequence of this sad day.

———

CITY OF BIRMINGHAM PROCLAMATION

Whereas the President of the United States of America has made the supreme sacrifice to which the courageous conduct of his office exposed him, as it has other great Americans and other Presidents; and

Whereas his death, in the very prime of life, at the hands of a traitorous assassin, strikes a blow not only to our Nation but to the whole free world; and

Whereas this city, its government and all its people, out of a deep and unalterable respect for the great office of the Presidency of the Nation, and out of sincere and human sympathy for the President's wife and his children and the members of their respective families, bows with them in sorrow; and

Whereas John Fitzgerald Kennedy's death in line of duty has wiped out, for these hours of mourning and remembrance, all temporal differences or partisan feelings and united the whole free world in regretful sorrow:

Therefore, I, Albert Boutwell, as mayor of Birmingham and by the privilege vested in that office, do proclaim, with the concurrence of the president of the City Council of Birmingham and such members of the council as I have been able to consult, and do declare that the 30 days, beginning November 22, 1963, and ending at sundown December 21, 1963, shall be for the city of Birmingham a period of mourning and respect, during which the flags of the United States flown upon public buildings and other official flagstaffs of the city shall be flown at half-mast; and, that the city hall of Birmingham, and all other of its buildings, not essential to the services of public protection, shall be closed Monday, November 25, 1963, in observance of a day of prayer for the comfort of the President's family, and the blessing and guidance of Almighty God for the newly succeeding President in his administration of the affairs of our Nation;

I hereby request the effects of this proclamation to be observed by all the boards and agencies of the city, not essential to the maintaining of necessary services to the people of this city;

I further order that a copy of this proclamation be engrossed by the city clerk of the city of Birmingham, affixing upon it the great seal of the city of Birmingham and that the same shall be forwarded to Mrs. John F. Kennedy so that the bereaved family may know the sympathy and sorrow of our city in their hour of personal grief;

And, finally, I order that copies, similarly engrossed and sealed, shall be posted, together with appropriate floral wreaths upon the principal doors of the city hall of Birmingham, and there remain until sundown, November 25, 1963.

Given under my hand at Birmingham, Ala., this 23d day of November 1963.

ALBERT BOUTWELL,
Mayor.

Attest:

JUDSON P. HODGES,
City Clerk.

STATEMENT OF THE MAYOR TO THE COUNCIL,
NOVEMBER 26, 1963

Mr. President and members of the council, I wish at this time to offer for your consideration a proposed joint resolution of the mayor and the council of the city of Birmingham.

There is no need to recall to anyone the tragic event of last Friday. Actions taken by your city government to express our deep and lasting sorrow and to condemn the senseless and inexpressably evil act of violence that took the life of President John F. Kennedy have already been conveyed to the last President's wife and widow and to the Nation.

The time of mourning that loss to ourselves and the Nation is not ended. Indeed, it will cast its shadow over a long time to come. But, mourning, as we still are, the undeniable reality of this hour is that a nation, reunited by tragedy, must now proceed upon its destiny under the leadership of the man the Nation chose, along with the martyred President, as its Vice President.

I, therefore, as mayor, offer the following resolution to the council for its concurrence, so that it may be presented to President Lyndon B. Johnson as a unanimous expression of our support and confidence as he proceeds in the tasks which destiny has thrust upon him.

"Whereas on November 22, 1963, the cowardly act of an assassin fatally struck down John F. Kennedy, President of the United States of America; and

"Whereas on that same day, by virtue of his earlier election by the people as Vice President of the United States, and by the provisions of the Constitution, Lyndon Baines Johnson, after illustrious service in both Houses of the Congress and in the Vice Presidency, has now assumed the highest office and honor of Chief Executive of the Nation, and leader of the free world; and

"Whereas in the performance of that office, he has earnestly and humbly evoked the support of this Nation, and the blessing and guidance of Almighty God for its successful accomplishment: Therefore be it

"Resolved by the government of the city of Birmingham, on behalf of all its citizens of all races and creeds, That we do hereby declare our unstinting support in all that he may seek to do to accomplish what is good for this Nation, and to lead it in the paths of peace and prosperity; and be it further

"Resolved, That we convey to the President of the United States our confidence in his leadership, and in the high ideals and principles that have characterized his public actions in the past, and predict his future direction; and, finally, be it

"Resolved, That we, as a government and a people, do join our prayers with his and with the Nation and with the prayers of free peoples everywhere, that Divine Providence may counsel him in wisdom, imbue him with unfaltering strength of mind and courage, and bless him with continuous good health against all the trials that lie before him, before us as a Nation. And finally do we pray that the God of peace and good will among men, will bless this Nation, under its new leadership, with lasting peace among the nations of the earth, and the material blessings of plenty to us and all mankind."

STATE OF ALABAMA,
Jefferson County:

I, Judson P. Hodges, city clerk of the city of Birmingham, do hereby certify that the above and foregoing is a true and correct copy of a resolution duly adopted by the Council of the City of Birmingham at its meeting held November 26, 1963, and as same appears of record in minute book C-1 of said city.

Given under my hand and corporate seal of the city of Birmingham, this the 26th day of November 1963.

Albert Boutwell, Mayor; John E. Bryan, Councilman; Alan T. Drennen, Jr., Councilman; John Golden, Councilman; Don A. Hawkins, Councilman; Judson P. Hodges, City Clerk; M. E. Wiggins, President of the Council; Nina Miglionieo, Councilman; Dr. Eleazer C. Overton, Councilman; George G. Seibels, Jr., Councilman; Tom W. Woods, Councilman.

Hon. Ben F. Jensen

OF IOWA

Mr. Speaker, tributes to our late President have taken many sensitive and touching forms. We are, after all, a mature nation, and the loss of a Chief Executive strikes deeply at our national consciousness.

Those who composed some expression of their grief have contributed much to the heartbeat of America, this blessed land.

One such contributor to the dramatic narratives that welled up throughout America when our citizens learned of John F. Kennedy's death was the Honorable Folsom Everest, of Council Bluffs, a judge of the 15th Iowa judicial circuit, and a friend of mine for more than a quarter of a century.

To my colleagues I commend this stirring eulogy to our late martyred President, and cite also Judge Everest's equally moving tribute to the genius of our form of government.

There will be fewer faint hearts about the future of this noble country if good people will strive to relearn and be fortified by the towering majesty of our Constitution as so earnestly illustrated by Judge Everest. The eulogy follows:

A TRIBUTE TO OUR LATE PRESIDENT, JOHN FITZGERALD KENNEDY

There are times when language is a totally inadequate method of expression. This is such an occasion. All over our country in places such as this men are trying to describe the gallant and admirable qualities of our murdered, martyred President, John Fitzgerald Kennedy. Few will succeed, and they, only because of a more intimate knowledge of him than can be gleaned from the columns of the press. This, coupled with true capacity to paint a word picture, may lead one or two toward the goal but for me to venture far in that area is to pretend to a knowledge I do not have and an eloquence I do not possess.

A few outstanding things all of us know. We understand that he possessed great physical courage. This he demonstrated through combat service in time of war and in facing up to excruciating pain and suffering since the war. These are qualities shared with many others. That he had a brilliant intellect is apparent from the manner in which he absorbed and digested facts about new and strange situations. Amazing qualities of leadership were essential to his success not only in his chosen field of politics but in his earlier Navy career. For a stranger to

go further than to point out these obvious characteristics would be presumptuous indeed.

The shocking but dramatic manner of his passing has been sufficiently depicted by radio, television, and press. The utter futility of the act committed can hardly be overemphasized. The motivation of the accused assassin may be suspected but never really known, for he in turn has been gunned down by a foolish man who could not wait for the orderly processes of the law to exact payment for so foul a crime. Oswald never admitted committing the assassination much less the reasons why he did it but if it be assumed that he sought to modify in some degree or fashion the attitude of our country toward Castro's Cuba the only result has been a worsening rather than a lessening of the severity of our attitude in that respect. If he sought to create confusion in Government by murdering the Chief of State then he failed of the objective for the act served to unite rather than disrupt the people responsible for our policy. We have already seen the almost instant transference of authority to President Johnson who took the oath of office within less than 2 hours of the shooting of President Kennedy. We have witnessed the wisdom with which he sought and has obtained the allegiance and support of the leaders of both parties in the Senate and House and you may be sure that during the opening weeks of his Presidency he will be free from partisan criticism while feeling out the strength and weakness of the opposing leadership in the cold war. If it be assumed that the killer sought modification of attitude on the civil rights program of legislation the issues there are too well drawn for Presidential attitudes to change them in any important respect. The Legislature and the courts will make the decision which the Executive can do little more than implement.

Perhaps it is not amiss for a moment to dwell briefly on the strength of the form of government devised for us by the Founding Fathers and implemented through the Constitution which they wrote and persuaded the States to adopt. It was not perfect. Being drawn by mortals it partook of their mortality. Like all legislation it was the product of compromise but as it went before the people it expressed the fundamentals of separation of church and state; separation of powers of the executive, the legislature, and the judiciary; delegation of powers by the States to the Federal Government and government of the people, by the people, and for the people. It required almost immediate amendment through the adoption of the Bill of Rights which assured protection of the individual against the arbitrary exercise of power. Through the years it has not only been amended but interpreted and as a written document it is properly the subject of interpretation. Seldom has this been done without arousing passionate protest on the part of some and this was true in early days as well as modern times but the essential elements remain. Other nations have similar documents but ours alone has stood the test of time and stress. It accommodates itself to crises such as the assassination of Presidents or their sudden demise. In all the times this has happened there has never been the suggestion of other than an orderly transference of power. The ugly head of dictatorship has never reared itself nor has the military sought to interfere with civilian authority. These have been common corollaries in other lands and other places.

In all probability we shall never know the true motives of the assassin but the result is a senseless killing, a depraved expression of hatred—incapable of rationalization. We deplore the deed and the reflection it casts on our vaunted civilization. Those of us who have been exposed to the intensities and passions of the battlefield recognize that the veneer of civilization is thin and rubs off under such pressures but this act has no such excuse. We are tempted to regard such a killer as insane but the stupid act of another killer makes such a determination impossible and leaves only the field of speculation. The answer we may never know.

The words of John Masefield, poet laureate of England, appeared in the press this morning:

"All generous hearts lament the leader killed,
The young chief with the smiling, radiant face,
The winning way that turned a wondrous race
Into sublimer pathways, leading on.
Grant to us life that though this man be gone
The promise of his spirit be fulfilled."

TRIBUTE BY

Hon. Charles S. Joelson

OF NEW JERSEY

Mr. Speaker, the enclosed article from the Paterson Evening News of December 6, 1963, was sent to me by my distinguished predecessor, the Honorable Gordon Canfield.

It well describes the reaction of Peace Corps volunters in Peru, as well as of the Peruvian people at the tragic death of President John F. Kennedy.

Mary Ellen Patterson, who is referred to in the article, is presently with the Peace Corps in Peru. She is the daughter of Mrs. Dorothy Patterson, who was formerly an aid to Congressman Gordon Canfield on Capitol Hill. Idealistic and deeply patriotic Peace Corps volunteers such as Mary Ellen Patterson make those of us who supported the Peace Corps most grateful.

The article follows:

PEACE CORPS VOLUNTEER REPORTS PERUVIAN SHOCK AT
KENNEDY'S DEATH

Weeping Peace Corps volunteers in Latin America were comforted by men and women in the villages they serve when word of President Kennedy's assassination reached their lonely outposts.

One such volunteer, Mary Ellen Patterson of 181 East 33d Street, in a letter home has told of the dark day and the spirit of kindness with which their Latin American friends reached out to them in their sorrow.

Miss Patterson lives in Urubamba (Quechua translation is Valley of Snakes), a tiny community 2 hours by jeep along a windy, steep-cliffed road in the Department of Cuzco, Peru.

She wrote: "The news hit hard here in South America. We did not find out until 5:30 p.m. and at first we thought the man was joking. Then another and another told us. Still unbelieving we went to the Normal School to see if Annie Achetelli, another PCV (Peace Corps volunteer) had heard anything. Upon arrival we found everyone huddled around a shortwave radio. We knew then it was no joke.

"SHED TEARS

"We joined Annie and the Peruvians, mourning with and for us. The school flag was lowered to half mast. We stayed and listened to the Voice of American and everything we could find. Our Peruvian friends were wonderful. They brought dinner to us and almost all were in tears.

"We were to have dinner that night with two PCV's in Yucan, and we started off very late. While we were walking, a truck stopped and asked if we wanted a lift to Urubamba. We told the driver we were going to Yucan and he said 'no importa,' turned his truck around and took us right to the door. If only all the world could always perform as our Peruvian friends did that day what a wonderful place it could be.

"My Peace Corps home for 2 years, Cuzco, was the capital of the Inca Empire, embracing in its most flourishing days territory which today constitutes all of Peru and the major part of Bolivia, Brazil, Argentina, Chile, Ecuador, Venezuela, and Colombia. It was in other words, the Rome of South America.

"Peace Corps volunteers cannot speak for such a large area nor do we consider ourselves experts in foreign aid, but as one lives in the hearts, homes, and towns of the recipients one gathers bits of knowledge.

"LIKE FREE AID

"The people without question like the free food for peace and the tractors. They like the new roads and the free schools built for their children. But Indians sometimes look at us with disdain and question, 'Why do you send your soldiers here to train our soldiers in the art of killing campesinos?' (Campesinos in general are Indians.)

"Yes, they like our profusion when it is in their favor.

"Today, many are worried it will stop.

"What isn't free means work, or do without.

"Some are grateful to the United States. Others are not. These see through the eyes of envy and not of friendship.

"Kennedy's death has brought fears and questions to many.

" 'When will you be called back?'

" 'Nixon will take over.'

" 'Your Government, it will collapse?'

" 'I cried all night. Your President, the good man is dead. The Communists did it. They will start a war.'

"These are some of the comments we hear.

"SOFT AMERICANS

"A young, gay-hearted teacher had this to say, 'You Americans are so forgiving that if there should be a war between you and Khrushchev and his side lost, you would be the first to send emergency relief to help put them back on their feet to start them all over again. Soft Americans.'

"One poltroon who would not come face to face with us shouted from a barroom door, 'Viva Fidel.' Our immediate reaction was to turn around and reciprocate. Instead we walked on in silence past the familiar adobe houses and the hungry little faces until we reached our own.

"As we sat on the front step in the hot sun, the day's conversations welded into a picture.

"PERUVIANS MOURN

"The normal school insisted we have a quiet dinner with them. They gave us a shortwave radio for as long as we wanted it. All schools canceled classes Saturday, and Monday was declared a day of national mourning. By Tuesday, 'Carretas,' a Peruvian magazine, had a front cover tribute to Kennedy with a picture on the inside of his son, saluting as his father's casket went by.

"Many of our friends sent letters of sympathy. Some tried to write in English, like this very sincere man, a principal and teacher in one of our mountain schools. He sent this note:

"'I express my profound sorrow for the assassination of Mr. Kennedy. He was a good man and friend of the Peru and all America.—Henry Aguirre Pacheco, teacher of School Maras.'

"This is one example of how many Peruvians felt the day of November 22, 1963.

"We are sad. I believe it has affected us more here because everyone comes to pay their respects. The hotel gave us a mourning dinner and another today. People are crying. Most everyone is worried. Most believe the end of the world is near."

Mr. Speaker, the Central of Polish Organizations of Passaic, N.J., on December 14, 1963, held a stirring and impressive memorial program for our late beloved President, John F. Kennedy.

At the end of the services, the chairman read to the assemblage the following letter to Mrs. John F. Kennedy which well sums up the feelings of all good Americans.

The letter follows:

DECEMBER 16, 1963.

Mrs. JOHN F. KENNEDY,
The White House,
Washington, D.C.

DEAR MRS. KENNEDY: The Central of Polish Organizations of Passaic, N.J., in the name of the Americans of Polish descent of Passaic and Bergen Counties, have held a memorial service for the late John Fitzgerald Kennedy at the Polish Peoples Home in Passaic, N.J., on December 15, 1963.

The tragic occurrence in Dallas has deprived the Nation of a true champion of democracy. The members of this organization have especially felt the sorrow of the passing of the late President since they feel they have lost one of their true friends of freedom and one of their mainstays and champions of freedom of oppressed peoples throughout the world.

The whole community of Polish-American descent, together with the societies which form this organization, wish to extend to you and your family their sincere sympathy in your hour of sorrow.

Respectfully yours,

MARIA BELESKI,
Secretary.
JOHN GRYWALKSKI,
President.
BRUNO SKRZYNSKI,
Chairman, Memorial Service.

TRIBUTE BY

Hon. Harold T. Johnson

OF CALIFORNIA

Mr. Speaker, Mr. Robert Vukajlovich, of Jackson, Calif., a historic community in the mother lode area which I represent, has put down on paper his thoughts concerning the assassination of our beloved President. Mr. Vukajlovich, in spite of his youth, is a poet of some distinction. I think he expressed the thoughts of all of us in this tribute to John Fitzgerald Kennedy. I have conveyed this work to President Kennedy's courageous widow.

A TRIBUTE TO JOHN FITZGERALD KENNEDY

(By Robert Vukajlovich)

Well, here it is, near Christmas time,
And soon '64's bells will chime;
But first, before we start the new,
Let's look back on what just got thru.
Yes, lest we plunge on aimlessly,
Let's give a look at '63:

Happy today, sad tomorrow.
Filled with joy, yet filled with sorrow,
'63 began a mere
Model of the previous year.
But tho the start was fool and fuss,
Look what the ending brought to us.

Yes, this year's life was held at bay
On November's 22nd day.
For on that day was Heaven sent
A man more than a President;
A man a god in ev'ry way,
Affectionately known as J.F.K.

Oh! When the shots rang out so clear
And ceased what was a day of cheer,
The sound they made, the death they dealt,
Was not just simply heard, but felt.
The world was stunned in utter shock
And lifeless as a morbid rock.

What feeble form of man or beast,
Yes, feeble form, to say the least,
Could ever be so bad a seed
To stoop to such a tragic deed?
Just one inhuman beyond belief
Could ever crawl to bring such grief.

He took a husband from his wife;
From a boy and girl, their father's life;
And from the world, this demon sent
Our prayer for peace, our President.
But one big thing he left, you see,
He left Kennedy's memory.

He left what's ahead in '64,
What Kennedy lived his whole life for.
The mem'ry of his smiling face
Putting faith in fear's old place.

Yes, the assassin can shoot and shoot
And kill the flower, but not the root.
And from the root, I'm sure you know,
Another flower soon will grow.

Yes, his mem'ry lives and speaks its piece,
And no assassin can make it cease.
We've lost the flower, but gained the root
And like his son, I give salute.

He lived and died for peaceful life,
For an end to wars, and fear, and strife.
So like he'd want it, let it be;
Let this go down in history

Not as the end of a tragedy,
Nor as the end of '63,
But rather as the noted start
Of the life he held in his heart:

The first big step to opened doors,
The first big step to no more wars,
The first big step to freedom's floor,
The step that starts in '64.

Yes, so will live the U.S.A.
In salute to the greatest:
J.F.K.

TRIBUTE BY

Hon. Frank M. Karsten

OF MISSOURI

Mr. Speaker, under leave to extend my remarks I include the following eulogy printed in
the Northwest County Journal on November 28,
1963.

JOHN FITZGERALD KENNEDY

If ye break faith with us who die we shall not sleep.—
"In Flanders Fields," Lt. Col. John McCrae.

Now he has taken his place with the thousands who for
an ideal have given their lives,
Left to our hands is a task uncompleted—our task is to
see that ideal survives;
Those who have fallen may rest from their labors in
honor forever—their course has been run—
If we would honor our heroes and martyrs, we dare not
seek rest till that task has been done.
Sorrow is fitting for those who have fallen, but mourning
is empty and sorrow is vain
If we forget to rekindle the fire we receive as a trust from
the hands of the slain.
Honored who died in the cause of our freedom—in
ground they made sacred forever they sleep,
We have been pledged by a courage unflinching, and
falter we dare not—that pledge we must keep.
Prayer may be said for the souls of the fallen, for much
good is wrought by the prayers which we say,
Searching our souls let us also beg pardon for sins we've
committed, if humbly we pray;
Ask that our eyes may see clearly, unblinded by pride of
possession, by hatred or fear,
Ask that our lives be made worthy the lives of the fallen,
whose deeds we revere.
Father of Mercy, in mercy forgive us our share in the
guilt for the blood that was spilled,
Grant us the grace and the strength and the courage to
put our weak hands to a task unfulfilled;
Grant that the faith which we have in this Nation be
vibrant and virile in glorious deed,
Grant us the strength and the courage and wisdom to
cherish and practice democracy's creed.
Now he has taken his place with the thousands this
Nation will honor while freedom shall live,
Will we begrudge—this example before us whatever our
country must ask us to give?
May we not ask for a nation united, our hearts purged of
envy and cankering hate?
Cannot we learn that as God is our Father, each man is
our brother—before it's too late?
Praise is becoming, but what shall come after, the echoes
of eulogy muted and still?
Man is but mortal, but man is a spirit and here is a task
for the mind and the will.
Grave is the challenge that faces this Nation, and caution
would bid us to falter and quail,
Those who have died dared the bright face of danger, and
these we must honor, for they did not fail.
Pray for the dead who with selfless devotion have counted
but lightly their strength and their youth,
Learn from the dead we need more than a gesture if we
would do homage to freedom and truth;
Pray we as well for ourselves, since we need it if we would
be worthy His choice for our part,
Never have tears stayed the dull hand of death, and He
only hears prayers when they're said with the heart.
Father of Mercy, in mercy forgive us, Thy children who
far from Thy precepts have strayed,

Dark are the clouds in a world filled with hatred, and
  Father, Thy children now seek Thee, afraid;
Grant us the peace which we hopefully seek for, but
  which lacking Thy help, we can never attain,
Grant us a cleansing of heart and of conscience, that those
  whom we honor have died not in vain.

—JOE HEADE.

TRIBUTES BY

Hon. Joseph E. Karth

OF MINNESOTA

Mr. Speaker, the reaction from the people of
the Fourth District of Minnesota to the assassination of President John Fitzgerald Kennedy was
instantaneous and profound. I received spontaneous expressions of grief and shock from many
ordinary citizens, from community and business
leaders.

I would like to share with the Congress and
the Nation just a sample of the communications
sent to me after the tragic event of November 22,
1963:

ST. PAUL, MINN.,
November 22, 1693.

Hon. JOSEPH E. KARTH,
House of Representatives,
Washington, D.C.

MY DEAR MR. KARTH: The entire 3M company is
shocked and saddened by the death of our President. The
death of John F. Kennedy is a loss to our Nation and to
the world. On behalf of all employees and stockholders
we wish to express our condolences to his family and
reaffirm our support to our Government in the difficult
days ahead.

MINNESOTA MINING & MANUFACTURING CO.,
WILLIAM L. MCKNIGHT,
Chairman of the Board.

———

NOVEMBER 22, 1963.

Congressman JOSEPH E. KARTH,
House Office Building,
Washington, D.C.:

The entire St. Paul labor movement was shocked and
grieved by the President's death. Please extend our
deepest sympathy to Mrs. Kennedy and the Kennedy
family. President Kennedy will be remembered by us for
his reawakening of the true ideals and values which are
America's heritage. We will continue to work for them
in tribute to his memory.

ST. PAUL AFL–CIO TRADES & LABOR ASSEMBLY.

ST. PAUL, MINN.,
November 22, 1963.

Congressman JOSEPH E. KARTH,
Washington, D.C.:

The St. Paul Area Chamber of Commerce is deeply
shocked at the untimely death of President Kennedy. We
want you to know that the business community of St.
Paul stands ready to serve in any way we can at this critical
time.

FREDERICK BJORKLUND,
President, St. Paul Area Chamber of Commerce.

———

NOVEMBER 22, 1963.

Congressman JOSEPH E. KARTH,
House Office Building,
Washington, D.C.:

Our hearts were saddened, our senses shocked by the
tragic death of our President John Fitzgerald Kennedy.
Our heartfelt sympathy goes out to Mrs. Kennedy and the
family in these hours of grief. We renew our pledge to
support the legislation which President Kennedy wanted
to help achieve his long-range goals to establish a just
peace in our time.

FOURTH DISTRICT, DEMOCRATIC-FARMER-
LABOR PARTY, EXECUTIVE COMMITTEE.

———

NOVEMBER 22, 1963.

Hon. JOSEPH E. KARTH,
House of Representatives,
Washington, D.C.:

The tragic death of our President profoundly shocks
and saddens us. We extend our most heartfelt sympathy
to Mr. Kennedy's family and to every representative of
our Government. We are outraged by this act and pledge
you our support during this most critical period.

R. M. HUBBS,
President, St. Paul Fire & Marine Insurance Co.

———

ST. PAUL, MINN.,
November 23, 1963.

Hon. JOSEPH E. KARTH,
U.S. Congressman,
Washington, D.C.:

On behalf of our management and employees please express our deep sympathy and grief to Mrs. Kennedy and
her family, as well as to the government staff, of the
loss of a great man and a great President. We share in
President Johnson's request for God's help for a united
support from all in the face of the tragedy that has befallen our country.

ELMER R. ERICKSON,
President, Northwestern Refining Co.

———

ST. PAUL POSTAL UNION,
St. Paul, Minn., November 22, 1963.

Hon. JOSEPH E. KARTH,
U.S. Congressman of Minnesota,
Washington, D.C.

DEAR CONGRESSMAN: The tragic death of our great
President came as a terrible shock to us. It is a sad

commentary on our country that something like this could happen and it saddens us.

This assassination is a tragedy beyond words for the President's family, his party, the country, and the world. The bullet fired from the assassin's rifle has stricken a brilliant and dedicated statesman at the very height of his career.

There must and should be a more careful way of protection from madmen and crackpots for our leaders. The man or men who have committed this heinous crime are totally unfit to live in our great country. Words cannot express our grief and we extend our most heartfelt sympathy to our martyred President's family and to every representative of our Government. We are outraged by this atrocious act and pledge our support during this most trying time.

Sincerely,

WILLIAM L. ULMER,
Legislative Representative.

Mr. Speaker, many people who have been touched by the tragedy of November 22, 1963, and the solemn funeral ceremonies for our late President Fitzgerald Kennedy have expressed the full intensity of their feeling in many ways.

I read and was especially moved by a sonnet written by Sister Marie David, C.S.J., who is an art instructor at the college of St. Catherine in St. Paul, Minn. I want very much to share the inspiration of these verses with my colleagues.

THE BURIAL AT ARLINGTON NOVEMBER 25, 1963

(By Sister Marie David, C.S.J.)

Death was not quick enough to close the door
Through which he captured you. We all have seen.
And now we come with gifts. Forevermore
This later land has its Andromache in
Whom it grieves. The Nation meditates.
The Nation mourns as one heart, broken, and
The whole world grieves. And prays. And waits
Drum beat, bagpiper, gunfire salute, and band,
Air Force and bird cry. Then the slow bugle, lonely
Crown of the dirge. High. Final. Bright
Rousing cry to a people who have this day, only
Followed a builder to this loveliest site.
Forever stay. Enrich our richest earth.
So from it spring your several dreams to birth.

TRIBUTE BY

Hon. Elizabeth Kee

OF WEST VIRGINIA

Mr. Speaker, our late beloved President, John Fitzgerald Kennedy, was idolized by the people of West Virginia. All in this great State are in deep mourning over his passing, and extend heartfelt sympathy to his bereaved family.

Mr. Speaker, my heart is heavy as I include in my remarks the following extremely fitting tribute paid to President Kennedy—this man of prayer and action—by the Reverend Robert E. Brengartner, Catholic chaplain at the U.S. Naval Medical Center, Bethesda, Md. Father Brengartner has so perfectly described the great spirit, the selfless dedication and spiritual depth of our late President that I want to share these expressions with President Kennedy's family, as well as with my colleagues in the Congress:

"Greater love than this no one has, that one lay down his life for his friends."—John 15: 13.

Nineteen hundred years ago our Blessed Lord not only expressed this idea, but exemplified it in His own life.

Through the ages men and women have heeded this call of love and laid down their lives for others. They are the martyrs of our faith; they are the martyrs of our country. They died for truth, for the love of God, for the freedom of man.

To this long list of heroes has been added the name of John Fitzgerald Kennedy, President of the United States. The day he took the oath of office is the day he accepted in all its stark reality not only the honors and powers of his office, but also the awesome responsibilities and the dangers to life connected with such a position. We are all aware of the courage and determination mingled with a constant cheerfulness with which he tackled every problem.

He seemed the ideal Christian man, combining the age-old Christian axiom of Ora et labora—pray and work. Pray, as if everything depended upon God, and work, as if everything depended upon yourself. He was a man of prayer and action.

If anyone was truly alive President Kennedy was. He lived life to the hilt. And I mean this in the good sense of making use of every talent and every moment God has given.

Born to high station—with a silver spoon in his mouth—John F. Kennedy could have spent his life in leisure and security—Switzerland in the winter—the Riviera in the summer. But with his God-given qualities of compassion and justice, wisdom, courage and decision, he was drawn into the battle for humanity—the ocean of human interests—to be the leader of a great people, and a friend to the peoples of the world.

As a John the Baptist, a voice crying in the wilderness, he would cry out for social justice, for equality, for the rights of the individual. And who cannot say that like John the Baptist he was murdered for speaking the truth—for defending the rights of God and man?

Who can say what brought about this hatred in the mind of a man who would kill our President? What influenced him to such an act of revenge? Was it some prejudice on our part—some hatred of ours—some act of rebellion against lawful authority—some sin of social injustice?

Look at the crucifix. There you can see what sin did to God's own Son.

Look at the broken body of our young President. There again you can see the effect of a sinful act.

Look at Mrs. Kennedy and Caroline and John, Jr., and you see the sorrow caused by one man who defied God's law—"Thou shalt not kill."

From the echo of that shot in Dallas last Friday waves of sorrow and misery have flowed over the world.

Perhaps President Kennedy can accomplish in death what he could not accomplish in life—to show that all men are created equal and that social justice must prevail. If this can be accomplished, then John F. Kennedy, President of the United States, will not have died in vain.

TRIBUTE BY
Hon. Edna F. Kelly
OF NEW YORK

Mr. Speaker, the tragedy of 1963 made the holy season of Christmas a sobering and thoughtful one. One which made all reflect and think, "for whom the bell tolls." Many words and letters have been written as a tribute to the late President Kennedy. The following meditation was written by the Reverend Michael Farina of St. Thomas the Apostle Church, in Washington, D.C. He gave it in place of a sermon on Sunday, November 24:

A MEDITATION: ON DEATH

Birth is an awesome mystery
A wondrous one
When mere man shares in the creative power of God.
Oh, it is a gift of love.
Yet, then does a man challenge why?
Asking, seeking?
When other wombs are barren and other arms unfilled
With such a gift of love
God has given him.
Then, they weep tears of joy.

Death is a terrifying mystery
A frightening one
When mere man must acknowledge the power of the Creator.
Oh, it is a gift of love
Yet, then does a man challenge why?
Asking, seeking?
When hearts, with an unspeakable loneliness, unfilled
With such a gift of love
God has taken from him.
Then they weep tears of sorrow.

God is a mystery
A loving one
Creator knowing, wisdomwise in purpose why and when
The seed quicken, the flower reach beauteous bloom
Time into eternity intrude,
Exchanging love for life and life for love
And this in love.

TRIBUTE BY
Hon. Eugene J. Keogh
OF NEW YORK

Mr. Speaker, we know that the tributes paid to our late President have come from all parts of the world. One such which has come to my attention is the tribute of Jose Maria de Areilza, formerly his country's Ambassador to Washington and presently Ambassador to France. This moving paper was published in the newspaper A B C, one of the significant Spanish newspapers. The approach of Ambassador Areilza is most impressive, and I would like to have it recorded along with the countless many other fine expressions of sympathy that have been made. The Ambassador adds much by reason of his personal friendship with the late President by whom, I know, he was held in high esteem:

A CRIME AGAINST THE YOUTH OF THE WORLD

Kennedy's death can be judged from various angles, according to whether one considers the origin of the crime, the repercussions of his disappearance from the political scene, the profile of his successor, or the outlook for the next U.S. election campaign. I would not want to take up any of these aspects here without another more direct, and at the same time remote aspect which may not have been sufficiently emphasized and which seems to me, however, rather suggestive.

When a public figure, a political leader, meets with violent death, people try afterward to form an idea of the symbol which he represented. The crime emotionally focuses attention on that person and his outstanding feature in the interest of evaluating the crime and appraising the loss. Abraham Lincoln thus was transformed into the man responsible for the emancipation of the slaves and for the government of the people for the people; Garcia Moreno, into the Catholic governor persecuted by the sects; Canovas, into the peacemaker in our 18th century discords; Jaures was the Socialist who hated war; Canalejas, the stubborn liberal, who fought for freedom; Calvo Sotelo, the implacable prosecutor responsible for the gradual disintegration of the Popular Front; Jose Antonio, the prophet and definer of a renewed patriotism.

What relevant symbol did the assassinated President represent? In my opinion, and in addition to other qualities, his political image was the visible incarnation of youth, not only of the physical strength of his young years—in his case damaged by the serious injury suffered during the war in the Pacific—but of the generous, open, and bold spirit which is so much a part of the American mentality.

J.F.K.—to use the popular sigla of his initials, had known the supreme tests of adolescence—first, university student, then, soldier. He felt on his body, torn by the machinegun bullet, the brutal impact of the war which rocked the world between 1939 and 1945. He returned to his home and to politics, with a maturity attained through pain and sacrifice. His best known book is "Profiles in Courage," and it is an excellent account of historic personalities whose outstanding quality was valor—courage.

He was the youngest member of the U.S. Senate when he entered the upper Chamber in 1953 as representative of the State of Massachusetts. But, in spite of his previous brief political career in the House of Representatives, he was not a greenhorn in public affairs.

He conveyed his boundless eagerness to learn in the intense interrogatory to which he subjected his questioners. His desire was to be informed, to accumulate information, to make up, with firsthand data, for his youth in contrast with the greater age of his distinguished senatorial colleagues.

Kennedy's entire campaign for his nomination as Democratic candidate for the Presidency, and later, for his election as President, was conducted under the symbol of youth. Although his opponent, Nixon, was also young, as he was, he did not succeed in accentuating that freshness and exuberance which Kennedy managed to put into speeches, his propaganda, and his person.

The generosity, tradition, and idealism in his makeup were not incompatible with an effective pragmatism and a coldness of steel in nerve-racking moments requiring stable nerves. The man who had mobilized his country's Armed Forces—including the nuclear forces—to support his demand for withdrawal of the Russian missiles from Cuba, had no trouble in negotiating with Russia, a few months later, an agreement for the suspension of nuclear tests in the atmosphere, thus clearing the way for a reduction of East-West tensions and holding out the promise of future solutions.

That is to say, his position was firm, but tolerant; aware of danger, but open to discussion; an enemy of communism, but opposed to the foolishness of the "antis." And that constructive understanding of human affirmation, which made him call out in a speech: "There are no indispensable persons. Only peace and justice are indispensable in this world," was what aroused in the hearts of his listeners, inside and outside the United States, expectation and enthusiasm, coupled with illusions—excessive, if you will—in a world laden with threatening clouds and prophetic omens.

"Merchant of hope" is what Napoleon called the statesman and the governor. Kennedy was one to the *n*th degree, and his words and his deeds had the capacity to project themselves into a tomorrow of promising horizons.

I believe that the youth of the world fully understood his simple and direct language; that is, not only the youth of the United States and of the West, but also the youth of the third world, that of the Socialist countries of the East and of the Soviet Union itself. Above—or below—the conflicting ideologies and doctrinal antagonisms which divide people, there was, when listening to him, a universal sensibility particularly, in the intuition of masses of young people for whom the figure of the assassinated President was a permanent focus of shining hope.

The impressive increase in the number of young people, as shown in the population statistics of different countries, is a well-known phenomenon. In the United States, in France, in the Soviet Union, in Spain, the number of persons under 30 years of age has become an increasingly important factor—so decisive, in fact, that the experts in public opinion and publicity—are giving serious consideration to this new circumstance. The majority likes and dislikes, the customs, the demands, and the consumer market are showing more and more a predominantly juvenile imprint. And the youth of today—rebellious and nonconformist and cut loose from the older generations—is ardently searching for channels through which the destiny of human events may be charted. The young people do not want any more hecatombs. They prefer facts and realizations to doctrines and abstractions.

Kennedy was a visible and universal symbol of that wish. He knew how to give shape and expression to general anxiety, and to bring about a climate of confidence which made it necessary for many governments, reluctantly, to yield to that irresistible policy of dialog in the interest of peace and harmony among nations.

Many people and many interests rose up against him and against what he represented: Inevitably those who opposed the future and things to come; those who continued to look back into the past, like Lot's wife; and those who stirred up hatred and fanaticism which would subsequently engender fighting, tragedy, and death.

To find out whether the deadly bullet was fired by a loner with an unbalanced mind, or by an executioner in the service of a conspiracy of one kind or another, has, in my opinion, relative rather than historical interest. And for understandable political reasons, it is unlikely that this whole question may [ever] be cleared up.

What is important is to record the enormous shock which the death of the President produced in the most remote corners of the globe, precisely because his message had been heard by large masses of the earth's population. It is also true—though it may be sad to say so—that the assassination was received with satisfaction by more than one group, sector, or party inside and outside the United States, which would only confirm what has been said above.

I think that I could condense my thinking on the subject into one phrase: The death of Kennedy was a crime against the youth of the world.

JOSE MARIA DE AREILZA.

TRIBUTES BY

Hon. John Lesinski

OF MICHIGAN

Mr. Speaker, I shall never forget that tragic and dark day of November 22 when, with you in the House restaurant here in the Capitol, I heard the dreadful news about the assassination of our 35th President, John Fitzgerald Kennedy. It was, and still is, extremely difficult to believe that such a terrible thing can happen in the United States today. But happen it did and a great leader was taken from us.

John Fitzgerald Kennedy was born to wealth and could have chosen a career in any field, but he chose the most difficult one of all, that of public service. And he served boldly and courageously, both in war and in peace. He was a strong and fearless leader, both in war and in peace.

The entire world recognized his outstanding character and qualities and our loss was also their loss, mourned even by our enemies.

To his bereaved widow and family I extend my heartfelt condolences.

The following poems by one of my constituents, Miss Bettie LaVeck, express much better the feelings of all Americans over this loss:

We the People of This United States

We the people of this United States of America live in the manner we so desire with the right to speak as we believe, live as we believe, pray as we so desire. We have more as a family than any other country of living people on this whole earth, and yet we are still greedy, filled with hate, hate for others that we envy and are jealous of not realizing that each family, each person has a cross to bear of their own to enter into heaven, the heaven created by God for those whom are worthy of entering this Kingdom of Heaven. With this in mind, I write a few words to try to bring out the true meaning of love, of life, of the meaning of togetherness for all mankind. The hunger of greed, lusts of life, not truly believing in ourselves can be our very downfall as a Nation. Destroying each other in inhuman acts.

Eternal Rest

The President's casket is now laying in state.
The murderer who has chosen his fate.
Noblemen pass to bid farewell
To their past President they knew so well.
Time passes.
Servicemen erect in form
Have their duties to perform.
The horses' hoofs beat upon the streets with time,
The drums beat with a rhythm rhyme.
In disbelief crowds gather and stare,
Time meaning nothing, they're going nowhere.
A small lad steps out in plain view,
Saluting his father in front of you.
Religion of all faiths busy with their prayer,
Each and every human willing to do their share.
Never in history have people turned to God as of this day,
No matter what color or age, they bow their heads to pray.
Time passes.

Each mourn the way he sees fit,
Throughout this vast world a small candle is lit.
The flag stands at half-mast, the bugle gives its call,
The stillness echoes through the air, the guns salute in all.
The sun slowly sinks into the west,
While we have placed our President to eternal rest.

—Bettie A. LaVeck,

Taylor, Mich.   *Age 35.*

We Mourn Our President

Today Mr. Kennedy with a smile on his face and a hand
     shake for all
Was shot and killed, into his wife's arms he did fall.
She cuddled him and cradled him while death came to
     call
Our Nation deeply saddened as bare trees in the fall.
Oh President, my President, what fate made you go?
The highest peak of your career was now that we know.
You worked each day for each of us, your courage never
     wavered,
Now I feel God chose you to sit beside your Saviour.
And as the years go by, little John and Caroline will know,
That the President, their daddy, really loved them so.
For his love will live in history, his accomplishs reread
     with time
And you will tell your children, that daddy he was mine.
Mrs. Kennedy I touched you though you felt me not,
Your bravery and your courage could never be forgot.
May a candle brightly glow and kindle in your heart,
For God walks close beside you, for you He is a part.
I'm sure that each American feels hurt, shocked and sad,
Indigent acts such as this make America look rather bad.
It takes just one to start a heavy stone to roll,
And soon several others start to take their toll.
We wonder and we ponder, we shiver and we cry,
We cannot find the answers no matter how we try.
Yet, it was our President that gave his life this day
And set our Nation mourning for God to show the way.

—Bettie A. LaVeck,

Age 35.

Taylor, Mich., *November 28, 1963.*

TRIBUTES BY

Hon. Roland V. Libonati

OF ILLINOIS

Mr. Speaker, Mr. Castleman, publicity director of the American Federation of Senior Citizens, delivered a eulogy to senior citizens groups throughout the Chicago area. The Senior Citizen is a publication devoted toward helping the aged attain a more secure life. The movement is affiliated with the Chicago Council and the

National Council of Senior Citizens. His rendition, as follows, was interesting and provocative:

A Eulogy to Martyrs

(By Wm. Castleman, chairman, Uptown Senior Citizens Association)

The world has a long list of martyrs, men, and women who gave their lives for the love of their fellow men. Over 3,000 years ago, Moses, a son of a slave, the first known emancipator of human slavery, became a Prince in the House of the Pharaohs of Egypt. He built a nation based on the freedom of the individual, with opportunity for his people to life and happiness was his greatest concern. His duty laid plainly before him; the effort to lay the foundation of a social state in which deep poverty and degrading want should be unknown—where men released from the meanest struggles that waste human energy should have the opportunity for intellectual and moral development.

This great leader of mankind, who could have had anything that his heart desired, gave up all the luxuries that wealth could give, to live among his people, who down through the centuries have stood steadfast to the belief in the Mosaic laws in the face of endless persecutions. To this day no one knows where the sepulcher of Moses is at. Yet, he left the people of the world laws of human behavior that will live to the end of time. These laws, the Ten Commandments, are as necessary to life and happiness today as they were 3,000 years ago, if humanity is to survive the great storms of life in this critical period.

Some of our historians record that some 1,932 years ago, a son of a carpenter, whose love for humanity, justice and peace, became a threat to the Roman oligarchy, who in their fears sentenced him to death. He was compelled to drag a heavy manmade cross over a long road to Calvary to be crucified. The jeers of the ignorant, the biased, and the uninformed, rent the air in glee, while others stood silently by with tears streaming down their faces in deep prayer.

And in our country, another emancipator of slaves, came forth to lead our Nation to greater freedom, justice, and opportunity, Abraham Lincoln, a son of a farmer. Having deep convictions, he was able to save our Nation in a bitter struggle between the forces of slavery and those of liberty. He tried hard to prevent a conflict and the loss of human life in seeking a solution toward preserving our Nation. He died at the hands of an assassin, cutting short his dream of building a better world. Had he lived a full lifespan, maybe we would not now need to face the grave problem of equal rights.

And again our Nation is in mourning. A young man, a millionaire's son, is shot by an assassin's bullet. Was his love for humanity, for liberty, and justice the cause of his destruction? Why has this occurred at a time when the world is so badly in need of a great leader for peace and humanity? John F. Kennedy had the courage, the capacity, and the love for his fellow men. He could have saved the Nation from internal strife, and brought peace to a world of chaos. Can his untimely death be a warning to us, that unless we abolish greed and selfishness we are doomed by the laws of nature and nature's God. Are we to be obliterated from the face of the earth? This was true of the dinosaurs some thousands of years ago. Nature's laws, God's laws, if you please, have no favorites.

May the light of reason direct us in this dark hour toward the laudable aims and aspirations of our late beloved President, John F. Kennedy. May his dream of a New Frontier for humanity be our inspiration to make his dream a reality in our day. He then shall not have given his life for his country in vain. His body has ceased to be with us, but his spirit lives on, ever reminding us that our duty is to make his dream of a New Frontier come true, that we may all enjoy a better and more peaceful world.

———

My President Is Dead

Oh, the wind is bitter cold tonight
  That moans through the cypress trees.
The moon is dark and has no face
  And gone is the gentle breeze,

So still is the song of the mockingbird,
  His music I hear no more.
And the angry waves cry out in the night
  As they beat on the ragged shore.

Oh, lift him gently and lay him down
  Beneath a blanket of snow,
Wrap him with love and tenderness
  For cold are the winds that blow.

He was only here for such a little while,
  He was much too young to die.
So find him a valley that's green again
  With a patch of blue for his sky.

Maybe he wasn't always right,
  But he fought for what he believed,
For a better world and the right to be free
  In a land that must not be deceived.

He looked like a boy when he smiled sometimes
  With a twinkle in his eye.
Yet he stood so tall in the world of men.
  Why did he have to die?

Bewilderment covers the earth tonight,
  A nation stands shocked and stunned.
How could the violent seed of hate
  Stop a life that has only begun?

Let not the good that he sought to do
  Lie now in the cold dark grave.
Let the peace on earth and the freedom of man
  Be the price for the life he gave.

Oh, cold is the wind from the mountain tonight
  And unknown the road ahead
For the wind wails out through the cypress trees
  My President is dead.

      —Billee Shoecraft.

TRIBUTES BY

Hon. Clarence D. Long

OF MARYLAND

Mr. Speaker, under unanimous consent to revise and extend my remarks I wish to include a short poem written by Maureen Norton, of Baltimore, Md.

The death of President Kennedy touched the hearts of all Americans. Even the teenage generation felt the impact of that great loss. Quite by accident, Mr. and Mrs. Bernard Norton, the parents of Maureen, came across this small ballad which their daughter had written. Maureen is a junior at the Institute of Notre Dame, and I feel this poem reflects both her own deep sentiments and the fine training she has received.

> With scarlet red roses,
> And a light pink suit,
> Walked Mrs. Kennedy looking cute.
> With a dark blue suit,
> And a smile so gay,
> Walked Mr. Kennedy through the day.
> All during the day,
> They walked with joy
> To only one's dismay.
> Though why we lost this great man
> No one will fully understand.
> God calls us when He sees fit
> That is the answer, that is it.

Mr. Speaker, I include a tribute of sympathy from the Second District Democratic Club, Baltimore County, to Mrs. Jacqueline Kennedy, upon the loss of her beloved husband, the late President, John Fitzgerald Kennedy. It is a tribute which expresses the feelings of all American citizens upon the untimely death of President Kennedy. It is with great pride, and a joining of my own personal sympathy with that of the Second District Democratic Club, that I insert the club's official resolution of sympathy. It is my high privilege, as well, to transmit an official copy of this resolution, under the seal of the club and signed by the club president in the name of all the members, to Mrs. Jacqueline Kennedy.

The resolution follows:

Whereas it is with profound regret and the deepest sorrow that the Second District Democratic Club, Inc., records the untimely demise of the late John Fitzgerald Kennedy, President of the United States of America, on November 22, in the year of our Lord one thousand nine hundred and sixty-three; and

Whereas the said John Fitzgerald Kennedy did faithfully serve our beloved Nation in war and in peace, and who by his heroic action in the time of war saved the lives of many of his countrymen, and in the time of peace gave his life in the service of his country; and

Whereas by his political activities he became the leader of our Democratic Party, and as a legislator and as President of this great Republic, had sponsored many important pieces of legislation for the benefit of this Nation and for mankind in general; and

Whereas in his passing this Nation has lost one of its most beloved and respected citizens, and we the individual citizens have lost a true and trusted friend: Now, therefore, be it

Resolved by the Second District Democratic Club, Inc., on this 16th day of December, in the year of our Lord 1963, That this expression of sorrow be spread on the minutes of this club and that the secretary be instructed to send a copy of this resolution to Mrs. Jacqueline Kennedy, the widow of our late beloved President.

As witness my hand and seal of the club this 16th day of December 1963.

CHARLES C. GLOS,
President.

TRIBUTE BY

Hon. Harris B. McDowell, Jr.

OF DELAWARE

Mr. Speaker, a recent sermon on the death of President Kennedy by the Rev. Donald J. Maccallum, pastor of the People's Congregational Church, Dover, Del., has evoked wide interest.

Former Senator J. Allen Frear of Delaware called me and spoke of his interest in this sermon.

I am including this sermon at this point in my remarks:

A SERMON ON THE DEATH OF PRESIDENT KENNEDY

(Delivered in People's Congregational Church, Dover, Del., by Rev. Donald J. Maccallum, November 24, 1963)

When bitter and senseless tragedy stuns not only a nation but the whole world, when a person whose life and office symbolize the finest in our national character and the highest aspirations of our people is cut down by the hand of a demented assassin, when the reward of conscientious public service and courageous devotion to duty is a bullet in the head, it is time for a people to think, it is time for a people to listen.

We are here to listen to what God might speak to us through this calamitous experience, and we are here to think deeply, honestly, and penitently about the society which must ever bear on its conscience the guilt of its own affliction.

In some other places in the world, the violent death of a chief magistrate would not occasion the alarm or the grief, the astonishment or the sorrow, the abhorrence or the sympathy that have accompanied the murder of the President.

For in some less favored lands, assassination is an expected instrument of political power. But not in the United States. We have protected ourselves from political violence by a common loyalty to peaceable constitutional procedures.

It is not yet possible to know what wildly twisted motive triggered the fatal shot. That it was an act of mental madness is self-evident. But the acts of a demented mind can be the execution of a fearful logic unswerved by civilized traditions or humane instincts. Behind violence is a stimulus to destroy what threatens self-will and personal desire.

And the question which the American people must ask themselves today is whether the social passions of these recent years have provided a climate stimulating to such abhorrent depravity as the murder of our Chief of State.

Whether the President was made a martyr to the principles of domestic justice and tranquillity or whether his death is another sacrifice on the altar of peaceful world relations which he protected with deliberate courage just a year ago, or whether he was the victim of some unsuspected personal vengeance, this fact remains:

We have breathed the foul fumes of a new and dangerous climate in our country in recent months and years. We have departed from our tradition of resolving momentous social issues by rational and peaceable constitutional procedures. We have tolerated shootings, bombings, murders, and mobbings as instruments of political decision. We have incited to riot in place of reason. We have substituted violence for vision. And even in those communities which have not been riven by hateful passions, we have been fed a steady stream of social poison by venomous purveyors of malice and hate.

This is not the kind of society for which our fathers labored. This is not the kind of society for which sons and brothers and husbands have fought as citizen soldiers and laid down their very lives. This is not the kind of society which has inspired other nations to seek for themselves the blessings of liberty and justice and peace. This is not the kind of society to which we have ourselves aspired. This is not the kind of society which reflects the true national character of our people. This is not the kind of society which our President symbolized. This is the kind of society which has a lunatic capacity to destroy our finest national qualities, to crush our noblest aspirations, and to return us to the dark reign of primitive passions, unbridled impulses, and social terror.

The assassination of the President hovers today over this whole Nation as an urgent question mark demanding instant answer: Is this the kind of society we want? Do we want a society in which political victories can be gained by personal violence? Do we want a society in which demented passions can direct our destiny? Do we want a society in which conscientious contributions to the public good endanger even life itself? Do we want a society stripped of those humane and civilized values which men have struggled long and painfully and with great sacrifice to achieve and to protect?

Yes, we have created a new and fearful climate in America—a climate which, if it did not direct the assassin's bullet on Friday, still stimulates the kind of depravity, the kind of insanity, the kind of violence, the kind of inhumanity, the kind of unbridled self-will, the kind of social irresponsibility, the kind of moral blindness so lamentably exalted in Dallas.

Is this what we want? Is this what we believe in? Is this the direction we shall pursue until our luster as a free and just and responsible people is tarnished dull? This is the time for sober self-examination, for probing appraisal of the flaws in our national character and certainly a time for penitence.

These days of universal sorrow should also be days when a new resoluteness of spirit stiffens the American character. The words of our first martyred President ring with renewed urgency across a century of time:

"It is for us to be here dedicated to the great task remaining before us—that from these honored dead we take increased devotion to that cause for which they gave the last full measure of devotion—that we here highly resolve that these dead shall not have died in vain—that this Nation, under God, shall have a new birth of freedom and that Government of the people, by the people and for the people, shall not perish from the earth."

However, history shall judge the brief administration of John Fitzgerald Kennedy, those of us who lived under his leadership will testify to its resolute purpose in those days of frightening nuclear crisis and to its resolute firmness in days of domestic discord. Whatever political evaluations the future may make, this President will stand with the Great Emancipator as a purposeful leader who, in the lonely hours of critical decision, chose "firmness in the right, as God gives us to see the right."

You may remember that after that address that asked of the American people a willingness to sacrifice, some cynically inquired, "What sacrifice?" Today we know what sacrifice.

There is only one sacrifice that any man is asked to make for the principles and purposes in which he believes—the sacrifice of his life. Some honored few give up their lives in the course of public duty and perhaps in the stillness of death far more than the vigor of life, they inspire in us, the living, a new spirit of dedication to "the unfinished work which they * * * so nobly advanced."

Life is sacrificed, life is made a holy offering, in some cases by giving it up, in others by living it out in devotion to the highest good we know, the finest purposes we perceive.

"Ask not what your country can do for you," he said. "Ask what you can do for your country." And when we ask, the answer comes: you can consecrate your life by the high resolution that these dead shall not have died in vain; you can dedicate your life "to the unfinished work which they * * * advanced"; you can sacrifice your life by engulfing self-will and self-interest in a consuming passion for liberty and justice for all.

These days of lamentation are also a time for renewed confidence in our Nation and in its destiny. "What are we coming to?" many a person asked when they heard of the sniper's fatal shot. "What are we coming to?" It is understandable that we should ask in the moment of shock. But when composure is regained such despair should vanish.

There is cause, indeed, for grief and sorrow and penitence that such a crime should happen. But there is no cause for despair. For "we know that in everything God works for good with those who love him."

Our Government is not so weak, our Nation is not so fragile, our people are not so resourceless, that we cannot endure, painfully it may be, this bitter assault on our principles, this awful personal tragedy.

The helm of Government has passed into skilled and experienced and devoted hands and the ship of state sails on. The seas may be rough and the winds may be fierce but the vessel is sturdy and the course is clear.

To a mourning people, tempted to despair, these words from an earlier time seem to speak the confident assurance we need:

> "Thou, too, sail on, O Ship of State!
> Sail on, O Union, strong and great!
> Humanity with all its fears,
> With all the hopes of future years,
> Is hanging breathless on thy fate!
>
> "Sail on, nor fear to breast the sea!
> Our hearts, our hopes are all with thee,
> Our hearts, our hopes, our prayers, our tears,
> Our faith triumphant o'er our fears,
> Are all with thee,—are all with thee!"
>
> —H. W. LONGFELLOW.

PASTORAL PRAYER

Eternal God, our Father, we bring unto Thee the solemn prayer of a sorrowing people.

Forgive us our sins, pardon our iniquities, comfort our afflictions, and renew in us a right spirit that while we mourn, we may not murmer and while we grieve we may not despair.

We give Thee thanks that Thou dost raise up leaders of the people, that Thou dost endow men with noble faculties of mind and spirit devoted to the public good.

Especially in these mournful days we thank Thee for the President now dead in whom we symbolized the hopes and aspirations of our people. For his faithful public service, his integrity of character, his strength of purpose and his breadth of vision, we offer to Thee the gratitude of a grieving nation.

Comfort those who intimately mourn his loss and strengthen those who must pursue the path he laid but did not tread.

Inspire by Thy spirit the President of the United States that he may bear the burdens of his heavy task and guide this people toward their long-sought destiny of liberty with justice, prosperity with peace.

And breathe upon a stricken land the consolation and the comfort which Thou alone canst give.

Save us from corroding bitterness and deliver us from formless fears that we may emerge from tragedy with deeper unity, profounder sympathies, and stronger devotion to this land we love.

Through Jesus Christ our Lord.

Amen.

TRIBUTES BY

Hon. Clifford G. McIntire

OF MAINE

Mr. Speaker, the various newspaper publications throughout our land have come forward with editorial offerings relating to the tragic assassination of President John Fitzgerald Kennedy.

Here are two articles in this respect from two newspapers in my State of Maine, one the Lewiston Daily Sun and the other the Lewiston Evening Journal. I commend their content to the attention of my colleagues:

[From the Lewiston (Maine) Daily Sun, Nov. 23, 1963]

PRESIDENT ASSASSINATED

An assassin's bullets have destroyed the life of the President of the United States, and changed the course of history.

The rifle shots which rang out as the official motorcade rode through the streets of Dallas, Tex., wrote a violent end to the career of President John F. Kennedy and plunged the Nation and the world into mourning.

In the brief moments of the terrifying sound of gunfire, the President and the Governor of Texas lay wounded. America's First Lady had flung herself in front of her husband in a brave but vain attempt to shield him from the bullets which already had found their mark.

President Kennedy was in Texas as part of an effort to strengthen the Democratic Party there. He had spoken out against factionalism and strife within his party. He did not foresee that a fanatical assassin would take matters into his own hands to strike a blow against life itself. Even the extraordinary precautions always taken to protect a President were not enough.

Violence is common to the politics of many countries. It is unusual and all the more shocking in the United States. That there were hotbeds of extremism in the West and Southwest has been a matter of common knowledge. That it would kindle the awful flames of assassination was unexpected.

The President's assassination cut short his brilliant career at its very height. He was in the preliminary stages of a campaign for another 4-year term, although he had made no official announcement of his candidacy. His visit to Texas, like the tours into other parts of the country, including the recent trip to the University of Maine, formed part of that background campaign.

Every American, regardless of party, has suffered a personal loss. America has lost an outstanding leader whose brave program for a peaceful world was the hope of all mankind.

There are no words to soothe the pain of his griefstricken wife and family. But an America in mourning strives to share that great sorrow.

[From the Lewiston (Maine) Evening Journal, Nov. 23, 1963]

THE BLACKEST DAY

Today we, the American people, mourn the death of President John Fitzgerald Kennedy. There are no words which can be written to describe adequately the depth of emotion we are feeling over the untimely, brutal, calculated murder of our youthful President.

His near 3 years as leader of our Nation were marked by severe international crises, domestic problems that featured racial bitterness in the South and in some of our larger cities and problems involving a Congress which did not always see eye to eye with him insofar as certain important legislative matters were concerned. Despite the complex and often irritating issues which faced President Kennedy these past 3 years, he maintained a basic good humor and a sense of purpose that made his political opponents like him as a man and admire him for his persistency.

The great warmth of the late President was exemplified many times during the course of his press conferences. Many Maine citizens had a recent opportunity to witness it upon his visitation to the University of Maine where he received an honorary degree. And most remembered of all, of course, were those pictures of John Kennedy which appeared in the press and on the television screen to show him the uninhibited, loving father and family man.

Friday, November 22, 1963, will go down in American history as one of the blackest days this Nation has ever faced. It definitely represents the most tragic single event since the surprise attack upon Pearl Harbor. It was a deed most obviously undertaken by one imbued with the stark, deadly hatred which moves only within those who have taken up the cause of the lunatic left or the radical right. The assassination of President Kennedy carries within it the curse of Cain as so often witnessed to by those who are extremists. May his death bring all who have veered over into paths of intolerance and hatred back to the reality demanded of all who have faith in God; back to a realization that intolerance and hatred solve nothing, and that only love of one's fellow man possesses the virtue to bring understanding.

There are no tears shed which can relieve us of a terrible sense of loneliness and lostness. There are no emotions sufficient to disclose the measure of our sympathy for Mrs. Kennedy, 6-year-old Caroline, and 3-year-old John. Only through our prayers and our faith may we hope to walk from the valley of shadow back into the light.

Today the world shares the bereavement of John Kennedy's family and friends. May the American people of the immediate tomorrow assure the end of any similar future tragedy by dedicating themselves to the sacred task of building and preserving peace for our time at home and abroad. Then and only then may the American people proclaim that the death of this dedicated American was not in vain.

Mr. Speaker, newspapers throughout my State of Maine have been making editorial comment on the untimely and tragic assassination of President John Fitzgerald Kennedy.

Just recently I had the opportunity of reading the editorials that appeared in the Bangor Daily News and the Portland Sunday Telegram. I have found these editorials eminently interesting and I commend them to the attention of my colleagues.

[From the Bangor (Maine) Daily News, Nov. 25, 1963]

FROM THE FOUR CORNERS OF THE EARTH

As John Fitzgerald Kennedy is laid to his eternal rest today, sorrowing Americans can find comfort and reassurance in the great outpouring of sympathy that has come from all parts of the world.

The formal diplomatic messages were to have been expected. But there has been much, much more.

France's Charles de Gaulle will attend today's services in Washington to bid final farewell to the man who was leader of the free world as well as President of the United States. Britain will be represented by Prince Philip and Prime Minister Sir Alec Douglas Home. Chancellor Ludwig Erhard of West Germany will be a mourner.

Their presence is a tribute to the late President and to the Nation. But most heart warming of all has been the spontaneous response of the world's common people.

In West Berlin, 80,000 free world men and women marched in a solemn torchlight parade, demonstrating their grief over the loss of the young and vigorous free world leader. Candles were burned in the windows of Berlin homes.

The commander of the Japanese naval craft that sunk Kennedy's PT boat in World War II—and thus very nearly taking Kennedy's life at that time—sent condolences to the Kennedy family. The cameldriver friend of President Lyndon B. Johnson sent his personal message of sympathy from Pakistan. A Russian woman—a private citizen—brought an armful of roses to the U.S. Embassy in Moscow.

And so it went after the news of the late President's assassination was flashed to the far corners of the earth. The plain and good people of the world were shocked and grieved.

More than that, their words signified encouragement to the Nation that has the task of leading the struggle for freedom and justice for all men everywhere. They were speaking from their hearts. They were expressing gratitude for what this Nation has done for them. And they were rallying behind the cause which John Fitzgerald Kennedy symbolized as the President of the United States.

Today's sorrow must be borne. Life must go on. The struggle must go on. The burden is made lighter by the outpouring of sympathy that has streamed into the Nation's Capital from the plain, good people of the world. They have faith in America. This strengthens the faith of Americans in themselves.

And so now to the sad task of saying farewell to John Fitzgerald Kennedy—whose dedicated service to his country was cut short by an assassin's bullet.

[From the Portland (Maine) Sunday Telegram and Sunday Press Herald, Nov. 24, 1963]

HISTORIC WARNING

As the Nation lifts itself from the shock of the President's assassination, it faces into a new chapter of American history.

Like a symphony repeating a grand theme, the story of the American Republic has almost looped back on itself to encompass the shooting of another noble President who had been catapulted into fame by his championship of Negro freedom. On Friday the Union acted out a muted version of those events of nearly a century ago, with a startling parallel—the succession of a Vice President named Johnson.

John Kennedy's brief administration was marked by one thing above all. It was his recognition of the disease of racial segregation that infects the whole country; his appraisal of its virulence; and his courage in speaking and acting to remedy the evil. More than any President in modern times, he took his stand for the rights guaranteed to Negroes in the U.S. Constitution. And that deliberate act made the parallel with Abraham Lincoln more than a mechanical one of date and fatal bullets and Vice Presidents named Johnson.

President Kennedy has fallen at a critical time in the evolution of the racial problem. Like Lincoln, he was greatly admired and bitterly hated for his words and actions in the cause of human freedom. He leaves a country divided, with a new presidential election approaching, in which the main issue may be "black and white."

Fortunately, the Nation is not wounded as it was 100 years ago by the Civil War. President Lyndon B. Johnson has a much greater chance to conciliate the opposing factions than did his namesake, President Andrew Johnson, who was the victim of bitter squabbling and vindictiveness in the days of Reconstruction. He is a southerner himself, but has shown a broad sympathy for the cause of civil rights. His career in the Senate was a lessonbook in bringing divergent groups together for effective action. He is no weakling.

But if he is to succeed in preventing America's most critical issue from once again tearing the Union apart, he must receive the help, the charity, the determination of millions of Americans that "this Nation, conceived in liberty and dedicated to the proposition that all men are created equal," shall endure. The historic parallel is a warning. This is a time for men of all factions to live by the legacy of John Kennedy: "Ask not what your country can do for you, but what you can do for your country."

Mr. Speaker, the American people continue to make sad reflections on the tragic assassination of President John Fitzgerald Kennedy. In recognition of these reflections I submit two appropriate articles, one a statement by State Senator Bill Boardman, of Calais, Maine, and another a front-page extract from the November 28 issue of the Penobscot Times.

PRESIDENT OF ALL THE PEOPLE—A NATION VOICES ITS SORROW, AND ITS HOPE

Several days have passed, and now it must be accepted that it was not a hideous dream: John Fitzgerald Kennedy, the brilliant and vigorous young President of the United States is dead.

People of this area, despite the evidence of news bulletins and television pictures, could not believe it: they could not believe that anyone could be capable of such a crime against the country, and they could not believe that the country was so suddenly bereft of its vital and buoyant young leader. People, it seemed, felt an almost fierce possessiveness toward this President, regardless of their political views.

The recent visit of President Kennedy to the University of Maine—which gave thousands of residents of this area their first and only opportunity to see a President in person—made it more difficult to accept the fact of his loss. People here, whether they saw him in person or on television, felt, after his visit, that he was uniquely our President. They had seen him break into a grin at the wit of University President Lloyd Elliott; they knew that he had actually tried, as a new alumnus, to sing the Stein Song; and many had seen him play his characteristic trick of darting suddenly from his planned route to shake hands with people in the crowd. It made people feel warm toward him that he had so apparently enjoyed himself on his visit to Maine. The President of the United States was no longer an awesome figure in the distant city of Washington, D.C.

The reasons for the great fondness of the people for President Kennedy were as varied as the many facets of his complex personality: from his calm, poised intelligence, to his enthusiasm for touch football; his ready handshakes for people lining a fence, to his vision of world peace; his steady but unobtrusive devotion to his religious faith, to his pride in his family. His youth made him singularly appealing: he was kin to all the young, and older people could take a fond, parental pride in him, even though they might shake their heads disapprovingly at times.

Whatever the reasons, John Fitzgerald Kennedy had, by some magic of personality, become uniquely the President of all the people, in the 2 years and 10 months of his leadership. It is for historians to attempt to explain how he accomplished this. The present can only mourn its great loss.

The words have all been said, by statesmen and politicians, by reporters and broadcasters, by people in all walks of life.

Everyone said the right words, to describe the shock and the horror and the sorrow of the events in Dallas, Tex.

They were said in Old Town and in Lincoln, in Washington and Los Angeles, in Boston and Tampa.

They were the words of a people who were stunned and disbelieving, who were unanimously outraged and sick at heart over the bullet in Dallas that took the life of John Fitzgerald Kennedy.

They were the words of a people who suddenly felt that part of them, too, had died in Dallas on that fateful

Friday afternoon. For John Fitzgerald Kennedy was a part of these people, as they were a part of him, because he was the Nation's chosen leader and every American felt that the tremendous burdens he carried were their burdens.

The words and the tears were those of people who had lost a relative or someone who was close to them, and in a sense this was true.

There were words that expressed the revulsion for a terrible deed that ripped the glitter from the vaunted civilization of which Americans proudly boast, and exposed the intolerance and hatred which too many of us have been willing to ignore.

There were the words of a minister who asked if this terrible event were not to be expected by a people who could ignore the callous bombing that wiped out the lives of children in Alabama.

There were the words, too, of millions of people who joined a stricken widow and her two young children in mourning for the death of a husband and father. They mourned, too, for a brave policeman's widow and children in Dallas, and they suffered with the black image which tarnished the Nation when "eye for an eye" revenge killed the man who had fired the assassin's bullet.

They were the words of strangeness and uneasiness, words of an entire people who were joined in the common bondage of sadness and sorrow.

But eventually, they were the words of hope and confidence in the future.

They were the words of a people drawn together by this tragic event, of a people who gained solidarity and strength in their common sorrow.

They were the words of Americans who believe in their country, who know that one chosen from among us has always met the test of the problems ahead.

They were the words of a people who know that the country goes on and the Government goes on.

They were the words of a people who recognized their good fortune in having Lyndon Johnson to succeed John Kennedy—a great man to succeed a great man in a great Nation.

———

PRESIDENT JOHN F. KENNEDY: "* * *; ASK RATHER WHAT YOU CAN DO FOR YOUR COUNTRY"

President John F. Kennedy at the age of 46 was in the prime of life, from the standpoint of youthful vitality, and in respect to the high office which he held. Our late President had the unique capacity to draw upon the talent of our country, and at the same time was able to project his image as the President of the United States in a manner which demanded respect. The personality of John F. Kennedy was such that he could draw people to him with remarkable ease. From the day he was sworn in as the 35th President of our great country he was beset by matters of extreme and grave importance to the welfare of our country—these have been trying times for our youthful President, and indeed trying times for the free world under his leadership as President of the United States. One by one the matters affecting our freedom, liberty, and civil rights had come to the front for consideration. Each of the matters came forth as

an incident which quickly spread to the knowledge of the people of the world—our integration problems, the Cuban situation which included the effort on the part of the Soviet Union to test our country to the maximum, and the many other incidents some of which may be known only to top officials of our country.

There are many things in this world which we mortals cannot seem to understand; things from the distant past and from the near present. The events of the past weekend, one of the blackest in my lifetime, are difficult to comprehend or fully realize. In a world which has become more civilized day by day how can it be that the President of the United States—a man respected by his own people, and by people throughout the world—has been cut down in one of our own cities at the hands of a brutal assassin?

As in any free country where expression of opinion is protected and freedom of action is a birthright the only safeguard is law and justice—the law as declared by society for the conduct of society, and the courts of our great land which are dedicated to the carrying out of the law of our land—to afford equal justice to all under the law.

When the people of any free nation, separate or in groups, disregard the law and the course of justice they are in deep trouble, as is their nation. The incidents of violence which have marked our past few years in complete, or sometimes partial disregard of the law, including the integration incidents, and the tragic death of our President, have stirred our Nation.

What course this new awareness will take I cannot say for sure, but I certainly hope it will start action in a proper direction. This is indeed a time to reexamine our own attitude and appreciation for the freedom which we are guaranteed under our law, and the protections we are given under the law.

Why at the prime of his career and his life was our President taken from us under such tragic circumstances? Could it be that the Divine Power, which has the ability to give life and to take it away, has been given no alternative but to indicate to us, in this tragic way, the grave error in the course we are following as individuals and from which we must change. To take from us a man who was exerting so great an effort toward peace, justice and equality, in a position where such action could do so much good, in the Divine Plan must have been of strong purpose to call for such action. The tragic passing of our President—occasioned by the anger or wrath of his attacker—by one of the most wicked acts that a mortal being is capable of, namely murder (the taking of the life of another), was in direct and complete disregard of the law of our society and the higher law of Almighty God. Taking the law of God and man into one's own hands, for the presumed purpose of administering justice, is contrary to any sense of justice; this sets up the assassin as the sole judge with no rules to follow except his own warped sense of value.

In the tragic death of President John F. Kennedy perhaps we will be able to see the course which has unfolded before us and what should be done to strengthen our sense of values and responsibility to others through the law of society and proper administration of justice. The whole episode of the past week has left me stunned, as it undoubtedly has many citizens of our country and the world; what the meaning of it all is in terms of history, and the will of Almighty God. I am not positive but I hope that as time unfolds we may be given insight into the whole picture of last weekend which claimed the life of our President, a police officer in pursuit of his suspected assassin, and finally the assassination of the man who was the prime suspect in the murder of our President. Violence has spread its full wings and struck with talons sharp, quick and deadly.

In the words of our late President, John F. Kennedy, "ask not what your country can do for you; ask rather what you can do for your country." These words are destined to go down in history—President John F. Kennedy gave the supreme sacrifice on November 22, 1963; he gave his life in the service of his country. May God grant that he has not died in vain, and may his soul rest in eternal peace.

Respectfully,

Senator BILL BOARDMAN.

CALAIS, MAINE.

TRIBUTE BY

Hon. Charles McC. Mathias, Jr.

OF MARYLAND

Mr. Speaker, under leave to extend my remarks I include the following: Thousands of words have been spoken and many thousands more written in eulogy of our late President, and many thousands more will be heard and read in the days ahead for Americans will not soon forget the terrible tragedy of the assassination.

Reactions to this incomprehensible act have appeared in print in newspapers all over the world, but, I believe no editorial presents the heart of America better than one entitled "Death Carries No Party Labels" written by Leo T. Paulin which appeared in the November 27 edition of the Bethesda-Chevy Chase (Md.) Advertiser.

I submit the text of this editorial and commend it to my colleagues:

Death carries no party labels: It was 8 o'clock when I walked out of my office and into Wisconsin Avenue last Friday night. The same amount of current as always flowed through the wires to the street lights that illuminate Wisconsin Avenue.

But on this night the intensity of their light could not penetrate the gray fog which enveloped everyone on the street. A man walked by holding an infant in his arms. His face, too, was fog-gray. He stared ahead—an empty

stare, uncomprehending, tragic. It was almost like a man walking into destination unknown with a dead son in his arms.

Traffic along the broad avenue moved reluctantly. Cars came to a gentle stop at the red light. When the light turned green they tiptoed on their way with reverence; like people leaving a funeral parlor. The drivers were intent. It seemed not at all important to beat the driver in the next lane away from the intersection.

An hour before I left the building I stood gazing into the street from my second-floor office. With me were Joan Winters, our fashion editor, and Bill Hantzis, one of our account executives. The windows were open and the distant wail of sirens told us that the awful tragedy that had befallen the United States, and most of the world, a few hours earlier would be coming even closer to us in a few minutes.

Helmeted police astride screeching motorcycles came first. Then the long light-gray naval hospital ambulance carrying the lifeless body of our President passed under our window. I made the sign of the cross; so did Joan. Bill Hantzis was silent, motionless.

In the ambulance also was courageous, magnificent Jacqueline Kennedy, still wearing the blood-stained suit against which she had cradled her dying husband.

At 2:25 p.m. on that fateful Friday, November 22, 1963, I walked out of Suburban Hospital where I had visited Jack Espey, a patient there and vice president of the Paulin Publishing Co. Minutes after I started my car I heard the frightening flash: "President Kennedy has been shot."

As the reality of the horrible act dawned, my eyes filled with tears. I stopped the car on Georgetown Road and listened to the developing details. When I arrived at our publishing building I went into my private office and found most of the staff there clustered around the TV set.

The women were crying openly; the men were red-eyed holding back tears. Somehow men are not permitted the release of sobbing unashamedly. The pall of tragedy was wrapped around us. Our work, so important minutes earlier, had become meaningless, absurdly insignificant.

The couple of dozen phones in our office which seem to ring incessantly were stilled. For a time America's heart had stopped beating. And America was as dead as John F. Kennedy, the strong, vibrant, dramatic personality who successfully challenged the greatest forces in life but succumbed to a piece of lead, pencil eraser size.

No writer anywhere can piece words together to adequately describe America's grief, shock, revulsion over the cowardly slaying of its beloved President. You reason, you rationalize, you ask, why? And there is no answer.

Was it part of God's design that this man, the great intellect, who pioneered new trails in the affairs of nations be taken from the world of mortals just 2 years and 10 months after he assumed the Presidency?

Was it part of divine design that John F. Kennedy missed by the narrowest of margins, yet missed, the nomination for Vice President in 1956? Had he captured that nomination and had been defeated along with

Adlai E. Stevenson, would he have been elected President in 1960? There is no answer.

Today, John F. Kennedy lies in a hero's grave in Arlington. The moment life passed from his body was a moment of deepest despair. All the Nation was grieved. His political opponents as completely so as his political supporters. And this is one of the marks of America's greatest. There are countries in the world, too many of them, where the passing of a head of state is a festive occasion for the opposition.

Only here, in America, can we detach political philosophy from the person espousing the philosophy. While he lived I did not subscribe to his New Frontier program and design for America. I opposed it at the polls and through my writings.

Yet when John F. Kennedy died I cried. I cried because I opposed only what he stood for and not what he was. I loved his warmth and gregariousness. His death revealed to all America the deep-seated affection for him which transcends all political antagonisms.

In the short span of his career John F. Kennedy has achieved greatness. He has left his mark on the world. His death, as no other single tragedy, not even World War II, awakened us once again to the true power of our beloved United States. Our unity, as a people, is our strength.

The office of the Presidency is sacred. The man who occupies it is our President.

And as the tears of sorrow dry and life returns to near normal, those of us who do not agree with the policies of his successor will marshal forces to oppose him. But let no man take his life. He's our President. We love him. This is America's greatness.

TRIBUTE BY

Hon. Spark M. Matsunaga

OF HAWAII

Mr. Speaker, much has been spoken and written in eulogy to our late beloved President, John Fitzgerald Kennedy, with such eloquence and thought-provoking sentiment that nothing I can say here can add to what has already been said or written. There is, however, an editorial which appeared on the front page of the Honolulu Advertiser of Saturday, November 23, which I believe worthy of the attention of this body.

JOHN F. KENNEDY

The tragedy of President Kennedy's assassination is almost beyond belief.

Here, one moment, was the young dynamic leader of the world's greatest power—driving through the crowds he enjoyed and from whom his personal magnetism always brought warm rapport.

Here, the next moment, was the fatally wounded victim of a madman whose ancestors-in-violence had slain Presidents Lincoln, Garfield, and McKinley and sought the deaths of Roosevelt and Truman.

President Lincoln was cut down within a week after the end of a war which had divided the Nation.

Ninety-eight years later, President Kennedy was slain in the midst of a struggle which divides the world.

History will write its appraisal of the 35th President as it already has of Lincoln, the 16th—"the finest product of democracy (and) its greatest exponent."

But even in the midst of shock and deep sadness, this can be said:

John Fitzgerald Kennedy was a President in the truest tradition of America. He had great intelligence. He had courage, as his action on Cuba a year ago so clearly showed. He had eloquence and he had wit.

Above all, he had faith in his Nation and in its ability to sustain a great destiny:

"In the long history of the world, only a few generations have been granted the role of defending freedom in its hour of maximum danger. I do not shrink from this responsibility—I welcome it."

He also said—this before his election 3 years ago—"we will need in the sixties a President who is willing and able to summon his national constituency to its finest hour, to alert the people to our dangers and our opportunities, to demand of them the sacrifices that will be needed."

In giving his life in the hazardous leadership of this Nation, he made the greatest sacrifice of all.

But in those words above, and those which follow, he left an inspiring and valid legacy to President Johnson:

"With a good conscience our only reward, with history the final judge of our deeds, let us go forth to lead the land we love, asking His blessing and His help, but knowing that here on earth God's work must truly be our own."

TRIBUTES BY

Hon. George P. Miller

OF CALIFORNIA

Mr. Speaker, one of the great tragedies of history occurred on November 22 when President John F. Kennedy was taken from us at the peak of his career. All of the American people were deeply affected and grieved by what happened.

The National Association of Letter Carriers by action of their executive council officially conveyed the sympathy of the membership of this organization to Mrs. Kennedy and her children. It also passed an official resolution pledging the prayers and loyalty of the 165,000 letter carriers to our new President Lyndon Johnson.

It gives me great pleasure to offer these resolutions because I believe they typify the feelings of all of us.

The National Association of Letter Carriers is to be highly commended for taking this action. The resolutions follow:

RESOLUTION BY NATIONAL ASSOCIATION OF LETTER CARRIERS

Whereas the cowardly and senseless assassination of President John Fitzgerald Kennedy has spiritually impoverished the entire free world; and

Whereas the cause of intelligent liberalism has suffered an irreparable blow through the sudden death of John Fitzgerald Kennedy; and

Whereas the National Association of Letter Carriers, its officers and its 165,000 members, feels a deeply personal loss in the death of a man whom they considered a very great President and a beloved friend; Be it

Resolved, That the Executive Council of the National Association of Letter Carriers convey to the widow of the martyred John Fitzgerald Kennedy and to his children the expression of their deep and personal grief, their abiding affection, their loyalty, their gratitude and their boundless admiration and sympathy.

> Jerome J. Keating, President; James H. Rademacher, Vice President; J. Stanley Lewis, Secretary-Treasurer; Charles N. Coyle, Assistant Secretary-Treasurer; George A. Bang, Director, Life Insurance; James P. Deely, Director, Health Insurance; Philip Lepper; James C. Stocker; Edward F. Benning; Carl J. Saxsenmeier; Thomas M. Flaherty; William T. Sullivan; J. Joseph Vacca; Glenn M. Hodges; Tony R. Huerta; George G. Morrow, Jr.; Dean S. Soverns; Austin B. Carlson; Fred Gadotti.

Mr. Speaker, many eloquent words have been expressed concerning various facets of the tragedy which faced our Nation last month.

One of my constituents has forwarded to me a copy of a poem which appeared in the Alameda, Calif., newspaper, the Times-Star.

This beautiful poem was written by Mr. Everett Johannes, of Alameda, and was inspired by the picture of the riderless horse following the caisson bearing the casket of our late President.

I am pleased to share this beautiful poem with my colleagues:

THE RIDERLESS HORSE

Young he was—my rider;
  A symbol of the land.
But he was slain—my rider.
  I cannot feel his hand.

Brave he was—my rider.
  He struggled for his men.
But he is dead—my rider.
  He cannot fight again.

A fire burns at his temple,
  A flag's at half its height,
A widow grieves in silence,
  Her veil is like the night.

We mourn your spur—my rider.
  We mourn your forceful hand.
The roses bloom, my rider,
  Like grief upon the land.
               —EVERETT JOHANNES.

Mr. Speaker, last November the world saw a brilliant life snuffed out when an assassin's bullet struck down our beloved President, John F. Kennedy.

Many millions of words have been spoken in tribute to what this great man accomplished during the 2 years and 10 months he served as our President. Many memorials are being prepared in his memory. However, the most lasting memorial will be the works he himself contributed to the greatness of our country.

One of these was his diligent effort on behalf of civil rights. This effort is clearly embodied in the civil rights bill now pending before the Congress.

I believe the American people share the sentiments which are expressed in the following excerpt from a newsletter published by the Alameda branch of the National Association for the Advancement of Colored People on December 19, 1963.

I am pleased to extend the remarks of the president of this branch, Mr. Carter Gilmore:

NEWSLETTER

The world will long remember John Fitzgerald Kennedy. Although we are saddened by his death, I know the world will be a better place because a man of his character lived among us.

The United States can at last take a long look at itself and realize what hate and bigotry can do, not only to one man but a nation, that is deprived by the tragic death of such a noble President—one who had so much he wanted to do for every American, white and Negro alike.

His beliefs shall live on, for men of good will will not let them die. His civil rights bill before Congress now makes our fight more intense, more dedicated.

Our hearts go out to his family, especially to his widow and children whose superb dignity made most children proud to be Americans.

The Negroes' quest for human right will go on, not only because we must, but because of men like Medger Evers and our late President John Fitzgerald Kennedy.

Sincerely,
               CARTER GILMORE,
                 President.

Mr. Speaker, many eloquent words have been spoken and lines of poetry have been written in tribute to the memory of our late President John F. Kennedy.

A good friend of mine, Mrs. Agnes Brown, of Oakland, Calif., has written her personal reflection on the greatness of President Kennedy and it is certainly a touching eulogy.

J.F.K.

The inauguration that snowy day,
The Cardinal, the Poet-Trumpets gay,
A challenging speech in staccatoed phrase
His wisdom and vision charting new ways.

The parents, brothers, sisters and cousins,
Peace Corpsmen circled the globe by dozens,
Vienna to Rio we heard acclaim.
The heroic Leader had won world fame.

New Frontiersmen were most everywhere
In quickened Space-age, that handsome pair
Children were playing in hallowed place
Beauty, Poetry, Song in White House grace.

Our Modern Lancelot Pursued his Grail
We watched him debate on his campaign trail
From West Virginia to the Golden Gate
He saw new ways to solve problems of state.

Who can ever forget the brilliant mind,
That eloquent voice and love of mankind,
The sparkling dry wit, ever flashing smile,
Was loved from Berlin to Emerald isle.

And a child shall lead them we've seen again,
Little John saluted him for all men,
We'll carry on as we know he would say,
I'll be thinking of all in the U.S.A.

—Agnes Brown.

TRIBUTE BY

Hon. Joseph G. Minish

OF NEW JERSEY

Mr. Speaker, one of the finest tributes to our late beloved President that has come to my attention was written by Mr. Jerry Bakst for the Suburban World which is published in several editions throughout the towns of Essex County, N.J. I know the Members will be interested in reading Mr. Bakst's moving eulogy which follows in full.

THE FALLEN EAGLE

(By Jerry Bakst)

No one in Verona, no one in Cedar Grove, regardless of political viewpoint or party preference, can have escaped the sense of shock, disbelief, dismay, and grief over the horrible news that the Nation's youngest elected President had been struck down by an assassin's bullet.

He was like a strong, young eagle, shot down in midflight on powerful wings by a senseless hunter, and the leaden thud when he fell was made stronger by the memory of him in the majesty of flight.

He was the first President—the first leader of the free world—born in this century, and an example of the best this country can produce. He had a keen mind, a curious and probing intellect, an energetic body, great and tremendous zeal for hard work, a monumental grasp of facts and figures, an appreciation of complex ideas, and a zest for life and service. He was the product of excellent family training and schooling.

He was seasoned and hardened by combat—in competitive sports, the horror of war, and the tough world of political campaigning—all of which served as a kind of crucible to fuse the fine natural gifts of heart and of mind and body into a personality of steel that was geared to cope with the dangerous and challenging world of the 1960's. He strove always for excellence.

He could have been a dilletante and a playboy. He chose public service. And he summed up his concept of how Americans should think in a dangerous and challenging age when he declared, in his superb inaugural address: "And so, my fellow Americans, ask not what your country can do for you; ask what you can do for your country."

He saw the challenge to his generation as "a call to bear the burden of a long twilight struggle—year in and year out—a struggle against the common enemies of mankind—tyranny, poverty, disease, war itself." And as he took on the most terrible burdens of responsibility that could rest on any American in the "long twilight struggle" in which this Nation is engaged, he declared bravely, for the world to hear: "I do not shrink from this responsibility; I welcome it."

He lived as he believed. "* * * Of those to whom much is given, much is required. And when at some future date the high court of history sits in judgment on each one of us—recording whether in our brief span of service we fulfilled our responsibilities to the state—our success or failure, in whatever office we may hold, will be measured by the answers to four questions—Were we truly men of courage * * * were we truly men of judgment * * * were we truly men of integrity * * * were we truly men of dedication * * *"

He believed in service and sacrifice to his country: "To maintain our freedom, to demonstrate that we are the truly revolutionaries, that their system is as old as Egypt—will require more discipline, sacrifice, and vitality than this country has ever shown." And on another occasion: "The New Frontier of which I speak is not a set of promises * * * it is a set of challenges. It sums up not what I intend to offer the American people, but what I intend to ask of them. It appeals to their pride, not their pocketbooks. It holds the promise of more sacrifice instead of more security."

John Fitzgerald Kennedy was the first of his religious faith to become President and in that sense he crossed an important New Frontier, as did his country in electing him. He pledged solemnly to defend our traditional separation of church and state. He lived up to that pledge, often in the face of bitter criticism from the very people who opposed him because they feared he would not.

In the loss of this young American eagle, this country has suffered a severe blow. But his own words of challenge, his own call to sacrifice, his own call to courage, judgment, integrity, and dedication will, if heeded, see this Nation through under its new Chief Executive, President Lyndon B. Johnson.

TRIBUTE BY

Hon. John S. Monagan

OF CONNECTICUT

Mr. Speaker, there is no place in the United States where President Kennedy was taken to the hearts of the people to a greater degree than in Connecticut, and no place in Connecticut where he was more beloved than in Waterbury and the adjacent communities of the Fifth Congressional District, which I represent.

I had the distinct and memorable privilege of accompanying President Kennedy on his campaign tour, in the early hours of the morning, through the Naugatuck Valley of Connecticut on the Saturday and Sunday just preceding the election day of 1960.

I recall riding with him in an open convertible in the chill late evening and early morning hours, through the towns of Ansonia, Derby, Seymour, Beacon Falls, Naugatuck, and on to Waterbury, where at 3 a.m. he was greeted by an estimated 50,000 enthusiastic people. In Naugatuck, where 4,000 residents waited to greet him after midnight, he smilingly cautioned the crowd to "not make so much noise—you might awaken the Republicans."

In the November 23, 1963, edition of the Waterbury Republican, there appeared, after the tragic death of President Kennedy, a touching review of that campaign tour, and a report of a subsequent visit to Waterbury by the President.

That 1960 visit to Waterbury had national impact.

In his book "The Making of the President, 1960," Theodore H. White reported on it at length.

With permission to extend my remarks, I include, for my colleagues and for posterity, the article "President Kennedy Had Special Place in Waterburians' Hearts," as it appeared in the Waterbury Republican, after the death of the President.

PRESIDENT KENNEDY HAD SPECIAL PLACE IN WATERBURIANS' HEARTS

Waterbury loved President John F. Kennedy.

Waterburians probably felt closer to Kennedy than to any other President in the history of this country.

This love and devotion sprang into full bloom when he came to the city at 3 o'clock in the morning in 1960 just days before the election. It flowered even more beautifully when he came back to Waterbury 2 years later and made a promise to come back still one more time.

This promise an assassin prevented him from keeping.

This promise to come back caught the imagination of the people of Waterbury, for it was not just an ordinary promise. It was a pledge to return to the city during the election campaign next year to return at the most improbable hour of 3 o'clock in the morning.

Just how much did Waterbury love Kennedy? Love can't be measured, but there is one statistic that can be used. It is the record-shattering plurality of almost 22,000 votes that the city gave him in supporting him for President.

TALK OF COUNTRY

This plurality—even more—the President's visit was an item of conversation in political circles throughout the country whenever the campaign was discussed. Reporters with Kennedy said there had been nothing like it at any time during the campaign.

It wasn't the size of the crowd. There had been far larger crowds. It wasn't the enthusiasm. There had been as enthusiastic audiences.

It was the combination—the unbelievable combination of Waterbury's biggest crowd in history turning out on the green at 3 a.m. in a wild, cheering display of affection for a man running for President.

The story of his trip to Waterbury did not get newspaper headlines around the country because it was long past the deadlines of morning newspapers. There were no afternoon papers because it was a Sunday, and by Monday, the Kennedy entourage had swept on to too many other communities, and too many other speeches had to be reported.

But the trip did have a national impact. It is mentioned at considerable length by Theodore H. White in his book "The Making of the President, 1960."

It has been mentioned by Connecticut political reporters whenever they discuss presidential campaigns. It was mentioned by national reporters on visits to Waterbury. They all wanted to know how Kennedy's 1962 visit to Waterbury compared with 1960.

TIME DIFFERENT

These newsmen realized, of course, that it couldn't be the same because in 1962 Kennedy spoke on The Green in the early evening.

But all newsmen—more important—all Waterburians, have been waiting. They have been waiting for a promise that cannot now be kept. They have been waiting for—as Kennedy said it on The Green:

"Our meeting here 2 years ago at 3 in the morning was the high point of the 1960 campaign, and we will meet at 3 o'clock in the morning the last week of the 1964 campaign and see what's going to happen then."

Waterburians have been waiting to "see what's going to happen then." They have already joked about standing on The Green after midnight on a morning early next November to greet the President. They have talked of having parties in their homes and then going to The Green to celebrate.

They have talked about taking their children, yes, even at 3 o'clock in the morning because they have been speculating that it would be something for history to remember.

Mass hysteria? Curiosity? Pride? Love and devotion? Perhaps a little bit of all, but mostly love and devotion for a President who has been close to Waterbury.

Waterburians have been waiting. They've been waiting to show the entire country just what kind of a reception they could really give.

The wait is over.

How did it start?

BEGAN IN 1956

Back in 1956 Kennedy first attracted more than normal attention in Waterbury and in the State. State Chairman John M. Bailey and then Gov. Abraham A. Ribicoff backed Kennedy for the nomination for Vice President. Because these two top Democratic leaders were for him, the Connecticut press paid more attention to the Massachusetts Senator than might have been normal at a national convention.

And Kennedy came close to making it. He was close but not close enough.

Waterburians had been reading of him. Soon they could see him. Kennedy made a campaign speech in 1956 in Library Park for Stevenson.

For 4 years Bailey and Ribicoff kept the Kennedy name before Connecticut. The thought of an Irish Catholic President had a particular appeal in this city where Irish Catholics have been prominent in the political field for generations.

Kennedy won the nomination. The campaign had more appeal, perhaps, than many to Waterburians, but a peculiar set of circumstances took it out of the ordinary.

The word came to Connecticut that Kennedy would campaign in the State. Connecticut's political leaders

were told one city could have him for a midnight rally only. The others would get him during the day.

The political leaders in the other cities were doubtful about a midnight visit. Mayor Edward D. Bergin stuck his neck out. He said Waterbury would produce a crowd.

SPECIAL FEELING

On Saturday afternoon, the city took on a special feeling. One could feel, if not see, that something big was happening. People walking on The Green walked differently. Bergin had his fingers crossed, hopeful that there would be a crowd, not at midnight as originally planned, but long after.

The crowd started far down the Naugatuck Valley and grew as the campaign motorcade drove north through Ansonia and Seymour and Beacon Falls and Naugatuck.

There was the policeman who forgot about traffic and turned to wave and cheer. There was the woman standing in her nightgown with a coat over it. And another. And still another. And pretty soon national newsmen stopped calling these women "nuts" and began to wonder.

And the motorcade hit Waterbury. Crowds jammed South Main Street from building across to building. It was impossible to drive. Security forces were almost helpless. The shouts completely drowned out the Mattatuck Drum Band—probably the only time in history the drum band has been drowned out.

Kennedy stepped out on the balcony of the Roger Smith Hotel at 3 a.m. and the city exploded.

Kennedy said: "I promised your mayor I would have you all in bed by 3 a.m."

And the crowd responded with a tremendous "No." Then they chanted, "We Want Kennedy."

The crowd was estimated at from 25,000 to 50,000. White sets it at 30,000 in his book on the campaign. Regardless of numbers, it was the biggest turnout in the city's history.

WENT TO MASS HERE

The next morning, November 6, Kennedy went to mass at the Immaculate Conception Church. From there he went to the Roger Smith to greet Democratic Party workers and others.

He spoke very briefly, saying the turnout in Waterbury had been "the greatest rally that we have had in this entire campaign." He said it was the "biggest crowd we have had in a city of this size in the United States," and it was not at noon but at 3 a.m.

In 1962 when he returned to Waterbury and spoke from a platform set up on the green, Kennedy looked over the mass of humanity which came a second time to see him and said:

"I must say, having been here at 3 o'clock (in the morning) and now at 6:30 (in the evening), that Waterbury is either the easiest city in the United States to get a crowd in, or it has the best Democrats in the United States."

Waterburians loved him.

They adored him when he added:

"In any case, our meeting here 2 years ago at 3 in the morning was the high point of the 1960 campaign, and we will meet at 3 o'clock in the morning the last week of the 1964 campaign and see what's going to happen then."

The President of the United States cannot keep that promise.

TRIBUTES BY

Hon. William S. Moorhead

OF PENNSYLVANIA

Mr. Speaker, I was privileged to read the eulogy by ex-Gov. David L. Lawrence delivered at the Allegheny County Bar Association memorial services in honor of President John F. Kennedy. If words could only fill the void—and, of course, they cannot—these remarks would certainly be adequate. The wisdom which Governor Lawrence imparts is one gained from long experience and close friendship with many Presidents. He rightly observes that all the renaming of streets, airports, and schools will not absolve us from working for the kind of America that John F. Kennedy worked for, fought for, died for. This is our legacy, this is our duty.

I commend the Governor's remarks for the perusal of my colleagues:

PRESIDENT JOHN F. KENNEDY

(Remarks of former Gov. David L. Lawrence)

Words still seem weak and weightless as a means of expressing the heavy burdens of loss and sadness—and, yes, of shame—which bear down upon us all.

Death, itself, we have been forced to expect.

But none of us could foresee it touching the man whose youth and enthusiasm, and hard courage had symbolized the world's new generation and humanity's brightening hopes.

Yet touch it did, and take it did, and the taking choked mankind's conscience and darkened the human spirit.

And only when it struck—brutally, maliciously, hatefully—did we realize the dimensions of the depth of our love for this man and the height of the hopes he inspired in us.

And only after the terrible deed was done did many recognize the lethal quality of poisonous hate which has infested so much of America's bloodstream and infected its mind and heart and spirit.

That hate has been cruelly apparent for some time and no one tried harder or more forcefully or more diligently to quiet its torment and to exercise its source.

A week before his visit to Texas, the President was in Florida, in his continuous effort to spur this Nation to the greatness he saw for it. And there he borrowed upon a dialog between Scrooge and Marley in Dickens' "A Christmas Carol" with this assessment of human responsibility:

"Mankind is our business," he said, "and if we work in harmony, if we understand the problems of each other and the responsibility that each of us bears, then surely the business of mankind will prosper, and your children and mine will move ahead in a secure world in which there is opportunity for all."

He had devoted all of the brilliance of his impressive intellect to the service of mankind. The sharp, crisp Presidential phrases caused a nation's ideals to soar, while the generosity of his compassion caused many of us to search our inward thoughts and summon up our strength and our devotion to commitments of service.

Yet, as the Scriptures tell us, "he that hateth his brother is in darkness, and walketh in darkness, and knoweth not whither he goeth, because that darkness hath blinded his eyes" (I John ii: 115).

And the valiant persuasion of brilliance and compassion, the clarity of reason and comprehension could not light up that darkness. The tragic irony is that the leader who appealed for reason, who called up the Nation's compassion, who devoted his intellect and his warmth to the highest ideals of national and human purpose—the tragedy struck at this man of peace and reason, of honor and strong courage.

That it occurred is our mantle of shame.

And that shame will weigh upon us long after the shock of tragedy passes.

It is a shame which comes, as Dean Moor said last Monday, from the knowledge that "this crime is possible in a world loaded with greed, hatred, and bigotry in religion, politics, race, and creed. In that atmosphere," Dean Moor reminded the conscience of us all, "anything that is vicious and reprehensible can and will happen until we have a change of heart."

Now that John Kennedy is gone, there are proposed memorials of every kind and nature—bridges and city squares, sports stadia and cultural centers, schools and hospitals. Each is appropriate.

But the only fitting memorial to his memory, to his life, and his work, will be the future course of this Nation, in removing hate and evil from our hearts and our lives, in achieving that secure world and the equality of opportunity he strived for, in restoring respect and human dignity as a way of life, and building a nation of high conscience and determined conviction—better, wiser, more united, more reasonable and more reasoned.

In short, the only fitting memorial to John F. Kennedy is the kind of America he worked for, fought for, died for.

He laid down the challenge in his inaugural in words that will ring in history and echo in every ear.

"And so, my fellow Americans, ask not what your country can do for you; ask what you can do for your country."

His answer has been indelibly inscribed for the ages.

Now, we must respond and by that response will future generations measure us and judge us.

Indeed, by that response will we measure and judge ourselves.

May God give us the wisdom, the courage, and the determination to see to it that the darkness is lifted, and the Nation's soul is cleansed, through the good deeds that are now ours to do.

Mr. Speaker, on January 30, 1964, the senior citizens of the Young Men and Women's Hebrew Association and Irene Kaufmann Centers, of Pittsburgh, held memorial services in honor of John Fitzgerald Kennedy. There were nearly 500 people represented at this meeting and they passed a resolution which is beautifully written and quite moving in its purpose. I commend the reading of this resolution to my colleagues:

Whereas we, Americans of all racial, religious, and national backgrounds, but Americans all, are here assembled to honor and reverence the memory of our great and beloved President, John Fitzgerald Kennedy; and

Whereas though our hearts are still weighted with grief, and sorrow still shadows our Nation, the image of John Fitzgerald Kennedy will forever cast its luminous glow of faith and courage, lighting the road to the better future he sought for his countrymen; and

Whereas his dreams and hopes for America, were not vague, unchartered visions, but rather, clearly articulated proposals in a program of action solidly based in his knowledge of his country's history and resources, and his undertaking of its people's needs; and

Whereas that program of action rightly emphasized— our Nation's responsibility in world peace and human betterment; the vigilant pursuit of freedom and equality for Americans of all races, creeds, and backgrounds; the spiritual and intellectual nourishment of our youth through increased educational opportunities, as well as the care of their bodies through more effective health and housing measures; the decent treatment of the aging through comprehensive medical service and constructive use of leisure time; "to add," as he put it, "not just more years to life, but more life to the years"; the obligation of this generation of Americans to cherish and guard America's soil, its rivers and forests, its wildlife and its natural resources, so that future generations, too, will know the blessing of this great land's abundance, its beauty and its variety; and

Whereas we recognize that we most truly honor the memory of John Fitzgerald Kennedy when we honor his great and living purpose by giving our own unstinting service to that purpose: Therefore be it

Resolved, That we here assembled pledge our determined efforts toward the realization of the goals he charted with unflagging labor and steady will; and be it further

Resolved, That copies of this resolution be sent to the press, our representatives in the Congress of the United States, and to Mrs. John Fitzgerald Kennedy, that she may know our resolve, that though his great light has been taken from the world, its glow will ever remain to show the way for his fellow Americans.

TRIBUTE BY

Hon. Thomas G. Morris

OF NEW MEXICO

Mr. Speaker, Americans throughout this country and abroad participated in countless memorial services as a mark of respect to the great heritage of our late and beloved President John F. Kennedy.

Just such a service was held at the Community Church of the Sandias in San Antonio, N. Mex., and the Reverend Arthur C. Opperman opened this sad occasion with a short but poignant message which I repeat today so that my colleagues may have the benefit of his wisdom and perception:

Today we bow our heads in sorrow and in shame. Our American sense of honor and dignity has been totally outraged. Our late President, John Fitzgerald Kennedy, of 2 years, 10 months, and 2 days, lies in state in our Nation's Capitol, the victim of a spirit of hate and violence which we as Americans shudder to contemplate.

Our deepest sympathy is with the Kennedy family, and our sincerest prayers are with our new President, Lyndon Baines Johnson.

Times of Bible prophecy of evil are upon us, and we are reaping the awful harvest, the first fruits of a national apathy in the face of the surging waves of secularism, pluralism, and the subtle brainwashing of godless communism.

All men do not have the capacity for freedom. In the slave world, assassination is the common way to remove men from office. One hundred years ago a great wave of hatred and violence produced a like man with the mark of Cain. Nourished on the godless doctrines of Marxist atheism from his youth, Lee Harvey Oswald, possessed by a weak, poisoned, un-American, freedom-hating mind, has engulfed our Nation in this horror ecumenical.

TRIBUTES BY

Hon. Abraham J. Multer

OF NEW YORK

Mr. Speaker, I commend to the attention of our colleagues the following memorial resolution adopted by the National Association of Letter Carriers relative to the death of our late President John Fitzgerald Kennedy and conveyed to the Congress by their executive council.

Whereas the tragic death of President John Fitzgerald Kennedy has deprived the free world of its most courageous, most powerful and most inspiring leader; and

Whereas the cause of liberalism and human freedom hangs trembling in the balance because of this mindless murder of its most forceful advocate: Be it

Resolved, That the Executive Council of the National Association of Letter Carriers convey to the leaders of both Houses of the Congress its fervent prayers that the legislative branch of Government carry through to a successful conclusion the liberal program initiated by our martyred President, including the program of raising the standards of Federal employment; and be it further

Resolved, That the Executive Council of the National Association of Letter Carriers convey to the leaders of both Houses of the Congress an expression of their deep friendship, respect, confidence and support in this time of tragedy and peril.

> Jerome J. Keating, President; Charles N. Coyle, Assistant Secretary-Treasurer; Philip Lepper, Carl J. Saxsenmeier, J. Joseph Vacca, George G. Morrow, Jr., James H. Rademacher, Vice President; George A. Bang, Director, Life Insurance; James C. Stocker, Thomas M. Flaherty, Glenn M. Hodges, Dean E. Soverns, Fred Gadotti, J. Stanley Lewis, Secretary-Treasurer; James P. Deely, Director, Health Insurance; Edward F. Benning, William T. Sullivan, Tony R. Huerta, Austin B. Carlson.

Mr. Speaker, I commend to the attention of our colleagues the following beautiful eulogy delivered at the memorial service held on Monday, November 25, 1963, at Temple Beth Emeth of Flatbush, a congregation of which I have been a proud member since 1931. Rabbi Samuel D. Soskin, our spiritual leader, delivered this moving evocation of the spirit of John F. Kennedy.

EULOGY FOR JOHN FITZGERALD KENNEDY, DELIVERED BY RABBI SAMUEL D. SOSKIN, AT THE MEMORIAL SERVICE ON MONDAY, NOVEMBER 25, 1963, AT TEMPLE BETH EMETH OF FLATBUSH, BROOKLYN

"Out of the fullness of the heart the mouth speaketh." * * * We are met in God's sanctuary to weep for a family which endures the cruel fellowship of sorrow and to mourn with all humanity the loss of one whose death diminishes all of us.

For John Fitzgerald Kennedy was the voice and conscience of a land which has stood as God's stake in human history. In this land millions of peoples have found something so unique, so magnificent that no words can adequately describe it. Perhaps it can best be named the flame of brotherhood in which men are given the right to speak freely and to worship in freedom. It is something Americans give to each other, in order that each may have it for himself.

That flame burned in the soul of our martyred President as he fought against those who would darken the bright landscape of our country with the wicked shadows of bigotry and intolerance. How much we owe to him who was the Ish Tam, the man whole in his integrity whose love for Nation was the reflection of our own love.

Though my soul is grieved, I think back on that event in Washington when the leaders of our Reform Jewish movement presented a Torah to our beloved President. Even now I am held captive to that moment when the descendant of Irish immigrants who had come to America to find freedom, took into his keeping the symbol of that tradition which echoed on Sinai's heights proclaiming that all men must be given freedom because all are God's children.

Surely we Jews should be the first to recognize that John Fitzgerald Kennedy lived by the ideals encased in that Torah and we can honor him only by seeking to match his consecration. It can be done if we are ready to labor and to sacrifice for the enrichment of the lives of fellow men. There are the hungry and the naked and the rejected of the world. They must be fed and clothed and redeemed. There are slums to be erased and bigotries to be wiped away. For what does it avail if men pray to God and do not deeds of justice?

John Fitzgerald Kennedy cherished a vision of a peaceful and righteous world. Within his soul he carried the gold of God which alone can forge the gates of the kingdom of heaven. The bullet which shattered his body could not destroy that vision. We, who are an ancient people and who have held that same vision, know that the coming of the kingdom may be far off. But, it is for us, despite the peril and our almost unbearable grief, to labor for that kingdom.

May the spirit of John Fitzgerald Kennedy, servant and leader of his people, friend of all mankind, quicken us for the task, that future generations may say of us as we say of him: "Zecher Tzadik Livrocho," may his memory be for an everlasting blessing.

Amen.

Mr. Speaker, typical of how our friends abroad feel about the tragic death of our late beloved President, John F. Kennedy, is the expression contained in the following letter received by my law partner and his wife, Mr. and Mrs. Barnett J. Nova, from one of their dear friends, Mrs. Peter Haddon, of London, England:

NOVEMBER 23, 1963.

MY DEAR GRACE AND BARNEY: I felt I had to write and tell you how completely shocked and horrified we are at President Kennedy's death and how deep and profound our sympathy is at this time.

It really doesn't make sense in any way and must be absolutely tragic for his wife and family.

We in England share this sad loss with Americans because in the short time President Kennedy held office a great warmth of affection grew up here toward him and everyone, without exception, talks of his great loss not only to America, but England, the world, and peace.

I still find it hard to believe and must hang on to the thought that God moves in strange ways, otherwise I would find it very difficult to go on believing in God because this all, seems so very pointless. Perhaps this is one of the supreme sacrifices which will cause all peoples of the world to move toward better understanding. I sincerely hope so.

Thinking of you.

Love,

ANN.

Mr. Speaker, on Sunday, December 15, 1963, I was privileged to participate in the annual blue and gold charter breakfast hosted by the parents committee of Cub Scout Pack No. 435 in my home district in Brooklyn.

The breakfast was held in the Oceanview Jewish Center and just before I presented the Scouter of the Year Award a poem in memory of our late beloved President, John Fitzgerald Kennedy, was recited by the members of the troops and the poem's author, Mr. James Vincent.

It is a beautiful tribute and I commend it to the attention of our colleagues:

ADIEU

(By James Vincent)

A young man was sent our way with a winning smile,
    handsome face, and a vision for his Nation's
    future.
We must "look ahead," said he, our eyes set on new
    horizons, on new frontiers for the sixties—
How old must you be to love your country?

So young a man for so big a plan—how can leadership
    be given to such as he—who will follow this
    young man?
Will the ancients, so set in their way change for him?
This Nation must walk slowly and softly they say,
How old must you be to lead your country?

But his voice rang true, his dreams were great; a nation
    he loved answered his call.
For less than 3 years this noble man planned and guided
    the course of his beloved land.
How old must you be to want greatness for your country?

At times the perils were great, with missiles, atoms, and
    a strange force so close to our gate.
The elders said to climb this mountain was wrong for
    you cannot come down—but a man went up and
    a giant returned and, this, made our Nation strong.
How old must you be to protect your country?

We say this is the land of the free—"not so," said he; not
    while we give some, second-class citizenry—
Not when these cannot earn their daily bread or find a
    school for their children or live in semislavery.
How old must you be to understand your country?

He would like to mingle with the average man; to learn
    of his thoughts, his fears and grasp his hand—
For after all, these are the many in our great land.
How old must you be to love the people in your country?

He fell among the many, on a bright November day;
    taken from us in one swift moment, to greet and
    smile no more.
How could this happen to such a man and in this land,
    and in this day and age.
How old must you be to die for your country?

To know men walk still among us, to whom life and
    love mean nil, is it but our neighbors that engen-
    dered this rage?
Each of us will have his part of the torch to bear.
How old must you be to cry for your country?

We will never know how far, how great, or how long
    would be the shadow this man cast;
Now we will wait for the historians and history to pass
    judgment on his deeds.
How old must you be to be remembered by your country?

For each to love one another was the Lord's plan; to live
    with all in peace and harmony; to respect and care
    about your fellow man.
Adieu; rest ye well, fallen eagle; though there is a new
    captain at the helm, the ship of state sails on, fol-
    lowing the course you charted.
Adieu.   Adieu.

TRIBUTE BY

Hon. John M. Murphy

OF NEW YORK

Mr. Speaker, under the leave to extend my re-marks I include a poem written by Vernon Boyce Hampton, of Staten Island, N.Y., in memory of our late President:

For our martyred President John Fitzgerald Kennedy.

FLAGS IN MOURNING

(By Vernon B. Hampton)

Old Glory flies in the spirit of mourning,
    Symbol of America's grief;
Greatening with each hour's drawing
    In the shock of loss of the Nation's Chief.

Anthemed in a colorful requiem,
    Ten million flags o'er land and sea
Wave in the breeze in solemn requiem
    For John Fitzgerald Kennedy.

The colors half-staffed, mutely flying,
    Speak of the world-wide loss deplored,
For the one struck down had a faith undying:
    That brotherhood promised world accord.

The flag that he loved, his life defended
    In war and peace and in martyrdom,
And our Nation, as his life is ended
    Must finish the tasks he would have done.

So we dedicate ourselves anew,
In the hour of his soul's release,
To consummate the dreams he dreamed
Of justice, brotherhood, and peace.

VERNON B. HAMPTON.

The period of national mourning is observed for 30 days from the date of President Kennedy's death November 22, 1963.

TRIBUTE BY

Hon. William T. Murphy

OF ILLINOIS

Mr. Speaker, we mourn, in our own way, the passing of President Kennedy, and it is not always easy to transmit our feelings. Some are gifted in expressing that which we may feel, and I offer here a poem written and composed by Mrs. Jessie M. Williams, of Chicago, Ill., on the day President Kennedy passed away:

ETERNAL LIGHT

Somewhere a candle flickers
Somewhere a vote is hushed
Somewhere all hearts are saddened
Somewhere a life was crushed

Somewhere the peace he fought for
On land and on the sea
Somewhere he gave his all
For his love of humanity

There's a mound upon a hillside
An eternal light to never cease
A Nation bows in reverence
For the man who fought for peace.

TRIBUTE BY

Hon. Ancher Nelsen

OF MINNESOTA

Mr. Speaker, a resident of Minnesota's Second Congressional District, Mrs. Dana Anderson, was so moved by the events following the assassination of our late President Kennedy that she composed an excellent poem entitled "The Eternal Flame."

I insert Mrs. Anderson's poem, written using her pen name Elsa Romberg.

THE ETERNAL FLAME

Think ye now that my light is out
That assassin hands have dealt a blow?
Think ye that all my lips have formed
Now lie with me in earth below?

Ideals that have their life from God
Die not at all when flesh it spent;
Philosophy the Bible gives
Lives on and to the world is lent.

See now the flame marking my grave,
Its voice is louder far than speech
For from its leaping tongues are heard
The ideals all the world would reach.

"Ask not," it says, "what should be done
For self or nations o'er the sea
But together ask how to attain
The best today—the best to be!"

My light burns on; my flame unspent
Leaps higher to declare my way!
Take from its energy some strength!
My light burns on for you today!

TRIBUTES BY

Hon. Barratt O'Hara

OF ILLINOIS

Mr. Speaker, "Man of His Century" was the tribute to President John F. Kennedy in a memorial radio address by President Nkrumah to the people of Ghana. I am extending my remarks to include President Nkrumah's radio message, honoring the memory of our martyred President:

PRESIDENT NKRUMAH IN RADIO MESSAGE HONORS MEMORY OF PRESIDENT KENNEDY

It is with deep sorrow that I speak to you today and pay tribute to the memory of the late President John F. Kennedy, a great world statesman, and a relentless fighter for equality and human dignity.

The whole world has been shocked and bewildered at President Kennedy's tragic death by assassination in the prime of his life. In spite of his brief term of office, President Kennedy has made an indelible mark on the history of our time. He will be remembered as a distinguished champion for peace and the rights of man. His inspiration, his tremendous courage, his integrity and the warmth of his feeling for his fellow men will be a beacon to those who share his convictions and aspiration.

John Kennedy's achievements in international affairs have been remarkable. We in Africa will remember him above all for his uncompromising stand against racial and religious bigotry, intolerance, and injustice. His courage and steadfastness in pursuing the objectives of racial equality in his own country will always remain as his greatest contribution to the struggle against racialism and racial arrogance.

*   *   *   *   *

President Kennedy was a remarkable man and a man of his century. Born to wealth, he was yet deeply sensitive to the problems and hopes of the common man and of the underprivileged. This aspect of his character was reflected both in his domestic and international policies.

His ideas on economic aid, social welfare, and world peace were far in advance of large sections of influential opinion in his own country. As the youngest President ever of the United States, he was truly a representative of our century—a century of expanding opportunities for all the elimination of poverty, ignorance, and disease, and the establishment of a new order of truth, equality, and social justice.

With a true sense of history John Kennedy carried on in a most dramatic manner what Abraham Lincoln began 100 years ago; like Lincoln he was prevented from carrying his endeavors to the great heights he had set for himself by an assassin's bullet. As a man endowed with great human warmth, his relationship with people was always friendly and sincere. I was privileged to meet President Kennedy and his wife in Washington in 1961 not long after he became President of the United States. In fact, I think I am right in saying that I was the first head of state to whom he granted audience immediately after he had been sworn in as the President of the United States. I was deeply impressed by his wisdom and sincerity.

His presence, his sense of understanding and appreciation of the grave issues confronting our world, and his genuine interest in the solution of the problems confronting developing countries made me regard him even then as a man from whom the world could expect great things, as a man who could become one of the most important leaders of our time. It really takes a man like John Kennedy to say, and I quote from his writings: "A man does what he must in spite of personal consequences, in spite of obstacles and dangers and pressures and that is the basis of all human morality." We in Africa can have no more appropriate epitaph to John Kennedy's memory than his own words spoken in his inaugural address: "Whether you are citizens of America or of the world, ask of us the same high standards of strength and sacrifice that we shall ask of you. With a good conscience our only sure reward with history, the final judge of our deeds, let us go forth to lead the land we love, asking His blessing and His help but knowing that here on earth God's work must truly be our own."

To his dear wife and children, I send deepest condolence on my own behalf and on behalf of the people of Ghana.

Mr. Speaker, by unanimous consent I am extending my remarks to include the sermon of Rabbi Jacob J. Weinstein at K.A.M. Temple in Chicago on November 25, 1963. It is worthy of a permanent place in the literature of this tragic period when in the presence of a shock and a grief that reached into all nations the whole world

seemed on the eve of recapturing its soul. Rabbi Weinstein's eulogy follows:

It is with a heavy heart I speak to you today. Our President has been taken from us—not by the gentle angel who comes to give us peace after the storms and strifes of life's weary years, not by the one who spares us the decay of age and the bemeaning of time—but by the violent one, the mad, distemperate one, the ignorant one of aggressive brawn and little brain—the satanic deputy of all that is raw and primitive in this land of ours—ignorant, violent and primitive, yet armed with telescopic sight, and able to kill from afar, send the arrow by night and speed the pestilence by day. Unhappy land, unhappy time—that preserves the jungle heart and the troglodytic mind and arms them with the shining armor and the long thrust of science.

John Fitzgerald Kennedy is cut down in the midst of life. Where was the like of him—Adonis with the mind of Nestor? A golden-haired youth who could have dallied in all the opulent pastures of great wealth and lived as riotously and elegantly as the Medicis—he gave himself rather to the service of our Republic. As a soldier, as Congressman, Senator, President, he revealed a remarkable insight into the political and economic order of our society. He knew the structure of power. He knew intimately the ways in which men are guided and goaded to action. He knew the play and counterplay of forces and the mysterious wheels within wheels which make up the chain of effective command. He was a political marvel who could learn and retain an infinite number of facts about an incredible number of subjects and could sift them and concentrate them upon the problems at hand. One day when the President's Committee on Equal Employment Opportunity was meeting at the White House, I was privileged to watch him as he walked from one meeting to another—some six in all—the Business Ethics Advisory Committee, the Labor and Management Conference, a joint committee on the new trade bill, a Committee on the Alliance for Progress, the White House Conference on the Aged—and relate himself to the complicated agenda of each group, make excellent suggestions on the work reported and present sound advice on the next steps for each committee. I was given to understand that this 3-hour stint was only a fraction of his working day and that before he would get to bed that night, there were several functions of state, several meetings with congressional leaders on thorny matters and a vast heap of legislative and State Department memos to read, amend and sign.

HIS HEART WAS NEVER ABSENT

But while his mind worked with incredible logic and remarkable speed, and his body sustained an energy expenditure that would have honored a platoon, his heart was never absent. He was one of the most contained men emotionally I have ever known. This was not because there was any lack of feeling. It was because he had suffused his heart into his mind. He could afford no wasteful drain of sentiment. He was completely bent on finding the necessary means to implement his vision of the good society. He would be the first to admit that he was no self-abnegating saint—that he relished ego satisfaction with the best of us; but he would likewise maintain, and rightly, that he had over the long and disciplined years sublimated that ego into community and that what remained of self-interest was enlightened and socialized.

He had style. There was grace in him and an instinct for the right measure for every purpose. His wit was dry, perceptive, often sharp but seldom cutting. He played politics as the young David played his harp—with artistry—so that the wiliest of old wolves and foxes of the Senate knew that his charm was never a substitute for strength, but merely the sense of ease with which he used his power. Together with Mrs. Kennedy he had made the White House a palace of grace and beauty. He removed the last remnants of the coonskin, the spittoon and the antimacassar and made it reflect, as it should, the ripe artistic heritage of our Nation.

I will never forget the visit Mrs. Weinstein and I made on the occasion of the centenary of the proclamation which ended slavery and saw these two beautiful people gracefully representing the youth, the vitality and the power of this Nation in this home which they had made beautiful and intimate without making it parochial.

BRIGHT BROTHER—FATHER TO OUR YOUTH

It is not an accident that so many young people have come to the synagogue to mourn our President. He was their assurance that youth was not allergic to maturity, that one did not have to spend all one's youth in apprenticeship, that one did not have to be dour and solemn to be profound. He was the great arbiter between the generations. He was David hitting bull's-eye the Philistine Goliaths of our time with the smooth round pebbles of his incisive logic. He made political battle as exciting as a gridiron contest, and the war for social security as dramatic as Gettysburg. Through the Peace Corps he developed a most effective moral equivalent for war. The youth of the Nation have lost a father who was also a brother.

It is still not possible to accept the fact that this handsome puissant statesman in whom the forces of nature had opulently conspired to channel incredible riches of strength and wisdom is no more, that the striking profile of courage which lifted our hearts on that bitter January day in 1961 and, bare-headed, cast its golden light was the target for an assassin's bullet. It seemed as he responded to the high challenge of the hour in his crisp New England speech, that he was aligned with the enduring forces of earth and that the bright armor of his genius would turn any adversary's noisome threat.

STAIN OF VIOLENCE IN OUR NATIONAL LIFE

This is not the time to consider the wild barbaric forces still loose in our land, the immaturity of the mass mind and the malevolent forces that play upon it—but we shall have to soon—or the gangsters, the atavistic radicals of right and left, the childish irritation with the inevitable disciplines of a highly interlaced social fabric such as ours will destroy us. There are altogether too many respectable people whose sins of omission and commission help to trigger the gunman's hand and supply the heady stimulation for the dynamiter's throw. We stand idly by the blood of our brother—not only when he is slain but when we encourage under specious slogans the lawless and anarchic and callous forces in our society.

You have seen the cartoon by Bill Mauldin—Abe Lincoln clutching his head in woebegone despair, as he contemplates this new martyrdom. What an ominous red thread of violence connects these century-separated assassinations! The lynch rope, the auto-da-fé faggots, the sniper's bullet—these are the blots on the bright face of the American dream. They are the present-day survivals of our jungle frontier in our land and in our hearts.

Happily we can point to the remarkable discipline of the Negro in the mass demonstrations of the past several years as evidence that even the most wronged and deprived people need not meet violence with violence, that there are great reservoirs of common decency and of Judeo-Christian reverence for life in the hearts of our people. Strange is it not that the most deprived and despoiled of our land can respond with non-violent dignity while those who are asked to share only a little of their wealth and power maul our dignitaries and cry for Judge Lynch? We must mobilize that decency to shrink the area in which the primitives can operate. Let the blood of two Emancipation Presidents be the seed of a new Nation dedicated to the proposition that all men are created equal and are entitled to their full heritage under God.

Someone has said that men are things that think a little but chiefly forget. One hundred years ago the rabbi of this congregation, the beloved Liebman Adler, the father of the more famous Dankmar Adler of the Adler-Sullivan team, said in his eulogy of Lincoln:

"The more and more thoroughly we reminisce about Lincoln, the more do we love him and the more do we find his murder aimless and the greater do we see the loss to his own family and the Nation."

What might this dark brooding man with the infinite weariness of the burden of man's inhumanity to man say to this golden-headed colleague who now belongs with him to the ages?

But this is the hour for mourning and for prayer in our heart that God will grant comfort to the sorrowing family—to the wife, to the children, to the parents—too intimate already with grief and to the brothers and sisters who constitute a Maccabean tribe and who in their various ways provided brilliant models of social consciousness and social service at their best.

We must take courage too, for ours is a nation too strong and resilient to be weakened by the loss of even its finest leader. It is the saving grace of a democratic check and balance system such as ours that a temporary blow to one of its powers only shifts the burden to the others until equilibrium is restored. And we have in our new President a man of great sagacity, one knowledgeable in all the varied manners and mysteries of politics and administration and one who faithfully subscribes to the national goals of our late President.

It remains only for us to do the unfinished work—to bind and heal the wounds of our Nation, to bring the Negro and all minorities into the family estate as full brothers in fact, to make the machine in its automated dimensions our servant and not our master, to give effective education and training to all our young and, finally, to keep open the channels of communication that we might achieve a just peace in the framework of a world government of the United Nations.

If we would transmute the pain of this hour into the substance of good, then must we here highly resolve that we shall achieve in our land an equality of opportunity and a general security without impounding the liberties of the people, without penalizing differences with death, without reducing the infinite variety of the human condition to the manageable categories of totalitarian necessity. This was the overreaching goal of John Kennedy's massive and brilliant thrust. Our achievement of that goal will be his most adequate and fitting memorial.

I hear an ancient voice speaking from the Book of Books—it comes from one intimate with grief and acquainted with sorrow. He spoke to a nation whose cup of woe had filled to overflowing.

Comfort ye, comfort ye my people—For ye have paid
    double for all your sins * * *
Bring now good tidings to the humble
And bind up the broken hearted
And proclaim liberty to the captives
And the opening of the eyes to them that are bound.
Proclaim the year of the Lord's good pleasure
Comfort all that mourn * * *
All that mourn in Zion * * *
Give them a garland for ashes
The oil of joy for mourning
The mantle of praise for the spirit of heaviness.

Mr. Speaker, Patrick Joyce is a top newsman whom I have known for 17 years, our friendship dating back to 1946 when he was working on an article for the International News Service on the freight subway system in Chicago's Loop. Mr. Joyce is a resident of the seventh ward which has been my home for more than half a century. Prior to coming to Chicago he lived in Massachusetts and as an active newsman several times interviewed President Kennedy's grandfather, "Honey" Fitzgerald, whom he described in a letter just received by me as "a grand man in every way."

With this preface, Mr. Speaker, I am extending my remarks to include a poem by Patrick Joyce that eloquently speaks a sentiment felt by all Americans:

In Memoriam: John F. Kennedy

(By Patrick Joyce)

No man can know the measure of
His nation's loss, the wide world's love.
Are all the yearnings of his years
Lost in the tumult and the tears?
Peace for this earth, and freedom's breath,
Have they, too, died our leader's death?
Or, sharp in sorrow, shall we learn
Goals that he sought, we cannot spurn:
Hope for our youth, aid for the old,
Help for the hungry and the cold?

One nation bound in brotherhood:
This was the cause for which he stood;
A world of freemen reaching far,
To the remotest sun or star;
A world of good, where men could find
God and their destinies entwined.
Now is the time to dry our tears:
He was a man for all the years.
Bear high his banner, heed his call:
Make this his brave memorial.

TRIBUTE BY

Hon. James G. O'Hara

OF MICHIGAN

Mr. Speaker, the Imlay City Times, in its December 13, 1963, issue, printed part of a letter written by Jens Brueckner describing his reaction and that of others in Germany to the tragic death of our late President Kennedy.

Mr. Speaker, I believe some of my colleagues may find Jens Brueckner's letter interesting and under unanimous consent I wish to offer an excerpt from the letter, as it appeared in the Imlay City Times.

GERMANY'S REACTION TO KENNEDY DEATH

Jens Brueckner, German exchange student who spent last year in the Herman Haedicke home, and attended Imlay City Community High School, recently wrote to the Haedicke family, following the assassination of President Kennedy.

Jen's letter follows, in part, telling of his reaction, and that of the German people, to the assassination of the President.

OLDENBURG,
November 30, 1963.

It was a deep shock last Friday when I heard about the assassination of the President. At first I just could not believe it, and when I heard that he was wounded, I surely thought that these wounds would not be mortal. The more I was shocked when the speaker announced after a period of silence, "Ladies and gentlemen, the President of the United States, John Fitzgerald Kennedy, is dead."

When I heard about the happenings in Dallas, I immediately switched to the AFN, an American station in Germany. They broadcasted all incoming news from Texas, described every detail, and so I got a very clear and accurate picture. All German radio programs were interrupted to present all news about the President.

It was a shock for the entire German people when they heard about the death of the President. You can say that no President was as popular as Kennedy here in

Germany. Through his visit to Germany in June he won so many friends, and so many people felt as if a member of their family had died.

Stations did not present anything else but serious and solemn music and news from America. The regular program was interrupted until 1 day after the funeral. The funeral itself was broadcast too, and you could even see it on television through Telstar.

The days from Friday to Monday were days of national mourning There was no sport, no movies, no dances, etc. You really can say that it was a shock for the entire nation, and that the people are really worried what the future will bring.

—Jens Brueckner.

TRIBUTE BY
Hon. Wright Patman
OF TEXAS

Mr. Speaker, religious tolerance is a cornerstone of the American public. John F. Kennedy was our first Roman Catholic President. It is most fitting that the editorial in the November 29, 1963, issue of the Baptist Standard be given the widest possible publication.

The words of Editor E. S. James are as follows:

THE PRESIDENT'S UNTIMELY DEATH

It is now 3 p.m., Friday, November 22. Two hours ago the President of the United States was assassinated on the streets of Dallas, and at this hour Gov. John Connally lies seriously wounded from the same brutal attack. The Baptist Standard joins multiplied millions over the whole earth in grief over the President's untimely death and the terrible manner by which it was effected. Texas citizens can never forget the shame that has been brought to this State and to the city of Dallas by the cowardly assault. It is not yet known who committed the crime, but whoever it was did not represent the level-headed and patriotic citizenship of this State and city.

President Kennedy was not a Baptist, but it is safe to say that southern Baptists have had no better friend in the White House. He defended the principle of religious liberty for which many Baptist forefathers gave their lives. The editor of this magazine probably knew him about as well as any gospel minister in America knew him. We gave it as our opinion last February that he was a man of courage, integrity, and faith in God; and we shall ever remember him as such.

We did not help elect him, and he knew it; but regardless of political differences we came to admire and respect him for standing by his convictions and doing it in the face of the strongest opposition. America has lost a leader whom it will not forget, and the Nation has now reaped the bitter harvest of unbridled political hatred.

The deceased President's faith in God is probably best expressed in a Thanksgiving Day proclamation issued by him November 7.

—E. S. JAMES.

TRIBUTE BY
Hon. Claude Pepper
OF FLORIDA

Mr. Speaker, Joseph B. Gregg, a teacher in Sunrise Junior High School, Fort Lauderdale, Fla., has composed and sent me a most venerable letter on the tragic circumstances of November 22, 1963. Under unanimous consent I offer the tribute written by Mr. Gregg.

AN OPEN LETTER TO ANYBODY WHO CARED

Every man, at some point in his life, acquires a hero—no, even more than that—an idol. And that, in the finest sense of the word.

Mine no longer walks this earth.

And in heretofore undiscovered reaches of my heart I have wept—and have suffered through the creation of a chasm of sorrow I did not know was capable of man.

I have sat in my Florida room with my wife, and watched and listened to the horror of it all unfold on TV, and I turned to hide the welling, glistening tears—because it is unmanly to cry. But through these hours I became a little lost boy at heart, and aren't little boys, at times like these, allowed to cry? Why then did I run, ashamedly, to the solitude of a room upstairs, to give lonely release to my heart?

These 2 days of timelessness I have gone to work and sat and stood and walked around wide eyed as a narcotic, yet as unseeing; concentrating on the "why," yet unthinking; stunned beyond the ability to believe, yet believing every one of the millions of words I have absorbed by now.

My idol has been toppled.

But deeper still in the recesses of my heart, where must dwell knowledge beyond attainment of a simple human brain, I know, as surely as I know his body is dead, he is not dead.

For as long as one man suffers from the cruelty of inequality; as long as one deranged mind calls for peace through war; for so long as one challenge to the salvation of mankind remains unbattled, the immortal soul and the unconquerable intellect of John Kennedy shall walk this earth—though he be embodied in us, the least of all his fellow men.

I pledge myself to carry on, in my fumbling way, and however I can, his noble, dedicated and sacred work.

My idol is not dead.

JOSEPH B. GREGG,
Sunrise Junior High School, Fort Lauderdale, Fla.

TRIBUTE BY

Hon. Carl D. Perkins

OF KENTUCKY

Mr. Speaker, under leave to extend my remarks I include the following editorial from the Hazard Herald, Hazard, Ky., of Thursday, December 12, 1963:

WE'VE LOST A FRIEND

(By Larry Caudill)

Whenever the scroll of human history is unrolled, it will reveal John Fitzgerald Kennedy in the forerank of history's greatest men.

This was evidenced only in small measure in the tribute paid the assassinated President by his people and the world.

The world mourned, but it scarcely knew the full stature of Kennedy.

The breadth of John Kennedy's knowledge and intelligence was amazing. He could speak with knowledgeable authority on almost any subject a common, average man could name.

He was such a gracious, tolerant, common man at first acquaintance that the average man's reaction might be "he's just another ordinary fellow." But within minutes the range of John Kennedy's intelligence and reactions would inspire amazed admiration.

In the winter of 1958–59 the "patriotarch," Joseph P. Kennedy, was in residence at his mansion at Palm Beach, Fla. Most of the time one or more of the Kennedy children was visiting the elder Kennedys.

Jack Kennedy was a Senator and came to Palm Beach during the Christmas holiday recess of Congress.

The civic and social organizations eagerly sought the younger Kennedys at their regular meetings. On this visit Senator Jack Kennedy was invited to the Everglades Club, a select social and civic group which numbers among its members not only plain millionaires but the supermillionaires like Joe Kennedy, whose financial valuation was something like $300 million.

Joe prevailed upon son Jack to speak to the Everglades Club. His speech in general was a report on the work of Congress.

The Palm Beach Post-Times city editor wanted a general interview with Senator Kennedy. The reporter found him relaxed on the lawn of the walled estate on Ocean Boulevard, near a small swimming pool. He had spent the morning on a cabin cruiser trolling for sailfish which were running along the Atlantic Ocean south toward Fort Lauderdale.

Fishing was quite a lengthy topic of conversation because we both were devoted fishermen. He noted that the current run on sails was on the small side, 3 or 4 feet long, whereas the more desirable 6- and 7-footers were scarce. His boat had caught and released unharmed about seven sailfish. It was apparent that Jack Kennedy was an expert fisherman, with a light trout rod in the mountain stream or a long outrigger trolling pole.

Now, a reporter with a willing and intelligent interviewee can ask a million questions with as many topics. Jack Kennedy fielded them all with quick, accurate information.

He was informed on space exploration: He expected that it would be feasible to send a man to the moon within 5 to 10 years. Now we are on the verge of it.

At the Everglades Club the night before, automation in American industry and its effect on employment of the individual worker.

Since he knew the reporter was from eastern Kentucky, Kennedy cited the automation in the coal industry. He said it was more advanced than the country realized.

In the Everglades Club audience, he recalled, mere tycoons of the coal industry where they had been employing 10 men, within 5 to 10 years they would be employing 2 men. The other eight men, replaced by machines, would be jobless.

He sought to impress upon the industrialists that it would be primarily their responsibility to look ahead to that situation and make provision for the 8 out of 10 "automated men."

So it has worked out, not only in the coal industry. Lack of job opportunity is a national problem in all American industry.

Senator Kennedy knew then the peculiar problems of eastern Kentucky and elsewhere in Appalachia from automation and undereducation to overpopulation and economic stagnation.

Eastern Kentucky's people lost a great good friend when President Kennedy died in Dallas.

Recently the Franklin D. Roosevelt, Jr., task force presented to President Kennedy its preliminary report of the first survey of the Appalachian Regional Commission.

The very next day Kennedy called in appropriate officials from every department of Government concerned. He instructed them to put in motion immediately a program for the help of eastern Kentucky, and at the same time to speed up the long-range program for all of Appalachia.

That's how great and how good and how humble was President John F. Kennedy.

What destiny would have dealt him in the future if he had lived can be only speculation. But it could not have been but grand.

His physical presence was long enough to leave his massive imprint on the Nation and the world.

TRIBUTES BY

Hon. John R. Pillion

OF NEW YORK

Mr. Speaker, the tragic death of President John F. Kennedy has engendered a sense of loss among the citizens of this Nation.

To most of us, his death was a shocking and personal tragedy.

To many, it meant the loss of a courageous Chief of State who sincerely sought to bring to this world a permanent peace.

To others, his death meant a loss of a political leader who sought to aid the oppressed, the ill, the needy among us.

Mr. Speaker, the citizens of the city of Buffalo and of western New York State join the people of this Nation and of the world in revering and in honoring the memory of our late President, John Fitzgerald Kennedy. The depth of sorrow and sympathy of the people of the Buffalo area over the loss of this great President is accurately expressed in editorials appearing in the two major newspapers published in the city of Buffalo, N.Y.

From the Buffalo Evening News, Saturday, November 23:

A MARTYRED PRESIDENT

The sense of incredulous shock and total tragedy that swept over a stunned Nation with yesterday's terrible news from Dallas has been so universally experienced and so widely articulated that further words today could add no more than a trite echo.

From the Buffalo Evening News, Monday, November 25:

THIS DAY OF MOURNING

This is the day officially designated for Americans to pay their final homage to the elected leader whom assassination has snatched from them.

It is a day, moreover, on which President Johnson has fittingly invited all "the people of the world who share our grief to join us in * * * mourning and rededication"— and in fact the heads of a score of major foreign states have flown in to Washington for the solemn occasion.

This funeral day is thus, as the President's proclamation suggests, a time for Americans not only to "pay their homage of love and reverence," but to turn from grief to rededication.

From the Buffalo Courier-Express, Saturday, November 23:

SNIPER'S SHOT A NATIONAL CALAMITY

Shots from a Dallas ambush have thrown a Nation into mourning for a martyred President. John F. Kennedy fell victim to an assassin's fusillade. The Nation and the world have lost an inspiring and admired leader.

From the Buffalo Courier-Express, Monday, November 25:

A LEADER DIES, ANOTHER CARRIES ON

Suffice it to say that the loss is incalculable, undoubtedly far greater than can be estimated at the moment. John F. Kennedy was a leader the United States and the world can ill afford to do without.

He came to the Presidency the youngest man and the first Roman Catholic ever elected to that high office. He came endowed with expert politicianship and with the advantage of valuable governmental experience as the result of legislative service in both the House of Representatives and the Senate of the United States. He entered into his duties as Chief Executive with enthusiasm and a display of leadership which probably culminated in his courageous handling of the crisis arising from the menacing presence of Soviet missiles in Cuba.

President Kennedy's accomplishments were many and impressive. History will well and truly record them. And history would have no way of knowing the heights he might have attained had he been spared.

The Nation mourns a valued President.

TRIBUTE BY

Hon. Adam C. Powell

OF NEW YORK

Mr. Speaker, under leave to extend my remarks I include the following:

FRANCE'S TRIBUTE TO THE LATE PRESIDENT KENNEDY— GENERAL DE GAULLE'S STATEMENT—OFFICIAL MESSAGES—GENERAL DE GAULLE ATTENDS THE FUNERAL— FRENCH PUBLIC OPINION

General de Gaulle's statement on the death of President Kennedy:

"President Kennedy died like a soldier, under fire, in the line of duty and in the service of his country.

"In the name of the French people, ever the friend of the American people, I salute his great example and his great memory."

OFFICIAL MESSAGES

Message to Mrs. Jacqueline Kennedy from General and Madam de Gaulle:

"The great sorrow that has just befallen you distresses my wife and myself to the bottom of our hearts. Rest assured that we are with you in our thoughts and in our prayers. President Kennedy shall never be forgotten."

Message to President Lyndon Johnson from General de Gaulle, President of the Republic:

"The death of President Kennedy is a source of deep sorrow to the French people, who held in the highest esteem this great head of state, illustrious servant of freedom and of the destiny of mankind.

"In the face of a misfortune which so profoundly affects your country and which concerns all the peoples of the world, and at a time when fate bestows upon you the highest responsibilities, rest assured, Mr. President, of the more than ever loyal and confident friendship of France for the United States of America."

Message to President Lyndon Johnson from M. Georges Pompidou, Premier:

"Deeply moved by the tragic loss experienced by the United States on the death of President Kennedy, whose courage and great gifts as a statesman were admired by all, the French people wish to convey to you the grief felt by all my fellow countrymen.

"Rest assured that at a time when under such cruel circumstances you take up your high office, my colleagues of the French Government and myself join with you in a feeling of most grieving and most loyal friendship."

Message to Secretary of State Dean Rusk from M. Maurice Couve de Murville, Minister of Foreign Affairs:

"Profoundly shocked by the news of the act which has just cost the life of the President of the United States, may I assure you that I deeply share in your mourning and in that of the Government and the American people. Mindful of the welcome that President Kennedy extended to me only a few weeks ago, I can appreciate the extent of your sorrow.

"All my countrymen join with me and share in the feelings of friendship toward your country which have existed for two centuries."

Message to Secretary of Defense Robert McNamara from M. Pierre Messmer, Minister of the Armed Forces:

"Upon hearing of the tragic death of President Kennedy, I ask you to accept the condolences of the French Armed Forces and also my own personal, sincerest, and grieving condolences."

Message to Gen. Maxwell Taylor, Chairman of the Joint Chiefs of Staff, from Gen. Charles Ailleret, Chief of Staff of the French Armed Forces:

"May I express to you, and request that you convey this message to the Joint Chiefs of Staff, the shock and the indignation of the French Armed Forces on hearing the news of the outrage against President Kennedy.

"May I also express to you my deepest personal sorrow at the death of the President of the United States who welcomed me such a short time ago with so much friendliness and warmth."

Statement by M. Roger Seydoux, permanent representative of France to the United Nations. Before a plenary session of the United Nations General Assembly, held on November 27, 1963, to pay homage to the memory of the late President Kennedy, M. Roger Seydoux, permanent representative of France to the United Nations, made the following statement:

"All my compatriots, for whom the visit in Paris of Mr. and Mrs. John Kennedy remains a bright memory, turn toward the people of the United States, our everlasting friend. We wish them to know that their trial is our trial, their sadness our sadness, their mourning our mourning. Ours also is, despite the heavy loss they must bear, their steadfast faith in the future as is steadfast our confidence in their great destiny."

Statement by the French Premier, M. Georges Pompidou. The following statement by the French Premier was broadcast over French television and transmitted to the United States by satellite via the Pleumeur-Bodou relay station:

"The stupefaction engendered by a despicable assassination, the indignation at seeing President Kennedy struck down by the side of his young wife in the fulfillment of his duties as a humane and liberal head of state, is accompanied by a great sadness also felt in our hearts: sadness because, once again, blind violence has triumphed; sadness because a great and friendly people is plunged into mourning; sadness because the free world has lost one of its surest guides.

"In these tragic hours, all France is at the side of the United States in anger, in grief, and, despite everything, in confidence also for the future."

Statement by French Foreign Minister, M. Maurice Couve de Murville. M. Couve de Murville made the following statement over the three major American television networks. It was transmitted by the communications satellite relay:

"It was with the most grievous impression of shock that we all, in Paris and in France, heard the appalling news of President Kennedy's cold-blooded murder. Many elements combined in our thoughts: the terribly premature disappearance of a statesman of the first magnitude, the death of a man who was the incarnation of youth and vitality, the awful tragedy that hit a glamorous and loveable family, the general feeling of a blow inflicted to a great country for which France has, from the beginning, felt the closest friendship, further reinforced by comradeship in three wars.

"For me, who had the privilege of long talks with President Kennedy, the memory will not pass of his friendliness, his eagerness, his wisdom, and his courage.

"Believe me when I say that we, the French people, today all grieve and pray together with the American people."

Statement broadcast over American television by Mr. Hervé Alphand, French Ambassador to the United States:

"The tragic death of President Kennedy has deeply moved the French people, forever the friend of the American people. Your sorrow is our sorrow and this sorrow we share with Mrs. Kennedy and her family, tonight we pray with them.

"The President had always displayed toward my country a great fondness, particularly on the occasion of his visit to Paris in 1961.

"For me it was also a personal friend who always showed me a profound affection and understanding.

"As General de Gaulle said today, he died as a soldier. We shall never forget his example or his memory, the memory of a great man."

GENERAL DE GAULLE ATTENDS PRESIDENT KENNEDY'S FUNERAL

The Presidency of the Republic issued a communique on November 23 announcing that General de Gaulle, President of the Republic, would attend the funeral of President Kennedy. He would be accompanied by M. Maurice Couve de Murville, Minister of Foreign Affairs; General Charles Ailleret, Chief of Staff of the French Armed Forces; and M. Etienne Burin des Roziers, General Secretary of the Presidency of the Republic.

France mourns President Kennedy

On the personal orders of General de Gaulle, all flags on public buildings were flown at half staff from 9 a.m., on November 23.

In paying this respect to the memory of President Kennedy, General de Gaulle departed from French tradition, which requires flags to be flown at half staff only during the funeral of a head of state of an allied or friendly power.

On November 23, the Paris Municipal Council sent a telegram to Mrs. Kennedy in which it told her that the city of Paris was in mourning. In addition, a member of the council proposed that the name of John F. Kennedy, defender of the fundamental freedoms of man and who fell for these freedoms, be given to a street in Paris. The council unanimously adopted this proposal on November 28.

In addition to messages of condolence addressed by official French circles to Mr. Charles Bohlen, many people from all walks of life, veterans associations, French-American associations and others sent messages of sympathy to the U.S. Embassy in Paris.

Among many expressions of sympathy, mention should be made of a group of between 2,000 and 3,000 students of all nationalities who went to sign the register of condolence in the U.S. Embassy in Paris.

A service in the memory of President Kennedy was held on November 25 in the cathedral of Notre-Dame de Paris. It was attended by the U.S. Ambassador and Mrs. Bohlen and by Madam Charles de Gaulle. M. Georges Pompidou, French Premier, the president of the senate and Madame Gaston Monnerville, members of the Government and members of the diplomatic corps in the French capital were also present in the great cathedral which was unable to hold the crowds of Parisians who wished to attend the service and who overflowed into the square in front of the cathedral, where members of the Garde Républicaine, swords unsheathed, formed an honor guard.

The French press

The entire French press without exception reflected the feeling of affliction among the French people at the death of President Kennedy. Raymond Aron in Le Figaro of November 23 wrote: "The assassination of J. F. Kennedy affects all mankind * * *. He wanted to be one of those statesmen whom history remembers because they accomplish their task * * *. He will leave a memory which will not be unworthy of the grandeur which he dreamed of achieving."

In an editorial of November 23, Combat wrote: "The crime committed yesterday is the worst one can imagine, since the man it struck down was a symbol in the eyes of hundreds of millions of our contemporaries."

Also on November 23, France-Soir wrote: "Like lightning, anguish and grief have hit the world. The hearts of men and women sank at the same moment, in every country and on all continents. * * * All peoples weep, also, and above all, for this man who, in the words of Pope Paul VI, 'defended the liberty of peoples and the peace of the world.'"

La Nation of November 25 published the following editorial comments: "He was one of the great men of this world. * * * A man with a personal fortune for whom it was possible therefore to have narrow views, and yet he was more aware than millions of others of man's fate, a man, above all, who had the courage to direct his actions in tune with his heart."

Paul Bastid, in l'Aurore of November 25, wrote: "There was in the personality of John Fitzgerald Kennedy a kind of lucid fire in the service of liberty and peace which commanded admiration and sympathy. He devoted himself entirely, with the energy of his temperament and of his age, to causes that are dear to us."

Le Monde, in an editorial in its November 26 issue, said: "He leaves an inspiration, a style, a line from which America will not easily stray." In the same issue, the French poet and Nobel prize winner Saint John Perse, wrote: "Kennedy * * * was an athlete running in a race against fate. He fought fairly and squarely always, and his encounter with death came with his face uncovered."

The next day Le Monde published an editorial containing the following comment: "The gesture by the President of the Republic who, right at the outset, decided to be present at the funeral of a man whom many considered his rival, has come opportunely to show that, in difficult times, he intends to behave as a loyal friend of the United States. He had already proved this during the Cuban crisis."

Eulogy pronounced by M. Jacques Chaban-Delmas, President of the French National Assembly

At the opening of the November 26 sitting, in the presence of Mr. Charles Bohlen, U.S. Ambassador to France, M. Jacques Chaban-Delmas, President of the French National Assembly, pronounced the following eulogy of the late President Kennedy:

"John F. Kennedy was not only the world's most powerful head of state. He was also an exceptional man.

"The murder of this hero, who fell in the flower of his youth, who knew what power and glory was, this murder in which the fate of the ancients finds expression, has already taken on an historic amplitude, and its echo will never die away. No, we shall not forget John F. Kennedy.

"Yesterday, in Washington, France expressed her grief through the presence of the most famous of her citizens, he who, without a doubt, already belongs to history and continues to forge the future.

"Today, the National Assembly shares as one in the mourning of the United States and of its Congress. It participates with emotion in the sorrow of the Kennedy family. Deeply shocked, it pays its respects before the anguish of this charming, worthy, and courageous young woman who brought a little of the gentleness of France into the harsh existence of America's first citizen.

"Tomorrow it will be up to each and every one to pursue his task in defending and expounding the great principles shared by our two countries, principles in whose respect President Kennedy lived and also died."

M. Maurice Couve de Murville, Minister of Foreign Affairs, associated the Government with the words of the National Assembly:

"The homage paid by the National Assembly marks the share taken by the French people in the mourning of the American people and shows the esteem and affection for the President who died in the line of duty."

More than 400 deputies stood and observed 1 minute's silence. Meetings were suspended for 1 hour as a sign of mourning.

Hon. Roman C. Pucinski

OF ILLINOIS

Mr. Speaker, during the past incredible 72 hours, like all Members of Congress, I, too, have received expressions of grief from many of my constituents. One in particular deserves the attention of my colleagues.

Following, Mr. Speaker, is a eulogy composed by Mr. Norman H. Kindlund, of my district in Chicago, Ill., whose beautiful words express the deep loss that we have all suffered in the untimely death of our President:

HAIL HEROIC SHADES

Centuries of statesmen
Leaders of all lands,
From your earned repose
Where your spirits rest,
Hearken for another
Has overcome the test.

Perservering virtue
Held 'gainst calumny,
Loneliness in cause—
Hard by lies oppressed,
Firm in his convictions,
Ne'er from these digressed.

Youth now stands before you
As our Nation is,
Dominant in mien
Resolute and free—
Bid him salutation
From your company.

Author of your exploits
Styled in eulogy,
Void of flowery praise
Yet with rev'rence due,
Tribute to your courage
Pass by in review.

Scorning all aloofness,
On his feet for all,
Example showing freely—
Mankind must be fit,
For survival's mandates
And no cringe admit.

Though he falls foreshortened
By a coward's stroke,
Honor shields forever
With invigorating rest
Youthful Chief of State;
Greet him as our best.

Penchant, trenchant style,
Uplift in word and deed,
Humanity's great burden
With sincerity made clear—
Welcome now his spirit
To your fearless ranks a peer.

Mr. Speaker, the Polish National Alliance and Polish American Congress, through its president, Mr. Karol Rozmarek, joined the entire Nation and the world in paying tribute to our late President John F. Kennedy. Mr. Rozmarek stated that "to Americans of Polish origin President Kennedy will always remain on lofty heights of reverence."

I believe it is well known to all Members of Congress what a tremendously high respect Americans of Polish descent had for President Kennedy, because of his deep understanding of the impressive contribution which these people have made to the growth of America. I should like, at this point, to include Mr. Rozmarek's entire statement:

An immense tragedy has struck our Nation and millions of Americans weep in sorrow and anger. In sorrow, for we have lost an enlightened leader, the youngest and most forward looking among the world's statesmen, in this era of the cold war and exploding international crises, which at the same time, is an era of terrifying nuclear weapons, and an era of human destiny involved in the discovery and exploration of the vastness of outer space.

A LEADER

Americans weep in sorrow because we have lost a leader, who would rather bring forth in international affairs a lighted torch of understanding, compassion, and patience.

And Americans weep in anger realizing that the young and purposeful life of our great President has been cut down by an assassin's bullet. A coward hidden in a warehouse, fired the shot which killed our President, plunged us into this mourning and reverberated shockwave.

A STATESMAN

I would like to quote the American journalist, Max Freeman who writes today of our late President Kennedy: "He was growing all the time in a tradition of spacious statesmanship, and excellence would have been his companion had more time been granted to him * * * and now he will be remembered as the man who broke the furrows and walked always to the far horizons."

To Americans of Polish origin the memory of the late President Kennedy will always remain on lofty heights of reverence. He was our true and tried friend. He understood our ancestry and the cultural, religious, and traditional values that link us with the land of our forefathers.

SYMPATHY FOR POLAND

To Poland and her people, the most ravaged and heroic in World War II, he has shown deep understanding and sympathy, eloquently expressed in his remarkable book "The Strategy of Peace," and in his Senate speeches and his several Presidential addresses.

His name will be hallowed forever in our memory. We express our deepest sorrow to Mrs. Kennedy and her children.

NEW CHIEF

Our ship of state has a new captain at the helm—in the person of President Lyndon B. Johnson, until last Friday, the Vice President of the United States. Like his predecessor, President Johnson has proven great qualities of leadership, first in the Senate of the United States and later in the greatly expanded office of the Vice President of the United States.

May God grant him strength and guidance in this most responsible and most powerful office in the free world, in these momentous times.

CHARLES ROZMAREK,

President, Polish National Alliance and Polish American Congress.

Mr. Speaker, I have taken this special order today in order to call to the attention of my colleagues a magnificent special memorial section published by the Chicago Sun-Times on December 29, 1963, in memory of our late President John Fitzgerald Kennedy.

Students of history for centuries to come will seek information about this tragic chapter of American history when President Kennedy was murdered.

It is my hope that by including the complete text of this special memorial section published by the Sun-Times, we may leave for posterity a permanent record of how one American publication interpreted and reported this tragic event of 1963.

The men and women who prepared this special memorial section are among America's most highly respected writers. Their words describing this entire tragedy graphically record the full impact of the tragedy.

It is with a sense of deep pride that I include in my remarks today the work of these outstanding men and women of American journalism.

The Chicago Sun-Times has performed a classic public service in compiling into a few pages the full scope of those tragic days in November which took from America one great President and gave to America another great President.

The Sun-Times Kennedy memorial section follows:

A BLACK FRIDAY IN DALLAS

(By Merriman Smith)

WASHINGTON.—It was a balmy sunny noon as we motored through downtown Dallas behind President Kennedy.

The procession cleared the center of the business district and turned into a handsome highway that wound through what appeared to be a park.

I was riding in the so-called White House press pool car, a telephone company vehicle equipped with a mobile radiotelephone. I was in the front seat between a driver from the telephone company and Malcolm Kilduff, acting White House Press Secretary for the President's Texas tour. Three other pool reporters were wedged in the back seat.

Suddenly we heard three loud, almost painfully loud cracks. The first sounded as if it might have been a large firecracker. But the second and third blasts were unmistakable—gunfire.

The President's car, possibly as much as 150 or 200 yards ahead, seemed to falter briefly. We saw a flurry of activity in the Secret Service followup car behind the Chief Executive's bubbletop limousine.

Next in line was the car bearing Vice President Lyndon B. Johnson. Behind that, another followup car bearing agents assigned to the Vice President's protection. We were behind that car.

Our car stood still for probably only a few seconds, but it seemed like a lifetime. One sees history explode before one's eyes and for even the most trained observer, there is a limit to what one can comprehend.

I looked ahead at the President's car but could not see him or his companion, Gov. John B. Connally, of Texas. Both men had been riding on the right side of the bubbletop limousine from Washington. I thought I saw a flash of pink which would have been Mrs. Jacqueline Kennedy.

Everybody in our car began shouting at the driver to pull up closer to the President's car. But at this moment we saw the big bubbletop and a motorcycle escort roar away at high speed.

We screamed at our driver, "Get going, get going." We careened around the Johnson car and its escort and set out down the highway, barely able to keep in sight of the President's car and the accompanying Secret Service followup car.

They vanished around a curve. When we cleared the same curve we could see where we were heading—Parkland Hospital, a large brick structure to the left of the arterial highway. We skidded around a sharp left turn and spilled out of the pool car as it entered the hospital driveway.

I ran to the side of the bubbletop.

The President was face down on the back seat. Mrs. Kennedy made a cradle of her arms around the President's head and bent over him as if she were whispering to him.

Governor Connally was on his back on the floor of the car, his head and shoulders resting in the arms of his wife, Nellie, who kept shaking her head and shaking with dry sobs. Blood oozed from the front of the Governor's suit. I could not see the President's wound. But I could see blood spattered around the interior of the rear seat and a dark stain spreading down the right side of the President's dark gray suit.

From the telephone car, I had radioed the Dallas bureau of UPI that three shots had been fired at the Kennedy motorcade. Seeing the bloody scene in the rear of the car at the hospital entrance, I knew I had to get to a telephone immediately.

Clint Hill, the Secret Service agent in charge of the detail assigned to Mrs. Kennedy, was leaning over into the rear of the car.

"How badly was he hit, Clint?" I asked.

"He's dead," Hill replied curtly.

I have no further clear memory of the scene in the driveway. I recall a babble of anxious voices, tense voices—"Where in hell are the stretchers * * *. Get a doctor out here * * *. He's on the way * * *. Come on, easy there." And from somewhere, nervous sobbing.

I raced down a short stretch of sidewalk into a hospital corridor. The first thing I spotted was a small clerical office, more of a booth than an office. Inside, a bespectacled man stood shuffling what appeared to be hospital forms. At a wicket much like a bank teller's cage, I spotted a telephone on the shelf.

"How do you get outside?" I gasped. "The President has been hurt and this is an emergency call."

"Dial 9," he said, shoving the phone toward me.

It took two tries before I successfully dialed the Dallas UPI number. Quickly I dictated a bulletin saying the President had been seriously, perhaps fatally, injured by an assassin's bullets while driving through the streets of Dallas.

Litters bearing the President and the Governor rolled by me as I dictated, but my back was to the hallway and I didn't see them until they were at the entrance of the emergency room about 75 or 100 feet away.

I knew they had passed, however, from the horrified expression that suddenly spread over the face of the man behind the wicket.

As I stood in the drab buff hallway leading into the emergency ward trying to reconstruct the shooting for the UPI man on the other end of the telephone and still keep track of what was happening outside the door of the emergency room, I watched a swift and confused panorama sweep before me.

Kilduff, of the White House press staff, raced up and down the hall. Police captains barked at each other, "Clear this area." Two priests hurried in behind a Secret Service agent, their narrow purple stoles rolled up tightly in their hands. A police lieutenant ran down the hall with a large carton of blood for transfusions. A doctor came in and said he was responding to a call for "all neurosurgeons."

The priests came out and said the President had received the last sacrament of the Roman Catholic Church. They said he was still alive, but not conscious. Members of the Kennedy staff began arriving. They had been behind us in the motorcade, but hopelessly bogged for a time in confused traffic.

Telephones were at a premium in the hospital and I clung to mine for dear life. I was afraid to stray from the wicket lest I lose contact with the outside world.

My decision was made for me, however, when Kilduff and Wayne Hawks of the White House staff ran by me, shouting that Kilduff would make a statement shortly in the so-called nurses room a floor above and at the far end of the hospital.

I threw down the phone and sped after them. We reached the door of the conference room and there were loud cries of "Quiet." Fighting to keep his emotions under control, Kilduff said "President John Fitzgerald Kennedy died at approximately 1 o'clock."

I raced into a nearby office. The telephone switchboard at the hospital was hopelessly jammed. I spotted Virginia Payette, wife of UPI's southwestern division manager and a veteran reporter in her own right. I told her to try getting through on pay telephones on the floor above.

Frustrated by the inability to get through the hospital switchboard, I appealed to a nurse. She led me through a maze of corridors and back stairways to another floor and a lone pay booth. I got the Dallas office. Virginia had gotten through before me.

Whereupon I ran back through the hospital to the conference room. There Jiggs Fauver, of the White House transportation staff grabbed me and said Kilduff wanted a pool of three men immediately to fly back to Washington on *Air Force 1*, the presidential aircraft.

"He wants you downstairs, and he wants you right now," Fauver said.

Down the stairs I ran and into the driveway, only to discover Kilduff had just pulled out in our telephone car.

Charles Roberts of Newsweek magazine, Sid Davis of Westinghouse Broadcasting and I implored a police officer to take us to the airport in his squad car. The Secret Service had requested that no sirens be used in the vicinity of the airport, but the Dallas officer did a masterful job of getting us through some of the worst traffic I've ever seen.

As we piled out of the car on the edge of the runway about 200 yards from the presidential aircraft, Kilduff spotted us and motioned for us to hurry. We trotted to him and he said the plane could take two pool men to Washington; that Johnson was about to take the oath of office aboard the plane and would take off immediately thereafter.

I saw a bank of telephone booths beside the runway and asked if I had time to advise my news service. He said, "But for God's sake, hurry."

Then began another telephone nightmare. The Dallas office rang busy. I tried calling Washington. All circuits were busy. Then I called the New York bureau of UPI and told them about the impending installation of a new President aboard the airplane.

Kilduff came out of the plane and motioned wildly toward my booth. I slammed down the phone and jogged across the runway. A detective stopped me and said, "You dropped your pocket comb."

Aboard *Air Force 1* on which I had made so many trips

as a press association reporter covering President Kennedy, all of the shades of the larger main cabin were drawn and the interior was hot and dimly lighted.

Kilduff propelled us to the President's suite two-thirds of the way back in the plane. The room is used normally as a combination conference and sitting room and could accommodate 8 to 10 people seated.

I wedged inside the door and began counting. There were 27 people in this compartment. Johnson stood in the center with his wife, Lady Bird. U.S. District Court Judge Sarah T. Hughes, 67, a kindly faced woman stood with a small black Bible in her hands, waiting to give the oath.

The compartment became hotter and hotter, Johnson was worried that some of the Kennedy staff might not be able to get inside. He urged people to press forward, but a Signal Corps photographer, Capt. Cecil Stoughton, standing in the corner on a chair, said if Johnson moved any closer, it would be virtually impossible to make a truly historic photograph.

It developed that Johnson was waiting for Mrs. Kennedy, who was composing herself in a small bedroom in the rear of the plane. She appeared alone, dressed in the same pink wool suit she had worn in the morning when she appeared so happy shaking hands with airport crowds at the side of her husband.

She was white faced but dry eyed. Friendly hands stretched toward her as she stumbled slightly. Johnson took both of her hands in his and motioned her to his left side. Lady Bird stood on his right, a fixed half-smile showing the tension.

Johnson nodded to Judge Hughes, an old friend of his family and a Kennedy appointee.

"Hold up your right hand and repeat after me," the woman jurist said to Johnson.

Outside a jet could be heard droning into a landing.

Judge Hughes held out the Bible and Johnson covered it with his large left hand. His right arm went slowly into the air and the jurist began to intone the constitutional oath, "I do solemnly swear I will faithfully execute the office of President of the United States * * *."

The brief ceremony ended when Johnson in a deep, firm voice, repeated after the judge "and so help me God."

Johnson turned first to his wife, hugged her about the shoulders and kissed her on the cheek. Then he turned to Mr. Kennedy's widow, put his left arm around her and kissed her cheek.

As others in the group—some Texas Democratic House members, members of the Johnson and Kennedy staffs— moved toward the new President, he seemed to back away from any expression of felicitation.

The 2-minute ceremony concluded at 2:38 p.m., and seconds later the President said firmly, "Now, let's get airborne."

Col. James Swindal, pilot of the plane, a big gleaming silver and blue fan-jet, cut on the starboard engines immediately. Several persons, including Sid Davis, of Westinghouse, left the plane at that time. The White House had room for only two pool reporters on the return flight and these posts were filled by Roberts and me, although at the moment we could find no empty seats.

At 3:47 p.m., the wheels of *Air Force 1* cleared the runway. Swindal roared the big ship up to an unusually high cruising altitude of 41,000 feet where, at 625 miles an hour, ground speed, the jet hurtled toward Andrews Air Force Base outside Washington.

When the President's plane reached operating altitude, Mrs. Kennedy left her bed-chamber and walked to the rear compartment of the plane. This was the so-called family living room, a private area where she and Mr. Kennedy, family, and friends had spent many happy airborne hours chatting and dining together.

Mr. Kennedy's casket had been placed in this compartment, carried aboard by a group of Secret Service agents.

Mrs. Kennedy went into the rear lounge and took a chair beside the coffin. There she remained throughout the flight. Her vigil was shared at times by four staff members close to the slain Chief Executive—David Powers, his buddy and personal assistant; Kenneth P. O'Donnell, appointments secretary and key political adviser; Lawrence O'Brien, chief Kennedy liaison man with Congress; and Brig. Gen. Godfrey McHugh, Mr. Kennedy's Air Force aide.

Mr. Kennedy's military aide, Maj. Gen. Chester V. Clifton, was busy most of the trip in the forward areas of the plane, sending messages and making arrangements for arrival ceremonies and movement of the body to Bethesda Naval Hospital.

As the flight progressed, Johnson walked back into the main compartment. My portable typewriter was lost somewhere around the hospital and I was writing on an oversized electric typewriter which Mr. Kennedy's personal secretary, Mrs. Evelyn Lincoln, had used to type his speech texts.

Johnson came up to the table where Roberts and I were trying to record the history we had just witnessed.

"I'm going to make a short statement in a few minutes and give you copies of it," he said. "Then when I get on the ground, I'll do it over again."

It was the first public utterance of the new Chief Executive, brief and moving: "This is a sad time for all people. We have suffered a loss that cannot be weighed. For me it is a deep personal tragedy. I know the world shares the sorrow that Mrs. Kennedy and her family bear. I will do my best. That is all I can do. I ask for your help—and God's."

When the plane was about 45 minutes from Washington, the new President got on a special radiotelephone and placed a call to Mrs. Rose Kennedy, the late President's mother.

"I wish to God there was something I could do," he told her, "I just wanted you to know that."

Then Mrs. Johnson wanted to talk to the elder Mrs. Kennedy.

"We feel like the heart has been cut out of us," Mrs. Johnson said. She broke down for a moment and began to sob. Recovering in a few seconds, she added, "Our love and our prayers are with you."

Thirty minutes out of Washington, Johnson put in a call for Nellie Connally, wife of the seriously wounded Texas Governor.

The new President said to the Governor's wife: "We are praying for you, darling, and I know that everything is going to be all right, isn't it? Give him a hug and a kiss for me."

It was dark when *Air Force 1* began to skim over the lights of the Washington area, lining up for a landing at Andrews Air Force Base. The plane touched down at 5:59 p.m.

I thanked the stewards for rigging up the typewriter for me, pulled on my raincoat and started down the forward ramp. Roberts and I stood under a wing and watched the casket being lowered from the rear of the plane and borne by a complement of Armed Forces bodybearers into a waiting hearse. We watched Mrs. Kennedy and the President's brother, Attorney General Robert F. Kennedy, climb into the hearse beside the coffin.

The new President repeated his first public statement for broadcast and newsreel microphones, shook hands with some of the Government and diplomatic leaders who turned out to meet the plane, and headed for his helicopter.

Roberts and I were given seats on another helicopter bound for the White House lawn. In the compartment next to ours in one of the large chairs beside a window sat Theodore C. Sorensen, one of Mr. Kennedy's closest associates with the title of special counsel to the President. He had not gone to Texas with his Chief but had come to the airbase for his return.

Sorensen sat wilted in the large chair, crying softly. The dignity of his deep grief seemed to sum up all of the tragedy and sadness of the previous 6 hours.

As our helicopter circled in the balmy darkness for a landing on the White House south lawn, it seemed incredible that only 6 hours before, John Fitzgerald Kennedy had been a vibrant, smiling, waving, and active man.

———

THREE LAST, BRIGHT HOURS—AND THE NIGHTMARE DESCENDS

(By Carleton Kent)

DALLAS.—It had rained in the early morning, but then the sky cleared into the livid blue of the Southwest; the air was cool, and every prospect pleased as John F. Kennedy rode into Dallas.

In neighboring Fort Worth, not notably a hotbed of liberalism, he had been extravagantly praised at a chamber of commerce breakfast meeting by "Mr. Fort Worth," Chamber President Raymond Buck.

"Our great, courageous, and brilliant leader of the world's strongest nation," Buck had called him. "Our hearts and our arms are open to you. May God bless you and cause His light to shine on you and your companions."

Three hours later, in the bright sun of Dallas, 30 miles away, the young President lay dying in the back seat of an open car, struck down by an assassin whose gun couldn't miss his russet-haired target in a slow-moving motorcade.

He had come to Texas the day before for precampaign politicking in a State whose 25 electoral votes would be important in 1964, whose Democratic Party was torn by a family feud, and in which conservative Republicans fanatically devoted to Senator Barry Goldwater, Republican, of Arizona, were boasting of their strength.

Overnight the President had smoothed over the public portions of the fight among Democrats. He had persuaded Senator Ralph W. Yarborough, the liberal Democrats' champion, to ride in the same car with Lyndon B. Johnson, his dearest Democratic foe, and Mrs. Johnson in the Fort Worth and Dallas motorcades.

This was something Yarborough had twice refused to do on Thursday, in San Antonio, and Houston.

Pleased over this demonstration, maybe only a gesture of Democratic unity, the President charged on Dallas, the citadel of right-wing Republicanism.

He had a speech in his pocket, to be delivered at an enormous luncheon meeting sponsored by top business executives of Dallas—almost to a man stanchly conservative—and it minced no words.

It accused his extremist foes of talking nonsense—of assuming that words will suffice without weapons, that vituperation is as good as victory, and that peace is a sign of weakness.

The assassin's bullet struck him down a half hour before he was to deliver his challenge, and while he was on his way to the luncheon date in the Dallas trade mart that ended on the grimmest of notes.

The crowd in downtown Dallas had been extra large and appeared extra friendly.

There were a few Goldwater signs. There was one in big capitals in an office building that said merely, "Bah." There was another, longer one: "Because of my respect for the Presidency, I despise you and your brand of socialism."

Reporters riding in a "White House press bus" 200 yards behind the President's car guessed Mr. Kennedy probably laughed at those.

After the sniper's bullet hit him, Mrs. Kennedy cradled his head in the lap of her raspberry-colored wool suit, the one he had kidded her about earlier in the joyous day at Fort Worth.

He had apologized to a crowd standing in the early morning rain of a parking lot across from the hotel, because his wife hadn't come with him.

"Mrs. Kennedy is organizing herself," he said. "It takes longer. But, of course, she looks better than we do when she does it."

And at the chamber of commerce breakfast later he complained that "nobody wonders what Lyndon and I wear."

Just before the shots rang out that killed him and gravely wounded Texas Governor, John B. Connally, riding in the seat ahead of him, the Kennedys were laughing at something Mrs. Connally turned around to say to them.

"You can't say Dallas wasn't friendly to you today," she said.

Then occurred the kind of nightmare the Secret Service always lives with.

And Senator Yarborough riding two cars behind will never forget the sight of the Secret Service man beating his fist on the presidential car in what he knew to be anger, frustration, and despair.

The President died without ever answering Mrs. Connally, or saying another word.

He could have had no intimation of what fate had in

store for him. He did know, of course, that his visit to Texas was begging political danger.

But that was the kind of America he preached. He felt it was better to come to Texas, to challenge the Republicans and to risk any damage accruing from the Democratic Party's factional fight, than to turn his back on it and pretend no trouble existed. He chose to go into difficult political terrain, and to face the most vociferous and unyielding foes of his administration in the fiercest citadel of conservatism in the Nation.

Of course, he didn't know one man, instead of arguing politics, would use a sniper's rifle.

––––

A GRAY SATURDAY IN CAPITAL

(By David Wise)

WASHINGTON.—The rain in Washington, cold, gray, and dismal, had begun soon after the dawn.

At each corner of the President's mahogany casket, four white candles cast flickering shadows in the hushed East Room of the White House.

John F. Kennedy, 35th President of the United States, reposed there, in his home, for the last time Saturday, 1 day after an assassin's bullet in Dallas had cut short his Presidency, his hopes, and his life at the age of 46.

A family mourned, a nation mourned, a world mourned, and as the rains came throughout the long, sorrowful day, it seemed as though the heavens mourned, too.

There was shock in Washington Friday when the President was murdered. Saturday there was only sadness.

The dead President's immediate family and the great men of power in Washington filed past the closed casket Saturday.

During the night, residents of the Capital could hear the sirens of the police escort as the casket containing the President's body moved through the dark streets from Bethesda Naval Hospital to the White House.

The blue-gray Navy ambulance left the hospital at 4 a.m. Inside were Mrs. Jacqueline Kennedy, still wearing the blood-spattered pink suit, stockings, and shoes she wore Friday, and the President's brother, Attorney General Robert F. Kennedy.

At 4:25 a.m., the ambulance, its window curtains drawn, moved through the northwest gate of the White House. A double line of marines led the way as the ambulance and three limousines moved under the elms, bare of leaves, up the driveway to the north portico of the White House.

Hundreds of persons who had waited in the darkness outside the White House gates watched silently. Men removed their hats. Mrs. Kennedy stepped out of the ambulance, waiting patiently for the flag-draped casket to be removed.

Then, she turned and walked steadily between the double line of marines, on the arm of Robert Kennedy.

Mrs. Kennedy, the Attorney General, and a few members of the President's staff gathered in the East Room before dawn. One of the priests in attendance said a short prayer.

At 10:30 a.m., a private Mass was conducted in the East Room, attended by Mrs. Kennedy, her 2 children, and about 75 close friends and members of the family.

And all day long they came to file silently into the East Room—the leaders of Congress, the military, members of the President's Cabinet, his close friends, the Justices of the Supreme Court, the members of the diplomatic corps, Governors, and mayors.

As the leaders of the Nation filed past the casket, two of President Kennedy's rocking chairs were taken out of the White House by workmen, to be placed in storage.

––––

AMID SORROW, THE STRENGTH TO CARRY ON

(By Thomas B. Ross)

WASHINGTON.—"Mrs. Kennedy has asked that this be as distinguished a tribute as we can possibly make it."

With those words of Attorney General Robert F. Kennedy, R. Sargent Shriver, Jr., began the preparations for the solemn and majestic ceremonies that ended when John Fitzgerald Kennedy was laid to rest Monday afternoon.

This is the story of how Mrs. Kennedy's anguished request was carried out.

It was then midafternoon Friday, Mr. Kennedy had been shot to death 3 hours before. Shriver had just talked by phone with Robert Kennedy, who was waiting for the body to be flown back from Dallas.

Shriver carried the Attorney General's words to a meeting in the White House of the late President's staff, his principal military aides, and the protocol chiefs of the State Department. Shriver was not to go to bed for another 30 hours.

He had been having lunch with his wife, Eunice, at a downtown restaurant when word came that his brother-in-law had been shot. Together, they returned to Shriver's office in the Peace Corps.

Robert Kennedy phoned for the first time a short while later. Shriver suggested the Attorney General stay with Mrs. Kennedy and let him handle the details. The Attorney General agreed and the Shrivers set out for the White House.

Mrs. Shriver left almost immediately with Senator Edward Kennedy, Democrat, of Massachusetts, to be with their parents in Hyannis Port, Mass.

Shriver went to work on the arrangements. Mrs. Kennedy had now returned to Washington with the President's body. Another call from the Attorney General conveyed her desire to have the East Room in the White House prepared as it was for the body of Abraham Lincoln.

Shriver had 8 hours to carry out the request and no one seemed to know how the East Room had been decorated for Lincoln.

Shriver called Richard Goodwin, a former aide at the Peace Corps who had recently been chosen as the President's special assistant on the fine arts. Within half an hour, Goodwin produced a photograph of Lincoln's body lying in repose in the White House.

Shriver then turned to William Walton, an artist friend of Mrs. Kennedy. Walton took Goodwin's picture and put the White House staff to work.

A furniture upholsterer, brought to the White House from Cape Cod, Mass., by the First Lady, stood on a 20-foot ladder for 9 hours arranging the black window curtains in the proper way.

Carpenters took down the aluminum storm doors to return them to their original form.

Walton removed the gay flower decoration and substituted white lilies. Also during the first night he managed to find the proper yellow candlesticks. Antique oil lights were located to illuminate the White House driveway.

At midnight, Shriver had a crucifix brought in from the bedroom of his home in nearby Maryland.

The military men were having great difficulty locating a ceremonial honor guard to receive the President's body with appropriate dignity and ceremony.

Finally, at 3 a.m., the White House naval aide, Capt. Tazewell T. Shepard, Jr., located two dozen members of a crack drill team at the marine barracks a couple miles from the White House.

They were roused from sleep and volunteered without hesitation. They arrived at the White House in time for Mrs. Kennedy's arrival from Bethesda Naval Hospital with the body at 4:30 a.m.

By then all was in readiness.

Everything, the First Lady said, had been done exactly as she would have done it.

The First Lady declared her resolve to walk behind the casket to the church and she asked that Mass be held at St. Matthew's.

Mrs. Kennedy, the Attorney General, and Shriver agreed that there should be a "low" spoken Mass rather than a "high" sung Mass with incense and more elaborate ceremony. The late President had not been a man for pomp and circumstance.

Mrs. Kennedy recalled how pleased she had been with the man who sang at her wedding. Within hours he agreed to come to Washington for the Requiem Mass.

The First Lady also remembered how moved she had been by Bizet's "Agnus Dei," which also had been played at the wedding. The piece was promptly included in the music scheduled for the Mass.

Mrs. Kennedy asked that there be no elaborate diplomatic display and so the State Department's chief of protocol, Angier Biddle Duke, sent out a worldwide request that the foreign representation be held down.

But the request was to no avail. By noon Saturday the State Department had been flooded with cables reporting that emperors, princes, queens, and presidents were determined to attend the funeral.

All afternoon Saturday Shriver and Duke worked out the invitation list and the seating arrangement in the cathedral. It was completed by nightfall.

And at 11 p.m., more than 30 hours after he had received his first call from the Attorney General, Shriver went home to bed.

A Mournful Sunday Procession

(By William Braden)

Washington.—The body of John Fitzgerald Kennedy was carried to the Capitol rotunda to lie in state Sunday in a ceremony that pulsed with the stark horror of a Greek tragedy.

The agony of the procession was made almost unbearable by the shooting in Dallas that ended the life of President Kennedy's accused assassin.

Lee Harvey Oswald, 24, was gunned down while the first elements of the cortege were forming around the north portico of the White House.

The news that Oswald had been shot spread quickly at the White House and along the cortege route, where it was picked up by spectators with transistor radios.

And then, as if events had been following some ironic script, word of Oswald's death electrified the mourners in the rotunda just as Mrs. Kennedy turned and left the casket of her husband.

There were no tears for Oswald. But it was plain that everyone in this stricken city had already had his fill of hate and violence. And even the supposedly hardened newsmen here were physically sickened by the new bloodshed, holding their stomachs as they turned away from White House radios and televisions sets.

With this added anguish, the cortege left the White House slightly behind schedule at 1:10 p.m.

The body of the murdered President was carried on the same black artillery caisson that bore Franklin Delano Roosevelt on a similar journey in 1945.

The four-wheeled caisson, draped in black, was pulled by six white horses. It was preceded by a mounted soldier on a seventh white horse. The caisson was followed by a soldier carrying a flag and by a riderless dark gray horse named Black Jack.

The gelding was fully saddled and a sword in a scabbard hung on the right side of the saddle. The silver stirrups were reversed and held a pair of black riding boots.

The casket, covered by the Stars and Stripes, was carried from the East Room of the White House by servicemen and placed on the caisson at the crepe-hung north portico.

To the beat of muffled drums, the procession left the White House by the northeast gate, the driveway lined by sailors who presented the flags of the 50 States.

Following an historic route, the cortege moved along Pennsylvania Avenue to 15th Street, and then turned right, taking 15th south until it rejoined Pennsylvania. Then, with the Capitol dome visible in the distance, it proceeded down Pennsylvania and Constitution Avenue to Delaware Avenue, where it turned right again to arrive at the East Plaza of the Capitol. The cortege covered the 1.8-mile route at a constant pace of 100 steps to the minute, the cadence set by the throb of the drums.

No one who was there is likely to forget those drums that thudded like a broken heart the entire length of the march.

An estimated 300,000 persons jammed the route, standing 10 to 20 deep at the curbs, leaning from windows, perched on walls and rooftops and wedged in trees.

The crowd was the largest he had ever seen in Washington, said Police Capt. Joseph V. Osterman.

It seemed that almost all of those along the way, adults and children, were wearing their Sunday best, in respect for the dead leader. And aside from the drums—always the drums—the silence seemed nearly perfect as the cortege moved down the broad eight lanes of Pennsylvania Avenue.

The skies were cloudless and painfully bright. A crisp wind blew from the west, whirling brown and yellow leaves from near-barren trees, bracing the flags that hung at half-staff all along the way.

To some, the procession sometimes seemed like a little lost ship making its way down the black river of pavement. It was not a small procession, but it looked diminutive on the vast, empty boulevard.

The cortege was headed by a police honor guard. This was followed by the escort commander, Maj. Gen. Philip C. Wehle; by the 20 drummers from the 5 services; by a company of Navy personnel, symbolizing Mr. Kennedy's service in that branch during World War II; by a special honor guard consisting of the Joint Chiefs of Staff; and, just ahead of the caisson, a color detail and clergymen.

Behind the caisson came a serviceman with the Presidential flag and then the horse and cars carrying dignitaries and members of Mr. Kennedy's family—among them President Johnson and Mrs. Kennedy with the two children, Caroline and John, Junior.

The rear was brought up by another police honor guard and by the White House press corps.

Their repressed emotions finally proved too much for the well-behaved spectators. And when the procession had passed, they suddenly broke from the curbs and moved into the street to join the reporters who brought up the rear of the cortege.

It was a startling and poignant sight. Looking back, the reporters abruptly found themselves joined by hundreds and then thousands of men, women, and children.

Running and trotting, the spectators swept after the cortege, following their fallen President.

But at Ninth Street, police threw a cordon across the avenue—holding spectators and reporters alike.

The reporters were finally allowed through. But minutes later they had been joined by a second wave of spectators.

Another police cordon was encountered at Seventh Street. Once again, the reporters eventually talked their way through. But at Fourth Street, the reporters and others came up against a line of Marines with fixed bayonets. And this time the newsmen were stopped cold, despite the protests of a White House press aid who pointed out that they were a part of the official procession.

The cortege continued along Constitution Avenue and then swung around to the East Plaza.

Again the crowds broke, and they moved like a wave toward the Capitol—thousands and thousands of them, literally engulfing the building and rushing up the stairs of the West Plaza.

Arriving at the East Plaza, the cortege was honored by a 21-gun salute. Drums sounded four ruffles and flourishes, and the Air Force band played "Hail to the Chief" and a naval hymn, "Eternal Father, Strong To Save."

The casket was then carried into the rotunda, under the great dome, where it was placed upon the black-draped catafalque that once supported the coffin of Abraham Lincoln.

John, Junior, was taken outside, but Caroline stood at her mother's right side in the rotunda as brief tributes were paid to Mr. Kennedy by Senator Mike Mansfield, of Montana, the Senate Democratic leader; Earl Warren, Chief Justice of the United States, and Representative John W. McCormack, of Massachusetts, Speaker of the House.

"There was the sound of laughter; in a moment, it was no more. And so, she took a ring from her finger and placed it in his hands," said Mansfield.

He eulogized Mr. Kennedy as a leader, as a patriot, as a father and as a husband.

"He gave us of his love that we, too, in turn—might give," said Mansfield. "He gave that we might give of ourselves, that we might give to one another until there would be no room, no room at all, for the bigotry, the hatred, prejudice and the arrogance which converged in that moment of horror to strike him down."

"We are saddened," said Warren. "We are stunned. We are perplexed.

"What moved some misguided wretch to do this horrible deed may never be known to us, but we do know that such acts are commonly stimulated by forces of hatred and malevolence, such as today, which are eating their way into the bloodstream of American life.

"What a price we pay for this fanaticism.

"It has been said that the only thing we learn from history is that we do not learn.

"But surely we can learn if we have the will to do so. surely there is a lesson to be learned from this tragic event.

"If we really love this country, if we truly love justice and mercy, if we fervently want to make this Nation better for those who are to follow us, we can at least abjure the hatred that consumes people, the false accusations that divide us and the bitterness that begets violence.

"Is it too much to hope that the martyrdom of our beloved President might even soften the hearts of those who would themselves recoil from assassination but who do not shrink from spreading the venom which kindles thoughts of it in others?"

"At each great crisis in our history," said McCormack, "we have found a leader able to grasp the helm of state and guide the country through the troubles which beset it."

Mr. Kennedy was such a man, said McCormack, and he added:

"Now that our great leader has been taken from us in a cruel death, we are bound to feel shattered and helpless in the face of our loss. This is but natural.

"But as the first bitter pang of our incredulous grief begins to pass, we must thank God that we were privileged, however briefly, to have had this great man for our President. For he has now taken his place among the great figures of our world history.

"While this is an occasion of deep sorrow, it should also be one of dedication. We must have the determination to unite and carry on the spirit of John Fitzgerald Kennedy for a strengthened America and for a future world of peace."

The acoustics were bad, and most of the speeches went unheard by the small group of mourners who had crowded into the rotunda. Former President Harry S. Truman stood behind the speakers with bowed head, his hands clasped in front of him.

Mrs. Kennedy was dressed in black, her head covered with black lace. Caroline wore a blue coat, red shoes, white gloves, and a ribbon in her hair. And those who do not have children her age wondered whether she understood what was happening there.

Her uncle, Robert F. Kennedy, the Attorney General, stood next to her.

It was warm in the rotunda. Representative Carl Vinson, Democrat, of Georgia was led out at the beginning of the ceremony. A physician said Vinson was overheated. And after being given a fluid, the Representative, who has been in Congress for more years than Mr. Kennedy lived, returned to hear the proceedings from a chair.

At 2:17 p.m., a serviceman and President Johnson carried a mounted floral tribute to the casket in the center of the rotunda. Mr. Johnson bowed his head briefly and then turned and walked back.

Then Mrs. Kennedy and Caroline walked hand in hand to the catafalque, kneeled and Mrs. Kennedy kissed the flag which covered her husband's casket.

The time—2:19 p.m.

The mother and daughter turned and walked from the bier, and then led the mourners out of the rotunda.

————

[From the Chicago (Ill.) Sun-Times, Dec. 29, 1963]

A Monday Walk in Gothic Gloom

(By William Braden)

WASHINGTON.—The casket moved through the streets followed by presidents and princes, dukes and prime ministers—even a king and an emperor.

But the eyes of thousands were on a woman in black.

She strode briskly to the cadence of the funeral drums, her head erect, her widow's veil tossed by the wind.

The passage of years may some day blur the memories of those who lined the curbs of the Nation's Capital Monday. Even the clatter of hooves and the beat of the drums may someday be forgotten.

But for those who stood and watched it, Mrs. John F. Kennedy's last walk with her husband can never be forgotten.

She strode with strength and purpose behind the caisson that bore the murdered President, the veil fluttering like a proud and terrible flag of honor. And those who watched shared both her sorrow, which was a nation's sorrow, and her strength, which was her own.

Surely it was her finest hour.

Many of the world's most powerful leaders, all on foot, kept step behind Mrs. Kennedy as her husband's casket was carried from the White House to the Requiem Mass in St. Matthew's Cathedral.

A separate procession a short time earlier had taken the casket to the White House from the Capitol rotunda, where Mr. Kennedy had lain in state since Sunday afternoon.

A final procession, following the mass, bore the casket to its resting place in Arlington National Cemetry.

The widow's unprecedented march to the cathedral followed a route of about a half mile.

The procession first moved west on Pennsylvania Avenue, turning north at 17th Street. Then it continued to the cathedral at 17th, Connecticut Avenue and Rhode Island Avenue.

The day was crisp and bright—very much as it was on Sunday when Mr. Kennedy was carried to the rotunda. The temperature was in the forties, the sky was cloudless, and the buildings along the way formed deep canyons of alternate sunlight and shadow.

Mourners jammed the sidewalks. Others stood on high ledges of office buildings and many more appeared to risk their lives by sitting on the edges of roofs, their feet hanging down.

The crowds waited silently, as they did Sunday. Then, in the distance, came the sound of the muffled drums.

Then the sound of pipes and then the dread music of military bands playing Chopin's funeral march.

And finally the long procession, far grander than Sunday's, headed by a police honor guard.

Close behind the police came the red jacketed Marine Band, its snare drums covered with crepe.

Spectators in the rear stood on boxes to see, and a well-dressed man hurried up carrying a newly purchased garbage can to use for a platform.

A phalanx of West Pointers marched by, followed by cadets and midshipmen from the Air Force, Navy, and Coast Guard Academies.

Next came contingents of enlisted men and a mixed contingent of servicewomen.

Above the unwavering rhythm of the drums, the chords of the funeral march echoed again and again.

The Navy Band passed, moving from the shadows into the sunlight that glistened on its instruments.

More contingents of servicemen, and then the Air Force Band.

From time to time the bands played "America" or "Onward, Christian Soldiers." But always they returned to Chopin's dirge.

Paratroopers swung past wearing jaunty berets, followed by marines in dress uniform.

Then the sound of pipes and the Black Watch marchers in kilts and busbies, the ribbons of their instruments flying in the breeze.

And then the black artillery caisson drawn by six white horses.

The three horses on the left side were ridden by soldiers in dress blues, and an outrider kept pace of a seventh white horse.

The casket was still covered by the U.S. flag that would not be removed until the burial ceremony, and it was secured to the lumbering four-wheeled caisson by two black bands.

Behind it marched a solitary bluejacket in white puttees, carrying the Presidential flag. And then once more the awesome sight of the riderless dark horse with two black boots placed in its reversed stirrups.

So far the stillness of the crowd had been almost unbroken.

But now, as the widow passed, a very faint sound rose, lost almost at once on the wind, like a low, collective moan.

Mrs. Kennedy was flanked on the right and left by her husband's brothers, Robert and Edward—the Attorney General and the junior Senator from Massachusetts.

She walked past at steady pace, her arms swinging free, her face hidden by the black veil.

Men, women, and children turned their heads to stare

after her. And they continued to stare after her until she was far up the street.

They seemed hardly to notice those who came behind her—Harry S. Truman, Dwight D. Eisenhower, Prince Philip, President Charles de Gaulle, President Johnson.

After the mass, Mrs. Kennedy and the dignitaries entered limousines for the hour-long procession through downtown Washington and across the Potomac River to Arlington National Cemetery in Virginia.

Newsmen here have remarked on the muteness and tearlessness of the spectators during Sunday's and Monday's processions.

But the reason for that is not hard to find. Tears spring from grief. And the grief here is deep.

But there is horror here, too. A horror that numbs and dumfounds and at times prevents the outward manifestations of sorrow.

It is a gothic gloom that pervades this ctiy.

The black bunting. The drums. The ringing of the bells at night and the shuddering of organs. The pomp and circumstance, out of another age.

And more than that, the memories. The constant reminders here, at every hand, of a happier time.

For it is here that he lived and worked and was seen. It is here that one walks past the White House at night and sees the crepe above the door in the lighted north portico.

The White House, with Caroline's swings and John, Junior's, sandbox back behind.

It is as if Poe's raven perched on every marble bust in this city of marble busts, calling "Nevermore."

The natural shock at the death of a President is multiplied beyond measure by the circumstances of that death—sudden and violent, unexpected and senseless. Not the natural death of a beloved and elder statesman but the murder of a young pioneer who promised a new frontier.

This is more than grief. This is deeper than grief.

"It's going to happen to the whole world," said an old woman who stood watching the final procession from cathedral to cemetery, her eyes glazed with unreasoning fear. "And it's going to happen overnight. It happened to him. And if it happened to him, it can happen to all of us."

In the passing procession, the limousine carrying the new President was escorted by a score of Secret Service men.

The men who walked beside the car seemed to be staring up at every window of every building along the way.

———

[From the Chicago (Ill.) Sun-Times, Dec. 29, 1963]

"THE TRUMPET SUMMONS US"—HIS BUOYANT WORDS ECHO

(By Carleton Kent)

WASHINGTON.—The soul of John F. Kennedy, martyred 35th President of the United States, was commended to God Monday in a simple Roman Catholic low mass in St. Matthew's Cathedral.

The hour-long ceremony, attended by 1,200 persons from all over the world, some of the highest and others of the most ordinary estate, was dominated in one sense by the heavy, harsh voice of Richard Cardinal Cushing, who performed the last rite.

But overriding Cardinal Cushing, the music and the ancient Catholic ritual were some of Mr. Kennedy's own words—and particularly those of his inaugural address of January 20, 1961.

They were delivered by the Most Reverend Philip Hannon, auxiliary bishop of Washington, along with a recollection of some of the slain President's favorite Bible quotations, from the pulpit.

Bishop Hannon read the inaugural address, and the words sounded as brave and buoyant as they had on that freezing winter's day less than 3 years ago when Mr. Kennedy took the oath as President:

"Now the trumpet summons us again—not as a call to bear arms, though arms we need—not as a call to battle, though embattled we are—but a call to bear the burden of a long twilight struggle, year in and year out, 'rejoicing in hope, patient in tribulation'—a struggle against the common enemies of man: tyranny, poverty, disease, and war itself.

"I do not shrink from this responsibility—I welcome it. I do not believe that any of us would exchange places with any other people or any other generation.

"And so, my fellow Americans: Ask not what your country can do for you—ask what you can do for your country."

In the congregation were Ethiopia's Emperor, the Queen of the Hellenes, the King of the Belgians, the Prime Minister and the Prince consort of the United Kingdom, the proud soldier-President of France, and the governmental rank—and the file—from America and all over the world.

White House office secretaries and petty-detail handlers were there, too, all joined together in a moving display of affection and grief.

At 11:45 a.m. the congregation, all but those who had walked behind Mrs. Kennedy in the sad procession from the White House, could hear through the open main doors a military band playing the hymn "Pray for Dead." Its strains clashed with those of the organ, playing softly inside.

Five minutes later came a mournful skirl from the famed Black Watch bagpipers, who only 2 weeks ago had staged a brave marching show on the south lawn of the White House for a grandstand full of Washington children, at the Kennedy's request.

And at noon Cardinal Cushing, followed by purple-garbed prelates, walked down the center aisle to the massive main doors.

He greeted Mrs. Kennedy, who had just been joined by her children, Caroline, 5, and John, Junior, 3, who had arrived by car. John cried a moment, but stopped when his mother comforted him. Later he was given a religious pamphlet to occupy his attention.

In turn, Mrs. Kennedy, dressed in black and wearing a long diaphanous veil, was comforted by the richly garbed and mitered Cardinal Cushing, who had officiated at her wedding and the baptism of the children.

He put his arm around her shoulders, as she genuflected

before him. Then he leaned down and gently patted the children.

Mrs. Kennedy, giving a hand to each child, walked down the aisle, closely followed by Attorney General Robert F. Kennedy, Senator Edward M. Kennedy, the late President's mother, Mrs. Rose Kennedy, and other members of the family.

The sounds of military protocol outside—the mournful muffled drum beats, the orders cracked out to - honor guards and other military units, continued to mingle with the liturgical music inside the cathedral.

Cardinal Cushing stood aside, his hands clasped in the attitude of prayer, as President Charles de Gaulle, of France, in his beige general's uniform, led the foreign dignitaries into the church. He was accompanied by Queen Frederika of Greece. Emperor Haile Selassie of Ethiopia also was in the front row.

De Gaulle's face was stern and solemn as he walked down the aisle, guided by ushers in the full-dress uniforms of the U.S. armed services.

Many of those who followed—the chiefs of state and heads of foreign delegations, the Supreme Court, the Cabinet, the diplomats, the congressional leaders of both parties—walked with downcast eyes.

The band outside played the traditional ruffles and flourishes, followed by "Hail to the Chief" that always greets the President on formal occasions—and President and Mrs. Johnson entered the church.

Then, after Cardinal Cushing had blessed the casket, the pallbearers bore it inside and walked slowly down the center aisle, behind altar boys carrying the crucifix and candles, their flames guttering in the cold wind blowing through the open door.

De Gaulle knelt during the entire service, his body erect, his face somber and seemingly frozen. Near him sat West Germany's Chancellor Ludwig Erhard, following the mass with absorption.

Toward the end, Cardinal Cushing doffed the vestments of the mass, resumed the scarlet cape and capella, and blessed the body in the simple wooden coffin and uttered the final prayer:

"I am the resurrection and the life. He who believes in Me, even if he die, shall live; and whoever lives and believes in Me shall never die."

The honor guard slowly carried the casket out of the cathedral. Tears coursed down the strong, angular face of the cardinal as he stood in the doorway, his raiment brilliant in the afternoon sun.

He wiped his eyes with a handkerchief while the Army band ranked outside played a dirge.

The young widow walked erect with her children. But under her black veil her eyes shone with tears. Mrs. Rose Kennedy lost her composure as she left the cathedral and wept. So did Senator Kennedy.

President Johnson's face was set in a grim, tragic mask as he reached the door—again to the sound of "Hail to the Chief."

Caroline, sobbing at her mother's side, and John, Junior, were turned over to the family nurse, Maud Shaw, and three Secret Service agents.

Former President Dwight D. Eisenhower and his wife walked out of the cathedral a few paces ahead of former President Harry S. Truman.

The Eisenhowers and Mr. Truman paused at the door to say a few words of comfort to Mrs. Kennedy. Then General Eisenhower and Mr. Truman, political feuding forgotten, conversed on the cathedral steps as they awaited their cars.

And the sad journey to Arlington National Cemetery and Mr. Kennedy's final resting place resumed.

———

Journey's End on Hillside

(By Thomas B. Ross)

Arlington Cemetery.—John Fitzgerald Kennedy was buried Monday at a modest graveside overlooking the majestic memorial to Abraham Lincoln.

It was a grand but simple ceremony in the eloquently understated manner of the 35th President of the United States who was killed by an assassin's bullets last Friday.

The burial place at the Arlington National Cemetery was close by the spot where the late President had paused on a quiet stroll early last spring and commented: "Imagine living out here. Wouldn't this be a wonderful place for the White House?"

At that time, accompanied by Defense Secretary Robert S. McNamara and his close friend Charles L. Bartlett of the Sun-Times Washington Bureau, President Kennedy had just completed an unpublicized tour of the cemetery and the Custis Lee mansion once the home of Gen. Robert E. Lee.

Monday afternoon, John Fitzgerald Kennedy was laid to rest in the hillside sloping down from the mansion to the Potomac River.

At the grave was his widow, Jacqueline, but his children, Caroline and John Jr., who had attended the requiem mass at St. Matthew's Cathedral, were not taken to the cemetery.

With the exception of the late President's ailing father, Joseph P. Kennedy, the rest of the large family was there—mother Rose, brothers Robert and Edward, sisters Eunice, Patricia and Jean.

Mrs. Kennedy, a black veil covering her beautiful face, stood a few paces from the grave as Richard Cardinal Cushing of Boston read the committal prayers of the Roman Catholic Church.

Mr. Kennedy's burial place is located in an open stretch of land more than 100 yards from the other closely ordered graves of this military cemetery.

The only other President buried here is William Howard Taft.

The late President's body was borne to the cemetery across the Lincoln Memorial Bridge. Mrs. Kennedy followed the black, horse-drawn caisson in a limousine. The Marine Band and a special military honor guard preceded the casket in slow cadence.

The cortege came to a halt 100 yards from the grave. Mrs. Kennedy stepped out of the limousine and the band sounded "Ruffles and Flourishes." Then the National Anthem was played.

Mrs. Kennedy approached the grave along a straw mat in company with Attorney General Robert Kennedy. The rest of the family followed immediately behind them, taking up positions to the right of the grave on a long grass-colored matting.

President Johnson stood inconspicuously behind the family, off to the side, and it was difficult to pick him out of the crowd of mourners.

Former Presidents Harry S. Truman and Dwight D. Eisenhower, alighting from the same car, assumed an equally inconspicuous vantage point in the throng of lofty national and international dignitaries.

The mourners made their way to the graveside between two columns of the Army's Special Forces, advanced by the late President to strengthen the fight against Communist guerrillas in such places as Vietnam.

Autumn leaves, dropped from planes at a high altitude, fell on the burial site as the mourners approached their places.

President Charles de Gaulle, of France, resplendent in a light brown general's uniform, took up a position at the foot of the grave. Emperor Haile Selassie of Ethiopia, on De Gaulle's left, was also in uniform, a bright kelly green sash across his chest.

Prior to the religious ceremony, the Irish guard, here on personal request of Mrs. Kennedy, performed a special manual at the foot of the grave.

De Gaulle removed his hat and glasses and made the sign of the cross as Cardinal Cushing began the prayers. The cardinal's vivid red robes stood in sharp contrast to the black lectern.

The prayers, alternately in Latin and English, included the Lord's Prayer and the Hail Mary. Twice the cardinal sprinkled holy water on the casket. Midway through the religious rites, Cardinal Cushing paused, the troops came to present arms, and a 21-gun salute was sounded.

Overhead 50 jet fighter planes zoomed by at low altitude. They were followed by *Air Force 1,* the plane which carried the late President to Dallas and brought his body back last Friday. The exhaust and the contrails of the jets left a gray smudge on the cloudless sky.

At the conclusion of the prayers, Mrs. Kennedy and the Attorney General moved closer to the grave beside Cardinal Cushing. The late President's brother-in-law, R. Sargent Shriver, Jr., of Chicago, took up the spot left by the Attorney General next to Mrs. Rose Kennedy.

Three volleys of musketry rang out, and taps were sounded. The band struck up a hymn, and the eight body bearers began to fold the American flag which they had been holding over the casket.

Mrs. Kennedy lit an "eternal flame," akin to the light that burns under the Arc d'Triomphe in Paris. Then she took the folded flag, paused momentarily as Cardinal Cushing offered a few words of comfort to her, and walked to her limousine.

At that point, for the first time in her 3-day ordeal, Mrs. Kennedy's public composure began to dissolve. Those close to the grave said she began to weep, and she approached Gen. Maxwell D. Taylor, Chairman of the Joint Chiefs of Staff.

Taylor put his arm about her and attempted to console her. Mrs. Kennedy, although still weeping, seemed to regain much of her composure as she departed for her limousine.

Cardinal Cushing moved to the side of the late President's mother, who had been leaning heavily on Shriver's arm. The cardinal raised his arm, as if to put it about Rose Kennedy's shoulder. But she straightened herself up, grasped his hands, and kissed the episcopal ring.

Then she rested her head on his shoulder for a brief moment, before leading the rest of the family to the waiting cars.

———

MRS. KENNEDY—A WOMAN EQUAL TO HER TASK

(NOTE.—This tribute to Mrs. John F. Kennedy was written on the 10th anniversary of her wedding to the late President by Charles Bartlett, a close personal friend. It is being reprinted because it reveals the qualities of character and personality that were so clearly revealed in her conduct during the tragic days of late November.)

(By Charles Bartlett)

WASHINGTON.—It would be impossible to imagine any state of life in which the companionship of marriage was more essential or any wife more ideally suited to this particular President.

An observer living among politicians is struck by the fact that the complexities which confront all wives are compounded for the wives of politicians and doubly compounded for the wife of a politician who manages to reach the White House. The difference is that the compartmentalization between home and office which is possible in private life becomes exceedingly difficult in public life. No private pursuit, however ambitious, carries an involvement for a wife that equals the demands placed upon a woman whose husband is seeking or holding high political office.

It is possible to love a politician without loving politics but it is impossible to marry one without becoming part of his career.

Jacqueline Kennedy's struggle to attain this compartmentalization has been the measure of her firmness and resourcefulness. A President lives as much in controversy as in the White House and his private life is a seclusion from the tempest and a respite from the pressures.

Mrs. Kennedy's greatest accomplishment has been to maintain this refuge and embellish it with the variety, warmth, and wit of her own personality.

As a young woman entering the White House, Mrs. Kennedy had many choices and much advice, but she chose a firm course of following her own best instincts. She set out to do the things she could do well for her family and the White House and to do them in her own style and with people she selected herself.

The zest and thoroughness with which she plunged into the task of refurbishing the White House were the mark of this spirit.

Starting almost on the first day of her residency, she sought out the people who could give her the knowledge that she needed, then the people who could find the things that she needed, and finally the people who would pay for them.

When the drive faltered, she swallowed her shyness and went before the television cameras in an appearance that will long stand as a classic in the medium. When donors faltered, she prodded them with charm and persistence that narrowed their avenues of escape.

Her effort developed a momentum that swiftly transformed the White House from simulated and meaningless elegance to gracious and authentic dignity. She created in less than 3 years a priceless museum of American treasures.

This same determination—to make the White House reflect the best in American life—was applied to a dogged and detailed assault on the pomposity of official functions. The effort did not spring from any desire to win fame as a hostess. It was simply a matter of doing something that had to be done in a fashion that would please her husband and enhance the country in the eyes of foreigners.

The cause of her public impact in an era when masses of women are struggling to be more beautiful and interesting is not difficult to discern. But the imitators of Mrs. Kennedy have missed the essence of her personality and success, which is an insistence on being herself.

Women are using their emancipation to go in many directions, but the most common fallacy of the sex is a tendency to watch each other and to do what the other is doing.

Mrs. Kennedy did not make the mistake of trying to be Eleanor Roosevelt or Dolly Madison. But by fidelity to her own individuality, she has become a unique figure in the White House and an enormous asset to the President.

———

The Man the Nation Lost

(By Charles Bartlett)

WASHINGTON.—John F. Kennedy was an intensely realistic man and he talked occasionally of assassination in the same analytical fashion in which he discussed the other hazards and opportunities of his Presidency. On the morning of the day it happened, he referred to the ease with which a President could be shot.

This may or may not have been a premonition, but it was certainly not a fear or any form of negative emotion. His mind dwelled constantly on the forces which could obstruct his purposes and this was simply one that had to be considered.

He was impelled into politics by a sense of the things that could be done for the country. He ran for President with a confidence that he could be a constructive force. His days in the White House were marked above all by a driving desire to do his best in the time that he had.

He could not have regretted, if the assassin's bullet left him any moments of reflection before death, any wasted time or missed opportunities. He could only have felt a deep sadness that he would not live to achieve his high hopes for his term of office.

It is ironic that a man so dedicated to tangible deeds is destined now to be remembered less for his accomplishments than for the intangible qualities of his spirit and character. He disciplined himself to be great in order to do great things and the waste of his death is that his greatness so far exceeded his time for achievement.

Discipline was a prime ingredient of his greatness. He rarely talked in abstract terms but he displayed over the years a firm determination to define for himself the strong and weak characteristics of man and to expand the strengths and reject the flaws that he found in himself. It was as if he had assessed the qualities that he would need for the challenges he saw ahead and determined to possess them through an exercise of will.

In this pursuit he had much to work with from the beginning. His mind was lightning fast from youth, his intuition was quick and precise, and his curiosity was limitless. His temperament was innately balanced between action and reflection, between gravity and humor, and between cold reason and human warmth.

He did not change as a personality. His burdens never eclipsed his broad streak of gaiety, his adversities did not encroach upon his optimism, and his honors and offices never managed to swell his solid assurance into anything that could be called conceit.

He inspired loyalty because he was loyal and because his personal qualities made associates and friends strive to show him their best. He projected an electricity that sought a spark of wisdom or wit and his presence, even as a young man, was always a challenge.

The zest and enthusiasm that he brought into the White House never flickered. He arrived with a burning sense of the good things that could be done and as he faced the difficulties of doing them, his determination deepened and his pace quickened.

Death caught him at a time when he was stimulated beyond all the past periods of his intense life by the varied challenges on the domestic and foreign fronts. He went off to Texas in a high spirit of confidence that he could meet these challenges despite all the disappointments of the past year.

His force stemmed from his belief that a great nation should not tolerate remediable shortcomings and no one who had the privilege of knowing him can ever accept the virtue of a passive attitude. To at least this one friend, his epitaph will be: "He was a gentle and fine man who possessed the will to meet the problems as he saw them."

———

America Weeps

President Kennedy lies dead, a martyr in the cause of democratic government.

His countrymen weep in sorrow and in anger.

The immensity of the crime can hardly be grasped in these hours of confusion that inevitably have followed the assassination of the Chief of the most powerful Nation in the world.

The Nation goes ahead with a new leader, Vice President Johnson has assumed the heavy burden of the Presidency and the policies of the Nation will undergo no imminent change. But inevitably the assassination will change the course of history, not only in the Nation but in the world.

And it should change the temper of our times. At the moment the motive that lurked in the twisted mind of the killer is not, of course, known.

But the deed in Dallas was different only in degree of importance from such acts of violence as the bombing of houses of worship, racial murders and only last month, in the same city, the degrading assault on U.N. Ambassador Adlai Stevenson.

All of these acts of violence are the work of persons who, fundamentally, do not believe in a democratic government operating under a rule of law.

The whisperers and preachers of hate and disunity, who undermine confidence in our Government and our public officials by irresponsible attacks on their sanity and loyalty, plant the motives in the heads of those who pull the triggers and toss the bombs.

Those who impugn the motives of our national leaders, who defy the courts, distort the operations of the United Nations, or advocate a change in our form of government, might not themselves do violence. But they engender the kind of hate that must have been in the eyes that lined up Mr. Kennedy's head in the crosshairs of a rifle sight yesterday.

The awful loss that hate visited upon the Nation and the world should inspire all Americans to join together in this hour of shock and mourning in a reexamination of the national conscience.

The right of dissent, the exercise of free speech, the criticism of the President and other public officials, high and low, must not corrode into sullen rebellion that breeds violence. All Americans, those who agree with their Government's policies and those who disagree, must stand together on this fundamental and demonstrate this unity by action as well as words. The purveyors of hate must acknowledge the danger they create.

When we speak of the purveyors of hate we obviously are not speaking of the President's regular political opposition, those persons in his own party and in the Republican Party who had disagreed with many of his views and policies and who also grieve for Mr. Kennedy. We are speaking of the extremists, left and right, who go beyond the pale in their opposition and criticism. The Nation owes a great debt to Mr. Kennedy who gave his life in the service of his country as surely as a soldier on the front line. And to Mrs. Kennedy and the President's family, the American people offer their hearts. The personal tragedy of an assassination seldom has been as heartbreakingly evident as in the scene that followed the shooting; Mrs. Kennedy holding the President's head in her lap and weeping "Oh, no."

No, it should never have happened in America. That it did must weigh heavily on America's conscience. And if it brings a reawakening and a real change in the temper of our times, Mr. Kennedy will not have died in vain. This is a prayer in which all Americans can join.

The Assassination of John F. Kennedy

(Gwendolyn Brooks, Chicago's Pulitzer Prize-winning poet, wrote these words upon the assassination of President Kennedy and sent them to the Sun-Times. "I was so very much upset, as everyone else is, I wanted to express what I felt," she said. "I started making notes during the first 2 hours after I heard of the President's death. Late Friday, after the house was quiet, I sat down and completed the poem.")

(By Gwendolyn Brooks)

"* * * this good, this decent, this kindly man."— Senator Mansfield.

I hear things crying in the world
A nightmare congress of obscure
Delirium uttering overbreath
The tilt and jangle of this death.

Who had a sense of world and man,
Who had an apt and antic grace
Lies lenient, lapsed, and large beneath
The tilt and jangle of this death.

The world goes on with what it has.
Its reasoned, right, and only code.
Coaxing, with military faith,
The tilt and jangle of this death.

The Deed That Freedom Bred

(By Walter Lippmann)

WASHINGTON.—The first need of the country is to take to heart the nature of this unspeakable crime. There is no public crisis at home or abroad that demands such instant attention that it cannot wait until we have collected ourselves and can proceed deliberately. But there is a searing internal crisis within the American spirit that we have first to realize and then to resolve.

The American future depends on it, and our capacity to govern ourselves. What we have to realize is that, though speech and gossip and rumor are free, the safety of the Republic is at stake when extremists go unrestrained. Extremists may profess any ideology. But what they all have in common is that they treat opponents as enemies, as outside the laws and the community of their fellowmen.

What happened in Dallas, to be sure, could have happened in another city. But it must be said that the murder of the President was not the first act of political violence in that city, but one in a series. The man who is now the President of the United States was manhandled by his fellow Texans. The man who represents the United Nations at the United Nations was spat upon.

In this atmosphere of political violence lived the President's murderer, himself addicted to the fascination of violence in his futile and lonely and brooding existence. The salient fact about him was his alienation from humanity, from country, family, and friends. Nothing within him, it would seem, bound him to the President or to the Governor as human beings. No human feeling stayed his hand.

In his alienation, Lee Harvey Oswald turned to the left. But that was incidental. Those who assaulted Mr. Johnson and Adlai E. Stevenson had turned to the right. The common characteristic of all of them was their alienation, the loss of their ties, the rupture of the community.

An extremist is an outsider. For him, the Government in Washington is a hated foreign power and the President in Washington is an invading conqueror. There is no limit, therefore, to his hatred that feeds upon the venom of malice, slander, and hallucination.

In Dallas today there is much searching of conscience, and well there should be. Dallas has long been conspicuous for its tolerance of extremists, and for the inability of its decent citizens, undoubtedly the great majority, to restrain the extremists and restore a condition of honest and temperate and reasonable discussion.

It was comforting to read Sunday that the mayor of Dallas, Earle Cabell, had said, "Each of us, in prayerful reflection, must search his heart and determine if through intemperate word or deed we might have contributed in some fashion to the movement of this mind across the brink of insanity."

We must all follow the mayor of Dallas in that prayerful reflection. It is only too easy to forget that in a free country there must be not only liberty and equality, but also fraternity.

The only solace for the Nation's shame and grief can come from a purge, or at least the reduction of, the hatred and venom that lie so close to the surface of our national life.

We have allowed the community of the American people to be rent with enmity. Only if and as we can find our way back into the American community will we find our way back to confidence in the American destiny.

We must stop the flow of the poison that leads men, in differing, say, about taxes or civil rights or Russia, to feel that those who take the other view are implacable enemies. In the light of this monstrous crime, we can see that in a free country, which we are and intend to be, unrestrained speech and thought are inherently subversive.

Democracy can be made to work only when the bonds of the community are inviolate, and stronger than all the parties and factions and interests and sects.

I wish I felt certain that the self-realization into which grief has shocked us will endure when we go back about our business.

The divisive forces of hatred and ungovernability are strong among us, and the habit of intemperate speech and thought has become deeply ingrained. It is deepened by the strains of war and the frustrations of this revolutionary age, by the exploitation of violence and cruelty in the mass media, by the profusion of weapons and by the presence of so many who know how to use them.

But I do have much hope in the healing arts of Lyndon B. Johnson. We can turn to him with confidence.

His great gift is in finding the consensus without which the American system of government with its States and regions, its checks and balances, is unworkable.

To find the concensus among our divided and angry people is his historic opportunity. To restore the internal peace of the United States in his unique mission.

That done, all else will be manageable.

His Legacy to the Nation

(By Milburn P. Akers)

President Kennedy's place in history will be established only in the perspective of the passing years. But his place in the hearts of his countrymen and free men everywhere has been manifest ever since word of the tragic happenings in Dallas was flashed throughout the world.

A nation deeply divided on many issues recoiled in shock and horror at his assassination; a nation which had long prided itself on determining devisive issues at the polls or in the courts was stunned by the realization that a gallant young President had been felled by an assassin. That nation, instantly united in its grief, paid tribute to John F. Kennedy in a manner such as has seldom, if ever, been accorded mortal man.

And then, following obsequies attended by the great and the near great from all over the world, they buried him at Arlington; not another unknown soldier but an American President who, in a relatively short span, had come to symbolize many of free men's aspirations. John F. Kennedy continues to live in the hearts of his countrymen.

What of the future—the future to which Mr. Kennedy so frequently alluded?

Many of its problems remain unresolved, the time allotted the stricken President having been too short to determine them.

President Johnson has a heritage of unsolved problems, even as did Mr. Kennedy and as have had most Presidents. For the great problems of the Nation and of the world are not speedily solved. Most Presidents can do little more than point in the direction of those solutions.

Mr. Kennedy did so in the nuclear test ban treaty. He was pointing toward an end to the cold war, to disarmament, and to a normalization of trade between the free world and the Soviet bloc. These things were seen by him as possibilities after he had boldly and successfully met Soviet Russia's missile challenge in Cuba.

President Johnson, whose methods are apt to differ vastly from those of his predecessor, will, no doubt, continue these efforts. For the world cannot afford to live dangerously in the atomic age.

Mr. Johnson is in general agreement with his predecessor's foreign policies. The difference will be largely in methods.

On the domestic front, Mr. Johnson, long experienced in the wiles of legislative leadership, is likely to settle for the possible in contrast to Mr. Kennedy's constant pressing for the desirable. Mr. Kennedy put the emphasis on the future. Mr. Johnson, more pragmatic than ideological, will doubtless put the emphasis on the present. In so doing, he may press for the adoption of quite a few of those measures which Mr. Kennedy advocated and, in advocating, brought enactment closer.

The race problem remains. Mr. Kennedy's solutions, northern and metropolitan in outlook, will now give way, insofar as White House leadership is concerned, to ones which, while southern and rural in origin, have been tempered and shaped in the national arena. This isn't to say that one view is superior to the other. It is merely to note that a new approach to his still unresolved problem is likely.

In John F. Kennedy the Nation had a youthful, gallant President to whom history beckoned; a President intent on reshaping the Nation's structure in many ways. He championed the cause of the aged and the infirm, of youth in need of educational opportunities, and of peace. He sought a nation in which opportunity was the right of all, irrespective of race. He established objectives with which few disagreed. Disagreement came largely in the methods he proposed to accomplish them.

Mr. Johnson agrees with many of those objectives. But his background, training, and experience are such that he will, while seeking the objectives to his utmost, settle for the possible, when he has satisfied himself what is possible and what is not possible.

Mr. Kennedy was the architect. Mr. Johnson's role, given time, will be that of the builder.

The President: How He'll Be Remembered

(By Eric Sevareid)

What was John F. Kennedy? How will he stand in history? As this is written, just after his death, it is hard even to assemble thoughts, easy to misjudge such a complicated human being.

The first thing about him was his driving intelligence. His mind was always on fire; his reading was prodigious; his memory almost total recall of facts and quotations. A friend of mine crossed the Atlantic on a liner with the Kennedy family, years ago. She remembered the day Jack was ill in the stateroom; there lay the thin, freckled little boy—12 years old, and reading Churchill's early life, other books scattered about his bed. His was a directed intelligence; he did not waste his energies; he always seemed to know where he was going and he put first things first.

John Kennedy's intellectuality was perhaps the hallmark of his nature, even more than his youth; the thing that made him different from so many Presidents. But few thought of him as an intellectual in the sense of one seeking truth for its own sake; he sought it, in order to act upon it. He was that rare and precious combination, the man of contemplation as well as the man of action. He had a sharp sense of history from his immense reading, and was acutely conscious of what his own place in history might be. In a sense, he lived for that; much of his personal correspondence as President suggested his awareness that those letters would be part of the American archives and story for all time.

He brought a new style into Government; he surrounded himself with intellectuals, as did Franklin D. Roosevelt in his first years; but in his personal style he was more like President Theodore Roosevelt. Like the first Roosevelt, President Kennedy believed in action; he had no patience with those who were tired or skeptical or cynical; no patience with those who could not keep up, mentally or physically.

He became, with his young and beautiful wife, the symbol of America as he and most of us like to think of America: Itself young, itself always hopeful, believing, and believing that Government could change the face of our land and our lives and that America could do more than any country in the world to change the face and the nature of the world itself.

He showed no signs, even after 3 years in office, of growing tired, either in body or spirit, but the built-in obstacles to practical achievement were—and remain—prodigious and complex. He began some new practical courses of Government action—as with the Peace Corps

and the Alliance for Progress; these, perhaps, were more imaginative than his domestic conceptions; in any case, it is in the domestic field that his difficulties were the greatest and progress the slowest.

Early on, he showed that his way would be to try to conciliate and persuade the Congress, and to compromise with it where he had to, rather than to try bulldozer tactics. Of his bold actions, his nuclear confrontation with the Soviet Union over Cuba was the boldest, one of the boldest, and most successful acts of statesmanship the history books will ever tell the future about.

But at bottom, President Kennedy was a cautious, prudent man. He liked to have all his ducks in a row before he fired. However vibrant in his political behavior, he was, in his deepest emotional nature, a conservative human being. Rarely did the people become aware of his deep feelings about anything. When he spoke to the country by radio or television, his head usually ruled his heart. Only in very special circumstances, as on the day of brutal events in Mississippi, did passion rise in his voice as he spoke. This is why some professional observers said that President Kennedy had opened his mind to us, but not his heart, that therefore, politically, he had not captured the heart of the people.

If that was so, it is so no longer; the heart of the people is with the young President in death; with all of his family.

Where the Eternal Flame Burns

(By James Hoge)

Washington.—Every 15 minutes, a city bus stops in front of the White House, picks up a load of passengers and wends its way through the Capital and across the river to the gentle slope where John F. Kennedy lies.

The buses, marked by wreaths of artificial flowers, half-staffed miniature American flags and signs reading "John F. Kennedy, Eternal Flame," have been carrying passengers free of charge to Arlington National Cemetery every day since the late President was buried there 3 weeks ago Monday.

The service has been taxed to its fullest. But that has also been the case with police who direct auto traffic to the cemetery and attendants who keep the throngs moving at the grave site.

Few officials expected such an outpouring and now few expect it to cease when the state period of mourning ends December 22.

The crowds are full of the kind of people John F. Kennedy knew well.

There are Roman Catholic nuns, once affectionately praised by the late President for being good Democrats while the Church's hierarchy leaned toward the Republicans.

There are teen-aged girls, the jumpers who hopped with excitement along parade routes during Mr. Kennedy's 1960 campaign, now giving in to tears as easily as they once gave in to joy.

There are Negroes who looked to the wealthy son of Massachusetts as their greatest presidential friend since Abraham Lincoln.

There are ministers and diplomats of foreign countries

who still come an average of one a day to lay wreaths.

And, as statistics confirm, there are the hundreds of thousands of Americans who were moved by John F. Kennedy's idealism, grace, and good cheer far more than anyone suspected while he was alive.

Those who take the 15-minute bus ride from the White House to Arlington pass many points in this historic city which bring to mind the late President and his family.

The sad trip begins in front of the main entrance to the Executive Mansion, now draped in black. It continues past the White House south lawn, where, last Christmas season, Mrs. Kennedy took her children for a sleigh ride in a horse-drawn buggy. Now there stands a darkened half-decorated Christmas tree.

The bus turns into Constitution Avenue just in front of the Washington Monument, its tip shrouded in mist these wintry days and its base ringed with flags at half staff.

It passes the marble headquarters of the Organization of American States, where many of Mr. Kennedy's ambitious plans for Latin America were enthusiastically received and at times ardently opposed. Off to the right looms the State Department, once home of the fast-paced, wit-infused Kennedy press conferences.

The bus turns into Lincoln Memorial Drive and then onto the bridge, which now begins at either end with a memorial to a martyred President.

Passengers strain to catch a view of the Kennedy grave site which lies on the hillside directly above the bridge and immediately below the Custis Lee Mansion. Mrs. Kennedy picked the location and stipulated that it be on a direct line with the Lincoln Memorial.

From the bridge, the white picket fence up as a temporary barrier around the grave is visible through the mist.

"I'm not sure I want to go any further," an elderly lady said out loud to no one in particular. The lines around her eyes seemed to crease with sorrow. "I cried so much that weekend. I don't want that again.

"But I promised myself I would come," she continued to a new-found listener. "He was always so good about getting out to see us. I feel I owe him this trip."

Another passenger asked the driver what it cost to run buses to the cemetery every 15 minutes for 9 hours each day. "About $500," he answered. "There are four buses. That takes six busdrivers, about $500 a day," he repeated.

Among the passengers was an agricultural expert from India, who for the last 5 months has been teaching at a Texas college. "I leave soon for home," he said in strained English. "I never see Mr. Kennedy. But I know he was a great man. I come to see how you bury great men. They will ask me in India if I have been here. They respected your President more than most."

It was a short uphill walk from the bus stop to the grave. As they walked, several people fidgeted with cameras, rolling in film and setting dials. But most just looked ahead.

A young naval officer shouldered a child and began the grade upward. "This is where the caisson came," he recalled for his son. "You remember Mrs. Kennedy lighting the flame? Well, that's it up ahead. It is sup-

posed to remind you of him and what he did for all of us." The child was silent, lost for a little while in a world where questions do not come easily.

Groups of people seemed to converge on the grave from many directions. They filed along temporary, matted walkways, laid over the cemetery grass, in the hope of minimizing the damage done by the feet of 1,200,000 mourners.

Recent rainy weather turned the walkway immediately around the picket fence into a pool of mud and forced the cemetery attendants to lay thick, black gravel.

The slopes on all sides still bear the marks of the crush of people who came immediately after the state funeral. But within the picket fence, the grass is deep green and the brilliant colors of floral wreaths abound.

"I want there to be flowers forever," said a young nun of the Sisters of Charity of St. Vincent de Paul. She and some 20 other Sisters, dressed in their quiet habits, journeyed to Arlington from Norfolk, Va., to place a single rose on the grave.

The grouping around the picket fence never seemed to be without a contingent of nuns, almost as if, like the four-man honor guard which stood at attention, the sisters meant to watch over John F. Kennedy.

There were nuns in blue garb, black and even red. They came from many places around the country. As one said, "We all sent representatives. This was not only a good man. He was a believing son of God."

Within the picket fence, the eternal flame, ordered by Mrs. Kennedy as a fitting remembrance of her husband, flickered brightly under the gray-clouded sky.

Many studied the flame, as if trying to decide if they liked it. "You know, I didn't think it was a very good idea when I heard about it," a middle-aged man mused.

"But now that I see it * * * well * * * you know it's really appropriate," he went on. "The guy was a light himself. And you see this thing flickering here, moving from side to side and it's like he's not all dead. Something right here has life."

The flame is presently produced by butane gas, stored in tanks under a nearby street. The city's gas and light company has begun engineering work on laying a pipe for natural gas that will be used in the permanent monument, now being designed under Mrs. Kennedy's direction.

Around the eternal flame have been tossed the hats of soldiers from several of the armed services. There is a green beret of the special guerrilla forces, greatly expanded during Mr. Kennedy's administration. There is an airman's cap, one from the Navy and an MP armband, a buffing strap from 3d Infantry and a light blue arm marking from the Marines.

The military mementos hark back to an ancient Grecian custom of paying tribute to a fallen warrior.

Most breathtaking sight at the grave is the view from behind the eternal flame over the Potomac to the Lincoln Memorial and beyond in a straight line all the way to the Capitol Building.

The view seems to catch everyone. People stop taking pictures, and just gaze or whisper about the panoramic vista. What they see is the view that John Kennedy, himself, once saw on a Sunday afternoon stroll and he reacted like them, awed, and pleased at the beauty and the majesty. "Imagine living out here!" he commented to his companions.

He is there now along with two of his four children. On either side of the eternal flame are stone markers, reading simply: "Patrick Bouvier Kennedy, August 7, 1963–August 9, 1963," and "Baby Girl Kennedy, August 23, 1956."

The shades of late afternoon began to deepen and a group of Mennonite college girls realized they must leave to catch the last bus back to Washington. They looked the part of mourners with their faces bare of cosmetics, and their long, uncut hair rolled in buns.

"It is important that we not forget," said a 19-year-old member of the group. "We must, must learn something from what this man gave up for us."

The bus was subdued. It started down the hill, through the cemetery gates and across the bridge to Washington. The time 4:45 p.m. Shortly, the sun would be down and the commuters heading the other way across the bridge would see above them the bright, flickering light meant to remind them of John F. Kennedy today, tomorrow, and forever.

TRIBUTE BY

Hon. Graham Purcell

OF TEXAS

Mr. Speaker, among the finest tributes to our late and beloved President Kennedy was a message delivered at the memorial service held at the National City Christian Church in Washington, D.C., on Monday, November 25, 1963.

The message was delivered by Dr. George R. Davis, minister. Dr. Davis is my dear personal friend. He served as minister of the First Christian Church of Wichita Falls, Tex., before coming to Washington to assume his present position of service.

Throughout my years of acquaintance with him, I have alway found that Dr. Davis has a remarkable capacity to speak the right words at precisely the right moment. His message in his memorial service for President Kennedy was no exception. I commend his message to my colleagues:

Shall we ever be the same again? Most of us never again. We do not wish to be. When we knew for certainty that the shadow had fallen across the path of our beloved Nation, that our young President had actually been lost to us, in one tragic, senseless moment, something died in us. A man may be judged and executed for the crime, but he will not have been the product of one State, one city, one family, not altogether. I was born a Kansan, and have lived in Oklahoma, Missouri, Texas, and now in the Nation's Capital. I have watched people everywhere, and have looked deep into my own heart. In the 12 years I ministered in Texas, I think I came to know something of the heart of the people, and the heart was sound. I had more than a passing interest in Dallas. It was and is a great city. These has been a "streak of viciousness, more than a streak, in certain kinds of radicals" running through the area. But I have found that same streak in Washington too. I refuse to let one State, one city assume the guilt for this tragedy, or to be a part of those who seek to fasten the guilt upon them. "Let the one without sin cast the first stone," the one who has not stooped by action, attitude, or even by indifference, to create the climate which was festering in America. All I have said in this regard, you will find to be true if you search your hearts and listen. You and I know this, in our deepest heart. Where did hate find birth in our time? Where was this evil spawned which sets loose such madness even in one person? Who are to be judge and jury? How expertly men have learned to hate in recent times, revealed in the mountains of cheap mail, whispered rumors, discord, and violence, idle stories, obscene humor so-called, racism, bigotry. And when some minds flounder on such a sea of spiritual sickness, who is really guilty? Perhaps a moment of greatness would be reached in the character of each of us, if we were able to respond with those men gathered about a table in upper room centuries ago, when on the edge of the darkness of guilt they cried out, each one for himself, "Lord, is it I?" Let us not imagine for one moment this would lessen the guilt of the hand which struck the devilish blow, it only widens the circle of involvement. This is a time for soul searching, a time for each of us to travel through the vast and hidden places of our own hearts, to open wide every window to those secret places, that the light may shine in every door that God may enter with cleansing and healing power.

We shall ever be remembering the face of a young and vigorous leader, his steadiness and his vibrant spirit. Millions had taken courage and hope, especially the young, but not the young alone, from his courage and hope. We shall be remembering for a long time a beautiful, gracious, and devoted young mother, and a little girl, and a little boy, a little boy who was just beginning to discover the wonderful ways of a happy father with a happy little boy. To so many they were like the family next door. This came not from an undue presumption of familiarity, rather from the genuine warmth of which the human heart is capable at the right times. Perhaps there were some who forgot how young they were, the family in the White House, and resented their breaking of the old customs, the customs for the old. But they were not old. Isn't it tragic what we so often do to the young, on the battlefields of a thousand wars, and often to their dreams by unconsciously resenting their youth. God grant that a new spirit may be born in us, that our President may not have died in vain, "that there shall be a new birth of freedom in our Nation, so that government of the people, by the people, for the people, shall not perish from the earth." Our prayers encompass President and Mrs. Lyndon B. Johnson and their daughters, as tasks too heavy for men to carry are laid upon his shoulders. We take heart in the continuity of our Nation's Government, which has been born out of the experience of the years, and out of other tragedies in peace and war. We take heart from the patient preparation which trained a tall and friendly Texan for such an unforeseen emergency, and that we were not left adrift when our captain fell. We take heart in the realization that though "tried, the Nation is not undone, though stricken we are not destroyed, though bowed in grief, we are comforted."

It is not out of place in time of such sorrow to remind ourselves the process of life must go on, and it goes on, undirected or directed, it goes on in chaos or with order. We rejoice that trained hands were there to take the helm, hands trained in the art of governing and politics. The times still confront us across the earth with dangers on every hand. We cannot be sure altogether of what to-morrow is to bring forth. But we believe a "sparrow does not fall to the ground without the Father's notice," that "great nations are not without His concern" in times of grave peril. And we know that in our peril we still have men and women adequate with the help of God, and who ask for the help of God even as the President now asked, "For your help, and God's."

"They that wait upon the Lord shall renew their strength, they shall mount up with wings as eagles, they shall run and not be weary. They shall walk and not faint."

Only the most callous would be insensitive now. Only the most politically partisan would raise an issue now about the rightness of our sorrow and our expressed appreciation for a great man who has fallen the victim of the violent in man, and in which many of us shared, if only by our indifference to a mood, a black and sinister mood, which had been fastening itself on the mind of the Nation in some quarters. God grant that mood has been shattered, though high the price. We may be thankful in these recent hours the partisan voice has not been raised. Americans have been Americans. Every hour, almost without exception, has been marked with dignity, by the press, the radio, and television, the public statements of public officials. There has been a greatness across the Nation. The family of John F. Kennedy in numerous ways during all these darkened hours gave character to the events, and in a sense saved the Nation from utter disgrace by the pattern of their conduct. Even the dramatic tones, which may have seemed to some overdone, were exalting. Our new President and his family, in ways which have marked their conduct during his years as Vice President and before, left nothing to be desired in them as great people. For all of this we are grateful.

We do not make a god of John Fitzgerald Kennedy. He walked on feet of clay as all mortals. Not all Americans, not by any means, on the day before he was shot down, stood in agreement with his policies, all his suggested programs. Far from it. And Americans of free mind will not all feel compelled in the high emotionalism

of deep sorrow to say, "Yes," to all he advocated. I am a little bothered by those who have begun to suggest that to clear our consciences of guilt, and to build a fitting memorial to him, all he wished for the Nation must now be immediately granted. I can think of no quicker way to ruin all he really stood for, if one reads carefully all he said, and he said much, and with a brilliance and clarity seldom if ever equaled in the American Presidency or elsewhere. I think it is true, men now will see him, his ideas, in a new light of appreciation, both his advocates and his opposition. And it is to be hoped down the years men of all views will express themselves toward each other with greater charity, greater tolerance, because his senseless death shocked men into taking a second, long look, always, at one another, and will somehow refuse to let their tongues become the instruments of hell in caustic judgments. It could be wildly hoped, with a kind of desperation, that his blood will wash out even the ugly scrawlings of the extremists, and that even they might be redeemed, and thus the Nation be saved from an eventual, awful judgment. But to surrender the right to oppose, to see either in the Congress or among our people in general an end to the right to differ, to see the end of men who go on saying, "no," unmoved even by the pressures from martyrdom, would be no true memorial to John F. Kennedy. That would be the death of all we cherish. Men will return to their debates. They should, with a new kindness let us pray, but return they should, unhindered by the charge that to do so is a betrayal of a fallen leader. Not so. Only let a new spirit be born, a true brotherliness. Only let us move onward toward those goals which the best men and women on both sides of the aisle really wish equally to see attained, goals of freedom, justice, dignity, for all people, our own, and across the whole earth. As we have heard the muffled drums, and the toiling of the solemn bells, let us again be reminded by John Donne, "No man is an island unto himself. Each man is a piece of the continent, a part of the main. A clod washed away by the sea, makes Europe the less. I am involved in mankind. Every man's death diminishes me. Therefore, never send to know for whom the bells tolls. It tolls for thee."

Mr. Speaker, the last public remarks by our late and beloved President Kennedy were made in Fort Worth, Tex., on that tragic day of his assassination. He spoke at a breakfast meeting of the Fort Worth Chamber of Commerce in the Texas Hotel.

It was my privilege to be in attendance that morning. I had accompanied the President to Texas, and had been with him on his visits to San Antonio and Houston on November 21, the day before his life was snuffed out.

On the morning of November 22, in Fort Worth, President Kennedy was in wonderful spirits. His trip had been a huge success, the large crowds had given him a warm welcome. His usual good humor was very much in evidence.

President Kennedy spoke that morning of confidence, confidence in many things. He spoke of the stature of our defenses, of the wonderful new TFX fighter plane, of Fort Worth Congressman Jim Wright, of the part Texas has played in the development of our Nation. I believe the full text of President Kennedy's remarks, the last he was to make in public, should be read and absorbed by all of us:

REMARKS OF THE PRESIDENT BEFORE THE FORT WORTH CHAMBER OF COMMERCE, TEXAS HOTEL, FORT WORTH, TEX.

I know now why everyone in Texas, Fort Worth, is so thin, having gotten up and down about nine times. This is what you do every morning.

Mr. Buck, Mr. Vice President, Governor Connally, Senator Yarborough, Jim Wright, members of the congressional delegation, Mr. Speaker, Mr. Attorney General, ladies and gentleman, 2 years ago, I introduced myself in Paris by saying that I was the man who had accompanied Mrs. Kennedy to Paris. I am getting somewhat that same sensation as I travel around Texas. Nobody wonders what Lyndon and I wear.

I am glad to be here in Jim Wright's city. About 35 years ago, a Congressman from California who had just been elected received a letter from an irate constituent which said: "During the campaign you promised to have the Sierra Madre Mountains reforested. You have been in office 1 month and you haven't done so." Well, no one in Fort Worth has been that unreasonable, but in some ways he has had the Sierra Madre Mountains reforested and here in Fort Worth he has contributed to its growth.

He speaks for Fort Worth and he speaks for the country, and I don't know any city that is better represented in the Congress of the United States than Fort Worth.

And if there are any Democrats here this morning, I am sure you wouldn't hold that against him.

Three years ago last September I came here with the Vice President, and spoke at Burke Burnett Park, and I called in that speech for a national security policy and a national security system which was second to none, a position which said not first but, if, when and how, but first. That city responded to that call as it has through its history. And we have been putting that pledge into practice ever since.

I want to say a word about that pledge here in Fort Worth, which understands national defense, and its importance to the security of the United States. During the days of the Indian War, this city was a fort. During the days of World War I, even before the United States got into the war, Royal Canadian Air Force pilots were training here. During the days of World War II, the great Liberator bombers, and which my brother flew with his copilot from this city, were produced here.

The first nonstop flight around the world took off and returned here, in a plane built in factories here. The first truly intercontinental bomber, the B–36, was produced here. The B–58, which is the finest weapons system in the world today, which was demonstrated most recently in flying from Tokyo to London, with an average speed of nearly 1,000 miles per hour, is a Fort Worth product.

The Iroquois helicopter from Fort Worth is a mainstay in our fight against the guerrillas in South Vietnam. The transportation of crews between our missile sites is done in planes produced here in Fort Worth. So wherever the confrontation may occur, and in the last 3 years it has occurred on at least three occasions, in Laos, Berlin, and Cuba, and it will again—wherever it occurs, the products of Fort Worth and the men of Fort Worth provide us with a sense of security.

And in the not too distant future a new Fort Worth product, and I am glad that there was a table separating Mr. Hicks and myself—a new Fort Worth product, the TFX. Tactical fighter experimental—nobody knows what those words mean, but that is what they mean, tactical fighter experimental—will serve the forces of freedom and will be the No. 1 airplane in the world today.

There has been a good deal of discussion of the long and hard fought competition to win the TFX contract, but very little discussion about what this plane will do. It will be the first operational aircraft ever produced that can literally spread its wings through the air. It will thus give us a single plane capable of carrying out missions of speed as well as distance, able to fly very far in one form or very fast in another. It can take off from rugged, short airstrips, enormously increasing the Air Force's ability to participate in limited wars. The same basic plane will serve the Navy's carriers, saving the taxpayers at least $1 billion in costs if they built separate planes for the Navy and the Air Force.

The Government of Australia, by purchasing $125 million of TFX planes before they are even off the drawing boards, has already testified to the merit of this plane, and at the same time it is confident in the ability of Fort Worth to meet its schedule. In all these ways, the success of our national defense depends upon this city in the Western United States, 10,000 miles from Vietnam, 5,000 or 6,000 miles from Berlin, thousands of miles from trouble spots in Latin America and Africa or the Middle East. And yet Fort Worth and what it does and what it produces participates in all these historic events. Texas, as a whole, and Fort Worth bear particular responsibility for this national defense effort, for military procurement in this State totals nearly $1¼ million, fifth highest among all the States of the Union. There are more military personnel on active duty in this State than any in the Nation, save one—and it is not Massachusetts—any in the Nation save one, with a combined military-civilian defense payroll of well over a billion dollars. I don't recite these for my partisan purpose. They are the result of American determination to be second to none, and as a result of the effort which this country has made in the last 3 years we are second to none.

In the past 3 years we have increased the defense budget of the United States by over 20 percent; increased the program of acquisition for Polaris submarines from 24 to 41; increased our Minuteman missile purchase program by more than 75 percent; doubled the number of strategic bombers and missiles on alert; doubled the number of nuclear weapons available in the strategic alert forces; increased the tactical nuclear forces deployed in Western Europe by over 60 percent; added 5 combat-ready divisions to the Army of the United States, and 5 tactical fighter wings to the Air Force of the United States; increased our strategic airlift capability by 75 percent; and increased our special counterinsurgency forces which are engaged now in south Vietnam by 600 percent. I hope those who want a stronger America and place it on some signs will also place those figures next to it.

This is not an easy effort. This requires sacrifice by the people of the United States. But this is a very dangerous and uncertain world. As I said earlier, on three occasions in the last 3 years, the United States has had a direct confrontation. No one can say when it will come again. No one expects that our life will be easy, certainly not in this decade and perhaps not in this century. But we should realize what a burden and responsibility the people of the United States have borne for so many years. Here a country which lived in isolation, divided and protected by the Atlantic and the Pacific, uninterested in the struggles of the world around it, here in the short space of 18 years after the Second World War, we put ourselves, by our own will and by necessity, into defense of alliances with countries all around the globe. Without the United States, South Vietnam would collapse overnight. Without the United States, the SEATO alliance would collapse overnight. Without the United States the CENTO alliance would collapse overnight. Without the United States there would be no NATO. And gradually Europe would drift into neutralism and indifference. Without the efforts of the United States in the Alliance for Progress, the Communist advance onto the mainland of South America would long ago have taken place.

So this country, which desires only to be free, which desires to be secure, which desired to live at peace for 18 years under three different administrations has borne more than its share of the burden, has stood watch for more than its number of years. I don't think we are fatigued or tired. We would like to live as we once lived. But history will not permit it. The Communist balance of power is still strong. The balance of power is still on the side of freedom. We are still the keystone in the arch of freedom, and I think we will continue to do as we have done in our past, our duty, and the people of Texas will be in the lead.

So I am glad to come to this State which has played such a significant role in so many efforts in this century, and to say that here in Fort Worth you people will be playing a major role in the maintenance of the security of the United States for the next 10 years. I am confident, as I look to the future, that our chances for security, our chances for peace, are better than they have been in the past. And the reason is because we are stronger. And with that strength is a determination to not only maintain the peace, but also the vital interests of the United States. To that great cause, Texas and the United States are committed.

Thank you.

TRIBUTES BY

Hon. Wm. J. Randall

OF MISSOURI

Mr. Speaker, thousands of words have been written since the tragic event of Friday, November 22. Perhaps the dominant or overbearing reaction even yet is one of disbelief.

First, it was incredible that a fanatic assassin could murder our President. Then this was made even worse by the act of a self-appointed prosecutor, judge, juror, and executioner who, during our mourning, fired another bullet ending the life of the President's assassin. Few will ever weep the death of Lee Oswald but these same persons realize that a man accused of the most heinous crime is entitled to a trial.

This is why it is so difficult to even classify or identify all the changing emotions of this past week. But one thing is beginning to take shape and that is the fact that even in death President John Kennedy will continue to serve his country. It is this thought that is dominant in a combined editorial-feature story appearing upon the front page of the Kansas City Star of Sunday, November 24, and written by the editor and publisher of that paper, Roy A. Roberts, one of the leading journalists in America today, the first half of which follows:

KENNEDY LEGEND WILL LIVE ON

I am confident that the legend of John Fitzgerald Kennedy, living after the man, will drive forcefully toward his two major goals: The peace of the world and the rights of mankind.

Even in the sorrow of the moment, it is possible to see that in the long course of history the legend may prove more effective than was the vibrant national and world leadership of John Kennedy.

But what a shocking price it is to pay. What a pointless sacrifice of a human life at the hands of an assassin.

If I know the American people—and I believe that I do—they are sentimental and they are fine. They cherish the memory of a man and oftentimes in their midst, the honored legend of one of their fallen fellows carries further than did his voice, however eloquent and powerful.

We can know, certainly, that the legend of John Kennedy will not quickly pass. In these few terrible hours it has been inscribed on the Nation's consciousness. Both the man and the legend have their place in history and both will grow with the decades. Violent death, pointless death, so often guarantees that it will be so.

And, in the case of the late President, it could be no other way. He was first in so many things.

He was the first President elected to the space age.

He was the first Roman Catholic President.

He was, almost unique in our history, a truly urban President.

He was the first President to carry for long—although Dwight Eisenhower knew the burden in his later years—the awesome responsibility of the finger on the button. He knew that the moment of decision could come and that civilization, in the push of a button, could be reduced to chaos.

Throughout the story of the Republic, there has always been the lonely man in the White House, ordained by his people to make the decisions. The Presidency has always been an assignment of terrible burden. But from the other day henceforth, until man learns to control these nuclear forces, the burden has grown and will continue to grow. It is a time of no second-guessing and beyond peace lies death.

Thus does the happenstance of time ennoble and enshrine the legend of the young President struck down because of some twisted mind's decision. In sorrow, animosities are buried. From grief grows the memory that works on for the cause.

Certainly the immediate impact of the tragedy has sobered the Nation. I hope, indeed, that it will erase permanently some of the fierce antagonisms of the forthcoming campaign. I do know that the American people, as they have always done in moments of emergency past, will close ranks in this dark time. Because it has always been thus, this Nation has reached its heights of freedom and democracy.

Mr. Speaker, since the tragic events of Friday, November 22, much has been written and much more will be written about President John F. Kennedy.

Undoubtedly there will come forth hereafter many articles, dissertations, and full-length books, and then the final pages of history will be written many years from now.

Right now, it seems to me, there is a sort of duty or obligation imposed on the membership of Congress, who served during this tragic week, to screen out or comb through the best in editorial comments, in their respective districts and, after a determination of what seems to be the best, make these editorials and comments part of a permanent record.

By so doing, there can be preserved a cross section of American thought from every corner of our United States. These spontaneous writings coming at a time when the writer feels the spirit in the air, of these last few days, should not be lost.

As a noteworthy instance, I have asked consent that there be printed the leading editorial from the Kansas City Times of Saturday morning, November 23, 1963, which follows:

JOHN F. KENNEDY, WHO GAVE HIS LIFE

This Nation and the world stand in shock today.

This Nation and the world have lost, in a few moments of terrible finality, a young and vigorous leader who had found his place on the stage of history. John F. Kennedy died for his country, as did his brother in a moment of wartime violence. More has been lost in the last few hours than could possibly be put into words. And with the loss there is a scar, now, across the face of the Republic.

Yet in finality there is a beginning. With the prayers and sympathy for Mrs. Kennedy and her children, there must be the hope and the prayers of the Nation and the world for President Lyndon B. Johnson. If the reins of democracy are dropped in the flash of an assassin's bullet, they must be seized at once. Death closes a chapter; it must open another.

We do not know what animated the wretched assassin. But we are struck by the comparison with another excruciatingly difficult period of history in which another President, Abraham Lincoln, gave his life.

Less than 3 years ago the youthful John F. Kennedy took over the heavy responsibilities of his office at a fateful time for the U.S. role in the world and for far-reaching decisions at home. He showed the courage to face down the threats and power of Soviet Russia. He carried forward the responsibilities of American world leadership against widespread misunderstanding and recrimination at home. He displayed beyond a doubt a deep conception of this world's problems, a deep understanding of the cold war and of the meaning of international communism.

In domestic affairs he had the courage to move forward, moderately but firmly, to carry out the mandates of the Constitution for all American citizens. For this, too, he encountered widespread recrimination, but he showed no fear of opposition at home or abroad.

A young man, arriving in the final hours of a generation of older world leaders, he quickly earned the respect of the people of other nations. But the years were to be tragically short.

Not for more than six decades—in those terrible 8 days when President McKinley struggled in vain for his life—has the Nation witnessed so awful an upheaval in its political life. It is the type of thing, the United States has told itself, that happens elsewhere; but not here in this mid-20th century. We know otherwise, now, and we should know, too, what fruit can grow from the seeds of hatred, whatever the source of hatred may be.

So it is the morrow of a day of death. History must move on. The mantle falls upon Lyndon B. Johnson and we can take heart in the fact that he is a man with training for this job. As majority leader of the Senate, he was close to the problems of nations and the cold war. As John F. Kennedy's Vice President, he was in the inner council, a man who has moved easily in the halls of state.

As was John F. Kennedy, Lyndon Johnson will be tested and probed by the Communists and other enemies of freedom. We can take comfort, however, in the knowledge that he has been prepared for the ordeal of fire.

The business of freedom and democracy must not end and it never will. John F. Kennedy died the death of a martyr for his country and Lyndon Johnson stands in his stead. For all Americans, it is a time to rally around their new President. For the Republic, it is a time of the deepest sorrow and a time of prayer.

Mr. Speaker, the 72 hours which elapsed from about noon of Friday, November 22, until just a little after noon on Monday, November 25, encompasses events which will be the subject matter of countless articles and scores of books written in the years to come.

Students of current history are now at work on their appraisal. With the passage of time, future historians will look back upon the events of these 3 days. They will carefully analyze all the facts and gain new insights by years of reflection and study. I suggest the foregoing will happen because such has been the course of history. This was the general outline that developed following the assassinations of Presidents Lincoln, Garfield, and McKinley.

It is with these thoughts in mind that I have asked consent today to include in my remarks some editorials which I have selected as among the best to appear in the papers published in the Fourth Congressional District of Missouri together with two others from outside the district which seemed to me to be of such quality as to deserve to be saved.

My purpose is not to single out these editorials to the omission and possible neglect or exclusion of others equally well written. The ones which have been included below, it seems to me, each contained some outstanding thought upon the tragic event of President Kennedy's assassination, which deserved to be perpetuated as a part of the literature written at the moment of this incredible happening. They should be made available for reference and review by students of history in the years ahead.

The editorials follow:

[From the Independence (Mo.) Examiner, Nov. 25, 1963]

HE DID NOT DIE IN VAIN

How does the death of a President affect the citizens of a small midwestern city like Independence?

It probably is no different than any other city in this great Nation.

Still, it is encouraging to witness the apparent surge of inner strength as people here began to comprehend the tragic news and realize the need for personal reflection and rededication of self and country.

Friday was perhaps the darkest day this Nation has known since the death of Franklin Delano Roosevelt. Today, as that day almost 20 years ago when Independence's Harry S. Truman assumed the grave responsibilities of the office of President, the American people are called upon to use their faith—in God, in their country, and in their fellow man.

It has been said in recent days and months that the United States, and the entire world, is losing its faith.

Feeling the pulse of Independence in the hour of the national crisis Friday, and again today during the sober hour of the funeral of its 35th President, the Examiner feels compelled to acclaim that this Nation has not lost its faith, but that it is a stronger nation, with a stronger people than ever before.

John Fitzgerald Kennedy did not die in vain.

———

[From the Independence (Mo.) Examiner, Nov. 26, 1963]

JOHN FITZGERALD KENNEDY

John Fitzgerald Kennedy came to the Presidency of the United States as the bearer of great change. He was the symbol of something new, but he died by something as old as time—the hand of the fanatic.

He was the first man born in the 20th century to hold the office—and the second youngest in history. He was the first Catholic in the White House. He came as a naval hero of World War II who narrowly had missed death in Pacific waters, and survived a second brush with death in a grave illness 9 years ago.

To the Nation's high politics he thus brought a fresh stamp. The well-remarked "Kennedy style" was a blend of intellect, vigor, wit, charm, and a clear talent for growth.

On the always shifting, often troubled world scene, he sometimes moved with more caution than expected in young leadership. Soon after entering the White House, he gamely took full blame for the Cuban Bay of Pigs fiasco as an enterprise sadly lacking in boldness.

Yet only his worst enemies withheld from him the label "courageous" when he moved resolutely against Soviet Premier Khrushchev in the great Russian missile crisis in Cuba in late 1962. And he boldly pressed for an East-West test ban treaty this year in the face of heavy charges that this imperiled our security.

In domestic affairs Kennedy won much of his program in beginning 1961, gained far less the following year, and encountered a major stalemate in 1963. The constant note against him was insufficient leadership.

But again, when 1963 brought the greatest racial crisis of this century, Kennedy—at acknowledged heavy political cost—committed himself to sweeping civil rights proposals that opened a vast new battleground.

Amid all his efforts to put the imprint of vigorous, imaginative youth upon the country's affairs in the 1960's, the last President found himself moving against a deepening background of protest, with an ugly underscoring of violence which he sought with only limited success to wipe away.

Much of this protest went to the steady encroachments of the Federal Government and its rising cost. But the bitterest reaction was white and Negro response to the enlarging racial struggle. The far right gave the mood its most perilous texture.

With the calamity in Dallas the lesson of the danger inherent in violent extremism now may be deeply implanted in America's conscience.

In this way, Kennedy in death may achieve what the living President could not do to curb the almost ungovernable rancor that increasingly discolored the politics of his brief time in power.

It was John Kennedy's good fortune to surmount many obstacles to rise to his country's highest office and bring with him the winds of a new era.

It was his final tragedy that as he labored in difficult times to use these forces for the Nation's and the world's gain, they were swiftly challenged by countering winds of bitter reaction. In Dallas, one swift gust struck him down.

The Nation thus loses a young leader whose great promise lived in the shadow of great controversy. The way he died must inescapably cost all Americans deeply in self-esteem as free men of good will.

That is the greater tragedy.

————

[From the Harrisonville (Mo.) Democrat-Missourian, Nov. 26, 1963]

JOHN F. KENNEDY

"And so, my fellow Americans: Ask not what America will do for you—ask what you can do for your country."

The incredible and tragic events of the weekend brought shame upon our house, and apprehension and sorrow to the rest of the world. In a few seconds in the city of Dallas, Tex., an insignificant 24-year-old agitator, lurking in a warehouse window with a $13 gun and 50 cents worth of bullets, altered the course of history.

Lee Harvey Oswald assassinated the President of the United States.

In a bizarre and almost ludicrous aftermath, a self-appointed judge, jury and executioner, in the person of an also insignificant nightclub operator and police character, shot the accused assassinator to death.

A stunned nation asks "Why?"

We may never know. We do know that events of the past few years have caused reasonable citizens to make unreasonable utterances. An atmosphere of intolerance, and even hate, upon which twisted minds flourish may have contributed to this world-shaking tragedy.

Now a shocked and confused nation is attempting to bring some semblance of order to its house. Within 80 minutes of the death of Mr. Kennedy, Lyndon B. Johnson was sworn in as the new President. He asked for our help, and for God's. Perhaps we, as ordinary citizens, can best help by pursuing our ordinary affairs in our ordinary manner, but practicing always in our daily lives those principles upon which our country was founded.

[From the Warrensburg (Mo.) Daily Star-Journal, Nov. 25, 1963]

OUR PRESIDENT

Today is one of the saddest in the long history of this community and the Nation. In every Warrensburg and Johnson County home and throughout the country hearts are heavy with grief as last rites are held for President John F. Kennedy.

All weekend the people were seeking comfort and reassurance as well as guidance and strength. Understandably, they turned to their churches. Morning worship services yesterday in Warrensburg were filled beyond capacity in most churches, as they very likely were in every town and city.

It was Friday during the noon hour when first news of the tragedy in Dallas struck. In Warrensburg, as news came in bit by bit while the seconds passed, every possible reaction and emotion occurred. A merchant who normally has the utmost composure stood with tears in his eyes. A young photographer's usual air of quiet, unaffected assurance turned to utter dismay. A newsman who works with remarkable equanimity said his stomach actually was churning inside.

Everywhere it was the same—the people could not believe the President of the United States no longer was John F. Kennedy, a young man with uncommon ability and a charmingly cordial way.

In uncivilized countries, differences in policies still are settled by violence. Surely, the assassination of the President could only have been the act of a person mentally ill.

(Here it must be injected that every man accused of a crime has the right in this country to fair trial by a court of law. Yesterday's fatal shooting of the prime suspect as he was being moved from the Dallas jail was a lawless act. It would not have been surprising had this occurred in the Congo or Nazi Germany, but this is the United States of America where every man is innocent until proven guilty. Even though this is a time of high emotion and extreme outrage, it is no time for anyone to take the law into his own hands.)

Was President Kennedy provided adequate protection? Yes, in our opinion it was made as safe as it could be. The only alternative would have been to keep him from the people at all times and this isn't the way a democracy works, or should work.

A week ago today when this writer was at the Americana Hotel in Miami Beach on the same day President Kennedy arrived, a vast amount of security measures were being taken for his safety. For 2 weeks, Secret Service men had checked every room and each occupant of the hotel. No taxicabs, no vehicles were permitted to park, load, or unload in front of the hotel at any time the President was inside. Even though demonstrations were expected by both pro-Castro and anti-Castro Cubans, it seemed to us then the precautions might be excessive.

We talked that day with newspaper publishers from the Dominican Republic, Argentina, Mexico, a former Prime Minister of Peru, and others about the stability of the U.S. Government in contrast to some Latin and South American countries where revolutions and assassinations of national leaders are not uncommon. It was disturbing to hear one or two sanction force as a means of changing governments.

In the United States, we are indeed blessed with stability of government which can only be upset between elections by such an act as occurred in Dallas.

Some of the President's domestic objectives we opposed. But this never lessened our great admiration for him as a man, as a forceful leader, as a Chief Executive who dealt extremely well with the constant Communist threat.

President Kennedy was gifted with the power of expressing his knowledge, and in an effective, pleasing manner. Even under trying circumstances he had a quick humor. The whole record of his life was that of unselfish generosity. We admired, too, his unshakable resolution in the face of adversity. He had a devotion to the Christian way of life that must have given him a courage and strength to enable him to carry out the tremendous tasks of President.

Along with all the prayers and messages of sorrow from over the world go those from this community. Of the late President, the people are speaking from their hearts when they say: "We will remember him well, and we will remember him worthy of high praise."

[From the Pleasant Hill (Mo.) Times, Nov. 28, 1963]

THANKFUL IN OUR DARKEST HOUR

This Thanksgiving Day, following so closely on the tragic horror and quick changing national scene of last weekend, may seem empty to many Americans but there can be and should be fervent prayers of gratitude for the dynamic and useful life of our dead President and for the fine qualifications of his successor.

Those who have read and heard the comment of newspapers and radio and TV commentators over the past days have digested the numerous eloquent eulogies of the late President John F. Kennedy by those who were close to him and they have heard the simple expressions of the average shocked and stunned American. They have also been filled in on the unusual qualities and ability of our new President, Lyndon B. Johnson.

Thus, we come to this Thanksgiving Day, many disheartened, sad, and grieved over the loss of a great President, but we should be lifted in spirit by the fact that the new President is well prepared for his awesome responsibilities so suddenly thrust upon him. President Johnson, in his first few remarks after he received the oath of office, said he needed the help of all the people of the United States and the help of God. We recall that former President Harry S. Truman made a similar plea when he was catapulted into the Presidency, and a hot war not yet over when former President Franklin D. Roosevelt died.

Today we should be thankful we had the benefit of the courageous leadership of John F. Kennedy for 3 years and that this country will be led by a man equally as courageous and patriotic—one who will meet the great challenges at home and abroad.

We should thank God that we live under a democratic Government which, through its constitutional processes, makes for an orderly and peaceful transition even in the electrified atmosphere of an assassination; that there will be no struggle for power and authority.

Thus, even in great public bereavement we can, through our belief in this democracy, stand firmly behind our new President and give him the support he asks and needs desperately.

[From the Windsor (Mo.) Review, Nov. 28, 1963]

A DAY NONE WILL FORGET

Few, if any, who are old enough to comprehend will forget the dramatic and tragic weekend that has just passed.

The present generation remembers reading about the assassination of President Lincoln. The thwarted attempt on President Truman's life at Blair House will be recalled by some. To a lesser degree some will remember the death of Mayor Cermak of Chicago while marching in a parade behind President Roosevelt's car.

The sudden death of President Kennedy by a sniper's rifle in Dallas, Tex., will ever remain in the memory of most Americans and in other countries as well.

Those who watched television over the weekend and virtually had front row seats for the assassination and the subsequent murder of the President's attacker.

Pictured were the happy events prior to the rifle shots that felled President Kennedy and Governor Connally of Texas; the swearing in of Lyndon Baines Johnson as the 36th President of the United States aboard the Presidential plane at the Dallas airport; arrival of the slain President's body and those on the plane in Washington; the procession from the White House to the Nation's Capitol where thousands walked by the casket; murder of the assassin in the Dallas police headquarters; arrival of leaders from all over the world to join in paying tribute to a great soldier of peace, and then the climax on Monday with the final tribute and burial in Arlington Cemetery.

These historic events were recorded on film and tape for the entire world to see.

Never has this Nation, or the world, been so moved or drawn together by a single interest, outside of world war, than by the dreadful death of President Kennedy.

From the time the world was electrified by the words, "President Kennedy has been shot," the thoughts of people everywhere were centered on this historic event.

There was no heart for the ordinary activities of life among most Americans, regardless of politics or religion. Our President had been killed.

From disbelief at first, followed shock and then grief—grief for the first family with two small children; for the President's family which has suffered tragedy before and whose father still is paralyzed from a stroke.

Why would anyone want to kill one of the world's foremost leaders in the cause for peace?

[From the Higginsville (Mo.) Advance, Nov. 28, 1963]

JOHN FITZGERALD KENNEDY, 35TH PRESIDENT, UNITED STATES OF AMERICA

Our Nation mourns the untimely death of our 35th President, slain in a violent act by a misguided fellow human being, November 22, 1963.

On November 25, with all the honors and tribute a nation and the world could bestow, he was put to rest with other heroes of our Nation in Arlington National Cemetery.

The ranks of politics, race, and creed immediately closed when this tragedy came, with the citizenry rallying under one patriotic belief—Americanism. Nations of the world see again that we can and do become one in time of tragedy and national disaster.

The 30-day period of national mourning will be but a fleeting moment in the eons of time, but history will forever record his service to his country as a military man, a Senator, and as the President.

Let it never be said of our Nation that we who populate it shall put profit and prejudice above our patriotism and respect. We will long endure as a free people so long as we retain these ideals and principles upon which our Nation is founded.

_____

[From the Rich Hill (Mo.) Mining Review, Nov. 29, 1963]

JOHN FITZGERALD KENNEDY

This past weekend—hectic, tragic, sad but historic—has most of us a bit confused. We are confused because it all seems so unreal, unbelievable, like a bad dream from which we expect to awaken, yet it did happen.

When the mad dog assassin struck down our brilliant, young President, the grief that followed seemed to unite not only our own country but the whole world. No eulogy that this column can produce will do justice to the occasion. It is interesting to note that some of the most sincere tributes paid to the late President, John F. Kennedy, came from those on the opposite side of the political fence. These contained no maudlin expressions and lacked the tinge of political overtones.

_____

[From the Kansas City (Mo.) Labor Beacon, Nov. 29, 1963]

JOHN F. KENNEDY

Historians in the future will assess the impact on America and the world of the tragically short administration of John F. Kennedy.

But the American people—and the people of the world—this week made their overwhelming assessment of the impact of John Fitzgerald Kennedy the man. No leader of modern times has received the spontaneous outpouring of respect and affection shown the fallen President.

The demonstration dramatically showed the effect of President Kennedy's youthful optimism, vigorous idealism and deep-seated understanding of the wants and needs of all people. The fact that around the world tributes were led by the young people proved that a common bond of sympathy and personal identification tied the people to their leader.

Regardless of the ultimate verdict on President Kennedy's 2 years, 10 months and 2 days in the world's most difficult post of responsibility, the effect of his great personality must be recognized as a tremendous force for good throughout the world. It will live on in the rededication of people—and particularly young people—toward the goals which he so precisely stated.

For it was in his vision of the future toward which the United States and the world must work that John F. Kennedy was at his greatest. He was an idealist to the extent that he sought a nation and a world of justice, dignity and peace. He was a realist in that he understood that such a world could not be realized in a hundred days; a thousand days; in "this administration"; or perhaps in our lifetime.

He made that goal a living goal and thereby provided a reason for patriotism, for dedication, and for effort by the young people of the world.

The reaction to President Kennedy's death must give small comfort to the bigots whose preachments of hatred have bewildered and confused many Americans. A Catholic, his death was mourned sincerely by Protestants, Jews, Moslems, Hindus; even some Communists. And this was fitting: President Kennedy felt his responsibility to all people, regardless of religion or color.

These are the lessons in the life of John Fitzgerald Kennedy. The American people this week showed that the majority have learned the lessons and approve. In tribute to President Kennedy, let us not forget what we have learned.

_____

[From the Roll Call, Washington (D.C.), Nov. 27, 1963]

FROM AN OFFICE WINDOW

I looked out of my window and saw history march by.

It was the same office window through which I have contemplated hundreds of bustling mornings, gloomy dusks. The vista from an office window over the years becomes a humdrum setting; it is hardly the place you expect to see—suddenly and unexpectedly—one of the most awesome spectacles of the age.

It was Monday and the funeral cortege of the late President Kennedy was mournfully surging up Connecticut Avenue.

It is impossible to sort out one's emotions, already so terribly assaulted by sudden violence, upheaval, and grief.

The overriding reaction, as so many said, is one of disbelief. Even looking down from a 12th story building directly upon the flag-draped coffin of the late President, some uncontrollable part of the mind keeps trying to tell you this can't be so. But it is. The muffled drums; the majestic marching troops, the horse-drawn caisson are real.

Real too is the story of how it happened—a lunatic's fanatic gesture, its incredible horror compounded by the vengeance of a self-appointed judge-executioner.

No man can sort and identify the tumbling, crowding, changing emotions of the past few days.

As things begin to even out a little, however, a few reactions begin to take shape.

One is, that in death John Kennedy continues to serve his country.

The world-shattering trauma of his sudden removal from the scene seems to have reached deep into the souls of men. The impotent anger at this disaster is being channeled, with the help of wise clergymen and clear-minded statesmen, where it properly belongs: toward all of us.

Will this rededication to decency and respect for law and order persist after the captains and the kings have departed and we have settled back to normality? The cynic may be doubtful but in this moment of history, we cannot afford to heed the cynic. There is abroad in our land a sudden realization that in our smug prosperity and the comfort of a great system of government we take too much for granted, we have permitted rot, moral decay, and hatred to exist and multiply.

The shock and shame over what has happened to our young, vital, and inspiring President has shaken us.

The example of his widow, his family, and even of his tiny innocent children, challenges those of us less directly bereaved to try to be better people.

We need new insights, new perspectives, along with new dedication.

Until this happened, the common view of Congress was one of a sprawling, ineffective body of men. This one took a junket somewhere; that one was stubbornly blocking this bill. Scandal and gossip shrouded the Hill. The image of our lawmakers was tarnished.

Then comes national crisis—calamity. These same men suddenly emerge to light as what they really are: Fine, dedicated statesmen. Patriots, resolute in helping carry forward this Nation under the new President. Men whose oratory we so often mock as florid and cynical—speaking wisdom and eloquence. We are comforted, reassured, and inspired by this view of our lawmakers, as we are by the conduct of the new President, by the Cabinet and staffs, by the family of the late President—and would it be hyperbole to say, most of all, by two little children whose conduct has been so gallant?

A great New England essayist once wrote that "nobleness enkindleth nobleness." Let us hope this proves true.

Because today I look out the same window and everything looks just as it was before that fatal hour in Dallas last Friday. Now comes the time for all good men to face the real test of putting into practice those good thoughts we have been jolted into expressing these past few terrible days.

———

[From the Huntington (Ind.) Our Sunday Visitor, Dec. 8, 1963]

JOHN F. KENNEDY: 1917–63

John Fitzgerald Kennedy, first Catholic President of the United States, is dead, the victim of an assassin's bullet in Dallas, Tex.

Tributes to the late President have poured in from all over the world, from heads of state as well as from the common people to whom he was dedicated.

President Kennedy's funeral in St. Matthew's Cathedral in the Nation's Capital was thronged with the great and near great from his native land and from nearly every member of the world's community of nations.

Seldom in our history have so many people from all walks of life been struck by the passing of the leader of a nation. And seldom have the tributes been so heartfelt and genuine.

In the 3 short years John F. Kennedy served as this Nation's Chief Executive, he showed the world an image of a man dedicated to his duties, to his family, and to his God.

The office of the Presidency of the United States is an exalted office, and the brutal attack on our late president, as former President Eisenhower pointed out, was the more despicable because it was an attack, not only on the person of the President, but upon the very dignity of the office.

But along with the dignity of the Presidency there goes an awesome responsibility and a duty more demanding than that in any other elective office.

John F. Kennedy measured up to the duty of his office—and he measured up to its dignity. He earned the tributes and the prayers of all the people of the world.

President Lyndon Johnson, who now assumes the Presidency, needs our prayers and our support in a special way. Pope Paul VI, in his message to President Johnson, summed up these thoughts when he wrote: "We pray God to grant Your Excellency, as you accede to the Presidency of the Nation, His choicest graces of guidance and strength."

In his message on the occasion of the late President's death, Pope Paul voiced the sentiments of all of us when he said: "We deplore this event with our whole heart. We express the hope that the death of this great statesman will not bring damage to the American people, but will strengthen its moral and civil sense and sentiments of nobility and concord. We pray God that the sacrifice of John Kennedy may help the cause promoted and defended by him of the liberty of peoples and of peace in the world."

May he rest in peace.

TRIBUTES BY

Hon. George M. Rhodes

OF PENNSYLVANIA

Mr. Speaker, from all corners of the earth, letters are still pouring into the White House expressing sorrow and sympathy to Mrs. John F. Kennedy and to the Nation on the death of our martyred President.

Expressions of sympathy also continue to come to my office from constituents who are saddened by the loss of a beloved and great President.

Following is a copy of an inspiring eulogy which was read over the public address system at Mount Penn High School, Reading, Pa., by Mr. Carl F. Constein, supervising principal:

EULOGY FOR PRESIDENT JOHN F. KENNEDY

(By Carl F. Constein, Nov. 26, 1963)

For most of us, time stood still over the last bizarre weekend. It is always so during times of great tragedy. It is still difficult for us to believe that President Kennedy is dead. Even though we may not have the heart to return to our books, we must do so, as all people must return to their work and life goes on. It seems appropriate in a school, where the study of history is so important, to mark this moment in history as we take up our separate lives again.

Regardless of our political and other convictions, we Americans unite in our shock that this deed should have happened, in genuine sympathy for the President's family, and in profound grief for our loss. Through the miracle of television, we have come to know Mr. Kennedy well. His face, his mannerisms, his personality were familiar to us all. Because of this familiarity, we feel the loss more keenly.

What qualities did the late President Kennedy possess that drew us to him? I believe courage was his most outstanding quality. PT–109 tells of his great physical courage in World War II. Even more important, he had the kind of courage that demands patience and restraint. He demonstrated this fortitude in overcoming a serious back ailment suffered in the war, in fighting hard in the Halls of Congress, and a little more than a year ago, in standing firm in the Cuban crisis.

History was his major interest; writing was an ambition of his; courage was his conviction. Out of this combination came a very readable book about Americans who faced decisions squarely and without flinching. The book is called "Profiles in Courage."

But courage alone isn't enough. A criminal, even an assassin, may have that. Mr. Kennedy had a tremendous ambition to be of public service. Born to great wealth, he could have chosen any number of less demanding careers and lived a life of ease. He chose to serve his fellow man, openly welcoming the awesome responsibilities of the office of President.

One of the burdens of that office is making far-reaching decisions daily. Mr. Kennedy had an unquenchable desire for detailed knowledge of all the operations of government. He was an avid reader and had an intellectual curiosity about many subjects. Yet somehow he managed to reserve a place for wit and friendly give-and-take with reporters and associates.

In spite of the terrible problems existing everywhere in the world, his attitude was optimistic, even idealistic. He would have us reach for the stars and make a start in attacking problems which might take a thousand years to solve. The important thing is to continue the struggle and to do it with good heart and courage.

These are qualities of greatness which deserve to be emulated. Our sorrow is increased when we realize that he was the youngest President ever to be elected and ever to die in office. He may not have reached the peak of his potential.

We ask ourselves, how could this monstrous deed of assassination have happened? Why would anyone take such desperate action? A democracy has an inherent problem in this regard, for a President must be available to the people. In truth, it is not possible to prevent attempts at assassination. We can conclude that the assassin was mad and dismiss it at that. But that is too easy. We all share the sorrow; we should all consider the guilt.

There was apparently much loose talk about the possibility of assassination in Dallas. Suppose, then, a person who has had this evil intent reads and hears this talk. Is he not encouraged to do the deed? Where does he read such inflammatory words? To our shame, he reads them in those magazines and newspapers which publish the unbridled words of hatred coming from some pens. Where does he hear such inflammatory words? He hears them in the street and in the shops from people who go too far in their hatred. It may take the form of sick humor, or smart satire, or extreme profanity.

For too long now we have taken the attitude that anything goes. Modern psychology tells us to get rid of our pent-up feelings. All of us see value in this advice in our personal relations. But there is a limit to which we can go, a limit far short of physical violence. There are standards to be followed and all of us know what they are. All of us have the moral law within. We don't have to be told what is right and what is wrong. We know when we are going too far in our thoughts, our words, and our deeds.

Here while we eulogize our late President, John F. Kennedy, let us resolve no longer to be part of the furthering of hatred of the kind that caused his death. In our own lives let us control our words in little things so that they don't grow into mass intolerance and hatred resulting in big, tragic deeds.

On Thursday we celebrate Thanksgiving Day. Our observance may be somber. Yet there is much for which to thank God. We thank him for our system of government which makes possible a smooth transition from one President to another. We thank him for the preparation and experience of our new President, Lyndon B. Johnson. Finally, we thank God for the life and example of President John F. Kennedy.

Mr. Speaker, following are letters sent from oversea business leaders to Mr. David Frankel, president of American Safety Table Co. of Reading, Pa., expressing deep sorrow and sympathy on the tragic death of President Kennedy:

VLAARDINGEN, NETHERLANDS.

DEAR SIRS: This weekend in the Netherlands was overclouded by what they feel as the loss of a good friend, your President, Mr. J. F. Kennedy.

Due to the medium television and some relay satellites everybody was confronted with the emotions in Washington.

In this hour I like to transmit my feelings of sympathy to you and your coworkers. God bless America.

Very truly yours,

BILL SCHIPPERS.

———

ATHENS, GREECE.

DEAR SIR: I would beg you to accept my personal sympathy as well as the sympathy of the people of my office for the unexpected death of the President of the United States, John Kennedy.

Be sure that the news of the end of his life touched us as if he would be a relative of ours.

Yours very truly,

GEORGE YANNAKOURAS.

———

AMSTERDAM, HOLLAND.

GENTLEMEN: The whole Dutch nation, and we who feel so close to the people of the United States of America, in particular, were deeply shocked by the sudden and violent death of your President, Mr. John F. Kennedy.

We share the sorrow of his family and of all American people and we shall keep him long in our memory. May he rest in peace.

Very truly yours,

L. C. VERBEEK.

———

SANTIAGO, CHILE.

GENTLEMEN: We wish to express our feelings of deep sorrow for the tragic decease of the President of your country, Mr. John F. Kennedy. His untiring efforts on behalf of world peace and progress have won him the respect and admiration of all human beings. His passing is a loss to mankind.

All of us here are with you and share your mourning.

Sincerely,

LOWENSTEIN & STEWART.

Mr. Speaker, running through all of the tributes that have been paid to President Kennedy since his tragic death has been the recognition that this young and brilliant man gave a new sense of dignity and purpose to both the Presidency and the Nation.

From those famous words in his inaugural address, "Ask not what your country can do for you, but what you can do for your country," to his remarks calling for an end to vituperation and a return to unity prepared for delivery in Dallas, John F. Kennedy gave eloquent voice to his country's highest ideals.

The young people of America were quickest to respond to this call for public dedication and public service and the Peace Corps has become a monument to President Kennedy's success in translating American idealism into gifted action, as well as into words.

Karl Meyer, staff reporter for the Washington Post, captured the new spirit of eloquence and dignity that marked President Kennedy's administration in an article written shortly after the tragic events in Dallas. I commend it to my colleagues:

A PROMISE OF POWER WISELY USED: JOHN F. KENNEDY GAVE US AN EXHILARATING VISION OF POLITICAL DIGNITY

(By Karl E. Meyer)

He came in with a snowstorm and the symbolism was flawlessly right on Inauguration Day, January 20, 1961. There was no premonition of tragedy, but rather a sense of rebirth in a Capital mantled in beauty as the oldest President yielded office to the youngest man ever elected Chief Executive of the United States.

It was much more than a change of administration. It was also a change of generations, a change of out-look—and, most immediately apparent, a change of style. When John Fitzgerald Kennedy became 35th President of the United States, he appeared to fulfill Robert Frost's augury that an age of poetry and power was commencing in Washington.

But the poetry is now hushed, and the promise of power wisely used is now an unfinished chapter of a history entitled, "Let Us Begin." We are left with memories of a singular and gifted man, memories that sustain us following a tragedy as unspeakable as it was incomprehensible. None of us suspected that in retrospect the inaugural snow would seem a shroud.

Every President is a bundle of men—the chief of state who admonishes us to be better than we are; the taskmaster of a bureaucracy; the champion of a party, and, not least, in this case the father of a family whose every trivial habit was watched and copied by the Nation. More than most, President Kennedy made of these fragments of official functions a harmonious whole.

This swiftly became apparent during the first 100 days. If he did not give us a new deal, he did provide an exhilarating vision of the dignity of political life. In every aspect of government—small and large—he insisted on trained competence, on grace and integrity, on idealism tempered with a shrewd awareness of the possible. If the substance of his program did not differ dramatically from his predecessor's, it surely contrasted in style.

A STANDARD OF ARTICULATENESS

The most obvious element of that style was articulateness. The clipped cadences of the inaugural address set the standard for his other great utterances as President. They also reflected the man, a man who could be ambiguous but who was seldom diffuse or banal.

"He brought an unsparing instinct for reality to bear on the platitudes and pieties of society," Mr. Kennedy once said of Robert Frost. The words applied to the President at his best.

Yet more fundamental than eloquence were Mr. Kennedy's sense of history, his courage, his temperance, his belief in reason and all of these were laced with a potent dram of wit. The President did not excel at slapstick or sarcasm; his weapon was irony, which he used like a rapier, and sometimes so deftly that the victim only slowly became aware that his head had been figuratively separated from his neck.

His favorite foil was the press, but, unlike some other great men, his sense of humor extended even to himself. He was never more memorably engaging than at the White House correspondents' banquet in May 1962, at which he mockingly protested the rise in ticket prices for the dinner—this, after the press had parodied his own attack on big steel.

Only the other day, though it feels like a chasm of time, Mr. Kennedy deflated Barry Goldwater by remarking that the Arizona Senator had spent a busy week in, among other things, selling the TVA and interfering in the Greek election. With his death, President Kennedy has left Washington not only a sadder but also a colder place.

The courage in office was untheatrical and was the more impressive for its understated quality. Though

President Kennedy had his share of Irish temper, his nature was not choleric and his anger seldom soured into rancor. But when he felt personally betrayed, or when he believed that a deep principle was involved, he could display a spinal fortitude that belied his need for a rocking chair.

As a presidential candidate, he made what was probably his greatest speech before an audience of Protestant clergymen. The subject was religious bigotry; his delivery blended passion and precision; the place, ironically, was Texas.

As President, his courage was twice tested by Cuba—first in failure, then in success. Perhaps the most morally impressive moment was his acceptance of full responsibility for the debacle at the Bay of Pigs—and his refusal to redeem a fiasco at the risk of American blood and a world war. And though the defeat cut cruelly and deeply into his self-esteem, he disdained making a ritual scapegoat of any adviser.

In what was at once his greatest and most perilous moment as Chief Executive, Mr. Kennedy forced Nikita Khrushchev to pull nuclear missile bases out of Cuba before the eyes of the world—but he did not push the Soviet leader into a corner. He honored his inaugural commitment: "Let us never negotiate out of fear. But let us never fear to negotiate." In triumph, he showed the same restraint that earlier had marked his acceptance of bitter defeat.

Domestically, the strength of his backbone was demonstrated during a summer of racial discontent. Though the President was aware that his support of a strong civil rights program could rend his party and cost him popularity, he accepted both risks with calm—with an almost awesome equanimity.

This detachment frequently drained the drama from his gestures and gave a misleading coldness to his Presidency. Yet that was also an indispensable element of the Kennedy style—an abhorrence of posturing. As President, he placed more confidence in the verdict of history than in the clamor of the crowd. And the sense of history was perhaps the secret of his serenity.

President Kennedy was a prodigious reader who was steeped in the records of the past and absorbed by the literature of the present. His chief military aide, Brig. Gen. Chester V. (Ted) Clifton, was astonished to discover that Mr. Kennedy even glanced critically over the monthly list of books recommended to service officers and that he read, in galley proof, books like Barbara Tuchman's "Guns of August."

From his reading, the President acquired a sense of detachment about himself and about the limits of his power. To his liberal friends, this trait was at once exasperating and winning; to them, he sometimes appeared more a Hamlet than a Hotspur. Like Lincoln, he seemed to feel that he was as much controlled by events as controlling events. In death, his view has acquired a poignant authority.

His favorite biography was Lord David Cecil's "Melbourne," a book about the urbane Whig who was Queen Victoria's first Prime Minister. In both the flattering and unflattering sense, the choice disclosed something of Mr. Kennedy's definition of himself. For the Whig aristocracy, like the President's own family, blended moderate liberalism, an attitude of noblesse oblige, a conventional if broad-ranging interest in the arts and a coolness about excessive commitments.

Above all, the leaders like Melbourne who dominated British politics in the early 19th century were temperate men. They wanted to civilize power as much as to use it. They regarded noisy public dispute as a mark of political failure, not as a device for compelling consent.

SYMPATHETIC POLITICIAN

In his relations with fellow politicians, as well as with the press, Mr. Kennedy showed a reluctance for turbulent combat. A gifted craftsman in politics himself, he understood the political problems of others.

When a President of Argentina campaigned for office on a platform calling for a cancellation of contracts with foreign oil producers, Mr. Kennedy's restrained reaction testified to his fraternal feeling for another elective official's need to keep a promise.

The same tolerance marked his relations with a Congress nominally dominated by his own party. He could be tough in private, but his voice was soft in public. Through all the vicissitudes of political life, he retained an abiding faith in the power of reason to affect the destiny of men. It was President Kennedy who saw to it that a "hot line" was installed in the White House to give reason a chance before mankind plunged over a brink.

His belief in human intelligence gave a glow to his style. More, perhaps, than any other President since Thomas Jefferson, Mr. Kennedy cherished not only learning but the learned. His ideal of government seemed to be part academy, part precinct club. His mind was open to fresh ideas, and his official residence was open to anybody—from Nobel laureates to lowly subordinates—who could impart a ferment.

THE CHILLING HEIGHTS

It may be that when he took the oath of office, John F. Kennedy was still the carefree playboy of hostile propaganda, though the evidence is to the contrary. Lincoln was also a more ambitious politician than a prophet of freedom when circumstances contrived to make him President on the eve of civil war.

But the heights chill as well as elevate, and before long Mr. Kennedy comprehended the responsibility in his hands. In two speeches—at the United Nations in 1961 and at American University only a few months ago—the President disclosed his troubled reflections about a world that modern weapons could turn into a flaming pyre.

In private discussions, the President tirelessly iterated his feeling that mankind walks a narrow ledge. However, he had to zig and zag, the goal he sought was peace, and his methods were those of reason. Those who admired him never doubted his earnestness, though they were sometimes impatient with his caution.

He now belongs to history, and his confidence that time would soon bear him out, bringing the country to where the land was bright, remains an imponderable. So does his buoyant faith in reason.

For the most savage irony is that this apostle of the enlightenment, this advocate of rational discourse, was cut down by the very fanaticism that as President he sought to contain.

He paid with his life in a cause that remains in doubt. The last page of his biography must be written with what Vergil called the tears of things.

Mr. Speaker, following is a letter sent to June F. Marsh, Pasadena, by Dr. Norman C. Cooper of Seal Beach, Calif.

With the permission of Dr. Cooper copies of this letter were reproduced. I feel sure that the sentiments expressed in the letter are shared by millions of our fellow citizens. Because it is a beautiful and deserving tribute to our late beloved President, I ask that it be included with my remarks:

SEAL BEACH, CALIF.,
November 25, 1963.

MY DEAR JUNE: I had your special delivery letter of Friday. I was glad to receive the letter expressing your feeling. I had thought of you and Alta both in the last 3 days and of the many conversations we have had about Senator and President and now former President Kennedy, and how often we had expressed how very much he had meant to each of us personally. I, too, was shocked and stunned by his needless and unexpected death. I presume that I had thought too much of him. When he went, something of me went with him. He was perfection to me and was all that I looked for in a human being.

I was numb all Friday afternoon and could only moan— Why did it have to happen. I couldn't cry or weep yet I felt like it. Saturday I was more relaxed and I could cry. I have never felt so badly about anyone or anything before.

He was young, strong and healthy, intelligent, handsome, well educated, an eloquent speaker, had high ideals, altrusim, and a sense of oughtness that was uncanny. He had an electrifying personality, a warmth of friendship, a glow and zest for life, a radiant and endearing smile, and was filled with charm, wit, and humor. He was a family man with a lovely, charming wife and two lovely children whom he adored and in turn by whom he was adored. He was a deeply religious man with the roots of his belief and faith penetrating all the ideals of history and one who applied his religion to everyday living. He was a leader leading all leaders. He, of course, was so far ahead of his contemporaries that few understood him or what he said or what he meant, as simple and straightforward as his words were.

I never thought of President Kennedy as a President or a political figure. I thought of him as a man walking among people trying to get them to do the right thing, a person who was looking after me and my rights and the other man's rights whether he be black or white, Catholic or Protestant, Jew or gentile, privileged or of low birth. I saw him as looking out for the teenage dropouts from school and for the aged in a medical program. I saw him lift the Negro to the status of a human being and give the underprivileged child a fair chance for his place in the sun.

I identified with him. In so doing I had comfort, and solace, and strength. I walked more proudly because he lived. I held my head higher because America produced him, because he was ours, because he belonged to me. I owned him. He was mine. He no longer belonged to Rose Kennedy or the Ambassador as a son— he belonged to me as much as he belonged to them. He belonged to all of us. Even the peoples of foreign countries never thought of him as an American—they thought of him as their own. He didn't belong to the Catholic Church—he belonged to every church. The Protestant Church would no more allow him to be buried without their services than would the Catholic Church.

The world, society, humanity and people will never be the same to me now. The pace of humanity in its progress from the caves will be slowed, culture will lapse, and civilization will walk towards its goal with a faltering tread. This was the greatest man since Christ. He was a Moses, a Socrates, a Savonarola, a Lincoln, all in one. The world gets a chance to have a man like this so seldom that it forgets from one man to the next how to treat him, how to accept him, how to use him, how to work with him. I was privileged to know him, to live in his age, and to see his worth. My own personal loss can never be compensated for.

A valiant hero is now a martyr. A profile in courage now lies slain by an assassin's bullet. My heart is heavy, my hopes dimmed, my sorrow great.

Sincerely yours,

NORMAN C. COOPER.

Mr. Speaker, last Sunday evening, December 15, the Berks County Historical Society adopted a resolution in memory of the late President John Fitzgerald Kennedy. Mr. Speaker, with permission of the House, I include the resolution.

RESOLUTION IN MEMORY OF PRESIDENT JOHN F. KENNEDY, ADOPTED BY THE BERKS COUNTY HISTORICAL SOCIETY, READING, PA., DECEMBER 15, 1963

Whereas the members of our Historical Society of Berks County in common with the citizenry of this Nation and of all nations have recently suffered an incomparable and most unexpected shock in the insensate and brutal assassination of John Fitzgerald Kennedy, late President of the United States; and

Whereas President Kennedy has a particular hold on the fealty and interest of our society in that he was himself a zealous and learned student of our American history and the author of books and brochures upon historical subjects:

Therefore, we, the members of this society, do hereby attest to a memory which looms across the whole spectrum of American life, economic and social, bequeathing to us a program, a practical dream whose fulfillment will be his lasting memory.

We direct that a minute of this resolution attesting our sense of loss of Mr. Kennedy's death be forwarded to the Secretary of State of the United States and be made a perpetual minute in the archives of our society.

TRIBUTE BY

Hon. R. Walter Riehlman

OF NEW YORK

Mr. Speaker, this past Sunday, I feel confident, the majority of Members of Congress, together with millions of other Americans, and people all around the world, attended their churches to worship. In most instances, I believe, at least a portion of each service was devoted to a memorial to our late President, John F. Kennedy.

At the service in the church of which I am a member, the pastor's remarks were most appropriate, and his approach to this terrible tragedy was helpful to me. Therefore, I would like to share these remarks with my colleagues and others.

"On the Passing of John F. Kennedy," by the Reverend Finley M. Keech, minister of the First Baptist Church, Tully, N.Y., follows:

ON THE PASSING OF JOHN F. KENNEDY

In the 2 days just past we have been cast low by the passing of President John F. Kennedy. But in order to have profound appreciation it is not necessary that his opinions be altogether ours, nor his politics and policies. It is necessary only to know that his country is our country and that his citizenship is ours as well; and because of this we can mourn his passing from mortal life in our midst.

We all have heard many details of the circumstances by radio and television which we need not duplicate here. But in order to describe adequately the enormity of the crime that has been committed we must say something like: "One person, it would seem, has taken unto himself the prerogative which is God's alone—to grant life to a human being or to take it"—and herein is the essence of the tragedy.

Beyond merely describing what has come to pass, however, we crave an understanding of what is happening in our midst.

First, we can observe that there is among us a national personality. For I believe that groups as well as persons express a personality. We belong to clubs or small groups which, by virtue of the persons comprising them, possess a corporate personality. The same, it seems, is true of larger groups, the church congregations we belong to, and even political parties. And a national personality now shows itself in grief and sorrow for the passing from this life of our President.

But just as surely a national personality will also be observed in the days before us as the Nation continues to direct its people's purposes.

Second, in seeking to understand what now happens among us and within us, we must bring to the surface of consciousness what is at least subconscious, to say that we are now struck with how mortal we are. That is to say, upon seeing that another is indeed mortal we have it dramatically impressed upon us that we, too, are mortal and that we can die as well as he.

But there is another side to this matter, namely, that somehow, in our humanity and human society, we are a part of the whole of life that creates human hatreds and promotes, albeit unwittingly, even psychopathic animosities among some of the population. It would be fitting in this circumstance, therefore, that persons of the church use the occasion more assuredly to dedicate themselves to the Kingdom of God in our midst and resolve therein to use the Christian gospel as a counterforce to the passions of hatred.

And last, in the happenings around us we are finding the true purpose of intercession, that is, of intercessory prayer in which we render prayer in another's behalf. Be assured that we are not offering prayer for a dead and inert body. We pray, rather, in the behalf of a living soul received of our Heavenly Father. We pray for a family now broken, for a young widow and her almost infant children, and for a family that has suffered much tragedy and is now cast into the consummate tragedy of human experience. It should be our high hope that, in praying in the face of tragedy, we shall be able to learn also of life in its goodness and blessings.

Involving ourselves, as we have done, in intercession for others, we may hope also that therein shall be found the strength and direction for our lives whereby we shall be able to live in behalf of others and all.

It is a Christian thing to do, to pray for others. It is a Christian thing also to be able to weep with those who weep and to mourn with those who mourn. So I ask that we join with others of our fellow citizens in prayer, silently each in his own way, and corporately too.

TRIBUTE BY

Hon. Ralph J. Rivers

OF ALASKA

Mr. Speaker, it was my privilege and honor to render the eulogy at the John Fitzgerald Kennedy Memorial Services held at Anchorage during those dark hours of November 23, following the assassination of our great President the day before.

The words are mine but they come from the hearts of the people of Alaska, as follows:

Fellow Alaskans, in simple words, we are gathered here as mourners to honor our honored dead, and with heavy hearts to pay a parting tribute to our beloved leader and fellow American, John Fitzgerald Kennedy, the 35th

President of the United States of America, whose life and dreams were ruthlessly taken from him—and from us—at the peak of his great career.

The consequent disruption of the lives of his lovely widow and children and sorrowing parents and other members of the Kennedy family calls forth from our hearts our deepest and most compassionate sympathy. Although we here are but a handful of grieving people, we symbolize the hearts and minds of Alaskans and Americans everywhere. We bespeak the tidal wave of admiration and affection for the memory of John F. Kennedy, which sentiments sweep across our land and indeed across the world. This admiration and affection, of course, stems from his own great personal courage, and friendliness and unflagging concern for the freedom and welfare of his fellow men. It is also directed toward his deep patriotism and dedicated and unstinting contribution of his great knowledge and talent for leadership to the service of his country, and in the interest of all of God's children everywhere.

Born at Boston, Mass., on May 29, 1917, he was reared by strong and farsighted parents to be strong, energetic, brave, industrious, knowledgeable, and wise, and these were the traits which characterized every crowded year of his full and rich and warm personal and public life. Reams will be written about his greatness, his achievements, his strength—but I want to remember, too, Kennedy the man—the devoted son, husband, and father—the good-humored way he met and talked to the people of the press at his news conferences, calling each by name—the way he shook his finger for emphasis—the way he said "Cuber" and "Alasker"—his big ready grin.

In terms of his public life, he was always way out in front—for example, his service in the Navy and heroism in World War II—his Membership in the U.S. House of Representatives and in the U.S. Senate at an early age—the fact that he was the youngest President of the United States in history, and the first President of the Catholic faith. In keeping with his great gifts, he grasped the meaning of our changing times from colonialism to freedom, from feudalistic systems to democracy, and the appalling threat of catastrophic nuclear war in a world seething with change in the midst of a worldwide population explosion. Thus, his strength was matched by his farsightedness and desire and effort to keep America ahead in the cold war and related events, and in the effort to secure world peace through strength, as the only long-range guarantee of our national security and a better world. For this we blend our affection and admiration of our so recently departed great President with gratitude for the benefits America has derived from his having lived and worked with and for us. Among those benefits, we count the heritage of the great inspiration he has left with us to lead more magnanimous and stronger and better lives. This is the inspiration left to our able and distinguished and patriotic new President, Lyndon Baines Johnson, and to others in high places who will proceed to guide the ship of state through turbulent waters, on an even keel. Let us then join in standing strongly behind our new President with confidence that the destiny of our great Nation is in strong and capable hands, to take the place of those of our late great brother, John F. Kennedy.

TRIBUTE BY

Hon. Howard W. Robison

OF NEW YORK

Mr. Speaker, on December 2, 1963, the Council of the City of Binghamton, N.Y., meeting in regular session, unanimously adopted the following resolution honoring the memory of the late John Fitzgerald Kennedy, which resolution was thereafter approved, on December 3, by the Honorable John J. Burns, mayor of Binghamton, and then forwarded to me.

Under leave to extend my remarks and to include extraneous material, the resolution is hereto appended:

IN COUNCIL OF THE CITY OF BINGHAMTON, STATE OF NEW YORK, A RESOLUTION HONORING THE MEMORY OF JOHN FITZGERALD KENNEDY

Whereas John Fitzgerald Kennedy, the 35th President of the United States of America, and the greatest leader of our time, has met his untimely death on November 22, 1963, at the hand of a cruel and cowardly assassin; and

Whereas his dedication to the cause of peace and the elevation of human dignity will always be remembered by the immortal words and work he left behind, which are not only known to this grieving Nation but to the world; and

Whereas President John Fitzgerald Kennedy, in all his public utterances, exhorted the people of this world to strive for the common good and with the best that is in each of us; and

Whereas he was a man whose private and public life was above reproach; who was sincere and equitable, honest and honorable; one to whom artifice and treachery were unknown, who was a stranger to bigotry and prejudice, an adviser of the indigent and a friend of all, regardless of race, color, or creed; and

Whereas at Gettysburg 100 years ago, that great and kindly man, Abraham Lincoln, most eloquently spoke to the people a few words which now in paraphrase, seem to express our thoughts about our deceased President:

"It is for us, the living, rather, to be dedicated here to the unfinished work which John Fitzgerald Kennedy who fought here has thus far so nobly advanced. It is rather for us to be here dedicated to the great task remaining before us—that from this honored dead President we take increased devotion to that cause for which he gave the last full measure of devotion—that we here highly resolve that this man shall not have died in vain;" and

Whereas we dedicate this meeting in memory of our compatriot, John Fitzgerald Kennedy, whose name is written in letters of gold upon the fleshy tablets of our grateful and appreciative hearts, and whose name is deeply engraved in the pure white marble of honest fame and whose name will be inscribed on the tablet of the immortals: Now, therefore, be it

Resolved, That this council when it adjourns tonight, it do so in the name and on behalf of the city of Binghamton and its citizens, with deep and sincere regret and in respect to the memory of John Fitzgerald Kennedy, the late President of the United States of America; and be it further

Resolved, That the clerk of the city of Binghamton forward a copy of this resolution to Mrs. Jacqueline Kennedy, the widow of John Fitzgerald Kennedy, and also that a copy be forwarded to Hon. Howard W. Robison, Congressman of the 33d District of the State of New York, with instructions that this resolution be made a part of the Congressional Record; and that the clerk of the city of Binghamton spread this resolution upon the minutes of this council.

Dated: December 2, 1963.

LEO J. KELLEY,
President of Council.
JOHN I. BURNS,
Mayor of the City of Binghamton.

TRIBUTES BY

Hon. Peter W. Rodino, Jr.

OF NEW JERSEY

Mr. Speaker, my words can add nothing to the eloquence of the editorials of the Newark newspapers about our beloved and great late President:

[From the Newark (N.J.) Evening News, Nov. 23, 1963]

HOUR OF DARKNESS

John F. Kennedy lies dead at the hand of an assassin. The Nation is prostrated with shock and grief and shame.

His death will have global consequences, but now there is room in our hearts only for sorrow at the death of a gallant young President.

The country's first thought goes to his near ones—to the anguished wife who sat at his side when gunfire struck him down in Dallas, to his children suddenly bereft of a father, to his parents and others of a large family knit by strong bonds of affection.

But we mourn also for the United States, which has lost a President who discharged his responsibilities with diligence and devotion, with grace and dignity. He had courage. He had magnanimity. For all who are underprivileged he had compassion.

John F. Kennedy's name is now added to a sad and tragic roll—Lincoln, Garfield, and McKinley.

His death is a grievous loss not only to his country, but to all the Western World.

He was the personification of the brave, youthful leadership to which the world looks for a more rational and tranquil existence. To him words like freedom and liberty and justice were not abstractions. They were ideals to be fought for and defended.

But for the moment all this is irrelevant. For most Americans, in this hour of darkness, the only reality is that, by an infamous act, a beloved President lies dead.

It is an hour when our thoughts turn backward to a brighter day, and we seem to hear again the inspiring words that concluded the inaugural address of our 35th President:

"Ask not what your country can do for you—ask what you can do for your country."

Now the President who spoke those memorable words has given his life for his country. No man can do more.

———

[From the Newark (N.J.) Star-Ledger, Nov. 23, 1963]

THE PRESIDENT IS DEAD

President Kennedy is dead, the victim of a shocking, senseless tragedy.

The first, almost reflex, reaction to the assassination of John Fitzgerald Kennedy is the chilling, grievous loss to our country and the free world.

Another reaction, almost as immediate, is heartfelt sympathy for his grief-stricken family.

In a sense, they are related—the loss to his family and the Nation—the loss is deeply personal and immeasurable.

It is difficult to measure words so soon after an incident of such catastrophic dimensions. The words come hard, haltingly because the shocking impact of this tragedy numbs the senses.

Mr. Kennedy was struck down at the height of his vigor. He was an articulate spokesman for the cause of world democracy, a symbol of hope for undeveloped nations and the new countries emerging into strange, new independence in Africa.

How can you measure his loss on the international scene? In his tragically short tenure in the White House, Mr. Kennedy became a beacon of hope for the free world. He was a vigorous exponent of foreign aid, the lifeblood to the future for less privileged nations.

It is ironic that the President should die at a time when his efforts to ease world tensions appeared to be taking firm hold, after months of wearing negotiations and anxiety.

Mr. Kennedy had matured greatly in office. He had the most difficult task in this uncertain, anxiety-ridden world, a world that is divided by two diametrically opposed political and economic philosophies.

The President had taken on new stature after the showdown in Cuba, when he stood up to the missile-waving Premier Khrushchev. This was a major breakthrough for American foreign policy; it gave fresh, new hope to free nations that were deeply concerned over Communist aggressions.

At home, Mr. Kennedy found greater obstacles to his legislative programs in recent months, an uneasy prelude to the national election next year.

There was stubborn resistance to his foreign aid program, his social legislation was stalled and he faced formidable opposition to his civil rights bill.

In recent months, it became apparent that Mr. Kennedy was moving slowly and inexorably to a centrist area on economic problems, in an effort to deal more effectively with the Nation's nagging unemployment problem.

Now Mr. Kennedy is dead.

How do we measure him as a President, as a leader of world opinion, as a catalyst for the free nations and the undeveloped countries?

It is still too early to fully evaluate him in this respect. His administration was shockingly brief; he was not able to carry through the difficult, painstaking international programs.

Many problems are still unsolved, at home and abroad. But much progress has been made in his short time in office.

The United States and the free world had come a long way under Mr. Kennedy's leadership—it has a long way to go. The road is long, tortuous and full of pitfalls. In his own way, the President made that road a little smoother, a little easier to traverse.

The assassin's bullet ruthlessly removed that heavy burden from the President's shoulder. This burden now is the awesome responsibility of Lyndon Baines Johnson, an experienced political leader of high competence and tireless energy.

Mr. Johnson is faced with a big job. We are fortunate he is a big man.

————

[From the Newark (N.J.) Sunday News, Nov. 24, 1963]

A MAN OF PEACE

Even now in this solemn period of mourning, it is difficult to comprehend the tragedy that has befallen the Nation in the assassination of President Kennedy.

Messages of condolence pouring in from all over the world reflect the disbelief of the American people that in this age such a thing could have happened here.

All Americans are united in a common sorrow, a sorrow that for many is deeply personal. For if there was political opposition to John F. Kennedy, there was, save in one malignant mind, little personal enmity.

He had won the hearts of millions not only in the United States, but around the world. Even in Moscow women wept when his death was announced.

This affection was a response to his personality and character. He had wit and intellect, grace and style, gallantry and idealism. He brought to the Presidency energy, imagination, and courage, and applied them all in his efforts to solve that which confronted him.

But above all else, in everything he did, Mr. Kennedy gave proof of his supreme dedication to the cause of peace and freedom. To him these were the transcendent needs of our time—at home as well as in the world.

His gravest economic problem was persistent unemployment. He sought to combat it by stimulating economic expansion through tax reduction. To improve social conditions, he worked for the implementation of constitutional guarantees on civil rights.

To meet want, he advocated programs of mental health and health insurance for the aged; for community betterment he offered redevelopment programs. He proposed Federal assistance in other areas, notably in education.

In most of this Mr. Kennedy was frustrated by congressional indifference or, as in the case of civil rights, by intraparty hostility. He encountered increasing difficulty with Congress over his foreign-aid programs. But

Congress supported his efforts to strengthen the Nation's defenses and the space program which made such rapid strides during his administration.

In foreign policy he achieved more evident success. Offsetting an initial defeat in the Bay of Pigs was his successful confrontation of the Soviet Union in the crisis arising over Russian missile bases in Cuba.

The President succeeded in lessening cold war tensions. He negotiated with the Russians a treaty banning atomic tests in the atmosphere, and authorized the sale of surplus American wheat grain to Communist countries, but he remained forever wary of their ultimate purposes.

Complicating Mr. Kennedy's efforts to provide rational and constructive leadership for the West was a new spirit of nationalism in Western Europe, which was largely the result of the economic rehabilitation that America had financed.

Personifying this spirit was President de Gaulle, whose dream of a Europe united under French leadership conflicts with the American ideal of a wider Atlantic community.

And America's generous foreign-aid program created another problem, an unfavorable balance of trade that threatened the stability of the dollar.

The President's noble concept, the Alliance for Progress, through which he hoped to bring an end to poverty and illiteracy in Latin America faltered largely because most of the beneficiaries have failed to do their part.

But if at his death much that he had begun remained unfinished, he had won the world's respect. He cared for people, he cared for the world, and he worked unceasingly that they might be prosperous and peaceful. And the people and the world, believing in the sincerity of his purpose, mourn the loss of one who had offered so much hope.

————

[From the Newark (N.J.) Star-Ledger, Nov. 25, 1963]

OF MOURNING AND REDEDICATION

Today has been proclaimed a day of mourning. Americans everywhere will join in a heartfelt, sorrowful tribute to the Chief Executive so ruthlessly and viciously shot down by an assassin.

Now that the initial shock has been somewhat worn away by the inexorable process of time, the terrible enormity of the crime—with all its farflung ramifications—is only beginning to dawn on the American people.

And they are realizing, too, that the deeper the tragedy the more difficult it is to truly do it justice.

The impact of the tragedy was further brought home to millions of Americans via the television sets in their living room. They saw the flag-draped casket bearing the remains of John Fitzgerald Kennedy move slowly on a horse-drawn caisson through the streets of Washington from the White House to the Capitol rotunda.

They heard the regular beat of the hushed drums—100 steps to the minute. And the mournful rhythm beat a tattoo the American people will not quickly forget. There have been few, if any, instances in history where so many people participated in a service marking so great a tragedy.

In many a living room yesterday it would have been hard to find a dry eye. The sight of Mrs. Kennedy, little

Caroline at her side, bravely kneeling to kiss the casket of her husband will be etched for a long time on the minds of millions of Americans.

The loss Mrs. Kennedy suffered is, of course, a great one. But all of us also have suffered a great loss.

Mr. Kennedy served but a brief period in the White House. But it was an eventful period. Historians may be reluctant to pass final judgment at this early date. It was clear, however, since shortly after his inauguration that the Kennedy administration was to be earmarked by youth, vigor, intelligence, and determination to make a fresh attack on accumulated problems at home and abroad.

Seeing their young President in action, the American people had a growing confidence in his ability. Not everyone agreed with him. But no one—least of all John F. Kennedy—would have expected or wanted unanimity. The American Government provides room for disagreement and diversity. This is one measure of its strength.

But there is no room for hatred of the type displayed by the assassin who ended the President's life. When it comes to hatred, there is only room for hatred of injustice and violence.

In his few years in the White House, President Kennedy sought to end injustice and inequality in the Nation and violence from abroad. And millions of American people are undoubtedly better off today because of his efforts.

By proclamation, today is a day of mourning. It is also, by proclamation, a day of rededication. In their mourning, the American people should not overlook the obligation to rededicate their efforts to help make their country a better place for all its citizens—in a world secure in justice and freedom, removed from the threat of violence.

Perhaps such a utopia—of which man has dreamed for centuries—cannot be achieved on this earth. But this was the aim of the Founding Fathers of this Nation. And it was the aim of John F. Kennedy.

Mr. Kennedy's tragic death may have helped sharpen the full realization of fundamentals to which Americans are accustomed to give lipservice. Now is the time for all to rededicate themselves to giving much more than lipservice to the high ideals on which this Nation was founded.

TRIBUTES BY

Hon. Paul G. Rogers

OF FLORIDA

Mr. Speaker, the entire world mourns the passing of our late President, as does our own Nation. We in Florida and the Sixth District feel the loss acutely, as we considered the President and his family as neighbors and friends. The winter White House at Palm Beach was a familiar place to all, and Palm Beach itself had witnessed not only the comings and goings of the President but his growth and development from childhood until the weekend prior to his tragic death.

Millions of words have already been written about the man and the act which has taken him from us at the prime of his life, when we know in our hearts words cannot express our feelings. To his family we can only say the prayer, God be with you, which has already manifested itself in the courage and strength which we have all witnessed and which will be an inspiration for years to come.

To the memory of John Fitzgerald Kennedy the American people should rededicate themselves to abolish from this land forever the hate and discord which created the atmosphere for this tragedy, and remember the warning of Lincoln that while no foreign power may ever conquer, we have within ourselves the power to destroy our own Nation. Every single citizen must take an active part in the work of returning our Nation to the rule of reason and of law.

Mr. Speaker, I include several representative editorials from Florida papers.

[From the Palm Beach Post, Nov. 23, 1963]

SHOCK AND MOURNING

America today is in mourning.

A great, good man is dead at the hands of an assassin. The youngest man ever elected to the Presidency of the United States, a brilliant statesman with a valorous war record, a beloved family man with an abiding faith in God—has been cut down in the prime of his career.

John Fitzgerald Kennedy has joined the martyrs. Like his illustrious predecessors, he now belongs to the ages.

In the Palm Beaches, which was to the President a "second home" and site of the "winter White House," shock prevails. Only a few days ago, he was among us, vigorous and smiling.

We join the universal hope that his assassin will be apprehended and properly punished. But this is a secondary consideration. Such a foul deed could have been conceived and executed only by diseased minds.

Our thoughts at this time are primarily of sympathy for the bereaved family, and of hope and concern for our new President, Lyndon B. Johnson.

May God be with them all, and with us.

———

[From the Fort Lauderdale (Fla.) News, Nov. 24, 1963]

WORDS UNSPOKEN AT DALLAS OFFER GUIDANCE TO NATION IN THE TRYING DAYS AHEAD

President John F. Kennedy was to have made a speech in Dallas on Friday. Before he reached the appointed place, the 35th President of the United States held a rendezvous with death and his voice was stilled forever, his words unspoken.

Although they were left unsaid, the words should be our guide in this awkward hour when a President of the United States rests this very day in state in the rotunda of the Capitol, and while the new President works in the heavy presence of death and mourning, to take over our Nation's affairs and chart the direction the ship of state shall sail for the next 14 months.

Well might President Lyndon B. Johnson heed those words unspoken. Well might every American citizen weigh them and accept them as counsel through the convulsions that must occur during the difficult transition.

What Mr. Kennedy had intended to say in his Dallas speech was an excerpt from the Bible, Psalm 124: "Except the Lord build the house, they labor in vain that build it. Except the Lord keep the city, the watchman waketh but in vain."

Mr. Kennedy was a master of oratory and there were those among us who believed that he often spoke wise counsel, but too often did not pay heed as he spoke. All of that is of consequence no longer, for in the martyrdom of his high office, the President rests expiated of human frailties, left to the judgment of his Maker and of history.

What is of consequence is that Mr. Kennedy had chosen to recite from a psalm which, through lamentable and shocking circumstances, should now become an echoing reminder for Americans through the remaining ages.

They are the words in which can be found the answer to the anguished question of House Speaker John W. McCormack, who, when informed of Mr. Kennedy's assassination, cried out: "My God, My God. What are we coming to?"

Both the question and the reply found in the psalm should serve as admonitions to each and every American citizen. Indeed, what were we coming to in the mounting tempest, calmed for now by the chill of death?

Irrefutably, we had become a divided nation; ultra-liberal against ultra-conservative, Democrat against Republican, northerner against southerner, atheist against religionist, black against white, American against American.

We had been caught up in an ugly web of opportunism, of materialism; placed at the mercy of outside influences that would bury us, sapped of resolve to pay any cost for the preservation of our inherited doctrine, caught in a crosscurrent of demands upon another without regard for one to the other.

We were a finely divided nation and we knew it; yet little of anything was accomplished in restoring our national unity. We were on a collision course with the future that awaited us in November 1963.

Our direction from that point on shall remain forever unknown, obliterated by a searing bullet triggered by one individual whose horrendous action may leave us uncertain and exposed to deepening schism, or spared the rendering that awaited at the point of collision.

That we never will know.

But this we do know: If this Nation is to be destroyed and, as Mr. Kennedy once said, become part of the debris of history, it is we, the living, who shall destroy it. If this Nation is to survive in strength, it is we, the living, who shall make that determination in the months ahead.

Thus, the admonition left unsaid by John Fitzgerald Kennedy assumes meaning far greater than had he pronounced from a speaker's platform in ill-fated Dallas: "Except the Lord keep the city, the watchman waketh but in vain."

And with humility, Lyndon B. Johnson gave the Nation encouragement for the future when he said as he was sworn as the 36th President of the United States:

"I will do my best—that's all I can do. I ask your help—and God's."

WILLIAM A. MULLEN.

————

[From the Fort Myers News-Press, Nov. 23, 1963]

"Ask What You Can Do"

"And so, my fellow Americans, ask not what your country can do for you—ask what you can do for your country."

In the shock and sorrow, in the confusion and uncertainty following the assassination of President John F. Kennedy, well may those words he uttered in his inaugural address be recalled now and pondered by his countrymen.

They were noble words and inspiring. But many came to take a cynical view of them in the weeks and months that followed their delivery on that freezing January day of 1960 by the 43-year-old President elected by a popular vote margin of only one-tenth of 1 percent. How much Kennedy himself, by the actions he took and the programs he espoused, contributed to that public cynicism need not be examined at this time of national bereavement but may be left to the later judgment of history.

It is appropriate instead to recall the achievements of Kennedy's short administration of less than 3 years, and there were many. There were notable successes in the space program, the creation of the Peace Corps, some tax revision, the bolstering of the United Nations through a bond issue and other means. The outstanding accomplishment of the Kennedy administration is certainly the negotiation and ratification of the treaty outlawing nuclear weapon tests in the atmosphere, which gives mankind good ground for hope, at least, that the poisonous pollution of the air will now cease and that further progress may be made in the international control of the awesome bomb.

Now in the aftermath of the tragedy in Dallas, many question marks arise over the Nation's future policies and programs which devolve upon President Lyndon B. Johnson. The initial impact of the tragedy is so overwhelming that none can venture to answer them with assurance, nor would care to undertake their consideration in this hour. Of only one matter can there be assurance now—that all segments of the Nation will uphold the hands of President Johnson in the difficult days of readjustment immediately ahead.

In this dark hour all Americans, of all persuasions, mourn the untimely death of the young President Kennedy. Their thoughts go out in sympathy to his wife and two little children and to the others of his family.

In this hour too Americans can find good guidance from their fallen leader in his words—"ask what you can do for your country."

TRIBUTE BY

Hon. Walter Rogers

OF TEXAS

Mr. Speaker, a resident of the district I have the honor to represent, George (Farmer) Schaeffer, of Box 418, Canyon, Tex., was one of the Texas Panhandle's stanchest admirers of the late President John F. Kennedy. Mr. Schaeffer, a lifelong student of history and current affairs, is as truly a patriotic American as I have ever known. His own deep sense of obligation to his country was reflected by his enlistment, at an advanced age, in the U.S. Army for service in France as an infantryman in World War I, and as a private soldier again in World War II, after recruiting officers chose to overlook the fact that he was well past 50 years of age.

Mr. Schaeffer shared with President Kennedy a love of his Nation's history and of literature, and the tragic death of the President inspired the following sorrowing lines from Mr. Schaeffer's pen.

I submit them as the heartfelt expression of grief from a private citizen who loved his President:

A shot rang out one sunny day,
    A nation plunged in grief,
Those silent throngs have gathered round,
    In shocking disbelief,
But yes, 'Tis true, alas, too true,
    Too late to call him back,
A grieving wife his only shield,
    From murderous attack.

A sober thought across the land,
    Our conscience now divulged,
A tragic sequence to the thoughts,
    We have so long indulged,
The fruits of hate, we now have plucked,
    And bitter though they be,
We must thereof, eat to the full,
    In sad humility.

His rendezvous with destiny,
    Although it was so brief,
The ship of State, in troubled waters,
    He guided by the reef,
His love of country knew no bounds,
    His works, They did suffice,
And for that love and loyalty,
    He paid the highest price.

The world has lost a giant, great,
    Who battled for the right,
This erring world pays tribute to,
    A brave man and his might,
The colored man has lost a friend,
    The poor an advocate.
We all have lost a captain bold,
    To guide the Ship of State.

Down Pennsylvania Avenue,
    The cortege wends its way,
Past weeping throngs of citizens,
    With silent lips that pray.
With measured tread the caisson rolls,
    The Stars and Stripes his shroud,
The flags are flying at half mast,
    The cannon boom so loud.

With muffled drum and sound of taps,
    In sorrow laid to rest,
We wonder why it had to be,
    God does things for the best.
In mystic ways He sometimes moves,
    His wonders to perform,
The foulest air is somehow cleansed,
    In wake of brutal storm.

Wistful children, so woebegone,
    A widow numbed with grief,
'Tis only through the grace of God
    That they have found relief.
The widow now, walks not alone,
    For God walks by her side,
Her children walk, also with her
    In understanding pride.

The lighted torch he carried high,
    Its flame will never dim,
Eternal flame of liberty
    For it was lit by him.
Ever onward this vision goes
    To far ends of the world,
To light the hopes of mortal man
    This challenge by him hurled.

Safe at last across the river,
    Beyond the pale of sorrow,
He left his stamp upon the world,
    Left a bright tomorrow;
We thank the Lord that we have had,
    Him with us for a while,
His steady hand upon the helm,
    His ready willing smile.

We know he had not lived in vain,
For he accomplished much,
We hope he has not died in vain,
He left that human touch;
A noble warrior for the right,
He shirked not from the fray,
We have a duty to the dead,
Let's start on it today.

All that is left are memories,
Wrote with a golden pen,
Memories that will ever live,
Live in the hearts of men;
Farewell, farewell John Kennedy,
But no, 'tis not farewell,
Just au revoir, our gallant chief,
He whom we loved so well.
—FARMER SCHAEFFER.

TRIBUTE BY

Hon. John J. Rooney

OF NEW YORK

Mr. Speaker, on Sunday last Mrs. Rooney and I attended holy mass at the hospital chapel at Walter Reed Army Hospital here in Washington. The celebrant of the mass was Rev. Eugene L. A. Fisher, C.S. Sp., chaplain—lieutenant colonel—AUS, retired. For his sermon during the sacrifice of this memorial mass, which was for the happy repose of the soul of the late President John F. Kennedy, Father Fisher read to the congregation the following beautiful prayer poem which he had written out in longhand the evening before:

JOHN FITZGERALD KENNEDY

(By Eugene L. A. Fisher, C.S. Sp., chaplain (lieutenant colonel), AUS, retired)

We know not track time or lone hour
When God will say, "Come see."
The great, the grand, with all their power
Can hardly set us free.

Within a triumphal parade
Mid shouts of joyous praise
The call may come in sudden raid
Or as explosive blaze.

Our President was jubilant
The crowds acclaimed with pride
Not knowing that the time was scant
Sad tragedy the ride.

Assassin's bullets turned the joy
To grim reality
It could have been his wife or boy
It hurt both you and me.

A great man, lover of world peace
Who kept our country strong
Given the time, would still increase
Our strength to right the wrong.

Cut down in virile prime of life
With aspirations high
To conquer in world's bitter strife
Keep flag safe in the sky.

A gifted man with talents rare
To help his fellow man,
He labored with that special care
As only masters can.

Our States have lost their greatest friend
The world a man most kind
Whose labors and great toil could lend
A key to freedom find.

He now rests in a hero's grave
Life's trials for him are o'er
A martyr's palm archangels wave
God blessed his latest chore.

His passing is our country's loss
God called him when ready,
Like you, we shall not shirk the cross—
John Fitzgerald Kennedy.

TRIBUTES BY

Hon. Donald Rumsfeld

OF ILLINOIS

Mr. Speaker, the following editorial comments indicate, as well as any words can, the depth of feeling, the profound shock, and the grief and sorrow which is felt by the people of Illinois.

A dedicated, valiant, and sacrificing leader has been taken from the Nation by an incomprehensible act of violence. With heavy hearts, we join with millions across the globe in mourning his loss, in extending our prayers for his family, and in pledging our support to our new President at this time of national crisis.

[From the Chicago Sunday American, Nov. 24, 1963]

THE PRESIDENT WE'VE LOST

America's change of Presidents from John F. Kennedy to Lyndon Johnson has been brought about by bullets—methods dreadfully familiar in some countries, but strange and deeply shocking in the United States. It is especially tragic that the victim of this assassination should have been the laughing and confident Kennedy.

While he lived, he was leader of the world—the free part of the world—and he led not only because he commanded the vast resources of the United States but also because he awakened faith in his purposes among those with whom he came in contact.

In his own country he led with imagination and courage. In this time of great and rapid change, he was well suited to his task because he was a believer in change; he looked for good to come out of it, so he was not timid about letting old values go. He felt the country would benefit by the change.

Although some of his suggestions were not acceptable to many conservative minds, the American people are indebted to him because, in general, he taught them to examine novel ideas for themselves instead of responding to them entirely as the teachings of tradition dictated.

The manner of his death is shocking as well as sorrowful because it shows the presence in this country of a mind that could not differ without hate, and did not hesitate to deal death to anyone who disagreed.

If this spirit of partisan hate is widespread in this country, let us have determined campaigns to trample it out. A free country cannot govern itself except by the exercise of friendly disagreement. America must be a land of open debate, not poisonous resentments living and growing in secret.

The American people mourn John F. Kennedy. Their sympathy goes to his wife and children, his mother and father. And so his death is as deeply felt by people who disagreed with his political philosophy as by those who agreed with it. That is the spirit in which free people can govern themselves.

———

[From the Sun Times, Nov. 23, 1963]

AMERICA WEEPS

President Kennedy lies dead, a martyr in the cause of democratic government.

His countrymen weep in sorrow and in anger.

The immensity of the crime can hardly be grasped in these hours of confusion that inevitably have followed the assassination of the chief of the most powerful nation in the world.

The Nation is left temporarily without a leader. Vice President Johnson will assume the heavy burden of the Presidency and the policies of the Nation will undergo no imminent change. But inevitably the assassination will change the course of history, not only in the Nation but in the world.

And it should change the temper of our times. At the moment the motive that lurked in the twisted mind of the killer is not, of course, known:

But the deed in Dallas was different only in degree of importance from such acts of violence as the bombing of houses of worship, racial murders and only last month, in the same city, the degrading assault on U.N. Ambassador Adlai Stevenson.

All of these acts of violence are the work of persons who, fundamentally, do not believe in a democratic government operating under a rule of law.

The preachers and whisperers of hate and disunity, who undermine confidence in our Government and our public officials by irresponsible attacks on their sanity and loyalty, plant the motives in the heads of those who pull the triggers and toss the bombs.

Those who impugn the motives of our national leaders, who defy the courts and distort the operations of the United Nations would not themselves do violence. But they engender the kind of hate that must have been in the eyes that lined up Mr. Kennedy's head in the crosshairs of a rifle sight yesterday.

The awful loss that hate visited upon the Nation and the world should inspire all Americans to join together in this hour of shock and mourning in a reexamination of the national conscience.

The right of dissent, the exercise of free speech, the criticism of the President and other public officials high and low, must not corrode into sullen rebellion that breeds violence. All Americans, those who agree with their government's policies and those who disagree, must stand together on this fundamental and demonstrate this unity by action as well as words. The purveyors of hate must acknowledge the danger they create.

When we speak of the purveyors of hate we obviously are not speaking of the President's regular political opposition, those persons in his own party and in the Republican Party who had disagreed with many of his views and policies and who also grieve for Mr. Kennedy. We are speaking of the extremists from both parties who go beyond the pale in their opposition and criticism.

The Nation owes a great debt to Mr. Kennedy who gave his life in the service of his country as surely as a soldier on the frontline. And to Mrs. Kennedy and the President's family the American people offer their hearts. The personal tragedy of an assassination seldom has been as heartbreakingly evident as in the scene that followed the shooting; Mrs. Kennedy holding the President's head in her lap and weeping "Oh, no."

No, it should never have happened in America. That it did must weigh heavily on America's conscience. And if it brings a reawakening and a real change in the temper of our times Mr. Kennedy will not have died in vain. This is a prayer in which all Americans can join.

TRIBUTE BY

Hon. Harold M. Ryan

OF MICHIGAN

Mr. Speaker, I would like to offer a poem composed by the Honorable Wade McCree, judge of the district court for eastern Michigan.

Judge Wade McCree presided at the memorial service on November 25, 1963, for our late President, John F. Kennedy, on the site of the old city hall at Detroit, Mich., which is now appropriately called Kennedy Plaza.

After the following very pertinent observation of Judge McCree, who said:

Regardless of any opinion we may entertain about Lee Harvey Oswald and Jack Ruby, we should include their grief-stricken families within the ambit of our compassion.

Judge McCree closed his remarks with the following poem which he composed for the occasion, and which I wish to bring to the attention of the Members of this honorable body as a further tribute to our beloved President, whose life was snuffed out at the height of his career.

In Memoriam—J.F.K.

What can we do, surviving him who died
   In selfless service to transform a world
From one of hate and war and vaunted pride
   To one of love with freedom's flag unfurled?

What can we do, surviving, to assure
   That his last gift shall not have been in vain?
What did his noble sacrifice procure
   Or must this tragic loss be void of gain?

To bow our heads in grief as we stand here
   To shed our tears and count ourselves bereft
Profanes this noble hero's flag-draped bier
   Unless we learn the lesson he has left.

If we would honor him we mourn today
We must forsake forever hatred's way.

Mr. Speaker, there is a young, talented, 15-year-old girl in my district who has stirred the hearts of all Detroiters through her sorrowful interpretation of the funeral tragedy as seen through the eyes of little John-John. Miss Candy Geer, of Grosse Pointe, Mich., deeply impressed with the reactions of the late President Kennedy's little son at the funeral proceedings, composed a poem in which she describes the bewilderment of a small boy who "wonders where his daddy has gone."

Her poem, which was printed in the Detroit News on January 21, has made the young and old sadly recall those bleak November days; but this time, those days are recalled through the eyes of a brokenhearted little boy who no longer has his daddy.

I would like to have the Members of Congress and every American read this poem which has truly made Detroit cry again.

Six White Horses

(By Candy Geer)

Six white horses came today
To take my Daddy far away.
Mommy said I must be good
And stand as big as Daddy would.
And now I am big, so I won't cry.
When I see Daddy wave goodby.
'Cause Daddy is my special friend.
He always comes back soon again.
I cannot wave, I don't see why?
There's just a black box moving by.
But Mommy says I should be still.
I'm a big boy now, and so I will.
I hear some drums; they're awful loud!
My Mommy's sad and so's the crowd.
And everybody's dressed in black.
But Daddy soon will hurry back.
We're going to take a walk to mass.
Then maybe I'll see Daddy pass.
I wonder why we're only three?
He always comes to church with me.
Two men are talking, I can see.
They said they're very proud of me.
They said my Daddy's in that box—
The black one, with the six gold locks.
I have on a big boy's suit.
And now it's my turn to salute.
I do it just like big boys do
Because I have to be one, too.
They're going to stop and then just leave.
But in that box how will he breathe?
'Though I do not understand
There's Mommy here to hold my hand.
He's going to leave and not come home!
We just can't leave him here alone.
I want to hear him laugh and say,
"John-John, come here so we can play."
I don't see Daddy anywhere.
I want to cry and I don't care!
He's in the ground—he cannot be.
He should be right here holding me!
But Mommy says I must be good—
So I'll just stand as Daddy would.

TRIBUTES BY
Hon. William F. Ryan
OF NEW YORK

Mr. Speaker, many tributes have been written in memory of our beloved President John F. Kennedy. One of the most moving tributes I have read appeared last Sunday, December 1, in the

Corpus Christi Calendar, the weekly bulletin published by Corpus Christi Church which is located in the Morningside Heights section of the district which I have the honor to represent. Msgr. Arthur A. Campbell is the pastor.

Father John Dwyer captured the spirit of John F. Kennedy when he observed:

One of the many amazing things about John F. Kennedy was that for our people he bridged the gap between the remote abstract thing, "the Government," and ourselves.

Mr. Speaker, I hope all of my colleagues will read the following:

OUR MAN, THE PRESIDENT

So many words have been written about our poor late President, and yet all of us realize that words are not adequate to express fully our sorrow and our shock. This is why so many grown men have shed tears once or several times in these last days. There are thoughts that lie too deep for words and yet must find expression; thus tears mixed with inadequate words brought forth the way we thought and felt about "our man," the President.

One of the many amazing things about John F. Kennedy was that for our people he bridged the gap between that remote abstract thing, the Government, and ourselves. When he walked into the White House, we walked in with him and it became our Washington residence, a place we maintained for our representative. When he spoke sharply or persuasively to foreign governments or to big business, he spoke for us, telling them how we felt.

Oh sure, we disagreed with some things he said or did even as we disagree with some of the things the other members of our family say and do. But even when we disagreed, we felt he was sincere, that he had his reasons, and that maybe he knew something he couldn't yet tell us which influenced his decision. Being human, we gave him room and allowed for his differences with us. Only the editorial writers of the Daily News, the New York Times, and the Wall Street Journal are infallible and all knowing, so they could be so consistently critical and harsh in their judgments of almost everything the President said or did. Fortunately we didn't elect them to represent us; we did elect "our man." He spoke for us, and when he died we lost part of our ability to express the way we think to the world.

The outpouring of affection at his death proved that although many of the high and the mighty opposed him because he opposed their self-centeredness, the vast majority of his fellow citizens loved him and respected him as a good man, aligned with his God, with his fellow man and with us. Perhaps we did not deserve him, so that God allowed him to be taken from us, that we might better appreciate a man like John F. Kennedy, if He should deign in His mercy to send us another to be "our man."

Mr. Speaker, on November 25, the day our beloved President John F. Kennedy was buried in Arlington Cemetery, memorial services were held in the synagogues and churches throughout the land. The overwhelming grief of our people was reflected in the words spoken that day.

On November 25, 1963, at Congregation B'nai Jeshurun in New York City, the Honorable Charles H. Silver, president of the congregation, delivered a moving address at memorial services for John F. Kennedy. I include that address at this time.

ADDRESS BY HON. CHARLES H. SILVER

Our land has endured an agonizing nightmare that even the most insane narrator of fiction could not conceive.

Unfortunately, it is no wild dream from which we can awake to comforting reality, nor a disturbing novel whose cover we can close with a sigh of relief.

Dark, indeed, is the glass through which we look back on the events of the past few days.

The President is dead. Even as we mourn the loss of America's first citizen, we lament, as well, the loss of a part of our national self-respect.

All we have left are the bitter dregs of our bereavement—a chance to examine the heartbreak and error of yesterday—the fault and sorrow today. Out of these, perhaps, we can somehow build a path to a brighter tomorrow.

But we must not forget. We must remember these things. We must remember these momentous days of dread and resolve—in the sight of our Creator—to make amends, to seek the truth, and, with sanity, justice, and mercy, to wipe this abomination from the blighted pages of history.

The first news came like a bolt from the sky. This, it truly was—shocking and numbing in its impact on people in their homes and offices—workers in factories and shops—children in their classrooms.

With moist eyes, unable to move from our television sets, we have watched, stunned and confounded by a series of unbelievable scenes, consumed by a sense of horror and disbelief.

As the original fact of the cowardly attack on our President struck home—and then struck again with the dreadful tidings of his death—the whole world came to a sudden shuddering halt. The crowded streets froze into screaming silence.

In every fearful heart there came a piercing grief, a pang of sorrow for Mrs. Kennedy and the children. In every city, freedom held its breath.

The day of infamy that was born in Dallas began to spread its darkness at noon across the tortured face of the earth.

From every farflung land, even from behind the Iron Curtain, where compassion seemed to have fled, there came a sound of sobbing. Humanity could not stem its tears.

The bleeding flesh of our heroic dead became a symbol of mankind's shame that civilization could breed the evil hand and eye that aimed that fatal shot.

Was this the terrible price of too much freedom?

Are the borders of constitutional protection too broad for those who despise our laws and desecrate our liberty?

Has our own lazy loyalty and indifferent Americanism played a part in this incredible pattern of events?

It is not easy to answer.

Our hearts are too heavy with the knowledge that our noble young warrior has been cut down in the prime of his days, in the very procession of his triumph, at the very beginning of his most notable achievements.

He can no longer lead us in the struggle for justice and decency. And yet, somehow, he leads us still.

John Fitzgerald Kennedy had a way of telling us his plans for the New Frontier that made the soul of America stand taller. There was deep conviction in his voice and intellectual authority in every glowing phrase.

His was a bold, uncompromising call to truth—a call to arms against injustice and oppression that keeps on ringing in our aching hearts.

We hear him yet. We see him as he stood before us, smiling, self-assured, and, oh, so tragically young. He is there—head high, waving to the cheering crowds, rushing forward to shake a friendly hand.

Such a man cannot be eliminated by a madman with a gun—no, nor by the madness that walks abroad in the world. Such a man lives in the hope of every citizen, growing with the growth of the great country he served, alive and indestructible in our memories of those few short years when his own stature grew to match those other great Americans to whose ideals John Kennedy devoted his life.

Time erects his monument and history will build it high. We weep that Israel has lost this cherished friend. We are outraged at the disgrace that befell our land and took away our leader.

But we are proud that our beloved President, in death as in life, stamped the profile of his magnificent courage across the conscience of mankind.

He asked not what his country could do for him. He asked only what he could do for his country—and no man could have done more.

On this untimely day of atonement, as we sit in the synagogue along with all the generations of Israel, we pay homage to our sacred dead.

We honor the image of his remembered glory, his wisdom, wit, and eloquence. Our spirit is warmed again by the fire that lighted his love of America.

In his name, let us resolve to strengthen the sinews of our national integrity, to protect the principles of liberty, justice, and equality for which he gave his life.

That is the greatest tribute we can pay our fallen hero in eternal gratitude for his ultimate sacrifice, while our hearts follow him, along with our fervent prayers, to that further New Frontier he is entering tonight.

Let us rise, beseeching eternal peace and the blessing of Almighty God, as we join in a minute of silent prayer, for the immortal soul of John Fitzgerald Kennedy, 35th President of the United States.

In the last paragraph of the last speech he ever wrote, he expressed some of this philosophy for himself, for his country, and for the world:

"We in this country, in this generation, are—by destiny rather than choice—the watchmen on the walls of world freedom. We ask, therefore, that we may be worthy of our power and responsibility—that we may exercise our strength with wisdom and restraint—and that we may achieve for our time and for all time the ancient vision of peace on earth, good will toward men. That must always be our goal—and the righteousness of our cause must always underlie our strength."

Mr. Speaker, I wish to bring to the attention of my colleagues a letter which appeared in the New York Times. The letter, written by Jay Newman, a second year law student, is a sensitive and eloquent analysis of the reactions of youth to the death of the late President Kennedy.

KENNEDY LEGACY TO YOUTH—STUDENT SAYS PRESIDENT RENEWED THEIR PRIDE IN AMERICA

To THE EDITOR OF THE NEW YORK TIMES:

The death of the young President who inspired and encouraged youth was a deep shock and will have a profound influence upon the students of America, who identified with him as he identified with them.

The high school and college generation has not experienced—as a group—tragedy, anguish, and frustration on a national scale. Pearl Harbor, the death of President Roosevelt are vaguely remembered; take their place as history, not of personalization. The late President united this youth for the first time into one being—a being guided and directed by his heart and mind.

For the first time the youth had a leader, for the first time they have seen their leader die. This will profoundly affect their generation. From it will arise a greater maturity and understanding of the amorphous concept called life. This generation never experienced defeat, injustice on such a grand scale. With the rise of J.F.K., the vigor, vitality, and creativity of American youth was centered around national goals and aspirations as never before. All too soon it is over.

At first it will appear as if the torch were wrested from their hands and given to another generation; but eventually this attitude will be replaced by a greater depth in youth due to the tremendous impact the late President instilled into this Nation: The renewed sense of pride in their country—the individual personalization with the highest office in the land—giving instead of taking—new dimensions to the word "flexibility" and making human dignity a reality. It will be realized that all this has not ended because of his death, but has just begun. Our leader is dead, but his leadership is within America, never to die.

This then is the legacy John Fitzgerald Kennedy has bequeathed to us, the students of America.

JAY NEWMAN,
Georgetown Law Center.

WASHINGTON, *December 7, 1963.*

Mr. Speaker, I wish to draw the attention of my colleagues to an eloquent tribute to the late President Kennedy. This tribute was presented to the joint board of the Millinery Workers Union by the union's manager, Nathaniel Spector.

The tribute follows:

A TRIBUTE TO THE MEMORY OF OUR MARTYRED PRESIDENT JOHN F. KENNEDY

(By Nathaniel Spector)

President Kennedy wanted to be President. He fought for it heroically—not for his own glory or power, but for the power of his office to advance the welfare and progress of the American people for disarmament and world peace.

With the rise of John F. Kennedy to the Presidency, new vigor, vitality, and creativeness were brought into the life of our Nation. President Kennedy's assumption of leadership of our Nation was a breath of fresh air, a reawakening—like life in spring. His fresh, youthful spirit captivated not only the people of his generation, but most Americans; he revitalized, invigorated and gave new hope for a better life for all Americans.

He was a great liberal humanitarian and a true believer of democratic principles and practices. He took decisive action where and when necessary. He was unafraid of new ideas; of problems—national or international; he welcomed those that he thought could bring benefits to the American people and peace to the democratic people all over the world. He was the symbol of a better future; of a new approach to national and world problems. He was the promise of a better tomorrow, free of poverty, prejudice, unemployment, inequality, injustice, and ignorance.

On November 22, the day of his assassination, his death inscribed itself deep in the hearts of all Americans for all time.

The day of his arrival in Dallas, Tex., a page ad appeared in the Morning News, sponsored by the American Fact-Finding Committee, which had as its purpose to arouse the people against the President.

Following the assassination of President Kennedy, a woman teacher wrote to the daily press, stating that the people of Dallas were responsible for the death of President Kennedy. She was dismissed. A traveling salesman was in a movie house when the assassination of President Kennedy was announced; the audience applauded. A priest stated that when the assassination of the President was announced in school, the children applauded.

The people in the South made it known now that they had no intention of voting for President Kennedy if he ran for office next year. They would rather vote for a Republican.

It is evident that the bloodstream of the people has been poisoned by bigotry, prejudice, falsehood, and hatred. President Kennedy was the captain of his soul. Courage and dedication do not die. Tonight we express our admiration, in sorrow, and pay homage to his lasting memory and, collectively, we pour our grief and tears in a common pool. Our leader is dead, but his leadership is with America—it shall never die.

To his courageous widow and his two lovely, fatherless children, our hearts go out.

Mr. Speaker, many, many words have flowed since the assassination of President John F. Kennedy, all expressing in some way the grief and sense of loss that people through the world felt about this tragedy.

James T. Farrell, a renowned author of many novels and stories, was a great admirer of President Kennedy. In his grief Jim Farrell penned a simple verse to give life to his feelings. He wrote this short poem in a moment of great emotion and then sent it to me to express his sorrow. I am sure that all of my colleagues will be moved by the words of a gifted novelist.

JOHN FITZGERALD KENNEDY

He rode, smiling, in sun and triumph
Six seconds of naked tragedy
And of the ultimate, terrible beauty of death—
He was no more.
We wept in the solitudes of our silence,
With the solidarity of grief.
—JAMES T. FARRELL.

Mr. Speaker, on November 25, the day of national mourning for our late President John F. Kennedy, Dr. Grayson Kirk, president of Columbia University, delivered an address at the memorial service in St. Paul's Chapel at Columbia. Among the many heartfelt eulogies to President Kennedy, I believe that Dr. Kirk's is one of the most inspiring I have read. I am sure my colleagues will be moved by Dr. Kirk's eloquent tribute which follows:

JOHN FITZGERALD KENNEDY

(Memorial address by Grayson Kirk)

On this sad day unnumbered millions of men and women have gathered together as we have done to pay a last word of respect and tribute to the memory of a great man. The earth that this afternoon receives the shattered body of John Fitzgerald Kennedy is wet with the unashamed tears of an outraged mankind. The world has been stunned by the effect of a single senseless and brutal act committed by a creature who at that moment forfeited his right to membership in the human race.

No greater blow can be dealt a nation than to strike down a chosen leader who had amply demonstrated a capacity for leadership rare among men of any generation. The entire Nation grieves, not merely out of a decent sympathy for a bereaved family and close personal friends, but because it knows that it, too, has suffered a crippling loss; that it, too, has been impoverished; that it, too, has been shamed before the world. And as our people bow their heads in their grief, they bow them also in shame that such a thing could have happened in our land and in our time.

The poignancy of our grief is all the more intense because we do not need to wait to be told by future historians that this was no mere and ordinary man thrust into high office by the chance results of democratic political process. We know in our hearts, and we know with deep and abiding conviction, that this was a man who possessed in abundance those special and unusual qualities of which our people at this time in their history stood in great need, from which they derived deep and lasting benefit, and without which they must look into a bleak and troubled future.

And on this afternoon of national mourning, it is fitting that we recall, for the benefit of all our citizens, some of the reasons why our loss is a national disaster, the like of which few generations have had to endure. So doing, we take some small measure of comfort in remembering what we have had; so doing, we set up in ourselves criteria by which we may measure those who would follow our President in this, the highest of all our offices.

We honor the memory of John Kennedy because he was a man of courage. He knew instinctively the importance of this quality among leaders. He wrote discerningly about it, in order that we might all be more aware of our national need for men who possessed it. In his youth he demonstrated that, in his own character, it was stronger than even the primal instinct for self-preservation. In his maturity he did not flinch from decisions that he knew would evoke hostility and abuse from men whose vision of the Nation's welfare was narrow, selffish, and distorted. From among all leaders he faced the terrible risk of nuclear war in order to protect the basic national interests of the people whom he had sworn to protect and defend.

But his was not the blind courage in face of danger which, happily, comes to many men in time of crisis. His was the courage derived from the intelligent evaluation of all facets of a complex and perilous situation and fortified by the strength of basic convictions. His was the courage of intelligence, the courage that goes beyond that of many intelligent men who, faced with a grave and unpleasant problem, lapse into the agony of indecision and the error of impulsive judgment.

Though as a young man he offered his life for his country, his final gift of this, the most precious of man's possessions, was more than a supreme sacrifice just in defense of his country. He wanted his country to become a land in which our democratic ideals would be more fully realized, a land in which we and our children could take ever greater pride, a land in which the old dreams of mankind might at last be realized. And he gave up his life because despicable and selfish men, hating this prospect, so filled the atmosphere with their venom that one mean creature became their tool and their agent. Now that the deed is done, and our President is gone, their protestations of innocence and even of grief ring hollowly upon our ears. John Kennedy died because he wanted a better America. Consciously he fought them, knowing as he must have, what the risks were. Bravely he died, not so much for the America of today as for the America of the future.

John Kennedy had more than courage and intelligence. He had compassion. Born to wealth and, had he so chosen, a life of ease and indolence, he elected a career of public service, one in which he could put his talents to work for his fellow men. Just as he was proud of the great qualities and achievements of his country, he was deeply troubled by the inequities and inequalities which still persisted in a society, ostensibly dedicated to their elimination. He was troubled, too, by the new injustices, the new hazards of life that grew out of social and technological change.

He saw a society in which men of one color were being denied that equality of opportunity which is the foundation stone of America. He saw a society in which the benefits of modern medical progress were on occasion denied to men and women because they lacked the means to pay for their needs. He saw a society in which aged men and women of limited resources were being ruthlessly pushed aside and allowed to live out their final years in that quiet helpless desperation that only poverty without hope can breed.

And because he was a man of compassion, he grieved over these cancers in the body politic. And because he was a man of action, he strove to exercise them and to heal their wounds. And because he was a determined man, not content to allow an affluent society to be so afflicted, he died.

Today, as we reflect with gratitude upon those great qualities, this constructively directed energy, this vision of what our country might be and must become, we must ask ourselves what good, what possible benefit, we as a people can derive from this man's life, what lessons we may take to our hearts from this crushing tragedy. Our grief must be tempered with the resolution that the sacrifice was not vainly made, that out of our national sorrow there may come some good, that from the shrine of this bloodstained soil in Arlington there may come a chastened and better America. In no other way can we justify to him what he did for us.

First and foremost, we must resolve to be more responsible in our thoughts and actions. This land of ours is plagued by men of small minds, men of vicious and uncontrolled emotions, men for whom hatred is greater than love, men whose concern for their fellow men is lost in insensate bigotry, men who in their hearts despise all that this Nation stands for, men who do not deserve the land in which they live. It does not matter whether they are of the reactionary right or the radical left, the menace which they present to this country is equally ominous because they would—in order to bring back a world that never was or one that betrays the cause of human freedom—destroy all our effort.

Since we are obliged by the imperatives of that freedom to permit such men to carry on, to a reasonable extent, their destructive activities, it is the obligation of those of us who really love our country to be more energetic, more alert to the danger, more willing to remind our citizens about the dangers implicit in the ravings of the extremists. When we are silent in the face of this danger, when we deride our chosen leaders or sit quietly by when others do so, when we allow ourselves to become irrational in our partisanship, when we allow others to sneer at our principles, we are unconscious accomplices in the sabotage of our country. Apathy in these circumstances is cowardice. If this experience through which we have passed does not chasten our hearts, and does not steel our determination to combat these forces of destruction about us, then may God help us, because we will not help ourselves.

It has been the historic pride of this country for the past century that our excesses of political partisanship have never reached the point when the conflict on either side jeopardized loyalty to our Constitution and our democracy. This is still true of the overwhelming majority of Americans, but we face today, in this respect, greater dangers than at any time since the Civil War. Respect for law is lost in the selfishness of men who try to cheat and evade its commands. Respect for law is lost in the organized resistance of men to the application of the Constitution under which they live. Respect for law is dead when our highest officers are physically assaulted, when their lives are threatened, and when such threats become grim reality. To these dangers we must become more alert. Against them we must devise countermeasures. From them we must learn and practice that self-discipline which has never been congenial to our people but upon which the future of our country depends. In this respect, we hang our heads in shame over the spectacle which we present to the world, a spectacle which ill accords with our boasting.

More energy against the extremists and their poison, more self-discipline—even these are not enough if we are to justify by the future health and progress of our society the sacrifice John Kennedy made for his country. Each segment of our society must reexamine its responsibilities. The press, radio, and television, through their emphasis upon the reporting of violence often go beyond their basic need to keep us informed; by these emphases they may condone and inflame still further violence, and they cannot escape social responsibility by saying that they are merely giving the public what it wants. In the home, the extreme permissiveness of our modern parents breeds in their children contempt for all authority, a contempt that takes its toll in broken youthful lives and bewildered parents who try to evade responsibility for their own failures by casting the blame on others. And, of course, our schools, our colleges, and our universities need to reexamine their functions and to try to discover how, along with their traditional duties, they can impart to their students a greater sense of social responsibility. The death of our beloved President carries a lesson to every part of our society and to every institution. In his memory we must heed it.

Thus, today, in our grief and our remorse, we look sadly, but with new resolve to the future. We are determined to create in this land the democracy in which he believed, one which applies the ancient principles of human dignity, equality, and opportunity to the conditions and necessities of modern life. As we do this, and as we bring nearer to reality, the dreams of men like the man we mourn today, we make out of his gallant life and its tragic ending a national treasure for the future. We can do no more, and we can do no less. His soul is in the hands of God, his heritage in the hearts of our people.

Mr. Speaker, at this time of tragedy there is much that all of us could say, yet in a sense there is nothing to say. In this hour of national and international grief let us dedicate ourselves to the principles and purpose of President John F. Kennedy; let us unite in common determination to cleanse our national life of bigotry and vituperation; in doing so, let us consider the words of our beloved President which he had prepared to deliver to the Dallas Citizens Council and the Dallas Assembly. In that speech, an eloquent statement of American policy, it is significant that President Kennedy intended with words of reason to caution against "voices preaching doctrines wholly unrelated to reality, wholly unsuited to the sixties, doctrines which apparently assume that words will suffice without weapons, that vituperation is as good as victory and that peace is a sign of weakness."

The text of the undelivered speech follows:

TEXT PREPARED FOR DALLAS

I am honored to have this invitation to address the annual meeting of the Dallas Citizens Council, joined by the members of the Dallas Assembly—and pleased to have this opportunity to salute the Graduate Research Center of the Southwest.

It is fitting that these two symbols of Dallas progress are united in the sponsorship of this meeting. For they represent the best qualities, I am told, of leadership and learning in this city—and leadership and learning are indispensable to each other.

The advancement of learning depends on community leadership for financial and political support—and the products of that learning, in turn, are essential to the leadership's hopes for continued progress and prosperity. It is not a coincidence that those communities possessing the best in research and graduate facilities—from M.I.T. to Cal Tech—tend to attract the new and growing industries. I congratulate those of you here in Dallas who have recognized these basic facts through the creation of the unique and forward-looking graduate research center.

LINK IN WORLD AFFAIRS

This link between leadership and learning is not only essential at the community level. It is even more indispensable in world affairs. Ignorance and misinformation can handicap the progress of a city or a company—but they can, if allowed to prevail in foreign policy, handicap this country's security. In a world of complex and continuing problems, in a world full of frustrations and irritations, America's leadership must be guided by the lights of learning and reason—or else those who confuse rhetoric with reality and the plausible with the possible will gain the popular ascendancy with their seemingly swift and simple solutions to every world problem.

There will always be dissident voices heard in the land, expressing opposition without alternatives, finding fault but never favor, perceiving gloom on every side and seeking influence without responsibility. Those voices are inevitable.

But today other voices are heard in the land—voices preaching doctrines wholly unrelated to reality, wholly unsuited to the sixties, doctrines which apparently assume that words will suffice without weapons, that vituperation is as good as victory and that peace is a sign of weakness.

At a time when the national debt is steadily being reduced in terms of its burden on our economy, they see that debt as the greatest single threat to our security. At a time when we are steadily reducing the number of Federal employees serving every thousand citizens, they fear those supposed hordes of civil servants far more than the actual hordes of opposing armies.

STEVENSON QUOTED

We cannot expect that everyone, to use the phrase of a decade ago, will "talk sense to the American people." But we can hope that fewer people will listen to nonsense. And the notion that this Nation is headed for defeat through deficit, or that strength is but a matter of slogans, is nothing but just plain nonsense.

I want to discuss with you today the status of our strength and our security because this question clearly calls for the most responsible qualities of leadership and the most enlightened products of scholarship. For this Nation's strength and security are not easily or cheaply obtained—nor are they quickly and simply explained.

There are many kinds of strength and no one kind will suffice. Overwhelming nuclear strength cannot stop a guerrilla war. Formal pacts of alliance cannot stop internal subversion. Displays of material wealth cannot stop the disillusionment of diplomats subjected to discrimination.

Above all, words alone are not enough. The United States is a peaceful nation. And where our strength and determination are clear, our words need merely to convey conviction, not belligerence. If we are strong, our strength will speak for itself. If we are weak, words will be no help.

STRENGTH OF AID PLAN

I realize that this Nation often tends to identify turning points in world affairs with the major addresses which preceded them. But it was not the Monroe Doctrine that kept all Europe away from this hemisphere—it was the strength of the British Fleet and the width of the Atlantic Ocean. It was not General Marshall's speech at Harvard which kept communism out of Western Europe—it was the strength and stability made possible by our military and economic assistance.

In this administration also it has been necessary at times to issue specific warnings that we could not stand by and watch the Communists conquer Laos by force, or intervene in the Congo, or swallow West Berlin, or maintain offensive missiles on Cuba.

But while our goals were at least temporarily obtained in those and other instances, our successful defense of freedom was due—not to the words we used—but to the strength we stood ready to use on behalf of the principles we stand ready to defend.

REVIEWS AREAS OF STRENGTH

This strength is composed of many different elements, ranging from the most massive deterrents to the most subtle influences. And all types of strength are needed—no one kind could do the job alone. Let us take a moment, therefore, to review this Nation's progress in each major area of strength.

First, as Secretary McNamara made clear in his address last Monday, the strategic nuclear power of the United States has been so greatly modernized and expanded in the last 1,000 days, by the rapid production and deployment of the most modern missile systems that any and all potential aggressors are clearly confronted now with the impossibility of strategic victory—and the certainty of total destruction—if by reckless attack they should ever force upon us the necessity of a strategic reply.

In less than 3 years, we have increased by 50 percent the number of Polaris submarines scheduled to be in force by the next fiscal year—increased by more than 70 percent our total Polaris purchase program—increased by 50 percent the portion of our strategic bombers on 15-minute alert—and increased by 100 percent the total number of nuclear weapons available in our strategic alert forces.

Our security is further enhanced by the steps we have taken regarding these weapons to improve the speed and certainty of their response, their readiness at all times to respond, their ability to survive an attack and their ability to be carefully controlled and directed through secure command operations.

But the lessons of the last decade have taught us that freedom cannot be defended by strategic nuclear power alone. We have, therefore, in the last 3 years accelerated the development and deployment of tactical nuclear weapons—and increased by 60 percent the tactical nuclear forces deployed in Western Europe.

Nor can Europe or any other continent rely on nuclear forces alone, whether they are strategic or tactical. We have radically improved the readiness of our conventional forces—increased by 45 percent the number of combat ready army divisions—increased by 100 percent the procurement of modern army weapons and equipment—increased by 100 percent our ship construction, conversion and modernization program—increased by 100 percent our procurement of tactical aircraft—increased by 30 percent the number of tactical air squadrons—and increased the strength of the Marines.

As last month's Operation Big Lift—which originated here in Texas—showed so clearly, this Nation is prepared as never before to move substantial numbers of men in surprisingly little time to advanced positions anywhere in the world. We have increased by 175 percent the procurement of airlift aircraft—and we have already achieved a 75 percent increase in our existing strategic airlift capability. Finally, moving beyond the traditional roles of our military forces, we have achieved an increase of nearly 600 percent in our special forces—those forces that are prepared to work with our allies and friends against the guerrillas, saboteurs, insurgents and assassins who threaten freedom in a less direct but equally dangerous manner.

But American military might should not and need not stand alone against the ambitions of international communism. Our security and strength, in the last analysis, directly depend on the security and strength of others—and that is why our military and economic assistance plays such a key role in enabling those who live on the periphery of the Communist world to maintain their independence of choice.

Our assistance for these nations can be painful, risky, and costly, as is true in southeast Asia today. But we dare not weary of the task. For our assistance makes possible the stationing of 3.5 million allied troops along the Communist frontier at one-tenth the cost of maintaining a comparable number of American soldiers. A successful Communist breakthrough in these areas, necessitating direct U.S. intervention, would cost us several times as much as our entire foreign-aid program, and might cost us heavily in American lives as well.

MOST FOR NINE COUNTRIES

About 70 percent of our military assistance goes to nine key countries located on or near the borders of the Communist bloc; nine countries confronted directly or indirectly with the threat of Communist aggression—Vietnam, Free China, Korea, India, Pakistan, Thailand, Greece, Turkey, and Iran. No one of these countries possesses on its own the resources to maintain the forces which our own chiefs of staff think needed in the common interest.

Reducing our efforts to train, equip, and assist their armies can only encourage Communist penetration and require in time the increased oversea deployment of American combat forces. And reducing the economic help needed to bolster these nations that undertake to help defend freedom can have the same disastrous result. In short, the $50 billion we spend each year on our own defense could well be ineffective without the $4 billion required for military and economic assistance.

Our foreign-aid program is not growing in size; it is, on the contrary, smaller now than in previous years. It has had its weaknesses, but we have undertaken to correct them, and the proper way of treating weaknesses is to replace them with strength, not to increase those weaknesses by emasculating essential programs.

Dollar for dollar, in or out of Government, there is no better form of investment in our national security than our much abused foreign-aid program. We cannot afford to lose it. We can afford to maintain it. We can surely afford, for example, to do as much for our 19 needy neighbors of Latin America as the Communist bloc is sending to the island of Cuba alone.

LOSS THROUGH BALLOTS

I have spoken of strength largely in terms of the deterrence and resistance of aggression and attack. But, in today's world, freedom can be lost without a shot being fired, by ballots as well as bullets. The success of our leadership is dependent upon respect for our mission in the world as well as our missiles—on a clearer recognition of the virtues of freedom as well as the evils of tyranny.

That is why our information agency has doubled the shortwave broadcasting power of the Voice of America and increased the number of broadcasting hours by 30 percent—increased Spanish-language broadcasting to Cuba and Latin American readers—and taken a host of other steps to carry our message of truth and freedom to all the far corners of the earth.

And that is also why we have regained the initiative in the exploration of outer space—making an annual effort greater than the combined total of all space activities undertaken during the fifties—launching more than 130 vehicles into earth orbit—putting into actual operation valuable weather and communications satellites—and making it clear to all that the United States of America has no intention of finishing second in space.

This effort is expensive but it pays its own way, for freedom and for America. For there is no longer any fear in the free world that a Communist lead in space will become a permanent assertion of supremacy and the basis of military superiority. There is no longer any doubt about the strength and skill of American science, American industry, American education, and the American free enterprise system. In short, our national space effort represents a great gain in, and a great resource of, our national strength—and both Texas and Texans are contributing greatly to this strength.

Finally, it should be clear by now that a nation can be no stronger abroad than she is at home. Only America which practices what it preaches about equal rights and social justice will be respected by those whose choice affects our future. Only an America which has fully educated its citizens is fully capable of tackling the complex problems and perceiving the hidden dangers of the world in which we live. And only an America which is growing and prospering economically can sustain the worldwide defense of freedom, while demonstrating to all concerned the opportunities of our system and society.

It is clear, therefore, that we are strengthening our security as well as our economy by our recent record increases in national income and output—by surging ahead of most of Western Europe in the rate of business expansion.

And the margin of corporate profits—by maintaining a more stable level of prices than almost any of our oversea competitors—and by cutting personal and corporate income taxes by some $11 billion, as I have proposed, to assure this Nation of the longest and strongest expansion in our peacetime economic history.

This Nation's total output—which 3 years ago was at the $500 billion mark—will soon pass $600 billion for a record rise of over $100 billion in 3 years. For the first time in history we have 70 million men and women at work. For the first time in history average factory earnings have exceeded $100 a week. For the first time in history corporation profits after taxes—which have risen 43 percent in less than 3 years—have reached an annual level of $27.4 billion.

My friends and fellow citizens, I cite these facts and figures to make it clear that America today is stronger than ever before. Our adversaries have not abandoned their ambitions—our dangers have not diminished—our vigilance cannot be relaxed. But now we have the military, the scientific and the economic strength to do whatever must be done for the preservation and promotion of freedom.

That strength will never be used in pursuit of aggressive ambitions—it will always be used in pursuit of peace. It will never be used to promote provocations—it will always be used to promote the peaceful settlement of disputes.

We in this country, in this generation, are—by destiny rather than choice—the watchmen on the walls of world freedom. We ask, therefore, that we may be worthy of our power and responsibility—that we may exercise our strength with wisdom and restraint—and that we may achieve in our time and for all time the ancient vision of peace on earth, good will toward men. That must always be our goal—and the righteousness of our cause must always underlie our strength. For as was written long ago, "Except the Lord keep the city, the watchman waketh but in vain."

TRIBUTES BY

Hon. Katharine St. George

OF NEW YORK

Mr. Speaker, the following cables have been received by me to transmit to the U.S. national group of the Inter-Parliamentary Union and to the Congress. They are the expressions of sympathy of the Inter-Parliamentary Union from its Secretary General, Mr. de Blonay, and from the same group on behalf of the Council, and the president of the Union, President Mazzilli; from the Spanish group through its president, Mr. De Ananequi; from the Brazilian group through its president, Mr. Rui Palmeira; from the Parliament of Monaco through its president, Mrs. Louis Aureglia; from the Italian group through its president, Mr. Vodacci Pisanelli, and from the French group through its president, Senator Moutet.

I ask unanimous consent to include the seven cables, with three translations.

I know that I interpret the sentiments of the Inter-Parliamentary Union in requesting you to transmit to the U.S. group our feelings of profound emotion and deep sympathy in the tragic passing of President Kennedy, a great champion of democracy and peace.

> BLONAY,
> *Secretary General.*

———

PARIS, *November 23, 1963.*

Mrs. St. GEORGE,
Inter-Parliamentary Group,
The Capitol, Washington, D.C.:

Suis certain interpreter sentiments union toute entiere en vous priant accepter et transmettre groupe American sentiments profonde emotion et sympathie emue a l'occasion tragique disparition President Kennedy grand serviteur de la Democratie et de la paix.

> BLONAY,
> *Secretaire General.*

November 23, 1963.

DEPUTADOS BRASILIADF,
House of Representatives,
Washington, D.C.:

Please accept my own name and behalf IPU Council expression deepest sympathy tragic event President Kennedy's death. Not only the United States but the whole world mourns one of its greatest leaders.

> RANIERI MAZZILLI.

———

VITORIA, *November 24, 1963.*

GEORGE B. GALLOWAY,
Library of Congress,
Washington, D.C.:

On behalf of Spanish group Interparliamentary Union please express American group our most sincere condolence.

> MANUEL DE ANANEGUI.

———

BRASILIA, *November 26, 1963.*

KATHARINE ST. GEORGE,
House of Representatives,
Washington, D.C.:

Deeply distressed tragical death President Kennedy I present name Brazilian group and my own expression our deepest sympathy.

> RUI PALMEIRA.

———

The Inter Parliamentary group of the Principality of Monaco is deeply shocked at the tragic event that has put the United States and the world in mourning. We express through you our profound condolences and the deep emotion of the members of the National Council and the whole population of Monaco.

> LOUIS AUREGLIA,
> *President.*

———

MONACOVILLE, *November 23, 1963.*

Mrs. KATHARINE ST. GEORGE,
U.S. Interparliamentary Group, House Office Building,
Washington, D.C.:

Groupe Interparlementaire Principaute de Monaco consterne par tragique evenement qui endeuille les etats unis et le monde vous exprime condooleances profoundement emues des membres conseil national et de la population Monegasque.

> LOUIS AUREGLIA,
> *President.*

———

ROMA, *November 25, 1963.*

Mrs. St. GEORGE,
Chairman, United States of America Group IPU, the
Capitol, Washington, D.C.:

Touched for the tragic lost President Kennedy on behalf of Italian group please accept deepest condolences while joining to the nations.

> VODACCI PISANELLI.

Deeply shocked by your national mourning. The French national group wishes to express its very sincere and deep compassion.

MOUTET.

PARIS, *November 25, 1963.*

Lt. Presidente ST. GEORGE,
House Office Building,
Washington, D.C.:

Profondement bouleverse par votre deuil national groupe Francais vous exprime sa tres sincere et bien vieve compassion.

MOUTET.

Mr. Speaker, the following letter and cable have been received by me as President of the U.S. national group of the Interparliamentary Union.

The letter is from General Dimoline, secretary of the British group, and expresses their heartfelt sympathy to us over the tragic death of our late President, John Fitzgerald Kennedy.

The cable is also a message of sympathy from Senator de Baeck, expressing the feelings of the Belgian group.

INTER-PARLIAMENTARY UNION,
PALACE OF WESTMINSTER,
London, December 4, 1963.

Dr. GEORGE B. GALLOWAY,
Executive Secretary of the U.S. Interparliamentary Group, Library of Congress, Washington, D.C.

MY DEAR GALLOWAY: At the first meeting of the executive committee of the British group, on behalf of all members of the group, I was instructed to write and convey to the American group our deepest sympathy in the tragic death of your late President.

We send you and Mrs. Kennedy and the peoples of the United States, whom you represent, our heartfelt sympathy in this senseless outrage against the cause of humanity which the President did so much to uphold. His death is not only a severe blow to his own countrymen but to all who watched with admiration his noble efforts for peace.

He was a great and human man and his loss will be felt by the world for a long time.

Yours sincerely,

W. A. DIMOLINE.

———

PALAIS DE LA NATION,
Bruelles, November 24, 1963.

CHAIRMAN OF THE GROUP OF THE UNITED STATES OF AMERICA OF THE INTERPARLIAMENTARY UNION,

State Department, Washington, D.C.:

It is with a feeling of real affliction that we heard of the tragical and irreparate loss of President Kennedy. This terrible misfortune that has just come upon the United States of America, and all the countries of the world, must have been the more cruel as it was un-

expected. Be assured that we feel most sincerely for the member of your group, and also for the American citizens in their affliction.

CARLOS DE BAECK,
Chairman of Belgian Group, Interparliamentary Union.

TRIBUTES BY

Hon. William L. St. Onge

OF CONNECTICUT

Mr. Speaker, the late President Kennedy's love for the U.S. Navy is well known. So is his bravery and the record of his gallant service in the Navy during World War II.

Several very worthy proposals have been made in the Halls of Congress and elsewhere to pay tribute to his memory and to immortalize the man and his deeds. In the 3 years that it was destined for him to lead our Nation, he was instrumental in building up our fleet of nuclear-powered submarines for the security of our country and of the free world.

I am, therefore, proposing that we name one of these nuclear-powered submarines, now under construction at Electric Boat, Groton, Conn., in honor of the late great President. I feel that this would be a very worthy tribute to him. Consequently, I am this day writing a letter to Acting Secretary of the Navy Paul B. Fay, Jr., suggesting that the U.S. Navy name one of its submarines the U.S.S. *John Fitzgerald Kennedy.*

Mr. Speaker, under leave to extend my remarks, I wish to offer the text of my letter to the Secretary of the Navy and several editorials from newspapers in my district in Connecticut commenting on the tragic and untimely death of our beloved President and its meaning for the Nation.

Hon. PAUL B. FAY, Jr.,
Acting Secretary of the Navy,
Department of the Navy,
Washington, D.C.

DEAR MR. SECRETARY: All of us are deeply grieved and stunned by the sudden death of our beloved President and many of us in Congress are thinking of ways to perpetuate his name and to honor his memory.

In view of the late President John F. Kennedy's great love for the U.S. Navy and his gallant service in the Navy during World War II, I propose to you that the next nuclear-powered submarine to be completed at

Electric Boat, Groton, Conn., be named the U.S.S. *John Fitzgerald Kennedy*. I believe this would be a most fitting and appropriate manner of paying tribute to the memory of our late President and at the same time it would also be a signal honor for the U.S. Navy to have one of its ships bear this illustrious name.

In recent months, I proposed that nuclear-powered submarines be named in honor of the Revolutionary War patriot, Haym Salomon, and the early American inventor, David Bushnell. I believe, however, that the present suggestion should take precedence over my earlier proposals for very obvious reasons.

I further suggest that when this submarine is completed and ready for launching, the courageous widow of our late President, Mrs. Jacqueline Kennedy, who bore up so graciously under the strain of this great tragedy, be invited to christen the new ship.

Sincerely,

WILLIAM L. ST. ONGE,
Member of Congress.

———

[From the Norwich Bulletin, Nov. 26, 1963]

IN HIS HONOR

Amid solemnity that was hushed, yet vibrant, John Fitzgerald Kennedy, the 35th President of the United States, yesterday was laid to rest in a martyr's grave in historic Arlington Cemetery. The words that John F. Kennedy spoke in his inaugural address some 34 months ago, "Ask not what your country can do for you, ask what you can do for your country," will be engraved on the pages of history. They were prophetic words—and John F. Kennedy fulfilled them to the last degree. He gave his all to his country.

Even though John Fitzgerald Kennedy is dead, struck down most foully by an assassin's hand, the cause he championed as acknowledged leader of the free world lives on. We who survive him can best honor his memory by doing all in our power to advance that cause which he held so precious, which is the very cause for which this Nation was founded—the liberty and dignity of all mankind.

As we thumb through the pages of history for guidance in a troubled time perhaps the best guidance for the difficult time ahead may be taken from the immortal words spoken by Abraham Lincoln on that solemn occasion at Gettysburg almost exactly 100 years ago. For President Kennedy died in defense of freedom as truly as did those who fell on that historic field of battle. In these days of profound national sorrow it is appropriate to recall and reflect on Mr. Lincoln's exhortation to his fellow Americans "that from these honored dead we take increased devotion to that cause for which they gave the last full measure of devotion— that we here highly resolve that these dead shall not have died in vain."

To resolve thus and to act thus—that is the task to which we must now turn our minds and our efforts. This is so even though grief and a deep sense of loss will far outlast the period of stunned and outraged shock of the past few days at the murderous acts that have occurred in Dallas. We cannot sink ourselves in a sea of heedless sorrow. The forces that work against the realization of man's highest dreams of liberty and dignity remain strong and malignant. Those are the forces which must now be countered with a new dedication of devotion so that John F. Kennedy's martyrdom in the fullness of life shall indeed not have been in vain.

All that was mortal of John F. Kennedy lies in Arlington Cemetery overlooking the banks of the Potomac for which he had such love, but his spirit of devotion to his country will remain forever with us as an inspiration to carry on the cause which he held so dear. The heaviest burden now falls upon Lyndon Baines Johnson, who became President of the United States at the moment John F. Kennedy's thread of life was cut by an assassin's bullet.

But all citizens of these American States in some measure must share the burden that now rests on the shoulders of President Johnson. In his first public utterance as Chief Executive President Johnson said this to the people of America and the world: "I will do my best. That is all I can do. I ask your help—and God's." His words were a commitment, and a challenge, worthy of the best that is in all of us.

The Nation must go on. The threads of the fabric that was so rudely torn apart that day in Dallas must be gathered and rewoven into an even stronger fabric of freedom and dignity. We must wear it with renewed consciousness that the entire world is watching us. We must so wear this garment of liberty and dignity so that in years to come the entire world will be wrapped in its folds. That is the least we can do to honor this man who gave so much that freedom should never perish from the face of the earth. That is our task and the task of future generations. We must not fail.

———

[From the Middletown Press, Nov. 25, 1963]

THE PRIDE AND THE SHAME

Unto the land he so dearly loved, President Kennedy was committed today. The last drum roll has dirged, the last caisson has rolled, the last 21-gun salute has echoed across Pennsylvania Avenue and the green hills of Arlington. The last chords of "Hail to the Chief" have drifted away, and now the land has hushed.

There were kings and queens, and princes, and prime ministers and presidents today in Washington, the largest assemblage of foreign dignitaries ever at once on our shores. And there were thousands of common people too, coming from near and far of this uncommon land where young men, many young men, have grown up to be President.

The pageantry and dignity of it all brought us closer to the national fabric and made us proud.

Steadfastly, Mrs. Jacqueline Kennedy has proved an example to us all. As her husband was a courageous man—which Ernest Hemingway once described as grace under pressure, so she has again proved to be a gallant lady. With her tiny children, she has borne with bravery the awful hours that began for her near noon on Friday. The ring she placed in her husband's dead hand, the kiss she bestowed upon our flag so proudly draped, are moments none of us will soon forget.

Would it be that this was the whole story. But yesterday in Dallas the terrible hours continued. In the police station of the city that formerly saw Vice President Johnson spat upon, Adlai Stevenson attacked by pickets, and our President murdered, the prisoner charged with assassinating the President was murdered in the full view of the Nation. And Dallas is worried about its image.

Whatever may be said about the wisdom of President Kennedy having gone to Dallas, or the security precautions taken there, what can be said about murder in the police station? What can be said about a nation that harbors so many people so conscious of its image, so oblivious to its laws, so willing to disregard its legal and moral precepts? Somewhere we are all failing, and not just in Dallas.

If the majesty of a young President who gave his life for his country cannot be obscured by such horrible events, the least we as citizens can do is to rededicate ourselves to all that is uniquely great about our country—that man does not take the law into his own hands, that man does follow the law of the land whether he likes it or not, that man should care for his substance and not his image. It is in the support of these ideals that we must persist.

[From the New London Day, Nov. 25, 1963]

NO ONE'S ABOVE THE LAW

"Why is everybody going around shooting each other?" the 8-year-old boy asked. Knowing only of the small world around him in which he is occupied chiefly with school and play, he is innocent of complex adult emotions. Perhaps, because of this, his reaction is uniquely objective. After the starkness of the weekend's reality has softened and the Nation is able to consider more fully what has happened, many of the boy's elders must try to find the answer to his question.

The shocking developments in Dallas culminated yesterday in the slaying of the President's alleged assassin, even while he was under heavy police guard. This deed was done by a man who walked unquestioned into the Dallas city jail and to within a foot of his quarry, still undergoing questioning as the prime suspect in the slaying of Mr. Kennedy.

As a result, we might well ask whatever became of the principles of law and order in America, or, with the little boy, "Why is everybody going around shooting each other."

The breakdown seems to have begun long before the assassination. It had been evident not only in Dallas but in hamlets and metropolises in many parts of the United States. It is apparent in contempt for the minor laws as well as in the studied disregard for basic concepts of human dignity and rights embodied in the Constitution.

Lee Harvey Oswald didn't act for humanity in his heinous crime on Friday. Jack Rubinstein, the Dallas nightclub operator who slew Oswald, didn't act for Americans. Both took the law into their own hands.

As a result of Rubinstein's shot there may always be doubt as to the origins, and the possibility of others being involved, in the tragedy of Friday. It did not avenge Mr. Kennedy or the American people. There can be no sympathy for those who place themselves above the law.

The terror of the past weekend can be answered only in one way: The American people must renew their belief in law and order in small matters and large. Freedom is based on principle and has its limits. The sober aftermath of the events in Dallas is the time to give deep thought about whether the Nation can afford to encourage or even tolerate those who would live above its laws.

[From the Leader, Rockville, Conn., Nov. 25, 1963]

A DAY OF MOURNING

Today is a day of mourning, not only for the Kennedy family, but for all the people of the United States and indeed the whole world.

Word Friday that President Kennedy had been assassinated spread quickly and stunned everyone. Certainly nothing has happened in the United States since Pearl Harbor that has come with such a shock.

To be sure, leaders have been assassinated in other countries of the world, and indeed three previous Presidents of the United States have died at the hands of assassins. However, most Americans have felt that we had reached a degree of civilization where such things could not happen.

President Kennedy was the youngest man ever to be elected to the Presidency. During his less than 3 years in office, he was called upon to face problems of a magnitude that few peacetime Presidents have had to face. He did this with initiative and courage.

Certainly at 46 his potential for many years of productive, useful service was great, and he most certainly would have found ways to continue his public service after his years in the Presidency were over.

In his inaugural address, President Kennedy said: "Ask not what your country can do for you—ask what you can do for your country." His own life was a personification of these words for his contributions in war and peace were many, including the greatest contribution of all—his own life.

The whole world is sorrowing with Mrs. Kennedy, the two Kennedy children whose relationship with their father was an ideal one, other members of his family, and his close associates.

TRIBUTE BY

Hon. George F. Senner, Jr.

OF ARIZONA

Mr. Speaker, each of us has mourned the passing of President Kennedy in our own way. It is not always easy or possible to articulate the grief we feel at a moment of great tragedy.

To some are given the gift of expressing that

which we may feel. For such comfort as my colleagues and my fellow Americans may derive therefrom, I offer here a poem written by a very dear friend in Arizona, Mrs. Willard "Billee" Shoecraft, on the day President Kennedy passed away:

My President Is Dead

Oh, the wind is bitter cold tonight
    That moans through the cypress trees.
The moon is dark and has no face
    And gone is the gentle breeze.

So still is the song of the mockingbird.
    His music I hear no more.
And the angry waves cry out in the night
    As they beat on the ragged shore.

Oh, lift him gently and lay him down
    Beneath a blanket of snow.
Wrap him with love and tenderness
    For cold are the winds that blow.

He was only here such a little while.
    He was much too young to die.
So find him a valley that's green again
    With a patch of blue for his sky.

Maybe he wasn't always right,
    But he fought for what he believed.
For a better world and the right to be free
    In a land that must not be deceived.

He looked like a boy when he smiled sometimes
    With a twinkle in his eye.
Yet he stood so tall in a world of men.
    Why did he have to die?

Bewilderment covers the earth tonight.
    A nation stands shocked and stunned.
How could the violent seed of hate
    Stop a life that had only begun?

Let not the good that he sought to do
    Lie now in a cold, dark grave.
Let the peace on earth and the freedom of man
    Be the price for the life he gave.

Oh, cold is the wind from the mountain tonight
    And unknown the road ahead
For the wind wails out through the cypress trees
    My President is dead.
                —*Billee Shoecraft.*

TRIBUTES BY

Hon. Don L. Short

OF NORTH DAKOTA

Mr. Speaker, an editorial in the Wall Street Journal of November 26, puts into frank perspective the question of where, if anywhere, the guilt should be established—or blame laid—for the tragic assassination of John Fitzgerald Kennedy, the 35th man to hold the highest office in the land as President of the United States of America.

I commend this editorial to the attention of Members of the House of Representatives, and the public, and under unanimous consent, I include the editorial with my remarks.

At this same time, I would also like to include a copy of my public statement, made shortly after this tragic event took place:

No Time for Collective Guilt

In the shock of these past few days it is understandable that Americans should find their grief mingled with some shame that these events should happen in their country. We all stand a little less tall than we did last Friday morning.

Yet, for our own part, we find past understanding the remarks of some otherwise thoughtful men who, in their moment of shock, would indict a whole nation with a collective guilt. It seems to us that they themselves have yielded to the hysteria they would charge to others, and in so doing show that their own country is past their understanding.

Anyone who has been reading the newspapers, listening to the radio or watching television has heard these men; they include public commentators. Members of our Congress, and men of God. And the substance of what they charge is that the whole of the American people—and by inclusion, the ways of the American society—are wrapped in a collective guilt for the murder of a President and the murder of a murderer.

A Senator said that the responsibility lay on "the people of Dallas" because this is where the events took place. A spokesman for one group of our people said the Nation was "reaping the whirlwind of hatred." One of our highest judges said the President's murder was stimulated by the "hatred and malevolence" that are "eating their way into the bloodstream of American life." A newspaper of great renown passed judgment that "none of us can escape a share of the fault for the spiral of violence." And these were but a few among many.

Such statements can only come from men who have not been abroad in the land, neither paused to reflect how the events came about nor observed in what manner the whole American people have responded to tragedy.

A President lies dead because he moved freely among the people. He did so because he was beloved by many people, respected by all, and because everywhere people turned out in great numbers to pay him honor. In a society of tyranny the heads of state move in constant fear of murder, cordoned behind an army of policemen. It is the fundamental orderliness of the American society that leads Presidents to move exposed to all the people, making possible the act of a madman.

In the tragedy there is blame, surely, for negligence. In retrospect, perhaps, it was negligent of a President himself not to be aware that there are ever madmen in the world; yet it is a negligence born of courage and confidence. It was negligent of the police authorities, perhaps, not to search and cover every corner, every window, which might shield a madman; yet it was a negligence born of years of proven trust in the crowds of Americans through which Presidents have safely moved.

It was most certainly a terrible negligence on the part of the local police authorities which permitted one man to take vengeance into his own hands. It was an outrageous breach of responsibility for them to have moved a man accused of so heinous a crime in so careless a fashion. It was outrageous precisely because all the American people were themselves so outraged by the crime of assassination that anyone who knew these people ought to have known that one among them might be deranged enough to do exactly what was done.

Yet the opportunity for negligence came because here the accused was being treated as any other accused, his detention in the hands of local police, the procedures those followed for the ordinary of murders. In another land he would have been efficiently buried by a secret police in a Lubyianka prison, never again to be seen or heard of until his execution.

One might say, we suppose, that some of this negligence could be laid to all of us. It is, after all, the eager interest of the people in the persons of their leaders that brings them into open caravans, and it is the desire of the people to follow the normal ways even in murders of state that left the accused to bungling local police.

In sum, there is in all of this—let there be no mistake—much to grieve, to regret, to blame. We can't escape remorse that there are madmen in our midst, that a President is dead, that we have been denied the right to show in open court the virtue of a free society. Now we pay the price of all sorts of negligence.

But this is something different from the charge in the indictment. It is more than nonsense to say that the good people of Dallas, crowding the streets to honor a President, share a murderous guilt; or that the tragic acts of madmen cast a shadow on the whole of America. Such an indictment is vicious.

Of reasons for shame we have enough this day without adding to them a shameful injustice to a mourning people.

STATEMENT RELEASED BY CONGRESSMAN DON L. SHORT, REPUBLICAN, OF NORTH DAKOTA, IMMEDIATELY AFTER LEARNING OF THE ASSASSINATION OF JOHN FITZGERALD KENNEDY, THE PRESIDENT OF THE UNITED STATES OF AMERICA, FRIDAY, NOVEMBER 22, 1963

All sane-minded Americans are shocked at the tragedy of the assassination of the President of the United States.

Democrats and Republicans, liberals and conservatives, people of all races and creeds, deplore this tragic happening on what will be recorded as a dark day in our Nation's history.

This is the work of a demented person, as similar attempts on the lives of former Presidents and high Government officials have been in the past. Americans believe in, and have accepted since our Nation was founded, the principle of rule by law.

Forceful overthrow of government is completely un-American, and this shameful incident in our history is completely contrary to the principles by which this Nation, under God, was founded—to give men a new and permanent opportunity for freedom.

Our President has truly laid down his life in the service of his country.

TRIBUTES BY

Hon. Carlton R. Sickles

OF MARYLAND

Mr. Speaker, Mr. R. H. Gardner, of the Baltimore Sun, has written a column in which he likens our late President, John Kennedy, to the great tragic heroes of literature. His parallel is striking and moving.

I submit this column, which appeared in the Baltimore Sunday Sun on December 1, 1963.

J. F. K. IN MOLD OF CLASSIC TRAGIC HERO

(By R. H. Gardner)

Apart from all its other consequences, the assassination of President Kennedy is significant for the light it sheds on the old question of whether or not tragedy, in the classical sense, can occur within the framework of the modern world.

Opinion has generally favored the negative side of this argument because of changes, since the time of Shakespeare, in both the form of governments and attitudes concerning the nature of man.

The tragic poets, you will recall, chose kings as their heroes on the theory that a monarch's actions, affecting thousands of people, assume greater importance than those of an average man. His death has greater impact on the universe.

By spreading the king's absolute authority among a number of institutions, democracy shifted the emphasis from the leader to the system. This and the growing belief that, instead of exercising free will, man was a slave to social and psychological conditionings, undermined, on the one hand, the individual's value to the social order and, on the other, the responsibility he formerly felt for his own actions.

Thus the reason why we have no modern tragedies is that playwrights have been unable to conceive of a contemporary figure strong and noble enough to qualify as a tragic hero. In my opinion, the late President has furnished them with an example.

Surely no king in history had the power to affect the lives of more people; yet it was not the power he wielded that made men all over the world, most of whom had never met him, cry in the streets when they heard of the assassination; nor was it this power that made his death a tragedy.

The distinguished scholar, A. C. Bradley, has defined the substance of tragedy—in the Shakespearean sense, at least—as the waste of the good. The death of a "bad" President—and we've had a few—would not, it seems, constitute tragedy. But what is meant by "good"? An examination of the masterpieces of the past indicates that the term implies something more than possession of the Christian virtues.

QUALITIES OF HERO

What do the majority of tragic heroes have in common? The answer is they display a superiority deriving not so much from their positions as kings, generals and demigods as from their qualities as human beings. They have, that is to say, a superabundance of talent, the courage to put it to bold use and the willingness to shoulder responsibility for such actions even when they prove to be disastrous.

In each of these areas, President Kennedy excelled. His keen intelligence, orderly mind, philosophic outlook, historical perspective, self-confidence and high moral purpose constituted a talent for government unparalleled in our time. His confrontation with Russia over the Cuban missiles demonstrated, as no other decision could, his courage; and his statement, following the Bay of Pigs disaster, illustrated a willingness to accept responsibility even when others were at fault.

I do not mean that these were Mr. Kennedy's only attributes, no more than I mean that the above-mentioned events were his only accomplishments; but they adequately illustrate his qualifications as a tragic hero. His death, therefore, represents not only the waste of good, but in view of the pitifully small pool of first-rate talent upon which humanity depends for survival, the wanton destruction of the precious, the liquidation of man at the level of the sublime.

SENSE OF INEVITABLE

Nor is this all. The President's life and death seem to embody that peculiar sense of the inevitable the Greeks called fate.

It is unlikely the American people will ever learn the whole story of Mr. Kennedy's assassination. After almost 100 years, we still don't know the details of Lincoln's. But legend will doubtless attribute it to Lee Harvey Oswald, and it is with this legend that we must deal now.

In the Gospels, Jesus is quoted as saying that it might have been better had Judas never been born; and one might argue that from the standpoint of classical tragedy, Lee Harvey Oswald was born only so that he could commit the monstrous deed the Dallas police attribute to him.

Though, on the face of it, he and the President had nothing in common, they were inextricably linked by a bond of antithesis: Kennedy represented everything that Oswald wasn't.

Reading his story, one perceives the pathetic sordidness of Oswald's life—his childhood concern because he could not add to the income of his widowed mother, his occupancy of an apartment with her above a New Orleans pool hall, his resentment of a society that seemingly had no place for a person such as he, his conversion to Marxism, his decision (born out of desperation) to join the marines, his failure to make a name for himself in this substitute for a normal education.

Yet he learned one thing: How to put a rifle to his shoulder, squint through the sights and shoot.

COULDN'T WIN

Oswald's determination not to be just another failure was manifested in his decision to go to Russia. But even there he was just another man. So he returned—to misery. His wife was not accepted by her new countrymen and, as one who had defected to communism, he was fired from one job after another. He was defeated at every turn.

Apart from his position as the head of a state Oswald considered immoral, President Kennedy must have struck him as an intolerable symbol of a man who had everything—money, family, position, social prestige, intelligence, wit, personal attraction, a lovely wife, beautiful children.

And all Oswald had was an ability to snipe.

Thus the President's tragic flaw—if indeed it can be called that—was his consummate perfection. In a world filled, if not yet dominated, by violence and hatred, he was too good to endure.

And so he fell. And so the reverberations—shaking this mechanized, atom-haunted universe like nothing since the murder of Agamemnon.

Mr. Speaker, I would like to submit a resolution recently approved by the City Council of Baltimore. The resolution honoring President Kennedy was read and adopted on November 26, 1963.

BALTIMORE CITY COUNCIL RESOLUTION 245

(Introduced by the President and Messrs. Bonnett, Duffy, Staszak, Panuska, Prucha, Ward, Arthur, Curran, Gallagher, Pica, Dixon, Parks, Soypher, Caplan, Edelman, Rubenstein, Schaefer, Hines, Leone, and Myers, November 26, 1963 (read and adopted).)

City council resolution expressing deepest sympathies over the passing of John F. Kennedy:

"John Fitzgerald Kennedy, the 35th President of the United States, has lost his life in the service of his country.

"Millions upon untold millions of people in the United States and in the farthest regions of the earth mourn his passing. The City Council of Baltimore, voicing the heartfelt sentiments of all of our people, expresses the deep and poignant feelings of this community over a terrible and vicious deed of assassination.

"John Kennedy was a great and a good man. Young, vital, compassionate, and able, he was a leader of men and of nations. He left his imprint upon his generation and upon the world. The City Council of Baltimore records its profound sorrow at his passing.

"In the spirit of the late President, who contributed so much to the vitality of the American Republic and who would have been the first to urge that this Nation move forward despite its grief, we express also our fervent and sincere good wishes to the new President, Lyndon B. Johnson: Now, therefore, be it

"*Resolved by the City Council of Baltimore,* That the deep sorrow of every resident of Baltimore City be expressed over the untimely and shocking death of John F. Kennedy; and be it further

"*Resolved,* That the sincere good wishes of this community be sent to his successor under trying circumstances, the Honorable Lyndon B. Johnson; and be it further

"*Resolved,* That the chief clerk of the council be instructed to send copies of this resolution to Mrs. Jacqueline Bouvier Kennedy, President Lyndon B. Johnson, and each member of the Maryland delegation in the Congress of the United States; and be it further

"*Resolved,* That when this body adjourns today on November 26, 1963, it do so in honor and respect for the memory of John F. Kennedy, and in dedication to the spirit of tenacity with which this country moves forward in a time of adversity."

Mr. Speaker, November 22 was a day of infamy for all Americans when the assassin's bullet took the life of our beloved President. That night, deep in sorrow and confusion over the loss of such a great man, a young recording artist sat quietly in his room and drafted the lyrics of a song to show in his own way the depth of the tragedy he felt.

John Stewart, a member of the Kingston Trio, deserves our praise for giving his generation a "Song for a Friend," in memory of John F. Kennedy.

The lyrics are as follows:

SONG FOR A FRIEND

When you sit and wonder why things
Have gone so wrong,
And you wish someone would tell us
Where our friend has gone.

Look then to the hills when there's
Courage in the wind,
And in the face of freedom and those
Who looked to him.

And search within the heart of
Every young man with a song,
Then I think we'll know
Where our friend has gone.

Summer takes the winter as
The good years take the pain.
There will be laughter in the land again,
But hearts won't be the same.

And I know I'll remember when
A chill wind takes the sky,
And speak of years he gave us hope
For they will never die.

And as we gaze at brave young men
When yesterday's grow long,
Then I think we'll know just
Where our friend has gone.

When you sit and wonder why things
Have gone so wrong,
It's then that we'll remember
Where our friend has gone.

—JOHN STEWART.

TRIBUTES BY

Hon. Samuel S. Stratton

OF NEW YORK

Mr. Speaker, the tragic assassination of President Kennedy has dealt a heavy and tragic blow to the people of the whole country, as well as to the people of my own district.

Expressive of that sentiment in my own area of upstate New York, Mr. Speaker, is an eloquent tribute paid to our late beloved President by the Reverend Edward O'Heron, assistant pastor of St. Mary's Church in Cortland, N.Y., which I now include in the form in which it appeared in the Cortland Standard of November 25, 1963.

FATHER O'HERON'S EULOGY TO PRESIDENT

Because a eulogy of the late President delivered several times in the past 2 days by the Reverend Edward O'Heron of St. Mary's Church has been so well received, the assistant pastor was asked this morning to repeat his words at the solemn high requiem mass held at the church.

Following is his tribute to John F. Kennedy:

"Speech is always inadequate to describe the thoughts and feelings of a human being. During these sorrowful hours since the news flashed of our national tragedy in Dallas, speech is never so inadequate as it is at this time. In a way it seems almost sacrilegious to say anything. It seems that there is nothing to be done and nothing to be said except to be quiet—and to reflect—and to pray.

"At the same time, however, as human beings we are compelled to speak. We are creatures of body as well as soul. Whenever we feel deeply, whenever we love deeply, whenever we mourn deeply, our nature demands that we express ourselves, even though it be ever so inadequate.

"In the opening words of the Gospel of St. John we read the following words, 'There was a man sent from God whose name was John.' Today we Americans can well apply those words of the evangelist to the President whose death we now mourn. 'There was a man sent from God whose name was John.' In recent months we have lost two men sent from God whose names were John, the one a Pope and now a President. In some ways they were so different from each other, the one the son of a millionaire, the other the son of a peasant share-cropper. Yet at the same time they were so much alike, so dedicated to the needs of others, so sensitive to the sufferings of others.

"We will leave to the world's orators the task of eulogizing John F. Kennedy as Chief Executive or poli-tician or supreme commander. We will leave it to the historians to assess his place in history. Today we wish only to speak of John F. Kennedy as a member of the family, a member of your family, a member of my family. Just how much a part of your family he was is seen by the fact that if you had been informed on Friday after-noon of the sudden death of one of your own blood relatives, your sorrow could hardly be any deeper or any more heartfelt than it is right now at the death of Presi-dent Kennedy. One concise sentence from the news wire service summed it all up with the words, 'Everyone's bright young brother has been killed.'

"This is perhaps the greatest lesson we can learn from the life of John F. Kennedy. He has shown us that in spite of our political differences, in spite of our religious differences, we are in fact members of the same human family, we are brothers with the same Father in heaven.

"On Friday morning at a breakfast talk in Fort Worth, Tex., John F. Kennedy had this to say, 'This is a very dangerous and uncertain world—We would like to live as we once lived but history will not permit it.' He went on to say, 'No one expects that our life will be easy—certainly not in this decade and perhaps not in this century.' John F. Kennedy was right. Our life will not be easy. As we realize today how much poorer we are without him, let us also not forget to be grateful for the fact that we are so much richer for having had him with us. How he took our narrow, self-centered attitude toward life and toward other people, and broadened our vision to encompass every human being on the face of the earth. How well he has given us the lesson and the challenge of the service of God not merely through prayers but the service of God through the service of men. Perhaps it all comes down to this. As we mourn the death of a great American, a member of our family, and pray for his soul, let us not forget to include prayers of gratitude, gratitude that for us Ameri-cans in the 1960's there was a man sent from God whose name was John. May the God who he served so well give eternal peace to his valiant soul."

Mr. Speaker, under leave to extend my remarks I include an eloquent and moving resolution in tribute to our late, beloved, martyred President, John F. Kennedy, adopted last December by the City Council of the City of Oneonta, N.Y., in my congressional district.

The resolution follows:

The following resolution was offered by Alderman Kreger, who moved for its adoption, seconded by Alderman Jeffrey:

"Whereas John Fitzgerald Kennedy, the 35th President of the United States of America, has met his untimely death on November 22, 1963, at the hand of a cruel and cowardly assassin; and

"Whereas his dedication to the cause of peace and the elevation of human dignity will always be remembered by this grieving nation and the world; and

"Whereas he was a man whose private and public life was above reproach; who was sincere and equitable, honest and honorable; who was a stranger to bigotry and prejudice, and a friend of all, regardless of race, color, or creed; and

"Whereas we dedicate this meeting in memory of our martyred President, John Fitzgerald Kennedy: Now, there-fore, be it

"*Resolved,* That this council, when it adjourns tonight, do so in the name and on behalf of the city of Oneonta, and its citizens, with deep and sincere regret and in respect to the memory of John Fitzgerald Kennedy, the late President of the United States of America; and be it further

"*Resolved,* That the clerk of the city of Oneonta for-ward a copy of this resolution to Mrs. Jacqueline Kennedy, the widow of John Fitzgerald Kennedy, and, also, that a copy be forwarded to Hon. Samuel S. Stratton, Con-gressman of the 35th District of the State of New York, with a request that this resolution be made a part of the Congressional Record; and that the clerk of the city of Oneonta spread this resolution upon the minutes of this council."

Voting ayes: Alderman Coddington, Alderman Feeney, Alderman Lettis, Alderman Matthews, Alderman Jeffrey, and Alderman Kreger.

Noes: none.

Absent: none.

Resolution duly adopted.

Mr. Speaker, in these sad days as we mourn our late President John F. Kennedy, all of us treasure anything that helps to fill out the full portrait of this great leader and warm and vital friend.

Prof. John Lydenberg, of Hobart College, Geneva, N.Y., in my district, once taught a sec-tion of an English literature course at Harvard College in which President Kennedy was a stu-dent. His recollections of that experience, pub-lished in the Geneva Times on December 17, will be of interest, I believe, to every Member of this body. Under leave to extend my remarks, I in-clude herewith Professor Lydenberg's eloquent memoir and personal tribute:

PROFESSOR LYDENBERG ALSO TAUGHT JOHN KENNEDY

John F. Kennedy had many teachers and two of them happen to be from Geneva. The reminiscences of J.F.K. by Harold Klue who taught Kennedy at the Riverdale Country School appeared in the Times last week.

They brought forth another set of memories by John Lydenberg who taught Kennedy at Harvard.

Professor Lydenberg, recently elected councilman in the first ward, recalls a somewhat more grown-up Kennedy than Mr. Klue.

As a freshman, Kennedy enrolled in Professor Lydenberg's section of an English literature course.

"Yes, I taught him at Harvard," said Mr. Lydenberg yesterday, "but I'm not sure he would have remembered me. He was a good student, full of bounce and curiosity.

"His bounce was physical as well as mental. He and his great friend Glenn Frank, Jr. (I don't suppose anyone now remembers Glenn Frank, Sr., then Governor of Wisconsin and before that president of the University of Wisconsin) used to pound up the shaky stairs in the old frame house in which our section met. And I recall the two of them once vaulting together out of a window of Weld Hall to attack me for something as I was innocently loping down the steps of Widener Library.

"There was always that urge for action, with John Kennedy, as well as the mind that eagerly absorbed the information on which action should always be based.

"I bitterly mourn his passing and can only hope that we will be able to find other men with somewhere near his potential for greatness. I dearly hope that perhaps we here, in Geneva, in our homes, in our jobs, and especially in our political activity, can somehow give the Presidents-to-come more help in realizing their potential.

"If we wish to honor John Kennedy's memory, we must not simply mourn, but we must, each and every one of us, follow his lead in searching for knowledge and in finding the courage to act upon that knowledge once we've found it."

TRIBUTE BY

Hon. Leonor Kretzer Sullivan

OF MISSOURI

Mr. Speaker, in what might seem to be a most unlikely place—in a periodical devoted largely to commodity futures prices, shipping schedules, insurance actuarial developments, and other vital but prosaic commercial news—I saw today a beautiful editorial on our late President which moved me deeply. It deserves a place among the finest tributes to John F. Kennedy and among the eloquent and incisive evaluations of the significance of his life upon our national life.

The editorial appeared today in the New York Journal of Commerce. Entitled "Recessional," it calls for action by all of us—the whole Nation—to keep alive, through sacrifice and effort and even some economic strain, if necessary, the bright hopes kindled in the youth of America in these past 3 years by the young President with whom they identified so closely—what the Journal of Commerce expressively described as "that largely intangible but strangely compelling spirit that flowed through the rotunda all Sunday night."

[From the New York Journal of Commerce, Nov. 26, 1963]

RECESSIONAL

To those who could not tear themselves away from their TV screens during that desolate weekend, one thing stood out over everything else, even over the murder of the suspected assassin. It was the faces of the thousands upon thousands of ordinary Americans moving slowly past the bier in the rotunda of the Capitol—all that cold night and well into the next morning.

These were mostly the young. Students, soldiers, sailors, young mothers with children, girls who knelt and crossed themselves, in a solemn procession that seemed to have no end.

It was impossible to watch this without being deeply moved. It was impossible to watch it without grasping its meaning. These young people—some stoic, some dabbing at their eyes, some preoccupied with cleaning their glasses—had a deep sense of identification with John F. Kennedy. He had fired them with enthusiasm and imagination. He was one of them and he was dead.

We think it vital that these young people should retain this sense of identification. The bright hopes kindled among them these past 3 years should not be dashed or diluted. They should not be made to feel that only when all other matters have been disposed of—economic and otherwise—will their future be given serious thought.

In a decade those who are now 20 will be 30; those who are 30 will be 40. This is the body of the whole Nation. It is worth some sacrifice, some extra effort, even some economic strain, if necessary, to keep alive that largely intangible but strangely compelling spirit that flowed through the rotunda all Sunday night.

TRIBUTE BY

Hon. Robert Taft, Jr.

OF OHIO

Mr. Speaker, it has come to my attention that the Ohio State University Young Republican Club adopted a very fitting and appropriate memorial statement on the assassination of President Kennedy. In order that others may share it, I am including it in my remarks today.

STATEMENT ON THE DEATH OF PRESIDENT JOHN FITZGERALD KENNEDY

1. The Young Republican Club of the Ohio State University expresses its profound grief at the dastardly assassination of President John Fitzgerald Kennedy.

2. The President of the United States is President of all the people, of all parties, and of every persuasion sanctioned by the rule of law. As Chief Magistrate he bears in his person the greatness and purpose of the Republic. The hand raised against him was raised not only against us all, but against that which makes our Union sacred and enduring.

3. The nobility of our form of government is equaled only by its difficulty. The President must at the same time be an effective leader of a party, and one who commands loyalties beyond party. Mr. Kennedy possessed to an extraordinary degree the quality which engendered friendship and respect even in the midst of highly partisan politics. He bore the dignity of his high office with a modesty and grace which reflected the best traditions of his great predecessors. He will long be mourned and long remembered.

Be it resolved that this statement be sent with our deepest sympathy to Mrs. John F. Kennedy.

Be it also resolved that copies of this statement be forwarded to the press.

On behalf of the Ohio State University Young Republican Club.

WILLIAM O. MARTIN,
President.

TRIBUTES BY

Hon. Albert Thomas

OF TEXAS

Mr. Speaker, under leave to extend my remarks I include the following:

AN ODE TO JOHN FITZGERALD KENNEDY, 35TH PRESIDENT OF THE UNITED STATES

(By Breckenridge Porter, Jr.)

In his heart a passion lived
That the world might be more amative.
Love of man his main concern;
Peace he spake, hate he spurned.
Throughout the world he made his plea,
For peace on earth, and unity.
And from those countries he traveled home,
Only to fall among his own.
Now our peoples are coterie,
And Heaven is the resting place, for
John Fitzgerald Kennedy.

Mr. Speaker, under unanimous consent, I include the following poem written by my distinguished constituent, Mr. Fizer M. Noe, of

Houston, Tex. This is a most moving tribute to our late beloved President John F. Kennedy:

OUR FALLEN HERO

Cold lies the wreath upon the snow.
　Beneath it a form smolders to dust.
Our fallen hero's life is spent;
　His soul lives on among the just.

Life's battle now is fought and won;
　In each conflict he was brave and strong.
An assassin's bullet cut him down;
　He lies a hero uncrowned, renowned.

He battled here for peace.
　Walked head high, with firm sure power;
Self-giving, poured life and love
　Into each passing hour.

Like the Chief Guardian of his soul
　Was told of impending danger;
He steadfastly set his face toward Dallas
　And in triumph rode her streets no stranger.

Our First Fair Lady by his side,
　Shared each moment with equal pride.
Tall, straight and strong;
　He cowered not before any wrong.

He lived and died, not in vain;
　Help us our Father in Thy Name,
That in the end we shall give back to Thee
　A life well spent for God and man!

A white wreath lies upon the glistening snow;
　Beneath our Chieftain's body goes back to dust.
The eternal why? screams for reply;
　God made us; He is just!

—Fizer Montague Noe.

TRIBUTE BY

Hon. Herman Toll

OF PENNSYLVANIA

Mr. Speaker, Rabbi Meir Lasker of Temple Judea Congregation, which is in my district in Philadelphia, delivered an unusual sermon in memory of John Fitzgerald Kennedy on Friday evening, November 22, the day that our late President was shot.

The sermon is so outstanding that I have included it for the Members to read:

SERMON DELIVERED FRIDAY EVENING, NOVEMBER 22, 1963, IN MEMORY OF JOHN FITZGERALD KENNEDY

Friends, I know that all of us were stunned beyond words at the tragic events of today. The startling echo of the phrases coming over the radios "the President has been shot," "the President of the United States is dead," still rings in my ears, and I am certain in your ears as well, and it has left all of us shaken and bewildered. Is there any real American in our midst whose soul is not now numbed, whose heart is not now mired in the valley of the shadow of death?

A fearful emptiness fills our being as our seared spirits cry out "Why?"

Here was a young man, gifted, educated to the concept of democracy. Whether we concurred with all of his ideas and ideals—or whether we failed to go along with them in part or in entirety—is of little consequence at the moment. All of us realized, and I am certain all of us sympathized with the tremendous tasks he faced, the heavy burdens he carried, and the innumerable crises that John F. Kennedy was confronted with.

He had a dream—this youthful President of ours, a wondrous magnificent dream—to bring America a little bit closer to the realization of the ideals set by the Founding Fathers of this country "that all men were created equal." He had a dream—that all men, regardless of tint of skin or race, or nationality or creed—might walk with dignity under the protection of the flag of our country. He had a dream—that all would be equal before the law both in the North and the South, in the East and the Western sections of our land. For this he lived, for this he fought, and because of this he was assassinated. And as I contemplate this tragedy, I can only say: "You, John F. Kennedy, the President of the United States, you unremittingly fulfilled the words of our sage Rabbi Tarfon: 'It is not incumbent upon you to complete the tasks'—but begin it you did—and others will pick up the bloody banner that fell from your hands so suddenly—and carry it to victory.

"For the dreamer dies—but never the dream
  Though death shall call the whirlwind to his aid
  Enlist men's passions, and trick their hearts with hate.
  Still shall the vision live."

Friends, I am certain that all of us tonight are engulfed with memories, emotions, thoughts. For this moment is not a sorrowful moment for Mrs. Kennedy alone—who lost her husband, nor for the Kennedy family who lost a son and a brother—but it is a moment of grief and soul searching for 180 million Americans. For in our hearts, we know, that we cannot throw the entire guilt upon the head of the young assassin, nor even upon the shoulders of the white council groups—who undoubtedly influenced, by their corrupt standards, this irrational act.

For in truth we are all somewhat responsible, all of us should proclaim "Hotonu"—we too have sinned in this—that we have sat by silently for days and weeks and years—permitting such conditions to develop—that lawlessness was bound to raise its ugly head.

If the death of our President is to have any meaning—and his life and blood that was shed—be not in vain—it should sound the alarm for us with new urgency. It should awaken us—shock us into the realization that we must act—and act now—not tomorrow—not next month and not next year, but now, that the lawlessness that has engulfed our Nation, the false concepts of first and second class citizens—superior and inferior citizen—may for all time be destroyed and vanish from the shores of our land.

Yes. I believe that John F. Kennedy had a dream. He was raised to the noble position of Presidency of the United States not merely because of the honor it entailed, but because he felt with and for the peoples of this land; the poor, the aged, the down-trodden. And because he sympathized with their hunger and their needs, he strived to initiate legislation that would aid them. Slum clearance, aid to students, and medicare. Having seen the crises that engulfed other nations, where the common man was neglected, he strived to stave this off in the country he loved. For this he was abused, for this he was hated, for this too, he died.

Time after time he called upon the American people to awaken from their lethargy; to meet the challenging needs of our time—but we, as a people, failed to rise to the challenge—we lagged behind, our Congress and Senate lagged behind—but I suspect that this bloody orgy—which struck today—may awaken us—that we must act now.

Here was a man, a real man—father of children—who shared with many parents the terrible fear, the haunting dread, that the nuclear arms race, unless quietly arrested, would doom us all.

And because of his position as President of the United States, he saw clearly what horrors might strike our civilization at any moment and blow our world out of existence. He strived to bring about a little light in the gloomy darkness—through a nuclear test ban. He hoped, as we all prayed, that we and our children and our children's children might live out our lives in peace—with none to make us afraid.

And now—he who sought peace for us—lies dead—dead by the bullet of an assassin. Shall we now fail him?

I should like to close with words paraphrased from the poet. Words that the spirit of John F. Kennedy, a martyr of our Nation, may ask us:

"What will you do with the world that I died for to make new
  With the strength and the beauty of life—and its Valor—
  What will you do
  Will you lead out of bondage the captives—
  Or fetter mankind?"

Rabbi Meir Lasker.

TRIBUTE BY

Hon. James W. Trimble

OF ARKANSAS

Mr. Speaker, I have this eulogy delivered by Maj. Gen. Teddy H. Sanford, commander at Fort Chaffee, Ark., in the district which I am honored to represent, at the memorial services held at Fort Chaffee on Monday, November 25, 1963, for our late President, John F. Kennedy.

GENERAL'S EULOGY

We the military of Fort Chaffee are gathered here this afternoon, with our friends and neighbors of this community, in the presence of God, to pay our last respects to our late Commander in Chief.

John Fitzgerald Kennedy is dead, cut down by an assassin's bullet—an act that has outraged decent men everywhere.

Mr. Kennedy brought to the head of our Government all the essential attributes of a great leader.

He was first of all a man of deep religious faith.

He brought to the White House not only the physical courage he had proven in combat, but also a great moral courage, so essential in the man who must make decisions.

Although he himself was born with wealth and high position, he brought with him a real concern for the average man, and the underprivileged everywhere.

He had an intimate knowledge of the world and its great problems.

He was a man of wisdom and peace and as our new President has said of him "he molded and moved the power of our Nation in the service of a world of growing liberty and order."

He did not shrink from his responsibilities but welcomed them.

He also brought with him a sense of humor, so essential to one shouldered with great responsibility.

His inaugural address was one of the greatest; lines from it have been quoted over and over again and they will be quoted for decades to come. Like the one in which he said, "Ask not what your country can do for you, ask what you can do for your country."

He upheld the faith of our fathers, which is freedom of all men. He broadened the frontier of that faith, and backed it with energy and courage.

Mr. Kennedy said in his inaugural address, "The energy, the faith, the devotion which we bring to this endeavor will light our country and all who serve it—and the glow from that fire can truly light the world."

History will be much kinder to Mr. Kennedy than we have been.

He shall live in song and story as long as man remains free.

We pray that God shall continue to shed His grace on this Nation as He has so generously in the past.

With God's help we shall pick ourselves up from this great national tragedy and shame, and move forward to new heights, and as Mr. Kennedy said "light the world."

We of the military have not only lost our Commander in Chief, we have, also, lost a great champion. He not only understood military power as an instrument in world politics, he also understood the men and women of the services who constitute that power. He supported their aspiration for a more equal sharing of the privileges of citizenship in this great Nation.

Now that he has been relieved of command and of the great burdens placed upon him, not only by this Nation, but by the whole free world, may he rest in peace.

For his widow and children, his mother and father, and all his loved ones, we pray that God in His mysterious way will bring peace to their broken hearts.

TRIBUTES BY

Hon. Al Ullman

OF OREGON

Mr. Speaker, the comment by Emmet John Hughes in this week's Newsweek needs no comment. I include it at this point:

AN ECHO IN THE SILENCE

(By Emmet John Hughes)

He belonged uniquely to us—to this time and place, to this Nation and generation—and to no other. In all history, what else could he have been, where else be seen, and when else be heard? A Hapsburg prince or a Bourbon sovereign? A minister to Victoria plotting designs of empire? A German Chancellor fretfully patching the Weimar Republic? Or some earlier American President slackly presiding over the 1920's? Each weird image confirms how wholly and how rightly he found his home in this—our—generation. He was ours as the first President to be born in this tempest of our century—to glimpse life during the First World War, to bear the ordeal of the Second, and to fight back the darkness of a Third. Sometimes it happens so: the instant of history and the instinct of the man appear almost to plot their meeting with secretly timed precision. So it seems with us. We were clearly meant to be together, for this while. And this is why the assassin, as he put a bullet in his brain, also put a scar upon our generation.

He did not find this place with us, of course, because he won universal assent and applause. He won something more important: a recognition of his person and his force. A student of history, he often quoted its earlier scanners, like Edmund Burke, to depict his own nation: "We sit on a 'conspicuous stage,' and the whole world marks our demeanor." And his demeanor indeed was so marked—down to the thrust of a finger and the flash of a smile. A student of the Presidency, too, he repeated the challenge of Woodrow Wilson: "The President is at liberty, both in law and conscience, to be as big a man as he can." We shall never know the laws this President might have signed. But we can be aware of the size of the man.

He cannot yet be measured, and he may never be measured, by the crises or debates that seemed—for fierce, fleeting moments—to stir his Presidency—steel prices and medical care, Peace Corps and "managed news," tax reform and test ban, missiles in Cuba and troops to Alabama. Now, all that he did and all that his death left undone seem to matter far less than what he knew—and felt—of himself and of his country.

He understood the Presidency. There was quiet proof of it on one occasion last year—with his formal White House dinner to honor 49 Nobel Prize winners. He warmly hailed the assembled poets and physicists and dramatists, peacemakers and mathematicians. He saluted them as "the most extraordinary collection * * * of human knowledge that has ever been gathered at the White House—with the possible exception of when

Thomas Jefferson dined alone." And so he let them know that he discerned the rare sign of Presidential greatness: the steady power to be, to believe, and to decide—alone.

He sensed the cruel paradoxes of democratic leadership, thus dismaying zealots and exasperating simplifiers. He knew a leader must summon his people to be with him—yet stand above, not squat beside, them. He knew that he must try to be resolute without being arrogant, patient without being timid, and compassionate without being maudlin. He detested cant but delighted in eloquence. He could appeal for conciliation without forswearing power. And he could respect ideas without confusing them with deeds, exhort action without unharnessing it from reason, and esteem words without becoming infatuated with his own.

He belonged uniquely to us—above all—in his joyful passion for political life. For by this he proved he knew the root and genius of his Nation. He knew it to be conceived and dedicated—not to the propagation of such faiths as once came out of Israel, nor the fostering of the arts of a new Greece, nor the spread of sovereignty in the way of ancient Rome—but to the matchless political art of governing men in freedom. And so he knew, too, that his Nation was born not of an accident of history but of an act of intelligence: the triumph of men who studied seriously, spoke articulately, wrote fearlessly, debated rationally, and concluded—intelligently.

He strove to do as they. And he had some of this on his mind and ready for his utterance as he met death. The speech he never would deliver warned against hucksters of "seemingly swift and simple solutions." He was ready to deplore the confusion of rhetoric with reality and the plausible with the possible. And he would firmly insist: "America's leadership must be guided by the lights of learning and reason."

He took lively pride in his native Massachusetts, of course, and its men of greatness. So his ear and his wit always and easily recognized the voice of the rebel of Concord, Henry David Thoreau. And he almost surely would have shared the philosopher's judgment, pertinent perhaps even to his own tragedy: "Better a monosyllabic life than a ragged and muttered one. Let its report be short and round like a rifle, so that it may hear its own echo in surrounding silence."

He leaves—lastingly—such an echo.

Mr. Speaker, across the Nation, and throughout the world, American citizens are still deeply mourning the loss of our President, John F. Kennedy. A poet constituent has written to express his feelings; one of his poems I wish to insert at this point in my remarks:

TO THE MEMORY OF PRESIDENT KENNEDY

He was guided, by a star unseen,
    And reached a height of fame;
And captivated the hearts of the world
    That very few attain.

His life was a testimony,
    For his love, of his country,
A hero, both in peace and war,
    This we all could see.

This was indeed a good man,
    Of courage and too of restraint;
He knew not conceit, nor intolerance,
    Always giving his energy and strength.

He typified the American mood,
    And the spirit of our day;
Guided by the unseen star,
    He never knew dismay.

He gave his life for his country,
    That a lesson to teach;
That we should go forward.
    And a higher goal to reach.

Hate has taken him from us,
    But ever let that shining light;
Point to an eternal pathway
    That will lead us from the night.
                        —*Charlie Hess.*
Klamath Falls, Oreg.

TRIBUTE BY

Hon. Lionel Van Deerlin

OF CALIFORNIA

Mr. Speaker, each of us has responded in his own way to the shocking event of November 22. One of my constituents in the city of La Mesa, Calif., sent me some especially moving poetry which seeks to suggest the magnitude of our loss in the death of President Kennedy.

Author of the following lines is Mrs. Linda Hurley, of 6155 Dalhart Street, La Mesa, Calif.:

ON THE DEATH OF JOHN F. KENNEDY

Out of west Texas
The Texas of Neiman-Marcus
Of oil wells and limousines
And barons without castles
And long-horned critters
Came the thunderbolt—the silver sliver
In the November noonday
The bullet that felled
The man who was humanity
To a city called Berlin
And a city called Saigon
And a score of other cities
In every latitude and longitude
Of every magnitude and multitude.

And humanity wept
The children wept
And the bankers wept
And the statesmen wept
Rivers of tears,
To wash away
The blood the bullet brought
The bullet in the brain of the man whose name was Hope.
Weep not for him, but weep for me
And for all the funny letter-words like NATO, SEATO,
       and U.N.,
And for the black-skinned people
And the white-skinned people
And the slant-eyed people
For the people of the cross and
The people of the star with six points.
Wrap the coffin in the red, white, and blue flag
That was his banner.
Let this be his shroud
Sound the salute not with cannon
Sound it instead with his own ringing words
For his words were hope
And his way was truth
And his manner was bold and his gift was manifold.
It did not belong to him—
The life the madman took.
It belonged, in part, to me
For I am an American
And he was my President.
He was not the President of the man who killed him for
      he was no real American—
Just some sick, sad, soul,
Some self-appointed Judas
With a mind incompetent
To comprehend
Even the ugly theory he embraces
And should he die a million deaths
And each with endless agony
He could not repay the loss
Nor could he heal the wound.
Oh, what is justice now.
The only justice is the future
And the burden we all bear
To mold our world as
Would the man we mourn.
So let us do our mourning
As we build
Our moaning as we plan
Our monument of living, acting faith
To this man who left his mark
Upon our land.
You cannot bury a soul
You cannot murder an ideal.
You cannot assassinate man's will to be free.
You cannot kill us all.
I love my bleeding
Nation even more.

In mourning there is solidarity
In dedication there is
Resolute strength
To mold the future with
Integrity
For words remembered
Shout their living challenge
And death gives way to martyrdom.
The only vengeance for
This grievous hour
Is what our Nation is
And will become.

TRIBUTE BY

Hon. Charles L. Weltner

OF GEORGIA

Mr. Speaker, I recently received a copy of a resolution by the De Kalb County Democratic Executive Committee, expressing its sorrow and loss at the death of our late President. I submit this resolution as follows:

A RESOLUTION ADOPTED BY THE DE KALB COUNTY DEMO- CRATIC EXECUTIVE COMMITTEE IN MEETING HELD DECEMBER 4, 1963

Whereas the assassination of President John F. Kennedy on November 22, 1963, has shocked the people of this State and Nation; and

Whereas President Kennedy had become a significant world leader and a capable President of the United States; and

Whereas he was the leader of the Democratic Party; and

Whereas the people of Georgia had given him overwhelming support in his campaign for election as President; and

Whereas his leadership in life has been lost to the people of Georgia, the United States and the world: Now, therefore, be it

Resolved by the De Kalb County Democratic Executive Committee, That our profound feeling of sorrow and of sympathy be communicated to his family and furthermore, that our appreciation for the outstanding services of John F. Kennedy, in war and in peace, is hereby expressed by the members of this committee; and be it further

Resolved, That a copy of this resolution be spread upon the minutes of this committee and that a copy be transmitted to Mrs. Jacqueline Kennedy.

KELSEY HOWINGTON,
Chairman.
Mrs. HARRY B. WILLIAMS, Jr.,
Secretary.

TRIBUTES BY

Hon. Basil L. Whitener

OF NORTH CAROLINA

Mr. Speaker, Rev. Albert Ambrose, pastor of the First Baptist Church at Drexel, N.C., recently delivered a very fine sermon during a memorial service arranged by the Burke County, N.C., Ministers Association for the late President John F. Kennedy. I believe there is a lesson in Reverend Ambrose's message for all of us, and I include it in my remarks.

AN ATMOSPHERE FOR MURDER

(By Rev. Albert Ambrose, Pastor, First Baptist Church of Drexel)

(EDITOR'S NOTE.—The following is from a memorial service at Calvary Lutheran Church, arranged by the Burke County Ministers Association, for a national day of mourning over the assassination of President John F. Kennedy.)

President Johnson has proclaimed that today shall be a day of mourning for our country.

In these few moments I would like for us to consider what comes after today. Will we spend today in mourning and then tomorrow it will be back to business as usual. We may try to do this, but we can't.

We can't hide our heads in the sand, and like the watchman of the night cry out all is well, and think that by our saying it that it is.

All is not well. Our failure to deal with the pressing problems of our day has created an atmosphere in which all things are possible. We go over the last several months and we find the groundwork for the sort of thing that happened in Dallas on Friday. The murder of a man whose only crime was standing up for his people. The murder of four young girls whose only crime was going to Sunday school. The shameful display that took place in and outside a hearing room in our Nation's Capital at the questioning of those who made an illegal visit to Cuba. The incident, also in Dallas, that surrounded the visit of our Ambassador to the U.N.

When people ask how can this happen, that our President can be assassinated, look back and you can see how.

As we look back we also need to look ahead. Do you see an America growing in strength, prestige, influence, and usefulness, or do we see an America increasingly wracked by violence, and disorder? The boys thought they would play a joke on the wise old man of the village. One held a bird in his hand. "Is the bird alive or dead." The wise man answered "As you will." It is all up to you. It is up to our people.

It is up to us to decide whether we shall let the hate-mongers and the apostles of violence continue to pour into the bloodstream of the life of America their poison. Shall we let the disciples of prejudice and class hatred have an influence far out of keeping with their number and which is far different from that which is held by a majority of our people.

What will the good people of our church do? Will we remain silent as, by and large, we have done, or will we seek to know the mind of the Lord. This is not the time to sit back and watch the world plunge into oblivion. This is the time for a moral and spiritual revolution that will shake the foundation of this land. It is the time for God's people to stand, to throw off the shackles of complacency and indifference. It is the time to put on the whole armor of God, and stand in the evil day.

Let our day of mourning also be a day of repentance. All of us share in the guilt of the slayer of our President. All of us share in the guilt of Jack Ruby. The Bible says "blessed is the Nation whose God is the Lord."

The Bible also says "If My people which are called by My name will humble themselves and pray, and turn from their wicked way, then I will hear from heaven, and I will heal their land."

Our only hope today is in God. But our hope in God must be expressed in terms of vital relationship with the living Lord, with Jesus Christ. To know Christ is to know God, and to know God aright is life eternal.

To know Christ is also to be committed to the struggle against the forces of evil. It is a battle, it is a life and death conflict, and the stakes are the souls of men.

Paul writes in Roman 13: 11 words that are especially fitting for our day:

"And this, knowing the season, that already it is time for you to awake out of sleep; for now is salvation nearer to us than when we first believed. The night is far spent, and the day is at hand; let us therefore cast off the works of darkness, and let us put on the armour of light: Let us walk becomingly as in the day; not in revelling and drunkenness, not in chambering and wantonness, not in strife and jealousy. But put ye on the Lord Jesus Christ, and make not provision for the flesh to fulfill the last thereof.

"Encamped along the hills of light, ye Christian soldiers rise, and press the battle ere the night shall veil the glowing skies. Against the foe in vales below let all our strength be hurled. Faith is the victory we know that overcomes the world.

"On every hand the foe we find draws up in dread array. Let tents of ease be left behind and onward to the fray. Salvation's helmet on each head, with truth all girt about. The earth shall tremble 'neath our tread and echo with our shout.

"Faith is the victory that overcomes the world."

I would like to read for you a poem, a tribute to John F. Kennedy, by Timothy Brendle, a young member of my church.

"(By Timothy T. Brendle)

"A clip is hooked, a chain is pulled
  And then a flag unfurls,
Half ascended, half descended,
  A message to the world.

"A volley sounds, and then again
  The sound lifts o'er and o'er.
A statesman from our midst departed
  Through life's immortal door.

"A family weeps, a nation mourns,
  But time erodes the pain.
And for the deeds he's done so well
  His country gives due fame.

"But onward time will go marching
  And praises will subside.
For in the shadow of his greatness
  The Nation's grief we hide.

"Will we really e'er forget him,
  Who served us day by day
By doing his best to master
  The task that came his way?

"Our Country often found great strength
  In his desire to serve
And now, in death, his challenge rings:
  'Go on and Peace preserve.' "

Mr. Speaker, on Friday, December 13, 1963,
Dr. Harry M. Moffett, pastor of the First Presbyterian Church, Gastonia, N.C., delivered a
memorial to the late President, John Fitzgerald
Kennedy. The occasion on which this address
was delivered was the annual dinner of the
Gaston County Democratic Party.

The memorial address was so impressive that
many of our friends have suggested that it should
be made available to the public. I concur in this
thought and, therefore, include it.

A MEMORIAL TO JOHN FITZGERALD KENNEDY

I accepted the invitation to offer this memorial because
I have long wanted to express, however clumsily, something of my faith and my conviction about our American
democratic process. These opinions and this faith have
been a part of my personal philosophy since long before
John Fitzgerald Kennedy became a public figure. However, in his experience in the Presidency many of my concerns and convictions about the conflicts, the tensions, the
challenges that are America came to light.

Any man who attains the world's highest and most
powerful office of leadership, the American Presidency,
can only achieve it by passing through the turbulent
channel of the American two-party political system.
There is no other way to the American Presidency save
this one, and it is a demanding and stormy path.

Our constitutional democratic Republic with its rights
and privileges—its high possibilities for human achievement—rests upon two equally important and essential but,
eternally conflicting, principles of political truth.

One is the right of private ownership of property and
the principle of the right to profit from one's labor and the
use of one's talent. Without this basic right, and this
unassailable principle, the stability, strength, and preservation of this great Nation cannot endure.

Equally essential to our way of life and our national
greatness is the second principle which is the right of all
citizens to life, liberty, and the pursuit of happiness. The
principles of equality before the law, and of freedom to
enjoy all the privileges and rights of American citizenship
that we can earn, whatever one's economic, racial, religious, or social background is inherent in our Constitution,
in our national ideals, in our popular assumptions, and
through all our history has been constantly pressuring for
fuller achievement and development in this land.

In every citizen, in every community, in every county
and State, in both political parties, the conflict between the
claims of property rights and privileges, as against the
extension or protection of personal rights and individual
liberties is in constant tension and debate—and this tension, I believe, to be the major source of our strength, our
progress, and our liberties.

No man can emerge as President of this country until
he has been subjected to all the practical pressures, the
sectional schisms, the public partisanship that creates the
fierce intraparty strife and political warfare that is inherent in our system.

No man can emerge from this fierce fight without being
marked and scarred by the ordeal through which he has
passed. Nor can he assume the gigantic responsibilities
of high office with the full support and assurance of the
Nation behind him. The very toughness of the pragmatic political battle that brought him victory raises question among many Americans as to the readiness of his
mind, his spirit, sometimes even his deep commitment to
the great ideals and principles that are imbedded in our
Nation's strength and unity.

John Fitzgerald Kennedy, youngest man to attain this
office, first of his religious faith, son of a wealthy and
powerful family, reared in privilege, and popularly believed to have been groomed for his achievement by an
ambitious father, entered his high office with more than
the usual burden of public doubt, fear and hostility bearing
down upon him.

Moreover, he took office in a period of awesome, terrifying world crisis and deep domestic discord.

Over a billion people of varying degrees of unreadiness
have shaken off serfdom, revolted against poverty and
indignity, and are crying for liberty and equality. In this
revolutionary age, confronted by a formidable ideology
embodied in two fanatically ambitious nations, John Kennedy faced the awesome task of identifying this Nation of
overwhelming power and wealth with the hunger and
need of a confused world being tempted by false promises
of social justice and freedom from Communist powers bent
on totalitarian world domination. In an age where he

had, at his command, enough destructive power to destroy civilization; in an age in which war is a horror not to be contemplated by rational men; with courage, vision and determination, he set out to strengthen his country's world leadership, to bring hope and help to bewildered humanity, and to confront, control, and conquer the ambitions of the Communist world by working toward some far distant but necessary world order of nations, while at the same time strengthening and expanding our national military might and security.

For his sensitivity to the new demands and terrible challenges of this new nuclear and space age, for conscientious statesmanship and courageous leadership in behalf of our great democracy, I give him honor and respect.

He inherited at home many formidable tasks. The most controversial, the most explosive, the source of the greatest and most dangerous disunity, was the critical struggle over the expansion of civil rights to a historically, discriminated against, racial minority. Held in subtle bondage to poverty, through limited educational and economic opportunity and discriminatory laws, their plight is supported by a vast complex of entrenched fears and privilege, of submerged guilt and open hate; of deep frustrations and accepted prejudices. Here, in this conflict, the fundamental principles of our constitutional democratic government are locked in a deadly struggle in which, not only our national respect for law, order, and justice, but our influence and leadership of the peoples and nations struggling for life and liberty, in our world is in serious jeopardy.

While I do not for one moment ask, or demand your entire approval of his approach to this problem, I am confident you will join me in honoring his courage and his commitment to the basic, but difficult, principles and ideals of our American dedication to liberty and justice for all men everywhere, as he saw them, and for his willingness to risk his political future in a bold confrontation of the problem, for he sought to create through law an area in legal and civil justice by which he hoped, I believe, to establish an atmosphere in which the subtle, more personal and intangible difficulties of racial desegregation could be confronted and adjusted in peace and order.

I would honor the memory of this man because I came to see in him an expression of, what I believe to be, a priceless and essential factor in the maintenance of our liberty and strength. He gave every evidence of being a devout, sincere, adherent of his religious faith who believed himself responsible to God for his conduct and life. He was loyal to his church and to his creed. At the same time, he was equally and fully committed to the vital American principle of religious liberty and the separation of church and state.

I respect him and honor his memory because of the way he conducted himself before the press, the public, and the world at large.

He was acutely aware of the presence around him of hate, vituperation, and vicious fanaticism, and of the ever-lurking possibility of death, yet he always bore himself with courage and courtesy, with consideration and honor.

He personified his faith in freedom, his confidence in his countrymen, his openness to the world about him, by the abandon with which he exposed himself, with the minimum protection, to the mercy of people wherever he went. This cost him his life, and it cost his country and the political party represented here their elected leader.

If, however, from the stunning shock of these events, there emerges a fresh awareness of the burdens, responsibilities, and demands of political leadership in our country in this revolutionary new era—

If, among all reasonable citizens of this land, there is awakened a new understanding of the need for honest, forthright, courageous debate on the part of partisans of differing public and private interests but at the same time a condemnation and repudiation of vituperation, of threats, of malicious unsupported attacks on the integrity and loyalty of those we oppose—

If, at last, we awaken to the vital importance of personal and community standards of high moral integrity, of respect for law and the rights of others, of need for protecting and encouraging responsible character and conduct in all our people and in all our affairs—

Then I am confident that not only the memory of this slain President, but all that is honorable, decent, just, and deeply and profoundly American in his faith, his philosophy, and his conduct of his office will live on to strengthen and enrich the dynamic stream of our democracy and the world leadership of this great Nation.

TRIBUTE BY

Hon. John W. Wydler

OF NEW YORK

Mr. Speaker, among the many fine tributes paid to our late President was one contained in remarks delivered at a memorial service for John F. Kennedy on November 25, 1963, by Rabbi Ralph P. Kingsley of the Garden City Jewish Center in Garden City, N.Y.

I believe these words are of importance and would be of interest to the Members of Congress.

REMARKS DELIVERED AT A MEMORIAL SERVICE FOR JOHN F. KENNEDY, NOVEMBER 25, 1963

For 3 days now I have wept and cried, as have many of us. I have wept and cried not only because a human being has died—for all humans must ultimately meet with death. I have wept and cried because the symbol of a new America, a new America which is really the pristine America, which our Biblically inspired founders had conceived, has been, at least temporarily, removed. For John F. Kennedy embodied so much of what our Founding Fathers brought to this land. Most important perhaps (and I quote here from the inaugural address) was "the belief that the rights of man come not from the generosity of the state, but from the hand of God." In other words, the state is the guarantor, not the giver of human rights. To the very end this was his concept—spelled out again in the quotation from Psalms with which he would have concluded his talk in Dallas on that fateful Friday afternoon:

"Except the Lord build the house, they labor in vain that built it: Except the Lord build the city, the watchman waketh but in vain."

We have had many church-going Presidents, but it has been a long time since we have had such a deeply religious President, in the profoundest meaning of the word "religious."

His every thought and act was pervaded by a commitment to a power which transcended the individual person, and even state. It was to this power we call God, that he pledged his allegiance. America (specifically, this generation of Americans) was in his eyes, to use the vocabulary of the Bible, God's instrument in bringing to pass the cherished dreams of the religious visionaries of the past. In like manner to the prophets of old, who spoke of Israel as being an אור לגוים John F. Kennedy spoke of America as being a light to the world. In speaking of our role as defenders of freedom, he said again in his inaugural address, "The energy, the faith, the devotion which we bring to this endeavor will light our country and all who serve it—and the glow from that fire can truly light the world." This was a religious concept. America had a divinely ordained task.

More than anything else the life of this man, and all that he stood for, was pervaded by a deeply religious fervor and conviction which overflowed, and which made itself felt. He made me proud to be an American when much that happened here had made me ashamed. Through his leadership, through the framework of modern liberalism, he sought to achieve the dream of our Founding Fathers.

We have asked ourselves again and again: what if this man had been given length of days; what might he have done? We wonder why one so young, so courageous, so full of vision and energy, had to meet so untimely an end?

We answer, that history is not determined by what might have been, but by what was and is. We answer that not the length of days, but their fullness, not the amount of years, but the accomplishments during those years, are what matters. A colleague of mine has said: "A bullet can end a man's life, but not his philosophy." To this I add, a bullet can prevent a man from doing more. It cannot destroy what he has done.

The legacy that John Kennedy has given us is ours to keep. Surely it will not—we must not let it—follow him to the grave. While he lived, John F. Kennedy was filled with a deep faith—a faith in the full potential of American democracy; a faith in man's ability to bring about a world in which there is peace and liberty; a faith in the ultimate triumph of truth and justice over the forces of evil; a faith in man's reasoning capacity, to help him solve the problems facing our world.

In his death, that faith to which he was so deeply committed, falls to us—to you, to me, to uphold. Not by more violence, but through the process of law and order; not by disillusionment and despair, but by yet greater commitment and dedication to freedom and to the pursuit of peace; not by eyes blinded by distrust and fear, but by yet greater vision and hope, must we carry on the task he left us.

And so, we conclude with those same words he spoke so movingly less than 3 years ago:

Finally—whether you are citizens of America or citizens of the world, ask of us here the same high standards of strength and sacrifice which we ask of you. With a good conscience our only sure reward, with history the final judge of our deeds, let us go forth to lead the land we love, asking His blessing and His help, but knowing that here on earth God's work must truly be our own.

INDEX

Addresses and Tributes in the Senate of the United States

George D. Aiken, of Vermont, address, 10

Gordon Allott, of Colorado, address, 196

Clinton P. Anderson, of New Mexico:
  Address, 14
  Requiem, poem by Jenie Burke, Jal, N. Mex., 563
  This Day, poem by Emma Lee McLeod, Los Alamos, N. Mex., 562

E. L. Bartlett, of Alaska:
  Address, 153
  Letter from Richard Gillam, Stuttgart, Germany, 638

Birch Bayh, of Indiana, address, 178

J. Glenn Beall, of Maryland:
  Address, 181
  Poem by Joseph F. Spalla, Baltimore, Md., 622
  Poem by Miss Diane Love, "And in a Moment It Was No More," 622

Wallace F. Bennett, of Utah, address, 194

Alan Bible, of Nevada:
  Address, 54
  Editorials from—
    Boulder City (Nev.) News, 63
    Carson City (Nev.) Appeal, 60
    Elko (Nev.) Daily Free Press, 59
    Elko (Nev.) Independent, 59
    Gardnerville (Nev.) Record-Courier, 64
    Hawthorne (Nev.) Independent-News, 58
    Henderson (Nev.) Home News, 63
    KOLO–TV Station, Reno, Nev., 64
    Las Vegas (Nev.) Review-Journal, 61
    Paradise Press, Las Vegas, Nev., 58
    Reno (Nev.) Nevada State Journal, 61
    Wells (Nev.) Progress, 61
    Yerington (Nev.) Mason Valley News, 61
  Eulogy by J. G. Earl, Moapa Valley High School, Overton, Nev., 55
  Eulogy by Joseph P. Trodd, Chaplain, U.S. Navy, at Dulce Nombre de Maria Cathedral, Agana, Guam, 56
  Letter from Charles K. Pulsipher, Moapa Valley Schools, 56
  Proclamation and statement by Manuel F. L. Guerrero, Governor of Guam, 56
  Sermon by Monsignor John Lambe, Our Lady of Las Vegas (Nev.) Catholic Church, 64
  Tribute by Grant M. Bowler, Moapa Valley High School, Overton, Nev., 55

J. Caleb Boggs, of Delaware:
  Address, 191
  Poem, "Tribute to a Fallen President," by Geraldine Marie Quigley, Wilmington, Del., 591

Daniel B. Brewster, of Maryland:
  Address, 160
  Eulogy by Very Rev. William-M. J. Driscoll at requiem mass, Georgetown Preparatory School, Washington, D.C., 620

Quentin N. Burdick, of North Dakota:
  Address, 19
  Article from Mandan (N. Dak.) Pioneer, 646
  Poem by H. A. Swenson, First Lutheran Church, Bismarck, N. Dak., 20
  Resolutions by pupils of Pekin, N. Dak., public school, 20
  The Sleeping Prince, tribute by Larston Farrar, 646

Harry Flood Byrd, of Virginia, address, 139

Robert C. Byrd, of West Virginia:
  Address, 73
  Article from St. Albans (W. Va.) Advertiser, 563

Howard W. Cannon, of Nevada, address, 72

Frank Carlson, of Kansas:
  Address, 12
  Article by Robert M. Schrag, assistant editor, Mennonite Weekly Review, entitled, "A Moment in History," 599
  Resolution by All-Student Council, University of Kansas, 13

Clifford P. Case, of New Jersey, address, 132

Frank Church, of Idaho:
  Address, 73
  Editorials from—
    Aberdeen (Idaho) Times, 77
    Boise (Idaho) Statesman, 77
    Grangeville (Idaho) Free Press, 77
    Idaho Falls (Idaho) Post-Register, 76
    Lewiston (Idaho) Morning Tribune, 77
    Moscow (Idaho) Idahonian, 76
    Pocatello (Idaho) Sunday Journal, 76
    Rexburg (Idaho) Standard, 78
  From letters and poems, 76
  Poem, "Muffled Drums in Washington," by Colen H. Sweeten, Jr., Malad City, Idaho, 76
  Tribute at memorial services at River Road Unitarian Church, Bethesda, Md., Nov. 24, 1963, 74

Joseph S. Clark, of Pennsylvania, address, 54

John Sherman Cooper, of Kentucky:
  Address, 48
  Newsletter written by Mrs. John Sherman Cooper, 628

Norris Cotton, of New Hampshire:
  Address, 195
  Tribute by Rev. Robert W. Little, copastor, United Church of Christ, Keene, N.H., at Cathedral of the Pines, Rindge, N.H., 624

Carl T. Curtis, of Nebraska, address, 195

Everett McKinley Dirksen, of Illinois:
  Address on Nov. 25, 1963, 2
  Address on Dec. 11, 1963, 7
  Tribute by Talmage S. Wilcher, Virginia State Elks Association, at memorial service Nov. 30, 1963, 600
  Tribute by William J. Simonini, U.S. Air Force (ret.), 601

Thomas J. Dodd, of Connecticut, address, 30

Peter H. Dominick, of Colorado, address, 198

Paul H. Douglas, of Illinois:

Address, 130

A Little Boy Named John-John, by Sid Landfield, editor, Mount Sterling (Ill.) Democrat-Message, 626

Editorial from Tazewell County (Ill.) Reporter, Nov. 28, 1963, 627

James O. Eastland, of Mississippi, address, 51

J. Howard Edmondson, of Oklahoma:

Address, 51

Poem by David Randolph Milsten, Tulsa, Okla., published in Tulsa (Okla.) World, 649

Allen J. Ellender, of Louisiana, address, 177

Clair Engle, of California, address, 152

Sam J. Ervin, Jr., of North Carolina:

Address, 78

A Prayer, by Dr. Roy E. Watts, minister, First Presbyterian Church, published in High Point (N.C.) Enterprise, 94

Articles from—

Benson (N.C.) Review, Nov. 28, 1963, 81

Clayton (N.C.) News of Nov. 27, 1963, 84

Coastland (N.C.) Times of Nov. 29, 1963, 97

Davidson (N.C.) Mecklenburg Gazette of Nov. 28, 1963, 118

Forest City (N.C.) Courier of Dec. 5, 1963, 88

Montgomery Herald, Troy, N.C., Nov. 28, 1963, 100

Newland (N.C.) Avery Journal, Nov. 28, 1963, 119

Rutherfordton (N.C.) County News, Dec. 4 and Dec. 11, 1963, 121, 122

Southern Pines (N.C.) Pilot of Nov. 28, 1963, 99

Stanly News & Press, Albemarle, N.C., Nov. 26 and Nov. 29, 1963, 80

Watauga Democrat, 81

Editorials from—

Asheboro (N.C.) Courier-Tribune, Nov. 25, 1963, 117

Bertie Ledger-Advance, Windsor, N.C., November 1963, 104

Brevard (N.C.) Transylvania Times, Nov. 28, 1963, 117

Caswell Messenger, Yanceyville, N.C., Nov. 28, 1963, 106

Charlotte (N.C.) News of Nov. 23, 1963, 83

Concord (N.C.) Tribune of Nov. 24, Dec. 1, and Dec. 3, 1963, 85

Durham (N.C.) Sun of Nov. 23 and Nov. 25, 1963, 86

Elizabethtown (N.C.) Bladen Journal of Nov. 28, 1963, 87

Elkin (N.C.) Tribune, Nov. 25, 1963, 119

Forest City (N.C.) Courier of Nov. 28, 1963, 87

Graham Star, Robbinsville, N.C., Nov. 29, 1963, 111

Greensboro (N.C.) Times of Nov. 28, 1963, 88, 89

Hamlet (N.C.) News-Messenger of Nov. 26, 1963, 89

Henderson (N.C.) Daily Dispatch of Nov. 23, 1963, 90

Henderson (N.C.) Times-News of Nov. 23, 1963, 91

Henderson (N.C.) Western Carolina Tribune of Nov. 28 and Dec. 5, 1963, 91

Sam J. Ervin, Jr., of North Carolina—Continued

Editorials from—Continued

Hickory (N.C.) Daily Record of Nov. 23, Nov. 26, and Nov. 27, 1963, 92, 93

High Point (N.C.) Enterprise of Nov. 24 and Nov. 25, 1963, 93, 94

Kinston (N.C.) Daily Free Press of Nov. 23 and Nov. 25, 1963, 95

Leaksville (N.C.) News of Nov. 28, 1963, 95

Lenoir (N.C.) News-Topic of Nov. 23, 1963, 96

Lincoln (N.C.) Times of Nov. 25, 1963, 96

Lumberton (N.C.) Robesonian of Nov. 25, 1963, 97

Marshall (N.C.) News-Record, Nov. 28, 1963, 114

Mebane (N.C.) Enterprise, Nov. 28, 1963, 115

Morehead City (N.C.) Carteret County News-Times, Nov. 26, 1963, 115

Mount Olive (N.C.) Tribune, Nov. 26, 1963, 116

Nashville (N.C.) Graphic, Nov. 28, 1963, 109

Newton (N.C.) Observer-News-Enterprise, Nov. 25, 1963, 110

North Wilkesboro (N.C.) Journal-Patriot of November 1963, 120

Raeford (N.C.) News-Journal, Nov. 28, 1963, 120

Raleigh (N.C.) Times, Nov. 23, 1963, 110

Reidsville (N.C.) Review, Nov. 25, 1963, 121

Rocky Mount (N.C.) Telegram, Nov. 23, 1963, 112

Roxboro (N.C.) Courier-Times, Nov. 25, 1963, 112

Rutherfordton (N.C.) County News, Nov. 27, 1963, 121

Salisbury (N.C.) Sunday Post, Nov. 24, 1963, 123

Sampson Independent of Nov. 28, 1963, 84

Sanford (N.C.) Herald, Nov. 22, 1963, 113

Sanford (N.C.) News Leader, Nov. 27, 1963, 113

Shelby (N.C.) Cleveland Times, Nov. 26, 1963, 113

Shelby (N.C.) Daily Star, Nov. 23, 1963, 114

Stanly News & Press, Albemarle, N.C., Nov. 26, 1963, 79

Station WBBB, Burlington-Graham, N.C., Dec. 11, 1963, 124

Station WBT, Charlotte, N.C., Nov. 23 and Dec. 4, 1963, 107

Station WHIT, New Bern, N.C., Nov. 29, 1963, 108

Station WRAL–TV, Raleigh-Durham, N.C., Nov. 22, 1963, 108

Station WSOC, Charlotte, N.C., Nov. 29, 1963, 107, 108

Station WTYN, Tryon, N.C., Nov. 22, 1963, 109

Twin City Sentinel, Winston-Salem, N.C., Nov. 23, 1963, 106

Warren Record, Warrenton, N.C., Nov. 29, 1963, 101

Washington (N.C.) Daily News, November 1963, 100

Watauga Democrat, Nov. 28, 1963, 82

Waynesville (N.C.) Mountaineer, Nov. 25 and Dec. 9, 1963, 123

West Jefferson (N.C.) Skyland Post of Nov. 28, 1963, 102

Whiteville (N.C.) News Reporter of Nov. 25, 1963, 102

Wilmington (N.C.) Morning Star of Nov. 23, Nov. 24, and Nov. 26, 1963, 102, 103

Sam J. Ervin, Jr., of North Carolina—Continued
    Editorials from—Continued
        Wilson (N.C.) Daily Times, November 1963, 104
        Winston-Salem (N.C.) Journal of Nov. 23 and Nov. 26, 1963, 105
    Eulogy by Rev. Charles Mulholland of Sacred Heart Catholic Church, published in Brevard (N.C.) Transylvania Times of Dec. 12, 1963, 118
    Poem, "A Nation Mourns," from Durham (N.C.) Sun, Nov. 23, 1963, 86
    Remarks by Rev. R. F. Smith, pastor, First Baptist Church, North Wilkesboro, N.C., Nov. 24, 1963, 590
    Resolution by Senate of Dialectic and Philanthropic Literary Societies, University of North Carolina, 591
    "Taps," poem from Durham (N.C.) Sun of Nov. 25, 1963, 86
Hiram L. Fong, of Hawaii, address, 189
J. W. Fulbright, of Arkansas:
    Address, 32
    Communications from—
        Enver Aka, President, Senate of the Turkish Republic, 36
        Thos. Amarasuriya, President, Senate of Ceylon, 36
        Ali Bengelloun, Ambassador of Morocco, 36
        Djaafor Charif-Emami, President, Iranian Senate, 35
        Julio de la Piedra, President, Peruvian Senate, 37
        Sir Howard d'Egville, secretary of British-American Parliamentary Group, 36
        Nils Langhelle, President, Norwegian Storting, 35
        A. M. McMullin, President, Australian Senate, 35
        Alfred Maleta, Director, Parliament of Austria, 35
        Cesare Marzagora, President, Senate of Italy, 36, 37
        Kaneshichi Masuda, Japanese Diet, 36
        Carlos H. Perette, President, Argentine Senate, 36
        Maurice Schumann, President, Foreign Affairs Commission, National Assembly, Republic of France, 35
        A. Van Acker, President, Chamber of Deputies of Belgium, 35
        Czeslau Wycech, President, Sejm of the Polish Peoples Republic, 36
    Editorial from Arkansas Traveler, 34
    "It Rained in Washington Today," poem by Harold C. Miller, 637
    Resolution of House of Commons, 34
    Tributes by—
        Mr. D. Del Bo, president of European Coal and Steel Community, 636
        Mr. E. Medi, vice president of Commission of European Atomic Energy Community, 636
        Mr. Gaetano Martino, president of European Parliament, 633
        Mr. L. de Block, Kingdom of the Netherlands, 634
        Mr. W. Hallstein, president of the Commission of European Economic Community, 635
    Tribute from Madison County Record, Huntsville, Ark., by Sam Faubus, 637
Barry Goldwater, of Arizona, address, 179
Albert Gore, of Tennessee, address, 128

Ernest Gruening, of Alaska:
    Address, 65
    Editorials from—
        Anchorage (Alaska) Daily News of Nov. 23, 1963, 67
        Anchorage (Alaska) Daily Times of Nov. 22, 1963, 67
        Cook Inlet Courier, Homer, Alaska, Nov. 22, 1963, 69
        Daily Alaska Empire, Juneau, Alaska, Nov. 24, 1963, 69
        Fairbanks (Alaska) Daily News-Miner of Nov. 23 and Nov. 25, 1963, 68
        Jessen's Weekly, Fairbanks, Alaska, Nov. 27, 1963, 69
        Nome Nugget, Nome, Alaska, Nov. 25, 1963, 70
Philip A. Hart, of Michigan:
    Address, 129
    Biography of John F. Kennedy written by fifth grade class of Central Grade School, Negaunee, Mich., 659
    Letter from Jo Ann Johnson, Negaunee, Mich., 659
    Resolution by United Nations League of Lawyers, 661
    Resolution of Capitol Hill Chapter, Federal Bar Association, 662
    Resolution of National Council of Federal Bar Association, 661
Vance Hartke, of Indiana:
    Address, 125
    Address by Rev. Charles W. Ridlen, pastor, Frankfort East Side Christian Church, at community memorial service, 593
    Editorial read over radio station WXLW, Indianapolis, Ind., Nov. 22, 1963, 592
    Eulogy by Rabbi Frederick A. Doppelt, Congregation Achduth Vesholom, Fort Wayne, Ind., 592
    Eulogy written by Bruce Kingery, Kokomo, Ind., 594
    Poem by Arthur Franklin Mapes, Kendallville, Ind., entitled "He Moved the World," 596
    Poem by Peggy Anna Moore, Georgetown, Ind., 596
    Resolutions by Young Democrats of Indiana, 592
    Tributes from article by Mrs. Mary D'Andrea in Logansport (Ind.) Pharos-Tribune, 596
Carl Hayden, of Arizona:
    Address, 32
    Resolution by Arizona State Legislature, 549
Bourke B. Hickenlooper, of Iowa, address, 140
Lister Hill, of Alabama, address, 11
Spessard L. Holland, of Florida, address, 199
Roman L. Hruska, of Nebraska, address, 198
Hubert H. Humphrey, of Minnesota:
    Address, 175
    A Deeper Reality, article by Dr. Rafael Squirru, Organization of American States, 681
    Alliance for Progress tributes to President John F. Kennedy, 664
    Article by Dr. Jerome B. Wiesner from Science magazine of Nov. 29, 1963, 676
    Article from Americas magazine, 683
    Editorial from high school paper by Joan Graham, Albert Lea, Minn., 673
    Eulogy by Bishop Kellogg, Cathedral Church of St. Mark, Minneapolis, Minn., 675

Hubert H. Humphrey, of Minnesota—Continued
  Poem by Linda Jean Miller, Northeast Junior High
    School, Minneapolis, Minn., 673
  Statement by Jerry Voohris, Cooperative League of
    the U.S.A., 674
  Tribute by Richard H. Rovere from New York Re-
    view of Books, Nov. 26, 1963, 680
Daniel K. Inouye, of Hawaii:
  Address, 37
  Sermon by Father John H. McDonald at Star of the
    Sea Church, Honolulu, Hawaii, Nov. 24, 1963, 617
Henry M. Jackson, of Washington, address, 16
Jacob K. Javits, of New York:
  Address, 133
  Eulogy by John H. Sheehan, National Association
    of Retired Civil Employees, 623
  Poem by James T. Farrell, 623
Olin D. Johnston, of South Carolina, address, 52
B. Everett Jordan, of North Carolina, address, 78
Len B. Jordan, of Idaho, address, 181
Kenneth B. Keating, of New York:
  Address, 168
  Expression of sentiments of Rochester, N.Y., Jewish
    community, 170
  He Left the World Richer, by Rev. Paul R. Hoover,
    pastor, Grace Evangelical Lutheran Church,
    Rochester, N.Y., 169
  Poem, "Ask Not," by Miss Kay Magenheimer, Amity-
    ville, N.Y., 623
  Sermon by Rev. William A. Sadler, Jr., Dover Plains,
    N.Y., 170
  Tribute by David A. MacLennan, Rochester (N.Y.)
    Rotary Club, 173
Edward M. Kennedy, of Massachusetts:
  Address, 200
  Resolution by Federal House of Deputies of Brazil, 631
Thomas H. Kuchel, of California:
  Address, 25
  Articles from—
    Sacramento (Calif.) Bee of Nov. 22 and Nov. 26,
      1963, 26
    Sacramento (Calif.) Union of Nov. 23, 1963, 25
    San Francisco (Calif.) Chronicle of Nov. 25, 1963,
      27
  Editorials from—
    Long Beach (Calif.) Independent-Press-Telegram of
      Nov. 24, 1963, 29
    Long Beach (Calif.) Press-Telegram of Nov. 22,
      1963, 29
    Los Angeles (Calif.) Times of Nov. 23 and Nov.
      25, 1963, 28, 29
    San Francisco (Calif.) Chronicle of Nov. 25, 1963,
      27
    San Francisco (Calif.) Examiner of Nov. 23, 1963,
      29
    San Francisco (Calif.) Monitor of Nov. 29, 1963,
      30
Frank J. Lausche, of Ohio, address, 135
Edward V. Long, of Missouri:
  Address, 183
  Legend Will Live On, article by Roy A. Roberts in
    Kansas City (Mo.) Star, Nov. 24, 1963, 185
Russell B. Long, of Louisiana, address, 199

Eugene J. McCarthy, of Minnesota:
  Address, 137
  Poem by Wendell Berry, from the "Nation," 590
  Tribute by Daniel F. Foley, American Legion National
    Commander, at memorial service in Minneapolis,
    Minn., Nov. 23, 1963, 589
John L. McClellan, of Arkansas, address, 50
Gale W. McGee, of Wyoming, address, 151
George McGovern, of South Dakota:
  Address, 142
  America's Loss, poem by Christine Olson, 149
  Article by Arthur Schlesinger, Jr., in Saturday Evening
    Post, Dec. 14, 1963, 656
  Editorials from—
    Argus Leader, Sioux Falls, S. Dak., Dec. 5, 1963,
      148
    Arlington (S. Dak.) Sun, 150
    Black Hills Press, Sturgis, S. Dak., Nov. 23, 1963,
      147
    Clark County (S. Dak.) Courier, 151
    Daily Republic, Mitchell, S. Dak., Nov. 26, 1963,
      146
    Exponent, Northern State Teachers College, Aber-
      deen, S. Dak., 147
    Freeman (S. Dak.) Courier, 151
    Lemmon (S. Dak.) Tribune, Nov. 28, 1963, 150
    Pep-A-Graph, Lennox (S. Dak.) High School paper,
      Nov. 28, 1963, 148
    Salem (S. Dak.) Special of Nov. 28, 1963, 149
    Tyndall (S. Dak.) Tribune and Register, 150
  Eulogy by Judge Francis Dunn before Sioux Falls (S.
    Dak.) Elks Lodge, 656
  Excerpts from letters, 144
  Excerpts from sermon by Rev. Charles Greene, pastor,
    Gettysburg, S. Dak., Episcopal Church, 146
  Excerpts from sermon by Rev. Edward A. Gilbertson,
    pastor, Grace Lutheran Church, Sisseton, S. Dak., 146
  Letter from Mrs. Olive Briles, 145
  Poem by Molly Kazan, 658
  Statement by a secretary in office of Senator McGovern,
    146
  Tribute by Bishop Edwin R. Garrison, Dakota area,
    Methodist Church, 652
  Tribute by Bishop James K. Matthews, Boston area,
    Methodist Church, 653
  Tribute by Bishop John Wesley Lord, Washington
    (D.C.) area, Methodist Church, 653
  Tribute by Emily Ann Barnes, Long Island, N.Y., 652
  Tribute by Mr. William Attwood in Look magazine,
    650
Thomas J. McIntyre, of New Hampshire:
  Address, 138
  Editorial from Portland (N.H.) Herald, Nov. 23, 1963,
    563
Pat McNamara, of Michigan:
  Address, 124
  Tribute by John Herling, Washington correspondent,
    637
Warren G. Magnuson, of Washington:
  Address, 22
  Address by Clarence C. Dill, of Spokane, Wash., 22
  Dies Irae, Dies Illa, poem by Mrs. Edna Leal Williams,
    644

Mike Mansfield, of Montana:
   Addresses, 1, 5
   Eulogy in the Rotunda, U.S. Capitol, 6
   Statement on death of John Fitzgerald Kennedy, 6
   Telegrams and letters of regret and condolence, 550
   Tribute by Mr. Eric Nicol, published in Vancouver (B.C.) Province, 555
   Tribute by Rabbi Henry Segal, B'nai Israel Synagogue, Washington, D.C., 555
Edwin L. Mechem, of New Mexico, address, 192
Lee Metcalf, of Montana, address, 190
Jack Miller, of Iowa:
   Address, 174
   Poem, A Psalm of Life, by Henry Wadsworth Longfellow, 175
A. S. Mike Monroney, of Oklahoma, address, 182
Wayne Morse, of Oregon:
   Address, 70
   Eulogy by Elder Bryant A. Alder, Church of Jesus Christ of Latter-day Saints, Portland, Oreg., 559
   Eulogy by Prof. Joseph F. Smith at Mormon Tabernacle, Honolulu, Hawaii, 561
   Resolution by Democratic Central Committee of Multnomah County, Oreg., 562
   Telegrams and letters received expressing sorrow, 557
   "The Kennedy Star," poem by Rex Trowbridge, Sisters, Oreg., 561
   Tribute by Mr. Howard C. Zimmerman, Eugene, Oreg., poem, "I Heard the Drums," 558
Thruston B. Morton, of Kentucky, address, 180
Frank E. Moss, of Utah:
   Address, 154
   Death of the President, poem by Clinton F. Larson, of Provo, Utah, 160
   Editorials from—
      Ogden (Utah) Standard-Examiner of Nov. 23, 1963, 157
      Provo (Utah) Daily Herald of Dec. 2, 1963, 158
      Salt Lake City (Utah) Deseret News of Nov. 23, 1963, 156
      Salt Lake City (Utah) Tribune of Nov. 23 and Nov. 24, 1963, 157, 158
   "Eternal Flame," poem by Louis W. Larsen, published in Salt Lake (Utah) Tribune, 644
   Letter from Highland High School, Salt Lake City, Utah, 158
   Letter from Horst A. Reschke of Salt Lake City, Utah, 159
   Memorial address by Hugh B. Brown, president, Church of Jesus Christ of Latter-day Saints, at Utah State University, 641
   Memorial tribute address by Senator Alan Bible at Young Democratic Clubs Convention at Las Vegas, Nev., Jan. 31, 1964, 639
   Poem by Mrs. Beatrice Bennett, 160
   Tribute by C. Sumpter Logan, moderator, Presbytery of Utah, 158
   Tribute from a schoolgirl, 159
Karl E. Mundt, of South Dakota:
   Address, 196
   Tribute by Pastor H. Clarence Johnson, Lutheran Church, 662

Edmund S. Muskie, of Maine:
   Address, 37
   Articles from—
      Bangor Daily News of Nov. 28, 1963, 46
      Portland Press Herald of Nov. 25, 1963, 43
      Portland Sunday Telegram of Nov. 24, 1963, 42
   Editorials from—
      Bangor Daily News of Nov. 23, Nov. 25, and Nov. 26, 1963, 42, 44, 45
      Bates News of December 1963, 47
      Daily Kennebec Journal of Nov. 23 and Nov. 26, 1963, 39, 40, 46
      Lewiston Daily Sun of Nov. 23, Nov. 25, and Nov. 26, 1963, 39, 44, 45
      Lewiston Evening Journal of Nov. 23, Nov. 25, and Nov. 26, 1963, 40, 44, 45
      Maine Campus of Dec. 5, 1963, 47
      Portland Evening Express of Nov. 23 and Nov. 25, 1963, 41, 42, 43
      Waterville Morning Sentinel of Nov. 23, 1963, 40
   Letter to Maine, 39
   Report to Maine, 38
   Statement upon assassination, 38
   Tribute by Cumberland County Women's Club, 48
   "Who Was This Man," poem by Miss Kathleen Watson, Bath, Maine, 625
Gaylord Nelson, of Wisconsin, address, 193
Maurine B. Neuberger, of Oregon:
   Address, 53
   Sermon, "Christmas Always Begins at Midnight," 53
John O. Pastore, of Rhode Island, address, 20
James B. Pearson, of Kansas, address, 71
Claiborne Pell, of Rhode Island:
   Address, 131
   Poem by Miss Mary McGann, of Newport, R.I., 633
   Poem by Rev. Jessie Koewing Brown, Providence, R.I., 632
   Poem by Robert E. Taylor, Providence, R.I., 632
Prayers by the Chaplain of the Senate, Rev. Frederick Brown Harris, D.D.:
   November 25, 1963, 1
   December 11, 1963, 5
Winston L. Prouty, of Vermont, address, 21
William Proxmire, of Wisconsin, address, 137
Jennings Randolph, of West Virginia, address, 127
Abraham A. Ribicoff, of Connecticut:
   Address, 17
   Editorials from—
      Ansonia (Conn.) Evening Sentinel, Nov. 23, 1963, 606
      Bridgeport (Conn.) Post, Nov. 23, 1963, 604
      Bridgeport (Conn.) Sunday Herald, Nov. 24, 1963, 605
      Bridgeport (Conn.) Telegram, Nov. 23, 1963, 604
      Bristol (Conn.) Press, Nov. 23, 1963, 606
      Danbury (Conn.) News-Times, Nov. 23, 1963, 607
      Greenwich (Conn.) Times, Nov. 25, 1963, 607
      Hartford (Conn.) Courant, Nov. 23, 1963, 602
      Hartford (Conn.) Times, Nov. 23, 1963, 602
      Manchester (Conn.) Evening Herald, Nov. 23, 1963, 607
      Meriden (Conn.) Journal, Nov. 23, 1963, 608

Abraham A. Ribicoff, of Connecticut—Continued
  Editorials from—Continued
    Meriden (Conn.) Morning Record, Nov. 23, 1963, 608
    Middletown (Conn.) Press, Nov. 23, 1963, 609
    Naugatuck (Conn.) Daily News, Nov. 23, 1963, 610
    New Britain (Conn.) Herald, Nov. 23, 1963, 610
    New Haven (Conn.) Journal-Courier, Nov. 25, 1963, 604
    New Haven (Conn.) Register, Nov. 25, 1963, 603
    New London (Conn.) Day, Nov. 23, 1963, 611
    Norwalk (Conn.) Hour, Nov. 23, 1963, 611
    Norwich (Conn.) Bulletin, Nov. 23, 1963, 612
    Stamford (Conn.) Advocate, Nov. 23, 1963, 612
    Torrington (Conn.) Register, Nov. 23, 1963, 612
    Waterbury (Conn.) American, Nov. 23, 1963, 605
    Waterbury (Conn.) Republican, Nov. 23, 1963, 605
    Willimantic (Conn.) Daily Chronicle, Nov. 23, 1963, 613
    Winsted (Conn.) Evening Citizen, Nov. 23, 1963, 613
  Jewish Community Tribute at Washington (D.C.) Hebrew Congregation, 614
  Memorial prayer, 617
  Poem by Judith Anne Wright, Bloomfield, Conn., 614
  Song, "America, the Beautiful," 617
  Tribute by Mr. Justice Arthur J. Goldberg, U.S. Supreme Court, 616
  Tribute by Hon. Myer Feldman, Deputy Special Counsel to the President, 616
A. Willis Robertson, of Virginia:
  Address, 179
  Sermon by Dr. R. B. Culbreth, pastor, Metropolitan Baptist Church, Washington, D.C., 564
  Telegram of sympathy from Mr. James F. Tindall, president, Virginia Press Association, 566
Richard B. Russell, of Georgia, address, 13
Leverett Saltonstall, of Massachusetts:
  Address, 8
  Poem by William F. McDonough published in Union Postal Clerk magazine, 645
  Tribute written by Lola Kramarsky, president, National Hadassah, 645
Hugh Scott, of Pennsylvania, address, 192
Milward L. Simpson, of Wyoming, address, 183
George A. Smathers, of Florida:
  Address, 9
  Editorial by Martin Andersen, publisher of Orlando (Fla.) Sentinel, 619
Margaret Chase Smith, of Maine, address, 139
John J. Sparkman, of Alabama:
  Address, 13
  Eulogy by Cam McCurry, Oneonta, Ala., 630
  Eulogy by Jim Williams, radio station WAMI, Opp, Ala., 630
  Tribute by Paul-Henri Spaak, Minister of Foreign Affairs, Belgium, 630
John Stennis, of Mississippi:
  Address, 141
  Telegram from Jack R. Reed, President, Mississippi Economic Council, 142

Stuart Symington, of Missouri:
  Address, 167
  The Young Champion, tribute by James W. Symington, 168
Herman E. Talmadge, of Georgia:
  Address, 19
  Message by Dr. James P. Wesberry, pastor, Morningside Baptist Church, Atlanta, Ga., Nov. 24, 1963, over television station, 598
Strom Thurmond, of South Carolina, address, 24
John G. Tower, of Texas, address, 196
Herbert S. Walters, of Tennessee:
  Address, 180
  Prayer by Mrs. Cora Taliaferro, St. Peter's Episcopal Church, Chattanooga, Tenn., 181
Harrison A. Williams, Jr., of New Jersey:
  Address, 162
  Address by Rabbi Gershon B. Chertoff, Temple B'nai Israel, Elizabeth, N.J., 648
  Article from Trenton (N.J.) Times, by William J. O'Donnell, 163
  Editorials from—
    Asbury Park (N.J.) Evening Press, 163
    Atlantic City (N.J.) Free Press, 166
    Camden (N.J.) Catholic Star-Herald, 165
    Jersey Journal, 165
    Newark (N.J.) Star Ledger, 164
    Time for Rededication, from Jewish News, 164
John J. Williams, of Delaware, address, 187
Ralph W. Yarborough, of Texas:
  Address, 136
  Invocation at President Kennedy's inauguration Jan. 20, 1961, by Rev. Dr. John Barclay, minister of Central Christian Church, Austin, Tex., 586
  Memorial service at First Methodist Church, Fort Worth, Tex., and eulogy by Dr. Gaston Foote, Nov. 24, 1963, 584
  Sermon by Dr. John Barclay, Central Christian Church, Austin, Tex., 587
  Speeches of President John F. Kennedy—
    At citizens' rally in front of Texas Hotel, Fort Worth, Tex., Nov. 22, 1963, 571
    At dedication ceremonies, Aerospace Medical Health Center, Brooks Air Force Base, Tex., Nov. 21, 1963, 567
    As prepared for delivery at dedication ceremonies, Aerospace Medical Health Center, Brooks Air Force Base, Tex., 568
    As prepared for delivery at the Trade Mart, Dallas, Tex., 573
    As prepared for delivery at Municipal Auditorium, Austin, Tex., 575
    At testimonial dinner for Congressman Albert Thomas, Houston, Tex., Nov. 21, 1963, 570
    Before Fort Worth Chamber of Commerce, Fort Worth, Tex., Nov. 22, 1963, 571
    Before League of United Latin American Citizens, Rice Hotel, Houston, Tex., Nov. 21, 1963, 569
  "Summing Up," article by J. Frank Dobie, published in Austin (Tex.) American-Statesman, Dec. 29, 1963, 583

Ralph W. Yarborough, of Texas—Continued
"The Incredible Tragedy," article by David Lawrence, in U.S. News & World Report, Dec. 2, 1963, 580
"The Poet and the President," article by Dr. Jenny Lind Porter, published in Austin (Tex.) American-Statesman, Dec. 15, 1963, 581
Tributes from France—
Article from Ambassade de France, 578
Editorials from French press, 579
Eulogy by M. Jacques Chaban-Delmas, President of French National Assembly, 580
France mourns President Kennedy, 579

Ralph W. Yarborough, of Texas—Continued
Tributes from France—Continued
Official messages of tribute from France, 578
Milton R. Young, of North Dakota:
Address, 48
Article by Theodore H. White, "For President Kennedy: An Epilog—For One Brief Shining Moment, Camelot," 49
Stephen M. Young, of Ohio:
Address, 188
Resolution by District of Columbia chapter of Federal Bar Association, 629

Addresses and Tributes in the House of Representatives of the United States

Watkins M. Abbitt, of Virginia, address, 381

Homer E. Abele, of Ohio, address, 454

Thomas G. Abernethy, of Mississippi, address, 425

Joseph P. Addabbo, of New York:
  Address, 402
  Editorial from Long Island (N.Y.) Press, Nov. 23, 1963, 725
  Poem by Maria Papa, of Ozone Park, N.Y., 403

Carl Albert, of Oklahoma:
  Address, 211
  "The Grief of Maria," article from Buenos Aires (Argentina) Herald, 690

Bruce Alger, of Texas, address, 512

John B. Anderson, of Illinois, address, 490

Mark Andrews, of North Dakota, address, 517

Appointment of Members to attend funeral services, 205

Leslie C. Arends, of Illinois, address, 221

Thomas L. Ashley, of Ohio, address, 405

Robert T. Ashmore, of South Carolina, address, 531

Wayne N. Aspinall, of Colorado, address, 431

James C. Auchincloss, of New Jersey:
  Address, 357
  Poem by Paul T. Flood, of Winter Park, Fla., 358

William H. Avery, of Kansas, address, 465

William H. Ayres, of Ohio, article by John Cosgrove from National Press Club Record, 726

John F. Baldwin, of California, address, 249

Walter S. Baring, of Nevada, address, 415

William A. Barrett, of Pennsylvania:
  Address, 388
  Sermon by Father George E. O'Donnell at Cathedral of SS. Peter and Paul, Philadelphia, Pa., Nov. 25, 1963, 727

Robert R. Barry, of New York, tribute to Alberto Gavasci from Home News & Times, Yonkers, N.Y., 728

Ross Bass, of Tennessee:
  Address, 276
  Sermon by Dr. Wallace E. Fisher, pastor, Lutheran Church of the Holy Trinity, Lancaster, Pa., 730
  Speech at memorial services, Columbia Military Academy, by Capt. Lewis E. Moore, Jr., 729

William H. Bates, of Massachusetts, address, 235

James F. Battin, of Montana, address, 352

Frank J. Becker, of New York, address, 359

Lindley Beckworth, of Texas:
  Address, 390
  Editorials from—
    Gilmer (Tex.) Mirror, Nov. 28, 1963, 392
    Longview (Tex.) News-Journal, Nov. 24, 1963, by Carl L. Estes, 391

Ralph F. Beermann, of Nebraska, address, 483

Page Belcher, of Oklahoma:
  Address, 365

Page Belcher, of Oklahoma—Continued
  Memorial to J. F. K., poem by Miss Carolyn Woods, Enid, Okla., 732

Charles E. Bennett, of Florida:
  Address, 314
  Editorial from Florida Times Union by Caleb King, Jr., Nov. 25, 1963, 723

E. Y. Berry, of South Dakota, address, 540

Jackson E. Betts, of Ohio, address, 372

John A. Blatnik, of Minnesota:
  Address, 302
  Editorials by—
    Marty McGowan, editor of Appleton (Minn.) Press, 303
    Miss Veda Pokikvar, editor of Tribune-Press, Chisholm, Minn., 302

Hale Boggs, of Louisiana:
  Address, 213
  A Scene Unduplicated, article by Richard L. Strout, in Christian Science Monitor, Nov. 27, 1963, 702
  Articles from—
    Christian Science Monitor, Nov. 27, 1963, 700, 702
    Denver (Colo.) Register, Dec. 8, 1963, 692
    New Orleans Times-Picayune, Nov. 25, Nov. 26, and Nov. 30, 1963, 694, 699
    New York Times, Nov. 23, 1963, by James Reston, 220
    Shreveport-Bossier City (La.) Journal, Nov. 25, 1963, 702
    Wall Street Journal, Nov. 26, 1963, 696
    Washington (D.C.) Daily News, Nov. 27, 1963, 691
    Washington (D.C.) Evening Star, Nov. 29, 1963, 698
    Washington (D.C.) Post, Nov. 25, Nov. 26, and Dec. 1, 1963, 695, 699, 701
  Editorials from—
    Baltimore (Md.) Sun, Nov. 23, 1963, 700
    New Orleans (La.) Clarion Herald, Nov. 28, 1963, 697
    New Orleans (La.) States-Item, Nov. 23, 1963, 692
    New Orleans (La.) Times-Picayune, Nov. 25 and Nov. 26, 1963, 693, 704
  Eulogy by Mrs. Hale Boggs before National Women's Democratic Club, Dec. 2, 1963, 216
  Eulogy by Richard Cardinal Cushing, 217
  For One Shining Moment There Was Camelot, article by Theodore H. White from Life magazine and published in Washington (D.C.) Daily News, Dec. 4, 1963, 219
  Frayed-Collar Friendship, article by Tom Fox in Clarion Herald, New Orleans, La., 705
  Proclamation by Mayor Victor H. Schiro, of New Orleans, La., 704
  Tribute by Joseph E. Le Blanc, Jr., of Lafayette, La., 217

Edward P. Boland, of Massachusetts:
  Address, 226
  Article by John Kenneth Galbraith, from Washington (D.C.) Post of Nov. 25, 1963, 228
  Editorial from Saturday Review, by Norman Cousins, 706
  Editorials from the French press, 713
  Eulogy by M. Jacques Chaban-Delmas, President, French National Assembly, 713
  Eulogy by Rev. Donald L. Garfield, rector, St. Peter's Episcopal Church, Springfield, Mass., at requiem mass, 710
  France mourns President Kennedy, 713
  France's tributes to President Kennedy, official messages, 712
  Letter from a member of the Christian Church, Three Rivers, Mass., 710
  Message by Richard Cardinal Cushing, from Boston (Mass.) Herald, Dec. 20, 1963, 714
  Poem by Brian F. King in Springfield (Mass.) Sunday Republican, 710
  Poem by Joseph A. Novak, Santurce, P.R., 709
  Poem by Rev. Thomas F. Curran, St. Patrick's Church, Chicopee Falls, Mass., 709
  Poem from New York (N.Y.) Herald Tribune by Mrs. Molly Kazan, 715
  President Kennedy's inaugural address, 227
  Tribute by Rev. David G. Granfield, in December issue of American Ecclesiastical Review, Catholic University of America, Washington, D.C., 714
Frances P. Bolton, of Ohio:
  Address, 455
  Memorial services Nov. 25, 1963, at Hue, Vietnam, 734
Herbert C. Bonner, of North Carolina, address, 250
Frank T. Bow, of Ohio, address, 455
John Brademas, of Indiana, memorial sermon by Rev. Dr. W. A. Visser 'T Hooft, at St. Pierre Cathedral, Geneva, Switzerland, 734
William G. Bray, of Indiana, address, 314
Jack Brooks, of Texas, tribute by State Senator Dorsey B. Hardeman at Park Heights Baptist Church, Nov. 25, 1963, 736
William S. Broomfield, of Michigan, address, 339
Donald G. Brotzman, of Colorado, address, 343
James T. Broyhill, of North Carolina, address, 492
Joel T. Broyhill, of Virginia:
  Address, 366
  Article from Falls Church (Va.) High School Jaguar Journal of Dec. 19, 1963, 737
  Poem and tribute by Janet Hess, Falls Church, Va., 737
  Sermon by Pastor H. Alvin Kuhn, Lutheran Church of the Redeemer, McLean, Va., Nov. 25, 1963, 736
Charles A. Buckley, of New York, address, 411
James A. Burke, of Massachusetts, address, 232
Everett G. Burkhalter, of California, address, 308
Omar Burleson, of Texas:
  Address, 358
  Proclamation by R. R. Kelley, mayor, Stamford, Tex., 358
Laurence J. Burton, of Utah:
  Address, 492

Laurence J. Burton, of Utah—Continued
  Letter to editor of Ogden Standard-Examiner from Mr. and Mrs. Donald D. Stout, Layton, Utah, 493
James A. Byrne, of Pennsylvania, address, 385
John W. Byrnes, of Wisconsin, address, 476
William T. Cahill, of New Jersey, address, 368
Ronald Brooks Cameron, of California:
  Address, 344
  Letter from Terry L. Worthylake, West Covina, Calif., 344
Clarence Cannon, of Missouri, address, 223
Hugh L. Carey, of New York:
  Address, 501
  Sermon by Rev. Raymond Shelvin, St. Francis Xavier, Brooklyn, N.Y., Dec. 21, 1963, 738
  Statement on Nov. 27, 1963, 502
  Tribute by Harry H. Kruener at Borough Hall, Brooklyn, N.Y., Dec. 6, 1963, 738
Bob Casey, of Texas, address, 412
Elford A. Cederberg, of Michigan, address, 354
Emanuel Celler, of New York:
  Address, 238
  Memoriam by Fur Center Synagogue, New York, N.Y., 739
Charles E. Chamberlain, of Michigan:
  Address, 523
  Article by David Lawrence, U.S. News and World Report, Dec. 3, 1963, 523
  Editorials from—
    Flint (Mich.) Journal, Nov. 23, 1963, 740
    State Journal, Lansing, Mich., Nov. 23, 1963, **740**
Frank Chelf, of Kentucky, address, 251
J. Edgar Chenoweth, of Colorado, address, 470
Frank M. Clark, of Pennsylvania:
  Address, 405
  Editorial from News Tribune, Beaver Falls, Pa., 741
Don H. Clausen, of California:
  Address, 324
  Poems by Joyce Torrence Conley, Crescent City, Calif., 324
James C. Cleveland, of New Hampshire, address, 454
Jeffery Cohelan, of California:
  Address, 420
  Letter from Prof. S. G. Raybould, University of Leeds, Leeds, England, 742
  Memorial tributes by students of Willard High School, Berkeley, Calif., 742
Harold R. Collier, of Illinois, address, 512
William M. Colmer, of Mississippi, address, 472
Silvio O. Conte, of Massachusetts, address, 230
Harold D. Cooley, of North Carolina, address, 488
James C. Corman, of California, address, 317
William C. Cramer, of Florida, address, 485
Glenn Cunningham, of Nebraska, address, 426
Willard S. Curtin, of Pennsylvania, address, 376
Emilio Q. Daddario, of Connecticut:
  Address, 243
  Poem by Wilbert Snow from Wesleyan Alumnus magazine, 743
  Tribute by Jerome B. Wiesner from Science magazine, 744
Paul B. Dague, of Pennsylvania, address, 353

Dominick V. Daniels, of New Jersey:
  Address, 364
  Poem by Frank Leanza, of West New York, N.J., 747
  Tribute by Cub Pack 43, Hoboken, N.J., 747
James J. Delaney, of New York, address, 414
John H. Dent, of Pennsylvania:
  Address, 490
  Resolution introduced in Pennsylvania State Senate by
    William J. Lane and James S. Berger, 748
Winfield K. Denton, of Indiana, address, 365
Steven B. Derounian, of New York, address, 359
Edward J. Derwinski, of Illinois:
  Address, 467
  Editorials from—
    Blue Island Sun-Standard, Nov. 28, 1963, 467
    Harvey Tribune, Nov. 24, 1963, 468
    Lemonter, Nov. 28, 1963, 468
    Markham Bulletin, Nov. 28, 1963, 468
    Park Forest Reporter, Nov. 27, 1963, 469
    Riverside Advertiser, Nov. 25, 1963, 469
    Sauk Village Review, Nov. 28, 1963, 469
    Suburbanite-Economist, Nov. 27, 1963, 469
    Worth-Palos Reporter, Nov. 28, 1863, 470
Samuel L. Devine, of Ohio, eulogy by Bob Sherman, news
  editor radio station WMNI, Columbus, Ohio, Nov.
  23, 1963, 748
John D. Dingell, of Michigan:
  Address, 370
  Memorial address by Rabbi Moses Lehrman, Oak Park,
    Mich., Nov. 25, 1963, 750
  Memorial tributes by—
    Broadus N. Butler, Wayne County (Mich.) Board
      of Supervisors, Nov. 26, 1963, 754
    Rabbi Richard C. Hertz, Temple Beth El, Detroit,
      Mich., Nov. 29, 1963, 751
    Rabbi Jacob E. Segal, Adas Shalom Synagogue, De-
      troit, Mich., 755
Bob Dole, of Kansas:
  Address, 463
  Tributes from western Kansas newspapers, 463
Harold D. Donohue, of Massachusetts:
  Address, 236
  Article from Worcester (Mass.) Evening Gazette, Nov.
    26, 1963, by Ivan Sandrof, 716
W. J. Bryan Dorn, of South Carolina, address, 525
John Dowdy, of Texas, address, 427
Thomas N. Downing, of Virginia, address, 371
Thaddeus J. Dulski, of New York:
  Address, 408
  Editorials from—
    Buffalo (N.Y.) Courier-Express, Nov. 26, 1963, 758
    Buffalo (N.Y.) Evening News, Nov. 23, 1963, 757
  Eulogy by Vincent M. Gaughan at Trinity Episcopal
    Church, Hamburg, N.Y., 760
  Poems by Joseph C. Carson, Buffalo, N.Y., 759
  Resolution by Frank E. Wendling, Board of Super-
    visors, Buffalo, N.Y., 758
Robert B. Duncan, of Oregon, address, 424
Florence P. Dwyer, of New Jersey, address, 518
Ed Edmondson, of Oklahoma:
  Address, 442
  Poem by David Randolph Milsten, 442

Don Edwards, of California, address, 389
Carl Elliott, of Alabama:
  Address, 380
  Resolution by mayor and city council of Vestavia Hills,
    Ala., 760
Robert F. Ellsworth, of Kansas, address, 465
Eulogies by—
  Chief Justice Earl Warren, in the Rotunda, U.S. Capi-
    tol, Nov. 24, 1963, 204
  Senator Mike Mansfield, of Montana, in Capitol Ro-
    tunda, Nov. 24, 1963, 203
  Speaker of the House, John W. McCormack, in the
    Rotunda, U.S. Capitol, Nov. 24, 1963, 204
Robert A. Everett, of Tennessee:
  Address, 333
  Letter from a University of Tennessee student, 333
  Telegram from Shannon D. Faulkner, superintendent
    of Tipton County schools, 334
Joe L. Evins, of Tennessee:
  Address, 253
  Memorial address by Hon. Weldon B. White, War
    Memorial Building, Nashville, Tenn., 761
George H. Fallon, of Maryland, address, 386
Leonard Farbstein, of New York:
  Address, 342
  Editorial by Abraham Schlacht, editor of East Side
    News, New York, N.Y., 763
  Eulogy by Rabbi Harry J. Kaufman, Beth Sholom Con-
    gregation, Washington, D.C., 763
Dante B. Fascell, of Florida:
  Address, 276
  Article from the Voice, publication of Diocese of
    Miami, Fla., Nov. 29, 1963, 279
  Broadcasts by WTVJ–TV, Miami, Fla., Nov. 25, 1963,
    281
  Editorials from—
    Diario Las Americas, Miami Springs, Fla., Nov. 24,
      1963, 765
    Hialeah-Miami Spring (Fla.) Home News, Nov. 27–
      29, 1963, 280
    Jewish Floridian, Nov. 29, 1963, 279
    Key West (Fla.) Citizen, Nov. 24, 1963, 765
    Miami Beach (Fla.) Daily Sun, Nov. 24, 1963, 765
    Miami (Fla.) Herald, Nov. 23, 1963, 278
    Miami (Fla.) News, Nov. 30, 1963, 280
    Miami (Fla.) Times, Nov. 30, 1963, 279
    News Leader, Homestead, Fla., Nov. 24 and Nov. 28,
      1963, 278
  Poems—
    A Prayer for a President, by Mrs. George A. Pikari,
      Miami, Fla., 277
    All the World Knows Why, by John L. Perry,
      Miami, Fla., 277
    Dolor, by J. Carlton Barnette, Miami, Fla., 278
    He Followed to Infinity, by Jean Quinn, Miami, Fla.,
      277
    His Chair is Still, by Donna Davis, Miami, Fla., 277
    John F. Kennedy, by Judy D. Cooper, Miami, Fla.,
      277
    Long May He Live, by Madelynne Cooper, Miami,
      Fla., 277
    Love or Hate, by Albert L. Citero, Miami, Fla., 277

Dante B. Fascell, of Florida—Continued
  We Mourn for Ourselves and for the World, editorial from Miami (Fla.) News, Nov. 23, 1963, 764
Michael A. Feighan, of Ohio, address, 251
A. Fernós-Isern, of Puerto Rico, address, 417
Paul Findley, of Illinois:
  Address, 522
  Editorials from—
    Illinois State Journal, Springfield, Ill., 522
    Illinois State Register, Springfield, Ill., 522
Edward R. Finnegan, of Illinois, address, 344
O. C. Fisher, of Texas, address, 473
Daniel J. Flood, of Pennsylvania, address, 398
John J. Flynt, Jr., of Georgia, address, 480
John E. Fogarty, of Rhode Island:
  Address, 394
  Articles from Providence (R.I) Cowl, 766, 767
  Eulogy by Rev. Vincent C. Dore, president, Providence (R.I.) College, 767
  Memorial address by Francis H. Horn, president, University of Rhode Island, 767
Gerald R. Ford, of Michigan, address, 425
Ed Foreman, of Texas, address, 539
L. H. Fountain, of North Carolina, address, 543
Donald M. Fraser, of Minnesota:
  Address, 478
  Article by H. O. Sonnesyn, editor, North Minneapolis (Minn.) Post, 770
  Meditation by Pastor Alton Motter, Minneapolis, Minn., 769
Samuel N. Friedel, of Maryland, address, 526
James G. Fulton, of Pennsylvania:
  Address, 480
  Editorial by John J. Edwards, West Side News, Kingston, Pa., 771
  Poem by Irvin R. Lindemuth, pastor, Birmingham Congregational Church, Pittsburgh, Pa., 770
  Television and radio editorial by station KDKA, Pittsburgh, Pa., 771
Richard H. Fulton, of Tennessee, address, 315
Don Fuqua, of Florida:
  Address, 321
  Remarks by Dr. Gordon W. Blackwell, president of Florida State University, at memorial convocation, 322
Cornelius E. Gallagher, of New Jersey:
  Address, 543
  Editorial by Eugene Farrell in Jersey Journal, Jersey City, N.J., Nov. 23, 1963, 771
  Editorial from Jersey Journal, Jersey City, N.J., Nov. 25, 1963, 772
Edward A. Garmatz, of Maryland:
  Address, 410
  Tribute by Joseph L. Manning, Independent Retail Grocers & Meat Dealers Association, Baltimore, Md., 773
J. Vaughan Gary, of Virginia, address, 362
Robert N. Giaimo, of Connecticut:
  Address, 241
  Memorial address by Richard C. Lee, mayor, New Haven, Conn., Nov. 24, 1963, 773
Jacob H. Gilbert, of New York, address, 418

Milton W. Glenn, of New Jersey:
  Address, 461
  Editorial by Charles E. Seel in the Atlantic City (N.J.) Reporter, 461
Henry B. Gonzalez, of Texas, address, 422
Charles E. Goodell, of New York, address, 535
George A. Goodling, of Pennsylvania:
  Address, 354
  Poem by Mrs. Sarah Ann Knaub, York, Pa., 355
Bernard F. Grabowski, of Connecticut, address, 248
Kenneth J. Gray, of Illinois, address, 283
Edith Green, of Oregon:
  Address, 505
  Editorials from—
    Portland Journal, Nov. 23, 1963, 507
    Portland Oregonian, Nov. 26, 1963, 507
    Portland Reporter, Nov. 23, 1963, 507
  Memorial service by Rabbi Emanuel Rose, Congregation Beth Israel, Portland, Oreg., 506
  Sermon by Rev. Robert H. Bonthius, pastor, Westminster Presbyterian Church, Portland, Oreg., 506
  Tributes by—
    Monroe Sweetland, of Portland, Oreg., 775
    Oregon Chapter of National Association of Claimants' Counsel of America, 775
William J. Green, Jr., of Pennsylvania:
  Address, 338
  Eulogy by Father O'Malley at Woodstock College, Md., 778
  Poem by Catherine Kennedy Haugh, Philadelphia, Pa., 777
Robert P. Griffin, of Michigan, address, 484
Martha W. Griffiths, of Michigan, address, 374
H. R. Gross, of Iowa, address, 511
Charles S. Gubser, of California, address, 327
Edward J. Gurney, of Florida:
  Address, 476
  Editorials from—
    Orlando (Fla.) Sentinel, Nov. 23, 1963, 477
    Titusville (Fla.) Star-Advocate, Nov. 25, 1963, 476
G. Elliott Hagan, of Georgia:
  Address, 443
  Editorials from—
    Bryan Countian, Pembroke, Ga., Nov. 27, 1963, 446
    Bulloch Herald and Bulloch Times, Statesboro, Ga., Nov. 28, 1963, 444
    Claxton (Ga.) Enterprise, Nov. 28, 1963, 447
    Darien (Ga.) News, Nov. 28, 1963, 446
    Metter (Ga.) Advertiser, Nov. 28, 1963, 448
    Millen (Ga.) News, Nov. 28, 1963, 448
    Montgomery Monitor, Mount Vernon, Ga., Nov. 28, 1963, 450
    Pembroke (Ga.) Journal, Nov. 28, 1963, 445
    Savannah (Ga.) Morning News, Nov. 23, 1963, 443
    Savannah (Ga.) Evening Press, Nov. 23, 1963, 443
    Screven County News, Sylvania, Ga., Nov. 28, 1963, 449
    Springfield (Ga.) Herald, Nov. 29, 1963, 446
    Swainsboro (Ga.) Forest-Blade, Nov. 27, 1963, 448
    Sylvania (Ga.) Telephone, Nov. 29, 1963, 449
    This Week in Savannah, Ga., Nov. 29, 1963, 447
    True Citizen, Waynesboro, Ga., Nov. 27, 1963, 444
Harlan Hagen, of California, address, 473

James A. Haley, of Florida:
  Address, 434
  Eulogy at requiem mass, St. Raphael's Church, Englewood, Fla., Nov. 25, 1963, 778
  Prayer at requiem mass, Church of the Epiphany, Venice, Fla., Nov. 24, 1963, 778
Charles A. Halleck, of Indiana, address, 212
Seymour Halpern, of New York, address, 254
Richard T. Hanna, of California, address, 537
Julia Butler Hansen, of Washington, address, 540
Ralph R. Harding, of Idaho:
  Address, 437
  Editorials from—
    Arco (Idaho) Advertiser, Nov. 28, 1963, 440
    Blackfoot (Idaho) News, Nov. 26, 1963, 438
    Gooding (Idaho) Leader, Nov. 28, 1963, 442
    Idaho Falls Post Register, 439
    Idaho Statesman, 441
    Idaho Sunday Journal, Nov. 24, 1963, 441
    Owyhee Chronicle, 441
    Rexburg (Idaho) Standard, Nov. 26, 1963, 440
    Rigby Star, 440
Porter Hardy, Jr., of Virginia:
  Address, 362
  "Shoulder High We Bring You Home," tribute from Norfolk (Va.) Ledger-Star, 363
  "To Light the Lamps of Our Time," editorial from Norfolk Virginian-Pilot, 363
Oren Harris, of Arkansas, address, 239
James Harvey, of Michigan:
  Address, 325
  Poem by Rev. Wilfred G. Sawyier, pastor, First Presbyterian Church, Ionia, Mich., 326
Wayne L. Hays, of Ohio:
  Address, 529
  Poem by Miss Marty Hale, Steubenville, Ohio, 779
James C. Healey, of New York:
  Address, 336
  Eulogy by Louis L. Schwartz at Jewish Center of Highbridge, New York, N.Y., Nov. 25, 1963, 779
F. Edward Hébert, of Louisiana, address, 483
Ken Hechler, of West Virginia:
  Address, 283
  Articles from—
    Charleston (W. Va.) Gazette, by Harry Hoffmann, 285
    Huntington (W. Va.) Herald-Advertiser, by Bill Belanger, Dec. 1, 1963, 290
    Huntington (W. Va.) Herald-Advertiser, by H. R. Pinckard, Nov. 24, 1963, 287
    Huntington (W. Va.) Herald-Dispatch, by Bill Wild, Dec. 2, 1963, 286
  Editorial from Huntington (W. Va.) Advertiser, Nov. 23, 1963, 287
Robert W. Hemphill, of South Carolina:
  Address, 416
  Article by Jim Oliphant from Spartanburg (S.C.) Journal, 781
David N. Henderson, of North Carolina, address, 435
A. Sydney Herlong, Jr., of Florida, letter by John F. May, principal, to student body of Mainland Junior High School, Daytona Beach, Fla., 781
Charles B. Hoeven, of Iowa, address, 472

Chet Holifield, of California, address, 256
Elmer J. Holland, of Pennsylvania:
  Address, 397
  Eulogy by Very Rev. Monsignor Basil N. Smochko at St. John's Byzantine Catholic Church, Munhall, Pa., Nov. 25, 1963, 782
  Tribute by Michael Roman, editor, Greek Catholic Union Messenger, Homestead, Pa., 783
Walt Horan, of Washington:
  Address, 317
  Sermon by Rev. Robert Clyde Curry, Chevy Chase Presbyterian Church, Washington, D.C., 784
Frank J. Horton, of New York, address, 359
Craig Hosmer, of California:
  Address, 352
  Poem by Blaine Nels Simons of Long Beach (Calif.) Bar Association, 787
George Huddeston, Jr., of Alabama:
  City of Birmingham (Ala.) Proclamation, 787
  Resolution adopted by mayor and city council of Birmingham, Ala., Nov. 26, 1963, 788
  Statement of Mayor Albert Boutwell of city of Birmingham, Ala., Nov. 22, 1963, 787
W. R. Hull, Jr., of Missouri, address, 320
Richard H. Ichord, of Missouri:
  Address, 405
  Tribute by Edward T. Sowers, editor, Rolla (Mo.) Daily News, 405
John Jarman, of Oklahoma, address, 409
W. Pat Jennings, of Virginia:
  Address, 368
  Editorial from Bristol (Va.) Herald-Courier, Nov. 24, 1963, 369
Ben F. Jensen, of Iowa:
  Address, 380
  Eulogy by Judge Folsom Everest, Council Bluffs, Iowa, 789
Charles S. Joelson, of New Jersey:
  Address, 319
  Article from Paterson (N.J.) Evening News by Hon. Gordon Canfield, 790
  Letter from Central of Polish Organizations, Passaic, N.J., 791
August E. Johansen, of Michigan, address, 485
Albert W. Johnson, of Pennsylvania:
  Address, 355
  Editorials from—
    Derrick, Oil City-Franklin-Clarion, Pa., Nov. 25, 1963, 355
    Kane Republican, Kane and Mount Jewett, Pa., Nov. 29, 1963, 355
    Warren (Pa.) Times-Mirror, Nov. 25, 1963, 357
    Warren County (Pa.) Observer, Nov. 25, 1963, 356
Harold T. Johnson, of California:
  Address, 379
  Poem by Robert Vukajlovich, Jackson, Calif., 791
Lester R. Johnson, of Wisconsin, address, 410
Charles R. Jonas, of North Carolina, address, 432
Paul C. Jones, of Missouri:
  Address, 260
  Editorial by Jack Stapleton, Jr., publisher of Daily Dunklin Democrat, Kennett, Mo., 261
Robert E. Jones, of Alabama, address, 384

Frank M. Karsten, of Missouri:
　Address, 378
　Eulogy from Northwest County Journal by Joe Heade, 792
Joseph E. Karth, of Minnesota:
　Address, 390
　Communications of sympathy from citizens of Fourth Congressional District of Minnesota, 793
　Sonnet by Sister Marie David, College of St. Catherine, St. Paul, Minn., 794
Robert W. Kastenmeier, of Wisconsin, address, 493
Elizabeth Kee, of West Virginia, tribute by Rev. Robert E. Brengartner, chaplain, U.S. Naval Medical Center, Bethesda, Md., 794
Hastings Keith, of Massachusetts:
　Address, 237
　Article from Provincetown (Mass.) Advocate, Nov. 28, 1963, 719
　Editorials from—
　　Cape Cod Standard-Times, 723
　　Cape Codder, Orleans, Mass., 720
　　Dennis-Yarmouth Register, 720
　　Hull-Nantasket Times, Nov. 28, 1963, 722
　　Nantucket Inquirer and Mirror, 720
　　New Beacon, Provincetown, Mass., Nov. 27, 1963, 719
　　Old Colony Memorial, Plymouth, Mass., 718
　　Standard-Times, New Bedford, Mass., Nov. 23, 1963, 717
　　Vineyard Gazette, Martha's Vineyard, Mass., 718
　Excerpts from article by John Bond, editor of Rockland Standard 722
　Poem from Barnstable Patriot, Hyannis, Mass., 721
　Poem from South Shore Mirror, Nov. 28, 1963, 722
　Resolution by Hyannis Board of Selectmen, 723
　Tribute by former Congressman Donald W. Nicholson from Wareham (Mass.) Courier, 719
　Tributes from—
　　Brockton Enterprise, 723
　　Otis Air Force Base newspaper, 718
　　Wareham (Mass.) Courier, 717
Edna F. Kelly, of New York:
　Address, 524
　Meditation by Rev. Michael Farina, St. Thomas the Apostle Church, Washington, D.C., 795
Eugene J. Keogh, of New York:
　Address, 337
　Tribute by Jose Maria de Areilza, former Ambassador to U.S., 795
Clarence E. Kilburn, of New York, address, 352
Joe M. Kilgore, of Texas, address, 482
Michael J. Kirwan, of Ohio, address, 400
John C. Kluczynski, of Illinois, address, 451
Victor A. Knox, of Michigan:
　Address, 334
　Poem by Betty Wojtaszek, of Roger City, Mich., 334
Horace R. Kornegay, of North Carolina, address, 433
John C. Kunkel, of Pennsylvania, address, 541
John Kyl, of Iowa, address, 487
Melvin R. Laird, of Wisconsin, address, 370
Phil M. Landrum, of Georgia, address, 503
Odin Langen, of Minnesota, address, 428
Delbert L. Latta, of Ohio, address, 457

Robert L. Leggett, of California, address, 297
Alton Lennon, of North Carolina, address, 541
John Lesinski, of Michigan:
　Address, 323
　Poems by Bettie A. LaVeck, of Taylor, Mich., 797
Roland V. Libonati, of Illinois:
　Address, 527
　Eulogy by Wm. Castleman, chairman, Uptown Senior Citizens Association, Chicago, Ill., 798
　"My President Is Dead," poem by Billee Shoecraft, 798
John V. Lindsay, of New York, address, 453
Glenard P. Lipscomb, of California, address, 429
Sherman P. Lloyd, of Utah, address, 335
Clarence D. Long, of Maryland:
　Address, 454
　Poem by Maureen Norton, Baltimore, Md., 799
　Resolution by Second District Democratic Club, Baltimore, Md., 799
Robert McClory, of Illinois, address, 342
John W. McCormack, of Massachusetts:
　Address, 207
　Eulogy in Rotunda, U.S. Capitol, Nov. 24, 1963, 204
　Memorial tribute by Bishop James K. Mathews, Methodist Bishop of New England, at Washington Cathedral, Washington, D.C., Nov. 2, 1963, 687
　Poem by George N. Welch, president, Charitable Irish Society of Boston, Mass., 689
　Poem by Miss Miriam Gilbert, "A Eulogy for President Kennedy," 690
William M. McCulloch, of Ohio, address, 455
Joseph M. McDade, of Pennsylvania:
　Address, 328
　Editorials from—
　　Canton (Pa.) Independent, Nov. 28, 1963, 330
　　Carbondale (Pa.) News, Nov. 28, 1963, 331
　　Forest City (Pa.) News, Nov. 28, 1963, 331
　　Sayre (Pa.) Evening Times, Nov. 23, 1963, 332
　　Scranton (Pa.) Times, entitled, "Nation Mourns," 332
　　Scranton (Pa.) Tribune, 328
　　Towanda (Pa.) Daily Review, Nov. 23, 1963, 329
　　Troy (Pa.) Gazette, Nov. 28, 1963, 330
　　Tunkhannock (Pa.) Republican and New Age, Nov. 28, 1963, 329
　　Wayne (Pa.) Independent, Nov. 25, 1963, 333
Harris B. McDowell, Jr., of Delaware:
　Address, 319
　Sermon by Rev. Donald J. Maccallum, pastor, People's Congregational Church, Dover, Del., 799
John J. McFall, of California, address, 484
Clifford G. McIntire, of Maine:
　Address, 458
　Article from Penobscot (Maine) Times, Nov. 28, 1963, 803
　Editorials from—
　　Bangor (Maine) Daily News, Nov. 25, 1963, 802
　　Lewiston (Maine) Daily Sun, Nov. 23, 1963, 801
　　Lewiston (Maine) Evening Journal, Nov. 23, 1963, 802
　　Portland (Maine) Sunday Telegram and Sunday Press Herald, Nov. 24, 1963, 803
　　Letter from State Senator Bill Boardman, of Calais, Maine, 804

Clifford G. McIntire, of Maine—Continued
  Memorial addresses by—
    Dr. Frederick W. Whittaker, president, Bangor Theological Seminary, Bangor, Maine, 460
    Rev. Peter M. Kemper, pastor, First Baptist Church, Pittsfield, Maine, 458
Robert T. McLoskey, of Illinois, address, 539
John L. McMillan, of South Carolina, address, 311
Torbert H. Macdonald, of Massachusetts, address, 224
Clark MacGregor, of Minnesota, address, 436
Ray J. Madden, of Indiana, address, 387
George H. Mahon, of Texas, address, 249
John O. Marsh, Jr., of Virginia, address, 451
Joseph W. Martin, Jr., of Massachusetts:
  Address, 231
  Tribute by Rev. William Foley, rector, Church of the Good Shepherd, Newton, Mass., 706
Charles McC. Mathias, Jr., of Maryland:
  Address, 300
  Editorial by Leo T. Paulin in Bethesda-Chevy Chase (Md.) Advertiser, Nov. 27, 1963, 805
Spark M. Matsunaga, of Hawaii:
  Address, 531
  Editorial from Honolulu (Hawaii) Advertiser, Nov. 23, 1963, 806
D. R. (Billy) Matthews, of Florida:
  Address, 424
  Letter to constituents, 424
Catherine May, of Washington, address, 427
George Meader, of Michigan, address, 430
Robert H. Michel, of Illinois, address, 542
George P. Miller, of California:
  Newsletter by Alameda (Calif.) branch National Association for the Advancement of Colored People, 807
  Poem by Everett Johannes in Alameda (Calif.) Times-Star, 807
  Poem by Mrs. Agnes Brown, Oakland, Calif., 808
  Resolution by National Association of Letter Carriers, 807
William E. Miller, of New York, address, 429
Wilbur D. Mills, of Arkansas, address, 239
Joseph G. Minish, of New Jersey:
  Address, 507
  Eulogy by Jerry Bakst from Suburban World, Essex County, N.J., 808
  Interview by WTOP Reporter Harold Walker with Daniel P. Moynihan, Assistant Secretary of Labor, 508
William E. Minshall, of Ohio, address, 324
John S. Monagan, of Connecticut:
  Address, 246
  Article from Waterbury (Conn.) Republican, 809
  Eulogy by Col. J. S. Chmielewski, chaplain, 8th Army, Seoul, Korea, 247
  Statement issued on Nov. 26, 1963, 247
Joseph M. Montoya, of New Mexico, address, 404
Arch A. Moore, Jr., of West Virginia, address, 485
William S. Moorhead, of Pennsylvania:
  Address, 292
  Eulogy by former Gov. David L. Lawrence at Allegheny County Bar Association memorial service, 811
  Resolution by Young Men and Women's Hebrew Association and Irene Kaufmann Centers, Pittsburgh, Pa., 812

Thomas E. Morgan, of Pennsylvania, address, 311
Thomas G. Morris, of New Mexico:
  Address, 413
  Memorial message by Rev. Arthur C. Opperman at Community Church of the Sandias, San Antonio, N. Mex., 812
James H. Morrison, of Louisiana, address, 313
F. Bradford Morse, of Massachusetts:
  Address, 225
  Editorial by Andrew A. Minahan, Merrimack Valley Advertiser, Tewksbury, Mass., 724
Rogers C. B. Morton, of Maryland, address, 474
Charles A. Mosher, of Ohio, address, 510
John E. Moss, of California:
  Address, 544
  Resolution by Sacramento (Calif.) Board of Education, 545
Abraham J. Multer, of New York:
  Address, 240
  Eulogies in the Rotunda, U.S. Capitol, Nov. 24, 1963, 203
  Eulogy by Rabbi Samuel D. Soskin at Temple Beth Emeth of Flatbush, Brooklyn, N.Y., Nov. 25, 1963, 813
  Letter of sympathy from Mrs. Peter Haddon, London, England, to Mr. and Mrs. Barnett J. Nova, 813
  Poem by James Vincent, Brooklyn, N.Y., 814
  Resolution by National Association of Letter Carriers, 813
  The Riderless Horse, poem by Louis I. Newman, 241
John M. Murphy, of New York:
  Address, 486
  "Flags in Mourning," poem by Vernon B. Hampton, Staten Island, N.Y., 814
William T. Murphy, of Illinois:
  Address, 538
  Poem by Mrs. Jessie M. Williams, Chicago, Ill., 815
William H. Natcher, of Kentucky, address, 252
Lucien N. Nedzi, of Michigan, address, 370
Ancher Nelsen, of Minnesota:
  Address, 493
  "The Eternal Flame," poem by Mrs. Dana Anderson, Minnesota's Second Congressional District, 815
Robert N. C. Nix, of Pennsylvania, address, 312
Walter Norblad, of Oregon, address, 367
Leo W. O'Brien, of New York, address, 408
Thomas J. O'Brien, of Illinois, address, 384
Barratt O'Hara, of Illinois:
  Address, 515
  Eulogy by Rabbi Jacob J. Weinstein at K.A.M. Temple, Chicago, Ill., Nov. 25, 1963, 816
  Memorial radio address by President Nkrumah to people of Ghana, 815
  Poem by Patrick Joyce, Chicago, Ill., 818
James G. O'Hara, of Michigan:
  Address, 491
  Letter from Jens Brueckner, Oldenburg, Germany, published in Imlay City (Mich.) Times, 818
Arnold Olsen, of Montana, address, 294
Alec G. Olson, of Minnesota, address, 536
Thomas P. O'Neill, Jr., of Massachusetts, address, 234
Frank C. Osmers, Jr., of New Jersey, address, 526
Harold C. Ostertag, of New York, address, 379
Otto E. Passman, of Louisiana, address, 385

Wright Patman, of Texas:
  Address, 519
  Editorial from Baptist Standard by Editor E. S. James, 819
Edward J. Patten, of New Jersey, address, 298
Thomas M. Pelly, of Washington, address, 345
Claude Pepper, of Florida:
  Address, 299
  Tribute by Joseph B. Gregg, Sunrise Junior High School, Fort Lauderdale, Fla., 819
Carl D. Perkins, of Kentucky:
  Address, 264
  Articles from—
    Journal Enquirer, Grayson, Ky., Nov. 28, 1963, 274
    Licking Valley (Ky.) Courier, Nov. 27, 1963, 272
    Maysville (Ky.) Daily Independence, Nov. 23, 1963, 268
    Pike County (Ky.) Times, Nov. 28, 1963, 273
    Sandy Hook (Ky.) Elliott County News, Nov. 26, 1963, 272
  Comparison of Two Presidents, article from Hazard (Ky.) Herald of Nov. 28, 1963, 268
  Death of a President, poem by Ida Lee Hansel, published in Hazard (Ky.) Herald, 268
  Editorials from—
    Ashland (Ky.) Daily Independent, Nov. 23, 1963, 275
    Bath County (Ky.) News Outlook, Nov. 28, 1963, 275
    Hazard (Ky.) Herald of Nov. 28, 1963, 267, 268
    Louisa (Ky.) Big Sandy News, Nov. 28, 1963, 266
    Louisville (Ky.) Courier-Journal, Nov. 23, 1963, 265
    Maysville (Ky.) Daily Independent, Nov. 23, 1963, 273
    Morehead (Ky.) News, Nov. 28, 1963, 269
    Paintsville (Ky.) Herald, Nov. 27, 1963, 274
    Prestonsburg (Ky.) Floyd County Times, Nov. 28, 1963, 270
    West Liberty (Ky.) Licking Valley Courier, Nov. 27, 1963, 271
  Eulogies by citizens of Lawrence County, Ky., 266
  Letter from mayor and citizens of Owingsville, Ky., 275
  "We've Lost a Friend," editorial by Larry Caudill, in Hazard (Ky.) Herald, Dec. 12, 1963, 820
Philip J. Philbin, of Massachusetts:
  Address, 233
  Poem by Dr. Charles H. Bradford, 725
Otis G. Pike, of New York:
  Address, 433
  Letter from Rev. Herbert Perry, missionary minister in southern Rhodesia, Africa, 433
John L. Pilcher, of Georgia:
  Address, 377
  Statement published in Thomasville (Ga.) Times-Enterprise, Nov. 22, 1963, 377
John R. Pillion, of New York:
  Address, 327
  Editorials from—
    Buffalo (N.Y.) Courier-Express, Nov. 23 and Nov. 25, 1963, 821
    Buffalo (N.Y.) Evening News, Nov. 23 and Nov. 25, 1963, 821

Alexander Pirnie, of New York, address, 372
W. R. Poage, of Texas, address, 422
Richard H. Poff, of Virginia, address, 326
Joe Pool, of Texas:
  Address, 479
  Letter from Mrs. Lottie Adams, Electra, Tex., 480
Adam C. Powell, of New York:
  France's tribute to President Kennedy—
    Eulogy by M. Jacques Chaban-Delmas, President of the French National Assembly, 823
    French public opinion—France mourns President Kennedy, 823
    Official messages, 821
    The French press, 823
Prayers by the Chaplain, Rev. Bernard Braskamp, D.D.:
  November 25, 1963, 203
  December 5, 1963, 207
Melvin Price, of Illinois, address, 376
Roman C. Pucinski, of Illinois:
  Address, 303
  Article from Washington (D.C.) Post of Nov. 24, 1963, by Karl E. Meyer, 305
  Editorial from Chicago (Ill.) Sun-Times of Nov. 23, 1963, by Robert E. Kennedy, 305
  Memorial section of Chicago (Ill.) Sun-Times, Dec. 29, 1963—
    A Black Friday in Dallas, article by Merriman Smith, 825
    A Gray Saturday in Capital, article by David Wise, 829
    America Weeps, editorial, 836
    Amid Sorrow, the Strength to Carry On, article by Thomas B. Ross, 829
    A Monday Walk in Gothic Gloom, article by William Braden, 832
    A Mournful Sunday Procession, article by William Braden, 830
    His Legacy to the Nation, article by Milburn P. Akers, 838
    Journey's End on Hillside, article by Thomas B. Ross, 834
    Mrs. Kennedy—A Woman Equal to Her Task, tribute by Charles Bartlett, 835
    The Assassination of John F. Kennedy, by Gwendolyn Brooks, 837
    The Deed That Freedom Bred, article by Walter Lippmann, 837
    The Man the Nation Lost, article by Charles Bartlett, 836
    The President: How He'll Be Remembered, by Eric Sevareid, 839
    "The Trumpet Summons Us"—His Buoyant Words Echo, article by Carleton Kent, 833
    Three Last, Bright Hours—And the Nightmare Descends, article by Carleton Kent, 828
    Where the Eternal Flame Burns, article by James Hoge, 839
  Poetic eulogy by Norman H. Kindlund, Chicago, Ill., 824
  President John F. Kennedy's inaugural address, 307
  Tribute by Karol Rozmarek, president, Polish National Alliance and Polish American Congress, 824

Graham Purcell, of Texas:
Address, 315
Eulogy at memorial service at National City Christian Church, Washington, D.C., by Dr. George R. Davis, Nov. 25, 1963, 841
Last public speech of President John F. Kennedy before Fort Worth Chamber of Commerce, Texas Hotel, Fort Worth, Tex., Nov. 22, 1963, 843
Albert H. Quie, of Minnesota, address, 428
Wm. J. Randall, of Missouri:
Address, 295
Editorials from—
Harrisonville (Mo.) Democrat-Missourian, Nov. 26, 1963, 847
Higginsville (Mo.) Advance, Nov. 28, 1963, 848
Huntington (Ind.) Our Sunday Visitor, Dec. 8, 1963, 850
Independence (Mo.) Examiner, Nov. 25 and Nov. 26, 1963, 846
Kansas City (Mo.) Labor Beacon, Nov. 29, 1963, 849
Kansas City (Mo.) Star, Nov. 24, 1963, by Roy A. Roberts, editor and publisher, 844
Kansas City (Mo.) Times, Nov. 23, 1963, 845
Pleasant Hill (Mo.) Times, Nov. 28, 1963, 848
Rich Hill (Mo.) Mining Review, Nov. 29, 1963, 849
Roll Call, Washington, D.C., Nov. 27, 1963, 849
Warrensburg (Mo.) Daily Star-Journal, Nov. 25, 1963, 847
Windsor (Mo.) Review, Nov. 28, 1963, 848
Charlotte T. Reid, of Illinois, address, 352
Ogden R. Reid, of New York, address, 259
Ben Reifel, of South Dakota, address, 367
Henry S. Reuss, of Wisconsin:
Address, 513
Article from Milwaukee (Wis.) Journal, Dec. 2, 1963, 514
George M. Rhodes, of Pennsylvania:
Address, 494
Articles from—
New Era, 500
Time magazine, 498
Washington (D.C.) Evening Star, Nov. 26, 1963, by Eric Sevareid, 496
Editorials from—
Harrisburg (Pa.) Patriot, 496
Pottsville (Pa.) Republican, 497
Reading (Pa.) New Era, AFL–CIO Paper, 497
Washington (D.C.) Post by Karl E. Meyer, 852
Eulogy by Carl F. Constein, supervising principal, Mount Penn High School, Reading, Pa., 850
Letter from Dr. Norman C. Cooper, Seal Beach, Calif., to June F. Marsh, Pasadena, Calif., 854
Letters of sympathy from overseas business leaders to David Frankel, president, American Safety Table Co., Reading, Pa., 851
Resolution by Berks County Historical Society, Reading, Pa., 854
John J. Rhodes, of Arizona, address, 366

R. Walter Riehlman, of New York:
Address, 521
Remarks by Rev. Finley M. Keech, minister, First Baptist Church, Tully, N.Y., 855
Ralph J. Rivers, of Alaska, eulogy at memorial services, Anchorage, Alaska, Nov. 23, 1963, 855
Kenneth A. Roberts, of Alabama, address, 489
Ray Roberts, of Texas, address, 453
Howard W. Robison, of New York:
Address, 393
Resolution by Council of City of Binghamton, N.Y., 856
Peter W. Rodino, Jr., of New Jersey:
Address, 517
Editorials from—
Newark (N.J.) Star-Ledger, Nov. 23 and Nov. 25, 1963, 857, 858
Newark (N.J.) Sunday News, Nov. 24, 1963, 858
Byron G. Rogers, of Colorado, address, 343
Paul G. Rogers, of Florida:
Address, 477
Editorials from—
Fort Lauderdale (Fla.) News, Nov. 24, 1963, 859
Fort Myers (Fla.) News-Press, Nov. 23, 1963, 860
Palm Beach (Fla.) Post, Nov. 23, 1963, 859
Walter Rogers, of Texas:
Address, 420
Poem by George Schaeffer, Canyon, Tex., 861
Fred B. Rooney, of Pennsylvania, address, 340
John J. Rooney, of New York:
Address, 252
Poem by Rev. Eugene L. A. Fisher, read at memorial mass, 862
James Roosevelt, of California, address, 383
Benjamin S. Rosenthal, of New York, address, 504
Dan Rostenkowski, of Illinois, address, 316
J. Edward Roush, of Indiana, address, 293
Edward R. Roybal, of California:
Address, 532
President Kennedy's inaugural address, 533
Donald Rumsfeld, of Illinois:
Address, 344
Editorials from—
Chicago (Ill.) Sun Times, Nov. 23, 1963, 863
Chicago (Ill.) Sunday American, Nov. 24, 1963, 862
Harold M. Ryan, of Michigan:
Address, 361
Poem by Judge Wade McCree, Detroit, Mich., 864
Six White Horses, poem by Miss Candy Geer, Grosse Pointe, Mich., 864
William F. Ryan, of New York:
Address, 296
Address by Hon. Charles H. Silver, Congregation B'nai Jeshurun, New York City, N.Y., 865
Letter from Jay Newman, Washington, D.C., published in New York (N.Y.) Times, 866
Memorial address by Dr. Grayson Kirk, president, Columbia University, 867
Poem by James T. Farrell, 867
Text of speech prepared for delivery at Dallas, Tex., by President John F. Kennedy, 869

William F. Ryan, of New York—Continued
  Tribute by Father John Dwyer in Corpus Christi Church bulletin, 865
  Tribute by Nathaniel Spector, Millinery Workers Union, 867
Katharine St. George, of New York:
  Address, 343
  Cable from Carlos de Baeck, Belgian member, Inter-Parliamentary Union, 873
  Expressions of sympathy from members of Inter-Parliamentary Union, 872
  Letter from Gen. W. A. Dimoline, British member, Inter-Parliamentary Union, 873
Fernand J. St Germain, of Rhode Island, address, 399
William L. St. Onge, of Connecticut:
  Address, 242
  Editorials from—
    Leader, Rockville, Conn., Nov. 25, 1963, 875
    Middletown (Conn.) Press, Nov. 25, 1963, 874
    New London (Conn.) Day, Nov. 25, 1963, 875
    Norwich (Conn.) Bulletin, Nov. 26, 1963, 874
  Letter to Secretary of Navy regarding naming submarine in honor of John Fitzgerald Kennedy, 873
Henry C. Schadeberg, of Wisconsin, address, 537
Paul F. Schenck, of Ohio, address, 456
Herman T. Schneebeli, of Pennsylvania, address, 359
Richard S. Schweiker, of Pennsylvania, address, 524
Ralph J. Scott, of North Carolina, address, 381
George F. Senner, Jr., of Arizona:
  Address, 531
  My President Is Dead, poem by Mrs. Willard "Billee" Shoecraft, 876
John F. Shelley, of California, address, 386
George E. Shipley, of Illinois, address, 395
Don L. Short, of North Dakota:
  Address, 475
  Editorial from Wall Street Journal, Nov. 26, 1963, 876
  Public statement released on Nov. 22, 1963, 877
Garner E. Shriver, of Kansas, address, 463
Abner W. Sibal, of Connecticut, address, 248
Carlton R. Sickles, of Maryland:
  Address, 413
  Article from Baltimore (Md.) Sun by R. H. Gardner, Dec. 1, 1963, 877
  Resolution by City Council of Baltimore, 878
  Song for a Friend, by John Stewart, member of Kingston Trio, 879
Robert L. F. Sikes, of Florida, address, 335
Eugene Siler, of Kentucky, address, 437
B. F. Sisk, of California, address, 475
Joe Skubitz, of Kansas, address, 466
John M. Slack, Jr., of West Virginia, address, 339
Neal Smith, of Iowa, address, 418
William L. Springer, of Illinois, address, 430
Neil Staebler, of Michigan, address, 299
Robert T. Stafford, of Vermont, address, 345
Harley O. Staggers, of West Virginia, address, 530
Tom Steed, of Oklahoma:
  Address, 406
  Memorial service at Oklahoma Baptist University, Shawnee, Okla., by Dr. James Ralph Scales, 406

Bill Stinson, of Washington, address, 529
Samuel S. Stratton, of New York:
  Address, 373
  Eulogy by Rev. Edward O'Heron, St. Mary's Church, Cortland, N.Y., 879
  Memoir by Prof. John Lydenberg, Hobart College, Geneva, N.Y., published in Geneva (N.Y.) Times, Dec. 17, 1963, 880
  Resolution by City Council of Oneonta, N.Y., 880
Leonor Kretzer Sullivan, of Missouri:
  Address, 374
  Editorial from New York Journal of Commerce, Nov. 26, 1963, 881
Robert Taft, Jr., of Ohio:
  Address, 458
  Memorial statement by Ohio State University Young Republican Club, 882
Burt L. Talcott, of California, address, 492
Roy A. Taylor, of North Carolina, address, 450
Charles M. Teague, of California, address, 328
Olin E. Teague, of Texas, address, 541
Albert Thomas, of Texas:
  Address, 540
  Our Fallen Hero, poem by Fizer M. Noe, Houston, Tex., 882
  Poem by Breckenridge Porter, Jr., 882
Clark W. Thompson, of Texas, address, 481
Frank Thompson, Jr., of New Jersey, address, 504
T. Ashton Thompson, of Louisiana, address, 315
Homer Thornberry, of Texas, address, 509
Herman Toll, of Pennsylvania:
  Address, 403
  Resolution by State Senate of Pennsylvania, 404
  Sermon by Rabbi Meir Lasker, Temple Judea Congregation, Philadelphia, Pa., 882
Thor C. Tollefson, of Washington:
  Address, 482
  Editorial from Bremerton (Wash.) Sun, 483
James W. Trimble, of Arkansas:
  Address, 408
  Eulogy by Maj. Gen. Teddy H. Sanford at memorial services at Fort Chaffee, Ark., 884
William M. Tuck, of Virginia, address, 382
Stanley R. Tupper, of Maine, address, 452
Al Ullman, of Oregon:
  Address, 509
  An Echo in the Silence, article by Emmet John Hughes in Newsweek, 884
  Poem by Charlie Hess, Klamath Falls, Oreg., 885
Lionel Van Deerlin, of California:
  Address, 436
  Poem by Mrs. Linda Hurley, La Mesa, Calif., 885
Charles A. Vanik, of Ohio, address, 388
William K. Van Pelt, of Wisconsin, address, 473
Carl Vinson, of Georgia, address, 222
Joe D. Waggonner, Jr., of Louisiana, address, 385
George M. Wallhauser, of New Jersey, address, 351
John C. Watts, of Kentucky, address, 382
James D. Weaver, of Pennsylvania:
  Address, 346
  Editorials from—
    Albion (Pa.) News, Nov. 27, 1963, 348

James D. Weaver, of Pennsylvania—Continued
    Editorials from—Continued
        Allied Newspapers, Grove City, Pa., by Frances Moore, editor, Nov. 25, 1963, 351
        Corry (Pa.) Journal, Nov. 23, 1963, 348
        Edinboro (Pa.) Independent, Nov. 28, 1963, 350
        Erie (Pa.) Lake Shore Visitor, Nov. 29, 1963, 349
        Erie (Pa.) Morning News, Nov. 26, 1963, 350
        Erie (Pa.) Times, Nov. 23 and Nov. 25, 1963, 346, 349
        Farrell (Pa.) Press, Nov. 29, 1963, 347
        Greenville (Pa.) Record-Argus, Nov. 25, 1963, 349
        Meadville (Pa.) Tribune, Nov. 26, 1963, 347
        Sharon (Pa.) Herald, Nov. 23, 1963, 347
        Titusville (Pa.) Herald, Nov. 23, 1963, 348
Charles L. Weltner, of Georgia, resolution adopted by De Kalb County Democratic Executive Committee, 886
J. Irving Whalley, of Pennsylvania, address, 325
Compton I. White, Jr., of Idaho:
    Address, 400
    Editorial by William Johnston, editor of Lewiston, Idaho, Morning Tribune, Nov. 23, 1963, 401
Basil L. Whitener, of North Carolina:
    Address, 421
    Memorial address by Dr. Harry M. Moffett, pastor, First Presbyterian Church, Gastonia, N.C., 888

Basil L. Whitener, of North Carolina—Continued
    Sermon by Rev. Albert Ambrose, pastor, First Baptist Church, Drexel, N.C., 887
    "Tribute to John F. Kennedy," poem by Timothy Brendle, Gastonia, N.C., 888
Victor Wickersham, of Oklahoma, address, 416
William B. Widnall, of New Jersey, address, 536
John Bell Williams, of Mississippi:
    Address, 471
    Editorial from Evening Post, Vicksburg, Miss., Nov. 23, 1963, 471
Charles H. Wilson, of California, address, 396
Earl Wilson, of Indiana, address, 538
James C. Wright, Jr., of Texas, address, 309
John W. Wydler, of New York:
    Address, 512
    Remarks by Rabbi Ralph P. Kingsley, Garden City (N.Y.) Jewish Center, 889
John Young, of Texas, address, 442
J. Arthur Younger, of California, address, 380
Clement J. Zablocki, of Wisconsin:
    Address, 262
    Editorials from—
        Milwaukee Journal of Nov. 23, Nov. 24, and Nov. 28, 1963, 263
        Milwaukee Sentinel of Nov. 23 and Nov. 25, 1963, 263, 264